Roman and European Mythologies

Roman and European Mythologies

Compiled by

YVES BONNEFOY

Translated under the direction of

WENDY DONIGER

by Gerald Honigsblum,
Danielle Beauvais, Teresa Lavender Fagan, Dorothy Figuiera,
Barry Friedman, Louise Guiney, John Leavitt,
Louise Root, Bruce Sullivan, and David White

The University of Chicago Press • *Chicago and London*

Y V E S B O N N E F O Y,
a scholar and poet of world renown, is
professor of comparative poetics, Collège de France.
Among his many works to have appeared in English, two
have been published by the University of Chicago Press—a
volume of poetry, *In the Shadow's Light* (1991), and a work
of criticism, *The Act and Place of Poetry* (1989), both
translated by John T. Naughton.

W E N D Y D O N I G E R
is the Mircea Eliade Professor in the
Divinity School, and professor in the Department of South
Asian Languages and Civilizations, the Committee on Social
Thought, and the College, at the University of Chicago.
Under the name of Wendy Doniger O'Flaherty she has written,
among other books, *Women, Androgynes, and Other Mythical
Beasts* (1980), *Dreams, Illusion, and Other Realities* (1984),
and *Tales of Sex and Violence: Folklore, Sacrifice, and
Danger in the Jaiminīya Brāhmaṇa* (1985), all published
by the University of Chicago Press.

The University of Chicago Press, Chicago 60637
The University of Chicago Press, Ltd., London

Printed in the United States of America

01 00 99 98 97 96 95 94 93 92   5 4 3 2 1

This paperback is drawn from *Mythologies,* compiled by
Yves Bonnefoy, translated under the direction of Wendy Doniger,
and published by the University of Chicago Press in 1991.
That work was originally published as *Dictionnaire
des mythologies et des religions des sociétés traditionnelles et
du monde antique,* sous la direction de Yves Bonnefoy
publié avec le concours du Centre National
des Lettres, © 1981, Flammarion, Paris.

The preparation of the complete English edition was
supported by grants from the French Ministry of Culture,
the Andrew W. Mellon Foundation, and the
National Endowment for the Humanities.

This book is printed on acid-free paper.

Paperback ISBN: 0-226-06455-7

Library of Congress Cataloging-in-Publication Data

Dictionnaire des mythologies et des religions des sociétés
traditionnelles et du monde antique. English. Selections.
Roman and European mythologies / compiled by Yves Bonnefoy;
translated under the direction of Wendy Doniger by Gerald Honigsblum
. . . [et al.].
p. cm.
Includes bibliographical references and index.
1. Mythology, European—Encyclopedias. 2. Mythology, Roman—
Encyclopedias. 3. Mythology, European, in literature—
Encyclopedias. I. Bonnefoy, Yves. II. Title.
BL689.D5313 1992
291.1'3'094—dc20   92-15402
CIP

Contents

PART 3
WESTERN CIVILIZATION IN THE CHRISTIAN ERA

Preface to the Paperback Edition

This is one of four paperback volumes drawn from the full, clothbound, two-volume English-language edition of Yves Bonnefoy's *Mythologies*. These paperbacks are not an afterthought, but were part of the publication plan from the very beginning. Indeed, one of the reasons why we restructured the original French edition as we did was in order ultimately to make these separate volumes available. For though there is of course a sweep and majesty in the full editions, both French and English, a breathtaking scope that is the true raison d'être of the work as a whole, there is also, in the English version, a pattern that allows readers to focus on one culture at a time. And it is with such readers in mind that the University of Chicago Press is issuing these paperbacks, which will include (in addition to the present volume) *Greek and Egyptian Mythologies*, *Asian Mythologies*, and *African and American Mythologies*. Each book draws from the full work not only the culturally specific material but also the two prefaces and the general introductory essays, which deal with methodological issues pertaining to all the cultures discussed.

Since each culture poses different problems, and each section of essays embodies the work of a different group of French scholars, each has its own methodological flavor and its own contribution to make to the more culturally specific study of mythology. The present volume begins with Roman mythologies and goes on to trace the ways in which Greek and Roman myths (known primarily in their Roman form) continued to inform and animate early Christian and later European literature. The particular innovation in these essays lies, I think, in the ways in which they apply the methods of mythologists to works that have previously been treated primarily by theologians and literary critics. This approach brings into focus an entirely new line of development in the great literary classics of the West and encourages us to take a fresh look at the problems of cultural and historical diffusion.

For example, there is one theme that several of the authors chose to select out of thousands of possibilities—the theme of the ways in which other cultures saw the links between their myths and those of others, and in particular the ways in which the dominant culture of the West, European Christianity, looked at the mythologies of the world. Thus, in the essay entitled "Christian Judgments on the Analogies between Christianity and Pagan Mythology," the author explains how the early Christian fathers came to terms with the striking resemblances between their own religion and the pagan myths of the dying and rising god. My favorite argument is this one:

> In [Justin's] eyes, demons find a choice ground for their manipulations in particular pages of the Scriptures: in the Messianic prophecies, inspired visionaries mysteriously described the Savior long before his coming. So the demons, in order to deceive and mislead the human race, took the offensive and suggested to the poets who created myths that they give Zeus many sons and attribute monstrous adventures to them, in the hope that this would make the story of Christ appear to be a fable of the same sort, when it came.

From these humble beginnings, European theologians continued to lock horns with Roman deities, even as European peasants continued, blissfully unaware of these theological battles raging over their heads, to incorporate ancient myths into their living folk traditions. And, on a rather different track, European poets continued to draw upon, and reinterpret, the great Greek and Roman myths to express their individual geniuses. We should hardly be astonished to find that French folklore and literature hold a central place in these essays, but almost equal time is given to the great English Romantic traditions up to the present. And the volume concludes with an argument for the relevance of these myths in our own lives and thoughts today.

Wendy Doniger

Preface to the English Edition of the Complete Work

Yves Bonnefoy in his preface (which follows this preface) explains why he organized his book—and after all, this is his book—as he did. He had good reasons, and he is eloquent in their defense. But it remains for me to explain the ways in which the English edition differs from the French in more than the language in which it is expressed, since some of what M. Bonnefoy will say does not in fact apply to this edition at all, particularly in what concerns the arrangement of the articles.

M. Bonnefoy graciously if reluctantly allowed me to restructure his work. As he put it, "Of course I will miss the formula of the dictionary, for the reasons that I indicate in my preface (the rupture with all the apriority of classification, the possibility of surprising juxtapositions, in short, the irony), *but I absolutely do not oppose* your choice, which is in response to very good reasons, and which is better adapted to the English-speaking world in which your edition will appear. I therefore give you carte blanche, with the understanding that you will publish my preface as is. For it is a good idea to point out that the book was originally what I indicate in that preface—this will bring in a supplementary point for reflection."[1] On another occasion,[2] he remarked that there was another consideration (one that, I must confess, had not occurred to me) that had persuaded him to organize his original version of the book in what he termed "the random way," while we might be able to rearrange our version in "the more organized way": French students, he pointed out, have only limited access to open stacks in the French libraries (since there is not enough room to accommodate them) and few of the bookstores are quiet enough to read in. French students therefore have apparently not formed the habit of browsing—except in a dictionary.

Without denying the validity of his arguments, let me state my reasons for the reorganization. And in order to justify the changes, I shall first state my conception of the strengths and weaknesses of the French work itself.

The Strengths and Weaknesses of the French Edition

To begin with, even in its French form, with all the articles arranged alphabetically, it is not a dictionary, nor even an encyclopedia, nor a dispassionate fact-book even for those topics that it covers (and many major items are omitted). It is a quirky and idiosyncratic set of essays, long and short, by a particular group of mythologists, most of whom are French and all of whom participate in the French school of mythology in its broadest sense. The patent omissions and biases have prompted a certain amount of criticism leveled at the French edition,[3] criticism of imbalances, of inconsistencies (in the selection of topics, in the manner of their treatment, in the style, in the methodologies, etc.), and of the choice of illustrations, as well as more substantive criticisms of the interpretations.

Some of these criticisms are just; some are not. The arguments about what *is* there (what is said about the mythologies that are discussed) are interesting; the arguments about what is *not* there are, I think, beside the point. Many of the scholars involved in the project chose not to write about what other people (including certain reviewers) regarded as "central" or "basic" themes of the mythologies they treated; they wrote long essays on the subjects they cared about personally, and gave short shrift to subjects to which other scholars might have given pride of place. The reader who continues perversely to look for ways in which the glass is half empty rather than half full will notice immediately, for instance, that there is almost nothing about Islam or Judaism in the book. This is primarily because Yves Bonnefoy had originally intended to save this material for another volume, on the mythologies of monotheistic religions—a volume that has not yet materialized. It might be argued that this justification is disingenuous, for some of the very best material in the extant volume is on Christianity, which is by most standards monotheistic. But on closer inspection it is quite clear that while the book does treat the appropriation of classical mythology by Christianity, and the incorporation of "pagan mythologies" into what might be called "rural Catholicism," it rightly does not treat mainstream, monotheistic Christianity as a mythology. Moreover, to have dealt with the central traditions of Islam and Judaism in this way would certainly have been tantamount to a betrayal of what the adherents of those religions regard as their basic tenets. Yet this Jewish and Islamic silence is also in part accounted for by the simple fact that the authors who were assembled to prepare this book did not choose to write articles on these subjects. Similarly, the African articles deal almost exclusively (though hardly surprisingly) with Francophone Africa; yet these articles constitute superb paradigms for the study of other African mythologies. So, too, there are only two articles on Buddhism per se, and there is virtually nothing about Buddhism (or Islam, for that matter) in Southeast Asia (though there is a great deal of wonderful material about indigenous Southeast Asian religions, and those two articles on Buddhism are fascinating). On the other hand, there is extensive coverage of the Turks and Mongols, whose mythologies are relatively unknown to Western readers. This sort of imbalance might be regarded as a kind of mythological affirmative action.

This is, therefore, certainly not an encyclopedia. In a famous painting by the surrealist René Magritte, a caption in his neat script, under a painting of what is clearly a pipe, declares, "This is not a pipe." I would have liked to write on the cover of this book, "This is not a dictionary of mythologies." Rather like the ugly duckling that turned out to be a terrific swan, as a dictionary this book leaves much to be desired, but as a book of mythologies it is superb, indeed peerless. If it is not a dictionary, what *is* it, then? It is a most exciting (far more exciting than an encyclopedia ought to be) collection of essays on *some* aspects of *some* mythologies, written by a group of brilliant and philosophically complex French scholars. It is highly opinionated and original, and should inspire hot, not cold, reactions. Like all multiauthored works, it is a mixed bag; there is some jargon, some wild theorizing, some boring surveys, some overclever interpretation, and some of what I would regard as simple errors of fact, but there is also an overwhelming proportion of very sound and/or brilliant articles about mythology in general and about a number of mythologies in particular. This is not primarily a book, for instance, to consult for all the stories about Apollo; one has Robert Graves for that (though this is a far better book with which to begin to formulate some ideas about the meaning of Apollo). It is, however, a book in which to discover the delightful and useful fact that in the ritual celebration of the Brazilian god Omolu, who is of Yoruba origin but came to be syncretized with Saint Lazarus, people dance to a beat called "he kills someone and eats him." I was thrilled to come upon a hauntingly sad and beautiful Inuit myth about the cycle of transmigration of a mistreated woman, a myth that agrees, in astonishing detail, with certain complex myths of transmigration that I know from medieval Sanskrit philosophical texts. Other readers will undoubtedly stumble upon strange stories that are curiously familiar to them—stumble upon them quite by chance, just as Yves Bonnefoy intended them to do.

But if the selection is not as complete as a dictionary should ideally be, neither is it as arbitrary as a nondictionary can be. Most of the great mythological traditions are covered, and within those areas most of the important myths are treated. But this is not the point. What is treated very thoroughly indeed is the problem of *how to understand a mythology,* what questions to ask, what patterns to look for. More precisely, this is a book that demonstrates what happens when a combination of two particular methodologies, those of Georges Dumézil and Claude Lévi-Strauss, is applied to *any* mythology. It is, as its title claims (in English as in French), not so much a book about myths (sacred narratives) as a book about mythologies (whole systems of myths, or even systems of ideas about myths). It is that rare and wonderful fusion, a book about methodology that simultaneously puts the methodology to work and shows you just what it can and cannot do. It is a mythodology.

Many of these articles tell the reader how to study mythology in general and, more important, how to study each particular body of mythology, how to solve (or, more often, to approach) the particular problems that each mythology presents. Some tell the reader why it is not possible to write an article about that particular mythology at all (a consideration that does not, however, prevent the author from writing the article in which this assertion is made). The most hilarious example of this (I will leave the reader to decide which article it is) is almost an unconscious satire on the pusillanimity of scholars in certain fields; in it, the author goes on for pages and pages (it is one of the longest articles in the book) telling us, over and over, why there are insufficient data, why the data that we have are skewed, why the extant interpretations of the data are skewed, why all hypotheses and generalizations about the data are worthless, why in fact it is impossible to make any valid statement about the mythology at all. This is in its way a masterpiece, a kind of Zen nonarticle on a nonsubject, a surreal piece of nonscholarship worthy of Samuel Beckett. And yet even this article has its value here as a striking example of one particular methodology, one approach to the subject, that argues in great detail, and rightly, the obstacles that oppose any truly responsible survey of the subject.

But this is the exception, not the rule. The book teems with marvelous primary material, both myths and rituals (with which many myths are inextricably linked), using the materials and the methodological considerations to animate one another, the soul of data within the body of theory, and the soul of theory within the body of data. Sometimes the methodology is in the foreground, sometimes the data; usually they are in a fine balance. In the Greek and European sections, for instance, there are startling reinterpretations of well-known stories, or new emphases on previously overlooked details in well-known stories; many of the articles on the Greeks demonstrate the cutting edge of French structuralism. As Arthur Adkins has remarked, "The dictionary in its French version is a truly remarkable work. The Greek section in particular is quite unlike any other dictionary known to me. [It] for the most part presents the views of the Paris school, and the writers come out fighting. The Paris school is undoubtedly producing the most interesting work in the field at present. . . . [The work] represents more of a *parti pris* than the title 'Dictionary' may suggest."[4] The Vietnamese section, by contrast, abundantly documents a fascinating mythology that is virtually unknown to the English-speaking world, and presents it, moreover, in the context of an enlightened political awareness that is almost unprecedented in scholarly treatments of mythology anywhere (but that is also a notable virtue of the articles in this volume that deal with the Americas and Oceania).

If this is a book as much about method as it is about myths, what is the method? It is a masterpiece of what might be called trifunctional structuralism, a joint festschrift for Claude Lévi-Strauss and Georges Dumézil, a vision of the world of mythology seen through their eyes, *la vie en* Lévi-Strauss and Dumézil. To combine the methodologies of these two scholars is in itself a most extraordinary and fruitful achievement. If I may oversimplify both approaches for a moment, Lévi-Strauss's basic method, a variant of Hegelian dialectic, is to seek the intellectual or logical framework of the myth in binary oppositions that are mediated by a third term; the Dumézilian approach is to gloss the main figures of a myth in terms of three functions that have social referents: religion and government, defense, and material production. These two theories are in no way contradictory, especially if one resolves the potential conflict between Dumézilian tripartition and Lévi-Straussian bipolarization by taking into account the mediating third term and thus making Lévi-Strauss, too, tripartite. In this sense, both of them operate with triads, though very different triads. Furthermore, they complement rather than contradict one another because they focus on different levels (Lévi-Strauss on abstract intellectual concepts, Dumézil on social functions). Combined as they are in this volume, they are startlingly innovative.

Indeed, the beauty of the book is that it is not doctrinaire in its application of the theories of these two great scholars, but rather creative and imaginative. Dumézil's trifunctional analysis of Indo-European mythology is applied, quite loosely to be sure, even beyond the bounds of the Indo-European world (where it is, properly speaking, no longer trifunctional but tripartite), and a general way of thinking in terms of oppositions and inversions forms the armature of many analyses in which the name of Lévi-Strauss is not actually invoked. The search for tripartitions of both sorts is the driving force behind many of the analyses in this book.

The book is so very French that I thought seriously of putting the word "French" in the title of the English edition: *Mythologies According to the Contemporary French School*, or *The View from France*, or *Essays in the French Style*, *A French Collection*, *A Paris Collection*, *The French Connection*, and so forth. Yves Bonnefoy's remarks, in his preface, explaining why he chose primarily French scholars are delightfully, if unconsciously, Francophile. He has maintained elsewhere that the preponderance of French scholars was simply a natural outcome of choosing to organize the scholarship from the geographical center of the project, Paris, rather than to range over the world at random. But as anyone who has ever had the privilege of working at the Sorbonne will immediately realize, most French scholars think that the only people who know anything are other French scholars. In this instance, at least, they would be right: such is the hegemony of French scholarship in the field of mythology right now that a well-read American or British mythologist would probably draw on precisely these same "French" approaches.

This is one of the great values of the book: it represents, as few other works in any field do, the achievements of the *crème de la crème* of an entire generation of French scholarship in a large and important field. Yves Bonnefoy himself has remarked that he loves the book because it freezes a moment in time, in history, and in space; it is the embodiment of the beauty of the Ecole Pratique.

But in a way, the guiding spirit of the book is not just that of the twin gods, Dumézil and Lévi-Strauss. It is the spirit of Yves Bonnefoy himself. This is, after all, a book put together by a poet, not by a philologist. The editor of this nondictionary is also, let me hasten to say, a scholar of the first rank, but he is at heart a poet. The reader who keeps this in mind is more likely to get from the book what it has to give than the reader who picks it up hoping that it will be a kind of mythological Guinness book of records.

The Restructuring of the English Edition

We decided to restructure the book in order to minimize its weaknesses, emphasize its sometimes hidden strengths, and make it useful to the English-speaking reader in new ways. Its primary weakness is, as I have admitted, that it is not a true encyclopedia. If the English edition were arranged alphabetically, as the French edition is, readers might look for things and not find them and get mad, as some of the French reviewers did; and, on the other hand, readers might overlook a lot of strange and beautiful essays that no one would ever dream of looking up on purpose at all.

Bonnefoy in his preface explains why he wanted to use a dictionary format: to avoid all prearranged categories, to let the reader find things by chance, to allow accidental juxtapositions to give rise to unexpected ideas. But to some extent this argues for a false naïveté on the part of the reader and even, perhaps, on the part of the editor, for both of them *are looking for something*. In choosing the arbitrariness of alphabetical order, Bonnefoy is indeed shuffling the deck; but he does still have a deck, which, like all decks, is highly structured. The alphabetical shuffle conceals the true order but does not destroy it. Thus, for instance, all the articles on a certain subject are written by a single author, an expert on that subject. Clearly the articles were originally commissioned in this way, and they are still listed this way in the front of the French edition. And each author does have his methodological presuppositions, which the reader encounters every time he or she wanders (arbitrarily, accidentally) into that territory. Bonnefoy chose to conceal the patterns that he saw in the material in order to let readers discover them by chance; I have chosen to set out in the open the patterns that I see, and to let readers decide whether or not they want to follow those patterns. The difference lies in what sort of browsing is encouraged, cross-cultural (through the French edition's physical juxtaposition of the major articles on creation or on sacrifice) or intracultural (through the English edition's grouping of all the Siberian or Celtic articles).

Several of the translators, the Honigsblums in particular, arranged the work according to geographic areas or cultures, which made it easier to check the consistent use of technical terms. Gradually it occurred to us that this arrangement would also be useful to readers. Bonnefoy chose to mix the cultures together to encourage cross-cultural *aperçus*; I chose to separate out each culture to encourage consecutive reading in each tradition. (Another, related advantage of the present arrangement lies in the fact that this arrangement will make it possible in the future to publish sections of the work as individual books, making them available to specialists in particular cultural fields.) For the overall structure I decided to use a kind of geographical swing: beginning with Africa, then traveling up through the Near East, the ancient Mediterranean, the Indo-European world; remaining in place geographically but moving forward in time to later European culture, then back in time to South Asia; on in both space and time to Southeast Asia, East Asia, Inner Asia; across the Bering Strait to North America, South America; and finishing the journey paradisiacally in the South Pacific. Within each category of culture (Greek, Celtic, etc.), I have put the long, meditative, general essays first, and the shorter, more straightforward dictionary entries second. Several pathbreaking essays that are not tied to a particular culture, and that immediately establish the Dumézilian and structuralist stance of the book, form an introductory sequence.

Of course, since both the French and the English editions have detailed indexes, and the French edition has an outline listing the articles according to cultures, it comes down to a matter of emphasis, for in either edition the reader can find materials that are arranged alphabetically (both in the index and in the body of the work in the French edition, and in the index in the English edition) as well as materials that are grouped according to the culture (in the outline of the French edition, and in the body of the work in the English edition). In the restructured English edition, the reader can still use the index as Bonnefoy suggests the French index might be used, to find his or her favorite Naiad or Norse god, and also to find all the articles on, say, creation, or sacrifice, which cut across methodological lines. This is, after all, the same book, and can ultimately be used in all the same ways.

New problems arise out of this rearrangement, however, for some cultures don't really fit into any of the large categories—Turks and Mongols, Armenians and Albanians, Ossets and Georgians, Siberians, Malagasy, Maghreb—and so I had to settle for putting them where they seemed least out of place. Another disadvantage of my rearrangement is the fact that it exposes repetitions, necessary in an encyclopedia (where the author of any one article, who cannot assume that the reader will have read any other article, may therefore have to resupply a certain amount of basic material), but rather jarring in a book such as this (where the reader may well find it annoying to read the same story, or the same theory, almost verbatim in consecutive articles). A good example of this recycling is provided by the very first part, on West Africa, with its recurrent motifs of twinning and sexual mutilation; another occurs in the South Asian section, which pivots around the sacrificial pole and the avatar.

I decided not to cut any of these repetitions, however, for several reasons. First of all, I decided not to abridge or revise (a decision I will attempt to justify below). Second, some readers may only pick up isolated articles and will therefore need the basic information that also appears in other articles. And, finally, these repetitions demonstrate how certain scholars always think in terms of a limited number of particular myths, dragging them into whatever other subject they are supposed to be discussing. For scholars, like their native informants, do just what Lévi-Strauss says they do: they continually rework the same themes in a kind of academic bricolage, and no two variants are ever *quite* alike.

For the most part, I think the rearrangement is a positive move. For one thing, it makes it possible to *read* the book, instead of merely browsing in it or looking things up in it (though, as I have said, readers can still engage in both of these activities in the English edition). For another, it may prove more useful in this form not only to mythophiles and area specialists, but to people interested in French anthropology and philosophy.

The book is therefore *re*structured, because of course it was originally highly structured, ideologically if not organizationally. Its English title, *Mythologies,* to me echoes the wonderful books by Roland Barthes and William Butler Yeats, both with the same title, and further resonates with the French title of the great Lévi-Strauss trilogy, *Mythologiques* (treacherously translated in one English edition as *A Science of Mythology*). *Mythologies* has, finally, the advantage of being simultaneously an English and a French word, a last attempt at bilinguality before the Fall into the English version.

The English Translation

This edition was prepared "under my direction" in not nearly so important a sense as the original was "sous la direction de Yves Bonnefoy." Certain parallel procedures probably exacerbated rather than minimized the inevitable slip twixt French cup and English lip, and one of these was the employment of a team of English scholars to translate the text that was originally composed by a team of French scholars.

Gerald Honigsblum translated the entire second volume of the French edition, with the editorial assistance of Bonnie Birtwistle Honigsblum. The first volume was translated by a group of professional translators (Danielle Beauvais, Teresa Lavender Fagan, Louise Guiney, Louise Root, Michael Sells) and another group consisting of some of my students in the history of religions (Dorothy Figueira, Barry Friedman, Daniel Gold, John Leavitt, and David White). Their initials follow those of the original authors of the French articles. Bruce Sullivan did the bibliographies.

The translated articles were then checked for accuracy (in the transliteration of names, technical terms, and so forth) by specialists in each of the particular fields. Arthur Adkins did by far the most difficult task, working painstakingly and courageously through the enormous and often very tricky articles on the Greeks and Romans. Lawrence Sullivan vetted Africa and the Americas for us; Robert Ritner, Egypt; Walter Farber, Mesopotamia; Dennis Pardee, Semites; Richard Beal, Hittites; Laurie Patton, Celts; Ann Hoffman, Norse; Zbigniew Golab, Slavs; Frank Paul Bowman, Richard Luman, and David Tracy, early Christianity; Anthony Grafton, medieval and renaissance Europe; Françoise Meltzer, modern Europe; Charles Keyes, Southeast Asia; Anthony Yu and Jane Geaney, China; Gary Ebersole, Japan; Bruce Cummings, Korea; Matthew Kapstein and Per Kvaerne, Tibet; Robert Dankoff, Turks and Mongols. I did the South Asian and Indo-Iranian sections.

There are thus several levels at which inconsistencies—in style, in format (citations of texts, abbreviations), in transliteration, in ways of dealing with specific untranslatable concepts—could have slipped in: differences between the technical languages (not to say jargons) and the methodologies employed by the various academic guilds that regard themselves as the proprietors of each culture (anthropologists in Africa, Sanskritists in India, archaeologists in Sumer, and so forth); differences between the approaches of individual French authors, between our several translators, between our experts; and, over the long haul, differences in my own decisions at particular stages of the final supervision, and in the decisions of our copyeditors at the Press. We have tried to minimize the inconsistencies, but we know that many remain.

We left the bibliographies basically in their original form, with the following exceptions: in some cases we have substituted English editions for French editions, or extended the dates of continuing series, and in several cases we have added supplementary bibliographies (clearly designated as such and distinguished from the original French text). But many bibliographies and articles still cite the French editions of texts that have subsequently appeared in English.

We did not follow the usual practice of citing standard English translations of Greek or Latin or Sanskrit works that the French, naturally enough, cited in French. Instead, we translated the French translation of the classical text into English. At first glance this procedure may seem unwise, but we found it necessary because the French version of the classical text (and the subsequent analysis, which depended upon that version) often differed so dramatically from any extant English translation that the sense of the discussion would be totally obscured by the introduction of such a translation. We made an occasional exception, using a standard English translation where there were long quotations not directly analyzed in the French text, or where the available English translation was very close to what the French author had made of the original. (We were also, unfortunately, forced to translate back into English a few citations from English primary and secondary sources that time and other constraints prevented us from obtaining in the original form, and to retranslate several entire French articles that we know were originally written in English, because the English originals were for one reason or another no longer available to us.)

We decided to give Greek and Roman names, wherever possible, in the form used by the *Oxford Classical Dictionary,* which unfortunately is inherently inconsistent. The *OCD* has the advantage of avoiding pedantry by spelling most names in the way that people in English-speaking countries are used to seeing them. This means Latinizing most of the familiar Greek names (not, of course, substituting Roman names: thus we have Heracles, not Herakles, for the Greek god, but Hercules only for the Roman god), but not Latinizing the unfamiliar Greek names, and not Romanizing any of the Greek words when they are not names. All words, including proper names, that are printed in the Greek alphabet in the French edition have here been transliterated. No accents are indicated, and macrons are used not to distinguish long and short *a, i,* and *u,* but only on *e* and *o,* to distinguish epsilon from eta and omicron from omega.[5]

We also sought to standardize the transliteration of non-Greek names and terms, such as Gilgameš (vs. Gilgamesh) and Śiva (vs. Shiva), and we used the Pinyin system for most Chinese names.[6] But this general policy was sometimes overruled by the demands of a particular article. We strove for consistency within each article—using English titles for Greek works where the meaning was needed and traditional Latinized titles where it was not, full citations or abbreviations as appropriate, and so forth. Assuming, perhaps snobbishly, that anyone who couldn't read French couldn't read Greek or Latin, I have translated many titles and quotations that my sanguine French colleague, Yves Bonnefoy, had left in their classical splendor. Except for the titles of certain works generally known to English speakers in their original form, and terms that either are familiar to readers or have no English equivalent, I have translated everything, even terms like *polis* (for the most part), and *savoir faire,* and, sometimes, *par excellence.* I fear that this may insult some readers, but I suspect that it will be a welcome (and in any case probably invisible) crutch to *hoi polloi.*

Despite everything, the book remains idiosyncratic, but the idiosyncrasies are in large part a true reflection of the original French edition. In general, we have not *corrected* the original text at all, since, as I noted above, the work is valuable not only for the information and ideas that it contains but for being *what it is,* a moment frozen in time, a fly in amber, an incarnation of the École Pratique as it was in 1981, warts and all. The warts include matters of style and politics, such as sexist and occasionally racist language in the original text. These problems were sometimes ameliorated and sometimes exacerbated by the transition from French to English. Thus, to ameliorate, we often chose to translate *homme* as "human" rather than "man"; but the English "savage" (often more apt than "wild" or "primitive") exacerbates the negative connotations of *sauvage,* which the French often use in a positive sense.

Our respect for the integrity of the French text made us resist the temptation to correct what we regarded as errors in that text. (Of course, we made our own errors, and unfortunately the reader who does not have the French edition will not know, if he or she finds a mistake, which side of the Atlantic it originated on.) We certainly made no attempt to correct such major problems as wrongheaded (in my opinion) opinions, nor to decipher the impenetrable semioticisms in one or two articles or to excise the unreadable lists in others. At the other end of the spectrum, however, we did correct typographic errors and a few outright howlers (such as a reference to the *Iliad* when the *Odyssey* was clearly intended). It was trickier to decide what to do about the middle ground: infelicities of expression, repetitions, and so forth. Of course we tried to clarify unclear thoughts, though we certainly did not always succeed. But for the most part, we respected our French colleagues' right to live with their own sins.

At first we made no attempt to smooth out the English, striving only to make the French thought accessible in English, leaving it awkward when it was awkward. We did try, however, to say well in English what was well said in French. In the end, however, our collective gorge rising again and again in response to such massive proportions of translatorese and the fatal attraction of the *cliché juste,* we did try to relax the translation a bit.

By and large, I opted for fidelity over beauty. This is rather a shame, for the original French text is, on the whole, very beautiful. Not for the first time I take comfort in Claude Lévi-Strauss's famous dictum that, whereas poetry may be lost in translation, "the mythical value of myth remains preserved through the worst translation."[7] I fear that we have lost much of Yves Bonnefoy's poetry; I can only hope that we have found, for the English reader, most of Yves Bonnefoy's mythology.

Wendy Doniger

NOTES

1. Yves Bonnefoy, personal communication, 28 June 1984.
2. Notes on a meeting with Yves Bonnefoy, 6 June 1988.
3. As, for example, by Robert Turcan, in "Mythologies et religions: Notes Critiques, à propos du *Dictionnaire des Mythologies . . . ,*" in *Revue de l'Histoire des Religions* 200, no. 2 (April–June 1983): 189–98.
4. Arthur Adkins, personal communication, 2 March 1988.
5. Our attempt to follow, consistently, the above rule resulted in the following apparent inconsistencies. A distinction is made between the treatment of two forms of the same word when it is used both as a name and as a noun: thus we have Eros (the god) and *erōs* (the emotion), Cyclops (plural: Cyclopes) for the individual and *kuklops* for the class of creature. Exceptions to the general Latinization occur in certain familiar spellings particularly with regard to *clk* (Clytemnestra, following the regular policy, but Kronos, following general usage); to *-osl-us* (Pontus, following the rule, but Helios, following general usage); and to certain plurals (Kronides, but Oceanids and Atreidae; Melissae, but Moirai). In general, upsilon is transliterated as *y* in Latinized names, such as Polyphemus, but as *u* in nouns, such as *polumētis.* And so forth.
6. For the Yoruba names, we chose to follow the French edition in using a simplified transliteration, for the system that is technically, and politically, correct is extremely cumbersome and incompatible with the methods used in other parts of the work.
7. Claude Lévi-Strauss, *Structural Anthropology* (New York 1963), 210.

Preface to the French Edition of the Complete Work

I

A few words of introduction, not in justification of the enterprise, but in order to clarify certain of its intentions and various points of method.

One of our primary convictions was of the need to adopt the dictionary format. Encyclopedias, invariably too lengthy to be read in a single sitting, are usually approached through the index, thereby functioning like dictionaries but with certain disadvantages that dictionaries do not have. For one thing, readers of encyclopedias are deprived of those sudden juxtapositions that alphabetical order can effect between two topics that may have something in common but occur in different contexts: chance encounters from which fresh insights can emerge. And for another thing, an encyclopedia, no matter how rationally intended the order of its contents, cannot but reflect the preconceptions of the time when it was written; it thus rapidly becomes dated and, even, from the very moment of its conception, imposes certain constraints on its readers. We have only to think of the treatises of the not very distant past and their way of drawing distinctions between the Mediterranean world and what is loosely referred to as the Orient, as if western Europeans lived at the center of the world! Progress has been made in this respect, but potentially dangerous prejudices are undeniably still at work in our thinking today. "Any classification of religions . . . will always in some way be factitious or one-sided; none is susceptible to proof," wrote Henri-Charles Puech.[1] Only alphabetical order, arbitrary by definition, can eliminate hidden dogmatism or prevent the consolidation of an error as yet unperceived as such.

Furthermore, and as a corollary to its primary task of rational organization, an encyclopedia also tends toward a kind of unity—if not homogeneity—of discourse; and because any work of this kind attempts to say the most in the least possible number of pages, there will be—in order to achieve coherent exposition of the most important material—an attenuation of what, in a monograph, would remain undiminished or would even be enhanced: diversity of viewpoint, the clash of ideas and methods, to say nothing of the irreconcilability of different scholars' feelings, aspirations, and temperaments. Even when there is consensus on some point, we cannot believe that this disparity, the nutrient on which all scholarship thrives, will have lost its seminal value. The advantage of a dictionary, which allows free rein to a greater number of authors, and which facilitates the juxtaposition of both detailed analysis and broad synthesis, is that it can more comfortably, or more immediately, accommodate a living science whose very contradictions and even lapses into confusion serve as a lesson that can inspire, and on which we can reflect. We might say that a dictionary can aspire to a totalization which, because it is still only potential, is less subject to the perils of dogmatic deviation. Within a dictionary's open-ended structure, every aspect of scientific research—classification or comparison, hypothesis or explanation, discovery of a law or conjecture as to its significance—will be allowed to reveal its specificity and find its own level. We may, therefore, regard the dictionary format as the most adequate expression of today's scholarship, which is suspicious of all systems, instinctively realizing the complexity and pluralities inherent in its objects of study as well as the interaction between these objects and its own methods.

There is, in short, a kind of spirit or "genius" in what might simply appear to be the way the subject matter is arranged; and in direct consequence of this conception came the following decision: that in making the choices rendered necessary by the limited space, preference would be given to the process of discovery rather than to what has already been discovered; to new challenges, new departures, and new divergences rather than to the syntheses of the past, even those still found acceptable today. In deciding what to include in the dictionary, our preference has been, in other words, for new problems rather than old (and hence overfamiliar) solutions, even major ones. *Research,* the only endeavor, today, to which we habitually apply the word "pure," has been our true objective. In this book the reader will find what are at this very moment the pivotal points being debated in regard to this or that myth or religious festival, and not a mere enumeration—the comprehensiveness of which would in any case be difficult to establish—of points already settled in the past. And let us remark in passing that, by so doing, we are merely making public, for the sake of a more general reflection, a practice that has already proved itself in certain scientific circles, but only to a privileged few. The introduction to the *Annuaire* of the École des Hautes Études (section V, religions), states that the teaching dispensed by the professors of this institution is a science "in process" and that "those responsible for teaching others will find no better way to exercise their function as the initiating and motivating force behind their students' research than by sharing . . . the results of their own, even if this means admitting to failures." In this dictionary we have not always been quite so radical as these admirable words advise, but we, too, have attempted not to "transmit what is already known, but to demonstrate as concretely as possible how knowledge is acquired, and how it grows."[2]

It should therefore come as no surprise to the reader that some of the assignments normally charged to works on mythology were eliminated from our project at the outset, notably those detailed accounts of demigods, nymphs, demons, genies, and heroes that occupy the forefront of less recent or more conventional studies. Insofar as these figures do not appear prominently among those chosen by contemporary scholars for reevaluation, merely to have listed them and added a few perfunctory remarks about each one—which, as there are thousands of them, is the best we could have done—would have been once again, and once too often, to present only the chaff instead of getting at the grain deep within, to rethrash the oversimplifications of yesteryear with an outward show of scientific objectivity. Apart from a few minor protagonists of Greek myth—retained because of their artistic or literary importance, through centuries of survival or revival or nostalgia for the gods of antiquity—we have chosen to deal, rather, with the innumerable minor characters in the drama of creation and the cosmos within the context of broader-based articles concerned primarily with *structures:* creation, cosmos, sacrifice, the divinity of the waters, divine animals or ancestors, etc.—the structures that modern science has taught us better to discern beneath the apparent disorder of myths. For only through these more active concepts, these more all-encompassing frameworks, can we realize the ultimate meaning of something that has always been only an element in the symbolic totality arising from man's desire to know; only in this way will we be able to perceive the differences, similarities, resonances, and, what is more, the perhaps hidden truth, the quality of mystery, even the power to terrify, that underlies figures who became, in the mirror of classical paintings or in the *Mythologies* of our grandparents, elegant Marsyas or lovable Flora. The reader will, however, be able to find the information that our articles do dispense about many of these tiny sparks from the larger fire, by referring to the index, where many names that he may have regretted not finding more prominently displayed in the columns of the text have been assembled.

We have, on the other hand, been generous in allotting space—and sometimes a great deal of space—to what at first glance might appear to be an excessively specific or technical development on a minor point in a remote religion, or an almost unknown tribe. We have done so because some important aspect of the most recent research in the field is thereby revealed, is therein at work, and the essay is therefore being offered, indirectly, as a concrete example of today's practical methods. In a situation of overwhelming possibility, the guiding principle presiding over the choices we did in fact make was consistently to prefer the illuminating example over the supposedly exhaustive enumeration; except on those occasions when a truly extensive, minutely scrupulous coverage of a field narrow enough to be included in the book in its entirety could also be made to serve as one of our major exemplary cases. This dictionary is in large measure a *network of examples,* each with some bearing on a particular level or category of religious experience or scientific method; if we have included a study of sacrifice in a religion in which sacrifice is especially important, we have deliberately omitted an article on sacrifice for another region of the world in which, by the same token, animals or the presence of the dead have been selected from a mythic narrative in which they are felt to be essential. The advantage of this principle is that it allows us to plumb the depths, which is one way to achieve universality and thus to speak of everything, despite the occasional appearance of superficiality. The reader will note that our articles are seldom very short; allowing for the stylistic terseness characteristic of dictionaries, we strove for an average length that would permit us to publish what are actually brief monographs; I am pleased to note that the present enterprise has served as the occasion for much research, some of it completely new, either in subject matter or in approach. The reader will thus be a witness to the creative process in action.

And if he should be annoyed because he cannot find in our table of contents or even our index some name or subject to which several lines have been devoted in the *Oxford Classical Dictionary* or the *Real-Encyclopädie,* he should also bear in mind the intellectual character of our endeavor, and should listen in the depths of our pages for the stirrings of research in process, that catalyst through which, from the womb of needs as yet unsatisfied, hypotheses as yet unproved, oppositions and even conflicts, are born the research projects, innovations, and ideas that tomorrow will provide the material for new articles in the still open dictionary and, later, for a whole new volume. Any dictionary worthy of the name must affirm, with real fervor, that it will continue thus; that is, that it will turn into a serial appearing twelve times a century, an institution whose past becomes future, a rallying ground that will help keep a discipline alive.

II

What is this discipline, exactly, in our own case? And how did we define or, rather, how were we able to recognize the subjects appropriate to our dictionary?

It is entitled *Dictionary of Mythologies and Religions in Traditional Societies and in the Ancient World*—thus, apparently, introducing two distinct subjects. What really is the subject, and what, in terms of specific content, will the reader find in the book?

Let us state at the outset that what our French publisher wanted was a "Dictionary of Mythologies," explanation enough in itself, because it refers to a specific area and one abundantly rich in problems of great scientific interest today. To quote again from section V of the *Annuaire:* the current tendency for the science of religion to assume a central place in anthropological studies is due to "the increasing importance being accorded to 'myth' for the interpretation and comprehension of the human phenomenon. On this point, the most diametrically opposed schools of contemporary thought are undivided. Religious myths have attained highest priority as objects of study by the most disparate scientific disciplines and schools of philosophy, whether they are regarded as images or projections of a system of communications among men; as manifestations of archetypes of the psyche; or as the special objects of a phenomenology of human consciousness . . ."[3] Certainly we no longer believe, as did the Socrates of Plato's *Phaedrus,* that there is no need to study myth because the important thing is to know ourselves—rather the reverse. Mythology appears to us ever more clearly as one of the great aspects of our relationship with ourselves, as well as being a conception of the world and the terrestrial environment that has been undoubtedly useful; we therefore ought to draw up a balance sheet—however provisional—of the discoveries made by the present century in the various chapters of man's reflection on myth. That there is still not complete agreement among scholars as to how myth should be defined matters little; that the problem of definition may even be premature also matters little, precisely because the plurality inherent in the enterprise of a dictionary as defined above actually makes the juxtaposition of contradictory propositions seem natural and allows them to be compared with one another. Neither in this introduction nor in the body of the book, where the actual choices have been made, will the reader find a definition of myth decreed as law, as if the die were cast. Our only methodological limitation, one that in our view safeguards the rights both of the study of myths as archetypes and of the methods appropriate to myths approached as systems of communication, is to apprehend myth on the level of collective representations, where, as one of our contributors writes, myth is "the form in which the essential truths of a particular society are articulated and communicated." Despite what may be the apparent freedom of the narrative, our task must be to seek within it a body of collective knowledge in contradistinction to the ephemeral creations of the individual consciousness, no matter how impressive these may be in great novels or poems. Apart from a few fleeting insights, included solely that we might better understand and recognize the limitations we have set for ourselves, there are in our dictionary none of the "personal myths" that come from art and the free play of imagination and that perhaps belong to a dialectic entirely different from those that unite human beings under the sign of their communications in the real world, of their confrontation with real necessities, and that are accompanied and made possible by rituals and beliefs. We have similarly omitted from the book what are sometimes referred to as "modern myths," representations that are circulated by popular literature or the media, myths that do indeed touch many spirits but that differ from the great majority of mythic narratives in that they are not so much the expressions of a society as they are the expressions of a yearning for a different society, or of the fear of forces that the structures of our societies have not integrated. In our view, the place for the study of these is, rather, in a dictionary devoted to the basic categories of religious experience as such, in particular, transcendence, eschatology, and salvation.

In short, the myths in this book have been culled only from the mouths of societies or groups. This does not indicate a refusal to study the connection between myth and the deep structures of the human psyche; it merely delimits, in order to avoid any confusion, an object of thought that could then be connected with others, or analyzed in other ways than has been done here. The one form of individual creativity we did consider appropriate to include, at least through a few major examples, is the reflection of those who, although they may have relied on highly subjective spiritual or philosophical preconceptions, nevertheless attempted—as did Plato, for example, or Cicero—to understand myths as society produces them or assumes them. Objective as contemporary scholarship aspires to be, there are a few preconceptions similar to theirs still at work today, perhaps; so who can tell if in these ancient interpretations of myth there is not some lesson that could be of use to future investigations either of myth as the expression of social relationships, or of mythological figures as spearheads cutting through local custom and belief toward more universal spiritual forms?

But assuming nothing about the essence or function of myth except its relationship to a society does not necessarily mean that erecting the boundaries for a dictionary of mythologies presents no further problems. For no myth exists in isolation; none is a narrative drawing only on itself for its terms and its conventions. We still had to decide what, precisely, from a given society or culture, and from among all its conscious or unconscious communal acts, ought to be included in the book so that none of the discussion or information would be elliptical or too allusive. In other words, what complementary studies must be integrated into a dictionary of mythologies to ensure that the overall statement that it makes will not be hobbled, giving only an impoverished and therefore dangerous idea of the field?

Here is where we can justify the ambiguous precision of our title, in which the word "religion" appears next to the word "mythology." Proceeding empirically, at no great philosophical risk, we may hold as evident that in every human society mythical narrative and religious practice are closely related; and thus, that everywhere, or almost everywhere, it is the historian or analyst of religions who also studies mythologies. As a corollary to this, surely we can affirm that it makes little sense to classify and analyze myths without reference to those aspects of religion that have determined them and will certainly clarify them. And, further, if we do so, in order to make room for this additional material we should also be prepared to sacrifice some of the data about myths properly speaking: what is lost in comprehensiveness will largely be regained in the comprehension of the place and the meaning of myth. This book deals with religions as well as with myths; or, rather, it stands at the intersection where the two roads meet—always with the proviso, however, that each of our contributors has been left free to decide for himself how to apportion the two concerns in practice, taking account of the vastly different forms that the same scientific goal can assume in areas as diverse as Indonesia, for example—that huge complex of societies, languages, and religious influences, where current research is still at the stage of amassing data that must subsequently be put in order—or Vedic India, or Greece, which we know plenty about.

We do not mean that all things religious are therefore in a relationship of complicity, or even of continuity, with the production of myths and the sometimes evanescent, sometimes enduring, figures of myth; there is a dividing point at which one must take sides; the consequences are bound to be great and it is important to justify them. It may come as a surprise to the reader that the religions of Sumeria, Egypt, and Persia are included in the book, while Judaism, Christianity, and Islam are not; that the divinities—if that is the right word—of Buddhism are included, but that no reference is made to the spiritual essence of this major religious experience as it occurs in China, Japan, or elsewhere. It may also cause surprise that, more specifically, the studies of the religions which have been included do not mention what has often made them forms of transcendental experience, mysteries, quests for the Absolute, arenas of soteriological ambition for the yearnings or the nostalgia of individuals or of sects. This is because, during such phases in a religion's development, the religious principle—in its essence, perhaps, a contradictory one—turns against the mythic narrative by which it is at other times nourished. When this happens, the spirit is no longer content to rest at the level of the gods but aspires to a transcendence that it senses as amounting to something more than the representations of it provided by myth; it rejects myth or creates in place of it a gnostic system to uncover its secret meaning. And the effort thus made by the religious spirit to reach the divine within mythical manifestations that it regards as paradoxical or imperfect consequently determines that this aspect of the religious experience has no place in a dictionary of myth and of the rituals and beliefs associated with myth. We have not taken into consideration here the aspect of religion that fights the gods, the mediating powers, that holds them to be paganisms; this aspect in itself is so complex and so rich that it would take another book at least the size of this one to do it justice. The reader will therefore not find among the religions introduced in this volume those whose essential vocation is—let us try to be succinct—the direct experience of transcendent divinity; nor those which tend to have a universal message, addressed to all people everywhere, no matter what their culture or where they live; not even those religions whose moorings in the history of a specific society or a specific people have enabled them, through a founder, a theophany, a prophet, or their reform of a previous paganism, to attach to themselves legends or histories closely resembling myths. In practice, we have excluded from this book the great religions of a Word, a Promise; and especially the mystery religions, Judaism, Christianity, Islam, Gnosticism, Taoism, and the legacies of the Buddha. The one exception to this rule consists of certain incursions justified by the "pagan" nature of some of their minor aspects, such as the cult of the saints in our own churches or the gods and demons of Buddhism.

Let us hope that these religions will one day form the subject of another dictionary, one dealing, as it were, with divinity, as opposed to gods; with universal theologies and experiences of unity, in contrast to the rivulets of myths, rituals, and holy places. Upon further reflection, we ought also to reserve for another volume certain problems of boundaries, such as the way in which past and present evangelistic missionaries have regarded the myths of societies they set out to convert, not without repercussions on Christian doctrine; or—to come closer to home—the way in which at certain moments Christianity itself has played the role of a myth: a myth of truth, or progress, even at the price of relinquishing a good part of its aptitude for genuine communion. As one of our authors writes, myths are never recognized for what they are except when they belong to others; it is therefore our duty to apply to our own behavior as people of the Western world the same methods that our science reserved only yesterday for so-called primitive societies. But a great religious experience must first be described before we can go beyond it and begin the task of distinguishing its ambiguities.

And yet certain religions which might be said to represent a quest for the Absolute as obvious as any other—those of India, for instance, and perhaps also of Egypt—have been included; but this is because in their search for unity they involve myth in a very intimate, almost ultimate, manner, if only in an initial stage and as one more form of illusion. We have not used the word "polytheism" to designate the religions whose myths are dealt with in this dictionary, despite its apparent reference to the differentiation, the polymorphy, of the divine. For although there are resolutely polytheistic religions, such as those of ancient Greece or Rome, in other cultures and other lands there are religions based on more complex intuitions, in which the multiplicity of representations at once clear-cut and diffuse exist in a sort of breathing of the spirit that seems to refute our own exaggerated distinctions between entity and nonentity, between the one and the many. Might we not, perhaps, call these religions "poetic" or "figurative," since an artist knows well the imaginary nature of the figures that, nevertheless, alone can express, in the artist's vision, the essential reality? In any case, such religions belong in this dictionary by virtue of their massive and continuing recourse to the logic of myth.

III

And now for a few words of clarification concerning the geographical and historical area covered by our enterprise. Or rather—since this dictionary by definition covers all terrestrial space and every era of terrestrial history—concerning the relative proportions we decided upon for the various parts of our inquiry.

First, one remark that may be useful: if we have designated and defined myth in the context of an inquiry that by rights extends to the farthermost regions of the globe, this in no way means that we wish to affirm, by emphasizing the most powerful of these mythologies—whose links with the languages in which they are expressed are obviously close—that there is any uniformity on earth in this mode of consciousness. As has frequently been pointed out, the word *myth* itself comes from the Greek, and the concept that we project into this word, although adjusted to accommodate overlappings and overflowings, also has a logic, a coherence, and still bears the mark of its origin; there is therefore no foundation for believing that what some other ethnic group has experienced under the forms that we call myth corresponds to the same laws with which we are familiar. Perhaps there are societies that do not tend to integrate their myths into some meaningful whole but leave them as fragments that flare up and then are extinguished without, in passing, casting any light on what we ourselves are tempted to look for or to find everywhere: the outline, if only a rough one, of the vault of a universe. If in these cases we can often see nothing but an incoherent babble opening the way to higher forms of consciousness, might it not also be possible for us to sense in them an entirely different mode of consciousness, one in which the discontinuous, the partial, the forever incomplete would themselves be perceived as the very being of human meaning? Could we not see them as an ontology of the superficiality of our inscription on the world—an ontology that the planet's recent history would tend rather to confirm than to deny—somewhere beyond the ruin of our own aspirations? The representation of the divine can obey laws as diverse as those of artistic representation, which extends from the controlled irrationality of a Poussin, who was, in fact, an heir to the Greeks, to the fugitive traces on the gray wall of some works of art of our time.

This should remind us if need be that a dictionary like ours, if it is to fulfill its task of describing the variety of mythologies, must supplement its descriptions of the religious data with additional material on the cultures, mental structures, languages, and functionings of the social collectivity. To the extent that myth is one of the forms of asking questions about mystery, it represents a relationship between the human consciousness—in its cognitive functions, its praxis, its historical memory, or its exploration of the outside environment—and the culture as a whole. Recent research has clearly demonstrated that myth's manifest complexity makes it one of the most useful tools for an archaeology of the imagination, of philosophy, or of science. It was therefore essential to the present undertaking that myth appear not only as an act of speech about the divine, but as a text in which the divine is infinitely embedded in signifiers; and it is the task of the ethnologist, the sociologist, and the linguist to decipher and analyze these signifiers. A background in the social sciences is much more than an imperative for this book; it is its natural and inevitable locus, and one from which many of our contributors, either explicitly or implicitly, have strayed but little. But this consideration even further restricts the space available for the purely mythological material within the finite number of pages at our disposal. When the whole world demands to be heard, the time for each part to speak must be allotted sparingly.

How to mitigate this disadvantage? It would have been tempting to reverse ethnocentric custom and to eliminate at a stroke every trace of exclusiveness, every hierarchy; to relinquish forever the specious charm of the old Greco-Roman monopoly, and its belated acceptance of Egypt and the Near East; and thus to have offered to each separate part of the world an equal number of pages. But rational and fair as this was in principle, we knew that in practice it could never be other than a utopian ideal, at least for the foreseeable future. The first and major reason is that the analysis of myths that is most familiar to us is the work of scholars who write or read in French, English, Italian, German, and more rarely in other languages, still mostly Western ones. With all of its virtues and all of its limitations, this linguistic given constitutes an intangible fact that we must first examine before our own consciousness can be raised, before it can be made to apprehend from within how to circumscribe its own difference so as to be more receptive to categories other than its own. If the mythology of Africa or of ancient Japan is an object of study for our language, the myths and divinities of Greece and Rome, not to mention those of the Celtic and Germanic worlds, survive through hidden symbolisms, overt conditionings, artistic or philosophical references, even—and above all—through concepts, in the most intimate being of mythology, that operate on the very level on which our language apprehends and analyzes the object. And these components, all too familiar but never sufficiently explored, never sufficiently distanced, therefore demand an almost excessive attention if we in the West are ever to achieve a valid understanding of the other civilizations of the world.

This invaluable opportunity to psychoanalyze our methods, we felt, should not be sacrificed by unduly abbreviating that portion of the book dealing with our own origins; so, an important place, even though in a most attenuated manner, should once again be given to the cults and mythologies of more or less classical antiquity and to their later effects on the religious, artistic, and intellectual life of Europe, of which we, of course, are a product. And because for other parts of the world we have also had to take into account the very variable degree of progress in the field, so that it would have been unfortunate to weigh each contribution equally, we have resigned ourselves without compunction to being biased in our allocation of space, believing that to define where we stand does not—or at least so we may hope—imply a valorization of what lies nearest to us or any dogmatism. We have reserved almost half the work for the Mediterranean world, the Near and Far East, and for the historical relations between their mythologies and the European consciousness, as demonstrated by such phenomena as the survival of the classical gods or the fascination with Egypt after the Italian Renaissance. The other half of the book is for the rest of the world, here again, however, taking into account the actual importance that one region or another may have today assumed in a field that naturally is not static and that will have fresh insights to contribute to future supplements to the present volume. It is unfortunately only too true that the vast societies of Africa and Asia have in our columns once again been given less space than the tiny population of Greece. But a particular problem concerning a particular, vanishing society in Vietnam has, on the other hand, merited more of our attention than many perhaps expected aspects of our classical world. We can only hope that the reader will not find our distribution of the materials too misinformed.

IV

Here now is some practical information to help the reader find his way through the labyrinth of the dictionary. [The rearrangement of articles in the English-language edition obviates the problems discussed in this paragraph, which we have therefore abridged.] Certain religions or cultures to which, regretfully, we could only allot a few pages are represented by a single article that can easily be found under the name of the country or geographical area, thus, *Albania* or *Crete*. Generally speaking, however, our contributors had more space at their disposal and were able to address various questions that they considered not only basic but exemplary, in articles spread throughout the book. A list of the names of all the authors, in alphabetical order of their initials, allows the reader to go from the initials at the end of each article to the complete name of the author.

This same list also indicates the academic affiliations of the hundred or so scholars who were willing to contribute to the dictionary; it will be noted that most of them teach at the Collège de France, the École Pratique des Hautes Études, or in French universities. Why this preference for the French, in a century when intellectual exchange is so abundant, between some countries at least, and in which we see so many publications—of, for example, papers delivered at colloquia—that mix together in their abstracts the names of professors from Tübingen or Yale with those from Tokyo or Nairobi? It may at once be pointed out that contributions to this type of publication are usually printed in the language in which the original paper was delivered, obviously requiring of the reader that he be made aware of the linguistic and conceptual apparatus presiding at their conception. French scholars know that, in dealing with ideas originally conceived in German, or in English, they must undertake the task of recognizing schools of thought, cultural or religious conditionings or customs, the influence exerted by the words themselves—since every language has its own semantic nodes, as complex as they are uncompromising; and they also know this task may take a long time, demanding further reading or travel abroad. They further understand that it is only in connection with these vast extratextual areas that they will be able to identify and appreciate the meaning of the text itself. It is of course always possible to translate, and to read a translation. But we must not forget that it takes more than a mere rendering of sentences into a new language for these backgrounds to be revealed and for the underlying meaning to be made clear.

This is precisely the risk that prevails when an enterprise such as ours is opened to authors who think and write in different languages—which would have to be many in number for all the major trends in international scholarship to be represented as they deserve. We believed that scholars who thus had to express themselves through translation would find their work deprived of a part of its significance at the very moment when we would seem to be listening to it. Moreover, the converse is also true: problems can best be differentiated, and even antagonistic methods best be revealed, through the widest possible deployment of the unity and diversity—the cluster of potentialities simultaneously contiguous and concurrent—that is embodied in a single language at a precise moment in its history. We therefore deemed it preferable to call primarily on French scholars and, since those responding to our call number among the most eminent and the most representative, thus to offer to the reader, as an adjunct to our panorama of mythologies and religions, a matching panorama of the contemporary French schools of history, sociology, and religious studies, all of which are of the first rank and deserve to be known as such. To sum up: while a few of the original contributions to the *Dictionary of Mythologies* were translated from languages other than French, for the most part the material can be viewed as a whole, produced by a single society—an ever evolving one, to be sure, and one not inattentive to other cultures—at a crucial juncture in the development of a scientific discipline that is still young. This dictionary is French, the expression of a group of scholars all working within reach of one another, as sensitive to their areas of disagreement as they are gratified by their points of convergence. It is our hope that, if it should be translated, the translator will find it vast enough to allow for the emergence, here and there within its mass, of the unstated concept of implied bias not readily discernible in briefer texts; and that these underlying elements will be revealed in a translation offering the reader, and serving as the basis for future debate, an intellectual effort seen whole: not just the visible tip of the iceberg, but its hidden, submerged bulk as well.

V

Such were the guiding principles determining how our work should be organized. It is only proper to add, however, that despite the great trust which it was the present editor's pleasure to encounter in his authors—who sometimes produced material for him equivalent in volume to a small book—the above principles are primarily the expression of his own concept of what scholarship is, and what it is that scholars are attempting to do. Only he can be held directly responsible for them.

I have just used the word "trust." Going back to the source from which all trust springs, however, I should rather have said "generosity," because this word, glossing "trust," better characterizes both the reception that I as editor was given by specialists in their fields who could so easily have refused to credit any but one of their own, and the quality of their contributions, which to me seems patent. I see this now that the enterprise has been achieved. Most of these scholars, all of them with many tasks competing for their time, have been with our project from the beginning, when, responding to my appeal, they consented to represent their respective disciplines in a dictionary that was still just an idea—an idea to which they themselves had to give meaning. Most of them also agreed to oversee the illustration of their articles, thereby enriching the text with a variety of often rare, sometimes previously unpublished, documents directly relevant to the text. Whenever minor vicissitudes befell the project thereafter, decisions were always made in a spirit of mutual understanding and cooperation. I am extremely grateful to all the authors of this book, and to those eminent individuals who were kind enough to advise me when initial decisions had to be made. Indeed, my only great regret is that I am unable to express this gratitude today to two men who are no longer with us, two men who possessed consummate wisdom, foresight, and discipline, and whose example will stand as an enduring one. Historian Eugène Vinaver's masterly command of Arthurian Romance, a borderline topic standing between myth and literature, is well known. So, too, is Pierre Clastres's intense involvement with the Indian civilizations of South America; the articles by him that we are publishing here were the last pages he ever wrote.

I now have the pleasure of thanking Henri Flammarion and Charles-Henri Flammarion, who wanted this dictionary to exist, and who showed such keen interest in the questions with which it deals. My thanks also to those who transformed typescripts, photographs, and graphics into the reality of the present book. First on the list of these is Francis Bouvet, a man attached to the project from the moment of its inception and now, regrettably, only a memory, but a cherished one. My thanks to Adam Biro, who took over the same functions and brought to them the same understanding and the same invaluable support. Thanks to Claire Lagarde, who from start to finish, and with intuitive devotion and unfailing good humor, sent out requests, acknowledged receipts, sent out requests again, read, filed, saved, and expedited contracts, typescripts, documents, and proofs, even at times when her other duties were pressing. And, finally, thanks to Pierre Deligny, who, simply because he was asked, since we had no legitimate claim to his assistance, unhesitatingly accepted in his own name as well as in that of Denise Deligny and Danielle Bornazzini the crushing responsibility for correcting three successive sets of proofs, with their intricate web of unfamiliar names, cross-references, rearrangements, accent marks, and emendations, and who brought the job to a successful conclusion, with Mesdames Deligny and Bornazzini specifically undertaking responsibility for compiling the index. Yes, to these other authors of the *Dictionary of Mythologies*, many thanks, in the name of the authors of the text.

Yves Bonnefoy/l.g.

NOTES

1. Preface, *Histoire des religions*, vol. 1 (Paris 1970) (Encyclopédie de la Pléiade).
2. *Annuaire* of the École des Hautes Études, Paris, vol. 83, no. 1 (1975–76), p. 4.
3. Ibid., p. 3.

Contributors

A.L.-G André LEROI-GOURHAN, professor, Collège de France.

B.B. Bernard BÖSCHENSTEIN, professeur ordinaire, University of Geneva.

C.Me. Claude METTRA, producer, France-Culture.

E.P. Evelyne PATLAGEAN, professor, University of Paris X.

E.V. Eugène VINAVER, professor, Manchester University.

F.C. Françoise COZANNET, cultural attachée, Ministère de la Recherche et de la Technologie.

F.Fl. François FLAHAULT, chargé de recherche, Centre nationale de la recherche scientifique.

F.S. François SECRET, directeur d'études, École pratique des hautes études, Ve section (sciences religieuses).

J.C. Jeannie CARLIER, chef de travaux, École des hautes études en sciences sociales.

J.-C.S. Jean-Claude SCHMITT, maître assistant, École des hautes études en sciences sociales.

J.E.J. John E. JACKSON, professor of French literature, University of Bern.

J.M. Jean MOLINO, professeur ordinaire, University of Lausanne.

J.P. Jean PÉPIN, directeur de recherche, Centre national de la recherche scientifique.

J.Ri. Jean RICHER, professor emeritus, University of Nice.

J.Se. Jean SEZNEC, member of the British Academy; formerly professor, Oxford University and Harvard University.

J.St. Jean STAROBINSKI, professor, Faculty of Letters, University of Geneva.

M.D. Marcel DETIENNE, directeur d'études, École pratique des hautes études, Ve section (sciences religieuses).

M.Ed. Michael EDWARDS, professor of English and comparative literature, University of Warwick.

M.El. Mircea ELIADE, professor in the Divinity School, University of Chicago.

M.O. Maurice OLENDER, attaché, Centre de recherches comparées sur les sociétés anciennes.

M.P. Massimo PALLOTTINO, member of the Institut de France and the Accademia dei Lincei; president, Institute of Etruscan and Italic Studies; professor emeritus, University of Rome.

M.T. Michel TARDIEU, directeur d'études, École pratique des hautes études, Ve section (sciences religieuses).

N.B. Nicole BELMONT, directeur d'études, École des hautes études en sciences sociales.

P.Br. Pierre BRUNEL, professor, University of Paris I.

R.C. Raymond CHRISTINGER, professor, University of Geneva.

R.R. Renée RICHER, professor, University of Nice.

R.S. Robert SCHILLING, professor emeritus, École pratique des hautes études and University II of Strasbourg.

PART

1

Introduction: The Interpretation of Mythology

Toward a Definition of Myth

From Plato and Fontenelle to Schelling and Bultmann, philosophers and theologians have proposed numerous definitions of myth. But all the definitions have one thing in common: they are based on Greek mythology. For a historian of religions, this choice is not the happiest one. It is true that myth, in Greece, inspired epic poetry and theater as well as the plastic arts; yet it was only in Greek culture that myth was subjected to prolonged and penetrating analysis, from which it emerged radically "demythologized." If the word "myth," in all European languages, denotes "fiction," it is because the Greeks declared it to be so twenty-five centuries ago.

An even more serious mistake in the eyes of the historian of religions is that the mythology that Homer, Hesiod, and the tragic poets tell us about is the result of a selective process and represents an interpretation of an archaic subject which has at times become unintelligible. Our best chance of understanding the structure of mythical thought is to study cultures in which myth is a "living thing," constituting the very support of religious life—cultures in which myth, far from portraying *fiction,* expresses the *supreme truth,* since it speaks only of realities.

This is how anthropologists have proceeded for more than half a century, concentrating on "primitive" societies. Reacting, however, against an improper comparative analysis, most authors have neglected to complement their anthropological research with a rigorous study of other mythologies, notably those of the ancient Near East, primarily Mesopotamia and Egypt; those of the Indo-Europeans, especially the grandiose and exuberant mythology of ancient and medieval India; and finally that of the Turco-Mongols, the Tibetans, and the Hinduized or Buddhist peoples of Southeast Asia. In limiting research to primitive mythologies, one risks giving the impression that there is a gap between archaic thought and that of peoples considered "of history." This gap doesn't exist; indeed, by restricting investigation to primitive societies, one is deprived of the means of measuring the role of myth in complex religions, such as those of the ancient Near East or of India. For example, it is impossible to understand the religion and, more generally, the style of Mesopotamian culture if one ignores the cosmogonic myths and the myths of origin that are preserved in the *Enūma Eliš* or in the epic of Gilgameš. Indeed, at the beginning of each new year, the fabulous events recounted in the *Enūma Eliš* were ritually reenacted; at each new year the world had to be re-created—and this requirement reveals to us a profound dimension of Mesopotamian thought. The myth of the origin of man explains, at least in part, the characteristic vision and pessimism of Mesopotamian culture: Marduk drew man out of the earth, that is, out of the flesh of the primordial monster Tiamat, and out of the blood of the archdemon Kingu. And the text specifies that man was created by Marduk in order to work the land and to ensure the sustenance of the gods. The epic of Gilgameš presents an equally pessimistic vision by explaining why man does not (and must not) have access to immortality.

Historians of religions therefore prefer to work on *all categories* of mythological creations, both those of the "primitives" and those of historic peoples. Nor do the divergences that result from too narrow a documentation constitute the only obstacle to the dialogue between historians of religions and their colleagues in other disciplines. It is the approach itself that separates them from, for example, anthropologists and psychologists. Historians of religions are too conscious of the axiological differences in their documents to put them all on the same level. Attentive to nuances and distinctions, they cannot be unaware that there are important myths and myths of lesser importance, myths that dominate and characterize a religion, and secondary, repetitive, or parasitic myths. The *Enūma Eliš,* for example, could not be placed on the same level as the mythology of the female demon Lamashtu; the Polynesian cosmogonic myth has a completely different weight from the myth of the origin of a plant, since it precedes it and serves as its model. Such differences in value do not necessarily command the attention of the anthropologist or the psychologist. Thus, a sociological study of the nineteenth-century French novel or a psychology of the literary imagination can make equal use of Balzac and Eugène Sue, Stendhal and Jules Sandeau. But for the historian of the French novel or for the literary critic, such mixing is unthinkable, for it destroys their own hermeneutic principles.

In the next generation or two, perhaps earlier, when we have historians of religions born of Australian or Melanesian tribal societies, I have no doubt that they, among other critics, will reproach Western scholars for their indifference to the scales of *indigenous* values. Let us imagine a history of Greek culture in which Homer, the tragic poets, and Plato were passed over in silence, while the *Interpretation of Dreams* by Artemidorus of Ephesus and the novel by Heliodorus of Emesa were laboriously analyzed under the pretext that they better clarified the specific characteristics of the Greek spirit, or helped us understand its destiny. To return to our subject, I do not believe it possible to understand the structure and function of mythic thought in a society in which myth still serves as a foundation without taking into account both the *body of mythology* of that culture and the *scale of values* that it implies or declares.

Indeed, wherever we have access to a still living tradition that is neither strongly acculturated nor in danger of disappearing, one thing immediately strikes us: not only does mythology constitute a kind of "sacred history" of the tribe in question, not only does it explain the totality of reality and justify its contradictions, but it also reveals a hierarchy in the sequence of the fabulous events it relates. Every myth tells how something came into existence—the world, man, an animal species, a social institution, etc. Because the creation of the world precedes all others, cosmogony enjoys particular prestige. As I have tried to show elsewhere (see, for example, *The Myth of the Eternal Return,* New York, 1954; *Aspects du mythe,* Paris 1963), the cosmogonic myth serves as a model for all myths of origin. The creation of animals, plants, or man presupposes the existence of a world.

Of course, the myth of the origin of the world is not always cosmogonic in the technical application of the term, like Indian and Polynesian myths, or the myth told in the *Enūma Eliš*. In a large part of Australia, for example, the cosmogonic myth in a strict sense is unknown. But there is still a central myth which tells of the beginnings of the world, of what happened before the world became as it is today. Thus one always finds a *primordial history,* and this history has a *beginning*—the cosmogonic myth properly so called, or a myth that introduces the first, larval, or germinal state of the world. This beginning is always implicit in the series of myths that tell of fabulous events that took place after the creation or the appearance of the world, myths of the origin of plants, animals, and man, or of death, marriage, and the family. Together these myths of origin form a coherent history, for they reveal how the world has been transformed, how man became what he is today—mortal, sexual, and obliged to work to sustain himself. They also reveal what the Supernatural Beings, the enculturating Heroes, the mythical Ancestors, did and how and why they moved away from the Earth, or disappeared. All the mythology that is accessible to us in a sufficient state of conservation contains not only a beginning but also an end, bounded by the final manifestations of the Supernatural Beings, the Heroes or the Ancestors.

So this primordial sacred history, formed by the body of significant myths, is fundamental, for it explains and justifies at the same time the existence of the world, of man, and of society. This is why myth is considered both a *true story*—because it tells how real things have come to be—and the exemplary model of and justification for the activities of man. One understands what one is—mortal and sexual—and one assumes this condition because myths tell how death and sexuality made their appearance in the world. One engages in a certain type of hunting or agriculture because myths tell how the enculturating Heroes revealed these techniques to one's ancestors.

When the ethnologist Strehlow asked the Australian Arunta why they celebrated certain ceremonies, they invariably replied: "Because the [mythical] Ancestors prescribed it." The Kai of New Guinea refused to modify their way of living and working and explained themselves thus: "This is how the Nemu [the mythical Ancestors] did it, and we do it the same way." Questioned about the reason for a certain ritual detail, a Navajo shaman replied: "Because the Sacred People did it this way the first time." We find exactly the same justification in the prayer that accompanies an ancient Tibetan ritual: "As has been passed down since the beginning of the creation of the earth, thus we must sacrifice. . . . As our ancestors did in ancient times, so we do today" (cf. *Aspects du mythe,* pp 16ff.). This is also the justification invoked by Hindu ritualists: "We must do what the gods did in the beginning" (*Śatapatha Brāhmaṇa,* 8.2.1.4). "Thus did the gods; thus do men" (*Taittirīya Brāhmaṇa,* 1.5.9.4). In sum, the governing function of myth is to reveal exemplary models for all rites and all meaningful human activities: no less for food production and marriage than for work, education, art, or wisdom.

In societies where myth is still living, the natives carefully distinguish myths—"true stories"—from fables or tales, which they call "false stories." This is why myths cannot be told indiscriminately; they are not told in front of women or children, that is, before the uninitiated. Whereas "false stories" may be told anytime and anywhere, myths must be told only *during a span of sacred time* (generally during autumn or winter, and only at night).

The distinction made between "true stories" and "false stories" is significant. For all that is told in myths *concerns the listeners directly,* whereas tales and fables refer to events which, even when they have caused changes in the world (for example, anatomical or physiological peculiarities in certain animals), have not modified the human condition as such. Indeed, myths relate not only the origin of the world and that of animals, plants, and humans, but also all the primordial events that have resulted in humans becoming what they are today, i.e., mortal, sexual, and societal beings, obliged to work for a living, and working according to certain rules. To recall only one example: humans are mortal because something happened in the beginning; if this event hadn't occurred, humans wouldn't be mortal, they could have existed indefinitely, like rocks, or could have changed their skin periodically, like snakes, and consequently would have been able to renew their life, that is, begin it again. But the myth of the origin of death tells what happened *in illo tempore,* and in recounting this incident it explains *why* humans are mortal.

In archaic societies, the knowledge of myths has an existential function. Not only because myths offer people an explanation of the world and of their own way of existing in the world, but above all because in remembering myths, in reenacting them, humans are able to repeat what the Gods, the Heroes, or the Ancestors did *ab origine.* To know myths is to learn not only how things have come into existence, but also where to find them and how to make them reappear when they disappear. One manages to capture certain beasts because one knows the secret of their creation. One is able to hold a red-hot iron in one's hand, or to pick up venomous snakes, provided one knows the origin of fire and of snakes. In Timor, when a rice field is growing, someone goes to the field at night and recites the myth of the origin of rice. This ritual recitation forces the rice to grow beautiful, vigorous, and dense, just as it was when it *appeared for the first time.* It is *magically forced to return to its origins,* to repeat its exemplary creation. Knowing the myth of origin is often not enough; it must be recited; knowledge of it is proclaimed, it is *shown.* By reciting myths, one reintegrates the fabulous time of origins, becomes in a certain way "contemporary" with the events that are evoked, shares in the presence of the Gods or Heroes.

In general one may say:

—that myth, such as it is lived by archaic societies, constitutes the story of the deeds of Supernatural Beings;

—that the story is considered absolutely *true* (because it refers to realities) and *sacred* (because it is the work of Supernatural Beings);

—that myth always concerns a "creation"; it tells how something has come into existence, or how a way of behaving, an institution, a way of working, were established; this is why myths constitute paradigms for every meaningful human act;

—that in knowing the myth one knows the "origin" of things and is thus able to master things and manipulate them at will; this is not an "external," "abstract" knowledge, but a knowledge that one "lives" ritually, either by reciting the myth ceremonially, or by carrying out the ritual for which it serves as justification;

—that in one way or another one "lives" the myth, gripped by the sacred, exalting power of the events one is rememorializing and reactualizing.

To "live" myths thus implies a truly "religious" experience, for it is distinct from the ordinary experience of daily life. This experience is "religious" because it is a reenactment of fabulous, exalting, meaningful events; one is present once again at the creative works of the Supernatural Beings. Mythical events are not commemorated; they are repeated, reiterated. The characters in myth are brought forth and made present; one becomes their contemporary. One no longer lives in chronological time but in primordial Time, the Time when the event *took place for the first time.* This is why we can speak of the "strong time" of myth: it is the prodigious, "sacred" Time, when something *new,* something *strong,* and something *meaningful* was made fully manifest. To relive that time, to reintegrate it as often as possible, to be present once again at the spectacle of divine works, to rediscover the Supernatural Beings and relearn their lesson of creation—such is the desire that can be read implicitly in all ritual repetitions of myths. In sum, myths reveal that the world, man, and life have a supernatural origin and history, and that this history is meaningful, precious, and exemplary.

M.El./t.l.f.

The Interpretation of Myths: Nineteenth- and Twentieth-Century Theories

If we fail to trace its outline clearly at the outset, the subject we discuss here risks either being merely a collection of rather curious interpretations accepted in their own periods, or else getting lost in the underbrush of the most varied hermeneutic enterprises. There are two indispensable points of reference. We must, first of all, distinguish interpretation from exegesis. We will define the latter as a culture's incessant but immediate commentary on its own symbolism and practices, its most familiar stories. There is no living tradition without the accompanying murmur of its exegesis of itself. Interpretation, on the other hand, begins when there is some distance and perspective on the discourse of a tradition based on memory. Its starting point is probably, as Todorov suggests, the inadequacy of the immediate meaning, but there is also the discrepancy between one text and another, from which the strangeness of the first can become evident. For, in the work of interpretation, it is the prefix *inter* of the Latin word *interpretatio* that designates the space of deployment of hermeneutic activity. In the Western tradition, from the Greeks to ourselves by way of the Romans and the Renaissance, the first hermeneutics appears in the gap opened up by what a new form of thought decided to call *muthos,* thus inaugurating a new form of otherness which makes one text the mythologist of the next. But this interpretive path required one more marker to give it its definitive orientation. From Xenophanes and Theagenes in the sixth century B.C. to Philo and Augustine, hermeneutics took as its privileged object the body of histories that a society entrusts to its memory, what today we call a mythology. But the play of allegory often based itself on nothing more than a name, a word, or a fragment of a text, on which it could graft the bourgeoning symbolism whose discourse became all the more triumphant when, with the affirmation of Christian doctrine, the certainty of possessing the truth unleashed the audacities of a hermeneutics like that of the *City of God.* It is only with Spinoza—as Todorov has recently stated—that a theory of interpretation takes shape on which our modern readings still largely depend. It was he who formulated rules whose mere application was enough to uncover the truth of a meaning, inside the text and within the bounds of a work. But before it could become philology in the nineteenth century, this theory of interpretation, which Spinoza applied to Scripture, still needed the presence of a cultural object with a clearly defined shape—mythology—understood as a discourse that is other, with its own distinctive traits.

Within these limits and for both of these reasons, an archaeology of theories of the interpretation of myth can restrict itself to the nineteenth and twentieth centuries. Travel accounts since Jean de Léry have traced an axis of otherness whose two poles are the savage and the civilized, between which the Greeks serve as mediator. It is the exemplary values of Greece that are evoked, in good Renaissance style, and Lafitau (1724)—while orienting it toward a deciphering of the present by the past—was merely to systematize the path already beaten, throughout the seventeenth century, by Yves d'Évreaux, Du Tertre, Lescarbot, and Brébeuf. One of the best understood differences—the importance of which has been shown by Michel de Certeau—is that between nakedness and clothing. The detour via the Greeks allows the naked body, which a purely and simply Christian education leads one to reject as belonging to paganism and noncivilization, to be made an object of pleasure, and it may also allow the surprise of a return to oneself. Savages are so handsome that they can only be virtuous. And men's stature, the proportion of their limbs, their nakedness in the midst of the forests, in the beauty of a nature not yet offended by civilization, remind most of these voyagers of the lineaments of Greek statues and the natural privilege which distinguished, in their eyes, the heroes of Homer and Plutarch. As a Jesuit father wrote in 1694, "We see in savages the beautiful remains of a human nature that is completely corrupted in civilized peoples." Nothing could be more like an American savage than a Greek of Homeric times. But this splendid animal, whose development has known no obstacles, whose body is not deformed by labor, evokes the citizen of Sparta or the contemporary of the Trojan war only on the moral and physical level. There is no meeting on an intellectual level; all that the travelers of the seventeenth century expected from savages was that they bear witness to a natural religion of which they were the last trustees. Never, it seems, is the mythology of Homer or Plutarch compared with the stories of these first peoples of nature. One reason is probably that classical mythology, thoroughly moralized, had by then been integrated into a culture dominated by belles lettres. Myths would remain masked as long as they were not assigned their own space.

The nineteenth century saw the discovery of language as the object of a comparative grammar and a renewed philology. In this linguistic space, which is to the highest degree that of the sounds of language, mythical discourse suddenly appeared. It did so in the modality of scandal, which would feed the passionate discussions and theories of two rival schools of the second half of the nineteenth century: the school of comparative mythology, and the anthropological school. As the Sanskritist and comparative grammarian Max Müller wrote, "The Greeks attribute to their gods things that would make the most savage of the Redskins shudder." Comparison defines the nature of the scandal. It is as if it were suddenly discovered that the mythology of Homer and Plutarch was full of adultery, incest, murder, cruelty, and even cannibalism. The violence of these stories, which seemed to reveal themselves brutally as "savage and absurd," appeared all the more unbearable since they were being read at the same time as the stories of distant lands, lands that colonial ethnography was both inventorying and beginning to exploit. The scandal was not that the people of nature told savage stories, but rather that the Greeks could have spoken this same savage language. For in the nineteenth century all that was Greek was privileged. The romantics and then Hegel affirmed this enthusiastically. It was in Greece, they said, that Man began to be himself; it was Greek thought that opened up the path leading from natural consciousness to philosophical consciousness; the Greek people were believed to have been the first to have attained "the uttermost limits of civilization," in the words of a contemporary of Max Müller, the anthropologist Andrew Lang. From the moment that the mythology of Greece could resemble the language spoken by "a mind struck temporarily insane" (Lang), neither our reason nor our thought is definitively safe from an unforeseeable return of the irrational element which, the voice of the savages teaches us, is buried at the very heart of those stories that once seemed so familiar.

The mythology that is subjected to the trial of interpretation is, primarily, nothing but an absurd, crazy form of speech which must be gotten rid of as quickly as possible by assigning it an origin or finding an explanation to justify its oddness. On this point, Max Müller and Andrew Lang are in full agreement. Their divergence appears from the time when the presence of those insane statements at the heart of language and in mythic discourse has to be justified. For Max Müller, a contemporary of the discovery of comparative grammar, the only possible explanation was a linguistic one. And his *Science of Language* argues that a stratigraphy of human speech reveals a mythopoeic phase in the history of language. Since 1816, when Franz Bopp published the first comparative grammar, language had been understood as a set of sounds independent of the letters that allow them to be transcribed; a system of sonorities, animated with its own life, endowed with continual activity and traversed by the dynamism of *inflection*. In the history of language, after what is called a thematic stage, in which terms expressing the most necessary ideas are forged, and what is called a dialectal stage, in which grammar definitively receives its specific traits, an age begins that Max Müller designates as mythopoeic, in which myths make their appearance in very specific circumstances.

At the beginning of its history, humanity possessed the faculty of uttering words directly expressing part of the substance of objects perceived by the senses. In other words, things awakened sounds in humans which became roots and engendered phonetic types. Humans "resonated" at the world, and thus had the privilege of "giving articulated expression to the conceptions of reason." As soon as the individual lost the privilege of emitting sounds at the spectacle of the world, a strange disease fell upon language: words like "night, day, morning, evening" produced strange illusions to which the human mind immediately fell victim. For as long as humans remain sensitive to the meanings of words, these first sonic beings are conceived of as powers, endowed with will, and marked by sexual traits, though the physical character of the natural phenomena designated by the words is not forgotten. As soon as the double meaning becomes confused, the names of the forces of nature break free: they become proper names, and from a spontaneous expression like "the sky rains," a myth abruptly emerges based on "Zeus makes the rain fall." There is an excess of meaning at the source of mythopoeic creation, an uncontrolled surplus of signification, which tricks the speaker, prey to the illusions of a language within which the play of these "substantive verbs" produces, in a burgeoning of images, the strange and often scandalous discourse of myths.

To this theory, which based the metaphors of language on natural phenomena and declared that a good mythologist should possess a "deep feeling for nature," without which linguistic knowledge is futile, the anthropological school immediately objected that comparative grammarians seemed to have forgotten somewhere along the way that "the Redskins, the Australians, and the lower races of South America" continued even today, in the forests and savannas, to tell the same savage tales, which can hardly be explained as the unwonted result of a few misunderstood phrases. The road the anthropological school would follow led in the opposite direction from that of the grammarians. It was no longer the past or origins that were to explain the present, but rather the mythology of contemporary savages that could account for the "savage" stories of the past. And Lang attempted to show that what shocks us in the mythology of civilized peoples is the residue of a state of thought once prevailing in all humanity. In contemporary primitives we can see the power of this state of thought as well as its coherence. At the same time, anthropologists began to investigate these gross products of the primitive human mind and to discover that things which to our eyes seem monstrous and irrational were accepted as ordinary events in everyday life. They soon came to the conclusion that whatever seems irrational in civilized mythologies (the Greco-Roman world, or India) forms part of an order of things that is accepted and considered rational by contemporary savages.

This position led to two orientations, which anthropology attempted to explore in parallel. For the first, which leads from Frazer to Lévy-Bruhl, mythology remains the discourse of madness or mental deficiency. In 1909, before he published the thousands of pages of *The Golden Bough*, the prolegomena to a history of the tragic errors of a humanity led astray by magic, James George Frazer wrote a small book (*Psyche's Task*) in which he asked how folly could turn to wisdom, how a false opinion could lead to "good conduct." And at the center of his reflection Frazer places a paradox:

primitive superstitions were the foundation of what now seems desirable to us in society: order, property, family, respect for life. Prejudice and superstition in fact served to strengthen respect for authority and thus contributed to the rule of order, the condition of all social progress. Frazer had given hundreds of examples in his already published works, and in this slim volume he is no less enthusiastic an admirer of the conduct of the son-in-law in a primitive society who avoids speaking to or being alone with his mother-in-law, surrounding her with taboos, as if these people, not yet capable of elaborating a thought-out set of laws, still had a sense that an intimate conversation between these two people could easily degenerate into something worse, and that the best way to prevent this from happening was to raise a solid wall of etiquette between them. Without knowing it, and almost reluctantly, primitive thought, even in its most obstinate errors, prepared the way for the triumphs of morality and civilization.

For Lucien Lévy-Bruhl, who published *Les fonctions mentales dans les sociétés inférieures* in 1910, primitive societies differed from ours in their mental organization: their thought, constituted differently from our own, is mystical in nature; it is ruled by a "law of participation" that makes it indifferent to the logic of noncontradiction on which our own system of thought is based. Lévy-Bruhl finds the characteristics of primitive thought, which surrenders itself to affectivity and to what he calls "mysticism," among both schizophrenics and children, who also think in an affective way and establish commonalities between things and beings whose mutual distinctiveness is obvious to the intelligence of a civilized adult. Lévy-Bruhl would increasingly identify this "prelogical" stage with "mystic experience," and Van der Leeuw, who extended his analysis, would try to show that primitive thought survives in every human mind, that it is a component of all forms of reason, an indispensable element whose symbolic load and image-making power help to balance the conceptual development of our thought. In the *Notebooks,* which were published after his death, Lévy-Bruhl found it necessary to revise his position on the mental and intellectual gap between ourselves and "savages." But his work, in profound accord with that of Frazer, seems to us today to be part of a fencing in of savage thought (*la pensée savage*), confining it in the prelogical and thus avoiding any contamination which might threaten our own reason.

At the very moment when these armchair anthropologists were interning primitive thought, others were setting out on voyages of discovery to Africa and Oceania, and so were discovering, alive and functioning, the rationality of a form of thought that operates through and in myth—a rationality different from our own, but no less impressive for that. The great living mythologies of the Pacific or the Sudan fulfill an indispensable function in these simpler cultures. Revealing a distinctive reality, guaranteeing the effectiveness of worship, myths codify the beliefs, found the moral rules, and determine every practice of daily life. When Marcel Griaule brought back the Dogon cosmology, with its astonishing architectures of symbolic correspondences, there could no longer be any doubt that mythology was indeed the keystone of archaic societies, the indispensable horizon of all cultural phenomena and of the whole pattern in which society is organized. Myths not only constitute the spiritual armature of human lives; they are bearers of a real "theoretical metaphysics." For the first time, then, myths came to be studied in their entirety, a study in which every detail, even the most insignificant, found its place in a holistic interpretation, an interpretation so rich, so exhaustive, that the ethnographer, once introduced into this polysymbolic world, is in serious danger of "having nothing more to say about Dogon society than the Dogon say themselves" (Pierre Smith, 1973).

In 1903, before Frazer and Lévy-Bruhl had begun their investigations, Marcel Mauss, following the French sociological school, set forth in a few pages a program of which Georges Dumézil would one day prove to be the master craftsman. Three points seem essential. 1. To determine the mechanism of the formation of myths means to seek some of the laws of the mental activity of man in society. 2. Mythology can be reduced to a small number of myths, and each type is made up of a certain number of combinations. 3. The apparent illogicality of a mythic narrative is itself the sign of its distinctive logic. For Mauss, Durkheim's nephew and collaborator, myths are social institutions, that is, ways of acting and thinking which individuals find already established and, as it were, ready to hand; they form a fully organized pattern of ideas and behaviors which imposes itself more or less forcefully on the individuals inscribed in a society. Myth is above all *obligatory* in nature; it does not exist unless there is a sort of necessity to reach agreement on the themes that are its raw material and on the way these themes are patterned. But the constraint comes solely from the group itself, which tells the myth because it finds its own total expression in it.

A symbol through which society thinks itself, mythology informs experience, orders ritual and the economy, and gives archaic societies their categories and classificatory frameworks. For the Durkheimian school, myths—which, incidentally, are hardly mentioned in the *Année sociologique*—are of the same order as language, "a property of which the proprietor is unconscious"; and, inseparable from this, just as a language continues to bear centuries-old vocabulary and syntax, mythology implies a certain traditional way of perceiving, analyzing, coordinating. The analogy is even more precise: like language, mythology is tradition itself, it is the symbolic system that permits communication beyond words; it is the historical unconscious of the society. In this perspective, the importance of myths derives from the common nature that links them to the most archaic element of language, in that domain where sociology hoped to discover some of the fundamental laws of the mind's activity in society.

It was Mauss once again who, against Lévy-Bruhl, in 1923 defended the thesis that considerable parts of our own mentality are still identical to those of a large number of societies called primitive. But it was first Marcel Granet, then Louis Gernet, who developed a sociological analysis of religion with its legends and myths. For the Sinologist Granet, attempting to proceed from language to the fundamental frames of thought, the mythology of the Chinese provided material in which the emotions characteristic of ancient festivals were recorded. Behind the legendary and mythic tales were ritual dances and dramas from which imaginative schemas emerged that imposed themselves on the mind and on action. Farther along, social contexts and great technical feats that crystallize the productions of the imaginary order could be glimpsed. For the Hellenist Gernet, in a break with the established positivist history that was content to note the gratuitous play of the imaginary, myths reveal a social unconscious. Just as semantic analysis gives access to the great social fact of language, the study of legends and of certain mythic themes allows one to go back to transparent or explicit social practices. The mythic image thus offers the most convenient means of access, not to a timeless memory, but to archaic behaviors and social actions and—going far beyond the social data that have, as Gernet puts it, "a direct relation to myth"—to fundamental phenomena of mental life, those that determine the most general forms of thought.

The specificity of the Greeks pointed Gernet in yet another direction. Myths, in their fragments, shining splinters, offer not only the prehistoric behaviors that were their reason for being; they are at the same time part of a global way of thinking, whose categories, classifications, preconceptual models exert a major influence on positive thought and its various advances. Thus Gernet, starting from a series of traditions about types of precious objects, attempts to show how money and the economy emerge from a set of behaviors linked to the mythical notion of value—a notion that involves domains which, though separate nowadays, used to overlap or merge together: the religious, the political, the aesthetic, the juridical. Mythology is thus part of a global religious system that is symbolic in character, with a web of multicorrespondences from which law, philosophy, history, and political thought will emerge and become progressively distinct. But since Gernet thought of myths as raw material for the thought that arose with and in the Greek city, in the space of the polis, he examined the mythic element only in terms of what was beyond it, in a break with its own nature and its functioning. By failing to separate mythology either from language or from the institutional system, the sociological model of myth culminated in the paradox of sometimes losing sight of the very object that seemed finally to have been recognized and legitimated.

More serious, certainly, was the misunderstanding between Freudian psychoanalysis and the anthropological problematic, which seems to give access to a form of the unconscious inscribed in myth. In his self-analysis, as recounted in his letter to Fliess of October 15, 1897, Freud discovers that his libido awoke between the ages of two and two and a half, and turned toward *matrem* (confessors' Latin for the name of the mother). Freud refers this desire for the mother to a Greek tragedy, *Oedipus the King,* a reference both cultural and paradigmatic. The first thing that Sophocles' Oedipus gives Freud is a better understanding of himself—but the choice of a Greek paradigm already announces the universal character of Freud's discovery of the heart of the matter. The early hypothesis, that little Sigmund is *like Oedipus,* shifts toward the Freudian thesis that Oedipus marrying his mother *must have been the same as ourselves.* While Freud's enterprise, by showing that there is no essential difference between the mentally ill person and the healthy person, seems to invert the separation marked by Lévy-Bruhl, it does assume, from the beginning, a segregation of Greek myths from those of other peoples. For Freud, *Oedipus the King* still excites us and exerts a profound effect on us because every man, always and everywhere, feels love for his mother and jealousy of his father; and from the day Freud first adopted this view, the Greek myth was invested with a new privilege: that of translating better than any other "an instinctual attraction which everyone recognizes because everyone has experienced it."

It was to Greek mythology that Freud would continue to turn in his quest for successive proofs of the reality of the unconscious, comparing the discourse of dreams and fantasies with the legends of Olympus, which his successors, stubbornly but not without fidelity, were to proclaim as the language in which we can most easily read the drives and works of desire. In asking for an admission of guilt within the Oedipal configuration, psychoanalysis indeed marks a return to myth and the religious; but in seeing both of these as merely the visible tip of the iceberg of the "Unconscious," forgetting that analytical space is that of free association, it has condemned mythology to being nothing but the symbolic and obsessive repetition of a few unconscious representations centered on sexuality.

It was in the direction opened up by Maussian sociology that theoretical work on myth became involved in the first structural analyses. Resuming the project of comparative mythology that had been wrecked by the excesses of Max Müller and his disciples, Georges Dumézil, thanks to a decisive discovery, founded the comparative study of Indo-European religions by ceasing to rely on purely linguistic concordances between divine names and adopting instead the more solid base of articulated sets of concepts. A factual discovery—in Rome, the three *flamines majores* corresponding to the Jupiter-Mars-Quirinus triad; in Iran, the tripartition of social classes—opened the way to structural analysis of the Indo-European world: the tripartite schema was an essential structure in the thought of the Indo-Europeans. Every organized society is based on the collaboration of three distinct but complementary functions: sovereignty, martial power, fecundity. Parallel to this, the gods form a functionally weighted triad, within which the Sovereign, the Warrior, and the group of divinities who preside over fecundity mutually define one another. Since there was never any question of reproducing a definitely Indo-European myth or ritual, Dumézil had to use precise and systematic correspondences to trace a ground plan of the chosen myth or ritual, indicating its articulations, its intentions, its logical significations, and then, on the basis of this schematic figure, projected into prehistory, to try to characterize the divergent evolutions which have led to analogous and diverse results in different places: Indian myth, Roman myth, Scandinavian myth, or Vedic ritual in relation to the Latin rite. For Dumézil, religions are whole patterns in which concepts, images, and actions are articulated and whose interconnections make a sort of net in which, by rights, the entire material of human experience should find its distribution.

By focusing his examination on the concept and on organized patterns, Dumézil radically parts company with a history of religions that thought in terms of genesis and affectivity. For historians like H. J. Rose and H. Wagenvoort, all religion is rooted in the sense of the "numinous" that the human race experiences spontaneously when confronting the phenomena of nature: there is no divine power who was not first one of these *numina,* in which magico-religious force, diffused in the natural world, is concentrated. For Dumézil, by contrast, the observer never reaches isolated facts, and religion is not a form of thought soaked in emotionality. It is in their mutual relations that the various elements can be apprehended, and there always remains, virtually or in action, a representation of the world or of human action that functions on different levels, under a particular type on each level. The religious system of a human group is expressed "first of all in a more or less explicit conceptual structure, which is always present, if sometimes almost unconscious, providing the field of forces upon which everything else comes to be arranged and oriented; then in myths, which represent and dramatize these fundamental intellectual relationships; and then, in turn, in rituals, which actualize, mobilize, and use the same relations." Independently of these gains in the Indo-European domain, Dumézil's method affirmed the virtues of the concept that can equally inform a myth or underlie a ritual. From this point on, "the surest definition of a god is differential, classificatory," and the object of analysis becomes the articulations, the balances, the types of oppositions that the god represents. Against the historians of genesis, Dumézil affirms the primacy of structure: the essential problem is not to determine the precise origin of the various elements that have been fitted together but to accept the *fact* of the structure. The important thing, Dumézil declares, is to bring the structure itself to light, with its signification. It would seem to follow that structures are there, that it is enough to be attentive to them, to avoid forcing them, and to show a little skill in disengaging them. Thus it is not necessary to construct structures as one would elaborate a model of the set of properties accounting for a group of objects. In a sense, structuralism is still in the age of hunting and gathering. Myths, for Dumézil, are the privileged theater that makes visible fundamental conceptual relations. But in the spirit of Mauss's sociology, to which he owes a curiosity for "total social facts" that causes him to explore simultaneously all the works produced by the human mind, myths cannot be deciphered until they have been put back into the totality of the religious, social, and philosophical life of the peoples who have practiced them. The mythology posited by the earlier comparativism of Frazerian inspiration as separate from language, as a more or less autonomous object, endowed with permanence and chosen to locate the common themes elaborated by the Indo-Europeans, was referred back to the language of which it formed a part and, through this language, to the ideology that grounds it and runs through it.

The structural analysis developed by Lévi-Strauss was established under the same kind of conditions as the comparative and philological analysis of the nineteenth century. The gratuitous and insane character of mythic discourse was again the point of departure. For Max Müller this was shocking; for Lévi-Strauss it was a challenge. He took up the challenge after he had shown that kinship relations, in appearance contingent and incoherent, can be reduced to a small number of significant propositions. If mythology is the domain in which the mind seems to have the most freedom to abandon itself to its own creative spontaneity, then, says Lévi-Strauss, to prove that, on the contrary, in mythology the mind is fixed and determined in all of its operations is to prove that it must be so everywhere. The structural analysis of myths thus finds its place in a wider project, which aims at an inventory of mental constraints and postulates a structural analogy between various orders of social facts and language.

This whole approach to myth applies to a new domain the methods of analysis and principles of division developed for linguistic materials in the methods theorized by the Prague school and more particularly by Roman Jakobson. But while myth is assimilated to a language from the outset, it is not identical either to the words of a text or to the sentence of communicative discourse. Mythology is a use of language in the second degree; it is not only a narrative with an ordinary linguistic meaning: myth is in language and at the same time beyond natural language. In the first stage of an ongoing investigation ("The Structural Study of Myth," 1955), Lévi-Strauss tries to define the constituent units of myth in relation to those of structural linguistics. Mythemes are both in the sentence and beyond it. In this perspective, the constituent unit is a very short sentence, which summarizes the essential part of a sequence and denotes a relation: "a predicate assigned to a subject." But this sentence is not part of the explicit narrative; it is already on the order of interpretation, the product of an analytical technique. These sentence relations, then, are distributed on two axes: one horizontal, following the thread of the narrative, the other vertical, in columns, grouping together relations belonging to the same "bundle." It is on the level of these bundles of relations that the real mythemes are located. At the same time, structural analysis poses two principles as essential to its practice: there is no authentic version of a myth in relation to others that are false; correlatively, every myth must be defined by the whole set of its versions. There thus takes shape the project of ordering all the known variants of a myth in a series forming a group of permutations.

The next stage of his investigation ("The Story of Asdiwal," 1958) led Lévi-Strauss to propose that myth makes full use of discourse, but at the same time situates its own meaningful oppositions at a higher degree of complexity than that required by natural language. In other words, myth is a metalanguage and, more precisely, a linked sequence of concepts. Attention will be turned, therefore, to registering the various levels on which myth can be distributed. The cutting up of the mythic narrative which in the first phase (1955) seemed to be entrusted to the whim or ingenuity of the model-builder, is now subject to testing—indispensable to all formal analysis—in terms of the *referent:* "the ethnographic context," which the later transformational orientation of the *Mythologiques* would cease to pursue. The surveying of pertinent oppositions in a mythic sequence thus finds the fundamental guarantee of its legitimacy in previous knowledge of an organized semantic context, without which the myth is in principle incomprehensible. Ritual practices, religious beliefs, kinship structures: the whole of social life and social thought is called upon to define the logical relations functioning within a myth, and at the same time to establish the different types of liaison between two or more myths. In the four-volume *Mythologiques* (1964–1971), the progressive analysis continues to show relations between myths, the social life of those who tell them, and the geographical and technological infrastructure, but it does not restrict itself to this back-and-forth between levels of signification and an ethnographic context that reveals the philosophy of a society. The meaning of a myth is no longer inscribed in its structures' reference to a social infrastructure; rather, the position the myth occupies in relation to other myths within a transformation group is henceforth the vector of an analysis that reveals the autonomy of a mythic thought in which every narrative refers back in the first instance to another, picking up and organizing its elements in a different way. Just as each term, itself without intrinsic signification, has no meaning other than a positional one in the context in which it appears to us, in the same way each myth acquires a signifying function through the combinations in which it is called upon both to figure and to be transformed. It is these transformations which, in the last analysis, define the nature of mythic thought.

It has been objected that this practice of mythological analysis makes a choice for syntax against semantics; and, likewise, that while it has been possible to apply the practice successfully to the mythologies of so-called totemic societies, since these are rich in classificatory structures, it excludes Semitic, Hellenic, and Indo-European societies from its field of interest, societies whose mythological thought is marked by renewals of meaning and by a semantic richness that exceeds the powers of structural analysis. One can reply, on the one hand, that for this type of analysis, which gets at the meanings of myths by multiplying the formal operations that allow us to uncover the logical framework of several narratives, the semantics of myths is necessarily enriched through the inventorying of the syntax. On the other hand, the practice of structural analysis is hardly alien to our familiar mythologies, such as that of the Greeks; one may, indeed, be surprised at the remarkable similarities between the way the Greeks themselves thought their mythology and the method used by ethnologists in approaching myths told by nonliterate peoples. More pertinent objections have come from anthropologists such as Dan Sperber, who denounces the semiological illusion of structuralism as well as the distance between the linguistic models invoked and an intuitive practice whose specific procedures, unlimited in number and nature, offer knowledge of the intellectual operations from which the stories we call "myths" are woven.

M.D./j.l.

BIBLIOGRAPHY

The titles listed are in the order and within the limits of the problems formulated by this article.

T. TODOROV, *Symbolisme et interprétation* (Paris 1978). M. DE CERTEAU, "Ethno-graphie: L'oralité, ou l'espace de l'autre," in Léry, *L'écriture de l'histoire* (Paris 1975), 215–48. G. CHINARD, *L'Amérique et le rêve exotique dans la littérature française du XVIIe au XVIIIe siècle* (Paris 1934). M. DETIENNE, "Mito e Linguaggio: Da Max Müller a Claude Lévi-Strauss," in *Il Mito: Guida storica e critica* (2d ed., Bari and Rome 1976), 3–21 and 229–31, with bibliography. H. PINARD DE LA BOULLAYE, *L'étude comparée des religions*, 1 and 2 (Paris 1925). J. DE VRIES, *Forschungsgeschichte der Mythologie*, Orbis Academicus, 1, 7 (Munich 1961). K. KÉRÉNYI, *Die Eröffnung des Zugangs zum Mythos* (Darmstadt 1967). G. VAN DER LEEUW, *L'homme primitif et la religion*, Étude anthropologique (Paris 1940). P. SMITH, "L'analyse des mythes," *Diogène* 82 (1973): 91–108. M. MAUSS, *Œuvres*, V. Karady, ed., 3 vols. (Paris 1968–69). L. GERNET, *Anthropologie de la Grèce antique* (Paris 1968). S. C. HUMPHREYS, "The Work of Louis Gernet," *History and Theory* 10, 2 (1971). J. STAROBINSKI, "Hamlet et Freud," preface to French trans. by E. Jones, *Hamlet et Œdipe* (Paris 1967), IX–XL. S. VIDERMAN, *La construction de l'espace analytique* (Paris 1970). S. FREUD, "Zur Gewinnung des Feuers," in *Gesammelte Werke* (London 1932–39), also in English. G. DELEUZE and F. GUATTARI, *L'anti-Œdipe* (Paris 1972), "Psychanalyse et familiarisme: La sainte famille," 60–162. H. FUGIER, "Quarante ans de recherches dans l'idéologie indo-européenne: La méthode de Georges Dumézil," *Revue d'histoire et de philosophie religieuse* 45 (1965): 358–74. M. MESLIN, *Pour une science des religions* (Paris 1973), "Psychanalyse et religion," 113–38. P. SMITH and D. SPERBER, "Mythologiques de Georges Dumézil," *Annales E.S.C.*, 1971, 559–86. J.-P. VERNANT, "Raisons du mythe," in *Mythe et société en Grèce ancienne* (Paris 1974), 195–250. P. RICŒUR, s.v. "Mythe (3. L'interprétation philosophique)," in *Encyclopædia Universalis* (Paris 1968), 11:530–37. CL. LÉVI-STRAUSS, *Structural Anthropology*, 2 vols. (New York 1963, 1976), originals in French; *Mythologiques*, 4 vols. (Paris 1964–71), = *Introduction to a Science of Mythology*, 4 vols., entitled *The Raw and the Cooked* (New York 1969), *From Honey to Ashes* (London 1973), *The Origin of Table Manners* (New York 1978), and *The Naked Man* (New York 1981).

MYTH AND WRITING: THE MYTHOGRAPHERS

The word *mytho-logy* is but one instance of many in which the proximity of myth and writing inevitably results in a kind of violence, its victim an original word, sacred in nature and condemned to fixity by a profane order. Beyond the words which by their very texture bear witness to this phenomenon (such as *mythography*), Greek privilege has held fast. When strange and unforgettable stories, which sounded very independent and yet bore obvious resemblances to the mythology of antiquity, were brought to us from all continents, early anthropologists turned instinctively to Greece, where a few centuries earlier great minds from Xenophanes to Aristotle had faced the problem of limiting the dominion of myths and had resolved it within their own intellectual activity by drawing a boundary at which mythical thought fades away before the rationality of scientists and philosophers. The split between the land of myth and the kingdom of *logos* served as a precedent for the decision made by Tylor and his disciples to impose a historical limit on the reign of mythology over the human mind. This opposition between two forms of thought and two stages of human intelligence, the latter canceling the former, took the form of a sharp contrast between reason, which used all the resources of the written, and a mythological activity tuned to the fantasy of an incessant babbling.

Henceforth, never the twain shall meet. For those practicing historians who tend to favor written traces, oral discourse has become so totally inaudible that it is quite illegible whenever it manifests itself as writing—a contrived writing, which masks the incoherence of traditions sustained through memory by imposing a factitious order of mythographical classifications. For others, the Greeks so thoroughly ensured the triumph of reason and *logos* that they ruined their former system of thought for good, allowing only frail remains to survive as witnesses of a lost state to which only two possible roads of access still remain: one is the discovery, by an ancient traveler in a forgotten village, of a tale saved from the contamination of writing thanks to a few natives unaware of the progress of culture; the other is the less hazardous road of historical and geographical investigation through which one gains access to a long-deferred vision of a landscape that authenticates the narrative or the myths of which it is the guarantor, the recovered witness.

Within this framework, the truth of the myth is enclosed in a speechlike nature, which writing more or less obliterates, at times by shackling the freedom of a self-expressive memory with the constraints of an interpretation subject to foreign rules; and at other times, more often than not, by reducing the myth's own speech to silence in order to speak on its behalf and to condemn it to an absolute otherness. In an attempt to rectify this division, structural analysis introduced a summary separation between cold and warm societies, the former deprived of a temporal dimension, the latter open to history and to the continual renewals of meaning that writing facilitates. The border thus drawn appeared all the more definite as it seemed to reiterate the distinction between oral and written literature, a distinction reinforced, if not justified, by the decision made by this type of analysis to look for the essential of the "myth" not in the narration but in the story transmitted by memory, a story whose narrative form was left to the discretion and talent of each narrator.

Yet another issue arises, for which the Greek model inspires a formulation that suggests the progressive emergence of writing in a traditional society. Since the time E. A. Havelock first published his studies, the Homeric epic, which Milman Parry had recognized as belonging to oral practice, can no longer be considered an enclave of a living tradition that made room for a culture of the written. The introduction of an alphabetical writing technique caused no immediate changes, nor did it produce any profound upheaval. Greece experienced not a revolution of writing but, rather, a slow movement with uneven advances depending on the areas of activity; by the turn of the fourth century, writing prevailed mentally and socially. Until the end of the fifth century, Greek culture had been essentially of the oral type. It entrusted to its memory all traditional information and knowledge, as do all societies unacquainted with written archives. And it is here that we must revise the notion of *mythology,* with which the Greeks encumbered us as a consequence of their entanglement with *logos.* For the unified concept "myth," which nowhere seems to be defined as a discrete literary genre, must fade away in favor of a set of intellectual operations fundamental to the memorizing of narratives that together make up a tradition. Claude Lévi-Strauss suggests the term *mythism* for the process by which a story, initially personal and entrusted to the oral tradition, becomes adopted by the collective mode, which will distinguish between the crystal clear parts of the narrative—that is, the levels that are structured and stable because they rest on common foundations—and the conjectural parts—details or episodes amplified or neglected at each telling, before being doomed to oblivion and falling outside the bounds of memory. Every traditional society develops, with varying success, a widely shared creative memory, which is neither the memory of specialists nor that of technicians. The narratives we agree to call myths are the products of an intellectual activity that invents what is memorable.

When writing appears, it neither banishes traditional memory to a state of decay nor sustains an oral practice in imminent danger of becoming extinct. Writing occurs at different levels and in different orders, but always at the encounter between an act of remembering and the works that memory creates. Writing was to introduce a new memory, word-for-word memory, which comes with the book and with education through the study of written texts. Competing ever so slowly with the former kind of memory, mechanical memory alone is capable of engendering the idea, familiar to us, of the *correct* version, a version which must be copied or learned exactly, word for word. In Greece between the sixth and fifth centuries, the first historians, those whom the Greeks call "logographers," selected writing as the instrument of a new kind of memory that would become an integral part of thought and political action. This new way of remembering was constructed on the boundary between a type of oral tradition with its remembrances, spoken narratives, and stories circulating by word of mouth, and, on the other side, the dominant obsession of the new investigators, who respected as knowledge only what had been seen, and who would ultimately condemn, without appeal, those who accepted traditions of the past that were transmitted without precise terminology or rigorous proof. This was the battleground, the wide open space of writing, for the confrontation between variants that became different versions of the same myth, usually examined from within the confines of a city in quest of self-image or political identity.

Elsewhere, other routes were taken that linked writing to the production of myths whose successive variations were inseparable from the hermeneutic activity of scribes and interpreters devoted to textual exegesis. From the moment the traditional narratives of the Bible, the Book of the Hebraic world, were committed to writing, they were swept away by the inner workings of a system of writing which, though initially consonantal, in its hollows called for a vocalic complement to bear its meaning, since one cannot read a consonantal text unless one understands it, that is, unless one attributes to it a meaning set apart from other possible meanings. In the continuity of interpretation thus opened up, the hermeneutics that was focused on the mythical accounts of Israel claimed a privileged place, which made it more sensitive to the permanence of fundamental themes endlessly revived and reevaluated, but also forced it to be the infinite exegesis, forever interned within its own symbolic wealth.

M.D./g.h.

BIBLIOGRAPHY

R. FINNEGAN, *Oral Poetry: Its Nature, Significance and Social Context* (Cambridge 1977). J. GOODY and J. WATT, "The Consequences of Literacy," *Comparative Studies in Society and History,* 1963, 304–45. J. GOODY, "Mémoire et apprentissage dans les sociétés avec et sans écriture: La transmission du Bagre," *L'homme,* 1977, 29–52. E. A. HAVELOCK, *Preface to Plato* (Cambridge, MA, 1963). R. KOENIG, "L'activité herméneutique des scribes dans la transmission du texte de l'Ancien Testament," *Revue de l'Histoire des Religions,* 1962, 141–74. CL. LÉVI-STRAUSS, *Mythologiques* 4 (Paris 1971): 560 (translated as *Introduction to a Science of Mythology,* New York 1969–). L. SEBAG, *L'invention du monde chez les Indiens Pueblos* (Paris 1971), 472–85. J. VANSINA, *De la tradition orale: Essai de méthode historique,* Musée royal de l'Afrique centrale (Tervuren 1961).

Some mythographic texts of ancient Greece: APOLLODORUS, *The Library,* J. G. Frazer, ed. (London 1921). DIODORUS OF SICILY, *The Library,* vol. 4, C. H. Oldfather, ed. (London 1935). ANTONINUS LIBERALIS, *Metamorphoses.* HYGINUS, *Astronomica,* B. Bunte, ed. (Leipzig 1875). HYGINUS, *Fabulae,* H. I. Rose, ed. (Leiden 1933). *Mythographi graeci,* 5 vols., R. Wagner, Martini, A. Olivier, and N. Festo, eds., Bibl. Script. graec. Teubneriana (Leipzig 1896–1926). *Mythographi Vaticani,* G. H. Bode, ed., vols. 1–2 (1834; reprinted Olms 1968). ACUSILAUS OF ARGOS, PHERECYDES OF ATHENS, and HELLANIKOS OF LESBOS, in *Fragmente der griechischen Historiker,* F. Jacoby, ed., I: *Genealogie und Mythographie* (Leiden 1922; 2d ed., 1957).

PREHISTORIC RELIGION

To speak of "prehistoric religion" without specifying time and place is tantamount to assimilating under modern thought facts and contexts that came to light at very different times and places, tantamount to creating a kind of average image that can only be validated by the judgment of our own way of thinking projected onto some arbitrarily chosen facts. Prehistoric religion no longer occasions a debate in which either pro- or anticlerical convictions are at stake. The science of prehistory has been enriched by much new data and major changes in methodological approaches. Rather than arguing about whether the atheist brute evolved first into the magician and then into the priest, scientists have given priority to inquiries that bring out the deep connections among play, aesthetics, social behavior, economic realities, and practices that rest on a metaphysical framework. The proofs that can be proliferated from a so-called religious approach are largely derived from the realm of the unprecedented, from the presence of peculiar facts found in a context where they are least expected, such as the discovery, on a Mousterian site inhabited by Neanderthal man, of fossil shells, which he collected and brought back to his dwelling place, or the discovery that he gathered red ocher or buried his dead. These diverse elements do not fit in with our vision of Neanderthal man. Yet how could there not be a striking contrast between this primal brute with his bulky brow ridges and the subtle quality of a religiosity polished by two millennia of Christianity and all of ancient philosophy? Neanderthal man was not, in the final analysis, as short of gray matter as was long believed, though the metaphysical level of his cultic activities was certainly very different from ours (at least, as we imagine ours to be).

What matters is the existence of practices within a psychological realm not directly tied to techniques of acquisition, manufacture, or consumption, even if these practices do flow back into material life. Man acquired religious behavior when he developed the whole system of symbolic thought, which cannot be separated from language and gesture as it works out a network of symbols that present a counterimage of the outside world. That Neanderthals had already developed this network of symbols is beyond doubt, but whether one can go on to distinguish evidence of a primordial religion or an extremely diffuse symbolic complex remains questionable. The gathering of magical shells and ocher supports the view that the pump had been primed for the simultaneous evolution of the fields of art, play, and religion, three fields which to this day cannot be separated.

Homo sapiens picked up where Neanderthal man left off, with regard to the gathering of "curios" (shells, fossils, crystals, iron pyrites, stalactite fragments, etc.) sometimes found together in the same pile. Ocher became much more plentiful. The first use of manganese dioxide, a black dye, coincided with the production of a greater number of drawings engraved on bone or stone surfaces. By the Aurignacian period, these drawings took the form of rhythmic incisions and figurative tracings. By 30,000 B.C., figurative art had developed to the point at which subjects could be divided into the following groups: female sexual symbols (sometimes also male), figures of animals, and regularly spaced incisions or punctuations. These themes predominated throughout the development of Paleolithic art, a subject to which we shall return.

Burial Grounds and the Cult of Bone Remains

Neanderthals buried their dead. The practice of inhumation is attested by several obvious tombs and, statistically, by the numerous finds of skeleton fragments. Shanidar in Iraq is the site of the only discovery of a Neanderthal laid out on a bed of flowers, from which a great number of fossilized pollens were found. In Monte Circeo (Italy), in a similarly convincing find, a skull was placed in the center of a cave chamber. In the face of such striking testimony, it is difficult not to ascribe to the immediate predecessors of humankind as we know it today sentiments analogous to our own regarding the afterlife in a parallel universe, a universe which may have been as inexplicit as that of the average subject of any of today's major religions. Difficult as it may be, given the available evidence, to describe Neanderthal man's attitude toward the supernatural, it is even more difficult to demonstrate the meaning of what falls into the category of the "cult of bone remains." Because bone is the only physical element (human or animal) that survives decomposition, any bones found as evidence in an unusual situation could have played a part in a cult. Whether with respect to Neanderthal man or to *Homo sapiens*, we have some evidence that can be explained in terms that are not at variance with an interpretation based on the supernatural. Separated by several scores of millennia, the skulls of Monte Circeo (Mousterian) and the skull from Mas-d'Azil (Magdalenian) attest the special character of the head (the whole head or merely the skull). Although the idea of "graves" of animals has been advanced repeatedly, it seems that natural phenomena were more often at issue than man himself, especially in the case of the remains of cave bears.

The burial graves of fossil *Homo sapiens* are rare, and hardly a single grave dating from the Upper Paleolithic Age (30,000–9000) has been excavated either with care or with all the technical means that would have assured its documentary value. We do, however, have a certain number of facts at our disposal (graves; bodies, either curled up or stretched out; a head protected by a stone; ocher dusting; and funereal household objects, including, at the least, clothing and ornaments worn by the dead person). In addition, the double children's tomb at Sungir, north of Moscow, where hundreds of ornamental elements adorn the bodies and large spears made of mammoth ivory were found in the grave, bears witness to the development of the concern to equip the dead, a development that occurred at a remote phase of the Upper Paleolithic Age. Obviously, graves do not all reflect identical religious intentions, nor can we be certain what kind of sentiments led to these emotional displays. Mortuary furniture is ordinarily less sumptuous. In several cases we might even speculate that the presence of certain vestiges was connected with accidental conditions surrounding the filling of the grave. But a rather constant factor is the presence of ocher, which varied according to the population's wealth in dyes. Ocher gave the soil and the skeleton that it covered a reddish coloration. This practice, common during the Upper Paleolithic Age, is the indisputable sign of acts whose meaning goes beyond a simple natural emotion. If the use of ocher supports various interpretations according to habitat, the sheer fact of its being brought into a grave where a body had been laid constitutes the most distinct feature of the belief in an afterlife, since the dead person was considered still capable of using what he was offered.

Personal Adornments

Jewelry appeared in the West around 35,000 B.C. Its prior origin is unknown. Throughout Europe, its appearance coincided with the first manifestations of the Upper Paleolithic Age. During the Châtelperronian epoch (35,000–30,000), it appears already quite diversified: at that same time we find annular pendants carved out of bone, as well as teeth from various animal species (fox, wolf, marmot, aurochs, etc.), made so that they could be hung by means of a perforation of the root or a slit. Fossil shells were treated in the same way. It may seem far-fetched to regard ornamental pendants as anything other than purely aesthetic objects, and, in fact, some may have had exclusively decorative functions. However, among the hundreds of pendants acquired from European sites, the majority reveal a preoccupation with magic at one level or another. Those that unambiguously represent male and female sexual organs must surely have had some sort of symbolic value (fig. 1). The cylindrical fragments of stalactite and points of belemnites designed to hang may have a meaning of the same order. This symbolic function of sexual images may have been extended to include fragments of shattered assegai spears that were perforated but otherwise untreated (see the symbolism of the assegai below). The role of teeth designed to hang must have been rather complex, at least in the early stages, for the teeth of some animals, the marmot for example, do not seem to have the characteristics of a trophy or a talisman. This is not true of the atrophied canines of reindeer, which even today are symbols of masculinity and

Pendants with genital designs. Left: series of female symbols; right: phalloid symbol. 7.5 cm. Isturitz (Pyrénées district). (Fig. 1)

were imitated in bone or soft stone when pendants first appeared.

The same applies to shells. For the most part they seem to have a purely aesthetic function, but the rather frequent discovery of porcelain (Cyprea), universally attested in prehistoric and historic times as a protective female symbol, makes it highly probable that the collection of shells served as talismans. In short, having gone beyond a strictly decorative function, long and oval pendants encompassed both the aesthetic and the religious realms, and probably the social realm as well, although we still have too little data to clarify the matter.

The Occurrence of Wall Painting

The development of personal adornments does not diminish the importance of the collections of natural curiosities; rather, it was an added feature that prevailed until the end of the Upper Paleolithic Age, ca. 9000. Adornments evolved throughout this period. But in the Aurignacian and the Perigordian Ages, the main event was the spread of pictorial works. Between 30,000 and 20,000, certain forms began to appear in engravings. These first forms were executed on blocks and probably on the walls of rock shelters as well. Despite their crudeness, they shed light on the concerns of their creators. The repertoire of these works is very limited; representation of the female genitalia, highly stylized, is the most widespread. A few representations of the male genitalia can be found, but they were apparently replaced quite early by abstract symbolic figures: dotted lines or bar lines that seem to accompany explicitly female figures. There are also highly geometrical figures of animals, parallel to one another and often juxtaposed or superimposed on one another. The Aurignacian-Gravettian bestiary includes the horse, the bison, the ibex, and other imprecise figures indicating that from the very beginning art made use of two clearly defined registers: human figures symbolically rendered, starting with the representation of the entire body and progressing, by way of genital figures and animals, to geometric figures. During the ensuing 20,000 years, the details may have varied but the basic figures, human and animal, remained in the same relationships. These relationships cannot easily be established on the basis of the engraved blocks alone; displacement in the course of time and, especially, following excavations has destroyed the spatial ties that might have guided us to their meaning. But something happened, perhaps by the Gravettian Age but certainly around 15,000: penetration deep into caves and the execution of paintings or engravings, sometimes more than a kilometer from the opening. This boldness on the part of Paleolithic men is of immediate interest to us because the works produced at such locations preserved their positions with respect to one another and with respect to the wall itself. We can therefore raise questions about the possible religious ideology of the creators of these figures. What motives could have inspired the Magdalenians of Niaux or Pech-Merle to their speleological adventure? It is hard to believe that it was just a matter of curiosity, and one is inclined to think that in their eyes the cave must have seemed a mysterious amalgam of female forms. Direct evidence is furnished by the numerous oval cavities or cleft lips painted on the inside in red ocher (Gargas, Font-de-Gaume, Niaux). The execution of numerous genital symbols in deep side passages indirectly reinforces the hypothesis of the woman-cave. To date, explicit male symbols are rare but one may find, on Aurignacian blocks, for instance, signs made up of series of dots or rods accompanying oval or triangular figures depicted with different degrees of realism. All stages of development come together, with regional nuances, from the whole female figure to the pubic triangle rendered as an empty rectangle. This tendency of male and female signs to conceal themselves behind abstract graphics may well have been a response to taboos of a socioreligious character. This hypothesis becomes all the more plausible as other figurative anomalies give evidence of the same meaning. Not only is there no known instance of human or animal mating anywhere in Paleolithic art, but sexual organs are explicitly represented on relatively few figures. At Lascaux (where, however, the bulls have obvious sexual characteristics), two figures appear (fig. 6): the "jumping cow" in the Axial Diverticulum and an engraved horse in the Passage, both of which have their hooves turned in such a way that the underbelly on both animals is visible and completely empty. This strange mannerism in figure drawing is not easily explained, but it does show the complexity of Paleolithic thought. Curiously, secondary sexual characteristics (the antlers of the cervidae, the thick withers of the bovidae, and

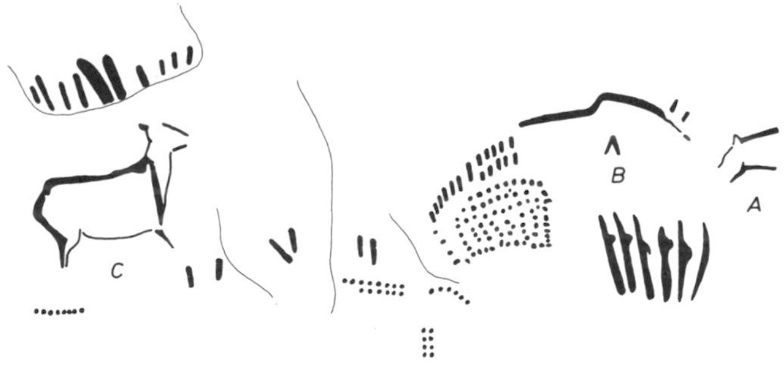

Middle part of the first great panel of the Cave of Pindal (Asturias). Animals A and B (horse and bison) are reduced to the minimal identifiable size: dorsal line and horns for the bison, which also bears a scar from a wound in the shape of an inverted V; central portion of the head and the neck and withers for the horse. Above the bison and the horse, S^2 line of the so-called claviform type (see fig. 5). The photograph includes only the right side of a series of red and black paintings. Between group A-B and the doe (C), there are several groups of S^1 and S^3 signs. The doe is 85 cm long. (Fig. 2)

the horns of the ibex) are rendered very exactly; and, moreover, the animals are frequently depicted in couples, the female in front and the male behind. It is certain that the figures basically connote what might be thought of as a "fertility cult," a generally banal statement that takes on a subtlety in the present instance by virtue of the apparent contradiction of the representation.

Animals

Paleolithic materials yield other peculiar data. The hundreds of figures that cover the walls of caves seem at first glance to defy any kind of order. Even though the idea of a coherent whole emerges from the way the figures are arranged, few prehistorians have used this possible organization to delve further into the ideology of the artists. One rather surprising fact stands out: the fauna that are represented display variations that seem to reflect the environment. In some caves the bison, together with the horse, is the principal subject (Font-de-Gaume, Niaux, Altamira), whereas in others the aurochs plays the main role (Lascaux, Ebbon). But in all the cases cited above, the complementary bovid (bison or aurochs depending on the site) is represented by one or more figures separated from the rest. Another point should also be mentioned: the reindeer that figure in great numbers among the food wastes of the hunters at the time of these works occupy little space in the iconography of certain grottoes such as Lascaux, Niaux, or Altamira. At Lascaux, rather paradoxically, though the bony remains of reindeer make up almost all the animal wastes, only one figure can be attributed to the reindeer, and even that is somewhat doubtful. Thus the fauna depicted do not always correspond to what Paleolithic man hunted. This fact is important because, if it were confirmed, it would lead us to conclude that at least some of the animals represented played a role unconnected with the food that people then lived on. The number of sites for which it was possible to draw up a list of the animals depicted and a parallel list of the animals consumed as meat is unfortunately too limited to verify this hypothesis.

Groupings

We referred above to groupings of animal figures and signs, starting with the Aurignacian Age (30,000). The most frequent, almost exclusive animal grouping is of horses (100%) and of bison (56%) (or of aurochs, 39%, in other words, 95% for bovidae). This initial dyad, moreover, occupies the center of all surfaces used, and may be repeated several times in the same cave. The groupings in wall paintings have a complexity that derives from the diversity of the caves in which the decorations appear. So, too, geographical location and chronological evolution are reflected in various applications of the initial figurative formula and in the more or less pronounced use of natural forms. In any case, it is likely that the cave or the surface of the shelter wall was the object of a deliberate choice, and that the figures were not piled one on top of another haphazardly.

The horse(A)-bovid(B) twosome appears at all sites (fig. 7.1). Although we must allow for the possibility of caves or shelters that might not fit the basic AB formula, practically speaking the AB group is always present and dominates the groupings both numerically and topographically. But rarely does the AB group appear alone. Another category of animals intervenes, namely, group C (stag, mammoth, and occasionally chamois and reindeer). Among the wall painting groups, the ibex is most often the accompanying animal, but the stag, hind, mammoth, and reindeer also play the same role, most often on the sidelines, on the outer perimeter of the central panel groupings, or in the intermediary sections. The most frequent formula is thus AB + C, making up a triad with one interchangeable element: the ibex at Niaux, the mammoth at Rouffignac, the stag at Las Chimeneas. In the same cave, we can also see "moving" animals, or the following: at Niaux, the stag marks the deepest part of the large painted surface, the rather numerous ibexes framing the AB figures; at Lascaux, the situation is similar—ibexes appear three or four times immediately to the side of a group of animals, stags being equal in number but farther to the side. In a cave like the Combarelles, in which the figures number into the hundreds, the "third animal" is represented by the reindeer, the ibex, and the mammoth, which are concentrated in the general area of the side panel of each decorated gallery.

Finally, there is also a D category to which fierce animals belong: the rhinoceros, the bear, and the big cats. The bear is a relatively rare animal in Paleolithic iconography and has no clearly defined place, but the rhinoceros and the big cats are marginal animals, most often situated in the deepest or most peripheral parts of the figured group. At Lascaux, Font-de-Gaume, the Combarelles, to cite only a few, the big cats are in this position. In these three places, the rhinoceros occupies an analogous position: at Lascaux, at the bottom of the Well; at Font-de-Gaume, at the end of the main gallery next to the big cat; and at the Combarelles, superimposed over the "lioness" from the end of the second gallery. The complete formula for the grouping is C + AB + C (+ D) in the case of a cave with a single composition, one that forms part of a series. In extreme cases, as in Lascaux or Combarelles, one may encounter a series of groupings with the basic formula repeated time and again.

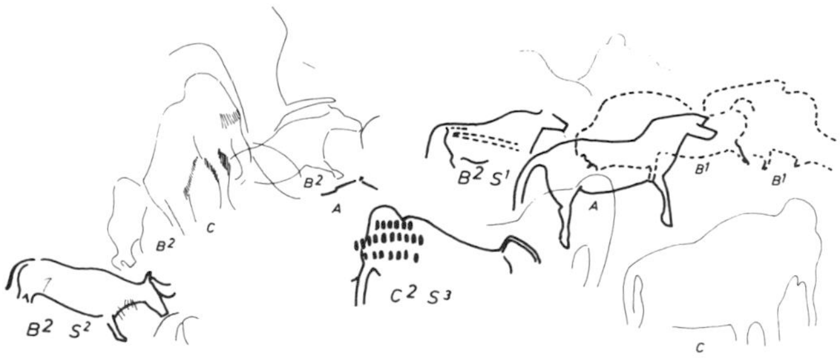

Cave of Pech-Merle (Lot). Middle and left of the great frieze painted in black. Two groups of animals can be seen: the group on the left and the group on the right each include a horse (A) and two bison on the right, two aurochs on the left. The mammoths present in both groupings make up group C. Between the two groupings, there are also three animals marked by signs: (1) a bull (B^2) bearing a sign (S^1) with a male connotation on his side (see fig. 5); (2) a cow (B^2) marked by wounds (S^2); (3) diagonally across from both animals, a mammoth bearing three rows of thick red dashes. The figures are between 60 and 120 cm long. (Fig. 3)

Signs

Signs seem to follow the same general patterns as animal figures. They fall into three categories (fig. 5). The first is made up of male symbols (S^1) ranging from the human body depicted in its entirety to a simple little stick. In between are sometimes very abstract transitions (lines branching out with two extensions at the base, as in Lascaux). The signs of the second group (S^2) correspond to female symbols. Like the signs of the first group, they range from a complete female representation to an empty or partitioned rectangle. The third group (S^3), in comparison with the other two, is homologous to the animals of group C or CD. It is made up of aligned dots or a series of little sticks aligned or clustered. In several cases, the S^3 signs are repeated at the beginning and the end of the figurative series. This phenomenon is quite evident at Lascaux, where the aligned dots are found at the entrance and at the far end of the Axial Diverticulum, between the Passage and the Nave, at the bottom of the Well, and at the end of the Diverticulum of the Big Cats. The signs of the third group, therefore, occupy a position rather set back, most often in the background, as at Font-de-Gaume, Pech-Merle, and El Castillo.

The relationship between signs and animals corresponds to the following broad lines: the S^1S^2 group is found juxtaposed with the animals of groups A and B (fig. 2), as in the case of the Diverticulum of the Big Cats at Lascaux (fig. 6), in which the S^1S^2 signs are in the central panel, right across from an AB group (horse-bison). But the signs may be independent of the animal figures, grouped in a separate diverticulum. Good examples can be found at Niaux (Black Room), at El Castillo, at La Pasiega, and, notably, at Cougnac. The relationship between animals and signs may thus be defined by the following formula:

$$\begin{array}{c} C + AB + C + D \\ S^3 + S^1S^2 + S^3 \end{array}$$

or

$$\begin{array}{c} C + AB + C + D/S^1S^2, \\ S^3 \qquad\quad S^3 \end{array}$$

Both formulas can even be found in the same cave (La Pasiega).

This complex arrangement must have encompassed an ideology whose elaborate character may be perceived through the arrangement. The situation is further complicated, however, by the role played by the cave itself. Natural caves have many accidental features that evoked, for Paleolithic man, sexual forms, generally female. These natural structures, fissures or stalagmitic formations, sometimes underscored in red (Gargas, Niaux), are also frequently completed with an S^1 sign (little sticks or dots: Gargas, Combel de Pech-Merle, Niaux), proving that the natural phenomenon was considered equivalent to S^2. This is particularly clear in Niaux, where two fissures in the inner gallery were marked at the entrance by a sign of male connotation (branching sign) accompanied in one of the two cases by a horse with its head extended in the direction of the fissure.

In the course of millennia and in a territory as vast as that of Paleolithic cave art, figurative traditions must have undergone numerous variations, and it is remarkable that we should come across an ideographic system that is so well constructed. Yet two rather important questions, concerning the role of wounds on animals and the role of hands, remain largely unresolved.

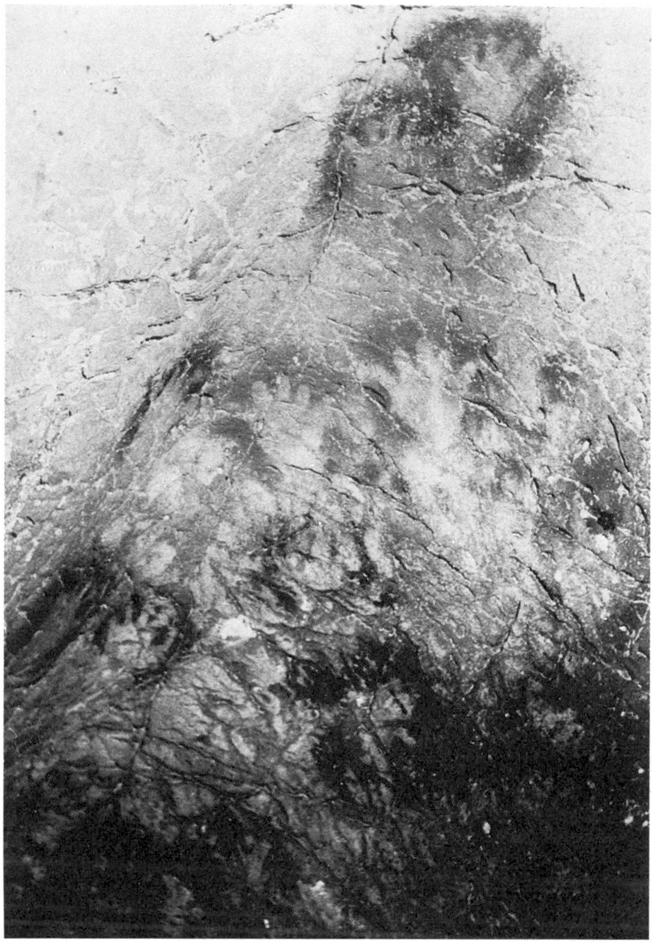

Cave of Gargas (Hautes-Pyrénées). Panel showing "negative" hands with "mutilated" fingers. Most such hands, colored red or black, are grouped in twos by subject, and appear to have been executed by folding in the fingers or by applying a stencil. (Fig. 4)

Wounds

In art objects as well as mural art, we find animals with wounds. Ever since research on prehistoric religion began, this detail has been thought to reveal the practice of magic spells. This explanation is not altogether impossible, but certain elements lead us to believe that it does not resolve the problem entirely. In fact, 96% of the animal figures on file (between 2,500 and 3,000) show no wounds. We might ask ourselves if the two series, animal and sign, really belong to the same symbolic system, or if two lines of symbols might have existed without any organic ties between them. Signs do seem to have played their role at the same times and in the same places as animals. What is more, both evolved synchronically, and both underwent parallel stylistic transformations. It is very unlikely that signs were slipped in among animals, with no connection to them, in the course of various rituals; too many signs are connected to animals by their position for the relationship not to be a close one, as the Pech-Merle paintings show (fig. 3). This does not preclude the claim that signs are sometimes independent, as at Altamira, where the signs and the animals of the Great Ceiling make up two distinct clusters; or as at El Castillo or La Pasiega, where, for one important portion, the painted

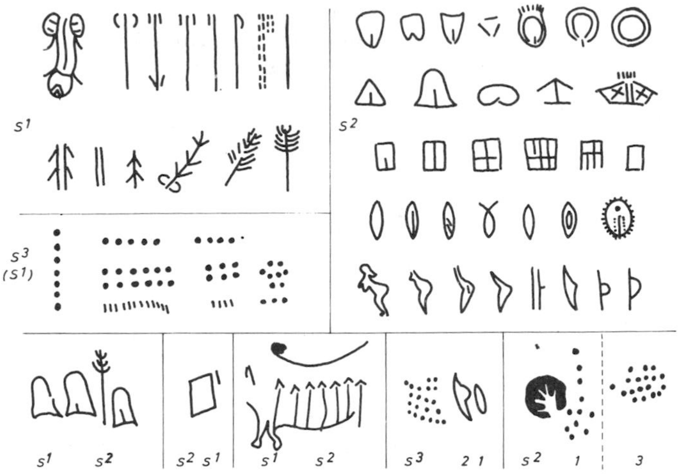

Geometrization of male and female symbols. S^1: phalloid derivatives. S^2: principal series of vulvar derivatives. S^3: rows of punctuation (dotted lines) and barred lines. Below, from left to right: S^1-S^2 groupings. El Castillo (Santander): triangle derivatives and branching sign. Lascaux (Dordogne): maximal geometrization and abstractions (empty rectangle and bar). Lascaux: crooked bar (S^1) and seven aligned wounds (S^2). S^1, S^2, S^3 groupings. Niaux (Ariège): bar (S^1), claviform (see same S^2 figure), cloud of dots (S^3). Pech-Merle (Lot): at the entrance of a deep side passage, three figures that appear to correspond in value to S^1: dotted line with four lateral dots (see same S^3 figure). The negative hand probably corresponds to S^2, and the cloud of dots, farther into the passage, probably corresponds to S^3. (Fig. 5).

Lascaux (Dordogne): (1) Engraved horse with rump turned such that the perineal region is exposed but devoid of primary sexual characteristics. 60 cm. (2) Paintings from the axial gallery, central part of the righthand wall. Aurochs in the same posture as the horse in front. Secondary sexual characteristics (general profile) are attributable to a cow, but primary characteristics, notably the udder, are invisible. This figure is included in the grouping formula A-B S^1-S^2 (horse-aurochs, bars, gridlike sign; see fig. 5). 1.70 m. (Fig. 6)

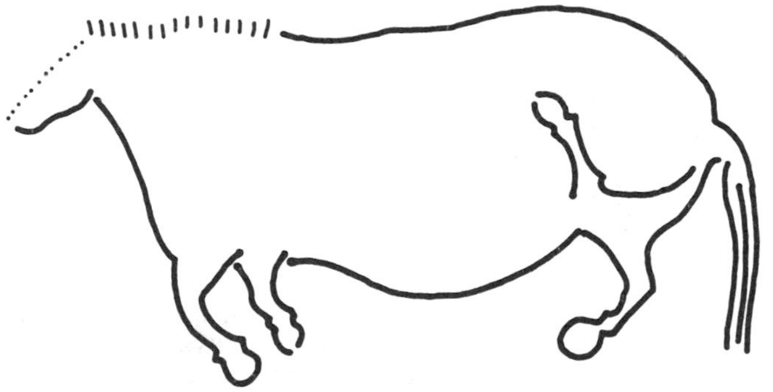

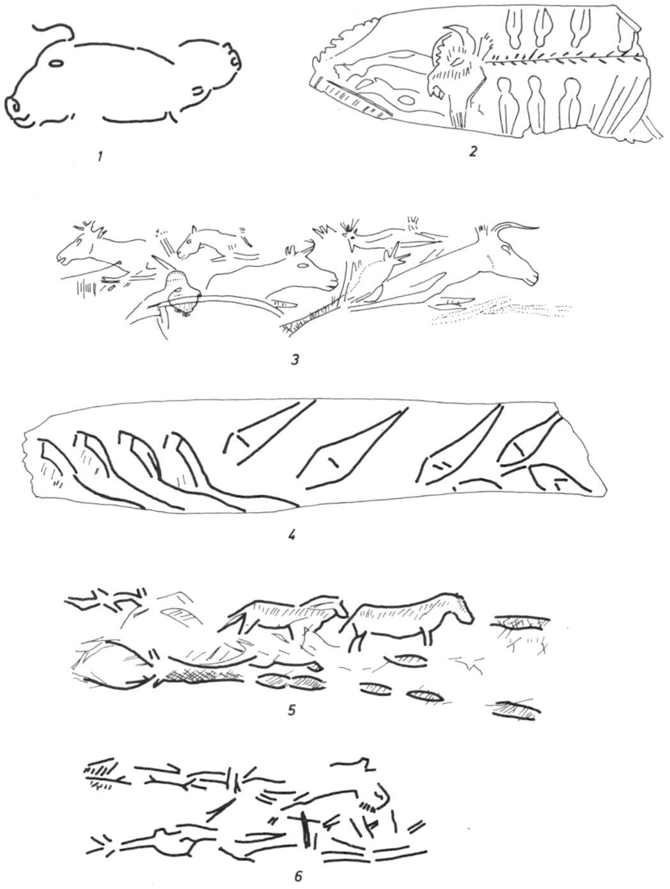

Gourdan (Haute-Garonne). The principle of association of animals A and B may also be applied to portable objects. This engraving on bone plaquette represents the aurochs-horse twosome with the heads of both animals assembled like the faces on playing cards. About 6 cm from nose to nose. (2) Raymonden (Dordogne). Partial pendant (or fish spatula). A scene of a religious nature seems to be unfolding: six or seven persons (perhaps more) are lined up on either side of a line resembling barbed wire at the end of which is the severed head of a bison and two paws with ill-defined hooves. Near the knee, one of these legs bears a "chestnut," a horny growth that is the vestige of the multifingered hoof of the ancestors of the *equidae*. It may indeed be a horse leg, and this grouping with its sacrificial look may refer to the A-B model. (3) Torre (Guipuzcoa). Roll of fine engravings around a bone tube. From left to right: stag, man, horse, chamois, two small ibex with frontal horns, and aurochs. This series of animals referring to A-B model + C is of more than purely artistic interest: between the subjects are abstract tracings (parallel or crossed strokes, beginnings of spherical figures, clouds made of fine dots, etc.) which must have ensured that Magdalenians could "read" this mythogram. (4) Mas-d'Azil (Ariège). Bone plaquette engraved with horses and fish, already strongly geometrized. Mythographic theme born out by several examples. (5) El Valle (Santander). Bone tube with engraved bird. Subject related to preceding one: two horses, one behind the other, a stag facing forward, numerous features with no apparent meaning, perhaps a snake, and some oval figures, probably fish. (6) El Pendo (Santander). Bone tube engravings, like the preceding ones, but virtually uninterpretable. There remains a part of the head and neck of a horse and a herbivore with visible horns (or antlers) and ears borne by a very long neck. Note that these two figures occupy the same situation as those of the El Valle tube. (Fig. 7)

signs are collected in a side passage; or at Cougnac (Lot), where S^1 and S^2 signs are located in a side alcove away from the animal figures, while the S^3 series occurs in the figured panels.

Whether these are two series of symbols executed simultaneously and experienced as forming the frame of a single ideological block, or whether they are two separate series with elements that were to enter one another on synchronic but distinct levels—either case presupposes a highly complex intellectual content, intimately tied to an elaborate social system. Could they be symbols of the propagation of humans and animals, a cosmogony that calls into play the complementary forces of male and female? It is difficult to reach a conclusion without going beyond the available data, but certainly we are in the presence of something quite different from what was long imagined about "the Paleolithic savages."

Of the 4% of animals showing wounds in the thoracic or the neighboring abdominal areas, if we do a percentage count by species, the greatest number goes to the bison (8%), then to the horse (2.5%), with zero or less than 1% for all other species. There is yet another striking fact. Although wounded animals are encountered throughout the Franco-Cantabrian region, most cases occur in the Ariège sector of the Pyrenees, with the greatest number represented at Niaux (25% of figured animals). The value of the wound as a testimony to magic spells for game might be merely an accessory phenomenon, but the hunting symbolism to which it refers is certain. The fact that wounds appear essentially only on the bodies of the basic twosome is perhaps connected with the AB = S^1S^2 equation, the wounds being the equivalent of S^2, that is, the female connotation. Three pieces of evidence may be invoked to support this contention: a horse at Lascaux bearing seven wounds on its body and an S^2 sign (fig. 5) on its neck and withers; a bison at Bernifal whose shoulder has an oval wound flanked by two little sticks; and a bison at Niaux engraved on clay, which has three wounds and two little sticks on its side. These parallel sticks belong to the highly varied portion of masculine symbols. One of the best examples of the relationship between signs and animals is that of the great panel of Pech-Merle (fig. 3) made up of two groupings that share the same C animal (C^2 mammoth). One is the aurochs-horse (AB^2), and the other the horse-bison (AB^1). Between the two groupings of figures are three animals: a bull, a cow, and a mammoth. Each bears different signs. The bull bears a double line of dashes with lateral extensions (S^1, of male character). The cow is riddled with wounds that seem to play the role of S^2 signs. The mammoth is covered with red spots aligned to form the equivalent of the S^3 sign. From this evidence we can hypothesize that "wounds" have the value of a female symbol. Establishing this symbolism would open a vast realm of possibilities for the symbolic system of Paleolithic art, one that involves the alternation of symbols of life and death.

Hands

While the problem of wounds allows us to do no more than hint at some kind of metaphysical solution, *positive* hand imprints (in which a hand is smeared with color and pressed flat against the wall) and *negative* hand imprints (in which a hand is laid flat against the wall and outlined in color) raise questions equally resistant to clear answers. Positive hands are substantially rarer than negative hands and show up infrequently in groupings, but the Bayol cave in the Ardèche region has a good example. It shows six positive hands in a grouping that includes an aurochs, two horses, and one big cat, all treated in a very particular style.

There are several types of negative hands, probably corresponding to several different traditions. The first category is made up of hands integrated in a grouping that includes, notably, dottings; this is the case in Pech-Merle, where in six instances hands are associated with dotted lines in close proximity to the two crisscrossed horses and once with eleven dotted lines above the opening of a very low side passage (fig. 5). The same arrangement of animal figures and dottings is found in El Castillo. In the Périgord, negative hands appear in isolation (one at Font-de-Gaume, one at Combarelles, several grouped at Bernifal, etc.). At Roucadour (Lot), the hands are superposed over the animals, and they have long pointed fingers incised on a black background. The Pech-Merle hands give the impression of being inserted in an arrangement where they play an important role, surely as important as the S^2 signs with their female connotation.

The hands in the cave of Gargas (Hautes-Pyrénées), like those in the neighboring grotto at Tibiran, are very different in nature (fig. 4). Repeated scores of times in different panels and hollows of the cave, they have the special feature of cut-off or, more likely, bent-in fingers. The various combinations of fingers might have been part of a kind of symbolic code of the animals most commonly represented in figurative art (horse, bison, ibex, etc.). The same digital formula appears again in side-by-side hands repeated twice and alternating between red and black (fig. 4). Examples can also be found at the openings of niches or fissures, in the position normally occupied by animals or signs of CD and S^1 groups. As strange as it may seem, the "mutilated hands" of Gargas, which include many children's hands, are not missing all five fingers. They seem to correspond to a fairly rational application of signals involving variably bent fingers, gestures that can still be observed today among certain groups of hunters, notably the Bushmen. Aside from the monumental aspect of the connections between the groups of hands and their natural support, the ideographic aspect is extremely impressive.

Animal and human figures make up the ground on which our tentative explanation of wall painting rests. This explanation calls on data which, in the way they are assembled, suggest a complex ideological construct. To what extent can objects that are found not on walls but on sites of living quarters corroborate this claim?

Objects

Caves contain particularly precious data, if only because the images have preserved their location on walls. A no less precious source of information, however, may be found on the surfaces of Paleolithic floors strewn with objects that bear human and animal figures. Some of these objects are fairly soft fragments of stone or fragments of bone on which figures have been incised or sculpted. No practical function can be attributed to them, and we are struck by their resemblance to the figures on walls. Given their iconographic content, we ask whether they could have played the same role in living quarters as the figures played in the cave, and whether they were used to reproduce the same combinations. These questions are difficult to answer decisively, for the possibilities of iconographic combinations are extremely varied. The figures (statuettes, plaquettes or blocks, weapons or tools, personal adornments) may have been assembled in a meaningful way (according to the C-A-B-C + D model), a configuration that may presuppose, for example, either several plaquettes each bearing one figure, or several plaquettes each bearing several animal figures. Unfortunately rare are the cases where portable objects are found in their functional places, and even rarer are sites where the excavators took the trouble to record the exact position of the relics. Yet we can begin by assuming that, since caves existed only in a limited number of areas while vast territories lent themselves only to open-air settlements, the plaquettes of stone, ivory, or bone or the statuettes which sometimes abound at such sites fulfilled the role that otherwise devolved upon cave walls.

We may also assume that the other decorated objects reflect, in whole or in part, the same ideological scheme that is displayed by the grouping of the figures on the walls.

Statuettes

Statuettes of animals are relatively rare in the Paleolithic art of western Europe. The cave of Isturitz (Basses-Pyrénées) stands out as an exception with its numerous animals (bison, horses, bears) incised in soft rock. The true domain of animal figures in round relief is central and eastern Europe. The pictorial repertory of Europe east of the Rhine is mostly made up of statuettes molded in clay mixed with powdered bone (Moravia), incised in bone or in mammoth ivory; and figurines of mammoth, horse, bison, and big cats. The functions of these statuettes are as yet unclear, but since they must have assumed the same role as that played by the engravings and paintings in the caves, they must have the same symbolic ranges.

One category of figures is made up of female statuettes, inaccurately called "Venus" figures, that appear in various forms depending on the stages of the Paleolithic epoch and the regions in which they were executed. The items discovered at Kostienki (on the Don River), on Ukranian sites, at Predmost in Moravia, Willendorf in Austria, and at Brassempouy and Lespugue in southwestern France show in the details of their execution that they belong to the same pictorial traditions. Were the religious traditions that they were supposed to illustrate of the same nature? That is hard to answer, for the good reason that female statuettes can only symbolize a limited number of functions, generally relating to fertility. Based on what we know today, it would be difficult to say any more about them, except perhaps that the statuettes discovered in living quarters may have played an identical role to that of the signs in the groupings of figures on the walls. Male figures by their very scarcity seem to have occupied a much more modest place.

In brief, plaquettes, which are far more numerous in the West than statuettes, and statuettes, which are more numerous than plaquettes in central and eastern Europe, seem to have had the same functions. Given the resemblances between portable art (on plaquettes and statuettes) and mural art, we can ascribe identical functions to them and assimilate them to the same religious process. Unfortunately, this does not entirely clarify the details of the process that we know to have borrowed the same basic symbols throughout all of Europe for twenty thousand years. The formula A-B, C, D + S^1, S^2, S^3 did not necessarily have the same ideological implications in the Urals as it did on the banks of the Vézère. The hundreds of plaquettes of engraved schist from Gönnersdorf (dating from the Magdalenian epoch ca. 10,000) left lying on the ground may not have had the same function as the heavy engraved blocks of the Aurignacian epoch around 30,000.

It seems possible nevertheless to discern in the groupings of art objects and mural art alike the systematic presence of two animals A-B, often associated with one or two animals from group C. Human figures and male and female symbols are also present, as they are in wall paintings. The specialized use of certain objects may have influenced the choice of the figures that were drawn on them. There were relatively few decorated objects during the first millennia; realistic figures, at least, were rare. It is not until the middle and late Magdalenian Age, from 12,000 to 9000, that objects made of reindeer horn and bone begin to be covered with figures. Propelling devices—hooked pieces probably designed to hurl assegais at game—most often depict a single animal, close to the hook. On objects in this category the most eclectic assortment can be found: horse, bison, mammoth, ibex, reindeer, big cat, fish, bird. The propelling devices (their real use is still unknown) thus fall in the same iconographic category as plaquettes and statuettes.

Perforated Sticks

Perforated sticks are a different story. A kind of lever made of reindeer horns, the stick consists of a cylindrical handle with a bifurcation at one end in which a hole three centimeters in diameter has been pierced at the thickest point. Its real use was to straighten out, while hot or cold, the long assegai spears that had kept the curvature of the horns from which they had been made. The class of perforated sticks includes a large number of carefully decorated objects. In a significant proportion of them, the handle is sculpted in the shape of a phallus. Sometimes both extensions of the head of the object have this decoration. There are also many perforated sticks that bear the A-B grouping (horse-bison) or the third animal, in the form of a stag, a reindeer, or an ibex. A whole series of perforated sticks are decorated on their lateral extensions with two heads of bison, highly geometrized and often reduced to two sets of parallel bars. This decorative element can be found from the Asturias to Switzerland. Some perforated sticks feature realistic scenes, such as the one at Dordogne in Laugerie-Basse, which on one side shows a man knocked over by a bison and on the other side a horse; or the one in La Madeleine, which has a man, a snake, and two horses on one side, and two bison on the other. Certainly these animals were not grouped in a fortuitous manner: the H-B + A formula (Human-bison + horse) is the same formula as in the famous scene on the Well at Lascaux (a man knocked over by a bison, with a horse on the opposite wall). The second scene, however, must refer to another mythic content, for its formula, H-A + B (+ S) (Human-horse + bison [and snake]), has no known equivalent, but it does highlight the imperative character of the representation of the complementary animal: in the first case, the horse; in the second, the bison. We should also note that, as at Lascaux, the second animal is on the side opposite to the one with the scene.

Assegais

Assegais make up a category of particularly expressive decorated items. The ornamentation on these spears appears relatively early, around 20,000, and consists of geometric patterns, sometimes of a highly simplified animal figure. These markings may correspond to different hunters in the same group. But as time went by, the animal figures multiplied on some of these assegais. During the late Magdalenian era, some were covered with rows of horses on a raised field, which suggests that they served as instruments for parades or rituals rather than as effective weapons. The ends of assegais are often perforated to make them into pendants. Such pieces may have been part of a particular assegai that was lucky in its hunting and thereby served as a "talisman." The numerous pendants found in the Upper Paleolithic Age are largely inspired by sexual symbolism (cowrie shell, oval pendants, stag canines, etc.). It is thus likely that the assegai played a dual symbolic role. A few indices seem to support this contention, namely, the probable assimilation in mural art of male symbols with the assegai and female symbols with the wound. Many details from the natural relief of walls, such as oval niches painted red and the wounds on certain animals, support such a hypothesis. But it is difficult to consolidate the ideological aspects of this symbolic frame of reference.

Other decorated objects that might shed light on the religious thought of Paleolithic man require an even more sensitive interpretation. Harpoon points with realistic decoration are extremely rare. Conversely, we do have a considerable number of spatulas in the shape of fish, often highly geometrized. They may bear symbolic meaning, but at what level? The scale of values may range from a representation of a primarily aesthetic character to an instrument indispensable for the execution of a ritual. The same may be said of the rings of bone, three or four centimeters in diameter, with a very eclectic range of animal engravings on both sides. The fish spatula with its inevitable iconographic base (usually a species of *Salmonidae*), and the rings of bone on which all species are represented (including the human species) provide us only with a basic assumption and certainly not with evidence for an entire superstructure of beliefs. It is therefore by reference to the figures on walls and plaquettes that the iconography of portable objects can be analyzed. We may also want to view in the same spirit the so-called silhouette outlines, small pendants carved out of a hyoid bone, of which there are many known examples showing heads of horses as well as a group of eighteen ibex heads and one bison head, which may remind us of the triad horse-bison-ibex, the model of wall depiction.

One last category of materials is made up of groupings of figures engraved mostly on cylindrical objects (tubes of bird bone, assegai shafts, etc.), similar to the perforated sticks referred to above. Some of these objects bear explicit figures, like the bone tube of Torre (Spain), which in the space of fifteen centimeters depicts a series of busts including a stag, man, horse, chamois, ibex, and aurochs (fig. 7.1). This grouping, which may also incorporate signs in parallel or converging lines cross-hatched inside with ladders, is not far removed from certain wall groupings, such as the diver of Portel (Ariège), whose middle part is occupied by a horse, a bison, and male and female signs, while the periphery is occupied by the third sign (S^3), an ibex, and a stag. It would be hard not to regard these various assembled animals as the protagonists of a mythical story, a mythogram rather than a catalogue of the presumed victims of a spell of hunting magic. But whatever the figures may designate precisely, we cannot yet afford to go outside the realm of fact to venture an explanation. Thus we have a whole series of groupings on cylinders or plaquettes, graphically explicit but just as mysterious as ever, such as the strange object found in Les Eyzies on which eight hunters carrying assegais on their shoulders seem to be parading in front of a bison, or another item from Chancelade (fig. 7.2) on which seven human silhouettes appear to surround a bison's head and severed front hooves. These two examples, probably variants of the same theme, show how the discovery of new versions might help us to decipher an increasingly important part of the Paleolithic message.

A significant number of specimens (figs. 7.4, 7.5, 7.6) bear an ornamentation that is very difficult to identify: a row of curves and ovoid figures including a recognizable horse here and there or a highly simplified stag, or sometimes a fish. Given the constancy with which geometric motifs replace explicit figures, we could almost speak of ideograms, though we need not see in these semigeometric figures the elements of "writing." We can assume that the geometrized symbols preserved their meaning, so that a grouping like "chevrons-broken lines" could be equivalent to, for instance, "horse-snake," chevrons being the tail end of a row of horses, and the broken line being the geometrization of the snake's body: both cases exist in an explicit form.

It might seem surprising to hear so little said about "prehistoric religion." As far as practices are concerned, our knowledge consists mainly of gaps. We may imagine that the caves were shrines in which highly elaborate rituals took place, but all we *have* is wall decorations. The fact that the dead were buried with ocher and, at least in some cases, with funerary personal effects, leads us to ascribe to Upper Paleolithic man some notion of an afterlife, but we know nothing about its modalities in any detail. The tablets or engraved blocks tell us about iconographic activities that must have had a religious purpose, but we are far from being able to assert what kind of purpose it was. The same applies to decorated objects (perforated sticks, propelling devices, spatulas, etc.) of which we cannot even claim to know the exact usage. Nevertheless, the wealth of the iconography and the constancy of certain relationships between figures and between figures and the surfaces on which they appear make it possible for us to sketch the bare outlines of a system of religious thought, though its background is still very murky. The complexity and quality of these groupings express feelings (with nuances tied to places and times) that reflect simultaneously the aesthetic and religious life of Paleolithic man.

A.L.-G./g.h.

BIBLIOGRAPHY

H. BREUIL, *Quatre cents siècles d'art pariétal* (Montignac 1952). P. GRAZIOSI, *L'arte dell'antica età della pietra* (Florence 1956). A. LAMING-EMPERAIRE, *La signification de l'art rupestre paléolithique* (Paris 1962). ANDRÉ LEROI-GOURHAN, *Préhistoire de l'art occidental* (Paris 1965); *Les religions de la préhistoire* (Paris 1971); "Les signes pariétaux de Paléolithique·supérieur franco-cantabrique," *Simposio intern. de arte rupestre* (Barcelona 1968), 67–77, fig.; "Considérations sur l'organisation spatiale des figures animales dans l'art pariétal paléolithique," *Actes del Symposium intern. de arte prehis.* (Santander 1972), 281–308; "Iconographie et interprétation," *Val Camonica symposium 72* (Capo di Ponte 1975), 49–55. ARLETTE LEROI-GOURHAN, "The Flowers Found with Shanidar IV, a Neanderthal Burial in Iraq," *Science* 190 (1975): 562–64. L. MEROC, "Informations archéologiques, Circonscription de Toulouse, Mas d'Azil," *Gallia Préhistoire* 4 (1961):256–57.

"Nomadic Thought" and Religious Action

When the rainy season comes, the mendicant monk stops wandering and heads back to his monastery.[1]

For some years now, nomadic societies have awakened strong and renewed interest among ethnologists. On an intuitive level, these societies scattered over the globe seem to be mutually comparable, and attempts have been made to construct models of such societies, that is, to go beyond the empirical diversity that science seeks to overcome. These attempts at synthesis, notably the collective work published under the direction of Lee and De Vore[2] on hunter-gatherers, and the works of B. Spooner[3] on pastoral nomads, are evidence of the special position that nomadic societies occupy today in ethnology.

The term "nomadism" covers quite diverse phenomena: hunter-gatherers and pastoral nomads move over greater or lesser distances, more or less frequently; hunter-gatherers make use of wild objects, and pastoral nomads domestic objects, to mediate their relation with the natural environment. Although nomadic societies differ among themselves in their type of economy and in the breadth and frequency of their movements, as a group they contrast with societies that do not move, settled societies, and it is in this light that we shall consider them for the purposes of this study, setting aside the ways in which the group could be subdivided. Dissimilar in many ways, both social and economic, these societies share not only itinerant behavior but also certain characteristics, which we will examine in order to determine whether they are reflected at the level of thought and worldview. Starting with a limited amount of work done on this subject, we can but suggest a direction of study and posit some hypotheses for research. To find pantheons common to nomads, if such a thing were possible, would require far more concerted and exhaustive studies. But it may already be possible to isolate from its various contexts an attitude to the supernatural world and religion that is common to nomads, and to define a framework within which we might study their mythology.

"Free, individualistic, subject to no state nor to any tyranny," such is the "traditional stereotype" of the pastoral nomad.[4] But it is also an objective piece of information to the extent that it is derived from the image that the nomad has of himself. When this self-image comes into close contact with settled societies, it may even be more pronounced, thus affirming in a deliberate way the difference between nomadic and settled ideologies. Pastoral nomads have a realistic vision of the world and a rather meager ceremonial life. They practice a great deal of divination but little witchcraft. Religion is centered on the individual rather than on the group; indeed, a pantheon comprising a great number of divine figures seems to be more common among farmers. If nomads show little interest in religion, and if they refer to manifestations of the supernatural in "stoic terms," this does not mean that they are any more "secular"[5] than any other group. The cosmology of pastoral nomads in the Middle East, for example, tends to be expressed in Islamic terms. Through this filter, as Spooner points out, it should be possible to see those elements of cosmology that antedate Islam or are not integral to it. When these are compared with other cosmologies from nomadic populations in regions lacking such a culturally dominant ideology, it may be possible to isolate the elements that derive from the nomadic adaptation.[6]

The mythology of hunter-gatherer societies presents notable similarities. The myths that retrace the origins of a society are apparently universal and come out of the same mold. In these myths, the culture hero creates mankind and its customs; he domesticates fire, teaches arts and crafts, and shapes the landscape and animals. In the cosmology, spirits are not gods: culture heroes or creator spirits no longer intervene in the affairs of men, and that is why they are not worshiped. They have to do with existential ideology and not with normative ideology. Just as the accent is placed on the person in nomadic society, so the world of spirits is strongly individualized; egalitarianism within the group is reflected in the absence of any hierarchy among the spirits. The individual deals directly with the world of the supernatural. Except for the shaman/doctor, there is no reliable mediation by specialized individuals.[7] The culture hero who offers the world to humans after he has created them is not totally absent from nomadic societies; but probably more characteristic of such societies is the strongly existential aspect of the ideology as well as egalitarianism. The absence of authoritarian chiefs and of a certain type of power excludes certain types of divine figures. Moreover, nomadic hunters pay little attention to what does not involve them directly. Accordingly, the Mbuti are more concerned with the present than with the past or the future. They are practical people. They eschew all speculation about the future or the hereafter on the grounds that not having been there they do not know what it is like and not knowing what it is like they cannot predict what their behavior will be. They say that to try to look into the future is to "walk blindly."[8] Knowledge is considered a way of living rather than a rule. And it is precisely in their behavior in the face of—rather than by the content of—myth or the supernatural that the clear outlines of a way of thinking peculiar to nomads begin to emerge. We see in hunter-gatherers certain features already observed in the pastoral nomads, and profoundly different from the religious attitudes of settled societies. Before we describe nomadic societies as nonreligious or hardly religious, we might first ask whether ethnologists hold too narrow a conception of ritual and symbolic behavior, and whether their analytic tools may be too closely tied to the categories of settled societies, which would hamper their perception of religious phenomena among nomads.

Among the Basseri, pastoral nomads of Iran, the paucity of ritual activity is striking;[9] they are indifferent to metaphysical problems and to religion. But is this really a lack, or are the descriptive categories that are being used incapable of describing the reality of the situation? The central rite of the society is migration itself. For the Basseri, migration is laden with meaning, though not expressed by means of technically unnecessary symbolic acts or exotic paraphernalia. The Basseri respond not to the utilitarian aspects of activities but to movement and its dramatic forms, to the meanings implicit in the sequence of their activities.[10] Is it not rather ethnocentric to assume that an activity that is important from an economic point of view cannot also be important from a ritualistic or symbolic point of view? The migrations of nomads are more than mere business trips; they are also ritually motivated and determined, and our difficulties in observation seem to be due to our conflation of these two domains.

In this discussion of the relationship between religious attitude (taken in a rather broad sense) and nomadism, societies with seasonal variations are both exceptional and typical because they are alternately nomadic and settled. The gathered habitat of the winter season contrasts with the scattered habitat of the summer season, with its mobility and the splintering of the group into families in the narrowest sense of the word. There are two ways of occupying land, but there are also two ways of thinking: "This contrast between life in winter and life in summer is reflected not only in rituals, festivals, and religious ceremonies of all sorts. It also profoundly affects ideas, collective representations, in a word, the whole mentality of the group.[11] . . . In summer, life is somewhat secularized."[12] The ecological constraints to which the group is subject make nomadism necessary, and the group's requirements come to restrict religious thought and practice. But just as we must consider the role of adaptation to the environment, we must also refine our categories of analysis, and when appearances evoke secularization, we must understand that the foundation has yet to be deciphered. The mobility that characterizes nomadic societies is indeed the central feature of their organization, but it is also the main obstacle to our understanding.

"We must beware of any tendency to treat fixed and permanent ties linking together aggregates of people as normal, and loose, impermanent bonds as abnormal and requiring special explanation."[13] The migrations of hunters or pastoral nomads by far exceed those that would be required by the demands of the natural environment and of access to natural resources. The fluidity and the constant coming and going, both of groups and of individuals within the groups, have a political function: they make it possible to ensure order, the resolution of conflicts, and, paradoxically, cohesion, because the lines of fusion and fission of groups and individuals do not necessarily follow the lines of kinship. Among nomads, social relations become activated through changes of place: proximity or distance are not relevant, and space is in a sense negated. Finally—and, in our view, this is an essential point—the changes of place have a religious function: they are highly valued, so highly that Barth sees them as the central rite among the Basseri. It is movement that leads nomads "into closer recognition of the one constant in their lives, the environment and its life-giving qualities. Under such conditions of flux where band and even family relations are often brittle and fragmentary, the environment in general, and one's own hunting territory in particular, become for each individual the one reliable and rewarding focus of his attention, his loyalty, and his devotion."[14] In other words, the nomad "does not have the impression of inhabiting a man-made world. . . . He is controlled by objects, not persons. . . . There is not an anthropomorphic cosmos. Hence there is no call for articulate forms of social intercourse with nonhuman beings and no need for a set of symbols with which to send and receive special communication."[15] The nomad does not seek to improve the environment in which he lives. In this sense, he is controlled by objects and a world that are *wild*, and he is in direct touch with nature. The domestic animals through whose intervention he exploits the wild objects, if he is pastoral, serve only to mediate this relationship with nature. Whether he is a hunter-gatherer or a shepherd, he does not impose his Culture on Nature as do settled peoples. Mobility and fluidity of groups and within groups; decentralized societies, or rather societies with multiple centers; egalitarianism; direct contact with nature—such are the poles that may affect the ideology of nomads and that may be reflected in collective representations and in rituals.

With a few examples, we have sought to come to terms with nomadism and its underlying ideology as a "certain type of behavior,"[16] rather than as a mode of economic production or as a variable determined by environment. This particular attitude, in the face of the supernatural and the symbolic world, is governed by what we might call a nomadic way of thinking that participates in the "primitive/wild/*sauvage*" way of thinking but preserves its own characteristics within it. The analysis of the content of the myths of various nomadic societies may indeed highlight the lines of force around which "nomadic thought" is organized, and will finally allow us to spell out the specificity of a way of thinking in which what is normal is not what is fixed, and the fluid and the moving are order and not chaos.

F.-R.P./g.h.

NOTES

1. M. MAUSS, "Étude de morphologie sociale," in *Sociologie et anthropologie* (Paris 1966), 472.
2. R.-B. LEE and I. DEVORE, eds., *Man the Hunter* (Chicago 1968).
3. B. SPOONER, "Towards a Generative Model of Nomadism," *Anthropological Quarterly* 44, no. 3 (1971): 198–210; "The Cultural Ecology of Pastoral Nomads," in *Addison-Wesley Module in Anthropology,* no. 45 (Reading, MA, 1973).
4. B. SPOONER, "Cultural Ecology of Pastoral Nomads," 35.
5. Ibid., 39.
6. Ibid.
7. E. R. SERVICE, *The Hunters* (Englewood Cliffs, NJ, 1966).
8. C. M. TURNBULL, *Wayward Servants* (Garden City, NY, 1965), 247.
9. F. BARTH, *Nomads of South Persia* (Boston 1961), 135.
10. Ibid.
11. M. MAUSS, "Étude de morphologie sociale," 447–48.
12. Ibid., 444.
13. J. WOODBURN, "Stability and Flexibility in Hadza Residential Groupings," in *Man the Hunter,* Lee and DeVore, eds., 107.
14. C. M. TURNBULL, "The Importance of Flux in Two Hunting Societies," in *Man the Hunter,* Lee and DeVore, eds., 137.
15. M. DOUGLAS, *Natural Symbols* (London 1970), 60–61; cited in Spooner, "Cultural Ecology of Pastoral Nomads," 40.
16. CL. LÉVI-STRAUSS, "Hunting and Human Evolution: Discussion," in *Man the Hunter,* Lee and DeVore, eds., 344.

PART 2

Rome

Italy

It is impossible to speak of a "religion of ancient Italy" in the same way that one might speak of "the Greek religion." In the traditional framework of the classical world, built on the two great civilizations of Greece and Rome, Italy does not represent a united and continuous historical reality as Greece does. Initially, during the first millennium B.C., Italy's territory was divided into zones inhabited by diverse peoples, each having their own beliefs and customs—zones to which were added the band of Greek colonies along the southern coasts of the peninsula and in Sicily. Later, beginning at the time of the Roman conquest and continuing to the end of antiquity, the religion of ancient Italy became identified with Roman religion. Therefore several articles should be consulted on this topic: the following article on pre-Roman Italy, along with the articles to which it refers, and those articles that deal with Roman religion.

M.P./d.b.

Religion in Pre-Roman Italy: The Historical Framework

Pre-Roman Italy occupies a special place in the general development of the religious conceptions of the Mediterranean peoples of antiquity, even if its role was much less important than that of the Greek world, by which it was greatly influenced. The term "pre-Roman" usually designates the period from the beginning of historical times around the eighth century B.C. to the political, linguistic, and cultural unification of Italy under Roman domination between the third and first centuries B.C. (obviously we must not forget the existence of Rome, then at the very beginning of its development—which took place in parallel with that of the other centers of culture of the Italic world).

The absence of unity and coherent progress is the essential characteristic of pre-Roman Italy, and one that clearly differentiates it from Greece at the same period. Italy can be seen as a mosaic of people distinct in origin, language, and culture, and of social groups at different stages of development. We know the historical names of the main ethnic groups which existed at the beginning of the Roman conquest (Latini, Campani, Apuli, Calabri, Lucani, Bruttii, Samniti, Sabini, Piceni, Umbri, Etrusci, Liguri, Veneti, Histri, Galli); these names reappear in the names of the regions of unified Italy at the time of the emperor Augustus (I. Latium and Campania; II. Apulia and Calabria; III. Lucania and Bruttii; IV. Sabini and Samnium; V. Picenum; VI. Umbria; VII. Etruria; VIII. [Gallia] Cispadana, then Aemilia; IX. Liguria; X. Venetia and Histria; XI. [Gallia] Transpadana), and some of these, sometimes with some alterations and displacements, survive to this day. But we must keep in mind that this subdivision only partly corresponds to the original ethnographic and historical conditions as these are revealed to us by linguistics and archaeology. In fact, except for some minor and heterogeneous groups hard to classify (such as the Liguri and the Alpine populations), we can list the following formations on Italian territory: (a) the Etruscans, with their own language, which is not Indo-European; (b) the Italic peoples who spoke Indo-European languages, but different ones from the Latins, the Apulians, the Umbro-Sabellians, and the Veneti; (c) the Greek colonies along the coasts of southern Italy (Magna Graeca) and Sicily. Toward the end of the archaic period, the double role of cohesion and diffusion that the cities played is superimposed on ethnic factors, particularly in the zones of the Greek colonies and in Tyrrhenian Italy (Etruria, Latium, Campania). In the fifth and sixth centuries B.C., the face of pre-Roman Italy would be profoundly changed by the expansion of the Sabellian-Umbrian peoples (that is, the Sabines, the Samnites, the Campanians or Osci, the Lucani, the Bruttii, the Piceni, the Umbrians, etc.) over a large part of the peninsula, and by the penetration of the Celts (Gauls) via the Alps into northern and central Italy.

It was necessary to pause for these historical preliminaries in order to understand the complexity and variety of religious experience in such a composite world. It is evident that each of the principal cultures should be the object of a separate study, suited to its own specific character: thus we

Pre-Roman Italy.

should deal with Hellenic Italy in terms of Greek religion, and with Rome from its origins in terms of Roman religion; for Etruria and the various Italic populations, we must refer to the most characteristic aspects that can be glimpsed behind what is known of their religions, and for the Gauls, to Celtic religion. At the same time, we must not neglect the insular territories (Sicily, Sardinia, and Corsica), which, while not part of Italy in the ancient sense of the word, that of continental Italy, had close historical and cultural relations with the mainland, while at the same time local cultures spread and Phoenician and Carthaginian colonies were established.

Yet from a more general, historical point of view, we must get the religions of all of Pre-Roman Italy into perspective in order to attempt to determine their place, functions, and consequences.

If we set aside the Roman sources, what is known on this subject is relatively restricted, fragmentary, and heterogeneous. The absence of an indigenous literature among the Italic peoples, or its loss (where it did exist, as it certainly did in Etruria) following the disappearance of the local languages and their replacement by Latin, constitutes a fundamental negative factor in comparison with other ancient civilizations. The data recorded by classical Greek and Latin writers are indirect, fortuitous, and often uncertain, especially when the sources are relatively late. Even for the Greek colonies, the literary accounts are full of gaps due to the loss of a large part of the works of local authors. Outside the Greek colonies, the few remaining documents, mainly epigraphs written in Etruscan, Umbrian, Oscan, Messapian, and Venetian, give us some useful data on beliefs and cults. But for the rest we only have the evidence of archaeological monuments and records—the remains of sanctuaries and necropolises, images and pictorial scenes, coins, furnishings, etc.

The most important general facts can be summarized as follows:

1. *The persistence of prehistoric traditions and primitive conceptions.* The transition to the historical period is not clearly marked. The innovations that characterize this transition (the formation and definition of the main ethnocultural units at the beginning of Greek colonization, the opening to the forms and ideas of the great civilizations of the eastern Mediterranean, evolution to urban structures, development of political and religious institutions, the adoption of writing, etc.) are gradual. At first they are limited—outside the Greek colonies, of course—to the Tyrrhenian coast and particularly to Etruria and the Etruscan sphere of influence; in most of the rest of Italy, that is, in the interior of the peninsula, on the Adriatic slope, and in the north, their penetration was very slow and remained marginal. These latter territories preserved, almost until the time of the Roman conquest, certain essential aspects of the way of life and organization characteristic of Iron Age cultures, as well as survivals of prehistoric ritual customs such as the celebration of cults in grottoes or rock sanctuaries, and the practice of pictorial engravings (characteristic of the Alpine valleys), anthropomorphic stelae, the proximity of houses and tombs, etc. But even in the more advanced cultural centers, except for the Greek colonies, traces survived of primitive conceptions and practices so distant from the rationality of the classical world that they sometimes provoked the astonishment and incomprehension of writers in the Hellenistic and Roman periods. Most striking are the suggestions of an animistic conception of the supernatural; the omnipresent importance of divine signs and divination; the high social and religious status of women (in Etruria and even in early Rome), which have been interpreted as survivals of matriarchy; and the tenacious belief in the material survival of the dead in their place of burial, and all the rites implied in such a belief (house-shaped urns and tombs, portrait images, rich funerary apparatus, funeral games, etc.).

2. *External influences, especially from Greece.* In addition to the conditions that it inherited from prehistory and protohistory, Italic religiosity was profoundly interwoven with Oriental and Greek themes that, in certain respects, marked it decisively. During the "Orientalizing" period between the eighth and sixth centuries B.C., along with a great number of objects and pictorial themes imported from the Aegean world and the Near East (Egypt, Syria, Mesopotamia, Urartu, Anatolia) via the great currents of Phoenician and Greek maritime traffic, probably echoes of the beliefs of the ancient Oriental civilizations and archaic Greece at the beginning of its development penetrated widely in Italy. Evidence of this is provided by certain divine or monstrous beings and their iconography ("mistress of animals," sphinx, griffin, centaurs, etc.), the legendary traditions that integrate the elements of the newly emerging Greek mythology, and symbolism in general. Certain characteristic phenomena, which were not manifested clearly until later, seem directly linked to the Asiatic world—for instance, Etruscan haruspicy used little models of animal livers, as in Mesopotamia and Anatolia. As for the influence of the Semitic religions, aside from their diffusion in the Phoenician and Carthaginian colonial domain of Sicily and Sardinia (discussed above), we can cite the unusual case of the consecration of a *sacellum* to the goddess Astarte, assimilated to the Etruscan goddess Uni, in the sanctuary of Pyrgi on the Tyrrhenian coast. But it was mostly Greek religion, directly transplanted to the

colonies of southern Italy and Sicily beginning in the eighth century B.C., that gave the Italic centers its divine models with their respective attributes (the local pantheon thus came to be identified with the Greek pantheon—the Etruscan god Tinia and the Latino-Italic [D]iove, for example, were assimilated to Zeus; the Etruscan and Latin goddess Uni [Juno] to Hera; the god Mars, recognized by all the Italic peoples, to Ares; and so forth), its myths, and the specific traits of its cult (forms of altars and temples, sacrificial rites, votive offerings). It is very interesting, finally, to see the development of an impressive store of legendary narratives and mythographic constructions linking the heroic world of the Greeks with local Italian traditions, either by mixing them or by linking them.

3. *Definitions of the different cultural environments.* The diversity of populations and cultures in pre-Roman Italy constitutes the fundamental historical perspective; it is manifested especially in the domain of the sacred, which by its very nature participates in the deepest heritage of every people and every community. Real and profound differences separate the religion of the Etruscans from that of the Latins and of primitive Rome, as well as from that of the colonial Greeks; the same is true for the religions of the other Italic peoples such as the Sabines, the Samnites, the Umbrians—indeed, each of these deserves to be treated separately, as noted above. The differences can be explained not only by the diversity of origins of all the religions, but also by the precise historical circumstances that emphasized the specific character and tendencies of each of them. In the Etruscan world, for example, the early rise of a dominant social class that drew its extraordinary economic power largely from the exploitation of considerable mineral resources, that emphasized the prestige of its noble origins, and that blended protohistoric funerary traditions with Oriental influences certainly favored the ideological and ritual development of a cult of the dead, the equal of which is not to be found, making all allowances, except in Egypt and, outside the Mediterranean world, in China. Later in Etruria, after both Etruscan decline and Roman supremacy became evident, the dominant oligarchies, having lost all economic and political initiative, shifted their interests to the ritual and speculative tradition of their priestly class, thus creating particularly favorable conditions for the elaboration and codification of the set of doctrines and norms called the *disciplina,* which for the ancients and for us represents the most peculiar expression of Etruscan religiosity. The Osco-Umbrian-speaking Italic populations probably inherited some of the essential traits of their religious conceptions and customs from prehistory and from the pastoral and warlike nomadism of their ancestors: thus there are traces of a tribal totemism and the rite, which is also a myth, of the *ver sacrum,* the "sacred springtime," that is, the migration of young men of the age to bear arms—a rite that was substituted for a primitive sacrifice of all living beings born in a certain year. But it is also clear that the great expansion of these peoples during the historical period and their increasingly frequent employment as mercenaries contributed to the warlike character of their religion, and notably to the cult of the god Mars or Mamers, from whom the military state of the Mamertini, founded by Campanian mercenaries in Sicily in the third century B.C., drew its name directly. Finally, there was the well-known connection between the political history of Rome and the predominance of juridical and public values in Roman religion.

Hercules and Mlacuch. Mirror from Atri. London, British Museum.

4. *Common aspects and unitary tendencies.* However different they may be, the religions of pre-Roman Italy have points in common. And if these resemblances do not define a distinctive global character that would allow us to oppose the Italic world as a whole to other culture areas, they nevertheless deserve to be examined carefully, especially since they ultimately converge toward the Roman religion. An elementary geographical reason, the contiguity of the lands lying between the seas and the Alps, made Italy necessarily a place of contacts and exchanges. In the course of prehistory and protohistory—and particularly at the time of the "Proto-Villanovian" culture, that is, between the twelve and ninth centuries B.C., at the end of the Bronze Age—Italy presents, from an archaeological point of view, a uniformity that suggests an underlying unity, even on the level of sociocultural structures, ideas, and customs. For example, the funerary equipment in the various cultures of the Iron Age has common aspects, whether cremation predominates (as in the north of Italy and in the central part on the Tyrrhenian side) or burial (as in the south of Italy and in the central part on the Adriatic side). The Oriental and Greek influences, which have already been discussed, constitute another source of inspiration that was more or less widely diffused beyond the limits of each ethnic group or culture: we can cite as examples in the domain of myths the voyages of Odysseus and Diomedes, and the propagation of the cult of Heracles, Pythagorean doctrines, Dionysian rites, etc. But Etruscan civilization at the time of its supremacy and expansion—even if it was secondary to Greece—also spread its ideas, images, and ceremonies over vast territories in peninsular and north-

The monster Volta emerging from a well. Urn. Volterra. Guarnacci Museum. Museum photo.

Hercules suckled by Uni. Florence, Archaeological Museum.

ern Italy. Archaeological data, literary sources, and epigraphic documents reveal the existence of bilateral and multilateral exchanges among the major cultural centers of the Italic world. Among the most significant examples: the Etrusco-Latin cultural *koine* of the sixth century B.C., whose presence in the religious domain is shown not only by the form and decoration of sacred buildings, but also by certain cults, legends, and miracles; the system of giving dual names to the gods, as well as to persons, a system that is shared by the Umbrian and Etruscan pantheons (Mars Grabovius, in the Iguvine Tables; or Fufluns Pachies in Etruria) and that is also found in Latium and Campania; the close resemblances between augural doctrines and practices in Umbria and Rome; and the fusion of Greek and Italic beliefs, notably in southern Italy. Campania, especially, is the meeting place and the melting pot in which the Greek, Etruscan, Samnite, and Latin traditions combine. Between the fourth and second centuries B.C., broad areas of integration and unification of religious ideas and practices existed throughout the peninsula (which explains the vulgarization of the cults of Mars and of Heracles-Hercules, the diffusion of terra-cotta and small bronze votives, certain types of temples, etc.). In the course of this process, the hegemony of Rome certainly also plays an important role in the acceleration and catalyzing of this process, which preceded the general assimilation of the Italic religions by Roman religion.

Etruscans and Italians: The Poverty of Mythic Narratives

The extraordinary development of mythological imagination and erudition among the Greeks seems to contrast with an extreme paucity of stories about gods and heroes among the peoples of ancient Italy. Naturally when we express a judgment—or, perhaps, an impression—of this kind, we must take into account the limits imposed on our knowledge by the loss of any original literatures, with the exception of Latin literature. We have only a few fragments of the Etruscan and Italic traditions, occasionally collected or summarized much later by classical and Byzantine authors, often with obvious alterations. A large proportion of these narratives suggest a legendary world already open to the influence of the Greek myths, if not thoroughly elaborated by the Greeks in terms of their interpretation of the origins of the Italic peoples, cities, and cults. In such a context it is difficult to isolate the local elements, and especially to evaluate their authenticity and age. The same problem exists for the interpretation of Etruscan artistic representations, in particular for the scenes engraved on mirrors and the reliefs on small cinerary urns and sarcophagi, sometimes with more or less obscure episodes from local legends, or, rather, elements of these legends inserted into Greek compositions. It is certainly always possible that orally transmitted sagas were at the origin of these scenes, but of these no evidence remains. We may, however, still find some echo of them in the enigmatic representations sculpted or engraved on funerary stelae of the Adriatic regions (those of Daunia in Apulia and the necropolises of Novilara on the frontier Marches), with their scenes of battles, ceremonies, navigation, monstrous beings, etc.; and on a few archaic narrative vessels and bronzes. But these traditions, even though they existed, must be considered isolated phenomena, specific to each ethnic group at the beginning of its historical development. The early diffusion of Greek mythology, with its gods and heroes, must have smothered any attempt to elaborate the indigenous legends into organized cycles, especially in the Tyrrhenian area (Etruria, Latium, and Campania), which, while more advanced, also came under Greek influence earlier. On the other hand, certain predispositions based on general ways of thinking and religious conceptions—like Etruscan ideas about the mysterious nature of the divine—caused a weak development of mythology, and especially of narratives that record the actions of the gods; this is clearly different from the extraordinary imagination that the Greeks demonstrated in this domain.

But modern researchers have focused their attention on a few pieces of pictorial or literary data, which allow us to locate, if not to reconstruct, certain Etruscan or Etruscan-Italic legends that can be grouped around divine, daemonic, or heroic figures. All, or almost all, of these seem to have been developed late, integrating Greek elements and also perhaps more or less altered memories of historical facts. The most significant are (1) Hercle (Heracles), "son of Uni (Juno-)," who was nursed by the goddess; (2) Maris (Mars), who was presented in a multitude of infantile or juvenile forms that his different epithets allow us to distinguish (Maris Halna, Maris Husrnana, Maris Ismithians); he was believed to be the son of Hercle; he was subjected by Minerva to a rite which was supposed to ensure his immortality—an episode that is probably connected to the stories of the longevity and the triple death and resurrection of the centaur Mares, the ancestor of the Ausones (Aelianus, *Varia Historia* 9.16); (3) Epiur and Tages, children who had the appearance and wisdom of old age; this same Tages was said to have been the inventor and master of the haruspicium, which came out of a furrow in the earth, and to have had connections with Tarchon, the eponymous hero of Tarquinia; (4) the probably parallel stories about the teaching of the nymph Vegoia (Lasa Vecu or Vecuvia) and her relations with a certain Arruns Veltymnus, probably from Chiusi; (5) the legend of Cacus, a singer whose songs were perhaps transcribed by a young man named Artile; both were threatened by the warriors Aule and Caile Vipinas (who themselves belonged to a cycle of historical events dating from the sixth century B.C. which were transformed into semilegendary tales); elsewhere Cacus is cited as Tarchon's ambassador to King Marsyas, the eponym of the Italic people of the Marsi (Sabinus, *Collectanea* 1.8), and by Virgil (*Aeneid* 8.184ff.) as a cruel shepherd turned bandit who was finally killed by Hercules; (6) the monster (V)olta, who appeared in the Volsinian area and was killed by King Porsenna (Pliny, *Naturalis Historia* 2.140), is undoubtedly the character whom we see springing out of a well in the reliefs on some urns, with the head or pelt of a wolf, and confronting men who are armed or performing rites of exorcism. Some of these mythic schemata are found beyond the specifically Etruscan domain, which implies relations with the Italic world. But we must assume that the connections and fusions between the traditions of different ethnic areas were realized only during an erudite and reflexive period, and that they remained subordinate to the process of Greco-Italic mythic elaboration that was mentioned at the beginning of this article. In the mythic aspects of the traditions of the "sacred springtime" we can sometimes find a relatively autonomous vein of legends proper to the Sabellians.

The Divinities

I. Ancient Italy in General

A student of the ancient Italian gods must never lose sight of the religious unity of classical civilization, that is, the fundamental unity of the Greek and Roman religions. Beyond the traits that, on the level of imagination, mentality, and behavior, differentiate the relations that Greece, Etruria, the Italic populations, and Rome maintained with the sacred, it is evident that their ideas of the personalities, functions, looks, and attributes of the main divinities are essentially the same. This cannot be explained solely within the perspective of comparative studies of Indo-European and Mediterranean divinities (the supreme god of light or of heaven, for example, or the mother goddess, etc.); it is necessary to take full account of concrete historical relationships. The fact that these divine figures are described anthropomorphically puts them within the domain of culture (that is, of mythographic imagination and erudition, of the creations and traditions of iconography) rather than of religious thought. By facilitating their diffusion, this characteristic allows an osmosis between areas that, while different in their initial religious conceptions, participated in the same civilization, as was precisely the case of Greece and Italy throughout antiquity. Of course Greek inspiration was initially and constantly determinant; but this did not go so far as to suppress certain local characteristics that were preserved in the Greek divinities who were assimilated. Although the names of the gods were different, both names often—but not always—conveyed the same reality (the Etruscan name Tin[ia], for instance, can be seen as a simple "translation" of the Greek Zeus, the Latin name Venus of the Greek Aphrodite, etc.). The degree of identification varies depending on the case, the place, and the period. But certain Greek gods, notably Apollo, kept their names when they were introduced into Italy: perceived as foreigners at first (the cult of Apollo was introduced in Rome only in the fifth century B.C.), they were finally more or less completely integrated into the Italic pantheon. Among these gods, the most popular was Heracles (in Oscan his name became *Herekle,* in Etruscan, *Hercle,* and in Latin, *Hercules*). This type of influence must be connected with the massive importation of Greek myths into Italy, which is attested on Etruscan monuments beginning in the archaic period.

The Greco-Italic theological koine, as a general phenomenon, was born of a process that began at the dawn of historic times, at least with the first Greek attempts to colonize southern Italy and Sicily, and culminated in the Hellenistic period with the Roman conquest of Greece. But it ran up against the persistence of certain local cults that totally or partly escaped Greek adaptations and transformations. This happened especially in out-of-the-way and peripheral zones, but also in some great religious centers in which very important divinities survived—divinities whose characters and traditions would not, and will not, allow them to be identified with Greek models. This is the case, for example, of Veltune-Voltumna, *deus Etruriae princeps* (Varro, *De Lingua Latina,* 5.46), at Volsinii in Etruria, and of the goddess Vesona in the Umbro-Sabellian world. There was a definite indigenous influence on certain particular conceptions of the divine, for example on the mysterious and anonymous collegial divinities (*di involuti, opertanei*) in Etruria, and on the *indigitamenta* in Rome. But there was also the importance of triads (which Greek and other ancient religions also had), such as the very famous Roman triad of Jupiter, Juno, and Minerva, or in Umbria the gods called "Grabovii," that is, Jupiter, Mars, and Vofiono. And finally there was the proliferation of minor divinities and daemons.

Double names constitute the most important characteristic of the divinities of the Italic world; in certain aspects this was connected with the normal usage, common also in Greece, of adding an attribute or *epiklesis* to the proper and current name of the god or goddess. But in Italy (i.e., in Umbria, in the Oscan-speaking areas, in Etruria, and even in Rome), this particularity appears with the frequency and especially the coherence of a system comparable to that of the onomastics of persons bearing double names (personal name and family name), a system found exclusively in the societies of ancient Italy, i.e., precisely among the Etruscans, the Latins, and the Umbro-Sabellians. It is, in fact, very likely that it was used to harmonize the relatively institutional character of the gods (as well as of demigods and daemons) with the model of human society and institutions, as is seen in other cases (for example, in the grouping of certain divinities into "colleges," and in the people's conception of the demigods, who could be clients, helpers, or servants). The first name, which corresponds to the individual or personal name in human onomastics, is naturally the god's principal name; but it can also be a name common to members of a certain category of demigods (in Etruria, for instance, the names *Lasa* or *Charu[n]* are sometimes followed by a second, more specific, designation), or a "concept" (as in the Umbrian ritual of the Iguvine Tablets: *Ahtu Marti* = "Oracle [of] Mars"), or simply the generic name indicating the divinity (of the type *Des Fortuna;* cf. the Etruscan *Flere Nethuns* = the god Neptune or the divinity of Neptune). As in noble names, the god's second name generally has an objective meaning; it can refer to a place (*Juno Populon[i]a*); to a family line—which suggests a family cult (for example, *Culsl Leprnal* = Culsu "of the Leprna family" in the funeral elegy of the Tarquinian priest Laris Pulenas); to a function (*Keri Arentikai* = Ceres the Avenger, in an Oscan curse [*tabella defixionis*] from Capua, and the parallel *Mars Ultor*); or to another divinity, whether by assimilation (as in *Fuflunsul Pachies*, in which the Etruscan name *Fufluns* is attached as an attribute to the name of the god Bacchus, who corresponds to Fufluns) or simply by association (*Deus Fidius, Janus Junonius,* etc.). To this last type of formation belongs the extraordinary interweaving of divine names that characterizes the Umbrian pantheon in the Iguvine Tablets (see below).

II. Etruria

Our knowledge of the Etruscan gods is based primarily on pictorial representations (chiefly engraved mirrors, but also funerary paintings, vases, statuettes, etc.), especially when these are accompanied by explanatory inscriptions; on other Etruscan texts, such as rituals, votive dedications, the miniature model of a liver from Piacenza, etc.; and on the comparison of information preserved in classical literary sources.

The great celestial divinities have characteristics and attributes analogous to those of the Greek divinities to whom they were assimilated. They were believed to inhabit all of the sixteen regions of heaven, particularly the first four regions located in the northeast, and they could hurl bolts of lightning. First was Tin or Tinia, the supreme god corresponding to Zeus (and to the Latino-Italic Jupiter); he threw three thunderbolts, one on his own, the second on the advice of the three Consentes, and the third, most terrible one, at the order of the enigmatic Superior and Obscure gods, *di Superiores et Involuti* (Seneca, *Quaestiones Naturales* 2.41). Next came Uni, the consort of Tin(ia) and homologue of the Greek goddess Hera and the Latin Juno—she was highly venerated in all the main Etruscan cities, in different forms, but especially as the goddess of maternity (in the sanctuary of Pyrgi she was equivalent to Ilithyia or Leucothea and was assimilated to the Phoenician goddess Astarte); Menerva, the homologue of Minerva and Athena; Maris, the homologue of Mars and Ares, whose epithets and manifestations were the most varied of all; Sethlans, the homologue of Vulcan (the name *Velch[an?]* is also attested) and Hephaestus. These two last-named divinities also appear in other celestial zones. In the northwest regions was another hurler of thunderbolts: Satres, the homologue of the Latin Saturnus and the Greek Ouranos. Other major divinities were Turan (literally "the Mistress"), the homologue of Aphrodite and Venus; Nethuns, the homologue of Neptune and Poseidon; Turms, the homologue of Hermes (the name *Herme-* is also attested) and Mercury. Finally there were some divinities who were borrowed directly from Greece: Hercle (that is, Heracles), Aritimi or Artums (Artemis), and Ap(u)lu (Apollo).

The divinities of nature (celestial and terrestrial) and of natural products seem to be located mainly in the southern regions of the celestial vault: there were the solar gods Ca(u)tha and Usil, and probably the moon Tiv(r) and the dawn Thesan, Selvans (= Sylvanus), and Fuflun(s), the homologue of Dionysus and Bacchus. Among the divinities of fate, death, and the netherworld who usually lived in the inauspicious western regions are Cilen(s), Letha(m), Calu, Vetis (who may be Veive, i.e., Veiovis, the Jupiter of the netherworld), and also the goddess Vanth, the god Mantus and his consort Mania, and, borrowed directly from Greece, Aita or Eita (Hades) and his consort Phersipnai (Persephone, Proserpina). But in this domain it is hard to make a clear distinction between the gods strictly speaking and certain infernal daemons. Finally we must note separately the two divinities of Volsinii, Voltumna (*Veltuna* or *Veltha* in Etruscan—as we said above, this divinity became the most important god of Etruria from the time the representatives of the Etruscan states began to meet periodically in his sanctuary) and Nortia, probably the goddess of destiny: a nail was driven into her temple each year (Livy, 7.3.7).

Alongside these divine figures who were defined and represented anthropomorphically under the influence of the Greek pantheon, some indigenous supernatural entities survived, often grouped in colleges of obscure and mysterious divinities, whose number, sex, and name are not known (Varro, in Arnobius *Adversus Nationes* 3.40). These included the *Involuti et Superiores* gods, and the *Favores Opertanei* (i.e., "hidden"). The writers of antiquity mention other "colleges" or categories of divinities; these were generally referred to in Etruscan by the word *aiser* or *eiser* (= "gods"); the expression *eiser śi-c śeu-c,* found in the ritual of the Zagreb Mummy, could refer either to all of these or to a specific cult. There may be a parallel in the *Consentes* or *Complices* (in Etruscan perhaps *Aiser Thuflthа*), counselors of Tinia-Jupiter, who were twelve in number; but there were also the Penates, who were divided into four classes of divinities, of the sky, the water, the earth, and human souls (Nigidius Figulus, in Arnobius 3.38); the Lares; and the Manes, that is, the spirits of the dead. The relations among all these groups are not clear: the *Consentes* may have been pairs of major divinities, but they are also sometimes identified with the Penates—who may represent, in another form, all Etruscan divinities.

III. The Italic Populations

Outside Etruria, the archaeological evidence provided by pictorial representations is very rare. We must therefore rely almost entirely on epigraphic documents, with the occasional help of information found in literary sources. In addition to the scarcity of data, another problem is the multiplicity and dispersion of ethnic groups speaking Indo-European languages and of their ritual centers. As a result, it is difficult to propose a synthesis of the data on the Italic divinities, not only for the marginal zones of the Adriatic and southern Italy, but also for the territories of the Umbro-Sabellian peoples, whose religious experience, that is, cultural experience in general, appears to have been very different. Undoubtedly there were fairly close relations between these peoples and the ancient Latin and Roman world, due to common underlying characteristics and to very early contacts between the Sabines and the inhabitants of Latium (a large number of Roman cults were supposed to be of Sabine origin, starting with that of the god Quirinus), but also to later influences—and notably that of the Roman religion in the frontier territories of the interior peninsula, especially after the territories began to fall under the political domination of Rome. But the Greek and Etruscan cults also exercised their influence.

Probably many of the basic figures of the common pantheon of Greece and Italy were adapted to the traditions and rituals of the Italic sanctuaries, beginning with Jupiter, who, under the name of *(D)iove-*, *(D)iuve-*, but also *Iupater*, accompanied by multiple epithets, is widely attested in the Umbro-Sabellian area. Even though we have no epigraphic document clearly proving the existence of a goddess corresponding to Juno, we cannot exclude the hypothesis that the goddess Hera, whose worship was extremely widespread in Italy, influenced the cults of the mother goddess, such as those practiced in the famous sanctuary of Capua—but unfortunately we still do not know the name of the divinity to whom this sanctuary was consecrated. Yet we find references to Ceres (*Kere*), at Capua, Agnone, and Rossano di Vaglio; and to Diana in the sanctuary of Diana

Right: Votive statue of a woman with a child. Fifth century. Capua, Museo Campano. Museum photo.

Votive statue of a woman with a child. Fifth to sixth century. Capua, Museo Campano. Museum photo.

Tifatina near Capua. In Campania and in the territory of the Pelignians, Aphrodite-Venus appears under the name *Harentas,* that is, "the goddess of desire." The cult of Heracles (*Herekle*) is also well known. But the preeminent Italic god, present everywhere and attested by both epigraphic and literary sources, seems to have been Mars (in the Oscan form *Mamers*), the god of war and migrations and the patron of mercenaries. The discovery of a very large number of small statues representing Mars and Heracles in the votive deposits of sanctuaries all over the peninsula is evidence of deep popular veneration for these divinities. There are other specifically Italic divinities who do not really have homologues in the Greco-Roman world, such as the goddess Mefitis, a great divine figure of the Sabellian peoples, known especially in Irpinia; it is certainly she who, with Jupiter (*Diove*), formed the couple that may have been named "the Sovereigns" (*rego*) in the dedications of Rossano di Vaglio. She seems to have been partly assimilated to Ceres and Venus. Ceres Jovia is also called "Queen" in the inscription of the Tablet of Rapino, near Chieti. Among the Umbrians (at Prestino) and the Picenians, the worship of another female divinity, Cupra, was widespread; a famous sanctuary was dedicated to her on the Adriatic (today's Cupra Maritima).

But the richest and most complete documentation on the Italic divinities worshiped in a particular place, in this case the Umbrian city of Gubbio, is provided by the Iguvine Tablets. The Tablets mention a large number of divine figures or entities, only some of whom are known, such as Jupiter, Mars, Pomono, Vesona, Cerfo, Fisovio, Holo, Hondo, Tefro, Trebo, Vofiono, etc. What seems most significant today is that each of these names, rarely used by itself, generally forms the first part of a double name, the second part being an adjective formed from the name of another divinity (for example, Cerfo Martio, Prestota Cerfia, Torsa Cerfia, Torsa Jovia, Fisovio Sancio, etc.). All of this makes up an extraordinary interweaving of reciprocal relations, a kind of genealogical tree. At the top of this tree is the triad of Jupiter Grabovio, Mars Grabovio, and Vofiono Grabovio, all of whom can be connected to a first entity, Grabo-, whose origin, according to G. Devoto, is as the personification of rocks or oak trees, and who is also found in the Etruscan divine name *flere in crapsti* (= god of the *grab-*, or in the *grab-*). This is evidently a system born of a complex theological elaboration, complicated all the more by the fact that some of these divine entities seem to be personifications of concepts or actions (*Vofiono-*, for instance, is "the shaker," *Trebo-* "the dwelling," etc.).

Nothing, or very little, can be said about the other Italic populations, more isolated and less known. On the indigenous divinities of the Apulians, there is no information at all; the names of the Greek goddesses Demeter and Aphrodite, which appear in the Messapian inscriptions, could be translations of one or several local female divinities, particularly since Demeter recalls the cult of Ceres, which was widespread among the Sabellians. On the other hand, Jupiter Menzana could be an ancient local god of horses. Once again, it is a female divinity who seems to prevail in these areas. We could also cite the Reitia of the Veneti, of whom we have a few representations, for example, in the reliefs on the bronze disks from Montebelluna, where she is portrayed as a *potnia theron,* with a large key. Among the epithets of Reitia attested in Venetian dedicatory inscriptions is *Tora,* probably one of the most ancient names of the goddess. In any case, the existence of a sanctuary of Argive Hera, like that of Juno at Padua, confirms that the Venetian cults were essentially connected with female divinities.

M.P./j.l.

BIBLIOGRAPHY

1. Introduction

G. MICALI, *L'Italia avanti il dominio de' Romani* (Florence 1810; 2d ed., 1821; reprinted Turin 1887). D. RANDALL MACIVER, *Italy before the Romans* (Oxford 1928). F. ALTHEIM, *Italia, Studi e Materiali di Storia delle Religioni,* 10 (1934): 125–55; *Italien und Rom,* 1: *Die Grundlagen* (Amsterdam and Leipzig 1941), = *Römische Geschichte,* 1 (Frankfurt am Main 1951). J. WHATMOUGH, *The Foundations of Roman Italy* (London 1937). M. PALLOTTINO, "Le origini storiche dei popoli italici," in *X Congresso Internazionale di Scienze Storiche, Relazioni* (Florence 1955), 2:3–60. G. M. A. RICHTER, *Ancient Italy* (Ann Arbor 1955). A. MAIURI, *Arte e civiltà dell'Italia antica* (Milan 1960); *Études étrusco-italiques* (Louvain 1963). G. RADKE, *Die Götter Altitaliens* (Münster 1965). G. DEVOTO, *Scritti minori,* 2 (Florence 1967). M. A. LEVI, *L'Italia antica,* 1 (Milan 1968). H. HEURGON, *Rome et la Méditerranée occidentale jusqu'aux guerres puniques* (Paris 1969). M. PALLOTTINO, *Civiltà artistica etrusco-italica* (Florence 1971); "Sul concetto di storia italica," in *L'Italie préromaine et la Rome républicaine: Mélanges offerts à Jacques Heurgon* (Paris 1976), 771–89; *Genti e culture dell'Italia preromana* (Rome 1980). R. BLOCH, *Recherches sur les religions de l'Italie antique,* Centre de recherche d'histoire et de philologie de l'École pratique des hautes-études (Geneva 1976); *Popoli e civiltà dell'Italia antica,* vols. 2–7 (Rome 1974–78); *I Galli e l'Italia,* catalog of the exposition (Rome 1978).

2. Etruscans and Italians

G. Q. GIGLIOLI and G. CAMPOREALE, *La religione degli Etruschi: Storia delle religioni* (6th ed., Turin 1971), 2:537–672, and especially 598ff. A. J. PFIFFIG, *Religio Etrusca* (Graz 1975), and especially 16ff., 198ff., 347ff., with all the references to earlier studies.

3. The Divinities

U. BIANCHI, "Gli dei delle stirpi italiche," in *Popoli e civiltà dell'Italia antica,* 7 (1978): 195–236. R. BLOCH, *Recherches sur les religions de l'Italie antique* (Geneva 1976). G. Q. GIGLIOLI and G. CAMPOREALE, *La religione degli Etruschi, Storia delle religioni* (6th ed., Turin 1971), 2:537–672. A. J. PFIFFIG, *Religio Etrusca* (Graz 1975). G. RADKE, *Die Götter Altitaliens* (Munster 1965).

See also other more specific works cited at the end of the other articles on Italy before Rome.

Sacrificial Cults and Rites in Pre-Roman Italy

Our knowledge about the cultic forms, especially the sacrificial forms, that were practiced by the populations of pre-Roman Italy comes to us from a few original documents of great importance. Among them, the most important document is the Umbrian text of the Iguvine Tables, the longest pre-Latin inscription ever discovered in Italy. Next in importance are the Etruscan text inscribed on the wrappings of an Egyptian mummy now in Zagreb and the clay tablet from Capua that also bears an Etruscan inscription. Finally, there are other documents, both Etruscan (the golden plates of Pyrgi, the lead disk of Magliano, etc.) and Oscan (the *iuvilas* inscriptions from Capua and the *Tabula Agnonensis*). It should be emphasized that the richest and deepest information that the epigraphic sources give us about the ancient cultures of the Italic world is information about ritual practices. The value of these epigraphic data surpasses that of archaeological data (the remains of shrines, temples and their decorations, scenes depicting sacred ceremonies, and so forth) and the fragmentary and indirect information supplied by classical literary sources.

Italic sacrificial rites are described in minute detail in the seven bronze tablets from Gubbio. Although their dates have been set at the second and first century B.C. and although they were written partly in the Umbrian alphabet and partly in the Latin alphabet, certain elements of their redaction go back to much earlier times. They consist in a set of sacred regulations that belong to the city-state of Gubbio (Iguvium). Mentioned among them are the city's acropolis (the Fisia acropolis), and the place set aside for the observation of auguries (a *templum*) and its roads and gates. Its institutions and its priests are named, notably the college of the Atiedii Brethren. The ritual prescriptions are connected with various kinds of ceremonies: a great sacrifice of expiation and purification of the city and the acropolis, a lustration of the people followed by the exile of foreigners, sacrifices to ward off ill fortune, the sacrifice of a dog, rites of assembly, and the rites of the festivals celebrated every two months. The liturgy took place in three phases: (1) the prayer ratifying the pact with the deity (*persklom*); (2) the observation of the flight of birds to determine auguries (*avie*); and (3) the sacrifice itself, or the offering (*esono*). Different ceremonies were invoked to gain the favor of different deities. The deities were quite numerous; some were well-known and common to all Italic religions (like Jupiter and Mars), while others, more obscure, personified sacred concepts. But almost all of them were characterized by a second name indicating the relationships of kinship or affiliation that united them. The victims of blood sacrifices could be oxen, calves, heifers, pigs, sheep, or dogs, all carefully selected for their age, sex, and color, and according to their breeding, which could be either sacred or profane. The bloodless offerings consisted of liquids, notably the "sacred beverage" and wine, which were used as an accompaniment to the sacrifice or poured as simple libations; finally, there were offerings of grain, cakes, fat, and so forth. The officiating priest, in addition to the augur, was the *arsfertor*, who corresponds to the Latin flamen. The supreme religious authority was vested in the *uhtur* (*auctor*, "maker").

This extraordinary heritage of knowledge (basically clear, even though there are still some problems in the interpretation of the texts) opens the way to a whole spectrum of comparisons with Greek and Roman sacrificial rites, to which the Umbrian rites seem to be closely tied by profound analogies. These analogies certainly go back partly to the origins, but they may also have come about through the progressive assimilation of ritual customs within the environment of Hellenistic civilization and through the immediate influence of Rome. Moreover, according to the method of "parallel texts" that K. Olzscha has applied in this area, the Iguvine Tables constitute the point of departure for any understanding of Etruscan ritual texts, primarily those of the Zagreb Mummy and the clay tablet from Capua. Indeed, there are close correspondences between the Umbrian document and the Etruscan text of Zagreb. The same entire formulas appear in both; indeed, in certain cases we can juxtapose them as if they were "bilingual." This demonstrates a basic unity in the mentality and sacred language that also applies to the Roman literary and epigraphic documents that deal with ritual prescriptions (for example, Cato's *De Re Rustica*, the *Acta Fratrum Arvalium*, the proceedings of the secular games, and so forth).

The ritual that one can read on the wrapping (*liber linteus*) of the Zagreb Mummy describes a series of ceremonies that took place in a particular religious center, the shrine of Cilth (*śacni cilth-*), in a chronological order that was fixed by a calendar of religious festivals. The most important part of the text is made up of three long, almost identical liturgical sequences, the first dedicated to a college of deities (*aiser*, that is, "the gods," *śi-c śeuc-*), the second to a god designated by the expression *flere in crapśti* (which may correspond to Jupiter Grabovius of Gubbio), and the third to Neptune (*flere nethuns*). These three sequences seem to be intended for the purification of the sanctuary, the city, and the people. There are also references to ceremonies in honor of the gods Culsu and Veive (and therefore probably funerary ceremonies) and rites of lustration. There is also a reference to a "royal palace" and to a temple of the goddess Uni. Sacrificial rites were designated by the term *ais(u)na* (= *res divina*), which is connected with the form *esono* found on the Iguvine Tables; these rites included dedications and offerings, with or without the shedding of blood. Given our uncertain knowledge of Etruscan vocabulary, it is difficult to state the exact nature of the victims (who are thought to be similar to the victims of the Iguvian ritual) or of the offerings. We can simply say that the offerings of liquids, notably wine (*vinum*), seem to have been very important. The Zagreb text is more or less contemporary with the Iguvine Tables and must therefore go back to the late phase of Etruscan civilization and to the time of the Roman Republic. On the other hand, the ritual prescriptions of the Capuan tile belong to a much earlier period (fifth century B.C.). These mention sacrifices and offerings to ancestors and to infernal deities. Both of these great documents of Etruscan ritual mention various officiating priests. The principal term designating a priest is *cepen*

Fragment from the Iguvine Table. Gubbio, Palazzio dei Consoli. Photo Garivati.

(in Capua, the archaic form *cipen),* often followed by an exact term indicating functions. Thus, a *cepen thaurch* was responsible for funerary tasks. Other terms indicating priestly functions appear on tomb inscriptions. The highest sacred office was apparently held by the *maru* (that is, the Maro, who in Umbria carried out civil functions—it was also Virgil's family name).

M.P./g.h.

BIBLIOGRAPHY

M. PALLOTTINO, "Questioni ermeneutiche del testo di Zagabria," *Studi Etruschi* 6 (1932): 273–81. G. DEVOTO, *Tabulae Iguvinae* (Rome 1937). K. OLZSCHA, *Interpretation der Agramer Mumienbinde* (Leipzig 1939). J. HEURGON, *Étude sur les inscriptions osques de Capoue dites Iúvilas* (Paris 1942). G. DEVOTO, *Le Tavole di Gubbio* (Florence 1948). M. PALLOTTINO, "Sulla lettura e sul contenuto della grande iscrizione di Capua," *Studi Etruschi* 20 (1948–49): 159–96; "Scavi nel Santuario etrusco di Pyrgi: Relazione preliminare della settima campagna, 1961, e scoperta di tre lamine d'oro inscritte in etrusco e in punico," *Archeologia Classica* 16 (1964): 76ff. A. J. PFIFFIG, *Religio Iguvina* (Vienna 1964); *Religio Etrusca* (Graz 1975).

Conceptions of the Afterlife among the Peoples of Pre-Roman Italy

I. Italian Protohistory

With the exception of the Etruscans, whom we will discuss further on, ancient sources tell us nothing directly about the beliefs of the peoples of pre-Roman Italy concerning the fate of human beings in the next world. All that one can vaguely deduce from the funeral customs and the tombs, that is, through archaeology alone, belongs to the general category of Mediterranean and European protohistories of the Bronze Age and the Iron Age, including those of primitive Greece. The data tend to demonstrate the persistence and the preeminence of a fundamental conception, common to the earliest stages of development in all human cultures: that of a direct relationship between the spirit of the dead—always understood as the survival in some way or another of their individuality—and their mortal remains in their resting place, that is, in the tomb. The tomb must therefore be a secure shelter, and, to the extent possible, garments, food, and objects of daily use will be placed near the body or the ashes of the deceased for use in the future life. Until the most recent periods, that is, approximately the Hellenistic period—and when Rome, after unifying Italy, imposed her civilization on it—the Italic necropolises almost without exception preserved this ritual custom. In fact, it continued until the time of the migrations among the European peoples who lived on the margin of the classical world, while in Greece it disappeared much earlier.

The simultaneous use of funerary practices as different as burial and cremation is also found in other civilizations of the antique world (including Greece and Rome), but it is so characteristic of pre-Roman Italy that it makes it possible to distinguish the different territories, ethnic milieus, cultural horizons, and chronological periods. From the perspective of a genuine historical reconstruction, it is not easy to describe the alternation of the two rites. We can say, nevertheless, that, essentially, the burial of bodies in a folded or straight position is the heritage of prehistoric customs that were widespread in Italy even during the Neolithic and the Bronze Age and survived in a large area of the Adriatic, interior, and southern zones of the peninsula; while the practice of cremation, linked to the great movement of European "fields of urns," became widespread at the end of the Bronze Age, and continued afterward, during the Iron Age and the historical period, to be the exclusive or preeminent patrimony of the inhabitants of northern and Tyrrhenian Italy. The phase of greatest expansion of the rite, in which it took over even southern Italy and Sicily (probably diffused from the north by land and from the Balkans and the Aegean world by sea), coincides in the final Bronze Age with the culture called "Proto-Villanovian," which is found in remarkable uniformity throughout Italy (eleventh to ninth century B.C.). At the beginning of the Iron Age (ninth to eighth century B.C.), we see that the zones where cremation predominates already correspond rather precisely to the territories of the Liguri (the culture of Golasecca), the Veneti (the culture of Este), the Etruscans (Villanovian culture), and in part to those of the Latins and the Umbrians. On the other hand, burial seems to characterize the Sabellian-Umbrian peoples (including the Piceni of the Adriatic), the Apulians, and the natives of Magna Graecia and Sicily. But the practice of burial gains ground throughout the Tyrrhenian slope beginning in the seventh century, in Latium and in Etruria, with the characteristic dugout tombs. Later, grave monuments, chambered tombs carved into the rock and imitating the interior of homes, and finally veritable mausoleums were superimposed upon, or rather, in many places, substituted for, the dugout tombs. In Etruria there was, in the end, a fairly clear boundary between the southern cities where burial predominated (Caere, Tarquinii, Vulci), and the northern cities where cremation predominated (Volaterrae, Clusium, and Perusia). It is known that in Rome in the historical period, the two rites coexisted and were linked to different familial traditions. It is probable that it was the same in other cities; for it is possible that the practice of one rite or the other depended upon the social status of the deceased.

The main ideological significance of cremation is still a matter of dispute; in any case, this does not concern the practice and the diffusion of the rite in Italy during the more recent historical periods. Nevertheless, it cannot be denied that there is some connection with the idea of a generative or regenerative power in fire, which might also suggest a relationship between the cinerary vase in the form of a cabin-urn—widespread in prehistoric Latium and in Etruria—the domestic hearth, and the cult of Vesta (Müller-Karpe). The form of the individual tombs would evidently differ according to whether one buried or cremated the body; but neither the rules about the nature and extension of the cemeteries nor the funerary furnishings seem to have differed in any other way—which leads one to think that there was a profound similarity between the conceptions of the next world. Noteworthy is the general tendency to make the urns or tombs look like a house (from the first cabin-urns to the little urns in stone, the sarcophagi, the tomb facades and *hypogea* carved into the rock), in order to offer the dead the continuation of their milieu, that is to say a *domus aeterna*, following the definition that the Romans would later give to the tomb. More significant still is the intention to reproduce the image of the deceased—probably in order to preserve a corporeal support for the spirit, in conformity with the Mediterranean tradition that went back to ancient Egypt.

This practice is manifest not only in the presence of figurines in the proto-Latin cremation tombs, and later in the Etruscan tombs, but especially in the fact that they tended to give human forms to the cinerary urns (such as the "canopic vases" of Clusium). The "portraits" of Etruscan funerary painting and sculpture, and the *imagines maiorum,* that is, the masks and busts of ancestors, of the Roman funerary custom (Pliny, *Naturalis Historia* 35.6) are evidently related to this tradition—even though, with time, what had originally borne the mark of magic or religion became a simple commemoration or proud aristocratic exhibition.

The separation, because of the "impurity" of the dead, between the locales of interment and the locales of habitation—a separation that characterizes all the major cultures but, generally speaking, seems alien to the world of prehistory—is already in operation in Italy between the Bronze Age and the Iron Age. However, it seems that in the beginning this separation was not rigorously demarcated: in many cases (for example, in Rome, in Villanovian Tarquinii and Bologna, in Este), groups of tombs are placed around centers of habitation. It was only when the movement of urbanization began to take hold, in the eighth and seventh centuries B.C., that this custom took the form of a ritual rule, confirmed by the Roman law of the Twelve Tables ("It is forbidden to bury or cremate a body in the city"), later to become a general and continuous tradition. The necropolises thus developed outside of the urban centers, along the major routes, and attained dimensions comparable to those of the cities, which they imitated in spacial planning and in the arrangement of the monuments (an exemplary case is that of Caere in Etruria, though one can cite precedents, admittedly embryonic, in protohistorical Latium, as well as the evidence of the recent discoveries at Decima, near Rome). The indigenous cities of Apulia constitute a singular exception, still unique in all of ancient Italy: the prehistoric heritage seems here to have crystallized into a system in which homes and tombs were mixed indiscriminately.

II. The Etruscans

A significant amount of information about Etruscan notions of the hereafter is furnished by archaeology, that is, by the tombs and their decoration; by the study of epigraphic documents; and finally by the echoes of their beliefs in the literary sources of the Roman and Christian periods. The tombs are among the most significant expressions, if not the most significant, of the culture of the ancient Etruscans. Contrary to other peoples of ancient Italy, they seem to have paid particular attention and devoted great economic resources to the care of their dead and to the furnishings of the sepulchers—for which no equivalents in monumentality and richness are found outside of certain cultures of the Near East. This concern should correspond logically to special psychological and ideological orientations.

The faith in the survival of the deceased in his tomb, common to all the religion of pre-Roman Italy—and to the preclassical cultures in general, as we have already seen—is indeed manifest in Etruria, especially in the archaic period, with remarkable clarity and intensity: the grandiose tumulus sepulchers of the Orientalizing period with their sumptuous furnishings (such as the famous tomb of the Regolini-Galassi of Caere, the contents of which are conserved in the Vatican museum), and the chamber tombs, filled with all kinds of riches (including an incalculable number of Greek vases), the immense necropolises at Caere (Cerveteri), Tarquinii, Vulci, Clusium, and, in particular, because of the importance of their decoration, the painted tombs, especially those of Tarquinii. This sudden and incomparable blossoming stands out clearly from the common base of the protohistorical funerary customs of the Iron Age customs which Etruria still knew in the Villanovian period (ninth to eighth century B.C.). The economic and political development of the Etruscan world must have played a predominant role in this process: the seventh and sixth centuries, its greatest period of expansion, witnessed the formation of a dominant class that controlled the wealth and wanted to glorify itself even in the realm of funerary rites. As for the concern that these barbarian potentates showed for their dead, it is probable that they were inspired in this by models and memories of the East. The funerary paintings of Tarquinii represent funerary ceremonies, games, hunting scenes, dances, and feasts in which the dead play a role, surrounded by their close friends and relatives and their servants: there are so many subjects borrowed from the visible reality that there are almost no allusions to the supernatural world or the hereafter. Evidently interest is entirely focused upon an immanent continuity of which the images themselves, in perpetuating the effectiveness of the funeral rites, offered a guarantee.

But between the fifth and fourth centuries, the atmosphere changes. Fantastic creatures begin to appear in the tombs, most often winged, and certainly belonging to a different world. In painting (at Orvieto) and in sculpture (the stelae of Bologna), the theme of a "voyage" of the deceased to another place emerges. The difference between the realm of the living and that of the dead also materializes. It is clear that traditional Greek beliefs about the underworld, and probably Orphic and Pythagorean influences as well, played a predominant role in this transformation. The realm of the hereafter was represented as a city lined with towers, whose door is guarded by demons. The dead arrive there by chariot or on horseback, also led by demons. Borrowing, in part, the iconography of archaic banquets, they would sometimes represent the stay of the dead in the underworld as a banquet. The rulers of the next world, Aita (Hades) and Phersipnai (Persephone), preside over the feast, while other demons play the role of servants and musicians. The influence of Greece is evident in the large scene of the Nekyia (the Homeric world of the dead) on the tomb of Orco II at Tarquinii, with Tiresias and other famous heroes of Hellenic mythology; it was inspired by an iconographic tradition that may go back to the tableau of Polygnotus of Thasos that was found in the Lesche of the Cnidians at Delphi (Pausanias 10.28.7). On the other hand, the menacing demons belong to the Etruscan imagination: Vanth and other beings armed with torches who resemble the Erinyes; the terrifying and omnipresent Charun, with his hammer; and the most monstrous of all, Tuchulcha, with his serpents.

The fact that the dead are submerged in a menacing atmosphere may indicate a pessimistic conception of the destiny of man in the next world. Nevertheless—in the representations of illustrious people (from the most noble families of Tarquinii or Orvieto), serenely lying down or sitting down for a banquet; or in the scenes where corteges of magistrates, with their retinue, march toward the beyond—the accent placed upon the human dignity of the dead seems to contrast with the basic desolation and theatrical horror, thus creating an ambiguity that is difficult to explain. Perhaps it is not unreasonable to seek an analogy with certain macabre conceptions in the funerary art of the European baroque (Pfiffig). In fact, we know from several literary sources that it was possible, by means of the appropriate blood sacrifices, to raise the souls of the dead to the condition

Canopic jar from Dolciano. Chiusi, Museo civico. Museum photo.

of "divine souls"; this is what is taught in the *libri acherontici* (Ateius Labeo is here cited by Servius in his Commentary on the *Aeneid*, 3.168; Arnobius *Adversus Gentes* 2.62). If the ritual text of the Etruscan inscription of the Capuan tile indeed refers, as we think it does, to the ceremonies performed in honor of the infernal gods, then one has, as early as the fifth century, evidence of ritual practices intended to facilitate the survival of the dead in the next world. On the one hand, such a document may illuminate the importance of the funerary rites known since the archaic period, of which we find a singular representation in the tomb of the funeral bed, in Tarquinii: people are depicted making offerings next to a majestic catafalque bed surmounted by two headdresses that symbolize the presence of a divine couple (who may perhaps be identified with the deceased themselves?). On the other hand, the document may proclaim all those beliefs and practices concerning the deification of the dead, which the *disciplina Etrusca* would later codify. However, as far as these last are concerned, one should probably consider the influence of the Greek mysteries and the Orphic, Pythagorean, and Dionysian doctrines, which, coming directly from Greece, or through the intermediary of Magna Graecia, had penetrated into Etruria.

Comparing the facts furnished by the Greek and Latin sources with the results of a careful analysis of the sacred and funerary texts of the Etruscans allows us to widen and make more precise our understanding of their eschatology. Thus, we can lengthen the list of all the deities and demons of destiny, of death, and of the hereafter that inhabit the deadly western regions of the sky, with the names of the gods Calu, Celi, Letha(m), Larun (or Laran), of the goddess Sur(i), of the goddess or god Culsu (or Culsan), of the demon Leinth (which might possibly mean "He who causes to die"), whose sex is undetermined, and of the female demon Nathum (or Natinusna)—and recalling the names of the infernal Jupiter, Veive or Vetis (Veiovis), and the divine couple Mantus and Mania, who were certainly associated with Manes. These last, whom the Etruscans also called *man(im),* are the dead themselves, but considered as spirits, demons, or even as gods. They are also recognized under the name *apher,* corresponding to the Latin *Parentes* (*Parentes* gods); this name denotes the ancestors who are the object of a cult in the inscription of the Capuan tile. The concept of soul or spirit is expressed in Etruscan by the term *hinthial* (for example: *hinthial Patrucles,* "the soul of Patrocles"). It was thought that the Etruscan name for the next world was Achrum, derived from the name of the river of the underworld among the Greeks, the Acheron—which would explain the title of the *Libri Acherontici* or *Acheruntici.*

M.P./m.s.

BIBLIOGRAPHY

B. NOGARA, *Gli Etruschi e la loro civiltà* (Milan 1933), 220–89. F. DE RUYT, *Charun, démon étrusque de la mort* (Rome and Brussels 1934). F. CUMONT, *Recherches sur le symbolisme funéraire des Romains* (Paris 1941). M. PALLOTTINO, "Sulla lettura e sul contenuto della grande iscrizione etrusca di Capua," *Studi Etruschi* 20 (1948–49): 159–96; "Il culto degli antenati in Etruria ed une probabile equivalenza lessicale etrusco-latina," *Studi Etruschi* 26 (1958): 49–83. J. BAYET, "Idéologie et plastique," 2: "La sculpture funéraire de Chiusi," in *Mélanges d'archéologie et d'histoire* (1960), 35ff. J. M. C. TOYNBEE, *Death and Burial in the Roman World* (London 1971). A. J. PFIFFIG, *Religio Etrusca* (Graz 1975).

ETRUSCAN RELIGION

I. Historical Premises

The historian Livy (5.1.6) evokes the Etruscans as "a nation that was devoted beyond all others to religious practices, and all the more because it excelled at them." According to a false etymology, their name of Tusci was derived from the Greek *thuoskooi,* "experts in sacrifices" (Dionysius of Halicarnassus, 1.30.3). This reputation is almost a commonplace in ancient literature. The Christian writer Arnobius (*Adversus gentes,* 7.26) called Etruria "the creator and mother of superstitions." It is clear that the Greeks and Romans were impressed by Etruscan religion, not so much by its intensity as by a particular characteristic which must have appeared quite strange to them. This was the Etruscans' obsessive search for contact with the supernatural world through the interpretation and scrupulous performance of the divine will—a search which, especially in the final phase of Etruscan civilization, became a technique for experts alone.

Literary sources of the Roman period, which report with sufficient breadth and which sometimes paraphrase and summarize data lost from the written tradition of the Etruscans, reveal the existence of doctrines that were claimed to have been handed down from an original teaching by superior beings, and that discuss the concept of the sacred, the relationships between the heavenly and terrestrial worlds, the gods, the destiny of men in time and after death, and the forms and rules of divination and worship. We do not know to what degree these concepts, which were arranged and codified much later, correspond to the earliest practices and beliefs of Etruscan religion, our direct knowledge of which is based on archaeological evidence and sometimes epigraphical documents. Insofar as our limited knowledge of the Etruscan language allows us to understand them, the most important extant Etruscan texts—dedicatory and ritual texts such as the Pyrgian tablets, the Capuan tile, the lead disk of Magliano, and especially the long manuscript written on the cloth of the Zagreb Mummy from Egypt (the sole example of a sacred *liber linteus* preserved from antiquity)—offer information that not only confirms what we have been able to learn from classical sources, but also adds further data, especially important because of their undeniable and immediate authenticity. What is more important, they demonstrate a continuity in the forms of worship and in the sacred language that goes back at least to the end of the archaic period, as is the case with the documents from Pyrgi. Nevertheless, if one hopes to undertake a "historical" reconstruction of Etruscan beliefs and their development, it remains difficult to distinguish between reality and erudite speculation.

In any case, the religion is indisputably the best known aspect of the civilization of ancient Etruria. Considered in a general perspective, it is one of the most interesting and original of ancient religions, with many characteristics that distinguish it from other Mediterranean religions. There has always been a wish to explain these peculiarities by a theory that the Etruscans came from the Orient. This theory, founded on the modern interpretation of an account in Herodotus (1.94) and other ancient sources, is buttressed by the fact that in Etruscan religion there was no dearth of elements having more or less direct ties with Oriental concepts (such as demonology, haruspicy, and funerary customs). Some scholars, most notably A. Piganiol, have supported this point of view. But in the past few years, following new archaeological discoveries and linguistic studies of greater depth, the problem of the origins of the Etruscans has opened onto ever broader, more complex and subtle perspectives. In spite of the distant ties that the Etruscans might have had with the Aegean world and Asia Minor, these new insights make it even more improbable that there ever was, at the dawn of historical times, a massive immigration of an already unified people from the eastern Mediterranean. At the same time, all evidence indicates that the Etruscan ethnic group had already taken form in Italy at the end of the Bronze Age at the latest. As for resemblances to Oriental religions, these are of so heterogeneous a nature (we find such elements at diverse periods and in relation to civilizations as distinct as those of Mesopotamia, Anatolia, and Egypt) as to make the idea of a common hereditary tradition unlikely; the resemblances are better explained one by one through cultural contacts.

It is better to refer to historical reality, that is, to characteristics and events in the life of the Etruscans, than it is to ask vague questions about their origins. We know that their civilization knew a sudden and early burgeoning between the eighth and sixth centuries B.C., bringing with it the formation of great urban centers and an expansion of political and economic power, especially in the maritime sphere—the celebrated Etruscan thalassocracy—which was very important around the Mediterranean. But its development ended as early as the fifth century, at the end of the archaic age, before Greece at her apogee imposed and affirmed the universal values of classicism that would come to be identified with the progress of the ancient world and with the very foundations of Western civilization. It is thus understandable that the essential and deepest characteristics of the spiritual world of the Etruscans remained fixed at the level of preclassical cultures, tied to prehistoric traditions and primitive ideas, and variously affected by Oriental and archaic Greek motifs. This explains why so many aspects of Etruscan beliefs would later appear distant, foreign, and obscure to Hellenist-Roman religious and philosophical thought.

The massive penetration of influences from Greek civilization in Etruria had noticeable repercussions in the realm of their gods and iconography and allowed for a diffusion of myths as well as of certain images of the afterlife. All of their art, not only temple art but also the art of funerary monuments and decorative objects (vases, engraved mirrors, jewelry, etc), is dominated by Greek mythological subjects. But it must be asked to what extent Hellenization was a decisive and determining factor in the development of Etruscan religion, and whether this was not more of an external veneer—a "cultural" phenomenon rather than an ideological essence.

The reality underlying these pictorial representations was revealed with incontestable clarity in the complex of notions and precepts collected in Roman literature. We must therefore trace the elaboration of this complex to the time when Etruria, after losing its capacity for maritime activity, was reduced to the limits of the Tyrrhenian territory, between the Tiber and the Arno. Caught there between the expansion of the Gauls and the Italic peoples of the interior of the peninsula, reduced to an essentially local economy, and finally subjected to the domination of Rome between the fourth and first centuries B.C., the Etruscans would in the end enclose themselves in the conservatism of their priestly oligarchies and in the cult of their traditions, before definitively bequeathing these vestiges and memories to Roman religion.

II. General Characteristics of Etruscan Religion

Given the present state of our knowledge—and taking account of the fragmentary and generally indirect character of our sources—it is difficult to form an overall idea of the religious ideas of the Etruscans and even more difficult to define them with simplistic formulas. Such elements as signs of the constant influence of supernatural forces in the world and on human actions, intense relationships between the living and the spirits of the dead, and apotropaic precautions and magical practices of evocation or disguise lead one to think of a persistence of animism. A fetishist theory, proposed by such authors as C. Clemen, appears more uncertain, as the venerated objects, such as weapons or worked rocks (somewhat analogous to the Semitic sacred stones and prehistoric menhirs), could also have been symbols or attributes of divinities or the dead. Although cults of water, trees, lightning flashes and the places struck by them, as well as cults of the gods of the sky, sun, moon, and sea are often cited, one cannot really call Etruscan religion a religion of nature or of heavenly bodies. It seems, however, that one might easily mark out a cosmological system founded on the material definition and the division of celestial space according to astronomical orientation and, in an analogous and recurrent manner, of terrestrial space, or better, of particular terrestrial spaces that may be identified with portions of territory or with the areas of cities and sacred places—i.e., the *templum,* which may be reduced to the microcosm of the viscera of sacrificed animals. The attributes, the localization, and the hierarchies of the major and minor divinities are inserted into such a system, and the favorable and unfavorable powers and presages (to the east and west, respectively, i.e., to the left and right of a subject looking toward the southerly sun) are distributed among them, thus concretely establishing the procedures of divinatory practices.

As far as the realm of the divine is concerned, one may simply define Etruscan religion as a polytheism similar to that of the other great religions of the ancient world—including the Greek and Roman religions—with personal divinities largely assimilated to the major gods of the Greek and Italico-Roman pantheon, but also to obscure divinities who are sometimes multiple and named collectively, and sometimes anonymous and enveloped in mystery. Furthermore, it is clearly possible to speak of an accentuated polydaemonism, understood in the sense of the belief in an incalculable number of supernatural beings who have affinities with the daemons and demigods of the Greek world, but regarding whom it is difficult to establish how far they partake of a truly divine nature (or whether these are individually minor gods). They have often been seen in the roles of attendants or servants of major divinities. Depending on whether they belong to groups of female, infant, or warrior genies, of daemons or of monsters of the hereafter, they present different characteristics, as much from the viewpoint of their appearance as of their localization.

In the way in which all of these superior beings are conceived, there are probable signs of primitive survivals, especially in the indeterminate and fleeting character of certain aspects of the divine. This may also explain the apparent weak development of a mythology in the sense of a narration linking together the actions of gods and demigods. Several transmitted accounts or episodes from local legend that may be inferred from artistic representations (on engraved mirrors, for example) seem to have developed under the influence of Greek myths or result from a late and scholarly fusion of Greek and local elements. But the deepest and most original import of Etruscan religion appears in the overwhelming importance of supernatural forces and in the nature of the relationship between men and gods. Every event and phenomenon, rather than being explained rationally, is thought to result from the direct intervention of a divinity. The following statement made by Seneca is particularly significant: "Between the Etruscans, the most skilled of men in the art of interpreting lightning, and ourselves [that is, the Hellenistic-Roman world] there are differences. We think that lightning is emitted because clouds collide; they hold that clouds collide in order that lightning may be emitted. They refer everything to the divinity: therefore they are convinced not that lightning flashes give an indication of the future because they are produced, but that they are produced because they have something to indicate" (Seneca, *Quaestiones naturales,* 2.32.2).

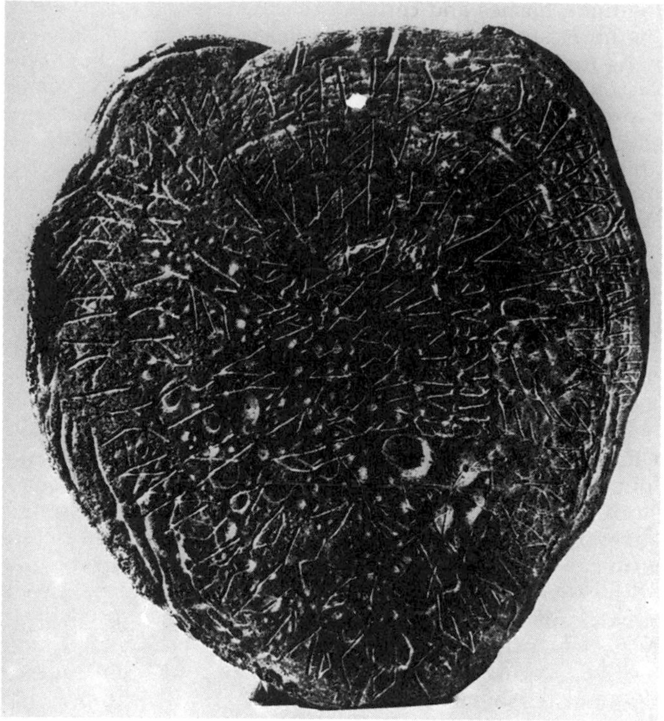

Lead disk from Magliano. Florence, Museo archeologico. Photo Sopr. Arch.-Firenze.

People are incessantly preoccupied with observing, recognizing, and understanding the signs of the divine will in order to derive auguries and prescriptions from them, and then with conforming to this will in the most scrupulous way possible by avoiding every fault, even one that is involuntary. If they nevertheless commit such a fault, they strive to apply a remedy to it as quickly as possible; all of this they do by means of extremely precise rituals of great formal rigor. Not only worship, but also every private or public form of conduct becomes concentrated and exhausted from this fearful dependence on the supernatural, in the face of which man is apparently bereft of both autonomous consciousness and a sphere of activity that is proper to his own will—and this is the basis for the ethical and juridical concepts that are inherent in the religion (it is in this that Etruscan religion is most clearly differentiated from Greek and Roman religion).

III. The Teachings of the Sacred Books

In order to apprehend divine injunctions with certainty and to conform to them, people needed precise instructions, instructions that were gathered together into the collection of teachings and norms defined by the Latin expression *disciplina Etrusca,* and that were collected and expounded in the numerous writings which constituted Etruscan sacred literature. The origin of the *disciplina Etrusca* and of the books relating to each of its parts was generally attributed to persons of a semidivine nature, such as the infant genius Tages for haruspicy or the nymph Vegoia for the doctrine of lightning flashes and certain other teachings. In this sense the Etruscan religion may be considered a revealed religion.

As for the study and interpretation of divine signs as a theory and technique entrusted to specialists, Etruria is especially distinguished in haruspicy and hepatoscopy (i.e., the reading of viscera—especially the liver—of sacrificed animals) and in the observation of lightning flashes, two arts that are expounded in the *libri haruspicini* and in the *libri fulgurales,* respectively. In addition, attention was given to all unusual events and marvels (monstrosities, inexplicable sounds, apparitions, etc.), which are described and explained in the collections known as *ostentaria.* At the same time, one must note the limited importance given to observing the flight of birds, which was, by contrast, highly developed in Rome and in Umbria and constituted the foundation for Roman augury. The essential aspect of divinatory practices—the aspect elsewhere connected with the values of the orientation of celestial and terrestrial space—is found in the study of auspicious or inauspicious omens, since these indicate the satisfaction or the wrath of the superior beings and thus are warnings about all future action.

The other aspect of the *disciplina Etrusca* is its general and ritual normativity. It encompasses every cultic performance, regardless of its origin or specialization. In more precise terms, we know that the *libri rituales* included precepts about the founding of cities, the establishment of sacred edifices, and even the political and military statutes of the state; this was, in other words, a code that was not only religious but also politico-institutional (a nondistinction that confirms the fundamental subordination of the human world to the divine world). The concept of "the law of the land of Etruria" and the sacred and intangible character of the boundaries of agrarian properties, which were defined by the supreme divinity, seem to have arisen in this context; the same is true for consecrated objects and places (sanctuaries, but also cities and tombs). Finally there was a whole collection of doctrines for the time, fate, and duration of the lives of men and of the nation (counted in "centuries"), which were to be found in the *libri fatales.* As for one's fate in the hereafter, this was treated in the *libri acherontici:* the normative portions of these writings indicate the rites necessary for the prolongation of life and the divinization of the dead.

Their forms of worship, at least according to what is known from the tradition of original Etruscan texts and from the monuments, do not seem to differ essentially from those of the Greeks and Romans. Sacred enclosures, altars, and temples, understood to be the dwellings of the divinity, are conceived and constructed in an analogous fashion, although with some typological peculiarities. Among the rituals, prayers, offerings without bloodletting, sacrifices of animals, and votive offerings are found everywhere; by contrast, consultation of the viscera of sacrificed animals is typically Etruscan. Certain kinds of ceremonies seem to be of particular importance, such as ceremonies of foundation, of consecration, and for the expiation of private and public sins, which were also most especially connected with the fundamental themes and imperatives of Etruscan religion. There were also calendars of festivals and celebrations, as is indicated in the series of prescriptions that are distributed according to the month and the day in the ritual text of the Zagreb Mummy. Cultic activities were performed by priests, and the different categories of priests are listed in Etruscan texts (documents of sacred content or funerary inscriptions containing biographies of the deceased). It is difficult, however, to specify their functions and specializations (a *cepen thaurch* mentioned in the Zagreb text is certainly a funerary priest), just as it is impossible to know with certainty to what degree "officiant" priests were distinguished from divinatory experts, especially the haruspices. The priesthood must often have received public support; the existence of priestly colleges is widely attested.

IV. The Problem of the Hereafter

The last sector that remains to be considered is the hereafter. But it would be wrong to separate this from the rest of Etruscan religion, since so many of the essential aspects of the afterlife are situated within the more general ideas of the religion. Among these aspects are the conformity of the chthonic or subterranean world with the cosmological system of correspondences between heaven and earth; the assimilation of the dead to certain divine entities, with resulting analogies in the sphere of worship; the definition of the tomb as a sacred place (*sacni*); and so on. The belief, inherited from prehistory and the great preclassical civilizations (or from civilizations foreign to the classical world), in the survival of the personalities of the dead along with the material remains of their bodies and in the places in which these were deposited, constitutes a fundamental ideological premise and implies the need to protect, feed, and honor the dead, according to their social rank. The continuity of life is to be insured by images that substituted for (and thus did not merely commemorate) effigies of the dead, by urns and tombs recalling the familiar household environment, and by the richest possible decoration of tombs with clothing, jewelry, weapons, instruments, and furniture, in addition to food and drink. These characteristics, as archaeology most suggestively indicates, are manifest especially in the earliest periods (independent of differences in funerary practices: from the beginning of historical times inhumation has tended to prevail over cremation), but the important fact, and the one that reveals a tenacious conservatism, is that these practices continued until the end of Etruscan civilization. The profoundly different idea of an afterlife conceived as a place of destination and reunion of the deceased diffused out of Greece and was to have notable repercussions on the Etruscan imagination, especially after the fifth century B.C. Images on funerary monuments show the development and refinement—more or less parallel with old customs and traditions—of the definition of an eschatological space based upon the concepts of the descent to the underworld and the kingdom (or city) of the dead. The description of the kingdom combines elements of Greek inspiration (the sovereignty of the gods Hades and Persephone and the presence of mythical characters) and purely local elements (monstrous demons, enormous banquets, the increased importance always given to the personality of the deceased in portraits and inscriptions). The atmosphere of sadness and fear in these Etruscan images of the hereafter is in the last analysis nothing but an interpretation that draws on the Greek idea of Hades. But at the same time the older forms of ritual obligation toward the dead, in tombs, continue to be refined and concretized in a cult of ancestors assimilated to divinities—a cult that implies, perhaps also under the influence of the mystery religions, ceremonies specifically destined to transform the human souls of the deceased into "divine souls."

M.P./d.w.

BIBLIOGRAPHY

K. O. MÜLLER and W. DEECKE, *Die Etrusker* (Stuttgart 1877; 2d ed., Graz 1965). C. O. THULIN, *Die etruskische Disziplin* (Göteborg 1905–9). F. MESSERSCHMIDT, *Griechische und etruskische Religion*, in *Studi e materiali di storia delle religioni* (1929), 5:21. B. NOGARA, *Gli Etruschi e la lora civiltà* (Milan 1933), 156–289. C. CLEMEN, *Die Religion der Etrusker* (Bonn 1936). R. ENKING, *Etruskische Geistigkeit* (Berlin 1947). M. PALLOTTINO, *L'origine degli Etruschi* (Rome 1947), 135–38. A. GRENIER, *Les religions étrusque et romaine*, in *Les religions de l'Europe ancienne* (Paris 1948), 3:1–233. A. PIGANIOL, *Les Étrusques, peuple d'Orient*, in *Cahiers d'histoire mondiale* 1, 2 (1953): 344. M. PALLOTTINO, *Deorum sedes*, in *Studi in onore di A. Calderini e R. Paribeni* (Milan 1956), 223–34. R. HERBIG, "Zur Religion und Religiosität der Etrusker," *Historia* 6 (1957): 123–32. L. BANTI, *Il mondo degli Etruschi* (Rome 1969), 235–54. G. Q. GIGLIOLI and G. CAMPOREALE, *La Religione degli Etruschi*, in *Storia delle religioni* (6th ed., Turin 1971), 2:537–672. G. DUMÉZIL, *La religion romaine archaïque* (2d ed., Paris 1974), 661–80. M. PALLOTTINO, *The Etruscans* (London 1975), 138–52 and 260–62. A. J. PFIFFIG, *Religio Etrusca* (Graz 1975). R. BLOCH, *Recherches sur les religions de l'Italie antique* (Geneva 1976). See also *Studi Etruschi*, 1–44 (1927–76).

Etruscan Daemonology

Etruscan demonology (more properly, daemonology) may be looked upon as one of the most interesting chapters of the history of religions of the Mediterranean world, provided, however, that it can be rid of certain simplistic and even naive interpretations—such as the all-too-obvious comparisons with demonologies of the Orient that aim to prove the Oriental origin of the Etruscans—and that it can be properly situated within the reasonable perspective of a comparison with the Greek world. In this essay it has been judged expedient to assemble all that has reference to the infradivine, that is, to those entities that might be defined in the Greek and Latin sense as "demigods": not forgetting, however, that in many cases it is difficult to specify whether a particular being is to be classed in the upper sphere, the sphere of divinities, or in the lower sphere, more populous and less definable, in which there are daemons. No cult, properly speaking, is connected with these daemons, except in a very limited fashion, for their principal characteristic is that they accompany the gods and serve as intermediaries between them and men. From this point of view one might say that the imagination of the Etruscans was given free rein, certainly more free than among the Greeks, as if it used images to enrich and render more comprehensible and fascinating the world of the supernatural. For in other respects, that world seemed distant and obscure to them—more distant and obscure, incidentally, than the Greek gods appeared to the Greeks, since myth had brought the gods nearer to men and nearly reduced them to the size of men—from which arose the Etruscans' obsession with understanding and interpreting the divine will through divinatory practices. The possibility cannot be entirely ruled out, however, that Etruscan "polydaemonism" may also have been the expression of primitive tendencies, more specifically a heritage or revival of ideas and creations characteristic of preclassical civilizations, such as those of the Near East or the Minoan and Mycenaean Aegean, which the Greeks had gone beyond sooner than the others, without, however, dispersing them entirely.

Most of our knowledge on this subject comes from mythological and funerary depictions and from written materials that identify individuals. By far the richest documentation is provided by scenes engraved on the backs of bronze mirrors, with the most variegated supernatural beings, posing or in action, mingled with images of gods and with episodes from Greek myth. Analogous compositions or isolated figures of demigods and daemons are found, though less systematically, in the representations on vases, reliefs, engraved stones, jewelry, etc. For the study of daemons of the world beyond the grave, one must take note of the frescoes of the sepulchers, but also the sculptures of sarcophagi and urns. The written sources, less numerous and less explicit, must be interpreted with care and have no value except to confirm archaeological data. They interest us in particular for their evidence about the semidivine beings who taught the Etruscan discipline, that is, Tages and Vegoia, or such other legendary matters as, for example, the figure of Cacus, the monster Volta, and other beings of this kind. One must also bear in mind the vast literary and epigraphical documentation (Latin) on the concept of the "genius," who is essentially the divinity who represents and guards the vital principle of men, institutions, and the gods themselves, but who may also be placed in an intermediate position between men and divinities: "son of the gods and father of men," notes Festus, who also calls him the son of Jupiter and the father of Tages! (Festus, 359, 452 L). These characteristics of the "genius" justify the traditional use of the word "genie" to designate the beings who are found on the level of the demigods and daemons.

A discussion of Etruscan daemonology must begin with a few observations about monsters and other fantastic figures of Oriental or Greek origin. These invade sculpture, painting, and the decoration of objects (bronzes, vases, jewels, etc.) in very large numbers, as if they were a favorite, obsessive object, beginning in the Orientalizing period, in the seventh century B.C.: quadrupeds winged or with a human head, sphinxes, centaurs, sirens, griffins, and particularly sea monsters. They continued to be present in diverse contexts until the latest periods of Etruscan art. But their link with particular figures specific to Greek myth, such as the Gorgon, the Chimera, the Sirens, Cerberus, etc., indicates that there is something there that is foreign to properly Etruscan conceptions. It is difficult to believe that all these images, generally used for decoration, corresponded to actual daemonic beliefs. But distortions in monstrous forms, the mixture of elements characteristic of diverse creatures, and the mixture of natural beings with artificial forms (like the forms of vases, in the objects called "canopic jars," otherwise called the anthropomorphic cinerary urns of Clusium) seem to be a specific trait of the mentality and artistic imagination of the Etruscans. An example of this is the winged monster with the head of a cock which recently appeared as a roof ornament of a religious edifice in the sanctuary of Pyrgi. The adding of wings is a favorite motif in the representation of human beings and gods, and of horses too, chiefly in archaic art. But that leads us back to the world of daemons that are properly Etruscan.

From a general point of view, which excludes the more specific analysis of particular cases, we can discern several

Infernal daemon with one of the deceased. Private collection. Manfredonia. Photo Pr Ferri.

categories of types and functions: and that leads us to the female, infant, martial, Dionysian, marine, and infernal daemons (or genies). The first class is extremely diversified and includes the figures of young women, clothed or nude, sometimes winged, wearing necklaces, and stamped by an ideal of beauty and elegance—an idea of the desirable. Their attitudes, their attributes (toilet articles), and their association with Turan often make them appear to be the companions and servants (to dress her, for example) of the goddess of love; this may be the meaning of the inscription *Snenath Turns,* "female assistant (?) of Turan." In some respects, these figures recall individuals from scenes of the women's chambers depicted on Greek vases. But we also encounter them in connection with other divinities, or crowning heroes (Heracles, Paris), or variously employed in quite diverse compositions, without notable coherence. In several cases, proper names accompany these figures, typically Etruscan names about which nothing else is known, such as Alpan, Evan, Zipna, Zirna, Zinthrepus, Mean, Mlacuch, Munthuch, Purich, Rescial, and Talitha. Some bear the name of Lasa, which also often appears as the first part of a double name, according to the system which is widely prevalent in systems of divine names: particularly Lasa Achununa, Lasa Vecu (or Vecuvia), Lasa Thimrae, Lasa Racuneta, and Lasa Sitmica. It might be possible someday to establish some kind of correspondence between Lasa and the Greek concept of nymph. One cannot, however, extend the term "lasa," as a generic designation, to all the female figures of the type being discussed, let alone to the female funerary spirits to be discussed farther on. Lasa Vecu or Vecuvia can easily be identified with the nymph Vegoia, whom the tradition continued to regard as the mistress and even author of a part of the *disciplina Etrusca.* This is an important argument in favor of the thesis that the female figures of these scenes, in addition to representing the collective and the secondary, sometimes correspond to well-known and well-defined individualities; this is also suggested by their presence in other depictions in which their nature is unfortunately no less indecipherable. Some of these figures are even probably, by virtue of their position of special dignity and their clothing, true divinities: this would be the case for Thalna, Ethausva, Thana or Thanr, and Malavis(ch).

Less frequent and clear is the evidence for other classes of demigods or demons, such as the masculine figures of the Apollonian type, or those who look like Silenus, or the warriors, or the small infant genies, who appear on mirrors, with more or less obscure Etruscan names. Among the infant or juvenile figures, the figure of Epiur, associated with Hercle (Heracles) and with Tinia (Jupiter), is especially interesting. In connection with this last divinity, one may recall the tradition concerning Tages, the nephew of Jupiter, a child or young man whose appearance and knowledge were those of an old man; born from the earth, he was supposed to have taught haruspicy to the Etruscans. Tages and Vegoia—Tages is represented on a mirror under the name Papa (or Pava) Tarchies, with the features of a young haruspex—exercised the characteristic function of "intermediaries" between the gods and men. Because of that they are fully contained in the category of Etruscan daemons (or genies): more particularly, those who reveal the divine will. One might add to them a young singer, perhaps a seer as well, who appears on another mirror and some urns; he is called Cacu, but he is clearly different from Cacus, the ferocious brigand of the Roman legend transmitted by Virgil.

The possibility that the daemons may have been conceived in other than anthropomorphic fashion, that is, as shadows without substance or in the aspect of a symbol, arises from some allusions to their connections with progeneration and sexuality. A peculiar tradition reported by the Neoplatonic philosopher Porphyry visualized Etruscan daemons as tenuous bodies living in the light of day, but doomed to be eclipsed at night, with the possibility, however, of being reborn in the scattering of their seed (Proclus, in his commentary on Plato's *Timaeus,* 142, D; Psellus *De oper. daemon.* 8). These are, of course, the later speculations of the learned, but they must preserve the memory of ancient beliefs about the existence of obscure forces of fecundity ultimately connected with the concept of Genius. One may recall the account, certainly of Etruscan origin, of the birth of the king of Rome Servius Tullius, who was born from the union of a slave with a *phallos* that appeared in the hearth of Queen Tanaquil, famous for her knowledge of the Etruscan discipline (Dionysius of Halicarnassus 4.2; Pliny *Nat. Hist.* 36.204). The same ancient authors explained this prodigious event as the fertilizing intervention of a god or daemon who could conceive his own materialization in the form of a simple sexual symbol. The mysterious connection between the shades and sexual power may well be associated with the scene of emaciated "animulae," hovering around a tree, that Tiresias evokes in the painting from the *Nekuia* of the tomb of Orco II of Tarquinii, and that are explicitly ithyphallic (Weinstock). The restorative fecundity of the daemons may also have been extended to the souls of the deceased, as a part of the beliefs that determined the complex rites whose function was to guarantee them immortality and to deify them.

This brings us to the hereafter, on which the daemonological imagination of the Etruscans seems to have lingered with particular pleasure. Even in this domain, it is difficult to distinguish clearly between divine figures (that is, Aita-Hades and Phersipnai-Persephone, "sovereigns" of the world of the dead, and, in other connections, Mantus and Mania, or Veive-Veiovis, etc.) and figures who are below the rank of gods. It is probable that Vanth was a goddess of fate, who recorded the fates of human beings. But the extraordinary frequency of her representations in tomb paintings and sculptures, in the costume of the Greek Erinyes (short tunic, fillets crossed over the bosom, buskins, and the attribute of a flaming torch) and often in the company of the daemon Charun, suggests that she belongs in the first rank, among the female daemons of the world beyond the grave, in exact correspondence with the Erinyes or Furies, on whom moderns have occasionally and mistakenly conferred the name "lasa." The same thing may be said of Culsu. It is probable that these Etruscan Erinyes, generally placed as guardians at the entrances to the infernal world, were also clearly individualized. The predominant role among the male daemons belonged to Charun, the preeminent personification of death, who is represented with a grey or greenish skin, a hooked nose, sometimes wings, and hair like serpents, and who is always armed with a heavy mallet. He certainly derives from the Greek Charon, whose name he bears. But he deviates from Charon in his appearance and functions. He can also appear in various other guises, differentiated by a second name, as can be seen at Tarquinii, in the Tomb of the Charons. The other clearly characterized daemon is Tuchulcha, who has the beak and feet of a bird of prey, long pointed ears, hair in the form of a nest of serpents, great wings, and enormous serpents for arms: a kind of monstrous humanoid griffin. A variety of beings with ape-like faces, more or less individualized, are also encountered, as are kinds of infernal servants or small orchestras of musicians of purely human appearance, except that they sometimes have wings. Finally recall the prevalence of infernal beings that look like animals, characterized by chthonic symbolism, from Cerberus and Scylla to dragons, and especially serpents. The intentionally terrifying appearance of many of these daemonic images, whose role is to frighten the deceased and also to torment them, has been connected with what is known of the somber and even desperate conception of the world beyond the grave among the Etruscans in the final period of their history, between the fourth and first century B.C. But infernal daemons of equally monstrous appearance had already been imagined in classical Greece in the fifth century, as is proven by the description of Eurynomos in the *Nekuia* of Polygnotus of Thasos (probably the distant prototype of the *Nekuia* on the tomb of Orco at Tarquinii), in the Lesche of the Cnidians at Delphi (Pausanias *Graeciae descr.* 10.28.7). As was stated at the beginning, this leads to the qualification of certain exaggerated hypotheses about the originality of Etruscan daemonology. It is also possible that certain Orphic and Pythagorean influences were transmitted by the Italiot environments of the Greek colonies of southern Italy. This last subject remains rather obscure, however, awaiting the future research that is so clearly desirable.

M.P./b.f.

Mirror showing Tinia and Epiur. Paris, Bibliothèque nationale.

BIBLIOGRAPHY

F. DE RUYT, *Charun, Démon étrusque de la mort* (Rome and Brussels 1934). R. HERBIG, *Götter und Dämonen der Etrusker* (Mainz 1965). S. WEINSTOCK, "Etruscan Demons," in *Studi in onore di Luisa Banti* (Rome 1965), 345–50. G. Q. GIGLIOLI and G. CAMPOREALE, "La religione degli Etruschi," in *Storia delle religioni* (6th ed., Turin 1971), 2:537–672. A. J. PFIFFIG, *Religio etrusca* (Graz 1975). M. PALLOTTINO, "Nome e funzione: A proposito di alcune divinità minori etrusche e romane," in *Saggi di antichità* (Rome 1979), 2:823–32.

Etruscan and Italic Divination

The mantic world of the Etruscans, and more generally of the Italic peoples, was fundamentally similar to that of the Greeks, at least as far as practices were concerned: these, like so many matters of religious life, enter into the general framework of classical antiquity. But certain aspects of them are distinguished characteristically—and were also seen by the ancients as being different—especially the consequences of certain essential ideas about the sacred and the relationship between men and gods on the level of their origins and their history. It is especially necessary to point out two phenomena that, in a way, epitomize the originality of divinatory practices in ancient Italy. The first is a desire to understand the obscure wishes of the gods through every possible sign—a desire that became so obsessive that it dominated all of Etruscan religious ideas and finally almost became identified with religion itself, justifying the existence of genuine technicians of divination, such as the haruspices and the interpreters of lightning flashes. The second was the development, through the observation of the flight of birds (*auspicium*), of the augural doctrine that becomes the fundamental doctrine of the sacred in Italico-Roman religion.

The first of these phenomena constitutes the essence of what was defined by the expression *disciplina Etrusca;* this was first taught by semidivine beings (Tages and Vegoia) and was transcribed into a series of books whose contents are more or less known to us. These deal with the observation of the viscera of animals (*haruspicina*), lightning flashes (*ars fulguratoria*), and portents (*ostenta*), and with their interpretation.

With respect to divination based upon auspices, it should be noted that the Umbrians practiced it at the same time as the Romans, as is witnessed by the ritual texts of the Iguvine Tablets; auspices served especially as introductions for sacrificial ceremonies.

M.P./d.w.

The Doctrine and Sacred Books of the *Disciplina Etrusca*

The Latin expression *disciplina Etrusca* is here meant to cover the whole complex of Etruscan doctrines and norms, in particular those concerning divination, but also, more generally, the ritual practices of the religion and the rules governing the civil life of the Etruscans. All of these elements are to be found in a series of sacred texts. This is a phenomenon that is wholly characteristic of Etruria but unique in the classical world. Their uniqueness may explain the extraordinary interest which the Etruscan treatises aroused among the Romans, who translated or summarized them and adopted some of their teachings. In certain cases, one may speak of a religious conception and a practice founded upon principles fixed by revealed and written traditions, as with the Hebraic religion. However, apart from the historical improbability of such an analogy, we do not know to what extent it is possible to trace back to the earliest stages of Etruscan religion the "system" of the *disciplinarum scripturae* (Vitruvius, 1.7.1) that appears to have been established later. But the *disciplina Etrusca* contains in itself motifs that may be viewed as belonging either to "science" or to "law," motifs that seem to encompass the sacred and profane aspects of one another in an inextricable fashion. It is probable, at least beginning from a certain time, that every human action was performed—or should have been performed—"in accordance with the *disciplina Etrusca*" (Servius, *Aen.*, 4.166). We may nevertheless conjecture, though only with great caution, that the original expression now lost, which was translated or paraphrased into Latin as *disciplina Etrusca,* corresponded to the Etruscan words *tesnś teiś raśneś* and *tesne raśne cei* (*raśna* = Etruscan, Etruria), which introduce and accompany the clauses of a land contract made between two families in the inscription of the Cippus of Perusia *CIE* 4538 (Mazzarino). It appears that the conclusion of the celebrated "prophecy of Vegoia"—which will be discussed later—makes a direct allusion to a rule of conduct, if not to a moral principle, in the phrase, "In this avoid all falsehood and duplicity: carry the discipline in your heart" (*Agrimensores,* Lachmann, 1, p. 350ff.).

Those writings on the *disciplina Etrusca* that were known to the Romans can be divided into three large groups: (1) the *libri haruspicini,* (2) the *libri fulgurales,* and (3) the *libri rituales* (Cicero, *On divination,* 1.72).

1. The first books deal with divination by observing and interpreting the viscera—particularly the liver—of sacrificed animals (*extispicium*). This practice was specifically attributed to the Etruscans and won them a particular renown. The priests who performed this divination were called the haruspices. The consultation of haruspices entered into Roman religion and continued to be practiced up to the end of pagan times, though its Etruscan origins were never forgotten. From artistic representations we know the characteristic dress of the haruspices, with a mantle hooked together at the chest and a hat with a cylindrical end. The origin of haruspicy was traced back to the teachings of Tages, a being of divine birth who was believed to be the son of Genius and the nephew of Jupiter; having arisen out of a furrow in the earth, he appeared to men as a young man with white hair. He is said to have taught his precepts to Tarchon, the hero from whom Tarquinii got its name, or to the twelve Etruscan kings and to the Etrurian people as a whole, so that he was regarded as the author of those writings which also go by the name of *Tagetici* or *Tagetinici.* A scene engraved on a Tuscan mirror that is conserved in the archaeological museum of Florence depicts him under the name of Papa or Pava Tarchies, wearing the dress of a haruspex, holding a liver in his hand, and teaching the discipline to Tarchon (*Avle Tarchunus*). The casuistry used in the examination of viscera for divine signs was particularly complicated, as evidenced by various ancient texts meticulously assembled and studied by C. O. Thulin. Readings were made with the help of patterns that can be seen in depictions of haruspices, but also and especially by means of the famous bronze lamb liver found near Piacenza. The surface of the liver is divided into squares in which the names of gods are found; it was believed that each divinity manifested itself in its own particular space. Around the edges there are sixteen squares corresponding to the sixteen zones of heavenly space and to their respective divinities. The interpreters' skill was thus exercised upon the microcosm of the liver as if upon a very small mirror of the celestial *templum.* The importance of the order of the haruspices—the famous college of Tarquinii counted sixty of them—was such that their authority apparently extended to every branch of Etruscan divination, and "haruspex" became the generic term designating the interpreter of the will of the gods. We are certain that the Etruscan equivalent of this name was *netśvis* (whereas the Latin expression *liber haruspicinus* reproduces and translates the Etruscan words *zich nethśrac* from the funerary inscription of the Tarquinian priest Laris Pulenas *CIE* 5430).

2. The *libri fulgurales* or *de fulguratura* contained the doctrine of lightning bolts and of their interpretation, which constituted the other great specific sector of Etruscan divination. This science was founded on the definition of the celestial expanse—which was called *templum*—in its orientation and its parts. The *templum* was thought to be divided into sixteen regions, each of which was the seat of one or several gods (Cicero, *Divin.*, 2.42; Pliny, *Hist. Nat.*, 2.143; Martianus Capella, *De nuptiis Mercuri et Philologiae*, 1.43ff.). The eastern sector was judged to be favorable (*pars familiaris*)

Bronze liver. Plaisance, Museo Civico.

and the western sector unfavorable (*pars hostilis*): the same concept applies to the small model of the liver found at Piacenza, where the favorable sector is indicated (on the convex side) by the word *usils* (= of the sun), i.e., the portion of the day, while the unfavorable sector is indicated by the word *tivs* (= of the moon), or the portion of the night. Yet this does not prove that the astral element would have had any particular importance. By collating the names of the divinities cited by Martianus Capella with those engraved in the squares on the liver of Piacenza, we may deduce that the supreme gods such as Tinia-Jupiter, Uni-Juno, Minerva, and Mars occupied the eastern sector and in particular the northeastern quarter of the celestial vault. Some of them were explicitly designated as throwers of the lightning bolt (*manubiae*): the god Tinia-Jupiter could throw three lightning bolts from three different celestial regions (and his name is repeated in three of the border squares on the liver of Piacenza). It was the nature gods in particular, such as Nethuns-Neptune, Catha (the sun), Fufluns-Bacchus, Selvans-Silvanus, who were found in the southern sectors. In the western sector, the *pars hostilis,* were the infernal divinities or the gods of fate, such as Letham, Cel, Culsu, Fortuna, the Manes, and Vetis-Veiovis. Naturally, the zone from which the lightning came indicated the divinity for which it was the sign. The interpretation was based on the intensity, form, and color of the lightning bolt, the noise that accompanied it, the place where it struck, and its effects. The casuistry was very complicated. Distinctions were made between good and bad and private and public lightning bolts, between those that gave advice or orders, commutable or fixed sentences, etc. Particular rites of purification were performed at the place where the lightning had struck and where it was thought to remain under the surface in the form of a small stone: this sacred place was called *bidental* in Latin. In his *Quaestiones naturales* II, Seneca left an ample and methodical summary of all of these doctrines, which ancient tradition dated back to the writings of the nymph Begoe or Vegoia (from which the name of the *libri Vegonici* also comes). The observation and interpretation of lightning bolts was left to a special priest called the *fulgurator,* from which it seems possible to deduce the Etruscan name (*trutnvt frontac*) from the bilingual Etrusco-Latin inscription of the priest L. Cafatius, which is preserved in the Pesaro Museum.

3. The contents of the *libri rituales* were much more varied and complicated. We know (especially from Festus, 285) that they contained a series of prescriptions for the rites of foundation of cities and the consecration of altars and temples, as well as for the civil and military organizations of the state. Among all of these precepts, there is one that seems to have been of particular importance to the social and economic structures of Etruria: according to ritual norms partly corresponding to those concerning the definition of the heavenly space, the earth was to be divided in order to permit its profitable use, following an ordered system of the division of property. It is clear that land surveying as a system is one of the fundamental factors in the technical and economic advances introduced by Greek colonization in Italy (as the most recent archaeological investigations, notably those undertaken in Metapontum and at Megara Hyblaea in Sicily, have shown), and one that was to play a fundamental role in the life of the Roman world. But in Etruria, the division and delimination of land, insofar as these depended on the will of the gods, had a significance that was clearly religious, as shown by the prophecy of Vergoia cited above, which, within a teaching to a certain Arruns Veltymnus, predicted for the last years of the Etruscan "eighth century" (i.e., the beginning of the first century B.C.) a series of disasters resulting from violations of the boundaries and passages of properties. This probably reflects the conservative tendencies of the Etruscan oligarchies in the face of the agrarian reforms promulgated at Rome by the Greeks and taken up later by M. Livius Drusus.

Among the ritual books, a more specific category of writings was established, which was called *libri fatales* and which was devoted to doctrines of time and of fate, i.e., to the durations of the lives of men, cities, and states. These books also treated of the concept of "centuries," understood as cycles that were not only natural but also religious, that brought renewal and were punctuated by portents, rendering obligatory the performance of particular rites of purification. Other writings, called *libri acherontici* (from the name of the river of hell, the Acheron), seem to refer more particularly to one's destiny after death; we know that they contained instructions for ceremonies by which men could gain immortality, i.e., transform themselves into "divine souls" or into "gods of the soul": *di animales* (Servius, *Aen.*, 3.168; Arnobius, *Adversus gentes,* 2.62). Then follows a very large section of the *disciplina Etrusca* that, if we go by what is written in it, should also enter into the category of *libri fatales,* i.e., the theory, classification, observation, and explanation of odd or portentous events: of *ostenta.* This is probably an occasional practice which, in unforeseeable cases, left everything to the interpreter's experience and verbal responses. Nevertheless, there were also written documents called *ostentaria* (a late collection or transcription, attributed at least in part to the Etruscan haruspex Tarquitius—the name comes from *libri Tarquitiani*) of which a few fragments remain, recorded in Latin literature, and which seem to have all the characteristics of a summary, as may be seen in the following example: "A ewe or a ram, if it is draped with purple or with gold, brings an increase of abundance to the head of the state or country, multiplies the progeny of the country, and makes it happier" (extract from the book of Tarquitius, cited by Macrobius, *Saturnalia,* 3.7.2). Signs may be of very different kinds; unusual celestial apparitions, rains of blood or of stones (and logically lightning bolts should be classified under this same heading, since they elsewhere constitute, as we have seen, a peculiar but essential chapter in Etruscan divination), earthquakes, the falling of statues, plants with unusual shapes or aberrant growth, animals that behave strangely or that have exceptional characteristics, monstrous beings, and so on. Obviously, under this heading were also

Mirror from Tuscany. Florence, Archaeological Museum.

classified the signs of the flight of birds, which otherwise does not seem to have been the object of a technically developed divinatory art in Etruria, nor to have had a primordial role in worship, as it did in the Roman and Umbrian religions. Portents announce the future, but in many cases they are the frightening manifestation of some private or public impurity or fault, which requires purification by special and extremely meticulous rites. Finally, we must stress the exceptional importance that Roman religion placed on the Etruscan traditions of the observation of the *ostenta* and the expiatory rites that they required. By contrast, the divination by oracles that was so typical of the Greek world seems to have been wholly foreign to the *disciplina Etrusca.*

We said at the beginning that there is no way of knowing when all that has been described so far became, even in substance, the heritage of Etruscan religion and culture. It is very probable—and this is the general opinion of researchers on the subject—that the *disciplina Etrusca,* as a written "corpus," was systematized mainly during the last part of the history of Etruria and thus resulted from the reflection and traditionalism of priestly circles that were already in contact with Hellenistic and Hellenistic-Roman scholarship. In the same way, accounts of primordial events, such as the "preachings" of Tages, are for the most part artificial reconstructions of a mythical or etiological type. Nevertheless, we cannot imagine that such a heritage of beliefs, practices, and speculations, some of which are analogically tied to ritual forms from distant times and places—such as the bronze model of the liver at Piacenza which evokes small terra-cotta models of livers used for haruspicy in Mesopotamia and Asia Minor—could have resulted solely from scholarly inventions from before the high point of Etruscan civilization, i.e., the archaic period. Numerous traditions whose origins can be traced back precisely to the archaic period (portents, prophecies, and especially the testimony of the "books" attributed to the Sibyl of Cumae—the *libri Sibyllini*—which are connected with King Tarquinius Superbus and also with the *libri fatales:* Livy, 22.9) and the fact that the existence of the fundamental elements of haruspicy from the fourth century onwards can be established on the basis of artistic representations suggest that the essential elements of the ideas, norms, and practices that became known to the Romans under the name of *disciplina* belong to the earliest stages of Etruscan religion; and we should attribute to the late periods little more than a better organization of the sacred laws, along with a general literary definition of the sacred.

The first ideas were probably transmitted orally and in the form of songs (Lucretius, 6.381; Censorinus, *De die natali,* 4.13). The attribution of these teachings to demigods such as Tages and the nymph Begoe or Vegoia probably goes back to fairly early local traditions. The attribution to Tages must be related to the city of Tarquinii because of its relationship with Tarchon, and the attribution to Begoe or Vegoia (whose Etruscan name is *Lasa Vecu* or *Vecuvia*) to the city of Clusium or a Vecu family—which might suggest that these cults and myths have noble origins. But these two cases, as well as other indications, seem to throw into relief the tendency of the Etruscan religion to seek the "sources" of doctrines and religious precepts in the authority of supernatural beings, which to some extent gives it the character of a "revealed" religion. It is likely that in the beginning these two teachings were not clearly distinguishable from one another. Not only haruspicy but also the ritual discipline was traced back to Tages, in particular all that concerned the *jus terrae Etruriae* and the *libri acherontici* (Servius, *Aen.,* 8.398). Vegoia is cited with regard not only to the doctrine of lightning bolts, but also to warnings about the intangibility of boundaries, as we have already seen. The idea that the books that circulated under the names of Tages (*Tagetici*) and Vegoia (*Vegonici*) were generally collections of their oral teachings emerges quite clearly from the body of citations found in literary sources. The legendary and semilegendary characters who collected and spread them, such as Tarchon or Arruns Veltymnus, must have been very important. In any case, the canonical attributions and divisions are undoubtedly fictive and late, especially since there are references to unknown authors, such as the Marcii, or authors completely foreign to the *disciplina Etrusca,* such as the Carthaginian Mago, all of whom are anachronistically associated with Vegoia (Servius, *Aen.,* 6.72; *Agrimensores,* Lachmann, p. 348). With these authors, we come to those historians who collect, develop, summarize, and translate (from Etruscan into Latin) traditional doctrines, first L. Tarquitius (Priscus), the author of the previously cited *libri Tarquitiani,* and then A. Caecina, Aquila, Nigidius Figulus, Umbricius Melior, Capito, Labeo, and several others into the late imperial period.

M.P./d.w.

BIBLIOGRAPHY

C. O. THULIN, *Die Götter des Martianus Capella und der Bronzeleber von Piacenza* (Giessen 1906); *Die etruskische Disziplin* (Göteborg 1906–9). M. PALLOTTINO, "Uno specchio di Tuscania e la leggenda etrusca di Tarchon," in *Rendiconti della Pontifica Accademia Romana di Archeologia*

6 (1930): 49–87. B. NOGARA, *Gli Etruschi e la loro civiltà* (Milan 1933), 189–219. M. PALLOTTINO, *Deorum sedes*, in *Studi in onore di A. Calderini e R. Paribeni* (Milan 1956–57), 223–34. S. MAZZARINO, "Sociologia del mondo etrusco e problemi della tarda etruscità," in *Historia* 6 (1957): 98–122. R. BLOCH, *Les prodiges dans l'Antiquité classique* (Paris 1963), 43–76. A. J. PFIFFIG, *Religio Etrusca* (Graz 1975). C. A. MASTRELLI, "Etrusco-piceno frontac e greco *Keraunos*," *Studi Etruschi* 44 (1976): 149–61.

The Religion of the Sabellians and Umbrians, Italics of Central and Southern Italy

I. Historical and Linguistic Background

The people who lived in the heart of the Italian peninsula, who belonged to a single linguistic stock of Indo-European origin (but different from Latin), and whom modern scholars designate by the general name of Sabellian-Umbrians or Osco-Umbrians, Eastern Italics, or simply "Italics," made up a fundamental element of the population and thereby of the history and the culture of pre-Roman, ancient Italy. Originally these people may all have had a common national name connected with the root *sabh-*, from which are derived the historical names of Sabines, Sabellians, and Samnium (*Safinim* in its indigenous form), whence comes the name of the Saunites or Samnites. Legends evoke very ancient kinship relations among them, as well as similarities in the area of their religious traditions. Yet from the dawn of historical times, this ethnic group appears to have been fragmented into many different populations and tribes, each having its own name and characteristic dialect, behavior, and history. Their contacts with the Tyrrhenian centers of Etruria, Latium, and Campania, and with the Greek colonial world, coupled with their expansion within the peninsula southward and toward the Tyrrhenian Sea, determined this vast process of cultural integration. As a result of this integration, the Eastern Italics benefited more and more from the imports from great urban civilizations, despite their own fundamental ties to pastoral and agrarian community structures and to primitive customs. This influence could not fail to have repercussions in the area of religion.

The people in question can be identified and classified more precisely in linguistic, historic, and geographic terms. Although they have a common origin, the Italic languages are divided into two main groups: the so-called Oscan language (named after the Oscans in Campania), widespread in southern Italy and documented by a significant number of inscriptions that use indigenous alphabets, Greek and Latin; and the Umbrian language, known almost exclusively through the texts of the Iguvine Tables of Gubbio, which use Umbrian and Latin alphabets. The first language is the heritage of those people whom we call Sabellians (Sabelli) in the broadest sense of the Latin term—people who included at the time of the Roman conquest small groups settled in what now is called Abruzzi (the Marsi, Paeligni, Praetuttii, Vestini, and Marrucini)—and farther south, the Samnites, and then the Frentoni, the Campani or Osci, the Hirpini, the Lucani, and the Bruttii, all the way to the Mamertini in Sicily. It is likely that the Sabines (Sabini) of central Italy and their neighbors the Aequi, the Hercini, etc., who were scattered around Latium since prehistory, as well as the Picenti or Piceni along the Adriatic slope, belonged to older strata of populations who spoke dialects of the Oscan type during a less-differentiated archaic phase. The Umbrians (Umbri), who made their way northward along the valley of the Tiber and beyond the Apennines to the outer limits of the Paduan plain, constituted a distinctly separate branch with their own innovations; but there were also some similar groups to the south, such as the Volsci in Latium.

If we consider this dispersion and the variety of geographical and historical conditions, we cannot speak of an Italic religion as a defined reality, understood as a unitary concept. Moreover, such an idea was totally alien to the ancients' way of thinking. Rather we must distinguish and evaluate the facts about the peoples and places of the cultures that are best known historically and that are most fully documented. We can thus realistically study the religion of the Sabines (which we know from Roman tradition) and the religion of the Sabellians of Abruzzi, Samnium, Campania, Irpinia, Lucania, etc. Our knowledge of the Sabellians is based essentially on local epigraphic evidence in the Oscan language, such as the Tabula Agnonensis, and the inscriptions of Capua, the Cippus of Abella, the collection of texts from Rossano di Vaglio; and inscriptions on the archaeological remains from shrines. We can also study Umbrian religion, or more exactly Iguvine religion, since we know it exclusively through the Iguvine Tables, from Iguvium, the ancient name for Gubbio. But for each of them, with the exception of the Umbrian religion, the fragments that we have are not sufficient to give a clear idea of their true character. This is partly due to the paucity of information provided by classical authors and scholars (in contrast with the great interest that the ancients took in Etruscan religion). As a result, a synthesis of all the data seems to be called for.

II. The Myth of the Animal Guide or Ancestor

At the oldest, undoubtedly communal, level there are traditions about the migrations of groups under the guidance or advice of a sacred animal that may also give its name to the ethnic group that claims it. For example, the Sabellians were guided by a bull; the Piceni, by a woodpecker (*picus*, from which they got their name); the Hirpini and the Lucani, by a wolf (*hirpus* in Italic, and *lukos* in Greek). The same relationship may have existed for other minor populations and tribes: thus the Frentani and the hart (whose Indo-European name *bhrento-* is attested particularly in neighboring Apulia), and the Ursentini and the bear. The ritual basis for these migrations was something called *ver sacrum* (the sacred springtime), that is, the propitiatory or expiatory offering to the god of all those beings who were born during a given period of time. Humans, however, were not sacrificed but were compelled to leave their original group to go and settle elsewhere and to find new means of subsistence, which in turn triggered the formation of new groups (see the article "Ver Sacrum," below). Clearly these are concepts peculiar to primitive societies of a pastoral-nomadic type. The theriomorphic element was important not only among these people but also in more advanced societies of the Eurasian world, as A. Alföldi has recently shown. There is some reason to believe, although hesitantly, that these are survivals of totemism.

The myth of the animal guide, or ancestor, feeder, and protector, was quite widespread in prehistoric Italy; it remained especially linked to pastoralism and transhumance; clear archaeological evidence supports the validity of this relationship in the culture of the so-called Apennine Bronze Age. We even find it in the oldest Latin and Roman legends.

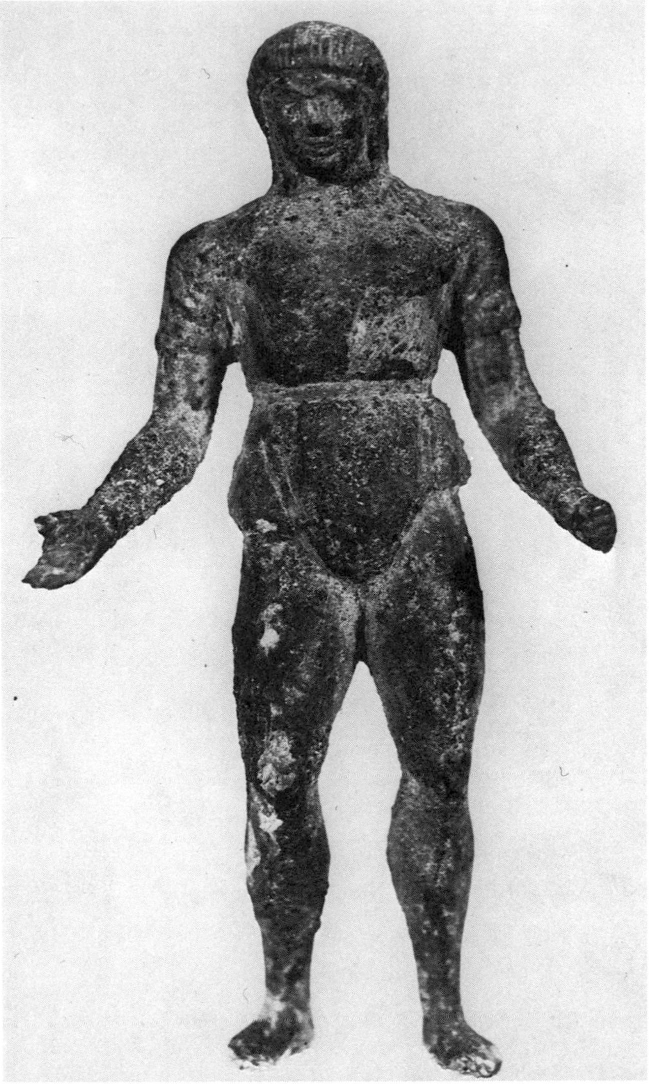

Etruscan *Tabula Agnonensis*. London, British Museum. Museum photo.

Right: Ex-voto. Avellino, Museo Irpino. Museum photo.

In the oldest Latin legends we may recall the sow who led Aeneas and his companions from Lavinium to Alba Longa, or the she-wolf of Rome. The traditions and rites of the Luperci may also be recalled. Even in prehistory these concepts must have clashed with the substantially different beliefs and rites of agrarian societies. They were probably permanently obliterated in the wake of the religious ideas that spread within the zones of proto-urban and urban cultures of coastal Italy, notably in the south and along the Tyrrhenian coast, under Greek and Etruscan influence. Even in the historical period, these ancient concepts seem to have characterized the people of inland Italy, who were still tied, at least in their place of origin, to pre-urban structures, to an essentially pastoral economy, and to a mobility that involved aggressive and warlike tendencies. This fits the description of the Sabellian-Umbrians exactly. What is most interesting is that the *ver sacrum* was an enduring rite that continued to be performed in later periods, as well as an etiological myth of the origins of the Italic people, a myth that later became part of the scholarly reconstruction of the legendary ethnography of Italy in the heroic era. Their very ancient relation with the god Mars (in the Oscan form Mamers) stressed this warlike feature, which must be connected with the increasing use of mercenaries. The sources explicitly attest that animal guides, particularly the bull and the woodpecker, were consecrated to this god. We may therefore assume that the original figures or the theriomorphic divine forces were gradually transformed into simple attributes or symbols. This secondary character is obvious, for instance, in the representations of the Italic bull (*viteliu*), which overcomes the Roman she-wolf on the coins of the federated Sabellians who rose up against Rome during the Social War (90–87 B.C.). That was the last attempt by these people to assert a "national" consciousness.

III. Personal Deities

Belief in more or less anthropomorphic, personal deities seems to have been the ancestral patrimony of the Sabellian-Umbrians, but it spread, becoming solidified and complicated as contacts developed with the Greek and Tyrrhenian (i.e., Etruscan, Latin, and Campanian) religious worlds.

Ex-voto. Avellino, Museo Irpino. Museum photo.

Ex-voto. Avellino, Museo Irpino. Museum photo.

Many of the most ancient centers and cult sites in southern Italy were subject to Italic occupation. Thus came into being a vast network of correspondences, identifications, and reciprocal influences, of common experiences and developments, which must have resulted in the diffusion of the cults of the supreme celestial deity (D)iove-Jupiter, of Mars-Mamers, of Herekle-Herakles, and of Kere-Ceres. But there were also specifically Italic deities, or deities peculiar to each Italic environment, such as the goddess Mefitis in the Sabellian area (Irpinia and Lucania), the goddess Cupra in Umbria and in the Picenum, and the god Cerfo in Gubbio. Our knowledge of the Umbrian pantheon is especially rich because of the Iguvine Tablets. This pantheon presents the characteristic system of double names for gods, in which the second element plays the role of a qualifying adjective (as in personal names) and is often derived from the name of another god, for example, Tefre Jovie (Tefro "of Jupiter"), Serfe Martie (Çerfo "of Mars"), Prestota Serfia (Prestota "of Çerfo"). This crisscrossing of direct or collateral kinship lines gives it the appearance of a large family of gods. This does not necessarily signify, however, a true mythological theogony such as existed among the Greeks and in other ancient religions. The abstract character of certain primary names, such as Saçi ("pact of sacred allegiance") in the expression *Iupater Saçe* (Jupiter "of Saçi"), suggests rather that this network of relationships was the fruit of a conceptual elaboration peculiar to the Iguvine religion. This does not alter the fact that the double name for gods is widely attested, though in a less typical and coherent way, outside Umbria, not only in all of the Sabellian country but also in Latium and Etruria.

IV. Forms of Worship

The frameworks within which people understood their connections with the gods, and therefore the forms of their worship, did not differ in essence from what we know about the religion of Rome and, more generally, of the Greco-Italic world. These forms include the observation of the signs of divine will; objects or living creatures dedicated and consecrated to the gods (*devotio*); private and public rites of propitiation and expiation, with prayers, offerings without bloodshed or sacrifices; votive gifts; places of worship, notably with open-air altars; later, temples built on Greek and Etruscan models. But in this general overview, we should note characteristics peculiar to each of the religious centers that we mentioned earlier. In Campania, for instance, at Capua, an important collection of Oscan epigraphs attests that sacred buildings called *iuvilas* (probably altars or small shrines) were the sites of ceremonies celebrated on certain days of fixed festivals, sometimes even with public magistrates officiating. Also in Capua, the imposing shrine of Fondo Patturelli with its strange stone statues depicting mothers seated with children in their arms, and with all its terra-cotta votive objects, is evidence of a cult devoted to the goddess of fertility. The inscription on the Tabula Agnonensis in Sannio describes a processional rite with stations in front of the numerous altars inside a sacred enclosure that were dedicated to Ceres, Flora, and other minor deities; in certain years a holocaust was celebrated. The shrine of the goddess Mefitis in the Ansanto Valley near Mirabella Eclano in the heart of Irpinia attests what was probably a chthonic cult. The shrine was rich in votive objects and may have been connected with the toxic emanations from this wild site, hence the more general meaning of the word *mephitis*, "foul-smelling." Also dedicated to Mefitis (who is identified with Venus and Ceres) is another shrine, possibly connected with an original cult of the waters and discovered at Rossano di Vaglio in Lucania. This shrine is interesting especially for its Oscan inscriptions in the Greek alphabet, which M. Lejeune has studied, as well as for the architechtonic structures that surround a large altar. The general feature of these Italic religious centers was the form of the sacred enclosure with its altars and votive monuments. True temples in the Greek and Etruscan-Latin style appeared late and in isolated places, for instance, in Paestum or in Pietrabbondante.

The Iguvine Tablets, the longest pre-Latin inscription yet discovered in Italy, bring us in themselves a profound and detailed knowledge of the rites of Umbrian religion. Each ceremony began with the observation of the flight of birds in an appropriate and precisely oriented part of the sky that corresponded to a part of the earth, recalling the Etruscan and Latin conception of the *templum*. As in Rome but not in Etruia, augury represents the sole form of divination, or at least its principal form. An expiatory purification preceded the sacred act. Real sacrifices were performed with animal victims obtained from sacred breeding farms (*sakri*) or profane ones (*perakni*), the animals differing according to the deities (oxen, lambs, pigs, etc.). There were also frequent bloodless offerings, i.e., offerings of food and drink. The rite was accompanied by vows and prayers invoking the protection of the gods for the city and the shrine. The curse placed on foreigners (Etruscans, Iapuzcus, Naharkus) was notable. The Tablets also provide information on the various priestly functions, particularly those of the college of priests known as the Atiedii Brethren.

Within the general framework of the conservatism of the Italic people, the cult of the dead and funerary practices were closely related to traditions widespread all over Italy in the course of protohistory, with a clear predominance of the rite of inhumation in ditch graves. In the Adriatic region of Picenum, and occasionally in burials of chiefs in lower Italy, the funerary furnishings have a particular opulence. Through contact with the Greco-Tyrrhenian world, a type of tomb appeared and spread later among the Campanians of Capua and the Lucanians of Paestum; the tombs had the shape of cases and were decorated with paintings featuring mostly martial subjects but also had references to the afterlife and conceivably echoes of Pythagorean doctrines. It does not appear, however, that the problem of death inspired a preoccupation and doctrinal reflection among the Sabellians and the Umbrians comparable to those found in Etruria.

M.P./g.h.

BIBLIOGRAPHY

F. VON DUHN, *Italische Gräberkunde*, 2 vols. (Heidelberg 1923, 1939); vol. 2 with F. MESSERSCHMIDT. J. WHATMOUGH, *The Foundations of Roman Italy* (London 1937). G. DEVOTO, *Tabulae Iguvinae* (Rome 1937). E. C. EVANS, *The Cults of the Sabine Territory* (New York 1939). J. HEURGON, *Étude sur les inscriptions osques de Capoue dite Iúvilas* (Paris 1942). E. VETTER, *Handbuch der italischen Dialekte* (Heidelberg 1953). J. HEURGON, *Trois études sur le "Ver sacrum"* (Brussels 1957). M. G. BRUNO, "I Sabini e la loro lingua," in *Rendiconti dell'Istituto Lombardo di Scienze e Lettere* 95 (1961): 501–41; 96 (1962): 413–42 and 565–640. V. PISANI, *Le lingue dell'Italia antica oltre il latino* (2d ed., Turin 1964). A. J. PFIFFIG, *Religio Iguvina* (Vienna 1964). G. RADKE, *Die Götter Altitaliens* (Münster 1965). G. DEVOTO, *Gli antichi Italici* (3d ed., Florence 1967); *Scritti minori*, vol. 2 (Florence 1967). E. T. SALMON, *Samnium and the Samnites* (Cambridge 1967). V. CIANFARANI, *Culture adriatiche d'Italia* (Rome 1970). D. ADAMESTEANU and M. LEJEUNE, *Il Santuario lucano di Macchia di Rossano di Vaglio*, Memorie delle'Accademia Nazionale dei Lincei, Classe di scienze morali, ser. 8, 16 (Rome 1971): 37–83; the complementary contributions of M. LEJEUNE have been published in the reports of the same academy, 1972, pp. 663–84; 1973, pp. 399–414. J. HEURGON, "I culti non greci della Magna Grecia," in *Le genti non greche della Magna Grecia* (*Atti dell'XI Convegno di Studi sulla Magna Grecia*, Taranto 1971) (Naples 1972), 55–75. A. ALFÖLDI, *Die Struktur des voretruskischen Römerstaates* (Heidelberg 1974). U. BIANCHI, "Gli dei delle stirpi italiche," in *Popoli e civiltà dell'Italia antica* 7 (1978): 195–236.

The Beliefs and Rites of the Apulians, an Indigenous People of Southeastern Italy

The Latin form *Apuli* is derived from, or at least related to, the term "Iapyges" used by the Greeks to designate the indigenous populations of southeastern Italy, i.e., ancient and modern Apulia, including the three groups of the Daunians, the Peucetians, and the Messapians (settled from north to south, respectively, in the present-day provinces of Foggia and Bari and in the Salentine peninsula). For the territory of the Messapians, names of other ethnic groups are also cited, such as the Salentines and the Calabrians—the source of the geographic term Calabria (which, beginning in the Middle Ages, spread to the southwestern extremity of Italy and took on its contemporary meaning); in the Roman period, the region was divided into Apulia in the north and Calabria in the south. All of these peoples, by their ethnolinguistic character, their traditions, and their cultural productions, constitute a well-defined group in the populations and cultures of ancient Italy. The language, today called Messapian and documented by a number of inscriptions discovered especially in the southern part of the country, is certainly Indo-European, but, unlike those of the other Italic peoples, it has important connections with the other side of the Adriatic, which in a way confirm the ancient traditions of an Illyrian origin of the Iapyges. On the other hand, their name is related, if not identical, to that of the Iapuzcus (or Iabusques) cited in the Umbrian inscription of the Iguvine Tablets, that is, people inhabiting central Italy and probably the Adriatic coast; it is also connected to the name of the Iapodes or Iapydes of northern Dalmatia—which confirms the original existence of important ethnic relationships between the two coasts of the Adriatic.

Priam surrounded by Trojan men and women. Stela from Daunia. Photo pr. Silvio Ferri, Pisa.

The culture and particularly the religion of the pre-Roman Apulians present, insofar as they can be known, a peculiar mixture of indigenous elements, chiefly connected with prehistoric and protohistoric traditions, and Greek elements from the colonies established on the margins of this territory by the eighth century B.C. but preceded by precolonial incursions going back to the Mycenaean age (the role of Taranto seems to have been important). Classical sources transmit the memory of a web of legends elaborated by the Greeks about the colonization of Apulia by the Arcadians, Cretans, Illyrians, etc., and about the eponymous heroes Iapyx, Messapus, Peucetius, and Daunus. Daunus was known not as a foreigner but as an indigenous king and must certainly be connected with a Paleo-Italic mythic source, as is proved by the etymological identity of his name with the Latin name Faunus. There are also legends about the Adriatic enterprises of Diomedes and his death in Daunia while he was returning from Troy, and about the founding of cities and sanctuaries, among which those of Athena Ilias at Luceria and of Calchas and Podalirius on Mount Gargano are especially famous. These tales preserve traces of local traditions, for example, of the curative powers of the waters of the *heroon* of Podalirius and the oracles granted during the sleep of anyone who slept wrapped in the skin of a sacrificed ewe. Behind the worship of Greek goddesses such as Demeter and Aphrodite, whose names are mentioned along with their special attributes in the Messapian inscriptions, we glimpse indigenous divine figures; to one god, Menzana, identified with Jupiter, these same Messapians, who were reputed as breeders of horses, sacrificed living horses.

Achilles, seated, playing a lyre; on the right, Priam; and on the left Andromache and Hecuba. Stela from Daunia. Photo pr. Silvio Ferri, Pisa.

The funerary domain is known exclusively through archaeology, which provides very abundant and diverse data. The principal rite is that of burial in stone tumuli (called "specchie") in pits or stone containers, and only later in room-shaped tombs that imitated houses, with rich funerary furnishings which attest to the traditional belief in the survival of the dead as long as their sepulcher lasts. The beautiful anthropomorphic stelae of Daunia, decorated with geometric designs, with customary or ritual scenes, and with representations of mythical episodes and monstrous animals, are connected with forms diffused in European prehistory and protohistory. Another remarkable expression of conservatism is the custom of burying the dead in inhabited zones—a custom which, even in the historical period, contrasts with the advanced character of the great urban centers girded with imposing defensive walls.

M.P./j.l.

BIBLIOGRAPHY

M. MAYER, *Apulien vor und während der Hellenisierung* (Leipzig and Berlin 1914). J. WHATMOUGH, *The Foundations of Roman Italy* (London 1937). J. BERARD, *La colonisation grecque de l'Italie méridionale et de la Sicile dans l'Antiquité* (2d ed., Paris 1957), 368ff., 426ff. O. PARLANGELI, *Studi messapici* (Milan 1960). G. GIANNELLI, *Culti e miti della Magna Grecia* (2d ed., Florence 1963).

Myths and Cults of the Ancient Veneti, an Indo-European People of Northern Italy

Among the peoples and cultures of ancient Italy, the Veneti constituted a unit well defined by the territory they occupied (between the Alps and the Adriatic, a territory that still bears their name); by the Indo-European language they spoke, which was quite close to Latin; and by their particular culture, which developed coherently from the end of the Bronze Age to the dawn of the Roman conquest (i.e., from the tenth to the third or second centuries B.C.), all the while preserving a basic protohistorical stamp. Consequently, the Paleo-Venetian world on the one hand had close natural ties to the central European domains of Hallstatt and Slovenia, as is understandable, and on the other hand remained open to all of the cultural influences of neighboring northern Etruria, particularly the Etrurian alphabet. But there were few influences from Greek culture. Venetian organization still continued to be tied to pre-urban and proto-urban structures. The major centers, which we know best, were Ateste (modern Este) and Patavium (modern Padua), which along with Vicentia (modern Vincenza) and Verona became "real" cities only considerably later. The port of Adria, near the mouths of the Po and the Adige, was the principal point of contact with Etruscans and Greeks. To the north, Venetian culture reached into the Alpine valleys, where it exerted its influence on the territories inhabited by the Rhaetians, who spoke another language. To the east, it encountered the local cultures of the Carni and the Istrians, with whom the Veneti mixed freely. Celtic expansion into the Alps and northern Italy did not reach the center of the Venetian cultural domain, but merely touched its margins.

The Veneti, like other ancient peoples of Italy, had their place in the legendary cycles of origins elaborated by Greek ethnography and mythology in contact with the Italic world. The Veneti were said to have originated in Asia Minor, which they left under the leadership of Antenor. Their legends account for the presence and cult of Diomedes, the preeminent Adriatic hero and the founder of Adria; they are full of elements revealing knowledge of local facts, such as the fame of the Veneti for horse breeding. At the mouth of the Timavo River, white horses were sacrificed to Diomedes, who was supposedly responsible for the origin of the shrines of Argive Hera and Aetolian Artemis; both of the shrines consisted of wooded enclosures that shut in wild animals. Livy (10.2) reports that the main temple in Padua in the fourth century was consecrated to Juno. All signs suggest that this was a

Deity of the Veneti. Bronze plaque. Este, Museo nazionale atestino. Photo Soprintendenza.

classical phenomenon of the transposition or interpretation of a native goddess, probably the most important deity of the Veneti: she protected fertility, tamed passions, and healed men. Her name, Reitia, is known principally through dedicatory inscriptions on a shrine in Este and is, moreover, followed by different epithets that are separately attested, such as Sainati. Note the analogy between her name and that of the Rhaetian people. In other places (in the Cadore) and in a different way, the goddess also appeared as Loudera (i.e., Libera). There was yet another deity with three forms, masculine (identified with Apollo) or feminine.

The cult took place in outdoor shrines adorned with votive gifts (statuettes, bronze plates that are illustrated or that bear inscriptions and alphabetical signs, vases, objects for women's use, etc.), in which libations and holocausts were carried out. Most of the evidence is archaeological. We know of various places of worship in Este, others in Padua, Vincenza, Lagole di Calalzo, in the Rhaetian territory in Magré, and in Sanzeno in the Valle di Non. There was a cult of sulfur water in Abano, connected with the god Aponus. As there are no extant literary sources, we can say little about the religion with respect to the dead or ideas of the afterlife. The funerary customs fit into the general framework of protohistoric traditions, with more or less elaborate funerary trappings, but generally with a close adherence to the rite of cremation.

M.P./g.h.

BIBLIOGRAPHY

J. WHATMOUGH, *The Foundations of Roman Italy* (London 1937). F. VON DUHN and F. MESSERSCHMIDT, *Italische Gräberkunde*, 2 (Heidelberg 1939). G. B. PELLEGRINI and A. L. PROSDOCIMI, *La lingua venetica* (Padua 1967). M. LEJEUNE, *Manuel de la langue vénète* (Heidelberg 1974). G. FOGOLARI, "La protostoria delle Venezie," in *Popoli e civiltà dell' Italia antica* (Rome 1975), 4:61–222, with a detailed bibliography on the religion of the Veneti, pp. 219ff.

Ver Sacrum: The Italic Rite of the "Sacred Springtime"

The Latin expression *ver sacrum* (sacred springtime) was used by Roman authors in a precise technical sense to designate an Italic rite that was attested several times by sources dealing with the origins and history of peoples classified today in the Sabellian-Umbrian linguistic branch. As far back as the time of the very first settlements by people known as the Aborigines (i.e., the Sabines) in central Italy in the Rieti basin and the time of their southward expansion toward Latium, there was a custom of consecrating to a god the entire generation born in a given year after wars, famines, or even overpopulation. Young men old enough to bear arms were compelled to leave their country and found "colonies" in new lands (Dionysius of Halicarnassus 1.16; Varro, quoted by Pliny the Elder, *Naturalis Historia* 3.109). The Sabines, who had reached the site of Rome, were accordingly called Sacrani "because they were born of a sacred springtime" (Festus, pp. 424–25 L.; Servius *Aen.* 7.796). Yet another event is connected with the legendary diaspora of the Sabines, one that showed all the essential features of the *ver sacrum:* during a long war against the Umbrians, a vow was made to sacrifice all the living creatures born during one year. Once victory was won, the vow was fulfilled in a different way: the children of men were exempt. When a famine struck, it was thought necessary to include humans, too, in the vow. They were consecrated to Mars, and on reaching adulthood were sent off, guided by a bull, to found a colony. When they arrived in the Oscan country (Campania), the bull suddenly curled up on the ground as if he had found his place. The newcomers stopped, chased the local inhabitants away, settled, and sacrificed the bull to the god Mars. Thus were born the Samnite people (Strabo 5.4.12). Similarly, the Sabines, guided by a green woodpecker (*picus*), who was also consecrated to Mars, emigrated to Picenum where they founded the Piceni (Festus, p. 235 L.; Pliny the Elder, *HN* 3.110).

There are probably many other stories of a mythical character similar to these, stories that deal with the origins of various Italic people and explain the migration of the Hirpini, Lucani, Ursentini, etc., and why their names evoke the names of animals. Associated with these stories is one that focuses on events of a later period in history but that also presents legendary features and is built on the same foundation as the earlier stories. In this story, a "princeps" of the Samnites named Sthennius Mettius is said to have consecrated to Apollo the *ver sacrum* of all those who would be born in the following year, in an attempt to avert a plague. But the plague raged again twenty years later; the oracle made it clear that no human sacrifice had taken place and therefore imposed emigration on all the young men born that year. The expatriates clustered in Sila (in modern Calabria), which they subsequently left to come to the aid of Messina. There they were welcomed and finally settled. They received their name, *Mamertini,* from the god Mamers (Mars) (Festus, p. 150 L.) according to the historian Alfius who had written an account of the Punic wars. This is surely an idealized version of the settlement in Sicily of Campanian mercenaries who founded the Mamertine state in the third century. Significantly, under Greek influence Apollo took the place of Mars as the god who received the vows. Mars, however, remained the eponymous god and guardian of the Mamertines, and his image appeared on all their coins. At this time, as a result of the diffusion of the martial traditions of the Sabellians, the idea of the *ver sacrum* as the ultimate remedy for public calamities must have become generalized. Even Rome, threatened by Hannibal, resorted to the rite in 217 B.C. after the battle of Lake Trasimene: a vow was made to Jupiter that involved only animals. But when it came to actually carrying out the vow in the years 195 and 194 B.C., because of various quibbles and restrictions they sacrificed only some of the animals (Livy 22.9, 23.44, 24.44). We can further speculate logically that the tradition must have stayed alive particularly among the Sabellians, as attested by the *ver sacrum* vowed by the Italic insurgents at the time of the Social War, which broke out early in the first century B.C. (Sisenna frag. 99, 102 P.).

In the history of this strange manifestation of Italic religiosity, we have to distinguish three aspects or "moments": first, the possible existence of a primitive ritual institution; second, its formal establishment and its legendary definition as an etiological saga of origins; and third, its perennial nature or its recurrence in the course of historical time. On the first point, it is difficult to say anything beyond forming

Poussin, *Spring*. Paris, Musée du Louvre. Photo Giraudon.

hypotheses. The basic themes of the legend, i.e., the migration of armed men, the proliferation of ethnic groups, the expiatory and purificatory character of the vow, the consecration only of living creatures, resulting in blood sacrifices (with exile substituting for slaughter in the case of humans), and the presence and the ambiguously divine meaning of an animal guide who also played an eponymous role for the new group—all of these themes together seem to correspond to the living conditions and mentality of a primitive society of herdsmen characterized by great mobility and aggressiveness and by theriomorphic conceptions of the divine that recalled totemism. This type of society has numerous elements that can be compared with those of other cultures. There are, moreover, definite signs of a spread of the pastoral economy to the more interior populations of the Italian peninsula during the Bronze Age. Conceivably the movements of the populations of the high Apennine valleys brought with them a wide range of beliefs and specific rites based partly on the idea of a necessity or a sacred vocation for migration, and in part on the attraction of more abundant grazing lands for the animals. For the continued growth of these populations forced them to look for new resources in order to survive, and during their greatest expansion, the Sabellian-Umbrian people occupied increasingly larger and richer areas.

But it is evident that the traditions tended to crystallize into myths in the course of the Italic diaspora, probably in cultural environments that had come under Greek influence. (In Campania the Samnites came into contact with the Greeks by the fifth century B.C.) The structure of the myth has characteristic and constant features, with three basic elements: (1) the consecration to the deity (notably to Mars, the god of the Sabellians) of all that was produced in a given year (in spring, during the month of Mars—March), because of a vow of purification or expiation after a scourge such as a war or a plague; (2) a migration for colonization, by young men old enough to bear arms; (3) the role of an animal guide (usually consecrated to Mars). Once established, the pattern was imposed retrospectively on legendary tales about origins, which were nourished by many additional facts remembered about real events. At the same time, the myth became the religious norm for rites performed later, in historically documented times. We may conclude that this is one of the most important examples of a dialectic relationship uniting ritual and myth.

The violent political and military events that shook Italy during the fourth and third centuries B.C. (the enormous spread of the conquering Sabellians as far as Apulia and Sicily; the invasions of the Gauls in the north; the enterprises of Greek chiefs from Alexander of Epirus to Pyrrhus; and the progressive assertion of the hegemony of Rome and the struggles against Carthage, which culminated dramatically with Hannibal's Italian expedition) undoubtedly provided many occasions to resort to this extreme and venerable remedy, the Italic rite of the *ver sacrum*. The evidence, as we have noted, lies in the semilegendary episode of the Mamertini and in the attenuated, peculiar version of the same rite that the Romans adopted after the shock of Hannibal's bold advances. But the substitution of Apollo (in the first instance) and Jupiter (in the second) for Mars, and the partial nature of the sacrifice in the *ver sacrum* celebrated in Rome, amply

Mars from Todi. Museo etrusco gregoriano. Rome, Vatican Museum. Museum photo.

demonstrates that the requirements of a particular time could impose a significant deviation from the model of the myth. Evidently, since times and circumstances had changed, it had become something of an anachronism to express in concrete terms a rite so ancient and so shrouded in legend—assuming that it had ever actually existed.

M.P./g.h.

BIBLIOGRAPHY

W. EISENHUT, *Ver sacrum,* in Pauly/Wissowa, *Real-Encyclopädie,* vol. 15 A (1955), col. 917. J. HEURGON, *Trois études sur le "ver sacrum"* (Brussels 1957).

The Latins and the Origins of Roman Religion

The Latins (*Latini*) were the inhabitants of a territory which once stretched to the south of the lower course of the Tiber up to the Pontine plain (*Pomptinus ager:* Livy 6.5.2). The *Latium antiquum* or *vetus* was bounded on the northwest by the Tiber and by the land of the Etruscans; on the northeast it was contiguous with the Sabine territory. It formed a vast expanse bordered on the east by the Alban range, from mounts Palombara, Tivoli (Tibur), Palestrina (Praeneste), and Cori (Cora), to Terracina (Anxur) and Circeo (Circeii); and was bordered on the west by the coast of the Tyrrhenian Sea. At the heart of this region are the hills that served as habitats, such as Alba Longa, which tradition places in the middle of the *populi Latini,* or Monte Cavo (*Mons Albanus*), which was the seat of a federal cult of Jupiter Latiaris.

To this *Latium vetus,* which took form in protohistory by the beginning of the first millennium B.C. (during the transition between the Bronze Age and the Iron Age), was later added a *Latium Adjectum* or *novum* made up of the territory conquered by the Romans in the historic period (starting in the sixth century B.C.), which included the Volscian, Aequi, Hernican, and Auruncan territories (see Pliny the Elder, *Naturalis Historia* 3.68–70).

These Latins, whom the tradition refers to as the *populi Latini* ("Latin nation") or by the collective name of *nomen Latinum,* settled on the hills in autonomous groups more or less tied to one another, *vicatim* ("by villages"). These territorial associations were basically founded on religious grounds, creating a feeling of community that was manifested later (in the historical epoch) by the existence of federations. These united the majority of the Latins around common cults, for instance, around the shrine of *Juppiter Latiaris* on Mons Albanus, or around the shrine of *Diana Aricia* in the *Nemus Dianae* ("the sacred grove of Diana"). Other federal cults played an important role in history. Most notable is the recently excavated city of Lavinium. Its necropolis dates back to the tenth century B.C., with remains of sixth-century ramparts, a federal cult which in historic times is attested by the discovery of thirteen archaic altars and of a *heroon* in memory of Aeneas, located near a tomb from the seventh century B.C.[1]

According to the latest archaeological discoveries, the oldest inhabitants of Latium devoted themselves principally to raising livestock and additionally to exploiting natural resources (salt, fruit, and game). The more the woodlands were cleared and the marshlands dried up, the more the Latins took to farming and to the making of pottery and iron tools.

Did these Latins, whose language belonged to the Indo-European family, drive back or subdue "autochthonous" populations? Recently it was common to contrast the Indo-European invaders, who practiced the ritual of cremation, to the natives, who were accustomed to the ritual of inhumation.[2] This schema is not consistent with the facts. Contrary to the hypotheses of the previous theory, archaeology has at least shown that the ritual of cremation (at the end of the Bronze Age and the beginning of the Iron Age) has almost always preceded the ritual of inhumation (in the late Iron Age: eighth through seventh centuries), though these practices did not necessarily take on any ethnic significance.[3]

The advances made by the community of the Latins can be

verified by the growing wealth and number of their centers, which multiplied throughout the eighth and seventh centuries: Satricum, Antium (Anzio), Ardea, Lavinium (Pratica di Mare), Politorium (possibly Decima), Ficana, Praeneste (Palestrina), and of course Rome. The first document in the Latin language is the inscription on the golden fibula of Praeneste (end of the seventh century): *manios med fhefhaked numasioi* (in classical Latin: *Manius me fecit Numerio,* "Marius made me [or "had me made"] for Numerius").[4]

Tradition commonly ascribes an increasingly dominant role to Rome. Starting with the "reigns" of Romulus and Numa, the Roman community extended its influence farther with the victory over Alba (under Tullus Hostilius) and the conquest of the coastal regions as far as Ostia at the mouth of the Tiber. This conquest brought about the elimination of the centers of Politorium, Tellenae, and Ficana.

Recent digs at Castel di Decima (which corresponds to Politorium) have confirmed the tradition of this community. The necropolis that was discovered includes tombs dating from the eighth century to the close of the seventh century B.C., a terminus corresponding to the destruction of Politorium by Ancus Marcius, according to Livy 1.33.3.[5]

Rome, which became the ruler of Latium, itself submitted to the domination of the Etruscans, as was reflected in the tradition of the last three kings, Tarquinius the Elder, Servius Tullius, and Tarquinius Superbus, all allegedly of Etruscan origin. After the expulsion of the Etruscans in 509 B.C., Roman dominance was consolidated following the battle of Lake Regillus in 496 or 499. The battle ended with the defeat of the Latins by the Romans and the signing of an alliance of "eternal peace" between the two partners in 493, the *foedus Cassianum.*[6] The founding of the federal Temple of Diana on the Aventine also took place in this context. One last uprising by the Latins who took up arms against Rome during the First War of the Samnites (343–341 B.C.) brought about the final defeat of the Latins. The Latin league was dissolved in 338 B.C. and incorporated into the Roman community.

R.S./g.h.

NOTES

1. Cf. Castagnoli, *Lavinium* 1: *Topografia generale, fonti e storia delle ricerche* (Rome 1972); *Lavinium* 2: *Le tredici are* (Rome 1975); with collaborators. P. Sommella, "La necropoli protostorica rinvenuta a Pratica di Mare," *Rendic. Pontif. Accad. Rom. Archeol.* 46 (1973–74): 34–48; "Heroon di Enea a Lavinium, Recenti scavi a Pratica di Mare," ibid. 44 (1971–72): 47–74.
2. Such are the conclusions of the work of A. Piganiol, *Essai sur les origines de Rome* (Paris 1916).
3. See, finally, M. Pallottino, in *Civiltà del Lazio primitivo* (Rome 1976), p. 45. It is thus that at Lavinium the oldest incineration tombs (10th century) predate the inhumation tombs: cf. P. Sommella, ibid., pp. 292–93.
4. On this document, cf. G. Colonna, ibid., pp. 372–73, and A. E. Gordon, *The Inscribed Fibula Praesnestina: Problems of Authenticity* (Berkeley 1975). Most recently M. Guarducci, *Memorie della Accademia Nazionale dei Lincei,* ser. 8, vol. 24, fasc. 4 (Rome 1980), 415–574, pl. I–XI, has reopened the discussion with an essay *La cosidetta Fibula Prenestina,* attempting to demonstrate that it is a forgery. Perhaps we should conclude with a paraphrase of a verse by Virgil (*Aeneid,* 7, 412): *Et nunc magnum manet* Fibula *nomen / sed fortuna fuit* ("Of this Fibula, only a great name remains, but his good fortune is gone").
5. Cf. F. Zevi, ibid., pp. 252–56.
6. Cf. Livy (2, 33, 34) and Dionysius of Halicarnassus (6, 95).

SUMMARY BIBLIOGRAPHY

A. ALFÖLDI, *Early Rome and the Latins* (Ann Arbor 1964). J. HEURGON, *Rome et la Méditerranée* (Paris 1969). *Popoli e Civiltà dell' Italia antica,* Biblioteca di Storia patria (3 vols., 1974), in particular, in vol. 2, G. COLONNA, *Preistoria e protostoria di Roma e del Lazio,* pp. 273–346. *Civiltà del Lazio primitivo* (Rome 1976) for the state of the problems and the most recent archaeological discoveries.

Greco-Italic Traditions and Legends, from the Bronze Age to Virgil

The initial deep penetration and diffusion of Greek cults and myths in Italy and the contacts that bound them to local traditions in a tangle of religious conceptions and legendary constructions that we can define by the expression "Greco-Italic"—all of this constitutes a particularly interesting aspect of the classical world, one that merits separate treatment. The Greek colonization of southern Italy and Sicily beginning in the eighth century B.C. certainly played a dominant part in this process. But we can suppose that the process began in the Bronze Age under the influence of Mycenaean civilization. On the other hand, the phenomenon spread well beyond the domain of Greek colonies, including all of the peninsula and part of northern Italy (besides the islands)—where populations lived who, without being Greek, were bound in some manner, more or less directly, to Greek culture.

I. Greek Evidence of the Lands of the West

It is natural that navigators of Aegean origin brought back from the oceans of the West and from mysterious lands encountered during their voyages around them marvelous impressions, which were spread little by little in the narratives that were gathered and poetically elaborated in the *Odyssey.* One can cite the episodes of the Cyclops, of Aeolus, of the Laestrygonians, of Circe, of the Land of the Dead, of the Sirens, of Scylla and Charybdis, and of the island of the Trident (as V. Bérard translates it) with the Cattle of the Sun. The entire subsequent classical tradition set these episodes in the framework of Italy and the neighboring islands and, more specifically, certain places that remained famous under these names during all of antiquity, like the Aeolian Islands, Mount Circe, the Lake of Avernus, and Cumae—which was the site for calling up the netherworld—the sanctuary of the Sirens at the tip of the peninsula of Sorrento, and the menacing Scylla and Charybdis in the Straits of Messina. The Homeric narrative of the adventures of Odysseus should be considered the point of departure and the almost unique source of all the identifications, interpretations, erudite speculations, and legendary constructions of antiquity about these places, with the characters, events, and cults that are connected with them. Nevertheless, without taking into account the traditions suggested by the ancients, modern criticism sought a geographic and historic verification of the particulars of the *Odyssey;* yet it arrived at conclusions which, hypothetical as some of them might seem because of the very excess of their details—as is the case for the grandiose reconstruction of Victor Bérard—confirm on the whole the veracity of the epic testimony concerning the knowledge that the Greeks of the Mycenaean Age had of the Italic world.

Independent of the Homeric narratives, however, the Greek legendary inheritance gives us other evidence of the most ancient contacts between the proto-Hellenic world and Italy, even though this evidence is profoundly transformed by myth. We are thinking of the insistence with which the enterprises of the Argonauts, the wanderings of Heracles, the colonizations of the Arcadians, and the migrations of the Pelasgi were connected with or extended to Italy. But the documents which seem to us to be the most significant for their more detailed geographic and chronological character—for their superior historical importance—are, on the one hand, narratives about the presence of Cretans, notably of King Minos and of the artist Daedalus, in Apulia and Sicily (that is, in the regions where relations with the Mycenaeans were the most frequent; but there are echoes of the activity of Daedalus in both Campania and Sardinia); and, on the other hand, the cycle of legends about the "Italian" adventures of the heroes of the Trojan cycle. These latter are Achaean heroes returned from the Trojan War (their return journeys, the *nostoi,* were sung by different Greek poets, among whom was Stesichorus of Himera, who lived in Sicily in the archaic period): there are references to Diomedes in Apulia, but also in other Adriatic regions and in Latium; Menestheus and his Athenians in the zone of the Straits of Messina; Epeus, the builder of the Trojan Horse, and Philoctetes, who inherited the weapons of Heracles, on the Ionian coast between Metapontum and Croton; Idomeneus and his Cretans at the same place as his predecessor, Minos, in Apulia; and Odysseus, who is the most illustrious of all. The Trojan heroes fleeing their sacked city joined the Achaean heroes: first Aeneas, who, after emigrating to Latium, was to acquire extraordinary renown in myth and poetry as the founder of the future greatness of Rome; then Antenor, who with his Veneti settled in northern Italy; there are also references to the Trojans who settled on the shores of the Ionian Sea at Siris, and in Sicily, where they were regarded as the ancestors of the nation of the Elymians. It should be noted that all of these stories, despite the diverse origins of their protagonists, are constructed according to several relatively uniform schemata (which argues against the system of analogies used in erudite elaborations), namely, the arrival by sea of a foreign hero with his companions, the encounter and the battle with an indigenous king whose daughter the hero eventually marries and whose kingdom he inherits, the founding of sanctuaries and of city-states according to the model of the colonial Greek *ktisis,* the death of the hero in his new country, and the cult at his tomb. These are the well-known cases of Aeneas, Diomedes, and Antenor.

But having reached this point, we are confronted with references—presented more or less explicitly in the Greek mythic narratives—to indigenous places, populations, and characters. Legend tends to assume an etiological character, that is, it tends to accept, describe, and interpret local situations and events. The latter are, moreover, better and better understood, beginning with the eighth century B.C., thanks to colonization, commercial exchanges (one thinks of the Greek settlement recently discovered at Graviscae, the port of Tarquinii), the stability of the great currents of commerce, and the presence of Greek entrepreneurs and artists in the Italic centers. Starting from the names of the peoples and city-states, complicated narratives are elaborated, eponymous heroes are invented who enter in turn into the legendary patrimony side by side with the heroes of the Greek myths, and even the Greek heroes are linked to the new heroes by genealogical bonds. Thus, in the *Theogony* of Hesiod (5.1014), Latinus, the eponym of the Latins, who appears in a different light in the saga of Aeneas, is mentioned with his brother Agrius as a son of Odysseus and Circe and king of the Tyrrhenians. And of Odysseus and Circe, Auson is born, the eponym of the Ausones; he in turn is the father of Liparus, the eponym and king of Lipara in the Aeolian Islands. Liparus was succeeded by Aeolus, who came from the peninsula and married Liparus's daughter (Diodorus Siculus 5.7–8). The eponyms of different peoples of southern Italy, such as Sicilus, Italus, Morges, Oenotrus, Peucetius, and Iapyx, seem to be interrelated and related to the Arcadians and the Pelasgi (Dionysius of Halicarnassus 1.11–13); but it is also said of Iapyx that he was Cretan and the son of Daedalus. Particularly complicated are the problems involving the name and origins of the Achaean city-state of Metapontum on the Ionian Sea. It was said that Metapontum was created by the hero named Metabus (who was also thought to be king of the Volsci, according to the *Aeneid,* 11.532ff.) or by Metapontus, according to the Thessalo-Boeotian legends about Arne, Melanippus, and Aeolus; or by Nestor, according to the Pylians (Diodorus of Sicily 4.67.3–6; Strabo, *Geog.,* 6.1.15). One might also mention the bonds that connect Tyrrhenus, the eponym of the Tyrrhenians (that is, the Etruscans), with the Lydian dynasty (in the classical narrative of Herodotus 1.94), with Telephus, the king of Mysia, and with the Pelasgi of the islands of Lemnos and Imbros (Dionysius of Halicarnassus 1.29ff.; Strabo 5.2.4).

II. The Indigenous Traditions and the Elaboration of a Common Patrimony

In the elaboration of this entire corpus of legends, important roles must have been played not only by the knowledge and imagination of the Greeks but also by the indigenous traditions and even, in a more or less active way, by the cultural environment of Italy, especially the sanctuaries. Bringing with them the cults of the motherland, Greek navigators and colonizers found in Italy sacred places, local beliefs, and customs of very ancient origin. It is probable that the new arrivals tried to understand and illuminate the indigenous elements in terms of their own conceptions, and that at the same time, in the centers that remained foreign to Hellenism, people wanted to ennoble the traditional patrimony of rites and relics by assimilating it to the prestigious models of Greek religion and mythology. The cults of Hera and in particular of Argive Hera were disseminated along all the coasts of Italy in the colonial and extracolonial zones (at Metapontum, at Croton, at the mouth of the Silarus near Posidonia in Latium, and in Etruria and Venetia). The spread of the cults of Hera and of other female divinities, such as Leucothea, Artemis, and especially Athena of Ilium (at Siris, at Lucera in Apulia, at Lavinium, and at Rome), whose origin is very ancient and is sometimes attributed to the founding action of a hero, harmonized with the diffusion of female cults, notably that of the mother goddess, among the indigenous populations of Italy. The goddess of the "Pelasgian" sanctuary of Pyrgi in Etruria, whom the Greeks referred to under the names of Ilythia or Leucothea, is today attested by Etruscan inscriptions under the name of Uni, that is, Juno or Hera. This lengthens the list of manifestations of this divinity on the Italian coast.

The long process of joining the local divinities with those of the Greek pantheon and assimilating them (Jupiter-(D)iove = Zeus = Tin(ia) in Etruscan, just as Venus =

Poussin, *Inspiration of the Poet,* detail. Paris, Musée du Louvre. Photo Flammarion.

Aphrodite = Turan in Etruscan, and others) must have developed and attained its completion in the archaic period, at least as far as the Tyrrhenian domain of the Etruscans, Latins, and Campanians is concerned. The same can be said for the penetration into Italy of typically Hellenic cults which had no local correspondences, such as those of Apollo, Artemis, or the Dioscuri (attested by the archaic epigraphy at Lavinium in Latium under the name of *qurois,* and at Tarquinii in Etruria under the name of *Tinascliniiaras* = *Dioskoroisin*), as well as the principal cycles and characters of Greek mythology, whose names were adapted into indigenous languages. Judging from the linguistic data, it seems to be a Doric cultural current, probably Corinthian (De Simone), which introduced these names into Etruria. One can site in this connection the famous narrative of the arrival at Tarquinii, toward the middle of the seventh century B.C., of the Corinthian Demaratus, who brought literature and the arts with him (Livy 1.34 and 4.3; Pliny, *HN,* 35.43; Tacitus, *Annales,* 11.14, etc.).

In establishing a common patrimony of Greco-Italic legends in the sanctuaries, one must not overlook the supposed tombs of the heroes and the cults that were established in their honor. Recall the funeral ceremonies in honor of the Nelides at Metapontum (Strabo 6.1.15), which made possible the diffusion of narratives and of songs about the foundation of the city by the Pylians; or the sacrifices to Antenor at the mouth of the Timavo (Strabo 5.1.9); similarly, the many narratives about the deeds of Diomedes must have flourished, when he had been deified, in places where he was assumed to have rested or disappeared—this is the case notably for the sanctuary tomb of the Tremiti in Apulia, as certain ancient authors attest. But the most significant example is the sepulcher of Aeneas at Lavinium, identified in a *heroon* recently discovered near this city, which can be ascribed to the fourth century B.C. and was constructed above a princely tomb in the Oriental style, dating from the seventh century B.C. This indicates that the Latin saga of Aeneas must have spread and developed between the sixth and fifth centuries B.C., probably around the sanctuaries of Lavinium (and concomitant with the first Greek versions of the coming of Aeneas to Italy: Hellanicus, in Dionysius of Halicarnassus 1.48).

III. The Role of Writers

The literary circles of Asiatic Ionia and the Greek and Hellenizing centers of Italy came into contact with popular gossip and communication between the political and sacerdotal milieus of the various city-states of the Tyrrhenian world and the Greek colonial domain. Together, they must have contributed, from the earliest period, to the diffusion and collation of knowledge about Greek and indigenous cults and about the stories transmitted in sanctuaries. Between the fifth and third centuries B.C., Italiot writers (that is, Greeks in Italy), and in particular Siciliots (Greeks in Sicily) played a very important role in the reconstruction, enrichment, and systemization of the Greco-Italic legends; these writers include Hippys and Lycus of Rhegium, Antiochus,

Philistus of Syracuse, and Timaeus of Tauromenium (Taormina), whose works were in large part lost but still survive in abundant extracts and expansions in subsequent literature. But of the historians, geographers, and essayists of the Greek mother country, like Thucydides, Ephorus, the Pseudo-Scylax, and Aristotle, we also have important documents that bear witness to their interest in the Italic world; and beginning in the Hellenistic period, poets, mythographers, historiographers, Greek and Latin men of letters, and compilers (from Lycophron to Diodorus Siculus, Dionysius of Halicarnassus, Strabo, Livy, Virgil, Pliny, Justin, and later the scholiasts such as Servius and Tzetzes) collected and elaborated this material in an essentially reflexive and erudite spirit, so well that their work resulted in a complete amalgam of opinions, versions, and interpretations.

The richest and most coherent picture of heroic Greco-Italic mythology that we have is found in the introduction to the *Roman Antiquities* of Dionysius of Halicarnassus and in the *Aeneid* of Virgil. These are two profoundly different works, even if they are almost contemporaneous. The first is the patient and abundant work of a historiographer who presents his subject diachronically, in the perspective of a historical reconstruction; he assembles and recomposes the very different traditions of earlier writers, especially emphasizing the thesis of the Greek origin of the Italic peoples—among whom and through whom the city "that dominates all the earth and all the sea" was to come into being. Virgil's poem, by contrast, is a mirror that synchronically reflects the image of the peoples and legendary characters of Italy in the heroic period, as well as the adventures of Aeneas. This is a tableau almost comparable to that of the heroic Greek world in the *Iliad*. But beyond all erudite research on origins, all of this is transfigured poetically in an evocation which, according to the prophecy of Anchises at Cumae, connects the past to the present, that is, to the glory of Rome. In both testimonies there is a consciousness of the religious and cultural unity of the Greek and Italo-Roman worlds, that is, of classical civilization, whose first manifestations go back to the beginning of historical time.

M.P./d.f.

BIBLIOGRAPHY

J. BERARD and H. LANGUMIER, *Odyssée* (Paris 1952). M. PALLOTTINO, "Le origini storiche dei popoli italici," *Xe Congresso internazionale di Scienze Storiche, Relazioni* (Florence 1955), 2:3–60. J. BERARD, *La colonisation grecque de l'Italie méridionale et de la Sicile dans l'Antiquité* (2d ed., Paris 1957). G. RADKE, *Die Götter Altitaliens* (Münster 1965). *Santuari di Magna Grecia. Atti dei IVe Convegno di studi sulla Magna Grecia,* Taranto, 1964 (Naples 1965); see especially the papers by G. Pugliese Carratelli, 19ff., and by W. Hermann, 47ff. H. HENCKEN, *Tarquinia, Villanovans and Early Etruscans* (Cambridge, MA, 1968), 2:603–18. C. DE SIMONE, *Die griechischen Entlehnungen im Etruskischen* (Wiesbaden 1968–70). *La Magna Grecia e Roma nell'età arcaica. Atti dell'VIIIe Convegno di studi sulla Magna Grecia,* Taranto, 1968 (Naples 1969); see especially the papers by J. Heurgon, 9ff., and by G. Pugliese Carratelli, 49ff. D. MUSTI, *Tendenze nella storiografia romana e greca su Roma arcaica: Studi su Livio e Dionigi d'Alicarnasso* (Urbin 1970). On Lavinium and the *heroon* of Aeneas, see P. SOMMELLA, in *Rendiconti della Pontificia Accademia Romana di Archeologia,* 44 (1971–72): 47–74, and *Gymnasium,* 81, 4 (1974): 273–97.

Roman Religion

Though the importance of religion in the ancient world seems self-evident to us today, this view is relatively recent. The seventeenth century was largely content to mobilize Greek and Roman deities on gala occasions at court without distinguishing between the two. When Montesquieu wrote his *Considerations on the Causes of the Grandeur of the Romans and of Their Decadence* (1734), he was thinking primarily of politics and morals. Not until the nineteenth century did Fustel de Coulanges give religion its true place at the very heart of ancient society. This scholar devoted his course at the University of Strasbourg to the notion of "the history of a belief" (1862–63), and in the following year he published a work which became a classic, *The Ancient City* (1864). For the first time, the study of religion was unequivocally acknowledged to be indispensable to the understanding of the institutions of the ancients. But this line of inquiry sometimes had to grope its way, and in their haste to propose overarching explanations, several theoreticians felt compelled to expound elaborate systems that subjected religious studies to intellectual fashions. For example, in Max Müller's system, deities were nothing but names (*Nomina numina*) given to various impressions aroused by the light of the sun. Then there was Wilhelm Mannhardt, who expounded his naturist theory in a book bearing the evocative title of *The Cult of the Tree among Germanic Peoples* (1875). Today we are more skeptical of systematic explanations; we prefer more matter-of-fact studies of the evidence.

Sociology unquestionably gave this method new currency toward the end of the last century by introducing the principle of comparison of ancient societies with modern-day "primitive" societies. Emile Durkheim's *The Elementary Forms of Religious Life* (1912) is a comparative study with the stated objective of defining religion in general. He wisely suggested that "only the comparison of facts of the same nature can have the value of proof." This advice has not always been heeded. The tendency was to drift imperceptibly toward a "universal" comparativism that all too often confused what is *archaic* with what is *primitive* (in the sense of *inferior*). Can one say that the remarkable work of James Frazer is immune to such a reproach? Through his vast erudition, this scholar rendered great service to the history of religions, and to Roman religion in particular, in his monumental commentary on Ovid's *Fasti.* He did, however, set forth a perilous principle when he said that "human nature is *much the same* throughout the world and at all times." This inspired some dangerous comparisons, drawn from that arsenal of sociological examples that is vast enough to produce apparent likenesses for almost anything: if the Hottentots will not do, the Zulus will!

By this kind of improper assimilation, a basically "primitivist" picture was projected onto the origins of early Roman society. Polynesian mana was used to explain a religion in the Indo-European tradition; gods and goddesses would suddenly rise out of a vague cloud in the name of progressive evolution.

Reactions were not long in coming. Georg Wissowa in his *Religion and Cult of the Romans* (1902; 2d ed. 1912) firmly established the importance of respecting homologous areas in the religious realm, and he painstakingly constructed a clear and precise catalog of the data. Nevertheless, description alone, however faithful, was not sufficient to make these data intelligible. Very early on, historians noted the benefit they could derive from the comparison of analogous religious structures, for instance, by noting resemblances between the Latin triad Jupiter-Mars-Quirinus of Rome and the Umbrian triad Jupiter-Mars-Vofionus of Iguvium (all three known as Grabovio, "of the oak tree"). But comparativism was destined to bear its fruits on an even grander scale as a result of the illuminating works of Georges Dumézil, who based his efforts on the existence of the original community of the ancient Indians and the ancient Italians (the probable equivalence of the Sanskrit term *Brahman* and the Latin term *flamen* to designate the priest is one sign among many to that effect). As a result of Dumézil's research, the Indo-European heritage could no longer be denied to ancient Rome. Contrary to the claims of evolutionists, it would seem that personal gods, classified according to a functional hierarchy that recalls an analogous distribution of functions in India, had existed in Rome since its origins. Contrary to the teachings of the "primitivists," Dumézil revealed that the Romans had inherited a millennial ideology that they had indeed subjected to a kind of metamorphosis: history was substituted for myth so that the same character could appear in a divine form in a mythology of Indo-European inspiration and in a human form in Roman history. An eloquent example is furnished by a double pair of "homologues": the Roman heroes Horatius Cocles, the One-Eyed, and Mucius Scaevola, the One-Handed, correspond to the Scandinavian duo of Óðinn, the one-eyed magician-god, and Týr, the jurist-god who sacrificed one hand. The results of this vast research were recorded by Georges Dumézil in his work *Archaic Roman Religion* (1966; English trans. 1970; 2d ed. 1974; hereafter *ARR*).

The comparativist insight could not, however, divert us from the main objective of the historian of Roman religion, namely, to define the originality of this religion as precisely as possible. Not all the facts can be explained, despite great scholarly effort, but the research that has been conducted for some hundred years helps us to formulate the problem with greater accuracy.

To what extent can we speak of the originality of Roman religion? Georg Wissowa tried to define it using chronological criteria. He thought that the Romans had succeeded in protecting their institutions from foreign influences until about the third century B.C., after which syncretism must have had a destabilizing effect. That the facts did not bear out this distinction is just as well. It would have been surprising to discover that Rome could have lived in isolation when in the sixth century B.C. she still constituted nothing but a modest cell compared with her rich neighbors, the Etruscans (who contributed to her urbanization under the dynasty of the last three kings of Rome, who are traditionally said to have come from Etruria) and the colonists of Magna Graecia (who had founded wealthy settlements in the southern part of Italy).

F. Altheim believed that he could oppose Wissowa on these grounds: he dismissed the idea of any Latin originality, on the premise that foreign influence, most particularly Greek influence, had been a factor since the beginning. In a sense, his treatise, *Greek Gods in Ancient Rome* (1930), is a polemic rather than a summation of individual studies.

Of course, this extreme position was open to criticism. It is risky even to attempt to reduce the Roman pantheon to a sort of carbon copy of the Hellenic pantheon, whether we admit the direct influence of Magna Graecia or indirect influence through the Etruscans. If Hellenic deities such as Apollo or the Dioscuri were familiar in Rome by the sixth century, they had been incorporated into the Latin pantheon under particular circumstances, conforming to the hospitable attitude of the polytheism of the ancients. Such admissions would not challenge the autochthonous traditions.

Representation of an offering. Bone bas-relief. Rome, City Museums. Photo Oscar Savio.

I. The Notion of *Religio* and Cult

We should first acknowledge that the term *religio,* which passed into most modern Western languages, is a Latin creation. It is a specific word that has no Greek counterpart; the "analogous" expressions that are invoked, including *to sebas* (respect for the gods), *hē proskunēsis* (adoration), *hē eulabeia* (reverential fear), and *hē thrēskeia* (cult or worship), only underscore the bankruptcy of a genuine translation for *religio* in that language.

This assertion is all the more remarkable because the Romans took great pride in being the most religious people in the world: "If we compare ourselves with foreign nations," wrote Cicero (*De natura deorum* 2.3), "we may appear to be equal or even inferior in various realms, except in religion, by which I mean the worship of the gods, in which we are by far preeminent" (*religione id est cultu deorum, multo superiores*). He states the same thing elsewhere (Cicero *De haruspicum responsis* 19) in a more concise form: *pietate ac religione omnes gentes superavimus* ("in piety and in religion we head the list of nations").

This claim may still have had some value at the end of the first century B.C., when it occasionally appeared as an expression of praise for individuals. Thus the author of a *Laudatio* of a Roman matron known by the name of Turia (end of the first century B.C.) mentions among this woman's qualities "her religious spirit free of superstition (*religionis sine superstitione*)."

What are we to understand by this term that the Romans coined in order to define a situation in which they proudly claimed to excel, a term that we inherited from the Latins and that made its way into every language of the Western world? Philologists agree that *religio* comes from a verbal root (like *legio* or *regio*), but they do not agree about which verb it comes from. Some derive the word from *relegere* and ascribe to the prefix an intensive value that gives the expression the meaning of "scrupulous observance." Others prefer to derive it from *religare*, with the meaning of "to bind oneself to the gods." Texts are quoted to support either hypothesis. The supporters of *relegere* invoke the ancient verse cited by Nigidius Figulus (Aulus Gellius 4.9.11): *religentem esse oportet, religiosus ne fuas* ("it is fitting to be religious but not excessively scrupulous"). The *religare* supporters recall the ritualistic use of sacred ribbons (*vittae*), as well as the numerous references to the idea of religious bonds, for example, Lucretius 1.931: *Religionum nodis animum exsolvere* ("Deliver the soul from religious bonds"); Livy 5.23.10: *Se domumque religione exsolvere* ("To free oneself and one's own from a religious obligation").

It would seem difficult to settle upon one or the other etymological explanation, especially in view of the fact that each represents a complementary aspect of the meaning of the expression. For it is indeed true that the *religio* of the Latins implies at the same time both a concern for scrupulous observance in worship and the idea of bonds that unite the gods and men.

We could say that the conviction of an inescapable interdependence between heaven and earth was the basis for Roman piety, the purpose of which was to assure the *pax veniaque deum*. Without the friendship and grace of the gods, a Roman felt crippled. He therefore took pains to maintain this "state of grace" through a meticulous cult, so meticulous that it has often seemed formalistic. He would be attentive to signs sent from heaven, and if unluckily the gods should vent their anger—*Iamque irae patuere deum* ("the wrath of the gods has already been revealed"; Lucan 2.1)—he would not rest until he had reestablished harmony. In Rome one would not think of rebelling against the gods; this theme was the privilege of the Greeks, particularly in the myth of the Titan Prometheus. Not until Lucretius do we see the first blasphemous overtones in Latin literature, and even then, when the Epicurean poet raises the flag of rebellion against religion and denounces the crimes committed in its name—*tantum religio potuit suadere malorum* (Lucretius 1.101)—he borrows his example from Hellenic religion by denouncing the sacrifice of Iphigenia.

Dioscuri. Paris, Bibliothèque nationale. Cabinet des Médailles. Photo BN.

Although the reverential fear of the gods was the basis of Roman piety, the concern for efficacy explains many features of the cult. First of all, there was that rather cautious tone in prayers when a Roman was unable to identify exactly which deity he was supposed to appease; accordingly, in the case of an earthquake the supplicant makes use of the following prudent formula: *si deo, si deae* (whether you be god or goddess; Aulus Gellius *Noctes Atticae* 2.28.2–3). When he gets into a fight with a deity, he does so with a precise stipulation, of which the *carmina* conveyed to us by Cato the Elder give us a good idea. This contractual propensity has often been interpreted in a pejorative sense, but in fact it can only be understood as a concern to establish an irreproachable covenant between men and the gods. Piety is justice toward the gods, says Cicero (*est enim pietas justitia adversum deos; Nat. D.* 1.41), and in the prayer addressed by Cato's peasant to an unidentified woodland deity, we find this important formula: *uti tibi jus est* ("in keeping with your right"; *De agr.* 139).

This preoccupation is often translated with an insistence that is excessive for our taste. Cato's peasant is not afraid of repeating ponderously the exact clauses within whose bounds he means to fight the deity. Perhaps we should even attribute to certain apparently descriptive adjectives a more practical meaning. Thus, adding the qualifier *inferium* to *vinum* is supposed to prevent the consecration of all the wine in the cellar, since the prayer concerns only wine as offering (this according to Trebatius, as cited by Arnobius, *Adversus nationes* 7.31). As a result, some have denounced the legalistic harshness of Roman piety that was supposed to be embodied by the motto "I shall give when you have given" (*dabo cum dederis*). Thus the gods are informed of the conditions that the Roman state required if it was to carry out its vow to consecrate, within a predetermined limit of time, all the firstfruits of the season—the *ver sacrum* (Livy 22.10).

The Romans certainly had a taste for precision, especially when it came to drawing up contracts, and the same legalistic mind can be seen in their prayers. But we should not disregard the other side of Roman piety, which is expressed by an unconditional appeal for divine kindness. When a Roman general "sacrifices" his own person along with the enemy army in the midst of battle, according to the act of *devotio*, he addresses an urgent prayer to the gods—*vos precor veneror, veniam peto feroque* (Livy 8.9)—and he puts himself entirely in their hands, without bothering with restrictive clauses.[1] This type of unconditional *votum* can often be found in Roman history, for example, when promises are made to build a temple. The *votum* is certainly not disinterested, but except for the quietist, what worshiper is ever disinterested in his devotion? The *votum* implies the hope of fulfillment, *do ut des* ("I give so that you may give"). Marcel Mauss argued that "the gift is the archaic form of exchange"; implicitly it provokes the recipient to restitution and, in the case of the gods, to an increased level of restitution. The Romans never stopped practicing this unconditional form of piety, which also appears to be its most ancient form. They expected some benefit from it in return in the name of the reciprocity of the "good offices" that were the basis of *pietas*.

II. Indo-European Tradition and Historical Evolution

Roman religion undoubtedly experienced various vicissitudes from the birth of Rome till the coming of the empire. The early stages of the development of the primitive city are reflected even in the liturgy; for the characteristics of certain festivals allow us to draw some conclusions about the relative extension of the physical area of Rome.

In this regard, the following three festivals represent three successive stages. The first, the Lupercalia, a public festival that fell every year on 15 February, reveals its archaic character in its ceremonial (see the article "Faunus" below) and in the role of its priests (*luperci,* wolfmen of sorts, clad in loincloths). The ceremony consisted primarily of a race run by these *luperci,* who carried goatskin thongs with which they struck passersby. This flagellation was said to guarantee fertility to women. Now this precautionary race was strictly confined to the Palatine, taking place on the outer limit of the ancient *oppidum Palatinum* that was the cradle of the *Urbs.* This feature alone might suggest that it was one of the oldest festivals of the Roman calendar, not to mention other characteristics that can be explained only by the pastoral customs of an older time.

The festival of the Septimontium that falls on 11 December is a ceremony that concerns only the inhabitants of the *montes* (*feriae non populi, sed montanorum mode,* as Varro says in *De lingua Latina* 6.24). Fortunately, ancient scholars preserved the list of these seven *montes* (which must not be confused with the seven hills of the future Rome). It consists of the heights of the Palatium, the Germal, the Velia (which later formed the Palatine), the Fagutaline, the Oppian, the Cispian (which would later be absorbed into the Esquiline), and the Caelian.[2] It is evident that this new topographical definition corresponds to a later stage, to a step intermediate between the isolated villages and the definitive organization of the city. It is interesting to note the use of the term *mons* to designate these hillocks, rather than the word *collis,* which was later applied to the northern hills.

The ceremony of the Argives brings us to the last phase. This festival, celebrated in two stages (on 16 and 17 March and on 14 May), began with a procession that was supposed to carry the *Argei,* or dolls made of rushes (Ovid *Fasti* 5.621), into the twenty-seven chapels prepared for that purpose. On 14 May they were fetched from these *sacraria* and thrown into the Tiber from the top of the Pons Sublicius. The meaning of the ceremony has been much discussed. Wissowa saw it as a ritual of substitution in which effigies replaced humans; whereas Latte instead compared these dolls made of rushes to the *oscilla,* figurines that were suspended from trees, for the purpose of absorbing all the city's impurities.

In any case, the festival included elements relevant to our discussion. The reference to the Pons Sublicius, the oldest bridge in Rome, built on piles as its name implies, may provide a starting date: tradition attributes it to King Ancus Marcius (Livy 1.33.6). But it is the route of the procession through the twenty-seven chapels, as reported by Varro (*Ling.* 5.45–54), that supplies the most precise information. The procession moved through the heights of the Caelian, the Esquiline, the Viminal, the Quirinal, and the Palatine, circling around the Forum, which was henceforth part of the city. This topographical description thus corresponds to the incorporation of the Forum into the city at the decisive phase of urban transformation, the Rome of *quattuor regiones.*

We have thus seen the circle grow larger from lustration to lustration. It first encompassed the *Roma Quadrata*[3] of the Palatine, then the seven hillocks, and finally the *Urbs* centered on the Forum. The conservatism of the Roman liturgy allows us to observe this progression step by step as the city developed. During the last phase, the Forum became the religious heart of the city with the shrine of Vesta and the dwelling place of the Vestal Virgins. The hill situated to the far west later formed the high point of this new unit, for it was on the Capitol that the most important public temple dedicated to the triad of Jupiter-Juno-Minerva arose. This building, which according to tradition goes back to the Tarquin kings, shows incontestable Etruscan influences.[4] This brings us to the end of the sixth century B.C.

Do these religious traditions go back only to the birth of Rome? Must we begin with this date as an absolute starting point? A certain primitivist school of thought not long ago supported this contention, which the comparativist work of Georges Dumézil has since rendered untenable. Ample evidence suggests that the origins of Rome had an Indo-European legacy, which explains many features of the legend. Thus political and religious initiatives were divided between the first two kings: the founding of the city was attributed to Romulus, and the religious organization to his successor Numa.

This stylization, as comparativist teaching tells us, is a mark of the Indo-European concept of sovereignty with its double face: on the one hand, we have the warlike and *ferox* side of Romulus, and on the other hand, we have the juridical and peace-loving side of Numa.

There is no doubt that this Indo-European heritage left its traces within institutions, both in the survival of rites that appear aberrant if we refuse to clarify them through the Indo-European ideology, and in the existence of hierarchical structures that can be explained only in terms of the same ideology.

By comparing several Latin goddesses with certain Vedic myths,[5] Georges Dumézil was able to develop the most suggestive results of his investigation. These goddesses, who once seemed to provide no hold for any satisfactory explanation, were the object of considerable controversy among scholars. Thus, Mater Matuta finally lost her meaning as a dawn goddess and became a mother goddess or a Good Mother; she was honored with two unusual rites on the day of the festival of the Matralia on 11 June. During the ceremony the Roman matrons bore in their arms and fondled, not their own children, but the children of their sisters; they would have a slave woman go into the temple of Mater Matuta and would beat her with sticks before expelling her. These rites certainly seem peculiar. But the dawn goddess is "one of the most striking feminine figures in the *Ṛgveda,*" in which she appears nursing and suckling the child who is either "the common child of Dawn and her sister Night" (India, as we know, is not bothered by contradictory conceptions), or "the child of Night alone."

All the evidence suggests that the most logical form of the theology—"Dawn fondling the child of her sister Night"—had reached as far as Rome, but here the myth vanished and only the rite survived, prescribing for matrons the behavior of the deity. Thus mothers do with their sisters' children what Dawn, the sister of Night, does with the Sun, the child of Night.

The ritual of expelling the slave woman can also be explained by the Vedic parallel. "Dawn the goddess marches, driving back by her light all the shadows, the dangers." The Vedic hymns "thus portray the natural phenomenon of the break of day as the violent driving back of the shadows, of the 'shadow,' assimilated to the enemy, to the barbarous, to the demoniac, to the 'formless,' to danger, etc.—by Dawn or the band of Dawns—noble goddesses, 'women of the *arya,*' . . . This is what the *bonae matres,* the *univirae* women, also act out in the Matralia, against a slave woman who must represent, in contrast with them, the wicked and baseborn element."[6]

The Matralia offer a telling example of the preservation of the rite independently of the myth. Indeed, Ovid, who knew nothing of this Indo-European theology, did not hesitate later to tack onto the archaic Roman liturgy an explanation borrowed from Hellenic fable. The syncretist interpretation had assimilated Mater Matuta to the Greek Ino-Leucothea. The poet managed to find in the tangled and contradictory web of fables about Ino-Leucothea a homologous situation that could justify the ritual schema of the Roman cult.

Ino-Leucothea may appear to be a kindly nurse for her nephew Bacchus, but she turns out to be an evil mother to her own children. Ovid justifies the liturgy of the Matralia with the following etiology, in which he addresses an exhortation to the mothers of Latium: "May mothers piously invoke the goddess not on behalf of their own offspring, for as a mother she herself has hardly brought good luck. May they commend unto her, rather, the children of others, for she has been more useful to her nephew Bacchus than to her own sons" (Ovid *Fasti* 6.559–62).[7]

By resorting to the same method that is the basis of the analysis of structural correspondences, the comparativist scholar succeeded in illuminating the meaning of Diva Angerona, "who saves the sun from the crisis of the winter solstice by the power of silence"; of Fortuna Primigenia, a primal goddess, simultaneously "mother and daughter of Jupiter"; and of Lua Mater, "the goddess Dissolution in the service of Roman order."

These rites had become unintelligible in Rome only because they had been detached from their mythological context. In rediscovering the symbolic meaning of these rites by confronting them with the Indo-European data, comparativism by the same stroke supplied a brilliant proof of its own legitimacy.

These are, moreover, marginal divinities that were increasingly regarded as relics in historic times. The Indo-European heritage in Rome is even more forcefully manifest in the fundamental structures. A tripartite ideology inspires the political system of the earliest times, as well as the hierarchy of the three principal gods, Jupiter, Mars, and Quirinus.

Tradition kept alive the memory of the three tribes that were thought to have provided the framework of the original society: the Ramnes, the Luceres, and the Titienses or Quirites. This division took on an ethnic value: the Ramnes were regarded as the companions of Romulus, the Luceres as the Etruscan allies led by Lucumon, and the Titienses as the Sabines of Tatius. Cicero characterized this tripartition precisely: "Romulus had divided the people into three tribes . . . by giving them his own name, the name of Tatius, and the name of Lucumon, who, serving as Romulus's ally, perished in the battle against the Sabines" (Cicero *De republica* 2.8).

The memory of this tripartition has never vanished. Its existence was acknowledged by the great scholar Varro (cited in Servius Danielis *ad Aen.* 5.560) and reiterated in the form of an aphorism of the abridger Florus (2.5.6): "The Roman people are made up of a mixture of Etruscans, Latins, and Sabines."

But this triple division can hardly be the result of a fortuitous addition. What is the explanation for the ethnic components? If the tripartition were valid, one would be surprised by its narrow limits; for other peoples, such as the Umbrians, who stand out among the Italics, or even the Greeks of Magna Graecia could have aspired (perhaps with a stronger claim) to the honor of supplying "valences" for Roman society.

In fact, the ethnic coloration of this threefold grouping barely conceals its functional scope. It is quite remarkable that the Ramnes correspond so precisely to the companions of the priest-king, the Luceres to the paradigmatic soldiers, and the Titienses to those who are herdsmen/farmers by traditional vocation. This reflection led Georges Dumézil to recall the existence of equivalent structures in Vedic India, with the difference that in India this distinction was frozen into hereditary classes: each Arya belongs by birth to one of the three groups, Brahmans, warriors, and herdsmen/farmers. The difference may be explained by the fact that India remained a royal society of the feudal type, whereas Rome, in the course of its history, never stopped evolving toward a democracy of citizens.

This functional tripartition can also be found in the hierarchy of the three principal gods, which preceded the Capitoline triad in Rome. Indeed, it is visible just below the surface in the ancient *ordo sacerdotum,* recorded by Festus (pp. 299–300 L^2), who saw the following hierarchical order: the king, the Flamen Dialis, the Flamen Martialis, the Flamen Quirinalis, the Pontifex Maximus. The three flamens, flanked by the king and the great pontiff, were assigned to the service of Jupiter, Mars, and Quirinus, respectively. Once a year these three flamens proceeded in an open chariot to a chapel of Fides, the goddess of good faith, who presided over the harmonious relationships among these three representatives. This divine triad can be explained only by the conceptual structure that Georges Dumézil called "the ideology of the three functions," which can be found over and over again in most of the ancient Indo-European societies, with variants and alterations peculiar to each society.

The same triad appears in the religious institutions of the archaic period. Thus the *Regia,*[8] the former "dwelling place of the king," which during the Republic became the seat of the Pontifex Maximus, housed three types of cults (besides the cults of Janus and Juno, who were honored as those who ushered in the new year and the new month). The first concerned Jupiter as principal god; the second, Mars, in the *sacrarium Martis;* and the third, in another *sacrarium,* concerned Ops Consiva, who belonged to a group of deities who are represented by Quirinus on the canonical list of the trilogy. Because the authority of Quirinus, the patron god of the community of the Quirites (who were responsible for productive tasks in time of peace, as opposed to the *milites* who were subject to Mars), could extend to all areas within his jurisdiction, his flamen could intervene whenever a specialized priest was not available. In this regard, Ovid (*Fasti* 4.910) remarks that the Flamen Quirinalis officiates during the ceremonies of Robigus (or Robigo), a deity invoked to prevent wheat blight.

The same association joins together—after Janus, the god of beginnings, and before the particular deities invoked on special occasions—Jupiter, Mars, and Quirinus in the old *carmen* of the *devotio,* a solemn prayer by which the Roman commander-in-chief "devoted" to the Manes gods his own person as well as that of the enemy (Livy 8.9.6). It also inspired the old rule of *spolia opima* recorded by Festus (p. 302 L^2), which provides for the *prima spolia* to be offered to Jupiter, the *secunda* to Mars, and the *tertia* to "Janus Quirinus." The tripartite scheme prevails, whatever interpretation one adopts for *prima, secunda,* and *tertia,* and whatever

Temple of Vesta. Rome. Photo Alinari.

meaning one gives to the expression "Janus Quirinus" (which I have tried to clarify in *M.E.F.R.*, 1960, p. 116ff. = *R.C.D.R.*, *Janus dieu introducteur. . .*). The association can also be found in the triple patronage of the college of the Salii, who were under the protection of the three deities, *in tutela Jovis Martis Quirini* (Servius Danielis *ad Aen.* 8.663).

Finally, these Roman facts are confirmed remarkably by the parallelism in the Umbrian pantheon. In Iguvium as in Rome, a triad brought together three gods: *Iov-*, *Mart-*, and *Vofiono-*, who were given the common modifier *Grabovio-* (in this list, *Vofiono-* has been interpreted by linguists as the etymological equivalent of *Quirinus:* see Georges Dumézil, *ARR*, p. 149, no. 3).

The memory of a tripartite ideology that reflects old Indo-European conceptions seems beyond dispute as far as the origins of Rome are concerned. It assumes that a society cannot function harmoniously unless it is structured by three hierarchical functions, namely, sovereignty (magical and juridical), force (physical and military), and fertility and prosperity (along with their pastoral and agrarian variants). But it seems that this scheme was in a constant state of decline from the time when the Latins settled on the Italic peninsula. By ending their itinerant status in order to become settled, they moved from prehistory to history.

This history was then marked by the tension of internal rivalries and by the pressure of outside influences. Tradition would have us believe that three monarchs of Etruscan origin were the last on the list of kings—Tarquinius the Elder, Servius Tullius, and Tarquinius Superbus—so that Etruscan influence dominated at the dawn of Roman history. In fact, Etruria, which gave its women a more important social role than Indo-European society did, was certainly familiar with the substitution of two goddesses, Juno and Minerva, for the masculine consorts of Jupiter. As early as the end of the sixth century B.C., the new association of Jupiter, Juno, and Minerva, to which a temple was dedicated on top of the Capitol, finally replaced the former triad of Jupiter-Mars-Quirinus.

In a sense, this change was made in a spirit of continuity. The keystone has remained, even though Jupiter took on the features of Tinia, thanks to the Etruscan artist Vulca of Veii (see Pliny [the Elder] *Naturalis Historia* 35.157).[9] Juno, the protecting goddess of the *Juniores*, particularly of the young men of military age, succeeded Mars, the god of war; and Minerva, the guardian of artisans, took over for Quirinus, the patron of economic activities.

III. The Principal Stages of Religious History

We will not attempt to cover all the meanderings of the religious history of Rome. We can, however, review the principal stages that stake out its development. The expulsion of the kings in 509 B.C. is an important event because it marks the collapse of the keystone that ensured the cohesion of the old system. Of course, in a manner of speaking the king survived on the religious level, in the role of Rex Sacrorum or Rex Sacrificulus, who inherited the liturgical functions of the former king. In this indirect way, the Romans thought they could escape the legitimate wrath of the gods—*ira deum*—who would not have accepted the complete overthrow of the religious traditions. However, this fossilized individual would no longer play any role in the life of the city. In the absence of a supreme arbiter, two classes, the patricians and the plebeians, initiated a rivalry that was to last for centuries. Their confrontation was expressed essentially in terms of an economic, social, and political struggle that can be explained by the opposition of their respective interests, but it was also manifest on the religious level. From the beginning, patricians and plebeians were far from enjoying religious equality. Patricians alone were entitled to enter traditional priestly orders such as the pontificate and the augurate. Not until 300 B.C. was the Ogulnia law passed, which guaranteed religious equality between the two classes by reserving for plebeians a good half of the seats recruited in each college. Even so, the archaic priesthoods, such as the Rex Sacrorum, the Flamines Majores, and the Salii, remained reserved for patricians.

This religion, so thoroughly structured in its origins, was quickly exposed to two perils that became increasingly menacing as time went by: the wave of syncretism and the monopolization of certain cults by the great conquerors of the first century B.C.

What is meant by syncretism? Stig Wikander[10] clarified the origin of the word, which dates back to Plutarch (*De fraterno amore* 19 = *Moralia* 3.271), where it has a different meaning, since *sunkrētismos*, meaning "union, federation," was applied to Cretans who had the custom of forming a sacred union when outside enemies approached. Through several incarnations (syncretism designated "sometimes the attempts made to reconcile protestors, sometimes the attempt to reconcile the various philosophies of antiquity, especially those of Plato and Aristotle"), a new usage that claimed to justify itself through a false etymology deriving the word from *sunkrēsis* or "mixture" used the term to denote "the mixture of myths and religions." In the realm of Roman religion in particular, it designated the contamination of autochthonous traditions and figures by elements of Greek or Eastern origin.

This phenomenon can be verified in the Roman liturgy of the lectisternia, which more or less assimilated Roman deities to Greek deities to a more or less pronounced degree. In all instances it presupposed a common denominator; thus, the concept of "spell," which at first in Rome had a religious essence (*veneror* < **venes-or* "I cast a persuasive spell [on such a deity]"),[11] drew together the Roman Venus and the Greek Aphrodite despite the fact that it had a more profane color in Greece.

Temple of Venus. Rome. Photo Anderson.

Syncretic action could have diametrically opposed effects. Thus, through the Trojan legend, the goddess Venus exerted a widespread influence that merely deployed all the implications of her primordial function. She gradually "became" what she fundamentally "was" all along, namely, the mediating power between the Romans and the gods.

Conversely, the Latin Diana, who was the deity of the light of night (close to Jupiter, by her semantic origin), experienced the vicissitudes of her political misfortunes. Her Latin identity became so evanescent[12] that in the time of Augustus she was regarded as no more than "Apollo's sister." As such, she appears next to "her mother" Latona in the Palatine temple that Augustus erected in honor of "her brother" Apollo (see Propertius 2.31.15–16).

Yet another peril threatened the Roman pantheon, a peril particularly noticeable during the last century of the Republic: the illegal solicitation of fashionable deities by anyone who aspired to power. Deep trouble prevailed internally and externally; social unrest (90–88 B.C.) and civil wars (88–86 B.C.) had shaken up Roman society. These troubles had been followed by the bloody proscriptions of Sulla (83–82 B.C.), which anticipated the prohibitions of the triumvirate of 43 B.C. In 73 B.C., the slaves rose in rebellion at the instigation of Spartacus.

In this climate of disarray, "saviors" appeared who, each in his turn, placed their ambition under the protection of a well-disposed deity within the scope of their family traditions and their level of culture, or lack of it.

The earliest and least cultured—Marius—offered the spectacle of utter incoherence.[13] He showed evidence both of a certain respect for tradition (after the victory over the Cimbri at Vercellae in 101 B.C., he dedicated a temple in honor of *Honos*, "Honor," and *Virtus*, "Courage") and a propensity for strange deviations: after the victory over the Teutons at Aix in 102 and over the Cimbri in 101, he let the Romans offer libations "both to the gods and to Marius" (Plutarch *Marius* 27.8). Long under the influence of a woman named Martha, a Syrian priestess, he turned his attention for a while toward the Magna Mater, the goddess Cybele; but his religion, which was steeped in superstition, never reached the level of a personal cult.

Sulla was altogether different.[14] He took the Trojan legend and turned it to his personal advantage, after rather eclectically soliciting the good graces of the Cappadocian goddess Ma as well as those of Hercules. He understood the benefit of Trojan patronage so clearly that he had himself surnamed Epaphroditos. This translation of the Latin cognomen Felix showed clearly that he intended to pass for the protégé of Venus Felix, the goddess who brings luck. Sulla was the one who was actually responsible for inaugurating the tradition of personal devotion to those in power.

Pompey tried to follow this example,[15] but the uncertainty of his character was reflected in his religious hesitations. He too tried to benefit from the Trojan mystique after his victory over Mithridates in 66 B.C. Upon his return to Rome, he raised above his theater—the first stone theater in Rome, built in 55 B.C.—a temple dedicated to Venus Victrix. Pompey's misfortune may have stemmed from having had Julius Caesar as his adversary. During the decisive battle of Pharsalus (48 B.C.), he first chose the watchword *Venus Victrix,* but had to abandon it to his adversary Caesar and instead use *Hercules Invictus*.

Julius Caesar was able to reclaim the tutelary patronage of Venus with the greatest "legitimacy,"[16] since he traced his lineage directly to Venus by way of Julus Ascanius, the son of Aeneas and grandson of Venus. But Caesar did not stop at founding a personal cult by erecting a magnificent temple to Venus Genetrix in his new Forum. His stroke of genius was to create a close association between the Roman nation and the Julian dynasty: Venus Genetrix may have been the mother of all the Romans, who were the descendants of Aeneas, but she was particularly the mother of those descendants of Aeneas known as the Julii, Caesar's descendants.

This "divine ancestry" made all the more feasible an innovation that would later be institutionalized during the empire: the deification of the deceased emperor (except in the cases of deposed emperors).

In 44 B.C., the Roman senators took the initiative and proclaimed Caesar's deification: "And finally they proclaimed him Jupiter Julius directly and ordered that a temple be dedicated to him as well as to the Clementia Caesaris by naming Anthony their priest, following the example of the flamen Dialis."[17] This initiative brings to mind a precedent: Aeneas had already been assimilated to Jupiter Indiges (Livy 1.2.6). But here the Senate had bestowed upon the living Caesar a privilege that the Latins had acknowledged in the founder of the nation only after he had vanished from the earth.

In any case, the cult of *divus Julius* was instituted after Caesar's death. The heavenly promotion benefited from a coincidence of exceptional circumstances: the appearance of a comet during the games in honor of Venus Genetrix, which was generally interpreted as the happy portent of Caesar's apotheosis.[18] We know that this title became official, since the adopted son of Caesar, Octavian, would later take the name of Divi Filius ("son of the deified").

Caesar's heir followed the customs of his times. He too practiced a cult of choice—his personal devotion to Apollo. But he was called upon by the fates to assume a more important task, namely, to reconcile the respect for the Julian heritage with the spirit of openness to necessary innovations.[19] The empire had been founded.

IV. Religion during the Imperial Era

By a quirk of fate, the last emperor of the Roman Empire of the West took the name of Romulus Augustulus (dethroned by Odoacer in A.D. 476), as though this double name were destined to call to mind one last time the first king of Rome and, with an ironic twist (recalling Graeculus against Graecus), the founder of the Roman Empire. The following is an attempt to isolate the essential characteristics that have marked the fundamentally religious fabric of this five-century period.

First, Roman polytheism was enriched by every new host as the frontiers of the empire were extended. By definition, this openness conformed to one of the fundamental tendencies of polytheism. This tendency had been encouraged by the syncretism that had enabled foreign deities to enter Rome. They came at first principally from Etruria and Magna Graecia, later from the Near East, and finally from Egypt. What was the Roman attitude toward this profusion of new deities?

Sometimes foreign deities were Romanized by virtue of the *interpretatio Romana* (a kind of renaming by equivalence), and at other times they kept their original names. This phenomenon can be verified throughout the empire.[20] Historians of religion therefore often encounter subtle cases of contamination. To what extent, for example, does the African Saturn bring to mind, through the affinities of the two gods, the Carthaginian Baal?[21] And to what extent was Caesar right in identifying the great god of Gaul with Mercury (*Gallic War* 6.17)?[22]

Another characteristic of the Imperial Era was the impact of various philosophical currents upon religion, a circumstance that has only recently been acknowledged. This philosophical ascendancy was applied selectively. It chose deities whose personalities inclined them to this process: from the first century, the Roman Hercules had attracted the attention of the Stoics and the Cynics.[23] In this case the philosophical exegesis was not corrosive; to the contrary, to the extent that it exalted Hercules's mission of salvation throughout the world and his triumph over human passions, it had the opportunity to introduce into the religious vision the dimensions that it had lacked in ancient Roman religion, namely, the ethical and eschatological dimensions.

But the very diversity of the philosophical schools (for instance, Marcus Aurelius had four chairs reserved at the University of Athens for followers of Plato, Aristotle, the Stoa, and Epicurus, respectively) generally brought about a very different result. It triggered a high level of skepticism among "enlightened minds," whereas all forms of superstition from astrology to magic exerted a seductive spell on the souls of the "simple-minded."[24] After that, the intelligentsia did not hesitate to adopt an altogether pragmatic attitude. Theoretical agnosticism coexisted with deference toward the establishment.

As early as the first century A.D., Pliny the Elder offers evidence in sharp contrast to the deism that was still professed by Cicero.[25] Not content to censure the "human frailty" (*imbecillitatis humanae*) that seeks "a representation and a form of god," he did not hesitate to propose a definition that reduced god to social service: *Deus est mortali juvare mortalem et haec ad aeternam gloriam via* ("To man, god means helping man and therein lies the way to eternal glory").[26] The same Pliny who derided "the even greater stupidity" which consisted in believing in innumerable gods found it altogether natural to approach the emperor "with religious respect" (*religiose*).[27]

This feature is significant. Whereas polytheism was running the double risk of discrediting itself through both incessant proliferation and the growing skepticism of the intellectuals, the most solid infrastructure of Roman religion appeared to be the imperial cult.

Augustus[28] saw to it that a close link was maintained in the provinces between the imperial cult and the cult of Rome. The cult of Rome reached its apogee under the Emperor Hadrian, who tied it to the Julian cult of Venus in the double temple with apses back-to-back. This temple had been erected in honor of Roma Aeterna and Venus Genetrix in A.D. 121.[29] This does not alter the fact that "the Antonine dynasty intensified and diversified the religious exaltation of the emperor and his family. In response to their wishes, the cult of the *divi* (emperors deified after their deaths) took up an increasingly larger segment of the liturgical calendar, and official propaganda proclaimed with increasing intensity the supernatural 'virtues' of the princes."[30]

The imperial mystique was nurtured inside certain priestly colleges, particularly within the close ranks of the Arval Brethren.[31] Such had been the intention of Augustus, who spearheaded a renewal of this archaic cult. The Arval Brethren saw to it that in the sacred grove of *Dea Dia*, sacrifices were also offered to the *divi*,[32] who were progressively added to the list of deities inscribed in their liturgy.

The Arval Brethren never missed a chance to show their loyalty to the princely house. At the start of every year, they uttered the *vota,* solemn prayers for the reigning prince. The following is an example, a *carmen* recited on 3 January of the year 91 on behalf of Domitian: "Jupiter, very kind, very great, if the Emperor Caesar, the son of the deified Vespasian, Domitian, Augustus, Germanicus, Great Pontiff, holder of tribunitan power, perpetual censor, father of the country, and Domitia Augusta, his wife whom I name expressly, if all these stay alive, grant that their house remain safe and sound on the third of January of the year about to close and for the next year, this for the Roman people and the Roman state, and grant that you watch over this day and their persons so as to keep them from whatever perils may exist or come about before that day, and grant them the joy of success, as I expressly state, by watching over their persons so that they may be kept in their current situation or else in an even better situation; if you will kindly grant this request, we hereby solemnly promise in the name of the college of the Arval Brethren that we will offer you an ox with golden horns."[33]

The development of this imperial mystique was to provoke conflict between Christians and pagans.[34] Whereas Roman tradition was founded on tolerance toward all forms of worship, the mandatory requirement of the imperial cult, which was interpreted by the Roman authorities as a proof of citizenship, met with refusal on the part of the Christians, who saw in it nothing but an act of idolatry. The famous exchange of letters (ca. A.D. 111–12) between Pliny the Younger, then governor of Bithynia, and the emperor Trajan[35] sheds some light on this historical misunderstanding. The governor had confessed his difficulty to the emperor. He had ordered the execution of Christians obstinate in their vows; he had ordered the release of those who had been "denounced by anonymous libels," and who had recanted "in front of the image of the emperor and the statues of the gods" and who had "blasphemed Christ." But since after investigating he had been unable to find anything other than "an unreasonable and inordinate superstition, he had suspended the hearing pending the advice of Trajan."

The emperor replied: "There is no need to investigate [the Christians]. If they are exposed and convicted, they must be punished, but with the following restriction: whosoever shall deny being a Christian and give concrete proof of his avowal, by which I mean offering sacrifice to our gods, even if he had been suspect in the past, he shall be granted a pardon in exchange for his repentance. As for the anonymous denunciations, they must not be entered as evidence in any proceedings involving accusation. This is a hateful example of behavior that is not becoming to our times."[36] Through the spread of the imperial cult, the religious policies of the Antonine dynasty tended to create a powerful link between Rome and the people of the empire, and it did so by exhibiting a wisdom of the kind that can be witnessed in Trajan's decisions. This policy left its mark throughout the empire. It is interesting to note that in the easternmost part of the Mediterranean basin, it was the imperial cult that left the strongest imprint. In fact, in Roman Palestine, out of the whole of "paganism" it was the imperial cult that attracted the greatest attention in the rabbinical commentaries, as has been demonstrated in a recent study.[37] The Jews may have obtained from the Roman emperors a dispensation from all cultic activity, but this "applied only to dead gods and not to the living gods who were the deified monarchs."[38] At the very least, the Jews were sworn to loyalty and to participating in the official festivals.

One important case cited with admiration by rabbinical sources—an exceptional case[39]—speaks of the "holy man" who through all his life had refused to look at the effigy of a Roman coin, in order to respect the prohibition against the imperial cult. This anecdote provides a striking contrast with the account in the Gospel of Matthew (22, 20, and 21), which tells of Christ's famous intervention with respect to the coin with the effigy of Caesar. It reveals the existence of a new climate. After the destruction of the Temple of Jerusalem (in A.D. 70), the hostility against Rome found additional nourishment in the extension of the imperial cult (Revelation, chapters 13 and 15, refers to the threat of death that hung over "all who would not worship the image of the Beast)."

Thus, the policy that had consisted in compounding the civic allegiance with the imperial cult had run up against serious difficulties. In any event, it left such an emptiness of spirit that a reaction spread more and more widely, on both the theological and the ethical levels. Moving in opposition to the traditional polytheism and its *national* gods, various initiatives asserted the primacy of a single *universal* deity. It was no accident that these initiatives revolved around deities of Oriental origin. Thus, the figure of Hercules, who from the first century had attracted philosophers, took on even greater visibility in the theology of Julian "the Apostate," who tried to make him into a pagan answer to Christ.[40] Similarly, the appeal of the Egyptian Isis took on a universalist character, as is attested in book 11 of the *Metamorphoses* of Apuleius, a kind of mystical document of Pan-Isiasm.[41] In it Isis is invoked as "the mother of all nature, the sovereign of all the elements, the primordial origin of the centuries, the supreme deity" (Apuleius *Metamorphoses* 11.5.1).

Finally, in the third century, the emperor Aurelian[42] tried to make the cult of the sun preeminent by erecting on the Field of Mars a splendid temple to Sol Invictus (the invincible sun), in A.D. 274.[43] The sun, which was already considered by the emperor to be his personal protector (Conservator Augusti), was hailed as "the sovereign god of the Roman

Mithra sacrificing a bull. Paris, Musée du Louvre. Photo Giraudon.

Empire" (Dominus Imperi Romani). Its festival (Natalis Solis) was set on 25 December, "the date on which the star resumes its ascending path for another year."[44]

This was certainly the last and the most impressive attempt by a Roman emperor to create a *universal* cult: pansolarism would later provide the foundation of the theology professed by Macrobius at the beginning of the fifth century A.D.[45] It also offers proof that the tendency toward henotheism had taken hold at the expense of polytheism. Moreover, the preeminence of a *single* deity of universal appeal must have appeared as the only chance paganism had from then on in the face of the success enjoyed by the mystery religions.

Indeed, these religions had gained popularity especially among the throng of disinherited people, because of their ethical prescriptions and eschatological promises, all dimensions alien to traditional Roman religion. The cult of Mithra had been spread by soldiers and had thrived particularly in the frontier provinces of the empire; the initiates who had entered into the "militia of goodness" by passing through seven degrees of mysteries were guaranteed eternal bliss.[46] As for Christianity, it had progressed in spite of—or perhaps because of—the persecutions.[47] More open than Mithraism, which was reserved for initiates, it offered an asceticism that was supposed to ensure to "all men of goodwill" salvation in the hereafter. The Roman world was heading for profound metamorphoses.

R.S./g.h.

NOTES

The brief references are to the bibliographic lists. Abbreviations that are not defined in the list below conform to the rules of the *Oxford Classical Dictionary.*

1. "I ask you and venerate you, I beg and even now I obtain your favor." The editors have had a tendency to replace the manuscript reading *feroque* by *oroque*. Georges Dumézil, *La religion romaine archaïque* (*Archaic Roman Religion; ARR*), 2d ed., p. 109, was right to reestablish it and provides an excellent commentary.

2. See in particular Festus, p. 458 L., who in affirming the number seven adds Subura to this list. See also Servius *ad Aen.* 6.783.

3. *Roma quadrata* (square Rome) designates, according to Festus, pp. 310–12 L., "the placement of the Palatine, situated in front of the temple of Apollo, where are found the objects that are customarily deposited to obtain good fortune at the time of the foundation of a town." The expression *Roma quadrata* figures in the *Annales* of Ennius (vol. 123, p. 42, of the Warmington edition).

4. Cf. the article "Roman Gods," below.

5. See Georges Dumézil, *Déesses latines et mythes védiques* (Latin goddesses and Vedic myths) (Brussels 1956), and more recently, *Archaic Roman Religion* (2d ed., Paris 1974), 66–68.

6. Cf. Georges Dumézil, *Archaic Roman Religion,* pp. 51–52.

7. The demonstration has been developed in my article "Ovide interprète de la religion romaine," *R.E.L.* 46 (1969): 230–34 (= *R.C.D.R.,* same title).

8. The monument is the site of recent excavations: see F. E. Brown, *La protostoria della Regia, Atti della Pontificia Accademia Romana di archeologia, Rendiconti* 47 (1976): 15–36.

9. On the cultic statue in terra-cotta from the Capitoline temple of Jupiter, see, most recently, O. W. von Vacano, "Vulca, Rom und die Wölfin, Untersuchungen zur Kunst des frühen Rom," *Festschrift Vogt* (= *A.N.R.W.*) 1, 4, pp. 523–83.

10. Stig Wikander, *Les "-ismes" dans la terminologie historico-religieuse,* in *Les Syncrétismes dans les religions grecque et romaine* (Paris 1973), 9–14.

11. Cf. the semantic analysis developed in my book *R.R.V.*, 33ff.

12. The assimilation of Diana to Artemis, in particular to Artemis Locheia, has led to a confusion between Diana *lucifera* ("she who brings light") and Juno *lucina* ("she who brings to light"), the protectress of those who give birth: cf. Catullus 34.13–14.

13. On the religious attitude of Marius, see my book *R.R.V.*, 268ff., as well as J.-C. Richard, "La Victoire de Marius," *M.E.F.R.* 77 (1965): 69–85.

14. Regarding the religious innovations of Sulla, see my book *R.R.V.*, 273ff. In a general way, cf. J. Carcopino, *Sylla ou la monarchie manquée* (Paris 1931). P. Jal, "Les Dieux et les guerres civiles," *R.E.L.* 40 (1962): 170–200.

15. See my book *R.R.V.*, 296ff.

16. On the religious attitude of Julius Caesar, see my book *R.R.V.*, 301ff. In general, cf., most recently, Stefan Weinstock, *Divus Julius* (Oxford 1971).

17. Dio Cassius 44.6.4. For commentary on this passage, see G. Dumézil, *La religion romaine archaïque,* 2d ed., p. 541.

18. On the apotheosis of Caesar, see the texts presented and the commentary in my book *R.R.V.*, 316–23.

19. Cf. the article "The Religious Policies of Augustus" below.

20. J. Toutain has devoted a series of works to "Cultes païens dans l'empire romain" (Bibliothèque de l'École des Hautes Études); in particular, vol. 3, fasc. 1: *Les cultes africains: Les cultes ibériques* (Paris 1917); vol. 3, fasc. 2: *Les cultes de la Gaule romaine* (Paris 1920).

21. Cf. M. Leglay, *Saturne Africain, Histoire* (Paris 1966); *Saturne Africain, Monuments* (Paris 1966). In general, cf. Gilbert Charles-Picard, *Les religions de l'Afrique antique* (Paris 1954).

22. Cf. P. M. Duval, *Les Dieux de la Gaule* (Paris 1957).

23. See my article "L'Hercule Romain et la réforme religieuse d'Auguste," *R.Ph.*, 1942, 31–57 (= *R.C.D.R.*, same title). In general, see M. Simon, *Hercule et le christianisme* (Strasbourg 1955). See also J. Bayet, *Hercule funéraire, M.E.F.R.*, 1921–22, 219–66,, and 1923, 19–102.

24. Cf. J. Festugière, *La révélation d'Hermès trismégiste* I: *L'astrologie et les sciences occultes* (Paris 1944).

25. See the article "Cicero as Theologian" below.

26. Pliny the Elder, *N.H.* 2.14 and 18.

27. Ibid., 2.14: *Innumeros quidem . . . majorem ad socordiam accedit.* Ibid., *Praef.* 11: "You (= Vespasianus) are approached only with religious respect, even by those who come to offer homage, I know."

28. Cf. the article "The Religious Policies of Augustus" below.

29. Cf. Wissowa, *Ruk*[2], 340–41. The anniversary of the temple, dedicated 21 April, coincides with the date of the birth of Rome.

30. J. Beaujeu, *La religion romaine à l'apogée de l'empire* (Paris 1955), 1:426.

31. Cf. J. Scheid, *Les Frères Arvales, Recrutement et origine sociale sous les empereurs Julio-Claudiens* (Paris 1975), 340–42.

32. Cf. G. Henzen, *Acta Fratrum Arvalium* (Berlin 1874), 148–49.

33. *CIL*, 6, 2068, lines 1–9: "Juppiter optime maxime, si imperator Caesar divi Vespasiani filius Domitianus Augustus Germanicus pontifex maximus tribunicia potestate censor perpetuus pater patriae et Domitia Augusta conjunx eius, quos me sentio dicere, vivent domusque eorum incolumis erit ante diem III Nonas Januarias quae proximae populo Romano Quiritibus, rei publicae populi Romani Quiritium erunt, et eum diem eosque salvos servaveris ex periculis si qua sunt eruntue ante eum diem eventumque bonum ita uti me sentio dicere, dederis, eosque in eo statu qui nunc est aut eo meliore servaveris, astu ea ita faxsis [*sic*], tunc tibi nomine collegi Fratrum Arvalium bovem auratum vovemus esse futurum." This *votum* written in the solemn style of the Imperial Chancellery is not presented in an *unconditional* fashion (like the prayer of the *devotio* of Decius who surrenders himself to the gods in total confidence): it is encumbered with clauses wherein prudence contends with guile (thus, even as it asks Jupiter to preserve the present situation—"eo statu qui nunc est"—it does not refuse the eventual improvement of a better situation—"aut eo meliore"). As in all good contracts, a date of expiration is fixed—3 January of the following year—for the contracting parties: the safeguarding of the imperial couple then would be "repaid" by the ritual sacrifice of the ox with gilded horns.

34. Cf. J. Moreau, *La persécution du christianisme dans l'empire romain* (Paris 1956), 40ff.

35. Pliny the Younger, *Epistulae* 10:96–97. The epistolary exchange between the governor and the emperor is cited and commented upon in J. Moreau, *La persécution,* 41–45.

36. Pliny the Younger, *Epistulae* 10:97 (trans. J. Moreau, except for

some corrections). We reproduce the last Latin phrase, which has the force of a lapidary formula: "Nam et pessimi exempli nec nostri saeculi est."

37. Cf. Mireille Hadas-Lebel, *Le paganisme dans la Palestine romaine d'après les sources rabbiniques.* Mémoire inédit de l'École des Hautes Études, section 5, 1976.

38. J. Juster, *Les Juifs dans l'empire romain* (Paris 1914; reprinted 1969), 2:338.

39. Cf. M. Hadas-Lebel, *Le paganisme,* 96–97.

40. Cf. M. Simon, *Hercule et le christianisme* (Strasbourg 1955), 145ff.

41. Cf. R. Merkelbach, *Roman und Mysterium in der Antike* (Munich and Berlin 1962). For the abundant bibliography on Isis, see J. Leclant, *Inventaire bibliographique des Isiaca* (Leiden 1972: A–D; 1974: E–K).

42. Of Illyrian origin and of modest extraction (he was born 9 September 214 or 215), Aurelian bore the official name of Imperator Caesar L. Domitius Aurelianus. We do not know under what conditions he had acquired Roman citizenship as well as the name L. Domitius. The cognomen Aurelianus is explained by the fact that his father was the tenant of a senator named Aurelius (cf. Groag, *R.E.,* s.v. Domitius no. 36, c. 1351–52). Aurelian is therefore foreign to the ancient Roman lineage called Aurelia, a lineage "that came from the Sabine and took its name from the Sun" (*Aureliam familiam ex Sabinis oriundam a Sole dictam putant:* Paulus-Festus, p. 22, 5 L.).

43. On the origin and extension of the solar cult created by Aurelian, see Groag, *R.E.,* s.v. Domitius no. 36, c. 1398–1400.

44. J. Bayet, *Histoire politique et psychologique de la religion romaine* (2d ed. 1969), 227.

45. Macrobius *Saturnales* 1.17ff.

46. On Mithraism, see E. Cumont, *Textes et monuments figurés relatifs aux mystères de Mithra,* 2 vols. (Brussels 1896 and 1899). St. Wikander, *Étude sur les mystères de Mithra,* vol. 1 (Lund 1951). We recall the celebrated phrase of E. Renan (*Histoire des origines du christianisme* 7: *Marc Aurèle et la fin du monde antique* [17th ed., Paris], p. 579): "If Christianity had been impeded in its growth by some mortal malady, the world would be Mithraist." The modern critic is far from ratifying this judgment: cf. M. Simon, *Mithra rival du Christ? Actes du second congrès international d'études mithraiques* (Tehran 1975).

47. See P. de Labriolle, *La réaction païenne: Étude sur la polémique antichrétienne du IIe au VIe siècle* (Paris 1934). J. Moreau, *La persécution,* passim.

BIBLIOGRAPHY

Principal Ancient Sources

Fasti: The Roman calendar: ed. TH. MOMMSEN, *CIL,* 1 (2d ed., 1893), for the Julian year; ed. G. MANCINI, *N.S.,* 1921, 73–141, for the pre-Julian year; complete calendar ed. DEGRASSI, *I.I.,* XIII, pars II (1963).

Acta fratrum Arvalium, ed. HENZEN (Berlin 1874); ed. PASOLI (Bologna 1950); proceedings from the first century B.C. to the fourth century A.D. of the college of the Arval Brethren. Proceedings of A.D. 218 include the *carmen Arvale,* which doubtless goes back to the end of the sixth century B.C.

Carminum Saliarium reliquiae, ed. B. MAURENBRECHER, *J. Ph.,* 1894, Sup. Band. 21:314–52; fragments of the ancient *carmen* of the Salii.

CATO, *De agricultura* (for the prayers and the sacrifices of the private cult).

S. P. FESTUS, *De verborum significatu quae supersunt cum Pauli epitome,* ed. LINDSAY (Leipzig 1913).

M. TERENTI VARRONIS, *Antiquitatum rerum divinarum libri* 1, 14, 15, 16, ed. R. AGAHD, *J. Ph.,* 1898, Sup. Band. 24:3–220; reconstitution of Varro's lost works, based on citations of the Church Fathers.

Acta ludorum saecularium, CIL, 6, 32323ff.; proceedings concerning the secular games, particularly the games of 17 B.C.

De Ludis saecularibus populi Romani Quiritium, Libri sex, by I. B. PIGHI (2d ed., Amsterdam 1965).

OVIDIUS, *Fastorum libri* 6; commentary on the liturgical calendar.

All the Latin authors, particularly Virgil, should be consulted by the historian of Roman religion.

Encyclopedias

DAREMBERG and SAGLIO, *Dictionnaire des antiquités grecques et romaines,* 10 vols. including index vol. DE RUGGIERO-CARDINALI, *Dizionario Epigrafico di antichità romane* (Rome 1885–). ROSCHER-ZIEGLER, *Ausführliches Lexikon der griechischen und römischen Mythologie,* 10 vols. (Leipzig 1884–1937). PAULY-WISSOWA, *Realencyclopädie der classischen Altertumswissenschaft* (Stuttgart 1893–).

General Studies

M. MARQUARDT, *Le culte chez les Romains,* 2 vols., trans. M. Brissaud (Paris 1889–90). W. WARDE FOWLER, *The Roman Festivals of the Period of the Republic* (London 1899); *The Religious Experience of the Roman People from the Earliest Times to the Age of Augustus* (London 1911; 2d ed., 1922). G. WISSOWA, *Religion und Kultus der Römer* (2d ed., Munich 1912). F. CUMONT, *Les religions orientales dans le paganisme romain* (Paris 1909; 4th ed., 1929). C. BAILEY, *Roman Religion and the Advent of Philosophy,* The Cambridge Ancient History 8:423–65 (1930); *Phases in the Religion of Ancient Rome* (Berkeley 1932). N. TURCHI, *La Religione di Roma antica* (Bologna 1939). F. ALTHEIM, *Römische Religionsgeschichte* (2d ed., Berlin 1965). J. BAYET, *Histoire politique et psychologique de la religion romaine* (2d ed., Paris 1969). K. LATTE, *Römische Religionsgeschichte* (Munich 1960). G. DUMÉZIL, *Idées romaines* (Paris 1969); *Archaic Roman Religion* (Chicago 1970); *La religion romaine archaïque* (2d ed., Paris 1974); *Fêtes romaines d'été et d'automne* (Paris 1975). A. KIRSOPP MICHELS, *The Calendar of the Roman Republic* (Princeton 1967).

ABBREVIATIONS

A.N.R.W. = *Aufstieg und Niedergang der römischen Welt* (Berlin).

CIL = *Corpus Inscriptionum Latinarum* (Berlin 1863–).*D.A.* = DAREMBERG-SAGLIO, *Dictionnaire des antiquités grecques et romaines* (Paris).

DEGRASSI, *I.I.* = A. DEGRASSI, *Inscriptiones Italiae,* vol. 13, part 2: Fasti anni Numani et Iuliani (Rome 1963).

DESSAU, *I.L.S.* = H. DESSAU, *Inscriptiones Latinae selectae,* 3 vols. (Berlin 1892–1916).

ERNOUT-MEILLET, *D.E.*[4] = ERNOUT-MEILLET, *Dictionnaire étymologique de la langue latine* (4th ed., Paris).

J. Ph. = *Jahrbücher für classische Philologie* (Leipzig).

M.E.F.R. = *Mélanges de l'École française de Rome. N.S.* = *Notizie degli scavi di Antichità* (Rome).

PLINY, *N.H.* = PLINIUS, *Naturalis Historia.*

R.E. = PAULY-WISSOWA, *Realencyclopädie der classischen Altertumswissenschaft* (Stuttgart).

R.E.L. = *Revue des études latines* (Paris).

SCHILLING, *R.C.D.R.* = R. SCHILLING, *Rites, cultes, dieux de Rome* (Paris 1979).

SCHILLING, *R.R.V.* = R. SCHILLING, *La religion romaine de Vénus depuis les origines jusqu'au temps d'Auguste* (Paris 1954).

VETTER, *H.I.D.* = E. VETTER, *Handbuch der italischen Dialekte* (Heidelberg).

WALDE-HOFMANN, *L.E.W.*[3] = WALDE-HOFMANN, *Lateinisches etymologisches Wörterbuch* (3d ed., Heidelberg).

WISSOWA, *Ruk*[2] = G. WISSOWA, *Religion und Kultus der Römer* (2d ed., Munich 1912).

Roman Gods

The word *deus* has undergone considerable phonetic change but has nonetheless been preserved by the various Romance languages to mean deity. Its origin is Indo-European and it designates a celestial being. *Deus* came phonetically from the old form of *deivos;* similarly, *dea* came from *deiva.* The ancients were aware of the derivation: thus, Varro (*De Lingua Latina* 3.2) contrasts the usual form *deos* with the "old" version *divos*. By virtue of this etymology, *deus* and *dea* are for the Latins superior powers connected with the luminous heaven (*divum*).

In this sense, the Latin word differs from its Greek homologue, *theos*, which has a different etymology, *theos*, which goes back to a prototype **thesos* ("having to do with the realm of the sacred"), an ill-defined term that leads in another direction. This difference in vocabulary between the Latin and the Greek words designating deity does not exist at the level of the supreme god, *Juppiter* (**Diou-pater*) and Zeus (**dyeus*), which correspond to the same Indo-European theme.

The semantic value of *deus* leaves little doubt that the Latins sought to represent the deity in the form of a personal and individual being. And yet this linguistic truth was challenged for a certain period in favor of an animistic conception according to which a "pre-deist" phase supposedly preceded the notion of a personal god. By virtue of "evolution," individualized deities were supposed to have disentangled themselves from the murky nebula of the origins. This tendency was represented in particular by H. J. Rose, who thought he had found support in the Latin word *numen*, which apparently corresponded to the Melanesian term *mana*. This latter term had gained currency in 1891 in *The Melanesians* by Bishop Codrington, who had defined it as "a supernatural power or influence . . . a force that produces everything that is beyond the ordinary power of men, outside of the common rules of nature."[1]

The alleged equivalence of *mana* and *numen* was later supported by H. Wagenvoort in his book *Roman Dynamism*,[2] whose title alone suggests the idea of a "diffuse force" which might have preceded the world of the gods. We need not enter into this debate, which appears to be closed. Georges Dumézil[3] has shown definitively that the Latin word *numen*, meaning "power" or "manifestation," was *always* used with the genitive of the deity in question during the Imperial Era. Thus it could not be "abstracted" from the god, without whom there would be no *numen*.[4] A further ironic point: in his last attempt to attribute to the word *numen* the meaning of "impersonal power" (*eine unpersönliche Kraft*),[5] in 1972, H. Wagenvoort cited as the "most ancient" proof of the use of the word a text by Accius: *Alia hic sanctitudo est, aliud nomen et numen Jovis* ("Here holiness is other, and other are the name and power of Jupiter").[6] Somehow he did not notice that he was proving Dumézil's point.

The etymological meaning of *deus* may indeed refer to a "luminous being," but the term itself was also applied by extension to divine powers that were not "celestial." Such is the case of the *di Manes*, a term that designated the infernal gods in the formula of the *devotio*, the prayer of consecration to the gods,[7] before it was replaced, toward the end of the first century B.C., by the expression *divi parentum* or *divi parentes*, which was reserved for the deceased in a family. These *di Manes*, for whom the meaning "Good Gods" most likely corresponds to a propitiatory euphemism, are by definition alien to the world of heavenly light. In the first case they evoked the spirits dwelling underground; in the second case they evoked the community of the dead.[8]

Moreover, we should note that if the word *deus* remained attached to the god "who is thought of as having existed forever," the form *divus*, which represents the old form of the term, was later reserved to designate the "deified" being, in this case the emperor who was given the honors of apotheosis.

Thus, the category of the *divi* (deified emperors) is distinguished from the world of the *dei* of the traditional pantheon. Other factors intervened in the use of the two terms: the influence of the Hellenistic cult explains, for instance, what Virgil may have had in mind far in advance of the "deification" of Octavian in the preamble of book 1 of the *Georgics*.[9] The specific use of *divus* that is theoretically reserved for an emperor deified after apotheosis is occasionally refuted: thus, an adulator of Nero proposed to the Senate that a temple be erected to *divo Neroni* (the divine Nero), who was still alive,[10] a case of anticipation later refuted by the course of events.

I. The Roman Pantheon

Let us return to the *dei* of the Roman pantheon and examine their charactistics. We should be on guard against a certain romanticism that had already developed in antiquity according to which the Roman deities corresponded merely to rough outlines of themselves before Etruria and Greece filled out their personalities. Thus, Pliny the Elder, who enjoyed the favor of the emperor Vespasian, evoked the following sylvan dream: "The forests were once the temples of the gods, and following the ancient rite, the countryside in its simplicity continues today to dedicate its most beautiful tree to a god. The statues in which gold and ivory shine do not inspire in us any more veneration than do the sacred groves and their very silence."[11]

This nostalgia for simplicity calls to mind a reflection by Varro, who also took delight in evoking the cult of yesteryear. "For more than one hundred and seventy years," he said, "the Romans worshiped their gods without statues. Had this practice prevailed, the gods would be honored in a purer way" (*quod si adhuc mansisset, castius di observarentur*).[12]

What is evident in both of these statements is the distinct belief of the Romans that their basically native deities had been different "in times past." The *castitas* praised by Varro was aimed directly at the Hellenic anthropomorphism that attributed human passions and vices to the gods, as in Homer's *Iliad* or in Hesiod's *Theogony*. A Roman deity is defined by a specific competence and is unfettered by the embellishments of a mythology more or less laden with the vicissitudes of life. In its origins it is therefore a stranger to the kind of anthropomorphism[13] that characterizes the Greek and Etruscan pantheons, a remarkable fact when one considers the cultural pressure exerted by the Greco-Etruscan environment.

This fact may be verified especially by the existence of a number of deified abstractions, such as Ceres or Fides, and also by the persistence of this tendency in historical times. I refer to the appearance of gods such as Aius Locutius or Rediculus. The voice that announced that the Gauls were coming ever closer to Rome was heard only once;[14] yet that was sufficient reason to raise an altar to the god called Aius Locutius ("he who speaks, he who says"). Similarly, a *fanum* was dedicated to Rediculus just outside the Capena Gate because Hannibal, who had almost reached the walls of Rome, "had turned away when he got to this place" (*ex loco redierit*).[15] These borderline cases nevertheless show clearly that in order to "exist" the deity merely had to manifest itself.

In addition to these exceptional examples, such a manifestation was translated into a permanent function. Those deities whose festivals are inscribed in the liturgical calendar all have a speciality, which is often indicated by the transparent meaning of their names. Thus, Ceres, for whom the Cerialia were observed on 19 April, is in charge of growth, in particular the growth of cereals; Consus, the god who

Mercury, Pallas, Apollo, and Diana. Rome, Villa Albani. Photo Alinari-Giraudon.

presides over the gathering of wheat, is celebrated during the Consualia of 21 August and during the Opiconsiva of 25 August, in association with Ops, the goddess who watches over abundance.

These deities were either masculine or feminine; at the beginning, Rome had no hierogamy. Any examples given to the contrary are mere fantasies. Consequently, Faunus,[16] the "wild" god who is involved in what may be the oldest ceremony in Rome, the Lupercalia of 15 February, had no feminine consort. Fauna certainly looks like an artificial construction of scholarly casuistics. Even the name is not certain, confused as it was sometimes with Fatua, sometimes with Bona Dea, a name which in turn refers to a Damia, originally from Tarentum.[17] Similarly, Pales, whose festival, the Parilia, fell on 21 April, a day that would later coincide with the anniversary of the birth of Rome, had no male consort. Virgil[18] only knew of the goddess: *Te quoque magna Pales (canemus).* (However, on 7 July two Pales goddesses were celebrated.)[19] The *god* Pales that Varro mentions[20] belonged to the Etruscan pantheon and had no liturgical existence in Rome.

What are we then to make of a formula such as *sive deus sive dea,* which reappears in several prayers?[21] It expresses not an uncertainty about the sex of an indeterminate deity, but merely an uncertainty about the *identity* of the deity to whom the invocation is addressed. Anxious to have his prayers answered, a Roman did not wish to mistake one deity for another, and when unsure of whom to address, he considered both possibilities and thus invokes either a god or a goddess.[22]

The same spirit of caution is evident in a formulaic prayer cited by Servius Danielis (*ad Aeneid* 2.351): *Et pontifices ita precabantur: Juppiter Optime Maxime, sive quo alionomine te appellari volueris* ("And the pontiffs said the following prayer: Jupiter most kind and great, or whatever be the name by which you prefer to be called"). For whatever reason, the pontiffs wanted to anticipate the case when Jupiter might opt for another appellation, although he was clearly identified by his Capitoline attributes.[23]

Roman polytheism by definition constituted an open pantheon made up of deities that in some cases go back to time immemorial and in other cases had been received at various dates, often following crises or epidemics. In this sense, Roman religion resembled a *Janus biceps* gazing simultaneously into the past and the future. The college of pontiffs, presided over by the Pontifex Maximus, looked after the traditional cults, while the college of *viri sacris faciundis* (who numbered successively two, ten, and fifteen, and whose general title "in charge of conducting ceremonies" did not reflect its special mission) were in charge of introducing foreign deities, often after consulting the Sibylline Books.

The status of deities differed depending on their origins. Their shrines were inside the *pomerium* (the sacred limits of the city) if they belonged to the native soil; conversely, their cults were relegated to the outside of the pomerial zone (the Aventine or the Field of Mars), if they came from outside. Vesta was the preeminent native goddess, protectress of the sacred fire in the heart of the city, while Juno Regina, a native of Veii, was a foreigner welcomed to Rome in 392 B.C. in a temple on the Aventine.[24]

Does this difference in origin and status correspond to the distinction between the Di Indigetes and the Di Novensiles? In the formula of the *devotio,* the expression appears in the reverse order without making things any clearer. The meaning is still disputed,[25] but there is agreement on the fact that the ancients and indeed several moderns (among them

Wissowa) made a semantic slip. They interpreted *indigetes* as *indigenae* and took *novensiles* (*-sides*) to be a compound of *novus* and *insidere,* thus contrasting the "native gods" and the "newly imported gods." This interpretation may be suspect *literally,* but it did nonetheless express an apparently real contrast.[26] In any case, the Romans were fully aware of the ancient or recent origin of their gods. I would be inclined to compare the term *Indigetes* to *Indigitamenta,* meaning a collection of litanies, and to *indigitare* (to invoke ritualistically), which would give it the sense of "one who has (always) been invoked." If the epithet admits of this nuance, namely, the recollection of a sustained fervor, its presence could then be explained in the Virgilian expression *Di patrii Indigetes,* in which, far from having a double meaning with *patrii,* it carries the meaning of persuasive insistence.[27]

It would be surprising if these gods, so closely tied to the ancient city, did not bear the political or social mark of its vicissitudes.[28] First of all, the Romans who had become masters over Italy had taken up federal cults that presupposed ritual equality among the participants, at least at the time of the old federation. Accordingly, every year the Roman consuls went up to the top of Mount Alban on the site of the former Alba Longa to celebrate the cult of Jupiter Latiaris. Locating the festival (*feriae Latinae*), which in historical time was a movable feast (*feriae conceptivae*), on the site of Alba Longa suggests that in former times it had not been under the jurisdiction of Rome. This federal cult of the Latins, presided over at that time by the Alban city, which was later destroyed, was originally celebrated in a sacred grove (Livy 1.31.3). Only later, probably during the rule of the last dynasty of the Roman kings, was a shrine built and dedicated to Jupiter Latiaris.

Forum. Temples to Castor and Pollux. Rome. Photo J. Roubier.

The substitution of Rome for Alba in the operation of this cult is instructive. The consuls, accompanied by the representatives of the state, had to proceed to the federal shrine a short time after taking office (and in any case, before their departure on a military campaign). They presided over the ceremony that was attended by delegates from every city. The essential act was the sacrifice of a white bull.[29] The *exta* (the consecrated entrails) were first offered to the god, and the *viscera* (the profane meat) were shared among all the representatives of the cities. This was a solemn celebration that tied together the Latin cities of the confederation with sacred bonds through their participation in a common sacrifice. For the duration of the ceremonies, all armed conflicts were suspended.[30] Rome thus respected a festival that sealed the bonds among the cities of Latium; she was content simply to claim the right to preside over it.

The Roman attitude toward the federal cult of Diana was altogether different. Tradition localized this cult in Aricia, near Lake Nemi, which was called the *speculum Dianae* (Diana's mirror).[31] At Aricia, as in the case of Jupiter Latiaris of Mount Alban, a sacred grove[32] preceded the shrine dedicated to Diana. This was the center of a federation of Latin cities that may have banded together after the dissolution of Alba Longa and that reunited around the federal altar that was dedicated at that time by the Latin dictator Egerius Laevius,[33] a native of Tusculum, when he was president of the Latin League. When the confederation shifted over to Roman control, the cult was transferred to Rome and set up on the Aventine Hill. At first it consisted of a simple altar,[34] and later of a temple that kept its federal character, according to Varro (*De Lingua Latina* 5.43), who refers to it as *commune Latinorum templum* (a temple common to the Latins).

But this cult continued to be federal only in appearance. Never is any gathering mentioned of Latin cities on the Aventine any more than in Aricia. The anniversary festival of its temple, which fell on the ides of August, bore the name of *dies servorum* (day of the slaves). Whatever interpretation[35] we may want to give to this designation, the Aventine cult reveals a gradual effacement of the Latin goddess. Diana became so evanescent that she was ripe for absorption by her Greek counterpart, Artemis.[36] In Horace's *Carmen Saeculare,* composed in 17 B.C. for the secular games held under Augustus, she is merely Apollo's sister. This shows how sharp a contrast there was between the fate reserved for the old tutelary deity of the Latins and the honors that the Romans bestowed on Jupiter Latiaris.

Yet another mark was made by the effects of social tensions. As long as there was no religious equality between plebeians and patricians (before the Lex Ogulnia of 300 B.C.), there was a serious rivalry between the two classes that explains certain ritual innovations.

Thus, at the beginning of the fifth century B.C., a kind of compensatory balance could be established. Two temples were founded, the first in honor of the triad of Ceres-Liber-Libera (493 B.C.), near the Circus Maximus, and the second only a few years later, in honor of Castor, in the middle of the Forum (484 B.C.). The promise (*votum*) to build these temples came from the same person, A. Postumius, the hero of the famous battle of Lake Regillus that the Romans won over the Latins in 499 B.C.

This battle became famous in the annals. It had a critical phase that was overcome only when the Roman cavalry was called in. While ordering his cavalry to enter the fray, the dictator Postumius at the same time made a vow to erect a temple to Castor (Livy 2.20.12), the reason being that Castor, originally a Greek god (whose presence in Lavinium, outside the ancient city, was verified by the recent finding of an archaic inscription associating him with Pollux), was, more specifically, the patron of horsemen, according to the Hellenic tradition that was itself based on the Indo-European tradition. A. Postumius had thus combined "human and divine" means, to quote Livy's expression, by addressing a *votum* to Castor while calling on his *equites*. Starting with the "historical" event of Lake Regillus, the god of the patrician class of horsemen became a national Roman god.

Before undertaking this military campaign, the same dictator also made another religious innovation to satisfy the common people. Dionysius of Halicarnassus (*Antiquitates Romanae* 6.17) reports that Postumius, preoccupied with the difficulties of getting fresh supplies, vowed to erect a temple to the triad of Demeter-Dionysus-Kore. This temple was consecrated by Postumius immediately after his victory, so that he could show his gratitude for the exceptionally abundant harvest (the Temple of Castor was to be dedicated nine years later by his son). Knowing that the management of the new cult of Ceres-Liber-Libera was entrusted to the plebs and that the temple also served as a meeting place for the councillors of the plebs,[37] one can no longer question Postumius's intentions: by balancing this plebeian cult with a patrician cult, the dictator wanted to guarantee an even mixture that would satisfy both classes, even while it marked the hierarchical order. The temple of Ceres and of her consorts was built outside the *pomerium* near the Circus Maximus; the sanctuary of Castor was then to be built inside the *pomerium*, in the very heart of the Forum.[38]

II. Foreign Influences

Along with internal factors, outside influences made their mark on the development of Roman religion. This process may be explained by the fact that Rome had direct connections with the Greek and Etruscan worlds. And we must not forget that Magna Graecia bordered on Roman territory just as the Etruscan confederation did. These connections would later be extended still further with the conquest of Greece and Asia Minor. Greek and Etruscan influences certainly enhanced the more anthropomorphic character of the cult. Tradition has it that the first terra-cotta statue of Jupiter in the Capitoline Temple was the work of an Etruscan sculptor, Vulca of Veii (Pliny [the Elder] *Naturalis Historia* 35.157), and that the bronze Ceres as well as the decoration of the plebeian temple were executed by Greek artists, Damophiles and Gorgasus (ibid. 34.15). Once the deity took on human form, it was logical for it also to obtain a home. Thus the *fanum*, the holy place that was often a sacred grove (*lucus*), was replaced by the *aedes* (shrine), which was meant to be the dwelling place of the deity. Ordinarily the shrine would appear later on the site formerly consecrated to the god. Thus Livy 3.63.7 indicates that the shrine of Apollo (*aedes Apollonis*) was built in 431 B.C. in the Prata Flaminia on a spot that already bore the name "Apollo's enclosure" (*Apollinare*).

New deities were not simply brought in capriciously. It required a serious event that could challenge the Romans' confidence in their national pantheon, or at least make them seek additional help from some new deity. The way in which the Greek Apollo was introduced is highly instructive. It was not the god of the Muses, nor the sun god, that attracted the Romans' attention, nor was it the prophet-god who would later watch over the Sibylline Books (these titles were to be solemnly evoked in Horace's *Carmen Saeculare* in the time of Augustus). It was, rather (probably right after an epidemic), the healing god.[39] Thus, the oldest invocation recorded in

Juno Sospita. Rome, Vatican Museum. Photo Anderson-Giraudon.

the prayers of the vestals was addressed to the "physician," "Apollo Medice, Apollo Paean" (Macrobius *Saturnalia* 1.17.15). The circumstances surrounding the building of his first temple in the Prata Flaminia explain why he was brought in: a serious epidemic inspired the dedication of the shrine *pro valetudine populi* in honor of the god who bore the official name of Apollo Medicus (Livy 4.25.3; 40.51.6).

Of no less interest are the circumstances surrounding the arrival in Rome of the Etruscan deity Juno of Veii, at the beginning of the fourth century. This event merits a retrospective look. The war that the Romans waged on Veii lasted longer than anyone expected and gave rise to alarming rumors. (Like the siege of Troy, the siege of Veii was supposed to have lasted six years [Livy 5.22.8].) After certain miracles ("Lake Alba had risen to an incredibly high level with no rain or any other explanation": Livy 5.15.2), the Romans named Marcus Furius Camillus dictator. The new chief, whom the Latin historian calls *fatalis dux* (for the ruin of the Etruscan city), did not merely take measures of military reorganization; he made a decision by directly addressing the tutelary goddess in the following prayer: "Queen Juno, now residing in Veii, I beg you to follow me after our victory into our city that soon will be your own. There you shall receive a temple worthy of your majesty" (Livy 5.21.3). An anecdote told by the Latin historian underscores the kind disposition of the goddess: To the question, "Will you go to Rome, Juno?" asked by a young Roman, the goddess is said to have agreed with alacrity (Livy 5.22.5). Thus Rome became the seat of two Queen Junos. One sat on her throne in the Capitoline temple next to Jupiter as a national deity; the other was placed on the Aventine Hill as a deity of foreign origin.

We should also mention the entry into Rome of Cybele, the Oriental goddess, at the end of the third century B.C. This example not only proves that the Romans cast their sights beyond the Greek and Etruscan worlds, but also reveals a certain constancy in their ways of doing this. Following the dramatic vicissitudes of the Second Punic War, the Romans saw only toward 204 B.C. the hope of putting an end to more than fourteen years of military campaigns. The historian Livy notes the series of wondrous events that stimulated the religious consciousness: "Two suns had been seen; intermittent lights had flashed through the night; a track of fire was seen stretching from sunrise to sunset. Lightning had struck a door at Terracina, a door at Anagnia, and walls in many places; in the shrine of Juno Sospita at Lanuvium a terrible din could be heard" (Livy 29.14.3). Hope had been born as much as a year before, from the proclamation of an oracle taken from the Sibylline Books. It spelled out the conditions of reorganization: "On the day when a foreign enemy wages war in the land of Italy, it will be possible to defeat him and drive him out of Italy, if the Idaean Mother is brought from Pessinus to Rome" (Livy 29.10.5).

This innovation, which led the Romans to turn finally to an Asiatic deity of a primitive nature (with the black stone that was supposed to embody the deity and the Galli, the eunuch-priests who attended her cult), may really be explained by the Trojan clarification that transformed the savage Magna Mater of Mount Ida into a "grandmother of the Roman people." Ovid stressed this when he attributed to the goddess a miraculous intervention that overcame the reluctant Attalus, king of Phrygia: "It is I who wanted to be sought out; do not delay but send me forth, I beg you; Rome deserves to have all deities go there." Frightened by this terrifying voice, the king cries out: "Leave, and you shall always remain one of ours; Rome can be traced back to Phrygian ancestors" (Ovid *Fasti* 4.269–72).

The installation of Cybele in the temple of Victory on top of the Palatine in 204 (while she awaited the construction of her own temple in 191) came eleven years after Venus Erycina was established in a temple built on the Capitoline. The introduction of the two cults had been triggered by the military reversals suffered by the Romans at the hand of the Carthaginian enemy. Both cults referred back to the same Trojan legend. The order in which they were introduced can be explained quite naturally. The Romans had in fact already encountered Venus, the mother of their legendary forefather, Aeneas, during the First Punic War. The consul Lucius Junius did not hesitate to "recognize" her in the person of Aphrodite of Mount Eryx; he had successfully occupied Mount Eryx in 248 in a definitive move that led to final victory. Consequently, during the Second Punic War, the Romans *first* had recourse to Erycina, who could have appeared to them to be a sure guarantee of victory, in the face of the *same* enemy. Later, still on the same "Trojan" track, to increase their chances, they thought of welcoming among them the "Great Goddess" who enjoyed enormous prestige in the land of their "ancestors."[40]

These innovations at the end of the third century B.C. prove that Roman religion, so foreign to Greek mythology in its origins, submitted to the influence of syncretism. The Trojan legend was undoubtedly present in Etruria from the end of the sixth century B.C. (statuettes of Aeneas carrying Anchises were found in Veii) and penetrated the religion from then on, to the point of providing it with an ideological framework that was able to justify the importing of new cults.[41] It was not just any legend; it was to become a kind of national dogma with Julius Caesar, who claimed to be a descendant of Julus Ascanius, the son of Aeneas. According to this myth, the Romans descended from Aeneas were the privileged beneficiaries of a propitiatory Venus who intervened on their behalf so that they might receive the gods' grace, *pacem Veniamque deum*. All of Virgil's *Aeneid* is based on this theology, which promises the Romans descended from Aeneas divine blessings in all of their enterprises, provided they keep the *pietas* of their illustrious ancestor.

The success of the legend of Troy also proves that the Romans, who were far from giving in to any sort of syncretist fascination, knew how to be selective. It seems that they welcomed suggestions from abroad . . . *ad majorem gloriam populi Romani*. What is most significant about this is the way in which Augustus was able to exploit the Greek idea of the couple Ares-Aphrodite to serve Roman purposes. The emperor did indeed set aside a place of honor for this divine couple not only in the Pantheon (built in 25 B.C.) but also in the pediment of the Temple of Mars the Avenger (built in 2 B.C.). But he had no intention of retaining the Hellenistic symbolism (Aphrodite, the principle of Love, pacifying the principle of Discord). To the contrary, he wanted to "link the father of the founder of Rome" with "the mother of the nation of the descendants of Aeneas" in the service of a dynastic mission. Mars thus took on a "Julian" character as an *ultor parentis patriae* ("Avenger of Caesar, the father of the country"), while Venus, still remaining Aeneadum Genetrix, took on a more military character in order to draw closer to Mars. Thus, it was no longer the Hellenistic myth of their love but rather their common commitment to serve Rome and her emperors that gave Mars and Venus their raison d'être as a couple. This metamorphosis tells us a great deal about the Roman reaction to foreign influences.

III. The Groupings of Divinities in the Course of Roman History

It might be useful to recapitulate the different groupings of deities who have marked the course of the religious history of Rome. This panoramic view across time will be instructive for more than one reason. First, the archaic triad of Jupiter-Mars-Quirinus was replaced by the Capitoline triad of Jupiter-Juno-Minerva, which had its seat in the Capitoline temple that was built under the Tarquin kings and dedicated, according to tradition, by the consul M. Horatius in 509 B.C.[42]

As time passed, Greek influence gave rise to different associations of deities in the official liturgy. Such was the case for the triad of Ceres-Liber-Libera, whose temple was located outside the *pomerium* on the slopes of the Aventine.[43] Greek influence was especially manifested in the institution of the lectisternium, which consisted of offering a meal to the statues of deities that were exhibited on display beds. This presentation of the deities on *pulvinaria* (couches) that could be approached made way for a more emotional form of devotion, the supplication.

A persistent and deeply disturbing epidemic[44] resulted in the call for the celebration of the first lectisternium in 399 B.C.,

Jupiter and Juno. Pompeii. Naples. Photo Alinari.

after a consultation of the Sibylline Books by the *duom viri sacris faciundis.* It grouped Apollo and Latona (his mother), Hercules and Diana, and Mercury and Neptune into heterogeneous pairs.

Even more dramatic circumstances, the disasters suffered at the hands of Hannibal, provoked the celebration of the second lectisternium in 217 B.C. For the first time in their history, the Romans offered sacrificial meals to a dozen deities, six gods and six goddesses, grouped into couples according to the Hellenic pattern, in the following order:[45] Jupiter and Juno; Neptune and Minerva; Mars and Venus; Apollo and Diana; Vulcan and Vesta; Mercury and Ceres.

Though this ceremony was celebrated in Rome[46] only once, it was the source of the idea of constituting an official circle of twelve principal deities. These *di consentes*[47] eventually had their own statues made of gilded bronze; these were placed, each in its own niche, inside the Portico that was built at the far western end of the Forum at the foot of the Capitol.[48]

What can these different groupings tell us?[49] If we consider the two oldest triads, we are struck by two facts. First, Jupiter remained the keystone of both the archaic and the Capitoline triad. He was hardly touched by the wave of assimilation, except to the extent that his associate during the second lectisternium was Juno, who was already one of his Capitoline consorts. Second, only one god bore a Latin name that did not yield to any syncretist operation: Quirinus (which is connected with *Quirites,* "citizens"). He has an Umbrian homologue but no Greek equivalent.[50]

On the list of the first lectisternium, half the names are of purely Greek origin (Apollo, Latona, Hercules), and the other half are Latin names that mask Hellenic deities: Diana (Artemis), Mercury (Hermes), and Neptune (Poseidon). Apollo is at the head of the list: a healing god, he was the first to be invoked during this period of epidemic.

As for the second lectisternium, it gives evidence of a concern for hierarchical groupings (which was alien to the first) in that it separated out twelve principal deities from the pantheon. The best proof of this is that Jupiter, who was absent from the first lectisternium, could not fail to be present in the second, where he occupied the expected place: the first. It is likely that the dignity of her role as Capitoline consort counted in favor of Minerva, who occupied the second rank in association with Neptune. Conversely, Latona was eliminated, her single claim to fame as "the mother of Apollo" being insufficient to win her a place in the Roman cult. Apollo may have lost "his mother," but he did regain "his sister," namely, Artemis, whose Latin counterpart was Diana.

The Greek inspiration of this list that pairs off gods and goddesses into couples is obvious. Thus one could see behind the first four couples Zeus-Hera, Poseidon-Athena, Ares-Aphrodite, and Apollo-Artemis. In the case of the final two couples, in the absence of any cultic or mythological link they can justify their presence in Rome as well as in Greece, as Georges Dumézil points out,[51] one by virtue of a common denominator (fire: Vulcan and Vesta, or Hephaestus and Hestia), and the other by virtue of related activities (commerce and grain: Mercury and Ceres, or Hermes and Demeter).

A word is in order about what is meant by "a couple." Although the Greek model may at first glance suggest marital bonds for Jupiter and Juno, and erotic bonds for Mars and Venus, no such thing could possibly apply to the other paired deities. The pairing of Neptune (Poseidon) and Minerva (Athena) evokes their rivalry in the naming of Athens (Servius Danielis *ad Georg.* 1.12); the association of Apollo and Diana (Artemis) is based on the genealogical ties that link brother and sister.

The pattern of mythological coupling was used in Rome to acclimatize the idea of association. This statement is valid not only for the divine pairs who are unknown to the plots of Greek mythology (Vulcan and Vesta; Mercury and Ceres); it also applies to the cases that at first glance seem to be the most thoroughly marked by Hellenism. It seems that the liturgical presentation of the lectisternium of the twelve gods made it possible to shed new light on an old truth. Jupiter and Juno had been king and queen of the city since they took their places side by side in the Capitoline temple, toward the end of the sixth century B.C.

As for Mars and Venus, in Rome they did not form a couple in the strict sense of the term. Mars was the old warrior god who presided over Roman arms, while Venus appeared more and more as the tutelary power of the nation of the descendants of Aeneas. The Greek precedent seems simply to have suggested to the Romans the idea of associating the two essential characters in their history: Aeneas, the founder of the nation, and Romulus, the founder of the city.[52]

Another problem concerns the selective list of the dozen deities of the second lectisternium. What about those who are missing? First there is Hercules, who had been one of the six deities worshiped during the first lectisternium. With great insight, Georges Dumézil has recalled the case of deities who had been "demoted" after military catastrophes: "except for the three great Capitoline divinities, the ceremonies after Trasimeno do not honor by name any of the divinities invoked after Trebbia; the new disaster has lowered them in rank, as if they had demonstrated their indifference or their inadequacy. An appeal is now made to other divinities, to Mens rather than to Fortuna, to Mars rather than to Genius, to Venus rather than to Juventas. Hercules' elimination itself is perhaps an expression of this same movement, not so much a demotion as a certified report of his incapacity to adjust to the circumstances."[53]

Besides limiting the selection to the twelve privileged gods, the lectisternium had even greater significance. All the chosen deities henceforth had a right to the city in the Greek world as in the Latin world. They were worthy to be honored with the zeal appropriate to the *ritus graecus.* They were important to all the people, men and women, in all their temples, who prayed to the gods to deliver them from their afflictions. Livy (26.9.7) describes the dramatic supplication that took place in 211 B.C. when Rome was at the mercy of Hannibal: "The wailing of women was heard not only in private houses, but everywhere matrons came to lie down across public ways; they ran around the shrines, swept the altars with their loosened hair, fell to their knees, raised their hands (*supinas manus*) to the god of heaven, and prayed to them to wrest the city of Rome from the hands of the enemy and to save the Roman mothers and their little children from violence."

Latona and Apollo under the palm tree of Delos. Amphora. Paris, Musée du Louvre. Photo Giraudon.

One other consequence resulted. These innovations indirectly stamped as archaic the deities who were resistant to syncretist assimilations. They did not disappear from the liturgy, thanks to Roman conservatism. But many were soon to become "fossilized," following the example of the Rex Sacrorum ("the king of the sacrifices"), who when political kingship collapsed had been perpetuated for no reason other than to avoid doing a disservice to the gods.[54]

First was Quirinus, whom the economic and social evolution of the city had already eliminated at the time of the Capitoline triad. Another was Janus, the god of beginnings, the god of transitions, who played a specific role in the Roman liturgy. Another was Genius, who enjoyed a revival only because of the initiative taken by Augustus. Another was Silvanus, the sylvan god who was related to Faunus. Another was Anna Perenna, who survived because of the festival that marked the passage from the old year to the new year. Finally there were the Penates, the gods who watched over supplies, and the Lares, the gods who protected cultivated land and who were particularly worshiped at the hearth of the Roman family.

Each of these gods corresponds to an original aspect of the divine representation of the Romans. They belong to the category of gods that are "difficult to pronounce in Greek," to borrow an expression from Dionysius of Halicarnassus (2.50.3). Witness the term "Lares," which for lack of an appropriate term was improperly translated by the Greeks as *hērōes* (for example, in Dion. Hal. 4.14.3), whereas Rome, recognizing only gods and men, was unaware of the intermediate being, the hero.[55]

Consequently, what had been challenged by the innovations of the end of the third century B.C. was the irreducible originality of the Roman pantheon. Some deities were relegated to the shadows. Others lost their onomastic privilege and were henceforth translatable into a "foreign" language. If their range of influence stood to gain by it, their identity was, on the other hand, exposed to syncretist overlays. One merely has to read Ovid's *Fasti* to get a measure of the ground covered in the first century A.D.[56] In this sense, the end of the third century B.C. corresponds to a decisive turning point in the religious history of Rome.

The following is a summary of the different groupings of deities in Rome. The groupings of a ritual nature are in roman type; the groupings of literary fabrication are in italics. I. The archaic triad: Jupiter-Mars-Quirinus. II. The Capitoline triad: Jupiter-Juno-Minerva (see Livy 1.38.7; 1.55.1–6). III. The triad Ceres-Liber-Libera (in 493 B.C.; see Dion. Hal. 6.17.2). IV. The first lectisternium of 399 B.C.: Apollo-Latona, Hercules-Diana, Mercury-Neptune (see Livy 5.13.4). V. The lectisternium of the twelve great gods of 217 B.C.: Jupiter-Juno, Neptune-Minerva, Mars-Venus, Apollo-Diana, Vulcan-Vesta, Mercury-Ceres (see Livy 22.10.9). VI. The list of twelve agricultural deities: *Juppiter-Tellus, Sol-Luna, Ceres-Liber, Robigus-Flora, Minerva-Venus, Lympha-Bonus Eventus* (see Varro *De Re Rustica* 1.1.4–7). VII. The list of twelve deities as arranged by Virgil (*Georgics* 1.5–25), Caesar being proposed as a thirteenth: *Sol-Luna (= clarissima mundi lumina), Liber-Ceres, Fauni-Dryads, Neptune, Aristaeus (= cultor nemorum), Pan-Minerva, Triptolemus (= unci puer monstrator aratri), Silvanus,* and at verse 25: *Caesar.* VIII. The list of twenty *Di Selecti* of Varro (cf. Augustine *De civitate Dei* 7.2): *Janus, Juppiter, Saturn, Genius, Mercury, Apollo, Mars, Vulcan, Neptune, Sol, Orcus, Liber pater, Tellus, Ceres, Juno, Luna, Diana, Minerva, Venus, Vesta.*

R.S./t.l.f.

NOTES

The abridged references refer to bibliographic collections. See the articles "Roman Religion" above, and "The Religion of the Roman Republic" below.

1. Text cited by G. Dumézil, *La religion romaine archaïque* (2d ed., 1974), 36.

2. The book *Roman Dynamism* (1947) by H. Wagenvoort is the translation by H. J. Rose of the book published originally in the Netherlands under the title *Imperium: Studien over het manabegrip in zede en taal der Romeinen* (1941). Note that the Dutch title makes explicit reference to the idea of mana.

3. G. Dumézil, *La religion romaine archaïque,* 2d ed., pp. 36–48.

4. It was only from the Augustan Age that the poets had occasionally used—by metonymy—*numina* in place of *dei;* but the older usage was not lost, as is attested by the Virgilian expression *quo numine laeso* (*Aeneid* 1, 8), which means "which will (of Juno) having been violated": cf. the exegesis of Th. Birt, *Zu Vergil Aeneis* I, 8: *quo numine laeso, B PhW,* 38 (1918): cols. 212–16 (ibid., 46–47).

5. H. Wagenvoort, *Wesenszüge altrömischer Religion,* in *Aufstieg und Niedergang der römischen Welt,* 1, 2, pp. 352ff.

6. *L. Accii tragoediarum fragmenta,* ed. Q. Franchella (Bologna 1968), § 596 (= 2d ed. Ribbeck, *Scaenicae Romanorum poesis fragmenta,* § 646 = H. Warmington, ed., *Remains of Old Latin,* 2:546, § 650).

7. Cf. Livy, 8.9.6.

8. The formula *D(is) M(anibus)* became usual on the epitaphs. It is followed by either the genitive or the dative of the form designating the deceased.

9. On this problem, see *Le culte des souverains dans l'Empire romain . . . Entretiens préparés et présidés par W. den Boer* (Geneva 1973), as well as the review by J. Béranger, *Gnomon* 48 (1976): 379–84. What are we to think of the *deus* of the first *Bucolic* of Virgil—a title which a shepherd gives to his benefactor Octavian? The shepherd promises to worship his god. The religious aspect is thus revealed here more than in the fervent eulogy of literary inspiration which is addressed by Lucretius (5.8) to Epicurus: "deus ille fuit, deus, inclute Memmi."

10. Tacitus, *Ann.* 15.74.3 (example cited by J. Béranger, *l.l.,* 383).

11. Pliny, *Natural History* (*N.H.*) 12.3: *Haec* (sc. *arbores et silvae*) *fuere numinum templa priscoque ritu simplicia rura etiam nunc deo praecellentem arborem dicant. Nec magis auro fulgentia atque ebore simulacra quam lucos et in iis silentia adoramus.*

12. Varro cited by Augustine, *City of God* (*C.D.*) 4.31.

13. Some have wanted to explain the absence of anthropomorphism by a "technical incapacity" of the Romans. This hypothesis does not stand up well to recent conclusions of archeology which have found figurines in the oldest tombs of Latium (these testify at least to the ability to represent the human figure); cf. E. Gjerstad, *Early Rome,* 4, 2 (Lund 1966), 579–81. See the observations of P. Boyancé, *REA,* 57 (1955): 66–67, and of G. Dumézil, *La religion romaine archaïque,* 2d ed., pp. 44ff.

14. Cf. Livy 5.32.6.

15. Cf. Festus, p. 354, 28 L.

16. The ancient etymology which had explained the name "Faunus" by *favere* (Servius *ad Georg.* 1.10) has been contested by the moderns, but perhaps we may return to it: cf. Latte, *R.R.G.,* 83, n. 3. In that case, one must understand the expression "Faunus" ("the propitious god") in the same way as "Di Manes," as a euphemism of propitiatory value.

17. Cf. G. Wissowa, *Ruk*^{2}, 216 (with indications of ancient sources); G. Dumézil, *La religion romaine archaïque,* 2d ed., p. 355.

18. Virgil *Georgics* 3.1 and 294.

19. Cf. G. Dumézil, *La religion romaine archaïque,* 2d ed., pp. 385–87: The Pales of the Parilia is concerned with small livestock, while the two Pales of 7 July are concerned with sheep and cows.

20. Varro, cited by Servius *ad Georg.* 3.1.

21. Wissowa (*Ruk*^{2}, 38, n. 1) has commented on the principal passages: Actes des Arvales (*CIL,* 6, 2099 2, 1, 3; 2104, 2; 2107, 9); Cato *De agricultura* 139, etc.

22. As G. Dumézil notes (*La religion romaine archaïque,* 2d ed., p. 59, n. 2), the case of Macrobius, *Saturnalia* 3.9.7, is different: *Si deus, si dea est cui populus civitasque Carthaginiensis est in tutela* (in the formula of the *evocatio*) corresponds to a known Latinism: "every one of the gods and goddesses who protect the people and the city of Carthage . . ."

23. The reference on the inscription of the shield of the Capitol, noted also by Servius (*ad Aen.* 2.351: *Genio Romae, sive mas sive femina),* calls on an analogous commentary. To the extent to which "Genius" can only be a masculine, the *sive mas sive femina* cannot apply to the divinized Rome. God or goddess? In ignorance, the formula allows either hypothesis.

24. This is the classic example—and, moreover, unique in the annals—of the transfer of a cult of foreign origin to Rome. Toward the end of the siege of the Etruscan city of Veii (in 396 B.C.), the Roman dictator M. Furius Camillus ensured the good graces of the tutelary goddess by the *evocatio*—a prayer in which he asked Juno Regina to abandon her city in exchange for a "temple worthy of her grandeur" in Rome. Cf. above, this article. As we know, the *pomerium* is the sacred frontier that delimits the zone of urban auspices in opposition to the *ager effatus* (= the adjacent ground made available for other auspices); the pomerial line was indicated by a series of cippus columns: cf. Aulus Gellius 13.14.1; Varro *L.L.* 5.143.

25. Cf. the argument made against Latte, *R.R.G.,* pp. 43 and 45, n. 1, by G. Dumézil, *La religion romaine archaïque,* 2d ed., pp. 108–10, an argument that bears on not only the meaning but also the antiquity of the formula.

26. G. Dumézil, *La religion romaine archaïque,* 2d ed., p. 110, n. 1, has noted a text of Ovid (*Metamorphosis* 15.861–70) in which the same typology appears, recalling the conjoint formula *Indigetes* and *Novensiles.*

27. Virgil *G.* 1.498. We note also the cult of Jupiter Indiges at Lavinium (Livy 1.2.6); the cult of Sol Indiges, which, very important at the origin, is entered in the calendar on the date of 11 December (for documentation, cf. Latte, *R.R.G.,* pp. 44 and 73). Pliny's reference to a *locus Solis Indigetis* near the Numicus at Lavinium (*N.H.* 3.56; for this reading of the manuscripts instead of the correction of Barbarus *lucus Jovis Ind.,* see Castagnoli, *Lavinium,* 1, p. 93, n. 10), as well as the comments of Dionysius of Halicarnassus (1.55.2), confirm the antiquity of the cult.

28. J. Bayet, *Histoire politique et psychologique de la religion romaine* (2d ed., Paris 1969), has rightly insisted on this aspect.

29. This detail of the bull "white as snow" offered to Jupiter Latiaris is due to Arnobius *Adversus nationes* 2.68 (*In Albano antiquitus monte nullos alios licebat quam nivei tauros immolare candoris*). The same author indicates that later a senatorial decision also authorized animals with red (*rufulos*) hair. If the account of Arnobius is correct, the sacrifice on Mount Alban departed from the ritual pattern that required castrated animals for Jupiter: cf. Ateius Labeo, cited by Macrobius (*S.* 3.10.4). It is true that according to Virgil (*G.* 2.146–48) and Servius (*ad locum*) the bull was also sacrificed to Capitoline Jupiter by the winners on the day of the ceremony of triumph.

30. The suspension of all war during the *feriae Latinae,* as well as the *communio sacrorum,* has suggested to Latte (*R.R.G.,* p. 145) the idea of a possible influence of the Greek amphictyony, which might have been transmitted by an Etruscan intermediary: the Etruscan confederation of the "twelve cities," which met near the sanctuary of Voltumna, located near the Volsinii (Livy 4.23.5; 4.25.7, etc.).

31. Servius *ad Aen.* 7.515.

32. In an inscription (*CIL,* 1, 2^2, 2444), Diana of Aricia is called *Diana af louco* ("Diana of the sacred forest").

33. Cato, *Orig. frag., H.R.F.,* 58, P. Cf. Festus, p. 128, 15 L; *Manius Egerius lucum Nemorensem Dianae consecravit* ("Manius Egerius consecrated to Diana the sacred forest of Nemi").

34. The statute of the cult, which served for those that followed as a model for other foundations, made an allusion to an altar: *lex arae Dianae in Aventino* ("regulation of the altar of Diana on the Aventine": *CIL,* 3, 1933).

35. Different interpretations have been proposed by G. Wissowa (*Ruk*^{2}, 250–51), L. Latte (*R.R.G.,* 173), and G. Dumézil (*La religion romaine archaïque,* 2d ed., 412–13).

36. Regarding the cult of Diana and the effacement of the Latin goddess under Roman hegemony, cf. R. Schilling, "Une victime des vicissitudes politiques: La Diane latine," *Coll. Latomus,* 70 (= *Hommages à Jean Bayet*), 1964, 650–67; reprinted with the same title in *R.C.D.R.*

37. Cf. H. Le Bonniec, *Le culte de Cérès à Rome des origines à la fin de la république* (Paris 1958), 277–311. For an opposing view, see A. Alföldi, *Il Santuario federale latino di Diana sull'Aventino e il tempio di Ceres, S.M.S.R.*, 32 (1961): 21–39. (This scholar moves the date of the foundation of the temple and of its political role after the reform of the Decemvirs back to the second half of the fifth century B.C.)

38. Cf. R. Schilling, *Les Castores romains à la lumière des traditions indo-européennes,* Collection Latomus (= Hommages à Georges Dumézil) (Brussels 1960); reprinted with the same title in *R.C.D.R.*

39. Cf. J. Gagé, *Apollon romain* (Paris 1955), 158ff.; 167.

40. Cf. Robert Schilling, *La religion romaine de Vénus* (Paris 1954), 242–66.

41. Regarding the statuettes of Aeneas and Anchises from Veii, the proposed date varies from the sixth to the fourth century B.C. It seems reasonable to accept at the latest the beginning of the fifth century. See, in particular, A. Alföldi, *Die trojanischen Urahnen der Römer* (Basel 1957). See, most recently, W. Fuchs, *Die Bildgeschichte der Flucht des Aeneas, A.N.R.W.*, 1, 4 (1973), 615–32.

42. With regard to the line of continuity that exists between the two triads, see the article "Roman Religion," above.

43. Cf. above, this article. The cult of Ceres is classed by Festus (p. 268, 31 L.) among the *sacra peregrina* ("foreign cults"). Although Indo-European in its structure, the triad here seems influenced by a Greek model. For a discussion, see H. Le Bonniec, *Le culte de Cérès à Rome,* 277–311; for an opposing view, see A. Alföldi, *Early Rome and the Latins,* 95–100.

44. Cf. Livy 5.13.4–6. This Hellenic rite, which came from the Etruscan town of Caere, was repeated four times consecutively in the course of the following years: cf. Wissowa, *Ruk*[2], p. 422 and n. 7.

45. An undifferentiated list is furnished by Ennius, *Annales,* 60–61 (ed. Warmington): *Juno Vesta Minerva Ceres Diana Venus Mars Mercurius Jovis Neptunus Vulcanus Apollo.* The hierarchical order is indicated by Livy (22.10.9; cf. also 22.9.10).

46. We know that the lectisternium of the twelve divinities must have inspired in Octavian one day the idea of organizing a joyous masquerade—the *cena dōdekatheos*—in the course of which the twelve guests were disguised as gods and goddesses (Suetonius *Aug.* 70).

47. The twelve *di consentes* of the Forum are cited by Varro (*R.R.* 1.1.4). The expression is unique: the term *consentes* ("who are together") was assimilated by the Latins to *consentientes* ("who decide in accord").

48. Cf. G. Lugli, *Roma antica: Il centro monumentale* (Rome 1946), 114–15.

49. We have retained here only the divine groupings that have a ritual existence. However, the number twelve influenced the group of twelve "agricultural divinities" imagined by Varro (*De re rustica* 1.1.4–6), as well as the semireligious, semimythological list of Virgil (*G.* 1.5–20). Elsewhere, Varro, cited by Augustine (*C.D.* 7.2), had drawn up a list of twenty principal divinities (*deos selectos*).

50. Regarding the equivalence of the Latin *Quirinus* and the Umbrian *Vofiono-,* see G. Dumézil, *La religion romaine archaïque,* 2d ed., p. 161 and n. 3.

51. Cf. ibid., p. 475.

52. These phrases reproduce a part of the commentary of my book *R.R.V.*, 207–8.

53. G. Dumézil, *La religion romaine archaïque,* 2d ed., p. 475.

54. Cf. Festus, p. 422 L.: "He who performs the ceremonies that the kings used to perform is named Sacrificulus Rex (or Rex Sacrorum)."

55. The word *heros,* copied from the Greek, appears only later, in the language of the poets, for example, in Virgil.

56. Cf. R. Schilling, "Ovide interprète de la religion romaine," *R.E.L.* 46 (1969): 222–35; reprinted in *R.C.D.R.*, same title.

Roman Sacrifice

In its intrinsic meaning, the term sacrifice (*sacrificium*) indicates that something is voluntarily taken away by man from the profane world to be offered to the gods (*sacrum facere*). To what end? Probably, in accordance with the worldview at the origin, the purpose was to comfort the gods, who in the Roman conception were allies of mankind. The Romans were tied to the gods by bonds of reciprocity defined by the notion of *pietas,* by virtue of which men had to honor (*colere*) the gods who in turn owed men protection.

Nothing illuminates the means and ends of sacrifice better than the accompanying prayer that a Roman peasant addressed to a particular god. In this case, Cato's formulation (*De Agricultura* 134) lists the arrangements that should be made to offer a propitiatory sacrifice to Ceres, the goddess of growth, before the harvest. First, the sacrifice could not be limited to Ceres alone. According to the rules of this polytheistic hierarchy, one must first address Janus, the god of beginnings, and then the sovereign god, Jupiter (the text also mentions Juno, a rather suspect addition). Once these preliminaries have been attended to, the offering to Ceres consists of the entrails of a sow and a libation of wine. This is already a Roman innovation, namely, that the part set aside for the god when a blood sacrifice is performed should be the *exta,* or entrails, of the animal, including the heart (*cor*), lungs (*pulmones*), liver (*jecur*), and gallbladder (*fel*).[1]

The wording of the prayer to Jupiter contains all the characteristic elements that recur in the other formulas: *Juppiter, te hoc ferto obmovendo bonas preces precor, uti sies volens propitius mihi liberisque meis domo familiaeque meae mactus hoc ferto* (Jupiter, in making this offering to you, I pray with good prayers that you watch over me and be gracious unto me, my children, my house, and all my household; may this offering be a comfort to you). This utterance is as clear as it is precise. He names the intended god, the offering (the *fertum* is a kind of cake), the legitimacy of the request (*bonas preces*), and the purpose of the sacrifice. Among all the specific terms in this text, so florid with its archaic language,[2] we should remark on *mactus,* which the ancients interpreted in the sense of *magis auctus;*[3] it seems to reflect the old concept that divine power had to be "comforted" with the sacrifice.

Thus, the sacrifice in the beginning seems to have consisted essentially in "sustaining" the god. This idea is confirmed by the epithet *dapalis* that is applied to Jupiter when he becomes the recipient of a meal (*daps*) that consisted of a "jug" of wine (*urna vini*) and an offering of sacred flour with the value of one *as* (a Roman coin or weight), *assara pecunia.*[4] The celebrant and the participants did not remain strangers to the ceremony, since a part of the food that was not consecrated was distributed for the use of laymen and consumed by the participants.[5]

Although the *daps* represents a sacrifice at the family level, the *epulum* corresponds to a more solemn meal organized and subsidized by the state. The *epulum Jovis* was offered to Jupiter every year on 13 November, on the Capitoline, starting at the end of the third century B.C. According to the description provided by Valerius Maximus (2.1.2), "The god was invited to take his place on a couch, Juno and Minerva on chairs." This *epulum* thus dealt with the Capitoline triad,

Sacrificial scene (relief). In the background: facade of the temple of the Capitoline Jupiter and wall topped with statues of men and animals fighting. In the foreground: Emperor Marcus Aurelius, *capite velato,* assisted by the *flamen Dialis* wearing his *apex* cap; he pours a libation on the flame of the tripod altar. Behind him, a bearded man wearing a toga and a crown of laurels, probably representing the senate. In front of him, a *camillus* holding a casket of incense (*acerra*) and a pipe player; the head of the victim hovers over them. To the right, sacrificers, one holding an ax, the other a jar (*situla*). Rome, Museo dei Conservatori. Photo Alinari-Giraudon.

and gods and goddesses conformed to the prevailing customs of the men and women of the times. The word *epulo* was hardly ever used as an epithet of Jupiter, which would have resulted in an expression symmetrical to *Juppiter Dapalis,* but it did serve to designate the priests specially charged with the responsibility to celebrate official sacrifices in order to relieve the pontifex; this college of priests was known as the *septemviri epulones.*

What kinds of food could one offer the gods? Particular preferences aside, the following list was drawn up by Verrius Flaccus, a great scholar in the time of Augustus, and preserved in a summary by Festus:[6] "commodities that can be offered in sacrifice: grain, pearl barley, wine, leavened bread, dried figs, pork, lamb, cheese, mutton, bran, sesame and oil, fish with scales except angelfish (a saltwater fish also known as monkfish)."

In addition to these foods, the firstfruits of the harvest were offered to the appropriate protective deities, for instance, the first must (*sacrima*) was offered to Liber Pater. We should also point out that the list drawn up by Festus is not complete. It mentions cheese, but it omits milk, for example, which was an older offering than wine: lukewarm milk was a favorite of one of the oldest deities, Pales, the goddess of shepherds and their flocks, whose festival, the Parilia (21 April), coincided with the anniversary of the founding of Rome.[7]

Alongside these bloodless sacrifices are blood sacrifices that can be traced back to equally ancient times.[8] The usual victims are animals belonging to the pig, sheep, or cow families. Perhaps we should distinguish between what are called *hostia*[9] (expiatory victims to appease the wrath of the gods) and *victima* (victims offered as signs of gratitude). But these fine distinctions seem to have disappeared in historical times.

On the other hand, the Roman liturgy seems to have been subject to precise general rules. The animal has to be of a certain age that varies depending on the circumstances. Thus, we can distinguish among victims that still suckle (*lactentes*), two-year-olds (*bidentes*), and adult victims (*hostiae majores*). Normally a god demands a male victim and a goddess, a female.[10] By the same principle of analogy, a sky god requires a light animal, and a netherworld god a dark one. But exceptions to these rules do occur.

There are particular sets of rules for certain deities. Jupiter is to receive a castrated animal,[11] whereas Apollo, Neptune, and Mars demand an intact male, such as a bull.[12] Mars has the honor of being the recipient of a triple offering that groups the representatives of the three animal species: boar, ram, and bull, designated by the term *suovetaurilia.*[13]

How does the sacrifice actually proceed? First it presupposes certain conditions on the part of the celebrant, who must be in a state of ritual purity. For example, he cannot perform his duties if a member of his family has just died, making the family *funesta* (in mourning).[14] Wearing a toga that is rolled up into a *cinctus Gabinus* (freeing the arms), the celebrant washes his hands in a bowl (*malluvium*) and dries them with a towel (*mantele*). So as not to be disturbed during the ceremony, he covers his head with a tail of his toga. He thus appears *capite velato,* which to the ancients was a peculiarly Roman attitude, in contrast with the uncovered head, *capite aperto,* of the Greek ritual.[15]

Among the sacrifices, some are performed within the family circle, for instance, the *Lemuria* which the paterfamilias celebrates according to an archaic liturgy that aims at expelling the *Lemures,* evil spirits, from the house.[16] Others are celebrated within the social group as constituted by the curia, among them the Fornacalia celebrated in honor of Fornax, the goddess of ovens, during the roasting of grain;[17] or the Fordicidia, the sacrifice of a pregnant cow (*forda*) to the goddess Earth, who is supposed to be full of seed on that day (15 April).[18] The most solemn sacrifices are the *publica sacra* "which are offered for the people at the expense of the state."[19]

These sacrifices require a ceremonial regulated by an ordering of several phases. First of all, the *probatio,* a kind of admission test—the chosen animal must be beyond reproach: it must be appropriate to the deity and have no physical defect; it must conform to precise norms. Thus, as Pliny the Elder reminds us, "a calf is admitted only if its tail reaches the knucklebone; if it is any shorter, the sacrifice will not please the gods."[20]

The victim is adorned with boughs (*verbenae*), and its head is decorated with white or scarlet headbands (*infulae*). Often if it is a cow or an ox, its horns are gilded (*taurus auratus et bos femina aurata,* in the liturgy of the Arval Brethren, designates a bull or heifer with golden horns);[21] cattle or pigs wear a kind of cover (*dorsuale*) on their backs, but not sheep, which are offered with their thick fleece (*altilanei*), which has never been sheared.[22]

Thus adorned, the victim is led near the altar (*ara*), in front of the temple; next to the altar is placed a movable hearth (*foculus*), often garnished with turf (*caespite*)[23] and intended to receive the preliminary libations of wine and incense.[24]

An order goes out calling for silence (*Favete linguis!*)[25] while a flutist (*tibicen*) "is heard trying to cover up all other sounds." The celebrant then proceeds to the *immolatio:* The victim's head is dusted with *mola salsa* (loose flour mixed with salt, prepared by the vestals),[26] an operation that is completed with a libation of wine.[27] The victim is then stripped of all its trappings, the *dorsuale* and the *infulae.* The celebrant passes his knife along the animal's backbone from head to tail. This symbolic gesture of possession completes the act of the *consecratio.*

Then the celebrant recites the formulaic prayer that an assistant reads to him "to avoid any omission or inversion."[28] The moment of death has arrived. It is achieved most often through the mediation of the celebrant's assistants. One assistant sacrificer (*victimarius* or *popa*) asks, *Agone?* ("Shall I go ahead?" meaning "Shall I perform the sacrifice?") He then strikes the forehead of the victim with a hammer or an ax, probably to daze it. Another assistant, the *cultrarius,* stabs the jugular vein with a knife (*culter*). The gushing blood is collected and spread over the altar. If the animal ever resists in the course of these operations, or worse yet, escapes (*hostia effugia*), it portends bad luck.

If the proceeding goes according to plan, the body of the animal is opened up to allow an inspection of its internal organs (*inspicere exta*). This examination is only to make certain that the organs are in good condition to ensure the approval of the gods (*litatio*). Thus, we find in the minutes of the Arval Brethren the elliptic expression: *hostiae litationem inspexerunt* ("they examine the victim for the purpose of *litatio*").[29] This procedure conforms to the prescriptions of the Roman liturgy and is therefore alien to the divinatory character of the consultation of the *exta,* which was introduced into Rome through Etruscan haruspicy.

If the results of the examination are good, the celebrant records the *litatio,* or the approval given by the gods for his sacrifice. If they are not good (if, for example, the heart or part of the liver is missing),[30] the sacrifice has to begin again, substituting a new victim (*hostia succidanea*) for the first animal. Roman tenacity is evident in a decision by the senate (in 176 B.C.) that enjoined the consuls who had failed to get a *litatio* (inspection had revealed a liver in a state of total decomposition) "to start sacrificing again with adult victims until they obtained the god's approval" (*usque ad litationem*).[31]

Marcus Aurelius offering a sacrifice. Bas-relief. Rome, Palazzio dei Conservatori. Photo Alinari-Giraudon.

Once the *litatio* is obtained, the next phase can proceed. The *exta* are removed from the victim; they are then dusted with *mola salsa;* a few additional pieces are thrown in, *augmenta* or *magmenta.*[32] These supplements must represent the rest of the victim. Both *exta* and *augmenta* are then cooked in a pot (*olla extaris*). This is the way they are ordinarily cooked in the historical period, but tradition also mentions broiling the *exta* on a skewer.[33]

The *exta* are then cut up (except in sacrifices of lustration offered by the censors).[34] These *prosecta,* or *prosicies,* can now be offered to the god. The whole offering is then burned on top of the altar that has already been sprinkled with the blood. *Exta porricere,* or *dare,* is the name of this operation. The ritual of the Arval Brethren uses a more suggestive expression, namely, *exta reddere:* in fact it is a matter of "rendering unto" the deity the consecrated part that is due that deity.[35] The celebrant and his assistants are entitled to consume the *viscera,* or "meat,"[36] which is set aside for profane use.

Roman liturgy thus clearly distinguishes the sacred part from the profane part. It understands the blood and the entrails to be the parts reserved for the gods, because these organs are reputed to be the seats of life itself, according to the principle defined by Trebatius: *sola anima deo sacratur* ("the soul alone is consecrated to the god").[37] Roman sacrifice differs fundamentally from Greek sacrifice, which calls for an *undifferentiated* distribution of all parts of the victim between the god and the worshipers,[38] not to mention the trick of Prometheus, who, to make matters even worse, sought to deceive the gods.[39]

But Rome also witnessed the *ritus graecus,* the Greek liturgy that was used notably for the cult of Hercules at the Ara Maxima,[40] where participants in the sacrificial offering were also permitted to consume the *exta.* On the other hand, the god could receive "all kinds of food and drink" (*Herculi autem omnia esculenta posculenta*).[41] The distinction was thus no longer made between the *exta,* reserved for the god (*deo dicata*), and the *viscera profana,* the profane meat left for consumption by the assistants. The vocabulary used in the liturgy at the Ara Maxima was specific: to Hercules of the Ara Maxima went an offering of the *decuma,* a tithe of grain that the god was supposed to have obtained for his followers; *pollucere,* "to offer," could apply both to the god and to men. In Plautus,[42] *polluctum* designates a lavish festival that delights both the god and the happy guests.

It is only by chance that we know of another form of sacrifice in Rome, namely, the holocaust, which consisted of burning the victim whole. In the *Aeneid,*[43] Aeneas offers to Pluto, "the king of the Styx," bulls burned whole. The practice of the holocaust is mentioned only in the minutes of the secular games. During the games celebrated by Augustus in 17 B.C., nine ewe lambs were apparently sacrificed to the Parcae (*deis Moeris*),[44] according to the Greek ritual (*Achivo ritu*), and similarly at the secular games of Septimus Severus in A.D. 204, a sow was sacrificed whole to the goddess Earth (*Terrae Matri*).[45]

These sacrificial forms of foreign origin highlight even more the originality of the Roman liturgy, which was never, however, completely free of contamination. Quite early, Etruscan haruspices practiced side by side with the Roman celebrant, when simply reporting the *litatio* was not felt to be sufficient, but curiosity to know the future demanded the practice of the divinatory consultation of the *exta*.

Cato's formularies and the minutes of the Arval Brethren preserved the original ritual of the Roman sacrifice most faithfully. In the final analysis, what is striking in this liturgy is its concern for efficacy, its temperance, and its precision. In order not to fail in its purpose, the liturgy multiplied its prescriptions for the dress, gestures, and utterances of the celebrant. For the same reasons, it strove to preserve the serenity of the ceremony through a propitiatory silence and the ritual sound of the flute.

The sacrifice was invariably accompanied by a prayer that addressed the deity by name, detailing the terms of the request. Frozen ritualism, one might claim. Certainly such a cautious framework had a rigidity about it. This is especially true when we think of the *supplicationes* surrounding the lectisternia, which gave free expression to a more passionate and tumultuous devotion. Livy several times evokes the spectacle of "Romans rushing into every shrine, women prostrated everywhere, sweeping the temples with their hair."[46] The senate itself encouraged this kind of devotion . . . in times of crisis.

But the official liturgy guarded its rights. If there was indeed ritualism,[47] this ritualism can be explained, in the last analysis, by a deep concern for *pietas,* the piety that Cicero (*De Natura Deorum* 1.116) defined as *justitia erga deos* ("justice toward the gods"). Unlike Prometheus, who did not hesitate to deceive Zeus in the sacrificial distribution, the Roman was imbued with a scrupulous respect for what was the gods' due. *Votum solvit libens merito* ("he carries out his vow wholeheartedly and deservedly") was the ritual formula.

This spirit of fairness also explains the innovation of one Scipio Aemilianus, who had a public prayer emended in a restrictive sense, the prayer being the one said during the closing ceremony of the census. Instead of asking the gods for "the betterment and growth of the Roman Republic," he said, "The Republic is strong enough and big enough; I therefore simply pray that the gods maintain it in good condition forevermore."[48]

R.S./g.h.

NOTES

1. Cf. Lucan, 1, 621. Sometime later the peritoneum (*omentum*) is added. It has been suggested that *exta* is from *ex-secta:* (organs) set apart (from the victim): cf. Ernout-Meillet, *D.E.*[4], s.v. *exta.* This is only a hypothesis.

2. Note the specific words: *fertum* (which the ancients had connected with *fero*), which may alternate with *strues,* designating also a sacrificial cake; *obmovere,* which is employed for solid offerings, in contrast with *inferre* (*vinum*). The order of precedence of the beneficiaries reflects the mentality of the ancient paterfamilias. What is the place of the wife? I believe that she is included in the final group of the *familia.*

3. This etymology has been taken up again by certain moderns who would like to derive the participle from a verb **magere* (cf. Walde-Hofmann, *L.E.W.*[3], s.v. *mactus*). Note that the corresponding verb, *mactare,* which in the historical period means "to honor by a sacrifice, to sacrifice," is well attested.

4. Cf. Cato, *De Agricultura* 132. On the interpretation of the text, see my "Sacrum et profanum," *Latomus,* 1971, pp. 960–61, reprinted in *R.C.D.R.*

5. Cf. my commentary on the text of Cato 50.2: *Ubi daps profanata comestaque erit . . . ,* ibid., pp. 961–62.

6. Festus, p. 298 L.: "Pollucere merces . . . liceat: sunt far, polenta, vinum, panis fermentatus, ficus passa, suilla, agnina, casei, ovilla, alica, sesama et oleum, pisces quibus est squama, praeter squatum . . ." The enumeration is obviously in disorder. (It ends by noting that all the provisions [*esculenta*] and all the beverages [*posculenta*] are permitted by Hercules.)

7. Cf. Ovid, *Fasti* 4.746.

8. Archeology has recovered, for the period of the Iron Age—the "preurban period"—sacrificial remains (no doubt from ceremonies for the dead) of sheep, pigs, and cows: cf. E. Gherstad, *Early Rome* (Lund 1966), 4, 1, p. 64.

9. Cf. Ernout-Meillet, *D.E.*[4], s.v. *hostia.*

10. Cf. Arnobius 7.19.

11. Cf. Macrobius 3.10.3.

12. Cf. ibid. 3.10.4.

13. Cf., for example, Cato 141, where Mars is gratified by a suovitaurilium of suckling beasts—*suovitaurilibus lactentibus.*

14. Cf. the anecdote related by Livy (2.8.7–8). At the moment when the consul Horatius went to the consecration of the temple of Capitoline Jupiter, his adversaries released the news that his son was dead. But Horatius sought to excuse this attempt at obstruction.

15. So, too, in the *ritus Graecus* of Hercules at the Great Altar, the officiant had his head uncovered (cf. Servius *ad Aen.* 3.407). In fact, the prescription of the "covered head" is not applied to two Roman divinities, either: Saturn (cf. Festus, p. 432 L., and Servius, *l.l.*) and Honos (cf. Plutarch *Quaestiones Romanae* 266).

16. Cf. Ovid, *Fasti* 5.421ff. The ceremony took place every year, at midnight, thrice repeated, 9, 11, and 13 May.

17. Cf. Ovid, *Fasti* 2.527. Though Ovid assigns this festival to the Curia, Festus (p. 298 L.) ranks it among the *popularia sacra, "quae omnes cives faciunt"*—which is not contradictory, to the extent that the *popularia sacra* are not to be confused with the *publica sacra* (see note 19).

18. Cf. Ovid, *Fasti* 4.629–34.

19. Cf. Festus, p. 284 L.

20. Pliny *N.H.* 8.183. In the preceding context, Pliny had remarked that of all the animals that have long tails, the cow is the only one whose tail continues to grow.

21. Cf. G. Henzen, *Acta Fratrum Arvalium* (Berlin 1874), 122.

22. Cf. ibid., p. 144, for examples.

23. Cf. ibid., p. 23.

24. On the significance of this *foculus,* cf. G. Dumézil, *La religion romaine archaïque,* 2d ed., pp. 321 and 549.

25. The Latin formula translates the meaning of the omen as "Be propitious in holding your tongue!" For all the information on the course of the sacrificial ceremonial, see Pliny *N.H.* 28.11.

26. Cf. Paulus-Festus, p. 97 L.: *Immolare est mola, id est farre mollito et sale, hostiam perspersam sacrare* ("To immolate is to consecrate the victim in the *mola* mixture, i.e., in wheat flour and salt").

27. Latte, *R.R.G.,* p. 387, interprets these preparations as a "Verstärkung der Segenskraft des Opfertieres" (a reinforcement of the beneficial potential of the victim).

28. Cf. Pliny *N.H.* 28.11.

29. Henzen, *Acta Fratrum Arvalium,* p. 26.

30. Paulus-Festus, p. 287 L.

31. Cf. Livy 41.15.1–4.

32. Cf. Varro *L.L.* 5.112.

33. Cf. Ovid, *Fasti* 2.362.

34. Cf. Servius Danielis *ad Aen.* 8.183. We note this exception to show the minutiae in the precision of Roman liturgy.

35. Cf. Henzen, *Acta F.A.,* p. 23.

36. *Viscera* means "all that is found between the skin and bone" (Servius *ad Aen.* 6.253). It is appropriate, however, to note two exceptions that pose a problem. (1) The reference in the proceedings of the Arval Brethren of A.D. 240, 29 May: *et de sangunculo porciliarum vesciti sunt* ("and they consumed the blood of young female pigs")—a tasting that follows the sacrifice of *porciliae* in the sacred wood of *dea Dia* (cf. *Notizie degli scavi,* 1914, fasc. 12, p. 464ff.). (2) The reference to *sanguinem gustare antea frequenter solebant,* in an indeterminate fragment of the calendar of Praeneste (cf. *Notizie d.s.,* 1921, p. 277ff.): O. Marucchi comments on the two texts, *Not. d.s.,* 1921, p. 277ff.

37. Trebatius, the author of a treatise *De religionibus,* is cited by Macrobius (*S.* 3.5.1). A. Magdelain (*Essai sur les origines de la Sponsio* [Paris 1943], pp. 35–41) had the merit of isolating the information of Trebatius and of arranging the texts on this problem.
38. Concerning these differences, see my *Sacrum et profanum,* pp. 963–64, reprinted in *R.C.D.R.*
39. Cf. Hesiod, *Theogony,* 535ff.
40. See Jean Bayet, *Les origines de l'Hercule romain* (Paris 1926), passim. On the particular point of the *ritus graecus,* see my "Sacrum et profanum," cited in note 38.
41. Cf. Festus, p. 298 L.
42. Cf., for example, Plautus, *Rudens,* 1419.
43. Virgil *Aeneid* 6.253: *Et* solida *imponit taurorum viscera flammis.*
44. Cf. *CIL.,* 6, 32323 = Pighi, *De ludis saecularibus* (2d ed., Amsterdam 1965), 113–14, lines 90–91: *Nocte insequenti, in Campo, ad Tiberim deis Moeris imp. Caesar Augustus immolavit agnas feminas IX prodigivas Achivo ritu* . . . "The following night, the emperor Caesar Augustus sacrificed, on the Field (of Mars), by the Tiber, nine *whole* lambs, according to the Greek rite . . ." Note the extension of the meaning of the verb *immolare,* "to sacrifice." For the meaning of *prodigivas,* cf. Festus, p. 296 L.: *prodiguae hostiae vocantur . . . quae consumuntur.* "One gives the name of *prodigivae,* 'victims,' to those who are destroyed by fire." See Latte, *R.R.G.,* p. 392.
45. *CIL,* 6, 32329 a, line 49 = Pighi, *De ludis saecularibus,* p. 162: *Geta Caesar immolavit Terrae matri suem plenam Graeco A(chivo) r(itu) prodigivam . . . :* "Geta Caesar (one of the sons of Septimus Severus) sacrificed to the goddess Earth a whole sow in the fire according to the Greek rite."
46. Livy 3.7.8. It was a matter of averting an epidemic in 463 B.C. Cf. ibid. 26.9.7 (in 211 B.C.): *undique matronae in publicum effusae circa deum delubra discurrunt crinibus passis aras verrentes, nisae genibus, supinas manus ad caelum ac deos tendentes* . . . "Most of the mothers of families rushed together in public; they gathered around the sanctuaries of the gods, sweeping the altars with their disheveled hair; prostrated on their knees, they turned their palms toward heaven and toward the gods . . ." (The panic was due to Hannibal's approach to Rome.)
47. The precision of ritualism was pushed to the point of anticipating a *profane* time (*fas* in liturgical terms) between the killing of the victim and the presentation of the internal organs (*inter hostiam caesam et exta porrecta*).
48. Cf. Valerius Maximus 4.1.10. The text adds: "And the censors of the following census adhered to this more modest formula."

ESSENTIAL BIBLIOGRAPHY

G. DUMÉZIL, *La religion romaine archaïque* (2d ed., Paris 1974), 545–51 (succinct, exact analysis, with bibliography). R. E. KRAUSE, *Suppl.* 5 (1931), s.v. "hostia," c. 236–82 (encyclopedic study). K. LATTE, *Römische Religionsgeschichte* (*R.R.G.*) (Munich 1960), 375–93 (detailed study, marred by an important error on p. 391: according to Latte, the participants in a Roman sacrifice had to have part of *all* the pieces of the victim; the author misses the distinction between *exta* and *viscera*). G. WISSOWA, *Religion und Kultus der Römer,* 2d ed. (*Ruk*[2]) (Munich 1912), 409–25 (a technical and well-documented study).

THE RELIGION OF THE ROMAN REPUBLIC: A REVIEW OF RECENT STUDIES

The twenty-five-year period between 1950 and 1975 was a fertile time for scholarship, as is indicated by the sheer size of the appended bibliography,[1] for it produced important editions of texts about the religions of Rome and many works of a broad scope. The quarrying of primary sources remains the basis for speculation in religious studies, a decision that bodes well for the strengthening of the groundwork and also demonstrates the interest generated by these studies among a wider and wider public. The many books and articles dealing with diverse subjects offer a further confirmation of the vitality of the field. We shall first focus on the year 1950 and then identify the themes and tendencies that emerge in the light of these works (noting some of their differences). We will then discuss the problems that have received the most attention.

We need only compare the titles of classical reference works from the nineteenth century with those of our own time to note the difference in perspective. The word "mythology" figures in the titles of L. Preller's work *Römische Mythologie* (Berlin 1858) and of W. H. Roscher's encyclopedia, *Ausführliches Lexikon der griechischen und römischen Mythologie* (Leipzig 1884). Georg Wissowa introduced the word "religion" only when he published the famous reference work *Religion und Kultus der Römer* (Munich 1902; 2d ed. 1912) on his own authority.[2]

"Religion" versus "mythology": the change is significant for modern exegesis because it corresponds to a decisive turning point. Instead of viewing Roman religion as a more or less faithful copy of Greek mythology—such was the implicit premise of the scholarship of the nineteenth century—we are now trying to establish the original legacy of Rome, which is manifest essentially in Roman cults and rites. Of course substituting "religion" for "mythology" does not in and of itself constitute a magic password, nor does it preclude basic and significant divergences. Kurt Latte, who succeeded Wissowa in the same series (*Handbuch der Altertumswissenschaft*), did not hesitate to take his own stance vis-à-vis his predecessor. In 1957 he wrote in a letter: "What I looked for in Rome were first of all new inscriptions and archaeological facts. . . . A modern treatment of the subject can no longer begin with the gods, a concession already made by Wissowa"—a conception "that dates back to the century of Louis XIV."[3] Latte's own position also triggered vigorous reactions. This is a fundamental issue, to which we will return, one that often surprises the layman: why is it that the most important contemporary scholars have frequently been inclined to criticize one another or to "ignore" one another with a disapproving silence? Does the personal coefficient affect research in religion so strongly that the research cannot find a ground of common concern in the midst of the facts?

Yet to the extent that they are perceptible and intelligible, facts are what matter. Latte was certainly right: archaeology and epigraphy have enriched our knowledge in this field. However one may judge the excavations of Einar Gjerstad, this scholar had the merit of opening up fruitful discussions on the dating of the religious events in the area of the Roman Forum. Carefully targeted research has yielded suggestive results. Thus, A. Bartoli was able to show in his report, *I pozzi dell'area sacra di Vesta* (c. 13ff.) that the material found in the "archaic well," primarily pots (*olle*), dates back to a time "between the seventh century and the beginning of the sixth." To take another example, P. Romanelli was able to settle a question about the cult of Cybele in Rome that had previously divided scholars. His publication *Lo scavo al tempio*

The Palatine. View from the Campanile of S. Francesca Romana. Rome. Photo Alinari-Giraudon.

della Magna Mater sul Palatino e nelle sue adiacenze (c. 281ff.) shows that the discovery of numerous statuettes of Attis from the first century B.C. left no room to doubt the presence of this consort god side by side with the Magna Mater.

No less interesting have been the epigraphic findings in Pratica di mare, a zone that corresponds to the ancient Lavinium. Prior to these discoveries, three inscriptions engraved on cippi that came from Tor Tignosa had already attracted attention to this region:

Parca Maurtia dono
Neuna dono
Neuna Fata

Dated in the third century and first published by M. Guarducci,[4] they were the object of commentaries by St. Weinstock[5] and L. L. Tels-de-Jong,[6] among others. Shortly after this discovery, M. Guarducci published research concerning another inscription engraved on a bronze plaque found in the same region and also dating from the third century.[7]

CERERE AULIQUOQUIBUS VESPERNAM PORO

Almost every word of this inscription has been read and interpreted in conflicting ways by various scholars.[8] CERERE is sometimes read as an accusative (with an M missing) and sometimes as a dative; VESPERNAM is sometimes taken to be a nominalized adjective or an adjective suggesting an implicit CENAM (which would designate an evening offering) and is sometimes taken to be a proper noun, VESPERNA, which would correspond to a goddess of food associated with Ceres; PORO to one scholar is an adverb (POR(R)O meaning "henceforth"); to another it is a verb (an altered form which should be corrected to read POR[RICIT]O); to still others, it is a noun—POR(R)O, "leeks," in the ablative singular with a collective sense. Only the term AULIQUOQUIBUS met with unanimity, as a result of a commentary by Paulus-Festus (*Glossaria Latina* p. 22 L) which helped identify these *aulicocia exta* as the sacrificial viscera boiled in a pot. After so many diverse attempts, it might seem foolhardy for us to propose the interpretation that seems most plausible.[9]

In 1958, Lavinium had already emerged as a likely place for archaeological exploration. In the same domain, Tor Tignosa—where the archaic inscriptions *Parca Maurtia, Neuna,* and *Neuna Fata* were discovered—was also the site of another inscription dating from the third century: LARE AINEIA.[10] The exceptional importance of this discovery was obvious: for the first time, on this site that was considered to be the cradle of the Trojan legend, an epigraph mentioning Aeneas appeared. He was no longer a simple hero whose praises were sung by poets, but a god honored by a cult. He is referred to by the term *Lar,* which dates back to the archaic vocabulary of Rome (e.g., the Lases of the *Carmen Arvale* and the *Lar familiaris*), though we should not jump to the conclusion that *Lar* was merely a synonym for "hero" (interpreted in the Greek manner).

In the same area in the same year (1958), at a place called Madonnetta, F. Castagnoli and L. Cozza unearthed a bronze plaque that dated from the sixth or fifth century and that bore the dedication *Castorei Podlouqueique qurois.*[11] The early date of this inscription, its association with the divine twins, and their designation by the expression *quroi* provided ample material for the reflection of scholars.[12] For it was known that originally Castor alone was admitted inside the *pomerium* in Rome: as the patron god of horsemen, he received the gratitude of the Roman authorities after the famous victory of Lake Regillus, which was won by A. Postumius, who enlisted the help of the Roman cavalry, at the beginning of the fifth century.[13] Henceforth, it was simple to prove that Rome had not needed to go very far to become familiar with the Dioscuri; their cult was celebrated near Lavinium, where it had come from Magna Graecia and not, as had been thought, from Etruria. The Roman attitude is even more interesting: Castor had been "chosen" because of his specialty as a "horseman" and because of a particular historical circumstance.

The epigraphic find on the site of Lavinium may presage further discoveries. At least that was what it suggested to the scholar who devoted himself to this task. F. Castagnoli wrote that the current investigations focus "on a part of the outer walls of the east side. These are walls in *opus quadratum* with remains of a gate and a street. Several phases can be identified, the oldest one going back to the sixth century."[14]

The new inscriptions were put together in a collection that is easy to consult, and was published through the efforts of A. Degrassi: *Inscriptiones Latinae liberae rei publicae*, vol. 1 (Florence 1957) and vol. 2 (Florence 1963). This excellent publication makes accessible for study the most important epigraphic texts with an updated bibliography. With a similar purpose, A. Pasoli reworked an edition of the *Acta Fratrum Arvalium* (Bologna 1950) by going back to the *Acta* published by G. Henzen (Berlin 1874) and completing them with inscriptions discovered since that date. We should note, however, that in this case the annotations are sparse; Henzen's commentary remains indispensable.

Following Th. Mommsen's publication (*CIL*, I²), a new edition of the Roman calendar was needed, especially since the discovery of the pre-Julian calendar of Antium (*N.S.* 1921, pp. 73ff.) had provided a document invaluable for a new inclusive study. This considerable work was completed with admirable care by A. Degrassi. It constitutes section 2 of volume 13 of the *Inscriptiones Italiae* devoted to *Fasti et Elogia* (Rome 1963) under the title *Fasti anni Numani et Juliani* (section 1 appeared in 1947 and included *Fasti consulares et triumphales*). In separate publications, the author presented all the epigraphic fragments, often reproduced in color facsimiles, before offering a general commentary that takes into account the principal works on the subject.

With regard to the calendar, we should mention A. Kirsopp-Michels, *Calendar of the Roman Republic* (Princeton 1967), which tried to settle the often intricate problems of calendrical practice during the Republic. Unlike her predecessors, Kirsopp-Michels suggests (pp. 160ff.) that the *mensis Intercalaris* or *Mercedonius* of the pre-Julian calendar always had twenty-seven days, as is shown by the epigraphic document of Antium (*Fasti Antiates majores*). The insertion of this month, which intervened every other year, would have been done sometimes after 23 February (Terminalia) and sometimes after 24 February (then considered an ordinary day and not the Regifugium). In this way, the author seeks to reconcile the Antium document with the remarks of Censorinus (*De die natali* 20.6) and Macrobius (*Saturnalia* 1.13.12), who mention an insertion (following the February Terminalia) which was sometimes twenty-two and sometimes twenty-three days long and which concluded each time with the last five days of February (hence the traditional hypothesis of an intercalary month that supposedly had twenty-seven or twenty-eight days alternatively). A. Kirsopp-Michels's new hypothesis is ingenious and more economical than the previous explanation, which faltered before the Antium document which features only one *intercalaris* of twenty-seven days. (The reader should refer to the work in question for a more detailed discussion.)

The hope of having in one collection the illustrated documents that concern Roman religion has not proved in vain. I. Scott Ryberg illustrated his book *Rites of the State Religion in Roman Art* (*MAAR* 22, 1955) with numerous photographs that make it possible to understand the concrete realities and sacrificial celebration in Roman religion far more precisely than is possible with mere lengthy descriptions.

In this overview of scholarship, it is appropriate to mention two recent editions of texts of religious interest. To the classic works of R. von Panta (*Grammatik der Oskisch-umbrischen Dialekten*, vol. 2, Strasbourg 1897), R. S. Conway (*The Italic Dialects*, Cambridge 1897), and G. Devoto (*Tabulae Iguvinae*) we must add the more recent publication of J. Wilson Poultney's *The Bronze Tablets of Iguvium* (*Mon. Am. Ph. Ass.* 17, 1959).

Finally, by far the most important commentary on Ovid's *Fasti* since Sir James George Frazer published *The Fasti of Ovid* (London 1920) is the work of F. Boemer[15] (*P. Ovidius Naso, Die Fasten, I, Einleitung, Text und Übersetzung*, Heidelberg 1957). This publication corresponds to the return to favor of Ovid as a "religious exegete." It seems to have been established long ago that the poet of the *Amores* should not be taken too seriously in matters of religion; I have attempted to show that this attitude lacked subtlety and seriousness.[16]

Works of general interest that have appeared during the two decades since 1955 and that establish certain basic positions within the field include, among others, G. Radke's book, *Die Götter Altitaliens* (Münster 1965), which takes the form of a dictionary that lists the different deities in alphabetical order. Each of the entries raises particular points which bear simultaneously on the work as a whole and on the interpretation of the particular elements. While we might discuss both the overall presentation of the work and its interpretation of the facts, we shall instead merely point out the author's principal idea. He claims (p. 8) to have wanted to return to Varro's objective, but under conditions improved by progress in linguistics, since Varro was noted for his "etymological investigations." Radke reasons that, "All too often antiquity left us nothing but a name."[17] While this method may seem altogether too restrictive in general, it may "pay" in difficult or hopeless cases. Take, for example, the two cases that seem to respond best, a priori, to the spirit of this method of inquiry: Falacer and Dea Dia. Indeed, we have almost no information about these two except for their names.[18]

The paradox of Falacer is that he is provided with a flamen even though no one knows anything about the significance of the god. We know no more after reading the paragraph devoted to him. And for Dea Dia the inadequcy of a method based solely on onomastics is also clear. Radke adopts—justifiably—Altheim's proposal of comparison with the root **diu-*, but he redirects this scholar's line of thought in a less fortunate direction, by assimilating the goddess to the moon. Then he has recourse to the altogether gratuitous "reconstruction" of a *Doppelnamen, Dia Luna.* Yet the opposite approach would seem to be demanded here, to avoid the excesses of a purely etymological exercise in the name of liturgy. In fact, Dea Dia enters into the principal liturgy of the Arval Brethren as the deity invoked in the season that is decisive for harvesting (the month of May), in order to dispense good light, in other words, good weather. Far from being confused with Diana, she is differentiated from the goddess of the night precisely because she is responsible for diffusing the daylight.[19]

An attempt in the opposite direction can be seen in Jean Bayet's *Histoire politique et psychologique de la religion romaine* (Paris ed. 1957; 2d ed. 1969), to the extent that the author in the course of his investigations attempts to deal with religious phenomena in the context of Indo-European traditions, the political institutions of the city, and the events of history, without neglecting the topographical features of the Roman site. Since I have already devoted a special review to this book,[20] I shall limit myself to recalling the broad outline. Nothing was more alien to Jean Bayet than complacency in pure abstraction; precisely because in Rome many deities have names with transparent meanings, such as Ceres or Fides, just to mention the oldest, he felt the need to "incarnate" them into the process by which they became real gods.

Hence he paid attention to history in the full sense of the term, to Roman religion from the migrations of the Italians and the settling of primitive Rome to the final stages. This "stratigraphic" preoccupation, borrowed from archaeology, works well throughout Bayet's book. It has the advantage of heightening the contrast between such archaic rites as the Lupercalia and later religious forms. It is counterbalanced by an awareness of the constants not only within the "religious mentality of the Romans" but also within the frameworks and institutions of public worship.

Not all of the proposed analyses have received the same high approval. Since the first edition in 1957, two points in particular deserve to be reexamined: the origin of the Dioscuri in Rome and the Ara Maxima cult of Hercules. On the first point, I indicated in my review[21] "that it is not certain that the Dioscuri had been 'evoked' from Tusculum." The discovery of the archaic dedicatory inscription to Castor and Pollux on the site of ancient Lavinium contributed substantially to this subject. The "evocation" itself seems improbable, for reasons stated in my article on the Dioscuri. On the second point, a new explanation was proposed by D. van Berchem, who dates the founding of the Great Altar to between the ninth and eighth centuries and attributes it to Phoenicians who came up the Tiber.[22] The author took care to explain several rites and taboos of this cult, as well as the name Potitii, which he interprets to mean "the possessed" by arguing that a *gens Potitia* did not exist.[23] It is, however, impossible to prove such an initiative on the part of Phoenicians that early.[24] Only later (in the sixth or early fifth century, according to scholars) is there evidence, in the golden plaques of Pyrgi discovered by M. Pallottino's archaeological team.[25] This provided both a document in the Phoenician language and two texts in Etruscan that the

Bearers of Lares. Rome, Vatican Museum. Museum photo.

specialists attribute to Punic colonists rather than to Phoenicians. This last discovery would have delighted K. Latte, who was always on the lookout for epigraphic novelties. Such documents are a great aid to research,[26] though we need not "leave the gods" in the name of a new sociological historicism.

We shall now turn to other syntheses that have appeared in the last twenty years, beginning with the published works of F. Altheim (works that precede this period, but there have been new editions of his *Römische Religionsgeschichte*).[27] Altheim's thesis is well known. It is most vividly expressed in his book, *Griechische Götter im alten Rom* (Greek gods in ancient Rome [Giessen 1930]), the title of which is in and of itself so telling. No one has ever doubted the usefulness of this reaction against the concept that dates back to Wissowa (*Religion und Kultus der Römer* [Munich 1902; 2d ed. 1912]), which tended to exaggerate the isolation of the Latin world from its neighbors, at least until the third century B.C. But often in such cases reaction goes to extremes. It seems less and less true that Rome did nothing but passively accept Greek or Etruscan concepts.[28] This exclusivity in orientation may have led K. Latte to write that a discussion with Altheim was hopeless, "aussichtslos."[29]

No one has criticized the principles affirmed by Latte at the time when he composed his own handbook, principles that recognized the value of epigraphy and archaeology. But this very tendency may have developed in an unwarranted manner in his hands. This state of mind had made Latte seemingly impervious to any notion of system. This latter-day doubting Thomas of the history of religions had an insatiable need for concrete proofs. Nothing is more revealing than his affected ignorance of the idea of an Indo-European substratum. He thus dismisses a priori the very enterprise of Dumézil, *weil die Pfeiler . . . auf denen sie [die Erneuerung dieser Versuche] ihr Gebäude errichtet, bei philologischer Kritik des Materials wegbrechen* (because the pillars on which it [the renewal of this attempt] built its structures falls apart at the philological criticism of the material).[30]

We have now reached the heart of the problem. What is the "right" method according to Latte? In the chapter dealing with sources,[31] he mentions the calendar, inscriptions, and literary sources. One can immediately see the drastic character of this limited list. Latte rejects comparativism by challenging the validity of the comparative method and by citing abuses committed by the nominalism of the nineteenth century (which had tried hard to identify deities through affinities suggested more or less by etymology).[32]

This line of thought led him to ignore the structures of religious organization, which make up one of the most original dimensions of Roman religion. For instance, he does not mention the archaic triad of Jupiter-Mars-Quirinus, nor does he mention the hierarchy of the three major flamens who each correspond to one of these three gods. In his estimation, these are *Ortsgottheiten* who, far from having been arranged in a complementary hierarchy, had been more or less attracted according to the vagaries of historical accident and were subjected to the counterblows of an internal rivalry. Thus we learn that Quirinus, *Gottheit vom Quirinal*, had been eclipsed by Mars in the minds of his worshipers.[33]

What is more, the very personalities of the deities become so malleable that they seem to be patterned from the vicissitudes of history. Nothing is more revealing than a sentence such as this one: *Dieselben Göttergestalten nehmen verschiedene Aspekte an, je nachdem sie aus den Nöten des bäuerlichen oder kriegerischen Lebens angerufen werden* (The same divine forms take on various aspects each time that they are called forth from the needs of peasant or martial life).[34] The result is that Mars represented for the peasant the wildness (*der Wilde*) that the peasant tries to keep away from his fields, while for the warrior Mars represented an accredited protector who would "later" become the god of war.[35]

This method confuses two different ideas: the identity of the deity and the realm of his competence. In Rome, there is no god with a variable definition in the way that, in our time, there are airplanes with a variable geometry. Gods were invariably identified. To go back to the example of Mars, Latte should have been alerted by an archaic document—the *Carmen Arvale*,[36] in which Mars is characterized as *ferus*. This episode, however, does not warrant referring to him as an *Exponent der unheimlichen, unvertrauten Welt draussen* (an exponent of the uncanny, unreliable world outside).[37] The best proof of this lies in the fact that Mars is summoned to the defense of the *ager Romanus* in a reference that leaves no doubt as to its meaning: *limen sali* (leap to the frontier).[38] Mars is invoked in this prayer, along with the Lases and the Semones, but in accordance with the definition of his own office. His task is to ensure the defense of borders, just as the task of the Lases is to protect the tilled land, and the task of the Semones is to promote the growth of seeds.

Ferus, therefore, does not mean "the savage against whom one wants to protect one's fields,"[39] but the god of strength, who is capable of unleashing his *furor* against a potential foe; thus, *ferus*, which is linguistically related to *ferox*,[40] characterizes the warlike nature of the god.

But we should take Latte to task not for the sources he advocates but for the ones he omits. In the case of literary sources, Latte is justified when he cautions scholars[41] to guard against the distortions of archaic documents by the Neoplatonic or Stoic schools. Yet it is surprising that in the table of contents one finds the names only of Nigidius Figulus, Varro, Lucretius, and Cicero, all of whom caught Latte's attention only because they represented the philosophical opinions or religious beliefs of their times.

Certainly Plautus is cited several times with reference to certain expressions formulated in religious language, and Livy with reference to certain institutions, such as the ritual of the fetiales or the *inauguratio*. But the treatises of Cicero, such as *De natura deorum*, *De divinatione*, and *De legibus*, deserve more consideration despite their author's tendency to rationalize. It is to Cicero that we owe the survival of precious fragments from the earliest times, precisely because he preserved them in quotations in his treatises. For example, Cicero cites a fragment from a tragedy by Ennius[42] that refers to a dialogue during which Cassandra speaks as follows:

> *Missa sum superstitiosis hariolationibus;*
> *Namque Apollo fatis fandis dementem invitam ciet.*[43]

This text is remarkable for its use of the expressions *superstitiosis hariolationibus*, which do not carry here the pejorative connotation that they would later have, and for the etymological figure *fatis fandis*, which can be invoked in the argument about the etymology of *fatum*.[44]

Equally surprising is the meager share allotted to Virgil and Horace, two poets whose vocabulary and allusions to cultic institutions constitute a mine of information for the historian of Roman religion. Finally, Latte's judgment of Ovid, the author of *Fasti*, must also be adjusted, indeed revised, particularly when it comes to such a statement as: *Altrömische Religiosität lag diesem modernsten unter den römischen Dichtern recht fern* ("Ancient Roman religious feeling remained far away from this most modern of Roman poets").[45] Elsewhere I have tried to show why and how Ovid can be of use to modern research. To counter Latte's condemnation of the *Fasti* one need only recall the impressive account that Ovid gives of the nocturnal ceremony of the *Lemuria*. He evokes an atmosphere of archaic times that is at once magical and religious, without yielding to literary embellishments or Greek fables.[46]

We should add that the poet gives clues that can be valuable in filling in the lacunae in our knowledge. Thus 1 January on the pre-Julian calendar lacks the name of a deity. Should one supply *CO[NS]O*, as Mancini would have it, or *CO[R]O(NIDI)*, as Degrassi suggests? Ovid's testimony allows us to resolve the question and opt for the second hypothesis.[47]

I have greatly criticized Latte's work, because the enterprise originally inspired equally great hope. It may still have significant value for research in the field. Latte put together a great mass of documents that make it possible to begin to establish files for problems yet to be solved. His principal concern was to be the first to offer to the scholarly world a fresh harvest of epigraphic and archaeological novelties that could fertilize research in the history of religions. In this he succeeded. He may not have supplanted the work of his predecessor Wissowa, but he did fill in a gap of fifty years' worth of information. His judgments may not have been infallible, but he did produce in his text and in his notes a number of relevant and suggestive thoughts. He is a scholar whose works, far from leaving the reader indifferent, make him think. He therefore deserves our thanks.

An altogether different spirit characterizes the works of Georges Dumézil. Not that this scholar disregarded archaeological or epigraphic documentation. On the contrary, he used it brilliantly when, for instance, he proposed an intelligible decipherment of the fragments of the archaic inscriptions of the truncated stela of the Forum.[48] But his main concern has always been to discern the structures that characterize a given religious situation or social organization. Since *La religion romaine archaïque, avec un appendice sur la religion des Étrusques* (Paris 1966),[49] Dumézil has published in succession *Idées romaines* (Paris 1969); *Mythe et Épopée*, vol. 1 (Paris 1968), vol. 2 (Paris 1971), vol. 3 (Paris 1973); and *Fêtes romaines d'été et d'automne* (Paris 1975); and he has revised and updated *La religion romaine archaïque* (2d ed. Paris 1974).[50]

This work is by far the most striking of those of these last twenty-five years, because of both its breadth and its originality. The last publications are the full harvest of over thirty years of fruitful labor and reflection. They represent a kind of balance sheet that this author has tried to draw up. The elements that were the object of the individual studies became integrated into the whole, so that the whole benefited from individual analyses, and conversely, comprehensive views often shed light on particular issues.[51]

For the first time the reader has access to an interpretation of Roman religion in the light of the comparative Indo-European tradition. This was the intended plan behind the whole enterprise. An important introduction that bears the modest title of *Primary Remarks* opens the discussion and gives the author a chance to define his line of inquiry. This section alone (151 pages) could have been a book. After that, the material is arranged into four parts. The first part introduces "The Great Gods of the Archaic Triad." The second part ushers us into Roman history—the end of the monarchy and the beginnings of the Republic—by discussing various aspects of "Ancient Theology," among them the Capitoline triad, the public cult of Vesta, and the forces and elements that characterize the "third, second, and first functions." (The notion of function has, of course, a particular character in Dumézil's language. On the basis that the archaic Roman triad Jupiter-Mars-Quirinus, which can also be found among the Umbrians at Iguvium, can only be explained by historical, topographical, and ethnic considerations, the author demonstrates the necessity of recognizing a three-level religious conception, a theological structure.) The third part is devoted to "Extensions and Mutations" of Roman religion. The fourth and last part deals with the cult (ceremonies, priests, *signa*, and *portenta*), with a chapter devoted to private cults. An appendix concerns the religion of the Etruscans.

The "Preliminary Remarks" give the reader a clear understanding of the author's method. The reader learns how comparativism was able to lift up the heavy hypothetical structure that seemed to weigh irretrievably on the archaic period of Roman history, ever since the eighteenth century, when Louis de Beaufort wrote his famous *Dissertation sur l'incertitude des cinq premiers siècles de Rome* (1738).

Beyond the hypercritical wave of the nineteenth century that was one of the logical consequences of this method of doubt, Dumézil opened up a new way, following a systematic investigation that revealed corresponding structures in the respective areas of the Indo-European realm, for instance, the comparable antitheses Romulus-Numa in Rome and Varuṇa-Mitra in Vedic India, and the parallel conjunctions of Cocles-Scaevola (or "the Cyclops and the Lefty") in Rome and Óðinn-Týr ("the one-eyed god and the one-armed god") in Scandinavian mythology.

The history of Rome need no longer be considered a doubtful fabrication coming out of the headquarters of fanciful annalists. It is actually a stylized history that exhibits—on the banks of the Tiber in a historical form—an ideology that is elsewhere mythical. Now, although there is an "Indo-European heritage" in Rome, it is no longer possible to reduce the divine, in the origins of the early Rome of Romulus, to an embryonic world of diffuse forces out of which, by virtue of a process of evolution, "numinal" deities emerged who were endowed with a numen not unlike the Melanesian mana.

Consequently the triad of Jupiter-Mars-Quirinus, which existed in both Rome and Iguvium (predating the Capitoline association of Jupiter-Juno-Minerva), can only be an accidental and late grouping. Wissowa had already recognized this archaic "Dreiverein" (Trinity), which Latte would later challenge. This may be a case of hairsplitting, but hairsplitting can lead to blindness: one cannot see the forest for the trees.

This threefold hierarchy can also be found in the priestly structures and the ritual institutions. The triple *flamonium* is in itself a veiled reference to the divine triad. The three priests who in the hierarchy of precedence come immediately after the Rex (turned Rex Sacrorum or Rex Sacrificulus during the Republic) are, in their respective order, the Flamen Dialis assigned to Jupiter, the Flamen Martialis assigned to Mars, and the Flamen Quirinalis assigned to serve Quirinus. These three flamens proceeded together once a year in an open chariot to a chapel of Fides, or Good Faith, who was necessary for harmonious relationships among people in all walks of life.

Dumézil also shows this threefold grouping[52] in the archaic forms of the cult. Thus, the Regia, the former "house of the king," which during the Republic became the seat of the Pontifex Maximus, accommodates three types of cult. The first concerns Jupiter (in addition to the cults of Janus and Juno, who were honored as those who usher in the new year and the new month); the second, Mars, in the *sacrarium Martis;* the third, in another *sacrarium*, Ops Consiva, who

Ara pietatis. Temple relief. Rome, Museo dei Conservatori. Photo Alinari-Giraudon.

belongs to the group of deities represented by Quirinus in the canonical list of the *flamines majores*.

The same grouping includes—after Janus, the god of beginnings, and before the specific deities invoked in special circumstances—Jupiter, Mars, and Quirinus in the ancient *carmen* of the *devotio* (Livy 8.9.6). It also inspires the old theory of *spolia opima* recorded by Festus (p. 302 L.[2]), who tells that the *prima spolia* are offered to Jupiter, the *secunda spolia* to Mars, and the *tertia* to "Janus Quirinus." The threefold scheme persists, no matter what interpretation we adopt for *prima, secunda, tertia,* whether it is based on time or rank. The choice is open. We should note that on this point[53] Latte agrees with Dumézil by accepting this evidence about the triad: Latte suggests an interpretation of the *prima, secunda, tertia* as a function of worth and not of time, which is consistent with the trifunctional explanation of the triad proposed by Dumézil.[54] Finally, the same scheme can be found in the triple patronage of the college of the Salii who are *in tutela Jovis Martis Quirini.*[55]

But does this tripartition correspond to anything that would not quickly dissolve through historical erosion, as the Capitoline triad replaced the old Indo-European triad as early as the sixth century B.C.? Dumézil's own definition of the "ideology of the three functions" applies here. "It can be observed," he states, "with the special peculiarities of each of the societies, among the Indians and Iranians as well as among the ancient Scandinavians and, with more pronounced alterations, among the Celts. To judge from some survivals which are to be found despite the early reorganization of the three traditions, it was also known to several waves of Greek invaders, the Achaeans and the Ionians. . . . The principal elements and the machinery of the world and of society are here divided into three harmoniously adjusted domains. These are, in descending order of dignity, sovereignty, with its magical and juridical aspects and a kind of maximal expression of the sacred; physical power and bravery, the most obvious manifestation of which is victory in war; and fertility and prosperity with all kinds of conditions and consequences, which are almost always meticulously analyzed and represented by a great number of related but different divinities, among whom now one, now the other, typifies the whole in formulary enumerations of gods. The 'Jupiter-Mars-Quirinus' grouping, with the nuances appropriate to Rome, corresponds to the lists found in Scandinavia and in Vedic and pre-Vedic India: Óðinn, Thor, Freyr; Mitra-Varuṇa, Indra, Nāsatya."[56]

Therein lies the very heart of a proof that in the course of its development took great pains to answer exhaustively all the criticisms raised against it. The reader is urged to refer to it. It is important to add that Dumézil also demonstrated the fertility of his comparativist method in the area of marginal cults. Their archaic rites had been incomprehensible to Romans of the classical era for most of the time. One example will suffice, namely, the festival of the Matralia on 11 June—a strange liturgy in which Roman ladies introduce a slave woman into the temple of Mater Matula (itself an exceptional act) and then drive her out, hitting her with sticks. During this rite the ladies hold in their arms not their own children but those of their sisters. These rites seem incomprehensible when viewed solely in a Roman context. But when compared with Vedic mythology, they become clear, because Mater Matuta represents Dawn.[57]

It is greatly to his credit that Dumézil was able to shed light on the function of a whole series of deities whose liturgy had become unintelligible because of the "lost mythology," and thus to give them their true identity. They were studied in the book appropriately entitled *Déesses latines et mythes védiques* (Brussels 1956), which was followed by studies on Carna (1960) and on the two Pales (1962). The reader who takes the trouble to follow these demonstrations will become aware of the "archaic dimension" of Roman religion, as well as the constants that emerge here and there in the religious mentality, despite great gaps in time.

Dumézil willingly took risks by the very method that he adopted. Because he exposed his thought step by step as it progressed, he was reproached for excessive fluidity and by some people for fickleness. "His latest state of mind," one such disparaging observer maliciously called it. Of course, a publication that proceeds by successive alterations and corrections is liable to be a problem. But to each his own rhythm. Dumézil has enjoyed inspiring critical reaction in an area in which he has often been a pioneer. Thus, his study of the inscription of the *lapis niger* benefited from suggestions and corrections of detail proposed by other scholars. The thrust of his argument, which revealed the augural prescription for the *juges auspicium,* was not diminished by it. We owe the fine collection *Idées Romaines* (Paris 1969) to this maturation of thinking. (In it, the author made every effort to use his entire experience as a scholar in formulating his fundamental ideas about Roman civilization. He also added several

Funeral procession. Aquila, Museo nazionale d'Abruzzo. Museum photo.

studies on the ideology of the three functions and some analyses outlining deities [Venus, Carna, Pales, Consus, and Ops].)

The preceding observations allow us at least to recognize certain broad outlines of research in the field of Roman religion. They are not so much contradictory as complementary. They emphasize approaches that attempt to solve problems in various ways. The bibliographies that follow allow the reader to take into account a wide variety of studies. It is not my intention to cast my lot for one work rather than another, but simply to offer a few final reflections.

First we must come to terms with the fact that many points in this vast field of investigation still remain obscure. Such ceremonies as the Lupercalia and the Argei may never be really explained. Of course some aspects of them have given rise to plausible or probable explanations, but the enduring mystery gives us some idea of the level of our ignorance. We may dream of an ideal colloquium of scholars concerned with the same problem: they would leave their egos aside and gather about a round table instead of working in isolation *pro virili parte* and subsequently making exclusive, rather polemical, pronouncements.[58]

But aside from the problems that remain unsolved, these two decades have undoubtedly been among the most fertile in the history of research on Roman religion, thanks to archaeological finds and the sustained efforts of many people. Unquestionably the problem of origins has benefited from a renewal of effort on a level unknown until now, through archaeological digs, philological inquiry, and the comparativists' contributions to the field.

Furthermore, the originality of Rome emerged far more clearly after the extreme swings of the pendulum represented by Wissowa and Altheim. Monographs that appeared in France and elsewhere during this period played a significant role in this respect. Not only have they contributed to the settling of specific issues but they have also often cast a new light on general problems through a kind of inverse reaction.

Luckily for researchers, many questions remain open. First is the problem of syncretism, which affects all societies that are not isolated from the rest of the world. This was true of Rome as much in the archaic period as in the classical and postclassical periods. Syncretism cannot be defined as a passive assimilation. The study of homologous deities in Greece, Etruria, and Rome shows clearly how the true question to understand is not so much the origin of the borrowing as the process by which the borrowing took place.[59]

The Augustan Age is particularly fascinating, though this is not always suspected. In the *Fasti,* Ovid confronted the awesome problem of reconciling the national tradition with an ideology of Greek inspiration. Although Ovid succeeded unevenly in this task, his modern critics have often failed to appreciate its inherent difficulties. The Imperial Age left some interesting liturgical documents, the *Acta* of the Arval Brethren. Nothing could be more revealing than the names of the dignitaries of the city who considered it an honor to be, along with the emperor, part of a college originally designed to promote an agrarian cult.[60] Nothing could be more instructive than sorting out archaic traits that demonstrate the great age of rites and invocations that were introduced later.[61]

Another question focuses on the connection between magic and religion. How is it possible that these two mentalities, which contradict each other in certain respects, managed to coexist within certain calendrical festivals?[62] How does one go about interpreting certain rites that clearly come under the rubric of magic, such as releasing foxes "with torches tied to their burning backs" during the festival of the Cerialia?[63] Are we to see in it "a magical/religious process to promote fertility"?[64] Or, on the contrary, are we to consider these foxes "the symbolic representatives of the solar heat which must be kept in check"?[65]

In general, it is not always easy to distinguish the boundaries between these two mentalities; sometimes they overlap, as in the formula of the *carmen* in the *devotio* of Decius, as reported by Livy (8.9.6), which partakes simultaneously of a religious supplication and a compelling magic: *vos precor veneror veniam peto feroque* ("I pray to you and I honor you, I ask for and I obtain your acceptance, your favor").[66]

Another of the questions Latte raised was, To what extent can one still speak of a living faith in historical times?[67] This formulation may perhaps reflect too modern a point of view. The Romans of the first century, for the most part (except Lucretius), seem to reconcile respect for traditions with great philosophical freedom. Their situation in the face of national religious institutions is thus not entirely comparable to that of the modern believer who separates himself clearly from the "unbeliever" by virtue of his belief.[68]

Nevertheless, we might ask the question in different terms. What religious ideals pervaded minds in the various periods? On the official level, Rome's ideological choice was manifested in particular by two remarkable initiatives. At a time when it was fully exposed to the syncretist movement of its neighbors Etruria and Magna Graecia, Rome adopted the Trojan legend. This was a choice with an enormous impact, which would later allow the city to use a myth of Greek origin *ad majorem gloriam populi Romani*. We know today how this myth, already present in Italy in the sixth century, inspired the Roman bards of the third century before it provided an official doctrine for the poets of the Augustan Age and for the regime that would later claim Julius Caesar as its authority.

Moreover, thanks to the teachings of the Etruscans, Rome was familiar with the doctrine according to which the *saecula* had to be pursued until they reached the end of a series of ten, which was supposed to fill out a great period. Rome was not indifferent to this doctrine, since the institution of the secular games, which materialized in the third century by the command of the *Sibylline Books*, had a sequel (especially the solemn celebration of 17 B.C.), which a reference to the "great series of centuries" in the fourth *Bucolics* places on the same level. But another theme was to eclipse the first: the theme of *Roma aeterna* that Virgil advanced as an official dogma in the *Aeneid* by having Jupiter utter the following verses for the benefit of the Romans, who traced their descent from Aeneas:

> *Hic ego nec metas rerum nec tempora pono:*
> *Imperium sine fine dedi*
> "I fix no limits for them in time or in space:
> I give them an empire without end."[69]

Here again the choice is significant and gives material for thought. One question often leads to another. It should not surprise us that several scholars go beyond their particular analyses to ponder this fundamental problem: what constitutes the basic innovation of the religious patrimony of Rome? This matter should not be dealt with by classifying types of explanations but rather by providing the bibliographic repertory. In any case, the answer cannot be easy nor can it exhaust the fascination of the historian of religions for a heritage of traditions several millennia old.

R.S./g.h.

NOTES

1. Among the reviews bearing upon the period before 1950, we emphasize N. Turchi, "Studi sulla religione Romana," 1940–50, *StudRom* 2 (1954): 570–77; A. Brelich, "Storia delle religioni: Religione Romana," 1939–48, *Doxa* 2 (1949): 136–66; H. J. Rose, "Roman Religion," 1910–60, *JRS* 50 (1960): 161–72. It is sufficient to mention for the rest the collections published from time to time in the journal *Studi Romani:* N. Turchi, "Recenti studi sulla religione Romana," *StudRom* 6 (1958): 591–94; U. Bianchi, ibid. 9 (1961): 301–7; ibid. 11 (1963): 581–89; ibid. 15 (1967): 70–78.

2. We must not forget that, collaborating on the *Handbuch der römischen Alterhümer* of J. Marquardt and Th. Mommsen, Wissowa had edited the third volume (2d ed., Leipzig 1885) under the generic title *Römische Staatsverwaltung,* which included the subtitle *Das Sacralwesen.*

3. Extract of a personal letter from K. Latte to me in French, dated 27 October 1957.

4. M. Guarducci, *BCAR* 72 (1946–48): 2ff. Cf. A. Degrassi, *Inscriptiones Latinae liberae rei publicae* (= *I.L.L.R.*), nos. 10–12.

5. St. Weinstock, *Festschrift,* A. Rumpf (Cologne 1952), 151ff.

6. L. L. Tels-de-Jong, *Sur quelques divinités de la naissance et de la prophétie* (Delft 1959), passim. Cf. my review of this work in *Gnomon* 32 (1960): 650–53.

7. M. Guarducci, Arch. Class 3 (1951): 99ff., and "Ancora sulla legge sacra di Lavinio," ibid. 11 (1959): 204ff. (cf. A. Degrassi, *I.L.L.R.*, no. 509).

8. We refer to St. Weinstock, *JRS* 42 (1952): 34ff., and *RE,* 8, 2 (1958): cc, 1712–13 s. v. Vesperna; R. Bloch, *CRAI,* 1954, 203ff.; H. Le Bonniec, *Le culte de Cérès à Rome* (Paris 1958), 463ff.; Ae. Peruzzi, *Un problema etimologico latino, Maia* 11 (1959): 212ff.; K. Latte, *Römische Religionsgeschichte* (Munich 1960), 70, n. 1.

9. In spite of the efforts of Weinstock (who cites elsewhere the passage of Festus, p. 505 L: *Vesperna apud Plautum* [fr. inc. 45] *cena intellegitur*), the divinity of Vesperna seems suspect to me. I will understand it as a matter of a *lex sacra,* until proof to the contrary (in particular, an irrefutable attestation of this supposed divinity): "presents to Ceres, in an evening offering, viscera boiled in the pot."

10. Published by M. Guarducci, *BCAR* 76 (1956–58), appendix pp. 3ff.; it is cited by A. Degrassi, *I.L.L.R.*, no. 1271, with an important bibliography from which it is advisable to single out A. Alföldi, *Die trojanischen Urahnen der Römer* (Basel 1957); *Early Rome and the Latins* (Ann Arbor 1963), 255ff.

11. F. Castagnoli, *SMSR* 30 (1959): 109ff.

12. Cf. A. Degrassi, *I.L.L.R.*, no. 1271a, with bibliographic references.

13. Cf. A. Alföldi, *Early Rome and the Latins,* 268ff., and my article "Hommages à Georges Dumézil," Coll. Latomus, 45 (1960), 177ff. (= *R.C.D.R., Les Castores romains . . .*).

14. In a letter of 15 March 1971, F. Castagnoli courteously informed me of the then impending publication of the results of the excavations at Lavinium, with cited details: "Nei due ultimi anni gli scavi hanno riguardato un tratto delle mura sul lato orientale: sono mura in opera quadrata con resti di una porta e una strada. Presentano più fasi, la più antica databile al VI secolo."

15. The same author is publishing a commentary on Ovid's *Metamorphoses,* of which the first volume, *Kommentar,* books 1–3 (Heidelberg 1969), has appeared. An edition "for the educated public" of *Fastes,* by H. Le Bonniec (text, translation, notes), 2 vols. (Catana 1969), has appeared.

16. Let me cite my two articles on Ovid, reprinted in *R.C.D.R.*

17. Radke, op. cit., p. 8: "Und doch bietet sich uns in immer wiederkehrenden Fällen kaum etwas Anderes als der Name."

18. It is by design that I have not included Venus, which would have given the discussion a very personal turn. Always appreciating the moral of the fable of La Fontaine, *The Miller, His Son, and the Donkey,* I will not here oppose Radke's denial of the public agreement accorded to me by Hans Herter, Kurt Latte, Jean Bayet, and Georges Dumézil.

19. Cf. the argument developed in my article on Dea Dia, Coll. Latomus, 102 (1969), 2: 675–79 (= *R.C.D.R., Dea Dia . . .*).

20. Cf. *R.E.L.* 35 (1957): 424–31.

21. Ibid., pp. 428–29. The idea of making the cult of Castor come from Tusculum was a common enough opinion (cf. Latte, *R.R.G.*, p. 23) before the discovery of the archaic dedication on the ancient site of Lavinium.

22. D. van Berchem, *Hercule Melquart à l'Ara Maxima, RPAA* 32 (1960): 61–68.

23. J. Carcopino (*Aspects mystiques de la Rome païenne* [Paris 1941]) sees in the Pontitii a function of Pythagorian origin, coming from Taranto after 370. In the second edition of his book ([1969], p. 289),

J. Bayet remarks with good reason that Hercules already appears in the first Roman lectisternium of 399.

24. "But what might attract them (the Phoenicians) into this poor region?" asks J. Bayet (ibid. [1969], 289).

25. Cf. M. Pallottino, *Scavi nel santuario di Pyrgi,* Arch. Class. 16 (1964): 58–63; 76–104; 104–17.

26. Cf. the observations of R. Bloch (*Un mode d'interpretatio à deux degrès: De l'uni de Pyrgi à Ilithye et Leucothée,* Arch. Class. 21 [1969]: 64–65) on the presence of Thesan on a bronze lamella discovered by M. Pallottino at Pyrgi and published by him: *Un'altra laminetta di bronzo con iscrizione etrusca recuperata dal materiale di Pyrgi,* Arch. Class. 19 (1967): 336–41. R. Bloch wrote: "Thesan is nothing but the dawn known in Rome under the characteristics of Mater Matuta and subsequently assimilated to the marine goddess Leucothea." This identification is all the more interesting because Mater Matuta—to whom G. Dumézil restored her true identity, transcending all the confused discussions (*La religion romaine archaïque* [2d ed., Paris 1974], 66ff.), at the same time that he explicated the rites of the Matralia of 11 June—had a temple not only at Rome and Satricum-Conca, as R. Bloch called it, but also a cult, precisely at Caere (to which Pyrgi served as port), as I have observed in *R.E.L.* 43 (1965): 74; cf. Ovid *F.* 6 475ff.

27. F. Altheim, *Römische Religionsgeschichte* (Baden-Baden 1951–53; 2d ed., Berlin 1956). It is advisable not to rely on a French work published by the same author, *La religion romaine antique* (Paris 1955). I have observed, in *RHR* 159 (1961): 242–45, that it is less a translation than an adaptation, presented in language often incorrect.

28. I refer, for example, to the work of H. Le Bonniec, for Ceres (1958); to my work for Venus (1954); and to my articles on the Castors (1960) and Diana (1964), reprinted in *R.C.D.R.*

29. K. Latte, *R.R.G.,* 15, no. 1.

30. Ibid., 9 and n. 3.

31. Ibid., 1ff.: Quellen.

32. Ibid., 9.

33. Ibid., 114: "Der Gott, der Quirinus im Bewusstsein seiner Verehrer zurückgedrängt hat, war Mars."

34. Ibid., 18: "The same divine figures appear under different aspects according to whether the invocation expresses the needs of agriculture or of military life."

35. Ibid., 18: "Mars, der Gott der Welt jenseits der Siedlung, ist für den Bauern der Wilde, von dem er wünscht, dass er seine Fluren verschonen möge, für die Krieger, die die Grenzen der eigenen Siedlung überschreiten, ist er der gegebene Schirmherr und wird so zum Kriegsgott."

36. Cf. Degrassi, *I.L.R.R.,* n. 4, with notes and bibliographic references.

37. Cf. Latte, *R.R.G.,* 114.

38. The complete verse *Satur fu, fere Mars; limen sali, sta berber* can be translated "Be satisfied, ferocious Mars; leap to the frontier and mount guard." Cf. the explicit explanation of G. Dumézil, *La religion romaine archaïque,* 2d ed., 239ff. It is possible that "be satisfied" should be understood with the implicit idea of "by our offerings," as H. J. Rose has suggested.

39. According to the terms of Latte, *R.R.G.,* 114: "Das Arvallied wünscht, der Wilde möge satt sein, und wenn man ihm beim Flurumgang opfert, so möchte man seine Felder gegen ihn schützen."

40. Cf. A. Ernout and A. M. Meillet, *Dictionnaire étymologique de la langue latine* (4th ed., Paris 1959), 230, s. v. *ferus.*

41. Latte, *R.R.G.,* 1.

42. Cicero *De divinatione* 1.66. The passage from Ennius is attributed to a tragedy by Ennius, "Alexander"; cf. the edition by A. S. Pease (Darmstadt 1963), 211.

43. "I had been sent to make prophetic predictions; Apollo impels me in spite of myself in my delirium to reveal fate."

44. A brief reference to this passage (Ennius, scen. 57 V^2) is made, among other texts, in a note by Latte (*R.R.G.,* 268, n. 1). For the meaning of *superstitiosus,* see, most recently, E. Benveniste, *Le vocabulaire des institutions indo-européennes* (Paris 1969): 2:274ff.; for the etymology of *fas, fatum,* cf. ibid., 133ff. (the author refuses the derivation from the theme *dhēs-* in favor of the link with *fari*).

45. Latte, *R.R.G.,* ("This poet, one of the most modern among his contemporaries, was quite a stranger to the spirit of old Roman religion").

46. Ovid *F.* 5.429–44.

47. Cf. A. Degrassi, *Inscriptiones Italiae,* 13, 2 (1963): 388, with reference to my article "Un passage lacunaire du calendrier préjulien d'Antium éclairé par le commentaire d'Ovide" (*F.* 1.289–94), Coll. Latomus, 44 (1960): 694–97; reprinted in *R.C.D.R.* In the *editio minor* of the *Inscriptiones Latinae liberae rei publicae* (Florence 1957), 1:23, Degrassi has again put a question mark after his restoration.

48. Cf., most recently, G. Dumézil, *La religion romaine archaïque,* 2d ed., 99–103.

49. Cf. my article *REA* 70 (1968): 83–91.

50. An English translation, *Archaic Roman Religion* (Chicago 1970), is based on the first French edition.

51. I return here to certain developments presented in my review (*RHR* 172 [1967]: 217–20) and in my article (*REA* 70 [1968]: 83–91). However, all the references on this subject are to the second edition, *La religion romaine archaïque,* 2d ed., and to the English translation. Kohlhammer at first expected to publish this work in German. But "the delays required by translation into German were prolonged," so it is the French edition which represents the latest state of the author's thought, and he has kept the book up-to-date.

52. G. Dumézil, *La religion romaine archaïque,* 2d ed., 183–86.

53. K. Latte, *R.R.G.,* 204–5.

54. G. Dumézil, *La religion romaine archaïque,* 2d ed., 178–80.

55. Cf. Servius, *ad Aen.* 8.663.

56. G. Dumézil, *Archaic Roman Religion,* p. 161.

57. Cf. ibid., pp. 51 and 337–39.

58. An experiment of this type has been carried out for the gold lamellae of Pyrgi: see "Tavola rotonda: Le lamine di Pyrgi" (Rome 1970).

59. In France, in the line of monographs devoted to divinities, Jean-Louis Girard, a former student of the E.N.S., intends to write a thesis on Minerva.

60. *Les Frères Arvales, recrutement et origine sociale . . .* (Paris 1975).

61. I have tried to cover some problems in the *Annuaire* de l'École des Hautes Études (Paris 1969–70), 256–57.

62. In the article on this question (*Annuaire* de l'École des Hautes Études [Paris 1967–68], 31–55 = *R.C.D.R., Religion et magie à Rome*), I have examined in particular the festival of the Robigalia.

63. Cf. Ovid *F.* 4.681–82. F. Bömer (*Die Fasten,* 2, ad loc.) has denied the reality of this rite, which most commentaries take into consideration.

64. This is the idea of J. Bayet (*RBPh* 29 [1951]: 5–32), whom H. Le Bonniec follows on this point (*Le culte de Cérès à Rome* [Paris 1958], 122).

65. This is the suggestion of K. Latte (*R.R.G.,* 19).

66. Cf. G. Dumézil, *Archaic Roman Religion,* p. 94, for the commentary on this *carmen.* It is advisable, this scholar demonstrates, to respect the reading *feroque,* for which most editors have arbitrarily substituted the conjecture *oroque.*

67. Latte, *R.R.G.,* 15: "Es gilt zu ermitteln, was in historischen Zeiten noch lebendiger Glaube war."

68. With respect to "respect for traditions," a supposed "remark" about an augur who could not look at another augur without laughing is often attributed to Cicero, who was himself an augur. In fact, Cato's remark, reported by Cicero, applies, not to the Roman augur, but to the diviner who in that era was still considered a priest of Etruscan allegiance. See the texts: Cicero *De divinatione* 2.51: "Vetus autem illud Catonis admodum scitum est, qui mirari se aiebat quod non rideret haruspex haruspicem cum vidisset"; *De natura deorum* 1.71: "mirabile videtur quod non rideat haruspex cum haruspicem viderit."

69. Virgil *Aen.* 1.278–79: "I have not fixed limits for them in time or in space: I have given them an empire without end."

PRINCIPAL BIBLIOGRAPHY

1. Editions of Texts of Religious Significance

F. BÖMER, *P. Ovidius, Naso, Die Fasten* 1: *Einleitung, Text und Übersetzung* (Heidelberg 1957); 2: *Kommentar* (Heidelberg 1958).
A. DEGRASSI, *Inscriptiones Italiae,* 13, *Fasti et Elogia,* fasc. 2, *Fasti anni*

Numani et Juliani (Rome 1963); this fascicle 2 completes the publication by the same author of fasc. 1, *Fasti consulares et triumphales* (Rome 1947). It is the most complete edition and the most important commentary on the Roman calendar; *Inscriptiones latinae liberae rei publicae,* fasc. 1 (Florence 1957); this edition, with interesting notes, concerns Roman religion especially in nos. 1 (*Tituli a saeculo septimo ad quartum*) and 4 (*Numina et sacerdotes;* ibid., fasc. 2 [Florence 1963]); this publication, conceived according to the same method, is to be consulted especially for nos. 9, (*Leges sacrae*); 14 (*Magistratus et sacerdotes civitatum, pagorum, vicorum*); 23 (*Tabellae defixionum*); *addit-amenta* (the most recent religious inscriptions). G. DEVOTO, *Tabulae Iguvinae* (3d ed., Rome 1962). A. ERNOUT, *Le dialecte ombrien: Lexique du vocabulaire des "Tables Eugubines" et des inscriptions* (Paris 1961). A. PASOLI, *Acta Fratrum Arualium* (Bologna 1950); this edition was completed by the inscriptions published afterward by G. HENZEN (*Acta Fratrum Arualium* [Berlin 1874]); but it does not replace his commentary, which remains indispensable. A. J. PFIFFIG, *Religio Iguvina: Philologische und religionsgeschichtliche Studien zu den Tabulae Iguvinae* (Vienna 1964). J. W. POULTNEY, *The Bronze Tablets of Iguvium,* Mon. Am. Ph. Ass. 17 (1959). E. VETTER, *Handbuch der italischen Dialekte* (Heidelberg 1953).

2. General Works and Summaries

A. ALFÖLDI, *Early Rome and the Latins* (Ann Arbor 1963). F. ALTHEIM, *La religion romaine antique* (Paris 1955) (mediocre translation). *Römische Religionsgeschichte* (Baden-Baden 1951–53; 2d ed., Berlin 1956). J. BAYET, *Histoire politique et psychologique de la religion romaine* (Paris 1957; 2d ed., Paris 1969); *Idéologie et plastique* (Rome 1974). E. BENVENISTE, *Le vocabulaire des institutions indo-européennes* 2: *Pouvoir, droit, religion* (Paris 1969). W. DEN BOER, *Le culte des souverains dans l'empire romain.* Entretiens sur l'antiquité class. 19 (Geneva 1973). P. BOYANCÉ, *Études sur la religion romaine* (Rome 1972). M. H. CRAWFORD, *Roman Republican Coinage,* 1–2 (Cambridge 1974). P. DE FRANCISCI, *Primordia civitatis* (Rome 1959). G. DUMÉZIL, *Les dieux des Indo-Européens* (Paris 1951); *L'idéologie tripartie des Indo-Européens* (Brussels 1958); *Archaic Roman Religion* (Chicago 1970); *Idées romaines* (Paris 1969); *Mythe et épopée,* 3 vols. (Paris 1968–73); *Fêtes romaines d'été et d'automne* (Paris 1975). J. FERGUSON, *The Religions of the Roman Empire, Aspects of Greek and Roman Life* (London 1970). H. FUGIER, *Recherches sur l'expression du sacré dans la langue latine* (Paris 1963). E. GJERSTAD, *Early Rome* 1: *Stratigraphical Researches in the Forum Romanum and along the Sacra Via* (Lund 1953); 2: *The Tombs* (1956); 3: *Fortifications, Domestic Architecture, Sanctuaries, Stratigraphic Excavations* (1960); 4: *Synthesis of Archaeological Evidence* (1966); 5: *The Written Sources* (1973). P. GRIMAL, *Dictionnaire de la mythologie grecque et romaine* (Paris 1951; 4th ed., Paris 1969). F. C. GRANT, *Ancient Roman Religion* (New York 1957). W. R. HALLIDAY, *Lectures on the History of Roman Religion* (New York 1950). J. HEURGON, *Rome et la Méditerranée occidentale jusqu'aux guerres puniques* (Paris 1969). H. HUNGER, *Lexikon der griechischen und römischen Mythologie* (5th ed., Vienna 1959). A. KIRSOPP MICHELS, *The Calendar of the Roman Republic* (Princeton 1967). K. LATTE, *Römische Religionsgeschichte* (Munich 1960). M. LEGLAY, *La religion romaine* (Paris 1971). R. M. OGILVIE, *The Romans and Their Gods in the Age of Augustus* (London 1969). R. E. A. PALMER, *Roman Religion and Empire* (Philadelphia 1974). A. PASTORINO, *La religione romana,* Problemi di storia 21 (Milan 1973). S. PEROWNE, *Roman Mythology* (London 1969). G. B. PIGHI, *La religione romana,* Lezioni Augusto Rostagni 3 (Turin 1967). J. POUCET, *Recherches sur la légende sabine des origines de Rome* (Kinshasa 1967). G. RADKE, *Die Götter Altitaliens* (Munich 1965). H. J. ROSE, *Ancient Roman Religion* (London 1949; New York 1950). I. SCOTT RYBERG, *Rites of the State Religion in Roman Art,* MAAR 22 (1955). R. SCHILLING, *The Roman Religion: Historia Religionum* (Leiden 1969). E. SYDENHAM, *The Coinage of the Roman Republic* (London 1952). R. THOMSEN, *Early Roman Coinage* (Copenhagen 1957). G. VAN DER LEEUW, *Phänomenologie der Religion* (Tübingen 1956). S. WEINSTOCK, *Divus Julius* (Oxford 1971), religion at the time of Caesar.

3. Monographs and Specialized Studies

A. ALFÖLDI, *Der frührömische Reiteradel und seine Ehrenabzeichen* (Baden-Baden 1952); *Studien über Caesars Monarchie* (Lund 1953); *Die trojanischen Urahnen der Römer* (Basel 1957). A. BARTOLI, *I pozzi dell'area sacra di Vesta* (Rome 1959). M. G. BERTINELLI ANGELI, *Nomenclatura publica e sacra di Roma nelle epigrafi semitiche* (Genoa 1970). R. BLOCH, *Les prodiges dans l'antiquité classique* (Paris 1963). M. BOLLINI, *Minerva medica minor: Atti del III Congresso di Studi Veleiati* (Milan-Varese 1969). F. BÖMER, *Rom und Troja* (Baden-Baden 1951). P. BOYANCÉ, *La religion de Virgile* (Paris 1963). A. BRELICH, *Tre variazioni sul tema delle origini* (Rome 1955). A. BRUHL, *Liber Pater: Origine et expansion du culte dionysiaque à Rome et dans le monde romain* (Paris 1953). P. CATALANO, *Contributi allo studio del diritto augurale,* 1 (Turin 1960). F. CRAMER, *Astrology in Roman Law and Politics* (Philadelphia 1954). L. DELATTE, *Recherches sur quelques fêtes mobiles du calendrier romain* (Liège 1957). W. DEONNA and M. RENARD, *Croyances et superstitions de table dans la Rome antique* (Brussels 1961). G. DUMÉZIL, *Aspects de la fonction guerrière chez les Indo-Européens* (Paris 1956); *Rituels indo-européens à Rome* (Paris 1954); *Jupiter, Mars, Quirinus* (Paris 1941); *Déesses latines et mythes védiques* (Brussels 1956). R. DUTHOY, *The Taurobolium: Its Evolution and Terminology,* Études prélimin. aux relig. orient. dans l'empire rom. 10 (Leiden 1969). L. FERRERO, *Storia del Pitagorismo nel mondo romano: Dalle origini alla fine della Repubblica* (Turin 1955). H. FREIER, *Caput velare* (diss., Tübingen 1965). J. GAGÉ, *Apollon romain: Essai sur le culte d'Apollon et le développement du "ritus graecus" à Rome, des origines à Auguste* (Paris 1955); *Matronalia, Essai sur les dévotions et les organisations cultuelles des femmes dans l'ancienne Rome* (Brussels 1963); *Basileia: Les Césars, les rois d'Orient et les mages* (Paris 1968). G. K. GALINSKY, *Aeneas, Sicily and Rome* (Princeton 1969). H. GESCHE, *Die Vergottung Caesars,* Frankfurter althist. Studien 1 (Kallmün 1968). U. GEYER, *Der Adlerflug im römischen Konsekrationszeremoniell* (diss., Bonn 1967). D. R. GORDON, *The Evidence for the Survival of Italian Agricultural Cult* (Madison, WI, 1968, microfilm). B. GRASSMANN-FISCHER, *Die Prodigien in Vergils Aeneis* (Munich 1966). F. GUIZZI, *Aspetti giuridici del sacerdozio romano: Il sacerdozio di Vesta* (Naples 1968). L. HALKIN, *La supplication d'action de grâces chez les Romains* (Liège 1953). G. H. HALSBERGHE, *The Cult of Sol Invictus* (Leiden 1972). J. HEURGON, *Trois études sur le "Ver sacrum"* (Brussels 1957). M. W. HOFFMAN LEWIS, *The Official Priests of Rome under the Iulio-Claudians* (Rome 1961). L. A. MAC KAY, *Janus* (Berkeley 1956). C. KOCH, *Der römische Iuppiter* (Frankfurt 1937; new edition Darmstadt 1968); *Religio, Studien zu Kult und Glauben der Römer* (Nuremburg 1960). D. LADAGE, *Städtische Priester- und Kultämter im lateinischen Westen des Imperium Romanum zur Kaiserzeit* (diss., Cologne 1971). H. LE BONNIEC, *Le culte de Cérès à Rome, des origines à la fin de la République* (Paris 1958). J. LE GALL, *Recherches sur le culte du Tibre* (Paris 1953). A. MAGDELAIN, *Recherches sur l'"Imperium": La loi curiate et les auspices d'investiture* (Paris 1968). R. J. MELLOR, *Dea Roma: The Development of the Idea of the Goddess Roma* (diss., Princeton 1967). R. MERKELBACH, *Isisfeste in griechisch-römischer Zeit, Daten und Riten* (Meisenheim-am-Glan 1963). M. MESLIN, *La fête des kalendes de janvier dans l'empire romain: Étude d'un rituel de Nouvel An* (Brussels 1970). W. MUELLER, *Die heilige Stadt, Roma quadrata, himmlisches Jerusalem und die Mythe vom Weltnabel* (Stuttgart 1961). R. M. OGILVIE, *The Romans and Their Gods in the Age of Augustus* (London 1969). D. G. ORR, *Roman Domestic Religion: A Study of the Roman Household Deities and Their Shrines at Pompeii and Herculanum* (diss, University of Maryland 1972, microfilm). R. E. A. PALMER, *The King and the Comitium: A Study of Rome's Oldest Public Document* (Wiesbaden 1969); *Roman Religion and Empire* (Philadelphia 1974). G. PICCALUGA, *Elementi spettacolari nei rituali festivi romani* (Rome 1965). G. B. PIGHI, *De ludis saecularibus populi Romani Quiritium* (Milan 1941; 2d ed., Amsterdam 1965); *La poesia religiosa Romana* (Bologna 1958). G. CHARLES-PICARD, *Les trophées romains: Contribution à l'histoire de la religion et de l'art triomphal à Rome* (Paris 1957). G. PFANNMUELLER, *Tod, Jenseits und Unsterblichkeit in der Religion, Literatur und Philosophie der Griechen und Römer* (Munich and Basel 1953). P. ROMANELLI, *Lo scavo al tempio della Magna Mater sul Palatino e nelle sue adiacenze* (Rome 1962). D. SABBATUCCI, *L'Edilità romana: Magistratura e sacerdozio* (Rome 1954). R. SCHILLING, *La religion romaine de Vénus, depuis les origines jusqu'au temps d'Auguste* (Paris 1954); *Rites, cultes, dieux de Rome* (Paris 1979). U. W. SCHOLZ, *Studien zum altitalischen und altrömischen Marskult und Marsmythos* (Heidelberg 1970). L. SCHUMACHER, *Prosopographische Untersuchungen zur Besetzung der vier hohen römischen Priesterkollegien im Zeitalter der Antonine und der Severer, 96–235 n. Chr.* S.J. SIMON (Mainz 1973). S. J. SIMON, *The Greater Official Priests of Rome under the Flavian and Antonine Emperors* (diss., University of Chicago 1973, microfilm). P. STEHOUWER, *Étude sur Ops et Consus* (diss., Groningen 1956). L. STORONI MAZZOLANI, *Sul mare della vita* (Milan 1969), on the conception of death in Rome. G. J. SZEMLER, *The Priests of the Republic: A Study of Interactions between Priesthoods and Magistracies* (Brussels 1972). L. TELS-DE-JONG, *Sur quelques divinités romaines de la naissance et de la prophétie* (Delft 1959). J. TRIER, *Venus: Etymologien um das Futterlaub*

(Cologne 1963). R. TURCAN, *Les sarcophages romains à représentations dionysiaques* (Paris 1966). H. S. VERSNEL, *Triumphus: An Inquiry into the Origin, Development and Meaning of the Roman Triumph* (Leiden 1970). H. WAGENVOORT, *Studies in Roman Literature: Culture and Religion* (Leiden 1956). A. WLOSOK, *Die Göttin Venus in Vergils Aeneis* (Heidelberg 1967). R. K. YERKES, *Sacrifice in Greek and Roman Religions and Early Judaism* (New York 1952).

Roman Festivals

The very word for festival is a Latin term that derives from *festa*—a neuter plural that corresponds to the classical expression *festus (dies)*. This leads us back to the root **dhe-*, which serves to form the stem **dhēs-*. This stem is the base both for the Latin noun *fanum* (with the root in its weak form) and the words *fesiae*—which renders *feriae*—and *festus (dies)* (with the root in its strong form). It is certainly difficult to define the stem **dhēs-*, which according to Benveniste[1] "designates some religious object or rite whose meaning we can no longer ascertain; in any case, it is related to the sacred sphere."

The lack of precision of this definition indicates the degree of present-day ignorance and induces us to learn about ancient beliefs on the subject. The following are the statements of Macrobius,[2] which go back to the origin of the institution of the calendar: "Numa, having divided the year into months, went on to divide each month into days, all of which were known as *dies festos* (festivals) or *profestos* (working days) or *intercisos* ("interruptions" or "intermittents": morning and evening are festivals, while the interval between them is a period for work). The festival days are dedicated to the gods, on working days men may transact their private and public business, and the 'interruptions' are days shared between gods and men."

This distinction remained in effect both for the calendar of the republican epoch, which is supposed to have been instituted by King Numa (and which is characterized by the periodic insertion, every two years, of an intercalary month, *mensis intercalaris* or *mercedonius*, to compensate for the deficit of the lunar year—355 days—in relation to the solar year of 365¼ days),[3] and for the Julian calendar, which was reformed in 46 B.C. by Julius Caesar and which, except for a correction made by Pope Gregory XIII in the sixteenth century, is still in use in societies of Latin tradition.

Nevertheless, the distribution of the days as presented by Macrobius does not appear in a direct reading of the distinctive marks of the calendar. As this document was edited for the use of men, the days bear a sign which indicates whether or not they are suitable for profane use: *F* designates the *dies fasti*, in which it is *fas*, "religiously legitimate,"[4] to attend to the concerns of everyday life: in particular, the praetor could pronounce the three sacramental words, *tria verba sollemnia*, "do, dico, addico"[5] which permitted the exercise of the *legis actio*, legal procedure. The letter C signifies comitial days (*dies comitiales*) on which the holding of *comitia* (assemblies) was also authorized.[6]

By contrast, the letter *N* marked the days (*dies nefastos*) on which *non licebat lege agere*,[7] because such days were reserved "for the will of the gods," *deorum causa*, to use Varro's expression.[8] The term *nefastus* thus does not have the pejorative sense that it took on later,[9] but simply indicates that the praetor was forbidden to pronounce the three sacramental words and the magistrate was forbidden to hold assemblies. These days had religious overtones only to the extent that if the praetor were to transgress the rule by mistake (*imprudens*), he would have to perform an expiatory sacrifice (*piaculari hostia*). And if, on the contrary, he violated the prohibition knowingly—*prudens*—he would be struck with *impietas*, an inexpiable wrong.[10] Otherwise these *dies nefasti* did not impede the holding of assemblies in the senate, the meetings of the *contiones*, or the activities of the markets.[11]

The true festival days—*dies fasti*—which carry proper names in capital letters on the calendar, generally[12] have the sign *NP*: these two ligatured letters have given rise to a series of debates which have never come to any certain conclusions.[13] But these are undoubtedly *feriae publicae* set aside for the gods, *dies deorum causa instituti* according to Varro's definition.[14] They are charaacterized by sacrifices to the gods as well as by ceremonies and rejoicing.[15] They imply an obligation to rest: these are *dies quieti*, declares Cicero (*De legibus* 2.55), days "exempted from all litigation," on which it is proper to celebrate "completed tasks, in the midst of one's servants."[16] Freemen are to renounce their lawsuits and quarrels, and slaves are to benefit from the right to rest from their labors and their troubles.[17] This prescription for rest was combined with a precise set of rules, if we are to believe Macrobius:[18] "The priests used to maintain that the celebration of the festival was desecrated if, after it had been officially proclaimed, anyone worked." In practice, exceptions were provided, for example for certain agricultural work,[19] and the lawmakers elaborated a kind of casuistry to this end. When asked what one was permitted to do on the day of a religious festival, Scaevola replied: "That which if omitted would do harm to someone."[20] Macrobius, who cites this response, immediately gives two concrete examples: "If an ox fell into a pit and the head of the household pulled it out with the aid of his laborers, he would not be thought to have desecrated the festival; nor a man who, seeing that the main beam of his roof was broken, propped it up to avoid its imminent collapse."[21]

It is nevertheless interesting to note that this prescription retained an absolute character vis-à-vis the high priestly dignitaries, the king of the sacrifices and the flamens (among whom the *flamen Dialis* was *quotidie feriatus*, "every day in a 'festive' state"). Macrobius in fact specifies that "the king of the sacrifices and the flamens did not have the right to see anyone working on festival days; they also had a public crier proclaim that all were to abstain from work; whoever neglected this prescription was fined. Besides the fine, the code provided that if a person did any work on these days through carelessness, he was to sacrifice a pig in expiation; on the other hand, if he had acted knowingly, there was no expiation for him, according to the opinion of Scaevola the pontiff."[22] Yet Macrobius mitigates this opinion of Scaevola with a corrective:[23] "There is no profanation, if the work concerned the gods or the cult, or if an urgent situation of vital interest presented itself."

Among the *feriae*, private festivals, *feriae privatae* (such as the *Lemuria* of 9, 11, and 13 May, which were celebrated by the head of the household to drive the *Lemures* from the house—or the *Denicales*, whose aim was to purify a family that had been in mourning),[24] are to be distinguished from public festivals, *feriae publicae*.

The latter, which were officially celebrated in the general interest, *pro populo*, were subdivided into fixed and movable feasts—*feriae conceptivae*, which were announced each year at a variable date but within the same season (these are especially agricultural festivals, such as, for example, the *Sementivae*)—and *feriae imperitivae*, ordained by the civil or religious authorities under exceptional circumstances (for example, upon the appearance of a prodigy or to celebrate a victory). Only fixed festivals, *feriae publicae stativae,* normally appeared on calendars (which were used by the *Corpus Inscriptionum Latinarum*).

It is appropriate at this point to examine the distribution of the various festivals over the course of the year. Their arrangement on the calendar, as well as their respective meanings, furnishes valuable information: the calendar constitutes an accurate mirror of the religious mentality of the Romans. Historians of Roman religion also have a document that is unique of its kind: the poet Ovid's liturgical commentary on the *Fasti.* In spite of its syncretist inspiration, which mixes Roman religion with Greek mythology, Ovid's poem constitutes a useful and valuable source by virtue of its internal stratification. This is because Ovid's method generally consists in presenting religious data on three levels: he describes rites, he situates their institutionalization in history, and he attempts to explain their meaning through a myth.

The question then arises as to whether the relationships between these three levels are arbitrary or whether, rather, they correspond to a complementary clarification of the religious reality. A general response is not possible. There are as many species as there are particular phenomena.[25] What must be emphasized is that as a born observer, Ovid is an incomparable witness to liturgy: in this respect he often helps us to elucidate the meaning of archaic ceremonies beyond his own interpretation, precisely because he did not hesitate to describe faithfully rites that appeared strange to his contemporaries.

The recognition of an Indo-European heritage at Rome, which in France has been the work of Georges Dumézil, has made it possible to decipher archaic rites whose mythological key had long been lost. I am thinking, for example, of the 11 June *Matralia* in which mothers of households, by fondling in their arms their sister's child rather than their own, carried out a ceremony whose meaning they did not know, but one that corresponds to a procedure of sympathetic magic in Vedic India: the goddess Dawn takes care of the Sun, who is the son of Night, her sister.[26]

These are nevertheless extreme cases; the majority of religious festivals clearly remained intelligible to Romans of the classical age.[27] It is sufficient to take a look at the calendar to realize that two groups emerge from the whole: the festivals of martial import in the month of March inaugurate military campaigns in the spring (14 March: *Equirria;* 17 March: *Agonium Martiale;* 19 March: *Quinquatrus;* 23 March: *Tubilustrium*), and the pastoral or agricultural festivals take place in the month of April (15 April: *Fordicidia;* 19 April: *Cerialia;* 21 April: *Parilia;* 25 April: *Robigalia*).

Corresponding to the festivals that celebrate the opening of the military year are the festivals that close it at the end of military operations: the purificatory ceremony of the *Tigillum Sororium* of 1 October, the sacrifice of the winning horse of the 15 October race, and the *Armilustrium* of 19 October.

As for agricultural or pastoral festivals, these take place during two further periods of liturgical intensity, in summer and winter. In the months of July and August they successively celebrated the *Lucaria* (19 and 21 July), the *Neptunalia* (23 July), the *Furrinalia* (25 July), the *Portunalia* (17 August), the *Consualia* (21 August), the *Volcanalia* (23 August), the *Opiconsivia* (25 August) and the *Volturnalia* (27 August). All of these summer festivals are intended to promote the harmonious arrival of the products of the land or the prosperity of the livestock. Then follows a liturgical recess: the months of September and October are absolutely "empty." The last agricultural festivals take place in December to ensure good preservation of the winter harvest: these are the *Consualia* of 15 December and the *Opalia* of 19 December.

Thus it is evident that in Roman society the liturgical year was modulated according to significant rhythms: for festivals pertaining to war, it was punctuated by two periods that corresponded to the opening and closing of the military campaigns. As for festivals of a pastoral or vegetable nature, the calendar was divided into three periods which corresponded to the three seasons of greatest importance to plants and animals: spring, summer, and winter.

While it may be that these two groups of festivals are concerned with the two great preoccupations of ancient society—defense and subsistence—they do not complete the religious tapestry. It would be especially interesting to study the greatest festival: the *Vinalia* addressed to Jupiter. This festival is exceptional in several ways—in its double articulation in the calendar (19 August and 23 April), in the quality of the god (he is the supreme god) and of the priest (the *flamen Dialis* is the chief priest in the city), and by its object, the annual renewal of the alliance between the sovereign god and the Roman people.[28]

One final aspect must be considered. Archaic festivals often lent themselves to a certain rejuvenation in the course of time. So it is that the liturgy of the *Consualia,* which included a horse race, set the style for the *ludi,* those chariot races that would animate the Great Circus. Thus the *ritus graecus,* with its lectisternia and its *supplicationes* of matrons invading the temples in times of panic, modified the hieratic appearance of the Roman ceremonies. But the basic end remained the same: *ferias observare*[29] always consisted of offering to the gods a time set aside from the profane tapestry in order to obtain, to use the oft-repeated words of Livy, *pacem veniamque deum,* "the favor and grace of the gods."

R.S./d.w.

NOTES

1. E. Benveniste, *V.I.I.,* 2:133.

2. Macrobius *S.,* 1.16.2: *Numa, ut in menses annum, ita in dies mensem quemque distribuit diesque omnes aut festos aut profestos aut intercisos vocavit. Festi dis dicati sunt, profesti hominibus ob administrandam rem privatam publicamque concessi, intercisi deorum hominumque communes sunt.* The *dies intercisi* are eight in number (cf. Varro *De Lingua Latina* 6.31). It is also necessary to mention the three *dies fissos* (24 March and 25 May, designated by the initials Q[uando] R[ex] C[omitiavit] F[as], and 15 June, designated by the initials Q[uando] St[ercus] D[elatum] F[as]), which are subdivided into a first, sacred, part and a second, profane, part: cf. Servius *ad Aen.* 6.37.

3. The economy of this pre-Julian calendar is well known because of the discovery of the *Fasti Antiates veteres,* a document found at Antium and published for the first time in the *N.S.,* 1921.

4. The etymology of *fas* is contested. E. Benveniste, *V.I.I.,* 2:133, following the suggestion of the ancients, brings together *fas* and *fari,* derived from the root **bhā-: fas* designates "divine speech," the divine law. On the other hand, G. Dumézil (*La religion romaine archaïque,* 2d ed., p. 144) prefers to connect *fas* with the root **dhē-* (zero grade: dhəs-), which is the base of *fanum* and *feriae,* in giving it the meaning "mystic basis," "which underlies all the arrangements and visible connections defined by the *ius.*"

5. *Do (iudicem), dico (ius), addico (litem):* cf. Macrobius *S.* 1.16.14. See A. Giffard, *Études de droit romain* (Paris 1972), 19.

6. Cf. Macrobius *S.* 1.16.14.

7. The expression is from Gaius *Institutiones* 4.29. Cf. Varro *L.L.* 6.53.

8. Varro *L.L.* 6 12.

9. By the second century A.D. Aulus Gellius (*Noctes Atticae* 5.17) indicates the evolution of meaning that has given *nefastus* the pejorative value of "inauspicious," which the modern language has conserved and which was expressed in the classical period by the adjective *ater* (or *religiosus*). See also Nonius Marcellus, p. 103 L.: *atri dies dicuntur quos nunc nefastos aut posteros vocant.*

10. Cf. Varro *L.L.* 6.30.

11. A. Kirsopp Michels (*The Calendar of the Roman Republic,* p. 68) has rightly stressed this aspect, in reaction against the interpretation of the classical manuals. For example, Wissowa (*Ruk*[2], p. 435) presents the following table: making a deduction of 11 special days (8 *intercisi* days and 3 *fissi* days), 344 days remain in the pre-Julian year; 235 belong to men (192 *dies comitiales,* 43 *dies fasti*), 109 to the gods (all the ides, half of the calends—February, March, June, July, October, December—a third of the nones—February, April, June, July)—and the 45 days that bear a particular name and correspond to the *feriae publicae.*

12. With the exception of some nine festivals: A. Kirsopp Michels (op. cit., pp. 76–77) tries to explain the initial *N* by the *Regifugium* (24 February), the three *Lemuria* (9, 11, 13 May), the *Vestalia* (9 June), and the *Matralia* (11 June), and the initial *F* by the *Feralia* (21 February). As for the *Vinalia* of 23 April marked by the letter *F* and the *Vinalia* of 19 August which bears the initials *FP,* the author reserves judgment. I have offered an explanation in my book *R.R.V.,* pp. 129–30, proposing, following a suggestion by Wissowa, to transcribe *FP* in *Feriae publicae* (I wrote *Feria publica,* but the plural *Feriae publicae* alone is used in the classical period); in this hypothesis, the stonecutter has omitted by error the *P* at least for the *Vinalia* of 19 August.

13. After Wissowa, who has proposed (*Ruk*[2], p. 438) the transcription *nefas (feriae) publicae,* A. Kirsopp Michels (op. cit., p. 76) suggests the reading *(dies) nefasti publici.*

14. Varro *L.L.* 6.12ff.

15. Cf. Macrobius *S.* 1.16.4.

16. Cf. Cicero *De legibus* 2.19: *Feriis jurgia amovento, easque in famulis, operibus patratis, habento . . .*

17. Ibid. 2.29: *cum est feriarum festorumque dierum ratio, in liberis requietem habet litium et jurgiorum, in servis operum et laborum.*

18. Macrobius *S.* 1.16.9: *affirmabant autem sacerdotes pollui ferias, si indictis conceptisque opus aliquod fieret.*

19. Cf. Cato, *De agric.* 138; Pliny *Naturalis historia* 18.40.

20. Macrobius *S.* 1.16.11: *Scaevola denique consultus quid feriis agi liceret, rspondit quod praetermissum noceret.*

21. Ibid.

22. Ibid. 1.16.9–10.

23. Ibid. This corrective is attributed to someone named *umbro,* who is otherwise unknown.

24. On the *Lemuria,* cf. Ovid *Fasti* 5.421–44. On the *Denicales,* cf. Festus, p. 61; 282, 16 L.

25. Cf. my study *Ovide, interprète de la religion romaine, R.E.L.,* 46, 1969, p. 222ff. Reprinted in *R.C.D.R.*

26. Cf. Ovid *F.* 6.475ff., for the description of Roman rites; G. Dumézil, *R.R.A.*[2], 66ff.

27. On the details of these festivals, see in addition to the classic work of G. Wissowa (*Ruk*[2]), the *R.R.A.*[2] of Georges Dumézil and his *Fêtes romaines d'été et d'automne.*

28. Cf. Robert Schilling, *R.R.V.,* p. 71ff., especially 124–55.

29. Cf. Macrobius *S.* 1.16.4.

SUMMARY BIBLIOGRAPHY

G. WISSOWA, *Religion und Kultus der Römer* (Munich 1912), 432–49, "Die Festzeiten" (= *Ruk*[2]). G. DUMÉZIL, *La religion romaine archaïque* (2d ed., Paris 1974), 551–58, "Sacra publica" (= *R.R.A.*[2]); *Fêtes romaines d'été et d'automne* (Paris 1975). ERNOUT-MEILLET, *Dictionnaire étymologique de la langue latine* (4th ed., Paris 1959), s.v. *feriae.* E. BENVENISTE, *Le vocabulaire des institutions indo-européennes* (Paris 1969), 2:133ff (= *V.I.I.*). A. KIRSOPP MICHELS, *The Calendar of the Roman Republic* (Princeton 1967), especially 69–83. MARQUARDT-WISSOWA, "Die Feiertage des römischen Kalenders," in *Römische Staatsverwaltung,* pp. 567–89. R. SCHILLING, *La religion romaine de Vénus . . .* (Paris 1954) (= *R.R.V.*), and *Rites, cultes, dieux de Rome* (Paris 1979) (= *R.C.D.R.*).

Roman Divination

1. Divination or Auspices: Roman and Italic Traditions

In Rome the expression *divinatio* is of rather recent date; it does not appear until Cicero, who defines it in the following manner: "According to an ancient belief that goes back to heroic times and that is confirmed by the general agreement of the Roman people and of all nations, there exists among men a certain form of *divinatio,* which the Greeks call *mantikē* (prophecy); that is, a faculty for knowing the future ahead of time—*praesensionem et scientiam rerum futurarum*" (*On Divination,* 1.1; *On Laws,* 2.32).[1]

The word is a substantive derived from *divinus,* which is itself connected with *divus* (= the ancient *deivos,* which, through the laws of phonetics, ends up as *deus*), "divinity." The meaning of *divinatio* may be explained by the semantic drift that took place in the case of *divinus:* this term, which originally meant "of divine nature," also took on the sense "inspired by the divinity."

It is in the writings of Cicero that the word *divinus* is first used in the sense of "diviner" (see, for example, *On Divination,* 2.9, 10, 11). The new meaning arises from the first, the diviner essentially passing for one of divine nature who is inspired. This relationship is strong enough for Cicero to commit the same semantic slippage on the level of the substantive: thus he uses *divinitas* in the place of *divinatio* (for example, *On Divination,* 2.80). It is true that the choice of the term in this context might have been influenced by a concern for stylistic symmetry: in this passage, the expression "experts in divination" (*divinitatis auctores*) designates men who are accused of being ignorant, "strangers to humanity" (*humanitatis expertes*). But ordinarily the idea of divinatory practices is rendered by the new word *divinatio.*

If the semantic extension of the word *divinus* (= diviner) and the creation of the substantive *divinatio* are recent, how are we to explain the discrepancy which seems to exist in Rome between this new vocabulary and a reputedly ancient set of practices? Did not Rome have a venerable institution that answered to this sort of preoccupation—the college of augurs?

In fact, the Romans of the first century B.C. did not agree on the significance of this augural institution. Did these "official interpreters of Jupiter" (*On Laws,* 2.20) simply have the task of revealing, through the elucidation of the auspices, Jupiter's approval or disapproval of any given human initiative? Or did they also have the charismatic virtue of being able to predict the future? This is the basic problem that beset the members of the college in the time of Cicero. And thanks to Cicero's allusions in his treatise *On Divination,* this debate remains accessible to us.

As the debate is presented to us, the augur App. Claudius Pulcher had no doubts at all about his divinatory powers when in 63 B.C. he announced to the consul Cicero "the imminence of a civil war that would be sinister and disturbing" (*On Divination,* 1.105): this prediction that foresees the Catiline conspiracy was based upon "incertitudes connected with the augury of prosperity"—*addubitato salutis augurio* (from Dio Cassius, 37.24.2, we know that this involved a kind of request addressed to the gods to find out if it was opportune to ask for prosperity for the people). He was ridiculed by his colleagues, who called him a charlatan augur (in the terms of the time: an "augur of Pisidia," "augur of Sora"). "He alone, over the past several years, has carried on an art that consisted not only in reciting an augural formula, but also in practicing divination"—*solus enim, multorum annorum memoria, non decantandi augurii, sed divinandi tenuit disciplinam.* Such is at least the version of Quintus, the brother of Cicero, who highly approved of this conception of the augural art.

By contrast, another augur, C. Claudius Marcellus, also a colleague of Cicero, professed quite a different opinion (*On Divination,* 2.75), which Cicero shared: "the right to augur—in which a divinatory power would have originally been acknowledged—has been subsequently maintained and preserved only in the interest of the state." Cicero attempts to justify this positivist conception, and in this sense he shows a critical liberty in *On Divination* that contrasts with the nuanced declarations of *On Laws:* "by the evolution and progress of learning." "Romulus, who founded the city after taking the auspices, was capable of thinking that the auguring science consisted of prediction (the ancients were mistaken on several points)" (*On Divination,* 2.70).

And to demonstrate the illusory character of the auspices, Cicero analyzes the procedure employed in the consultation of the sacred chickens who, when little pellets of food fell from their beaks—but how could they not fall?—were expected to furnish the consultant with the favorable auspices of the *tripudium solstimum* (*On Div.,* 2.71). He denounces the mechanical nature of the questions and answers exchanged between the magistrate-consultant and the augur and waxes ironic about the automatic results of these "auspices obtained through constraint."

It is true that this "auspicial simulation" (Cicero's own expression) had already been denounced in equally categorical terms by Quintus (*On Div.,* 1.28). But Cicero's brother had explained this decadence in augural practices as being the result of ignorance and the negligent laxity of those in charge at the college. Cicero, by contrast, goes much further in his criticism, by denying the existence of any divinatory value in the augural institution: "I am not one of those augurs who presumes himself capable of telling the future by observing birds and other signs" (*On Div.,* 2.70).

The time has now come to ask whether the argument that arose in the first century B.C. in the heart of the college of augurs and that is reflected in Cicero's treatise did not originate from a certain confusion, the same confusion that caused several very different modes of divine consultation to be classified under one and the same heading. It is a fact that the title of Cicero's treatise covers some quite varied divining techniques. When he introduces the different *divinandi genera* (*On Div.,* 1.12), Cicero finds it quite natural to group the augurs together with the haruspices (specialists in the examination of victims' viscera as well as of portents and lightning flashes), the interpreters of the *Sibylline Books,* the astrologers, and the interpreters of oracles and dreams: a heterogeneous list, if ever there was one.

From this the question arises of the possible existence here of a kind of improper contamination that wrongly classified the official Roman augurs among those specialists reputed to possess prophetic powers. Certainly, a kind of golden legend exalted the role of certain augurs. So it is that tradition kept alive the memory of the augur Attus Navius, who lived during the reign of Tarquinius the Elder (*On Div.,* 1.31–32) and who became famous for his exceptional gifts. "In order to test his knowledge, the king had asked him if what he was thinking could come to pass. After taking the augury, Attus responded that such was possible. Tarquinius then told him that he had thought that a piece of flint could be sliced in half with a razor, and ordered Attus to perform the experiment. Thus, a piece of flint was brought to the meeting place of the Comitium, and before the eyes of the king and the people, it was cut by the razor. Following this, Tarquinius made Attus Navius his augur and the people began to consult him about their affairs. As for the flint and the razor, they were buried in the Comitium and covered with a *puteal* [a sacred enclosure], according to tradition."

What is striking in this account is that the reputation of Attus was created by means of an incident that owes its renown less to the practice of the augural art than to the "miracle" of the flint cut by the razor. Undoubtedly Attus had consulted the auspices ahead of time, but his success owes more to the "marvelous" fracturing of the flint by the razor than to the confirmation of his augural performance.

Quite a different impression is made by the account of an auspicial consultation, as it appears, for example, in the narration by the poet Ennius of what took place under the conditions that preceded the founding of Rome. The passage was cited by Cicero (*On Div.,* 1.107–8) and merits an attentive reading. It depicts Romulus and Remus who, as augurs, ask for a decision from the gods: "Then, with great care, the aspirants for the ruling power apply themselves at the same time to solicit the auspices and the sacred investiture (*dant operam simul auspicio augurioque*) . . . On the hill (not specified further), Remus consecrates himself to the auspices and sees only one favorable bird. As for the fortunate Romulus (*at Romulus pulcher*), he waits on the summit of the Aventine and sees the winged brood on its heights. The city will be called Roma or Remora: this is what is at stake. Everyone is concerned to know which of the two will be the master . . . In the meantime, the white sun (*sol albus*) has hidden itself in the depths of the night. Then, surging forth in the brilliance of its rays, the light appears. And at the same time as a beneficent bird (*pulcherrima avis*), winging swiftly away from the distant heights, veers to the left, the golden sun appears. From the sky three times four birds descend, sacred messengers, who direct themselves toward the place blessed by the omens (*praepetibus sese pulchrisque locis dant*). Romulus then perceives (*conspicit*) that he is the one who has been accorded, with the guarantee of the auspices, a seat and land to rule over." (We know that in the language of augury *pulcher* means either "beneficent," in the active sense, or "beneficiary of the auspices," in the passive sense).

There is nothing in this account that allows us to interpret the Roman augur as a diviner who foretells the future. For what did "the two augurs" who were candidates for the Roman throne ask? To be chosen for the sacral investiture (*augurium*), which each of them solicited by observing the birds (*auspicium*). The appearance of the *greater number* of birds (such appears to be the version adopted by Ennius), on the *left* side (which is, according to augural techniques, the favorable side), manifested the divine decision in favor of Romulus.

Thus, the only goal of taking auspices is to obtain from Jupiter the indication of his will: if the auspices are favorable, the sovereign god is expected to approve the request and confer the investiture. (The same goes for the inauguration of King Numa, as described by Livy, 1.18.6–10.) If, on the contrary, the auspices are absent or unfavorable, it is better to suspend the process that is under way.

Thus our impression is verified: the institutional augur, as he conforms to the portrait drawn by Ennius and Livy, makes no pretensions about being able to predict the future but limits himself to announcing the will of Jupiter by making use of a consultation based upon a rigorous technique. To him might well be applied the definition that Cicero claims for himself (*On Div.*, 2.70): "I am not among those augurs who pretend to be able to foretell the future." These did in fact exist, but they do not belong to the official college: they are designated by the scornful term "Marsian augurs," and they are found in the list enumerated by Quintus (*On Div.*, 1.132), along with village haruspices, traveling astrologers, worshipers of Isis who tell the future, interpreters of dreams; that is, "the imposter clairvoyants" (*impudentes harioli*), according to Ennius's expression. A rigorous technique? Actually, a great concern for sobriety in the practice of the augural function is revealed by the numerous precautions taken in the rules. There seems to have been a desire to forewarn against any manifestation that might be too personal, or against any tendency toward a "mystic" *furor.*

First of all, the augur never acts alone, on his own initiative. He must be in liaison with a magistrate who himself has the right to take the auspices, while the augur has only the right to collect and announce them (in the case of Romulus evoked by Ennius, there was the unusual combination of the two functions in the same person).

Next the augur must lay out an enclosed and oriented area—the *templum*—within which he claims to make his observations, according to specific conditions.

Note, finally, that all operations may be protected from contrary or unforeseen circumstances. In other words, it is possible to arm oneself in advance against unfavorable auspices. Pliny the Elder speaks of this (*Natural History,* 28.17): "In the augural tradition, it is a rule that neither imprecations nor auspices of any sort can affect those who, before an undertaking, declare their refusal to take account of them: there exists no greater sign of the goodness of the gods." The behavior of the augur M. Marcellus (third century B.C.) is revealing: "When he wished to undertake something, he would travel in an enclosed palanquin so as not to be hindered by the auspices" (*On Div.*, 2.77).

It would thus seem wise to limit ourselves to the historical period and not to reconstruct, after the manner of Cicero, "the augur of the origins," who would have had "a power to see into the future" (*On Div.*, 2.77). Nothing seems less certain than this. Everything points, on the contrary, to the fact that public augury in Roman religion had always contented itself, according to the official definition, with being the "interpreter of the very great and very good Jupiter." After this, what is left of Cicero's criticism? First of all, the denunciation of certain deviations which had, for example, transformed the consultation of the sacred chickens into a "simulation of the auspices."

Next let us consider the remark that the conventions of augury appear to be rather arbitrary. "Why," observes Cicero (*On Div.*, 2.82), "is there disagreement about the favorable side, which is situated on the left for the Romans and on the right for the Greeks?" And he cites a verse from Ennius: *Tum tonuit laevum bene tempestate serena* ("Then it thundered on the left side when the weather was clear: a happy omen") and a verse from Homer, translated into Latin (*Prospera Juppiter his dextris fulgoribus edit* ("Favorable omens: Jupiter throws his lightning bolts to the right").

Moreover, there is even a disparity within the Roman discipline of augury. "Why," Cicero asks again (*On Div.*, 2.80), "do certain birds have the privilege of furnishing a favorable auspice when they fly to the left, while for others, it is when they fly to the right?" This sort of opposition, which may seem strange, is recorded in the tradition. In the "Comedy of the Asses" (*Asinaria,* 259–61) of Plautus, the slave Libanus tries to find a solution to his financial problems; using the language of augury, he cries:

> *"Impetritum, inauguratumst; quovis admittunt aves.*
> *Picus et cornix ab laeva, corvus, parra ab dextera*
> *Consuadent; certum herclest vestram consequi sententiam."*
> ("Omens asked for, auguries taken. Good: every direction is allowed for by the birds. Green woodpecker and crow to the left, raven and nightjar to the right agree. It's decided; by Jove, I'll take your advice.")

That the disagreement between the Greeks and the Romans over the favorable side was common knowledge seems normal. But the fact that the most subtle knowledge about a division of birds into favorable and unfavorable categories according to their species had spread beyond the milieu of the specialist shows to what extent the public mentality was sensitive to this sort of preoccupation (Horace offers us an analogous example at the beginning of Ode 27 of book 3).

It is not the task of modern scholars to respond to the criticisms raised by the augur Cicero. Nevertheless, it is perhaps possible to glimpse certain elements of a response. It may be that the contradiction between the Greeks and the Romans regarding the favorable side is only an apparent one. Varro (cited by Festus, p. 454 L) gives the following commentary: "When one looks, from the home of the gods, toward the south, the eastern part of the world is found on the left and the western part on the right; it thus follows, in my opinion, that the auspices of the left were judged to be better than the auspices of the right." Thus, all is clear for Varro: the Romans located the abode of the gods to the north; in the performance of his functions (see Varro, *On the Latin Language,* 7.7) the augur ordinarily faced south and thus placed the east, the region of the rising sun, of birth and of life, to his left.

Now the situation is reversed for the Hellene. He "*turns towards the gods* to question them" (Bouché-Leclercq, *Histoire de la divination dans l'antiquité,* 4, p. 23, Paris 1882). Thus the Hellene oriented himself toward the north and from this perspective placed the east to his right. Here again the favorable direction corresponds to the direction of the rising sun, toward which the doors of the temples opened. But in relation to the observer, the orientation is reversed. These notions of left and right thus appear to be quite relative, because with reference to the basic orientation both of them designate the same eastern direction, the source of favorable omens.

But what about birds that give contradictory signs according to whether they appear to the left or the right? The example from the *Asinaria* shows clearly that, in order to be favorable, the green woodpecker and the crow should be to the left, and the raven and the nightjar to the right. It must be admitted that this harmonious conjunction of opposites is more surprising. We might surmise that the general Roman rule remains in force for the green woodpecker and the crow (we should remember that the green woodpecker is the preeminent bird of auguries: the "bird of Mars"; to cite

Ovid's definition [in *F.*, 3.37], according to legend he helped to feed Silvia's twins when they were abandoned in the wilderness), while the raven and the nightjar were the exception—an exception that can be explained by the intrinsic nature of these birds.

It is hardly possible to develop such hypotheses here. Would the raven, who passes for the official messenger of Apollo (see Aelianus, *On the Nature of Animals,* 1.48), thus conform for this reason to the Greek perspective? As for the *parra* (which we hesitantly identify here as the nightjar), it is often considered by Latin authors to be a bird of evil omen, by its very nature (see Horace, *Odes,* 3.27.1, and Varro, *On Agriculture,* 3.5.18). Are we to imagine, then, that by passing from the left to the right it changes its sign so that the unfavorable becomes favorable?

It is evident that these questions cannot be resolved in the absence of the *libri augurales.* Nothing remains but the very minutiae of every prescription to prove the extent to which the augural institution was "protected" by a network of rigorous rules. In the end, it was the augurs alone who were responsible for the interpretation of the auspices: it fell to them to know whether the city would enjoy the *pax veniaque deum:* in other words, whether or not it would have the blessing of the gods. We can thus understand why their function, far from being abandoned to the improvisations of prophets, was tightly regulated.

In the end, the function of the official augur of Roman religion does not include a divinatory role in the prophetic sense of the word: the priest is charged only with transmitting to the city the signs that manifest the agreement or disagreement of the gods (and principally of Jupiter) with a particular human initiative or undertaking. The native Roman tradition thus presents a great contrast with the Greek institution of oracular consultation. The Delphic Pythia was not content merely to make Apollo's opinion known by prescribing purifications or dictating moral maxims; she also gave oracles, which contributed the most to her prestige, "and one must suppose that the god of Delphi would not have enjoyed the reputation he had if he had never given authentic answers."[2]

Does this tradition that is so marked by sobriety and rigor characterize Rome alone in ancient Italy? Actually, it is found elsewhere in Italy. Is it necessary to cite the "Marsian augurs"? But these are mentioned by Cicero (*On Div.*, 1.132; 2.70) only as charlatans who do not deserve to be taken seriously. They claim to be the descendants of the son of the sorceress Circe[3] and chiefly have a reputation as healers and snake charmers.

History has also preserved the name of a confraternity which, according to Tacitus,[4] was created by King Titus Tatius to maintain the Sabine rites: these are the Sodales Titii, who "derive their name from the birds of Titus (*ab avibus Titiis*), which they customarily observe according to prescribed augural procedures."[5] But these *sodales* hardly offer a foothold for further investigation, and if the "birds of Titus" prove the existence of an augural consultation, it is one which remains full of mystery.

At Iguvium, the Umbrian city that corresponds to the modern Gubbio, it is quite another story. In 1444 seven bronze tablets were found there, designated the Tabulae Iguvinae ("Iguvine Tablets"; *Eugubio* is a synonym for *Gubbio*). These contain, in the Umbrian language, precise prescriptions for the Iguvium rite, concerning the various ceremonies of lustration and sacrifice.[6] These ceremonies are placed under the authority of the confraternity of the twelve Atiedii Brethren, who name an *arfertur* (the equivalent of the Latin *flamen*) to preside over them.

The interest that these documents (in particular, tablets 6a and b) hold for our purposes is that they provide us with the terms of the formulas for taking auspices (6a.1–7), for determining the *templum* (6a.8–11), and for setting the limits of the *pomerium* (6a.12–16). Even if there are divergences on details, the analogy of homologous terms and ritual situations is striking enough to make the Tabulae Iguvinae a precious document that provides, at another point in the Italic domain, an instructive parallel to the tradition of auspices and the institution of augurs that developed in Rome.[7] In Iguvium as in Rome, there was a ritual observation of birds (*aveis aseriater,* 6a.1, corresponding to the Latin *avibus observatis*) before anyone began a ceremony or an important undertaking.

2. Divination: Sibyl, Haruspicy, *Sortes*

The sibyl, haruspicy, and *sortes* are techniques that came from foreign lands and introduced extensive divination into Rome as a means of predicting the future. In this regard, two civilizations exerted a preponderant influence from a very early period: the Hellenic and the Etruscan. They gave Rome the benefit of their respective gifts of the *Sibylline Books* and haruspicy.

In a striking formula, Pliny the Elder defines the unique gifts of the Sibyl: *divinites et quaedem caelitum societas nobilissima* (*N.H.*, 7.119), "a power of divination and a kind of glorious communication with the celestial world." According to an often-cited legend, the Sibyl of Cumae offered her books for sale to King Tarquinius Superbus. The king bought three, which he had deposited in the temple of Capitoline Jupiter. It was there that the *libri Sibyllini* could later be consulted, on order of the Senate, by priests specially appointed for that office, the *viri sacris faciundis.*[8] They were especially consulted in case of serious crises or panic brought about by military disaster or by an epidemic: so it was in 217 B.C., when Rome, battered by the defeat at Lake Trasimene, feared "Hannibal at the walls of the city."[9] The consultation of the Sibyls ordinarily involved expiatory sacrifices and sometimes the introduction of new cults with a potential for remedying the situation: for example, in 217 B.C., the report of the *viri sacris faciundis* recommended that the Senate, among other things, erect a temple to Venus Erycina and another to Mens. The allusion is obvious: Venus from Mount Eryx in Sicily, who had "patronized" the Roman victory in the First Punic War, was entreated to intercede once again in favor of her protégés, the Romans, who were now fighting against Hannibal, the son of Hamilcar who was defeated in the first war. As for Mens, the goddess of lucidity, the Romans appealed to her in this time of disarray in conformity with the old instinct that led them to invoke the functional divinity that appeared to be the most appropriate to a given situation.

This example shows that the use of these "prophetic books" entailed no risk for the Roman state. Contrary to the oracle of Apollo, which sometimes gave out ambiguous declarations,[10] the response of the Sibyl was always "filtered" and submitted to verification and censorship by the Senate. The measures prescribed following the consultation of the books are always precise and reassuring. Cicero (*On Div.*, 2.112) credits this to the wisdom of the ancients and the role played by the Senate. He adds this significant observation: "Let us thus leave the Sibyl well protected in her retreat

Relief from the forum of Trajan. The scene on the left represents an *extispicium* (examination of the vital organs) carried out by a victimary under the supervision of the haruspex. On the right, carved onto the facade of the Capitoline Temple of Jupiter, a group of figures wearing togas (and, in the background, a figure wearing a cap with apex, designating the *flamen Dialis*) surround a figure facing forward—probably the emperor Trajan. This group awaits the result of the divination before departing on a military campaign. Paris, Musée du Louvre. Photo Giraudon.

(*Quamobrem Sibyllam quidem sepositam et conditam habeamus*) . . . and, conforming to the example of our ancestors, let us use the *Sibylline Books* to calm religious fears rather than to incite them."

Along with the *Sibylline Books*, Rome also knew of other "prophetic" books, at least episodically, in the *Carmina Marciana*. Livy (25.12.1) attributes these versified predictions to a Marcius who was said to have been an "illustrious diviner" (*vates illustris*). In fact, his identity is imprecise: although Livy, in agreement with Festus (p. 438 L) and Pliny the Elder (*N.H.*, 7.119), cites a single Marcius, another tradition, represented by Cicero (*On Div.*, 1.89; 2.113), mentions "brothers by the name of Marcius" (*Marcios quosdam fratres*), except in one passage (ibid., 1.115) where he uses the singular.

Whatever may have been their source of inspiration, these *Carmina Marciana* were collected in 213 B.C. among the superstitious works seized by order of the Senate during that time, when Rome lived in terror of the approach of Hannibal. But Livy states (1.1), "of two predictions, the confirmation given to the one which had been published after the event (i.e., the disaster at Cannes in 216) conferred a certain authority upon the other (i.e., the promised defeat of Hannibal), whose time had not yet come." In the second prediction, an injunction was made to the Romans to celebrate games in honor of Apollo, games which were to be renewed each year; and the *decemviri sacris faciundis* were commanded to perform sacrifices according to the Greek rite. This last prescription brought the intervention of the Senate, which asked the *decemviri* to consult the *Sibylline Books:* so the annual games in honor of Apollo, the *ludi Apollinares,* were introduced in 212 B.C.

The allusion in the *Carmina Marciana* to priests specially appointed for the consultation of the *Sibylline Books* gives rise to the suspicion that the "Marcian prophecy," far from being of native stock as Pliny the Elder claimed, was born in a Hellenic milieu.[11] It is thus possible that this prophetic manifestation played a part in the inspiration of the *Sibylline Books*.[12]

The other divinatory technique is of Etruscan origin and has the name *haruspicinae disciplina,* "the teaching of haruspicy." According to a legend told most fully by Cicero, a man ploughing his fields at Tarquinii one day saw "a certain Tages" arise out of the earth from under the blade of his plow and speak to him: his instructions were to constitute the source of haruspicy.[13] In broad terms, this art is divided into three spheres: the examination of *exta* (i.e., the viscera of sacrificed animals) or extispicy;[14] the observation of lightning flashes (*fulgura*); and the interpretation of portents (*prodigia* or *portenta*).[15] We also know of the *libri haruspicini,* the *libri fulgurales,* and the *libri rituales.*[16] These works are indicative of the great effort exerted by the Etruscans to divine the future by scrutinizing every available "sign" in the world.

For this was their major concern. To this end, the Etruscans distinguished between these omens that were solicited (*impetrita*) and the signs offered by the gods (*oblativa*), particularly those portents that were the object of special treatises, *ostentaria* (one of these was translated into Latin by someone named Tarquitius).[17]

Nothing reveals the Etruscans' mentality more than their attitude toward the observation of birds. Where the Roman augur contented himself with recording Jupiter's agreement or disagreement according to the flight of birds (*alites*) or the sound of their cries (*oscines*), the Etruscan saw a basis for prediction. Such was the case with Tanaquila of Tarquinia, the wife of the Lucumon who would become the first Etruscan king of the Romans under the name of Tarquinius the Elder. She had succeeded in persuading her husband to leave Tarquinia to try his luck in Rome. "We had nearly arrived at Janiculus, when Lucumon, seated with his wife on his chariot, saw an eagle glide slowly downward, take off his headgear, swoop upward above the chariot crying loudly, and, as if invested with a divine mission, adroitly replace the headgear on his head; then the eagle flew away across the sky. Tanaquila, it is said, greeted this omen (*id augurium*) with joy, being a woman who was expert, as the Etruscans generally are, in celestial portents. Kissing her husband, she exhorted him to expect a high and noble destiny: 'This bird, coming from that region of the sky on this day, has brought a message; the auspice which it has given concerns the highest part of the person: he took off an ornament placed on a human head and put it back by divine order.'"[18]

This is far from the simple Roman style of taking auspices. All of the elements in this scene lend themselves to a symbolic interpretation: the localization of Janiculus designates the place of election; the eagle, consecrated to Jupiter, authenticates the message of the sovereign god; the choice of the head of Lucumon, which is successively bared and covered by the bird, augurs a future coronation. Whatever the case, this new manner of taking auspices opens much richer and more precise perspectives on the knowledge of the future.

It is quite understandable from this that the Romans would have hoped to benefit from these *genera divinandi.* Cicero admits this at the beginning of his treatise on divination:[19] "As the teachings of the haruspices seemed to be quite valuable for the solicitation and observation of presages (*in impetriendis consulendisque rebus*) and for the interpretation and conjuration of portents (*in monstris interpretandis ac procurandis*), the Romans used all of this knowledge originating from Etruria so as not to appear to have neglected any divinatory procedure."

Thus, the Roman state became accustomed to relying occasionally upon the help of the Etruscan haruspices. When they appealed to their good offices, it was generally for extispicy. It is true that this latter had something seductive about it. According to its basic postulate, everything in the world was joined together by virtue of a fundamental harmony (*sumpatheia*); in particular, the liver of a victim offered to the gods constituted a microcosm which was divisible into different zones corresponding to as many homologous zones in the macrocosm of the world.[20] An attentive consultation of the state of the liver was thus expected to lead to conclusions about the situation in the corresponding regions of the world. This use of extispicy was not without certain consequences for the Roman ritual of sacrifice, which included an important stage in its order of different operations: the examination of the *exta,* which had to be flawless, or the sacrifice would be null and void. The simple inspection-report of the *exta,* which was the task of the sacrificer, seems to have had superimposed upon it, in the course of time, a consultation of a divinatory nature. This contamination may be verified in the description of sacrificial ceremonies in Livy. Thus, before going into the decisive battle with the Latins at Veseris, on the foot of Mount Vesuvius, in 340 B.C., the Roman consuls offered a sacrifice. A haruspex was there who announced to one of the consuls, Decius, "that, in the part of the liver that concerned him, there was a lesion at one end" (*Decio caput jocineris a familiari parte caesum haruspex dicitur ostendisse*).[21]

This was the prediction of an unhappy event. In fact, in the course of the engagement, the left wing commanded by the consul Decius collapsed and its leader had recourse to the most extreme solution for such a case: in order to save his Roman legions he "devoted himself" by the official procedure of the *devotio,* by linking his own death to the destruction of the enemy army.[22] Thanks to this self-sacrifice, "he turned against his own person all the dangers and all the threats of the gods of heaven and of hell."[23]

By contrast, the haruspex had given Manlius, Decius's colleague, the assurance that his sacrifice had been wholly successful (*Manlium egregie litasse*).[24]

This account is highly instructive. It allows us to understand why the use of haruspicy could have seemed useful. According to Roman liturgical rules, the sacrifice would have had to be declared null and void because of the defective state of the victim's liver. The officiant would have been reduced to declaring: *non litatum est* ("the gods have not given their agreement"). And the consuls would have been barred from doing the sacrifice again: at any rate, they would not have been authorized to go into battle on the same day.

The intervention of the haruspex set a much more subtle and nuanced procedure in motion, which allowed for the possibility of success in spite of the announcement of dangers. According to this exegesis, the sacrifice was far from being a total failure: although Decius was threatened, Manlius was "wholly successful." It was up to Decius to be cautious. And in fact Decius was able to avert this danger, to remedy it with a *procuratio.* At the critical moment of the battle he saved the general situation by turning upon himself alone (and upon his enemies) the dangers that the diviner had announced.

Such a flexible and subtle procedure captivated the spirit of the time. Of course feelings must have been mixed: to what extent was this "foreign" technique credible? Cicero's reflections are revealing: "How were the haruspices able to decide that a certain part of the liver belonged to the enemy and another to the consultant; that a certain lesion presaged a danger and another an advantage?"[25] There are other allusions in the same vein. Even if people wanted to use the haruspices, they would still always be "foreign and barbarian."[26] Who does not know the famous saying of Cato, twice cited by Cicero: "It is amazing that one haruspex can keep from laughing when he sees another haruspex"?[27]

Cicero was so free with his language here only because he found himself within a circle of friends that were open to argument (*Soli sumus: licet verum inquirere . . . :* "We are alone, ourselves, free to seek the truth . . .").[28] And it would be anachronistic to attribute the same critical spirit to the Romans of the third and second centuries B.C. History shows that the Senate became accustomed to consulting the haruspices more than once.

It must nevertheless be noted that the Senate addressed itself at the same time to haruspices and to the interpreters of the *Sibylline Books,* as if, impelled by an instinctive distrust, it wanted to verify the accuracy of one procedure by checking it against the other. One of these double consultations enters into the period of tension that preceded the war against Perseus, the king of Macedonia. This was provoked in 172 B.C. by a portent: the fall of a rostral column that stood upon the Capitol (which preserved in its *rostra*—made of the prows of captured ships—the memory of a naval victory).

Immediately, "the Senate gave the order to the haruspices

to give a report and to the *decemviri* to consult the *Sibylline Books*."[29] It is interesting to note the differences between the two "answers." The Sibylline interpreters limited themselves to proposing measures of purification and religious devotion.[30] The haruspices did not hesitate to predict the future: "this portent would be for the better; it predicted an extension of the frontiers and the extermination of enemies; for the *rostra,* which the storm had blown over, were spoils of the enemy that would be taken in the future."[31] By resolutely adopting different perspectives, these two most representative divinatory procedures ran little risk of conflicting with one another.

Were there other divinatory perspectives in Italy which might have enjoyed some authority in the eyes of the Roman Senate? It seems that there were not, even though Italy knew important cults of the goddess Fortuna, whose oldest and most renowned sanctuaries were situated in Praeneste and in Antium.[32] There certainly was, especially in Praeneste, a means to consult Fortuna by using tablets called *sortes.* Cicero recalls the legend that was connected with the origin of their discovery.[33] A Praenestian of noble family, Numerius Suffustius, had a dream in which he was commanded to carve a notch in a rock whose location was told to him. From the crack, "wooden tablets (*sortes*) covered with ancient lettering poured out." Following a consultation by the haruspices, the *sortes* were enclosed in a box made of olive wood. When a consultant received a warning from Fortuna, they drew lots: a child mixed up the tablets with his hand and drew them out of the box.

Cicero hastens to add the following: "The beauty of the sanctuary and the antiquity of the tablets of Praeneste continue to be renowned to the present day—at least by the masses. What sort of person is in fact their administrator, what sort of prominent man consults them? Everywhere else the *sortes* have fallen into disuse."[34]

The official discrediting was not peculiar to Cicero's time. The inscriptions found at Praeneste at the time of the archaeological excavations of the temple, which had been sumptuously restored by Sulla, reveal only the devotion of lesser people at the place of the goddess.[35] In a general way, Lattus is correct in summarizing his evaluation in the following fashion: "It is not the interests of the state, but the questions of people worried about being tricked or preoccupied with the outcome of some undertaking that receive an answer here."[36]

What was the real role of these *sortes,* which some have seen as "Italic oracles"? Perhaps it is best first to indicate the centers that may be considered authentic repositories of prophetic tablets.

Nothing indicates that we should include Antium, which was the seat of a cult of two Fortunas whom Martial would later name "the truthful sisters."[37] In fact, we know very little about how they were consulted, except for a late piece of information from Macrobius, who mentions a procession of statues for divinatory purposes.[38]

Neither does it seem that Padua should enter into this category, even taking into account the fact that Tiberius drew lots with tablets there.[39] Apart from Praeneste, the only cities that are explicitly mentioned in connection with *sortes* are Caere and Falerii. But in neither case is there any consultation of tablets. The tablets are mentioned by Livy each time in the context of a group of portents that manifested themselves during the Second Punic War, by which it was learned that Hannibal would inflict heavy defeats upon the Roman armies.

During the winter of 218 B.C., the Romans were alarmed by a series of events that were at once disparate and extraordinary. Among signs as diverse as "In the Picenum, a rain of stones fell" and "In Gaul, a wolf carried off the sword of a sentinel by pulling it out of its scabbard," the following account appeared: "At Caere, the divinatory tablets have shrunk"—*Caere sortes extenuatas.*[40] The following year, in the spring of 217, the scene painted by Livy is even darker. (The consul Flaminius, who had gone out on a military campaign without regularly taking the auspices, had been killed in the course of the disaster at Lake Trasimenus.) The portents increased everywhere. In particular, "at Falerii, the sky split open as if torn, and from this opening a great light surged forth; the divinatory tablets shrank spontaneously, and one, bearing the inscription 'Mars shakes his lance,' fell."[41]

This is a portent which repeats itself in two different cities a year later. Neither in Caere nor in Falerii are the tablets connected with a cult of Fortuna. Even if we could assume that the *sortes* should ordinarily have been consulted there in the same way as in Praeneste, there is no question of a divinatory consultation here. It is only the miraculous character of the shrinking of the tablets that is emphasized, along with, at Falerii, the aggravating circumstance of the fall of a tablet bearing the announcement that Mars has been set in motion. The best proof of this is that in both cases the Senate ordered a consultation of the *Sibylline Books* in order to provide for the *procuratio* of all of these manifestations of the anger of the gods.

For—and we must make no mistake on this subject—the attitude of the official authorities about the *sortes* reveals deep tendencies that would only develop in the future. The *sortes* might well have been devalued as far as their prophetic function was concerned—their discredit would be complete by Cicero's time—but they still retained some importance as warning signs. Thus, the shrinking of the *sortes* of Caere and Falerii no longer involves their divinatory credibility: it enters directly into the category of portents.

3. Divination: Portents and Omens

Approaching the first century B.C., we come to a turning point. In appearance, the procedures are still the same: the apparatus of the state goes into action when the destiny of Rome seems to be in question. Portents are reported from everywhere in Italy (they were scrupulously gathered by the annalists), and the alert is given to the city leaders. These are addressed to the haruspices or the *decemviri* (and sometimes to both priestly bodies). The consultation of specialists resulted in diverse prescriptions: sometimes the offering of expiatory sacrifices and sometimes the introduction of new cults. The whole scenario is founded upon one basic postulate: through portents, the city was warned that it had incurred the wrath of the gods; it should now place itself once more in the favor, peace, and blessing of the gods—*pacem veniamque deum.*

So it was that once again the events of 169 B.C. unfolded. It is the eve of the war that will be fought against Perseus, the king of Macedonia. Livy gives a complete picture of the portents: "At Anagnia, two portents were announced this year: a torch appeared in the sky, and a cow spoke—she is now being kept at the expense of the city. Also at Minturnae, the sky was illuminated for several days with a brilliant light. At Reate, it rained stones. At Cumae, the statue of Apollo in the citadel wept for three days and three nights. At Rome, temple guards gave reports: one, that a crested serpent had been seen by several persons in the sanctuary of Fortuna, and another, that two portents were seen in the sanctuary of Fortuna Primigenia on the hill (of the Quirinal): a palm tree had grown there, and in the middle of the day it had a rained blood."[42] (A consultation of the *Sibylline Books* was made which prescribed that sacrifices be offered and that a solemn *supplicatio* be made.)

But this time Livy prefaced his report with a confidence that was out of character for him: "I am not unaware of the fact that, because of the indifference that makes people generally disbelieve in the portents given by the gods, portents are no longer publicly announced nor are they entered any more into the annals. As for myself, as I am treating of an ancient subject, I have taken on an antique mentality; a kind of religious scruple keeps me from rejecting as unworthy of putting in my annals those events which our ancestors, in their great wisdom, judged worthy of being officially recorded."[43]

What are we to understand by this diagnosis by Livy, who lived in the reign of Augustus (he wrote from 27 B.C. until his death in A.D. 17)? There is no reason to doubt the growing skepticism that he denounces. But the skepticism is mostly about the procedures and processes that claim to reveal the future. The basic elements used in their elaborate literary works would continue to impress people. As we can see, religious indifference curiously allied itself with an increase in superstitious attention to portents.

People laughed at the haruspices and greeted the recommendations of the *Sibylline Books* with circumspection, but they still paid attention to phenomena that were out of the ordinary, to *prodigia* or *ostenta*. People were still sensitive to omens: this was a constant of the Roman mentality.

What are we to understand by the word omen? A recent etymological essay suggested that it should be given the meaning of "truthful presage."[44] A famous example of an omen was cited by Cicero.[45] When Crassus was embarking his army at Brindisi (for the expedition against the Parthians which would end miserably with the disaster of Carrhae in 53 B.C.), he heard a merchant praising his figs from Caunus (a city in Caria), crying, "Cauneas!" ("figs of Caunus"). If he had grasped the omen, Crassus would have understood: *Cave ne eas* ("Take care not to go there").

Remember that Cicero, who permits himself to criticize such matters openly among his friends in *On Divination*, cannot keep from adding this commentary: "Once we take this path, a stubbed toe, a broken bridle strap, and a sneeze all become omens." But Cicero may have been alone in his desire to draw the line clearly between superstition and religion.[46] His theoretical protests did not correspond to general practice.

Omens invade all aspects of everyday life: they are accepted independent of any religious attachments and are thought to have a certain internal necessity.[47] Significant in this regard is Suetonius's presentation of the omens that announced the murder of Julius Caesar.[48] First, there was the discovery made by the colonists who were established at Capua under Julian law (regarding the division of lands into lots): they found the tomb of the founder of Capua, Capys, which contained a bronze tablet bearing the Greek inscription: "When the bones of Capys see the light of day, a descendant of Julus (i.e., Ascanius) shall perish under the blows of close relatives, and following this, his vengeance shall give rise to great disasters in Italy."

Next there was the announcement made to Caesar: the horses that he had previously consecrated to the river Rubicon obstinately refused all food and wept copiously. Then it was the warning given by the haruspex Spurinna during his sacrifice: "Caesar should watch for a peril that will come no later than the ides of March." And then: "On the eve of the ides, a wren carrying a laurel branch flew up toward the curia of Pompey (i.e., the Senate), where it was pursued by birds of every species, who had come out of a nearby grove; and in the curia itself the bird was torn to pieces." Finally, "the night before the day of the murder, Caesar saw himself in a dream sometimes flying above the clouds, sometimes shaking the hand of Jupiter; as for his wife Calpurnia, she dreamed that the peak of the roof had caved in and that her husband was pierced through by the debris as he lay in her arms. Then, suddenly, the door of the bedroom opened by itself."

This list enumerates some very different kinds of omens: to the *omina*—in the prophetic sense of the word—are added the haruspex's prediction, the decisive omen of the wren torn apart by members of its own species, and finally the premonitory dreams of Caesar and Calpurnia, interrupted by the sudden opening of the door.[49]

What was Caesar's reaction? In a sense, whether or not he believed in all of these "signs" is of little importance. (At one point, Suetonius notes that Caesar "pondered for a long time whether he should go to the Senate, because of these omens and because of his poor state of health." But later on he stresses, on the contrary, Caesar's indifference to the ritual failure of his own sacrifices—*cum litare non posset*—as well as his mockery of the haruspex Spurinna.) In this fatalistic perspective, the omens had to come true in any case. There is no longer any question of claiming the privilege of the institutional augur that Pliny the Elder recalled—the right to protect oneself in advance against unfavorable signs.[50]

In fact, even the most powerful men of the period succumbed to the obsession for omens. Although Caesar manifested, more than once, an aloof skepticism that sometimes bordered on insolence, his successor Augustus could hardly be classified among the "strong-willed."[51] From the very beginning, Suetonius indicates to what degree Augustus was attentive to signs and omens—*auspicia et omina*.[52] The same Cicero who railed against the mania that consisted in taking as an omen every incident of everyday life (every time we "stub our toes") did not doubt for a moment that the founder of the Roman Empire was subject to this very weakness.[53] In fact the first example that Augustus's biographer gives to justify his point is the following: "In the morning, if he (i.e., Augustus) unthinkingly put his left shoe on his right foot, he saw this as a menacing omen."[54]

The evidence about the life of Augustus shows to what extent he was subject to all sorts of superstitions. He was more receptive to *omina* than Crassuso was; thus "he never undertook anything serious on the day of the nones, because of the evil omen inherent in the word" (*Nonis* = *non is*, i.e., "Don't you go there").[55] The omen could be favorable: the future Augustus had the joy of encountering an ass and his master before the battle of Actium. The animal's name was Nicon and his master's was Eutychus.[56] Another omen led him to understand that he was nearing the end of his life. "When in the midst of a great popular competition he closed the lustration ceremonies on the Field of Mars, an eagle described several circles above him and then flew toward the next sanctuary and alighted above the first letter of the name of Agrippa": Augustus immediately charged his colleague (who held the position of censor) to take his place in the reading of the vows that would normally have been read for the following lustrum.[57]

As for the *prodigia*, they studded the whole of Augustus's life, even from before he was born. Was it not reported that "some months before his birth, a prodigy was produced before the eyes of all announcing that Nature was to give birth to a king for the Roman people"?[58] In the same vein, the following story circulated: Atia came by night to a ceremony in honor of Apollo. She had her palanquin placed in the temple and "knew" a serpent while she slept. On the following day, she had a spot in the shape of a serpent on her body, which proved to be indelible: "Thus Augustus, born nine months later, was considered to be the son of Apollo."[59]

And a series of portents accompanies his entire infancy and adolescence: when he was still a little baby, he disappeared one day from his cradle and was found again at dawn, "stretched out on the top of a tower, facing the rising sun."[60] He hardly knew how to talk when he ordered the frogs that were disturbing his family's country house to be silent: "after that day, it is said, the frogs never croaked again."[61]

Other portents indicated that his rise to glory was near. At the moment when he first put on his toga of manhood, the laticlave became unsewn on both sides and fell to his feet-"which clearly signified that the Senate, which was distinguished by this dress, would one day submit to him."[62]

The biographer reminds us of another similar prodigy: when Julius Caesar, in order to set up his camp close to Munda, had several trees cut down, he spared a palm tree, as an omen of victory—*ut omen victoriae;* this plant immediately put forth a shoot that in a few days outgrew its mother stock and attracted a flock of doves that nested in it; this *ostentum,* it is said, was Caesar's main motive for designating his grandnephew as his successor."[63]

After the murder of Caesar, Octavian returned to Apollonia (in Illyria) to come to Rome; he "suddenly saw, at a time of clear and peaceful weather, a kind of rainbow that ringed the solar disk."[64]

In the list of portents that tradition has transmitted, lightning and thunder appear more than once. In his native city of Velitrae, it was remembered "that the lightning once struck a point on the ramparts: it was prophesied that one of its citizens would one day attain the supreme power."[65]

Apparently Augustus had a pathological terror of thunder and lightning.[66] He erected a temple to Thundering Jupiter to thank him for having spared him when lightning had brushed his palanquin during an expedition and killed the slave carrying the torch in front of him.[67] Nevertheless, he knew how to get information from such manifestations—often by relying on the arts of the haruspices.

Lightning had struck the tomb of Julia, the daughter of Julius Caesar, several times on the same day that Octavian had seen the sun crowned by a rainbow on his way back to Apollonia.[68] It had struck a part of his own house, on the Palatine: following the advice of the haruspices, Augustus had a temple erected to Apollo in the same place.[69] At about the same time as the eagle had described its ominous circles above him, lightning had struck his statue and erased the first letter of his name, Caesar: according to the haruspices, the letter C foretold "that he had no more than a hundred (*centum*) days to live, but that he would join the ranks of the gods, because *aesar,* formed by the rest of the letters of his name Caesar, meant 'god' in the Etruscan language."[70]

These wholly classical manifestations of *prodigia* and *signa* did not constitute the only elements that made up the golden legend of Augustus. His life set the stage for other divinatory testimonies, above all for predictions drawn from astrology—which was foreign to the old Roman tradition.

While attending a meeting of the Senate in 63 B.C., the Pythagorean P. Nigidius learned of the birth of the future Augustus from his father Octavius, and "as soon as he knew the hour of the childbirth, he announced that a master of the universe had been born."[71] Later, during his stay in Apollonia, Octavian accompanied Agrippa to the observatory of the astrologer Theogenes. As Theogenes had made marvelous predictions about his companion, Octavian refused to give information about his own birth. He ended up consenting: "Then Theogenes leapt from his seat to adore him."[72] Augustus must have drawn great confidence from his horoscope, as he "later had his astrological chart published" and struck silver coins bearing the image of Capricorn.[73]

Other divinatory forms appear in the course of Augustus's exceptional life. These enter into a different category, according to Cicero, who separates those interpretations based on a technique (*ars*) from those made under the impetus of a natural force (*natura*).[74] The latter designated oracles and dreams.

In fact oracular consultations almost never occurred. Suetonius cites only one example, and this originates in an initiative taken not by Augustus but by his father Octavius. While the latter led his army across the wastes of Thrace, he had a consultation on the subject of his son, participating in a "barbarian ceremony" (*barbara caerimonia*) in a forest consecrated to Bacchus. The libation of wine caused a flame to shoot up so high that it went beyond the roof of the temple—an omen of sovereignty (the priests assured him) that until then only Alexander the Great had received.[75]

As for *somnia,* prophetic dreams, they are abundant in this "edifying" literature. First it is Atia "who, before going into childbirth, saw in a dream her entrails rising up to the heavenly bodies and spreading out over the perimeter of all of the earth and sky." Octavius "himself dreamed that the light of the sun was coming out from the womb of his wife."[76] Later, during the night that followed his visit to the oracle of Bacchus in Thrace, Octavius had another dream: "He saw his son, clothed in a superhuman majesty, carrying the thunderbolt, the scepter, and the attributes of the very great and good Jupiter, as well as a radiating crown, on a chariot decorated with laurels and drawn by twelve horses of a brilliant whiteness."[77]

Outside of the narrow family circle, other people are mentioned as having been witnesses in this review of premonitory dreams. In 63 B.C., Q. Catulus, who had just dedicated the new Capitoline temple (the old one had been burned in 83 during the civil war), dreamed two nights in a row. The first time he saw Jupiter choose from among children who were dressed in praetexta (magisterial togas) and were playing around his altar, to present an image of the state to one of them; the second time, he saw the same child on the lap of Capitoline Jupiter, and when he tried to take him down, Jupiter held him back, explaining that he was bringing this child up for the salvation of the state. "The next day, Catulus happened to meet the future Augustus, whom he did not know; greatly astonished, he contemplated him and proclaimed his perfect resemblance to the child of his dreams."[78]

Even Cicero is cited among the witnesses. According to Suetonius, Cicero confided the following dream to Julius Caesar: he had seen a child with very distinguished features, who had come down out of the sky by means of a long gold chain, stopped before the door of the Capitol, and received a whip from the hands of Jupiter.[79] When he later saw Octavian, who was still unknown to most people, in Caesar's entourage, he immediately identified him with the figure in his dream.

Augustus himself benefited from a premonitory dream that saved his life in the battle of Philippi, undertaken in 42

B.C. against the murderers of Julius Caesar. Once when he had decided to stay in his camp because of the state of his health, he was dissuaded from this by one of his friends who had had a dream. He did well to take his advice: the enemy pillaged his camp, threw itself upon the palanquin where he normally would have been resting, and completely tore it apart.[80]

Such was the vast array of *divinandi genera* that flourished at the advent and during the reign of Augustus. To all appearances, the picture is quite varied. Yet on closer inspection, the traditional forms of divination had not been submerged, in spite of the invasion of oneiromancy and the (more timid) incursion of astrology. Anything else would have been astonishing during the reign of an emperor who looked to maintain balanced quantities of the traditional and the innovative in his religious policies. When his biographer writes that he was particularly sensitive to *ostenta*, it must not be forgotten that in order to interpret them, he almost always turned, following the old custom that had been adapted to Roman ways, to qualified experts, the haruspices, for the interpretation of lightning flashes as well as of the *exta* (the victim's viscera) and the *auspicia* (the observation of birds).[81]

For most of the portents provoked by lightning that have been enumerated, the haruspices were consulted both to interpret the event and to stave off its unpleasant consequences.

The same specialists allowed Augustus to benefit from their competence in extispicinary consultations. Thus, in the course of a sacrifice that Octavian offered during his first consulate, "the haruspices unanimously interpreted as an omen of prosperity and grandeur the fact that the livers of all of the victims were folded inward."[82] In the same way, they interceded near Perusia in the course of a sacrificial celebration—and here the way that they acted shows with what rapidity they could adapt themselves to circumstances. Augustus, who had not been able to obtain the *litatio* (the gods' approval of his sacrifice), had given the order to increase the number of victims, when suddenly the enemy rushed in and carried off all the sacred preparations. The reaction of the haruspices: "All the perils and evils foretold to the sacrificer would fall upon those who held the *exta* (the viscera of the victims), and so it came to pass."[83]

The observation of birds also allowed for exegeses "in the Etruscan style," i.e., for symbolic interpretations that went beyond the functions of the Roman augur. On several occasions the appearance of an eagle is noted in the course of Augustus's career.

The first time is particularly significant. "While Octavian was having his lunch in a forest close to the fourth milestone on the way to Campania, an eagle suddenly stole the bread from his hand; it flew high into the sky and then suddenly descended slowly (*leniter*) and returned the bread to him."[84] This "miracle," which bore the promise of a heavenly consecration, recalls the analogous portent of the eagle that took away and returned Lucumon's headgear on the road to Rome.[85]

Another omen carries an equally transparent symbolism. The triumvirate had just been established (in 43 B.C.) between Antony, Lepidus, and Octavian, when the troops of the three were witness to the following sight at Bologna: "An eagle, perched on the tent of Octavian, struck down and killed two crows that had been harassing it from either side; the entire army noted that one day there would be discord—as had been shown—between the three colleagues, and foretold the outcome."[86]

Recall the ominous eagle of the ceremonies of the lustrum, when Jupiter's bird sent three omens that corresponded to as many crucial events in the life of Augustus: his supernatural consecration (for he would become Augustus), his victory over his rivals (for he would triumph definitively at Actium in 31 B.C.), and his end, which was not far off (for his fate would be sealed in A.D. 14).[87]

But in the end, this is a distortion of the ancient meaning of the auspices. Certainly the allegorical interpretation of the behavior of birds is foreign to the strict rules of augury. Yet this practice, favored by the activities of the haruspices, did not obliterate the respect for ancestral practices. Augury lost none of its official importance.

The best proof of this is the following testimony: "During his taking of the auspices, at the time of his [Octavian's] first consulate, twelve vultures appeared to Octavian as they had to Romulus in the past."[88]

The exceptional character of these auspices, which were reserved for only two personages in Roman history, was stressed by Augustan propaganda. The connection between Romulus and Augustus, beneficiaries of the same heavenly favor, held a clear meaning for the contemporaries of the latter: at a distance of several centuries, the founder of the empire had raised himself up to the glorious rank of the founder of the city.

Furthermore, Augustus would never have dreamed of disdaining the dignity of augury. Not only did he himself hold this office—which would appear to have been the earliest of his priestly positions[89]—but he also scrupulously respected the Julian tradition which included giving major power to the augural office.[90] And when he would later erect a sanctuary to his deified father, he would take care not to forget the attribute of the augur: on a gold denarius that represented the cultic statue of the emperor standing beneath the portico of his temple, Caesar appears with the *lituus*.[91]

4. Divination and Syncretism

Although the reign of Augustus reveals a kind of equilibrium between the ancient traditions and new forms of divination, it must be added that this equilibrium was precarious. It would not take long to accomplish an evolution that would make the old opposition disappear. We have already shown the fundamental difference between Roman augury and Etruscan haruspicy.

Roman augury was not divinatory in the strict sense of the word: its task was to guard the good relations between gods and men. The highest magistrate alone (who was clothed in the *imperium*) was invested with the right to take auspices: he relied on the technical assistance of the augur to ascertain the agreement or disagreement of heaven with an enterprise. The initiative taken by the king-augur Romulus retained an exemplary value over the centuries: it is not by chance that Augustus insisted on enjoying the same celestial privilege.

Haruspicy, by contrast, manifested divinatory pretensions from the very start. To this end, it used three principal procedures: the examination of the *exta*, essentially of the liver; the interpretation of portents; and the observation and conjuration of lightning. In contrast with the sobriety of the augural art, haruspicy profited from the prestige of a technique that was more perfected and richer in promises: it could predict the future!

As such, it aroused both the mistrust and the curiosity of the Romans. Being realists, the Romans did not intend to be deprived of the services of haruspicy any more than of the "predictions" offered by the *Sibylline Books*, which, even though they were of Hellenic origin, had come to them, according to tradition, through the interposition of an Etruscan king, Tarquinius Superbus. But they subjected the requests made to the haruspices, as well as the consultations of the interpreters of the *Sibylline Books,* to strict control by the Senate—who always could make decisions, as a last resort.

Thus, throughout all of the Roman Republic, the priestly body of augurs was placed in a kind of rivalry with the "foreign" priests. Our sources indicate that there was a certain tension between the native priests and the foreign "diviners." The anecdote about the haruspex reported by Cicero is symptomatic of this. Cicero, who had been an augur and who was not a man who would make fun of a Roman priest, recounted with great delectation the saying attributed to Cato, that "one haruspex cannot look at another haruspex without laughing."[92] This shows how wrong some modern scholars can be when they interchange augur and haruspex.

The trench between the indigenous and migratory priestly bodies would soon be filled up, however. Cicero had drawn a clear line between Roman priests and augurs on the one hand and Sibylline interpreters and haruspices on the other.[93] This boundary would become blurred after the reign of Augustus. In the syncretist climate that came to characterize the empire more and more, the poets sometimes anticipated institutional reforms.

So it was that Tibullus, on the occasion of the election of his friend Valerius Messalla as *quindecimvir sacris faciundis,* appealed to Apollo as the god who would thenceforth be thought to concentrate all of the divinatory powers in himself.[94] The poet does not even hesitate, in pushing the spirit of "contamination" to the extreme, to place the Roman augur under the obedience of the god: "Phoebus, be propitious: a new priest enters into your sanctuary . . . You, you see far into the future; it is to you that the augur who knows the fate announced by the prophetic bird consecrates himself; you govern the oracles; by your grace, the haruspex can see into the future, when the still throbbing viscera carry the stamp of the god; it is through your inspiration that the Romans have never been misguided by the Sibyl who announces hidden destinies in six-footed verses."[95] Thus he brought to heel the Roman augur who, althought he was not long before "the interpreter of Jupiter," now enters into the service of a god of foreign origins; in addition, he incorporated all divinatory forms exclusively under Apollo.

It fell to the emperor Claudius to proceed with the institutional reorganization. He gave a speech to the Senate reminding them of the merits of the college of the haruspices, and after a *senatus consultum,* he obtained their incorporation into the official priestly order.[96] It is characteristic that, in his arguments for haruspicy, Claudius placed this "most ancient knowledge in Italy" in opposition to "foreign superstitions."

But this reinforcement and consolidation of the Italic priestly body did not impede the development of another phenomenon which was to grow more and more powerful: the "savage" superstition that would win over at every level. Cicero's brother, who admitted the legitimacy of the official means of divination, at the end of his report denounced the charlatans of the profession: "drawers of lots, diviners greedy for profit, calling up souls [psychomancy]." He rejected equally "Marsian augurs, village haruspices, circus astrologers, prophet-votaries of Isis, and interpreters of dreams"—all of whose prophecies were based on nothing but imposture.[97]

When Claudius alluded to the *externae superstitiones,* he was probably thinking in particular of the diviners of Isis and possibly of the Jews.[98] After various changes in fortune, between the years A.D. 36 and 39 the Egyptian Isis had finally obtained an official temple in Rome, which was situated on the Field of Mars.[99] This was quite an exceptional rise, since this cult was still being persecuted under Tiberius (in A.D. 19, after a scandal, this emperor had a chapel to Isis destroyed and its cultic image thrown into the Tiber). This was only a beginning, considering the expansion that it must have known in the second century, during which there flourished a mysticism of Isis to which book 11 of the *Metamorphoses* of Apuleius is a literary witness.

In a general sense, the structures of the official religion could not hold out against the seductions of Oriental currents of thought. In a reversal of the program that Cicero had previously sanctioned, religion gave way to superstition.[100]

A form of superstition whose hold over the mind became stronger and stronger was astrology. While it had held the attention of Augustus only episodically (by the chance visit to Theogenes' observatory),[101] it played a greater role in the life of Tiberius, who admitted the astrologer Thrasyllus into his circle of intimate friends.[102] Suetonius's remark about Tiberius is quite illuminating:[103] "Unconcerned with gods and cults, since he was a fervent believer in astrology (*quippe addictus mathematicae*) and was entirely persuaded that all was ruled by fate (*fato*), he nevertheless had an excessive fear of thunder; when the sky was stormy, he never failed to place a laurel crown on his head because that foliage, it is said, cannot be touched by lightning." In the same way, Caligula relied on the good offices of the astrologer Sulla.[104]

It is nevertheless true that the Julian emperors did not reject the legacy of the Augustan traditions. Thus, Claudius remained loyal to the memory of the founder of the dynasty to the point of considering the vow in the name of Augustus the most sacred.[105] It was in the same spirit that he interceded in his role of supreme pontiff in ordering propitiatory prayers when a bird of evil omen was reported at the Capitol.[106]

Nevertheless, the wave from the East would finally submerge everything by progressively undermining the official organs of divination (which continued to be regimented) in favor of a savage and uncontrolled form of prophecy. Soon Juvenal would write the famous verses:[107] "I cannot, citizens, tolerate a Greek Rome; and yet, what is the proportion of the Achaean element in these dregs? It has been a long time now that the river of Syria, the Orontes, has been pouring into the Tiber." For Juvenal, a Greek is capable of practicing any kind of trade; to be, among other things, "masseur, augur, doctor, magician."[108] And the poet adds a sarcastic confession: "What would I do with Rome? I cannot tell a lie . . . I do not wish to nor could I promise a son the death of his father. I have never examined the viscera of frogs."[109] Whatever excesses of language we allow a satirical poet, he stigmatizes a divination that had been degraded into all sorts of deviant forms—a phenomenon that was all too real.

R.S./d.w.

NOTES

1. The word "auspice" used in the title of this section and later in the text is to be understood in the etymological sense: "observation of birds" (*auspicium* from *avis* and *specio*).

2. J. Defradas, *La divination en Grèce,* in *La divination* (Paris 1968), 1:194.

3. Pliny, *N.H.,* 7.15.

4. Tacitus, *Ann.*, 1.54.

5. Varro, *L.L.*, 5.85. Cf. the note by J. Collart in his edition of book 5 of Varro (Paris 1954), 198, n. 5.

6. The most important editions of the Iguvine Tablets are: G. Devoto, *Tabulae Iguvinae* (2d ed., Rome 1940); *Le tavole di Gubbio* (Florence 1948); J. W. Poultney, *The Bronze Tables of Iguvium* (Baltimore and Oxford 1959); see also the linguistic commentary by E. Vetter, *Handbuch der italischen Dialekte*, 1 (Heidelberg 1953). The text has been elucidated, except for certain specific points.

7. For example, the observation of omens of the Iguvine Tablets (6a, 1–7) includes the following distribution of birds: in one category the *parra* (Umbrian *parfa*) and *cornix* (Umbrian *curnase*); in the other, the *picus* (Umbrian *peiqu*) and *pica* (Umbrian *peica*). On the other hand, the text of Plautus (*Asinaria*, 259–61) arranges in the same category the green woodpecker *(picus)* and the crow *(cornix)* and in another category the nightjar *(parra)* and the raven *(corvus)*. Thus, two differences appear from the beginning between these two divinatory formulae: (1) the magpie *(pica)* of the Umbrian text takes the place of the raven *(corvus)* of the Latin text, the two birds otherwise belonging to the same family of Corvidae; (2) a reversal is observed in the distribution: contrary to the Latin text, which groups *cornix* and *picus*, the Umbrian text associates *cornix* and *parra*; corresponding symmetrically to the Latin group *corvus* and *parra* is the Umbrian pair *pica* and *picus*. With regard to the respective orientations of these pairs of birds, the obscurity of certain Umbrian words makes it impossible to resolve the problem: thus the dispute over the meaning of *dersua* continues between G. Devoto (*Tab. Iguvinae*, 1940, p. 142), who favors the Latin translation *dextra*, and E. Vetter (*Handb. der ital. Dial.*, 1953, 1:229–31), who opts for the Latin translation *prospera*, excluding the meaning of "right."

8. Cf. Pliny, *N.H.*, 13.88; Dionysius of Halicarnassus, 4.62; Aulus Gellius, *N.A.*, 1.19. The Sibyl had first proposed nine books to Tarquin the Proud. When the king found the price too high, she burned three and offered the six others at the same price. Refused again by the king, she destroyed another three books. Impressed, the king decided to buy the three remaining books at the price set for the set of nine. The *Sibylline Books* deposited in the temple of Capitolinus Jupiter were lost when this monument burned in 83 B.C. More or less reconstructed, they were subject to a selection under Augustus and were transferred to the Palatine, where they were placed "under the statue of Palatine Apollo" (Suetonius, *Aug.*, 31.1). They remained there until the time of Honorius: then the regent of that emperor, Stilicho, burned the "Sibylline oracles," which in the eyes of Roman traditionalists were regarded as "pledges of the Empire's eternity given by Fate"—*aeterni fatalia pignora regni* (Rutilius Namatianus, *De Reditu Suo*, 2.52–55). The *viri sacris faciundis* successively increased in number from two to ten, and finally to fifteen.

9. Cf. Livy, 22.9.7–8. On this subject see my book *La religion romaine de Vénus* (Paris 1954), 96ff., 228–29.

10. Cicero (*De divin.*, 2.116) gives as precedent a verse by Ennius (*Ann.*, 174–76, ed. Warmington), a Latin transposition of Apollo's response to King Pyrrhus: *Aio te, Aeacida, Romanos vincere posse*. The meaning may be either "I affirm, O descendant of Aeacus, that you can vanquish the Romans," or "I affirm . . . that the Romans can vanquish you."

11. Pliny the Elder, *N.H.*, 7.119. Bouché-Leclercq, *Histoire de la divination dans l'Antiquité*, 4:129–30, has expressed, with good reason, the hypothesis of a Hellenic influence. With respect to the plural *Marcios quosdam fratres* (Cicero, *De divin.*, 1.89), which competes with the singular *Marcius* (of the tradition represented by the majority of authors), it seems arbitrary to reduce it to duality. Contrary to the statement of Bouché-Leclercq (*Histoire de la divination:* "Cicero attributes the prophesies to the collaboration of *two* brothers of that name"), Cicero has sometimes used an indeterminate plural (ibid., 1.89; 2.113), sometimes the singular (ibid., 1.115).

12. This is the suggestion made by G. Wissowa (*Encycl. of Relig. and Ethics*, 4:821 [1912]), who proposed a Latin verse transposition drawn from the *Sibylline Books*.

13. *De divin.*, 2.50. Servius cites (*ad Aen.*, 6.72) a nymph Begoë *quae artem scripserat fulguritarum [sic] apud Tuscos*.

14. In France there is a tradition of translating *exta* by *entrailles* (entrails). This word seems wrong to me, however, because it merely designates "l'ensemble des organes enfermés dans l'abdomen" ("the group of organs enclosed in the abdomen") (Dict. Robert). I prefer the translation *fressure* (viscera), which has the advantage of designating a set of visceral organs including the heart, liver, lungs, and spleen. Except for the spleen, which the ancients replaced by the gall bladder *(fel)*—but in ancient medicine "the spleen was thought to secrete the bile"—these are exactly the organs that the Romans understood (adding sometimes the peritoneum, *omentum*) under the name *exta: cor, jecur, pulmones*.

15. Cf. Cicero, *De divin.*, 1.12 and 35.

16. Cf. ibid., 1.72.

17. Cf. Macrobius, *S.*, 3.7.2.

18. Livy, 1.34.8–9.

19. Cicero, *De divin.*, 1.3.

20. Cf. the report by Cicero, *De divin.*, 2.34.

21. Livy, 8.9.1.

22. On the process and the finality of the *devotio*, cf. G. Dumézil, *La religion romaine archaïque* (2d ed., Paris 1974), 108–10; R. Schilling, *Religion et magie à Rome, Annuaire de l'École des Haute Études, Sciences religieuses* (1967–68), 39–40; reprinted in *R.C.D.R.*

23. Cf. Livy, 8.10.8.

24. Ibid., 8.9.1.

25. Cicero, *De divin.*, 2.28.

26. *An vos Tusci ac barbari auspiciorum populi Romani jus tenetis?* ("Do you, Etruscans and barbarians, possess the right of divination of the Roman people?"), wrote the father of the Gracchi, Tiberius Sempronius Gracchus (consul in 177 B.C.), in his address to the diviners who came to report to the Senate the illegality which he had committed in the course of presiding over the meetings. It is a cry from the heart, inspired by anger (*Tum Gracchus . . . , incensus ira . . .*). The scene is reported by Cicero (*N.D.*, 2.11).

27. Cicero, *De divin.*, 2.51. In the treatise *N.D.*, 1.71, Cicero cites the "saying" without referring to Cato. This citation has been remembered incorrectly by moderns, who have substituted the augur for the diviner. This is a contradiction that violates the "spirit" more than the "letter" of the text of Cicero.

28. Cicero, *De divin.*, 2.28. In the preceding context, Cicero had wanted to give reassurance in advance, by declaring "that it is necessary to respect the diviner out of regard for the interests of the state and the communal religious practices."

29. Livy, 42.20.

30. Ibid., 42.20.3: The *decemviri* made the following recommendations: "It is necessary to proceed to a lustration of the city, to organize supplications and solemn prayers, to sacrifice victims of great size on the Capitoline in Rome and at the Promontory of Minerva in Campania; the games should be celebrated for ten days as soon as possible in honor of Jupiter, the good and great." (On the Promontory of Minerva, facing the Isle of Capri, is a temple of Minerva.)

31. Ibid., 42.20.4.

32. For the two cults of Praeneste and Antium, see the recent restatement with the essential bibliography of K. Latte, *Römische Religionsgeschichte*, 176ff. On the interpretation of *Fortuna Primigenia*, cf. G. Dumézil, *Déesses latines et mythes védiques* (Brussels 1956), 71–98.

33. Cicero, *De divin.*, 2.85.

34. Ibid., 86–87.

35. These investigations have been published by F. Fasolo and G. Gullini, *Il santuario della Fortuna Primigenia a Palestrina* (Rome 1953).

36. K. Latte, *Römische Religionsgeschichte*, p. 177: "Nicht Sorgen des Staats, sondern Fragen von Leuten, die Angst haben, getäuscht zu werden, oder um den Ausgang einer Unternehmung besorgt sind, werden hier beantwortet." Latte then wonders, "Vielleicht war es in alter Zeit anders." I do not think that it was different long ago: with his customary conscience, Livy would not have omitted to mention an official consultation of the *sortes*. But he does not cite this in the outline of a set of marvels: see the documentation cited below.

37. Martial, 5.1.3: *Tua responsa veridicae discunt sorores*. Since the *tua responsa* refers to Domitian, these "sisters" contented themselves with repeating "the truth" of the emperor.

38. Suetonius (*Caligula*, 57.6) limits himself to noting that Caligula was warned by the Fortunes of Antium to take precautions against Cassius (*Monuerunt et Fortunae Antiatinae ut a Cassio caveret*). As for

Macrobius (1.23.13), he says that at Antium they take the statues of the Fortunes out on procession "to get answers," and he makes the connection with the statue of the god of Heliopolis, carried on a litter by the notables who advance "not according to their whim, but under the influence of the god who guides them as he wills."

39. Patavium (Padua) was the seat of an oracle of Geryon. Tiberius went to consult him: "He drew out a tablet which invited him to throw golden dice into the source of the Aponus; it happened that the dice he threw indicated the highest figure" (Suetonius, *Tiberius,* 14.4). It was a good omen for his future reign.

40. Livy, 21.62.5. Further on, § 8, Livy takes up the expression again with a variant: *Caere, ubi sortes adtenuatae erant.* With regard to the miracle of the shrinking of the *sortes,* Pliny the Elder (*N.H.,* 34.137) cites an analogous case: the family of the *Servilii* possessed a *triens* (one-third of an *as*) that had the property of increasing and decreasing.

41. Livy, 22.1.11: *Et Faleris caelum findi velut magno hiatu visum, quaque patuerit, ingens lumen effulsisse; sortes sua sponte adtenuatas unamque excidisse ita inscriptam: Mavors telum suum concutit.*

42. Livy, 43.13.3–6. With respect to the two sanctuaries of Fortuna in Rome, it is probable that the first is designated the sanctuary of the *Forum boarium.* Cf. J. Lugli, *Roma antica, Il centro monumentale* (Rome 1946), 554. With respect to the second, *Fortuna Primigenia,* which is situated on the hill (of Quirinal), cf. J. Lugli, *Fontes ad topographiam veteris urbis Romae pertinentes* (Rome 1957), 4:207, nos. 39, 40.

43. Livy, ibid., 43.13.1–2.

44. E. Benveniste, *Le vocabulaire des institutions indo-européennes* (Paris 1969), 2:256: "the Latin radical *ō* (of *omen*) may be directly compared with the Hittite verbal theme *hā* 'to believe; to hold as true'; consequently, *omen* is interpreted as 'declaration of truth.' A fortuitous word, pronounced in a decisive circumstance, may be accepted as an omen, as a true presage, as a sign of destiny." In the same chapter the author analyzes "the series of words with precise meaning: *miraculum, monstrum, ostentum, portentum, prodigium.* The curious reader who is eager to grasp the semantic nuances that distinguish these different terms should consult this book. The relative abundance of similar terms in Latin, in the face of the unique Greek word *teras,* is a fact symptomatic of the state of mind that we are describing: E. Benveniste has restored the contrast on the linguistic level.

45. Cicero, *De divin.,* 2.84.

46. Cf. the text of *De divin.,* 2.148, discussed in the article "Cicero as Theologian" below.

47. J. Bayet, in the chapter "Présages figuratifs déterminants dans l'antiquité gréco-latine," in *Croyances et rites dans la Rome antique* (Paris 1971), 60 and 63, rightly emphasized this aspect.

48. Suetonius, *Julius,* 81.

49. Incontestably a more menacing omen. Recall that in time of war the doors of the temple of Janus are also open.

50. Cf. the text of Pliny, *N.H.,* 28.17, cited above in § 1, "Divination or Auspices?"

51. Cf. Suetonius, *Julius,* 77.2: "He (Caesar) had the insolence to say one day when the haruspex announced a bad omen after examining organs in which the heart was lacking: the omen could have been favorable if it had pleased him; it was not necessary to interpret as a wonder the fact that the beast had no heart."

52. Suetonius, *Aug.,* 92.1: *Auspicia et omina quaedam pro certissimis observabat* ("He considered certain signs and omens to be absolutely true").

53. Cf. the text of Cicero, *De divin.,* 2.84, cited above.

54. Suetonius, *Aug.,* 92.1: *si mane sibi calceus perperam ac sinister pro dextro induceretur, ut dirum (observabat).*

55. Ibid., 93.5. The nones correspond to the fifth day of the month, except in March, May, July, and October, in which they fall on the seventh day. But they are always on the ninth day (hence their name) before the ides of the month (i.e., the thirteenth or fifteenth).

56. Ibid., 96.5. In Greek *Nikon* means "victor," and *Eutychus,* "fortunate, happy." The battle of Actium (31 B.C.), by eliminating Antony, the ally of Cleopatra, confirmed the supremacy of Octavian, the future Augustus. The biographer adds that later, Augustus had a bronze statue of the ass and ass driver made (in the temple that he built) at the site of his camp.

57. Ibid., 97.2. The "adjacent sanctuary" must be the Pantheon, whose frieze door (even today) bears the inscription of the founder in large capitals: M. AGRIPPA L(ucii) F(ilius) COS. TERTIUM FECIT. By alighting above the letter A, the eagle, the messenger of Jupiter, designates Augustus, who is believed to have been "called" by heaven.

58. Ibid., 94.3. Suetonius invokes the testimony of Julius Marathus for this *prodigium.*

59. Ibid., 94.4. Recall that, through his mother Atia—the daughter of Julia, who was the sister of Julius Caesar—the future Augustus was the grandnephew of Julius Caesar before becoming his adopted son.

60. Ibid., 94.9.

61. Ibid., 94.10.

62. Ibid., 94.15. The *laticlavus* was a tunic with two large bands of purple that was reserved for senators. The anecdote is explained by the fact that the children of senators also had the right to wear the *laticlavus* (cf. ibid., 38.2).

63. Ibid., 94.16. The battle of Munda (45 B.C.) won over the sons of Pompey and assured the definitive victory of Caesar. Later Augustus transplanted to the interior of his home, near the Penates and the opening of the *compluvium,* a palm that had grown in front of his house (ibid., 92.3).

64. Ibid., 95.1. This marvel implied an omen of victory (the crowned sun) by playing on the same symbolism many times: Octavian, who was considered a *son of Apollo* (see the text of Suetonius cited in note 59), returns to *Apollonia* and sees a *solar* phenomenon.

65. Ibid., 94.2. The biographer adds that on the strength of this promise, the inhabitants of Velitrae fought a series of unfortunate wars against the Romans. "It was only later that events revealed that the omen (of the thunderclap) had announced the power of Augustus."

66. Ibid., 90.1. "To remedy it, he always carried with him a bit of sealskin."

67. Ibid., 29.5.

68. Ibid., 95.1.

69. Ibid., 29.4.

70. Ibid., 97.3. Recall that after his adoption by Julius Caesar, he bore the name *C. Julius, C(ai) f(ilius) Caesar.* His contemporaries (and after them the moderns) named him *Octavianus,* although he had never borne this cognomen that named his family of origin. After 27 B.C. his official name had been *Imperator Caesar Augustus.*

71. Ibid., 94.6.

72. Ibid., 94.17 . . . *exiluit Theogenes adoravitque eum.*

73. Ibid., 94.18. The sign of Capricorn still appears on the side of the emperor's head on the large cameo of Vienna; it also served as the emblem of the legions created by Augustus: cf. F. Cumont, *Dictionnaire des antiquités grecques et romaines,* s.v. "zodiacus," p. 1054a. The interpretation of this sign seems to have led to confusion. Suetonius (ibid., 94.18) wrote: "He coined pieces of silver in the effigy of Capricorn, under which he was born" (*nota sideris Capricorni, quo natus est . . .*). F. Cumont (*Dictionnaire*) has observed with good reason that the sign of Capricorn, which corresponds to January, can only designate the month of his *conception* and not that of his birth (23 September of the year 63).

74. Cicero, *De divin.,* 1.11–12: *Duo sunt enim divinandi genera, quorum alterum artis est, alterum naturae.* In the first category he classes haruspicy (subdivided into the examination of the viscera, the interpretation of marvels and omens, and lightning), augury, astrology, and the interpretation of the *sortes;* in the second, oneiromancy and predictions from dreams (*somniorum aut vaticinationum praedictio*). See further ibid., 1.34.

75. Suetonius, *Aug.,* 94.7.

76. Ibid., 94.5. The same dreams are recorded by Dio Cassius, 45.1.3.

77. Ibid., 94.8. The "transfiguration" of Augustus recalls the ritual aspect of the conqueror during the victory ceremonies, even while it suggests "by the air of superhuman majesty" (*mortali specie ampliorem*) a very marked assimilation to Jupiter.

78. Ibid., 94.12. The report of the first dream of Catulus includes variants: cf. ibid., 94.13, and Plutarch, *Cic.*, 44.
79. Ibid., 94.14. The same dream is reported, with some variations of detail, by Dio Cassius, 45.2.2.
80. Ibid., 91.1. Cf. the similar accounts of Velleius Paterculus, 2.70, and of Valerius Maximus, 1.7.1.
81. Ibid., 92.2: *Sed et ostentis praecipue movebatur.*
82. Ibid., 95.2. Cf. the version (which gives a variant reading) of Dio Cassius, 46.35.
83. Ibid., 96.3.
84. Ibid., 94.11. Cf. Dio Cassius, 45.2.1.
85. Cf. above, § 2, for the commentary on the text of Livy, 1.34.8–9.
86. Suetonius, ibid., 96.1. Cf. Dio Cassius, 47.1.3.
87. Cf. above.
88. Cf. Suetonius, ibid., 95.2. With regard to Romulus, see above, § 1.
89. Octavian had been *augur* in 37 B.C. at the latest; *quindecimvir sacris faciundis*, between 37 and 34; *septemvir epulonum*, in 16; *Pontifex maximus*, in 12 B.C. Cf. R. Cagnat, *Cours d'épigraphie latine* (Paris 1914), 177.
90. On the exceptional character that Julius Caesar, like Sulla, attributed to the law of auspices, see my book *La religion romaine de Vénus*, p. 304.
91. The type of this *aureus* is described in the passage cited in the preceding note.
92. Cf. above, § 2, especially note 7.
93. Cicero, *N.D.*, 3.5: "Roman religion is divided into celebrations and auspices; a third part has been added to it that consists of warnings of a divinatory nature made by the oracles of the Sibyl or the diviners, after marvels and omens."
94. M. Valerius Messalla Messallinus appeared as Quindecimvir of the secular games of 17 B.C.: cf. Pighi, *De ludis saecularibus* (2d ed., Amsterdam 1965), 236, n. 35. On his personality, see D. von Lunzer, in Pauly/Wissowa, *Real-Encyclopädie*, s.v. Valerius Messalla Messallinus, (sic), no. 264, cols. 159–62.
95. Tibullus, 2.5.1 and 11–16. According to this text Valerius Messalla also had to be an "interpreter of the Sibyl." The sanctuary to which verse 1 alludes is called the temple of Palatine Apollo, where Augustus had deposited the rest of the *Sibylline Books*.
96. Cf. Tacitus, *Annales*, 11.15.
97. Cicero, *De divin.*, 1.132. The last phrase paraphrases the expression of Ennius, cited by Quintus, the brother of Cicero: *impudentesque harioli.*
98. Cf. Suetonius, *Claud.*, 25.11: "As the Jews were agitated continually at the instigation of someone named Chrestos (*impulsore Chresto*), he expelled them from Rome." Orosius (*Adversus paganos*, 7.6.15) has cited and commented on this passage, substituting *Christo* for the reading *Chresto* of Suetonius. When Tacitus (*Annales*, 15.44.5) speaks of Christ, he uses the form *Christus*. Egyptian and Jewish cults are associated in the repression ordered by Tiberius: see Suetonius, *Tib.*, 36.1.
99. Cf. the sources indicated by G. Wissowa, *Religion und Kultus der Römer* (2d ed., 1912), 352–55.
100. Cicero, *De divin.*, 2.148: "it is necessary to spread religion at the same time as the study of nature, as much as it is necessary to extirpate all the roots of superstition."
101. Cf. Suetonius, *Aug.*, 94.17. Text cited in § 3 above, "Divination," especially note 72.
102. Cf. Suetonius, *Tib.*, 14.6. Cf. ibid., 14.3: a promise had been made to Livia by the astrologer Scribonius that one day Tiberius would rule.
103. Ibid., 69.
104. Suetonius, *Calig.*, 57.5.
105. Suetonius, *Claud.*, 11.3.
106. Ibid., 22.2.
107. Juvenal, *Satir.*, 3.60ff.
108. Ibid., 76–77.
109. Ibid., 41–45.

BIBLIOGRAPHY

(See also the bibliography at the end of the article "Augurs and Augury" below)
J. BAYET, "Présages figuratifs déterminants dans l'antiquité gréco-latine," in *Croyances et rites dans la Rome antique* (Paris 1971), 44–63. R. BLOCH, *Les prodiges dans l'antiquité classique* (Paris 1963). P. CATALANO, *Contributi allo studio del diritto augurale*, 1, Memorie dell'Istituto giuridico (Turin 1960). F. CUMONT, *Astrology and Religion among the Greeks and Romans* (New York and London 1912). S. WEINSTOCK, *Diuus Iulius* (Oxford 1971).

Roman Religion and Greek Philosophy

The Romans have never been noted for their "philosophical brains." This commonplace, though it has some basis of truth, should be tempered. Pliny the Elder (in *Naturalis Historia* 7.112) tells a famous anecdote about the reaction of Cato the Elder to the first Greek philosophers who were heard in Rome. There were three of them, who had come on a mission in 155 B.C. to plead the cause of the city of Athens, which at the time was in conflict with the Attic city of Oropus. They represented three philosophical tendencies: Carneades, the Academy; Diogenes, Stoicism; and Critolaus, the Peripatetic school. After listening to Carneades, Cato the censor cried out, "The ambassadors have to be sent back immediately, for the dialectic of such a man (*illo viro argumentante*) makes it impossible to discern the truth." (Pliny cannot help adding that the censor's great grandson, Cato Uticensis, brought two Greek philosophers back with him at the end of his missions abroad. *Quanta morum commutatio!* comments the natural scientist.)

In another testimony dating from a time close to this mission of the Greek philosophers, the Greek historian Polybius, who happened to be staying in Rome and was a friend of P. Cornelius Scipio Aemilianus, pronounced an admiring judgment on the Roman institutions that seemed to him to represent a happy balance among elements that were monarchical (the Consuls), aristocratic (the Senate), and democratic (the Roman people assisted by the tribunes of the Plebeians). What did he regard as the secret of the Roman success? Certainly he gave it no philosophical basis; no code such as that of Athens inspired by the "wise" Solon was to be found anywhere here. Polybius (6.56) did not hesitate to say: "One of the greatest advantages of the Roman constitution stems from its conception of divinity. The strength of Roman domination comes from a thing that is considered a flaw among other men, and by that I mean the *deisidaimonian.*" (The Greek term is ambiguous; it can mean both "reverential fear" and "superstitious fear" of the gods.)

Let us turn to the Roman sources. In the second century B.C., the Latin adaptations of the poet Ennius (239–169), *Epicharmus* and *Euhemerus sive Sacra Historia*, helped to spread the philosophical ideas of Epicharmus, a philosopher-poet from Cos (540–450), and of Euhemerus, a rationalist theoretician (born ca. 340 B.C., and of uncertain origin). For both, the gods were nothing but former mortals worshiped by mankind as a result of their good deeds. Flagrantly contradicting the Roman traditions which must have impressed Polybius with their force, these ideas probably did not overstep the limits of the circles of "initiates," such as "the circle of the Scipios" (see P. Grimal, *Le Siècle des Scipions* [2d ed., Paris 1975]). Paradoxically, it is in the work of this "enlightened" author that attempts have been made to find a formula that would "explain" the mentality of the average Roman. Someone named Neoptolemus cries out in a tragedy of Ennius (*Tragoediae* § 400, ed. E. H. Warmington [1967], vol. 1, p. 368): *philosophari mihi necesse, paucis, nam omnio haud placet* (I must philosophize—sometimes; but I cannot keep doing it always and in everything). This remark of a character with a Greek name, which is taken from a fragment of a lost tragedy, tells us nothing specific about the state of the Roman mind, any more than another remark gleaned from the same author enlightens us about the motives behind the poetic inspiration of Ennius: *numquam poetor, nisi si podager* (I never indulge in poetry unless I am suffering from gout: *Saturae* § 21, ibid. 1, p. 390). Neoptolemus's observation was later to give Cicero (*Tusculanae Disputationes* 2.1–2) the opportunity to oppose this assertion (which he explained in terms of class: Neoptolemus "was a military man absorbed in his career") and to proclaim the benefits of the permanent practice of philosophy.

The contrasts revealed in the second century B.C. (the reaction of Cato the Elder to Ennius, who was open to Hellenism) show at least that ancient Rome, at last victorious over the most formidable enemy in its history (the victory of Scipio Africanus over Hannibal at the battle of Zama in 202 B.C. was to be capped by the total defeat and solemn destruction of Carthage in 146), the Rome which had until that date lived on strong ancestral traditions (*Moribus antiquis res stat Romana virisque,* "Thanks to the customs and to the men of the past, the Roman state stands firm"—another verse of Ennius [*Annals* § 467, ed. W., vol. 1, p. 174])—that very Rome would face outside influences, especially the influence of Greek schools of philosophy, after the conquest and surrender of Greece in 146 B.C. following the destruction of Corinth.

Although the second century B.C. showed evidence of barely perceptible stirrings only in educated circles—and this ideological current could not have disturbed the *mos maiorum,* on the evidence of Polybius—such was no longer the case in the first century, and for a number of reasons. First, the contacts between Rome and Greece and the Near East became more frequent following the military campaigns of Sulla and Pompey in Greece and in Asia Minor. Pliny the Elder (*Naturalis Historia* 7.112) tells a revealing anecdote that shows how a great Roman war chief was not impervious to the charm of Greek wisdom. When Pompey returned from the war against Mithridates, he stopped to visit the Stoic Posidonius (who lived on the island of Rhodes), paid him his respects, and "made his troops bow before the gate of wisdom."

Moreover, a practice had become established, of completing the education of a young Roman who had begun his studies with a *litterator* (who taught him reading and writing) and a *grammaticus* (who started him in the interpretation of "classical" texts, Greek as well as Latin) by sending him to spend some time in Greece to receive training in philosophy. Cicero is a good example of this.

Cicero applied himself to the task of transmitting the heritage of Greek thought to his Roman contemporaries. The choice that he made is instructive, especially because the whole Ciceronian enterprise belongs chronologically after the Epicurean poem of Lucretius, the *De rerum natura* (before 55 B.C.). When *De natura deorum,* written by Cicero in 45 B.C., insists in its preamble on the opportunity, indeed the necessity, for theological reflection, it rapidly circumscribes the debate between three major tendencies: Epicureanism (represented by C. Velleius), Stoicism (by Q. Lucilius Balbus), and the new Academy (by C. Aurelius Cotta). Above all, the discussion pits the Epicurean teaching against the Stoic doctrine, while the representative of the new Academy assumes the role of a moderator who claims to be free of all dogmatic prejudice.

In the course of this discussion, the fundamental contrast between Epicureanism and Stoicism in minds steeped in Roman traditions is revealed in a sudden burst. The more the religious posture of Epicureanism seemed alien to them, even deviant, the more Stoicism seemed close to certain essential aspects of Roman theology. First of all, there was the conception of the gods. Epicureanism is known to have localized them in the *intermundia,* the spaces between the worlds. They are supposed to have a human appearance, but without any function corresponding to the organs; above all, they are bereft of any activity and are reputed to enjoy eternal happiness.

Nothing could have shocked a Roman more, accustomed as he was to conceive of a deity with a function. Thus the spokesman for the new Academy did not hesitate to mock these gods "deprived of any reality" (Cic. *Nat. D.* 1.75), "without solidity or three-dimensional features" (ibid. 1.105–6), who cannot even be happy, since they have permanent instability (by definition, their existence depends on a precarious balance based on the incessant flow of atoms, compensated for by the perpetual emission of "images" from their own being: ibid. 1.114).

Then there was the notion of piety. This was not overlooked by Epicurus, who devoted a treatise to it, *Peri Hosiotētos,* which the academician Cotta mentions (ibid. 1.115). Epicurus advised the wise to hold "pious opinions about the gods" (*Letter to Menoeceus* 133). According to him, "The impious person is not the one who destroys the mob's belief in the gods, but the one who attributes to the gods the characteristics bestowed on them by the mob's opinions" (ibid. 123). Epicurean piety consists in the wise man's modeling of himself on divine beatitude: "You shall thus never experience trouble, either dreaming or waking, but you shall live like a god among men" (ibid. 134).

Cotta's reaction to this teaching was a function more of his role as the Roman pontifex than of his position as an exponent of the new Academy. "How can you expect," he cries to Velleius, "that men will *honor* gods who not only do not *treat men with honor,* but have no concern for them whatever and do nothing?" In Latin the formulation is more forceful because it underscores the reciprocity of the relationship (which *necessarily* exists between men and gods in Roman religion) through the *univocal* use of the word *colere,* "to honor" applied to both gods and men: *Quid est enim cur deos ab hominibus "colendos" dicas, cum di non modo homines non "colant," sed omnino nihil curent, nihil agant?* (Cic. *Nat. D.* 1.115).

After that, the solipsistic indifference of the Epicurean gods could only scandalize a Roman's mind. Although it is true that piety for him manifests a reverential and equitable gratitude toward the kindly gods (*est enim pietas justitia adversum deos:* ibid. 1.116), Epicureanism appears to be merely harmful and destructive. Therefore Cotta, who had at first granted the sincerity of Epicurus's belief in the gods (ibid. 1.86), finally concludes by rallying behind the Stoic Posidonius (ibid. 1.123), for whom Epicurus was only an atheist in disguise who professed faith in the immortal gods only in order to avoid becoming odious: *invidiae detestandae gratia.* After that any reconciliation becomes impossible. Cotta seems to be raising his voice in the name of all of Roman tradition when he launches this final judgment: "Epicurus completely eradicated religion from men's hearts when he deprived the immortal gods of the possibility of granting them help and grace" (ibid. 1.121).

Stoic theology is presented quite differently. At first it does not seem any closer to Roman tradition. On the contrary, its cosmic conception deifies the world and the stars, relegating the traditional deities to the rank of mendacious inventions of fable: *ad commenticios et fictos deos,* to quote the expression of Balbus, the spokesman for Stoicism (Cic. *Nat. D.* 2.70). But by affirming the divine oneness which he defines as "an artful and creative fire that penetrates the world methodically" (*ignem artificiosum ad gignendum progredientem via:* ibid. 2.57), Stoicism proves to be highly flexible in the face of polytheistic pluralism. In fact, although divine power is primarily revealed "in the admirable order and the incredible regularity of the heavenly bodies" (ibid. 2.56), it is also manifest in other ways. All one has to do is set aside the fables to rediscover philosophic truth. One can then know the god who penetrates all reality in the world (*deus pertinens per naturam cuiusque rei*), no matter what name custom may have dressed him up in (*quoque eos nomine consuetudo nuncupaverit*): "Ceres for the lands, Neptune for the seas, or whatever other name for whatever other realm" (ibid. 2.71).

In this way, the traditional gods and the Stoic conception of divinity are reconciled: all these names correspond to various aspects of the same divine breath of life that goes through the world, *pneuma noeron kai purōdes ouk echon morphēn:* "a fiery and intelligent breath, free of any form" (identified with the heavenly ether). For a Roman, this definition had the great merit of going beyond Hellenic anthropomorphism to join an ancestral idea. Varro (cited by Augustine, *De Civitate Dei* 4.31) reminds us "that for more than 170 years the ancient Romans worshiped gods *without statues.* If this practice had prevailed until the present day," he added, "the cult of the gods would be purer" (*quod si adhuc mansisset, castius dii observarentur*).

In this perspective, the cult of deified abstractions in Roman religion becomes entirely justified (Cic. *Nat. D.* 2.79): *Mens* (intelligence), *Fides* (loyalty), *Virtus* (active virtue), *Concordia* (harmony). These refer to virtues inherent in the divine power. Stoicism did not intentionally limit itself to these special cases. It meant to demonstrate its ability to explain everything at the heart of a world penetrated by the divinity. Balbus does not fail to show that the subtle exegeses of a Zeno, a Cleanthes, and a Chrysippus went so far as to discover the deep meaning of a sometimes scabrous mythology (*phusica ratio non inelegans inclusa est in impias fabulas:* ibid. 2.64). He cites the myth of Caelus (= Ouranos), who is mutilated by his own son Jupiter (= Zeus); this narrative symbolizes the fact that "the ether, that is, the fire of the highest region, capable of engendering all things by itself, does without that part of the body that requires union with the opposite sex to procreate."

By this method, Stoicism finally subsumed the entire traditional heritage. It cleverly managed to find the right equations between religious names and physical or philosophical concepts. Thus Jupiter corresponds to the ether, and Juno represents the air between the sea and the sky (ibid. 2.66). Finally, Cicero viewed the entire world as a city common to both gods and men (ibid. 2.78), in which all the elements—earth, water, air, and fire—are maintained in perfect cohesion because of the divine spirit that penetrates everything.

The idea of a world wholly controlled by divine providence (*omnia regi divina mente atque providentia:* ibid. 2.80) is at the opposite end of the spectrum from the Epicureanism that postulates indifferent gods in an infinity of worlds. It is very close to the traditional religious vision and therefore is not in danger of running up against the Roman *pietas,* which was based on the notion of mutual exchange. On the contrary, it calls for a more refined form of piety for the believer, one that allows him to distinguish between religious attitudes and acts of superstition (ibid. 2.71).

It recommends an inner piety in addition to the mere formal purity of time past. The old way is illustrated by an anecdote that Livy (1.45.6) tells about the Roman who reminds the Sabine of his obligation to wash his hands before offering his marvelous heifer in sacrifice, a stratagem which allows the Roman to benefit, by way of substitution, from the prediction of prosperity tied to this sacrifice. Thus, "the cult of the gods will be stamped with a greater purity and a more perfect piety, if our worship is expressed through prayers that reveal an irreproachable state of mind" (ibid. 2.71).

Furthermore, Stoicism went beyond the traditional religions, which had exposed themselves to criticism. In the name of divine prediction and providence, it rehabilitated the legendary accounts of the interventions of the gods in human affairs, for example, the appearance of Castor and Pollux "who in the course of the Battle of Lake Regillus (in 496 B.C.), were seen lending a hand to the Roman troops" (ibid. 2.6). Similarly, it credited the predictions of divination in its various forms. Thus, the augur Attus Navius was said to merit the prestige that tradition bestows on him, since the revelation of the future may be granted by the gods to certain men (ibid. 2.9). The existence of augurs even gives Balbus the chance to propose a new proof of the existence of the gods, in the form of this curious syllogism (ibid. 2.12): "If someone has interpreters, he must himself exist. Now, the gods have interpreters. Let us therefore recognize that the gods exist." (In fact, this "proof" is gratuitous, since "the existence of the gods is a notion innate to all men, in some way carved into the soul": *omnibus enim innatum est et in animo quasi insculptum, esse deos.*)

Of course, Epicureanism and Stoicism were not the only philosophies to thrive in Rome, but they certainly elicited much stronger reactions than all the other movements (for example, the Euhemerism that is present in the works of Ennius or the Pythagoreanism that supposedly influenced Nigidius Figulus). Nevertheless, they had quite different audiences among the Romans. Because of the relative chronology (the dialogue of the protagonists in *De natura deorum* is believed to have taken place between 77 and 75 B.C.), neither Velleius, nor Balbus, nor Cotta, makes any reference to the poem by Lucretius. How interesting it would have been to record their feelings about the magnificent profession of Epicurean faith in the *De rerum natura.*

In any case, the poem by Lucretius appears to be an isolated flash of lightning in the literary sky. For reasons mentioned earlier, the Roman mind in the end remained stubbornly resistant to Epicureanism. On the other hand, in more than one instance, Stoicism struck sympathetic chords deep in the Roman soul. By its tone, it attracted Cicero, for one (*Nat. D.* 3.95), who became its advocate despite his attachment to the probabilism of the new Academy. It fertilized the entire philosophical and dramatic production of Seneca, to cite only one famous example.

Instead of rejecting the Roman pantheon outright, as Epicureanism did, Stoicism was able to subsume all the gods of the tradition by interpreting them as just so many manifestations of the same divine power. That is how it succeeded in reconciling the philosophical requirement that postulated the oneness of the divinity with the practices of traditional polytheism. Above all, by developing the notion of providence, Stoicism reinforced the basis of Roman piety, which could only conceive of beneficent gods. One revealing fact among others: as Cicero (*Nat. D.* 2.64) points out, popular interpretation had always mocked the etymology proposed by scholars, who saw in the supreme god *Juppiter* a *Juvans pater,* a "helpful Father."

R.S./g.h.

The Decline and Survival of Roman Religion

It is a well-known fact that the Roman Empire was progressively invaded by Eastern religions, among them Christianity, which was to triumph in the fourth century. But it may be well to present some of the nuances connected with this fact. On the eve of its victory, Christianity was inclined to aim its polemic less against traditional Roman religion than against the scandalous fictions of Greek mythology and the extravagances of the mystery religions. At least that is the impression left by an anonymous pamphlet drafted a few years after 394, the *Carmen Contra Paganos,*[1] which discharges its most virulent shafts against the cults of Isis, Mithra, and the Magna Mater, all of which were merely foreign cults, *sacra peregrina,* in ancient Rome (except for the Magna Mater, who was *also* of Roman "kinship" through her role in the Trojan legend).

In any case, the death agony of Roman religion was prolonged throughout the entire fourth century, beginning when Constantine proclaimed himself the protector of Christianity in 313 with the Edict of Milan, though he did not abolish paganism. Various episodes marked the confrontation between the new religion and the ancient institution. The case of the statue of Victory, which matched Symmachus, the pagan prefect of Rome, against Saint Ambrose, Bishop of Milan, is perhaps the most important symbolically. The statue of Victory was finally removed from the the altar of the Senate. Others attacked the old religion with even more force. In A.D. 375, the Emperor Gratian renounced the title of Pontifex Maximus and in A.D. 382 he withdrew the subsidies of the pagan temples and the salaries of their priests.

The emperor Theodosius delivered the decisive blows. He had already decreed the closing of the temples, forbidden the celebration of public sacrifices, and ordered an end to the domestic cults of the Lares, Genii, and Penates; his victory over Eugenius in 394 assured the triumph of Christianity once and for all. Toward the year 400, Saint Jerome was able to write that "the gold of the Capitol is peeling, soot and cobwebs cover all the temples of Rome" (*Epistolae* 107.1). Around the same time, Stilicho, the minister of the emperor Honorius, whom the poet Rutilius Namatianus (*De reditu suo* 2.41 and 52) calls the *dirus Stilicho* (sinister Stilicho), had the prophetic books of ancient Rome, the *Sibylline Books,* burned.

From that point on, is it correct to speak of the survival of a religion that had begun to wane some fifteen hundred years before? The slow pace of its demise, however, speaks for the strength of its deep entrenchment. Indeed, surprising resurgences prove that the death warrant issued by Theodosius at the end of the fourth century was not the last word. Thus, the calendar of Polemius Silvius, dated A.D. 449, still refers to "pagan" festivals, despite the author's Christian faith. It refers, for example, to the Carmentalia in January and the Lupercalia in February (see A. Degrassi, *Inscriptiones Italiae,* vol. 13, 2, pp. 264–65). At the end of the fifth century, a pope was compelled to protest against the celebration of the Lupercalia in Rome.[2] And even in the sixth century, when Belisarius, Justinian's general, held out in Rome against a difficult siege by the Goths, Romans remembered the archaic rite that prescribed opening the gates of the sanctuary of Janus Quirinus in time of war, and in order to conform to the ancient prescription they secretly undertook to force open the gates of the temple, which had been closed since the abolition of paganism.[3]

Christianity thus found itself in close combat with pagan vestiges alive enough to provide it with useful substitutions. The mutations provide, in their way, evidence of the old institutions. Thus, a whole school of research was born in the wake of *Antike und Christentum* by E. J. Dölger. For example, the idea of purification that inspired the festival of the Lupercalia was taken up again in the festival of the Purification of the Virgin. The Ambarvalia, which were meant to ensure the lustration of the fields, were transposed into the processions on Rogation Days. Even the cult of the dead preserved the ancient piety; there was no longer a taste for libations (which Monica, the mother of Augustine, still practiced), but people used flowers—Ovid (*Fasti* 4.539) recommends violets. And the cult of the saints is known often to have taken over the cult of the local deity.

Another legacy of Roman religion remains in the sacred vocabulary. Beginning with the second century, when Latin replaced Greek in the liturgy of the Western church, the wealth of the Latin language became available to Christians. The transfer was not made directly, of course. (There are no rules without exceptions: the invocation *Regina caeli* addressed to Isis by Apuleius was taken up again in the paschal anthem in honor of the Virgin Mary.) Often the adopted word no longer carried its exact original meaning but took on a new range of colors, as a bronze is colored by a patina through the passage of time. Thus, in the classical language, the word *religiosus* evokes the idea of taboo or scruples, and therefore can be applied to an inanimate object (a *locus religiosus* is inviolable) or to a personal subject (a *religiosus* man is exceedingly scrupulous). But in the language of Apuleius, the term seems to have lost this altogether negative value. The author of *Metamorphoses* (11.13.6) delights in contrasting the common people (*populi*) or the impious (*inreligiosi*) with the *religiosi,* who are the faithful worshipers of the divinity of Isis. This "positive" meaning remained associated with the word after Christianity adopted it. Saint Jerome (*Epistulae* 107.2) certainly meant to compliment his correspondent when he said he regarded her as *religiosissima in Christo filia.*

Scene from the Isiac ritual. Painting from Herculaneum. Naples, National Museum. Photo Alinari-Giraudon.

Coin with likeness of Theodosus. Photo Arthaud/Martin.

Another term worth noting is *sacramentum*. Again Apuleius, a magician in the art of stretching vocabulary, seems to have played the role of intermediary. Speaking of the holy *militia* of Isis into which his hero is to enlist the next day, he calls the enlistment a *sacramentum* (Apuleius *Metamorphoses* 11.15.5). Used in this way, the word still retained a link with the military meaning appropriate to its classical usage, while revealing its religious vocation through its context. *Sacramentum* in the mystical sense then became possible for the Christian language.

This example also shows that when it was necessary, Christians knew how to transpose onto the sacred register words that were originally profane. The method of "recycling" appears as frequently in vocabulary as it does in paleo-Christian architecture and sculpture. An investigation into the Leonine sacramentary yields much insight.[4] We discover the *vota* that the Lord is asked to receive with favor, and the *hostia* that ceases to be bloody and becomes *salutaris* or *spiritualis* and designates Christ.[5] Even the most sacred vocabulary of Rome appears with specific words like *venerari* and *venia*, along with the ritual practice of associating prayer and sacrifice: "Ecclesiae tuae, quaesumus, Domine, *preces* et *hostias* apostolica commendet oratio ut quod pro illorum gloria celebramus prosit ad *veniam*."[6]

But Rome did not limit itself to a lexicographical legacy whose most prestigious term was *religio*. The Roman spirit strongly marked the style of Christianity, a style that is visible in the structure of the prayers that preserved the qualities of sobriety and clarity that had distinguished the *carmina* of older times, avoiding all dull sentimentality and establishing relationships based on a clear confidence between men and heaven. According to one formula of Augustine (*De Doctrina Christiana* 3.11), Christianity was able to carry away the "gold and silver vases" of its adversaries and use them in its own way. The style is perhaps even more striking (it shows up, if not at the beginning, at least at the time of the turmoils and heresies) in its sense of order and in its spirit of organization. One fact seems to take on a profoundly symbolic value. It is well known that the first popes simply bore the title of bishop (*episkopos*); but it is not just an accident that the tradition later revived the title of Pontifex Maximus and gave it to the ruler of Christendom. Consciously or unconsciously, it was a way of paying magnificent homage to the traditions of ancient Rome.

R.S./g.h.

NOTES

1. *Carmen contra paganos* is a satirical poem directed against Virius Nicomachus Flavianus, *praefectus Italiae, Illyrici et Africae,* who had exercised his functions first under Theodosius, in A.D. 390–91, and then in the reign of the usurper Eugenius in 393–94. The author of *Carmen* attacks, without naming him, the *praefectus* who had restored the pagan rites at Rome and made war "on the true God," before "dying a miserable death" (Flavianus committed suicide during the battle of the river Frigidus, 5–6 September A.D. 394). The identification proposed by Mommsen and the date (a little after 394) have since been confirmed: see A. Chastagnol, *Hommages à Marcel Renard,* 2:143, and J. F. Matthews, "The Historical Setting of the Carmen contra Paganos," *Historia,* 1970, 464–79. See the edition of the poem (with Italian trans. and notes) by G. Manganaro, in *Nuovo Didaskaleion* 11 (1961): 23–45 (but the author wishes to propose—wrongly—too late a date).

2. Usually the treatise on the Lupercalia is attributed to Pope Gelasius. Recent criticism has tended to attribute the authorship to Pope Felix III: cf. P. Nautin, *Dict. d'hist. et de géogr. eccl.,* no. 32, Felix III, col. 894.

3. Cf. Procopius, *De Bello Gothico* 1.25, ed. Comparetti (Rome 1895), 1:184–85.

4. We have kept the name "Leonine sacramentary," which is the one most widely used to designate the collection that contains the most ancient prayers of the Latin church. It is under this title (which attributes it to Pope Leo the Great) that it has been published, notably in volume 55 of Migne's *Patrologiae Cursus Latina*. One edition, more recent and more learned, has been produced by L. C. Mohlberg under the title *Sacramentarium Veronense*, in the collection *Rerum ecclesiasticarum documenta*, where it constitutes volume 1 of the *Fontes* (2d ed., Rome 1966). This new title refers to the source, a manuscript from Verona (no. 85 of the Capitulary Library) which, written in uncial script, dates from the first half of the seventh century and originates from Italy—no doubt from Verona.

5. Cf. *Sacramentarium Veronense*, ed. Mohlberg (2d ed., Rome 1966), p. 33, 1.10ff. (= Migne, *P.L.*, 55, c. 46): "Remotis obumbrationibus carnalium victimarum, *spiritalem* tibi, summe Pater, *hostiam* supplici servitute deferimus . . . " (Abandoning the gloomy sacrifices of bloody victims, we offer, O sovereign God, as humble supplicants, a spiritual sacrifice . . .).

6. Cf. ibid., p. 43, 1.9ff. (= Migne, *P.L.*, 55, c. 53–54): "O Lord, may the intercession of the apostles commend the prayers and sacrifices of thy Church, in order that the festival that we celebrate in your honor may serve to gain us thy favor." See the index to the words *venerari* and *venia* in Mohlberg's work, pp. 430–31.

Anna Perenna

The double name of this Roman goddess is clarified by a commentary from Macrobius (*Saturnalia*, 1.12.6): *Eodem quoque mense (= Martio) et publice et privatim ad Annam Perennam sacrificatum itur ut annare perennareque commode liceat.* "It is also in the same month (of March) that both in public and in private sacrifices are offered to the wood of Anna Perenna in order to live happily through the entire year." (The sacred wood, *nemus*, of Anna Perenna is mentioned by Martial, 4.64.17.) If *Anna* is the personification of the new year, *Perenna* (**perennus*, doublet of *perennis*) must allude to the whole year (by reference to the verb *perennare* or *perannare*), but may also by extension designate a period of time without end (for this meaning, see Ovid, *Fasti*, 1.721).

The "joyous festival" of Anna Perenna (cf. Ovid, *F.*, 3.523) was celebrated on 15 March in a *nemus* situated at the first milestone of Rome, near the banks of the Tiber. It was a *festum geniale* of the ancient and official type, vividly described by Ovid (*F.*, 3.525–42):

> The crowd arrives, and scattered here and there over the green grass they drink, every lad reclining beside his lass. Some camp under the open sky; a few pitch tents; some make a hut of boughs and leaves. Others set up reeds in the guise of rigid pillars and stretch out their togas on the reeds. But they grow warm with sun and wine, and they pray for as many years as they take cups, and they count the cups they drink. There you will find men who drink as many cups as the years of Nestor, and women who would live to be as old as Sibylls, by the number of cups they drink. There they also sing all the songs that they learned in the theater, beating time to the words with their hands. A man sets a bowl down on the ground and begins a few clumsy steps, while his sweetheart, all dressed up, dances around with streaming hair. They stagger home, a public spectacle: "How happy you are!" cries the crowd as they meet them. I met a procession lately, worth mentioning: a drunk old woman dragging a drunk old man.

This joyous festival, animated by general carousing and spiced with obscene words (*obscena:* Ovid, *F.*, 3.695) surely of apotropaic significance, inaugurated the new year on a date that was notable on the ancient calendar: the ides of March, the brightest day of the first month of the ancient year. It was consecutive (according to the calendar of Philocalus) or concomitant (according to Lydus, *De Mensibus*, 4.49) with another popular, if not official, ceremony: the Mamuralia, a festival that consisted of the expulsion of Mamurius Veturius. This double name (which appears in the song of the Salians: cf. Varro, *De Lingua Latina*, 6.49) is interpreted to mean the "old Mars"; that is, the "old year" (cf. A. Degrassi, *Inst. Iust.*, 13.2, pp. 422–23). Thus the articulation of the two ceremonies takes on a transparent meaning.

As for the character of Anna Perenna, ancient etiology connects her with several different legendary or historical figures. Ovid (*F.*, 3.449ff.) lists diverse attempts at identification: the goddess was assimilated to the sister of Dido, the Anna who became "the Nymph of Numicius" at Lavinium (*F.*, 3.557–656)—or to Anna of Bouillae, an old woman from an area near Rome, who fed the common people with "rustic cakes" during her retreat on the Sacred Mountain (ibid., 3.661–74), as well as other associations that the poet barely touches upon (*Luna, Themis, Io, Atlantis:* ibid., 3.657–60).

R.S./d.b.

Apollo in Rome

Apollo is the barely Latinized transcription for the Greek god *Apollōn*. He was introduced to Rome as a healer. *Apollo Medicus* was his official title in the temple dedicated to him in 433 and consecrated in 431 B.C. during a serious epidemic (Livy, 4.25.3; 40.51.6). The location of the temple, in the Flamen Fields to the southwest of the Capitol (and thus outside the pomerial zone), was already called the *Apollinare* (Livy, 3.63.7): it is impossible, however, to say whether this "Apollonian enclosure" indicated an official or a private cult.

In the prayers of their litany (*Indigitamenta*), the vestal virgins referred to Apollo as *Apollo Medice, Apollo Paean* (Macrobius, *S.*, 1.17.15). The second invocation corresponds to the invocation *iē Paiēōn*, addressed to the god of healing of the Greek cult (cf. von Blumenthal, *R.E.*, s.v. Paian, ca. 2341). He again appears in the capacity of healer, in the first place, accompanied by his mother Latona, in the first lectisternium of 399 B.C. (Livy, 5.13.4).

In 217 B.C., during the celebration of the lectisternium of

the twelve divinities, which was ordered, among other religious measures, after the disaster of Trasimenus, Apollo was honored in the company of Diana. At that date the god was no longer confined solely to the domain of medicine. In 212 B.C., at the instigation of the "diviner" Marcius, and with the approval of the *Sibylline Books* (Livy, 25.12.15), the games were celebrated for the first time in honor of the god, *ludi Apollinares,* "to attain victory" (the Latin historian specifies: *victoriae, non valetudinis ergo*).

The cult of Apollo was most widespread during the reign of Augustus. In 23 B.C., Octavian, who would in the next year take the title Augustus, had a magnificent temple to Apollo built on the Palatine, near his own palace: at that date he had the *Sibylline Books* transferred there from their previous place in the temple of Capitoline Jupiter (Suetonius, *Aug.,* 31.1)—a symbolic gesture through which the emperor, in restoring the "inspired books" to the god, officially recognized his prophetic nature.

In 17 B.C., Apollo (with Diana-Artemis) was at the center of the celebration of the Secular Games; in addition to written accounts of this festival (cf. J. B. Pighi, *De ludis saecularibus,* 2d ed., Amsterdam, 1965, pp. 107–30), we have the official hymn composed by Horace: the *Carmen saeculare.* (For the Roman Apollo in general, consult J. Gagé, *Apollon romain: Essai sur le culte d'Apollon et le développement du "ritus graecus" à Rome, des origines à Auguste,* Paris 1955.)

R.S./d.b.

The Arval Brethren

The title "Fratres Arvales" (*arva* = field) designates the priests whose domain is the fields, or rather the priests charged with assuring the mystical protection of the fields. The peculiarity of this brotherhood, which consists of twelve members, lies in its return to the archaic period in certain characteristics of its cult, although its effective functioning dates from a restoration by the emperor Augustus.

The cult of the Arvals is particularly well known to us from the *Acta fratrum Arvalium,* official records that were engraved in stone and that extend in layers from the Augustan Age (the first inscription appears to date from 20 B.C.) to the middle of the third century A.D. (there is an epigraphic text from A.D. 304 that mentions the name of the president in charge of the college). The prestige of the brotherhood is measured by the quality of its recruitment: besides the emperor, who was a kind of honorary member, it included men of the best society and of senatorial rank. It is paradoxical that these urban people should have preserved a cult dedicated to the prosperity of the fields and the harvests: in this way, the rites of the Arvals perpetuated the old cult of the Ambarvalia, which consisted in leading around the fields those animals that were to be sacrificed to Mars. Traditionally, these animals formed in groups of three, called *suovetaurilia*—boar, ram, bull—as we know from the famous prayer addressed to Mars by the peasant, which Cato recorded in chapter 14 of his treatise *De Agricultura.*

But the cult of the Arvals differs from this ancient rite not only in the character of its ceremonies but also in its orientation: the central place was no longer occupied by Mars but by a divinity invoked under the name of *dea Dia.* This goddess, whose predominance among other divinities is attested by numerous official acts, does not appear in the official hymn, the *carmen Arvale,* which the Brethren sing at the end of the principal ceremony. This is an interesting discordance which indicates that the *carmen Arvale* merits closer examination.

Although the twelve Arval Brethren incontestably owe their organization or their resurrection to an initiative of Augustus, legend carries their institution back to the "time of Romulus." According to Masurius Sabinus (quoted in Aulus Gellius, *Noctes Atticae* 7.7.8), they were originally twelve brothers born of Acca Larentia; since one among them was dead, Romulus was substituted for him in the role of an adopted son. A more convincing proof of the archaism of the institution lies in certain cultic prescriptions and allusions. The college is presided over by a *magister,* assisted by a priest, a flamen; the presidency, *magisterium,* of one year's duration, does not coincide with the civil year, but extends from one Saturnalian Festival (17 December) to another (*ex Saturnalibus primis ad Saturnalia secunda*)—a festival that the Romans celebrated after the harvest, according to Dionysius of Halicarnassus (3.32.4): this time lag could be explained by old agrarian traditions.

Other indications point in the same direction: the cult excludes the use of iron, and any introduction of this metal—for example the chisel used to engrave the report—regularly necessitated expiatory sacrifices, *ob ferrum illatum.* Similarly, in their ceremonies the Brethren used earthen pots made by a rudimentary technique—*ollae*—several of which have been found in the sacred woods of the Arvals. All of these characteristics, in conjunction with the chant of the archaic hymn, *carmen Arvale,* suggest great antiquity.

Nevertheless, this brotherhood carries the imperial stamp. Conforming to his general plan, Augustus wanted to restore a cult that could claim a venerable antiquity, for this corresponded to one of his major plans: to restore agriculture to a place of honor after the great impoverishment of the fields provoked by the civil wars. One only has to bear in mind the general ambiance that favored the production of Virgil's *Georgics* to understand the honors and privileges accorded to the Arval Brethren: these high-ranking people, who counted the emperor one of their own, benefited from official subventions (in the form of *sportulae*) and had the official documents of their liturgy engraved in stone each year.

Imperial intervention is revealed first in the organization of the cult around the principal goddess, *dea Dia,* who appears there for the first time. She was a divinity of the "clear sky" (*Dia* is a reference to the ritual prescription to announce in January the May ceremonies *sub divo culmine,* "under the celestial vault"), of the "good weather" necessary for the ripening of the harvests. In time, imperial intervention led to the introduction of divinities of recent origin. Thus, in the documents of A.D. 224, Mars is invoked in the expression *Mars pater Ultor,* in his aspect of an avenging god—a cult instituted by Augustus; similarly, the emperors deified after their death (the *divi*) are regularly mentioned after the other gods. The Arvals developed the habit of inserting official prayers, *vota publica,* in their January liturgy to safeguard the imperial house; and they manifested their loyalty fervently on other occasions, such as births of princes or the departures and returns of the emperors.

The fundamental object of the cult was clearly defined by Varro (*De Lingua Latina* 5.85): *fratres Arvales dicti, qui sacra publica faciunt propterea ut fruges ferant arva . . .* "The Arval Brethren are so named because they celebrate public sacrifices so that the fields bear their harvests." This definition always corresponds to reality, despite innovations of recent date. The ritual no longer involves, as did the older Ambarvalia, a circumambulation of the Roman territory—*ager Romanus*—by the sacrificial animals. Conforming to the etymology of the term, the Ambarvalia assured the lustration of the domain (the *lustratio agri* recorded by Cato represents a kind of minor ritual on a personal scale) by a peripheral promenade of representative animals—boar, ram, bull—who would afterwards be sacrificed. The Arvals celebrate their principal liturgy only at a specific place in Roman territory, "at the fifth milestone of the Via Campana," where the sacred woods and the sanctuary of *dea Dia* are located.

The date of the ceremonies is fixed by the president, *magister*, in January, during the first month of his term: like the festival of sowing (*Sementivae*), these are movable feasts (*feriae conceptivae*) that last for three days. The records show that since Vespasian, the dates coincide alternatively with 17, 19, and 20 May or else with 27, 29, and 30 May. (There is thus a regular interval of one day between the first and second day of the festival, conforming to Roman usage: the second day is reserved for the official ceremony, in the *lucus* of *dea Dia*, while the first begins the opening ceremonies at Rome, and the third, designated by an even number, marks its completion at Rome. A parallel is offered by the *Feralia* of 21 February, the public festival of the dead, followed on 22 February by the *Caristia*, private family gatherings.)

Let us return to the essential rites. On the first day, beginning at dawn, the Brethren offer incense and wine to *dea Dia*; then they consecrate by their touch "dry, green ears of grain" (*fruges aridas et virides contingerunt*). In the afternoon they gather for a banquet, followed by a distribution of perfumes and crowns. These ceremonies usually take place in the Roman home of the president. On the second day several sacrifices are made in the woods consecrated to *dea Dia*. First come expiatory sacrifices of young sows (*porcilias piaculares*)—to bring about the successful completion of diverse works, in particular the pruning of the woods—together with the honorary offering of a cow. Then the Brethren, clothed in the *toga praetexta*, their heads veiled and garlanded with ears of grain, proceed to the woods to carry out the solemn sacrifice of a fattened ewe (*agnam opimam*) in honor of *dea Dia*. Afterwards, two of them go to look for the ears of grain that were consecrated on the preceding evening: these ears of grain are going to be passed from hand to hand, from right to left, before being handed over to attendant slaves. Then, the Brethren enter the sanctuary to fulfill different holy obligations, occasionally mysterious. (What is, for example, the precise significance of the prayers to pots [*ollas precati sunt*] and of the throwing of these pots through the doors of the sanctuary?) Finally the temple is closed to all except the Brethren, who, little books in hand, their *toga praetexta* tucked up, then begin to entone the traditional hymn, dancing to a three-beat rhythm (*carmen descindentes tripodaverunt*). The rest of the day is devoted to the reappointment of the president and the flamen for the following year, the celebration of games, and a banquet on the return to Rome. On the third day the ceremonies are completed in Rome, in the president's house. After an offering of incense and wine, the ears of grain are presented to *dea Dia*.

In a general way, the symbolism of these ceremonies is transparent: these "dry and green" ears of grain, which are successively consecrated, passed from hand to hand, and offered to *dea Dia*, express the preoccupations of the officiants: the ear of grain of the past should respond in some way to the ear of grain of the future. To this end, the propitiatory sacrifice is offered to none but *dea Dia*.

What is the role of *dea Dia?* She could not double for Ceres, the goddess of growth, or Tellus, the goddess Earth. But she collaborates with them as "divinity of the clear sky": is it by chance that she is given prayers and sacrifices in May, the crucial season for future harvests? It is certain that she does not figure in the official hymn, the *carmen Arvale*. We have the extraordinary good fortune—because of a record from A.D. 218—of knowing the text of this hymn, which appears to date from the end of the sixth century B.C. It is the only archaic Latin text that has come to us in a form that is at all intelligible, despite difficulties in the text—or in the transmission. It runs as follows:

> E nos, Lases, iuvate, [e]nos, Lases, iuvate e nos lases iuvate. Neve lu[e], rue, Marma, sins incurrere in pleores, neve lue, rue Marmar, [si]ns incurrere in pleoris, neve lue, rue, Marmar, sers incurrere in pleoris.
>
> Satur fu, [f]ere Mars; limen [sal]i, sta berber.
> Satur fu, fere Mars; limen sali, sta berber.
> Satur fu, fere Mars; limen sa[l]i, s[t]a berber
>
> [Sem]unis alternei advocapit conctos, Semunis alternei advocapit conctos, Simunis altern[ei] advocapit [conct]os.
>
> E nos, Marmor, iuvato, e nos, Marmor, iuvato, e nos, Ma[r]mor, iuvato
>
> Triumpe, triumpe, triumpe, trium[pe, tr]iumpe.

An approximate translation would be:

> Help us, O Lares, help us, O Lares, help us O Lares! Mars, O Mars, don't let Dissolution, Destruction pounce upon the people (?). Mars, O Mars, don't let Dissolution, Destruction pounce upon the people (?). Mars, O Mars, don't let Dissolution, Destruction pounce upon the people (?).
> Be surfeited, savage Mars; leap to the frontier, take your position;
> Be surfeited, savage Mars; leap to the frontier, take your position;
> Be surfeited, savage Mars; leap to the frontier, take your position.
>
> You will invoke the Semones one by one, all together, you will invoke the Semones, one by one, all together, you will invoke the Semones, one by one, all together.
>
> Help us Mars, O Mars, help us, Mars, O Mars, help us, Mars, O Mars.
>
> Victory, victory, victory, victory, victory!

It would not be possible to point out here all the problems which merit discussion (see the bibliography). But it is striking that the hymn, although it invokes the *Lares*, protective gods of the soil, and the *Semones*, gods of the seed (*semina*), is addressed chiefly to Mars in his role of defender: the god is begged to take up a position at the frontier of the Roman domain, to preserve it from visible and invisible enemies. Thus a remarkable contrast is revealed between the archaic period and the imperial age. Mars the Protector hardly appears any longer in the imperial liturgy of the Arvals, except in an episodic fashion (Mars the Avenger) and in the exceptional sacrifices of the *suovetaurilia* offered to conjure up marvels: he has ceded his place of honor to *dea Dia,* doubtless because minds were more preoccupied with prosperity than with defense in a time in which there was apparently no longer need to fear an invasion of the Roman *arva.*

R.S./d.f.

BIBLIOGRAPHY

G. HENZEN, *Acta fratrum Arualium* (Berlin 1874). E. PASOLI, *Acta fratrum Arualium* (Bologna 1950). "Aruales fratres," in G. WISSOWA, *Real-Encyclopädie* (1895), cols. 1463–87; "Zum Ritual der Arvalbrüder," *Hermes* 52 (1917): 321–47. E. NORDEN, *Aus altrömischen Priesterbüchern* (1939): 109–280, on the *carmen Aruale.* R. SCHILLING, *Dea Dia dans la liturgie des Frères Arvales: Hommages à Marcel Renard* (1969), 2:91–96; reprinted in *R.C.D.R.*

AUGURS AND AUGURY

Augur is a masculine derivative of an old neuter root **augus,* which also provided the noun *augurium* and the adjective *augustus.* The masculine term *augur, -ris* is obviously connected with the neuter noun *augurium.* The augur is the priest who is permitted to perform *auguria.* The two words cannot be explained unless we go back to the old neuter root **augus* (of the type of *genus* or **venus*), which seems to have referred to what was "full of mystic force" (Georges Dumézil). If the *augurium* represents the sign of supernatural manifestation, the augur is the priest who confirmed the presence or absence of this mystic force, at least during the historic era (it is not possible to say whether his function originally had more to do with operation than with confirmation). As for the adjective *augustus,* it could be applied to a thing or person that is imbued with mystic plenitude (the adjective was at first used only for objects: Octavian, upon becoming emperor, was the first person to bear the surname Augustus, following a vote of the Roman Senate in 27 B.C.).

Thus it can be demonstrated that the French noun *augure* has an equivocal meaning, in that it can refer to either the priest or the sign. Another kind of ambiguity stems from the related word *auspicium,* which is not irrelevant to the art of the *augur,* even though its semantic origins differ. *Auspicium* refers to the observation (*specere*) of birds (*aves*), which allowed the augur to know the will of the gods. Everyone knows that Rome was founded after an *auspicium:* Romulus, after having a vision of twelve vultures, was chosen by the gods as king and founder of the city. Thus, he was the first augur in Roman tradition.

The institution of the College of Augurs was, however, attributed to his successor, King Numa (Livy, 4.4.2). The number of its members was successively three, six, nine (in 300, during the advent of the plebians), fifteen (under Sulla), and finally sixteen (after Julius Caesar's reform). Their official definition has a clear meaning: *Interpretes Jovis Optimi Maximi, publici augures* (Cicero, *Laws,* 2.20), or: "The augurs of the state are the interpreters of all-powerful Jupiter."

Their work consisted essentially only in interpreting the signs that were sent by Jupiter; the right to conduct the auspices was reserved for the magistrate. This fundamental distinction is particularly clear in a text of Cicero, who was himself an augur: "We [augurs] only have the right to announce the auspices (*nuntiationem*), while the consuls and other magistrates have in addition the right to conduct them (*spectionem*)" (*Second Phillipic,* 81). Thus, during the entire period of the Republic, the public auspices (*auspicia populi Romani*) were entirely monopolized by the magistrates: the ritual formula *auspicium imperiumque* shows how much their power of command was based on the so-called guarantee of the auspices.

What actual role has fallen to the augurs since that time? "To carry out the office of augury" can be said in different ways: *augurium agere* (Varro, *Ling.* 6.42), *augurare,* and *inaugurare.* But we have only incomplete information on the *disciplina augurum,* first because the science of augury was supposed to be kept secret, known only to its initiates, and also because most of the ancient works on this subject have been lost. The following activities can be distinguished, however. First, the augurs were charged with performing certain archaic rituals, the goal of which, at least, can be determined. Thus the *auguria vernisera* (Festus, p. 520 L.) and the *augurium canarium* (Pliny, *Natural History,* 18.14) both concerned the outcome of the harvest. Another ceremony, called the *augurium salutis* (Dio Cassius, 37.24.1), was celebrated annually if the Roman army was not on campaign: should this be connected with another rite mentioned by Varro (*Ling.,* 5.47) in which the augurs, starting from the Capitoline citadel, go down the Via Sacra and perform their office?

There is more complete information about the inauguration of people and places. Livy (1.18.6–10) has supplied us with an account of the inauguration of King Numa, whom the Fathers had just proclaimed king. "Then he was led by the augur into the citadel and sat on a stone, facing the south. The augur, with his head veiled, took a place on his left, holding in his right hand a bent stick without knots, called a *lituus.* Then after he had looked over both city and fields, he prayed to the gods and pointed out the directions from east to west, declaring the region on the right to be the south, the region on the left to be the north; in front of him, as far as he could see, he mentally marked a spot. Then he passed the *lituus* to his left hand and placed his right hand on Numa's head, saying the following prayer:

> O revered Jupiter (*Juppiter pater*), if it is mystically right (*si est fas*) that Numa Pompilius, whose head I touch, be king of Rome, send us clear and certain signs (*uti tu signa nobis certa adclarassis*) within the boundaries that I have marked.

Then he stated distinctly (*peregit verbis*) the auspices (*auspicia*) that he wanted to be sent. When they had been sent, Numa was proclaimed king and he descended from the place of augury (*templum*)."

In this account, the augur appears in ritual dress (his head is veiled and he holds the bent *lituus*). Facing east, he defines the *templum,* which is a quadrangular space from whose interior he intends to look out. (This orientation of the augur toward the east is not obligatory, as we learn in Varro, *Ling.,* 7.7; here the augur turns toward the south and the *four* parts of the *templum* are referred to as follows: "the region to the left [*sinistra*] is the east; the region to the right [*dextra*] is the

Altar from the second century A.D. from the Sandals Quarter (*vicus sandaliarus*) in Rome. Decorated with a victory on one face and two lares on the other. Shown here is the back face, which depicts a youthful augur (perhaps the young Lucius Caesar) holding a *lituus*, flanked by Augustus and Livia (the only known commemoration of a dynastic event). Photo Alinari-Giraudon.

west; the region in front [*antica*] is the south; the region behind [*postica*] is the north.") Also note the precautions and prudence used in this consultation with Jupiter. Not only does the augur precisely define the field of observation, but he lists restrictively the auspices that he wants to get (see Pliny, *Natural History*, 28.17)—this was a known procedure, called the *legum dictio* (the statement of conditions).

The ancients distinguished between signs that were solicited under precise conditions within the *templum* (*auspicia impetrativa* or *impetrita*) and signs that occurred on their own (*auspicia oblativa*). With respect to the origins of these *signa* or *auspicia*, they were divided into five categories (see Festus, p. 316 L.): celestial signs, *ex caelo* (particularly lightning and thunder); signs provided by birds, *ex avibus* (in certain birds, *alites*, the flight was observed, in others, *oscines*, the song); signs given by the hopping of sacred chickens, *ex tripudiis* (this form of consultation degenerated very early because of abusive practices); signs from the behavior of animals, *ex quadrupedibus;* and finally, threatening portents, *ex diris*.

Another function of the augurs was to inaugurate places. During the historical era, the Capitoline citadel where Livy placed the inauguration of Numa bore the name of *auguraculum*—this place of augury was itself a *templum*. The exact definition of this word is given in Varro (*Ling.*, 7.8): "On earth a place is called a *templum* when it is defined by a precise formulation for the duties of augury or the taking of auspices (*augurii aut auspicii causa*)"—the first activity concerns augurs and the second, magistrates. Through augury the place would become "exorcized and available"—*locus liberatus et effatus*.

These *templa* included not only most divine sanctuaries (the round *aedes* of Vesta was not inaugurated, however), but also secular structures, such as the Curia and the Comitium. In a larger sense, the city of Rome itself formed an immense *templum* which was reserved for urban auspices (*auspicia urbana*). The augurs ranked the territories in five categories (according to Varro, *Ling.*, 5.33): the territory of Rome, the territory of Gabii, foreign territory, hostile territory, unknown territory. These boundaries had great importance in conducting auspices. As for Rome itself, the urban area was considered to be separated from the rest of the territory (*ager Romanus*) by a boundary called the *pomerium*. This explains why each addition to the city had to be sanctioned by the inauguration of a new *pomerium*.

The College of Augurs came right after the Pontifical College. Despite its noble titles, its decadence in the last century of the Republic was very advanced: this was due both to the increasing ignorance of the augurs in practice and to the abuse caused by political interventions. Note, for example, this reproach by Cicero (*Second Phillipic*, 81) directed at the augur Antony: "See his insolence. Many months before, he (Antony) declared in the Senate that he would *use the auspices* to block the election of Dolabella . . ." The college did gain a certain respite through the reforms of Augustus: the last augurs cited date from the end of the fourth century A.D.

R.S./d.b.

BIBLIOGRAPHY

A. BOUCHÉ-LECLERCQ, *Histoire de la divination dans l'antiquité*, 4 (Paris 1882). G. WISSOWA, *Religion und Kultus der Römer* (2d ed., Munich 1912), 523–34. P. CATALANO, *Contributi allo studio del diritto augurale*, 1 (Turin 1960). A. MAGDELAIN, *Auspicia ad patres redeunt* (Brussels 1964), 427–73. G. DUMÉZIL, *Idées romaines* (Paris 1969), 80–102; *La religion romaine archaïque* (2d ed., Paris 1974), 98–103, 584–89; = *Archaic Roman Religion* (Chicago 1970).

The Religious Policies of Augustus

To President Léopold Sédar Senghor

A subject as vast as the religious policies of Augustus might lend itself to a bibliographic review of the various judgments made by historians of antiquity; such a review would be in danger of swelling to indefinite proportions. Such is not the intention of this discussion. The most I will say about this subject is that the pendulum of opinion appears to be swinging, in that the position of Ronald Syme (*The Roman Revolution*, Oxford 1939; 2d ed., 1952), which was very critical of Augustus, has recently been contested by Hans Erich Stier (*Augustusfriede und römische Klassik*, A.N.R.-W., 2, 2, pp. 49ff. [1975]).[1]

Beyond such bibliographic methods, I will base my discussion essentially on ancient sources, in order to isolate the major lines of the religious work of Augustus and thus to facilitate a critical and objective consideration of the issue. What are the principal documents at our disposal? Along with the precious *Index rerum a se gestarum*, attributed to Suetonius[2]—or the *Res gestae divi Augusti*[3]—we also have the information furnished by historians[4] and the numerous allusions made by the poets of the Augustan era, particularly Virgil, Horace, and Propertius.

We will first try to summarize the various stages in the career of this heir of Julius Caesar, then to study his religious work in general, and finally to examine his essential character.

In 44 B.C., when Octavian, the adopted son of Caesar—*Divi filius*—appears on the political scene, he shows no signs of his destiny as the future Augustus. The strong contender appears to be Antony: in this sense, Shakespeare was not mistaken, in his play *Julius Caesar*, in giving the principal role to Mark Antony; his "historical accuracy" agrees with the events.

It is, however, Octavian's political ascension that will allow the religious initiative to progress. Three different periods can be distinguished:

(*a*) From 44 to 31 B.C., Octavian behaves as Caesar's loyal heir. It is in this role, in 44 B.C., that he spends his own money to celebrate the festivals in honor of the dedication of the temple of Venus Genetrix, to make up for the insolvency of the magistrates normally responsible for this duty.[5] Then, after the world is divided between the three triumvirs, he soon finds himself facing Antony alone: Lepidus, who had received Africa, was eliminated in 36 (after the victory over Sextus Pompey at Naulocus). Octavian, who rules the West, keeps his distance from Antony, who has the East. As Antony becomes more and more Orientalized, to the point of marrying Cleopatra (after repudiating Octavia, the sister of his rival), Octavian presents himself as the champion of the West. We know the result of the conflict which ended in 31 B.C., during the battle of Actium, which would be placed by Octavian's eulogists under the sign of Venus and Caesar.[6]

(*b*) From 31 to 12 B.C., Octavian's religious policies become more personal. It is then that the head of the Roman state accords an official place to Apollo, to whom he attributes most of the credit for the victory of Actium: he builds a sanctuary of Apollo on the Palatine Hill (in 28 B.C.). In 27 B.C., he acquires unprecedented religious prestige when he is given the name *Augustus* by Senate decision.[7] And in 17 B.C., he celebrates, as *magister das decemviri sacris faciundis*, the secular games, which are essentially under the auspices of Apollo and Diana.

(*c*) In 12 B.C., Augustus finally becomes *Pontifex maximus*, at the death of Lepidus, whom he did not wish to strip of this dignity during his lifetime—out of respect not for the man but for the supreme priesthood. At this date, Augustus has all the titles that he lists in the *Res Gestae*:[8] *Pontifex maximus, augur, quindecimvirum sacris faciundis, septemvirum epulonum, frater Arvalis, sodalis Titius, fetialis fui.*

I. The Religious Work

Let us now look at the work he did. At first this consisted of basic reconstruction, following all the devastation of the civil and foreign wars. First, material reconstruction: Augustus himself declares[9] that he reconstructed eighty-two religious buildings that had been damaged or destroyed. Restoration of cultic practices followed, such as the *augurium salutis* and the ceremony of the Lupercalia.[10] Various institutions were restored to honor. He increased the prestige of the vestal virgins, and noting that a vacancy caused by the death of one of the members was not being filled and that the citizens were slow to suggest their daughters as replacements, he swore that "if one of his granddaughters were old enough, he would have proposed her."[11] He ended the scandalous vacancy—lasting seventy-five years—of the *flamonium Dialis*, a position last held in 87 B.C. by L. Cornelius Merula, who took refuge in the sanctuary of Jupiter to escape his enemies and left his priestly insignia there before committing suicide.[12]

In the same spirit, Augustus took care to reestablish the normal functioning of the great colleges of pontiffs, augurs, the *quindecimviri sacris faciundis*, the *septemviri epulones*, and the sodalities. While restoring them, he was careful to update the institutions in keeping with changed circumstances.

A recent study[13] has revealed the intentions of Augustus in restoring the college of the Arval Brethren. He made this reform at a time when people wanted to "give honor to the plow," as Virgil indicates:[14] *O fortunatos nimium, sua si bona norint, agricolas.*[15] The Arval Brethren were charged, both by name (*arva*) and by office, with insuring the mystical protection of the fields. But they were also responsible for praying to the gods for the prosperity and salvation of Caesar and the Roman Empire, particularly at the beginning of each year, in the month of January. Augustus succeeded in making this college as representative as possible of Roman society, through a wise measure of social recruitment: patricians from old families, noble Republicans, old partisans of Pompey and Antony, and loyal subjects of Augustus were "fraternally" put in service to the same cause, *ad majorem gloriam populi Romani*. According to Augustus's plan, the title of *Brother* would emphasize the relationship that would, like the ties of a family, hereafter unite this new nobility to the person of the *princeps*.[16]

This example shows how wisely Augustus reconciled the spirit of reform with a respect for tradition. Roman religion always had this double allegiance: although it was anchored in traditions that could be traced back to Indo-European origins, the logic of polytheism allowed it to incorporate new cults as well: take, for example, the introduction of Aphrodite of Mount Eryx on the Capitoline in 215 through the assimilation of this goddess with the Roman Venus, or the establishment of Cybele on the Palatine Hill in 204 through her connection with the Trojan legend. It was all a matter of degree, especially since more than one conqueror—from Sulla to Antony—had more or less succumbed to Oriental seductions. At a time when Rome, which had just succeeded in extending the boundaries of its empire, might have yielded to the easy terms of the *interpretatio Romana*, Augustus showed a remarkable concern for balance between traditional and innovative tendencies. The same impression can be drawn from an examination of most of his initiatives.

For this reason, and to appeal to a people tired of wars, he reinstated the ancient rite that closed the sanctuary of Janus in times of peace. With pride he proclaimed in his will:[17] "The temple of Janus Quirinus, which according to the will of our ancestors is to be closed when victorious peace reigns over all of the Roman Empire, both on land and at sea, in the memory of man has been closed only twice before my birth: under my principate, the Senate has closed it three times."

When in 12 B.C. Augustus assumed the office of Pontifex Maximus, he resolved the resulting conflict of interests elegantly: since as head of state he could not live in the Regia, the official residence of the supreme pontiff, he had a chapel consecrated to Vesta built in his palace on the Palatine: henceforth the goddess, represented by the sacred flame that was never extinguished, a symbolic token of the eternity of Rome, appeared even closer to the prince and more closely involved in the fate of the Empire.

Augustus was also cleverly able to combine certain Hellenic features with Roman traditions. In 28 B.C. he had a temple to Apollo erected on the Palatine Hill; upon becoming supreme pontiff in 12 B.C., he transferred there the *Sibylline Books,* which had previously been in the care of Jupiter in the cellars of the temple of Capitoline Jupiter; Augustus had the prophetic books placed under the statue of Apollo, after subjecting them to a rigorous selection process.[18] Thus he maintained the old Roman tradition that allowed him, by order of the Senate, to consult the *Sibylline Books;* at the same time he made an innovation by reestablishing the logical connection between the inspired books and their source of inspiration.

The same preoccupation with balance appears in the organization of the secular games in 17 B.C.: the games were under the exclusive authority of the master of the *quindecimviri s.f.* (Augustus was not yet supreme pontiff at that date). In this way Augustus restored an ancient rite that until then had been addressed to *Dis Pater* or Pluto and that had a funereal quality. Augustus gave it a double meaning. First, he retained the nocturnal aspect (the invocation of the Parcae, divinities that presided over fate; of the Eileithyiae, who presided over births; and of Tellus, who presided over prosperity); then he added a diurnal aspect: the invocation of the gods who were the protectors of Rome, Jupiter and Juno, in particular, but especially Apollo and Diana, who were called upon to provide Rome with "a new century of still greater happiness."[19]

Perhaps the best example of this renovation of ancient cults is the new light which Augustus wanted to shed on the association between Mars and Venus. Mars had been worshiped originally as the "fiery god" (*fere Mars* is one of the invocations of the *carmen Arvale*) and as the father of the founder of the *Urbs,* Romulus. Venus had been honored for centuries, in connection with the Trojan legend, as the mother of the nation of the Romans descended from Aeneas. Certainly the two divinities had already been associated during the lectisternium of 217 B.C., *graeco ritu,* based on the model of Ares and Aphrodite. Instead of borrowing from the Hellenic pattern, Augustus proposed a new formula. Mars, the father of the founder of the City, became its dynastic protector as well, *Mars Ultor,* the god who would be the avenger of the assassination of Caesar and the honor of Rome. As for Venus, she stopped begging for peace at any price, as in the preamble to Lucretius's poem, and was mobilized into the service of the Romans descended from Aeneas. Thus the two gods appeared in the prophetic vision that Virgil attributed to Vulcan, when he forged and embossed the shield of Aeneas at the request of Venus: both gods were engaged in the battle of Actium at the sides of Octavian "against the monstrous gods of the Nile and the barking Anubis."[20]

This explains why Mars and Venus often appeared together in official art. When M. Vipsanius Agrippa built the Pantheon, dedicated to all the gods and goddesses (in 25 B.C.), their statues appeared side by side.[21] Later, in 2 B.C., when the great temple of Mars Ultor was dedicated in the forum of Augustus, Venus was shown at the side of Mars on the facade: *stat Venus Ultori juncta.*[22]

After this, it is not surprising that Augustus had the statue of Venus in the Pantheon decorated with two huge pearls that had belonged to the queen of Egypt:[23] it was a way of consecrating the "best spoils" taken from the "enemy" to the Roman Venus. What a contrast, however, to the action of Julius Caesar, who had placed a "beautiful statue of Cleopatra" (Appian) in the temple of *Venus Genetrix,* an act which represented an incontestable homage to the queen of Egypt.[24]

Augustus and a Vicomagister. Altar from the Belvedere. Rome, Vatican Museum. Museum photo.

II. The Personality of Augustus and the Spirit of Reform

Perhaps the moment has come to devote some attention to the personality of the emperor himself. Many anecdotes about his behavior are reported by his biographers: they reveal, besides goodwill and humor, a certain simplicity and a sense of moderation. Not only did Augustus disdain all flattery, he resisted the seductions of a propaganda meant to provide him with a halo of legend. At least three examples are conclusive.

One legend reported that his mother Atia conceived the future emperor from Apollo when he had metamorphosed into a serpent.[25] Octavian put so little stake in his reputation as *Apollinis filius* that, unlike Julius Caesar, who claimed at an early age to be *Veneris nepos,* he did not hesitate to compromise it during the masquerade of the *cena dōdekatheos* ("the dinner of the twelve gods"): during this sacrilegious feast, he disguised himself as Apollo, "regaling his friends, also dressed as gods and goddesses, with new adulteries of the gods."[26] Of course this youthful episode was later erased by his devotion to Apollo at Actium: his devotion then retained nothing of the old legend.

Another episode is also significant. On the day of the birth of the future Augustus (in 63 B.C.) the Pythagorean P. Nigidius Figulus hurried to proclaim: *dominum terrarum orbi natum* ("a master of the universe is born").[27] Far from exploiting this theme "of public notoriety," Augustus later forbade by special edict the use of the word *dominus* to refer to him—following a public demonstration that reflected this theme: when an actor cried, during a play: *O dominum aequum et bonum!* the public rose to its feet in an ovation to the emperor.[28]

The last example is cited by Suetonius:[29] "During his first consulate, Augustus was taking the auguries, when twelve vultures appeared to him, as had once happened to Romulus." Again, he refused to take advantage of the omen. In 27 B.C., during the famous session of the Senate when some people wished to honor him with the title of *Romulus* or *novus conditor,* he refused them in favor of the name Augustus.[30]

These facts help us to understand the spirit that inspired the most personal initiatives of Augustus. As a Roman who would not allow his image to be inflated, despite the obvious opportunities to do so, he must have often remembered the phrase that the slave repeated to his conqueror during the triumphal procession: "*memento te hominem esse.*" From this came a sort of wisdom of the soil, doubled by an instinctive mistrust of foreign influences, particularly Oriental influences. Of course he respected cults that had been sanctified by time: he was initiated into the mysteries of the Athenian Demeter in Athens, for example.[31] On the other hand, he refused Isis access to Rome (in 28 B.C.), even though some years earlier (in 43 B.C.) the triumvirs had authorized the erection of a temple consecrated to Isis and Serapis in Rome. Similarly, when traveling across Egypt he refused to make the slightest "detour to go to see the ox Apis."[32]

Regarding the Jews, the following facts easily demonstrate his attitude to them. He congratulated his grandson Gaius for having crossed Judea without offering a sacrifice in Jerusalem.[33] And when he learned that among the children under two years old who were massacred in Syria on the order of Herod, King of the Jews, was Herod's own son, he cried: "I would rather be Herod's pig than his son" (*mallem Herodis porcus esse quam filius*).[34]

His caution toward accepting honors offered him by foreigners is also significant. His reaction to the extraordinary veneration shown by the sailors of Alexandria whom he happened to meet on the coast of Puteoli is revealing: Augustus was *admodum exhilaratus*—"charmed and amused"—according to his biographer,[35] and he had pieces of gold distributed to his companions so that they could buy Alexandrian wares.

Of course the cities of Asia Minor conferred divine honors upon him, in accordance with Hellenistic tradition: he was called *sōtēr* in a decree of the confederation of Greek cities of Asia Minor (in 9 B.C.), as well as in an inscription from Halicarnassus (in 2 B.C.). Augustus, however, "accepted no temple in the provinces that did not associate the name of Rome with his own, and obstinately refused this honor in Rome itself."[36] Thus the altar of Rome and Augustus was erected in Lyon in 12 B.C., and an altar of Rome and Augustus was built in Cologne (*civitas Ubiorum*), in the first century A.D.

This sense of moderation was linked with an deep understanding of the Roman spirit. With a sure instinct, Augustus gave new life to the cult of deified abstractions like *Fides* or *Ceres*, which were characteristic of ancient Roman religion. *Fortuna Augusta, Clementia Augusta, Justitia Augusta, Pietas Augusta, Salus Augusta* all reappeared, now marked with an epithet showing their imperial connection.

Pax Augusta stands out in this list of divinities. The *ara Pacis Augustae* still exists today beside the Tiber, near the Mausoleum of Augustus which was once crowned with a statue of the emperor. Its majestic simplicity is striking, particularly in contrast with the tortuous art on the altar of Pergamum.[37] The Augustan altar offers a faithful image of the art and religion of the Augustan Age. Here it shows the processions of the Vestals, of the victims accompanied by the sacrificial priests; there it shows the cortege of the household of Augustus, the priests, the magistrates, the prince himself, *capite velato,* surrounded by three major flamens; then follow the senators and some of the Roman people.

Elsewhere, images of the rising Rome appear: the Lupercal cave, and Aeneas sacrificing to the Penates, the household gods. Still elsewhere are the goddess Roma, and Tellus, who holds two children in her arms and is accompanied by two Horae. Everything celebrated the majesty of Rome, as interpreted by Romanized Greek art: all of Roman society was present, from the founder Aeneas to the representative of the Julian dynasty, with Augustus attracting all the attention as the auspicious guarantor of prosperity. It was to Peace, the Augustan Peace won after so many civil and foreign wars, that the Romans owed their happiness. And it was to Augustus that they expressed their gratitude, as did the poet who at almost the same time addressed the prince in these terms: *Lucem redde tuae, dux bone, patriae.*[38]

III. The Beginnings of the Imperial Cult

Augustus knew how to direct popular fervor progressively into an official form without upsetting Roman customs. He had undoubtedly reflected on the precedent of Julius Caesar who, when he was still very young, at the funeral oration of his aunt Julia, had claimed "a royal lineage on his mother's side; a divine lineage on his father's side."[39] The career savagely broken on the ides of March in 44 B.C., of the *Venere prognatus,* gave food for thought.

With a sure instinct, Augustus was inspired by an old Italic custom that honored the Genius of the father of the family in every household. The one whom Horace had just hailed as the *dux bonus,* and who several years later (in 2 B.C.) was to receive the official title of *Pater Patriae,* made it possible for the people to venerate their Genius surrounded by *Lares compitales.* A coincidence worthy of note: the poet's dream

Sacrifice offered by Aeneas. Rome, Altar of Peace (*ara Pacis*). Photo Anderson-Giraudon.

had preceded the institution of the cult, which dates from 12 B.C. Indeed, in an ode (written between 16 and 13 B.C.),[40] Horace had evoked the devotion of the Roman citizen in the following terms: "By offering you in profusion their prayers and their libations of wine so pure, everyone venerates your divine spirit at the same time as the Lares." A reform of 7 B.C. would create 265 *collegia compitalicia* who would be responsible for maintaining this cult. From then on, the Roman populace could see at all cross-roads the two Lares surrounding the figurine of the *Genius Augusti* and exposed to its fervor. It is thus, through a slow process, that the concept of deifying the imperial personage became more familiar.

Because the stroke of genius consisted in instilling this concept into a way of life, rather than imposing it in the name of a right. By virtue of his Julian lineage, the *Divi filius* could have demanded deification: he would not want to fully accept it . . . until the hour of apotheosis. Augustus had understood that if a divine law could constitute a powerful bond of dynastic allegiance, it was still necessary that the law be recognized by the majority of the people.

We also see a politico-theological mystique being established, according to which the reigning prince was Jupiter's representative on Earth. In this capacity he was expected to see that justice reigned—different behavior from that of an *autokratōr* or an omnipotent *dominus*. For if there is a conviction anchored in the Roman mentality, it is that all power ultimately depends on the gods: *Dis te minorem quod geris imperas* ("It is because you submit to the gods that you rule"), Horace proclaimed in his address to the Roman.[41]

The prince who concentrated in his person the true power and the auspices, so as to leave to the generals only the technical command (*ductus*) of war, appeared to all to be the appointed intermediary between the gods and the Roman people. It is of this hierarchy that Horace is thinking in his prayer to Jupiter:[42] "Father and protector of the human race, son of Saturn, the fates have entrusted great Caesar to your care: may you reign with Caesar as your second in command!" And further on he recommends Augustus to Jupiter in more detail:[43] "He will submit to you and will govern the vast world with justice."

This is how the essential traits of the religious work of Augustus appear to us. It is characterized by a strong effort to fuse Hellenism and Romanism more firmly together: it is true that the former was often used in the service of the latter. The religious work is also characterized—this time in contrast to the initiatives of Julius Caesar—by a more noticeable reserve toward Oriental influences: Egyptian gods in particular are ostracized, which can be explained by the aftermath of the victory of Actium.

This policy reveals Augustus to be above all a profound realist. Although open to philosophy,[44] the emperor was as superstitious as any good Roman.[45] He was certainly not a mystic. But he understood the Roman mentality so well that he succeeded where Julius Caesar had failed: he knew how to make the minds of his time accept an imperial mystique. By encouraging the upsurge of Augustan deities, that is, the launching of deified ancient abstractions, he created a new religious dynamism.

Above all, he founded this theology on an ethic: placed under the direct authority of Jupiter, the emperor was subject to the rule of equity and was destined for apotheosis, but only insofar as he respected the duties of his office (the bad emperor, on the other hand, would be struck down by the *damnatio memoriae*).

It is certainly difficult to judge this work without running the risk of falling into anachronism. In his reflections, [46] Jean

Senatorial procession. The senators are preceded by two lictors wearing togas and crowned with laurel wreaths. The figure with his head covered and carrying a small box serves to emphasize the religious element. Rome, Altar of Peace. Photo Anderson-Giraudon.

Imperial procession. Augustus as high priest (the central figure, with his head covered) is preceded by lictors and flamines, each wearing the priestly cap (*galerus*) with apex. Augustus is followed by members of the imperial family—perhaps the young Caius Caesar, Livia (wearing a *stola*), and Agrippa (crowned with a laurel wreath). Rome, Altar of Peace. Photo Alinari-Giraudon.

Bayet reproaches Augustus for having disregarded the resources of philosophy, the appeal of his time to aspirations of greater universalism. But after so much trouble and confusion, could Augustus have done any better? It seems to me that such work should be judged not from an "intellectual" point of view but by taking into account the weight of history and the social organization of the time.

Certainly the imperial religion comprised rites, such as the offering of incense and libations of wine,[47] which were to create a great obstacle for Christians. But could Augustus have anticipated the emergence of an exclusive monotheism?

In any event, at the beginning of the fifth century A.D., Orosius insisted on testifying for Augustus and proposed two arguments in his defense:[48] (1) By a providential arrangement, the emperor had established a durable and true peace which served the coming of Christ; (2) although he was at the summit of power, Augustus had refused the title of *dominus hominum* just at the time when the true *dominus* of mankind was to be born. It should be stressed that the refusal to be an absolute *dominus* was contrary to the entire Hellenistic and Oriental tradition.

The judgment of the Christian Orosius deserves to be taken into account by modern historians.

R.S./d.b.

NOTES

1. For a partial bibliography for recent years, see also B. Haller, *Augustus und seine Politik, Ausgewählte Bibliographie, A.N.R.W.*, 2:55–74 (= *Aufstieg und Niedergang der römischen Welt*).

2. Suetonius, *Divus Augustus*, 101, 5. The will was entrusted to the protection of the vestals in A.D. 13, one year before the death of Augustus.

3. J. Gagé, ed., *Res Gestae divi Augusti* (Paris 1935), 9.

4. In particular, Nicolas of Damascus, who is probably biased (see Jacoby, *Fr. Hist. Graec.*, n. 90); Tacitus, *Annales*, passim; Pliny, *Naturalis Historia*, 7, 147–50 (very critical of Augustus); Suetonius, *Divus Augustus;* Appian; Dio Cassius.

5. See Dio Cassius, 45, 6, 4, and Suetonius, *Aug.*, 10, 2. See my book *La religion romaine de Vénus* (Paris 1954), 313 and 325; = *R.R.V*.

6. See Virgil, *Aeneid*, 8, 679–81, in particular: *patriumque aperitur vertice sidus* ("the paternal star revealed itself above the head" [of Augustus] [at the zenith of heaven]). See Propertius, 4, 6, 59: *At pater Idalio miratur Caesar ab astro: sum deus: est nostri sanguinis ista fides* ("and his father Caesar contemplated the scene of the height of the Idalian star [i.e., Venus]: I am God; behold the proof of my [divine] lineage").

7. On *Augustus*, see my article "L'originalité du vocabulaire religieux latin," *Rev. belge de phil. et d'hist.* 49 (1971): 48–49; reprinted in *R.C.D.R.*

8. *Res Gestae*, ed. J. Gagé, § 7.

9. Ibid., § 20, 4.

10. Suetonius, *Aug.*, 31, 4–5.

11. Ibid.

12. See Velleius Paterculus, 2, 22, 2.

13. J. Scheid, *Les Frères Arvales: Recrutement et origine sociale sous les empereurs julio-claudiens* (Paris 1975).

14. See Virgil, *Georgics*, 2, 458–59.

15. Ibid., 1, 506.

16. M. J. Scheid has cleverly remarked that the Greek translation of *Frater Arualis* that figures in the *Testament* of Augustus is revealing: the Latin expression (*Res Gestae*, 7, 3) is translated by *adelphos aroualis* (which affirms fraternity by blood, while the subsequent tradition chose the words *phratēr aroualis*), which in Greek merely designates belonging to a single community (the phratry).

17. *Res Gestae*, 13.

18. See Suetonius, *Aug.*, 31, 1.

19. See Horace, *Carmen Saeculare*, 66–68.

20. See Virgil, *Ae.*, 8, 698–702.

21. See Dio Cassius, 53, 27, 2.

22. Ovid, *Tristia*, 2, 296.

23. Pliny, *N.H.*, 9. 121.

24. On this subject see my book *R.R.V.*, 328, n. 1. See Appian, *Bella Civilia*, 2, 102.

25. See Suetonius, *Aug.*, 94, 4.

26. Ibid., 70, 1. This dinner is dated 39–38 or 38–37 B.C. See J. Gagé, *Apollon romain*, 487.

27. See Suetonius, *Aug.*, 94, 6.

28. Ibid., 53, 1.

29. Ibid., 95, 2.

30. Ibid. Of course Octavius knew that the names of Romulus and Remus had been disparaged in the polemic of the recent civil wars (see Horace, *Epodi*, 7, which deplores the fact that a kind of "original sin" had weighed upon the destiny of Rome since the fratricide of Remus by Romulus).

31. See Suetonius, *Aug.*, 93, 1.

32. Ibid., 93, 2.

33. Ibid.

34. Macrobius, *Saturnalia*, 2, 4, 11.

35. Suetonius, *Aug.*, 98, 2.

36. Ibid., 52, 1.

37. This is the reflection of H. E. Stier (*A.N.R.W.*, 2, 2:49). The Pergamum altar dates from the second century B.C. On the *ara Pacis*, see the articles of Pietrangeli and Bianchi-Bandinelli, *Enciclopedia dell'arte antica*, 523–28, *ara Pacis Augustae*. The altar was built in 13 B.C. and dedicated in 9 B.C.

38. Horace, *Carmina*, 4, 5, 5 (the date of the ode is between 16 and 13 B.C.

39. See Suetonius, *Div. Iul.*, 6, 2.

40. Horace, *C.*, 4, 5, 33–34: *Te multa prece, te prosequitur mero / defuso pateris et Laribus tuum / miscet numen . . .*

41. Horace, *C.*, 3, 6, 5.

42. Horace, *C.*, 1, 12, 49–52: *Gentis humanae pater atque custos, / orte Saturno, tibi cura magni / Caesaris fatis data;* tu *secundo / Caesare* regnes!

43. Ibid., 1, 12, 57: *Te minor latum reget aequus orbem.*

44. See Suetonius, *Aug.*, 89, 2. Augustus had a wide and varied culture thanks to the philosopher Areus and his sons Dionysius and Nicanor.

45. Ibid., 90–92.

46. J. Bayet, *Histoire politique et psychologique de la religion romaine* (2d ed., Paris 1969), 191.

47. Augustus was certainly not indifferent to this type of rite: the proof is that he ordered the senators "to burn incense and pour wine before the altar of the god in the temple at which the meeting of the Senate took place," in order to induce them to discharge their duty *religiosius*, "with more religious conscience." See Suetonius, *Aug.*, 35, 4.

48. Orosius, *Adversus paganos*, 6, 22, 5 (the author recalls that in the course of a demonstration, Augustus had refused the title of *dominus* that an enthusiastic public wanted to give him: see Suetonius, *Aug.*, 53, 1: "Igitur eo tempore, id est eo anno *quo firmissimam verissimamque pacem ordinatione Dei Caesar composuit,* natus est Christus, *cuius adventui pax ista famulata est,* in cuius orto audientibus hominibus exultantes angeli cecinerunt 'Gloria in excelsis Deo et in terra pax hominibus bonae voluntatis.' Eodemque tempore hic (= Augustus) ad quem rerum omnium summa concesserat, *dominum se hominum appellari non passus est,* immo non ausus, quo verus dominus totius generis humani inter homines natus est."

Ceres

The word *ceres* is formed from the root **ker-*, "growth." The notion became personified and deified; the goddess Ceres "presides over growth," especially the growth of cereal grains. M. Valerius Probus, a grammarian of the first century A.D., already gives this definition (*ad.* Verg. G. 1.7): *Cererem a creando dictam* ("Ceres comes from *to cause to grow*").

There is a masculine form, *Cerus* (cf. Degrassi, *Inscr. Latin*, no. 63, *Keri pocolom*, "cup of Cerus"). The expression *Cerus manus*, which is used in the song of the Salians, is interpreted by the ancients as *creator bonus* (Festus, p. 109 L.). But this rare and archaic masculine form was never a "competitor" of the goddess.

The goddess is also said to be worshiped by the Oscans (cf. Vetter, *H.I.D.*, no. 147) and by the Faliscans (ibid., no. 241). In spite of this Italic occurrence and this ancient origin, Ceres underwent an intensive Hellenization very early. It may be

Ceres. Paris, Bibliothèque nationale, Cabinet des Médailles. Photo BN.

Ceres. Paris, Bibliothèque nationale, Cabinet des Médailles. Photo BN.

possible to indicate the ancient elements of her cult, but it is more difficult to detect exactly how they were distorted. The study of Jean Bayet, "The Cerialia: The Alteration of a Latin Cult through a Greek Myth" (*R.B.Ph.H.*, 1951, pp. 5–32, 341–66; reprinted in *Croyances et rites dans la Rome antique,* Paris 1971, pp. 89–129), is very suggestive in this connection.

The great age of the goddess is beyond doubt. Her name enters into the category of deified abstractions, characteristic of the religious spirit of Rome. She has a flamen, and her festival, the Cerialia, which falls on 19 April, is included in the ancient cycle of the liturgical calendar. Another archaic trait may be that Ceres carries out her functions with the help of lesser specialists whom her priest invokes when he sacrifices to Tellus ("the Earth") and to Ceres, according to Fabius Pictor (cited by Servius Danielis, *ad. Georg.*, 1.21). The lesser specialists are Veruactor (for plowing fallow land), Reparator (for the renewal of cultivation), Imporcitor (for marking the furrows), Insitor (for sowing), Obarator (for surface plowing), Occator (for harrowing), Sarritor (for clearing and weeding), Subruncinator (for hoeing), Messor (for the harvest), Convector (for hauling the harvest), Conditor (for bringing in the harvest), Promitor (for taking the harvest out of storage).

Ceres fulfills her mission throughout the whole vegetative cycle. She acts sometimes alone and sometimes in conjunction with Tellus. In January the Feriae Sementivae were celebrated after sowing, a movable feast (cf. Ovid, *Fasti,* 1.657ff.) in honor of Ceres and Tellus, respectively. On 19 April was the festival inscribed in the archaic cycle as the Cerialia (which follows the Fordicidia of 15 April, consecrated to Tellus), which were paired with the games, the Ludi Ceriales (cf. Ovid, *Fasti,* 4.679–82). These included a strange rite with magical significance: the release of foxes with flaming torches on their backs. Ceres was also present at the Ambarvalia, the lustration of the fields (cf. Tibullus, 2.1; Virgil, *Georgics,* 1.338). Before the harvest the *porca praecidanea* was sacrificed to Ceres and Tellus (Cato, *De Agricultura,* 134; Varro, cited by Nonius, p. 240 L.). It was to Ceres that the first harvested ear of grain, the *praemetium* (Festus, p. 423 L.), was offered.

Taking root in the native religion in this way did not save the goddess from an early contamination by Hellenism. In the public cult she was associated with two other divinities to form the triad Ceres-Liber-Libera. According to tradition (cf. Dionysius of Halicarnassus 6.17.2–3), a temple comprising three *cellae* was erected in honor of this triad in accordance with the injunction of the *Sibylline Books.* Promised in a vow by the dictator A. Postumius in 496 B.C., it was dedicated in 493 by the consul Sp. Cassius. Interpretations diverge on the meaning and the date of this cult (cf. H. LeBonniec, *Le culte de Cérès à Rome des origines à la fin de la république,* Paris 1958, p. 277–311. For an opposing view, see A. Alföldi, *Early Rome and the Latins* [1964], p. 92ff.). But there can be no doubt about the influence of the Hellenic model of Demeter-Dionysus-Kore, by whatever roads these divinities may have entered Rome.

From a political point of view, the sanctuary was of great importance, since it served as a depository for the plebeian archives and as a center of administration, the *cura annonae.* It is from this *aedes* that the plebian magistrates, the *aediles,* took their name.

As for the cult of Ceres itself, which held first rank in the triad ("temple of Ceres" was sufficient to designate the triadic temple), its Hellenization only increased with the passage of time. In 217 B.C., the goddess was associated with Mercury-Hermes at the lectisternium of the twelve great divinities. In 191 B.C., a "fast in the honor of Ceres," *jejunium Cereris,* was decreed by the *Sibylline Books* in order to conjure the appearance of marvels (Livy, 36.37.4). In 174 B.C., "supplications" at the temple of Ceres were prescribed by the *Sibylline Books* (Livy, 41.28.2), "at the news that a great earthquake had occurred in the land of the Sabines."

Other events point to the same tendency: the annual celebration of a lectisternium in honor of Ceres on 13 December (Arnobius, 7.32); a single sacrifice to both Hercules and Ceres on 21 December according to the *graecus ritus* (Macrobius, *S.*, 3.11.10).

An even more revealing sign is that Demeter was purely and simply substituted for Ceres in certain ceremonies. Thus, the *sacrum anniversium Cereris,* celebrated by married women in the month of August, commemorated the kidnapping and return of Persephone (cf. Festus, p. 86 L.). It is significant that the only "mysteries" into which Cicero permits the admission of women in his treatise *The Laws* (2.21) are the mysteries of Ceres.

Thus, a general question arises about interferences between Demeter and Ceres. The Hellenization of Ceres might explain why a ceremony that should logically concern Tellus ("the Earth") was credited to Ceres, to a Ceres-Demeter. For example, the sacrifice of the *porca praesentanea* (Festus, pp. 296–98 L.), when a family is in mourning for one of its members; or the opening of the *mundus Cereris*, on certain days of the year (24 August, 3 October, 8 November: Festus, p. 126 L.). Wissowa (*Ruk*^{2} p. 194) had already rightly noted that it was not Ceres but Tellus who was in contact with the divine Manes and the subterranean world (Livy, 10.28.13: *Telluri ac dis Manibus*).

R.S./d.w.

Cicero as Theologian

Who is not inclined to be surprised on seeing the word "theologian" applied to Cicero? Nevertheless, the illustrious orator, "who won the greatest laurels for eloquence," according to the ringing praise that Pliny the Elder bestowed on him over a century after his death (*Natural History* 7.117), is perhaps most representative of the period insofar as religious thought is concerned.

First of all, he has left us the most important works of that period on this theme, works that have become even more important to present-day readers because of the loss of so many works of famous philosophers (to cite only examples of opposing schools, the treatise of Epicurus on *Piety* is lost, as well as the work in five books on *The Gods* by the Stoic Posidonius).

These works were composed during the same expanse of time and form a kind of trilogy: *De Natura Deorum* ("On the Nature of the Gods" = *Nat. D.*) in the year 45 B.C., *De Divinatione* ("On Divination") in 44 B.C., and *De Fato* ("On Fate") also in 44 B.C.

Moreover, Cicero did not limit himself to composing mere compilations as the product of his reading of Greek authors. Perhaps it is not useless to go into detail on this point, in the light of what Cicero himself has confided here and there. "From my earliest youth," he writes in response to those who were surprised at "the sudden outburst of philosophical reflection on my part, I have been devoted to the study of philosophy" (*Nat. D.* 1.6), and he cites the teachers who contributed to his education, in the following order: the Stoic Diodotus (who lived in Cicero's own house until his death, in 59), the follower of the new Academy; Philo, the partisan of the old Academy; Antiochus; and the Stoic Posidonius of Rhodes (whom Cicero heard in 77 during his sojourn on that island). This list proves that Cicero sought every opportunity to perfect his knowledge by profiting from the irreplaceable exchanges of oral teaching.

Cicero's list omits certain others, the representatives of the Epicurean school that he had also frequented since his adolescence: Phaedrus, author of a treatise on the gods, whom he knew first in the year 90 and found again in 79 in Athens. At this time he had spent six months in the Athenian city and had the further opportunity to hear Zeno of Sidon, who was the head of the Epicurean school, as well as his disciple Philodemus, who struck up a friendship with the Roman guest.

Because of the variety of these philosophical associations, some scholars have come to hasty conclusions: to them, Cicero is a mere eclectic spirit, a kind of aesthete of thought. He is supposed to have chosen the academic trend because it was the only one that allowed him to reserve judgment, even perhaps to contradict himself.

Indeed, the academic school said that the wise man should limit himself to *probable* opinions, since he cannot distinguish the true from the false (*Nat. D.* 1.12). Cicero insists, however, that this does not consist in denying the existence of truth, but only in avoiding any precipitous judgment. But the problem of the nature of the gods is extremely arduous and full of mystery (*perdifficilis . . . et perobscura quaestio est de natura deorum: Nat. D.* 1.1).

If one reads attentively the preamble of the treatise *Nat. D.*, in which there is a discussion between three interlocutors (who are supposed to be holding their conversation between the years 77 and 75 B.C.)—a preamble that constitutes the only personal intervention of Cicero, aside from the final reflections of the last book—the author is far from giving any impression of an amiable skepticism that is content to attend jousts of contradictions. On the contrary, he shows that this is a debate that can leave no one indifferent, and although he wants the controversy to develop freely, he cannot refrain from warning of the risks. Thus, grappling with the Epicurean position, he declares: "If it is true that the gods exercise no control whatsoever over human affairs, what will become of piety, reverence, and religion?" (*Nat. D.* 1.9).

This is a cry from the heart that betrays the ambiguity of Cicero's position. On the one hand he is passionately attached to the pursuit of the one truth—*ad veri investigandi cupiditatem*—and refers to the freedom of examination of the Socratic method (*Nat. D.* 1.11: he goes back expressly to Socrates in enumerating the links of the chain: Arcesilas in the third century, Carneades in the second; in the first century, Philo of Larissa was the representative of this trend). On the other hand, he is so indebted to Roman categories of thought that he is alarmed in advance at the upheaval (*perturbatio vitae . . . et magna confusio: Nat. D.* 1.3–4) that would be caused by a discussion which would end by establishing that "the gods cannot or do not wish to concern themselves with men."

This is far from a gratuitous aestheticism. What then are the motives that caused the orator of old to devote himself to an inquiry that threatened to be so thorny? Chronology offers a first answer. Cicero's entire "work of philosophical reflection" comes between the years 46 and 43: *The Paradoxes of the Stoics* (*Paradoxa Stoicorum*) in 46; *The Academics* (*Academica*) in 45; *Definitions of Good and Evil* (*De Finibus Bonorum et Malorum*) in 45; *Tusculan Disputations* (*Tusculanae Disputationes*) in 45; *Cato the Elder, or On Old Age* (*Cato Maior, De Senectute*) in 44; *Laelius, or On Friendship* (*Laelius, De Amicitia*) in 44; *On Duties* (*De Officiis*) in 43. In this flowering, which does not take into account the lost treatises (such as the *De Gloria* or the *De Virtutibus*), is found the trilogy of theological books cited above.

In a fairly short expanse of time, Cicero thus produced an impressive number of books of a philosophical character. The dating is explained by circumstances. Cicero was kept at a distance from political affairs from the time of the establishment of the dictatorship of Julius Caesar in 46; he had leisure time at his disposal, which had not been available until then to the orator and statesman; at the same time, he wondered whether his studious retreat would not be interrupted suddenly by new events (the ides of March, 44, are near . . .). This was an additional reason to hurry and transmit to his fellow citizens the lessons of Greek wisdom in Latin (*Tusc.* 1.1) and to give his country a new jewel, philosophy (ibid. 1.5).

So far we have only discussed general reasons, which can explain why the "amateur" who is open to ideas (*ipse et magnus quidem sum opinator, non enim sum sapiens*, he writes in *Lucullus* 20, which constitutes the second book of the first *Academica*) has resolved to make his great plan come true. But there was a more personal reason: in February of 45 a cruel bereavement struck Cicero: the death of his daughter Tullia whom he cherished above all else (*Tulliola, deliciolae nostrae,* he wrote, in one of the Letters to Atticus [1.8.3]). More than any other motive, this immense sorrow must have prompted Cicero to ask questions about final ends and to meditate about problems of the immortality of the soul and the nature of the gods (*Nat. D.* was probably written in August of 45).

We would know more about the state of his soul were it not for the loss of the treatise *On Consolation* that he wrote under the sway of grief. But allusions made to this treatise by Cicero himself in his other works should be sufficient to warn us against coming to premature conclusions about the "skeptical tendencies" which are supposedly systematic in Cicero.

Perhaps we have failed to take a necessary precaution: when speaking of Cicero, it is important to separate his critical spirit, so avid for theoretical discussion conducted with a demand for total liberty, from the personal quest of a man who is attempting to arrive at the most reasonable form of belief, in the midst of all the contradictions of the philosophers.

From this perspective, it is indeed possible to resolve several contradictions that are only apparent.

Thus at one level—at which, moreover, only the practice of augury is concerned—some people have thought it possible to oppose "Cicero the augur" to "Cicero the philosopher." In the treatise *On Laws* (2.32), the augur recognizes the solid foundation of divination, which would be justified in a world governed by gods who are careful to warn men by signs. In the treatise *On Divination* (2.70 and 148), by contrast, Cicero makes an incisive criticism and denies any prophetic value to the signs of the auspices. A careful reading shows, however, that in both passages the positions which seem to be contradictory are accompanied by a commentary of identical meaning: in the first passage, the author points to the changes and negligence which had distorted the art of augury from the time of Romulus (*On Laws* 2.33); in the second, he confines himself to disputing the power of prediction which some people wanted to grant, in his time, to the office of the augur, which should not be questioned as an official institution (*On Divination* 2.70; see the article "Roman Divination," above).

Now we come to the crucial questions. Is there really a wavering on the doctrine of the soul? Cicero dealt with the question especially in the first book of the *Tusculan Disputations*. The author is confronted with two contradictory positions and tries to show that in either position death cannot be considered an evil. If the soul is immortal, it is assured of happiness in the heavenly life (*Tusc.* 1.74–75). Or if it is mortal (as is conceded by the Epicureans and even the Stoic Panaetius, who differs in this from Plato), then, deprived of all sensation, it would not be able to experience suffering

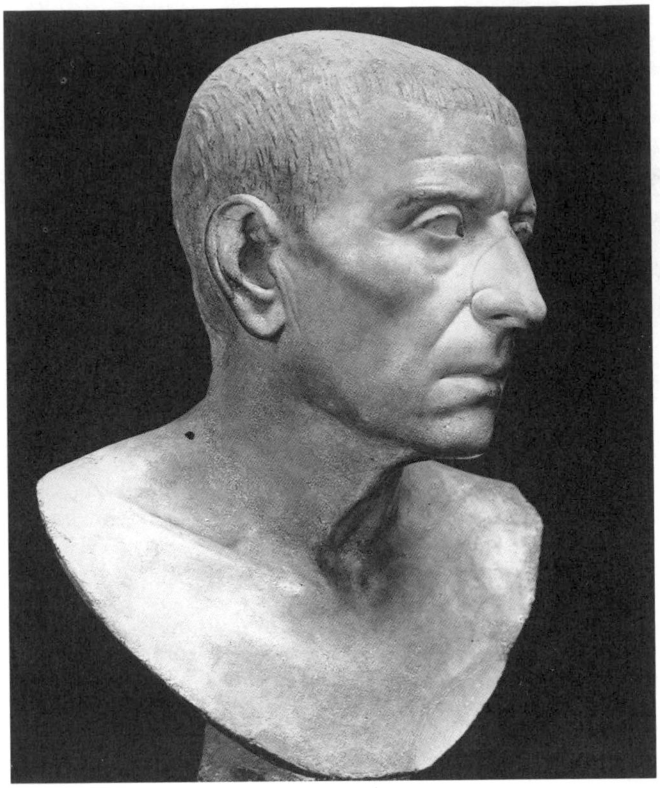

Cicero. Florence, Uffizi. Photo Alinari-Giraudon.

(ibid. 1.82ff.). In fact, Cicero merely takes up two academic exercises in philosophizing which he examines and then comes to the conclusion that in either case death is not to be feared.

This objective and methodical approach to the discussion does not keep him from revealing his own opinion, for there is no uncertainty as far as he is concerned. Conscious of the importance of his own testimony, he cites a passage from his *Consolation* which still remains his credo: "The soul has an essence that is heavenly and divine and consequently eternal."

The question of the destiny of the soul is connected with the problem of the gods. Here again there is a contrast that leads to reflection. In the *Nature of the Gods,* Cicero freely adopted an attitude of discretion, situating the debate in a fairly remote period (between 77 and 75 B.C.). Since he was an *adulescens* at that time, he shows self-effacement before the champions of the two great schools, Velleius for the Epicureans and Balbus for the Stoics; they hold their discussion under the critical arbitration of the academician Cotta. But—and what a surprise—at the end of this long debate, in which Greek philosophy and Roman religion sometimes confront each other directly, Cicero forgets his connections with the academic school and finds the conclusions of the Stoic Balbus "closer to the truth," *ad veritatis similitudinem.*

What has happened then? We can already see the beginnings of a solution in the last exchange of arguments. Cotta has just finished a critical examination of Balbus's thesis, and has emphasized how "obscure and laborious" the problem of the nature of the gods still remains (*Nat. D.* 3.93). It is then that these words of correction make Balbus leap to the defense. This time he reacts more as a Roman pontifex than as a Stoic philosopher and says with some emotion to his adversary: "You should give me another day to answer. For this debate involves our altars and our hearths, the temples and shrines of the gods, and the walls of our city: and do you pontiffs declare that these are sacred and that their protection depends more upon their religious character than their value as enclosing fortifications?" (*Nat. D.* 3.94: *Dabis diem nobis aliquem, ut contra ista dicamus. Est enim mihi tecum pro aris et focis certamen et pro deorum templis atque delubris proque urbis muris, quos vos, pontifices, sanctos esse dicitis diligentiusque urbem religione quam ipsis moenibus cingitis*). Is it surprising that after this Cicero shares in this profession of faith?

An even more decisive answer is given by Cicero himself. In the passage from the *Tusculan Disputations* cited above (1.66), he follows his profession of faith from the *Consolation* with this explicit declaration: "And indeed the divinity itself, as we conceive it, can be understood in no other way than as a mind autonomous and free, separated from all perishable matter, conscious of all and moving all, and having perpetual motion."

This declaration, delivered in a tone of pure deism, does not keep Cicero from remaining faithful to Roman traditions any more than his adherence to Stoicism keeps Balbus from reacting as a responsible pontifex when the skepticism of his adversary Cotta risks undermining the foundations of the Roman patrimony and of sowing a *perturbatio vitae et magna confusio,* to quote Cicero's own terms (*Nat. D.* 1.3). It is true that Cicero, who maintains a lively curiosity for new ideas, remains profoundly convinced of the superiority of the ancestral tradition. In the preamble of the *Tusculan Disputations* (1.1), he wrote: ". . . it has always been my conviction that our ancestors made wiser discoveries than the Greeks, and although our ancestors borrowed some of their material from the Greeks, they improved it until they judged it worthy of their efforts."

Another piece of evidence is given at the end of the discussion on divination. This time, Cicero assumes the role of critic in opposition to his brother Quintus in the debate about the prophetic pretensions of the art of divination. He has rejected all forms of this art (*On Divination* 2.148), only to affirm immediately and forcefully that by suppressing this superstition, he intends to preserve religion all the better: *nec vero—id enim diligenter intelligi volo—superstitione tollenda religio tollitur.* "And also," he adds, "just as it is a duty to weed out every root of superstition, so it is a duty to spread the influence of religion, in harmony with the knowledge of nature."

R.S./l.r.

Diana

The etymology of Diana's name is transparent: it is formed on the adjective *dius* ("luminous"); the neuter *dium* designates "the luminous sky." *Diana* means "the luminous one" and therefore comes from the same root *diu-* as Jupiter: she dispenses nocturnal light, alternating with Jupiter, the god of day. Cicero (*De Natura Deorum,* 2.27.69) gave a precise definition of her name: "Diana is associated, it is thought, with the moon . . . she is called Diana because at night she makes the day (*diem*)."

The identity of the goddess is confirmed by her cult: throughout Italy (Statius, *Silvae,* 3.1.59–60), the anniversary of her cult falls on 13 August, the ides, which formerly coincided with the day of midsummer. It is therefore no accident that the ides designated both the anniversary of the temple of Diana on the Aventine (13 August) and the anniversary of the temple of Jupiter on the Capitol (13 September). There is also the rite: even in Ovid's time (*Fasti,* 3.270) women carried torches from Rome to Aricia, "carrying the light" (Propertius, 2.32.9–10) to the goddess, as if to stimulate her essential function through sympathetic magic.

Diana was originally worshiped in the sacred woods of this Latin city situated at the foot of the Alban Hills. After various changes in fortune (see R. Schilling, *Une victime des vicissitudes politiques: La Diana latine,* in *R.C.D.R.*), her cult was moved to the Aventine in Rome. Tradition dates this transfer at the time of Servius Tullius, but it is more likely that it took place during the fifth century B.C., after the Roman victory over the Latins near Lake Regillus (496 B.C.).

Diana was exposed to Hellenic influence very early (probably because of the circumstances of her introduction, she became especially the protectress of slaves: the anniversary of her temple on the Aventine is called *dies servorum,* "the day of the slaves"; see Festus, p. 460 L.). Her personality became so evanescent that she was ready to be remodeled to her Greek homologue, Artemis.

Diana was associated with Hercules during the first lectisternium of 399 B.C., which attempted to ward off an epidemic (Livy, 5.13.6). The association may perhaps be explained by reference to the homologous Greek divinities: Artemis *Locheia* was originally not a lunar goddess but essentially the

Altar of Diana. Paris, Bibliothèque nationale, Cabinet des Médailles. Photo BN.

Diana. Paris, Bibliothèque nationale, Cabinet des Médailles. Photo BN.

Diana Nemorensis (Diana-Hecate-Selene). Paris, Bibliothèque nationale, Cabinet des Médailles. Photo BN.

protectress of feminine life; Heracles had the evocative surname of Alexicacus ("he who repels evils"), as the Latins knew (see Varro, *De Lingua Latina*, 7.82). At the lectisternium of 217 B.C., Diana-Artemis returned to her natural mythological family and was coupled with "her brother" Apollo.

The influence of Artemis *Locheia* explains, in our opinion, certain artifacts that were foreign to the virginal nature of Diana (ex-votos in the form of vulvas or phalluses, found at Aricia), as well as the presence, in the Arician woods, of Virbius, who was nothing but Hippolytus in disguise (Virgil, *Aeneid*, 774–77).

During the time of Augustus, Diana's absorption by Artemis was almost total. But in striking contrast, the old custom of *rex Nemorensis* continued in the Arician woods, where Diana's priest performed this office (most often a fugitive slave) until a more vigorous claimant came to murder him in order to take his place. Various explanations attempt to make sense of this barbarous custom (see A. Alföldi, "Diana Nemorensis," *AJA* 64, 1960, pp. 137–44; G. Dumézil, *R.R.A.*[2], 410). It still existed at the height of the Imperial Era (see Suetonius, *Caligula*, 35.6) as evidence of a prehistory that had ended.

R.S./d.b.

Faunus

The name *Faunus* is the subject of considerable discussion. The ancient authors (Cornelius Labeo, cited by Macrobius, in *Saturnalia*, 1.12.21; Servius, *ad G*, 1.10) explain it by the verb *favere* ("to favor")—an etymology that appeared "popular" to modern authors. The attempt by von Blumenthal (*Hesychstud.*, 1930, p. 38) to interpret the name by reference to *thaunon-thērion*, thus giving it the meaning "wolf," was taken up by other scholars (F. Bömer, *Fasti, Kommentar*, p. 100) who drew upon the meaning of the root **dhau-*, "strangle": Faunus would thus be "the strangler." But this interpretation ran into other objections (since this meaning of the term is attested only in the Phrygian domain: cf. K. Latte, *R.R.G.*, p. 83, n. 3)—so the ancient meaning has once again come into favor, except for the debate as to whether the true meaning of Faunus is to be taken as a positive qualifier or a euphemistic expression.

Uncertainty also arises from the fact that the association of Faunus with the cult of the Lupercalia, undoubtedly the most archaic of Roman cults, is relatively recent. (It is thus irrelevant to argue from the meaning of *lupercus* to explain the nature of Faunus.) In fact, the name of this festival bears only a semantic correspondence to Lupercal, which designates the cave of the she-wolf (Virgil, *Aeneid*, 8.342), and the Luperci, the officials of this "truly savage brotherhood" (*fera quaedam sodalitas:* Cicero, *Pro Caelio*, 26) who, on 15 February, ran around the Palatine as if to trace all around it a circle of magic protection; this was a purifying rite, which logically fell during the month of purification (*februa*), which is the month of Februarius.

What does *Lupercus* mean? Undoubtedly "wolf-man" (according to a formation analogous to *noverca*, "new" [mother], through the connection with *nova*). Furthermore, these Luperci are nearly naked (Ovid, *Fasti,* 2.287), wearing only a loincloth (ibid., 5.101). Clearly, these Luperci, since they are divided into two groups, the Quinctiales (who are connected with Romulus) and the Fabiani (who are connected with Remus), are situated at a stage before civilization.

In this whole ceremony there is nothing that refers to a god Lupercus. It is noteworthy that when Virgil (*Aeneid,* 8.344) and Ovid (*F.,* 2.271) want to put the festival under the patronage of a divinity, they suggest a Greek god, Pan of Arcadia. Faunus Bicornis was indeed regarded as the Latin homologue of Pan in this period. But the equation does not go back much earlier. In the third century B.C., the Latin interpretation of Pan was not Faunus, but Silvanus (as in Plautus, *Aulularia,* 674, 766; cf. F. Bömer, *Ovid, Fasti, Kommentar,* p. 101). It was not until the time of Ovid that the syncretic translation of Pan took precedence over Faunus in the Latin accounts: on his arrival in Arcadia on the site of the future Rome, Evander is said to "have taught about many cults, the first being that of the two-horned Faunus" (*Fasti,* 5.99). In this vein, Ovid does not hesitate to explain the word *Lupercus* through the Arcadian Mount Lycaeus: "in Arcadia, Faunus of Mount Lycaeus has his temple" (ibid., 2.423–24).

Furthermore, the Latin name should deceive no one. Faunus is merely a Latin disguise for Pan. His identity as a foreigner would not fool anyone. Ovid gives us proof of this in the following testimony (ibid., 2.194): "On the ides of February, smoke rises from the altar of Faunus on the Tiberine island." In fact, in 194 B.C. a temple had been erected to Faunus on this island through fines levied upon the *pecuarii* ("owners of herds": cf. Livy, 33.42.10). The date of the celebration (which did not coincide with the Lupercalia), as well as the location of the temple outside the *pomerium,* point to the fact that Pan-Faunus had once been foreign to the primitive ceremony of the Lupercalia.

However, because of the later syncretism, he came to be regarded as the patron of the Luperci (Ovid, *F.,* 5.101). His reputation as a lecherous god (ibid., 2.346) qualified him to patronize the procedure that had been advocated in advance "by the voice of Juno" (ibid., 2.441): *Italidas matres sacer hircus inito* ("Let a sacred goat penetrate the Italian mothers!"). The god also bears the evocative surname of *Inuus* (Livy 1.5.2), which should throw light on the rite of the Luperci, who strike the backs of passersby (Ovid, *F.,* 2.445) with thongs made from the hide of the sacrificed goat (ibid., 2.446). According to Festus (p. 75 L.), these thongs are made from the hide of a she-goat; and the she-goat is immolated for Faunus (Ovid, *F.,* 2.362). Thus the "recommendation of Juno," as explicated by an "Etruscan augur," could be put into practice.

Faunus also has magical powers (ibid., 3.323). In a general sense, he is the *agrestis* god who eludes the "culture" of the cities. Following the model of the Panes of Hellas, the Fauni multiplied in the works of the Latin poets; they form joyous corteges with the Nymphs and Satyrs (cf. Ovid, *Metamorphoses,* 1.193). But here we are no longer in the territory of ritual but in the domain of mythological fantasy.

R.S./d.w.

Genius

Genius is an authentically Roman notion: it has no Greek equivalent. Ancients and moderns have differed on its exact meaning. It comes from the verb *genere,* a rarer form than the reduplicating verb *gignere.* Censorinus (*De Die Natali* 3.1) proposed three explanations: Genius is responsible for our birth (*ut genamur curat*), or it is born at the same time as we are (*una genitur nobiscum*), or it welcomes us and protects us after our birth (*nos genitos suscipit ac tutatur*). Modern scholars have in general been drawn to the first orientation; most (for example, Wissowa, *Religion und Kultus d. Römer,* 2d ed., p. 175) have given an active meaning to *genius* and have interpreted it as the deification of genetic power. G. Dumézil (*Religion romaine archaïque,* p. 364) has observed, on the other hand, that "the compound *ingenium,* which is of a more current type but was undoubtedly ancient as well, has only a passive sense: property, innate quality, *quod ingenitum est.* Genius in the animate genre is exactly that, personalized and divinized."

Two arguments militate in favor of this last interpretation. First, the parallelism with other semantic formations: the *Venus-venia-venerare (-ri)* series (to which can be associated, analogically, *Fides-[Dius] Fidius-fidere*) is similar to the *genus-Genius-generare* series. In all of these series, the derivatives in *-io-* come from a religious vocabulary, having to do with deified notions (Genius, Fidius) or with a sacred word (*venia*). Venia indicates the favor acquired from the gods by the *venerans.* Fidius designates the god who guards and guarantees Good Faith. Similarly, Genius must designate the deification of the personality with its innate qualities.

There is also another reason: a text by Servius (*ad Aen.* 3.607) that Otto (*R.E.,* s.v. Genius, ca. 1158) had the merit of bringing out of obscurity points out that "the forehead is consecrated to Genius; let us also touch our forehead to venerate the god" (*venerantes deum tangimus frontem*). Rather than personifying sexual activity, Genius incarnates the personality of each human being. Genius is common to men and women (cf. Censorinus, ibid. 3.3). The parallelism Genius-Juno is merely a later construction, found for the first time in Tibullus (3.12.1) in the form of a Juno Natalis that is the mirror image of the Natalis identified with Genius (3.6.48). In the theater of Plautus, no allusion to Genius is of a sexual nature: it is the vital principle that is strengthened by good living.

A purely Latin notion, Genius was nevertheless subject to Greek influence, which is already discernible in Lucilius (cited by Censorinus, ibid. 3.3). Varro (cited by Augustine, *De Civitate Dei* 7.13) sees in Genius a principle more rational than fundamental. Horace (*Epistulae* 2.2.187ff.) proposes a more ethical conception, by distinguishing a variable *Genius* (*mutabilis*), sometimes white (*albus,* which inclines us toward good), sometimes black (*ater,* which incites us to do evil). This Genius is presented chiefly as a companion (*comes*) who directs our destiny (*natale astrum*).

Next to the private Genius there exists a Genius Publicus that is first mentioned in 218 B.C. (Livy 21.62.9). Later a Genius Populi Romani is indicated, around which Sulla is said to have hoped to reunite Roman citizens during the

Household shrine, with a depiction of two lares on either side of the genius. Pompeii, the Vettii house. Photo Anderson-Giraudon.

Social War. The Genius Publicus is presented as a symbol of prosperity and success: on 9 October he is honored along with Fausta Felicitas and Venus Victrix in Capitolio.

The Genius Augusti appears as a double legacy: Augustus understood the benefit that he could derive from a cult both deeply rooted in Latin mentality and capable of an official status. He hoped to associate the cult of his own Genius with that of the Lares in all the crossroads of Rome (Ovid, *Fasti* 5.145–46).

With an extension of meaning that is at first sight surprising, the Genius Loci has been borrowed for many special uses. The notion was also extended to collectivities, for example, Genius Coloniae or Genius Municipii. At the time of the Empire, there was a Genius Senatus that constituted a kind of mirror image of the Genius Populi Romani.

R.S./d.b.

BIBLIOGRAPHY

G. DUMÉZIL, *La religion romaine archaïque,* 2d ed., 362–69. R. SCHILLING, *Genius at Ange, R.C.D.R.*

HERCULES

The Latin name Hercules is a derivation from the Greek, *hēraklē̄s: *Herkles,* then **Hercoles* (the dative *Hercolei* is attested several times), then *Hercules.* The name is found in various forms all over Italy—in the Etruscan domain: *Hercle* (M. Pallottino, *Testimonia linguae etruscae,* no. 399); in the Oscan dialect: *herekleis* (= *Herculis;* E. Vetter, *H.I.D.,* no. 1, B); in the Vestinian dialect: *herclo* (= *Herculi,* ibid., no. 220); in the Praenestine dialect: *hercle* (= *Hercules;* cf. ibid., no. 367b), *hercles* (= *Hercules;* ibid., no. 367c), and *hercele* (= *Hercules;* ibid., no. 366d).

The ubiquity of his name is in keeping with the legend of the Greek voyager. His acclimatization to Rome as a god gave rise to a thorough study by Jean Bayet (*Les origines de l'Hercule Romain,* Paris 1926) that remains the definitive work on the subject.

The legend that was imposed in Rome in the classical era is a version of the victorious battle of a hero/benefactor against maleficent "Evil." This is how Livy (1.6.4ff.), Dionysius of Halicarnassus (1.31–40), Virgil (*Aeneid* 8.193ff.), and Ovid (*Fasti* 1.541ff.) have presented the arrival of the "hero, carrier of the club," on the banks of the Tiber: after coming from the fabulous island of Erytheia, near Spain, with a herd of cattle taken from the giant Geryon, he is the victim of the theft of several head of cattle by a certain Cacus, who appears to be a shepherd (Livy), a bandit (Dionysius of Halicarnassus), or a "horrible" monster (Virgil and Ovid).

Hercules kills Cacus (which popular etymology interprets as *kakos,* "the evil one") and wins the general sympathy of the inhabitants of the region. In particular, Evander, the king of the Arcadians in Pallantium, the future site of Rome, shows his gratitude by building an altar to Hercules (Livy; Dionysius of Halicarnassus)—the Ara Maxima, located at the Forum Boarium. According to other versions (Virgil, *Aen.* 8.271; Ovid, *Fasti* 1.581), Hercules himself established the altar and the cult of the Ara Maxima.

Such is the general theme of the legend, if one disregards "aberrant" variants (thus, according to Diodorus [4.21], Hercules is received by two hospitable characters, Pinarius and . . . Cacius; he establishes his own cult at the "Great Altar" by instituting the practice of offering the "tithe": there is no mention of a monstrous Cacus). The legend tells us nothing about the historical antiquity of the cult.

The cult was made up of two groups in the classical era, in the north and the south of the Forum Boarium, which was both a cattle market and a commercial center. To the north, more precisely at the northwest corner of the Circus Maximus, was the Ara Maxima, which had been built later from a round temple devoted to Hercules Victor, whose annual celebration fell on 12 August. The epithet Victor appears in the pre-Julian calendar of Antium; in other calendars and literary sources there is a vacillation between Victor and Invictus; cf. A. Degrassi (*Ins. Ital.,* 13.2, p. 494). Tacitus (*Annales* 12.24) thinks that the Ara Maxima was included within the pomerium of the Romulan city.

In the south, between the banks of the Tiber and the Aventine hill, is another temple of Hercules Victor or Invictus, situated near the Porta Trigemina (Varro, cited by Macrobius, *Saturnalia* 3.6.10). This temple, placed outside the pomerium, had its annual celebration on 13 August; it had the status of a foreign cult, *sacra peregrina* (Festus p. 268 L.).

The essential difference between the two locations of the cult was as follows: that of the Ara Maxima was from the beginning private and overseen by two gentes, the Potitii and, in a subordinate position, the Pinarii; that of the Porta Trigemina was an establishment of Greek merchants, who honored one of their gods who was believed to be the distributor of health and prosperity.

In 312 B.C. the cult of the Ara Maxima underwent a radical change; it became nationalized at the instigation of the censor Appius Claudius, and the Potitii abandoned their *familiare sacerdotium* to the state, at a cost of 50,000 *as*—a transaction that must not have pleased the god, if one

Hercules and the Nemean lion. Paris, Bibliothèque nationale, Cabinet des Médailles. Photo BN.

believes the tradition: the twelve Potitii of that period died within thirty days (Festus, p. 270 L.), and Appius Claudius became blind and passed to posterity with the cognomen Caecus (cf. Livy 9.29.9–11).

Before this date Hercules had already participated in an official ceremony in Rome. In 399 B.C. he had appeared at the first lectisternium in the company of Diana-Artemis. After 312 B.C. he was a "Romanized" god, after the Roman state took over the cult of the Great Altar, resorting to public slaves who were put under the authority of the urban praetor. Nevertheless, the rite practiced there differed from the Roman liturgy: the *ritus Graecus* (cf. my article, "*Sacrum et profanum*," *Latomus* 1971, pp. 963–68; reprinted in *R.C.D.R.*). It included a practice which met with great success: the offering made to the god, the *polluctum,* was followed by a lavish feast, the *polluctura,* which was open to all participants.

Other innovations of the cult attest to the influence of Hercules: in 218 B.C. (Livy 21.62.9), a *supplicatio* was addressed to him (at the same time as a lectisternium to Juventas—Hebe, who in mythology is believed to be his wife: Ovid, *Fasti* 6.65). But the disaster of Trasimenus, which occurred shortly thereafter, must have provoked a certain disenchantment: Hercules no longer appears at the big lectisternium of the twelve gods in 217 B.C.

It was not long before he came back into favor: the epithets that epigraphy has recorded (Wissowa, *Ruk*[2], p. 282, and J. Bayet, *op. cit.*, p. 487)—*Defensor, Conservator, Salutaris* (*Alexicacus,* "he who drives away evil," is cited by Varro, *De Lingua Latina* 7.82) demonstrate the confidence in the god's aid and protection. Nevertheless, it was the dispenser of success and prosperity who received the greatest devotion. Moreover, the establishment of the tithe at the Ara Maxima was preferred by merchants and soldiers: by promising the god a tenth of their profit or of their spoils of war, they supported the prestige of Hercules Victor. In this context we may cite the ostentatious gesture of a former flautist who had become a merchant, M. Octavius Herrenus, who offered a tithe and a feast in honor of Hercules (Marius Sabinus of the first century B.C., cited by Macrobius, *Sat.* 3.6.11). There was also the innovation of a general, M. Fulvius Nobilior, who in 189 B.C., when he returned from a victorious campaign in Aetolia, had the temple of Hercules Musarum constructed near the Circus Flaminius (the general had brought back from the capture of Ambracia nine statues of the Muses, which he wanted to entrust to Hercules Musagetes, "leader of the Muses"; Pliny, *Naturalis Historia* 35.66).

The popularity of Hercules was eclipsed toward the end of the first century B.C., after the founding of the empire by Augustus: the god was in disgrace for "supporting" the unfortunate rival of the conqueror, Anthony (see my article "L'Hercule Romain en face de la réforme religieuse d'Auguste," *R.Ph.*, 1942, p. 39; reprinted in *R.C.D.R.*). But it was not long before Hercules emerged from the shadows where political circumstances had put him (ibid., p. 52ff.). One day, at the time of the dispute between paganism and Christianity, he even became a rival of Christ (M. Simon, *Hercule et le christianisme,* Belles Lettres, Paris, n.d.).

R.S./t.l.f

JANUS

The name Janus has an etymology that is accepted by most linguists: it comes from the root *iā-*, which is an enlargement of the Indo-European root *ei-* ("to go"), and which appears as an abstract term corresponding to the notion of "transition."

As for its form, *janus* is a stem originally in *-u-* that has shifted to a stem in *-o-*: this explains the form of the ancient derivatives Januarius ("January"), *janu-al* ("cake reserved for Janus"), *janua* ("door"), as well as the more recent derivatives *jani-tor* ("doorkeeper"), Jani-culum ("the Janiculum hill"), Jani-gena ("daughter of Janus").

This etymology corresponds to the thinking of the ancients, which was clearly formulated by Cicero (*De Natura Deorum* 2.27.67): "the name (of Janus) comes from the verb 'to go' (*ab eundo*); this is why passages that open to the street are called *jani,* and the doors of profane buildings are called *januae.*"

If this definition sins by the letter, still it faithfully expresses the spirit of the word. It is preceded by an important specification: the characteristic trait of "transition" that Janus incarnates is that of being initial. Cicero evokes Janus's special trait of being "the first" (*De Natura Deorum* 2.27.67) in sacrificial ceremonies. But this quality applies generally as well, as is attested in Varro's formula (cited by Augustine, *De Civitate Dei* 7.9): *penes Janum sunt prima, penes Jovem summa* ("Janus presides over all that begins, Jupiter over all that culminates").

Although the Indo-European origin of Janus "remains the most likely" (E. Benveniste, personal communication), his

Janus. Paris, Bibliothèque nationale, Cabinet des Médailles. Photo BN.

Latin origin is no less certain. Greece has no homologous figure (this was already noticed by Ovid, *Fasti* 1.90; the possible influence of the "Double Hermes" on the sculptured representation of *Janus Bifrons* does not affect his definition), and the Etruscan *ani* portrayed on the liver of Piacenza is a borrowing (from the Latin word: cf. Skutsch, *R.E.*, s.v. Etrusker, c. 767; or from another Italic language: cf. G. Dumézil, *A.R.R.*,[2] p. 338).

The functional definition of the god explains his role in both legend and liturgy (I repeat here the central points of my article "Janus le dieu introducteur, le dieu des passages," in *M.E.F.R.*, 1960, pp. 89–131; reprinted in *RCDR*). In his legend, which in Rome must be fairly late, Janus assumes all the "initial" roles. This is clear from the first canto of Ovid's *Fasti*, where he is said to have been identical to Chaos "in olden days" (*Fasti* 1.103ff.). Similarly, he is supposed to have been the "first ruler" of the banks of the Tiber: the Janiculum, which bears his name and lies on the edge of *archaic* Rome, perpetuates the memory of his ancient citadel (*Fasti* 1.245–46). And it is Janus once again who offers generous hospitality to Saturn so that he can "hide" in Latium after his expulsion from the heavenly realm (*Fasti* 1.235ff.).

While these fantasies only have the merit of fitting the description of the god, the evidence from his cult is of greater weight. Janus has no flamen of his own, but the *rex sacrificulus* ("king of sacrifices") offers him a sacrifice in certain circumstances (at the beginning of each month, for instance: cf. Macrobius *Saturnalia* 1.15.10, and Wissowa's commentary, *Ruk*,[2] p. 103). This royal intervention recalls that Janus is the initiator of time. It is for him that the public sacrifice first celebrated in the first month of the year is performed: the Agonium of 9 January. And it is he who, in association with Juno (whence his surname Junonius), is the patron of the calends of all the months of the year.

Under the name of Janus Curiatius, the god also presides over a rite of passage which, within the curiae, involved young men of arms-bearing age. But because of its archaism and the lack of information about it, it is extremely difficult to define this cult clearly.

Such is not the case for Janus Quirinus, who is cited from the time of the "royal laws" (Festus, p. 204 L.) and whose worship Augustus attempted to revitalize. It was at the temple of Janus, founded, according to tradition, by Numa (cf. Varro *De Lingua Latina* 5.165; Livy 1.19.2), that a symbolic rite was carried out. This temple, which was both a sanctuary with an altar (*ara . . . parvo conjuncta sacello:* Ovid *Fasti* 1.275) and a door (*porta Janualis:* Varro *Ling.* 5.165), was the visible sign of the state of peace or war, *index pacis bellique* (Livy 1.19.2), depending on whether the doors were closed or open. (In the absence of archaeological data, it is impossible to specify the workings of this *sacellum-porta* complex.) Here Janus was called Geminus (his statue is *biceps*, two-faced) or Quirinus. It is the latter name, the older one since it goes back to a "royal law," that was preferred under Augustus. The emperor boasted (*Res Gestae Divi Augusti* 13) that he had closed the temple of Janus Quirinus three times. In this way the association Janus-Quirinus served to exalt the "peaceful" values that Quirinus embodied. Here Janus assured the "transition" from war to peace. At least this is suggested by two pieces of evidence from Horace. The poet wanted to stress the "quirinal" side of Janus when he coined the expressive variant *Janum Quirini* (*Carmina* 4.15.9), an idea that he took up again (*Epistulae* 2.1.255) in the more prosaic form *custodem pacis . . . Janum* ("Janus, guardian of peace").

R.S./j.l.

JUNO

The name *Juno* "supports only one etymology: it is a derivation in *-on-* from *jun-*, a syncopated form of *juven-* which is also found in *junix*, 'heifer' . . . and in the comparative *junior*" (G. Dumézil, *R.R.A.*,[2] p. 299).

Juno is active at the birth of human beings and of the moon. One of the most important festivals on the calendar, which takes place on 1 March, the Matronalia, concerns Juno Lucina, "she who gives birth": the goddess is invoked under this name by pregnant women (as described in Plautus, *Aulularia* 692, and in Terence, *Adelphoe* 487). In association with Janus, under the name of Juno Covella (see my article "Ianus, le dieu introducteur, le dieu des passages," in *M.E.F.R.*, 1960, pp. 102–8; reprinted in *R.C.D.R.*), she patronizes the calends of every month: this patronage should probably be explained as a function of an ancient ritual that stipulated resorting to the goddess of "youth," of "vital strength," in order to encourage the "work" of the young moon, from the calends to nones.

Other ancient cults of Juno fall on the first of their respective months: February (Juno Sospita), June (Juno Moneta), September (Juno Regina, on the Aventine), and October (Juno Sororia). All of these dates correspond to archaic and autonomous cults of Juno. The only exceptions to this generalization result from a loss of autonomy in worship:

Juno Sospita, a crow on her shoulder, crowning Cornuficius. Paris, Bibliothèque nationale, Cabinet des Médailles. Photo BN.

Juno Caprotina is honored on 7 July, on the nones, because this festival is dependent on the cult in honor of Jupiter on 5 July, at the Poplifugia (on this ceremony, see G. Dumézil, "Les nones Caprotines," in *Fêtes romaines d'été et d'automne* Paris 1975, p. 271–83); Juno Regina of the Capitol is celebrated on 13 September, on the ides, because here she is subordinate to Jupiter, whose temple is honored annually on this day.

Juno plays a role in legendary history: in 390 B.C., the Capitol had been saved from a surprise attack by the Gauls (Livy 5.47.3–4) by the cries of geese, birds consecrated to Juno. Was it because of the intervention of Juno Moneta, "the Warner"? She is mentioned under this title by Cicero (*De divinatione* 1.101). A temple was erected to her in 345 B.C. by the dictator L. Furius Camillus on the Capitoline citadel (Livy 7.28.4; later, the installation next to this sanctuary, *ad Monetae,* of a monetary workshop, gave *moneta* the meaning "money").

During the historical period Juno is closely associated with Jupiter: in the Capitoline triad, Juno Regina sits at the side of the ruling god in the *cella* to the left (Livy 7.3.5); in the lectisternium of 217 B.C. she forms a couple with Jupiter, in the manner of Hera and Zeus. Rome knew of a second Juno Regina, the ancient Uni, protectress of the Etruscan city of Veii: in 396 B.C. she had been transferred to Rome, to the Aventine hill, following an *evocatio* of the dictator L. Furius Camillus, after the siege of the city (Livy 5.21.3 and 22.4–6).

R.S./t.l.f.

JUPITER

Jupiter is the supreme god. His name, which is of Indo-European origin, signals his quality as a celestial god, the god of light. The Latin *Juppiter* is really a vocative form that, through its frequent use in this way, served as a nominative. (Indeed, there is a rarer form of the nominative, *Diespiter,* for example, in Plautus, *Poenulus* 739). The name comes from *Jou-pater* (with expressive gemination of the first consonant of the second element and apophony of the interior vowel): *Jou* comes from **dyeu* (the same root is at the base of *dies,* "day"). *Juppiter* thus has a semantic relationship with the Greek Zeus, since the nominative *Zeus* is based on **dyeus.* This name is also found in all Italic dialects, particularly in Umbrian and Oscan.

In Rome, Jupiter is the principal divinity of the archaic triad (which associates Mars and Quirinus with him) and of the Capitoline triad (which assigns Juno and Minerva to him as consorts). He is also named first (with Juno) in the lectisternium of 217 B.C. His cult was maintained from its beginnings by the first priest of the sacerdotal body, the *flamen Dialis.* On the ides of each month (which fall on the 13th of most months, but on the 15th of March, May, July, and October), a lamb is sacrificed to him (Festus, p. 93 L.). In the historical era, the principal festivals in his honor were the Vinalia, which were celebrated on 19 August (the consecration of grapes) and on 23 April (the offering of wine). At that time he was honored as the ruling god, the protector of the Romans descended from Aeneas, according to the "Trojan" interpretation that claimed to explain the liturgy (see my book *R.R.V.*, p. 131–48). The *ludi Romani,* celebrated in his honor (from 15 to 18 September), follow the anniversary of the temple (on the ides of September and after the interval of the 14th). These games are accompanied by an *epulum Jovis,* a solemn meal offered to the god.

Jupiter is given several qualifiers depending on which of his aspects is to be highlighted. Thus the celestial and meteorological aspect is expressed by Jupiter Tonans or Jupiter Fulgur; the aspect of magical intervention, by the epithet Stator ("he who immobilizes": see Livy 1.12.4–6) or

Votive relief. Munich, Staatliche Antikensammlungen und Glyptothek. Photo Koppermann.

Capitoline triad (Jupiter-Juno-Minerva) represented on an oil lamp. Rome, City Museum. Photo Oscar Savio.

Jupiter Feretrius (Livy 1.24.7–8; the Roman fetial who concluded a treaty with the Alban people invokes Jupiter Feretrius, he who must strike, *ferire,* the first one who backs away; see Festus, p. 81 L.). He is qualified as Jupiter Optimus Maximus on the Capitolium (on the ethical meaning of these adjectives, see G. Dumézil, *Archaic Roman Religion,* p. 200).

It is at the temple of the Capitol that his role as the protector god of the city is exercised fully. It is there, on the calends of January, that the new consuls go, accompanied by senators, magistrates, priests, and the populace. It is there that the consul designated for a military campaign pronounces the *vota,* the prayers and solemn promises made for a successful outcome. It is there that, when he returns, the victorious and triumphant general pays his debt of gratitude to the ruling god.

R.S./t.l.f.

The Lares

The name Lar has no clear etymology. In the singular, but more often in the plural, Lares, it designates the deities who protect a piece of land. This basic feature was rightly underscored by Wissowa (*Ruk*^{2}, p. 169): "The primary importance of the Lares is as deities attached to a locality."

This definition, supported by ritual evidence, was obscured by the speculations of ancient and modern scholars who tended to confuse the Lares with the "infernal spirits" (Festus, p. 273 L., repeated by Ernout-Meillet, *D.E.*^{4}, s.v. Lares). The issue was further obscured by a later mythological interpretation that resulted in the invention of a "Mother of the Lares," who was called Mania in Varro (*De Lingua Latina* 9.61) and in Macrobius (*Saturnalia* 1.7.35), Lara in Ovid (*Fasti* 2.615), Mater Larum in the liturgy of the imperial period of the Arval Brethren (Henzen, *Acta Fratrum Arvalium,* p. 145). Her antiquity must be challenged, since early Roman religion does not recognize genealogical ties.

In the archaic *Carmen* of the Arval Brethren, the Lares are referred to (in the form Lases, without the rhotacism of the internal *s*) as protectors of the *ager Romanus* (plowed fields of Rome). In the singular, the Lar Familiaris is the protector of the family estate, whom the paterfamilias greets first when he arrives in his country home (see Cato *De Agricultura* 2.1). He protects all the *familia,* freemen and slaves alike. The master of the house also offers a crown to the Lar Familiaris so that "this home may be for us a source of wealth, blessing, happiness, and good fortune" (see Plautus *Trinummus* 40–41).

In the country, the cult of the Lares was practiced at crossroads (*compita*), special meeting places. These Lares Compitales were worshiped in particular at the beginning of the month of January in a movable feast, the Compitalia.

In Rome itself, the Lares were honored on 1 May as Lares Praestites ("tutelary Lares"); Ovid (*Fasti* 5.129–36) recalls their office as protectors and defenders of the ramparts. The popularity of their cult (at crossroads, they were represented as two young men accompanied by a dog) was so great that Augustus seized the opportunity to place a statue of his own Genius among them. Thus, to borrow Ovid's expression (*Fasti* 5.146), "each quarter honored three deities."

To this list a new cult should be added, attested by a recent

Lares. Paris, Bibliothèque nationale, Cabinet des Médailles. Photo BN.

Representation of two snakes at the base of a lararium. Photo Boudot-Lamotte.

discovery, an archaic inscription on a cippus (a low column) of the fourth century B.C. found in the vicinity of Lavinium: *Lare Aenia d[ono]*, "offering to the Lar Aeneas"; see *Roma medio republicana* (Rome 1973, p. 321, no. 472). For the first time the singular word *Lar* is apparently followed by a proper noun; and for the first time epigraphy seems to provide proof of a cult of Aeneas, specifically in the area of Lavinium where a *heroon* was discovered which tradition attributes to Aeneas (see P. Sommella, "Heroon di Enea a Lavinium, Recenti Scavi a Pratica di Mare," *Rendic. Pontif. Accad. Archeol.* 44 [1971–72]: 47–74).

R.S./g.h

The Manes

The word Manes has given rise to various exegeses. We must reject the popular etymology *manare,* cited by Festus (p. 146 L.): "The name *Manes (di)* may be explained by the fact that these gods were thought to spread (*manare*) throughout the aerial and earthly elements"; we must also reject the arbitrary connection with the Phrygian word *mēn* made by Kurt Latte (*Römische Religionsgeschichte,* p. 99, n. 3). We should probably accept the explanation based on the euphemism, *manis* (or *manus*), "good," "kindly," as opposed to *immanis.* The expression is said to have been applied to the infernal gods (*di inferi*) in order to gain their favor. This explanation, accepted by most modern scholars, was proposed by Aelius Stilo (cited by Festus, p. 132 L.): "The infernal gods were called Manes with the meaning "kindly" (*boni*) by people who venerated them in a suppliant tone, for fear of death."

The use of the expression is ancient. It appears in the ritualistic formula of the *devotio,* which the consul Decius pronounced in 340 B.C. He consecrated himself, at the same time as the enemy army, "to the Manes gods and to the Earth goddess" (*Deis Manibus Tellurique:* Livy 8.9.8). It was also to the "Manes gods" that M. Curtius devoted himself in 361 B.C., when he plunged on horseback into a chasm which had opened in the Forum following an earthquake (Livy 7.6.4). Cicero evokes the "laws of the Manes" in his treatise on laws (Cicero *De legibus* 2.22 and 2.45).

But the expression *di Manes* does not appear to have been widely used in ancient times to designate the deceased of the family. These were named *di* or *divi parentum* in a passage from the "royal laws" (Festus, p. 260 L.). Similarly, the funeral ceremonies around the family tombs that lasted for nine days (*dies parentales*), starting on 13 February and ending on 21 February with a public holiday, the Feralia, were called Parentalia; the substantive *parentatio* and the verb *parentare* were the specific words for the cult of dead ancestors.

Only toward the end of the first century B.C. was the custom established of using the inscription *D(is) M(anibus)* for the dead of the family. Dedications to the Manes gods were made on tombstones (see R. Cagnat, *Cours d'épigraphie latine,* Paris 1914, pp. 280–81: before this, epitaphs were "very brief"; "the names of the deceased, first in the nominative, then in the genitive case, made up the entire inscription; not a word or a formula could be found that recalled death, even indirectly"). The dedications were followed by the names of the deceased in the nominative, genitive, or dative case.

Nevertheless, the phrase *di Manes* took on other meanings through metonymy. Thus, it can designate the home of the dead (Virgil *Aeneid* 4.387), or simply corpses (Livy 31.30.5).

The Virgilian formula, *quisque suos patimur Manes* (Virg. *Aen.* 6.743: We each suffer our own Manes), has inspired a number of interpretations. The ancient commentator on Virgil, Servius (schol. ad Virg. *Aen.* 7.643), understood it to mean "the judgment" that awaits us during the visit of the Manes, and by way of justification, he advanced the following philosophic view: At our birth two genies welcome us; one incites us to good, the other to evil; after our death, they are the witnesses of our fate—of our freedom or our reincarnation. It is hard to see how such a Neoplatonic concept harmonizes with Virgil's thought. It is, in any case, alien to Roman traditions.

R.S./g.h.

Mars

The name of the god Mars has no Indo-European etymology. Mars is the Latin form that comes from *Mavors*, an ancient form sometimes used by poets (an intermediate form, *Maurs*, is also attested: *CIL*, I^2, 49). In the official *Carmen* of the Arval Brethren, Mars is still invoked by the names Marmar (from *Marmart-s*) and Marmor (a foreign form). In the Oscan dialect, the god has a related name, Mamers (see A. G. Ramat, *Studi intorno ai nomi del dio Marte, Arch. Glottol. Ital.*, 47, 1962, p. 112ff.).

The antiquity of Mars, the god of war, is attested by the fact that he belongs to the archaic triad of Jupiter-Mars-Quirinus, and by the cult office of the *flamen Martialis*. His character as a warrior god is apparent in the liturgy. The Salii, a brotherhood of priests consecrated to him, opened and closed the military calendar year with martial dances. Among the ancients, this calendar would begin in the spring (the festivals of the Equirria of 27 February and 14 March, consisting of horse races on the Field of Mars; the Agonium Martiale on 17 March; the lustration of arms during the Quinquatrus on 19 March; and the lustration of war bugles during the Tubilustrium on 23 March) and would finish in the autumn (the ritual of purification during the Tigillum Sororium on 1 October; the sacrifice of the war horse, the October Equus, on 15 October; and the lustration of arms, Armilustrium, on 19 October). Mars had his places of worship outside the city's pomerium, which was under the jurisdiction of the *imperium militiae* (see Vitruvius 1.7.1). Accordingly, on the Field of Mars an ancient altar, *ara Martis*, was raised, near which D. Junius Brutus Callaicus built a temple in 138 B.C. South of the city wall near the Appian Way was the most important sanctuary, the *templum Martis extra portam Capenam*, which was dedicated on 1 June 338 B.C. This was the point of departure for the annual parade known as the *transvectio equitum*, a cavalry procession (see Dionysius of Halicarnassus 6.13.4).

Within the city walls, on the other hand, the talismans of Mars were kept in a chapel inside the Regia (the *sacrarium Martis*). These objects were the twelve shields, the *ancilia* (one was reputed to have fallen from heaven, and the remaining eleven were said to be indistinguishable reproductions: see Ovid *Fasti* 3.369ff.), and also the spears, the *hastae Martis* (the spears were able by their "spontaneous" movement to provide omens—*Mars suum telum concutit*, "Mars shakes his spear": see Livy 22.1.11). Before setting out for

Representation of a *suovetaurilia* sacrifice combining the boar (*sus*), the ram (*ovis*), and the bull (*taurus*). Paris, Musée du Louvre. Photo Giraudon.

Mars bearing a lance and a shield. Pompeii fresco. Photo Boudot-Lamotte.

war, the commander-in-chief would come to touch these sacred objects while shouting: *Mars vigila* (Mars be vigilant!).

If the military character of the god is well established, why have certain modern scholars (see G. Hermansen, *Studien über den italischen und römischen Mars,* Copenhagen 1940) tried to establish the existence of an "agrarian Mars"? The ambiguity resulted from an incorrect interpretation of certain activities of Mars outside the strictly military domain; it led to long discussions, of which G. Dumézil has given a balanced account (*Archaic Roman Religion,* pp. 224–45). We shall only cite two particularly revealing examples. Mars is invoked in the *carmen Arvale,* which tries to assure mystical protection of the fields. The Arval Brethren, who also address themselves to the Lases (= the Lares, guardians of the farm) and to the Semones (the gods in charge of the growth of seeds, *semina*), ask the "savage Mars" (*fere Mars*) only for a service that corresponds to his definition as a defender (cf. *limen sali,* "leap to the frontier!"): the service of protecting the *ager Romanus* against all enemies.

Similarly, the peasant who comes to the lustration of his field in Cato (*De Agricultura* 141) walks the animals of the *suovetaurilia* (boar, ram, and bull)—a sacrifice that belongs to Mars—while begging the god to stop, repel, and ward off (*prohibessis, defendas averruncesque*) visible and invisible ailments (*morbos visos invisosque*), dearth and desolation (*viduertatem vastitudinemque*), calamities (the destruction of stalks of grain, *calami* taken in the sense of *culmi*), and inclement weather (*calamitates intemperiasque*). Here again Mars is asked to act in keeping with his function: this action will make possible the growth of harvests and the prosperity of the herds and people.

During the lectisternium of 217 B.C., Mars was associated with Venus on the Greek model of Ares-Aphrodite, and this Hellenic couple played a rather catalytic role in the service of the Roman cause (the reasons can be seen in my article "Roman Gods," above). Therefore Mars came under little influence from the Greek god of war.

The religious policies of Augustus only confirmed this process by proclaiming Mars Ultor, "the avenger." The god earned this name for two reasons: as the avenger of the assassination of Julius Caesar (the victory at Philippi in 42 B.C.) and as the avenger of the disaster suffered by the Romans at Carrhae in 53 B.C. (a negotiation with the Parthians, followed by a surrender of the Roman flag, had been presented as a victory). As a result, the emperor ordered that a round temple be raised on the Capitol in honor of Mars Ultor (in 20 B.C.: Dio Cassius 54.8.3) and then had the great temple installed in the middle of his own Forum (in 2 B.C.: Dio Cassius 60.5.3). Mars enjoyed a new glory. The "father" of Romulus, the founder of Rome, he was associated with Venus, the "Mother" of the Romans descended from Aeneas. He was no longer simply a god of war, camping on the outskirts of the city; he had solemnly entered the interior of his city to receive the honors given him on top of the Capitol and in the heart of the new Forum.

R.S./g.h.

Mercury

The name of the god Mercury cannot be disassociated from the word *merx,* which means merchandise. Such was the sentiment of the ancients (Festus, p. 111 L.: *Mercurius a mercibus est dictus*). The word *Mercurius* is based on a *u* stem. In addition to the consonantal stem of the Latin word *merx,* the *u*- stem is attested in an Oscan dedication from Capua (*Mirikui* = *Mercurio,* Vetter, *H.I.D.,* n. 136) and in several Faliscan inscriptions (e.g., *tito mercui efile* = *Tito Mercu aediles,* Vetter, ibid., n. 264; this is a dedicatory inscription of merchants; the first name placed before the name of the god seems foreign).

Mercury, the patron of merchants, was introduced to Rome at least by the early fifth century B.C. A temple dedicated to him was built in 495 B.C. (Livy 2.27.5) outside the pomerium, near the Circus Maximus on the slope of the Aventine. His anniversary fell on the ides of May (Livy 2.21.7).

Mercury entered Rome in the midst of social upheavals caused by the debts incurred by the plebeians and by problems of food storage (Livy 2.27.5). The consecration of the temple was therefore associated with the creation of a brotherhood of merchants, the *mercatorum collegium*.

It is likely that the temple was dedicated at the behest of the *Sibylline Books,* given its extramural location and the circumstances. The year before, similar circumstances had, at the prompting of the *Sibylline Books,* called upon the dictator A. Postumius to dedicate a temple to the triad of Ceres-Liber-Libera. Later Mercury was associated with Neptune in the first lectisternium of 399. Mercury-Hermes represented trade, which benefited from the maritime help of Neptune-Poseidon. This commercial vocation was again affirmed in the lectisternium of 217, which this time linked Mercury and Ceres in an even more striking economic association.

When he is presented in the preamble of Plautus's *Aulularia,* the god stresses his commercial function, even while he alludes to another aspect of his Greek model, one that is required by the plot of the play, namely the role of messen-

Right: Mercury. Paris, Bibliothèque nationale, Cabinet des Médailles. Photo BN.

Below: A group consisting of Mercury, Attis, and the Sibyl on an oil lamp. Rome, City Museum. Photo Oscar Savio.

ger: "I preside over messages and profits" (Plautus *Aulularia* 12). In a scene from Ovid (*Fasti* 5.681–90), a merchant addresses a prayer to the god of commerce, who does not trouble himself with scruples. The prayer ends on the following casual note: "Grant me only that I can earn a lot; grant that I may enjoy my gains! Grant me the pleasure of tricking the buyer with fine words!"

During the Augustan Age Mercury extended his field of action under the influence of his Greek counterpart, among the poets. He "became," following the example of Hermes, "the son of Zeus and Maia" (*Homeric Hymn to Mercury* 1); this same Maia, the daughter of Atlas, is merely a homonym of Maia, the entity associated with Volcanus (Aulus Gellius *Noctes Atticae* 13.23.2). In Virgil (*Aeneid* 4.239), he puts on his golden heel-wings to transmit Jupiter's messages; he also acts as the psychopomp—the conductor of souls into the netherworld (ibid. 4.242). Horace (*Carmena* 1.10) celebrates the god as the inventor of the lyre and the conductor of souls into the next world. On one occasion he happens to greet Mercury as an avatar of Augustus (ibid. 2.41). There is a striking contrast between the poet Ovid (*Fasti* 5.665–70), sensitive to the civilizing qualities of Hermes, and the merchant that he so carefully depicts, who asks Mercury only to assuage his appetite for profit.

Still another role awaited Mercury in the Roman world. He was to take up again his mission of traveler, no longer as a messenger of Zeus, but as an "interpreter" of deities who appeared too mysterious to the Romans. For example, Caesar (*Gallic War* 6.17.1) gave the name of Mercury to the principal god of the Gauls, as Tacitus (*Germania* 9.1) did to the Germanic god Óðinn.

R.S./g.h.

Minerva

The name of the goddess Minerva (*Menerva* is the oldest epigraphical form, and *Minerva* is the classical Latin form) can be traced back to an Indo-European root **men-*, which indicates the activities of the mind (see J. L. Girard, "Étude onomastique: Le nom de Minerve en Italie," *Annuaire de l'E.P.H.E.*, section 5, vols. 80–81, fasc. 2 [1971–73], pp. 64–65). It has no Indo-European parallels outside of the Italic languages.

Minerva was originally a native of southern Etruria (Wissowa, *Ruk*², p. 253, thought it might have been Falerii, a city of Italic origin, conquered very early by the Etruscans). In fact, one of her most ancient temples, whose anniversary fell on 19 March (the year is uncertain), is on the Aventine, which stood outside the pomerium (compare the *Fasti Praenestini*, on 19 March). Another shrine on the Caelian Hill was a chapel containing the statue of Minerva of Falerii that was captured when the city was taken by the Romans in 241 B.C. It bore the name *sacellum Minervae captae* (see Ovid *Fasti* 3.843ff.). Unlike Juno of Veii, who had been "invited" after an *evocatio* to "surrender" to Rome, the Minerva of Falerii was treated simply as a prisoner.

In the Capitoline triad, Minerva, like Juno, is the consort of Jupiter and sits at the supreme god's right hand (see Livy 7.3.5). At the lectisternium of 217 B.C., she was associated

Minerva. Paris, Bibliothèque nationale, Cabinet des Médailles. Photo BN.

with Neptune—an obvious reference to the confrontation between Athena and Poseidon.

Her principal festival falls on 19 March, the day of the Quinquatrus (the fifth day after the ides; see Festus, p. 304 L.), which is also the anniversary of her temple. In the calendar of Praeneste, this day is called *artificum dies*, "the day of craftsmen." It is celebrated by artisans, artists, and schoolmasters (see Ovid *Fasti* 3.809–34). In this aspect, the Latin Minerva was akin to Athena Ergane.

Perhaps another aspect of her personality may also be explained by a Hellenic influence transmitted by the Etruscans. On a basket from Praeneste, Minerva appears in a mysterious scene involving Mars (see G. Dumézil, *Archaic Roman Religion*, pp. 243–44). In light of this, the coincidence of the feast of Minerva with the Quinquatrus of March, which was originally dedicated to the lustration of arms (see the calendar of Praeneste), cannot be considered fortuitous. In any event, the Latin Minerva seems to be strongly marked by Etruscan and Hellenic influence. (Research is in progress: J. L. Girard, *R.E.L.* 48 [1970], pp. 469–72.)

R.S./g.h.

Neptune

Neptune is an ancient god. The Neptunalia were registered on 23 July in the cycle of festivals of the old liturgical calendar. The etymology of Neptune's name is controversial. Certain philologists (P. Kretschmer, *Einleitung in die Geschichte der griechischen Sprache*, Göttingen 1896, p. 133) have explained the word as a derivative from the stem **neptu-*,

Neptune. Paris, Bibliothèque nationale, Cabinet des Médailles. Photo BN.

"moist substance." But the word **neptu* "is not attested in any other Indo-European language"; "the root **nep-*, which barely survives in Vedic and Avestan, is unknown in Latin" (Georges Dumézil, *Mythe et épopée*, vol. 3, p. 41).

The comparative approach would explain it by way of "the important Indo-Iranian religious figure of the Vedic *apām napāt*, Avestan *apąm napà*, descendant of the waters" (Ernout-Meillet, *D.E.*[4], s.v. "Neptunus"). By comparing the mythical depiction of the god common to the Indo-Iranian Apām Napāt and the Irish god Nechtan with the historicized legend about Neptune, Dumézil (ibid., p. 87) proposed to derive the three nouns from the Indo-European root **nepot-* (**nept-*), "descendant, sister's son."

The Latin god must have been the patron of *all* the waters before he presided essentially over the open seas, under the influence of the Greek god Poseidon. Though it is not possible to form a clear notion of his functions, in the absence of a flamen or of any commentary in Ovid's *Fasti*, Dumézil has gathered enough evidence to suggest Neptune's role by constructing a converging series of "lines of fact" (ibid., pp. 21–89). The Neptunalia took place on 23 July, that is, at the beginning of the summer heat, when the earth, vegetation, and human beings were most in need of water. On that day, in order to have protection from the heat of the sun, it was customary to put up huts made of foliage (*casae frondeae*), which were called *umbrae* (shades: Festus, p. 519 L.). In the exercise of his functions, Neptune is assisted by two abstract entities (which are in a way his personified potentialities), Salacia (see Aulus Gellius *Noctes Atticae* 13.23) and Venilia (see Varro *De Lingua Latina* 5.72). Salacia evokes gushing water (the verb *salire*); Venilia, still or flowing water.

This supports the idea that Neptune first ruled over fresh water, an idea that is further buttressed by the fact that the Neptunalia were preceded and followed by two festivals that had similar concerns, the Lucaria on 21 July and the Furrinalia on 25 July. The first deals with the condition of the *luci*, woods subject to drought; the second involves the action of Furrina, who was probably the goddess of deep waters (for the elucidation of these two festivals, see Dumézil, *Fêtes romaines d'été et d'automne*, pp. 32–37 and 42–52).

Nevertheless, Neptune was exposed to the Greek influence of Poseidon quite early. He was associated with Mercury, the god of commerce, in the first lectisternium of 399 B.C., an alliance that shows that Mercury, the god of the sea (*mare*), was henceforth supposed to extend his dominion to fresh water, in the manner of Poseidon. Hellenization was even more marked at the lectisternium of 217 B.C. This time the couple Neptune-Minerva barely concealed the Hellenic model of Poseidon-Athena.

All of this explains a noteworthy contrast. While ancient historiographers seem to have been preoccupied with the marvel of water primarily with regard to *fresh* water (the overflowing of Albanus Lacus [now called the Lago di Albano] toward the end of the Roman war against the Veii: see Livy 5.15.12 and G. Dumézil, *M.E.*, vol. 3, pp. 40–62), Neptune later followed Poseidon in being dragged into the open sea. Classical authors were therefore accustomed to consider Neptune essentially as the god of the sea. Varro (*De Lingua Latina* 5.72) gives the following explanation of the names of Neptune: "By virtue of the fact that the sea veils (*obnubit*) the land as clouds (*nubes*) veil the sky, Neptune derives his name from *nuptu*, the ancient word for *opertio* (veiling)." The only merit of this "explanation" is to reveal the link between Neptune and the sea that after that appeared natural. Virgil (*Georgics* 1.29) refers to the god only with one significant periphrasis: *deus immensi maris*, "the god of the boundless sea" (see the commentary of Servius Danielis, ad loc.).

R.S./g.h.

The Penates

The *di Penates* are the "gods of the indoors" (*penates* formed like *Arpinates*). This etymology seems the most likely, even though Cicero (*De Natura Deorum* 2.68) hesitates between this explanation (*penitus insident, ex quo etiam penetrales a poetis vocantur:* "they dwell inside [houses], from which also comes their designation of *penetrales* by the poets") and another explanation that would derive the word from *penus* in the sense of "provisions" (in his time, *penus* or *penum* had only this meaning). In fact, the older meaning of *penus* is attested in a commentary by Festus (p. 296 L.): *penus vocatur locus intimus in aede Vestae tegetibus saeptus* ("*penus* designates the most secret place in the shrine of Vesta, which is closed off by curtains").

Precisely because of this semantic shift of the word *penus*, these gods were thought to watch over the welfare of the family. The hearth was considered their altar (Servius Danielis on *Aeneid* 11.211), and they shared in the family meal: one part was reserved and thrown into the fire; total silence would prevail until a slave announced, *deos propitios* ("the gods are propitious") (ibid. 1.730).

The Penates gods were also closely associated with Vesta, the goddess of the hearth (Cicero *Nat. D.* 2.68; Servius Danielis on *Aen.* 2.296), and with the Lars Familiaris. In the *Mercator* (834) of Plautus, when Charinus goes into exile, he bids farewell both to the Penates gods of his parents and to the family Lar.

Corresponding to this private cult was a cult of public Penates, who were thought to have been brought by Aeneas to Lavinium (Ovid *Fasti* 3.615; Servius Danielis on *Aen.* 2.296). Varro (*De Lingua Latina* 5.144) recalls that "Lavinium is the first city of Roman stock founded in Latium. This is where our Penates gods are" (*nam ibi Penates nostri*). Therefore, "when they leave office, Roman magistrates go to Lavinium to sacrifice to the Penates and Vesta" (Servius Danielis l.l.).

In Rome near the Palatine, on the slopes of the Velia, there was also a shrine of the Penates gods (Varro *Ling.* 5.54; Livy 45.16.5). Dionysius of Halicarnassus (1.68.1–2) tells of seeing "the statues of Trojan gods, which are visible to all and which an inscription identifies with the Penates: they are two seated young men holding a lance, the work of ancient craftsmanship."

We might be tempted to conclude that these statues were transferred from Lavinium to Rome. But it is more likely that these were relics, as is implied in the account of Dionysius of Halicarnassus, who states that he has "seen many other statues of these gods, in the same military attitude, in ancient temples" (ibid.).

In any event, a relief of the Ara Pacis represents a shrine that fits the description of Dionysius of Halicarnassus: "Inside a small temple were two sitting gods, half naked, with lance in hand" (see I. Scott Ryberg, "Rites of the State Religion in Roman Art," *American Academy in Rome* [1955], pp. 40–41 and plate 10, fig. 21). Resolutely adopting the Roman viewpoint, Dionysius of Halicarnassus called the official Penates "Trojan gods." As a Greek witness he did not succumb to the temptation to confuse these two young "soldiers" with the Dioscuri. On the contrary, he proposed a series of Greek synonyms to translate for his compatriots "these gods that the Romans call Penates" (*ibid. 1.67.3: tous de theous toutous Rōmaioi men Penatas kalousin*).

R.S./g.h.

Penates. Paris, Bibliothèque nationale, Cabinet des Médailles. Photo BN.

Priapus: The Last of the Gods

The Romans knew Priapus as the god of gardens where they could see him in the pose of *anasurma* ("exposing oneself"), rolling up his robe filled with fruit in order to expose his huge phallus. From the time when he first appeared at the dawn of the Hellenistic era until well into the Christian Middle Ages, Priapus was able to encompass very different realities. From the great retinue of Ptolemy II Philadelphus (Athenaeus 5.201c), in which Priapus held a mythico-political position, to the epigrams of the *Anthologia Palatina*, in which he is the god of fishermen, or even in the kitchen gardens of Alexandria and Rome, where Priapus was made into an obscene scarecrow (*Anthologia Planudea* 236; Horace *Satirae* 1.8), this god did not rate a place among the theological definitions advanced by the ancients. Apparently they did not see fit to assign him his own space in their pantheon, even though Priapus could be part of the Dionysian *thiasos*, and tradition often referred to him as the son of Dionysus and Aphrodite or a nymph. Consequently, when Diodorus Siculus (4.6.4) and Strabo (13.1.12) attempt to describe Priapus, they can do so only by mentioning his "resemblance" to such Attic gods as Ithyphallus, Orthanes, Conisalus, and Tychon, all ithyphallic deities of whom we know virtually nothing except for the Priapic "resemblance" that characterizes them.

Even though the ancients (and the moderns) often confused Priapus alternately with Pan, with Dionysus, with a Satyr, or even with Hermaphroditus, the ancient sources make it possible to discern a specific figure for this *divus minor* (*Corpus Priapeorum* 53), whose iconography reveals at the very least a radical difference: unlike his phallic companions, Pan and Satyr, Priapus is completely human. He does not have horns, animal feet, or a tail. In fact, his only anomaly, his only defect, is the outrageous phallus that defines him, from his birth, as *amorphus*, or deformed, and that prompted his mother, Aphrodite, to disown this monstrous child who was born to her on the banks of the Hellespont at Lampsacus (schol. on Apollonius of Rhodes *Argonautica* 1.932; schol. on Pseudo-Nonnus 147.29, ed. S. Brock). Indeed, his huge penis, described in Latin texts as *terribilis* (Columella *De Re Rustica* 10.33), makes it possible to recognize Priapus in pictures and to identify him in writings by giving him the physical shape essential to one of his major functions, namely, that of a god who protects small farms against thieves or the evil eye by threatening sexual violence against anyone who came close to the property that he guarded (*Anthologia Planudea* 241; *Corp. Priap.* 11.28, 44, 59,

Priapus. Bronze statuette. Augsburg, Römisches Museum. Museum photo.

and 71). Thus the stage was set for the cult of a Priapus who was a guardian of the fields and whose exercise of phallic authority was a subject of derision in the Priapea (*Anth. Pl.* 86; *Corp. Priap.* 10). In these Greek and Latin epigrams, the ithyphallic effigy of the god, often crudely carved out of cheap fig tree wood and carelessly daubed with red, assumes a voice to utter obscene threats.

But Priapus is all talk and no action. Unlike other deities who intervene in agricultural matters by conceiving of an instrument that mediates between man and his environment, Priapus himself never makes anything. He participates in the everyday world of silent practices, in which the god becomes a functional object for personal use, an amulet. Thus, when the statue of Priapus was stationed in a small orchard or a modest kitchen garden, the ancients acknowledged his double function, prophylactic and apotropaic. First, Priapus must sympathetically infuse the soil with the hyperfertility conveyed by his excessive sexuality; the ithyphallic figure of the god is then required to protect the fenced-in garden against intruders, through a kind of antiseduction coupled with threats that always remain verbal but nonetheless constitute a program of graphic sexual violence and corporal punishment, the instrument of which is always his aggressive phallus. Priapus is a god whose obscene sign assures magical efficacy, a god who belongs to that realm of concrete sexual representations that, although it seldom aroused the interest of ancient theology and historiography and was not often registered, even less often changed, assured for itself in this way a long existence. Thus, we find this same deity in one of his ancient functions, keeping evil at bay, in the *Chronicle of Lanercost* (1268), where a "lay Cistercian brother" erects a statue of Priapus (*simulacrum Priapi statuere*) to put an end to an epidemic that is destroying cattle.

The reading of ancient texts reveals, alongside this apotropaic Priapus, another feature of the god that conveys the Priapic *corpus* as a whole. Inside the gardens of Priapus, nothing, or almost nothing, grows. Whether there are a few meager vegetables (*Anth. Pl.* 236) or some withered vines (*Anth. Pl.* 238), this god, as Virgil (*Eclogues* 7.34) recalls, is the guardian of a poor garden. Moreover, Priapus, in keeping with his sorry environment, is usually poorly fashioned in cheap wood by a clumsy peasant (*Anth. Pal.* 9.437; *Corp. Priap.* 10). The descriptions of this rustic deity that the poets provide in their Priapea are verified and confirmed by Columella (*De Re Rustica* 10.32), when he advises horticulturists to revere Priapus in the "trunk of an old tree hacked down at random" (*forte*). Finally, it may even happen that Priapus serves no purpose at all, and if he is still placed in gardens, it is merely by force of habit and simple convention (*nomou charin*: *Anth. Pl.* 238).

The offerings made to Priapus are generally as mediocre as his effigy or the crops he is supposed to be watching: figs with shriveled skins (*Anth. Pal.* 6.102) and an occasional fruit or two (*Corp. Priap.* 53); or else the unlucky god is pitied and receives as a sacrifice, instead of fruits, verses of poets (*Corp. Priap.* 60). As for offerings from fishermen, they are no more abundant than those of the gardeners: old refuse from a catch (*Anth. Pal.* 6.192), the shell of a turtle or crayfish, in exchange for which the god is asked for very little (*me polla*), just enough to abate the supplicant's hunger (*Anth. Pal.* 6.89), enough to warm his weary bones (*Anth. Pal.* 6.193). Priapus is also offered fruit made of wax and is asked to be content with the mere image of fruit (*At tu sacrati contentus imagine pomi: Corp. Priap.* 42). Yet the supplicant expects real fruit in return.

But the troubles of Priapus reached their peak when he expressed his anxiety about castration and his fear that he, Priapus, whose essential attribute is the phallus, might end up as Gallus (*Corp. Priap.* 55); or worse yet, when Priapus had to beg the thief to come and steal from his garden, so that by fulfilling his mission as an aggressive guard, he might relieve himself (*Corp. Priap.* 17.77). But would he ever be able to do it?

The gardens of Priapus are thus located at the opposite pole from the fertile groves of Aphrodite in which Dionysus yearned to be the gardener (Nonnus *Dionysiaca* 42.274ff.). Whereas Dionysus rightfully claims the title of Eukarpus ("the god of good fruits"; *Anth. Pal.* 6.31), Priapus, who is known for his ugliness and small size, is not Eukarpus but congenitally *amorphus,* ugly and deformed. We can better understand this aspect of Priapus, who is said to be the last of the gods (*Corp. Priap.* 63), when we appreciate his close connections with the fig tree and the ass throughout the stories in which he appears.

During both the Hellenistic and the Roman eras (*Anth. Pal.* 9.437; Horace *Satirae* 1.8), the wood of the fig tree was reserved for carving statues of Priapus. While "protecting" the fruits of this tree, the god makes numerous puns on the word *ficus*, "fig," which also means "hemorrhoid" or "anus" (*Anth. Pl.* 240–41; Martial *Epigrammaton libri* 6.49). The semantic field of the fig throughout all of antiquity, and even well beyond, conveyed numerous sexual and obscene images with which Priapus is closely associated. Thus, Aristophanes (*The Peace* 1348) uses the verb *sukologein*, "to pick figs," to mean "copulate," and Ovid (*Fasti* 5.433) recalls the apotropaic function of the *fica*, a gesture to ward off the evil eye, which one makes by placing the tip of the thumb between the index finger and the middle finger. The multiple scatological and obscene connotations of the fig form a meaningful network surrounding Priapus. The wood of the fig tree (of which statues of the god were made) was

The birth of Priapus and Aphrodite's rejection. Sideview of an altar. Aquileia, Museum. Photo Vermaseren.

considered a second-rate material (*inutile lignum:* Horace *Satirae* 1.8), good to burn for heat for the poor; and its fruit, the fig, was the daily food of the poorest people. Such facts show even more clearly what meager crops this god was supposed to protect.

Simultaneously participating in this realm of the hypersexual and reflecting the drudgery of everyday life, the ass, the poor man's horse, was, like Priapus, part of the Dionysian *thiasos* and as such paraded, like Priapus, in the great retinue of Ptolemy II Philadelphus. Both Priapus and the ass are represented as ithyphallic, and the ass, considered lustful (*salax asellus: Corp. Priap.* 52), sometimes even assumed the god's place and his functions by performing violent sexual acts on a poor thief. In confirmation of this close relationship, a myth tells how the two had a contest to see which of them, Priapus or the ass, had the biggest penis. Priapus turned out to be a poor loser and killed the ass (Lactantius *Divinae Institutiones* 1.21.28). Since then, an ass has been sacrificed to Priapus at Lampsacus (Ovid *Fasti* 1.440).

But the identification of Priapus with the ass reaches its zenith when a Latin poet of the second century B.C., Afranius, makes Priapus say: "Contrary to popular belief, I was not born of an ass" (Macrobius *Saturnalia* 6.5.6). That Priapus might have been the son of an ass and denies it only reinforces the known affinities between the god and the animal. These affinities are further emphasized when people mock the ass just as they mock Priapus (Aesop *Fables* 274), and when the clumsy animal, totally devoid of cunning, wants to do something and fails. Recall that it was the ass who caused humanity to lose its eternal youth by misplacing the precious *pharmakon* with which Zeus had entrusted him (Aelianus *De natura animalium* 6.51). In Lucian (*Dialogi Meretricii* 14.4), "the ass who plays the lyre" becomes the symbol of an aged, toothless, and inept lover. We recognize the same clumsiness in Priapus when he tries to seduce the beautiful Lotis, or in another version of the same myth, when Vesta escapes his embrace like a shadow, and the god suffers a crushing disappointment. He comes away empty-handed, his penis exposed, impotent, the object of everyone's laughter (Ovid *Fasti* 1.391–440 and 6.319–48).

To this file of correspondences among Priapus, the fig tree, and the ass, we must add certain important facts that are supported by ethnography. Aristotle points out that "the bodies of asses are all but sterile" and that their semen is by nature cold (Aristotle *De Generatione Animalium* 748a–b). The same author, speaking of animals with large penises, says that they are "less fertile than those that have average-sized penises, because cold sperm is not fertile and it grows cold covering too great a distance" (ibid. 718a). Furthermore, Aristotle reasons that nature has endowed the male organ with the capacity to be or not to be erect and that "if this organ were always in the same state, it would constitute a real inconvenience" (Aristotle *De Partibus Animalium* 689a). But such is precisely the case with Priapus, who is always ithyphallic and never experiences the slightest seminal discharge, let alone any sexual relief (*Corp. Priap.* 23).

That Priapus's erection was considered pathological by the ancients is confirmed by their writings about disease. The physicians of antiquity named a terrible disease after Priapus: *priapismus*, which starts with an inflamed, relentless, and painful erection that eventually causes sterility and death for the patient, whose organ remains forever erect (Alexander of Tralles 11.8). Galen (7.728, 10.967, and 13.318, ed. C. G. Kühn), who also describes this disease, classifies it among the *emphysēmata* and compares it to a disease that the "ancients" called *saturiasis*. But Galen also establishes an

Ithyphallic Priapus in a small temple. Cameo. Berlin, Staatliche Museen. Museum photo.

important distinction between the two diseases. While priapism is an incurable ailment precluding even the slightest relief, satyriasis can produce a seminal discharge accompanied by pleasure (ibid. 19.426). Just as Galen (8.439) points out that *priapismus* was named after Priapus, we may surmise that the term *saturiasis* comes from Satyr. It would seem then that an erection of a satyrian nature, even though it is excessive, does not preclude desire or pleasure (*hēdonē*), whereas priapism, always involuntary, can only end in death.

The difference between the ithyphallicism of Priapus and that of the Satyr might also correspond to another division, which ranks Satyrs among the daemons of nature, hybrid creatures that mix human and animal elements, whereas Priapus is always integrally anthropomorphic and is ranked among humans. We might be tempted to read here a double lesson that would illuminate many points about the numerous misfortunes that Priapus experiences from his birth: first, the impossibility of excessive sexuality for a human (Priapus), the impossibility of that single-minded sexuality which, Aristotle tells us, goes against nature; second, that unending sex might be viable for animals or semihumans, but it would only lead men to impotence, to the kind of painful and joyless erection that is the sign of priapism.

But perhaps Priapus, whom the ancient doctors semantically struck with priapism, instructs us about one last failure, that of a god who in the final analysis integrates himself poorly into the Dionysian space where, next to the Satyrs and the Pans whose ithyphallicism seems obvious, Priapus alone suffers from a pathological erection. Similarly, we might argue that the unbridled sexuality of Priapus, far from being intentionally subversive, calls rather for a return to the established norms. Thus the obscenity of this god becomes almost institutional and generative of the conservative power that is conveyed by the world of fertility, a world in which Priapus, in his own way, has long participated.

M.O./g.h.

BIBLIOGRAPHY

H. HERTER, *De Priapo* (Giessen 1932); by the same author, the article "Priapos" in *Paulys Real-Encyklopädie der klassichen Altertumswissenschaft,* 22 (1954): col. 1914–42. *Corpus Priapeorum* (= *Corp. Priap.*), in *Grattius Faliscus. "Priapeorum" poetae, Scriptorum Romanorum quae extant omnia* 263 (Pisa 1976). M. OLENDER, *Éléments pour une analyse de Priape chez Justin le Gnostique*, in *Hommages à M. J. Vermaseren* (Leiden 1978), 2:874–97; *Études sur Priape*, forthcoming from E. J. Brill of Leiden in the series *Études préliminaires aux religions orientales dans l'empire romain.*

Psyche

There once lived a king and a queen who had three daughters of great beauty, but Soul, or Psyche, the youngest, was so beautiful that men were at a loss for words to describe her perfections. To look at her was like contemplating Venus herself, a Venus fresh from the sea foam and in the flower of her virginity; people flocked from far and wide to admire her.

But the real Venus, angered to see her altars abandoned in favor of a mortal, instructed her son Amor to avenge her by inspiring in her rival a burning passion for the most miserable of men. The very excess of Psyche's beauty daunted all her suitors; her sisters had already married successfully, leaving Psyche, the forsaken virgin, weeping in her solitude. Fearing some curse, the king consulted the oracle of Apollo. "On a sheer cliff, O King, abandon your daughter, sumptuously dressed for the wedding with death. Wait not for a son-in-law born of mortal blood, but a fierce monster that flies in the air." In tears, they all prepared for the girl's marriage with death. A funeral procession escorted her to the cliff and left her there. But as she waited, trembling, for the approach of the monster, a gentle breeze embraced her, inflated her robe, carried her to the bottom of the rocky wall, and gently set her down on the grass, where she fell asleep. When she awoke, an enchanted palace opened before her; a disembodied voice invited her in; and tables appeared, magically filled with wines and delicious foods. Psyche fell asleep. In the dark of night the mysterious husband came; he made Psyche his wife but left hastily before dawn. Days and nights passed in this way. Although she was quite fulfilled, Psyche yearned for the sight of humans. She persuaded her husband to let her sisters (who were looking for her) come to

Sixteenth-century stained glass window from the Château de Chantilly (Oise), a very faithful rendering of the story of Psyche according to Apuleius. Musée Condée. Photo Monuments historiques.

visit her, but on one condition: she must never try to find out what he looked like. Such curiosity would be sacrilege, a temptation to which she must never yield, even if her sisters gave her wicked advice: "If you see my face even once," he said, "you will never see it again." Furthermore, she must neither listen to nor reply to her sisters' questions.

The sisters arrived, carried by the same zephyr. First they marveled and admired, but soon, mad with envy, they persuaded the naive Psyche to penetrate the mystery of this strange husband. Perhaps he was a devouring monster or a horrible snake hiding in the dark. Armed with a lamp and a sharp razor, she was to cut his throat while he slept. The wicked sisters went away, leaving Psyche disturbed and irresolute, for she both "hated the monster and loved the husband." Nevertheless, in the still of the night, she did what could never be undone. Bringing her lamp close, she gazed in astonishment and rapture upon the sweetest and most lovable monster, Cupid himself. Suddenly a drop of scalding oil fell from the lamp onto the god's shoulder; he flew away in a rage while Psyche, clinging to him, tried in vain to accompany him, lost her grip, and fell back to earth in despair. When she tried to drown herself in a river, compassionate Pan consoled and calmed her. She thanked him and worshiped him. Then began Psyche's long wandering in search of Amor.

While Psyche traveled over the surface of the earth, Amor lay in bed in his mother's room, nursing the painful wound inflicted by the burning lamp. A gull revealed to Venus the disobedience of her son, the cause of his ailment, and the name of his beloved. Full of rage, the goddess heaped reproaches on her son and set out in search of the fleeing Psyche to seek her own vengeance.

Meanwhile the wretched girl found refuge in a temple of Ceres full of tools in disorder, which she tidied up with care. Ceres appeared and congratulated her but refused to conceal her despite Psyche's entreaties. Psyche then prayed to Juno in her temple, but to no avail. In despair, pursued over the world like a fugitive slave, Psyche decided to hand herself over voluntarily to the implacable goddess. Venus had her tortured and whipped by her servants, Worry and Melancholy, and then gave her four impossible tasks to carry out. First, she had to sort out a huge mound of cereal grains, a task she completed with the help of a colony of ants. Then she had to approach a herd of sheep with golden fleece and steal a tuft of their precious wool, even though they were known to attack humans. As she was about to give up and throw herself into a river, a talking reed dissuaded her and advised her to approach the sheep, not at high noon when they were dangerous, but when the evening had quieted them. Psyche brought the golden fleece to Venus. Then the goddess demanded that she fetch water that gushed from the top of a mountain and emptied into the Styx, water that talked, uttered threats, and was guarded by dragons. But an eagle, a friend of Cupid, completed this third task for her.

The last test was the hardest. She had to descend into Hades and ask Proserpina to put "a bit of beauty" into a small box for Venus. When Psyche once again attempted to escape by throwing herself from the top of a tower, the tower gave her sound advice on how to descend into Hades: hold a cake in each hand; keep two coins in your mouth; do not give or say anything to the lame donkey driver; do not come to the aid of the putrified old man swimming in the river; do not help the old women weaving linen; sit only on the floor next to Proserpina; refuse fine foods; eat only coarse bread; above all, do not open the box—do not yield to curiosity. Thus counseled, Psyche subdued Cerberus with the cakes on her arrival and departure; similarly, she paid the boatman of Hades and accomplished all the tasks. But as she reentered the light of day, she succumbed to her reckless curiosity and opened the little box. Inside was no beauty but a deadly sleep which overcame her.

Meanwhile Cupid, who had recovered, rushed to her aid. He put the slumber back in its box and prayed to Jupiter. Before the assembled gods, the master of the universe pronounced Cupid and Psyche united by the bonds of a legitimate matrimony. He appeased Venus and offered ambrosia to Psyche; the mortal woman henceforth became a goddess.

This is a tale of miracles. Its folk motifs are clearly revealed, and, without major distortion, we can analyze it in the manner of Propp (M. Bossard, *Les Cahiers de Fontenay* [1978],

9–10), rightly emphasizing the close ties between certain "services rendered" by Psyche and the "help" she received in her impossible tasks. Thus, the ants helped her to sort the grain, as she set the temple of Ceres in order. She honored Pan, the god of herds and god of the reed flute; accordingly, a reed helped her to collect the wool from the sheep. A closer analysis would reveal a connection between the eagle and Cupid, and perhaps between the tower and Juno.

But beyond this inquiry into the structure of the narrative, we should examine the meaning. The tale of Psyche forms the center part (4.28–6.24) of another "episodic" story, the *Metamorphoses* of Apuleius, a Platonic philosopher of the second century A.D. Although no other versions are extant, it surely must have been a widely popular story, for Plotinus knew it through *several* pictures and *several* tales (*muthois*), and we have various pictorial representations of the union of Eros and Psyche (usually with wings). But although Apuleius did not actually invent the story of Psyche out of whole cloth, he chose to include it in a much broader account, and we must begin by interpreting this choice.

The *Metamorphoses,* a work of eleven books, tells the story of Lucius, the victim of his own curiosity, whom a sorceress transformed into an ass. After lengthy wanderings and numerous ordeals, he was restored to human form, initiated, and saved by the grace of the kindly goddess Isis.

Now the itinerary of Psyche recalls on several points and in a way retraces the itinerary of Lucius. Both of them sin through *curiositas,* have to submit to terrible trials, face death, wander in search—one in search of his true form, the other in search of her husband—and serve a goddess. At the end of the road, both rise to a higher status: he is saved, and she becomes a goddess.

The *Metamorphoses* culminate in book 11 with the initiation of Lucius into the mysteries of Isis. R. Merkelbach (*Amor and Psyche,* p. 392ff.) has rightly pointed out that there are close ties between the story of Psyche and the initiatory ritual that takes place at the end of the work. Thus the wedding with death promised to Psyche refers back to the widespread concept of initiation as death, rebirth, and a whole mystical marriage. An oracle orders Psyche, and a dream sends Lucius to his initiation, for, as the priest of Isis asserts, no one can be initiated who has not been called by the deity. The leap into the void also belongs to the ritual of mysteries. Thrice happy those who enter Cupid's palace; thrice happy he whom Isis has called (11.6). The union with Amor refers to an attested rite: the initiates of Isis are united with Horus, her priest. The silence that is repeatedly urged on Psyche when her sisters visit her in Hades, the refusal to communicate with the ungodly (the donkey driver, the weavers, and the old man)—each has a counterpart in the mysteries; and Lucius insists that he will tell only what can be revealed to the uninitiated without sacrilege (11.23). Like Lucius, Psyche is warned against sacrilegious *curiositas.* The revelation of Eros, radiant with light as Psyche looks on, has as its counterpart Lucius's vision of Horus, a brilliant sun shining in the dark of night. We need not multiply such comparisons; it has been done. The background of mystery is undeniable, making the story of Psyche, among other things, an initiatory tale, a symbolic figure of initiation into the mysteries of Isis.

But the initiatory ritual itself is on the one hand a reproduction, a representation of a myth, the myth of Isis as we know it from Plutarch (*De Iside et Osiride*); and on the other hand, in terms of the process, the initiate is not only saved, but has become Isis; he identifies himself with the goddess. It should therefore come as no surprise that a close analysis establishes a definite parallelism between the myth of Isis and the tale of Psyche. Like Psyche, Isis confronts a violent and angry adversary, Typhon; she leaves in search of her husband; offers to be a servant of the Syrian Venus, Astarte; overcomes obstacles; finds her husband again; and sees her child legitimized. Psyche thus appears in book 4 as a symbol or a coded sign that is a precursor of Isis, who will reveal herself in all her radiance in book 11.

Finally, in the *Metamorphoses,* the story of Psyche is addressed to a young woman, Charity, who was kidnapped from her husband by robbers on the morning of her wedding day; who is ready, like Psyche, to surrender to death; and who is saved, like Psyche, by her husband. It is clear that the *Metamorphoses* weave very subtle but close ties between parallel itineraries: Charity and Psyche, each first a mortal woman and then a goddess; Lucius, man then ass, then man again, and finally an initiate into the mysteries of Isis; and last of all, Isis herself. All of them complete a journey that involves loss, wandering and quest, rediscoveries, and the achievement of a better status.

We can push our interpretation further: the name of the heroine, "Soul," is not simply a name when uttered by a Platonist, who would call his interpretation allegorical. Such is the interpretation advanced by Plotinus (6.9) when (I do not go into the details of the narrative) he identifies Psyche with the human soul, which, separated from God, descended to earth and experienced the "fall," the "exile," and the "loss of wings." But having come from God, the soul necessarily loves God and seeks him, and even here on earth it can find him and be united with him if it purifies itself and detaches itself from all that is earthly. One is then "filled with the light of knowledge, or rather one is pure light, weightless, buoyant, become god, or rather still being god, all aglow . . . but if once again one grows heavy, it is as if one goes out like a light." This is the itinerary not of a mystery but of a mysticism in which the language and the symbolism of the mysteries is merely the least ineffective symbol available to speak what is unspeakable about the union with God.

Thus the story of Psyche, through or beyond its connections with Isiac initiation, remains open to other past, present, or future interpretations, foreseen or unforeseen by Apuleius.

J.C./g.h.

BIBLIOGRAPHY

G. BINDER and R. MERKELBACH, *Amor und Psyche* (Darmstadt 1968).
M. BROSSARD, "Conte ou mythe? Apulée, *Métamorphoses* (4.28–6.24)," *Des mythes, Les Cahiers de Fontenay,* nos. 9–10 (March 1978): 79–134.

QUIRINUS

The form Quirinus appears as an adjective used as a noun. Its kinship with Quirites (citizens) had already been recognized by the ancients (see Varro *De Lingua Latina* 5.73: *Quirinus a Quiritibus*). Modern philology plausibly explains how it was formed: Quirinus (**Couiri-no-*) is the adjective that qualifies the god who patronizes the community of the citizens (see G. Dumézil, *Archaic Roman Religion,* p. 246).

Quirinus ranked third in the archaic triad of Jupiter-Mars-Quirinus, and like his two divine associates, he had his own priest, the *flamen Quirinalis.* Significantly, the situation of Quirinus within the Roman triad recurred in the Umbrian triad in which Vofionus, his counterpart, holds the same rank. In fact, the semantic equivalence of the two names has been convincingly demonstrated (see G. Dumézil, *Archaic Roman Religion,* p. 149, no. 2), so well that the two series (Roman and Iguvine), both of which also include Jupiter and Mars, are entirely parallel. The god had been honored since early antiquity on the hill that bears his name, in a *sacellum* located near the Porta Quirinalis (Festus, p. 303 L.). This *sacellum* gave way to a temple built in 293 B.C. by L. Papirius Cursor. The Quirinalia, the festival that bears the name of the god in it, fell on 17 February in the cycle of the oldest festivals in the liturgical calendar. It coincided with the last day of the Fornacalia that were devoted to the roasting of the grain (this day was called *dies stultorum* because it gave the *stulti,* or "scatterbrains," who had missed their curia's scheduled day of roasting, a chance to recover the loss). This brings into sharper focus the vocation of a god whose duty was to watch over supplies and the material well-being of the community.

However, this god, whose functional profile seems fairly clear as far as very early times are concerned, was open to many ambiguities in historical times. First of all, he is classed among the "Sabine" deities whom Titus Tatius is supposed to have introduced into Rome (see Varro *Ling.* 5.74). A "historical" presentation stamped with ethnic coloration has tended to turn Quirinus into a Sabine symmetrical with Mars. Thus, ancient historiography attributed the first twelve Salii, the Salii Palatini, to Mars Gradivus (Livy 1.20.4) and the other twelve, the Salii Collini, to Quirinus (Dionysius of Halicarnassus, *Antiquitates Romanae* 2.70.1 and 3.32.4).

The outcome was a second ambiguity, of a functional kind. Once "syncretism had been brought about after the reconciliation of the Romans and the Sabines," it was necessary to define and distribute the respective tasks of each god. Hence the formulas written down by Servius: "When Mars rages uncontrolled (*saevit*), he is called Gradivus; when he is calm (*tranquillus*), he is called Quirinus" (Servius Danielis on *Aeneid* 1.292). Later in his text, the same commentator accentuates the contrast even more explicitly: "Quirinus is the Mars who presides over peace and is worshiped inside the city, for the Mars of war (*belli Mars*) has his temple outside the city" (Servius Danielis on *Aen.* 6.859).

But this distribution was probably too subtle to be understood clearly. The proof is that when the Greeks tried to "translate" Quirinus, all they could come up with was a surname of Ares: Enyalius, "the bellicose," is the Greek name which serves as the *interpretatio graeca* of Quirinus from Polybius (3.25.6) to Dionysius of Halicarnassus (2.48, 9.60).

One last ambiguity stems from the assimilation of Romulus to Quirinus. When was the founder-king of the city promoted to god? Historians have disagreed on the date. G. Dumézil (*ARR,* p. 249) argues that it was at the beginning of the third century B.C. It may be true that the Romulus-Quirinus assimilation was still presented by Cicero (*De Natura Deorum* 2.62) as a special tradition: *Romulum quem quidam eundem esse Quirinum putant* ("Romulus who, *according to some,* is identical with Quirinus"). By the time of Augustus, however, it was no longer an issue. Thus, Virgil refers to it in the *Aeneid* (1.292). (In the *Georgics* 3.27, the poet applied the expression *victor Quirinus* to Octavius, who was not yet Augustus; this fact may be connected with the initiative taken around the same time by certain senators who proposed the surname "Romulus" for the *Divi filius* [see Suetonius *Divus Augustus* 7.4].) In any event, the assimilation of Romulus to Quirinus is the result of the same process that earned Aeneas the privilege of being identified with Jupiter Indiges after his disappearance from the face of the earth (Livy 1.2.6).

Quirinus. Paris, Bibliothèque nationale, Cabinet des Médailles. Photo BN.

These ambiguities of Quirinus blur rather oddly in the light of comparative analysis, which assigns to Quirinus the role of the "third function." If the god is the patron of prosperity and fertility, we can understand how he may be said to be of "Sabine origin," since the Sabines were regarded as specialists in this area. We can understand how his priest, the *flamen Quirinalis,* could intervene in the various cults of this domain (Larentia: see Aulus Gellius *Noctes Atticae* 7.7.7; Robigo, the deity of the "blight of grain": see Ovid *Fasti* 4.910ff.; Consus, the god of "harvesting": see Tertullian *De Spectaculis* 5). Finally, we may begin to see both the opposition and the complementarity of Mars and Quirinus, of the *milites* and the *Quirites.* Following Jean Bayet, G. Dumézil (*ARR,* p. 260) draws our attention to a telling passage from the *Commentarii Consulares,* copied by Varro (*Ling.* 6.88). This document shows that the contrast between *Quirites* (citizens) and *exercitus* (army) must be of long standing and that it has legal and political implications (for example, the contrast between the *comitia curiata* of a civil nature and the *comitia centuriata* of a military nature).

R.S./g.h.

Silvanus

The name of Silvanus is derived from *silva,* "forest," and appears to be a nominalized adjective. This seemingly obvious form has awakened doubts among exegetes. Some reject it outright, among them Deecke (*Etrusk. Forsch.*, vol. 4, p. 54), who proposed that Silvanus is derived from the Etruscan Selvans. Others contend that this "adjective" must have been the epithet of another god. Thus, following Ursinus, philologists have taken Mars Silvanus as it appears in Cato's text (*De Agricultura* 83) to be a unitary expression. Wissowa (*Ruk*^{2}, p. 213) considered Silvanus a qualifier of the Silvicola Faunus.

We need not accept all of these hypotheses, nor need we discuss here the Etruscan Selvans, which may well be borrowed from the Latin (see Georges Dumézil, *Archaic Roman Religion,* p. 616). And H. Keil proved decisively that the two names in Mars Silvanus were grouped in an asyndeton for "Mars and Silvanus" (*Commentarius in Catonis . . . librum,* Leipzig 1894, p. 110). Cato pointed out that offerings meant for both gods could be placed in the same receptacle, *in unam vas.* So to make Silvanus a qualifier for Faunus seems rather gratuitous. Virgil (*Aeneid* 10.551) specifically wrote "Silvicola Faunus" and not "Silvanus Faunus."

Despite a common bond with the forest, the two gods differ in more ways than one. Silvanus, and not Faunus, was chosen by Plautus (*Aulularia* 674, 676, 766) and by Accius (cited in Cicero *De natura deorum* 2.89) to serve as the Latin counterpart of the Greek god Pan. Faunus has a reputation for acts of gallantry, whereas Silvanus is characterized by a clear allergy to women. No women are allowed to be present at his ceremonies, though a freeman or a slave may celebrate them (Cato loc. cit.). Silvanus was so frightening to young women in childbirth that "three guardian gods were placed on duty, represented by three men who made the rounds of the house at night, so that the god Silvanus would not come in to torment them during the night" (Varro cited by Augustine, *De Civitate Dei* 6.9.2).

The forest was Silvanus's domain. That is why the ceremony celebrated in his honor in daylight took place *in silva* (Cato loc. cit.). It was in the forest of Arsia, *ex silva Arsia,* that the voice of Silvanus was heard by the Romans in 503 B.C. heralding their victory over the Etruscans (Livy 2.7.2). Plautus (*Aulularia* 674) refers to a "forest of Silvanus (*Silvani lucus*) outside the walls at a distance, all overgrown by a willow grove." Even if the allusion in the original Greek is to one of "Pan's caves," the information given by Plautus retains its value. In describing the grove near Caere "girded like a small valley by a belt of black fir trees," Virgil (*Aeneid* 8.600) indicates that "it was consecrated by the old Pelasgians to Silvanus, the god of the fields and the herd."

This last definition (*arvorum pecorisque deus*) might come as something of a surprise unless we remember that Italic forestlands included clearings suitable for grazing and cultivation. This further explains the association of Mars and Silvanus in Cato's *votum* (loc. cit.; on the respective roles of the two gods, see Dumézil, *ARR,* pp. 235–36). To the extent that Silvanus is the patron god of the sylvan pasture, he is the protector of cattle; as the guardian of the family estate, he extends his protection to the fields and their outer reaches (cf. *Silvanus domesticus:* examples cited by Wissowa, *Ruk*^{2}, p. 214; *Silvanus tutor finium:* Horace *Epodi* 2.22). But at the height of the Augustan Age, he *also* remained the "shaggy god of the thickets" (*horridi dumeta Silvani:* Horace *Carmina* 3.29.22–23).

Thus, Silvanus presents an original profile. He enjoyed no public cult. He had neither temple, nor festival, nor official priest. He was honored on a strictly private basis. It was the syncretist wave that blurred his otherwise strong personality; the poets multiplied the Silvani following the example of the Fauni so that they too might take part in the joyful procession of nymphs and satyrs (Ovid *Metamorphoses* 1.193).

R.S./g.h.

Venus

Venus may well be the most original creation of the Roman pantheon. Originally the term was merely a neuter noun, like *genus* and *opus.* The word is part of a remarkable semantic series *venus-venia-venerari* (sometimes *venerare* in Plautus) which is comparable to the series *genus-genius-generare* (see the article "Genius," above). The use of the verb derived from this neuter **venus, venerari* (<**venes-ari*) in Plautus and the authors of the Republican era shows that it is exclusively reserved for the religious realm. What does it signify? It does not lend itself to a direct and exhaustive translation. The way Plautus uses *veneror ut* (which is not retained in classical usage) suggests the following transposition: "I exert [on some deity] a spell [to obtain something] so that . . ."

In this sense, the verb conveys an attitude of seduction toward the gods, an attitude of unconditional confidence that distinguishes this type of prayer from the contractual type, based on the legal postulate *dabo cum dederis* ("I shall give when you have given"). The persuasive charm that the *venerans* uses on the gods corresponds to the correlative *venia* that has the meaning "grace" or "favor" (this word comes from "the technical vocabulary of the pontiffs," according to Schol. Dan. *Aen.* 1.519).

The neuter **venus,* which was set in the preeminent religious verb, *venerari,* was personified, in keeping with the Roman genius for deifying abstractions. This metamorphosis, which must have taken place in Lavinium (see the author's book *La religion romaine de Vénus,* pp. 75–83), came about with a shift from neuter to feminine. The Greek Aphrodite and the Etruscan Turan had certainly not been strangers to this process of deification. But the process remains unique in that nowhere else has the root **ven-,* which is attested in Oscan, Venetian, and Hittite references (see *La famille sémantique des mots apparentés à Vénus* in *R.C.D.R.*), resulted in a deity (the Oscan counterpart to the Latin *Venus* is *Herentas,* formed from a different root, **her-,* "to wish.").

The promotion to divine status (from the neuter **venus* to the goddess Venus) was enhanced by the goddess's encounter with the Trojan legend, which exalted the *Aeneadum Genetrix,* the "mother of the descendants of Aeneas," into the role of tutelary mother. The myth corresponded faithfully

Venus on the sea shell. Pompeian fresco. Photo Boudot-Lamotte.

(one time does not establish a pattern) to the rite: it made explicit in discursive language the toll levied by the *venia deum,* "the favor of the gods," that the *venerans* Roman imposed and collected. It suggested that the Roman citizen was privileged in this respect, since the specialist in the *captatio veniae* mediated between the Romans descended from Aeneas and the gods. That is what lies behind the famous declarations of the Romans in which they claim the title of "the most religious people in the world" (Cicero *De natura deorum* 2.3.8; *De haruspicum responsis* 9.19). These professions of *pietas* and *veneratio* implied the hope of obtaining *pacem veniamque deum,* "the favor and grace of the gods," as Livy frequently put it.

The tutelary role of Venus is verified in the official religion. She is associated with the cult of Jupiter in the Vinalia, which are supposed to have been instituted by Aeneas. The first temple founded in her honor (at the beginning of the third century B.C.) is dedicated to Venus Obsequens (Venus the propitious). It had been promised by Q. Fabius Gurges in the heat of battle in 295 B.C., in the hope of obtaining victory over the Samnites.

The role of Venus as an intercessor crystallized dramatically in the third century at the time of the first two Punic wars. During the first, the Romans lost no time in withdrawing the goddess of Eryx from the control of the Punic adversary and placing themselves under her protection; to do this, they capitalized on the Trojan legend that was very much alive among the Elymians and on their victorious resistance at the summit of Mount Eryx.

Indeed, syncretism served the Roman cause well. It furthered the victorious mystique in Sicily by assimilating Aphrodite Erycina to Venus. The Romans also had recourse to the *same* goddess during the second war against the *same* enemy. And in this same context the association between Venus and Mars took hold during the lectisternium of 217 B.C.

Mars and Venus. Pompeian fresco. Naples, National Museum. Photo Giraudon.

The "Trojan" interpretation of the goddess of Mount Eryx explains that the cult of Venus Erycina involved a double religious status in Rome. On the Capitol, inside the pomerium, Venus Erycina was venerated as a Roman goddess; outside the pomerium, near the Porta Collina, she called to mind her foreign origin.

The lesson was not lost in later times. Venus came to follow Latin lines in her propitiatory role, while yielding to extensions of Mediterranean syncretism. Thus, Sulla pretended to recognize Aphrodite of Aphrodisias as an ally of the Romans. He even succeeded in having the oracle of Delphi validate the religious claims of the Romans descended from Aeneas.

By the first century B.C., the only novelty was that political adventurers rose to power and sought to turn the situation to personal advantage. Venus Felix (Sulla), Venus Victrix (Pompey), Venus Genetrix (Caesar)—each attempted to reconcile himself with the goddess by giving her an epithet that marked her with an original label. Caesar, who claimed a direct descent, was the best placed to exploit the Trojan mystique for his own profit. Through the cult of Venus Genetrix, he gave definitive form to the national *credo* that proclaimed Venus to be Mother of the Romans and Mother of the Caesars. The improvements that Augustus, Caesar's adoptive son, made on his father's canvas do not lack respect for the essential dogma. By then, the theological work was complete.

R.S./g.h.

Vesta

The name of the goddess appears to be a derivative of the root *ə$_1$*eu-*, "to burn," with the archaic suffix *-ta*. It supplied two stems (E. Benveniste, quoted by G. Dumézil, *Rituels indo-européens à Rome* from the collection "Études et Commentaires" [Paris 1954], vol. 19, pp. 33–34). Stem 1 of this root (*ə$_1$*eu-s*) is found in the Greek *euō*, the Latin *uro*, "I burn"; stem 2, *ə$_1$*u-es*, is found in the Latin *Vesta* and probably in the Greek *Hestia*.

Cicero (*De natura deorum* 2.27.67) asserts the semantic kinship of the two goddesses, but he believed that Vesta had been borrowed from the Greeks. In contrast with the "devouring" Volcanus, Vesta exercised a salutary action on "altars and hearths" (*ad aras et focos pertinet:* ibid. 2.27.67).

The shrine of Vesta was a round building "similar to a globe; thus the goddess was identified with the earth" (Festus, p. 321 L.; see Ovid *Fasti* 6.267). This shape distinguished it from the temple, which was quadrangular and oriented to the four cardinal points. The comparative method sheds much light on this contrast. Vedic religion distinguished the "fire of the master of the house," which is "this world" and "as such is round" (G. Dumézil, *Archaic Roman Religion*, pp. 312–13), from the "fire of the offerings . . . whose smoke bears the gifts of men to the gods . . . it is oriented to the cardinal points, and consequently is quadrangular" (ibid. p. 313).

Vesta, who bears the official name *Vesta publica populi Romani*, constitutes *quasi focum urbis* (the hearth of the city: Cicero *De legibus* 2.29). She is the eternal flame rekindled only once a year, on 1 March, i.e., at the beginning of the ancient calendar year (Ovid *Fasti* 3.143–44). If by misfortune the fire entrusted to the care of the vestals were allowed to go out, "the virgins were whipped by the pontifex, and were required by custom to rekindle it by the friction of 'fertile' wood (*felicis materiae*) until one of them was able to carry the resulting fire into the sanctuary in a bronze sieve" (Festus, p. 94 L.).

This "eternal flame" therefore had a symbolic value that was reinforced by the presence of sacred talismans (see Livy 26.27.14; Ovid *Fasti* 6.445). Among the talismans was the Palladium, a statue of Pallas that was thought to have come from Troy (see Cicero *Pro Scauro* 48). In the "eternal flames of Vesta" (*aeternis Vestae ignibus*) and in the Palladium that was considered the preeminent talisman among the *pignora fatalia* (Ovid loc. cit.), Rome saw the proof of its power (see Livy 5.52.7).

Maintaining the "primordial" fire was primarily the responsibility of the six vestal virgins, the priestesses who were sworn to absolute chastity for the entire duration of their service (Ovid *Fasti* 6.283ff.). They also kept watch over the talismans, or *pignora*, which were kept in the *penus Vestae* (Festus, p. 296 L.), the most secret part of the sanctuary. In the front of the sanctuary, the *penus exterior* (Festus, p. 152 L.), the vestals kept a reserve supply of the various ingredients that they prepared for the celebration of sacrifices: *muries* (Festus, p. 152 L.), or brine used for salting, and *mola*, the sacred flour. We know that the heads of sacrificial animals were sprinkled (*immolare*) with *mola salsa* before the sacrifice.

In general, Vesta took part in all sacrifices. Cicero (*De natura deorum* 2.27.67) points out that she was invoked last of all in "all prayers and sacrifices," just as Janus was, by contrast, first on the list of divinities. It is interesting to note that this liturgical rule is the exact opposite of the Greek custom which counseled "starting with Hestia," *aph Hestias archesthai*. Curiously, Ovid (*Fasti* 6.303–4) treats Vesta in the Greek manner.

The festival of the goddess, the Vestalia, took place on 9 June according to the ancient cycle of the liturgical calendar. From 7 to 15 June, the sanctuary of Vesta was open exclusively to women, who were allowed to enter barefoot. On the last day, the sanctuary was ritually swept. The end of this operation was marked on the calendar by the letters *Q(uando) ST(ercus) D(elatum) F(as)*, meaning "Once the dung is carried away the sacred day is over." This ancient note, which seems out of place in the then urbanized setting, must reflect a time "when an encamped pastoral society had to clean the *stercus* of its herds from the location of its sacred fire" (Georges Dumézil, *Archaic Roman Religion*, p. 318).

This goddess, who went back to the very origins of the city, had long escaped the widespread anthropomorphism of the Etruscans and the Greeks. Ovid (*Fasti* 6.295–98) points out that even in his time the *ignis Vestae* (the expression comes from Festus, 94 L.), being self-sufficient, had no ritual statue. Cicero (*Nat. D.* 3.80) mentions a statue of Vesta in front of which the Pontifex Maximus Q. Mucius Scaevola had been massacred, but it must have been an honorary statue placed in the vestibule or in front of the sanctuary.

Through syncretism, however, Vesta was considered the counterpart of the Greek goddess Hestia. In this capacity, she formed a couple with Vulcan-Hephaestus during the lectisternium of 217 B.C. In this association the "beneficent fire" and the "devouring fire" were united for the greater good of the city.

R.S./g.h.

Banquet of the Vestals. Altar of the Pietà. Rome. Palazzio dei Conservatori. Photo Barbara Malter.

Temple of Vesta. Paris, Bibliothèque nationale, Cabinet des Médailles. Photo BN.

Virgil's Religious Vision

Every true reader of Virgil dreams of forgetting for a moment the vast literature that has been written about the poet over so many centuries and of getting at the secret of his fascinating presence. This need seems even more compelling when his religious vision is at issue. This vision paradoxically seems to survive the dead gods, as if it had managed to preserve for posterity the essential component of a spirituality that went far beyond the structures of the ancient city, and as if it had managed to escape the rather negative prejudice of many toward Roman religion, which is often said to be dry and formalistic.

To what can we attribute Virgil's privilege? It cannot be explained simplistically by resorting to the three-tiered classification devised by Varro,[1] which distinguished the gods of poets, the gods of philosophers, and the gods of the city. Nor does it demonstrate any system—far from it—since the poet developed from the little poems of the *Catalepton* to the overwhelming fresco of the depiction of the underworld in book 4 of the *Aeneid:* the disciple of the Epicurean Siro became a bard with a Stoic accent.

We will have to distinguish between the circumstantial element, through which Virgil was marked by his own time and place, and the eternal element, through which he transcended the bondage of his historical slot. To that end, it may prove useful to follow the poet on the three different levels of the religious customs of his time, his own religious sensibility, and his philosophical and eschatological speculations.

I. Virgil and Roman Tradition

Virgil (71–19 B.C.) lived in an unusual period that witnessed the end of the civil wars and the establishment of the Roman Empire, when Octavian, victorious at Actium in 31 B.C., was proclaimed Augustus by the Senate in 27 B.C. Henceforth Rome assumed the entire Greek heritage. Religion was dominated by a syncretism that not only equated the principal Roman deities with their Hellenic counterparts, but went on to give the deities of Rome a dimension of mythological storytelling borrowed from those counterparts.

It is therefore not surprising to find Virgil, true to the custom of his time, indiscriminately mixing old Italic deities with Greek gods: Silvanus is flanked by Pan and the nymphs (Virgil *Georgics* 2.494), and Pales the goddess of herdsmen and their flocks is associated with Apollo and Pan (ibid. 3.1–2).

Greek mythology made it possible for Virgil to give the gods profiles and legends that made them available for poetic creation. Thus, Neptune, who was only the governing god of the waters within the framework of the Roman liturgy,[2] travels on the high seas in a wheeled chariot in Virgil's epic (Virgil *Aeneid* 1.147–55). When he notices that the sea has been stirred up on the orders of Aeolus, "He gazes forth on the deep with a pacific mien" (ibid. 1.127; trans. C. Day Lewis, *The Aeneid of Virgil* [Garden City, New York, 1952], throughout this article), and he rebukes the winds, saying, "Do you really dare, you Winds, without my divine assent to confound earth and sky, and raise this riot of water?" (ibid. 133–34). The allusion is a discrete recollection of the Hesiodic legend that makes the Winds the sons of the Titan Astraeus, who rebelled against Zeus. It also invokes the hierarchical principle by virtue of which the realm of the sea belongs to Neptune and not to "Aeolus, the king of the Winds."

Consequently, while he still used the mythological storytelling that somehow assimilates Neptune to Poseidon, Virgil was able to keep a certain distance. Neptune intervenes on behalf of Aeneas, the victim of the storm, whereas Poseidon *enosichthōn,* "the shaker of the depths," displays a constant hostility toward Odysseus in Homer. He intervenes in the sarcastic tone of a superior officer of the Roman army when he reminds Aeolus of the limits of his competence: "His domain is the mountain rock. . . . Let Aeolus be king of that castle and let him keep the winds locked up in its dungeon" (ibid. 140–41).

Mythology supplied the poet with those elements of the supernatural epic that are indispensable for the literary story line. Often this mythology had only a decorative value that the poet uses with a dash of nonchalance. Thus, Venus, who elsewhere plays an essential role in religious ideology, benefited from all the Mediterranean heritage that belonged to Aphrodite. She is the sovereign ruler of the island of Cythera and of the shrines of Amathus, Idalia, and Paphus on Cyprus (ibid. 10.51). According to the interlocutor, she is regarded as "the daughter of the deep" (ibid. 5.800–881, where she is summoned by Neptune), or "the daughter of Jupiter" (ibid. 1.256; 10.30, where she has to deal with Jupiter).

We must not forget that Virgil was unable to finish the *Aeneid* (in his will he had ordered it destroyed because it was incomplete). Although it is possible that in the final analysis he would have adopted a single genealogical linkage, the initial choices (the Hesiodic or the Homeric legend) are obviously inspired by an aesthetic of correspondences whereby the god of the sea faces the daughter of the waves, and the sovereign god faces his "beloved daughter" (*Nata,* ibid. 1.256, highlights the nuance of emotion; *Tua progenies,* 10.30, highlights the nuance of a claim).

This selective aesthetic promoted the blending of mythological elements per se with precise allusions to Roman ritual. These allusions abound to the point where the Roman reader could not feel cut off from familiar territory when he confronted the behavior of Aeneas and his entourage. The hero was idealized by virtue of the backward leap in time, and he was given a sort of halo by a golden legend. But he acted according to the reflexes and religious habits of a contemporary of Virgil. One example: the attention given to the auspices and the prodigies. The traitor Sinon explains to the Trojans that the reason why the Greeks intend to go back to their own country of Argos (ibid. 2.178) is to take the auspices in response to the warnings of the soothsayer Calchas. He is sure of being believed by the Trojans (who are supposed to have a Roman mentality), so common was the practice in the Roman liturgy of taking the auspices again (*auspicia repetere*) in case of failure. Similarly, Venus disguised as a huntress points out to Aeneas "those twelve swans flying in jubilant formation," and tells him of the good omen: it is a sign that his twelve ships, saved from the storm, have reached safe harbor (ibid. 1.393–400).

The same goes for the prodigies. More than in Livy's account, they seem "natural" in a narrative in which the supernatural is part of daily reality. The Trojans no longer hesitate to allow the fatal horse inside their city when they see their priest Laocoön (who had been opposed to it) and his two children choked by two serpents, which then glide away toward the shrine of Athena (ibid. 2.219–27).

A prodigy prevents Aeneas from throwing himself into a hopeless battle: a feathery tongue of flame appears above the head of Ascanius (in Livy 1.39.1, an analogous prodigy designates the child Servius Tullius as heir to the throne). Anchises asks Jupiter to confirm an omen: "From our left hand came a sudden crash of thunder, and a shooting star slid down the sky's dark face, drawing a trail of light behind it" (Virgil *Aen.* 681–94). This accumulation of prodigies (in augury, the left side or *laevum* is favorable) was needed to prevent Aeneas from rushing into a senseless death and to convince his father Anchises to leave Troy. There are many more examples attesting Virgil's knowledge of liturgy, which inspired the admiration of the participants in the *Saturnalia* of Macrobius.

What about theology? How was Virgil to adapt himself to the institutions of the state while avoiding the trap set by the Trojan legend? The triad of Jupiter-Juno-Minerva formed the core of Roman religion, just as the temple of the Capitoline triad occupied the place of honor in every Roman city. Beyond that, the outline of the legend was based on the abandonment of the city of Troy by the gods, particularly by the tutelary divinity Athena-Minerva (the ominous sign was the serpents who murdered Laocoön and took refuge in her shrine), and the declared hostility of Juno toward the Trojans.

Here time has been Virgil's accomplice. Once Jupiter had decreed the destiny of the Trojans—the *fata* that promised that they would found a new Troy—the "reconciliation" of the two goddesses with the Roman descendants of Aeneas was bound to come about in the course of events. Such a turnabout by hostile deities had been anticipated within the regulations of the Roman pontiffs: the procedure of the *evocatio* (the invitation to abandon the city in exchange for a temple in Rome) hastened the fall of the enemy city by depriving it of its protecting deity. Virgil explicitly refers to this when Troy falls (ibid. 2.351–52).

As for Minerva, she wasted no time in leaving the Greeks after their victory. Was she angry because of the theft of her cultic statue, the Palladium (which later became one of the talismans of Rome), which was stolen by Diomedes and Odysseus (ibid. 2.163)? According to the traitor Sinon, this sacrilege was precisely what led the Greeks to offer the horse to the goddess as a replacement (ibid. 2.183–84). This version, involving a trick, leaves the issue unresolved. But in any case, Minerva did not forgive the Greek Ajax for having abducted Cassandra from her sanctuary, where Cassandra had put herself under Minerva's protection during the sack of Troy (ibid. 2.403–15). So Minerva smashed the Greek fleet to pieces as it was returning home (ibid. 1.39–41).

After this, it is not surprising that she should then resume her former role of tutelary goddess of the descendants of Aeneas. With Neptune, Venus, and Mars, she belongs to the group of Roman gods who battled against the "grotesque deities of the Nile" in the scene that depicts the battle of Actium on the shield wrought by Vulcan (ibid. 8.698–700). Thus, the Minerva of the legend has joined the Capitoline goddess of Roman religion.

The change of heart of the *aspera Juno* (ibid. 1.279) is strewn with many more obstacles, even though Jupiter announces immediately (ibid.) his intention to rally behind the cause of Rome in the future. Of course, like other deities, she had a shrine in Troy (ibid. 2.761). But throughout the action of the epic, she is depicted as the relentless enemy of the Trojans.

Why? Because she is the special protectress of Carthage, the city which she prefers to any other dwelling place (ibid. 1.11ff.), and she knows it will be threatened by a future race of Trojan blood. Needless to say, Virgil embellishes the legend with a historical account of the Punic wars. Juno knows in advance (ibid. 1.39) that she will have to bow to fate, but she multiplies the setbacks for the Trojans, starting with the storm that she "ordered" from the king of the winds, Aeolus. The tenacity of the goddess reminds the reader of the three long wars that the Romans and Carthaginians waged with one another for control of the Mediterranean.

The principal examples of the goddess's interventions start with Aeneas's initial contact with King Latinus, who is ready to welcome the Trojans to Italian soil. Minerva inspires Turnus, the king of the Rutulians, to raise the flag of war (ibid. 7.406ff.) and she herself opens the doors of the sanctuary of Janus (ibid. 7.601ff.), a ritual act that openly announces the hostilities (in his testament, Augustus is known to have recalled with pride that he succeeded in *closing* the doors of Janus on three occasions). Yet Aeneas, aware of this animosity, tries to appease the goddess. In accordance with the prophetic announcement, he sacrifices to her the wild sow and the young wild boars that he finds in the forest of Hesperia.

But all for naught. After the unhappy episode of the sojourn of Aeneas in Carthage, in the course of which the goddess tries to cheat fate by making Aeneas marry Queen Dido (ibid. 4.90ff.), she is more than ever determined to postpone the day of reckoning. She intervenes vehemently in favor of Turnus at the assembly of the gods (ibid. 10.63ff.) and does not hesitate to shield him from the dangers of combat (ibid. 10.606ff.).

Minerva makes a final attempt by calling Turnus's sister, Juturna, to come to her brother's rescue (ibid. 12.134ff.), before she obeys Jupiter's command not to do anything more (ibid. 10.804–6). She then obtains Jupiter's promise that by uniting with the Trojans, the Ausonians will keep their language and customs. "All will be Latins . . . . No other nation will pay such reverence to Juno. The goddess bowed and agreed, glad now to change her own policy" (ibid. 12.834–41). Thus the goddess rejoined the Roman cause and the poet recovered the orthodoxy of the official religion.

II. The Originality of Virgil

We cannot overlook the constraints that weighed on the poet: Virgil was subject to the conventions of the epic form that went back to Homer. The ancients had already acknowledged that on the literary level, the *Aeneid* corresponded to both the *Odyssey* (the wanderings of Aeneas in the first six books) and the *Iliad* (the struggles on Italian soil in the last six books). In particular, Virgil had relied on the anthropomorphic polytheism that Varro had repudiated. But although it may not be obvious, he was able to go beyond these contingent frameworks to express his own religious sensibility.

First of all, Virgil's polytheism is not the same as Homer's. Two deities in particular—Jupiter and Venus—break out of the conventional mold, because Virgil reinterpreted them in the light of a new theology. Although the sovereign god, too, inherits the full panoply of Homeric titles,[3] he nonetheless differs from his Greek counterpart in several ways. Though he is a figure of majesty, he is not described in the image of Zeus with his "black brows and ambrosial locks" (Homer *Iliad* 1.538). He has more mystery: a mere sign from him is enough to cause all of Olympus to tremble (Virgil *Aen.* 9.106).

Above all, whereas in Homer Zeus is subordinate to Fate—to the *heimarmenē*—Jupiter exercises real sovereignty: the *fata* become intermingled with his own decrees. There is nothing more instructive than the answer given by Jupiter to Venus when she worries about the fate of her Trojans, victims of the terrible storm: "Fear no more, Cytherea. Take comfort, for your people's destiny is unaltered. . . . I have not changed my mind" (ibid. 1.257–60). The Latin text is even more explicit. The expression *tuorum fata* is later taken up again by the verb *fabor* (by which Jupiter is to reveal the secret of this fate), in visible semantic correspondence to the substantive *fata*. These *fata* consist of the announcement of the reign of Aeneas in Lavinium for three years, the reign of Ascanius in Alba for thirty years, the reign of the kings of Alba for three hundred years, and finally the promise of an eternal reign given to the Romans as "successors to the Trojan nation": *imperium sine fino dedi* ("I gave them an empire without end").[4]

As for the Virgilian Venus, her character is even more marked by this theological metamorphosis. She probably borrowed her smile from Aphrodite when she annexed her Mediterranean sanctuaries. But here we have no scandalous adventures (in Homer, Aphrodite is caught in a blatant act of adultery with Ares); nor do we have any concession to Hellenistic affectation (in Apollonius of Rhodes, Cypris admires herself in a mirror). Venus appears with the dignity appropriate for the mother of the descendants of Aeneas and the future Caesars.[5]

Venus first assumes a maternal role, watching over Aeneas and Ascanius: *mea maxima cura* ("my dearest care": ibid. 1.677). She also assumes the role of a guide; from the time of the departure from Troy, the star of Venus shows Aeneas the way: *matre dea monstrante viam,* Aeneas says to Dido (ibid. 1.382).[6] She assumes the role of intercessor; in books 2 and 10 she pleads the cause of the Trojans before Jupiter or before the assembled gods. This role of intercessor is more than a literary fiction, since it corresponds to certain cultic institutions. By the beginning of the third century B.C., Fabius Gurges had shown his gratitude to Venus Obsequens (the propitious), and in the first century, the cult of Venus Genetrix founded by Julius Caesar illustrated brilliantly the maternal role of the goddess who mediated between the gods and the Romans.[7]

So it is not surprising that Virgil gives Venus a properly theological role, for despite all the syncretism, she always embodied the effective enchantment that is expressed by the preeminent religious verb *venerari.*[8] It is she who obtains from Jupiter the right of the Trojans to come to the end of their trials *in the name of their piety: hic pietatis honos?* ("Is this the reward for being true?" ibid. 1.253). She invokes the piety that is based on an equitable exchange between men and gods, an equity richly deserved by the *pius Aeneas.*[9]

It is Venus who explains to Aeneas the supernatural reasons for the fall of Troy: in the name of *pietas*-equity, Troy had to succumb, for the city was remiss in *pietas* when King Laomedon deprived the gods (Poseidon-Neptune, in particular) of their promised rewards. The "revelation" that Venus makes to Aeneas is explicit: "It is not the beauty of hated Helen, it is not Paris, though you hold him to blame—the gods, the gods, I tell you, are hostile (*divum inclementia, divum*), it's they who have undermined Troy's power and sent it tumbling" (ibid. 2.601–3). When Venus takes the veil of fog from Aeneas's eyes, the hero sees a supernatural vision beyond Neptune, Juno, and Pallas: the vision of Jupiter himself ardently participating in the destruction of Troy.[10]

In this way, Virgil entirely transformed the epic that until that time had been purely narrative (the travels of Odysseus in the *Odyssey,* the episodes of the Trojan War in the *Iliad*) into a spiritual adventure. Jupiter may have condemned ancient Troy, but he was also the guarantor of the resurrection of a new Troy. Virgil creates a striking symbol: whereas Anchises, his limbs paralyzed, represents the misfortune that struck ancient Troy ("For years now I have been lingering, obnoxious to heaven," he cries out)[11] and must die in Sicily rather than entering the promised land, the pious Aeneas, invested with the favor of the gods, is charged with the responsibility of founding the new city. Aeneas is entrusted with a mission.

This is where Virgil expressed a preoccupation crucial to the Roman mentality: since men are necessarily dependent

Rome: relief of the altar of the Pietà representing a scene of sacrifice. The head of the victim is held up by a kneeling assistant. Behind the victim are two lictors; on the right is a flute player. Photo Alinari-Giraudon.

on heaven, it is paramount that they not lose the benevolence and grace of the gods, *pacem veniamque deum,* an expression that recurs frequently in Livy. Evoking the relentlessness of the battle of Troy, Aeneas cries out: "Ah well, there's no trusting the gods for anything, once they're against you!"[12]

Any error committed against the gods triggers their resentment, *ira,* and demands expiation. That is why the length of the civil wars of the first century B.C. finally brought about a religious anguish: could Rome have been struck by a divine curse? One had to wonder whether a kind of original sin were not weighing heavily on the destiny of Rome. In book 1 of the *Georgics* (written around 36 B.C.), after a fervent prayer—"Gods of our homeland, invoked from the beginning, and you Romulus and venerable Vesta"[13]—Virgil implores the protecting deities of Rome to allow the young Octavian to devote himself to the common welfare. He justifies his prayer by adding: "We have long atoned for the perjury of Laomedon's Troy with our blood."[14]

Horace does not refer to the Trojan fault when he expresses the same anguish. He places "the original sin" at the origins of Rome, in the fratricide of Remus by Romulus: "A cruel fate has been awaiting Romans since the sacrilegious murder of the brother."[15] Whatever reference is adopted, the idea of the necessity for an expiation weighed on the minds of everyone.

But there is a counterbalance: the assurance that piety gives of receiving the favor of the gods. It was not without reason that from among all the possible epithets, Virgil chose *pius* to describe Aeneas. This virtue of the Trojan chief was the key to his success. The poet again captured a fundamental belief of the Romans. Recall the verse that Horace addresses to the Roman: "Because you submit to the gods, you command."[16] Cicero has his spokesman Cotta pronounce an even more explicit speech: "Rome would never have been able to reach such grandeur if it had not enjoyed the extreme indulgence of the immortal gods."[17] Elsewhere, Cicero claimed on behalf of the Roman people the title of the "most religious people in the world."[18]

Consequently we can appreciate the magnificent song of hope which, with time, was enlarged upon in Virgil's work. The fourth *Bucolic* (written ca. 40 B.C.) heralded the coming of a new golden age with the imminent birth of a messianic child.[19] But this hope was still fragile, fettered by "the persistent traces of the crime."[20] In book 6 of the *Aeneid,* the ghost of Anchises makes the following triumphant revelation to Aeneas (Augustus has been ruling for many years): "Caesar is there and all Ascanius's posterity, who shall pass beneath the arch of day. And here, here is the man, the promised one you know of—Caesar Augustus, son of a god, destined to rule where Saturn ruled of old in Latium, and there bring back the age of gold."[21] Henceforth, hope did not rest on a *nascenti puero;* rather it became incarnate with the coming of a prince, Augustus, who considered himself the representative of Jupiter on earth.[22] All the vows had thus been kept and Anchises was able to formulate the celebrated program: "But, Roman, never forget that government is your medium! Be this your art: to practice men in the habit of peace, generosity to the conquered, and firmness against aggressors."[23]

III. The Universality of Virgil

A question now arises. Virgil has appeared to us to be profoundly imbued with "Romanness" both in the choice of his themes and in the expression of his feeling. But where is the universality which made him go beyond the narrow limits of the ancient framework?

Virgil's polytheism has shown itself different from Homer's Olympus. The fact that Jupiter acquired his full sovereignty by determining the *fata* instead of submitting to them is not insignificant. His prestige is no longer challenged by the other gods (as Zeus battled with his rivals). Thus, the polytheism is shifting, if not toward monotheism, at least toward the henotheism that asserts the supremacy of one god among several.

The poet lets slip some expressions that may provide an illustration: *Dabit* deus *his quoque finem* ("The god will end these sorrows too": Virgil *Aen.* 1.199), Aeneas cries out at the height of the storm. This invocation could be translated without revision into the form of a modern prayer: "God will also end our trials."

Although this god reminds us of the Jupiter Optimus Maximus of the official religion, he embodies above all the idea of providence. This is the meaning of Jupiter's action in the *Georgics.* Apparently the god whom Virgil designates here solely by the name of Pater[24] made the human condition more painful, since, when he became successor to Saturn, he replaced the Golden Age with the Iron Age. But he sought in this way to rescue the intelligence of mortals from a passive torpor (*gravi veterno*), and to inspire it instead with a desire to live "so that necessity would gradually bring about, thanks to experience, variety in the arts and crafts."[25]

This is far from the fatality of a hostile nature which leaves man helpless, as in Lucretius. "God helps those who help themselves" is the new message. At the same time, it is far from a nostalgic dream of the Golden Age, an age in which man has nothing to do, as "the earth produces everything liberally,"[26] while "the hardwood oak trees ooze with honey dew."[27] And although Virgil later evokes a new Golden Age in the *Aeneid,* that Golden Age differs from the mythical one by the direct connection of man—although a "providential" man—with the work of Providence.

From this point of view, the *Aeneid* constitutes a hymn to the glory of Providence that leads the chosen people through all sorts of trials and then, at the end of their wanderings, to the promised land. Faith in Providence presupposes the acceptance of trials on the part of the faithful. Are these trials not the ransom of expiation for the "Trojan error"?

In this context, the extraordinary resignation of the Virgilian heroes can be understood. When the best sons of Troy fall at the hands of the Greeks, the poet sometimes seems to delight in emphasizing the scandalous character of their death. "Then Rhipeus fell, he who of all the Trojans was most fair-minded, the one who was most regardful of justice: the god's ways are inscrutable . . . . And Panthus—not all his goodness, nor the headband he wore as Apollo's priest saved him from death."[28]

When King Priam sees his son Polites slaughtered before his very eyes, he cannot help but appeal to heaven: *si qua est caelo pietas* ("If there is any justice in heaven").[29] This is a cry of human distress, but it is in vain, because the decree is ruthless: whatever may be their *personal* piety, the Trojans cannot escape the *collective* punishment of the condemned city. Priam's appeal has a tragically derisory tone, since the penalty inflicted upon Troy by heaven results precisely from the violation of *pietas* by the ancestor. The fallen king's fate is therefore of little importance. However, Providence is attending, since the essential is saved: Aeneas receives promises for the future. Thus Virgil invites the reader to a meditation that goes beyond the bounds of an era. Is the world governed by a benevolent Providence, or is it subject to blind chance? To what extent is the individual responsible for collective transgressions?

In his inquiry into fate, the poet was led to ask questions that Roman religion was not accustomed to raise: What is death? What is the meaning of the world?

The liturgical calendar did not forget the ceremonies in honor of the dead. It even had two kinds of celebrations: one was the Feralia, held on 21 February, which called for offerings and libations on the tombs of the deceased; the other was the Lemuria, which was repeated on three separate days—9, 11, and 13 May—and which was intended to expel deadly ghosts (Lemures) that could haunt a home.[30] But whether it was a liturgy of veneration or a rite of exorcism, none of these ceremonies provided any insight into the world of the beyond.

Faced with this silence, Virgil was forced to sketch an eschatology that took into account philosophical ideas from Greece but was not altogether alien to Italic traditions. He proposed to resort to the offices of the Sibyl in order to guide Aeneas to the netherworld. By this choice, he not only left behind the modest Homeric model[31] but he also gave new life and strength to a venerable figure: the Sibyl was supposed to have inspired the *Sibylline Books* which were consulted ritually by the Roman authorities on the order of the Senate.

First, the Sibyl demands that Aeneas make a preparatory sacrifice and also that he acquire a mysterious object, the golden bough. Then he can descend into Pluto's kingdom of Shades by entering the cave of Avernus. Here commentators have scrutinized, and will continue to scrutinize, the possible influences on the poet.[32] But Virgil guarded himself from all rigid dogmatism. He describes a vision of hell; he offers a description to his reader, who will be gradually initiated into a new teaching.

The novelty is the idea of a distributive justice in the kingdom of the Shades. Until Virgil, the only distinction familiar to Romans was the separation of the dead into the *Di parentes,* who from the first century are called the *Di Manes*—the spirits of the ancestors considered benevolent—and the Lemures or Larvae, evil spirits. This distinction is alien to any idea of merit or demerit.

Aeneas, guided by the Sibyl, first discovers the *Campi lugentes* (fields of wailing), the abode of the dead who have not fulfilled their destiny (Virgil *Aen.* 6.418–547). He then manages to avoid visiting Tartarus, but the Sibyl describes it to him as the place of torture reserved for the criminals of mythology and history (ibid. 6.548–625).[33] The two of them then arrive at the palace of Pluto, where Aeneas sees the golden bough. A little further on they discover "a happy place, the green and genial glades where the fortunate live, the home of the blessed spirits," the Elysian fields (ibid. 6.635–65).

There Aeneas meets Anchises, who reveals to his son the secrets of the universe. Virgil was visibly inspired here by various influences. The world presented as "sustained by a spirit within" (ibid. 6.725–28) conforms to the teachings of the Stoics. The souls who drink the water of Lethe and forget their past lives recall Plato. The souls who "for a thousand years" undergo successive reincarnations until their final purification recall the Orphics and the metempsychosis of Pythagoras.

Does this mean that Virgil was content to juxtapose miscellaneous elements like the multicolored pieces of a mosaic? Aside from the finishing touches that he might have made to his unfinished poem, the general impression is altogether different. Virgil suggests and proposes. His role is to be a guide for the reader, as the Sibyl is for Aeneas. The fiction of the kingdom of the Shades has a symbolic value: everything remains wrapped in mystery.

It is precisely because Virgil knew how to respect the mystery of things that he maintained a power of incantation. He owes this first of all to a gift of expression commensurate with his genius. It is impossible to exaggerate the allusive power of Virgilian verse, which cannot be conveyed in translation.

But above all he bequeathed to posterity the themes that survived the ruin of the ancient city. Some of these themes reappeared in Christian teachings: the idea of an original sin that affects a community; the idea of reward for one's merits after death; the nostalgia for a lost Golden Age; the reconciliation of humanity with a Providence-God; mankind's hope of reaching a new Golden Age or paradise.

None of these themes had a greater impact than the one that would be provoked during the Middle Ages by the messianism of the fourth *Bucolic.* Thanks to the magic of the Virgilian word, expressions wrought for the Roman context were again ready for use, as if their thin shell had burst open under the delayed effect of a time bomb. *Iam redit et Virgo* ("Lo the Virgin has returned": *B.* 4.6);[34] *Iam nova progenis caelo demittitur alto* ("Lo an exceptional child comes down from on high": *B.* 4.7);[35] *Si qua manent sceleris vestigia nostri* ("If traces of our crime remain": *B.* 4.13);[36] *Ille deum vitam accipiet* ("He shall attain divine life": *B.* 4.15).[37] For new generations, all these expressions seemed charged with a Christmas message, to the glory of "the child to be born" (*nascenti puero: B.* 4.8).[38]

Thus Virgil enjoyed a new prestige: he took his place among the prophets who foretold the coming of Christ. In fact, this stirring mirage can be explained both by the fascination of the words and by the breadth of Virgil's vision, for the authentic poet belongs to his time even while he transcends it.

By the fifth century A.D., the African-born author Fulgentius[39] undertook a strictly allegorical reading of Virgil that neglected the subject matter of the narrative in favor of its symbolic meaning. Thus he gave three words of the first verse of the *Aeneid*—*arma, virum,* and *primus*—the meaning "to have," "to govern," and "to adorn," these three words referring to "nature," "science," and "happiness." The fashion was set.

Though we cannot here follow the successive commentators on Virgil, it would be fitting to reserve a special place for Dante, who saluted Virgil as "his master and his inspirer."[40] The poet from Mantua became the guide to the poet from Florence in the *Divine Comedy.* When he was plunged in anguish on Good Friday of the year 1300, Dante saw himself "in the middle of a dark wood," whereupon Beatrice sent to his aid the ghost of his brilliant predecessor. Virgil carried out his mission by guiding Dante through the netherworld and purgatory; and then, with great delicacy,[41] he entrusted this mission to Beatrice at the gates of paradise. Nothing proves the universality of Virgil's vision better than this consecration, across the ages, by Dante. We are among those who believe that in the long chain of admirers, Dante was not the last.[42]

R.S./g.h.

NOTES

1. Varro, cited by Augustine, *C.D.,* 6, 5.

2. The festival of the Neptunalia was on 23 July. See the convincing exegesis of G. DUMÉZIL, *Fêtes romaines d'été et d'automne* (Paris 1975), 25–31.

3. Among the following expressions, some are close to the Homeric model (not to mention *regnator Olympi*), while others are more novel: *divum pater atque hominum rex* ("father of the gods and king of men": *Aen.* 1.65; 2.648; 10.2, etc.); *hominum rerumque aeterna potestas* ("eternal power that reigns over men and the world": ibid. 10.18); *pater omnipotens, rerum cui prima potestas* ("all-powerful father, sovereign power of the world": ibid. 10.100); *hominum rerumque repertor* ("creator of men and the world": ibid. 12.829).

4. This text is not invalidated by the role of arbiter that Jupiter takes in book 10 of the *Aeneid.* Grappling with the recriminations of Juno, he proclaims his neutrality (verse 112) . . . knowing that "the Fates will find an ending"—*fata viam invenient* (verse 113).

5. Thence the *virginal* aspect under which she appears to Aeneas (*Aen.* 1.315); the dignity of her clothing ("the folds of her robe flowed down to her feet": ibid. 1.404): she evokes not a nude Aphrodite of Praxiteles but the draped Venus of Arcesilaus that Caesar placed in the temple of Venus Genitrix.

6. See *Aen.* 2.801. In the commentary on this passage, Servius Danielis notes that, according to Varro, "the star of Venus was always visible to Aeneas until he arrived at the country of the Laurentes; after he arrived, it was no longer visible: thus he knew that he had arrived."

7. Regarding these two cults, see my book *La religion romaine de Vénus* (Paris 1954), passim.

8. On the semantic relationship *Venus-venerari,* see ibid., 30–42.

9. In different circumstances, Priam (*Aen.* 2.536) and Dido (*Aen.* 4.382) would appeal to this *pietas* on the basis of equity.

10. Cf. *Aen.* 2.604–18. The presence of Jupiter sanctions the legitimacy of the "punishment" of Troy, which is inflicted in particular by Neptune (the divinity frustrated by Laomedon), by Juno (the sworn enemy), and by Pallas-Minerva (the divinity that was formerly the protectress).

11. *Iam pridem invisus divis* (*Aen.* 2.647).

12. *Heu nihil invitis fas quemquam fidere divis!* (*Aen.* 2.402).

13. *Di patrii, Indigetes, et Romule Vestaque mater* (*G.* 1.498). For *Indigetes,* which is not to be confused with *indigenae,* I understand the word in connection with *Indigitamenta* ("litanies" or "lists of invoked gods").

14. *Satis iampridem sanguine nostro / Laomedonteae luimus perjuria Troiae* (*G.* 1.501–2).

15. Horace, *Epod.* 7.17.

16. *Dis te minorem quod geris, imperas* (Horace *C.,* 3.6.5).

17. Cicero *N.D.* 3.2. (The last words of my translation are a transposition of the idiomatic expression *sine summa placatione deorum immortalium.*)

18. Cicero ibid. 2.3.8. In comparison with other peoples, the Romans are *religione, id est cultu deorum, multo superiores.*

19. There have been innumerable efforts to identify this child since the book by J. CARCOPINO, *Virgile et la IVe Bucolique* (Paris 1930).

20. Virgil *B.* 4.13: *Si qua manent sceleris vestigia nostri . . .*

21. Virgil *Aen.* 6.789–94. *Divi genus,* son of a god, recalls that Augustus is the adopted son of Julius Caesar, who was deified after his death. A mythical Golden Age (in the reign of Saturn) was succeeded by a real Golden Age (in the reign of Augustus): the joy of the style is explained by the end of the civil wars which had marked the last century of the Republic.

22. See the article "The Religious Policies of Augustus," above.

23. Virgil *Aen.* 6.851–53: *Tu regere imperio populos, Romane, memento; / hae tibi erunt artes: pacisque imponere morem, / parcere subjectis et debellare superbos.*

24. Virgil *G.* 1.121.

25. Ibid. 1.133: *Ut varias usus meditando extunderet artes paulatim . . .*

26. Ibid. 1.128.

27. Cf. Virgil *B.* 4.30: *Et durae quercus sudabunt roscida mella.*

28. Cf. Virgil *Aen.* 2.426–30: *. . . cadit et Rhipeus, justissimus unus / qui fuit in Teucris et servantissimus aequi / (dis aliter visum) . . . / . . . nec te tua plurima, Panthu, / labentem pietas nec Apollinis infula texit.*

29. Ibid. 2.536. Note the use of *pietas* applied to the gods, conforming to the idea of reciprocity included in the Latin word. We know that Laemedon, father of Priam, hence grandfather of Polites, had aroused the anger of the gods by neglecting his obligations to them.

30. For the dates in question, see Ovid's commentary, *Fasti,* on books 2 and 5, respectively.

31. In the *Odyssey* 11.206ff., Odysseus calls up the dead in order to consult the prophet Tiresias: he is content to dig a ditch, which makes it possible for him to perform the magic rites.

32. The most important commentary on the descent to hell remains the work of E. NORDEN, *P. Vergilius Maro, Aeneis, Buch VI* (3d ed., Leipzig 1927).

33. In *Aen.* 8.666–70, Catilina appears also in Tartarus, on the representation of the shield forged by Vulcan. Note that to cross the stagnant waters of the Cocytus to the spirits that crowd the shore of Acheron, the boatman Charon required only the burial of their bodies. Unburied, these spirits had to wander "for a hundred years" (*Aen.* 6.325–30): the idea that the lack of burial deprived the dead of rest conforms to an old Italic tradition.

34. Our translation of these different texts voluntarily shows an inflection with a Christian meaning, to emphasize the new interpretation that one may give them; Virgo—interpreted as the Virgin Mary—designates in Virgil's text Astraea, the daughter of Zeus and Themis, who rose to heaven at the advent of the Iron Age: her return announces the return of the Golden Age (*redeunt Saturnia regna*).

35. In keeping with the set purpose announced in the preceding note, I have translated *nova progenies* by "an exceptional child" (= Christ)—a possible translation, although the context of the *Bucolic* suggests rather "a new generation"—(by allusion to the generation of the Golden Age which was thought to have descended from heaven with the aid of a rope; Lucretius [2.1153] scoffs at this myth).

36. The allusion, interpreted as a reference to the original sin of Adam and Eve, concerned, in the passage of the *Bucolic,* the aftereffects of the civil wars (in 40 B.C., the fleet of Sextus Pompey, who was only defeated in 36 B.C., was still capable of starving Italy by preventing the arrival of grain from Africa).

37. In the Christian perspective: Christ made human will return to heaven. A more literal fidelity would require the translation: "he will attain the life of the gods"—men leading the same life as the gods in the Golden Age.

38. The *nascens puer* was applied to the Infant Jesus. Many attempts have been made to remove the mystery of the 4th *Bucolic*. Finally, an intriguing identification—M. Claudius Marcellus, posthumous son of C. Claudius Marcellus and Octavia—has been proposed by J. PERRET, *Virgile* (Paris 1965), 45–48.

39. Fulgentius, *Expositio Virgilianae continentiae.*

40. Dante, *Inferno* 1.85: "Tu se' lo mio maestro e'l mio autore."

41. Of course, this delicacy belongs to Dante, who found the elegant solution that avoids denying Virgil access to the Christian paradise.

42. Virgil has always been appreciated in England, France, and Italy. In Germany, the renewal of Virgilian studies is more recent; this is in part due to the work of TH. HAECKER with the meaningful title *Vergil Vater des Abendlandes* (7th ed., Munich 1952).

VULCAN

Vulcan is the god of fire. The etymology of the name is difficult to determine. G. Dumézil (*Fêtes romaines d'été et d'automne* [Paris 1925], pp. 72–76) reviews all the principal attempts to elucidate it and shows how precarious they are. They include a comparison with the Cretan *welchanos;* an explanation by way of the Ossetic noun (*Kurd-alae)-waergon;* and an Etruscan hypothesis based on the abbreviation *Vel* from the Piacenza liver, which is arbitrarily completed to yield *Vel(chans),* whereas the Etruscan homologue of Hephaestus is *Sethlans.* Dumézil prefers a derivation from the Vedic *várcas* ("brightness," or "flash," one of the properties of Agni, the god of fire), but as a good comparativist, he hastens to point out the difficulty: "no verbal or nominal derivative of this version of the root exists in Latin" (ibid., p. 74).

Vulcan had a flamen and a festival, the Volcanalia, on 23 August (i.e., at the end of the dog days of summer, which begin with the Neptunalia of 23 July), that was inscribed in the ancient cycle of the liturgical calendar. The site of the cult, which consisted of an altar and was designated by the expression *Volcanal* or *area Volcani,* was southeast of the Capitol and thus outside the pomerium of the old city. Later a temple to Vulcan was built that predates the reference to the temple by Livy (24.10.9) in 214 B.C. It too was outside the new pomerial boundaries, near the Circus Flaminius. Its anniversary fell on 23 August, the festival of the Volcanalia.

All signs indicate that Vulcan, the very opposite of Vesta, embodied the *destructive* fire, which is why his cult was "outside the walls" (Vitruvius 1.7.1). He was attended by two entities: Maia (Gellius 13.23.2) and Stata Mater (Festus, p. 146 L). Maia (probably derived from **mag-ia*) suggests extension, whereas Stata Mater (cf. the epithet *Stator* for Jupiter) suggests immobilization or cessation. These two notions thus express symmetrically two opposite faculties: fire may spread or go out.

There are specific references to this devouring nature of fire: Vulcan helped to destroy the enemy's arms (Livy 1.37.5; 23.46.5; 30.6.9; 41.12.6). Another custom is less clear; every year "on the other side of the Tiber in the month of June" (according to Festus, p. 274 L.) or "during the festival of the Volcanalia" (according to Varro *De Lingua Latina 6.20)* small live fish (*genus pisciculorum vivorum*) were tossed into the fire in honor of Vulcan "instead of human souls" (*pro animis humanis:* Festus) or "in order to redeem themselves" (*pro se:* Varro). What could have been the significance of combining the idea of redemption (see Ovid *Fasti* 5.438: the Lemuria) and the demand for living beings (see Ovid *Fasti* 3.342: Jupiter demands a life; Numa offers a fish)?

Vulcan was presented in the company of Vesta at the lectisternium of 217 B.C. Although the meaning of this association is transparent, it also proves that toward the end of the third century B.C., even Roman deities as ancient as Vulcan and Vesta did not escape the Hellenization that compared them with Hephaistos and Hestia. This process was to be confirmed later: in 64 B.C., after the great fire of Rome, a *supplicatio* in accordance with the *ritus graecus* was called for on the orders of the *Sibylline Books,* on behalf of Vulcan, Ceres, and Proserpina (Tacitus *Annales* 15.44.2).

Hellenization had other repercussions of a mythological nature. Vulcan was regarded as the father of Cacculus, the founder of Praeneste (Virgil *Aeneid* 7.678–79; schol. Servius ad loc.), and according to a version collected by Ovid (*Fasti* 6.627), the father of the Roman king Servius Tullius.

For the poets, Vulcan is merely the Latin name for Hephaestus. The epithet Mulciber, the smelter (which Festus [p. 219 L.] explained through the act of "making iron

Vulcan. Paris, Bibliothèque nationale, Cabinet des Médailles. Photo BN.

malleable," *a molliendo ferro*), refers to the smith, the patron of the Cyclops. That is how Virgil (*Aeneid* 8.724) designates him when Vulcan, at the request of his "wife" Venus, consents to forge the armor of Aeneas. The entire scene is inspired by Greek mythology, which had united Hephaestus with Aphrodite (for Mulciber see again Cicero's *Tusculanae Disputationes* 2.23: the adjective is applied to Hephaestus in the Latin translation of Aeschylus's *Prometheus Unbound*).

Despite this pervasive syncretism, the ritual definition was not lost. To commemorate the burning of Rome under Nero at the end of the first century A.D., the emperor Domitian ordered altars built "to prevent future fires" (*incendiorum arcendorum causa*). Each year, on the day of the Volcanalia, a reddish-brown calf and a boar were to be sacrificed there (*Corpus Inscriptionum Latinarum* 6.826).

R.S./g.h.

PART

3

Western Civilization in the Christian Era

The Survival of Myths in Early Christianity

The Old Testament

I. Hellenistic Judaism

The Old Testament is no less important to Christianity than it is to Judaism, although each does a different reading of it. It follows that any inquiry into the mythical foundation that may have persisted in early Christianity must take into account early Christianity's view of the Law and the Prophets. When it comes to biblical hermeneutics, we know that the Church Fathers were often influenced by the Hellenized Jews who lived just before the Christian era. This is what makes the testimony of the most prominent of these Hellenized Jews, Philo of Alexandria, so interesting.

Philo evokes a contemporary trend which he himself condemns—that of reducing certain biblical episodes to the level of Greek myths that were deemed comparable. The identity of these comparativists is not certain, but it is hard to know who they could have been if not those free-thinking Jews, a few examples of whom are known to us. At all events, Philo has them say to the pious Jews: "The Books that you claim to be sacred also contain those myths that you are accustomed to laugh at when you hear others tell them." By way of proof, they offered the Homeric myth of the Aloadae piling up mountains to reach the sky (Homer, *Odyssey* 11.305–20), "in place of which Moses introduces" the construction of the tower of Babel, although the biblical episode of the confusion of languages (Gen. 11.1–9) may have been "similar to the [pagan] myth" of the original community of language among all living beings (*De confusione linguarum* 2.2–4, 9). Shortly before the Christian era, therefore, some exegetes were convinced of the mythical quality of at least a few pages of the Old Testament. Philo reports concurrent examples that probably illustrate the same orientation: when Moses speaks of giants (Gen. 6.4), he is alluding to myths by poets on the same subject (*De gigantibus* 13.58); systematic detractors minimize the sacrifice of Isaac and Abraham's consent to it (Gen. 22.1–19) by comparing it to the practice among Greeks, private citizens or even kings (here one can discern a reference to Iphigenia sacrificed by Agamemnon), of sacrificing their children in the hope of gaining military success (*De Abrahamo* 33.178–34, 183); Philo finally points to certain demented slanderers of the Scriptures who claim that the story of the various animals cut in half by Abraham (Gen. 15.9–17) actually describes an act of divination, with a sacrificial victim and the inspection of its entrails (*Quaestiones in Genesin* 3.3). Such information was recognized as historically significant by H. A. Wolfson[1] and J. Daniélou.[2]

The adjectives and other qualifiers that Philo uses show that he does not support this tendency. But he does admit that a number of passages from the Bible are mythical, provided, he insists, that they are taken literally—a restriction which, though his adversaries had no use for it, greatly changes the perspective. He gives examples of biblical texts of this type: the planting of paradise by God (Gen. 2.8), imagined as the work of a careful gardener arranging a place in which to relax, is a "mythopoeisis" which would not occur to anyone (*Legum allegoriae* 1.14.43); the creation of Eve out of a rib taken from the sleeping Adam (Gen. 2.21–22), taken literally, "resembles a myth" (*Legum allegoriae* 2.7.19–20); if one stops to think about them, the anthropomorphisms that Moses applied to God in his pedagogic endeavor (such as Gen. 6.7: God regrets having created man and thinks of destroying him; Deut. 8.5: like a man, God educates his son) become absurd in themselves and in their consequences, for they are the "mythopoeses" of impious men (*Quod deus sit immutabilis* 12.59).

This last text suggests that there were literalists among the exegetes who, probably unintentionally, went so far as to call certain pages of the Bible myths, thereby objectively joining the cause of the aforementioned comparativists, although their intentions and methods were quite different. To avoid the risk of seeing the Bible concede part of its territory to myth, one merely had to renounce extreme literalism: by the miracle of allegory, mythical appearance dissolves and makes way for a more respectable theoretical meaning. Such is the rejoinder with which Philo responds to the threat of the mythicization of Scripture. Take, for instance, the two biblical serpents, the serpent in paradise, who speaks and seduces the woman (Gen. 3.1–5), and the bronze serpent, who procures the welfare of anyone who merely looks at him (Num. 21.9). On the face of it, "They look like wonders and monsters, . . . but if one explains them by allegory, the resemblance to myth vanishes, and the truth reveals itself

The baptism of Christ. Mosaic in the nave of the church of Daphni, ca. 1100. Photo Hans Hinz—Skira.

with all clarity'': the mortal knots of the first serpent are the knots of pleasure; the bronze of the second serpent is the strength of the soul that nothing can attack (*De agricultura* 22.96–97). So the myth that one might on occasion be tempted to suspect in the Bible is just an illusion that vanishes in the light of allegory. The *De opificio mundi* (56.157) repeats this idea with an example close to the preceding one: the passage of Genesis that refers to the planting of paradise with two trees, the enticing serpent, the fall, the punishment—despite all appearances (Gen. 2.7–3, 24), these "are not the mythical fictions dear to the race of poets and Sophists, but rather examples of figures that invite one to allegory, in accordance with implied meanings.'' These are some of the ideas about myth in Philo's hermeneutics that have been discussed by G. Delling,[3] and by me in a previous work.[4]

II. Patristic Christianity

As P. Heinisch[5] has pointed out (along with many other scholars), Philo had an enormous influence on the exegesis of the Church Fathers. Among the teachings that were handed down in this way are his views that although certain biblical texts appear to be mythical, such an appearance is shattered by the allegorical interpretation, which virtually exercises a demythologizing function, as J. Daniélou has wisely observed.[6] Another way of formulating this principle is to say that without allegorical exegesis, one remains unarmed before all the appearances of myth. That is how Gregory of Nyssa dealt with the verses from Genesis (2.16–17) concerning the tree of knowledge; without actually naming the allegory, he designated it in no uncertain terms: "If one does not contemplate the truth in the narrative by means of philosophy, the unsuspecting reader will find the narrative inconsistent and similar to myth'' (*Commentary on the Song of Songs*, prologue, ed. Langerbeck, pp. 11, 5–7).

Origen had previously given yet another presentation of the same concept. He claimed that the Old Testament was both myth and truth (or, following the classical dichotomy, *mythos* and *logos*) depending on the quality of its readers: it was myth for the Jews, who perceived only its surface, but it became truth for Christians who through allegory penetrated to its deep meaning. The following are two texts taken from Origen that typify this way of seeing things. First from *Contra Celsum* 2.4 and 5.42: Christians "bestow greater honor on the Books of the Law by showing what depths of wise and mysterious teachings are enclosed in these texts, whereas their meaning has escaped the Jews, whose contact with them is too superficial and mythical.'' "To Jews, children with the intelligence of children, the truth was still proclaimed in the form of myth; but now, for the Christians who seek instruction and wish to make progress, what were formerly myths, to call them by their name, are now metamorphosed into those truths that were hidden in the myths.'' (The Bible read by Jewish eyes is still described as "myth'' and "mythology'' in 2.5–6, and 52 of the same treatise.) We can see how these various authors solved the problem of myth in the Bible by subjectifying it: myth that was nothing but myth could not be found in the Holy Scriptures, which is why the comparativists' illusion was false; Scripture merely contains apparent and provisional myths destined to wither away under the effect of the allegorical reading. This is precisely the ideology that was held in common by many Hellenized Jews and by the Church Fathers. Origen took a step forward where Philo obviously could not follow him when he made the appearances of myth the lot of the Jews and profound truth the privilege of Christians.

III. The History of Religions

The tendency toward comparativism that Philo denounced nevertheless continued, in a slightly different form. For it is not Greek myths that today provide us with counterparts to the Old Testament (although there are plenty of examples of those); rather, we turn to more ancient cultures, Babylonia and Phoenicia, where we pick up striking parallels, notably between biblical narratives of the creation and the flood, and the Babylonian poem of the *Enūma eliš* and the epic of Gilgameš. It used to be accepted without argument that this coincidence could be explained by an influence exerted on Israel; this view was championed by H. Gunkel[7] among others. Since then, scholars have become more circumspect; see, for example, the works of A. Heidel[8] and E. O. James.[9] People still resort to analogies that indicate the presence of considerable mythical segments in the Old Testament. But these episodes are marked by a particular coloration because of the monotheism basic to the the Jewish tradition.

We shall not attempt to give an inventory here of all the episodes with mythical dimensions in the Bible, but rather limit ourselves to a typical example, myths of water, referring the reader for more details to the work of P. Reymond.[10] Hebrew cosmology rests essentially on the myth (not exclusively Jewish) of a primordial ocean that surrounds the dry earth boundlessly, threatens its existence, and gives birth to all the waters on earth, below (rivers and springs) and above (rain). The origin of time is marked by Yahweh's struggle with this hostile element, often personified by the sea monsters Rahab

(Job 26.12) and Leviathan (Isa. 27.1; Ps. 74.13–14, etc.). The primordial struggle of God against the forces of the sea also develops against the Nile and its incarnation the Pharaoh, himself assimilated to the crocodile of Egypt. This amalgam is admirably depicted in Ezekiel 29.3–4: "These are the words of the Lord God: I am against you, Pharaoh king of Egypt, you great monster, lurking in the streams of the Nile. You have said, 'My Nile is my own; it was I who made it. I will put hooks in your jaws,' " etc.

The mythical ocean of the Bible is not only liquid; it is also dark. This dual quality excellently describes the formlessness of original chaos. Yahweh's creative action consists in his victory over the dark ocean; this victory is marked at the beginning of Genesis (1.2, 6–7) by two important features of domination: the spirit of God prevails over the waters by hovering over them (or is it perhaps that he watches anxiously over the nascent world which the waters still threaten?), and God divides the waters in two by interposing the firmament. The sea is henceforth "held back with two doors" (Job 38.8). The mythical water is domesticated by God, who uses it to punish men (the flood, Gen. 6–9) or to serve them (the water that springs forth from the cleft rock during the exodus from Egypt, Ps. 78.15–16, 105.40, etc.). Numerous analogies to this sequence of grandiose depictions occur outside of Israel: Yahweh's victorious struggle with the ocean evokes Marduk's struggle against Tiamat in the *Enūma eliš;* the sea monster Leviathan also appears in the Canaanite legend of Ba'al and Anat known through texts excavated at Ras Shamra-Ugarit. But, as before, we should not hasten to infer an influence on biblical authors; rather, we should think of parallel roots going down into a common mythical background.

The New Testament

I. Keeping Myth at Bay

> For we did not follow cleverly devised myths (*sesophismenois muthois*) when we made known to you the power and coming of our Lord Jesus Christ, but we were eyewitnesses of his majesty.

Such is the profession of faith by which the Second Epistle of Peter (1.16) defines the antimythical position of the New Covenant. Nothing could be clearer, even if the word "myth" does not have there exactly the same meaning that we have seen until now. The designation "eyewitnesses" (*epoptēs*) applied to the beneficiaries of a revelation is in the context all the more peculiar since it comes from the technical language of the Greek mysteries. Saint Paul's hostility toward myth is equally well known: his precept to Timothy is to "have nothing to do with those godless myths, fit only for old women" (1 Tim. 4.7), to warn the Ephesians "to give up . . . studying those interminable myths . . . which issue in mere speculation and cannot make known God's plan for us, which works through faith" (1 Tim. 1.3–4), for the time will unfortunately come when "they will stop their ears to the truth and turn to mythology" (2 Tim. 4.4). He asks his other disciple Titus to insist that the Christians of Jewish origin in Crete not "lend their ears to Jewish myths and commandments of merely human origins, the work of men who turn their backs upon the truth" (Titus 1.14). These are the only five passages in which the New Testament refers to myth by that name. They consistently define a wholly negative attitude. In particular, the last two Pauline texts cited pose myth and truth as opposites, such that any belief in one constitutes a denial of the other.

The theologian's reflection on Christian specificity moves in the direction of these biases. The Greek philosophers who lived during the period of Christian expansion defined myth by its ability to give a temporal appearance to the timeless. Plotinus thus said that "myths, in order to be truly myths, must parcel out their content over time and separate from one another many beings who are together and can only be distinguished by virtue of their rank or their powers" (*Enneades* 3.5 [50] 9.24–6). A similar view may be found in the philosopher Sallust, a friend of the emperor Julian, when he interprets the myth of Cybele and Attis. A strikingly different approach is taken by Christianity, which, particularly in the first few centuries, placed at the very heart of faith the reality of time and newness in historical progress. No one has more accurately described the contrast between these two mentalities than H.-Ch. Puech (in a lecture[11] that I unfortunately did not know about when I wrote my own study of this subject).[12]

Because the content of myth is indifferent to temporality, myth presents itself as a model capable of indefinite repetition. By contrast, the redemptive incarnation and passion constitute a single and nonrepeatable fact. The Jewish high priest who once a year entered into the most secret sanctuary of the Temple or the Holy of Holies foreshadowed the sacrificed Christ. Christ in turn accomplished what the high priest had only begun, offering himself up, not once a year, but once and for all in the totality of history. This is the lesson of chapter 9 of the Epistle to the Hebrews (see also 1 Peter 3.18), where there is a recurrence of the adverbs *hapax, ephapax,* (Latin *semel*), marking the absolute singleness of the sacrifice. It must be added that this conviction surely rested in large measure on the eschatological perspective of a nascent Christianity: since the end of time was expected in the near future (Paul thought he would be a witness to this event; we shall return to this below), there was no room for an eventual repetition of the passion.

One might object that Christianity itself provides the setting for a certain repetition of previous situations, and to this extent it is allied to the world of myth. For instance, the liturgical cycle annually reproduces the principal events in the life of Jesus (his conception, his birth, various episodes of his public life, his passion and death, his resurrection, and his ascension). Furthermore, the ritual celebration of the sacraments often recalls either the episodes of sacred history that prefigure them—what Saint Paul called its "types" (thus the flood and the crossing of the Red Sea are recalled in memory by the ceremony of baptism)—or the scenes from the life of Jesus during which they were instituted (the celebration of the Eucharist somehow reactualizes the Last Supper). One may therefore discern, notably in the conception of sacramental practice as a reactivation of the founding elements, a phenomenon not without analogy in the mysteries of the Hellenistic East, in which the ritual reenactment of original myths allowed the initiate to relive, through participation, the destiny of the deity. Baptism, for instance, is conceived by Saint Paul as a burial with Christ, an assimilation into his death and resurrection, the privilege of putting on Christ as a garment (Rom. 6.3–5; Gal. 3.27), whereas Johannine theology sees as the effect of the Eucharist the mutual dwelling of the faithful in Jesus and of Jesus in the faithful (John 6.56). But we should not lose sight of the fact that, unlike myths, biblical "types" and scenes of institution are regarded by Christianity as historical events. Moreover, anyone who hesitates to admit to the necessarily temporal nature of this religion and, hence, its nonmythical character has at his disposal some evidence to the contrary, which H.-Ch. Puech has brilliantly demonstrated, namely, the confrontation with Christian Gnosticism, which conceived time as essentially bad and salvation as deliverance from time: by thus severing Christianity from any temporal and historical perspective, Gnosticism, unlike the Church, fully embraced myth.

II. New Testament Mythology and Demythologization

This is not to say that early Christianity is free of any mythical factor, however steeped in history it is supposed to be. There is convincing evidence to that effect in the New Testament itself, despite the denials we have mentioned. For the sake of continuity, let us return to the example given above with respect to the Old Testament. There is little doubt that myths of water lie in the background of the Gospels. Thus, the scene described in the synoptic Gospels (Mark 4.35–41, etc.) when Jesus quells the storm on Lake Gennesaret must be viewed as yet another episode of the struggle between God and the primordial ocean, which persists in rebelling despite its defeat. In the fourth Gospel, the most level-headed exegetes, such as A. Jaubert,[13] detect several fairly well developed references to the original mythical water. The same would apply to the water flowing from Jesus' side on the Cross (John 19.34), and especially to the idea of "living water" mentioned in the dialogue with the Samaritan woman (John 4.6–15) and in Christ's comparing the gift of the Holy Spirit to the streams of living water flowing out from within him (John 7.37–39).

In the 1950s the surviving mythical elements in the New Testament were brought to light by the brilliant exegete Rudolph Bultmann in a series of remarkable scholarly works.[14] Bultmann discovered many mythological elements (he preferred "mythological" to "mythical") in the teaching of Christ. Among them is the conception of the "Kingdom of God" as an eschatological reality about to come. "There are some of those standing here who will not taste death before they have seen the Kingdom of God already come in power," said Jesus (Mark 9.1), and Saint Paul was convinced he was among those whom the coming of the Lord would find still living (1 Cor. 15.51–52; 1 Thess. 4.15–17). Other similar depictions include the splitting up of the universe into three storeys (which explains Christ's descent into hell and his ascension into heaven; see Acts 1.9–11, Eph. 4.9–10), the belief in miracles and in the intervention of supernatural forces, the idea that Satan and the demons rule the world and men's souls, and so forth. All these conceptions are thought to be mythological insofar as they differ from scientific conceptions.

No less mythological, in Bultmann's eyes, is the picture that the early Christian community had of its founder. At issue are not miracles like virgin birth but two major images applied to Jesus. First, he is proclaimed the "Son of Man" who at the end of time is supposed to come back on the clouds of heaven to judge the world in a thunderous cosmic blaze (see for instance Matt. 25.31–32; Thess. 4.16–17; 2 Pet. 3.10–12). But this is a title, usage, and setting that are usual in late Jewish apocalyptic, as is seen, for example, in the Book of Daniel (7.13–14). Second, Jesus is presented as the preexisting Son of God who abandons the divine pleroma, becomes man, descends on earth by breaking down the dividing wall, accomplishes his mission of reconciliation and salvation, and finally reascends into heaven. Those are the categories of Pauline christology (for example, Eph. 2.13–16; Col. 1.13–22 and 2.9–15) and Johannine christology (John 1.1–18). But they are also the categories of the Gnostic myth of the primordial man who is a savior; from him too, as from Jesus, flows the living water that revives the universe, according to the Naassenes, the Gnostics described by Hippolytus (*Refutatio omnium Haeresium* 5.9, 19). This double kinship of the christology of the New Testament with apocalyptic and Gnosis seems to Bultmann to be the very signature of its mythological nature.

Such cosmological and religious representations belong to their own time; we cannot expect today's believer to hold them to be true; even if he wished to do so, he would not willingly choose a defunct image of the world. Similarly, the truth of Christian preaching is to be found not in these mythologies but in the fact that it is fundamentally a *kerygma*, a personal message to the human conscience, a universalist challenge which cannot be compromised by the necessarily contingent and now outgrown cultural context in which it was heard. This is the definition of *kerygma* that Bultmann finds formulated precisely in Paul's statement to the Corinthians: "Only by declaring the truth openly do we recommend ourselves, and then it is to the common conscience of our fellow men and in the sight of God" (2 Cor. 4.2). We must not, however, deny that mythological statements have any function, for they do contain a meaning, which they also hide, that is deeper than they are themselves. To discover this meaning, we must accomplish the work for which Bultmann coined a word that has since then come into general usage: "demythologization" (*Entmythologisierung*).

The appropriate function of mythology in general is to bring divine reality down to the human level, and to endow transcendent subjectivity with "worldly" objectivity. According to Bultmann's famous definition, "the mode of representation in which the nonworldly, the divine, appears worldly and human, the beyond as the here below, is mythological."[15] Furthermore, this misconstruction through mythology is more or less the lot of all religion, which, in its attempt to express the divine, can only resort to a language and categories that are incapable of expressing it. J. Sperna Weiland[16] rightly believes that Bultmann is reiterating in his own way the rationalist criticism which, in the early stages of Greek thought, denounced the anthropomorphic theology of the poets. The task of demythologization must therefore be to identify behind the screen of an outdated cosmology the religious intention from which it emerged. For science, it is absurd to speak of a top and a bottom of the universe; but if the biblical assertion that God resides in heaven is devoid of immediate meaning, it does endeavor to translate divine transcendence indirectly. Similarly, to situate hell under the earth is a way of depicting the terrifying character of evil, and so forth. If the image of "heaven" thus serves as the spatial expression of God's transcendence, then the idea of the "end of the world" is its temporal expression. Behind the apparent content of eschatological preaching can be heard an exhortation to the availability by which human beings open themselves up to the future of God. New Testament mythology also speaks to human beings about themselves. As we have seen, the function of the cosmological myth is not to define an objective image of the universe but to shed light on the divine nature; its function is also to reveal the way in which people experience their condition in the world—in other words, to express a certain understanding of human existence. This is an existential interpretation, and Bultmann does not attempt to conceal the fact that he has borrowed it from Heidegger.

These theses of Bultmann on demythologization and its premises have awakened considerable interest and won many disciples. It matters little that some of them, like R. A. Johnson,[17] have tempered the originality of his positions by demonstrating the philosophical roots and historical anticipations of *Entmythologisierung*. But Bultmann's arguments have also met with much resistance. More recently, the *religionsgeschichtliche* perspective adopted by Bultmann—that the preexisting Son of God was a category predating Pauline christology, which then borrowed it—has been strongly and cogently criticized by M. Hengel.[18] But it was not the assertion of the presence of mythical elements in the New Testament that upset exegetical scholars. H. Schlier,[19] who is not a Bultmann exponent, has no difficulty in recognizing the double influence of Jewish apocalyptic and the Gnostic primordial man, to which he even adds the influence of Hellenistic mysteries; but this triple concession is clearly equivalent to abandoning to myth a considerable portion of the Gospels and the Epistles. No, what is really disturbing is that Bultmann does not contain mythology within any limits, however broad, but rather absorbs into it everything in the New Testament that is not specifically kerygmatic. Thus O. Cullmann, in an important book,[20] first endorses the way Bultmann applies demythologization to the entire history of salvation and not just to its extremities. But later he begins to fear that this history, in which we can see the essence of early Christianity, may be totally dissolved in the process.[21] We should add to this major objection our own sense of the importance of the notion of an irreversible unfolding of time in the definition of Christian reality. The same challenge is expressed, sometimes colored by confessional preoccupations, by L. Malevez[22] and R. Marlé,[23] the latter with the additional interest of having prompted a response from Bultmann himself.[24] The controversy is probably not over, but Bultmann's contribution thus far has been to draw attention, more than anyone else before him, to the reality of a mythical component in the New Testament. We can and must discuss the dimensions of this component; we can no longer deny its existence.

The good shepherd. Rome, catacombs.

Liturgy

I. Myths of Water in Baptism

It is widely recognized that the mythical function of consciousness operates even more freely in liturgical practice than in literature or in the realm of speculation. G. P. Zacharias[25] has shown that Christian liturgy is an excellent testing ground for Jung's analyses of the workings of the psyche. Mythical elements could probably be detected behind many liturgical gestures or formulas of early Christianity. To avoid spreading ourselves too thin, we shall focus on two fairly representative examples, the first one connected to the Jewish myth (mentioned earlier) of the primordial ocean as the enemy of god.

Baptism, as it is practiced in the New Testament (for example, Matt. 3.13–16: the baptism of Jesus in the Jordan River; Acts 8.38–39: the baptism of the Ethiopian eunuch), involves descending into water and rising out of it. Pauline theology (Rom. 6.3–9) sees baptism as a double assimilation, first to the death and burial of Christ, then to his resurrection and his victory over death. The two pairs of acts can be perceived as parallel: the baptismal candidate both immerses himself in, and escapes from, a mythical water, a sea of death.

Two observations support this contention. First, in the earliest form of Christianity there is a connection between baptism and Christ's descent into hell immediately after his death. According to the Jewish cosmology that was still powerful at that time, to go underground among the dead leads to the realm of the original Ocean. Second, the theology and liturgy of the first centuries A.D. claimed to discern figurative interpretations or "types" of baptism in episodes in the Old Testament. Among these, the three principal ones were the flood (Gen. 6–8), the crossing of the Red Sea by the Israelites in the flight from Egypt (Exod. 14.15–31), and the crossing of the Jordan into the Promised Land (Josh. 3.9–17). We can see that all three of these accounts illustrate the confrontation between the primordial ocean and Yahweh, and the latter's victory over the former. We are led to conclude that baptism too, in the unfolding of its ritual, is regarded as the last skirmish in this mythical struggle, which is as old as history. In the liturgical and doctrinal texts of the patristic era, numerous indices can be found of this conjunction of baptism with the *descensus ad inferos* and the three episodes in the Old Testament; they have been admirably collected by P. Lundberg.[26] But we must also realize that the New Testament bears witness to the same phenomenon. The first Epistle to the Corinthians (10.1–2) is a clear example: "Our ancestors were all under the pillar of cloud, and all of them passed through the Red Sea; and so they all received baptism into the fellowship of Moses in cloud and sea." The first Epistle of Peter (3.19–21) is more obscure; but in these few lines we can recognize the descent into hell, the flood, and baptism: "In the spirit he [Christ] went and made his proclamation to the imprisoned spirits. They had refused obedience long ago, while God waited patiently in the days of Noah and the building of the ark, and in the ark a few persons, eight in all, were brought to safety through the water. It is the 'antitype' of this water, baptism, that now will save you too."

II. Orientation and Solar Myths

Early Christians prayed facing east, where the sun rises. This differs from the custom of the Jews, who pray facing Jerusalem, as Daniel does in the biblical book that bears his name (6.11); so important is this difference that Elkesai, the

Orpheus Christ. Sabbartha alabaster. Tripoli Museum. Photo Baudot-Lamotte.

founder of a Judeo-Christian sect, dissociated himself from Christianity by prescribing that his followers face Jerusalem and forbidding them to face east. The Scriptures contain many details confirming each in its own way the special position of the east: the earthly paradise was planted "to the east" (Gen. 2.8); it is believed that Christ's ascension took an eastward course, for the Latin version of Psalm 68 (67), verse 34, applies to the Lord the phrase *qui ascendit super caelum caeli ad orientem* ("who ascended above heaven, to the east of heaven"), and his return is also expected to come from the east; the angel in the Revelation of John (7.2) rises out of the east, and so forth.

These coincidences result not from mere chance but from the early assimilation of Christ to the sun, in particular the rising sun. The classical work on this subject remains that of F. J. Dölger.[27] Already in the hymn of Zachariah (Luke 1.78–79), Jesus is called "the morning sun from heaven [who] will rise upon us, to shine on those who live in darkness, under the cloud of death." This has the ring of a prophetic naming of Christ as the "sun of righteousness" referred to in Malachi (4.2); Tertullian summarizes an entire past and future tradition when he writes (*Adversus Valentinianes* 3.1): *orientem, Christi figuram* ("the east, the figure of Christ"). The metaphor was already well implanted when, at the end of the third century, it became even more firmly rooted and was used to thwart the cult of *Sol invictus* imposed by the Emperor Aurelian. Thus, the pagan festival of the *dies natalis Solis invicti* ("the day of the birth of the unvanquished Sun"), celebrated on 25 December when the exhausted sun is reborn, made way for the nativity of the solar Christ.

One can understand how such grandiose imagery could not work its way into early Christianity without bringing in with it a fringe of mythical cosmology. Here again, it may be in certain details of the liturgy and worship that the contamination can most easily be identified. For example, in the ritual of baptism, between the renunciation of the devil and the profession of faith in Christ, the catechumen would suddenly turn around, pivoting from west to east; for the west was taken to be the realm of darkness ruled by the Prince of Darkness, and so the baptismal candidate looked in that direction to repudiate Satan, but he turned to face east at the moment he joined Christ. This ceremonial detail, commented upon by several ancient authors and also studied by F. J. Dölger,[28] may certainly be regarded as a vehicle of the mythical mentality. On the other hand, as J. A. Jungmann[29] has demonstrated, the depiction of the solar Christ required an eastward orientation not only for prayer but, consequently, for church building and even for the layout of cemeteries; Greek and Roman temples also faced east. It was finally concluded that this orientation of the church, when added to that of the Christians inside, made it difficult both for the congregation and for the celebrant to position themselves. As a result, starting in the fourth century, church builders turned the apse rather than the facade of the church toward the east, probably without awareness of the ancient images that prompted these architectural concerns from afar.

J.P./g.h.

NOTES

1. H. A. WOLFSON, *Philo: Foundations of Religious Philosophy in Judaism, Christianity and Islam* (Cambridge, MA, 1948), 1:82–84 and 124.
2. J. DANIÉLOU, *Philon d'Alexandrie,* Les Temps et les Destins (Paris 1958), 107–10.
3. G. DELLING, "Wunder-Allegorie-Mythus bei Philon von Alexandreia," *Wissenschaftliche Zeitschrift der Martin-Luther—Univ. Halle—Wittenberg,* Gesellschafts- und Sprachwiss. Reihe, 6 (1956–57): 727ff., and 737ff., n. 139ff. The article is reprinted in *Gottes ist der Orient,* Festschrift für O. Eissfeldt (Berlin 1959).
4. J. PÉPIN, "Remarques sur la théorie de l'exégèse allégorique chez Philon," in *Philon d'Alexandrie,* Actes du colloque de Lyon de 1966 (Paris 1967), 143–46.
5. P. HEINISCH, *Der Einfluss Philos auf die älteste christliche Exegese (Barnabas, Justin und Clemens von Alexandria),* Alttestamentl. Abhandlungen, 1, 1–2 (Münster 1908).
6. J. DANIÉLOU, "La démythisation dans l'école d'Alexandrie," in E. Castelli, ed., *Il Problema della demitizzazione, Archivio di Filosofia* (Rome 1961), 45–49.
7. H. GUNKEL, *Schöpfung und Chaos in Urzeit und Endzeit: Eine religionsgeschichtliche Untersuchung über Gen 1 und Ap Joh 12* (Göttingen 1895).
8. A. HEIDEL, *The Babylonian Genesis: The Story of Creation* (2d ed., Chicago 1951); *The Gilgamesh Epic and Old Testament Parallels* (2d ed., Chicago 1949).
9. E. O. JAMES, *Myth and Ritual in the Ancient Near East* (London 1958).
10. PH. REYMOND, *L'eau, sa vie et sa signification dans l'Ancien Testament,* Supplements to *Vetus Testamentum* 6 (Leiden 1958), 123–24, 182–98.

11. H.-CH. PUECH, "Temps, histoire et mythe dans le christianisme des premiers siècles," in C. J. Bleeker et al., eds., *Proceedings of the 7th Congress for the History of Religions* (Amsterdam 1951), 33–52.

12. J. PÉPIN, "Le temps et le mythe," *Les études philosophiques* 17 (1962): 55–68, reprinted in *Mythe et allégorie: Les origines grecques et les contestations judéo-chrétiennes* (2d ed., Paris 1976), 503–16.

13. A. JAUBERT, *Approches de l'Évangile de Jean*, Parole de Dieu (Paris 1976), 58–63, 140–46. See also C. H. DODD, *The Interpretation of the Fourth Gospel* (2d ed., Cambridge 1970).

14. R. BULTMANN, "New Testament and Mythology," in H. W. Bartsch, ed., *Kerygma and Myth* (London 1953), 1–44; "Zum Problem der Entmythologisierung," in H. W. Bartsch, ed., *Kerygma und Mythos* (Hamburg 1952), 2:177–208; *Jesus Christ and Mythology* (New York 1958); "Zum Problem der Entmythologisierung" (bis), in *Glauben und Verstehen* (Tübingen 1965), 4:128–37. These are the principal works of R. Bultmann on New Testament myth.

15. BULTMANN, "New Testament and Mythology."

16. J. SPERNA WEILAND, "La théologie de la démythisation est-elle une idéologie?" in E. Castelli, ed., *Démythisation et idéologie* (Paris 1973), 180.

17. R. A. JOHNSON, *The Origins of Demythologizing: Philosophy and Historiography in the Theology of Rudolf Bultmann,* Studies in the History of Religions 28 (Leiden 1974).

18. M. HENGEL, *Der Sohn Gottes: Die Entstehung der Christologie und die jüdisch-hellenistische Religionsgeschichte* (2d ed., Tübingen 1977), 32–93; English translation, *The Son of God* (Philadelphia, 1st ed. 1975).

19. H. SCHLIER, *Essais sur le Nouveau Testament,* Lectio divina, 46 (Paris 1968), chap. 5, pp. 97–112: "Le Nouveau Testament et le mythe."

20. O. CULLMANN, *Christ and Time: The Primitive Christian Conception of Time and History* (rev. ed., Philadelphia 1964), "The Connections between History and Prophecy."

21. O. CULLMANN, "Le mythe dans les écrits du Nouveau Testament," in K. Barth et al., *Comprendre Bultmann: Un dossier* (Paris 1970), 15–31.

22. L. MALEVEZ, *Le message chrétien et le mythe: La théologie de Rudolf Bultmann,* Museum Lessianum, section théol., 51 (Brussels and Paris 1954).

23. R. MARLÉ, *Bultmann et l'interprétation du Nouveau Testament,* Théologie, 33 (Paris 1956).

24. R. BULTMANN, "In eigener Sache," in *Glauben und Verstehen* (Tübingen 1960).

25. G. P. ZACHARIAS, *Psyche und Mysterium: Die Bedeutung der Psychologie C. G. Jungs für die christliche Theologie und Liturgie,* Studien aus dem C. G. Jung–Institut, Zürich, 5 (Zurich 1954).

26. P. LUNDBERG, *La typologie baptismale dans l'ancienne Église,* Acta Seminarii Neotestam, Upsaliensis, 10 (Leipzig and Uppsala 1942); see also J. DANIÉLOU, *Bible et liturgie: La théologie biblique des sacrements et des fêtes d'après les Pères de l'Église,* Lex orandi, 11 (Paris 1951), 97–155.

27. F. J. DÖLGER, *Sol salutis: Gebet und Gesang im christlichen Altertum,* Liturgiegeschichtliche Forschungen, 4–5 (Münster 1925).

28. F. J. DÖLGER, *Die Sonne der Gerechtigkeit und der Schwarze: Eine religionsgeschichtliche Studie zum Taufgelöbnis,* Liturgiegeschichtliche Forschungen, 2 (Münster 1918).

29. J. A. JUNGMANN, *The Early Liturgy, to the Time of Gregory the Great* (South Bend, IN, 1959).

Christian Judgments on the Analogies between Christianity and Pagan Mythology

I. The Problem

1. *Insertions and dissimilarities.* When nascent Christianity had to define itself in the face of Greek culture, especially of pagan theology, it hesitated between two contrary responses. As A. J. Festugière has demonstrated,[1] both responses were offered by the apostle Paul. In his Athenian discourse, of which the Acts of the Apostles (17.16–34) describes the setting and preserves the outline, Paul manipulated the language and ideas of the philosophers of the time, who were his listeners, and showed how the new religion had come to fulfill their expectations: the place that paganism held vacant for the "unknown god" was claimed for the Christians' God, whom Paul introduced by leaning heavily on Stoic stereotypes. But this attempt at harmonization ended in almost total failure; so when Paul left Athens for Corinth, he chose a quite different method, which is echoed in the beginning of the First Epistle to the Corinthians (1.17–25; 2.1–5). No longer is there any attempt to fit the new religion into a continuity with pagan theology; instead, pagan earthly wisdom and pagan logical and rhetorical knowledge are brutally confronted with the scandal of the Gospel and the folly of the Cross.

It can be claimed, without exaggeration, that this two-sided approach in Pauline preaching gave rise to two opposing currents which run through the whole of Christian history. These are recognizable from the time of the Church Fathers; certain authors strive to present their belief as the realization of what was best in pagan theology, while others, by contrast, accentuate the antagonism between the two. This cleavage is no doubt due to several circumstances: the diversity of temperaments, which is the first thing one thinks of, was not all-determining; one should also take into consideration the historical situation as well as political and social conditions. Minds tended in different directions as persecution became rife, or as tolerance reigned, or as the Christian empire triumphed. For whatever reasons, this duality of attitudes is undeniable, though some defend one or the other position while many hesitate between the two or temper the one with the other.

In the pages which follow we shall apply this schema to a particular problem—the existence and import of characteristics common to Christianity and to preceding theologies. The intransigent attitude would be to deny, in the name of Christian transcendence, the very fact of such analogies; Tertullian, for example, is content to contrast the purity associated with the virgin birth of the Son of God to the squalor in which the sons of Jupiter were born: "The Son of God was not born in such a way that he had to blush at the name of son or at his paternal lineage; he did not have to submit to the affront, through incest with a sister or the debauching of a daughter or of another man's wife, of having a divine father covered with scales, horned or feathered, or changed into a shower of gold like the lover of Danaë. The human infamies that you commit are Jupiter's infamies! But the Son of God does not have a mother as the result of unchastity; and even the mother that you see him to have was not married" (*Apologeticus* 21.7–9).

Contrary to what one might expect, however, such a flat refusal is not the prevailing attitude among the Fathers. More often, they admit that certain intersections are possible between the gods and heroes of paganism (including their myths and ceremonies) on the one hand, and the figures and events of biblical history (including Christian beliefs and life) on the other. They are led to make such a concession for varied reasons: for one, their pagan adversaries, as we shall see more than once in this context, had drawn their attention to many of these similarities, and it was safer to admit to them in order to defuse them than to close one's eyes to them. Indeed, the uses to which the Christians put these intersections with paganism, the explanations they give for them, and the importance they accord to them vary greatly, ranging from a simple figure of speech to the Christianization of a pagan element. We must attempt to distinguish between these different styles of comparative thought, starting from the most superficial, which are of no consequence, and progressing toward those which bring into play an entire view of history. Here, then, is the bottom rung of the ladder.

2. *Comparisons without theological intent.* An example of such comparisons is the one that the earliest Christian apologists made between the Noah of Genesis (5.29–9.29) and the Deucalion of classical mythology (cf. among others Ovid, *Metamorphoses* 1.313–415). It is, in fact, less a comparison of these two figures than the reduction of the latter to the former. Theophilus of Antioch rejects the legend of Deucalion and Pyrrha surviving the flood and throwing stones behind them, which turn into men; but he retains the name of Deucalion as one that the pagans, by means of a bizarre etymology, gave to Noah (*Ad Autolycum* 3.18–19; see also 2.30, and the earlier Justin Martyr, *Second Apology* 7.2). This amounted to an admission of a certain homogeneity between the two cultures. It would be two centuries before Christian specialists in chronology, Eusebius of Caesarea and his translator Jerome, would distinguish between the localized flood of Deucalion and the older, universal flood of Noah, which was completely unknown to pagan history. This new outlook is described and adopted in Augustine's *City of God* (18.8, 10).

On other occasions, in the case of Christian authors raised on Greek culture, a biblical episode spontaneously evokes a mythic episode, or vice versa. In an attempt to stir the hardened hearts of the idolaters, Clement of Alexandria compares them to Niobe (turned into a rock, cf. *Iliad* 24.602–17), then catches himself and, "in order to speak more in the language of our mystery," replaces Niobe by Lot's wife (who became a pillar of salt, Genesis 9.26) (*Protrepticus* 10.103–4). The pagan Platonist Celsus wanted to keep only the blameworthy traits in the story of Joseph, and forgot that this person preferred prison to the burning passion his master's wife had for him (Genesis 39.7–20); the Christian Origen reproaches Celsus for his omission, while the virtue of Joseph reminds him of the quite analogous, yet to his eyes inferior, virtue ascribed to Bellerophon (who rejected, at the peril of his life, the advances of Anteia, wife of his protector King Proetus, cf. *Iliad* 6.155–70) (*Contra Celsum* 4.46). Such parallels, which today continue to strike us with their pertinence, came automatically to the minds of the Christians of Alexandria, though hardly above the level of free association.

A comparison of the same order, destined to endure for a long time, was established by Eusebius between Heracles and the Samson of the Book of Judges (13.24–16.31); he claimed he collected it from the Jewish tradition. The comparison is naturally based on the physical strength common to both individuals, who were, Eusebius adds, almost contemporaries, close to the time of the fall of Troy (*Chronica,* preface, in the translation by Saint Jerome; and again in *Praeparatio Evangelica* 10.9.7). The art and literature of the Middle Ages and the Renaissance would popularize the analogy, retaining in particular the episode of Heracles slaying the Nemean lion, since this has a homology in the biography of Samson (Judges 14.5–6). Medieval sculpture would similarly metamorphose Heracles into Saint Christopher and Heracles slaying Geryon into Saint George slaying the dragon. On the medieval Christianization of Heracles, which remains superficial throughout, we may refer to a study by M. Simon,[2] and, with respect to pictorial representations of Heracles, a book by J. Adhémar.[3] This concern to provide a biblical figure corresponding to the Greek hero continues down to Dante: David's combat with Goliath (1 Samuel 17.4–51) finds its replica in that of Heracles with Antaeus (cf. Ovid, *Metamorphoses* 9.183–84; Lucan, *Pharsalia* 4.597–660) (Dante, *De Monarchia* 2.9.11; cf. 2.7.10, and *Convivio* 3.3.7–8).

II. Rhetorical Uses

1. *The language of the mysteries.* The preceding parallels may be imputed to mere reminiscences, natural to authors at the crossroads of two cultural traditions. Others are more premeditated, responding to the need felt by certain Christian apologists to address themselves to pagan listeners in the religious language of pagans.

Such a design is perhaps nowhere better expressed than at the end of the *Protrepticus* (12.119.1), when Clement of Alexandria announces to his pagan interlocutor: "Come . . . and I shall show you the Word and the mysteries of the Word by transposing your own imagery (*kata tēn sēn diēgoumenos eikona*)." Following this resolution, which Hugo Rahner[4] rightly considers an exemplary statement, Clement presents the essence of Christianity in the technical language of the Dionysian mysteries: baptism and eucharist thus lend themselves to a description in which the *dadouchoi* (torch bearers), the *epoptia* (supreme revelation), the initiation, the hierophant (in this context the Lord), the *muste* (initiate), the seal, the lighting, etc., all play a part (12.120.1–2). Christian authors, from Saint Paul to Pseudo-Dionysius the Areopagite and Maximus the Confessor (sixth and seventh centuries), indulge freely in these borrowings from the vocabulary and notions of the Greek mysteries; the reader may consult E. Hatch's classic work and a more recent work by Arthur Darby Nock.[5]

There is yet another way of speaking to pagans in the language of their own religion. It consists in extracting some of the more popular episodes from the mythical biographies of pagan gods or heroes, and transposing their meaning in such a way as to render more accessible a given aspect of the Christian mystery. This procedure assumes a recognition on the part of the Christian authors of parallels between their own religion and classical mythology. Such parallels remain quite superficial, and their manipulation does not essentially differ from the point-for-point comparisons treated above. The procedure may, however, be extended into a rhetorical orchestration, in which different episodes from the mythological account take on a meaning determined by the principal theme. This assertion may be verified in a famous example.

2. *The Christian Odysseus.* As A. Wifstrand[6] has noted, the New Testament is still quite restrained in its use of *exempla* borrowed from Greek culture; second-century Christian apologists use a few of these, but most often with hostile intentions. A much more hospitable attitude appears in the third century with Clement of Alexandria—perhaps because the Gnostics had, in the meantime, taken the Christian amalgam with Greek mythology as far as it could go. We could go on citing forever the rhetorical uses of paganism

made by Clement and his successors in order to formulate Christian ideas; rather, we shall take a particular case—to wit, the legend of Odysseus and the Sirens—and follow it through part of the tradition. This too has been masterfully studied by Hugo Rahner,[7] as well as by P. Courcelle[8] and Jérôme Carcopino.[9]

Shortly before the passage we just examined on the reemployment of the language of the mysteries, Clement of Alexandria evokes the famous episode of Odysseus's encounter with the Sirens and with Charybdis (*Odyssey* 12.39–123, 154–259). In his eyes, the Sirens symbolize the misdeeds of habit and the appeals of pleasure, and Odysseus, when he thwarts them by tying himself to his mast, is the image of the Christian who triumphs over perdition by embracing the wood of the Cross (*Protrepticus* 12.118.1–4). A little later than Clement, Hippolytus of Rome draws attention to a detail, neglected by his predecessor, in the same account and endows it with meaning: before having himself tied up to the mast, Odysseus plugs his companions' ears with wax; here we are to understand that faithful Christians are to remain deaf to the insidious propaganda of heretics, and become one in body with the wood of the Cross so as to conquer agitation and remain firm (*Refutatio omnium Haeresium* 7.13). Toward the end of the third century, Bishop Methodius of Olympus was nourished on Homer, as V. Buchheit has shown;[10] his principal work, *The Symposium*, not only imitates that of Plato but, starting in the prologue (§ 4), refers to the banquet of the Olympians in the *Iliad* (4.1–4). In another work, a *Treatise on Free Will* (1.1–3), the same author contrasts the fatal song of the Sirens to the salutary chorus of the Prophets and Apostles, in the presence of whom one need not plug one's companions' ears with wax nor gird oneself with ropes. Methodius nevertheless abstains, unlike his two predecessors, from comparing the mast of Odysseus with the tree of the Cross. A century later, however, Saint Ambrose renews these ties with tradition: for him, the sea is the deceitful world, the Sirens the sensuality that enthralls the soul, the rocky shore the body; far from blocking one's ears, one should open them to the voice of the Christ; one should attach oneself, not like Odysseus to a mast with material bonds, but to the wood of the Cross with spiritual bonds. Ambrose is not loath to innovate on several points: among the circumstances that delay the voyage of Odysseus he cites, apart from the Sirens, the sweet fruits of the Lotus Eaters and the gardens of Alcinous (*Odyssey* 7.112–32; 9.82–104). As is natural for a Latin author, he mixes his Homeric memories together with certain recollections of the voyage of Aeneas according to Virgil (*Aenead* 1.536; 2.23). Especially important for the viewpoint under consideration here is the fact that Ambrose himself notes traffic between Greek mythology and the Bible when he observes that the Bible speaks of Giants and the Valley of the Titans (Genesis 6.4; 2 Samuel 5.22; 23.13), and that the prophet Isaiah (13.21) names the Sirens. (This whole passage from Saint Ambrose is found in his *Exposition of the Gospel According to Saint Luke* 4.2–3.)

The last important representative of this tradition was the fifth-century bishop Maximus of Turin, who probably took his inspiration from the passage from Ambrose just cited. The term-for-term correspondence between the episode in the *Odyssey* and its Christian application is now carried to its extreme: the sea is a representation of the hostile world, the pleasures of which are represented by the Sirens; Ithaca is the celestial land where the true life will be lived; the means to enter it is the Church, whose image has traditionally been the boat; here, as in Neoplatonist allegory, Odysseus incarnates the human condition; secured to his mast, which symbolizes the Cross, he naturally stands for the Crucified, but also for every Christian, and even all of humanity; his companions evoke the more distant adepts who nevertheless are within the shadow of the Cross, such as the penitent thief: finally, even the wax stuck into their ears is given a meaning—it is the Scriptures. In this detailed paralleling, Maximus capitalizes on nearly all of the contributions of his predecessors; his personal appetite for rhetoric makes him the ideal representative of this mode of using myths. Unlike the writing of Clement, Hippolytus, Methodius, and Ambrose, his text has never been translated into French. For these varied reasons, he is worth presenting in translation here, in spite (or because) of his inflated and prolix style. He begins with an account of the danger threatening Odysseus and of the hero's expedients for protecting himself against it:

> The pagan fables relate the story of the famous Odysseus who, tempest-tossed upon a wayward course over the sea for ten years, could not reach his homeland; his navigation had brought him to a place in which there arose, in its cruel sweetness, the suave song of the Sirens; they charmed those who came there with a melody so seductive that instead of taking in this sensual delight, they threw away their lives in shipwreck; such was the seduction of this song that hearing the sound of their voices was enough to make a man a prisoner to their magic charm: he would stop steering toward his desired port and rush into undesired ruin. Odysseus, it is said, having come to the brink of this exquisite shipwreck and wishing to escape from the perils of its sweetness, filled the ears of his companions with wax and then tied himself to the mast of his ship; thus his men would be deaf to the fatal charm, and he would deliver himself from the danger of changing his ship's course.

Then follows the Christian application:

> If, then, this fable relates that for this man Odysseus to tie himself to the mast was to be delivered from peril, how much more necessary it is to proclaim what truly came to pass; to wit, that today it is the whole of the human species that has been wrested from the threat of death by the tree of the Cross! Indeed, from the moment Christ the Lord was nailed to the Cross, from that very moment, we have been able to traverse with closed ears, so to speak, those critical points at which the world unfolds its seductions; for we do not stop to listen to the fatal messages of this world, nor do we deviate from our path toward a better life and fall astray upon the reefs of pleasure. For not only does the tree of the Cross allow the man who is nailed to it to see his homeland once again, but it also protects, by the shadow of its might, his companions who are grouped around him. That the Cross returns us to our homeland after much wandering is proclaimed by our Lord when he says to the crucified thief: "Today shalt thou be with me in paradise" (Luke 23.43). This thief, who had for so long been wandering and shipwrecked, certainly could not have returned to the homeland of paradise, which the first man had left, other than tied to the mast. For the mast on the ship is, in a sense, the Cross in the Church, which alone keeps itself safe and sound amid the seductive and mortal shipwrecks which shake the world from one end to the other. Thus anyone who, in this ship, attaches himself to the tree of the Cross or whose ears have been closed by means of the Holy Scriptures does not fear the sweet tempest of lust. For the comely features of the Sirens may be said to be the

cowardly cupidity of the pleasures, a cupidity which by its pernicious seductions softens the firmness of the spirit that has become its prisoner.

The beginning of the next paragraph is important from a methodological standpoint: in his Christian preaching, the author does not refrain from drawing on the imagery of myths in the same way that he draws on the *exempla* of the Old Testament; but he takes care to contrast the pure fiction of myths to the historical context of the biblical accounts: "Thus Christ the Lord was hung on the Cross to free the entire human race from the shipwreck toward which the world is heading. But let us forget the fable of Odysseus, which is an invention without reality; let us see if we can find in the Holy Scriptures some similar example, which Our Lord, before accomplishing it himself, first initiated through his prophets!" (These passages from Maximus of Turin may be found in his *Sermon* 37.1–3, in vol. 23, pp. 145–46, of the Mutzenbecher edition in the *Corpus christianorum;* and in *Homily* 49 in vol. 57, col. 339B–340B of the *Latin Patrology* of Migne.) The last sentence cited offers a remarkable definition of the relationship between the person of Jesus and the figures who announce him in the Old Testament: this is the typological perspective, which is clearly distinguished from the allegorical exegesis of myth. When it comes to substituting a biblical "type" for the fable of Odysseus, whose rhetorical use he has exhausted, Maximus cites the bronze serpent: affixed by Moses on the top of a pole (Numbers 21.6–9), this apotropaic object was seen, from New Testament times onward (John 3.14), as an image of the salvation procured by the Crucified. Here it is contrasted, in an equally traditional way, to another biblical serpent—that of Paradise, who is also wound around a tree.

III. The Chronological Quarrel

1. *Newness and oldness.* It is according to these categories, need it be said, that the New Testament defines itself with regard to the Old. This antithesis is not absent from the Gospels (the old skins and the new wine of Matthew 9.17, etc.); but it is with Paul that it takes on its true dimension: the Christian is invited to take off the "old man" to put on the "new man" (Colossians 3.9–10; Ephesians 4.22–24); he shall serve in the newness of the spirit and no longer in the oldness of the letter (Romans 7.6); he shall be a new creature in Christ, for whom *vetera transierunt, ecce facta sunt omnia nova* ("the old things are passed away; behold, all things are become new"; 2 Corinthians 5.17. Taking its cue from this Pauline theme, one of the earliest documents of noncanonical Christian literature, the *Epistle of Barnabus* (5.7; 7.5), twice calls Christians "the new people" (*ho laos ho kainos*).

Saint Paul defined Christian newness with regard to Judaism. Next came the tendency to cast Hellenism together with Judaism as two parallel expressions of oldness. This is what we find in a second century apocryphal text, the *Kerygma Petri:* "It is in a new way that you worship God through the Christ. . . . The Lord has laid down a new covenant for us; for the ways of the Greeks and Jews are old, but we Christians worship him in a new way in a third generation." Clement of Alexandria, citing this text, accentuates this ternary aspect immediately afterward: "(Peter), it seems to me, clearly showed that the one and only God is known by the Greeks in pagan fashion, by the Jews in Jewish fashion, but by us in a new and spiritual fashion" (*Stromateis* 6.5.41.4–7). In the *Protrepticus,* which is addressed to the Greeks, Clement retains only the Greeks and omits the Jews: "Today, even your myths seem to have aged. . . . But where is Zeus himself? He has aged, like his wings," and lost the ardor and cleverness which marked his amorous exploits (*Protrepticus* 2.37.1–3). Paganism, Clement says further, has fallen into superstition in its old age: it may find youth, and even innocent childhood, if it comes to worship the true God (*Protrepticus* 10.108.3).

This glorification of Christian newness must have grated on many followers of traditional paganism. Some of them said so themselves: the Platonist Celsus, cited by his adversary Origen (*Contra Celsum* 7.53), lets slip, in an address to the Christians, a "you who are so taken with innovation"; earlier, the historian Suetonius had identified Christianity as a *superstitio nova* ("new superstition"; *Nero* 16.3). Judgments of the same sort may be inferred through the retorts of the Christian apologists; the latter defended themselves against being considered as "newcomers," *hesterni,* as may be seen in A. Casamassa's classic article.[11] The unknown Christian author of the *Letter to Diognetes* asserts that people would ask such questions as: "Why do [the Christians] not accept the gods recognized by the Greeks, nor keep the religious observances of the Jews? . . . And why has this new race of men (*kainon genos*), this new way of life, come into the world only now and not earlier?" (1.1). The arguments exchanged between Christians and pagans on this theme have recently been studied once again in N. Zeegers-Vander Vorst's work.[12]

Perhaps it was to silence this objection that the Christians, without tempering their claims to newness, also attempted to connect themselves with ancestors of indisputable antiquity, who were none other than the Jews. This connection was difficult to make, not only because the Christians professed themselves to be the "new people," but also because the Gospels and especially the Pauline writings strove to dissociate them from a Judaism that was judged to be outdated. A passage from Tertullian, himself somewhat of an anti-Semite, conveys this ambiguity: "But since we have stated that our religion is founded upon the documents of the Jews, which are so old, though it is generally known (and we ourselves agree) that our religion is itself comparatively new, belonging as it does to the time of Tiberius, perhaps one might on this ground discuss its nature and say that, under the cover of a religion that is very illustrious and certainly authorized by law, our religion conceals certain new ideas that are its own, for aside from the question of age we do not agree with the Jews about abstaining from certain foods, or about the sanctity of festival days, or about their distinctive bodily mark, or sharing their name, which would of course be our duty if we were the servants of the same God" (*Apologeticus* 21.1–2). Nor did the false situation in which the Christians found themselves escape their adversaries; this is the reproach put in the mouth of the Jew in Celsus's *True Discourse:* "How can you trace your beginnings back to our sacred texts and yet, in doing so, scorn them, while you have no other origin to claim for your doctrine than our Law?" (in Origen, *Contra Celsum* 2.4).

2. *Antiquity and truth.* Given that the Christians could validly claim their antiquity through Judaism, just as a young grafted branch acquires the age of the old stock of the wild olive (a metaphor that Tertullian, in *De Testimonio Animae* 5.6, takes up, not without alterations, from Saint Paul in Romans 11.17–24), the Church Fathers increased their efforts to prove that Jewish prophecy was older than Greek culture. They concentrated on the person of Moses, who was regarded as the most outstanding figure of early Judaism: they

had to show that he, more than all others, preceded the earliest representatives of pagan tradition. As for the pagans, the dominant tendency was to take Homer as exemplary, so that the chronological debate often took the form of a man-to-man combat between these two individuals; I have attempted to show this in another work.[13] It was for this reason, among others, that Christian authors became so closely interested in the Greek poet, as may be verified in the works of Jean Daniélou[14] and G. Glockmann.[15]

In fact, the way had been opened by late Judaism itself, at least among those of its representatives who were the most influenced by Hellenism—for example, the historian Josephus at the end of the first century (*Contra Apionem* 2.2.14). Among Christians themselves, this theme appears briefly in Justin (*First Apology* 59.1). Even more concerned with it was his disciple Tatian, who inaugurated a demonstrative schema that was to become classic: in the opinion even of historians who adhered neither to Judaism nor to Christianity, Moses was the contemporary of the Argive king Inachus, who preceded the Trojan War by four centuries (*Oratio ad Graecos* 31.35–36, 38–41). The same argumentation may be found in the long chapter (*Stromateis* 1.21, especially §§ 101–2) which Clement of Alexandria, in acknowledging his debt to Tatian on the point, devotes to a comparative chronology of the Hebrew people and the neighboring civilizations. His conclusion is peremptory: "Moses was at the height of his powers even before the date at which the Greeks place the creation of man"; or, "It is thus proved that Moses preceded not only the Greek sages and poets, but also the majority of their gods" (ibid. §§ 106.2 and 107.6). At about the same time, Tatian's schema makes its appearance in the Latin world with Tertullian (*Apologeticus* 19.1*–2* and 3; the whole of chapter 19 wrestles with the problem). In the first half of the fourth century the historian Eusebius, a specialist in chronology, places so much value in the debate that he puts together an entire dossier with the texts we have just seen in Tatian, Clement, Josephus, and others (*Praeparatio Evangelica* 10.9.12–13.13). Eusebius adopts the now classic demonstration of Tatian and inserts complementary elements derived from other sources: Moses was earlier than the Phoenician historian Sanchuniathon of Beirut, who was himself a contemporary of Queen Semiramis and, like her, much earlier than the Trojan war (ibid., 10.9.13–17).

What was it that motivated the Christians to forget temporarily the prerogatives of their newness and to link themselves, at whatever cost, to the early age of Judaism? What made their adversaries determined to deny Judaism this anteriority with regard to their own history? Surely it was the conviction, which reigned everywhere at the time, that the antiquity of a doctrine guaranteed its truth. It is striking that, in the space of a few pages, Theophilus of Antioch associates these two notions four times in the same terms: our Scriptures and our beliefs, he repeats, are "older and truer" (*archaiotera kai alēthestera*) than those of every other people (*Ad Autolycum* 2.30; 3.16, 26, 29). The Latin Fathers had their own formula to lend authority to that which is connected with antiquity: *auctoritas vetustatis* (Minucius Felix, *Octavius* 20.2; Lactantius, *Divinae Institutiones* 2.6.7; Ambrose, *Exameron* 1.1.3; etc.)—a formula that Tertullian, better than anyone else, developed when speaking of the Jewish and Christian Scriptures: "The authority of these documents is assured them first of all by their extreme antiquity. Among you also the credibility of something is proved by its antiquity, which is as respectable as religion. Authority is given to the Scriptures by their extreme antiquity" (*Apologeticus* 19.1 and 1*.

By claiming, to their advantage, the chronological priority of the Jews over the Greeks, the Christian authors also conformed to the spirit of the time in another respect. There was a belief, maintained by Plato and Aristotle, that became more and more deeply engrained in the Hellenistic and Roman periods, as many works have shown:[16] that barbarian wisdom preceded and inspired Greek culture. Tatian (*Oratio ad Graecos* 35) and Clement of Alexandria (*Stromateis* 1.15.71.3; 1.29.180.5) shared this outlook of the period; but they put it to a use that was quite uncommon (outside of Christian and, naturally, Jewish circles): they held that the prophets of Israel themselves were to be counted among those barbarian sages, of whom they were the earliest and most eminent. Tatian thus calls Moses "the initiator of the whole of barbarian wisdom" (ibid., 31), while Clement, after enumerating the prophets of Egypt, the Assyrian Chaldeans, the Gallic Druids, the Persian Magi, the Indian Gymnosophists, and various others, notes that the Jewish people are by far the oldest of all (ibid., 1.15.71.4–72.4). Furthermore, the two authors are not afraid to treat Christianity as a "barbarian philosophy," nor to speak of themselves as "we Barbarians" (Tatian, ibid. 42; Clement, ibid. 1.29.180.3, etc.). The famous article by J. H. Waszink should be consulted on these various points.[17]

IV. The Explanation by "Theft"

1. *Borrowing, theft, adulteration.* We have dwelled on the confrontation of comparative chronology since it seems to have weighed heavily on the Christians' evaluation of the features they shared with classical paganism. From the moment they thought that, by virtue of their connection to the Jewish people, they preceded Greek history, they were able to consider resemblances to their adversaries only as cases of plagiarism committed against them by the latter. The direction of influence seemed beyond all doubt; as Justin unambiguously puts it, "It is not we who think like the others, but all of them who imitate us in what they say" (*First Apology* 60.10). Tertullian would recall the determining role played by chronology: "That which first existed is necessarily the origin of what followed. And this is why you have things in common with us or things that resemble ours"; so it is, he continues, that our Wisdom (*sophia*) gave you your philosophy, and our prophecy your poetic divination (*Apologeticus* 19.1.5*–6*). This slide from posteriority to dependence, in Judaism as well as in Christianity, has been studied by K. Thraede.[18]

Such an overview is susceptible to subtle variations, according to the polemical temperament. When this becomes heated, the pen is moved to write the word "theft" (*klopē*). Thus Theophilus of Antioch: "These tortures were predicted by the prophets, but later poets and philosophers stole them from the Holy Scriptures in order to make their own teaching seem trustworthy" (*Ad Autolycum* 1.14; 2.37, trans. Robert M. Grant, Oxford 1970). But the true theoretician of this sort of explanation--as A. Méhat[19] and R. Mortley[20] have suggested—was Clement of Alexandria. Here is one of his programmatic texts on this point, in which he attempts (in rather unconvincing fashion) to found the accusation of "theft" upon a verse from John (10.8) and asserts that the plagiarism committed by paganism extended beyond the miracle accounts to a large part of their theology and ethics:

> Let us now see, since the Scriptures treat the Greeks as "thieves" who stole barbarian philosophy, how we may briefly prove that they were indeed thieves. Not only shall we establish that it was by copying the miracles of our

history that they described their own, but we shall also convict them of digging up and falsifying the most important of our dogmas—our Scriptures are older than theirs and we have shown this—concerning faith, wisdom, gnosis, and knowledge, hope and charity, repentance, continence, and in particular the fear of God. (*Stromateis* 2.1.1.1)

This page introduces, with one word, another important notion: that the supposed theft perpetrated by the Greeks is at the same time a falsification. Clement had already observed that they had not understood all of the Hebraic doctrines which they had purloined and coopted as being their own: some of these they altered, while they applied an indiscreet and incompetent sophistry to others (*Stromateis* 1.17.87.2). In the same period, the same accusations of unwarranted appropriation, of curiosity, of incomprehension, and of adulteration are leveled against the same "men of glory" by Tertullian (*Apologeticus* 19.1.6*; 47.3). The resemblance between the two authors undoubtedly derives from the fact that both were dependent upon Tatian, who explains the formation of Greek mythology as follows:

> With much indiscretion, the sophists of Greece applied themselves to altering all that they borrowed from Moses . . . , first in order to appear as if they were making a personal statement, and, second, in order that, in camouflaging by I know not what false rhetoric all that they had not understood, they might bring truth down to the level of mythology. (*Oratio ad Graecos* 40)

Justin had also expressed the same idea in a more summary fashion, and saw the fact that the pagans contradicted each other as proof that each had, in his own way, misunderstood Moses (*First Apology* 44.10).

2. *Greek and Latin examples.* The Fathers furnished these general views with a plethora of illustrations, often taken by one author from another, so that it is difficult to select samples. According to Justin (*First Apology* 69.3,6), the darkness of Genesis (1.1) is the source of the Erebus of the poets (Hesiod, *Theogony* 123). The creation account recorded by Moses is, in the eyes of the Christians, one of the Jewish texts most impudently pirated by the Greeks: the notion of the seventh day; the falling out between Ocean and Tethys; the Greeks reduced by Menelaus to the water and earth from which they were made; the cosmic ornamentation of the shield of Achilles—all that these scattered disparate traits of epic poetry have in common, according to Clement of Alexandria (*Stromateis* 5.14.99.4–107.4), is that they came from a distorted reading of the beginning of Genesis. We have seen the same author challenge the originality of the Greeks not only on points of doctrine, but also in the accounts of miracles: Clement holds that the famous prayer of the pious Ajax, which brought rain during a catastrophic drought (Apollodorus Mythographus, *Bibliotheca* 3.12.6, 9–10), merely plagiarizes a prayer (of very different inspiration, it must be said) of Samuel (1 Samuel 12.17–18) (*Stromateis* 6.3.28.1–29.3).

In the same line of thought, Origen saw the episode of the Tower of Babel (Genesis 11.1–9) as the source of the Homeric narrative of the scaling of heaven by the Aloidae, who threatened the gods (*Iliad* 5.385–91 and *Odyssey* 11.305–20), and the burning of Sodom and Gomorrah (Genesis 19.1–29) as the starting point of the legend of Phaethon (Euripides, *Hippolytus* 735–41, etc.) (*Contra Celsum* 4.21). It is undoubtedly the same Alexandrian milieu that produced, about the same time, an *Exhortation to the Pagans*, spuriously attributed to Justin. In this unknown author, we again encounter several examples of the sort we have seen in Clement and Origen and in others as well—thus the wonderful garden of Alcinous (*Odyssey* 7.114–26) manifestly imitates the Paradise of Genesis (2.8–9), while the fall of Lucifer in Isaiah 14.12 gave rise to the punishment of Ate, who was thrown down from Olympus in *Iliad* 19.126–31 (§ 28).

Further removed from Greek culture, Latin patristics takes less pleasure in accumulating illustrations of this sort; yet these are not rare. Serapis, the Hellenized Egyptian god whose head is crowned with a modius, is really the Jew Joseph, the judicious counselor to the Pharaoh on matters concerning wheat (Genesis 41.25–57) and the object of a cult inspired by gratitude for this advice; but Joseph was the great grandson of Sarah, Abraham's wife, from which his name of "child of Sarah," *Sarras paîs* in Greek, became Serapis. The reduction of a Greco-Egyptian divinity to a biblical personage, with the aid of etymology in the finest tradition, is found in the fourth century in the works of the Christian apologist Firmicus Maternus (*De errore profanarum religionum* 13.2). It had begun earlier with Tertullian, who undoubtedly drew on a Jewish source (*Ad nationes* 2.8.9–19). We saw at the beginning of this article that Samson, the hero of the Book of Judges, evoked, in the eyes of certain Fathers, the figure of Heracles; at that time Heracles was certainly not seen as a true *copy* of Samson. By the end of the fourth century, with the heresiologist Filaster of Brescia, it was a foregone conclusion that by drawing on the figure of Samson the pagans had come to call valiant men "Heracles" (*Liber de Haeresibus* 8.2).

3. *A widespread accusation.* The thesis of theft appears less extraordinary if it is recalled that late Judaism had pointed early Christianity in this direction. In the second century B.C. the Jewish historian Artapanos makes Moses the inspiration for Orpheus (Eusebius, *Praeparatio Evangelica* 9.27.4); his contemporary and coreligionist Aristobulus had preceded Clement of Alexandria in postulating that the celebration of the seventh day in Homer and Hesiod had been taken from the Scriptures (Eusebius, *ibid.* 13.12.13). N. Walter argues strongly for this view.[21] An influence so stubbornly asserted was bound in the end to convince a few Greek philosophers; such a conviction was undoubtedly behind the well-known statement by the Neophythagorean Numenius of Apamea, who regarded Plato as none other than "a Moses speaking Greek" (cited by Clement of Alexandria, *Stromateis* 1.22.150.4).

On the other hand, it must be realized that the Christian apologists, in alleging such seemingly incongruous examples of "theft," were often just replying to their adversaries, who proffered the same examples—naturally in support of the reverse lineage. Thus, the pagan Celsus saw the Tower of Babel and the burning of Sodom and Gomorrah as mere caricatures of the Greek legends of the sons of Aloeus and of Phaethon, and Origen (*Contra Celsum* 4.21) merely reverses the argument. As I have attempted to show elsewhere,[22] Celsus similarly held that Christian views regarding the devil are nothing but counterfeits of various Greek myths. But we know from the works of C. Andresen[23] that the positions taken by Celsus had the opportunity to reply to Justin's *Apology*; so a great polemic arose between successive generations, who did not dispute the proposed analogies but drew their arguments from them in opposing fashions.

Furthermore, wholly analogous controversies are to be found even within Greek culture. For example, Herodotus (*History* 2.53) echoes a debate on the question of whether or not Homer and Hesiod had preceded, i.e., informed, the ancient poet-theologians. Elsewhere, certain philosophers were accused of plagiarizing poets who were their compatriots, as the biblical authors would be accused by Celsus; "Epicurus is caught red-handed in the act of stealing; he has taken his most solid theories from the poets"; such is the grievance formulated by Sextus Empiricus (*Adversus Grammaticos* 273).

V. The Thesis of Demonic Imitation

1. *The intercession of demons.* Clement of Alexandria presents an important variant of the theory of theft: the theft was committed not directly by the Greeks but by a disobedient angel for their benefit. Here is a very clear text: "Philosophy . . . comes to us stolen or given to us by a thief. Some Power, some Angel, learned a shred of truth, without himself remaining faithful to the truth, and he breathed this knowledge to men, teaching them the fruit of his theft" (*Stromateis* 1.17.81.4).

Tertullian also implicates demons in this theft, calling them "spirits of error," but he attributes much subtler intentions to them: by falsifying the true doctrine, demons established fables similar to it and offered these to poets and philosophers; since they would not be believed by the public, these fables would discredit the Christian faith, which was similar to them—but when doubt would thus have destroyed the faith, there would be a return to the poets' and philosophers' fables, which are the alternative to faith. This truly diabolical calculation is made clearer through the examples which follow: if there is general mirth when Christians predict the judgment of God, Gehenna for the punishment of souls and paradise for their recompense, it is because people are laughing about the pagan replicas—the tribunal of hell, the Pyriphlegethon, and the Elysian Fields. But Tertullian is able to throw back these arguments and defuse their malice: "Where, I pray you, did the poets and philosophers get these things that are so like ours? Only from our mysteries. Now, if they got them from our mysteries because these are more ancient, then our mysteries are more reliable and more to be believed, for even what is nothing but a copy of them finds credence." As for supposing that they might have been taken from their own soil, how then could our mysteries, which preceded them, be a copy of them (*Apologeticus* 47.11–14)?

2. *The counterfeiting of Christian prophecies.* Demons held an important place in the theology of the apologist Justin. In agreement with a thesis that was current in the first centuries of the common era, he holds the false gods of paganism to be demons: it was these demons who committed the horrors which poets and mythologists ignorantly assign to the king of the gods and to his brothers Pluto and Poseidon (*Second Apology* 5.3–5).

Another misdeed on the part of the demons was, according to Justin, to travesty the Scriptures so as to supply mythology with traits that have perceptible parallels with the Christian and Jewish faiths. For example, the reason people place the image of Kore, the daughter of Zeus, over springs is that demons imitated the verse from Moses (Genesis 1.2) about the spirit of God moving upon the face of the waters. The demons, furthermore, knew that God had conceived in his thought the world that was to be created; from this primordial thought, with equal perversity, they had Athena, another daughter of Zeus, born without sexual intercourse. Justin formulates an unexpected grievance against this supposed perversion: he holds that it is ridiculous for thought to be represented by a female form. He seems to ignore the fact that, starting with the Presocratics, Athena had never ceased to be regarded as an image of thought, and even of divine thought, as F. Buffière has demonstrated.[24] In any case, Justin has no difficulty in showing that the behavior of Zeus's other children can be explained in the same way (*First Apology* 64.1–6).

Justin had used such an explanation not long before for some of these gods. In his eyes, demons find a choice ground for their manipulations in particular pages of the Scriptures: in the messianic prophecies, inspired visionaries mysteriously described the Savior long before his coming. So the demons, in order to deceive and mislead the human race, took the offensive and suggested to the poets who created myths that they give Zeus many sons and attribute monstrous adventures to them, in the hope that this would make the story of Christ appear to be a fable of the same sort, when it came. We recognize in this strategy imputed to the demons the very strategy Tertullian had imputed to them, no doubt in following Justin's analyses. The only problem, continues Justin, is that the demons did not exactly understand these prophecies, which they wished to realize in their own way—and the imitations they made of them are filled with errors, as Justin undertakes to show with some highly interesting examples (*First Apology* 54.1–4).

Moses (Genesis 49.10–11) relates a prophecy of Jacob that the Messiah would bind his foal to a vine and wash his garments in wine. The demons made two imitations of this: on the one hand, Dionysus, the son of Zeus and Semele, the inventor of the vine, who was cut into pieces and resuscitated and then ascended into the sky, and whose mysteries involve an ass; on the other, Bellerophon, the son of a man, who ascended into the sky on the horse Pegasus. This duality alone demonstrates for Justin that the demons had not entirely understood the prophecy, which did not specify whether the Messiah would be the son of God or of a man, nor whether he would ascend on the foal of an ass or of a horse. They did know from Isaiah (7.14; 52.13) that he would be born of a virgin and would ascend into heaven by his own power; they then inspired the story of Perseus, born of the virgin Danaë, and of Zeus, who had transformed himself into a rain of gold. When it is said that Heracles, the son of Zeus and of Alcmene, valiantly traveled over the world and ascended into the sky after his death, how is it not possible to see this as an imitation of the Christian prophecy of Psalm 19, (verse 5): "rejoiceth as a strong man to run a race"? Finally, having learned from the same source (Isaiah 35.5–6) that the Messiah would heal the sick and raise the dead, the demons staged the story of Asclepius (*First Apology* 54.5–10; a parallel and sometimes more complete development of this is found in Justin's other work, the *Dialogue with Trypho* 67.1–2; 69.1–5; 70.5, in which the demons give way to the devil, called the "serpent of error"; on Heracles, see M. Simon's[25] excellent commentary).

There is nevertheless in the prophecies, Justin continues, an episode that the demon imitators never credited to a single son of Zeus because it was announced in a purely symbolic fashion, which made it unthinkable for them: it is the crucifixion (*First Apology* 55.1). All the same, the evil-doing of the demons was not limited to inventing sons of Zeus before the coming of the Christ; when he had come, they recognized him as the prophesied Messiah, and set magicians against him (ibid. 56.1).

No other Christian author would take up in such breadth this sort of explanation for the resemblances which come to light between the person of Christ and certain mythological figures. But there are various resurgences of such argumentation. In the fourth century, Firmicus Maternus announced his intention to "review successively all the formulas of pagan religion, to prove that the worst enemy of the human race borrowed them from the holy and venerable predictions of the prophets to serve his filthy crimes" (*De errore profanarum religionum* 21.1). These "formulas," which Firmicus calls *symbola*, are those of the mysteries, of which he gives a few examples. He also considers some pagan rites, which he denounces as misleading imitations of prophecies; contrary to Justin, according to whom the demons had in no way penetrated the prophets' allusions to the Cross, Firmicus holds that it was in order to counterfeit the material of the Cross that the devil had wished to make wood the instrument of rites of renewal (citing the pine in the cult of Cybele and Osiris, the tree trunk in that of Proserpine, etc.) (ibid. 27.1–2).

3. *Mithra and Jesus.* Among the formulas of profane worship, Firmicus Maternus cites the following: "the god born of stone," which, as we know from other sources, designates Mithra. In his eyes, this stone evokes another stone—that by which God promises to strengthen the foundations of the future Jerusalem (according to Isaiah 28.16), and which prophetically designates the Christ. In the perspective that we have just seen, the first of these elements could only have come from the second by theft, fraudulent transfer, adulteration of the faith—and this is, indeed, the author's judgment (*De errore profanarum religionum* 20.1).

Justin had preceded him on this precise point: the initiators into the mysteries of Mithra speak of the god "born of a stone" and call the place of initiation a "cave" because, under the influence of devils, they are imitating the prophecies of Daniel (2.34: the stone that was hewn from the mountain in the dream of Nebuchadnezzar) and of Isaiah (33.16: the righteous one in a cave of solid rock). Justin counters this satanic counterfeiting of Isaiah's prophecy by pointing out the true symbolic import of the verse, which, he contends, refers to the cave of the Nativity at Bethlehem (*Dialogue with Trypho* 70.1–3; 78.5–6).

According to the same verse from Isaiah, the righteous one will receive an inexhaustible supply of bread and water in his cave, which is, Justin continues, a clear prophecy of the eucharist in its two forms (ibid. 70.4); but initiation into the mysteries of Mithra also entails the presentation of bread and a cup of water, accompanied by certain formulas. This coincidence too comes from an imitation imputable to perverse demons (with the difference that here the object of their counterfeiting is no longer prophecy but the actual Gospel accounts of the institution of the eucharist) (*First Apology* 66.4). The same resemblance would be recorded, and explained in identical fashion, by Tertullian: the office of the devil is to pervert the truth and imitate the divine sacraments in the mysteries of idols. The devil too has his baptism, through which he promises the expiation of misdeeds, and Mithra marks the foreheads of his soldiers, celebrates the oblation of bread, gives an idea of the resurrection, crowns his martyrs, etc. (*De praescriptione haereticorum* 40.2–4).

VI. An Apologetic Starting Point

1. *Homogeneity constituted as an argument.* In the writings of Tertullian (*Apologeticus* 47.11–14), we have encountered the idea that paganism had manufactured myths similar to Christian doctrines in order that the obvious falsity of the former should cast doubt, by reason of their similitude, on the latter. The African priest skillfully defused this calculation without relinquishing the presupposition: if the pagan myths inspired belief, how much more should our mysteries, of which theirs are copies, do so! These two arguments, which run in opposite directions, both rely on certain analogies between the two beliefs. More than once, Christian apologists used the same assumption for the same advantage, in various ways. Tertullian himself, in treating of the incarnation and the virgin birth, requires that the pagans first accept them simply because of their resemblance to the myths which they themselves had forged out of the corresponding prophecies: "For the time being accept this 'fable,' which is like your own, until I show you how he is proved to be Christ and who they are among you who have previously circulated fables of this genre, to destroy this truth" (*Apologeticus* 21.14); shortly thereafter (ibid., 21.23), the same author would have them admit that the Christian ascension is "much truer" than (which implies "comparable to") those of Romulus and other Romans.

But this sort of argument goes back farther than Tertullian, for Tatian, wishing to substantiate the incarnation, evokes certain mythic metamorphoses (of Athena as Deïphobus [*Iliad* 22.226–27], of Apollo as the cowherd of Admetus, of Hera as an old woman in the presence of Semele), and authorizes himself, on the basis of this parallel, to take the Greeks to task: "You who insult us, compare your myths to our accounts. . . . Considering your own legends, accept our teachings, if only on the basis of their being myths similar to your own" (*Oratorio ad Graecos* 21). Furthermore, the last passage cited from Tatian turns out to be based, almost word for word, on Justin. Justin has just cited a mass of practices, events, authors, and texts, all borrowed from Greek tradition, which imply a belief that souls remain sentient after death. He refers, for example, to necromancy, the conjuring of the dead, possession, the great oracles of Dodona and of Delphi, philosophers favorable toward the idea of reincarnation, Homer's trench and Odysseus's descent to the underworld (*Odyssey* 11.24ff.), and so forth. After enumerating these pagan testimonies to a belief also held by Christians, Justin demands an at least equal adherence to the Christian version: "If only on the basis of its resemblance to this teaching, accept ours" (*First Apology* 18.3–6).

A comparable attitude appears in Origen, although with a slightly different application. His adversary Celsus refused to accord any meaning other than the literal one to the biblical pages on the creation of woman from the rib of the sleeping Adam (Genesis 2.21–22) and on the garden of different trees planted by God, with its serpent who rebels against the divine commands (ibid., 2.8–9; 3.1–5). In both accounts, Origen opportunely cites as parallels the Hesiodic myth of Pandora (*Works and Days* 53–98, most of which he cites); the first woman, given by Zeus to men as "an evil thing and the price paid for fire" (the comparison with Eve, who alone has a historical reality, had already been instituted by Tertullian, *De corona militum* 7.3); and the Platonic myth (*Symposium* 203b–204c, also cited in great part) of the birth of Eros, who was conceived in the garden of Zeus (the importance of this last text to the Platonist tradition, both pagan and Christian, was revealed by J. M. Rist).[26] Confident of this convergence, Origen feels justified in demanding that the two biblical accounts and the two Greek myths be read in the same light. If, as one would be correct in doing, one recognized a doctrinal import hidden in the depths of the Greek myths, it would be unreasonable to deny such an import to the biblical accounts and merely to retain their surface meaning (*Contra Celsum* 4.38–39). We recognize here the procedure of using analogies with paganism as an authorization to demand at least the same treatment for Christian beliefs. The reality of this argument stands out even more in the two examples that we are about to look at.

2. *The Christ and the sons of Zeus.* We have recalled how the Christians of the first generations insisted that the "newness" of their religion be recognized. A passage from Justin that speaks of the most miraculous aspects of the person and life of Jesus is therefore surprising: "We offer nothing new with respect to those among you who are considered the sons of Zeus." What follows shows that this declaration is to be taken literally: if Jesus is the Word of God, it must be known that this is something he holds in common with Hermes, the Word of Zeus; if he was born of a virgin, so was Perseus; if he healed the sick and raised the dead, it must be admitted that Asclepius did the same; if he was crucified, the sons of Zeus too had their passions (Asclepius struck by lightning, Dionysus dismembered, Heracles throwing himself into fire); and finally, if he ascended into heaven, such was also the case with Asclepius, the Dioscuri, Perseus, Bellerophon on the back of Pegasus, and Ariadne who was placed among the stars—to say nothing of the deceased emperors (*First Apology* 21.1–3; 22.2–6).

Further pages in the *Apology* as well as the *Dialogue with Trypho* again take up many of these episodes pertaining to the sons of Zeus, as we have seen; but in these instances their purpose is to illustrate the fraud perpetrated by the demons who travestied the messianic prophecies because they misunderstood them. Justin's purpose here is quite different and even more surprising: he appears to be overcome by a comparativist frenzy at which even the most reductionist historians of religions would balk. He sets himself to taking the edge off the most salient points of Christology in order to dissolve them in their assimilation to the mythological biographies. No doubt his strategy is an apologetic one: by maximizing the parallels between Christ and the Greek gods, he may legitimately claim the same welcome among the pagans for Christ as for the Greek gods. A little later, Justin clearly declares his aspirations—and his chagrin at failing to see them realized—when he says: "While we say the same things as the Greeks, we alone are hated!" (ibid., 24.1). Naturally, this desire to gain a foothold, even at little cost, among the pagan masses, can only represent an initial and minimal phase in the apologetic enterprise. As Justin himself notes, Christ has arguments other than this in his favor: "All of our teachings received from Christ . . . are alone true . . . , and if we judge them worthy of being welcomed by you, it is not because of these resemblances but because we speak the truth." As for explaining the analogies in question, the chapter ends with the thesis dear to this author: "Before the Word became man among men, some took the initiative under the influence of evil demons and, through the intermediary of the poets, presented as reality the myths they had invented" (ibid., 23.1, 3).

3. *Heracles and Jonah.* A short branch of the tradition concerning Heracles, first represented in the third century B.C. by the Alexandrian poet Lycophron (as noted by M. Simon),[27] credits the hero with having spent three days in the belly of a fish with no harm done except for the loss of his hair. Apart from this last detail, the parallelism with the prophet Jonah is striking; several Christian commentators on the Book of Jonah (2.1–11) referred to it, and used it in the service of an argument which closely follows those we have just seen. Here, in the first half of the fifth century, is the conclusion of Cyril of Alexandria: "It is out of the question for us to give credence to divine prodigies on the basis of the Greek fables, but we retain them to our benefit, to convince the incredulous that the scope of their own legends does not allow them to reject such elements in our accounts" (*Commentary on Jonah* 11; *Patrologia Graeca* 71.616C–617A). In other words, coincidences such as those between Heracles and Jonah, which are unimportant for Christians in their own practice, are useful for making an impression on the incredulity of the Greeks. In the eleventh century the same conclusion is reached through the same comparison by the Byzantine exegete Theophylact, archbishop of Achrida: the story of Jonah is apparently incredible, especially to minds steeped in Greek errors, but the parallel from Heracles creates a dilemma for them: "Either they will also accept our miracles, or they will also reject their own. But we must not use the decay of their myths to reinforce the solidity of our own truth" (*Exposition on the Prophet Jonas* 2.1; *Patrologia Graeca* 126.932 BC).

VII. A Propaedeutic to Christianity

1. *Providential Greek culture.* At the beginning of this study, we saw various Church Fathers refer to certain mythological situations which were more or less comparable to Christian truths, in order, they thought, to speak to their pagan interlocutors in their own language; they were taking advantage of these parallels on a merely rhetorical level, without dealing with underlying questions. But to base an apologetic procedure on such parallels, even at the level we have just described, was to imply recognition of a certain reality in them. There is, however, a third Christian view of the analogies with paganism, which invests them with eminent value since it gives them a foundation that is nothing less than a design of Providence. This perspective must at least be noted in conclusion; it is part of a far broader view, that of the function of Greek culture in the economics of Christian salvation.

This function might be said to be propaedeutic—the word used by Clement of Alexandria, the principal representative of this theology of history. Saint Paul, he says, gives the "rudiments of the world" (Epistle to the Colossians 2.8) as a symbol of Greek philosophy because that philosophy is, so to speak, "elementary," and because it is a "propaedeutic" (*propaideia*) of the truth (*Stromateis* 6.8.62.1). But the function that fell to Greek philosophy is to be understood in two very different ways, neatly distinguished by Clement in an earlier passage: in a more banal sense, philosophy is today a "propaedeutic" (*propaideia*) in the direction of the true piety for minds desirous of reaching faith through demonstration; in a more profound and fundamental sense, it was given to the Greeks in the beginning, before the Lord extended his call to them, "because it was, itself, the educator of Hellenism, just as the Law was that of the Jews, for moving toward the Christ" (*Stromateis* 1.5.28.1, 3).

Several pages of the *Sixth Stromatis* are devoted to this vision of history. In discussing the consciousness of Christian newness we cited a sentence on the three modes—Greek, Jewish, and Christian—of the knowledge of God. Clement accentuates the strict parallelism between the two kinds of "evangelical preparation": on the one hand, the Law and the Prophets were given in their time to the barbarians (i.e., the Jews); and, on the other, philosophy was given to the Greeks, in order to habituate the ears of both to the Good News (6.6.44.1). Here, "philosophy" takes on a broader meaning than it has today, extending to the whole of culture.

Clement is bold enough to conceive of a Greek prophetism corresponding to the Jewish: "Just as God, wanting to save the Jews, gave them prophets, he also inspired among the Greeks the most prominent personalities to be their own prophets in their language, according as they were capable of receiving the gift of God, and he distinguished them from ordinary people" (6.5.42.3). Concurrent texts by the same author have been cited by J. Daniélou.[28] It is easy to understand, within this very particular perspective, how any intersection, however approximate or superficial, between the Greek religious corpus on the one hand and Jewish or Christian beliefs on the other would stand out and assume meaning in a way quite unlike those we have previously seen.

2. *Heiliger Homer* ("holy Homer"). The proof that Clement includes both poetry and mythology in his understanding of "Greek philosophy" is to be found first of all in the fact that he considers Homer primarily a Greek prophet. In his *Paedagogus,* in which he gives a commentary on the numerous scriptural texts in which milk is introduced as a symbol of spiritual nourishment, Clement first thinks of the beginning of book 13 of the *Iliad* (lines 5–6) in which the righteous (in fact, the noble Scythian tribes) are called "milk eaters" (*galactophagoi*), and he infers from this that Homer "prophesies involuntarily" (ibid. 1.6.36.1). There also appears to be a distinction, in the *Odyssey* (9.275, 410–11), between a "Zeus with the aegis," about whom the Cyclops hardly concern themselves, and a "great Zeus," whom they dread. In this god, of whom there are apparently two persons, Clement sees an allusion to the Christian duality of the Father and the Son, and he again concludes that Homer "was favored with an authentic gift of prophecy" (*Stromateis* 5.14.116.1; this feature was pointed out by F. Buffière).[29]

It seems as if, parallel to the Hebraic tradition, which of course remains the privileged channel, part of the Revelation had flowed into Greek culture; it is to the reality of this double current arising from a single source that we must relate—both in their indices and in their consequences—the coincidences that leave the present-day reader skeptical, though they impressed Clement. Homer, the principal prop for this demonstration, emerges from it as sacralized as the Jewish prophets—a canonization that H. Rahner[30] characterized so well with the formula he borrowed from Goethe: *Heiliger Homer!* It should also be noted how, under different guises, comparing Homer with the Holy Scriptures was a favorite pastime of certain humanists and scholars of the modern era; the works of N. Hepp[31] are persuasive on this point.

To return to the first centuries A.D., it would appear that this Christian Homer was more attractive to marginal currents of thought than to the orthodox tradition. The Gnostic Naassene sect is said to have founded itself upon a harmonization between the Homeric poems and the Jewish Scriptures, a harmonization made possible in both cases through the application of a highly inventive allegorical exegesis. This is what Hippolytus had to say in their regard: "Following the new method of interpretation of literary works which they have invented, they attribute to Homer, their prophet, the glory of having first, in a mysterious way, revealed these truths, at the same time as they mock those who have not been initiated into the Holy Scriptures, in pressing such ideas upon them" (*Refutatio omnium haeresium* 5.8.1). Among the many examples of this amalgamation, here is another, which long held the attention of H. Leisegang[32] and, later, J. Carcopino:[33] at the beginning of the last book of the *Odyssey* (24.1ff.), we see the souls of the dead suitors of Penelope being conducted to the Mead of Asphodel by the golden wand of Cyllenian Hermes. Now, the Naassenes not only identify this god with the Logos, which is unremarkable, but they identify him precisely with the Christian Word; his golden wand is none other than the iron rod of Psalm 2 (verse 9); it awakens the drowsing souls, conforming to the role reserved for the Christ in the Epistle to the Ephesians (5.14); as for the suitors, they are really men who, awakened from sleep, recall the bliss from which they have fallen and hope for their redemption, according to the Christian perspective (Hippolytus, *Refutatio omnium haeresium* 5.7.29–33).

3. *The Sibyl and Virgil.* The *Sibylline Oracles,* to which our attention has been drawn anew by V. Nikiprowetzky,[34] are today regarded as a highly composite work, in which elements that are very diverse in both date and source are found side by side. A basic corpus of pagan oracles was augmented between the second century B.C. and the second century A.D.—in imitation of primitive literary patterns, for purposes of propaganda to paganism—by a Jewish contribution (not without Christian interpolations) and then by a fully Christian contribution. But the Fathers of the second and third centuries, who often cite this collection (sometimes associating the Sibyl with the name of Hystaspis, the Iranian pseudo-magus, as do, for example, Justin, *First Apology* 20.1, 44.12, and Clement of Alexandria, *Stromateis* 6.5.43.1), conceived of it quite differently. For them it was an exclusively pagan work in which they admiringly discovered a mass of Jewish and even Christian parallels, whence their conviction that here once again they were dealing with a manifestation of the Revelation, and their habit of paralleling its testimony with Jewish prophecy. On this line of thought, which continued to perpetuate itself in the Middle Ages in the first strophe of *Dies irae: Teste David cum Sibylla,* see the works of K. Prümm.[35]

Their very title suggests that the *Sibylline Oracles* should not be considered without recalling the celebrated Virgilian *Fourth Eclogue,* for Virgil there makes reference to a prophecy by the Sibyl of Cumae, and the two texts are, in the eyes of many other Christians, to be placed in a somewhat comparable situation. The content of this short poem is well known; the salient points are as follows: the Virgin returns, a new generation descends from heaven, a child is born who will receive the divine life and will govern the globe pacified by his father, the golden age begins in spite of the fact that there remains in the hearts of men something of the ancient malice, etc. As J. Carcopino[36] has shown, this is a work adapted to circumstances, in which all of these traits are fully explicable through reference to the historical situation; that is, to local history.

But, especially if one believes that these verses date from 40 B.C., such a concentration of details charged with evocation for the Christian consciousness could only lead to reading it as a non-Christian but true prophecy. In fact, as has been shown by P. Courcelle's scholarly investigation,[37] a number of authors—often, it must be admitted, second-rate ones—identified the Virgilian child with the Infant Jesus, the new generation with the Christian people or with the incarnated Word, and so forth. Some nevertheless hesitated to bestow the title of prophet upon Virgil because it was totally without understanding it that he conveyed the annunciation of the Christ, which he received from the Sibyl, herself a true prophetess. Virgil, the unconscious prophet: this, roughly, is how Saint Augustine and the grammarian Philargyrius thought of the author of the eclogue, just as Clement of Alexandria saw Homer as an "involuntary prophet."

In spite of their appeal, these harmonizing interpretations

met with resistance among the Christians themselves. The most famous, and most severe, was that of Jerome: "These are puerilities, like charlatans' tricks, teaching what one does not know; even worse—to use an unpleasant expression—than not even to know what one does not know" (*Letter* 53, to Paulinus, 7). The partisans nevertheless remained more numerous than the adversaries, and would continue to be so down to the Middle Ages, when Abelard and then Dante were the most celebrated defenders of the messianism of the eclogue. Both of these writers, in line with Augustine's thought, also see Virgil as having announced the incarnation without realizing it, and therefore without believing it himself. Abelard compares him in this regard to Caiaphas; Dante, as I showed in another study,[38] expresses the same conviction by the compelling image of a man walking while holding behind his back a torch that sheds light upon those who follow him but leaves the man himself in darkness (*Purgatorio* 22.67–69). It matters little whether these authors made Virgil a conscious or merely an "objective" prophet, since, in the latter case, the prophetic function in the full sense of the word belonged to the Sibyl. What is significant is that the existence of analogies such as those we have discussed—some of them real, but most of them superficial or even illusory—fueled the conviction that classical paganism, from Homer to Virgil, never ceased to lead toward Christianity.

J.P./d.w.

NOTES

1. A.-J. FESTUGIÈRE, "Saint Paul à Athènes et la Ire Épître aux Corinthiens," *L'enfant d'Agrigente* (Paris 1941), 88–101; on the Athens discourse, see the classic thesis by B. GÄRTNER, *The Areopagus Speech and Natural Revelation* (Uppsala 1955).

2. M. SIMON, *Hercule et le christianisme* (Paris 1955), 170–73.

3. J. ADHÉMAR, *Influences antiques dans l'art du Moyen Age français: Recherches sur les sources et les thèmes d'inspiration* (diss., Paris; London 1937; 2d ed., 1975), notably 221–22 and pl. XXIII 72. For pagan survivals in primitive Christian art, see also W. ROTHES, "Heidnisches in altchristlicher Kunst und Symbolik," in *Festgabe A. Ehrhard* (Bonn and Leipzig 1922), 381–406.

4. H. RAHNER, *Griechische Mythen in christlicher Deutung* (Zurich 1945; 2d ed., 1957), p. 21, etc.

5. E. HATCH, *The Influence of Greek Ideas on Christianity;* 2d ed. by F. C. Grant (New York and Evanston 1957), 283–309; A. D. NOCK, *Early Gentile Christianity and Its Hellenistic Background* (New York 1964), 116–45.

6. A. WIFSTRAND, *L'église ancienne et la culture grecque,* trans. from Swedish (Paris 1962), 107–34.

7. RAHNER, *Griechische Mythen in christlicher Deutung,* 414–86. See also the well-documented articles that the same author published in the *Zeitschrift für Katholische Theologie* from 1941 through 1964 under the general title of "Antenna crucis"; these studies have been conveniently reassembled in H. RAHNER, *Symbole der Kirche: Die Ekklesiologie der Väter* (Salzburg 1964), 237–564; titles include: "Odysseus am Mastbaum," "Das Meer der Welt," "Das Schiff aus Holz," "Das Kreuz als Mastbaum und Antenne," "Das Mystische Tau," "Der Schiffbruch und die Planke des Heils," "Das Schifflein des Petrus: Zur Symbolgeschichte des römischen Primats," "Die Arche Noe als Schiff des Heils," and "Die Ankunft im Hafen."

8. P. COURCELLE, "Quelques symboles funéraires du néoplatonisme latin: Le vol de Dédale; Ulysse et les Sirènes," *Revue des études anciennes* 46 (1944): 65–93; "L'interprétation evhémériste des Sirènes-courtisanes jusqu'au XIIe siècle," in *Mélanges L. Wallach* (Stuttgart 1975), 33–48.

9. J. CARCOPINO, *De Pythagore aux Apôtres: Études sur la conversion du monde romain* (Paris 1956), 192–221. It is now known that one of the Gnostic Copt writings discovered at Nag Hammadi, *L'Exégèse de l'âme,* also exploits the legend of Odysseus, in concurrence with biblical texts; cf. M. SCOPELLO, "Les citations d'Homère dans le traité de *L'Exégèse de l'âme,*" in M. Krause, ed., *Gnosis and Gnosticism* (Leiden 1977), 3–12.

10. V. BUCHHEIT, "Homer bei Methodios von Olympos," *Rheinisches Museum* 99 (1956): 19–36.

11. A. CASAMASSA, "L'accusa di 'Hesterni' e gli scrittori cristiani del II secolo," *Angelicum* 20 (1943): 184–94.

12. N. ZEEGERS-VANDER VORST, *Les citations des poètes grecs chez les apologistes chrétiens du IIe siècle* (Louvain 1972), 184–86 and 272. For Christian attitudes in the first three centuries toward the part of pagan authors, see more generally W. KRAUSE, *Die Stellung der frühchristlichen Autoren zur heidnischen Literatur* (Vienna 1958).

13. J. PÉPIN, "Le 'challenge' Homère-Moïse aux premiers siècles chrétiens," *Revue des sciences religieuses* 29 (1955): 105–22.

14. J. DANIÉLOU, *Histoire des doctrines chrétiennes avant Nicée,* 2: *Message évangélique et culture hellénistique aux IIe et IIIe siècles* (Tournai 1961), book 1, pp. 73–101, "Homère chez les Pères de l'Église."

15. G. GLOCKMANN, "Das Homerbild der altchristlichen Literatur in der Forschung der Gegenwart," *Klio* 43–45 (1965): 270–81; by the same author, *Homer in der frühchristlichen Literatur bis Justinus* (Berlin 1968).

16. For example, A. J. FESTUGIÈRE, *La révélation d'Hermès Trismégiste,* 1: *L'astrologie et les sciences occultes* (Paris 1944), 19–44; H. DÖRRIE, "Die Wertung der Barbaren im Urteil der Griechen: Knechtsnaturen? Oder Bewahrer und Künder heilbringender Weisheit?" in *Antike und Universalgeschichte, Festschrift H. E. Stier* (Munster 1972), 146–75.

17. J. H. WASZINK, "Some Observations on the Appreciation of 'The Philosophy of the Barbarians' in Early Christian Literature," in *Mélanges C. Mohrmann* (Utrecht and Anvers 1963), 41–56.

18. K. THRAEDE, "Erfinder," part 2, in *Reallexikon für Antike und Christentum* (1962), cols. 1242–61.

19. A. MÉHAT, *Étude sur les "Stromates" de Clément d'Alexandrie* (Paris 1966), 356–61.

20. R. MORTLEY, *Connaissance religieuse et herméneutique chez Clément d'Alexandrie* (Leiden 1973), 162–66.

21. N. WALTER, *Der Thoraausleger Aristobulos: Untersuchungen zu seinen Fragmenten und zu pseudepigraphischen Resten der jüdisch-hellenistischen Literatur* (Berlin 1964), 44–51 and 150–71.

22. J. PÉPIN, *Mythe et allégorie: Les origines grecques et les contestations judéo-chrétiennes* (2d ed., Paris 1976), 448–52.

23. C. ANDRESEN, *Logos und Nomos: Die Polemik des Kelsos wider das Christentum* (Berlin 1955), 352–55.

24. F. BUFFIÈRE, *Les mythes d'Homère et la pensée grecque* (Paris 1956), 279–89.

25. SIMON, *Hercule et le christianisme,* 111.

26. J. M. RIST, *Eros and Psyche: Studies in Plato, Plotinus and Origen,* "Phoenix," supplement vol. 6 (Toronto 1964).

27. SIMON, *Hercule et le christianisme,* 174–75.

28. DANIÉLOU, *Histoire des doctrines chrétiennes avant Nicée,* 2: *Message évangélique et culture hellénistique aux IIe et IIIe siècles,* book 1, pp. 53–55.

29. BUFFIÈRE, *Les mythes d'Homère et la pensée grecque,* 361 and note 86.

30. RAHNER, *Griechische Mythen in christlicher Deutung,* 357.

31. N. HEPP, "Les interprétations religieuses d'Homère au XVIIe siècle," *Revue des sciences religieuses* 31 (1957): 34–50; *Homère en France au XVIIe siècle* (Paris 1968).

32. H. LEISEGANG, *La gnose,* trans. from German (Paris 1951), 89–90.

33. CARCOPINO, *De Pythagore aux Apôtres,* 180–81.

34. V. NIKIPROWETZKY, *La troisième Sibylle* (Paris and The Hague 1970).

35. K. PRÜMM, "Das Prophetenamt der Sibyllen in kirchlicher Literatur mit besonderer Rücksicht auf die Deutung der VI. Ekloge Virgils," *Scholastik* 4 (1929): 54–77, 221–46, and 498–533.

36. J. CARCOPINO, *Virgile et le mystère de la VIe Églogue* (2d ed., Paris 1943).

37. P. COURCELLE, "Les exégèses chrétiennes de la quatrième Églogue," *Revue des études anciennes* 59 (1957): 294–319.

38. J. PÉPIN, *Dante et la tradition de l'allégorie* (Montreal and Paris 1970), 103–5.

The Euhemerism of the Christian Authors

I. Euhemerus and His Doctrine

We have very little precise information about Euhemerus, a Greek known only from a small number of testimonies which often disagree with one another (these may be found in the collections of G. Némethy[1] and G. Vallauri[2]). He is most often said to be a native of Messene in Peloponnesos, or Messina in Sicily, but he is also said to come from Agrigento, or Tegea, or Chios. According to Diodorus the historian, it was King Cassandra of Macedonia (316–297) who sent Euhemerus on an expedition to the Red Sea; on the other hand, Euhemerus seems to be cited by the poet Callimachus in works that must date from 275–270. It can thus roughly be estimated that Euhemerus went on his travels as early as 300–298, and wrote about them around 280. On these data, see Jacoby's 1907 article, which is still valuable.[3]

In Euhemerus, the author is always identified with the voyager. Returned from his exploration, he draws from it a geographical novel in which real memories rub shoulders with affabulation; this combination is given free reign in the description of Panchaia, an imaginary island off the coast of Arabia. Euhemerus would have it that he found there "a temple of Zeus Triphylian, in which a golden column stood whose inscription indicated that it had been erected by Zeus himself; on this column, the god had inscribed the details of his greatest deeds, in order that posterity be informed of them" (fgt 23 Nemethy = *testim* 4 Vallauri = Lactantius, *Divinae Institutiones* 1.11.33). It is this testimony by the gods about their own exploits that Euhemerus comments on in a *Sacred Record* (*Hiera Anagraphē*), a clever title that reminds one that what is being treated is mainly an "inscription." Nothing remains of this work, but some Greek authors mention it, especially Diodorus of Sicily. The Roman poet Ennius translated (or adapted) it into Latin, and the Christian Lactantius preserved fragments of that translation, whose title was probably *Sacra Historia*.

This is enough to yield a rough idea of the theology of Euhemerus. The central idea is connected to the inscription in the temple of Zeus: it is that the gods of mythology were at first men, who were divinized *post mortem* in recognition of eminent services that they had rendered to humanity. As Lactantius also says (*De ira dei* 2.7.8 = *testim* 15N = *testim* 5mV), "It is beyond doubt that all those who receive worship as gods were men, and that the first and the greatest among them were kings; but that by virtue of the courage with which they had served the human race, they were gratified with divine honors after their death; or else following the good deeds and inventions with which they had embellished the life of humankind, they ensured for themselves an imperishable memorial. Who does not know this? . . . Those who hold to this teaching are primarily Euhemerus and our Ennius." But the popular pantheon also included gods of lesser morality who were, according to the preceding principle, difficult to identify with public benefactors; they too, however, could be explained by the same principle, provided that violence and deceit were substituted for good deeds and gratitude. On this subject, Sextus Empiricus (*Adversus Mathematicos* 9.17 = fgt 1N = *testim* 5c5) seems to have preserved the express formulations of the *Sacred Record:* "Euhemerus, known as 'the Atheist,' says this: 'When men lived in disorder, those whose superiority in strength and intelligence permitted them to make everyone carry out their orders, wishing to receive more admiration and respect, falsely attributed to themselves a superhuman and divine power, which caused the masses to regard them as gods.'"

In reducing the shimmering of mythology to the more prosaic realities of history, Euhemerus joined the current of rationalist criticism applied to popular religion, a current that has been studied by P. Decharme[4] and A. B. Drachmann;[5] this is why he was known as "the Atheist." He was an innovator; the Sophists, especially Prodicus, are sometimes considered his predecessors. But Prodicus, although he explained divinization in terms of utility, was thinking mainly of the benefits offered by the great natural realities—the sun, rivers, springs, fruits of the earth, etc.—which men turned into gods; it was only at a later point that he extended this principle to the inventors of beneficial crafts themselves, and this thesis was not as well documented as the first. On the other hand, as G. Vallauri has shown,[6] Euhemerus was not a sniper. His great idea incontestably corresponds to the spirit of his age; it is clearly related (and we shall see that the Christians were not mistaken about this) to the cult of sovereigns which was instituted in the Hellenistic period. Several authors or currents more or less contemporaneous with Euhemerus (the uncertainty of our chronology does not permit us to say whether he influenced them or was indebted to them) offered, as he did, a theory of the gods as former great servants of humanity. We do not know the exact moment at which ancient Stoicism adopted this explanation for certain gods—or, more accurately, for certain heroes, such as Heracles, Castor and Pollux, Asclepius, Dionysus. It is in any case a foregone conclusion with Zeno's student Persaeus of Citium (certainly posterior to Euhemerus by a few years), whose thesis was formulated by Cicero (*De natura deorum* 1.15.38) as follows: "Those who had devised something of great usefulness were honored as gods." There was another author, Hecataeus of Abdera (or of Teos), probably slightly earlier than Euhemerus, who proposed altogether analogous views on the origins of the Egyptian gods, if in fact he was, as is generally asserted (but see the counterargument of W. Spoerri),[7] the source, in the Egyptian domain, of the historian Diodorus of Sicily.

Euhemerus, therefore, was certainly not the only person of his time to defend the thesis we have just described. But it was his name that remained coupled to it for posterity, notably for the Christian writers of the first centuries. For these writers broadly explored the possibilities Euhemerism offered, and we shall see why and how they did so. Works on this subject are rare, but we should at least point out the articles by F. Zucker[8] and K. Thraede,[9] and the dissertation by J. W. Schippers,[10] to which we might add my own earlier studies;[11] we should also add that the works of J. D. Cooke[12] and of P. Alphandéry[13] on the medieval developments of Euhemerism, and by J. Seznec[14] on survivals of ancient theologies down to the Renaissance, contain much data on their use in the patristic age.

II. Christian Formulations

1. *Defense and illustration of Euhemerus.* The pagan gods are false gods; but what are they really? Christian theologians could not evade a response to this question. This response often takes the form, as with Saint Augustine, of describing the gods of the nations as "foul demons who wish to pass as gods": *deos gentium esse inmundissimos daemones . . . deos se putari cupientes* (*City of God* 7.33). Euhemerism, however, offered an alternative, which Christians hurried to adopt. In spite of the atheism attached in classical tradition to the name

of Euhemerus, Theophilus of Antioch (*Ad Autolycum* 3.7 = *testim* 19–20N = *testim* 5lV) was perhaps the only Christian who noted his impiety. Many Church Fathers, on the other hand, absolve him along with other supposed "atheists," and compliment him on his clairvoyance. The African Arnobius of Sicca (late third to early fourth century) illustrates this outlook: "We surely cannot show here that all those whom you introduce under the name of gods were men: it suffices to open Euhemerus of Agrigento—whose books Ennius translated into an Italic language that everyone understands—or else Nicagoras of Cyprus, or Leo of Pella, or Theodore of Cyrene, or Hippo and Diagoras, both of Melos, or a thousand other authors who, attentive to scrupulous accuracy and as the free men that they were, brought to the light of day facts that had been left in shadow" (*Adversus nationes* 4.29 = *testim* 14N = *testim* 5iV). Elsewhere, Clement of Alexandria (*Protrepticus* 2.24.2 = *testim* 13N = *testim* 5hV) makes a very similar comment, which may have been Arnobius's model. At the beginning of the third century, Minucius Felix (*Octavius* 21.1 = *testim* 9N = *testim* 5fV) counts Euhemerus among historians and sages; Saint Augustine (*City of God* 7.27 = fgt 20N = *testim* 5n2V), calling history to the aid of poetry, associates his name with that of Virgil, who is also taken as a witness to the fact that Saturn was a mere dethroned king (*Aeneid* 8.319ff.). This last text shows that the Christian author was at pains to find Euhemerism in texts other than those of its founder; he would see another of his partisans in the person of the Egyptian Hermes Trismegistus, who, he says, "testifies that the gods of the Egyptians are men who have died" (*City of God* 8.26, using as an illustration the Hermetic *Asclepius* § 24).

The haste with which Christian authors adopted the theses of Euhemerus may be explained in part by the fact that they found similar theses in some of their scriptures. Such is the case with the Wisdom of Solomon, to which attention has been drawn by J. D. Cooke (see note 12); here are the terms in which the genesis of idolatry is traced in it: "For a father, consumed with grief at an untimely bereavement, made an image of his child, who had suddenly been taken from him; and now he honored as a god what was once a dead human being, and handed on to his dependents secret rites and initiations. Then the ungodly custom, grown strong with time, was kept as a law . . . and the multitude, attracted by the charm of his work, now regarded as an object of worship the one whom shortly before they had honored as a man" (*New Oxford Annotated Bible*, Wisdom of Solomon 14.15–20). This development (undoubtedly from the first century B.C.) on the origin of the gods is incontestably linked to Euhemerism, from which it probably takes its inspiration. Eight centuries later, Isidore of Seville would recall it, perhaps in order to describe the same kind of retrogression: after the death of certain great men, their friends represented them by means of an effigy simply as a means of consoling themselves and honoring their memory; it was only the following generations which, with the help of demonic influences, fell into the error of making gods of these men (*Etymologiae* 8.11.4).

In their portrayal of Euhemerism, the Christians accentuated particular aspects of it. The original humanity of the gods is less striking to them than the death through which they have passed, which continues to cling to them; more than divinized men, they are "corpses": "we, who are alive, do not sacrifice to corpses who are gods, and we do not worship them," is what we read in the Second Epistle (3.1), attributed (wrongly) to Saint Clement, one of the first bishops of Rome; "You have ended up as corpses yourselves, for having put your trust in corpses," is the warning given to the pagans by Clement of Alexandria (*Protrepticus* 3.45.5); "They never manufacture gods except from corpses," writes the historian Eusebius (*Praeparatio Evangelica* 3.3.17), echoing the same idea. They fear beings that are twice dead, "more dead than the dead": such is already the statement attributed to the Apostle Peter in the *Clementine Homilies* (10.9).

In explaining by what error men came to worship those who had previously been their peers, Clement stresses the aura of prestige with which the distant past is so easily endowed, while the present remains ignored for its banality. The historian Thucydides (*Peloponnesian Wars* 1.21.1) had earlier observed that "with the passing of time, most historic facts pass into the region of myths that no one can believe." Clement again takes up this idea of the complicity of time and myth: "Those whom you worship were once men, who afterwards died. But myth and time have loaded them with honors . . . For the past, being cut off from immediate control by the obscurity which time brings, is invested with a fictitious honor . . . That is how the dead men of old, made venerable by the authority that time concedes to error, are believed to be gods by those who come after" (*Protrepticus* 4.55.2–3). It was, moreover, a Jewish explanation before it became Christian; we find it on the lips of another Clement, a cultivated Greek converted to Judaism and the protagonist of the *Clementine Homilies* (6.22); these homilies themselves belong to a Jewish apologetic tradition which may go back as far as the beginning of the second century. It takes time to forget that the gods were once men; but too much time results in a weakening of the legend. As Clement of Alexandria says (*Protrepticus* 2.37.1–3), the myths and gods of paganism "have aged" today, and Zeus himself is no longer the intrepid lover he once was (Tatian, *Oratio ad Graecos* 21, already spoke in a like fashion: "Why does Hera no longer bear children? Has she grown old, or does she lack someone who might announce it to you?"). But it is the discovery of Euhemerus that consummates this decadence, described by Clement by means of a metaphor familiar to ancient theories of myth, that of "laying bare" (the verb *gumnoun*)—the truth "lays bare" the mass of gods by tearing away their masks (*Protrepticus* 2.27.5); the myth of Zeus is "laid bare" before the eyes of the pagans (2.37.3)—which is all another way of saying that the Euhemerist explanation strips the Greek pantheon of its finery and reduces it to its mere human expression.

Thus Christian thought tried to accredit Euhemerus's hypothesis by analyzing the process of divinization. Other authors offer equally enlightening examples. Lactantius, the principal witness to the Latin adaptation of Euhemerus, reduces the classical pranks of Jupiter to purely human dimensions: the golden rain with which the god showered Danaë's breast was nothing more, in a concrete sense—if one subtracts from it all the poetic amplification—than the wages of a common courtesan, just as "rain of iron" is used for a volley of arrows; the eagle of Ganymede was originally simply the insignia of the legion sent out to kidnap the young shepherd; as for the bull of Europa and the heifer into which Io metamorphosed herself, we are to understand these ruminants, in a more prosaic way, as figureheads on the prows of the ships used to transport the two maidens (*Divinae Institutiones* 1.11.17–22; in the same vein, *Epitome divin. instit.* 11; certain of these explanations are taken up again by Augustine, *City of God* 18.13).

2. *The divinization of emperors and pharaohs.* We have seen that the appearance of Euhemerism was probably not uncon-

nected with the cult of the Hellenistic sovereigns. This *Sitz im Leben* could not escape the Christian authors, who associated the theses of Euhemerus with the apotheoses of princes which were taking place before their eyes or had occurred recently. This is what Athanasius of Alexandria does, for example, in a *Discourse against the Pagans*. His Euhemerist convictions are well established: the gods are very ancient leaders, upon the loss of whom (along with their relatives) there was lamentation—such was the case with Zeus, Hermes, Osiris, etc. (*Contra Gentes* 10, *Patrologia Graeca* 25.24A). Thus was constituted the antique pantheon, its principal author being Theseus, the legendary king of Attica (10.21BC). Athanasius clearly refuses to take such divinities seriously; as he says in a well-turned phrase, "Their mythology is not a theology" (19.40C). For him, the process of divinization unveiled by Euhemerus evokes the apotheosis bestowed upon emperors and claimed by some of them for third parties (as by Hadrian for his favorite Antinous) (9.20CD). Against such pretensions, Athanasius simply observes that, since the worker should be superior to his work, mortal men are incapable of making gods (9.21A; an analogous argument had previously been more amply developed by Tertullian, *Apologeticus* 11.1–3).

The passages from Athanasius are undoubtedly the most synthetic, but they are not the only ones to be found in patristic literature on the subject. The author of the *Clementine Homilies* (6.23) bases his arguments on Euhemerism, recalling that down through the Ptolemaic period the Egyptians had made gods of their pharaohs even while they were still alive. As for Saint Augustine, he would note that Euhemerus's explanation is rendered probable by the spectacle of different episodes in Roman history: "What then is surprising in the fact that the earliest men did for Jupiter, Saturn, and the rest the very thing that the Romans did for Romulus and wanted to do, in a more recent time, for Caesar himself?"(*De consensu evangelist.* 1.23.32).

This pretension to legal apotheosis on the part of great individuals naturally rankles the Christians, who are sometimes presented as adversaries of Euhemerism; we have seen that such is not the case, except to the extent that Euhemerus might have appeared to them as being partial to aspirations to divinization on the part of sovereigns. Whatever the case, it must be said that, in their rejection of apotheosis, the Christian authors, as often happened, followed in the footsteps of certain Greek philosophers. We saw above that the Stoic Persaeus of Citium, regarding the phenomenon of heroization, held a doctrine related to, and probably dependent upon, that of Euhemerus. And Cicero, describing the thesis of Persaeus in his dialogue *De natura deorum* (1.15.38), puts his account in the mouth of an Epicurian philosopher named Velleius, who no sooner formulates the doctrine than he condemns it with great verve: "What could be more absurd than . . . to raise men to gods once death has destroyed them?"

3. *The "letter of Alexander to Olympias."* Even though Euhemerus never, properly speaking, founded a school, his theses were exhibited in works other than his own. Among the latter, a text should be noted here for the echo it finds among Christian listeners; that is, a so-called letter from Alexander of Macedonia to his mother Olympias, discussed in an article by F. Pfister.[15] Various Christian apologists (Tertullian, Minucius Felix, Cyprian, Augustine) believe that the author really was Alexander, to whom the Euhemerist theory was thought to have been revealed in Egypt. Here, for example, is how Athenagoras, the earliest among them, associates the Macedonian king with the historian Herodotus, who precedes him by a century: "Herodotus and Alexander, the son of Philip, in his letter to his mother, say that they have learned from the priests that these gods were once men. Each of them is said to have had conversations with the priests in Heliopolis, Memphis, and Thebes" (Athenagoras, *Supplication to Marcus Aurelius* 28).

Other Fathers of the Church (Tatian, Tertullian again, Clement of Alexandria, Eusebius, Arnobius), commenting on the same subject, evoke a certain Leo. That all of these writers had the same text in mind is demonstrated by the fact that Augustine (*City of God* 8.5, 27; *De consensu evangelist.* 1.23.33) makes Leo the Egyptian priest from whom Alexander received the revelation of the original humanity of the gods. Such divergencies lead one to believe that this was a document of which the Christians had only heard tell, and that its author was neither Alexander nor Leo but an unknown individual whose ideas and lifetime were close to those of Hecataeus of Abdera and of Euhemerus; he was probably later than they and influenced by them. Of all of the Christian writers, only Arnobius, in a passage cited above, speaks of Leo *of Pella;* this geographical detail might lead one to believe that he was a real individual; but this does not accord with the testimony of Augustine, who sees Leo as a *sacerdos Aegyptius.* The situation being so confused, especially if one remembers that Pella was the capital of the kingdom of Macedonia and the birthplace of Alexander, one is tempted to subscribe to F. Pfister's hypothesis, that Arnobius's "Pellaeus Leon" was merely a metaphor designating Alexander, the "lion of Pella!"

III. The Arguments Set Forth

1. *The "synonymy" of the gods.* Accepting Euhemerism, the Christian authors muster various arguments in favor of this doctrine; some were their own, but most had been formulated before them. So it is that Clement of Alexandria, in order to "refute the imaginations" that presided over the constitution of the pagan pantheon, invokes what he calls the "synonymies" (*Protrepticus* 2.27.5), and what today we would call homonymy: the fact that the names of the greatest gods refer to several distinct divinities. By way of illustration, he recalls that there were three Zeuses, five Athenas, six Apollos, and many an Asclepius, Hermes, Hephaestus, and Ares (2.28.1–29.2). Many other Christian authors made sport of the fact that several would-be gods could bear the same name, especially that of Zeus (Theophilus of Antioch, *Ad Autolycum* 12.10; Minucius Felix, *Octavius* 22.6; Arnobius, *Adversus nationes* 4.14, etc.); but none could exploit these circumstances to the advantage of the Euhemerist thesis as well as Clement did. The way had nevertheless been opened by the pagan philosophers themselves; Cicero, for example, in the third book of his dialogue *De natura deorum,* borrows from Cotta, the spokesman for skepticism in the New Academy, a long elaboration on the plurality, not only of Jupiters, but also of Vulcans, Mercuries, Apollos, etc. (*Nat. D.* 3.21.53–23.60). This fact had already been interpreted there as an argument in favor of the human origin of these gods, as the first sentence of his declamatory passage shows: "We ought also to fight those who argue that these beings who came from the human race and were transported to heaven are not really, but only by convention, the gods whom we all honor with our most devout veneration" (3.21.53).

2. *The traces left by the gods.* It could have been predicted that the bodily peculiarities of the gods would be seen as

indices of their human origin. In his treatise *On Isis and Osiris* (chap. 23), Plutarch shows himself to be personally hostile to Euhemerism; he nevertheless notes (chap. 22) that, according to the Egyptians, Hermes had short arms, Typho was red-headed, Horus blond, Osiris brunette; and he gives voice to the following conclusion: "This is because, by nature, they were men." The Christian Eusebius makes no mistake; in searching in his *Praeparatio Evangelica* (3.3.15–16) for confirmations for his Euhemerist convictions, he sees how he can make good use of Plutarch's text on the bodily characteristics of the gods. He cites that text as "witness to the fact that they were mortal men." The details of their physical appearance are just part of the picture, and Clement of Alexandria invokes other concrete data that point in the same direction: "May the lands they dwelled in, the arts they practiced, the record of their lives, yes, and even their tombs, convince you that they were only men" (*Protrepticus* 2.29.1).

In drawing out this argument, Clement and Eusebius followed Euhemerus's lead directly, as several sources show: "Euhemerus and our Ennius show the birth, marriage, progeniture, power, exploits, death, and tomb of all the gods" (*testim.* 15N = *testim.* 5mV = Lactantius, *De ira dei* 2.7.8; cf. on the same *testim.* 9N = *testim.* 5fV = Minucius Felix, *Octavius* 21). The last element mentioned, the tomb as an attestation of death, is the most important of all; it is the only one retained by Cicero (*Nat. D.* 1.42.119 = *testim.* 2N = *testim.* 5dV): *ab Euhemero autem et mortes et sepulturae demonstrantur deorum* ("Moreover, both the deaths and the tombs of the gods are demonstrated by Euhemerus"). Euhemerus was especially concerned with Zeus, narrating his death in Crete, the funerary rites performed by his sons the Curetes, and the placing of the body in the sepulcher in Cnossos (fgt 29N = fgt 24V = Lactantius, *Divinae Institutiones* 1.11.46). Thus the poet Callimachus, wishing to dismantle nascent Euhemerism, would choose to refute it on this ground (*Hymn to Zeus* 8–9 = *testim.* 1bV): "The Cretans are always liars; for the Cretans even built your tomb, O king, but you did not die, for you exist forever."

The Christian authors take care not to side with Callimachus; several of them expressly rebuke him and say that the Cretans are right rather than he, as shown in the texts brought together by N. Zeegers-Vander Vorst.[16] Tatian (*Oratio ad Graecos* 27) and Clement of Alexandria (*Protrepticus* 2.37.4) took this line. The interpellation of Athanagoras, which comes at the end of three chapters on the human origin of the gods, merits a citation; it points out the contradiction of the poet, who denies that the god is dead but recognizes that he was born, without realizing that he who is born must die: "You believe, Callimachus, in the birth of Zeus but you do not believe in his tomb. And thinking to conceal the truth, you proclaim his death, even to men who are unaware of it; if you see the cave you recall Rhea's giving birth, but if you see the funerary urn you throw darkness over the death of the god, not knowing that the only eternal being is the God without a beginning" (*Supplication* 30). Origen took up the same argument—that death necessarily follows birth—but his text is notable in that he gives the floor to his adversary, the pagan Celsus, who says to the Christians: "You mock those who worship Zeus, giving as a reason the fact that his tomb is displayed in Crete, and yet you honor Him who came out from the tomb, without knowing how and under what authority the Cretans act in this way" (*Contra Celsum* 3.43). It is a sentence exceptionally rich in information: this Platonist of the second century knew the Christian argument derived from the tomb of Zeus; he found little coherence between it and faith in a resurrected God; and he knew (unfortunately without making it known) an allegorical justification of the myth of the sepulcher of Zeus. Whatever the case, Origen maintains the historicity of the tomb of Zeus while alleging that the learned Callimachus was ignorant of any allegory of this kind.

Aside from the reference to Callimachus's *Hymn to Zeus,* which seems to be limited to the four authors we have just seen, there is no end to the list of Christians who advance the argument of the tomb. The *Clementine Homilies* nevertheless are worth singling out for the fact that they do not merely turn the tomb of Zeus in Crete to their account, but feel that their Euhemerist convictions will be more widely shared if they add the tombs of Kronos in the Caucasus, Ares in Thrace, Hermes in Egypt, Aphrodite in Cyprus, Dionysus at Thebes, Asclepius in Epidaurus, etc. (5.23 and 6.21; the theses are proposed by the Jewish or Judeo-Christian Clement). A passage taken from Tertullian is of interest because it adds to these sepulchers the consideration of other "monuments of antiquity" from which we learn about the gods, the cities in which they were born, the lands in which they left traces of their activities: Tertullian hopes that the pagans will succumb in the face of such proofs and recognize that all their gods were formerly men (*Apologeticus* 10.3–4). This conclusion leads to Euhemerism, which Tertullian next develops (10.6–11) by using Saturn and Jupiter as illustration. After much hesitation over which one of the two contemporaneous authors influenced the other, it is generally thought today that it was Tertullian who served as model for Minucius Felix. In fact, the latter offers an elaboration on Saturn and Jupiter very similar to the one we have just seen (*Octavius* 23.9–13). With admirable clarity he mobilizes Jupiter—to whose tomb he adds, as we have seen Athenagoras do, the cave of Ida—to the cause of Euhemerism: "Even today people visit the grotto of Jupiter and show his tomb, and the very sites that he consecrated prove his human nature (*ipsis sacris suis humanitatis arguitur*)" (23.13; M. Pellegrino's edition of *Octavius* is valuable for its copious annotation, especially on the chapter in question).[17]

3. *The existence of rites.* Many historians of religions today conceive of the relationship between myth and ritual in such a way that myth appears to justify ritual a posteriori. An example of these etiological myths is provided by M. Eliade: "Preconjugal ceremonial unions preceded the appearance of the myth of the preconjugal relations between Hera and Zeus, the myth which served to justify them."[18] This is a point on which the Fathers of the Church were not very "modern." For they believed in general that the cultic activities of paganism bore witness to the historical reality of myths, in other words, to the human origin of the gods.

The argument begins with Tertullian, who parallels the names of the gods, which are an element of their civil status as mortals, with their histories, which are confirmed by rites: "With regard then to your gods, I see only the names of certain dead men of the past, about whom I hear tales, and I identify their sacred rites from the tales (*sacra de fabulis recognosco*)" (*Apologeticus* 12.1; we have just encountered the word *sacra,* "sacred rites," in the work of Minucius Felix—*ipsis sacris suis*—who invokes the cave and tomb of Jupiter while thinking of the rites that were performed there). The same reasoning would soon become more explicit with Arnobius, as we see in this passage: "How then, do we prove that all these stories are records of actual events? From the solemn rites, of course, and the mysteries of initiation, either those which take place at stated times and days or those which the people hand down in secret, preserving the perpetuity of their special customs. For it must not be believed that these practices are without their origins, that they take place without rhyme or reason, that they do not submit to motives that link them with primitive institutions." Here Arnobius offers examples of the way in which today's sacred liturgies are rooted in yesterday's human episodes, thus rendering them incontestable: the pine introduced in procession in the sanctuary of Cybele is the image of the one under which Attis emasculated himself; the annual phallophoria reflect the castrating mission of Liber; the secret ceremonies of Eleusis contain the memory of the wanderings of Ceres in search of Proserpina and some of her stopping places. Whether or not they are correct, Arnobius continues, these examples leave no loopholes: "If these mysteries have another cause, that is nothing to us, so long as they are produced by some cause. For it defies belief that these practices were all undertaken without antecedent causes; or we must judge the people of Attica to be crazy for having forged a religious rite that has no motive. And if our conclusion is clearly established, if the causes and origins of the mysteries derive from actual events (*e rebis actis mysteriorum causae atque origines effluunt*) . . ." (*Adversus Nationes* 5.39; cf. 5.5–7 for the development of his examples; on this passage, as well as for the whole of Arnobius's apologetic treatise in general, see the commentary by George E. McCracken).[19]

4. *The dilemma of Xenophanes.* While they are the principal index of the original humanity of the gods, the tombs also become the favored place for their worship. In a text of Jewish apologetics from the end of the second century or the beginning of the first century B.C., introduced into the Greek Bible under the title of the *Letter of Jeremiah,* we read that the offerings presented to the pagan gods are assimilated to those placed on tombs (verse 26).

A saying that gained great currency in the first Christian centuries was that the temples of false gods were tombs, their own tombs. Athenagoras (*Supplication* 28) attributes this saying to the Euhemerist theologians of Egypt, and also to a Greek grammarian of the second century B.C., Apollodorus, the author of the treatise *On the Gods,* which was known, perhaps directly but more likely indirectly, to several Christian authors (on this last point, see the works of Zucker[20] and Geffcken[21]). "They despise the temples as if they were tombs" (*templa ut busta despiciunt*), says Cecilius, the pagan interlocutor in Minucius Felix's dialogue (*Octavius* 8.4), of the Christians; in the fourth century, Firmicus Maternus, another apologist, found these words to his taste and put them to his own use: *Busta sunt haec, sacratissimi imperatores, appellanda, non templa* ("These should be called tombs, most sacred emperors, not temples"; *De errore profanarum religionum* 16.3). It was primarily Clement of Alexandria who gave credence to this theme: "These temples . . . are euphemistically called temples, but they are really tombs . . . Be ashamed to honor these tombs" (*Protrepticus* 3.44.4); and later, with regard to the temple of Antinous, which was consecrated by the emperor Hadrian: "Just like temples, so also tombs, pyramids, mausoleums, and labyrinths seem to be objects of reverence; they are temples of the dead, just as temples are tombs of the gods" (4.49.3).

This parallel was not pushed any farther. But it has an important corollary: if it is true that the temples are nothing but tombs, then it follows that the mourning connected with tombs should invade and alter the worship offered in temples. This critique had been formulated by Greek philosophy itself; we find it in Cicero's *De natura deorum* in the mouth of the spokesman for Epicureanism, Velleius, who addresses it to the Stoic Persaeus, having just described the latter's theory on divinization, which is close to Euhemerism: by thus introducing deceased men among the gods, "the whole cult of the gods becomes an expression of mourning" (*quorum omnis cultus esset futurus in luctu,* 1.15.38; here, as elsewhere, we may read this Ciceronian dialogue, a fundamental document in the religious philosophy of antiquity, in A. S. Pease's edition,[22] which is irreplaceable, especially for its fabulous wealth of notes).

This incompatibility, strengthened by the similarity in sound of the Latin words *cultus* and *luctus,* led Christian authors to argue in the form of a dilemma. Once again, they do not reject Euhemerism; they continue to be indebted to it for having shown them the human origin of the pagan gods; but, like Velleius, they clearly spurn the idea that gods so conceived could be anything but false gods. It is in this sense that they exploit the principle whereby an authentic cult could not be exclusively funerary: if your gods are gods, do not mourn for them; if you mourn for them, admit that they are men.

This schema is first established by Athenagoras, when he writes of the gods of Egypt: "If they are gods, they are immortal; but if they are wounded and if their sufferings constitute their mysteries, they are men" (*Supplication* 28; the dilemma is veiled by the fact that the author passes from the notion of mortality to that of suffering, which the mysteries perpetuate). Earlier (14), Athenagoras had similarly referred to the incoherence of the cults celebrated in Egyptian temples, in which everyone beats his breast in unison as if at a funeral, and everyone offers sacrifices such as are made to gods. The same reasoning attains its greatest limpidity in Clement of Alexandria: "If you believe they are gods, do not lament them, nor beat your breast; but if you mourn for them, stop thinking that they are gods" (*Protrepticus* 2.24.3). Among Latin authors, the memory of the Ciceronian antithesis between *cultus* and *luctus* persists. After recalling the demonstration of grief which colors the legend of Isis and governs her annual mysteries, Minucius Felix asks: "Is it not ridiculous to mourn what one worships or to worship what one mourns?" (*vel lugere quod colas vel colore quod lugeas*) (*Octavius* 22.1). In the fourth century, this dilemma takes a plainly scholastic turn with Firmicus Maternus: "If they are gods whom you worship (*colitis*), why do you mourn them (*lugitis*)? Why do you celebrate annual ceremonies of mourning for them? If they deserve tears, why do you heap divine honors on their heads? Do either one thing or the other: either do not weep for them if they are gods, or, if you think they deserve grief and tears, do not call them gods any longer, lest your lamentations and tears should defile the majesty of the divine name." (*De errore profanarum religionum* 8.4; on this apologetic treatise, the author of which is a converted pagan, see the commentaries of the editor A. Pastorino,[23] as well as that of the French translator G. Heuten[24].)

This consensus of the Christian apologists on the incompatibility of worship and mourning may be surprising, coming as it does from the followers of a religion in which the central figure of the cult is precisely that of a man-God who has been put to death. The explanation may derive from the fact that these authors could not themselves define the dilemma in question, but had merely borrowed it unsuspectingly from a Greek philosophical tradition. Clement of Alexandria makes no mystery of this source; for he does not offer the formula we have just seen as his own, but cites it as a warning addressed to the Egyptians by someone he does not name. He does imply that it is one of those philosophers reputed to be "atheists" because of the insight with which they brought to light the errors concerning the gods; to this end he cites some names, including that of Euhemerus (*Protrepticus* 2.24.2, as indicated at the beginning of this study).

In fact, the author of this dilemma is the pre-Socratic Xenophanes of Colophon, well known for his biting critique of the theology of Homer, a critique that the Christians would also use to their advantage. It was an apothegm to which the earliest witness was Aristotle, who saw it as an illustration of a certain rhetorical procedure: "To the people of Eleus who asked whether or not they should offer a sacrifice to Leucothea and mourn her death, Xenophanes counseled that if they thought her a goddess, they should not mourn her, but, if they thought her a woman, they should not sacrifice to her." We are certainly in the presence of the antithesis between divinity and humanity and, in parallel fashion, between a religious cult and mourning; lacking, however, are two elements which are characteristic of the text cited by Clement—i.e., that there the remark is addressed to the Egyptians, and that there the dilemma is altered by a form of chiasmus. But these differences disappear in another tradition of the sayings of Xenophanes, attested by Plutarch: "Xenophanes of Colophon was thus right to judge that the Egyptians, if they believed in the gods, should not mourn their death, but that if they did mourn them, they should not believe them to be gods" (the texts of Aristotle and Plutarch—and two other analogous texts, also by Plutarch—may be found in H. Diels and W. Kranz, *Die Fragmente der Vorsokratiker*, 6th ed. [Berlin, 1951], vol. 1, p. 115; see also p. 180, in which the same apothegm is attributed by an ancient author, aberrantly, to Heraclitus). So it was in the version known to Plutarch that the saying of the pre-Socratic reached Clement of Alexandria and his successors. This episode illustrates the skill with which the Christian apologists often use the Greek philosophers themselves to refute the theology of paganism: they hasten to Euhemerus for demonstration that the gods are deceased men, in other words, they think, false gods. And if anyone should be tempted to take this kind of divinization seriously and to believe that those lamented dead have become real gods (it is improbable but not impossible that such was the personal opinion of Euhemerus), then the apologists call on Xenophanes to support their assertion that one cannot mourn a dead man and worship a god in the same person.

J.P./d.w.

NOTES

1. G. NÉMETHY, *Euhemeri reliquiae* (Budapest 1889).

2. G. VALLAURI, *Evemero di Messene* (Turin 1956).

3. F. JACOBY, "Euemeros," 3, in Pauly-Wissowa, *Real-Encyclopädie*, vol. 11 (1907): 952–72. Jacoby also compiled a collection of *testimonia* concerning, and fragments of, Euhemerus (in which, unfortunately, many of the texts are mentioned instead of being cited in full) in his monumental work *Die Fragmente der griechischen Historiker* (Berlin 1923), under no. 63, vol. 1:300–313.

4. P. DECHARME, *La critique des traditions religieuses chez les Grecs, des origines au temps de Plutarque* (Paris 1904); on Euhemerus and Euhemerism, 371–93.

5. A. B. DRACHMANN, *Atheism in Pagan Antiquity* (London, Copenhagen, and Christiania 1922), 111–13.

6. G. VALLAURI, *Origine e diffusione dell'evemerismo nel pensiero classico* (Turin 1960).

7. W. SPOERRI, *Späthellenistische Berichte über Welt, Kultur und Götter: Untersuchungen zu Diodor von Sizilien* (Basel 1959).

8. F. ZUCKER, "Euhemeros und seine *hiera anagraphē* bei den christlichen Schriftstellern," *Philologus* 64 (1905): 465–72.

9. K. THRAEDE, "Euhemerismus," in *Reallexikon für Antike und Christentum* (1966), 6:877–90.

10. J. W. SCHIPPERS, *De Ontwikkeling der Euhemeristische Godencritiek in de Christelijke Latijnse Literatuur* (diss., Utrecht; Groningen 1952). For the euhemerism of the Latin Fathers, essentially Arnobius and Lactantius, see G. L. Ellspermann, *The Attitude of the Early Christian Latin Writers toward Pagan Literature and Learning* (Washington 1949), 58–59 and 72–74.

11. J. PÉPIN, *Mythe et allégorie: Les origines grecques et les contestations judéo-chrétiennes* (2d ed., Paris 1976), index I, see "Evhémère."

12. J. D. COOKE, "Euhemerism: A Mediaeval Interpretation of Classical Paganism," *Speculum* 2 (1927): 396–410.

13. P. ALPHANDÉRY, "L'evhémérisme et les débuts de l'histoire des religions au moyen âge," *Revue de l'histoire des religions* 109 (1934): 5–27.

14. J. SEZNEC, *The Survival of the Pagan Gods: An Essay on the Role of the Mythological Tradition in the Humanism and Art of the Renaissance*, Studies of the Warburg Institute, 11 (London 1940; Paris 1980), especially 13–18.

15. F. PFISTER, "Ein apokrypher Alexanderbrief: Der sogenannte Leon von Pella und die Kirchenväter," in *Mullus, Festschrift Th. Klauser* (Münster 1964), 291–97.

16. N. ZEEGERS-VANDER VORST, *Les citations des poètes grecs chez les apologistes chrétiens du IIe siècle* (Louvain 1972), 103–4.

17. M. MINUCII FELICIS, *Octavius*, con introd. e commento di M. Pellegrino (Turin 1947).

18. M. ELIADE, *The Myth of the Eternal Return, or Cosmos and History* (Princeton 1954), 27.

19. ARNOBIUS OF SICCA, *The Case against the Pagans*, translated and annotated by G. E. McCracken, 2 vols. (Westminster, MD, 1949), 2:583–84.

20. E. ZUCKER, *Spuren von Apollodoros peri theōn*, bei christlichen Schriftstellern der ersten fünf Jahrhunderte (diss., Munich; Nuremberg 1904).

21. J. GEFFCKEN, *Zwei griechische Apologeten* (Leipzig and Berlin 1907), pp. XVII and 225–26; on the dilemma of Xenophanes in Athenagoras, p. 225.

22. M. TULLUS CICERO, *De natura deorum*, A. S. Pease, ed., 2 vols. (Cambridge, MA, 1955; 2d ed., Darmstadt 1968), 1:263–64.

23. JULIUS FIRMICUS MATERNUS *De errore profanarum religionum*, a cura di A. Pastorino (Florence 1956), 116.

24. JULIUS FIRMICUS MATERNUS, *De errore profanarum religionum*, G. Heuten, trans. (Brussels 1938), 64 and 161–62.

Christianity and Mythology in the Greek Church

By the year 313, when the Edict of Milan marked a decisive rapprochement between the Roman Empire and the Church, the Church already had behind it two centuries of existence at the heart of a Hellenism which had itself been drawn into the flow of history during that time. To be sure, that ancient religious system was still in place, under the benevolent aegis of the reigning power and elites and in the collective conservation of tradition. The place and times of rites persisted, with their developments, their mythic justifications punctuated by major or minor names from the classical pantheon. This picture, however, needs some important retouchings. The first is the increasing attraction of sources of wisdom attributed to the East. These initiate one into paths to a happy personal and stellar immortality, founded on terrestrial asceticism, and are placed under the patronage

Saint George killing the dragon. Sculpture on two panels of pine. Nicosia, Cyprus Folk Art Museum. Museum photo.

of long adopted exotic gods and goddesses such as Isis, or, at least, gods renewed by exoticism such as the Egyptian Thoth-Hermes. Next, there is the flowering, on various levels, of symbolic speculations fueled by the Greek myths, portrayals of episodes invested with new hope (such as the labors of Hercules on sarcophagi, or the flight of the Dioscuri on the subterranean vault of the Porta Maggiore in Rome), as well as the extensive philosophical constructions of a Plotinus in the third century. In such a perspective, one is confronted less by the continuity of ancient mythology than by the fabrication of a contemporary mythology in the second and third centuries, produced by imperial Hellenism in response to the questions of the time. The ancient traditions and their symbolic interpretations are combined with borrowings of varying antiquity from cultures bearing little or none of the stamp of Hellenism from the Roman or Persian East. Among these cultures is Judaism in its diverse currents, which at that time was elaborating its theory of angels and defining the figure of Satan, itself undergoing influences from Persia. This was also the time when an obsession with demons, invisible and omnipresent assailants, was developing, an obsession that Christianity would claim for its own from the very start. Finally, the myths taught in the Gnostic sects, of which some existed within Christianity itself, are perhaps the most striking monument to the powers of invention that were manifesting themselves at the time. These would have a medieval posterity of their own.

It was in this cultural context that the young Christian Church had to find its place. An Origen or a Clement of Alexandria were deeply imbued, on a philosophical level, with the very culture they found so easy to combat on a literally narrative or naively ritual level. This leads to an essential, secular ambiguity. The Byzantine elite, whether or not it was of the Church, would not abandon the philosophical approach, the rhetorical discipline, and the literary baggage of ancient Hellenism: the teaching it received assured its cultural preservation, with greater or lesser success from one period to another, and its distinctive social value remained intact as a result. On the other hand, Hellenic Christianity as a whole integrated into its new faith those traditions whose function remained necessary, such as the annual cycle of festivals. As a result, the encounter of the Eastern Church with the complex mythology that existed around the year 313 is not an encounter between a scholarly culture and a popular culture, but rather the beginning of a thousand-year coexistence of cultural practices at different levels of society and different levels of consciousness, levels whose respective scope and depth would vary according to the efficacy of the official repression imposed upon the ancient religion.

We may thus pass quite quickly over the well-known dates and facts that serve as landmarks in the battle against the old gods carried out publicly in the fourth century by the Church, which was associated with the ruling power except during the short restoration under Julian (361–363). The repression that had begun with Constantine reached its official end with the general prohibition against the ancient religion proclaimed by Theodosius I in 392. Nevertheless, the reign of Justinian I (527–565) was still marked by the confiscation of sanctuary properties and the prohibition of teaching by pagans. And although Bishop Porphyry tore down the sanctuary of Marneion of Gaza at the end of the fourth century, the last internal missions, notably those in the mountains of Asia Minor, were established around 542, and the last matters involving personalities of the capital, including the patriarch himself, occurred around 570. The whole of the sixth century is still marked by skirmishes that erupt in the cities on the days on which the old festivals, the *Vota* and *Bromalia,* provoke excitement. The seventh century marks the real threshold, for in Byzantium this was the period of invasions perpetrated by peoples who were in every way non-Christian—Arabs, Avars, and Slavs. The result is a definitive identification between the Christian cause and that of the political Roman-ness of Hellenic culture. In 626, the Virgin appears on the walls of the capital under siege by the Avars and their troops, and saves it. The historical data of Christian Hellenism are complete thenceforth and for all time.

The realm of Christian Hellenism would be immense if it were defined as that of churches born, directly or indirectly, of the Eastern Roman Empire, from Alexandria to Kiev and Moscow, from the Caucasus to the Balkans. We thus focus on lands which remained, for all intents and purposes, Hellenic in language and, at least predominantly, Hellenic in culture—for to venture further, especially into Slavic lands, would be to pursue the identical Christianization of too different a substratum. Delimited in this way, the history of Christian Hellenism presents three great continuities on three cultural levels: the elite, the Church, and the Christian people.

Most manifest is the great secular culture of an elite in which service to the State is closely associated with service to the Church: both are taught at the same desks, and in a language whose mythological allusion remains a sign of recognition all the more appreciable for the fact that it is scholarly. To be sure, the formalism of an Agathias, in the century of Justinian, is not the scholarship of a Photius in the ninth century, nor the classical mastery of Psellus and his friends in the following period. But literary references to mythology adorn even sacred speeches, even episcopal correspondence, and even a Life of a saint of the eleventh or twelfth century that likens the struggle of the missionary saint Nikon in the region of Sparta to the labors of Hercules. In the same way, though to a lesser degree, the iconographic setting of secular life draws on the ancient repertory. The Neoplatonist current flows without interruption from Plotinus, from Proclus and the Athenian Academy of the fifth century, to the philosophers of the capital of the eleventh century, and finally to Mistra and the person of Georgius Gemistus Plethon as the empire dragged to its close and the Renaissance dawned. There was always a very fine line, right down to ideas which were suspect and subject to prosecution, as in the case of John "The Grammarian" and of Leo the Philosopher in the ninth century, the difficulties experienced by Michael Psellus, the accusations he himself made against the patriarch Michael Cerularius, and the trials of John Italos in the eleventh century. It is difficult to plumb the depth of the temptations thus denounced. But it must not be forgotten that people like Psellus and, it would seem, Cerularius drew from ancient Hellenism more than merely the forms and ideas of that great cultural tradition. They were also nourished with its obscure and dangerous curiosities, and recovered from it the magical or divinatory practices which the end of antiquity had developed against demons—for demons continued to offer the same face to people of the eleventh century, arousing in them the same obsession.

The greatest source of information on the relations of the Greek Church and its people with Hellenic mythology is to be found not here but in the documents written by clerical or monastic scribes. Such information thus has a twofold application, to the practices of the Christian people but first and foremost to the clerics themselves. We find it in accounts of martyrs (increasingly flamboyant in more recent periods), in the Lives of the saints (which range from quite fictional works of spiritual edification to biography), in the observations and interdictions of Church councils (of which the most significant takes place in 692), and in the commentaries of later canonists. Finally, liturgical books, notably those of southern Italy, like the collections of magic formulas that continue an earlier tradition, throw light on the marginal areas in which the Church accepts and absorbs the practices of its people, and in which Christianity imprints its own forms on ancient responses. With the end of the Middle Ages, ordinary ecclesiastical culture ceases to constitute a distinct and significant stratum, and the distance between the observer and the observed collectivity reaches its present dimension. Such is the case with Leo Allatius (1586–1669); a Uniate Greek born on Chios who settled in Rome, he left an important testimony within the framework of his work in favor of a union of the churches. In the nineteenth century, with the national self-reassertion of Greece and the general renewal of the study of ancient Hellenism, Christian Greek culture was scrutinized in a search for continuity. Information collected at the end of the nineteenth century and the beginning of the twentieth century is thus attributable to Greek or foreign scholars, who came for different reasons to a single path, the quest for the ancient stratum of contemporary Greek culture. The first of these scholars were mobilized by the fundamental debate provoked by the assertions of Fallmerayer (1842) on the historical rupture inflicted upon the populations of Greece by the medieval influx of Slavs. The next group left their libraries and universities to search in the field for still living traces of ancient Hellenism. All of these enterprises put together a mass of data in which the survival of ancient Hellenism naturally occupies an important position. Although marred by an overly vertical penetration downward through historical strata, the data nevertheless make possible a better method for analyzing the religious system into which Christianity and the vestiges of the ancient cults were integrated. We thus remain in the direct line of our medieval sources, and can verify their correctness.

There is certainly a continuity between the medieval sources and contemporary observations, and its course may be traced back to antiquity. Yet the true extent of this continuity must be appreciated. The most immutable grounding, and undoubtedly the oldest even with regard to the ancient religion, is that of the calendar, the annual cycle of festivals. The council held in 692 in the capital to extirpate the heretical contagion, whether Judaizing or Hellenic, still fully recognizes the ancient rituals in the traditional festivities that mark the year: the Calends of January 1st, the *Vota* of the 6th, the *Bromalia* of November-December, and March 1st. The council condemns the wild dancing that drives women out into the streets, encourages costumes and masques, and is performed, according to the Fathers, in the name of the false gods of the Greeks (i.e., the pagans). The Fathers refrain from naming these gods, with one exception: their explicit prohibition against proclaiming the name of the "infamous Dionysus" while trampling grapes in the press. The hagiography of Steven the Younger, martyred in 764 for his defense of icons, gives his date of death as November 28th—the day on which the iconoclastic emperor, by his own testimony hardened in his Hellenism (i.e., paganism), celebrates the *Bromalia,* proclaiming the names of Dionysus and Bromius, the fathers of seed grains and wine. Commenting on these canons in the twelfth century, Theodorus Balsamon asserts that the practices they condemn have not yet disappeared. Demetrius Chomatianus, archbishop of Achrida at the beginning of the thirteenth century, mentions the same festivities while also giving details about the *Rousalia* carnival, which Balsamon indicated as a practice found on the borders of the Empire. This immemorial cycle, in which the dead and living take part in the succession of the agrarian seasons, persists in the Greek islands today. Its culminating periods are the Twelve Days that separate Christmas from the Epiphany, the three weeks of Carnival (during which the pantomimes of the Kalogheroi reproduce an archaic Dionysian ritual of death and resurrection), Saint George's Day in April (a festival of shepherds, like the ancient Parilia), Pentecost in its connection with the dead, and the night of Saint John in June. The sites bear witness to the same permanence, especially the sanctuaries dedicated to Christian saints to which people still come in search of healing, most often through the ancient ritual of spending the night there (incubation): the practice is attested to without a break through the medieval and modern periods.

This victorious perenniality was bought at the price of the almost total obliteration of the names of the gods themselves. At the beginning of the Greek Middle Ages, a lesser power, often malevolent, doomed to defeat in the end but uncontested in the present, was the lingering sign of the old gods in the Hellenic Christian consciousness (starting with that of the clergy itself). But the names of those gods were quickly repudiated, which is equally significant; the council of 692 passed over their names in silence in reference to their festivals, but also in the important and oft-renewed prohibition against ancient forms of oath-taking and especially of divination. In the stories of martyrs composed after the triumph of the Church, the gods are named wrongly, or driven into anonymity. These tales recount the victory of their hero over the Hellenic gods his persecutor has ordered him to worship, gods whose statues crumble to dust at the invocation of a Christian. The designation of the gods shows to what extent their memory had become blurred in the mind of the ordinary cleric. Sometimes a single god, such as Apollo, is designated as superior to all the others. Sometimes they are degraded collectively as anonymous "demons." In the same vein, the Lives of the saints up to the sixth century relate militant episodes of destruction of local sanctuaries. But in the same period, and even later, they also evoke victories over demons of the countryside, phantoms without name or any semblance of a condemned past (as pagan gods), who perch in trees or lurk in isolated tombs or ancient ruins. The action taken by the Church thus represented the other side of a general belief that it shared, and with which it was imbued, at both a popular and a local level, even in its own ritual: an example is the late repertory of Italo-Greek prayers preserved in a sixteenth-century manuscript, which continues to place demons that are to be avoided in trees and ancient tombs, as well as at crossroads—while references to names drawn from the ancient repertory remain insignificant, especially in proportion to those of a Judaizing tinge, such as are found especially in amulet texts. Dionysus constituted a lasting exception. One should not, however, succumb to the nineteenth-century authors' obsession with explicit ancient lineages, such as the story of Saint Diony-s(i)us who brought the first vine stock to Naxos, or the story of Saint Demetra, honored at Eleusis, and of her daughter ravished by a Turkish magician, and of the young man who would go to her rescue. Whatever interest these tales may hold, they are perhaps less significant than the survival of Charon, of the bogey-woman Gyllu, or of the troop of Nereids. It should be noted that the aquatic and sylvan seductresses recur in Slavic folklore, and that the Slavic presence or influence in Hellenic territory is hardly taken into account by Fallmerayer's adversaries.

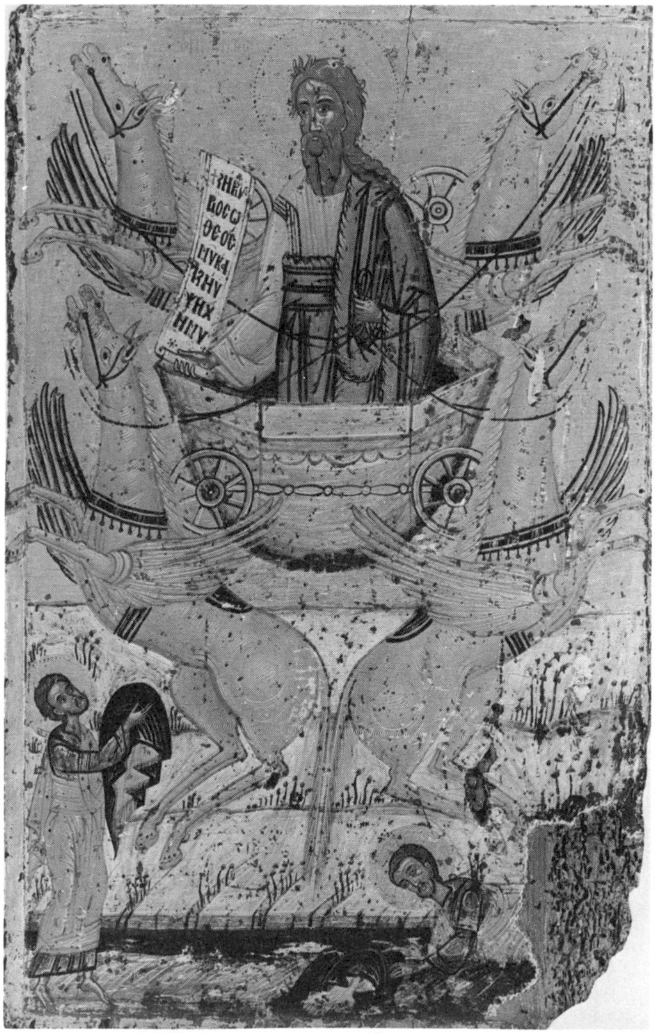

Elijah in his chariot of fire. 1655. Amberg-Herzog collection. Geneva, Musée d'Art et d'Histoire de Genève. Museum photo.

Christian Hellenism, then, did not forget the ancient religious strand but eclipsed the names of the gods under whose patronage the old rituals were performed and, by that act, dissolved the mythic accounts that explained those rituals. Does this mean that Christian Hellenism was bereft of a mythology? The question primarily involves a portion of the ancient heritage which is not that of classical or Romanized Hellenism, but that of Gnosticism. Its medieval posterity in Byzantium—the Paulicians and Bogomils—preserve or enrich the myths about Creation, the first man, and the role of Satan in the created world. The cults of the saints and of the Virgin are more difficult to analyze.

The first answers, formulated at the turn of the twentieth century, proposed direct and simple identifications, of the "Mithra = Saint George" type. But such identifications do not stand up to examination. First of all, they can never be justified by an exhaustive and point-for-point coincidence; their authors tied them hastily to various partial similarities, places of worship, attributes, and festival dates. Next, and more important, this collection of facts, however interesting it may be, has never accounted for the initial and major innovation developed by Christianity, which is the cult devoted to the saints, to their living person, to their tomb, to their images, and, in a comparable fashion, to the Virgin. Hence, the temple of Athena Parthenos became a church of the Virgin; shepherds celebrated Saint George's Day on a date which was more or less that of the Parilia; Saint Elijah, whose festival day falls in July, exercises from the heights of the hills an atmospheric power that justifies his biblical assumption but also recalls that of Zeus and of Helios; Saint Michael took Hermes' role as conductor of souls to the afterworld. But all of this is secondary. What must first be analyzed is the constitution of a network of supernatural mediators—nearly all, reputedly, of human birth, but of whom the most widely honored nevertheless have no history, nor even any legend, apart from the collection of their miracles; it is a repertory of rites of supplication, of the motifs and mechanics of these miracles. Research needs to be undertaken starting from local data. It will thus be found that the saints offer no myths, new or old—if the term "myth" is taken to mean an account which is at once explanatory and reversible—but merely fragments of earlier myths, as well as fragments of rituals, some more coherent than others. To go beyond this would mean questioning the whole history of the Christian religion.

E.P./d.w.

BIBLIOGRAPHY

1. General History

K. S. LATOURETTE, *A History of the Expansion of Christianity* (London 1947), vols. 1–2. G. OSTROGORSKY, *A History of the Byzantine Empire* (Oxford 1968). A. PIGANIOL, *L'Empire chrétien,* new ed. by A. CHASTAGNOL (Paris 1972). E. STEIN, *Histoire du Bas Empire,* vol. 1: *A.D. 284–476* (Paris 1959); vol. 2: *A.D. 476–585* (Paris 1949). A. E. VACALOPOULOS, *The Greek Nation, 1453–1669: The Cultural and Economic Background of Modern Greek Society* (New Brunswick, NJ, 1976).

2. History of Culture

a) General Studies

H. G. BECK, *Kirche und theologische Literatur im byzantinischen Reich* (Munich 1959). J. GOUILLARD, *Le Synodikon de l'Orthodoxie,* Centre de rech. d'hist. et civil. byzant., Travaux et mémoires 2 (1967): 1–316. J. M. HUSSEY, *Church and Learning in the Byzantine Empire, 867–1185* (Oxford and London 1937). P. LEMERLE, *Le premier humanisme byzantin: Notes et remarques sur enseignement et culture à Byzance des origines au Xe siècle* (Paris 1971).

b) The End of Antiquity

J. CARCOPINO, *La basilique pythagoricienne de la Porte Majeure* (Paris 1927). F. CUMONT, *Recherches sur le symbolisme funéraire des Romains* (Paris 1942). A.-J. FESTUGIÈRE, *La révélation d'Hermès Trismégiste,* 4 vols. (Paris 1944–54). J. GEFFCKEN, *Der Ausgang des griechisch-römischen Heidentums* (Heidelberg 1920). H. JONAS, *The Gnostic Religion* (2d ed., Boston 1963; reissued 1970). W. E. KAEGI, "The Fifth-Century Twilight of Byzantine Paganism," *Classica Medievalia* 27 (1966): 243–75. M. MESLIN, *La fête des Kalendes de janvier dans l'Empire romain: Étude d'un rituel de Nouvel An* (Brussels 1970). A. MOMIGLIANO, ed., *The Conflict between Paganism and Christianity in the Fourth Century* (Oxford 1963). A. MOMIGLIANO, "Popular Religious Beliefs and the Late Roman Historians," *Studies in Church History* 8 (1971): 1–18. R. REITZENSTEIN, *Poimandres: Studien zur griechisch-ägyptischen und frühchristlichen Literatur* (Leipzig 1904).

c) Aspects of Byzantine Neoplatonism

A. H. ARMSTRONG, ed., *Cambridge History of Later Greek and Early Medieval Philosophy* (Cambridge 1967). A. CAMERON, "The Last Days of the Academy at Athens," *Proceeds. Cambridge Philol. Society* 145 (1969): 7–29. J. GOUILLARD, *La religion des philosophes,* Centre de rech. d'hist. et civil. byzant., Travaux et mémoires 6 *(Recherches sur le XIe siècle)* (1976): 305–24. F. MASAI, *Pléthon et le platonisme de Mistra* (Paris 1956).

d) Myths of Heresy

G. FICKER, *Die Phundagiagiten* (Leipzig 1908). M. LOOS, "Certains aspects du bogomilisme byzantin des XIe et XIIe siècles," *Byzantinoslavica* 28 (1967): 39–53; "Satan als erstgeborener Gottes: Ein Beitrag zur Analyse des bogomilischen Mythus," *Byzantino-Bulgarica* 3 (1969): 23–35.

3. Beliefs and Rituals

a) Sources Mentioned

Council of 692: text in F. LAUCHERT, *Die Kanones der wichtigsten altkirchlichen Concilien nebst den apostolischen Kanones* (Freiburg and Leipzig 1896), 97–139; comm. of Theodore Balsamon, *Patrol. Graeca,* vol. 137 passim.

Life of Stephen the Younger, in *Patrol. Graeca,* vol. 100, 1069–1186. DEMETRIOS CHOMATIANOS, J. Pitra, ed., *Analecta* 6 (1891): 509–10ff. MICHEL PSELLOS, "Accusation du patriarche Michel Cérulaire devant le synode," L. BRÉHIER, ed., *Rev. Et. Grecques* 16 (1903): 375–416; 17 (1904): 35–76.

Prayers, amulets, exorcisms: F. PRADEL, *Griechische und süditalienische Gebete, Beschwörungen und Rezepte des Mittelalters* (Giessen 1907). A. A. VASILIEV, *Anecdota graeco-byzantina,* vol. 1 (Moscow 1893).

b) Studies

S. P. KYRIAKIDES, *Two Studies on Modern Greek Folklore* (Salonika 1968). J. C. LAWSON, *Modern Greek Folklore and Ancient Greek Religion: A Study in Survivals* (1910), reprint with foreword by A. N. OIKONOMIDES (New York 1964). G. MEGAS, *Greek Calendar Customs* (Athens 1958). N. G. POLITIS, *Meletē epi tou biou tōn neōterōn Hellēnōn* (Essay on the life of the modern Greeks) (Athens 1871–74). B. SCHMIDT, *Das Volksleben der Neugriechen und das hellenische Altertum* (Leipzig 1871). K. SVOBODA, "La démonologie de Michel Psellos" (diss., Brno 1927).

4. Cult of the Saints

a) General Studies

P. BROWN, "The Rise and Function of the Holy Man in Late Antiquity," *Journ. Rom. Studies* 61 (1971): 80–101. P. E. LUCIUS and G. ANRICH, *Die Anfänge des Heilgenkults in der Christlichen Kirche* (Tübingen 1904); also in French.

b) Particular Studies

G. ANRICH, *Haghios Nikolaos,* 2 vols. (Berlin 1913). J. B. AUFHAUSER, "Das Drachenwunder des Hl. Georg in der griechischen und lateinischen Überlieferung," *Byzant. Archiv.* 5 (1911). A. D. DE GROOT, *Saint Nicholas: A Psychoanalytic Study of His History and Myth* (The Hague 1965). S. GEORGOUDI, "Sant'Elia in Grecia," *Studi e Materiali di Storia delle Religioni* 39 (1968): 293–319. K. KRUMBACHER, *Der heilige Georg in der griechischen Überlieferung* (Munich 1911). *Millénaire monastique du Mont Saint-Michel,* 3: *Culte de Saint Michel et pèlerinage au Mont,* M. Baudot, ed. (Paris 1971). W. VON RINTELEN, *Kultgeographische Studien in der Italia Byzantina: Untersuchungen über die Kulte des Erzengels Michael und der Madonna di Costantinopoli in Süditalien* (Meisenheim 1968).

The Naassenes' Use of Pagan Mythologies

Known only from the account in the *Elenchos* (V, 6, 1–10, 2), the Naassenes never went by that name, which was invented by some polemicist who wanted people to believe that they were worshipers of the snake (*naḥaš* in Hebrew), like those who were called Ophites in Greek and *Ḥēwē* in Syriac. They referred to themselves as Gnostics, as we learn from several passages (V, 2, p. 77, 4–5 Wendland; V, 6, 4, p. 77, 30–78, 1; V, 11, p. 104, 4–5). Two of the sacred writings they used were the *Gospel according to the Egyptians* (V, 7, 9) and the *Gospel according to Thomas* (V, 7, 20), the first belonging to the pagan branch of Gnosticism, the second to a primitive literary form of Christian Gnosis. That they were connected, as has also been pointed out (V, 7, 20), with the apostolic tradition of James, "brother of the Lord," transmitted to Mariamme (Mary Magdalene), is a conventional argument added by the Christian editor of the pamphlet used by the polemicist in composing his account of the Naassenes. The document of pagan Gnosis that underlies it may go as far back as the waning of the first century B.C. The title of this earlier document as well as that of its reinterpretation, which has come down to us, remain unknown. In the eyes of the Eastern author of the *Elenchos* compilation, the absurdity of this particular form of Gnosis comes from the systematic use of "Greek and barbarian" pagan mythology (V, 7, 1, p. 79, 3–5), these two denominations designating a Gnostic interpretation—through the language of mysteries—of myths that Greek esotericism attributed to the Assyrians, Egyptians, and Phrygians.

In this type of pagan Gnosis, reinterpreted in the Christian manner, the primordial man, Adamas, defined the principle of the universe as one because it was male, and as triple because it was composed of breath (spirit), soul, and earth. Breath and earth have a precise status, above and below, male and female. But what is this soul, which occupies the intermediary position? The essence of Gnosis was to answer this question. The median position of the soul, the passage that each being had to make, descending toward existences and rising again toward being, makes the soul the principle of becoming; it is Phusis, the universal cosmic nature, the Gnostic replica of the Platonic Soul of the world.

The Naassenes' interpretation of the three myths of Adonis, Endymion, and Attis allows us to determine the soul's status precisely. Because Adonis means both the desire of the soul to tend toward generation and its withdrawal toward death through its inability to procreate, the soul is at once fertile and infertile, Aphrodite and Persephone (Kore). Endymion, the beloved of Selene (the moon), expresses the desire of the beings from above to unite with the male beauty of the soul. Rhea, the mother of the gods, castrating her lover Attis, shows symbolically that the spiritual part of the soul, the object of Selene's desire, is the original and heavenly element that comes from Adamas and is thus intellectual and male because it rejects the perceptible, which is both inferior and female. The three myths complement each other and must be read together. The sterility of the soul—its Persephone side—is what relates it to the material of the bodies in which it is held prisoner; the fertility of the soul—its Aphrodite side—is what allows it to initiate the chain of life of those who exist and, after that, to rejoin and conjoin its origin.

All that is retained from the myth of Isis and Osiris, the "Egyptian" version of the "Assyrian" myth of Attis, is the sequence dealing with Isis's search for the sexual organ of Osiris. Isis is dressed in seven black robes, for which there is a triple interpretation. The first is astrological: the seven robes of Isis designate the realm of nature (*phusis*) and of generation (*genesis*), governed by the world of planets in a state of perpetual movement and change. The second is cosmological: Osiris is the symbol of water or "the seminal substance," the first element of life and of becoming. And the third is liturgical: the sexual organ of Osiris, lost and found again, henceforth naked, erect, and crowned with fruit in temples and on streets and paths, evokes the initiation ritual of the soul, which is first abandoned and then returned unto itself, made fertile through identification with its original male principle.

Hermes with his erect sexual organ, interpreter of the gods, psychopomp, holding sway over time, in opposition to the dividing and separating word of the demiurge Ialdabaoth, represents the function of a Logos that succeeds in achieving communication, a Logos of revelation because it allows a descent from above to the realm below, a Logos of redemption because it achieves the passage of the souls from the country of death—Egypt or the Ocean—to the mother earth of the living—Jerusalem or Jordan—that is, from the mixed world, which is inferior and material, to the unified world, which is superior and spiritual.

This passage marks the end of the soul's wandering, the moment when "the unfortunate one [the soul] whose wanderings have led it into a labyrinth of ills" (V, 10, 2, p. 103, 10–11) has reached its celestial homeland. Its primitive unity restored, the soul belongs henceforth to the "kingless race" of those who have definitively broken with the world of forms and appearances. This state of beatitude, characteristic of the perfect possessor of Gnosis, is described in a series of images borrowed from the hierogamic ritual of the mysteries of Cybele: the drunkenness from the cup of Anacreon, a cup filled with wine from the wedding at Cana; statues from the temple of Samothrace, with hands raised and sexual organ erect, symbolizing the plenitude of the inner kingdom where all androgyny disappears in the identification with the primordial being; an allegorical interpretation, in the homiletic style, of a hymn in which all the names of Attis are proclaimed: Adonis, Osiris, Mene-Selene, Adamna, Corybas, Papas, the corpse (*nekus*), the god, the fruitless one (*akarpos*), the goatherd, the harvested ear of corn, and the fluteplayer born of an almond. Each of these terms is explained in detail and is applied to the Gnostic, who has in a sense become initiated into the mysteries and is the seer of his own essence. In this Eleusis of the world above, the Gnostic regards himself as an initiate and as Demeter's husband, stripped of all his clothes and then reclothed, at once virginal, because the hemlock made him into a eunuch, and fertile, because he wears the yellow, harvested ear of corn, in other words because he has assimilated the immeasurable fertility that comes from the castration of Attis: "I will sing of Attis, the son of Rhea, not to the thin sound of little bells, nor to the languishing flute of the Curetes of Mount Ida, but with the song of Phoebus's lyres I will mingle my cries of Evoe Evan! For he is Pan, he is Bacchus, he is the shepherd of the shining stars."

Such language harks back to a liturgical practice in the tradition of Greek mysteries that was in active use in an ancient pagan form of Gnosis, and was later reused in a purely fictitious way by the Christian author of the Gnostic pamphlet attributed to supposed Naassenes.

M.T./g.h.

BIBLIOGRAPHY

R. REITZENSTEIN, *Zwei religionsgeschichtliche Fragen* (Strasbourg 1901), 95–96; *Poimandres* (Leipzig 1904), 81–102. W. BOUSSET, *Hauptprobleme der Gnosis* (Göttingen 1907), 183–86. R. REITZENSTEIN and H.-H. SCHAEDER, *Studien zum antiken Synkretismus aus Iran und Griechenland* (Leipzig and Berlin 1926), 104–73. R. P. CASEY, "Naassenes and Ophites," *Journal of Theological Studies* 27 (1926): 374–87. A. D. NOCK, "Iranian Influences in Greek Thought," *Journal of Hellenic Studies* 49 (1929) = *Essays on Religion and the Ancient World*, Z. Stewart, ed. (Oxford 1972), 200–201. M. SIMONETTI, "Qualche osservazione sulle presunte interpolazioni della Predica del Naasseni," *Vetera Christianorum* 7 (1970): 115–24. TH. WOLBERGS, *Griechische religiöse Gedichte der ersten nachchristlichen Jahrhunderte* (Meisenheim 1971), 1:37–82; to be completed by A. Kehl, *Jahrbuch für Antike und Christentum* 15 (1972): 95–101.

THE GNOSTICS AND THE MYTHOLOGIES OF PAGANISM

At first sight, the pagan heritage of the Gnostics appears less monolithic than their Christian adversaries would have it. The constant accusation brought against them of having systematically transposed the gods and myths of the Greeks with the help of "barbarian names" is an all-purpose argument that proves nothing. To show, for example, that Valentinus is nothing but a vulgar imitator of Hesiod, Epiphanius points out the parallels between the ordering into syzygies of the set of thirty aeons of the Valentinian pleroma, which are born of the Abyss (Bythos), and a series of entities of the *Theogony* born of Chaos, which are also set up in opposing pairs and reduced for practical purposes to thirty in number (see *Panarion* 31.2.4–4.9). In fact, only the parallel between the Valentinian Bythos and the Hesiodic Chaos is operative; all the rest is artificial.

From their self-proclaimed proofs that Gnosticism was merely camouflaged paganism, searching, according to the formula of Irenaeus, to "adapt to myths the sayings (*logia*) of God" (*Adversus Haer.* 1.8.1 = Epiphanus, *Panarion* 31.24.6), the heresiologists drew the conclusion that the practices of the Gnostics were as contrary to the ethos of Christianity as their thought was to the "orthodoxy." And now the Gnostics are accused pell-mell of eating meat consecrated to idols, of participating in the festivals and games of the pagans, of practicing adultery and incest (Irenaeus, *Adversus Haer.* 1.6.3 = Epiphanius, *Panarion* 31.21.1–6), of organizing, under the cover of sacred rituals, carousings, drinking parties, orgies, abortions, and manducations of sperm, menstrual blood, and fetuses (Epiphanius, *Panarion* 26.4.3–5.8)! These facts were manifestly evoked to prove that deliquescent thought and dissolute practice go hand in hand.

In fact, the paganism of the Gnostics is not to be found where the Church Fathers placed it. It does exist, but elsewhere. Documents on the subject, which came to Europe in the eighteenth and nineteenth centuries or were discovered after the Second World War near Nag Hammadi, show it to be subtler than what was presented by the authors of heresy catalogs, who were eager to drive out those who contested from within, and more compact than is admitted by modern critics, whose knowledge is clouded by Jewish sources alone, following a long, fruitless search in the direction of Babylon or Iran for an explanatory frame-myth. As it appears to those who read the Gnostics' texts today and are familiar with what the Gnostics themselves read, the paganism of the Gnostics, who were more or less Christianized, is linked to the powerful influence exerted on their thinking by the literary, ideological, and practical models of the magical papyruses, of Hermeticism, of Middle Platonism, and of the Mystery religions.

As for the gods of paganism themselves, those who were taken back and integrated by the Gnostics into their own pantheon were adopted in order to feed the Gnostic astrological demonology and Platonizing panallegorism. They were transformed in both cases, either into planetary categories of fate as among the Astrologers, or into figures of the wandering and saved soul as among the Platonists. The Gnostic interpretation of the gods and myths of paganism is thus founded upon the interpretation that was operative in the popular and scholarly philosophy of their time. But only rarely did they reproduce it as such; most often they brought to it an increase of signification, even as they tried to compress myth to the utmost. The Gnostic reading of the myth of the phoenix remains a good example of this method (see *Revue de l'Histoire des Religions* 183 [1973]:117–42).

Another example is the Gnostic habit of attributing to the planetary entities of paganism the status and role of the angels in the Jewish demonology of the apocalypses. Already reduced to an astral function by the Mathematicians, the Greek god as reused by the Gnostics gains a renewal of personality as the archon of intermediate space. In the description of the sphere of destiny that ends the *Pistis Sophia*, the five gods—Kronos, Ares, Hermes, Aphrodite, and Zeus—are appointed by Ieu to oversee all the archons of the cosmic system. Each of them bears a double name and is connected to a consort power; the one that belongs to Zeus, who is good, has the duty of holding the tiller of the world (p. 356, 2–357, 17 of the Coptic text, ed. Schmidt, Copenhagen 1925). This primary function of the guardians of the circular celestial motions enables the five planetary gods to be guides to souls after their death. Under the guidance of Hermes as psychopomp, they cause the soul to circle the earth three times, so that it can rejoice in the spectacle of creation; next they make it descend into the Amentos (Hades), so that it can be afflicted by the sight of the infernal fire; then they cause it to rise again to the "middle way," the sphere of destiny, in which the flame of punishment also burns; and finally it is led up to the Virgin of Light to be judged. Zeus and Aphrodite stand in front, Kronos and Ares behind. If the soul is needful of supplementary purification, it is then thrown into the water below the sphere, which is a boiling fire. Only after this ordeal may it drink of the cup of forgetfulness and the cup of sobriety, which cause it to enter a new and luminous body (p. 381, 24–383, 11 of the Coptic text). Among the Manichaeans, too, the luminaries become vehicles for souls, and Hermogenes makes the sun a refuge for resurrected bodies.

Paganism, while providing the soul with its escorts in the particular otherworldly zone in which they exert their authority, also provides it, more generally, with the images of its condition as a traveler who has left a far distant land to fall to this world below. In order to describe the fate of the wandering soul in search of its true homeland and delivered in this existence into the seductions and tribulations of the world, the Gnostics took up some of the allegories used by the Platonists in their own time. Two characters from Homer, Helen and Odysseus, were used as motifs for allegorical transpositions.

Held prisoner in Ilion (= matter), where she appears as a reflection (*eidōlon*) of the beauty of Hellas, her homeland, which is the intelligible world (see Hermias, *In Plat. Phaedrum*, p. 77, 13–78, 1 Couvreur), Helen incarnates, in a type of Christian Gnosis attributed to Simon Magus, the splendor of the first thought (*Ennoia-Epinoia*) of the intellect (*Nous*) of the Father. But she is also the lost lamb of the Gospel (Luke 15:4), wandering among the angels and the luminaries—her own creatures, who have forced her to live successive lives in the bodies of women. It is she who caused the Trojan War. The poet Stesichorus, who attacks her in his verse, goes blind; he recovers his sight while writing his *Palinodia.* Helen ends her long transmigration in a brothel in the city of Tyre in Phoenecia. It is there that Simon discovers her, and by means of a ransom he frees her from her bonds and marries her. They thus form, as a couple, "the perfect love," "the Holy of Holies," procuring salvation for humans through the revelation of Gnosis. The myth, told by Irenaeus (*Adv. Haer.* 1.23.2–3, pp. 191–93 Harvey) and his continuators (among others, *Elenchos* VI, 19, 1–7), rests upon a traditional mystic

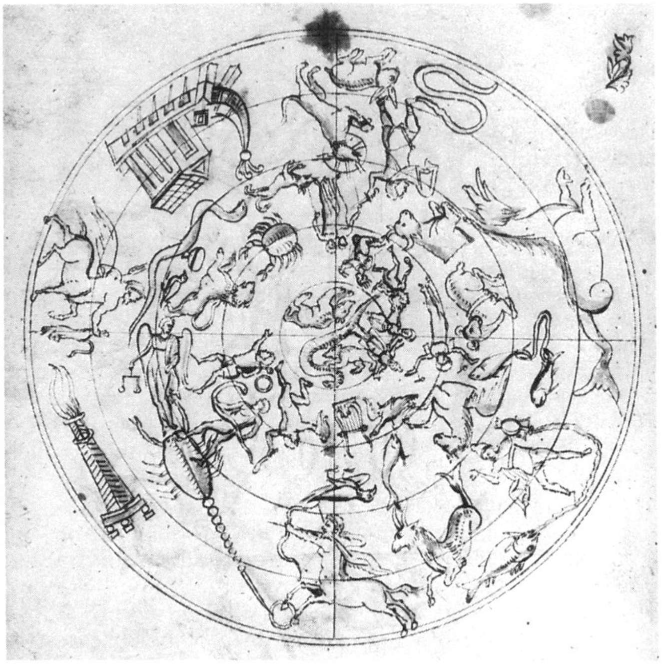

The zodiac. Rome, Biblioteca apostolica vaticana, MS gr. 1087, folio 310v. Library photo.

(Right) Gnostic papyrus from Nag Hammadi (Codex II, no. 10544, p. 136). Cairo, Coptic Museum, Museum photo.

(Far right) Hermaphrodite. Rome, Capitoline Museum. Photo Oscar Savio.

interpretation, from the late period, of the *Iliad* and the Trojan War: the kidnapping of Helen (= the divine part of the soul), torn from her own people and nostalgic for them, provokes a combat of powers, as a result of which this soul will be restored to its original homeland.

In a non-Gnostic work read by the Gnostics, which was discovered at Nag Hammadi (II, 6) and entitled *Exegesis on the Soul,* the tears of Odysseus, whom Aphrodite has deceived and brought to Calypso, express this same nostalgia for one's lost homeland: "No one is worthy of salvation if he still loves the place of his wanderings. This is why it is written by the poet, 'Odysseus sat on the island, prey to his tears and his sorrow; he turned his face from the words of Calypso and from her impostures; he wished to see his homeland and the smoke of its hearths and, above all, wished for the assistance of heaven to return to his homeland.' The soul, in turn, says, 'My man has turned away from me; I want to return once more to my homeland.' For the soul groaned, saying, 'It is Aphrodite who deceived me; she made me leave my homeland; I left my firstborn behind me, along with my husband who is good, wise, and handsome' " (p. 136, 25–137, 5). As a prisoner in a world subjected to the heavenly bodies and to fate (= Calypso, the daughter of Atlas) and trapped inside a body enslaved by sex (= Aphrodite), the soul will seek to "flee" and to free itself from the double bond of microcosm and macrocosm to reach its "true place," which is Gnosis, as quickly as possible.

In the *Apophasis Megalē,* a treatise placed under the authority of Simon Magus and related in the *Elenchos,* the *molu* plant with the black root and the milk white flower (*Odyssey* 10.304–6), the magical herb given by Hermes to Odysseus to protect him from the enchantments of Circe, is an allegory on the transformation made by Moses (= the Logos) when he turned the bitter water of the desert into fresh water (Exodus 15:22–24). It is thus the image of the metamorphosis of the wandering soul, restored to itself by Gnosis, which has been brought to it by the Logos and brings it to the knowledge of life in its movement (exodus) through the desert of the difficulties and bitter things of this world (VI, 15, 3–4). The *molu* procures the knowledge of all things and restores the soul to its primal "character," which properly belongs to it (VI, 16, 1). The Stoic philosopher Cleanthes associated the *molu* of Odysseus with the logos, that is, with reason, whose role is to calm the ecstatic leaps and passions of the soul (*SVF* 1.526 Arnim). For Porphyry, the *molu* represents the virtue of prudence and wisdom (*sōphrosunē*), which allows the soul that is thrown into the "*kukeōn* of generation," the mixture that is this world, to escape from its "miserable and bestial form of life" (Stobaeus, *Anthologion* 1.49.60 Wachsmuth).

The allegorical interpretation of the tale of Eros and Psyche, transmitted by Apuleius, is connected with the mystic exegesis of the *Iliad* and the *Odyssey.* Eros draws Psyche into the machinations of existence: sensuality, marriage, procreation, and death (*Nag Hammadi Coptic* II/5, p. 109, 19–25). For Justin the Gnostic, Psyche is under the power of Naas the serpent; incited by him, she sows corruption among the beings (*Elenchos* V, 26, 26). But the blood that flows from Psyche after her intercourse with Eros, which then spreads over the earth, gives birth to roses "for the joy of the light" (*Nag Hammadi Coptic* II/5, p. 111, 8–14). This twofold aspect of the dark and light soul is connected, in the same work, with the ambivalence of an Eros established in the middle of paradise, at the origin of all life and all death.

Heracles also becomes a Gnostic hero as the traditional figure of the Stoic sage before he comes to symbolize in Plotinus the fate of the double soul divided between the darkness of Hades (= the body and the world) and the light of the gods (= the intelligibles), a reflection (*eidōlon*) that is separated yet remembers its true being, which is "above" (*Enneads* 1.1.12.31–39; 4.3.27.7–23). In the mythology of Justin's *Book of Baruch,* he appears as a link in a chain of prophets sent by Elohim to try to recuperate the divine element—breath (*pneuma*)—that dwells in men (see *Elenchos* V, 26, 27–28). Following the messengers Baruch and Moses, the one sent to Adam and the angels of heaven and the other to the circumcized (the Jews), Heracles is portrayed as the "prophet coming from the uncircumcized peoples" (p. 131.5); the pagans will be the object of his mission. His twelve labors are allegories of the battles he fought against the twelve planetary angels of the Earth called Edem. Seduced by Omphale, however, whom Justin assimilates to Babel and to Aphrodite, he puts on the robe of Edem, which shuts him into the universe of lesser powers. "It is in this way," the myth concludes, "that the prophecy and works of Heracles had no effect." The Heracles of Justin the Gnostic, as savior and then prisoner, and the divided Heracles of

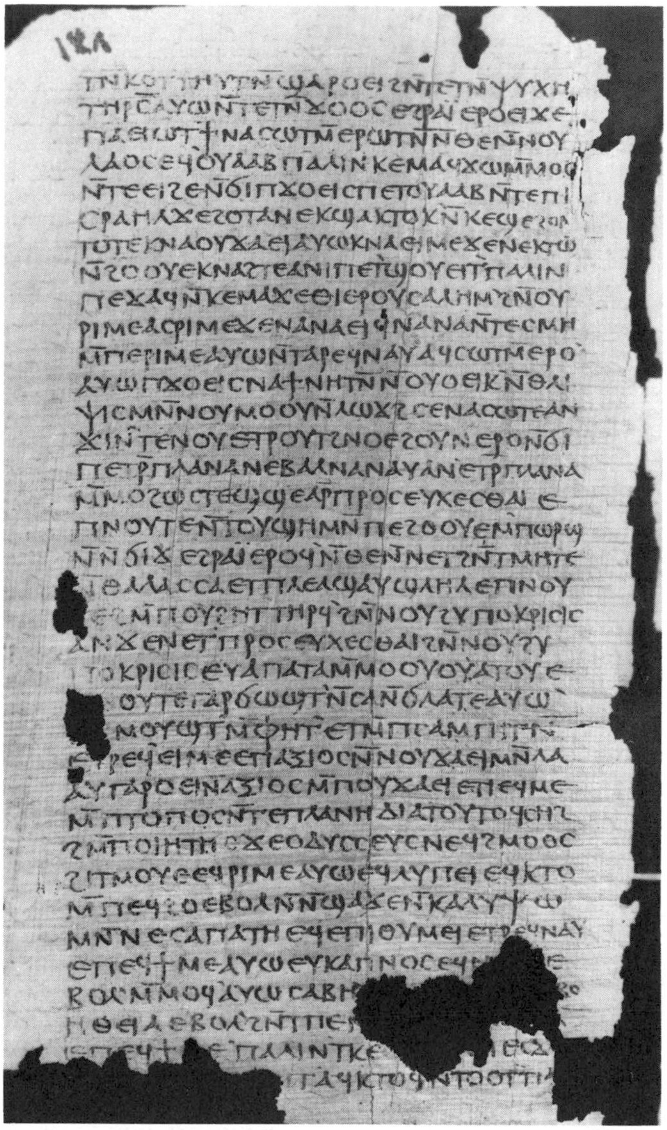

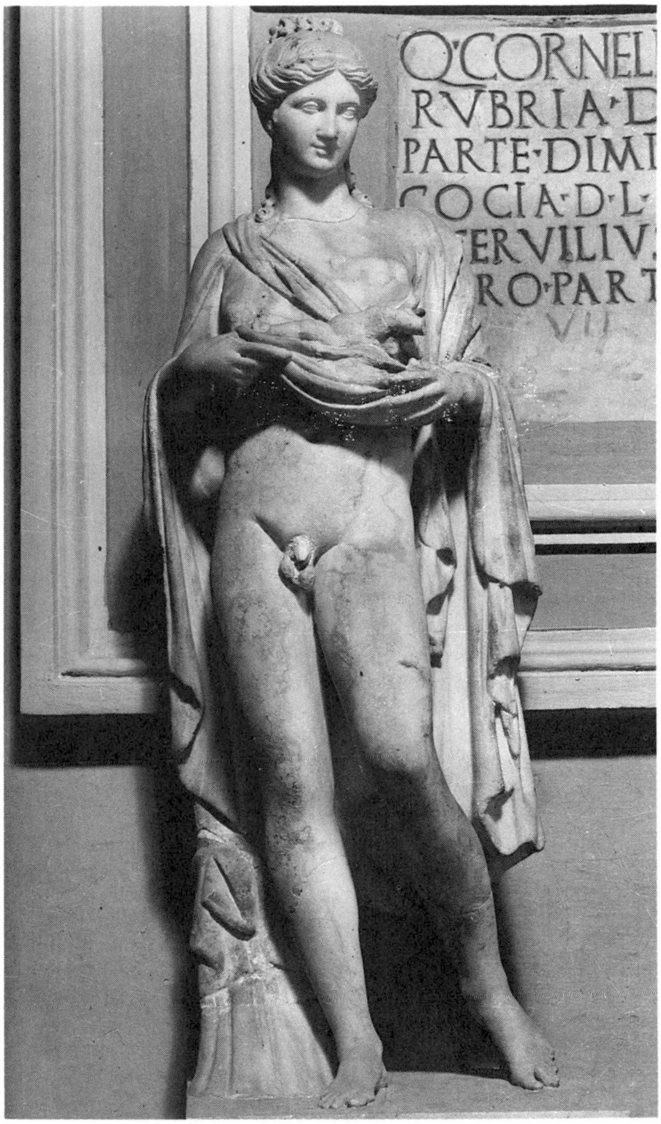

Plotinus, the reader of Homer, belong very much to the same period in the history of ideas.

The Egyptian myth in its Greek reinterpretation of the wanderings and tears of Isis, who is searching for her twin brother and lover Osiris (Plutarch, *Moralia* 356a–358b), served as the starting point for the Valentinian myth of the wanderings and tears of Sophia, abandoned to the sorrows and passions of this world, "a supplicant to the Father," because she has lost the unity of her origin and suffers from love of her twin (Irenaeus, *Adv. Haer.* 1.2.2 = Epiphanius, *Panarion* 31.11.4). Similarly, in the version of the myth presented in the *Elenchos,* the offspring of the Sophia above, himself called the "external" or "lower Sophia," overcome by sorrow and anxiety, looks for his twin everywhere and begs that he who has abandoned him return to him; it is then that the "common fruit of the pleroma," Jesus, who makes the sadness of Sophia into the "material substance" of the universe (*Elenchos* VI, 32, 3–6), is sent to him. Transformed by the creative Logos of Osiris and rendered capable of "receiving all bodily and spiritual forms," Isis incarnates, by her nature, the female principle of the universe; it is she who contains the whole (*pandechēs*) and who presides over all of generation (see Plutarch, *Moralia* 372e). Hence she is assimilated to Platonic matter, as the support and recipient of all things (*Timaeus* 49a; 51a). In the same way, among the Gnostics, the Valentinian Sophia, having surrendered to passion, becomes the principle of the constitution and essence of matter, out of which the world is born (Irenaeus, *Adv. Haer.* 1.4.2 = Epiphanius, *Panarion* 31.16.7). The child of Isis, Horus (= Harpocrates), "debased by matter through the bodily element" (*Moralia* 373b3–4), corresponds to the deformed offspring of the Valentinian Sophia, and is described as a "substance disorganized and without form," analogous to the primordial earth of Genesis and called "the runt" (*Elenchos* VI, 30, 8–31, 2). But just as the Isis of the Platonic tradition has an innate love for the first principle, which is the Good (Plutarch, *Moralia* 372e), so the Valentinian Sophia feels passion and desire for the Father (Irenaeus, *Adv. Haer.* 1.2.2 = Epiphanius, *Panarion* 31.11.4). Just as Isis is called "the seeking of Osiris," *zētēsis Osiridos* (*Moralia* 372c20), Sophia is "the seeking of the Father," *zētēsin tou Patros* (*GCS* 25, p. 403, 13). The joy of Isis, who carries in her the seeds of the world (Plutarch, *Moralia* 372e13–14), corresponds to the laugh of Sophia, who gives birth to light (*GCS* 25, p. 410, 22). The prostrate and weeping Isis, whose tears fecundate the soil of Egypt with floodwaters (Pausanias, *Periegēsis* 10.32.18), corresponds to the sorrow of Sophia, whose tears are the source of the sea, springs, and rivers, from which all the elements of the world come (Irenaeus, *Adv. Haer.* 1.4.2–4 = Epiphanius, *Panarion* 31.16.7–17.8). Last, the sequence of the myth about Isis's search for the phallus of Osiris (*Moralia* 358b) becomes the object, in Naassene Gnosis, of a triple interpretation, which is astrological, cosmological, and initiatory.

The portrait of Isis "of manifold names," *muriōnumos* (Plutarch, *Moralia* 352e), who is hermaphroditic by nature because of her identification with the moon (368c), underlies the portrait of this universal Mother of living creatures, who among the Gnostics is called Sophia, Eve, or Barbelo. Following the pattern of aretalogies which enumerate the titles and virtues of Isis, the Gnostics composed hymns, of which certain fragments have been found at Nag Hammadi (II/4, p. 89, 16–17; II/5, p. 114, 8–15); an entire treatise was even constructed upon this literary genre (*Nag Hammadi Coptic* 6/2; see, for example, p. 13, 27–14, 14). After the fashion of Isis, the mother goddess of the Gnostics encompasses what for humanity are opposites; she is at once virgin and mother, father and mother, prostitute and virgin, male and female, whole and part, self and other: "My husband is he who engendered me, and I am his mother and he is my father and my lord." The soul of each is henceforth engulfed in this soul of the world. With the Gnostics as with their contemporaries, the myth of the soul that wanders across the multiplicity of this world has for its corollary the myth of the repose of this soul in the fullness of the transcended division. The dispersion (*diaspora*) of the soul that is in submission to the planetary god is answered by the coming together (*sullexis*) of the Isian and sovereign soul.

The gods of paganism thus served the Gnostics merely as a means to illustrate this dialectic. In the same way that they are used by their contemporaries who are magicians, philosophers, and astrologers, so the Gnostics use these henceforth supernumerary entities of a drama, whether classifying them in catalogs of demons or dissolving them in allegorism. With the exception of Eros, none of the pagan gods that pass into Gnosis provides a new myth. Mythos and logos are no longer balanced. On the other hand, the fact that certain Gnostics, such as the Perates, the Naassenes, and, to a lesser extent, Justin, chose this very field of Hellenism to satisfy their appetite for allegory made possible the efflorescence of surprising systems of thought—the truly original and most successful forms of the Gnostic interpretation of the gods of paganism.

M.T./d.w.

BIBLIOGRAPHY

A. DIETERICH, *Abraxas: Studien zur Religionsgeschichte des späteren Altertums* (Leipzig 1891). H. USENER, *Götternamen: Versuch einer Lehre von der religiösen Begriffsbildung* (Bonn 1895; 3d ed., Frankfurt 1948). W. BOUSSET, "Die Himmelsreise der Seele," *Archiv für Religionswissenschaft* 4 (1901): 136–69, 229–73. R. REITZENSTEIN, *Poimandres: Studien zur griechisch-ägyptischen und frühchristlichen Literatur* (Leipzig 1904). E. NORDEN, *Die Geburt des Kindes* (Warburg 1924). R. P. CASEY, "Two Notes on Valentinian Theology," 1: "Valentinian Myths," *Harvard Theological Review* 23 (1930): 275–90. A. TORHOUDT, *Een onbekend gnostisch systeem in Plutarchus' De Iside et Osiride* (Louvain 1942). M. TARDIEU, *Trois mythes gnostiques* (Paris 1974).

The Perates and Their Gnostic Interpretation of Paganism

In the first half of the second century A.D., some Christian Gnostics were connected with the Ophite branch of Gnosticism by virtue of the important role of the serpent (Greek *ophis*) in their system of symbols. Known only from the account of them in the *Elenchos* (V, 12–18), the Perates are presented as adepts of the Chaldean science, devoting themselves to "allegorizing the order of the astrologers" (V, 15, 4, pp. 110, 29–30 Wendland) and to "transforming the names" (V, 13, 9, p. 107, 9–10; V, 15, 2, p. 110, 22) of Chaldean categories of stars into entities for their own pantheons. We are also told that they called themselves Perates because they alone, being aware of the laws that fix the "necessity of becoming" and the "ways by which man came into the world," were "able to cross over and go beyond (*perasai*) corruption" (V, 16, 1), in other words the planetary spheres that determine the fate of any individual that is subject to generation. Only the names of their founders are known: Euphrates the Peratic (a surname added by the heresiologist) and Celbes of Carysta, also known as Acembes or Ademes (V, 13, 9; IV, 2, 1; X, 10, 1). In the *Contra Celsum* (VI, 28, 31–2), Origen points out that "those who call themselves Ophites (*Ophianoi*) boast of having a certain Euphrates as the instigator of their ungodly doctrines." As this comment comes right after the refutation of the astrological chart that Celsus attributed to some Christians, we may surmise that Euphrates and Celbes represented the primitive layer of what the heresiologists called "Ophitism." In fact, "Ophitism" was nothing more than a form of theological reflection within Christianity itself; it used astrological terminology just as Bar-Daisan did, and the Peratic system was to become one of its later variants, marked by a specifically Gnostic character.

The books that the Perates read were the "Book of Moses" (V, 16, 8, p. 112, 14)—that is, Genesis, Exodus, and Numbers—in the Old Testament, and the Gospel according to John in the New Testament. Among the books they drew from "ignorance" (a Gnostic term for Hellenism) to support their theses, the Perates used Homer, Heraclitus, Aratus, and the Sibylline oracles among other "poets" and "sages." They also used short astrological treatises analogous to those recorded on magical papyruses. By way of example, the author of the *Elenchos* cites a long excerpt (V, 14), purposely chosen for its particular obscurity, from one of the books "held in high esteem among them," which was entitled *Hoi Proasteioi heōs Aitheros* ("The Suburbanites up to the Ether") (IV, 14, 10, p. 110, 12–13). As the content of the treatise reveals, such a title designates the gods and demons assigned to each of the planetary spheres that in some way constitute the periphery (*proasteion*) of the ethereal realm in which the first principle resides. Each god is introduced with his various names, consorts, functions, and signs. The first among them, Kronos, "tied in ropes after having locked up the dense, nebulous, obscure, and dark network of Tartarus," is assimilated to the power of the sea, Thalassa, who came from chaos and the slime of the abyss and is the mother of the Titans. Chorzar, the androgynous daughter of the sea, guardian of the waters, which she soothes by playing twelve small flutes, corresponds to Poseidon. The Curetes are associated with the rising of the sun; Ariel is chief of the winds; Osiris and Isis, the latter identified with the constellation of the Dog, designate the keepers (Archons) of the hours of night and day. Rhea, Demeter, Mēn, and Hephaestus, presiding over food, fruit, and fire, represent the dual movement, upward and downward, right and left, of the signs of the Zodiac on the ecliptic. The Moirai, cause of generation, are three powers of the middle air. Finally, at the lower extremity of the circles, and therefore the closest to us, is Eros, "forever a child" and androgynous, the "principle of beauty, pleasure, freshness, youth, concupiscence, and desire"; he brings to a close the catalog of the gods who are rulers (*toparchai*) of the planets.

The content of such a document has nothing Gnostic about it and can in no way be considered the source of the whole account of the Perates in the *Elenchos*, as the critics unanimously claim. The Christian polemicist in fact used two separate books. The first was the *Proasteioi* of the fragment summarized above, which was read by the Perates and belonged to the pagan literature of magic and astrology. The second, the title of which is not given (citations being always introduced by "said he"), was a document of genuinely Peratic revelation, an apocryphon placed under the name of an Old Testament revelatory figure, perhaps Moses, by virtue of the place it occupies in the excerpts cited in the *Elenchos* as well as in late Greek esotericism in general.

The world according to the Perates, like that of the Valentinians, is a triadic emanative system but, unlike the Valentinian world, does not fit into any syzygies. The triad forming the unity of the whole includes the first principle, the Perfect (*teleion*), which is the Good or the Unbegotten, followed by the Unlimited (*apeiron*), constituting the self-begotten world (*autogenēs*) of the powers of the intermediary space, and finally, in third place, the Particular (*idikon*), that is, our own world, begotten by flow (*kata aporroian*) originating in the stars, the causes of generation.

Unlike the third, the first two worlds are essentially incorruptible and imperishable. Furthermore, each part of the triad defines a class of gods, of logos, of intellect, of man, of nature, of the body, of power, and therefore of Christ, who, "starting with the three parts of the world, possesses within him all compounds and all powers" (V, 12, 4). His function will be to "cause to go back upward what had come down from on high" (V, 12, 6), that is, to restore to its fullness the original unity of being.

For the Perates, this basic outline corresponded to the triadic models used by the Astrologers (center or monad, a universe of powers subject to declination and ascension, generation), by Physicians (brain, cerebellum, spinal cord), and by Platonists (Father, Son, matter).

Matter (*hulē*), defined as having no quality (*apoios*) and no shape (*aschēmatistos*), is the work of the homicidal demiurge, the Archon of this world, "an aborted being who was born in the night and will perish in the night" (V, 17, 6). Because water is the fundamental constituent of matter, matter is identified with the Kronos of astrology, the consort of Thalassa. Thalassa is the power of disorder and mud that has come from the eternal humid element, always in motion and in convulsions, mistress of becoming and of death, analogous to Thalatth-Omorka (Homoroka) in the cosmogony of Berossos (FGrH III C no. 680 F 1[6] Jacoby) or to the Gūḥra' of Qūq, the gaping cavern of the waters of death swallowing the seven virgins who are the companions of the Mother of living creatures (cf. Theodore bar Konai, p. 334, 20–25 Scher).

Precisely by virtue of the position that he occupies in the triad, the Autogenēs, identified with the Johannine Son and Logos, is declared to be in "perpetual movement," attracted simultaneously upward by the immobile Father and downward by moving matter (V, 17, 2), like Hermes ferrying "downward all that belongs to the Father" (p. 114, 34) and "from here below to points beyond" (p. 115, 17). From the Father he receives powers, impressions, and ideas, which he transmits to matter, somehow channeling their flow, like a painter mixing on his tablet (= matter) forms and colors, that is, that which comes from the Father (V, 17, 5). This same function is described with the help of another "proof" (*apodeixis*, p. 116, 1) drawn from the nature of the cerebellum, the intermediary between the encephalon and the spinal cord; the cerebellum "attracts through the pineal gland the spiritual and life-giving substance that flows from the brain" (V, 17, 12), and from there directs it into the spinal cord, where it is changed into semen and at the end of its flow is expelled through the phallus.

The character of this second principle, defined as "always in motion" and analogous to the serpentine cerebellum (*drakontoeidēs*), connects it with the bronze serpent in Numbers 21.6–9, trained by Moses in the desert, that is, on the other side of the Red Sea (= Thalassa), which stands for the water of corruption and death (= Kronos) of this world, in which "little Egypt" (= the body) swims. The soteriological function of this serpent, which is called "universal" (p. 112, 18), "true and perfect" (p. 112, 7–8), is described with a remarkable profusion of allegories. It is the rod of Moses, the vanquisher of the rods of the magicians of Egypt, and it stands for the power within the very person of Moses. It is

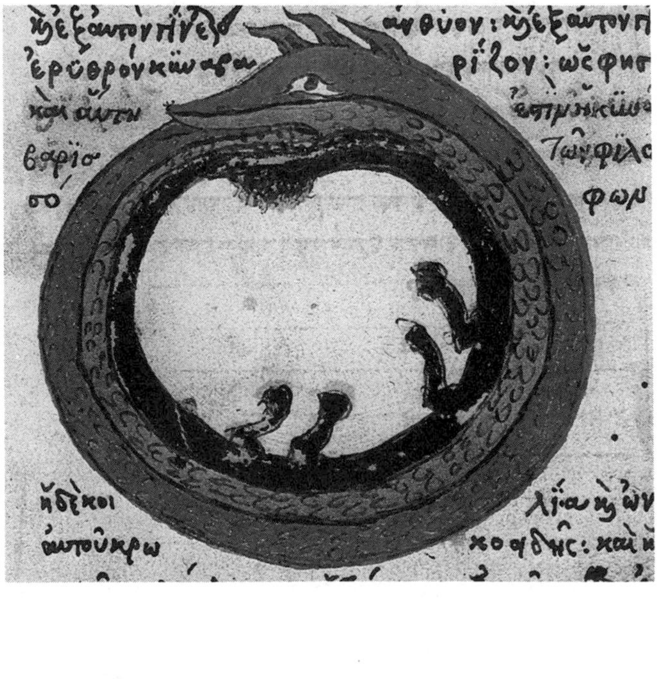

The serpent Ouroboros (ms. gr. 2327, fol. 196). Paris, Bibliothèque nationale. Photo BN/S.R.D.

Brass serpent. Milan, Basilica of Saint Ambrose. Photo Segre.

Eve, universal distributor of Logos, wisdom, and life, the "common nature" (*koinē phusis*, p. 113, 6) of the world above, as opposed to the particularity (*idikon*) of our world. It is the very mystery of Eden, whose river carries the waters of life. It is the emblem of the victims of the God of the Old Testament: Cain, the just slayer of a brother sullied by a bloody sacrifice; Esau of the blessed robe, who saw the face of God; Nemrod the builder of the Tower of Babel, "giant and hunter before the Lord"; and finally Jesus, "betrayed by his brothers" and "raised up" on the wooden cross. It is the constellation of the serpent-bearer (Ophiuchus, Serpentarius), which "shines eternally in the sky" and was described by Aratus as holding east and west, merged together, near its head (V, 16, 15). Finally, it is identified with the motionless *ouroboros*, closed upon itself, holding its tail in its mouth and thus symbolizing the completeness of the Father, the conjunction of the beginning and the end. It is thus the supreme anti-Kronos, countering the bond of death, which holds the world in its grip, with the bond of knowledge (*gnōsis*) and of the vision of the first unity: "By gazing up at the sky, someone with blessed eyes will see the splendid image of the serpent coiled up at the great beginning (*archē*) of the sky, becoming the principle (*archē*) of all movement for all who are born" (V, 16, 14). Thus there are three serpents corresponding to the three elements that make up the triad: the *ouroboros* for the Father; the bronze serpent for the Son; and the burning and venomous serpents of the desert for matter. The first two evoke life and Gnosis; the third evokes the ruin that is bound up with this world.

Peratic mythology drew from the thought of Egyptian astrologers and magicians. It took the possibility of multiple allegorical combinations, which the Jewish Platonistic current of Alexandria offered it, and made that possibility its own. But unlike other Gnoses, which chose one side or the other, proceeding by way of selective elimination or retrieval, Peratic mythology simultaneously had recourse to Judaism by way of anti-Judaism, to astrology by way of anti-Chaldaism, to Greece by way of anti-Hellenism, and to the Gospel by way of anti-Christianity. In this, it is Gnostic. It is highly unlikely that it was the expression of a school or a church. Between Valentinus and Bar-Daisan, Heracleon and Qūq, its inventor occupies a profoundly original position in the history of thought.

M.T./g.h.

BIBLIOGRAPHY

A. HILGENFELD, *Die Ketzergeschichte des Urchristentums* (Leipzig 1884), 263–67. FR. BOLL, *Sphaera: Neue griechische Texte und Untersuchungen zur Geschichte der Sternbilder* (Leipzig 1903), 309–10. W. BOUSSET, *Hauptprobleme der Gnosis* (Göttingen 1907), 124–25. H. LEISEGANG, *Die Gnosis* (4th ed., Stuttgart 1955); K. PREISENDANZ, "Ostanes," in PAULY-WISSOWA, *Real-Encyclopädie*, vol. 18 (Stuttgart 1942), cols. 1625–26.

EROS AMONG THE GNOSTICS

The sole writing that speaks of the mythic itinerary traveled by Eros (*Nag Hammadi Coptic* II 5, p. 109, 1–111, 28) concentrates, as do most descriptions of the period, on the genealogy and function of the god. Eros is the son of Pronoia, the *paredros* (consort) of the demiurge Ialdabaoth. Upon seeing the beauty of the angel of light, still called the primordial Adam or Light-Adam, that creature arisen out of the splendor of the ogdoad—i.e., from the Father, who is the principle of all things—Pronoia ardently wishes to unite with him. But the angel refuses, and she herself is too weighed down by her tenebrous element to be able to mount up to him. So she tears the luminous particles away from the angel, mixes them with her blood, and spreads them over the earth. By this act Pronoia responds, in kind, to that of her husband, who had flung his sperm "into the center of the earth's navel," whence the terrestrial Adam of the Garden of Eden had arisen. It is in the very middle of paradise that Eros is born as the fruit of the moist desire of his mother and the astral fire of the angel: he is thus androgynous by nature. "His masculine nature is Himeros, because he is a fire that comes from the light. The femininity within him is a soul of blood and comes from the substance of Pronoia" (p. 109, 3–6).

Because he unites in himself the two antagonistic forces of the primal Adam and of Pronoia, and because he is the place in which the union of love-desire (Himeros) and the beloved soul (Psyche) is realized, Eros produces sensual pleasure (*hēdonē*), which will lead to marriage, procreation, and death (p. 109, 20–25). Apart from the discrete allusion to the popular tale of Amor and Psyche, the Gnostic myth of the origin of Eros refers especially to the hermaphroditic conception of the Orphic Eros, whom the *Pseudoclementine Homilies* assert to have been formed "by Pronoia of the divine breath (*pneuma*)": "This living being Orpheus calls Phanes, because, when he appeared, the whole universe was illuminated by his splendor, Phanes having been brought to perfection in the womb of the liquid element by the brilliance of fire, the most magnificent of the elements; and there is nothing incredible about this, for in glow-worms, for example, nature has given a watery light for us to see" (6.12.4). Born of the mingling of the dry and the wet, of male fire and female blood, under the aegis of a Pronoia who was the bearer of light and of the divine breath, the Gnostic Eros governs the fusion of the primordial elements. According to an expression in the *Oracles,* he is their bond and their unifier, he who by projecting all things unifies them (pp. 25–26 Kroll). But, at the same time, this role of the conjoiner of opposites played by Eros does not give him in the Gnostic pantheon the eminent status which he enjoyed among the Orphics. He remains at the very source of the death that is transmitted by his daughter, sensual pleasure. Like the Eros of the Platonic myths of the *Symposium,* who is shared between heaven and earth, Poros and Penia, and gods and men, the Gnostic Eros is halfway between the light of the Father and the darkness of chaos, a daemonic intermediary being, situated neither above in the ogdoad nor below on earth, but in a space described by Plato as the garden of the gods (203b6); the Gnostic author specifies that this place is "in the center of the navel of the earth," in Eden, which is the garden (*paradeisos*) of the biblical god, beyond the sun and the moon.

Installed in paradise, Eros inaugurates his function as intermediary by stimulating all beings by the sight of his splendor: "He is very handsome in his beauty, having more loveliness than all the creatures of chaos. When all the gods and their angels saw Eros, they became enamored of him. But when he appeared to them all, he set them on fire. Just as many lamps are kindled from a single lamp, and the light is one light, and the lamp is not diminished, so Eros was scattered in all the creatures of Chaos, and he was not diminished. In the same way that he appeared in the midpoint (*mesotēs*) between light and darkness, so Eros appeared between angels and men" (p. 109, 6–19). Here we find a series of themes common to the whole period. In the *Poimandres,* personified Nature "smiles with love" upon seeing the "inexhaustible beauty" of the primordial man reflected in the water (§ 14). As a means to express the idea of the nondepletion of the primal energy of a God who gives his knowledge, Numenius would employ the same terms as the Gnostic author: "It is in this way that one can see a lamp lit from another lamp, bearing a light which did not deprive its source of light: only its wick was lit by that fire" (fr. 23 Leemans = 14 Des Places). Justin too uses the same image to describe the inexhaustible character of the Logos, which communicates itself: "Just as we see that from a first fire another fire is produced, without diminishing the fire from which the other was lit, the first fire in fact remaining the same, even so the new fire too which is lit here is seen to be entirely real without having diminished the one from which it was lit" (*Dialogue with Trypho* 61.2). Furthermore, by placing Eros between light and darkness, the Gnostic author brings together, in an erudite syncretism, the Greek genealogy of Eros, who is born of the night and is a transmitter of fire, and the activity of the God of Genesis, who separates light from darkness and night from day. Like a lamp that makes visible what is indistinct in darkness, Eros illumines beings submerged in the confusion of chaos. By allowing the elements to be distinguished, he is a reference mark and a center (*mesotēs*). As a sign of recognition and a principle of order, he is also that being who transmits the fire and blood from which he comes, and from which the disorders of the world are born. Born of the night, he remains a child of the night, communicating to beings and things the irrationality of his mother.

The luminary function of Eros was linked to his dependence on light and fire, and his sexual function to his connection with the "blood of the virgin" (p. 109, 1–2), by virtue of which Eros would govern all of the watery sphere, in the fecundated woman as much as in the fertilized ground: "Thus the intercourse (*sunousia*) of Eros was accomplished. The first sensual pleasure sprouted upon earth, woman followed earth and marriage followed woman, procreation followed marriage and death followed procreation. After that particular manifestation of Eros, the grapevine sprouted up from the blood which was poured upon the earth. Therefore those who drink it (the vine) engender in themselves the desire for intercourse. After the grapevine, a fig tree and a pomegranate tree sprouted up on earth, together with the rest of the trees, according to their kind, having their own seed within them derived from the seed of the powers and their angels" (p. 109, 19–110, 1). As principles of fertility and destruction, earth and woman represent the two aspects of the ambivalence of Eros. This is nothing new to the Greek world. Yet the way in which our Gnostic draws a correspondence between the three consequences of the sensual pleasures of woman (marriage, procreation, and death) and the three trees (vine, fig, pomegranate)—all three connected with Eros and possessed of a precise sexual symbolism—is entirely original. Wine, the drink of Aphrodite and Dionysus, composed like Eros of fire and boiling blood, leads man to the "desire for coitus" (p. 109, 29). The fig tree, a tree that is always green because it provides, according to Pliny, four harvests each year, is the phallic symbol par excellence; Dionysus uses a branch of the fig tree as a substitute for a phallus in a myth told by Clement of Alexandria (*Protrepticus* 2.34.3–4). Later Judaic writings would designate the fig tree as the tree of the forbidden fruit. Its leaves would serve to cover the nakedness of Adam and Eve. The pomegranate, which is filled with a multitude of grape seeds that ferment beneath its skin, contains a wine that is particularly recommended for the pleasures of love. Like his mother Aphrodite, Eros is portrayed holding pomegranates in his hands. But this fruit is also associated in the Greek world with Hera, the goddess of marriage and of procreation. Thus, the ancient myths still have their say when the Gnostic author wishes to name three plants associated with the sexual function of Eros. And it is not by mere chance that the mythic horticulture of Eros is built upon these three trees alone, for each one, within a single semantic field, portrays a particular aspect of the sexual function (fig tree–phallus–Dionysus; wine–sensual pleasure–Aphrodite; pomegranate–fecundity–Hera) and recapitulates through the perspective of the vegetal code the semantic totality of the cosmogonic and anthropological manifestation of Eros. It is thus in a very coherent fashion that the Gnostic author constructed, by reusing traditional schemata, the picture of an Eros who rules over both woman and earth.

While the cosmogonic epiphany of Eros, which separates light from darkness, remains positive, that of the Eros who

Androgynous winged Eros. Vienna, Kunsthistorisches Museum. Museum photo.

Gnostic papyrus from Nag Hammadi (Codex II no. 10544, p. 109). Cairo, Coptic Museum. Museum photo.

appeared "between angels and men" would, through recourse to woman, cause a principle of death to enter the world. The Coptic Gnostic text calls this death a dissolution of beings, a *bōl ebol* (p. 109, 24; the term is also found in *The Dialogue of the Savior, Nag Hammadi Coptic* III, 5, p. 122, 3). One consequence of this manifestation was the expulsion of Adam and Eve from paradise. But if, by reason of his fundamental duplicity, Eros is the most dreaded of the gods, he is also the most beautiful and most desirable, since his ambivalence, composed of fire and blood, expresses the totality of the primordial elements, the dry and the wet, from which the world was born. At once a principle of the dissolution of things and a principle of their reintegration, he both originates the sensual pleasure of copulation and, at the same time, according to the elegant formula of the *Pseudoclementine Homily,* "realizes the culmination of the beauty of the world" (p. 111, 16–17 Rehm). After the description of Eros's function as source of the madness that carries away the world, there is a description of this same function organizing what is beautiful in the world: paradise.

The Eden of Eros was created by Justice, an entity belonging to the ogdoad of the Father, "outside the circuit of the moon and the circuit of the sun in the luxuriant earth, which is in the east in the midst of the stones. And desire (*epithumia*) is in the midst of the trees that are beautiful and tall" (p. 110, 2–7). Paradise is situated beyond the time determined by the luminaries of day and night, in a mythic east of the Age of Gold in which precious stones abound. Because they are made up of the antagonistic elements of the wet and the dry, solar fire and river waters, precious stones belong to the biological and sexualized world, as do animals and plants, and consequently, just like trees, enter the semantic field of Eros. The plants of paradise, named by the Gnostic author, conform to the data of Jewish and apocalyptic tradition: to the north is planted the tree of life and immortality, which has a solar brilliance and is identified with the cypress-olive pair; near it is the tree of knowledge, which has a lunar brilliance and is identified with the fig-palm pair (p. 110, 6–11, 8). The relationship between Eros and paradise is also illuminated by the threefold reference to Eden as the land of beauty, of delights, and of desire—three titles that are eminently related to the god of Love. The description of paradise ends with an interpretation of the myth of Amor and Psyche. Just as Pronoia had spread her blood over the earth, from which Eros was born, so Psyche unites with Eros in paradise and spreads her blood over the earth, from which roses and lilies will be born (p. 111, 8–12). And then each of the daughters of Pronoia, one at a time, comes to unite with Eros, to give birth to all of the plants (p. 111, 14–24). By a skillful, harmonious syncretism, the editor of the Gnostic text seeks to present symmetrically the two universes—or rather the two gardens (*paradeisoi*)—in which the beauty and the desire of Eros dwelled: first the biblical Eden, from which evil powers are excluded and where, consequently, all the trees and fruits are beautiful and desirable; then the Greek paradise of Eros, in which the powers connected with sexual defilement appear. These two paradises, the Judaic and the Greek, constitute the two faces of an ambivalent Eros, whose androgyny, made of blood and fire, implies that his work will itself be ambiguous, being male and good on the one hand (fire = biblical Eden) and female and evil on the other (blood = Greek garden).

Eros is the only Greek god to have escaped an astrological and daemonological reduction among the Gnostics because he remained omnipresent and in fashion during this period—the end of the second century B.C.—when the system of which this treatise speaks was being constructed. Romances, oracles, and epigrams take possession of him; depictions of him abound in sarcophagi as well as in private homes as a companion at every moment in this life and the life beyond. Plotinus commented on him in his lectures as tending toward the beauty of the One, and the *Chaldean Oracles* proclaim him to be the son of the paternal intellect and the unifier of the totality of being. So it is not surprising that this god, familiar in the popular and scholarly mythology of Roman Egypt, should have furnished Gnostic thought with one of its least obscure and most brilliant pages. From the Eros of the ancient theogonies, who arose out of the earth, from chaos, or from an egg, to the beautified Eros of Gnosticism, placed in the midst of the stones and trees of paradise, we can trace the history of a single idea: that this world bears within itself the force that makes it survive.

M.T./d.w.

BIBLIOGRAPHY

M. TARDIEU, *Trois mythes gnostiques: Adam, Éros et les animaux d'Égypte dans un écrit de Nag Hammadi 2, 5* (Paris 1974).

Hecate in Greek Esotericism

To the Christian Gnostics, who believed that magic had been brought to the earth by fallen angels, Hecate represents one of the five Archons appointed to rule over the 360 demons (or daemons) of the "Middle," the aerial place below the zodiacal sphere or the circle of the sun, which fixes the Heimarmene. She has three faces and twenty-seven demons under her command. She occupies the third level in the hierarchy of the "Middle," between two female demons, long-haired Paraplex and Ariouth the Ethiopian, and two male demons, Typhon and Iachtanabas (*Pistis Sophia,* chap. 140; Coptic text: p. 363, 8–364, 6 Schmidt).

During the same period, this secondary figure of Gnostic daemonology is also an omnipresent personage in the pantheon of magical papyruses, because of the range of meanings attributed to her emblems and because of the system of associations which link her to, and even identify her with, other gods and goddesses.

Her three forms (*trimorphos* PGM XXXVI, 190) and her three faces (*triprosōpos,* IV, 2119, 2880) make her, as in classical Greek tradition, the goddess of crossroads (*triodites,* IV, 27, 2962) and the protectress of roads; but they express above all the "abundance of all magical signs" (XXXVI, 190–191), possessed by the "sovereign" goddess (*kuria,* IV, 1432) "of many names" (*poluōnumos*, IV, 745). The three-faced Hecate of the love charm of Pitys, contained in the magical Greek codex of Paris, has the head of a cow on the right, the head of a female dog on the left, and the head of a girl in the center (IV, 2120–2123). The Hecate engraved in a magnetized rock (IV, 2881–2884) also shows three faces: a goat on the right, a female dog on the left, and in the middle a girl with horns.

Her mouth exhales fire (*puripnoa,* IV, 2727); her six hands brandish torches (IV, 2119–2120). Hence, engraving her name with a bronze styletto on an ostracon (XXXVI, 189) or on a lead tablet (IV, 2956) will have the effect of a fire "burning" and "consuming" the beloved woman (XXXVI, 195, 200), so that she is deprived of sleep forever (IV, 2960, 2965–2966). Furthermore, the fire that inhabits Hecate, as the most subtle of the four elements, characterizes her keen intelligence and the extreme sharpness of her perception (*puriboulos,* IV, 2751). Her whole being radiates with the brilliance of the fire from the stars and from the ether. The *Chaldaean Oracles* made this Hecate "of the breasts that welcome storms, of resplendent brilliance" into an entity "descended from the Father," associated with the "implacable thunderbolts" of the gods, with the "flower of fire," and with the "powerful breath" of the paternal Intellect (p. 20 Kroll). Because she carries and transmits fire from above, she is the supreme goddess of vivification. The reason Hecate's womb is so remarkably "fertile" (*zōogonon,* p. 19 Kroll) is that she is filled with the fire of paternal Intellect, the source of life or the strength of thought, which it is her duty to communicate and to disseminate.

Through her emblems and her triadic conception, Hecate is associated with another goddess of time and destiny, Mene or Selene, the goddess of the moon. The prayer to the moon of P IV, 2785 invokes them as one and the same entity; epithets and attributes of the two goddesses are interchangeable. Hecate/Selene also has three heads, carries torches, presides over crossroads: "You who in the three forms of the three Charites dance and fly about with the stars . . . You who wield terrible black torches in your hands, you who shake your head with hair made of fearsome snakes, you who cause the bellowing of the bulls, you whose belly is covered with reptilian scales and who carry over your shoulder a woven bag of venomous snakes" (IV, 2793–2806). She has the eye of a bull, the voice of a pack of dogs, the calves of a lion, the ankles of a wolf, and she loves fierce bitches: "This is why you are called Hecate of many names, Mene, you who split the air like Artemis, shooter of arrows" (IV, 2814–2817). She is the mother (*geneteira*) of gods and men, Nature the universal mother (*Phusis panmetōr*): "You

Hecate. Paris, Bibliothèque nationale, Cabinet des Médailles. Photo BN.

come and go on Olympus and visit the vast and immense Abyss: you are beginning and end, you alone rule over all things; it is in you that all originates, and in you, eternal, that all ends" (IV, 2832–2839). Another hymn in the Paris codex used as a love charm shows the same joy in piling up titles of the goddess, who has this time become Aphrodite, the universal procreator (*pangennēteira*) and mother of Eros (IV, 2556–2557), at once below and above, "in the Hells, the Abyss, and the Aeon" (IV, 2563–2564), chthonic (IV, 1443), holding her feasts in tombs (IV, 2544) and associated with Ereskigal, the Babylonian queen of Hells (LXX, 4), but also the "celestial traveler among the stars" (IV, 2559), nocturnal, but also the bearer of light (IV, 2549–2550).

Her ring, scepter, and crown represent the power of the one who, possessing the triad, embraces all. Above and below, to the right and to the left, at night as during the day, she is the one "around whom the nature of the world turns" (IV, 2551–2552), the very Soul of the world, according to *Chaldaean Oracle* "the center in the middle of the Fathers" (p. 27 Kroll), occupying, according to Psellus, an intermediary position and playing the role of the center in relation to all the other powers: to her left the source of virtues (p. 28 Kroll), to her right the source of souls, inside, because she remains within her own substance, but also directed to the outside with a view to procreation.

Whether invoked in love charms to bring to oneself the woman one desires (the *agōgai* of the magic papyruses) or evoked by the "constraints that subdue the gods" (the *theiodamoi anankai* of the Chaldaen philosophers, p. 156, v. 190 Wolff), Hecate is henceforth inscribed in a table of correspondences and combinations which go far beyond her proper function as a goddess of enchantment and magic. It is from this Hecate, the product of the syncretism of the papyruses, that the tradition of the Hecate of the Neoplatonic commentators on the *Oracles* takes shape.

M.T./t.l.f.

BIBLIOGRAPHY

R. GANSCHINIETZ, *Hippolytos' Capitel gegen die Magier,* TU 39/2 (1913): 64–70. TH. HOPFNER, *Griechisch-ägyptischer Offenbarungszauber,* SPP 21 (1921): 259 d; "Hekate-Selene-Artemis," in *Pisciculi . . . Franz Joseph Dölger dargeboten,* T. Klauser and A. Rücker, eds. (Münster in Westf 1939), 125–45. M.-P. NILSSON, *Die Religion in den griechischen Zauberpapyri* (1947), reprinted in *Opuscula selecta,* 3 (1960): 143–45. H. LEWY, *Chaldaean Oracles and Theurgy: Mysticism, Magic and Platonism in the Later Roman Empire* (Cairo 1956), 47–56, 83–98, 269–73, 292–93, 353–55, 361–66. TH. KRAUS, *Hekate: Studien zu Wesen und Bild der Göttin in Kleinasien und Griechenland* (Heidelberg 1960); "Alexandrinische Triaden der römischen Kaiserzeit," *Mitteilungen des Deutschen Archäologischen Instituts,* 19 (1963): 97–105.

JUSTIN THE GNOSTIC: A SYNCRETISTIC MYTHOLOGY

Justin the Gnostic is artificially linked by heresiology to the Christian Gnostics through a triadic system superficially analogous to that of the Sethians or the Perates, and through the very secondary role that Jesus plays in the final phase of the soteriology. In the single account by the Christian polemicist who speaks of him (*Elenchos,* V, 23–28), he is described as the author of a treatise on revelation entitled *The Book of Baruch,* written in the second half of the second century A.D. Nothing is said of the individuality of the author, but the passages cited from his book lead one to believe that his was a personality that remained profoundly Oriental, closer to Qūq, to Monoïme, or even to Elchasaï than to the representatives of the schools of Platonizing Gnosticism.

Three principles (*archai*), roots (*rhizai*), or sources (*pēgai*) dominate the universe, all three of them uncreated (*agennētoi*). Above is the innately good being, male, endowed with foresight (*prognōstikos*) and identified with Priapus. His ithyphallic symbol, in charge of guarding the ripe autumn fruit (*opōrai*), represents all of creation, which he protects. From then on, according to one of those etymologies of which the Gnostics were very fond, he becomes "the one before (*prin*) whom there was nothing," "the one who created whereas nothing existed before" (*priopoein*), the source of the inexhaustible fertility of the universe (V, 26,

33). In the middle of the triad is the Father, identified with the Jewish Elohim, endowed with will (*thelēsis*) and split between the extreme limits of the triad. As in the Valentinian myth of the ignorance of the demiurge, he at first has no idea of the existence of the first principle and believes himself to be the only God (V, 26, 15). In the third place is a young girl who is a goddess, half earth, half snake, to whom is given the Hebrew name of paradise, Edem, land of origins where the snake lives, also called Israel, endowed with anger (*orgē*), deceitful and perverse, jealous and evil. With a double intelligence and a double body (*dignōmos* and *disōmos*), she incarnates the duplicity of all women, simultaneously drawn toward men, whom she pollutes, and attracted by Elohim, whom she makes her lover. But, unlike the Valentinian Sophia at the boundaries of the two worlds, the origin of evil but also of salvation, the unique function of Justin's sly and lubricious Edem is to be forever responsible for all misfortunes that befall men; this perfidious goddess of the earth is the "prostitute" (V, 27, 4, p. 133, 13) who chains everyone she approaches, both God and men, to his destiny of death. The three principles being outside of time and without any descendants, the sole object of the myth is thus to explain how one of the divine elements—the breath (*pneuma*) of Elohim—escaped from the control of its owner (the fall) and was then restored to him (salvation).

In Justin's mythology, the story of the fall does not describe, as does the Valentinians' version, a second time frame for the process of organizing the universe; it takes place not outside the triad of the principles but inside it, coextensive with the primordial order itself. Indeed, the demiurgic scenario takes place at the beginning of things through the desire that instantaneously carries the second principle (= the Father, or Elohim) toward the young girl Edem, a union that is allegorically represented by the two loves of Zeus, in the form of a swan for Leda and of golden rain for Danaë (V, 26, 34–35). It is thus a metamorphosed Elohim who unites with Edem. But the account of the Christian polemicist does not indicate the particular form of metamorphosis undergone by virtue of the will to dissimulate, since desire (*epithumia*) and will (*thelēsis*) are the Gnostic constant at the origin of all faults. Thus smitten with each other, Elohim and Edem unite and give birth to twelve angels, who form the astral structure of the universe, or the paradisiac land of origins. Thus the paradise of Genesis is merely an allegorical interpretation proposed by Moses for those angelic seeds planted in Edem by Elohim (*Genesis* 2.8). The two trees in paradise allegorically designate the two angels which appeared in the third rank of the zodiacal entities: Baruch, the tree of life, on the side of the father; Naas (= the snake), the tree of the knowledge of good and evil, on the side of the mother. Similarly, the four rivers in paradise are an allegory used by Moses to describe the tetradic organization of the angels: "These twelve angels, which are intertwined with the four parts of the universe, surround and rule the world, holding it in a kind of satrapic power which they derive from Edem; they do not always stay in the same places, but surround the world as in a dancing circle, moving from place to place, and gradually leaving to others the places that were established for them" (V, 26, 11–12). The first consequence of Elohim's reciprocal love for Edem is the installation of the Heimarmene, an uninterrupted torrent that rolls its stream of distress and vice around the world, chaining all beings to "the necessity of evil" (p. 129, 1). The Valentinians had responded to the problem of the origin of evil by adopting the Platonic solution; Justin adopts the determinism of the astrological conception, whose materialism he radicalizes by transferring it to ontology: evil is nothing but the product of a movement in the very center of the triad. The evil being, engendered by nature and materialized by the astral sphere, comes directly from the unbegotten themselves, Elohim and Edem, under the indifferent eye of Priapus.

The emergence of the sphere of planetary angels will set the entire anthropogonic process in motion. The angels of Elohim pull an animal body, heavy and lifeless, out of the earthly part of Edem—a variant of the Valentinian myth of Sophia's abortion. Elohim and Edem then undertake to make it the "seal and memorial of their love, the eternal symbol of their union" (p. 128, 4). Edem gives it a soul (*psuchē*), the principle of existence (*bios*); Elohim gives it breath (*pneuma*), the principle of life (*zōē*). Thus arises the primordial couple, Eve and Adam, each "in the image" of their model. The centripetal mobility of the astral angels, circling around the world, corresponds to the centrifugal force of the human microcosm trying to escape the circle of destiny in order to rejoin the point of origin.

The myth of the fall, which opens with the union of Edem and Elohim, ends with the story of their separation. Curious to know the secrets of the universe, and by nature drawn toward the heights (*anōpherēs*, p. 129, 5), Elohim climbs with his angels into the upper reaches of the sky, where he discovers the perfect light of Good. Without his angels, since they are Edem's sons, he then enters into the luminous depths of the supreme principle, and sits down on its right. But from that moment it is no longer possible for him to regain his breath (*pneuma*), which is trapped in humans. Sad to have been abandoned, Edem attempts one last time to seduce Elohim, and surrounds herself with all the cosmic beauty of her angels. All is in vain. Furious, she avenges herself by striking at what remains of Elohim in humans, the breath-spirit. In order to make Elohim experience in his turn the torture of separation and sadness, she enjoins Aphrodite-Babel, the first of her demons, to inspire in humans the dramas of love—broken hearts, adultery, and divorce. She then commands Naas (the snake), the third of her angels, to unite with Eve and then with Adam, as a result of which the spirit of Elohim in man is brought to lewdness and pederasty.

As in all the systems of the time, a corollory of the myth of the fall states that salvation will consist in seeing to it that the breath-spirit of Elohim, which resides in humans, is detached first from the multiple degradations, mutilations, and humiliations that it underwent through the power of the inventor of sexuality, Edem-Israel of the double and earthly body, so that it can then reascend, pure and light, to its originating principle. To this evil action of Edem—striking, through her intervening angels (Aphrodite-Babel and Naas), the breath of Elohim inherent in the human spirit—Elohim will set up a counteroffensive of salvation in four stages, each marked by the dispatch of a prophet and dominated by the antagonism of Psyche (on Edem's side) and Pneuma (on Elohim's side)—the anthropological version of the antagonism inherent in the macrocosm (the angels of the father against the angels of the mother).

Elohim first sends Baruch, the third of his angels (= the anti-Naas), to the children of Edem-Israel, the Jews. The voice of Baruch, calling the people of the circumcised to conversion, is stifled by the hissing of Naas. Elohim sends Baruch off a second time, but this time only to the Jewish prophets. They are seduced by Psyche, who is manipulated by Naas, and make a mockery of Baruch's words. Two dispatches, two failures. For the third mission, Elohim chooses Heracles, whom he sends among the uncircumcised (= the pagans) to fight the twelve angels of Edem. In twelve gigantic battles, Heracles triumphs over the lion, the hydra, the boar, and so forth, allegorical names of the mother's angels. Seduced by Omphale, however, who is none other than Aphrodite-Babel, Heracles is stripped of his strength, that is, of the orders transmitted to Baruch by Elohim, and puts on Edem's own robe. Unsatisfied by this partial victory, Elohim sends Baruch off once again, "in the days of King Herod," to a boy of twelve, Jesus of Nazareth, the son of Joseph and Mary, who is busy tending sheep. He reveals to him the Gnosis—the knowledge of the past (the loves of Edem and Elohim, and the repentance of the latter), the present (Naas's fight against Baruch), and the future (the return of Pneuma to the Good). Furious at seeing Jesus resist all his attempts at seduction and remain faithful to Baruch, Naas has him crucified. But Jesus, "abandoning on the wood the body of Edem" (p. 131, 31–32), "gives back the spirit (*pneuma*) into the hands of the Father (= Elohim) and rises up to the Good" (p. 132, 23). The death of Jesus thus marks the end of the antagonism of Psyche and Pneuma and the definitive victory of Elohim over Edem. Justin's tritheist system is therefore a camouflaged dualism: above, the male universe of good, the domain of Priapus-Elohim; and below, the female universe of evil, the domain of Edem. To classify such a Gnostic system among the Christian Gnostics, as the author of the *Elenchos* followed by later criticism has done, is not acceptable.

The anti-Judaic bias of a Justin so taken by Jewish Scriptures is obvious. On the other hand, when Christian heresiology accuses Justin of "following word for word the myths of the Greeks" (p. 125, 8) by simply applying the myth of the union of Heracles with the young girl/snake "to the generation of the universe" (V, 25, 1–4), this constitutes a polemical argument invented for the sake of the cause. The myth of the half-earth/half-snake woman associated with the biblical Edem was not borrowed from Herodotus, as is said in the *Elenchos;* according to Van den Broek, it emerged from speculations that are connected with the cult of Isis-Thermouthis in Hellenistic Egypt. But it is more likely that the goddess of the earth, described by Justin as a young girl or a young virgin (*korē*, p. 127, 4), the wife (*suzugos*, p. 129, 6) of an astral god, comes from the esoteric tradition of the "Hellenized Magi," according to whom the earth is a young virgin betrothed to Parnsag (Theodore bar Konai, *Liber scholiorum*, 11, p. 297, 12–14 Scher). Moreover, the chain-of-prophets theory recalls the theory that is found in pseudo-Clementine writings or among the Elchasaites. Unlike the latter, Justin lacks the essentially Christian element almost entirely; at the same time, the uncreated and eternal character of the elements of the triad appears incompatible with the "Judeo-Christian" theses in the strict sense. However, the importance given to water symbolism (stagnating waters below the firmament; living waters above) is connected with Eastern baptist trends. Finally, Justin's Christological Docetism recalls that of the *Apocalypse of Peter,* in which Jesus "the carnal" is nailed to the cross while Jesus "the living" is joyful and laughs (*Nag Hammadi Coptic* VII, 3, p. 81, 10–22), just as his diatribe against the Jewish prophets is related to that of the *Second Logos of the Great Seth* (*Nag Hammadi Coptic* VII, 2, p. 62, 27–64, 12). This pagan-dominated Elchasaism, which is Justin's system, is the response to a desire for synthesis between a syncretist mythology stemming from the Chaldean astrologers and a baptist practice impregnated by Gnosticizing Docetism.

M.T./t.l.f.

BIBLIOGRAPHY

W. VÖLKER, *Quellen zur Geschichte der chrislichen Gnosis* (Tübingen 1932), 27–33. E. HAENCHEN, "Das Buch Baruch: Ein Beitrag zum Problem der christlichen Gnosis," *Zeitschrift für Theologie und Kirche* 50 (1953): 123–58; reprinted in *Gott und Mensch: Gesammelte Aufsätze* (Tübingen 1965), 299–334. M. SIMONETTI, "Note sul Libro di Baruch dello gnostico Giustino," in *Vetera Christianorum* 6 (1969): 71–89. A. ORBE, "La cristología de Justino gnóstico," *Estudios Eclesiásticos* 47 (1972): 437–57. R. VAN DEN BROEK, "The Shape of Edem according to Justin the Gnostic," *Vigiliae Christianae* 27 (1973): 35–45. W. SPEYER, "Das gnostische Baruch-Buch," *Jahrbuch für Antike und Christentum* 17 (1974): 190.

The Medieval West and "Mythic Thought"

The conjunction of the terms "Christianity" and "mythology" was not at all shocking to the *philosophes* of the eighteenth century: on the contrary, analogous to their unfavorable judgments on the myths of other civilizations, the "great minds" saw in Catholicism a tissue of errors and affabulations that strained the limits of Reason, a "Christian mythology" relegated by the Enlightenment to the dark centuries of the Middle Ages.

In the nineteenth century, this "Christian mythology" entered the fields of study of historians and folklorists. But, though it partially avoided polemic in order to become an object of knowledge, it was still not apprehended through a unified vocabulary and precisely defined concepts: each author, it seems, could furnish his own definition of myth. Agreement was reached on one point: no one questioned the use of the word "myths" and "mythologies" when treating of the Middle Ages.

A primary procedure, which is generally recognized as outmoded today, was the search for the *origins* of "myths" spread by medieval Christianity. In his *Essays on Christian Mythology* (1907), Paul Saintyves was especially concerned with the Greco-Roman origins of the "Christian mythology" of the Middle Ages. More recently, Henri Dontenville has connected "French mythology" with an ancestral Celtic mythology, which he claims to have recovered from eleventh- to sixteenth-century documents and from more recent folklore.

Commenting on the title of his great work *The Saints as Successors to the Gods,* Saintyves strongly asserts that "the cult of martyrs and saints is of pagan origin," though he does go on to say more precisely that "this does not mean that they are not Christian." Churches have been built on numerous sites of pagan cults, and the pagan festivals yielded to the great Church festivals (Christmas, All Saints', etc.) on the same days. Similarly, the gods or heroes of antiquity were transformed into saints of the Church, and ancient myths are found to lie at the origin of certain hagiographic legends. For example, the legend of Saint Julian the Hospitable seems to reproduce the myth of Oedipus (page 269). It is true that the same might be said of the apocryphal legend of Judas, who was never—far from it—assimilated to a saint; but Saintyves never explains this contradiction in his thesis. His hypotheses nevertheless have the merit of being applied to long periods of time, necessary in the study of narrative traditions, and of taking account of an important part of the cultural heritage from which Christianity progressively arose. But these merits should not obscure the fact that the function of the saints who interceded with God was, simply because of the central presence of God, radically different from that of the pagan gods.

On the other hand, Dontenville's reconstitution of a "French mythology" bears the stamp of the "Celtic school": this is organized around the "mythic" giant Gargantua, to whom are connected the great legendary characters of the Middle Ages—Merlin, Morgan Le Fay, King Arthur, the serpent woman Mélusine, the horse Bayard, Tarasca, etc. One may wonder about the validity of a method which rests more on phonetic analogies than on a genuine scientific etymology. Elsewhere, though it is true that these narrative traditions were quite widespread, it is doubtful that they operated on a "national" or even a pan-European scale: it is likely that no narrator, let alone any listener, was ever aware that Gargantua could have been connected both to Mount Gargan in Italy and to Mont Saint-Michel in Normandy. The perspective that time and the scholarly work of Rabelais offer to the modern Celticist should not make him forget that the social context in which these folkloric traditions functioned was certainly much narrower. Our opinion is that this framework should be brought back to the scale of village or urban communities, or even to lineages such as that of the Lusignans, who explain their origins by reference to the legend of Mélusine.

A second methodology tends to reserve the expression "Christian mythology" solely for those medieval narrative traditions that were concerned with the world beyond. This is the implicit procedure followed by Sabine Baring-Gould in his *Curious Myths of the Middle Ages* (1866–88), and especially by Arturo Graf in his great book *Myths, Legends and Superstitions of the Middle Ages* (1892): myths, and not mere legends, were those accounts which, in the twelfth century, placed in the East the earthly Paradise to which Seth, the son of Adam, went to ask in vain for his father's pardon. In the same period, other "myths" relate that Morgan Le Fay carried the wounded Arthur to the Isle of Fortune (according to Geoffrey of Monmouth); if we are to believe Gervase of Tilbury, this Arthurian court was in Sicily in the depths of Mount Etna, where purgatory was located.

Graf sees a connection between these representations of the world beyond, which is nevertheless located on earth, and the "myth" of the land of Cockaigne. Cockaigne is also situated on earth, but it is made for the living, for people who enjoy good living, in fact, since it spares its inhabitants from eating the overly delicate food of paradise, "where it is prohibited to eat anything other than fruits or to drink anything other than water," according to a fourteenth-century German poem. Cockaigne—whose name evokes cakes (the German *Kuchen* or the English *cake* have the same root)—is the world of the carnival inversion of rules about eating and of the Church calendar, signifying the definitive triumph of "Carnage" over "Lent." Thus Lent is only observed once every twenty years, while the festival of Easter is repeated four times each year! As František Graus (1967) has shown so well, Cockaigne, essentially conceived as a village region or, less often, as a manor, is one of the

Paris, Bibliothèque de l'Arsenal. Photo Giraudon.

three great forms of the medieval utopia. Another is the pursuit of the ancient utopian traditions, which continue to be known in literate circles; the third, by contrast, is "popular," and represents the medieval version of the Golden Age. This is pushed back into a past that is never as distant as that of the earthly Paradise before the fall, and is generally connected with the name of a more or less legendary saint-king whose reign remains the symbol of peace and opulence. Cockaigne is thus the expression neither of the most scholarly culture nor of folkloric culture; it is associated with the intermediate milieu of Goliards and students, who were aware of both village traditions and the Latin culture of the clergy. It expresses the utopia of a world in which, thanks to the fountain of youth that is at the center of this land, sensual pleasure and youth are perpetually renewed.

We must dispute Graf's use of the word "myth," but we should recognize that the author did not devote himself to the traditional quest for "origins." On the contrary, he grounded his research in history, demonstrating—with regard to the image of the devil, for example—how these representations are the product of a constantly evolving society, and are not reducible to "origins" containing all of their future developments in advance. If, however, he seems to have sensed the need for a typology of narrative genres, he was never explicit about it; if he distinguished "myths" from "legends," he never really gave his reasons for doing so. He assimilated utopia into myth, which, as we shall see, is unjustifiable.

The word "myth" is also employed by historians of medieval heresy when they speak of a "Cathar myth." Here the observer is presented with a body of structured and apparently autonomous beliefs (some have even spoken of "another religion" rather than a heresy, which is merely a deviation from Christianity) which express essential truths about the origin of the world, of evil, of man, and about the fate of the soul after death. The principal theme of this "Cathar myth," such as it appeared in the south of France and in northern Italy from the twelfth to the fourteenth centuries, is the rivalry between the two principles of Good (God) and Evil (Satan). This opposition underlies the story of the origin of souls: by means of the charms of his creature, Woman, Satan succeeds in seducing the majority of the spirits of God, who leave Paradise through a hole. When the Father notices what is happening, he puts his foot over the hole, but in vain; it is too late and nearly all of the spirits have gone away. These spirits, however, in the presence of Satan, remain nostalgic for the celestial glory they once knew. To make them forget it, Satan gives them a carnal envelope, the body, which is thus a creation of Evil; upon the death of the body, the soul leaves it and goes to dwell within another body, that of an animal or a man. This transmigration of souls is the only hell that exists, and here too it is situated on earth. When a soul eventually enters the body of a Cathar Perfectus, it is assured its salvation, for the death of this man will allow it to return to the Father. And when all of the souls have returned to God, it will be the end of the world. Legends were grafted upon this basic narrative, and those concerned with the migration of souls play an important role. One of these relates that a Perfectus found in a ravine a horseshoe that he had lost in that very spot when he was previously a horse. All of these accounts have multiple functions: they offer an explanation for the history of the world, from its beginning to the end of time, and a unified representation of this world and the world beyond. At the same time, they justify the internal divisions between the heretical groups, between Perfecti and Believers, and the alimentary and sexual taboos of the Cathars, for whom all that concerns the flesh is diabolical. This group of narratives, organized into a coherent whole, does resemble what might be understood as a "mythology." But first the illusion of its autonomy must be dissipated: Like orthodoxy, this body of narratives was constituted out of an interpretation of the Scriptures. Furthermore, it would be a mistake not to see it as a complete theology, seeking, through the same rational avenues as does the theology of the Church, arguments it might use to counter the Church. Under these conditions, is it legitimate to speak of "myths"?

Although historians of medieval Christianity have not hesitated to use the words "myths" and "mythologies," they have given them widely varying contents. Beyond these divergences there is the basic question of whether it is legitimate to speak of "myths" with reference to medieval Christianity, regardless of the particular meanings one might give the word. This question demands that the word be given as clear a definition as possible, to ensure its applicability to the Middle Ages. The clarification demanded of the medievalist is all the more urgent for the fact that the analysis of myths has constituted one of the most dynamic branches of research in the human sciences for at least thirty years.

Myth defines itself at the heart of a structured narrative system according to its own logic, constituting the sole form of articulation and reception for the essential truths of a given society: myth tells what is known about the world, the cosmos, human society, animals, and gods. The logic of myth is that of "savage thought," which keeps reorganizing the same elements ("mythemes") according to symbolic codes of affinities, in the same way, according to Lévi-Strauss, that a *bricoleur* (a kind of professional scrap collector and fix-it man) assembles given materials already at hand. Furthermore, myth, as opposed to legend, does not claim to be the account of a historical tradition; nor does it express, as opposed to a utopia, an aspiration for a different society: on this subject, the reader may refer to Pierre Vidal-Naquet's pertinent remarks. We should also note, along with Jean-Pierre Vernant, that mythic thought, which is the totality of the thinking of a society at a given moment of its historical development, may yield its place to another kind of thinking, as occurred in ancient Greece, when political reason and philosophy came to birth at the same time as the polis.

These definitions seem to exclude from the outset any evocation of a medieval "Christian mythology." In fact, the essential verities of medieval Christianity were uttered not by the voice of myth but by the Book, which reproduces the revealed and immutable Word of a unique God and is interpreted by the clergy. Far from engaging in a discussion that was closed on itself and founded on combinations of ever-repeated images, the clergy found, in the very distance they placed between their reason and the Word of God, the possibility of a continuous transcendence of their thought. As faith in quest of understanding (*fides quaerens intellectum*), and as a refusal to take pleasure in the play of oppositions or in the opposing will to reduce all contradictions (the meaning of Abelard's *Sic et Non*), theological reason excludes myth.

Paris, Bibliothèque des Beaux-Arts. Photo Giraudon.

Of course, medieval Christianity did inherit myths, starting with the Semitic myths of Genesis, the Flood, etc., which the Bible had bequeathed to it. Deposited as they were in the Bible, however, and spread and explained by the Church, these myths were not lived as such: they constituted the *historia* par excellence, sacred History, and Moses, as the Dominican Vincent de Beauvais stated in the thirteenth century, "was the first among us to write the history of the beginning of the world" (*Speculum Doctrinale* 3.127). What has elsewhere been stated by myth is now attested to by the historian.

Historia, which enumerates in chronological order those events which in fact took place (*res factae, res gestae*), is set against *fabulae,* the artifices of language—that is, according to Saint Augustine, against the myths of pagan antiquity (known to the authors of the Middle Ages through the mythographers of late antiquity, especially through the *Mythologiae* of Fulgentius), against entertaining fables (those of Aesop above all), and against the false beliefs of the Manicheans (*Contra Faustum Manichaeum,* ed. Migne, *Patrologia Latina,* vol. 42, col. 374). Here we can see just how much the "Cathar myths" of the modern historians are in fact inherited from the clerical tradition of the Middle Ages. Thus, not only is it impossible to assimilate medieval Christianity to a "Christian mythology," but medieval Christianity itself took its distance from all the accounts that it perceived as myths (*fabulae*) in order to pass judgment on them.

Medieval Christianity is not to be identified, however, with the religion of the clergy alone. The clergy designated as *fabulae* the oral traditions of the *illiterati,* that is, all persons—long including the lay members of the aristocracy—who had no access to writing, to the Latin language, in a word, to the culture of the clergy. Is it appropriate, at least at this level, which by convention we call folkloric, to speak of "mythology" and "myths"?

Historically, it is true, the roots of medieval folklore are to be found in a pre-Christian past, which at that time had until quite recently been on the fringes of Christianity for the Slavic, Scandinavian, Celtic, and Germanic populations who had just been Christianized or were being Christianized. This pagan past was more complex in the case of Gaul, where Romanization had preceded Christianization. But here the collapse of the social structures of the Late Empire may have favored a Celtic "revival" with which Christianity, still not firmly established, would have found itself in brutal confrontation. Whatever the case, folkloric culture is not reducible to these "origins": it was perpetually taking shape and transforming itself in symbiosis with the scholarly culture of the clergy; it became Christianized even as it folklorized official Christianity.

These reciprocal borrowings were not, however, the products of chance; nor were they at all symmetrical. We know that hagiography borrowed heavily from folkloric legends. In the same way, even if the Church had a definite view of the Creation and of the origin of time, it was less comfortable about concrete descriptions of the last things: here there was a certain deficiency or at least a perceptible rift between the account of Genesis, which was realistic but set in the past, and the eschatological symbolism of the Apocalypse, set in the future. Thus it was particularly with regard to the last things that a need was felt to complete and render more concrete the beliefs and even the dogma of the Church: whence the success of the resulting commentaries on the Apocalypse, elucidations that were scholarly but which, quickly vulgarized, fueled a popular millennialism from the thirteenth to the fifteenth centuries that easily slipped into heresy (Spirituals and Beguines, Hussites, etc.). There was a consequent pressure for folkloric depictions, soon assimilated by the clergy, which A. Graf calls "myths." Jacques LeGoff has shown that from the twelfth century onward, under pressure from folk culture, the Christian afterlife became definitively organized, and purgatory took its place between hell and paradise. An analogous deficiency could also be found in the case of the figure of the devil; to be sure, Satan is present in the New Testament, where he comes to tempt Christ himself; and antiquity also had its demons. But it is only with the high Middle Ages that the devil becomes ever-present, obsessive, and tyrannical, which had never previously been the case. It should be further noted that one of the reasons for this medieval diabolical proliferation is the attribution, from the time of Christian antiquity, of a demonic character to certain pagan divinities. It must be clearly recognized, Saintyves to the contrary, that the devil too, and not only the saints, succeeded the gods.

Inversely, what was the effect of Christianization on folk culture? Clerical culture was not content with vulgarizing its topics, baptizing legends, and informing traditional rites. It had especially dispossessed folk culture of its preeminent knowledge: knowledge of the other world, an ear for supernatural beings, and the interpretation of visions, the control of which the clergy meant to reserve for itself alone. The constitution of a "white magic" domesticated by the Church and the increasing repression of all folk demonology followed the same pattern.

Under these conditions, it is difficult to see how medieval folklore could have spoken through myths, for it is the function of myths to constitute and transmit such knowledge. Since this function was monopolized by the Church, the clergy could no longer speak of myths, for their efforts tended in the opposite direction, toward a rational explanation of the Word of God.

Folklore, then, was left with the other narrative genres, which, though far from negligible in importance and function, do not go to the heart of the matter as myth does. Specialists in the study of popular narrative genres strove to give them definitions, which were sometimes too rigid: folktale, whose function is to offer a "naive ethics" (A. Jolles); legend, which has a familial thematization and is anchored to a particular topography and history (H. Bausinger), etc. These narrative genres were allowed to develop freely, and it is they rather than myths that are revealed to us in the written documents of the Middle Ages.

At the same time, although we should not speak of "mythology" or of "myths" in this connection, we may perhaps find "mythic thought" in these folktales and legends. The originality of medieval folk culture resides not only in its contents but also in the way it has organized those contents. Current studies on the narrative traditions of medieval folklore all show that this folklore operated according to a logic that was different from the theological reasoning of the clergy, at least of the most scholarly fraction of the clergy. The structural transformations revealed by the variants of a single account also allow us to speak here, like the ethnologists, of "savage thought" and, like the historians of ancient Greece, of "mythic thought." It is in this sense, we believe, that medieval studies can and should take their place in the now open field of the analysis of myths and oral traditions.

The prudent position we are adopting is also dictated by the state of the documents with which we are constrained to work: it is on the local scale, as we have shown, that one must reconstitute the narrative system of a thirteenth-century village community, for example. But through the written texts of the scholarly culture we can grasp only dispersed shreds of oral traditions, rescued from oblivion by the zeal of an inquisitor or the curiosity of an "intellectual" of the Middle Ages. We are also unable to restore narrative systems, and without them it is difficult to speak of "mythology" and "myths"; Dontenville's attempt is too ambitious in its geographical scope to be convincing. However, sometimes the documentation seems more favorable: using the inquisition register of Jacques Fournier, bishop of Pamiers, Emmanuel Le Roy Ladurie recently brought back to life an entire village community of the upper Ariège in the early fourteenth century. This case is a peculiar one in many regards: at Montaillou, the Cathar heresy had, so to speak, restored to the laity the knowledge of the essential truths, and the "Cathar myth," unlike the interpretations of the Perfecti in the twelfth century, who were so well versed in theological debates, had been reinterpreted in the light of local folklore and inserted into the narrative traditions of the village. In this way, the respect that the Perfectus of the time inspires in the simple Believer is compounded by the attractiveness of his eternal word, for he knows all about Good and Evil, the Creation and the end of the world, and the fates of the souls of deceased family members who, in the ravines close to the villages, search for a body to enter. He knows all about the social order, too. In the beginning was incest: brothers and sisters married freely. Today, on the contrary, the village is a collection of neighboring *"domus,"* familial groups which are at once rivals and relatives since they practice the exchange of women between them. The marriage of dowried girls threatens the material equilibrium of each *"domus."* It creates a permanent danger and inspires nostalgia for a bygone day when girls were not expected to leave their homes, and gave themselves to their brothers. But that primordial incest set brother against brother, and had to be put to an end: by imposing exogamy and marriage, the Church instituted the present social order, which, for the sake of peace, sacrifices these peasants' ideal of self-sufficiency. One would like to find other versions of this account, so as to compare it with all of the parallel accounts that must have been circulating at that time. One may at least ask a question: on the inner fringes of Christianity, where folklore and heresy were intermingled and the ascendancy of the Church was less strong, is it not possible that the medieval West also knew myth?

J.-C.S./d.w.

BIBLIOGRAPHY

1. For a general introduction to the history of medieval Christianity: J. LE GOFF, *La civilisation de l'Occident médiéval* (Paris 1964). K. THOMAS, *Religion and the Decline of Magic: Studies in Popular Beliefs in Sixteenth and Seventeenth Century England* (London 1971); all of part 1 concerns the Middle Ages.

2. On the theoretical problems posed by the analysis of myths: CL. LÉVI-STRAUSS, *The Savage Mind* (Chicago 1966). J.-P. VERNANT, *Mythe et société en Grèce ancienne* (Paris 1974), especially 195–250, "Raisons du mythe"; *Les origines de la pensée grecque* (Paris 1969). P. VIDAL-NAQUET, "Esclavage et gynécocratie dans la tradition, le mythe, l'utopie," *Recherches sur les structures sociales dans l'Antiquité classique* (Paris 1970), 63–80.

3. On narrative genres: A. JOLLES, *Einfache Formen: Legende, Sage, Mythe, Rätsel, Spruch, Kasus, Memorabile, Märchen, Witz* (Tübingen 1930). H. BAUSINGER, *Formen der Volkspoesie* (Berlin 1968).

4. Ancient mythology in the scholarly culture of the Middle Ages: J. SEZNEC, *La survivance des dieux antiques: Essai sur le rôle de la tradition mythologique dans l'hymanisme et dans l'art de la Renaissance* (Paris 1939). A. RENAUDET, *Dante humaniste* (Paris 1952). F. SAXL and E. PANOFSKY, *Classical Mythology in Medieval Art* (New York 1933).

5. Mythology and folklore: N. BELMONT, *Mythes et croyances dans l'Ancienne France* (Paris 1973), which is justly critical of H. DONTENVILLE, *La mythologie française* (Paris 1948). The opposite is true in the case of the Tarasque: L. DUMONT, *La Tarasque: Essai de description d'un fait local d'un point de vue ethnographique* (Paris 1951).

6. Hagiography and "mythology": P. SAINTYVES, *Les saints successeurs des dieux: Essais de mythologie chrétienne,* 1 (Paris 1907); *En marge de la Légende Dorée. Songes, miracles et survivances. Essai sur la formation de quelques thèmes hagiographiques* (Paris 1931). Suggestive in a different way: B. DE GAIFFIER, "Mentalité de l'hagiographe médiéval d'après quelques travaux récents," *Analecta Bollandiana* 86 (1968): 391–99. See especially: F. GRAUS, *Volk, Herrscher und Heiliger im Reich der Merowinger* (Prague 1965). J. LE GOFF, "Culture cléricale et traditions folkloriques dans la civilisation mérovingienne," *Niveaux de culture et groupes sociaux* (Paris 1968), 21–32; "Culture ecclésiastique et culture folklorique au Moyen Age: Saint Marcel de Paris et le dragon," *Ricerche storiche ed economiche in memoria di Corrado Barbagallo* (Naples 1970), 2:53–90.

7. The world beyond and utopias: A. GRAF, *Miti, Leggende et superstizioni nel Medio Evo* (Turin 1892); *Il diavolo* (Milan 1889). S. BARING-GOULD, *Curious Myths of the Middle Ages* (New Hyde Park and New York 1866–88). A. MAURY, *Croyances et légendes du Moyen Age* (Paris 1896). C. G. LOOMIS, *White Magic: An Introduction to the Folklore of Christian Legends* (Cambridge, MA, 1948). F. GRAUS, "Social Utopias in the Middle Ages," *Past and Present* 38 (1967). J. LE GOFF, *The Birth of Purgatory,* trans. Arthur Goldhammer (Chicago 1984). Finally, on the millenarian movements of the low Middle Ages: N. COHN, *The Pursuit of the Millennium* (London 1957). And especially: B. TÖPFER, *Das kommende Reich des Friedens: Zur Entwicklung chiliastischer Zukunftshoffnungen im Hoch mittelalter* (Berlin 1964).

8. On the "Cathar myth": A. BORST, *Die Katharer* (Stuttgart 1963), also in French. *Cathares en Languedoc,* Les Cahiers de Fanjeaux 3 (Toulouse 1968). E. LE ROY LADURIE, *Montaillou, village occitan de 1294 à 1324* (Paris 1975).

9. Folklore and oral traditions in historical studies today: besides the above cited studies by J. Le Goff, see: J. LE GOFF and E. LE ROY LADURIE, "Mélusine maternelle et défricheuse," *Annales E.S.C.*, 1971, 587–622. J. LE GOFF and P. VIDAL-NAQUET, "Lévi-Strauss en Brocéliande," *Critique* 326 (June 1974): 541–71. J. C. SCHMITT, "Religion populaire et culture folklorique. A propos d'une réédition: La piété populaire au Moyen Age d'Etienne Delaruelle," *Annales E.S.C.*, 1976, 5. On the particular relations between folklore and learned literature in the vernacular: E. KÖHLER, *L'aventure chevaleresque: Idéal et réalité dans le roman courtois,* French trans. (Paris 1974). Outside the period and in a different context see also: C. GINZBURG, *Il formaggio e i vermi* (Turin 1976). M. BAKHTIN, *Rabelais and His World* (Cambridge, MA, 1968), trans. from Russian.

The Survival of the Ancient Gods in the Middle Ages and the Renaissance

I. The Middle Ages

Before inquiring how mythology was interpreted in the Middle Ages, we should remember that it had survived on different levels, mainly in folklore. It was among the *pagani,* in rural areas, that polytheism had most tenaciously persisted. With the advent of Christianity, the cult of sylvans and nymphs was not annihilated along with the temples knocked down by the first apostles in Gaul. "Immutable at the depths of rivers, in the eternal twilight of forests, the spirit of the old days lived on." Regarding this tenacity we have the testimony of the capitularies and the councils who up to the Carolingian period denounced superstitious practices and condemned as sacrilegious those who continued to light flares and fires near trees, rocks, and fountains. Their anathemas remained powerless. Gregory the Great had already recognized the impossibility of extirpating the layers of beliefs rooted "in such stubborn minds"; the only way to fight superstition was to assign the pagan vestiges to the new cult, to put pious images on trees, to carve crosses on menhirs, to place fountains under the invocation of the Virgin—in a word, to cover the ancient venerations with a cloak of orthodoxy. Indeed, strange assimilations had made the saints the successors of the gods. Saint Christopher, for example, had become the heir of Mercury, Hercules, and even Anubis. Having lent him their attributes and practices, they continued to be honored under the saint's name. These amalgams and avatars were further means of survival. But demons, too, took over guard duty from the gods, so to speak. "It was foolishly said: the great Pan is dead; then, seeing that he lived, he was made into a god of evil." The pagan origins of the sabbath were denounced by the Council of Aix-la-Chapelle, which found Diana, *panagorum dea* ("goddess of the pagans"), among the wicked women straddling animals, along with Satan. Michelet describes sorcery, a pact with the powers of instinct, as a rebellion, a revenge of nature oppressed by Christian asceticism.

But it was the Christians who, paradoxically, preserved mythology and even taught it. For it remained well above rustic superstitions; it was an integral part of classical culture, a culture adopted by the Church in the first centuries. The Church Fathers, who were imbued with it, were aware of the difficulty and the danger of preserving in education a literature and an art indissolubly linked to polytheism; but they accepted the necessity of permitting their youth to be instructed in schools of the Greco-Roman type. Tertullian himself recognized this necessity. In the fourth century, Christian children and adolescents were raised as pagans; despite the immorality of fable, they entered with Virgil into a familiarity with the gods, for the essence of the grammarian's schooling remained the explication of the poets; it was, moreover, from the list of the gods' names that one learned to read. The last generation to receive this instruction was the one raised by Ausonius. With the invasions that destroyed the ancient school, an eclipse began which lasted until the eighth century. In the middle of the sixth century, scholastic life was perpetuated in Rome and in Africa, and then came the collapse of culture and the decadence of letters. However, the ancient sources had not dried up; beyond the barbarian rupture, seeds of renewal survived. The Carolingian "renaissance," to which the name of Alcuin is linked, flourished in the twelfth century, when Chartres and Orleans became the great seats of classical studies. But each renewal was accompanied by a rise in neopaganism—witness the popularity of Ovid in the twelfth century (the preeminent *aetas Ovidiana*). The correspondence of monks is full of mythological allusions, and the goliards, who resuscitated paganism even in their mores, dedicated poems to Narcissus, to Philomela, and to Pyramus and Thisbe. At the end of the century, Alexander of Villedieu complained that old gods were being worshiped in Orleans, that Venus,

Deianira being abducted by Nessus. Fragment from a small column in Chartres Cathedral. Photo Giraudon.

Bacchus, and Faunus had their altars and their festivals there: the path to Paradise was lost.

Medieval art shows signs of these "renaissances." Here, too, antiquity once again became inspirational. When the first churches rose from the ruins of pagan sanctuaries, and oratories replaced shrines to the Lares, the vestiges were incorporated into new constructions and were put to use for the new religion. Sarcophagi were transformed into altars, their fragments into stoups or baptismal fonts; diptyches and ivory cases served as reliquaries; images of the Olympians were encrusted in the ambo of Aix-la-Chapelle. The sculptors who copied these pagan relics looked to them first for decorative forms and formulas, for lessons in technique and style—but also for profane themes, which they would combine with sacred representations. In decorating Christian tombs, the sculptors of Arles had already introduced mythological motifs on the covers of their sarcophagi: Castor and Pollux, Eros and Psyche, and so forth. In Roman art, ancient allegories of the Earth and the Ocean, and of the Moon and the Sun on their chariots, accompanied the crucifixion and the apparition of Christ in his glory. Sirens and centaurs reappeared on tympana, lintels, and capitals. Chiron's education of Achilles is depicted at Vezelay. The same scene was formerly depicted at Chartres, together with the abduction of Hippodamia. And on a column of the western portal one even sees Deianira carried away by Nessus. The end of the twelfth century offers one of the most unexpected examples of a pagan monument in the interior of a cloister—the famous fountain that was constructed to serve as a washbowl for the monks of Saint-Denis. Its mutilated basin stands today in the courtyard of the École des Beaux-Arts in Paris; the rim is decorated with medallions, perhaps copied from cameos, on which about thirty heads are sculpted in relief. Among the heroes and allegories one can distinguish Jupiter, Neptune, Thetis, Ceres, Bacchus, and pastoral divinities. Gothic art, which abandoned ancient forms, seemed to retain from antiquity only its prophetic prefigurations: antiquity is scarcely represented in cathedrals except by the Sibyl. However, at the base of the portal of Auxerre there is a sleeping Eros.

In the last analysis, the survival of the gods through the Middle Ages, up to the dawn of the *Rinascimento,* can be explained by an important and general reason: they were protected by the interpretations that antiquity itself proposed for their origin and nature. These various interpretations, corresponding to various representations, can essentially be reduced to three.

The first is Euhemerism, popularized by Ennius: the gods were only humans, raised from the earth to heaven by the idolatry of their contemporaries. Christian apologists and the Church Fathers willingly adopted this interpretation and used it as a weapon against paganism—a two-edged sword, for though it relegated the gods to the level of mortals, it confirmed their existence and allowed them a place in history. Paulus Orosius, Isidore of Seville, and their successors would later attempt to assign them a place in time. Going back to the primitive ages in Egypt, Assyria, Greece, and Rome, Isidore discovered mythological dynasties; every single chronicler after ranked the gods among ancient kings and heroes, and at the same time sought to connect them with the great figures of the sacred History in lineages parallel to those of the patriarchs, judges, and prophets. As a result of these synchronisms, the prestige of the gods was restored. Moreover, to make a place for characters of fable in the annals of humanity was to recognize that they had been its benefactors. They had earlier obtained the honors of apotheosis because they had destroyed monsters, built cities, invented arts. Prometheus, Atlas, Hercules, Theseus, Isis who taught writing, and Minerva who taught women weaving were the venerable precursors of civilization.

In the twelfth century, the *Historia Scholastica* of Petrus Comestor codified the parallelism between profane history and the history of the people of God. In its translation by Guyart des Moulins it became a sort of scholastic manual of mythology, providing Vincent de Beauvais with the essence of what he wrote about the gods in his *Speculum Historiale.* Iconography illustrates this diffusion, and this direction, of Euhemerism. In Florence, Giotto's bell tower, on which the prophets are represented, depicts on the first section of the bas-reliefs, near Daedalus the first aeronaut, Orpheus the father of Poetry, and Hercules the conqueror of Cacus.

On the other hand, pride of race prompted scholars of the Middle Ages to seek ancestors and forebears for their people in the fabulous past. Thus the Franks claimed to be descended from the Trojan Francus, as earlier the Romans had claimed to have been from the Trojan Aeneas; the Italians had Janus and then Saturn and his sons for their first kings. The prodigious success of the *Romance of the Rose* is explained in part by its ethnogenic character. Mythological characters became the patrons of such and such a people, the stock from which it was born. They were also founders of dynasties; princes discovered ancestors for themselves among them, and boasted of having at least a demigod as the originator of their house. Thus Brutus, the Trojan hero, became the ancestor of the kings of England; and that is why the abduction of Helen is portrayed in a thirteenth-century genealogical scroll illustrating that royal lineage. The chronicles and world histories thus became vehicles of a mythographic tradition that would flourish in the Renaissance.

The physical interpretation, according to which the gods were heavenly bodies, perpetuated another tradition. Anyone discerning a governing intelligence behind the movement of the spheres is inclined to place divinity in the sky; but astronomical nomenclature, which attached each planet, each constellation, each sign of the zodiac to a character from fable, had encouraged the Greeks and the Romans to identify celestial bodies with gods. This "mythologization" of the sky was the result of a long evolution, complicated by the intrusion of exotic "signs" from Egypt or Chaldea: the *sphaera graecanica* was rivaled, or fed upon, by a *sphaera barbarica,* whose elements became mixed up with classical elements.

The definitive fusion of astronomy and mythography shows the influence of the Stoics, who were satisfied with a rationalist interpretation that seemed to legitimize and purify the gods by reducing them to cosmic symbols; but the major influence was that of Oriental cults (particularly the cult of the Sun, in Persia, and the Babylonian cult of the planets), which were prevalent in the Greco-Roman world. Not only was the belief in sidereal gods confirmed; it took on an extraordinary religious intensity. Indeed, the stars were alive; they had a face, a gender, a personality, and their power was awesome, for they were the arbiters of destiny: they determined the fate of men and of empires. Thus, toward the end of the pagan era, the gods who were dethroned on earth became all-powerful once again, thanks to astrology, in the sky. But here, too, Christians preserved what they wished to abolish. Astrology, which they ought to have abhorred, maintained its partisans and supporters among them; even its adversaries made important concessions to it. Neither Lactantius nor Saint Augustine questioned the influence of the stars; but they maintained that the will of man and the grace of God could conquer this

Monks' wash basin in the Abbey of Saint-Denis. Thirteenth century. École des Beaux Arts. Photo Giraudon.

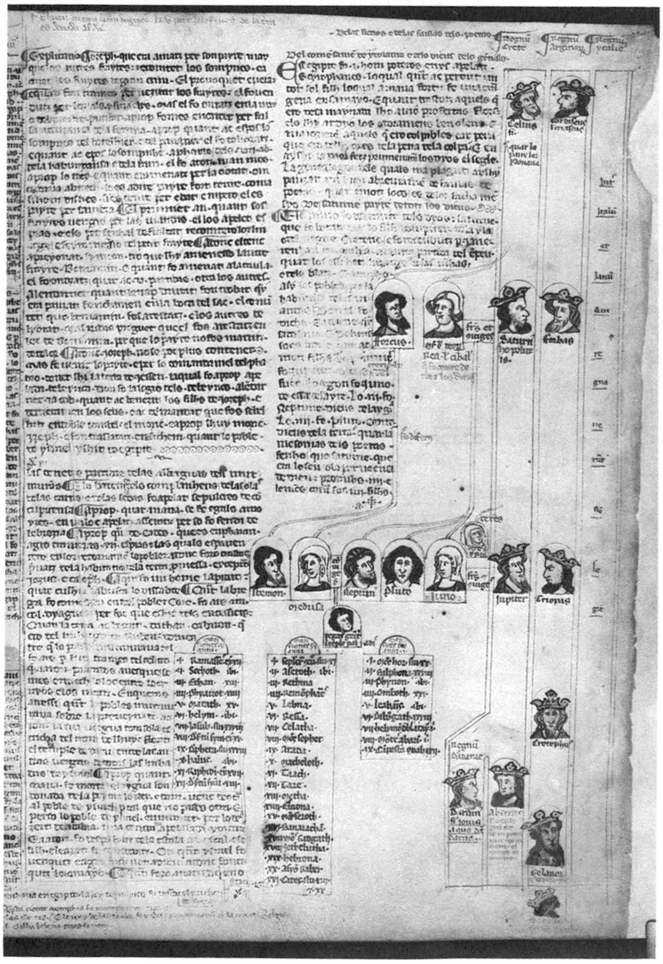

Caelus and his descendants (Ms. Egerton, 1500, fol. 6). London, British Library. Library photo.

influence. Others saw the coercion of the stars as merely an expression of the doctrine of predestination, or at least as the intermediary through which God manifested his immutable decrees. Indeed, even when they condemned astrology, the apologists and the Church Fathers kept its deep root intact; the fear of demons and their evildoing haunted the popular imagination, but the astrological conception of causality dominated the greatest minds.

After the twelfth century, the influx of Arabic science into the West gave astrology a renewed virulence. The *Ghāya*, a manual of practical magic composed of Oriental and Hellenistic materials, was translated into Spanish at the court of Alfonso X; about twenty Latin manuscripts of it are known under the title of *Picatrix*—"the Reverend Father Picatrix, rector of the Diabological Faculty," as Rabelais would call him. This manual taught how to conjure up celestial powers and render them favorable; it taught formulas of prayer and invocation and prescribed instruments for the purpose: images of Jupiter, Venus, Mars, and Saturn, engraved on rocks, gained the influence of the corresponding divinities. As we have seen, gemstones bearing effigies of the gods had never ceased to be used; now they served as amulets and talismans; this time it was in the lapidaries that the gods found refuge.

The third system of interpretation consisted of discovering a spiritual meaning in the figure of the gods, and a moral lesson in their adventures. This sort of allegory had been applied by the first critics of Homer, such as Heraclitus, and, at the end of the pagan era, by Stoics such as Cornutus, to justify the apparent impiety of the myths by distinguishing

Juno-Memory (Vat. ms. Palat. lat. 1066, fol. 223v). Vatican, Biblioteca apostolica vaticana. Library photo.

their literal meaning from their deep or secret meaning. Since that time, the old legends had gradually been elevated: in the *Aeneid* the Olympians regained their dignity; with his genius for deifying moral ideas, Virgil moralized the gods. But in the hands of the Neoplatonists, allegory became a means of sanctifying them. They studied fable in depth as if it were a sacred text. In his treatise, *On the Gods and the World,* "a veritable pagan catechism," Sallust, a friend of the emperor Julian, chose the most shocking myths in order to reveal a philosophic content in them—accessible, it is true, to initiates alone. Julian himself applied the method in his hymns to Helios and to the Great Mother, with the intention of contrasting the mythology thus regenerated to the Christian cult.

The Church, for that reason alone, should have been hostile to allegory. But the apologists and the Church Fathers themselves applied the method to holy books; and they employed it in education. Having conserved profane poetry in their own education, they were inevitably led to moralize mythology in their turn. In the sixth century, the *Moralia* of Gregory the Great, biblical allegories, had their counterpart in the *Mythologiae* of Fulgentius, profane allegories. In the Middle Ages, the fable as a whole became a *philosophia moralis.* Thus the three goddesses between whom Paris had to choose were, according to Fulgentius, symbols of the active life, the contemplative life, and the amorous life. In the Carolingian period a poem by Theodulf, bishop of Orleans, explained how wise men could turn the lies of poets, beginning with Ovid, into truths.

Beginning in the twelfth century, this type of exegesis reached stunning proportions. It was then that Bernard de Chartres and John of Salisbury meditated on pagan religion, "not out of respect for false divinities, but because they disguised sacred teachings, incomprehensible to the common man." It was above all the time when the rehabilitation of Ovid—who was proclaimed *Ethicus* and even *Theologus*—was affirmed. Arnolphe d'Orleans and John Garland rigorously demonstrated the edifying nature of the *Metamorphoses.* In the first years of the fourteenth century the immense *Moralized Ovid* appeared, whose author distinctly declared that if one knew how to read the poems, "everything is for our edification." The eyes of Argus on the tail of Juno's peacock are the vanities of the century; Phaethon is Lucifer; Ceres searching for Proserpina is the Church beckoning the souls of sinners. To the same century belonged (among other commentaries) Robert Holkot's *Morulia super Ovidii metamorphoses* and Thomas Waleys's *Metamorphosis Ovidiana moraliter explanata.* Rabelais would mock the allegorizers who claimed to discover "the Sacraments of the Gospel" in Ovid; Luther, who denounced allegory as a seductive courtesan, would thunder against those who "turned Apollo into Christ, and Daphne into the Virgin Mary." But they would not halt the popularity of these aberrations.

Allegories and conventional moralizations are again found in the works of Dante, where mythology holds a place that is at first sight surprising. With Dante, too, fable, a repertory of passions, is full of edifying meanings. In the *Purgatorio,* the stories of Aglaurus, Progne, Midas, Meleager, and Pasiphaë become so many examples of human deviation. But Dante's attitude toward pagan divinities is profoundly original. He treats them seriously, even with reverence. Not only does he accept the reality of these supernatural beings, but he suggests that between the Fall and the Redemption they played a premonitory role, so that they sometimes elucidated the lessons of the Old Testament. In the "Bible of the Gentiles," the great gods, the *superi,* veiled intelligences, were instructed to make the world aware, in a disguised form, of the authority of the true God. Through the sanctions that Jupiter or Apollo inflicted on sinful mortals they gave human creatures a presentiment of the absolute submission owed to the Creator. Hence the importance, in the *Commedia,* of the "titanic" theme of insubordination, revolt, and the punishments for these transgressions. Dante confirms the judgment by condemning to hell the rebels struck down by the gods. As for the demons that torment them, the most notorious—Charon, Pluto, Minos—are taken from among the *inferni.* Whereas the *superi,* the heavenly spirits, acted for a yet hidden God, these fallen spirits were invested with infernal functions; they passed into the service of Satan.

In the following century, the most extravagant and systematic monument of Christian allegory applied to mythology is a revised version of a treatise by Fulgentius—the *Fulgentius Metaforalis* by the Franciscan John Ridewall. The order of the chapters is governed by the identification of the gods with virtues, an identification stretched by analysis to the most minute subtleties. Thus Saturn is Prudence; the elements that compose this virtue are Memory, Intelligence, and Foresight. Ridewall examines these children of Saturn one by one: Juno ("Memoria"), Neptune ("Intelligentia"), and Pluto ("Providentia"). The respective attributes of these gods are explained precisely by the ideas they represent. Juno's veil is meant to hide the shame of sin, fostered by Memory; the rainbow that crowns her is the sign of her reconciliation with

God, obtained through remembrance and repentance; the scepter she holds indicates that the pardoned soul has regained control of itself, another benefit of Memory.

It was through these three systems of interpretation that the gods ultimately survived. The three systems, however, were not mutually exclusive. At the risk of proposing contradictory explanations, scholars of the Middle Ages frequently applied all three of them to the same character or to the same fable. Pierre d'Ailly, who affirmed the concord between astronomy and history, maintained that the gods were both stars and rulers. On the other hand, there were points of contact as well as of interference between the three cycles. When mythological heroes were taken as examples, morality came to the aid of history. Each planet had its temperament; it determined not only the destiny but the character and the abilities of those born under its influence, who, through this transmission from the physical to the moral, truly became its "children." The ambition of medieval culture, its concern with embracing the totality of knowledge, confined within the *Summaries* the *naturale,* the *morale,* and the *historiale.* In this reduction to unity, numerals played a primordial role: by reason of their number, the planets, the signs of the zodiac, and the elements were placed in concord with the virtues, the months, and the humors, in order to

Venus, Juno, Pallas (ms. fr. 143, fol. 198v). Paris, Bibliothèque nationale. Photo BN.

establish the interdependence of all parts of the cosmos and all forms of knowledge. Scholasticism further develops these tables of concord. In his *De natura rerum,* Alexander Neckham codified the relationship, established in the ninth century, between the planets and the virtues. In the *Convivio,* Dante compares these same planets "by reason of their properties" to the liberal arts: the Sphere of the Moon corresponds to Grammar; that of Mercury, to Dialectic; that of Venus, to Rhetoric; that of Jupiter, to Geometry, etc. As for the sphere of fixed stars, it showed "manifest" resemblances to Physics, Metaphysics, Morals, and Theology.

Diagrams graphically express these relationships, by circles containing smaller circles that form a tracery of symmetrical compartments. At the center of these microcosms is written the name of Man, himself an abridgment of the Universe. But the gods have their role in these correspondences, which is why they are first found in the miniatures in encyclopedias, before reappearing in Italian monumental art. In Florence they are seated on Giotto's bell tower with the Sibyls and the prophets, in the same row as the virtues, the sciences, and the sacraments; they dominate the entire cycle of figures that recount the creation of man and the invention of the arts. At the Trinci palace in Foligno, frescoes painted around 1420 also developed the great encyclopedic theme; the gods are once again in evidence, and once again historic and cosmic traditions intersect; mythical characters and stellar powers make an essential contribution to this decorative whole.

The Renaissance gathered together and developed these various interpretations; when the gods reappeared in full daylight, it was first in one of these frameworks. In this matter the Renaissance is greatly indebted to the Middle Ages. The reason the continuity long remained unsuspected is that the classical form of the gods was lost in the meantime; they had become unrecognizable. The history of their metamorphoses can nevertheless be followed from the Carolingian period up until the fifteenth century, mainly because of the extremely rich documentation furnished by miniatures in astrologic-mythological manuscripts. These illustrations can be divided into two groups, according to whether they had a visual model as a prototype or were derived from a simple descriptive text.

The "visual" tradition may be further broken down into several families. The first had a purely Western origin and character and flourished until the thirteenth century or thereabouts. Essentially it included the *Aratea,* that is, the manuscripts of that poem (translated by Cicero), the *Phaenomena,* in which Aratus describes the constellations as a mythographer rather than as an astronomer. The Carolingian copies of the *Aratea* restored the ancient model with striking fidelity. But new and strange versions appeared at the end of the Middle Ages, which came from the Orient. They are found in two contexts—first, in Arabic astrological manuscripts, where Hellenistic figures had been profoundly altered by the transcribers who were ignorant of mythology. Hercules, for example, is dressed as a Turk, with a scimitar and a turban; Medusa, decapitated by Perseus, becomes a bearded demon. Second, they are encountered in illustrations in Michael Scot's treatise, composed in Sicily around 1250. This treatise, of which we have more than thirty manuscripts, shows the strangest constellations, borrowed from the "barbaric sphere." The drawings of the planets are even more bizarre: Jupiter is represented as a scholar, Saturn as a warrior, and Mercury as a bishop. This last series of figures goes back, by way of the *Ghāya,* to a Babylonian tradition. It, too, played a role in fourteenth-century Italian monumental art: in the Spanish Chapel in Florence, in the Eremitani of Padua, on the capitals of the Doges' Palace—it is in this extraordinary iconography that the Olympians were disguised.

Apart from astronomical manuscripts, examples of the "visual" tradition are rarely found outside of Byzantine art, though miniatures of profane manuscripts and ivory caskets with mythological motifs still remain very close to Hellenistic models. There is, however, a surprising Western illustration of Raban Maur's *De rerum naturis* in the copy by Montecassino. However crude the divinities represented may be, an ancient model can still be detected behind each one of them.

The types derived from a descriptive text, a "literary" source, constitute a distinct group. Here the Byzantines were privileged; they had the "Library" of Apollodorus, and perhaps even an illustrated manuscript of the work that served as a mythographical manual from the ninth to the fourteenth century. In the West, this family of gods is found in allegoric treatises. These treatises contained two parts, the first descriptive and the second moral. The descriptive elements were generally taken from early mythographers and scholiasts such as Macrobius, Servius, Lactantius Placidus, Martianus Capella, and Fulgentius: it was their erudition that served as a basis for the medieval compilers. After 1100, illustrations appeared in the margins of treatises of this kind. A manuscript of Remi d'Auxerre's *Commentaries* on Martianus Capella shows a series of gods: Cybele, Apollo, Saturn, Mercury, and others; but they are difficult to identify, for the miniaturist had only one text to guide him, and this text, slavishly followed, engendered only barbaric images. This also applies to Ridewall's *Fulgentius metaforalis,* whose illustrations are grossly anachronistic caricatures.

The *Liber imaginum deorum* of Albricus deserves special attention, for it was to have a lasting influence on iconography. Albricus, who has been identified with the *Mythographus Tertius,* may have been Alexander Neckham, who died in 1217. His work, called the *Poetarius* or the *Scintillarium poetarum,* enjoyed great popularity as an aid to reading the profane poets; but it is encumbered by a heavy allegorical critical apparatus, and there is no illustrated manuscript of it available. Two centuries later an abridgment, the *Libellus de imaginibus deorum,* would become a useful aid to artists. Between the *Liber* and the *Libellus* came an eminent intermediary, Petrarch himself, who in describing the images of the gods decorating the palace of Syphax, in his *Africa,* followed Albricus step by step, though retaining only his pictorial elements. In this pared-down form, the *Libellus* was taken up again in 1340 by a friend of Petrarch's, Pierre Bersuire, who put it in the Fifteenth Book of his *Redictorium morale.* This Fifteenth Book, in which Bersuire "moralizes" Ovid, includes a series of "portraits" of the gods, borrowed, says the author, from Petrarch, "for I was unable to find images of the gods themselves anywhere else." It was Bersuire's "portraits," collected and rid once again of their commentaries, that finally, around 1400, constituted the *Libellus.* This time the result was pure iconography, and the same formula kept recurring: *pingebatur* ("it is painted"). The Codex Reginensis 1290 of the Vatican, which contained the text of the *Liber,* also contained that of the *Libellus,* illustrated with ink drawings executed around 1420. The images were lively and charming, but they showed only a distant kinship with the ancient forms, for they were only "reconstructions" of the gods following a text, or rather a mosaic of texts; indeed, as we have seen, all the descriptions come from disparate sources.

Nonetheless, these composite figures in the *Libellus,* which "codify" the gods' traits and fix them in an immutable attitude, were to establish a lineage in art. The *Libellus* was to become a repertory, as is attested not only by a rich series of Italian, Flemish, and French miniatures but by representations of all sorts: tapistries, enamels, and sculptures. On a capital at Autun on which Luxuria is depicted, Vulcan, Venus, and Eros appear as they are described in the *Liber.* The illustrated book, as we shall see, helped propagate the *Libellus,* which, while it continued to serve as a source for mythographers and as a reference for humanists, was to furnish artists with guiding examples during the entire Quattrocento, and even after.

In sum, by the end of the Middle Ages the "visual" and "literary" traditions had profoundly altered the classical forms of the gods. Unfaithful copies, substitutions, disguises, or naive reconstructions—it is hard to tell from which procedure they suffered most, not to mention the mistakes, blunders, and misconceptions that further aggravated this corruption and that can be explained by their peregrinations from east to west, and from north to south.

The gods were gradually to regain their shape. By examining certain series it is possible to follow the stages of this restoration. Some factors delayed it, however, of which the most important were the influence of the printing press and the illustrated book. The printing press first published only the mythographers that the Middle Ages had drawn from (aside from the *De natura deorum*), and medieval compilations

Microcosm (ms. lat. 13002, fol. 7v). Munich, Bayerische Staatsbibliothek. Library photo.

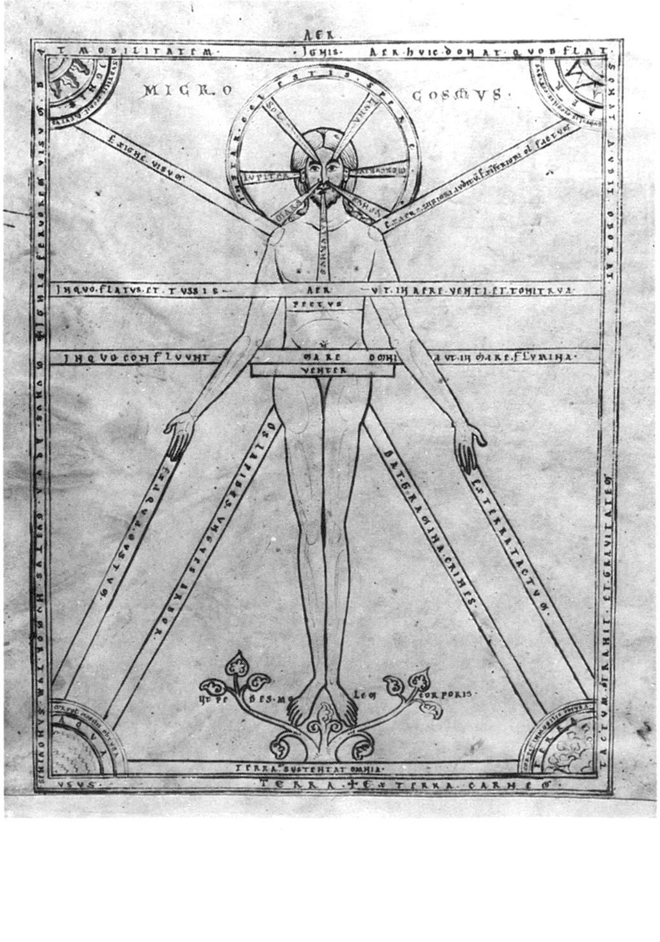

themselves, beginning with the *Liber* of Albricus. Boccaccio's *Genealogia deorum,* heir to this tradition, would be the great repertory during the first half of the Cinquecento. It underwent eight printings between 1473 and 1532, whereas Apollodorus's *Library* (used, as we have seen, by the Byzantines) was not published—in Greek and Latin—until 1555. Above all, the illustrated book served to disseminate an iconographic tradition that was still completely medieval. The great mythological incunabula were Boccaccio's *De Casis* (Ulm 1473) and his *De la ruyne des nobles hommes et femmes* (Bruges 1476). During the same period there appeared, in Anvers and Paris, the *Recueil des Histoires de Troie,* the *Faits et Prouesses de Jason,* and the *Destruction de Troie la Grant,* which had nine printings from 1484 to 1526. The tradition that was perpetuated through these books was that of the *Libellus*—a Norse tradition, not a classical one—and the woodcuts could just as well have illustrated romances of chivalry. It was these woodcuts, however, that first assured the graphic diffusion of the favorite themes of the Renaissance: the abductions of Europa and Proserpina, and so forth. Toward the end of the fifteenth century these models, still Gothic in appearance, could be found everywhere, whereas the archaeological discovery of antiquity had begun long before. The unique role of the Renaissance would be to restore to ancient subjects their ancient forms.

II. The Renaissance

Collectors, among whom the prototype was Cyriacus of Ancona, brought together copies of medals, inscriptions, and fragments of sculpture and architecture. And two camps were formed in elegant society and among patrons: admirers of courtly romances, and antiquarians. The *Hypnerotomachia Poliphili,* published by Aldo Mannucci in 1499, is a compromise combining a love story—a story which also conceals an initiation into the most serious mysteries—with a repertory of classical archaeology. This strange book, magnificently illustrated, was to have a deep and lasting influence not only on the appearance and the decoration of books to come, but also on architecture and painting. It can be compared to Petrarch's *Triumphs,* another great book, which underwent several printings before 1500 and whose illustrations were inspired by classical sculpture, such as Mantegna's "Triumph of Caesar."

Another category of illustrated books, the *Emblemata,* engendered a long tradition. Their principal sources were old medals—especially the reverse sides (from whose figures Pisanello drew his inspiration)—as well as hieroglyphics engraved on obelisks. Scholars had believed that they could decipher them ever since Cristoforo de Buondelmonti had returned from Andros, in 1419, with the manuscript of the *Hieroglyphica* by Horus Apollo. Their influence exploded in the *Hypnerotomachia.* Aldo printed them in 1505, and Piero Valeriano provided them with a monumental commentary in 1556. The humanists, who believed them to be the key to a sacred language, fabricated cryptograms in turn. The first collection of *Emblemata* was the one by Alciat, in 1531, which underwent more than fifty printings in all languages. And mythology had an important place in works of this genre; the countenances and attributes of the gods in them were interpreted as signs concealing truths or moral maxims. In turn, these alleged hieroglyphics (which drew from several sources in addition to Horus) introduced a curious deviation into figurative mythology, a deviation with major consequences. For the time would come, toward the end of the sixteenth century, when it would once again be necessary to reconcile the pagan fable with Christian teachings, and the *Emblemata* were to become the ideal instrument for this compromise.

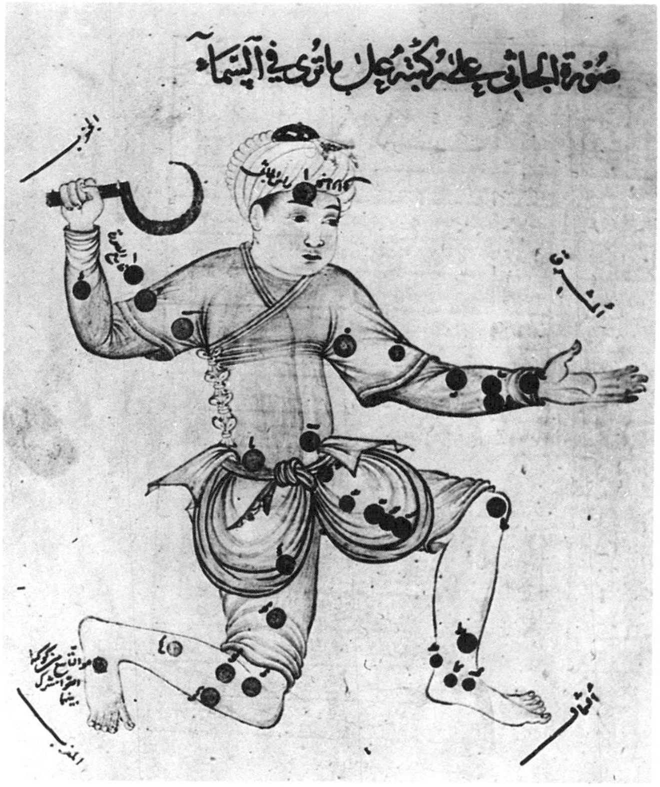

Hercules (ms. arab. 5036). Paris, Bibliothèque nationale. Photo BN.

Around 1500 in Italy the gods seemed omnipresent: they were on the ceilings of palaces, sometimes on the cupolas of churches, on marriage chests, almanacs, and suits of armor; they participated in the ceremonial entrances of rulers and in carnival processions; they presided over fountains in public squares and haunted garden grottos. But their role was not always purely decorative. They often reappeared, as we have said, in particular frameworks, systems of ideas elaborated in the Middle Ages, whose encyclopedic spirit still breathed in works such as the Malatesta temple and the Stanza della Segnatura. Raphael's "Parnassus" can be fully understood only as an element of a design in which all parts are connected even in their details: Poetry combines with Philosophy, Theology, and Justice to compose the four human understandings; on the ceiling the four elements are represented by episodes arranged in pairs: in each, a mythological scene is combined with a historic scene, and these diverse cycles are intertwined. The elements are attached to the sciences by way of the virtues, according to a diagram which at the same time makes apparent the relationship between the sciences: Theology and Philosophy have the same relationship as fire and water; Jurisprudence and Poetry have the same relationship as the earth and the sky.

But fable also played a part in real life: certain programs allied politics with morality. Aside from their edifying intentions—the triumph of Reason over the passions, of mind over matter—they contained (and always under a

Venus and the Graces. "The Tarots of Mantegna."

mythological cloak) allusions to contemporary events. In the decoration of the Palazzo del Te, Jupiter whipping the Giants illustrated the punishment of those who rebel against divine authority; at the same time it was a tribute to the efforts of Charles V for having reestablished imperial power in Italy. Likewise, in the Doges' Palace, Mercury and the Graces, Bacchus and the Ariadne of Tintoretto sing the praises of the Most Serene Republic, of its prosperity, and of the wisdom of its government. In the ballets given at the French court for Catherine de Medicis, Circe represented the horror of civil wars, and Minerva the return of order and peace. The Renaissance assigned a pagan demeanor even to Christian themes. On a candelabra in the basilica of Saint Anthony of Padua, Riccio portrays the pascal sacrifice of the lamb in front of an altar on which an Olympian Christ is standing; conversely, the *Sacrifice to Priapus* by Jacopo de' Barbari utilizes the elements of a Presentation to the Temple. These overlappings are not blasphemous; rather they express a sense of harmony and continuity. While Bellini's Redeemer pours his blood into a chalice, behind him, on a bas-relief, a drinking scene is taking place. The famous example of the Maenad transformed into a holy woman at the foot of the Cross reminds us that the Renaissance employed ancient models not only in a different context but also with a meaning totally different from the original.

Nor should the omnipresence of the gods be regarded as the boasting expression of liberated instinct and joy of life. With their beauty, certainly, they recovered their power of heroic or sensuous contagion. But at the same time they regained a singular dignity. This restitution of form is also a reconsecration, for fable is theology as much as it is poetry. It is no longer bound by a lying religion; for the pagans it was true. Such is Boccaccio's argument; and it followed that the poetry of the ancients, like their philosophy, maintained its legitimacy even in a Christian century. Hence the attitude of the humanists toward pagan beliefs. The fervor of their mythological erudition, like the archaeological and philological fever that consumed them, was a form of piety, *docta pietas.* They pursued the dream of a syncretism or a universal theism, with Platonism for a gospel; and they elaborated a religion of initiates.

Nothing is more expressive of this ambition than the great mythological creations of the Renaissance, many of which are enigmatic—such as Botticelli's "Primavera" and "The Birth of Venus," Piero di Cosimo's "Mars and Venus," Michelangelo's "Leda" and "Bacchus," and Titian's "Sacred and Profane Love." To clarify these works completely it is not enough to indicate their immediate sources; one must find a spirit, a climate—that of the humanists among whom they were born. The iconological studies by Panofsky and Chastel, and Wind's *Pagan Mysteries of the Renaissance,* have proved the worth of this method. The Neoplatonists of the Quattrocento, Pico della Mirandola, and Marsilio Ficino, who saw Plato through the eyes of the final representatives of paganism—Iamblichus, Proclus, Porphyry, and Plotinus—borrowed their notions about the mysteries and the rites of initiation; and they elaborated a theory of cryptic expression, which was applied to the visual arts. The artists whom they counseled, or who came under their influence, deliberately clouded the profound meaning of their works: the works only become fully intelligible when one is aware of the intentions and secret "doctrines" that they contained in abundance.

The principal key is to be found in the "Orphic theology," to which Plato, according to Proclus, was the heir. It was a Trinitarian system, a philosophy of transmutation. The development of the unity into a triad; the coincidence of opposites in the unity; *discordia concors*—these maxims were the clue to the mythological compositions that were the most hermetic in appearance; they formed their hidden structure. For mythology, too, has its triads of the Parcae and the Charites, illustrating procession, conversion and return; and Paris sees perfection divide into three goddesses. Every god was ambiguous, encompassing two extremes: the eloquent Mercury was the god of silence; Apollo inspired both madness and moderation; Minerva was peaceful and warlike; and Pan was hidden in Proteus. Their duplicity engendered infinite combinations, for they were alternately divided and united by a dialectical movement. As for Marsyas and Psyche, their stories, illustrated by Raphael, hide essentially the same lesson: purification through trial. The terrestrial Marsyas is tormented so that the celestial Apollo may be crowned; the misfortunes of Psyche are merely stages of a mystical initiation and redemption.

Raphael. *Apollo and Marsyas.* Rome, Vatican. Photo Anderson-Giraudon.

Other nuances remain inexplicable as long as one fails to appreciate the role of paradox and irony in the intentions of the artist and his advisers. The Neoplatonists learned from Plato himself how to speak of sacred subjects playfully; Apuleius and Lucian taught them the art of *serio ludere.* The facetious note is evident in Bellini's "The Feast of the Gods"; and Mantegna himself, serious as he was, created his "Parnassus" in a spirit less heroic than mocking. The unique accent of the great mythologies of the Renaissance, their singular splendor, may reside in what radiates through the veils, the soothsaying, and the smiles.

J.Se./t.l.f.

BIBLIOGRAPHY

For the essential bibliography on the subject, see J. SEZNEC, *The Survival of the Pagan Gods* (New York 1953). The present list, which follows the order of the questions treated in the article, includes the most important among recent publications.

H. MARROU, *Histoire de l'éducation dans l'Antiquité* (Paris 1948). E. MÂLE, *La fin du paganisme en Gaule et les plus anciennes basiliques chrétiennes* (Paris 1950). P. FRANCASTEL, *L'humanisme roman* (2d ed., Paris 1970). R. PFEIFFER, *History of Classical Scholarship from 1300 to 1850* (Oxford 1976). H. WADDELL, *The Wandering Scholars* (new ed., New York 1961). J. HUBERT, J. PORCHER, and W. F. VOLBACH, *Carolingian Art,* chap. 3 (London 1970). W. OAKESHOTT, *Classical Tradition in Medieval Art* (London 1959). R. RENUCCI, *Dante, disciple et juge du monde grégo-latin* (Clermont-Ferrand 1954). K. WEITZMANN, *Greek Mythology in Byzantine Art* (Princeton 1951). G. BOAS, *The Hieroglyphics of Horus Apollo* (New York 1950). D. C. ALLEN, *Mysteriously Meant: The Discovery of Pagan Symbolism and Allegorical Interpretation of the Renaissance* (Baltimore 1970). E. PANOFSKY, *Renaissance and Renascences in Western Art,* chap. 4 (Stockholm 1960). E. GOMBRICH, *Botticelli's Mythologies,* Warburg Institute Studies 26 (London 1945). E. WIND, *Bellini's Feast of the Gods* (Cambridge, MA, 1948); *Pagan Mysteries in the Renaissance* (London 1958; new ed., 1968).

Alchemy and Mythology

"It is easy to be a poet among the gods."

All other things being equal, it might be said of history, especially the history of the Renaissance, what the Cabalists, uncovered by the Phoenix of that period, said of the book of Revelation, that each of its letters presents seventy faces, meaning by that number the inexhaustible totality of the words of God.[1] One after the other, various modes of thought of that time, rejected by a history that based itself on a science rendered still darker in the occultist night,[2] have been studied by historians of science,[3] of art, of religions: magic, astrology, hermetism, lapidary, the science of numbers, physiognomy, in a word, the cabala. And although the history of these strange researches has not always escaped the frowns of the historian for such an episode of "menschlichen Narrheit,"[4] people have nonetheless discovered in it the poetry that makes all things new.

Though alchemy scarcely appears in works on the Renaissance,[5] historians of alchemy[6] have long made room for it in the *Mytho-Hermetic Dictionary in which One Finds the Fabulous Allegories of the Poets, the Metaphors, the Enigmas and the Barbarous Terms of the Hermetic Philosophies Explained,* the complement and table to the *Egyptian and Greek Fables* of Antoine Joseph Pernety (1716–1801), and in several other works of his predecessors. The most famous, because of the beauty of Matthäus Merian's engravings, is Michael Maier (1568–1622), physician to Rudolph II and friend of the Rosicrucian Robert Fludd, whose entire program is displayed on the title page of the *Arcana arcanissima, hoc est Hieroglyphica Aegyptio-Graeca vulgo necdum cognita, ad demonstrandam falsorum apud Antiquos Deorum, dearum heroum, animantium et institutorum pro sacris receptorum originem, ex uno Aegyptiorum artificio, quod aureum animi et corporis medicamentum peregit, deductam, unde tot poetarum allegoriae, scriptorum narrationes fabulosae et per totam encyclopaediam, errores sparsi clarissima veritatis luce manifestantur, quaeque tribui singula restituuntur, sex libris exposita* (The most secret secrets, i.e. the Greco-Egyptian hieroglyphics not yet widely known, are here set forth in six books, in order to show the origin among the ancients of the false gods, goddesses, heroes, and living beings, and the received institutions for sacred matters, deduced from the art of the Egyptians, which produced the golden remedy of the body and the soul, whence come so many allegories of the poets, the fabulous narratives of the ancient writers, and the errors that are scattered through the entire encyclopedia, and which are here shown in the clearest light of truth and are individually restored in order to be assigned). There is also the fabulous Salomon Trismosin, author of the *Vellus aureum* (the *Golden Fleece*); Jacob Tollius, author of the *Fortuita, in quibus praeter critica nonnulla, tota fabularis historia graeca, aegyptiaca ad chemiam pertinere asseritur* (Chance occurrences: in which, in addition to several critical

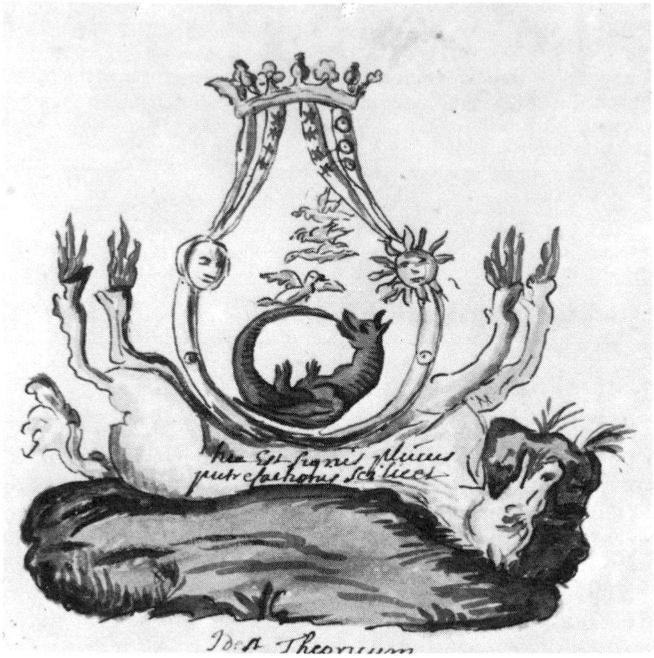

Treatise on alchemy, *La clef de la grande science* (MS Ars. 6577, fol. 8v). Paris, Bibliothèque de l'Arsenal. Photo BN.

matters, the entire Greek, Egyptian history of fable is asserted to pertain to alchemy); and, in the sixteenth century, Giovanni Bracesco, Cesare della Riviera. It is nevertheless important to know the history of the interconnections between alchemy and mythology.

The first witnesses to alchemical mythology cited in the Renaissance[7] are medieval authors: Suidas, whose *Lexicon* mentions alchemy, notably the Golden Fleece, three times; Eustathius, the commentator on Homer; Albert the Great, whose *De mineralibus* alchemicizes the myth of Pyrrha and Deucalion and the myth of the Gorgon; and the *Pretiosa novella margarita,* written around 1330 A.D. by Petrus Bonus Lombardus,[8] which allegorizes the *Bucolics,* the *Georgics,* and the *Aeneid,* as well as the *Metamorphoses.* It is the same fire that hardens clay and melts wax; it is Proteus, the golden bough, Phaethon, the Labyrinth, Medea, the Dragon whose teeth Jason sows, Pyramus and Thisbe. Nicolas Flamel evokes[9] "those serpents and dragons that the ancient Egyptians painted in a circle . . . they are those dragons that the ancient poets set to guard, never sleeping, the golden apples in the gardens of the Hesperidean nymphs. They are those upon whom Jason, in the adventure of the Golden Fleece, poured the potion prepared by the beautiful Medea . . . they are the two serpents sent by Juno, who is metallic by nature, which the mighty Hercules, that is, the sage, must strangle in his cradle." Or:[10]

. . . These of Mythology
In whom the ancient knowledge shines,
As seen in Jason, Cadmus,
Hercules, Aesacus, Achilles,
Then in the two monsters of Perseus.

Giovanni Aurelio Augurelli (ca. 1454–ca. 1537) was the first Renaissance poet to extol alchemy under the veil of fables. He is supposed to have been imitated by Gianfrancesco Pico della Mirandola (1469–1533), if we may judge by the poems included in the *De auro libri tres,* long suspect because of the late date of its publication. With the testimony of Lilio Gregorio Giraldi (1479–1552), who took refuge in the castle of Mirandola after the sack of Rome, we can no longer neglect valuable information about the readings: Giraldi, who had brought with him a manuscript of Psellus on the royal art, read the *Argonautics* with his friend, who had an alchemical eye.

About the same time in France, a Norman alchemist, Vicot, who worked in Flers like Nicolas de Grosparmy and Nicolas Valois, composed in verse, unfortunately rather prosaic, *The Great Olympus, or Poetic Philosophy Attributed to the Much Renowned Ovid.* The "initiated," who claim that this work dates from the time of Flamel, have not read, among other things, a precise reference to the French translation of Alciat's *Emblemata,* of which it constitutes, moreover, the first alchemical interpretation. Moreover, one of the numerous copyists of these works by the Flers alchemists, another Norman, Jean Vauquelin des Yveteaux (1651–1716), proposed—well before Pernety—a mytho-hermetic dictionary that remains in manuscript: *Fabulous Truths, a Curious Treatise on the origin of the Sciences and on the Progress of their Communication, with the Exposition and Explanation of the Fictions of the First Savants. The Whole for the Comprehension of Ancient and Modern Authors Who Treat of Theology, Morality, Philosophy, Physics, Alchemy, History, Fables, Romances, Stories and Poetic Fictions, Magic and the Early Sciences, Divine Cults.*[11]

Meanwhile, in the realm of dictionaries more properly alchemical, Giovanni Bracesco da Iorci Novi in *La espositione di Geber* of 1544 supplied the alchemical meaning of several important fables. Another Norman, Robert Duval, recopied the whole, sanctioning these interpretations with the examples of Pico della Mirandela and Flamel, whose enigmas he had seen at the cemetery of the Innocents. Most of the symbols of the period are found in two folios published in 1591 by Antonio Ricciardi (ca. 1520–1610), a friend of P. Bongo, the author of *Mysticae numerorum significationis liber: Commentaria symbolica in duos tomos distincta, in quibus explicantur arcana pene infinita ad mysticam, naturalem et occultam rerum significationem attinentia, quae nempe de abstrusiore omnium prima adamica lingua: tum de antiquissima Aegyptiorum coeterarumque gentium orphica philosophia, tum ex sacrosancta veteri mosaica et prophetica, nec non coelesti nova christiana, apostolica et sanctorum patrum evangelica theologia depromta sunt. Praeterea quae etiam celeberrimorum vatum fragmentis et denique in chymistarum secretissimis involucris continguntur* (The book of the mystical meaning of numbers: symbolic commentaries separated into two volumes, in which are explained almost infinite secrets pertaining to the mystical, natural, and secret meaning of things, which are derived from the more abstruse, first Adamic language of all peoples; both with relation to the most ancient Orphic philosophy of the Egyptians and other peoples; then from the time of ancient Mosaic and prophetic theology; and especially from the heavenly new Christian Apostolic and evangelical theology of the holy fathers. Besides which, these matters are also touched upon in fragments of the most celebrated prophets and finally in the encased and most secret beliefs of the chemists).[12]

Jacques Gohory Parisien (ca. 1520–76) added to these interpretations those from the romances of the Middle Ages. In dedicating the translation of the thirteenth book of *Amadis of Gaul* to the duchess of Nevers, Gohory, who published a translation of the *Poliphilus,* wrote: "But it is not to be forgotten in connection with Poliphilus (whose lover Polia is said to have been born in the Trevisane border region), and with the goldsmith Augurel, who also throws light on the matter, and with Count Bernard Trevisan, that Merlin tells among his prophecies how at Tarvis a person is to be born who will make gold and silver." And Gohory, who also published *The Perilous Fountain . . . Containing the Cryptography of the Secret Mysteries of Mineral Science,* added: "It is not a ridiculous absurdity that princesses are carried away by Magicians, Giants, and Giantesses, at the beginning of this book, in an azure chariot conducted by four harpies, and the fortunate virgin in the chariot of swans, nor that Medea of Colchis is mounted on her chariot that is yoked to two dragons, nor that Juno the goddess of wealth goes in her chariot drawn by two peacocks. For the preceding wonders are set forth by the Englishman Bacon in the book *On the Admirable Power of Art and Nature.*" Gohory was well-read, because in the preface he states: "Here you see the infernal Rock on which Jason's rich weapons are found, and the terrible serpent like the dragon of Columna and his dark cavern, things also treated by our authors François Guillaume de Lorris and Jean de Meun, the poet of the *Amorous and Perilous Fountain,* and Nicholas Flamel, who has left notable signs of them in his pictures in Paris at various temples in the form of dragons and angels of certain colors. Two gilt leaves from that work have lately been carried off by curious people, from the two ossuaries of the town's public cemetery."

Blaise de Vigenère (1523–96), who was in the service of the Gonzagues de Nevers (who were kindly disposed toward alchemy) and who praised the romances of the Middle Ages, has added many digressions on alchemy in a work of a translator likened at that time to Amyot. And we must set in its proper place *The Images or Pictures from the Flat Painting of Philostratus,* which Michael Maier knew, Goethe appreciated, and Tollius cited. Clovis Hesteau de Nuysement (ca. 1560–ca. 1624) is our greatest alchemical poet, but we will have to make room at his side for Nicolas Barnaud (ca. 1538–ca. 1607), who gave an alchemical interpretation to the famous inscription from Bologna of Aelia Laelia Crispis, as well as to the *Enigmas* of C. Symposius, which François Bérolade de Verville included in *The Voyage of the Fortunate Princes, a Cryptographic Work,* but which he criticized in his *Palace of the Curious.* Let us not forget Claude Barthélémy Morisot (1592–1661), a friend of Rubens, who dedicated his alchemical romance *Peruviana* to Gaston d'Orléans. It was about the same time that Pierre Jean Fabre de Castelnaudary (1588–1658), whose *Hercules Piochymicus* became part of Pernety's *Dictionary,* dedicated to the same prince and his adepts his *Summary of Alchemical Secrets.*[13]

Another figure in this history was one Angelo Ingegneri,[14] who published at Naples, in 1606, *Contra l'Alchimia e gli Alchimisti, paliodia dell'Argonautica, con la stessa Argonautica dichiarata da copiose postille del proprio autore.* A friend of Cesare della Riviera, the author of the *Mondo magico degli Heroi,* and of an ambassador for Charles V, Giacom' Antonio Gromo surnamed Ethereo, who had composed a *Medea ricamata,* an alchemical work illustrated with drawings, Ingegneri had at first extolled alchemy in the myth of Jason and Medea, through which a symbolism often difficult to grasp could be assessed. Giving an account of the *Fortuita* of Tollius, one of the collaborators of the *News from the Republic of Letters* noted:[15] "To tell the truth, I might never have believed that an idea of alchemy could be extracted from the speeches of Sophocles, . . . but everything changes in the hands of a clever man," while one of the admirers of Tollius in our time,[16] who presents himself as an "adept," could write: "The mythologies of the gods and heroes, like the religion of Christ, the Apostles, and the evangelical annals, have solid meaning and real value only in the undeniable and numerous connections that they show with alchemy, its materials and its operations."

F.S./b.f.

Title page of *Arcana Arcanissima* by Michael Maier. Paris, Bibliothèque nationale. Photo BN.

NOTES

1. G. G. SCHOLEM, "La signification de la Loi dans la mystique juive," G. Vajda, trans., *Diogène* 15 (1956): 14.

2. F. SECRET, "Du 'De occulta philosophia' à l'occultisme du XIXe siècle," *Revue de l'histoire des religions,* 1975.

3. It suffices to mention the Warburg Institute studies: L. THORNDIKE's *History of Magic and Experimental Science,* published in 8 vols. beginning in 1923; *Ambix, the Journal for the Study of Alchemy and Early Chemistry,* founded by F. Sherwood Taylor; *Isis,* founded by George Sarton; etc.

4. Cf. review by J. DE BALTRUSAITIS, "La quête d'Isis," *L'oeil* 161 (1968): 38.

5. One need only consult the bibliography in the English translation of J. SEZNEC's classic work, *The Survival of the Pagan Gods: The Mythological Tradition and Its Place in Renaissance Humanism and Art* (New York 1953); M. TURKER, *Bibliographie zur Symbolik, Ikonographie und Mythologie* (Baden-Baden 1960); and *Bibliographie zur Symbolkunde* from 1964.

6. See, among others, the bibliography in J. VAN LENNEP's *Art et alchimie* (Paris and Brussels 1966) and the preface to the Italian edition of PERNETY's *Dictionary* (Milan 1971) (this dictionary was reissued in the *Bibliotheca hermetica,* under the direction of R. Alleau, who wrote the article "Alchimie" in the *Encyclopaedia universalis*).

7. F. SECRET, "Notes sur quelques alchimistes italiens de la Renaissance," *Rinascimento* 23 (1973); "Gianfrancesco Pico della Mirandola,

Lilio Gregorio Giraldi et l'alchimie," *Bibliothèque d'humanisme et Renaissance* 38 (1976).

8. L. THORNDIKE, *A History of Magic and Experimental Science* (New York 1934), 3:155.

9. *Bibliotheca Hermetica* (Paris 1970), 104; cf. 110.

10. Ibid., 144.

11. F. SECRET, *Annuaire de l'École pratique des Hautes Études* (Sciences religieuses) 83 (1974–75).

12. *Annuaire* 79 (1971–72).

13. F. SECRET, "Claude Barthélemy Morisot, chantre de Rubens et romancier chymique," *Studi francesi* 40 (1970).

14. "Littérature et alchimie au XVIIe siècle: L'écusson harmonique de Jacques Sanlecque," *Studi francesi* 47 (1972).

15. *Nouvelles de la République* (April 1687), 400.

16. E. CANSELIET, *Les douze clefs de la philosophie* (Paris 1971), 18, and *Mutus Liber,* 79.

Cabala and Mythology

It is well known that the Cabala was much in vogue[1] after the scandal of Giovanni Pico della Mirandola's *Conclusiones* and after the publication of *De arte cabalistica,* when secretive men were in open dispute. Equally well known are the relationships that were established between this current of new ideas and astrology, alchemy, etc. Consequently, it is hardly surprising that mythology was "Cabalized," in other words, that fables born among the Gentiles were interpreted with the help of a tradition peculiar to the Chosen People. Nor is it surprising that the Church Fathers had been able to interpret paganism, and that Peter the Venerable,[2] alerted by the denunciations of the Karaites, had judged the Talmudists, who read their fables literally, to be more foolish than the Ethnics. After the *Apologia* and the *Conclusiones,* the Orphic Hymns, "fables and pure nonsense" in appearance, took on meaning, thanks to the mysteries of the Cabala, which were not "imaginary nonsense or tales of charlatans" but more deeply rooted meanings hidden under the outer crust of the Law.[3] The same can be said for the Curetes in the service of Orpheus, for the Powers in the service of Dionysus, for Orpheus and Night, and for *Ensof* in the Cabala.[4]

The *Theologia poetica,* which was supposed to interpret the *Graecia mendax* (Greek lie) according to the purest *veritas Hebraica* (Hebrew truth) and the principle of correspondences hailed by the *Heptaplus,* was never written. Circumstances were such that the work of Egidio da Viterbo (1469–1532),[5] who tried to bring the *Theologia poetica* to fruition in his own way, remained in manuscript form.

Indeed, this hermit from Saint-Augustin, general of the order at the time of Luther's revolt, left a work that should not be too hastily judged as clashing with the religious reform brought about by Luther, but should be closely studied in order to be understood. Egidio da Viterbo became a cardinal and preached the urgent need for reform at the Lateran Council; according to him, it was up to *homines per sacra immutari, non sacra per homines* ("men to be changed through sacred things, not sacred things through men"). After the sack of Rome, he wrote that God had not permitted sacred things to be profaned, but the profaning of sacred things was to be avenged. Recalling that it was on hearing the cardinal preach on the Virgin that Jacopo Sannazaro conceived the idea for his *De partu Virginis,* a historian insisted with Erasmus that Sannazaro should have sacrificed less to paganism when treating an altogether Christian subject. The historian, however, quoted the cardinal as saying to the poet, "When I received your divine poem, I wanted to become better acquainted immediately with this marvelous creation. God alone, who inspired it with his breath of life, can reward you worthily, not by giving you the Elysian fields, the fabulous retreat of the likes of Linus and Orpheus, but by giving you blessed everlasting life."[6]

It is still unclear how Egidio da Viterbo, perfect Hellenist that he was, became the most erudite Christian scholar of Hebraic literature. Yet from *De Ecclesiae incremento,* written in 1507 on the occasion of the discoveries made by Portugal, to his last work, the *Scechina,* in which the last of the Sephirot reveals to Clement VII and Charles V the mysteries of the Aramaeans (whose language was that of the *Zohar*), Egidio da Viterbo seems to have followed a path opened by his compatriot, the Dominican Giovanni Nanni, known as Annius of Viterbo (1432–1502). This Etruscan bard maintained that the Greeks had corrupted not only the true origins of the Latins, but also the truths that had been transmitted by the offspring of Noah or Janus, which in Aramaic means wine. It seems that one of the parties responsible for Annius's etymological delirium was a physician to Alexander VI by the name of Samuel Zarphati. Annius had projected a *Historia hetrusca pontificia a Pontifice Noa qui est Janus in Vaticano coepta* (The Pontifical Etruscan history from the Pontifex Noa, who is Janus, begun in the Vatican). This is the theme of the *Historia XX saeculorum* (History of Twenty Centuries) that Egidio dedicated to Leo X, in which knowledge of the Cabala informed an Etruscan subject matter. We do not possess the promised treatises—*De symbolis* (On Symbols) and *De Etruscorum arcanis* (On the Secrets of the Etruscans)—but we do have a rich corpus of themes barely sketched in completed works preserved in the series of glossaries *Glossarium chaldaicae linguae et Cabalae vocabula* (The Glossary of the Chaldean Language and the Words of the Cabala), or *Caldea Babylonica et Aramaea fratris Aegidii* (The Babylonian Chaldean and Aramaean of Brother Aegidius).[7] Even Aegidius Viterbiensis, who sometimes signed his name Aegidius Palaeologus, followed in the footsteps of Annius, who claimed that Palaeologus was the Greek translation of Viterbiensis or Lucumo. These *arcana* (always called *cana* following Solon's apostrophe to the Greeks, who remained children) are worthy of study.[8] Among them are the Sibyl; *semita Dei* (the footpath of God)[9]; Cybele, wife of the Etruscan king Jasius, whose nuptials Isis[10] attended and who was named for the Hebrew word that means Cabala; Camilla,[11] who in Virgil's *Aeneid* (7.803) moves ahead of the advancing winds and is so named for the Chasm of Ezekiel, where holy animals moved with the velocity of thunder; and Paris,[12] so called by Priam, the descendant of Dardanus, because he would break the reign, since his name means "to burst in," according to Hebraic etymology. There are also interpretations of fables according to their biblical models or the great themes of Plato, Homer, and Virgil. Father de Lubac, after describing as "a strange polyphony" a sermon in which Egidio "calls on Minerva, Odysseus, Venus, Juno, Paris, Helen, Pallas, Ajax for help," went so far as to assert that the fifth book of the *Scechina* "ends on a few lines that are perhaps one of the most beautiful poems of renascent Christian humanism."[13]

Drawing on common sources but proceeding along different paths and in an altogether different setting, Guillaume Postel (1510–81) systematized a craze of which the *Cratylus* is the masterwork and invented the word *emithology* to characterize it. The usual term *etymology* is in fact a metathesis of the word *emithology,*[14] craftily effected by the Greeks. In the language of creation and revelation, its root *emeth* means truth (*veritas*), which Postel, according to his method, wrote as *Berritas,* meaning "a well."

Being an admirer of the etymologies of Annius of Viterbo and, like him, dead set against the *Graecia mendax* (Greek lie) and in favor of Etruria, Postel undertook to eliminate fables from calendars, geography, and astronomy. He made his purpose clear in the title: *Signorum caelestium vera configuratio aut Asterismus, stellarumve per suas imagines aut configurationes dispositio, et in eum ordinem quem illis Deus praefixerat restitutio et significationum expositio, sive Caelum repurgatum* (The true configuration of the celestial signs, or Asterism, or the disposition of the stars through their images and configurations, both restored in the very order in which God previously established them and explained in their meanings, or, finally, Heaven Recleansed). Cleansing this heaven of Greek fables and restoring the order willed by God, Postel expressed ideas he discovered by translating the *Sefer Bahir,*[15] which ridiculed the theme of the thirty-six decans. When Postel was not measuring his sky, he was busy rediscovering in Capricorn the scapegoat sent to Azazel and in Taurus the bull that Adam sacrificed (according to the Cabalists) or the bull that is the fourth leg of the Merkabah.[16] In 1572, when a new star appeared in the constellation of Cassiopeia, Postel inflated ancient mythology with the emithology of Cassiopeia that comes both from Cush, the firstborn conceived by Ham in the ark in violation of the law of abstinence,[17] for which he stole the books of magic composed by Adam; and from Aph, the face. The new star heralded the coming of Christ "in us," and the end of the black faces of tyrants. Determined to refer to Africa as Chamesia, Asia as Semia, and Europe as Japetia, in order to abolish the fable of the cow and the "abominable ne'er-do-well,"[18] Postel occasionally indulged in altering the spelling of the word Asia[19] in the holy tongue, in order to recapitulate his sermon. With aleph and samekh, Asia means remedy, for God instituted in Asia the mysteries of salvation. With aleph and shin, Asia means founding, for the world was peopled by colonies that had come from Asia. With ayin and shin, Asia further means realization, for everything will be brought about through the mystery of Christ contained in Asia, spelled with a samec and a hain, meaning the bread of the Eucharist, which the firstborn of the Restitution consecrated at Venice for the whole world.

Postel multiplied these emithologies in his *De Etruriae originibus,* included them in the *Galliade,* and sprinkled them throughout his works, which he signed at the end of his life with the name of Pos-tel or Rorisperge, which in the holy tongue means distributor of dew.

Postel was not the last to play with the ways of Cabalistic art set forth in *De arte cabalistica.* Cesare della Riviera, who mixed the Cabala with his alchemy, found in Diana[20] *Diem, cioe lucem afferens naturae* ("Bringing the day, namely, the light of nature"). At the very least a new world, endowed with the genius of the Hebrew language and with the amazing parables of the Rabbis, had been opened up, and poetry flowed from it. One need only open *De harmonia mundi* by Franciscus Georgius Venetus (1460–1540), later translated by the poet Guy Le Fèvre de la Boderie; the *Scechina* by Egidio da Viterbo; the wonderful digressions of Blaise de Vigenère, who was an astrologer, an alchemist, and a Christian Cabalist; and, last but not least, the reveries of Athanasius Kircher as found in the *Iter extaticum,* which is at the heart of J. Baltrusaitis's fine book on the quest of Isis.

F.S./g.h.

NOTES

1. F. SECRET, *Les kabbalistes chrétiens de la Renaissance* (Paris 1965).
2. H. DE LUBAC, *Exégèse médiévale,* IV, II (Paris 1964), 187. This fine book has a whole chapter on symbolism; cf., by the same author, *Pic de la Mirandole* (Paris 1974).
3. *Conclusiones* (Paris 1532), 12.
4. *Conclusiones,* ed. B. Kieszkowski (Geneva 1973), 81, 82.
5. J. W. O'MALLEY, *Giles of Viterbo on Church and Reform: A Study in Renaissance Thought* (Leiden 1968). Cf. *Annuaire de l'École pratique des Hautes Études* 83 (1974–75).
6. M. AUDIN, *Histoire de Léon X* (Paris 1846), 513.
7. Ms B.N.F. *lat. 596 et 597.*
8. *Historia,* fol. 198 v.
9. Ibid., fol. 229.
10. Ibid., fol. 223.
11. *Scechina* (Rome 1959), 2:229.
12. *Historia,* fol. 42 v.
13. H. DE LUBAC, *Pic de la Mirandole,* 102 and 306.
14. F. SECRET, *L'émithologie de G. Postel, Umanesimo e Esoterismo* (Padua 1960).
15. *Notes sur G. Postel, B.H.R.,* 1977.
16. *Signorum . . .* (Paris 1552).
17. F. SECRET, *De quelques courants prophétiques et religieux sous Henri III, R.H.R.,* 172 (1967).
18. *De universitate* (ed. 1635), 31.
19. M. S. BRIT, *Sloane 1409, Commentarius in Apocalypsim,* fol. 238.
20. *Il mondo magico,* ed. J. Evola (Bari 1932), 47.

PAN AMONG THE CABALISTS AND ALCHEMISTS OF THE RENAISSANCE

There have been many reproductions of the hieroglyphic representation of Jupiter or of Pan as put forward by Athanasius Kircher in his *Oedipus Aegyptiacus.*[1] He may have taken the idea from the *De harmonia mundi,* a wonderful work, which Guy Le Fèvre de la Boderie translated. We shall cite the passage from his great poem *La Galliade* in which the theme of Pan is Cabalized:[2]

To show a Whole that bounds all things,
He depicts a Pan who has two horns
On his head, designating by this obvious sign
Both the channel of the east and the channel of the west.
A large deerskin bespeckled with stars
He wears on his back; it is the vaulted tent
Of the glittering firmament wherein shine brightly
More eyes than ever-watchful Argos had.
From his chin his beard hangs down to his belt,
Which radiates influence upon the heart of nature:
He plays a flageolet with seven pipes,
Which are the seven pitches of the seven glowing lights

That make the world dance round and round,
All the different feet falling into step.
He delights in hearing, from the caves and the woods,
The answering voice of Echo repeating his own seven voices,
Because the influence of each part
Harmonizes with the Whole of which it is a part.
From his waist to his cloven-hoofed feet
He is all covered with thick-layered hair
To show that the bottom of the round machine
Under his cloven hooves is made of earth and water
And that the elements, mingling into one another,
Seem to be unequal, hairy and bristly,
And Syrinx who feigned to be his friend
Was Nature organized in sweet alchemy.
Because he had read on Chaldean monuments[3]
That wines were kept within grapes
Ever since the seven days when the world was created,
And that we are intoxicated by the wine abounding
In the house of God who pours his liquors
Into the vessels of hearts through nine pure pipes,
Therefore he invented nine Bacchuses and nine Muses
Who with their sweet infusions go about intoxicating
The divine poets who have drunk of them.

And Clovis Hesteau de Nuysement, who, like La Boderie, was in the service of François d'Alençon, was able to alchemize this theme by citing Orpheus. After he had presented his Demogorgon,[4]

Virgil, perfectly well versed in all these mystic secrets, gave to this Spirit or soul of the world the name of Jupiter, whom he has his shepherd Damete invoke for the sake of his songs since, he claims, all things are filled with him. This god of the forests, Pan, worshiped by shepherds, may be taken to be the same thing. For, aside from his name, which means "all," he is also made into the lord of the forests because the Greeks considered him the priest of Chaos, which they otherwise called Hile, meaning a forest. In his hymn, Orpheus calls on him as follows:
Pan the strong, the subtle, the whole, the universal;
All air, all water, all earth, and all immortal fire,
Thou who sittest upon the same throne with time,
In the lower, middle, and upper kingdom,
Conceiving, begetting, producing, guarding all;
First in all and of all, thou who comest to the end of all,
Seed of fire, of air, of earth, and of the waves,
Great spirit enlivening all the limbs of the world,
Who goest about from all to all changing natures,
Lodging as the universal soul within all bodies,
To which you give existence and movement and life,
Proving by a thousand effects thy infinite power.

F.S./g.h.

NOTES

1. *Oedipus,* tomus secundus, pars prima (Rome 1653), 204.
2. *La Galliade ou de la révolution des arts et des sciences* (Antwerp 1578), 115. Cf. F. SECRET, *L'ésotérisme de Guy Le Fèvre de la Boderie* (Geneva 1969), 136.
3. The wine kept in its grapes since the six days of creation (Talmud, *Berakot* 34 b) symbolizes the delights of the world to come; cf. G. VAJDA, *Le commentaire d'Ezra de Gérone sur le Cantique des cantiques* (Paris 1969), 262, n. 40.
4. Ed. Matton, p. 279.

Fables and Symbols from Sixteenth- and Seventeenth-Century Hermeticism

I. The Mytho-Hermetic Dictionary

Henri de Linthaut's *Commentary on the Treasure of Treasures of Christophe de Gamon* glosses this brief outline of the main Hermetic fables, following G. Bracesco:[1]

"I know (a) that we must cover up, as our Poems,
This heavenly secret with a heap of allegories.
I know that this scholarly knowledge of Nature
Wants soundlessly to encircle her sacred forehead with laurel,
To maintain her greatness in secret silence
And to admire the excellences of her high secrets.

"(a) The ancient philosophers were admirable for their ability so dexterously to cover over all their science with the pleasant veil of poetical fables. For if we believe Empedocles, the entire practice and matter of this art is hidden under the fable of Pyrrhus and Deucalion, and, in particular, the preparation of Sulphur is hidden under the story of Hercules and Anthea. The conversion of Jupiter into a shower of gold hides the distillation of philosophical gold; the eyes of Argus converted into a peacock's tail hide sulphur changing its color. Under the fable of Orpheus is hidden the sweetness of our quintessence and drinkable gold. With the Gorgon turning those who look at her to stone they have covered the fixation of the Elixir, and have hidden philosophal sublimation under Jupiter converted into an eagle, carrying Ganymede off to the heavens. Under the fiction of the golden tree that grows a new branch when a branch is cut off they have hidden the distillation of philosophers' gold, which they have also covered with Jupiter cutting off his father's genitals. They called Mercurial water the chariot of Phaethon. By Minerva armed they meant this distilled water, which has in itself very subtle portions of Sulphur. By Vulcan whom Minerva follows, they have hidden the Sulphur following this same water, and its salt in putrefaction. By the cloudy cover with which Jupiter surrounded Io, they meant the little skin that appears at the beginning of the congealing of the Elixir: and it is said that the black particles that follow are the black sails with which Theseus returned to Athens. By the flood and the generation of animals, they meant the generation and distillation of Sulphurs. By Mars our Sulphur, by Juno the air, and sometimes the element of earth. Under Vulcan hurled down to Lemnos for his deformity they depicted the preparation of our first black Sulphur. With Atalanta they covered our Mercurial water, quick and fugitive, whose race is arrested by the golden apples thrown by Hippomenes, which are our fixing and coagulating Sulphurs. And that with which Theseus anointed the mouth of the Minotaur are the different kinds of Labyrinthine Sulphurs, that is the Mercurial water of our limed vessel, which is the true Minotaur, being both mineral and animal and thus sharing two natures.

"Here is a part of the fictions of poets that hide the main points of our science. If you desire a fuller interpretation of them, consult Bracesco in his Dialogue of Demogorgon and Geber. . . ."[2]

One can in any case consult the little "Dictionary" that we have put together here; Hercules, Orpheus, and Pan, however, are treated in other parts of this work.

II. The Chariot

Giovanni Piero Valeriano Bolzani (1477–1558), who dedicated to Cardinal Egidio da Viterbo, his protector, the hieroglyph of the stork, the symbol of piety chosen by the Cabalist,[3] echoes, in the *Hieroglyphica seu de sacris Aegyptiorum aliarumque gentium literis commentarius* (Hieroglyphics, or commentary on the sacred writings of the Egyptians and other peoples), one of the main themes of the successor of Annius of Viterbo:[4] "The sovereign Majesty (so majestic and great that it is seen in the celestial regions) is borne in a chariot, not a Platonic chariot in which the great Jupiter, constructor and sovereign governor of heaven, rides lightly about, but a chariot that we can see in the venerable old monuments of the Tuscans, a chariot of which Giles of Viterbo, a figure strong in doctrine, has drawn out the deepest secrets or mysteries of the Aramaeans and made us see it in our day in a public form. The Aramaeans said that one and the same book had two ordinances or laws: one written, the other delivered from God to Moses: the former is for the people, the latter for the wise: the former represents human things in common shapes, while the latter represents the luminous forms of divine things: and the former reveals the history of the creation of the world and the way to rule it, the latter the instrument, even the image of divinity drawn from life. Plato seems to mention the two kingdoms of Jupiter and Saturn as the happiest and most perfect, in that by Jupiter he means human life and action, but by the kingdom of Saturn he means the contemplation of divine things. . . ."

Then, after citing the *Georgics* (1.125) on Jupiter and *Metamorphoses* (1.89) on the Golden Age, he continues: "To return to our theme, Hebrew has two different names for these two: the first is Bresit, that is, the work of creation: the latter is called chariot, that is, secret knowledge. So this secret second law, which must be unveiled by the Messiah and by his own, is hieroglyphically described by them in the figure of the chariot. This is Ezekiel's chariot in his vision of the four images by which, like precious pearls and seals, the Lord created four leading angels and princes of all the heavenly intelligences. The first pearl is on the right hand, whence come beautiful, pleasant things, and is called Michael. On the left hand is another pearl from which things of strong, austere complexion come, and which is called Gabriel. Raphael is like a medicine mixed and tempered by these first two. In the fourth place is Uriel, the closest to the earth as dispenser of the three above-mentioned. Thus Michael and Gabriel are taken for the two wheels, Raphael for the seat, which is in the middle, and Uriel for the axle. The Greek theologians call the power of Michael in God Venus, Gabriel Mars, Raphael Jupiter, to whom the seat is dedicated. The fourth, the sun, which has the power of the male and the female, source of all generation, in Hebrew is called Uriel and Adonim. Orpheus cites all four of these in a verse calling him male/female, geniture and Adonis; it is thus not so fabulous that Plutarch should have remarked on the honor and service the Jews pay to Bacchus . . . for he holds that they solemnize their feast of the Tabernacles in honor and praise of Bacchus, and that Adonis and Bacchus are the same. . . ."

The chariot is one of the themes most often evoked by Egidio da Viterbo. In the Golden Age, the Tyrrhenians, the Etruscans, who were not fixed to one place like trees or mollusks, had chariots for houses, acorns for food, springs and brooks for drink, and the sky for a roof. The patriarchs of Etruria devoted themselves to contemplation, despising wealth, and it was to those who practiced contemplation that the *sella currilis*[5] was reserved, which the Romans, who for a long time sent their children to learn among the Etruscans, borrowed from them. The chariot, which symbolizes the contemplation of divine realities, is contrasted to the horse, which symbolizes the arrogant philosophy of the Greeks,[6] as is witnessed in one of the last lines of the first *Georgic*, echoing the considerations of the *Pheadrus*: *"Fertur equis auriga, neque audit currus habenas"* ("The driver is carried away by the horses, and the chariot does not heed the reins").

The chariot theme is linked to the four mysterious letters F A V L, which were earlier deciphered by Annius of Viterbo and designate the sacred wood where the Lucumons taught the doctrine proclaimed by Ezekiel for the fourth age, when he saw a human Face (*Facies*), an Eagle (*Aquila*), a Calf (*Vitulus*), and a Lion (*Leo*); and he saw these initials, which designated—with the names of the tribes of Faluceres, Arbanos, Vetulonios, and Longolanos—the Fountain (*Fons*) of sovereign good, whose Dawn (*Aurora*) it announced, which heroic Virtue (*Virtus*) loved in order to receive Light (*Lux*) from it.[7] And because of the arcane nature of its transmission, they gave it the name of "Faulas" or fables.[8]

Two centuries later, a French Jesuit, Joachim Bouvet (1656–1730), rediscovered the Mercava in the Chinese tradition.[9] This missionary, who presented Louis XV with the portrait of the Emperor Kangxi, whose envoy he was, and who corresponded with Leibniz, was called the father of the symbolic system, who discovered in Chinese traditions—particularly in the *Yi Jing*, "the Book of Changes,"—the mysteries of Christianity. In a magnificently illustrated text of 1724, *Pro expositione figurae sephiroticae Kabalae Hebraeorum, et generatim*

Page from a manuscript by the Jesuit priest Joachim Bouvet in which he shows concordances between Cabala and the *Yi Jing*. Chantilly, Archives of the Society of Jesus, MS Fonds Brotier.

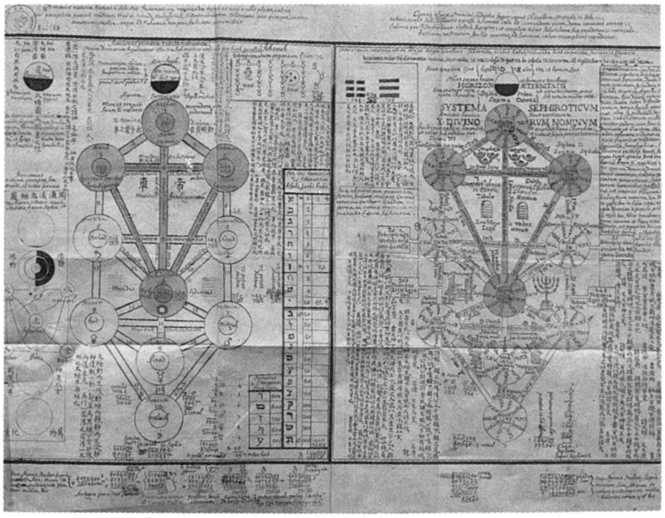

demonstranda mira conformitate primaevae Sinarum sapientiae hieroglypicae cum antiquiore et sincera Hebraeorum Kabala ab ipso mundi primordio, per sanctos Patriarchas et Prophetas successive propagata (Through the exposition of the figure of the sephirot in the cabala of the Hebrews wondrous things are demonstrated, in general, by the conformity of the ancient hieroglyphyic wisdom of the Chinese with the ancient and true cabala of the Hebrews from the very beginning of the world, propagated successively by the holy fathers and the prophets), he uncovered, masked under the figure of the monarch Huang Di on his chariot drawn by six winged spirits or six dragons, the Lord of the Mercava of Ezekiel and the Cabala.[10]

III. Demogorgon

The word Demogorgon appears in the *Mytho-Hermetic Dictionary,* but Pernety attributes to Raymond Lull a treatise on operations on stone, entitled *Demogorgon,* in the form of a dialogue in which Demogorgon is one of the interlocutors. In fact, it was Giovanni Bracesco degli Orsi novi who in 1544 published *La Espositione di Geber filosofo,* in which Geber, in a dialogue with Demogorgon, recounts the meaning of this ancestor of the gods according to the "genealogia delli Dei de Gentili."[11] And Jean Seznec,[12] following Carlo Landi's book,[13] which is extremely rare in France, has summarized the fortunes of this invented god. Also to be noted is some later research, since Landi forgot Leo Ebreo[14] in his list of vulgarizers of Demogorgon, and since citation of Demogorgon can upon occasion help us to date a work which "initiates" situate a century earlier.[15] I am referring to the *Five Books, or the Key to the Secret of Secrets*[16] of Nicolas Valois, who speaks of the calcination of the body, "which the Ancients symbolized by a Dragon asleep in the fire, guarded by an old man who is the virtue of sulphur retained in the soul, which Demogorgon awakens from the earth by our Mars." And among those who followed Bracesco we may note Clovis Hesteau de Nuysement, who, repeatedly citing Bracesco, was not shy about returning to this new character several times.[17]

"But in order for me to tell my portion of the meaning hidden under these Mythologies, do we not see clearly that the ancient Demogorgon, father of all the gods, or rather of all the members of the world, who is said to live at the center of the earth, covered with a green and iron-bearing cloak, feeding animals of all sorts, is none other than the universal Spirit who from the womb of Chaos, obeying the voice of the Lord, lights up the heavens, the elements, and all that is in them, which he has since then always maintained and quickened; for he truly does live in the middle of the earth, as I have amply declared at the beginning of this book, that is, at the center of the world, where he is placed as on his throne, and whence like the heart of this great body and seat of universal life, he produces, animates, and nourishes all. But this green and ferruginous coat in which he is dressed can hardly be anything but the surface of the earth which envelopes him, blackish and iron-colored, enameled and painted with grasses and flowers of all sorts."

And Nuysement ends up by assimilating him to Pan.

IV. Memnon

Memnon, who made harmonious sounds at the break of day, does not figure in the *Mytho-Hermetic Dictionary,* but Raymund Minderer (ca. 1570–1621), a doctor from Augsburg as unknown as his contemporary Michael Maier is famous, did not fail to produce an alchemical exegesis of him. Minderer, who is neglected in Ferguson's *Bibliotheca chemica* but who discovered ammoniac acetate, did not claim that the ancients intended to teach alchemy under a veil. In the *De calcantho seu vitriolo . . . disputatio iatrochymica* (in which he studies, in turn, Proteus, Hercules, and Memnon), the Memnon of the *Theogony,* of the *Aeneid,* of the *Metamorphoses,* and of Tzetzes' *Chiliades,* is connected with vitriol.[18] This black king of the Ethiopians shows the power of vitriol over the black fumes of atrabile, as does the fact that he is the son of Dawn. Memnon's expedition to Troy and the struggle against Achilles allow us to glimpse the battle of vitriol against the worst enemies of the human race, and Achilles is the Hermetic artisan who by fire and his alchemical art kills the calcanthum. The fight also demonstrates the weapons of Memnon, who like Hercules vanquishes monsters. His sword, hanging in the temple of Asclepius, completes the proof. His metamorphosis into a bird on the pyre perfectly illustrates the transformation of vitriol into volatile spirit. And the funeral column that made sounds at the break of day evokes, for those familiar with alchemical operations, the droplets tinkling at the beaks of retorts, which require the operator to keep watch lest there be an explosion.

V. The Phoenix

The phoenix has its place in the Hermetic bestiary,[19] but its place in the illumination of Guillaume Postel seems all the more worthy of note in that it appears only in manuscript works, which illuminate, along with the profound myth of the firstborn son of Mother Jeanne, a totally Gnostic way of thinking, based particularly on certain monuments of Hebraic literature.

It is in the form of a prophecy of the Venetian Virgin that Postel presents the Palma or Thamar, explaining only that [20] "since among the elementary things there is no thing living that lasts longer than the Palma while producing such fruits, perfect in sweetness and nutritive value, the Lord desired to be recognized here in this world in the substance of this Palma not only as the supreme example of sweetness and nutrition, temperament and long life, but also for the sake of perfect love. For nothing better shows the disposition of the upper world toward the lower than the nature of the palm tree, which is made in such a way that it is impossible that it be found or survive in any place unless both male and female are found there . . ." Now, at the time when Postel met Mother Jeanne at her hospice in Venice, he was translating a certain number of texts from Hebrew literature. This is where he found, after the current etymology of Jehochanna, the grace of the Lord, the theme of the "god with a human face," interpreted as Tipheret, the Messiah who has a dual character as both male divinity and female humanity. Then he discovered the story of the bird[21] as immense as its egg, the Bar Yukne, which with Leviathan and the Ox will be served at the feast of the just. Postel, who himself was the egg laid by this "advice," rejected the reading Bar Iucneh, and, sure that it was really his own Jehochanna, he immediately interpreted it as the Gan Eden, the garden that God planted, which he rediscovered in the word "Wecanah" in Psalm 80, verse 15: "that which your right hand has planted." From here on we must follow Postel's glossed translation of the passage from the *Commentary on Genesis:* "Rabbi Simlai said: Chavah (Eve) (after she had eaten the fruit of the tree) came to Adam and said: Do you think that I am dead? Behold, another Chavah has been created for thee (she was predicting the Mother of the World for the new Adam) for there is nothing new under the sun (everything returns) [and Postel uses the word 'revolvuntur,' which translates 'Gilgul,' the recirculation of souls]. If I were dead, you would remain alone. But as Isaiah writes [but Postel replaces 'the earth' in the text with 'woman']: It is not in vain that I have created even woman, I formed her so that she might endure (so that, restored, she might remain inseparably with Adam and her sons). The masters said: She began to say, 'There is an abundance of food.' Domestic and wild animals and all the flying things heard her, with the exception of one bird (*avem unam*) called Chul, as it is written in Job: I will have days as many as Chul." Postel, who translated this text twice, points out that literally the word means sand, and that it may thus be read as the Canah from which all Israel came, without noting that the Vulgate translated it "*sicut palma*" ("as if it were a palm"). In the other translation he claims that this Chul is the Phoenix, a bird imagined on the basis of the genius of the province of Phoenicia, whence everything comes and to which everything returns, but that here the Phoenix really seems to be, not a "chimeric goat-stag" bird, but a unique intelligence which rises above all other creatures, and Postel finishes the translation: "Rabbi Inai said: This bird lived for a thousand years. And at the end of the thousand years, a fire came out of its nest and burned it up. An egg remained in this fire, and the bird came back, grew up, and lived (thus under the image of the phoenix they represent what I have called Jochana, who comes back to life from the dust and gives life to the whole human race). Rabbi Iodan, son of Rabbi Simeon, said: It has lived for a thousand years; at the end of the thousand years its body is consumed and its wings come off its body; what remains of it is like an egg, which produces new limbs."

And Postel concludes: "All things, but men above all, are restored by this bird in every age, for it is similar to the Chul or Phoenix, who for this reason is called Chaliah, which means 'revolution.'"

VI. Sagittarius

Fulcanelli's *Mystery of the Cathedrals* does not mention the representation that Pierre Jean Fabre de Castelnaudary (1588–1658) was still able to see at Saint-Sernin in Toulouse, for which he offered an alchemical interpretation in the *Alchymista christianus*:[22] "A centaur, or a Sagittarius, armed with his bow, fires an arrow against a monster whose face is that of a woman, the body that of an eagle, the feet and tail those of a dragon. An enigma which could receive a Christian interpretation, but which should be interpreted chemically and alchemically because it is such, allowing us to contemplate under the surface the admirable correspondence of the natural and divine arcana. Chemically the Sagittarius represents mercurial water. As in the Sagittarius, in this volatile piece of rock one can distinguish two natures: one igneous and sulphurous, overcoming other natures and essences by its power, just as human nature overcomes all others; and the Mercury of the philosophers, which like the equine nature of the centaur is characterized by the rapidity of its movement. And just as the horse is consecrated to the celestial sun, mercurial water is consecrated to the terrestrial sun. As for the bow and arrows, they represent the effects of mercurial water, which through putrefaction poisons and kills the metallic substance or chemical chaos represented by the monster, who contains three natures: sulphur, mercury, and salt, or animal, vegetable, and mineral natures. The animal nature, which has the color of fire, is indicated by the human face. The vegetable or mercurial nature is indicated by the eagle's body. This nature the alchemists call eagle, which is of the nature of air, for in air is hidden the greatest abundance of the vital spirit. The mineral nature or salt of the philosophers is represented by the lower part of the monster, which is that of the venomous and murderous dragon. Just as the dragon dwells in the bowels of the earth, where it feeds and grows, so does the mineral nature or salt of the philosophers occupy the bowels of the earth, where it feeds and grows, and like the dragon devours everything and renews itself. This is the secret of the chemical art: chemical chaos or the metallic nature must be destroyed, put to death, and putrefied by the deadly poisoned arrows of mercurial water, so that everything may convert itself into an eagle and finish as a dragon, that is, be completed in earthy matter, fixed and permanent, which is the fixed salt of the philosophers, which converts everything into itself, as is said in the Table of Emerald: it is the strength of all strength, the strong strength, when it has been converted into earth. This can also be mystically understood of Christ and his Church, who should constitute one body, strong to resist tempests, as is said in the two verses carved in marble:

Juncta simul faciunt unum duo corpora corpus,
Sic est in toto fortius orbe nihil,

the two bodies joined together make a single body and there is nothing stronger in the world."

VII. The Scarab

Athanasius Kircher (1602–82), the hero of the quest of Isis,[23] even while attacking alchemy magnified its purely spiritual doctrine, finding it in concord with the true Cabala, which he did not condemn along with the Cabala of the rabbis. Dazzled by John Dee's discovery, copied by Cesare della Riviera, of the hieroglyph of Mercury, Kircher perceived the hieroglyph of the scarab as the key to the chemical art, in perfect concordance with the famous exegesis of *bereshit*, the first word of the Hebrew Genesis, at the end of the *Heptaplus*.

The scarab signifies the raw material of the metallic art: rolling up the bodies of the whole world, it produces an egg, visible above its tail. The seeds of all the metals that hide there eventually rise up to the seven spheres of the planets: besides the five spheres of the minor planets, the head of Horus designates the sun, and the segment of a circle above it designates the moon, and inside it is the cross, natural symbol of the elements. Between its forelegs the scarab holds a tablet bearing (in Greek script) the word *phulo* which signifies love. If like doctors we dissect this hierogrammatism into its parts, we obtain this phrase: The soul of the world or the life of things is hidden in the machine of this lower world, where rests the egg fertile in seminal reasons, which, exercising its power over the spheres of the metallic planets, animates them with its heat and makes them act, so that Horus, that is, the sun and the moon, emerges through the dissolution of the elements and the separation of pure from impure things. When this is done, each thing is linked to every other thing by a natural and sympathetic love, and this is the completion of the work.

Kircher, before explaining a discourse too obscure for novices, referred to his *Prodomus Coptus*, in which, after analyzing the hieroglyph of the scarab, he connected it with Pico della Mirandola's analysis of the first word of Genesis:[24] "The father to the Son or by the Son, beginning and end or rest, created the head, the fire, and the foundation of the great man by good accord or alliance." "What can the winged

Scarab. In Kircher, *Oedipus Aegyptiacus*. Paris, Bibliothèque nationale. Photo BN.

globe in the hieroglyph signify other than the famous circle whose center is everywhere and whose circumference is nowhere, to speak with Trismegistus, which is the supermundane abstract Intellect, first Intelligence, celestial Father. What could the body of the scarab signify other than the Son whom his Father has constituted principle, rest, and end of all things, by whom all was made and without whom nothing is made. Lest someone be angered at seeing God himself, who surpasses all admiration, being compared to the most vile, the most horrible, the most stinking of all beings, let us hear what Saint Augustine, the great light of the Church, has said of the admirable humanity of Christ in his *Soliloquies:* 'He is my good scarab, not so much because he is the only son of God, author of himself who took on our mortal form, but because he rolled in our filth, whence he sought to be born a man.' By this son, then, eternal Wisdom and true Osiris, the world was created, this great man, whose head is the angelic world, source of knowledge, whose heart is the sun, source of movement, life, and warmth, and whose foundation is the sublunary world. What could the character signifying love designate but this Spirit, who, '*meharephet peney ha-maym,* floating on the waters,' gives life to all things by the fire of his most fertile love, and ties all together in a good alliance."[25]

VIII. The Sirens

Egidio da Viterbo dealt with this theme a number of times, in the *Sententiae ad mentem Platonis* (Opinions According to the Mind of Plato), the *Historia XX saeculorum* (History of Twenty Centuries), and in the *Scechina.* In the *Sententiae,*[26] the Sirens represented the three powers of the soul—memory, intelligence, and will—since, according to Cicero, they are teachers of knowledge. Indeed, in the *De finibus* (On the Ends), Cicero, after translating the passage from the *Odyssey* about the Sirens, adds: "Homer could see that his fable would be without value if the Sirens sang nothing but little songs to catch a man like Ulysses in their net: it is, then, knowledge that the Sirens promise." In the *Historia XX saeculorum,*[27] speaking of Naples, "ornament of the Tyrrhenian sea, which breathes the sweetness of the sky and the winds, which blossoms with the wealth of the sea and the land, born for leisure, the fine arts and the pursuit of wisdom," Egidio da Viterbo evokes Virgil who, though from Mantua, sang of Parthenope, one of the Sirens, whose body, when cast up on the shore, marked the birth of Naples. And he repeats Cicero's judgment, but in order to specify that the true knowledge is arcane wisdom, which was cultivated by the ancient Tyrrhenians. At that time it was forbidden to divulge this knowledge to the people, who, by hearing talk about several degrees of the divine realities, would have been separated from the Unity. This is what was taught by the Hebrews in their Cabala, by Pythagoras in his Symbols, Plato in his Epistles, Virgil in the fourth book of the *Aeneid,* and the Romans when they forbade disclosure of the Books of Numa. But if divine wisdom is salutary, why were Ulysses' sailors drowned? What is good for the wise harms those who are not. It is like the sun, pleasant to our eyes, unbearable for the sick. The same is true of the Sirens' song, heard only by Ulysses and not by his troop of companions, like a warning given by the son of God not to cast holy things before dogs. He wanted to be the rock of foundation for some, but for others, according to the word of the Apostle, a rock of scandal. Or, as Paul says (2 Corinthians 2.16): "To the one we are the savor of death unto death; and to the other the savor of life unto life." A signification that Egidio picks up again in the *Scechina*[28] concerning the Talmud's interdiction, in the treatise *Haghiga,* against revealing this divine wisdom to the vulgar, "neither to several nor to two, but only to the single pious, wise, and full-grown man," and he sees as a parallel to the Sirens' reefs the mysterious stones, *lapides Bohu, mephulot,* plunged into the abyss,[29] which represent the desires of the body.

IX. Vesta

In the *Treatise on Fire and Salt,* published after his death, Blaise de Vigenère evokes Vesta, along with Pallas, as follows:[30]

"These two deities, Pallas and Vesta, both virginal and chaste, as is fire, represent to us the two fires of the sensible world: Pallas, that is, is the celestial, and Vesta the elemental fire of this lower world: which, although cruder and more material than that of the upper world, nevertheless always tends contrariwise, as if it sought to separate itself from the corruptible substance to which it remains attached, to return free and exempt from all these hindrances to its first origin whence it came, like a soul imprisoned in the body:

> *Igneus est ollis vigor, et caelestis origo*
> *Seminibus, quantum non noxia corpora tardant,*
> *Terrenique herbetant artus, moribundaque membra.*
> (Fiery energy is in these seeds, their source is heavenly; but they are dulled by harmful bodies, blunted by their own earthly limbs, their mortal members).[31]

"The other, on the contrary, while more subtle and essential, throws itself toward the earth here below, as if these two ceaselessly aspired to meet and come before each other, like two pyramids, the upper one with its base firmly in the Zodiac, where the sun completes its annual journey through the twelve signs. From the peak of this pyramid, all that is born and has its being drops down here below, according to the doctrine of the ancient Astrologers of Egypt; therefore nothing appears on earth or in the water that is not sown there from heaven, which is like a laborer who cultivates it. And marking this world below with its warmth, with the efficacy of its influences, it leads the whole to its complete perfection and maturity: which is also confirmed by Aristotle in his books *De ortu et interitu*.[32] But the fire of this lower world, on the other hand, has the base of its pyramid attached to the earth, making one of the six faces of the cube, to which the Pythagorians attribute its form and figure because of its form and invariable stability: and from the point of this pyramid arise contrariwise the subtle vapors that serve to nourish the sun, and all the other celestial bodies; according to what Phurnutus, following others,[33] has written: an inextinguishable fire, he says, is attributed to Vesta, because the fiery power that is on earth takes from its nourishment from Vesta; and on this the sun sustains itself and consists. This is also what Hermes implied in his Table of Emerald: '*Quod est inferius, est sicut quod est superius; et e converso, ad perpetranda miracula rei unius*' ('What is below is just like what is above; and the reverse, for the sake of accomplishing the miracles of the one world'). And Rabbi Joseph, son of Carnitol, in his *Gates of Justice*:[34] 'The foundation of all lower edifices is placed on high; and their peak or their summit here below, like a tree inverted. As if man were nothing but a spiritual tree planted in the paradise of delights, which is the earth of the living, by the roots of his hair, according to what is written in the *Canticles* 7: *Comae capitis tui sicut purpura Regis juncta canalibus*.'

"These two fires, the high and the low, which in this way recognize each the other, were not ignored by the Poets, for Homer in book 18 of the *Iliad*[35] put Vulcan's forge in the eighth starry heaven, where he is accompanied by his artisans, endowed with a singular prudence, who know all sorts of works, which have been taught them by the immortal Gods in whose presence they labor. In book 8 of the *Aeneid*, however, Virgil put this workshop here below on earth, on an island called Vulcanian,

> *Vulcani domus, et Vulcania nomine tellus*[36]

to show that fire is in both of these regions, the celestial and the elementary, but in diverse ways."

F.S./j.l.

NOTES

1. *Commentaire de H. de Linthault de Mont-Lion sur le Trésor des trésors* (Lyon 1610), 97.
2. *La espositione di Geber* (Venice 1544); Latin translation in 1548; cf. "Notes sur quelques alchimistes italiens de la Renaissance," *Rinascimento* 23 (1973): 203.
3. F. SECRET, "Le symbolisme de la kabbale chrétienne dans la Scechina d'Egidio da Viterbo," *Archivio di filosofia* (Rome 1958), p. 150.
4. Trans. J. de Montlyard (Lyon 1615), 579.
5. *Historia XX xaeculorum* (ms. Naples IX.B.14), fol. 208 v: "Domos urbesque aspernente curru contenti vitam traducerent ut currum semper ad decus currulis contemplationis allicerentur. Quare Chabala quae de divinis agit a Talmudistis doctoribus: et veterum sapientibus Maase Mercava: opus currule assidue nuncupatur. Statuas vero tam equestres: quam currules ab Ethruscis accepisse Romanos."
6. Ibid., fol. 244 v: "Graecus philosophus superbiam philosophiam indicat equo: italicam Tyrreni plaustro curruque significat."
7. Ibid., fol. 55 v, 181, etc.: *De Ecclesiae incremento, Traditio*, 25 (1969).
8. *Historia*, fol. 231 v "illis occultis narrationibus: quas a Faul faulas vocabant."
9. Cf. *Annuaire École pratique des hautes études (sci. religieuses)*, 86 (1977–78).
10. Ms. Fonds Brotier of the archives of the Society of Jesus (Chantilly), fol. 183 "de mystico ipsius curru, super nubes et alas sex spirituum (quales spectantur in ipsa figura sephirotica) seu sex draconum, qui sunt spirituum seu angelorum typi."
11. *La espositione*, p. 71 v.
12. *The Survival* (Harper, ed. 1961), 221.
13. *Demogorgone, con saggio di nuova edizione delle Genealogie deorum gentilium del Boccacio e silloge dei frammenti di Teodonzio* (Palermo 1930) (an. VIII).
14. *Dialoghi d'amore*, S. Caramella, ed. (Bari 1929), 106ff.
15. N. VALOIS, *Les cinq livres*, Bernard Roger, ed. (Paris 1975).
16. Ibid., p. 265.
17. *Traictez du vray sel secret*, Matton, ed. (Paris 1974), 278.
18. *De calcantho* (Augsburg 1617), 44.
19. PERNETY, *Dictionnaire*, s.v.; J. VAN LENNEP, *Art et alchimie*, p. III; bibliography in M. TARDIEU, *Trois mythes gnostiques, Adam, Éros et les animaux d'Égypte dans un écrit de Nag Hammadi*, II, 5 (Paris 1974).
20. *Le prime nove del altro mondo . . . inititulata La Vergine Venetiana* (Padua 1555), French trans. (Paris 1928), 42.
21. *Sloane 1411*, fol. 388 v: "Quare in psalmo 80 scripta est faeminea vox Canah et hortum"; *Sloane 1409* (translation of the *Beresith Rabba*), fol. 133, 135 v; *Sloane 1411* (*Commentaire du Recanati*, fol. 84, 98 v; cf. on the sources, J. BUXTORF, *Lexicon Chaldaicum talmudicum et rabbinicum* (Basel 1639), fol. 720 Hwl, and 952; cf. G. SCHOLEM, *Les origines de la kabbale* (Paris 1966), s.v. Palmier and M. Tardieu.
22. Cf. *Alchymista* (Toulouse 1632), 232; cf. *Littérature et alchimie*, B.H.R., 35 (1973): 520.
23. J. BALTRUSAITIS, *La quête d'Isis*.
24. F. SECRET, "Beresithias ou l'interprétation du premier mot de la Genèse chez les kabbalistes chrétiens," in *In principio: Interprétation des premiers versets de la Genèse* (Paris 1973).
25. *Œdipus Aegyptiacus* (Rome 1654), 3:405. *Prodromus coptus* (Rome 1636), 263.
26. Cf. text in E. MASSA, *I fondamenti metafisici della Dignitas hominis* (Turin 1954), 86.
27. *Historia*, ms. Naples, IX.B.14, fol. 148 v; see also fol. 53 v.
28. *Scechina* (Rome 1959), 2:83.
29. Ibid., 1:178; on these stones see G. SCHOLEM, *Les origines*, s.v.
30. *Traicté* (Paris 1617), 69.
31. *Aeneid* 6, c. 730, trans. Allen Mandelbaum (New York 1961).
32. This is the title of the translation by J. PERION (Paris 1552).
33. Cf. CORNUTUS (L. Annaeus) in *C. Julii, Augusti liberti fabularum liber* (Paris 1578), 164 v (in Teubner, ed., 1881, p. 53).
34. *Cant.* VII, 5; cf. JOSEPH IBN GIQATILIA, *Sha'arey Tsedeq* (Riva 1561), f. 18 v; cf. on the theme G. VAJDA, *Le commentaire d'Ezra de Gérone sur le Cantique des cantiques* (Paris 1969), 301.
35. *Iliad* 18.370.
36. *Aeneid* 8.423.

HERCULES IN ALCHEMY

One of the last historians of the theme of Hercules,[1] Marc René Jung, offered a note on Hercules in alchemy. He cited[2] Michael Maier and Pierre Jean Fabre, whose *Hercules piochymicus* was summarized by Pernety. It is enough to observe that Hercules appears to be everywhere for alchemists who are eager to find Diana under veils. Blaise de Vigenère, quite unjustly neglected, spoke a lot about it in his *Philostrate*: "If we want to apply this fantasy or poetic fiction to natural philosophy, we have already said in the preceding portrayal that Hercules is none other than the Sun, which by its heat and its rays, acting as arrows, exterminates the Hydra with all of its reborn heads, that is, the cold, the quality proper to water, of which this serpent is born and whose name it bears."[3] But it was Nuysement who dealt with all of the labors:

The labors of Hercules that are regarded as vain fables
Are by this secret art true symbols.
Geryon with his three bodies, terrifying and powerful,
Is the triple quicksilver embracing the ground and the moon.
The giant born of the earth, the indestructible Antaeus,
Whose power no one could supplant
As long as he touched his mother the Earth,
Is the spirit, living and hot,
Of our gold, which our water draws out and raises on high.
The Hydra that is constantly reborn, with seven horrible heads,
Is water, mother of gold and of all fusible bodies,
The water that never dampens, nor extinguishes the fire,
The serpent that the sun must kill little by little.
The monstrous species of the light Centaurs
Are the hideous matter of the two joined seeds.
The treacherous Diomedes with his cruel horses
Is the Artist hiding his cache of metals
In the secret room where his water devours it.
The shield of the Amazon Hippolite is Iris who decorates
This water with a hundred colors. The sickening dung
Of the Augean stable is the stinking blackness
That covers corpses after their putrefaction.
The birds of Stymphalus that ravage the pasture
Of the ill-fated Phineus, coming to defile him,
Are the strong vapors that come out of bodies.
The pursuit and capture of the wild boar
Is when matter enters the color grey
And leaving its darkness in order to become white
Gives a sign for the worker of its good fortune.
The skin of the great lion that this demigod wears
Is the red color that puts on the whiteness.

The bull he subdues is the body that is fixed.
The stag with golden horns is the yellowing fixed body.
Cerberus with the three throats is the newborn child, who asks
That someone feed it with new meat.

F.S./d.w.

NOTES

1. Cf. H. DE LUBAC, *Exégèse médiévale* 4, 2, p. 228, on Hercules and the theses of M. Simon, R. Trousson, and Pierre Sage.
2. *Hercule dans la littérature française du XVIe siècle* (Geneva 1966), p. 202.
3. *Poeme philosophic de la vérité de la phisique minerale,* Matton, ed., p. 95, v. 1600.

Orpheus in the Renaissance

Orpheus was so much in vogue during the Renaissance that a number of chapters could easily be added to the studies[1] already devoted to the subject. One Joannes Goropius Becanus (van Gorp, 1518–72), who was a friend of Christophe Plantin and Benito Arias Montano, both artisans of the Royal Polyglot of Philip II, and who is generally derided for having found that Flemish was more ancient than Hebrew in his bizarre *Origines Antwerpianae sive Cimmeroriorum Becceselana* (1568), accumulated in his *in-folios* the substance of an Orphic theology, which revealed the meaning of poetry to the Bishop of Antwerp, Laevinius Torrentius.[2] We should at least recall that the sixteenth century opens with a *Vellus aureum* by G. A. Augurelli, who in his *Chrysopoeia* evoked the *Argonautica*[3] which Lilio Gregorio Giraldi later read by the fireside in the company of Gianfrancesco Pico della Mirandola:

And in this place the most happy Nymphs
Through these treasures lush and rich
Untangle with a beautiful ivory comb
The Golden Fleece. There,
To acquire glory,
Prince Jason came first, by boat,
With his men, to carry off this fleece.
The noble youths did not fear,
Under Hercules and Jason,
Skillfully to wend their course
Through so many ocean waves
To reach the wealthy isle of Colchis.

According to the Reverend Vicot, chaplain to the lord alchemists of Flers, in the commentary to his *Grand Olimpe,*[4]

Some believed that this fleece was a book made of a sheepskin, so named for that reason, a book in which this noble secret was inscribed. Others allegorizing more subtly believed that the reference was to the first lord of this work, namely, Aries. Still others speak about a potent medicine consisting of fine wool gathered and fleeced from the back of a sheep. But whatever the case, at least we know that some time ago a brave young person, who by means of this divine powder had faithfully served one of our neighboring states, was rewarded by having an Order established in memory of him in this present state, which is still today called the Order of the Golden Fleece.

It is to a knight of the Golden Fleece that the Doctor from Antwerp, Guillaume Mennens, dedicated his *Aurei velleris sive sacrae philosophiae vatum selectae ac unicae mysteriorumque Dei, naturae et artis admirabilium libri tres* (Three books, of the golden fleece or the sacred philosophy, unique and chosen by the prophets, and of the mysteries of God, and of the nature and art of wondrous things), in which there are many references to the *De harmonia mundi* (On the harmony of the world) of Franciscus Georgius Venetus, who like many of his contemporaries was as much interested in astrology and alchemy as he was in the Cabala. Nor should we overlook the *Aureum Vellus, oder Güldin Schatz und Kunstkammer* by the great Salomon Trismosin, translated by Pierre Victor Palma Cayet (1525–1610), known as Petrus Magnus because he was interested in alchemy and the Cabala, and because he introduced Doctor Faustus to France.[5]

Orpheus, in whom Guy Le Fèvre de la Boderie found the "Mouth of Light" according to his teacher's emithology, is enthroned right in the middle of the temple of Intelligence engraved by Bartolomeo del Bene in his *Civitas veri,* which was published by his nephew Alphonse del Bene, bishop of Alby (1538–1608).[6] Del Bene attacked the alchemists in this

Orpheus. From Bartolomeo del Bene, *Civitas veri* (1609). Paris, Bibliothèque nationale. Photo BN.

Orpheus. From Bartolomeo del Bene, *Civitas veri* (1609). Paris, Bibliothèque nationale. Photo BN.

work and wrote a poem in Italian in which he showed that it was because of their longing for the divine poets David and Orpheus, the bards of immortality, that the Furies invented the alchemists, who boast of making men immortal during their own lifetimes.[7]

It is, moreover, for the same reason that Jean de Sponde (1557–95) praised Paracelsus, actually "Aureolus," for having resumed the conquest of the Golden Fleece in his own time. Jean de Sponde mentions this in *Homeri quae extant omnia*, dedicated to Henri III in 1573, in which he expounds on alchemy, having come to study this science at Basel, notably with one Theodor Zwinger.[8]

F.S./g.h.

NOTES

1. Cf. D. P. WALKER, "Orpheus the Theologian and Renaissance Platonists," *Journal of the Warburg Institute* 16 (1953), reprinted in *The Ancient Theology* (London 1972); F. JOUKOVSKI, *Orphée et ses disciples dans la poésie française et néo-latine du XVIe siècle* (Geneva 1970).
2. F. SECRET, *Annuaire de l'École pratique des hautes études* (sciences religieuses), 82 (1973–74): 257ff.
3. F. HABERT DE BERRY, trans., *Les trois livres de la Chrysopée* (Paris 1550), 69.
4. Ms. F. FRANC, 12299, fol. 115, cf. *Notes sur quelques alchimistes italiens*, p. 209.
5. *Alchimie et littérature*, in *Bibl. d'Hum. et Ren.* 35 (1973): 516.
6. *Civitas*, p. 249, "In medio intelligentiae templo suo . . . Statua est Orphei vatis theologi"; the attack on the alchemists is on p. 153.
7. Le Mans, ms. 7, fol. 94 v; cf. M. E. COUDERC, "Les poésies d'un Florentin," *Giornale storico dell. Let. ital.*, 1891.

"Poi che dal ciel la bella donna et pia
Qual manna o mele hybleo
Di Liban piovve infra gran cedri pria
Et detto il carme al pastorello Hebreo
. . .
Et con la Tracia poscia, et dolce lyra
Mosse le piante, e sassi . . ."

8. F. SECRET, "Notes pour une histoire de l'alchimie en France," *Australian Journal of French Studies* 9 (1972): 222.

King Arthur, the Romances of the Round Table, and the Legend of the Grail

I. The Arthurian Legend

The term "Arthurian legend" has existed in scholarly French usage only since the publication of Edmond Faral's famous work by this title dealing with the genesis of certain Latin texts from the Middle Ages. The title is somewhat paradoxical, for according to Faral these texts, rather than recording a legend, fabricate one from bits and pieces, and stem from no particular folk tradition. Such is the case of the *Historia Regum Britanniae* composed by Geoffrey of Monmouth in 1137, the earliest date for the imaginary chronicles of the reign of King Arthur, from his great conquests to his heroic death on the battlefield in 542. This chronicle and its adaptation in French verse by Wace (1155) were already part of the Arthurian stories that had as their protagonist the fabulous king surrounded by his knights, who owed him, according to feudal custom, their homage and faith. In order to explain the appearance of these texts and their many derivatives, need we hypothesize the existence of a true legend transmitted orally from generation to generation? The theory of folk origins has never been anything more than a succession of postulations which are often contradictory and almost always unverifiable, since no positive proof can be summoned in favor of the existence of a preliterary Arthurian myth. This does not mean that Celtic or Scandinavian folklore lacks parallels and analogies to certain narratives which are connected with the legendary figures of King Arthur and his knights. The point is, however, that none of these parallels is recorded within the Arthurian framework, none is linked to the characters or themes as the literary texts of the Middle Ages present them, and so none can be properly called "Arthurian." Literary scholarship has persisted in cultivating this type of speculation because it has been unable to propose an alternative explanation which would even begin to do justice to the texts. Such an explanation was not possible until the day that the narrative literature of the Middle Ages gained the right to be treated as a body of work subject to the laws of literary creation. Before giving up the search for the myth, however, we must be convinced that the blossoming of stories grouped around the character of King Arthur and his Round Table can explain one another, as so many other analogous traditions do, through the autonomous and spontaneous effort of the authors of our texts, and notably through the use of two distinct and yet complementary procedures. One consists of gathering together all the elements already in existence, which until now have appeared only in isolation. Like a magnetic field, the work thus becomes the locus where, once reunited, these elements form a new structure, acquiring an original significance. This procedure underlay the formation of epic and fictional cycles that dominated all French narrative literature in the thirteenth century. The other procedure, a term used here in no pejorative sense, is a timeless one. It consists of rethinking a given body of work to give it a new meaning, more profound, more subtle, or simply more in keeping with the tastes of the public to whom it is addressed. The pseudo-chronicle of Geoffrey of Monmouth was only the beginning of the myth of the greatness and the fall of the Arthurian monarchy, a myth that was elaborated over the course of the last three centuries of the Middle Ages through the successive contributions of French and English writers. According to Geoffrey, as in all the chronicles derived from his *Historia* (Wace's *Brut*, Layamon's *Brut*, and the fourteenth-century English poem *Morte Arthure*), Arthur dies a victim of the treachery of Mordred. This is a fortuitous incident which is unexpected and unjustified. French prose writers of the thirteenth century, authors of the great Arthurian cycle (1220–25), applied themselves to creating a motive for this major event, making it the culmination of a whole series of intelligently developed themes. This process continued until the third quarter of the fifteenth century, in the hands of the greatest of the Arthurian prose writers, Sir Thomas Malory. We move from a single episode in a chronicle to the tragic drama of *Morte Arthur saunz guerdon*, just as, in a work of romantic fiction, we move from a single fact to a structured work. Insofar as the main Arthurian themes have undergone this evolution, it may be said that Arthurian mythology as a whole springs from the dual movement that forms wholes and continuously renews their meaning. This mythology is found in English-speaking countries at all levels of oral and written culture, from stories still told aloud today in Wales and Cornwall to the works of poets and prose writers of our times.

King Arthur. Vision of the holy grail. Paris, Bibliothèque nationale, MS fr. 112. Photo Bibliothèque nationale.

At what precise moment was the idea of the great king's survival and eventual return to the country he had once made the most beautiful kingdom on earth added to this already rich and fertile collection of romantic themes? Here again we encounter a very general belief, which appears in the folklore of many other countries: the refusal to accept as final the disappearance of a savior, a liberating hero, who must return to ensure the salvation of his people. It is in the logic of things that tales of the glorious exploits of a great king lead to the hope for his return, and there is nothing to contradict the view that, in the British tradition, this hope itself was also of literary origin. Its first expression is found in the chronicles based on the work of Geoffrey of Monmouth and those of Wace and Layamon, and the Latin formula *Rex quondam rexque futurus* ("the Once and Future King") continued to appear even in the fourteenth-century *Morte Arthure*. In the fifteenth century, Malory described this belief, while at the same time indicating that he did not share it: "This," he said, "is what some think; all we really know is that in this world the great king changed his life."

Two other themes developed in an analogous manner: the theme of the Grail and that of the romance of Lancelot and Guinevere. Clearly, it is within an Arthurian framework—in the stories of Chrétien de Troyes—that they appear for the first time, one in the *Conte de Graal* (*Story of the Grail*, ca. 1181), and the other in the *Conte de la Charrette* (*Story of the Cart*, ca. 1172). But these stories are actually foreign to the Arthurian "legend" proper. The King Arthur to whom they refer is no longer the fabulous warrior of Geoffrey of Monmouth and Wace. The King Arthur of Chrétien de Troyes does not even remember the exploits attributed to that warrior. His role consists solely in encouraging the adventures that take place around him; he has no thoughts of becoming involved himself. It was not until the thirteenth century, in the great Arthurian cycle in prose attributed to Walter Map, that the epic of Arthur's kingdom, the Grail, and the passionate love affair of Lancelot and the queen all came together. In this context, the latter two themes acquired new meaning and depth. From that moment on, their true value appears as a chance phenomenon born of the imagination of remodelers and adapters rather than deriving from the mysterious depths of popular traditions. Sequences created in this manner sometimes seem to be preliterary myths, such as the theme of the kingdom transformed into a wasteland (*terre gaste*). Recent research has shown that this story was formed through the agglutination of diverse elements originally independent of one another; so we cannot regard them as parts of a single original myth. Simply by respecting the chronology of our texts from the twelfth and thirteenth centuries, we see how the true architects of the legend of the *terre gaste* worked their material. And this work did not cease with the vogue of French Arthurian novels; it continued through the work of Thomas Malory in the fifteenth century right up to one of the greatest poems of the twentieth: Eliot's *The Waste Land*. If Chrétien de Troyes had lived to see the extraordinary development of the Grail motif, he might have asked himself, like Boaz: How could this have come from me? Such a question would remain unanswered if we forgot to take into account the creative imagination of the writers of the thirteenth-century prose cycle, who used the Grail as a symbol of divine grace without asking what it meant.

II. The Grail

We do not even know the meaning of the Grail in the poem by Chrétien de Troyes that bears its name (ca. 1181). The pageant of the Grail as he described it has caused rivers of ink to flow in our time. For the young knight Percival who saw it, as well as for all readers of this passage, it provides an opportunity to look in wonder at two mysterious objects: the Grail itself, that is, the sacred vessel carried by a maiden, and the bleeding lance in the hands of a young man who leads the procession. If, when that procession passed before him, Percival had only asked its significance, the *méhaigné* king, the wounded king who lived in the castle, would have been cured of his wounds. But Percival, interpreting too literally the advice given him by a wise man named Gornemant, was careful not to ask that question. If he had asked it, who knows what the people of the castle would have told him? Did Chrétien de Troyes himself know the exact meaning of the object he introduced into his poem? We do not know, just as we do not know whether a Grail legend ever existed before Chrétien de Troyes. The evidence suggests that if there was a legend, it was of strictly literary origin like the Arthurian legend, created and propagated by writers. Chrétien de Troyes was followed at the end of the twelfth century by Robert de Boron, the author of a poem called *Estoire du Graal* (*The Story of the Grail*) or *Joseph of Arimathie*. According to Robert de Boron, the Grail was the vessel in which Joseph had collected a few drops of Christ's blood after the crucifixion, and which Joseph's brother-in-law Bron, and his son Alan, were to carry to England—a symbol of the faith which would spread through the Western world. Did Robert de Boron compose a *Percival* as well? No record remains of such a work, but it is possible that the *Perlesvaus*, a prose text from the beginning of the thirteenth century, was an adaptation of a lost poem of Robert de Boron.

The main event in the evolution of the Grail theme in the thirteenth century is the substitution of Galahad for Percival in the role of the hero of the Grail. Galahad, the pure knight and natural son of Launcelot, appears for the first time in the great Arthurian cycle composed between 1220 and 1225, where he seems to play the role of a liberator charged with delivering the Arthurian kingdom from the sin of lust. He alone would be able to see the Grail clearly and openly and to achieve his quest. He alone, because of his character and his behavior, would be able to give human incarnation to the magic light which emanated from it. Furthermore, the Grail here has a very specific meaning, as Etienne Gilson has demonstrated in a famous study (*Romania*, 1925). Before this symbol of divine grace, the knights of King Arthur are somehow ranked according to their degree of perfection or imperfection. Galahad attains the highest knowledge of the divine mystery, which can be obtained through a pure mind (*pura mens*). At a lower level are Percival and Bohort, who arrive at this knowledge through their senses, while Launcelot reaches it only through dreams: three mystic states admirably described in the preceding century by Saint Bernard of Clairvaux. The cycle in which Galahad's quest first appeared was followed by a composition almost as extensive as what is now called the *Roman du Graal* (1235). While the quest for the Grail was only an episode of relatively limited scope in the great Arthurian cycle, in the *Roman du Graal*, Arthur's kingdom, "the adventurous kingdom," is destined from the beginning to face this magical object, whose mere presence seems to condemn the kingdom as much as the ideology of chivalry it embodies. In the same period, Wolfram von Eschenbach in his *Parzival* reestablished the eponymous hero in the role of knight of the Grail and transformed the Grail itself into a magical stone with a profoundly moral significance. Wagner was visibly inspired by Wolfram, whose source seems to be none other than Chrétien de Troyes. This had a curious consequence: for most modern readers, the Grail legend is a legend of Percival, while for readers in the last three centuries of the Middle Ages the Grail legend was essentially that of Galahad, inseparably linked to the prose poem about Lancelot. Because this story survived to modern times only through Sir Thomas Malory's adaptation (published in 1485 by William Caxton), only English-speaking countries retain the memory of the pure knight Galahad. As with the Arthurian legend or the legend of Tristan and Isolde, the Grail legend became diversified according to the various forms and interpretations given to it by the poets and prose writers of the late Middle Ages. As a poetic theme, or as a religious or moral symbol, the Grail has never been anything but the product of their imagination.

We have no reason to search elsewhere for the secret of its emotional power and its prodigious and widespread influence.

III. *Terre Geste* (Wasteland)

In its most complete and latest form, this theme includes four elements: a miraculous weapon, a serious wound suffered by a great man (king or knight), the devastation of a kingdom, and the healing of the wounded man. The blow that inflicts the wound—the "dolorous stroke"—is almost always given by the miraculous weapon, while the other elements of the narrative are often separated from one another. They are found together for the first time in one of the branches of the *Roman du Graal,* sometimes called the *Suite du Merlin* and dating approximately from 1230–35.

The four elements of the theme of the wasteland in this work form a continuous narrative whose protagonist is Balain, an unfortunate knight who seems destined to bring sorrow to all he meets. The "dolorous stroke" which causes the devastation of the country is dealt by him while he is defending himself against the powerful king Pelles, a king mysteriously linked to the theme of the Grail, since it is the Grail in the hands of the pure knight Galahad that will heal him. The architects of the legend of the *terre gaste* not only constructed a perfectly coherent and well-balanced scenario; they knew how to enhance in a new way the theme of the Grail within the Arthurian cycles, as the hapless knight was contrasted to the fortunate knight Galahad. The one plunges Arthur's kingdom into gloom and misfortune, while the other floods the kingdom with a new light and shows it the way to salvation.

E.V./d.b.

BIBLIOGRAPHY

1. Texts

GEOFFROI DE MONMOUTH, *Historia Regum Britanniae,* Acton Griscom, ed. (New York 1929); *Historia Regum Britanniae: A Variant Version,* J. Hammer, ed. (Cambridge, MA, 1951).

WACE, *Le roman de Brut,* Ivor Arnold, ed., 2 vols. (Paris 1938–40).

LAYAMON, *Brut,* G. L. Brook and R. F. Leslie, eds. (London 1963).

CHRÉTIEN DE TROYES: two editions: (1) W. Foerster, *Sämtliche erhaltene Werke nach allen bekannten Handschriften,* 4 vols. (Halle 1884–99); Wörterbuch (1914). (2) An edition based on Guiot's copy (Bibl. Nat. franç. 794): *Erec et Enide,* Mario Roques, ed. (1955); *Cligés,* A. Micha, ed. (1957); *Le Chevalier de la Charrette,* M. Roques, ed. (1958); *Le Chevalier au lion (Yvain),* M. Roques, ed. (1960); *Le conte du Graal* (Perceval), F. Lecoy, ed., 2 vols. (1975); *Le conte du Graal et les continuations: Der Percevalroman,* Alfons Hilka, ed. (Halle 1932); *Le Roman de Perceval ou le Conte du Graal,* W. Roach, ed. (2d ed. revised and augmented, 1959); *The Continuations of the Old French Perceval of Chrétien de Troyes,* W. Roach, ed., 4 vols. (Philadelphia 1949–71); GERBERT DE MONTREUIL, *La continuation de Perceval,* Mary Williams, ed., vol. 1 (1922), vol. 2 (1925); vol. 3, Marguerite Oswald, ed. (1975); *The Elucidation: A Prologue to the Conte du Graal,* A. W. Thompson, ed. (New York 1931); *Bibliocadran,* L. D. Wolfgang, ed., *Beihefte zur Zeitschrift für romanische Philologie,* 150 (1976).

ROBERT DE BORON, *Le roman de l'estoire dou Graal,* W. A. Nitze, ed. (Paris 1927).

Der Prosaroman von Joseph Arimathia, G. Weidner, ed. (Oppeln 1881); *The Modena Text of the Prose Joseph d'Arimathie,* W. Roach, ed. *Romance Philology* 9 (1955–56): 313–42.

The Didot Perceval, According to the Manuscripts of Modena and Paris, W. Roach, ed. (Philadelphia 1941).

Perlesvaus: Le haut livre du Graal, W. A. Nitze and T. Atkinson Jenkins, eds., 2 vols. (Chicago 1932–37).

La queste del Saint Graal postérieure à la Vulgate, Critical Ed., F. Bogdanow, ed., forthcoming.

WOLFRAM VON ESCHENBACH, *Parzival,* text (after Lachmannschen's 5th ed., 1891; narrative and glossary by Werner Hoffman), Gottfried Weber, ed. (Darmstadt 1967).

The Vulgate Version of the Arthurian Romances, H. O. Sommer, ed., from *Manuscripts in the British Museum,* vol. 1: *L'estoire del Saint Graal;* vol. 2: *L'estoire de Merlin;* vols. 3–5: *Le livre de Lancelot del Lac;* vol. 6: *Les aventures ou la Queste del Saint Graal: La mort le Roi Artus;* vol. 7: *Supplement: Le livre d'Artus, with Glossary* (Washington 1908–16). Partial editions: *La Queste del Saint Graal,* A. Pauphilet, ed. (1924); *La mort de Roi Artu,* J. Frappier, ed. (1936; 4th ed., 1968).

G. PARIS and J. ULRICH, *Merlin, roman en prose du XIIIe siècle publié avec la mise en prose du poème de Merlin de Robert de Boron d'après le manuscrit appartenant à M. Alfred H. Huth,* 2 vols. (Paris 1886).

La folie Lancelot, F. Bogdanow, ed. (Tübingen 1965).

SIR THOMAS MALORY, *The Works,* Eugène Vinaver, ed., 3 vols. (2d ed., Oxford 1967).

La demanda del Sancto Grial, Primera Parte: *El Baladro del sabio Merlin con sus profecias;* Segunda Parte: *La demanda del Sancto Grial con los maravillosos fechos de Lanzarote y de Galaz su hijo, Libros de Caballerias,* part 1 of *Ciclo arturico,* by ADOLFO BONILLA Y SAN MARTIN (Madrid 1907). *El Baladro del sabio Merlin segun el texto de la edicion de Burgis de 1498,* Pedro Bohigas, ed., 3 vols. (Barcelona 1957–62). *A Demanda do Santo Graal,* Augusto Magne, ed., 3 vols. (Rio de Janeiro 1944).

2. Critical Studies

J. D. BRUCE, *The Evolution of Arthurian Romance from the Beginnings Down to the Year 1300,* 2 vols. (Göttingen and Baltimore 1923); 2d ed. (1928, 1958), with a bibliographic supplement by A. Hilka. E. K. CHAMBERS, *Arthur of Britain* (London 1927); reprinted with bibliographic supplement (Cambridge 1964). E. FARAL, *La légende arthurienne,* Études et documents, 3 vols. (Paris 1929). J. FRAPPIER, *Chrétien de Troyes* (Paris 1957; 2d revised ed., 1971); *Étude sur la mort le Roi Artu, roman du XIIIe siècle, dernière partie du Lancelot en prose* (Paris 1936; 2d ed. revised and augmented, 1961). R. S. LOOMIS, ed. *Arthurian Literature in the Middle Ages: A Collaborative History* (Oxford 1959).

F. LOT, *Étude sur le Lancelot en prose* (Paris 1918); reprinted with a supplement (1954). J. S. P. TATLOCK, *Legendary History of Britain* (Berkeley and Los Angeles 1950). E. VINAVER, *A la recherche d'une poétique médiévale* (Paris 1970); *The Rise of Romance* (Oxford 1971). P. ZUMTHOR, *Merlin le Prophète: Un thème de la littérature polémique de l'historiographie et des romans* (Lausanne 1943).

F. BOGDANOW, *The Romance of the Grail* (Manchester and New York 1966). A. C. L. BROWN, "The Bleeding Lance," *Publications of the Modern Language Association* 25 (1910): 1–59. K. BURDACH, *Der Graal* (Stuttgart 1938); reprinted (Darmstadt 1974). R. S. LOOMIS, *Arthurian Tradition and Chrétien de Troyes* (New York 1949); *Celtic Myth and Arthurian Romance* (New York 1927); *The Grail, from Celtic Myth to Christian Symbol* (Cardiff and New York 1963). *Lumière du Graal: Etudes et textes présentés sous la direction de René Nelli* (Paris 1951). W. GOLTHER, *Parzival und der Gral in der Dichtung des Mittelalters und der Neuzeit* (Stuttgart 1925). J. MARX, *La légende arthurienne et le Graal* (Paris 1952); *Nouvelles recherches sur la littérature arthurienne* (Paris 1965). A. PAUPHILET, *Études sur la queste del Saint Graal attribuée à Gautier Map* (Paris 1921). *Les romans de Graal dans la littérature des XIIe et XIIIe siècles* (Paris 1956).

E. VETTERMANN, *Die Balen-Dichtungen und ihre Quellen,* supplement to *Zeitschrift für romanische Philologie,* 60 (1918). J. WESTON, *From Ritual to Romance* (Cambridge 1920).

Tristan and Isolde

We have many texts pertaining to the legend of Tristan and Isolde, among them fragments of two great French poems of the twelfth century, one attributed to Béroul, the other to Thomas; a German poem of the same period composed by Eilhart von Oberg; a Norwegian saga; a German poem of the thirteenth century by Gottfried von Strassburg; an English poem entitled *Sir Tristrem;* a prose version in Italian; and finally a prose romance in French preserved in a very large number of manuscripts as well as in a few printed editions of the late fifteenth and early sixteenth centuries. In an attempt to explain both the origin and the vast diffusion of this legend, scholars first applied to the legend of Tristan the general theory of the mechanical formation of epic, just as they had done for other literary traditions including the Homeric poems and the French *chansons de geste.* This theory, conceived and developed by the great German romantic thinkers, was tinged by the mystique of the spontaneous and the primitive, which saw poetry as an impersonal product of popular genius created by virtue of an immediate intuition, presumably the manifestation of the divine in man. According to the theory, all narrative poetry was originally a tradition of short songs, each devoted to an isolated event. These songs were not frozen by writing. Rather, expert singers peddled their wares, so to speak, on street corners, and the songs thus passed on from generation to generation by simple word of mouth. Finally, collectors gathered them, set them down in writing, and developed them with the view toward putting together vast collections of narratives. According to this hypothesis, what was preserved of the legend of Tristan may well be just such a series of assemblages. Behind it all was a theme of singular strength and vitality, namely, the illegitimate and guilty love of Tristan for Isolde, a love whose fatal and indestructible nature was symbolized by the love potion that Tristan and Isolde drink by mistake during their voyage from Ireland to Cornwall. According to Gaston Paris, to this basic theme were added progressively the various components of what we now call the romance of Tristan: the dangers met by the lovers, the attempts by their enemies to destroy them, the episode of their joint exile and their life in the forest, then their summons by the king to return, their renewed indiscretions, their forced separation, Tristan's exile in Brittany, his futile effort to forget Isolde the Fair by marrying Isolde of the White Hands, the poisoned wound that he suffers in combat and that Queen Isolde alone can cure, her own departure for the distant land where Tristan is dying, her arrival at the moment after his death, and finally her own sudden death on the dead body of her lover. According to the romantic canon, this theme did not take shape in its overpowering simplicity inside the soul of a single poet. Separate poems joining together and breaking up into various groups may have made up the first phase of the life of the legend. During the next phase, an attempt may have been made to group into one coherent story the adventures of Tristan and Isolde until their deaths. A late nineteenth-century German scholar by the name of Golther described the poem of Eilhart von Oberg as a "conglomerate of disparate scenes and episodes artificially linked together." In the same period, Novati, an Italian scholar, was writing: "Béroul's poem, although it can be said that it is rather solidly constructed, at every moment reveals the solderings between the pieces from which it was made." Against the background of this doctrine, the great medievalist of our century, Joseph Bédier, put forward his findings with all the strength of his talent and erudition. He claimed that the basis of the whole poetic tradition has always been a single poem, the common archetype of all the known romances that speak of Tristan and Isolde. This archetype is not an aggregate of collected pieces, but a spontaneous work of art resplendent in the unity of its creation. Few people seriously challenge this hypothesis today. There are of course divergent views regarding the content of the common archetype. Again it was Bédier who first attempted to reconstruct the archetype by adopting a very simple method that he explained in the following terms. First, one compares the four "primary" versions derived from the original romance, i.e., the poems of Béroul, Eilhart, and Thomas, and the prose romance. When these versions yield differing accounts, one must ask by what criteria the antiquity of a particular feature may be determined: its archaic "turn," its intrinsic value, its conformity to the overall work? We are aware of how precarious such determinations may be. Nonetheless, Bédier's work led him to make the following statement:

> Every time the comparison could apply to at least three of the texts, the features which, for reasons of taste, feeling, and logic, we deemed original were features attested by three versions or by at least two of them. Conversely, the features which for reasons of taste, feeling, and logic we deemed to have been revised and of more recent date, appeared to be isolated in a single version of the ones compared.

Bédier was able to make the important claim that the compared versions were independent from one another for

Le roman de Tristan et Yseult (ms. fr. 103, fol. 1). Paris, Bibliothèque nationale. Photo BN.

the following reason: since each time two or three of them were in agreement, they were faithful to their source, whereas each time that they were not in agreement, they were at variance with the source. Hence, our texts allow us simultaneously to establish the existence of an archetype and to reconstruct it in its broad outlines. Béroul and Eilhart, according to recent investigations, were probably the most faithful to the archetype. Their adaptations most clearly assert the essential theme of the original romance, namely, the juxtaposition, forever unresolved, of the two irreconcilable powers, that of the love potion and that of the social law which the lovers never repudiate. This does not alter the fact that if we are to understand the evolution of the legend into the modern period, we must consult Thomas's version and the French prose version, which implicitly or explicitly proclaim the sovereign rights of love. Thomas inspired, among others, the German poet Gottfried von Strassburg, from whose work, in turn, Wagner learned the legend of Tristan. The prose romance (1230), itself widespread in medieval Europe, made the legend of Tristan into one of the romances of the Round Table. In a collection of English prose romances published in 1485 by William Caxton under the title of *Le morte d'Arthur,* Sir Thomas Malory gave us an abridged version of the romance that serves as the source for most modern English versions.

Should we assume that a popular legend, predating the first Tristan romance, was disseminated by the Celts from across the Channel and passed on by Breton bards, as certain French poets claim? The existence of a legend featuring Mark, his wife, and his swineherd Tristan in love with the wife is attested in a very ancient Welsh triad, a plain, unpolished story in which there is talk neither of a love potion nor of the social order that the lovers are destined simultaneously to violate and to respect. It is not of this story that one thinks when postulating an original Celtic Tristan, but of something as complete and as profoundly poetic as the French archetype of our earliest romances. But we have no proof that such a work ever existed. A romance of Tristan composed in France toward the middle of the twelfth century is, outside of our texts, the sole tangible reality. Given the current state of our knowledge, we cannot deny the most compelling poem of the French Middle Ages its profound and startling originality.

E.V./g.h.

BIBLIOGRAPHY

1. Texts

Béroul's *Tristan:* E. Muret, ed., 4th ed., revised by L.-M. Defourques (Paris 1970); A. Ewert, ed., *The Romance of Tristan* by Béroul (Oxford 1939), introduction and commentary, vol. 2 (1970).

Thomas's *Tristan:* J. Bédier, ed., *Le roman de Tristan par Thomas,* 2 vols. (Paris 1902–5); B. H. Wind, ed., *Les fragments du Tristan de Thomas* (Paris 1960).

Folies Tristan: J. Bédier, ed., *Les deux poèmes de la Folie Tristan* (Paris 1907); E. Hoepffner, ed., *La Folie Tristan de Berne,* 2d ed., revised and corrected (Strasbourg 1949); *La Folie Tristan d'Oxford,* 2d ed., revised and corrected (Strasbourg 1943).

EILHART VON OBERG, *Tristrant,* ed. fr. Lichtenstein (Strasbourg 1877).

GOTTFRIED VON STRASSBURG, *Tristan und Isolt,* F. Ranke, ed. (Berlin 1930); idem, G. Weber, ed., with G. Utzmann and Werner Hoffmann (Darmstadt 1967).

The Romance in Prose (partial editions): R. L. Curtis (Munich 1963); J. Blanchard, *Les deux captivités de Tristan* (Paris 1976).

Tristram saga, E. Kölbing, ed. (Heilbronn 1878).

2. Critical Studies

Arthurian Literature in the Middle Ages, R. S. Loomis, ed. (Oxford 1959), chaps. 12–14, 26. EMMANUÈLE BAUMGARTNER, *Le Tristan en prose: Essai d'interprétation d'un roman médiéval* (Geneva 1975). DANIELLE BUSCHINGER, *Le Tristan d'Eilhart von Oberg* (Paris 1975). M. DELBOUILLE, DENIS DE ROUGEMONT, and E. VINAVER, *Tristan et Iseut à travers le temps* (Brussels 1961). A. FOURRIER, *Le courant réaliste dans le roman courtois en France au Moyen Age,* 1: *Les débuts* (12th century) (Paris 1960). W. GOLTHER, *Tristan und Isolde in den Dichtungen des Mittelalters und der neuen Zeit* (Leipzig 1907). P. JONIN, *Les personnages féminins dans les romans français de Tristan au XIIe siècle,* Publ. de la Faculté des Lettres (Aix-en-Provence 1958). J. KELEMINA, *Untersuchungen zur Tristansage* (Leipzig 1910); *Geschichte der Tristansage nach den Dichtungen des Mittelalters* (Vienna 1923). E. LOESETH, *Le roman en prose de Tristan, le roman de Palamède et la compilation de Rusticien de Pise, analyse critique d'après les manuscrits de Paris* (Paris 1891); reprinted by B. Franklin (New York 1970). W. RÖTTIGER, *Der heutige Stand der Tristanforschung* (Hamburg 1897). G. SCHOEPPERLE, *Tristan and Isolt: A Study of the Sources of the Romance* (Frankfurt and London 1913); reprinted by B. Franklin (New York 1958). A. VAVARO, *Il roman di Tristan di Béroul* (Turin 1963). E. VINAVER, *Études sur le Tristan en prose, les sources, les manuscrits, bibliographie critique* (Paris 1925).

Gypsy Myths and Rituals

Of all the ethnic minorities scattered throughout the world, Gypsies are perhaps one of the most original by virtue of their life-style and their adherence to tradition. In the heart of our developed and urbanized countries, this wandering people manifests a profound will to survive despite all attempts to assimilate it and despite the countless harassments and persecutions of which it have been the target. The last such attempt resulted in the extermination of nearly five hundred thousand Gypsies in Nazi concentration camps.

One of the basic factors of this resistance is the Gypsies' religious sense. We say religious sense rather than religion, because it is above all a general state of mind and a specific ethical and religious behavior rather than a system of dogmatized beliefs and institutionalized ritual practices. This kind of religious life is closely tied to the history of the Gypsies and to their culture, which it nurtures and endows with meaning. We therefore begin with a brief overview of the origins of the Gypsies and the originality of their nomadism.

I. Nomadism and Gypsy Life

In order to understand the Gypsy soul, we must never lose sight of the close link between the history of this people and the type of nomadism within which it has preserved its identity to this day. Gypsy myths and rites may then be perceived in the context of their true nature and of their functioning.

Originally from India, Gypsies reached Europe at the beginning of the modern era (fifteenth and sixteenth centuries), after long wanderings through the Near East. Many invasions have swept over Europe and shaped its population. The Gypsies constitute the last such invasion, the most peaceful and by far the least numerically significant. They came too late into a world already organized politically, so that there was no place left for them, and no hope of occupying some vacant territory. They were compelled to scatter throughout all civilized countries, cornered as they were by two necessities: first, they had to be accepted by native populations despite the suspicion they aroused by the alien character of their ethnic type, language, and customs, marking them as intruders or undesirables; second, they had to live. They did so by preserving their originality and continuing in the path of nomadism that had always worked for them, which we have elsewhere called "parasitic nomadism" (without any pejorative overtones). Whereas most nomadic people are largely self-sufficient, hunting or raising cattle on lands that they know, such could not be the case for the Gypsies. To survive, they had to establish a trading pattern with settled populations, often by limiting their nomadism to a single country. To make such commerce possible, Gypsies learned many small trades compatible with their wandering life and incorporated them into the old rural world: tin-plating of kitchen utensils, basket weaving, pot and pan making, saddlery, handicrafts, door-to-door retailing, horse trading, metal scrapping, circuses, bear training, popular and veterinary medicine, musical entertainment for festivals and country weddings, fortune-telling, etc.

Needless to say, such trades have become less and less profitable. The advent of industrial and urban society has brought about considerable change in the rural world with which the Gypsies lived in a symbiotic relationship. The rural world has shrunk quantitatively; industrialization has reached the farmer; the standard of living has increased; and widespread education and the pervading influence of the mass media have transformed needs and made obsolete the small-scale trading (except for metal scrapping and the secondhand market) which allowed Gypsies to survive while continuing to practice their ancestral nomadism. This has led to the crisis of acculturation that now threatens the very survival of this people's cultural identity (see my article, "Les Tsiganes face au problème de l'acculturation," *Diogène*, 1976, no. 4).

II. Christianity and Animism

When speaking of the religion of the Gypsies, we should distinguish clearly between two things. On the one hand, Gypsies officially profess a particular religion, usually the Christian faith. On the other hand, a backdrop of animistic religion survives tenaciously in an abundance of ancient myths and in the practice of magic rites, more or less integrated into the official religion.

Gypsies have usually adopted the faith of the country in which they wandered, be it Islam or Christianity (Eastern Orthodoxy, Roman Catholicism, Protestantism, and today Pentecostalism in many instances). Here again, it has been a question of survival. On arriving as aliens in the Christian West, to take one example, where being a pagan was the worst of all disgraces (the same may be said of the Muslim areas in the Balkans, where the Gypsies adopted Islam), Gypsies saw that adopting the local religion was in their best interest, especially in view of the fact that baptism constituted the only real form of identity. Insecure as Gypsies were and uncertain of the welcome they might receive, they were afraid of being expelled or persecuted (even today the precariousness of camping zones reserved for nomads perpetuates this form of racism), and of being unable to practice their indispensable trades. Belonging to the local religion thus became a basic guarantee for the Gypsies. It alone could confer on them the minimum of credibility that they needed to be accepted by the settled populations. We should not, however, think that joining the official religion was merely a superficial act. Though initially an act of self-interest, it was most often incorporated into the Gypsy religious mentality, which, as we shall show below, was of an animistic type.

Gypsies reinterpreted Christian beliefs and rites from a more primitive and fundamental religious structure. This animistic base indicates an overarching religious mentality that pervades all of Gypsy life, even while leaving it open to other religious beliefs experienced in an original style. To summarize this basic religious sense, we could say that for the Gypsies there are not two realms—that of everyday, secular life, and that of far-off, extraterrestrial deities. Rather, the world in which the Gypsies lead their daily existence is peopled with mythical and supernatural beings—kindly and evil spirits, demons, fairies—who bear various names and assume all sorts of bodily features and appearances.

At every moment of their life, Gypsies feel that they are in contact with those beings on whom their personal fate rests, beings who are hidden behind the most familiar events, persons, and things. This attitude is a form of the "law of participation" that characterizes people who live close to nature, who feel that they have a special bond with the cosmos and are subject to the influence of the mythical beings that control the generally menacing cosmic forces. Knowing that they are in communication with this supernatural universe, the Gypsies try to make it work on their behalf by performing specialized rites (of purification, exorcism, prophylaxis, healing, divination, etc.). This religious element has played a major role in the Gypsies' resistance to a hostile environment, as it is the soul of their very own nomadism. Openly despised by sedentary populations, under constant threat of persecution, the Gypsies could reach deep inside themselves for the strength of their conviction that they are part of a superior world dominating the real world. Moreover, the pride they experience in their destitution and the mystery with which they shroud their magic rites make them respected and feared, and thus encourage others to accept their meager services.

III. The Gypsy Religious Sense

It is difficult to isolate the original religious elements of the Gypsy world from the successive contributions of religions adopted at a later time. Certainly, with the progress of evangelization the earlier elements have gradually become blurred or, at best, have survived within a kind of reinterpretation of Christain dogmas that they themselves have influenced. Ethnologists of the previous century, H. von Wlislocki among them, who managed to live in close touch with Gypsy groups in central Europe, collected a number of mythical narratives, especially cosmogonies. With respect to the creation of the world, we can observe a basic dualism, conceivably of Iranian origin (after leaving India, the Gypsies stayed in Persia for a long time), whereby God opposes the devil in a kind of contest, but with a clearly Christian tone, for the devil ultimately submits to God. This cosmogony contains many elements common to most such accounts, including primeval waters, the tree as the source of life, and the separation of heaven and earth.

Underlying the Gypsy religious mentality, one thing we know for certain: Gypsies believe in the existence of a benevolent God (Del, Devel) who is a creator-god. Far from any pantheistic concept, he is very much a personal god, the almighty whom Gypsies often invoke for his kindness in connection with every event, even in the midst of magic rites.

Specifically Christian elements seem to coexist happily with the older, animistic core. In particular, belief in Jesus Christ (Baro Devel) is hardly distinguishable from belief in God the creator and protector of mankind. In their quest for a happy existence, Gypsies have a great cult of the saints and particularly of the Virgin Mary (see § V below, on the mediating importance of femininity). Accustomed as they are to believing in a myriad of superior beings, benevolent or malevolent, they are comfortable with devotion of the saints (hence the success of pilgrimages, such as that of the Saintes-Maries in Provence). They are likewise serious about exorcising the devil; hence the importance attributed to Christian baptism, understood to fall under the general rubric of exorcism.

Two features of Gypsy religiosity seem to be carryovers of a pre-Christian stage: the problem of death and salvation, and the existence of numerous spirits that influence daily life.

The god of the Gypsies may be God the Creator, Providence, who loves mankind, but he is by no means the God who redeems from sin (little importance is given to this redemptive aspect of the mission of Christ), nor is he the God who rewards or punishes after death. The absence of the idea of repayment in the afterlife is connected with a fatalism characteristic of Gypsy psychology. It is undeniable that the Gypsies believe in the immortality of the soul, the soul being conceived of in a rather material way. This afterlife, however, is not the salvation that concludes existence in the Christian sense. It is not an immortality capable of bringing about total happiness (or the misery of hell). It is, rather, a kind of painful peregrination of the soul in a mysterious world full of terror and fright. This bodily soul or vital principle remains in death until it reaches putrefaction. Accordingly, numerous funerary customs assume that the dead person slumbers and that the living have the obligation to help him in his laborious peregrinations in the Kingdom of the Dead, particularly through libation, meals, and festivals. The best known funerary festival is the famous Pomana, celebrated a year and six weeks after the burial. Whereas the meal that is eaten in the presence of the deceased before his burial takes place in an atmosphere of jubilation, of licentiousness even, the meal of the Pomana assumes a certain dignity and takes place in accordance with a precise ritual. The deceased who is being celebrated is represented by a living being, of approximately the same age, who is washed and dressed in new clothes and assumes the role of the deceased by imitating his or her tastes and mannerisms. The objective of the Pomana is twofold. On the one hand, it is an act of solidarity toward the deceased, who is thought to be still living elsewhere and who needs help and consolation in his painful new roaming. But the Pomana also has a prophylactic purpose (and here we are introduced into the real mythological universe of the Gypsies), namely, to protect the living from the harmful influences that every dead person releases in the form of evil spirits.

IV. Gypsy Mythology

Gypsies indeed believe in a multitude of supernatural beings, good and evil spirits, who exercise their influence throughout the course of life. This belief comes across in numerous tales and magic rites.

The importance of these numerous spirits would lead us to believe in a kind of polytheism among the Gypsies, one that stands out against the background of monotheism referred to above, which it does not contradict. Adopting an official monotheistic religion (Christianity or Islam) kept Gypsies from seeing these spirits as "gods" in the classical sense. These beings, however, participate no less in the divine absolute, for they influence the existence of mortals. Their functional character further explains their multiplicity. The general acculturation of Gypsies today makes it difficult to pinpoint the origins of these mythical beliefs, strata of a layered religious consciousness that bears the traces of influences of various populations among whom Gypsies once lived.

Among these countless spirits, all of whom have more or less physical features, we can distinguish several groups that are often confused even by modern Gypsies themselves. The main group is made up of the famous goddesses of fate, the Oursitori (or Ursitory, called Ourmes by certain tribes) or "white women," because they wear white dresses. Their descriptions and life-styles vary greatly from tribe to tribe. In general, they are connected with the plant kingdom and regarded as kinds of souls of trees. They go in groups of three and intervene mainly at the birth of a Gypsy, determining the child's fate. One of these fairies is good, another is bad, and the third plays an intermediary role. Some historians see a link between this belief and that of the ancient Parcae. Most magic rites prescribed by this belief aim to influence these goddesses of fate on the occasion of a birth by offering them the appropriate food and by invoking them with numerous prayers whispered by a magician at the entrance to the house in which the delivery has taken place. A contemporary Gypsy has written a novel (Mateo Maximoff, *Les Ursitory,* Paris 1946), later produced as a movie, which popularized this belief.

Beside these goddesses, the Gypsy world of the supernatural is peopled by many other spirits whose actions are revealed mainly at the time of illness or death. Convinced that they live symbiotically with all of these spirits, Gypsies see them in all natural phenomena. Accordingly, they explain illness as the invasion of a pathogenic spirit struggling against the vital spirit that every man bears within him.

Gypsies generally believe in the existence of an individual protective spirit, a sort of guardian angel, which is often difficult to distinguish from the breath of life (what we might call the soul), and which the Gypsies of southeastern Europe call Butyakengo (etymologically, "he who has many eyes," to be better able to spot dangers threatening his protégé). This protective spirit helps to unite the generations. Every person who dies leaves on earth part of his vital or protective spirit, which goes on to live in the body of a descendant (generally the oldest). The other descendants are not shortchanged, however, because the protective spirit of the departed remains on earth and continues to protect the descendants. In so doing, this spirit acts as a portion of the soul of the departed which generations pass on to one another. Each individual, whose body is enlivened by his own spirit or soul, is also visited by a portion of the spirit of his descendants. Herein lies a fine point: to the extent that this portion is distinct from the spirit that belongs strictly to a given person, it constitutes within him a protective spirit, which can leave him for a while.

The protective spirit actually watches over the man in whom it dwells, even though it leaves his body while he sleeps in order to protect him from impending danger. Whereas a dying man gives up his soul (his individual vital spirit) through the mouth, it is through the ears that the protective spirit inherited from the ancestors moves in. It warns its protégé by a ringing in the ear. If it should leave the body momentarily, it does so out of the right ear, the left ear being the port of entry; hence the care Gypsies take in cleaning their left ear with their little finger, also known as the auricular finger because it is small enough to be introduced into the ear. For that purpose, Gypsies carefully file the fingernail of their auricular finger. It is essential to facilitate the return of the protective spirit and its warning messages on which the protégé's life may depend. Since the deceased has no more need of a protective spirit (being destined to roam in a parallel and mysterious world), certain Gypsy tribes break the little finger of the corpse and tie a coin to it with a red thread.

Many such beliefs and rites must have been borrowed from the prevailing folklore in a more or less distant time. Traces of some have come down to us in popular language, for example, in the French expression *Mon petit doigt me l'a dit* ("My little finger told me," equivalent to "A little bird told me" in the English-speaking world). Such borrowings are undeniable even if the demands of Gypsy life have resulted in the integration or reinterpretation of these alien elements. We could find many other examples in beliefs in evil spirits as causes of illness and misfortune. Among them, we can cite those spirits who are freed by death and who explain why, for Gypsies, death is laden with curses and taboos that affect those who remain. Though often mixed together, these evil spirits are of two sorts, the Moulo and the vampires.

The Moulo, synonymous with "ghost" or the "moving dead," designates the spirit of a dead person that can make itself manifest and reincarnate itself in another person or animal. It is often translated as the "living dead." The origin of the Moulo is revealing. Not every dead person becomes a Moulo, only a stillborn child. For some Gypsy tribes, the Moulo has no bones, and both hands lack the middle finger, which he left in the tomb. He lives in the mountains and often visits houses to steal what he needs. He can become visible to the eye, which is always a bad sign.

In other tribes where belief in the Moulo is less pronounced, it is more or less subsumed into the belief that the souls of the dead transmigrate to animals—a dog, a cat, a frog—in the form of evil spirits.

This brings us to the other kind of spirits freed by death, the vampires. The myth we are encountering here is not endemic to Gypsies but is found in the folklore of many Indo-European branches (especially Slavs and ancient Germans). Historians have established a clear link between the *lukanthropos* of the Greeks, the *versipellis* of the Romans, the werewolf of the ancient Germans, and the Gypsy vampire, an evil spirit that possesses the body of a deceased man. Hence the precautions taken by Gypsies when one of their own dies, lest such a harmful spirit escape and bring misfortune. This further explains certain libations during the funerary meal, particularly the Pomana (see above): to ward off evil spirits from the tomb, wine or aquavita is poured over it.

Also widespread among the Gypsies is the belief in witches, conceived of as women endowed with evil powers rather than as supernatural beings, fairies or goddesses, like the Oursitori. A woman turns into a witch after having sexual relations with a demon that causes disease. (Etymologically, the Gypsy word for witch means a woman who becomes irritated by the delight of her human brothers.) Their special feature is that they can transmit this demoniacal spirit to a man or an animal, for instance, to a worm or a small snake, which in turn may transmit the spirit to a man sleeping with his mouth open.

In their great variety, these beliefs have also often been borrowed from the prevailing, even Christianized folklore. Accordingly, many Gypsy tribes schedule their great annual festival of the witches during the night of Whitsunday. Similarly, the connection between many dietary taboos and the belief in witches is probably attributable to a reinterpretation of ancient taboos, the meaning of which has been lost. Incorporating these taboos into the mythology of witches gave them a new vitality. This carryover was in fact made within a context dominated by sexuality. For example, the broad bean is a forbidden food because it looks like a testicle. Besides the sexual origin of the witch's powers (relations with demonic spirits), the renewing of such powers takes place in a similar context, namely, the blood vow. In classical Christian demonology, this vow can be made by a man or a woman, and involves giving the devil a little blood taken from one's arm after inflicting a wound on oneself. In the case of the witch, she revives her power by giving the devil her menstrual blood to drink. Obviously, the Christianization of many Gypsies often eliminated these older mythical elements. But belief in the power of witches, in their capacity to cast spells, to cause misfortune by giving someone the evil eye or by breathing on someone, was bound to create an aura of mystery surrounding the Gypsies, especially among gullible people, susceptible to superstition and thereby more likely to respect these strange nomads and to supply them with a few resources.

V. Magic Rites and Femininity

Myths condition rites. The multiplicity of myths and their highly varied origins explain the variety of ritual practices, some examples of which we have already seen. We should now look at the major place occupied by women in Gypsy mythology. On the one hand, we have the intermediaries between evil spirits and men, namely, witches. On the other hand, the benevolent Oursitori are goddesses. The intermediaries between the supernatural world and the human world are mostly women performing a magic function, be it divination, healing, or propitiation. Although the Gypsy world knows no priestly function (not even in the person of the tribal chief), sorceresses perform the functions that are ordinarily relegated to the priestly castes in most religions (telling fortunes, exorcising, invoking the gods, healing, etc.).

A Gypsy woman usually becomes a sorceress by inheriting such powers and the knowledge of the rites from an ancestor. Some Gypsies compare sorceresses with witches (for example, when the sorceress has sexual relations with water spirits), but the connotation of sorceress is less pejorative and does not involve the blood vow.

Living in a symbolic universe peopled by evil forces and taboos, Gypsies know that their fate is controlled by the random alternation of good luck (*Bacht*) and bad luck (*Bibacht*). They therefore engage in more and more rites in an effort to know what their fate may be and to redirect it to the extent that they can. Hence the rites of purification performed against the impurities carried by a woman at the time of her period or by a child at birth, or at the moment of death when numerous impure spirits are freed. This impurity is not ethical. It is mostly involuntary and connected with an existential situation. The rites of divination that have popularized fortune-tellers reflect the need to scrutinize inexorable fate. Best known is the use of Tarot cards, but other more esoteric techniques also apply, for instance, the use of an animal's scapula. For healing rites, various dialectics are used, the best known being "signs," in which the apparent properties of an animal or plant designate that animal or plant as a remedy for a given sickness. For instance, a stiff joint is wrapped in the supple skin of an eel. Other rites refer to Christian symbolisms: the ass that had the privilege of carrying Christ may show up in certain therapeutic techniques.

All these myths and rites certainly suggest a syncretising of religious elements that originated in very different sources. But from a more phenomenological point of view, we should rather be talking of symbiosis. For these borrowings are not purely artificial, nor have they been artificially preserved. Once incorporated into the mythical universe of the Gypsies, they took on new life, allowing this marginalized people to preserve its identity to this day.

F.C./g.h.

BIBLIOGRAPHY

In general, see F. COZANNET, *Mythes et coutumes religieuses des Tsiganes* (Paris 1973), which contains all the desired references.

There are many monographs, most of which are to be found in two specialized journals: *Journal of the Gypsy Lore Society* (Edinburgh) and *Études tsiganes* (Paris).

See also the analyses in the following general works: J. BLOCH, "Que sais-je?" *Les tsiganes* (3d ed., Paris 1969). M. BLOCH, *Mæurs et coutumes des tsiganes* (Paris 1936), originally in German. F. BOTEY, *El Gitano* (Barcelona 1970). J.-P. CLEBERT, *Les tsiganes* (Paris 1961). A. COLOCCI, *Gli Zingari* (Turin 1889). C. DUFF, *A Mysterious People: An Introduction to the Gypsies of All Countries* (London 1965). E. FALQUE, *Voyage et tradition: Les Manouches* (Paris 1971). R. LIEBICH, *Die Zigeuner in ihrem Wesen und in ihrer Sprache* (Leipzig 1883). J.-P. LIÉGEOIS, *Les tsiganes* (Paris 1971); *Mutation tsigane* (Brussels 1976). W. IN DER MAUR, *Die Zigeuner, Wanderer zwischen den Welten* (Vienna 1969). P. SERBOIANU, *Les tsiganes: Histoire, ethnographie, linguistique,* trans. from Romanian (Paris 1930). W. SIMSON, *A History of the Gypsies* (London 1961). F. VAUX DE FOLETIER, *Les tsiganes dans l'ancienne France* (Paris 1961); *Mille ans d'histoire des tsiganes* (Paris 1971). G. E. C. WEBB, *Gypsies, the Secret People* (London 1961).

The following vocabularies are also very useful: M. COLINON, *Les Gitans, vocabulaire, tradition et images* (Manosque 1975). S. A. WOLF, *Grosses Wörterbuch der Zigeunersprache* (Mannheim 1960).

Fable and Mythology in Seventeenth- and Eighteenth-Century Literature and Theoretical Reflection

For anyone who hopes to define the status of ancient myths in the seventeenth and eighteenth centuries, there are two extremely dissimilar domains for consideration. One domain includes all the events of culture (poetry, theater, ballet, painting, sculpture, decorative arts) in which mythological motifs are recognizable; the other comprises the historical, critical, and speculative texts that attempt to elaborate a knowledge of myths, a science of myths. In the period in question, this distinction was clearly expressed by terms that demarcated to the fullest extent the difference established by contemporaries between the free use of mythological motifs and the studied knowledge of myths: for the former, *fable,* and for the latter, *mythology.*

I. The Function of Fable in Classical Culture

Fable is the body of received ideas about the gods of paganism. Largely founded on Hesiod, Ovid, Apollodorus, and more recent popularizers (such as Natale Conti), it is a repertory of genealogies, adventures, metamorphoses, and allegorical correlations. And as the motifs of fables are omnipresent—among the ancients read in secondary schools, in the tragedies seen at the theater, in historical presentations, in decorations and dwellings—fable is an obligatory discipline in the education of a respectable man. Thus a circle is formed: it is necessary to know fables in order to understand the works offered by recent and ancient culture; and, because fable is learned, and the ancient model remains alive, new works that are composed go back to fable either to borrow its subject matter or to use its ornamentation—in depictions, emblems, and phrases.

Rollin, in the sixth book (part four) of his *Treatise of Studies* (1726), which remained authoritative for more than a century, mentions fable and justifies its study in a subtle way:

> There is hardly a subject in the study of belles lettres that is either of a greater utility than that of which I speak here, or that lends itself better to profound scholarship. . . .

Without knowledge of fable, there can be no knowledge of literature:

> It is (an advantage) of great application . . . for the understanding of authors, be they Greek, Latin, or even French, in the reading of whom one is stopped short if one does not have some tincture of fable. I am not only speaking of poets, of whom we know this to be almost the natural language: it is also often employed by orators; and it sometimes furnishes, through favorable application, the liveliest and most eloquent touches. . . . There are other kinds of books to which everyone is exposed: paintings, engravings, tapestries, and statues. These are so many enigmas to those who are ignorant of fable, which often serves as their explanation and their key. It is not rare for people to speak of such matters in conversation. It seems to me not at all agreeable to remain silent and to appear stupid in a group for lack of instruction in a matter that may be learned in youth at little expense.

Knowledge of fable is the very condition for the legibility of the entire cultural world. It is one of the prerequisites for participation in the "conversations" in which an educated man is called on to play a part. Fable, for Rollin, is indispensable to anyone who would understand the aesthetic milieu in its entirety, and who would be accepted into a chosen "group." It thus serves a double function; it is an imaginal language offering access to a certain type of organized speech, and this language functions as a social sign of recognition between individuals who can decipher in the same fashion the universe of mythic fictions.

Jaucourt, in his *Encyclopedia* article on "Fable," is in emphatic agreement:

> This is why knowledge, at least superficial knowledge, of fable is so common. Our plays, both lyric and dramatic, and every genre of our poetry allude to it perpetually; the engravings, paintings, and statues that adorn our cham-

Oedipus. From Mme. de Genlis, *Arabesques mythologiques* (1810–11), vol. 2, pl. 4. Paris, Bibliothèque nationale. Photo BN.

Perseus. From Mme. De Genlis, *Arabesques mythologiques* (1810–11), vol. 2, pl. 2. Paris, Bibliothèque nationale. Photo BN.

> bers, our galleries, our ceilings, and our gardens are nearly always drawn from fable: finally, it is so widely used in all of our writings, our novels, our pamphlets, and even in our ordinary conversations that it is impossible to be unaware of it at least to a degree without having to blush at one's lack of education.
>
> . . . Fable is the heritage of the arts; it is a source of ingenious ideas, of humorous images, of interesting subjects, of allegories and emblems whose use—whether more or less favorable--responds to genius and taste. Everything is active and endowed with breath in that enchanted world where intellectual beings have bodies, where countrysides, forests, and rivers have their particular divinities: I know that these are chimerical characters, but the role they play in the writings of the ancient poets, and the frequent allusions made to them by modern poets, have almost made them real for us. Our eyes are so accustomed to them that it is difficult for us to see them as imaginary beings.

The author of an *Elementary Encyclopedia,* which appeared in 1775, betrays irritation with fable but nevertheless maintains its necessity. His way of recommending Chompré's *Dictionary of Fable* (which Rollin had already hailed) clearly shows that this work, being at once an allegorical iconology and a repertory of fabulous heroes, aims not so much to examine the substance of myths as to decipher the *attributes* used by artists: at most, it is a semiological code that serves to express an "intention" in a consecrated language:

> It is an assemblage of puerile tales bereft of verisimilitude, which would be worthy of scorn were these chimeras not absolutely necessary in order to understand the ancient authors, to be moved by the beauties of poetry, of pictures and allegories, and even to make use of an infinity of conventional expressions, such as "She's a Megara, a Fury, a Muse." . . . I invite my readers to equip themselves with the small portable *Dictionary* by M. Chompré. It is very useful to young people and, indeed, to everyone. Whether one is looking, for example, for the subject of a tapestry, a picture, or an allegorical piece, with this book one is certain of finding it.
>
> If there is an eagle, look up this word, and it will refer you to *Jupiter,* to *Periphas,* and to *Ganymede.* If it is a scythe, you will find *Saturn* or *Time.* If a figure is holding a trumpet, the word trumpet will refer you to *Fame.* . . . Through the attributes you will come to know the subjects: and with a little judgment you will come to guess the artist's intention.[1]

This dictionary enables one to slip from one language into another; it is a translation tool, permitting artists and poets to find the appropriated "figures" and, furthermore, ensuring that readers will be able to go back from the figure to the original idea. Recourse to the dictionary postulates a disjunction between appearance and meaning, which is immediately nullified by a system of fixed correlations, a system that makes all possible strangeness vanish from allegory. For this reason, the use of mythological figures is reduced to a stylistic procedure: the reader or spectator is to translate the image of trumpet by the concept of Fame; and if a particular image of the trumpet holds our attention by the elegance of its form or the shine of its brass, an informed reading will avoid tarrying over this literalness whose only function is to be temporary, to indicate the "elevated" or "noble" register of the expression.

Reduced to this sort of lexicon, fable—even as it refers back to a fictive past located in Greco-Latin space—takes on an ahistorical appearance: in it, everything becomes simultaneous, even genealogies. Fable develops its networks synchronically, as if it were the vocabulary of a single state of language. The internal chronology of fable is not inscribed in the historical passage of time. From the moment that the gods, their names, their cults, their connections with people and places, etc., become the object of historical research, fable becomes an object of scholarship, and is no longer the closed and self-sufficient system we have described. It then becomes a matter for "antiquaries" (if they restrict themselves to inventories of exhumed documents: statues, altars, medals, side by side with written sources such as inscriptions, literary texts, etc.) or for mythologists (if they develop hypotheses on the origin of fables, and on the differences or resemblances between the religious beliefs of various peoples, etc.). This is a difficult and dangerous domain, and Rollin advises educators to halt at its threshold: "It would be best, it seems to me, to avoid what is related only to scholarship and would render the study of fable more difficult and less agreeable; or, at least, to relegate reflections of this kind to brief notes."

Jaucourt ends his *Encyclopedia* article on "Fable" by drawing up a program of mythological knowledge that goes beyond a mere familiarity with the figures of fables:

> But to carry one's curiosity to the point of attempting to pierce the diverse meanings or the mysteries of fable, to understand the different theological systems, and to know the cults of the pagan gods is a branch of learning reserved for a small number of scholars; and the branch of learning that constitutes a very large part of belles lettres, and is absolutely necessary in order to have an understanding of the monuments of antiquity, is what is called *Mythology.*

It is thus a matter of interpreting the figures of fable according to the exigencies of a historical, genetic, and systematic understanding. Whereas fable itself, in a vulgarized and facile form, is a universal means for "poetizing" everything, "mythology" questions it about its origins, its intellectual import, its revelatory value, and its ties with institutions and customs. In short, the semantic opposition between fable and mythology may be enunciated as the difference between a generalized and stabilized interpretive system, and a rational type of reflection that makes this interpretive system an object to be interpreted according to other criteria of validity.

The renewal of myth at the end of the seventeenth century arose from this type of scholarly reflection, which applied itself to understanding mythic inventiveness in a new way since stereotyped recourse to fable had revealed itself to be sterile and tedious. Nevertheless, before reviewing the development of mythological theories, we must define, more clearly than we have done thus far, the function of fable in the "classical" European—especially French—culture of the seventeenth and eighteenth centuries.

In a culture that tolerates the coexistence of the domains of the sacred and of the profane, fable clearly occupies the profane area: it inhabits the world of mundane diversions. We may even go so far as to say that, by its avowed absence of truth value, fable is the very index of the futility of mundane existence. Fable desires to be nothing more than fiction or ornament, or, at most, scholarly remembrance. Its authority is declared to be nil vis-à-vis religious authority from the very start. As aestheticized paganism, claiming no more than beauty or grace, it is not a dangerous rival to the Christian orthodoxies—unless souls allow themselves to be unduly controlled by it and to become inflamed by the impure examples of the pagan pantheon.

Let us return to Rollin, the perfect spokesman for the religious institution at the beginning of the eighteenth century. When he includes fable in his educational program, it is not only in order to enhance the understanding of literary or pictorial works. It should also serve as a warning, as a counterproof to Christian truth:

> This study, when followed with the caution and wisdom that religion demands and inspires, may be of great utility to the young.
>
> First, it teaches them what they owe to Jesus Christ their liberator, who freed them from the powers of darkness and allowed them to move into the admirable light of the Gospel. What were men before him . . . ? Fable gives us the answer. They were blind worshipers of the devil who knelt before gold, silver, and marble; who offered silver to deaf and dumb statues; who recognized gods in animals, reptiles, and even plants. . . . Every story told in fable, every circumstance in the life of the gods, should at once fill us with confusion, admiration, and recognition. . . . A second advantage of fable lies in the fact that, in disclosing the absurd ceremonies and impious maxims of paganism, it inspires in us a new respect for the august majesty of the Christian religion, and for the sanctity of its morality.

Belief is thus to be reserved for the sole legitimate authority, revealed dogma; whereas these pagan figures are to be censured, even though in everyday life—as Rollin recognizes—their visual images, ever-renewed, surround us. At the very least, and in spite of its power to seduce, the unreality of fable leaves no doubt about the vanity of worldly existence. The presence of fable is a sure indication that worldly desires lead one astray into "false" objects. Thus the necessity of directing one's love toward its true object—God, Christ—becomes all the more urgent.

But the demarcation between the sacred and the profane has its own legitimacy, for it is postulated by religious authority itself. By way of determining the exact domain of its own jurisdiction, religious authority tolerates the existence of an external domain, which it watches over without forcing it to comply with its strictest rules. In order not to break the ties with the sacred order, human life is permitted to unfold, in part, in a profane time and space; and the figures inherited from a sacred order that has come to an end—the order of paganism—may innocently serve as ornaments to a part of existence that is not directly governed by the truths of the faith. Certainly, the imaginary is dangerous, and the images of desire constitute a grave peril to Christian souls: but in one way—in the form of a pantheon to which no one could try to attach any serious belief—orthodoxy permits a *superficial* survival of what is, in another way, censured and repulsed by Christian ethics. Hence, in a more or less balanced compromise, Christianity (and especially the Catholicism of the Counterreformation) allowed the entire universe of polytheistic drives and undercurrents—which it had historically supplanted and which its true believers were invited to deny and surpass—to coexist by its side, though in the form of a gratuitous image and a defused fiction. This compromise authorizes a certain duplicity: "worldly" people (including the king himself) could taste of profane diversions, surround themselves with pagan scenes, and even become actors in mythological ballets, but they had to listen to the preachers and receive the sacraments.

Love and ambition—the two great provinces in which worldly concupiscence operates (*libido sentiendi, libido dominandi*)—celebrate their triumphs in the disguise of fable. In love poetry, recourse to the code of fable is a part of a system of distancing which, in transposing feeling into heroic or pastoral fiction, allows desire to be made manifest, while giving it a glorious, purified expression which is detached from trivial contingency. In this sense, fable ensures a displacement of all of the elements of discourse in the direction of a register that is entirely ludic and "polite"—which is exactly what defines the "gallant" attitude. When we recall that the principal corpus of myths—Ovid's *Metamorphoses*—already has a strong ludic component, it is obvious that in order to satisfy the taste for novelty, for the "piquant," which held sway in cultivated circles, artists and poets strove to outdo one another in playing this game. This competitive bidding is particularly perceptible in the art of the European rococo, with its proliferation of the decorative, its supple sinuousity, and its ornamental use of miniatures. But this element of the intellectual game, at times combined with more authentically experienced components, is already apparent in mannerism and in the vogue for literary conceits (as, for instance, in the *Adonis* of Marini); we find it again in the affectation of the seventeenth century, and it is still present in the badinages of the end of the eighteenth century. Benserade and his *Metamorphoses of Ovid Set in Rondeaux* are an excellent example of this excess of affectation: the work was seen as "piquant" because it was a well-tempered paraphrase that made use of a small, regular form to abridge and rework a Latin text whose mythic content had itself already been made the object of playful levity. The game is thus doubled. The rondeau is a miniature in comparison to the model it imitates: all is made to turn in a tight circle of twelve verses, of which the first four syllables reappear two more times—concluding the poem in their final appearance. At the end of the ancien régime, in C. A. Demoustier's *Letters to Emilie about Mythology,* the mythic narrative is reduced to banter interspersed with verse: the versified elements are sometimes episodes or commentaries from the narrative, sometimes gallant compliments to the person addressed. This form, inherited from the seventeenth century, becomes so light as to be meaningless. Here again, the mythology, which is told letter by letter, undergoes a paring down, an attenuation, turning it into the minimal substance of an adventure story and the excuse for a facile pedagogy whose aim is merely to please. It is only one step away from that work patronized by Madame de Genlis, in which all that remains of the gods is their names, represented by calligraphy in the form of an emblem.

Yet the mythic repertory that is capable of transcribing current events or feelings in a fictive register may also serve to magnify and celebrate them in a triumphant mode. Miniaturization is just one of the propensities of the joyous imagination, the one in which play seeks to ally itself with the conquest of innocent levity. When play, on the other hand, becomes charged with glorifying intentions, it magnifies without allowing itself to be restrained by the regulations of the real world. The mythological fiction makes possible the laudatory hyperbole, which would otherwise be unpronounceable within the bounds of Christian order. For a victory in battle, the Christian festival culminates in the adoration of the God of armies: *Te Deum laudamus.* But the Christian festival has as its double a profane and thus mythological festival, which exalts the prince himself: he is compared with Mars or Hercules, he is the favorite of Bellona, and so forth. For a princely birth, Christian baptism has its double in ceremonies or poems of fabulous inspiration, in which announcements are made of nothing less than the imminent return of Astraeus and the Golden Age. The apotheosis of the prince may set the stage for his lawful representatian within a system of divine figures, the validity of which is established, from the start of the game, as belonging to the past and which is now pure appearance. This "white" divinization allows the energies of celebration to blossom; and while these powers remain captives of the Greco-Roman model, they allow for every sort of extravagance, for they pretend to be nothing but pure show. The Sun King is allowed to dance in the costume of Apollo. Jupiter can descend from the sky, in a stage machine, to announce to future centuries an illustrious lineage of sovereigns.

Although the conventional system of Greco-Roman mythology favors a purifying or glorifying transmutation, it is no less vulnerable for this, since the authority upon which it is founded is nothing more than an aesthetic habit. There is nothing to protect it against parody, or against the ebb of tastes, which would abandon mythic embellishment to return to the ordinary reality of desire.

The direction taken by satire and comedy in the seventeenth century was to remove the masks, to reverse the trajectory of the mythological enterprise with its purifying trends (affectation) or glorifying trends (the ideal of the nobility), and to return to literalness all that the mythological code had previously transferred into the metaphorical dimension. In contrast to the tableaux in which desire is exalted and divinized, satire brings us down again into the world of everyday life and into the reality of instinct in its brutal state. The following episode from the *Discourse on the Journey of Saint-Germain in Laye,* which figures in the *Satirical Cabinet* (1618), is exemplary in this regard: the mythic decor is read as an erotic stimulant:

Mais faisons, je vous pry, pour saouler nostre veuë,
Dans la chambre du Roy encore une reveuë.
Voyez, en cest endroit, comme Mars et Venus
Se tiennent embrassez, languissans et tous nuds;
Voyez les à ce coing, en une autre posture:
Avez-voux jamais veu si lascive peinture?
Haussez un peu les yeux, et voyez les encore
En une autre façon, dessus ce plancher d'or;
Voyez les ici pres, tous deux encore aus prises.
Quoy! tout est plain d'Amours et de flames éprises,
Dans ceste belle chambre! Allons, fuyons ces lieux:
Sortons-en, je vous prie, ou bien faisons comme eux!

But I pray you, to proclaim our vows,
Let us meet again in the bedroom of the King.
Look over there, as Mars and Venus
Embrace, languishing and entirely nude;
Look at them over here, in a different position:

Have you ever seen such a sexy painting?
Raise your eyes a bit, and look at them again
In a different form, above this golden floor-board;
Look at them close by here, the two of them still locked together.
O my! Everything is full of love-making and heated passion,
In this beautiful bedroom! Come on, let's get out of here:
Let's leave, I beg you, or else do what they are doing!

One may be sacrilegious with impunity when dealing with the pseudo-sacred. Burlesque plays freely upon such license. The great mythic images that are used to ennoble the circumstances of public and private life are the means of transmutation and travesty. By disfiguring and caricaturing them, one realizes a return to their trivial reality: to travesty what was a means of travesty is to nullify its depicted purity and glory, and to return to the grit and smell of the world as it exists for those who have lost their illusions. Dassoucy's *Ovid in a Good Mood,* Scarron's *Virgil Travestied,* the young Marivaux's *Homer Travestied,* and Blumauer's late *Virgil's Aeneas Travestied* (Vienna 1732–94) constitute more than attacks on the most highly respected literary models. Through those models, they assault the very virtues that were exalted by the epico-mythic tradition: warlike exploits, the sacrifice of one's life for country and glory. Their mockery, which took aim at the heroes and gods of antiquity, was more generally directed against the heroic ideal. The simple pleasure of living is of far greater value. What is denounced, then, is fictive immortality, a deal offered to fools, counterfeit money whose mythic celebration pays those who shed their blood on the field of battle. Following the wars of Louis XIV, parody, as employed by Marivaux, attacked not only the ancients and their partisans but, even more, the illusions of military glory. Verses such as these (addressed by Andromache to Hector) are demobilizing. They "demystify" the common ground of the undying memory:

Oh! great gods! when I contemplate
The afflicted state of widowhood,
I find a bed to be quite fearsome,
When in that bed we are no longer two!
Once the bloody Achilles
Killed my father in a town . . .
Well then! What was its name?
I do not remember its name.
He buried him himself, it is said,
With great sumptuousness:
But when a body is buried,
What is the good of honoring it?
No matter what glory one is buried with,
One has nothing but the earth for cover.

This resolutely worldly confession of faith (which reduces death to mere interment), in challenging a "pagan" image of immortality,[2] implies disbelief in Christian immortality. We might even say that parody is a burlesque of mythic narratives and pastoral or warlike fables which does not limit its destructive effect to the aesthetic dimension alone, or even to the hierarchy of "official" values: indirectly it directs itself against the highest authority. For, even though fictive, the world of fable nonetheless offers images of a sovereignty that is homologous to the ruling sovereignty but is, so to speak, legal tender. To attack Jupiter and the gods of fable is, according to one's insinuations, to attack in *effigy,* and with impunity, the king and the powerful, the holiness of God, of the Pope, and so forth. Since the world of fable is, by the decree of the spiritual powers that be, a profane world without any true sacred content, there can be no blasphemy or lèse-majesté in disfiguring it. The critique leveled by libertinism against religion or against the centralizing monarchy can thus be effected obliquely by attacking (in appearance) only those powers which the least suspect Christian tradition had never ceased to condemn. As may be seen, the duality of the (Christian) sacred and the profane (placed in its "mythological" setting) is arranged in such a way as to make it possible to play sometimes upon their separation and their mutual exclusion and sometimes upon their parallelism and their isomorphism. If pagan and Christian sovereignty are considered in their formal similarity (an identical structure in which all is dependent upon a supreme divinity; an identical presence of the miraculous), then a polemic against Christianity (or against the superstitious aspects of Christianity) may be developed in total safety by directing its darts only against what at first sight appears to be the gods of paganism (for example, the article "Jupiter" in Bayle's *Dictionary*). If Christianity and paganism are viewed as incompatible, hos-

Louis XIV as the Sun God in the ballet *La nuit,* 1653. Anonymous watercolor. Paris, Bibliothèque nationale. Photo Giraudon.

tility to Christianity may be manifested by the more dangerous means of resolutely favoring the world of fable. Under the cover of an aesthetic tradition that had become acclimated to mythological fiction and had given it its noble pedigree, the rebellious mind would proclaim its preference for the pagan fable over the doctrine imposed by the Church, which was no less fabulous and lying but was a thousand times less agreeable. This was the time when anti-Christian feeling first showed its face unveiled: that open antipathy recurred several times after the Renaissance, but especially in the seventeenth century. In the case of a Voltaire, the option of paganism—in his *Apology for Fable*—does not so much attest an authentic sentiment in favor of the world of myth as it attests the opportunism of a method of propaganda that is capable of putting barbs on anything:

Savante antiquité, beauté toujours nouvelle,
Monument du génie, heureuses fictions,
Environnez-moi des rayons
De votre lumière immortelle:
Vous savez animer l'air, la terre, et les mers;
Vous embellisez l'univers.
Cet arbre á tête longue, aux rameaux toujours verts,
C'est Atys, aié de Cybèle;
La précoce hyacinthe est le tendre mignon
Que sur ces prés fleuris caressait Apollon. . . .

Wise antiquity, beauty always new,
Monument of genius, happy fictions,
Surround me with the rays
Of your immortal light:
You know how to animate the air, the earth, and the seas;
You embellish the universe.
This tree with the high head, with branches always green,
It is Atys, loved by Cybele;
The precocious hyacinth is the tender darling
Whom Apollo caressed in these flowering meadows. . . .

Another series of examples follows, and Voltaire continues:

Tout l'Olympe est peuplé de héros amoureux.
Admirables tableaux! séduisante magie!
Qu'Hésiode me plaît dans sa théologie
Quand il me peint l'Amour débrouillant le chaos,
S'élançant dans les airs, et planant sur les flots!
Vantex-nous maintenant, bienheureux légendaires,
Le porc de saint Antoine, et le chien de saint Roch
Vos reliques, vos scapulaires,
Et la guimpe d'Ursule, et la crasse du froc;
Mettez la Fleur des saints à côté d'un Homère:
Il ment, mais en grand homme; il ment, mais il sait plaire;
Sottement vous avez menti:
Pour lui l'esprit humain s'éclaire:
Et, si l'on vous croyait, il serait abruti.
On chérira toujours les erreurs de la Grèce;
Toujours Ovide charmera.

All of Olympus is peopled with amorous heroes.
Admirable scenes! Seductive magic!
How Hesiod pleases me with his theology
When he depicts Love disentangling chaos,
Bounding in the air and soaring on the waves!
Praise us now, you fortunate creatures of legend,
The pig of Saint Anthony, and the dog of Saint Roch,
Your relics, your scapulars,
And the wimple of Ursula, and the squalor of the monk's robe;
Put the Flower of the saints next to a Homer:
He lies, but like a man; he lies, but he knows how to please;
You have lied stupidly:
With him, the human mind is enlightened:
But if anyone believed you, he would be made stupid as a brute.
People will always cherish the errors of Greece;
Ovid will always charm.

Voltaire appears less inclined actually to enter the world of fable than to make an ally of it in his battle for the Enlightenment and for a civilization of earthly happiness. His *Apology for Fable*, far from taking him out of his own element, only confirms his choice—in favor of an urban civilization and the pleasures to be had through the arts—which is proclaimed in his famous poem *The Man of the World.* Voltaire's Homer, through whom "the human mind is enlightened," has nothing "primitive" about him. Fable, as sung by Voltaire, comes down to a modern, profane diversion, in clear contrast to religious practice. The dichotomy of the sacred and the profane, to which we have alluded from the start, is nowhere more noticeable than in the final verses of the poem:

Si nos peuples nouveaux sont chrétiens à la messe,
Ils sont païens à l'Opéra.
L'almanach est païen, nous comptons nos journées
Par le seul nom des dieux que Rome avait connus;
C'est Mars et Jupiter, c'est Saturne et Vénus,
Qui président au temps, qui font nos destinées.
Ce mélange est impur, on a tort; mais enfin
Nous ressemblons assez à l'abbé Pellegrin,
"Le matin catholique, et le soir idolâtre,
Déjeûnant de l'autel, et soupant du théâtre."

If our new peoples are Christians at Mass,
They are pagans at the Opera.
The almanac is pagan, in which we measure our days
Only with the name of the gods that Rome knew;
It is Mars and Jupiter, it is Saturn and Venus,
That preside over time, that make our destinies.
This mixture is impure, it is wrong; but in the end
We resemble rather closely the Abbé Pellegrin:
"Catholic in the morning, and idolatrous in the evening,
Lunching at the altar, and dining at the theater."

Up to this point we have considered myth only in its formal and most general aspect; that is, as the agent of an aesthetic transformation on the profane level, under the assumption that the starting point of myth was regularly presented in a circumstance of life that one wished to celebrate, to purify, or to magnify. But the mythological code, with its variants and its multiple branches, also exists for itself, independent of those embellishments to which it might serve as a vehicle. It presents a broad canvas abounding in passionate connections, extreme situations, and monstrous acts. Upon this preexisting material, imagination and desire may freely project their most authentic energies by making use of its choices and scenarios. Certain seventeenth- and eighteenth-century works may be regarded as reinterpretations of great mythical themes—with the proviso that these artists were less interested in modifying the meaning of myths than in using them as a field for the free play of their faculties. In its received form, of course, myth remains a "subject" that demands respect. But in an aesthetics which, contrary to our own, did not place a premium on the kind of "originality" that could produce content, subject, and style (i.e., the entirety of a work's constituent parts) ex nihilo, the freedom of expression left to the artist in treating a known fable in whichever way he desired was enough to liberate, in certain cases, some very deep-seated forces. Even the most apparently frivolous narrative or tragedy can be intensely seductive in its hidden meanings. As told by LaFontaine, the story of Psyche, in its playful and free form, is charged throughout with symbols that are piled upon the primary data and revolve around the themes of the secret and of instant recognition. *Andromache, Iphigenia,* and *Phaedra* are plays in which the mythic element is psychologized, thus allowing for the free play of the dark forces of passion. The abandoned Ariadne or Dido present lyricism as well as music with an occasion for the melodious *lamento,* the mournful lament. Under the safeguard and the cover of an existing myth, which offers it a form of reception, desire is allowed to live out its imaginary satisfaction impersonally. The traditional mythic structures are perceived as obstacles only from the time when the exigencies of personal expression are to prevail. The role played by the mythic universe as foundation for and receiver of projections of desire is complemented by a more intellectual function, which may build pedagogical, political, or ethical constructs upon the epico-mythical schemata. The mythic framework allows for the embellishment, enlargement, and "detemporalization" of moral lessons for the edification of young princes. Fénelon's *Telemachus* is at once a prose poem, a "Bildungsroman," and a political utopia. The Odyssean setting, with its foam-capped sea, its apparitions of Amphitrite, and its nymphs lying under verdant arbors, ensures a harmonious fusion of these composite elements. Mentor, who is Minerva, in the guise of a profane fable lavishly distributes a lesson of wisdom in which the most rigorous precepts of Christian doctrine are protected, decanted, universalized, and rendered agreeable.

Furthermore, in examining the choices made by seventeenth- and eighteenth-century writers and artists working within this mythic complex, one cannot help but observe the emphasis on certain themes, according to the period in question, that point to a common anxiety often related to the preoccupations to which that particular time was sensitive. It is fair to say that the baroque, haunted by the changeableness of appearances, enjoyed fables of metamorphosis (Bernini's *Daphne* is one case among many). *Pygmalions* abounded in the eighteenth century, not only because that century posed the question of the animation of matter, but also because its artists dreamed of an imitative perfection for which they might be rewarded by a loving embrace from their own work come to life. It is no coincidence that the sole writing of Jean-Jacques Rousseau on a mythical subject is a *Pygmalion,* in which the writer's fundamental narcissism is given free play: the artist's desire is paid back by the being formed by him as the image of his ideal. A limit has been reached here. The fable of Pygmalion represented, in a language that was still mythic, a demand for self-expression whose next manifestation would consist of a rejection of any mythic mediation, any recourse to preexisting fable. Similarly, in a later period (around 1800), certain heroic myths (Prometheus, Heracles, Ganymede) would be called upon to express hope and revolt: the apotheosis of the human hero makes it possible to glimpse a future in which the rule of the ancient gods will have collapsed, giving way to man. Here again, mythic language tends toward its own abolition, to the extent that the disappearance of the authority of the gods carries with it the fall of traditional imagic discourse as this was organized around them. This would lead, ultimately in Wagner's *Twilight of the Gods,* to recourse to a total myth culminating in the fall of the mythic universe, conceived as a now inoperative expression of an ancient law of the world.

But this tendency, far from being the only one, is mirrored—as we shall see—by an exactly opposite tendency.

II. The Growth of Mythological Theories

Fable, stabilized in the form of a body of fixed accounts and symbols which are indefinitely repeatable, can thus, in the most favorable cases, be relived, reanimated, and given presence by a fiery imagination capable of projecting its dream upon a preexistent image. A musician or painter (more often than a poet) could at times, in the eighteenth century, breathe new life, a passionate shiver, a seemingly invented strangeness, into the theme of a fable.

But the renaissance of mythic material took place via a more circuitous path which, paradoxically, at first sight seemed to be leading to the death and final expulsion of fable. It was mythology—that is, scholarly discourse applied to myths—that put the world of fable to death, but even in doing so it gave it the grounds, in an unexpected way, for a new, enlarged, and rejuvenated efflorescence.

It was a case of a progressive evolution, whose stages are not difficult to trace.

The mythology of the eighteenth century fuses, in variable proportions, the learning of the antiquarians (concerning the attributes of the gods, places of worship, written sources, coins, etc.) and the conjectures of the theologians: the convenient hypothesis, which goes back to Clement of Alexandria, is that the pagan gods are the pluralized and degenerate reflections of the true God of which Genesis speaks, or of the kings of the sacred scriptures. For infidels and sinners, primordial Revelation has been progressively obscured. After the dispersion of Babel, when people had forgotten the first and only God, nothing held them back from divinizing their princes, their rivers, their animals. But, in the same way that the pagans' languages, in the eyes of the etymologists, are corrupt derivatives of the Hebrew, so one can divine in their deities, though falling short, the holy religion of which they are the distorted reflection. The Abbé Banier perfectly summarizes this common view:

> In the earliest times, men worshiped one God. Noah preserved in his family the devotion his fathers had offered to the creator; but it did not take his descendants long to corrupt its purity. The crimes to which they abandoned themselves soon weakened the idea of the Divine, and people began to associate it with perceptible objects. What appeared to them to be the brightest and most perfect in nature moved them to homage; and for this reason the sun was the first object of their superstition. From sun worship, they moved to the worship of other celestial bodies and planets, and the entire heavenly troop . . . attracted a religious cult to itself, as did the elements, the rivers, and mountains. Things did not stop there; nature itself was regarded as a divinity, and under different names she became the object of worship for different nations. Finally, great men were seen as meriting, either by their conquests or by their invention of the arts, honors due only to the Creator of the Universe: and this was the origin of all the gods adored by paganism.

Such a mythological system places the various traditional theories of the origins of myths (Euhemerism, astral symbolism, etc.) on an equal footing in order to explain the false religions even as it indicts them, all the while maintaining, intact, the authority of a primary Revelation, of which the Church has remained the depository.

But this orthodox mythology, in developing a psychological explanation for the cause of the crimes and the impiety of the infidel nations, engendered an even bolder line of thought directed at the very motives of every faith and every form of devotion: the skeptics would use it to undercut the authority that orthodoxy thought to preserve and reinforce. The weapons used by the Church against superstition could easily be turned against the Faith, and the most common ruse was to attack Church dogma itself, in the guise of carrying on the fight led by the defenders of the Faith against idolatry. From this point on, the God of the Hebrews was to be submitted to a causal interpretation analogous to the one that the theologians reserved for the pagan gods. The explanation given by Lucretius, "inborn dread" (*insitus horror,* 5.1160–1239), would hold for every cult without exception. (The "libertine" current of the seventeenth century had widely cultivated this return to the Epicurean doctrine.) Fable, instead of being secondary and derivative, would appear as the primary response of men to the terrors of dreams, to great natural events, to all that amazed them.

Fontenelle's short dissertation *Origin of Fables* connects myths and polytheism with simple causes: ignorance, wonder, terror in the face of the powers experienced everywhere in nature, and the propensity to explain the unknown by the known. Fables offer us "the history of the errors of the human mind." It follows that one should not hesitate to learn every aspect of fable; mythology is to be practiced as Fontenelle does it in order that we may be set right: "To fill one's head with all the excesses of the Phoenicians and the Greeks is not a science, but to know what led the Phoenicians and the Greeks to these excesses is indeed a science. All mankind is so alike that there is no people whose idiocies should not make us tremble."

Here we see the meeting between scorn for fable and the affirmation of the great epistemological value of reflecting on the beginnings of our relationship to the world and on the errors committed by the mind when it was first left to its own devices. Everything began, for the savage as well as for the infant, with a deplorable propensity for false explanations, up to the time when our intelligence, as it was slowly and progressively disabused, became capable of laughing at its childish beliefs, and even of knowing why it allowed itself to be drawn into the world of fable. The cultivated mind sees a warning here too: the "primitive" errors into which every people has fallen are also errors of every period, and nothing is easier than falling back into error. One must always be on one's guard against yielding to the ever-renewed temptation of myth. Our imagination ever remains receptive to myth even when our reason denies it: "While we may be incomparably more enlightened than those whose crude minds invented the Fables in good faith, we all too easily return to that same way of thinking that made Fables so agreeable to them. They passed them on because they believed them, and we pass them on with just as much pleasure even though without belief; all of which proves that imagination and reason can have little to do with one another, and that matters of which reason has been disabused from the start lose nothing of their attractiveness as regards the imagination." The dichotomy of the sacred and the profane, which allowed fable to subsist on the periphery of sacred history, is thus replaced by the dichotomy of reason and imagination. Once again, fable is regarded as stripped of all truth, all authority; it is reason (and not revelation) that is master. But the imaginary and the pleasure that attaches to it are not branded with any moral reprobation: they are perfectly legitimate so long as they do not usurp the prerogatives of reason. Illusion has the right to enchant us as long as we know that we are in the realm of poetry and not science: when we give in to the seductions of myth, by playing its game we tarry in a world that we were capable of leaving behind forever. The poets of the childhood of the world—Homer and Hesiod—are certainly admirable, but their great images are nothing but the reverse side of their ignorance. In the perspective of a progressive becoming in which reason perfects itself from one century to the next, myth is the innocent witness to the first babblings of the mind, starting from the time when the soul could speak only in metaphor to voice its terrors and its wonders. This general theory of myth places all faiths on an equal footing: it makes an exception for the "true religion" only as a precaution and for the sake of style. The intellectual education of men should lead them to shed all prejudices, all errors, all cults. (Such disillusionment leads to poetry that makes use of fable without admitting to it, in a cold, spiritual, and mocking tone: the entire antipoetic eighteenth century defines itself in this way.)

But not everyone bore witness to the same confidence in the powers of cultivated reason. Hume, who interprets the birth of fables more or less in the way of Fontenelle, betrays doubt about the constructs of reason. It is possible that these constructs are no more solid than the polytheistic cosmogonies—in which case our "progress" becomes precarious, and the pleasure that we derive from ancient myths is less childish than it might appear. In our uncertainty regarding the true, myth can at least claim the privilege of beauty, without being any more of a lie than the things we take to be reasonable. Reason that is divested of illusions about its own powers can still show indulgence for the first creatures produced by the imagination.

The complete rehabilitation of myth would soon follow in this vein. But in order for this to occur, the primary experience of the mind, instead of being assigned the mark of imperfection, had to become endowed with the character of plenitude, the prerogative of unity. In this reevaluation of myth it is easy to see a return of theological thought, which would come to be combined with the psychological explanation of the production of primary ideas and primary feelings. *Genesis* reappears behind (or in) the simple impulses of the mind, which constitute the first stage of the genetic reconstruction of the intellectual faculties of the human race. However "stupid" we may call the child, the savage, or early man, they nevertheless lived in immediate contact with the world: they were like Adam in paradise. Revelation was not given to them from the outside like a doctrine; it ruled from within. Their knowledge consisted not in reflection but in participation: they lived in familiarity with the world and its forces. In this image of primordial community (which is itself based in myth), a primary role falls to those powers attributed to primitive language: it is at once speech and song (Strabo says this; Vossius and Vico repeat it;[3] Rousseau and Herder develop its theoretical consequences). It carries in itself the "almost inevitable impression of passion seeking to communicate itself" (Rousseau). Speech and feeling are not dissociated; expressive fidelity is absolute; there is no longer any place for lying or abstraction. The heart and speech of humans no longer make two. As for the gods that humans imagine, in the grip of terror or in a playful spirit, they are but the face of a living nature that turns toward them—a nature to which they are not strangers. Immediate to themselves, immediate to nature, humans manifest, in early lyricism and in the first great epics, the impulse in which the

Bernini, *Apollo and Daphne*. Rome, Villa Borghese Museum. Photo Alinari-Giraudon.

greatness and the limits of their mortal condition are inscribed. Such is the new conviction which restores to myths a legitimacy at once ontological and poetic, and which lends equal attention to the testimonies of every primitive literature. As if in response to this new attention, entire mythologies come to light or are partially invented: the Edda, Ossian, the sacred books of the East, the songs of the American Indians. These works reveal an art that preceded art, a poetry anterior to any rule of composition. And people took delight in recognizing, in this "barbarism," a grandeur and an energy no longer possessed by the civilized languages.

The result was not only a broadening of the field of mythological knowledge, nor a mere increase in the repertory of epic or naive texts made available to people of good taste who were weary of the frivolities of their own century. For those who experienced the power of these texts, the idea of a regenerated poetry, a language restored to its primitive vigor, inevitably prompted the desire for a new way of living and feeling which would recover the fullness of primitive times. In its nostalgia for the high language that has been lost, the mind turns toward the beginnings of societies in the hope of drawing out an enthusiasm that will give birth to songs capable of restoring to peoples, in the immediate future, the boiling impetus and the unanimous soul that have deserted them. The resurrected notion of genius is an invitation to listen to the voice which speaks out of the depths of nature and the collective consciousness. In a project of this sort, the poet, having recognized that all of the peoples of the world, at the time of their first self-affirmation, glorified themselves in their gods and heroes, felt himself drawn toward a past which he could offer to his fellow citizens in order to unite them in the state of mind of the reinvented community. Thus, it is once again toward the Greek and Roman (and, subordinately, Celtic or "Gallic") models that the French poets turned: but the traditional models themselves—after the revelation of the Nordic and Oriental antiquities—now offered a new face. Now it was no longer bad taste that was to be found in Homer, Aeschylus, Pindar, or even Virgil, but a gigantic, savage sublimity, contact with which could only be revivifying. Marked by an idealistic conviction of Neoplatonist inspiration, the Neoclassical system aspired not only to bring together the atemporal forms of the Beautiful, but also, following Winckelmann, to affirm that the archetypes of "beautiful nature" could only manifest themselves by virtue of the flowering of political liberty in the Greek city-states. At the cost of certain displacements and condensations, the deities presented in Greek statuary appear as the incarnation of this ideal, as it was fashioned by free citizens. To be sure, this perspective causes the primitive world to lose much of its harshness and ferocious savagery: the all too smooth serenity celebrated by Winckelmann as the reflection of an intelligible heaven cannot be the vehicle for energies that are meant to erupt from the mysterious depths of living nature. But for an André Chénier there is no contradiction in seeking the juxtaposition, in the Hellenic past as a whole, of a formal harmony, the heat of young desire, and, especially, the great breath of freedom. This to the extent that the imitation of the ancients amounted to more than a mere repetition of names or images: it was to be a second conquest of fire, a transfusion of energy. "Let us light our torches at their poetic fires." Herder, about the same time, hoped that the poetry of the ancients, without being made the object of a servile imitation, could become the source for a modern "heuristic poetry" which would allow for the invention of "an entirely new mythology." But he quickly recognized the difficulty there would be in reconciling "the spirit of reduction with the spirit of fiction," the "dismembering of the philosopher" with the "ordered reassembling of the poet."

The appeal is thus addressed to the poet, who is expected to awaken the collective impulse by exalting the hearts of men and restoring the presence of forgotten divine forces. At stake is society itself, people's search for renewed awareness of the bond that unites them. The figure of the ancient gods becomes charged with a political significance here. They are witnesses to what the popular soul needs in order to recognize itself; they must again become what they were: respondents and guarantors whom the social group imagined in its own image, and in whom it discovered its truth, its own nature. The privileged theater for the return of the gods as evoked by the poets is human celebration (national or universal celebration, according to whether one generalizes or particularizes its scope).

We see here the formation of a "myth of mythology" (H. Blumenberg), which makes the uncertain origins of myths coincide with the origin of the nation (or of humanity), and shows the people in a world in crisis their duty to reunite themselves with their lost origins (with lost nature) lest they lose their souls and perish. No sooner is this new myth formulated and this duty enunciated than questions are raised. Is it possible for the people of an age of science and of reasoned reflection to recover the naive wonderment of a young humanity that peopled nature with deities that were changeable and not slaves to the principle of identity (K. Ph. Moritz)? In the ode entitled *The Gods of Greece,* Schiller evokes at length the ancient host of gods: but they were banished and will never return; nature is thenceforth *entgöttert,* bereft of gods. Our poetry can only live by coming to grips with this absence, by saying that we miss them: "What must live immortally in song must perish in life." Incapable of recovering naive simplicity, modern poetry devotes itself to sentimental nostalgia. Jean-Paul would restate it in his own way: "The beautiful, rich simplicity of the child is enchanting not to another child but to someone who has lost it. . . . The Greek gods are but flat images for us, the empty clothes of our feelings, and not living beings. And while there were no false gods on earth at that time—and every people could be received as a guest at the Temple of another people—today we hardly know anything but false gods. . . . And whereas in the old days poetry was an object of the people, just as the people were the object of poetry, today we sing only while going from one office to another. . . ."

Falconet, *Pygmalion and Galatea*. Baltimore, Walters Art Gallery. Museum photo.

The impossibility of bringing ancient mythology back to life (not because we no longer admire it, but because we admire it too much and because the present time has become incapable of accepting it) merely accentuates the desire to see the birth of a new mythology. We find this idea at the end of a text (copied in Hegel's hand in 1796, but perhaps the work of Schelling, and certainly inspired by Hölderlin) known as "the oldest systematic program of German idealism": "We need a new mythology, but this mythology should be placed in the service of ideas, it should become a mythology of *reason.* Those ideas which do not present themselves in an aesthetic form—that is, a mythological form—are without interest for the people; and conversely, a mythology that is not reasonable is an object of shame for the philosopher. Thus the enlightened and those who are not enlightened will end up joining hands: mythology must become philosophical in order to make the people reasonable, and philosophy mythological, in order to make the philosophers sensitive. Then will we come to see the establishment of an eternal unity between us." In many of his writings (*Bread and Wine, Archipelagus,* etc.), Hölderlin chose to speak of the intermediate moment, the time of anxious waiting, between the irreversible disappearance of the ancient gods and the rise of a new god, a Dionysus or a Christ of the final hour. In 1800, Friedrich Schlegel in turn called for a new mythology, arising not, as had the old, from a contact with the perceptible universe, but "from the most profound depths of the spirit," just as harmonious order unfolds "when chaos is touched by love."

Though it may have been disappointed, this expectation of a new flowering of myth (a myth which would once again become the kingdom of unifying imagination, but also the triumph of sensible reason, and which would no longer borrow the face of the ancient gods) attributes to the future, to history that is to come, a function whose equivalent may be found only in religious or gnostic eschatologies. And even when myth seems still to be lacking, both human time and history as made by humans are profoundly mythicized by this hope. In awaiting the coming of a new mythology as if it were to be a veritable Parousia, this thought was already mythically defining the present as the deaf gestation of a new Adam, as the nocturnal examination of the point from which the universal dawn would shine forth: the present was a time of working and testing, moving forward, forced halts, attempts at new beginnings. Human history, the object of the new mythopoesis, reveals an intelligible meaning; it is the reconquering, under a still unknown appearance, of the lost wholeness, the collective reintegration into a unity, the return to the oldest truth, at the cost of bringing an entirely new world into being. Conceived in this way, myth, which at the beginning of the eighteenth century had been purely profane ornamentation, becomes the sacred par excellence, the ultimate authority—a sacred that imposes its laws in advance and judges human values in a final tribunal. Having never come to pass, it is nevertheless the judge of all that comes to pass. Such a change is but the corollary of another change: what had been the sacred at the beginning of the eighteenth century—written revelation, tradition, dogma—is submitted to a "demystifying" critique which reduces it to a mere human work, a fabulous work of the imagination. The sacred is reduced to a psychological function, while certain human faculties (feelings, consciousness, imagination) or certain collective acts (the common will) become endowed with a sacred function. In the intellectual history of this century, the sacralization of myth is closely associated with the humanization of the sacred. It is no longer sufficient, as has so often been done, to see the philosophy of the Enlightenment as a process of "secularization," in which human reason laid claim to prerogatives which had previously belonged to the divine *logos*. A reverse movement is also apparent, whereby myth, at first cast aside and held to be absurd, was now seen as having a deep and full meaning, and valued as revealed truth (Schelling). This double transformation effects a redistribution of the contrasting elements of the profane and the sacred. The old sacred sheds its skin and the profane order becomes charged with a mythic hope for a liberating progress. In the expectation of a ruling myth which will invent the humanity of the future, the old myths are taken up again as prefigurations—myths of Prometheus, Heracles, Psyche, and the Titans—but now they are used to designate rebellion, desire, and the hopes of those who aspire to become masters of their destiny. The myth that is to come, as sketched in advance by a diffuse expectation, will not only be imagined by man (by the poet-prophet, the people-poet, or humanity at work), but will also have man himself as its hero. The awaited Myth—born neither of the truth of history nor of the truth of poetry—is no longer a theogony but an anthropogony. It is one that will celebrate in song, in order to assemble the peoples, the Man-God who produces himself from his own song or by the work of his hands. All the mythologies of the modern world are but the substitutes and small change of this unfinished Myth.

J.St./d.w.

NOTES

1. Revised, amplified, transformed, Chompré's *Dictionnaire* became F. Noël's *Dictionnaire de la fable* (1801), which was used by artists and poets of the nineteenth century. Noël's *Dictionnaire de la fable* includes the mythologies of the Norse, Asia, etc.; the Greco-Roman world, while remaining predominant, ceased then to be the sole purveyor of imagery.

2. Of course, it is not a matter of the afterlife as the Homeric poems present it, but rather as it is promised by the mythological convention current in the seventeenth century.

3. Vico proposes a false etymology according to which *muthos* is related to *mutus* (mute), indicating that fable appeared in silent times and was the earliest form of speech, which came to be joined with an earlier language consisting of gestures and mute signs.

BIBLIOGRAPHY

Seventeenth- and Eighteenth-Century Authors (in Chronological Order)

G.-J. VOSSIUS, *De gentili theologia . . .* (Amsterdam 1668). A. VAN DALE, *Dissertationes de progressu idolatriae et superstitionum et de prophetia* (Amsterdam 1696); *De oraculis veterum ethnicorum* (Amsterdam 1700). P. JURIEU, *Histoire critique des dogmes et des cultes, depuis Adam à Jésus-Christ* (Amsterdam 1704). W. KING, *A Discourse concerning the Inventions of Men in the Worship of God* (5th ed., London 1704). J. TOLAND, *Letters to Serena* (London 1704). J. TRENCHARD, *The Natural History of Superstition* (London 1709). B. LE BOVIER DE FONTENELLE, *De l'origine des fables* (Paris 1724). C. ROLLIN, *Traité des études*, 4 vols. (Paris 1726); *Histoire ancienne*, 13 vols. (Paris 1730–38). S. SHUCKFORD, *The Sacred and the Profane History of the World Connected . . .* , 2 vols. (London 1728). A. RAMSAY, *The Travels of Cyrus, to Which Is Annexed a Discourse upon Mythology of the Ancients* (London 1728). T. BLACKWELL, *An Enquiry into the Life and Writings of Homer* (London 1735). T. BROUGHTON, *Bibliotheca historico-sacra, or an Historical Library of the Principal Matters Relating to Religion Ancient and Modern, Pagan, Jewish, Christian and Mohammedan*, 2 vols. (London 1737–39). A. BANIER, *La mythologie et les fables expliquées par l'histoire*, 3 vols. (Paris 1738). N. PLUCHE, *Histoire du ciel . . .* , 2 vols. (Paris 1739). G. VICO, *La scienza nuova* (3d ed., Naples 1744). R. LOWTH, *De sacra poesi Hebraeorum praelectiones* (London 1753). P. H. MALLET, *Introduction à l'histoire de Dannemarc . . .* (Copenhagen 1755); *Edda . . .* (3d ed., Geneva 1787). D. HUME, *The Natural History of Religion* (London 1757). A. PERNETY, *Les fables égyptiennes et grecques dévoilées* (Paris 1758). P. CHOMPRÉ, *Dictionnaire abrégé de la fable* (Paris 1759). C. DE BROSSES, *Du culte des dieux fétiches . . .* (1760). A. COURT DE GÉBELIN, *Le monde primitif . . .* , 9 vols. (Paris 1773–83). R. WOOD, *An Essay on the Original Genius and Writings of Homer* (London 1775). J. BRYANT, *A New System or an Analysis of Ancient Mythology* (London 1775–76). J.-S. BAILLY, *Lettres sur l'origine des sciences* (Paris 1777); *Lettres sur l'Atlantide de Platon* (Paris 1779). J. G. LINDEMANN, *Geschichte der Meinungen älterer und neuerer Völker im Stande der Roheit und Kultur, von Gott, Religion und Priesterthum* (Stendal 1784–85). C. G. HEYNE, *Opuscula academica* (Göttingen 1785–1812). C. A. DEMOUSTIER, *Lettres à Émilie sur la mythologie* (Paris 1786–98). R. P. KNIGHT, *A Discourse on the Worship of Priapus . . .* (London 1786). J.-P. RABAUT DE SAINT-ÉTIENNE, *Lettres à M. Bailly sur l'histoire primitive de la Grèce* (Paris 1787). P. C. REINHARD, *Abriss einer Geschichte der Entstehung und Ausbildung der religiösen Ideen* (Jena 1794). C. F. DUPUIS, *Origine de tous les cultes*, 12 vols. (Paris 1796). W. JONES, *Works*, 6 vols. (London 1799). F. NOËL, *Dictionnaire de la fable*, 2 vols. (Paris 1801). K. P. MORITZ, *Götterlehre . . .* (3d ed., Berlin 1804). J. A. DULAURE, *Des divinités génératrices, ou des cultes du phallus chez les anciens et les modernes* (Paris 1805). F. CRUEZER, *Symbolik und Mythologie der alten Völker, besonders der Griechen* (Leipzig and Darmstadt 1810–12). F. C. BAUR, *Symbolik und Mythologie, oder die Naturreligion des Altertums*, 3 vols. (Stuttgart 1824–25). J. G. HERDER, *Sämtliche Werke*, 33 vols. (Berlin 1877–1913). W. BLAKE, *Complete Poetry and Prose* (London 1948). JEAN-PAUL, *Vorschule der Aesthetik* (Munich 1963). F. HÖLDERLIN, *Sämtliche Werke*, 6 vols. (Stuttgart 1943–61), *Œuvres*, edited by P. Jaccottet (Paris 1967). F. SCHLEGEL, *Kritische Schriften* (Munich 1970).

Modern Studies on the History of Mythology (in Chronological Order)

F. STRICH, *Die Mythologie in der deutschen Literatur von Klopstock bis Wagner* (Halle 1910). O. GRUPPE, *Geschichte der klassischen Mythologie und Religionsgeschichte* (Leipzig 1921), important. R. SCHWAB, *La renaissance orientale* (Paris 1950). W. REHM, *Götterstille und Göttertrauer* (Berlin 1951); *Griechentum und Goethezeit* (Bern 1952). F. E. MANUEL, *The Eighteenth Century Confronts the Gods* (Cambridge, MA, 1959), important. J. DE VRIES, *Forschungsgeschichte der Mythologie* (Freiburg and Munich 1961). R. TROUSSON, *Le thème de Prométhée dans la littérature européenne* (Geneva 1964). J. BALTRUŠAITIS, *La quête d'Isis* (Paris 1967). Y. F.-A. GIRAUD, *La fable de Daphné* (Geneva 1968). P. ALBOUY, *Mythes et mythologies dans la littérature française*. M. FUHRMANN, ed., *Terror und Spiel: Probleme der Mythenrezeption* (Munich 1971), important. B. FELDMAN and R. D. RICHARDSON, *The Rise of Modern Mythology* (Bloomington and London 1972), an important anthology of documents, commentaries, and bibliographies. K. KERENYI, *Die Eröffnung des Zugangs zum Mythos: Ein Lesebuch* (Darmstadt 1976), a collection of texts on myth, from Vico to W. F. Otto.

The Mythology of Ancient Switzerland

Despite occasional hypercriticism, archeological discoveries made in Switzerland lead us to conclude that there was a ritual life in the area even in Paleolithic times.[1] But it is not until the Bronze Age that we find evidence of a mythology, of which certain vestiges are reflected even in contemporary Switzerland.

With the Roman presence on Helvetian soil, documents bearing on native beliefs or on great Celtic deities multiplied: Lugh, Sucellus, and Epona all had their devotees, as did local deities such as Artio, Mars Caturix, Genava (protectress of Geneva), and Aventia (patron goddess of Avenches). An inscription from this last locality mentions the "Lugavi"; this inscription is analogous to the one at Uxama (Osma) in the Spanish province of Soria and supports the view that Lugh was a "multiple" god, perhaps triple. An Irish story alludes to triplicity. Like Danaë, Ethnē—Lugh's mother—is locked up in a tower. McKineely, the owner of a blue cow, disguises himself and manages to rescue the young woman. From that union triplets are born; two die by drowning, and Lugh is the sole survivor.[2]

The great Celtic myths have not left clear traces on Swiss folklore; yet a curious coincidence should be mentioned. The city of Bern, founded in 1191 by the Zaehringen family following a successful bear hunt, is adjacent to a site called Muri, where in 1832 a votive statuette dedicated to the goddess Artio was discovered: she is depicted sitting, facing a large bear, which seems to be climbing down from a tree. To this day, the city of Bern raises bears in pits, but the present inhabitants' affection for their ursine heraldry cannot be connected with the goddess Artio or with any kind of totemism. Yet various popular traditions, of which some are still alive and others disappeared during the past few centuries, must have connections with myths of ancient Switzerland, though it is not possible to establish whether these myths are Celtic or Germanic. There are carnival customs common to youth groups that existed among both the Celts (for example, the Irish *feinid*) and the Norse (for example, the Scandinavian *berserkir*). The "Punchiadurs" of Grisons indulged in ritual combats analogous to those that took place on the occasion of the Roman Caprotine Nones. The Roitschegetten of Lötschental (Valais) or the Klausen of Appenzell still indulge in a kind of wild hunt in carnival season.

A custom still observed in Sursee (Lucerne) on Saint Martin's Day, 11 November, consists of decapitating, blindfold, a goose hanging from a string; this custom cannot merely be connected with a memory of the days of the tithe.[3] Each competitor must wear a blindfold in the shape of the sun and a loose-fitting red cape. In other places, "wild men" appear, whether at carnival time, in tales and legends, or on inn signs. Sometimes they wear bear costumes. This ancient heritage was formerly neglected because of its popular character, and the related mythical stories were treated with contempt like old wives' tales.[4] In central Switzerland and in Valais, legends have been recorded that correspond to the story of the death of the great Pan told by Plutarch in his treatise on the disappearance of the oracles. Since Switzerland is hardly an isolated case, Plutarch may have recorded the Greek version of an ancient popular European theme.[5]

Stories about giants and dragons also show how arbitrary it often is to speak of French or German mythology. Gargantua has left his traces in French-speaking areas, whereas in German-speaking Switzerland the giants have a rather Norse look about them. All these giants really look alike. Similarly, the legendary dragons of Switzerland remind us of Tarasques or Mélusines as much as monsters from the Germanic epic stories. Celtic and Norse sources, similar in background, interpenetrate and cannot be told apart.

The bear goddess Artio. Votive statuette. Bern, Historisches Museum. Museum photo.

One Swiss theme, however, the best known by far, has origins that must be sought in northern Europe—the theme of William Tell.

Several historians of religions have recently demonstrated that certain Indo-European heroes, formerly considered historical characters, in fact belong to mythology. A striking case, and probably the most recent, is that of William (Wilhelm) Tell. It had long been noted that the stories about Tell, Toko, Puncker, William of Cloudesly, and others were very much alike, and it was agreed that the theme of the remarkable archer came from a Scandinavian source. But this case study had generally been limited to the episode of the apple placed on the head of a child and hit with a shot from a crossbow.[6]

Skill in archery was thought to have a supernatural quality. The *Malleus maleficarum* devotes several pages to this subject, and if he had actually lived, the skillful crossbowman would certainly have brought down upon himself the thunderbolts of the Inquisition.[7] Fairies and witches were credited with the power of unleashing magic, harmful arrows. The esoteric symbolism of the bow and arrow may also be at play here.

Shadows also obscure the episode of Tell's escape as a prisoner navigating a lake. Norse heroes comparable to Tell have also escaped, but on skis. Such is the case of Toko, Heming, and Geyti Aslaksson. Toko ends up at sea, but the two Scandinavian deities famous for their bowmanship, the god Ullr (Ollerus) and the goddess Skadi, move about on skis. Furthermore, Ullr navigates on bones as well as he does in a boat; a picture in the *Historia de gentibus septentrionalibus* by Olaus Magnus illustrates the practice of supernatural waterskiing.

Sucellus. Viège bronze. Geneva, Musée d'Art et d'Histoire. Museum photo.

The very name Wilhelm (*helm* means helmet) and the episode of the hat shows that the headdress plays a significant role—its magic value in several myths is well known—and also that Tell (or Toll, i.e., crazy) by his very name belongs to a troublesome category, that of madmen. Tell's refusal to take off his own hat to a piece of headgear hooked onto the end of a pole is interpreted as the political gesture of a madman, that is, of an individual quasi-ritualistically authorized to express popular sentiment and unpleasant truths. This interpretation takes no account of ethnographic or religious facts such as the worship of the symbol of a deity placed on top of a pole (a fact mentioned by Olaus Magnus, book 3, chapter 2), or belief in magic arrows. In this realm of ideas, we should also mention the rock engravings of northern Europe that depict horned or masked skiers and a remarkable sorcerer shooting numerous arrows at another figure.[8] Nor should we forget that the fool and the archer have played a prominent role in the British Morris dances and mystery plays.

The story of Tell is a composite of several stories, one of which, the skier-archer, might be of Paleo-Finnish origin. In the nineteenth century, the historian Jean de Müller wrote that Tell's male line of descent ended in 1684 with Jean Martin's death, and his female line ended in 1720 with Vérena's death. Today, this Swiss national hero has left the bounds of history and entered, full-grown, the realm of myth.

R.C./g.h.

NOTES

1. For the cult of the bear, see CHRISTINGER and BORGEAUD, *Mythologie de la Suisse ancienne* (Geneva 1963), 29ff. The excavations of the Petit Chasseur at Sion (Valais) and those of the Carschenna (Grisons), for example, have brought to light important documents on cultural life prior to the Roman occupation or the arrival of the Celts, but these documents cannot be linked to particular myths.
2. Ibid., p. 88.
3. Another game played in Switzerland, *marelle* (hopscotch), is probably connected to ancient initiatory rites and to the myth of the labyrinth (ibid., 2:107ff.).
4. This is, for example, the attitude of Apuleius with regard to the tale of Psyche and Cupid (*Metamorphoses,* 4.27).
5. PLUTARCH, *De defectu oraculorum.* J. MULLER, *Sagen aus Uri* (Basel 1969), 3:207–10. L. COURTHION, *Les veillées des mayens* (Geneva), 197–201.
6. *Quellenwerk zur Entstehung der schweizerischen Eidgenossenschaft III Chroniken,* Band 1 (Aarau 1948). H. DE BOOR, *Die nordischen, englischen und deutschen Darstellungen des Apfelschussmotivs.* M. DELCOURT, "The Legend of Sarpedon and the Saga of the Archer," *History of Religions* 2, 1 (1962).
7. H. INSTITORIS and J. SPRENGER, *Le marteau des sorcières (Malleus maleficarum)* (Paris 1973).
8. H. KÜHN, *Die Felsbilder Europas* (Stuttgart 1952). W. J. RAVDONIKAS, *Les gravures rupestres des bords du lac Onega et de la mer Blanche* (Moscow 1938), vol. 2.

MYTHIC ELEMENTS IN FRENCH FOLKLORE

It may appear surprising, if not paradoxical, that France is covered in this book. France does not have, and probably never has had, its own mythology in the sense of an organized system of narratives about origins and supernatural beings. The mythology of France is not really French, for it is an emanation and complement of the Christian religion. First, therefore, we must demonstrate the historical absence of a "French mythology" while at the same time justifying its presence in this work.

I. The Absence and Presence of a French Mythology

Historians caution us against any temptation to make Celtic or, later, Roman Gaul the prefiguration of modern France, which would thus be the end of a linear evolution. It took many centuries for the political, linguistic, cultural, and religious differences between the diverse ethnic strata to be effaced and for a certain national cohesion to develop. Popular French consciousness nevertheless tends to place the Gauls in a special position as the ancestors of the French, but this Gallic "myth" is of scholarly origin and does not appear before the sixteenth century. Gallic religion, mythology, and culture left very few material traces, and we know that the political structures of Gaul were replaced by those of the Romans after the conquest, and then by those of the Franks. Latin was quickly imposed over all of the Gallic territory, both because it was the language of the conquerors and because it could be written. The invasions and implantations of the barbarians finally drove out all that may have remained Celtic in Gaul. It is not our purpose here to explain the Celtic vestiges: that subject is treated in other articles in the present work.

The instrument that turned out to be most effective in concealing a potential and precocious French mythology was incontestably Christianization. Its action was twofold, positive on the one hand and negative on the other. It was negative when, over several centuries, it strove to condemn, combat, and extirpate those beliefs and practices which the Church held to be pagan. This struggle changed the two known forms of such belief, through the organic processes of rejection and assimilation. In 452 the Council of Arles condemns worshipers of rocks; in 538 the Synod of Auxerre stigmatizes those who worship fountains, forests, and rocks. In 567 the Council of Tours recommends that all those who, before rocks, do things unrelated to the ceremonies of the Church be driven from the Church. In the seventh century, Saint Eligius, in the homilies related in his *Vita*, written by Saint Owen, stigmatizes the practices denounced as pagan. The continuing struggle was apparently quite ineffective, since the Church was obliged to pursue it until well after the Council of Trent. The assimilative method met with much greater success, but it was a success that sometimes turned against the victor. It consisted in Christianizing practices that were—or were considered to be—of pagan origin. "It is the same with sacred forests as with the Gentiles," declared Saint Augustine; "one does not exterminate the Gentiles but one converts them, changes them; in the same way one does not cut down sacred groves; it is better to consecrate them to Jesus Christ." In the same way, local deities that watch over springs and fountains are replaced by the names of missionaries and local saints (Sébillot, 1904–7). From the texts of the councils and synods that have come down to us, the essential objects of persistent paganism appear to have been water, rocks, and forests. We may thus speak of survivals, even though the forms of the beliefs and practices may have changed considerably over the centuries.

Christianity acted much more positively, however, when it offered the Gallo-Roman peoples a self-sufficient mythic and religious system. Here we find the main reason for the absence of a French mythology, since the needs of the majority of the people were satisfied by the Christian system. But because not all of the people were completely satisfied, a number of beliefs, stories, and practices managed to slip through the cracks of the Christian religion, while others thrived independently, parallel to Christianity. Whether grasped in its state of syncretism with Christianity or in an independent state, this ensemble belongs to the domain known as folklore. In comparison with "authorized" mythologies which are learned as relatively well organized systems, folklore, by its very nature, often appears in pieces. To anyone first encountering it, folklore presents itself in the form of crumbs, debris, and fragments, in which it conceals its mythic nature. Folklore thus carries forward those mythic materials to which Christianity and later scholarly culture refused to give a noble expression, so that they had to appear in seemingly harmless forms—tales, legends, beliefs, and "popular" practices—although the inoffensive appearance of such forms did not always shelter them from the condemnation of the Church or the dominant culture.

Festival of the Tarasca at Tarascon (1946), a good example of a popular festival inserted into the Christian liturgical calendar. Paris, Musée des Arts et Traditions populaires. Museum photo.

This is, in all likelihood, the only mythology France has known—although it does not belong to France alone in all of its expressions, since European folklore is divided not according to strict national boundaries but into broader areas. An attempt has nevertheless been made to bring to light a French mythology, by attributing Celtic origins to it: we are referring to Henri Dontenville's work (1948). The central character of this recovered mythology is Gargantua—not so much Rabelais's hero as the Gargantua of a great number of stories and beliefs which are essentially topographical. To Gargantua is attributed the creation of numerous mountains, hills, buttes, menhirs, lakes, swamps, etc. (Sébillot, 1883). According to Dontenville, Gargantua is the son of the Celtic god Belen (Bélénos), but this divine origin is demonstrated by an etymological elaboration that lacks rigor. Other supernatural personages, such as the fairies Morgana and Mélusine, also gravitate around this mythology. It is incontestable that Gargantua was a popular character before becoming a literary figure thanks to Rabelais. On the other hand, it is quite difficult to make him the hero of a French mythic system postulated through beliefs and accounts called survivals and vestiges. Mythology has not reached the scientific level of linguistics, which is able to reconstruct with some accuracy the earlier state of a language. According to Émile Benveniste's formulation, linguistics has succeeded "in restoring the wholes that evolution has broken up, in bringing buried structures to light" (Benveniste, 1969, 1:9). The science of mythology, unlike the science of etymology, is not ready to produce reconstructions of an earlier stage on the basis of present-day elements: it does not have laws that direct the evolution of mythic systems, for the evolution is the function of too many variables for all to be studied at the same time.

The theory that folklore consists of the vestiges of vanished mythologies is not a new one. Set forth more or less explicitly earlier, the theory did not spread until the beginning of the nineteenth century, when it became the foundation of the vast undertaking of the brothers Grimm. The folktales that they collected and published under the title of *Kinder- und Hausmärchen* (1812–15) were thought to have preserved the beliefs and customs of the ancient Germanic peoples, after they had given them a poetical form which was the product not of scholarly poetry but of "natural" poetry which, through the intermediary of creative people, was of divine origin. In Jacob Grimm's *Deutsche Mythologie* (1835), the theory becomes more explicit. It surmises that a mythology and a pantheon which were highly developed in the pre-Roman era were destroyed by the medieval Church and survive only in the form of the fragments found in folklore.

While the brothers Grimm gave this theory the fame and influence that are so well known to us, they did nothing but express—albeit in a work of great importance—a current of European ideas which was to be found in France from the first quarter of the nineteenth century. The first systematic collection of what was not yet called folklore was undertaken by members of the Celtic Academy—transformed after 1815 into the Society of the Antiquarians of France—whose expressed goal was to collect dialects, patois, and jargons, place names, monuments, usages, and traditions, in order to "explicate ancient times by modern times." It was the same doctrine—which we will call the ideology of survivals—that governed both the French venture (which declined after 1825–30) and that of the brothers Grimm, which was more abundant and prolonged.

It should be noted that this current of ideas in the Europe of the first half of the nineteenth century was characterized by strong nationalism, as it was in France in the second half of the century, after the research was temporarily eclipsed between 1830 and 1860–70. This nationalism would seek its foundation in the camp of the Gauls and the Celts, so it was natural that the historians and archaeologists should determine its theoretical foundation. The foundation is accepted without discussion by folklorists such as Paul Sébillot and all those who worked on the *Review of Popular Traditions,* while the Celticists, archaeologists and historians such as Henri Gaidoz, Alexandre Bertrand, and Alfred Maury, turn into folklorists the better to affirm their thesis. As far as Henri Gaidoz is concerned, refer to the article "Popular Customs and Rituals in France," in which one of his studies is presented and discussed. As for Alexandre Bertrand, in his book *The Religion of the Gauls* (1897) he writes the following lines, which the brothers Grimm themselves could not have disavowed:

> There exist, or there existed in human memory, in our country, as in Ireland, Germany, and the Scandinavian countries, old customs, old traditions, and old superstitions, which are faint but still recognizable echoes of primitive times. "Driven from their temples," H. Gaidoz could write, "the Gallic gods took refuge in our countryside"; we shall go in search of them. The very care taken by the Church very early to stigmatize the old beliefs, to anathematize them, or to Christianize them by changing their spirit—most often without visibly modifying their form—in its inability to uproot them, strongly attests to the important role that they played in the country before Christianity and to the people's lively attachment to them. (Bertrand, 18–19)

In order to elucidate the problems arising from the connections between mythology and folklore, we must criticize the notion of survivals. Despite its fragility, it has constituted the founding principle of folklore studies until recent times, for in France it was only with the works of Arnold van Gennep that the notion was abandoned, even though his contemporary Pierre Saintyves continued to use it. Note that van Gennep was a man of the soil and Saintyves was not. Ethnology has taught us that a belief or custom can never be a pure survival. It may sometimes be an archaism with respect to the dominant culture, but it is never an anachronism. In order to be maintained, traditions must have a function in the culture of which they are a part. Claude Lévi-Strauss expresses this very clearly concerning the beliefs and customs of Christmas:

> Explanations by survivals are always incomplete; for customs neither disappear nor survive without reason. When they persist, the cause is to be found less in the viscosity of history than in the permanence of a function which modern analysis should be able to disclose. . . . We are, with the rites of Christmas, in the presence not only of historical vestiges, but also of forms of thinking and of behavior which reveal more general conditions of life in society. The Saturnalias and the medieval celebration of Christmas do not contain the final ground for a ritual otherwise inexplicable and devoid of meaning; but they do offer comparative material which is useful for drawing out the deep meaning of recurrent institutions. (Lévi-Strauss, 1952)

Even assuming that a practice might have been preserved without much change from Gallo-Roman antiquity to the nineteenth century, its meaning could not be exactly the same, since its cultural context is fundamentally dissimilar, and the greatest differences are found in the diversity of the religion and the economy.

Although it is inadmissible that popular beliefs, practices, and narratives are pure vestiges or survivals of an earlier state, they should not be divested of all reference to the past. The past is essential not as an explanatory principle but as a given in the material. It is a constant in folklore, at whatever historical time one observes and collects, to be at once caught in the present moment and reflected into a more or less distant past. The term "popular traditions," which is sometimes used for folklore, is a good indication of the nostalgic component of these materials. A reality observed *hic et nunc* always refers to a tradition; that is, to a past. But this past is

Steps of the ages. Gangel, Metz. Paris, Musée des Arts et Traditions populaires. Museum photo.

The twelve months of the year. Calendar from Epinal, Pellerin. Paris, Musée des Arts et Traditions populaires. Museum photo.

not truly historical: it is reflected from generation to generation back to distant origins which are difficult to inscribe in history. But the quest for origins is by definition not historical but mythic. In this sense folklore, by its very nature, includes mythic fragments whose importance varies according to the form and technique by which it is expressed. Clearly, popular beliefs, practices, and stories are likely to serve as vehicles for mythic fragments. These are the three forms we have chosen to study.

It is thus evident what separates us from the early folklorists of France and Europe, but also what we hold in common. They regarded folklore as the vestiges of ancient mythological systems altered, mutilated, and even corrupted by the wear of time, as archaeological monuments may be. As with such monuments, it became necessary to submit them to reconstruction, a mental reconstruction that would invest them with meaning. Failing this reconstruction, "survivals" were regarded as freaks, curiosities, if not aberrations. Throwing them back into the past provides them with a meaning, a meaning that cannot always be restored to them, but which exists because it did exist: this kind of meaning may be called retrospective.

On the other hand, we believe—without denying the phenomena of transmission—that folkloric acts are bearers of a *present* mythic component, even if this component is viewed as ancient and archaic both by observers of the acts and by those who practice them. It is not possible for depictions and practices bereft of a current meaning, and thus of a function, to continue to exist: in the case of folklore the current sense and function are constituted by a throwback into the past. Curiously, this throwback is accompanied by a feeling of extreme precariousness. All folklorists, regardless of the age for which they gather folklore, insist on the urgency of their work and on the inevitability of the disappearance of what they collect. The same fragility is attributed to the collected folklore as is attributed to archaeological fragments which are freed from their earthly gangue and thus likely to crumble because of their great age.

II. Popular Beliefs, Rituals, and Narratives

The forms of folklore from which we will attempt to extract the underlying mythic forms are popular beliefs, rituals, and narratives. It is not that folklore is manifested only in these three forms, but they are easier to decipher than popular art, dress, or dance, whose apparently greater technical material and social function mask their mythic component even more.

In their techniques, popular narratives are obviously closest to myths, yet are not myths, since this "fluid oral literature" involves only folktales and legends. The folkloric taxonomy which distinguishes them is useful from a formal point of view inasmuch as it introduces terms of reference. This taxonomy is certainly less clear-cut on the level of meaning. The legend is an account which appears to be inserted into time or space, and usually into time *and* space. It presents real places and a cast of characters which are supposed to have existed. This historico-topographical insertion essentially occurs through the presence of proper names: personal names and place names. An example is the Charlemagne of epic legends, who is imagined to be the king of the Franks who was crowned emperor of the West at Aix-la-Chapelle in 800. The folktale, by contrast, appears as a purely fictional account; people and places are impersonal, and its temporality is not historical but narrative, i.e., internal to the account. Although popular legends and folktales are narratives, as opposed to beliefs, rituals, and practices, we will not examine them all together. Legends have a more fundamental relationship with beliefs than with folktales, in the sense that the relationship between them is generative: beliefs generate legends in forms of varying complexity. As for popular folktales, we will treat only those which are elegantly, and rightly, called *contes merveilleux* ("supernatural stories" or "fairy tales"), i.e., numbers 300 to 749 in the Aarne and Thompson classification (1961).

Of all of the folkloric expressions, the most difficult to comprehend are undoubtedly folk beliefs, since these offer the least material support. They are also often apprehended under a form other than their own: i.e., that of the legends they engender, or of the practices and rituals they underlie. These practices are characterized by the fact that they exclude—or try to exclude—language, and only use objects and actions. Of course, no practice or ritual has ever totally eliminated language, but the words or formulas used in them are to be assigned to what Claude Lévi-Strauss calls implicit mythology.

Formally, these diverse expressions are distinct from one another. From the point of view of their contents, this is not completely the case. There are slippages from one form to another. A motif from a popular folktale may be found in a legend. A practice refers to a belief. Another belief may have been collected as a legend in another time or place or from another informant. But the most developed form of the legend allows for the identification of a generative or contracted core, reduced to its most basic expression by a reverse movement. In the schema of a ritual, one may recognize the theme of a popular folktale, to which this form clearly gives a much greater freedom.

These movements, these shifts, these comings and goings have at least two causes. We know from the works of Lévi-Strauss that "mythic thought is essentially transformational," as testified by the mythic fragments that are carried in this way. The other cause is the particular nature of this mythology "in crumbs," which could not be expressed in the form of a coherent whole because Christianity occupied, and not without a certain aggression, almost the entire authorized field of expression. Forced to be fragmented in order to be expressed, this "implicit" mythology became perhaps even more fluid than the others.

In spite of its fundamental fluidity, we will attempt to grasp its most important aspects under the following rubrics: "French Fairy Tales, Folktales, and Myths"; "Folk Beliefs and Legends about Fairies in France"; and "Popular Customs and Rituals in France."

N.B./d.w.

BIBLIOGRAPHY

A. AARNE and S. THOMPSON, *The Types of the Folk-Tale: A Classification and Bibliography* (Helsinki 1961). A. AUDIN, "Les rites solsticiaux et la légende de S. Pothin," *Revue de l'histoire de religions* 96 (1927): 147–74. N. BELMONT, *Mythes et croyances dans l'ancienne France* (Paris 1973). E. BENVENISTE, *Le vocabulaire des institutions indo-européennes*, 2 vols. (Paris 1969). A. BERTRAND, *La religion des Gaulois: Les druides et le druidisme* (Paris 1897). J. F. BLADÉ, *Contes populaires de la Gascogne*, 3 vols. (Paris 1886). P. DELARUE, "Les caractères propres du conte populaire français," *La pensée*, no. 72 (March–April 1957), 39–62. P. DELARUE and M. L. TENEZE, *Le conte populaire français*, 2 vols. (Paris 1957–64). D. DERGNY, *Usages, coutumes et croyances*, 2 vols. (Abbeville 1885–88; 2d ed., Brionne 1971). H. DONTENVILLE, *La mythologie française* (Paris 1948). G. DUBOIS, *Celtes et Gaulois au XVIe siècle: Le développement littéraire d'un mythe nationaliste* (Paris 1972). G. DUMÉZIL, *Légendes sur les Nartes* (Paris 1930); *Mythe et épopée*, 3 vols. (Paris 1968–73). L. DUMONT, *La Tarasque: Essai de description d'un fair local d'un point de vue ethnographique* (Paris 1951). C.-M. EDSMAN, *Ignis divinus. Le feu comme moyen de rajeunissement et d'immortalité. Contes, légendes, mythes, rites* (Lund 1949). P. FORTIER-BEAULIEU, *Mariages et noces campagnardes dans le département de la Loire* (Paris 1937). H. GAIDOZ, *Études de mythologie gauloise: Le dieu gaulois du soleil et le symbolisme de la roue* (Paris 1886), published first in the *Revue archéologique* (1884–85). C. GAIGNEBET, *Le carnaval: Essais de mythologie populaire* (Paris and Payot 1974). J. GRIMM and W. GRIMM, *Kinder- und Hausmärchen*, 2 vols. (Berlin 1812–15); the 3d ed. (1856) includes a third volume of commentaries; often translated into English, e.g., M. HUNT and J. STERN, trans., *Grimm's Fairy Tales* (New York 1944). J. GRIMM, *Deutsche Mythologie* (Berlin 1835); in English as *Teutonic Mythology* (London 1882–88). H. HUBERT, "Étude sommaire de la représentation du temps dans la religion et la magie," in H. Hubert and M. Mauss, *Mélanges d'histoire des religions* (Paris 1909). A. LE BRAZ, *La légende de la mort chez les Bretons armoricains*, 2 vols. (Paris 1923). C. LÉVI-STRAUSS, "Le Père Noël supplicié," *Les temps modernes*, no. 77 (1952); "L'analyse morphologique des contes russes," *Cahiers de l'Institut de science économique appliquée* 9 (March 1960): 3–36; reprinted in *Anthropologie structurale* (Paris 1973), 2:140–73, under the title "La structure et la forme." A. MAURY, *Croyances et légendes du Moyen Age* (Paris 1896). E. MÉLÉTINSKY, "Marriage: Its Function and Position in the Structure of Folktales," in P. Maranda, ed., *Soviet Structural Folkloristics* (The Hague and Paris 1974), 61–72. M. MONNIER, "Vestiges d'antiquité observés dans le Jurassien," *Mémoires de la Société des Antiquaires de France*, 4 (1823). V. PROPP, *Morphology of the Folk-Tale* (Bloomington, IN, 1958), original in Russian. P. SAINTYVES, *Essais de mythologie chrétienne: Les saints successeurs des dieux* (Paris 1907); *Les contes de Perrault et les récits parallèles* (Paris 1923); *En marge de la Légende dorée* (Paris 1931); *Corpus du folklore des eaux en France et dans les colonies françaises* (Paris 1934); *Corpus du folklore préhistorique en France et dans les colonies françaises*, 3 vols. (Paris 1934–36); *L'astrologie populaire* (Paris 1937). P. SÉBILLOT, *Le paganisme contemporain chez les peuples celto-latins* (Paris 1908); *Gargantua dans les traditions populaires* (Paris 1883); *Le folklore de France*, 4 vols. (Paris 1904–7; reprinted Paris 1968). M. TEISSIER, "Recherches sur la fête annuelle de la roue flamboyante de la Saint-Jean, à Basse-Kontz, arrondissement de Thionville," *Mémoires de la Société des Antiquaires de France* 5 (1823): 379–93. A. VAN GENNEP, *The Rites of Passage* (Chicago 1960; originally Paris 1909); *Le folklore* (Paris 1924); *Le folklore de la Bourgogne: Côte d'Or*, Contributions au folklore des provinces de France (Paris 1934); *Manuel de folklore français contemporain* (Paris 1937–58); in books 3 and 4 there is a systematic and critical bibliography on the folklore of France. A. VARAGNAC, *Civilisation traditionnelle et genres de vie* (Paris 1948).

Journals

Mélusine: Recueil de mythologie, Littérature populaire, traditions et usages. Founded by H. Gaidoz and E. Rolland in 1877 (10 vols. between 1877 and 1912).

Revue des traditions populaires. Founded by P. Sébillot in 1886 (32 vols. through 1918).

Revue d'ethnographie et des traditions populaires. Founded by M. Delafosse in 1920 (10 vols. through 1929).

Revue de folklore français et de folklore colonial. Edited by P. Saintyves (13 vols., 1930–42).

Arts et traditions populaires. Journal of the Société d'ethnographie française (1953–70).

Ethnologie française. Journal of the Société d'ethnologie française. Founded in 1971.

French Fairy Tales, Folktales, and Myths

Vladimir Propp's contribution to the study of the folktale, especially to the study of the tale as myth, is both important and unsatisfying. His well-known analysis of the functions of the folktale provided the fundamental schema for the folktale but at the same time constituted a reductionist approach. And while Propp is convinced that the fairytale derives from myth, he sees this process as what could be called devolutionist. Propp's works on this problem are not sufficiently known in France, but what he says here and there in his *Morphology of the Folktale* is explicit enough. "If we define these tales from a historical point of view, they deserve the old, now abandoned, name of mythical tales" (p. 122, alluding to Wilhelm Wundt's terms *Mythusmärchen* and *Märchenmythus*). The tale derives from the myth through the intermediary of an historical evolution: "It is quite possible that there is a relationship, governed by laws, between the archaic forms of culture and religion on the one hand, and between religion and folktales on the other hand. A culture dies, a religion dies, and their content is transformed into a folktale. The traces of archaic religious representations that are preserved in folktales are so obvious that they can be isolated before any historical study" (pp. 131–32).

Once more we find the historical problematic as the theoretical foundation of folklore. Unfortunately, there is nothing to indicate that French fairy tales are derived from ancient religion and mythology, either Celtic or Gallo-Roman. We know, on the other hand, that they are variants of tales found throughout the Indo-European domain, so their origin goes back much earlier, perhaps to the beginning of the Neolithic—in which case we cannot say anything about them at all. On the other hand, if one is willing to admit that fairy tales include still-meaningful mythical fragments within a structure that has lost its coherence, then an attempt at decoding becomes possible.

Another Russian formalist, E. Meletinsky, sees the opposition between myth and folktale as based on an opposition between the collective and the individual: the myth is concerned with the collective fate of the universe, of humanity, of the local community, while the folktale is concerned with the fate of individuals. This remark is very helpful and does not contradict Claude Lévi-Strauss's proposition that the difference between myth and folktale is a difference of degree. On the one hand, "folktales are built on weaker oppositions than those of myths: not cosmological, metaphysical, or natural, but more often local, social, or moral ones"; on the other hand the folktale "is less subject than the myth to the triple exigencies of logical coherence, religious orthodoxy, and collective pressure. . . . The folktale's permutations become relatively freer and progressively acquire a certain arbitrariness" (1960). Folktales may be considered myths that are weakened in their structure and expression, but this does not make the meaning of their content any less mythic. It is only harder to grasp.

In this analysis of the contents of French fairy tales, which represents only a preliminary outline, we will make use of a remark of Propp's. In the *Morphology of the Folktale* he says "The voyage, one of the main structural foundations of the folktale, is the reflection of certain representations of the voyages of the soul into the other world" (p. 132). The motif of the voyage, particularly the voyage into the other world—but is it just one motif among others, or is it rather the very essence of the fairy tale?—sometimes appears quite explicitly, sometimes more obscurely, and sometimes in an insignificant guise. It certainly reflects an eschatology which, in spite of sometimes having a Christian appearance, has little to do with Christianity.

One tale type (T471, *The Bridge to the Other World* in the Aarne-Thompson classification) has the French name of the *Voyage dans l'autre monde* (journey into the other world). Its distribution in France is uneven: sixteen of the twenty-six known versions are from Brittany, seven others are from Gascony, and the others from Alsace and Nevers. The initial

Wedding party leaving a church. Lithograph, Laruns. Paris, Musée des Arts et Traditions populaires. Museum photo.

"Mardi Gras is dead; shrovetide follows without regret." Paris, Musée des Arts et Traditions popularies. Museum photo.

motif makes it possible to divide them into two groups. The young hero's journey is provoked either by an unknown person who asks him to bear a message to the other world or by his decision to visit his sister, who is married to a foreigner who took her to a distant land. We will summarize what seem to be the richest versions from the second group.

A girl who does not want to get married finally marries a foreigner, who appears in different guises depending on the version: a young man dressed all in white and as handsome as an angel; a beggar, when she is the king's daughter; the *Ankou*, death personified, in a Breton version; a magnificently dressed lord who turns out to be a dead man; a young man as bright as the sun; a man with red teeth, or simply the Sun in person. After the wedding he takes her far away to his kingdom. Her brother decides to visit her, but his journey turns out to be long, difficult, and full of challenges and strange spectacles. When he arrives at the castle where his sister lives, she tells him that her husband is gone all day long, leaving early in the morning and only coming back in the evening. The husband agrees to let his brother-in-law go with him on this daily trip, on condition that he remain completely silent while they travel. In some versions it is during this journey that he sees strange spectacles whose

Mardi Gras procession. Woodcut (Second Empire). Paris, Musée des Arts et Traditions populaires. Museum photo.

Handing on the distaff to the new bride. Sketch by Jules Lecoeur in *Le Monde illustré* of 1865. Paris, Musée des Arts et Traditions populaires. Museum photo.

meaning is revealed to him only when he comes back in the evening: these are always Christian allegories, the main one being that he visits Heaven and sees Purgatory and Hell as he goes by them. He returns to his village; certain versions indicate that his voyage seemed short to him but really lasted several hundred years. He dies soon after his return.

The archaic appearance of this tale is especially striking in the least-Christianized versions. It readily evokes cosmogonic myths, since we understand that the husband of the hero's sister is the Sun, even in the most Christianized versions in which he is not designated as such: his daily trip is sufficiently explicit in this respect. The Christianization of the story has caused a shift in the axis of the narrative: it is no longer centered on the marriage with the Sun, which now serves as a subsidiary motif to the Christian journey of the hero.

This fairy tale, perhaps better than any other, gives the impression of being the result of a complex labor of stratification. Around its archaic kernel (the motif of the Sun, his wife, and his daily journey) Christian allegorical motifs have been assembled, most of which were probably created in the Middle Ages, at the time of the formation and fixing of the representations and images concerning the triple localization of the world beyond, in Heaven, Purgatory, and Hell. The form proper to the fairy tale has included all of these motifs within a single narrative.

Among the other archaicizing traits of the story, note the motif of the journey itself, which is used to express a temporal problematic. The voyage to the other world, that is, a spatial displacement, has the function of translating a temporal category, that of eternity. We have said that in certain versions the time the hero spent in the other world seemed very short to him, but in fact he had spent several centuries there. No one recognizes him when he comes back to his village: "They looked in the old record books and found that about three hundred years earlier there had been a family of that name which had since completely died out." This way of expressing time by space and the unfolding of time by displacement in space are used a second time in the tale. For the husband, the Sun (whether he is named as such or not), goes on a daily journey which requires him to leave early in the morning and return only in the evening. The story rarely justifies these regular absences; if it does so, it says that he goes around the world, or that he goes to Heaven. The daily displacement thus expresses a daily periodicity, while the hero's long and laborious journey conveys, by contrast, a long duration, covering several generations, which is too much for human memory to master and which is revealed only in written documents (inscriptions in record books or on tombstones), the image of eternity. The time of a human life lies in between these two times, one of which is periodic and the other, by definition, not periodic. It shares something of the qualities of both: it is periodic in the sense that generations follow one another but is of a longer periodicity than the succession of days and nights, though its prolongation never lasts until its abolition, that is, for eternity. In most of the versions, the end of the hero's journey and (sometimes) his return home are followed by his death, which is the promise of the eternal joys of Heaven for him—since at this point Christianity takes over the narrative again.

The mythic character of the principal motifs of the tale is beyond doubt. If necessary, we can confirm this by comparing the tale with a story collected among the Ossets, a population of the northern Caucasus, among whom a piece of ancient Indo-European mythology has survived in the form of legends about people called the Narts (Dumézil 1930 and 1968–73, and "Popular Customs and Rituals in France"). Sozryko, the hero of the story, is equally well known among the populations neighboring the Ossets, the Chechens and Kabardinians. The tale possesses obvious solar traits.

One day while hunting, Sozryko pursues a hare and shoots all his arrows at it, but it vanishes before his very eyes. The hunt leads him into the Black Mountains, to a black castle of iron, where the daughter of the Sun dwells, guarded by her seven brothers. He immediately asks for her hand, which is granted to him on two conditions: he must bring a hundred deer, a hundred wild sheep, and a hundred head of various kinds of game; and he must fill the four quarters of the castle with leaves from the Aza tree, a tree of heaven. His mother advises Sozryko to go first to the Master of Game and then to his own first wife, now dead, who will ask the Master of the Dead for the leaves. He sets out for the land of the dead; on his way he sees strange spectacles whose meaning he does not understand: a man and a woman lying under the skin of a bull which, although it is enormous, cannot cover the one without uncovering the other, while farther along he sees another couple who fit comfortably under the skin of a hare; he sees two shoes, one of goatskin, the other of pigskin, fighting and jumping on one another. When he finally reaches his late wife she explains the meaning of the strange visions: they are the punishments and rewards for actions on earth. But other encounters are allegories for the future: the puppies lying on a heap of rags who barked at him were announcing the coming insolence of the young. In addition, his wife gives him the leaves from the tree of heaven. To shake off the dead who try to follow him back, Sozryko shoes his horse backward and bursts through the gates of the infernal kingdom. With his game and his leaves he returns to the castle of the seven brothers, who give him their sister, the daughter of the Sun, in marriage (Dumézil, 1930, no. 28).

Despite a great deal of remodeling, this narrative is highly evocative of the French folktale version of the "journey into the other world." The same characters appear, although their distribution is different: a girl, sister, wife or future wife, a brother or brothers, a hero who is clearly solar in the French story, who has solar traits if we consider the whole set of Caucasian stories about him. All of these characters are involved in a voyage to the world beyond. In both cases the journey is crowded with strange spectacles which are only explained afterward in the form of allegories. The allegories are not at all the same in the French folktale and the Caucasian legend, although there are elements common to both, such as the couple united or divided on the ground, or the battle of the two shoes, which is worth comparing with one of the encounters in the French tale. Most versions of that tale say that the hero finds his way blocked by two goats violently butting their heads together, ravens fiercely fighting, two trees banging together with such fury that pieces of wood shoot out of them, and two stones smashing each other brutally. According to the explanation at the end of the story, these are generally two brothers who were enemies during their lifetimes, or two quarreling spouses. The motif of two objects that crash together violently, and through which the hero must pass—the rocks of the Symplegades—is found in a great number of mythologies and designates the perilous entrance to the other world. In what is certainly a weakened form, we find it both in the French folktale and in the Caucasian legend.

Both of these narratives, then, bring together comparable or similar motifs to tell the story of a voyage to the other world, while each orders the motifs in a somewhat different way. While the Caucasian legends have probably undergone less remodeling than the folktales in relation to the ancient stock of Indo-European mythology, they probably do not represent an archaic, original, and primitive state in comparison with the folktales: the Caucasian stories have at least undergone a considerable change in form, since they have passed from myth to legend. But the comparison shows that the common theme and motifs of the two stories are indeed mythic, even if their form is not.

The theme of the voyage to the other world occupies the whole narrative space of this particular story. But it also appears frequently in other French fairy tales, where it does not present the same irreversible character and is often linked instead to the quest for, or a reconquest of, a husband or wife.

In *The Love of Three Oranges* (T408), the initial explicit motif is the quest for a wife.

A young prince breaks a container that belongs to an old woman; she puts a curse on him: he will never be happy until he finds and marries the Love of Three Oranges; or else he desires to marry a girl who is "rosy, black, and white"; or else he simply wants to get married. He goes off on his search; he walks for months or years and finally meets one or more supernatural beings (the Mother of the Winds, for example) who advise him to arm himself with certain objects: their usefulness will be revealed at the castle where the old woman with the three oranges lives. He arrives there after an exhausting voyage, and thanks to the objects, which are exactly right for the job, manages to get to the old woman's room; he steals the three oranges from her and runs away. On the way back he cuts one of the three oranges in two, and a marvelously beautiful girl comes out of it, asks him for something to drink, and dies, since he has no water to give her. The same thing happens with the second orange, so he waits until he finds a fountain to open the third. This time the girl quenches her thirst and survives. But he leaves her by the fountain in order to go and find clothing and ornaments for her worthy of the rank she is going to have. During his absence a witch, black woman, or Moorish woman takes her place after turning the girl into a dove or a fish. The prince, surprised to find her so ugly, marries her anyway, or gets ready to marry her, since she blames her transformation on her long wait. But the dove attracts the prince's attention, and he breaks her enchantment.

This lovely tale is typical of the stories of the quest. That it is a journey into the other world is hardly in doubt: the great length of the journey, its difficulties, and the meetings with supernatural characters mark it clearly, as does the marvelous origin of the girl whom he desires. Indeed, the very motive of the journey is desire, desire for a woman without even knowing whether she exists, desire inflicted on the hero by an old woman. In this sense we can speak of a journey of initiation, if initiation consists of the adolescent's tearing himself away from the influence of his mother to become integrated into the society of men. Success in this transitional passage is rewarded with the possibility of marriage. In so-called primitive societies, this passage takes place by means of rituals that are often demanding, long, and complex. European societies, on the other hand, in which initiation rites as such have never existed or have not existed for a very long time, nevertheless maintain the idea of an initiation, a purely imaginary one, since it appears more or less clearly in folktales. The initiation essentially consists of a journey, beginning with a departure from home in which can be seen the symbolic rupture of the Oedipal ties. The voyage leads to another world which is not necessarily conceived of as a world of the dead: strictly speaking, it is a world that lies beyond the human world. A young Ojibwa Indian leaves his family and village to retire to a deserted place where he fasts and meditates until a supernatural being appears to him and becomes his guardian spirit. In fact, all initiation rituals have a phase in which the initiate is supposed to be dead, that is, they always include a passage to the world beyond.

The theme of the voyage in fairy tales thus represents, on the one hand, the adolescent's flight from and break with his Oedipal feelings and, on the other hand, the winning of magical objects and a beautiful bride who brings gifts; she is often the daughter of a king. The journey is thus charged with the possibility for him to become a hero, often by triumphing over his own brothers: thus in the version of *The Love of Three Oranges* from Guyenne, only the youngest of the three brothers receives from an old woman the fruits (here they are apples) containing the marvelous young women, since only he was kind to her; his two older brothers, who set off with him "to seek their fortune as if it were something you could pick up along the side of the road," come back empty-handed, since they refused to help the old woman in distress.

In all these tales the hero is male. Are there any in which he is replaced by a heroine, and do they show the same narrative pattern? There are, of course, stories in which the main character is a girl or a young woman, but while they too contain the motif of the voyage to the world beyond, their lesson is quite different. The most important of these tales in terms of the number of versions and the beauty, variety, and richness of the story is entitled *The Search for the Lost Husband* (T425). The ancient story of Psyche as told by Apuleius in *The Golden Ass* is one of its European forms, although it is not the prototype. *Beauty and the Beast* is another of its forms. Here is the version from Gascony collected by J. F. Blade (1886).

A Green Man with one eye has three daughters, each more beautiful than the next. One evening the King of the Ravens comes to ask for one of the daughters in marriage, and to force him to agree he puts out the Green Man's one eye. The youngest daughter accepts him in order to restore her father's sight; the marriage is celebrated and the bridegroom carries her off to his castle, which lies three thousand leagues away, "in the land of cold, in the land of ice, where there are no trees or greenery." At midnight, in the darkness, the King of the Ravens reveals that he and his people were changed into ravens by a sorceror. His penance must last for seven more years, and until then his bride must not try to see him at night when he takes off his feather clothing and lies down next to her, separated by a sword. In the morning before daybreak he gets up and goes out. During the day the poor bride wanders around, always alone, in the ice and snow; but one day she comes to a poor hut; next to it a wrinkled old woman is washing linens as black as soot and singing a refrain that says she is waiting for the "married virgin" to come. The girl helps her wash her clothes, which become as white as milk. The old woman foretells trials for her, but promises to help her in the day of her greatest need. Seven years, less one day, pass, and that night the girl decides to see what her husband looks like. He is as beautiful as the day. She brings the candle closer, and a drop of wax falls onto him; he wakes up and sadly tells her that since she has violated the prohibition, he has fallen back into the power of the sorceror. The sorceror chains him to the peak of a high mountain on an island and sets two wolves to guard him: one is white and keeps watch during the day; the other is black and keeps watch at night. The young wife leaves the castle and goes back to the old washerwoman's cottage. The washerwoman tells her where her husband is being held prisoner and gives her magical objects: an inexhaustible sack and an inexhaustible gourd, iron slippers, and a golden knife for cutting "the blue grass, the grass that sings night and day, the grass that breaks iron." When her slippers break, it will be almost time for her to rescue her husband. She walks for one year through the land "where there is neither night

"Fairy tales." Cover of a chapbook. Woodcut. Épinal, Pellerin. Paris, Musée des Arts et Traditions populaires. Museum photo.

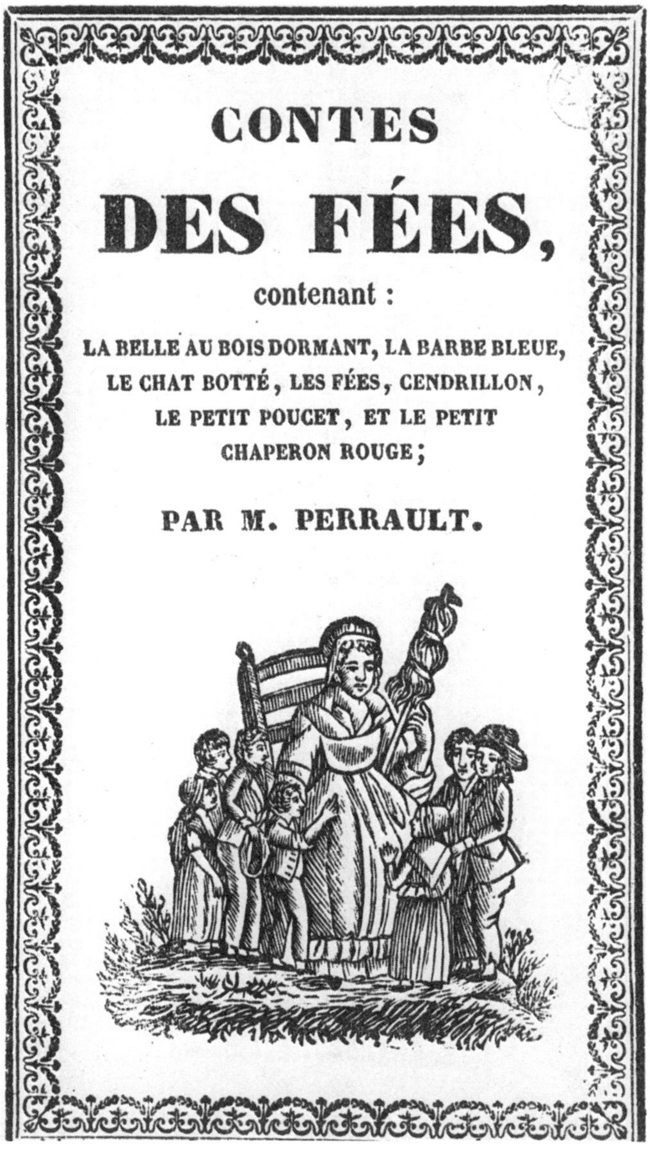

nor moonlight, where the sun always shines"; then for another year in the land "where there is neither day nor night, where the moon always shines"; finally for a third year in the land "where there is neither sun nor moon, and it is always night." There she finds the grass that cuts iron: her iron slippers are broken. She gathers the grass and sets off again, walking until she finds the sun. At the edge of the sea she takes a boat, disembarks on the island where her husband is being held prisoner, puts the wolves to sleep with the singing grass, kills them with the golden knife, breaks the chain of seven hundredweight with the grass that breaks iron, and frees her husband and all his people, who had been turned into ravens.

In this story, then, it is the young girl who must undertake the journey to the world beyond, characterized in this version by cold, ice, darkness, emptiness, and great distance. But unlike what we see when the hero is male, marriage is not the result of the adventure, its crown and reward: marriage represents, rather, something already given at the beginning of the narrative. For the heroine the marriage is acquired almost from the start, but it appears to be an unhappy union with a repulsive creature, a monstrous animal, whom she agrees to marry through filial piety to free her father from a terrible evil or even to save him from death. By overcoming a terrible trial she succeeds in transforming the monstrous marriage into a happy union with a prince "as beautiful as the day." But first she violates a prohibition, and this greatly delays her final happiness.

We see then that the lesson of this story is different from those in which the hero is male. The adolescent boy must undergo an initiation before he can find a bride and accede to the married state; the girl undergoes the same kind of initiation during marriage and through her own fault, because she violates the taboo laid down by her husband. While the nature of the initiation may be the same for both—a voyage full of difficulties to the other world—its meaning is different in the second case: it seems that for girls it is marriage itself that constitutes the initiation. The *Laws of Manu,* the early collection of texts from ancient India compiled between the second century B.C. and the second century A.D., confirms this hypothesis: "For a woman, marriage replaces initiation. Her zeal to serve her husband is for her what study and discipline under the Brahman are for a man, her care in keeping house is equivalent to his maintenance of the sacred fire." For the woman must transform the attachment she has to her father into affection for and devotion to her husband, who appears to her, in a patriarchal society like that of the ancient Indo-Europeans and the cultures that developed from it, as a horrifying monster. One of the forms of the prohibition laid down by her husband consists, in a fairly large number of versions, of not staying too long with her family when she goes to visit them, as she is permitted to do after her marriage. She obeys this rule once, twice, but the third time she goes she forgets the time. That is, the taboo the heroine transgresses is that against remaining too attached to her natal family. As punishment she must suffer a long trial to win her husband back and so to prove her devotion to him. In patrilineal societies, such as Indo-European societies past and present, brides are usually foreigners: they come from a different family, a different lineage. They are introduced into a family that is not their own to fulfill a duty that is essential to the future of this family, i.e., to bear children. It is thus necessary to test their loyalty, devotion, and zeal toward their husbands; this trial constitutes their initiation which, unlike that of the boy, takes place at the time of marriage. This initiation, which has disappeared from the rituals of the Indo-European peoples (assuming that it ever existed), is no longer present except in the popular realm of the imaginary, in the myths underlying their fairy tales. The motif of the voyage to the world beyond, which thus goes back to the initiation of young people, girls or boys, is not, of course, the only mythical motif that appears in these stories, but it is certainly the most important, the richest, and the most persistently fascinating.

N.B./j.l.

BIBLIOGRAPHY

See "Mythic Elements in French Folklore," above.

Folk Beliefs and Legends about Fairies in France

Although they are different in form, beliefs and legends are comparable in their modes of production and their functions. It has often been observed that beliefs engender legends through a process of narrative development: a belief may be expressed in a sentence or unfolded in an account. Such an account always includes specific information about time and place, which are often nearby. Anatole Le Braz, who had noted this phenomenon in his investigations, states it very clearly in the introduction to his book, *The Legend of Death among the Armoricain Bretons* (1923):

> The legend is a local product: we have seen it take root, grow, and flower. It is perpetually in the course of formation and transformation: it is alive. The actors that it brings into play are known or have been known to all. They are the people of the canton, of the parish; they are your neighbors, they are you yourselves. . . . The setting is also real: it lies before your very eyes, at your door. It is the sunken road you have passed over a hundred times, the moor that you see here made fuzzy by gorse, the cemetery enclosed in the dark greenery of great yew trees; it is the sea.

In his book, one can see clearly how the mechanism functions by which belief engenders legend. For example, Le Braz relates the following belief (which is not peculiar to Brittany, since it is certainly found throughout all of France): "As long as a dead person is lying out on the funeral platform, it is an offense to him to send the people of the house out to work in the fields, as if nothing had happened" (1, p. 220). After setting forth this prohibition, he goes on to cite the account of one of his female informants, an account which she had related as a personal reminiscence:

> While she was a servant girl at Kersaliou, the master of the house died. It was the beginning of July, and the eldest son was out haying with the household staff. They

Farmhouse mill and raised stone. Saint-Pierre, Morbihan. Photo Musée des Arts et Traditions populaires.

heard the news at the three o'clock collation. When this was over, the eldest son sent the servants back to work, in spite of being told that such was not the custom. Returning to the field, they perceived a man trampling down the hay, whom they recognized to be their deceased master. The vision disappeared. They finished their work and brought in the hay. The time came a few months later to begin using that hay as forage for the animals. But within a few days all the animals in the stable died, and the veterinarian was unable to do anything for them. The ruined son began drinking, and hanged himself on Christmas night: his failure to respect his dead father had brought about his misfortune.

We can see very clearly in this account the narrative development which has the initial belief for its object. This belief, far from being fixed like a dogma, plays a part in everyday experience and produces its events, which only take on their meaning when they are reconstituted in a narrative form. Here we encounter once again what Henri Hubert affirmed in his study "The Representation of Time in Religion and Magic" (1909): "Myths are rejuvenated in history. They draw out from it elements of reality which serve to consolidate the belief of which they are the object as myths. . . . The rejuvenation of myths is not a phenomenon that is different from the general phenomenon of their localization in the past, but a particular form of the same phenomenon."

"Myths rejuvenated in history" are nothing but legends. It is precisely by virtue of this phenomenon of renewal in and through history that legends are diverse, unstable, and abundant. As the collection of Anatole Le Braz so clearly shows, the same belief may give rise to a great number of different accounts. But one nevertheless always finds in them the generative mythic core that is the belief.

The same phenomenon of the engendering of legends from beliefs is also found in what may be called the topographic mythology of France, in which the principal protagonists are fairies, supernatural beings characterized by their small or Gargantuan size.

Beliefs about fairies are an excellent example of the interpretation of folkloric facts in terms of survivals. A. Maury forcefully declares that "fairies appear to us to be the last and most persistent of all of the vestiges that paganism left imprinted on peoples' minds" (1896). For him, fairies are the inheritors of the characteristics and functions of the Parcae and of the name of Fatum or the Fata, these being no more than the Roman designation for the Parcae. The etymology from *fatum, fata* is certain. As for the attributes of fairies, it cannot be denied that they greatly overlap those of the Parcae.

Like the Parcae, fairies preside over childbirth and decide the fate of the newborn child. They are, as was once said, "wombmates." In Brittany, they were served a meal in a room next to that of the mother who had given birth, as a means of conciliating them. They are also spinners. Van Gennep reports in his *Folklore of Burgundy* (1934, p. 175) that at Clamerey, a fairy named La Beuffenie formerly came to thread her distaff at midnight in a secluded place, on a crag that dominated Armançon. It is sometimes said that menhirs or rocks are distaffs planted in the ground by fairies. The association made about the Parcae between their function as dispensers of fate and their character as spinners is not found explicitly for fairies, although such an association may be postulated on the basis of the great importance of the symbol of the thread of destiny in Europe. But fairies have characteristics that the ancient Parcae do not have. Fairies are connected with the megaliths. The relationship is sometimes only toponymic, resulting in the appellations of the Rock of the Fairies, the Stone of the Fairies, the Cabin of the Fairies, the Cave of the Fairies, etc., to describe menhirs, dolmens, and shady walks throughout France. At times the designations are accompanied by legends:

> Long ago, a fairy traveling through Sainte-Colombe (Landes) carrying the Peyre-Lounque (a rock located in the region) attached to her distaff, met an unknown old man who said to her: "Where are you going?" "To Dax." "You will, if you say, 'And may it please God.'" "Whether or not it pleases Him, the Peyre-Lounque is going to Dax." The old man, who was none other than God himself, ordered her to abandon her rock at that very place, which she had to do, and he added, "Until it pleases God, it will not leave this place." (Sébillot, 1904–7, vol. 4, p. 6)

Sometimes they carry these enormous rocks in their aprons: a rockslide near Ailly in the Vosges is called the Burden or the Fairies' Load—it fell from their aprons. But they are not content merely to spread megaliths around: they are also builders. Near Remiremont, a causeway built with Cyclopean masonry which joins Saint-Mont to the mountain of Morthome bears the name of the Bridge of the Fairies. The amphitheater of Cimiez is called the "Tub of the Fairies." In Poitou, the fairy Mélusine constructed the old roads of the region, as well as the arenas and aqueducts of Poitiers and a great number of chateaux: one night was sufficient for her to build the castle of Lusignan.

This role of builder is totally unknown among the Parcae. It is thus incorrect to see fairies as the heirs of the Parcae merely on the basis of two shared characteristics. The other characteristics of fairies should connect them on the one hand with the popular figure of Gargantua, and on the other with the supernatural and innumerable populations of goblins, elves, sprites, imps, etc.

In French topographical beliefs and legends, Gargantua shapes the countryside, particularly irregularities in terrain.

> In the canton of Châtillon-sur-Indre, people give the name of "foot scrapings of Gargantua" to large mounds, of which the largest is the Footstep of Bourges, located near Clion. It is maintained that once, when Gargantua had one foot in Bourges and the other in this place, he shook one of his shoes, and thus flung his foot-scraping (the mass of clayey soil that sticks to the bottom of the shoes of people who walk in the rainy season) next to the church of Murs, two leagues from Clion, while the other shoe dropped another scraping in the vineyards of Château, close to Bourges, which has been called Mottepelous from time immemorial. (Sébillot, 1883, p. 197–98)

Gargantua is the source of the elevation upon which the city of Laon is built: finding his basket to be too full, he emptied part of it onto the plain, which became a mountain. But it was not only by unloading that he shaped the irregularities in the terrain; it was also, as Rabelais himself said, "en fyantant et compissant (in shitting and pissing)." "In the Chartreuse range, the Aiguille de Quaix is known in the area by the name of l'Etron de Gargantua (Gargantua's Turd). The giant, needing to stop to satisfy a bodily need, placed one foot on the helmet of Nero and the other on Mount Rachais. The needle (Aiguille) does seem to resemble this object from a certain angle. Gargantua pissed at the same time, which is what produced the cascade of Vence." His appetite is not described as any less formidable in popular tradition than it is in Rabelais. He is a glutton who swallows, without noticing them, enormous boats, which he takes to be small flies. But he is sometimes nauseated and vomits them, thus forming the rock of Bé near Saint-Cast, for example.

All of these beliefs and the accounts that develop them are to be found in nearly identical form throughout France, in which Gargantua mythically modeled not so much the landscape in its totality as the most remarkable accidental landforms. The means he uses for this are of an oral and anal nature, so that a mythic character may be seen in him that comes from those two stages of infantile development. His gigantic size has its source in the inverted projection of the disproportionate view that children have of adults and the world.

Tradition often stresses, on the other hand, fairies' diminutive size. They manipulate—it is said—materials which, if they are not always construction materials, are nevertheless hard and resistant. They sometimes carry them in the form or manner of distaffs, or else in their aprons: Gargantua carries malleable materials in his basket or in his stomach (earth, excrement). These characteristics of fairies are clarified if, in opposition to the character of Gargantua, one sees in them phallic figures which would thus belong to the following stage of infantile sexual development.

In their contacts with humans, fairies manifest a certain ambivalence, just like the numerous populations of various goblins, who resemble them in their diminutive size. They render services to humans, but it is difficult to have social ties with them because of their sensitive and skittish character. In the Alps and Pyrenees, those supernatural beings of small stature who help the herders are called servants; in exchange, they are left small offerings in kind, such as the first skimming of the best cream. If one neglects to leave them their share, they may take cruel vengeance, for example, by leading the herd over a cliff and leaving the region forever.

Sometimes the relations between fairies and humans extend to marriage: the legend of Mélusine is the best known of these, but there are a great number of others which always include a prohibition which the husband must scrupulously respect. The nature of the prohibition is quite varied: not to see his fairy-wife while she is bathing, not to see her on Saturday, not to look at her naked shoulder, not to call her a "bad fairy," etc. The union brings prosperity, but one day the husband violates the prohibition and the fairy disappears forever. It is striking to note the frequency of this denouement in accounts which relate the variety of relationships between humans and the small supernatural beings. They disappear, leave the country, and never appear again. The pattern is so marked that one cannot help but wonder whether the etiology of these accounts does not reside precisely in this matter: they exist to explain the disappearance of fairies, goblins, and other sprites, which is due to a fault of men who are unable to maintain good relations with them over long periods of time, in spite of the advantages of such associations. What we see here is a schema similar to that of the great origin myths of primitive peoples, which place at the beginnings of humanity a golden age in which all things were realizable and death did not exist. As the result of a sin, the violation of a taboo, all of the advantages

Mélusine returning to suckle her child. Couldrette, Bibliothèque nationale MS fr. 12575, folio 89. Photo BN.

enjoyed by humanity are withdrawn, and relations with the supernatural beings are interrupted or grow difficult. This is a particularly good example of the process of weakening from mythology to folklore: it is no longer a question of the fate of humanity or the social community, but of the fate of an individual and the outcome of his conjugal union and prosperity.

These legends also manifest, more or less explicitly, a symbolic teaching: the world of fairies and sprites disappeared in the face of Christianity because they belonged to paganism. Once again the ideology of survivals is at work: legends about fairies and their relations with humans are very much of the present, but they tell of a past regarded as finished. The past nevertheless remains inscribed in various places which thus serve as the basis for remembering it.

N.B./d.w.

BIBLIOGRAPHY

See "Mythic Elements in French Folklore."

Popular Customs and Rituals in France

In the preface to his book *Les Saints successeurs des dieux* (The saints: successors of the gods) (1907), P. Saintyves let it be known that his work would be followed by another volume entitled *La Mythologie des rites* (The mythology of rituals), in which he intended to examine the pagan rites that persisted in the cult of the saints and led to the development of certain hagiographic legends. This work never saw the light of day, but its suggestive title raises the question of whether it is proper to speak of a mythology of rituals.

For Saintyves, the transition from myth to ritual was never in question. Referring to the tales of Perrault, he maintains that "a myth is but the exegesis of or the commentary on a ritual," which allows him to regard the stories as the narrative relics of ancient seasonal or initiation rituals that have fallen into disuse. Cinderella is thus the Bride of the Cinders, paraded around on Shrove Tuesday and promised to the young sun, while her stepmother is the old year, and the stepmother's daughters are the months preceding spring. Tom Thumb is the young boy who must undergo initiation rites; he is led by his father into the initiation enclosure, the forest, where he must undergo a number of trials.

I. The Popular Rituals of Marriage

This theory assumes a historical process of degeneration and argues that the evolution proceeds from ritual to myth. If we make an effort to avoid this historicizing point of view, and if we consider the materials of ritual and myth to be coupled in an ongoing relationship, we may then argue that myths and rituals are, in the words of Claude Lévi-Strauss, "different transformations of identical elements." We shall attempt to show this by taking as an example a popular ritual of marriage that was quite widespread in France at least until the end of the nineteenth century, a ritual that is called the "hidden bride," the "false bride," or the "substitute bride." The following description was published in 1823, but its author observed the ritual in Bresse before the Revolution (Monnier, pp. 355–56).

> The day set for signing the contract is commonly the eve of the marriage celebration. Before supper, a peculiar scene unfolds among the Bressans: the bride-to-be invites several of her girlfriends to her house where they put on one another's clothes and move into a separate room. The groom-to-be then shows up with his friends and his brothers and finds the house locked up. They knock at the door and ask about a ewe they have lost. They are told that there is no ewe there that belongs to them, but they are persistent and finally gain entry into the house and search every room. When they get to the door to the room with the girls in it, they knock, ask again, and receive the same answer as before. Finally, one person comes out and, after asserting that he has just checked to see that there was no strange ewe in his flock, makes all the young maidens file out one by one. The husband-to-be makes them dance successively, and if he fails to recognize his bride-to-be, he becomes the object of banter for the rest of the evening.

There are many parallels to this amusing description, among them one that George Sand recounts in the appendix to *La Mare au Diable,* and another, more recent one that originated in the province of the Loire and was in practice until about 1920 (Fortier-Beaulieu).

The young men on the groom's side show up at the door of the bride's house on the morning of the wedding. Everything is locked. They climb over the wall and sing in the courtyard so that the door may be opened for them. They finally get in, but the bride-to-be hides in the hayloft, behind her grandmother's bed, in the kneading trough, or in the covered tipcart, or else she is disguised as a pipe-smoking beggar sitting by the fireplace or as an old woman. In some villages, they used to throw down a dummy called "the ghost," or "the first bride," to the young men assembled in front of the house and then burn it in the farmyard.

These scenes surely have a playful element, but they could not have been enacted for the sole purpose of entertaining the wedding guests, especially the young men. An apparently insignificant clue suggests that this ritual was so important that just as it was disappearing a new element came to pick up a part of the meaning of the former practice. At the time when the custom was waning in the country in France, i.e., between 1870 and 1880, the bridal gown as we know it today came into fashion: the white dress and veil. The function of the veil may have been to conceal the bride temporarily, when the ritual of the hidden bride was no longer performed; for the veil harkens back through the centuries to the custom in ancient Rome, where *nubere* meant both to veil and to marry.

The symbolism of this ritual may first be deciphered on the social level. It is meant to express and play upon the reservations felt by the "wife givers," which is what at that moment the parents and friends of the bride happen to be, toward the "wife takers," the groom's party. This can only be a game, since it takes place at a moment in the long process of betrothal and marriage when the marriage agreement has

Peasants carrying firebrands in the fields on Christmas Eve. Tonneins (Lot-et-Garonne). Drawing by Gustave Janet. Photo Musée des Arts et Traditions populaires, Paris.

The lamb cart at Christmas. Les Baux. Photo Musée des Arts et Traditions populaires, Paris.

long since been concluded and would be very difficult to undo.

But the ritual has a deeper symbolic level that reaches down to the underlying myth. To bring it to light, we must call on a set of supernatural stories known in the international typology as the substitute bride (T403). One of the finest versions in French was collected by J. F. Bladé in 1886 and is entitled *Le Drac*.

By his first wife, a man has two strong, brave sons and a daughter as beautiful as the morning. His wife dies, and he marries a wicked, ugly widow who has a daughter who resembles her in every way. She persecutes her stepchildren until the two exasperated brothers leave for the war in order to distinguish themselves; they promise to find a husband for their sister, and they take a little statue with them made in her likeness (in other versions, it is a portrait). They demonstrate such courage in war that the son of the king of France summons them. He sees the statuette, falls in love with their sister, and orders them to fetch her so that he may marry her. The jealous stepmother, with her daughter, escorts the two brothers and the bride-to-be, who is dressed in her wedding gown. On the way, the stepmother intercepts the communication between the brothers and the sister and forces the sister to take off her wedding clothes. She puts them on her own daughter and throws the bride-to-be into a mud pit. The king's son, furious to see such an ugly girl arrive, sends the two brothers, the stepmother, and her daughter to their deaths. (In other French versions the prince marries the homely girl because he falls victim to the stepmother's magic spell.) The true bride-to-be is first rescued by a gardener's wife and then carried off by the Drac into his underwater kingdom. He ties her to a long gold chain that allows her to reach the shore. For three days she sings a riddling song that intrigues the prince's servants. The prince is alerted, breaks the chain, and recognizes the girl as his promised bride. (In the versions in which the prince kept the false bride and the stepmother, he expels the intruder and punishes her mother severely.)

In this story as in the ritual, a bride is temporarily hidden from her groom and replaced by a false bride. This thematic core is enriched in the tale with important imaginary developments that the ritual cannot afford. The theme, however, is the same. What is its meaning?

If we accept Claude Lévi-Strauss's contention that men exchange women in the same way that they exchange words, it is easy to recognize in the tale of the substitute bride the transfer of a woman to a man, the prince, her future husband, a transfer brought about by another man, her brother; the transfer is interrupted by the stepmother and then reestablished. The interruption of the transfer is achieved by the interruption of communication between the brother and sister. Coming as an intermediary between them, the stepmother alters the brother's words and is thus able to eliminate the sister and to substitute her own daughter, the false bride-to-be. But if women stopped circulating among men, marriages could only be incestuous. The false bride-to-be of the ritual and the tale is a representation of the imaginary incestuous bride-to-be and is substituted in play for a brief moment in place of the true bride-to-be, the one whom it is socially permissible to marry.

This interpretation of the tale, and later of the ritual, is confirmed by a story that is not French but most certainly belongs to the Indo-European mythical heritage. We are referring to a story that is part of the Nart epic that was made known to us by G. Dumézil (1930, 1968–73). This collection of popular epic legends is characteristic of some populations of the northern Caucasus, from the Black Sea to the Caspian Sea, and most particularly of the Ossets, the probable descendants of the ancient Scythians, among whom the narrative tradition has proved to be the most long-lived, though their neighbors, the Chechen-Ingush, Cherkess, and Abkhaz have sizable fragments in the form of variants. The saga of the Narts, fabulous heroes who lived in very ancient times, is of considerable interest: in a "folklorized" form, it has preserved to this day features of ancient Indo-European mythology, particularly the trifunctional organization of society identified by Georges Dumézil.

This epic presents an extremely popular female character, remarkable for her birth, beauty, and intelligence: the Prin-

The new fire of Holy Saturday. Copperplate. Paris, Picard, 1724. The rekindling of the fires is prescribed by the Roman rite, but it is also a ritual found in a large number of religious systems and carries a cosmological meaning and function. Paris, Musée des Arts et Traditions populaires. Museum photo.

cess Satana. The story of her wedding may be viewed as a parallel to the ritual and tale of the substitute bride. This reading of the story is much more direct, much cruder, but all the more interesting in that we are dealing with a tradition that originates in Indo-European mythology and is better preserved, less worked over and altered, than the French tradition.

Satana is the sister of the two high-ranking heroes from one of the three principal families of the Nart epic, the Äxsärtägkats, characterized by valor and strength; one of the other two families is distinguished by abundant cattle and the other by intelligence. When she is old enough to marry, Satana asks herself who is the man most worthy of her and concludes that only her own brother, Uryzmäg, is bold and intelligent enough for her. She sees only one obstacle to this project: he is already married. Nevertheless, she shares her project with him: "No one gives away his finest possession as a gift. Would it not be a pity for me to go over to another family? So I can marry only you." He repels her indignantly; she must therefore practice deceit. Some time later, Uryzmäg sets out on an expedition for a year and orders his wife to prepare food and drink for his return. When the year has nearly elapsed, she dutifully proceeds to prepare the intoxicating beverage of the Narts. Try as she may, she cannot make the liquid, because Satana has prevented this by a magic spell. The desperate wife asks her sister-in-law to come to her aid. Satana consents on condition that her brother's wife will lend her her wedding gown and veil for one night. The wife agrees and soon the drink is ready. Uryzmäg comes home; a great feast takes place and at night Satana dressed as the wife takes the wife's place in the conjugal bedroom. Through magic she prolongs the wedding night beyond its normal duration. When the legitimate wife dies of a broken heart, Satana reveals her true identity to her brother, who is at first horrified and then resigned.

Carnival in Paris. Woodcut by Gangel in Metz. Photo Musée des Arts et Traditions populaires, Paris.

It would be hard not to see in this account one of the primitive forms of the French tale and ritual despite the alterations they have undergone, alterations that change the reading but not the meaning. The tale and the ritual show that in all marriages there is the risk and temptation of incest, which is conjured up and played out in this manner to make it easier to avoid it. The Ossetic account shows this incest as having been realized, but it is realized by supernatural heroes and not by human beings, since the narrative form is that of a legend: this is another way to avoid incest.

This example of the deciphering of a ritual through a story need not imply that the myth predates the ritual and serves as its basis. These are two different forms of expression, one of which, myth, enjoys greater freedom in the realm of the imaginary and thus allows us to register a greater number of elements that may lead to an interpretation. On the other hand, what ritual loses in the imaginary realm, it gets back in the form of the considerable affective impact of enactment. In this light, the old debate about the priority of one of the forms or the other is no longer at issue.

This popular ritual of marriage, which seems to stem from

a common Indo-European source, may be classified in the very important category of rites of passage. The inventor of this heuristic concept, Arnold van Gennep (1909), placed under this rubric not only the rituals that mark the course of a human life from the cradle to the grave but also those that mark the passage of time, that is, periodical and cyclical, seasonal and calendrical ceremonies. Among the first kind, marriage was certainly the most important and the most developed. Baptism, which marked the newborn child's entrance into the social and religious community, long remained a ceremony restricted to a very small number of individuals. And although funerals sometimes brought the entire local community together, the authority of the Church acted as an obstacle to any significant development of popular rituals on these occasions.

II. Bonfires, Stakes, Firebrands, Fire Wheels, Christmas, Lent, and Midsummer Day

Among the numerous periodic rituals, those that involve the use of fire, whether bonfires or firebrands, are particularly noteworthy because of the mythical content one is tempted to see in them. In France, as in most European countries, rituals of fire were performed during the cycles of Christmas, Lent, and Midsummer Day (24 June). The dates of Christmas and of Midsummer Day fall close to those of the winter and summer solstices (21 December and 21 June). As a result, authors have viewed these holidays as Christianized forms of pagan solar cults. Despite the denials by van Gennep, who insisted that these were *not* solstitial ceremonies, the near coincidence of the dates is striking, though it does not fully explain the content of the rituals as they were performed.

The bonfires of the cycle of Shrove Tuesday–Lent are, within the general schema, related to those of Midsummer Day. In fact, in most instances they are mutually exclusive: wherever fires are made during Lent, they are not made on Midsummer Day, and vice versa. The rule is not absolutely general, since there are some folkloric zones where the practice takes place at both times of the year. Such places, however, are rare and are situated mostly at points of contact between areas of Midsummer Day bonfires (northwestern, western, southwestern, southeastern France) and areas of Shrove Tuesday–Lent fires (eastern, central-eastern France). The general schema of ceremonies of bonfires and firebrands calls for a celebration at each solstice except when the summer celebration is replaced by another one scheduled halfway through the cycle, at around the time of the equinox. This very general arrangement shows that the part of the year that is ceremonial in this respect begins at the moment when the day begins to grow longer and ends when it stops growing longer; the beginning of the period is marked by a bonfire ritual at home and the end—or the midpoint—by a communal bonfire ritual.

During the Twelve Days of Christmas, that is, the period from Christmas to Epiphany, there were few localities where bonfires or firebrands were lighted. The custom practiced at Pertuis in the Vaucluse is therefore noteworthy because of its rarity. The feast of the Beautiful Star, fully described in the eighteenth century by the Abbé Achard, was celebrated on the eve of Epiphany. This is how an observer at the beginning of the twentieth century described it: "The star is nothing but a cart with its rear carriage loaded with flammable material. In front sits a man who seems to drive the team. The cart is drawn by ten or twelve animals and crosses the town at full gallop to the acclaim of all the people. Buckets of water are poured at every moment over the firebox so as to prevent the flame from reaching the driver. If the fire flares up, it is a sure sign of a good crop. . . . But if the fire goes out or does not rise in a spiral, the crop will be poor, and everyone goes home unhappy. After the ride, the cart is unloaded in the town square and whoever gets hold of a burning firebrand first and carries it home to his hearth will bring good fortune there" (van Gennep, 1937–58, p. 3043). This curious moving bonfire, which represents the star followed by the Magi, thus determines whether crops will be good or bad, while its firebrands protect the house.

In some festivities in the Christmas cycle, firebrands are carried as individual torchlights. In and around Dreux, the processions of the Flaming Coals took place on Christmas Eve. The torches were pieces of wood dried in an oven and split lengthwise down the middle. The children's torches were mullein stems dipped in oil. All the townspeople would gather by neighborhoods around five in the afternoon and assemble at the Town Hall, where the clergy and the magistrates would join them. From there they would all walk three times around the covered market and the Church of Saint-Pierre, shouting "Noël, nolet, nolet." Upon returning to their neighborhoods, the people would lay down their torches to form a bonfire with the nonburning ends facing outward. They would then bring the remainder of that end piece back home with them to ward off misfortune. "This procession would take place in surprising order and with great respect, considering the size of the crowd." It was also said that the fire from the torches did not scorch or hurt. The circumambulation of the market and the presence of shepherds who had brought lambs with them from nearby farms suggest that the ritual was meant to attract prosperity.

The custom of the Yule log, though not practiced everywhere, was nevertheless much more widespread than the custom of the firebrands. The earliest description of this ritual comes from a student from Basel who was working on a doctorate in medicine at Montpellier. It dates back to 1597.

> On 24 December, Christmas Eve . . . a large log is placed on the andirons in the fireplace, over the fire. When it starts burning, the entire household assembles around the fire and the youngest . . . is supposed to hold a glass full of wine, a piece of bread, and a little salt in his right hand and a lighted candle in his left hand. Then all the boys and the men remove their hats and the youngest (or his father in his place) speaks thus: "Wheresoever the master of the house comes and goes / may God grant him much good / And no evil at all / And may God grant him childbearing women / kidding goats / lambing ewes / foaling mares / kittening cats / rat-bearing rats / And no evil at all, but plenty of good." It is said that the live coals cannot burn through a tablecloth on which they are placed. The people carefully keep the coals the year round. . . . When this has been done, they sit down to an ample meal, without fish or meat, but with excellent wine, preserves, and fruit. The table is set and left overnight, and on it are placed half a glass of wine, bread, salt, and a knife. (van Gennep 1937–58, pp. 3101–5)

This precise description requires only a few additional bits of information that are easily furnished by the accounts of countless regional witnesses. It is sometimes said that the log must be big enough to burn for three days (in which case it is called *Tréfoué*), or even for all twelve days of the cycle. Usually it is supposed to come from a fruit-bearing tree; in this connection, it is not hard to understand the choice of a log from an oak tree, since acorns once were human and animal food, and oak is a hard and slow-burning wood.

The half-burned logs are kept and used in often well-defined magical ways: they protect people and animals from illness; they keep harmful animals away from the house and the fields; they forewarn against the evil spells of sorcerers. Like the fire of Midsummer Day, the fire of the Yule log does not cause burns, nor do its sparks. Sometimes people would hit it with a firebrand in order to make as many sparks fly as possible, while uttering the following formula of prosperity: "So many bushels of wheat, so many jugs of wine" (Auvergne); "As many sparks as little chicks" (Poitou); "As many sheaves and sheaflets as sparks and sparklets" (Côte d'Or). The children would also hit it with a stick to get out the preserves and dried fruits that had been hidden in it for them. People would then say in Burgundy and in Franche-Comté that the log was "vomiting," "pissing," "shitting," or "giving birth."

The ritual of the Yule log is designed to promote prosperity, human, animal, and agricultural. The ritual is in most cases celebrated inside the home and within the family circle. Furthermore, it does not appear as if the Church tried to eradicate it as being superstitious, nor did it try to Christianize it. The few observable Christian embellishments seem to have been added spontaneously and rather late in the process without altering the essence of the ritual. In all of these matters, the fires of Midsummer Day differ from the Yule log. The Church fought long and hard against the Midsummer fires and, unable to eradicate them, tried to give them a Christian veneer through the presence of the clergy and through a process of rationalizing the ritual by assimilating it to the feast of Saint John the Baptist. Moreover, the fires are lighted by the whole local community and out of doors, in the most public way possible: the site is often chosen so that the fire can be seen from a great distance. Thus, not only do the Midsummer Day bonfires differ from the Yule logs in a number of characteristics, but they also have a much more highly developed and much richer ritual. A great number of descriptions of the Midsummer fires are listed in a bibliography in the *Manuel* by van Gennep (1937–58). The following one comes from the marshlands of Poitou; it was published at the beginning of the nineteenth century.

> The eve of Midsummer Day is a great festival throughout the countryside. After sunset, each brings his piece of firewood to the square; the firewood is shaped into a pyramid; the priest then comes forward in a solemn procession and lights the fire. The crackling fire thrills every heart; everyone looks joyful. Young men and women hold hands and are eager to start dancing around the new fire. But the heads of the families are there, and before they give way to the impatient young people, everyone must pass through the salutary flame the thick clump of mullein plants and walnut tree branches which, before the following dawn, must be placed above the door of the main cattleshed. Finally the ceremony is over, the young people remain in possession of the arena, the silence is broken, the groups spring forward, shouts of joy are heard, and there is dancing and singing. In the meantime, the old people warm themselves and place cinders in their clogs to ward off a multitude of ills.

From these descriptions, a certain number of general features of rituals can be identified that are pertinent to this particular ceremony. First, the entire local community participates in the preparation of the bonfire, and each person, even the poorest, contributes a piece of firewood. Sometimes, but more rarely, all the young people are charged with collecting the wood. Second, the lighting is performed by the clergy so that the Church may appear to be in control of what it could not prevent. Third, there is a procession around the fire, sometimes once, sometimes repeatedly, either before, or more often after, the lighting. The procession may make three, nine, or, rarely, fourteen (as in Bresse) full circles around the fire, or it may last until the fire dies out. Rounds are danced by "young people of both sexes" according to the reports of almost all observers. In some localities, the dances predicted and assured a prompt marriage. Fourth, the people made the fire give off as much smoke as possible by throwing herbs and green branches (sometimes bones) on the fire, and people and animals would be exposed to the smoke. Finally, when the fire began to die down, there were still two ritual acts to be performed. The participants, especially the young men and women, would jump over the bonfire once or several times, in order to get certain benefits: to protect themselves from illness, to get married within the year, to enjoy general prosperity. Then the half-burned pieces of firewood would be retrieved and kept in the house throughout the year so they would protect all those who lived in the house, human and animal alike, against lightning, fire, thieves, and sickness. The remains of the Yule log had the same power, and the fire of Midsummer Day, like that of Christmas, is not supposed to scorch.

The other forms of the ritual fires of Midsummer are relatively rare but all the more noteworthy. The most beautiful description, published in 1822, recounts the festival of the fire wheel of Basse-Kontz, in the district of Thionville (Teissier). This village is built halfway up the slope on the left bank of the Moselle River. The top of the slope forms a plateau called the Stromberg. The men and boys of the village go to the top at nightfall, while the women and the girls remain halfway up by the fountain. The wheel is on top; it is a straw cylinder "weighing four to five hundred pounds with a pole going through its center and sticking out three feet on either side. The pole is the rudder which the two drivers of the wheel hold on to." Every inhabitant has willingly provided a bale of straw: refusal to do so would bring certain misfortune in the course of the year. The surplus straw is used to make firebrands. As soon as the wheel is set on fire, two young men grab the ends of the pole and send it rolling down the slope. The goal is to dive into the Moselle river and extinguish what is left of the flaming wheel. But they rarely manage to do it. Success means that there will be a good crop. During this time, the men light straw firebrands, hurl them into the air, and relight them as long as the wheel continues to roll. Some run alongside the wheel. When it passes by the women assembled halfway down, they greet it with shouts.

This ritual clearly reveals an agrarian magic. The proper guidance of the wheel and its immersion in the river are the guarantors and omens of a plentiful harvest in the vineyard. This feature is also present in the bonfires of Midsummer Day, but often more diffusely and less explicitly.

Authors have identified these festivals as the remnants of a pagan cult of the sun. In this regard, the most interesting study was Henri Gaidoz's work on the Gallic sun god (1886). Some Gallic statues represent an individual often naked, bearded, with a full head of hair, and carrying a six-spoked wheel in his hand. More highly Romanized in southeastern Gaul, he seems to have been assimilated to Jupiter. For Gaidoz, the wheel is the image of the sun. There is no shortage of evidence in Indo-European (particularly Indian) mythologies to convince one of this. Furthermore, "the principal Christian festivals were substituted," he claims, "for festivals predating Christianity by quite some time, and for dates that for many centuries had already been devoted to popular cults." Since the two solstices were the most striking dates in popular imagination, the two great festivals of the year must have been scheduled at these times. In fact, we know of only one, the great feast of Mithra, the *Sol invictus,* which was celebrated on December 25. We must not forget, however, that Mithraism, which came from the East, was adopted by the Roman legions at the beginning of the Christian era and was not firmly established among the populations among whom they were camping. As far as the feast of Midsummer Day is concerned, Gaidoz is content to assert that it is "the continuation, under a Christian label, of the feast of the summer solstice, that the wheel, the symbol of our Gallic god, played a major role in these rites, and that our memories of it are not yet lost, though they are becoming fainter every day." This course of development is difficult to prove, for there is no known ancient ceremony celebrated on the summer solstice. Moreover, the first reference to the feast of Midsummer Day dates from the seventh century and appears in a homily of Saint Eloy, who says: "Let no one on Midsummer Day or on certain solemn occasions honoring the Saints practice the observance of the solstices, dances, carols, and diabolical songs." A survival of Germanic paganism is excluded from this, since the oldest reference to the fires of Midsummer Day in Germany dates from 1181. What remains is the problematic Celtic origin. No document indicates that solstitial fires existed in Gaul. Nothing proves that the god of the wheel, most likely a solar deity, was indeed associated with rituals of this kind. To account both for the Gallo-Roman deity and for the popular rites of Midsummer Day, it is enough to see in the wheel and particularly in the flaming wheel an Indo-European symbol of the sun.

It is, however, difficult to exclude totally from the data concerning the popular festivals of Midsummer Day the fact that at this time in the solar year the sun is at its apogee and that it is about to wane. In certain communities of the Auvergne, Bourbonnais, Languedoc, the Vosges, and the Bouches-du-Rhône, people would climb to the top of a hill during the night of June 23–24 to watch the sun rise and to greet it, often with shouts of joy. In this way, they would topographically mark the most extreme point of the sun's summer rising. Curiously, the Church in its efforts to Christianize these moments of rejoicing rationalized their connection with the summer solstice through the hallowed character of John the Baptist. In John 3:30, Saint John the Baptist, speaking of Jesus and introducing himself as his precursor, says, "He must increase and I must decrease," while Saint Augustine, making an error of a few days, says, *"In Johannis nativitate dies decrescit"* (on John's nativity the day decreases). We can see in this an example of the complex process by which French folklore was formed, probably mostly during the high Middle Ages according to the repeated claims of van Gennep. This formation, this invention, is by and large the result of the encounter, sometimes even the collision, between the Christian tradition, well established by that time, and popular mythical creativity.

Symbolically, the fires of Midsummer Day thus represent the sun at the height of its strength, just before it starts decreasing. The symbolism is quite clear in the case of the flaming wheels, since many mythologies represent the sun in this form. But the French rituals of the summer solstice are neither the reflection nor the relic of an improbable solar mythology. They can only really be explained if we consider

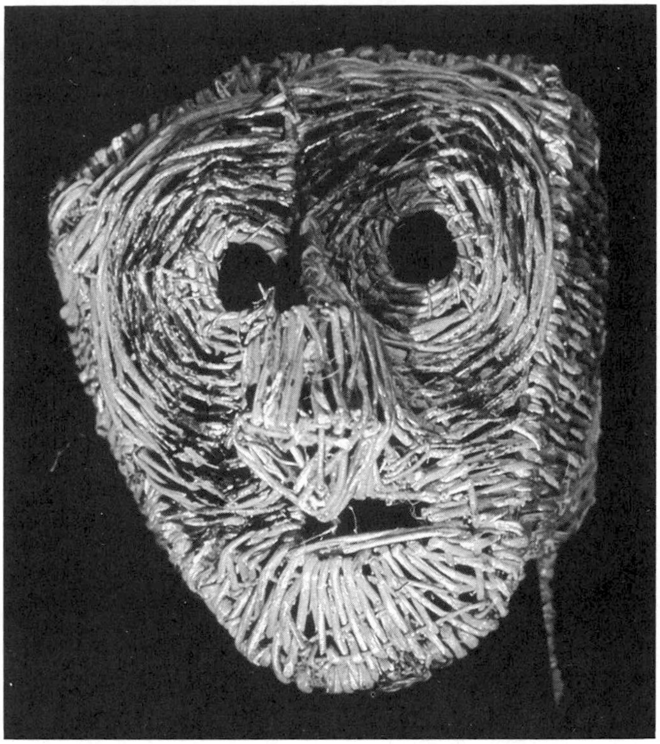

Mask. Aubrac. Photo Musée des Arts et Traditions populaires, Paris.

Midsummer Day bouquet above a cowshed door (Doubs). Photo Musée des Arts et Traditions populaires, Paris.

the general annual system of fires and bonfires: at Christmas, Shrove Tuesday–Lent, and Midsummer Day. It has been said that these rituals defined, in a way, one-half of the ceremonial year. Not that the second part of the year has no calendrical festivals, but they are much rarer and of lesser importance. As a result, the ritual organization of the year does not follow the Celtic calendar that divided the year into two parts in terms of two great festivals: Samain (November 1) and Beltaine (May 1), to which were added two other divisions determined by the festivals called Imbolc (February 1, Feast of Saint Bridget) and Lugnasad (August 1). This calendar did not follow the movement of the sun like the French popular calendar, the key to which rests not so much in solar symbolism as in the accompanying agrarian magic. The increasing sun, represented and supported by fire rituals, is the symbol, the guarantor, and the omen of the growth of plants, the propagation of domestic animals, and the prosperity of human beings. As the youngest in the family in Montpellier would say after the lighting of the Yule log: "And may God grant him childbearing women / kidding goats / lambing ewes / foaling mares / kittening cats / rat-bearing rats / And no evil at all, but plenty of good." All the fires that were lighted between Christmas and Midsummer Day, including Shrove Tuesday and Lent, involved formulas and rituals with an agrarian function. Within this general frame of reference, the rituals of Shrove Tuesday–Lent are partly the doublets of those of Midsummer Day. Of course, they also involve other elements, which the reader will find described in Gaignebet's book on the subject, a book full of erudition, but sometimes questionable from the theoretical point of view.

In the underlying mythology of the calendar ritual system, bonfires and firebrands represent the sun increasing from the winter solstice to the summer solstice, not as the symbols of a forgotten pagan deity but because the nature of fire enables it to materialize the idea of growth and the irresistible burgeoning of plants. Like the plant kingdom, fire moves upward and defies gravity. The Church accorded only a limited place to agrarian rituals (ember days and Rogation Days), but popular mythical thinking spontaneously created those forms of ritual for which it felt the need.

N.B./g.h.

BIBLIOGRAPHY

See the article "Mythic Elements in French Folklore."

Romanticism and Mythology: The Use of Myths in Literary Works

I. In France

According to Schelling, the products of mythology "by their depth, their endurance, and their universality are comparable only to nature itself." Nineteenth-century French literature sought a grand epic synthesis, philosophical and social; this is evident in Balzac's *Human Comedy,* the works of Ballanche, Lamartine's *Visions,* Victor Hugo's *Legend of the Centuries* and *God,* Michelet's *History of France,* and Auguste Comte's *Course of Positive Philosophy.*

Moreover, myths, as Mircea Eliade has pointed out, "reveal the structures of the real and the multiple modes of being in the world." Archaic myths are generally simplifications, designed to facilitate the understanding of the real, whereas later myths, by contrast, complicate forms and relations. The myths elaborated by nineteenth-century writers generally fall into the second category, whether they consciously modified an old myth to give it a new meaning or created a wholly or partially new myth.

At the beginning of the nineteenth century, a debate was launched between supporters of Greek and Roman mythology and partisans of the Christian supernatural. In Germany (see references to Herder below) and in France, many pondered over the origins of mythologies and over the meaning that they should be given.

For our purposes, the century begins with Goethe and Schiller in Germany, with William Blake in England, and in France with Chateaubriand's publication of *The Genius of Christianity* in 1802. This date, a milestone, also happens to be the year of Victor Hugo's birth. From then until 1825 there was a veritable war of mythologies. In a work entitled *On Literature,* which appeared before 1800, Madame de Staël called upon the Olympian Zeus, also known as the celestial Jupiter, to make way for Óðinn. She proposed to replace the fables of the Greeks and Romans with fables by Scottish, Icelandic, and Scandinavian bards, which she mixed together, designating them under the general rubric of Norse Mythology. In fact, as early as 1756, Paul-Henri Mallet had published his *Monuments of the Mythology and the Poetry of the Celts, particularly of the Ancient Scandinavians [sic].* In this work he brought to French readers the poems of the *Edda,* which he introduced as the "Bible of the Norse God Odin." In 1760, James MacPherson published his *Fragments of Ancient Poetry,* which inspired the pseudo-Ossian fashion. According to Madame de Staël, again in *On Literature,* "the shock to the imagination that the Ossianic poems cause inclines one's thought toward the deepest meditations." She thought that this mythology prepared the way for the acceptance of Christianity among the Norse peoples, because she did not understand the violent and bloody character of most of the gods in the *Edda.* It was not by chance that Ossian was one of Napoleon's favorite readings and remained in vogue throughout his reign.

In England, people never stopped reading the Bible. In France, Chateaubriand in the *Genius of Christianity* (1802) took up the defense of the Christian supernatural and recommended that poets seek inspiration in the Bible, in Milton, and in Tasso. It was partly through his influence that the Old Testament was rediscovered and became one of the bedside books of the French romantics.

Germanic influences helped to give the Christian supernatural its full vigor. Among these influences were Gessner's *Idylls* and Friedrich Klopstock's *Messiah* (1758–73). Vigny owed his "Jewish poems" to them, and by 1823 he was ready to institute in France a "Christian theogony" modeled, he claimed, on that of Hesiod. During the Empire, Edward Young's *Night Thoughts* (1742–45) made the Last Judgment a fashionable subject. Milton's *Paradise Lost* was translated into verse by Delille in 1804, and into prose by Chateaubriand in

1836. But Chateaubriand's theories led poets on a false trail. Chateaubriand criticized the epics of Dante, Milton, and Klopstock, condemning any poem in which religion constituted the central subject and not the subordinate theme, "where the supernatural is the *basis* of rather than incidental to the image." In his pamphlet *The Literary Scruples of the Baroness Mme de Staël* (1814), Alexandre Soumet opposed this theory; he wrote: "Could it be that subjects almost entirely based on the supernatural such as *The Messiah* and *Paradise Lost* are the only ones that can henceforth be apprehended by the stern imagination of the moderns? Our epic concepts must touch throughout upon the mysteries of another world." When in 1840 he published *The Divine Epic,* he stated in his preface that he had turned the Muse into a "mystical initiate," adding: "The supernatural, which is only incidental in ancient epics, almost always becomes the very subject of the songs of a modern epic poet. A wholly spiritualist religion commands him."

In order to avoid the sublime monotony that such a conception of an epic might engender, writers resorted to national traditions, fairies, magicians, and witches for the sake of variety. From 1813 to 1817, Marchangy published his eight-volume *Poetic Gaul,* devoting a large part of it to Scandinavian mythology and to an enchanting supernatural derived from Tasso. He claimed that the French national epic was organized around the figure of Charlemagne and that France's national epics might well rival Homeric literature. Charles Nodier emerged as the promoter of this "national" supernatural. In the *Journal of Debates* of 27 November 1817 (an article collected in book 2 of the *Mélanges de littérature,* pp. 317–24), he enthusiastically hailed the completion of the publication of *Poetic Gaul,* and he wrote:

> Look at your fables, your mythology, your old customs, poems, and tragedies: sublime subjects among which we merely have to make a choice, to give the seal of genius, so that in the empire of drama and epic they can take the place of the lamentable and eternal stories of Troy, Argos, Thebes, and Mycenae.

Nodier himself later illustrated the mythology of superstitions with *Trilby* and *The Crumb Fairy.*

The coexistence of Christianity with popular beliefs, some of which go back to prehistoric times, can be astonishing. Nonetheless, Madame de Staël pointed out in *De l'Allemagne* (1810) that popular superstitions are always analogous to the dominant religion, and she added: "A host of beliefs ordinarily attach themselves to religion and history alike." Joseph de Maistre went even further: "Man's worth can only be measured by what he believes. That does not mean that one should believe in nonsense, but it is always better to believe too much than to believe nothing." Moreover, in the tenth homily in the *Soirées in Saint Petersburg* the same author declares that superstition, as the term implies, is something beyond legitimate belief, and that, as such, it is "an advanced work of religion that must not be destroyed." This is a kind of paraphrase of the Gospel parable of the good and bad seed. Notes published by E. Dermenghem argue: "Superstition is the excess of religion . . . We must not believe that religion is one thing and superstition another, rather we should seriously ask ourselves if superstition might not be a necessary advance post of religion" (*Joseph de Maistre the Mystic,* p. 28).

Nodier always claimed that the supernatural answered a fundamental human need, the need to believe. He was later saddened to see popular beliefs on the wane, and would take great pains to preserve their memory. He showed clearly how the frenzied supernatural and the fantastic were born of the decadence of faith. Several works present the confrontation of mythologies. In *The War of the Gods* (1797), Evariste Parny burlesqued the confrontation of gods from various regions. Curiously, this mythological hodgepodge foreshadowed the parades of divine characters in Flaubert's *Temptation of Saint Anthony.* Chateaubriand, looking back with irony on his early work, *The Natchez,* later said, "It shows the supernatural in all its forms—the Christian supernatural, the mythological supernatural, the Indian supernatural: muses, angels, demons, spirits." In *The Martyrs* (1809), too, episodes associated with the religions of the Gauls and the Norse are added to the central struggle between Greco-Roman mythology on the one side and Christianity on the other.

Marchangy suggested as a subject for an epic the reestablishment of the empire by Charlemagne, precisely because it offered an opportunity to depict the gods of various religions. This is what the Vicomte of Arlincourt referred to in the second canto of his epic *Charlemagne, or the Caroleid* (1818), in which the gods Teutates, Óðinn, and Irminsul foment a rebellion against Charlemagne for his role in the spreading of Christianity. Throughout the epic (which has no less than twenty-four cantos), many mythologies are brought together. One step farther and it would be syncretism. This can already be found in Fabre d'Olivet, the author of *The Loves of Rose and Ponce de Meyrueis* (1803), who wrote a poem entitled *The Troubadour,* made up of five cantos and written in the archaic French of the langue d'oc. In this last work, the angel Gabriel is assimilated to Cupid, and Mary to Juno; Mary Magdalene becomes a figure of Mylita-Astarte as well as Aphrodite-Venus, and the deadly sins bear Hebrew names.

Vico's *New Science* appeared in 1725, although its influence in France was not felt until Michelet's translation in 1827. According to Vico, myths could be viewed as a kind of summary of primitive history. He saw in Homer a collective being, a symbol of the Greek people chanting their own story in national epics. In eighteenth-century France, Vico had a heterodox disciple in Nicolas Boulanger, who in his *Antiquity Unveiled by Customs* (1766) claimed to have found the source of all mythologies in the revolutions in nature, especially in the memory of the great geological catastrophes.

The nine-volume *Primitive World* of Court de Gébelin (1773–84) exerted a considerable influence. In this work, all myths were endowed with a historical meaning, often closely related to the history of agriculture. But the etymological dictionaries included in this work also engage in a deep meditation on language, an extension of some of the speculations of Father Athanasius Kircher.

In year III of the First Republic (A.D. 1794), Charles-François Dupuis published his *Origin of All Cults,* which set forth the thesis that the adventures of the gods describe the phenomena of nature, primarily celestial phenomena, such as the revolutions of the sun and the moon, their movements with respect to the constellations, etc. Although these theories have a measure of truth, they cannot account for the totality of all myths.

The idea of a universal revelation, which already appears in Lafitau's work in the eighteenth century, was quite widespread in the nineteenth century. With the development of secret societies and Illuminism, some authors claimed to recognize a prefiguration of Masonic rituals in the mysteries of Egypt and Eleusis. They traced the universal tradition step by step, and in their view myths had multiple and deep meanings. One work was particularly representative: *Freemasonry Traced to Its True Origin, or the Antiquity of Freemasonry*

Proved by the Explication of the Ancient and Modern Mysteries, by Alexandre Lenoir (1814).

Joseph de Maistre shared with these authors the belief in a primitive revelation identical with Hebrew and Christian monotheism. In his *Essay on Indifference in the Matter of Religion* (4 volumes, 1817–23), Lammenais later claimed to have rediscovered the original monotheism hidden behind the gods of polytheism. Baron Eckstein later introduced Hindu mythology into France in his newspaper *The Catholic,* and Lamartine then used his translations from the Sanskrit in his *Plain Course in Literature.* According to Eckstein, paganism was nothing but a corrupted and degenerate Catholicism, and he searched everywhere for the old sources of beliefs, doctrines, and symbols that could make up what might be called "the catholicism before Catholicism." He laid the groundwork for the comparative history of religions by comparing the myths of India, Iran, Greece, Scandinavia, and ancient Germany. Some of these studies foreshadow astoundingly the works of George Dumézil.

Eckstein's role was considerable. He introduced into France the ideas of his master, Frederick Kreuzer, the author of the celebrated *Symbolism and Mythology of Ancient Peoples* published in 1810–12. In 1824, Benjamin Constant, who had read the work in German, predicted in the first volume of his book *On Religion* the triumph of Kreuzer's book over "the narrow and arid system of Dupuis," and Constant added, "It will be a triumph for the imagination and in certain ways a gain for science." In fact, Kreuzer's work marked the dawn of the science of myths; Joseph-Daniel Guigniaut would later devote his life to translating him, to completing and rectifying him, and thus he became in France the true founder of religious studies, as Michelet pointed out. The French edition of Guigniaut's work, thus enriched, appeared in ten volumes between 1825 and 1851, with an extremely suggestive volume of plates. Entitled *Religions of Antiquity Considered Principally in Their Symbolic and Mythological Forms,* it fascinated the poets because it supplied them with a whole repertory of symbols and analogies. Drawing upon Schelling's philosophy of nature, Kreuzer claimed that the symbol is "the primitive form of human intelligence" and that it makes it possible to give finite intelligences an image of the infinite. By this means the priestly caste in the Orient received the primitive revelation and transmitted it to still uncultivated peoples. The symbol, which is "the idea made palpable and personified," gives birth to the myth, which explains and illustrates the idea through a narrative. Primitive revelation is preserved in mysteries. The Neoplatonists alone were able to penetrate the real spirit of paganism and the meaning of its secret rites.

The notion of a language of nature, of the primitive spoken word, formulated by Kreuzer, is related to certain speculations of Court de Gébelin, Claude de Saint-Martin, and Fabre d'Olivet.

In the December 1823 issue of *The French Muse* (thus before Guigniaut's publication), Alexandre Soumet echoed these doctrines. He claimed that poetry "explains and completes the work of the Creator." Everything is symbolic in the eyes of the poet. Through a continuous exchange of analogies and comparisons, he seeks to rediscover some traces of the primitive language, revealed to man by God, of which modern languages are but a flimsy shadow. Thus the faith in the truth of the imagination arose. Pierre Leroux, and later Charles Baudelaire, took this doctrine as far as it could go; Baudelaire went on to speak of the inexhaustible depths of the universal analogy.

This led to the flowering of epics, mentioned earlier, which owed as much to Vico as to Kreuzer in their conception.

The proponents of syncretism—Thalès Bernard, Gérard de Nerval, and Louis Ménard—must also be counted among the disciples of Kreuzer. They could claim to belong simultaneously to all religions (Nerval is said to have espoused seventeen) because they interpreted them symbolically. In their eyes, the symbol redeemed both religion and poetry. Beginning in 1828, Victor Cousin developed his brand of syncretism, which was thoroughly imbued with Neoplatonism and would later influence Quinet, Vigny, and Nerval. In *The House of the Shepherd, The Death of the Wolf,* and *The Bottle in the Sea,* Vigny appeared as the creator of modern myths. In *Daphne,* he reproached Christianity for having adulterated pure ideas, but after he had dreamed of a religion without images, he came to realize that he was dreaming an impossible dream.

French romanticism essentially fed on myths. This is especially true of the work of Victor Hugo, who dominated this period.

II. In Germany

Goethe deserves special attention here because his work served in many respects as a prelude to romanticism in Germany. A large number of great mythic themes gravitate around *Wilhelm Meister* and *Faust.* In his dramatic works, Goethe treated such subjects as Pandora and Iphigenia, which go back to classical antiquity. *The Green Serpent* is an allegory of human life inspired by *The Alchemical Wedding of Christian Rosencreutz* by Johann Valentin Andreae.

With *The Robbers* (1781), Schiller made current a modern myth with an extraordinarily promising future, the myth of the "noble bandit." Works like *Maria Stuart* (1800) and *Wilhelm Tell* (1804) give a mythical dimension to historic characters. Finally, his *Letters on the Aesthetic Education of Man* (1793) reflect on the proper use of mythology.

Although Bonald, Fabre d'Olivet, Joseph de Maistre, Saint-Martin, and Ballanche exerted a great deal of influence on literature in France, German Romanticism was imbued with occult doctrines to an even greater extent than was French romanticism. The loftiest ideas of Neoplatonism had been reintroduced in Germany by Meister Eckhart, Paracelsus, Agrippa von Nettesheim, and finally Jakob Böhme. Such poets as Ludwig Tieck and Novalis, and after them the storyteller E. T. A. Hoffmann, were deeply marked by their reading of Böhme.

For Johann Georg Hamann, the "magus of the north," all of creation is "a discourse addressed to the creature by means of the creature." Another great stimulus was Johann Gottfried von Herder, who took an interest in popular traditions and who in his quest for syncretism arrived at immanentism (the perception of God in the universe). The German romantics conceived of nature as an animate being. One of their fundamental myths is the quest for the primitive language from which all languages were differentiated and for the original religion which was at the origin of multiple beliefs.

Herder began his essay *On the Germano-Oriental Poets* by condemning all imitation of Oriental poetry, by which he meant imitation of the Old Testament. Converted for a time to Eastern aesthetics between 1769 and 1774, while he was preparing his *Oldest Document of the Human Race,* he returned to the idea of the supremacy of the language, mythology, and poetry of Greece. Later both Friedrich von Schlegel and his brother August Wilhelm Schlegel helped to acquaint Europe with Hindu literature. Numerous German scholars, among them J. A. Kanne, F. Majer, Görres, Karl Ritter, and Gottfried Müller, took myths seriously and encouraged others to do so.

But from the standpoint of our concern, the most important statement comes from Friedrich Schelling's *On the Philosophy of Art* (1802–3), in which he asserts that "the gods are the absolute itself seen through the particular and considered as real," that mythology "is the necessary condition and raw material of all art," and, further, that

> mythology is the universe in holiday dress, in its absolute state, the true universe per se, the image of life and supernatural chaos in divine imagination, already poetry by itself and in turn poetic matter and poetic elements. It is the world and in a sense the earth, the only place where works of art can flourish and live. Only in a world of this kind are immutable and determined forms possible, the only forms through which eternal ideas may be expressed.

Herder's ideas came to be known in France primarily through Edgar Quinet. Since works by Goethe, Schiller, and E. T. A. Hoffmann were also translated and discussed, their influence became, oddly enough, more significant than that of Sir Walter Scott and James Fennimore Cooper. Novalis, Tieck, Arnim, and Kleist were also translated and appreciated, but only later.

III. In Great Britain

With regard to the gradual swing into romanticism that took place in England—a writer like William Blake (1757–1827) may already be identified with romanticism—Louis Cazamian spoke of the phenomenon of collective paramnesia. Indeed, the English merely discovered within themselves latent tendencies that had already prevailed in their literature during the Elizabethan era. This explains why sensational statements or manifestos were almost entirely absent. The preface that Wordsworth and Coleridge wrote for the anonymous *Lyrical Ballads* (1798), or Shelley's *Defense of Poetry* (1821), cannot really be compared with Stendhal's *Racine and Shakespeare* let alone with Hugo's *Preface to Cromwell*.

Endowed with an exceptional imagination, William Blake was a prophet and visionary who elaborated a whole mythology in which he objectified the powers of his mind. He associated the imagination with the sun in the air and the ego, and called it *Los-Urthona;* sentiment, connected with fire, was *Luvah-Orc;* sensation and water were *Tharmas;* cold reasoning, connected with the earth, was *Urizen*. A throng of secondary figures, no sooner noticed than named, came to make up a personal mythology parallel to the Old Testament and Greek mythology. Blake was convinced that he was the reincarnation of Milton. His Gnosticism persuaded him that Satan was man's true friend, and he identified Christ with the human Imagination.

The most vigorous mind of the first generation of romantics was Samuel Taylor Coleridge, but since he was addicted to opium, he completed virtually nothing of what he began. In both of his most successful poems, *Kubla Khan* (1791) and *The Rime of the Ancient Mariner* (1798), he assumed the role of a maker of myths. Poe's *Adventures of Arthur Gordon Pym* later derived partly from *The Rime of the Ancient Mariner.*

In Byron's sizable oeuvre, *Manfred* and *Cain* were conceived according to the system of philosophic symbolism. Shelley transmuted his ideas into poetry and traversed a brief trajectory that allowed him to pass from anarchistic individualism to the meaning of human brotherhood and the meaning of the authority of sages. He disavowed rationalism and affirmed intuitive truths, finally espousing an idealistic pantheism. Like Vigny's *Moses,* his poem *Alastor* is devoted to the theme of the solitude of the superior individual. John Keats, in his majestic though unfinished masterpiece *Hyperion,* sought to rival Milton by describing the heavenly revolutions of pagan mythology, as Milton had described the Christian cycle of paradise lost and regained. Even the imagination of Thomas Carlyle, eloquent prose writer though he was, was of a mythicizing nature, and he was imbued with German idealism. His *Sartor Resartus* (The tailor retailored) (1833–34), based on a philosophy of clothes reminiscent of Balzac, is a transposed autobiography in which he expresses his contempt for his time by setting appearances in opposition to essences.

IV. A New Renaissance?

The return to myth that characterizes romanticism in France, Germany, and Great Britain appeared in all the countries of Western Europe in the nineteenth century. In Spain, José Zorilla y Moral gave the Don Juan myth its definitive form with *Don Juan Tenorio* (1844); Leopardi, who treats Prometheus with irony in *The Wager of Prometheus,* also wrote *Sappho's Last Song*. This poem may explain the mental leap that poets always make, the step that binds them to myths: "The happiest days of our lives are the first to wither away."

The glance backward constituted by the recourse to myths may well be at the same time the quest for a lost happiness, for a golden age when the young gods revealed themselves to humans. Maier later defined Sanskrit poems as "the dreams of children of our own species." The nineteenth century was for Europe the period of a true "Oriental Renaissance." In 1841, Edgar Quinet entitled a chapter of his *Genius of Religions* "The Oriental Renaissance." The following year, L. Dussieux, the author of the remarkable *Essay on the History of Oriental Erudition,* published in *The New Encyclopedia,* emphasized the fact that this renaissance had its roots in the previous century and was complementary to the first Renaissance.

In 1800, Friedrich Schlegel wrote, "It is in the Orient that we should look for the supreme romanticism," and before the end of the century, the inquiry of the elite takes on a planetary character. The goal of all the great Western poets was to rival the Hindu epics, the *Rāmāyaṇa* and the *Mahābhārata,* which explains in part the immense though only partially complete projects to which we alluded at the beginning of this article.

An oneiric text by the English writer De Quincey (translated into French successively by Musset in 1828 and Baudelaire in 1860) gives a probing account of the way in which Oriental mythologies, largely conflated and mixed together, invaded Western consciousness. In his book *The Oriental Renaissance* (p. 215), Raymond Schwab cites a passage from *The Confessions of an English Opium Eater* (chapter 4, "Pains of Opium," originally published in 1822): "I ran into pagodas, and was fixed for centuries at the summit or in secret rooms; I was the idol; I was the priest; I was worshipped; I was sacrificed. I fled from the wrathe of Brahma through all the forests of Asia; Vishnu hated me; Seva lay in wait of me. I came suddenly upon Isis and Osiris: I had done a deed, they said, which the ibis and the crocodile trembled at" (*The Collected Writings of Thomas de Quincey*, vol. 3, London: A & C Black, 1897, p. 412).

For all the poets of this time, the knowledge of Egyptian religion, Zoroastrianism, Hindu mythology, the Vedanta as expressed in the *Upaniṣads*, and Buddhism informed their work and supplied points of reference and comparisons. Such references, even when they remain implicit, help us to understand not only Lamartine, Vigny, Hugo, Nerval, and Michelet, but also Wordsworth, Coleridge, Shelley, Goethe, and Novalis.

J.Ri./g.h.

BIBLIOGRAPHY

P. ALBOUY, *La Création mythologique chez Victor Hugo* (Paris 1963). R. AYRAULT, *Heinrich von Kleist* (Paris 1966); *Genèse du romantisme allemand*, 4 vols. (Paris 1961–76). A. BÉGUIN, *L'ame romantique et le rêve* (Paris, repr. 1946). J. BUCHE, *L'école mystique de Lyon* (Paris 1935). N. BURTIN, *Un semeur d'idées au temps de la Restauration: Le baron d'Eckstein* (Paris 1931). R. CANAT, *L'Hellénisme des romantiques*, 3 vols.(Paris 1951–55). P.-G. CASTEX, *Le conte fantastique en France, de Nodier à Maupassant* (Paris 1951). L. CELLIER, *Fabre d'Olivet, contribution à l'étude des aspects religieux du romantisme* (Paris 1953). J.-A.-S. COLLIN DE PLANCY, *Dictionnaire infernal*, 4 vols. (Paris 1825–26). A. COURT DE GÉBELIN, *Monde primitif analysé et comparé avec le monde moderne*, etc., 9 vols. (Paris 1773–84; repr. Paris 1787). F. CREUZER, *Religions de l'Antiquité, considérées principalement dans leurs formes symboliques et mythologiques*, trans., partly recast, completed, and developed by DANIEL GUIGNIAUT, 10 vols. (Paris 1825–51). É. DERMENGHEM, *Joseph de Maistre mystique* (repr. Paris 1946). M.-J. DURRY, *Gérard de Nerval et le mythe* (Paris 1956; reissued 1976). E. EGGLI, *Schiller et le romantisme français*, 2 vols. (Paris 1927; index 1928). E. ESTÈVE, *Byron et le romantisme français, essai sur la fortune et l'influence de l'œuvre de Byron en France de 1812 à 1850* (Paris 1907). A. FABRE D'OLIVET, *Histoire philosophique du genre humain*, 2 vols. (Paris 1824). E. FRENZEL, *Stoffe der Weltliteratur* (2d ed., Stuttgart 1963). R. GÉRARD, *L'Orient et la pensée romantique allemande* (Paris 1963). F. GERMAIN, *L'imagination d'A. de Vigny* (Paris 1962). B. D'HERBELOT DE MOLAINVILLE, *Bibliothèque orientale* (Paris 1697). A. KOYRÉ, *La philosophie de Jacob Boehme* (Paris 1929). A. H. KRAPPE, *La genèse des mythes* (Paris 1938). J. LARAT, *La tradition et l'exotisme dans l'œuvre de Charles Nodier* (Paris 1928). M. MARACHE, *Le symbole dans la pensée et l'œuvre de Goethe* (Paris 1960). A. MONCHOUX, *L'Allemagne devant les lettres françaises de 1814 à 1835* (Paris 1953). H. PEYRE, *Bibliographie critique de l'hellénisme en France de 1843 à 1870* (New Haven 1932). M. PRAZ, *The Romantic Agony* (New York 1956). J. F. RICCI, *E. T. A. Hoffmann, l'homme et l'œuvre* (Paris 1941). J. RICHER, *Gérard de Nerval et les doctrines ésotériques* (Paris 1947); *Nerval, expérience et création* (2d ed., Paris 1970). J. ROOS, *Aspects littéraires du mysticisme philosophique* (W. Blake, Novalis, Ballanche) (Strasbourg and Paris 1951). R. SCHWAB, *La renaissance orientale* (Paris 1950). VAN TIEGHEM, *Le Romantisme dans la littérature européenne* (Paris 1948). A. VIATTE, *Les sources occultes du romantisme, 1770–1820* (Paris 1928).

N.B.: This bibliography is complemented by those of the individual articles listed and by references to a number of works in the text.

ROMANTICISM AND MYTH IN BLAKE, NERVAL, AND BALZAC

For the second time, the gods have deserted the earth. Almost two thousand years ago, a cry went out, "The great Pan is dead." A second cry that proclaims that God is dead now answers that first cry. How are we to think about the world, to give meaning to our individual histories, to the history of mankind, to the history of the universe? We must somehow attempt to recover from the shock caused by the brutal challenge to a conception of the world that made it possible for everything to have meaning, from suffering to war, from birth to death, from individual fate to collective destiny. Suddenly it all collapses. What are we to do in such times of anguish? It is not a matter just of believing, but of thinking, of living. But it is no longer possible to believe or think for others: "I must create a system, or be enslaved by another man" (Blake). And all of these systems can be constructed only with the debris of the lost gods.

Some people limit themselves to acknowledging the absence of the gods and try to live in remembrance of the times when the gods were here. Others stand still, waiting for a new epiphany on the edge of the promised land which they herald but will not see. Still others become hardened in a refusal that rejects all possible forms of myth; but the refusal is coupled with a pathos that owes everything to struggle and to the minerality of absence. Nietzsche still struggles with the gods and is unable to get beyond the point where the struggle against the gods is also a struggle among the gods, Dionysus against Christ on the Cross. The deniers are not so far from the prophets. The downfall of mythology and religion assures that they will be diffused everywhere and inscribed within everyone's vision. The great Christian schemata that until now constituted a place forbidden to mythical elaboration are freed through the power of religious criticism and come to merge with the schemata of all other mythologies; the Christian religion lends all of its underground strength to the reactivation of the old myths. And the great figures of the denying prophets who arise are the figures of giants, who, worn out from fighting the gods in their attempts to replace them, can only be recognized in the dark forms of Satan, Prometheus, or Dionysus. Among these figures are not only Byron, Blake, and Hugo, but also Marx and Nietzsche.

Still others choose to hear Nerval when he asks, "Will I see myself compelled to believe everything just as our fathers the philosophers felt compelled to deny everything?" But whether they refuse myth or want to believe in it at any cost, they all confront the same problem: we must, by whatever means, respond to the threat of seeing all meaning disappear. And the poet responds by asserting the omnipotence and omnipresence of meaning. To ward off the advent of a disenchanted and empty world, he constructs a wholly meaningful nature, and two thousand years later he renews the bonds with the pre-Socratic world in which myth is possible. For myth cannot develop from a desacralized nature; it demands a new way of conceiving what exists. Nature is not inanimate matter. It is energy: "Attraction and Repulsion, Reason and Energy, Love and Hate, are necessary to Human existence" (Blake). Thus invested with productive power, nature is all activity and movement. The materialist Engels seeks to rediscover in matter the dynamism that produces history and gives it meaning. We must go beyond the dualism that separates body and soul: "Man has no Body distinct from his Soul" (Blake). The body is nothing but a degenerate, heavy form of energy, which is, in contrast, wholly spiritual. The body is only an envelope, below which acts the dynamic essence that informs it. If Balzac believes in phrenology, it is because he sees at work everywhere the traces left by energy in its incessant activity, in man's brain as well as in social organization. Energy is present everywhere, in the inanimate world as in the human world: "A pure spirit grows larger under the outer crust of stones" (Nerval).

There are two worlds, a corporeal world and a spiritual world, that correspond point for point and make up the outer and inner components of whatever exists. Between the two worlds gates are erected that open to all who have the courage to cross the threshold: the gates of dreams, the gates of revelation, the gates of madness, the gates of artistic creation. These are the gates crossed by Milton and Blake, Louis Lambert and Balzac, Nerval and Aurélia. On this now animated world supernatural beings can multiply, beings who are nothing but the various shapes taken by various aspects of nature and history. There is no longer any break between the history of the earth and the history of humanity: once again, the universe is full of gods. In reading Buffon like a theogony, Blake and Nerval unfold the mythical stages in the life of the earth, and Balzac sees the gods and heroes in the street, in the office, in the store, and in jail. He does not enlarge the stature of his characters to make them closer to the gods; he makes them great only because he sees myths and gods in them. Balzac does not proceed from the fantastic to realism; he embodies myths progressively in the raw material offered to him by history and society. Esther Gobseck is an incarnation of Seraphita, and together with Lucien de Rubempré they reconstitute the couple Seraphitus-Seraphita; Vautrin is the devil, he is Cain, he is part of an infernal family whose demons are named Attila, Charlemagne, Robespierre, and Napoleon. The big city—Blake's London or Balzac's Paris—is a myth only because one projects upon it the vision of infernal cities that make it bear witness to the Apocalypse.

Nor is there a break between the history of humanity and individual history. Since the explanatory model is that of the organism, of the Great Animal, there is a direct relationship between ontogenesis and phylogenesis: simultaneous lives, successive lives, reincarnations, parallelisms of existences weave the fabric of historical and social events. If Vautrin is Cain, if Lucien de Rubempré is Abel, why should Nerval not be Lusignan or Napoleon? Once again, everything has meaning, right down to the slightest incidents, or perhaps the most fortuitous encounters in the life of an individual. The soldier who comes into Blake's garden and makes him stand trial is also a character of universal history, like the soldier of Africa whom Nerval meets and who becomes the sublime interpreter, the predestined confessor, the mediator between man and the supernatural. Each encounter has a meaning just as, for Balzac, each facial feature, each idiosyncrasy, each habit of the body and the mind carries a determined meaning. And these are the same mythical schemata that regulate the rhythm of individual existence and social life: masculine and feminine poles, grandeur and decadence, the descent into hell and the ascent back into the light, condensation and diffusion, separation and reconciliation; dualist schemata in which two opposite terms introduce the contradiction in being while awaiting the synthesis that is to reconcile them. This explains the importance of the Double, which haunts all creators: for Blake, all personalities are divided into Emanation and Specter, the feminine and masculine parts of the soul, which one day will rediscover their fruitful unity, in opposition with the hermaphroditic horror of Satan. Nerval sees himself threatened with dispossession

William Blake, *The Eternal*. Etching. Manchester, Whitworth Art Gallery. Photo Manor, Kay, and Foley.

by a Double who takes his place: "Am I the good one? Am I the bad one?" Balzac, also threatened by his own Double, gets rid of him and has all the characters into whom he put much of himself die: Louis Lambert, Valentin, Savarus, Z. Marcas. An obsession with the Double, but also a writing technique to overcome it.

In this world animated by mythical forces, in this figurative history, the poet and the artist—double beings—occupy a central place. The poet is the seer, one who, like Blake, perceives the soul of beauty in the forms of matter; one who, like Balzac, penetrates deep into the soul of a stroller, to recover his share of the gift of life; one who, like Nerval, sees once again the unknown relatives that make up his genealogy. Knowledge through sensation is deceptive; it is the result of the contraction of a human being reduced to the state of opaqueness (Blake) and made insensitive to supernatural realities. Beyond the realm of knowledge through sensation, knowledge of another order flashes like lightning; this is the knowledge that Blake awaited for twenty years before he recovered the intellectual vision which intoxicated him. Within the scope of this exceptional experience, "objects and bodies are luminous in themselves" (Nerval). Then contact is established between the two parts of the universe, the material part and the supernatural part. The artist knows how to read and understand the signs of the language that is spoken by nature and that guarantees the existence of correspondences between microcosm and macrocosm. The poet is the intermediary between these two worlds, and his dwelling place is "the house of the Interpreter," the name that Blake's friends gave to his house. The paths of the communication may vary: Blake enters directly into contact with supernatural beings: "I am under the direction of heavenly Messengers day and night." Nerval can only see the gates of the Great Beyond open through the converging experiences of dream and madness. Balzac creates intermediaries who ensure passage to the two realms or who, like Seraphita, themselves participate in both realms. It is essential that these moments of contact leave enduring traces, for what is transmitted must be set down. The revelation must be inscribed on the page—by drawing or writing—both to allow the poet to ensure the vision for himself and to bear witness before men of the presence of the gods. "I wanted to have a material sign of the vision that had consoled me" (Nerval). Blake, Nerval, and Balzac rediscover what Swedenborg did when he gave the name of *Memorabilia* to the story of his mystical inspirations. Nerval edited the *Memorabilia,* which he placed at the culmination of *Aurélia;* Blake inserted "memorabilia" ("A Memorable Fancy") in the *Marriage of Heaven and Hell,* and "memorabilia" would be a fitting word for the Sibylline phrases recorded from the mouth of Louis Lambert, who had gone mad in the eyes of the world. A special intermediary with the world Beyond, the poet is himself a maker of myths. Thus he shares responsibility for creation, before which he experiences the anxieties of the demiurge, anxieties and agonies that are recapitulated in Blake's *Milton, Aurélia,* or *Unknown Masterpiece.*

Blake, Balzac, and Nerval faced a common spiritual dilemma, and many others could have appeared beside them: Hölderlin and later Nietzsche, to mention only two. Clearly it would be illusory to expect to understand them solely on the basis of the particular conditions of their visions, on the basis of their peculiarities, excesses, or madness. What matters is not excessiveness or madness in itself, but this excessiveness or that madness. Both date from a time of crisis when myth alone, both in reason and in madness, could respond to the anxieties of someone who sought and asked.

J.M./g.h.

The Mythology of European Decadent and Symbolist Literature

Nothing could be more baffling than the history of decadence and symbolism. Of symbolism, Valéry said that it was "a certain region of the literary universe, that is, in France between 1860 and 1900." This says too much if we define symbolism strictly; too little if we mean decadence and symbolism taken as a whole that extends in space beyond France and in time beyond 1900. Valéry finally became aware of this and stated that "nothing in what has been written, nothing within the memory of those who experienced this period ever went by that name at any given date." Symbolism is therefore just "a myth."

Introducing the new term "myth" only adds to the general state of confusion. It can be invoked only if its full meaning is restored and if a study of the myths in symbolist and decadent literature replaces the vain attack on some ill-defined "myth of symbolism." This new alliance of decadence and symbolism under the sign of myth should be more enlightening than the quarrels and reconciliations of tiny groups within the literary arena.

I. The Glamour of a Word

Ancient, vague, inevitably the bearer of a potentially negative nuance and yet offering access to the fullness of the sacred, the word "myth" could not help but fascinate the men of that time. It swept their imagination into a dream of universality. "Myth is a tree that grows everywhere, in any climate, under any sun, spontaneously and without cutting," wrote Baudelaire in his article "Richard Wagner and *Tannhaüser* in Paris." "Religions and poetry from the four corners of the world provide us with overwhelming proof on this subject." But precisely because myth is in essence religious, it also contributed to this "vague sort of aesthetic spiritualism," which is, according to Valéry, the main characteristic of symbolism.

The great variety of mythological flora bears witness to the universality of myth. Although the Greco-Roman pantheon and its appendages have the lion's share, poets did not hesitate to make their contributions with Hebrew mythology (Herod, Salome) and national mythologies (Celtic myths in Yeats, Maeterlinck, and Apollinaire; legends of the *Kalevala* in Leino; the Cid in Manuel Machado; Indian myths in Rubén Darío), when they were not forging personal myths, such as Stefan George's Maximin or Blok's Beautiful Lady. It was no longer a matter of collecting myths in the manner of Leconte de Lisle or gathering up "all the gods the world has known" in the manner of Louis Ménard, but rather of molding them into boldly synthetic figures. Baudelaire had already noted that Wagner's Elsa was none other than "the ancient Psyche, who was also the victim of demonic curiosity, and who was also unwilling to respect her divine spouse's anonymity; she too lost all her happiness upon penetrating the mystery." For Gabriele d'Annunzio the "royal Herodias" was at the same time "the ancient Gorgon with her full head of hair . . . Circe, Helen, Omphale, and Delilah, the courtesan with a horrible laugh" (prelude to the *Intermezzo di rime,* 1884).

The sampling might be deemed superficial and the mix ornamental. They are, however, indicative of a quest that can be said to be spiritual. The Monsieur de Phocas of Jean Lorrain left society and abandoned the salons and the boudoirs of young women in order to find in the solitude of his townhouse on the rue de Varenne, in the contemplation of the jewels of Barruchini, or in Oriental self-annihilation, the gaze that he sought: it was "the gaze of Dahgut, daughter of the king of Ys, the gaze of Salome too; but especially the limpid and green clarity of the gaze of Astarte, of Astarte who is the demon of lust and also the demon of the sea." Similarly, J. K. Huysmans's des Esseintes thinks he has discovered in Salome, as Gustave Moreau represented her, "the ancient Helen," "Salammbô," Isis, Kālī, in other words, always "the deity symbolic of indestructible lust, the goddess of immortal Hysteria, the cursed Beauty," the one that Swinburne had celebrated under the name of Dolores.

Symbolic? Allegorical rather—allegory being only a "chilled symbol," as Hegel pointed out. The mythological syncretism of Jean Lorrain or Huysmans seems to have but

Gustave Moreau, *L'Apparition*. Paris, Musée Gustave Moreau. Photo Giraudon.

one aim, the triumph of a single deity, or better still, the triumph of a principle identified with the obsession of the decadent individual. When Tédor de Wyzewa stressed in *La Revue wagnérienne* of 8 June 1886 that for moderns, legends and myths are "nothing but symbols," he meant "allegories." And when Baudelaire defined his wretched swan which escaped from its cage as a "strange and fatal myth," he made it an allegory of fate that compelled man to exile. The exile of a mythological character (Andromache) and of a paradigmatic figure (the consumptive Negress) confirms this all the more, and confirms as well the compulsion that acts upon the poet himself, exiled from the ideal and immersed in the world of the spleen. The myth of the swan is indeed his myth—and the myth of himself—since he takes from it only one meaning, his own, identifying it with himself. Baudelaire wastes no time in recognizing it: "everything for [him] becomes allegory."

Such is the jeopardy into which decadent and symbolist literature casts myth, reducing it, as Henri de Régnier said, to "the conch shell that resounds with *one* Idea." For Yeats, Helen represents the fatal power of all beauty. In this respect, no example is more characteristic than Henri de Régnier himself. He made the birds of Lake Stymphalis into an allegory of passing time (*Epigram* in *Les Jeux rustiques et divins* [Rustic and divine games]), and he made the trials of Ulysses into the poet's martyrdom (*L'Homme et la Sirène* [The man and the siren]). Symbolic rather than symbolist, this treatment of myth is not new. It recalls Vigny's Moses, Shelley's Prometheus, Leconte de Lisle's Niobe, and Victor Hugo's Satyr, all of whom also embody an idea. And for Ballanche the ultimate meaning of all myths could be reduced to a single idea. Baudelaire treated the issue no differently when he discovered the universal meaning of sin in the Wagnerian myths and, more generally, in the "allegory created by the people," which is myth.

To ward off this danger, the "overly precise meaning" condemned by Verlaine in his famous *Art poétique* had to be erased. The use of myth becomes truly symbolic when the writer attempts to apprehend a mystery that is never completely discovered and must never be solved. "The perfect use of the mystery constitutes the symbol" was Mallarmé's answer to Jules Huret's question. And in the Manifesto of 18 September 1886, Jean Moréas took care to point out that "the essential character of symbolist art consists in never going as far as conceiving of the idea in and of itself." Mallarmé's faun and Mallarmé himself hesitate among diverse interpretations of the nymphs that appear to them. Everything begins with questions about a myth. Doubt, "heap of ancient night," is the very reason for the length of the discourse which will try in vain to exhaust the bulk of the mystery: "I, proud of my repute, I will long speak of goddesses."

The result is a fondness for ambiguous mythological figures—monsters, sphinxes, chimeras; a fondness also for the central and ever-dissolving figures of mystery cults (Orpheus, Isis, Dionysus) or of the celebration of mystery (the Grail); a fondness for myth to the extent that, more mysterious than discourse, myth gropes its way tentatively closer and closer into the zone of the unknowable.

The danger this time is that myth will express nothing but the quest itself. For Cavafy, for instance, the trials and tribulations of Odysseus are no longer, as they were for Henri de Régnier, merely the sufferings of the martyr-poet. They are the stages of an Orphic initiation through which the poet must pass:

> You will never meet the Lestrygonians,
> the Cyclopes and the fierce Poseidon,
> if you do not carry them within your soul,
> if your soul does not raise them up before you.
> (Trans. Rae Dalven, *The Complete Poems of Cavafy*, New York: Harcourt Brace Jovanovich, 1976, p. 36)

For Mallarmé, myths of the voyage to the world beyond play an essential role that can only be explained by such an imaging of the poetic quest. Although in *Le Guignon* (Bad luck), the *Mendieur d'azur* (The azure beggar), the *Martyrs de hasards tortueux* (Martyrs of tortuous perils), and the vultureless *Prométhée* (Prometheus), there are still the romantic mannerisms of Odysseus, we are on the other hand dealing with an Odysseus who faces the mystery of death and nothingness, the Odysseus of the *Nekuia* (The journey to the dead), when we deal with the poet of the *Tombeaux* (The tombs) or "the one who went to draw tears from the river Styx." A flash of union between decadence and symbolism, the "Prose pour des Esseintes" emerges as the annihilating evocation of another voyage, seemingly more Platonic than Homeric, toward the isle of Ideas. But the inquiry about myth makes room this time for the negation of a Utopia (the land of Pulcheria) where myth itself self-destructs.

II. The Rebirth of Myth

In July 1885, after Baudelaire and before Claudel, Mallarmé dedicated to Richard Wagner his *Rêverie d'un poète français* and thereby found himself led by his very subject to return to myth. To avail himself of another mythological motif dear to him, namely, the Phoenix, he established for his own time and in his country a death and resurrection of myth. In fact, "the French mind, strictly imaginative and abstract, therefore poetic . . . , loathes legend, and as such is at one with art, the inventor, in its integrity." And yet "this century or our nation which extols it have dissolved myths through conceptions only to make new ones."

The model which the French mind was supposed to spurn was Wagnerian drama. In giving preference to myth over history, Wagner fulfilled the vow of the first German romantics, Schlegel, Arnim, and Brentano. "Myth is the primitive and anonymous poem of the people," he wrote. "In myth, human relations shed their conventional form almost completely . . . and reveal what makes life truly, eternally, understandable." At issue, therefore, is not an ascent into the increasingly thick mists of the unknowable, but the revelation of what could be termed the essence of life. Baudelaire, who thoroughly understood that Wagner's poems "borrowed in large measure from the romantic spirit," also saw clearly that the ambition of the German master was to discover "the universal heart of man," and all this through myth.

The rebirth of myth did not happen without major modifications, which significantly transformed mythological figures, as in the case of *Tannhäuser.* "Radiant ancient Venus, Aphrodite born of white foam, has not crossed the horrifying shadows of the Middle Ages with impunity. She no longer dwells on Olympus nor on the shores of a fragrant island. She has withdrawn deep inside a magnificent cave, to be sure, but one illuminated by fires that are not those of kindly Phoebus. By going underground, Venus draws close to Hell, and with certain loathsome ceremonies is undoubtedly about to pay steady homage to the archfiend, prince of the flesh, and lord of sin." It is as if, after the death of Venus (her disappearance from Cythera in *Les Fleurs du mal* [The flowers of evil], her corpselike stillness in Swinburne's *Laus Veneris*), one could witness the weird spectacle of her resurrection (the Venus in furs of Sacher-Masoch), the birth of an ambiguous deity, simultaneously statue and woman, hetaera and goddess, Greek and barbarian.

Odilon Redon, *Brunehilde,* "Twilight of the Gods," final scene. Lithograph. Illustration for *La Revue wagnérienne,* 8 August 1885. Photo Martine Pont.

The use of mythology in theater also changed. Wagnerian drama sought to reinstate the mythic force of Greek tragedy. Nietzsche wrote his famous book *The Birth of Tragedy* in order to hail the rebirth of tragedy thanks to Wagner, tragedy in the post-Euripidean and post-Socratic sense of the term. For Nietzsche, myth remained a temporary and necessary concession to the Apollonian, since society would not tolerate the eruption of the purely Dionysian. Between music and our musical feelings carried to their utmost, "myth and the tragic hero arise, both being fundamentally nothing but symbols of universal realities of which music alone can speak directly. If we could feel as purely Dionysian beings, myth as symbol would have no effect on us; we would pay it no heed and would not stop lending an ear to the echo of the universals *ante rem.* But it is at this point that the Apollonian force erupts and, restoring our almost annihilated individuality, brings to it the balm of a delightful illusion." Jean Lorrain felt free to create a pretty vignette from the love of Tristan and Isolde (*Yseut,* in *Le Sang des dieux* [The blood of the gods]). Gabriele d'Annunzio felt free to turn the cup of tea, which had become as ritualistic in Rome as in London, into the modern avatar of Tristan's love potion. According to Nietzsche, Wagner introduced the mythical couple only to bring us to the moment when the image fades out, when the phenomenal world reaches its limit, and when Isolde's song of the love-death rises like a "metaphysical swan song." Myth proceeds on its course of self-destruction. Yet, curiously enough, this self-destruction cannot be articulated without recourse to mythological language. The paradox of Wagner's *Tristan* is renewed with Nietzsche's commentary, a vast fresco of Apollo and Dionysus which must nonetheless suggest that what exists beyond these images is as illusory as the others.

One would like to believe that Mallarmé understood the difficulty. Instead of indulging in philological erudition, as Nietzsche did, instead of bantering heavy-handedly, as Claudel did over that *gros édredon d'Isolde* ("stout eiderdown of Isolde"), he favored an abstract concept of myth, as if it had become disembodied, a mental myth stripped even of the prop of a name. At the very most, one will see "awaken" in this setting "the Figure which is None," and art admiring itself in the empty space it has opened up for itself.

III. The Myth of Decadence

People often compare the *Néant* (Nothingness) of Mallarmé to Stefan George in *Algabal* (1892), particularly where the Roman emperor Heliogabalus represents the despotic and inhuman soul which in its omnipotence can find only loneliness and sterility. This figure is very characteristic of what can be called the myth of Latin decadence or simply the myth of decadence.

Since for quite some time Edward Gibbon, Montesquieu, and others had applied the word "decadence" to the degradation of the Roman Empire, the switch to the empire of Badinguet and to the years which followed its collapse was easy. When the Sâr Péladan (Joséphin Péladan, 1859–1918) entitled his vast epic novel, his "éthopée," *Latin Decadence*, he meant to represent and condemn modern customs that had been corrupted by materialism. We all know Verlaine's famous statement, so characteristic—considering its date (1883)—of a general state of mind:

Je suis L'Empire à la fin de la Décadence
Qui regarde passer les grands Barbares blancs
En composant des acrostiches indolents
D'un style d'or où la langueur du soleil danse.

I am the Empire at the end of Decadence
looking at the great white Barbarians passing through
All the while composing indolent acrostics
In a golden style in which the languishing sun dances.
(*Langueur* in *Jadis et naguère*)

Often explicit, as in this sonnet by Verlaine, the comparison with the decadence of the Roman Empire is a constant. Baudelaire, in his study of the painter Constantin Guys, had already spoken of "decadences," i.e., troubled, transitional times "when democracy is not yet all-powerful, when the aristocracy is only partially tottering on the edge and degraded." The decadence he lived was of just such a kind, and he recognized himself just as easily in the Apulean era, the second century A.D. Toward this century and those that followed, which were even gamier, were drawn men like des Esseintes in Huysmans's *A Rebours* (Against the grain) (1884): "Stormy times, jolted by horrendous troubles, . . . while the Roman Empire shook at its foundations, while the lunacies of Asia, the filth of paganism, overflowed its bounds."

Many writers of the decadent and symbolist era felt surrounded by barbarians. For Huysmans, it was "the new generations, those hotbeds of hideous boors who feel the need to speak and laugh loudly in restaurants and cafés; who without apologizing push you around on the sidewalk; who without even excusing themselves or even addressing you, stick a set of baby carriage wheels between your legs." For Maurice Barrès, it was other people, those who surround Philippe (his double in *Le Culte du moi* [The cult of me]), people who have a conception of life diametrically opposed to his (*Sous l'oeil des Barbares*, [Under the eye of the barbarians]) (1888). In act 2 of *Tête d'Or* (The head of gold) (1889), Claudel's first masterpiece, Simon Agnel triumphs over the redheaded barbarians. The helpless watchmen who were supposed to guard the palace show up again, ten years later, in *Le Poème des décadences* (The poem of decadences) by Milosz, in which courtesans discuss precious stones to the roar of "the ocean of barbarian hordes from afar." Some people resist, withdraw into their splendid solitude, or declare themselves ready for the supreme fight. Others, however, accept, or even with loud cries call the barbarians liberators. There is the new aristocracy of Nietzsche, the Pleiades of Gobineau; there are also the patrician dandies of Milosz and the d'Annunzio of the *Intermezzo di rime*, who does not answer the call of cohorts fighting against the barbarians and who would rather forget his happy fate in idleness, "amidst mad or treacherous pleasures."

Simple imagery of the time, one might claim; but it is more than that. The myth of decadence, the myth of the barbarians, betrays the haunting obsession that the doomsday myth (or at least doomsday for a certain kind of world) imposed on the imagination of turn-of-the-century writers. As early as 1866, the Goncourt brothers spoke of "the end of societies." In *Le Crépuscule des dieux* (The twilight of the gods) (1884) of Elémir Bourges, the duke, attending a performance of *Götterdämmerung* in Bayreuth, sees in it the symbol of the end of the world as he knows it: "All the signs of destruction were visible on the old world, like angels of wrath, above a condemned Gomorrah." A critic praising Marcel Schwob writes, "Magically you evoke antiquity, this Heliogabalesque antiquity toward which flow the imaginations of thinkers and the brushes of painters, these decadences and these doomsdays, mysteriously perverse and macabre."

But the modern age is just as Heliogabalesque. Must we condemn it, or must we, on the contrary, delight in it? The same hesitation recurs. Despite the "pagan school," myth, in any case, is not an opportunity for a return to "naked eras," for a "renewal of resources"; it proclaims a forthcoming *eschaton* for which setting suns are the decor. In "a world worn threadbare where the most beautiful things on earth seem to fall into pieces by themselves," as Walter Pater writes in *Marius the Epicurean* (1884), is there any possible hope of starting over beyond chaos or mere exhaustion?

IV. Back to Basics

To answer this question after the fact, we will deliberately set aside the revival of Christian literature and aesthetic consolation and for the moment concentrate on the way in which the decadent and symbolist period conceived myth. Mallarmé's *Les Dieux antiques* (The ancient gods) happens to be an extremely loose adaptation of a manual attributed to the Reverend George William Cox and published in 1867: *A Manual of Mythology in the Form of Question and Answer.* But the manual and its French adaptation are inseparable from the school of comparative mythology, which ever since the mid-nineteenth century posits a so-called naturalist conception of mythology. The assumption made by Ludwig Preller is that "nature was the maternal foundation and the starting point for the representation of gods." The names of the principal exponents of this school—Preller, Bréal, Adalbert Kuhn—figure prominently in the foreword to *Les Dieux antiques*. The only name missing is that of Max Müller, the most important of all.

The great merit of the naturalistic conception of myth is to pull it away from an allegorical system and give it back to an archetypal system. For the aforementioned scholars and for the popularizers who came later, mythology reenacted the spectacle of the primordial elements. These are the elemental forces of nature and its dazzling manifestations—sun, rain, lightning, the flow of rivers, the growth of plants, all "represented as the varied actions, the changing states of living beings" and expressed "in narratives full of imagery" in the great divine myths. The foreword to *Les Dieux antiques* further states: "What pleasure is added to our sense of surprise at the sight of familiar myths slowly evaporating in water, light, and elemental wind, through the very magic that analysis of the ancient word implies!" Hence a new task that might well be assigned to the poet: to reenact the great spectacles and permanent conditions of life that stand behind mythological figures and to reveal in them elemental symbols.

Adalbert Kuhn preferred the archetype of the storm. Max Müller, G. W. Cox, and after him Mallarmé inclined rather toward the sun. For Cox, "the epic poems of the Aryans are merely versions of one and the same story, and this story originates in the phenomena of the natural world and in the course of each passing day and year." In a more concise and striking form, Mallarmé presents the same idea. The poems "are never anything but one of the numerous narrations of the great solar drama performed under our eyes each day and each year." Zeus is the pure sky; Athena, dawn; Hermes, the wind accompanying daybreak; Paris, the dark power of night that robs the western sky of the beautiful twilight. The desertion of Ariadne, and of Brunhild, means nothing but the fact that the sun cannot be delayed in the east by dawn. And if "Oedipus proves to be overcome by a power he cannot resist," it means that "the sun cannot rest in its course: the heavenly body does not act freely; in the evening, it must join the dawn from whom it was separated in the morning."

In Claudel's first drama, the parallel between the fate of Tête d'Or (Head of gold) and the course of the sun is too clear to conceal a new paraphrase of what Mallarmé would call "the solar act." (Claudel was one of Mallarmé's audience on the rue de Rome.) The victorious hero attempts in vain to forget that sun "whose first rays would in olden times make him sing / like a stone cast against bronze," and he attempts instead to see in it nothing but a "cow's lung floating at a butcher shop door." He comes back to fetch it, however, to take it with him finally on his expedition toward the gates of Asia, toward the land of the dawn. The death of Tête d'Or takes place at the end of a long death struggle, which is also the dying of the sun in the sky.

Ô soleil! Toi, mon
Seul amour! ô gouffre et feu! ô sang! ô
Porte! Or, or! Colère sacrée!
. . .
Je meurs. Qui racontera
Que, mourant, les bras écartés, j'ai tenu le soleil sur ma poitrine comme une roue?

O sun, Thou, my
Only love! O abyss and fire! O blood! O
Gate! Gold, gold! Holy wrath!
. . .
I die. Who shall tell
That, dying, arms outstretched, I held the sun on my chest like a wheel?

Reappearing quite explicitly this time is the myth of Memnon, the famous black statue that sings under the influence of the sun's first rays.

Many other examples could be cited: Odysseus appearing as the "avenging sun" in *Anciennetés* (Antiquities) by Saint-Pol Roux ("Le Palai d'Itaque au retour d'Odysseus métamorphosé en mendiant" [The palace of Ithaca on the return of Odysseus disguised as a beggar]) (1885); the inspiring sun in *The Seventh Ring* (1907) by Stefan George; the murderous sun in Bély's "A mes amis" (To my friends) (1907); the Herculean sun in Rubén Darío's "The Optimist's Greeting" in *Cantos of Life and Hope* (1905); the menstrual sun in Apollinaire ("Merlin et la vieille femme" [Merlin and the old woman] in *Alcools* [Alcoholic spirits]) (1913); the sun of "light and life" which the Jewish poet Chernichovsky in his indefatigable hope sought in an extraordinary collection of the most diverse myths leading up to a "face-to-face encounter with the statue of Apollo."

The end point of this solar quest through myths might well be the astonishing *Cantique de la connaissance* (Hymn of knowledge) by Milosz, in *La confession de Lémuel* (The confession of Lémuel) (1922), fruit of "the teaching of the sun-bright hour of the nights of the Divine." Here again the sun is the primal element; from it "gold draws its substance and its color; man draws the light of his knowledge." The sun

Alexandre Séon, *Le sar Mérodack Joséphin Peladan,* Catalogue of the Salon de la Rose-Croix, 1892. Photo Martine Pont.

Frontispiece for the Androgyne, from the cycle "la décadence latine" ("Ethopée"), 1891, by Alexandre Séon. Catalogue of the Salon de la Rose-Croix, 1892. Photo Martine Pont.

makes it possible for the new poet to reach the knowledge of archetypes: "being of the nature of our mind," they "are situated, as he is, in the consciousness of the solar egg." This immediate knowledge must lead to the abolition of symbols, instruments of a mediating knowledge:

> The poets of God saw the world of archetypes and described it piously through the precise and luminous terms of the language of knowledge.
>
> The decline of faith is manifest in the world of science and art by a growing dimness of language.
>
> The poets of nature sing the imperfect beauty of the world of the senses according to the ancient sacred mode.
>
> However, struck by the secret discordance between the mode of expression and the subject,
>
> And powerless to rise up to the only special place, I mean Patmos, the archetypes' land of vision,
>
> In the night of their ignorance, they imagine an intermediary world, floating and sterile, the world of symbols.

We pass from what Gilbert Durand calls the "numinosity" of myths to the luminosity of archetypes. The "Idea" sought by the symbolist mystique descends from heaven to return to earth, less ideal than "surreal," or perhaps even just simply real. For deep down, Milosz seems to be dreaming of the abolition of the dualism phenomenon/noumenon, and with him all those poets who are referred to as "naturistic" and who were often nothing but repentant symbolists. This milestone in literary history, for which the turn of the century could easily be made responsible, is more likely explained by the ambiguities of symbolism. There is no better example of this than a poem from *Chants de pluie et de soleil* (Songs of rain and sun) (1894) by Hugues Rebell, in which the poet persists in speaking of the "Idea" when he really means "things":

Je ne m'occuperai point de ces petites agitations
qui commencent sur un vagissement,
Et se terminent par un râle,
Mais de l'Idée qu'elles révèlent.
Je regarde les larmes, je regarde les sourires,
Ainsi que la pluie et le soleil;
Et les rugissements, les cris, les clameurs joyeuses,
les appels désespérés,
Passent en moi comme le vent dans les branches
d'un grand chêne.
Je n'étudierai point une passion, une âme, un visage,
Mais je monterai sur la Tour qui domine l'horizon,
Pour découvrir les peuples en marche,
Voir la forêt, la plaine et la mer
Et entendre des milliers de voix célébrer l'harmonie.

I will no longer busy myself with these trifling agitations
that begin with a wail
and end with a death rattle,
but with the Idea that they reveal.
I regard tears, I regard smiles,
like rain and sunshine;
and the bellowings, the cries, the joyous outcries, the desperate calls,
are to me like wind in the branches of a great oak tree.
I will no longer study a passion, a soul, a face,
but I will climb the Tower that dominates the horizon
in order to discover the peoples on the march,
to see the forest, the plain, and the sea,
and to hear the thousands of voices celebrate harmony.

After Whitman, writers like André Gide and Vicente Huidobro came to an agreement in their appeal to the things of the earth. In a famous mythological poem, *Les Muses* (The Muses) (the first of the *Cinq Grandes Odes* [The five great odes], 1900–1905), Claudel assigned to the second creator, namely, himself, the task of discovering the gold buried in the heart of each element, the gold of divine presence hidden by the Wagnerian myths. As if in accordance with the wish of Saint-Pol Roux, the renewal of the Word corresponded to "l'Age du Soleil" (The age of the sun), "the star bursting like a ripe fruit whose seeds of sensitive and moral clarity must be welcomed."

A decadent art could easily be accused of being epigonal, of giving too much attention to works and traditions of the past. Thus, at the end of the nineteenth century a mythology of the times, mythological bric-a-brac, emerged. It went against the grain of a modernity deemed vulgar; but curiously enough, it also went hand in hand with it. Nietzsche had a brilliant explanation for this phenomenon: deprived of myths, modern man is starving for myths, and he "rummages in all past eras to find his roots, even if he has to rummage back to the farthest reaches of antiquity." Accumulation is not the only characteristic of the turn-of-the-century use of myth. Ornamental, allegorical, symbolic, it tends to cut itself off from its archetypal roots, at least among second-rate writers. The Rimbaud of *Illuminations* constitutes a remarkable exception. And Nietzsche proposed for the myth of Prometheus simultaneously an allegorical interpretation (the need for crime that is imposed on the titanic individual) and an archetypal interpretation: "the hyperbolic value which a naive humanity attributes to fire as it does to the true palladium of a nascent civilization." The poets of life, the "naturists," whom literature textbooks present as the grave-diggers of symbolism, benefited nevertheless from a current that was not interrupted during the second half of the nineteenth century, namely, comparative mythology, with an original attempt to return to the elemental meaning of myths. Was this the finish or the rebirth of myths? The end has all the makings of a renewal. The poetic quest, seemingly reaching out to a "beyond," reverts to a "here below." It remains, like the myth in what is alive, the locus of a contradiction.

P.Br./g.h.

BIBLIOGRAPHY

General Works on Decadence and Symbolism

Symbolism: A Bibliography of Symbolism as an International and Multi-Disciplinary Movement, ed. D. L. Anderson (New York 1975). A. BALAKIAN, *The Symbolist Movement: A Critical Appraisal* (New York 1967). G. MICHAUD, *Message poétique du symbolisme* (Paris 1954).

General Works on Mythology in the Period

P. ALBOUY, *Mythes et mythologies dans la littérature française* (Paris 1969). M. PRAZ, *La carne, la morte e il diavolo nella letteratura romantica* (Milan 1930; new ed., Florence 1976). P. BRUNEL, "L'au-delà' et l''en-deçà': Place et fonction des mythes dans la littérature 'symboliste'," *Neohelicon* 3–4 (1974).

Works on Mythology

L. PRELLER, *Griechische Mythologie* (Leipzig 1854). G. W. COX, *The Mythology of the Aryan Nations* (1870). S. MALLARMÉ, *Les dieux antiques* (Paris 1880); reprinted in Mallarmé's *Œuvres complètes*, ed. H. Mondor and G. Jean-Aubry (Paris 1945).

Texts

C. BAUDELAIRE, "Richard Wagner et *Tannhaüser* à Paris," in *La revue européenne*, 1 April 1861. C. P. CAVAFY, *Poiemata* (Ikaros 1952); English trans., K. P. Kabaphes, *Poems* (New York 1952). P. CLAUDEL, *Tête d'or,* Librairie de l'art indépendant (1890); reprinted in *Théâtre,* ed. J. Madaule and J. Petit, vol. 1 (Paris 1967). G. D'ANNUNZIO, *Intermezzo di rime* (1883), in *Tutte le Opere di Gabriele D'Annunzio,* ed. E. Bianchetti (1950–64). J. K. HUYSMANS, *A Rebours, new ed., U.G.E., coll. 10/18, no. 975.* J. LORRAIN, *Monsieur de Phocas,* new ed., Le Livre Club du Libraire (1966); *Le sang des dieux* (1882), new ed., Édouard-Joseph (1920). O. V. DE L., MILOSZ, *Poésies,* new ed., A. Silvaire (1960), 2 vols. H. REBELL, *Chants de pluie et de soleil,* Librairie Charles (1894). L. VON SACHER-MASOCH, *Venus im Pelz* (Stuttgart 1870); English trans., *Venus in Furs* (Boston 1925). P. VALÉRY, "Existence du symbolisme" (Maestricht 1939), reprinted in vol. 1 of *Œuvres,* ed. J. Hytier (Paris 1962). W. B. YEATS, *The Collected Poems* (London 1933).

The Androgyne

There is no one myth of the androgyne, but rather a family of myths. Should these be considered different variants of the same original or fundamental myth? Probably not. It is better to speak of a mythic theme, whose actual unity we cannot affirm but which functions as an exemplary case. All the constitutive elements of myth are encountered in this theme, as in a microcosm, and all the explanations, all the patterns of analysis of myth, find their justification in it.

The androgyne theme is extremely widespread, one might almost say universal: it is recognized everywhere, from Greece to China, from Egypt to pre-Columbian America, from Africa to Oceania. It does not occupy the same position everywhere and almost never takes the same shape; but there is hardly a mythical construction in which a trace of the androgyne is not found. The theme is extremely polymorphous and appears not only in the form of mythical narratives: it is a complex in which the observation of nature, rituals, personal fantasies, the figures of gods, and narratives are blended. The point of departure is surely the consideration of an essential given of human existence: there are distinct sexes with corresponding physical and psychological characteristics. But nature everywhere offers to observation the presence of beings of uncertain sex, bisexual beings, the whole gamut of intersexual states. The recognized limits and forms of the states may vary from culture to culture, as the characteristics of each sex vary: their presence poses a problem and requires an explanation, since the irreducible presence of the two sexes demands it.

Thus a combination of three terms is formed—masculine, feminine, androgynous—which appears in the form of a myth that is lived and represented, a myth in action. A whole series of rituals, in particular those that are called rites of passage, give ample place to bisexuality: disguises in which one sex assumes the dress and attributes of the other, and operations such as subincision by which a man is symbolically endowed with the sexual organs of both sexes. Ceremonies of initiation, marriage rites, mourning ceremonies, fertility festivals, agrarian rites, and carnivals play upon the inversion of the sexes, mingling them in order to institute, if only for an instant, a symbolic androgyny. Multiplying and perhaps explaining the effect of these rites, almost everywhere there are fantasies of bisexuality, which belong to the most archaic foundation of our representations. For each sex, the presence of the other constitutes a source of anxiety, a threat, and a complement at once desired and feared. Accordingly, having both sexes is a recurrent fantasy, present in dreams, stories, works of art, and alchemy: simultaneously *animus* and *anima,* a human being is double and oscillates between the two poles of a totality that he seeks to reconstitute.

The androgyne also appears in the form of gods, double deities who have both masculine and feminine powers. These gods may be the origin of cosmologies, representing the primordial confusion before beings separate, divided according to the categories of the organized world as we know it, but also incarnating the double aspect of power and fertility, Zeus Labraundos, bearded and with six breasts on his chest, or Dionysus the man-woman. Besides the gods there are androgynous heroes, such as Tiresias, who passes successively through the two sexes; and something of a mythic fascination endures in the interest taken in an Aeonian knight. The priests themselves may be androgynes: devotees who castrate themselves in order to reconstitute the bisexuality of their god, shamans who dress and live as women in order to incarnate the cosmic totality. The rites and gods are associated with mythical accounts, in which the androgyne serves to explain the birth of the world and its development. More or less elaborate, the accounts are gradually transformed into mythical allegories or explicit philosophico-religious systems (the myth of Plato's *Symposium,* Orphism).

Can the mythological complex of the androgyne be explained by a single schema? People have claimed to account for it by ritual, by the psychology of archetypes, by a function of mediation: between the two poles of masculine and feminine there is a mediating category, androgyny, that makes it possible to pass from one pole to the other and to reflect at the same time on both terms of the opposition; might not the serpent of Genesis be the hermaphroditic intermediary between Adam and Eve, as the androgynous shaman is the intermediary between earth and heaven? It is certainly imprudent to reduce a mythical complex to its formal surface structure: the semantics of a myth is richer than its basic combinatory organization, as is demonstrated by the diverse forms of its preservation and its revivals in occidental tradition.

Although polytheistic religions everywhere grant androgyny an important place, the situation is completely different with the monotheistic religions of salvation: androgyny is not only put aside, it is systematically concealed. And we can understand why: the one god, refusing the empirical determinations of the gods of polytheism, cannot participate in one sex or the other without contradiction. As the object of a negative theology, he can be neither masculine, nor feminine, nor androgynous. But, concealed by the orthodoxies, androgyny continued to live on their margins, in the esotericisms of the Jewish, Christian, and Muslim traditions. Recurrent themes circulated in these traditions, in which Gnosticism, Neoplatonism, cabala, alchemy, and mysticism came to meet: an androgynous god, a god of origins, the product of an unbegotten forefather, the primary celestial power that gives birth to a series of aeons symmetically distributed in male and female pairs; the first androgynous human, who possesses both sexual powers and is thus truly

Khnopff. *The Sphinx.* Brussels, Musées royaux des Beaux-Arts de Belgique. Museum photo.

made in the image of god; the fall of man, who finds himself separated from the universal life and for whom the division of the sexes marks the origin of evil, which is separation; finally the ascension toward the light that at the end of time must reconstitute the androgyny of the origins. Androgyny thus marks the beginning and the end of history, to which it gives a meaning.

At the end of the eighteenth century, esoteric traditions emerged from the shadows and converged with two other movements to reactivate the theme of androgyny. On the one hand, with Winckelmann artistic neoclassicism accorded a central place to the hermaphrodite, regarded as the incarnation of ideal beauty, in which the partial beauties of the two sexes are harmoniously merged; and, after the heroic nudity of David and his school, plastic arts from the turn of the century offered a new type of nude: the clear-cut opposition between the male and female canons of beauty is succeeded by a beauty in which sexual contrasts are subdued, in which the body assumes the uncertain forms of the androgyne (Girodet, J. Broc, Granger, Dubufe). From another quarter, nascent biology lent a new force to the masculine-feminine pair, which became one of the fundamental categories of the romantic *Naturphilosophie:* the pair of terms, separated and tending to reconstitute an original unity, constitutes a polarity, a model particularly able to account for the physical and social world. At the same time, scientific observation multiplies the cases of intersexuality that exist now with all the force of scientific affirmation, while literature takes an interest in homosexuality or ambiguous sexuality. In this way, physical hermaphroditism and psychological androgyny reconstitute the double effect produced by mythical androgyny—horror and the holy, repulsion and adoration—reactivated by scientific understanding of living forms.

Throughout the nineteenth century, the theme of androgyny assumed greater prominence. Two types of androgyny succeeded one another and intermingled. In the first half of the century, the androgyny of synthesis and totality was theorized by F. von Baader and appeared in the works of Michelet, Balzac, and Wagner. In the second half of the century, the androgyne became a central figure of literature and the arts, from Swinburne and Peladan to G. Moreau and Stefan George: this was a more ambiguous androgyne, who lives only on the hesitation and indecision between the two poles, while adorning himself in the glamours of erotic or even satanic provocation. Does this revival of androgyny involve a real myth or only a fantasy reserved for a few creators? But the diffusion of the fantasy is itself a sign, the sign of a reflection on identity and sexual roles, thus proclaiming that mutation which leads us to question the masculine-feminine duality in our culture. Androgyny became again a myth; after Fliess, Freud affirmed the existence of a primal bisexuality: the human being is, at at least one moment in his development, woman-man and man-woman (Groddeck). And if, as Freud has said, the theory of instinct is our mythology, it was reserved to psychoanalysis to restore to the androgyne his function as myth, that is, as the paradigmatic narrative that makes sense of the world for a whole culture.

J.M./b.f.

The Androgyne, the Double, and the Reflection: A Few Myths of Romanticism

I. The Androgyne

Nineteenth-century writers generally accepted the dogma that the original Adam or "Kadmon Adam" of the Hebraic tradition was androgynous—the Platonic myth of the first androgyne furnishing, moreover, confirmation from a different tradition.

Fabre d'Olivet made Isha, the wife of Adam, a representation of human will, a notion that Ballanche was to take up again. Ballanche saw the descendants of Seth as the Orientals, representing the male, active, and initiating principle, in opposition with the Cainites or Occidentals, associated with the female, passive, and initiated principle. From another point of view, in which he followed Vico, he held that the patrician principle must regenerate the female and plebeian principle through initiation.

Father Enfantin saw himself as representing only half of the revelatory couple, while his imitator Ganneau ("the one-who-was-Ganneau") claimed to be Mapah (father and mother), the perfect androgyne. In 1829, H. de Latouche published *Fragoletta,* a clever and rather vulgar romantic treatment of the theme of a creature who is both man and woman. The heroine of *Mademoiselle de Maupin* (1836) of Théophile Gautier is an ambiguous being, a woman nevertheless, whose androgyny is chiefly mental. A late story from the same author, *Spiritist* (1865), describes a search for the union of souls that results in the creation of a new being, according to the doctrine of Swedenborg, who had also inspired Balzac's *Seraphîta* (1835).

Novalis, who always dreamed of total fusion with the loved one, found the image of the hermaphrodite prominent in the works of J. Boehme. But in both Balzac and Novalis, the process of angelization takes place through carnal ecstasy, which assumes absolute monism, the identity of body and spirit.

Though Balzac clearly describes "two creatures reunited in an angel, lifted by the wings of pleasure," the writer's degree of sincerity in *Seraphîta* poses a problem. He badly wanted to seduce Mme Hanska, and it is somewhat disturbing to note that in the same period he described a case of lesbianism in *The Girl with the Golden Eyes.* The invention of the character of Seraphîtus-Seraphîta suggests a misunderstanding of Swedenborg. For Swedenborg had not imagined that such a hypostasis could assume human form and become incarnate.

II. The Theme of the Double

The theme of the Double, in its various aspects—the Dioscuri, the Menechmes, Narcissus, and Amphitryon—has close connections with the theme of the Androgyne, but nevertheless gave rise, in the nineteenth century, to a whole series of works which must be mentioned separately. In a sense, the link between the theme of the Double and the recollection of a primordial Androgyne, or the myth of Narcissus, is established through the Gnostic belief that Adam lost his celestial nature because he became enamored of his own image. But in the Occidental conscience, at least, every work is born at first from the author's interest in himself, and it is with good reason that A. W. Schlegel saw Narcissus as an image of the poet.

In the foreground of romantic works pervaded by the theme of the Double must be placed the work of Jean-Paul Richter. In *Siebenkäs* he had defined the *Doppelgänger* (or *Doppeltgänger*): "It is what people call those who see themselves." Of course, a psychic phenomenon so exceptional (and one to which alcoholics seem especially inclined) has given birth to a modern myth, illustrated by numerous and important works. In Jean-Paul's novel *Siebenkäs,* the protagonists Leibgeber and Siebenkäs are "a single soul in two bodies," which is the very definition of the mystic androgyne. The same conception is found in *Titan* (1800), by the same author; however, in this work Albano commits the fatal error of believing that the demonic Roquairol is his soul brother. In this story, there are no less than five pairs of doubles, several women have the same appearance and are substituted for one another, and, in this gratuitously complicated plot, Jean-Paul finally also introduces the Menechmes of his *Siebenkäs. Flegeljahre* (The mad years, 1804) depicts the twins Walt and Vult, whose personalities are portrayed as complementary.

Goethe, in book 11 of *Poetry and Truth,* relates the vision of his double that he had after he had left Frederica Brion. In *Wilhelm Meister,* he multiplied the family resemblances and the doubles. He approved the analysis of J. J. Ampère, who saw in Faust and Mephistopheles the complementary aspects of his self.

In *Isabelle of Egypt* (1812) Achim von Armin introduced an original variant of the Double: Bella Golem, a magical double of the protagonist. In *Peter Schlemihl* (1814) Chamisso told the story of the man who sold his shadow. The theme of the double, in all its aspects, is a fundamental idea in the work of E. T. A. Hoffmann, whose stories abound in split personalities, transfers of personality, and malevolent doubles, in keeping with the interest of the times in "magnetism" and somnambulism. Especially characteristic is *The Devil's Elixirs* (1814), which was influenced by the theories of G. H. Schubert; there the storyteller produced counterparts who also serve as doubles. The hero is a young Capuchin friar, Médard, whose double is his half brother Victorin. Beside the satanic woman, Euphemia, is Aurelia, who is eventually identified with Saint Rosalie. In *Princess Brambilla* (1820), the protagonists suffer from "chronic dualism." Finally, it is striking to see Hoffmann, in *The Adventure of the Night of Saint Sylvester,* introduce Schlemihl, who no longer has a shadow, bringing him together with Spikher, who abandons his reflection.

The underlying idea throughout is that madness is a form of wisdom, that dream and fantasy alone may permit us to connect the external aspects and the mysterious aspects of our existence. In many respects, the character of Kreisler, the genial musician and fool, the hero of *Kater Murr,* is the double of Hoffmann himself.

Hoffmann's work (especially *The Devil's Elixirs* and *The Night of Saint Sylvester*) exerted a profound influence on Gérard de Nerval. The memory of the *Elixirs* reappears in *The Chimeras,* especially in *Aurelia* (1855). Moreover, the theme of the double also intrudes repeatedly in this story; Neval gives it the Oriental name of *ferouer* (*farvāsis*). Previously, in "The Story of Raoul Spifame," from the *Illuminati,* and in "The Story of Caliph Hakem," from the *Voyage to the Orient,* Nerval had treated several aspects of the theme of the double. For him, the obsession with resemblances is linked to paramnesia and the quest for personal identity; *Corilla* and the scenario of *Polygamy Is a Hanging Matter* are equally characteristic. For both Hoffmann and Nerval, the problem of the double is associated with the problem of literary creation. It is by looking at his self in a crystal with multiple facets that the creator brings forth his characters, who themselves nearly always appear in pairs, the laws of the human spirit being in this respect consistent with those of biology: Balzac and Dostoyevski, for example, conceived their characters both in twos and in fours. Dostoyevski treated the theme in his early novel *The Double* (1846), and in *The Brothers Karamazov* (1880) he depicts Ivan conversing with the Devil, an objectification of the obscure part of his being, before coming to grief in madness. The counterpart, the real person, should not be confused with the double, a projection or reflection that has only a potential existence; on the literary plane, however, the two themes are closely connected. It is the double that is treated in Heinrich Heine's poem *The Double* ("I am the fruit of your thoughts"), Coleridge's poem *Transformation,* Musset's *The Night of May* (1835); in Edgar Allen Poe's *William Wilson* (1839), somewhat as in the work of Hoffmann, the theme of the double is combined with the theme of the counterpart.

Heinrich von Kleist wrote of "tragic somnambulism"; his characters are subject to the absence of their selves (as was their creator). His *Amphitryon* (1807) depicts Jupiter endeavoring to make Alcmene understand that there are two distinct selves in her husband's personality. The principal characters of his great plays *Penthesilea* (1808), *Catherine of Heilbronn* (1810), and *The Prince of Homburg* (1821, posth.) contain two antagonistic personalities, and the conflict between the conscious personality and the suppressed tendencies plunges them at times into a sort of hypnosis, at which point they lose consciousness of their actions.

Ralph Tymms has pointed out that Zacharias Werner, at about the same time, created characters subject to similar divisions of consciousness in *Attila, King of the Huns* (1808) and *Wanda, Queen of the Sarmatians* (1810), and Grillparzer saw in Zacharias Werner an image of Narcissus. In a different vein, Charles Nodier told the *Legend of Sister Beatrice:* this is a pious story from the work of Abraham Bzovius, according to which the Virgin was supposed to have assumed, for some years, the appearance and the place of a nun unfaithful to her vows, while awaiting the return of the nun to the convent from which she had fled.

In the background of all these literary works lurks, transposed onto the plane of individual consciousness, the long Indo-European and biblical tradition of legendary twins, one of whom is usually inferior to the other: Pollux must assign half of his immortality to Castor, Zethus dominates Amphion, Romulus kills Remus, Cain slays Abel. Always one is sacrificed and the other becomes a founding hero. All of these myths express the same truth, conveyed in parallel terms by novels and stories: that the resolution of antagonisms is necessary for survival.

But, in another formulation, the image of the soul is conceived as a double (on the same scale or smaller). Thus, in several ways, the myth of the Double appears to be quite fundamental, and there is no reason to be surprised that this myth assumed such importance in the nineteenth century.

J.Ri./b.f.

BIBLIOGRAPHY

I. The Androgyne

P. ALBOUY, "Le mythe de l'androgyne (à propos de *Mademoiselle de Maupin*)," *Mythologiques,* 1976, 324–33. A. J. L. BUSST, "The Image of the Androgyne in the Nineteenth Century," in Jan Fletcher, ed., *Romantic Mythologies* (London 1967), 1–95. M. ELIADE, *Méphistophélès et l'androgyne* (Paris 1962). H. EVANS, *Louis Lambert et la philosophie de Balzac* (Paris 1951). T. GAUTIER, *Mademoiselle de Maupin,* Marcel Crouzet, ed. (Paris 1973). M. PRAZ, *The Romantic Agony.*

II. The Double

J. LHERMITTE, "Clinique et physiopathologie," *Les hallucinations* (Paris 1951), chap. 4. J. PERROT, *Mythe et littérature sous le signe des jumeaux* (Paris 1976). O. RANK, *Don Juan: Une étude sur le double* (Paris 1932). A. STOCKER, *Le double: L'homme à la rencontre de soi-même* (Geneva 1946). R. TYMMS, *Doubles in Literary Psychology* (Cambridge 1949).

Romantic Myths of the Rebel and the Victim: Satan, Prometheus, Cain, Job, Faust, Ahasuerus, Don Juan, and Empedocles

In his *Introduction to Universal History* (1830), Michelet in a strange mixture of ideas placed Prometheus at the origin of a wholly romantic lineage: "Liberty without God, impious heroism, in literature, the satanic school that was heralded in Greece in Aeschylus's *Prometheus Bound,* and was revived by Hamlet's bitter doubts, is idealized in Milton's Satan and with Byron falters into despair" (*OEC,* vol. 35, pp. 457–58). A "titanic" tradition flourished in nineteenth-century Europe in numerous works: next to the Titan Prometheus, Satan, as remodeled by Milton, participates as chief of the rebels and, curiously enough, is identified with Pan.

We have long known that the romantics never ceased to draw from the ancient well, which explains the parallel development of myths borrowed from Judeo-Christian books (the Bible, the *Book of Enoch*) and of Greek and Latin myths. In an attempt to assess the contemporary, apparently fallen, condition of man, myths of the fall develop along several parallel tracks, with the oppressor god sometimes called Jehovah and sometimes Zeus-Jupiter.

I. Satan

In the aftermath of Milton's *Paradise Lost* (book 1), Satan's successors go in several directions. One of his descendants, Karl Moor in Schiller's *The Robbers* (1781), was to be the original model for the "noble bandit," whose extraordinary literary posterity included Vautrin and Jean Valjean. Another track consists of mysterious and domineering men, rebels of high caliber such as Montoni in Ann Radcliffe's *Mysteries of Udolpho* (1794), Schedoni in *The Italian, or the Confessional of the Black Penitents* (1797) by the same author, Ambrosio in Lewis's *The Monk* (1796). In Germany, the figure of the mysterious bandit inspired Heinrich Zchokke's *Abellio* (1794), which in turn inspired Charles Nodier's *Le Voleur* (1805) and *Jean Sbogar* (1818). These are all dual characters, so that the theme of the noble bandit is tied to that of the dual personality, of which we shall speak later.

But it was probably Byron who carried the type of the rebel to its peak of perfection by conceiving a whole series of gloomy heroes, all prey to a mysterious fate, in works that bear their names: *Lara, The Corsair, The Giaour.* Byron wanted to be like his heroes, which led him to playact his life and to waste it away sedulously. We may recognize the debased forms of the Byronic hero in the protagonist of Alexandre Dumas's *Antony* and in certain characters created by Eugène Sue or Paul Féval, late incarnations of the noble bandit who, in Satanic disguise, represent the Good and aim to save the state. But Médard, the hero of E. T. A. Hoffmann's *The Devil's Elixirs* (1816), had great trouble in distinguishing good from evil. Moreover, Paul Féval puts Byron himself on stage in *The Mysteries of London* (1844), where he appears under the name of the Marquis de Rio Santo.

Hugo's Satan has an intense dramatic presence, and yet he is by definition the one-who-does-not-exist, since the poet does not really believe in the existence of the Devil and identifies evil with matter. All the incarnations of Evil in the work of Hugo, as Pierre Albouy has shown, are envious or jealous before they are wicked.

II. Prometheus

Resorting to an ancient image, Byron (*Prophecy of Dante*) and Hugo (*The Genius, Odes and Ballads,* IV, 6) turn

Prometheus into the image of the misunderstood genius, bringing men the fire from heaven, that is, inspiration. According to P. S. Ballanche (*Orpheus*, book 8), man, thanks to Prometheus, "has acquired the capacity for good and evil." The romantic Prometheus is the foremost example of Titanism; he protests and rebels against the state of things imposed on earth by the Deity, which strikes him as neither rational nor moral. This rebellious posture directed against the apparent reign of evil on earth often involves writers in a kind of Neognosticism that leads to the rehabilitation of beings heretofore considered guilty, such as Cain and, more particularly, Satan, who are then depicted as man's helpers (Byron, *Cain;* Vigny, *Eloa*).

With Lamartine, the pendulum swings constantly from revolt to resignation and back. Resignation seems to be an idea formulated in *The Desert* to mean a God conceived as unknowable. In the piece entitled *Man*, the second of the *Poetic Meditations* (1820), dedicated to Byron, he takes a position with regard to the English poet, saying to him: "Leave doubt and blasphemy to the son of night." But the significant inversion of the roles of God and Satan had already appeared in William Blake, who finally identified himself with Milton, pointing out that Milton "was on the devil's side without realizing it," and who saw Jesus Christ as representing the human imagination.

The romantics' misinterpretation, in part deliberate, of Aeschylus's *Prometheus* was further encouraged by the fact that only the first part (*Prometheus Bound*) of the Greek playwright's trilogy has survived. Of *Prometheus Unbound*, which showed the Titan's reconciliation with Zeus, we have only fragments, and on *Prometheus the Fire Bringer* we can merely conjecture.

In his preface to *Prometheus Unbound*, Shelley explains that reconciliation was inconceivable: the sufferings and endurance of Prometheus, and his opposition to a tyrannical god, seemed to Shelley to constitute the very essence of the myth. Shelley's *Prometheus Unbound* is a lyric masterpiece; in it, the Titan simultaneously represents the human spirit and, in certain respects, Christ. Jupiter appears as the objectification of man's base desires, an incarnation of evil. To free himself from oppression, it is enough to will it by depending on reason and science; this is what makes the work a hymn to human freedom. Demogorgon, a complex character difficult to analyze, seems to represent Necessity seen as a chain of events. The fourth and final act reaches the cosmic dimension; its last verses express recurring optimism in the face of sufferings and evils:

> To suffer woes which Hope thinks infinite;
> To forgive wrongs darker than death or night;
> To defy Power which seems omnipotent;
> To love and bear; to hope till Hope creates
> From its own wreck the thing it contemplates;
> Neither to change, nor falter, nor repent;
> This, like thy glory, Titan, is to be
> Good, great and joyous, beautiful and free;
> This is alone Life, Joy, Empire, and Victory.

In thus expressing his hope in man, Shelley, as M. Raymond Trousson has shown, established the prototype of the romantic Prometheus. In *The Bible of Humanity*, Michelet makes Prometheus the first democrat and extends the inspiration of the English poet. Edgar Quinet summarized his own conception of Prometheus in the preface to his trilogy *Prometheus*, after indicating that in his opinion this hero "is the image of religious humanity." He goes on to say: "But not only does he have this historical character, he also encompasses the inner drama of God and man, of faith and doubt, of creator and creation; because of that, this tradition can be applied to all times and this divine drama shall thereby never end." In accordance with Herder's philosophy of history, whereby each form is born of the one preceding it, Edgar Quinet makes Prometheus the pagan forerunner of Christ. Such a conception of the religious evolution of humanity clearly implies that religions are mortal, as are all things human ("as the eagle grows old, so will the dove"). Quinet never lacked inspiration, but his power of expression was never quite commensurate with his ideas, which explains why he is seldom read.

In *God* (4, *The Vulture*), Hugo contemplates the character of Prometheus at length, and sees him as the awakener of consciousness and reason, the man of progress, who pushed back superstitions and ignorance. In a short early poem entitled *Prometheus* (1816), Byron had already hailed the Titan who rebelled against the deity, the Titan whose "divine crime was to be good." Louis Ménard's early work *Prometheus Unbound* (1843) is also the apotheosis of progressive faith: "The Ideal is within you: Behold the supreme God." As M. R. Trousson pointed out, what attracted the romantics to the character of Prometheus is the fact that he was not content to limit himself to an egocentric revolt, but managed to be regarded as a philanthropist, building a new world with the help of reason and knowledge. With the exception of Nerval, the theme of Pandora disappears almost entirely, since Prometheus is no longer considered guilty. The romantic *Christ* becomes a Promethean figure. But it was Madame de Staël who provided an incomplete translation of Jean-Paul Richter's *The Dream* in her *On Germany* (1810), and who must surely be held chiefly responsible for the fact that Vigny (*The Mount of Olives*, 1843) and Nerval (*Christ among the Olive Trees*, 1844) almost simultaneously made Christ a purely human figure, rebelling against the ruthless Jehovah.

III. Cain

The romantics place Cain among the great rebels or great victims, and in 1821, Byron devoted to him the "mystery" that we have already mentioned. This character, interpreted within a more traditional framework, inspired Hugo to write his celebrated *Conscience* in *The Legend of the Centuries*. *Conscience* was first intended for *Chastisements*, because Hugo was identifying the accursed Cain with Napoleon III, as is evident from the piece entitled *Sacer esto* (Let it be holy) in *Chastisements* and from numerous fragments that have been preserved.

IV. Job

In the Bible, the Book of Job raises the problem of divine justice and the relation of man to the divine (who takes the form of a hurricane). It inspired Edward Young's *Night Thoughts on Life, Death, and Immortality*, and was widely commented upon during the nineteenth century. Chateaubriand spoke of Job in his *Genius of Christianity*, Pierre Baour-Lormian includes in his *Poetic Evenings* a *Job, a Lyrical Poem*. In 1842, P. Christian prefaced a new edition of a translation of Young's *Night Thoughts* and Hervey's *Graves* with an "Essay on Jobism." In 1851, Isidore Cahen states in his *Sketch on the Philosophy of the Poem of Job:* "Job is more modern and timely than Prometheus himself because he better expresses the bitter disenchantment that is the fruit of a more advanced civilization." In his *Book of Job* (1826), William Blake had explained the sufferings of Job through an exhausting literal interpretation of the text. Only upon accepting his misfortunes and understanding that the spirit alone brings life will Job again find grace in the eyes of Jehovah.

In Ballanche's *Orpheus,* the story of Job runs parallel to that of Prometheus. Whereas Prometheus inaugurated the mode of revolt, Job was the first to raise the moral problem of evil. Ballanche sees the doctrine of the immortality of the soul as emerging from the very despair of Job. Quinet in turn says that Job heralds Christianity (*The Genius of Religions,* V, 4); he does, however, consider that Job "stops at doubt" and contrasts him with Prometheus, "who goes so far as to curse." According to P. Leroux (*Job,* 1866; prologue published in 1860), God answers the plea of his creature with the theory of progress. Lamartine put Job among his "faithful books"—whenever he feels sad and evokes the problems of suffering and death, an irresistible propensity leads his inspiration back to the Book of Job, as we see in some of the most famous poems in *Poetic Meditations* (The Vale, *Despair, Providence for Man,* and *Autumn*). In *Harmonies,* the poem *Why Is My Soul Sad?* is in the same vein; other examples can easily be found. All of this culminates in the magnificent pages on Job in the *Familiar Course of Literature* in 1868.

Hugo's Job is sometimes seen as an actual character and sometimes perceived from within. According to Hugo, Job is superior to Prometheus; we read in *The Unfortunates* (from *Contemplations*): "Even when Prometheus is there, it takes only you, Job, / To make the manure heap higher than the Caucasus." Everywhere one looks one finds this gigantic manure heap or "homo humus." In *William Shakespeare,* in which Hugo articulated his *ars poetica* most explicitly, he stresses the fact that "Job's resignation completes Prometheus's revolt," but he also emphasizes Job's titanic character and power: "Fallen, he becomes gigantic. He crushes the vermin on his open wounds, while calling out to the stars." And, like Quinet, Hugo concludes, "Job's manure heap, once transformed, will become Christ's hill of Calvary."

As P. Albouy has rightly asserted, one might expect Hugo to come up with a wretched but pugnacious character who would embody both Job and Prometheus—and this he did in *The Laborers of the Sea* (1866), with Gilliatt: "A struggling Job, a fighting Job, who faces scourges squarely, a conquering Job, and if such words were not too lofty for a poor fisherman of crabs and crawfish, a Promethean Job." As Hugo intended, Gwynplaine in *The Laughing Man* is a thunderstruck Titan, part Job and part Prometheus. He represents the misshapen people ripe for liberation and rebellion. After Villequier, moreover, Hugo relived Job's drama for himself, and an entire part of his poetry may be deemed "Jobian." This holds true particularly for *Contemplations,* book 4 (*Pauca mea*).

The same inspiration can also be found in numerous poems. It was already evident in *Interior Voices* (1836) with the poem *Sunt lacrymae rerum* (Things Have Tears), for example, and it can still be seen in *Lux* (in *Chastisements*), in *All of the Past and All of the Future* (in *The Legend of the Centuries*), in *The Donkey,* and, in fact, every time Hugo takes up the theme of the Almighty overwhelming his human creature. The Jobian theme of God's unfathomable grandeur also appears in *At the Window through the Night* (in *Contemplations*). Among the fragments published by René Journet and Guy Robert under the title *Things of the Bible,* which appear in P. Albouy's second volume of *Poetic Works* (Bibliothèque de la Pléiade, 859–63), many lines translate or paraphrase passages from the Book of Job. These fragments are sketches for *Contemplations.*

V. Faust

Faust is one of the rare modern myths. For many French romantics, the first reading of Goethe's *Faust* in Gerard de Nerval's translations of 1828 and 1835 was a kind of initiation. And when in 1840 the second part of *Faust* began to be known in France, it became apparent to what extent writers were projecting their hopes and dreams on this one work. Faust as a character took his place beside Hamlet among the heroes of knowledge and understanding and was considered to be a typical representative of the conscience of the Western world as it had been affirmed since the Renaissance. The profound remarks formulated in 1840 by Nerval in his preface to the new edition of *Faust,* parts I and II, had endless repercussions: of particular significance were Nerval's comments on the Helen episode, which he saw as an attempt to reconcile the ancient and modern worlds.

Parallel to Goethe's version of the story of Faust, a popular version of the legend was evolving. This version was preserved by Friedrich von Klinger, who wrote a novel based on it, in which the protagonist travels in many countries and meets with one disaster after another, trying to use the power of Mephistopheles to good ends. Klinger's account inspired Byron's unfinished work *The Deformed Transformed* (1822) as well as Méry and Nerval's joint work *The Image-Maker of Harlem* (1851), which they complicated with ideas about reincarnation. Many other works and characters owe more than one element to Goethe's *Faust.* They include William Beckford's *Calif Vathek* (1786) and numerous rebellious characters: Byron's Giaour mentioned above, the hero in *Manfred* (1817), and Ambrosio in M. G. Lewis's *The Monk.*

Next to Quinet's *Ahasvérus* belongs George Sand's *The Seven Strings of the Lyre* (1839), a symbolic drama in which Albertus, Mephisto, and Helen encounter one another around a lyre, whose strings embody man's noblest inspirations. Honoré de Balzac parodied the theme of the pact with the devil in *Melmoth Reconciled,* which superimposed the memory of Maturin on that of Goethe; but he treated it seriously in *Lost Illusions* (1842), in which Vautrin proposes the diabolic pact to Lucien de Rubempré. And Nikolaus Lenau wrote a lyric and pessimistic *Faust* (1835, definitive edition 1840) in which the hero, like Lucien, commits suicide. This last example represents what one might call a contamination of the character of Faust by that of Werther. The Faust theme was also taken up by composers: Berlioz produced his *Eight Scenes from Faust* in 1828 and *The Damnation of Faust* in 1846. Gounod's *Faust* is dated 1859. To his credit, Robert Browning chose a character closer to the legendary Faust than to the historical Faust (if we are to believe Trithemius and Melanchthon's contention that Faust was an imposter and a sodomite) in his *Paracelsus* (1835).

VI. Ahasuerus, the Wandering Jew

In his youth, Goethe had sketched the outline of an epic poem on Ahasuerus, but the extant fragments have no direct bearing on the character himself. In the seventh canto of Shelley's *Queen Mab* (1813), Ahasuerus speaks out: he curses Jehovah and the priests and derides Jesus. Shelley's Wandering Jew prefers "the liberty of Hell to the servitude of

William Blake, *Job.* London, British Museum. Photo Fotomas.

Heaven"—a good demonstration of juvenile illusions. Friedrich Schubert also chose this character to express his own pessimism.

Perhaps because it was written in his youth, Edgar Quinet's *Ahasvérus* (1833) remains one of this writer's most readable works, characterized by a kind of fresh, youthful inspiration not always evident in his later writings. The principal character is the Wandering Jew, and in the first part there are numerous literary echoes and imitations of the first part of Goethe's *Faust.* Many of Quinet's characters speak with voices unfamiliar to us: Leviathan, the great serpent, the Vinateya bird, the Ocean, the rivers, the Valley of Josaphat, the desert, the stars, sphinxes, and griffins, but also mules, chariots, and birds, not to mention angels and demons. The interweaving sometimes becomes forced when not only Strasbourg Cathedral but even the characters on its stained glass window (including the symbols of the Evangelists) are endowed with the ability to speak! This may well be a poetic idea applied too systematically, although some of the curious dialogues show real strokes of inspiration.

As for doctrine, Quinet begins with Herder's philosophy of history; he then places at the center of his concerns the phenomenon of religion and ends by refuting God and deifying man. Ahasvérus is saved by the love of Rachel, a fallen angel, because she took pity on him and became a servant of Mob (death). In the scene of the Last Judgment, which precedes the conclusion, Ahasvérus is forgiven and becomes the image of mankind to come, whereupon the Eternal Father says to Christ the Judge: "Ahasvérus is the eternal man. All the others are like unto him. Your judgment of him will serve us as the judgment of them all. Our work is now ended, as is the mystery. Our city is closed. Tomorrow we shall create other worlds." The last word is given to Annihilation and Nothingness. The conclusion as a whole must be interpreted within the framework of a pessimism for which, on a cosmic scale, the sum total of all human lives constitutes but a brief moment in time before man makes way for a better-endowed or different species or else Nothingness. In this regard, Quinet never wavered, for he wrote at the end of his *Genius of Religions:* "In the rapid course of our lives, we are barely granted a moment to get to know this universe, and then we must die. Let us then take a hurried glimpse at the spectacle of what people have thought, invented, believed, hoped, and worshiped before our time. By tying all this past to our brief existence, it will seem that we ourselves grow in scope and that, starting from an imperceptible point, we too are making an infinite line."

These words help us to understand why writers, particularly eighteenth-century writers, have so often chosen to express themselves through myths. For myths give the individual a feeling of belonging to a long tradition and thus of overcoming solitude.

VII. Don Juan

Faust is in search of both love and knowledge. The romantic interpretation of the character of Don Juan, formulated in a tale by E. T. A. Hoffmann (1813), tended to turn Don Juan, the mythical hero, into a hero in quest of love and thirsting for the infinite, which went beyond the explicit intentions of Mozart and his librettist Da Ponte. Henceforth, parallels and comparisons between the two heroes recur everywhere, notably in Hugo's *Preface to Cromwell* (1827), in Musset's *Rolla* (1833), and in Théophile Gautier's *Comedy of Death* (1838). It was Christian Dietrich Grabbe who wrote a *Don Juan and Faust* (1829), which superposed two plots and tied together, without actually mixing them, Da Ponte's libretto and Goethe's *Faust.* The main idea was to contrast two heroes who aspired to be superhumans, one typical of the Latin temperament, and the other representing the Germanic mind and soul ("I would not be Faust if I were not German").

Meanwhile the figure of Don Juan, born in Spain, continued his career in the various literatures. Byron used him as a transparent mask for his ironic, sometimes burlesque, and largely autobiographical epic *Don Juan* (1819/1824), which he said he wrote "without any plan but with materials." It is often regarded as his masterpiece; in any case, it is the only work in which Byron succeeded in casting an almost lucid gaze upon himself. In the same year, 1830, Don Juan was the subject of Pushkin's *The Stone Guest* and of Balzac's *The Elixir of Longevity.* In *Namouna* (1832), Musset made him an artist in search of beauty, and in the following year, in *The Morning of Don Juan,* he focused on the confrontation between reality and life. In 1834, Blaze de Bury in *The Commandant's Dinner Party* created a single character combining Don Juan Tenorio and Don Juan Mañara, and absolved the sinner.

In 1834, Prosper Mérimée published his narrative *Souls in Purgatory;* in 1836 Alexandre Dumas staged *Don Juan de Mañara or the Fall of an Angel.* In Lenau's play of 1844, Don Juan, grown old, is killed by the Commander's son; it is really a suicide in disguise. We should also mention Levasseur's *Don Juan the Graybeard* (1848); J. Viard's *The Old Age of Don Juan* (1853); and Baudelaire's 1846 poem, *Don Juan in Hell* (1846, in *The Flowers of Evil,* 15).

As might be expected, Spain is where the play that established the theme was written, *Don Juan Tenorio* by José Zorilla y Moral (1844), acted communally on All Soul's Day. It is a large-scale play in two parts, in which Don Juan is saved through the intercession of Doña Inés.

VIII. Empedocles

Among the pre-Socratic philosophers, Empedocles was probably the one whose life lent itself most readily to a romantic interpretation. That explains why several nineteenth-century authors counted him among the heroes of knowledge. Like Hamlet, about whom Hugo wrote substantially in *William Shakespeare,* he is a victim of the constant replay of melancholy thoughts. Unlike Faust, he does not succeed in freeing himself through pleasure and action and finally throws himself into the crater of Mount Etna. Hölderlin persistently lends this character some of his own fundamental questions. The successive versions of his *Empedocles,* unfortunately never finished, are strikingly beautiful. The character is depicted as unable to resign himself to having lost the direct contact with the divine which he once possessed and which deified him. "He through whom the spirit has spoken, must depart on time," we read in the first version in 1798. The third version (1799) features a moving dialogue with his disciple Pausanias. The ode that the poet dedicates to the death of Empedocles starts as follows: "Searching and searching for life, you see / A divine fire shooting forth in brilliance deep beyond the earth."

In 1829, Count Jean Labensky (whose pen name was Polonius) published in French a poem of a thousand lines, entitled *Empedocles,* in which he states: "But man chose error over ignorance. / He was meant only to love, but he wanted to know." Louis Ménard, in a poem bearing the same title published in 1851, endows Empedocles with a belief in metempsychosis.

If only because of its romanticism, Matthew Arnold's "Empedocles on Etna" (1852) may well be his masterpiece; after its completion he reverted to a kind of neoclassicism. Arnold's character has read *Hamlet, Faust,* and *Manfred,* as well as Obermann and Amiel. He is a lonely man because of his very superiority. His philosophy is borrowed from Lucretius and Epictetus. He is nothing but knowledge; a particularly beautiful line captures the sense of the poem: "Nothing but a devouring flame of thought."

In Hugo's *God* (*The Ocean from Above*), a spirit challenges him in these admirable terms: ". . . curious about the abyss. Empedocles from God."

J.Ri./g.h.

BIBLIOGRAPHY

1. Satan

M. MILNER, *Le diable dans la littérature française de Cazotte à Baudelaire,* 2 vols. (Paris 1960).

2. Prometheus

A. PY, *Les mythes grecs dans la poésie de Victor Hugo,* P. B. SHELLEY, *Prometheus Unbound* (London 1820). R. TROUSSON, *Le thème de Prométhée dans la littérature européenne,* 2 vols. (Geneva 1964). See also the works by P. ALBOUY and M. PRAZ cited in the text.

3. Cain

C. GRILLET, *La Bible dans Victor Hugo* (Lyon 1910).

4. Job

P. ALBOUY, *La création mythologique chez Victor Hugo* (Paris 1963). C. GRILLET, *La Bible dans Victor Hugo* (Lyon 1910). A. WRIGHT, *Blake's Job: A Commentary* (Oxford 1972).

5. Faust

E. M. BUTLER, *The Fortunes of Faust* (Cambridge 1952). A. DABEZIES, *Le mythe de Faust* (Paris 1972). C. DÉDÉYAN, *Le thème de Faust dans la littérature européenne,* 6 vols. (Paris 1954–67).

6. Ahasvérus

G. VABRE PRADA, *La dimension historique de l'homme ou le Mythe du Juif errant dans la pensée d'Edgar Quinet* (Paris 1960–61).

7. Don Juan

M. BERVEILLER, *L'éternel Don Juan* (Paris 1961). G. GENDARME DE BÉVOTTE, *La légende de Don Juan,* 2 vols. (Paris 1911). L. WEINSTEIN, *The Metamorphoses of Don Juan* (Stanford 1959).

8. Empedocles

M. ARNOLD, *Empedocles on Etna* (London 1852). F. HOLDERLIN, *Empedokles* (Zurich 1949), in many editions and translations. V. HUGO, *Dieu,* R. Journet and G. Robert, eds., 2 vols. (Paris 1960), with a valuable index of proper names. The line cited, in the volume *L'Océan d'en haut,* is no. 3426.

Spirits of the Elements in the Romantic Period: Sylphs, Water Sprites, Salamanders, Gnomes, and Elves

At the confluence of popular traditions with Neoplatonism and the cabala is situated the belief, at least a poetical belief, in the spirits of the elements, which appeared in the writings of numerous nineteenth-century authors. The relevant texts include the writings of certain Fathers of the Church (Lactantius, Cyprian, Clement of Alexandria), Neoplatonists, and cabalists such as Macrobius and Philo, and the Byzantine Michael Psellus (eleventh century), the restorer of Neoplatonism. In 1566, Paracelsus published a *Liber de nymphis, sylphis, pygmaeis et salamandris et de caeteris spiritibus* (Book of nymphs, sylphs, pygmies, and salamanders, and of various spirits); various Christian cabalists of the Renaissance, such as Pico della Mirandola, R. Fludd, G. Postel, and Thomas Heywood in England, also spoke of the spirits of the elements.

In 1670, the Abbé of Villars, in a humorous tone, set out in the *Comte de Gabalis* the theory of elementary spirits, thus constituting what would come to be called the "philosophy of the Rosacrucians": this distinguished the ondines, water sprites; salamanders, spirits of fire; sylphs, associated with the air; and gnomes or elves, connected with the earth. But in narratives, these inventions become superimposed upon the fairy wonderlands of folktales or upon the belief in other beings of the intermediate world, ghosts, spirits, and demons.

Superimposed upon the influence of the various authors

already mentioned was the influence of Jacques Cazotte's novel, *The Amorous Devil* (1772), in which the incarnation of a demon, Biondetta, in order to seduce and tempt Alvare, pretends to be a sylph who needed to be loved by a man in order to attain immortality. Schiller left an unfinished work, *The Visionary* (1786–89), which was inspired by this theme. La Motte-Fouqué published *The Mandragore* in 1810 and *Ondine* in the following year. In order to be reunited with Eros, Psyche must become immortal; the love of Huldbrand of Ringstetten can immortalize Ondine.

But Huldbrand falls in love with Bertelda, with disastrous results. As early as 1812, Achim von Arnim, in *Isabella of Egypt,* develops the theme of the Mandrake, a wicked little magician born from the tears (or the sperm) of an innocent man who is hanged. From La Motte-Fouqué's Ondine is directly derived the White Lady of Avenal in *The Monastery,* by Sir Walter Scott (1820); the very idea of a "white woman" may have come from one of the bedside books of the romantics, Collin de Plancy's *Infernal Dictionary,* which says that this is a name given to certain sylphs or nymphs. In Scott's *Peveril of the Peak* (1822), there is a Fenella who seems to be a caricature of Goethe's Mignon. Finally, *Anne of Geierstein* (1829) tells the story of a complex being, Hermione, who partakes simultaneously of the nature of the sylphs and that of the salamanders.

In 1821, Alexis-Vincent-Charles Berbiguier de Terre Neuve du Thym published his astonishing work *The Elves, or All the Demons are not in the Other World.* Charles Nodier, in *Trilby* (1822), set in the Scotland of Sir Walter Scott, creates an enigmatic being who is something of a synthesis of the spirits of the elements since, depending on the episode that he is in, he is connected with air, fire, or water. E. T. A. Hoffman, who had read *The Amorous Devil* and *Gabalis,* both of which were translated into German, introduced references to the spirits of the elements into his narratives, which are directly influenced by La Motte-Fouqué and also by Louis Tieck, the author of the *Runenberg* and *The Elves* (1811). In this way the archivist Lindhorst in Hoffman's *The Golden Pot* is the incarnation of Oromasis, the prince of igneous substances (who duly added to the repertory of Collin de Plancy). *The Mines at Falun* (1819), the subject of which was hinted at in a story by Johann Peter Hebel (*The Unhoped-for Meeting,* 1808), combines the theme of the mines, evoked by Novalis in *Henry of Ofterdingen,* and the influence of the *Runenburg* of Tieck; the great Venus of Tieck corresponds to the Queen of Metals in Hoffman.

Finally, it is appropriate to connect the spirits of the elements with the figure of the queen of Sheba. In *The Crumb Fairy* (1832), by Charles Nodier, the hero, Michel, is protected in his waking state by the Fairy, who has singular powers. But he also lives a kind of dream from one night to the next, in which the Crumb Fairy, so wise in the daytime, at night becomes the wife of Solomon, the radiant Makeda. This can be traced back to the Platonic concept that identifies Wisdom and the Good with Beauty. And it is said that Michel becomes "the emperor of the seven planets." Nerval's queen of Sheba in his *Voyage to the Orient* (1851) is an authentic "daughter of fire," who also commands the spirits of the air through the mediation of the Hudhud hoopoe bird.

One wonders about the deep motivations of all these authors, who depicted the spirits of the elements as representations of a cruder creation relative to human beings, but with an element of purity that is associated with their very nature. A detailed study of each author would make possible an exposition of the compensatory mechanisms or projections that came into play. A study of the group as a whole remains to be done.

J.Ri./d.w.

BIBLIOGRAPHY

ACHIM VON ARNIM, *Isabelle d'Égypte,* introduction, translation and notes by Reneza Guignard (Paris), translation reprinted in book 2 of *Romantiques allemands* (Paris 1973). A. CHASTEL, "La légende de la Reine de Saba," *R.H.R.,* 1939, F. CONSTANS, "Deux enfants du feu, la Reine de Saba et Nerval," *Mercure de France* (April–May 1948). F. DE LA MOTTE-FOUQUÉ, *Ondine,* appears in a translation by Jean Thorel in book 1 of *Romantiques allemands* (Paris 1963), Maxime Alexandre, ed. In the same volume are: TIECK, *Le Runenberg et Les Elfes; Le vase d'or* by HOFFMANN; LA MOTTE-FOUQUÉ, *La mandragore.* E. T. A. HOFFMANN, *Le vase d'or,* Paul Sucher, ed. (Paris 1942). GÉRARD DE NERVAL, *Œuvres,* vol. 2 (contains *Le voyage en Orient* and *Les illuminés*). C. NODIER, *Contes,* P. G. Castex, ed. (includes *Trilby* and *La fée aux miettes*). O. PARSONS COLEMAN, *Witchcraft and Demonology in Scott's Fiction* (Edinburgh and London 1964).

ORPHEUS AND THE POETIC AND SPIRITUAL QUEST OF ROMANTICISM

In the romantic period, the figure of Orpheus shone with particular intensity. All the great poets referred to the singer and magus of Thrace, and Brian Juden could with good reason place much of the literature produced in France from 1800 to 1855 under the patronage of Orpheus. But in fact, all of European romanticism corresponds to a rebirth of Orphism, understood in a broad sense, insofar as religious aspirations were expressed in terms of lyricism. And in many respects the romantics joined the spirit of the Renaissance when, for them, the figure of Orpheus served to support the expression of a spiritualist philosophy that allowed the poet to be affirmed as both a magus and a leader of peoples. Indeed, each episode of the myth of Orpheus—the loss of Euridice, the descent into the underworld, the death of Euridice, Orpheus dismembered by the Maenads—is apt to receive diverse interpretations, and as a whole these exemplary situations form something like the breviary of the existential condition of the poet in the world. In other respects it was understood, from the time of Kircher, Dupuis, and Kreuzer (translated by J. D. Guigniaut), that the Orphean Lyre represented not only the constellation of that name, but planetary harmony, and even the entire universe, while the animals charmed by Orpheus represented the constellations (as Lucian of Samosata had already stated in his treatise, *On Astrology*).

Saint-Martin and Fabre d'Olivet made Orpheus a great theosophist. According to Fabre d'Olivet, the love of Orpheus for Euridice represented the love of true science, and the loss of Euridice was associated with a collapse in personal and descriptive lyricism when the first inspiration, prophetic and philosophical, had become inaccessible. In his *Orpheus* (1829), P. S. Ballanche turns the character into a pontiff and a theologian, whose teaching prefigures Christianity. Orpheus is a northerner and a plebeian by choice. In his misfortunes Ballanche sees above all the pain of a failure in love (which results in giving the myth a personal meaning), and the descent into the underworld seems to him to represent an initiation. Generally, Orpheus expresses "universal lamentation." Nevertheless, through suffering, the magus reaches the transcendent vision, the fullness of knowledge, and his gaze acquires the power to transfigure Nature.

Victor Hugo, in the preliminary passage of the *Odes* (*The Poet in the Revolutions*), saw a modern Orpheus in André Chénier ("Who knows how to love, knows how to die"), and he regrouped all the aspects of the myth—the social role of the poet, prophecy, purity, sublime love, the martyr—all the abysses. In *The Satyr* he put the great cosmic lyre into the hands of the main character, turning him into a complete Titan, simultaneously Pan and Orpheus. And in the Idyll of *The Legend of the Centuries* dedicated to *Orpheus* one reads: "I am the human soul that sings / And I love." In poem 50 of the third book of the *Four Winds of the Spirit, Sacred Horror,* Hugo has this phrase: "The serene poet contains the obscure prophet / Orpheus is black." And in *God,* he depicts Orpheus releasing Prometheus, whereas according to the traditional story Heracles was the author of this deed. This means that the poet represents the spirit triumphing over matter and tyranny. The character of Orpheus is often, for Hugo, the pretext for fruitful comparisons with Job, Jacob, Moses, and Dante.

Indeed, one could establish a long list of characters who, in the works of this period, represent the poet. We should add at least Amphion, Arion, Homer, Pythagoras, and Faust.

In the *Voyage to the Orient* Nerval took too seriously the episodes of the *Sethos* by the Abbé Jean Terrasson (followed also by A. Lenoir) who, claiming to tell of the initiation that Orpheus received in Egypt, described the trials by the elements, also present in the libretto of Mozart's *Magic Flute* by Emmanuel Schickaneder. But exhuming, in *The Illuminated,* the *Thrace* of Quintus Aucler, a title that refers to the *Threicius vates* ("Thracian prophet," the name given to Orpheus, not by Virgil, but by Ovid, *Metamorphoses* 11.2), he cited numerous pages from it, which summed up the complete doctrine of the *Orphica.* In *El Desdichado,* identifying in turn with the poet-magus, he would use the expression "constellated lute" for the human element subject to celestial influences (a meaning that he had found in the *Three Books on Life* by Marsilio Ficino, and in Guy Le Fèvre de La Boderie, the translator of the Florentine Neoplatonist). Orphism and neo-Pythagoreanism nurtured the best of the inspiration of the author of the *Chimeras.* Finally, *Aurelia* describes a modern "descent into Hell"; the second part has the epigraph: "Euridice! Eurydice!"

In Germany the theories of J. G. Hamann and J. G. Herder laid the foundations for a new Orphism. The theme of the hero's descent into hell was taken up and developed in *Heinrich von Ofterdingen* by Novalis (Friedrich von Hardenberg) and in Goethe's *Faust,* part 2. Hölderlin was truly spellbound by ancient and modern Greece, and most of his work is essentially Orphic. The titles of some of his poems

Delacroix, *Eurydice Picking Flowers.* São Paulo, Museu de Arte. Photo Giraudon.

Gustave Moreau, *Dead Poet Being Carried by a Centaur.* Paris, Musée Gustave Moreau. Photo Musées nationaux.

Gustave Moreau, *Orpheus on Eurydice's Grave.* Paris, Musée Gustave Moreau. Photo Musées nationaux.

are revealing (*To the Heavens; To the Parcae; To the Morning; The Poet's Vocation; To Mother Earth*). Recall the surprising beginning of *Patmos:* "So near. And difficult to grasp, the god!"

Shelley, author of *Hymn to Apollo* and *Hymn to Pan,* also, in 1820, dedicated a poem to *Orpheus.* In it he depicted plants forming a natural sanctuary around the singer who mourns Eurydice and whose lament imposes silence even on the nightingale. Finally, John Keats was the author of *Ode to Apollo, Hymn to Apollo,* and *Endymion.* His most ambitious work, *Hyperion,* remained unfinished. In order to celebrate the Greek gods it was truly something of Orphic inspiration that the poet, in his Miltonic lines, was trying to recapture.

The Orphic vision of the universe should be connected with certain prose poems by Alphonse Rabbe and Maurice de Guérin. The former, in *The Centaur,* describes the loves of the Centaur and of Cymothoë. Visits to the antiquities in the Louvre, in the company of Trébutien, are the source of Maurice de Guérin's prose poem *The Centaur* (1836), upon which his posthumous glory long rested. *The Maenad* came shortly afterward. Guérin relived something of the pagan intuition of the ancient poets; he juxtaposed in himself two irreconcilable traditions, and at the last moment he chose Christianity. But in his *Journal* he had noted on 10 December 1834: "I live with the interior elements of things." And in a text of the same year he evoked the fable in which the forests departed in Orpheus's footsteps, seeing in it the memory of a time when nature understood the language of man and obeyed him. His prose poems, inspired by statues, have a Dionysian rather than a truly Orphic character. One may say the same of Keats's *Endymion* and of Kleist's striking *Penthesilia.*

J.Ri./t.l.f.

BIBLIOGRAPHY

QUINTUS-NANTIUS AUCLER (for: GABRIEL-ANDRE AUCLERC): *La Thréicie, ou la seule voie des sciences divines et humaines, du culte vrai et de la morale* (Paris, year 7). M BESSET, *Novalis et la pensée mystique* (Paris 1947). L. CAZAMIAN, *Histoire de la littérature anglaise* (Paris 1929), part 2; part 1 is by Émile Legouis. L. CELLIER, "Le romantisme et le mythe d'Orphée," *Cahiers de l'association internationale des études françaises,* no. 10 (1958). B. JUDEN, *Traditions orphiques et tendances mystiques dans le romantisme français,* 1800–1855 (Paris 1971).

The Isis of Romanticism: The Myth of the Wife-Mother—Helen, Sophia, Mary

In the works of many writers, especially poets, of the nineteenth century, a great female character, mother or wife or both, appears. Many, even if they are detached from Christianity, retain an attachment to the Virgin Mary. Goethe introduces into the *Faust* of 1824 the descent to the Mothers, who have preserved the essence of Helen, who represents the archetype of Beauty. Helen contributes to Faust's reconciliation with fate. In Faust's dream, the feminine ideal moves from Margarethe to Helen and then to the Virgin Mary. The final chant of the celestial choir says: "The eternal feminine leads us upward." George Sand, in her anti-Faustian novel *The Seven Strings of the Lute* (1840), gives the name Helen to the character who represents human love.

At the root of the importance of Isis to the romantics is the romantic interpretation of the Egyptian mysteries proposed by various scholars and writers of the eighteenth century, as well as the Masonic rituals (often derived from the works in question), which gave importance to the figure of the goddess, making her a representation of Nature. The libretto of Mozart's *Magic Flute* by Schikäneder was derived from the *Sethos* of the Abbé Jean Terrasson (1731) and from Liebeskind's Hindu story, *Lulu, or the Magic Flute;* the tests by the elements which are described there represent what was believed at the time to have constituted the Isiac mysteries. Goethe was so interested in them that in 1798 he wrote a *Second Part of the Magic Flute.* It was in 1798 as well that Novalis began his *Disciples of Saïs,* in which we read: "To understand Nature, one must recreate Nature within oneself in her complete cycle."

In the philosophy of Jakob Böhme, Sophia represented not only Wisdom, the mystical spouse, half of the androgynous Adam, but also the Virgin of Light, identified with Logos. Poets such as Novalis explored both the Masonic tradition and Boehme, combining Isis and Sophia. After the death of his young financée, Sophie von Kühn, Novalis recorded in his journal the phrase "Christ and Sophia." His *Hymns to the Night* (1800), with their stunning sensuality, represent the triumph of the nocturnal and feminine side of being, much like the famous sonnet *Artemis* in Nerval's

Chimeras. In both cases, the love object is identified not only with Nature but also with Night and Death ("C'est la Mort ou la Morte . . . [It is death or the dead woman]," wrote Nerval). In Novalis's *Henri d'Ofterdingen* (1800), the central moment of the novel is marked by the love of Henri and Mathilde, and Mathilde can be identified with both Sophia and the Virgin of Saïs.

An important episode in Ballanche's *Orpheus* (1829) retraces the initiation of Thamyris—a disciple of Orpheus—into the mysteries of Isis. Alfred de Vigny's extremely maternal conception of the character of Kitty Bell in *Chatterton* (1835) corresponds to this same search for the feminine ideal. His great poem *The House of the Shepherd* (1844) deals with the whole problem of man's relationship with Nature ("On me dit une mère et je suis une tombe [They call me a womb, and I am a tomb]"), which is well described by the two fundamental aspects of the Earth (Demeter and Persephone), while Eva, the companion of man, is seen as a mediator between him and nature. Even in the posthumous poem *The Anger of Samson,* we read: "L'homme a toujours besoin de caresse et d'amour / Sa mère l'en abreuve alors qu'il vient au jour [Man always needs caresses and love; his mother drenches him in them when he comes into the world]." In the poem *Helen* (1821), as well as in the narrative *Daphne* (1837), Vigny applauds the feminine incarnations of the divine: the Virgin, Venus, the houris in the case of Helen and Thea in the case of Daphne, Ceres-Deo, Minerva-Pronoë, and Venus-Ourania, who correspond to the religious orientations of the poet even more than to those of his hero, Julien.

It would be possible to include many excerpts from Alphonse de Lamartine here too, since his entire life was colored by the memory of his mother. One excellent example is *The Tomb of a Mother* (circa 1829–30) in *Harmonies.* And the force of the maternal image in Lamartine's work is responsible for the grandeur of his admirable poem *The Vine and the House* (1857).

J.Ri./d.b.

BIBLIOGRAPHY

See the bibliography of the article "Orpheus and the Poetic and Spiritual Quest of Romanticism" and also: J. BALTRUŠAITIS, *Essai sur la légende d'un mythe. La Quête d'Isis: Introduction à l'Egyptiomanie* (Paris 1967). J. CHAILLEY, *La flûte enchantée, opéra maçonnique* (Paris 1968). P. NEWMAN-GORDON, *Hélène de Sparte, la fortune du mythe en France* (Paris 1968). NOVALIS (F. DE HARDENBERG), *Petits écrits,* trans. Geneviève Bianquis (contains *Les Disciples à Saïs*), Paris 1947; *Hymnes à la nuit,* Paris 1943. A. ROLLAND DE RENÉVILLE, *L'expérience poétique* (Paris 1938; reprinted 1965), chap. 4: "Le sens de la nuit."

Isis. From Kircher, *Oedipus Aegyptiacus,* 1652. Photo X.

JULIAN THE APOSTATE IN ROMANTIC LITERATURE

The mythic transfiguration of the emperor Julian II, also called Julian the Apostate, is a remarkable case in the history of ideas. For after he had been, for a dozen centuries, associated with Satan and the Antichrist, he was to become from the sixteenth century onward a model of tolerance and good government, mainly because of the influence of Erasmus, Bodin, and Montaigne. Two historic traditions, parallel and contradictory, explain these differing viewpoints—that of the Fathers of the Church (with Saint Gregory of Nazianze and Saint John Chrysostom), who accused him of all possible crimes, and that of the witnesses and panegyrists Ammianus Marcellinus and Libanius. By giving credence to the testimony of one group of witnesses or to the other, it is possible to arrive at diametrically opposed conclusions, which explains how Julian, over the centuries, could serve as a pretext and support for the expression of the most diverse ideologies.

In 1817 Charles Nodier, in an account published in the *Journal of Debates,* made Julian an image of Bonaparte, a tyrant without religion, and himself the image of the Antichrist. But twenty years later, in the *Dictionary of Conversation,* he used a portion of the same text to make him into a kind of Voltaire: "There was a certain affinity of character and intention between these two men, the most violent enemies that hell could raise against Christ." Thus, by a clever shifting of the scales, Nodier returned to the image of Julian which had prevailed for so long.

In 1822, Aubrey De Vere Hunt wrote a dramatic poem whose main character was Maximus of Ephesus, the magician and theurgist, who appears throughout the work and is presented as the "emperor's evil genius." Julian, bereft of personality, is but a puppet in his hands: his only free act, in the end, is to kill Maximus. Maximus, seeing luck turn against him, passes over to the Persian camp. The best scenes of the play are lyrical, as when the genie of the empire appears to Julian. Victor-Joseph Étienne de Jouy (en-Josas) in 1827 wrote *Julian among the Gauls,* a classical tragedy in five acts in verse; this play recalls one of Voltaire's tragedies because it has all the qualities of a pastiche by Corneille, to the point of textual borrowing. Julian and the Gallic prince Bellovese are both in love with the beautiful Greek slave Theora. She dies by poison at the end of the play. The chauvinism of the author is given free reign in his conception of the character of Bellovese, who has all the noble virtues of his race.

In the first two discourses of his *Historical Studies,* a late work (1831), Chateaubriand discusses Julian at length, and the second discourse is entirely devoted to him. Documentation is plentiful and the author seems to force himself to judge equitably this emperor who "brought his erudition into his life." But in fact, Chateaubriand proceeds without much critical spirit, by an accumulation of evidence of very uneven worth, and collects, without objection or reservation, the commentaries of Christian historians—detractors of the emperor—and the tales of persecution that they invented.

In his youth Alfred de Vigny (1816) wrote a tragedy about Julian which he later destroyed. Beginning in 1832 he dreamed of writing a *Second Opinion of Dr Black,* which, like the first play, would consist of three narratives, dealing, respectively, with Julian, Melanchthon, and Rousseau, each ending with a "suicide." The general problem envisioned was to have been the influence of religion on ethics. The plan was reworked several times, but the definitive work never took form. The part of the work that was written was entitled *Daphne,* from the name of the region near Antioch, and dates essentially from 1837.

Vigny introduces Julian in this work, although the main character is Libanius, the Old Sage of Antioch (known in history for having been Julian's friend and panegyrist). In *Daphne,* Julian comes to ask Libanius's advice and, surprisingly, the philosopher discourages his efforts to restore paganism: one cannot go back in history. Julian's longest speech is a summary of his treatise *On Helios the King.* When he has come to understand the futility of his efforts, Julian, despairing, leaves for his Persian campaign. His death is presented as a disguised suicide (which, in fact, it may have been). For years Vigny meditated on the character of Julian, and a great deal of material for his unfinished work can be found in his *Journal.* In 1833 he confessed to the process of identification in these words: "If metempsychosis exists, I was this man. He is the man whose role, whose life, and whose character would have suited me best of any in history."

In 1853, the German poet Eichendorff wrote an epic poem on Julian, focusing on his wars against the Germans. In his posthumous poem *The Dove* (*Last Songs,* 1872), L. Bouilhet depicted Julian mourning the death of paganism, and he himself announced the impending end of Christianity. Louis Ménard's *Dreams of a Mystic Pagan* (1876) contained *The Last Night of Julian;* in his poem the genie of the empire exhorts Julian to resign himself to the inevitable.

Henrik Ibsen first planned a trilogy on Julian, but then replaced the whole section about the battle of Strasbourg with a narrative and divided his work, published in 1873, into just two parts. The general title was *Emperor and Galilean: A Drama of World History.* Each part had five acts; the first part was *Caesar's Apostasy* and the second *Emperor Julian.* Among the primary sources, Ibsen had read only Ammianus Marcellinus and the *Life of Maximus* by Eunapius of Sardis. For the rest he turned to modern historians—first, the Germans Neander, J. E. Auer, and David Strauss, then to Albert de Broglie, author of *The Church and the Roman Empire in the Fourth Century* (1856). Ibsen put whole pages copied from these sources into the mouths of his characters, but at the same time he invented the character of Helena, the wife of Julian, a cruel and sensual woman who reveals to Julian at the moment of her death by poison that she has been the mistress of his brother Gallus.

Ibsen was unaware of the fact that Julian was raised in Arianism, nor did he seem to know, although it was indicated by all his sources, that Julian quickly returned to paganism and had hidden the fact for ten years, not proclaiming it publicly until he became emperor. A passage written by Neander on the Cainites probably inspired the major scene of evocation, in act 3 of *Caesar's Apostasy:* Maximus of Ephesus causes Cain and Judas to appear and indicates that Julian is the reincarnation of the same principle. Another possible source for this scene was the memory of canto 34 of Dante's *Inferno,* in which Judas, Brutus, and Cassius are crushed by the three mouths of Lucifer. The Manichaean schema which Ibsen implicitly proposes is the following:

Cain—Abel (and his "substitute" Seth)
Judas—Christ
The pagan Julian—the Christian Jovianus

Maximus is presented as the apostle of the "third reign"; he respects Christ because he is a prophet, but he announces the arrival of a religion superior to Christianity. This is where we must look for the philosophy of history which underlies the work. Ibsen had been very much affected by the Franco-Prussian war and by the Commune. He adopted the belief that events and men are directed by a "will," the agent of a rigorous determinism. According to him, the advent of the "third reign" would be the reconciliation of the spirit and the flesh, of paganism and Christianity.

The second part of the work, *Emperor Julian,* was perhaps written too rapidly. It covers the eighteen months of Julian's reign, while the first part dealt with a period of ten years. Only the negative side of Julian is developed here; he is shown as a personal enemy of the Galilean; he pursues the Galilean's disciples in his hatred and cruelly persecutes them, all the while remaining unable to detach himself completely from Christianity. He is reduced to bad temper, hypocrisy, and vanity, to the point where one wonders if he is really the same character as in *Caesar's Apostasy.* Ibsen modifies the historical order of events in order to make Julian's order to burn his fleet on the Tigris appear an act of madness. The play ends with an inquiry about predestination and the fact that some people can be "damned by obedience," an idea that is already present in the poem *Judas* ("And if Judas had been refused?").

Whatever point of view is adopted and unless only one specific episode in the life of the emperor is treated (as was done by de Jouy), every romantic writer who told the history of the emperor was forced to end in a stalemate: Julian was out of step with history.

J.Ri./d.b.

BIBLIOGRAPHY

E. FRENZEL, *Stoffe der Weltliterature* (2d ed., Stuttgart 1963), article "Julian Apostata." H. IBSEN, *Œuvres complètes,* P. G. La Chesnais, trans., vols. 9 and 10 (Paris 1937). A. DE VIGNY, *Stello, Daphné* (Paris 1970).

Napoleon as Myth

Napoleon, who had a keen sense of propaganda, was the architect of his own legend. During his reign, the press, literature, and painting were systematically placed under his control and gave a glorious and embellished image of him that tended to present him as a pacifist and the restorer of Catholicism and, outside France, as the liberator of oppressed peoples. As soon as Napoleon fell, there was a change. Caricatures of the emperor dominated for a while, making him the Corsican Ogre; they were circulated far and wide by his opponents. Satirical drawings thus joined the anti-Bonapartist propaganda that was already present among German nationalist poets such as Arndt, Theodor Körner, and Rückert. The condemnation is blatant in Chateaubriand's *De Buonaparte et des Bourbons* (1814) and also in Byron's *Ode to Napoleon* (1814). The same year Senancour protested openly in his "Letter from an inhabitant of the Vosges," and was one of the first to depict Napoleon as the man who, after conquering fate, was in the end overcome by it. This eventually became the essential idea behind the romantic myth.

The transition to the level of myth finally came with his death on Saint Helena on 5 May 1821, making the emperor a victim, which accounts for his frequent identification with Prometheus. His death occasioned Manzoni's poem *Il cinque maggio* (The fifth of May) and Grillparzer's *Ode to Napoleon.* Lamartine's *Bonaparte,* in his *Nouvelles Méditations* (New meditations) of 1822, is a poem that coldly questions Bonaparte and his fate and that echoes Manzoni. There is also Béranger's poem *Le Cinq mai,* in his *Souvenirs du peuple* (Memories of the people) (1828), and his famous *Parlez-nous de lui, Grand-mère* (Tell us about him, Grandmother). The *Mémorial de Sainte Hélène* (Memorial of Saint Helena), published in 1823, went on to enrich the legend. In it, Bonaparte poses as the liberator and unifier of the people, whereas in reality he had fought against liberalism and nationalism in all their forms.

There was then a progressive turnabout by certain writers. Hugo's mother may have taught her son to hate Napoleon and his crimes; but with his poem *Les Deux Iles* (The two islands) (1826), resentment gave way to pity, and the life of Napoleon was compared to the sun in its passage from east to west. The *Ode à la Colonne* (Ode to the pillar) (1827) was Hugo's response to an affront directed at four marshals of the empire during a reception at the Austrian Embassy.

Nerval, the son of a military doctor of the Grand Army, thought of himself as (or wished he had been) a "Napoleonite." He was sixteen years old when he wrote his own "Cinq mai" (The fifth of May, 1824), and in 1827 he published *Napoleon et la France guerrière, Elégies nationales* (Napoleon and France at war, national elegies), dedicated to Napoleon and for the most part written before 1825. The memory of the emperor haunted numerous texts by Nerval, particularly the six sonnets known by the title of *Autres Chimères* (Other fancies). Stendhal is known to have "fallen with Napoleon"; the heroes of his novels refer constantly to the emperor. Julien Sorel in *The Red and the Black* (1831) reads the *Mémorial,* and Fabrice in *The Charterhouse of Parma* (1839) is present at the battle of Waterloo. Balzac helped reinforce Napoleonic legend by the place he gave the emperor in *The Human Comedy.* Moreover, he conceived his opus as an imitation of Napoleon in which he intended "to achieve with the pen what he began with the sword." Already in *The Country Doctor* (1833), he presented an unforgettable "Napoleon seen by the people."

After the Return of the Ashes to Paris on 15 December 1840, the infatuation became widespread. Napoleon appeared in Balzac's work again: *The Vendetta* (1830), *A Shadowy Affair* (1841), *The Thirty-Year-Old Woman* (1844). Balzac admired Napoleon as a remarkable example of energy and of the sublime. In 1835, Vigny published *Military Servitude and Greatness,* in which a hovering presence of the emperor appeared. In *Memories from beyond the Grave* (1818), Bonaparte became "the colossal man," and Chateaubriand described his epoch as though it had consisted of a long dialogue between Napoleon and him. In 1844, Carlyle devoted a chapter of his *Cult of Heroes* to Napoleon. In 1845, Thiers began to publish his *History of the Consulship and the Empire,* completed in 1862.

A day in the reign of Napoleon, or the sun personified. Paris, Bibliothèque nationale. Photo D.R.

Franque, *La France dans l'attente du Retour d'Egypte*. Paris, Musée du Louvre. Photo Musées nationaux.

The first history of what was then a recent period, it was to have great success. Hugo sang the praises of the Return of the Ashes; in *The Chastisements* he included the *Expiation* (1852), in which he exalted Napoleon in order to humiliate his nephew. In his novel *Les Misérables* (1862), he chose to reenact Waterloo. Although Tolstoy in *War and Peace* (1864) made the emperor into a kind of soulless marionette, its strings pulled by fate, and although Proudhon, Littré, Erckmann, and Chatrian (*The Conscript of 1813*, 1864) saw Napoleon as a *condottiere* without scruples, Goguelat's account in *The Country Doctor* already suggested the deification of Napoleon, who was identified with the messiah. As early as 1816, Wendel Wurtz had given the black legend a mythical extension by identifying Napoleon with Appolyon, the destructive genie of the apocalypse. Mickiewicz, in *Pan Tadeusz* (1834), paid Poland's respects to Napoleon; later, under the influence of Towianski, he would make him the new messiah. Nerval took J. B. Pérès's hoax seriously: Pérès, in *How Napoleon Never Existed* (1827), satirized the theories of Dupuis and turned Napoleon into the new Apollo.

One problem remains that has never received a satisfactory solution. The objectively verifiable elements of Napoleon's career—the names of individuals, the general course of events—spontaneously organized themselves according to the structure of the solar myth. Although Napoleon is not entirely identified with the sun, it is nevertheless true that the myth built around his historical personality is of a complexity seemingly born of the resolution of certain opposites. He represents both liberty and authority; the messiah and, at the same time, the antichrist; warrior and also legislator. And if one tries to understand how, after his death, many of his contemporaries changed their attitudes toward him from hostility or resentment to admiration, one reaches the conclusion that they subconsciously made Napoleon into an image of the father bigger than life—at the same time simple and mysterious, kindly and terrifying. Since many of their fathers or paternal uncles had fought in Napoleon's armies, this image is not hard to explain.

The extension of the myth over the whole world came later and goes beyond the limits of this essay.

J.Ri./g.h.

BIBLIOGRAPHY

J.-B. PÉRÈS, *Comme quoi Napoléon n'a jamais existé*, 1827. See the reprint in *La Tour Saint-Jacques* (July–August 1956), with a study by Robert Amadou. J. TULARD, *Le mythe de Napoléon* (Paris 1971). R. WHATELY, *Historic Doubts Relating to Napoleon* (1st ed. anonymous, 1819), presents Bonaparte as a collective being representing the "better part" of the people and the army of France and insists on the *improbable* character of his life.

Modernity's Challenge to Myth, in the Poetry of Hölderlin, Heine, Baudelaire, Mallarmé, T. S. Eliot, and Rilke

Hölderlin

Two-thirds of the way through *Patmos* (1803), one of his last great hymns, Hölderlin, who has just evoked the disappearance of the evidence from the mythic time of Christ, the destruction of the temples, and the invisibility of the gods both in heaven and on earth, abruptly interrupts his evocation to ask about the meaning of these deficiencies that he has identified with his own time. The question, "What is it?," with which the tenth stanza of the poem ends, is answered by some lines as simple as they are essential in their attempt to repossess the truth of a historic becoming:

It is the cast
Made by the sower when he scoops
Wheat into the shovel and sweeps it
In an arc
Toward the clear
Void over the threshingfloor,
The husk falls at his feet, but
The grain does reach its goal,
And no bad thing it is, if
Some disappears, the live sound
Of speech
Fades, for divine work too is akin
To ours, the Highest does not want
All things at once. . . .
(Translated by Christopher Middleton from Friedrich Hölderlin and Eduard Mörike, *Selected Poems*, Chicago: University of Chicago Press, 1972, pp. 83–85.)

The reader will have recognized in this response the condensation of at least three biblical passages: the image of the preaching of John the Baptist (Matthew 3:12): "Whose fan is in his hand, and he will thoroughly purge his floor, and gather his wheat into the garner; but he will burn up the chaff with unquenchable fire"; the story of Ruth and Boaz (Ruth 2:2–17); and, perhaps especially, the passage from the Gospel (John 12:24): "Verily, verily, I say unto you, Except a corn of wheat fall into the ground and die, it abideth alone: but if it die, it bringeth forth much fruit."

What should nevertheless arrest us even more than this syncretism is the use that is made here of a parabolic language on the level of poetry. The question posed at the end of the preceding stanza bears fundamentally upon the meaning of a history whose upheaval Hölderlin could indicate as few others could. The night of the absence of the gods, in the writing of this poet, is far more than a simple metaphor: it is the declaration, the sharp act of perception, of a historical and metaphysical reality, which seems at first to lack the support of a transcendence that might assure its redemption. Nothing could be more serious, less "metaphoric," for Hölderlin, than this declaration.

It is precisely this seriousness that makes the lines we have cited so interesting. What the poetry achieves here is nothing less than a mythical repossession of the real. Just as the grain dies in order to be reborn as wheat, after failing to reach its goal, so too we are to understand that this night of history is called upon to cut across the proof of its negativity so that, in the end, the day will dawn that will mark the return of the gods. The concrete image, invested with the authority of the sacred text, makes it possible to signify the historical process by anchoring it in a natural rhythm. Existence and its meaning are one: we are in the poetic universe of myth.

What Hölderlin succeeded in affirming once more in 1803, at the price of great tension and an unequaled dialectic force, constitutes the model—at once dreamed of and inaccessible—of what has since been called modern poetry. Whoever inclines to the history of the poetic texts of the last 170 years or so cannot help but be struck by the progressive movement by which the gesture of confidence in the use of a mythic model loses if not its validity at least its force of credibility. The few remarks that follow certainly do not aim to exhaust the subject, but propose to illustrate this movement.

Heine

In his poem, *The Gods of Greece,* composed in 1825–26, Heinrich Heine reverses the order of the certainties that we saw at work in Hölderlin. In Heine, myth no longer serves as a foundation for history, but rather submits to history. The gods of Greece, which the imagination identifies in clouds at night, in this poem are made "suppressed and defunct" figures; Zeus appears here with "extinguished lightning" in his hand and with his face marked by "unhappiness and sorrow"; Aphrodite, "once golden, now silver," here has no more than an "appalling" beauty and is said to be the "goddess of corpses," "Venus Libitina." The founding nature of the gods in Hölderlin is succeeded here by a series of figures born of history and subject to its finitude: "For even the gods do not reign forever; the young ones take the place of the old ones." The relativization of mythic beings leads them to become no more than the supports for an entirely immanent vision of history, in which the struggle of antagonistic forces, far from representing a metaphysical confrontation, has taken a clearly political turn: man, in this poem, becomes morally superior to the gods because, unlike them, he does not side with those who are strongest, but joins in solidarity with those who are conquered.

Baudelaire

This feeling of a lost mythic integrity is found again, though in a rather different sense, at the beginning of the work of the one who, together with Georg Büchner in the medium of theater, could be said to be the founding poet of modernity: Charles Baudelaire. From his earliest poems, Baudelaire seems to long for the "naked epochs / When Phoebus amused himself gilding statues," and when "Cybele, fertile in generous fruits, / Did not find her sons too heavy a weight"; yet he does not hesitate to point out the contemporary truth of myth in those "poor twisted bodies, thin, pot-bellied, or flaccid," which "the god of Utility, implacable and serene, / swaddles as children in their bronze diapers," in other words, we understand, in the allegorical vision of a reality dispossessed of its mythic fullness.

In *The Swan,* for example, Baudelaire evokes the "strange and fatal myth" of the animal "that has escaped from its cage," in which he sees the image of the human condition of exile. But, except for the fact that this poet does not distinguish the term "myth" from the term "symbol," or "emblem," or even "allegory," his use of the swan does not so much reactualize a sphere of meaning or a mode of being that belongs to myth as it transforms the creature—just like Andromache, to whom it is compared—into a sign of the loss of or separation from myth. Baudelaire's swan is not an identity whose presence is sufficiently solid to suggest, if not to found, a poetic order in which signs are organized according to their own essence—which would be the very definition of a poetry of myth; on the contrary, it marks a division that allows only divided realities and the image of that division to become linked to it. And it is precisely in this division that Baudelaire deciphers the modernity with which, in opposition to romanticism, to pantheism, or to metaphysical Manicheanism in the style of Hugo, he will identify his poetry.

One could argue that some of his poems, some of his essays (on Poe, on Hugo, on Gautier), express the idea of a "shadowy and profound unity" that is able to bring together and to integrate the whole of reality into a network of "correspondences" which assure it of meaning in the manner of a myth. The importance accorded to the imagination, to the dream, is a sign of this meaning. But though these tendencies are incontestable, they do not go beyond the stage of intention. The only genuine figure that can really claim the status of a unifying locus of the real in Baudelaire is, paradoxically, death. The Baudelairean One is the unity of what perishes; death, moreover, is the only absolute that can measure itself against the absolute of the exigency of infinity. And if certain poems in the *Flowers of Evil* seem to reach a mythic dimension, despite everything—notably the great passages in the *Parisian Pictures*—they do so precisely because their repossession of finitude raises death to the level of a necessity that is visibly constitutive of what is real.

This recognition of death as a presence that is simultaneously intimate and universal is also what leads Baudelaire to attempt to make the work of art the only place the other side of death. Beyond his macabre Petrarchism, this view of death underlies a poem such as *A Piece of Carrion*—even though, against the avowed intention of the author, it could also be read as the expression of the triumph of a poetics designed to speak of the perishable part of existence (cf. the letter from Rilke to Clara of October 7, 1907). The architectural will of the poet of *Flowers of Evil,* his insistence on the independence and immanent logic of form, constitute an extension of and a response to the consciousness of a reality that could formulate no other myth than finitude. What ultimately characterizes the poetics of the *Flowers of Evil* is a tension—the tension between a palpable reality accepted in its opacity, its irreducibility to any idealization, and a (formal) dream in which the imaginary is able to recompose the network of identities that are as much material as they are spiritual.

Mallarmé

It might be supposed that the thinking of the greatest French disciple of Baudelaire, Stéphane Mallarmé, developed from a tension of the same kind. At least his early poems, as well as certain documents dating from his formative period, suggest such a connection. But, unlike his master, Mallarmé was to situate his place of choice in the realm of dream: "Yes, I know," he wrote to Henri Cazalis in April of 1866,

> we are nothing but vain forms of matter, but quite sublime for having invented God and our soul. So sublime, my friend, that I want to give myself this spectacle of matter, being conscious of it and nevertheless rushing passionately into the Dream that matter cannot be, singing of the Soul and all the parallel divine impressions that have accumulated in us since the earliest times, and proclaiming before the Nothing, which is truth, these glorious lies! Such is the plan of my lyric volume, and such perhaps will be its title, the Glory of the Lie or the Glorious Lie.

As one can see in these lines, the degenerating structure of Mallarmé's vision, which affirms in the same stroke the idealistic orientation of matter and the unreality of that orientation, hardly lends itself to a mythical apprehension. Moreover, even when Mallarmé did resort to mythic motifs in his poems, his use of myth remained marked by his vision of the real as a fiction. This is certainly true of the two great poems sketched during those years, the "Herodiade" and "The Afternoon of a Faun."

Mallarmé's Heriodiade is not the temptress that Flaubert would describe ten years later, in a dazzling page of his *Three Tales,* in the act of seducing Herod Antipas. She is the figure of a poetry dedicated to reflexivity, a poetry incarnate in his image of a woman looking at herself in a mirror. Her narcissism, her fierce refusal of any nubility (cf. "Yes, it is for me, for me, that I have blossomed, alone!"), are the image of Mallarmé's (mythic) desire for a language restored to its purity of a musical essence. A "dyad," in that her concern for herself determines her both as the desiring subject and as the image of her own desire, this "heroine"—even in her name—suggests the recoiling inward in which Mallarmé sought the salvation of language through poetry.

The mythic subjugation of the Faun is still more subtle. Since for Mallarmé the solar and musical figure of this fabulous creature is manifestly nothing but the image of the poet, or of poetic power, this poem too reveals the desire for reflexivity that was already at work in the "Herodiade." At the same time, however, the artifice by which the Faun feigns possession of the nymphs, whom he really has only desired, ends with the evocation of a reality which, for being fictive, is no less endowed with a charge of concretion and even of a sensuality of which there are few other examples in French poetry:

> As for me, proud of my voice, I'll speak at length
> Of those divinities and by idolatrous
> Depictions strip yet more veils from their shade.
> Thus, when I've sucked the brightness out of grapes,
> To chase regret deflected by my feint,
> I lift the empty cluster to the sky,
> Laughing, and, wild to be drunk, inflate
> The shining skins and look through them till night.
> (Translated by Patricia Terry and Maurice Z. Shroder, in *Stéphane Mallarmé, Selected Poetry and Prose,* ed. Mary Ann Caws, New York: New Directions, p. 37.)

The use of a mythical figure (a Faun) makes it possible to question what is immediately real ("Did I dream that love?") but leads here to the emergence of a poetic reality all the more absolute for being manifestly more fictive.

The gesture by which fiction was identified with the very site of reality, this absolute poetic idealism—which Mallarmé himself later went beyond by transforming his negative theology into a kind of theology of the twenty-six letters of the alphabet—set off one of the two currents which, following the turn-of-the-century symbolism, were to fertilize the poetry of the twentieth century and notably its use of myth: a Valéry, a Saint-John Perse, in France, a Stefan George, a Rilke, in Germany, would tap into that current, each in his own way.

Eliot

But this would not happen without the close parallel development of another current, which should be identified here. The end of the nineteenth century set the stage for an exacerbated and mythicizing idealism in the realm of literature; yet it also saw the development of works which, following the upheaval stirred up by Schopenhauer and Nietzsche, manifested a kind of renaissance of materialism. Starting in 1896, Freud wrote his *Interpretation of Dreams* (published in 1899), which is practically contemporary with the first volumes of Sir James George Frazer's *The Golden Bough,* the pioneering work in the field of mythic ethnology. Significantly, once Freud's fundamental concepts had been developed, the interest of psychoanalysis was to shift into the field of myth (*Totem and Taboo* dates from 1913, one year after Otto Rank's great book *The Incest Motif in Literature and Folktale*), that very myth whose historical origin and nature Frazer, after others, had demonstrated. Despite the general crisis of values in European society and civilization that led to the first World War—a crisis that was expressed in art by an impressive spate of inventiveness (cubism and futurism in painting, the Vienna school, Stravinsky in music)—writers were strongly stimulated by this challenge to their range of choice. This helps to explain how the great poem that would attempt to draw up the double balance sheet of civilization and literature, once the war was over, at the same time presents itself as a profound questioning of mythic speech.

We refer to T. S. Eliot's *The Waste Land,* published in 1922. *The Waste Land* signifies any barren land, ravaged land, but the title is also a direct reference to the land stricken with sterility in the legend of the Grail, in which Eliot, influenced by a book by an English medievalist who was a disciple of Frazer, learned to recognize a medieval, Christianized transposition of certain myths of fertility borrowed mainly from Egyptian and Mesopotamian antiquity. At its simplest level, use of the Grail myth tends to establish an equivalence between the medieval symbol of a land awaiting its deliverance and the ruined condition of postwar Europe. Such was, one might say, the mythic analogy of this text.

But this analogy constitutes only one of the levels of meaning in this poem—the most apparent, perhaps, but not the most profound. Aside from the fact that the mythic narrative is borrowed only in a most discontinuous manner (and is used much less closely, for example, than the myth of the *Odyssey* in Joyce's *Ulysses,* which had appeared in the previous year), *The Waste Land* is concerned less with the theme of mythic desolation than with questioning an entire series of previous poetic discourses, which are themselves quite often connected with a myth, for which this poem constitutes a kind of museum.

As Eliot himself indicated in the notes that accompany his poem, and as has often been remarked since, *The Waste Land* is largely made up of quotations. These quotations, borrowed from sources as diverse as Dante's *Inferno,* the *Satyricon* of Petronius, Elizabethan drama, the Bible, the *Upaniṣads,* the *Confessions* of Saint Augustine, and the *Flowers of Evil,* actually have less to do with a unified way of thinking—in this case a way of thinking about desolation—than they signify, through the often ironic or parodying use that is made of them, the decrepitude of the mythic design of their original context. "I had not thought death had undone so many," says one of the speakers of this poem (quoting Dante), as he watches a crowd of resigned pedestrians file over London Bridge—people who are so many metaphors for speech. As much as it is the enactment of a myth, *The Waste Land* is the properly Babelian actualization of the impossibility of a founding speech. The "death" of the inhabitants of the waste land, a synonym for the spiritual collapse of Europe of 1920, here also prefigures the end of the demiurgic period of poetry. Or, to put it differently, the figures who speak in the poem are not the only ones stricken by death, but through them the integrity of the poetic source or realm of which they have been made the symbols is also stricken.

Rilke

The fact that death is necessarily connected with the very possibility of myth is something few poets, after Eliot, have failed to realize. Rilke, for example, though he rejected Eliot's method of collage and fragmentation, in that same year 1922 could let his Orpheus emerge only by specifying in characteristic fashion that "Only one who has lifted the lyre / among shadows too, / May divining render / the infinite praise" (*Sonnets to Orpheus,* translated by M. D. Herter Norton, New York: W. W. Norton and Company, 1942, p. 33). When one turns to the poets of France, Italy, the United States, or Latin America, it seems that this is a universal experience, one that World War II made even more oppressing.

The historic relativization of spiritual horizons and social ideals, the affirmed will of a critical attitude of the mind, combined with the collapse of the sacred rhetorics and orders of speech, contributed more than a little to take apart what Western poetry since Homer had never ceased to put together. Belief in myths, as Paul Ricoeur has remarked, has for many people ceded its place to the interpretation of myths and of modes of belief that connect us with myth. Is it not time to close this chapter of our history, even if it is a principal chapter?

For two reasons, beyond all the skepticisms and all the rationalizations, it may be too early to do so. First, despite the immense deployment of efforts to objectivize, formalize, and grasp the origin and the nature of language, language continues, in the final analysis, to refuse to reveal its essence other than in a movement of the invention and creation of images which, while integrating ever more extended levels of reflexivity, keep their metaphoric essence. Nor must we forget that this growing reflexivity has come to be joined, by a kind of necessary counterpoint or compensation, with a simultaneous liberation of the unconscious which, while ruining certain conventional poetic forms, has not stopped and still does not stop formulating its truth by the creation of new structures that find in myth one of their most profound resources. The averred impossibility of a metalanguage that could formalize the essence, in the last analysis a metaphoric essence, of language returns dialectically to a consciousness of the mythic founding of that metaphor. As a result, in the connections that unite (and disunite) man with his human environment, earthly or cosmic, the need for the fiction through which the first connections with the world are avowed and formulated remains perceptible.

Despite all the impasses of literature today, at least the hope of giving voice, through the language of myth, to the always difficult harmony of an enchanted flute beyond all disenchantments may thus continue to affirm itself.

J.E.J./g.h.

BIBLIOGRAPHY

B. HEDERICH, *Gründliches mythologisches Lexicon,* 1770. J. FRAZER, *The Golden Bough: A Study in Magic and Religion,* 12 vols. (London 1890–. J. WESTON, *From Ritual to Romance* (Cambridge 1920).

F. SCHELLING, *Philosophie der Mythologie* (Stuttgart 1856). F. NIETZSCHE, *The Birth of Tragedy* (New York 1967). S. FREUD, *The Interpretation of Dreams* (New York 1927); *Totem and Taboo* (New York 1927), trans. from German. H. VON HOFMANNSTHAL, "Ein Brief," 1901–2, in *Gesammelte Werke,* Prosa I (Frankfurt 1959). S. MALLARMÉ, *La musique et les lettres* (Paris 1894). O. RANK, *Das Inzest-Motiv in Dichtung und Sage* (Leipzig 1912). P. VALÉRY, "Sur Phèdre femme," in *Variétés IV* (Paris 1944). T. S. ELIOT, "Tradition and the Individual Talent," *Selected Essays* (London 1932). M. BLANCHOT, *L'espace littéraire* (Paris 1955).

E. CASSIRER, *The Philosophy of Symbolic Forms,* 3 vols. (New Haven 1953–57). W. BENJAMIN, *Ursprung des deutschen Trauerspiels* (Berlin 1928). P. RICOEUR, *The Symbolism of Evil* (Boston 1969). *Terror und Spiel: Probleme der Mythenrezeption,* H. R. Jauss, ed. (Munich 1971).

HÖLDERLIN'S DIONYSUS

Dionysus became the god of poetry at the very moment when poetry itself analyzed its own status with the greatest precision, namely, in Germany in the work of Friedrich Hölderlin (1770–1843). In answer to Klopstock, who was content with rather superficial identifications, Hölderlin proposed a much more finely tuned connection between poetry and the god of wine, who in his eyes was also the god of joy, as attested by his translation of the last great chorus of Sophocles' *Antigone.* He writes:

The banks of Ganges heard how the god of joy
Was hailed when conquering all from far Indus came
The youthful Bacchus, and with holy
Wine from their drowsiness woke the peoples.
And you, our own day's angel, do not awake
Those drowsing still?
("The Poet's Vocation," 1800, translated by Michael Hamburger, from *Friedrich Hölderlin: Poems and Fragments,* Cambridge: Cambridge University Press, 1980, p. 173)

"Day's angel" is the mediator between the gods and men in the sphere of temporal action where contemporary history is made. He is the poet who, like Dionysus, stirs the soul of people by reinterpreting the moments when, according to tradition, God has revealed himself, seeing these moments in the light of great movements of the present, such as the French Revolution. But while he renewed the sacred chant of the Old Testament prophets and of the Greek poets, and made his own poetry the equivalent of the Revolution, Hölderlin must indeed have feared that he was not on the level of his god, since in the same ode he reminds us of the humiliating scene in Euripides' *Bacchae* when Dionysus, in bonds, is dragged about by the servants of Pentheus "like a captured wild animal," a "tame beast." The poet is almost tempted to take advantage of the god's docility to gain control over him, thus usurping the authority of the divine message. He would then have used the innocence and purity of the god for the benefit of his own arbitrary and idle humors, and would not have listened to him. Hölderlin is thus compelled to create an equivalent of the ancient song, but one that is renewed by modern-day events so that it might keep alive the fire that glows in the countenance and actions of Dionysus.

Hölderlin is the only modern poet who attempted to conform scrupulously to the Pindaric and Sophoclean modes, not by imitation, which would be a reduction, but *a fundamento*. Since Dionysus was no longer the god of a large community, his re-creation could be achieved only by song, or, to put it more precisely, he would be the fruit of the components of song, that is, a metaphor of song itself. In the quasi-Pindaric hymn "As on a holiday" (1800), the poet's attention was called to "the signs and deeds of the world"—the Revolution and the coalition wars that resulted from it. He is struck by the thunderbolt of Zeus as if, in Hölderlin's language of mythical metaphors, he were himself Semele, the mother of Dionysus. The thunderbolt engenders his poem, which is therefore identical with Dionysus, the synthesis of heavenly fire and maternal earth. In this frame of reference, the god appears both as the sign reverting to the pure elements of father and mother, and as the shelter offered by the earth against the danger of paternal fire. He is the god of encounter, exchange, of the mutual appeasement of two powers that men cannot receive without something to mediate between them; and this mediation comes about through language, which has a dual character: it reveals the burning immediacy of the spirit, but it also reveals the structuring and legislating form produced by word order and the laws of syntax and rhythm.

Dionysus may thus be the model for the union of opposites. But he is also the mediator between the origin and the developments which are indicated throughout the tradition right up to the threshold of a future not yet realized. Wine, the sign of his double birth, is a promise. Friends are seen feasting together—something Hölderlin frequently evokes, as in the *Stuttgart* elegy, which is thoroughly imbued with the spirit of Dionysus; the friends not only recall with rapture the presence of Zeus but also express ardent hope for a return of his presence in a new form. The French Revolution initiates a movement that could renew the times to the point at which community spirit would again be possible, the spirit of brotherhood of an entire people. This future heralded by wine, by Dionysus, is in keeping with the festivities that Dionysus inspired in ancient times. "Bacchus is the spirit of community"; here we have a renewal of what the Greeks knew. Hence the poem, Dionysus, and the wine which is his sign, are all three at the pivot where the past is called upon to transmute itself into the future. All three both recall and announce the mediation that they ensure between spirit and language, heaven and earth, masculine and feminine, ancient and modern, north and south, east and west, ancient community and future community. All told, Hölderlin bestowed on Dionysus the same status as that of his poem. He is a demigod always moving between Hellas and Hesperia, who sweeps his disciples along in his voyage "from land to land in the holy night."

In the elegy "Bread and Wine" (1800), Dionysus appears as someone who attracts creatures that have fallen prey to holy delirium, leading them beyond all bounds. He also appears as the conciliator of night and day, guiding the stars upward, downward, eternally joyful, "like undying verdure . . . because he remains." This god of awakening is the dynamic principle that pushes its devotees beyond all finitude, but it is also the principle of stability that resists the night of forgetfulness through the firmness of its attachment to the fullness of life past or to come.

In this period, Hölderlin charges the poet with the mission of delivering the German spirit from the torpor of its wintery slumber, which makes Dionysus above all the incarnation of the heavenly fire. Later, starting in 1803 when he began to be debilitated by illness, Hölderlin thought that he could see hovering over the world the threat of total collapse, anarchy, a new reign of the Titans; he then saw Dionysus in a very different aspect, as a guide capable of restraining nations intoxicated with death, of keeping them in shape, helping them curb their elemental forces. His fear of imminent universal dissolution inspired a Dionysus of stability and bounds, henceforth brother to two other demigods, Heracles and Christ. Their three labors forge, in heroism, a new permanence in the relation between man and the earth, which becomes habitable again by virtue of the institution of an order and of its law ("Unique," 1803). This Dionysus, guarantor of the people's stability through the grace of the rites and words born of his fire—tragedies, for instance—is finally merged into Christ, the founder of religious orders and communities.

Here is a dual dimension, already hinted at in the hymn "The Rhine" (1801), in which Rousseau is first interpreted in the light of the "divine delirium" of the god without law but later appears as the man in the background, like the recluse who prefers obscurity to profusions of joy, in order to relearn a weak song. This second dimension, the aspect of moderation, aspires to the security of a refuge and goes hand in hand with Hölderlin's belated image of the god who recovers from his perilous birth in the shade of German forests among the flowers, but who at the same time brings to the Northmen the virtues of the children of the sun.

B.B./g.h.

BIBLIOGRAPHY

1. Ancient Mythology in German Literature

F. STRICH, *Die Mythologie in der deutschen Literatur von Klopstock bis Wagner* (Halle a.S. 1910). J. G. ROBERTSON, *The Gods of Greece in German Poetry* (Oxford 1924). A. BECK, *Griechisch-deutsche Begegnung: Das deutsche Griechenerlebnis im Sturm und Drang* (Stuttgart 1947). R. BENZ, *Wandel des Bildes der Antike in Deutschland* (Munich 1948). W. REHM, *Götterstille und Göttertrauer* (Bern 1951); *Griechentum und Goethezeit* (3d ed., Bern 1952). W. F. OTTO, *Die Gestalt und das Sein* (Darmstadt 1955). K. REINHARDT, *Tradition und Geist* (Göttingen 1960). W. SCHADEWALDT, *Hellas und Hesperien* (Zurich and Stuttgart 1960). K. ZIEGLER, "Mythos und Dichtung," in *Reallexikon der deutschen Literaturgeschichte* (2d ed., Berlin 1962), 2:569–84. K. HAMBURGER, *Von Sophokles zu Sartre: Griechische Dramenfiguren antik und modern* (Stuttgart 1962). W. EMRICH, *Protest und Verheissung* (2d ed., Frankfurt am Main and Bonn 1963), 67–94. H. HATFIELD, *Aesthetic Paganism in German Literature: From Winckelmann to the Death of Goethe* (Cambridge, MA, 1964). W. KOHLSCHMIDT, "Die

Antike in der modernen Dichtung," in *Dichter, Tradition und Zeitgeist* (Bern 1965), 112–27. H. J. MÄHL, *Die Idee des goldenen Zeitalters im Werk des Novalis* (Heidelberg 1965). M. FUHRMANN, *Terror und Spiel: Probleme der Mythenrezeption* (Munich 1971).

2. Dionysus in Germany

M. MOMMSEN, "Dionysos in der Dichtung Hölderlins," *Germanisch-Romanische Monatsschrift*, n.s., 13, 4 (1963): 345–79. M. DIERKS, *Studien zu Mythos und Psychologie bei Thomas Mann* (Bern and Munich 1972). J. SCHMIDT, *Heinrich von Kleist: Studien zu seiner poetischen Verfahrensweise* (Tübingen 1974). B. BÖSCHENSTEIN, "Die *Bakchen* des Euripides in der Umgestaltung Hölderlins und Kleists," in *Aspekte der Goethezeit* (Göttingen 1977), 240–54; *Leuchttürme* (Frankfurt am Main 1977), 44–63.

Myth in Twentieth-Century English Literature

The problem of myth, of how we should deal with it and how it might deal with us, has troubled English-language writers in this century, as it has troubled writers everywhere. It is not a problem that will go away; it has at least been given several new twists. It would seem appropriate to begin considering it by looking at Yeats, the writer who appeared, at times, the most willing to allow myth to persuade him.

Yeats turned first to the mythology of Ireland, participating in the Celtic Revival of the end of the last century, which followed from several decades of work on the old Irish legends by scholars and translators and which coincided with a general renewal of interest in myth and folklore. He was twenty-five years old when Frazer's *The Golden Bough* appeared in 1890. Myth represented for him a kind of hygiene of the spirit. It was a means of seeing, utterly opposed to science, to materialism, and to Anglo-Saxon abstraction. The illuminist tradition of the eighteenth and nineteenth centuries relives in his work, offering to the imagination a universe saturated with dream and symbol, and allowing a return to origins, "to the roots of the Trees of Knowledge and of Life." Yeats even entertained the hope at one point that Celtic mythology would spread with the same force as the Germanic mythology of Wagner and others, being convinced that "every new fountain of legends is a new intoxication for the imagination of the world." It is true that, at first, he distorted Irish legends by assimilating them to a fin-de-siècle revery and to the melancholy of an infinite longing, reliving in a way that earlier Celtic revival that had penetrated European romanticism via the writings of Chateaubriand and Goethe, having been launched by Macpherson's so-called translations from Ossian.

Myth was also the possibility of recreating the Irish nation. Yeats desired to nourish the memory of his compatriots with the tales of Cúchulain, Ossian, Deirdre, and also of the fairies, witches, and ghosts of popular belief that he celebrated in *The Celtic Twilight*. He claimed that the Irish had a particular aptitude for myth: that stories of meetings with supernatural creatures were more numerous in Ireland than in the whole of the rest of Europe, that peasant and nobleman alike, to the end of the seventeenth century at least, respected those legends, and that even in his own day country people spoke with the dead "and with some who perhaps have never died as we understand death." The aim was in part political: in its myths, legends, and folklore could be discovered an Ireland utterly free of English contamination, at a moment when the relationship between the two countries was intensely at issue. But the aim above all was to discover place. By speaking "out of a people to a people," Yeats endeavored to reunite the Irish nation to the Irish land. Mythology, he believed, bestows on a race its first unity, "marrying" it "to rock and hill," and so giving birth, one might say, to a meaningful geography and to a geography of meaning. Even Christianity was not to be excluded. Although in "The Wanderings of Oisin" he opposed the druidic Ireland of Ossian to the Catholic Ireland of St. Patrick, he recognized elsewhere that the "places of beauty or legendary association" had also been impregnated for centuries with the Christian faith.

Mythology also provided a place for his own poetry, preserving it from what he saw as a false subjectivity, a fragmentary individualism inherited from the Renaissance. One of the deep aspirations of modern poetry expresses itself in a passage like the following: "I filled my mind with the popular beliefs of Ireland . . . I sought some symbolic language reaching far into the past and associated with familiar names and conspicuous hills that I might not be alone amid the obscure impressions of the senses." Nevertheless, despite this belief in locality, Yeats combined Celtic myths with others in the gradual elaboration of a cosmology that in the end was heterogeneous and personal. A member of the Theosophical Society and an initiate of the Order of the Golden Dawn, he studied Oriental religions, occult systems, magic, astrology, alchemy, the cabala, Neoplatonism, the "correspondences" of Swedenborg and Blake, and out of this eclectic brew produced *A Vision*. This preposterous and unforgettable book, whose concepts and images feed into many of his greatest poems and plays, emerged, according to Yeats, from revelations communicated to him by certain spiritual masters through the automatic writing of his wife. They taught him that everything was governed by the twenty-eight phases of the moon, which could be represented by a geometrical construction of wheels and "gyres." Each period of history had its phase, as did each individual, and as the whole of history passed again and again through all the phases, so each individual followed the same sequence in a series of reincarnations. Hence the existence of an *anima mundi*, a great general memory of the race, a notion that is clearly related to the collective unconscious of Jung.

Rather than delving further into this intriguing "phantasmagoria" (the word is Yeats's own), it is worth noting the attraction of a cyclical, lunar system for other writers of the period—it is to be found, in one form or another, in Joyce's *Finnegans Wake*, Pound's "Pisan Cantos," and Graves's *The White Goddess*—and also the apocalyptic nature of Yeats's version, since he worked out the cycles of history in such a way that the moment of his own life would correspond to a cataclysm. Around 1927 our period of civilization, founded by Christ, was to encounter, in war and terror, its antithesis, the Antichrist, the "rough beast" slouching toward Bethlehem to be born. Yeats's thinking here corresponds to that of his age. From Mallarmé ("the trembling of the veil") to Spengler's *Decline of the West*, Eliot's *The Waste Land*, and D. H. Lawrence's *Apocalypse*, apocalypse became the myth of an

W. B. Yeats. Photo BBC/British Council.

epoch. In the imagination of many, of course, the myth was actually lived through.

So myth also represented a possiblity of order, when "Things fall apart; the center cannot hold." Hence Yeats's preoccupation with the "unity of being" and "unity of culture." Yet to meditate on the unity of culture is arguably to recognize that such unity no longer exists; and to meditate on myth is surely to reduce it to an object of culture, to a series of objects exhibited in the imaginary museum. The irony is that Yeats, who could not endure "an international art, picking stories and symbols where it pleased," exploited mythologies for his poems and other works with the same cosmopolitan and skeptical erudition as Joyce, Eliot, or Pound (or Thomas Mann, for instance, since the phenomenon was not exclusive to writers in English). It is true that Yeats believed that the parallelism between Celtic and, say, Indian mythology was not fortuitous, and that every symbolic system derived from a single original belief. The result is nonetheless a mythology blatantly synthetic. As Eliot wrote, in *After Strange Gods:* "Mr. Yeats was in search of a tradition, a little too consciously perhaps—like all of us."

With Eliot too the exploitation of myth is a late-cultural phenomenon, and our distance from myth is suggested in his work even more decisively. The theme of *The Waste Land* could be seen as the sterile multiplicity of mythologies that we find at our disposal, fragments of an excessive and shattered past that we no longer know what to do with. The notes added to the poem refer to two works of anthropology, Frazer's *The Golden Bough* and Jessie Weston's *From Ritual to Romance. The Golden Bough,* which exerted a profound influence on Eliot's generation, derives religion from sympathetic magic, studying the persistence, in the Middle Ages and even in modern folklore, of ancient fertility rites, whose purpose was to ensure the rebirth of spring after the death of nature in winter, and whose focus was the death and resurrection of a vegetation god such as Adonis, Attis, or Osiris. Eliot's poems may be read in this perspective. At the beginning the vegetation god is buried, and there is talk of his dog, that is to say, Anubis, the jackal-headed god who aids Osiris's restoration, and of the hyacinth that is associated with him. In the fourth part Adonis is submerged in water in accordance with a parallel rite, in the person of a sailor who shares his Phoenician nationality, while at the end the rain falls, and it does so by the Ganges, the source of the most ancient of all vegetation myths. The poem is also a descent into Hades, like that which the golden bough made possible for Aeneas.

Jessie Weston sees in this fertility cult the origin of the Grail story, with even the miraculous cup itself representing a cultic object. She also associates the four symbols of the Grail: cup, lance, sword, stone or dish, with the four suits of the Tarot pack (having, as it happens, consulted Yeats). In *The Waste Land,* accordingly, the quest of the Grail and the laying down of Tarot cards become further spectral paradigms of the narrative. The place of the poem is a land laid waste and infertile partly by the sexual inadequacy of its inhabitants, like the Fisher King's territory in the Grail stories, where the vegetation fails because of his mysterious wound. At the end of the voyage, Eliot's reader finds himself, like the Grail knight, in the Perilous Chapel and the Perilous Cemetery, so as to be initiated into the mysteries of physical life (the rain falls) and spiritual life (the thunder speaks). It is the Tarot which predicts the entrances of a hanged god, of Adonis, and of the Fisher King.

These readings, however, are inexact, because of the dysfunctioning of the various narratives. The Tarot pack, for example, is interpreted by a charlatan who has "a bad cold." The reference to Parsifal's ritual purification occurs in a line quoted from the "Parsifal" of Verlaine, a poem which duly celebrates a man who has "overcome Women" but which is dedicated to a notorious homosexual. The reference is followed in Eliot's poem by another homosexual encounter. This derision of narrative can be partly explained by the fact that the modern victims of sterility, and the "hypocritical reader" who observes them, do not desire the regeneration promised by the myth. But the derision is also internal: narrative itself, as well as its "content," is in question. The narration breaks down. The rain falls, yet the plain remains arid; the quester's voyage is accomplished, yet he seems to lose his reason. The quest is even rendered null in the very first line of the poem, since April, the month which in Chaucer's *Canterbury Tales* encourages people by its sweet showers to go on pilgrimages, has become "the cruellest month."

The derision is clearest in the famous assembling in the text of juxtaposed and contradictory fragments. The quester is the reader himself who, confronted by these impenetrable objects, must ask their meaning. In another mythical perspective, the fragments are also the leaves of the Sibyl, who appears in the epigraph and elsewhere—shards of an oracle blown about by the wind. One might argue that traditional narrative is a kind of Grail quest, since it seeks its accomplishment in its ending. *The Waste Land,* on the contrary, mocks linear and teleological narrative in a text deliberately incoherent, a kind of waste land of writing. And at the deepest point of the poem another myth, of dispersal and confusion, is being recreated: the myth of Babel. Babel is present in the poem through a number of allusions—above all, its tower is "abolished" in the ending, precisely at the moment when the text crumbles into five different languages—and its effect is everywhere. A variety of languages seethes disquietingly throughout the text; the notes employ as many, and not always the same ones; the short epigraph and dedication contrive to use Latin, Greek, English, and Italian; and the translation of the *Upaniṣads* that a note recommends is in German. Even within individual languages, syntax dislocates and words fall apart.

If there is a derision of narrative, in fact, there is also derision of language. Language is one of the themes of the poem (the most *superficial*) so that cultural and psychological alienation are accompanied by a linguistic alienation, a fall of language that reflects the fall of man. In the Babel of the poem everything is dispersed: mythologies, places, historical moments, literary works quoted in fragments. According to this text built from the ruins of other texts, the Great Memory is a plethoric jumble, and historical consciousness a "heap of broken images." The last part of the poem, it is true, seeks a remedy for Babel. The thunder pronounces a restorative syllable, "Da," and the three words of salvation which derive from it are taken from Sanskrit, the oldest Indo-European language and the one which might serve to gather the scattered tongues. Yet the last lines are fixed in a definitive ambiguity, a juxtaposition of the rain of Sanskrit and the aridity of the numerous dialects.

The myth of Babel is at the center of *The Waste Land*, as of the whole of Eliot's work. And isn't Babel, a language myth, the fundamental myth in modern literature? Polyglot writing is one of its signs, in *The Waste Land* but also in the *Cantos* of Pound and, among more recent works, in *Renga*, a quadrilingual poem preoccupied with languages, texts, myths, composed by three Europeans of different nationalities and a Mexican. Above all, writers since Mallarmé ("languages imperfect through being several, there lacks a supreme one") recognize in one way or another the failure of language, and aspire to its renewal. Hence, in so many poets, novelists, and dramatists, a voluntary dilapidation of writing and the elaboration of new idioms.

This effort to recreate language is even more striking in Joyce, whose use of a multivariety of myths seems an attempt at an encyclopedic complexity. *Ulysses*, a rewriting of the *Odyssey*, has its main characters—Stephen-Telemachus, Bloom-Ulysses and Molly-Penelope—travel through a storyworld abounding in other reminiscences of the Homeric tale, while also involving them in numerous further myths of Greek, Jewish, Christian, and other origins. *Finnegans Wake*, a *summa* patient of a plurality of readings, enacts the myth of universal fall and resurrection, centering it on the original fault of the hero, H.C.E., on his dream and his awakening. The book also uses the theory in Vico's *The New Science* of the three phases of history and their eternal recurrence. It relives the dream of the whole of humanity, which at the end begins anew, and more particularly the dream of Finn MacCool, a mythical Irish hero asleep on the banks of the Liffey in Dublin, whose awakening or return is the awakening of all the heroes of the past. One finds in *Finnegans Wake* a use of Irish mythology quite different from that of Yeats, and one sees above all the oneiric nature of the narrative, dream being the natural domain of myth, for Jung as for others.

One also sees that the mythology is accompanied by a topography. Mythographer of the city of Dublin, Joyce makes the Irish capital a kind of *omphalos;* as the author of novels at once intensely realist and densely symbolic, he furnishes universal myths with a quotidian site. This concentration on Dublin distances him again from Yeats, and links him with that wider literary opening of the modern City to the insinuation of myth, other major expressions of which are the Paris of Baudelaire and the London of Eliot.

Joyce was far from considering myth as an initiation to knowledge, or a form of being. According to Eliot, the presence of myth in *Ulysses* is "a way of controlling, of ordering, of giving a shape and a significance to the immense panorama of futility and anarchy which is contemporary history." (This comment dates from the year following the publication of *The Waste Land*.) "It is a method already adumbrated by Mr. Yeats . . . It is, I seriously believe, a step toward making the modern world possible in art." Certainly, *Ulysses* offers itself as a kind of cosmos, where Joyce has endeavored to transpose myth *sub specie temporis nostri* (under the vision of our time), and where he has articulated a single story through several "stories" in parallel series: episodes of the *Odyssey*, organs of the body, Jewish rites, colors, etc. In the same way, the abundant material of *Finnegans Wake* is organized in a highly concentrated cyclic order (which recalls Yeats's *A Vision*, about which Joyce said, moreover: "What a pity he did not put all this into a creative work"). Nevertheless, the order that myth imposes upon a refractory world is far from secure. *Ulysses* even seems as problematic in this respect as *The Waste Land*, and its symbolism of lost keys suggests our distance at once from the novel and from a common mythology that reader, author, and characters might share. Its relations with the *Odyssey* are in any case in part burlesque, and the entanglement of mythic and literary reminiscences—Bloom is a rerun of Ulysses, Moses, the Wandering Jew, Sinbad the Sailor, Rip Van Winkle, and God the Father, among others—is as much a marvelous hotch-potch as an encyclopedic order. As for *Finnegans Wake*, it describes itself explicitly as "Chaosmos" and "Microchasme."

Parody and self-parody would seem to be a sure sign of a troubled relation to myth. A possible resolution, for a modern mind assailed by knowledge, is the comedy which, at the deepest level of the works, maybe absorbs that irony; and another, in terms of the myth itself, is in the heroines of the two novels, Molly Bloom and Anna Livia Plurabelle. These women are also, with due allowance for mirth, goddesses, feminine principles, who absorb everything into themselves. Molly "is" *Gea Tellus* or Cybele, the Earth and the universal mother; Anna Livia, the river, the sea, the maternal waters.

Like Eliot, Joyce also uses myths of language, as of art, and his use is equally ironic. Stephen, the future writer, is associated in *A Portrait of the Artist as a Young Man* with the Egyptian god Thoth, who was accused of theft and impiety for having invented writing. In both *A Portrait* and *Ulysses* he also represents Icarus, son of Daedalus. His father is not only the architect of the labyrinth—the labyrinth of Dublin, of Ireland, of his own past, and perhaps of the book itself, where Stephen wanders in search of a way out—but a forger, and thereby, according to the paronomasia which presides over Joyce's writing, a maker of false coin, a fabricator of texts and of stories. One finds in Joyce, as in Eliot, the same persistent and uneasy mockery of one's craft.

This irony too, however, seems resolved in *Ulysses*, by the fact that all the characters, events, symbols, and so on, are united by metempsychosis in language, "metempsychosis" being a word that actually circulates in the book; while *Finnegans Wake*, which is set "by the waters of babalong" and

Khnopff, *The Silver Headdress*. Pencil sketch. Private collection. Photo Dulière-Skira.

which, to return to another myth, is a kind of apocalypse of language, nevertheless finds its beginning, like Proust's *In Search of Lost Time,* in its end: the last word of the book is a definite article which seems to introduce the sentence-ending that opens the book. The Egyptian serpent bites its own tail, Vico's eternal recurrence is enacted by the story itself, and the whole book becomes a noun.

Other writers have explored various strata of the land's mythology. David Jones in particular, a poet and painter of both English and Welsh extraction, was preoccupied with "the Island of Britain" and with King Arthur, "the central figure of our island myth." Like Yeats, and like the Joyce of *Finnegans Wake,* he explored "the Celtic cycle that lies, a subterranean influence as deep as water troubling, under every tump in this Island, like Merlin complaining under his big rock." Also like them he founded his myths on a topography. The body of the hero in *The Sleeping Lord,* who is in part Arthur, is also the landscape, as are the bodies of Finn, and of the giant Albion in Blake.

In *The White Goddess,* Robert Graves excavated the prehistoric mythologies of Britain, examining the conflicts that existed among them and speculating on the cults that existed at Avebury and Stonehenge, in quest of the White Goddess, who gave to the island, he surmised, its early names of Samothea and Albion. In her capacity of goddess of the moon and the universal mother, he claimed to trace her worship from the Mediterranean to northern Europe, before her displacement by male gods and by the logic of Socrates. To rediscover the White Goddess, with whom Molly Bloom and Anna Livia Plurabelle are not unconnected, would be, for Graves, to recover the possibility of myth and also of poetry. For the goddess is equally the Muse (she was ousted in this role too by the male Apollo), and the center of the most widespread myth to do with literature. In Graves's version, however, she is creative and yet destructive, the goddess of death as of inspiration, demanding from her adept total sacrifice, and what she recalls most in modern times is the "belle dame sans merci" of the romantic agony.

Lawrence too was concerned with pre-Olympian mythologies, in his search for the openness to the cosmos, the veneration of the body of the universe, which he saw as chronologically prior to the cult of gods. It is true that, before Graves, he referred to the White Goddess, "the great cosmic Mother crowned with all the signs of the zodiac," and to "the great dark God, the ithyphallic, of the first dark religions"; and that *The Plumed Serpent* envisaged the return of a pre-Columbian Mexican god. Yet this further attempt to recover a mythic consciousness in a way bypassed the gods, whom, at the deepest level of his conviction, he "refused to name." He studied rather a kind of cosmic sensitivity, among the Etruscans, among the American Indians, and in what he considered the primitive and pagan substratum of the *Apocalypse* of Saint John. Inspired by a cyclic conception of time, he even foresaw a return to the living cosmos, via the apocalyptic crisis through which our civilization was passing, by means of certain ancient rites that mime a descent into the underworld followed by rebirth. It may be that *Lady Chatterley's Lover* enacts the seven phases of a rite of initiation in the domain essential to Lawrence, that of sexuality.

During a period covering about two generations, writers questioned mythology with something like fear and trembling. Their readers are bound to ask, as they asked, whether it is still possible, and vitally useful, for a modern European to place himself in contact with mythic sensibility, and it is not surprising to find among certain contemporary writers an impatient hostility to myth. Myth continues, however, in the work of a writer like Ted Hughes, who turns to mythology and folklore to make contact with "the bigger energy, the elemental power circuit of the Universe," and who also refers to "the great goddess of the primeval world." In *Crow* he creates a mythology, yet without overtly deploying myths drawn from a diversity of times and places: his poem does more or less without history and anthropology. He has declared that he wanted to produce "something autochthonous and complete in itself . . . with the minimal cultural accretions of the museum sort . . . hoarded as preserved harvests from the past." The words could be aimed at many of the texts we have considered, especially *The Waste Land* and *Ulysses.* A whole period of literature seems to be concluded when he demands that his myth should be the springing of "essential things . . . from their seeds in nature . . . after the holocaust and demolition of all libraries."

M.Ed.

BIBLIOGRAPHY

I. Texts

T. S. ELIOT, *Collected Plays* (London 1962); *Collected Poems, 1909–1962* (London 1963). ROBERT GRAVES, *The White Goddess* (London 1961). TED HUGHES, *Crow* (London 1972). DAVID JONES, *In Parenthesis* (London 1937); *The Anathemata* (London 1952); *The Sleeping Lord* (London 1974). JAMES JOYCE, *A Portrait of the Artist as a Young Man* (London 1916); *Ulysses* (Paris 1922); *Finnegans Wake* (London 1939). D. H. LAWRENCE, *The Plumed Serpent* (London 1926); *Mornings in Mexico* (London 1927); *Lady Chatterley's Lover* (London 1928); *Apocalypse* (London 1931); *Etruscan Places* (London 1932). EZRA POUND, *The Cantos of Ezra Pound* (London 1964). W. B. YEATS, *Collected Poems* (London 1950); *Collected Plays* (London 1952); *A Vision* (New York 1956); *Mythologies* (London 1959).

II. Critical Studies

MICHEL BUTOR, *Répertoire* (Paris 1960), chapters on Joyce and Pound. EDMUND WILSON, *Axel's Castle* (New York 1931), chapters on Eliot, Joyce, Yeats. MICHAEL EDWARDS, *Eliot/Language* (Skye 1975). HUGH KENNER, *The Invisible Poet: T. S. Eliot* (New York 1959). F. O. MATTHIESEN, *The Achievement of T. S. Eliot* (New York 1935). D. E. S. MAXWELL, *The Poetry of T. S. Eliot* (London 1952). MICHAEL KIRKHAM, *The Poetry of Robert Graves* (London 1969). JOHN PRESS, *Rule and Energy* (london 1963), chapter on Hughes. KEITH SAGAR, *The Art of Ted Hughes* (Cambridge 1975). BERNARD BERGONZI, *Heroes' Twilight* (London 1965), chapter on Jones. HARRY BLAMIRES, *David Jones* (Manchester 1971). UMBERTO ECO, *L'oeuvre ouverte* (Paris 1965), chapters on Joyce. STUART GILBERT, *James Joyce's Ulysses* (London 1930). CLIVE HART, *Structure and Motif in Finnegans Wake* (Evanston 1962). HARRY LEVIN, *James Joyce* (Paris 1950). JEAN PARIS, *James Joyce par lui-même* (Paris 1957). GRAHAM HOUGH, *The Dark Sun: A Study of D. H. Lawrence* (London 1956). FRANK KERMODE, *Modern Essays* (London 1971), chapter on Lawrence. DONALD DAVIE, *Ezra Pound: Poet as Sculptor* (London 1965). GEORGE DEKKER, *Sailing After Knowledge: The Cantos of Ezra Pound* (London 1963). DENIS DONOGHUE and J. R. MULRYNE, *An Honoured Guest: New Essays on W. B. Yeats* (London 1965). RICHARD ELLMANN, *The Identity of Yeats* (New York 1954). T. R. HENN, *The Lonely Tower: Studies in the Poetry of W. B. Yeats* (London 1950). KATHLEEN RAINE, *Yeats, the Tarot and the Golden Dawn* (Dublin 1972). PETER URE, *Towards a Mythology: Studies in the Poetry of W. B. Yeats* (London (1946).

The Survival of Ancient Myths in Modern Greek Poetic Consciousness

Though modern literature frequently refers to and uses ancient myths, in modern Greece such practices are, understandably, matters of special concern. The Greek spirit, naturally disposed to create myths, continues to use, maintain, and illustrate legends that belong to the national heritage, and it sometimes does so in the simplest aspects of everyday life. Frequent visits to sites where mythological events occurred and habitual contemplation of the heights on which a particular hero performed his exploits help make legends familiar. When a Greek names his child Athena or Dionysus, when a vine grower from Nemea refers to his wines as the "blood of the lion," he does not feel that he is adopting elements of culture. There is no intellectual search, no artifice, no affectation in those choices. Their lives are simply imbued with an idea that is not acquired but passed down from ancestors, with subconscious memories and with a tradition as old as the memory of their country. That is why myth, rather than being an object of metaphor, is the essential element and building block of Greek literary thought.

Prior to the rebirth of the Greek state in the early nineteenth century, popular Greek song, the constant expression of the thought of the Hellenic people, included legendary subjects, although its content was often based on current reality, that is, on the misfortune of the enslaved Greek people. In many different versions, one can discern the recollection of a minor mythological act or references to great legends. In a song portraying the rape of a woman by the Saracens (Isle of Symi version), the sun goes to warn the husband, Yannakis, of his misfortune, thus playing the role of the "guardian of gods and men" who warned Demeter of the abduction of Persephone (in the *Homeric Hymn to Demeter*). The exploits of the heroic frontier guardian Digenis Acritas are sung all over Greece. When Digenis kills a snake or, by the command of his king, stands up to a monstrous and ravaging crab, the song refers to the legend of Saint George and, further back, to an adaptation of the Labors of Heracles or an exploit of Apollo. The theme of the sacrifice of a woman, necessary for the success of a human enterprise, inspired by the legend of Iphigenia, is developed in numerous versions of the Panhellenic song of the "Bridge of Arta." The bridge can be built only if the master mason immures his wife in its foundation. The adventure of the husband returning after a long absence and bent on testing his wife's faithfulness before he is recognized is also widespread throughout Greece, on the islands as well as on the mainland. In versions from the Aegean islands of Zante and Thessaly, the meeting occurs at a fountain where the wife is washing clothes. Here the song alludes to two episodes in the *Odyssey:* Odysseus coming back to Ithaca and Odysseus discovered by Nausicaa on the beach. In a popular song, most likely from mainland Greece but widespread from Corfu to the Pontus, a murderous mother serves her husband the liver of their son, who had discovered the mother's infidelity. This recalls the feasts of Atreus and Tantalus. Yet, true to the very nature of popular songs, the ancient inspiration is never obvious but always implicit.

Modern Greek poetry, which was born with the independent Greek state, reserves a rather large place for ancient myths, elements of a national wealth that the newly freed Greeks had their hearts set on illustrating and developing. The way legends are treated varies both with the individual temperament and situation of each author and as a function of the evolving new Hellenism.

Andreas Kalvos (born 1792 on Zante, died 1867 in London; author of twenty *Odes* that appeared in 1824 and 1826) wrote a work, often compared to that of Pindar, in which he celebrates the high points of the War of Independence by simulating a war of antiquity through the use of ancient terms and forms, and through constant recourse to allusions and comparisons that create an intensely mythological climate. In the *Odes*, he often uses allegory and invokes the Muses, Graces, Friendship, Wealth, Wisdom, Virtue, Victory, and Liberty, "brilliant daughters of Zeus." By personifying them, the poet commemorates the sites of martyrdom: Chios, Psará, Samos, Souli. He evokes mythological traditions: the feasts of the gods (*To the Muses*), the nourishment of immortals whose mouths have the fragrance of ambrosia (*To Parga*), and the dwellings of Olympus (*To Liberty*). Deities and heroes appear: Kypris, whose touch was so sweet (*To Psará*); Icarus, whose wings freed him (*To Samos*); the Maenads and Eros, who made way for Ares on the devastated island (*To Psará*); but also the Erinyes summoned to punish the Turk (*To Chios*). The constant intention of Kalvos was to ennoble the act of war by applying to the modern event the meaning and the symbolic value of the ancient myth and to restore to the newly freed land the poetic beauty that legends had conferred upon it.

Konstantinos Kabaphēs (Cavafy) (born 1863, died 1933 in Alexandria; author of nearly 150 short published pieces, *Poems*) wrote a scholarly work, often difficult, in which ancient history and mythology occupy a major place. Allegory is there too. In *Dionysus and His Crew* (trans. Rae Dalven, *The Complete Poems of Cavafy,* New York: Harcourt Brace Jovanovich, 1976, p. 23), seated next to the god are License, Drunkenness, Song, Feast, as well as Telete, goddess of rituals; Sleep and Death take part in *The Funeral of Sarpedon* (ibid. p. 21). Sometimes the poet's intention is essentially aesthetic, in specific scenes such as the description of the handsome young man, the son of Zeus, killed by Patroclus (see Homer *Iliad* 16.665–83) in *The Funeral of Sarpedon.* From another perspective, starting with the experience of life, of the eternal human problems that arouse his pessimism, the author conceives his poem as a recollection and transposition of a moral premise or a philosophical universal into the world of mythology. In *Ithaca* (ibid. p. 36), the poet invites man, the new Odysseus, to face courageously the assaults of the Laestrygones, the Cyclops, and Poseidon. Sometimes he develops the theme of man abandoned by the gods: in *Infidelity* (ibid. p. 20), Thetis, who has been assured of Apollo's protection for her child, Achilles, learns that it was this god himself who killed her son; the original version of the poem bore in epigraph an excerpt from Plato's *Republic* that refers to this incident as recorded in Aeschylus's *Tragic Iliad.* When the hour has come, Antony loses the protection of the gods, and the poet invites him to resign himself to his fate in *The Gods Forsake Antony* (ibid. p. 30). In *Footsteps* (ibid. p. 15), when the Furies enter Nero's home, the "wretched" Lares hide. The sadness of death is illustrated by the grief of the immortal horses pulling the body of Patroclus in *The Horses of Achilles* (ibid. p. 24: see *Iliad* 17.423–55). The impotence and ignorance of mortals are very briefly and laconically illustrated in *Interruption* (ibid. p. 12), a poem that shows Metanira preventing Demeter from making her child immortal and Peleus terrified by the exploits of Thetis when she is trying to make Achilles invulnerable (cf. Apollonius of Rhodes *Argonautica* 4.865–79 and Apollodorus *On the Gods* 3.13). The notion of opposition can be expressed at another level, namely, that of the relationship between a dying paganism and a rising Christianity, illustrated by the seven poems devoted to the Emperor Julian, but also by isolated works such as *Supplication* (ibid. p. 5) or *Kleitos' Illness* (ibid. 133), in which the meaning and the image of the myths more or less disappear behind the historical antagonism of the two religions. Whether it is a philosophical thought, an invitation to Stoicism, or the mere description of an aesthete, the use of the mythological element in Cavafy's work, sometimes allusive, sometimes explicit, sometimes intimately tied to historical recollection, is never based on an overarching view, but on the analysis of a particular fact or of an exact detail.

The often scholarly aspect of the expression of myth and its occasionally artificial application are characteristics common to Kalvos and Cavafy, perhaps due to the same cause: their lack of contact with Greek soil. When he published his *Odes,* Kalvos had lived mostly abroad (in Italy and England). Cavafy spent his life in Alexandria.

Wholly different is the inspiration of Kōstēs Palamas (born 1859 in Patras, died 1943 in Athens; author of numerous collections of poems, two epics, a drama, etc.), who always lived in Greece and took part in the political and social evolution of the young state. This was a time when events and intellectual movements were causing a global dread of Hellenism and of the traditions of Hellenism, which follow one another without conflict. In the *Hymn to Athena,* a long poem, the author evokes the bond that in his mind ties the ancient world to the modern world. Indeed, Palamas treats myths as did the romantics who influenced him, but he also often expresses the strictly Hellenic attitude that takes possession of the indivisible elements of the whole Greek domain. In the poem *My Fatherlands* from the collection *Life Immovable,* Palamas projects allegorical forms of beauty onto the landscape of Missolonghi, where he grew up, and later onto the site of Attica. He presents a personified Pentelicus and Olympus, and he sings of the sites "where Homer's Phaeacians still live" and of the bliss that the specter of Solomos finds in the Elysian fields. In a single burst and in the same poem, he aims to celebrate the works of Digenis and the exploits of the heroes of the Independence, and then to evoke the maidens with baskets on the Acropolis, carrying Athena's cloak to the temple; thus he gathers together the immortal beauties from the history of Hellenism. He draws another parallel, rather unusual in the eyes of a Western reader but natural to the mind of a Greek artist, which goes beyond apparent distinctions to link notions common to paganism and Christianity, especially Eastern Orthodoxy. In *Sibyl,* after a reference to Virgil's *Aeneid* 6.65, he compares the prophetess to the *Panagia Odigitria* or "Guiding Virgin," a type of Byzantine virgin frequently found in religious iconography.

Assimilations on the same order were to be widely developed by Angelos Sikelianos (born 1884 in Leneade, died 1951 in Athens; author of a massive poetic work, *Lyrical Life* [trans. Edmund Keeley and Philip Sherrard, *Selected Poems,* Princeton: Princeton University Press, 1979], and of tragedies). He was an intellectual, an author exceptionally sensitive to the spirit and meaning of myths, a man for whom the gods had never left Greece. He told the story that, as a young child, during an earthquake he was filled with joy at the thought that the earth was speaking to him. Sikelianos's eagle eye saw through material appearances and was able to reach down to the deep meaning and eternal value of each scene. The spectacle—so common—of a he-goat in the midst of a herd of she-goats grazing by the shore of the Aegean Sea is for the poet the pure and simple materialization of a myth, so obvious that only the title, *Pan,* makes an explicit reference to the legend. He makes *The Greek Funeral Banquet,* inspired by a ceremony to which he was invited, an occasion to evoke the libations and banquets of initiation; with the "blood of Dionysus" he calls forth the souls of the dead and invokes the protection of Dionysus-Hades. Sikelianos's imagination exalts ordinary moments of life, finding a hidden meaning for them that links them to the most ancient traditions. In *Sacred Way* (ibid. p. 99), the showman's she-bear who stands erect on the Sacred Way at Eleusis in front of her cub suffers at the sight of his young nostrils wounded by the iron ring, and becomes the symbol of the weeping mother in the poet's consciousness:

> One of them,
> the larger—clearly she was the mother—
> her head adorned with tassels of blue beads
> crowned by a white amulet, towered up
> suddenly enormous, as if she were
> the primordial image of the Great Goddess,
> the Eternal Mother, sacred in her affliction,
> who, in human form, was called Demeter
> here at Eleusis, where she mourned her daughter,
> and elsewhere, where she mourned her son,
> was called Alcmene or the Holy Virgin. (Ibid. p. 101)

The kinship of faiths and religions and the hidden unity of symbols—marked by a number of titles: *Conscience of My*

Fresco from the facade of the refectory of the Great Laura, Mount Athos. Upper righthand corner: Artemis withdraws at the moment of the Annunciation. Photo Paul Huber, Bern.

Land, Conscience of My Race, Conscience of Faith—such were the convictions that animated Sikelianos when in 1926 he established the Delphic Feasts and attempted to create a center, a spiritual "omphalos," at Delphi, where he also had the tragedies staged in interpretations that allowed room for the neo-Hellenistic tradition.

George Seferis (born 1900 in Smyrna, died 1971 in Athens; author of *Poems* and *Essays*) lived through the painful experience of the catastrophe of Asia Minor. Endowed with a nature easily inclined toward melancholy, he was twenty-two when the Greeks were expelled from Ionia, and he lost his native land forever. Like all the Greeks born at the turn of the century in Turkey, he was to remain deeply marked by this misfortune; a significant part of his work is colored by melancholy, nostalgia, and the sentiment of parting, loss, frustration, shipwreck, and death. In this framework, he uses many mythological themes to illustrate the permanence of their symbolic value and the endurance of the Greek spirit. In *Mythistorema* (trans. Rex Warner, *Poems,* London: Bodley Head, 1960), allusions to myths are numerous, sometimes expressed in subtitles such as *Argonauts* (ibid. p. 13), *Astyanax* (ibid. p. 27), and *Andromeda* (ibid. p. 29), sometimes very discreetly indicated by a single proper name: Odysseus, Adonis, Orestes, the Symplegades. The collection ends with a wish borrowed from Homer's *nekuia* (journey to the dead):

> Those who one day shall live here where we end,
> If ever the dark blood should rise to overflow their memory,
> Let them not forget us, the strengthless souls among the asphodels.
> Let them turn towards Erebus the heads of the victims.
> We who had nothing shall teach them peace. (Ibid. p. 31)

In a long mythological poem from *Log Book 3, Helen* (bearing inscriptions of verses from Euripides' *Helen*), the heroine reveals that only her shadow went to Troy and that the war was a snare:

> Great pain had fallen on Greece.
> So many bodies thrown
> To jaws of the sea, to jaws of the earth:
> . . .
> That so much suffering, so much life
> Fell into the abyss. (Ibid. pp. 115–16)

Through these lines, it is easy to see the memory of another Ionic war, the massacres at Smyrna in September

1922. Numerous references to the tragedies and to Homer could also come from a more purely intellectual attitude. In *The Thrush* (ibid. p. 15), a man—simultaneously Odysseus and Seferis—seized by the dizziness of imagination and dreams, recalls "the lustful Elpenor." In *The Light*, Seferis evokes the fate of Oedipus deprived of the sight of the sun before the Nereids and the Graiae who "come running at the sight of scintillating Anadyomene" Aphrodite. A poem written in the Transvaal in 1942, *Stratis the Sailor among the Agapanthi*, from *Log Book 2*, is in a most significant way thoroughly permeated with mythological memories and traditions: the Agapanthi; "asphodels of the Negroes," who demand silence and prevent the author from speaking to the dead; and the goatskin bottle of the winds, which deflates itself (the author tries in vain to fill it); the memory of the house and of the old dog who waits until the voyager returns to die—all these are so many separate elements that illustrate an idea expressed by Seferis in *In the Manner of G.S.*, included in *An Exercise Book:* "Wherever I travel, Greece keeps wounding me" (ibid. p. 51).

But in modern Greek literature, all the genres use myths. Nikos Kazantzakis (born 1883 in Heraclion, died 1957 in Fribourg-en-Brisgau; author of novels, essays, dramas, and poems) wrote a drama in three parts, *Prometheus*, in which the gods appear on stage; also a tragedy, *Theseus*, or *Kouros*, directly inspired by the legend; and a very long epic of 33,333 lines, *The Odyssey*, which begins at the moment when the hero returns to Ithaca, an epic that can be interpreted as the adventure of modern man.

George Theotokas (born 1905 in Constantinople, died 1966 in Athens; author of essays, novels, and plays) narrated the venture of ambitious young idealists in his novel *Argo*. In his drama *The Bridge of Arta*, he takes up the theme of the popular song. In a brief tragedy, *The Last of the Wars*, he deals with the departure of the captive women after the Trojan War. He also wanted to create a "myth of Alcibiades" in his long play *Alcibiades*.

Pandelis Prevelakis (born 1909 in Rethymnus; author of essays, novels, plays, poems), without borrowing his title from tradition, created in his novel *The Sun of Death* the character of Aunt Roussaki, a deeply Christian Cretan peasant woman who serenely adopts and embellishes legends such as that of Demeter and Persephone, and the exploits of ancient heroes (by a device similar to that of Sikelianos), and whose daily life is illuminated by a familiar, intimate, and intuitive knowledge of the meaning and value of each plant, animal, and heavenly phenomenon. In her world where all is spirit, Roussaki lives out in utter calm both the pagan myth and the orthodox Christian myth. She creates them and maintains them and deserves to be regarded as a feminine image of Hellenism.

In their attempts to become part of world literature, modern Greek authors since World War II have had a slight tendency to withdraw gradually from traditional Greek fields, and thus from the world of mythology, in order to devote themselves instead to the universal problems of twentieth-century man.

R.R./g.h.

BIBLIOGRAPHY

In French

S. BAUD-BOVY, *La chanson populaire grecque du Dodécanèse* (Paris 1936). C. CAVAFY, *Poèmes* (Paris 1958). And on Cavafy: M. YOURCENAR, *Présentation critique de Constantin Cavafy* (Paris 1958, 2d ed.). C. DIMARAS, *Histoire de la littérature néo-hellénique* (Athens 1965). D. HESSELING, *Histoire de la littérature grecque moderne* (Paris 1924). N. KAZANTZAKIS, *L'Odyssée* (Paris 1968); *Théâtre I* (Paris 1974). And on Kazantzakis: C. JANIAUD-LUST, *Nikos Kazantzaki* (Paris 1970). P. PREVELAKIS, *Le soleil de la mort* (Paris 1966). And on Prevelakis: A. CHAMSON, "Prévélakis et la Crète," *Mercure de France* 1148 (April 1959): 579–88. G. SEFERIS, *Poèmes* (Paris 1963); *Trois poèmes secrets* (Paris 1970).

In Greek

G. THEOTOKAS, *Argō* (Athens, 2 vols.); *Theatrika Erga* (Athens 1965–67, 2 vols.). A. KALVOS, *Ōdai* (Athens 1970). K. PALAMAS, *Hapanta* (Athens, 16 vols.). A. POLITH, *Historia tēs Neas Hellēnikēs Logotechnias* (Thessalonika 1972). A. SIKELIANOS, *Lyrikos Bios* (Athens 1946–47, 3 vols.).

IMAGINATION AND MYTHOLOGY IN CONTEMPORARY LITERATURE (TOLKIEN, LOVECRAFT) AND SCIENCE FICTION

Every human being has two umbilical cords: one, made of flesh, is cut at birth; the other, even before conception, weaves a person into language. But not only can this second cord never make up for the cutting of the first, it is itself an ambiguous, or paradoxical, umbilicus: it connects only by keeping apart; it plunges each person into the immense universe of meaning only at the price of an irrevocable break (marked particularly by the proper name), a gulf that forever separates every subject from what would fulfill him. Moreover, the object of fulfillment, of completion, is constituted only within the universe of meaning (although the body is always determinative for its elaboration). And language thus comes between the object that it has itself helped to create and the subject who desires this object.

Fictional narratives are one of the forms of compromise (sexual life is another, and the most basic) which seek to reduce this paradox. They portray a thousand figures of fulfillment, figures which external reality would find it hard to provide; but the narratives offer the possession and full enjoyment of the figures only on condition of raising a symbolic barrier, which they announce: "This is a story, it's not true."

Fictional narratives, like myths and religions, are responsible for producing a link with fulfillment for man: an umbilicus of replacement. There is, however, a wide gap between a discourse, presented as fiction, that aims to produce wonder and a sense of pleasure, and another, presented as true, that regulates the individual's relations with the social body and writes his destiny on a register whose absolute points of reference are established and expressed by myths or religions.

The symbolic barrier in this second type of mythic discourse is marked above all by the fact that nothing can be changed by an individual: the truth is believed to escape the grasp of any particular person. Furthermore, one cannot possess and use the truth as one likes, but only according to the order of particular rituals and institutions, within the limits which the doctrine assigns to human beings. In the fictional narrative, by contrast, everything is permitted, since "it's not true." Someone who renounces telling the truth gains in return the right to make worlds out of the materials that language and symbolic representations provide for him.

Subjection to verisimilitude is not much of a constraint: quite simply, the fictional narrative must not maintain a discourse that is more unlikely than religious discourse. This is the limit within which it must remain (even if it sometimes narrows this limit to align itself with a positive discourse—psychological observation, history, the sciences, etc.—as, for example, in the classical novel). The literature that is called imaginative always stays the closest to its function as a pseudo-umbilicus, and thus to the broadest of its conditions of verisimilitude: it invents myths.

But this type of literature does not, any more than any other, escape the necessity to give some density to the representations evoked by the words of the narrative. To this end, one convenient procedure consists in dipping into the vast storehouse of already existing religious discourses, with the reservation that these discourses must cease to be taken as true, or rather as true for everyone; religions that have come to be considered beliefs, representations labeled folklore or superstitions, myths reduced to the level of fables or fairy tales, all these materials are able to provide grist for imaginative narratives. The narratives do not take up these materials as such: they acclimatize them to their new function; they use the pieces to make something different; they parody them, betray them, disown them (in brief, they use them), and this both to make them function in conformity with the representations in force among the category of readers to which they are addressed and to give the texts the character of a creation, to make the reader share in the pleasure of mastery: the reader must always be able to see that he is dealing with a created work, even when its artificiality is elaborated by the author so as to be "true to life."

Thus, while all narratives can be considered, in one way or another, to be bearers or creators of myths, only some, by the expedient of borrowing or parody, are linked with already existing beliefs, religions, or myths. But even a category limited in this way remains far too vast to cover here. I will therefore touch on only a few points to mark certain of the most representative directions of this use of mythology; with J. R. R. Tolkien first of all (a British author who died in 1973), whose work is addressed both to children (*The Hobbit*) and to adults (*The Lord of the Rings*, a long narrative in an archaic style, reminiscent of a medieval saga). We will then look at H. P. Lovecraft, the American author of horror stories who wrote between the two world wars. I would like, finally, to sketch the position of the gods in the problematic of the narratives of science fiction (or futuristic fiction).

I. *The Hobbit* by J. R. R. Tolkien

With *The Hobbit*, Tolkien joins the tradition of J. M. Barrie, whose hero Peter Pan is still famous; but Tolkien differs notably in that his fantasies are systematically based on beings whose names, at least, come from folklore (although he adds characters of his own invention, such as "hobbits"): dwarfs (with beards and hoods, naturally), giants (ferocious ones), elves, goblins, a sorcerer (old and wise, with a long white beard), a dragon (who, of course, breathes fire), raven messengers, etc.

With a cast like this, a setting made up of vast regions with varied landscapes, the wondrous possibilities provided by spells, enchantments, a ring of invisibility, and an attractive goal (a well-guarded treasure), Tolkien has the makings of a story with innumerable ups and downs—but a story that offers pleasure of what kind? In other words, where in this tale are the figures of fulfillment? According to what modalities do narratives like Tolkien's put their readers into some sort of relationship with fulfillment?

For the beginnings of an answer to this question, I will first note the following: the writing in *The Hobbit* supports the consistency of characters and plot by basing itself essentially upon the recollection of a convention, and the establishment of a connivance, between reader and author. To read *The Hobbit* is to enter into a game in which you enjoy a kind of guarantee: that however horrible certain episodes may be in themselves, they will not impose, they will never absorb the reader completely. For the author is constantly reminding us that he is there, in the wings of the story that he is telling; although his commentaries to the reader can be called humorous, it is precisely in this sense: although they are presented as serious and useful explanations of particular points in the narrative, they really have the effect of placing in the foreground the author's connivance with the reader, indicating that "at bottom, none of this is really true," and that the only ground on which the characters are standing is precisely that of the complicity between the author and the reader.

In this narrative mode, the fact that the names of many characters, along with some of their semiological traits, have been taken from a tradition external to the narrative itself is important and effective. For dwarfs, elves, and goblins constitute a set of representations shared by the author and his readers (since they know that these representations exist outside them). To introduce them by name is to ask the reader more or less explicitly to place himself within the frame of a convention. This procedure is the inverse of the one that consists of introducing a character through the weight of his (pseudo-) reality, i.e., through the multiplicity of semiological traits which engage him in a discourse of verisimilitude. It is as if at the moment of bringing a new character into play, Tolkien announces: "What about an elf—that suggests something to you, doesn't it? Here is my variation on the theme of an elf's traditional descriptive traits. Now here are the modifications entailed in this new element's entry into the current conjecture of the story."

Alongside these shared representations, explicitly introduced as such, the author calls upon others, which act as if there were nothing out of the ordinary about them and so come to portray reality. For example, while Bilbo the Hobbit is a being of pure fantasy (that is, the fruit of an accepted convention), he nevertheless presents the "reality" of a child. Not that he objectively displays the same types of motivations and feelings as children; rather, he evinces the same reactions of pleasure and fear as those which the child reader can suppose are characteristic of his own nature. This, then, is a bridge which connects not the reader to the author but the subject of the enunciation (the reader in the act of consuming the narrative) to the subject of the enunciated (Bilbo, for example). This link is not the register of connivance, but of analogy, identification. It is reinforced by all the indications that surround the daily life of the hero: Bilbo's lodgings, for instance, with all that a comfortable life re-

Elric the Necromancer. Drawing by Philippe Druillet. © Dargaud éditeur, Paris, 1975.

Dead Gods. Drawing by Philippe Druillet. Photo D.R.

quires, like the house of the three bears in the fairy tale, and especially with all the fixings for breakfasts and teas that leave nothing to be desired. The indications of comfort (or, by contrast, of insecurity) used in the narration function as an echo and amplification of the comfort felt by the child in the very act of consuming the narrative (especially when the story is read to him by an adult).

The connection with fulfillment which narratives like *The Hobbit* establish is thus nothing but the deployment, in the imaginary space of the enunciated, of the connection that is the basis of the very possibility of their enunciation. The voice of the storyteller, or the very pages of the book, are the concentrated site of a possibility of comfort; they establish the reader or listener in a position where all reality calls a truce; it lets him suck the milk of a story (a story of hidden treasure, for instance) at the breast of the storyteller. Elves and dwarfs, goblins and dragons—precisely because everyone knows that they have no existence other than their names—help to maintain this truce by reminding us that here (in the enclosed space of the enunciation of the narrative), the linguistic convention is law and has the power to suspend the dangers and privations that a confrontation with reality involves.

II. H. P. Lovecraft

Of all the authors classed in the genre of fantastic fiction or science fiction, Lovecraft is the one who has had the most systematic recourse to a pantheon. A pantheon purely as a parody: Lovecraft speaks of his gods as if they were generally recognized as gods. He carefully respects his own conventions, the same pantheon being common to all of his fiction (here too, as with Tolkien, we find that dimension of play by which the author simultaneously creates a universe and explicitly marks its conventional character, based on language).

At the apex, at the deepest level of the hierarchy, Azathoth, the unbounded, the sultan of demons, dwells in Primal Chaos. Among the mute gods who surround him are Nyarlathotep, the Crawling Chaos; in Outer Chaos, Yog-Sothoth, the Protoplasmic, also from the stars; Cthulhu, emprisoned inside a submerged city. Less horrific than Cthulhu is Dagon, another marine divinity. Minor gods include Umr-Attawil, Tsathoggua, Ghatanothoa, Hastur, and the Shub-Niggurath mentioned in an undiscoverable book of black magic, the *Necronomicon:* for along with these deities there are secret books that perpetuate their worship, as well as worshipers, dark and deviant personalities or degenerate human groups.

Maurice Lévy has called this effort at consistency the "myth of Cthulhu." But any kinship of Lovecraft's work with a myth or a religious system is entirely external. Defined as they are by their names and descriptions, the gods of the Lovecraftian pantheon are not differentiated like those of a genuine religious mythology: they repeat one another in a redundant way; all are representatives of more or less unfathomable regions of Chaos.

Lovecraft's knowledge of mythology may have helped him to enrich the description of his deities: Cthulhu, for instance, has many traits in common with Typhon, who is, like him, akin to the powers of Chaos, to "those who came before" (Hesiod's formula, but it could have been Lovecraft's), those cut off from the orderly world by a gate forever sealed (although for Lovecraft this gate opens often enough).

These imaginary deities are of a type with whom human beings cannot connect themselves by any symbolic and institutional mediation. Contact with them is a transgression, a short-circuit, an encounter which "normally" should not take place (Lovecraft's narrative is always the story of an exception). They are sacred pollution, the omnipotence of a glutinous and eternal matter; in brief, Lovecraft evokes a sense of the religious that overflows any symbolic inscription, and tongue-ties the universe of signs. Phrases such as "daemon activity," "shocking rituals," "outlaw sect," and "devilish exchange" are frequent and are used to amplify the word "blasphemous" (one of the author's favorite adjectives). In their constant repetition, these stereotyped phrases themselves become elements in a litany of incantation that reactivates a holy terror for each story, the evocation of powers which, like the pagan deities attacked by Christianity, come from the register of the diabolical.

Lovecraft's mythological base thus presents a very different sense from that of an author like Tolkien. The representations that Lovecraft gathers around his nonhuman entities are supported more by a paradoxical use of language than by the simple conventions of play: here language seeks to point out its own insufficiency in the face of the ineffable, the unnameable. Lovecraft portrays (by means of language, of course) various figures of the power that overflows and silences all language and all convention. Far from extending and illustrating the cozy fulfillment created by the reader's position in the enunciation (the reader, reading, lives only events of language), the sites of fulfillment in Lovecraft are those where, eluding the grasp of language, the real bursts forth.

For those who reach them, these forbidden places offer a restoration of the umbilicus of flesh; but this time it is an umbilicus whose circulation, to be restored, must be reversed: no longer nourishing and constructive, it is now a destructive suction, going toward the mother, toward the hero's absorption into flesh and into a lineage of the dead (from which he has only temporarily emerged). The power of Lovecraft's gods thus lies not in their science, laws, or wisdom (since for this they would have to recognize their subjection to some symbolic instance): it lies in their monstrous flesh, their power of contagion, a result of their crushing disproportion to any human order.

If Lovecraft abundantly, repetitiously, portrays sites of fulfillment, the subject of those that he has enunciated, the narrator, is plunged into these sites, to benefit from the experience. In these tales the author never marks himself as the subject of the enunciated: the reader must be alone in his confrontation with the site of fulfillment, for the goal of the narrative is to produce dread, not comfort. Here, language wants to restore conditions in which it would not have existed, but does so, and can do so, only from the moment that it exists. The enterprise is thus simultaneously serious (fascinating, extreme) and not serious, since it plays tricks and knows that it is playing them. Although in the enunciated no barrier now separates the hero from the divine (which, *by this fact,* is transformed into the diabolic), the reader is nevertheless in contact with the abyss of fulfillment only through the mediation and the screen of the narrative.

III. On Mythologies in Science Fiction

In science fiction, fulfillment is signified primarily in the form of the mastery of the immeasurable, the domination and spanning of enormous distances of space and time. Scientific discourse comes in, on the one hand, to connect reality (as well as it can) with the elaborations which otherwise would remain simply phantasmic. On the other hand, the presence of scientific discourse also serves to affirm the power of symbolic activity over what tends to go beyond it.

The introduction of fragments of discourse that parody the discourse of the exact sciences is thus never a sufficient reason to discount the presence of the divine. One need only peruse the titles of works of science fiction to be convinced of this: the struggle for omnipotence, faced with the obstacles of immensity and death, calls for the use of the vocabulary of religion and the cosmic.

The theme of a disproportion to be surmounted is everywhere present in science fiction, sometimes depicted in a problematic close to that of Lovecraft: the awesome omnipotence of the aliens, masters of vast distances in space and time, a diabolical invasion by creatures of flesh dominated by eyes or tentacles, threatening the measured universe of men. But, more specifically, the gods in science fiction are large-scale human beings, freed from the limits of death, possessing science and power on a universal scale; and yet never quite certain of having the last word in the struggles and rivalries that oppose them to other gods. Men become gods (in the work of Roger Zelazny, for example), or gods with a human face (in the work of A. E. Van Vogt), must keep up a constant outbidding for symbolic mastery: they must constantly be foiling plots, inventing machines that outclass those of the enemy, defeating the totalitarian rationality of a power (religious, political, technological) that bears all the earmarks of a fulfillment against which the hero must measure himself. Thus the figures of fulfillment presented to the reader are based on the disproportion between the reader himself and the material universe of which he is part, and *inseparably,* on discourses that, in their totalizing vocation, offer simultaneously the means of portraying this disproportion and the means of measuring up to it.

F.Fl./j.l.

BIBLIOGRAPHY

J. R. R. TOLKIEN, *The Hobbit* (Boston and New York 1938); *The Lord of the Rings,* 3 vols. (Boston 1954–56). H. P. LOVECRAFT, *Dagon; The Shadow out of Time; The Outsider; The Color out of Space; Beyond the Wall of Sleep.*

Science Fiction

Gods and god-men are frequently employed by authors such as O. STAPLEDON (the first one to tackle this theme), P. J. FARMER, M. MOORCOCK, A. E. VAN VOGT, D. F. GALOUYE, and R. ZELAZNY.

Among the numerous works on science fiction, I suggest *63 auteurs, bibliographie de science-fiction,* by A. VILLEMUR (Paris 1976); and the work of D. WOLHEIM, *Les faiseurs d'univers* (Paris 1974), who stresses more than others the theme of gods in science fiction.

General

The most general work on fantasy literature is no doubt that of P. VERSINS, *Encyclopédie de l'Utopie, des voyages extraordinaires et de la science-fiction* (Lausanne 1972).

On ghost stories, see the book by M. LEVY, *Le roman "gothique" anglais, 1764–1824* (Toulouse 1972). On fantasy literature in general see *Introduction à la littérature fantastique,* by T. TODOROV (Paris 1970).

Myth and Political Theory: Nationalisms and Socialisms

Although the nineteenth century is the century of the rebirth of myth and of mythology, this is a renaissance only of the myths of pagan antiquity and the mythologies revealed by the curiosity of travelers and the discoveries of scholars. Poets and artists use these mythologies to construct their own symbolic universe and to restore meaning to a world from which the gods seem to have retired. But many do not stop at a purely individual perspective, and attempt to build collective myths. Since the beginning of the nineteenth century, the poet, and more generally the intellectual, has felt that he was invested with a mission that is situated at the crossroads of two traditions: the tradition of the *philosophes* of the eighteenth century, who assert that they are fighting for enlightenment and progress, and the tradition of unknown prophets, those obscure interpreters of history who read the characters of the divine tongue in the symbols of the world and comment on its revelation (Hamann, Saint-Martin, Court de Gébelin, Fabre d'Olivet). The intellectual picks up where the disqualified clergy left off and claims a capacity to create myths and religions. When waiting for the gods—old or new—ends in disappointment, an ersatz mythology appears: the myth of religion as art and revelation as art. Thus, for the first time, the great literary and artistic works of the tradition are regarded as myths: Faust, Don Juan, and Don Quixote become the bearers of a universal and sacred meaning of which their creators were unaware. This religion of art may take all forms, from the artistic socialism of William Morris to the lofty and hopeless religion of Mallarmé. But more often the writer seeks to take on a social responsibility and perceives himself as being invested with authority; this involves intervening in social struggles, bringing the judgment of history to bear on events, and pointing out the just course of action. The intellectual has just discovered a new territory over which he seeks to become an expert, namely, political territory: "Political Science, which is the Science of Sciences," writes Blake. The new gods will be the gods of political struggle.

It is on the political terrain that truly collective myths arise; not the personal myths of poets and writers, but the myths of social prophets, which are born of a cross between the ambitions of the intellectuals and the new social entities that appeared at the beginning of the nineteenth century. These entities include on the one hand the nation, in the modern sense of the term, of which all the inhabitants are at least by right equal citizens, and on the other hand, the social classes, the distant legacy of the Estates of the ancien régime. The situation of both protagonists is quite comparable. Just as the classes struggle for power within the nation, so the nations fight for the conquest of the universal empire. The two entities are thus inseparable, by virtue of their birth and their meaning. History explains the development of nations by the struggle and the oppression of peoples (A. Thierry), just as Karl Marx explains it by the struggle and the oppression of classes. But the two new actors are the ones in whose hands the fate of all is played out: these new fighters need new conceptions of the world. Moreover, the very appearance of these actors and their awareness of their roles are symbolic facts, the result of a mythological construction as well as of the material evolution of societies. Heroes of new struggles, the people and the social class need narrative paradigms to define their function and remind everyone of their significance. Naturally they need myths. An enormous effervescence of ideas is thus produced, the creators of which are the intellectuals, but also the marginal intellectuals, the semiliterate and the self-taught, as well as established writers and ideologues. We are dealing with something like a "primitive soup" of modern ideologies, comparable to the flowering of philosophical and religious sects at the beginning of the Christian era, out of which a selection of ideas unfolded, similar to the natural selection of species: the fittest survived in the end.

Out of the period of ideological creation that spans the years between 1800 and 1850, two great mythical complexes emerged, the complex of the people and nationalism and the complex of the class and socialism, with a largely identical structure. To begin with, myth includes actors: on one side, the people (as described by Michelet or Hugo), and, on the other, the social class—whether the captains of industry of Saint-Simon or the proletariat of Marx. This mythical actor, who is not individual but collective, becomes incarnate in a series of mythical heroes: the Grand Ferré, Joan of Arc, or Gavroche as seen by Michelet and Hugo, or Spartacus and Thomas Münzer regarded as the martyrs of the oppressed classes. What matters is that the actors are aware of their lives and their roles: on the one hand, *Volksgeist*, the spirit of the people, in which the profound vocation of a culture is crystallized (Herder, Humboldt, Hegel); on the other hand, class consciousness, as a result of which the proletariat can see itself as the bearer of an exemplary fate. The fact is that the actors, people and class alike, have a mission to accomplish, which they carry within themselves and which historical development must let them bring to fruition. This realization is revealed in an ambiguous and contradictory form. It is the result of a struggle (the people's war, the class struggle) and at the same time aims for a universal reconciliation. Each country believes that it is invested with a providential mission, just as each class believes that it is destined to triumph over the others in the end; but in the universal fatherland, individual countries will find a "melting pot," just as the classes will all disappear in the classless society. It is thus a matter of bringing about peace, but peace can be achieved only at gunpoint. The transition to the final state must take place in a sudden mutation, conquest, or revolution by which all values are transmuted. Thus a new form of government is set up, an unprecedented era that inaugurates the end of history, the end of separate nations and classes. The linear time of human history is broken; the rupture puts an end to it and at the same time goes beyond it without recourse to transcendence.

In order to recognize the movement of history and hasten its development, a man of knowledge and action is needed, a prophet-theoretician, heralding the change to come. The moment he appears, he founds a school around him, with disciples and institutions that guarantee the spread of the doctrine (Saint-Simonists, Fourierists, positivists, Marxists). The party is only the organized and conscious form of this militia of disciples.

This myth rests on a scientific component (largely pseudoscientific at that) whereby the prophet-theoretician is a man of science, a historian, a geographer, a sociologist, an anthropologist, an economist, or a politician, and his theoretical construction is seen as scientific, science being the only orthodox model of knowledge. To the scientific component a technical component is added, the one already inscribed in the myth of Faust: science can make us the absolute owners and masters of nature. This technique of domination must also be exercised on society and history: the myth of the real Utopia, according to which a complete and coherent organization of the social world is possible. There is, however, a difference between the two mythical complexes. Originally the socialist complex favored the technical and scientific models, and the nationalist complex favored organic models; but in both cases, the concern for organization and coherent domination is the same. Gradually the two types of models tend to combine, as can be seen in today's nationalisms and socialisms. In the same way, the two complexes and the two great mythical actors tend to overlap thanks to notions such as imperialism (Lenin) and proletarian nations (Mussolini): the relations between nations are the exact equivalents of the relations between classes.

Thus a new kind of myth arose, which came to take its

place next to the traditional myths in the repertory of the historian of religions and which led to a new conception of mythology. For the correct understanding of myth had been blocked by two obstacles: the refusal to consider revealed religions as myths and the affirmation of modern rationality, which would empty heaven of its gods. In fact, there are three kinds of myths. First there is the traditional myth of polytheistic religions, sacred history that took place in a primordial time and space and that ritualistically guarantees the creation and preservation of man and the world. Next there is a myth characteristic of religions of salvation with a universalist vocation. This is a historical myth, anchored in the history of men by the presence of a prophet or a founder who has perforated human time with transcendence; the relationships between time and myth are thus transformed. The historical time of the founder partakes of the sacred time that he exemplifies, but it simultaneously introduces into sacred time the linear dimension of a time divided up between before and after, between creation, annunciation, and salvation. Finally there is the myth of modern ideologies, not what is incorrectly called modern myths, but mythic history in which it is no longer gods but ideas that guide the movement of the real and guarantee the second coming. Here again the essential dimension is the organization of human, individual, and collective time; this is why it is better to speak of ideological myth than ideology—which is a confusing and misleading notion—when one wishes to designate the third form of myth. In any case, myth is defined as a specific organization of time.

At the end of each mythical cycle, some people have believed that all mythical thought had to be effaced before the splendor of what is true: each time the myth has begun anew, but in a guise in which no one could recognize it any more. If we are at the end of the age of ideological myth—and nothing could be less certain—then surely somewhere, unbeknownst to anyone, the myth of tomorrow is already crystallizing.

J.M./g.h

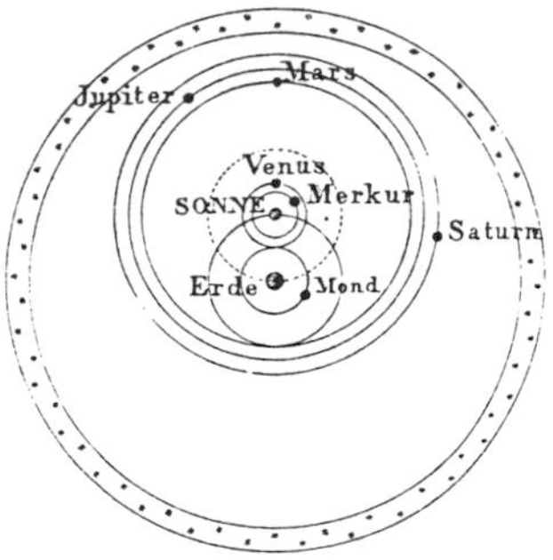

Epilogue: The Contemporary Need for Myths—a Testimonial

On a woodcut from Dürer's studio, the cosmos is represented by three circular spaces: in the center is the earth that is our place and its sky studded with stars; on the edge is the luminous space in which God reigns alone; and separating them both, a circle of dark fire. Between the divine kingdom and the human world there is no passage. Such was undoubtedly the initial state of creation. The tragic abandonment of the human species is balanced by the solitude of the deity. But it was man's task to bore a hole through the circle of dark fire. It is a long adventure, the last phase of which the Gnostic Clement of Alexandria has clearly depicted for us: "The knowledge of what we are and of what we have become, of the place from which we came and the place into which we have fallen, of the objective toward which we hasten and of what we are redeemed from, of the nature of our birth and our rebirth." On this path of knowledge, men separated from the divine have undertaken first to make the divine descend among them.

Thus the gods were born from the tears of mankind; men invented myths to console themselves, for the gods were all silence and opacity. They had no regard for the strangeness of our condition, and any compassion for our sufferings was alien to them. All creatures therefore had to force them to exist fully and to manifest themselves; a single path presented itself to the human imagination: to forge a history for them so that they might be engulfed in time and space like living creatures and, like us, be both actors and spectators in the savage theater of life and death. This foundation of mythic adventures was not achieved haphazardly. Well before the first rigors of reason defined our earthly existence as a line staked out by our birth and our demise, men had a premonition of those disastrous abysses which are the upstream and downstream flow of our belonging to the earth. Since these forever impenetrable areas of nothingness nurture anxiety and madness, there remains only one way out, which is to restore time's circular deployment, to enclose fate within a sequence of events either lived or dreamed, closely intertwined and eternally tied together by the miracle of metamorphoses. That is, furthermore, what plant life shows us: from the tiny fruit rotting in the mud is born the luxuriant bough, whose seed will return into the depths of the earth when the season comes.

This mythical imagination appears as a revolt against the basic perversity of matter, against creation's profound indifference toward us. It is a way to force nature to recognize our necessity, for the only justification for our long and painful history is that we are not in any sense a useless suffering nor the last link of an itinerary destined for destruction; we mortals are what makes nature immortal. If matter is perverse, if nature is indifferent, and as indifferent to itself as it is to our human destiny, it is because they are unaware of the heart that underlies them and gives them life. In their blindness, they are unaware of what makes them act within the vast unfurling of time.

I. The Hidden Creation

It is incumbent upon human inventiveness to reveal the heart that hides what mythic dreaming calls the Word, the Logos, the breath of life. This revelation is the object of myths. Through them, men reveal to creation what, in its depths, makes it live. The projection of the human spirit toward nature is not a game: it is born of the certainty, inherent in our condition, that the Word hidden within matter is also the word hidden within our being. And all revelation concerning the secret energy of nature is a revelation concerning our own essence.

Thus, far from being an explanation of the organization and the movement of the universe, mythology appears as a voyage toward knowledge, as an ever fresh approach to a knowledge of which the ephemeral character of our existence will allow us to discover only fragments. Far from shedding light on this mystery, myths are, on the contrary, designed to deepen it. An image common to all mythical representations introduces us to this nocturnal expedition: the image of the cave.

The first habitat of the human being, who alone in the entire realm of the living finds himself at birth bereft of everything and constrained to seek help from his environment, the cave is also the image of the maternal dwelling from which we are torn to be thrown into the harsh light of day. But the cave is a place of mixed associations in which all the opposing figures of our condition coexist: the white of the sky and the black of the earth, the dryness of the rock wall and the wetness of the spring. It is open like a shelter, yet closed like a tomb. The cave is the very image of our endurance; it is the fortress within which both life and death are enclosed. It is in a cave that Aphrodite reveals to human beings the mystery of love, but it is also in a cave that the Buddha meditates for millennia to give rise to as yet unimagined worlds.

We are inside the cave, as Plato says. All we can know of the world is that there is fire below us and above us, that there is also air outside, water inside, and the earth. But existence in the cave is tolerable only if we see it as the center of the universe; thus the blind, unknowable forces that whirl about far from the cave are directed around it, and for us. Such is the meaning of mythologies: to give the house of men its true dimension, to make our dwelling the Temple. In this way, depending on its time and place, every tribe invents what is necessary for its own coherence. Every element of creation is a sound or a word, and out of the totality of elements a language must be made which is audible to everyone, for if words go off on their own wandering paths, creation has no aim and slips toward absurdity and suicide.

These mythological dramas cannot be enclosed in the strictures of rational analysis. All attempts of contemporary scholarship to account for the enormous load of mythical materials carried along by the human past may lock up heroic adventures in the frozen compartments of learning. The vast inventories are like greenhouses in which wild plants have been imprisoned: their lively shoots break through the glass and proliferate skyward far from the guardians' watchful eyes, or their roots sink cunningly into the darkness of the virgin soil. It is better to regard myths as theater that is meant to carry a different message at each performance. The text of the play can remain the same, but each performance constitutes a different event because the acting conditions, the actors, the spectators, and also the immediate story of which they are the witnesses have changed.

II. The Masks of Mystery

If we look at these cosmogonies as integral parts of life as it was experienced in its intensity or endured in its daily round by the peoples of long ago, if we restore their movement and the passionate charge that was once theirs in the city, we can see that they were felt to be "revelations of being," that they allowed each participant in the community to become an active witness of those energies which by their confrontations and connections determined the metamorphoses of creation. The image at the center of archaic ritual celebrations is an image whose emotional force we can still entirely grasp, because, whether provoked or refuted, it remains at the core of our existence. It is the image of sacrifice. The sacrificial theme is directly involved in the most innocent contemplation of natural life, in which mortal and nascent forms, destruction and change, putrefaction and desiccation are endlessly exchanged. At the community level, any form of sacrifice is an alliance with the moving landscapes of nature, a humble participation in the vast holocaust which is the very condition of the survival of creation. In primitive communities, human blood is an object of exchange with the gods, just as gold is an object of exchange among the powerful in mercantile societies. Any blood that is shed is a tribute paid to the fertility of the earth; it is the promise of things to come. The values attached to particular kinds of blood, female blood, animal blood, the blood of certain special plants, are inscribed within this general concern with a pact between men and the powers of the Elsewhere. The gods must also take this pact very seriously since, if they fail to keep their word, men can exclude them from their kingdoms and make dead gods of them, never again to be celebrated in ritual.

Mythical representation has abandoned the wide stage of the tribe to be devoted entirely to each being in all his intimacy. The gods are no longer shared by a multitude. They have become the exclusive property of anyone who invents them. What once functioned on the collective level is now achieved on the personal level. Although today the only nameable progress is one that frees the individual from the constraints of the social body and hands him over totally to his true identity, imagination allows each person to explore the depth of his hidden source and to nurture his own mythology. But since we are not born of nothing, since we are but one parcel of the immense experience accumulated in time and space by our fellow creatures, the mythological corpus is revealed to be a treasure cave in which we mine riches meant especially for us.

For the divine adventures reported by myths are not the errant or aberrant fruits of a primordial imagination led astray by enthusiasm or the anxiety of solitude. On the contrary, they mirror the adventures experienced by men in a universe laden with meaning, a universe in which human destinies take their positions on a more general stage on which all the figures of creation, those of the plant, mineral, and animal kingdoms alike, play their roles. The stories present the dialogue between living beings and the basic mystery of life that no rational knowledge could ever hope to bring to light and of which the fundamental incarnations are birth, dreams, love, and death.

This dialogue, however, since the earliest days of our species, has been able to change its outer face as the material field of our history has undergone its own changes. The dialogue has not changed its nature. It has no object other than to open our eyes to the back country that is beyond words, beyond explicit communication, but where true fusion is achieved between the beings that we are in our turbulent individuality and the being of the world.

Images of fire provide the classic illustration. All mythologies give them a key place in their accounts of the origin. Two characteristics are common to all these mythical narratives. On the one hand, the stories dramatize an artisan's imagination, which is the very condition of the survival of the species. On the other hand, they put flesh on the heroic energies that made the mystery of fire familiar and gave it its place in the community. The artisan's imagination, for which men have often sought a model in animal society or in the secret lives of plants and stones, functions the same way in modern times as it did in antiquity. Only the instruments with which we invest reality have changed. Instead of having a direct relationship with fire, we usually experience it in the secondary form transmitted to us abstractly by machines.

The figures that serve as masks for the mystery have lost, perhaps provisionally, the carnal resonance that people bestowed on them in earlier times and have instead donned conceptual garments. But the garments of modern rationality do not delve into the depth of the enigma, and the loss of divine flesh makes us experience it as an impoverishment, conducive to solitude.

Rubens, *The Festival of the Gods*. Prague, Narodni Galeri. Photo Prokop Paul.

The permanence of our intimate tie with fire has been underscored by Gaston Bachelard in the single evocation of the flame of a candle. Before a candle or the brightly burning log in the fireplace, the daydreams of a child of today are just like those of the Neolithic, just like those of Mary Magdalene, whom Georges de la Tour painted in the humble smock of a peasant girl of seventeenth-century Lorraine. The universe experienced and the universe represented are confused in the uncertain territory of our inalienable intimacy. In the depths of our being, inaccessible to social constraint, sheltered from the curse that reduces us to being merely another person among others, the amalgam of forces unfolds, and the confrontation or the connection of these forces writes the history of life. We must turn for a moment to the imagery of Paracelsus when he describes each human creature as a microcosm that reflects the totality of the macrocosm, that is, all that the cosmos bears within itself as a creative spark, as a passion to exist, as anguish, as contradiction, as uncertainty.

To return to the realm of fire, this macrocosm, whose imagination has no bounds, figures in all the accounts that have nurtured the dreams of human tribes since the beginning. Its memory retains others, those that history has buried under its ruins, those that the eyes that we have now do not yet know how to excavate, and beyond memory are all the narratives yet to come. Although we are microcosms, we have the potential to recreate the totality of these accounts in ourselves, but our nature is fragmented and immature. As Michelet pointed out, we are far from being complete; we are, as the Greeks said, "not sufficiently cooked." We can therefore explore only a very small part of the timber yards of the imagination during our personal itineraries.

But however partial our course, our elementary connection with the flame of a log fire introduces us to the sum total of the values in which daily existence is invested. Through fire, time is manifested. The evening fireplace stands against the heat of the sun; the winter hearth protects against the harshness of the cold. Beyond this temporal relationship, fire defines our dietary mode, that is, our feelings about our own bodies. Within the secret of the unconscious, the presence of Eros is also experienced as a secret permanence of fire, while Thanatos is perceived as the absence of all igneous elements.

In archaic societies where cosmogony is directly implicated in the essential moments in the life of the tribe, the various representations of fire govern a certain number of daily rituals and practices and roughly define the boundaries that separate the forbidden from the permitted. These rituals and practices make ancient societies into communities invested with the sacred. Into this fabric of the sacred is woven a series of ties between man and the universe. It is through these ties that men are protected from anguish and solitude. When the boundaries of the sacred collapse, when the ties that bind creatures to the sky and the earth are annihilated, men are reduced to their own company, and the foundations of the community are based merely on ethics. The primordial image of life, the only one that can be the point of convergence of all ancient mythologies, is replaced by images of good and evil, underground figures that leave a living creature helpless before the opacity of his development.

By nature, ethics reduce the mental field of individuals to the measure of city life or throw individuals into what Ronald Laing calls "ontological insecurity," an insecurity that arises as soon as the being feels or anticipates that a part of him is moving far from the play of social requirements. Anyone who wishes to recuperate his being in its fullness must found his own sacredness, create his own myths and rituals. He must experience a new birth, he must be reborn to himself and the world, as the hermetic philosophers whisper. But this new spiritual birth is precisely comparable to a carnal birth. It is inscribed within a long heredity, whose different elements constitute traditional knowledge. Of this knowledge, myths are the underpinnings.

III. The Seeds of the Sun

There is opaque matter. Beyond Darkness is the Word. Between matter and the Word that is enclosed in it are the gods, and the gods live in our flesh. They are our flesh. "We dream of voyages through the universe," Novalis tells us. "Is not the universe within us then? The depths of our spirit are unknown to us. The mysterious road leads within. It is within us, if anywhere, that we find eternity with its worlds, the past and the future." In this way, all human experience is a metaphysical experience. It engages the totality of the human being within the historical totality of the world; it is the confrontation between an ephemeral and unique destiny and the multiple eternity that is the obligatory scene of our earthly existence. And in this way, the experience of each of us is similar to the experience of the great mythical figures whose trials prefigured our own trials, whose glory prefigured our own glory. Oedipus the orphan, Oedipus the lame, Oedipus the assassin and the incestuous—these various forms of the same living creature herald our own difficulties with our birth, our feet, our desires for love and for murder. Jason's quest for the fleece is also ours, in the face of the need for possession and power, in the face of the evil or benevolent forces of the feminine, in the face of the difficulties of brotherhood, conjugal love, and fatherhood.

These distant images are not alien to us because we are in the same situation as the men of antiquity, in whose midst the first cosmogonies were elaborated. We need a world which speaks to us, and the only road that ends where the world can begin to speak to us is that of poetry.

Poetry of this kind is Gnostic; in the extreme, it is gnosis itself, the ultimate heart of the knowledge that is the shape of our destiny. Gnosis is not a slow and difficult discovery of the reality of beings and elements; it is the creation of reality. It is the breath of life that founds and unveils in a single movement the various geologies of the real. Geology moves like life itself: the gods curled up in front of the central hearth of things are born, grow, die, and change, but the immediate appearance of reality is never transformed. The twilight forests and hillsides that the Celts peopled with deities associated with the sun that kept them warm, the water that made them fruitful, the winds that disturbed them, and the turf that sustained them, address us with an urgency as clear as the urgency with which they addressed the first tillers of the soil. It is wrong to say that these deities are dead because they have been covered over by three millennia of history. They are dead only as winter leaves are dead, torn from the immutable tree, mixed with mud, decaying in the humus the better to nourish the roots and to be reborn in the mad joy of spring on branches through which new blood flows. All that separates our excursion from that of the Celts of the past is that the very nature of their community led them all to look with the same gaze on the face of these deities. Our gaze is more solitary, and this solitude is largely intolerable. Men have not yet learned to know gods other than those of the city, to recognize temples other than those in which the faithful confuse their own piety with that of their fellow men. Our long series of trials is the story of this slow conquest of our differences, and the inability of so many people to recognize their inner sovereignty impels them to embark blindly on the vast ships of fools that contemporary society builds with the same blind perseverance with which it builds the monstrous factories of human labor.

But little by little, in anguish and in contradiction, the image of this imaginative genius within each creature, depicted for millennia by the Oriental tradition, is affirmed within each creature. Brahma can be seen founding his own being and the being of the world, not by a deliberate act of the will but by a meditative fathoming of his very flesh, whose hidden richness he will slowly penetrate in the course of millennia, a richness that is inexhaustible because it is multiplied in a series of unpredictable childbirths. In the progress that each being, magnified in his solitude, makes toward the exploration of his own labyrinth, in the fascination that leads each to his own Minotaur or Ariadne, the great mythical imageries are familiar landscapes. They help us not to lose our way; thanks to them, as Victor Hugo suggests, "the extent of the possible is, in a way, in front of our eyes. The dream you have within yourself can be found outside yourself . . . You hold your head in your hands, you try to see and understand; you are the window looking out on the unknown . . . The man who does not meditate lives in blindness; the man who meditates lives in obscurity. We only have the choice of darkness."

This diving into our own shadows, far from pushing us into darkness, vividly illuminates the banality of our worry-bound existences. First of all, it forces us to make our lives a drama that retraces, according to our limits and needs, the great tragedies that myths are able to stage. The passionate attachment that ties Merlin and Vivian together in the dense forest of Brittany is the medieval stage of the misfortunes that temporarily separated Eurydice from Orpheus, and the loves to which we are condemned are themselves the stage of the enchantments of which Vivian and her companion were victims. Like actors, facing the turmoil and disasters of their time, we take on a role that humanity has never stopped interpreting since its beginnings. But the text of the role, this unwritten word more imperative than any writing, is merely a prop, comparable to the mask and the set in a theatrical performance. It is the warmth of a memory that helps to warm up the present. But the essence of the play is found within ourselves, and the particular virtue of theatrical performance lies in the fact that within the daily accomplishment of individual passion, the individual bursts out beyond his limits and transforms into eternity the irremediably instantaneous element that he bears within himself.

What is theatrical in this mythical crossing within ourselves, and within all those who, before us, invented the hidden history or manifesto of the species, is the inherent capacity for doubling or splitting into two. On the one hand, we are a body enclosed in its sufferings and its desires, and we will forever collide with the suffering and the desires. On the other hand, we are a sign of the general breath of the universe. We carry within us the dreams and accomplishments of those who have begotten us; and we are heavy, like a pregnant woman, with the dreams and works of those whom we shall beget. Myths show us the path of this connivance with the past and the future—a connivance which is knowledge.

IV. The Word of the Stars

Astrology as a field bears witness to that connivance. For astrology has been throughout the millennia the burning consciousness of the tie that binds human time and space to eternity and infinity. Since the tragic agony of the Renaissance, astrology has been swept away by the undertow of the Reformation and the Counterreformation and dumped into the dubious traps of occultism, from which it reemerges timidly only in the mists of personal divination. Other vistas gradually become apparent. The major mythical figures both in the East and West join in astrology, as can be seen in the admirable manuscripts or imageries that are gradually emerging from the shadows to which they have been confined for four centuries.

The circle of the zodiac describes the union of the undying forms of creation (the earth and the sky) and the divine adventures. In the radiant meadow of the stars, the wrenching upheavals and frenzies of the gods find their coherence. Human fates, which duplicate divine fates, are displayed in the same way as so many signs of the imaginative freedom of the being. The reading of the stars had no purpose other than to allow every creature, existing in one well-defined place and century, to discover the special territory of his journey.

The astrological quest is the nostalgic quest for our origins. There is no greater misery than that of being orphaned, and we must know those who have begotten us in spirit so that we may be able to beget ourselves, that is, to survive, according to the spirit. To fathom the untold night of knowledge is to draft the map of the sky; it is the need to reveal this hidden geography that has led us to the shores on which we now stand. Through fascination with the stars, we gain access to the kingdom of the Mothers; and on the faces of all those nocturnal queens, we must recognize those who gave us birth, surrounded by the divine lovers in whose embrace they became fruitful. The zodiacal sky with its complex cartography of signs, planets, and divisions is there only to inform us of our native land, of which the gods are the emblematic symbol. The metaphysical landscape that it sets forth for our fulfillment is replete with dwellings: in some we shall be welcomed as honored guests and we shall experience joy; in others, we shall be received as undesirable strangers, and we shall have only heartache and nightmares as our share.

For such is the pitiless price that we must pay for our presence on this clod of earth: he who has not found his native land, his original fatherland, in the perplexing fires of the stars may never discover, here below, the land that was destined for him. Among the Hellenes, Apollo brought fortune to some and misfortune to others; Aphrodite opened the doors of the paradises of love to some, but for others, under the mask of desire, she flung open the gates to the stronghold of murder. The Christian pantheon with its complex interplay of virgins, saints, and black angels spoke the same language to the people of the Middle Ages. That is why these gods whose indelible imprint is visible in the sky accompany us on all our journeys. The decipherment of their adventures guides us on our way and keeps us from being forever aimless vagabonds. Many men standing before Isolde have taken themselves to be Tristan and have ended up in shame, when it was the role of King Mark or of the traitor that was meant to be theirs.

But this metaphysical landscape does not cross the fragmented course of our journey episodically; it is our day and our night, our dawn and our twilight. And the exploration of the shadows of being, to which every reading of myths refers us, opens our eyes to another realm, that of daily life. People of the earliest times attempted to put order and harmony into the movements of the universe, dreamed up sumptuous epics that reveal the gradual taking shape of what would eventually become civilization, because they wanted to rediscover in the innermost depth of their being the harmony and order that existed in the cosmos. The inner is the mirror of the outer, and the outer is the mirror of the inner. Between the outer and the inner, in the continent that is the locus of our condition, the faces that cross our days and our nights find their place: the landscapes, the houses, the humblest of objects that accompany our gestures and our attention. These backdrops are not naked, transparent surfaces. They refer us constantly to their interiority. And it is this interiority that all the ancient rituals reveal to us. In a community where myths are experienced as incarnations, the slightest fragments of reality are charged with meaning.

These meaningful fragments do not drift aimlessly. They are carriers of the language addressed to us by the multiplicity of created things. From one civilization to another, they bear witness to certain common characteristics, whose permanence has made it possible to constitute a vast symbolic "corpus." This forest of symbols translates the fundamental obsessions of the species in a rather similar manner, and it is on this similarity that contemporary psychology has relied in order to show how the images that flow through our dreams reveal the conflicts and obstacles that trouble our waking hours. What applies to symbolism also applies to astrology. In no way does it constitute a rigorous configuration. It offers the human imagination a network of paths upon which each of us can venture at our own pace and according to our own thirst.

For the symbolic figures that are, as it were, the shadows, the material projections of the divine or heroic avatars that we are told about in myths do not represent fixed forms, set in their original meaning, anymore than those original avatars did. Like myths, they belong to life and to metamorphosis. They have an original tie with creation, a tie that is reflected in our spirit, but that our own inventive genius can constantly enrich and transform. Each symbol needs to be experienced at the level of the most trivial and the most personal existence in order to become precisely the kind of bud that each of us causes to flower according to the inclination of his inalienable need. For instance, if we refer to the color red and to the meaning that it may have taken on in various cosmological representations and ancient rituals, we can see that it is both the same red and a different red, here beneficent, there maleficent, here associated with fertility, there with decay. We carry within us all the contradictions of a symbol that has been experienced differently in time and in space. And among the various scenarios that it offers us, we are given the choice and the chance to find the one which is irreducibly attached to our own nature.

V. The Inner Gold

The subtle artisans who built the bridge spanning the collective myths of the ancient civilizations and the personal mythologies that find their fulfillment in poetic exploration are obvious to us. They are the alchemists. In the ruins of the great ancient religions, haunted by the tragedy of the rupture between rationality and symbolism, between the idea and the image, which took place in the classical Mediterranean world, alchemy fosters in consciousness itself the happy conjunction of the spirit and the flesh. *Solve et coagula.* Matter is penetrated by spirit, and spirit cannot create anything without matter. But the dissolution of matter is not a work of destruction; it is the fruit of an intimate sympathy, and this encounter, as destructive in its own way as the encounter of love, parcels out all the sufferings, anxieties, and nightmares of matter itself. Each one of us human beings in the fullness of our development is this supreme alchemist capable of taking charge of the misfortunes and joys of matter and those of spirit, so that in their always ephemeral conciliation the creative breath of life may continue to inspire them.

At the inaccessible end of the alchemic road, in the last action of the Great Work, lies gold, the gold of time and also the gold of space. Called together in the garden of Eden are all the people of whom history spoke, as well as all those whom silence has entombed forever, but also all those who will come after us, lost like us within the narrow boundaries of the flesh, within the density of their hopes and despairs. This garden, so dazzlingly present in the mythologies that have now disappeared, is also present in the opacity of our modern existences. The voice that calls us to it has remained the same since the beginning, and this voice tells us that the field of knowledge is inexhaustible, for in our hearts the peaceful gold of the Mystery abides, hidden only under the disquieting passion of the blood.

C.Me./g.h.

BIBLIOGRAPHY

R. ALLEAU, *La science des symboles* (Paris 1976). J. EVOLA, *La tradition hermétique* (Paris 1973). T. BURCKHARDT, *Alchimie* (Basel 1974). N. O. BROWN, *Life against Death* (Middletown, CT, 1959); *Love's Body* (New York 1966). C. GAIGNEBET, *Le carnaval* (Paris 1974). H. LEISEGANG, *Die Gnosis* (Leipzig 1924; 4th ed., Stuttgart 1955). R. LEWINTER, *Groddeck et le royaume millénaire de Jérôme Bosch* (Paris 1975). J. C. POWYS, special issue of the journal *Granit* (Paris 1973). J. VAN LENNEP, *Art et alchimie* (Brussels 1966).

Two-headed Hermes. Third to second century B.C. Marseille, Musée Borély. Museum photo.

Index

Italicized numbers denote pages containing illustrations

O

P

Q

R

S

T

U

V

W

The Developing Person
Through Childhood and Adolescence

The Developing Person
Through Childhood and Adolescence
NINTH EDITION

KATHLEEN STASSEN BERGER

Bronx Community College
City University of New York

WORTH PUBLISHERS

Executive Publisher: Catherine Woods
Executive Editor: Jessica Bayne
Developmental Editor: Tom Churchill
Executive Marketing Manager: Katherine Nurre
Supplements and Media Editor: Sharon Prevost
Assistant Editor: Lukia Kliossis
Associate Managing Editor: Lisa Kinne
Director of Print and Digital Development: Tracey Kuehn
Production Editor: Vivien Weiss
Supplements Production Editor: Jennifer Chiu
Art Director: Barbara Reingold
Interior Designer: Lissi Sigillo
Photo Treatments: Lyndall Culbertson
Layout Designer: Paul Lacy
Photo Editor: Cecilia Varas
Photo Researcher: Jacqui Wong
Senior Illustration Coordinator: Bill Page
Illustrations: Todd Buck Illustrations, MPS Limited, TSI Graphics, Inc.
Production Manager: Barbara Seixas
Supplements Production Manager: Stacey Alexander
Composition: TSI Graphics, Inc.
Printing and Binding: RR Donnelley
Cover Art: Katherine Dunn

Library of Congress Control Number: 2011942454
ISBN-13: 978-1-4292-4351-3
ISBN-10: 1-4292-4351-1
ISBN-13: 978-1-4292-4376-6 (ppbk.)
ISBN-10: 1-4292-4376-7 (ppbk.)

Printed in the United States of America
First printing 2012
Worth Publishers
41 Madison Avenue
New York, NY 10010
www.worthpublishers.com

Credit is given to the following sources for permission to use the photos indicated:

Part Openers

Jose Luis Pelaez Inc./Jupiter Images, p. xxxii
Jose Luis Pelaez Inc./Jupiter Images, pp. vii, ix, 1
Alex Cao/Getty Images, p. 124
John Lund/Annabelle Breakey/Jupiter Images, pp. vii, x, 125
BLOOM Images/Getty Images, p. 222
© Vinicius Ramalho Tupinamba/istockphoto, pp. vii, xi, 223
Ronnie Kaufman/Larry Hershowitz/Getty Images, p. 320
George Doyle/Getty Images, pp. vii, xi, 321
Tyler Edwards/Getty Images, p. 408
Mark Anderson/Getty Images, pp. vii, xii, 409

Chapter Openers

Hugh Sitton/Photolibrary, pp. ix, 2
Fancy/Alamy, pp. ix, 34
David M. Phillips/Photo Researchers, Inc., pp. ix, 62
Rick Gomez/Corbis, pp. x, 92
Angelo Cavalli/Robert Harding, pp. x, 126
Getty Images/Dorling Kindersley, pp. x, 160
Bruce Yuan-Yue Bi/Lonely Planet, pp. x, 190
Joanne Lane/Photographers Direct pp. xi, 224
Dynamic Graphics/Creatas, pp. xi, 256
Little Blue Wolf Productions/Photolibrary, pp. xi, 288
Cindy Miller Hopkins/DanitaDelmont, pp. xii, 322
Holger Winkler/Corbis, pp. xii, 350
Sean Sprague/The Image Works, pp. xii, 376
Paul Miles/Axiom, pp. xii, 410
Hill Street Studios/Blend Images/Corbis, pp. xii, 438
Digital Vision/Getty Images, pp. xiii, 470
Exotica IM/Age Fotostock, pp. xiii, 504

About the Author

Kathleen Stassen Berger received her undergraduate education at Stanford University and Radcliffe College and earned an M.A.T. from Harvard University as well as an MS and PhD from Yeshiva University. Her broad experience as an educator includes directing a preschool, serving as chair of philosophy at the United Nations International School, teaching child and adolescent development to graduate students at Fordham University and undergraduates at Montclair State University in New Jersey and at Quinnipiac University in Connecticut, as well as teaching social psychology to inmates at Sing Sing Prison.

Throughout most of her professional career, Berger has taught at Bronx Community College of the City University of New York, first as an adjunct and for the past two decades as a full professor. She has taught introduction to psychology, child and adolescent development, adulthood and aging, social psychology, abnormal psychology, and human motivation. Her students—who come from many ethnic, economic, and educational backgrounds and who have a wide range of ages and interests—consistently honor her with the highest teaching evaluations.

Berger is also the author of *The Developing Person Through the Life Span* and *Invitation to the Life Span*. Her developmental texts are currently being used at more than 700 colleges and universities worldwide and are available in Spanish, French, Italian, and Portuguese, as well as English. Her research interests include adolescent identity, multigenerational families, immigration, and bullying, and she has published many articles on developmental topics in the *Wiley Encyclopedia of Psychology* and in publications of the American Association for Higher Education and the National Education Association for Higher Education. She continues teaching and learning every semester and in every edition of her books.

BRIEF CONTENTS

CONTENTS

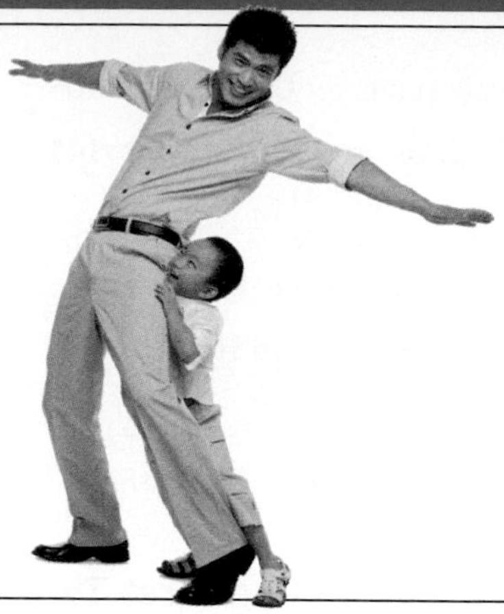

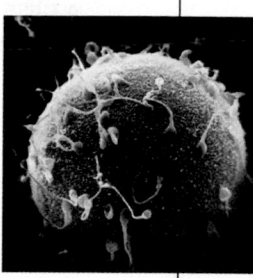

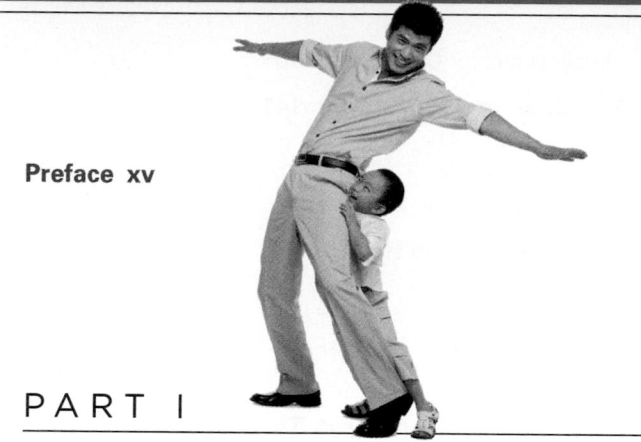

PART III

Early Childhood 223

Chapter 8 Early Childhood: Biosocial Development 225

Chapter 9 Early Childhood: Cognitive Development 257

Chapter 10 Early Childhood: Psychosocial Development 289

PART IV

Middle Childhood 321

Chapter 11 Middle Childhood: Biosocial Development 323

Preface

"Another edition? Has anything really changed?" people often ask.

I suppress the impulse to tell them that if they understood child development from infancy through adolescence, they would realize that change is pervasive. Scientists know more about the brain, culture, genes, education, and much else today than they did just a few years ago. Humans themselves change, too, as each cohort experiences new events around the world—electronic media, chemicals in the food supply, globalization, HIV, longer lives, fewer babies . . . . The list of sociocultural shifts that affect all our lives is long indeed.

Instead I talk about my own life, a small window on the larger changes around us. For example, in the past two years, my first grandchildren, Asa and Caleb, were born. As I watch them develop, I learn, again, about early childhood and motherhood. Among the dramatic changes since I first became a mother are recommendations to breast-feed longer, heightened worry about toxins, anticipated maternal employment, saving for college some day. And some of the accoutrements are new: bigger and better strollers and paper diapers, no-slip slippers, automatic rockers, books for babies, attractive mobiles.

Where does the science of child development fit into all this? Consider my experience.

When my daughter Bethany was pregnant, she knew of my extensive knowledge of development and asked me to be her birth partner, a great honor. We went to classes together, and I felt ready for the big day. She was told to also find a good midwife and doula—fortunate for me because, although I knew what was happening, understood the monitored vital signs, and had confidence in the professionals taking care of my daughter in labor, tears flowed down my cheeks as I watched.

I stayed in a corner, where Bethany could not see how emotional I was. At the birth, I helped her push, holding one leg as a nurse held the other—just as the midwife had told us. Caleb was born, small and perfect; Bethany cradled and fed him. A miracle.

And then I fainted.

I suddenly found myself on the floor, with six medical people clustered around me instead of attending to my daughter and new grandson.

"I'm fine," I assured them, telling them to focus on Bethany. They did not. They insisted that, per hospital policy, I'd have to be wheeled down to emergency intake. I protested until one nurse said, "You can refuse treatment when you're there."

So, to get them to focus on Bethany, I sat in the wheelchair—and soon told a triage nurse that a night of high emotion without food, water, or sleep made me faint. Then, I said, "I refuse treatment." She checked with her supervisor and then allowed me to return to Bethany. The midwife was patiently waiting for the placenta to be expelled.

How does all this relate to development? In three ways:

1. Emotions can overtake reason. As you will read, we are all dual-process thinkers. My knowledge led me to ignore my emotions—big mistake.
2. Knowledge helps. I have since learned that many family members faint at births. If I had been aware of this, I would have nourished my body rather

My Youngest at 8 Months When I look at this photo of Sarah, I see evidence of Mrs. Todd's devotion. Sarah's hair is washed and carefully brushed, her jumper and bloused are clean and pressed, and the carpet and stepstool are perfect equipment for standing practice. Sarah's legs—chubby and far apart—indicate that she is not about to walk early; but, given all these signs of Mrs. Todd's attention to caregiving, it is not surprising, in hindsight, that my fourth daughter was my earliest walker.

than deprived it in solidarity with Bethany (she could not eat). I would have noticed that I felt dizzy and lightheaded and thus would have sat down. Lack of knowledge is harmful in many ways—sharing vital information is why I write this book, and why you study development.

3. Development brings change. Personal changes were evident: Giving birth to four wonderful daughters (without ever fainting) is quite different from witnessing one of those daughters give birth herself. Cohort changes are evident as well: Now that fathers, friends, and grandmothers are often allowed in delivery rooms, new education is needed—like how to avoid fainting. I did not know; now I do. That is why updating developmental textbooks is necessary.

All this makes me remember again why I study human development. We all need to know more; it will help us, our loved ones, and every person develop with more joy and fulfillment and less harm and despair.

Teaching and writing remain my life's work and passion. I strive to make this text both challenging and accessible to every student, remembering that my students were the inspiration for writing a developmental text in the first place. Students deserve a book that respects their intellect and experiences, without making development seem dull or obscure.

Overall, I believe that a better world is possible because today's students will become tomorrow's leaders. My hope is that the knowledge they gain from reading this book will benefit all their family members—children and adults alike—from one generation to the next.

To learn more about the specifics of this text, including the material that is new to this edition, read on. Or simply turn to the beginning of Chapter 1 and start your study.

New Material

Every year, scientists discover and explain new concepts and present new research. The best of these are integrated into the text, including hundreds of new references on many topics—among them the genetics of delinquency, infant nutrition, bipolar and autism spectrum disorders, the importance of early attachment, high-stakes testing, drug use and drug addiction, brain development throughout childhood and into emerging adulthood. Cognizant of the interdisciplinary nature of human development, I reflect research in biology, sociology, education, anthropology, political science, and more—as well as in my home discipline, psychology.

Genetics and social contexts are noted throughout. The variations and hazards of infant day care and preschool education are described; the implications of various family structures (single parents, stepparents, same-sex parents) are explored; the pivotal role of middle school is noted; and so on.

Research on the Brain

Every page of this text reflects new research and theory. Brain development is the most obvious example: Every trio of chapters includes a section on the brain, often enhanced with charts and photos to help students understand its inner workings. The following list highlights some of this material:

Correlation between MAOA production and violent crime, p. 7
A Case to Study feature on brain plasticity, pp. 9–10
A View from Science feature on mirror neurons, pp. 20–21
Piaget's sensorimotor intelligence, pp. 47–49

Fronto-striatal deficits and ADHD, p. 49
Phenylketonuria and harm to the brain, p. 89
Prenatal brain development and age of viability, p. 97
Head-sparing and malnutrition, pp. 129, 154–155
Development of axons, dendrites, and cortex in infancy, pp. 133–135
A View from Science feature on the fusiform face area and face recognition, pp. 137–138
Neurological effects of stress, pp. 138–139
Social deprivation and brain growth, pp. 139–140
Sources of harm to the infant brain, including stress and deprivation, pp. 138–140
Techniques for measuring infant brain activity, pp. 167–168
Infant cognition and information-processing theory, pp. 169–176
Chomsky's language acquisition device, p. 188
Brain maturation and infants' emotional development, pp. 194–195
Synesthesia, pp. 195–196
Brain development, myelination, and speed of thought in early childhood, pp. 229–231
The corpus callosum and lateralization, pp. 232–233
Maturation of the prefrontal cortex, pp. 233–234
The limbic system, pp. 235–237
Stress and the brain, pp. 236–237
A View from Science: Witness to a Crime explores early cognitive competency, p. 265
Brain maturation as basis for theory of mind, pp. 267–269
Gender differences in brain development and emotional regulation, pp. 293–294
Reaction time, attention, automatization in middle childhood, pp. 333–336
Brain scans and IQ, pp. 336–337
Pituitary, hypothalamus, and puberty, pp. 412–414

© DOLI AKTER

Worlds Apart This day center in Dhaka, Bangladesh, shows that daycare is needed all over the world.

SCOTT ELLIS / THE NEW YORK TIMES / REDUX

A Religious Experience Buddha taught that life is suffering, but this young Buddhist monk might prefer to avoid it. He lives in a remote region of Nepal, where, until recently, measles was a fatal disease. Fortunately, a UNICEF porter carried the vaccine over mountain trails for two days so that this boy—and his whole community—could be immunized.

Sleep and the brain, p. 414
Brain development in adolescence, pp. 431–435
Drug abuse and the brain, pp. 497–500
Risk taking in emerging adulthood, pp. 508–509
Combining subjective and objective thought, pp. 510–517
Stereotype threat, pp. 511–512

New Pedagogical Aids

This edition incorporates learning objectives at the beginning of each chapter: The "What Will You Know?" questions indicate important concepts for students to focus on. There is also a new element at the end of each chapter: The "What Have You Learned?" questions help students assess their learning in more detail. Some further explanation follows.

Learning Objectives

Much of what students learn from this course is a matter of attitude, approach, and perspective—all hard to quantify. In addition, there are specific learning objectives, which supplement the key terms that should also be learned. In this edition, for the first time, two sets of objectives are listed for each chapter. Each question in the first set ("What Will You Know?"), asked at the beginning of each chapter, correlates with a major heading in the chapter and focuses on general ideas that students might remember and apply lifelong. At the end of each chapter are more specific learning objectives ("What Have You Learned?") that also connect to each major heading in the chapter but ask more specific questions about the chapter content.

Ideally, students answer the learning objective questions in sentences, with specifics that demonstrate knowledge. Some items on the new lists are straightforward, requiring only close attention to the chapter content. Others require comparisons, implications, or evaluations. Suggestions and grading rubrics for these questions are available in the test bank that goes along with the book.

Balancing the Range of Difficulty

To illustrate, the first "What Have You Learned?" question in Chapter 5 is straightforward: *What specific facts indicate that infants grow rapidly in the first year?* But the nineteenth question is more difficult: *What are the reasons for and against breast-feeding until the child is at least 1 year old?*

The first question might be answered simply as follows: *Birthweight doubles in four months and triples by one year, while infants grow about a foot*—or with several other specific details. However, students may, at first, be stumped by question 19, since the chapter is overwhelmingly in favor of breast-feeding. A good answer might be:

> *There are dozens of strong reasons for breast-feeding, including protection against disease, early immunity, better digestion, easier bonding, and perhaps a positive long-term effect on intellectual ability. Breast-feeding has advantages for the mother and family as well. Disadvantages are more difficult to find. However, if the mother is taking drugs or is unable to breast-feed, formula may be best. And if a woman or culture insists that no other foods, supplements, or vitamins are needed for a year or more, an infant might become malnourished, as occurred with Kiana. [See* A Case to Study *on p. 153.]*

As you can see from these examples, good answers may vary, but students should always use their own words and critical thinking skills, referring to specifics in the chapter.

Content Changes in the Ninth Edition

Child and adolescent development, like all sciences, builds on past learning. Many facts and concepts are scaffolds that remain strong over time: stages and ages, norms and variations, dangers and diversities, classic theories and fascinating applications. However, the study of development is continually changed by discoveries and experiences, so no paragraph in this ninth edition is exactly what it was in the eighth edition, much less the first. Some major revisions have been made, and hundreds of new examples are cited.

Since many of the students in this class are preparing to be teachers, every chapter now has an "Especially for" question for teachers. Other questions are especially for nurses, parents, police officers, and so on. Some students are planning for careers in early childhood development. To help them, we have provided an alignment of the text in the book with the standards provided by the National Association for the Education of Young Children, in an appendix developed by Wendy Bass Kerr from Pierce College.

Highlights of this updating appear below.

No More Playpens Much has changed since Jacqueline watched a temper tantrum in a playpen. "Little scientists" still "experiment" in order to see, but this 14-month-old uses a digital tablet and may protest if it is taken away.

Part I: The Beginnings

1. Introduction

- Scientific method explained at the outset of the book, with research on SIDS as example of a mystery that became hypotheses and then life-saving practices
- Nature–nurture interaction and critical versus sensitive periods explained in Chapter 1
- Cultural/ethnic differences made clear with example of Chinese and U.S. mothers reading books to toddlers
- Juvenile delinquency as example of multidisciplinary perspective, including genetics, neuroscience, child rearing, and social context
- Critical and sensitive periods brought forward from Chapters 4 and 5; illustrated via language learning
- *A View from Science* feature on mirror neurons

2. Theories of Development

- Distinction between theories, facts, and norms
- Examples of behaviorism include a *Thinking Critically* feature on toilet training
- Information processing now introduced in this chapter
- Humanism highlighted as a major theory
- Evolutionary theory explained, including *A View from Science* feature on sex differences in romantic jealousy

3. Heredity and Environment

- Epigenetics explained in more detail, including methylation and gene expression
- *Thinking Critically* feature on sex selection includes the United States, China, and India
- *Thinking Critically* feature on IVF insemination
- Stem cells explained; possible applications
- ART and multiple births
- Controversy regarding genetic testing for psychological conditions illustrated in *A View from Science* feature that focuses on schizophrenia

4. Prenatal Development and Birth

- Section on birth now directly follows section on prenatal development (in the previous edition, the section on Risk Reduction separated these sections)

- *Thinking Critically* feature on home births, including international comparisons
- Research on the benefits of the doula for high-risk infants and low-risk births
- Greater emphasis on father involvement (or absence) during pregnancy and birth, including couvade
- Various measures of newborn health—weight, age, Apgar score, Brazelton assessment scale, and reflexes
- Teratogens and innate vulnerability
- Complications of risk analysis and advice (e.g., alcohol, fish, prenatal testing)

Part II: The First Two Years

5. The First Two Years: Biosocial Development

- Bed-sharing, co-sleeping, and infant sleep patterns as issues for critical thinking
- New discussion of pain as an aspect of the sense of touch
- The fusiform face area of the brain and the effect of experience on specialized and differentiated recognition of human faces
- Current infant immunization, including California's 2010 whooping cough epidemic
- Infant survival worldwide; specifics include breast-feeding to combat malnutrition, vitamin D to prevent rickets, and bed nets to reduce malaria

6. The First Two Years: Cognitive Development

- Sharper yet more sympathetic coverage of limitations of Piaget's research
- Applications of information processing, especially for infant memory
- Stress on developing language before the first words, including in bilingual families
- *Thinking Critically* feature on the value of educational videos for infants
- Norms and theories of language learning explained with practical examples

7. The First Two Years: Psychosocial Development

- Extensive discussion of the influence of brain maturation on the emotional development of infants and toddlers
- Description of synesthesia and how it might differ in infancy and later on
- Variations in age of toilet training and how toilet-training approaches reflect theories of infant development
- *A View from Science* feature on the persistence or changeability of temperament and the effects of family and culture
- Impact of personal theories and how they can be changed
- Expanded discussion of infant day care, including comparison of day-care policies in 10 nations as well as possible positive and negative effects

Part III: Early Childhood

8. Early Childhood: Biosocial Development

- Expanded discussion of brain development, including maturation of the prefrontal cortex and a reorganized and expanded section on the limbic system and the effects of stress
- *A View from Science* feature on the long-term effects of child maltreatment
- Comparison of social understanding in humans and chimpanzees
- *Research Design* feature, in a section on environmental hazards, presents compelling new research on asthma risk

9. Early Childhood: Cognitive Development

- Role of imitation in children's learning, comparing non-Western and Western children
- New research on early intervention strategies that are effective in enhancing reading ability years later in elementary school.

CORBIS / AGE FOTOSTOCK

Words, Don't Fail Me Now Could you describe how to tie shoes? The limitations of verbal tests of cognitive understanding are apparent in many skills.

- Updated research on preschool programs, including Montessori schools and Reggio Emilia schools, and federal evaluation of Head Start programs
- *A View from Science* looks at cognitive competency through children as witnesses to crime

10. Early Childhood: Psychosocial Development

- Expanded discussion of play, including cultural differences and learning from peers
- Major section on moral development, with types and origins of prosocial and antisocial behavior and the moral lessons learned from methods of punishment
- New research on cultural differences in disciplinary practices, including *A View from Science* feature on cultural determinants of effective discipline
- Updated research on the impact of the new media

Part IV: Middle Childhood

11. Middle Childhood: Biosocial Development

- *A Case to Study* looks at SES influences on asthma
- International data on obesity and stress on macrocosm influences
- Variations of intelligence and IQ, including data from brain scans
- Bipolar disorder in childhood explained and contrasted with ADHD
- In psychopathology, examples of equifinality and multifinality
- Discussion of children with special needs expanded, including new section on gifted and talented students

12. Middle Childhood: Cognitive Development

- Cultural differences in methods of learning (individual versus collaborative; discovery versus direct instruction)
- Advent of universal primary education (e.g., India)
- Updates on various measures of learning—TIMSS, PIRLS, NAEP, NCLB
- Who decides what is part of the curriculum (e.g., religion, charter schools, vouchers)

13. Middle Childhood: Psychosocial Development

- Self-esteem presented as complex; problems with high self-esteem and international variations explained
- Updated data on family structures—nuclear, step, extended, single parents, same-sex parents, and others
- SES effects on children from both high- and low-income families
- Moral values, including peer influence, bullying, retribution, and restitution

Part V: Adolescence

14. Adolescence: Biosocial Development

- Specifics about the role that weight and stress play in the onset of puberty
- Problems with early teen sex as contrasted with later teen sex (pregnancy, STIs)
- Complications and benefits of brain development in adolescence
- Eating disorders now in this chapter; drug use now in Chapter 16

15. Adolescence: Cognitive Development

- Logical fallacies now include base rate neglect
- Contrast clarified between college-bound students and high school dropouts
- Methods of student engagement critically examined
- Technology and cognition discussed, with recent data on social networking, cyberbullying, computers in instruction
- International contrasts include results from the PISA

AP PHOTO / MOSCOW-PULLMAN DAILY NEWS, GEOFF CRIMMINS

Fourth Grade Challenge How much weight can a bridge hold? Thirty-three students in gifted classes at an elementary school in Idaho designed and built toothpick bridges and then tested them. David Stubbens (shown here) added 61 pounds to the bucket before his bridge collapsed.

ZUMA PRESS / NEWSCOM

Who and Where? As Erikson explained in 1968, the pride of self-discovery is universal for adolescents: These could be teenagers anywhere. But a closer look reveals gay teenagers in Atlanta, Georgia, where this march could not have occurred 50 years ago.

16. Adolescence: Psychosocial Development

- Identity crisis refers to gender identity and identity politics
- Norms, expectations, and roles of parents and peers presented in cross-cultural contexts—variations by region (e.g., Hong Kong), by SES, and by ethnicity
- Updated data on drug use, including brain changes, depression, anxiety

Epilogue: Emerging Adulthood

- Debate among scholars as to whether contemporary emerging adults are more selfish or more transformative than those of earlier generations
- Risk taking explained as a benefit to society as well as a problem
- Connection between social understanding and maturation of the prefrontal cortex
- New *A Case to Study* feature describes one professor's journey to postformal thought
- Updated data on college, including statistics on 25- to 34-year-olds who are college graduates, in many nations
- Impact of recent cultural and economic changes on ethnic and vocational identity
- Crucial role of parental support during emerging adulthood

Ongoing Features

Many characteristics of this book have been acclaimed since the first edition and have been retained in this revision.

Writing That Communicates the Excitement and Challenge of the Field

An overview of the science of human development should be lively, just as real people are. Each sentence conveys tone as well as content. Chapter-opening vignettes bring student readers into the immediacy of development. Examples and explanations abound, helping students make the connections among theory, research, and their own experiences.

ISSEI KATO / REUTERS

Just Like Me Emerging adults of every ethnicity take pride in their culture. In Japan, adulthood begins with a celebration at age 20, to the evident joy of these young women on Coming of Age Day, a national holiday.

Coverage of Diversity

Cross-cultural, international, multiethnic, sexual orientation, wealth, age, gender—all these words and ideas are vital to appreciating how children develop. Research uncovers surprising similarities and notable differences: We have much in common, yet each human is unique. From the discussion of social contexts in Chapter 1 to the coverage of cultural differences in family dynamics in the Epilogue, each chapter highlights possibilities and variations. New is inclusion of genetic susceptibility, another source of variation.

New research on family structures, immigrants, bilingualism, emerging adults, and ethnic differences in health are among the many topics that illustrate human diversity. Listed here is a smattering of the discussions of culture and diversity in this new edition. Respect for human differences is evident throughout. You will note that examples and research findings from many parts of the world are included, not as add-on highlights, but as integral parts of the description of each age.

Inclusion of all kinds of people in the study of development, pp. 10–11
Discussion of sex differences, p. 11
Culture, ethnicity, and race, as well as SES, defined, pp. 11–14
Sociocultural theory, pp. 50–53
Humanism and evolutionary theory, pp. 53–58
Male and female chromosomes, p. 67
Sex-selection policies in China, India, and other countries, p. 68
National differences in incidence of twin births, pp. 70–71
Nature–nurture interaction in nearsightedness among children in Britain, Africa, and Asia, pp. 80–81
Sex-chromosome abnormalities and sex-linked genetic problems, pp. 82–85
Rates of cesarean births internationally, pp. 101–102
Birthing practices in various cultures, pp. 102–105
Low-birthweight rates in different nations, pp. 115–116
Co-sleeping and bed-sharing customs, pp. 131–132
Ethnic variations in development of motor skills, pp. 147–148
Cultural values and practices in infants' language learning, pp. 179–182
Cultural divergence in emotions encouraged in toddlers, p. 193
Erikson on autonomy versus shame, p. 199
Ethnotheories in emotional development, pp. 201–202
Proximal and distal parenting, pp. 202–204
Latino fathers as toddlers' social references, pp. 212–213
International variations in parental leave policies (after a birth), pp. 214–215
Ethnic differences in young children's height, p. 226
National and ethnic differences in attitudes about nutrition, pp. 226–227
Influence of culture on young children's theory of mind, p. 269
Bilingualism in infants and young children, pp. 181–182, 272–274
Early-childhood bilingual education in the United States, pp. 282–283
Gender differences in emotional regulation, pp. 293–294
Cultural differences in young children's play, pp. 295–296
Ethnic differences in parenting styles, pp. 301–302
A View from Science feature on cultural differences in child discipline, pp. 310–311
Theories regarding sex differences, pp. 315–316
Childhood obesity in various countries, pp. 328–330
Vygotsky on cultural variations in school-age children's learning, pp. 353–355
Second-language learning in middle childhood, pp. 361–362, 366–367
International differences in math achievement scores, pp. 365–367, 369
Gender and SES differences in the "gifted and talented" designation, pp. 368
Cultural differences in self-esteem as social construction, p. 380
Same-sex families, pp. 389–390
Cultural differences in family structure, p. 392
The culture of children, pp. 395–397
Shyness versus arrogance among children in China, p. 396
Gender differences in bullying, pp. 397–398
Cultural influences on children's moral values, pp. 400–403
Gender differences in reactions to early or late puberty, pp. 418–419
Internet use among adolescents, by ethnicity, p. 451
Immigrant teens entering new schools, pp. 459–460
Gender identity and sexual orientation in adolescence, pp. 475–476, 486–487
Political/ethnic identity in adolescence, pp. 473–474
Immigrant adolescents' relationships with parents, pp. 478–480
Immigrant adolescents' relationships with peers, pp. 483–484

Same-sex relationships in adolescence, pp. 486–487
International variations in teenage pregnancy rates, p. 489
Gender differences in adolescent depression, pp. 490–491
Gender differences in suicide, pp. 491–494
Ethnic differences in adolescent arrest rates, pp. 494–496
International differences in adolescent drug use, p. 497
Gender differences in drug use, pp. 497–498
Cultural and national differences in health, sex, and reproduction and risk taking among emerging adults, pp. 506–509
Stereotype threat, pp. 518–519
Influence of culture on cognition in emerging adulthood, pp. 513, 515
International rates of college attendance, pp. 512–513, 515–516
Ethnic identity in emerging adulthood, pp. 518–519

Up-to-Date Coverage

My mentors welcomed curiosity, creativity, and skepticism; as a result, I am eager to read and analyze thousands of articles and books on everything from autism to zygosity. The recent explosion of research in neuroscience and genetics has challenged me, once again, first to understand and then to explain many complex findings and speculative leaps. My students continue to ask questions and share their experiences, always providing new perspectives and concerns.

Topical Organization within a Chronological Framework

The book's basic organization remains unchanged. Four chapters begin the book with coverage of definitions, theories, genetics, and prenatal development. These chapters function not only as a developmental foundation but also as the structure for explaining the life-span perspective, plasticity, nature and nurture, multicultural awareness, risk analysis, gains and losses, family bonding, and many other concepts that yield insights for all of human development.

The other four parts correspond to the major periods of development. Each part contains three chapters, one for each of the three domains: biosocial, cognitive, and psychosocial. The topical organization within a chronological framework is a useful scaffold for students' understanding of the interplay between age and domain. The chapters are color-coded with tabs on the right-hand margins. The pages of the biosocial chapters have blue tabs, the cognitive chapters have purple tabs, and the psychosocial chapters have green tabs.

Three Series of Integrated Features

Three series of deeper discussions appear as integral parts of the text, and only where they are relevant. Readers of earlier editions will remember the *A View from Science* feature; new to this edition are *Thinking Critically* and *A Case to Study.*

End-of-Chapter Summary

Each chapter ends with a summary, a list of key terms (with page numbers indicating where the word is introduced and defined), "What Have You Learned?" questions, and three or four application exercises designed to let students apply concepts to everyday life. Key terms appear in boldface type in the text and are defined in the margins and again in a glossary at the back of the book. The outline on the first page of each chapter, the new learning objectives, and the system of major and minor subheads facilitate the survey-question-read-write-review (SQ3R) approach.

A "Summing Up" feature at the end of each section provides an opportunity for students to pause and reflect on what they've just read. Observation quizzes inspire readers to look more closely at certain photographs, tables, and graphs. The "Especially for . . ." questions in the margins, many of which are new to this edition, apply concepts to real-life careers and social roles.

Photographs, Tables, and Graphs That Are Integral to the Text

Students learn a great deal from this book's illustrations because Worth Publishers encourages authors to choose the photographs, tables, and graphs and to write captions that extend the content. Appendix A furthers this process by presenting numerous charts and tables that contain detailed data for further study.

DAVID R. FRAZIER / DANITADELMONT.COM

And If He Falls . . . In this example of secondary prevention, the French teacher stands in front of the car, protecting the preschool children from oncoming traffic, which could do serious injury.

Supplements

As an instructor myself, I know that supplements can make or break a class. I personally have rejected textbook adoptions because I knew that a particular publisher historically had provided inaccurate test banks, dull ancillaries, and slow service. That is not the case with Worth Publishers, which has a well-deserved reputation for providing supplements that are extensive and of high quality, for both professors and students. With this edition you will find the following.

NEW! *Developing Lives:* An Interactive Simulation

The study of child development fully enters the digital age with *Developing Lives.* Using this interactive program, each student raises his or her own unique "child," making decisions about common parenting issues (nutrition choices, parenting style, type of schooling) and responding to realistic events (divorce, temperamental variations, and social and economic diversity) that shape a child's physical, cognitive and social development.

At the heart of this program is interactivity—between students and the simulation as well as among classmates. While the core experience happens on the computer, students can get notices or check in with their child "on the go" on a variety of mobile devices; they can even share photos of their baby with friends, family, and classmates. *Developing Lives* has a student-friendly, "game-like" feel that not only engages students in the program but also encourages them to learn. It features these helpful resources to reinforce and assess student learning: integrated links to the eBook version of your Worth text; readings from *Scientific American;* more than 400 videos and animations, many of them newly filmed for *Developing Lives;* and links to easy-to-implement assessment tools, including assignable quizzes on core topics, discussion threads, and journal questions.

NEW! *LearningCurve:* Formative Quizzing Engine

Developed by a team of psychology instructors with extensive backgrounds in course design and online education, *LearningCurve* combines adaptive question selection, personalized study plans, and state-of-the-art question analysis reports.

LearningCurve is based on the simple yet powerful concept of testing-to-learn, with game-like quizzing activities that keep students engaged in the material while helping them learn key concepts.

A team of dedicated instructors—including Lisa Hager, Spring Hill College; Jessica Herrick, Mesa State College; Sara Lapsley, Simon Fraser University; Rosemary McCullough, Ave Maria University; Wendy Morrison, Montana State University; Emily Newton, University of California, Davis; Curtis Visca, Saddleback College; and Devon Werble, East Los Angeles Community College—have worked together closely to generate more than 5,000 quizzing questions developed specifically for this edition of *The Developing Person Through Childhood and Adolescence.*

NEW! *Launch Pad:* Pre-loaded Assignments for Easy Startup

Launch Pad offers a set of prebuilt assignments, carefully crafted by a group of professors and instructional designers. Each assignable unit contains videos, activities, and formative assessment pieces to build student understanding for each topic, culminating with a quiz to hold students accountable for their work.

Human Development: A Video Tool Kit

This edition of *The Developing Person Through Childhood and Adolescence* is supplemented with the vast library of human development video and student activities on the Human Development Tool Kit. There are **more than 30 new student activities** especially for this edition. The tool kit was prepared by a talented team of instructors, including: Victoria Cross, University of California, Davis; Sheridan Dewolf, Grossmont College; Pamela B. Hill, San Antonio College; Lisa Huffman, Ball State University; Paul Kochmanski, Erie Community College; Thomas Ludwig, Hope College; Cathleen McGreal, Michigan State University; Martina Marquez, Fresno City College; Amy Obegi, Grossmont College; Michelle L. Pilati, Rio Hondo College; Tanya Renner, Kapiolani Community College; Kathleen Ringenbach, Brandman University—Antelope Valley Campus; Catherine Robertson, Grossmont College; Michelle Ryder, Daniel Webster College; Raechel Soicher, California State University, Davis; Stavros Valenti, Hofstra University; and Pauline Zeece, University of Nebraska, Lincoln.

The collection of student activities offers a full range of material, from investigations of classic experiments (like the visual cliff and the Strange Situation) to observations on children's play and adolescent risk taking. For instructors, the tool kit includes more than 400 video clips and animations, along with discussion starters and PowerPoint slides available to download for free. The kit also offers a selection of videos taken from the online library (215, to be exact) on a DVD called "The Human Development Video Collection," as well as a DVD with 40 of the most popular student activities, packageable for students.

PsychPortal

This is the complete online gateway to all the student and instructor resources available with the textbook. PsychPortal brings together all the resources of the video tool kits, integrated with an eBook and powerful assessment tools to complement your course.

The ready-to-use course template is fully customizable and includes all the teaching and learning resources that go along with the book, preloaded into a ready-to-use course; sophisticated quizzing, personalized study plans for students, and powerful assessment analyses that provide timely and useful feedback on class and individual student performance; and seamless integration of student resources, eBook text, assessment tools, and lecture resources. The quiz bank features more than 100 questions per chapter.

eBook

The beautiful and interactive eBook fully integrates the complete text and its electronic study tools in a format that instructors and students can easily customize—at a significant savings on the price of the printed text. It offers easy access from any Internet-connected computer; quick, intuitive navigation to any section or subsection, as well as any printed book page number; a powerful notes feature that allows you to customize any page; a full-text search; text highlighting; and a full, searchable glossary.

Companion Web Site

The companion Web site (at www.worthpublishers.com/bergerca9e) is an online educational setting for students and instructors. It is free, and tools on the site include interactive flashcards in both English and Spanish, a Spanish-language glossary, quizzes, and crossword puzzles. A password-protected Instructor Site offers a full array of teaching resources, including PowerPoint slides, an online quiz gradebook, and links to additional tools.

"Journey Through the Life Span" Observational Videos

Bringing observational learning to the classroom, this video series allows students to watch and listen to real children as a way of amplifying their reading of the text. "Journey Through the Life Span" offers vivid footage of people of all ages from around the world (North America, Europe, Africa, Asia, and South America), as seen in everyday environments (homes, hospitals, schools, and offices) and at major life transitions (birth, marriage, divorce, being grandparents).

Interviews with prominent developmentalists—including Charles Nelson, Barbara Rogoff, Ann Peterson, and Steven Pinker—are integrated throughout to help students link research and theory to the real world. Interviews with a number of social workers, teachers, and nurses who work with children, adults, and the aged give students direct insight into the practical challenges and rewards of their vocations. One hour of unedited footage helps students sharpen their observation skills. Available on VHS and DVD.

Child Development Telecourse

Stepping Stones, developed by Coast Learning Systems and Worth Publishers, teaches fundamentals of human development. The course also explores the variety of individual and developmental contexts that influence development, such as socioeconomic status, culture, genetics, family, school, and society. Each video lesson includes specific real-life examples interwoven with commentary by subject matter experts. The course includes 16 half-hour video lessons, a telecourse study guide, and a faculty manual with test bank. The test bank is also available electronically.

Instructor's Resources

This collection of resources written by Richard O. Straub (University of Michigan, Dearborn) has been hailed as the richest collection of instructor's resources in developmental psychology. The *Lecture Guides* preview learning objectives, springboard topics for discussion and debate, handouts for student projects, and supplementary readings from journal articles. Course planning suggestions, ideas for term projects, and a guide to audiovisual and software materials are also included.

Study Guide

The *Study Guide* by Richard O. Straub helps students evaluate their understanding and retain their learning longer. Each chapter includes a review of key concepts, guided study questions, and section reviews that encourage students' active participation in the learning process. Two practice tests and a challenge test help them assess their mastery of the material.

Interactive Presentation Slides for Human Development

A number of different presentation slides are available. There are two prebuilt slide sets for each text chapter—one featuring chapter outlines, the other featuring all chapter art and illustrations. These slides can be used as is or can be customized to fit individual needs. Video presentation slides provide an easy way to connect chapter content to the selected video clip and follow each clip with discussion questions designed to promote critical thinking.

In addition, a new extraordinary series of "next generation" interactive presentation lectures gives instructors a dynamic yet easy-to-use new way to engage students during classroom presentations of core developmental psychology topics. Each lecture provides opportunities for discussion and interaction and enlivens the psychology classroom with an unprecedented number of embedded video clips and animations from Worth's Video Tool Kit for Human Development Psychology.

Test Bank and Computerized Test Bank

The test bank, prepared by Rosemary McCullough (Ave Maria University) and Wendy Morrison (Montana State University), includes at least 100 multiple-choice and 70 fill-in, true-false, and essay questions for each chapter. Each question is keyed to the textbook by topic, learning objective, and level of difficulty.

The Diploma computerized test bank, available on a dual-platform CD-ROM for Windows and Macintosh, guides instructors step by step through the process of creating a test. It also allows them to quickly add an unlimited number of questions; edit, scramble, or resequence items; format a test; and include pictures, equations, and media links. The accompanying gradebook enables instructors to record students' grades throughout the course and includes the capacity to sort student records, view detailed analyses of test items, curve tests, generate reports, and add weights to grades.

The CD-ROM is also the access point for Diploma Online Testing, which allows instructors to create and administer secure exams over a network or over the Internet. In addition, Diploma has the ability to restrict tests to specific computers or time blocks. Blackboard- and WebCT-formatted versions of each item in the Test Bank are available on the CD-ROM.

Thanks

I'd like to thank the academic reviewers who have read this book in every edition and who have provided suggestions, criticisms, references, and encouragement. They have all made this a better book. I want to mention especially those who have reviewed this edition:

Melanie Arpaio, *Sussex County Community College*
Elaine Barry, *Penn State Fayette, The Eberly Campus*
Kris Bliss, *Mesa Community College*
Paul Boxer, *Rutgers University*
Natasha Fratello Breitenbach, *American River College*
Jamie Brown, *UNC–Charlotte*
Melinda Burgess, *Southwestern Oklahoma State University*
Dominic Carbone, *Sussex County Community College*
Ron Craig, *Edinboro University of Pennsylvania*
Timothy Croy, *Eastern Illinois University*
Laura Dell, *University of Cincinnati*
Patricia Dilko, *Canada College*
Elaine Francisco, *Skyline College*
Kate Fletcher, *University of Florida*
Heather Gelhart, *Cypress College*
Michael Goldblatt, *Bucks County Community College*
DeDee Goldsmith, *Oakton Community College*
Myra Harville, *Holmes Community College*
Tywanda Jiles, *Governors State University*
Jennifer Kampmann, *South Dakota State University*
Deena Kausler, *Jefferson College*
Megan Kelly, *University of Maryland*
Regina Kijewski, *Naugatuck Valley Community College*
Margaret King, *Ohio University*
Larry Kollman, *North Iowa Area Community College*
Kathryn Kotowski, *Cuyamaca College*
Michael Leffingwell, *Tarrant County College*
Kris Leppien-Christensen, *Saddleback College*
Martina Marquez, *Fresno City College*
Krista McClain-Rocha, *Skyline College*
Martha Myklebust, *Mendocino Community College*
Lori Nanney, *Cleveland Community College*
Sherri Palmer, *Truman State University*
Nicole Porter, *Modesto Junior College*
John Prange, *Irvine Valley College*
Melita Baumann Riddle, *Glendale Community College*
Joel Shapiro, *Green Mountain College*
Donna Sims, *Fort Valley State University*
Latoya Smith-Jones, *University of Texas at Arlington*
Cecilia Jane Spruill, *Pensacola State College*
Valerie Taylor, *Washtenaw Community College*
Peggy Thelen, *Alma College*
Sharron Thompson, *Chaminade University of Honolulu*
Tara Vargas, *Lewis and Clark College*
Anne Christine Watson, *Chapman University*
Lois Wedl, *College of Saint Benedict*
Julia Yoo, *Lamar University*

I also need to thank the instructors who reviewed our online materials. We've tried to apply the insights gained from their experiences with using our media materials in the last edition to make materials we've designed for this new edition better.

Patty Dilko, *Canada College*
Tony Fowler, *Florence Darlington Tech College*
Heather Gelhart, *Saddleback College*
Lisa Hagan, *Metropolitan State College of Denver*
Brantlee Haire, *Florence-Darlington Technical College*
Vicky Hammer, *Cloud County Community College*
Kris Leppien-Christensen, *Saddleback College*
Angela Lily, *Houston Community College*
Cheryl McGill, *Florence Darlington Tech College*
Lynn McKinley, *Grossmont College*
Wendy Bianchini Morrison, *Montana State University*
Patricia Puccio, *College of DuPage*
Rodney Raasch, *Normandale Community College*
DeAnna Timmerman, *Eastern Oregon University*
Curtis Visca, *Saddleback College*
Bridget Walsh, *University of Nevada-Reno*

In addition, I wish to thank the instructors who participated in our online survey. We've tried to apply their feedback as well, to further improve this new edition.

Farah Alam, *De Anza College*
Sindy Armstrong, *Ozarks Tech Community College*
Sherri Black, *Western Nevada College*
Deborah Barton, *York College of Pennsylvania*
Don Bower, *University of Georgia*
Diane Brown, *Everett Community College*
Sandra Broz, *Northeast Community College*
Stephen Burgess, *Southwestern Oklahoma State University*
Lanthan Camblin, *University of Cincinnati*
Catherine Camilletti, *University of Texas at El Paso*
Toni Campbell, *San Jose State University*
Donna Carey, *Keystone College*
Maria Casey, *Immaculata University*
Carolyn Cohen, *Northern Essex Community College*
Lauren Cooley, *Napa College*
Catherine Currell, *Central Michigan University*
Jennifer DeCicco, *Hunter College*
Gretchen DeHart, *Community College of Vermont*

Sorah Dubitsky, *Florida International University*
Natalie Ebner, *Yale University*
Robert C. Gates, *Cisco College*
Amy Gerney, *Misericordia University*
Zebbedia Gibb, *University of Northern Iowa*
Margie Goulden, *Pierce College*
Troianne Grayson, *Florida State College at Jacksonville*
Jerry Green, *Tarrant County College*
Christine Grela, *McHenry College*
Robert Hagstrom, *Northern Arizona University*
Danielle Hodge, *California State University–San Bernardino*
Kristin Homan, *Grove City College*
Alishia Huntoon, *Oregon Institute of Technology*
Matthew Isaak, *University of Louisville at Lafayette*
Mehraban Khodavandi, *Lakeland College*
Timothy L. Kitzman, *Blackhawk Technical College*
Kristina Klassen, *North Idaho College*
Jennifer King-Cooper, *Sinclair Community College*
Charles P. Kraemer, *LaGrange College*
Alison Kulak, *Concordia University of Alberta*
Karen Kwan, *Salt Lake Community College*
Krista Morris Lehman, *LeTourneau University*
Kathy Lein, *Community College of Denver*
Pei-Wen Ma, *William Paterson University*
Alisha Marciano, *Lynchburg College*
Dorothy Marsil, *Kennesaw State University*
Kris McAleavey, *Longwood University*
Alex McEntire, *Penn Valley Community College*
Kittie Myatt, *Argosy University–Nashville*
Nancy Neveau, *Northeast Wisconsin Technical College*
Liz O'Dell, *Northwest State Community College*
Alan Oda, *Azusa Pacific University*
Nancy Ogden, *Mount Royal University*
Bonnie Ortega, *Trinidad State Junior College*
Andrea Phronebarger, *York Technical College*
Cynthia Putman, *Charleston Southern University*
Cyd Quarterman, *Toccoa Fall College*
Jennifer Reid Reichert, *Marquette University*
Nancy E. Rizzo, *Valencia Community College*
Michael Rhoads, *University of Northern Colorado*
George Sayre, *Seattle University*
David J. Schieffer, *Minnesota West Community and Technical College*
Sheryl R. Schindler, *University of Utah*
Pamela Schuetze-Pizarro, *Buffalo State College*
Robert Schwartz, *Bergen Community College*
Deborah Sedik, *Bucks County Community College*
Sean Seepersad, *California State University*
Jane Tiedt, *Gonzaga University*
Tonya Toutge, *Bethel University*
Anne Unterkoefler, *Delaware County Community College*
Michel Vallante, *Quinsigamond Community College*
Ruth A. Wallace, *Butler Community College*
Steve Wisecarver, *Lord Fairfax Community College*
Susan Wolle, *Kirkwood Community College*
Rebecca Wood, *Center Connecticut State University*

The editorial, production, and marketing people at Worth Publishers are dedicated to meeting the highest standards of excellence. Their devotion of time, effort, and talent to every aspect of publishing is a model for the industry. I particularly would like to thank Stacey Alexander, Jessica Bayne, Tom Churchill, Lyndall Culbertson, Lukia Kliossis, Tracey Kuehn, Paul Lacy, Katherine Nurre, Sharon Prevost, Babs Reingold, Barbara Seixas, Ted Szczepanski, Cecilia Varas, Vivien Weiss, Jacquelyn Wong, and Catherine Woods.

Dedication

Every edition of this book is dedicated to people who made this textbook better than I could have alone. I dedicate this edition to Cele Gardner, my editor for more than ten years, who died in April 2010. We all miss her.

New York, October 2011

The Developing Person
Through Childhood and Adolescence

PART

I

CHAPTERS 1•2•3•4

the beginnings

The first part of this book describes many beginnings: first definitions, research designs, and theories that have become the science of human development and then the beginnings of human life, when two cells become one zygote, eventually becoming a baby (or, rarely, babies).

To be more specific, Chapter 1 introduces what, why, and how we study human development, explaining some basic research strategies and methods. Chapter 2 introduces several theories of development, both grand theories and newer ones. Chapter 3 describes the interacting genes and surrounding chemicals that influence everything from the thickness of toenails to the swiftness of brain waves. And finally, Chapter 4 describes early growth, from one dividing cell to the moment of birth.

The next four chapters, then, begin our study of child development. In all four chapters, it is evident that a swirling multiplicity of disciplines, ideas, and people create the context for a new person.

1

CHAPTER

Introduction

WHAT WILL YOU KNOW?

1. What makes the study of children, with all their variability and unexpected actions, a science?
2. How does culture change the way children develop?
3. Why is development considered dynamic, not static?
4. Why is comparing people of several ages not considered the best way to understand how people change as they grow older?
5. Is it unethical to study children scientifically?

A blizzard overwhelmed the U.S. mid-Atlantic states on December 26, 2010. Was it a force of nature, unrelated to human development? Only at first. Then people reacted, each according to age, history, family, and context.

Workplaces closed, hardware stores sold out of shovels, gloves were lost in frozen drifts, plows became stuck, cars and buses were abandoned mid-block, political leaders' approval ratings soared or plummeted. The mayor of Newark (Cory Booker, age 41, not married) responded to constituents on Twitter. He brought diapers to a snowed-in resident, rebuked another for cursing, shamed a third who was inside tweeting while his mother and wife shoveled. The governor of New Jersey (Chris Christie, age 48, married, father of four), however, flew to Florida because he had promised to take his family to Disney World. He replied to a reporter that his marriage would be in trouble if his wife went without him. Across the river, the mayor of New York (Michael Bloomberg, age 68, divorced) did not declare a Snow Emergency; many streets were impassable for days. Booker was praised, gaining a million Twitter followers; Christie was both defended and attacked; Bloomberg was soundly criticized, and his deputy resigned.

Meanwhile, children of all ages were overjoyed. My toddler grandson eagerly donned mittens and boots to play in Hudson River Park. Remembering my own childhood, I laid him down on virgin snow to make a snow angel and built a small snowman. But he cared little for angel wings or snowmen; he threw lumps of snow into the river.

A father nearby built a big snowman, complete with pine-needle hair and sculpted nose. His 6-year-old son ignored the creature until it was finished and then prepared to topple it. The man wanted to preserve his creation "for other people to admire"; his son argued that "a bully might come and knock it down." Developmental science to the rescue: I had just read about child guidance in China—praise *before* action, not only afterwards.

"You are not a bully; you are a good boy," I told him.

That snowman stayed erect for five days, until it melted.

Development is like weather. Birth, growth, and death come to everyone, and then individuals respond. This chapter describes universals and particulars, beginning with laws of science and sweeping definitions, and then detailing methods and applications. We can all soar, or at least come to the rescue, when needed.

Joy or Trouble? When the forecast is snow, many city children celebrate, as these two do at Columbus Circle in Manhattan. Adults are less enthusiastic.

>> Understanding How and Why

The **science of human development** *seeks to understand how and why people—all kinds of people, everywhere, of every age—change over time.* This definition has three crucial elements: science, people, and change.

Developmental study is a *science.* It depends on theories, data, analysis, critical thinking, and sound methodology just like every other science. Developmentalists ask questions and seek answers, to ascertain "how and why"—that is, to discover the processes of development and the reasons for those processes. In seeking answers, scientists gather evidence on whatever they are studying, be it chemical elements, rays of light, or, here, child behavior. One of the hallmarks of the science of human development is that it is *multidisciplinary;* that is, scientists from many academic disciplines (biology, psychology, sociology, anthropology, economics, and history among them) contribute to our understanding.

Science is especially needed when we study humans because lives depend on the answers. People disagree vehemently about what pregnant women should eat, when babies should cry, how children should be punished, whether teachers should explain sex. Such subjective opinions arise from emotions, culture, and upbringing, not necessarily from evidence. Scientists seek to progress from opinion to truth, from subjective to objective, from wishes to results.

When science concerns development, it leads to practical applications. The first experts on childhood opened schools, advised parents, founded community centers, and legislated to halt child abuse. Some scientists distinguish between basic and applied research, arguing that basic discoveries are valid for their own sake, whether or not applications are forthcoming. However, most developmentalists are eager to apply science to life's problems. As one scientist explains:

> After more than 40 years of concurrent advances in the science of early childhood development, the challenge facing policy makers at the end of the first decade of the 21st century is clear—it is time to leverage new scientific knowledge in the service of generating new intervention strategies.
>
> *[Shonkoff, 2010, p. 361]*

As you surely realize, facts may be twisted and applications may spring from assumptions, not from data. Because the study of development is a science, it is based on *objective* evidence, such as the neuroscience of brain activation, the data on family structure, the specifics of how learning occurs. At the same time, because it concerns human life and growth, it is also laden with *subjective* perceptions, which are open to bias. This interplay of the objective and the subjective, of facts and possibilities, of the universal and the unique makes developmental science challenging, intriguing, and even transformative.

The Scientific Method

To avoid unexamined opinions and to rein in personal biases, researchers follow five steps of the **scientific method:**

1. *Begin with curiosity.* On the basis of **theory** (a comprehensive set of ideas, as explained in Chapter 2), prior research, or a personal observation, pose a question.
2. *Develop a hypothesis.* Shape the question into a **hypothesis,** which is a specific prediction that can be tested.
3. *Test the hypothesis.* Design and conduct research to gather **empirical** (observable, verifiable) evidence (data).
4. *Draw conclusions.* Use the evidence to support or refute the hypothesis.
5. *Report the results.* Share the data, conclusions, and alternative explanations.

science of human development The science that seeks to understand how and why people of all ages and circumstances change or remain the same over time.

scientific method A way to answer questions using empirical research and data-based conclusions.

theory A comprehensive set of ideas.

hypothesis A specific prediction that can be tested.

empirical Based on observation, experience, or experiment; not theoretical.

Verification

Developmentalists begin with curiosity and then seek the facts, drawing conclusions only after careful research. **Replication**—repeating the procedures and methods of a study with different participants—is often a sixth step. Everyone wants to know more about his or her personal issues; that is one reason the study of human life is fascinating. But we need answers that are beyond the personal, valid answers that may or may not confirm our hunches and assumptions. Replication, either exactly or with modifications, can do that.

replication Repeating a study, usually using different participants, perhaps of another age, SES, or culture.

Scientists study the research procedures and reported results of other scientists who are working on the same issues. They read publications, attend conferences, send e-mails, and sometimes move from one nation to another to collaborate. Conclusions are revised, refined, and replicated. Then, especially when the topic is child development, other people analyze and apply the results.

SIDS, an Example

Coverage of every topic in this book is based on research that follows the scientific method. Here we present just one issue, **sudden infant death syndrome (SIDS),** to illustrate the process. Every year until the mid-1990s, tens of thousands of infants died of SIDS, called *crib death* in North America and *cot death* in England. Tiny infants smiled at their caregivers, waved their arms at rattles that their small fingers could not yet grasp, went to sleep seemingly healthy, and never woke up. As parents mourned their dead babies, scientists asked why (*step 1*) and tested hypotheses (the cat? the quilt? natural honey? homicide? spoiled milk?) to no avail: Sudden infant death was a mystery.

sudden infant death syndrome (SIDS) A situation in which a seemingly healthy infant, usually between 2 and 6 months old, suddenly stops breathing and dies unexpectedly while asleep.

A scientist named Susan Beal studied every SIDS death in South Australia for years, noting dozens of circumstances, seeking factors that increased the risk. Some things did not seem to matter (such as birth order) and others seemed to increase the risk (such as maternal smoking and lambskin blankets). A breakthrough came when Beal discovered an ethnic variation: Australian babies of Chinese descent died of SIDS far less often than did Australian babies of European descent. Genetic? Most experts thought so. But Beal's scientific observation led her to note that Chinese babies slept on their backs, contrary to the European or American custom of stomach-sleeping. She developed a new hypothesis (*step 2*): that sleeping position mattered.

To test her hypothesis (*step 3*), Beal convinced a large group of non-Chinese parents to put their newborns to sleep on their backs. Almost none of them died suddenly. After several years of gathering data, she drew a surprising conclusion (*step 4*): Back-sleeping protected against SIDS. Her published reports (*step 5*) (Beal, 1988) caught the attention of doctors in the Netherlands, where pediatricians had told parents to put their babies to sleep on their stomachs. Two Dutch scientists (Engelberts & de Jonge, 1990) recommended back-sleeping; thousands of parents took heed. SIDS was reduced in Holland by 40 percent in one year—a stunning replication (*step 6*).

Replication and application spread. By 1994, a "Back to Sleep" campaign in nation after nation cut the SIDS rate dramatically (Kinney & Thach, 2009; Mitchell, 2009). In the United States, in 1984, SIDS killed 5,245 babies; in 1996, that number was down to 3,050; in the past decade, it has decreased to about 2,000 a year (see Figure 1.1). Such results indicate that, in the United States alone, about 40,000 children and young adults are alive today who would be dead if they had been born before 1990. The campaign has been so successful that physical therapists report

And If I Die Not likely. Death "before I wake" occurred too often in many nations before 1990, but not in Mongolia (shown here) or other Asian countries. The reason, as scientists hypothesized and then confirmed, is that Asian parents put their infants "back to sleep."

Observation Quiz Back-sleeping babies sometimes squirm, making the blankets covering them come loose—another risk factor for SIDS. What detail makes that unlikely here? (see answer, page 6)

SEAN SPRAGUE / THE IMAGE WORKS

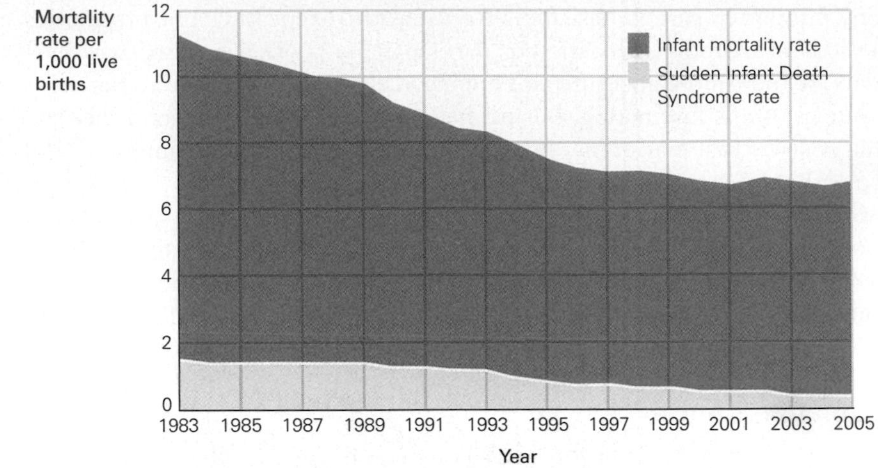

FIGURE 1.1

Rates of SIDS Death The dramatic decrease in SIDS deaths is a direct result of a scientific discovery that babies are more likely to survive if they sleep on their backs. The next challenge is to reduce the other causes of infant mortality. These rates are from the United States—some nations have much lower rates and others much higher. As with SIDS, international comparisons may increase survival.

Observation Quiz About what percent of infant mortality in the United States is the result of SIDS? (see answer, page 8)

that babies now crawl later than they used to; they therefore advocate *tummy time*—putting awake infants on their stomachs to develop their muscles (Zachry & Kitzmann, 2011).

Stomach-sleeping is a proven, replicated risk, but it is not the only one: SIDS still occurs. Currently, the rate is much lower in Canada and Japan than in the United States but higher in New Zealand, for reasons not yet known. Beyond nationality and sleeping position, other risks include low birthweight, a brain-stem abnormality that produces too little of a particular brain chemical (serotonin, a neurotransmitter), cigarette smoking in the household, soft blankets or pillows, and bed-sharing (when infants sleep in their parents' bed) (Duncan et al., 2010; Ostfeld et al., 2010). Most SIDS victims experienced several risks: Virtually never do babies with none of these risks die from SIDS (Ostfeld et al., 2010).

The Nature–Nurture Debate

This example highlights a historic puzzle, often called the *nature–nurture debate.* **Nature** refers to the influence of the genes that people inherit. **Nurture** refers to environmental influences, beginning with the health and diet of the embryo's mother and continuing lifelong, including family, school, culture, and society. For SIDS, nature includes serotonin in the brain and physiological maturation; nurture includes parental smoking and sleeping position.

nature In development, nature refers to the traits, capacities, and limitations that each individual inherits genetically from his or her parents at the moment of conception.

nurture In development, nurture includes all the environmental influences that affect the individual after conception. This includes everything from the mother's nutrition while pregnant to the cultural influences in the nation.

The nature–nurture debate has many other names, among them *heredity–environment, maturation–learning, nativist–empiricist.* Under whatever name, the basic question is: How much of any characteristic, behavior, or emotion results from genes and how much from experience? Note that the question is *How much?* not *Which?* Both genes and the environment affect every characteristic. Nature always affects nurture, and nurture always affects nature.

Indeed, some scientists think that the ongoing interaction between genes and experiences is so varied, explosive, and profound that *How much?* is not a valid question (Gottlieb, 2007; Meaney, 2010; Spencer et al., 2009). It implies proportions, as if each part contributes a share. But babies die of SIDS not because of nature added to nurture or vice versa, but because of multiplying risks: No genetic or environmental factor acts in isolation.

>> Answer to Observation Quiz (from page 5) The swaddling blanket is not only folded under the baby but is also tied in place.

Now consider a more complex example, which further illustrates that not only *How much?* but also *Which?* are the wrong questions regarding nature and nurture.

JEFF GREENBERG / ALAMY

Doing Good Someone threw that garbage onto this beach in south Miami, but these two teen volunteers are cleaning it up. It is easy to trace such good behavior to culture, family, and community, but genes may also play a role. Some people are naturally more caring about other people.

Genetics

Some young people become violent, hurting others as well as themselves. Indeed, if a person is ever going to kill someone, he (or less often, she) is most likely to do so between ages 15 and 25. Researchers in medicine, psychology, and sociology have found many factors that contribute to youth violence, including past child abuse and current circumstances. The violent delinquent is often a boy who was beaten in childhood, troubled in school, living in a drug-filled, crowded neighborhood (Maas et al., 2008).

Yet some such boys never harm anyone. A fourth discipline—genetics—suggests why. One genetic variant occurs in the code for an enzyme (monoamine oxidase A, abbreviated MAOA) that affects several neurotransmitters. This gene comes in two versions, dubbed short and long, producing people with lower or higher levels of that enzyme. Both versions are normal.

A famous developmental study began with virtually every child born in Dunedin, New Zealand, between April 1, 1972, and March 31, 1973. The children and their families were examined on dozens of measures from early childhood on, yielding literally hundreds of published studies based on a wealth of data, including parental practices and variants of the MAOA gene. About one-third of them had the short gene and thus had lower levels of MAOA. Researchers found that boys who were mistreated by their parents were about twice as likely to be overly aggressive (to develop a conduct disorder, to be violent, to be antisocial, and eventually to be convicted of a violent crime) if, *and only if,* they had the gene for low levels of the enzyme instead of the high-MAOA version (Caspi et al., 2002; see Figure 1.2). Some maltreated boys—usually those with high MAOA—nonetheless became model citizens.

Does this mean that becoming violent is inevitable for those with less of that enzyme? No. As Figure 1.2 shows, *if* they were not maltreated, boys with low MAOA were *more* likely than those with high MAOA to become law-abiding, peaceable adults. Such results were surprising at the time, but recently many other scientists have found genes, or circumstances, that work both ways—they predispose people to be either unusually successful or pathological (Belsky et al., 2011; Keri, 2009).

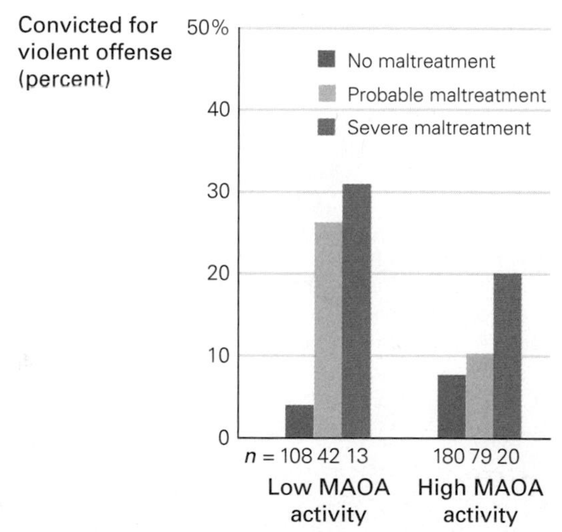

Source: Caspi et al., 2002.

FIGURE 1.2

Genetic Origins for Violent Crime Two variables—parental treatment and a variant of the gene that produces the enzyme MAOA—interact to affect the likelihood that a child will commit a violent crime. Of the boys in the "probable maltreatment" category, 10 percent were convicted of a violent crime if their MAOA level was high, but 26 percent were convicted if their MAOA was low.

Differential Sensitivity

Such differential sensitivity is now recognized, especially among developmentalists: Certain versions of particular genes may make it more likely for people to develop specific problems *or* specific strengths. Replications of the Dunedin study have not always confirmed the direct link between MAOA and violence. However, the general finding that genes can act in opposite ways depending on the environment has been confirmed by many other researchers. The social context—including the pregnant mother's diet, the affection bestowed on the infant, the intellectual stimulation of early childhood, bullying or friendship in middle childhood—affects how genetic codes work. Inherited risk influences later behavior, but the impact varies from one place, age, and background of participants to another.

Now consider a study of a very different population: African American 11-year-olds in rural Georgia, the United States (Brody et al., 2009). In this program, parents and children were randomly divided into two groups: (1) a group that had

>> Answer to Observation Quiz (from page 6) It depends on the decade. About 18 percent from 1983 to 1995, but only about 3 percent in 2005.

no intervention and (2) a group that attended seven seminars designed to increase racial pride, family support, honest communication, and compliance with house rules. (These features are in keeping with replicated research that finds that pride and parental involvement protect against early sex and drug use.) A follow-up study found that some participants had the short version of a particular gene (called 5-HTTLPR); others had only the long version.

That small genetic difference turned out to be critical: Those with the long version developed just as well whether they were in the intervention group or not. However, teenagers with the short version who attended the seminars were less likely to have early sex or to use drugs than were those who also had the short gene but not the family training. More of the latter broke the law. (This study is further explained in Chapter 16.) The interaction of nature and nurture was crucial: The special nurture without the sensitivity nature made no difference.

That often seems true regarding the two versions of this particular gene. The short version is fairly common—almost half of those with European ancestors and as many as three-fourths of those with Asian ancestors may have it—but culture and family affect whether it becomes an asset or a liability (Chiao & Blizinsky, 2010). Considering all the research on aggression, both nature and nurture are pivotal, sometimes in complex interactions (Tremblay, 2011).

Critical and Sensitive Periods

The interaction of nature and nurture brings up another issue: timing. Babies are most likely to die of SIDS about a year after conception, usually from 2 to 4 months after birth, when the breathing reflex undergoes a shift. People are most likely to take dangerous risks during adolescence, thus making early adolescence the best time for parents to set guidelines. Late adolescence is the most likely time for violent death. Immigrants who arrive as children are most likely to identify with their new nation; arrival in late adulthood makes identification less likely (Cheung et al., 2011). These are a few examples of the basic theme of development: Age matters. In fact, there are *critical periods* and *sensitive periods* for particular growth.

The Only Time or the Best Time

critical period A time when a particular type of developmental growth (in body or behavior) must happen for normal development to occur.

A **critical period** is a time when something *must* occur to ensure normal development or the only time when an abnormality might occur. For example, the human embryo grows arms and legs, hands and feet, fingers and toes, each over a specific few days between 28 and 54 days after conception. After that it is too late: Unlike some insects, humans never grow new limbs. Tragically, between 1957 and 1961, thousands of newly pregnant women in 30 nations took *thalidomide,* an antinausea drug. This change in nurture (via the mother) disrupted nature (the genetic program). If an expectant mother ingested thalidomide during that critical period, her baby's limbs were malformed or absent (Moore & Persaud, 2007). Specifics depended on the precise day she swallowed the drug. Surprisingly, if a woman took thalidomide only before day 28 or after day 54, no harm occurred.

sensitive period A time when a certain type of development is most likely, although it may still happen later with more difficulty. For example, early childhood is considered a sensitive period for language learning.

Life has very few such critical periods. Often, however, a particular development occurs more easily—but not exclusively—at a particular time. Such a time is called a **sensitive period.** An example is language. If children do not start speaking their first language between ages 1 and 3, they might do so later (hence the first three years are not a critical period), but their grammar is often impaired (hence, these years are a sensitive period). Similarly, childhood is a sensitive period for learning to pronounce a second or third language.

As is often the case with development, sweeping generalizations (like those in the preceding sentences) do not apply in every case. Accent-free speech *usually*

must be learned before puberty, but some teenagers or adults with exceptional nature and nurture (naturally adept at speech and then immersed in a new language) master a second language flawlessly (Birdsong, 2006; Muñoz & Singleton, 2011).

Childhood and Adulthood

Language is not the only thing that is best learned in childhood. As you will find out, early development is often the foundation for later life. For example, children who are severely malnourished at age 1 are more likely to become overweight and thus develop diabetes or heart disease in middle age. That makes early life a sensitive period for nutrition. Emotional control is best learned before age 6: Without it, adults typically have quick outbursts that they later regret. Early human relationships—with parents in infancy, with friends in school, with romantic partners in adolescence—affect adults' reactions to their children.

All these connections indicate that childhood is a sensitive period. However, **plasticity** is evident as well. Plasticity denotes two complementary aspects of development: Human traits can be molded (as plastic can be), yet people maintain a certain durability of identity (as plastic does). The concept of plasticity in development provides both hope and realism—hope because change is possible over the life span and realism because development builds on what has come before, for better or for worse. Malnourished children need not become diabetic: Nature and nurture may protect them. An adult whose childhood relationships were troubled may nonetheless become a loving, responsive parent. But in both cases, the adult is at increased risk.

plasticity The idea that abilities, personality, and other human characteristics can change over time. Plasticity is particularly evident during childhood, but even older adults are not always "set in their ways."

Plasticity works in the other direction as well: Early potential does not necessarily come to fruition. For instance, a review of children who are extraordinarily gifted (fascinated by numbers at age 3, or fluent readers by age 5, or expert violinists at age 9) found that genes, training, talents, and motivation very early in life affected the child's brain and abilities. However, early giftedness did not necessarily endure: Some child prodigies became ordinary adults, and some children who were not notably talented became so later on (Horowitz et al., 2009).

There is a crucial concept here. As is already evident, our understanding of development often benefits from neuroscience and genetics. Once, misbehavior was thought to be caused by bad parenting; we now believe parenting is only one factor. But currently people sometimes blame a child's behavior exclusively on brain immaturity or destructive genes. The crucial concept is that any human behavior has multiple causes and that plasticity is possible, especially in the early years but also lifelong (Nelson, 2011). That is true for everyone, but it is especially apparent when a baby is born with multiple disabilities, as I know from my nephew David.

A CASE TO STUDY

Plasticity and David

My sister-in-law had rubella (called German measles) early in her third pregnancy, a fact not recognized until David was born, blind and dying. Heart surgery two days after birth saved his life, but surgery at 6 months to remove a cataract destroyed that eye. Malformations of his thumbs, ankles, teeth, feet, spine, and brain became evident. Predictions were dire: Some people wondered why his parents did not place him in an institution. He did not walk or talk for years.

Fortunately, the traditional view of handicapped children was shifting: Specialists were beginning to recognize plasticity. For example, at 9 months David did not crawl because his parents kept him safe in their arms. Then a consultant from the Kentucky School for the Blind put him on a large rug, teaching him to feel the boundaries and crawl safely. At age 2 he did not talk, but an audiologist found that he could hear, and teachers encouraged my brother and his wife to sing to him. At age

2½ he did not chew, but a nutritionist showed his parents how to force him to eat food that was not pureed. In middle childhood, doctors repaired his heart, removed the remaining cataract, realigned his jaw, replaced the dead eye with a glass one, and straightened his spine. Dozens of other professionals also improved his life. David attended three specialized preschools, then a mainstreamed public school, then a special high school, then the University of Louisville—each with educators guided by research that confirmed plasticity.

Remember, plasticity cannot erase genes, childhood experiences, or permanent damage. David's disabilities are always with him. But the interaction of nature and nurture meant that, by age 10, David had skipped a year of school and was a fifth-grader, reading at the eleventh-grade level. He learned German and Russian, with some Spanish and Korean, and he learned how to circumvent his handicaps—for example, swimming to keep his body fit since he could not play basketball (as most Kentucky boys do).

David now works as a translator of German texts, which he enjoys because, as he says, "I like providing a service to scholars, giving them access to something they would otherwise not have." The child whose birth was a reason for despair has become an adult who contributes to his family and his community. My brother and his wife, their two other sons (see the accompanying photo), hundreds of educators and medical professionals, decades of research, new laws, and David's own determination have enabled him to overcome the odds. He still is dependent on others for reminders to wash his hair, for guidance in social situations, and for scheduling doctor's appointments. However, plasticity is possible; David proves that.

GLEN STASSEN

Family Bonds Note the friendly smiles of these three brothers; from left to right, Mike, Bill, and David. No wonder I am proud of my nephews.

SUMMING UP

Human development can be studied in many ways because each person is unique as well as similar to every other human being. The scientific study of development begins with curiosity and then follows a specific sequence, from hypothesis to data collection to conclusions that are based on empirical evidence, not on wishful thinking or prejudice.

Nature and nurture always interact. A critical period is a time when something *must* occur to ensure normal development or the only time when an abnormality might occur. A sensitive period is a time when a specific development can occur most easily. Although many constraints affect development, people alter and transcend their situations, demonstrating plasticity: Change is possible throughout life. ■

>> Including All Kinds of People

The second element of our definition of the science of development—*all kinds of people*—is equally important. Developmentalists study young and old; rich and poor; people of every ethnicity, background, sexual orientation, culture, and nation. To help organize their study, they segment people into discrete age divisions, such as infancy, childhood, adolescence, and adulthood, each with approximate ages (see Table 1.1).

The challenge is to identify both universalities and differences and then to describe them in ways that simultaneously unify humanity and distinguish each individual. The danger is in drawing conclusions based on a limited group or, worse, to consider one's own group normal and every other group abnormal. This is called the **difference-equals-deficit error,** the human tendency to notice differences and then to jump to the conclusion that something important is lacking. In a flash, every

difference-equals-deficit error The mistaken belief that a deviation from some norm is necessarily inferior to behavior or characteristics that meet the standard.

KUTTIG-RF-KIDS / ALAMY

Family Pride Grandpa Charilaos is proud of his tavern in northern Greece (central Macedonia), but he is even more proud of his talented grandchildren, including Maria Soni (shown here). Note her expert fingering. Her father and mother also play instruments—is that nature or nurture?

difference is perceived as a deficit (Gernsbacher, 2010). By studying all kinds of people, of every age and background, developmentalists recognize and try to avoid this danger. Many diversities are differences to be welcomed, not deficits to be remedied.

TABLE 1.1 Age Ranges for Different Stages of Development

Infancy	0 to 2 years
Early childhood	2 to 6 years
Middle childhood	6 to 11 years
Adolescence	11 to 18 years
Emerging adulthood	18 to 25 years
Adulthood	25 to 65 years
Late adulthood	65 years and older

Sex Differences

Consider the differences between males and females. Of course, both sexes are alike in many ways: In modern nations, boys and girls eat the same foods, learn the same lessons, and wear many of the same clothes—unless the culture insists otherwise. Yet humans tend to focus on differences, evident in the popularity over the past two decades of John Gray's book *Men Are from Mars, Women Are from Venus* (1992/2004) and repeated spinoffs, most recently *Venus on Fire, Mars on Ice* (Gray, 2010). Exaggerating human sex differences is a distortion that developmentalists seek to avoid. As Janet Hyde (2007) puts it, people are from neither Mars nor Venus; they are from Earth, where the similarities among the sexes far outweigh the differences.

The importance of accepting differences in sexual development is apparent when considering sexual orientation. Historically, people who were attracted to others of the same sex were considered deficient, and 50 years ago their suicide rate was much higher than the suicide rate of heterosexual people (Herek, 2010). Gay activism, scientific data, and other factors combined to cause a dramatic reversal: In the 1970s, psychiatrists and psychologists declared, "Homosexuality per se implies no impairment in judgment, stability, reliability" (Conger, 1975, p. 633). The gay suicide rate has plummeted, more in some nations than others.

Culture, Ethnicity, and Race

Confusion about diversity often results when anyone—scientist or nonscientist—refers to *cultures, ethnic groups,* or *races.* These terms are **social constructions,** which means they are terms constructed, or made, by a society. Social constructions can be powerful, affecting how people think, but since they arise from society, they can be changed by society.

When the terms *culture, ethnicity,* and *race* are misused, they lead to the difference-equals-deficit error. The following definitions may help us avoid that mistake.

social construction An idea that is built on shared perceptions, not on objective reality. Many age-related terms (such as *childhood, adolescence, yuppie,* and *senior citizen*) are social constructions, connected to biological traits but strongly influenced by social assumptions.

A System of Shared Beliefs

culture A system of shared beliefs, norms, behaviors, and expectations that persist over time and prescribe social behavior and assumptions.

For social scientists, **culture** is "the system of shared beliefs, conventions, norms, behaviors, expectations and symbolic representations that persist over time and prescribe social rules of conduct" (Bornstein et al., 2011, p. 30). Culture is far more than food or ritual; it is a powerful social construction.

Each family, community, and college has a particular culture, and these cultures may clash. For example, decades ago my friend from a small rural town arrived for her first college class wearing her Sunday best: a freshly pressed skirt and blouse with a matching striped jacket. She looked around, embarrassed, and went directly to a used-clothing store to buy jeans and a T-shirt.

Often people use the word *culture* to refer to large groups of other people, as in "Asian culture" or "Hispanic culture." That invites prejudice, since within large groups are many cultures. For instance, people from Korea and Japan are aware of notable differences between them, as are people from Mexico and Guatemala. Furthermore, individuals within those cultures sometimes rebel against their culture's expected "beliefs, conventions, norms, behaviors." It is a short step from generalizations about cultures to the difference-equals-deficit error: Culture needs to be understood in all its fluidity and variations.

JUPITER IMAGES

What's for Dinner? Markets are universal, but each culture has a unique mix of products, stores, and salespeople. Compare this floating food market in Bangkok, Thailand, with a North American supermarket.

Book Reading: An Example

Cross-cultural research uncovers shared behaviors that people are unaware of. One example is reading books to toddlers, a behavior that advances language development. Indeed, a European American criticism of Mexican Americans is that parents rarely read to their children. This criticism may reflect the difference-equals-deficit error, since cross-cultural research finds that many Mexican American families use other ways to foster literacy (Hammer et al., 2011).

Even when parents read to toddlers, they do not necessarily convey the same messages. Scientists designed a picture book (no words) and asked middle-class parents from different nations to look at it with their 20-month-olds. Everything said was recorded and analyzed (see the Research Design).

▶ Research Design

Scientists: Cheri C. Y. Chan, Amanda C. Brandone, and Twila Tardif.

Publication: *Journal of Cross-Cultural Psychology* (2009).

Participants: A total of 49 mother–toddler pairs, 25 of them from a city in the United States and 24 of them from Beijing, China. The two groups were comparable in age and education.

Design: Each pair was brought into a playroom and recorded in three 10-minute play sessions (1) with mechanical toys, (2) with regular toys, and (3) looking at the same picture book. (To equalize both groups, the book was created for this study by laminating an equal number of pages from books used in the United States and China.)

Major conclusion: Some universals were evident. For example, all the mothers were influenced by context—using more verbs when the toys were mechanical, for instance. Differences also emerged. The U.S. mothers gave fewer commands, such as "sit down" and "listen," and allowed children to express more irrelevant comments. During the joint book reading, Chinese mothers used more verbs than nouns (about 20 percent more), but U.S. mothers used more nouns than verbs.

Comment: This study shows cultural similarities as well as differences. All mothers encourage their children to play and talk. Yet prior research had shown that U.S. children learn object names more rapidly than children elsewhere and that Chinese culture encourages people to see themselves in active relationship to others rather than as isolated individuals. Many Asians tend to perceive objects and experiences in context rather than detached from their uses and surroundings. Might these cultural differences be reflected when mothers explain pictures to toddlers?

A notable cultural difference surfaced. The U.S. mothers used more nouns than verbs; the opposite was true for the Chinese. For example, in a picture of a dandelion, some U.S. mothers pointed out the petals, leaves, and stem, and added colors, as the "yellow flower" and "green leaves." In contrast, the Chinese mothers stressed actions: A dandelion could be picked or smelled, and since this particular dandelion was in a book, the child would need to go outside to pick one (Chan et al., 2009).

It is tempting to see that difference as a deficit. Indeed, the initial data from this study were reanalyzed because some researchers assumed the Chinese mothers were too strict and hypothesized that their frequent verbs were often commands ("sit down," "pay attention"). A detailed reanalysis, excluding all words not relevant to book reading, revealed otherwise. The difference was not a deficit; all the parents were teaching vocabulary and attitudes related to their cultures.

WANG JIANKAG / IMAGINE CHINA

Not the Same At first glance, this seems a standard scene; educated mothers the world over often read books to their toddlers. A closer look reveals differences—in the billboard, in hairstyles, in the mother's ring. However, the pivotal cultural variation cannot be seen: her words and his focus (see text).

Ethnic and Racial Groups

People of an **ethnic group** share certain attributes, almost always including ancestral heritage and usually national origin, religion, and language (Whitfield & McClearn, 2005). Ethnic group is not the same as cultural group: Some people of a particular ethnicity may not share a culture (consider people of Irish descent in Ireland and in North America), and some cultures are widespread, including people of several ethnic groups (consider British culture).

ethnic group People whose ancestors were born in the same region and who often share a language, culture, and religion.

Ethnicity is a social construction, affected by the social context. For everyone, ethnic identity is strengthened if (1) other members of the same group are nearby, and (2) other groups exclude the person. For example, African-born people who are longtime residents of North America typically consider themselves African, but African-born people living on that continent identify with a more specific ethnic group. Similar identities are evident for everyone: Ethnic identity becomes more specific and more salient (Sicilian, not just Italian; South Korean, not just East Asian) when others of the same ethnic group are nearby and when members of other groups focus on differences.

The term **race** has been used to categorize people on the basis of physical differences, particularly outward appearance. However, appearance is not a reliable indicator of biology, genetics, or development (Race, Ethnicity, and Genetics Working Group of the National Human Genome Research Institute, 2005). Skin color (often used as a racial marker) is particularly misleading, since dark-skinned people with ancestors from Africa have "high levels of genetic population diversity" (Tishkoff et al., 2009, p. 1035). And dark-skinned people whose ancestors were not African are typically distinct from Africans in genes as well as culture.

race A group of people who are regarded by themselves or by others as distinct from other groups on the basis of physical appearance, typically skin color. Social scientists think race is a misleading concept, as biological differences are not signified by outward appearance.

Social scientists reject the concept that race is genetic. As one team of psychologists explains: "Race is a social construction wherein individuals [who are] labeled as being of different races on the basis of physical characteristics are often treated as though they belong to biologically defined groups" (Goldston et al., 2008, p. 14). Unlike genetic differences, social constructions can disappear within a few decades: This has occurred with race (Rothenberg, 2010). For instance, Greek and Italian Americans were considered Black in the nineteenth century and White in the twentieth (Jacobson, 1998).

Socioeconomic Status

Another difference between one person and another relates to **socioeconomic status,** abbreviated **SES,** sometimes called *social class* (as in *middle class* or *working class*). SES reflects family income, but not income alone. The education and

socioeconomic status (SES) A person's position in society as determined by income, occupation, education, and place of residence. (Sometimes called *social class.*)

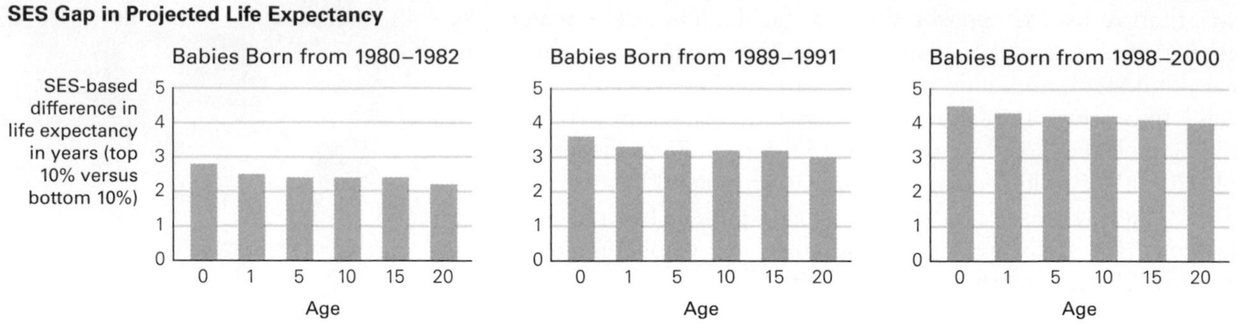

Source: Singh & Siahpush, 2006.

FIGURE 1.3

Everyone Lives Longer, But . . . The advances of medical science and public health have added years to life for everyone, no matter what their SES (not shown). However, for those in the top 10 percent and the bottom 10 percent, the gap between years of life expected has increased in the United States. As this graph shows, the most advantaged baby born in 2000 is expected to live 4½ years longer than the least advantaged (about 80 years compared to 75). Economic equality is not keeping pace with health improvements.

occupation of the head of the household, or of both parents, and sometimes the average education or income of the other residents of the neighborhood, are also used to determine SES.

SES affects every aspect of development, even life itself (see Figure 1.3). Social scientists have many theories as to why SES is so influential, some of which are explored later in the text. Not surprisingly, those trained as economists and sociologists tend to emphasize SES differences more than those trained in neuroscience or psychology. However, all developmentalists appreciate that SES impacts each person's life, perhaps even more in the early years than the later ones.

Finding the Balance

As already noted on page 0, the science of human development attempts to find the right balance between the universal and the particular. All humans are the same, yet each individual is unique. Sex, culture, ethnicity, and SES make that abundantly clear. Is that a paradox, a dilemma, or a fascinating challenge?

Be forewarned: Some data from many sources (e.g., the 2010 U.S. Census, United Nations reports, research studies) group people in categories that might be considered races, such as by African, European, Hispanic, and Asian ancestry. Other data distinguish people by gender, sexual orientation, national origin, and SES. Such social constructions are sometimes important to the scientist, the community, and the individual. This is not a criticism: Differences among people need to be noted so that "all kinds of people" are studied, thereby avoiding the assumption that everyone develops in the same way. This point was forcefully made by a leading developmentalist:

> Psychologists and psychiatrists are fond of writing sentences such as "individuals with the short allele of the serotonin transporter [the 5-HTTLPR mentioned earlier] are vulnerable to depression if they experience past stressors." . . . I suggest that they should more often write sentences such as "women with a European pedigree possessing the short allele of the serotonin transporter who live in a large city far from their family, and grew up as a later born child in an economically disadvantaged family are at risk for depression."
>
> *[Kagan, 2011, p. 111]*

Kagan's suggestion is meant to be an exaggeration: The right balance between generalizations and specifics is not obvious, but developmental conclusions should not be "contextually naked," as Kagan explains (2011, p. 112). We must guard against simple conclusions, across groups or within them. A child of one group may develop unlike another child of another group or of that same group. Such differences are not necessarily deficits; all these categories are social constructions, not enduring divides. This leads to the third aspect of our definition, *change over time.*

SUMMING UP

Developing persons of every age, culture, and background teach us what is universal and what is unique. Differences among people are not necessarily deficits, although some people mistakenly assume that their own path is best for everyone. Ethnicity, race, and socioeconomic status all impact development, with much variation and overlap. ■

>> Observing Changes over Time

Individuals, cultures, and societies *change over time.* Continuity and discontinuity, consistencies and transformations, sudden eruptions and gradual shifts—these are the focus of developmental science. Developmental study would be easier if people grew gradually, at the same pace every year (called *linear growth*), or at least if growth occurred in distinct stages, like steps. Traditionally, developmentalists debated which of those two patterns—continuity or discontinuity—was more accurate. But there are far more patterns of growth than these two (see Figure 1.4).

No matter what the pattern, for developmentalists age is always significant. Is it normal for a boy to throw himself down, kicking and screaming, when he is frustrated? Yes, if he is 2 years old; no, if he is 12. Is it normal for a girl to be interested in boys? Yes, at age 16; no, at age 6. More broadly, children think, play, and learn differently depending partly on their age: Specific patterns and norms at each age are the backbone of developmental science and are significant for anyone who works with children.

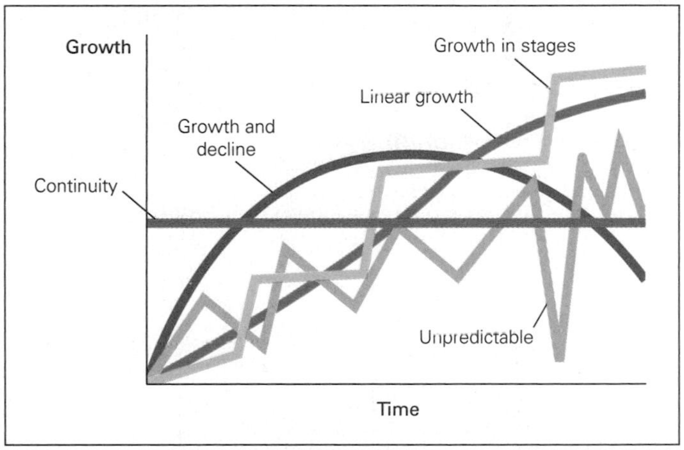

FIGURE 1.4

Patterns of Developmental Growth Many patterns of developmental growth have been discovered by careful research. Although linear (or nonlinear) progress seems most common, scientists now find that almost no aspect of human change follows the linear pattern exactly.

Dynamic Systems

Every aspect of development repeatedly interacts with every other; every person interacts with other people; all conditions and experiences interact continuously over time; each developmental change in a person affects every other aspect of that person as well as everyone else in that person's family, community, and beyond.

Consequently, scientists now envision development as the result of **dynamic systems.** The word *systems* captures the idea that a change in one aspect of a person, family, or society affects all the other aspects because each part is connected to all the other parts (Thelen & Smith, 2006) (see Figure 1.5). The body itself is a system, made up of many other systems (cardiovascular, respiratory, reproductive, and so on); a family is a system; so are neighborhoods, cities, nations, the world. Each small aspect of each person is connected to many systems within that person and affects many other people, and thus many other systems, as time goes on. To pick a simple example, a first birth turns a woman into a mother and a man into a father, a dramatic transformation of the individuals and of the family system that contributes to many other changes—in habits, goals, sleep, sibling rivalry, neighborhood interactions, national birth rates, and so on.

dynamic systems A view of human development as an ongoing, ever-changing interaction between the physical, cognitive, and psychosocial influences. The crucial understanding is that development is never static but is always affected by, and affects, many systems of development.

As explained by Esther Thelen (one of the leaders of the dynamic-systems perspective) in the *Handbook of Child Psychology,* "the application of dynamic systems to developmental processes is relatively new" (Thelen & Smith, 2006, p. 258) for social scientists but not for natural scientists. For decades, natural scientists have studied how

> . . . seasons change in ordered measure, clouds assemble and disperse, trees grow to certain shape and size, snowflakes form and melt, minute plants and animals pass through elaborate life cycles that are invisible to us, and social groups come together and disband.
>
> *[Thelen & Smith, 2006, p. 271]*

Given the way the natural world changes over time, it should not be surprising that human growth follows diverse patterns and paces. The assumptions that growth is linear and that progress is inevitable have been replaced by the idea that both continuity and discontinuity are part of every life, that gains and losses are apparent at every age, that changes proceed in many ways (see Figure 1.5).

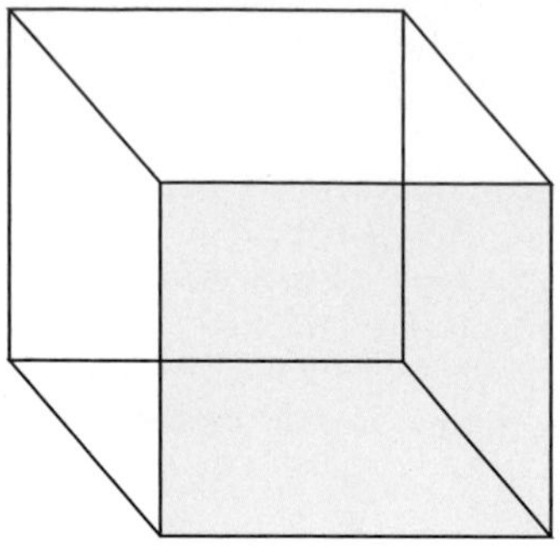

FIGURE 1.5

Dynamic Systems, Simplified Would it still be a box without one of the twelve lines? Which is the front, the top, or the bottom? And if someone flipped it around, would it be the same or not? Hopefully this simple example helps you grasp the complications of dynamic systems—every aspect of development is connected to every other, and the result might change at any moment.

Although the dynamic-systems approach is "relatively new" to the science of development, similar approaches were evident earlier. One of the most famous and forceful developmentalists of the later twentieth century was Urie Bronfenbrenner, who recommended an **ecological-systems approach** to developmental study (1977). He argued that developmentalists must consider all the systems that surround each person, just as a naturalist examines the ecology of each organism, considering the interrelationships between it and its environment. Toward the end of his life, Bronfenbrenner renamed his theory *bioecological* to ensure that the name reflected the natural settings and biological processes that the theory includes (Bronfenbrenner & Morris, 2006).

ecological-systems approach A perspective on human development that considers all the influences from the various contexts of development. (Later renamed *bioecological theory.*)

Bronfenbrenner described three nested levels that affect each person (diagrammed in Figure 1.6): *microsystems* (elements of the immediate surroundings, such as the family system), *exosystems* (local institutions such as school and workplace), and *macrosystems* (the larger contexts, including cultural values, economic

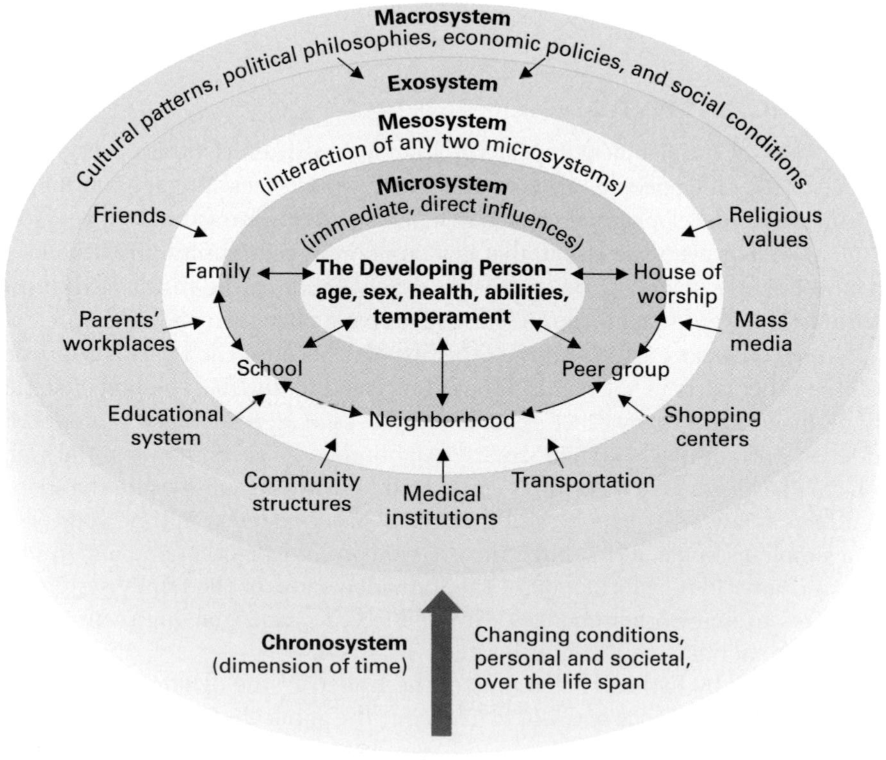

FIGURE 1.6

The Ecological Model According to developmental researcher Urie Bronfenbrenner, each person is significantly affected by interactions among a number of overlapping systems, which provide the context of development. *Microsystems*—family, peer groups, classroom, neighborhood, house of worship—intimately and immediately shape human development. Surrounding and supporting the microsystems are the *exosystems,* which include all the external networks, such as community structures and local educational, medical, employment, and communications systems, that influence the microsystems. Influencing both of these systems is the *macrosystem,* which includes cultural patterns, political philosophies, economic policies, and social conditions. *Mesosystems* refer to interactions among systems, as when parents and teachers coordinate to educate a child. Bronfenbrenner eventually added a fifth system, the *chronosystem,* to emphasize the importance of historical time.

AP PHOTO / JIM MOORE

Dynamic Interaction A dynamic-systems approach highlights the ever-changing impact that each part of a system has on all the other parts. This classroom scene reflects the eagerness for education felt by many immigrants, the reticence of some boys in an academic context, and a global perspective (as demonstrated by the world map). These facets emerge from various systems—family, gender, and culture—and they have interacted to produce this moment.

Observation Quiz What country is this? (see answer, page 20)

policies, and political processes). To reflect the dynamic interaction among the microsystem, exosystem, and macrosystem, Bronfenbrenner named a fourth system, the *mesosystem,* which encompasses the connections between the other systems.

One example of a mesosystem is the interface between school and family. Some elements of this mesosystem, such as parent–teacher conferences, are obvious. Others, such as promotion standards, curriculum choices, or school schedules that still assume one parent is home at 3 P.M., originate in the macrosystem, as nations recognize the connection between education of the population and economic growth.

Especially for Future Teachers Does the classroom furniture shown in the photograph above affect instruction? (see response, page 21)

The Historical Context

Change over time occurs not only within each person but also in families, communities, nations, and the entire world. Recognizing this, Bronfenbrenner coined the term *chronosystem* (literally, "time system"). Many other developmentalists also emphasize the historical context, for good reason. Children who are 10 years old today have thoughts and experiences—with technology, climate change, globalization, AIDS, school curriculum, and many other phenomena—unlike those their grandparents experienced at age 10. Their bodies differ as well (see Figure 1.7).

All persons born within a few years of one another are said to be of the same **cohort,** a group who travel through life together, experiencing similar circumstances. Members of each cohort are affected by the values, events, technologies, and culture of their era. For instance, young children in developed

cohort People born within the same historical period who therefore move through life together, experiencing the same events, new technologies, and cultural shifts at the same ages. For example, the effect of the Internet varies depending on what cohort a person belongs to.

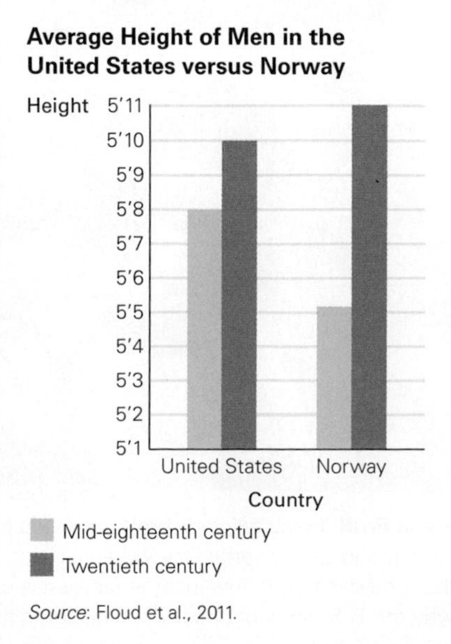

FIGURE 1.7

Systems and Cascades A change in any one part of a system affects all the other systems over time. Machines that made farming more efficient beginning in the eighteenth century improved the nutrition of pregnant women and added height, health, and decades of life to the average adult. This chart shows height specifics for two nations, but similar data are found in every nation that has longitudinal records. Another result is that the average human life span has more than doubled since 1800. Yet another is the population explosion of the twentieth century, which has led to dramatic reductions in average family size in the twenty-first century. So if you wish you had brothers and sisters, don't blame your parents, blame the tractor.

VINCE DEWITT / STOCK, BOSTON

Not the Typical Path This woman's lifelong ambition is to walk the 2,160-mile Appalachian Trail from Maine to Georgia. She is considerably more active than the average member of her cohort.

WILLIAM HAEFELI / THE NEW YORKER COLLECTION / WWW.CARTOONBANK.COM

"Hey! Elbows off the table."

Twenty-First-Century Manners If he obeyed his father but kept texting, would Emily Post be pleased?

nations in the twenty-first century almost always attend an early-childhood-education program, where they increase their vocabulary and make friends of their own age, often friends from other ethnic groups. This was not true for the cohort born 50 years ago, and this one historical change affects the intellect, motivation, and values of the current generation in ways older generations never imagined.

If you doubt that national trends and events touch individuals, consider your first name—a word chosen especially for you. Look at Table 1.2, which lists the most popular names for boys and girls born into cohorts 25 years apart, beginning in 1910. Your name and your reaction to it are influenced by the era. Research has found that, in the United States, names are influenced by when a person's birth state entered the union: Controlling for ethnic background, babies born in the "frontier" states of the Pacific Northwest or in "mountain" states (Montana, Oregon, Nebraska, and so on) are less likely to be given popular names than babies born in the original 13 states (Varnum & Kitayama, 2011).

A more general example of historical change is evident in the economy. Changes in SES are common and significant for child development. This is true for each child born into the same family. Typically, over the life of a family, income rises and falls, education and job status change (especially for children born to teenage parents), employment begins or ends, and families move from one neighborhood to another. Having many children reduces the resources for each child; moving into or out of a two-parent family structure changes SES as well. For many reasons, the SES of a first-born child may be quite different from that of a child born to the same parents 20 years later (Conley & Glauber, 2008).

Economic changes in an entire society also affect the development of the people within that society. For example, the global economic crisis that began around 2007 has meant fewer babies born, more children in each school classroom, later marriages, and much more. Each of these affects human development in ways detailed later in this book.

AP PHOTO / MAIL TRIBUNE, BOB PENNELL

Fresh Fruit Many religious groups provide food for low-income families. Lisa Arsa is fortunate to have found this Seventh Day Adventist food pantry for herself and her son, Isaac. Unfortunately, the food donated to low-income families is usually high in salt, sugar, and fat—among the reasons why the U.S. rates of obesity and diabetes rise as income falls.

TABLE 1.2 Which First Names for U.S. Girls and Boys Were Most Popular in 1910, 1935, 1960, 1985, and 2010?

Year	Top Five Girls' Names	Top Five Boys' Names
______	Mary, Susan, Linda, Karen, Donna	David, Michael, James, John, Robert
______	Mary, Helen, Margaret, Dorothy, Ruth	John, James, William, Robert, George
______	Isabella, Sophia, Emma, Olivia, Ava	Jacob, Ethan, Michael, Jayden, William
______	Mary, Shirley, Barbara, Betty, Patricia	Robert, James, John, William, Richard
______	Jessica, Ashley, Jennifer, Amanda, Sarah	Michael, Christopher, Matthew, Joshua, Daniel

Source: Social Security Administration Web site (http://www.ssa.gov/OACT/babynames), retrieved May 16, 2011.

Guess First If your answers, in order from top to bottom were 1960, 1910, 2010, 1935, and 1985, you are excellent at detecting cohort influences. If you made a mistake, perhaps that's because the data are compiled from applications for Social Security numbers, so the names of those who did not get a Social Security number are omitted.

The Three Domains

Obviously, it is impossible to simultaneously examine all the dynamic changes that occur over the years. Instead, scientists study one aspect of development at a time and then combine many aspects to describe a person. Developmentalists often segment their study into three domains—*biosocial, cognitive,* and *psychosocial.* (Figure 1.8 describes each domain.) Each domain includes several academic disciplines: biosocial includes biology and medicine, cognitive includes psychology and education, and psychosocial includes sociology and anthropology. The two newest disciplines, neuroscience and genetics, contribute to every domain.

Every aspect of growth touches on all three domains. This dynamic reality is expressed with a single word, **biopsychosocial,** a term that expresses the interaction of domains. Biopsychosocial does not imply that biological changes precede the other changes—sometimes the opposite sequence seems more accurate

biopsychosocial A term emphasizing the interaction of the three developmental domains (biosocial, cognitive, and psychosocial). All development is biopsychosocial, although the domains are studied separately.

FIGURE 1.8

The Three Domains The division of human development into three domains makes it easier to study, but remember that very few factors belong exclusively to one domain or another. Development is not piecemeal but holistic: Each aspect of development is related to all three domains.

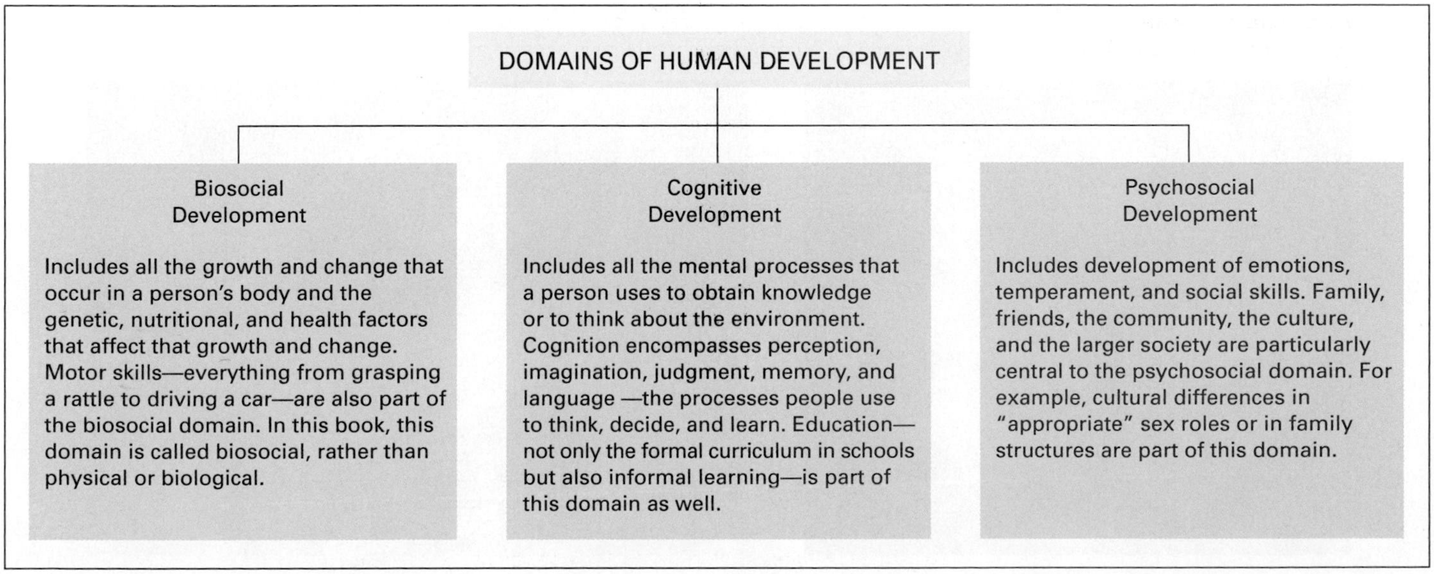
DOMAINS OF HUMAN DEVELOPMENT
Biosocial Development
Includes all the growth and change that occur in a person's body and the genetic, nutritional, and health factors that affect that growth and change. Motor skills—everything from grasping a rattle to driving a car—are also part of the biosocial domain. In this book, this domain is called biosocial, rather than physical or biological.
Cognitive Development
Includes all the mental processes that a person uses to obtain knowledge or to think about the environment. Cognition encompasses perception, imagination, judgment, memory, and language —the processes people use to think, decide, and learn. Education—not only the formal curriculum in schools but also informal learning—is part of this domain as well.
Psychosocial Development
Includes development of emotions, temperament, and social skills. Family, friends, the community, the culture, and the larger society are particularly central to the psychosocial domain. For example, cultural differences in "appropriate" sex roles or in family structures are part of this domain.

>> Answer to Observation Quiz (from page 17) The three Somali girls wearing headscarves may have thrown you off, but these first-graders attend school in Minneapolis, Minnesota, in the United States. Clues include the children's diversity (this school has students from 17 nations), clothing (obviously Western), and—for the sharp-eyed—the flag near the door.

(Cohen, 2010). For example, although babies start speaking because of maturation of the brain and vocal cords (*biosocial*), which allows them to express connections between objects and words (*cognitive*), such developments would not lead to speech unless people talked to the baby (*psychosocial*). In other words, the biology must precede the speech, but if the baby didn't hear speech, brain maturation would not occur. This is literally true: If profoundly deaf infants begin hearing years after the language-learning time, they never talk normally because some brain areas never developed (Buckley & Tobey, 2011).

You can see the quagmire here: Words and pages follow in linear succession and the mind thinks one thought at a time, making it impossible to consider ongoing development in all domains simultaneously. Yet because changes in everything and everybody are connected as time goes on, developmental discoveries from one line of research have the potential to raise questions among scholars in every other discipline. One example comes from **mirror neurons**—the term for parts of the brain that react to actions people see as if the people were actually performing the actions themselves—as explained in the following.

mirror neurons Cells in an observer's brain that are activated by watching an action performed by someone else as they would be if the observer had personally performed that action.

A VIEW FROM SCIENCE

Mirror Neurons

About two decades ago, scientists were surprised to discover that a particular region of a macaque monkey's brain responded to actions the monkey had merely observed as if the monkey had actually performed those actions itself (Gallese et al., 1996). For example, when one macaque saw another reach for a banana, the same brain areas were activated (lit up in brain scans) in both monkeys. Certain neurons, dubbed *mirror neurons,* in the F5 area of the observing macaque's premotor cortex, responded to what was observed. Using increasingly advanced technology, neuroscientists now are finding mirror neurons in several parts of the human brain (Keysers & Gazzola, 2010). Neurons fire in the same action sequences in both actor and observer, as is evident from studies in which ballerinas watch a ballet or soccer players watch another team's game.

Human brains mirror much more than reaching for bananas or scoring a goal. Indeed, the "human mirror neuron system may allow us to go beyond imitating the observed motor acts of others to infer their intentions and perhaps even their states of mind"

Lighting Up In the photograph at left, the arrow points to a web of neurons that are activated not only when a monkey uses motor abilities (as in reaching for a banana) but also when the monkey sees another monkey perform that action. At right, these toddlers in Buenos Aires may be exhibiting mirror neurons at work as they get ready to join other fans in cheering on Argentina's soccer team in a match against Peru.

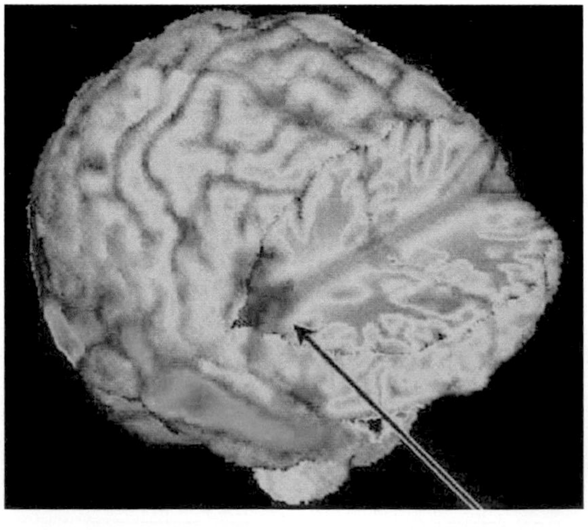

NATACHIA PISARENKO / AP

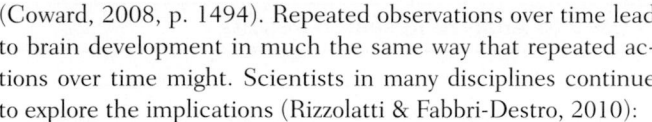

(Coward, 2008, p. 1494). Repeated observations over time lead to brain development in much the same way that repeated actions over time might. Scientists in many disciplines continue to explore the implications (Rizzolatti & Fabbri-Destro, 2010):

- Anthropologists hypothesize that mirror neurons might explain cultural transmission and social organization (Losin et al., 2009).
- Psychopathologists describes autism as a "broken mirror" (Marsh & Hamilton, 2011).
- Psychiatrists believe that abnormalities in the mirroring function of the brain may trigger the symptoms of schizophrenia (Buccino & Amore, 2008).
- Linguists believe mirror neurons aid language learning (Corballis, 2010; Rossi et al., 2011).
- Cognitive psychologists suggest that mirror neurons explain newborns' ability to imitate what they see, learning from observation (Diamond & Amso, 2008).
- Social psychologists think mirror neurons help people empathize with one another (Decety, 2011; Iacoboni, 2009).

Although scientists are excited by these multidisciplinary possibilities, they are cautious as well. Research on human brains is notoriously difficult. Neural networks are complex; mirror neurons certainly do not explain all of human learning, or social responsiveness (Plotkin, 2011; Wheatley et al., 2007). Yet because developmental research is multidisciplinary, thousands of scientists studying childhood are pursuing implications and applications suggested by an unexpected discovery in a monkey brain.

Especially for Parents Who Want Their Children to Enjoy Sports While your baby is still too young and uncoordinated to play any sports, what does the research on mirror neurons suggest you might do? (see response, page 22)

SUMMING UP

A dynamic-systems approach finds continuity as well as discontinuity, erratic change as well as linear progress, gains as well as losses throughout life. Developmentalists are interested in learning about the factors that influence a person's biosocial, cognitive, and psychosocial development. Urie Bronfenbrenner's bioecological approach notes that each person is situated within larger systems of family, school, community, and culture. Cohort, culture, and socioeconomic status affect each person's development, and biological factors are always influential. One example is in mirror neurons, which amplify human learning and development. Infants, children, and adults watch what other people do and, neurologically, experience it themselves.

>> Response for Future Teachers (from page 17) Yes. Every aspect of the ecological context affects what happens. In this classroom, tables and movable chairs foster group collaboration and conversation—potent learning methods that are difficult to achieve when desks and seats are bolted to the floor and the teacher sits behind a large desk.

>> Using the Scientific Method

Now we focus on the crux of the scientific method: designing research and analyzing evidence. Statistical measures often help scientists discover relationships between various aspects of the data they collect. (Some statistical perspectives are presented in Table 1.3.) Every research design, method, and statistical measure has strengths as well as weaknesses. You will notice that every chapter in this text includes a Research Design that explains the details of a particular study to help you see the variations and shortcomings that, when properly understood, add to our understanding of development. Now we describe three basic types of research designs—observation, the experiment, and the survey—and in the next section explore three ways developmentalists learn more about change over time.

Observation

We are all observers. Developmentalists have made observation a science, finding many ways to limit subjectivity so that conclusions are based on data, not assumptions. **Scientific observation** requires researchers to record behavior systematically and objectively, using behavioral definitions (noting instances of hitting, for instance, not instances of aggression) and timed data (e.g., what happens every 10 seconds, not just what captures attention). Observations often occur in a naturalistic setting (such as a home, school, or public park), where people behave as

scientific observation A method of testing a hypothesis by unobtrusively watching and recording participants' behavior in a systematic and objective manner—in a natural setting, in a laboratory, or in searches of archival data.

TABLE 1.3 Statistical Measures Often Used to Analyze Research Results

Measure	Use
Effect size	Indicates how much one variable affects another. Effect size ranges from 0 to 1: An effect size of 0.2 is called small, 0.5 moderate, and 0.8 large.
Significance	Indicates whether the results might have occurred by chance. A finding that chance would produce the results fewer than 5 times in 100 is significant at the 0.05 level. A finding that chance would produce the results once in 100 times is significant at 0.01; once in 1,000 times is significant at 0.001.
Cost-benefit analysis	Calculates how much a particular independent variable costs versus how much it saves. This is particularly useful to analyze public spending. For instance, one cost-benefit analysis showed that an expensive preschool program cost $15,166 per child but saved $215,000 by age 40, in reduced costs of special education, unemployment, prison, and so on (Belfield et al., 2006).
Odds ratio	Indicates how a particular variable compares to a standard, set at 1. For example, one study found that, although less than 1 percent of all child homicides occurred at school, the odds were similar for public and private schools. The odds of such deaths occurring in high schools, however, were 18.47 times that of elementary or middle schools (set at 1.0) (MMWR, January 18, 2008).
Factor analysis	Hundreds of variables could affect any given behavior. In addition, many variables (such as family income and parental education) may overlap. To take this into account, analysis reveals variables that can be clustered together to form a factor, which is a composite of many variables. For example, SES might become one factor, child personality another.
Meta-analysis	A "study of studies." Researchers use statistical tools to synthesize the results of previous, separate studies. Then they analyze the accumulated results, using criteria that weight each study fairly. This approach improves data analysis by combining the results of studies that used so few participants that the conclusions did not reach significance.

Who Participates? For all these measures, the characteristics of the people who participate in the study (formerly called the subjects, now called the participants) are important, as is the number of people who are studied.

they usually do and ideally where the observer can be ignored or even go unnoticed. Scientific observation can also occur in a laboratory, where scientists record human reactions in various situations, often with wall-mounted video cameras and the scientist in another room.

Observation is the mainstay of anthropologists, who live within a community while they take meticulous notes on its culture. Historians use observation when they pore over old records to gain insight, and many social scientists analyze data collected for some other reason, such as census data. Nonetheless, even with careful training, controlled timing, and the motivation to be objective, observation is limited: It cannot prove what *causes* human behavior.

Remember Beal's observations of Australian infants? She developed an important hypothesis, based on hundreds of detailed observations, but she needed more than observational data. Every observation has several plausible explanations. For SIDS, among the observed differences between Chinese and Australian infants were prenatal care, maternal diet, breast-feeding, facial features, baby blanket fabrics, and more. Proof was needed to support Beal's hypothesis that the crucial difference was sleeping position.

>> Response for Parents Who Want Their Children to Enjoy Sports (from page 21) The results of mirror-neuron research imply that people of all ages learn by observing body movements in others. This suggests that such parents should make sure their baby gets many chances to watch them (or someone else) throwing balls, running, and playing sports.

The Experiment

The experiment is the research method that scientists use to establish cause. In the social sciences, experimenters typically give people a particular treatment or expose them to a specific condition and then note whether their behavior changes.

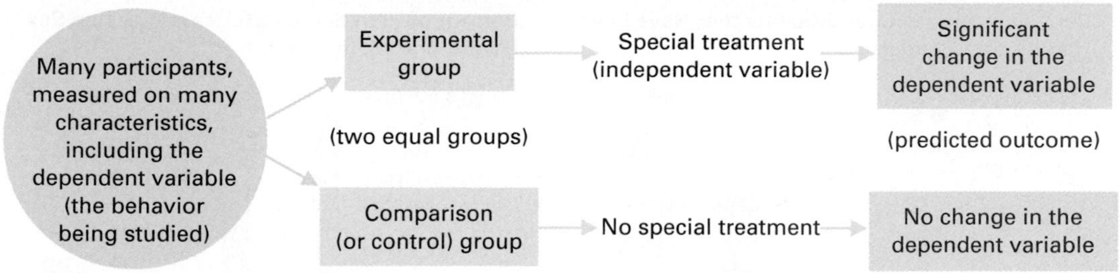

Procedure:

1. Divide participants into two groups that are matched on important characteristics, especially the behavior that is the dependent variable on which this study is focused.
2. Give special treatment, or intervention (the independent variable), to one group (the experimental group).
3. Compare the groups on the dependent variable. If they now differ, the cause of the difference was probably the independent variable.
4. Publish the results.

FIGURE 1.9

How to Conduct an Experiment The basic sequence diagrammed here applies to all experiments. Many additional features, especially the statistical measures listed in Table 1.3 and various ways of reducing experimenter bias, affect whether publication occurs. (Scientific journals reject reports of experiments that were not rigorous in method and analysis.)

In technical terms, experimenters manipulate an **independent variable,** which is the imposed treatment or special condition (also called the *experimental variable*). This independent variable may affect whatever they are studying, called the **dependent variable** (which *depends* on the independent variable). Thus, the independent variable is the new, special treatment; any change in the dependent variable is the result. If the experiment is carefully done, the researcher can conclude that the independent variable caused whatever changes occurred in the dependent variable. Beal convinced thousands of non-Chinese parents to put their babies to sleep on their backs (the independent variable) and then tallied infant deaths (the dependent variable).

The purpose of an experiment is to find out whether an independent variable affects the dependent variable. Usually, if an experiment is well designed (see Figure 1.9), at least two groups of participants are studied, with both groups similar in background characteristics (same ages, gender proportions, ethnic backgrounds, and so on). Typically, one group is designated to be the *experimental group,* which gets the particular treatment (the independent variable). The other group is the *comparison group* (also called a *control group*), which does not. The dependent variable in both groups is measured after the experiment, to make sure the independent variable (and not some other variable, such as time or circumstances) caused any change in the dependent variable.

Especially for Nurses In the field of medicine, why are experiments conducted to test new drugs and treatments? (see response, page 24)

The Survey

A third research method is the **survey.** Information is collected from a large number of people by interview, questionnaire, or some other means. The survey is a quick and direct way to obtain data, which is why it is used in the U.S. Census, political polls, and corporate customer surveys.

However, acquiring valid data is far more problematic than it appears. For example, elections would be easy to predict (never "too close to call") if people always voted as they said they would, if the undecided followed the trends, and if those who refused to tell or who were not asked were similar to those who responded. But none of that is true: People lie or change their minds; the undecided

independent variable In an experiment, the variable that is introduced to see what effect it has on the dependent variable. (Also called *experimental variable.*)

dependent variable In an experiment, the variable that may change as a result of whatever new condition or situation the experimenter adds. In other words, the dependent variable *depends* on the independent variable.

survey A research method in which information is collected from a large number of people by interviews, written questionnaires, or some other means.

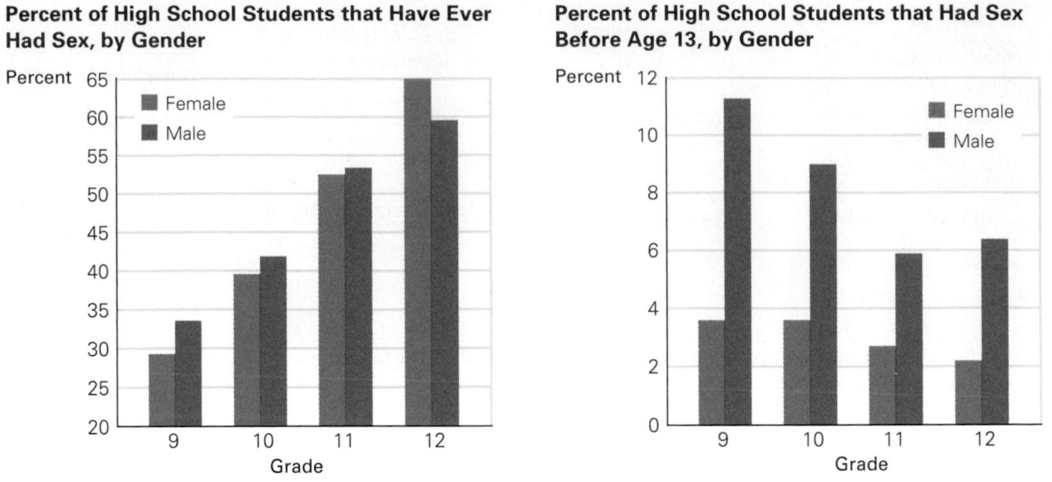

Source: MMWR, June 4, 2010.

FIGURE 1.10

Is Everybody Doing It? No. About one-third of high school seniors and half of all students in grades 9 through 12, both boys and girls, are still virgins. The data for this graph are from the Youth Risk Behavior Survey, a national survey that asks the same questions of thousands of U.S. students in the ninth through twelfth grades each year.

react in unexpected ways; those who never speak to strangers are unlike those who talk freely; college students, prisoners, and cell phone users are less likely to be surveyed but tend to be younger and less predictable than average. Good scientists correct for all this, but some uncertainty is inevitable.

Furthermore, answers are influenced by the wording and the sequence of the questions as well as by selective memory. For example, every year since 1991, thousands of high school students throughout the United States have been asked if they had sexual intercourse before age 13. Every year, about twice as many ninth-graders (8 percent in 2009) as twelfth-graders (4 percent) say yes (see Figure 1.10). How could that be? Do twelfth-graders forget, do ninth-graders lie, does "intercourse" have different meaning, or do sexually active ninth-graders drop out of school? Surveys of more than 200,000 students over the years cannot tell.

>> Response for Nurses (from page 23) Experiments are the only way to determine cause-and-effect relationships. If we want to be sure that a new drug or treatment is safe and effective, an experiment must be conducted to establish that the drug or treatment improves health.

Studying Development

Social scientists from every discipline use these same three methods (observations, experiments, and surveys) to explore human behavior. Typically, before conclusions are accepted, not only does replication occur, but so does research on the same topics using other methods.

Developmentalists have an added requirement: to consider dynamic change, not static results. To study change over time, they design cross-sectional, longitudinal, or cohort-sequential research (see Figure 1.11).

Cross-Sectional and Longitudinal Research

cross-sectional research A research design that compares groups of people who differ in age but are similar in other important characteristics.

The most convenient (quickest and least expensive) way to study developmental change over time is with **cross-sectional research,** in which a group of people of one age are compared with a similar group of people of another age.

For example, in the United States a repeated national survey tallies various medical measures (blood tests, weight, height, and so on) on a cross section of people of many ages. In 2007–2008, the incidence of childhood obesity was about 12 percent for 2- to 5-year-olds, almost 20 percent for 6- to 11-year-olds (Ogden, 2010) (see Figure 1.12), and 32 percent for adults. These data suggest that people get fatter as they grow older, a result found in other nations as well.

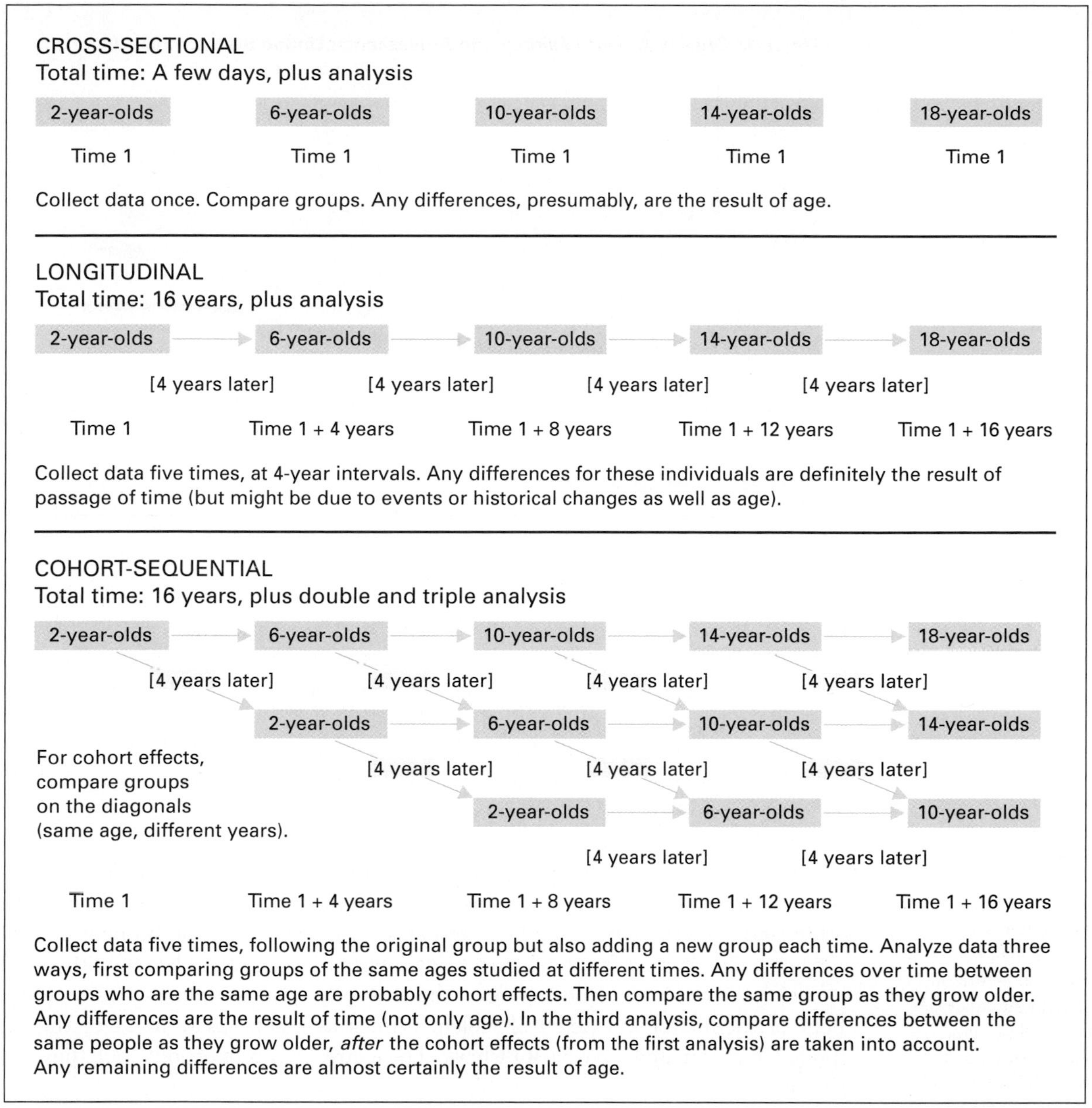

FIGURE 1.11

Which Approach Is Best? Cohort-sequential research is the most time-consuming and complex, but it yields the best information. One reason that hundreds of scientists conduct research on the same topics, replicating one another's work, is to gain some advantages of cohort-sequential research without waiting for decades.

However, cross-sectional data do not always reliably indicate the processes of development: It is not necessarily true that the current cohort of 2- to 5-year-olds will follow what seems to be the age-related trend. Their experiences may be different. When they reach adulthood, in 2030 or so, they may be thinner or fatter than adults now are. (In fact, 50 years ago, adults were lighter as well as shorter, on average, than they are now.)

To discover whether age itself, not historical trends, causes developmental change, scientists undertake **longitudinal research,** collecting data repeatedly on the same individuals. Longitudinal research is particularly useful in studying development over many years (Elder & Shanahan, 2006; Hofer & Piccinin, 2010). For instance, to predict the long-term effects of childhood obesity, one study recorded the childhood weight of almost 5,000 American Indians born between 1945 and 1984 (29 percent were obese) and then noted which ones died before

longitudinal research A research design in which the same individuals are followed over time, as their development is repeatedly assessed.

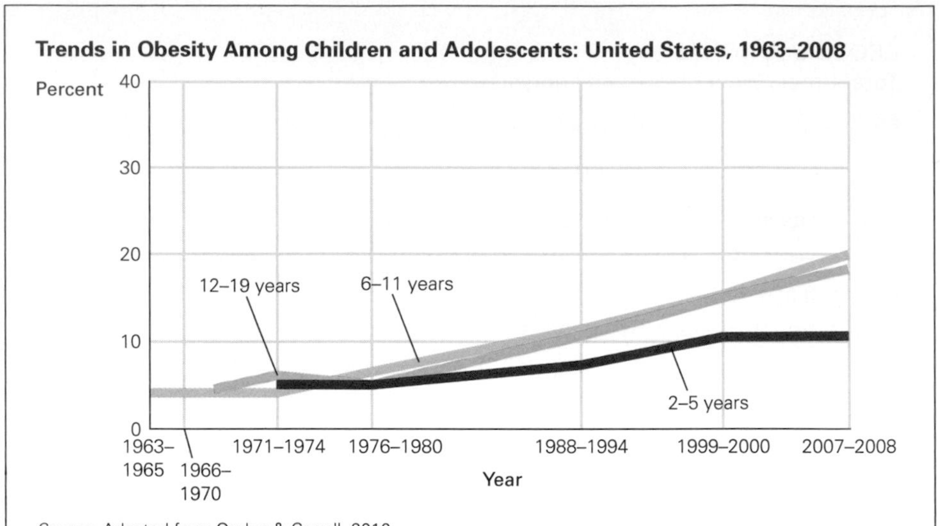

Source: Adapted from Ogden & Carroll, 2010.

FIGURE 1.12

And It Gets Worse Rates of obesity in the United States rise with age and cohort. Adults are increasingly overfeeding their children as well as themselves—about one-third of all adults are obese while another one-third are overweight but not yet obese.

late adulthood. Those 11-year-olds who were in the top quartile of weight (the heaviest 25 percent) died prematurely at twice the rate of those in the bottom quartile (Franks et al., 2010). However, the reasons for the higher death rate were not the expected ones such as diabetes but rather alcohol-related liver disease.

Are obese adolescents more likely to abuse alcohol? Is the interaction between obesity and alcoholism more deadly than either one alone? Will the higher death rates be apparent in late adulthood and will diabetes then become more lethal? More research is needed, but the questions themselves would not have been asked without longitudinal research.

Developmentalists agree that longitudinal research uncovers links that cross-sectional research does not. However, longitudinal studies require much more effort and time than cross-sectional research, and that limits the number of participants. The famous New Zealand study mentioned on page 7 began with 1,037 participants, but only 13 boys were in the severely maltreated, low-MAOA group. Four of them were convicted of violent crimes as adults, as were 11 of the 42 "probably maltreated" low-MAOA boys. These are high proportions, but they are low numbers.

Compare These with Those These diverse groups seem ideal for cross-sectional research. The younger ones have their hands all over each other and express open-mouth joy—but with age, even smiling classmates, like these graduating high school seniors, are more restrained. However, with cross-sectional research, it is not certain whether such contrasts are the direct result of chronological age or the result of other variables—perhaps income, cohort, or culture.

©CORBIS FLIRT / ALAMY

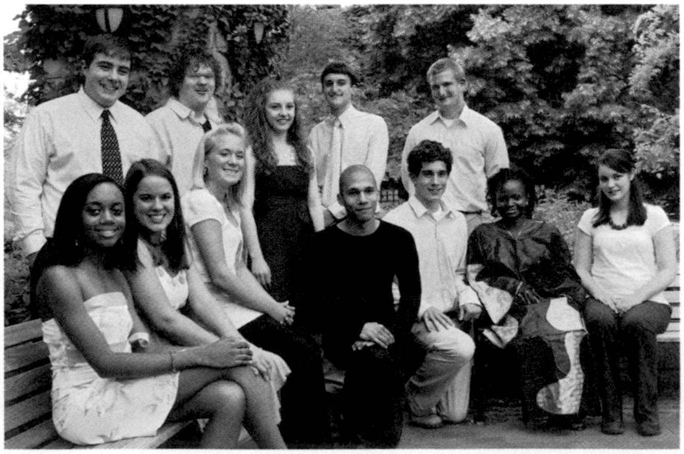

SYRACUSE NEWSPAPERS / LI HAU-LAN / THE IMAGE WORKS

ALL: MARILYN GENTER / THE IMAGE WORKS

Six Stages of Life These photos show Sarah-Maria, born in 1980 in Switzerland, at six stages of her life: infancy (age 1), early childhood (age 3), middle childhood (age 8), adolescence (age 15), emerging adulthood (age 19), and adulthood (age 30).

Observation Quiz Longitudinal research best illustrates continuity and discontinuity. For Sarah-Maria, what changed over 30 years and what didn't? (see answer, page 28)

Moreover, when developmentalists want to know the eventual effects of childhood experience, they need to wait decades for conclusions from longitudinal research. Waiting can have disastrous consequences. For example, until the results from longitudinal research were in, millions of teenagers started smoking because their parents, their schools, and their friends thought cigarettes were harmless. Currently, because of fears about adult cancer from industrial compounds (called *phthalates*) in plastic, many parents use glass baby bottles. Might the risk of occasional shattered glass hurt more people than chemicals in plastic? Longitudinal research can tell us—in 50 years.

Combining Methods and Strategies

As you can see, cross-sectional and longitudinal research each have advantages that compensate for the other's disadvantages. Scientists have discovered a third research strategy that involves using these two together, often with complex statistical analysis. In **cohort-sequential research** (or *cross-sequential* or *time-sequential research*), researchers study several groups of people of different ages (a cross-sectional approach) and follow them over the years (a longitudinal approach). A cohort-sequential design lets researchers compare findings for a group of, say, 25-year-olds with findings for the same individuals at ages 20, 15, 10 and 5—as well as with findings for groups who are *currently* age 20, 15, 10, and 5. Cohort-sequential research thus allows scientists to disentangle age and historical context.

cohort-sequential research A research design in which researchers first study several groups of people of different ages (a cross-sectional approach) and then follow those groups over the years (a longitudinal approach). (Also called *cross-sequential research* or *time-sequential research*.)

One well-known cohort-sequential study (the Seattle Longitudinal Study) discovered something about schoolchildren: Older adults are better at math than younger adults, not because number sense improves with age (it does not) but because decades ago schools emphasized math—a finding that neither cross-sectional nor longitudinal research alone could reveal. For parents and teachers, this is significant: Lessons learned before age 12 can affect intellectual abilities 50 years later.

Especially for Future Researchers What is the best method for collecting data? (see response, page 28)

>> Answer to Observation Quiz (from page 27) Of course, much changed and much did not change, but evident in the photos is continuity in Sarah-Maria's happy smile and discontinuity in her hairstyle (which shows dramatic age and cohort changes).

>> Response for Future Researchers (from page 27) There is no best method for collecting data. The method used depends on many factors, such as the age of participants (infants can't complete questionnaires), the question being researched, and the time frame.

SUMMING UP

Social scientists use many research methods, each with advantages and disadvantages. Observational research requires careful and systematic recording of whatever actually occurs. Experiments seek to establish cause and effect, as revealed by change in the dependent variable. A true experiment compares at least two groups, similar in many ways except that one receives a particular treatment (the independent variable) that the other does not. A third method, the survey, is useful for large groups. However, the accuracy of a survey depends on factors not always evident, including the wording of the questions and who responds.

Developmentalists need to study change over time, so they use additional strategies. Cross-sectional and longitudinal research designs are both useful, yet each has serious limitations. A combination of these two, often called cohort-sequential, is ideal but complicated statistically and logistically. ■

>> Cautions and Challenges from Science

The scientific method illuminates and illustrates human development. Facts, hypotheses, and possibilities have emerged that would not be known without science—and people of all ages are healthier and more capable because of it. For example, infant death, childhood malnutrition, adolescent suicide, and racism and sexism at every age are much less prevalent today than a few decades ago. Primarily because more children survive to adulthood, the average life span in developed nations is about 80, not 50, as it was a century ago. Science contributed to this; many of us would not be alive without it.

Developmental scientists have also discovered unexpected sources of harm. As detailed in later chapters, sugary drinks, television, lead paint, video games, and parental divorce are less benign in childhood than people first thought. New protections, and newly discovered dangers, are examples of the benefits of science.

However, science can be misused and misinterpreted. We now discuss three possible problems: correlation, quantification, and ethics.

Correlation and Causation

correlation A number between +1.0 and −1.0 that indicates the degree of relationship between two variables, expressed in terms of the likelihood that one variable will (or will not) occur when the other variable does (or does not). A correlation indicates only that two variables are somehow related, not that one variable causes the other to occur.

Probably the most common mistake in interpreting research is to think that correlation means causation. It does not. Scientists try to remember the mantra: *Correlation is not causation.* A **correlation** exists between two variables if one variable is more (or less) likely to occur when the other does. A correlation is *positive* if both variables tend to increase together or decrease together, *negative* if one variable tends to increase while the other decreases, and *zero* if no connection is evident.

To illustrate: From birth to age 9, there is a positive correlation between age and height (children grow taller as they grow older), a negative correlation between age and hours of sleep (children sleep less as they grow older), and zero correlation between age and number of toes (barring a rare accident or late-life diabetes, after the eighth prenatal week, humans have 10 toes lifelong). (Now take the quiz on correlation in Table 1.4.)

Expressed in statistics, correlations vary from +1.0 (the most positive) to −1.0 (the most negative). Totally positive or totally negative correlations are virtually never found because there are always exceptions that reduce the strength of the correlation. Indeed, a correlation of +0.3 or −0.3 is noteworthy; a correlation of +0.8 or −0.8 is amazingly high.

Many correlations are unexpected. For instance, first-born children develop asthma more often than later-born children, teenage boys commit suicide more

TABLE 1.4 Quiz on Correlation

Two Variables	Positive, Negative, or Zero Correlation?	Why? (Third Variable)
1. Ice cream sales and murder rate	positive	
2. Reading ability and number of baby teeth	negative	
3. Sex of adult and his or her average number of offspring		

For each of these three pairs of variables, indicate whether the correlation between them is positive, negative, or nonexistent. Then try to think of a third variable that might determine the direction of the correlation. The correct answers are printed upside down below.

often than teenage girls, and, at least in North America, babies born to immigrants are healthier than other babies. (These findings are discussed in later chapters.) Why? Correlations do not answer that question because, as the mantra says, correlation is not causation.

Quantity and Quality

A second caution concerns how heavily scientists rely on data produced by **quantitative research** (from the word *quantity,* such as more or less, higher or lower, in rank order, in percents, or in numerical scores). Because quantitative data are numerical, they can be translated across cultures and applied to diverse populations. One example of quantitative research is school test scores, used to measure the effectiveness of teachers, or to determine whether a child must repeat a grade, or to decide whether a particular school should win a grant or be shut down.

quantitative research Research that provides data that can be expressed with numbers, such as ranks or scales.

Since quantities can be easily summarized, compared, charted, and replicated, many scientists prefer quantitative research. Quantitative data are said to provide "rigorous, empirically testable representations" (Nesselroade & Molenaar, 2003, p. 635). Without numbers to measure ability or achievement, students might unfairly be denied college admission because of their ethnicity, religion, or SES.

Answers:
1. Positive; third variable: heat
2. Negative; third variable: age
3. Zero; each child must have a parent of each sex; no third variable

However, when data are reduced to numbers, nuances and individual distinctions are lost. Many developmental researchers thus turn to **qualitative research** (from *quality*)—asking open-ended questions, reporting answers in narrative (not numerical) form, and generating "a rich description of the phenomena of interest" (Hartmann & Pelzel, 2005, p. 163). Qualitative research reflects diversity and complexity, but it is vulnerable to personal bias and hard to replicate. Particularly if one person, *a single case study,* is used, conclusions may be idiosyncratic. (Earlier in this chapter, I referred to one case, my nephew David. Is he atypical, a misleading example, giving false hope? Would I have been equally likely to tell his story if he had died or remained unable to walk, talk, or think?)

qualitative research Research that considers qualities, not quantities. Narrative accounts and individual variations are often stressed in qualitative research.

Especially for People Who Have Applied to College or Graduate School
Is the admissions process based on quality or quantity? (see response, page 31)

The solution: a combination of quantitative and qualitative methods. Sometimes scientists translate qualitative research into quantifiable data; sometimes they use qualitative studies to suggest hypotheses for quantitative research. In this we return to the scientific method. Although news reports sometimes headline an unexpected result from one study, scientists do not accept a finding as verified until several groups of scientists, ideally after replication and then several qualitative and quantitative methods with diverse groups of participants, reach the same conclusion.

Ethics

All scientists, especially those studying humans, need to uphold ethical standards. Each academic discipline and professional society has a **code of ethics** (a set of moral principles).

code of ethics A set of moral principles or guidelines that members of a profession or group are expected to follow.

By federal law in the United States, most educational and medical institutions have an **Institutional Review Board (IRB),** a group that permits only research that follows certain guidelines. Although IRBs often slow down scientific study, some research conducted before IRBs were established was clearly unethical, especially when the participants were children, members of minority groups, prisoners, or animals (Blum, 2002; Washington, 2006).

Institutional Review Board (IRB) A group within most educational and medical institutions who ensure that research follows established ethical guidelines. Unlike in prior decades, most research in human development cannot begin without IRB approval.

Protection of Research Participants

Central to every IRB is the attempt to ensure that participation in research is voluntary, confidential, and harmless. In Western nations, this entails the *informed consent* of the participants—that is, their understanding of the research procedures and of any risks involved. If children are involved, consent must be obtained from the parents as well as the children. The children and the parent must be allowed to opt out at any time with no penalty. For instance, if children are given toys or parents are paid for participation, those who quit before the study is over must receive the same payment as those who complete the study, and any gifts or payments must be small so that people will not participate merely in order to get the incentive.

Implications of Research Results

Once a study has been completed, additional ethical issues arise. Scientists are obligated to "promote accuracy, honesty, and truthfulness" (American Psychological Association, 2010). That precludes distortions to support any political, economic, religious, or cultural position. Results must be carefully presented (Principle 14).

Especially for Future Researchers and Science Writers Do any ethical guidelines apply when an author writes about the experiences of family members, friends, or research participants? (see response, page 32)

Deliberate distortion is rare, but insidious dangers include unintentionally slanting the conclusions or withholding publication, especially when there is "ferocious . . . pressure from commercial funders to ignore good scientific practice" (Bateson, 2005, p. 645). Similarly, nonprofit research groups and academic institutions may pressure scientists to produce publishable results.

For this reason, scientific training, collaboration, and replication are essential. Numerous safeguards are built into scientific methodology, including the fact that reports in professional journals are typically "peer reviewed," meaning that before an article can be published, it must be evaluated by scientists not connected with the author(s). Reports often include (1) researchers' affiliations and sources of funding, (2) sufficient details to allow for replication, (3) limitations of the research, and (4) alternative interpretations.

off the mark.com
by Mark Parisi
... AND I FIGURE BY GENETICALLY COMBINING TREES AND PITBULLS, THE RAIN FORESTS MIGHT HAVE A FIGHTING CHANCE...
offthemark.com
MARK PARISI / ATLANTIC FEATURE SYNDICATE

A crucial question for all scientists is whether their research is ethical and will help solve human problems.

What Should We Study?

Long before designing and publishing research, the first ethical question for every developmental scientist is: "What research is needed to enable more humans to live satisfying and productive lives?" Consider these questions, for instance:

- Do we know enough about prenatal drug abuse to protect every fetus?
- Do we know enough about poverty to enable everyone to be healthy?
- Do we know enough about sexual drives to eliminate AIDS, unwanted pregnancy, and sexual abuse?
- Do we know enough about learning so that all children develop basic skills and values?

The answer to all these questions is a resounding *NO*. The reasons are many, but a major one is that these topics are controversial. Some researchers avoid them, fearing unwelcome and uninformed publicity (Kempner et al., 2005). Few funders eagerly support scientific studies of drug abuse, poverty, sex, or values, partly because the data may conflict with popular assumptions. Yet developmentalists should study whatever helps the human family. Many people suffer because questions go unanswered—or even unasked. More research and more application are needed (Keating, 2011).

The next cohort of developmental scientists will build on what is already known. The challenge is to find answers to many urgent questions that could improve life for the world's 6.9 billion people. This chapter and this text are only the beginning.

>> Response for People Who Have Applied to College or Graduate School (from page 29) Most institutions of higher education emphasize quantitative data—the SAT, the GRE, GPA, class rank, and so on. Decide for yourself whether this is fairer than a more qualitative approach.

SUMMING UP

Science has helped people in many ways over the past century, contributing to longer and happier lives. However, there are several potential pitfalls in scientific research. For instance, although correlations are useful, people may mistakenly assume that they prove cause, not simply connection. Quantitative research is more objective and easier to replicate than qualitative research, but it loses the nuances that qualitative research can reveal.

Scientists follow codes of ethics to make sure they fully inform research participants and safeguard their well-being. Research codes have become more stringent in recent years. Scientists also must be "mindful of implications," which means they must take care that results are not misinterpreted. The most urgent developmental issues are controversial and therefore difficult to study objectively or to report honestly. That is precisely why further scientific research is needed. ■

SUMMARY

Understanding How and Why

1. The study of human development is a science that seeks to understand how people change or remain the same over time. As a science, it begins with questions and hypotheses and then uses various methods to gather empirical data. Researchers draw conclusions based on the evidence.

2. Replication confirms, modifies, or refutes the conclusions of a scientific study. In child development, first replication and then application of research often helps the next generation, as in the application of research that led to far fewer sudden infant deaths.

3. The universality of human development and the uniqueness of each individual's development are both evident in nature (the genes) and nurture (the environment); no person is quite like another. Nature and nurture always interact, and each human characteristic is affected by that interaction. Neuroscience has discovered differential susceptibility—that certain genes increase or decrease the likelihood that a child will be affected by the environment.

4. Time is a crucial variable in studying human development. A critical period is a time when something *must* occur to ensure normal development or the only time when an abnormality might occur. Often a particular development can occur more easily—but not exclusively—at a particular time, called a sensitive period.

5. Throughout life, human development is plastic. *Plasticity* emphasizes that it is possible for individuals to change their characteristics and behavior as they develop, although it is also true that their childhood experiences affect later development.

Including All Kinds of People

6. All kinds of people, of every age, culture, and background, are studied by developmental scientists, who recognize that many variations are the result of social constructions, not biological facts. The goal is to find the universal patterns of human growth while also recognizing that each person is unique.

7. In studying human variations, one pitfall to avoid is the difference-equals-deficit error. For example, the concept that males and females are opposites may lead to the distorted idea that one sex is better than the other.

8. *Culture, ethnicity,* and *race* are social constructions, concepts created by society. Culture includes beliefs and patterns; ethnicity refers to ancestral heritage. The social construction of "race" has been so misused that social scientists prefer not to use it.

9. Socioeconomic status (SES) is an important influence on human development, affecting a person's opportunities, health, and even abilities at every stage. As with other differences among people, developmentalists seek to find the balance between recognizing similarities and respecting differences.

Observing Changes over Time

10. A dynamic-systems approach to development emphasizes that change is ongoing in life, with each part of development affecting every other part. The assumption that growth is linear and progress is inevitable has been replaced by the idea that both continuity (sameness) and discontinuity (sudden shifts) are part of every life, that gains and losses are apparent at every age.

11. Urie Bronfenbrenner's ecological-systems or bioecological approach notes that each child is situated within larger systems of family, school, community, and culture. Changes within a person, or changes in the context, affect all other aspects of the system.

12. Certain experiences or innovations shape people of each cohort because they are members of a particular generation who share the experience of significant historical events. Mirror neurons suggest that observing other people's experiences has a powerful effect on each individual, which may be one reason why cohort effects are strong.

Using the Scientific Method

13. Commonly used research methods are scientific observation, the experiment, and the survey. Each can provide insight and discoveries that were not apparent before the research.

14. An additional challenge for developmentalists is to study change over time. Two traditional research designs are often used: cross-sectional research (comparing people of different ages) and longitudinal research (studying the same people over time). Each has limitations, and for that reason cohort-sequential research (combining the two other methods) is also used. Every method of research has advantages and disadvantages.

Cautions and Challenges from Science

15. A correlation shows that two variables are related. However, it does not prove that one variable *causes* the other: The relationship of variables may be opposite to the one expected, or both may be the result of a third variable.

16. Quantitative research provides data that is numerical, and thus it is best to compare children in different contexts and cultures. By contrast, in qualitative research, information is reported without being quantified. Qualitative research best captures the nuance of individual lives, but quantitative research is easier to replicate, interpret, and verify.

17. Ethical behavior is crucial in all the sciences. Not only must participants be protected and data kept confidential (primary concerns of IRBs), but results must be fairly reported and honestly interpreted. Scientists must be mindful of the implications of their research.

18. Appropriate application of scientific research depends partly on the training and integrity of the scientists. The most important ethical question is whether scientists are designing, conducting, analyzing, publishing, and applying the research that is most critically needed.

>> Response for Future Researchers and Science Writers (from page 31) Yes. Anyone you write about must give consent and be fully informed about your intentions. They can be identified by name only if they give permission. For example, family members gave permission before anecdotes about them were included in this text. My nephew David read the first draft of his story (see pages 9–10) and is proud to have his experiences used to teach others.

KEY TERMS

science of human development (p. 4)
scientific method (p. 4)
theory (p. 4)
hypothesis (p. 4)
empirical (p. 5)
replication (p. 5)
sudden infant death syndrome (SIDS) (p. 5)
nature (p. 6)
nurture (p. 6)
critical period (p. 8)
sensitive period (p. 8)
plasticity (p. 9)
difference-equals-deficit error (p. 10)
social construction (p. 11)
culture (p. 12)
ethnic group (p. 13)
race (p. 13)
socioeconomic status (SES) (p. 13)
dynamic systems (p. 15)
ecological-systems approach (p. 16)
cohort (p. 17)
biopsychosocial (p. 19)
mirror neurons (p. 20)
scientific observation (p. 21)
independent variable (p. 23)
dependent variable (p. 23)
survey (p. 23)
cross-sectional research (p. 24)
longitudinal research (p. 25)
cohort-sequential research (p. 27)
correlation (p. 28)
quantitative research (p. 29)
qualitative research (p. 29)
code of ethics (p. 29)
Institutional Review Board (IRB) (p. 30)

WHAT HAVE YOU LEARNED?

Understanding How and Why

1. What makes the study of human development a science?

2. What are the five steps of the scientific method?

3. How does research on SIDS illustrate the replication and application of the science of child development?

4. What is known and unknown about the causes of sudden infant death?

5. What is the difference between nature and nurture?

6. Why is it a mistake to ask whether a human behavior stems from nature or nurture?

7. What is an example from neuroscience that illustrates differential susceptibility?

8. What is the difference between a critical period and a sensitive period?

9. Why is it important to know when a sensitive period in development occurs?

10. How can both plasticity and the long-term effects of childhood be true?

Including All Kinds of People

11. How is exaggeration of male–female differences an example of the difference-equals-deficit error?

12. How can people of several ethnic groups share a culture?

13. What is the difference between race and ethnicity?

14. What factors comprise a person's SES?

Observing Changes over Time

15. What is implied about human development when it is described as dynamic?

16. Why is it more accurate to consider the systems of development rather than each part in isolation?

17. What did Bronfenbrenner emphasize in his ecological-systems approach?

18. Why does it matter what cohort a particular person belongs to?

19. What are the differences among the three domains of development?

Using the Scientific Method

20. How do scientific observation and experimentation differ?

21. Why do experimenters use a control (or comparison) group as well as an experimental group?

22. How do independent and dependent variables make it easier to learn what causes what?

23. What are the strengths and weaknesses of the survey method?

24. How do cross-sectional and longitudinal research differ?

25. What are the advantages and disadvantages of cross-sequential research?

Cautions and Challenges from Science

26. Why does correlation not prove causation?

27. Why do some researchers prefer quantitative research and others qualitative research?

28. Why do most colleges and hospitals have an IRB?

29. What are the primary ethical principles used when scientists study humans?

30. Why are some important questions about human development not yet answered?

APPLICATIONS

1. It is said that culture is pervasive but that people are unaware of it. List 30 things you did *today* that you might have done differently in another culture. Begin with how and where you woke up.

2. How would your life be different if your parents were much higher or lower in SES than they are? Consider all three domains.

3. Design an experiment to answer a question you have about human development. Specify the question and the hypothesis and then describe the experiment. How would you prevent your conclusions from being biased and subjective? (Look at Appendix B.)

4. A longitudinal case study can be insightful but is also limited in generality. Describe the life of one of your older relatives, explaining what aspects of their development are unique and what aspects might be relevant for everyone.

>>ONLINE CONNECTIONS

To accompany your textbook, you have access to a number of online resources, including quizzes for every chapter of the book, flashcards (in English and Spanish), critical thinking questions, and case studies. For access to any of these links, go to www.worthpublishers.com/bergerca9e. In addition to these free resources, you'll also find links to podcasts, video clips, diagnostic quizzing with personalized study advice, and an ebook. Some of the videos and activities available online include:

- *Ethics in Human Research: Violating One's Privacy?* This video introduces the controversies around a research project in Iceland that collects the genetic and health information about private citizens.
- *What's Wrong with This Study?* This activity allows you to review some of the pitfalls in various research designs.

CHAPTER 2

Theories

WHAT WILL YOU KNOW?

1. How is a theory different from a fact?
2. Does development occur in stages or more gradually, day by day?
3. What limitations do Freud, Erikson, Watson, Skinner, and Piaget all share, according to newer theories of development?
4. Why is it better to use several theories rather than just one?

When I was little, on special occasions we drove to my grandparents' farm, the childhood home of my father, his three brothers, and one sister. My mother sang, "Over the river and through the woods, to grandmother's house we go." When we arrived, my brother and I played with our twelve cousins, including three other girls my age. I remember turkey, mashed potatoes, and lemon meringue pie; horses and hay in the barn; grandma wearing an apron; grandpa resting his big hands over a huge coffee mug; enormous wooden rocking chairs in the sitting room. But my strongest single memory is a bitter one: One Christmas, Grandma gave us girls presents—precursors of Barbie dolls. Mine had a peach-colored gown; my cousin's had a white bride's dress and veil.

Why did I feel rejected? In hindsight, I can think of several laudable reasons that particular cousin got the bride doll. But when I was 6, my simple theory about presents and brides led to resentment.

This chapter outlines five theories of human development, or actually ten, since each theory has at least two versions. There are hundreds more theories about the human life span, some explained later. Before beginning, however, you should know that theorizing is part of human nature. In fact, according to "theory theory," young children spontaneously develop theories to explain whatever they observe, because that is what humans do (Gopnik & Schulz, 2007). My theory led me to believe that Grandma loved my cousin more than me.

>> What Theories Do

A **developmental theory** is a systematic statement of general principles that provides a coherent framework for understanding how and why people change as they grow older. "Developmental theorists try to make sense out of observations . . . [and] construct a story of the human journey from infancy through childhood or adulthood" (Miller, 2011, p. 2). Such a story, or theory, connects facts and observations with patterns and explanations, weaving the details of life into a meaningful whole. A developmental theory is more than a hunch or a hypothesis and is far more comprehensive than my childish theorizing about bride dolls. My assumptions were not "systematic" and did not add up to a "coherent framework." Developmental theories provide insights that are both broad and deep, making them more comprehensive than the many observations and ideas from which they arise.

developmental theory A group of ideas, assumptions, and generalizations that interpret and illuminate the thousands of observations that have been made about human growth. A developmental theory provides a framework for explaining the patterns and problems of development.

As an analogy, imagine building a house. A person could have a heap of lumber, nails, and other materials, but without a plan and labor, the heap cannot become a building. Furthermore, not every house is alike: People have theories (usually not explicit) about houses that lead to preferences for the number of stories, bedrooms, entrances, and so on. Likewise, the observations and empirical studies of human development are essential raw materials, but theories pull them together.

As Kurt Lewin (1943) once quipped, "Nothing is as practical as a good theory." Theories differ; some are less comprehensive or adequate than others (why did we forget a back door?), some are no longer useful (no bathrooms?), some reflect one culture but not another (entrance facing east?), but without theory we have only a heap.

Questions and Answers

As we saw in Chapter 1, the first step of the science of human development is to pose a question, which often springs from a developmental theory. Among the thousands of important questions are the following, each central to one of the five theories described in this chapter:

1. Do early experiences—of breast-feeding or attachment or neglect—linger into adulthood, even if they seem to be forgotten?
2. Does learning depend on specific instruction, punishment, and examples?
3. Do children develop moral principles, even if they are not taught right from wrong?
4. Does culture guide behavior? Is that why Okinawa has more voters than Oklahoma?
5. Is survival a basic instinct, underlying all personal or social decisions?

Each of the five questions above is answered "yes" by one of the five major theories—in order: question 1 by psychoanalytic theory, question 2 by behaviorism, question 3 by cognitive theory, question 4 by sociocultural theory, and question 5 by the two universal theories (humanism and evolutionary theory). Each question is answered "no" or "not necessarily" by several others. For every answer, more questions arise: Why or why not? When and how? So what? This last question is crucial for the science of human development; the implications and applications of the answers affect everyone's daily life.

To be more specific about what theories do:

- Theories produce *hypotheses.*
- Theories generate *discoveries.*
- Theories offer *practical guidance.*

A popular book of child-rearing advice, *Battle Hymn of the Tiger Mother* (Chua, 2011), seems to advocate a parenting style that insists on high achievement. For example, Amy Chua rejected a birthday card, hastily handmade by her 4-year-old daughter, saying:

> I don't want this. . . . I want a better one—one that you've put some thought and effort into. . . . I deserve better.
>
> *[p. 103]*

Reactions to Chua's book are very positive (five-star rating) or very negative (one-star rating). Six months after it was published, of the first 500 reader reviews on Amazon, 42 percent were very positive, 23 percent very negative, with less extreme evaluations (two to four stars) from only 7, 11, and 17 percent of responders. Explaining these reactions, one professional reviewer wrote:

> There was bound to be some pushback. All the years of nurturance overload simply got to be too much. The breast-feeding through toddlerhood, nonstop baby wearing, co-sleeping, "Baby Mozart" . . . After "free range" parenting . . . [and] "simplicity parenting" [came] a kind of edgy irritation with it all: a new stance of get-tough-no-nonsense, frequently called—with no small amount of pride—being a bad mother.
>
> [*Warner, 2011, p. 11*]

Chua herself seems surprised at the extreme reactions. Although many people do not realize it, everyone has strong opinions about child development, sometimes promoted with fierce intensity. These opinions sometimes spring from the five theories soon to be described.

Facts and Norms

A **norm** is an average or usual event or experience. And while it is related to the word *normal,* the term has a slightly different meaning. For instance, it is a norm for brides to wear white in Western culture, symbolizing purity; but in Asian culture, brides wear red to symbolize celebration. And describing something as "abnormal" (not normal) implies that it is wrong, yet norms are not meant to be right or wrong. Norms are averages, though not merely an arithmetical mean or median. Rather, a norm is a mode, a common behavior that results from biological or social pressure. Norms reflect facts and can be calculated (such as the norm for babies beginning to walk or for brides to wear a certain color), but deviations are not necessarily deficits.

norm An average, or typical, standard of behavior or accomplishment, such as the norm for age of walking or the norm for greeting a stranger.

Do not confuse theories with facts, either. Theories raise questions, suggesting hypotheses, leading to research that gathers empirical data. Those data are facts that may lead to conclusions. Each developmental theory to be explained soon has led to research, data, and conclusions that have verified as well as refuted aspects of that theory, thereby advancing developmental science.

Thus, a theory is neither true nor false, good nor bad. Ideally, a theory is provocative and useful, leading to hypotheses and exploration. For example, some people dismiss Darwin's theory of evolution as "just a theory," while others believe it is a fact that explains all of nature since the beginning of time. No and no. Good theories should neither be dismissed nor equated with facts. Instead, theories deepen thought; they are useful (like a house plan), leading to new interpretations, studies, and perspectives.

As already explained, developmental theories are comprehensive and detailed, unlike the simple theories of children or the implicit theories that underlie the customs and assumptions of each culture. But to clarify the distinction between theory and fact, we return to the simple theory of the bride doll. My bitterness was one outcome of the dominant theory in my childhood culture—a pro-family theory. The theory led to a series of assumptions, including that everyone should leave their parents by age 20, marry one person and stay married lifelong, have at least two children, and visit their parents periodically. Furthermore, the parents should stay in their own house, not only so the children can visit but also because alternatives were sad and shameful. That led to norms, followed by my paternal grandparents' five offspring and by nine of my maternal grandparents' twelve children. We pitied my mother's unmarried sisters, Aunt Ida and Aunt Marie, as well as Aunt Alma, who had only one child.

True to the dominant theory of my childhood, I fantasized about my wedding, named my seven imagined children, and rejoiced when my Aunt Marie finally married but was sad when my mother said Marie was too old to have children. That theory was reflected in the laws and assumptions of my community: Having

AP PHOTO / THE ADVOCATE-MESSENGER, CLAY JACKSON

ASTAPKOVICH VLADIMIR ITAR-TASS PHOTOS / NEWSCOM

Backpacks or Bouquets? Children worldwide are nervous on the first day of school, but their coping reflects implicit cultural theories. Kindergarten girls in Kentucky bring many supplies, while elementary children in Russia bring flowers for their teachers.

more than one spouse was wrong (bigamists went to jail), divorce meant a "failed" marriage and "broken" family, and "only" children had psychological problems.

However, research has now shown that differences are not deficits, and none of the assumptions above is necessarily true. As flaws in the theory have been revealed, norms have changed accordingly. Longitudinal data found that singleton children (no longer called "only") are often high achievers with successful lives (Falbo et al., 2009) and that China's "one-child" policy led to economic success. Consequently, in some nations (Italy and Japan among them), having one child is the norm.

Some say that the pro-family theory I knew as a child has been replaced, at least in Western middle-class culture, by another untested theory: that personal happiness is the goal of life. This led to an alternate set of ideas: that parents should strive to make their children happy, that unhappy spouses should divorce, that self-esteem is more important than academic success—all of which led to the tiger-mother pushback.

Obviously, more science is needed. Realizing that theories are not facts and that "each theory of developmental psychology always has a view of humans that reflects philosophical, economic, and political beliefs" (Miller, 2011, p. 17), scientists question norms, develop hypotheses, and design studies. Science has thus led to conclusions that undercut some theories and modify others, to the benefit of all.

Theories do more than raise questions. They give insight and guidance, especially when developmental problems (such as a crying infant, an aggressive toddler, a bullied preschooler, a failing schoolchild, a drunk adolescent) occur. Without theories, we would be merely reactive and bewildered, adrift and increasingly befuddled, blindly following our culture and our prejudices. Theories are useful, leading to verification, exploration, and application. Eventually, better theories are developed: Without them we might be stuck with limiting, childish assumptions—as I was with the doll.

SUMMING UP

Theories provide a framework for organizing and understanding the thousands of observations and daily behaviors that occur in every aspect of development. Theories are not facts, but they allow us to question norms, suggest hypotheses, and provide guidance. Thus, theories are practical: They frame and organize our millions of experiences. ■

>> Grand Theories

In the first half of the twentieth century, two opposing theories—psychoanalytic theory and behaviorism (also called *learning theory*)—began as general theories of psychology, each with applications in child development. By mid-century, cognitive theory had emerged, becoming the dominant seedbed of research hypotheses. All three theories are "grand" in that they are comprehensive, enduring, and widely applied (McAdams & Pals, 2006), although they are not universally accepted (as you will soon read).

psychoanalytic theory A grand theory of human development that holds that irrational, unconscious drives and motives, often originating in childhood, underlie human behavior.

Psychoanalytic Theory: Freud and Erikson

Inner drives, deep motives, and unconscious needs rooted in childhood are the foundation of **psychoanalytic theory.** These basic underlying forces are thought to influence every aspect of thinking and behavior, from the smallest details of daily life to the crucial choices of a lifetime.

AKG / PHOTO RESEARCHERS, INC.

Freud at Work In addition to being the world's first psychoanalyst, Sigmund Freud was a prolific writer. His many papers and case histories, primarily descriptions of his patients' bizarre symptoms and unconscious sexual urges, helped make the psychoanalytic perspective a dominant force for much of the twentieth century.

Freud's Ideas

Psychoanalytic theory originated with Sigmund Freud (1856–1939), an Austrian physician who treated patients suffering from mental illness. He listened to their accounts of dreams and fantasies and to their uncensored streams of thought, and he constructed an elaborate, multifaceted theory. Early childhood, he thought, was crucial.

According to Freud, development in the first six years occurs in three stages. He called each stage *psychosexual* because children derive erotic pleasure from whatever body part is central at each stage. This idea (infantile sexuality) was one reason psychoanalytic theory was rejected at first, because Victorian sensibilities led to the dominant theory that children were innocent, asexual beings. According to Freud, in infancy, the erotic body part is the mouth (the *oral stage*); in early childhood, it is the anus (the *anal stage*); in the preschool years, it is the penis (the *phallic stage*), a source of pride and fear among boys and a reason for sadness and envy among girls. Two more developmental periods then follow early childhood. After the phallic stage, *latency* occurs, and then, at puberty, the *genital stage* arrives, lasting throughout adulthood. (Table 2.1 describes the stages in Freud's theory.)

SUSAN LAPIDES / DESIGN CONCEPTIONS

Childhood Sexuality The girl's interest in the statue's anatomy may reflect simple curiosity, but Freudian theory would maintain that it is a clear manifestation of the phallic stage of psychosexual development, when girls are said to feel deprived because they lack a penis.

Freud maintained that at each stage, sensual satisfaction (from stimulation of the mouth, anus, or penis) is linked to major developmental needs and challenges. During the oral stage, for example, sucking provides not only nourishment but also erotic delight for the baby and attachment to the mother. Kissing in adulthood is a vestige of the oral stage. Next, during the anal stage, pleasures that arise from control and self-control—initially with defecation and toilet training—are paramount.

One of Freud's most influential ideas was that each stage includes its own potential conflicts. Conflict occurs, for instance, when mothers try to wean their babies (oral stage) or teachers expect kindergartners to become independent of their parents (phallic stage). According to Freud, how people experience and resolve these conflicts—especially those related to weaning, toilet training, and sexual pleasure—determine personality patterns because "the early stages provide the foundation for adult behavior" (Salkind, 2004, p. 125).

Freud did not believe that new stages occurred after puberty; rather, he believed that adult personalities and habits were influenced by earlier stages. Unconscious conflicts rooted in a childhood stage may be evident in adult behavior—for instance, smoking cigarettes (oral) or keeping careful track of money (anal) or becoming romantically attracted to a much older partner (phallic). For all of us, psychoanalytic theory contends, childhood fantasies and memories remain powerful lifelong, particularly as they affect the sex drive (which Freud called the *libido*). If you have ever wondered why lovers call each other "baby" or why many people refer to their spouse as their "old lady" or "sugar daddy," then Freud's theory provides an explanation: The parent–child relationship is the model for all forms of intimacy.

Many other aspects of psychoanalytic theory are thought to explain behavior. According to Freud, the personality has three parts: the *id* (unconscious drives, inborn and animal-like, mostly sexual and aggressive), the *superego* (the moral ideal, the conscience, learned from parents and society), and the *ego* (the conscious self). The id is dominant in infancy, the superego develops in the phallic stage, and throughout life the ego defends itself against attacks from the id and superego. That defense occurs with *defense mechanisms* that keep the id and superego under control. Ideally, during childhood, parents help their children develop a strong ego so that impulses from the id and superego are kept in check.

TED STRESHINSKY / TIME LIFE PICTURES / GETTY IMAGES

A Legendary Couple In his first 30 years, Erikson never fit into a particular local community, since he so frequently changed nations, schools, and professions. Then he met Joan. In their first five decades of marriage, they raised a family and wrote several books. If he had published his theory at age 73 (when this photograph was taken) instead of in his 40s, would he still have described his life as a series of crises?

Erikson's Ideas

Many of Freud's followers became famous theorists themselves. They acknowledged the importance of the unconscious and of early childhood experience, but each of them expanded and modified Freud's ideas. One of them, Erik Erikson (1902–1994), is well respected for his theory of development.

Erikson never knew his Danish father. He spent his childhood in Germany, his adolescence wandering through Italy, and his young adulthood in Austria, working with Freud. He married an American, fleeing to the United States just before World War II. His experiences in many nations—as well as his studies of Harvard students, Boston children at play, and the child-rearing methods of Sioux and Yurok Indians—led Erikson to stress cultural diversity, social change, and psychological crises throughout life (Erikson, 1969).

Erikson described eight developmental stages, each characterized by a particular challenge, or *developmental crisis* (summarized in Table 2.1). Although Erikson named two polarities at each crisis, he recognized a wide range of outcomes between those opposites. For most people, development at each stage leads to neither extreme but to something in between. The resolution of each crisis depends on the interaction between the individual and the social environment.

In the stage of *initiative versus guilt,* for example, children between ages 3 and 6 often want to undertake activities that exceed the limits set by their parents and culture. They jump into swimming pools, pull their pants on backwards, make cakes according to their own recipes, and wander off alone. Such efforts to act independently leave them open to feelings of pride or failure, producing guilt if adults are too critical.

SAMANTHA SCOTT / ALAMY

Who Are We? The most famous of Erikson's eight crises is the identity crisis, during adolescence, when young people find their own answer to the question "Who am I?" Erikson did this for himself by choosing a last name that, with his first name, implies "son of myself" (Erik, Erik's son). These *hara juko* girls in Japan are among the millions of teenagers worldwide who display an identity unlike that of their parents.

TABLE 2.1 Comparison of Freud's Psychosexual and Erikson's Psychosocial Stages

Approximate Age	Freud (Psychosexual)	Erikson (Psychosocial)
Birth to 1 year	*Oral Stage* The lips, tongue, and gums are the focus of pleasurable sensations in the baby's body, and sucking and feeding are the most stimulating activities.	*Trust vs. Mistrust* Babies either trust that others will care for their basic needs, including nourishment, warmth, cleanliness, and physical contact, *or* develop mistrust about the care of others.
1–3 years	*Anal Stage* The anus is the focus of pleasurable sensations in the baby's body, and toilet training is the most important activity.	*Autonomy vs. Shame and Doubt* Children either become self-sufficient in many activities, including toileting, feeding, walking, exploring, and talking, *or* doubt their own abilities.
3–6 years	*Phallic Stage* The phallus, or penis, is the most important body part, and pleasure is derived from genital stimulation. Boys are proud of their penises; girls wonder why they don't have one.	*Initiative vs. Guilt* Children either want to undertake many adultlike activities *or* internalize the limits and prohibitions set by parents. They feel either adventurous *or* guilty.
6–11 years	*Latency* Not really a stage, latency is an interlude during which sexual needs are quiet and children put psychic energy into conventional activities like schoolwork and sports.	*Industry vs. Inferiority* Children busily learn to be competent and productive in mastering new skills *or* feel inferior, unable to do anything as well as they wish they could.
Adolescence	*Genital Stage* The genitals are the focus of pleasurable sensations, and the young person seeks sexual stimulation and sexual satisfaction in heterosexual relationships.	*Identity vs. Role Confusion* Adolescents try to figure out "Who am I?" They establish sexual, political, religious, and vocational identities *or* are confused about what roles to play.
Adulthood	Freud believed that the genital stage lasts throughout adulthood. He also said that the goal of a healthy life is "to love and to work."	*Intimacy vs. Isolation* Young adults seek companionship and love *or* become isolated from others because they fear rejection and disappointment. *Generativity vs. Stagnation* Middle-aged adults contribute to the next generation through meaningful work, creative activities, and/or raising a family, *or* they stagnate. *Integrity vs. Despair* Older adults try to make sense out of their lives, either seeing life as a meaningful whole *or* despairing at goals never reached.

As you can see from Table 2.1, Erikson's first five stages are closely related to Freud's stages. Erikson, like Freud, believed that problems of adult life echo unresolved conflicts of childhood. For example, an adult who has difficulty establishing a secure, mutual relationship with a life partner may never have resolved the first crisis of early infancy, *trust versus mistrust*. Even in late adulthood, one older person may be outspoken, while another fears saying the wrong thing, because they resolved their initiative-versus-guilt stage in opposite ways. However, in at least one crucial way, Erikson's stages differ significantly from Freud's: They emphasize not sexual urges but rather each person's relationships to family and culture.

Especially for Teachers Your kindergartners are talkative and always moving. They almost never sit quietly and listen to you. What would Erik Erikson recommend? (see response, page 43)

Behaviorism: Conditioning and Social Learning

The second grand theory arose in direct opposition to the psychoanalytic notion of the unconscious. John B. Watson (1878–1958) argued that if psychology was to be a true science, psychologists should examine only what they could see and measure: behavior, not irrational thoughts and hidden urges. In his words:

> Why don't we make what we can *observe* the real field of psychology? Let us limit ourselves to things that can be observed, and formulate laws concerned only with those things. . . . We can observe behavior—what the organism does or says.
>
> [*Watson, 1924/1998, p. 6*]

ARCHIVES OF THE HISTORY OF AMERICAN PSYCHOLOGY, THE UNIVERSITY OF AKRON

An Early Behaviorist John Watson was an early proponent of learning theory. His ideas are still influential and controversial today.

According to Watson, if psychologists focus on behavior, they will realize that everything can be learned. He wrote:

> Give me a dozen healthy infants, well-formed, and my own specified world to bring them up in and I'll guarantee to take any one at random and train him to become any type of specialist I might select—doctor, lawyer, artist, merchant chief, and yes, even beggar-man and thief, regardless of his talents, penchants, tendencies, abilities, vocations, and race of his ancestors.
>
> *[Watson, 1924/1998, p. 82]*

Other psychologists, especially in the United States, agreed. They developed **behaviorism** to study actual behavior, objectively and scientifically. Behaviorism is also called *learning theory* because it describes how people learn and develop habits, step by step. For every individual at every age, behaviorists describe laws detailing how simple actions and environmental responses shape complex competencies, such as reading a book or making a family dinner.

Learning theorists believe that development occurs in small increments: A person learns to talk, read, or anything else bit by bit over a long time. Because change is cumulative, behaviorists, unlike Freud and Erikson, describe no specific stages of development (Bijou & Baer, 1978). Rather, they focus on the laws of **conditioning,** the processes by which responses become linked to particular stimuli, sometimes called *S–R (stimulus–response) conditioning.* In the first half of the twentieth century, behaviorists described only two types of conditioning: classical and operant.

behaviorism A grand theory of human development that studies observable behavior. Behaviorism is also called *learning theory* because it describes the laws and processes by which behavior is learned.

conditioning According to behaviorism, the processes by which responses become linked to particular stimuli and learning takes place. The word *conditioning* is used to emphasize the importance of repeated practice, as when an athlete *conditions* his or her body to perform well by training for a long time.

classical conditioning The learning process in which a meaningful stimulus (such as the smell of food to a hungry animal) is connected with a neutral stimulus (such as the sound of a tone) that had no special meaning before conditioning. (Also called *respondent conditioning.*)

Classical Conditioning

A century ago, Russian scientist Ivan Pavlov (1849–1936), after winning the Nobel Prize for his work on animal digestion, began to examine the link between stimulus and response. While studying salivation, Pavlov noted that his experimental dogs drooled not only at the smell of food but also, eventually, at the footsteps of the people bringing food. This observation led Pavlov to perform a famous experiment: He conditioned dogs to salivate upon hearing a particular noise.

Pavlov began by sounding a tone just before presenting food. After a number of repetitions of the tone-then-food sequence, dogs began salivating at the sound even when there was no food. This simple experiment demonstrated **classical conditioning** (also called *respondent conditioning*).

SOVFOTO

A Contemporary of Freud Ivan Pavlov was a physiologist who received the Nobel Prize in 1904 for his research on digestive processes. It was this line of study that led to his discovery of classical conditioning.

Observation Quiz In appearance, how is Pavlov similar to Freud, and how do both look different from the other theorists pictured? (see answer, page 43)

In classical conditioning, a person or animal is conditioned to associate a neutral stimulus with a meaningful stimulus, gradually responding to the neutral stimulus in the same way as to the meaningful one. In Pavlov's original experiment, the dog associated the tone (the neutral stimulus) with food (the meaningful stimulus) and learned to respond to the tone as though it were the food itself. The conditioned response to the tone (no longer neutral but now a conditioned stimulus) was evidence that learning had occurred.

Behaviorists see dozens of examples of classical conditioning in human development. Infants learn to smile at their parents because they associate their mother and father with food and play; toddlers become afraid of busy streets if the noise of traffic frightens them; schoolchildren enjoy—or fear—sitting at their desks, depending on past experiences.

>> Response for Teachers (from page 41) Erikson would note that the behavior of 5-year-olds is affected by their developmental stage and by their culture. Therefore, you might design your curriculum to accommodate active, noisy children.

Operant Conditioning

The most influential North American proponent of behaviorism was B. F. Skinner (1904–1990). Skinner agreed that psychology should focus on the scientific study of behavior. His famous contribution to the science of psychology was to recognize another type of conditioning—**operant conditioning** (also called *instrumental conditioning*)—in which animals (including people) act and then a consequence occurs. If the consequence is enjoyable, the animal will repeat the behavior. If the consequence is unpleasant, the animal might not repeat that behavior. Usually, learning occurs only after several repetitions with consequences.

operant conditioning The learning process by which a particular action is followed by something desired (which makes the person or animal more likely to repeat the action) or by something unwanted (which makes the action less likely to be repeated). (Also called *instrumental conditioning.*)

SAM FALK / PHOTO RESEARCHERS, INC.

Rats, Pigeons, and People B. F. Skinner is best known for his experiments with rats and pigeons, but he also applied his knowledge to human behavior. For his daughter, he designed a glass-enclosed crib in which temperature, humidity, and perceptual stimulation could be controlled to make her time in the crib enjoyable and educational. He wrote about an ideal society based on principles of operant conditioning, where, for example, workers in less desirable jobs would earn greater rewards.

Pleasant consequences are sometimes called *rewards,* and unpleasant consequences are sometimes called *punishments.* Behaviorists hesitate to use those words, however, because what some call punishment may actually be a reward, and vice versa. For example, parents punish their children by withholding dessert, by spanking them, by not letting them play, by speaking harshly to them, and so on. But a particular child might dislike dessert, so being deprived of it is no punishment. Or a child might not mind a spanking, especially if that is the only time the parent gives the child attention. Thus, the intended punishment is actually a reward.

Similarly, teachers sometimes punish misbehaving children by sending them out of the classroom or even suspending them from school. However, if a child hates the teacher, leaving class is rewarding. In fact, recent research on school discipline finds that some measures, including school suspension, *increase* later misbehavior (Osher et al., 2010). The true test is the *effect* a consequence has on the individual's future actions, not whether it is intended to be a reward or a punishment. A child, or an adult, who repeats an offense may have been reinforced, not punished, for the first infraction. Consequences that increase the frequency or strength of a particular action are called *reinforcers,* in a process called **reinforcement** (Skinner, 1953).

Especially for Teachers Same problem as previously (talkative kindergartners), but what would a behaviorist recommend? (see response, page 45)

reinforcement When a behavior is followed by something desired, such as food for a hungry animal or a welcoming smile for a lonely person.

One of the discoveries arising from behaviorism is that each person responds differently to reinforcements and punishments, as already mentioned with spanking. In another example, a longitudinal study of children's physical activity (playing sports, exercising, and so on) found that, for boys, the father's praise was especially important. For girls, reinforcement helped, but the mother's own physical activity was the more powerful influence (Cleland et al., 2011).

>> Answer to Observation Quiz (from page 42) Both are balding, with white beards. Note also that none of the other theorists in this chapter have beards—a cohort difference, not an ideological one.

Social Learning

The importance of the mother's example leads to another insight from behaviorism. At first, behaviorists interpreted all behavior as arising from a chain of learned responses, the result of conditioning based either on the associations between one stimulus and another (classical) or on the consequences an individual experienced (operant). Such conditioning does occur, as has been demonstrated by many studies confirming this part of learning theory. However, humans are social and active, not just reactive. Instead of responding merely to their own direct experiences, "people act on the environment. They create it, preserve it, transform it, and even destroy it . . . in a socially embedded interplay" (Bandura, 2006, p. 167).

FIGURE 2.1

Three Types of Learning Behaviorism is also called *learning theory* because it emphasizes the learning process, as shown here.

Learning occurs through:

- **Classical conditioning** Through association: neutral stimulus becomes conditioned stimulus.
- **Operant conditioning** Through reinforcement: weak or rare response becomes strong, frequent response.
- **Social learning** Through modeling: observed behaviors become copied behaviors.

This insight led to **social learning theory** (see Figure 2.1), which holds that humans sometimes learn without personal reinforcement. This may occur through **modeling,** when people copy what they see others do (also called *observational learning*). Modeling is not simple imitation. Instead, people model only some actions, of some individuals, in some contexts. As an example, you may know adults who, as children, saw their parents hit each other. Some such adults abuse their own partners, while others scrupulously avoid marital conflict. These two responses seem opposite, but both are social learning produced by childhood observation. Still other adults may seem unfazed; differential susceptibility (explained in Chapter 1) may be the reason.

social learning theory An extension of behaviorism that emphasizes the influence that other people have over a person's behavior. Even without specific reinforcement, every individual learns many things through observation and imitation of other people. (Also called *observational learning.*)

modeling The central process of social learning, by which a person observes the actions of others and then copies them.

self-efficacy In social learning theory, the belief of some people that they are able to change themselves and effectively alter the social context.

Generally, modeling is most likely to occur when the observer is uncertain or inexperienced (which explains why modeling is especially powerful in childhood) and when the model is admired, powerful, nurturing, or similar to the observer (Bandura, 1986, 1997). If your speech, hairstyle, or choice of shoes is similar to those of a celebrity, ask yourself what made you model that person's behavior. Admiration? Similarity? If children's language includes curses that their parents never utter, who were the models and why are they admired?

Social learning is connected to perceptions and interpretations of experience. One crucial interpretation involves a sense of **self-efficacy,** the belief that personal achievement depends on personal actions. People develop a sense of efficacy when they see other people solve problems successfully, which teaches them to have high aspirations and to strive for notable accomplishments (Bandura et al., 2001). The same applies to ethnic groups, cultures, and nations. Whether or not one nation intervenes in the actions of another depends partly on the national sense of self-efficacy.

Applications of learning theory often combine strategies suggested by all three aspects of behaviorism. In one study, for example, when children (aged 5 to 10) had sleep problems, their therapy involved classical conditioning (a quiet room with blue walls), operant conditioning (encouragement from peers), and the self-efficacy aspect of social learning (convincing children and their parents that improved sleep was possible). According to the researchers, the combination led to markedly fewer arousal problems or nightmares (Schlarb et al., 2011).

BIG CHEESE / GLOW IMAGES

His Pride and Joy This father is proud of his muscles, but he is even more proud of his son—and didn't want to be photographed showing off his biceps alone. The pride is mutual: The boy hopes to become a man like his dad.

Observation Quiz Behind the posturing, what indicates that this boy models himself after his parent? (see answer, page 46)

Psychoanalytic Versus Behaviorist Theories

Psychoanalytic and behaviorist theories were provocative, innovative, comprehensive, and surprising; they have endured because they offer insights into important aspects of development. Until these theories were developed, few imagined that childhood exerts such power (psychoanalytic) or that adult behavior arises from earlier reinforcement (behaviorist) or observation (social learning).

with time and experience, and their thought processes affect their conclusions and actions. According to cognitive theory, to understand human behavior one must understand thinking.

Piaget maintained that cognitive development occurs in four age-related periods, or stages: *sensorimotor, preoperational, concrete operational,* and *formal operational* (see Table 2.3). Each period fosters certain cognitive processes; for instance, infants think with their senses, and abstract logic is absent in children but possible at puberty (Inhelder & Piaget, 1958; Piaget, 1952b).

According to Piaget, intellectual advancement occurs because humans at every age seek **cognitive equilibrium**—a state of mental balance. The easiest way to achieve this balance is to interpret new experiences through the lens of preexisting ideas. For example, infants grab new objects in the same way as they grasp familiar objects, children interpret their parents' behavior by assuming that adults think in the same way that children do.

However, achieving equilibrium is not always easy. Sometimes a new experience or question is jarring or incomprehensible. Then the individual experiences *cognitive disequilibrium,* an imbalance that creates confusion. As Figure 2.2 illustrates, disequilibrium can cause cognitive growth if people change their thinking. Piaget describes two types of cognitive adaptation:

- **Assimilation:** New experiences are reinterpreted to fit into, or *assimilate* with, old ideas.
- **Accommodation:** Old ideas are restructured to include, or *accommodate,* new experiences.

Accommodation is more difficult than assimilation, but it produces intellectual advancement. For example, if a friend's questions reveal inconsistencies in your own opinions, or if your favorite chess strategy puts you in checkmate, or if your mother says something completely unexpected, disequilibrium occurs. In the last example, you might *assimilate* by deciding your mother didn't mean what she said. You might tell yourself that she was repeating something she had read or that you misheard her. However, intellectual growth would occur if, instead, you changed your view of your mother to *accommodate* a new, expanded understanding.

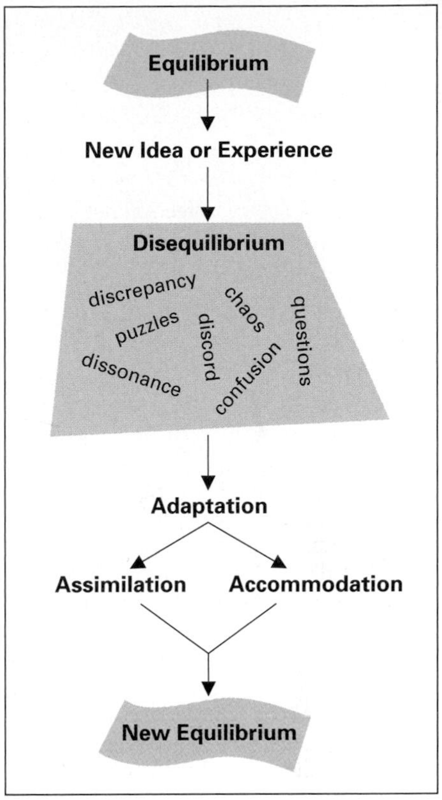

FIGURE 2.2

Challenge Me Most of us, most of the time, prefer the comfort of our conventional conclusions. According to Piaget, however, when new ideas disturb our thinking, we have an opportunity to expand our cognition with a broader and deeper understanding.

TABLE 2.3 Piaget's Periods of Cognitive Development

Age Range	Name of Period	Characteristics of the Period	Major Gains During the Period
Birth to 2 years	Sensorimotor	Infants use senses and motor abilities to understand the world. Learning is active; there is no conceptual or reflective thought.	Infants learn that an object still exists when it is out of sight (*object permanence*) and begin to think through mental actions.
2–6 years	Preoperational	Children think magically and poetically, using language to understand the world. Thinking is *egocentric,* causing children to perceive the world from their own perspective.	The imagination flourishes, and language becomes a significant means of self-expression and of influence from others.
6–11 years	Concrete operational	Children understand and apply logical operations, or principles, to interpret experiences objectively and rationally. Their thinking is limited to what they can personally see, hear, touch, and experience.	By applying logical abilities, children learn to understand concepts of conservation, number, classification, and many other scientific ideas.
12 years through adulthood	Formal operational	Adolescents and adults think about abstractions and hypothetical concepts. They reason analytically, not just emotionally, and can be logical about things they have never experienced.	Ethics, politics, and social and moral issues become fascinating as adolescents and adults take a broader and more theoretical approach to experience.

GAIL JUSIDMAN

DAVINA GRAHAM / ISTOCKPHOTO

RANDY DUCHAINE, BROOKLYN, NY

PHOTODISC / PUNCHSTOCK

How to Think About Flowers A person's stage of cognitive growth influences how he or she thinks about everything, including flowers. *(a)* To 7-month-old Maya, in the sensorimotor stage, flowers are "known" through pulling, smelling, and even biting. *(b)* At the concrete operational stage, children become more logical. This boy can understand that flowers need sunlight, water, and time to grow. *(c, d)* At the adult's formal operational stage, flowers can be part of a larger, logical scheme—either to earn money or to cultivate beauty. Thinking is an active process from the beginning of life until the end.

Ideally, when two people disagree, or when they surprise each other by what they say, adaptation is mutual. For example, when parents are startled by their children's opinions, the parents may revise their concepts of their children and their ideas, accommodating to new perceptions. If an honest discussion occurs, the children, too, might accommodate. Cognitive growth is an active process, dependent on clashing and challenging concepts.

Information Processing

Piaget is credited with discovering that people's thoughts and perceptions affect their development, an idea now accepted by most social scientists. However, many think Piaget's theories were inadequate. Neuroscience, cross-cultural studies, and step-by-step understanding of cognition have revealed the limitations of Piaget's theories. Here we introduce one newer version of cognitive theory, *information processing,* a theory inspired by the many processes by which computers function so efficiently. According to this theory, the human mind is similar in many ways to a sophisticated computer.

information-processing theory A perspective that compares human thinking processes, by analogy, to computer analysis of data, including sensory input, connections, stored memories, and output.

Information-processing theory "is not a single theory but, rather, a framework characterizing a large number of research programs" (Miller, 2011, p. 266). Instead of merely interpreting responses by infants and children, as Piaget did, information processing explores the processes of thought, that is, how minds work before responding. The underlying theoretical basis of information processing is that the details of process shed light on the specifics of outcome.

For information-processing scientists, cognition begins with input picked up by the five senses; proceeds to brain reactions, connections, and stored memories; and concludes with some form of output. For very young infants, output consists of moving a hand, making a sound, or staring a split second longer at one stimulus than at another. With the aid of sensitive technology, information-processing research has overturned some of Piaget's findings, as explained in later chapters.

Information processing also describes the relationship between one person's thinking and another's. For instance, under some conditions, thinking improves when people are part of a group, but under other conditions, groups slow down thought. Information processing helps us understand the difference (De Dreu et al., 2008). Similarly, some people say that watching television is destructive for young children; others disagree. Information-processing studies help researchers weigh in on this debate: Such studies can pinpoint exactly which cognitive processes are impaired by which images on the screen and at what age (Roseberry et al., 2009).

This approach to understanding cognition has many other applications. For example, it has long been recognized that children with ADHD (attention-deficit/hyperactivity disorder) are not simply excessively active but also tend to have difficulties learning in school, obeying their parents, and making friends. Information processing has led to the discovery that certain brain circuits (called *fronto-striatal systems*) do not function normally in children with ADHD. Consequently, they have difficulty reading facial expressions and voice tone in order to understand emotions (Uekermann et al., 2010). They may not know whether their father's "Come here" is an angry command or a friendly suggestion. Information processing helps in remediation: If a specific brain function can be improved, children may learn more, obey more, and gain friends.

YVES DEBRAINE/ BLACK STAR

Would You Talk to This Man? Children loved talking to Jean Piaget, and he learned by listening carefully—especially to their incorrect explanations, which no one had paid much attention to before. All his life, Piaget was absorbed with studying the way children think. He called himself a "genetic epistemologist"—one who studies how children gain knowledge about the world as they grow up.

SUMMING UP

The three grand theories originated decades ago, each pioneered by men who are admired for their ability to set forth psychological theories so comprehensive and creative that they deserve to be called "grand." Each grand theory has a different focus: emotions (psychoanalytic theory), actions (behaviorism), and thoughts (cognitive theory) (see Figure 2.3).

Freud and Erikson thought unconscious drives and early experiences form later personality and behavior. Behaviorists stress experiences in the more recent past and focus on learning by association, by reinforcement, and by observation. Cognitive theory holds that to understand a person, one must learn how that person thinks. According to Piaget, cognition develops in four distinct stages; according to information-processing theory, a multiplicity of components eventually result in crucial ideas and perceptions. ■

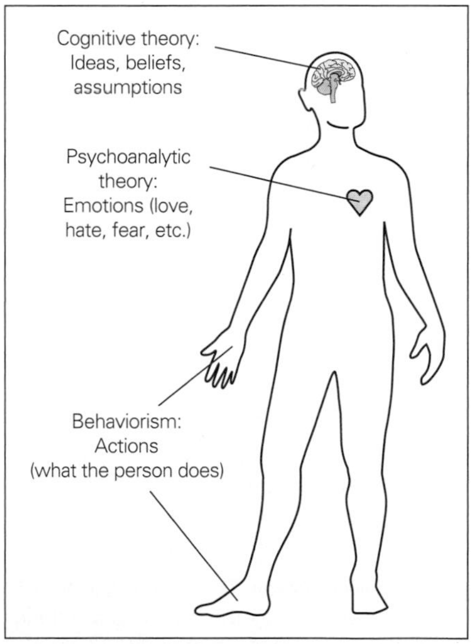

FIGURE 2.3

Major Focuses of the Three Grand Theories This simplified figure emphasizes that although all three of the grand theories recognize that thoughts, emotions, and actions interact within each person, each theory focuses on a different aspect of the person.

>> Newer Theories

You have surely noticed that the seminal grand theorists (Freud, Erikson, Pavlov, Skinner, Piaget) were all men, scientists from western Europe or North America, born more than a hundred years ago. These background variables are limiting. (Of course, female, non-western, and contemporary theorists are limited by their backgrounds, too.) Despite their impressive insights, the three grand theories no longer seem as comprehensive as they once did, in part because their limitations have become more apparent in the twenty-first century.

New theories have emerged that, unlike the grand theories, are multicultural and multidisciplinary and thus are more in accord with the current view of the science of human development. The first theory described here, sociocultural theory, draws on research in education, anthropology, and history; the second one, universal theory, arises from theology, political science, and history (humanism) or from archeology, ethology, and biology (evolutionary theory).

Sociocultural Theory: Vygotsky and Beyond

COURTESY OF DR. MICHAEL COLE, LABORATORY OF COMPARATIVE HUMAN COGNITION, UC, SAN DIEGO

The Founder of Sociocultural Theory Lev Vygotsky, now recognized as a seminal thinker whose ideas are revolutionizing education and the study of development, was a contemporary of Freud, Skinner, Pavlov, and Piaget. Vygotsky did not attain their eminence in his lifetime, partly because his work, conducted in Stalinist Russia, was largely inaccessible to the Western world and partly because he died young, at age 38.

The central thesis of **sociocultural theory** is that human development results from the dynamic interaction between developing persons and their surrounding society. Culture is viewed not as something external that impinges on developing persons but as integral to their development every day via the social context (all the dynamic systems described in Chapter 1).

Social Interaction

The pioneer of the sociocultural perspective was Lev Vygotsky (1896–1934), a psychologist from the former Soviet Union. Vygotsky was a leader in describing the interaction between culture and education. He noted that each community in his native Russia (which included Asians and Europeans, of many faiths and languages) taught its children whatever beliefs and habits its culture valued.

Vygotsky studied cognitive competencies of people of many ethnic groups as well as of children with and without special needs. He studied how farmers used tools, how illiterate people used abstract ideas, and how children of all abilities learned in school. In his view, each person, schooled or not, develops with the guidance of more skilled members of the society, who are tutors or mentors in an **apprenticeship in thinking** (Vygotsky, 1934/1986).

To describe this process, Vygotsky developed the concept of **guided participation,** the method used by parents, teachers, and entire societies to teach novices the skills and habits expected within the particular culture. Tutors engage learners (also called *apprentices*) in joint activities, offering not only instruction but also "mutual involvement in several widespread cultural practices with great importance for learning: narratives, routines, and play" (Rogoff, 2003, p. 285). Active apprenticeship is a central concept of sociocultural theory because each person depends on others to learn. This process is informal, pervasive, and social.

For example, one of my students came to my office with her young son, who eyed my candy dish but did not take any.

"He can have one if it's all right with you," I whispered to his mother.

She nodded and told him, "Dr. Berger will let you have one piece of candy."

He smiled shyly and quickly took one.

"What do you say?" she prompted.

"Thank you," he replied, glancing at me out of the corner of his eye.

"You're welcome," I said.

In that brief moment, all three of us were engaged in cultural transmission. We were surrounded by cultural traditions and practices, including my authority as professor, the fact that I have an office and a candy dish (a custom that I learned from one of my teachers), and the direct authority of the mother, who had taught her son to be polite and obedient. As an apprentice, he needed to be reminded to say "thank you." I guided him as well, in part by saying he could have one piece (encouraging math, authority, and moderation all at once). Specifics differ, but all adults teach children skills expected in their society and culture.

All cultural patterns and beliefs are social constructions, not natural laws, according to sociocultural theorists. They find customs to be powerful, shaping the development of every person, and they also find that some assumptions need to shift to allow healthier development of all people. Vygotsky stressed this point, arguing that mentally and physically disabled children should be educated (Vygotsky, 1925/1994), a cultural belief that has emerged in the United States in the past few decades but is not accepted in many other nations (Rogoff, 2003).

sociocultural theory A newer theory that holds that development results from the dynamic interaction of each person with the surrounding social and cultural forces.

apprenticeship in thinking Vygotsky's term for how cognition is stimulated and developed in people by more skilled members of society.

guided participation The process by which people learn from others who guide their experiences and explorations.

zone of proximal development In sociocultural theory, a metaphorical area, or "zone," surrounding a learner that includes all the skills, knowledge, and concepts that the person is close ("proximal") to acquiring but cannot yet master without help.

The Zone of Proximal Development

According to sociocultural theory, all learning is social, whether people are learning a manual skill, a social custom, or a language. As part of the apprenticeship in thinking, a mentor (parent, peer, or professional) finds the learner's **zone of proximal development,** the skills, knowledge, and concepts that the learner is close to acquiring but cannot yet master without help.

Through sensitive assessment of the learner, the mentor engages the mentee; together, in a "process of joint construction," new knowledge is attained (Valsiner, 2006). The mentor must avoid two opposite dangers: boredom and failure. Some frustration is permitted, but the learner must be actively engaged, never passive and never overwhelmed (see Figure 2.4).

To make this seemingly abstract process more concrete, consider an example: a father teaching his daughter to ride a bicycle. He begins by rolling her along, supporting her weight while telling her to keep her hands on the handlebars, to push the right and left pedals in rhythm, and to look straight ahead. As she becomes more comfortable and confident, he begins to roll her along more quickly, praising her for steadily pumping. Within a few lessons, he is jogging beside her, holding only the handlebars. When he senses that she could maintain her balance by herself, he urges her to pedal faster and slowly loosens his grip. Perhaps without even realizing it, she is riding on her own.

Note that this is not instruction by preset rules. Sociocultural learning is active: No one learns to ride a bike by reading and memorizing written instructions, and no good teacher merely repeats a prepared lesson. Because each learner has personal traits, experiences, and aspirations, education must be individualized. Learning styles vary: Some people need more assurance than others; some learn best by looking, others by hearing. A mentor needs to sense when support or freedom is needed and how peers can help (they are sometimes the best mentors). Teachers know how the zone of proximal development expands and shifts.

Excursions into and through the zone of proximal development, as illustrated by the boy prompted to say "thank you" and the girl learning to balance on a bike, are commonplace for all of us. Examples are everywhere. At the thousand or so science museums in the United States, children ask numerous questions, and adults guide their scientific knowledge (Haden, 2010). The same process is evident when children are learning to drum in rhythm with another drum: Children need practice, but they learn faster when the other drummer is not a machine but a person, older than they and presumably better at synchronizing a beat (Kleinspehn-Ammerlahn et al., 2011).

In general, mentors, attuned to ever-shifting abilities and motivation, continually urge a new level of competence; learners ask questions, show interest, and demonstrate progress, thereby guiding and inspiring the mentors. When education goes well, both are fully engaged and productive within the zone of proximal development. Particular skills and processes vary enormously from culture to culture, but the overall social interaction is the same.

DAVE KING / GETTY IMAGES

Gourmet Cook in the Making Some children have skilled mentors who engage them in learning. It would be much easier for this cook to cut, dip, and fry without help, but the child is an apprentice and will soon learn the skill himself.

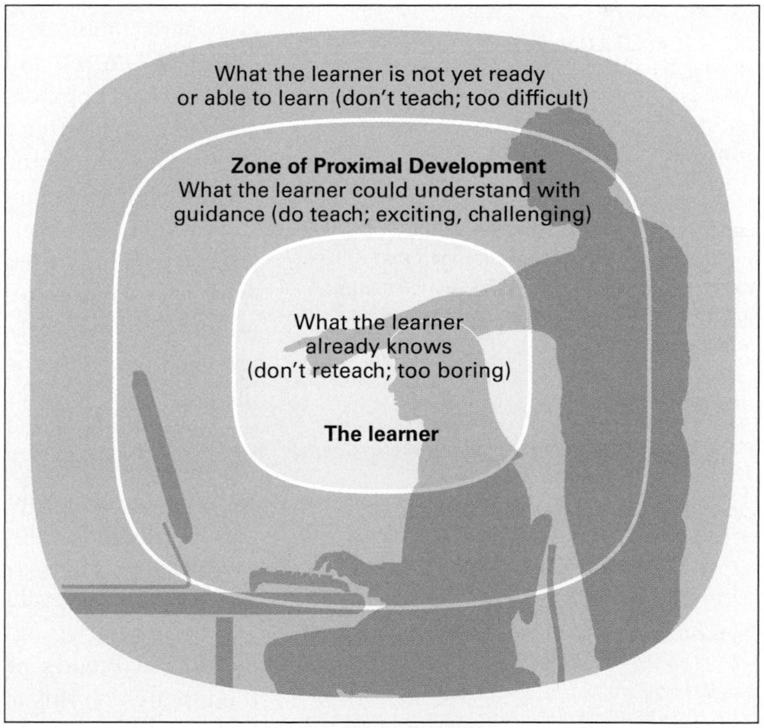

FIGURE 2.4

The Magic Middle Somewhere between the boring and the impossible is the zone of proximal development, where interaction between teacher and learner results in knowledge never before grasped or skills not already mastered. The intellectual excitement of that zone is the origin of the joy that both instruction and study can bring.

Taking Culture into Account

The sociocultural perspective has led contemporary scientists to consider social context in every study. Earlier theorists and researchers are quickly criticized for having failed to do so.

Research on attachment provides an easy example. As you will see in Chapter 7, a major topic in development is the relationship between infant and caregiver, a social bond that may affect the child lifelong. Secure attachment at 12 months correlates with the mother's responsiveness earlier in the infant's life, a finding that led to "attachment parenting" (the theory that parents should respond to every cry) and then to the "nurturance overload" mentioned early in this chapter.

At first, only attachment between mother and child was studied: It was thought that secure infants (about two-thirds of all babies studied) will play happily when mother is nearby, showing affection but not clinging. This early research was heavily influenced by psychoanalytic theory; it was Freud (1940/1949) who wrote that the mother–infant relationship is "unique, without parallel, established unalterably for a child's lifetime as the first and strongest love-object and as the prototype of all later love-relations" (p. 45).

Later research acknowledged fathers, grandparents, and other caregivers (Hrdy, 2009). Some infants are equally attached to both parents or are more securely attached to their fathers than to their mothers. Indeed, "in the United States and elsewhere, multiple attachment relationships are normative" (Thompson, 2006, p. 43). When researchers began exploring attachment in various cultures, they found a higher proportion of Japanese infants clinging to their mothers rather than exploring (suggesting these infants were insecurely attached) and a higher proportion of German infants exploring but seemingly indifferent to their mothers (also suggesting insecure attachment).

Especially for Adoptive Families Does the importance of attachment mean that adopted children will not bond securely with nonbiological caregivers? (see response, page 55)

However, the sociocultural perspective has shed new light on cultural differences such as these. The attachment bond is universally important, but the expression of it depends on cultural context. Unless that context is considered, infants who are developing well may be misjudged, as many Japanese and German infants were. Responsiveness of the mother to the infant in the first months of life is thought to influence attachment at 1 year, but it is now apparent that how the mother responds is strongly influenced by her culture (Kärtner et al., 2010). Moreover, the goal of the early actions of the caregiver varies by culture: Most Western families value language and thus respond to infant vocalization; many African families value social responsibility and thus teach sensitive interaction (Super et al., 2011). Attachment is just one of dozens of developmental concepts that have been reevaluated in research with participants from various cultures.

Another intriguing area of research is gender and ethnic prejudice, which may increase at Freud's phallic stage or Piaget's concrete operational stage. Most of the research on this topic has occurred in the United States, where, over the past half-century, research has found that children are increasingly aware of prejudice against Black Americans, yet they are more vulnerable to becoming prejudiced themselves depending not only on cognitive maturation but also on the particular circumstances of their lives (Brown & Bigler, 2005; Nesdale et al., 2005).

In the United States, studies indicate that by adolescence, personal experience counts: Children who attend schools that are almost exclusively European American are less likely to oppose prejudice than are children with more diverse experiences (Killen at al., 2010). The sociocultural perspective, however, reminds us that cultures may differ on such matters.

For example, a recent study among children in Denmark found that they all soundly disapproved of excluding a child from an activity because of that's child's gender or ethnic background (the outgroup were children born in Denmark to

Muslim parents who had immigrated in the 1960s) (Møller & Tenenbaum, 2011). Contrary to behaviorism and the conclusions of U.S. research, this study found that attitudes were not affected by whether a child's school had Muslim children or not; and contrary to Piaget, this study found few age differences in attitude. It did find, however, that children distinguished justice from custom—a sociocultural distinction (see the Research Design).

The Universal Perspective: Humanism and Evolutionary Theory

No developmentalist doubts that each person is unique. Yet many social scientists contend that focusing on cultural (or ethnic, or sexual, or economic) differences results in an unbalanced vision of humanity. We are one species, sharing universal impulses and needs. This universal perspective has been articulated in many developmental theories, each time expressed in particular ways but always contending that humans are, at the basic level, alike. Here we describe two of the most prominent of such perspectives: humanism and evolutionary theory.

Humanism

Many scientists are convinced that there is something hopeful, unifying, and noble in the human spirit, something ignored by psychoanalytic theory (which stresses the selfish id and infantile sexuality) and by behaviorism (which seems to ignore free will). The limits of those two major theories were especially apparent to two Americans: Abraham Maslow (1908–1970) and Carl Rogers (1902–1987), both deeply religious. They had witnessed the Great Depression and two world wars and concluded that traditional psychological theories underrated human potential by focusing on evil, not good. They founded a theory called **humanism** that became prominent after World War II, as millions read Maslow's *Toward a Psychology of Being* (1962/1999) and Rogers's *On Becoming a Person* (1961/2004).

As he expressed it first in 1943, Maslow believed that all people—no matter what their culture, gender, or background—have the same basic needs and drives. He arranged these needs in a hierarchy (see Figure 2.5):

1. Physiological: needing food, water, warmth, and air
2. Safety: feeling protected from injury and death
3. Love and belonging: having loving friends, family, and a community (often religious)
4. Esteem: being respected by the wider community as well as by oneself
5. Self-actualization: becoming truly oneself, fulfilling one's unique potential while appreciating all of humanity

At the highest level, when basic needs have been met, people can be fully themselves—creative, spiritual, curious, appreciative of nature, able to respect everyone else. One sign of self-actualization is that the person has "peak experiences" when life is so intensely joyful that time stops and self-seeking disappears. Given the stresses and deprivations of modern life, humanists believe that relatively few people reach the self-actualization of level 5. But everyone *can*—that is the universality of humanism.

Rogers also stressed the need to accept and respect one's own personhood as well as that of everyone else. He thought that people should give each other *unconditional positive regard*, which means that they should see (regard) each other with appreciation (positive) without conditions (unconditional). He did not think that everything people do is good, but he believed that people themselves are good, as in "Hate the sin but love the sinner." Rogers spent the last years of his life trying to

Research Design

Scientists: Signe J. Møller and Harriet R. Tenenbaum.

Publication: *Child Development* (2011).

Participants: Questions were asked of 282 Danish majority children, ages 8 to 12, attending seven schools—four of which had no ethnic minority children enrolled and three of which had some ethnic minority children enrolled. The schools were located in the suburbs, not where ethnic differences were most salient.

Design: Children, individually and privately, responded to eight hypothetical vignettes in which a child was excluded by teachers or children because of the child's gender or ethnicity. For example, "Shahar wants to play Ludo, but the teacher says she cannot play because there are already three Danish boys and girls playing. Instead, the teacher says that a Danish classmate can play."

Results: The children not only recognized the prejudice, they were strongly opposed to it. This was true even when the exclusion was based on gender and even when a child was the perpetrator. But opposition was most adamant when a teacher excluded an ethnic minority child (as in the example). Such teachers were strongly criticized by children of all experiences.

Conclusion: Although age and daily life affect children's awareness of discrimination in the United States, because Danish values strongly endorse egalitarian practices, the children with no personal experience of other ethnicities judged ethnic exclusion as morally wrong, especially when perpetrated by a teacher.

Comment: Studies in other nations have also found that children are aware of discrimination and generally oppose it. The strength of these children's attitudes, with little effects of age and experience, suggest that national culture can have a powerful impact. Similar studies need to be performed in cultures in which prejudice is more acceptable, to learn how much children independently seek to be inclusive and how much children respond as a result of sociocultural values.

humanism A theory that stresses the potential of all humans for good and the belief that all people have the same basic needs, regardless of culture, gender, or background.

BETTMAN / CORBIS

Hope and Laughter Maslow studied law before psychology, and he enjoyed deep discussions with many psychoanalytic theorists who escaped Nazi Europe. Nonetheless, he believed in the human spirit and that it could overcome oppression and reach self-actualization, where faith, hope, and humor abound.

reconcile the factions in Northern Ireland, South Africa, and Russia; he believed all sides needed to learn to listen to each other.

As you can see, humanists emphasize what all people have in common, not their national, ethnic, or cultural differences. Maslow contended that everyone must satisfy each lower level of the hierarchy of needs before moving higher. A starving man, for instance, may not be concerned for his own safety when he seeks food (level 1 precedes level 2), or an unloved woman might not care about self-respect because she needs love (level 3 precedes level 4). Destructive and inhumane actions that prevent people from self-actualization may be the consequence of unmet lower needs. At the end of his life, Maslow explained that the highest level transcended selfishness and became selflessness, when a person is able to appreciate all of humanity (Maslow, 1971).

Although humanism does not postulate stages, a developmental application of this theory is that the satisfaction of childhood needs is crucial for later self-acceptance. Thus, when babies cry in hunger, that basic need should be satisfied. People may become thieves or even killers, unable to reach their potential, to self-actualize, if they were unsafe or unloved as children. Rogers agreed that adults who were deprived of unconditional positive regard in childhood might become selfish and antisocial. He developed a widely used method of psychological therapy to help people become more accepting of themselves and therefore of other people.

This theory is still prominent among medical professionals because they now realize that pain can be physical (the first two levels) or social (the next two) (Majercsik, 2005; Zalenski & Raspa, 2006). Even the very sick need love and belonging (family should be with them) and esteem (the dying need respect).

Especially for Nurses Maslow's hierarchy is often taught in health sciences because it alerts medical staff to the needs of patients. What specific hospital procedures might help? (see response, page 56)

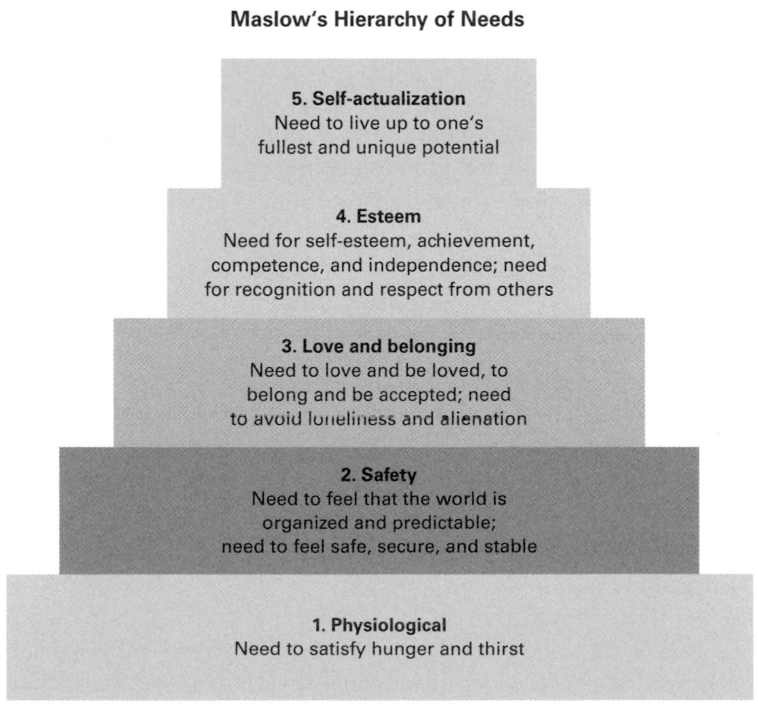
Maslow's Hierarchy of Needs
5. Self-actualization
Need to live up to one's fullest and unique potential
4. Esteem
Need for self-esteem, achievement, competence, and independence; need for recognition and respect from others
3. Love and belonging
Need to love and be loved, to belong and be accepted; need to avoid loneliness and alienation
2. Safety
Need to feel that the world is organized and predictable; need to feel safe, secure, and stable
1. Physiological
Need to satisfy hunger and thirst

Source: Maslow, 1954.

FIGURE 2.5

Moving Up, Not Looking Back Maslow's hierarchy is like a ladder: Once a person stands firmly on a higher rung, the lower rungs are no longer needed. Thus, someone who has arrived at step 4 might devalue safety (step 2) and be willing to risk personal safety to gain respect.

Echoes of humanism are also evident in education and sports: The basic idea here is that people are more effectively motivated when they try to master a body of knowledge or a skill to achieve a "personal best"—that is, to reach the peak of their own potential—than when they strive to be the best in their class or on their team (Ravizza, 2007).

Evolutionary Theory

You are familiar with Darwin and his ideas, first published 150 years ago—essentially that plants, insects, birds, and animals developed over billions of years, as life evolved from primitive cells to humans (Darwin, 1859). But you may not realize that serious research on human development inspired by this theory is quite recent. As two leaders in this field write:

> During the last two decades, the study of the evolutionary foundations of human nature has grown at an exponential rate. In fact, it is now a booming interdisciplinary scientific enterprise, one that sits at the cutting edge of the social and behavioral sciences.
>
> *[Gangestad & Simpson, 2007, p. 2]*

Evolutionary theory has intriguing explanations for many issues in human development, including women's nausea in pregnancy, 1-year-olds' attachment to their parents, puberty in young adolescents, emerging adults' sexual preferences, and parents' investment in their children. According to this theory, many human impulses, needs, and behaviors evolved to help humans survive and thrive over millions of years, with children particularly protected (Konner, 2010).

To understand human development, this theory contends, humans need to acknowledge the power of emotions that evolved thousands of years ago. For example, why are some people terrified of snakes (which cause 1 death in a billion), but virtually no one fears automobiles (which cause about 1 death in 5,000)? Evolutionary theory suggests that the fear instinct evolved over millennia to protect life when snakes killed people. Now we need to recognize that our fears have not caught up to modern inventions, so we need to use our minds, not be slaves of our emotions. That is happening: The motor-vehicle death rate has been cut in half by better-designed roads, laws, and cars. Other killers—climate change, drug addiction, obesity—are also difficult to manage because instincts are contrary to knowledge: Evolutionary theory contends that recognizing the origins of destructive urges helps to control them.

According to evolutionary theory, every species has two long-standing, biologically based drives: survival and reproduction. Understanding these two drives provides insight into protective parenthood, the death of some newborns, infant dependency, child immaturity, the onset of puberty, and much more (Konner, 2010). Later chapters will explain how in more detail, but here is one example. Human and nonhuman adults find babies appealing—despite the reality that babies (not only human, but also puppies, kittens, and so on) have little hair, no chins, stubby legs, and round stomachs—all of which are considered ugly in adults. The reason, evolutionary theory contends, is that adults of all species are instinctually attuned to protect and love the young.

A basic idea from evolutionary theory—**selective adaptation**—proposes that humans today react in ways that helped survival and reproduction long ago. In one version of selective adaptation, genes for traits that aid survival and reproduction are selected over time to allow the species to thrive (see Figure 2.6). Some of the best human qualities—cooperation, spirituality, and self-sacrifice—may have originated more than a hundred thousand years ago when groups of people endured because they took care of one another. Childhood itself, particularly the

>> Response for Adoptive Families (from page 52) Not at all. Attachment is the result of responsiveness, not biology. In some cultures, many children are adopted from infancy, and the emotional ties to their caregivers are no less strong than for other children.

Especially for Teachers and Counselors of Teenagers Teen pregnancy is destructive of adolescent education, family life, and sometimes even health. According to evolutionary theory, what can be done about this? (see response, page 57)

selective adaptation The process by which living creatures (including people) adjust to their environment. Genes that enhance survival and reproductive ability are selected, over the generations, to become more prevalent.

FIGURE 2.6

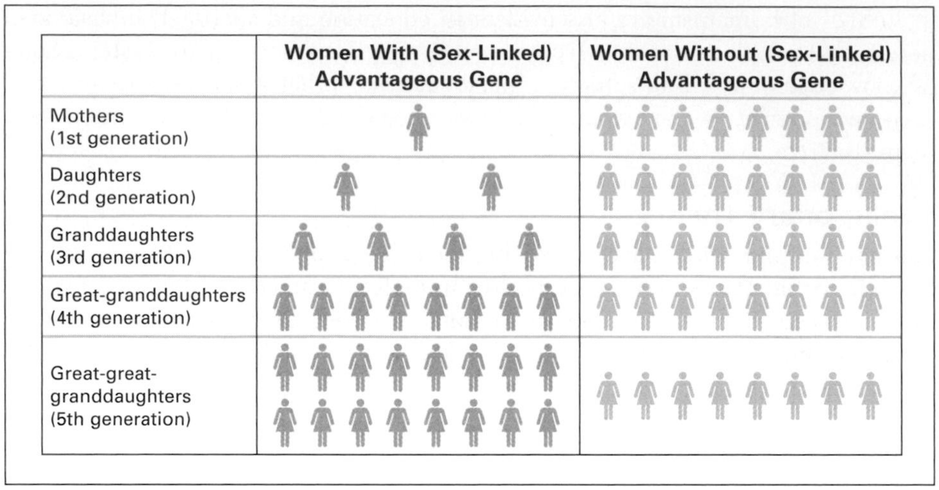

Women With (Sex-Linked) Advantageous Gene
Women Without (Sex-Linked) Advantageous Gene
Mothers (1st generation)
Daughters (2nd generation)
Granddaughters (3rd generation)
Great-granddaughters (4th generation)
Great-great-granddaughters (5th generation)

Selective Adaptation Illustrated Suppose one of a group of nine mothers happened to have a gene that improved her daughter's survival rate. Suppose most women merely replaced themselves each generation (as was generally historically true), but this gene mutation meant more births and therefore more surviving children, such that each woman who had the gene bore two who survived to womanhood instead of one. As you see, in 100 years, the "odd" gene becomes more common than the normal one—a new normal.

long period when children depend on their parents, can be explained via evolution (Konner, 2010).

The process of selective adaptation works like this: If one person happens to have a gene that makes survival more likely, that gene is likely to be passed on to the next generation (because the person has survived long enough to reproduce). Such a beneficial gene might have arisen as a mutation, or it might simply be one end of the natural variation in height, body type, anxiety, or any other characteristic that varies from one person to another. Anyone who inherits such a gene would be more likely to survive to adulthood, to be chosen as a mate, and to have several children—half of whom would inherit that desirable gene.

For example, originally all humans probably got sick after drinking cow's milk, a trait called *lactose intolerance* (Suchy, 2010). Then in a few regions, cattle were domesticated and raised for their meat. In those places, "killing the fatted calf" provided a rare feast for the entire community when a major celebration occurred. In such cattle-raising locations, if a hungry child chanced to have an aberrant gene for the enzyme that allowed digestion of cow's milk, and that child drank some milk intended for a calf, he or she had a better chance of surviving long enough to have children, since malnutrition was a common cause of death among early humans. Indeed, a girl with that gene might become fat enough to experience early puberty, then to sustain many pregnancies, and then to breast-feed her thriving babies longer than her lactose-intolerant, malnourished sisters could. In that way, the next generation would include more people who inherited that gene.

STOCK IMAGE / INA AGENCY

Got Milk! Many people in Sweden (like this pair) and the other Scandinavian countries regularly drink cow's milk and digest it easily. That may be because their ancient occupation of cattle herding coincided with a genetic tendency toward lactose tolerance.

This process of selective adaptation continues over many generations. That odd gene allowing digestion of cow's milk would become widespread in cold climates where plant proteins were scarce and cow's milk meant survival. This might explain why few Scandinavians are lactose-intolerant but many Africans are—a useful fact for Wisconsin dairy farmers who want to ship milk to starving children in Ethiopia. When the farmers realize that their milk might make some children sick, they can find other ways to relieve hunger. Although malnutrition is still a global problem, fewer children are starving than a few decades ago, partly because nutritionists now know which foods are digestible and nourishing for whom.

>> Response for Nurses (from page 54) Reassurance from nurses (explaining procedures, including specifics and reasons) helps with the first two, and visitors, cards, and calls might help with the next two. Obviously, specifics depend on the patient, but everyone needs respect as well as physical care.

For groups as well as individuals, the interaction of genes and environment affects survival and reproduction, the two basic drives recognized by evolutionary theory. Genetic variations are particularly beneficial when the environment changes, which is one reason the genetic diversity of humans throughout the world benefits humanity as a whole. If a species' gene pool does not include variants that allow survival in difficult circumstances (such as exposure to a new disease or to an environmental toxin), the entire species may become extinct. This explains why biologists are concerned when a particular species becomes inbred—diversity is protective of all creatures. About 90 percent of all species that ever existed have disappeared because as conditions changed, every member died without progeny (Buss et al., 1998).

Genetic variation among humans and inherited flexibility (the plasticity explained in Chapter 1) enable humans to survive and multiply. This is probably true not only for biological traits (such as digestion of milk) but also for traits that originate in the brain (Tomasello, 2009). For example, certain genes foster socialization, communication, and language, which helped humans in the Paleolithic era talk to one another and allowed societies a few thousand years ago to develop writing, then books, and then universities. As a result of this burgeoning of education and communications, humans now learn from history and from the experiences of people on the other side of the globe.

Because of humans' genetic inheritance, therefore, people have come to understand the importance of clean water, good nutrition, and immunization, and the average life expectancy worldwide has increased from about 20 years a thousand years ago, to 35 years a century ago, to about 75 years today (85 years in some nations and only 50 in others, but everywhere much longer than a few decades ago). The very fact that you are reading this book, accepting some ideas and rejecting others, is part of the genetic heritage that will aid future generations, according to evolutionary theory.

In developmental science, evolutionary theory is now considered insightful and intriguing, but some interpretations are hotly disputed. For instance, an evolutionary account of mental illness suggests that disorders are extremes of adaptive traits, such as a vivid imagination or feelings of anxiety. The implications of this interpretation include more acceptance of the unusual people among us. This is controversial. More controversial are evolutionary explanations of the emotional differences between men and women, as the following explains.

>> Response for Teachers and Counselors of Teenagers (from page 55) Evolutionary theory stresses the basic human drive for reproduction, which gives teenagers a powerful sex drive. Thus, merely informing teenagers of the difficulty of caring for a newborn (some high school sex-education programs simply give teenagers a chicken egg to nurture) is not likely to work. A better method would be to structure teenagers' lives so that pregnancy is impossible—for instance, with careful supervision or readily available contraception.

A VIEW FROM SCIENCE

If Your Mate Were Unfaithful

Universally, males seek more sexual partners than females do, and brides are younger than grooms. These are norms, not followed in every case, but apparent in every culture. Why? The evolutionary explanation begins with biology. Since females, not males, become pregnant and breast-feed, in most of human history, a woman needed a mature, strong man to keep predators away from her and her children. This would allow her to fulfill her evolutionary destiny, to survive and pass on her genes to children who would live long enough to reproduce. Consequently, a woman kept her man near the campfire with home-cooking and sex.

By contrast, men had a better chance of living on genetically by having as many offspring as possible, which meant having multiple sexual partners of prime childbearing age. That may explain why powerful kings had dozens of young wives and concubines, spreading their genes to many descendents. Because of those ancient needs, men still are more likely to stray, especially with younger women, whereas women seek one steady marriage partner.

Evolutionary psychologists have some research to support this interpretation. They asked people of many ages, nationalities, and religions to imagine their romantic partner either "forming a deep emotional attachment" or "enjoying passionate sexual intercourse" with someone else. After imagining that, people were asked which of those two possibilities would distress them more (Buss, 2003). One recent replication involved 212 college students, all U.S. citizens, whose parents were born in Mexico (Cramer et al., 2009). As with every other study of this kind, more women (60 percent) were distressed at the emotional infidelity and more men (66 percent) at the sexual infidelity.

Evolutionary theory explains this oft-replicated result by noting that for centuries a woman has needed a soul mate to be emotionally committed, to ensure that he will provide for her and her children, whereas a man has needed a woman to be sexually faithful to ensure that her children are also his. Indeed, worldwide, men are more likely to fly into a jealous rage if they suspect infidelity, sometimes beating their sex partners to death, which women never do (Mize et al., 2009).

This evolutionary explanation is rejected by many women, who contend that patriarchy and sexism, not genes, lead to mating patterns. Similar controversies arise with other applications of this theory.

People sometimes act in ways that are counter to evolutionary predictions: Parents sometimes abandon newborns, adults sometimes handle snakes, and so on. In the survey just cited of Mexican American college students, more than one-third did not follow the typical pattern for their sex (Cramer et al., 2009). Nonetheless, evolutionary theorists contend that, for the future of humankind, developmentalists need to understand people in order to mitigate destructive impulses (e.g., by establishing laws against "crimes of passion") and encourage the best of human nature (Ackerman & Kenrick, 2009; Bulbulia, 2007; Gintis et al., 2007).

Many hypotheses from evolutionary theory have not been scientifically tested, much less accepted, partly because this is the newest theory to be applied to development. Some critics contend that evolutionary theory is an unscientific leap from current behavior to imagined conditions before written history. Nonetheless, this theory offers intriguing explanations for universal human tendencies that are difficult to explain in other ways.

SUMMING UP

Newer theories of development are more multicultural, expansive, and multidisciplinary than the earlier grand theories. Sociocultural theory emphasizes the varied cultural contexts of development, suggesting that even such basic behaviors as caring for infants and educating children are guided by the community. Learning occurs within the zone of proximal development, as the result of sensitive collaboration between a teacher (who could be a parent or a child) and a learner who is ready for the next step.

Universal theories include humanism and evolutionary theory, both of which stress that all humans have the same underlying needs. Humanism holds that everyone merits respect and positive regard in order to become a fully self-actualized human being. Evolutionary theory contends that thousands of years of selective adaptation have led humans to experience emotions and impulses that satisfy two universal needs of every species: to survive and to reproduce. These primitive reactions need to be recognized and understood in order for the species to progress, according to this theory. ■

>> What Theories Contribute

Each major theory discussed in this chapter has contributed a great deal to our understanding of human development (see Table 2.4):

- *Psychoanalytic theories* have made us aware of the impact of early-childhood experiences, remembered or not, on subsequent development.
- *Behaviorism* has shown the effect that immediate responses, associations, and examples have on learning, moment by moment and over time.
- *Cognitive theories* have brought an understanding of intellectual processes and how our thoughts and beliefs affect every aspect of our development.
- *Sociocultural theories* have reminded us that development is embedded in a rich and multifaceted cultural context, evident in every social interaction.
- *Universal theories* stress that human differences are less significant than those characteristics that are shared by all humans, in every place and era.

No comprehensive view of development can ignore any of these theories, yet each has encountered severe criticism. Psychoanalytic theory has been faulted for

TABLE 2.4 Five Perspectives on Human Development

Theory	Area of Focus	Fundamental Depiction of What People Do	Relative Emphasis on Nature or Nurture?
Psychoanalytic theory	Psychosexual (Freud) or psychosocial (Erikson) stages	Battle unconscious impulses and overcome major crises	More nature (biological, sexual impulses, and parent–child bonds)
Behaviorism	Conditioning through stimulus and response	Respond to stimuli, reinforcement, and models	More nurture (direct environment produces various behaviors)
Cognitive theory	Thinking, remembering, analyzing	Seek to understand experiences while forming concepts and cognitive strategies	More nature (person's own mental activity and motivation are key)
Sociocultural theory	Social context, expressed through people, language, customs	Learn the tools, skills, and values of society through apprenticeships	More nurture (interaction of mentor and learner, within cultural context)
Universal perspective	Needs and impulses that all humans share as a species	Develop impulses, interests, and patterns to satisfy needs and survive as a species	More nature (needs that apply to all humans; genetic evolution)

being too subjective; behaviorism, for being too mechanistic; cognitive theory, for undervaluing emotions; sociocultural theory, for neglecting individuals; and universal theory, for slighting cultural, gender, and economic variations. Most developmentalists prefer an **eclectic perspective,** choosing what they consider the best aspects of each theory. Rather than adopt any one of these theories exclusively, they make selective use of all of them.

eclectic perspective The approach taken by most developmentalists, in which they apply aspects of each of the various theories of development rather than adhering exclusively to one theory.

Being eclectic, not tied to any one theory, is beneficial because everyone, scientist as well as layperson, tends to be biased. It is easy to dismiss alternative points of view, but using all five theories opens our eyes and minds to aspects of development that we might otherwise ignore. As one overview of seven developmental theories (including those explained here) concludes, "Because no one theory satisfactorily explains development, it is critical that developmentalists be able to draw on the content, methods, and theoretical concepts of many theories" (Miller, 2011, p. 437).

As you will see in many later chapters, theories provide a fresh look at behavior. Imagine a parent and a teacher discussing a child's actions. Each suggests a possible explanation that makes the other say, "I never thought of that"; if they listen with an open mind, together they understand the child better. Having five theories is like having five perceptive observers. All five are not always on target, but it is better to use theory to expand perception than to stay in one narrow groove. A hand functions best with five fingers, although each finger is different, and some are more useful than others.

SUMMING UP

Theories are needed to suggest hypotheses, to spur investigation, and, finally, to find answers so that empirical evidence can replace untested personal assumptions. All five of the major theories have met with valid criticism, but they have also all helped to move the scientific process forward. Most developmentalists are eclectic, making selective use of all these theories and more. This helps guard against bias and keeps scientists, parents, students, and everyone else open to alternative explanations for the complexity of human life. ■

SUMMARY

What Theories Do

1. A theory provides a framework of general principles to guide research and to explain observations. Each of the five major developmental theories—psychoanalytic, behaviorist, cognitive, sociocultural, and universal—interprets human development from a distinct perspective, and each provides guidance for understanding how human experiences and behaviors change over time.

2. Theories are neither true nor false. They are not facts; they suggest hypotheses to be tested. Good theories are practical: They aid inquiry, interpretation, and daily life.

3. A norm is a usual standard of behavior. Norms are not theories, although they may result from theories if a theory suggests that a certain behavior is proper; and norms are not necessarily good or bad, although sometimes differences from the norm are falsely considered deficits.

Grand Theories

4. Psychoanalytic theory emphasizes that human actions and thoughts originate from unconscious impulses and childhood conflicts. Freud theorized that sexual urges arise during three stages of childhood development—oral, anal, and phallic—and continue, after latency, in the genital stage.

5. Erikson described psychosocial, not psychosexual, stages. He described eight successive stages of development, each involving a crisis as people mature within their context. Societies, cultures, and family members respond to each person's development.

6. All psychoanalytic theories stress the legacy of childhood. Conflicts associated with children's erotic impulses have a lasting impact on adult personality, according to Freud. Erikson thought that the resolution of each crisis affects adult development.

7. Behaviorists, or learning theorists, believe that scientists should study observable and measurable behavior. Behaviorism emphasizes conditioning—a lifelong learning process, as association between one stimulus and another (classical conditioning) or the consequences of reinforcement and punishment (operant conditioning) guide behavior.

8. Social learning theory recognizes that people learn by observing others. Children are particularly susceptible to social learning. Self-efficacy is apparent in societies as well as individuals.

9. Cognitive theorists believe that thoughts and beliefs powerfully affect attitudes, actions, and perceptions. Piaget proposed four age-related periods of cognition, propelled by an active search for cognitive equilibrium. Information processing focuses on each aspect of cognitive input, processing, and output.

Newer Theories

10. Sociocultural theory explains human development in terms of the guidance, support, and structure provided by knowledgeable members of the society, via culture and personal mentoring. Vygotsky described how learning occurs through social interactions, when mentors guide learners through their zone of proximal development.

11. The universal perspective focuses on the shared impulses and common needs of all humanity. One universal theory is humanism. Maslow believed that all humans have five basic needs, which he arranged in sequence beginning with survival and ending with self-actualization. Rogers believed that each person merits respect and appreciation, with unconditional positive regard.

12. Evolutionary theory has recently been applied to development. It contends that contemporary humans inherit genetic tendencies that have fostered survival and reproduction of the human species for tens of thousands of years. Some hypotheses from this theory are particularly provocative, such as the explanation for male–female differences in romantic liaisons.

What Theories Contribute

13. Psychoanalytic, behavioral, cognitive, sociocultural, and universal theories have each aided our understanding of human development, yet no one theory is broad enough to describe the full complexity and diversity of human experience. Most developmentalists are eclectic, drawing upon many theories.

KEY TERMS

developmental theory (p. 35)
norm (p. 37)
psychoanalytic theory (p. 39)
behaviorism (p. 42)
conditioning (p. 42)
classical conditioning (p. 42)
operant conditioning (p. 43)
reinforcement (p. 43)
social learning theory (p. 44)
modeling (p. 44)
self-efficacy (p. 44)
cognitive theory (p. 46)
cognitive equilibrium (p. 47)
assimilation (p. 47)
accommodation (p. 47)
information processing (p. 48)
sociocultural theory (p. 50)
apprenticeship in thinking (p. 50)
guided participation (p. 50)
zone of proximal development (p. 51)
humanism (p. 53)
selective adaptation (p. 55)
eclectic perspective (p. 59)

WHAT HAVE YOU LEARNED?

What Theories Do

1. How can a theory be practical?

2. What is the relationship between norms and facts?

3. How do theories differ from facts?

Grand Theories

4. What is the basic idea of psychoanalytic theory?

5. What is Freud's theory of infantile sexuality?

6. What body parts are connected to the oral, anal, and phallic stages?

7. In what two ways does Erikson's theory differ from Freud's?

8. What is the basic idea of behaviorism?

9. In what way is behaviorism considered "in opposition" to psychoanalytic theory?

10. How do classical and operant conditioning differ?

11. What reinforcers are emphasized by social learning theory?

12. What is the basic idea of cognitive theory?

13. How are Piaget's stages similar to, and different from, Freud's stages?

14. In what ways are assimilation and accommodation similar?

15. Why is information processing not a stage theory?

Newer Theories

16. What are the underlying differences between the newer theories and the grand theories?

17. How is "apprenticeship in thinking" an example of sociocultural theory?

18. What do mentors do when mentees are in their zone of proximal development?

19. How is the religious background of both Rogers and Maslow related to humanism?

20. How does Maslow's hierarchy of needs differ from Erikson's stages?

21. How does evolutionary psychology explain human instincts?

22. Why are aspects of evolutionary theory of human emotions controversial?

23. What does the idea of selective adaptation imply about the nature–nurture controversy?

What Theories Contribute

24. What is the key criticism and key contribution of psychoanalytic theory?

25. What is the key criticism and key contribution of behaviorism?

26. What is the key criticism and key contribution of cognitive theory?

27. What is the key criticism and key contribution of sociocultural theory?

28. What is the key criticism and key contribution of universal theories?

29. What are the advantages and disadvantages of an eclectic perspective?

APPLICATIONS

1. Developmentalists sometimes talk about "folk theories," which are theories developed by ordinary people, who may not know that they are theorizing. Choose three sayings commonly used in your culture, such as (from the dominant U.S. culture) "A penny saved is a penny earned" or "As the twig is bent, so grows the tree." Explain the underlying assumptions, or theory, that each saying reflects.

2. Behaviorism has been used to change personal habits. Think of a habit you'd like to change (e.g., stop smoking, exercise more, watch less TV). Count the frequency of that behavior for a week, noting the reinforcers for each instance. Then, and only then, develop a substitute behavior, reinforcing yourself for it. Keep careful data for several days. What did you learn?

3. Ask three people to tell you their theories about male–female differences in mating and sexual behaviors. Which of the theories described in this chapter is closest to each explanation, and which theory is not mentioned?

>>ONLINE CONNECTIONS

To accompany your textbook, you have access to a number of online resources, including quizzes for every chapter of the book, flashcards (in English and Spanish), critical thinking questions, and case studies. For access to any of these links, go to www.worthpublishers.com/bergerca9e. In addition to these free resources, you'll also find links to podcasts, video clips, diagnostic quizzing with personalized study advice, and an ebook. Some of the videos and activities available online include:

- *Modeling: Learning from Observation.* This activity includes clips from Albert Bandura's classic Bobo doll experiment on observational learning.
- *Harlow's Studies of Infant Monkeys.* Original footage from Harry Harlow's lab of his studies.

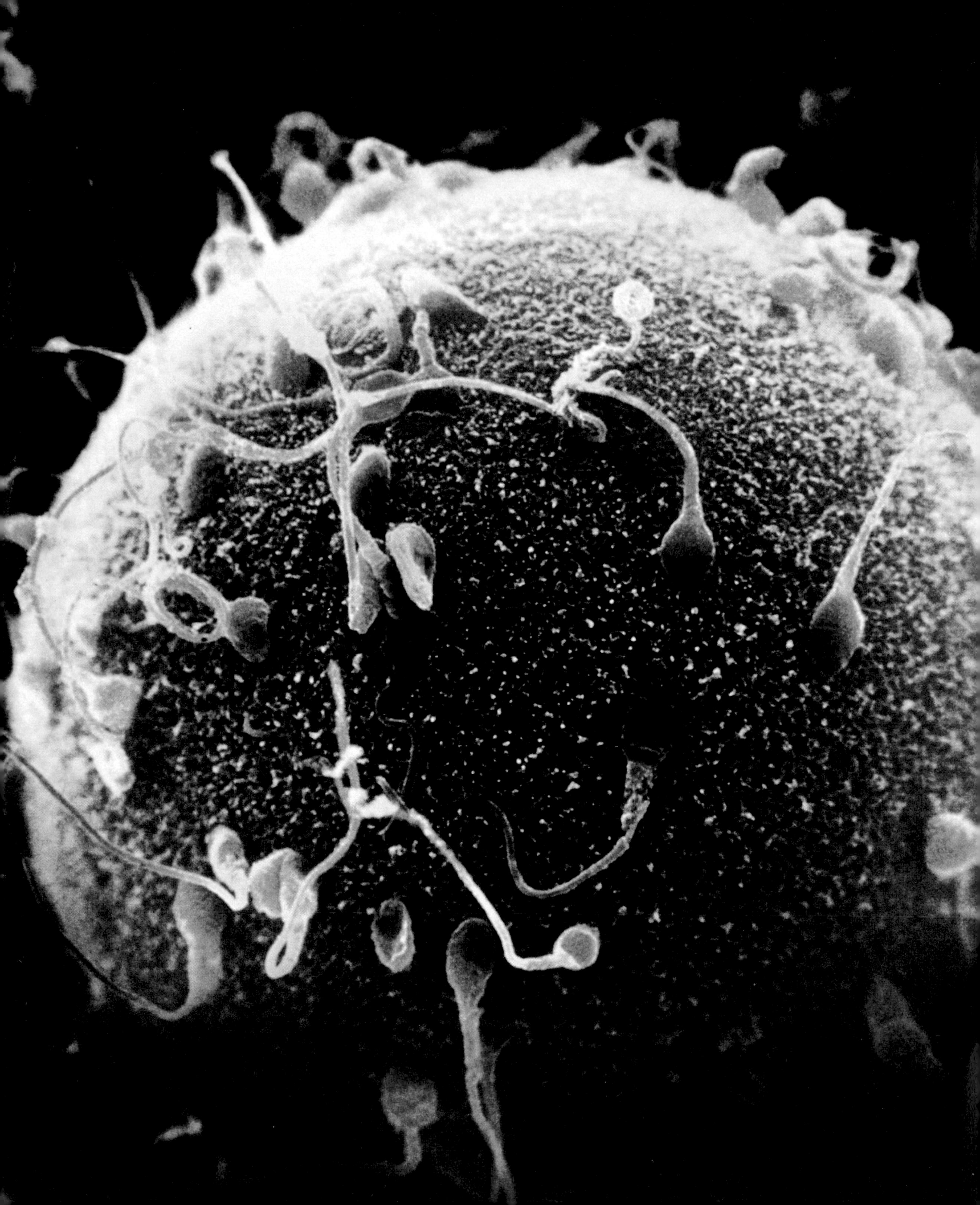

3

CHAPTER

Heredity and Environment

WHAT WILL YOU KNOW?

1. What is the relationship between genes and chromosomes?
2. Do sex differences result from chromosomes or culture?
3. How can a child have genetic traits that are not obvious in either the mother or the father?
4. If parents are alcoholic, will their children, because of genetics, be alcoholics too?
5. Why are some children born with Down syndrome, and what can be done for them?

"She needs a special school. She cannot come back next year," Elissa's middle school principal told us.

Martin and I were stunned. Apparently the school staff thought that our wonderful daughter, bright and bubbly (Martin called her "frothy"), was learning-disabled—more specifically, spatially disorganized. We had noticed that she misplaced homework, got lost, left books at school, forgot where each class met on which day—but we thought those were insignificant compared to her strengths in reading, analyzing, and friendship.

I knew the first lesson from genetics: Genes affect everything, not just physical appearance, diseases, and cognitive abilities, so I wondered what Elissa had inherited from us. Our desks were covered with papers, and our home had assorted objects everywhere. If we needed masking tape, or working scissors, or silver candlesticks, we had to search in several places. Could that be why we were oblivious to Elissa's failings?

The second lesson from genetics is that nurture always matters. My husband and I had both learned to compensate for innate organizational weaknesses. Since he often got lost, Martin did not hesitate to ask strangers for directions; since I was prone to mislaying important documents, I kept my students' papers in clearly marked folders. Despite our genes, we both were successful; we thought Elissa was fine.

Once we recognized our daughter's nature, we changed her nurture. Martin attached her bus pass to her backpack; I wrote an impassioned letter telling the principal it would be unethical to expel her; we hired a tutor who helped us teach Elissa to make a list of her homework assignments, check them off when done, put them carefully in her bag, and then take the bag to school. Elissa herself began to study diligently. Our efforts succeeded. Elissa aced her final exams, and the principal allowed her to return. She became a master organizer; 15 years later, she was valedictorian of her law school class.

This chapter begins with nature and then emphasizes nurture. Throughout, we note some ethical and practical choices regarding the interaction of genes and environments. I hope you recognize that interaction long before you have a seventh-grade daughter.

>> The Genetic Code

You already know that one sperm and one ovum combine to begin human life and that each newly created cell contains genes that affect every aspect of development. Remember, however, that development is dynamic, ongoing, and interactional; individuals are much more than the product of their genes.

For example, genes dictate the maximum life span for each species: For mice it is 4 years; for humans, 122; for the bowhead whale, about 200 (Austad, 2010). If you were a mouse, you couldn't live past age 4. But the factors that determine whether one person outlives another are dynamic and interactional, depending much more on where each person lives than on his or her genes.

Genes are not the main reason people in some nations live decades longer than those in other nations. From the shortest to the longest average life span, the range is about 40 years—for instance, age 45 in Afghanistan and age 84 in Japan (United Nations, 2011). As you can see, most people die decades before their inherited potential. Similarly, genes for language fluency, diabetes, strong teeth, and even organizational skills are expressed—or not—depending on nurture. To understand development, begin with genes. But never forget: Genetics describes possibilities (you *could* live to 122), not outcomes (you probably won't).

What Genes Are

First, we review some biology. All living things are composed of cells. The work of these cells is done by *proteins*. Each cell manufactures certain proteins according to instructions stored by molecules of **deoxyribonucleic acid (DNA)** at the heart of each cell. These DNA molecules are on a **chromosome.**

deoxyribonucleic acid (DNA) The chemical composition of the molecules that contain the genes, which are the chemical instructions for cells to manufacture various proteins.

chromosome One of the 46 molecules of DNA (in 23 pairs) that virtually each cell of the human body contains and that, together, contain all the genes. Other species have more or fewer chromosomes.

gene A small section of a chromosome; the basic unit for the transmission of heredity. A gene consists of a string of chemicals that provide instructions for the cell to manufacture certain proteins.

Humans have 23 pairs of chromosomes (46 in all), which contain the instructions to make all the proteins that a person needs (see Figure 3.1). The instructions in the 46 chromosomes are organized into genes, with each **gene** usually located at a specific spot on a particular chromosome. Humans have between 18,000 and 23,000 genes, and each gene contains the chemical recipe for making a specific protein (Brooker, 2009).

What exactly is a protein? A protein is composed of a sequence of chemicals, a long string of building blocks called *amino acids*. The recipe for manufacturing a protein consists of instructions for stringing together the right amino acids in the right order.

These instructions are transmitted to the cell via pairs of four chemicals called *bases* (adenine, thiamine, cytosine, and guanine; abbreviated A, T, C, and G). The bases pair up in only four possible ways (A-T, T-A, C-G, and G-C). Humans have more than 3 billion base pairs, which are arranged in triplets (three base pairs) on those 20,000 or so genes.

Especially for Scientists A hundred years ago, it was believed that humans had 48 chromosomes, not 46; 10 years ago, it was thought that humans had 100,000 genes, not 20,000 or so. Why? (see response, page 66)

Variations

Most genes have thousands of base pairs that make the 20 types of amino acids needed to create a human being. The triplets of each particular gene can vary, although usually they do not. Some genes have transpositions, deletions, or repetitions of the triplets not found in other versions of the same gene. Each of these variations is called an **allele** of that gene, and genes that have various alleles are called *polymorphic* (literally, "many forms") or, more formally, *single-nucleotide polymorphisms* (abbreviated SNPs). Most alleles cause only minor differences (such as the shape of an eyebrow); some seem inconsequential; some are notable, even devastating.

allele A variation that makes a gene different in some way from other genes for the same characteristics. Many genes never vary; others have several possible alleles.

The interaction of genes from the mother and genes from the father affects the embryo's growth in many ways (more about genetic interaction soon). This complex interaction actually begins the moment a zygote is formed, because everyone inherits alleles from the sperm and the ovum that make him or her unique. Thus, each person has some base pairs that differ from those of other people, and everyone has some extra repeats of a piece of a gene or sometimes of a whole gene. Consequently, each person has several gene pairs that do not quite match. One expert said: "What's cool is that we are a mosaic of pieces of genomes. None of us is truly normal" (Eichler, quoted in Cohen, 2007, p. 1315).

Furthermore, everyone has additional DNA and RNA (another molecule) that are not genes but that are critical to life: In a process called *methylation,* this material enhances, transcribes, connects, empowers, and alters genes (Shapiro, 2009). This nongenetic material used to be called *junk*—no longer. Thousands of scientists seek to discover what these molecules do, but no one thinks they are junk anymore (Wright & Bruford, 2011). It is clear that methylation can stop a gene's expression in a process that begins at the moment of conception or later—even after the person is born.

The entire packet of instructions to make a living organism is called the **genome.** There is a genome for every species and variety of plant and animal—even for every bacteria and virus. Knowing the genome of the human species is only a start (it was fully decoded in 2001). Even before 2001 it was apparent that, with the exception of monozygotic twins, each person has a slightly different code, although the *human genome* is 99.9 percent identical for any two persons. For instance, all humans have two eyes, two legs, linguistic abilities, and much more—major characteristics and capacities ordained by genes. Despite all the shared genes that make humans one species, small differences between individuals make each one of us unique.

genome The full set of genes that are the instructions to make an individual member of a certain species.

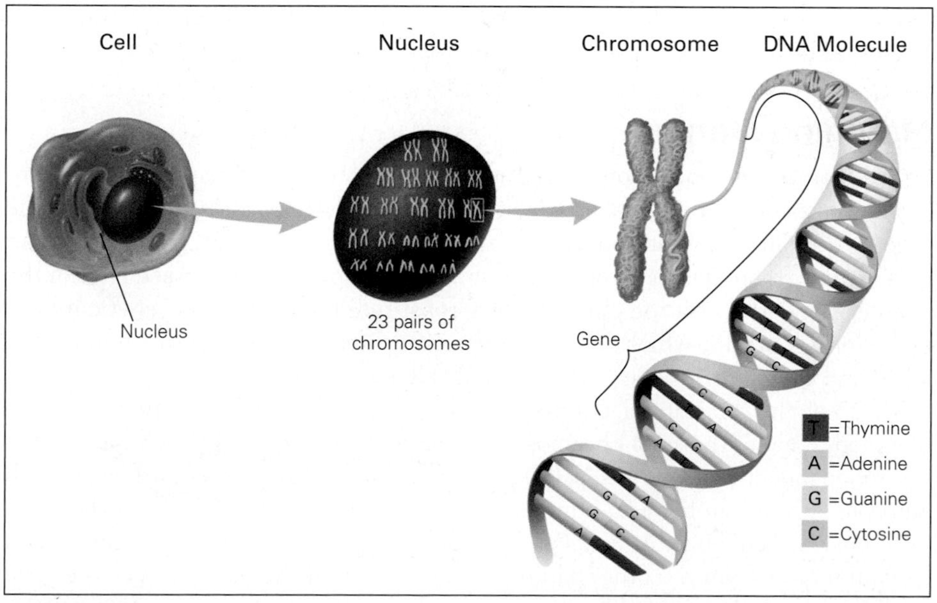

FIGURE 3.1

How Proteins Are Made The genes on the chromosomes in the nucleus of each cell instruct the cell to manufacture the proteins needed to sustain life and development. The code for a protein is the particular combination of T-A-G-C.

>> Response for Scientists (from page 64) There was some scientific evidence for the wrong numbers (e.g., chimpanzees have 48 chromosomes), but the reality is that humans tend to overestimate many things, from the number of genes to their grades on the next test. Scientists are very human: They are inclined to overestimate until the data prove them wrong.

SUMMING UP

The human genome contains hundreds of thousands of molecules, forming about 20,000 genes on 46 chromosomes, using 3 billion base pairs of 4 chemicals to instruct production of 20 amino acids to create proteins that make a human being. Some genes, called alleles, are polymorphic. Because of small differences in their genetic codes (perhaps a change of only one base pair), each future person is unlike any other. Other material, once called junk DNA, affects the expression of the genes—sometimes stopping expression completely, sometimes increasing the power of that gene. The result is that each person is unique yet similar to all other humans. The entire instruction code is the genome, contained in a single cell, smaller than the head of a pin. ■

>> The Beginnings of Life

A reproductive cell is called a **gamete** whether it is a *sperm* or an *ovum*. Each gamete contains 23 chromosomes. When two gametes combine, they create a **zygote,** a single cell of 46 chromosomes that begins a human life.

That one-celled zygote copies itself again and again, creating an embryo, a fetus, a baby, and eventually an adult with trillions of cells, each with the same 46 chromosomes and same thousands of genes of the original zygote. When sperm or ova are created, the parent cell splits neatly in half so that each gamete has only one of the two chromosomes at each location. Thus, for instance, a gamete has only one chromosome number 10 although the man or woman who formed it has two chromosomes at the 10th site. The new zygote will have a pair of number 10 chromosomes as well—one from the sperm and one from the ovum.

The particular member of each chromosome pair from each parent on a given gamete is randomly selected. A man or woman can produce 2^{23} different gametes—more than 8 million versions of his or her own 46 chromosomes. If a given couple conceived a billion zygotes, each would be genetically unique because of the chromosomes of the particular gametes that created them. Alleles, methylation, and other genetic interactions would add even more variations.

gamete A reproductive cell; that is, a sperm or ovum that can produce a new individual if it combines with a gamete from the other sex to make a zygote.

zygote The single cell formed from the union of two gametes, a sperm and an ovum.

genotype An organism's entire genetic inheritance, or genetic potential.

homozygous Referring to two genes of one pair that are exactly the same in every letter of their code. Most gene pairs are homozygous.

heterozygous Referring to two genes of one pair that differ in some way. Typically one allele has only a few base pairs that differ from the other member of the pair.

Matching Genes

At the moment of conception, the father's chromosomes match up with the mother's chromosomes—his number 10 with her number 10, for instance—so that the zygote's 23 pairs of chromosomes are arranged in father–mother pairs. (This can go awry if a zygote has more or fewer than 46 chromosomes, discussed later in the chapter.) The genes on the chromosomes constitute the organism's genetic inheritance, or **genotype,** which endures throughout life. Growth requires duplication again and again of the code of the original cell.

In 22 of the 23 pairs of chromosomes, both members of the pair are closely matched. Each of these 44 chromosomes is called an *autosome,* which means that it is independent (*auto* means "self") of the sex chromosomes (the 23rd pair). Each autosome, from number 1 to number 22, contains hundreds of genes in the same positions and sequence. At conception, each gene on each autosome matches with its counterpart from the other parent. If the code of all the base pairs of the gene from one parent is exactly like the code on the same gene from the other parent, the gene pair is **homozygous** (literally, "same-zygote").

However, the match is not always letter perfect because the mother might have a different allele for that particular gene than the father has. If a gene's code differs from that of its counterpart, the two genes still pair up, but the zygote (and, later, the person) is **heterozygous.** Usually this is no problem: Indeed, it is better to be

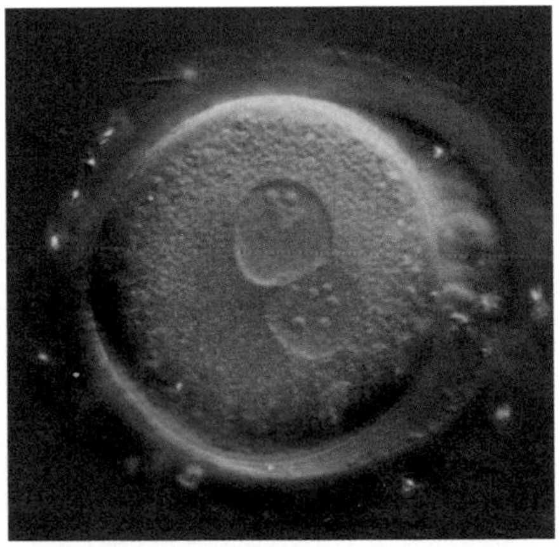

COURTESY OF LENNART NILSSON / BONNIER FAKTA/STOCKHOLM

The Moment of Conception This ovum is about to become a zygote. It has been penetrated by a single sperm, whose nucleus now lies next to the nucleus of the ovum. Soon, the two nuclei will fuse, bringing together about 20,000 genes to guide development.

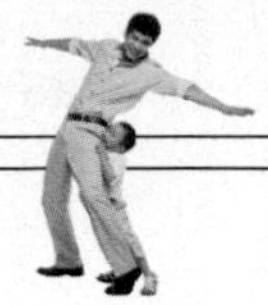

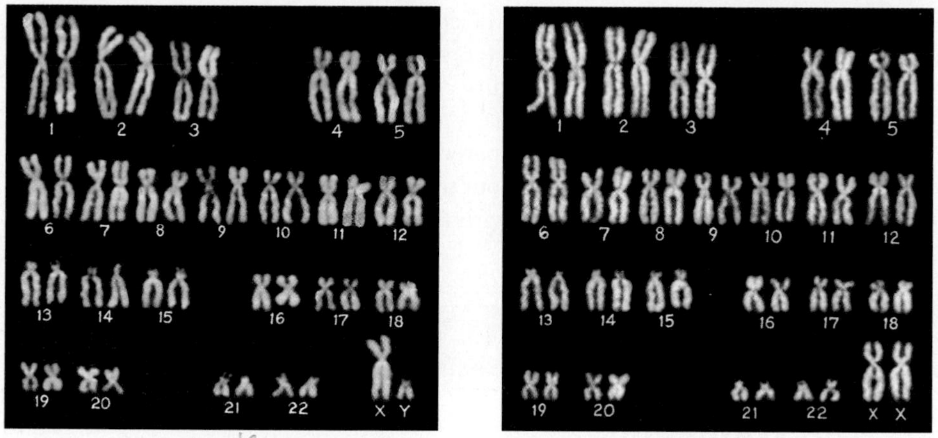

BIOPHOTO ASSOCIATES / PHOTO RESEARCHERS, INC.

Uncertain Sex Every now and then, a baby is born with "ambiguous genitals," meaning that the child's sex is not abundantly clear. When this happens, a quick analysis of the chromosomes is needed, to make sure there are exactly 46 and to see whether the 23rd pair is XY or XX. The karyotypes shown here indicate a normal baby boy *(left)* and girl *(right)*.

heterozygous than homozygous for some traits, as we will soon explain. But first, let us explain the most dramatic example of a disparate pair, the 23rd chromosomes.

Male or Female?

The chromosomes that make up the **23rd pair** are the sex chromosomes. In females, the 23rd pair is composed of two X-shaped chromosomes. Accordingly, it is called **XX.** In males, the 23rd pair has one X-shaped chromosome and one Y-shaped chromosome. It is called **XY.**

Because a female's 23rd pair is XX, every ovum contains either one X or the other—but always an X. And because a male's 23rd pair is XY, half of his sperm carry an X chromosome and half a Y. The X chromosome is bigger and has many more genes, but the Y chromosome has a crucial gene, called *SRY,* that directs the embryo to make male hormones and organs. Thus, the sex of the zygote depends on which sperm penetrates the ovum—a Y sperm with the SRY gene, creating a boy (XY), or an X sperm, creating a girl (XX) (see Figure 3.2). Since Y sperm are smaller, they can swim faster, so slightly more male than female zygotes are conceived.

23rd pair The chromosome pair that, in humans, determines sex. The other 22 pairs are autosomes; inherited equally by males and females.

XX A 23rd chromosome pair that consists of two X-shaped chromosomes, one each from the mother and the father. XX zygotes become females.

XY A 23rd chromosome pair that consists of an X-shaped chromosome from the mother and a Y-shaped chromosome from the father. XY zygotes become males.

Possible Combinations of Sex Chromosomes

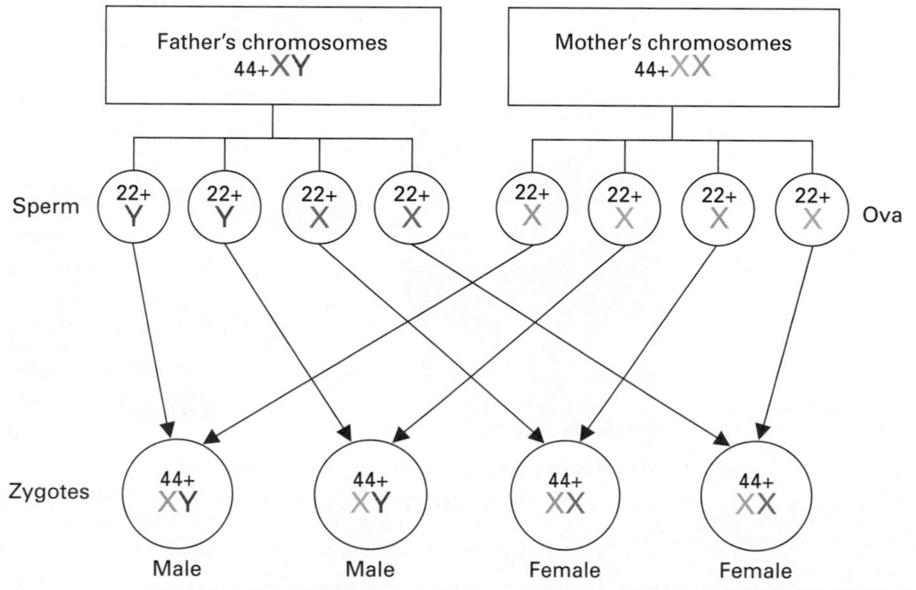

FIGURE 3.2

Determining a Zygote's Sex Any given couple can produce four possible combinations of sex chromosomes; two lead to female children and two, to male. In terms of the future person's sex, it does not matter which of the mother's Xs the zygote inherited. All that matters is whether the father's Y sperm or X sperm fertilized the ovum. However, for X-linked conditions it matters a great deal because typically one, but not both, of the mother's Xs carries the trait.

Observation Quiz In the chapter-opening photograph (page 62), can you distinguish the Y sperm from the X sperm? (see answer, page 69)

Thus, for humans, at the moment of conception the future embryo is either XX or XY. In some other species, however, sex is not determined at conception. In certain reptiles, for instance, temperature during incubation affects the sex of the embryo (Hare & Cree, 2010). But humans are male or female from the moment of conception, even though traditionally parents did not know their child's sex until birth. Now, however, parents can find out much earlier, making it easier to choose names, decorate nurseries, and bond with the future child—or not, as the following explains.

THINKING CRITICALLY

Too Many Boys?

Prenatal sex selection is possible; millions of couples do it. Is this a problem?

Historically, some newborns were killed in every culture. One of the moral advances of Islam, in the seventh century, was to forbid female infanticide. Currently, killing a newborn girl is rare because there are three other ways used to prevent female births—(1) inactivating X sperm before conception, (2) in vitro fertilization (IVF), or (3) aborting XX fetuses.

In China, a "one-child" policy initiated in 1990 cut the birth rate in half and increased the number of Chinese newborn girls available for adoption because parents wanted their one child to be a boy. This policy (sometimes enforced with sterilization and abortion) alleviated poverty but also skewed the sex ratio, as many Chinese couples aborted female fetuses. Since 1993, the Chinese government has forbidden prenatal testing to reveal sex, but many aspects of prenatal care (e.g., sonograms) reveal sex, and female fetuses were more often aborted. Recently, the one-child policy has become a two-child policy, and the sex ratio may be more balanced (Greenhalgh, 2008).

Parents elsewhere also prefer boys. The Indian government forbids abortion to prevent female births, but India nonetheless has only 92 girls for every 100 boys. One elderly Indian man said, "We should have at least four children per family, three of them boys" (quoted in Khanna, 2010, p. 66). Worldwide, one estimate is that 100 million fetuses have been aborted since 1990 because they were female (Sharma, 2008), perhaps 20,000 of them in the United States (Abrevaya, 2009).

Many nations forbid abortion solely because of sex. Some nations also forbid sorting sperm to change the proportion of X and Y sperm before insemination, a technique that works for humans about 85 percent of the time (Karabinus, 2009).

In the United States, individuals make their own choices before and after conception. Most fertility doctors and some parents believe that sex selection is a reproductive right and that couples who can afford it should be able to decide to have either a boy or a girl (Puri & Nachtigall, 2010). Some people who themselves would not abort a fetus because it is the less desired sex nonetheless oppose laws that forbid personal freedom—in this case, freedom to "balance" the family.

One consequence of sex selection in China has been a much higher mortality rate for young men than young women, perhaps because many men cannot find wives. Unmarried young men in every culture take risks to show their bravery, become depressed or drug-addicted, or neglect medical advice (Kruger & Polanski, 2011). From what is known about male–female differences, male-heavy societies might have more learning disabilities, drug abusers, violent crimes, wars, heart attacks, and suicides but fewer nurses, day-care centers, or close family bonds.

But wait: Chromosomes and genes do not determine behavior. Every male–female difference mentioned in the preceding paragraph is influenced by culture. Even traits that originate with biology, such as the propensity to heart attacks, are affected more by environment (in this case, diet and stress) than by sex. Answers to this issue are not obvious, which is why this feature is titled Thinking Critically. Is sex selection the parents' right or a social wrong?

AP PHOTO / MANISH SWARUP

My Strength, My Daughter That's the slogan these girls in New Delhi are shouting at a demonstration against abortion of female fetuses in India. The current sex ratio of children in India suggests that this campaign has not convinced every couple.

New Cells, New Functions

Within hours after conception, the zygote begins *duplication* and *division*. First, the 23 pairs of chromosomes carrying all the genes duplicate, forming two complete sets of the genome. These two sets move toward opposite sides of the zygote, and the single cell splits neatly down the middle into two cells, each containing the original genetic code. These two cells duplicate and divide, becoming four, which themselves duplicate and divide, becoming eight, and so on.

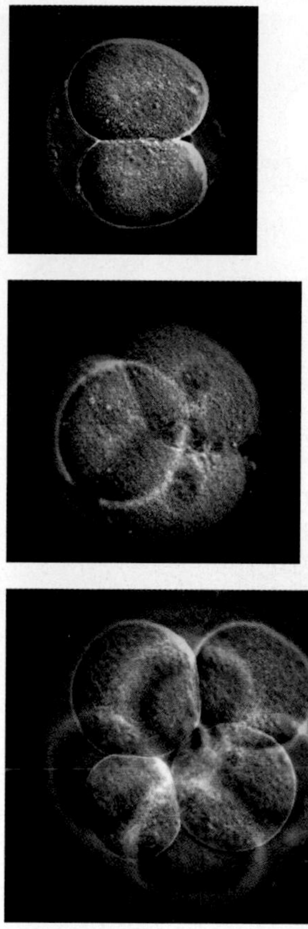

ALL: ANATOMICAL TRAVELOGUE / PHOTO RESEARCHERS, INC.

First Stages of the Germinal Period The original zygote as it divides into *(a)* two cells, *(b)* four cells, and *(c)* eight cells. Occasionally at this early stage, the cells separate completely, forming the beginning of monozygotic twins, quadruplets, or octuplets.

Every Cell the Same

By the time a baby is born, the zygote has become about 10 trillion cells, all influenced by the material that was once called junk and by whatever nutrients, drugs, hormones, viruses, and so on came from the pregnant woman. By adulthood, those cells become more than 100 trillion—again, all affected by the environment.

But no matter how old a person, how large the total number of cells, or how much division and duplication occur, almost every cell carries a complete copy of the genetic instructions of the one-celled zygote. This explains why DNA testing of any body cell, even from a drop of blood or a snip of hair, can identify "the real father," "the guilty criminal," "the long-lost brother."

DNA lingers long after death, evident in living African Americans who claimed Thomas Jefferson as an ancestor: DNA testing proved some of them right and some of them wrong (Foster et al., 1998). Indeed, because the Y chromosome is passed down to every male descendent, men have the Y of their male ancestors who died thousands of years ago. Tracing that Y chromosome suggests that thousands of East Asian men are descendants of Genghis Khan—although that twelfth-century leader's bones and thus his DNA have never been found (Stoneking & Delfin, 2010).

Stem Cells

If the two-celled organism is artificially split apart and each of those two separated cells duplicates, divides, and survives (an illegal practice for humans, successful with mice), that creates twins who begin as one zygote. Every cell of both of them would have the same DNA. However, barring dangerous and radical intervention, cells can become a complete creature *only* during the first few hours after conception—not later, even though they still have the same DNA as the original zygote.

The first cells are called **stem cells,** able to produce any other cell and thus to become a complete person. After about the eight-cell stage, duplication and division continue and a third process, *differentiation,* begins. Cells specialize, taking different forms and reproducing at various rates, depending on where they are located. For instance, some cells become part of an eye, others part of a finger, still others part of the brain. As one expert explains, "We are sitting with parts of our body that could have been used for thinking" (Gottlieb, 1992/2002, p. 172).

stem cells Cells from which any other specialized type of cell can form.

Scientists have discovered ways to add genes to differentiated cells in a laboratory process that reprograms those cells, making them like stem cells again. However, using those reprogrammed stem cells to cure genetic conditions is not yet feasible because inserting reprogrammed stem cells into a person may wreak havoc, causing cancers and even death. Although thousands of scientists are seeking to overcome that problem, currently reprogrammed cells are used only for testing drugs to treat diseases that are caused by genes, either directly (such as sickle-cell anemia) or indirectly (such as heart disease, diabetes, and dementia) (Vogel, 2010).

Some U.S. restrictions on stem cell research were lifted in 2009, and some states (e.g., California) and nations (e.g., South Korea) allow more extensive research, but

>> Answer to Observation Quiz (from page 67) Probably not. The Y sperm are slightly smaller, which can be detected via scientific analysis (some cattle breeders raise only steers using such analysis), but visual inspection, even magnified as in the photo, may be inaccurate.

everywhere many ethical and practical issues remain. As the head of the Michael J. Fox Foundation for Parkinson's Research said, "All my exposure was pop media. I thought it was all about stem cells. I have not totally lost hope on cell replacement, I just don't think it's a near-term hope" (Hood, quoted in Holden, 2009).

Politics and Genetics If life is the ability to grow, then life begins at conception. The question, of course, is at what point developing cells become human. Most zygotes, created inside a woman, do not implant—but this is largely irrelevant because the fact that they did not implant means no one knew they existed in the first place. Laboratory researchers, however, do notice when zygotes do not implant. This is significant to many because zygotes have the potential to produce stem cells that could be used to cure fatal disease—the ethics of which is a subject of considerable ongoing debate.

Twins

One "near-term hope" two decades ago has become reality. Millions of infertile couples have babies, often twins, increasing the demand for twin strollers, rhyming names, and newborn intensive care. To understand this, you need to know the difference between monozygotic and dizygotic twins.

Monozygotic Twins

Although every zygote is genetically unique, about once in 250 human conceptions, a complete split occurs after duplication, creating two, or four, or even eight separate zygotes, each identical to the first single cell. Such a split is illegal in a laboratory, but nature does it occasionally in the womb. (An incomplete split creates *conjoined twins,* formerly called Siamese twins.)

If each of those separated cells duplicates, divides, differentiates, implants, grows, and survives, multiple births occur. One separation results in **monozygotic (MZ) twins,** from one (*mono*) zygote (also called *identical twins*). Two or three separations create monozygotic quadruplets or octuplets. Because monozygotic multiples originate from the same zygote, they have identical genetic instructions for appearance, psychological traits, disease vulnerability, and everything else affected by genes.

Genetic identicals are blessed in at least one way: Monozygotic twins can donate an organ for surgical implantation in their twin with no organ rejection, thus avoiding a major complication with such transplants. They also befuddle their parents and teachers, who may use special signs (such as different earrings) to tell them apart. Usually, the twins themselves find their own identities while enjoying twinship. They might enjoy inherited athletic ability, for instance, with one playing basketball and the other soccer.

As one monozygotic twin writes:

> Twins put into high relief *the* central challenge for all of us: self-definition. How do we each plant our stake in the ground, decide how sensitive, callous, ambitious, cautious, or conciliatory we want to be every day? . . . Twins come with a built-in constant comparison, but defining oneself against one's twin is just an amped-up version of every person's life-long challenge: to individuate, to create a distinctive persona in the world.
>
> *[Pogrebin, 2010, p. 9]*

monozygotic (MZ) twins Twins who originate from one zygote that splits apart very early in development. (Also called *identical twins.*) Other monozygotic multiple births (such as triplets and quadruplets) can occur as well.

dizygotic (DZ) twins Twins who are formed when two separate ova are fertilized by two separate sperm at roughly the same time. (Also called *fraternal twins.*)

Dizygotic Twins

Among naturally conceived twins, only about one in three pairs is monozygotic. Most are **dizygotic (DZ) twins,** also called *fraternal twins.* They began life as two separate zygotes created by two ova fertilized by two sperm at the same time. (Usually, women release only one ovum per month, but sometimes double or triple ovulation occurs.) When dizygotic twinning occurs naturally, the incidence varies by ethnicity. For example, about 1 in 11 Yorubas in Nigeria is a twin, as are about 1 in 45 European Americans, 1 in 75 Japanese and Koreans, and 1 in 150 Chinese. Age matters, too: Older women more often double-ovulate and thus have more twins.

DAVID YOUNG-WOLFF / PHOTOEDIT

JOHNER IMAGES/ GETTY IMAGES

Same Birthday, Same (or Different?) Genes Twins who are of different sexes or who have obvious differences in personality are dizygotic, sharing only half of their genes. Many same-sex twins with similar looks and temperaments are dizygotic as well. One of these twin pairs is dizygotic; the other is monozygotic.

Observation Quiz Can you tell which pair is monozygotic? (see answer, page 73)

Like all full siblings, DZ twins have about half of their genes in common; they can differ markedly in appearance or they can look so much alike that only genetic tests can determine whether they are monozygotic or dizygotic. Chance determines which sperm fertilizes each ovum, so about half are same-sex pairs and half are boy–girl pairs.

Assisted Reproduction

When a couple are unable to conceive (true for about 12 percent of U.S. couples; international rates vary primarily because of health care), some choose **assisted reproductive technology (ART).** A woman can take drugs to cause ovulation, often of several ova, which may lead to multiple births (see Figure 3.3). Or ova can be surgically removed from an ovary, fertilized in a glass lab dish, and then inserted into the uterus. This is **in vitro fertilization (IVF)**—*in vitro* literally means "in glass." Younger women and women of normal weight are more likely to have successful IVF pregnancies, but even among healthy young women, less than half of IVF cycles result in a baby.

assisted reproductive technology (ART) A general term for the techniques designed to help infertile couples conceive and then sustain a pregnancy.

in vitro fertilization (IVF) Fertilization that takes place outside a woman's body (as in a glass laboratory dish). The procedure involves mixing sperm with ova that have been surgically removed from the woman's ovary. If a zygote is produced, it is inserted into a woman's uterus, where it may implant and develop into a baby.

Rate of Triplet and Higher-Order Births, by Age Group of Mother—United States, 1980–2008

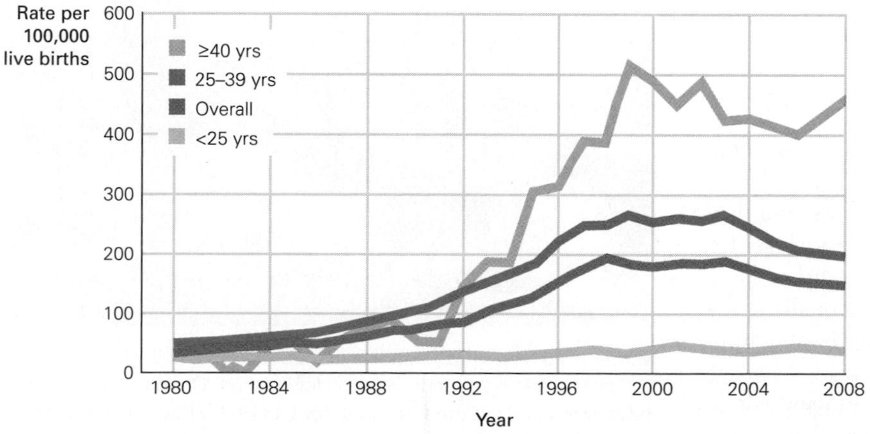

Source: Martin et al., 2011.

FIGURE 3.3

Why More Multiple Births? Historically in the United States, the natural rate of multiple births, particularly triplets and higher orders, tended to increase as mothers aged. Women in their mid- to late 30s were more likely to have twins than those who were younger. The advent of assisted reproductive technology (ART) led to a dramatic increase in multiple births overall starting in the early 1990s; it is now women aged 40 and over who are most likely to experience this phenomenon. After peaking in the late 1990s, rates of triplet and higher-order births seem to be on the decline, as the hazards of multiple births are more apparent.

JEFF STEINBERG / MATT SMITH, PACIFIC COAST NEWS / NEWSCOM

Perfectly Legal Nadya Suleman takes 10 of her 14 children to the park. She was a medical miracle when her eight newborns all survived, thanks to expert care in a Los Angeles hospital. Soon thereafter, however, considerable controversy began: She was dubbed "Octomom" because—even though already a single mother of six children, including twins—she still opted to undergo in vitro fertilization, which resulted in implantation of her octuplets. Many believe implanting more than two zygotes is unethical and should be illegal. The license of Suleman's doctor was revoked, but the debate continues.

In IVF, to improve the odds of fertilization, a sperm can be inserted directly into each ovum, a procedure called *intra-cytoplasmic sperm injection (ICSI)*, which is now standard. Then technicians can insert only one zygote, or only XX or XY zygotes, or as many zygotes as seem viable. Since the first "test-tube" baby in 1973, IVF has produced 4 million babies worldwide; in 2010, between 1 and 3 percent of all newborns in developed nations and thousands more in developing nations were the result of IVF.

Couples who once were childless now have children, sometimes children who are not biologically theirs if others provide the sperm and the ova. Donated sperm have been used for decades, resulting in millions of babies born after intrauterine insemination (formerly called *artificial insemination*). Donor ova and donor wombs (when an IVF embryo is implanted in a woman who did not provide the ovum) are increasingly common, although providing donor ova is more difficult for a woman than providing donor sperm is for a man. The word *donor* may be misleading, since people are paid for their sperm (up to $1,100), ova (up to $10,000 per ova), or surrogate pregnancies (up to $22,000) in addition to medical expenses.

Birth defects and later illnesses increase slightly with IVF (Kalra & Barnhart, 2011; Williams et al., 2011). Nonetheless, the risk is small: About 97 percent of all IVF newborns have no apparent defects.

Not small, however, is the risk of prematurity and low birthweight. In the United States, almost half of all IVF babies are low-birthweight twins or triplets (MMWR, June 12, 2009). Many couples who feared they could never have children suddenly have two tiny ones. Is this a problem? Consider the following.

THINKING CRITICALLY

Two Babies for the Price of One?

If you were infertile, would you welcome twins? Most scientists and doctors wish the answer was no, but most couples say yes. Couples want to avoid the cost (psychological and financial) of a second IVF cycle, so twins seem a bonus. If you were in a committed same-sex relationship, would you consider donor sperm, donor ova, or a donor womb? Many such couples say yes, to the consternation of many politicians.

Why do doctors hope for singletons and why do some people find IVF unethical? Ethics are a matter of culture and belief, and thus can be debated without obvious answers. But doctors have good reasons to hope for single births. Multiple births cause medical complications for mothers and infants, and they are costly for fathers, other siblings, and society as a whole. Indeed, twins and triplets have higher rates of death, disease, and disabilities lifelong. Even when compared with equally small singletons, multiples tend to develop more slowly and form weaker social bonds (Feldman & Eidelman, 2004).

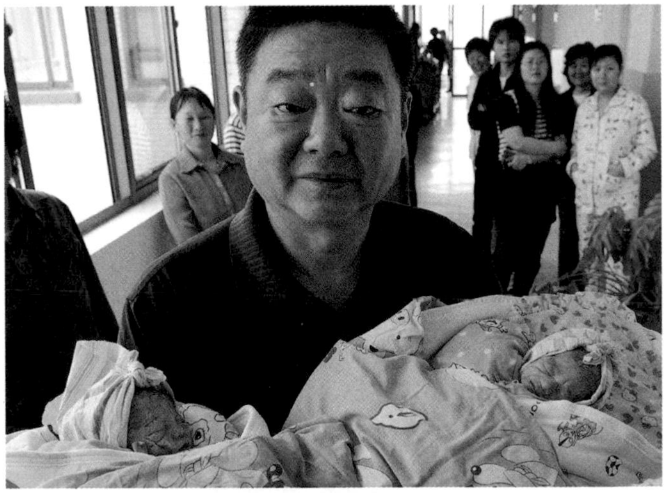
STR / AFP / GETTY IMAGES

Mama Is 60 Wu Jingzhou holds his newborn twin daughters, born to his 60-year-old wife after in vitro fertilization. Ordinarily, it is illegal in China, as in most other nations, for women to have children after menopause. But an exception was made for this couple since the death of their only child, a young woman named Tingling, was partly the government's fault.

Some nations make IVF twins a rare event. Finland allows insertion of only one IVF embryo per cycle, a move that did not reduce the rate of successful pregnancies but did increase the rate of full-term single births (Yli-Kuha et al., 2009). Similar results were found in the United States when an experiment funded only single-embryo transfer (Stillman et al., 2009). Most European nations limit numbers per IVF cycle when government health care pays for the procedure. China now allows more than one IVF zygote if a couple is infertile or if their only child died—as was the case for one 60-year-old woman who had twins (see photo).

Governments vary in other restrictions, as cultures differ regarding ethics. Switzerland requires that ART be used only "when future child welfare can be guaranteed," which usually means that low-income couples are not eligible. An Italian law in 2004 outlawed donor sperm or ova, required that couples be married and heterosexual, and insisted that three embryos be inserted if three were viable, thereby increasing medical complications and fetal deaths and limiting births (Italy already had the lowest birth rate in the world).

The Italian courts in 2009 lifted some of those restrictions, and more infertile Italian couples gave birth (Levi Setti et al., 2011). U.S. laws vary by state. Many wealthy couples travel to different states or nations if ART is not available where they live.

In the United States, IVF can be costly, but even when it is not, as when military insurance pays for it, Latino couples hesitate whereas rates increase among African and European Americans (McCarthy-Keith et al., 2010). When three or more embryos implant, doctors often recommend selective reduction (abortion) of some embryos to protect the others. Not every woman agrees, as was dramatically illustrated by the eight fragile infants born in California in 2009—a miracle or a disaster? (See photo on page 72.) Is ART an issue for elected officials, for judges, for medical ethicists? Or is every aspect of reproduction a personal choice?

SUMMING UP

People usually have 23 chromosomes from their mother and 23 from their father, with all the genes and chromosomes matched up into mother–father pairs—although the match may not be letter perfect because of alleles. The father's 23rd chromosome pair is XY, which means that half his sperm are X and half are Y, determining the future baby's sex. The genes of the zygote duplicate themselves, as that first single cell becomes two cells, four, eight, and so on. Although those early cells are stem cells, and each could become a whole person, soon the cells begin to differentiate as they multiply. Each cell becomes a particular type, traveling to the location on the body where it will perform whatever is needed, becoming skin, blood, bone, part of the brain, and so on.

Twins are monozygotic (one zygote, from the same stem cells) or dizygotic (two zygotes). Assisted reproduction technology has increased the rate of multiple births. Modern reproductive measures, including IVF, have led to millions of much-wanted, healthy infants but also to new dilemmas, including whether people should be able to choose the sex, the genetic and biological parentage, and the number of newborns they have. ■

>> Answer to Observation Quiz (from page 71) The Japanese American girls are the monozygotic twins. If you were not sure, look at their teeth, their eyebrows, and the shape of their faces, compared with the ears and chins of the boys.

>> From One Cell to Many

As already explained, when sperm and ovum combine into a zygote, they establish the *genotype:* all the genes that the developing person has. Creation of a person from one cell involves several complex processes that form the **phenotype**—the person's appearance, behavior, and brain and body functions. Nothing is totally genetic, not even such obvious traits as height or hair color, but nothing is untouched by genes, not even social traits such as political views or propensity to marry and divorce (Rutter, 2011).

The genotype instigates body and brain formation, but the phenotype depends on many genes and on the environment, influenced from the moment of conception until the moment of death through "the organism's encounters with its prenatal and postnatal environments" (Gottlieb, 2010, p. 26). Most traits are **polygenic** (affected by many genes) and **multifactorial** (influenced by many factors, including biological and psychological ones). A zygote might have the genes for becoming,

phenotype The observable characteristics of a person, including appearance, personality, intelligence, and all other traits.

polygenic Referring to a trait that is influenced by many genes.

multifactorial Referring to a trait that is affected by many factors, both genetic and environmental, that enhance, halt, shape, or alter the expression of genes, resulting in a phenotype that may differ markedly from the genotype.

say, a musical genius, but that potential is not usually realized. Some crucial factors in development of the zygote are in the genome itself, because

> genes occupy only about 1.5 percent of the genome. The other 98.5 percent, dubbed "junk DNA," was regarded as useless scraps . . . most of this supposedly useless DNA now appears to produce transcriptions of its genetic code, boosting the raw information output of the genome to about 62 times what the gene alone would produce.
>
> *[Barry, 2007, p. 154]*

Almost daily, researchers describe additional complexities in polygenic and multifactorial interaction. It is apparent that "phenotypic variation . . . results from multiple interactions among numerous genetic and environmental factors." To unravel this "fundamental problem of interrelating genotype and phenotype in complex traits" (Nadeau & Dudley, 2011, p. 1015), we begin with epigenetics.

Epigenetics

Research over the past two decades has found that every trait—psychological as well as physical—is influenced by genes. At first, some scientists thought that genes *determined* everything, that humans became whatever their genes destined them to be—heroes, killers, or ordinary people. Research quickly revealed the limitations of this hypothesis.

Even monozygotic twins are not totally identical—biologically, psychologically, or socially. Many people mistakenly believe that genes determine biology, but hundreds of factors after conception, beginning with the effects of the nongenetic material surrounding the zygote and the nutrition that results from the particular placement of the embryo in the womb, influence the biology of the person. Genes affect everything but determine nothing.

epigenetic Referring to environmental factors that affect genes and genetic expression—enhancing, halting, shaping, or altering the expression of genes and resulting in a phenotype that may differ markedly from the genotype.

Instead, all important human characteristics are **epigenetic.** The prefix *epi-* means "with," "around," "before," "after," "beyond," or "near." The word *epigenetic,* therefore, refers to the environmental factors that surround the genes, affecting genetic expression. Some "epi" influences occur in the first hours of life as biochemical elements silence certain genes in methylation that results from the material surrounding the genes. The details of this process are not yet clear: Thousands of biologists are trying to understand exactly how methylation develops and in what ways it alters genetic expression (Margueron & Reinberg, 2010).

For developmentalists, one fascinating finding is that methylation changes over the life span (Mazin, 2009). Another important finding is that all the diseases known to be genetic (including cancer, schizophrenia, and autism) are actually epigenetic (Saey, 2008). Certain environmental influences (such as injury, temperature extremes, drug abuse, and crowding) can impede genetic development, whereas others (nourishing food, loving care, play) can facilitate it. No trait—even one with strong, proven, genetic origins, such as blood pressure or social anxiety—is determined by genes alone because "development is an epigenetic process that entails cascades of interactions across multiple levels of causation, from genes to environments" (Spencer et al., 2009, p. 80).

The inevitable epigenetic interaction between genes and the environment (nature and nurture) is illustrated in Figure 3.4. That simple diagram, with arrows going up and down over time, has been redrawn and reprinted dozens of times since it was first published in 1992, reiterating that genes interact with environmental conditions again and

FIGURE 3.4

An Epigenetic Model of Development
Notice that there are as many arrows going down as going up, at all levels. Although development begins with genes at conception, it requires that all four factors interact.

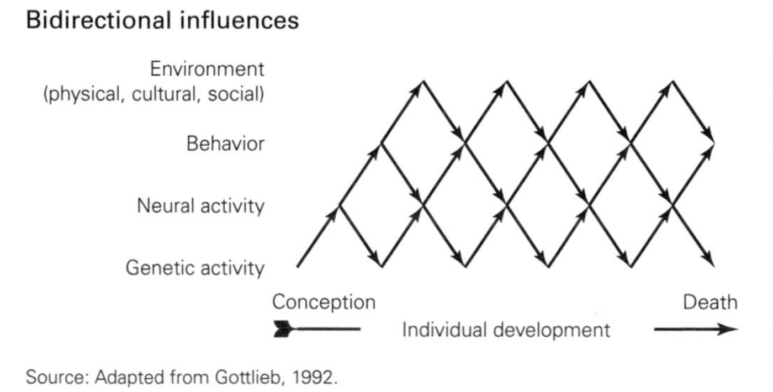

Source: Adapted from Gottlieb, 1992.

again in each person's life (Gottlieb, 2010). All this is a prelude to the explanation of genetic interaction: Epigenetics reminds us that genes are only the beginning.

Gene–Gene Interactions

Many discoveries have followed the completion of the **Human Genome Project** in 2001. One of the first surprises was that humans have far fewer than 100,000 genes, the number everyone believed throughout the twentieth century. The total number of genes in a person is between 18,000 and 23,000. The precise number is elusive because—another surprise—it is not always easy to figure out where one gene starts and another ends, or even if a particular stretch of DNA is actually a gene (Rouchka & Cha, 2009).

Human Genome Project An international effort to map the complete human genetic code. This effort was essentially completed in 2001, though analysis is ongoing.

Another unexpected finding is that all living creatures share many genes. For example, the eyes of flies, mice, and people all originate from the *Pax6 gene*. Similarly, the legs in many species—including the butterfly, the cat, the centipede, and the person—all begin with the same gene. Perhaps even odder is that chimpanzees have 48 chromosomes and people merely 46, yet humans and chimpanzees have almost all (an estimated 99 percent) of their genes in common. What makes humans unlike other animals? The answer lies partly in that "junk" around the genes (lower creatures have far less of it) and partly in 100 or so "regulator" genes, all of which influence thousands of other genes (Shapiro, 2009), directing formation of a creature who talks in words, walks on two legs, and thinks as people do.

The crucial factor that differentiates humans is in the brain. Adult brain size (about 1,400 cubic centimeters) is highly heritable (monozygotic twins are very alike) and is quite similar among humans worldwide, especially when compared with the small chimpanzee brains (about 370 cubic centimeters). Bigger animals (elephants) have bigger brains, but the proportion of brain to body is much greater for humans than for other creatures.

One caution here: Although brain size among humans correlates with body size (women, on average, have smaller brains than men), human brain size does not correlate with intelligence. Furthermore, some animals have brain capacities that people do not, such as an acute sense of smell. Nonetheless, something genetic in the way our brains function makes us uniquely human (Allen et al., 2008; Damasio, 2010; Ramachandran, 2011).

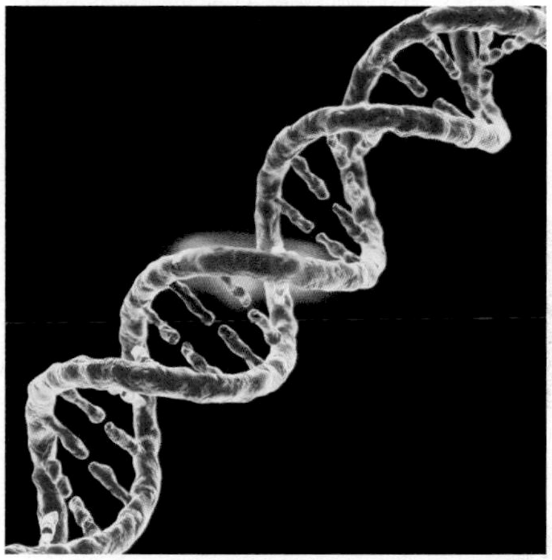

HYBRID MEDICAL ANIMATION / PHOTO RESEARCHERS, INC.

Twelve of Three Billion Pairs This is a computer illustration of a small segment of one gene, with several triplets. Even a small difference in one gene, such as a few extra triplets, can cause major changes in the phenotype of a person.

Additive Heredity

Some alleles are *additive* because their effects *add up* to influence the phenotype. When genes interact additively, the phenotype usually reflects the contributions of every gene that is involved. Height, hair curliness, and skin color, for instance, are usually the result of additive genes. Indeed, height is probably influenced by 180 genes, each contributing a very small amount (Enserink, 2011).

Most people have ancestors of varied height, hair curliness, skin color, and so on, so their children's phenotype does not mirror the parents' phenotypes (although it does always reflect their genotypes). I see this in my family: Our daughter Rachel is of average height, shorter than my husband or I but taller than our mothers. Rachel evidently inherited some of her grandmothers' height genes from us. And none of my children have exactly my skin color—apparent when we borrow clothes from one another and realize that a particular tint is attractive on one of us but not on the other.

How any additive trait turns out depends partly on all the genes a child happens to inherit (half from each parent, which means one-fourth from each grandparent). Some genes amplify or dampen the effects of other genes, aided by all the other DNA and RNA (not junk!) in the zygote.

Especially for Future Parents Suppose you wanted your daughters to be short and your sons to be tall. Could you achieve that? (see response, page 77)

Dominant–Recessive Heredity

dominant–recessive pattern The interaction of a heterozygous pair of alleles in such a way that the phenotype reflects one allele (the dominant gene) more than the other (the recessive gene).

carrier A person whose genotype includes a gene that is not expressed in the phenotype. The carried gene occurs in half of the carrier's gametes and thus is passed on to half of the carrier's children. If such a gene is inherited from both parents, the characteristic appears in the phenotype.

Not all genes are additive. In one nonadditive form, alleles interact in a **dominant–recessive pattern,** in which one allele, the *dominant gene,* is more influential than the other, the *recessive gene.* The dominant gene controls the characteristic even when a recessive gene is the other half of a pair. When someone inherits a recessive gene that is not apparent in the phenotype, that person is said to be a **carrier** of that gene because the recessive gene is *carried* on the genotype.

Most recessive genes are harmless. For example, blue eyes are determined by a recessive allele and brown eyes by a dominant one, which means that a child conceived by a blue-eyed person and a brown-eyed one will usually have brown eyes. "Usually" is accurate, because sometimes a brown-eyed person is a carrier of the blue-eye gene. In that case, in a blue-eye/brown-eye couple, every child will have at least one blue-eye gene (from the blue-eyed parent) and half will have the blue-eye recessive gene from the other parent and thus have blue eyes. The other half will have a brown-eye dominant gene and thus have brown eyes, like the parent who is the carrier of the blue-eye gene. If two brown-eyed parents both have the blue-eye recessive gene, they could have a blue-eyed child (one chance in four)—and no one should raise doubts about the child's paternity (see Figure 3.5).

X-linked A gene carried on the X chromosome. If a male inherits an X-linked recessive trait from his mother, he expresses that trait because the Y from his father has no counteracting gene. Females are more likely to be carriers of X-linked traits but are less likely to express them.

A special case of the dominant–recessive pattern occurs with genes that are **X-linked** (located on the X chromosome). If an X-linked gene is recessive—as are the genes for most forms of color blindness, many allergies, several diseases, and some learning disabilities—the fact that it is on the X chromosome is critical in determining whether it will be expressed in the phenotype (see Table 3.1).

Since the Y chromosome is much smaller than the X, an X-linked recessive gene almost never has a counterpart on the Y chromosome. Therefore, recessive traits carried on the X affect the phenotypes of sons more often than those of daughters because the daughters have another X chromosome, usually with the dominant gene. This explains why males with an X-linked disorder inherited it from their mothers, not their fathers. Because of their mothers, 20 times more boys than girls are color-blind (McIntyre, 2002).

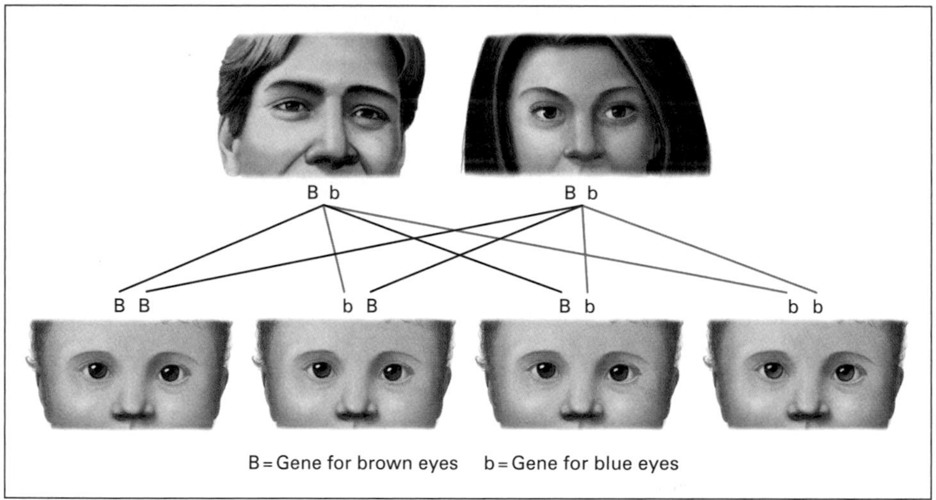

FIGURE 3.5

A Changeling? No. Many brown-eyed people carry a recessive gene for blue eyes. The only way to know for sure is if they have a blue-eyed parent (who gives one gene for blue eyes to every child) or if they have a blue-eyed child. Other recessive genes include red hair, Rh negative blood, and many genetic diseases.

More Complications

As complex as the preceding explanation may seem, it simplifies genetic interaction by making genes appear to be separately functioning entities. But remember that genes merely direct the creation of 20 types of amino acids, which combine to produce thousands of proteins. Those proteins then interact with other proteins, nutrients, and toxins, beginning with thousands of RNA molecules and other material at conception, continuing throughout prenatal development and throughout life.

Copy Number Variations

For any living creature, the outcome of all the interactions involved in heredity is difficult to predict. A small deletion, repetition, or transposition in any of the 3 billion base pairs, or several extra repetitions of a triplet, may be inconsequential, lethal, or something in between. When the human genome was first mapped in

TABLE 3.1 The 23rd Pair and X-Linked Color Blindness: Six Possibilities

23rd Pair	Phenotype	Genotype	Next Generation
1. XX	Unaffected woman	Not a carrier	No color blindness from mother
2. XY	Unaffected man	No color-blind gene	No color blindness from father
3. XX	Unaffected woman	Carrier from mother or father	Half her children will inherit her color-blind X. Half her girls will be carriers; half her boys will be color-blind.
4. XX	Unaffected woman	Carrier from mother	Half her children will inherit her color-blind X. Half her girls will be carriers; half her boys will be color-blind.
5. XY	Color-blind man	Inherited from mother	All his daughters will carry his color-blind X. None of his sons will have his color-blind X. All his children will have normal vision, unless their mother also had an X for color blindness.
6. XX	Color-blind woman (rare)	Inherited from both parents	Every child will have one color-blind X from her. Therefore, every son will be color-blind. Daughters will only be carriers, unless they also inherit a color-blind X from the father.

2001, headlines trumpeted that accomplishment. It was hoped that a specific gene could be located for each genetic disorder and that a cure would soon follow.

That "one gene/one disorder" hope proved to be fantasy, disappointing many doctors who hoped that personalized medicine was imminent (Marshall, 2011). Molecular analysis found, instead, that thousands of seemingly minor variations in base pairs turn out to be influential—each in small ways. Since there are 3 billion base pairs, accumulated variations have notable impact.

Attention has focused on **copy number variations,** which are genes with various repeats or deletions of base pairs. Copy number variations correlate with almost every disease and condition, including heart disease, intellectual abilities, mental illness, and many cancers. Such variations are partly developmental, in that they are often more influential prenatally than in adulthood because that is when the basic brain structures are formed. But remember plasticity—changes can occur lifelong (Chaignat et al., 2011).

copy number variations Genes with various repeats or deletions of base pairs.

Copy number variations are "abundant"—we all have some of them (Mills et al., 2011). Detecting and interpreting such variations may be crucial for the personalized medicine of the future. For instance, many drugs work differently depending on the genetic structure of the recipient; specific factors that lead directly to effective treatment of individual patients need to be better understood (Marshall, 2011).

Parental Imprinting

Sometimes one half of a gene pair switches off during prenatal development, allowing the other free rein but potentially causing a problem if that remaining gene has a deleterious variation. In fact, for girls, one X of the 23rd pair is deactivated early in prenatal life.

Switching-off probably happens during differentiation. This gives rise to a new hope: Perhaps making cells return to the stem cell stage of embryonic development will counter the problem of inactivation and solve some problems of genetic medicine (Lengner, 2010). For girls, it seems random whether the inactive X is

>> Response for Future Parents (from page 75) Yes, but you wouldn't want to. You would have to choose one mate for your sons and another for your daughters, and you would have to use sex-selection methods. Even so, it might not work, given all the genes on your genotype. More important, the effort would be unethical, unnatural, and possibly illegal.

MARIA PLATT-EVANS / SCIENCE PHOTO LIBRARY

She Laughs Too Much No, not the smiling sister, but the 10-year-old on the right, who has Angelman syndrome. She inherited it from her mother's chromosome 15. Fortunately, her two siblings inherited the mother's other chromosome 15 and are normal. If she had inherited the identical deletion on her father's chromosome 15, she would have developed Prader-Willi syndrome, which would cause her to be overweight as well as always hungry and often angry. With Angelman syndrome, however, laughing, even at someone's pain, is a symptom.

from the ovum or sperm, but geneticists wonder if reactivating genes on that inactive X could treat genetic diseases.

A related complexity is *parental imprinting:* Some genes are affected by whether they came from the mother or the father. The best-known examples of imprinting are two syndromes, Prader-Willi and Angelman. Both result in cognitive impairment, and both are caused by a deletion of the same small part of chromosome 15. However, if that deletion is inherited from the father's chromosome 15, the child will have Prader-Willi syndrome and be obese, slow-moving, and stubborn. If that deletion is from the mother's chromosome 15, the child will have Angelman syndrome and be thin, hyperactive, and happy—sometimes too happy, laughing when no one else does.

Parental imprinting is quite common. Early in prenatal development (day 15), an estimated 553 genes act differently if they come from the mother or from the father—a much higher frequency than previously thought. It is possible that imprinting may differ for XX versus XY embryos. For instance, women are more likely to inherit multiple sclerosis from their mothers than from their fathers, and men are less likely to develop it at all (Gregg, 2010): Could imprinting be involved? Many other traits affect one sex more than the other: Imprinting is one of the dozens of plausible biological and cultural explanations.

SUMMING UP

The distinction between genotype (heredity) and phenotype (manifest appearance and observed behavior) is only one of the many complexities involved in trying to understand the influence of genes on development. All traits are epigenetic, the product of nongenetic influences, beginning with methylation at conception and continuing lifelong. Furthermore, most traits are polygenic, the result of many genes that interact—some additively and some in a dominant–recessive pattern, with thousands of minor variations in base pairs. Some genetic effects vary in ways not yet understood, depending on which genes came from the mother and which from the father. ■

>> Genotype and Phenotype

The goal of this chapter is to help every reader grasp the complex interaction between genotype and phenotype. This is not easy. For the past 100 years in virtually every nation, a million scientists have struggled to understand this complexity. Each new decade brings advances in statistics and molecular analysis, as well as data that uncover various patterns. Each decade also raises new questions.

Current Consensus

Developmentalists today accept four generalities that were surprising when first reported (Gottlieb, 2010; Plomin et al., 2008; Rutter, 2011; Worthman et al., 2010):

1. Genes affect every aspect of behavior, including social interactions, intellectual abilities, even political values and reactions.
2. Most environmental influences on children raised in the same home are *not shared* (more on this in Chapter 13).
3. Genes elicit responses that shape development. Thus, personality may be partly the cause of a person's experiences, not merely the result.

4. Lifelong, people choose friends and environments that encourage their genetic predispositions (called *niche-picking*). Thus, genetic effects *increase* with age.

Every trait, action, and attitude has a genetic component: Without genes, no development could occur. Yet every trait, action, and attitude has an environmental component; without context, genes have no power. An easy example is height, powerfully influenced by genes. However, although Koreans, for instance, share many genes, adults in North Korea are on average 3 inches shorter than those in South Korea. The probable reason is chronic famine in North Korea (Johnson, 2010; Schwekendiek, 2009). A more surprising example is political ideology: Several researchers report that a particular allele of a dopamine receptor gene (DRD4-R7) correlates with being liberal, but one recent study finds this connection only if a person has many friends. Loners with the liberal-leaning gene tend to be more conservative (Settle et al., 2010).

Now we examine two complex traits: addiction and visual acuity. As you read about specific expressions of those traits (alcoholism and nearsightedness), you will see that understanding the progression from genotype to phenotype has many practical implications for child development.

MARCO C. PEREIRA / SARA WONG / 4SEE / REDUX

Hidden Husband Shyness is inherited, but this mother seems not to have the gene. Probably her husband is the shy one—unless nurture has taught the daughter to be shy and the mother to be outgoing.

Alcoholism

At various times, people have considered the abuse of alcohol and other drugs to be a moral weakness, a social scourge, or a personality defect. Historically, attention has been on alcohol, since that drug occurs naturally from fermentation and people everywhere have drunk it. In diverse times and places, alcoholics were locked up, doused with cold water, or burned at the stake. Alcohol has also been declared illegal (as in the United States from 1919 to 1933) as well as deemed a sacred part of religious observance (as in many Judeo-Christian rituals). We now know that, because inherited biochemistry affects alcohol metabolism, laws, treatments, and traditions have varied impacts on individuals.

Genes create an addictive pull that can be overpowering, extremely weak, or somewhere in between. To be specific, each person's biochemistry reacts to alcohol, causing sleep, nausea, aggression, joy, relaxation, forgetfulness, sex urges, or tears. How bodies metabolize alcohol allows some people to "hold their liquor" and therefore drink too much, whereas others (including many East Asians) sweat and become red-faced after just a few sips—an embarrassing response that may lead to abstinence. Candidate genes for alcoholism have been identified on every chromosome except the Y chromosome (ironic, since, internationally, more men than women are alcoholics) (Epps & Holt, 2011). Every research scientist agrees: Alcoholism is polygenic and culture is pivotal.

Although the emphasis has been on metabolism, inherited psychological characteristics may be as influential for alcoholism (Macgregor et al., 2009). A quick temper, sensation seeking, or high anxiety encourage drinking. Moreover, some contexts (such as fraternity parties) make it hard to abstain; other contexts (a church social in a "dry" county) make it difficult to swallow anything stronger than lemonade.

AP PHOTO / PELLE RINK / POLFOTO

Is He Drunk? This worker at Carlsberg Breweries in Copenhagen was one of many who benefited from company policy—beer available all day long from coolers placed throughout the work floor. In 2010, the policy changed: No more coolers, and beer could be consumed only at lunch. Many employees walked off their jobs in protest. Social attitudes about alcohol added intensity to this labor–management conflict.

Biological sex (XX or XY) and gender (cultural) also affect the risk of alcoholism. For biological reasons (body size, fat composition, metabolism), women become drunk on less alcohol than men, but how much a woman drinks depends on her social context. For example, in Japan, both sexes have the same genes for metabolizing alcohol, yet women drink only about one-tenth as much as men. When Japanese women live in the United States, their alcohol consumption increases about fivefold (Higuchi et al., 1996). It seems as if people of Asian descent who are born in the United States take on the drinking patterns of their fellow Americans, perhaps to the detriment of Japanese American women (Makimoto, 1998).

Especially for Future Drug Counselors
Is the wish for excitement likely to lead to addiction? (see response, page 81)

Nearsightedness

Age, genes, and culture affect vision as well. First consider age. Newborns focus only on things within 2 feet of their eyes; vision improves steadily until about age 10; the eyeball changes shape at puberty, increasing nearsightedness (myopia), and again in middle age, decreasing myopia, hence distance vision improves.

Now consider genes. A study of British twins found that the Pax6 gene, which governs eye formation, has many alleles that make people somewhat nearsighted (Hammond et al., 2004). This research found *heritability* of almost 90 percent, which means that if one monozygotic twin was nearsighted, the other twin was almost always nearsighted, too.

Heritable?

heritability A statistic that indicates what percentage of the variation in a particular trait within a particular population, in a particular context and era, can be traced to genes.

However, **heritability** is a statistic that indicates only how much of the variation in a particular trait *within a particular population* in a particular context and era can be traced to genes. For example, the heritability of height is very high (about 95 percent) when children receive good medical care and ample nourishment, but it is low (about 20 percent) when children are malnourished. Thus, the 90 percent heritability of nearsightedness among the British children may not apply elsewhere.

Indeed it does not. Visual problems may be caused by the environment. In some African nations, heritability of vision is close to zero because severe vitamin A deficiency is the main reason some children see less well than others. Scientists are working to develop a strain of maize (the local staple) high in vitamin A. If they succeed, heritability will increase and overall vision will improve (Harjes et al., 2008). But what about children who are well nourished? Is their vision entirely inherited? Cross-cultural research suggests that it is not.

STEPHEN SHAVER / POLARIS

Bright-Eyed and Nearsighted These are star students from Beijing, China, waiting in line for visas to the United States. If they had spent less time studying, would they be here?

One report claims "myopia is increasing at an 'epidemic' rate, particularly in East Asia" (Park & Congdon, 2004, p. 21), and another cites "very strong environmental impacts" on Asian children's vision (Morgan, 2003, p. 276). The first published research on this phenomenon appeared in 1992, when scholars noticed that, in army-mandated medical exams of all 17-year-old males in Singapore, 26 percent were nearsighted in 1980 but 43 percent were nearsighted in 1990 (Tay et al., 1992).

Further studies found nearsightedness increasing from 12 to 84 percent between ages 6 and 17 in Taiwan, with increases in myopia during middle childhood also in Singapore and Hong Kong (cited in Grosvenor, 2003). Some of this may be the natural increase in myopia at puberty, but not this much. Nurture must somehow be involved. But how?

Outdoor Play?

One possible culprit is homework. In Chapter 12, you will learn that, unlike earlier generations, contemporary East Asian children are amazingly proficient in math and science. Fifty years ago, most Asian children were working; now all attend school and study more than their peers in other nations. As their developing eyes focus on the print in front of them, those with a genetic vulnerability to myopia may lose acuity for objects far away—which is exactly what nearsightedness means.

A study of Singaporean 10- to 12-year-olds found a correlation between nearsightedness (measured by optometric exams) and high achievement, especially in language (presumably reflecting more reading). Correlation is not causation, but statistics (odds ratio of 2.5, significance of 0.001) suggest a link (Saw et al., 2007).

Ophthalmologists believe that the underlying cause is not time spent studying but inadequate time spent in daylight. Perhaps if Asian children spent more time

outside playing, walking, or relaxing, fewer might need glasses. This recommendation is supported by an editorial in a leading U.S. journal for ophthalmologists:

> The probability of becoming myopic by the eighth grade is about 60% if a child has two myopic parents and does less than 5 hours per week of sports/outdoor activity. . . . [It is] about 20% if a two-myopic-parent child does 14 hours or more per week of sports/outdoor activity.
>
> *[Mutti & Zadnik, 2009, p. 77]*

>> Response for Future Drug Counselors (from page 79) Maybe. Some people who love risk become addicts; others develop a healthy lifestyle that includes adventure, new people, and exotic places. Any trait can lead in various directions. You need to be aware of the connection so that you can steer your clients toward healthy adventures.

Between the early 1970s and the early 2000s, nearsightedness in the U.S. population increased from 25 to 42 percent (Vitale et al., 2009). Urbanization, television, and fear of strangers have kept many U.S. children indoors most of the time, unlike earlier generations who played outside for hours each day. To prove a causal link, a longitudinal experiment that keeps some children indoors while their siblings (to control for genes) play outside would be helpful, but that is impossible. Nonetheless, the correlational data on nearsightedness, as well as on alcoholism and on other genetic conditions, has many implications.

Practical Applications

Since genes affect every disorder, no one should be blamed or punished for inherited problems. However, knowing that genes do not act in isolation can lead to preventive measures when genetic vulnerability is apparent. For instance, if alcoholism is in the genes, parents can keep alcohol out of their home, hoping their children become cognitively and socially mature before drinking. If nearsightedness runs in the family, parents can make sure that children play outdoors every day.

Of course, outdoor play and abstention from alcohol are recommended for every child, as are dozens of other behaviors, such as flossing the teeth, saying "please," getting enough sleep, eating vegetables, and writing thank-you notes. However, no parent can enforce every recommendation. Awareness of genetic risks helps parents set priorities and act on them.

Ignoring the nature–nurture interaction can be lethal. Consider baseball superstar Mickey Mantle, who hit more home runs in World Series baseball than any other player. Most of his male relatives were alcoholics and died before middle age, including his father, who died of Hodgkin disease (a form of cancer) at age 39. Mantle became "a notorious alcoholic [because he]believed a family history of early mortality meant he would die young" (Jaffe, 2004, p. 37). He ignored his genetic predisposition to alcoholism.

At age 46 Mantle said, "If I knew I was going to live this long, I would have taken better care of myself." He never developed Hodgkin disease, and if he had, chemotherapy developed since his father's death would likely have saved him—an example of environment prevailing over genes. However, drinking destroyed his liver. He understood too late what he had done. When he was dying, he told his fans at Yankee Stadium: "Please don't do drugs and alcohol. God gave us only one body, keep it healthy. If you want to do something great, be an organ donor" (quoted in Begos, 2010). Despite a last-minute liver transplant, he died at age 63—15 years younger than most men of his time.

SUMMING UP

Genes affect every trait—whether it is something wonderful, such as a wacky sense of humor; something fearful, such as a violent temper; or something quite ordinary, such as a tendency to be bored. The environment affects every trait as well, in ways that change as maturational, cultural, and historical processes unfold. Genes themselves can be modified through epigenetic factors, including drugs and nutrition. Furthermore, genetic expression can be directed or deflected, depending on the culture and the society as well as on the individual and the family. This is apparent in height, alcoholism, nearsightedness, and almost every other physical and psychological condition. All have genetic roots, developmental patterns, and environmental triggers. ■

>> Chromosomal and Genetic Problems

We now focus on conditions caused by an extra chromosome or a single destructive gene. These are abnormalities in that they are not the norm (hence called *ab*normal). Three factors make these conditions relevant to our study:

1. They provide insight into the complexities of nature and nurture.
2. Knowing their origins helps limit their effects.
3. Information combats prejudice: Difference is not always deficit.

Not Exactly 46

As you know, each gamete usually has 23 chromosomes, creating a zygote with 46 chromosomes and eventually a person. However, some gametes have more or fewer than 23 chromosomes. One variable that correlates with chromosomal abnormalities is the parents' age, particularly the age of the mother. A suggested explanation is that, since ova begin to form before a girl is born, older mothers have older ova, less likely to be 23–23.

These miscounts are not rare. One estimate is that about 5 to 10 percent of all conceptions have more or fewer than 46 chromosomes (Brooker, 2009); another estimate suggests that the rate is as high as 50 percent (Fragouli & Wells, 2011). Far fewer of such zygotes are born, less than 1 percent, primarily because most such organisms never duplicate, divide, differentiate, and implant. If implantation does occur, many are aborted, spontaneously (miscarried) or by choice. Birth itself is hazardous; about 5 percent of stillborn (dead-at-birth) babies have 47 chromosomes (O. J. Miller & Therman, 2001), and many abnormal but living newborns die within the first few days.

Each abnormality leads to a recognizable *syndrome,* a cluster of distinct characteristics that tend to occur together. Usually the cause is three chromosomes (a condition called a *trisomy*) at a particular location instead of the usual two. Once in about every 200 births, a newborn survives with 45, 47, or, rarely, 48 or 49 chromosomes.

Down Syndrome

Down syndrome A condition in which a person has 47 chromosomes instead of the usual 46, with 3 rather than 2 chromosomes at the 21st site. People with Down syndrome typically have distinctive characteristics, including unusual facial features, heart abnormalities, and language difficulties. (Also called *trisomy-21.*)

The most common extra-chromosome condition that results in a surviving child is **Down syndrome,** also called *trisomy-21* because the person has three copies of chromosome 21. According to one estimate, a 20-year-old woman has about 1 chance in 800 of carrying a fetus with Down syndrome; a 39-year-old woman, 1 in 67; and a 44-year-old woman, 1 in 16. (Estimates vary, although all the data show marked increases with maternal age).

Some 300 distinct characteristics can result from that third chromosome 21. No individual with Down syndrome is identical to another, but most have specific facial characteristics—a thick tongue, round face, slanted eyes—as well as distinctive hands, feet, and fingerprints. Many also have hearing problems, heart abnormalities, muscle weakness, and short stature. They are usually slower to develop intellectually, especially in language, and they reach their maximum intellectual potential at about age 15 (Rondal, 2010). Some are severely retarded; others are of average or above-average intelligence. That extra chromosome affects the person lifelong, but family context, educational efforts, and possibly medication can improve the person's prognosis (Kuehn, 2011).

Problems of the 23rd Pair

Every human has at least 44 autosomes and one X chromosome; an embryo cannot develop without those 45. However, about 1 in every 500 infants is born with only one sex chromosome (no Y) or with three or more (not just two) (Hamerton & Evans, 2005). Having an odd number of sex chromosomes impairs cognitive and psychosocial development as well as sexual maturation. The specifics depend on the particular configuration as well as on other genetic factors. Sometimes only a part of that 23rd chromosome is missing, or a person with an extra chromosome is relatively unaffected by it. In such cases, the person seems to be a normal adult but typically is infertile (Mazzocco & Ross, 2007).

REUTERS/ CLAUDIA DAUT

Universal Happiness All young children delight in painting brightly colored pictures on a big canvas, but this scene is unusual for two reasons: Daniel has trisomy-21, and this photograph was taken at the only school in Chile where normal and special-needs children share classrooms.

Gene Disorders

Everyone carries alleles that *could* produce serious diseases or handicaps in the next generation (see Table 3.2). Most such genes have no serious consequences because they are recessive. The phenotype is affected only when the inherited condition is dominant or when a zygote is homozygous for a particular recessive condition, that is, when the zygote has received the recessive gene from both parents.

Especially for Future Doctors Might a patient who is worried about his or her sexuality have an undiagnosed abnormality of the sex chromosome? (see response, page 84)

Dominant Disorders

Most of the 7,000 *known* single-gene disorders are dominant (always expressed). They are usually easy to notice because their effects are evident in the phenotype. Severe dominant disorders are rare because people with such disorders rarely live long enough to reproduce and thus do not pass the gene on to children.

One exception is *Huntington disease,* a fatal central nervous system disorder caused by a genetic miscode—more than 35 repetitions of a particular triplet. Unlike most dominant traits, the effects do not begin until middle adulthood. By then a person could have had several children, and odds are that half would have inherited the same dominant gene. This was true for the original Mr. Huntington (Bates et al., 2002). Another exception is a rare but severe form of Alzheimer disease that causes dementia before age 60.

Especially for Teachers Suppose you know that one of your students has a sibling who has Down syndrome. What special actions should you take? (see response, page 88)

Recessive Disorders

Several recessive genetic disorders are sex-linked. The most famous of these is hemophilia, a blood disorder carried by Queen Victoria of England. She passed it on to her descendants, including Empress Alexandra, who bore the only male heir to the Russian throne, Crown Prince Alexi (Rogaev et al., 2009). Some historians suggest that X-linked hemophilia was a pivotal cause of antimonarchy revolutions, including the one that led to Communism in Russia in 1917. Alexi's parents were distracted from leading the nation and listened to irrational advice from Rasputin, a psychopathic "healer."

Especially for Historians Some genetic diseases may have changed the course of history. For instance, the last czar of Russia had four healthy daughters and one son with hemophilia. Once called the royal disease, hemophilia is X-linked. How could this rare condition have affected the monarchies of Russia, England, Austria, Germany, and Spain? (see response, page 88)

Another X-linked condition, **fragile X syndrome,** is caused by more than 200 repetitions of one triplet on one gene (Plomin et al., 2003). (Some repetitions are normal, but not this many.) The cognitive deficits caused by fragile X syndrome are the most common form of *inherited* mental retardation (many other forms, such as trisomy-21, are not inherited).

Since this is an X-linked, single-gene disorder, fragile X syndrome may be recessive; however, the exact inheritance pattern of fragile X is more complex than that

fragile X syndrome A genetic disorder in which part of the X chromosome seems to be attached to the rest of it by a very thin string of molecules. The cause is a single gene that has more than 200 repetitions of one triplet.

TABLE 3.2 Common Genetic Diseases and Conditions

Name	Description	Prognosis	Probable Inheritance	Incidence*	Carrier Detection?†	Prenatal Detection?
Albinism	No melanin; person is very blond, pale	Normal, but must avoid sun damage	Recessive	Carriers more common among Native and African Americans	No	No
Alzheimer disease	Memory loss; increasing mental impairment	Eventual death, often after years of dependency	Early onset—dominant; after age 60—multifactorial	Fewer than 1 in 100 early onset; more common in late adulthood	Yes, for early onset; yes, for risk factors.	No
Cancer	Tumors that can spread	Each type has different rates of cure and fatality	Multifactorial; almost all cancers have a genetic component	Most people eventually develop some type; about one-fourth die	No	No
Cleft palate, cleft lip	The two sides of the upper lip or palate are not joined	Correctable by surgery	Multifactorial	1 in every 700 births; more common in Asians and U.S. Indians	No	Yes
Club foot	The foot and ankle are twisted	Correctable by surgery	Multifactorial	1 in every 200 births; more boys than girls	No	Yes
Cystic fibrosis	Mucous obstructions, especially in lungs, stomach	Most live to middle adulthood	Recessive gene; also spontaneous mutations	1 in 3,200; 1 in 25 European Americans is a carrier	Sometimes	Yes, in most cases
Deafness (congenital)	Inability to hear	Language possible via signs, or cochlear implants	Multifactorial; some forms are recessive	1 in 1,000 births; more common in people from Middle East	No	No
Diabetes	Abnormal sugar metabolism; insufficient insulin	Early onset (type 1) fatal without insulin; later onset (type 2), variable	Multifactorial; for later onset, body weight is significant	Type 1: rare; type 2: 1 in 6, especially non–European Americans	No	No
Hemophilia	Absence of clotting factor in blood	Death from bleeding; blood transfusions prevent damage	X-linked recessive; also spontaneous mutations	1 in 10,000 males; royal families of Europe had it	No	No
Hydroceph-alus	Obstruction causes excess fluid in the brain	Brain damage and death; surgery allows normal life	Multifactorial	1 in every 100 births	No	Yes
Muscular dystrophy (30 diseases)	Weakening of muscles	Inability to walk, move; wasting away; death	Recessive or multifactorial	1 in every 3,500 males develops Duchenne's	Yes, for some forms	Yes, for some forms

>> Response for Future Doctors (from page 83) That is highly unlikely. Chromosomal abnormalities are evident long before adulthood. It is quite normal for adults to be worried about sexuality for social, not biological, reasons. You could test the karyotype, but that may be needlessly alarmist.

of other X-linked conditions. Repetitions of the damaging triplet increase when the affected X chromosome passes from one generation to the next; more repetitions correlate with lower IQ, especially in boys.

Most recessive disorders are on the autosomes and thus are not X-linked. For example, cystic fibrosis, thalassemia, and sickle-cell anemia are all equally common and devastating in both sexes (see Table 3.2). About 1 in 12 North Americans is a carrier for one of these three. That high incidence occurs because carriers benefit from the gene (Brooker, 2009).

Name	Description	Prognosis	Probable Inheritance	Incidence*	Carrier Detection?†	Prenatal Detection?
Neural-tube defects (open spine)	Anencephaly (parts of the brain missing) or spina bifida (lower spine not closed)	Anencephalic—severe retardation; spina bifida—poor lower body control	Multifactorial; folic acid deficit and genes	Anencephaly:1 in 1,000; spina bifida: 3 in 1,000; more common in Welsh, Scots	No	Yes
Phenylketo-nuria (PKU)	Abnormal digestion of protein	Mental retardation, preventable by diet begun soon after birth	Recessive	1 in 100 European Americans is a carrier; higher among Irish, Norwegians	Yes	Yes
Pyloric stenosis	Overgrowth of muscle in intestine	Vomiting, weight loss, death; corrected by surgery	Multifactorial	1 boy in 200, 1 girl in 1,000; less in African Americans	No	No
Rett syndrome	Neurological developmental disorder	Boys die at birth; at 6–18 months, girls lose speech and motor skills	X-linked	1 in 10,000 female births	No	Sometimes
Schizo-phrenia	Severely distorted thought	Drugs, therapy ease symptoms	Multifactorial	1 in 100 people develop it by early adulthood	No	No
Sickle-cell anemia	Abnormal blood cells	Painful "crisis"; heart, kidney failure; treated with drugs	Recessive	1 in 11 African Americans and 1 in 20 Latinos are carriers	Yes	Yes
Tay-Sachs disease	Enzyme disease	Healthy infant becomes weaker, usually dying by age 5	Recessive	1 in 30 U.S. Jews and 1 in 20 French Canadians are carriers	Yes	Yes
Thalassemia	Abnormal blood cells	Low energy, vulnerable to infections, slow growth	Usually recessive, occasionally dominant	1 in 10 from Italy, Greece, India, Egypt are carriers	Yes	Yes
Tourette syndrome	Uncontrollable tics, body jerking, verbal outbursts	Appears at about age 5; worsens, then improves	Dominant, but variable penetrance	1 in 250 children	Sometimes	No

*Incidence statistics vary from country to country. For instance, the rate of PKU is 1 in 119,000 in Japan but is 26 times that in Ireland. Those given here are approximate for the United States, but all these diseases can occur in any ethnic group in any nation. Many affected groups limit transmission through genetic counseling; for example, the incidence of Tay-Sachs disease is declining because many Jewish young adults obtain testing and counseling before marriage.

†"Yes" refers to carrier detection. Family history can also reveal genetic risk.

Sources: Benacerraf, 2007; Butler & Meaney, 2005; Cruz-Inigo et al., 2011; Haydon, 2007; Hemminki et al., 2008; Klug et al., 2008; McKusick, 2007; K. L. Moore & Persaud, 2007; Shahin et al., 2002.

The most studied example of the benefits of recessive genes is sickle-cell anemia. Carriers of sickle-cell die less often from malaria, still prevalent in parts of Africa. Indeed, four distinct alleles cause sickle-cell anemia, each originating in a malaria-prone region. Selective adaptation allowed the gene to become widespread because it protected more people (the carriers) than it killed. About 11 percent of Americans with African ancestors are carriers. Similarly, cystic fibrosis is more common among Americans with ancestors from northern Europe; carriers may have been protected from cholera.

Genetic Counseling and Testing

Until recently, after the birth of a child with a disorder, couples blamed witches or fate, not genes or chromosomes. Today, many young adults worry about their genes long before they marry. Virtually everyone has a relative with a serious condition, and everyone wonders what their children will inherit. Researchers now know much more than they did about genes even a few years ago: Not every scientist believes the public is ready for that knowledge, as the following explains.

A VIEW FROM SCIENCE

Genetic Testing for Psychological Disorders

Might your genes increase your chances of developing a psychological disorder—say, schizophrenia, dementia, bipolar disorder, autism, or addiction? Should you seek genetic testing to learn more? The answer from science to these two questions is yes for all five conditions, and then no to testing.

No doubt genes are part of every psychological disorder. Thankfully, parents are no longer blamed for causing their children's autism. Yet the environment is crucial for every disorder—not only what the parents do but also what the community and governments do. You have already seen this with alcoholism. The same is true for almost every psychological condition.

Consider, for example, schizophrenia, a devastating condition that distorts thought and gives rise to hallucinations, delusions, garbled talk, and irrational emotions. When one monozygotic twin becomes schizophrenic, often—but not always—the other identical twin also develops a psychological disorder. For dizygotic twins and other siblings, the risk is much lower—about 12 percent for schizophrenia—but higher than the 1 percent incidence of schizophrenia for people who have no relatives with the disease. This leaves no doubt that genes are one factor (Castle & Morgan, 2008), and some genetic-testing companies advertise an ability to detect vulnerabilities.

COURTESY OF EDNA MORLOK

Too Cute? This portrait of the Genain sisters was taken 20 years before they all developed schizophrenia. However, from their identical hair ribbons to the identical position of their feet, it is apparent that their unusual status as quadruplets set them apart as curiosities. Could their life in the spotlight have nurtured their potential for schizophrenia? There is no way to know for sure.

Yet note that even monozygotic twins differ, which means that schizophrenia cannot be simply genetic. That is apparent for non-twins as well. Children born to schizophrenic parents are at genetic risk but might not develop the disease. One careful study of the entire population of Denmark found that if both parents have the disease, 27 percent of their children develop it; if one parent has it, 7 percent of their children develop it. These same statistics can be presented another way: Even if both parents have schizophrenia, almost three-fourths (73 percent) of their children do not (Gottesman et al., 2010) (see the Research Design).

Among the known environmental causes are undernutrition of the mother during pregnancy, birth in the summer, use of psychoactive drugs in adolescence, emigration to another nation as a young adult, and family emotionality during adulthood. Because environment is crucial and many genes that increase vulnerability to schizophrenia remain to be found, few scientists advocate genetic testing for schizophrenia. Some worry that a positive test would lead to depression, lack of therapy, and more stigma for those who have mental illness than already exists (Mitchell et al., 2010).

In several U.S. states (California and New York among them), selling genetic tests is illegal without a physician's request, and most doctors test only to confirm diagnosis of a problem they already suspect. Nonetheless, many companies profit from genetic testing, and some people break the law to get the information they want. If they learn that they could develop a mental disorder, they might buy term-care insurance—a good investment for them but a bad one for insurance companies (D. H. Taylor et al., 2010). That might lead to more costly insurance for the general population and inferior care for those who cannot afford insurance. Another possibility is that people who learn they have a higher risk of illness or dementia might leave their families or even kill themselves. No wonder some places make genetic testing illegal.

However, any restriction seems unfair to people who want more information. The opposite problem often occurs: Children might be required to get genetic tests they do not want. The most obvious example comes not from tests for psychological conditions but from tests for known physical conditions. Some students who want to play sports in school must be tested for heart abnormalities and for the sickle-cell trait, both of which can cause sudden death if an otherwise healthy student becomes physically exhausted.

However, most young people who test positive never have a problem. If a positive test keeps someone off the team, is that fair? If that is fair, what about a test for behavior disorders? Should kindergartners be tested for antisocial behavior or attention-deficit disorder so that their teachers or parents can be forewarned? But might that information itself cause a problem?

Finally, marked ethical issues are raised regarding a new blood test for pregnant women that reveals, through cells discarded by the embryo, if the future baby might have any of 100 or more genetic or chromosomal conditions (Greely, 2011). Will that lead to more abortions or more stress? If the test is not recommended and a baby is born with a genetic condition, will that lead to a lawsuit?

It is easy to understand why scientists hope that people will rely on behavior change (e.g., more exercise) to make us all healthier, not on genetic tests. On the other hand, people want information about themselves. Many researchers debate what data people should have and how they should get it (Couzin-Frankel, 2011). Science has revealed much more about genes than anyone imagined a decade ago. Laws and ethics have not kept up with the possibilities.

PHOTO BY GARY W. GREEN. USED WITH PERMISSION OF THE ORLANDO SENTINEL. © 2010

Praying Too Late The coaches of this high school football team wish they had known that 15-year-old Oliver Louis was a carrier for sickle-cell anemia. Perhaps then his death could have been prevented before he collapsed in practice, due to exertional sickling. His teammates pray before they play—should they also be tested for genetic vulnerability?

Research Design

Scientists: Irving I. Gottesman, Thomas Munk Laursen, Aksel Bertelsen, and Preben Bo Mortensen.

Publication: *Archives of General Psychiatry* (2010).

Participants: Everyone born in Denmark between 1968 and 1997 whose parents were listed in the Denmark population archives.

Design: The researchers examined the psychiatric records of all the children in the study (more than 2 million of them), who were aged 10 to 52 at the time the study was done. The researchers also traced the medical records of the children's parents, noting hospital admission for psychiatric disorders. They found 196 couples (with 270 children) in which both the mother and father were hospitalized for schizophrenia and 83 couples (with 146 children) who were both admitted for bipolar disorder.

Results: Children born to parents with psychological disorders had much higher rates than average of developing a disorder. When both parents were schizophrenic, 27 percent of the children were hospitalized for schizophrenia and 12 percent had other severe disorders. Of those with only one schizophrenic parent, 7 percent developed that disorder. When neither parent was hospitalized for schizophrenia, less than 1 percent (0.86 percent) of the children were. Children whose parents had bipolar disorder had higher rates of other disorders (including depression) than the average person, but their illness rate was lower than that for children whose parents had schizophrenia.

Major conclusion: Genes confer vulnerability for serious mental disorders, especially schizophrenia. However, more than half of the children born to a schizophrenic mother and father escaped serious disorders themselves, and about 20,000 Danes who were hospitalized for schizophrenia had neither parent with the disorder.

Comments: This is an impressive study, since it included both parents of more than 2 million children. Such powerful research on a large population group with verified records (not just a selected sample with the researchers' assessment) is possible only in relatively small, developed nations with accurate records. Note, however, that the data are a correlation, not longitudinal. Even in Denmark, where every child gets good medical care, social services, and education, some of the burden of family schizophrenia may result from nurture, not nature.

ROBERT SPENCER / THE NEW YORK TIMES

"The Hardest Decision I Ever Had to Make" That's how this woman described her decision to terminate her third pregnancy when genetic testing revealed that the fetus had Down syndrome. She soon became pregnant again with a male fetus that had the normal 46 chromosomes, as did her two daughters and as will her fourth child, not yet born. Many personal factors influence such decisions. Do you think she and her husband would have made the same choice if they had had no other children?

genetic counseling Consultation and testing by trained experts that enable individuals to learn about their genetic heritage, including harmful conditions that they might pass along to any children they may conceive.

Genetic counseling relieves some worries by providing facts and helping prospective parents discuss sensitive issues. Genetic counselors usually favor testing, reasoning that knowledge is better than ignorance. However, high-risk individuals (who might hear bad news) do not always agree.

Many people, especially when considering personal and emotional information, misinterpret words such as *risks* and *probability* (O'Doherty, 2006). Even doctors do not always understand. Consider the experience of one of my students. A month before she became pregnant, Jeannette was required to have a rubella vaccination for her job. Hearing this, her prenatal care doctor gave her the following prognosis:

> My baby would be born with many defects, his ears would not be normal, he would be mentally retarded. . . . I went home and cried for hours and hours. . . . I finally went to see a genetic counselor. Everything was fine, thank the Lord, thank you, my beautiful baby is okay.
>
> *[Jeannette, personal communication, 2008]*

It is possible that Jeannette misunderstood what she was told, but one of the jobs of the professional is to make sure that the client understands. If sensitive counseling is available, then preconception, prenatal, or even prenuptial (before marriage) testing is recommended for everyone, especially for:

- Individuals who have a parent, sibling, or child with a serious genetic condition
- Couples who have had several spontaneous abortions or stillbirths
- Couples who are infertile
- Couples from the same ethnic group, particularly if they are relatives
- Women over age 35 and men over age 40

Genetic counselors follow two ethical rules: (1) Tests are confidential, beyond the reach of insurance companies and public records, and (2) decisions are made by the clients, not by the counselors.

However, these guidelines are not always easy to follow. One quandary arises when genetic tests reveal that the husband does not carry the gene that caused a recessive disease in a child. Should the counselor tell the couple that they have zero chance of having another baby with this problem because the husband is not the biological father? Counselors vary in how they handle this (Lucast, 2007).

Another quandary arises when DNA is collected for one purpose—say, to assess the risk of heart disease—and analysis reveals another problem, such as an extra sex chromosome or a high risk of breast cancer. This problem is new: Even a few years ago, testing was so expensive that researchers did not discover any conditions except those for which they were testing. Now, DNA collected a few years ago, from people who did not expect to be tested for the condition that was found, often reveals a genetic risk. Must the researcher inform the person?

The current consensus is that information should be shared if and only if (1) the person wants to hear it, (2) the risk is severe and verified, and (3) treatment is available (Couzin-Frankel, 2011). However, scientists and physicians disagree as to how severe, and how treatable, various conditions are. This is particularly true for psychological disorders. Moreover, many researchers are not able to provide the careful and patient counseling necessary. We all are carriers. Do we all want to know the specifics?

Sometimes couples make a decision (such as to begin or to abort a pregnancy) that is not what the counselor would do. People with identical genetic conditions often make opposite choices. For instance, 108 women who already had one child with fragile X syndrome were told they had a 50 percent chance of having another such child. Most (77 percent) decided to avoid pregnancy with sterilization or excellent contraception but some (20 percent) had another child (Raspberry &

>> Response for Teachers (from page 83) As the text says, "information combats prejudice." Your first step would be to make sure you know about Down syndrome, reading material about it. You would learn, among other things, that it is not usually inherited (your student need not worry about his or her progeny) and that some children with Down syndrome need extra medical and educational attention. This might mean you need to pay special attention to your student, whose parents might focus on the sibling.

>> Response for Historians (from page 83) Hemophilia is a painful chronic disease that (before blood transfusions became feasible) killed a boy before he could reach adulthood. Though rare, it ran in European royal families, whose members often intermarried, which meant that many queens (including England's Queen Victoria) were carriers of hemophilia and thus were destined to watch half their sons die of it. All families, even rulers of nations, are distracted from their work when they have a child with a mysterious and lethal illness. Some historians believe that hemophilia among European royalty was an underlying cause of the Russian Revolution of 1917 as well as of the spread of democracy in the nineteenth and twentieth centuries.

Skinner, 2011). Always the professional explains facts and probabilities; always the clients decide.

Sometimes people have no choice because testing is legally required. This is the case for **phenylketonuria (PKU)** in the United States. Newborns with the double recessive gene for PKU become severely retarded if they consume phenylalanine, an amino acid found in many foods. But if their diet has no phenylalanine, they develop almost normally (Hillman, 2005). Newborns need to start the special diet immediately (which is why testing is required), but parents whose child has PKU might treat that child differently (which is why the information needs to be sensitively transmitted).

phenylketonuria (PKU) A genetic disorder in which a child's body is unable to metabolize an amino acid called phenylalanine. Unless the infant immediately begins a special diet, the resulting buildup of phenylalanine in body fluids causes brain damage, progressive mental retardation, and other symptoms.

N03 / ZUMA PRESS / NEWCOM

Reach for the Sky Gavin and Jake Barker both have cystic fibrosis, which would have meant early death had they been born 50 years ago. Now their parents pound on their chests twice a day to loosen phlegm—and they can enjoy jumping on the trampoline while wearing special pneumatic vests under their shirts.

Tests for dozens of other conditions are routinely administered to newborns (specifics vary by U.S. state and by nation). Although early diagnosis can reduce problems, counseling is needed. In one study of newborn testing, some parents wanted facts and others wanted emotional support. They were distressed if they sought one yet received the other (Tluczek et al., 2006).

Counseling must be individualized because each adult's perceptions are affected by his or her partner, present and future children, work, religion, and community (McConkie-Rosell & O'Daniel, 2007). Without careful explanation and comprehension checking, misunderstanding is common. For example, half of a large group of women misinterpreted an explanation (written for the general public) about tests for genes that make breast cancer more likely (Hanoch et al., 2010).

Some leaders in genetic research stress that changes in the environment, not in the genes, are the most promising direction for "disease prevention and more effective health maintenance" (Schwartz & Collins, 2007, p. 696). Much depends on the family and society. Genes are part of the human story, influencing every page, but they do not determine the plot or the final paragraph.

SUMMING UP

Every person is a carrier for some serious genetic conditions. Most of them are rare, which makes it unlikely that the combination of sperm and ovum will produce severe disabilities. A few exceptional recessive-gene diseases are common because carriers were protected by a recessive gene against some lethal conditions in their communities. They survived to reproduce, and the gene spread throughout the population. Most serious dominant diseases disappear because the affected person dies before having children, but a few dominant conditions continue because their effects are not evident until after the childbearing years are over.

Often a zygote does not have 46 chromosomes. Such zygotes rarely develop to birth, with two primary exceptions: those with Down syndrome (trisomy-21) and those with abnormalities of the sex chromosomes. Genetic counseling helps couples clarify their values and understand the genetic risks, but every fact and decision raises ethical questions. Counselors try to explain probabilities. The final decision is made by those directly involved. ■

SUMMARY

The Genetic Code

1. Genes are the foundation for all development, first instructing the living creature to form the body and brain and then influencing thought and behavior. Human conception occurs when two gametes (an ovum and a sperm, each with 23 chromosomes) combine to form a zygote, 46 chromosomes in a single cell.

2. Genes and chromosomes from each parent match up to make the zygote. The match is not always perfect because of genetic variations called alleles.

The Beginnings of Life

3. The sex of an embryo depends on the sperm: A Y sperm creates an XY (male) embryo; an X sperm creates an XX (female) embryo. Virtually every cell of every living creature has the unique genetic code of the zygote that began that life. The human genome contains about 20,000 genes in all.

4. Twins occur if a zygote splits into two separate beings (monozygotic, or identical, twins) or if two ova are fertilized in the same cycle by two sperm (dizygotic, or fraternal, twins). Monozygotic multiples are genetically the same. Dizygotic multiples have only half of their genes in common, as do all siblings who have the same parents.

5. Assisted reproductive technology (ART), including drugs and in vitro fertilization, has led not only to the birth of millions of much-wanted babies but also to an increase in multiple births and infants who have a higher rate of medical problems. Several aspects of ART raise ethical and medical questions.

From One Cell to Many

6. Genes interact in various ways—sometimes additively, with each gene contributing to development, and sometimes in a dominant–recessive pattern. Environmental factors influence the phenotype as well. Epigenetics is the study of all the environmental factors that affect the expression of genes, including the DNA that surrounds the genes at conception.

7. The environment interacts with the genetic instructions for every trait, even for physical appearance. Every aspect of a person is almost always multifactorial and polygenic.

8. The first few divisions of a zygote are stem cells, capable of becoming any part of a person. Then cells differentiate, specializing in a particular function.

9. Combinations of chromosomes, interactions among genes, and myriad influences from the environment all ensure both similarity and diversity within and between species. This aids health and survival.

Genotype and Phenotype

10. Environmental influences are crucial for almost every complex trait, with each person experiencing different environments. Customs and contexts differ markedly.

11. Genetic makeup can make a person susceptible to a variety of conditions; nongenetic factors also affect susceptibility. Examples include alcoholism and nearsightedness. Cultural and familial differences affecting both of these problems are dramatic evidence for the role of nurture.

12. Knowing the impact of genes and the environment can be helpful. People are less likely to blame someone for a characteristic that is inherited; realizing that someone is at risk of a serious condition helps with prevention.

Chromosomal and Genetic Problems

13. Often a gamete has fewer or more than 23 chromosomes. Usually zygotes with other than 46 chromosomes do not develop.

14. Infants may survive if they have three chromosomes at the 21st location (Down syndrome, or trisomy-21) or one, three, or more sex chromosomes instead of two. In such cases, the affected child has physical and cognitive problems but can live a nearly normal life.

15. Everyone is a carrier for genetic abnormalities. Genetic disorders are usually recessive (not affecting the phenotype); if they are dominant, the trait is usually mild, varied, or inconsequential until late adulthood. When the gene is recessive and carrier status is protective, selective adaptation results in the carried gene becoming widespread, as has been shown with the sickle-cell gene that protects against malaria.

16. Genetic testing and counseling can help many couples. Testing usually provides information about possibilities, not actualities. Couples, counselors, and cultures differ in the decisions they make when risks are known.

KEY TERMS

deoxyribonucleic acid (DNA) (p. 64)
chromosome (p. 64)
gene (p. 64)
allele (p. 64)
genome (p. 65)
gamete (p. 66)
zygote (p. 66)
genotype (p. 66)
homozygous (p. 66)
heterozygous (p. 66)
23rd pair (p. 67)
XX (p. 67)
XY (p. 67)
stem cells (p. 69)
monozygotic (MZ) twins (p. 70)
dizygotic (DZ) twins (p. 70)
assisted reproductive technology (ART) (p. 71)
in vitro fertilization (IVF) (p. 71)
phenotype (p. 73)
polygenic (p. 73)
multifactorial (p. 73)
epigenetic (p. 74)
Human Genome Project (p. 75)
dominant–recessive pattern (p. 76)
carrier (p. 76)
X-linked (p. 76)
copy number variations (p. 77)
heritability (p. 80)
Down syndrome (p. 82)
fragile X syndrome (p. 83)
genetic counseling (p. 88)
phenylketonuria (PKU) (p. 89)

WHAT HAVE YOU LEARNED?

The Genetic Code

1. How many pairs of chromosomes and how many genes does a person usually have?

2. What is the relationship among genes, base pairs, and alleles?

The Beginnings of Life

3. In nature, what determines a person's sex and how can nurture affect that?

4. What are the advantages and disadvantages of being a monozygotic twin?

5. Why does in vitro fertilization increase the incidence of dizygotic twins?

From One Cell to Many

6. Why is a person's genotype not usually apparent in the phenotype?

7. What is the difference between an epigenetic characteristic and a multifactorial one?

8. Why do polygenic traits suggest that additive genes are more common than dominant–recessive ones?

9. What surprises came from the Human Genome Project?

Genotype and Phenotype

10. Regarding heritability, why is it important to know which population at what historical time provided the data?

11. What nature and nurture reasons make one person an alcoholic and another not?

12. What nature and nurture reasons make one person nearsighted and another not?

13. What can be learned from Mickey Mantle's life?

Chromosomal and Genetic Problems

14. Why does this textbook on normal development include abnormal development?

15. What usually happens when a zygote has fewer or more than 46 chromosomes?

16. What are the consequences if a newborn is born with trisomy-21?

17. Why are relatively few genetic conditions dominant?

18. Why are a few recessive traits (such as sickle-cell) quite common?

19. What are the advantages and disadvantages of genetic testing?

20. Why do people need genetic counselors, not merely fact sheets about genetic conditions?

APPLICATIONS

1. Pick one of your traits, and explain the influences that both nature *and* nurture have on it. For example, if you have a short temper, explain its origins in your genetics, your culture, and your childhood experiences.

2. Many adults have a preference for having a son or a daughter. Interview adults of several ages and backgrounds about their preferences. If they give the socially preferable answer ("It does not matter"), ask how they think the two sexes differ. Listen and take notes—don't debate. Analyze the implications of the responses you get.

3. Draw a genetic chart of your biological relatives, going back as many generations as you can, listing all serious illnesses and causes of death. Include ancestors who died in infancy. Do you see any genetic susceptibility? If so, how can you overcome it?

4. List a dozen people you know who need glasses (or other corrective lenses) and a dozen who do not. Are there any patterns? Is this correlation or causation?

>>ONLINE CONNECTIONS

To accompany your textbook, you have access to a number of online resources, including quizzes for every chapter of the book, flashcards (in English and Spanish), critical thinking questions, and case studies. For access to any of these links, go to www.worthpublishers.com/bergerca9e. In addition to these free resources, you'll also find links to podcasts, video clips, diagnostic quizzing with personalized study advice, and an ebook. Some of the videos and activities available online include:

- *Genetic Code.* This activity includes animations of basic genetic processes in our earliest development.
- *Identical Twins.* This video features footage of two identical twins, separated at birth and unknown to each other until adulthood.

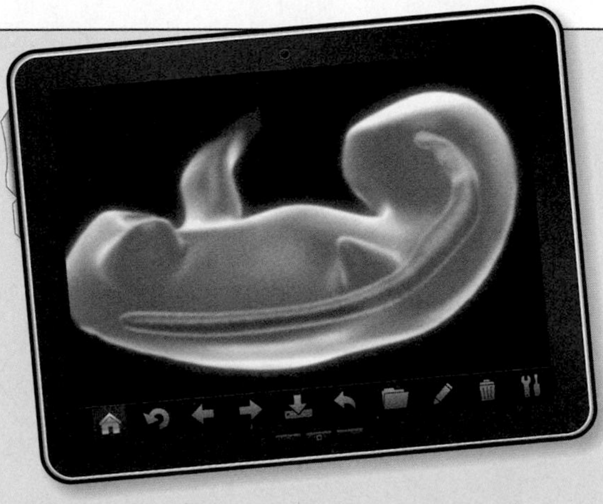

4

CHAPTER

Prenatal Development and Birth

WHAT WILL YOU KNOW?

1. When does a fetus become a baby?
2. Does medical assistance safeguard or impede the birth process?
3. What must a pregnant woman do to keep all toxins away from the developing person?
4. Is low birthweight the result of nature or nurture?
5. Why do some new mothers feel depressed after the birth of a baby, and what should fathers do about it?

Birthdays are important. Every February 28, I send a birthday card to my older brother, a 6-foot-tall grandfather of six, born in 1936.

Prenatal care is important, too. Although my brother was full term, he was born underweight because my mother was told to be hungry when she was expecting. Seventy-three years later, when my daughter was pregnant, she was told to eat as much as she wanted. In mid-pregnancy she baked a cake for her husband's birthday and decorated it with a metal figure of Superman. She wrapped Superman's legs in plastic before sticking it on the cake: She worried the figurine might be made of lead and wanted to ensure that slice would be safe to eat.

I think both my mother and my daughter were irrational mothers-to-be, heeding advice that they didn't need to. There are other foolish warnings—no spicy foods, no reaching, no sex, no exercise—that women have followed, and I took some unnecessary precautions myself. There is one universal here: Women everywhere hope for healthy and happy children, and they change their habits to that end.

My brother often asked my mother what time he was born. She said she didn't remember. Finally, when she was in her 90s, he told her "a story."

> When your first precious baby was beginning to be born, it was February 28th. But labor was slow, so your baby was born on the 29th. You felt sorry for your little boy, with a birthday only once in four years, so you persuaded the doctor to lie.
>
> "Yes," Mom replied. "That is just what happened."

I was shocked; my mother was scrupulously honest. I thought that she would never lie and that no doctor would sign a false birth certificate. But this illustrates another universal truth: Parents imagine their newborn's future lives and do what they can to protect them.

In this chapter, you will learn about the amazing growth of the embryo and fetus, and you will learn how family members and medical professionals try to protect every developing fetus and every newborn. Possible harm is noted, too—causes and consequences of diseases, malnutrition, drugs, pollution, stress, and so on. Birth places and practices vary, from a high-tech operating room to a lowly hut, in a tub of water at home or in a bed in a birthing center. Despite the many variations, remember the universals: We all develop for months before birth, nurtured by our mother's bodies and by thousands of people, who have hopes, plans, and fantasies for the future.

>> Prenatal Growth

The most dramatic and extensive transformation of the entire life span occurs before birth. To make it easier to study, prenatal development is often divided into three main periods. The first two weeks are called the **germinal period;** the third through the eighth week is the **embryonic period;** the ninth week until birth is the **fetal period.** (Alternative terms are explained in Table 4.1, which also explains why sometimes pregnancy is dated from the woman's last menstrual period rather than from conception).

germinal period The first two weeks of prenatal development after conception, characterized by rapid cell division and the beginning of cell differentiation.

embryonic period The stage of prenatal development from approximately the third through the eighth week after conception, during which the basic forms of all body structures, including internal organs, develop.

fetal period The stage of prenatal development from the ninth week after conception until birth, during which the fetus gains about 7 pounds (more than 3,000 grams) and organs become more mature, gradually able to function on their own.

Germinal: The First 14 Days

You learned in Chapter 3 that the one-celled zygote, traveling slowly down the fallopian tube toward the uterus, begins to duplicate and multiply (see Figure 4.1). At about the eight-cell stage, differentiation begins as those early cells take on distinct characteristics and gravitate toward particular locations.

About a week after conception, the multiplying cells (now numbering more than 100) separate into two distinct masses. The outer cells form a shell that will become the *placenta* (the organ that surrounds and protects the developing creature), and the inner cells form a nucleus that will become the embryo.

The first task of the outer cells is to achieve **implantation**—that is, to embed themselves in the nurturing lining of the uterus. This is far from automatic; about 50 percent of natural conceptions and an even larger percentage of in vitro conceptions never implant (see Table 4.2): Most new life ends before an embryo begins (Sadler, 2009).

implantation The process, beginning about 10 days after conception, in which the developing organism burrows into the placenta that lines the uterus, where it can be nourished and protected as it continues to develop.

Embryo: From the Third Through the Eighth Week

The start of the third week after conception initiates the *embryonic period,* during which the formless mass of cells becomes a distinct being—not yet recognizably human but worthy of a new name, **embryo.** (The word *embryo* is often used loosely, but each stage of development has a particular name; here, embryo refers to the developing human from day 14 to day 56.)

embryo The name for a developing human organism from about the third through the eighth week after conception.

First, a thin line (called the *primitive streak*) appears down the middle of the embryo, becoming the neural tube 22 days after conception and eventually developing into the central nervous system, the brain, and spinal column (Sadler, 2009). The head appears in the fourth week, as eyes, ears, nose, and mouth start

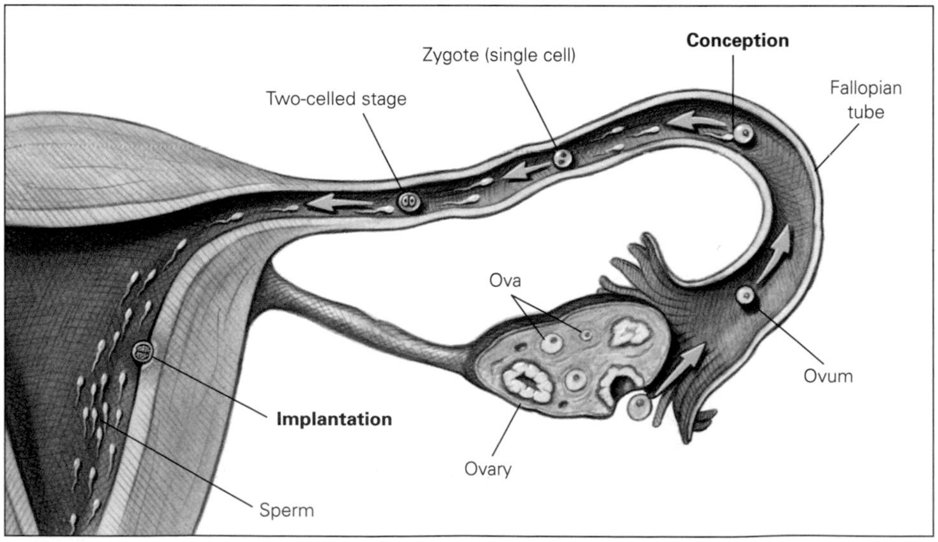

FIGURE 4.1

The Most Dangerous Journey In the first 10 days after conception, the organism does not increase in size because it is not yet nourished by the mother. However, the number of cells increases rapidly as the organism prepares for implantation, which occurs successfully about one-half of the time.

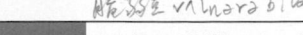

TABLE 4.1 Timing and Terminology

Popular and professional books use various phrases to segment the stages of pregnancy. The following comments may help to clarify the phrases used.

- *Beginning of pregnancy:* Pregnancy begins at conception, which is also the starting point of *gestational age.* However, the organism does not become an *embryo* until about two weeks later, and pregnancy does not affect the woman (and is not confirmed by blood or urine testing) until implantation. Perhaps because the exact date of conception is often unknown, some obstetricians and books for laypeople calculate from the woman's last menstrual period (LMP), usually about 14 days *before* conception.
- *Length of pregnancy:* Full-term pregnancies last 266 days, or 38 weeks, or 9 months. If the LMP is used as the starting time, pregnancy lasts 40 weeks, sometimes expressed as 10 lunar months. (A lunar month is 28 days long.)
- *Trimesters:* Instead of *germinal period, embryonic period,* and *fetal period,* some writers divide pregnancy into three-month periods called *trimesters.* Months 1, 2, and 3 are called the *first trimester;* months 4, 5, and 6, the *second trimester;* and months 7, 8, and 9, the *third trimester.*
- *Due date:* Although doctors assign a specific due date based on the LMP, only 5 percent of babies are born on that exact date. Babies born between three weeks before and two weeks after that date are considered *full term,* although labor is often induced if the baby has not arrived within 7 days of the due date. Babies born more than three weeks early are *preterm,* a more accurate term than *premature.*

to form. Also in the fourth week, a minuscule blood vessel that will become the heart begins to pulsate. By the fifth week, buds that will become arms and legs emerge. The upper arms and then forearms, palms, and webbed fingers grow. Legs, knees, feet, and webbed toes, in that order, are apparent a few days later, each having the beginning of a skeletal structure. Then, 52 and 54 days after conception, respectively, the fingers and toes separate (Sadler, 2009).

As you can see, prenatally, the head develops first, in a *cephalocaudal* (literally, "head-to-tail") pattern, and the extremities form last, in a *proximodistal* (literally, "near-to-far") pattern. At the end of the eighth week after conception (56 days), the embryo weighs just one-thirtieth of an ounce (1 gram) and is about 1 inch (2½ centimeters) long. It has all the basic organs and body parts (except sex organs) of a human being, including elbows and knees. It moves frequently, about 150 times per hour, but such movement is random and imperceptible (Piontelli, 2002).

TABLE 4.2 Vulnerability During Prenatal Development

The Germinal Period

About half* of all conceptions fail to grow or implant properly and thus do not survive the germinal period. Most of these organisms are grossly abnormal.

The Embryonic Period

About 20 percent of all embryos are aborted spontaneously,** most often because of chromosomal abnormalities.

The Fetal Period

About 5 percent of all fetuses are aborted spontaneously before viability at 22 weeks or are stillborn (defined as born dead after 22 weeks).

Birth

About 31 percent of all zygotes grow and survive to become living newborn babies.

*The rate of very early pregnancy failures could be higher, as often no one realizes that pregnancy occurred when it stops so early.

**Spontaneous abortions are also called miscarriages. The rate of induced abortions varies depending on availability of contraception and on culture; induced abortions are not included in this table.

Sources: Bentley & Mascie-Taylor, 2000; Sadler, 2009; Schorge et al., 2008.

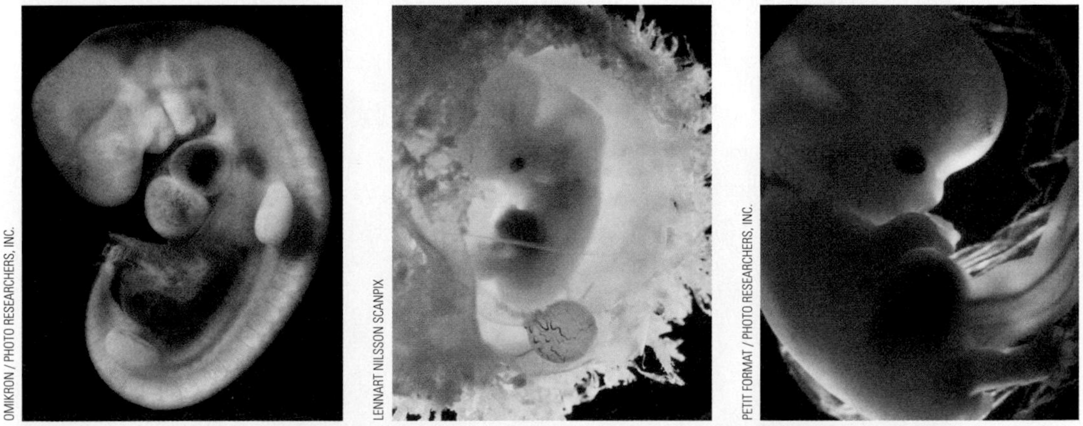

The Embryonic Period *(a)* At 4 weeks past conception, the embryo is only about ⅛ inch (3 millimeters) long, but already the head has taken shape. *(b)* At 5 weeks past conception, the embryo has grown to twice the size it was at 4 weeks. Its primitive heart, which has been pulsing for a week now, is visible, as is what appears to be a primitive tail, which will soon be enclosed by skin and protective tissue at the tip of the backbone (the coccyx). *(c)* By 7 weeks, the organism is somewhat less than an inch (2½ centimeters) long. Eyes, nose, the digestive system, and even the first stage of toe formation can be seen.

Fetus: From the Ninth Week Until Birth

fetus The name for a developing human organism from the start of the ninth week after conception until birth.

ultrasound An image of a fetus (or an internal organ) produced by using high-frequency sound waves. (Also called *sonogram.*)

The organism is called a **fetus** from the ninth week after conception until birth. The fetal period encompasses dramatic change, from a tiny, sexless creature smaller than the final joint of your thumb to a boy or girl about 20 inches (51 centimeters) long.

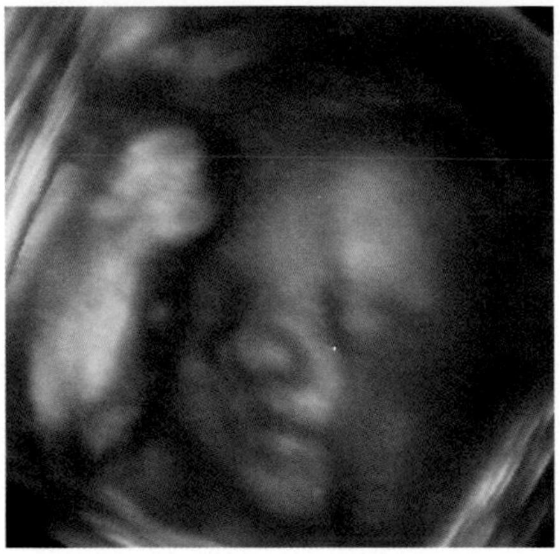

ROBIN MORGAN

There's Your Baby For many parents, their first glimpse of their future child is an ultrasound image. This is Alice Morgan, 63 days before birth.

The Third Month

In the ninth week, if a fetus is male (XY), the SRY gene triggers the development of male sexual organs. Otherwise, female organs develop. The male fetus experiences a rush of the hormone testosterone, affecting the brain (Morris et al., 2004; Neave, 2008). Of course, the range of brain and behavioral variations *among* males and *among* females is greater than the variations *between* the average man and woman. Nonetheless, some neurological sex differences begin in the third month. The brain of the male fetus is slightly different from that of the female fetus.

By the end of the third month, the sex organs are visible via **ultrasound** (also called *sonogram*), which is similar to an X-ray but uses sound waves instead of radiation. Fetal similarities far outweigh any gender differences, however. For instance, the head of the developing human of any sex or ethnicity comprises about half of the total body weight, and facial features appear human in placement and shape by the third month.

The 3-month-old fetus weighs about 3 ounces (87 grams) and is about 3 inches (7.5 centimeters) long. Early prenatal growth is very rapid, with considerable variation, especially in body weight, from fetus to fetus (Sadler, 2009). The numbers just given—3 months, 3 ounces, 3 inches—are rounded off for easy recollection. (For those on the metric system, "100 days, 100 grams, 100 millimeters" is similarly imprecise but useful.)

Especially for Biologists Many people believe that the differences between the sexes are sociocultural, not biological. Is there any prenatal support for that view? (see response, page 98)

The Middle Three Months

In the fourth, fifth, and sixth months, the heartbeat becomes stronger. Digestive and excretory systems develop. Fingernails, toenails, and buds for teeth form, and hair grows (including eyelashes). The brain increases about six times in size and develops many new neurons (*neurogenesis*) and synapses (*synaptogenesis*). Indeed,

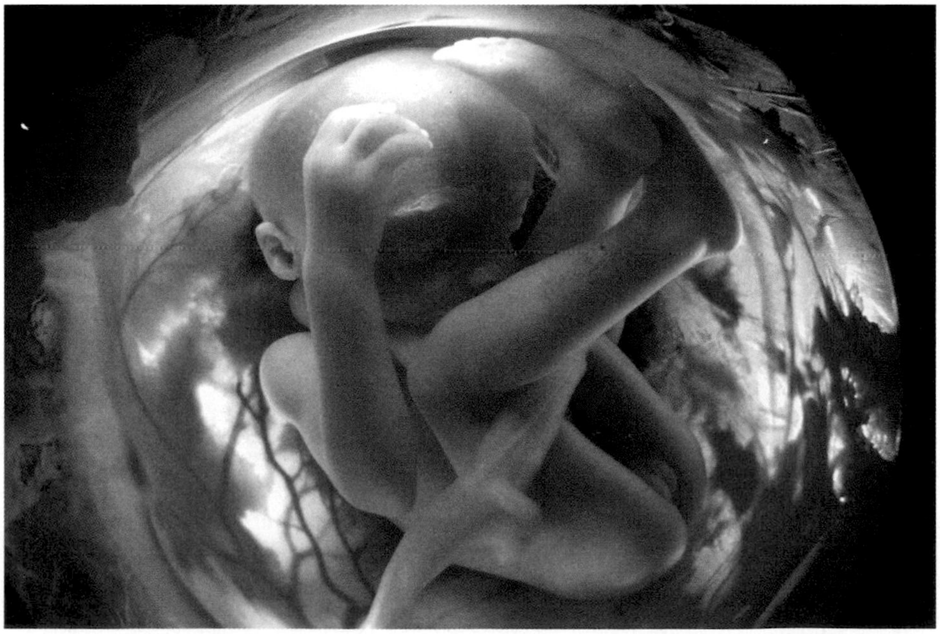

LENNART NILSSON SCANPIX

The Fetus At the end of 4 months, the fetus, now 6 inches long, looks fully formed but out of proportion—the distance from the top of the skull to the neck is almost as long as that from the neck to the rump. For many more weeks, the fetus must depend on the translucent membranes of the placenta and umbilical cord (the long white object in the foreground) for survival.

up to half a million brain cells per minute are created at peak growth during mid-pregnancy (Dowling, 2004). Some neurons extend long axons to distant neurons, and, following the proximodistal sequence, first the brain stem above the back of the neck, then the midbrain, and finally the cortex develop and connect. Crucial brain development occurs in every prenatal month, but these three months may be the most important of all (Johnson, 2011).

age of viability The age (about 22 weeks after conception) at which a fetus might survive outside the mother's uterus if specialized medical care is available.

The reason brain growth is critical at this point is that the entire central nervous system becomes responsive during mid-pregnancy, beginning to regulate basic body functions such as breathing and sucking. That means that advances in neurological functioning allow the fetus to reach the **age of viability,** when a preterm newborn can survive. With intensive medical care, some babies survive at 22 weeks past conception, although many hospitals worldwide do not routinely initiate intensive care unless the fetus is at least 25 weeks old. The age of viability decreased dramatically in the twentieth century, but it now seems stuck at about 22 weeks (Pignotti, 2010) because even the most advanced technology cannot maintain life without some brain response. (Reports of survivors born earlier than 22 weeks are suspect because the date of conception is unknown.) Figure 4.2 indicates survival rates for extremely preterm newborns with advanced medical care.

As the brain matures and axons connect, the organs of the body begin to work in harmony, so the heart beats faster during activity. Both fetal movement and heart rate quiet down during rest (which may not be when the mother wants to sleep). It is during these months that the mother usually feels the first signs of life.

Percentage of Preterm Infants Who Survive to One Year

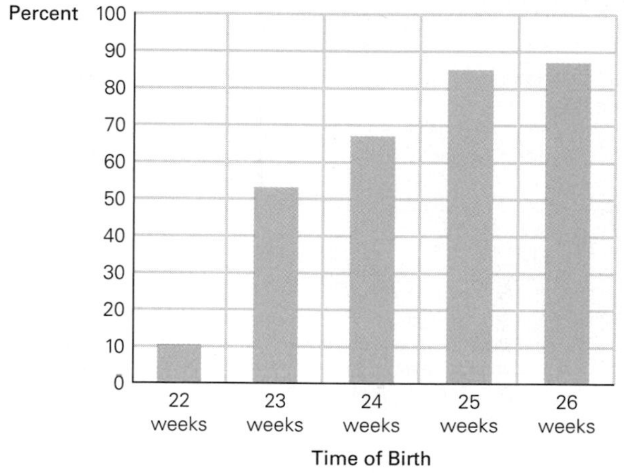

Source: The EXPRESS Group, 2009.

FIGURE 4.2

Each Critical Day Even with advanced medical care, survival of extremely preterm newborns is in doubt. These data come from a thousand births in Sweden, where prenatal care is free and easily obtained. As you can see, the age of viability (22 weeks) means only that an infant *might* survive, not that it will. By full term (not shown), the survival rate is almost 100 percent.

The Final Three Months

Attaining the age of viability simply means that life outside the womb is *possible*. Each day of the final three months improves the odds, not only of survival but also of life without disability (Iacovidou et al., 2010). (More on that later in this chapter.) A preterm infant born in the seventh month is a tiny creature requiring intensive care for each gram of nourishment and every shallow breath. By contrast, after nine months or so, the typical full-term newborn is ready to thrive at home on mother's milk—no expert help, oxygenated air, or special feeding required. For many thousands of years, that is how humans survived: You and I would not be alive if any one of our ancestors required intense newborn care.

The critical difference between life and death, or between a fragile preterm baby and a robust newborn, is maturation of the neurological, respiratory, and cardiovascular systems. In the last three months of prenatal life, the lungs begin to expand and contract, and the fetus exercises breathing muscles by swallowing amniotic fluid as a substitute for air. The valves of the heart go through a final maturation, as do the arteries and veins throughout the body. Among other things, this helps to prevent "brain bleeds," one of the hazards of preterm birth in which paper-thin blood vessels in the skull collapse.

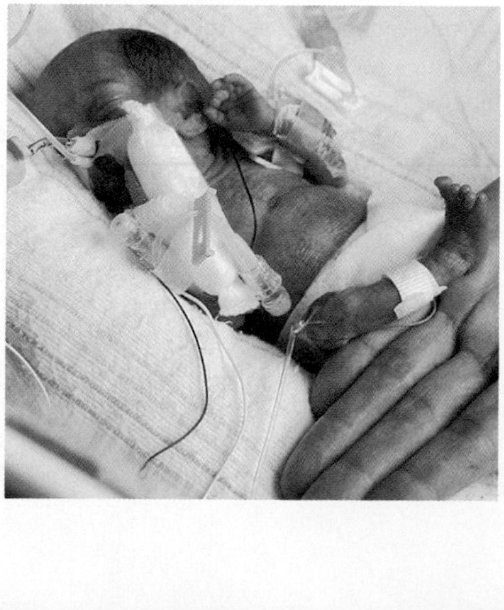

LOYOLA UNIVERSITY HEALTH SYSTEM HO / AP PHOTO

One of the Tiniest Rumaisa Rahman was born after 26 weeks and 6 days weighing only 8.6 ounces (244 grams). Nevertheless, she has a good chance of living a full, normal life. Rumaisa gained 5 pounds (2,270 grams) in the hospital and then, six months after her birth, went home. Her twin sister, Hiba, who weighed 1.3 pounds (590 grams) at birth, had gone home two months earlier. At their one-year birthday, the twins seemed normal, with Rumaisa weighing 15 pounds (6,800 grams) and Hiba, 17 pounds (7,711 grams) (CBS News, 2005).

AT ABOUT THIS TIME
Average Prenatal Weights*

Period of Development	Weeks Past Conception	Average Weight (nonmetric)	Average Weight (metric)	Notes
End of embryonic period	8	1/30 oz.	1 g	Most common time for spontaneous abortion (miscarriage).
End of first trimester	13	3 oz.	85 g	
At viability (50/50 chance of survival)	22	20 oz.	570 g	A birthweight less than 2 lb., 3 oz. (1,000 g) is extremely low birthweight (ELBW).
End of second trimester	26–28	2–3 lb.	900–1,400 g	Less than 3 lb., 5 oz. (1,500 g) is very low birthweight (VLBW).
End of preterm period	35	5½ lb.	2,500 g	Less than 5½ lb. (2,500 g) is low birthweight (LBW).
Full term	38	7½ lb.	3,400 g	Between 5½ lb. and 9 lb. (2,500–4,000 g) is considered normal weight.

*To make them easier to remember, the weights are rounded off (hence the imprecise correspondence between metric and nonmetric). Actual weights vary. For instance, normal full-term infants weigh between 5½ and 9 pounds (2,500 and 4,000 grams); viable preterm newborns, especially twins or triplets, weigh less than shown here.

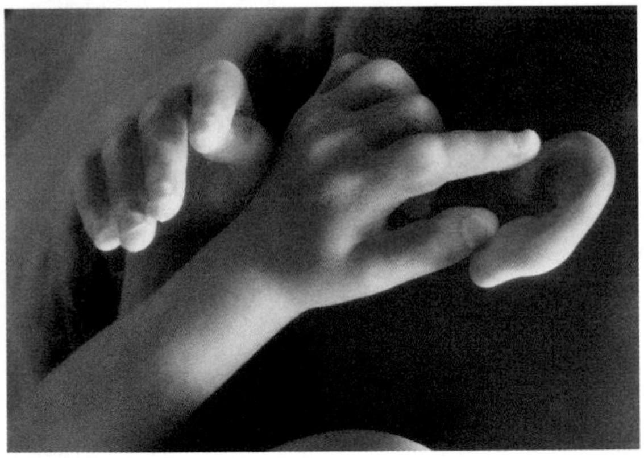

N. BROMHALL / PHOTO RESEARCHERS, INC.

Can He Hear? A fetus, just about at the age of viability, is shown fingering his ear. Such gestures are probably random; but, yes, he can hear.

The fetus usually gains at least 4½ pounds (2.1 kilograms) in the third trimester, increasing to almost 7½ pounds (about 3.4 kilograms) at birth (see At About This Time). By full term, human brain growth is so extensive that the *cortex* (the brain's advanced outer layers) forms several folds in order to fit into the skull (see Figure 4.3). Although some large mammals (whales, for instance) have bigger brains than humans, no other creature needs as many folds as humans do, because the human cortex contains much more material than the brains of nonhumans.

The relationship between mother and child intensifies during the final three months, for fetal size and movement make the pregnant woman very aware of it. In turn, her sounds, the tastes of her food (via amniotic fluid), and her behavior patterns become part of fetal consciousness. Auditory communication from mother to child begins at the 28th week and improves each week as fetal hearing (or newborn hearing if a baby is born early) becomes more acute (Bisiacchi et al., 2009). The fetus startles and kicks at loud noises, listens to the mother's heartbeat and voice, and is comforted by rhythmic music and movement, such as when the mother sings as she walks. If the mother is fearful or anxious, the fetal heart beats faster and body movements increase (DiPietro et al., 2002).

>> Response for Biologists (from page 96) Only one of the 46 human chromosomes determines sex, and the genitals develop last in the prenatal sequence, suggesting that dramatic male–female differences are cultural. On the other hand, several sex differences develop before birth.

SUMMING UP

In two weeks of rapid cell duplication, differentiation, and finally implantation, the newly conceived organism is transformed from a one-celled zygote to a many-celled embryo. The embryo soon develops the beginning of the central nervous system (3 weeks), a heart and a face (4 weeks), arms and legs (5 weeks), hands and feet (6 weeks), and fingers and toes (7 weeks) while the inner organs take shape. By 8

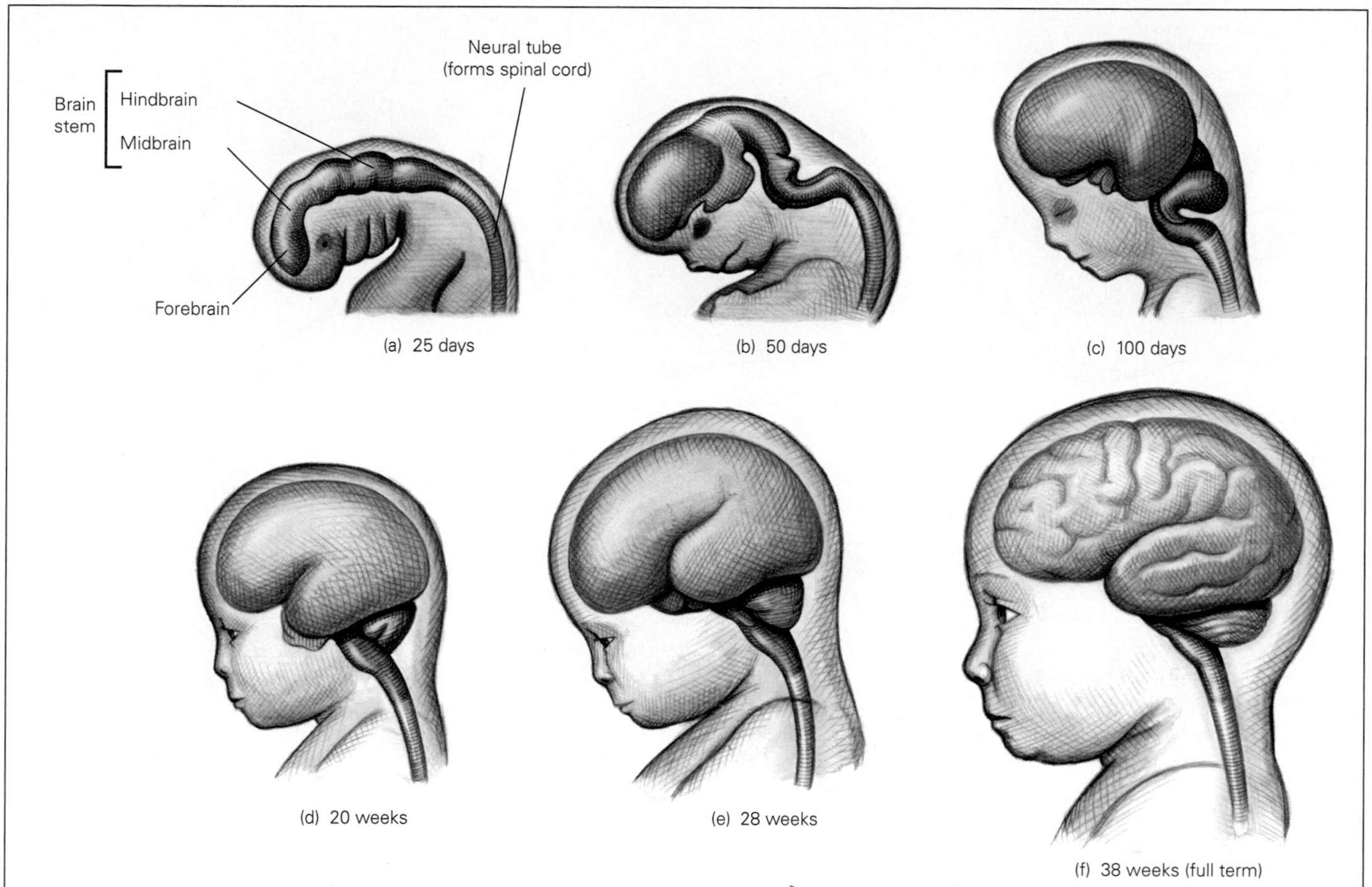

Source: Adapted from Cowan, 1997, p. 116.

FIGURE 4.3

Prenatal Growth of the Brain Just 25 days after conception *(a)*, the central nervous system is already evident. The brain looks distinctly human by day 100 *(c)*. By the 28th week of gestation *(e)*, at the very time brain activity begins, the various sections of the brain are recognizable. When the fetus is full term *(f)*, all the parts of the brain, including the cortex (the outer layers), are formed, folding over one another and becoming more convoluted, or wrinkled, as the number of brain cells increases.

weeks, all the body structures, except male and female sex organs, are in place. Fetal growth then proceeds rapidly, including mid-trimester weight gain (about 2 pounds, or 1 kilogram) and brain maturation, which make viability possible. By full term, all the organs function well in the 35- to 40-week newborn, who weighs about 7 pounds (about 3,200 grams).

>> Birth

About 38 weeks (266 days) after conception, when the fetus weighs 6 to 8 pounds (3,000 to 4,000 grams), the fetal brain signals the release of hormones, specifically *oxytocin,* which prepares the fetus for delivery and starts labor. The average baby is born after 12 hours of active labor for first births and 7 hours for subsequent births (Moore & Persaud, 2003), although labor may take twice or half as long. The definition of "active" labor varies, which is one reason some women believe they are in active labor for days and others say 10 minutes.

Women's birthing positions also vary—sitting, squatting, lying down. Some women give birth while immersed in warm water, which helps the woman relax (the fetus continues to get oxygen via the umbilical cord). However, some physicians believe water births increase the rate of infection, and the final emergence of the head is difficult for the medical team to monitor (Tracy, 2009). Preferences and opinions on positions are partly cultural and partly personal. In general,

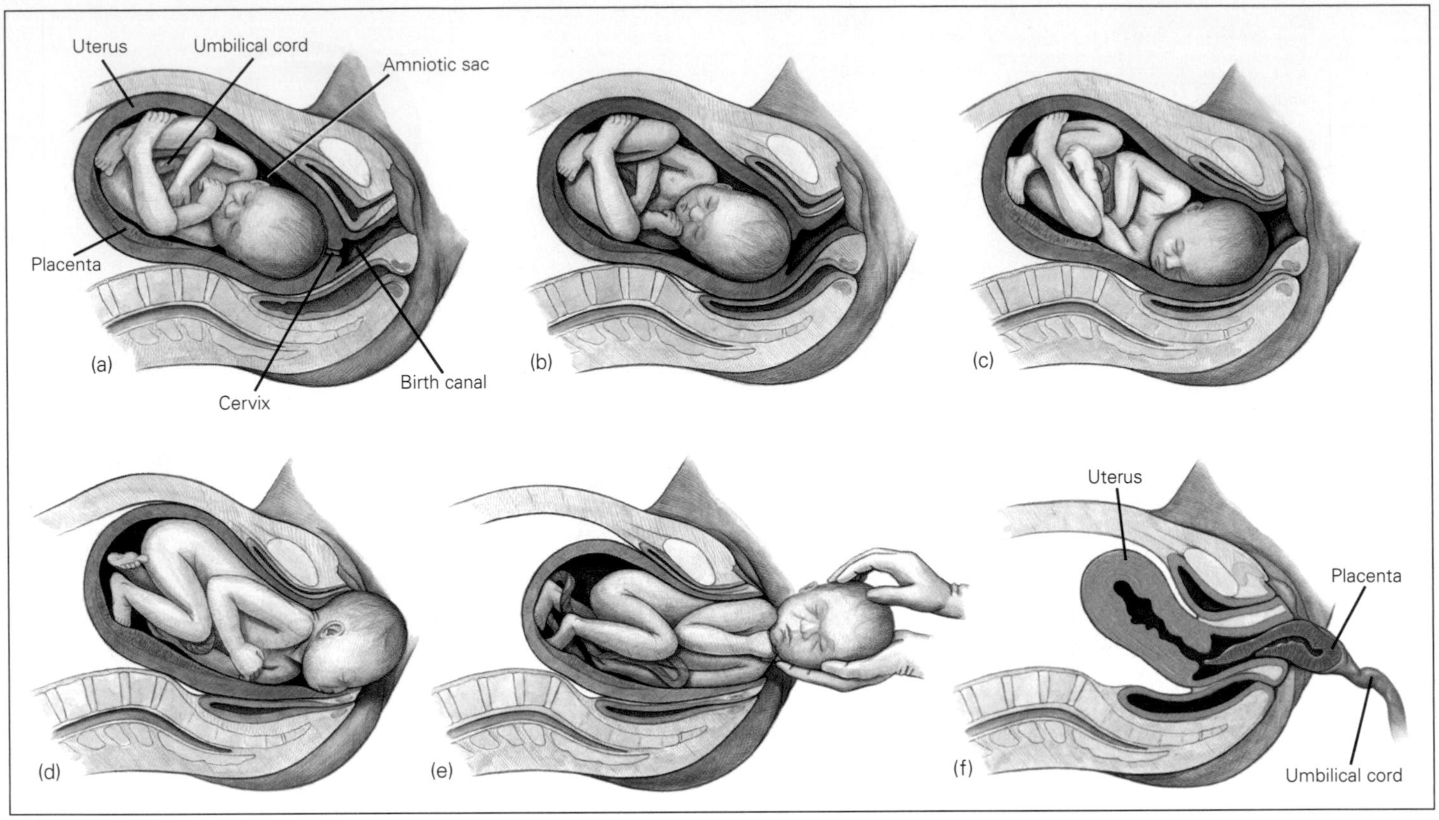

FIGURE 4.4

A Normal, Uncomplicated Birth *(a)* The baby's position as the birth process begins. *(b)* The first stage of labor: The cervix dilates to allow passage of the baby's head. *(c)* Transition: The baby's head moves into the "birth canal," the vagina. *(d)* The second stage of labor: The baby's head moves through the opening of the vagina ("crowns") and *(e)* emerges completely. *(f)* The third stage of labor is the expulsion of the placenta. This usually occurs naturally, but it is crucial that the whole placenta be expelled, so birth attendants check carefully. In some cultures, the placenta is ceremonially buried, to commemorate the life-giving role it plays.

Observation Quiz In drawing *(e)*, what is the birth attendant doing as the baby's head emerges? (see answer, page 102)

Apgar scale A quick assessment of a newborn's health. The baby's color, heart rate, reflexes, muscle tone, and respiratory effort are given a score of 0, 1, or 2 twice—at one minute and five minutes after birth—and each time the total of all five scores is compared with the maximum score of 10 (rarely attained).

physicians find it easier to see the head emerge if the woman lies on her back and many women find it easier to push the fetus out if they sit up, but these generalities do not hold for every individual. Figure 4.4 shows the universal stages of birth.

The Newborn's First Minutes

Newborns usually breathe and cry on their own. Between spontaneous cries, the first breaths of air bring oxygen to the lungs and blood, and the infant's color changes from bluish to pinkish. (Pinkish refers to blood color, visible beneath the skin, and applies to newborns of all hues.) Eyes open wide; tiny fingers grab; even tinier toes stretch and retract. The newborn is instantly, zestfully, ready for life.

Nevertheless, there is much to be done. Mucus in the baby's throat is removed, especially if the first breaths seem shallow or strained. The umbilical cord is cut to detach the placenta, leaving an inch or so of the cord, which dries up and falls off to leave the belly button. The infant is examined, weighed, and given to the mother to preserve its body heat and to breast-feed a first meal of colostrum, a thick substance that helps the newborn's digestive and immune systems.

One widely used assessment of infant health is the **Apgar scale** (see Table 4.3), first developed by Dr. Virginia Apgar. When she graduated from Columbia medical school with her MD in 1933, Apgar wanted to work in a hospital but was told that only men did surgery. Consequently, she became an anesthesiologist. She saw that "delivery room doctors focused on mothers and paid little attention to babies. Those who were small and struggling were often left to die" (M. Beck, 2009, p. D-1). To save those young lives, Apgar developed a simple rating scale of five vital signs—color, heart rate, cry, muscle tone, and breathing—to alert doctors

TABLE 4.3 Criteria and Scoring of the Apgar Scale

	Five Vital Signs				
Score	Color	Heartbeat	Reflex Irritability	Muscle Tone	Respiratory Effort
0	Blue, pale	Absent	No response	Flaccid, limp	Absent
1	Body pink, extremities blue	Slow (below 100)	Grimace	Weak, inactive	Irregular, slow
2	Entirely pink	Rapid (over 100)	Coughing, sneezing, crying	Strong, active	Good; baby is crying

Source: Apgar, 1953.

to newborn health. Since 1950, birth attendants worldwide have used the Apgar (often using the name as an acronym: Appearance, Pulse, Grimace, Activity, and Respiration) at one minute and again at five minutes after birth, assigning each vital sign a score of 0, 1, or 2.

If the five-minute Apgar is 7 or higher, all is well. If the five-minute total is below 7, the infant needs help. If the score is below 4, a neonatal pediatrician is summoned to the delivery room (the hospital loudspeaker may say "paging Dr. Apgar").

Medical Assistance

How closely any particular birth matches the foregoing depends on the parents' preparation, the position and size of the fetus, and the customs of the culture. In developed nations, births almost always include sterile procedures, electronic monitoring, and drugs to dull pain or speed contractions.

Surgery

Midwives are as skilled at delivering babies as physicians, but only medical doctors are licensed to perform surgery. More than one-third of U.S. births occur via **cesarean section** (**c-section,** or simply *section*), whereby the fetus is removed through incisions in the mother's abdomen. Cesareans are controversial: The World Health Organization suggests that c-sections are medically indicated in only 15 percent of births.

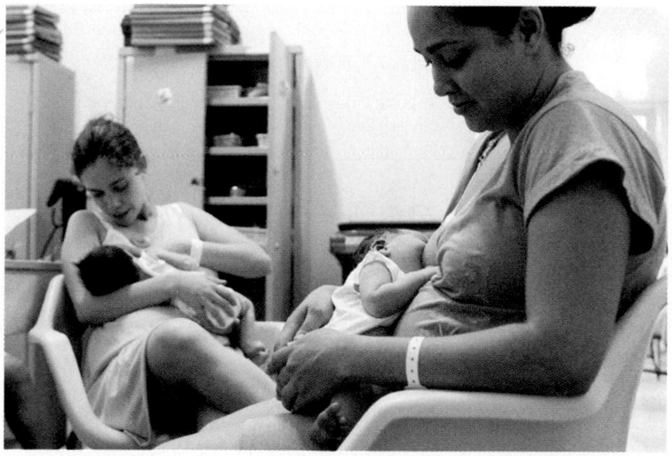

DOUGLAS ENGLE / MCT

From Day One For various reasons, some countries have much higher rates of cesarean deliveries than others. These new mothers in Brazil, which has a high cesarean rate, have safely delivered their babies and, with the encouragement of the hospital, are breast-feeding them from the very beginning.

Culture and cohort affect the rates: Most nations have fewer cesareans than the United States, but some—especially in Latin America—have more (see Figure 4.5). In every nation, both the safety and the incidence of cesareans have increased over the past two decades, with the most dramatic increases in China. In that nation, rates were 5 percent in 1991, 20 percent by 2001, and 46 percent in 2008 (Guo et al., 2007; Juan, 2010). In the United States, the rate rose every year between 1996 and 2008 (from 21 percent to 34 percent). Cesareans are usually safe for mother and baby and have many advantages for hospitals (easier to schedule, quicker, and more expensive than vaginal deliveries), but they also bring more complications after birth and reduce breast-feeding (Malloy, 2009).

cesarean section (c-section) A surgical birth, in which incisions through the mother's abdomen and uterus allow the fetus to be removed quickly, instead of being delivered through the vagina. (Also called simply *section.*)

Less studied is the *epidural,* an injection in a particular part of the spine of the laboring woman to alleviate pain. Epidurals are often used in hospital births, but they increase the rate of cesarean sections and decrease the readiness of newborn infants to suck immediately after birth (Bell et al., 2010). Another medical

Rates of Cesarean Sections in Selected Countries

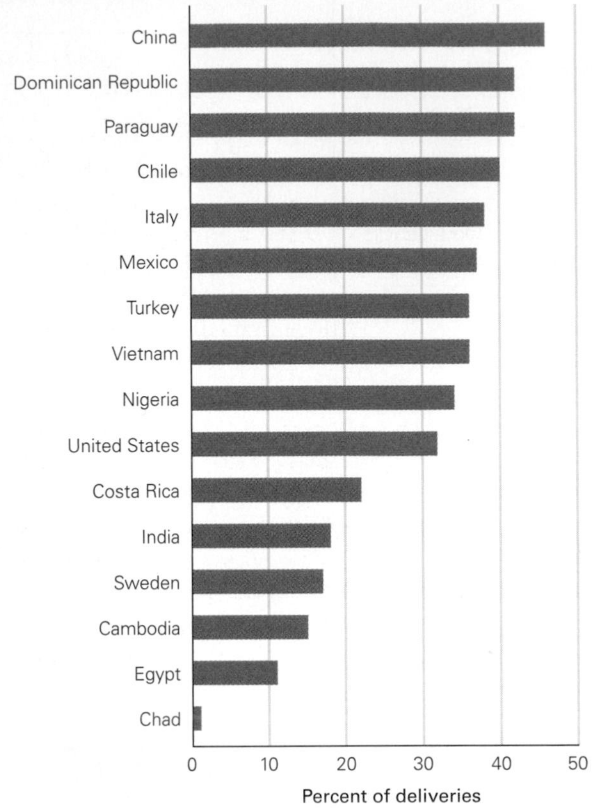

Sources: Various from 2000–2010. Percentages vary by source and year. The range is always dramatic, as shown here.

FIGURE 4.5

Too Many Cesareans or Too Few? Rates of cesarean deliveries vary widely from nation to nation. Latin America has the highest rates in the world (note that 40 percent of all births in Chile are by cesarean), and sub-Saharan Africa has the lowest (the rate in Chad is less than half of 1 percent). The underlying issue is whether some women who should have cesareans do not get them, while other women have unnecessary cesareans.

intervention is *induced labor*, in which labor is started, speeded, or strengthened with a drug. The rate of induced labor in the United States has tripled since 1990 and is now close to 20 percent.

Newborn Survival

Every year worldwide, obstetricians, midwives, and nurses save millions of lives. A century ago, at least 5 of every 100 newborns in the United States died (De Lee, 1938). Currently in the United States, newborn mortality is about 1 in 250—a statistic that includes very fragile newborns weighing only 1 pound. In advanced nations, fewer than 1 in 10,000 women die as a result of complications from abortion or birth; in poor nations, the rate is 100 times higher.

The primary reason birth is still hazardous in the least developed nations is the lack of medical attention. In sub-Saharan Africa, where only one-third of all births are attended by a doctor or trained midwife and the average mother has four children, about 1 in 16 women dies from complications of pregnancy or birth (Kruk et al., 2008). Worldwide, almost 2 million newborns die each year (Rajaratnam et al., 2010). The main cause of maternal death is uncontrolled bleeding, and the main cause of neonatal death is lack of oxygen and nutrition. Both are routinely prevented in hospitals.

Nonetheless, several aspects of hospital birth arise from custom or politics, not from necessity (Selin & Stone, 2009). A particular issue concerns attention lavished on "miracle babies" who require intensive care, microsurgery, and weeks in the hospital. Those who survive often—but not always—need special care all their lives. Only happy outcomes are published, but critics note the public expense of keeping them alive and then the lifelong burden borne by the parents.

The American Academy of Pediatrics recommends careful and honest counseling for parents of very preterm babies so that they understand the consequences of each medical measure. As an obstetrics team writes, "We should be frank with ourselves, with parents and with society, that there are gaps of knowledge concerning the management of infants born at very low gestational ages . . . including ethical decisions such as . . . when to provide intensive care and how extensive this should be" (Iacovidou et al., 2010, p. 133).

Alternatives to Hospital Technology

Questions of costs and benefits abound. For instance, c-section and epidural rates vary more by doctor, hospital, day of the week, and region than by the circumstances of the birth—even in Sweden, where obstetric care is paid for by the government (Schytt & Walderenström, 2010). A rare complication (uterine rupture), which sometimes happens when women give birth vaginally after a previous cesarean, has caused most doctors to insist that after one cesarean, subsequent births be cesarean. Juries blame doctors for inaction more than for action; to avoid lawsuits, doctors intervene.

Most U.S. births now take place in hospital labor rooms with high-tech operating rooms nearby. Another 5 percent of U.S. births occur in *birthing centers* (not in a hospital), and less than 1 percent occur at home (illegal in some jurisdictions). About half of the home births are planned and half not, because of unexpectedly rapid labor. The latter are hazardous if no one is nearby to rescue a newborn in distress (Tracy, 2009).

>> Answer to Observation Quiz (from page 100) The birth attendant is turning the baby's head after it has emerged; doing this helps the shoulders come out more easily.

THINKING CRITICALLY

Home Births

Compared with the United States, planned home births are more common in many other developed nations (2 percent in England, 30 percent in the Netherlands), where midwives are paid by the government. In the Netherlands, special ambulances called *flying storks* speed mother and newborn to a hospital if needed. Dutch research finds home births better for mothers and no worse for infants than hospital births (de Jonge et al., 2009).

In the poorest nations, almost all babies are born at home: Doctors are called only for emergencies, often arriving too late. Many women avoid hospitals unless they think they are dying. The following describes a birth in Ghana:

> Huddled in a corner of the hut, she was lying on the floor. . . . She lay curled into a small ball on her left side, her pregnant and contracting uterus protruding from her thin frame. No sound came from her. No sound came from the midwife either. She was seated in the corner of the dark, hot hut, waiting. Suddenly, Emefa gave a low whimper and hauled herself into a sitting and then squatting position. The midwife crept over to her and gently supported Emefa's back as she bore down. No words, no commands, no yelling. . . . The baby's head appeared gradually, slowly making its progress into the world. How did the midwife know that it was time? . . . A soft whoosh and the baby's body was born into the steady and confident hands of the midwife. And still there was no sound. The baby did not cry, not because there was any problem, but because it was a gentle birth. The baby was breathing as he was handed to his mother.
>
> *[Hillier, 2003, p. 3]*

The idea of a "gentle birth" is appealing, but this newborn may have been lucky. The infant mortality rate in Ghana is at least 10 times higher than in North America. Some people wish gentle home births would become more common in the United States; others shudder at the thought. Two opposite risks are apparent. On the one hand, home births might become emergencies and taking an ambulance to the hospital would delay care; on the other hand, hospital births might cause needless intervention, harming the new family.

One crucial question is how supportive the medical professionals are. One committee of obstetricians decided that planned home births are acceptable because women have "a right to make a medically informed decision about delivery," but they also insisted that a trained midwife or doctor be present, that the woman not be high-risk (e.g., no previous cesarean), and that speedy transportation to a hospital be ready (American College of Obstetricians and Gynecologists Committee on Obstetric Practice, 2011).

Some studies in England, Canada, Sweden, and the United States report that home births entail risks for the baby: The stillborn and newborn death rate, although very low, is higher than for a delivery room birth (home birth advocates dispute these conclusions). Every study finds benefits for the mother: fewer medical interventions and quicker recovery, and thus stronger mother–infant bonds, more successful breast-feeding, and less maternal depression—all of which benefit fathers and other children as well.

Probably the crucial phrase from the U.S. obstetricians is "medically informed." Unfortunately, many people are uninformed and, consequently, either unduly suspicious or irrationally appreciative of every hospital procedure. As one review of home births concluded: "Contradictory professional and public policies reflect the polarization and politicization of the controversy surrounding this birth option" (Wax et al., 2010, p. 132). Instead of polarization, critical and informed thinking is needed.

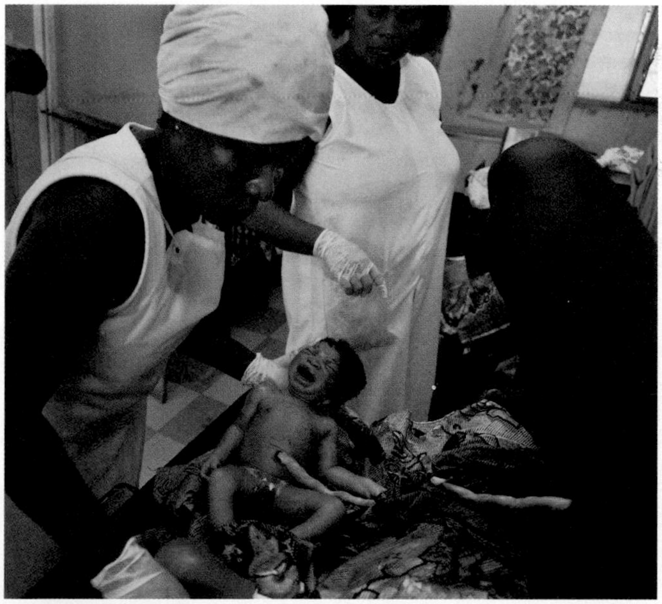

RANDY OLSON / NGS IMAGE COLLECTION

Celebration? The lusty cry of this infant is a good sign, as is his color (not bluish) and muscle tone. Moreover, this birth occurred in a clinic, which bodes well for the mother's recovery—unlike many other births in Ghana.

Observation Quiz Is this infant minutes, hours, or days old? (see answer, page 105)

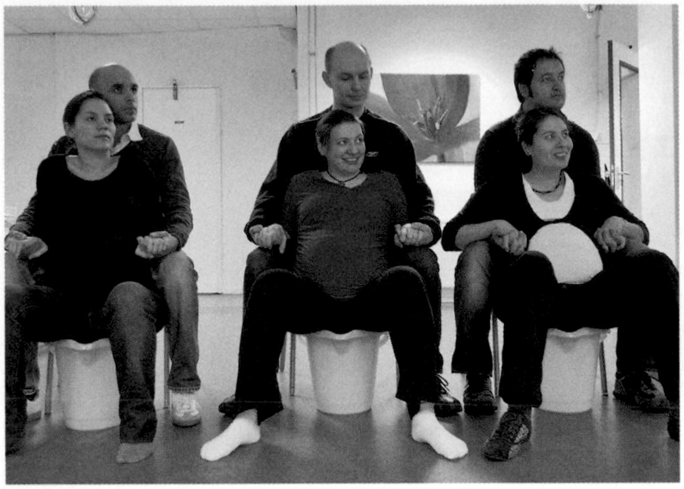
REUTERS / TOUSSAINT KLUITERS

AP PHOTO / LYNNE SLADKY

The Same Situation, Many Miles Apart: Getting Ready There are many similarities here: Six adults and three fetuses on the left and six adults and two fetuses (twins) on the right. But the differences are tragic, evident in the face of the expectant mother on the right. The husbands in the Netherlands are learning how to help their wives give birth at home, as most Dutch couples do. The Afghan doctor on the right, however, is explaining why this woman's labor will be induced, with neither baby expected to survive—a devastating blow this woman has already faced, having twice lost a baby less than a week old.

In the first part of the twentieth century, in advanced nations, women in hospitals labored by themselves until birth was imminent; fathers and other family members were kept away. Almost everyone now agrees that a laboring woman should never be alone. However, family members may not know what to do, and professionals focus more on the medical than the psychological aspects of birth, so some women do not get the emotional support they need. To meet this need, more women now have a **doula,** a woman trained to support the laboring woman by timing contractions, doing massage, providing ice chips, or doing whatever else might be helpful.

doula A woman who helps with the birth process. Traditionally in Latin America, a doula was the only professional who attended childbirth. Now doulas are likely to arrive at the woman's home during early labor and later work alongside a hospital's staff.

Often doulas begin their work before active labor, and then, as the moment of birth approaches, they work beside the midwives or doctors. Many studies have

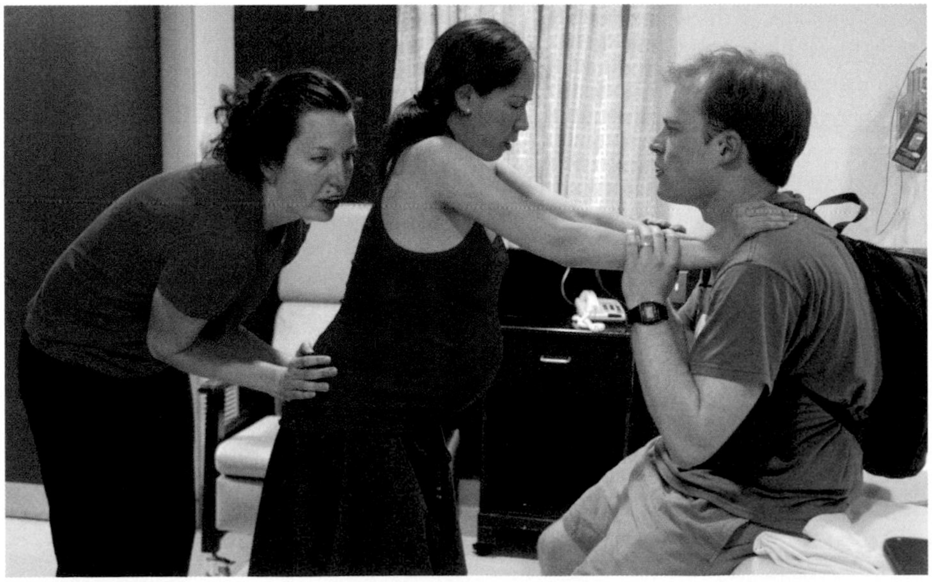
JADA SHAPIRO / BIRTHDAY PRESENCE

Pressure Point Many U.S. couples, like this one, benefit from a doula's gentle touch, strong pressure, and sensitive understanding —all of which make doula births less likely to include medical intervention.

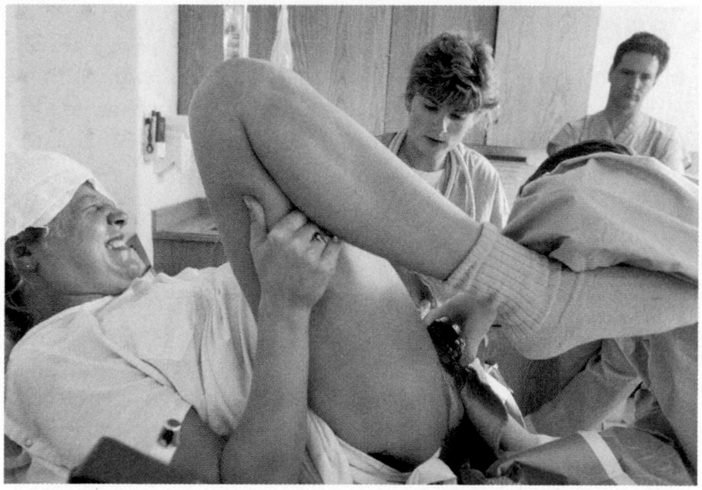

CUSTOM MEDICAL STOCK PHOTO

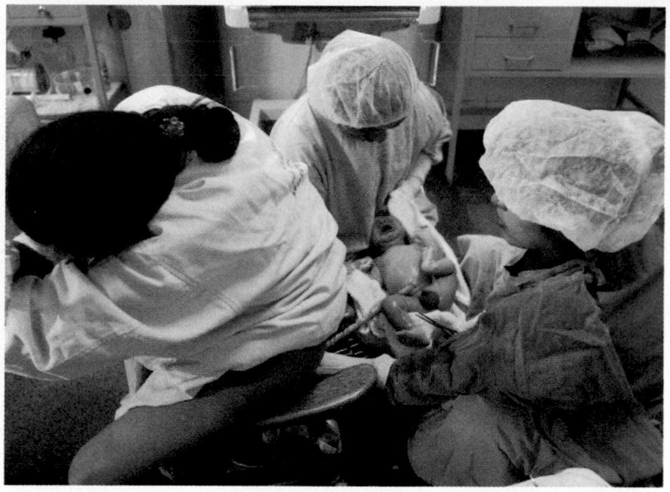

REUTERS / ENRIQUE CASTRO-MENDIVIL

The Same Situation, Many Miles Apart: A Better Position The most obvious difference between these births in Chicago, Illinois (*left*), and Cuzco, Peru, is the mother's body position. In the United States, the horizontal position was designed to give doctors a better view when the head emerges (*left*). In Peru, women prefer "vertical births," and this maternity center boasts more patients as a result of its willingness to perform them. Note other differences—the father present in Chicago, the protective head coverings in Cuzco. It is not so clear-cut which practices make better medical sense and which are simply social customs.

Research Design

Scientists: Susan McGrath and John Kennell.

Publication: *Birth* (2008).

Participants: A total of 420 pregnant women, all healthy, middle class, and accompanied by their male partner when they arrived in labor at a major hospital in Cleveland, Ohio. They gave birth to their first baby, attended by their obstetrician or midwife.

Design: All 420 received the usual medical care as well as the support of their partners, but, on admission to the hospital, half were randomly assigned a doula. The doula stayed with the couple, providing physical care (e.g., massage), expertise, and reassurance until the birth. Mothers and their partners were questioned 24 hours and 6 weeks later.

Major conclusion: The doula births were less often cesareans (13 versus 25 percent) and involved fewer epidurals (65 versus 76 percent). More than 99 percent of the women and their partners rated the doula's help positively or very positively. The conclusion: "Continuous labor support by a doula is a risk-free obstetric technique that could benefit all laboring women" (p. 97).

Comments: Three factors in this design add confidence to the conclusion: (1) Random assignment avoided selection factors (women who choose doulas tend to be healthy and well-educated); (2) the fathers' presence for all women proved that not merely the presence of a support person caused the benefits; (3) the doula appeared only when the couple arrived at the hospital (avoiding the confounds of doula help in early labor).

found that doulas benefit low-income women with no partner, decreasing the disparity in birth outcomes between middle-class and poor women (Vonderheid et al., 2011). It is now believed that doulas benefit anyone giving birth, rich or poor, married or not. For example, in one study, 420 middle-class married women were randomly assigned a doula (McGrath & Kennell, 2008). Those with doulas needed less intervention (see the Research Design).

SUMMING UP

Most newborns score at least 7 out of 10 on the Apgar scale, and thrive without medical assistance. If necessary, neonatal surgery and intensive care save lives. Although modern medicine has reduced maternal and newborn deaths, many critics deplore treating birth as a medical crisis rather than a natural event. Responses to this critique include women choosing to give birth in hospital labor rooms rather than operating rooms, in birthing centers instead of hospitals, or even at home. The assistance of a doula is another recent practice that reduces medical intervention. ■

>> Answer to Observation Quiz (from page 103) Probably ten minutes or less. His umbilical cord is still attached to the placenta, which is still inside the woman. Usually placentas are expelled with contractions a few minutes after birth.

>> Problems and Solutions

The early days of life place the developing person on the path toward health and success—or not. Fortunately, resilience is apparent from the beginning; healthy newborns are the norm, not the exception. However, if something is amiss, it is often part of a cascade that may become overwhelming.

Harmful Substances

teratogens Agents and conditions, including viruses, drugs, and chemicals, that can impair prenatal development and result in birth defects or even death.

behavioral teratogens Agents and conditions that can harm the prenatal brain, impairing the future child's intellectual and emotional functioning.

Such a cascade begins before the woman realizes she is pregnant, as many toxins, illnesses, and experiences can harm a new pregnancy. Every week, scientists discover an unexpected **teratogen,** defined as anything—drugs, viruses, pollutants, malnutrition, stress, and more—that increases the risk of prenatal abnormalities. But do not be alarmed. Many abnormalities can be avoided, many potential teratogens do no harm, and much damage can be remedied. Thus, prenatal development is not a dangerous period to be feared as much as a natural process to be protected.

Some teratogens cause no physical defects but affect the brain, making a child hyperactive, antisocial, or learning-disabled. These are **behavioral teratogens.** About 20 percent of all children have difficulties that *could* be connected to behavioral teratogens, although the link is not straightforward: The cascade is murky. One of my students described her little brother as follows:

> I was nine years old when my mother announced she was pregnant. I was the one who was most excited. . . . My mother was a heavy smoker, Colt 45 beer drinker. . . . I asked, "Why are you doing it?" She said, "I don't know."
>
> During this time I was in the fifth grade and we saw a film about birth defects. My biggest fear was that my mother was going to give birth to a fetal alcohol syndrome (FAS) infant. . . . My baby brother was born right on schedule. The doctors claimed a healthy newborn. . . . Once I heard healthy, I thought everything was going to be fine. I was wrong, then again I was just a child. . . . My baby brother never showed any interest in toys . . . he just cannot get the right words out of his mouth . . . he has no common sense . . .
>
> *[J., personal communication]*

My student asks, "Why hurt those who cannot defend themselves?" As you remember from Chapter 1, one case proves nothing, and as you just read, teratogens often cascade with murky connections. J. blames her mother for smoking and drinking beer, although genes, postnatal experiences, and lack of preventive information and services may be part of the cascade as well. Nonetheless, J. is right to wonder why her mother took a chance.

Behavioral teratogens can be subtle, and their effects may last a lifetime. That is one conclusion from research on pregnant women exposed to flu in 1918. Some miscarried; some babies were stillborn. Most survivors seemed unharmed and lived long lives—but not as long as the average baby born a year earlier. By middle age, the flu-exposed babies averaged less education, more unemployment, and lower income than their peers (Almond, 2006).

Risk Analysis

Life entails risks. *Risk analysis* discerns which chances are worth taking and how risks are minimized. To pick an easy example: Crossing the street is a risk, yet it would be worse to avoid all street crossing. Knowing this, we cross carefully, looking both ways.

Sixty years ago, no one applied risk analysis to prenatal development. It was assumed that the placenta screened out all harmful substances. Then two tragic episodes showed otherwise: (1) On an Australian military base, an increase in babies born blind was linked to a rubella (German measles) epidemic on the same base seven months earlier (Gregg, 1941, reprinted in Persaud et al., 1985), and (2) a sudden rise in British newborns with deformed limbs was traced to maternal use of thalidomide, a new drug for nausea that was widely prescribed in Europe in the late 1950s (Schardein, 1976). Thus began *teratology,* a science of risk analysis. Although all teratogens increase the *risk* of harm, none *always* cause damage. The impact of teratogens depends on the interplay of many factors, both destructive and protective, an example of the dynamic-systems perspective described in Chapter 1.

The Critical Time

One crucial factor is *timing*—the age of the developing organism when it is exposed to the teratogen (Sadler, 2009). Some teratogens cause damage only during a *critical period* (see Chapter 1) (see Figure 4.6). Obstetricians recommend that *before* pregnancy occurs, women should avoid drugs (especially alcohol), supplement a balanced diet with extra folic acid and iron, and update their immunizations. Indeed, preconception health is at least as important as health during pregnancy.

FIGURE 4.6

Critical Periods in Human Development The most serious damage from teratogens (green bars) is likely to occur early in prenatal development. However, significant damage (purple bars) to many vital parts of the body, including the brain, eyes, and genitals, can occur during the last months of pregnancy as well.

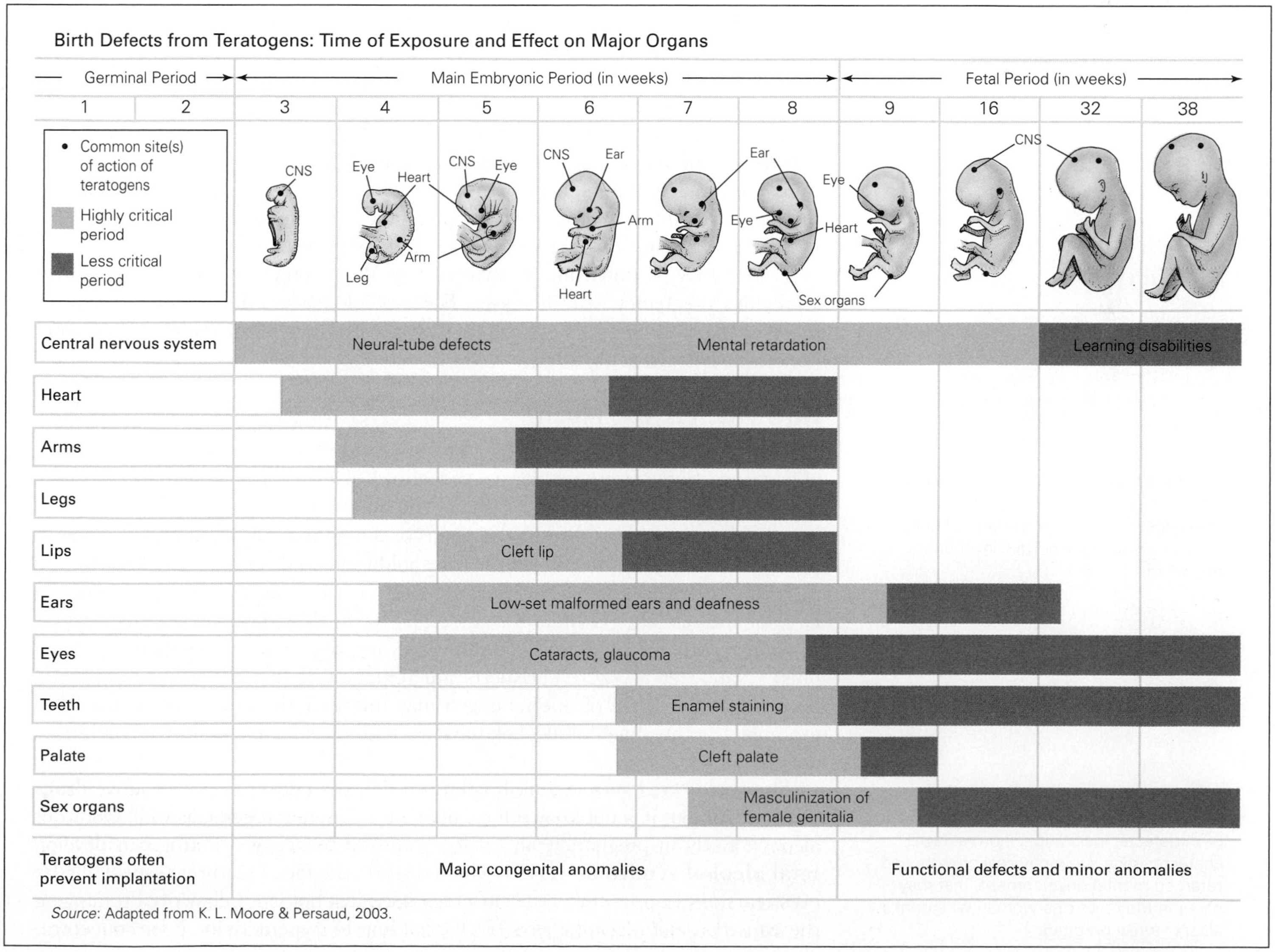

FIGURE 4.7

No One is Perfect Blaming pregnant women is easy, but almost no one avoids all drugs and stresses, sleeps and eats well, weighs just the right amount, exercises at least an hour each day, and completely avoids fried or salty foods. If you are the exception, could you keep it up for a year, while gaining 35 pounds; sometimes feeling nauseous; coping with stares and the questions of friends, relatives, and strangers; and going to the doctor every few weeks?

Preconceptual Practices of New Mothers in the United States, 2004

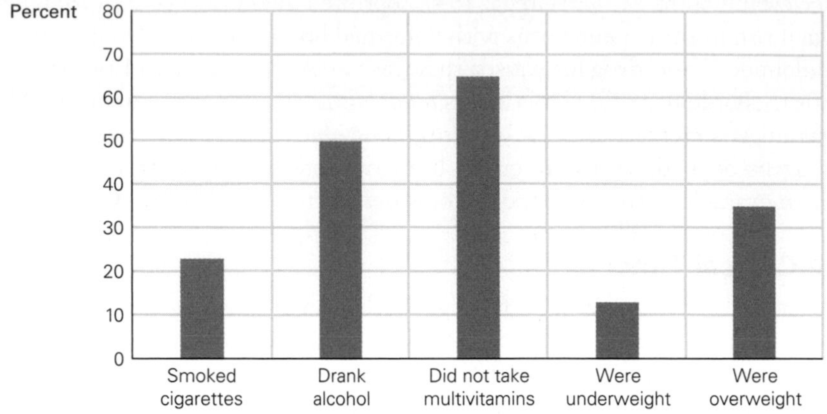

Source: D'Angelo et al., 2007.

Unfortunately, almost half the births in the United States are unplanned, often to women who are not in the best of health before conception (D'Angelo et al., 2007) (see Figure 4.7).

The first days and weeks after conception (the germinal and embryonic periods) are critical for body formation, but health during the entire fetal period affects the brain. Some teratogens that cause preterm birth or low birthweight are particularly harmful in the second half of pregnancy. Indeed, one study found that, although smoking cigarettes throughout prenatal development can be lethal for the fetus, smokers who quit in the first weeks of pregnancy had no higher risks of birth complications than did women who never smoked (McCowan et al., 2009).

Timing may be important in another way. When pregnancy occurs soon after a previous pregnancy, risk increases. For example, second-born children may be twice as likely to be autistic if they are born within a year of the first-born child (Cheslack-Postava et al., 2011).

How Much Is Too Much?

A second factor affecting the harm from any teratogen is the dose and/or frequency of exposure. Some teratogens have a **threshold effect;** they are virtually harmless until exposure reaches a certain level, at which point they "cross the threshold" and become damaging. This threshold is not a fixed boundary: dose, timing, frequency, and other teratogens affect when the threshold is crossed (O'Leary et al., 2010).

threshold effect In prenatal development, when a teratogen is relatively harmless in small doses but becomes harmful once exposure reaches a certain level (the threshold).

A few substances are beneficial in small amounts but fiercely teratogenic in large quantities. One is vitamin A, essential for healthy development but a cause of abnormalities if the dose is 50,000 units per day or higher (obtained only in pills) (Naudé et al., 2007). Experts are reluctant to specify thresholds, partly because the presence of one teratogen may intensify the effects of another. For example, the threshold for alcohol, tobacco, and marijuana is lower when all three are combined.

Thresholds are controversial. It is known that high doses of psychoactive drugs are harmful, but it is not known if small amounts are teratogenic as well. Consider alcohol. Early in pregnancy, an embryo exposed to heavy drinking can develop **fetal alcohol syndrome (FAS),** which distorts the facial features (especially the eyes, ears, and upper lip). Later in pregnancy, alcohol is a behaviorial teratogen, the cause of *fetal alcohol effects (FAE)*, leading to hyperactivity, poor concentra-

fetal alcohol syndrome (FAS) A cluster of birth defects, including abnormal facial characteristics, slow physical growth, and retarded mental development, that may occur in the fetus of a woman who drinks alcohol while pregnant.

tion, impaired spatial reasoning, and slow learning (Niccols, 2007; Streissguth & Connor, 2001).

However, some pregnant women drink alcohol in moderation with no evident harm to the fetus. If occasional drinking during pregnancy always caused FAS, almost everyone born in Europe before 1980 would be affected. As for FAE, hyperactivity and slow learning are so common that FAE cannot be blamed for every case. Currently, pregnant women are advised to avoid all alcohol, but women in the United Kingdom receive conflicting advice about drinking a glass of wine a day or two a week (Raymond et al., 2009), and French women are told to abstain but many do not seem to have heard that message (Toutain, 2010). Total abstinence requires that all women who might become pregnant avoid a legal substance that most adults use routinely. Wise? Probably. Necessary?

DAVID H. WELLS / CORBIS

Yes, But . . . An adopted boy points out something to his father—a positive interaction between the two. The shapes of the boy's eyes, ears, and upper lip indicate that he was born with fetal alcohol syndrome (FAS). Scientists disagree about the strength of the correlation between FAS and drinking alcohol during pregnancy.

Innate Vulnerability

Genes influence the effects of teratogens. When a woman carrying dizygotic twins drinks alcohol, for example, the twins' blood alcohol levels are equal; yet one twin may be more severely affected than the other because their alleles for the enzyme that metabolizes alcohol differ. Genetic vulnerability is suspected for many birth defects (Sadler et al., 2010). (Remember differential sensitivity.)

One particular chromosome, the Y, may be crucial. Male fetuses are more likely to be spontaneously aborted and, if born, more likely to have been affected by teratogens than female fetuses. Are those extra genes on the second X chromosome protective, or does the Y chromosome carry genes that increase vulnerability? Scientists do not know.

Genes are important in another way, in that the mother's genes affect the prenatal environment she provides. One maternal allele results in low levels of folic acid during pregnancy, which can produce *neural-tube defects*—either *spina bifida,* in which the tail of the spine is not enclosed properly (in healthy embryos, enclosure occurs at about week 7), or *anencephaly,* when part of the brain is missing. Neural-tube defects are more common in certain ethnic groups (Irish, English, and Egyptian) than in others (most Asian and African groups) because that maternal allele is rare among Asians and Africans (Mills et al., 1995).

A U.S. law required that, beginning in 1998, folic acid be added to packaged cereal. That initiative is credited with reducing neural-tube defects by 26 percent (MMWR, September 13, 2002). But some women rarely eat cereal and do not take vitamins. In 2010, in the Appalachian region of the United States (parts of West Virginia, Tennessee, and Kentucky), about 1 newborn in 1000 had a neural-tube defect.

Especially for Nutritionists Is it beneficial that most breakfast cereals are fortified with vitamins and minerals? (see response, page 111)

Applying the Research

Risk analysis cannot precisely predict the results of teratogenic exposure in individual cases. However, much is known about destructive and damaging teratogens and what individuals, family members, and society can do to reduce the risks. Table 4.4 on pages 110–111 lists some teratogens and their possible effects, as well as preventive measures.

Remember that the effects of teratogens vary. Many fetuses are exposed with no evident harm. The opposite occurs as well: About 20 percent of all serious defects occur for reasons unknown. Women are advised to maintain good nutrition and avoid teratogens, especially drugs and chemicals (pesticides, cleaning fluids, and many cosmetics contain teratogenic chemicals). Some medications are necessary (e.g., for women who have epilepsy, diabetes, severe depression) and should continue, but caution should begin *before* pregnancy is confirmed (Haas et al., 2011).

Sadly, the cascade of teratogens is most likely to begin with women who are already vulnerable. For example, cigarette smokers are more often drinkers (as was J.'s mother); those whose jobs involve chemicals and pesticides are more often malnourished (Ahmed & Jaakkola, 2007; Hougaard & Hansen, 2007).

Advice From Doctors

While prenatal care can be helpful to women who need to know how to protect the developing person, even doctors are not always as careful as they could or should be. According to a massive study of 152,000 new mothers in eight health maintenance organizations (HMOs) in the United States, doctors wrote an average of three prescriptions per pregnant woman, including drugs that had not been

TABLE 4.4 Teratogens: Effects of Exposure and Prevention of Damage

Teratogens	Effects of Exposure	To Prevent Harm
Diseases		
Rubella (German measles)	In embryonic period, causes blindness and deafness; in fetal period, brain damage.	Immunization before pregnancy.
Toxoplasmosis	Causes brain damage, loss of vision, mental retardation.	Avoid eating undercooked meat and handling cat feces, garden dirt.
Measles, chicken pox, influenza	May impair brain functioning.	Immunization before pregnancy; avoid infections during pregnancy (wash hands).
Syphilis	Baby born with syphilis; may damage brain and bones; eventual death.	Get early prenatal diagnosis and treatment with antibiotics.
HIV/AIDS	Baby may catch the virus during birth. If so, drugs may prevent illness and death.	Prenatal drugs and cesarean birth limit HIV transmission.
Other sexual infections, such as gonorrhea	Not harmful prenatally but may cause blindness and infections after vaginal birth.	Get early diagnosis and treatment; if necessary, cesarean section, treatment of newborn.
Infections, including infections of urinary tract, gums, teeth	May cause premature labor, which increases vulnerability to brain damage.	Get infection treated, preferably before pregnancy.
Pollutants		
Lead, mercury, PCBs, dioxin, pesticides, cleaning compounds	May cause spontaneous abortion, preterm labor, and brain damage.	Most substances are harmless in small doses. Avoid unwashed fruits, toxic chemicals, fish from polluted waters.
Radiation		
Massive or repeated exposure to radiation, as in medical X-rays	Early in pregnancy, may cause small head (microcephaly), retardation; late, may damage brain.	Get ultrasounds, not X-rays; reassignment suggested for women who work directly with radiation
Social/Behavioral		
Very high stress	Early in pregnancy, may cause cleft lip or cleft palate, spontaneous abortion. Later may cause preterm labor.	Adequate relaxation, rest, and sleep; reduce hours of employment; get help with housework and child care.
Malnutrition	When severe, interferes with conception, implantation, fetal development, and birthweight.	Consume balanced diet,extra folic acid, and iron; women with normal weight, gain 25–35 lbs (10–15 kg) during pregnancy.
Excessive, exhausting exercise	Can affect fetal development when it interferes with woman's sleep or digestion.	Maintain regular, moderate exercise.

declared safe during pregnancy (prescribed for 40 percent) and drugs with proven risks to fetuses (prescribed for 2 percent) (Andrade et al., 2004). Perhaps these doctors did not know their patients were pregnant and perhaps these women did not take the medications, but even a few pills early in pregnancy may be harmful.

Another problem is that not every doctor takes the time to understand the woman's life patterns, some of which may be harmful. For example, one Maryland study found that almost one-third of pregnant women were not asked and counseled about their alcohol use (Cheng et al., 2011). Those who were over age 35 and college-educated were least likely to be counseled, perhaps because their doctors assumed they knew the dangers, but in this study at least, they were also most likely to drink during pregnancy.

>> **Response for Nutritionists** (from page 109) Useful, yes; optimal, no. Some essential vitamins are missing (too expensive), and individual needs differ, depending on age, sex, health, genes, and eating habits. The reduction in neural-tube defects is good, but many women don't eat cereal or take vitamin supplements before becoming pregnant.

Teratogens	Effects of Exposure	To Prevent Harm
Medicinal Drugs		
Lithium	Can cause heart abnormalities.	Avoid all medicines, whether prescription or over-the-counter, unless essential and approved by a medical professional who understands recent research.
Tetracycline	Can harm the teeth.	
Retinoic acid	Can cause limb deformities.	
Streptomycin	Can cause deafness.	
ACE inhibitors	Can harm digestive organs.	
Phenobarbital	Can affect brain development.	
Thalidomide	Halts ear and limb formation.	
Psychoactive Drugs		
Caffeine	Normal use poses no problem.	Avoid excessive use: Limit beverages containing caffeine (coffee, tea, cola, cocoa).
Alcohol	May cause fetal alcohol syndrome (FAS) or fetal alcohol effects (FAE).	Stop or severely limit alcohol consumption during pregnancy; binge drinking is dangerous.
Tobacco	Decreases birthweight. May harm lungs, heart, urinary tract.	Stop smoking. If not, severely limit consumption.
Marijuana	Heavy exposure may affect the central nervous system; may hinder fetal growth.	Avoid or strictly limit use of marijuana.
Heroin	Slows fetal growth, starts preterm labor; addicted newborns require treatment to prevent convulsions.	Stop before pregnancy; if already pregnant, gradual methadone withdrawal is better than sudden abstinence.
Cocaine	May cause slow fetal growth, preterm birth, slow learning in infancy and childhood.	Stop before pregnancy; children may need special medical and educational attention
Inhaled solvents (glue or aerosol)	May cause abnormally small head, crossed eyes, and other indications of brain damage.	Stop sniffing before pregnancy; serious damage occurs during first weeks after conception.
Antipsychotic drugs (e.g., Haldol, Risperdal)	May cause movement abnormalities or withdrawal symptoms in newborns.	Caution needed. Sudden stopping is harmful; such drugs may make the woman a better prospective mother.

Note: This table includes only relatively common teratogens. As the text makes clear, many individual factors interact to determine harm. Some of these generalities will change with new research. Pregnant women should consult with their physicians.

Sources: Briggs et al., 2008; R. D. Mann & Andrews, 2007; Sadler, 2009; U.S. Food and Drug Administration, 2011.

Advice from Scientists

Scientists interpret the research in contradictory ways. For instance, pregnant women in the United States are told to eat less fish, but those in the United Kingdom are told to increase fish consumption. The reason for these opposite messages is that fish contains both mercury (a teratogen) and DHA (an omega-3 fatty acid needed for fetal brain development) (Oken & Bellinger, 2008; Ramón et al., 2009). Scientists in the two nations weigh the benefits and risks of fish differently, and few women can assess each mouthful, which would require them to know each kind of fish and where it swam.

Another dispute involves bisphenol A (commonly used in plastics), banned in Canada but allowed in the United States. The effect of bisphenol A is disputed because research on mice, not humans, finds it teratogenic. Should people be guided by mouse studies? Undisputed epidemiological research on humans is logistically difficult because exposure must be measured at several different time points, including early gestation, but the outcome may not be manifest for many years. No doubt pregnant women are more exposed to bisphenol A than they were a decade ago, and perhaps exposure correlates with hyperactive 2-year-olds, but those facts can be interpreted in at least a dozen ways (Braun & Hauser, 2011; Diamanti-Kandarakis et al., 2009).

No one doubts that prenatal teratogens can cause behavioral problems, reproductive impairment, and several diseases many years after birth. Almost every common disease, almost every food additive, most prescription and nonprescription drugs (even caffeine and aspirin), many trace minerals in the air and water, emotional stress, exhaustion, and poor nutrition *might* impair prenatal development—but only at some times, in some amounts, in some mammals. Most research is with mice; harm to humans is rarely proven to everyone's satisfaction, and even when it is, the proper response can be controversial.

Some people worry that research is misapplied, making every woman worry and causing evident harm to a few. For example, since 1998, five states (Minnesota, North Dakota, Oklahoma, South Dakota, and Wisconsin) have authorized "involuntary commitment" (jail or forced residential treatment) for pregnant women who drink alcohol or use other psychoactive drugs. The legal basis is that the fetus is a future child and that therefore drinking during pregnancy is child abuse.

If a baby is stillborn, women who took drugs during pregnancy can be convicted of second-degree murder, as occurred for an Oklahoma woman, Theresa Hernandez, who took methamphetamines while pregnant and was sentenced to 15 years (Fentiman, 2009). Advocates for women consider such laws discriminatory, especially since women who are poor or American Indian are most likely to be imprisoned (Schroedel & Fiber, 2001). The threat of jail may cause women who most need prenatal care to avoid it altogether.

Prenatal Diagnosis

Especially for Social Workers When is it most important to convince women to be tested for HIV: before pregnancy, after conception, or immediately after birth? (see response, page 114)

The benefits of early prenatal care are many: Women can be told which substances to avoid, they can learn what to eat and what to do, and they may be diagnosed and treated for some conditions (syphilis and HIV among them) that harm the fetus only if early treatment does not occur. Prenatal tests (of blood, urine, and fetal heart rate as well as ultrasound) reassure the parents long before fetal movement is apparent.

In general, early care protects fetal growth, makes birth easier, and renders parents better able to cope. When complications (such as twins, gestational diabetes, infections) arise, early recognition increases the chance of a healthy birth. Unfortunately, about 20 percent of early pregnancy tests *raise* anxiety instead of reducing it. For instance, the level of alpha-fetoprotein (AFP) may be too high or too low, or ultrasound may indicate multiple fetuses, abnormal growth, Down syndrome, or a mother's narrow pelvis. Many such warnings are **false positives,** which means they falsely suggest a problem that does not exist. Any warning, whether false or true, requires further testing but also leads to worry and soul-searching. Some choose to abort, some not, with neither option being what the parents assumed before prenatal testing. Consider the following.

false positive The result of a laboratory test that reports something as true when in fact it is not true. This can occur for pregnancy tests, when a woman might not be pregnant even though the test says she is, or during pregnancy when a problem is reported that actually does not exist.

A CASE TO STUDY

"What Do People Live to Do?"

John and Martha, both under age 35, were expecting their second child. Martha's initial prenatal screening revealed low alpha-fetoprotein, which could indicate Down syndrome.

> Another blood test was scheduled. . . . John asked:
>
> "What exactly is the problem?" . . .
>
> "We've got a one in eight hundred and ninety-five shot at a retarded baby."
>
> John smiled, "I can live with those odds."
>
> "I'm still a little scared."
>
> He reached across the table for my hand. "Sure," he said, "that's understandable. But even if there is a problem, we've caught it in time. . . . The worst case scenario is that you might have to have an abortion, and that's a long shot. Everything's going to be fine." . . .
>
> "I might *have to have* an abortion?" The chill inside me was gone. Instead I could feel my face flushing hot with anger. "Since when do you decide what I *have* to do with my body?"
>
> John looked surprised. "I never said I was going to decide anything," he protested. "It's just that if the tests show something wrong with the baby, of course we'll abort. We've talked about this."
>
> "What we've talked about," I told John in a low, dangerous voice, "is that I am pro-choice. That means I decide whether or not I'd abort a baby with a birth defect. . . . I'm not so sure of this."
>
> "You used to be," said John.
>
> "I know I used to be." I rubbed my eyes. I felt terribly confused. "But now . . . look, John, it's not as though we're deciding whether or not to have a baby. We're deciding what *kind* of baby we're willing to accept. If it's perfect in every way, we keep it. If it doesn't fit the right specifications, whoosh! Out it goes.". . .
>
> John was looking more and more confused. "Martha, why are you on this soapbox? What's your point?"
>
> "My point is," I said, "that I'm trying to get you to tell me what you think constitutes a 'defective' baby. What about . . . oh, I don't know, a hyperactive baby? Or an ugly one?"
>
> "They can't test for those things and—"
>
> "Well, what if they could?" I said. "Medicine can do all kinds of magical tricks these days. Pretty soon we're going to be aborting babies because they have the gene for alcoholism, or homosexuality, or manic depression. . . . Did you know that in China they abort a lot of fetuses just because they're female?" I growled. "Is being a girl 'defective' enough for you?"
>
> "Look," he said, "I know I can't always see things from your perspective. And I'm sorry about that. But the way I see it, if a baby is going to be deformed or something, abortion is a way to keep everyone from suffering—especially the baby. It's like shooting a horse that's broken its leg. . . . A lame horse dies slowly, you know? . . . It dies in terrible pain. And it can't run anymore. So it can't enjoy life even if it doesn't die. Horses live to run; that's what they do. If a baby is born not being able to do what other people do, I think it's better not to prolong its suffering."
>
> ". . . And what is it," I said softly, more to myself than to John, "what is it that people do? What do we live to do, the way a horse lives to run?"
>
> *[M. N. Beck, 1999, pp. 132–133, 135]*

The second AFP test was in the normal range, "meaning there was no reason to fear . . . Down syndrome" (p. 137).

As you read in Chapter 3, genetic counselors help couples discuss their choices *before* becoming pregnant. John and Martha had had no counseling because the pregnancy was unplanned and their risk for Down syndrome was low. The opposite of a false positive is a false negative, a mistaken assurance that all is well. Amniocentesis later revealed that the second AFP was a false negative. Their fetus had Down syndrome after all. Martha decided against abortion.

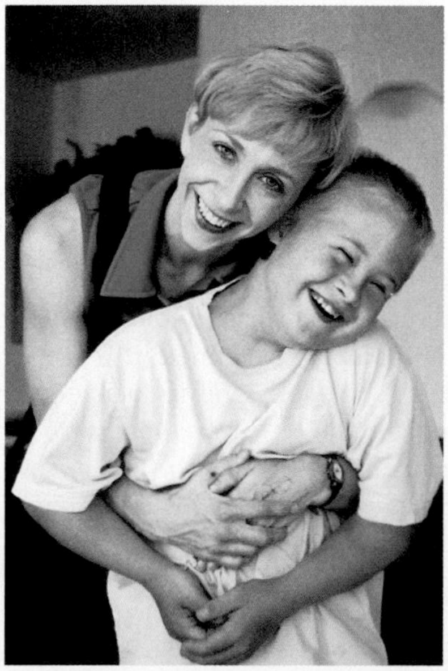

COURTESY KAREN GERDES

Happy Boy Martha Beck not only loves her son Adam (shown here), but she also writes about the special experiences he has brought into the whole family's life—hers, John's, and their other children's. She is "pro-choice"; he was a chosen child.

Low Birthweight

Some newborns are small and immature. With modern hospital care, tiny infants usually survive, but it would be better for everyone—mother, father, baby, and society—if all newborns were in the womb for at least 35 weeks and weighed more than 2,500 grams (5½ pounds). (Usually, this text gives pounds before grams, but hospitals worldwide report birthweight using the metric system, so grams precede pounds and ounces here.)

low birthweight (LBW) A body weight at birth of less than 5½ pounds (2,500 grams).

very low birthweight (VLBW) A body weight at birth of less than 3 pounds, 5 ounces (1,500 grams).

extremely low birthweight (ELBW) A body weight at birth of less than 2 pounds, 3 ounces (1,000 grams).

preterm A birth that occurs 3 or more weeks before the full 38 weeks of the typical pregnancy—that is, at 35 or fewer weeks after conception.

Low birthweight (LBW) is defined by the World Health Organization as under 2,500 grams. LBW babies are further grouped into **very low birthweight (VLBW),** under 1,500 grams (3 pounds, 5 ounces), and **extremely low birthweight (ELBW),** under 1,000 grams (2 pounds, 3 ounces).

Maternal Behavior and Low Birthweight

Remember that fetal weight normally more than doubles in the last trimester of pregnancy, with 900 grams (about 2 pounds) of that gain occurring in the final three weeks. Thus, a baby born **preterm** (three or more weeks early; no longer called *premature*) is usually, but not always, LBW. Preterm birth correlates with many of the teratogens already mentioned, an example of the cascade that leads to newborns with evident problems. When the environment of the womb is harmful, the hormones of the fetus may begin birth early.

small for gestational age (SGA) A term for a baby whose birthweight is significantly lower than expected, given the time since conception. For example, a 5-pound (2,265-gram) newborn is considered SGA if born on time but not SGA if born two months early. (Also called *small-for-dates.*)

Early birth is only one cause of low birthweight. Some fetuses gain weight slowly throughout pregnancy and are *small-for-dates,* or **small for gestational age (SGA).** A full-term baby weighing only 2,500 grams and a 30-week-old fetus weighing only 1,000 grams are both SGA, even though the first is not quite low birthweight. Maternal or fetal illness might cause SGA, but maternal drug use is a more common cause. Every psychoactive drug slows fetal growth, with tobacco implicated in 25 percent of all low-birthweight births worldwide.

Another common reason for slow fetal growth is maternal malnutrition. Women who begin pregnancy underweight, who eat poorly during pregnancy, or who gain less than 3 pounds (1.3 kilograms) per month in the last six months are more likely to have an underweight infant. Malnutrition (not age) is the primary reason teenagers often have small babies. Unfortunately, many of the risk factors just mentioned—underweight, undereating, underage, and smoking—tend to occur together.

What About the Father?

The causes just mentioned of low birthweight focus on the pregnant woman: If she takes drugs or is undernourished, her fetus suffers. However, the more we learn about birth problems, the more important fathers—and grandmothers, neighbors, and communities—are discovered to be. As an editorial in a journal for obstetricians explains: "Fathers' attitudes regarding the pregnancy, fathers' behaviors during the prenatal period, and the relationship between fathers and mothers . . . may indirectly influence risk for adverse birth outcomes" (Misra et al., 2010, p. 99).

As already explained in Chapter 1, each person is embedded in an ecosystem of other people who influence every action. Since the future mother's behavior impacts the fetus, everyone who affects her also affects the future baby. For instance, one correlate of low birthweight is whether the pregnancy was intended (Shah et al., 2011). Obviously, a mother's intentions are in her mind, not her body. Just as obviously, her intentions are affected by the father, and his intentions as well as hers affect her diet, drug abstinence, prenatal care, and so on.

>> Response for Social Workers (from page 112) Testing and then treatment are useful at any time because women who know they are HIV-positive are more likely to get treatment, reduce the risk of transmission, or avoid pregnancy. If pregnancy does occur, early diagnosis is best. Getting tested after birth is too late for the baby.

Not only fathers, but the entire social network and culture are crucial influences (Lewallen, 2011). This is most apparent in what has been called the *Hispanic paradox*. In general, low socioeconomic status (SES) correlates with low birthweight.

Immigrants average lower SES than the native-born, and low-SES babies are often small. But, paradoxically, newborns born in the United States to immigrants are generally healthier in every way, including in birthweight, than are newborns of American-born women of the same ethnicity. Thus, although Hispanic Americans born in Mexico or South America average lower SES than Hispanics born in the United States, their pregnancies and newborns have fewer problems because their husbands, their mothers, and their culture keep them healthy.

Consequences of Low Birthweight

You have already read that life itself is uncertain for the smallest newborns. Ranking worse than most developed nations—and similar to Poland and Malaysia—the U.S. infant mortality rate (death in the first year) is about 7 per 1000, primarily because of low birthweight. When compared with newborns conceived at the same time but born later, very-low-birthweight infants are later to smile, to hold a bottle, to walk, and to communicate.

As months go by, cognitive difficulties as well as visual and hearing impairments emerge. Survivors who were high-risk newborns become infants and children who cry more, pay attention less, disobey, and experience language delays (Aarnoudse-Moens et al., 2009; Spinillo et al., 2009). Longitudinal research studies find that, compared with the average child in middle childhood, formerly SGA children have smaller brain volume, and those who were preterm have lower IQs (van Soelen et al., 2010). Even in adulthood, risks persist: Adults who were LBW are more likely to have heart disease and diabetes.

Longitudinal data provide both hope and caution. Remember that risk analysis gives odds, not certainties—averages that are not true in every case. Some ELBW infants, by age 4, are normal in brain development and overall (Claas et al., 2011; Spittle et al., 2009).

Comparing Nations

In some northern European nations, only 4 percent of newborns weigh under 2,500 grams; in several South Asian nations, more than 20 percent do. Worldwide, far fewer low-birthweight babies are born than 20 years ago, and neonatal deaths have been reduced by one-third as a result (Rajaratnam et al., 2010). Some nations, China and Chile among them, have shown dramatic improvement. In 1970, about half of Chinese newborns were LBW; recent estimates put that number at 3 percent (UNICEF, 2011). By contrast, in other nations, notably in sub-Saharan Africa, the LBW rate is steady or rising because global warming, AIDS, food shortages, wars, and other problems affect pregnancy.

Another nation with a rising LBW rate is the United States, where the rate fell steadily throughout most of the twentieth century, reaching a low of 7.0 percent in 1990. But then it rose again, with the 2008 rate at 8.2 percent—higher than that of virtually every other developed nation (see Figure 4.8 for a sampling).

Many scientists have developed hypotheses to explain the rising U.S. rates. One logical possibility is assisted reproduction, since ART often leads to low-birthweight twins and triplets (and other multiples). However, LBW rates are rising even for naturally

FIGURE 4.8

Getting Better Some public health experts consider the rate of low birthweight to be indicative of national health, since both are affected by the same causes. If that is true, the world is getting healthier, since the estimated LBW world average was 28 percent in 1980 but is now 15 percent. When all nations are included, 47 report LBW at 6 per 1000 or lower, which suggests that many nations (including the United States and United Kingdom) could improve.

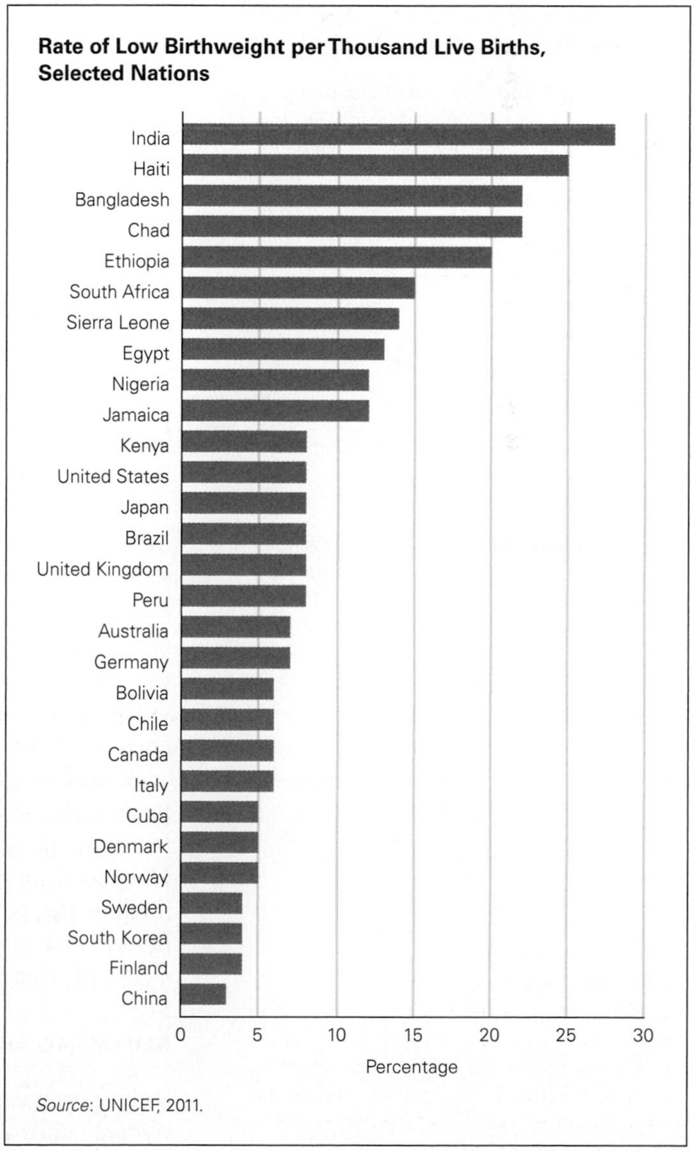

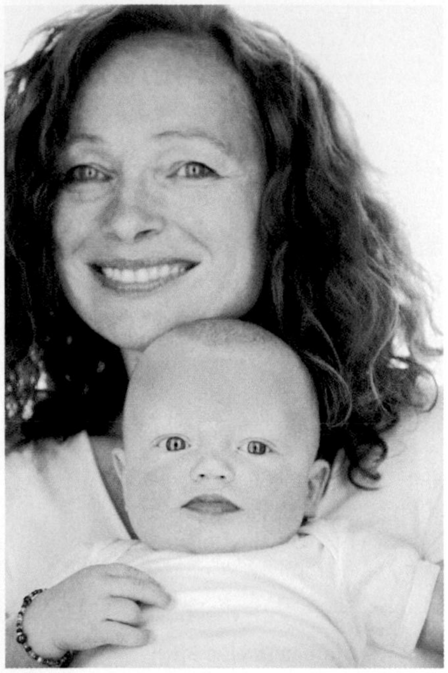
RADIUS IMAGES / ALAMY

A Growing Trend The rate of first births to women in their 40s tripled from 1990 to 2008, although most newborns (96%) have mothers under age 40. Nonetheless, prenatal testing and medical advances have made late motherhood less risky than it was, with some happy results. This mother is 42.

conceived babies (Pinborg et al., 2004), so the ART hypothesis cannot be the only explanation. Added to the puzzle is the fact that several changes in maternal ethnicity, age, and health since 1990 should have decreased LBW, not increased it.

For example, African Americans have LBW newborns twice as often as the national average (almost 14 percent compared with 7 percent), and younger teenagers have smaller babies than do women in their 20s. However, the birth rate among African Americans and young teens was much lower in 2010 than it was in 1990. Furthermore, maternal obesity and diabetes are increasing; both lead to heavier babies.

Something must be amiss. One possibility is nutrition. Nations with many small newborns are also nations where hunger is prevalent, and increasing hunger correlates with increasing LBW. In both Chile and China, LBW fell as nutrition improved. As for the United States, the Department of Agriculture found an increase in *food insecurity* (measured by skipped meals, use of food stamps, and outright hunger) between 2000 and 2007. Food insecurity directly affects LBW, and it also increases chronic illness, which itself correlates with LBW (Seligman & Schillinger, 2010). In 2008, about 15 percent of U.S. households were considered food insecure, with rates higher among women in their prime reproductive years than among middle-aged women or men of any age. These rates increased with the economic recession of 2008–2010; if this hypothesis is accurate, rates of LBW will continue to increase.

Another possibility is drug use. As you will see in Chapter 16, the rate of smoking, drinking, and other drug use among high school girls reached a low in 1992, then increased, then decreased. Most U.S. women now giving birth are in a cohort that experienced rising drug use; they may still suffer the effects. If that is the reason, the current decrease in drug use will mean that LBW should fall again in the United States. Sadly, in developing nations, more young women are smoking and drinking than a decade ago, including in China, where LBW decreased dramatically. Will rates rise in China soon?

Complications During Birth

When a fetus is at risk because of low birthweight, preterm birth, genetic abnormality, or teratogen exposure, or when a mother is unusually young, old, small, or ill, birth complications become likely. As an example, **cerebral palsy** (difficulties with movement control resulting from brain damage) was once thought to be caused solely by birth procedures (excessive medication, slow breech birth, or use of forceps to pull the fetal head through the birth canal). However, we now know that birth procedures are not the sole cause: Cerebral palsy results from genetic vulnerability, teratogens, and maternal infection (J. R. Mann et al., 2009), worsened by insufficient oxygen to the fetal brain.

cerebral palsy A disorder that results from damage to the brain's motor centers. People with cerebral palsy have difficulty with muscle control, so their speech and/or body movements are impaired.

A lack of oxygen is **anoxia,** which often occurs for a second or two during birth, indicated by a slower fetal heart rate. To prevent prolonged anoxia, the fetal heart rate is monitored during labor and the Apgar is used immediately after birth. How long anoxia can continue without harming the brain depends on genes, birthweight, gestational age, drugs in the bloodstream (either taken by the mother before birth or given during birth), and many other factors. Thus, anoxia is part of a cascade that may cause cerebral palsy.

anoxia A lack of oxygen that, if prolonged, can cause brain damage or death.

SUMMING UP

Risk analysis is a complex but necessary aspect of prenatal development because the placenta does not protect the fetus from all teratogens. Many factors reduce risk, including the mother's health and nourishment before pregnancy, her early prenatal care

(to diagnose and treat problems and to teach the woman how to protect her fetus), and the father's protection. The timing of exposure to teratogens, the amount of toxin ingested, and the genes of the mother and fetus may be crucial. Low birthweight, slow growth, and preterm birth increase vulnerability: Maternal illness, drug use, and malnutrition are among the most common causes of these complications. The birth process can add to the problems of the vulnerable infant, especially if anoxia lasts more than a moment or two. ■

>> The New Family

Humans are social creatures, seeking interaction with their families and their societies. Each person is affected by every other person, particularly within each family. We have already seen how this is true in fetal development; if anything, social interactions become even more important once the child is born.

The Newborn

Before birth, developing humans already contribute to their families via fetal movements and hormones that cause protective impulses in the mother early in pregnancy and nurturing impulses at the end. The appearance of the newborn (big hairless head, tiny feet, and so on) stirs the human heart, evident in adults' brain activity and heart rate when they see a baby. Fathers are often enraptured by their scraggly newborn and protective of the exhausted mothers, who may appreciate their husbands more than at other times.

Newborns are responsive social creatures in the first hours of life. They listen, stare, cry, stop crying, and cuddle. In the first day or two, a professional might administer the **Brazelton Neonatal Behavioral Assessment Scale (NBAS),** which records 46 behaviors, including 20 reflexes. Parents who watch their infant perform on the NBAS are amazed at the newborn's responses—and this fosters early parent–child connection (Hawthorne, 2009).

Brazelton Neonatal Behavioral Assessment Scale (NBAS) A test often administered to newborns that measures responsiveness and records 46 behaviors, including 20 reflexes.

reflex An unlearned, involuntary action or movement in response to a stimulus. A reflex occurs without conscious thought.

Technically, a **reflex** is an involuntary response to a particular stimulus. That definition makes reflexes seem automatic, with the new person having no role. Actually, the strength of reflexes varies from one newborn to the next, an early indication that each person is unique. Humans of every age instinctively seek to protect themselves (the eyeblink is an example). Newborns do this also, with three sets of reflexes (12 are cited here in italics) that protect them:

- *Reflexes that maintain oxygen supply.* The *breathing reflex* begins even before the umbilical cord, with its supply of oxygen, is cut. Additional reflexes that maintain oxygen are reflexive *hiccups* and *sneezes,* as well as *thrashing* (moving the arms and legs about) to escape something that covers the face.
- *Reflexes that maintain constant body temperature.* When infants are cold, they *cry, shiver,* and *tuck their legs* close to their bodies. When they are hot, they try to *push away* blankets and then stay still.
- *Reflexes that manage feeding.* The *sucking reflex* causes newborns to suck anything that touches their lips—fingers, toes, blankets, and rattles, as well as natural and artificial nipples of various textures and shapes. The *rooting reflex* causes babies to turn their mouths toward anything that brushes against their cheeks—a reflexive search for a nipple—and start to suck. *Swallowing* is another reflex that aids feeding, as are *crying* when the stomach is empty and *spitting up* when too much has been swallowed quickly.

Other reflexes are not necessary for survival but signify the state of brain and body functions. Among them are the following five:

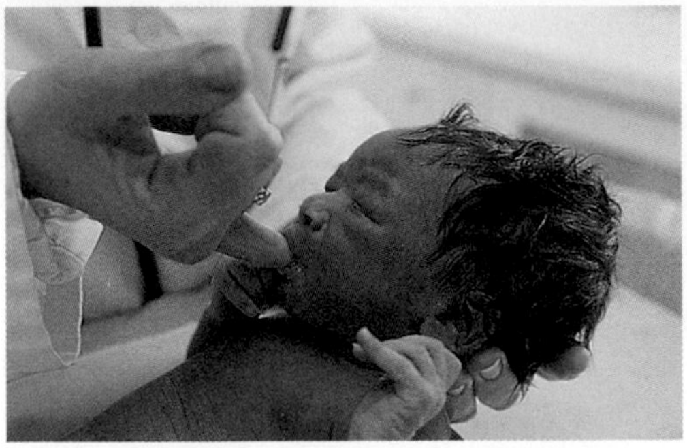

ASTIER / BSIP / SCIENCE SOURCE / PHOTO RESEARCHERS, INC.

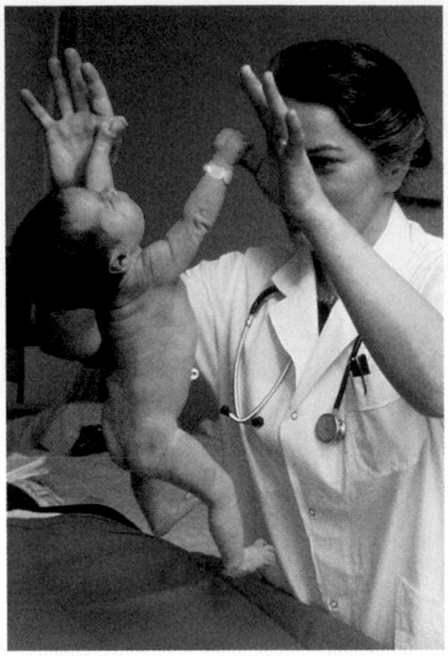

PETIT FORMAT / PHOTO RESEARCHERS, INC.

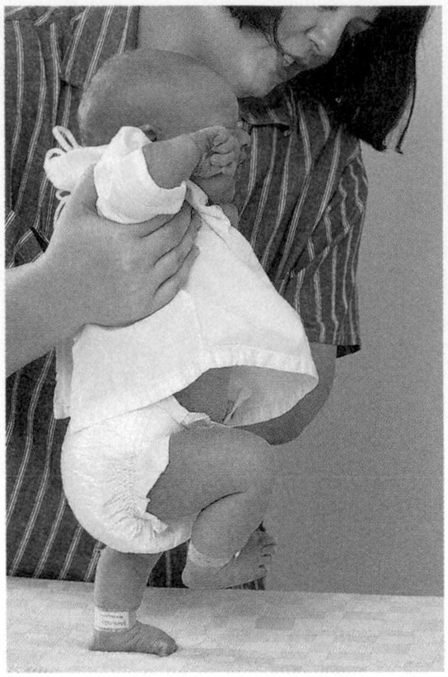

JENNIE WOODCOCK, REFLECTIONS PHOTOLIBRARY / CORBIS

Never Underestimate the Power of a Reflex For developmentalists, newborn reflexes are mechanisms for survival, indicators of brain maturation, and vestiges of evolutionary history. For parents, they are mostly delightful and sometimes amazing. Both of these viewpoints are demonstrated by three star performers: a newborn boy sucking peacefully on the doctor's finger, a newborn grasping so tightly that his legs dangle in space, and a 1-day-old girl stepping eagerly forward on legs too tiny to support her body.

- *Babinski reflex.* When a newborn's feet are stroked, the toes fan upward.
- *Stepping reflex.* When newborns are held upright, feet touching a flat surface, they move their legs as if to walk.
- *Swimming reflex.* When held horizontally on their stomachs, newborns stretch out their arms and legs.
- *Palmar grasping reflex.* When something touches newborns' palms, they grip it tightly.
- *Moro reflex.* When someone bangs on the table they are lying on, newborns fling their arms outward and then bring them together on their chests, crying with wide-open eyes.

Especially for Scientists Research with animals can benefit people, but it is sometimes wrongly used to support conclusions about people. When does that happen? (see response, page 120)

These reflexes are responses to experiences, not unlike an adult's sudden fear, or lust, or anger. The senses are also responsive: New babies listen more to voices than to traffic, for instance. Thus, in many ways newborns connect with the people of their world, who usually respond. If the baby performing these actions on the Brazelton were your own, you would be proud and amazed; that is part of being human.

New Fathers

Fathers affect a newborn's development. As we have seen, fathers-to-be help mothers-to-be stay healthy, nourished, and drug-free. The father's role in birth may also be crucial.

Father Presence

At birth, the father's presence reduces complications, in part because his presence helps his wife. I observed this with my own daughter, whose anxiety rose when the doctor and midwife discussed a possible cesarean without asking her opinion. Her husband told her, "All you need to do is relax between contractions and push when a contraction comes. I will do the rest." Elissa listened. No cesarean.

Especially for Nurses in Obstetrics Can the father be of any practical help in the birth process? (see response, page 120)

The father's actual presence is helpful, but present or not, his legal acceptance of the birth is important to the newborn. A study of all live single births in Milwaukee from 1993 to 2006 (151,869 babies!) found that medical complications correlated with several expected variables (e.g., maternal cigarette smoking) and one unexpected one—no father listed on the birth record. This was especially apparent for European American births: When the mother did not list the father, she was more likely to have long labor, a cesarean section, or other complications (Ngui et al., 2009).

Currently, about 40 percent of all U. S. women are not married when their baby is born (U.S. Bureau of the Census, 2010), but fathers may still be on the birth certificate. Apparently, when fathers acknowledge their paternity, birth is better for mother and baby.

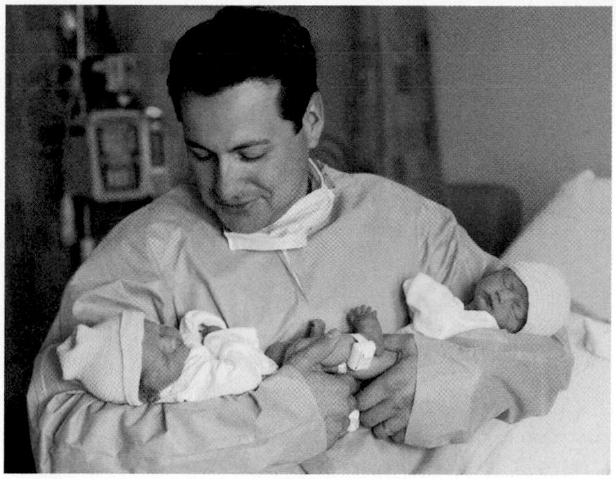

BLEND IMAGES / ALAMY

Paternal Pride Twins mean trouble—less sleep, less money, more worry. Yet, like most parents of newborns, no matter what special complications they entail, this father is enraptured with his 1-day-old sons.

Couvade

Pregnancy and birth may be biologically (not just psychologically) experienced by fathers. For example, levels of the stress hormone cortisol correlate between expectant fathers and mothers, probably because they make each other anxious or relaxed (Berg & Wynne-Edwards, 2002). Beyond that, many fathers experience symptoms of pregnancy and birth, including weight gain and indigestion during pregnancy and pain during labor. Indeed, among some Latin American Indians, fathers go through the motions of labor when their wives do, to help ensure an easy birth.

Paternal experiences of pregnancy and birth are called **couvade,** expected in some cultures, a normal variation in many, and considered pathological in others (M. Sloan, 2009). In developed nations, couvade is unnoticed and unstudied, but researchers find that fathers are often intensely involved with pregnancy and birth (Brennan et al., 2007).

couvade Symptoms of pregnancy and birth experienced by fathers.

Parental Alliance

Remember John and Martha, the young couple whose amniocentesis revealed that their fetus had trisomy-21 (Down syndrome)? One night at 3:00 A.M., after about seven months of pregnancy, Martha was crying uncontrollably. She told John she was scared.

> "Scared of what?" he said. "Of a little baby who's not as perfect as you think he ought to be?"
>
> "I didn't say I wanted him to be perfect," I said. "I just want him to be normal. That's all I want. Just normal."
>
> "That is total bullshit. . . . You don't want this baby to be normal. You'd throw him in a dumpster if he just turned out to be normal. What you really want is for him to be superhuman."
>
> "For your information," I said in my most acid tone, "I was the one who decided to keep this baby, even though he's got Down's. You were the one who wanted to throw him in a dumpster."
>
> "How would you know?" John's voice was still gaining volume. "You never asked me what I wanted, did you? No. You never even asked me."
>
> *[M. N. Beck, 1999, p. 255]*

This episode ended well, with a long, warm, and honest conversation between the two prospective parents. Each learned what their fetus meant to the other, a taboo topic until that night. Adam, their future son, became an important part of their relationship. Their lack of communication up to this point, and the sudden eruption of unexpressed emotions, is not unusual, because pregnancy itself raises memories from childhood and fears about the future. Yet honest and intimate communication is crucial throughout pregnancy,

A Good Beginning The apparent joy and bonding between this expectant couple and their unborn child is a wonderful sign. Although this couple in Germany may experience social discrimination—one reason the divorce rate is higher among multiracial couples than monoracial ones—their own parental alliance is crucial for their child. Many multiracial children become adults with higher achievement, greater self-understanding, and more tolerance than others.

MIKA / CORBIS

parental alliance Cooperation between a mother and a father based on their mutual commitment to their children. In a parental alliance, the parents support each other in their shared parental roles.

birth, and child rearing, helping to create the foundation for a **parental alliance,** a commitment by both parents to cooperate in raising the child.

The parental alliance is especially beneficial when the infant is physically vulnerable, such as having a low birthweight. The converse is also true: Family conflict when a newborn needs extra care increases the risk of child maladjustment and parental divorce (Whiteside-Mansell et al., 2009).

New Mothers

postpartum depression A new mother's feelings of inadequacy and sadness in the days and weeks after giving birth.

About half of all women experience physical problems after birth, such as healing from a c-section, or painfully sore nipples, or problems with urination (Danel et al., 2003). However, worse than any physical problems are psychological ones. When the birth hormones decrease, between 8 and 15 percent of women experience **postpartum depression,** a sense of inadequacy and sadness (called *baby blues* in the mild version and *postpartum psychosis* in the most severe form) (Perfetti et al., 2004). With postpartum depression, baby care (feeding, diapering, bathing) feels very burdensome, babies are not always comforted, and the mother may have thoughts of neglecting or abusing the infant.

Sometimes the first sign that something is amiss is that the mother is euphoric after birth. She cannot sleep, or stop talking, or keep from worrying about the newborn. Some of this is normal, but family members and medical personnel need to be supportive yet alert to the mother's moods. Maternal depression can have a long-term impact on the child, one of the many reasons that postpartum depression should be quickly recognized and treated. Fathers are usually the first responders; they may be instrumental in getting the help the mother and baby need (Cuijpers et al., 2010; Goodman & Gotlib, 2002). This is easier said than done: Fathers may become depressed as well; in such cases, other people need to help.

>> Response for Scientists (from page 118) Animal research should not, by itself, confirm an assertion that has popular appeal but no scientific evidence. This occurred in the social construction that physical contact was crucial for parent–infant bonding.

From a developmental perspective, some causes of postpartum depression (such as financial stress or marital problems) predate the pregnancy; others occur during pregnancy; others correlate with birth (especially if the mother is unprepared or alone or if she fantasized a very different birth process than actually occurred); and still others are specific to the particular infant (health, feeding, or sleeping problems). Successful breast-feeding mitigates maternal depression, one of the many reasons a lactation consultant is an important part of the new mother's support team.

Bonding

parent–infant bond The strong, loving connection that forms as parents hold, examine, and feed their newborn.

To what extent are the first hours crucial for the **parent–infant bond,** the strong, loving connection that forms as parents hold, examine, and feed their newborn? It has been claimed that this bond develops in the first hours after birth when a mother touches her naked baby, just as sheep and goats must immediately smell and nuzzle their newborns if they are to nurture them (Klaus & Kennell, 1976).

Although the concept of bonding has been used to argue against the impersonal medicalization of birth, research does not find that early skin-to-skin contact is essential for humans (Eyer, 1992; Lamb, 1982). Unlike sheep and goats, most mammals do not need immediate contact for parents to nurture their offspring. In fact, substantial research on monkeys begins with *cross-fostering,* a strategy in which newborns are removed from their biological mothers in the first days of life and raised by another female or even a male. A strong and beneficial relationship sometimes develops (Suomi, 2002).

>> Response for Nurses in Obstetrics (from page 118) Usually not, unless he is experienced, well taught, or has expert guidance. But his presence provides emotional support for the woman, which makes the birth process easier and healthier for mother and baby.

However, although mother–infant contact is not essential for bonding, the active involvement of both parents in pregnancy, birth, and newborn care nonetheless benefits them and their baby. Factors that encourage parents (biological

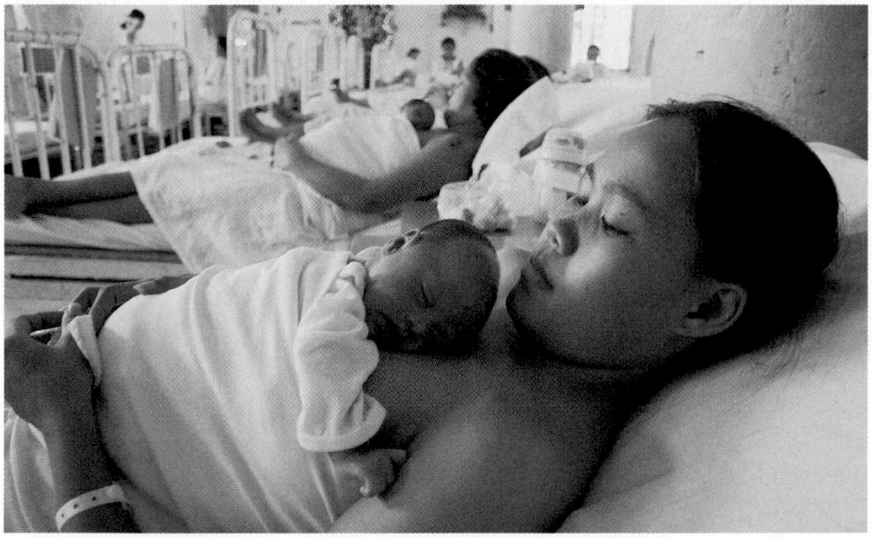

ALEX BALULUT / OMASA.COM

A Beneficial Beginning These new mothers in a maternity ward in Manila are providing their babies with kangaroo care.

or adoptive) to nurture their newborns have lifelong benefits, proven with mice, monkeys, and humans (Champagne & Curley, 2010).

The role of early maternal care has recently become apparent with **kangaroo care,** when the newborn lies between the mother's breasts, skin-to-skin, listening to her heartbeat and feeling her body heat. Many studies find that kangaroo-care newborns sleep more deeply, gain weight more quickly, and spend more time alert than do infants with standard care (Feldman et al., 2002; Ferber & Makhoul, 2004; Gathwala et al., 2008).

kangaroo care A form of newborn care in which mothers (and sometimes fathers) rest their babies on their naked chests, like kangaroo mothers that carry their immature newborns in a pouch on their abdomen.

Kangaroo care was first used with low-birthweight newborns and resulted in faster weight gain and fewer medical complications. Recently, it has also been successful with healthy newborns and with fathers providing the care—evidence that the entire new family is affected by early contact (Thomas, 2008). All the research finds that kangaroo care benefits babies, not only in the hospital but months later, either because of improved infant adjustment to life outside the womb or because of increased parental sensitivity and effectiveness. Which of these two is the explanation? Probably both.

Implementation of many strategies, especially for fragile infants and their parents, is especially needed in developing nations, where kangaroo care and other measures could reduce infant deaths by 20 to 40 percent (Bhutta et al., 2008). From a developmental perspective, the most difficult time for high-risk infants occurs when they leave the hospital, in the days and weeks after birth. At this time, measures to involve parents in early care are crucial. As we will see in later chapters, the relationship between parent and child is mutual, developing over months, not merely hours. Birth is one step of a lifelong journey.

SHEZAD NOORANI / PETER ARNOLD, INC.

A Teenage Mother This week-old baby, born in a poor village in Myanmar (Burma), has a better chance of survival than he might otherwise have had because his 18-year-old mother has bonded with him.

SUMMING UP

Every member of the new family contributes to their shared connection, enabling them all to thrive. The new baby has responsive senses and many reflexes. Close observation and reflection reveal how much the new baby can do. Father support of the new family is crucial, sometimes being the reason for a healthy, happy newborn and mother. Postpartum depression is not rare; factors before and after birth affect how serious and long-lasting it is. Family relationships begin before conception, may be strengthened throughout pregnancy and birth, and continue throughout the life span. ■

SUMMARY

Prenatal Growth

1. The first two weeks of prenatal growth are called the germinal period. During this time, the single-celled zygote multiplies into more than 100 cells that will eventually form both the placenta and the embryo. The growing organism may travel down the fallopian tube and implant.

2. The period from the third through the eighth week after conception is called the embryonic period. The heart begins to beat, and the eyes, ears, nose, and mouth form. By the eighth week, the embryo has the basic organs and features of a human, with the exception of the sex organs.

3. The fetal period extends from the ninth week until birth. In the ninth week, the sexual organs develop. By the end of the third month, all the organs and body structures have formed. The fetus attains viability at 22 weeks, when the brain is sufficiently mature to regulate basic body functions. Babies born before the 26th week are at high risk of death or disability.

4. The average fetus gains approximately 5 pounds (2,268 grams) during the last three months of pregnancy and weighs 7½ pounds (3,400 grams) at birth. Maturation of brain, lungs, and heart ensures survival of more than 99 percent of all full-term babies born in developed nations.

Birth

5. Birth typically begins with contractions that push the fetus out of the uterus and then through the vagina. The Apgar scale, which rates the neonate's vital signs at one minute and again at five minutes after birth, provides a quick evaluation of the infant's health.

6. Medical assistance can speed contractions, dull pain, and save lives. However, many aspects of medicalized birth have been criticized as impersonal and unnecessary, including about half the cesareans performed in the United States. Contemporary birthing practices are aimed at finding a balance, protecting the baby but also allowing more parental involvement and control.

Problems and Solutions

7. Some teratogens (diseases, drugs, and pollutants) cause physical impairment. Others, called behavioral teratogens, harm the brain and therefore impair cognitive abilities and affect personality traits.

8. Whether a teratogen harms an embryo or fetus depends on timing of exposure, amount of exposure, and genetic vulnerability. To protect against prenatal complications, good public and personal health practices are strongly recommended. Some specifics are debatable, but it is always the case that fathers and other family members affect the pregnant woman's health.

9. Doctors differ in the advice they give to pregnant women about avoiding teratogens, partly because they interpret the research differently and partly because of culture.

10. Low birthweight (under 5½ pounds, or 2,500 grams) may arise from multiple births, placental problems, maternal illness, malnutrition, smoking, drinking, drug use, and age. Compared with full-term newborns, preterm and underweight babies experience more medical difficulties. Fetuses that grow slowly (small for gestational age, or SGA) are especially vulnerable.

11. Birth complications, such as unusually long and stressful labor that includes anoxia (a lack of oxygen to the fetus), have many causes. Long-term handicaps, such as cerebral palsy, are not inevitable for such children, but careful nurturing from their parents may be needed.

The New Family

12. Humans are social animals. Newborns respond to others in many ways. The Brazelton Neonatal Behavioral Assessment Scale measures 46 newborn behaviors, 20 of which are reflexes.

13. Fathers can be supportive during pregnancy as well as helpful in birth; such support correlates with shorter labor and fewer complications. Some fathers become so involved with the pregnancy and birth that they experience couvade.

14. Many women feel unhappy, incompetent, or unwell after giving birth. Postpartum depression gradually disappears with appropriate help; fathers are crucial to the well-being of mother and child. Ideally, a parental alliance supports the child's well-being from birth on.

15. Kangaroo care is especially beneficial when the newborn is of low birthweight. Mother–newborn interaction should be encouraged, although the parent–infant bond depends on many factors in addition to birth practices.

KEY TERMS

germinal period (p. 94)
embryonic period (p. 94)
fetal period (p. 94)
implantation (p. 94)
embryo (p. 94)
fetus (p. 96)
ultrasound (p. 96)
age of viability (p. 97)
Apgar scale (p. 100)
cesarean section (c-section) (p. 101)
doula (p. 104)
teratogens (p. 106)
behavioral teratogens (p. 106)
threshold effect (p. 108)
fetal alcohol syndrome (FAS) (p. 108)
false positive (p. 113)
low birthweight (LBW) (p. 114)
very low birthweight (VLBW) (p. 114)
extremely low birthweight (ELBW) (p. 114)
preterm (p. 114)
small for gestational age (SGA) (p. 114)
cerebral palsy (p. 116)
anoxia (p. 116)
Brazelton Neonatal Behavioral Assessment Scale (NBAS) (p. 117)
reflex (p. 117)
couvade (p. 119)
parental alliance (p. 120)
postpartum depression (p. 120)
parent–infant bond (p. 120)
kangaroo care (p. 121)

WHAT HAVE YOU LEARNED?

Prenatal Growth

1. What are three major developments in the germinal period?
2. What body parts develop during the embryonic period?
3. What major milestone is reached about halfway through the fetal period?
4. What are three major reasons for why pregnancy continues months after the fetus could live outside the uterus?

Birth

5. Why has the Apgar scale increased newborns' survival rate?
6. Why has the rate of cesarean sections increased?
7. Why are developmentalists concerned that surgery is often part of birth?
8. Why is the newborn mortality rate much higher in some countries than in others?
9. What are the differences among a doula, a midwife, and a doctor?

Problems and Solutions

10. What teratogens harm the developing body structure?
11. Why is it difficult to establish the impact of behavioral teratogens?
12. How does timing affect the risk of harm to the fetus?
13. Why does risk analysis not predict precise damage to a fetus?
14. What factors increase or decrease the risk of spina bifida?
15. What are the potential consequences of drinking alcohol during pregnancy?
16. What are the differences among LBW, VLBW, and ELBW?
17. List at least four reasons why a baby might be born LBW.
18. How have U.S. LBW rates changed in the past decade?
19. What is the long-term prediction for a very tiny or vulnerable newborn who survives?
20. How do culture and customs affect one's exposure to teratogens?

The New Family

21. What do newborns do to aid their survival?
22. What impact do fathers have during and after birth?
23. How do fathers experience pregnancy?
24. What are the signs of postpartum depression?
25. What affects the parent–infant bond?
26. What are the results of kangaroo care?

APPLICATIONS

1. Go to a nearby greeting-card store and analyze the cards about pregnancy and birth. Do you see any cultural attitudes (e.g., variations depending on the sex of the newborn or of the parent)? If possible, compare those cards with cards from a store that caters to another economic or ethnic group.

2. Interview three mothers of varied backgrounds about their birth experiences. Make your interviews open-ended—let them choose what to tell you, as long as they give at least a 10-minute description. Then compare and contrast the three accounts, noting especially any influences of culture, personality, circumstances, and cohort.

3. People sometimes wonder how any pregnant woman could jeopardize the health of her fetus. Consider your own health-related behavior in the past month—exercise, sleep, nutrition, drug use, medical and dental care, disease avoidance, and so on. Would you change your behavior if you were pregnant? Would it make a difference if you, your family, and your partner did not want a baby?

>>ONLINE CONNECTIONS

To accompany your textbook, you have access to a number of online resources, including quizzes for every chapter of the book, flashcards (in English and Spanish), critical thinking questions, and case studies. For access to any of these links, go to www.worthpublishers.com/bergerca9e. In addition to these free resources, you'll also find links to podcasts, video clips, diagnostic quizzing with personalized study advice, and an ebook. Some of the videos and activities available online include:

- *Brain Development: In the Beginning.* Three-dimensional animation follows brain development from the formation of the neural tube until birth. Animations of microscopic changes in the brain include synaptic pruning.
- *Periods of Prenatal Development.* A series of detailed animations show the stages of prenatal development from fertilization to birth.

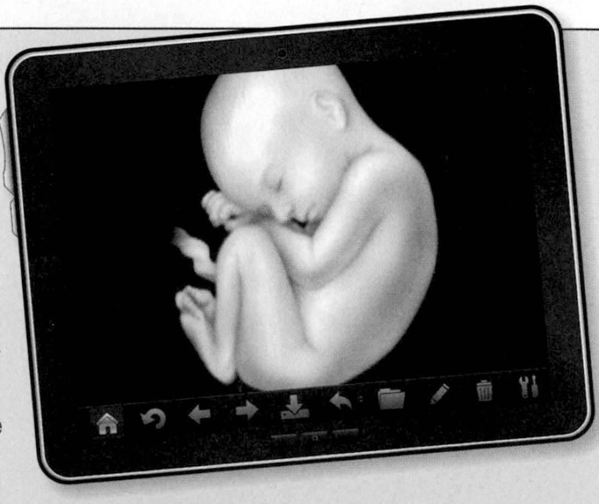

P A R T

II

CHAPTERS 5•6•7

the first two years

Adults don't change much in a year or two. Their hair might grow longer, grayer, or thinner; they might gain or lose weight; they might learn something new. But if you saw friends you hadn't seen for two years, you'd recognize them immediately.

By contrast, if you cared for a newborn 24 hours a day for a month, traveled for two years, and came back, you might not recognize him or her. The baby would have quadrupled in weight, grown a foot taller, and sprouted a new head of hair. Behavior and emotions would have changed, too—less crying, but new laughter and fear—including fear of you.

A year or two is not much compared with the 70 to 85 years of the average life. However, in those first two years humans reach half their adult height, start to talk in sentences, and begin to express almost every emotion—not just joy and fear but also love, jealousy, and shame. The next three chapters describe these radical and awesome changes.

5

CHAPTER

The First Two Years: Biosocial Development

WHAT WILL YOU KNOW?

1. How can you tell if a baby is growing normally in the first year of life?
2. Does brain wiring in the first two years depend on genes or experience?
3. When do babies see clearly, hear well, and walk on their own?
4. Why did more than half the newborns die a century ago, and almost all thrive now?

Our first child, Bethany, was born when I was in graduate school. I studiously memorized developmental norms, including sitting at 6 months, walking and talking at 12. At 14 months, though, Bethany spoke a dozen words but had not yet taken her first step. Instead of worrying, I decided genes were more influential than anything I did. I also read that French babies are among the latest walkers in the world, and my grandmother was French. My speculation was confirmed when our next two children, Rachel and Elissa, were also slow to walk.

Fourteen years later, when Sarah was born, I could afford a full-time caregiver, Mrs. Todd, from Jamaica. I cautioned her that Berger children walk late.

"Sarah will be walking by one year," Mrs. Todd told me. "My daughter Gillian walked at 10 months."

"We'll see," I replied, confident of my genetic explanation.

I underestimated Sarah and Mrs. Todd, who bounced my baby on her lap, day after day, and spent hours giving her "walking practice"—to Sarah's great delight. My fourth child took her first step at 12 months, late for a Todd baby, early for a Berger, and a humbling lesson for me.

This chapter describes physical development in the first two years of life, emphasizing changes in the body and brain, including cortex maturation, perceptions, and muscle control. All these changes make toddlers quite different from newborns. Individual variations in development abound, some genetic and some contextual, including, as I now believe, many resulting from cultures and caregivers. This chapter is titled *biosocial*, not merely biological or physical, because biological development is closely connected to the social context.

HAZEL HANKIN

My Youngest at 8 Months When I look at this photo of Sarah, I see evidence of Mrs. Todd's devotion. Sarah's hair is washed and carefully brushed, her jumper and blouse are clean and pressed, and the carpet and stepstool are perfect equipment for standing practice. Sarah's legs—chubby and far apart—indicate that she is not about to walk early; but, given all these signs of Mrs. Todd's attention to caregiving, it is not surprising, in hindsight, that my fourth daughter was my earliest walker.

>> Body Changes

In infancy, growth is so rapid and the consequences of neglect are so severe that gains are closely monitored. Medical checkups, including measurement of height, weight, and head circumference, occur often in developed nations because those measurements provide the first clues as to whether an infant is progressing as expected—or not.

Body Size

Exactly how rapidly does growth usually occur? Infants typically double their birthweight by the fourth month and triple it by age 1. For example, a 7-pound newborn might weigh 14 pounds at 4 months and 21 pounds at 12 months (from 3,250 to 6,500 to 9,750 grams). Physical growth then slows somewhat, but it is still rapid. By 24 months, most children weigh almost 28 pounds (13 kilograms) and have grown from about 20 inches at birth to about 34 inches tall (51 to 86 centimeters). This means that 2-year-olds are half their adult height and about a fifth of their adult weight, four times heavier than they were at birth (see Figure 5.1).

Much of the weight increase in the early months is fat. Often, in the *birth catch-up,* small babies experience extra gain to catch up to the norm. Baby fat is

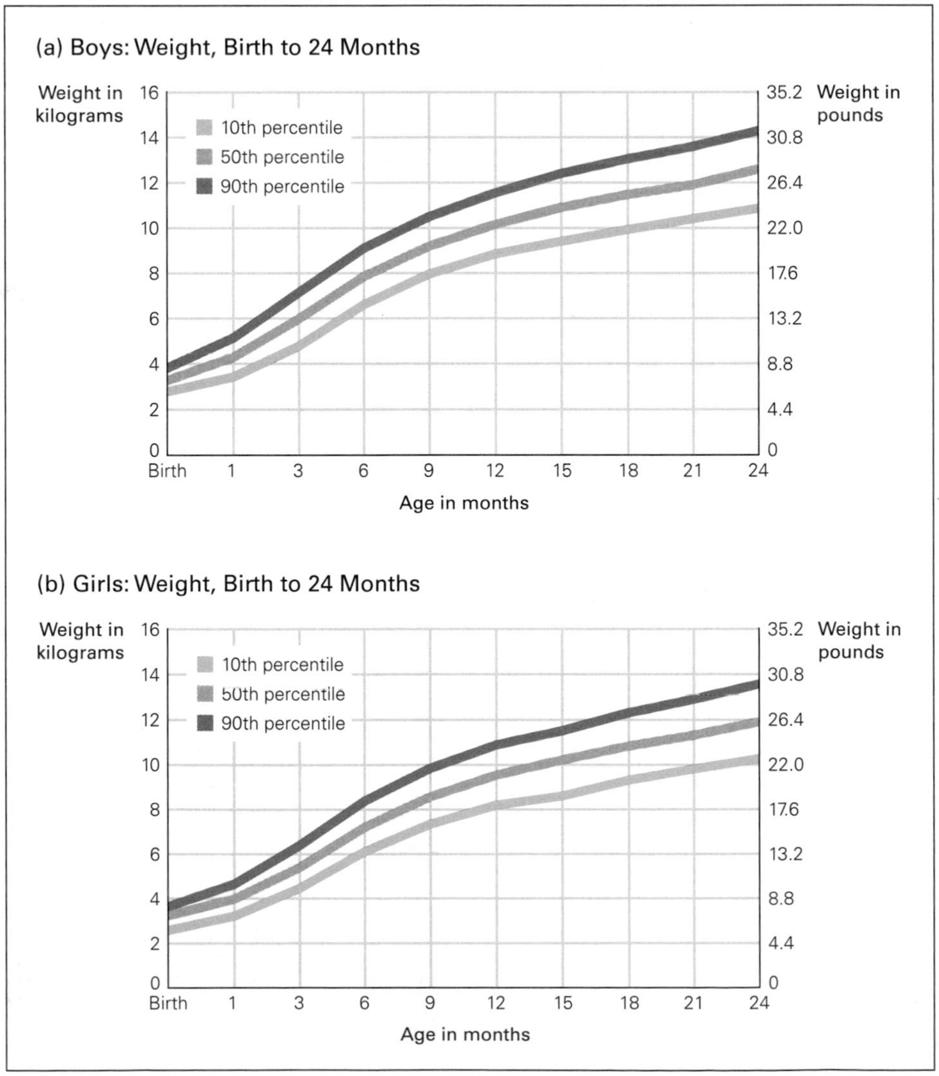

FIGURE 5.1

Eat and Sleep The rate of increasing weight in the first weeks of life makes it obvious why new babies need to be fed, day and night.

stored to keep the brain nourished if teething or the sniffles interfere with sucking. If nutrition is temporarily inadequate, the body stops growing but not the brain—a phenomenon called **head-sparing.** (Chronic malnutrition is discussed later in this chapter.)

head-sparing A biological mechanism that protects the brain when malnutrition affects body growth. The brain is the last part of the body to be damaged by malnutrition.

These norms are averages; individuals vary. Ethnic differences are common: Babies of South Asian ancestry tend to be somewhat smaller than babies from Africa if both groups of babies are well nourished (Nightingale et al., 2011). Of course, those are generalities: There are dozens of ethnic groups in South Asia and Africa, and even within groups, genes vary. A better predictor of expected growth for a particular infant is the average growth of both parents and all siblings. Even so, each infant shares only half of the genes of any one of these family members; some well-nourished children differ not only from their ethnic group but also from their relatives.

To decide whether a particular baby is growing well, it is best to know that infant's **percentile,** a number that indicates rank compared to other similar people of the same age. Percentiles range from zero to 100. Thus, a child of average weight would be close to the 50th percentile. Some children would be heavy (above the 75th percentile) and some quite light (below the 25th). Although half of all babies would weigh below the 25th or above the 75th percentile, most of them would be fine if they always ranked relatively high or low.

percentile A point on a ranking scale of 0 to 100. The 50th percentile is the midpoint; half the people in the population being studied rank higher and half rank lower.

Percentiles allow a given child to be compared not only to others the same age but also to his or her own past growth. Thus, 6-month olds whose weight *and* height are at the 90th percentile are quite normal if their newborn weight and height were also at the 90th percentile. Also growing normally is the child who is consistently at the 20th percentile.

Percentiles alert professionals and parents when something is amiss. If a newborn is at the 50th percentile in height and weight but 6 months later is at the 40th percentile in height but the 80th percentile in weight, that infant may be getting too heavy. Neither the 40th nor the 80th percentile is worrisome alone, but the combination and the change are warning signs. Losing weight compared to one's former percentile is also worrisome, as is being markedly underweight throughout the first two years. That is worse than being born underweight, since many small newborns catch up. Continual underweight in infancy correlates with becoming a short adult and, for females, with becoming overweight (Wang et al., 2010).

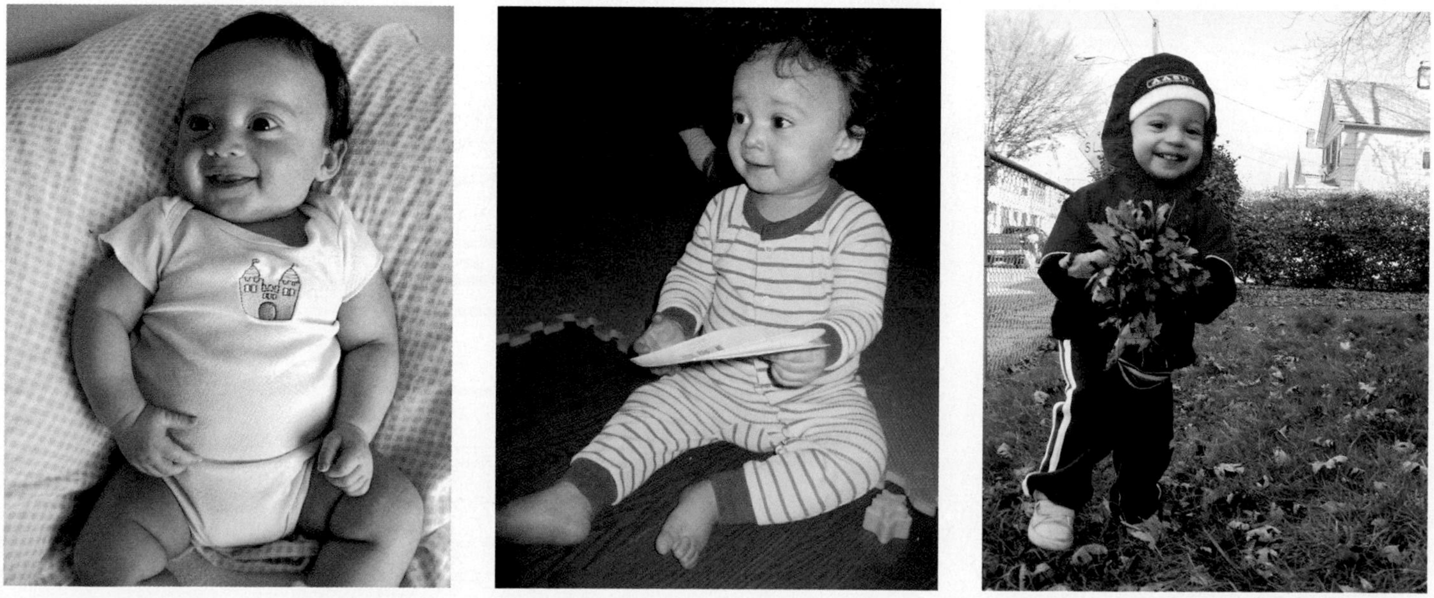

ALL: DIAN LOFTON

Same Boy, Much Changed All three photos show Riley, first at 3 months, then at 12 months, and finally at 24 months. Note the rapid growth in the first two years, especially apparent in proportions of the head and use of the legs—sprawling while propped against a pillow, steadying while sitting upright, or racing across an autumn lawn.

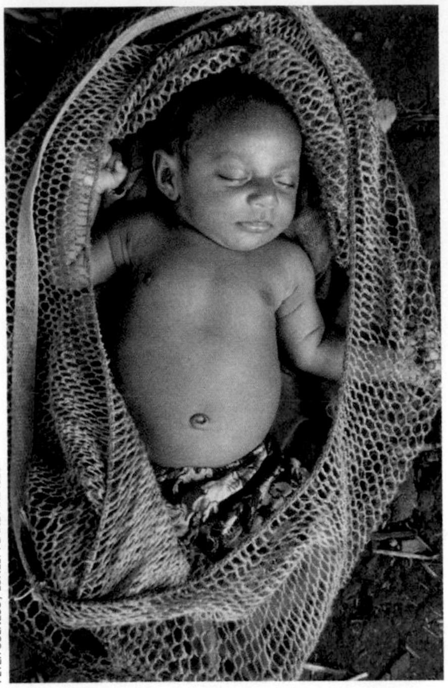

Protective Sleeping It matters little what infants sleep in—bassinet, cradle, crib, or Billum bag made from local plants in Papua New Guinea, as shown here. In fact, this kind of bag is very useful since babies can easily be carried in it. It can also be used for carrying food, tools, and much else. What does matter is the infant's sleeping position—always on the back, like this healthy infant.

Sleep

Newborns spend most of their time sleeping, about 15 to 17 hours a day. Hours of sleep decrease rapidly with maturity: The norm per day for the first 2 months is 14¼ hours; for the next 3 months, 13¼ hours; for 6 to 17 months, 12¾ hours. Variation is particularly apparent in the early weeks: One new baby in 20 sleeps nine hours or fewer per day and one in 20 sleeps 19 hours or more, according to parents' reports (Sadeh et al., 2009) (see Figure 5.2).

Sleep specifics vary not only because of biology (age and genes) but also because of the social environment. With responsive parents, full-term newborns who are well-fed sleep more than low-birthweight newborns, who need to eat every two hours. Babies who are fed cow's milk and cereal sleep more soundly—easier for parents but not necessarily good for the baby. Social environment matters more directly: If parents respond to predawn cries with food and play, babies learn to wake up early night after night, which is not necessarily good for anyone (Sadeh et al., 2009).

Throughout childhood, regular and ample sleep correlates with normal brain maturation, learning, emotional regulation, academic success, and psychological adjustment (Mindell & Owens, 2010). Children who wake up frequently and sleep too little often have other physical or psychological problems. Lifelong, sleep deprivation can cause poor health, and vice versa (Murphy & Delanty, 2007).

Over the first months, the relative amount of time spent in each type or stage of sleep changes. Babies born preterm may always seem to be dozing. Full-term newborns dream a lot; about half their sleep is **REM sleep** (rapid eye movement sleep), with flickering eyes and rapid brain waves. That indicates dreaming. REM sleep declines over the early weeks, as does "transitional sleep," the dozing, half-awake stage. At 3 or 4 months, quiet sleep (also called *slow-wave sleep*) increases markedly.

REM sleep Rapid eye movement sleep, a stage of sleep characterized by flickering eyes behind closed lids, dreaming, and rapid brain waves.

By about 3 months, all the various states of waking and sleeping become more evident. Thus, although newborns often seem half asleep, neither in deep sleep nor wide awake, by 3 months most babies have periods of alertness (when they are neither hungry nor sleepy) and periods of deep sleep (when noises do not rouse them).

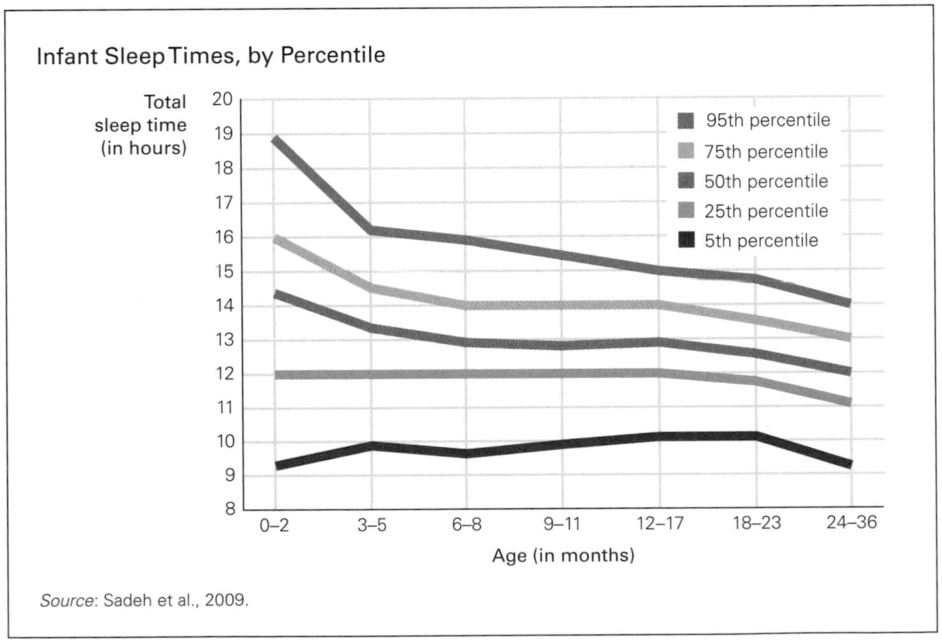

FIGURE 5.2

Good Night, Moon Average sleep per 24-hour period is given in percentiles because there is much variation in how many hours a young child normally sleeps. Other charts from this study show nighttime sleep and daytime napping. Most 1-year-olds sleep about 10 hours a night, with about 2 hours of napping, but some sleep much less; by age 3, about 10 percent have given up naps altogether. Note that these data are drawn from reports by U.S. parents, based on an Internet questionnaire. Actual sleep monitors or reports by a more diverse group of parents would probably show even more variation.

First-born infants typically "receive more attention" (Bornstein, 2002, p. 28), which may be why they have more sleep problems than do later-borns. Overall, an Internet study of more than 5,000 North American children under age 3 found that, according to their parents, sleep was a problem for 25 percent (Sadeh et al., 2009). Of course, sleep problems are more troubling for parents than for infants. This does not render them insignificant; overtired parents may be less patient and responsive (Bayer et al., 2007).

Developmentalists agree that insisting that infants conform to the parents' sleep–wake schedule can be frustrating to the parents and difficult for infants, whose brain patterns and digestion are not ready for a long night's sleep. However, when children frequently interrupt the adults' sleep, parents suffer. Parent reactions to infant sleep shape the baby's sleep patterns, which in turn affect the parents (Sadeh et al., 2010), as the following explains. Ideally, families interact and adapt until everyone's needs are met.

Especially for New Parents You are aware of cultural differences in sleeping practices, and this raises a very practical issue: Should your newborn sleep in bed with you? (see response, page 132)

co-sleeping A custom in which parents and their children (usually infants) sleep together in the same room.

THINKING CRITICALLY

Where Should Babies Sleep?

Traditionally, most Western infants slept in cribs in their own rooms; it was thought that they might be traumatized by the parents' sexual interactions. By contrast, traditional parents in Asia, Africa, and Latin America slept beside their infants, a practice called **co-sleeping.** They thought that parent–child separation at night was cruel. Even today, Asian and African mothers worry more about separation, and European and North American mothers worry more about sex. A recent study in 19 nations confirms those differences: The extremes were 82 percent of babies in Vietnam sleeping with their parents compared to 6 percent in New Zealand (Mindell et al., 2010).

Co-sleeping is becoming more common among Western parents, although reports differ as to the rates. About half of a group of British parents slept with their infants some of the time (Blair & Ball, 2004). A North American Internet survey found that 20 percent of the youngest babies were put to sleep in the parents' bed, as were 18 percent of the toddlers (Sadeh et al., 2009). Those parents who did not begin the night with their babies in the same room were asked, "What do you do if your infant wakes during the night?" "Bring child to parents' bed," answered 21 percent.

Both those who advocate co-sleeping and those who oppose it cite evidence (Hormann, 2007). With co-sleeping, breast-feeding is easier and more common. But so is sudden infant death (Gettler & McKenna, 2010; Ruys et al., 2007). For both these statistics, co-sleeping sometimes means *bed-sharing,* and that may be one reason the controversy rages. Everyone agrees that sharing a bed with a newborn is dangerous if the adult is drugged or drunk—and thus in danger of "overlying" the baby. It may be that co-sleeping is beneficial but bed-sharing is not, partly because adult beds, unlike cribs, are often soft, with comforters, mattresses, and pillows that increase a baby's risk of suffocation (Alm, 2007). (In cultures where bed-sharing is the norm, most people sleep on the floor.) Manufacturers, noting this dilemma, have designed "co-sleepers," which fit on the side of a bed, allowing newborns to be safe but also next to parents.

Obviously, culture affects sleep customs (in many cultures, husbands and wives do not share a bed). In addition, adults are influenced by their past experiences as infants, a phenomenon called *ghosts in the nursery* because the parents bring decades-old memories into the bedrooms of their children. One study found that, compared to Israeli adults who had slept near their parents as infants, those who had slept communally with other infants (as sometimes occurred on a kibbutz) were more likely to interpret their own infants' nighttime cries as distress, requiring comfort (Tikotzky et al., 2010).

Developmentalists hesitate to declare any particular pattern best (Tamis-Lemonda et al., 2008) because the issue is "tricky and

STEPHEN CHANG / JUPITER IMAGES

Danger or Safety? Will Susan roll over on newborn Anisa as they sleep? Some physicians fear that co-sleeping poses a risk of suffocation, but others believe that it is protective.

complex" (Gettler & McKenna, 2010, p. 77). Sleeping alone may encourage a child's independence and individuality—traits appreciated in some cultures, abhorred in others. Past experiences—the ghosts in the nursery—affect adult thinking; developmentalists do not want to welcome some ghosts while dismissing others.

A crucial issue is sleep deprivation. A videotape analysis found that, although co-sleeping infants awakened twice as often as solo-sleeping infants (six versus three times a night), co-sleeping babies got as much sleep as solo sleepers because they went back to sleep more quickly (Mao et al., 2004). One of the main reasons parents opt for co-sleeping—and a powerful argument for it—is that adults are less exhausted if they can stay in bed all night, simply reaching over to give a nighttime feeding.

This choice may backfire, however: If children become accustomed to co-sleeping, they may continue to crawl into their parents' bed when they are long past infancy. Thus, in the long run parents might lose sleep for years because they wanted more sleep when their babies were small. Of course, that concern reflects a cultural norm as well. According to an ethnographic study, by the time Mexican Mayan children are 5 years old, they choose "when, how long, and with whom to sleep" (Gaskins, 1999, p. 40), a practice that bewilders many other North Americans.

Logical arguments on both sides are many, but they are usually overwhelmed by cultural practices and personal ghosts. Whatever you think best, do your conclusions reflect values and emotions that are disconnected from developmental considerations?

>> Response for New Parents (from page 131) From the psychological and cultural perspectives, babies can sleep anywhere as long as the parents can hear them if they cry. The main consideration is safety: Infants should not sleep on a mattress that is too soft, nor should a baby sleep beside an adult who is drunk or drugged or sleeps very soundly. Otherwise, the family should decide for itself where its members would sleep best.

SUMMING UP

Birthweight doubles, triples, and quadruples by 4 months, 12 months, and 24 months, respectively. Height increases by about a foot (about 30 centimeters) in the first two years. Such norms are useful as general guidelines, but personal percentile rankings over time indicate whether a particular infant is growing appropriately, with brain growth more critical than body growth. With maturation, sleep becomes regular, dreaming becomes less common, and distinct sleep–wake patterns develop. The youngest infants sleep more hours in total but for less time at a stretch; by age 1, most babies sleep longer at night, with a nap or two during the day. Cultural and caregiving practices influence norms, schedules, and expectations.

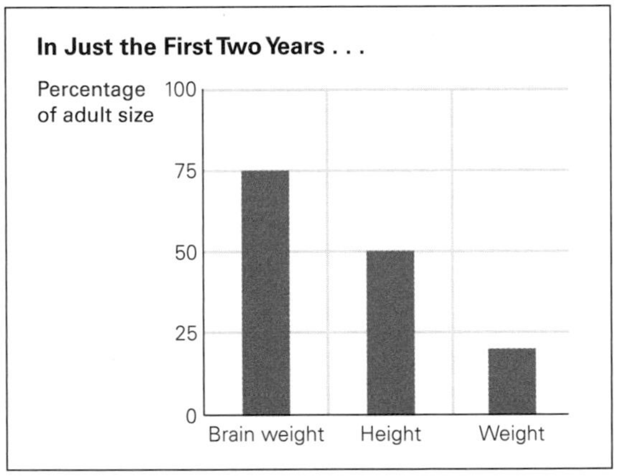

FIGURE 5.3

Growing Up Two-year-olds are barely talking and are totally dependent on adults, but they have already reached half their adult height and three-fourths of their adult brain size. This is dramatic evidence that biosocial growth is the foundation for cognitive and social maturity.

neurons The billions of nerve cells in the central nervous system, especially the brain.

>> Brain Development

Recall that the newborn's skull is disproportionately large. That's because it must be big enough to hold the brain, which at birth is already 25 percent of its adult weight. The neonate's body, by comparison, is about 5 percent of adult weight. The brain continues to grow very rapidly in the first years of life. By age 2, it is almost 75 percent of adult brain weight (see Figure 5.3).

Connections in the Brain

Head circumference provides a rough idea of how the brain is growing, which is why medical checkups include measurement of skull circumference. The distance around the head typically increases about 35 percent (from 13 to 18 inches, or from 33 to 46 centimeters) in the first year. Much more significant (although harder to measure) are changes in the brain's communication system. To understand this, we review the basics of neurological development (see Figure 5.4).

Communication within the central nervous system (CNS)—the brain and spinal cord—begins with nerve cells, called **neurons.** Most neurons are created before birth, at a peak production rate of 250,000 new cells per minute in mid-pregnancy (Purves et al., 2004). In infancy, the human brain has billions of neurons. Some are deep inside the brain in a region called the *brain stem,* which controls automatic responses such as heartbeat, breathing, temperature, and arousal. Others are in the

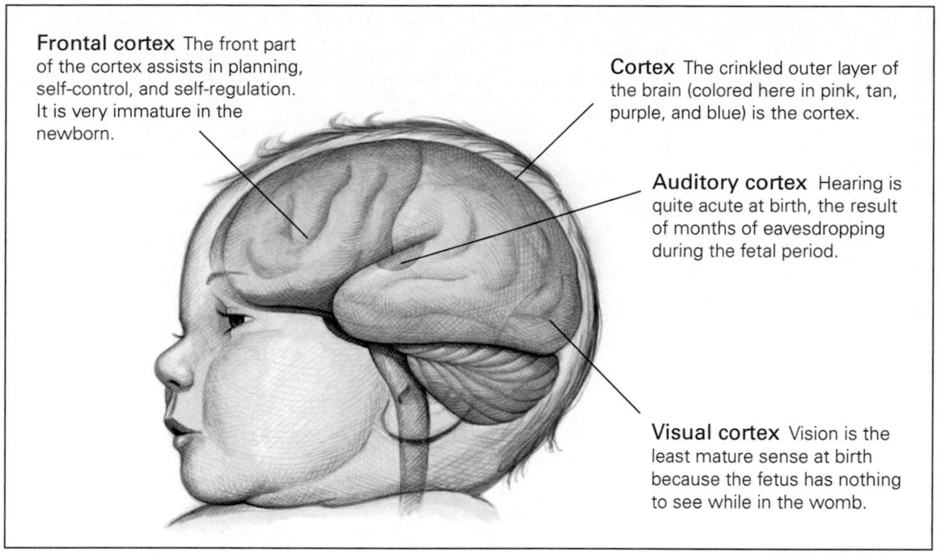

Frontal cortex The front part of the cortex assists in planning, self-control, and self-regulation. It is very immature in the newborn.
Cortex The crinkled outer layer of the brain (colored here in pink, tan, purple, and blue) is the cortex.
Auditory cortex Hearing is quite acute at birth, the result of months of eavesdropping during the fetal period.
Visual cortex Vision is the least mature sense at birth because the fetus has nothing to see while in the womb.

FIGURE 5.4

The Developing Cortex The infant's cortex consists of four to six thin layers of tissue that cover the brain. It contains virtually all the neurons that make conscious thought possible. Some areas of the cortex, such as those devoted to the basic senses, mature relatively early. Others, such as the frontal cortex, mature quite late, after age 20.

midbrain, in areas that affect emotions and memory. And most neurons (about 70 percent) are in the **cortex,** the brain's six outer layers (sometimes called the *neocortex*). The cortex is crucial: Most thinking, feeling, and sensing occur in the cortex, although parts of the midbrain join in (Johnson, 2011).

The last part of the brain to mature is the **prefrontal cortex,** the area for anticipation, planning, and impulse control. It is virtually inactive in the first months of infancy and gradually becomes more efficient in childhood and adolescence (Wahlstrom et al., 2010). (The prefrontal cortex is discussed in later chapters.) Various areas of the cortex specialize. For instance, there is a visual cortex, an auditory cortex, and an area dedicated to the sense of touch for each body part—including for each finger of a person or each whisker of a rat (Barnett et al., 2006).

cortex The outer layers of the brain in humans and other mammals. Most thinking, feeling, and sensing involve the cortex. (Sometimes called the *neocortex.*)

prefrontal cortex The area of cortex at the front of the brain that specializes in anticipation, planning, and impulse control.

Dendrites Sprouting

Within and between areas of the central nervous system, neurons are connected to other neurons by intricate networks of nerve fibers called **axons** and **dendrites** (see Figure 5.5). Each neuron has a single axon and numerous dendrites, which spread out like the branches of a tree. The axon of one neuron meets the dendrites of other neurons at intersections called **synapses,** which are critical communication links within the brain.

To be more specific, neurons communicate by sending electrochemical impulses through their axons to synapses, to be picked up by the dendrites of other neurons. The dendrites bring the message to the cell bodies of their neurons, which, in turn, convey the message via their axons to the dendrites of other neurons.

Axons and dendrites do not touch at synapses. Instead, the electrical impulses in axons typically cause the release of chemicals called *neurotransmitters,* which carry information from the axon of the sending neuron, across the *synaptic gap,* to the dendrites of the receiving neuron, a process speeded up by myelination (described in Chapter 8).

axon A fiber that extends from a neuron and transmits electrochemical impulses from that neuron to the dendrites of other neurons.

dendrite A fiber that extends from a neuron and receives electrochemical impulses transmitted from other neurons via their axons.

synapse The intersection between the axon of one neuron and the dendrites of other neurons.

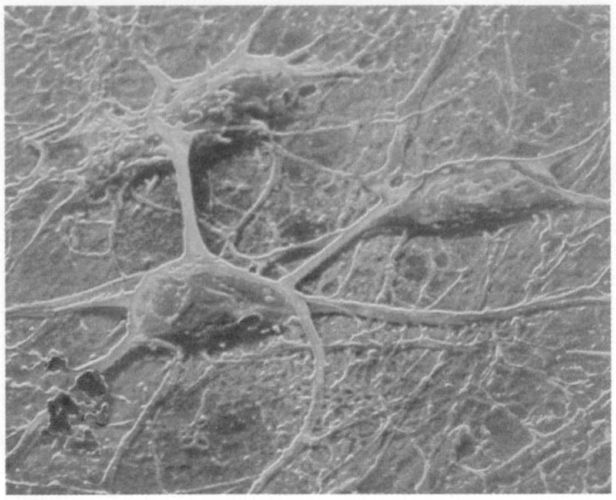

CNRI / PHOTO RESEARCHERS, INC

FIGURE 5.5

How Two Neurons Communicate The link between one neuron and another is shown in the simplified diagram at right. The infant brain actually contains billions of neurons, each with one axon and many dendrites. Every electrochemical message to or from the brain causes thousands of neurons to fire, each transmitting the message across the synapse to neighboring neurons. The electron micrograph directly above shows neurons greatly magnified, with their tangled but highly organized and well-coordinated sets of dendrites and axons.

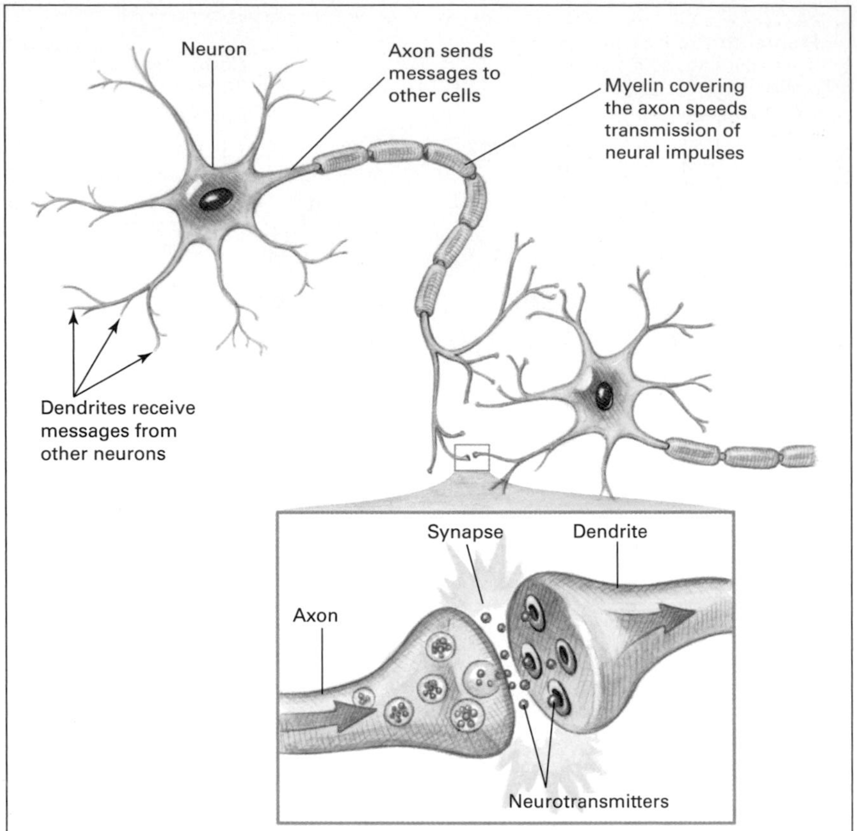

In the synapse, or intersection between an axon and dendrite, neurotransmitters carry information from one neuron to another.

Exuberance and Pruning

At birth, the brain contains at least 100 billion neurons, more than a person needs. By contrast, the newborn's brain has far fewer dendrites and synapses than the person will eventually possess. During the first months and years, rapid growth and refinement in axons, dendrites, and synapses occur, especially in the cortex. Dendrite growth is the major reason that brain weight triples from birth to age 2 (Johnson, 2011).

An estimated fivefold increase in dendrites in the cortex occurs in the 24 months after birth, with about 100 trillion synapses being present at age 2. This extensive postnatal brain growth is highly unusual for mammals. It is biologically necessary, given the large human brain and the relatively small human pelvis, but it also requires lengthy protection and feeding from adults, not needed by other animals (Konner, 2010). This early dendrite growth is called **transient exuberance:** *exuberant* because it is so rapid and *transient* because some of it is temporary. The expansive growth of dendrites is followed by **pruning** (see Figure 5.6), in which unused connections atrophy and die (Stiles & Jernigan, 2010), just as a gardener might prune a rose bush by cutting away parts to enable more, or more beautiful, roses to bloom.

transient exuberance The great but temporary increase in the number of dendrites that develop in an infant's brain during the first two years of life.

pruning When applied to brain development, the process by which unused connections in the brain atrophy and die.

Transient exuberance enables neurons to connect to, and communicate with, a greatly expanding number of other neurons within the brain. Synapses, dendrites, and probably neurons continue to form and die throughout life, more rapidly in infancy than at any other postnatal time (Stiles & Jernigan, 2010). Thinking and learning require connections among many parts of the brain. For example, to understand any sentence in this text, you need to know the letters, the words, the surrounding text, the ideas they convey, and how they relate to your other thoughts and experiences. Baby brains have the same requirements—no wonder it takes years to learn to read (see the Thinking Critically feature in Chapter 6).

Experience Shapes the Brain

The specifics of brain structure and growth depend on genes and maturation but even more on experience (Stiles & Jernigan, 2010). Infant brain organization itself depends partly on input, and some dendrites wither away because they are never used—that is, no experiences have caused them to send a message to other neurons. Expansion and pruning of dendrites occur for every aspect of early experience, from noticing musical rhythms to understanding emotions (Scott et al., 2007).

Strangely enough, this loss of dendrites increases brainpower. The space between neurons in the human brain—especially in regions for advanced, abstract thought—is far greater than the space in chimpanzee brains (Miller, 2010). It may seem logical that the more densely packed neurons of chimps would make them smarter than people, but the opposite is true. The probable explanation is that having more space for dendrite formation allows more connections as well as more pruning, thus fostering complex thinking. Further evidence of the benefit of cell death comes from one of the sad symptoms of fragile X syndrome (described in Chapter 3), "a persistent failure of normal synapse pruning" (Irwin et al., 2002, p. 194). Affected children become mentally retarded without this pruning; their dendrites are too dense and long, making thinking difficult.

Thus, pruning is essential. Normally, as brains mature, the process of extending and eliminating dendrites is exquisitely attuned to experience, as the appropriate links in the brain are established, protected, and strengthened. As with the rose bush, pruning needs to be done carefully, allowing further growth. Without certain experiences, some pruning may occur that limits later thought rather than aiding it. One group of scientists speculates that "lack of normative experiences may lead to overpruning of neurons and synapses, both of which may lead to reduction of brain activity" (Moulson et al., 2009, p. 1051).

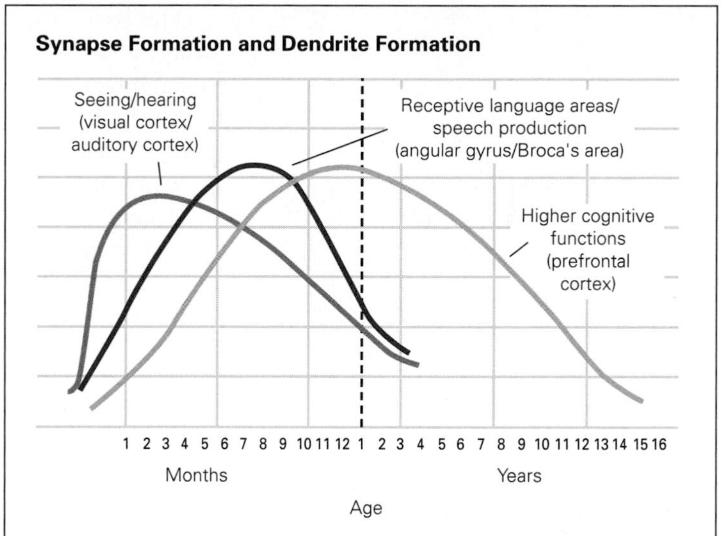

Source: Adapted from R. A. Thompson & Nelson, 2001, p. 8.

FIGURE 5.6

Brain Growth in Response to Experience These curves show the rapid rate of experience-dependent synapse formation for three functions of the brain (senses, language, and analysis). After the initial increase, the underused neurons are gradually pruned, or inactivated, as no functioning dendrites are formed from them.

Observation Quiz Why do both "12 months" and "1 year" appear on the "Age" line? (see answer, page 137)

Necessary and Possible Experiences

What are those needed "normative experiences"? A scientist named William Greenough identified two experience-related aspects of brain development (Greenough et al., 1987):

- **Experience-expectant brain function.** Certain functions require basic experiences in order to develop, just as a tree requires water. Those experiences are part of almost every infant's life, and thus almost every human brain grows as human genes direct. Brains need and expect such experiences; development would suffer without them.
- **Experience-dependent brain function.** Some brain functions depend on particular experiences. These specific experiences are not essential: They happen to infants in some families and cultures but not in others. Because of experience-dependent experiences, humans can be quite different from one another, yet all fully human.

experience-expectant brain functions Brain functions that require certain basic common experiences (which an infant can be expected to have) in order to develop normally.

experience-dependent brain functions Brain functions that depend on particular, variable experiences and that therefore may or may not develop in a particular infant.

The basic, expected experiences *must* happen for normal brain maturation to occur, and they almost always do. For example, in deserts and in the Arctic, on isolated farms and in crowded cities, almost all babies have things to see, objects to manipulate, and people to love them. Babies everywhere welcome such experiences: They look around, they grab for objects, they smile at people. As a result, baby brains develop.

In contrast, dependent experiences *might* happen; because of them, one brain differs from another. Experiences vary, such as which language babies hear, what faces they see, whether curiosity is encouraged, or how their mother reacts to frustration. *Depending* on those particulars, infant brains are structured and connected one way or another; some dendrites grow and some neurons thrive while others die (Stiles & Jernigan, 2010). Consequently, experience-expectant events make all people similar, yet everyone is unique because each undergoes particular experience-dependent experiences as well.

One of the conclusions from research using twins to ascertain the effect of socioeconomic status (SES) and intelligence is that early on, until about 10 months, experience-expectant circumstances (things to see, people to love) are as likely to be provided—or not—in families of every income level. After that age, however, babies from high-SES families are more likely to be encouraged to explore, talk, and play. Consequently, for them, genetics, which vary more than context (which is adequate for all high-SES twins) causes intellectual differences between one twin and another.

However, some low-SES families encourage cognition and some do not, differences that may emerge especially when the families have toddler twins to raise. Because of wide variations among low-income families, the family context is a more powerful influence than genes on the IQ of low-income toddlers. In other words, all 1-year-olds need some basic stimulation and attention to develop their full genetic capacity, and those basic requirements are usually met by wealthy families (who can afford individualized child care, even with twins) but not necessarily by poorer families (perhaps especially those with twins) (Tucker-Drob et al., 2011). (See the Research Design.)

Research Design

Scientists: Elliot M. Tucker-Drob, Mijke Rhemtulla, K. Paige Harden, Eric Turkheimer, and David Fask.

Publication: *Psychological Science* (2011).

Participants: The data for this study came from 750 pairs of twins (about one-fourth of them monozygotic) who were part of the Early Childhood Longitudinal Study, which began with 14,000 newborns from throughout the United States who were chosen to be representative of all economic levels and ethnicities. As you remember from Chapter 3, comparing monozygotic and dizygotic twins enables researchers to track genetic similarities and differences.

Design: Mothers and fathers were asked about their education, occupation, and income, and SES was calculated on a continuum from very low (e.g., no more than a sixth-grade education, both parents) to very high (e.g., professional degrees, both parents). Infants were tested on the Bayley Scales (tests developed by Nancy Bayley to measure development in the first years of life) at 10 months and again at 24 months. The mental scores (such as whether the infant could pull a string to ring a bell, could put three cubes in a cup on demand), not the motor scores (such as whether the infant could walk and run), were used to calculate intelligence.

Results: All the infants were much more capable at 24 months than at 10 months, as expected. Average intelligence did not correlate with SES at 10 months, but it did at 24 months. The variances in mental ability (i.e., the differences between one infant and another) at 10 months of age were traced primarily to the family environment (called a *shared environment,* the same for both twins), no matter what the SES; however, by 24 months of age, genetic differences were an important source of variance among high-SES but not among low-SES families. For them, environmental influences remained pivotal.

Comments: Remember from Chapter 3 that genetic differences emerge when basic needs are met, since a certain foundation is necessary before a child's genes can be fully expressed. (For example, genetic differences in height are obvious when every child is well fed.) This research suggests that, between 10 and 24 months, some low-income families do not provide the expected experiences for both twins that would enable all the brain growth that the genes allow.

As with conclusions from any one study, caution is needed. This research may overestimate SES similarities and differences for two reasons: (1) Intellectual tests are less reliable at 10 months than later in childhood, and (2) all families are challenged by twins, so low-income families may provide "expected experiences" for the brains of single-born toddlers, even if not for twins.

Nonetheless, the basic conclusion—that genes are more influential on the intellectual growth of advantaged children and environment is more crucial for the intellectual growth of low-income children—may be valid. Research on older children also finds notable variability in low-income households in opportunities for intellectual growth (Harden et al., 2007; Turkheimer et al., 2003). Might some low-SES children, born to become intellectual stars, never reach their potential? That is a conclusion reached by many experts on gifted children (Dai, 2010).

Examples from Bird Brains

The distinction between essential and variable input to the brain's networks can be made for all mammals. Some of the most persuasive research has been done with songbirds. All male songbirds have a brain region dedicated to listening and reproducing sounds (experience-expectant), but birds of the same species that happen to live in different locations produce slightly different songs (experience-dependent) (Konner, 2010). This is not unlike regional accents, as with English-speaking adults who grew up in Kingston or Kansas, or, for that matter, one neighborhood of Boston or another.

Birds inherit genes that produce the brain cells they need, which might be neurons dedicated to learning new songs (canaries) or to finding hidden seeds (chickadees). For the dendrites and neurons to connect, birds depend on specific experiences with song-learning or seed-finding (Barinaga, 2003). A human example comes from face recognition: All infants need to see faces (experience-expectant), but which particular face differences they learn to notice depends on who they see (experience-dependent), as the following explains.

>> Answer to Observation Quiz (from page 135) "One year" signifies the entire year, from day 365 to day 729, and that is indicated by its location between "12 months" and "2 years."

A VIEW FROM SCIENCE

Face Recognition

If you were in an unfamiliar city, walking down a strange street with thousands of other people, and you chanced to see a close friend from your hometown, would you recognize him or her? Of course (unless you are one of those unfortunate few who have an impairment called prosopagnosia, or face blindness). A part of the brain is astonishingly adept at face recognition, and past experiences trigger immediate recognition, as in this example when an adult sees a friend.

The *fusiform face area* is that crucial part of the brain, both experience-expectant and experience-dependent. The specifics are fascinating, which is why "face perception remains one of the most intensively researched areas in psychology" (Slater et al., 2010, p. 205). Most research has occurred in the past decade, as scientists try to figure out why a person would recognize a friend (one in 7 billion humans who might be on that street)—an awesome, taken-for-granted ability.

We now know that the fusiform face area of the brain is active in newborns, who respond to monkey faces as well as human ones and to visual stimuli (e.g., photos and toys with faces) as well as live faces. Soon, experiences refine face perception (de Heering et al., 2010). For example, 2-month-olds recognize their mothers and fathers, 3-month-olds pay close attention to faces they have never seen before, 6-month-olds ignore details of monkey faces because they have learned not to care (M. H. Johnson, 2005). (Researchers have learned all this by showing infants several faces and timing how long they look at each one.)

Before their first birthday, infants more readily notice differences among faces from their own species and their own ethnic group (called *own-race effect*) than among faces of other species and groups, and most distinguish female faces more readily than male ones (Slater et al., 2010). The own-race effect persists throughout life, handicapping adults who have always known people of one ethnicity if they try to recognize individuals from another group or even to read facial expressions of joy or anger in people from an unfamiliar culture.

Research finds that the own-race effect is the result of limited multiethnic experience, not innate prejudice against those who look different from oneself. One study found that genetic Koreans who were adopted early in life by European Americans were better at distinguishing non-Asian faces than Korean ones (Sangrigoli et al., 2005). Many adoptive parents now seek out members of their children's ethnic group, to help their children with ethnic identity later on. That may explain the result of a recent study of Asian adoptees: It was found that they were adept at distinguishing faces of both their native and adopted ethnic groups, unlike people who had been raised in communities that included only one ethnic group (de Heering et al., 2010).

The importance of early experience is also evident in two more studies. In one (Scott & Monesson, 2010), infants from 6 to 9 months were repeatedly (more than 30 times) shown a book of pictures of six monkey faces, each with a name written on the page (see photo). For one-third of the babies, the parents were told to read the names as they showed the pictures; another one-third of the parents were told to say only "monkey" as they showed each page; and for the final one-third, no verbal label was given. At 9 months, all the infants were shown pictures of six other monkeys, and their gaze patterns were closely tracked. Those infants who were repeatedly exposed to named monkeys were better at distinguishing one new monkey from another than were the infants who saw the same picture book but did not hear each monkey's name.

The second example begins with the fact that many children and adults fail to notice the individuality of newborns. Some even claim that "all babies look alike." However, one study found that 3-year-olds with younger siblings were much better at recognizing differences between photos of unfamiliar newborns than were 3-year-olds with no younger brothers or sisters (Cassia et al., 2009). Experience mattered.

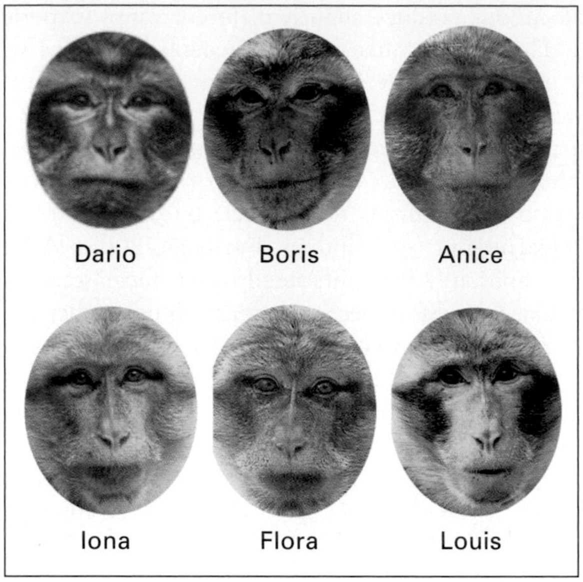

REPRINTED FROM NEUROPSYCHOLOGIA, FIG. 1. EXPERIENCE-DEPENDENT NEURAL SPECIALIZATION

Iona Is Not Flora If you heard that Dario was quite different from Louis or Boris, would you stare at unfamiliar monkey faces more closely in the future? For 6-month-olds, the answer is yes.

The ability to differentiate faces improves with age—you are now quicker to recognize your best friend than you were as a child. Distinguishing individual faces is best learned via early exposure, but adults can learn to recognize individuals of other ethnic groups or even individual animals of the same species or breed. This recognition takes slightly longer without early experience involving dozens of named individuals from that group, but it is never too late to learn. Infancy is a sensitive period, but plasticity is lifelong.

Harming the Infant Brain

Thus far, we have focused on the many normal variations that families offer babies; most infants develop well within their culture. For brain development, it does not matter whether a person learns French or Farsi, or expresses emotions dramatically or subtly (e.g., throwing themselves to the floor or merely pursing their lips, a cultural difference). However, the research has also found that infant brains do not develop well if they do not have the basic experiences that all humans need.

Lack of Stimulation

To begin with, infants need stimulation. Playing with a young baby, allowing varied sensations, and encouraging movement (arm waving in the early months, walking later on) are all fodder for brain connections. Severe lack of stimulation stunts the brain, as has been shown many times, not only with mice but also with humans. As one review explains, "enrichment and deprivation studies provide powerful evidence of . . . widespread effects of experience on the complexity and function of the developing system" (Stiles & Jernigan, 2010, p. 345).

This does not mean that babies require spinning, buzzing, multitextured and multicolored toys. In fact, infants can be overstimulated as well; they usually cry or go to sleep when that happens, as a way of avoiding the bombardment. Perhaps for that reason, there is no evidence that overstimulation harms the brain. It may, however, be wasted time and money; an infant can be fascinated by a simple object, intrigued by a smiling face.

Stress and the Brain

In addition to lack of stimulation, some specific experiences are particularly harmful, especially in the first six months (Jansen et al., 2010). If the brain produces an overabundance of stress hormones early in life (as when an infant is frequently terrified, or when the whole family experiences a massive earthquake and flood), sometimes that damages the brain's later functioning. The brain might produce either too many stress hormones, making the child and then the adult hypervigilant (always on the alert), or too few, making the person emotionally flat (never happy, sad, or angry). Note that this is an emotional response, not necessarily caused by physical pain: An infant might be terrified (by yelling, frightening faces, witnessed abuse) without directly being hurt.

Exactly how and when this happens is not yet clear; research finds conflicting conclusions (Jansen et al., 2010). Some stress seems part of every infant's life: It may even be experience-expectant. But there is a limit to how much stress an infant can accommodate. Years later, a kindergarten teacher might notice that one child becomes furious or terrified at a slight provocation and another child seems indifferent to everything. Why? In both cases, the underlying cause could be excessive stress-hormone production in infancy, changing how that child's brain responds to stress. It is also possible, with differential sensitivity, that some infants are unharmed by a stressful early life—but, of course, no infant should experience that risk (Sapienza & Masten, 2011).

Shaken Baby Syndrome

Another example is much more direct, the consequence of adults who do not understand the immaturity of the infant brain. Because the prefrontal cortex has not yet developed, telling infants to stop crying is pointless because they cannot *decide* to stop crying. Such decisions require brain maturity not yet present. Some adults react by shaking a baby. This can cause **shaken baby syndrome,** a life-threatening condition that occurs when infants are shaken back and forth sharply and quickly. Shaking stops the crying because blood vessels in the brain rupture and neural connections break. Pediatricians consider shaken baby syndrome an example of *abusive head trauma* (Christian et al., 2009).

shaken baby syndrome A life-threatening injury that occurs when an infant is forcefully shaken back and forth, a motion that ruptures blood vessels in the brain and breaks neural connections.

Not every infant who has neurological symptoms of head trauma is the victim of abuse. Nonetheless, in the United States, brain scans show that more than one in five of all children hospitalized for maltreatment (broken bones, burns, and so on) also suffers from shaken baby syndrome (Rovi et al., 2004).

Severe Social Deprivation

The developmental community was stunned and saddened by the discovery of a girl named Genie, born in 1957. Genie spent most of her childhood tied to a chair, never hearing human speech (her father barked and growled at her) or feeling love, because her parents were severely disturbed. After being rescued at age 13, she eventually responded to affection and learned to speak, but she never developed normally. Most developmentalists concluded that her normal experiences came too late; her brain had already passed the sensitive period for development of many abilities.

But Genie was just one person, and as you remember from Chapter 1, one case is not proof of any general principle. Perhaps Genie had been born brain-damaged. Or perhaps her early care after the rescue was itself traumatic (Rymer, 1993).

More research, with more participants, was needed but would be unethical to perform with humans. Consequently, Marion Diamond, William Greenough, and their colleagues studied some "deprived" rats (raised alone in small, barren cages) and compared them with "enriched" rats (raised in large cages with other rats as well as toys). At autopsy, the brains of the enriched rats were larger and heavier, with more dendrites (M. Diamond, 1988; Greenough & Volkmar, 1973). Much

A Fortunate Pair Elaine Himelfarb (shown in the background), of San Diego, California, is shown here in Bucharest to adopt 22-month-old Maria. This joyous moment may be repeated through Maria's childhood—or maybe not.

research with other mammals confirms that isolation and sensory deprivation harm the developing brain, including social and emotional development. This is further explored with longitudinal studies of orphans from Romania, as described in Chapter 7.

Intervention

The fact that infant brains respond to their circumstances suggests that waiting until a young child is evidently mistreated is waiting too long. In the first months of life, babies adjust to their world, becoming withdrawn and quiet if their caregivers are depressed or becoming loud and demanding if that is the only way they get fed. Such adjustments help babies survive but set patterns that are destructive later on. Thus, understanding development as dynamic and interactive means helping caregivers from the start, not waiting until destructive patterns are established (Tronick & Beegly, 2011).

A program to do this, beginning with high-risk mothers *before* any evidence of problems arose and including individualized support that did not require the mothers to leave their homes, resulted in less stress for the mothers and improved language development in the infants (Lowell et al., 2011). Developmentalists want this for every infant, either formally as in this program, or informally as when a relative or a neighbor helps a new mother with whatever she needs.

Implications for Caregivers

Developmental discoveries about early brain development have many implications for loving, low-risk caregivers as well as those at high risk. First, since each brain region follows a sequence of growing, connecting, and pruning, it helps to know which developmental events are experience-expectant and when those expectations arise.

For example, proliferation and pruning begin at about 4 months in the visual and auditory cortexes, which explains why very young infants are attentive to sights and sounds. Consequently, remedies for blind or deaf infants should occur early in life to prevent atrophy of those brain regions that expect sights and sounds. Hearing-impaired infants whose difficulties are recognized and remediated with cochlear implants become more adept at understanding and expressing language than those with the same losses but later implants. Brain expectancy is the reason (Kennedy et al., 2006).

The language areas of the brain develop most rapidly between the ages of 6 and 24 months; that is when infants need to hear speech in order to talk fluently. In fact, speech heard between 6 and 12 months helps infants recognize the characteristics of their local language long before they utter a word (Saffran et al., 2006). On the other hand, some stimulation is meaningless before the brain is ready. A 6-month-old might be uninterested in looking at a book, but a few months later book-reading may be a favorite activity. Infants respond to whatever their brains need; that's why musical mobiles, cars on the street, and, best of all, animated caregivers are fascinating.

This preference reflects **self-righting,** the inborn drive to remedy deficits. Infants with few toys develop their brains by using whatever is available. They do not need the latest educational playthings—their brains expect human interaction and whatever objects their parents find that interest them. Human brains are designed to grow and adapt; plasticity is apparent from the beginning of life (Tomalski & Johnson, 2010).

self-righting The inborn drive to remedy a developmental deficit; literally, to return to sitting or standing upright, after being tipped over. People of all ages have self-righting impulses, for emotional as well as physical imbalance.

Thus, how people respond to infants echoes lifelong. This means that caressing a newborn, talking to a preverbal infant, and showing affection toward a toddler may be essential to developing the child's full potential. If such experiences are missing, lifelong brain damage may result.

SUMMING UP

Brain growth is rapid during the first months of life, when dendrites and the synapses within the cortex increase exponentially. By age 2, the brain already weighs three-fourths of its adult weight. Pruning of underused and unconnected dendrites begins in the sensory and motor areas and then occurs in other areas. Although some brain development is maturational, experience is also essential—both the universal experiences that almost every infant has (experience-expectant brain development) and the particular experiences that reflect the child's family or culture (experience-dependent brain development). Infant brains need stimulation—though not so much as to become overwhelming—for the dendrites to grow and neurological connections to proliferate. ■

>> Sensation and Movement

You learned in Chapter 2 that Piaget called the first period of intelligence the *sensorimotor* stage, emphasizing that cognition develops from the senses and motor skills. The same concept—that infant brain development depends on sensory experiences and early activity—underlies the discussion you have just read. Experience molds the brain, and the brain allows sensory and motor experiences to occur (Fox et al., 2010).

The Senses

Every sense functions at birth. Human newborns have open eyes; sensitive ears; and responsive noses, tongues, and skin. Throughout their first year, infants use the senses to sort and classify everything they experience. Indeed, "infants spend the better part of their first year merely looking around" (Rovee-Collier, 2001, p. 35). As they look, they also listen, smell, taste, and touch anything they can, seeming to attend to everything without much focus or judgment. For instance, in the first months of life, they smile at strangers and put almost anything in their mouths (Adolph & Berger, 2005).

Why are they not more selective? Because sensation precedes perception. **Sensation** occurs when a sensory system detects a stimulus, as when the inner ear reverberates with sound or the retina and pupil of the eye intercept light. Thus, sensations begin when an outer organ (eye, ear, nose, tongue, or skin) meets anything that can be seen, heard, smelled, tasted, or touched. But what appear to be simple responses to every stimulus actually show some selection: Even newborns are attracted to social stimuli, preferring sensations from people over sensations from objects (Lloyd-Fox et al., 2009). They would rather suck your finger than a scrap of cloth; they settle for cloth when no finger is available.

sensation The response of a sensory system (eyes, ears, skin, tongue, nose) when it detects a stimulus.

Perception occurs when the brain notices and processes a sensation. This happens in the cortex, usually as the result of a message from one of the sensing organs. That message connects with past experience to suggest that a particular sensation might be worth interpreting (M. E. Diamond, 2007).

perception The mental processing of sensory information when the brain interprets a sensation. Perception occurs in the cortex.

Some sensations are beyond comprehension at first. A newborn has no idea that the letters on a page might have significance, that Mother's face should be distinguished from Father's, or that the smells of roses and garlic have different connotations. Perceptions require experience, either direct experience or messages from other people.

Infants' brains are especially attuned to their own repeated social experiences. Thus, a newborn named Emily has no concept that *Emily* is her name, but she has the brain and auditory capacity to hear sounds in the usual speech range (not the high sounds that only dogs can hear) and an inborn preference for repeated patterns and human speech, so she attends to people saying her name. At about 4 months, when her auditory cortex is rapidly creating and pruning dendrites, the repeated word *Emily* is perceived as well as sensed, especially because that sound emanates from the people Emily has learned to love (Saffran et al., 2006). Before 6 months, Emily may open her eyes and turn her head when her name is called. It will take many more months before she tries to say "Emmy" and still longer before she knows that *Emily* is indeed her name.

Especially for Parents of Grown Children Suppose you realize that you seldom talked to your children until they talked to you and that you never used a stroller or a walker but put them in cribs and playpens. Did you limit their brain growth and their sensory capacity? (see response, page 145)

Thus, perception follows sensation, when senses are noticed by the brain. Then cognition follows perception, when people think about what they have perceived. (Later, cognition no longer requires sensation: People imagine, fantasize, hypothesize.) The sequence from sensation to perception to cognition requires that an infant's sense organs function. No wonder the parts of the cortex dedicated to the senses develop rapidly: That is the prerequisite for human intellect. Now some details.

Hearing

The sense of hearing develops during the last trimester of pregnancy and is already quite acute at birth, when certain sounds trigger reflexes, even without conscious perception. Sudden noises startle newborns, making them cry; rhythmic sounds, such as a lullaby or a heartbeat, soothe them and put them to sleep.

A newborn's hearing can be checked with advanced equipment, routine at most hospitals in North America and Europe, since early remediation benefits deaf infants. Screening is needed later as well because some infants develop hearing losses in the early months (Harlor & Bower, 2009). Normally, even in the first days of life, infants turn their heads at a sound. Soon they can pinpoint the actual source of the noise.

Because of maturation of the language areas of the cortex, even 4-month-old infants particularly attend to voices, developing expectations of the rhythm, segmentation, and cadence of spoken words long before comprehension (Minagawa-

Kawai et al., 2011). As time goes on, sensitive hearing combines with the maturing brain to distinguish patterns of sounds and syllables. Infants become accustomed to the rules of their native language, such as which syllable is stressed (various dialects have different rules), whether changing inflection matters (as in Chinese), whether certain sound combinations are repeated, and so on. All this is based on very careful listening to human speech, even speech not directed toward them with words they do not yet understand.

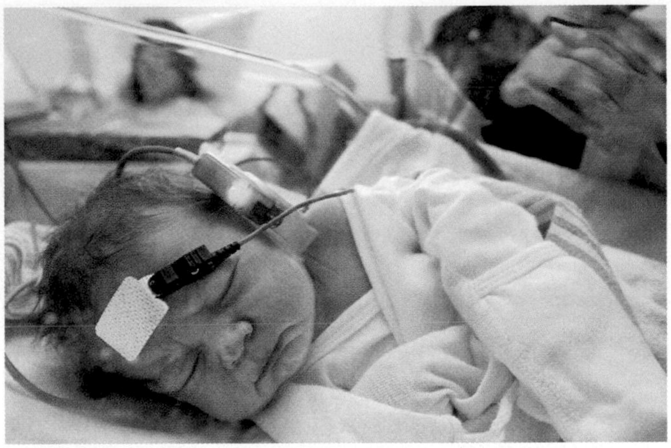

AP PHOTO / THE PLAIN DEALER, DAVID I. ANDERSEN

Before Leaving the Hospital As mandated by a 2004 Ohio law, 1-day-old Henry has his hearing tested via vibrations of the inner ear in response to various tones. The computer interprets the data and signals any need for more tests—as is the case for about 1 baby in 100. Normal newborns hear quite well; Henry's hearing was fine.

Seeing

Vision is the least mature sense at birth. Although the eyes open in mid-pregnancy and are sensitive to bright light (if the pregnant woman is sunbathing in a bikini, for instance), the fetus has nothing much to see. Newborns are legally blind; they focus only on things between 4 and 30 inches (10 and 75 centimeters) away (Bornstein et al., 2005).

Almost immediately, experience combines with maturation of the visual cortex to improve the ability to see shapes and then notice details, with vision improving so rapidly that researchers are hard-pressed to describe the day-by-day improvements (Dobson et al., 2009). By 2 months, infants look intently at a human face and, tentatively and fleetingly, smile at the person. (Smiling can occur earlier, but not as a direct response to something the baby sees.) Soon visual scanning becomes organized and more efficient, centered on important points. Thus, 3-month-olds look closely at the eyes and mouth, the parts of a face that contain the most information, and they prefer photos of faces with features over photos of faces with the features blanked out. They pay attention to patterns, colors, and motion (Kellman & Arterberry, 2006).

Binocular vision is the ability to coordinate the two eyes to see one image. Because using both eyes together is impossible in the womb (nothing is far enough away to need two eyes), many newborns seem to focus with one eye or the other, or to use their two eyes independently, momentarily appearing wall-eyed or cross-eyed. At about 14 weeks, the underlying brain mechanisms are activated, allowing binocular vision, with both eyes focused on a single thing (Atkinson & Braddick, 2003).

binocular vision The ability to focus the two eyes in a coordinated manner in order to see one image. This ability is absent at birth.

Smelling and Tasting

As with vision and hearing, the senses of smell and taste function at birth and rapidly adapt to the social world. Infants learn to appreciate whatever their mothers eat, first through the breast milk and then through smells and spoonfuls of whatever the family has for dinner. Some herbs and plants contain natural substances that are medicinal. The foods of a particular culture may aid survival: Bitter foods seem to provide some defense against malaria, spicy ones preserve food and thus work against food poisoning, and so on (Krebs, 2009). Thus, an infant's preference for whatever foods the family eats may be life-saving.

Families who eat foods that protected their community pass on those preferences to their children throughout childhood. Taste preferences endure when a person migrates to another culture or when historical circumstances change so that a particular food that was once protective is no longer so. Indeed, one reason for the obesity epidemic may be that when starvation was a threat, families sought high-fat foods; now their descendants still enjoy French fries, whipped cream, bacon, and so on.

Similar adaptation occurs for the sense of smell. As babies learn to recognize each person's scent, they prefer to sleep next to their caregivers, and they nuzzle

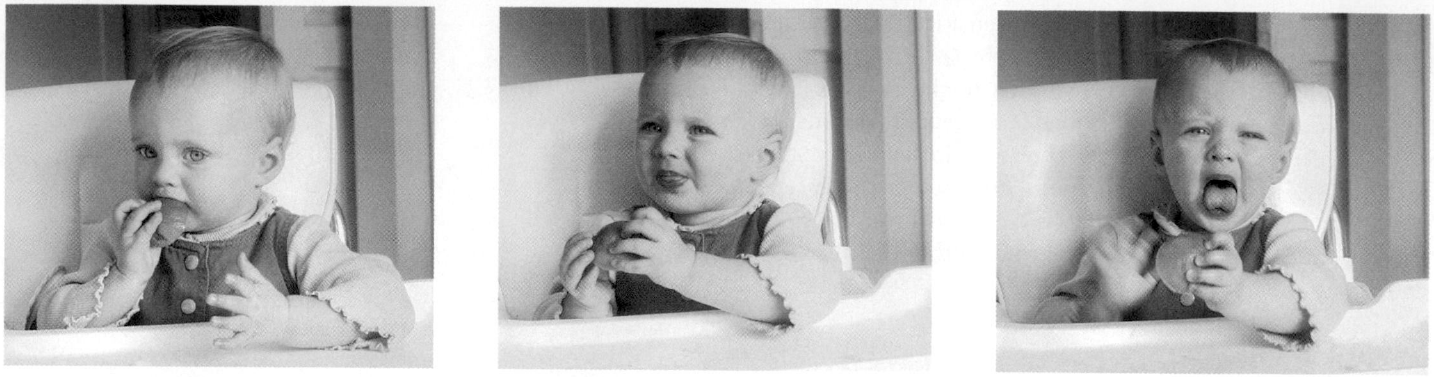

CINDY CHARLES / PHOTOEDIT, INC.

Learning About a Lime As with every other normal infant, Jacqueline's curiosity leads to taste and then to a slow reaction, from puzzlement to tongue-out disgust. Jacqueline's responses demonstrate that the sense of taste is acute in infancy and that quick brain reactions are still to come.

into their caregivers' chests—especially when the adults are shirtless. One way to help infants who are frightened of being given a bath (some love bathing, some hate it at first) is to take the baby into the bath with the parent. The smells of the adult's body mix with the smell of soap, making the experience comforting.

Touch and Pain

The sense of touch is acute in infants, with wrapping, rubbing, and cradling all soothing to many new babies. Some infants relax when held by their familiar caregiver, even when their eyes are closed. The ability to be comforted by touch is one of the important skills tested in the Brazelton Neonatal Behavioral Assessment Scale (NBAS, described in Chapter 4). Although almost all newborns respond to being securely held, over time they perceive what each touch communicates. Caressing, swaddling, kissing, massaging, tickling, bouncing, and rocking are each comforting to some infants, all involving the sense of touch as well as motion.

Pain is not usually considered one of the five senses, but it is often connected to touch. Some babies cry when being changed because cold on their skin is distressing, and some are upset when they need clean diapers, not because wetness itself is distressing but because a diaper rash is sensitive. Scientists are not certain about when and why infants feel pain. Certainly some things that are painful to adults (circumcision, setting a broken bone) seem much less so to newborns. For many medical procedures, from a pin-prick to minor surgery, a taste of sugar syrup right before the event is anesthetic: Infants typically cry lustily when their heel is pricked (routine after birth), but some remain calm if they have had a drop of sucrose (Harrison et al., 2010).

Basic Infant Care In many cultures, infant massage is considered an essential part of daily care, no less important than diapering or feeding. In other cultures, mothers attend classes to learn how best to touch their infants—firmly on the stomach, as shown here, or rhythmically moving the arms and legs, as these mothers will soon practice.

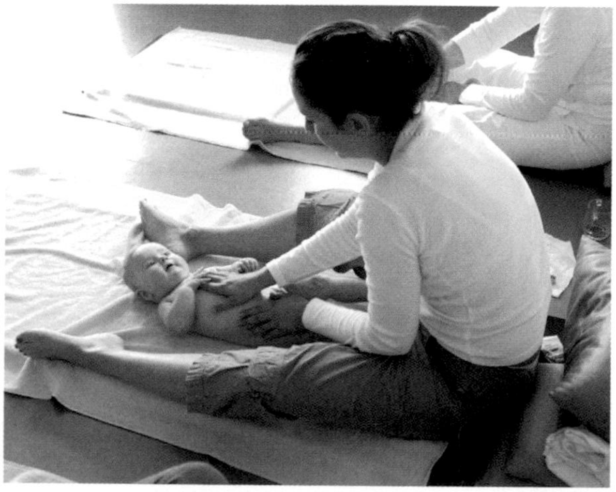

PICTURE PARTNERS / ALAMY

Some people argue that even the fetus can feel pain; others say that the sense of pain does not mature until months or years after birth. Many young infants cry for 10 minutes or more, with no obvious reason or effective consolation: Digestive pain is the usual explanation. Many infants seem distressed and in pain before their first tooth erupts: Teething is the explanation. That is difficult to ascertain, however, because crying may not reliably indicate pain. Certainly it does not in adults.

Many physiological measures, including stress hormones in the bloodstream and erratic beating of the heart, are being explored to measure infant pain. Recent research has focused on brain patterns as indicators of pain in premature infants, who typically experience numerous procedures that would be painful to an adult (Holsti et al., 2011). Some argue that infants should be given anesthetics; others say this would slow down breathing, a needless risk. We know from developmental studies that infants are unlike adults in many ways: It is a mistake to assume that they never feel pain, and it is equally wrong to assume that they feel pain as an adult might.

>> Response for Parents of Grown Children (from page 142) Probably not. Experience-expectant brain development is programmed to occur for all infants, requiring only the stimulation that virtually all families provide—warmth, reassuring touch, overheard conversation, facial expressions, movement. Extras such as baby talk, music, exercise, mobiles, and massage may be beneficial but are not essential.

Dynamic Sensory Systems

The entire package of sensations furthers two goals: social interaction (to respond to familiar caregivers) and comfort (to be soothed amid the disturbances of infant life). The most important experiences are perceived with interacting senses, in dynamic systems (see Chapter 1). Breast milk, for instance, is a mild sedative, so the newborn literally feels happier at mother's breast, connecting that pleasure with taste, touch, smell, and sight. Young human infants are, physiologically, an unusual combination of immaturity (they cannot walk) and sensitivity (their senses function at birth, unlike the many animals who are born with eyes closed). This combination aids social connections between infants and adults (Konner, 2010).

Infants respond to motion as well as to sights and sounds. Many new parents soothe their baby's distress by rocking, carrying, or even driving (with the baby in a safety seat) while crooning a lullaby; here again, infant comfort is connected with social interaction. Massage is especially calming when infants realize that the touch comes from a familiar caregiver who simultaneously provides auditory and visual stimulation. Even vacuuming the carpet with the baby in a sling may quiet a fussy baby because steady noise, changing sights, and carrying combine to soothe distress.

By 6 months, infants have learned to coordinate the senses, expecting lip movements to synchronize with speech, for instance (Lewkowicz, 2010). In sum, infant senses are immature, but each is part of a dynamic system of stimulation, functioning together as babies join the human family.

Motor Skills

We now come to the most visible and dramatic advances of infancy, those that ultimately allow the child to "stand tall and walk proud." Thanks to ongoing changes in size and proportion and to increasing brain maturation, infants markedly improve their **motor skills,** the movement abilities that are needed to control actions.

motor skills The learned abilities to move some part of the body, in actions ranging from a large leap to a flicker of the eyelid. (The word *motor* here refers to movement of muscles.)

Gross Motor Skills

Deliberate actions that coordinate many parts of the body, producing large movements, are called **gross motor skills.** These emerge directly from reflexes (discussed in Chapter 4) and proceed in a cephalocaudal and proximodistal direction. Infants first control their heads, lifting them up to look around or turning them from one side to another. Then they control their upper bodies, their arms, and finally their legs and feet.

gross motor skills Physical abilities involving large body movements, such as walking and jumping. (The word *gross* here means "big.")

Crawling is one example. As you remember from Chapter 4, when placed on their stomachs, many newborns reflexively lift their heads and move their arms and legs as if they were swimming. As they gain muscle strength, infants wiggle, attempting to move forward by pushing their arms, shoulders, and upper bodies against whatever surface they are lying on. Usually by 5 months or so, they become able to use their arms, and then legs, to inch forward (or sometimes backward) on their bellies. That is a gross motor skill.

Between 8 and 10 months after birth, most infants become able to lift their midsections and crawl (or *creep,* as the British call it) on "all fours," coordinating

CATHARINA VAN DEN DIKKENBERG / ISTOCKPHOTO

Young Expert This infant is an adept crawler. Note the coordination between hands and knees as well as the arm and leg strength needed to support the body in this early version of push-ups. This boy will probably become an expert walker and runner, as do many babies who bypass the crawling phase altogether.

the movements of their hands and knees in a smooth, balanced manner. Crawling is experience-dependent. Some normal babies never do it, especially if the floor is cold, hot, or rough, or if they have always lain on their backs (Pin et al., 2007). It is not true that babies *must* crawl to develop normally. All babies figure out some way to move before they can walk (inching, bear-walking, scooting, creeping, or crawling), but many resist "tummy time" by rolling over and fussing (Adolph & Berger, 2005). Overweight babies master gross motor skills later than thinner babies do (Slining et al., 2010).

Sitting also develops gradually, a matter of developing the muscles to steady the top half of the body. By 3 months, babies have sufficient muscle control to be lap-sitters if the lap's owner provides supportive arms. By 6 months, they can usually sit unsupported. Walking progresses from reflexive, hesitant, adult-supported stepping to a smooth, coordinated gait. Some children step while holding on at 9 months, stand alone momentarily at 10 months, and walk well, unassisted, at 12 months. Three factors combine to allow toddlers to walk (Adolph et al., 2003):

1. *Muscle strength.* Newborns with skinny legs and infants buoyed by water make stepping movements, but 6-month-olds on dry land do not; their legs are too chubby for their underdeveloped muscles.
2. *Brain maturation within the motor cortex.* The first leg movements—kicking (alternating legs at birth and then kicking both legs together or one leg repeatedly at about 3 months)—occur without much thought or aim. As the brain matures, deliberate leg action becomes possible.
3. *Practice.* Unbalanced, wide-legged, short strides become a steady, smooth gait after hours of practice.

RICK GOMEZ / MASTERFILE

Bossa Nova Baby? This boy in Brazil demonstrates his joy at acquiring the gross motor skill of walking, which quickly becomes dancing whenever music plays.

Once the first two developments have made walking possible, infants become passionate walkers, logging those needed hours of practice. They take steps on many surfaces, barefoot or wearing socks, slippers, or shoes. They resist being pushed in their strollers when they can walk.

> Walking infants practice keeping balance in upright stance and locomotion for more than 6 accumulated hours per day. They average between 500 and 1,500 walking steps per hour so that by the end of each day, they have taken 9,000 walking steps and traveled the length of 29 football fields.
>
> *[Adolph et al., 2003, p. 494]*

Fine Motor Skills

fine motor skills Physical abilities involving small body movements, especially of the hands and fingers, such as drawing and picking up a coin. (The word *fine* here means "small.")

Small body movements are called **fine motor skills.** Finger movements are fine motor skills, enabling humans to write, draw, type, tie, and so on. Movements of the tongue, jaw, lips, and toes are fine movements, too.

Actually, mouth skills precede finger skills by many months, and skillful grabbing with the toes sometimes precedes grabbing with the hands (Adolph & Berger, 2005). However, hand skills are more valued by society. Every culture encourages finger dexterity, so children practice finger movements. By contrast, skilled spitting or chewing is not praised; even mastery of blowing bubble gum is admired only by other children.

Regarding finger skills, newborns have a strong reflexive grasp but lack hand and finger control. During their first 2 months, babies excitedly stare and wave their arms at objects dangling within reach. By 3 months, they can usually touch such objects, but they cannot yet grab and hold on unless an object is placed in their hands, partly because their eye–hand coordination is limited.

By 4 months, infants sometimes grab, but their timing is off: They close their hands too early or too late. Finally, by 6 months, with a concentrated, deliberate stare, most babies can reach for, grab at, and hold almost any object that is of the right size. Some can even transfer an object from one hand to the other. Almost all can hold a bottle, shake a rattle, and yank a sister's braids. Once grabbing is possible, babies practice it enthusiastically: "from 6 to 9 months, reaching appears as a quite compulsive behaviour for small objects presented within arm's reach" (Atkinson & Braddick, 2003, p. 58).

Toward the end of the first year and throughout the second, finger skills improve, as babies master the pincer movement (using thumb and forefinger to pick up tiny objects) and self-feeding (first with hands, then fingers, then utensils) (Ho, 2010). In the second year, grabbing becomes more selective. Toddlers learn when *not* to pull at a sister's braids, or Mommy's earrings, or Daddy's glasses. However, as you will learn in Chapter 6, the curiosity of the "little scientist" may overwhelm this inhibition.

RADIUS IMAGES / GLOW IMAGES

Sensory Exuberance Human animals are unusual in that all the senses function at birth, but motor skills develop slowly. This Toronto boy loves to taste and bite the toy designed for looking (that bull's eye) and grabbing (those plastic rings), even though he cannot yet sit up unsupported.

Cultural Variations

All healthy infants develop skills in the same sequence, but the age of acquisition varies. At About This Time shows age norms for gross motor skills, based on a large, representative, multiethnic sample of U.S. infants. When infants are grouped by ethnicity, generally African Americans are ahead of Latinos, who are ahead of babies of European descent. Internationally, the earliest walkers are in Africa, where many well-nourished and healthy babies walk at 10 months. The latest walkers may be in France.

What accounts for this variation? The power of genes is suggested not only by ethnic differences but also by identical twins, who begin to walk on the same day more often than fraternal twins do. Striking individual differences are apparent in infants' strategies, effort, and concentration in mastering motor skills, again suggesting something inborn (Thelen & Corbetta, 2002).

But much more than genes contribute to variations, as the example that opened this chapter shows. Cultural patterns affect acquisition of every sensory and motor skill. For instance, early reflexes may not fade if culture and conditions allow extensive practice. This has been demonstrated with legs (the stepping reflex), hands (the grasping reflex), and crawling (the swimming reflex). Senses and motor skills are part of a complex and dynamic system in which practice counts (Thelen & Corbetta, 2002). Nutrition makes a difference as well: Both malnourished and overweight children are slower to develop motor skills.

AT ABOUT THIS TIME
Age Norms (in Months) for Gross Motor Skills

Skill	When 50% of All Babies Master the Skill (months)	When 95% of All Babies Master the Skill (months)
Sit, head steady	3	4
Sit, unsupported	6	7
Pull to stand (holding on)	9	10
Stand alone	12	14
Walk well	13	15
Walk backward	15	17
Run	18	20
Jump up	26	29

Note: As the text explains, age norms are affected by culture and cohort. These are U.S. norms, mostly for European Americans. Mastering skills a few weeks earlier or later does not indicate health or intelligence. Being very late, however, is a cause for concern.

Source: Coovadia & Wittenberg, 2004; based on Denver II (Frankenburg et al., 1992).

Observation Quiz Which of these skills has the greatest variation in age of acquisition? Why? (see answer, page 148)

YOUNG-WOLFF PHOTOGRAPHY / ALAMY

Modern Equipment She sleeps peacefully in San Diego in 2010. A cradle board is designed to keep infants safe, warm, and near their parents—a more mobile piece of baby furniture than the crib or playpen.

Cross-cultural research finds that some caregivers (including Jamaican ones like Mrs. Todd, who cared for my youngest daughter) provide rhythmic stretching exercises for their infants as part of daily care; their infants are among the world's youngest walkers (Adolph & Berger, 2005). Other cultures discourage or even prevent infants from crawling or walking. The people of Bali, Indonesia, never let their infants crawl, because babies are considered divine and crawling is for animals (Diener, 2000). Similar reasoning appeared in colonial America, where "standing stools" were designed for children so they could strengthen their legs without sitting or crawling (Calvert, 2003).

By contrast, the Beng people of the Ivory Coast are proud when their babies start to crawl but do not let them walk until at least 1 year. Although the Beng do not recognize the connection, one reason for this prohibition may be birth control: Beng mothers do not resume sexual relations until their baby takes a first step (Gottlieb, 2000).

Although variation in the timing of the development of motor skills is normal, slow development relative to the norm within an infant's ethnic group suggests that attention should be paid: Early visual, auditory, and motor difficulties are much easier to remedy than the same problems discovered later in childhood. Remember the dynamic systems of senses and motor skills: If one aspect of the system lags behind, the other parts may as well. On the other hand, early walkers are thrilled to have within reach dozens of objects they were unable to explore before—caregivers beware.

>> Answer to Observation Quiz (from page 147) Jumping up, with a three-month age range for acquisition. The reason is that the older an infant is, the more impact culture has.

SUMMING UP

The five senses (seeing, hearing, smelling, tasting, touching) function at birth, although hearing is far superior to vision, probably because of experience: The fetus has much more to hear than to see. After birth, vision develops rapidly, leading to binocular vision at about the 14th week. The sense of pain seems less acute in newborns than in adults, with sugar often an effective analgesic. More research is needed to measure infant pain—and to relieve it. By one year, infants heed stimuli from all the sense organs; sensitive perception and preferences for the familiar are evident. The senses work together and are particularly attuned to human interaction.

Motor skills begin with reflexes but quickly expand to include various body movements. Infants lift their heads, then sit, then stand, then walk and run. Sensory and motor skills interact in dynamic systems, with each ability affecting all the others. Skills follow a genetic and maturational timetable, but they are also powerfully influenced by experiences, guided by caregivers and culture, and by practice, which infants do as much as their immature and top-heavy bodies allow. Fine motor skills, especially hand skills, mature over the first two years, although many more years of practice and maturation are needed before children can do the simple actions that adults take for granted. ▪

>> Surviving in Good Health

Although precise worldwide statistics are unavailable, at least 10 billion children were born between 1950 and 2010. More than 2 billion of them died before age 5. Although 2 billion is far too many, twice as many would have died without recent public health measures. As best we know, in earlier centuries more than half of all newborns died in infancy.

In the twenty-first century, most people live to adulthood. In the healthiest nations, 99.9 percent who survive the first month (when the sickest and smallest newborns may die) live to age 15, and most live for decades more. Even in the poorest nations, where a few decades ago half the children died, now about three-fourths live (see Table 5.1).

The world death rate in the first five years of life has dropped about 2 percent per year since 1990 (Rajaratnam et al., 2010). Improvements in public health measures (clean water, nourishing food, immunization) are the main reason for increased survival, which in turn has led to many other benefits—lower birth rates, less starvation, and more education worldwide. Further reductions would occur if there were more doctors and nurses in underserved parts of the world: That would reduce infant deaths by 15 percent immediately (primarily because of healthier births and increased immunization) and by 50 percent over a few decades (primarily because of society-wide improvements in disease prevention) (Farahani et al., 2009).

One particular medical treatment, oral rehydration therapy (giving restorative liquids to sick children who have diarrhea), is now widely used, saving 3 million young children *per year.* Most such children are in developing nations, but oral rehydration saves lives in developed nations as well (Spandorfer et al., 2005).

Every year in Africa, 1 million people die of malaria, most of them undernourished children. Immediate drug treatment can save lives, but many victims live far from medical help. Furthermore, some anti-malaria drugs are no longer effective (Kun et al., 2010). One innovation has cut the malaria death rate in half: bed nets treated with insect repellant that drape over sleeping areas (Roberts, 2007). Better drugs are also urgently needed.

TABLE 5.1 Deaths of Children Under Age 5 in Selected Countries

Country	Number of Deaths per 1,000
Singapore	3**
Iceland	3**
Sweden	3**
Japan	3**
Italy	4**
Spain	4**
Australia	5*
United Kingdom	6*
Canada	6*
New Zealand	6*
United States	8*
Russia	12*
Vietnam	24**
Mexico	17**
China	19**
Brazil	21**
Philippines	33**
India	66**
Nigeria	138*
Sierra Leone	192*
Afghanistan	199

*Reduced by at least one-third since 1990.
**Reduced by half or more since 1990.
Source: You et al., 2010.

This table shows the number of deaths per 1,000 children under age 5 for 21 of the 192 members of the United Nations. Most nations have improved markedly on this measure since 1990. Only when war destroys families and interferes with public health measures (as it has in Afghanistan) are nations not improving this statistic.

Immunization

No immunization is yet available for malaria. However, measles, mumps, whooping cough, smallpox, pneumonia, polio, and rotavirus no longer kill hundreds of thousands of children each year, because targeted **immunization** primes the body's immune system to resist a specific contagious disease. Immunization (also called *vaccination*) is said to have had "a greater impact on human mortality reduction and population growth than any other public health intervention besides clean water" (J. P. Baker, 2000, p. 199).

When people catch a contagious disease, their immune system produces antibodies to prevent recurrence. In a healthy person who has not had the disease, a vaccine—a small dose of inactive virus (often via a "shot" in the arm)—stimulates the same antibodies. (Immunization schedules, with U.S. recommendations, appear in Appendix A, page A-4. Most of the vaccines listed are advised for infants in every nation. However, specifics vary; caregivers need to consult local public health authorities.)

immunization The process of protecting a person against a disease, via antibodies. Immunization can happen naturally, when someone survives a disease, or medically, usually via a small dose of the virus that stimulates the production of antibodies and thus renders a person immune.(Also called *vaccination.*)

Dramatic Successes

Stunning successes in immunization include the following:

- Smallpox, the most lethal disease for children in the past, was eradicated worldwide as of 1971. Vaccination against smallpox is no longer needed.
- Polio, a crippling and sometimes fatal disease, is rare. Widespread vaccination, begun in 1955, eliminated polio in the Americas. Only 784 cases were reported anywhere in the world in 2003. In the same year, rumors halted immunization in northern Nigeria. Polio reappeared, sickening 1,948 people in 2005, almost all in West Africa. Then public health workers and community

SCOTT EELLS / THE NEW YORK TIMES / REDUX

A Religious Experience Buddha taught that life is suffering, but this young Buddhist monk might prefer to avoid it. He lives in a remote region of Nepal, where, until recently, measles was a fatal disease. Fortunately, a UNICEF porter carried the vaccine over mountain trails for two days so that this boy—and his whole community—could be immunized.

leaders campaigned to increase immunization and Nigeria's polio rate plummeted. Meanwhile, poverty and new conflicts in South Asia prevented immunization: 1,606 worldwide cases were reported in 2009, primarily in Afghanistan, India, and Pakistan (MMWR, May 14, 2010). (See Figure 5.7.)

- Measles (rubeola, not rubella) is disappearing, thanks to a vaccine developed in 1963. Prior to that time, 3 to 4 million cases occurred each year in the United States alone (Centers for Disease Control and Prevention, 2007). In 2010, in the United States, only 61 people had measles, most of them born in nations without widespread immunization (MMWR, January 7, 2011).
- In 2006, a vaccine was introduced against rotavirus, which causes severe diarrhea. Before the vaccine, about 35 children died from rotavirus each year in the United States, but that rate is dropping (Pitzer et al., 2009). For technical and economic reasons (the vaccine is relatively expensive, about 30 cents per dose), it is not yet widely used in developing nations. Annually, more than half a million children die of rotovirus (Santosham, 2010).

FIGURE 5.7

Not Yet Zero Many public health advocates hope polio will be the next infectious disease to be eliminated worldwide, as is the case in almost all of North America. However, this graph shows a discouraging increase in polio rates from 2003 to 2005.

Observation Quiz Was the polio rate cut in half between 1989 and 2003? (see answer, page 152)

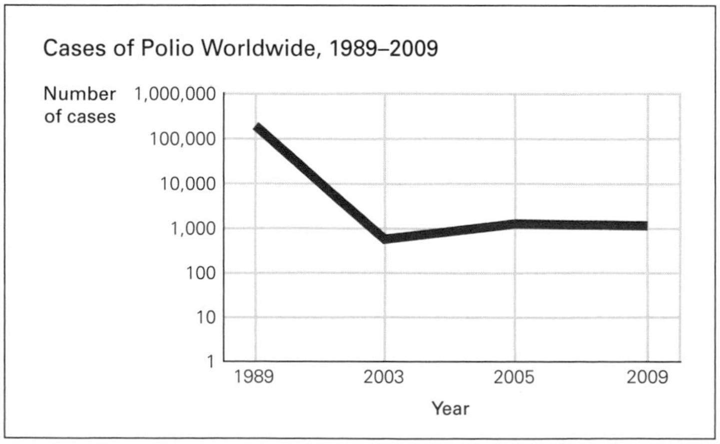

Immunization protects children not only from temporary sickness but also from serious complications, including deafness, blindness, sterility, and meningitis. Sometimes the damage from illness is not apparent until decades later. Childhood mumps, for instance, can cause sterility and doubles the risk of schizophrenia (Dalman et al., 2008).

Furthermore, each vaccinated child stops the spread of the disease and thus protects others, a phenomenon called *herd immunity.* Some people cannot be safely immunized, including: (1) embryos exposed to rubella (German measles), who may be born blind, deaf, and brain-damaged; (2) newborns, who may die from a disease that is mild in children; (3) people with impaired immune systems (HIV-positive, aged, or undergoing chemotherapy). All these are protected if they are part of a community (a herd) in which 90 percent of the people are immunized, because then the disease does not spread to those who are vulnerable. Without herd immunity, adults can die of a "childhood" disease.

Problems with Immunization

Some infants react to immunization by being irritable or even feverish for a day or so, to the distress of their parents. However, parents do not notice if their child does *not* get seriously ill. One doctor laments, "No one notices when things go right" (Bortz, 2005, p. 389). Before the varicella (chicken pox) vaccine, more than 100 people in the United States died each year from that disease and 1 million were itchy and feverish for a week. Now almost no one dies, and far fewer get chicken pox.

Many parents are concerned about potential side effects; the rate of missed vaccinations has been rising over the past decade. This frightens public health workers and most developmentalists, as the specter of an epidemic is more terrifying to them than to parents who want to avoid the distress after each round of shots. Developmentalists, taking a longitudinal and society-wide perspective, consider the risks of the diseases far greater than the risks from immunization.

Doctors agree that vaccines "are one of the most cost-effective, successful interventions in the history of public health" and lament that that success has made parents, physicians, and governments less vigilant (Hannan et al., 2009, p. S571). A hypothesis that the MMR (measles-mumps-rubella) vaccine causes autism has been repeatedly disproved (Mrozek-Budzyn et al., 2010; Shattuck, 2006). (More on autism in Chapter 11.)

The biggest problem with immunization is that no effective vaccine has been found for AIDS, malaria, cholera, typhoid, and shigellosis—all devastating diseases in the developing world. Another problem is that public health measures have not reached many rural areas of the world: About 2 to 3 million children die each year from diphtheria, tetanus, and measles because they have not been immunized (Mahmoud, 2004). This problem can occur in every nation. Late and inadequate immunization is blamed for a spike in infant whooping cough deaths in California in 2010, especially among farm families, prompting California to declare an epidemic (McKinley, 2010). Failure to immunize infants constitutes medical neglect.

Nutrition

Infant mortality worldwide has plummeted in recent years. Several reasons have already been mentioned: fewer sudden infant deaths (explained in Chapter 1), advances in prenatal and newborn care (explained in Chapter 4), and, as you just read, immunization. One more measure would make a huge difference: better nutrition.

Breast Is Best

Ideally, nutrition starts with *colostrum,* a thick, high-calorie fluid secreted by the mother's breasts at birth. After about three days, the breasts begin to produce milk. Compared with formula based on cow's milk, human milk is sterile; always at body temperature; and rich in iron, vitamins, and other newly discovered nutrients for brain and body (Drover et al., 2009).

Babies who are exclusively breast-fed are less often sick. This is true in infancy because breast milk provides antibodies against any disease to which the mother is immune and decreases the risk of allergies and asthma. Disease protection continues lifelong, because breast-fed babies are less likely to become obese adults and are thus less likely to suffer from diabetes and heart disease.

Breast milk is especially protective for preterm babies; if a preterm baby's mother cannot provide breast milk, physicians recommend milk from another woman (Schanler, 2011). (Once a woman has given birth, her breasts produce milk if they continue to be stimulated; women can therefore produce breast milk for years after giving birth.)

TABLE 5.2 The Benefits of Breast-Feeding

For the Baby	For the Mother
Balance of nutrition (fat, protein, etc.) adjusts to age of baby	Easier bonding with baby
Breast milk has micronutrients not found in formula	Reduced risk of breast cancer and osteoporosis
Less infant illness, including allergies, ear infections, stomach upsets	Natural contraception (with exclusive breast-feeding, for several months)
Less childhood asthma	Pleasure of breast stimulation
Better childhood vision	Satisfaction of meeting infant's basic need
Less adult illness, including diabetes, cancer, heart disease	No formula to prepare; no sterilization
Protection against childhood diseases, since breast milk contains antibodies	Easier travel with the baby
Stronger jaws, fewer cavities, advanced breathing reflexes (less SIDS)	**For the Family**
Higher IQ, less likely to drop out of school, more likely to attend college	Increased survival of other children (because of spacing of births)
Later puberty, less teenage pregnancy	Increased family income (because formula and medical care are expensive)
Less likely to become obese or hypertensive by age 12	Less stress on father, especially at night

Sources: Beilin & Huang, 2008; Riordan & Wambach, 2009; Schanler, 2011; U.S. Department of Health and Human Services, 2011.

The specific fats and sugars in breast milk make it more digestible and better for the brain than any formula (Drover et al., 2009; Riordan, 2005). The composition of breast milk adjusts to the age of the baby, with breast milk for premature babies distinct from breast milk for older infants. Quantity increases to meet the demand: Twins and even triplets can grow strong while being exclusively breast-fed for months. In fact, breast milk appears to have so many advantages over formula (see Table 5.2) that one might question the validity of the research. Are breast-feeding mothers better in some other, non-measured, ways that lead to such positive outcomes?

In the United States, parents of breast-fed babies are more likely to be married, college graduates, and/or immigrants (Gibson-Davis & Brooks-Gunn, 2006). Could one of those variables account for the advantages of breast-feeding? Perhaps somewhat, but the evidence in favor of breast-feeding seems overwhelming.

Formula-feeding is preferable only in unusual cases, such as when the mother is HIV-positive or uses toxic or addictive drugs. Even then, however, breast milk without supplementation may be advised. In some African nations, HIV-positive women are encouraged to breast-feed because their infants' risk of catching HIV from their mothers is lower than the risk of dying from infections, diarrhea, or malnutrition as a result of bottle-feeding (Cohen, 2007; Kuhn et al., 2009). Pediatricians agree that it "is clear and incontrovertible that human milk is the best nutritive substance for infants during the first year" (Wagner et al., 2008, p. 1148).

>> Answer to Observation Quiz (from page 150) No, much better than that. Note that this graph is on a log scale. The 2003 rate is less than one percent of the 1989 rate.

JENNIE HART / ALAMY

ALAIN EVRARD / ROBERT HARDING

The Same Situation, Many Miles Apart: Breast-Feeding Breast-feeding is universal. None of us would exist if our foremothers had not successfully breast-fed their babies for millennia. Currently, breast-feeding is practiced worldwide, but it is no longer the only way to feed infants, and each culture has particular practices.

Observation Quiz (see answer, page 154) What three differences do you see between these two breast-feeding women—one in the United States and one in Laos?

For all these reasons, doctors worldwide recommend exclusive breast-feeding, with the only dispute being whether other foods should be added at about 4 months or 6 months (Fewtrell et al., 2011). Successful breast-feeding involves some learning (how to latch on and off, for instance) and often some pain (cracked nipples) in the early weeks. Encouragement from family members, especially new fathers, is crucial.

Breast milk should remain in the diet for a year or more, according to the World Health Organization, although other easily digested foods should be added by at least 6 months. Some supplemental vitamins may also be needed, as the following explains.

A CASE TO STUDY

Breast-Fed Kiana, Close to Death

Thinking his 10-month old daughter, Kiana, had a bad case of flu, Ian Barrow took her to the emergency room earlier this year. Doctors immediately noticed something more serious: soft bones, an enlarged heart, and organs close to shutting down. The diagnosis was a shock: rickets. Barrow, a technician at the National Cancer Institute, says, "Rickets is something that has supposedly disappeared."

[Stokstad, 2003, p. 1886]

Rickets is caused by severe deficiency of vitamin D, a vitamin naturally produced by the body in response to sunshine. For light-skinned adults, even a few minutes of direct sun exposure three days a week is enough to make adequate vitamin D. Rickets was once common in children who rarely played outside; that is why vitamin D is added to milk. Although almost no older children get rickets, the disease has not disappeared: Exclusively breast-fed babies, aged 6 to 18 months, are at highest risk. Rickets is the worst consequence, but people of all ages may suffer from inadequate vitamin D, resulting in reduced immunity and less energy (Wagner et al., 2008).

Many modern mothers prevent the exposure of even an inch of infant skin to direct sunlight in order to avoid later cancer. Many also believe that breast milk provides complete nutrition. But if this latter belief prevents infants from getting vitamin D (88 percent of U.S. mothers do not give vitamin D to their babies), serious deficiencies may occur (J. A. Taylor et al., 2010).

Some researchers "blame public health experts who have urged women to breast feed without emphasizing the need for supplements. And they're even more angry at those who recommend that infants under 6 months avoid all sunlight to reduce cancer risks" (Stokstad, 2003, p. 1887). Many pediatricians do not prescribe vitamin D for breast-fed babies, and, even if they do, about half of their breast-feeding mothers do not follow that advice. Actually, only a blood test reveals how much vitamin D an infant has; many babies need no extra dose, but others do—rickets should never occur.

Remember how shocked Ian Barrow was. He knew that his child should be breast-fed, and he was proud of his wife for doing so. However, he did not know that rickets was still possible or that Kiana's dark skin meant that more sunlight was needed. Fortunately, this case ended well, because an alert father noticed that something was wrong and took his daughter to doctors who diagnosed her quickly and provided vitamin D immediately. Kiana not only survived; she thrived.

Experts are still debating how much vitamin D a person needs. In 2008, the American Academy of Pediatrics doubled its recommendation (from 200 to 400 IU a day) (Wagner et al., 2008). Not every doctor or parent agrees (J. A. Taylor et al., 2010), but "Ian Barrow, for one, says that he's making sure that Kiana and her brothers spend more time outside" (Stokstad, 2003, p. 1888). No expert doubts that breast is best, but that does not mean that breast-fed children always have every nutrient they need.

SCIENCE FACTION / SUPERSTOCK

Beach Baby Infants need to be protected from the sun, as this child is with hat and coverup designed especially to keep him safe from ultraviolet rays. Infants also need vitamin D, which the body produces naturally in response to sunlight on the skin. It can be obtained with vitamin supplements.

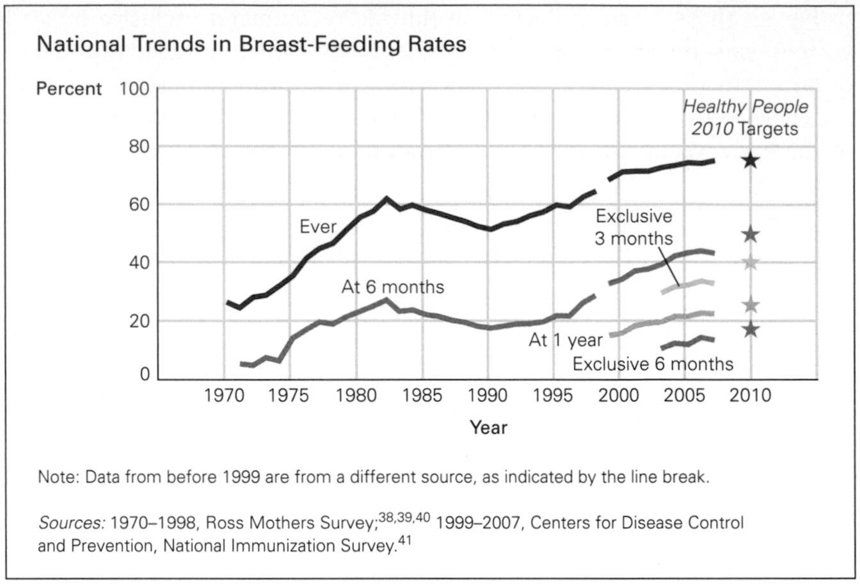

FIGURE 5.8

A Smart Choice In 1970, educated women were taught that formula was the smart, modern way to provide nutrition—but no longer. Today, more education for women correlates with more breast milk for babies. About half of U.S. women with college degrees now manage three months of *exclusive* breastfeeding—no juice, no water, and certainly no cereal.

Breast-feeding dramatically reduces infant disease and death. In the United States 75 percent of infants are breast-fed at birth, 46 percent at six months (most with other food as well), and 22 percent at a year (virtually all with other food and drink) (see Figure 5.8). Developmentalists and public health workers wish all these percentages were higher (U.S. Department of Health and Human Services, 2011). Worldwide, about half of all 2-year-olds are still nursing, usually at night.

How long a mother breast-feeds is strongly affected by her experiences in the first week, when encouragement and practical help are most needed (DiGirolamo et al., 2005). Ideally, nurses visit new parents weekly at home; such visits (routine in some nations, rare in others) increase the likelihood that breast-feeding will continue.

Malnutrition

Protein-calorie malnutrition occurs when a person does not consume sufficient food to sustain normal growth. That form of malnutrition occurs for roughly a third of the world's children in developing nations: They suffer from **stunting,** being very short for their age because chronic malnutrition kept them from growing (World Bank, 2010). Stunting is most common in the poorest nations (see Figure 5.9).

An even worse indicator of severe malnutrition is **wasting,** when children are severely underweight for their age and height (2 or more standard deviations below average). Many nations, especially in East Asia, Latin America, and central Europe, have seen improvement in child nutrition in the past decades; but in some other nations, primarily in Africa, wasting has increased since 2000. Several nations in South Asia also have high rates of malnutrition, with about half the children over age 5 stunted and almost half the children under age 5 wasted, at least for a year (World Bank, 2010).

One common way to measure a particular child's nutritional status is to compare weight and height with the detailed norms presented in Figure 5.10 and Appendix A, pages A-6 and A-7. Remember that percentiles may be more indicative of underweight than absolute numbers. A child may simply be genetically short or thin, but a decline in percentile ranking during the first two years is an ominous sign—and being in the bottom 3 percent is almost always a sign of malnutrition.

protein-calorie malnutrition A condition in which a person does not consume sufficient food of any kind. This deprivation can result in several illnesses, severe weight loss, and even death.

stunting The failure of children to grow to a normal height for their age due to severe and chronic malnutrition.

wasting The tendency for children to be severely underweight for their age as a result of malnutrition.

>> Answer to Observation Quiz (from page 152) The babies' ages, the settings, and the mothers' apparent attitudes. The U.S. mother *(left)* is indoors in a hospital and seems attentive to whether she is feeding her infant the right way. The mother in Laos *(right)* seems confident and content as she feeds her older baby in a public place, enjoying the social scene.

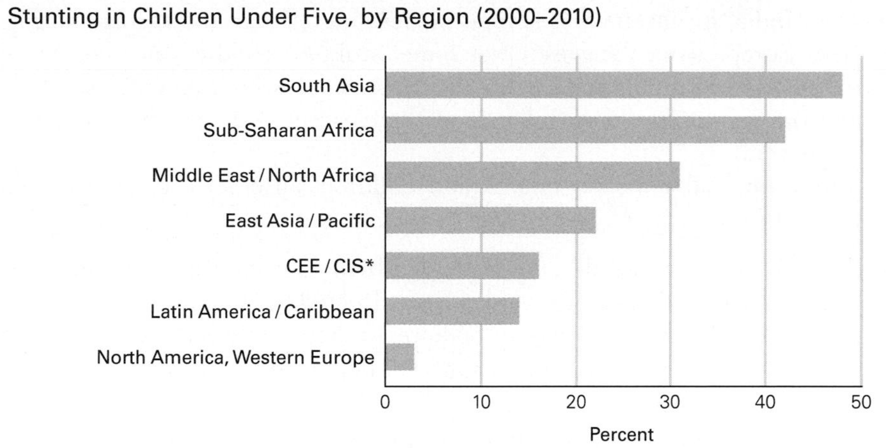

*Refer to Central and Eastern Europe Fund (CEE) and Commonwealth of Independent States (CIS), which together comprise the countries of central Europe as well as those that made up the former Soviet Union.

Source: UNICEF, 2011.

FIGURE 5.9

Genetic? The data show that basic nutrition is still unavailable to many children in the developing world. Some critics contend that Asian children are genetically small and therefore that Western norms make it appear as if India and Africa have more stunted children than they really do. However, children of Asian and African descent born and nurtured in North America are as tall as those of European descent. Thus, malnutrition, not genes, accounts for most stunting worldwide.

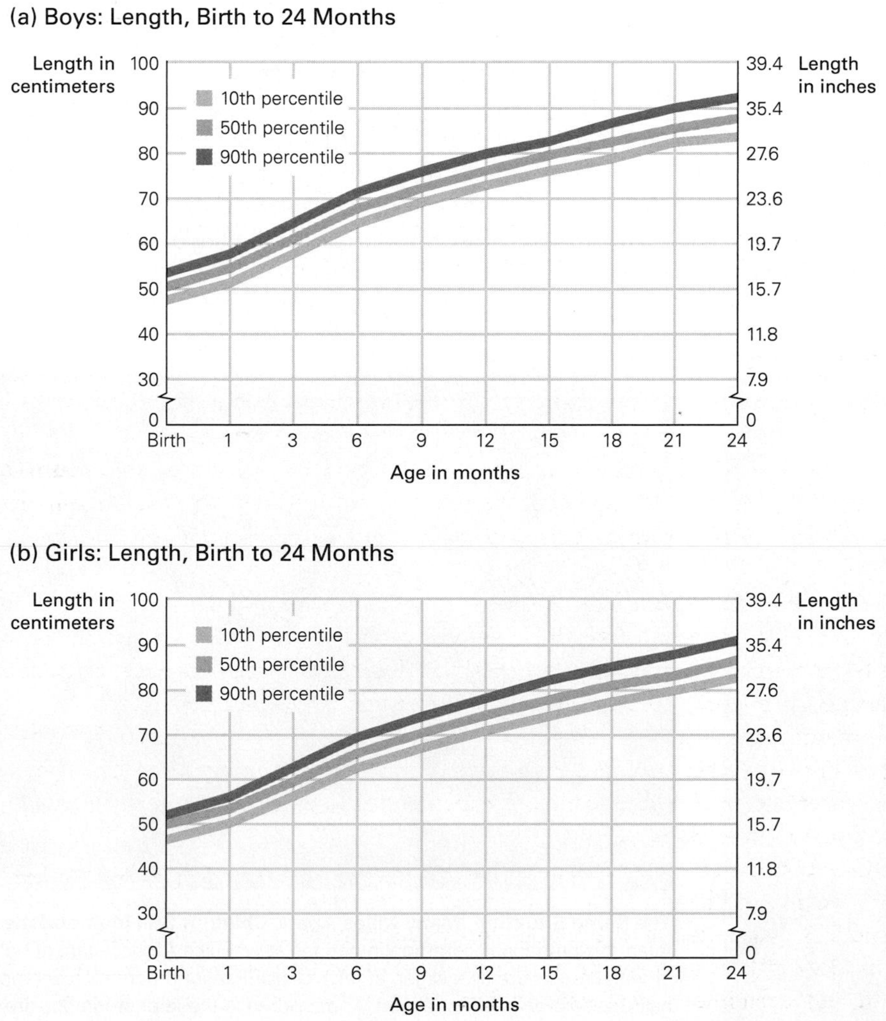

FIGURE 5.10

Gender Differences Boys and girls grow at almost the same rate throughout childhood—until age 11 or so, when girls temporarily grow faster than boys. Compare these graphs to the ones on weight, and note that already by age 2, genetic growth patterns are disturbed by overfeeding and underfeeding.

Also remember that there are ethnic differences among children. The average height in India, for instance, is several inches shorter than the average height in northern Europe, which suggests that some "stunted" children may not be malnourished. However, children born in North America whose parents were immigrants from India often grow taller than their parents—a sign that the parents were underfed.

Chronically malnourished infants and children suffer in three ways (World Bank, 2010):

1. Their brains may not develop normally. If malnutrition has continued long enough to affect height, it may also have affected the brain.
2. Malnourished children have no body reserves to protect them against common diseases. About half of all childhood deaths occur because malnutrition makes a childhood disease lethal.
3. Some diseases result directly from malnutrition.

marasmus A disease of severe protein-calorie malnutrition during early infancy, in which growth stops, body tissues waste away, and the infant eventually dies.

The worst disease directly caused by malnutrition is **marasmus.** Growth stops, body tissues waste away, and an infant victim dies. Prevention of marasmus begins long before birth, with good nutrition for the woman before and while she is pregnant. Then breast-feeding on demand (10 or more times a day) and frequent checkups to monitor the baby's weight prevent marasmus. Infants who show signs of "failure to thrive" (they do not gain weight) can be hospitalized and treated before brain damage occurs.

kwashiorkor A disease of chronic malnutrition during childhood, in which a protein deficiency makes the child more vulnerable to other diseases, such as measles, diarrhea, and influenza.

Malnutrition after age 1 may cause **kwashiorkor.** Ironically, *kwashiorkor* means "a disease of the older child when a new baby arrives"—signifying cessation of breast-feeding and less maternal attention. Although it may be that lack of protein is not the sole cause, the symptoms of kwashiorkor are unmistakable: Growth slows down; the liver is damaged; the immune system is weakened; the face, legs, and abdomen swell with fluid (edema); energy is reduced (malnourished children play less); hair becomes thin, brittle, and colorless; skin becomes blotchy (Osorio, 2011).

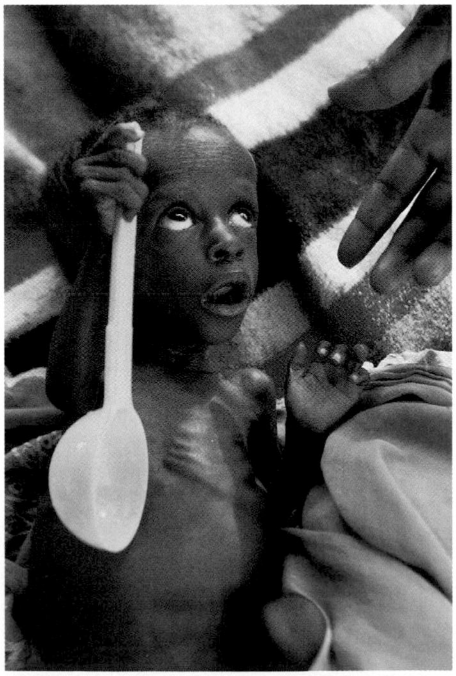

AP PHOTO / SCCHALK VAN ZUYDAM

DANG NGO / ZUMA PRESS / NEWSCOM

The Same Situation, Many Miles Apart: Children Still Malnourished Infant malnutrition is common in nations at war (like Afghanistan, at right) or with crop failure (like Niger, at left). UNICEF relief programs reach only half the children in either nation. The children in these photographs are among the lucky ones who are being fed.

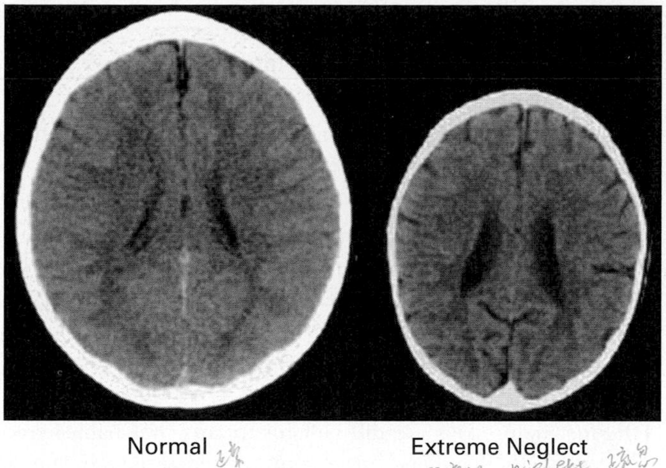

BRUCE D. PERRY / THE CHILD TRAUMA ACADEMY

Lifelong Deprivation These images illustrate the negative impact of neglect on the developing brain. The CT scans on the left are from healthy 3-year-old children with an average head size (FOC: 50th percentile). The image on the right is from a series of three 3-year-old children following severe sensory-deprivation neglect in early childhood. Each deprived child's brain is significantly smaller than average and each has abnormal development of cortex (cortical atrophy) and other abnormalities suggesting abnormal development of the brain.

Treatment includes providing protein that the body has long lacked. However, perhaps because the bodies of children with kwashiorkor have become less efficient at digestion, or perhaps because some other toxins or viruses have taken hold as the immune system has slowed down, when children are hospitalized with kwashiorkor they have a higher death rate than those hospitalized with marasmus (Badaloo et al., 2006; Osorio, 2011).

Prevention, more than treatment, stops childhood malnutrition. Prenatal nutrition defends against marasmus after birth; breast-feeding protects against marasmus in infancy; ongoing breast-feeding and ample food with iron and vitamin A prevent kwashiorkor in childhood. A study of two poor African nations (Niger and Gambia) found several specific factors that reduced the likelihood of wasting and stunting: breast-feeding, both parents at home, water piped to the house, a tile (not dirt) floor, a toilet, electricity, immunization (for measles, polio, and several other diseases), a radio, and the mother's secondary education (Oyekale & Oyekale, 2009).

Several items on this list are taken for granted by readers of this book. However, two themes apply to everyone at any age: (1) Prevention is better than treatment, and (2) people with some knowledge are more likely to protect their health and that of their loved ones. The next chapters continue these themes.

SUMMING UP

Many public health practices save millions of infants each year. Immunizing children and breast-feeding are simple yet life-saving steps. These are called public health measures rather than parental practices because they are affected by culture and national policies.

An underlying theme of this chapter is that healthy biological growth is the result not simply of genes and nutrition but also of a social environment that provides opportunities for growth: lullabies and mobiles for stimulating the infant's senses, encouragement for developing the first motor skills, and protection against disease. Each aspect of development is linked to every other aspect, and each developing person is linked to family, community, and the world. ■

SUMMARY

Body Changes

1. In the first two years of life, infants grow taller, gain weight, and increase in head circumference—all indicative of development. The norm at birth is 7½ pounds in weight, 20 inches in length (about 3,400 grams, 51 centimeters). Birthweight doubles by 4 months, triples by 1 year, and quadruples by 2 years, when toddlers weigh about 30 pounds (13½ kilograms). Even if babies are temporarily slow to gain overall, brain weight continues to increase.

2. Sleep gradually decreases over the first two years. As with all areas of development, variations in sleep patterns are normal, caused by both nature and nurture. In developed nations, co-sleeping is increasingly common for very young infants, and many (but not all) developmentalists consider it a harmless, or even beneficial, practice.

Brain Development

3. The brain increases dramatically in size, from about 25 to 75 percent of adult weight, in the first two years. Complexity increases as well, with cell growth, development of dendrites, and formation of synapses. Both growth and pruning aid cognition.

4. Experience is vital for dendrites and synapses to link neurons. In the first year, the parts of the cortex dedicated to the senses and motor skills mature. If neurons are unused, they atrophy, and the brain regions are rededicated to processing other sensations. Normal stimulation, which almost all infants obtain, fosters experience-expectant maturation.

5. Most experience-dependent brain growth reflects the varied, culture-specific experiences of the infant. Therefore, one person's brain differs from another's. However, in the basic capacities that humans share—emotional, linguistic, and sensory—all normal infants are equally capable.

6. Infant brains are designed to grow and mature, but deprivation, excessive stress, physical shaking, and lack of stimulation can all harm an infant brain, with impairment evident lifelong.

Sensation and Movement

7. At birth, the senses already respond to stimuli. Prenatal experience makes hearing the most mature sense. Vision is the least mature sense at birth, but it improves quickly, including onset of binocular vision at about 14 weeks. Infants use all their senses to strengthen their early social interactions.

8. The senses of taste, touch, smell, and motion are all apparent in young infants, and all are affected by the social context. Babies' sense of pain is controversial.

9. Infants gradually improve their motor skills as they begin to grow and brain maturation increases. Gross motor skills are soon evident, from rolling over to sitting up (at about 6 months), from standing to walking (at about 1 year), from climbing to running (before age 2). Practice and cultural encouragement affect development of gross motor skills.

10. Fine motor skills are difficult for infants, but babies gradually develop the hand and finger control needed to grab, aim, and manipulate almost anything within reach. Experience, time, and motivation allow infants to advance in fine motor skills.

Surviving in Good Health

11. About 2 billion infant deaths have been prevented in the past half-century because of improved health care worldwide, including relatively simple measures such as oral rehydration therapy and insect-repellant bed nets. More medical professionals are needed to prevent, diagnose, and treat the diseases that still cause many infant deaths.

12. Immunization has eradicated smallpox and virtually eliminated polio and measles in developed nations. In recent years, some parents worry about potential side effects of immunization, but the social benefits have consistently been shown to greatly outweigh any risks.

13. Breast-feeding is best for infants, partly because breast milk helps them resist disease and promotes growth of every kind. Most babies are breast-fed at birth, but not all are exclusively breast-fed for six months, as many doctors worldwide recommend. Supplemental food and vitamins are needed as well.

14. Severe malnutrition stunts growth and can cause death, directly through marasmus or kwashiorkor and indirectly through vulnerability if a child catches measles, an intestinal disorder, or some other illness. Malnourished infants become shorter (stunted) children than their genes would have otherwise programmed them to be.

KEY TERMS

head-sparing (p. 129)
percentile (p. 129)
REM sleep (p. 130)
co-sleeping (p. 131)
neurons (p. 132)
cortex (p. 133)
prefrontal cortex (p. 133)
axon (p. 133)
dendrite (p. 133)
synapse (p. 133)
transient exuberance (p. 134)
pruning (p. 134)
experience-expectant brain functions (p. 135)
experience-dependent brain functions (p. 135)
shaken baby syndrome (p. 139)
self-righting (p. 141)
sensation (p. 142)
perception (p. 142)
binocular vision (p. 143)
motor skills (p. 145)
gross motor skills (p. 145)
fine motor skills (p. 146)
immunization (p. 149)
protein-calorie malnutrition (p. 154)
stunting (p. 154)
wasting (p. 154)
marasmus (p. 156)
kwashiorkor (p. 156)

WHAT HAVE YOU LEARNED?

Body Changes

1. What specific facts indicate that infants grow rapidly in the first year?

2. Why is it OK for an infant to be consistently at the 20th percentile in height and weight?

3. How much do newborns usually sleep and dream?

4. What are the reasons for and against co-sleeping?

Brain Development

5. What is the difference between the cortex and the rest of the brain?

6. How does the brain change from birth to age 2?

7. What factors increase the accuracy of perception in the fusiform face area?

8. How can pruning increase brain potential?

9. What is the difference between experience-expectant and experience-dependent brain function?

10. What is the effect of stress hormones on early brain development?

11. What should caregivers remember about brain development when an infant cries?

Sensation and Movement

12. What is the relationship between perception and sensation?

13. What particular sounds and patterns do infants pay attention to?

14. How does an infant's vision change over the first year?

15. What suggests that infants experience less pain than adults?

16. What is universal and what is cultural in the development of gross motor skills in infancy?

17. Which fine motor skills are developed in infancy?

Surviving in Good Health

18. Why do public health doctors wish that all infants worldwide would get immunized?

19. What are the reasons for and against breast-feeding until a child is at least 1 year old?

20. What is the relationship between malnutrition and disease?

21. As an indication of malnutrition, which is better, stunting or wasting? Why?

APPLICATIONS

1. Immunization regulations and practices vary, partly for social and political reasons. Ask at least two faculty or administrative staff members what immunizations students at your college must have and why. If you hear, "It's a law," ask why that law is in place.

2. Observe three infants (whom you do not know) in public places such as a store, playground, or bus. Look closely at body size and motor skills, especially how much control each baby has over legs and hands. From that, estimate the age in months and then ask the caregiver how old the infant is. (Most caregivers know the infant's exact age and are happy to tell you.)

3. *This project can be done alone, but it is more informative if several students pool responses.* Ask 3 to 10 adults whether they were bottle-fed or breast-fed and, if breast-fed, for how long. If anyone does not know, or if anyone expresses embarrassment about how long they were breast-fed, that itself is worth noting. Do you see any correlation between adult body size and infant feeding?

>>ONLINE CONNECTIONS

To accompany your textbook, you have access to a number of online resources, including quizzes for every chapter of the book, flashcards (in English and Spanish), critical thinking questions, and case studies. For access to any of these links, go to www.worthpublishers.com/bergerca9e. In addition to these free resources, you'll also find links to podcasts, video clips, diagnostic quizzing with personalized study advice, and an ebook. Some of the videos and activities available online include:

- *Infant Reflexes.* Watch video clips of some of the most common infant reflexes, from the Babinski to the Moro.
- *Nutritional Needs of Infants and Children.* Including video footage from UNICEF of children around the world, this activity provides an overview of the nutritional needs and challenges children face in both developed and developing countries.

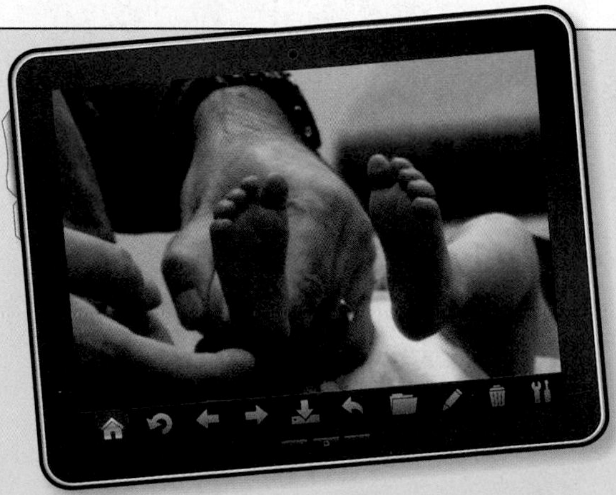

6

CHAPTER

The First Two Years: Cognitive Development

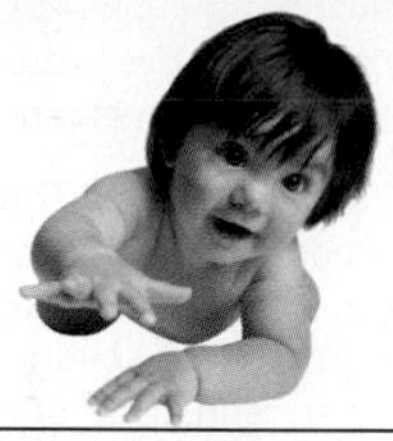

WHAT WILL YOU KNOW?

1. Why isn't Piaget's theory of sensorimotor intelligence universally recognized as insightful?
2. What factors influence whether infants remember what happens to them before they can talk?
3. When and how do infants learn to talk?

My aunt Anna's husband, Uncle Henry, boasted that he did nothing with his three children—all boys—until they were smart enough to talk. He may have found an excuse to avoid diapering, burping, and bathing, but he was wrong about infant cognition. Babies are smart from the first days of life; they think about people and things, communicating long before they say their first words. His sons grew up to be devoted to their mother and much more interactive with their own infants than Uncle Henry had been with them, a marked improvement in fathering. The research presented in this chapter explains why.

Newborns seem to know nothing. Two years later they can make a wish, say it out loud, and blow out their birthday candles. Thousands of developmentalists have traced this rapid progression. We begin with Piaget's six stages of intellectual progression over the first two years and his overall understanding of early cognition. We then describe another approach (information processing) with some intriguing research, using habituation and brain scans, that reveals preverbal memory and communication. The most dramatic evidence of early intellectual growth—the talking that Uncle Henry waited for—is then described. The final topic of this chapter may be the most important one: How do early cognitive accomplishments, particularly language, occur? The implications for caregivers are many—none of which Uncle Henry knew.

>> Sensorimotor Intelligence

As you remember from Chapter 2, Jean Piaget was a Swiss scientist, born in 1896. He was "arguably the most influential researcher of all times within the area of cognitive developmental psychology" (Birney et al., 2005, p. 328). When Piaget was growing up, most scientists thought infants were capable of only eating, crying, and sleeping, not learning and exploring. Contrary to conventional wisdom (including that of Uncle Henry), Piaget realized that infants are active learners, adapting to experience. That realization, with scientific observation to support it, has earned Piaget the admiration of developmentalists.

Adaptation, according to Piaget, is the core of intelligence. Piaget described four distinct periods of cognition, ending with formal operational thought at adolescence. The first period lasts until about 24 months, when words and thoughts become symbols, not merely labels.

sensorimotor intelligence Piaget's term for the way infants think—by using their senses and motor skills—during the first period of cognitive development.

primary circular reactions The first of three types of feedback loops in sensorimotor intelligence, this one involving the infant's own body. The infant senses motion, sucking, noise, and other stimuli and tries to understand them.

Piaget called cognition in the first two years **sensorimotor intelligence** because infants learn through the senses and motor skills that were developing before birth and continue to develop throughout infancy, as described in Chapters 4 and 5. Sensorimotor intelligence is subdivided into six stages (see Table 6.1).

Stages One and Two: Primary Circular Reactions

In every aspect of sensorimotor intelligence, the brain and the senses interact with experiences, each shaping the other as part of a dynamic system (Ambady & Bharucha, 2009). Piaget described this interaction of sensation, perception, and cognition as *circular reactions,* emphasizing that, like a circle, there is no beginning and no end (see Figure 6.1). The first two stages of sensorimotor intelligence are **primary circular reactions,** involving the infant's own body.

Stage one, called the *stage of reflexes,* lasts only a month. It includes senses as well as motor reflexes, the foundations of infant thought. The newborn's reflexes evoke some brain reactions, and soon reflexes become deliberate; sensation leads to perception, perception leads to cognition, and then cognition leads back to sensation. Sensorimotor intelligence begins.

As reflexes adjust to whatever responses they elicit, stage two, *first acquired adaptations* (also called the *stage of first habits*), begins, usually at about 1 month. Adaptation is cognitive; it includes both assimilation and accommodation (see page 47), which people use to understand their experience. Infants adapt their reflexes as repeated responses provide information about what the body does and how each action feels.

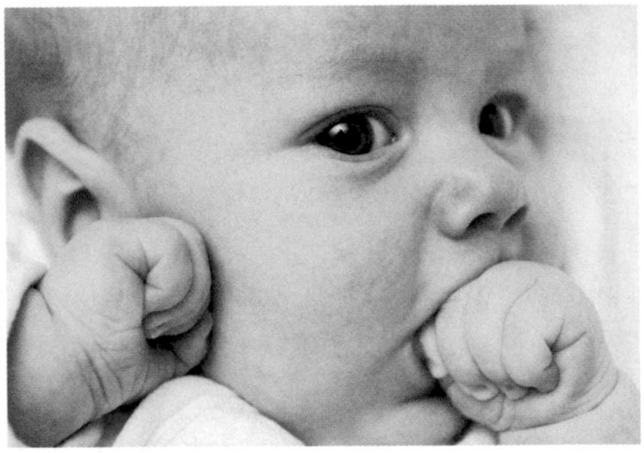

FSTOP / PUNCHSTOCK

Time for Adaptation Sucking is a reflex at first, but adaptation begins as soon as an infant differentiates a pacifier from her mother's breast or realizes that her hand has grown too big to fit into her mouth. This infant's expression of concentration suggests that she is about to make that adaptation and suck just her thumb from now on.

TABLE 6.1 The Six Stages of Sensorimotor Intelligence

For an overview of the stages of sensorimotor thought, it helps to group the six stages into pairs. The first two stages involve the infant's responses to its own body.

Primary Circular Reactions	
Stage One (birth to 1 month)	*Reflexes:* sucking, grasping, staring, listening
Stage Two (1–4 months)	*The first acquired adaptations:* accommodation and coordination of reflexes *Examples:* sucking a pacifier differently from a nipple; grabbing a bottle to suck it
The next two stages involve the infant's responses to objects and people.	
Secondary Circular Reactions	
Stage Three (4–8 months)	*Making interesting sights last:* responding to people and objects *Example:* clapping hands when mother says "patty-cake"
Stage Four (8–12 months)	*New adaptation and anticipation:* becoming more deliberate and purposeful in responding to people and objects *Example:* putting mother's hands together in order to make her start playing patty-cake
The last two stages are the most creative, first with action and then with ideas.	
Tertiary Circular Reactions	
Stage Five (12–18 months)	*New means through active experimentation:* experimentation and creativity in the actions of the "little scientist" *Example:* putting a teddy bear in the toilet and flushing it
Stage Six (18–24 months)	*New means through mental combinations:* considering before doing, which provides the child with new ways of achieving a goal without resorting to trial-and-error experiments *Example:* before flushing, remembering that the toilet overflowed and mother was angry the last time, and hesitating

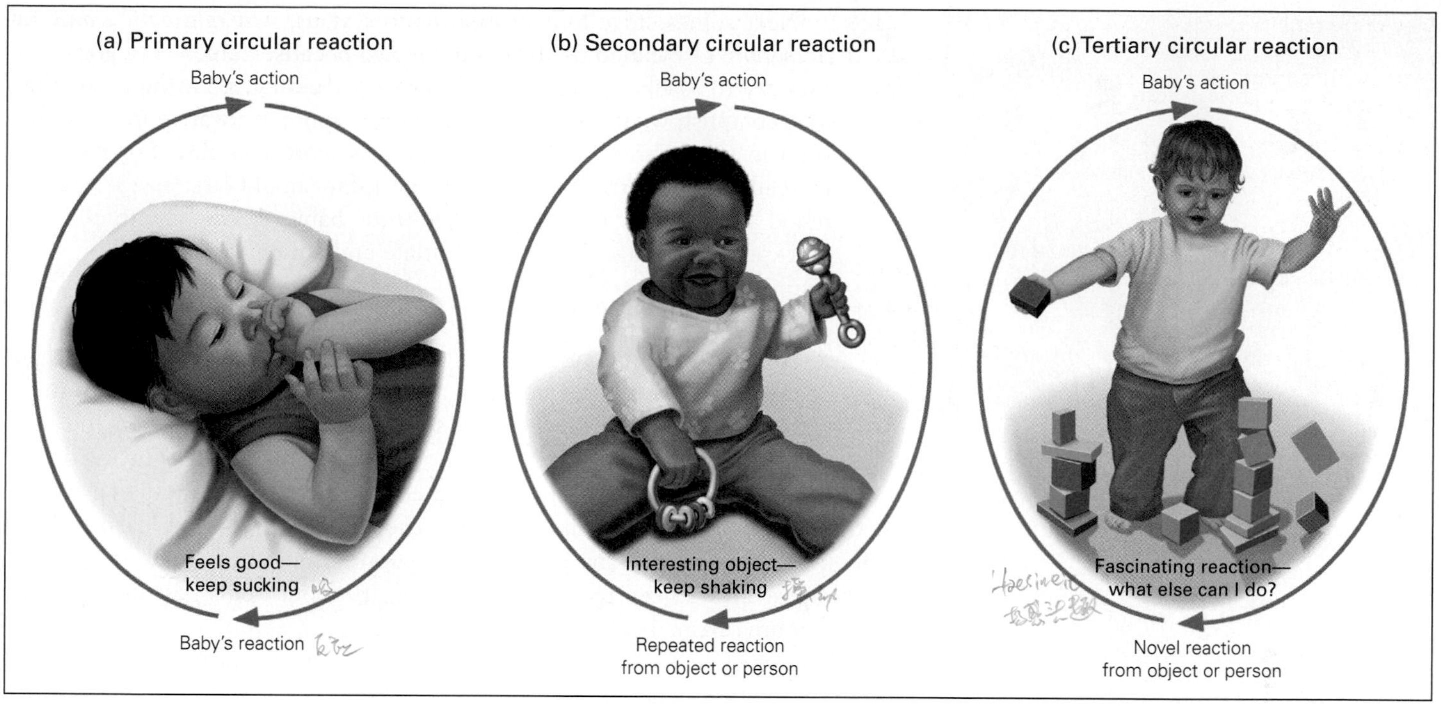

FIGURE 6.1

Never Ending Circular reactions keep going because each action produces pleasure that encourages more action.

Here is one example. In a powerful reflex, full-term newborns suck anything that touches their lips. By about 1 month, infants adapt this reflex to bottles or breasts, pacifiers or fingers, each requiring specific types of tongue pushing. This adaptation is a sign that infants have begun to interpret their perceptions; as they accommodate to pacifiers, they are "thinking."

During stage two, which Piaget pegged from about 1 to 4 months of age, additional adaptation of the sucking reflex is evident. Infant cognition leads babies to suck in some ways for hunger, in other ways for comfort—and not to suck fuzzy blankets or large balls. Once adaptation is successful, it sticks. For instance, breast-fed babies may reject milk from the nipple of a bottle (one reason breast-feeding mothers should offer breast-milk in a bottle occasionally in the early months). Likewise, if parents of a 6-month-old thumb-sucker decide that a pacifier would be better, they may be too late. The infant may refuse to adapt, spitting out the pacifier and finding the thumb instead. Piaget believed that people of all ages tend to be stuck in their ways for cognitive reasons; the adaptation of the young infant is one example.

Especially for Parents When should parents decide whether to feed their baby only by breast, only by bottle, or using some combination? When should they decide whether or not to let their baby use a pacifier? (see response, page 164)

Stages Three and Four: Secondary Circular Reactions

In stages three and four, development advances from primary to **secondary circular reactions.** Those reactions are no longer confined to the infant's body; they are an *interaction* between the baby and something else. One explanation for this advance is neurological; it seems that mirror neurons begin to function, as infants observe closely whatever they see someone do.

secondary circular reactions The second of three types of feedback loops in sensorimotor intelligence, this one involving people and objects. Infants respond to other people, to toys, and to any other object they can touch or move.

During stage three (4 to 8 months), infants attempt to produce exciting experiences, *making interesting events last.* Realizing that rattles make noise, for example, they wave their arms and laugh whenever someone puts a rattle in their hand. The sight of something delightful—a favorite book, a smiling parent—can trigger active efforts for interaction.

RUBBERBALL / ALAMY

Intelligence in Action At four months, he has already learned that every sense and motor skill connects with Daddy—or is it the other way around?

Next comes stage four (8 months to 1 year), *new adaptation and anticipation,* also called the *means to the end* because babies have goals that they try to reach. Often they ask for help (fussing, pointing, gesturing) to accomplish what they want. Thinking is more innovative in stage four than in stage three because adaptation is more complex. For instance, instead of always smiling at Daddy, an infant might first assess Daddy's mood and then try to engage. Stage-three babies know how to continue an experience; stage-four babies initiate and anticipate.

Pursuing a Goal

A 10-month-old girl might crawl over to her mother, bringing a bar of soap as a signal to start her bath, and then remove her clothes to make her wishes crystal clear—finally squealing with delight when the bath water is turned on. Similarly, if a 10-month-old boy sees his mother putting on her coat to leave, he might drag over his own jacket to signal that he wants to go along.

At that age, babies learn to indicate that they are hungry—and learn to keep their mouths firmly shut if the food on the spoon is something they do not like. If the caregivers have been using sign language, 10-month-olds gesture that they want food or are finished eating.

These examples reveal *goal-directed behavior*—that is, purposeful action. Neurological maturation makes this possible. The baby's obvious goal seeking stems from (1) an enhanced awareness of cause and effect, (2) memory for actions already completed, and (3) understanding of other people's intentions (Behne et al., 2005; Brandone & Wellman, 2009; Willatts, 1999). These cognitive advances benefit from new motor skills (e.g., crawling, grabbing), skills which themselves are the result of brain maturation—dynamic systems again.

Object Permanence

object permanence The realization that objects (including people) still exist when they can no longer be seen, touched, or heard.

Piaget thought that, at about 8 months, babies first understand the concept of **object permanence,** the realization that objects or people continue to exist when they are no longer in sight. As Piaget predicted, not until about 8 months do infants search for toys that have fallen from the crib, rolled under a couch, or disappeared under a blanket. Blind babies also acquire object permanence toward the end of their first year, reaching for an object that they hear nearby (Fazzi et al., 2011).

As they grow older, toddlers become better at seeking hidden objects, which Piaget again considered symptomatic of their advanced levels of sensorimotor intelligence. Piaget developed a basic experiment to measure object permanence: An adult shows an infant an interesting toy, covers it with a lightweight cloth, and observes the response. The results:

- Infants younger than 8 months do not search for the object (by removing the cloth).
- At about 8 months, infants search immediately (removing the cloth) after the object is covered but not if they have to wait a few seconds.
- By 2 years, children fully understand object permanence, progressing through several stages of ever-advanced cognition (Piaget, 1954).

>> Response for Parents (from page 163) Both decisions should be made within the first month, during the stage of reflexes. If parents wait until the infant is 4 months or older, they may discover that they are too late. It is difficult to introduce a bottle to a 4-month-old who has been exclusively breast-fed or a pacifier to a baby who has already adapted the sucking reflex to a thumb.

This research provides many practical suggestions. If very young infants fuss because they want something they see but cannot have (keys, a cigarette, candy), the solution is to put that coveted object out of sight. Fussing stops. By contrast, for toddlers, merely hiding a forbidden object is not enough. It must be securely locked up or discarded, lest the child later retrieve it, climbing onto the kitchen counter or under the bathroom sink. The fact that object permanence develops

BOTH: LAURA DWIGHT

Peek-a-Boo The best hidden object is Mom under an easily moved blanket, as 7-month-old Elias has discovered. Peek-a-boo is fun from about 7 to 12 months. In another month, Elias will search for more conventionally hidden objects. In a year or two, his surprise and delight at finding Mom will fade.

gradually lets caregivers know that games such as peek-a-boo and hide-and-seek are too advanced in the first months but are fun once infants understand object permanence. For older children, peek-a-boo is boring, but hide-and-seek becomes more complex (longer waiting, more imaginative hiding) as children's comprehension of hidden objects matures.

Piaget believed that an infant's failure to search before 8 months of age was evidence that the baby had no concept of object permanence—that "out of sight" literally means "out of mind." That belief has been questioned. As one researcher points out, "Amid his acute observation and brilliant theorizing, Piaget . . . mistook infants' motor incompetence for conceptual incompetence" (Mandler, 2004, p. 17). A series of clever experiments in which objects seemed to disappear behind a screen while researchers traced babies' eye movements and brain activity revealed that long before 8 months, infants are surprised if an object vanishes (Baillargeon & DeVos, 1991; Spelke, 1993).

The idea that such surprise indicates object permanence is accepted by some scientists, who believe that "infants as young as 2 and 3 months of age can represent fully hidden objects" (Cohen & Cashon, 2006, p. 224). Other scientists are not convinced (Kagan, 2008). Perhaps an eager researcher too quickly interprets shifts and pauses in infant eye gaze as evidence of thought.

Further research on object permanence continues to raise questions and produce surprises. For instance, many other creatures (cats, monkeys, dogs, birds) develop object permanence at younger ages than Piaget found. Does this reflect slower development of the human brain or simply slower maturation of motor skills (Bruce & Muhammad, 2009)?

Stages Five and Six: Tertiary Circular Reactions

In their second year, infants start experimenting in thought and deed—or, rather, in the opposite sequence, deed and thought. They act first (stage five) and think later (stage six). **Tertiary circular reactions** begin when 1-year-olds take independent actions to discover the properties of other people, animals, and things. Infants no longer respond only to their own bodies (primary reactions) or to other people or objects (secondary reactions). Their cognitive pattern is more like a spiral than a closed circle, increasingly creative with each new discovery.

tertiary circular reactions The third of three types of feedback loops in sensorimotor intelligence, this one involving active exploration and experimentation. Infants explore a range of new activities, varying their responses as a way of learning about the world.

The first stage of tertiary circular reactions, Piaget's stage five (ages 12 to 18 months), is called *new means through active experimentation,* which builds on the accomplishments of stage four. Now goal-directed and purposeful activities become more expansive and creative. Toddlers delight in squeezing all the toothpaste out of the tube, taking apart an iPod, or uncovering an anthill, activities they

Especially for Parents One parent wants to put all the breakable or dangerous objects away because a toddler is now able to move around independently. The other parent says that the baby should learn not to touch certain things. Who is right? (see response, page 167)

"little scientist" The stage-five toddler (age 12 to 18 months) who experiments without anticipating the results, using trial and error in active and creative exploration.

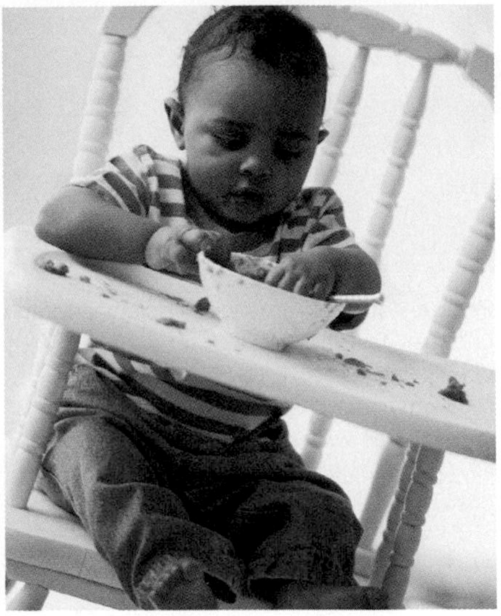

ARIEL SKELLEY / AGE FOTOSTOCK

Exploration at 15 Months One of the best ways to investigate food is to squish it in your hands, observing any changes in color and texture and listening for any sounds. Taste and smell are primary senses for adults when eating, but it looks as if Jonathan has already had his fill of those.

deferred imitation A sequence in which an infant first perceives something done by someone else and then performs the same action hours or even days later.

TOOGA PRODUCTIONS, INC. / GETTY IMAGES

No More Playpens Much has changed since Jacqueline watched a temper tantrum in a playpen. "Little scientists" still "experiment in order to see," but this 14-month-old uses a digital tablet and might protest if it is taken away.

have never seen an adult do. Piaget referred to the stage-five toddler as a **"little scientist"** who "experiments in order to see." Their scientific method is trial and error. Their devotion to discovery is familiar to every adult scientist—and to every parent.

Finally, on reaching the sixth stage (ages 18 to 24 months), toddlers begin to anticipate and solve simple problems by using *mental combinations,* intellectual experimentation via imagination that sometimes supersedes the active experimentation of stage five. Thankfully, the stage-six sequence may begin with thought (especially if the toddler remembers that something was forbidden) and then move on to action. Of course, the urge to explore may overtake memories of prohibition: Things that are truly dangerous (poisons, swimming pools, open windows) need to be locked and gated, not simply forbidden.

Another major cognitive accomplishment at the sixth stage is that toddlers can pretend. For instance, they know that a doll is not a real baby, but they can strap it into a stroller and take it for a walk. If an adult pretends to eat imaginary food (my nephew enjoyed giving me "shoe ice cream"), they may laugh—unlike older children, who no longer find that funny because they are long past stage six.

Evidence of an advance in cognition at about 18 months occurs in language as well: Instead of just uttering one word at a time, the stage-six child can combine two words to express more complex thoughts, an impressive intellectual accomplishment discussed later in this chapter. Because they combine ideas, stage-six toddlers think about consequences, hesitating a moment before yanking the cat's tail or dropping a raw egg on the floor. Of course, their strong drive to discover may overwhelm reflection; they do not always choose wisely.

Piaget describes another stage-six intellectual accomplishment, involving both thinking and memory. **Deferred imitation** occurs when infants copy behavior they noticed hours or even days earlier (Piaget, 1945/1962). A classic example is Piaget's daughter, Jacqueline, who observed another child

> who got into a terrible temper. He screamed as he tried to get out of a playpen and pushed it backward, stamping his feet. Jacqueline stood watching him in amazement, never having witnessed such a scene before. The next day, she herself screamed in her playpen and tried to move it, stamping her foot lightly several times in succession.
>
> *[Piaget, 1945/1962, p. 63]*

Piaget and Modern Research

As detailed by hundreds of developmentalists, many infants reach the stages of sensorimotor intelligence earlier than Piaget predicted (Oakes et al., 2011). Not only do 5-month-olds show surprise when objects seem to disappear (evidence of object permanence before 8 months, as described earlier), but also some babies younger than 1 year pretend and defer imitation (both stage-six abilities, according to Piaget) (Bauer, 2006; Fagard & Lockman, 2010; Hayne & Simcock, 2009; Meltzoff & Moore, 1999). How could a gifted scientist be so wrong? There are at least three reasons.

Sample Too Small

First, Piaget's original insights were based on his own infants. Direct observation of three children is a start, and Piaget was an extraordinarily meticulous and creative observer, but no contemporary researcher would stop there. Given the immaturity and variability of babies, dozens of infants must be studied. For instance, as evidence for early object permanence, Baillargeon (2000) listed 30 studies involving more than a thousand infants younger than 6 months old.

Methods Too Simple

Second, infants are not easy to study; there are problems with "fidelity and credibility" (Bornstein et al., 2005, p. 287). To overcome these problems, modern researchers use innovative statistics, research designs, sample sizes, and strategies that were not available to Piaget—often finding that object permanence, deferred imitation, and other sensorimotor accomplishments occur earlier, and with more variation, than Piaget had assumed (Hartmann & Pelzel, 2005; Kolling et al., 2009). For instance, if an infant looks a few milliseconds longer when an object seems to have vanished, is that evidence of object permanence? Many researchers believe the answer is yes—but only advanced measurement can prove it.

One particular research method has been a boon to scientists, confirming the powerful curiosity of very young babies. That research method is called **habituation** (from the word *habit*). Habituation refers to getting accustomed to an experience after repeated exposure, as when the school cafeteria serves macaroni day after day or when infants repeatedly encounter the same sound, sight, toy, or so on. Evidence of habituation is loss of interest (or, for macaroni, loss of appetite).

habituation The process of becoming accustomed to an object or event through repeated exposure to it, and thus becoming less interested in it.

Using habituation as a research strategy with infants involves repeating one stimulus until babies lose interest and then presenting another, slightly different stimulus (a new sound, sight, or other sensation). Babies indicate that they detect a difference between the two stimuli with a longer or more focused gaze; a faster or slower heart rate; more or less muscle tension around the lips; a change in the rate, rhythm, or pressure of suction on a nipple. Such subtle indicators are recorded by technology that was unavailable to Piaget (such as eye-gaze cameras and heart monitors).

By inducing habituation and then presenting a new stimulus, scientists have learned that even 1-month-olds can detect the difference between a *pah* sound and a *bah* sound, between a circle with two dots inside it and a circle without any dots, and much more. Babies younger than 6 months perceive far more than Piaget imagined.

Brain Activity Unseen

Third, several ways of measuring brain activity now allow scientists to record infant cognition long before any observable evidence is found (see Table 6.2) (M. H. Johnson, 2011). In functional magnetic resonance imaging, or **fMRI,** a burst of electrical activity measured by blood flow within the brain is recorded, indicating that neurons are firing. This leads researchers to conclude that a particular stimulus has been noticed and processed. As time goes on, changes in the blood flow indicate that habitation has occurred. Based on such advanced methods, scientists are convinced that infants have memories, goals, deferred imitation, and even mental combinations well in advance of Piaget's stages (Bauer et al., 2010; Morasch & Bell, 2009).

fMRI Functional magnetic resonance imaging, a measuring technique in which the brain's electrical excitement indicates activation anywhere in the brain; fMRI helps researchers locate neurological responses to stimuli.

Brain imagery of normal children is not only difficult and expensive to acquire, but CT scans in particular raise questions about long-term effects (Schenkman, 2011). Brain scans may be essential if an infant is ill or injured, but many parents are cautious about allowing such measures with healthy infants. Such caution is understandable, even admirable, but it slows down neurological confirmation of infant cognition.

As detailed in Chapter 5, it is known that early brain growth is rapid and wide-ranging: Dendrites proliferate, and pruning is extensive. The first months and years of life are filled with mental activity, prime time for cognitive development (M. H. Johnson, 2011), although, of course, neurological maturation and cognitive advances continue long past infancy. Despite many valid criticisms of Piaget's work, he was correct in many ways. For instance, significant new connections

>> Response for Parents (from page 165) It is easier and safer to babyproof the house because toddlers, being "little scientists," want to explore. However, it is important for both parents to encourage and guide the baby, so it is preferable to leave out a few untouchable items if that will help prevent a major conflict between husband and wife.

TABLE 6.2 Some Techniques Used by Neuroscientists to Understand Brain Function

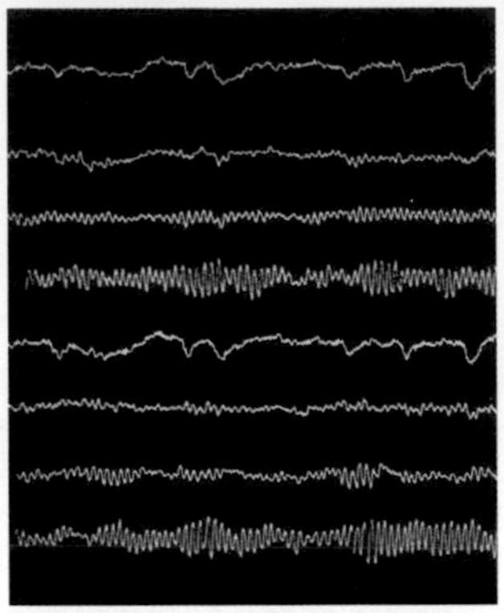
SPL / PHOTO RESEARCHERS

EEG, normal brain

Technique
EEG (electroencephalogram)

Use
Measures electrical activity in the top layers of the brain, where the cortex is.

Limitations
Especially in infancy, much brain activity of interest occurs below the cortex.

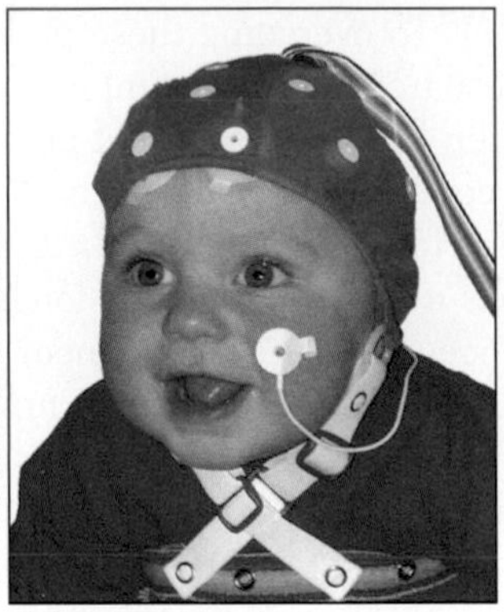
© 2001 UNIVERSITY OF WASHINGTON, INSTITUTE FOR LEARNING AND BRAIN SCIENCES

ERP when listening

Technique
ERP (event-related potential)

Use
Notes the amplitude and frequency of electrical activity (as shown by brain waves) in specific parts of the cortex in reaction to various stimuli.

Limitations
Reaction within the cortex signifies perception, but interpretation of the amplitude and timing of brain waves is not straightforward.

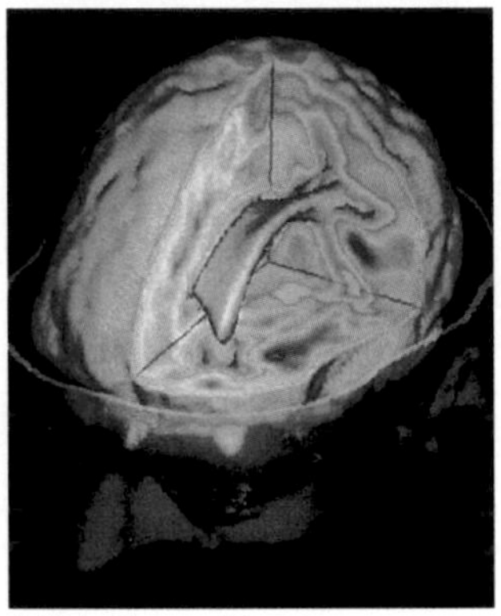
VOLKER STEGER / PETER ARNOLD

fMRI when talking

Technique
fMRI (functional magnetic resonance imaging)

Use
Measures changes in blood flow anywhere in the brain (not just the outer layers).

Limitations
Signifies brain activity, but infants are notoriously active, which can make fMRIs useless.

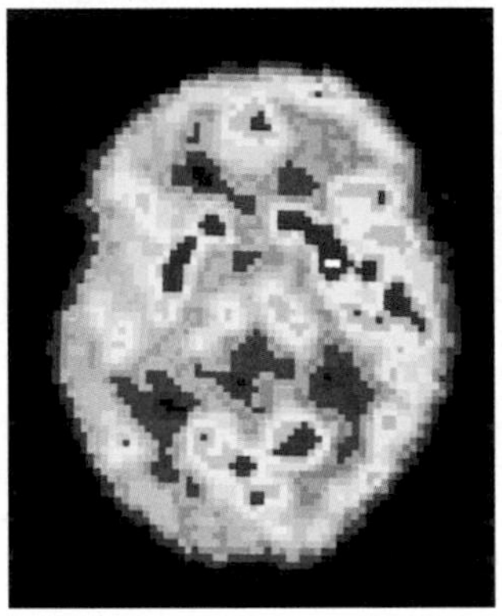
HANK MORGAN / PHOTO RESEARCHERS

PET scan of sleep

Technique
PET (positron emission tomography)

Use
Also (like fMRI) reveals activity in various parts of the brain. Locations can be pinpointed with precision, but PET requires injection of radioactive dye to light up the active parts of the brain.

Limitations
Many parents and researchers hesitate to inject radioactive dye into an infant's brain unless a serious abnormality is suspected.

For both practical and ethical reasons, these techniques have not been used with large, representative samples of normal infants. One of the challenges of neuroscience is to develop methods that are harmless, easy to use, and comprehensive for the study of normal children. A more immediate challenge is to depict the data in ways that are easy to interpret and understand.

in brain networks and functions seem to occur at years 2, 4, 6, and throughout puberty (Kagan, 2008)—all ages when Piaget described cognitive growth. Furthermore, there is "ample data to suggest that learning and memory are correlated with changes in the brain at multiple levels" (Nelson, de Haan et al., 2006, p. 17). Piaget was also correct to describe babies as avid learners. His main mistake was underestimating how rapidly their learning occurs.

SUMMING UP

Piaget discovered, studied, and then celebrated active infant learning, which he described in six stages of sensorimotor intelligence. Babies use their senses and motor skills to gain an understanding of their world, first with reflexes and then by adapting through assimilation and accommodation. Piaget's description of active infant learning was a welcome contrast to earlier assumptions that babies did not think until they could talk.

We now know that object permanence, pursuit of goals, and deferred imitation all develop before the time Piaget assigned to his stages. The infant is a "little scientist" not only at 1 year, as Piaget described, but months earlier. Thinking develops before infants have the motor skills to demonstrate their thoughts; eye movements and brain scans find that babies have active minds. ■

>> Information Processing

As explained in Chapter 2, Piaget's sweeping overview of four periods of cognition contrasts with **information-processing theory,** a perspective originally modeled after computer functioning, including input, memory, programs, calculation, and output. For infants, the output might be moving a hand to uncover a toy (object permanence), saying a word to signify recognition (e.g., *mama*), or simply glancing at one photo longer than another (habituation). As you remember, sensation leads to perception, which may lead to cognition.

information-processing theory A perspective that compares human thinking processes, by analogy, to computer analysis of data, including sensory input, connections, stored memories, and output.

For example, instead of the newborn's reflexive cry in response to the sensation of hunger, a slightly older hungry infant might perceive a bottle, grab, and then suck, or see Mother coming, reach to be picked up, and then nuzzle at her breast. Each step of this process requires information to be processed; older infants are much more thoughtful and effective than newborns because of more advanced information processing. Researchers have demonstrated that these advances occur week by week or even day by day in the first year, contrary to Piaget's notion of six discrete stages (Cohen & Cashon, 2006).

Especially for Computer Experts In what way is the human mind not like a computer? (see response, page 171)

With the aid of the sensitive technology just described, information-processing research has found impressive intellectual capacities: Concepts and categories seem to develop in infants' brains by about 6 months (Mandler, 2007; Quinn, 2004). Research inspired by information processing finds detailed sequences in number sense. For instance, habituation and brain scans reveal that 6-month-olds can detect the difference between a display of 8 dots and one of 16 dots but not the difference between 8 and 12 dots. This number sense advances within the next 3 months, so that by 9 months of age, babies can distinguish a display of 8 dots from one of 12 dots (Lipton & Spelke, 2003). It will be years before they can count, and even longer before they can add, subtract, and so on, but some number sense may appear as early as 3 months (Libertus & Brannon, 2009).

Knowing the incremental details of such cognitive development has many practical implications. For example, information processing pinpoints ways to avoid the later intellectual deficits many preterm children experience (Rose et al., 2008). The information-processing perspective helps tie together many aspects of infant cognition. We review two of these now: affordances and memory. Affordances concern perception or, by analogy, input. Memory concerns brain organization and output—that is, information storage and retrieval.

Affordances

Perception, remember, is mental processing of information that arrives at the brain from the sensory organs. It is the first step of information processing. One puzzle of development is that two people can have discrepant perceptions of the same situation, not only interpreting it differently but actually observing it differently.

Decades of thought and research led Eleanor and James Gibson to conclude that perception is far from automatic (E. J. Gibson, 1969; J. J. Gibson, 1979). Perception—for infants, as for the rest of us—is a cognitive accomplishment that requires selectivity: "Perceiving is active, a process of obtaining information about the world. . . . We don't simply see, we look" (E. J. Gibson, 1988, p. 5). Or, as one neuroscientist said, "You see what you expect or are trained to see, not what is there" (Freeman, quoted in Bower, 2007, p. 106).

The Gibsons contend that the environment (people, places, and objects) *affords,* or offers, many opportunities for interaction with what is perceived (E. J. Gibson, 1997). Each of these opportunities is called an **affordance.** Which particular affordance is perceived and acted on depends on four factors: sensory awareness,

affordance An opportunity for perception and interaction that is offered by a person, place, or object in the environment.

immediate motivation, current development, and past experience. As an example, imagine that you are lost in an unfamiliar city. Whom will you ask for directions? Not usually the first person you see: You will look for someone who seems knowledgeable and approachable. Both avoiding one person and choosing another are affordances, connected to the strangers' expressions, body language, gender, dress, and more (Miles, 2009).

BSIP / PHOTOTAKE USA

Chewable? Motivation is crucial for affordances. This baby's toy was designed to afford pulling, but he is teething, so he is motivated to recognize that it also affords chewing.

Age affects the affordances a person perceives. Toddlers enjoy running as soon as their motor skills enable it. Then they seek places to run: a meadow, a long hallway in an apartment building, or a road. To an adult eye, the degree to which these places afford running may be restricted by such factors as a bull grazing in the meadow, neighbors behind the hallway doors, or traffic on the road. Adults may restrict the toddler for those reasons. Furthermore, they are unlikely to start running themselves because motivation is pivotal in affordances: Many adults prefer to stay put.

Selective perception of affordances is characteristic not only of every age but also of every culture. Just as a baby might be oblivious to something adults consider crucial—or vice versa—an American in, say, Thailand might miss an important sign of the social network. In every nation, foreigners are considered rude because of their thoughtless behavior, but that rudeness may simply be evidence that their affordances are not what the native people perceive. That applies within cultures as well. Residents of Manhattan complain that tourists walk too slowly: Natives see sidewalks as affording rapid progress, not views of architecture.

Research on Early Affordances

The fact that experience affects which affordances are perceived is quite apparent in studies of depth perception. Research that demonstrates this fact began with an apparatus called the **visual cliff,** designed to provide the illusion of a sudden drop-off between one horizontal surface and another. Mothers were able to urge their 6-month-olds to wiggle toward them over the supposed edge of the cliff, but even with their mothers urging them on, 10-month-olds fearfully refused to budge (E. J. Gibson & Walk, 1960).

MARK RICHARDS / PHOTOEDIT

Depth Perception This toddler in a laboratory in Berkeley, California, is crawling on the experimental apparatus called a visual cliff. She stops at the edge of what she perceives as a drop-off.

visual cliff An experimental apparatus that gives the illusion of a sudden drop-off between one horizontal surface and another.

Scientists once thought that a visual deficit—specifically, inadequate depth perception—prevented the 6-month-olds from seeing the drop. According to this hypothesis, as the visual cortex matured, 10-month-olds could see that crawling into the gap afforded falling. Later research (using more advanced technology) disproved that interpretation. Even 3-month-olds notice a drop: Their heart rate slows and their eyes open wide when they are placed over the cliff. But until they can crawl, they do not realize that crawling over an edge affords falling, perhaps with a frightening and painful consequence.

The infant's awareness of the affordance of the visual cliff depends on past experience. The difference is in processing, not input; in affordance, not mere stimulus. Further research on affordances of the visual cliff included the social context, with the tone of the mother's encouragement being a significant indicator of whether the cliff affords crawling or not (Kim et al., 2010). The same sequence happens with walking: Novice walkers are fearless and reckless; experienced walkers are more cautious and deliberate (Adolph & Berger, 2005).

Especially for Parents of Infants When should you be particularly worried that your baby will fall off the bed or down the stairs? (see response, page 172)

Movement and People

Despite the variations from one infant to another in the particular affordances they perceive, all babies are attracted to two kinds of affordances. Babies pay close attention to things that move and to people. **Dynamic perception** focuses on movement and change. Infants love motion. As soon as they can, they move their

dynamic perception Perception that is primed to focus on movement and change.

bodies—grabbing, scooting, crawling, walking. To their delight, such motion changes what the world affords them. As a result, infants work hard to master the next motor accomplishment (Adolph & Berger, 2005). They also look at things that move—passing cars, flickering images on a screen, mobiles.

Other creatures that move, especially an infant's own caregivers, are among the main sources of pleasure, again because of dynamic perception. It's almost impossible to teach a baby not to chase and grab any moving creature, including a dog, a cat, or even a cockroach. Infants' interest in motion was the inspiration for another experiment that sought to learn what affordances were perceived by babies too young to talk or walk (van Hof et al., 2008). A ball was moved at various speeds in front of infants aged 3 to 9 months. Most tried to touch or catch the ball as it passed within reach. However, marked differences appeared in their perception of the affordance of "catchableness."

MARINA RAITH / PHOTOLIBRARY

The Next Move These infants are intrigued by things and people, as would be expected. However, they have much to learn about how to grab a ball or play with a friend. It would not be surprising if, a minute later, the ball rolled away, one child cried, and the wide-eyed redhead hit her playmate.

Sometimes younger infants did not reach for slow-moving balls yet tried to grasp the faster balls. They tried but failed, touching the ball only about 20 percent of the time. By contrast, the 9-month-olds knew when a ball afforded catching. They grabbed the slower balls and did not try to catch the fastest ones; their success rate was almost 100 percent. This "follows directly from one of the key concepts of ecological psychology, that animals perceive the environment in terms of action possibilities or affordances" (van Hof et al., 2008, p. 193).

The other universal principle of infant perception is **people preference.** This is in accord with another key principle of evolutionary psychology: that over the centuries, humans of all ages survived by learning to attend to, and rely on, one another. You just read that the affordance of the visual cliff depends partly on the tone of the mother's voice (Kim et al., 2010). Infants soon recognize their caregivers and expect certain affordances (comfort, food, entertainment) from them.

people preference A universal principle of infant perception, specifically an innate attraction to other humans, evident in visual, auditory, and other preferences.

Very young babies are particularly interested in emotional affordances, using their limited perceptual abilities and intellectual understanding to respond to smiles, shouts, and so on. Infants connect facial expressions with tone of voice long before they understand language. This ability led to an interesting hypothesis:

> Given that infants are frequently exposed to their caregivers' emotional displays and further presented with opportunities to view the affordances (Gibson, 1959, 1979) of those emotional expressions, we propose that the expressions of familiar persons are meaningful to infants very early in life.
>
> *[Kahana-Kalman & Walker-Andrews, 2001, p. 366]*

>> Response for Computer Experts (from page 169) In dozens of ways, including speed of calculation, ability to network across the world, and vulnerability to viruses. In at least one crucial way, the human mind is better: Computers wear out within a few years, while human minds keep advancing for decades.

Building on earlier studies, these researchers tested their hypothesis by presenting infants with two moving images side by side on one video screen (Kahana-Kalman & Walker-Andrews, 2001). Both images were of a woman, two views each of either the infant's own mother or of a stranger. In one image, the woman was joyful; in the other, sad. Each presentation was accompanied by an audiotape of that woman's happy *or* sad talk.

Previous studies had found that 7-month-olds could match emotional words with facial expressions, but younger babies could not. At 7 months, but not earlier, infants looked longer at strangers whose voice matched the emotion shown on their face and less at strangers whose facial expression did not match the tone they heard.

These researchers first replicated the earlier experiments, again finding that 3½-month-old babies could not match a stranger's voice and facial expression. However, when the 3½-month-olds saw two images of their *own* mother and heard

Especially for Parents This research on early affordances suggests a crucial lesson about how many babysitters an infant should have. What is it? (see response, page 173)

>> Response for Parents of Infants (from page 170) Constant vigilance is necessary for the first few years of a child's life, but the most dangerous age is from about 4 to 8 months, when infants can move but do not yet fear falling over an edge.

her happy or her sad voice, they correctly matched visual and vocal emotions. They looked longest when their smiling mother talked happily; but when their mother sounded sad, they stared more at the video of their sad-faced mother than at the video of their happy mother—thus connecting sound and sight, presumably based on their past experience with that person.

The researchers noticed something else as well. When infants saw and heard their happy mothers, they smiled twice as fast, seven times as long, and much more brightly (cheeks raised and lips upturned) than for the happy strangers. Experience had taught them that a smiling mother affords joy. The affordances of a smiling stranger are more difficult to judge.

Memory

Both a certain amount of experience and a certain amount of brain maturation are required in order to process and remember anything (Bauer et al., 2010). Infants have difficulty storing new memories in their first year, and older children are often unable to describe events that occurred when they were younger. Many adults have what Freud called "childhood amnesia"—they forget experiences, people, and even languages they knew when they were young. One reason is linguistic: People use words to store (and sometimes distort) memories, so preverbal children have difficulty with recall (Richardson & Hayne, 2007) while adults cannot access early memories because they did not have words to solidify them.

Calvin & Hobbes

Selective Amnesia As we grow older, we forget about spitting up, nursing, crying, and almost everything else from our early years. However, strong emotions (love, fear, mistrust) may leave lifelong traces.

However, a series of experiments reveals that very young infants *can* remember, even if they cannot later put memories into words. Memories are particularly evident in these circumstances:

- Experimental conditions are similar to those of real life.
- Motivation is high.
- Retrieval is strengthened by reminders and repetition.

The most dramatic evidence for infant memory comes from innovative experiments in which 3-month-olds were taught to make a mobile move by kicking their legs (Rovee-Collier, 1987, 1990). The infants lay on their backs, in their own cribs, connected to a mobile by means of a ribbon tied to one foot (see photograph on the next page). Virtually all the infants began making some occasional kicks (as well as random arm movements and noises) and realized, after a while, that kicking made the mobile move. They then kicked more vigorously and frequently, sometimes laughing at their accomplishment. So far, this is no surprise—self-activated movement is highly reinforcing to infants, a part of dynamic perception.

When some infants had the mobile-and-ribbon apparatus reinstalled in their cribs *one week later,* most started to kick immediately. Their reaction indicated that they remembered their previous experience. But when other 3-month-old infants were retested *two weeks later,* they began with only random kicks. Apparently they had forgotten what they had learned—evidence that memory is fragile early in life. But that conclusion needs revision, or at least qualification.

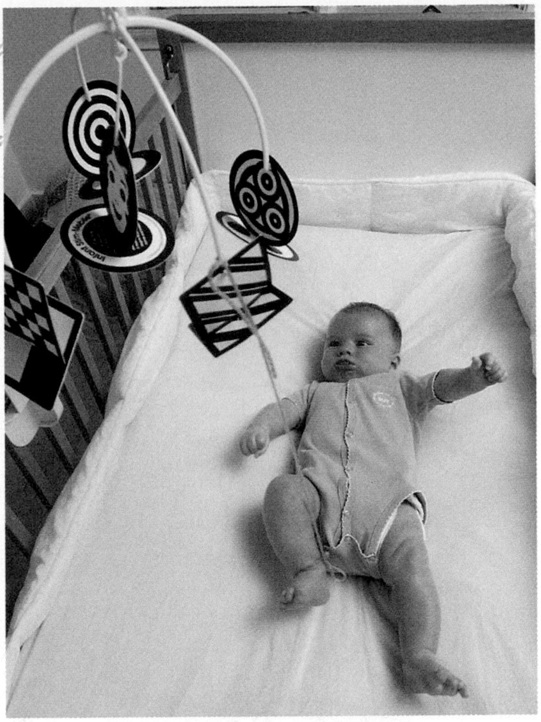

MICHAEL NEWMAN/ PHOTOEDIT

He Remembers! In this demonstration of Rovee-Collier's experiment, a young infant immediately remembers how to make the familiar mobile move. (Unfamiliar mobiles do not provoke the same reaction.) He kicks his right leg and flails both arms, just as he learned to do several weeks ago.

Observation Quiz How and why is this mobile unlike those usually sold for babies? (see answer, page 175)

Reminders and Repetition

The lead researcher, Carolyn Rovee-Collier, developed another experiment that demonstrated that 3-month-old infants *could* remember after two weeks *if* they had a brief reminder session before being retested (Rovee-Collier & Hayne, 1987). A **reminder session** is any experience that helps people recollect an idea, a thing, or an event.

In this particular reminder session, two weeks after the initial training the infants watched the mobile move but were *not* tied to it and were positioned so that they could *not* kick. The next day, when they were again connected to the mobile and positioned so that they *could* move their legs, they kicked as they had learned to do two weeks earlier. Apparently, watching the mobile move on the previous day had revived their faded memory. The information about making the mobile move was stored in their brains, but they needed processing time to retrieve it. The reminder session provided that time.

Other research finds that repeated reminders are more powerful than single reminders and that context is crucial, especially for infants younger than 9 months of age: Being tested in the same room as the initial experience aids memory (Rovee-Collier & Cuevas, 2009a). Six-month-old infants, who went through only two half-hour sessions with a novel puppet on one day, remembered the experience four weeks later—an amazing feat (Giles & Rovee-Collier, 2011). Many other studies have found that infant memory is fragile but that reminders, repetition, and retrieval cues may help very young infants remember (S. P. Johnson & Shuwairi, 2009).

reminder session A perceptual experience that helps a person recollect an idea, a thing, or an experience.

A Little Older, a Little More Memory

After about 6 months of age, infants retain information for a longer time than younger babies do, with less training or reminding. Toward the end of the first year, many kinds of memory are apparent. For example, suppose a 9-month-old watches someone playing with a toy he or she has never seen. The next day, if given the toy, the 9-month-old will play with it in the same way as he or she had observed. Younger infants will not.

Many experiments show that toddlers can transfer learning from one object or experience to another and that they learn from various people and events—from parents and strangers, from other babies and older siblings, from picture books and family photographs (Hayne & Simcock, 2009). The dendrites and neurons of the brain change to reflect their experiences and memories even in the first years of life.

In one series of experiments, 15-month-old infants were shown a toy, with an adult acting on it in a particular way. A day later, they were given another toy they had never seen, and they tried to act on it in the same way they remembered from the day before. This was true even if they had merely watched the action and if nothing had happened as a result of the action; it was even more true, though, if the action had produced a reaction (e.g., a noise), especially if the baby had also been allowed to manipulate the toy (Yang et al., 2010).

>> Response for Parents (from page 171) It is important that infants have time for repeated exposure to each caregiver, because infants adjust their behavior to maximize whatever each particular caregiver affords in the way of play, emotions, and vocalization. Parents should find one steady babysitter rather than several.

Note that these experiments are further evidence of several facts already mentioned: Babies observe affordances carefully; they are especially attuned to actions and people; and deferred imitation is possible before 18 months, when Piaget's stage six begins.

Aspects of Memory

NANCY SHEEHAN / PHOTOEDIT

Memory Aid Personal motivation and action are crucial to early memory, which is why Noel has no trouble remembering which shape covers the photograph of herself as a baby.

Brain activity patterns shown on fMRI and PET scans indicate that one region of the brain (the fusiform face area, explained in Chapter 5) is devoted to memory for faces, another to memory for sounds, another to memory for sights. While memories for many specific kinds of things are located in particular clusters of neurons, several additional brain regions also participate in these various memories: Particularly early in life, brain organization varies depending on the particular experiences to be remembered (Rovee-Collier & Cuevas, 2009b). An infant could lose one part of the brain yet still remember things that supposedly were stored there. As the brain matures and dendrites are formed, some kinds of memories are consolidated more than others. Again, memory for movement and for people is particularly strong.

Memories need not be of any specific object or experience but may instead be general notions of how the world works. In one experiment, 11-month-olds viewed a jumble of blocks, then some saw a face and some saw a ball, and then they all viewed the same blocks they'd seen earlier, except this time stacked in some order. The length of time they looked at the third view suggested that they realized that a person (the face) could organize blocks but an inanimate ball could not (Newman et al., 2010).

Many other studies show that infants not only remember specific events but also develop memories for patterns (Keil, 2011). Some examples come from research, such as what syllables and rhythms are heard and how objects move in relation to others; additional examples arise from close observations of babies at home, such as what behaviors are expected from Mommy as compared to Daddy or what details indicate it is time to go to sleep (e.g., a particular blanket, book, or crib). All this is evidence that every day of their young lives, infants are processing information and storing conclusions.

implicit memory Unconscious or automatic memory that is usually stored via habits, emotional responses, routine procedures, and various sensations.

explicit memory Memory that is easy to retrieve on demand (as in a specific test). Most explicit memory involves consciously learned words, data, and concepts.

One reason earlier scientists underestimated memory is that they failed to distinguish between **implicit memory,** which is memory that remains hidden until a particular stimulus brings it to mind (like the mobile reminder session), and **explicit memory,** which is memory that can be recalled on demand. Explicit memories are usually verbal, and therefore "although explicit memory *emerges* sometime between 6 and 12 months, it is far from fully developed" (Nelson, de Haan et al., 2006, p. 23). The particular part of the brain on which explicit memory depends is the hippocampus (explained in Chapter 8), present at birth but very immature until about age 5 or 6. It is no surprise that this timing coincides with the beginning of formal education, because children are much better at memorizing at that age.

Implicit memories, by contrast, begin in infancy or perhaps even before birth. Implicit memories are evident in all the examples just mentioned, when evidence of memory comes from the situation, not from the answer to a spoken question. For instance, adults who knew a language in childhood often have no explicit memory of it: They claim to have forgotten all the Spanish, French, Chinese, or whatever they knew. When asked the word for a common object such as table or apple in that language, they quite honestly reply that they do not know (Bowers et al., 2009). Moreover, when first tested, such adults do no better than those who never knew that language.

Especially for Teachers People of every age remember best when they are active learners. If you must teach fractions to a class of 8-year-olds, how would you do it? (see response, page 177)

However, repeated exposure reveals implicit memories from infancy. For example, a student who has forgotten all the Spanish he ever knew seems to catch on much more quickly in Spanish class than does the student who never heard Spanish as an infant. Apparently, the first weeks of Spanish class served as a reminder session. Reminders may also explain the phenomenon of déjà vu; people, places, and smells sometimes seem familiar or emotionally evocative, even if never experienced before, because something very similar occurred in infancy and was stored implicitly.

>> Answer to Observation Quiz (from page 173) It is black and white, with larger objects—designed to be particularly attractive to infants, not to adult shoppers.

Infants probably store in their brains many emotions and sensations that they cannot readily retrieve. The information-processing approach finds that infant memory is crucial for later development—far more so than are other components of early thought, such as attention and processing speed (Rose et al., 2009). Extensive research finds that memories help in early word learning, and those words in turn help encode later memories (Richardson & Hayne, 2007).

SUMMING UP

Infant cognition can be studied using the information-processing perspective. Information processing analyzes each component of how thoughts begin; how they are organized, remembered, and expressed; and how cognition builds, day by day. Infants' perception is powerfully influenced by particular experiences and motivation; affordances perceived by one infant differ from those perceived by another. Memory depends on brain maturation and on experience. For that reason, memory is fragile in the first year (although it can be triggered by dynamic perception and reminders) and becomes more evident, although still fragile, in the second year. ■

>> Language: What Develops in the First Two Years?

No other species has anything approaching the neurons and networks that support the 6,000 or so human languages. The human ability to communicate, even at age 2, far surpasses that of full-grown adults from every other species, including dolphins and chimpanzees, both of which have much better communication mechanisms than was formerly believed. Here we describe the specific steps in early language learning and then raise the crucial question: How do babies do it?

The Universal Sequence

The timing of language acquisition varies; the most advanced 10 percent of 2-year-olds speak more than 550 words, and the least advanced 10 percent speak fewer than 100 words—a fivefold difference (Merriman, 1999). But, although timing varies, the sequence is the same worldwide (see At About This Time on page 177). Even deaf children who become able to hear before age 3 (thanks to cochlear implants) follow the sequence. If they could not hear for the first months, their first words appear later, but they often catch up to their age-mates within a year or so (Ertmer et al., 2007). If they learn sign language, they also follow the sequence of word by word, then sentences of increasing length and complexity.

Listening and Responding

Infants begin learning language before birth, via brain organization and hearing. Habituation to noises has been demonstrated in

Who Is Babbling? Probably both the 6-month-old and the 27-year-old. During every day of infancy, mothers and babies communicate with noises, movements (notice the hands), and expressions.

ARIEL SKELLEY / GETTY IAMGES

CORBIS / ANTHONY BANNISTER

Too Young for Language? No. The early stages of language involve communication through noises, gestures, and facial expressions, very evident here between this !Kung grandmother and granddaughter.

fetuses several weeks before birth, which suggests that listening and remembering are inborn, basic to being human (Dirix et al., 2009). They even learn to prefer the language their mother speaks over an unheard language, with newborns of bilingual mothers preferring both languages and differentiating between them (Byers-Heinlein et al., 2010). (See the Research Design.)

Newborns look closely at facial expressions and prefer to hear speech over other sounds, a preference that is evident by 4 months (Minagawa-Kawai et al., 2011). By 6 months of age, infants can distinguish, just by looking at someone's mouth movements (no sound), whether that person is speaking their native language or not (Weikum et al., 2007). In fact, infants' ability to distinguish sounds and gestures in the language, or languages, most often heard improves over the first year, whereas the ability to hear sounds never spoken in their native language deteriorates (Narayan et al., 2010).

Careful analysis has found that adult communication with babies is distinct from communication with other adults (Falk, 2004). For instance, adults use higher pitch, simpler words, repetition, varied speeds, and exaggerated emotional tones when they speak to infants (Bryant & Barrett, 2007). This special language form is sometimes called *baby talk,* since it is talk directed to babies, and sometimes called *motherese,* since mothers universally speak it. Non-mothers speak it

Research Design

Scientists: Krista Byers-Heinlein, Tracey C. Burns, and Janet Werker.

Publication: *Psychological Science* (2010).

Participants: In three experiments, data were collected from 94 newborns (0–5 days old) in a large hospital in Vancouver, Canada. Half were born to mothers who spoke both English and Tagalog (the native language of Filipinos), one-third to mothers who spoke only English, and one-sixth to mothers who spoke English and Chinese.

Design: The infants sucked as they listened to 10 minutes of recorded sentences matched for pitch, duration, and number of syllables, alternating each minute in English or Tagalog. When they sucked at "high amplitude" (predetermined for each infant), the recording played. More frequent sucking was taken as a preference for one language or the other. The total number of intense sucks for English was subtracted from the Tagalog sucks.

Major conclusion: Most of the bilingual newborns preferred Tagalog, whereas the monolinguals preferred English. The Chinese bilinguals (who had not heard Tagalog in utero) were tested to rule out alternate explanations. As you see in the figure, newborn preferences were affected by language heard before birth. The researchers believe it is the rhythm of the language that becomes familiar, and they note that the rhythm of Chinese is somewhat similar to that of Tagalog, leading to the results of the Chinese bilinguals.

Comments: Other research had already shown that the fetus responds to the language spoken by the mother; this study suggests that some children begin to become bilingual before they are born. One advantage of this study is that all the participants were born in a large Canadian hospital, and thus all probably had adequate prenatal nutrition, health care, and birth experiences. More details, controls, and replication would help confirm the results. For example, although the bilingual mothers said they spoke both languages, with the less common one spoken at least 30 percent of the time, direct observation may have found otherwise. Until these results are replicated with other bilingual infants, it is possible that these results are related to something specific in Tagalog or English or are related to when and how much the mothers spoke each language, such as at work or at home. Nonetheless, this study confirms and extends a conclusion from thousands of studies: Infants have an amazing ability to learn languages, evident long before their first spoken word.

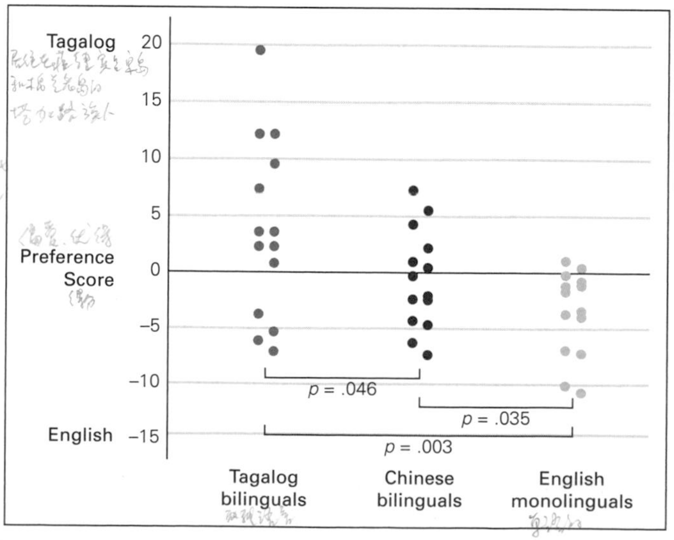

AT ABOUT THIS TIME
The Development of Spoken Language in the First Two Years

Age*	Means of Communication
Newborn	Reflexive communication—cries, movements, facial expressions.
2 months	A range of meaningful noises—cooing, fussing, crying, laughing.
3–6 months	New sounds, including squeals, growls, croons, trills, vowel sounds.
6–10 months	Babbling, including both consonant and vowel sounds repeated in syllables.
10–12 months	Comprehension of simple words; speechlike intonations; specific vocalizations that have meaning to those who know the infant well. Deaf babies express their first signs; hearing babies also use specific gestures (e.g., pointing) to communicate.
12 months	First spoken words that are recognizably part of the native language.
13–18 months	Slow growth of vocabulary, up to about 50 words.
18 months	Naming explosion—three or more words learned per day. Much variation: Some toddlers do not yet speak.
21 months	First two-word sentence.
24 months	Multiword sentences. Half the toddler's utterances are two or more words long.

*The ages of accomplishment in this table reflect norms. Many healthy children with normal intelligence attain these steps in language development earlier or later than indicated here.

Sources: Bloom, 1993, 1998; Fenson et al., 2000; Lenneberg, 1967.

as well. In fact, both "baby talk" and "motherese" may be misleading terms; scientists prefer the more formal designation, **child-directed speech.**

No matter what term is used, child-directed speech fosters learning. Even at 7 months of age, infants begin to recognize words that are highly distinctive (Singh, 2008): *Bottle, dog,* and *mama,* for instance, might be distinguished from one another before words that sound alike (such as *baby, Bobbie,* and *Barbie*). Infants respond vocally to adult noises and expressions (as well as to their own internal pleasures and pains) in many ways—with crying, cooing, and a variety of other sounds. Their responses gradually become more varied. By 4 months, most babies squeal, growl, gurgle, grunt, croon, and yell, telling everyone what is on their minds.

Also within the first months, infants' listening becomes more selective. Not only do infants prefer child-directed speech, they like alliteration, rhymes, repetition, rhythm, and varied pitch (Hayes & Slater, 2008; Schön et al., 2008). Think of your favorite lullaby (itself an alliterative word); obviously, babies prefer sounds over content.

Babbling

Between 6 and 9 months of age, babies begin to repeat certain syllables (*ma-ma-ma, da-da-da, ba-ba-ba*), a phenomenon referred to as **babbling** because of the way it sounds. Babbling is experience-expectant; all babies do it, even deaf ones. Responses from other people encourage babbling (this is the age of "making interesting events last"). Deaf babies stop babbling because they cannot hear responses; hearing babies continue.

All babies make rhythmic gestures, again in response to the actions of others (Iverson & Fagan, 2004). Toward the end of the first year, babbling begins to sound like the infant's native language; infants imitate what they hear in accents,

child-directed speech The high-pitched, simplified, and repetitive way adults speak to infants and children. (Also called *baby talk* or *motherese.*)

>> Response for Teachers (from page 174) Remember the three principles of infant memory: real life, motivation, and repetition. Find something children already enjoy that involves fractions—even if they don't realize it. Perhaps get a pizza and ask them to divide it in half, quarters, eighths, sixteenths, and so on.

babbling An infant's repetition of certain syllables, such as *ba-ba-ba,* that begins when babies are between 6 and 9 months old.

Especially for Nurses and Pediatricians The parents of a 6-month-old have just been told that their child is deaf. They don't believe it because, as they tell you, the baby babbles as much as their other children did. What do you tell them? (see response, page 178)

NEWSCOM

Happy Talk Ty's mother and the teacher demonstrate the sign for "more" in a sign language class at the public library in Hudson, Florida. Ty takes the lesson very seriously: Learning language in any form is crucial for 1-year-olds.

IMAGE SOURCE / GETTY IMAGES

Show Me Where Pointing is one of the earliest forms of communication, emerging at about 10 months.

cadence, consonants, and so on. Videotapes of deaf infants whose parents sign to them show that 10-month-olds use about a dozen distinct hand gestures in a repetitive manner similar to babbling. All babies express concepts with gestures sooner than with speech (Goldin-Meadow, 2006). Many caregivers, recognizing the power of gestures, teach "baby signs" to their 6- to 12-month-olds, allowing them to communicate with hand signs months before the infants master the fine motor skill of moving tongue, lips, and jaws to make specific words (Pizer et al., 2007).

One early gesture is pointing, typical in human babies at 10 months. Pointing is an advanced social gesture that requires understanding another person's perspective. Most animals cannot interpret pointing; most 10-month-old humans can look toward the place another person is pointing and can point themselves, even at the place where an object should be but no longer is (Liszkowski et al., 2009). Pointing with the index finger is a different and more advanced signal than doing so with a full hand, as if reaching (Liszkowski & Tomasello, 2011).

First Words

Finally, at about 1 year of age, the average hearing baby utters a few words. Caregivers usually understand the first words before strangers do, which makes it hard for researchers to pinpoint exactly what a 12-month-old can say. For example, at 13 months, Kyle knew standard words such as *mama,* but he also knew *da, ba, tam, opma,* and *daes,* which his parents knew to be, respectively, "downstairs," "bottle," "tummy," "oatmeal," and "starfish" (yes, that's what *daes* meant!) (Lewis et al., 1999).

>> Response for Nurses and Pediatricians (from page 177) Urge the parents to begin learning sign language immediately and investigate the possibility of cochlear implants. Babbling has a biological basis and begins at a specified time, in deaf as well as hearing babies. However, deaf babies eventually begin to use gestures more and to vocalize less than hearing babies. If their infant can hear, sign language does no harm. If the child is deaf, however, noncommunication may be devastating.

Gradual Beginnings

In the first months of the second year, spoken vocabulary increases gradually (perhaps one new word a week). However, 6- to 15-month-olds learn meanings rapidly; they understand about 10 times more words than they can say (Schafer, 2005; Snow, 2006). Initially, the first words are merely labels for familiar things (*mama* and *dada* are common), but some early words are soon accompanied by gestures, facial expressions, and nuances of tone, loudness, and cadence that are precursors of the first appearance of grammar (Saxton, 2010). A single word can convey various messages. Imagine meaningful sentences encapsulated in "Dada!" "Dada?" and "Dada." Each is a **holophrase,** a single word that expresses an entire thought.

holophrase A single word that is used to express a complete, meaningful thought.

Intonation (variations of tone and pitch) is extensive in early babbling and again in holophrases, with a temporary reduction in the range of intonation at about 12 months. Apparently, at 1 year of age infants reorganize their vocalization from universal to language-specific (Snow, 2006). They are no longer just singing and talking to themselves; they are trying to communicate in a specific language. Uttering meaningful words takes all their attention—none left over for intonation.

Careful tracing of early language from the information-processing perspective finds other times when vocalization seems to slow down before a burst of new talking, as perception and action are interdependent (Pulvermüller & Fadiga, 2010). That means that sometimes, with a new perceptual understanding, it takes time for verbal output to reflect that neurological advance. This slowdown before a language spurt is not evident in every infant, but many seem temporarily quieter before a burst of new words (Parladé & Iverson, 2011).

The Naming Explosion

Once vocabulary reaches about 50 *expressed* words (understood words are far more extensive), it builds rapidly, at a rate of 50 to 100 words per month, with 21-month-olds saying twice as many words as 18-month-olds (Adamson & Bakeman, 2006). This language spurt is called the **naming explosion** because many early words are nouns, although the word *noun* is a linguistic category, not an infant's preference (Waxman & Lidz, 2006).

naming explosion A sudden increase in an infant's vocabulary, especially in the number of nouns, that begins at about 18 months of age.

In almost every language, the name of each significant caregiver (often *dada, mama, nana, papa, baba, tata*) and sibling (and sometimes each pet) is learned between 12 and 18 months (Bloom, 1998). (See Appendix A, page A-4.) Other frequently uttered words refer to the child's favorite foods (*nana* can mean "banana" as well as "grandma") and to elimination (*pee-pee, wee-wee, poo-poo, ka-ka, doo-doo*). No doubt you notice that all these words have two identical syllables, each a consonant followed by a vowel. Many more words follow that pattern—not just *baba* but also *bobo, bebe, bubu, bibi*. Other early words are only slightly more complicated—*ma-me, ama,* and so on.

Especially for Caregivers A toddler calls two people "Mama." Is this a sign of confusion? (see response, page 180)

Cultural Differences

Cultures and families vary a great deal in how much child-directed speech children hear. Some parents read to their infants, teach them signs that communicate, and respond to every noise, including a burp or a fart, as if it is an attempt to talk. Others are much less verbal, using gestures, touch, and tone, saying "hush" and "no" instead of trying to teach vocabulary. As young as 5 months of age, babies prefer adults who often engage in child-directed speech, revealing their preferences even if, for the moment, those adults are silent. Apparently, just as infants seek to master physical skills as soon as they can, they seek to learn language from the best teachers available (Schachner & Hannon, 2011).

The idea that children should be "seen but not heard" is contrary to the emphasis on communication in most American families; however, an emphasis on listening respectfully, not talking, is common in other families, including many Latino ones (Cabrera et al., 2006), and among many fathers, especially those of low socioeconomic status (SES). Nonetheless, all infants listen to whatever they can and appreciate the sounds of their culture. Even musical tempo is culture-specific: 4- to 8-month-olds seem to like their own native music best (Soley & Hannon, 2010).

WOLFGANG KAEHLER / CORBIS

Cultural Values If they are typical of most families in the relatively taciturn Otavalo culture of Ecuador, these three children hear significantly less conversation than children elsewhere. In most Western cultures, that might be called maltreatment. However, each culture encourages the qualities it values, and verbal fluency is not a priority in this community. In fact, people who talk too much are ostracized and those who keep secrets are valued, so encouragement of talking may constitute maltreatment in the Otavalo culture.

Parts of Speech

Although all new talkers say names, use similar sounds, and say more nouns than any other parts of speech, the ratio of nouns to verbs and adjectives varies from place to place. For example, by 18 months, English-speaking infants use relatively more nouns but fewer verbs than Chinese or Korean infants do. Why?

One explanation goes back to the language itself. Mandarin and Korean are "verb-friendly" in that verbs are placed at the beginning or end of sentences, which makes them easier to learn. In English, verbs occur in various positions within sentences, and their forms change in illogical ways (e.g., *go, gone, will go, went*). This irregularity makes English verbs harder to learn than nouns.

An alternative explanation considers the entire social context: Playing with a variety of toys and learning about dozens of objects are crucial in North American culture, whereas East Asian cultures emphasize human interactions—specifically, how one person responds to another. Accordingly, North American infants are expected to name many objects, whereas Asian infants are expected to act on objects (as explained in Chapter 1) and respond to people. Thus, Chinese toddlers might learn the equivalent of *come, play, love, carry, run,* and so on before Canadian ones. (This is the result of experience, not genes. A toddler of Chinese ancestry, growing up in an English-speaking Canadian home, has the learning patterns of other English toddlers.)

A simpler explanation is that young children are sensitive to the sounds of words, with some sounds more salient than others. Verbs are learned more easily if they sound like the action (Imai et al., 2008), and such verbs may be more common in some languages than others. In English, most verbs are not onomatopoeic, although perhaps *jump, kiss,* and *poop*—all learned relatively early on—are exceptions. The infant preference for sounds may be one reason why many English-speaking toddlers who have never been on a farm nonetheless know that a cow says "moo" and a duck says "quack."

Every language has some words and concepts that are difficult. English-speaking infants confuse *before* and *after;* Dutch-speaking infants misuse *out* when it refers to taking off clothes; Korean infants need to learn two meanings of *in* (Mandler, 2004). Learning adjectives is easier in Italian and Spanish than

>> Response for Caregivers (from page 179) Not at all. Toddlers hear several people called "Mama" (their own mother, their grandmothers, their cousins' and friends' mothers) and experience mothering from several people, so it is not surprising if they use "Mama" too broadly. They will eventually narrow the label down to one person.

in English or French because of patterns in those languages (Waxman & Lidz, 2006). Specifically, adjectives can stand by themselves without the nouns. If I want a blue cup from a group of multicolored cups, I would ask for "a blue cup" or "a blue one" in English but simply "uno azul" (a blue) in Spanish. Despite such variations, in every language infants demonstrate impressive speed and efficiency in acquiring both vocabulary and grammar.

Putting Words Together

Grammar includes all the methods that languages use to communicate meaning. Word order, prefixes, suffixes, intonation, verb forms, pronouns and negations, prepositions and articles—all of these are aspects of grammar. Grammar can be discerned in holophrases but becomes obvious between 18 and 24 months, when two-word combinations begin (Hollich, 2010).

grammar All the methods—word order, verb forms, and so on—that languages use to communicate meaning, apart from the words themselves.

For example, "Baby cry" and "More juice" follow the proper English word order rather than the reverse. No child asks, "Juice more," and by age 2 children know that "cry baby" has an entirely different meaning. Soon the child combines three words, usually in subject–verb–object order in English (for example, "Mommy read book"), rather than any of the five other possible sequences of those words.

Children's grammar correlates with the size of their vocabulary (Snow, 2006). The child who says "Baby is crying" is advanced in language development compared with the child who says "Baby crying" or simply the holophrase "Baby." Comprehension advances as well. Their expanding knowledge of both vocabulary and grammar helps toddlers understand what others are saying (Kedar et al., 2006).

Young children can master two languages, not just one. The crucial variable is how much speech in both languages the child hears. Listening to two languages does not necessarily slow down the acquisition of grammar, but "development in each language proceeds separately and in a language specific manner" (Conboy & Thal, 2006, p. 727). Indeed, some evidence suggests that children are statisticians: They implicitly track the number of words and phrases and learn those expressed most often. That is certainly the case when children are learning their mother tongue; it is probably also true for knowing which sounds are most often

GETTY IMAGES

Look Who's Talking Men have a reputation for being strong and silent, but these three are more typical of today's men—sharing the joys and tribulations of fatherhood. Such conversations are distinctly human; other animals communicate, but only people use language so extensively.

Observation Quiz Which of these three prams is best for encouraging infant language? (see answer, page 182)

>> Answer to Observation Quiz (from page 181) The one on the left, which allows the baby to listen, watch, and talk to the father. One-on-one interaction is pivotal for learning language no matter which theory is right—reinforcement, social interaction, or brain maturation.

combined in two or three languages (Johnson & Tyler, 2010). Bilingual toddlers soon realize differences between languages, adjusting tone, cadence, as well as vocabulary when speaking to a monolingual person. Most bilingual children have parents who are also bilingual; hence, these children mix languages because they expect their parents to understand.

Theories of Language Learning

Worldwide, people who are not yet 2 years old already speak their native tongue. They continue to learn rapidly: Some teenagers compose lyrics or deliver orations that move thousands of their co-linguists. How is language learned so easily and so well?

Answers come from three schools of thought, each connected to a theory (behaviorism, sociocultural theory, and evolutionary psychology). The first says that infants are directly taught, the second that social impulses propel infants to communicate, and the third that infants understand language because of brain advances thousands of years ago that allowed survival of our species.

Theory One: Infants Need to Be Taught

The seeds of the first perspective were planted more than 50 years ago, when the dominant theory in North American psychology was behaviorism, or learning theory. The essential idea was that all learning is acquired, step by step, through association and reinforcement. Just as Pavlov's dogs learned to associate the sound of a tone with the presentation of food (see Chapter 2), behaviorists believe that infants associate objects with words they have heard often, especially if reinforcement occurs.

Especially for Nurses and Pediatricians Bob and Joan have been reading about language development in children. They are convinced that because language is "hardwired" they need not talk to their 6-month-old son. How do you respond? (see response, page 184)

B. F. Skinner (1957) noticed that spontaneous babbling is usually reinforced. Typically, every time the baby says "ma-ma-ma-ma," a grinning mother appears, repeating the sound as well as showering the baby with attention, praise, and perhaps food. These affordances are exactly what infants want, so babies repeat "ma-ma-ma-ma"; via operant conditioning, talking begins.

Skinner believed that most parents are excellent instructors, replying to their infants' gestures and sounds, thus reinforcing speech (Saxton, 2010). Even in preliterate societies, parents use child-directed speech, responding quickly with high pitch, short sentences, stressed nouns, and simple grammar—exactly the techniques that behaviorists would recommend.

The core ideas of this theory are the following:

- Parents are expert teachers, although other caregivers help.
- Frequent repetition is instructive, especially when linked to daily life.
- Well-taught infants become well-spoken children.

Behaviorists note that some 3-year-olds converse in elaborate sentences; others just barely put one simple word with another. Such variations correlate with the amount of language each child has heard. Parents of the most verbal children teach language throughout infancy—singing, explaining, listening, responding, and reading to them every day, even before age 1 (Forget-Dubois et al., 2009).

In one detailed U.S. study, researchers analyzed the language that mothers used with their 9-month-old infants (Tamis-LeMonda et al., 2001). Although all the mothers were middle class, from the same nation (to control for cultural and SES factors), in 10 minutes one mother never imitated her infant's babbling; another mother imitated 21 times, babbling back in conversation. All mothers described things or actions (e.g., "That is a spoon you are holding—spoon"), but one mother offered only 4 descriptions while another gave 33.

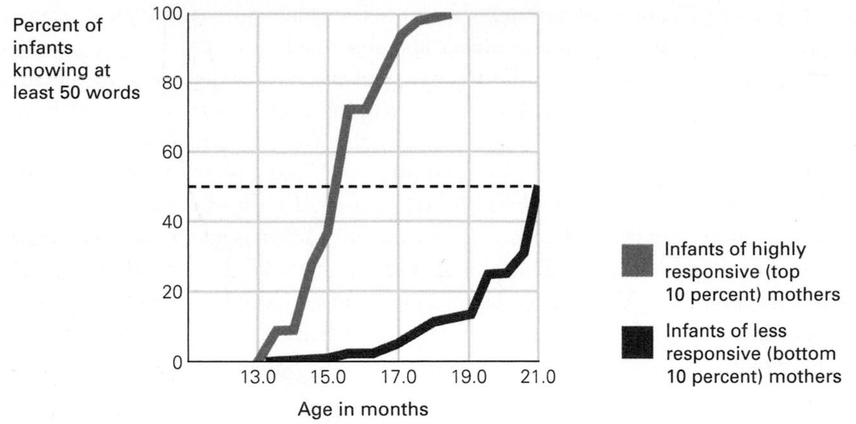

Source: Adapted from Tamis-LeMonda et al., 2001, p. 761.

FIGURE 6.2

Maternal Responsiveness and Infants' Language Acquisition Learning the first 50 words is a milestone in early language acquisition, as it predicts the arrival of the naming explosion and the multiword sentence a few weeks later. Researchers found that the 9-month-old infants of highly responsive mothers (top 10 percent) reached this milestone as early as 15 months. The infants of nonresponsive mothers (bottom 10 percent) lagged significantly behind.

Observation Quiz Why does the blue line end at 18 months? (see answer, page 185)

The frequency of maternal responsiveness at 9 months predicted language acquisition at 17 months (see Figure 6.2). It was not that noisy infants, whose genes would soon make them verbal, elicited more talk. Some quiet infants had mothers who frequently suggested play activities, described things, and asked questions. Quiet infants with talkative mothers usually became talkative later on. Those results are found in many nations. For example, in one large study in Australia, parents who provided extensive language to their preverbal infants had children who spoke early and well (Reilly et al., 2006).

According to behaviorists, if adults want children who speak, understand, and (later) read well, they must talk to their infants. A recent application of this theory comes from commercial videos, designed to advance toddlers' vocabulary. Typically, such videos use repetition and attention-grabbing measures (sound, tone, color) to encourage babies to learn new words (Vaala et al., 2010). Such videos, and Skinner's theories, have come under attack from many developmentalists, as explained in the following.

THINKING CRITICALLY

My Baby Can Read?

Toddlers can learn to swim in the ocean, throw a ball into a basket, walk on a narrow path beside a precipice, dial a phone, cut a melon with a sharp knife, play a guitar, say whatever word is on a flashcard, and much else—if provided appropriate opportunity, tools, encouragement, and practice. Indeed, toddlers in some parts of the world do each of these things—often to the dismay, disapproval, and even shock of adults in other cultures. Infants attempt to do what they see others doing, a trait that fosters rapid learning. The same trait challenges caregivers, who find it is not easy to keep "little scientists" safe.

In the past decade, many commercial companies have recognized this learning and have packaged videos, toys, and instructions for parents to teach babies to sort objects by shape, to recognize colors, or to say a word when they see a particular sign. Parents buy such products in order to accomplish two goals: to keep the baby safely entertained and to foster learning. The commercial products are expensive, advertised with testimonials, and named to appeal to parents, such as *Baby Einstein, Brainy Baby,* and *My Baby Can Read.* Contemporary toddlers are impressive learners. Is this because of educational videos? Probably not.

The learning abilities and accomplishments of toddlers have always been astonishing. Piaget is acclaimed for recognizing that; ignoring that made Uncle Henry a fool. Remember from Chapter 5 the face recognition skills that develop over the first year? A 1½-year-old can see another child on one occasion, hear his or her name, and then call that child by name a week later. Astonishing. Could you call that reading?

Similarly, 1-year-olds can reproduce actions demonstrated only once, can use a new toy in ways they have seen similar toys being used, can remember things that adults have forgotten. They are fascinated by dynamic activity, especially when it includes movement, sound, and people. This explains the popularity of child-directed videos—"like crack for babies," as one mother said (DeLoache et al., 2010, p. 1572). Not only are 1-year-olds "little scientists," experimenting with everything they can to reach conclusions about the natural world, they are also little linguists, mastering words at a rapid clip by age 2.

Thus, the abilities of toddlers have always been impressive. Since computers, talking toys, and commercial videos are pervasive in Western culture, and since many parents believe that their child's eventual achievement rests on what they do, many adults buy programs that are supposed to advance knowledge. Once people spend money and time on something, they tend to believe it works: Parents buy learning tools and then are impressed by their toddler's advances.

A rebuttal comes from research, which finds that the more video exposure a 6-month-old has, the slower the infant's cognitive and linguistic development (Tomopoulos et al., 2010). This study was not explicitly about "educational" videos, but there is no evidence that videos designed for infants improve later intellectual achievement. Before age 3, children's visual, auditory, symbolic, and conceptual skills render them less likely to learn with a video than without it—unless the video is a prop for parental involvement, in the same way a book or a trip to the store might be (Richert et al., 2011). In that case, learning would occur as well or better *without* the video (DeLoache et al., 2010). The crucial factor for intellectual growth seems to be caregiver responsiveness and encouragement.

Many developmentalists fear that advertisements take advantage of parents' wish to do everything they can for their child's future success (Yang et al., 2010). If toddlers exposed to a video express new words and concepts, parents tend to attribute that accomplishment to the video, not to the typical, amazing cognitive advances just described.

If a particular toddler does *not* master new skills at the advertised rate, few parents ask for a refund or complain of false advertising, instead blaming themselves or their baby. In 2009, developmentalists, pediatricians, and parents won a lawsuit against *Baby Einstein,* the source of most of the child-directed videos. As a result, *Baby Einstein* advertisements can no longer claim that their products are educational (Lewin, 2009).

Much depends on how a video is used (Courage & Setliff, 2010). Scientists might not criticize the parent who wrote a comment about the lawsuit against *Baby Einstein*:

> It's not a substitute for parental interaction or being read to, it's just a good way to spend 30 minutes in a long day being a baby. The more experiences babies have and the more things they see and hear, the more of a framework they have on which to hang further learning. Walks down the block, playing with parents, being read to, being spoken to, playing at anything, and yes, watching a TV screen that shows something that your child finds engaging, all contribute to that framework of experience, knowledge and understanding the world.
>
> My daughter, whom we adopted from China, had not been bathed in a bathtub in her orphanage. She did *not* like baths, or swimming pools (held by mommy or daddy) *at all.* One day we were watching Baby Neptune together. She was about 18 months old. After one scene with a kid playing in water, she got off of my lap (video still playing) and marched right into the bathroom, up her step stool, turned on the water in the sink and started to play in the water. Since that moment, she has turned into a true fish, loving baths, the sprinkler, her kiddie pool and now, at 8, she loves to swim all day. Not that she wouldn't have eventually found her love for water, but I saw the light go on!
>
> *[comment on Lewin, 2009]*

This seems to be a battle between most experts and many businesses, with parents on both sides and infants caught in the middle. Which side are you on? More important, why?

>> Response for Nurses and Pediatricians (from page 182) While much of language development is indeed hardwired, many experts assert that exposure to language is required. You don't need to convince Bob and Joan of this point, though—just convince them that their baby will be happier if they talk to him.

Especially for Educators An infant day-care center has a new child whose parents speak a language other than the one the teachers speak. Should the teachers learn basic words in the new language, or should they expect the baby to learn the majority language? (see response, page 186)

Theory Two: Social Impulses Foster Infant Language

The second theory is called *social-pragmatic*. It arises from the sociocultural reason for language: communication. According to this perspective, infants communicate because humans are social beings, dependent on one another for survival and joy. Each culture has practices that further social interaction; talking is one of those practices.

It is the emotional messages of speech, not the words, that are the focus of early communication, according to this perspective. In one study, people who had never heard English (Shuar hunter-gatherers living in isolation near the Andes Mountains) listened to tapes of North American mothers talking to their babies. The Shuar successfully distinguished speech conveying comfort, approval, attention, and prohibition, without knowing any of the words (Bryant & Barrett, 2007). Thus, the social content of speech is universal, which is why babies learn whatever specifics their culture provides.

Suppose an 18-month-old is playing with an unnamed toy and an adult utters a word. Does the child connect that word to the toy? A behaviorist, learning-by-association prediction would be yes, but the answer is no. In an experiment, when toddlers played with a fascinating toy and adults said a word, the toddlers looked up, figured out what the adult was looking at, and assigned the new word to that, not to the fascinating toy (Baldwin, 1993). This supports theory two: The toddlers wanted to know what the adults intended.

Another study also suggests social learning. Many 1-year-olds enjoy watching television and videos, but the evidence implies that they learn from it only when adults are actively involved in teaching (see Thinking Critically). In a controlled experiment, 1-year-olds learned vocabulary much better when someone directly taught them than when the same person taught on a video (Roseberry et al., 2009). This suggests personal, social, language acquisition, not impersonal learning.

According to theory two, then, social impulses, not explicit teaching, lead infants to learn language "as part of the package of being a human social animal" (Hollich et al., 2000). Those same impulses are evident in all the ways infants learn: According to this theory, people differ from the great apes in that they are social, driven to communicate. Thus, every infant (and no chimpanzee) masters words and grammar to join the social world in which he or she finds himself or herself (Tomasello & Herrmann, 2010).

OCEAN PHOTOGRAPHY / VEER

College Grad, Class of '33? Reading to an infant correlates with talking at age 1, reading at age 5, and college graduation at age 21. Of course, correlation is not causation, but in any case, this shared joy bodes well for the future.

Theory Three: Infants Teach Themselves

A third theory holds that language learning is innate; adults need not teach it, nor is it simply a by-product of social interaction. It arises from the universal human impulse to imitate. As already explained in the research on memory, infants and toddlers observe what they see and apply it—not slavishly but according to their own concepts and intentions. According to theory three, this is exactly what they do with the language they hear as well (Saxton, 2010).

The seeds of this perspective were planted soon after Skinner proposed his theory of verbal learning. Noam Chomsky (1968, 1980) and his followers felt that language is too complex to be mastered merely through step-by-step conditioning. Although behaviorists focus on variations among children in vocabulary size, Chomsky focused on similarities in language acquisition—the universals (see Chapter 2), not the differences.

>> Answer to Observation Quiz (from page 183) By 18 months, every one of the infants of highly responsive mothers (top 10 percent) knows 50 words. Not until 30 months do all the infants with quiet mothers reach the naming explosion.

Noting that all young children master basic grammar at about the same age, Chomsky cited this *universal grammar* as evidence that humans are born with a mental structure that prepares them to seek some elements of human language—for example, the use of a raised tone at the end of an utterance to indicate a question. Chomsky labeled this hypothesized mental structure the **language acquisition device (LAD).** The LAD enables children to derive the rules of grammar quickly and effectively from the speech they hear every day, regardless of whether their native language is English, Thai, or Urdu.

language acquisition device (LAD) Chomsky's term for a hypothesized mental structure that enables humans to learn language, including the basic aspects of grammar, vocabulary, and intonation.

Other scholars agree with Chomsky that infants are innately ready to use their minds to understand and speak whatever language is offered. All babies are eager learners, and language may be considered one more aspect of neurological maturation (Wagner & Lakusta, 2008). This idea does not strip languages and cultures of their differences in sounds, grammar, and almost everything else, but the basic idea is that "language is a window on human nature, exposing deep and universal features of our thoughts and feelings" (Pinker, 2007, p. 148).

The various languages of the world are all logical, coherent, and systematic. Infants are primed to grasp the particular language they are exposed to, making caregiver speech "not a 'trigger' but a 'nutrient'" (Slobin, 2001, p. 438). There is no need for a trigger, according to theory three, because words are expected by the developing brain, which quickly and efficiently connects neurons to support whichever language the infant hears. Thus, language itself is experience-expectant, although obviously the specific language is experience-dependent.

Research supports this perspective as well. As you remember, newborns are primed to listen to speech (Vouloumanos & Werker, 2007), and all infants babble *ma-ma* and *da-da* sounds (not yet referring to mother or father). No reinforcement or teaching is required; all infants need is for dendrites to grow, mouth muscles to strengthen, neurons to connect, and speech to be heard.

Nature even provides for deaf infants. All 6-month-olds, hearing or not, prefer to look at sign language over nonlinguistic pantomime. For hearing infants, this preference disappears by 10 months because their affinity for gestural language is not necessary for communication (Krentz & Corina, 2008). Deaf infants are signing by then.

A Hybrid Theory

Which of these three perspectives is correct? Perhaps all of them. In one monograph that included details and results of 12 experiments, the authors presented a hybrid (which literally means "a new creature, formed by combining other living things") of previous theories (Hollich et al., 2000). Since infants learn language to do numerous things—indicate intention, call objects by name, put words together, talk to family members, sing to themselves, express their wishes, remember the past, and much more—some aspects of language learning may be best explained by one theory at one age and other aspects by another theory at another age. Although originally developed to explain acquisition of first words, mostly nouns, this theory also explains learning verbs: Perceptual, social, and linguistic abilities combine to make that possible (Golinkoff & Hirsh-Pasek, 2008).

One study supporting the hybrid theory began, as did the study previously mentioned, with infants looking at pairs of objects that they had never seen and never heard named. One of each pair was fascinating to babies and the other was boring, specifically "a blue sparkle wand . . . [paired with] a white cabinet latch . . . a red, green, and pink party clacker . . . [paired with] a beige bottle opener" (Pruden et al., 2006, p. 267). The experimenter said a made-up name (not an actual word), and then the infants were tested to see whether they assigned the new word to the object that had the experimenter's attention (the dull one) or to the one that was interesting to them.

Unlike the previous study, which involved 18-month-olds, the participants in this one were 10-month-olds. The results differed from those involving older infants: The 10-month-olds seemed to assign the word to the fascinating object, not the dull one. These researchers' interpretation was that *how* language is learned depends on the age of the child as well as on the particular circumstances. Behaviorism may work for young children, social learning for slightly older ones: "The perceptually driven 10-month-old becomes the socially aware 19-month-old" (Pruden et al., 2006, p. 278).

After intensive study, another group of scientists also endorsed a hybrid theory, concluding that "multiple attentional, social and linguistic cues" contribute to early language (Tsao et al., 2004, p. 1081). It makes logical and practical sense for nature to provide several paths toward language learning and for various theorists

>> **Response for Educators** (from page 184) Probably both. Infants love to communicate, and they seek every possible way to do so. Therefore, the teachers should try to understand the baby, and the baby's parents, but should also start teaching the baby the majority language of the school.

to emphasize one or another of them (Sebastián-Gallés, 2007). It also seems that not only are some aspects of language learned in one way or another at certain ages, but also that each child learns differently; that is, some children learn better one way, and others, another way (Goodman et al., 2008). Parents need to talk often to their infants (theory one), encourage social interaction (theory two), and appreciate the innate abilities of the child (theory three).

As one expert concludes:

> In the current view, our best hope for unraveling some of the mysteries of language acquisition rests with approaches that incorporate multiple factors, that is, with approaches that incorporate not only some explicit linguistic model, but also the full range of biological, cultural, and psycholinguistic processes involved.
>
> *[Tomasello, 2006, pp. 292–293]*

The idea that every theory is correct in some way may seem almost idealistic. However, a similar conclusion was arrived at by scientists extending and interpreting research on language acquisition. They contend that language learning is neither the direct product of repeated input (behaviorism) nor the result of a specific human neurological capacity (LAD). Rather, from an evolutionary perspective, "different elements of the language apparatus may have evolved in different ways," and thus a "piecemeal and empirical" approach is needed (Marcus & Rabagliati, 2009, p. 281). In other words, a single theory that explains how babies learn language does not reflect the data: Humans accomplish this feat in many ways.

What conclusion can we draw from all this? That infants are active learners, not only of language, concepts, objects, and goals as explained in this chapter but also of the motor skills detailed in Chapter 5 and the social understanding to be described in Chapter 7.

Now back to Uncle Henry: My cousins loved their mother because she knew instinctively that her infant boys were ready to learn. When they grew up they realized, as developmentalists all recognize, that even in the first weeks of life, every caregiver—fathers as well as mothers—can be the first, and perhaps the best, teacher.

SUMMING UP

From the first days of life, babies attend to words and expressions, responding as well as their limited abilities allow—crying, cooing, and soon babbling. Before age 1, they understand simple words and communicate with gestures. At 1 year, most infants speak. Vocabulary accumulates slowly at first, but then more rapidly with the naming explosion and with the emergence of the holophrase and the two-word sentence.

The impressive language learning of the first two years can be explained in many ways: that caregivers must teach language, that infants learn because they are social beings, that inborn cognitive capacity propels infants to acquire language as soon as maturation makes that possible. Because infants vary in culture, learning style, and social context, a hybrid theory contends that each theory may be valid for some aspects of language learning and at different ages. ■

SUMMARY

Sensorimotor Intelligence

1. Piaget realized that very young infants are active learners, seeking to understand their complex observations and experiences. Sensorimotor intelligence, the first of Piaget's four periods of cognitive development, involves early adaption to experience.

2. Sensorimotor intelligence develops in six stages, beginning with reflexes and ending with mental combinations. The six stages occur in pairs, with each pair characterized by a circular reaction, or feedback loop, as infants first react to their own bodies (primary), then respond to other people and things (secondary). Finally, in the stage of tertiary circular reactions, infants become more goal-oriented, creative, and experimental as "little scientists."

3. Infants gradually develop an understanding of objects. As shown in Piaget's classic experiments, infants understand object permanence and begin to search for hidden objects at about 8 months. Other research, using brain scans and other new methods, finds that Piaget underestimated infant cognition, in object permanence and many other ways.

Information Processing

4. Another approach to understanding infant cognition involves information-processing theory, which looks at each step of the thinking process, from input to output. The perceptions of a young infant are attuned to the particular affordances, or opportunities for action, that are present in the infant's world.

5. Objects that move are particularly interesting to infants, as are other humans. Objects as well as people afford many possibilities for interaction and perception, and therefore these affordances enhance early cognition.

6. Infant memory is fragile but not completely absent. Reminder sessions help trigger memories, and young brains learn motor sequences long before they can remember with words. Memory is multifaceted; explicit memories are rare in infancy.

Language: What Develops in the First Two Years?

7. Language learning may be the most impressive cognitive accomplishment of infants, distinguishing the human species from other animals. The universal sequence of early language development is well known; there are alternative explanations for how early language is learned.

8. Eager attempts to communicate are apparent in the first weeks and months. Infants babble at about 6 to 9 months, understand words and gestures by 10 months, and speak their first words at about 1 year. Deaf infants make their first signs even before a year.

9. Vocabulary begins to build very slowly until the infant knows approximately 50 words. Then the naming explosion begins. Toward the end of the second year, toddlers put words together in short sentences, evidence that that they understand basic grammar.

10. Various theories explain how infants learn language as quickly as they do. The three main theories emphasize different aspects of early language learning: that infants must be taught, that their social impulses foster language learning, and that their brains are genetically attuned to language.

11. Each theory of language learning is confirmed by some research. The challenge for developmental scientists has been to formulate a hybrid theory that uses all the insights and research on early language learning. The challenge for caregivers is to respond to the infant's early attempts to communicate, expecting neither too much nor too little.

KEY TERMS

sensorimotor intelligence (p. 162)
primary circular reactions (p. 162)
secondary circular reactions (p. 163)
object permanence (p. 164)
tertiary circular reactions (p. 165)
"little scientist" (p. 166)
deferred imitation (p. 166)
habituation (p. 167)
fMRI (p. 167)
information-processing theory (p. 169)
affordance (p. 169)
visual cliff (p. 170)
dynamic perception (p. 170)
people preference (p. 171)
reminder session (p. 173)
implicit memory (p. 174)
explicit memory (p. 174)
child-directed speech (p. 177)
babbling (p. 177)
holophrase (p. 177)
naming explosion (p. 179)
grammar (p. 181)
language acquisition device (LAD) (p. 185)

WHAT HAVE YOU LEARNED?

Sensorimotor Intelligence

1. Why did Piaget call his first stage of cognition *sensorimotor* intelligence?

2. How do the first two sensorimotor stages illustrate primary circular reactions?

3. If a parent speaks and a baby babbles in response, how does that illustrate stage three of sensorimotor intelligence?

4. How is object permanence an example of stage four of sensorimotor intelligence?

5. In sensorimotor intelligence, what is the difference between stages five and six?

6. What steps of the scientific method does the "little scientist" follow?

7. Why is becoming bored a sign of infant cognitive development?

8. Why did Piaget underestimate how rapidly early cognition occurs?

Information Processing

9. How do the affordances of this book, for example, differ at age 1 month, 12 months, and 20 years?

10. What are several hypotheses to explain why infants refuse to crawl over visual cliffs?

11. What two preferences show that infants are selective in early perception?

12. What conditions help 3-month-olds remember something?

13. What is the crucial difference between implicit and explicit memory?

14. Why is explicit memory difficult for babies under age 2?

Language: What Develops in the First Two Years?

15. What communication abilities do infants have at 6 months?

16. What aspects of early language development are universal, apparent in babies of every culture and family?

17. What is typical of the rate and nature of the first words that infants speak?

18. What have developmentalists discovered about the way adults talk to babies?

19. What are the early signs of grammar in infant speech?

20. According to behaviorism, how do adults teach infants to talk?

21. According to sociocultural theory, why do infants try to communicate?

22. What does the idea that child speech results from brain maturation imply for caregivers?

23. How does the hybrid theory of language development compare to the eclectic approach to developmental study described in Chapter 2?

APPLICATIONS

1. Elicit vocalizations from an infant—babbling if the baby is under age 1, using words if older. Write down all the baby says for 10 minutes. Then ask the primary caregiver to elicit vocalizations for 10 minutes, and write these down. What differences are apparent between the baby's two attempts at communication? Compare your findings with the norms described in the chapter.

2. Piaget's definition of intelligence is adaptation. Others consider a good memory or an extensive vocabulary to be a sign of intelligence. How would you define intelligence? Give examples.

3. Many educators recommend that parents read to babies even before the babies begin talking. What theory of language development does this reflect?

4. Test an infant's ability to search for a hidden object. Ideally, the infant should be about 7 or 8 months old, and you should retest over a period of weeks. If the infant can immediately find the object, make the task harder by pausing between the hiding and the searching or by secretly moving the object from one hiding place to another.

>>ONLINE CONNECTIONS

To accompany your textbook, you have access to a number of online resources, including quizzes for every chapter of the book, flashcards (in English and Spanish), critical thinking questions, and case studies. For access to any of these links, go to www.worthpublishers.com/bergerca9e. In addition to these free resources, you'll also find links to podcasts, video clips, diagnostic quizzing with personalized study advice, and an ebook. Some of the videos and activities available online include:

- *The Visual Cliff.* Includes footage from Joseph Campos's lab at the University of California, Berkeley.
- *Language Development in Infancy.* How easy is it to understand a newborn's coos? Or a 6-month-old's babbling? But we can almost all make out the voice of a toddler singing "Twinkle, Twinkle." Video clips from a variety of real-life contexts bring to life the development of children's language.

7

CHAPTER

The First Two Years: Psychosocial Development

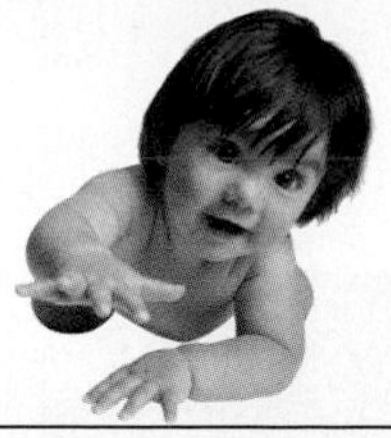

WHAT WILL YOU KNOW?

1. How do smiles and tears change from birth to age 2, and what difference does it make?
2. How much do various theories and cultures differ in their perceptions of infant emotions?
3. What are the signs of the parent–infant bond in infancy?

My 1-week-old grandson cried. Often. Again and again. Day and night. For a long time. Again. He and his parents were living with me while they looked for an apartment. I was the dog walker and cook, not caregiver, so I didn't mind for myself. But I did mind for my sleep-deprived daughter.

"Give him a pacifier," I told her.

"No, that causes 'nipple confusion,'" she said.

"I never heard of that. What have you been reading? Give him a pacifier."

My daughter knows that I value research and evidence, not hearsay or anecdote. She replied, "The American Academy of Pediatrics says no pacifiers for breast-fed babies in the first month. Here it is on their Web site."

That quieted me, but in the next few months I developed another worry—that my son-in-law would resent fatherhood. He spent many hours, day and night, carrying my unhappy grandson while my daughter slept.

"It seems to me that you do most of the baby comforting," I told him.

"That's because Elissa does most of the breast-feeding," he answered with a smile.

I learned a good deal in those months. In the decades since my children were infants, pediatricians have made new recommendations and fathers have become more active partners.

This chapter opens by tracing infants' emotions as their brains mature and their experiences accumulate, noting temperamental and cultural differences. Then we apply each of the five theories introduced in Chapter 2. Infant feeding and ethnotheories are included when we compare theories, as many practices are applications of general assumptions. This leads to an exploration of caregiver–infant interaction, particularly *synchrony, attachment,* and *social referencing.* For every aspect of caregiving, fathers as well as mothers are included.

We then consider infant day care, paying special attention to its impact on psychosocial development. The chapter ends with practical suggestions, reflecting what I have learned from my experiences, old and new, as well as from thousands of researchers, parents, and infants. Many specifics vary depending on culture and cohort, but some universal psychosocial needs are apparent. With or without pacifiers or patient fathers, most infants (including my now-happy grandson) thrive, as long as their basic emotional needs are met.

>> Emotional Development

Within the first two years, infants progress from reactive pain and pleasure to complex patterns of social awareness (see At About This Time) (Lewis, 2010). This is a period of "high emotional responsiveness" (Izard et al., 2002, p. 767), expressed in speedy, uncensored reactions—crying, startling, laughing, raging—and, by toddlerhood, in complex responses, from self-satisfied grins to mournful pouts.

CHRISTOPHER HERWIG / LONELY PLANET IMAGES

Smiles All Around Joy is universal when an infant smiles at her beaming grandparents—a smile made even better when the tongue joins in. This particular scene takes place in Kazakhstan in central Asia, an independent nation only since 1991.

Infants' Emotions

At first, there is pleasure and pain. Newborns look happy and relaxed when fed and drifting off to sleep. They cry when they are hurt or hungry, tired or frightened (as by a loud noise or a sudden loss of support). About one-third of infants have bouts of uncontrollable crying, called *colic*—probably the result of immature digestion.

Smiling and Laughing

Soon, additional emotions become recognizable (Lavelli & Fogel, 2005). Curiosity is evident as infants (and people of all ages) respond to objects and experiences that are new but not too novel. Happiness is expressed by the **social smile,** evoked by a human face at about 6 weeks. Preterm babies are later to smile at people because the social smile is affected by age since conception.

social smile A smile evoked by a human face, normally evident in infants about six weeks after birth.

Infants worldwide express social joy, even laughter, between 2 and 4 months (Konner, 2007; Lewis, 2010). Among the Navajo, whoever brings forth that first laugh gives a feast to celebrate the baby's becoming a person (Rogoff, 2003). Laughter builds as curiosity does; a typical 6-month-old laughs loudly upon discovering new things, particularly social experiences that have the right balance between familiarity and surprise, such as Daddy making a funny face.

Anger and Sadness

The positive emotions of joy and contentment are soon joined by negative emotions, more frequent in infancy than later on (Izard, 2009). Anger is evident at 6 months, usually triggered by frustration. Anger is obvious when infants are prevented from grabbing an object they want or from moving as they wish. For instance, when researchers wanted to see how infants responded to frustration, they "crouched behind the child and gently restrained his or her arms for 2 minutes or until 20 seconds of hard crying ensued" (Mills-Koonce et al., 2011, p. 390). "Hard crying" was not infrequent: Infants hate to be strapped in, caged in, closed in, or even just held tightly when they want to explore.

As always, culture and experience influence the norms of development. This is especially true for emotional development after the first eight months.

AT ABOUT THIS TIME

Ages When Emotions Emerge

Birth	Crying; contentment
6 weeks	Social smile
3 months	Laughter; curiosity
4 months	Full, responsive smiles
4–8 months	Anger
9–14 months	Fear of social events (strangers, separation from caregiver)
12 months	Fear of unexpected sights and sounds
18 months	Self-awareness; pride; shame; embarrassment

Anger in infancy is a healthy response to frustration, unlike sadness, which also appears in the first months. Sadness indicates withdrawal and is accompanied by an increase in the body's production of *cortisol,* the primary stress hormone. In a series of experiments, 4-month-olds were taught to pull a string to see a picture, which they enjoyed—not unlike the leg kicking that made the mobiles move, discussed in Chapter 6. Then the string no longer made the picture appear—and most of the babies reacted by angrily pulling the string. Some babies, however, quit trying and looked sad (Lewis & Ramsay, 2005); they were the ones for whom cortisol increased. This suggests that anger relieves stress, but some babies had learned, to their sorrow, that anger was not appropriate.

Since, in this study and others, sadness is shown to be accompanied by stress, sorrow is probably not a superficial emotion. Many researchers believe that the infant brain is shaped by the early social emotions, particularly sadness and fear (Fries & Pollak, 2007; S. C. Johnson, 2010).

Fear

Fully formed fear in response to some person, thing, or situation (not just distress at a surprise) emerges at about 9 months and then rapidly becomes more frequent as well as more apparent (Witherington et al., 2004). Two kinds of social fear are obvious:

- **Stranger wariness,** evident when an infant no longer smiles at any friendly face but cries if an unfamiliar person moves too close, too quickly
- **Separation anxiety,** expressed in tears, dismay, or anger when a familiar caregiver leaves

stranger wariness An infant's expression of concern—a quiet stare, clinging to a familiar person, or sadness—when a stranger appears.

separation anxiety An infant's distress when a familiar caregiver leaves, most obvious between 9 and 14 months.

Separation anxiety is normal at age 1, intensifies by age 2, and usually subsides after that. If it remains strong after age 3, it is considered an emotional disorder (Silverman & Dick-Niederhauser, 2004). Fear of separation may interfere with infant sleep; for example, if infants have learned to expect the presence of familiar objects and people when they go to sleep, they may wake up terrified if they are alone (Sadeh et al., 2010). Unless the parents also are fearful of their child sleeping alone, eventually children learn to do so.

Many 1-year-olds fear not only strangers but also anything unexpected, from the flush of a toilet to the pop of a jack-in-the-box, from the closing of elevator doors to the tail-wagging approach of a dog. With repeated experiences and caregiver reassurance, older infants might themselves enjoy flushing the toilet (again and again) or calling the dog (crying if the dog does *not* come).

JOURNAL-COURIER / TIFFANY HERMON / THE IMAGE WORKS

Stranger Wariness Becomes Santa Terror For toddlers, even a friendly stranger is cause for alarm, especially if Mom's protective arms are withdrawn. The most frightening strangers are men who are unusually dressed and who act as if they might take the child away. Ironically, therefore, Santa Claus remains terrifying until children are about 3 years old.

Toddlers' Emotions

Emotions take on new strength during toddlerhood (Izard, 2009). For example, throughout the second year and beyond, anger and fear become less frequent but more focused, targeted toward infuriating or terrifying experiences. Similarly, laughing and crying become louder and more discriminating.

New emotions appear: pride, shame, embarrassment, disgust, and guilt (Stevenson et al., 2010; Thompson, 2006). These emotions require social awareness, which emerges from family interactions and is influenced by the culture (Mesquita & Leu, 2007). For example, North American parents encourage pride in their toddlers (saying, "You did it yourself"—even when that is untrue), but Asian families discourage pride and cultivate modesty and shame (Rogoff, 2003). Disgust is strongly influenced by other people: Many 18-month-olds (but not younger infants) express disgust at touching a dead animal, but none are yet disgusted when a teenager curses at an elderly person, something that parents and older children may find disgusting (Stevenson et al., 2010).

By age 2, children can display the entire spectrum of emotional reactions. They have been taught what is acceptable in their family and culture—sometimes fear, sometimes boldness (Saarni et al., 2006). For example, if a toddler hides his face in his mother's skirt when a friendly dog approaches, the mother could hastily pick the child up or enthusiastically pet the dog, teaching fear or welcome the next time a dog appears.

Especially for Nurses and Pediatricians Parents come to you concerned that their 1-year-old hides her face and holds onto them tightly whenever a stranger appears. What do you tell them? (see response, page 195)

Self-Awareness

self-awareness A person's realization that he or she is a distinct individual, whose body, mind, and actions are separate from those of other people.

In addition to social awareness, another foundation for emotional growth is **self-awareness,** the realization that one's body, mind, and activities are separate from those of other people (Kopp, 2011). Closely following the new mobility that results from walking, at about age 1 an emerging sense of "me" and "mine" leads to a new consciousness of others.

Very young infants have no sense of self—at least of *self* as most people define it (Harter, 2006). In fact, a prominent psychoanalyst, Margaret Mahler, theorized that for the first 4 months infants see themselves as part of their mothers. They "hatch" at about 5 months and spend the next several months developing their sense of self (Mahler et al., 1975).

Some aspects of selfhood emerge even before age 1, but

> more complex self-representations are reflected [in] . . . self-referential emotions . . . . By the end of the second year and increasingly in the third [ages 1 and 2] the simple joy of success becomes accompanied by looking and smiling to an adult and calling attention to the feat; the simple sadness of failure becomes accompanied either by avoidance of eye contact with the adult and turning away or by reparative activity and confession . . .
>
> *[Thompson, 2006, p. 79]*

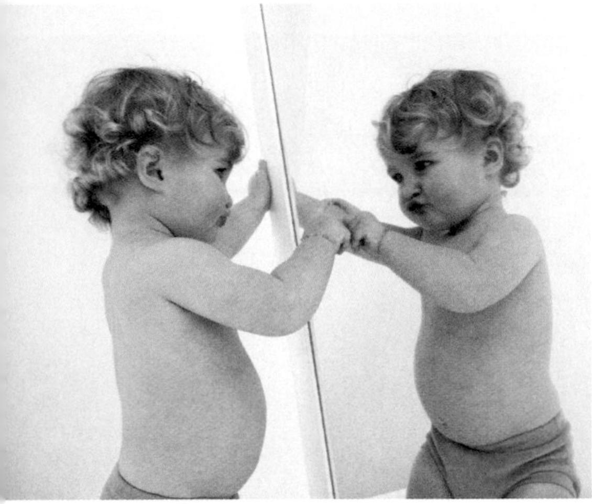

ANTOINE JULIETTE / AGE FOTOSTOCK

Who Is That? At 18 months, he is at the beginning of self-awareness, testing to see whether his mirror image will meet his finger.

In a classic experiment (M. Lewis & Brooks, 1978), babies aged 9 to 24 months looked into a mirror after a dot of rouge had been surreptitiously put on their noses. If the babies reacted by touching their noses, that meant they knew the mirror showed their own faces. None of the babies younger than 12 months old reacted as if they recognized themselves (they sometimes smiled and touched the dot on the "other" baby in the mirror). However, between 15 and 24 months, babies usually showed self-awareness, touching their own noses with curiosity and puzzlement.

Self-recognition in the mirror/rouge test (as well as in photographs) usually emerges at about 18 months, along with two other advances: pretending and using first-person pronouns (*I, me, mine, myself, my*) (Lewis, 2010). Therefore, some developmentalists connect self-recognition in the mirror with self-understanding, although "the interpretation of this seemingly simple task is plagued by controversy" (Nielsen et al., 2006, p. 176).

For example, one study found that self-recognition in the mirror/rouge test *negatively* correlated with embarrassment when a doll's leg fell off (it had been rigged to do so) as each toddler played with it (Barrett, 2005). Many 17-month-olds who recognized themselves, particularly boys, were *less* embarrassed at this mishap and more likely to tell the examiner about it. Does a sense of self diminish shame as it increases pride? Perhaps. Pride may be linked to the maturing self-concept, not necessarily to other people's opinions (Barrett, 2005).

Brain Maturation and the Emotions

Brain maturation is involved in all the emotional developments just described. There is no doubt that varied experiences, as well as good nutrition, promote both brain growth and emotional development. Nor is there any doubt that emotional reactions begin with neurons connecting to other neurons (M. H. Johnson, 2011).

Social Impulses

Many specific aspects of brain maturation support social emotions (Lloyd-Fox et al., 2009). For instance, most developmentalists agree that the social smile and the first laughter appear as the cortex matures (Konner, 2007). The same is probably true for nonreflexive fear, self-awareness, and anger. The maturation of a particular part of the cortex (the anterior cingulate gyrus) is directly connected to emotional self-regulation, which allows a child to moderate these emotions (Posner et al., 2007). (Several other parts of the brain comprise the limbic system, where many emotions originate. This is described in Chapter 8.)

One aspect of the infant's emotional development is that particular people (typically those the infant sees most often) arouse specific emotions. This is the result not only of past experience but also of neurological maturation, as a sequence of neurons that fire together become more closely and quickly connected in the brain. In the first weeks after birth, babies are content to be cared for by any competent person—a biological relative or a stranger. Soon preferences form, which is one reason adopted children are, ideally, placed with their new parents in the first days of life—unlike 100 years ago, when adoptions began after age 1.

All emotional reactions, particularly those connected to self-awareness, depend partly on memory (Harter, 2006; Lewis, 2010). As already explained in Chapter 6, memory is fragile at first and gradually improves as dendrites and axons connect. No wonder children over age 1 are more quickly angered than younger children when teased by an older sibling or are more obviously reluctant to enter the doctor's office. Toddlers remember the previous time a sibling frustrated them or the doctor gave them a shot. (As already noted, anger appears earlier when an infant is restricted or frustrated—not much memory needed for that.)

>> Response for Nurses and Pediatricians (from page 193) Stranger wariness is normal up to about 14 months. This baby's behavior actually sounds like secure attachment!

Stress

Chapter 5 suggested that excessive stress impairs the brain, particularly in areas associated with emotions (Adam et al., 2007). Brain imagery and cortisol measurements suggest that the hypothalamus (part of the brain that regulates bodily functions and hormone production, discussed further in Chapter 8) grows more slowly if an infant is often stressed.

The brain damage from abuse in infancy is difficult to prove experimentally, for obvious ethical reasons. However, brain scans of maltreated children reveal abnormal activation in response not only to stress and other emotions but even to photographs of frightened people (Gordis et al., 2008; Masten et al., 2008). Such abnormal neurological responses are likely caused by early abuse.

As first mentioned in Chapter 5, this research has important biosocial applications. Here we focus on the psychosocial aspects, which show how the social context relates to infant emotions. Since infants are learning emotional responses from the beginning of life, it is crucial that new parents be supported by the community so that they can respond consistently and lovingly to the newborn.

One study found a cascade of stress throughout development: Fathers affect mothers' stress levels, and, if a mother is highly stressed, that stress can harm their child (Talge et al., 2007). Contemporary fathers also directly affect infants' stress: If they are intrusive and critical caregivers, already by 7 months their babies have higher cortisol levels in response to challenges, such as the restraint described above (Mills-Koonce et al., 2011).

ALAMY

On Top of His World This boy's blissful expression is evidence that fathers can prevent or relieve stress in infants, protecting a baby's brain and promoting the mother's peace of mind.

Synesthesia

Brain maturation may affect an infant's ability to differentiate emotions—for instance, distinguishing between fear and joy. Some infants seem to cry at everything. Early emotional confusion seems similar to *synesthesia,* a phenomenon in which one sense triggers another in the brain. For older children and adults, the most common form of synesthesia is when a number or letter evokes a vivid color. Among adults, synesthesia is unusual; often, it is partly genetic and indicates artistic creativity (K. J. Barnett et al., 2008).

Synesthesia seems more common in infants because the boundaries between the sensory parts of the cortex are still forming (Walker et al., 2010). Textures seem associated with vision, sounds with smells, and the infant's own body seems connected to the bodies of others. The sensory connections are called *cross-modal perception;* the interpersonal connections may become the basis for early social understanding (Meltzoff, 2007).

The tendency of one part of the brain to activate another may also occur for emotions. An infant's cry can be triggered by pain, fear, tiredness, surprise, or excitement; laughter can turn to tears. Discrete emotions during early infancy are more difficult to recognize, differentiate, or predict than the same emotions in adulthood; infant emotions erupt, increase, or disappear for unknown reasons (Camras & Shutter, 2010). Brain immaturity is a likely explanation.

Temperament

Every human emotion is influenced by a person's genotype. Thus, an infant might be happy or fearful not only because of maturation but also because of the combination of various alleles on many genes. Among each person's genetic predispositions are traits of **temperament,** defined as the "biologically based core of individual differences in style of approach and response to the environment that is stable across time and situations" (van den Akker et al., 2010, p. 485). "Biologically based" means that these traits originate with nature (genes). Confirmation that temperament is constitutionally, not experientially, based comes from an analysis of newborn cries after the hepatitis B inoculation: Cry variations correlated with later temperament (Jong et al., 2010).

temperament Inborn differences between one person and another in emotions, activity, and self-regulation. Temperament is epigenetic, originating in genes but affected by child-rearing practices.

Temperament may overlap with personality, but the two terms are not synonymous. Personality traits (e.g., honesty and humility) are thought to be primarily learned, whereas temperamental traits (e.g., shyness and aggression) are considered primarily genetic. Of course, even though temperament originates with the genes, the actual expression of the traits is modified by experience—the result of child-rearing methods, culture, and learning (Rothbart & Bates, 2006).

The New York Longitudinal Study

In laboratory studies of temperament, infants are exposed to events that are frightening. Four-month-olds might see spinning mobiles or hear unusual sounds. Older babies might confront a noisy, moving robot or a clown who quickly moves close. At such experiences, some children laugh (and are classified as "easy"), some cry ("difficult"), and some are quiet ("slow to warm up"). These three categories come from the *New York Longitudinal Study* (NYLS). Begun in the 1960s, the NYLS was the first among many large studies to recognize that each newborn has distinct inborn traits (Thomas & Chess, 1977).

According to the NYLS, by 3 months, infants manifested nine temperamental traits that could be clustered into four categories (the three described above and a fourth category of infants who are "hard to classify"). The proportion of infants in each category was as follows:

- Easy (40 percent)
- Difficult (10 percent)
- Slow to warm up (15 percent)
- Hard to classify (35 percent)

Later research has confirmed that newborns differ in temperament and that some babies are unusually difficult. However, although the NYLS began a rich research endeavor, the nine dimensions of the NYLS have not held up to later research (Caspi & Shiner, 2006; Zentner & Bates, 2008). Generally, only three (not nine) dimensions of temperament are clearly present in early childhood (Else-Quest et al., 2006; van den Akker et al., 2010). Although each study of infant temperament uses somewhat different terms, the overall conclusions are similar, and the following three dimensions are apparent:

- Effortful control (able to regulate attention, balanced)
- Negative mood (fearful, angry, unhappy)
- Surgency (active, social, not shy, exuberant)

Especially for Nurses Parents come to you with their fussy 3-month-old. They say they have read that temperament is "fixed" before birth, and they are worried that their child will always be difficult. What do you tell them? (see response, page 198)

A VIEW FROM SCIENCE

Still Frightened?

One longitudinal study (Fox et al., 2001) identified three distinct types among 4-month-olds—exuberant, negative, and inhibited (fearful). We report this study in detail partly because these researchers used many methods to measure infant emotions: experiments within a laboratory, measures that varied depending on the age of the babies, detailed reports from the mothers, and brain scans. Moreover, they studied the same children at 4, 9, 14, 24, and 48 months and also followed up years later (Williams et al., 2010).

In the original study, half of the participants did not change much from 4 months to 4 years, reacting the same way and having similar brain-wave patterns when confronted with frightening experiences every time they were tested. The other half exhibited altered responses as they grew older. Inhibited, fearful infants were most likely to change and exuberant infants, least likely (see Figure 7.1). That speaks to the influence of child-rearing methods: Adults coax frightened children to be brave and encourage exuberant children to stay happy. The longitudinal research also speaks to the influence of culture: The formerly inhibited boys, as teenagers, were more likely to use drugs, but the inhibited girls were less likely to do so (Williams et al., 2010).

Similar results were found in another study that described temperament using three traits (typical, fearful, and expressive). Continuity was common, but the fearful children (already only 14 percent at age 2½) were most likely to change. By age 3, only 5 percent of the 3-year-olds were classified as fearful (van den Akker et al., 2010). Parental attitudes and actions were likely to cause the changes.

Other longitudinal studies of the relationship between infant temperament and adolescent personality (especially antisocial traits) again confirm these results: Continuity is evident, but so is the effect of family and culture, which sometimes diminish difficult or negative traits (Kagan et al., 2007; Zentner & Bates, 2008). Science repeatedly finds that many factors, both nature and nurture, underlie every trait of temperament or personality.

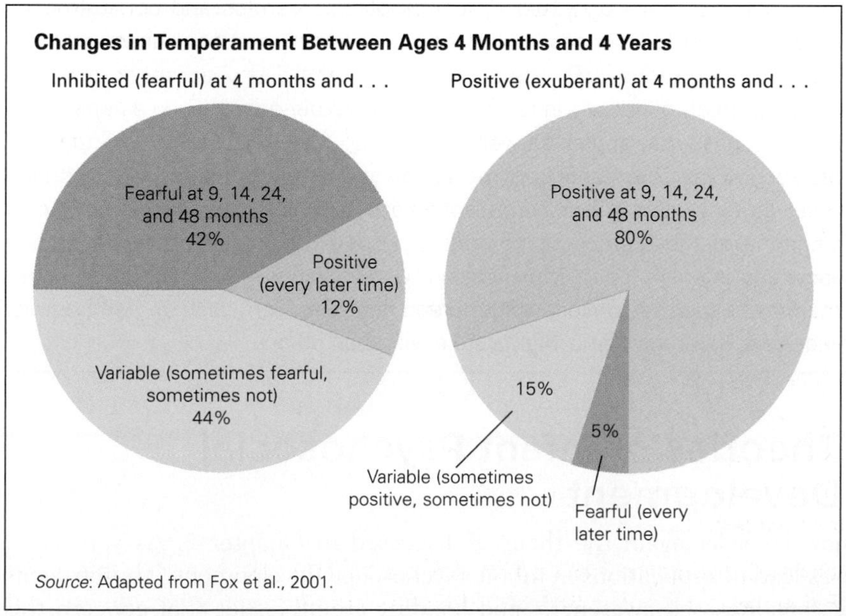

FIGURE 7.1

Do Babies' Temperaments Change?
The data suggest that fearful babies are not necessarily fated to remain that way. Adults who are reassuring and do not act frightened themselves can help children overcome an innate fearfulness. Some fearful children do not change, however, and it is not known whether that's because their parents are not sufficiently reassuring (nurture) or because they are temperamentally more fearful (nature).

Observation Quiz Out of 100 4-month-olds who react positively to noises and other experiences, how many are fearful at later times in early childhood? (see answer, page 198)

Goodness of Fit

All the research finds that traces of childhood temperament endure, blossoming into adult personality, but all the research also confirms that innate tendencies are only part of the story. Context always shapes behavior. Ideally, parents find a **goodness of fit**—that is, an adjustment that allows smooth infant–caregiver interaction. With a good fit, parents of difficult babies build a close and affectionate relationship; parents of exuberant infants learn to protect them from harm; parents of slow-to-warm-up toddlers encourage them while giving them time to adjust. Parents must do most of the accommodating, evident in this father and daughter episode:

goodness of fit A similarity of temperament and values that produces a smooth interaction between an individual and his or her social context, including family, school, and community.

> Kevin is a very active, outgoing person who loves to try new things. Today he takes his 11-month-old daughter, Tyra, to the park for the first time. Tyra is playing alone in the sandbox, when a group of toddlers joins her. At first, Tyra smiles and eagerly watches them play. But as the toddlers become more active and noisy, Tyra's smiles turn quickly to tears. She . . . reaches for Kevin, who picks her up and comforts her. But then Kevin goes a step further. After Tyra calms down, Kevin gently encourages her to play near the other children. He sits at her side, talking and playing with her. Soon Tyra is slowly creeping closer to the group of toddlers, curiously watching their moves.
>
> *[Lerner & Dombro, 2004, p. 42]*

>> Response for Nurses (from page 197) It's too soon to tell. Temperament is not truly "fixed" but variable, especially in the first few months. Many "difficult" infants become happy, successful adolescents and adults, especially if their parents are supportive.

Tyra needed Kevin. In general, anxious, difficult children are more affected by their parents' responsiveness than are easygoing children (Belsky & Pluess, 2009; Leerkes et al., 2009; Pauli-Pott et al., 2004). Ineffective or harsh parenting *combined with* a negative temperament creates antisocial, destructive children (Cicchetti et al., 2007).

Childhood temperament is linked to the parents' genes and their personality, which often is assessed using five dimensions, called the **Big Five**—openness, conscientiousness, extroversion, agreeableness, and neuroticism. Adults who are high in extroversion (surgency), high in agreeableness (effortful control), and low in neuroticism (negative mood) tend to be warmer and more competent parents (de Haan et al., 2009).

Big Five The five basic clusters of personality traits that remain quite stable throughout life: openness, conscientiousness, extroversion, agreeableness, and neuroticism.

SUMMING UP

Newborns seem to have only two simple emotions, distress and contentment, expressed by crying or looking peaceful. Very soon curiosity and obvious joy, with social smiles and laughter, appear. By the second half of the first year, anger and fear are increasingly evident, especially in reaction to social experiences, such as encountering a stranger. Sadness may appear as well.

In the second year, as infants become self-aware, they express emotions connected to themselves—including pride, shame, embarrassment, and guilt—and to other people. Maturation makes these emotions possible, but context and learning affect the timing, frequency, and intensity of their expression. Underlying all emotional development is brain maturation and the connections between neurons. From birth on, temperamental differences are apparent; some infants are easier than others. ■

>> Answer to Observation Quiz (from page 197) Out of 100 4-month-olds who react positively, 20 are fearful at least occasionally later in childhood, but only 5 are consistently fearful.

>> Theories of Infant Psychosocial Development

We now consider again the theories discussed in Chapter 2. As you will see, theories lead to applications in infant psychosocial development. Thumb sucking, crying, spoiling, self-awareness, and bonding are all issues that concern theory and practice.

Psychoanalytic Theory

Psychoanalytic theory connects biosocial and psychosocial development. Both major psychoanalytic theorists, Sigmund Freud and Erik Erikson, described two distinct stages of early development. Freud (1935, 1940/1964) wrote about the *oral stage* and the *anal stage*. Erikson (1963) called his first stages *trust versus mistrust* and *autonomy versus shame and doubt*.

Freud: Oral and Anal Stages

According to Freud (1935), the first year of life is the *oral stage,* so named because the mouth is the young infant's primary source of gratification. In the second year, with the *anal stage,* the infant's main pleasure comes from the anus—particularly from the sensual pleasure of bowel movements and, eventually, the psychological pleasure of controlling them.

Freud believed that the oral and anal stages are fraught with potential conflicts that have long-term consequences. If a mother frustrates her infant's urge to suck—weaning the infant too early, for example, or preventing thumb and finger sucking—the child may become distressed and anxious, eventually becoming an adult with an *oral fixation.* Such a person is stuck (fixated) at the oral stage and therefore eats, drinks, chews, bites, or talks excessively, in quest of the mouth-related pleasure denied in infancy.

Especially for Nursing Mothers You have heard that if you wean your child too early, he or she will overeat or become an alcoholic. Is it true? (see response, page 200)

Similarly, if toilet training is overly strict or if it begins before the infant is mature enough, parent and infant may become locked into a conflict over the toddler's refusal, or inability, to comply. The child develops an anal personality—as an adult, seeking self-control with an unusually strong need for regularity in all aspects of life. Most developmentalists no longer agree with this part of Freud's theory, although diverse opinions flourish about the optimal timing and method of toilet training, as you remember from Chapter 2.

trust versus mistrust Erikson's first psychosocial crisis. Infants learn basic trust if their basic needs (for food, comfort, attention, and so on) are met.

autonomy versus shame and doubt Erikson's second crisis of psychosocial development. Toddlers either succeed or fail in gaining a sense of self-rule over their own actions and bodies.

Erikson: Trust and Autonomy

According to Erikson, the first crisis of life is **trust versus mistrust,** when infants learn whether the world can be trusted to satisfy basic needs. Babies feel secure when food and comfort are provided with "consistency, continuity, and sameness of experience" (Erikson, 1963, p. 247). If social interaction inspires trust and security, the child (and later the adult) confidently explores the social world.

The second crisis is **autonomy versus shame and doubt,** beginning at about 18 months, when self-awareness emerges. Toddlers want autonomy (self-rule) over their own actions and bodies. Without it, they feel ashamed and doubtful. Like Freud, Erikson believed that problems in early infancy could last a lifetime, creating adults who are suspicious and pessimistic (mistrusting) or easily shamed (lacking autonomy).

JOSE LUIS PELEAZ, INC. / CORBIS

A Mother's Dilemma Infants are wonderfully curious, as this little boy demonstrates. Parents, however, must guide as well as encourage the drive toward autonomy. Notice this mother's expression as she makes sure her son does not crush or eat the flower.

Erikson was aware of cultural variations. He knew that mistrust or shame could be destructive or not, depending on norms and expectations. Some cultures encourage independence and autonomy; in others (e.g., China), "shame is a normative emotion that develops as parents use explicit shaming techniques" to encourage children's loyalty and harmony within their families (Mascolo et al., 2003, p. 402). Westerners expect toddlers to go through the stubborn and defiant "terrible twos"; parents elsewhere expect toddlers to be docile and obedient. Autonomy may be prized among North Americans, but it is considered immature by many other peoples (Morelli & Rothbaum, 2007).

>> Response for Nursing Mothers (from page 199) Freud thought so, but there is no experimental evidence that weaning, even when ill timed, has such dire long-term effects.

Behaviorism

From the perspective of behaviorism, emotions and personality are molded as parents reinforce or punish a child's spontaneous behaviors. Behaviorists believe that parents who smile and pick up their infant at every glimmer of a grin will have children with a sunny disposition. The opposite is also true, according to behaviorist John Watson:

> Failure to bring up a happy child, a well-adjusted child—assuming bodily health—falls squarely upon the parents' shoulders. [By the time the child is 3] parents have already determined . . . [whether the child] is to grow into a happy person, wholesome and good-natured, whether he is to be a whining, complaining neurotic, an anger-driven, vindictive, over-bearing slave driver, or one whose every move in life is definitely controlled by fear.
>
> *[Watson, 1928, pp. 7, 45]*

social learning Learning that is accomplished by observing others.

Later behaviorists recognized that infants also experience **social learning.** Albert Bandura conducted a classic experiment: Children watched an adult hitting a rubber Bobo clown with a mallet and then treated the doll the same way (Bandura, 1977). In this experiment, those children had good reason to follow the example; they were frustrated by being told they could not play with some attractive toys and were then left alone with a mallet and the Bobo doll, having just seen an adult hit the doll. Both boys and girls pounded and kicked Bobo.

Hammering Bobo These images are stills from the film of Bandura's original study of social learning, in which frustrated 4-year-olds imitated the behavior they had observed an adult perform. The children used the same weapon as the adult, with the same intent—whether that involved hitting the doll with a hammer, shooting it with a toy gun, or throwing a large ball at it.

Since that experiment, developmentalists have demonstrated that social learning occurs throughout life (Morris et al., 2007; Nielsen, 2006), a theme expressed many times in the latter half of this chapter. In many families, toddlers express emotions in various ways—from giggling to cursing—just as they have seen their parents or older siblings do. A boy might develop a hot temper, for instance, if his father's outbursts seem to win his mother's respect. Social learning theory acknowledges inborn temperament but stresses parental example: Shyness may be inborn, for instance, but parents who model social interaction will help a withdrawn child become more outgoing (Rubin et al., 2009).

Cognitive Theory

Cognitive theory holds that thoughts and values determine a person's perspective. Early experiences are important because beliefs, perceptions, and memories make them so, not because they are buried in the unconscious (psychoanalytic theory) or burned into the brain's patterns (behaviorism). Early relationships help infants develop a **working model,** a set of assumptions that become a frame of reference for later life (S. C. Johnson et al., 2010). It is a "model" because these early relationships are a prototype, or blueprint, for later relationships; it is "working" because, although it is used, it is not necessarily fixed or final.

working model In cognitive theory, a set of assumptions that the individual uses to organize perceptions and experiences. For example, a person might assume that other people are always trustworthy and be surprised when this working model of human behavior is proven inadequate.

Ideally, infants develop "a working model of the self as valued, loved, and competent" and "a working model of parents as emotionally available, loving, sensitive and supportive" (Harter, 2006, p. 519). However, reality does not always conform to this ideal. A 1-year-old girl might develop a model, based on her parents' inconsistent responses to her, that people are unpredictable. She will continue to apply that model to everyone: Her childhood friendships will be insecure and her adult relationships will be guarded.

To use Piaget's terminology, such a girl develops a cognitive *schema* to organize her perceptions. According to cognitive theory, an infant's early experiences themselves are not necessarily crucial, but the interpretation of those experiences is (Olson & Dweck, 2009). Remembered childhood echoes lifelong. A hopeful message from cognitive theory is that people can rethink and reorganize their thoughts, developing new models. Our mistrustful girl might marry a faithful and loving man and gradually develop a new model. Plasticity applies to cognition.

BILL BACHMANN / DANITADELIMONT.COM

Stranger Danger Some parents teach their children to be respectful of any adult; others teach them to fear any stranger. No matter what their culture or parents say, each of these two sisters in Nepal reacts according to her inborn temperament.

Sociocultural Theory

No one doubts that "human development occurs in a cultural context" (Kagitcibasi, 2003, p. 166). The crucial question is *how much* influence culture has. Sociocultural theorists argue that the influence is substantial, that the entire social and cultural context shapes infant emotional development.

Ethnotheories

An **ethnotheory** is a theory that is embedded in a particular culture or ethnic group. Although people are rarely aware of it—as you have already seen with breast-feeding, co-sleeping, child-directed speech, and toilet training—many child-rearing practices arise from ethnotheories (H. Keller et al., 2006). The motor skill and language timetables detailed in the previous chapters may be a result of parental encouragement, based on their ethnotheories. For example, part of the ethnotheory of the Kokwet in Kenya is that mothers should

> teach their babies to sit, stand, and walk. What would happen, they were asked, if a mother somewhere, for some reason, did not teach these things. The common answer, after a moment to assimilate such an outrageous idea, was that the child would not learn them.
>
> [*Super & Harkness, 2009, p. 93*]

ethnotheory A theory that underlies the values and practices of a culture but is not usually apparent to the people within the culture.

Ethnotheories are apparent with emotional development. A simple example comes whenever an infant cries: Is the baby expressing pain, anger, or just normal activity? Adults interpret it through their own culture's lens (Holodynski & Friedlmeier, 2010), with some adults rushing to comfort a crying baby and others believing the baby should "cry it out" to strengthen lungs and independence.

A more elaborate ethnotheory arises from cultures that believe that ancestors are reincarnated in the younger generation. In such a case, "children are not expected to show respect for adults, but adults [are expected to show respect] for their reborn ancestors." Consequently, children are allowed to express many emotions. Such cultures favor indulgent child rearing with no harsh punishment, a practice that "Western people perceive as extremely lenient" (Dasen, 2003, pp. 149–150).

Remember from Chapter 1 that cultures change when circumstances do. This was found in a study of the values of grandmothers and mothers of 3-month-olds (Lamm et al., 2008). The grandmother–mother pairs were from four contexts: urban Germany, urban India, and urban and rural West Africa. Women in each locale held ethnotheories unlike women living elsewhere. In all four cultures, generational differences were apparent, with the mothers valuing children's autonomy more than the grandmothers did.

Especially for Linguists and Writers U.S. culture has given rise to the term *empty nest*, signifying an ethnotheory about mothers whose children have grown up and moved out of the family home. What cultural values are expressed by that term? (see response, page 204)

The generation gap was smallest, however, in the two cultures that were most different from each other. Among urban Germans, grandmothers tended to agree with mothers in valuing autonomy; among rural Africans, mothers tended to agree with grandmothers in valuing obedience. The greatest mother–grandmother gap was in urban Africa, probably because dramatic social change meant that the grandmothers' traditions were quite unlike those learned by their daughters (Lamm et al., 2008).

Personal Theories

Parents are influenced not only by the theories of their ethnic group, but also by personal theories that arose from their own family or personal history. For instance, some parents blame their infants for crying, not realizing that young infants have no control over their crying or much else. As you just read, expressions such as crying and smiling, and emotions such as anger and fear, first arise because of maturation, not because of how the infant feels about the caregiver. Caregivers can respond to such emotions, but they cannot eliminate them.

Since theories of development are open to change, parents who are tempted to be abusive—either because of their own stresses or because their infants are difficult—can reframe their perceptions. They can stop blaming the infant and instead become more responsive, as cognitive theory would hope (Bugental & Schwartz, 2009). That is exactly the goal of the NBAS (Brazelton Neonatal Behavioral Assessment Scale, described in Chapter 4), in which the parents watch as a clinician encourages a baby to respond to sights, sounds, and people.

For example, Lucas was born with one foot that turned out. His parents were distant and dismayed, perhaps going by the theory that they were being punished through his deformity. The clinician demonstrated to them how they could listen and react better to Lucas. Soon Lucas looked at his mother when she spoke, which "elicited intense emotion in his mother, who took him in her arms and looked at him as if she had never realized until that moment that, behind his deformed foot, there was a little guy eager for her attention and her care" (Bruschweiler-Stern, 2009, p. 76).

Proximal and Distal Parenting

proximal parenting Caregiving practices that involve being physically close to a baby, with frequent holding and touching.

distal parenting Caregiving practices that involve remaining distant from a baby, providing toys, food, and face-to-face communication with minimal holding and touching.

Another example of ethnotheory involves a culture's ideas about how frequently parents should carry and cuddle their babies. **Proximal parenting** involves being physically close to a baby, often holding and touching. **Distal parenting** involves keeping some distance—providing toys, feeding by putting finger food within reach, and talking face-to-face instead of communicating by touch. Caregivers who believe that one of these is better are usually unaware that they are expressing an ethnotheory, but such differences begin to emerge early in life, when the infant is about 2 months old (Kärtner et al., 2010).

A longitudinal study comparing child-rearing methods of the Nso people of Cameroon with those of Greeks in Athens found marked differences in proximal and distal parenting (H. Keller et al., 2004). The researchers videotaped 78 mothers as they played with their 3-month-olds. Coders (who did not know the study's hypothesis) counted frequency of proximal play (e.g., carrying, swinging, caressing, exercising the child's body) and distal play (e.g., face-to-face talking) (see Table 7.1). The Nso mothers were proximal, holding their babies all the time and almost never using toys or bottles. The Greek mothers were relatively distal, using objects almost half the time.

TABLE 7.1 Infants in Rural Cameroon and Urban Greece

	Cameroon	Athens, Greece
I. Infant–mother play at 3 months		
Percent of time held by mother	100%	31%
Percent of time playing with objects	3%	40%
II. Toddler behavior at 18 months		
Self-recognition	3%	68%
Immediate compliance with request	72%	2%

Source: Adapted from Keller et al., 2004.

The researchers hypothesized that proximal parenting would result in toddlers who were less self-aware but more compliant—traits needed in an interdependent and cooperative society such as that of rural Cameroon. By contrast, distal parenting might produce children who were self-aware but less obedient, as needed when a culture values independence and self-reliance. The predictions were accurate. At 18 months, the same infants were tested on self-awareness (via the mirror/rouge test) and obedience to their parents. The African toddlers didn't recognize themselves in the mirror but were compliant; the opposite was true of the Greek toddlers.

Especially for Pediatricians A mother complains that her child refuses to stay in the car seat, spits out disliked foods, and almost never does what she says. How should you respond? (see response, page 205)

Replicating their own work, these researchers studied a dozen mother–infant pairs in Costa Rica. In that Central American nation, caregiver–infant distance was midway between the Nso and the Greeks, as was later toddler behavior. The researchers reanalyzed all their data, child by child. They found that, even apart from culture, proximal or distal play at 3 months was highly predictive: Greek mothers who, unlike most of their peers, held a personal theory that they should hold their infants often (they were proximal parents) had more obedient toddlers (H. Keller et al., 2004) (see the Research Design). Research with German father–infant pairs replicated these results (Borke et al., 2007).

Every aspect of early emotional development interacts with cultural beliefs, expressed in parental actions. Other research has found more separation anxiety in Japan than in Germany because Japanese infants "have very few experiences with separation from the mother," whereas in Germany "infants are frequently left alone outside of stores or supermarkets" while their mothers shop (Saarni et al., 2006, p. 237).

Still other research has found that Italian mothers and infants seem more intensely responsive to each other compared to U.S. and Argentinean mother–infant pairs and that rural mothers are more intrusive in that they are likely to stop an infant from exploring something in order to get him or her to do something else (Bornstein, Putnick et al., 2011). Despite such differences, no culture anywhere encourages caregivers to be indifferent to infant emotions: If such a culture existed, it probably would not endure for more than a generation. Babies everywhere need responsive adults.

Research Design

Scientists: A team of six from three nations (Germany, Greece, Costa Rica): Heidi Keller, Relindis Yovsi, Joern Borke, Joscha Kärtner, Henning Jensen, and Zaira Papaligoura.

Publication: *Child Development* (2004).

Participants: A total of 90 mothers participated when their babies were 3 months old and again when they were 18 months old (32 from Cameroon, 46 from Greece, 12 from Costa Rica). In Greece and Costa Rica, researchers recruited mothers in hospitals. In Cameroon, permission was first sought from the local leader, and then announcements were made among local people.

Design: First, mothers played with their 3-month-olds, and that play was videotaped and coded for particular behaviors by researchers who did not know the hypothesis. Fifteen months later, the toddlers' self-recognition was assessed with the mirror/rouge test, and compliance with preset maternal commands was measured. The mother's frequency of eye contact and body contact with the infant at 3 months was compared with the toddler's self-awareness and compliance at 18 months.

Major conclusion: Toddlers with proximal mothers were more obedient but less self-aware; toddlers with distal mothers tended to show the opposite pattern.

Comments: This is a good comparison study of child-rearing practices in various cultures in that it is longitudinal, using the same measures in each nation. However, with only three locations and relatively few mother–infant pairs (12 in Costa Rica), it is possible that factors unrelated to proximal/distal parenting affected the results. For example, the mothers in Athens were wealthier and more urbanized than the ones in Cameroon. However, if wealthier urban parents are also more distal parents, that itself would be a cultural difference.

>> Response for Linguists and Writers (from page 202) The implication is that human mothers are like sad birds, bereft of their fledglings, who have flown away.

Cultural differences may become encoded in the infant brain, called "a cultural sponge" by one group of scientists (Ambady & Bharucha, 2009, p. 342). It is difficult to measure how infant brains are molded by their context, but one study of adults born either in the United States or in China found that in both groups, a particular area of the brain (the medial prefrontal cortex) was activated when the adults judged whether certain adjectives applied to them. However, only in the Chinese was that area also activated when they were asked whether those adjectives applied to their mothers. The researchers consider this to be "neuro-imaging evidence that culture shapes the functional anatomy of self-representation" (Zhu et al., 2007, p. 1310) and speculate that the Chinese learned, as babies, that they are closely aligned with their mothers, whereas the Americans learned to be independent.

From the beginning of life, families dampen some emotions and fuel others. Another cross-cultural study found that culture affected how mothers in Germany and in India talked to their 3-month-olds, but even when a particular mother was unlike others in her community, all mothers tended to be quite stable in their responses as their infants grew: Their specific practices changed by age, but the underlying ethnotheories remained (Keller et al., 2010).

We noted earlier that infants become angry when they are restrained. Some Western parents rarely hold their infants *except* to restrain them (and the purpose of the restraint is often to enforce parent–infant separation). Parents strap protesting toddlers into strollers, buckle them into car seats, put them in cribs or behind gates that they cannot climb over—all examples of distal parenting. If toddlers do not passively allow diapers to be changed (and few do), some parents simply hold the protesting child down to get the task done. Compare this approach to that of Roberto's parents, who used nursing (very proximal) and the threat of separation to get their son diapered and dressed.

A CASE TO STUDY

"Let's Go to Grandma's"

Mayan parents from Mexico and Guatemala hold the ethnotheory that children should not be forced to obey their parents. Roberto, at 18 months, was playing with a ball and did not want to wear a diaper or put on his pants.

> "Let's put on your diaper . . . Let's go to Grandma's . . . We're going to do an errand." This did not work, and the mother invited Roberto to nurse, as she swiftly slipped the diaper on him with the father's assistance. The father announced, "It's over."

Roberto's mother felt

> increasing exasperation that the child was wiggling and not standing to facilitate putting on his pants. Her voice softened as Roberto became interested in the ball, and she increased the stakes: "Do you want another toy?" They [father and mother] continued to try to talk Roberto into cooperating, and handed him various objects, which Roberto enjoyed. But still he stubbornly refused to cooperate with dressing. They left him alone for a while. When his father asked if he was ready, Roberto pouted "nono!"
>
> After a bit, the mother told Roberto that she was leaving and waved goodbye. "Are you going with me?" Roberto sat quietly with a worried look. "Then put on your pants, put on your pants to go up the hill." Roberto stared into space, seeming to consider the alternatives. His mother started to walk away, "OK then, I'm going. Goodbye." Roberto started to cry, and his father persuaded, "Put on your pants then!" and his mother asked, "Are you going with me?"
>
> Roberto looked down worriedly, one arm outstretched in half a take-me gesture.
>
> "Come on, then," his mother offered the pants and Roberto let his father lift him to a stand and cooperated in putting his legs into the pants and in standing to have them fastened. His mother did not intend to leave; instead she suggested that Roberto dance for the audience. Roberto did a baby version of a traditional dance.
>
> [*Rogoff, 2003, p. 204*]

This is an example of an ethnotheory that "elders protect and guide rather than giving orders or dominating" (Rogoff, 2003, p. 205). A second ethnotheory is apparent as well: The parents readily used deception to get their child to do what they wanted.

SHEZAD NOORANI / PETER ARNOLD

SYLVAN GRANDADAM / AGE FOTOSTOCK

The Same Situation, Many Miles Apart: Intimate Parenting Some parents are proximal, encouraging mutual touch, as shown by this pair in the Sudan *(left)*; other parents are distal, as shown by this father in Germany *(right)*. Each is part of a cultural pattern that teaches values essential to that society—in this case, intimate family interdependence or individual self-sufficiency.

SUMMING UP

Theories differ in their explanations of the origins of early emotions and personality. Psychoanalytic theory stresses a mother's responses to an infant's need for food and elimination (Freud) or for security and independence (Erikson). Behaviorism also stresses caregiving—especially as parents reinforce the behaviors they want their baby to learn or as they thoughtlessly teach unwanted behaviors.

Cognitive theory highlights the child's concept, or working model, of the world. Sociocultural theory emphasizes that the diversity of nurture explains much of the diversity of emotions. According to sociocultural theory, child-rearing practices arise from ethnotheories, implicit and unexpressed but very powerful. ■

>> Response for Pediatricians (from page 203) Remember the origins of the misbehavior—probably a combination of the child's inborn temperament and the mother's distal parenting. Blended with ethnotheory, all contribute to the child's being stubborn and independent. Acceptance is more warranted than anger. On the other hand, this mother may be expressing hostility toward the child—a sign that intervention may be needed. Find out.

>> The Development of Social Bonds

You surely have noticed that the fifth theory was omitted from the preceding discussion. It is evident, however, in the following discussion, as both humanism and evolutionary theory stress the social interaction of infant and parent. Both the "love and belonging" and "unconditional positive regard" in humanism, and the urgency of species survival central to evolutionary psychology, are best explained within the context of social bonds.

Synchrony

Synchrony is a coordinated interaction between caregiver and infant, an exchange in which they respond to each other with split-second timing, evident in the first three months and then more frequently and elaborately as the infant matures (Feldman, 2007). Parents and infants average about an hour a day in face-to-face play. That is an average: Some parents play several hours a day, and others rarely play.

synchrony A coordinated, rapid, and smooth exchange of responses between a caregiver and an infant.

JGI / AGE FOTOSTOCK

MONALYN GRACIA / AGE FOTOSTOCK

Learning from Mother Lessons in emotion endure longer than do intellectual ones. The 9-month-old *(top)* knows she can make her mother laugh, and the 12-month-old *(bottom)* knows he should sometimes worry, although he does not know why.

still-face technique An experimental practice in which an adult keeps his or her face unmoving and expressionless in face-to-face interaction with an infant.

Mutual Responding

Detailed research reveals the mutuality of the interaction: Adults rarely smile at newborns until the infants smile at them, at which point adults grin broadly and talk animatedly (Lavelli & Fogel, 2005). Infants are more sensitive than mothers to the specific timing of their interactions, which makes synchrony especially important (Henning & Striano, 2011). Synchrony is evident not only through careful observation but also via computer calculation of the timing of smiles, arched eyebrows, and so on (Messinger et al., 2009). Via synchrony, infants learn to read others' emotions and to develop the skills of social interaction, such as taking turns and paying attention.

Although infants imitate adults, synchrony usually begins with parents imitating infants (Lavelli & Fogel, 2005). Careful research finds that they do so not only with split-second timing but also with tone and rhythm (Van Puyvelde et al., 2010). It is not surprising that the metaphors for synchrony often are musical: Synchrony has been called a dance, a duet, and improvised jazz. When parents detect an emotion from an infant's facial expressions and body motions and then respond, the infant learns to connect an internal state with an external expression. Such responsive parenting is particularly apparent in Asian cultures, perhaps because interpersonal sensitivity is crucial, and thus very young infants begin to learn it (Morelli & Rothbaum, 2007).

In Western cultures as well, parents become partners to their infants. This is especially important when the infant is at medical risk and the parent may ignore psychosocial needs because of urgent and time-consuming biological needs (Newnham et al., 2009). A study of emotional responsiveness among U.S. parents and infants found that those mothers who spent more time to bathe, feed, diaper, and so on were also those mothers who were most responsive. Apparently, some parents combine caregiving with emotional play, which takes longer but also provides more synchrony. Note that synchrony is exactly what Maslow and the other humanists would recommend. If basic needs (safety, food) are satisfied, people need love and belonging (responsiveness) without conditions, judgment, or rejection. That is synchrony.

When Synchrony Disappears

Is synchrony necessary? If no one plays with an infant, what will happen? Experiments using the **still-face technique** have addressed these questions (Tronick, 1989; Tronick & Weinberg, 1997). An infant is placed facing an adult, who responds normally while video cameras record each partner's reactions. Frame-by-frame analysis typically reveals that parents instinctively synchronize their responses to the infants' movements, with exaggerated tone and expression. Babies reciprocate with smiles and moving limbs. Long before they can actually reach out and grab an object, they respond by waving their arms—and are delighted if the adult moves in such a way that the waving arm touches the face or, even better, the hand grabs the hair.

In the still-face experiments, on cue, the adult erases all facial expression and stares with a "still face" for a minute or two. Sometimes by 2 months, and clearly by 6 months, babies are very upset by the still face, especially from their parents (less so from strangers). Babies frown, fuss, drool, look away, kick, cry, or suck their fingers. By 5 months, they also increase their babbling, as if to say, "Pay attention to me" (Goldstein et al., 2009).

Many research studies such as those using the still face lead to the same conclusion: Responsiveness to an infant aids development, measured both psychosocially and biologically—by heart rate, weight gain, and brain maturation (Moore & Calkins, 2004; Newnham et al., 2009). Particularly in the first year of life (more than later on), if a mother is depressed, her child suffers. Fathers, other relatives, and day-care providers need to help (Bagner et al., 2010). Young brains need social interaction—an essential, expected stimulant—to develop to their fullest.

Attachment

Toward the end of the first year, face-to-face play almost disappears. Once infants can move around, they are no longer content to respond to adult facial expressions and vocalizations. Another connection, called *attachment,* overtakes synchrony.

Attachment is a lasting emotional bond between people. It begins before birth, solidifies by age 1, and influences relationships throughout life (see At About This Time). Adults' attachment to their parents, formed decades earlier, affects their behavior with their own children as well as their relationship with their partners (Grossmann et al., 2005; Kline, 2008; Simpson & Rholes, 2010; Sroufe et al., 2005).

attachment According to Ainsworth, an affectional tie that an infant forms with a caregiver—a tie that binds them together in space and endures over time.

Infants show their attachment through *proximity-seeking* (such as approaching and following their caregivers) and through *contact-maintaining* (such as touching, talking, snuggling, and holding). Contact can be visual or verbal: A securely

AT ABOUT THIS TIME

Stages of Attachment

Birth to 6 weeks	*Preattachment.* Newborns signal, via crying and body movements, that they need others. When people respond positively, the newborn is comforted and learns to seek more interaction. Newborns are also primed by brain patterns to recognize familiar voices and faces.
6 weeks to 8 months	*Attachment in the making.* Infants respond preferentially to familiar people by smiling, laughing, babbling. Their caregivers' voices, touch, expressions, and gestures are comforting, often overriding the infant's impulse to cry. Trust (Erikson) develops.
8 months to 2 years	*Classic secure attachment.* Infants greet the primary caregiver, show separation anxiety when the caregiver leaves, play happily when the caregiver is present. Both infant and caregiver seek to be close to each other (proximity) and frequently look at each other (contact). In many caregiver–infant pairs, physical touch (patting, holding, caressing) is frequent.
2 to 6 years	*Attachment as launching pad.* Young children seek their caregiver's praise and reassurance as their social world expands. Interactive conversations and games (hide-and-seek, object play, reading, pretending) are common. Children expect caregivers to comfort and entertain.
6 to 12 years	*Mutual attachment.* Children seek to make their caregivers proud by learning whatever adults want them to learn, and adults reciprocate. In concrete operational thought (Piaget), specific accomplishments are valued by adults and children.
12 to 18 years	*New attachment figures.* Teenagers explore and make friendships on their own, using their working models of earlier attachments as a base. With more advanced, formal operational thinking (Piaget), physical contact is less important; shared ideals and goals are more influential.
18 years on	*Attachment revisited.* Adults develop relationships with others, especially relationships with romantic partners and children, influenced by earlier attachment patterns. Past insecure attachments from childhood can be repaired rather than repeated, although this does not always happen.

Source: Adapted from Grobman, 2008.

attached toddler is curious and eager to explore but maintains contact by occasionally looking back at the caregiver, or calling, "Mama?" Caregivers show attachment as well. They keep a watchful eye on their baby and maintain contact by initiating and responding to expressions, gestures, and vocalizations ("Here I am"). Many parents, awakening in the middle of the night, tiptoe to the crib to gaze at their sleeping infant, evidence of proximity-seeking. During the day, in contact-maintaining, they may absent-mindedly smooth their toddler's hair or caress the child's hands.

Attachment is a reflection of a universal trait, as expressed in evolutionary theory. Over humanity's history, proximity-seeking and contact-maintaining fostered the survival of the species by keeping toddlers near their caregivers and the caregivers vigilant. All of us inherited these impulses from our great-great- . . . grandparents, who would have died without them (Hrdy, 2009).

Although this evolutionary explanation of attachment rings true, we should also note that psychoanalytic and sociocultural theories are evident here as well. The original concept of attachment was developed by John Bowlby (1969, 1973, 1988), a British developmentalist influenced by both psychoanalytic theory and *ethology,* the study of animals. His thinking on mother–infant bonding inspired Mary Ainsworth, then a young graduate student, who spent more than a year in Uganda and wrote the first book on attachment based on her African research (Ainsworth, 1967).

Since then, research on attachment has taken place in dozens of nations. Attachment seems to be universal, but not everyone expresses it in the same way. Specific manifestations of attachment vary by culture (e.g., Ugandan mothers never kiss their infants but often massage them, contrary to Western custom), and some scholars believe that Ainsworth's descriptions are not equally relevant in every culture (Molitor & Hsu, 2011). Keep that in mind as you read about secure and insecure attachment.

Secure and Insecure Attachment

Most scholars now agree that attachment can be classified into four types, labeled A, B, C, and D (see Table 7.2). Infants with **secure attachment** (type B) feel comfortable and confident. The caregiver becomes a *base for exploration,* providing assurance that enables exploration. A toddler might, for example, scramble down from the caregiver's lap to play with an intriguing toy but periodically look back, vocalize a few syllables, or return for a hug.

On the other hand, insecure attachment (types A and C) is characterized by fear, anxiety, anger, or indifference. Some insecure children play independently without maintaining contact with the caregiver; this is **insecure-avoidant attachment** (type A). By contrast, another insecure child might be unwilling to leave the caregiver's lap; this is **insecure-resistant/ambivalent attachment** (type C). Ainsworth's original schema differentiated only A, B, and C, but later researchers discovered a fourth category (type D), **disorganized attachment.** Type D infants may shift from hitting to kissing their mothers, from staring blankly to crying hysterically, from pinching themselves to freezing in place.

In developed nations, almost two-thirds of all infants are secure (type B). Their mothers' presence gives them courage to explore. A caregiver's departure causes distress; the caregiver's return elicits positive social contact (such as smiling or hugging) and then more playing. A balanced reaction, being concerned but not overwhelmed by comings and goings, is an indication of secure attachment.

In those same nations, about one-third of infants are insecure, either indifferent (type A) or unduly anxious (type C). As already mentioned, although type B

secure attachment A relationship (type B) in which an infant obtains both comfort and confidence from the presence of his or her caregiver.

insecure-avoidant attachment A pattern of attachment (type A) in which an infant avoids connection with the caregiver, as when the infant seems not to care about the caregiver's presence, departure, or return.

insecure-resistant/ambivalent attachment A pattern of attachment (type C) in which anxiety and uncertainty are evident, as when an infant becomes very upset at separation from the caregiver and both resists and seeks contact on reunion.

disorganized attachment A type of attachment (type D) that is marked by an infant's inconsistent reactions to the caregiver's departure and return.

TABLE 7.2 Patterns of Infant Attachment

Type	Name of Pattern	In Play Room	Mother Leaves	Mother Returns	Toddlers in Category (%)
A	Insecure-avoidant	Child plays happily.	Child continues playing.	Child ignores her.	10–20
B	Secure	Child plays happily.	Child pauses, is not as happy.	Child welcomes her, returns to play.	50–70
C	Insecure-resistant/ ambivalent	Child clings, is preoccupied with mother.	Child is unhappy, may stop playing.	Child is angry; may cry, hit mother, cling.	10–20
D	Disorganized	Child is cautious.	Child may stare or yell; looks scared, confused.	Child acts oddly—may scream, hit self, throw things.	5–10

predominates in almost every published study of normal children, in some regions, the insecure infants are usually type A while in others, they are type C.

About 5 to 10 percent of infants fit into none of these categories and are classified as disorganized (type D). Disorganization prevents them from developing a strategy for social interaction (even an avoidant or resistant one, type A or C). Sometimes they become hostile and aggressive, difficult for anyone to relate to (Lyons-Ruth et al., 1999). This is evident in observational studies of the emotional reactions of type D children and also in hormonal assays. Unlike the first three types, disorganized infants have elevated levels of cortisol in reaction to stress (Bernard & Dozier, 2010).

Measuring Attachment

Ainsworth (1973) developed a now-classic laboratory procedure called the **Strange Situation** to measure attachment. In a well-equipped playroom, an infant is closely observed for eight episodes, each lasting three minutes. First, the caregiver and child are together. Then, according to a set sequence, the caregiver and a stranger come and go. Infants' responses indicate which type of attachment they have formed to their caregivers. (Reactions to the caregiver indicate attachment; reactions to the stranger are influenced more by temperament than by attachment.)

Strange Situation A laboratory procedure for measuring attachment by evoking infants' reactions to stress in eight episodes of three minutes each.

Researchers are trained and certified as able to distinguish types A, B, C, and D. They focus on the following:

- *Exploration of the toys.* A secure toddler plays happily.
- *Reaction to the caregiver's departure.* A secure toddler notices when the caregiver leaves and shows some sign of missing him or her. Depending on the child's temperament and past experiences, this sign may be loud crying or merely a pause in playing.
- *Reaction to the caregiver's return.* A secure toddler welcomes the caregiver's reappearance, usually seeking contact, and then plays again.

Attachment is not always measured via the Strange Situation, especially when researchers want to study a large number of people (Andreassen & West, 2007). Instead, surveys and interviews are used. Sometimes parents sort out 90 questions about their children's characteristics, and sometimes adults are interviewed extensively (according to a detailed protocol) about their relationships with their own parents, again with various specific measurements (Fortuna & Roisman, 2008).

Research measuring attachment has revealed that some behaviors that might seem normal are, in fact, a sign of insecurity. For instance, an infant who clings to

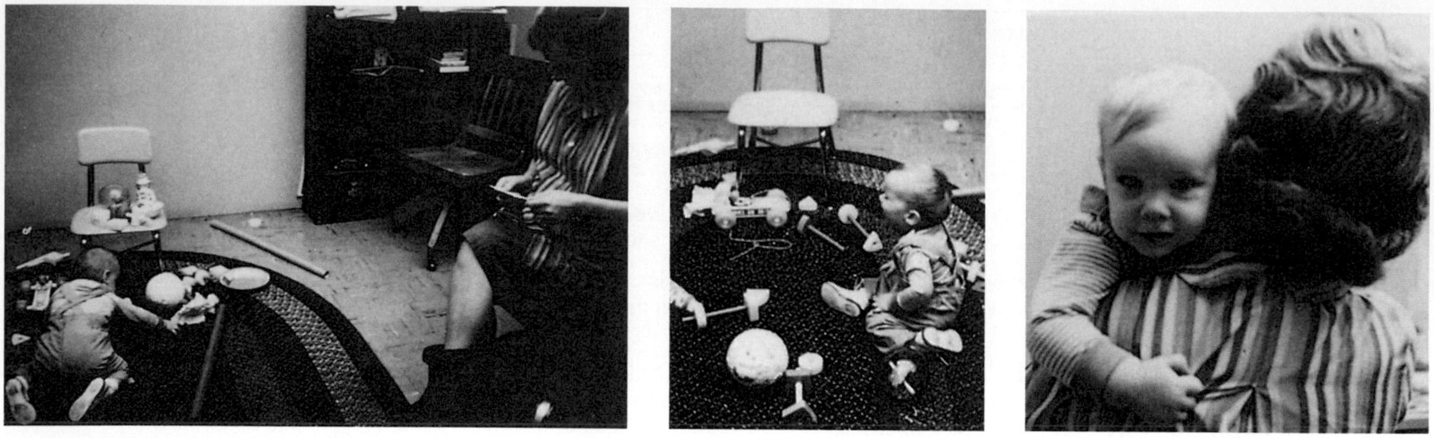

ALL: COURTESY OF MARY AINSWORTH

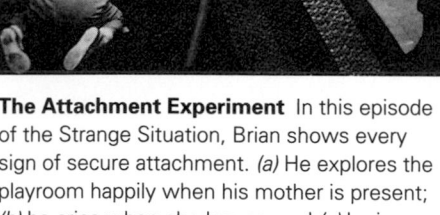

The Attachment Experiment In this episode of the Strange Situation, Brian shows every sign of secure attachment. *(a)* He explores the playroom happily when his mother is present; *(b)* he cries when she leaves; and *(c)* he is readily comforted when she returns.

the caregiver and refuses to explore the toys in the new playroom might be type A, not the secure type B. Likewise, adults who say their childhood was happy and their mother was a saint, especially if they provide few specific memories, might be insecure. And young children who are too friendly to strangers may never have formed a secure attachment to one familiar person (Tarullo et al., 2011).

Insecure Attachment and Social Setting

At first, developmentalists expected secure attachment to "predict all the outcomes reasonably expected from a well-functioning personality" (R. A. Thompson & Raikes, 2003, p. 708). But this expectation turned out to be invalid.

Securely attached infants *are* more likely to become secure toddlers, socially competent preschoolers, high-achieving schoolchildren, and capable parents (R. A. Thompson, 2006) (see Table 7.3). Some researchers find that secure attachment affects early brain development, one reason these later outcomes occur (Diamond & Fagundes, 2010). However, attachment status may shift with family circumstances as children grow older and parents change. Furthermore, harsh contexts,

TABLE 7.3 Predictors of Attachment Type

Secure attachment (type B) is more likely if:

- The parent is usually sensitive and responsive to the infant's needs.
- The infant–parent relationship is high in synchrony.
- The infant's temperament is "easy."
- The parents are not stressed about income, other children, or their marriage.
- The parents have a working model of secure attachment to their own parents.

Insecure attachment is more likely if:

- The parent mistreats the child. (Neglect increases type A; abuse increases types C and D.)
- The mother is mentally ill. (Paranoia increases type D; depression increases type C.)
- The parents are highly stressed about income, other children, or their marriage. (Parental stress increases types A and D.)
- The parents are intrusive and controlling. (Parental domination increases type A.)
- The parents are active alcoholics. (Alcoholic father increases type A; alcoholic mother increases type D.)
- The child's temperament is "difficult." (Difficult children tend to be type C.)
- The child's temperament is "slow to warm up." (This correlates with type A.)

especially the stress of poverty, make secure attachment less likely (Seifer et al., 2004; van IJzendoorn & Bakermans-Kranenburg, 2010), which means that later problems can be blamed on socioeconomic status (SES), not specifically on attachment. The underlying concept of attachment—that responsive parenting early in life leads to a secure parent–child relationship that buffers later stress and encourages later exploration—provides important insights into early psychosocial development, but exceptions may occur.

Insights from Romania

No scholar doubts that close human relationships ideally begin in the first year of life. Unfortunately, this has now been proven by thousands of children born in Romania. When Romanian dictator Nicolae Ceausesçu forbade birth control and abortions in the 1980s, illegal abortions became the leading cause of death for Romanian women aged 15 to 45 (Verona, 2003), and more than 100,000 children were abandoned to crowded, impersonal, state-run orphanages. The children experienced severe deprivation, including virtually no normal interaction, play, or conversation (Rutter et al., 2007).

In the two years after Ceausesçu was ousted in 1989, thousands of these children were adopted by American and western European families. Those who were adopted before 6 months of age fared best; most of them developed normally. For those adopted after age 1, early signs were encouraging: Skinny infants gained weight and grew faster than other 1-year-olds, developing motor skills they had lacked (Park et al., 2010). However, for many, but not all, of those who had been adopted *after* they were 6 months old, deprivation was evident in emotional and cognitive abilities. At age 11, they scored an average of only 85 on a standard IQ test (the WISC, described in Chapter 11), 15 points below normal (Rutter et al., 2010). Many were overly friendly to strangers throughout childhood, a sign that early attachment to a caregiver did not occur (Tarullo et al., 2011).

These children are now approaching adulthood, and ongoing research finds that most of them have emotional or conduct problems as they navigate adolescence and emerging adulthood. Initially it was thought that many of their problems resulted from malnutrition—that their brains as well as their bodies were deprived. The recent research, sadly, disputes this. Even those who were relatively well nourished, or who caught up to normal growth once they were adopted, nonetheless have had psychosocial problems in adolescence. The research question now is: What can modify or remedy early deprivation? Answers are not yet known (Rutter et al., 2010).

Romanian infants are no longer available for international adoption, but some are still abandoned by their parents. Research on them confirms that early experience, not genetics, is the main problem. Romanian infants develop best in their own families, second best in foster families, and much worse in institutions (Nelson et al., 2007). Research on institutionalized toddlers from many nations of eastern Europe, Asia, Africa, and South America who were adopted by western European or North American families still finds that they have a higher rate of emotional problems, especially evident at puberty. However, more recent adoptees develop better than those severely deprived Romanian orphans (Merz & McCall, 2010).

All infants need basic love and stimulation; all seek attachment—secure if possible, insecure if not. Without this sort of support, an infant becomes disorganized and adrift, emotionally troubled because extreme early social deprivation is very difficult to overcome.

Given that synchrony and attachment develop over the first year, and given that some parents have difficulty establishing secure attachments with their children, many developmentalists now seek to discover what impairs the parents and what can be done. It is apparent that secure attachment is more elusive when the parents were abused as children, the families are socially isolated, or the infants are unusually difficult (Berlin et al., 2011).

The most effective prevention must begin before problems start. Success has been reported by having skilled professionals come to the home to help build secure relationships between infant and caregiver (Lowell et al., 2011). In fact, if a professional helps parents in the first days after birth, perhaps by using the NBAS (first mentioned in Chapter 4) to encourage bonding, that can stop problems before they start (e.g., Nugent et al., 2009).

Social Referencing

social referencing Seeking information about how to react to an unfamiliar or ambiguous object or event by observing someone else's expressions and reactions. That other person becomes a social reference.

At every age, people want to know what other people feel about the experiences they themselves encounter. **Social referencing** refers to seeking appropriate emotional responses or information from other people, much as a student might consult a dictionary or other reference work. A glance of reassurance or words of caution or an expression of alarm, pleasure, or dismay—each becomes a social reference.

After age 1, when infants reach the stage of active exploration (Piaget) and the crisis of autonomy versus shame and doubt (Erikson), the need to consult others becomes urgent. Toddlers search for clues in gazes and facial expressions, paying close attention to emotions and intentions to understand what people do. Toddlers are selective in their social referencing: Even 16-month-olds notice which strangers are reliable references and which are not (Poulin-Dubois & Chow, 2009).

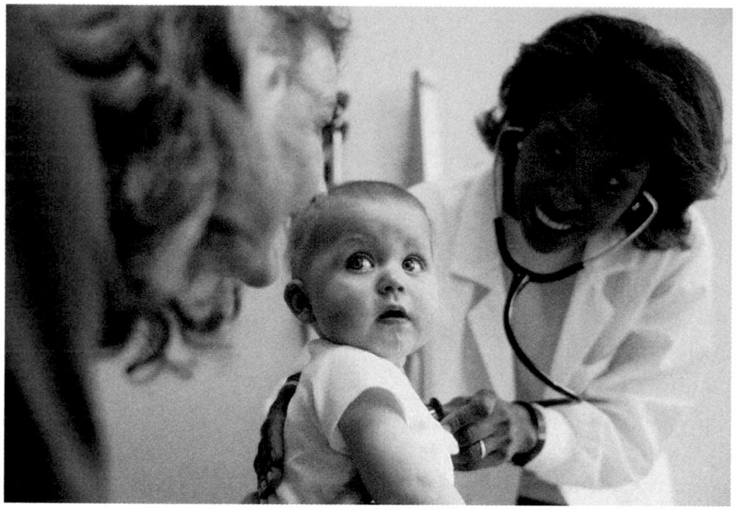

MICHAEL MALYSZKO / GETTY IMAGES

Whose Smile to Believe? Logically, the doctor is the one to watch: She has the stethoscope, and she is closer. But this baby references her mother, as any securely attached 1-year-old would.

Social referencing has many practical applications. Consider mealtime. Caregivers the world over smack their lips, pretend to taste, and say "yum-yum," encouraging toddlers to eat and enjoy their first beets, liver, or spinach. For their part, toddlers become astute at reading expressions, insisting on the foods that the adults *really* like. Through this process, children in some cultures develop a taste for raw fish or curried goat or smelly cheese—foods that children in other cultures refuse. Similarly, toddlers are able to use their mothers' cues to understand the difference between real and pretend eating (Nishida & Lillard, 2007).

Fathers as Social Partners

In most nations and ethnic groups, fathers spend much less time with infants than mothers do (Parke & Buriel, 2006; Tudge, 2008). Ethnotheories often limit father–child involvement, with some mothers believing that child care is the special domain of women (Gaertner et al., 2007) and some fathers thinking it unmanly to dote on an infant. That is not true everywhere. In Denmark, for instance, researchers report that 97 percent of fathers are present at the delivery of their babies; and, in a survey when the infants were 5 months old, 98 percent played with their infants every day, 83 percent changed diapers every day, and 61 percent fed the baby every day (Munck, 2009).

In many nations, ethnotheories about fathers are changing. One obvious example is Latino fathers, who were said to be less involved with their infants than many other fathers. Research refutes this assumption (Cabrera et al., 2006; Tamis-LeMonda et al., 2009). In the United States, many fathers of Mexican, Cuban, and Dominican heritage are active caregivers for their infants. Similar findings occur worldwide: Brazilian fathers seem to spend more time caring for their infants than do fathers in any other nation (Tudge, 2008). Among low-income families in the United States, the best predictor of a father's involvement with his infant is his relationship with the mother, and young Latina mothers are more likely to be married to their baby's father than are other young mothers of the same SES. Thus, many Latino infants begin life with a very involved male caregiver.

The normative involvement of Latino fathers has an unfortunate downside. If a biological Hispanic American father is absent, single Latinas seem to demand more from and respond less to their infants than do other single mothers (Cooper et al., 2009). Similar findings come from rural Mexico, where most infants are born to married parents, with fathers helping with infant care. However, when fathers are absent (usually because they have migrated to the United States to alleviate family poverty), infants are significantly more likely to become sick—a sign that the mothers find infant care more difficult when the fathers are gone (Schmeer, 2009).

Comparing Fathers and Mothers

Fathers enhance their children's social and emotional development in many ways (Lamb, 2010). Synchrony, attachment, and social referencing are all apparent with fathers. Indeed, fathers are more likely to elicit smiles and laughter from their infants than mothers are. Close father–infant relationships can teach infants (especially boys) appropriate expressions of emotion (Boyce et al., 2006), particularly anger.

The results of father–infant care may endure: Teenagers are less likely to lash out at friends and authorities if, as infants, they experienced a warm, responsive relationship with their father (Trautmann-Villalba et al., 2006). Close relationships with infants help the men, too, reducing the risk of depression (Borke et al., 2007; Bronte-Tinkew et al., 2007).

Contemporary fathers feed, diaper, and bathe infants, but typically "mothers engage in more caregiving and comforting, and fathers in more high intensity play" (Kochanska et al., 2008, p. 41), such as moving their infant's limbs in imitation of walking, kicking, or climbing, or swinging the baby through the air, sideways, or even upside down. Fathers provide excitement; mothers caress, read, or sing.

Research on father–infant care has focused on three different questions over the past two decades (Bretherton, 2010; Lamb, 2010). The first and second questions were: Can fathers provide the same care as mothers? Is father–infant interaction different from mother–infant interaction? As you just read, many studies found that the answer to both questions was yes.

The third question is: How do fathers and mothers interact to provide infant care? The answer seems to be that, in a well-functioning family, they cooperate and complement each other, each giving the infant what the other does not (Bretherton, 2010). Mothers are the usual caregivers and fathers are usually the best playmates, but not always—each set of parents, given their circumstances (which might include being immigrant, gay, low-income, or having a premature or disabled infant), finds their own way to make sure their infant thrives (Lamb, 2010).

HILL STREET STUDIOS / AGE FOTOSTOCK

Up, Up, and Away! The vigorous play typical of fathers is likely to help in the infant's mastery of motor skills and the development of muscle control. (Of course, fathers must be careful not to harm fragile bones and developing brains.)

Infant Day Care

About 134 million babies were born worldwide in 2011. Most of them are cared for exclusively by their mothers over the first two years, with the rest usually cared for by relatives, typically fathers in the United States and grandmothers in most other nations (Leach, 2009). Worldwide, only about 15 percent of infants receive regular care from a nonrelative who is both paid and trained to provide it. Statistics on the precise incidence and consequences of such care in each nation are difficult to interpret because "informal in-family arrangements speak to the ingenuity of parents trying to cope but bedevil child care statistics" (Leach, 2009, p. 44).

International Comparisons

It is known that the proportion of infants in nonrelative care varies markedly from nation to nation (Leach, 2009; Melhuish & Petrogiannis, 2006). Center-based care is common in France, Israel, China, and Sweden, where it is heavily subsidized by the government, and scarce in South Asia, Africa, and Latin America, where it is not. North America is in between these extremes, but variation from place to place is apparent.

Involvement of relatives other than mothers in infant care also varies. Worldwide, fathers are increasingly involved in baby care, but this varies by culture. Most nations do not yet have policies in place to facilitate father care. Some nations provide paid leave for new fathers as well as mothers; several nations provide paid family leave that can be taken by either parent or shared between them; some nations mandate that a job be kept available when mothers take an unpaid maternity leave; and most nations in the developing world provide limited paid leave for mothers (India does not allow women to be employed in the first six weeks after birth) but not fathers.

Some employers are more generous than the laws require. To help you grasp the variations in paid paternal leave, here is a list of policies in a few nations:

- Canada: 50 weeks of shared leave (either parent), at about three-fourths pay.
- Sweden: 16 months, close to full pay, shared (e.g., both parents can take 8 months) but at least 2 months is reserved for the father.
- Denmark: 52 weeks, shared, full pay; at least 2 weeks is reserved for the father and at least 18 weeks for the mother.
- Bulgaria: 52 weeks, full pay; shared by mother, father, and grandmother.
- Brazil: 5 days for the father and 120 days for the mother at full pay.
- Kenya: 2 weeks for the father and 2 months for the mother at full pay.
- Indonesia: 2 days for the father and 3 months for the mother at full pay.
- Lebanon: 1 day for the father and 7 weeks for the mother at full pay.
- Australia: 18 weeks for the father and 18 weeks for the mother at minimal wage.

In the United States, marked variations are apparent by state and by employer, although paid paternal leave is rare. Federal policy mandates that a job be held for a parent who takes unpaid leave of up to 12 weeks, unless the company has fewer than 50 employees. The U.S. military allows 10 days of paid paternal leave.

Cultures vary a great deal, as one would expect from the variations in ethnotheories. In some places, mothers of young children are discouraged from working; in others, they are refused public benefits unless they work. In England, many mothers return to work after 6 months, and day care is relatively common: One British survey found that only 9 percent of 4-month-olds were in regular nonmaternal care but 48 percent of 1-year-olds were (Leach, 2009).

In Germany, few mothers of young children are employed, not only because the ethnotheory discourages it but also because for decades a federal law mandated store closings (even for grocery, drug, and convenience stores) by 6:30 P.M. on weekdays, by 3:00 P.M. on Saturdays, and all day Sunday, which meant that an

TABLE 7.4 Percentage of U.S. Wives in the Labor Market by Ethnicity and Age of Child: 2008

	Ethnic Background			
Age of Child	European	African	Asian	Latina
Birth to 24 months	59	62	58	45
24 to 36 months	59	64	58	46
3 to 6 years	65	81	61	53
6 to 13 years	74	83	70	66
14 to 17 years	79	82	80	66

Source: U.S. Bureau of the Census, 2010.

Culture or Economy? Note that this table includes only married women. In most cases, their husbands are employed, which means that these are families who have two incomes. Obviously, economic necessity is not the only reason most U.S. mothers are in the labor force. Latino families tend to have relatively low income, but many Latina mothers stay home until the youngest child enters school.

Observation Quiz In which ethnic group does it make a difference whether the youngest child is in primary school or secondary school? (see answer, page 217)

adult family member (usually the mother) had to shop during the day. That law was changed in 2006, and now stores in many places are allowed to stay open longer, but the culture still expects mothers of infants to care for them 24/7.

In the United States, paid leave depends on the employer and is scarce and short; unpaid leave is legally mandated for mothers whose employers have more than 50 workers. Fifty-nine percent of married mothers of babies younger than 12 months old are in the labor force (rates are higher for mothers who are not married or who have slightly older infants) (U.S. Bureau of the Census, 2010). (See Table 7.4.)

Of course, paid leave is not the only factor; some unemployed mothers take time for themselves or for volunteer work. Father, grandmother, and paid caregivers are common: In the United States, only 20 percent of infants are cared for *exclusively* by their mothers (no other relatives or babysitters) throughout their first year. By contrast, in Canada (similar in ethnic diversity but with lower rates of maternal employment), 70 percent of Canadian infants are in exclusive maternal care (Côté et al., 2008). Obviously, these national differences are affected by ethnotheory more than by essential psychosocial needs of babies and parents.

Types of Nonmaternal Care

Most North American mothers who want someone else to help with infant care prefer that the caregiver be the baby's father. Many parents coordinate their work schedules so one or the other parent is always present, an arrangement that may help the infant and the budget but not the marriage, as parents have much less time together (Meteyer & Perry-Jenkins, 2010). Grandmothers are also often caregivers in the first year, less so in the second as infants become more mobile and social (Leach, 2009).

When parents turn to paid nonrelatives, wealthier families may hire someone to come to the home, but most parents find **family day care,** in which the caregiver looks after a small group of young children in her (almost never his) home. The quality of family day care varies; if ages vary, infants and toddlers may get less attention than older children, who resent them (Kryzer et al., 2007). As you know, providing physical care and ensuring safety are only the beginning of quality caretaking; ideally, the caregiver spends many hours each day talking to and playing with each baby.

family day care Child care that occurs in the home of someone to whom the child is not related and who usually cares for several children of various ages.

A better option than family day care may be **center day care,** in which licensed and educated adults care for several infants in a place designed especially for children. Most centers separate infants from older children. Ideally, the center has ample safe space, appropriate equipment, trained providers, and two adults

center day care Child care that occurs in a place especially designed for the purpose, where several paid adults care for many children. Usually the children are grouped by age, the day-care center is licensed, and providers are trained and certified in child development.

TABLE 7.5 High-Quality Day Care

High-quality day care during infancy has five essential characteristics:

1. *Adequate attention to each infant.* A small group of infants (no more than five) needs two reliable, familiar, loving caregivers. Continuity of care is crucial.
2. *Encouragement of language and sensorimotor development.* Infants need language—songs, conversations, and positive talk—and easily manipulated toys.
3. *Attention to health and safety.* Cleanliness routines (e.g., handwashing), accident prevention (e.g., no small objects), and safe areas to explore are essential.
4. *Professional caregivers.* Caregivers should have experience and degrees/certificates in early-childhood education. Turnover should be low, morale high, and enthusiasm evident.
5. *Warm and responsive caregivers.* Providers should engage the children in active play and guide them in problem solving. Quiet, obedient children may indicate unresponsive care.

for a group of five or fewer infants (de Schipper et al., 2006) (see Table 7.5). Such a setting advances cognitive and social skills: Toddlers are intrigued by other toddlers, and they learn from interaction. No matter what form of day care is chosen, responsive, individualized care with stable caregivers seems best (Morrissey, 2009). Caregiving change is difficult for babies, because each infant gesture or sound not only merits individualized response but also requires interpretation by someone who knows that baby well.

The Effects of Infant Day Care

The evidence is overwhelming that good preschool education (discussed in Chapter 9) benefits young children, especially in cognition. However, when it comes to infants, "disagreements about the wisdom (indeed, the morality) of non-maternal child care for the very young remain" (NICHD Early Child Care Research Network, 2005, p. xiv). A major problem is that quality varies a great deal. Some caregivers with no training look after many infants, and the result is inadequate care.

The consequences of nonmaternal care are a subject of debate. The concern is that infants with extensive nonmaternal care tend to become more aggressive later on (Jacob, 2009), although some babies seem far more affected than others (Phillips et al., 2011; Pluess & Belsky, 2009). As one review explained: "This evidence now indicates that early nonparental care environments sometimes pose risks to young children and sometimes confer benefits" (Phillips et al., 2011). Differential effects are evident: For genetic and familial reasons, the choice about how best to care for an infant varies from case to case.

Consider some of this "evidence" in detail. In England, one study found that infants who were not exclusively in their mothers' care were less advanced emotionally (Fergusson et al., 2008). Proof? No. Most of those infants were cared for by grandmothers, especially when the mothers were young and poor. As you know from your understanding of correlation, SES accounts for several variables in addition to nonmaternal care. In this case, the relevant variables probably include the grandmothers' low education, the mothers' immaturity, and the households' financial stress. Any of those could be the reason for emotional immaturity.

A large study in Canada found that when children were cared for by someone other than their mothers (usually relatives) in their first year, girls seemed to develop equally well in various care arrangements. However, boys from high-income families whose mothers were not their only caregivers fared less well than similar boys in exclusive maternal care: By age 4, they were slightly more assertive or aggressive and had more emotional problems (e.g., a teacher might note that a boy "seems unhappy"). The opposite was true for boys from low-income families: On average, they benefited from nonmaternal care, again according to teacher reports. The researchers insist that no policy implications can be derived from this study, partly because care varied so much in quality, location, and provider (Côté et al., 2008).

Research in the United States on low-income families also finds that center care is beneficial (Peng & Robins, 2010). For less impoverished children, an ongoing longitudinal study by the Early Child Care Network of the National Institute of Child Health and Human Development (NICHD) has followed the development of more than 1,300 children from birth to age 11. It has found many cognitive benefits of early day care, especially in language development.

The social consequences are less clear (Loeb et al., 2005). Most analyses find that secure attachment to the mother was as common among infants in center care as among infants cared for at home. Like other, smaller studies, the NICHD research confirms that the mother–child relationship is pivotal. The NICHD study and the consensus of other research in the United States is that infant day care, even for 40 hours a week before age 1, has much less influence on child development than does the warmth of the mother–infant relationship (Phillips et al., 2011).

The NICHD study has also found that infant day care seems detrimental when the mother is insensitive *and* the infant spends more than 20 hours a week in a poor-quality program with too many children per group (McCartney et al., 2010). Again, boys sometimes become more quarrelsome, having more conflicts with their teachers than did the girls or other boys with a different mix of maternal traits and day-care experiences.

As you see, the research does not provide a simple answer about nonmaternal care. Each study is complex: International variations, uncertainty about quality and extent of care (both at home and elsewhere), and the fact that choices are not random make it hard to draw general conclusions. Family income, culture, and education affect choice of care, and those same variables affect child development. The fact that boys are more affected than girls may indicate something about biological sex, but it simply may be that difficult boys are more often in day care because mothers do not want exclusive care of their active, difficult sons. That selection effect may explain why the average 5-year-old boy who was in family or center care at age 1 is slightly more aggressive than his classmate who had full-time maternal care in his early years.

>> Answer to Observation Quiz (from page 215) Asian Americans. One of every four Asian American wives who were unemployed when their children were of school age enters the labor market when the children become teenagers.

Especially for Day-Care Providers A mother who brings her child to you for day care says that she knows she is harming her baby but must work out of economic necessity. What do you say? (see response, page 218)

The Same Situation, Many Miles Apart: Universal Day Care? Casper, Wyoming *(left)*, is on the opposite side of the earth from Dhaka, Bangladesh *(right)*, but day care is needed in both places, as shown here.

Observation Quiz What three cultural differences do you see? (see answer, page 218)

AP PHOTO / STAR-TRIBUNE, SARAH BETH BARNETT

© DOLI AKTER

>> Response for Day-Care Providers (from page 217) Reassure the mother that you will keep her baby safe and will help to develop the baby's mind and social skills by fostering synchrony and attachment. Also tell her that the quality of mother–infant interaction at home is more important than anything else for psychosocial development; mothers who are employed full time usually have wonderful, secure relationships with their infants. If the mother wishes, you can discuss ways in which she can be a more responsive mother.

>> Answer to Observation Quiz (from page 217) The Bangladeshi children are dressed alike, are the same age, and are all seated around toy balls in a net—there's not a book in sight, unlike the Wyoming setting.

A careful summary of the longitudinal outcomes of nonmaternal infant care finds that "externalizing behavior is predicted from a constellation of variables in multiple contexts . . . and no study has found that children of employed mothers develop serious emotional or other problems *solely* because their mothers are working outside the home" (McCartney et al., 2010, pp. 1, 16).

Another complication in the United States is that children generally benefit if their mothers are employed (Goldberg et al., 2008), in part because maternal income reduces parental depression and increases family wealth, both of which correlate with happier and more successful children. Many employed mothers make infant care their top priority, sometimes at the expense of their own self-care or marriage.

A time-use study found that mothers who worked full time outside the home spent almost as much time playing with their babies (14½ hours a week) as did mothers with no outside jobs (16 hours a week) (Huston & Aronson, 2005). To make more time for their babies, they spent half as much time on housework, less time with their husbands, and almost no time on leisure. The study concludes:

> There was no evidence that mothers' time at work interfered with the quality of their relationship with their infants, the quality of the home environment, or children's development. In fact, the results suggest the opposite. Mothers who spent more time at work provided slightly higher quality home environments.
>
> *[Huston & Aronson, 2005, p. 479]*

That is a comforting conclusion for working mothers, but again other interpretations are possible. It may be that the women who were able to find worthwhile work were more capable of providing a "quality home environment" than the women who were unemployed. Every study reflects several possible variables and consequently researchers find mixed evidence on infant day care. Many factors are relevant: infant sex and temperament, family income and education, and especially the quality of care at home and elsewhere.

As with many topics in child development, questions remain. What is definitive is that each infant needs personal responsiveness from at least one person—ideally from both mother and father—who is the infant's partner in the synchrony duet, the base for secure attachment, and then the social reference who encourages exploration. If the baby has that, development should go well.

SUMMING UP

Infants seek social bonds, which they develop with one or several people. Synchrony begins in the early months: Infants and caregivers interact face-to-face, making split-second adjustments in their emotional responses to each other. Synchrony evolves into attachment, an emotional connection. Secure attachment allows infants to learn; insecure infants are less confident and may develop emotional impairments. As infants become more curious and encounter new toys, people, and events, they use social referencing to learn whether such new things are fearsome or fun.

The emotional connections evident in synchrony, attachment, and social referencing may occur with mothers, fathers, other relatives, and day-care providers. Nations and families vary in how much nonmaternal infant care they use, as well as in the quality of that care. Consequences also vary, with neither exclusive maternal care, family day care, nor center care necessarily best. Problems with later development may occur if an infant receives unresponsive care (as when one caregiver has too many infants or a depressed mother is the sole caregiver). Quality and continuity of care matter. ■

SUMMARY

Emotional Development

1. Two emotions, contentment and distress, appear as soon as an infant is born. Smiles and laughter are evident in the early months. Anger emerges with restriction and frustration, between 4 and 8 months of age, and becomes stronger by age 1.

2. Reflexive fear is apparent in very young infants. Fear of something specific, including fear of strangers and of separation, appears toward the end of the first year.

3. In the second year, social awareness produces more selective fear, anger, and joy. As infants become increasingly self-aware, emotions emerge that encourage an interface between the self and others—specifically, pride, shame, and affection.

4. Brain maturation has an obvious impact on emotional development, although specifics are not yet known. Synesthesia (when a sense or emotion in one part of the brain spreads to other parts) is apparent early in life. Self-recognition (on the mirror/rouge test) emerges at about 18 months.

5. Stress impedes early brain and emotional development. Some infants are particularly vulnerable to the effects of early mistreatment.

6. Temperament is a set of genetic traits whose expression is influenced by the context. Inborn temperament is linked to later personality, although plasticity is also evident.

7. Parental practices inhibit and guide a child's emotions. Ideally, a good fit develops between the parents' actions and the child's personality.

Theories of Infant Psychosocial Development

8. According to all major theories, caregiver behavior is especially influential in the first two years. Freud stressed the mother's impact on oral and anal pleasure; Erikson emphasized trust and autonomy.

9. Behaviorists focus on learning; parents teach their babies many things, including when to be fearful or joyful. Cognitive theory holds that infants develop working models based on their experiences.

10. The sociocultural approach notes the impact of social and cultural factors on the parent–infant relationship. Ethnotheories shape infant emotions and traits so that they fit well within the culture. Some cultures encourage proximal parenting (more physical touch); others, distal parenting (more talk and object play). Personal theories also affect how parents respond to infants.

The Development of Social Bonds

11. Sometimes by 2 months, and clearly by 6 months, infants become more responsive and social, and synchrony begins. Synchrony involves moment-by-moment interaction. Infants are disturbed by a still face because they expect and need social interaction.

12. Attachment, measured by the baby's reaction to the caregiver's presence, departure, and return in the Strange Situation, is crucial. Some infants seem indifferent (type A attachment—insecure-avoidant) or overly dependent (type C—insecure-resistant/ambivalent), instead of secure (type B). Disorganized attachment (type D) is the most worrisome.

13. Secure attachment provides encouragement for infant exploration. As they play, toddlers engage in social referencing, looking to other people's facial expressions to detect what is frightening and what is fun.

14. Fathers are wonderful playmates for infants, who frequently use them as social references, learning about emotions and exploration. If a man thinks that infant care is unmanly, or a woman thinks only women can care for babies, that may inhibit father involvement. Many modern fathers, however, complement the mother's infant care—and babies are happier because of it.

15. The impact of non-maternal care depends on many factors; it varies from one nation to another and probably from one child to another. Quality of care (responsive, individualized) is crucial, no matter who provides that care.

KEY TERMS

social smile (p. 192)
stranger wariness (p. 193)
separation anxiety (p. 193)
self-awareness (p. 194)
temperament (p. 196)
goodness of fit (p. 198)
Big Five (p. 198)
trust versus mistrust (p. 199)
autonomy versus shame and doubt (p. 199)
social learning (p. 200)
working model (p. 200)
ethnotheory (p. 201)
proximal parenting (p. 202)
distal parenting (p. 202)
synchrony (p. 205)
still-face technique (p. 206)
attachment (p. 207)
secure attachment (p. 208)
insecure-avoidant attachment (p. 208)
insecure-resistant/ambivalent attachment (p. 208)
disorganized attachment (p. 208)
Strange Situation (p. 209)
social referencing (p. 212)
family day care (p. 215)
center day care (p. 215)

WHAT HAVE YOU LEARNED?

Emotional Development

1. What are the first emotions to appear in very young infants?

2. What are 1-year-olds afraid of?

3. How do the emotions of the second year of life differ from those of the first year?

4. How does stress during infancy affect brain development?

5. Why does synesthesia seem to be more common in infants than in adults?

6. Why are temperamental traits more apparent in some people than others?

Theories of Infant Psychosocial Development

7. What are the similarities and differences between the oral stage and the trust stage?

8. What are the similarities and differences between the anal stage and the autonomy stage?

9. How would behaviorists explain family and cultural patterns of personality traits?

10. Why does "working model" arise from cognitive theory instead of the other theories?

11. What would be the beliefs of an ethnotheory that supports proximal parenting?

12. What would be the beliefs of an ethnotheory that supports distal parenting?

The Development of Social Bonds

13. How does synchrony help infants learn about emotions?

14. Is it possible to overemphasize the importance of secure attachment? Why or why not?

15. In what circumstances would an infant develop type A attachment?

16. In what circumstances would an infant develop type C attachment?

17. In what circumstances would an infant develop type D attachment?

18. For infants, how is father care different from, and similar to, mother care?

19. Why are most infants, in most nations, cared for exclusively by their mothers?

20. What are the differences between grandmother care, family day care, and center day care?

21. For which infants does early day care correlate with aggression in kindergarten?

22. Why is it difficult to draw definite conclusions about infant day care?

APPLICATIONS

1. One cultural factor influencing infant development is how infants are carried from place to place. Ask four mothers whose infants were born in each of the past four decades how they transported them—front or back carriers, facing out or in, strollers or carriages, car seats or on mother's laps, and so on. Why did they choose the mode(s) they chose? What are their opinions and yours on how that cultural practice might affect infants' development?

2. Observe synchrony for three minutes. Ideally, ask the parent of an infant under 8 months of age to play with the infant. If no infant is available, observe a pair of lovers as they converse. Note the sequence and timing of every facial expression, sound, and gesture of both partners.

3. Telephone several day-care centers to try to assess the quality of care they provide. Ask about such factors as adult–child ratio, group size, and training for caregivers of children of various ages. Is there a minimum age? If so, why was that age chosen? Analyze the answers, using Table 7.3 as a guide.

>>ONLINE CONNECTIONS

To accompany your textbook, you have access to a number of online resources, including quizzes for every chapter of the book, flashcards (in English and Spanish), critical thinking questions, and case studies. For access to any of these links, go to www.worthpublishers.com/bergerca9e. In addition to these free resources, you'll also find links to podcasts, video clips, diagnostic quizzing with personalized study advice, and an ebook. Some of the videos and activities available online include:

- *Attachment Behaviors in the Strange Situation.* You'll get a chance to watch—and take your best guess about attachment states—as some infants are left in the company of strangers.
- *Child Care.* A variety of videos showcase different types of early child care and different strategies for best practices.

PART II The Developing Person So Far:

The First Two Years

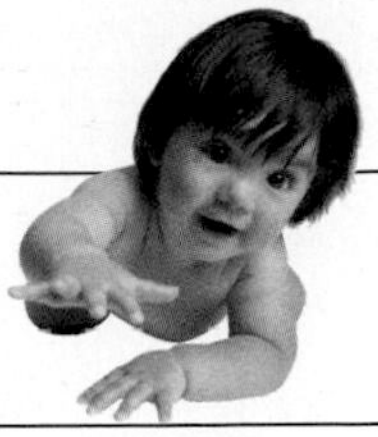

BIOSOCIAL

Body Changes Over the first two years, body weight quadruples and brain weight triples. Connections between brain cells grow dense, with complex networks of dendrites and axons. Neurons become coated with myelin, sending messages more efficiently. Experiences that are universal (experience-expectant) and culture-bound (experience-dependent) aid brain growth, partly by pruning unused connections between neurons.

Senses and Motor Skills Brain maturation underlies the development of all the senses. Seeing, hearing, and mobility progress from reflexes to coordinated voluntary actions, including focusing, grasping, and walking. Culture is evident in sensory and motor development, as brain networks respond to the particulars of each infant's life.

Public Health Infant health depends on immunization, parental practices (including "back to sleep"), and nutrition. Breast milk protects health and has so many other benefits that the World Health Organization recommends exclusive breast-feeding for the first six months. Survival rates are much higher today than even a few decades ago, yet in some regions, infant growth is still stunted because of malnutrition.

COGNITIVE

Sensorimotor Intelligence and Information Processing As Piaget describes it, in the first two years, infants progress from knowing their world through immediate sensory experiences to "experimenting" on that world through actions and mental images. Information-processing theory stresses the links between sensory experiences and perception. Infants develop their own ideas regarding the possibilities offered by the objects and events of the world. Research over the past two decades finds traces of memory at 3 months, of object permanence at 4 months, and of deferred imitation at 9 months—all much younger ages than Piaget described.

Language Interaction with responsive adults exposes infants to the structures of communication and language. By age 1, infants usually speak a word or two; by age 2, language has exploded—toddlers talk in short sentences and add vocabulary each day. Language develops through reinforcement, neurological maturation, and social motivation; all three processes combine to create a very conversational toddler.

PSYCHOSOCIAL

Emotions and Theories Emotions develop from newborn reactions to complex, self-conscious responses. Infants' self-awareness and independence are shaped by parents, in a transition explained by Freud's oral and anal stages, by Erikson's crises of trust versus mistrust and autonomy versus shame and doubt, by behaviorism's focus on parental responses, and by cognitive theory's working models. Much of basic temperament is inborn and apparent throughout life. Sociocultural theory stresses cultural norms, evident in parents' ethnotheories in raising their infants; some parents are more proximal (encouraging touch), others more distal (encouraging cognition).

The Development of Social Bonds Parents and infants respond to each other by synchronizing their behavior. Toward the end of the first year, secure attachment to the parent sets the stage for the child's increasingly independent exploration of the world. Insecure attachment—avoidant, resistant, or disorganized—signifies a parent–child relationship that hinders learning. Infants actively participate socially, using social referencing to interpret their experiences. Mothers, fathers, and day-care providers encourage infants' social confidence.

P A R T

III

CHAPTERS 8•9•10

early childhood

From age 2 to age 6, children spend most of their waking hours discovering, creating, laughing, and imagining, as they acquire the skills they need. They chase each other and attempt new challenges (developing their bodies); they play with sounds, words, and ideas (developing their minds); they invent games and dramatize fantasies (learning social skills and morals).

These years have been called the *preschool years,* but that has become a misnomer. School no longer means sitting at desks in rows. Many 2- to 6-year-olds are in "school," learning and playing. These years have also been called the *play years.* The young child's delight in play seems magical—whether quietly tracking a beetle through the grass or riotously turning a bedroom into a shambles. Young children's minds seem playful, too; they explain that "a bald man has a barefoot head" or that "the sun shines so children can go outside to play." But people of all ages play, so these are not the only play years.

Therefore, these three chapters are called *early childhood,* the traditional term for this period. Early childhood is a period of extraordinary growth, learning, and play, joyful not only for young children but also for anyone who knows them, a time for impressive growth in every domain.

CHAPTER 8

Early Childhood: Biosocial Development

WHAT WILL YOU KNOW?

1. Do children eat too much, too little, or both?
2. How does brain maturation affect emotional development in early childhood?
3. What do children need for their gross motor skills to develop?
4. When and how should child abuse be prevented

When I was 4, I jumped off the back of our couch again and again, trying to fly. I did it many times because I tried it with and without a cape, with and without flapping my arms. My laughing mother wondered whether she had made a mistake in letting me see *Peter Pan*. An older woman warned that jumping would hurt my uterus. I didn't know what a uterus was, I didn't heed that lady, and I didn't stop until I decided I could not fly because I had no pixie dust.

When you were 4, I hope you also wanted to fly and someone laughed while keeping you safe. Protection, appreciation, and fantasy are all needed in early childhood. Do you remember trying to skip, climb a tree, or write your name? Young children try, fail, and try again. They become skilled and wise, eventually understanding some of life's limitations, including that humans have no wings. Advances in body and brain, and the need for adult protection, are themes of this chapter. Amazing growth, unexpected injury, and sobering maltreatment are all described.

>> Body Changes

In early childhood as in infancy, the body and brain develop according to powerful epigenetic forces, biologically driven and socially guided, experience-expectant and experience-dependent (as explained in Chapter 5). Bodies and brains mature in size and function.

Growth Patterns

Just comparing a toddling, unsteady 1-year-old with a cartwheeling 6-year-old makes some differences obvious. During early childhood, children slim down as the lower body lengthens and fat turns to muscle. In fact, the average body mass index (BMI, the ratio of weight to height) is lower at ages 5 and 6 than at any other time of life. Gone are the toddler's protruding belly, round face, short limbs, and large head. The center of gravity moves from the breast to the belly, enabling cartwheels, somersaults, and many other motor skills. The joys of dancing, gymnastics, and pumping a swing become possible; changing body proportions enable new achievements year by year. Toddlers often tumble, unbalanced: It is fortunate they are close to the floor. Kindergartners race and rarely fall.

Size and Balance These cousins are only four years apart, but note the doubling in leg length and marked improvement in balance. The 2-year-old needs to plant both legs on the sand, while the 6-year-old cavorts on one foot.

Increases in weight and height accompany this growth. Over each year of early childhood, well-nourished children gain about 4½ pounds (2 kilograms) and grow almost 3 inches (about 7 centimeters). By age 6, the average child in a developed nation:

- Weighs between 40 and 50 pounds (between 18 and 22 kilograms)
- Is at least 3½ feet tall (more than 100 centimeters)
- Looks lean, not chubby (ages 5 to 6 are lowest in body fat)
- Has adultlike body proportions (legs constitute about half the total height)

When many ethnic groups live together in a nation with abundant food and adequate medical care, children of African descent tend to be tallest, followed by those of European descent, then Asians, and then Latinos. However, height differences are greater *within* ethnic groups than *between* groups.

Nutrition

Although they rarely die of malnutrition, preschool children may be at greater nutritional risk than children of any other age, primarily because it is easy to satisfy their small appetites with unhealthy foods, leaving no room for the nutrition they need. Over the centuries, low-income families encouraged their children to eat, protecting them against famine. This saved lives. Even today in the poorest nations, malnutrition beginning in infancy and continuing through early childhood contributes to one-third of all child deaths (UNICEF, 2008) and slows later growth, including growth of the brain. For instance, according to a study of hungry young children in Ghana, many became depressed or mentally impaired adolescents, although few became delinquents—perhaps they lacked the energy (Appoh, 2004; Appoh & Krekling, 2004).

Unfortunately, the well-intentioned tradition of encouraging young children to eat becomes destructive when food is abundant. This is true in many nations: In Brazil 30 years ago, the most common nutritional problem was undernutrition; now it is overnutrition (Monteiro et al., 2004), with low-income Brazilians particularly vulnerable (Monteiro et al., 2007).

A study of 2- to 4-year-olds in low-income families in New York City found many overweight children: Weight increased as family income fell (J. A. Nelson et al., 2004) and as children grew older (14 percent at age 2; 27 percent at age 4). This age pattern suggests that eating habits, not genes, were the cause. In that study, overweight children were more often Latino (27 percent) or Asian American (22 percent) rather than of African (14 percent) or European (11 percent) descent.

One explanation for these ethnic differences is that many of these children lived with grandparents who knew firsthand the dangers of malnutrition. This possibility is supported by generational data: Latino and Asian American grandparents are unlikely to be obese themselves but often have overweight grandchildren (Bates et al., 2008). Of course, this varies depending on the background, culture, and community of the particular grandparents, but for every group children's nutritional needs have changed faster than customs have.

An epidemic of heart disease and diabetes is spreading worldwide as overfed children become overweight adults (Gluckman & Hanson, 2006). An article in

The Lancet (the leading medical journal in England) predicted that by 2020, 228 million adults worldwide will have diabetes (more in India than in any other nation) as a result of unhealthy eating habits acquired in childhood. This article suggests that measures to reduce childhood overeating in the United States have been inadequate and that "U.S. children could become the first generation in more than a century to have shorter life spans than their parents if current trends of excessive weight and obesity continue" (Devi, 2008, p. 105).

Appetite decreases between ages 2 and 6 because, compared with infants, young children need fewer calories per pound. This is especially true for the current generation since children get much less exercise than their parents or grandparents did. They do not feed the animals, walk miles to school, or even go outside often to play. However, instead of accepting this generational change, many parents foolishly fret, threaten, and cajole their children to overeat ("Eat all your dinner and you can have ice cream"). Pediatricians have found that most parents of infants, toddlers, and preschoolers believe that relatively thin children are less healthy than relatively heavy ones, a false belief that leads to overfeeding (Laraway et al., 2010).

HOWARD BARLOW / ALAMY

Victory! Well, maybe not quite yet, but he's on his way. This boy participates in a British effort to combat childhood obesity; mother and son exercising in Liverpool Park is part of the solution. Harder to implement are dietary changes—many parents let children eat as much as they want.

Nutritional Deficiencies

Although most children in developed nations consume more than enough calories, they do not always obtain adequate iron, zinc, and calcium. For example, children now drink less milk than formerly, which means less calcium and weaker bones later on.

Another problem is sugar. Many customs entice children to eat sweets—in birthday cake, holiday candy, desserts, and other treats. Sweetened cereals and drinks (advertised as containing 100 percent of daily vitamins) are a poor substitute for a balanced, varied diet, partly because some nutrients have not yet been identified, much less listed on food labels. This means that eating a wide variety of foods may be essential for optimal health.

Compared with the average child, those preschoolers who eat more dark-green and orange vegetables and less fried food benefit in many ways. They gain bone mass but not fat, according to a study that controlled for other factors that might correlate with body fat, such as gender (girls have more), ethnicity (people of some ethnic groups are genetically thinner), and income (poor children have worse diets) (Wosje et al., 2010).

An added complication is that an estimated 3 to 8 percent of all young children are allergic to a specific food—almost always a common, healthy one: Cow's milk, eggs, peanuts, tree nuts, soy, wheat, fish, and shellfish are the usual culprits. Diagnostic standards vary (which explains the range of estimates) and treatment varies even more (Chafen et al., 2010). Some experts advocate total avoidance of the offending food—there are peanut-free schools, where no one is ever allowed to pack a peanut butter sandwich for lunch—but others suggest that tolerance to the offending food should be built up, beginning by giving babies a tiny bit of peanut butter (Reche et al., 2011). Fortunately, many childhood food allergies are outgrown, but since young children are already at nutritional risk, allergies make it even harder to achieve a balanced diet.

Healthy Eating Children eat the way their culture teaches them to-about ⅓ with hands, ⅓ with forks, and ⅓ with chopsticks. They also eat whatever their community presents, establishing lifelong tastes that might predict their health as well. This boy in Beijing may be fortunate: Traditional Chinese cuisine (brown rice and many vegetables) is among the healthiest in the world. However, with rising income, more meat and more obesity have become a trend in China. Has it reached this preschool?

ELLEN B. SENISI

Oral Health

Too much sugar and too little fiber cause tooth decay, the most common disease of young children in developed nations, affecting more than one-third of all U.S. children under age 6 (Brickhouse et al., 2008). Sugary fruit drinks and soda are prime causes; even diet soda contains acid that makes decay more likely (Holtzman, 2009).

Fortunately, "baby" teeth are replaced naturally at about ages 6 to 10. The schedule is primarily genetic, with girls averaging a few months ahead of boys. However, tooth care should not be postponed until the permanent teeth erupt. Severe tooth decay in early childhood harms those permanent teeth (which form below the first teeth) and can cause jaw malformation, chewing difficulties, and speech problems. Teeth are affected by diet and illness, which means that the state of a young child's teeth can alert adults to other health problems.

Most preschoolers visit the dentist if they have U.S.-born, middle-class parents—but not if their parents were born elsewhere. A study in San Francisco found that fear of the dentist was common among immigrants from China, who were unlikely to take their young children for an oral health checkup (Hilton et al., 2007). Young parents (below age 22 at the child's birth) of every ethnicity are more likely to have poor oral health habits themselves, and their children more often have cavities (Niji et al., 2010).

Of course, many low-income parents of all ethnic groups are overwhelmed with work and child care and do not realize that tooth brushing is a vital habit, best learned early in life (Mofidi et al., 2009). But in many countries, ignorance is not the problem; access is. In the United States, free dentistry is not available to most poor parents, who "want to do better" for their children's teeth than they did for their own (Lewis et al., 2010).

Hazards of "Just Right"

Many young children are compulsive about their daily routines, insisting that bedtime be preceded by tooth brushing, a book, and prayers—or by a snack, sitting on the toilet, and a song. Whatever the routine, children expect it and are upset if someone puts them to bed without it. Similarly, mealtime can become a time for certain foods, prepared and placed in a particular way, on a specific plate. This rigidity, known as the "just right" or "just so" phenomenon, might be a sign of a pathological obsessive-compulsive disorder in older children and adults. However, a wish for continuity and sameness is normal and widespread among young children (Evans et al., 2006; Pietrefesa & Evans, 2007). For example:

Especially for Nutritionists A parent complains that she prepares a variety of vegetables and fruits, but her 4-year-old wants only French fries and cake. What should you advise? (see response, page 231)

> Whereas parents may insist that the child eat his vegetables at dinner, the child may insist that the potatoes be placed only in a certain part of the plate and must not touch any other food; should the potatoes land outside of this area, the child may seem to experience a sense of near-contamination, setting off a tirade of fussiness for which many 2- and 3-year-olds are notorious.
>
> *[Evans et al., 1997, p. 59]*

Most children's food preferences and rituals are far from ideal. (One 3-year-old I know wanted to eat only cream cheese sandwiches on white bread; one 4-year-old, only fast-food chicken nuggets.) According to a survey of 1,500 parents of 1- to 6-year-olds (Evans et al., 1997), the "just right" phase peaked at about age 3, when children:

- Preferred to have things done in a particular order or in a certain way
- Had a strong preference to wear (or not wear) certain articles of clothing
- Prepared for bedtime by engaging in a special activity, routine, or ritual
- Had strong preferences for certain foods

VAHAN SHIRVANIAN / CARTOONSTOCK

"I'm not hungry. I ate with Rover."

Eat Your Veggies On their own, children do not always eat wisely.

By age 6, this rigidity faded somewhat (see Figure 8.1). Another team of experts put it this way: "Most, if not all, children exhibit normal age-dependent obsessive-compulsive behaviors [that are] usually gone by middle childhood" (March et al.,

2004, p. 216). The best reaction may be patience: A young child's insistence on a particular routine, a preferred pair of shoes, or a favorite cup can be accommodated for a year or two. After all, adults also have preferred routines, keeping their obsessions in check with rational thinking (Evans & Leckman, 2006). For preschool teachers, this means that routines need to be simple, clear, and followed by all the children—otherwise, every child will want to be an exception.

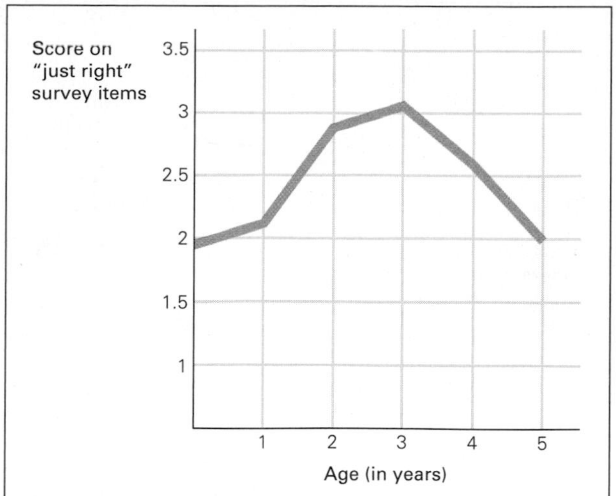

Source: Evans et al., 1997.

FIGURE 8.1

Young Children's Insistence on Routine This chart shows the average scores of children (who are rated by their parents) on a survey indicating the child's desire to have certain things—including food selection and preparation—done "just right." Such strong preferences for rigid routines tend to fade by age 6.

Childhood Overeating

Overeating can become a serious problem: Indulgence and patience—necessary for "just right"—may be destructive if the result is an overweight child. Our major discussion of childhood obesity occurs in Chapter 11 because the problem is most obvious in middle childhood, but the origins are found in early childhood.

As already mentioned, many adults entice young children to eat more than their small bellies want, developing habits and appetites that are destructive decades later. Caregivers are not the only ones at fault. The social context of early childhood (television commercials, store displays, other children's eating habits) encourages overconsumption, yet childhood obesity leads to later illness.

Pediatricians need to provide parents of 2- to 5-year-olds with "anticipatory guidance" (Collins et al., 2004), since prevention is better than putting a 6-year-old on a diet (as some pediatricians do). Preschool educators (sometimes via guidelines for parents or requests to food providers) can also influence children's nutritional intake, affording them more opportunities to expand their knowledge and experience—and ensuring that they have nutritious food (no candy).

SUMMING UP

Between ages 2 and 6, children grow taller and proportionately thinner, with variations depending on genes, nutrition, income, and ethnicity. Nutrition and oral health are serious concerns, as many children eat unhealthy foods, developing cavities and too much body fat. Young children usually have small appetites and picky eating habits. Unfortunately, many adults encourage overeating, not realizing that overweight leads to life-threatening illness. ■

>> Brain Development

Brains grow rapidly before birth and throughout infancy, as you saw in Chapter 5. By age 2, most neurons have connected to other neurons and substantial pruning has occurred. The 2-year-old's brain already weighs 75 percent of what it will weigh in adulthood. (The major structures of the brain are diagrammed in Figure 8.2).

Since most of the brain is already present and functioning by age 2, what remains to develop? The most important parts! Although the brains and bodies of other primates seem better than humans in some ways (they climb trees better, walk faster, and so on), and although many animals have abilities humans lack (dogs' sense of smell, for instance), humans have intellectual capacities far beyond those of any other animal. Considered from an evolutionary perspective, because of our brains, the human species developed "a mode of living built on social cohesion, cooperation and efficient planning . . . survival of the smartest" seems more accurate than survival of the fittest (Corballis, 2011, p. 194).

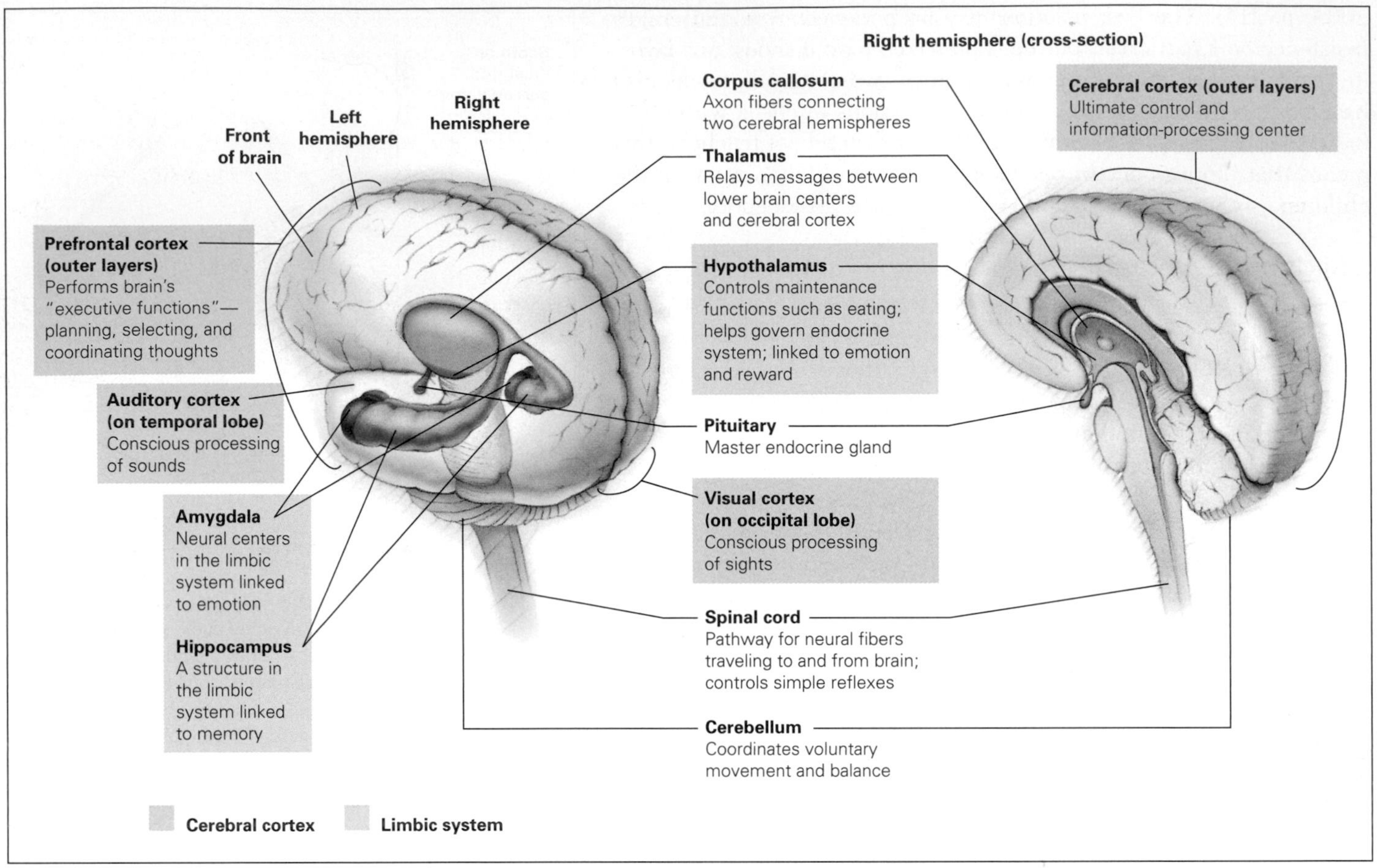

FIGURE 8.2

Connections A few of the dozens of named parts of the brain are shown here. Although each area has particular functions, the entire brain is interconnected. The processing of emotions, for example, occurs primarily in the limbic system, but many other brain areas are involved.

Those functions of the brain that make us human, not merely apes, begin in infancy but develop notably after age 2, enabling quicker, better-coordinated, and more reflective thought (Johnson, 2005; Kagan & Herschkowitz, 2005). Between ages 2 and 6, the brain grows from 75 percent to 90 percent of its adult weight, with increases particularly in the areas that allow advanced language and social understanding. The size of the cortex—brain regions where planning, thinking, and language occur—is a crucial difference between humans and other animals. Elephants, crows, chimpanzees, and dolphins have all recently surprised researchers with their intelligence, but none come close to *Homo sapiens* in the relative size of their cortex and their social understanding (Corballis, 2011).

For example, a careful series of tests given to 106 chimpanzees, 32 orangutans, and 105 human 2½-year-olds found that young children were "equivalent . . . to chimpanzees on tasks of physical cognition but far outstripped both chimpanzees and orangutans on tasks of social cognition" such as pointing or following someone's gaze (Herrmann et al., 2007, p. 1365).

Especially for Early-Childhood Teachers You know you should be patient, but you feel your frustration rising when your young charges dawdle on the walk to the playground a block away. What should you do? (see response, page 232)

Speed of Thought

After infancy, some brain growth is the result of proliferation of the communication pathways (dendrites and axons). However, most increased brain weight occurs because of **myelination.** *Myelin* (sometimes called the *white matter* of the brain) is a fatty coating on the axons that speeds signals between neurons (see Figure 8.3). Although myelination continues throughout childhood and adolescence, the effects of myelination are especially apparent in early childhood (Silk & Wood,

myelination The process by which axons become coated with myelin, a fatty substance that speeds the transmission of nerve impulses from neuron to neuron.

2011), partly because the areas of the brain that show greatest early myelination are the motor and sensory areas (Kolb & Whishaw, 2008).

Speed of thought from axon to neuron becomes pivotal when several thoughts must occur in rapid succession. By age 6, most children can see an object and immediately name it, catch a ball and throw it, write their ABCs in proper sequence, and so on. In fact, rapid naming of letters and objects—possible only when myelination is extensive—is a crucial indicator of later reading ability (Shanahan & Lonigan, 2010). Of course, adults must be patient when listening to young children talk, helping them get dressed, or watching them write each letter of their names. Everything is done more slowly by 6-year-olds than by 16-year-olds because the younger children's brains have less myelination, which slows information processing. However, thanks to myelination, older preschoolers are much quicker than toddlers, who sometimes forget what they were doing before they finish.

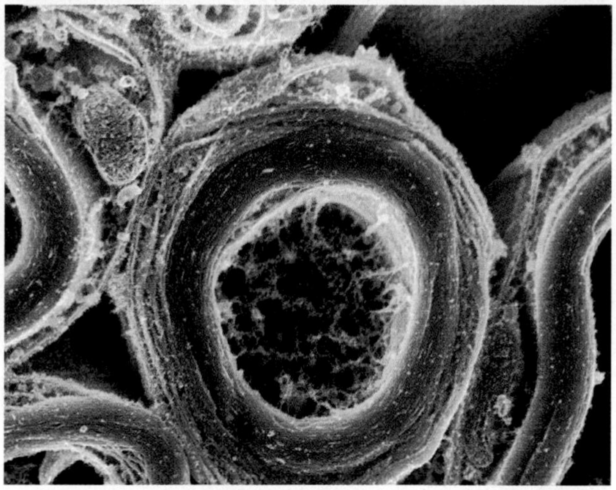

DR. DAVID FURNESS, KEELE UNIVERSITY / PHOTO RESEARCHERS, INC.

FIGURE 8.3

Faster and Faster Myelination is a lifelong process. Shown here is a cross section of an axon (dark middle) coated with many layers of Schwann cells, as more and more myelin wraps around the axon throughout childhood. Age-related slowdowns in adulthood are caused by gradual disappearance of myelin layers.

Connecting the Brain's Hemispheres

One part of the brain that grows and myelinates rapidly during early childhood is the **corpus callosum,** a long, thick band of nerve fibers that connects the left and right sides of the brain. Growth of the corpus callosum makes communication between the hemispheres more efficient, allowing children to coordinate the two sides of the brain or body. Failure of the corpus callosum to develop results in serious disorders: This is one of several possible causes of autism (Frazier & Hardan, 2009).

To understand the significance of the corpus callosum, note that the two sides of the body and of the brain are not identical. Each side specializes, being dominant for certain functions—the result of **lateralization,** literally, "sidedness." The entire human body is lateralized, apparent not only in right- or left-handedness but also in the feet, the eyes, the ears, and the brain itself. Genes, prenatal hormones, and early experiences all affect which side does what. Lateralization advances with development of the corpus callosum (Boles et al., 2008).

corpus callosum A long, thick band of nerve fibers that connects the left and right hemispheres of the brain and allows communication between them.

lateralization Literally, sidedness, referring to the specialization in certain functions by each side of the brain, with one side dominant for each activity. The left side of the brain controls the right side of the body, and vice versa.

Left-handed people tend to have thicker corpus callosa than right-handed people do, perhaps because they need to readjust the interaction between the two sides of their bodies, depending on the task. For example, most left-handed people brush their teeth with their left hand because using their dominant hand is more natural, but they shake hands with their right hand because that is what the social convention requires.

Some research a decade ago found that, relatively speaking, the corpus callosum was thicker in females than in males, a finding that led to speculation about women's superior emotional understanding. However, research using more advanced techniques now finds that this sex difference is far from universal. Some individual males and females have notably thicker corpus callosa than others, but gender does not seem relevant (Savic-Berglund, 2010). Much brain research, including data on the corpus callosum, has led some scientists to jump to conclusions—conclusions that are later proved wrong. Another male–female difference is that male brains are bigger and heavier. However, researchers are understandably cautious about interpreting this difference.

>> Response for Nutritionists (from page 228) The nutritionally wise advice would be to offer only fruits, vegetables, and other nourishing, low-fat foods, counting on the child's eventual hunger to drive him or her to eat them. However, centuries of cultural custom make it almost impossible for parents to be wise in such cases. A physical checkup, with a blood test, may be warranted to make sure the child is healthy.

The Left-Handed Child

Infants and toddlers usually prefer one hand over the other for grabbing spoons and rattles, and by age 2 most children have a dominant hand used for scribbling and throwing. Preschool teachers notice that about 1 child in 10 prefers the left

No Correction Needed The teacher in this preschool does not correct the left-handed children, one of whom happily draws beside her friends. Why does the word *correct* literally mean "to make right"?

hand. Handedness is partly genetic (Goymer, 2007), but many cultures have tried to make everyone right-handed, with some success. When left-handed children were forced to use their right hands, most learned to write right-handedly. However, neurological success was incomplete: Their brains were only partly reprogrammed (Klöppel et al., 2007).

Even today, many cultures endorse the belief that being right-handed is best, an example of the *difference-equals-deficit error,* explained in Chapter 1. Consider language. In English, a "left-handed compliment" is insincere, and no one wants to have "two left feet" or to be "out in left field." In Latin, *dexter* (as in *dexterity*) means "right" and *sinister* means "left" (and also "evil"). *Gauche,* the French word for *left,* means "socially awkward" in English. Many languages are written from left to right, which is easier for right-handed people.

The design of doorknobs, scissors, baseball mitts, instrument panels, and other objects favor the right hand. (Some manufacturers have special versions for lefties, but few young children know to ask for them.) In many Asian and African cultures, the left hand is used only for wiping after defecation; it is an insult to give someone anything with that "dirty" hand.

Developmentalists advise against switching a child's handedness, not only because this causes adult–child conflicts and may create confusion in the brain but also because left lateralization is an advantage in some professions, especially those involving creativity and split-second actions. A disproportionate number of artists, musicians, and sports stars were/are left-handed, including Michelangelo, Seal, Jimi Hendrix, Paul McCartney, Larry Bird, and Sandy Koufax. Four of the past six presidents of the United States were/are lefties: Ronald Reagan, Jimmy Carter, Bill Clinton, and Barack Obama (John McCain is also left-handed).

Acceptance of left-handedness is more widespread now than a century ago. That might explain why more adults in Great Britain and the United States claim to be left-handed today (about 10 percent) than in 1900 (about 3 percent) (McManus et al., 2010). There also seem to be more left-handed men than women, as well as more left-handers in North America than elsewhere.

The Whole Brain

Astonishing studies of humans whose corpus callosa are severed in a procedure that relieves severe epilepsy, as well as research on humans and other vertebrates with intact corpus callosa, have revealed how the brain's hemispheres specialize. Typically, the brain's left half controls the body's right side as well as areas dedicated to logical reasoning, detailed analysis, and the basics of language; the brain's right half controls the body's left side and areas dedicated to emotional and creative impulses, including appreciation of music, art, and poetry. Thus, the left side notices details and the right side grasps the big picture—a distinction that provides a clue in interpreting Figure 8.4.

This left–right distinction has been exaggerated, especially when broadly applied to people (Hugdahl & Westerhausen, 2010). No one is exclusively left-brained or right-brained (except severely brain-damaged individuals); moreover, the brain is flexible, especially in childhood, so a lost function of one hemisphere is sometimes replaced in the other hemisphere.

For most people, both sides of the brain are involved in almost every skill. That is why the corpus callosum is crucial: It connects the left and right hemispheres. As myelination of the corpus callosum progresses, signals between the two hemispheres become quicker and clearer, enabling children to become better thinkers

>> Response for Early-Childhood Teachers (from page 230) One solution is to remind yourself that the children's brains are not yet myelinated enough to enable them to quickly walk, talk, or even button their jackets. Maturation has a major effect, as you will observe if you can schedule excursions in September and again in April. Progress, while still slow, will be a few seconds faster in April than it was in September.

and less clumsy. To pick an easy example: No 2-year-old has the balance to hop on one foot, but most 6-year-olds can do it—an example of brain balancing. Many songs, dances, and games that young children love involve moving their bodies in some coordinated way—difficult, but fun because of that.

Planning and Analyzing

You learned in Chapter 5 that the *prefrontal cortex* (sometimes called the *frontal cortex* or *frontal lobe*) is an area in the front part of the brain's outer layers (the cortex), just behind the forehead. The prefrontal cortex is crucial; it is called the *executive* of the brain because the planning, prioritizing, and reflection that occur in the prefrontal cortex govern the rest of the brain.

For example, someone might feel anxious on meeting a new person whose friendship could be valuable. The prefrontal cortex can calculate and plan, not letting the anxious feelings ruin the interaction. Young children are much less adept than adults at social understanding and planning because their prefrontal cortexes are immature (Kolb & Whishaw, 2008). For example, when a stranger greets them, many 2-year-olds are speechless, hiding behind their mothers if possible; adults may feel equally shy, but they bravely respond.

Brain maturation is partly genetic, but early experience matters (Lenroot & Giedd, 2008). Control of anxiety, for instance, depends not only on age and temperament but also on caregiver patience and guidance. Brain scans of the prefrontal cortex and amygdala (soon described) taken at age 18 may show inhibition, but most inhibited adults no longer act in extremely anxious ways (Schwartz et al., 2010). Emotional regulation is further discussed in Chapter 10.

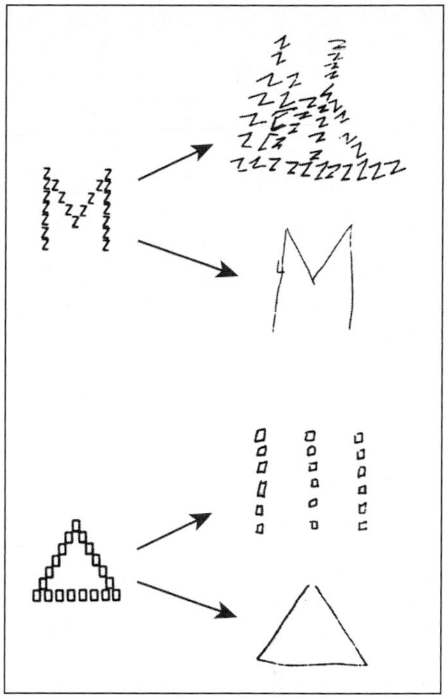

FIGURE 8.4

Copy What You See Brain-damaged adults were asked to copy the leftmost figure in each panel. One person drew the top set; another, the set at the bottom.

Observation Quiz Which set was drawn by someone with left-side damage and which set by someone with right-side damage? (see answer, page 234)

Maturation of the Prefrontal Cortex

The frontal lobe continues to develop for many years after early childhood; dendrite density and myelination continue to increase in emerging adulthood (Johnson, 2005). Nonetheless, advances in neurological control between ages 2 and 6 are evident in several ways:

- Sleep becomes more regular.
- Emotions become more nuanced and responsive.
- Temper tantrums subside.
- Uncontrollable laughter and tears are less common.

One example of the maturing prefrontal cortex is how children play the game Simon Says. Players are supposed to follow the leader *only* when orders are preceded by the words "Simon says." Thus, if leaders touch their noses and say, "Simon says touch your nose," players are supposed to touch their noses; but when leaders touch their noses and say, "Touch your nose," no one is supposed to follow the example. Young children quickly lose at this game because they impulsively do what they see and hear. Older children can think before acting. The prefrontal cortex works!

Such advances can be observed in every child. Might experience rather than brain maturation be the reason? A convincing demonstration that something neurological, not experiential, is the primary reason for these changes comes from a series of experiments in which 3-year-olds consistently make a stunning mistake that disappears by age 5. Children are given a set of cards with clear outlines of trucks or flowers, some red and some blue. They are asked to "play the shape game," putting trucks in one pile and flowers in another. Three-year-olds (and even some 2-year-olds) can do this correctly.

Then children are asked to "play the color game," sorting the cards by color. Most children under age 4 fail. Instead they sort by shape, as they had done before. This basic test has been replicated in many nations; 3-year-olds usually get stuck in their initial sorting pattern. Most older children make the switch.

When this result was first obtained, experimenters thought perhaps the children didn't know their colors; so the scientists switched the order, first playing "the color game." Most 3-year-olds did that correctly. Then, when they were asked to play "the shape game," they still sorted by color. Even with a new set of cards, such as yellow and green or rabbits and boats, 3-year-olds still tend to sort however they did originally, either by color or shape.

Researchers are looking into many possible explanations for this result (Marcovitch et al., 2010; Müller et al., 2006; Yerys & Munakata, 2006). All agree, however, that something in the cortex must mature before children are able to switch from one way of sorting objects to another. (Maturation of the prefrontal cortex is also discussed in Chapters 5, 11, and 14.)

Impulsiveness and Perseveration

Neurons have only two kinds of impulses: on–off, or activate–inhibit. Each is signaled by biochemical messages from dendrites to axons to neurons. Both activation and inhibition are necessary for thoughtful adults, who neither leap too quickly nor hesitate too long. (A balanced brain is most effective throughout life: One explanation of cognitive loss in late adulthood is that older people are too cautious or too impulsive.)

Many young children have not yet found the balance. They are impulsive, flitting from one activity to another. That explains why many 3-year-olds cannot stay quietly on one task, even in "circle time" in an early-childhood preschool, where each child is supposed to sit in place, not talking or touching anyone else. In another example, some young children want a toy that another child has but then lose interest when the toy becomes available. Few 3-year-olds are capable of the sustained attention that is required in most primary schools.

perseveration The tendency to persevere in, or stick to, one thought or action for a long time.

During the same age period, some children play with a single toy for hours. **Perseveration** refers to the tendency to persevere in, or stick to, one thought or action—evident in the card-sorting study just described (Hanania, 2010). Although many explanations are plausible, the fact that young children sometimes perseverate is apparent to anyone who hears a young child repeat one phrase or question again and again or who witnesses a tantrum when a child is told to stop something he or she was doing. (Wise teachers give a warning—"Cleanup in five minutes"—which sometimes helps.) The tantrum itself may perseverate. Crying may become uncontrollable; the child seems stuck in the emotion that triggered the tantrum.

Impulsiveness and perseveration are opposite manifestations of the same underlying cause: immaturity of the prefrontal cortex. No young child is perfect at regulating attention; impulsiveness and perseveration are evident in every 2-year-old (Else-Quest et al., 2006).

>> Answer to Observation Quiz (from page 233) In each pair, the copy on the top, with its careful details, reflects damage to the right half of the brain, where overall impressions are formed. The person with left-brain damage produced the copies that were just an M or a △, without the details of the tiny z's and rectangles. With a whole functioning brain, people can see both "the forest and the trees."

Over the years of childhood, from ages 2 to 12, brain maturation (innate) and emotional regulation (learned) increase: Most children become able to pay attention and switch activities as needed. By early adolescence, children change tasks at the sound of the bell—no perseveration allowed. Exceptions include children diagnosed with attention-deficit/hyperactivity disorder (ADHD), who are too impulsive for their age as well as too resistant to change. An imbalance between the left and right sides of the prefrontal cortex and abnormal growth of the corpus callosum seem to underlie (and perhaps cause) ADHD (Gilliam et al., 2011).

As with all biological maturation, some of this is related to culture—hence the reason this chapter is called *biosocial development,* not simply *physical development.* A study of Korean preschoolers found that they had earlier attention control and less perseveration than a comparable group of English children (Oh & Lewis, 2008). This study included the shape–color task: Of the 3-year-olds, 40 percent of Korean children but only 14 percent of British children successfully shifted from sorting by shape to sorting by color. The researchers explored many possible explanations, including genes, but concluded that "a cultural explanation is more likely" (Oh & Lewis, 2008, p. 96).

ZUMA PRESS PHOTOS VIA NEWSCOM

Ashes to Ashes, Dust to Dust Many religious rituals have sustained humans of all ages for centuries, including listening quietly in church on Ash Wednesday—as Nailah Pierre tries to do. This is developmentally difficult for young children, but for three reasons she probably will succeed: (1) gender (girls mature earlier than boys), (2) experience (she has been in church many times), and (3) social context (she is one of 750 students in her school attending a special service at Nativity Catholic church).

Emotions and the Brain

Now that we have considered the prefrontal cortex, we turn to another region of the brain, sometimes called the *limbic system,* the major region for emotions. Emotional expression and emotional regulation advance during early childhood (more about that in Chapter 10). Crucial to that advance are three major areas of the limbic system—the amygdala, the hippocampus, and the hypothalamus.

Three Brain Parts

The **amygdala** is a tiny structure deep in the brain, named after an almond because it is about the same shape and size. It registers emotions, both positive and negative, especially fear (Kolb & Whishaw, 2008). Increased amygdala activity is one reason some young children have terrifying nightmares or sudden terrors, overwhelming the prefrontal cortex and disrupting reason. A child may refuse to enter an elevator or hide when it thunders. The amygdala responds to comfort but not to logic. If a child is terrified of, say, a lion in the closet, an adult should not laugh but might open the closet door and command the lion to go home.

amygdala A tiny brain structure that registers emotions, particularly fear and anxiety.

Another structure in the brain's limbic system, the **hippocampus,** is located right next to the amygdala. A central processor of memory, especially memory for locations, the hippocampus responds to the anxieties of the amygdala by summoning memory. A child can remember, for instance, whether previous elevator riding was scary or fun. Memories of location are fragile in early childhood because the hippocampus is still developing. Nonetheless, deep emotional memories from early childhood can interfere with expressed, rational thinking: An adult might have a panic attack but not know why.

hippocampus A brain structure that is a central processor of memory, especially memory for locations.

The interaction of the amygdala and the hippocampus is sometimes helpful, sometimes not; fear can be constructive or destructive (LaBar, 2007). Studies performed on some animals show that when the amygdala is surgically removed, the animals are fearless in situations that should scare them; for instance, a cat will stroll nonchalantly past monkeys—something no normal cat would do (Kolb & Whishaw, 2008).

Especially for Neurologists Why do many experts think the limbic system is an oversimplification? (see response, page 237)

A third part of the limbic system, the **hypothalamus,** responds to signals from the amygdala (arousing) and to signals from the hippocampus (usually dampening) by producing cortisol and other hormones that activate parts of the brain and body (see Figure 8.5). Ideally, this hormone production occurs in moderation (Tarullo & Gunnar, 2006).

hypothalamus A brain area that responds to the amygdala and the hippocampus to produce hormones that activate other parts of the brain and body.

As the limbic system develops, young children watch their parents' emotions closely. If a parent looks worried when entering an elevator, the child may fearfully cling to the parent when the elevator moves. If this sequence recurs often

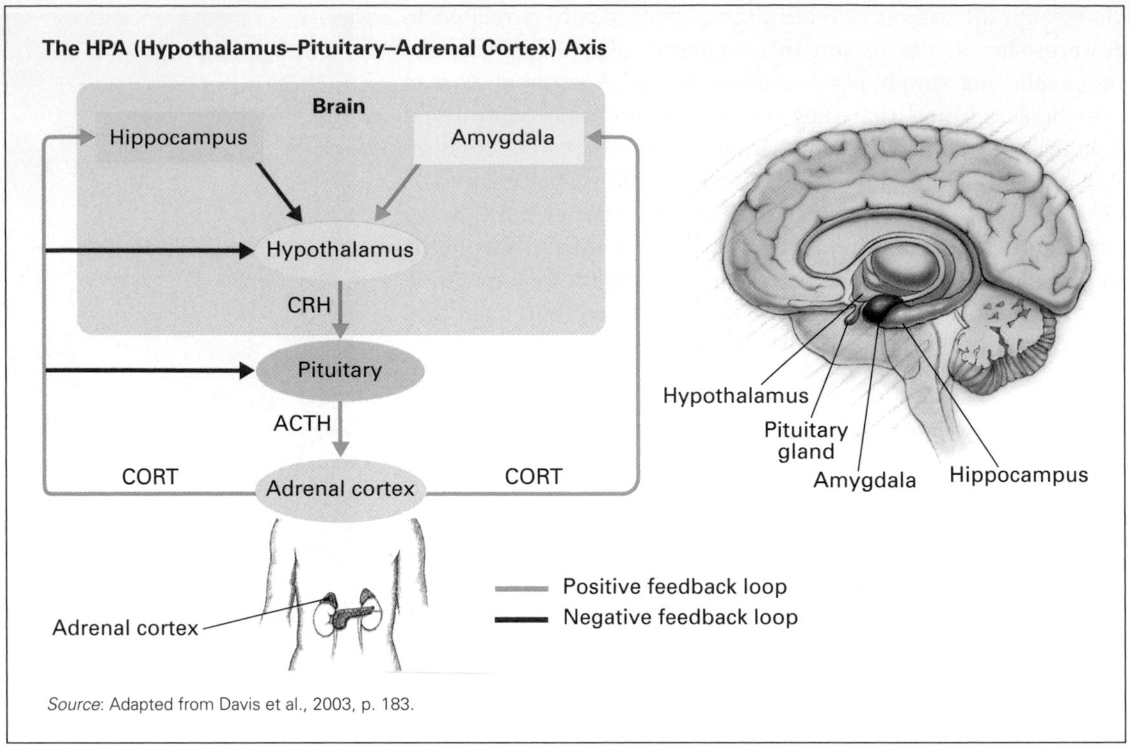

FIGURE 8.5

A Hormonal Feedback Loop This diagram simplifies a hormonal linkage, the HPA (hypothalamus–pituitary–adrenal) axis. Both the hippocampus and the amygdala stimulate the hypothalamus to produce CRH (corticotropin-releasing hormone), which in turn signals the pituitary gland to produce ACTH (adrenocorticotropic hormone). ACTH then triggers the production of CORT (glucocorticoids) by the adrenal cortex (the outer layers of the adrenal glands, atop the kidneys). Fear may either build or disappear, depending on other factors, including how the various parts of the brain interpret that first alert from the amygdala.

enough, the child's amygdala may become hypersensitive to elevators, as fear joins the hippocampus in remembering a specific location, and the result is increased cortisol. If, instead, the parent seems calm and makes elevator riding fun (letting the child push the buttons, for instance), the child will overcome initial feelings of fear, and the limbic system will be aroused to enjoy elevators—even when there is no need to go from floor to floor.

Knowing the varieties of fears and joys is helpful when a teacher takes a group of young children on a trip. To stick with the elevator example, one child might be terrified while another child might rush forward, pushing the close button before the teacher enters. Every experience (elevators, fire engines, animals at the zoo, a police officer) is likely to trigger a range of emotions, without much reflection, in a group of 3-year-olds: A field trip requires several adults, ready to respond to whatever the experience evokes.

Stress and the Limbic System

As you remember from previous chapters, excessive cortisol (the primary stress hormone) may flood the brain and destroy part of the hippocampus. Permanent deficits in learning and memory may result as "children exposed to traumatic or stressful events have an increased probability of developing major depression, post-traumatic stress disorder, and attention-deficit/hyperactivity" (Garcia-Segura, 2009, p. 169).

Yet stress may be helpful instead of harmful. Ongoing research seeks to discover exactly how and when stress harms the human brain (Loman et al., 2010). Emotionally arousing experiences—meeting new friends, entering school, visiting a strange place—seem beneficial if a young child has someone or something to moderate the stress.

In an experiment, brain scans and hormone measurements were taken of 4- to 6-year-olds immediately after a fire alarm. Some children were upset; some not, as measured by their levels of cortisol. Two weeks later, either a friendly or a stern adult questioned them about the event. Those with higher cortisol reactions to the alarm remembered more details than did those with less stress, which suggests that some stress aided memory. Another finding was that, for all the children, memory was better with a friendly interviewer (Quas et al., 2004).

Other research also finds that preschoolers remember experiences better when an interviewer is warm and attentive (Bruck et al., 2006). Context is crucial: Stress can facilitate memory and cognitive growth if adults are reassuring.

However, because developing brains are fragile, "prolonged physiological responses to stress and challenge put children at risk for a variety of problems in childhood, including physical and mental disorders, poor emotional regulation, and cognitive impairments" (Quas et al., 2004, p. 797). Such problems originating in early development of the limbic system may impair health decades later (Shonkoff et al., 2009).

"I would share, but I'm not there developmentally."

Good Excuse It is true that emotional control of selfish instincts is difficult for young children because the prefrontal cortex is not yet mature enough to regulate some emotions. However, family practices can advance social understanding.

Studies of children who have been maltreated suggest that excessive stress hormones in early childhood may permanently damage the limbic system, blunting or accelerating emotional responses lifelong (Wilson et al., 2011). But this research is not definitive because, as you remember from Chapter 1, correlation does not prove causation. Ethics precludes experiments that severely stress children. However, research with mice suggests that the relationship between early stress and abnormal brain development is causal, not merely correlational.

Sadly, this topic leads again to research on those adopted Romanian children mentioned in Chapter 7. When they saw pictures of happy, sad, frightened, or angry faces, their limbic systems were less reactive than were those of Romanian children living with their biological parents. Their brains were also less lateralized, suggesting less specialized, less efficient thinking (Parker & Nelson, 2005). Thus, early stress had probably damaged their brains.

Romania no longer permits wholesale international adoptions. Nonetheless, there are still many Romanian children in institutions. In one study, some were randomly assigned to foster homes at about age 2 whereas others were not. By age 4, those in foster homes were smarter (by about 10 IQ points) than those who remained institutionalized (Nelson et al., 2007). This research suggests that ages 2 to 4 may be a sensitive time for the brain, at least for the brain growth that is measured by IQ tests, primarily language and memory.

SUMMING UP

The brain continues to mature during early childhood. Myelination is notable in several crucial areas. One is the corpus callosum, which connects the left and right sides of the brain and therefore the right and left sides of the body. Increased myelination speeds up bodily actions and reactions. Furthermore, the prefrontal cortex enables a balance between action and inhibition, allowing children to think before they act as well as to stop one action in order to begin another. As impulsiveness and perseveration decrease, children become better able to learn.

Several key areas of the brain—including the amygdala, the hippocampus, and the hypothalamus—make up the limbic system, which matures from ages 2 to 6, aiding emotional expression and control. Children whose early experiences were highly stressful and who lacked nurturing caregivers may have impaired limbic systems. ■

>> Response for Neurologists (from page 235) The more we discover about the brain, the more complex we realize it is. Each part has specific functions and is connected to every other part.

The Joy of Climbing Would you delight in climbing on an unsteady rope swing, like this 6-year-old in Japan (and almost all his contemporaries worldwide)? Each age has special sources of pleasure.

>> Improved Motor Skills

Maturation of the prefrontal cortex improves impulse control, while myelination of the corpus callosum and lateralization of the brain permit better physical coordination. No wonder children move with greater speed and grace as they age from 2 to 6, becoming better able to direct and refine their actions. (At About This Time lists approximate ages for the acquisition of various motor skills in early childhood.)

Mastery of gross and fine motor skills is one result of the extensive, active play of young children, true everywhere. A study in Brazil, Kenya, and the United States tracked how young children spend their time. Some cultural variations and differences based on socioeconomic status (SES) emerged—for example, compared to their peers, middle-class European American children did the most talk-

AT ABOUT THIS TIME
Motor Skills at Ages 2–6*

Approximate Age	Skill or Achievement
2 years	Run for pleasure without falling (but bumping into things) Climb chairs, tables, beds, out of cribs Walk up stairs Feed self with spoon Draw lines, spirals
3 years	Kick and throw a ball Jump with both feet off the floor Pedal a tricycle Copy simple shapes (e.g., circle, rectangle) Walk down stairs Climb ladders
4 years	Catch a ball (not too small or thrown too fast) Use scissors to cut Hop on either foot Feed self with fork Dress self (no tiny buttons, no ties) Copy most letters Pour juice without spilling Brush teeth
5 years	Skip and gallop in rhythm Clap, bang, sing in rhythm Copy difficult shapes and letters (e.g., diamond shape, letter *S*) Climb trees, jump over things Use knife to cut Tie a bow Throw a ball Wash face, comb hair
6 years	Draw and paint with preferred hand Write simple words Scan a page of print, moving the eyes systematically in the appropriate direction Ride a bicycle Do a cartwheel Tie shoes Catch a ball

*Context and culture are crucial for acquisition of all these skills. For example, many 6-year-olds cannot tie shoelaces because they have no shoes with laces.

ing with adults, and working-class Kenyan children did the most chores. But at every income level in all three nations, children spent more time playing than doing anything else—chores, lessons, or conversations with adults (Tudge et al., 2006).

JEFFREY L. ROTMAN / CORBIS

Could Your Child Do This? Perhaps. If acrobatics was your family's profession and passion, you might encourage your toddler to practice headstands, and years later, your child could balance on your head. Everywhere, young children try to do whatever their parents do.

Observation Quiz Was this photo taken in the United States? (see answer, page 241)

Gross Motor Skills

Gross motor skills improve dramatically during early childhood. When playing, many 2-year-olds fall down and bump clumsily into each other, but some 5-year-olds are skilled and graceful, performing coordinated dance steps or sports moves.

Specific Skills

Most North American 5-year-olds can ride a tricycle, climb a ladder, and pump a swing, as well as throw, catch, and kick a ball. Some can skate, ski, dive, and ride a bicycle—activities that demand balance and coordination of both brain hemispheres. In some nations, 5-year-olds swim in oceans or climb cliffs. Brain maturation, motivation, and guided practice make these skills possible.

Adults need to make sure children have safe spaces, time, and playmates; skills will follow. According to sociocultural theory, children learn best from peers who demonstrate whatever skills the child is ready to try—from catching a ball to climbing a tree. Of course, culture and locale influence which skills children display—some small children learn to ski, others to sail.

Recent urbanization concerns many developmentalists. Compared with a century ago, when almost all children played together in empty lots or fields without adult supervision, half the world's children now live in cities. Many of these are "megacities . . . overwhelmed with burgeoning slums and environmental problems" (Ash et al., 2008, p. 739). Crowded, violent streets not only impede development of gross motor skills but also add to the natural fears of the immature limbic system.

The next generation of young children may have few older playmates and no safe space to practice motor skills. Gone are the days when parents told their children to go out and play, expecting them safely back when hunger, weather, or nightfall brought them home. Now parents fear strangers, cars, trucks, and stray animals and therefore keep their 3- to 5-year-olds inside, perhaps watching television or playing video games but not developing gross motor skills (Taylor et al., 2009). Preschool programs have many things to recommend them: Motor-skill development is one.

Exploring the Great Outdoors Two children climb over a rock outcrop in Shenandoah National Park in Virginia. Such outdoor play is important for the development of motor skills, even though many parents are tempted to try to keep their children safer by keeping them indoors.

JEFF GREENBERG / THE IMAGE WORKS

Environmental Hazards

Pollutants do more harm to young, growing brains and bodies than to older, more developed ones; they are of particular concern for urban young children. Much depends on local regulations. For example, in India, one city of 14 million (Kolkata, formerly Calcutta) has such extensive air pollution that childhood asthma rates are soaring and lung damage is prevalent. In another Indian city (Mumbai, formerly Bombay), air pollution has been reduced and children's health improved through several measures, including an extensive system of public buses that are required to use clean fuels (Bhattacharjee, 2008).

Asthma has many causes, and, once it occurs, attacks can be precipitated by several substances and circumstances that almost every child experiences, from dust to cold weather. Causes and consequences of childhood asthma are discussed in detail in Chapter 11, but connecting asthma and pollution in India requires mention of the complexity of pinpointing the effects of pollution on health. One major complication is that children from low-SES families are more likely to live in areas of high pollution—in cities with smog, near major highways or industrial plants, and so on. If they are in poor health, or slow to talk, or low in school achievement, that could be the direct result of air pollution on their bodies and brains, or it could be the result of several other circumstances that are more common in low-SES families.

Scientists have grappled with this complication and found that environmental substances cause as well as correlate with health problems in young children of families at every SES level. For example, one study in British Columbia, where pollution is relatively low and universal public health care and birth records allow solid research, found that air pollution from traffic and industry early in life was a cause, not just a correlate, of asthma during the preschool years (Clark et al., 2010). (See the Research Design.)

One complication is that the particles in the air that harm health are not necessarily the particles that people consider to be pollution. For example, burning wood makes smoke that is easy to see and smell, but according to that British Columbia study, wood smoke did not increase asthma. Of course, this conclusion may apply only to the particular kind of wood that is burned in western Canada—another research complication.

Respiratory problems are not the only early-childhood complications that may be caused by pollution. Research on lower animals suggests that hundreds of substances in the air, food, and water affect the brain and thus impede balance, finger dexterity, and motivation. The data are not clear-cut, leading one research team to implore that "developmental researchers direct basic and applied research about the effects of pollutant exposures and ways to reduce children's pollutant burdens" (Dilworth-Bart & Moore, 2006, p. 264). These researchers particularly stress the need to examine the effects of low doses of lead and pesticides on children of low-income and ethnic-minority families, as such children are most likely to be exposed as well as most vulnerable for a host of reasons.

Some substances—including lead in the water and air, pesticides in the soil or on clothing, bisphenol A (BPA) in plastic, and secondhand cigarette smoke—are already proven to be harmful to any child. Lead has been thoroughly researched at high exposure and has been found to reduce intelligence and increase behavior problems in young children.

Over the past 20 years, U.S. regulations have reduced the amount of lead in paint, gasoline, and manufacturing, and

Research Design

Scientists: Nina Annika Clark, Paul A. Demers, Catherine J. Karr, Mieke Koehoorn, Cornel Lencar, Lillian Tamburic, and Michael Brauer.

Publication: *Environmental Health Perspectives* (2010).

Participants: This study began with all births in southwest British Columbia (which includes Vancouver) in 1999 and 2000, a total of 59,917 babies. After excluding newborns with characteristics known to increase asthma risk (e.g., low birthweight) and those without sufficient data, 37,401 newborns were studied for three years. Among those, the researchers found 3,482 who, by age 4, had been hospitalized for asthma at least once,or had been diagnosed with asthma at least twice by a physician. As part of the research, each of those 3,482 was matched by SES, gender, and so on with five other children from the same cohort.

Design: Exposure to air pollution was measured by detailing the air pollution on the particular block where each child with asthma and his or her five matches lived. Many pollutants were included: carbon monoxide (CO), nitrogen oxides (nitric oxide [NO] and nitrogen dioxide [NO_2]), particulate matter ($\leq$ 10 micrometers and $\leq$ 2.5 micrometers in aerodynamic diameter [PM_{10} and $PM_{2.5}$]), ozone (O_3), sulfur dioxide (SO_2), black carbon, and wood smoke. Researchers also noted whether the mother smoked cigarettes as well as how close the residence was to major roads and factories that released pollutants in the air. The exposure of the children with asthma was compared with the exposure of the matched controls.

Major conclusion: Every subgroup category (such as high, middle, or low SES; breast- or formula-fed; ethnic background) had some children with asthma, although rates varied. For example, high-SES, breast-fed girls had lower rates of asthma than did low-SES, formula-fed boys. However, no matter what a particular child's background, air pollution, particularly from cars and trucks, increased the incidence of asthma. The extensive controls and matching in this study also revealed that some factors hypothesized to increase asthma did not do so, among them proximity to highways, birth to a First Nations family, birth to a mother not born in Canada, exposure to wood smoke, and having a mother who smoked. (On exposure to cigarette smoke, the researchers note that, unlike most of the measures, the only indicator of maternal smoking was the mother's admission.)

Comments: Strengths of this study include the conscientious and detailed measures, including air pollution block by block, wood smoke by season, an entire cohort with government health and population records, and the matched-control design. This raises a question: What results would be found in a region with higher pollution? Perhaps genes protect most children, even in high pollution areas, or perhaps the advantages of being a girl or being breast-fed disappear if pollution reaches a certain level. Further research is needed.

children's blood lead levels have dropped sharply—in some states (e.g., Colorado and Wyoming) the average is now close to zero. In other states (e.g., Michigan and Ohio) average lead levels are still too high, defined as above 10 micrograms per deciliter of blood among children under age 6 (MMWR, May 27, 2005). Some sources of lead remain unregulated, including lead in city water (from old pipes), in manufacturing, and in jet fuel. It is not known precisely how high blood levels of lead must be before harm occurs, but some scientists are convinced that even 5 micrograms per deciliter is probably too much (Cole & Winsler, 2010).

>> Answer to Observation Quiz (from page 239) No—not because of ethnicity (many U.S. citizens are of Indian descent) but because of child labor laws. This duo is part of a circus (note the rigging), and no child in North America is allowed to perform such feats for pay.

Lead must be reduced by laws and policies, but parents can take action as well. Specifics include increasing children's consumption of calcium, wiping window ledges clean of dust, testing drinking water, and making sure the child never eats peeling chips of lead-based paint (still found in old buildings) (Dilworth-Bart & Moore, 2006). Although scientists, laws, and parents have raised awareness about the dangers of lead exposure for young brains, the administrator of environmental public health for the state of Oregon says, "We simply do not know—as scientists, as regulators, as health professionals—the health impacts of the soup of chemicals to which we expose human beings" (Shibley, quoted in Johnson, 2011). Whether you think Shibley is needlessly alarmist or stating the obvious depends on your own perspective.

Fine Motor Skills

Especially for Immigrant Parents You and your family eat with chopsticks at home, but you want your children to feel comfortable in Western culture. Should you change your family's eating customs? (see response, page 243)

Fine motor skills, especially small movements of the hands and fingers, are harder to master than gross motor skills. Pouring juice into a glass, cutting food with a knife and fork, and achieving anything more artful than a scribble with a pencil all require a level of muscular control, patience, and judgment that are beyond most 2-year-olds.

Many fine motor skills involve two hands and thus both sides of the brain: The fork stabs the meat while the knife cuts it; one hand steadies the paper while the other writes; tying shoes, buttoning shirts, cutting paper, and zipping zippers require both hands. An immature corpus callosum and prefrontal cortex may be the underlying reason that shoelaces get knotted, paper gets ripped, and zippers get stuck. Short, stubby fingers add to the problem. As with gross motor skills, practice and maturation are key; thus, making things with glue, markers, and scraps of cloth are part of the curriculum for preschools. Puzzles—with large pieces of splinter-proof wood—are essential supplies.

Admirable Skill Lenny feeds herself with knife and fork, using carefully placed fingers. This fine motor skill is achieved by 5-year-olds worldwide if their culture encourages it and if they have time to practice and observe (as Willy does).

Observation Quiz How can you tell that this does not depict American culture? (see answer, page 243)

AP PHOTO / MATTHIAS RIETSCHE

Traditional academic learning also depends on fine motor skills and body control. Writing requires finger control, reading a line of print requires eye control, sitting for hours at a desk requires bladder control, and so on. These are beyond most young children, so even the brightest 3-year-old is not allowed in first grade, and some slower-developing 6-year-olds are frustrated if their teachers expect them to write neatly and cut straight.

Fine motor skills—like many other biological characteristics, such as bones, brains, and teeth—typically mature about six months earlier in girls than in boys. This may be one reason why girls typically outperform boys on elementary school tests of school achievement and many young girls consider boys "stupid." Some educators suggest waiting until a child is "ready" for school; others suggest that school expectations should adjust to the immaturity of the child, a controversy explored in Chapter 9.

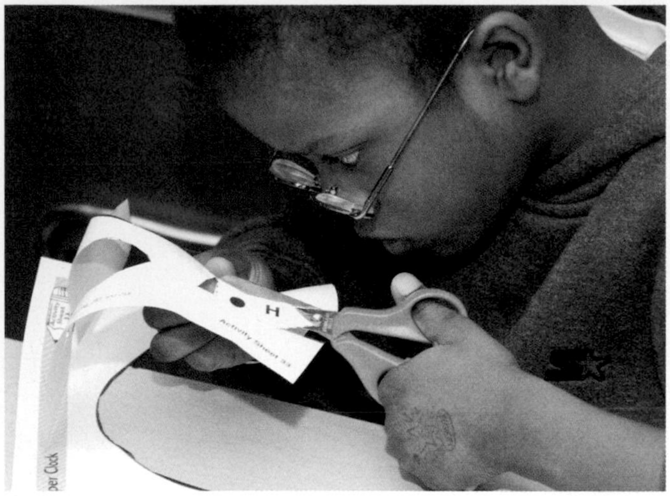

Careful Cutting For a left-handed 5-year-old with poor vision, is this task necessary practice or needless frustration?

Artistic Expression

Young children are imaginative, creative, and not yet self-critical. They love to express themselves, especially if their parents applaud their performances, display their artwork, and otherwise communicate approval. The fact that their fine motor skills are immature, and that their drawings thus lack precision, is not yet important. Perhaps the immaturity of the prefrontal cortex is a blessing: It allows creativity without anxiety (an older child might say, "I can't draw" or "I am horrible at dancing").

All forms of artistic expression blossom during early childhood. Psychologists disagree as to whether drawings reflect children's emotions (Burkitt, 2004). But there is no doubt that 2- to 6-year-olds love to dance around the room, build an elaborate tower of blocks, make music by pounding in rhythm, and put bright marks on shiny paper. In every artistic domain, skill gradually comes with practice and maturation. For example, when drawing a person, 2- to 3-year-olds usually draw a "tadpole"—a circle head, dots for eyes, sometimes a smiling mouth, and then a line or two beneath to indicate the rest of the body. Gradually, tadpoles get bodies, limbs, hair, and so on.

Cultural and cohort differences are apparent. For the most part, Chinese culture incorporates the idea that drawing benefits from instruction, so young children are guided in how best to draw a person, a house, and—most important for the Chinese—a word. By age 9, Chinese children draw more advanced pictures than children of other cultures, where artistic guidance is uncommon. Adult encouragement, child practice, and developing technical skill correlate with more mature, creative drawings a few years later (Chan & Zhao, 2010; Huntsinger et al., 2011).

Singing or Screaming Don't judge a picture by what you see, judge it by the intent of the artist. This 4-year-old's smiling pride and the heart-shaped head suggest a happy picture.

SUMMING UP

Maturation of the brain leads to better hand and body control. Gross motor skills advance every year as long as young children have space to play, older children to emulate, and freedom from environmental toxins. Pollution and fear of strangers reduce the opportunity many contemporary children have to develop gross motor skills. Children also develop their fine motor skills, which prepares them for the many requirements of formal education. They love to dance, draw, and build, which help in the gradual mastery of finger movements, which will in turn be essential when they start to write. ■

>> Injuries and Abuse

In almost all families of every income, ethnicity, and nation, parents want to protect their children while fostering their growth. Yet more children die of violence—either accidental or deliberate—than from any specific disease.

The contrast is most obvious in developed nations, where medical prevention, diagnosis, and treatment make fatal illness rare until late adulthood. In the United States in 2007, out of every 100,000 1- to 4-year-olds, only 2.2 died of cancer (the leading fatal disease at this age), but 9.6 died accidentally and 2.5 were murdered (National Center for Health Statistics, 2011). Some nations have fewer violent deaths than the United States. In Canada, the comparable rates for 1- to 4-year-olds were 2.6 (cancer), 5.2 (accidents), and 0.5 (murder) (Statistics Canada, 2011). In every nation, more young children die from accidents than from any other specific cause.

Avoidable Injury

Worldwide, injuries cause millions of premature deaths among adults as well as children: Not until age 40 does any specific disease overtake accidents as a cause of mortality, and worldwide 14 percent of all life-years lost are caused by injury (World Health Organization, 2010). In some nations, malnutrition, malaria, and other infectious diseases *combined* cause more infant and child deaths than injuries do, but everywhere children die from preventable accidents.

Nations with high rates of child disease also have high rates of child injury: India, for example, has one of the highest rates worldwide of child motor-vehicle deaths; most children who die in such accidents are pedestrians (Naci et al., 2009). Everywhere, 2- to 6-year-olds are at even greater risk than slightly older children. In the United States, for instance, children are twice as likely to be seriously hurt in early childhood as in middle childhood (Safe Kids USA, 2008).

>> Response for Immigrant Parents (from page 241) Children develop the motor skills that they see and practice. They will soon learn to use forks, spoons, and knives. Do not abandon chopsticks completely, because young children can learn several ways of doing things, and the ability to eat with chopsticks is a social asset.

Age-Related Dangers

Why are 2- to 6-year-olds so vulnerable? Some of the reasons have just been explained. Immaturity of the prefrontal cortex makes young children impulsive; they plunge into danger. Unlike infants, their motor skills allow them to run, leap, scramble, and grab in a flash. Their curiosity is boundless; their impulses are uninhibited; if they do something forbidden, such as playing with matches and causing a fire, their limbic systems might cause them to hide instead of getting help.

Age-related trends are apparent in particulars. Falls are more often fatal for the very young (under 24 months) and very old (over 80 years); motor-vehicle deaths peak from ages 15 to 25. In developed nations, safety seats are required for children in cars, helmets protect bike riders, and cities have sidewalks, but fatal accidents in early childhood often involve poison, fire, or drowning (Safe Kids USA, 2008).

>> Answer to Observation Quiz (from page 241) Lenny is using the fork with her left hand, as all good Germans do. This school is in Dresden.

Injury Control

Instead of using the term *accident prevention,* public health experts prefer **injury control** (or **harm reduction**). Consider the implications of this terminology. *Accident* implies that an injury is a random, unpredictable event; if anyone is at fault, it's a careless parent or an accident-prone child. This is called the "accident paradigm"—as if "injuries will occur despite our best efforts," allowing the public to feel blameless (Benjamin, 2004, p. 521).

injury control/harm reduction Practices that are aimed at anticipating, controlling, and preventing dangerous activities; these practices reflect the beliefs that accidents are not random and that injuries can be made less harmful if proper controls are in place.

A better phrase is *injury control*, which implies that harm can be minimized with appropriate controls. Minor mishaps (scratches and bruises) are bound to occur, but serious injury is unlikely if a child falls on a safety surface instead of on concrete, if a car seat protects the body in a crash, if a bicycle helmet cracks instead of a skull, if swallowed pills come from a tiny bottle.

Only half as many 1- to 5-year-olds in the United States were fatally injured in 2005 as in 1985, thanks to laws that govern poisons, fires, and cars. Control has not yet caught up with some newer hazards, however. For instance, as more homes in California, Florida, Texas, and Arizona have swimming pools, drowning has become a leading cause of unintentional death among young children (Safe Kids USA, 2008).

Prevention

Prevention begins long before any particular child, parent, or politician does something foolish. Unfortunately, no one notices the injuries and deaths that did not happen. For developmentalists, two types of analysis are useful to uncover the primary causes of injuries.

One is called an *accident autopsy.* When a child is seriously injured, analysis can find causes in the microsystem and exosystem as well as in the macrosystem. For example, when a child is hit by a car, an autopsy might point to parental neglect (microsystem), but it might also note that there were no nearby parks, that cars drove too fast and traffic lights were absent, that sidewalks were too narrow and curbs too low (exosystem), or that the entire nation valued speedy vehicles more than slow pedestrians (macrosystem).

The second way to analyze is to look at statistics. For example, the rate of childhood poisoning has decreased since pill manufacturers adopted bottles with safety caps that are difficult for 2-year-olds to open—a statistic which supports that regulation when anyone complains about the cost and inconvenience. Some adults say that children today are overprotected, with fewer swings and jungle gyms, more safety surfaces and mandated car seats, and so on. Statistics, not anecdotes and memories ("I loved the metal playground equipment, and I am still alive"), can quiet such complaints.

primary prevention Actions that change overall background conditions to prevent some unwanted event or circumstance, such as injury, disease, or abuse.

secondary prevention Actions that avert harm in a high-risk situation, such as stopping a car before it hits a pedestrian.

tertiary prevention Actions, such as immediate and effective medical treatment, that are taken after an adverse event (such as illness or injury) occurs and that are aimed at reducing the harm or preventing disability.

Levels of Prevention

Three levels of prevention apply to every childhood health and safety issue, including injuries, neglect, and abuse.

- In **primary prevention,** the overall situation is structured to make harm less likely. Primary prevention fosters conditions that reduce everyone's chance of injury.
- **Secondary prevention** is more specific, averting harm in high-risk situations or for vulnerable individuals.
- **Tertiary prevention** begins after an injury has already occurred, limiting the damage it might cause.

In general, tertiary prevention is most visible, but primary prevention is most effective (Cohen et al., 2010). A good example of this comes from data on pedestrian deaths. Fewer people in the United States die after being hit by a motor vehicle than did 25 years ago (see Figure 8.6). How does each level of prevention contribute?

FIGURE 8.6

While the Population Grew This chart shows dramatic evidence that prevention measures are succeeding in the United States. Over the same time period, the total population has increased by about one-third, making these results even more impressive.

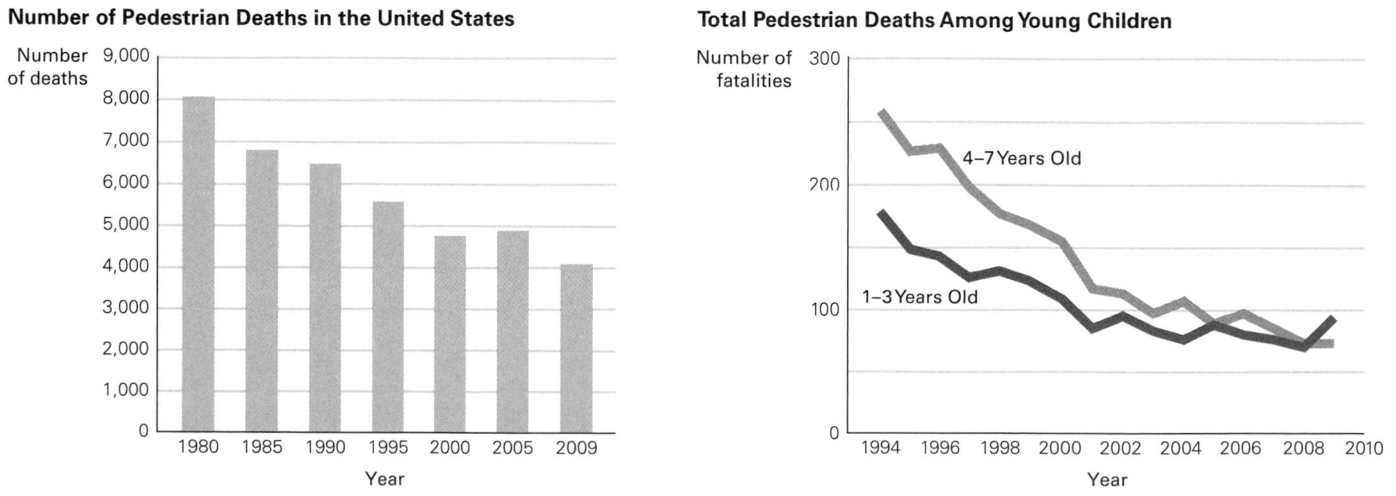

Source: United States Department of Transportation, 2010.

Primary prevention includes sidewalks, speed bumps, pedestrian overpasses, streetlights, and traffic circles (Retting et al., 2003; Tester et al., 2004). Cars have been redesigned (e.g., better headlights, bumpers, and brakes), and drivers' competence has improved (e.g., with stronger drunk-driving penalties and tougher licensing exams). If congestion is reduced via traffic regulations and improved mass transit, that is additional primary prevention.

Secondary prevention reduces danger in high-risk situations. Teachers know that they must hold the hand of a particular child when the group goes near the street. Flashing lights on stopped school buses and school-crossing guards are also secondary prevention. Salt on icy roads, warning signs before blind curves, and walk signals at busy intersections are also examples of secondary prevention because each is a high-risk situation that has special intervention.

Finally, *tertiary prevention* reduces damage after crashes, such as laws against hit-and-run drivers. Speedy ambulances, efficient emergency rooms, and effective rehabilitation are also tertiary. Medical personnel speak of the *golden hour* following an accident, when a victim should get to emergency care. Of course, there is nothing magical about 60 minutes in contrast to 61 minutes, but the faster an

Especially for Urban Planners Describe a neighborhood park that would benefit 2- to 5-year-olds. (see response, page 247)

MANOR PHOTOGRAPHY / ALAMY
(a)
ITAR-TASS/ MARINA LYSTSEVA / LANDOV
(b)
DAVID R. FRAZIER / DANITADELIMONT.COM
(c)

And If He Falls . . . These could all be considered secondary prevention, as children need playgrounds away from cars *(a)*, five-point buckles in infant seats *(b)*, and adult supervision when they cross the street *(c)*. Furthermore, the children in photos *(b)* and *(c)* are well-protected—the Russian child wears a snowsuit, and the French teacher blocks traffic as the schoolchildren cross. But the U.S. child in photo *(a)* is climbing a seemingly rusted metal ladder, which could do serious injury. Fortunately, more current playground equipment is plastic.

Especially for Economists In the feature below, how did Kathleen Berger's SES protect Bethany from serious harm? (see response, page 248)

injury victim reaches a trauma center, the better the chance of survival (Bansal et al., 2009). Speed becomes part of tertiary prevention, reducing permanent harm, but primary and secondary prevention halt harm before it occurs.

A CASE TO STUDY

"My Baby Swallowed Poison"

The first strategy that most people think of to prevent injury to young children is to educate the parents. However, public health research finds that laws that apply to everyone are more effective than education, especially if parents are so overwhelmed by the daily demands of child care and money management that they do not realize they need to learn.

For example, infant car seats have saved thousands of lives. However, use of car seats is much less common when it is voluntary than when it is mandated. For that reason, car seats are now legally required.

Parents often consider safety a lower priority than everyday concerns. That explains two findings from the research: (1) The best time to convince parents to use a car seat is before they take their newborn home from the hospital, and (2) the best way to make sure a car seat is correctly used is to have an expert show the parent how it works—not simply tell them or make them watch a video (Tessier, 2010).

Motivation is key, yet "too often, we design our physical environment for smart people who are highly motivated" (S. P. Baker, 2000). But in real life, everyone has moments of foolish indifference, when automatic safety measures save lives.

I know this firsthand. Our daughter Bethany, at age 2, climbed onto the kitchen counter to find, open, and swallow most of a bottle of baby aspirin. Where was I? A few feet away, nursing our second child and watching television. I did not notice what Bethany was doing until I checked on her during a commercial.

Bethany is alive and well today, protected not by her foolish mother but by all three levels of prevention. Primary prevention included laws limiting the number of baby aspirin per container, secondary prevention included my pediatrician's written directions when Bethany was a week old to buy syrup of ipecac, and tertiary prevention was my phone call to Poison Control.

I told the helpful stranger who answered the phone, "My baby swallowed poison." He calmly asked me a few questions and then advised me to give Bethany ipecac to make her throw up. I did, and she did. I still blame myself, but I am grateful for all three levels of prevention that protected my child. I am also well aware that my SES helped avert a tragedy. I had chosen a wise pediatrician and I followed his advice; I had a phone and knew who to call. As I remember all the mistakes I made in parenting (only a few of them detailed in this book), I am grateful for every level of prevention.

Culture and Injury Prevention: Baby on the Plane

I once was the director of a small preschool, and I was struck by the diverse fears and prevention measures of the parents, some helpful and some not. Some were thrilled that our children painted, but others were worried about the ingredients of the paint, for instance. I know that all children need to grab, run, and explore to develop their motor skills as well as their minds, yet they also need to be prevented from falling down stairs, eating pebbles, or running into the street—as many are inclined to do. Adults may not know the best strategies to prevent injury. Consider what one mother wrote about her flight from Australia to California:

> I travelled with my 10-month-old daughter and was absolutely and thoroughly disappointed in the treatment we received from the flight crew captain at the time. I was told or more like instructed that I was to "restrain" my child for the whole flight, which was 13 hours.
>
> I said that other people were able to move around the plane freely, why wasn't she? I was told that due to turbulence she would have to be restrained for the whole trip. On several occasions the flight crew captain would make a point of going out of his way to almost scold me for not listening to him when I would put her down to crawl around.
>
> *[Retrieved April 3, 2011, from Complaints.com]*

This same mother praised her treatment on other long flights, specifically on Asian airlines, when her child was allowed to move more freely and the crew was helpful. Which culture is better at protecting children without needlessly restraining them?

My sympathies were with the mother, and I had praise for the Asian crew, until I read this response:

> Consider the laws in the U.S. regarding child safety in an automobile. Nobody thinks a child should be free to crawl around in a car. No parent thinks their rights have been violated because their child is prevented from free flight inside a car when it impacts. Why not just put the child in the bed of a truck and drive around? . . . Her child could get stepped on, slammed against a seat leg, wedged under a seat, fallen on, etc.

Both sides in this dispute make sense, yet both cannot be right. The data prove that safety seats in cars save lives, but "impact" in planes is unlike that in a car crash. Statistical analysis is needed, or at least a case study of injured children on airplanes. Do passengers on planes step on crawling children? If so, is that controllable harm or a serious hazard?

>> Response for Urban Planners (from page 245): The adult idea of a park—a large, grassy open place—is not best for young children. For them, you would design an enclosed area, small enough and with adequate seating to allow caregivers to socialize while watching their children. The playground surface would have to be protective (since young children are clumsy), with equipment that encourages both gross motor skills (such as climbing) and fine motor skills (such as sandbox play). Swings are not beneficial, since they do not develop many motor skills. Teenagers and dogs should have their own designated area, far from the youngest children.

Child Maltreatment

The next time you read headlines about some horribly neglected or abused child, think of these words from a leading researcher in child maltreatment:

> Make no mistake—those who abuse children are fully responsible for their actions. However, creating an information system that perpetuates the message that offenders are the only ones to blame may be misleading. . . . We all contribute to the conditions that allow perpetrators to succeed.
>
> *[Daro, 2002, p. 1133]*

"We all contribute" in the sense that the causes of child maltreatment are multifaceted, involving not only the parents but also the neighbors, the teachers, the medical community, the culture, and even the maltreated children themselves. Difficult infants (fragile, needing frequent feeding, crying often) are at greatest risk of being maltreated, especially if their mothers are depressed and feel they have no control over their lives. Family financial stress adds to the risk (Bugental & Happaney, 2004). Each of these factors could be mitigated or prevented by the community, through laws, practices, or direct help.

MISHAWAKA POLICE DEPARTMENT / GETTY IMAGES

Nobody Watching? Madelyn Gorman Toogood looks around to make sure no one is watching before she slaps and shakes her 4-year-old daughter, Martha, who is in a car seat inside the vehicle. A security camera recorded this incident in an Indiana department store parking lot. A week later, after the videotape was repeatedly broadcast nationwide, Toogood was recognized and arrested. The haunting question is: How much child abuse takes place that is not witnessed?

Maltreatment Noticed and Defined

Noticing is the first step. Until about 1960, people thought child maltreatment was rare and consisted of a sudden attack by a disturbed stranger. Today we know better, thanks to a pioneering study based on careful observation in one Boston hospital (Kempe & Kempe, 1978): Maltreatment is neither rare nor sudden, and 80 percent of the perpetrators are one or both of the child's own parents (Children's Bureau, 2010a). That makes the situation much worse: Ongoing maltreatment, with no protector, is much more damaging than a single incident, however injurious.

With this recognition came a broader definition: **Child maltreatment** now refers to all intentional harm to, or avoidable endangerment of, anyone under 18 years of age. Thus, child maltreatment includes both **child abuse,** which is deliberate action that is harmful to a child's physical, emotional, or sexual well-being,

child maltreatment Intentional harm to or avoidable endangerment of anyone under 18 years of age.

child abuse Deliberate action that is harmful to a child's physical, emotional, or sexual well-being.

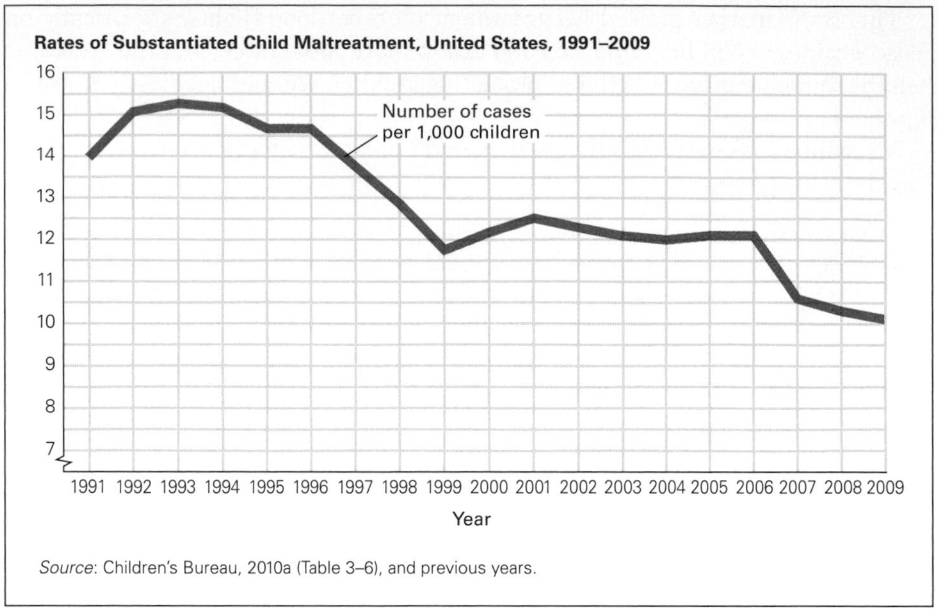

FIGURE 8.7

Still Far Too Many The number of reported and substantiated cases of maltreatment of children under age 18 in the United States is too high, but there is some good news: The rate has declined significantly from its peak in 1993.

Observation Quiz The data point for 2009 is close to the bottom of the graph. Does that mean it is close to zero? (see answer, page 251)

child neglect Failure to meet a child's basic physical, educational, or emotional needs.

reported maltreatment Harm or endangerment about which someone has notified the authorities.

substantiated maltreatment Harm or endangerment that has been reported, investigated, and verified.

and **child neglect,** which is failure to meet a child's basic physical or emotional needs. The more that researchers study the long-term harm of child maltreatment, the worse neglect seems to be, especially in early childhood.

Reported maltreatment means that the authorities have been informed. Since 1993, the number of *reported* cases of maltreatment in the United States has ranged from about 2.7 million to 3.5 million a year (Children's Bureau, 2010b). **Substantiated maltreatment** means that a reported case has been investigated and verified (see Figure 8.7). With the exception of sexual abuse (discussed in Chapter 14), most victims are under age 6. The substantiated annual maltreatment rate in early childhood is about 1 maltreated child in every 80; the reported rate is triple that (U.S. Bureau of the Census, 2009).

The overall ratio of 3-to-1 for reported versus substantiated cases can be attributed to three factors:

1. Each child is counted once, even if repeated maltreatment is reported. Thus, five reports that are verified can lead to one substantiated case.
2. Substantiation requires proof in the form of unmistakable injuries, severe malnutrition, or a witness willing to testify. Such evidence is not always available.
3. A report may be deliberately false (though few are) (Kohl et al., 2009) or may describe a circumstance that was not the result of maltreatment.

Frequency of Maltreatment

How often does maltreatment occur? No one knows. Not all cases are noticed; not all are reported; not all reports are substantiated. Similar issues apply in every nation, city, and town, with marked variations in reports and confirmations. Reports have increased since 1950, but that does not mean that abuse has increased. U.S. laws now require teachers to report suspected maltreatment—reports have increased because of those laws. Official U.S. statistics find that substantiated child maltreatment increased from about 1960 to 1990 but decreased by 18 percent between 2000 and 2009 (see Figure 8.8). During those years, physical and sexual abuse declined but neglect increased. Other sources also report declines over the past two decades.

>> Response for Economists (from page 246) Children from families at all income levels have accidents, but Kathleen Berger's SES allowed her to have a private pediatrician as well as the income to buy ipecac "just in case." She also had a working phone and the education to know about Poison Control.

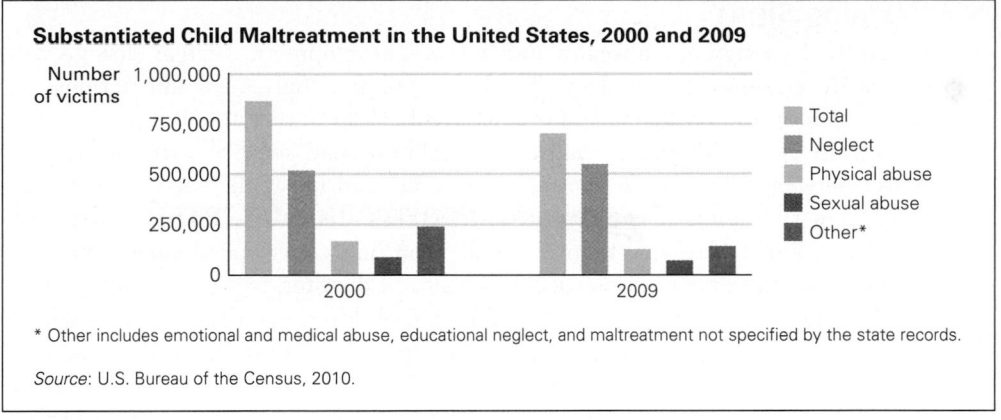

Substantiated Child Maltreatment in the United States, 2000 and 2009

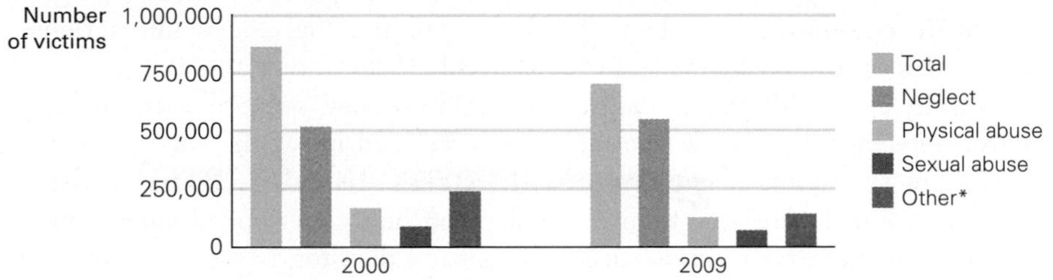

* Other includes emotional and medical abuse, educational neglect, and maltreatment not specified by the state records.

Source: U.S. Bureau of the Census, 2010.

FIGURE 8.8

Getting Better? As you can see, the number of victims of child maltreatment in the United States has declined in the past decade. The legal and social-work response to serious maltreatment has improved over these years, which is a likely explanation for the decline. Other, less sanguine, explanations are possible, however.

Observation Quiz Have all types of maltreatment declined since 2000? (see answer, page 251)

That is good news, but unfortunately official reports leave room for doubt. For example, Pennsylvania and Maine reported almost identical numbers of substantiated incidents of maltreatment in 2009 (4,084 and 4,073), but the child population of Pennsylvania is ten times that of Maine (U.S. Bureau of the Census, 2010). No one thinks that Maine children suffer ten times more than Pennsylvania ones; something in the reporting and substantiating process must differ between those two states. Furthermore, whether or not a person reports maltreatment is powerfully influenced by culture (one of my students asked, "When is a child too old to be beaten?") and in personal willingness to report. The United States has become more culturally diverse in the past decade—could that be why the rate of reported abuse has declined?

Especially for Criminal Justice Professionals Over the past decade, the rate of sexual abuse has gone down by almost 20 percent. What are three possible explanations? (see response, page 252)

Finally, some professionals are more likely to notice and report maltreatment than others. The most marked variation occurs for teachers. The percent of maltreatment reports from educators is 10 times higher in Minnesota than in North Carolina (24 percent versus 2.5 percent) (Children's Bureau, 2010). There are many plausible reasons for why teachers in North Carolina report less often, but no one thinks Minnesota schoolchildren are much more often abused.

In a confidential nationwide survey of young adults in the United States, 1 in 4 said they had been physically abused ("slapped, hit, or kicked" by a parent or other adult caregiver) before sixth grade, and 1 in 22 had been sexually abused ("touched or forced to touch someone else in a sexual way") (Hussey et al., 2006). Almost never had their abuse been reported. The authors of this study think these rates are *underestimates* (Hussey et al., 2006)!

One reason for these high rates of unreported abuse may be that the respondents were asked if they had *ever* been mistreated by someone who was caring for them; most other sources report annual rates. Another reason is that few children report their own abuse; many do not know that they are mistreated until later, when they compare their experiences with those of their friends. Indeed, some adults who were slapped, hit, or kicked in childhood do not think they were abused. Reinterpretation of childhood experiences is controversial: Some memories are false and others are accurate, finally recognized as abuse (McNally & Geraerts, 2009).

post-traumatic stress disorder (PTSD) An anxiety disorder that develops as a delayed reaction to having experienced or witnessed a profoundly shocking or frightening event, such as rape, severe beating, war, or natural disaster. Its symptoms may include flashbacks to the event, hyperactivity and hypervigilance, displaced anger, sleeplessness, nightmares, sudden terror or anxiety, and confusion between fantasy and reality.

Warning Signs

Often the first sign of maltreatment is delayed development, such as slow growth, immature communication, lack of curiosity, or unusual social interactions. All these difficulties may be evident even at age 1 (Valentino et al., 2006).

During early childhood, maltreated children may seem fearful, startled by noise, defensive and quick to attack, and confused between fantasy and reality. These are symptoms of **post-traumatic stress disorder (PTSD),** first identified in combat veterans, then in adults who had experienced some emotional injury or shock (after a serious accident, natural disaster, or violent crime, for example), and more recently in some maltreated children, who suffer neurologically as well as behaviorally (Neigh et al., 2009; Yehuda, 2006). Table 8.1 lists signs of child maltreatment, both neglect and abuse. None of these signs are proof that a child has been abused, but whenever any of them occurs, it signifies trouble.

REUTERS / SANJIB MUKHERJEE

Abuse or Athletics? Four-year-old Budhia Singh ran 40 miles in 7 hours with adult marathoners. He says he likes to run, but his mother (a widow who allowed his trainer to "adopt" him because she could not feed him) has charged the trainer with physical abuse. The government of India has declared that Singh cannot race again until he is fully grown. If a child, the parent, and the community approve of some activity, can it still be maltreatment?

Consequences of Maltreatment

The impact of any child-rearing practice is affected by the cultural context. Certain customs (such as circumcision, pierced ears, and spanking) are considered abusive in some cultures but not in others; their effects on children vary accordingly. Children suffer if their parents seem to love them less than most parents in their neighborhood. If a parent forbids something other children have (from candy to cell phones) or punishes more severely or not at all, children might feel unloved. However, although culture is always relevant, the more longitudinal research is published, the more widespread and long-lasting the impact of maltreatment is found to be.

TABLE 8.1 Signs of Maltreatment in Children Aged 2 to 10

Injuries that do not fit an "accidental" explanation, such as bruises on both sides of the face or body; burns with a clear line between burned and unburned skin; "falls" that result in cuts, not scrapes
Repeated injuries, especially broken bones not properly tended (visible on X-ray)
Fantasy play, with dominant themes of violence or sexual knowledge
Slow physical growth, especially with unusual appetite or lack of appetite
Ongoing physical complaints, such as stomachaches, headaches, genital pain, sleepiness
Reluctance to talk, to play, or to move, especially if development is slow
No close friendships; hostility toward others; bullying of smaller children
Hypervigilance, with quick, impulsive reactions, such as cringing, startling, or hitting
Frequent absence from school
Frequent changes of address
Turnover in caregivers who pick up child or caregiver who comes late, seems high
Expressions of fear rather than joy on seeing the caregiver

Especially for Nurses While weighing a 4-year-old, you notice several bruises on the child's legs. When you ask about them, the child says nothing and the parent says the child bumps into things. What should you do? (see response, page 253)

A VIEW FROM SCIENCE

Emotions Are Hard to Heal

The biological and academic impairment from maltreatment is substantial and thus relatively easy to notice—the teacher sees that a child is bruised, broken, or failing despite ability. However, when researchers follow maltreated children over the years, enduring deficits in social skills seem more crippling. Children continue to hate themselves, and they hate everyone else, too.

To be specific, many studies have found that mistreated children typically regard other people as hostile and exploitative; hence, they are less friendly, more aggressive, and more isolated than other children. The earlier abuse starts and the longer it continues, the worse their peer relationships are (Scannapieco & Connell-Carrick, 2005). Neglected children may have greater social deficits than abused ones, because they were unable to relate to their parents (Stevenson, 2007). The best cure is a warm and enduring friendship, but maltreatment makes this unlikely.

Deficits are lifelong. Maltreated children may become bullies or victims or both, not only in childhood and adolescence but also in adulthood (Dietrich, 2008). They tend to dissociate, that is, to disconnect their memories from their understanding of themselves (Valentino et al., 2008). Adults who were severely maltreated (physically, sexually, or emotionally) often abuse drugs or alcohol, enter unsupportive relationships, become victims or aggressors, sabotage their own careers, eat too much or too little, and engage in other self-destructive behavior (M. G. Smith & Fong, 2004). They also have a much higher risk of emotional disorders and suicide attempts, even after other risk factors (e.g., poverty) are considered (Afifi et al., 2008).

In the current economic climate, finding and keeping a job is a critical aspect of adult well-being; adults who were maltreated suffer in this way as well. One study carefully matched 807 children who had experienced substantiated abuse with other children who were of the same sex, ethnicity, and family SES. About 35 years later, the employment rates of those who had been mistreated were 14 percent lower than the rates of those who had not been abused. The researchers concluded that "abused and neglected children experience large and enduring economic consequences" (Currie & Widom, 2010, p. 111). In this study, the women were more impaired than the men: It may be that self-esteem, emotional stability, and social skills are even more important for female than for male workers.

This is just one of hundreds of longitudinal studies, all of which find that maltreatment affects children decades after the broken bones, or skinny bodies, or medical neglect disappear. Some people feel sorry for mistreated children; others blame parents, or poverty, or racism. But an emotion more universal than sympathy or anger may be enough. If our instinct for self-preservation leads to thoughts about our future, we might prevent child maltreatment. The health of the entire society a few decades from now depends on every child.

Three Levels of Prevention, Again

Just as with injury control, there are three levels of prevention of maltreatment. The ultimate goal is *primary prevention* that focuses on the macrosystem and exosystem (see Chapter 1). Examples of primary-prevention include increasing stable neighborhoods and family cohesion,and decreasing financial instability, family isolation, and teenage parenthood.

Secondary prevention involves spotting warning signs and intervening to keep a risky situation from getting worse (Giardino & Alexander, 2011). For example, insecure attachment, especially of the disorganized type (described in Chapter 7), is a sign of a disrupted parent–child relationship. Someone needs to help repair that interaction. Secondary prevention includes home visits by helpful nurses or social workers, as well as high-quality day care that gives vulnerable parents a break while teaching children how to make friends and resolve conflicts. Secondary prevention notes that families with several young children are at risk, especially when the family head is a single parent with money problems. If a nation has free health care for everyone, vulnerable children can be protected before serious harm occurs.

>> Answer to Observation Quiz (from page 248) No. The number is actually 10.1 per 1,000. Note the little squiggle on the graph's vertical axis below the number 10. This means that numbers between 0 and 9 are not shown.

>> Answer to Observation Quiz (from page 249) Most types of abuse are declining, but not neglect. This kind of maltreatment may be the most harmful because the psychological wounds last for decades.

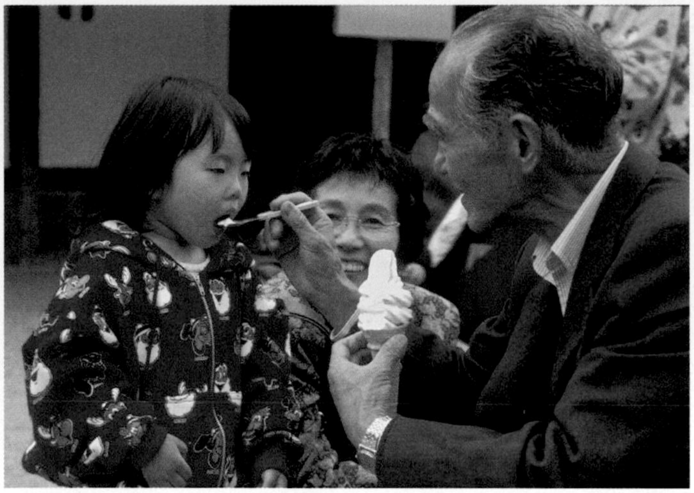

PHOTO JAPAN / ALAMY

JOACHIM LADEFOGED / VII

The Same Situation, Many Miles Apart: Fun with Grandpa Grandfathers, like those shown here in Japan and Sweden, often delight their grandchildren. Sometimes, however, they protect them—either in kinship care, when parents are designated as neglectful, or as secondary prevention before harm is evident. (The grandparents in Sweden are refugees from Iraq.)

Tertiary prevention includes everything that limits harm after maltreatment has already occurred. Reporting and substantiating abuse are only the first steps. Often the caregiver needs help to provide better care. Sometimes the child needs another home. If hospitalization is required, that signifies failure: Intervention should have begun much earlier. At that point, treatment is very expensive, harm has already been done, and hospitalization itself further strains the parent–child bond (Rovi et al., 2004).

Children need caregivers they trust, in safe and stable homes, whether they live with their biological parents, a foster family, or an adoptive family. Whenever a child is legally removed from an abusive or neglectful home and placed in foster care, **permanency planning** must begin, to find a family to nurture the child until adulthood. This is a complex task, requiring cooperation among social workers, judges, and psychologists as well as the caregivers themselves (Edwards, 2007). Sometimes the child's original family can become better; sometimes a relative can be found who will provide good care; sometimes a stranger is the best caregiver.

In **foster care,** children are officially removed from their parents' custody and entrusted to another adult or family; foster parents are reimbursed for the expenses they incur in meeting the children's needs. In every year from 2000 to 2009, about half a million children in the United States were in foster care. More than half of them were in a special version of foster care called **kinship care,** in which a relative—usually a grandparent—becomes the caregiver. This estimate is for official kinship care; three times as many children are unofficially cared for by relatives.

In every nation, most foster children are from low-income, ethnic-minority families, a statistic that should alert everyone to problems in the macrosystem as well as the microsystem. In the United States, children officially in foster care often have a history of severe maltreatment and multiple physical, intellectual, and emotional problems (Pew Commission on Children in Foster Care, 2004). Despite these problems, most develop better in foster care (including kinship care) than with their original abusive families if a supervising agency screens foster families effectively and provides ongoing financial support and counseling (MacMillan et al., 2009; Oosterman et al., 2007).

Adequate support is not typical, however. One obvious failing is that many children move from one foster home to another for reasons that are unrelated to the child's behavior or wishes. Foster children average three placements before permanent placement is achieved (Pew Commission on Children in Foster Care, 2004). Each move increases the risk of a poor outcome (Oosterman et al., 2007). Another

permanency planning An effort by child-welfare authorities to find a long-term living situation that will provide stability and support for a maltreated child. A goal is to avoid repeated changes of caregiver or school, which can be particularly harmful to the child.

foster care A legal, publicly supported system in which a maltreated child is removed from the parents' custody and entrusted to another adult or family, which is reimbursed for expenses incurred in meeting the child's needs.

kinship care A form of foster care in which a relative of a maltreated child, usually a grandparent, becomes the approved caregiver.

>> Response for Criminal Justice Professionals (from page 249) Hopefully, more adults or children are aware of sexual abuse and stop it before it starts. A second possibility is that sexual abuse is less often reported and substantiated because the culture is more accepting of teenage sex (most victims of sexual abuse are between ages 10 and 18). A third possible explanation is that the increase in single mothers means that fathers have less access to children (fathers are the most frequent sexual abusers).

REX FEATURES VIA AP IMAGES

A Missing Piece This British couple was told they would not be able to adopt a non-White British child, so they traveled to Mexico to find their new family. Some adoptive parents bond with their children, no matter what the differences. This mother said that when she first saw her daughter, "A piece of me that was missing suddenly clicked into place."

problem is that kinship care is sometimes used as an easy, less expensive solution. Kinship care may be better than stranger care, but supportive services are especially needed since the grandparent who gets the child is also the parent of the abusive adult (Edwards, 2010; Fechter-Leggett & O'Brien, 2010).

Adoption (when an adult or couple unrelated to the child is legally granted parenthood) is the preferred permanent option when a child should not be returned to a relative, but adoption is difficult for many reasons. Among those reasons: Judges and biological parents are reluctant to release children for adoption; most adoptive parents prefer infants; some agencies screen out families not headed by a heterosexual married couple; some professionals insist that adoptive parents be of the same ethnicity and religion as the child.

adoption A legal proceeding in which an adult or couple unrelated to a child is granted the joys and obligations of being that child's parent(s).

As detailed many times in this chapter, caring for young children—from making sure they brush their teeth to keeping them safe and active—is not easy. Parents shoulder most of the burden, and their love and protection usually result in strong and happy children. Teachers can be crucial during these years, working closely with the parents. The benefit to the entire community of having well-nurtured children is obvious; the ways to achieve that seem less clear.

>> Response for Nurses (from page 250) Any suspicion of child maltreatment must be reported, and these bruises are suspicious. Someone in authority must find out what is happening so that the parent as well as the child can be helped.

SUMMING UP

As they move with more speed and agility, young children encounter new dangers and are seriously injured more often than older children. They are also more often mistreated, either deliberately (abuse) or because essential care is not provided (neglect). Three levels of prevention are needed. Laws and customs can protect everyone (primary prevention); supervision, forethought, and protective care can prevent harm to those at risk (secondary prevention); and when injury or maltreatment occurs, quick and effective medical and psychosocial intervention, as well as prevention of further harm, are needed (tertiary prevention). Putting an end to maltreatment of all kinds is urgent but complex because the sources are often the family, the culture, the community, and the laws.

SUMMARY

Body Changes

1. Children continue to gain weight and add height during early childhood. One reason this occurs is that many adults overfeed children, not realizing that young children are naturally quite thin.

2. Culture, income, and family customs all affect children's growth. In contrast to past decades, children of low-income families are twice as likely to be overweight as their wealthier counterparts. Worldwide, an increasing number of children are eating too much, risking heart disease and diabetes.

3. Many young children consume too much sugar and too little calcium and other nutrients. One consequence is poor oral health. Children need to brush their teeth and visit the dentist years before the permanent teeth erupt.

Brain Development

4. The brain continues to grow in early childhood, reaching 75 percent of its adult weight at age 2 and 90 percent by age 5.

5. Myelination is substantial during early childhood, speeding messages from one part of the brain to another. The corpus callosum becomes thicker and functions much better. The prefrontal cortex, known as the executive of the brain, is strengthened as well.

6. Brain changes enable more reflective, coordinated thought and memory, better planning, and quicker responses. Left–right specialization is apparent in the brain as well as in the body, although the entire brain and the entire body work together for most skills.

7. The expression and regulation of emotions are fostered by several brain areas, including the amygdala, the hippocampus, and the hypothalamus. Childhood abuse may cause overactivity in the amygdala and hippocampus, creating a flood of stress hormones that interfere with learning. Some stress aids learning if reassurance is also present.

Improved Motor Skills

8. Gross motor skills continue to develop; clumsy 2-year-olds become 6-year-olds who move their bodies well, guided by their culture. Play is their main activity. By playing with other children in safe places, they practice the skills needed for formal education.

9. Urbanization and chemical pollutants hamper development. More research is needed, but it is already apparent that high lead levels in the blood can impair the brain and that opportunities to develop gross motor skills are restricted when play space is scarce.

10. Fine motor skills are difficult to master during early childhood. Young children enjoy expressing themselves artistically, developing their body and finger control as well as self-expression. Fortunately, self-criticism is not yet strong.

Injuries and Abuse

11. Accidents cause more child deaths than diseases, with young children more likely to suffer a serious injury or premature death than older children. Close supervision and public safeguards can protect young children from their own eager, impulsive curiosity.

12. Injury control occurs on many levels, including long before and immediately after each harmful incident. Primary prevention protects everyone. Secondary and tertiary prevention also save lives.

13. Child maltreatment includes ongoing abuse and neglect, usually by a child's own parents. Each year, about 3 million cases of child maltreatment are reported in the United States; less than 1 million are substantiated.

14. Physical abuse is the most obvious form of maltreatment, but neglect is more common and may be more harmful. Health, learning, and social skills are all impeded by abuse and neglect, not only during childhood but also decades later.

15. Tertiary prevention may include placement of a child in foster care, including kinship care. Adoption is much less common, although often the best solution for the child. Permanency planning is required because frequent changes are harmful to children. Primary and secondary prevention help parents care for their children and reduce the need for tertiary prevention.

KEY TERMS

myelination (p. 230)
corpus callosum (p. 231)
lateralization (p. 231)
perseveration (p. 234)
amygdala (p. 235)
hippocampus (p. 235)
hypothalamus (p. 235)
injury control/harm reduction (p. 243)
primary prevention (p. 244)
secondary prevention (p. 244)
tertiary prevention (p. 244)
child maltreatment (p. 247)
child abuse (p. 247)
child neglect (p. 248)
reported maltreatment (p. 248)
substantiated maltreatment (p. 248)
post-traumatic stress disorder (PTSD) (p. 250)
permanency planning (p. 252)
foster care (p. 252)
kinship care (p. 252)
adoption (p. 253)

WHAT HAVE YOU LEARNED?

Body Changes

1. About how much does a well-nourished child grow in height and weight from ages 2 to 6?

2. Why do many parents overfeed their children?

3. The incidence of what adult diseases increases with childhood obesity?

4. What specific measures should be part of oral health in early childhood?

5. When is it normal for children to be picky about eating and other daily routines?

Brain Development

6. How much does the brain grow from ages 2 to 6?

7. Why is *myelination* important for thinking and motor skills?

8. What is the function of the corpus callosum?

9. What should parents do if their toddler seems left-handed?

10. How does the prefrontal cortex affect impulsivity and perseveration?

11. What are the functions of three areas of the brain that are part of the limbic system?

12. Is stress beneficial or harmful to young children? Explain why.

Improved Motor Skills

13. What factors help children develop their motor skills?

14. What is known and unknown about the effects on young children of chemicals in food, air, and water?

15. How does brain and body maturation affect children's artistic expression?

Injuries and Abuse

16. Why is the term *injury control* preferred over the term *accident prevention*?

17. What primary measures prevent childhood injury, abuse, and neglect?

18. What secondary measures prevent childhood injury, abuse, and neglect?

19. What tertiary measures prevent further childhood injury, abuse, and neglect?

20. Why did few people recognize childhood maltreatment 50 years ago?

21. Why is neglect in childhood considered more harmful, in the long term, than abuse?

22. Why is it difficult to know exactly how often childhood maltreatment occurs?

23. What are the signs that a child may be mistreated?

24. What are the long-term consequences of childhood maltreatment?

25. Why would a child be placed in foster care?

APPLICATIONS

1. Keep a food diary for 24 hours, writing down what you eat, how much, when, how, and why. Then think about nutrition and eating habits in early childhood. Do you see any evidence in yourself of imbalance (e.g., not enough fruits and vegetables, too much sugar or fat, eating when you are not really hungry)? Did your food habits originate in early childhood, in adolescence, or at some other time?

2. Go to a playground or other place where young children play. Note the motor skills that the children demonstrate, including abilities and inabilities, and keep track of age and sex. What differences do you see among the children?

3. Ask several parents to describe each accidental injury of each of their children, particularly how it happened and what the consequences were. What primary, secondary, or tertiary prevention measures would have made a difference?

4. Think back to your childhood and the friends you had at that time. Was there any maltreatment? Considering what you have learned in this chapter, why or why not?

>>ONLINE CONNECTIONS

To accompany your textbook, you have access to a number of online resources, including quizzes for every chapter of the book, flashcards (in English and Spanish), critical thinking questions, and case studies. For access to any of these links, go to www.worthpublishers.com/bergerca9e. In addition to these free resources, you'll also find links to podcasts, video clips, diagnostic quizzing with personalized study advice, and an ebook. Some of the videos and activities available online include:

- *Brain Development in Early Childhood.* Animations illustrate the macroscopic and microscopic changes as children's brains grow.
- *Stolen Childhoods.* Some children, because of poverty or abuse, never have the opportunities for schooling and nurture that many of us take for granted. Children in a variety of difficult circumstances, from sex work to work in carpet factories, tell their stories in a variety of video clips.

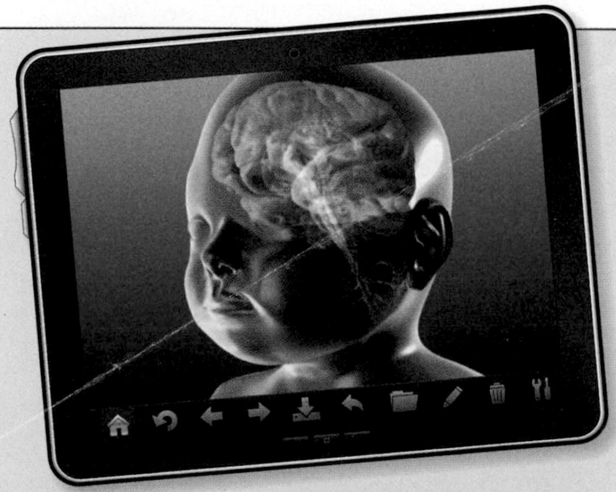

CHAPTER 9

Early Childhood: Cognitive Development

WHAT WILL YOU KNOW?

1. Are 2- to 6-year-olds focused mostly on their own perspective (egocentric) or are they strongly influenced by others?
2. Why is it much easier to fool a 3-year-old than a 5-year-old?
3. Are children confused if they hear two languages?
4. Are there important differences between one preschool program and another?

I was one of dozens of subway riders who were captivated by a little girl, about age 3, with sparkling eyes and many braids. She sat beside a large man, her legs straight out in front of her. Her mother was standing about 6 feet away, on the other side of the man. The little girl repeatedly ducked her head behind him, saying, "You can't see me, Mama," unaware that her legs (in colorful striped stockings) were constantly visible to her mother.

Like that little girl, every young child has much to learn. Young children are sometimes *egocentric,* understanding only their own perspective. Among their developing ideas is a *theory of mind,* an understanding of how minds work (as in knowing that your mother would never lose sight of you on a subway).

Early childhood is a time of prodigious new learning. Examples abound. Toddlers' simple block towers become elaborate cities, with tunnels, bridges, and houses designed and built by kindergartners. The youngest children are easy to fool; by age 5, they do the fooling. The halting, simple sentences of a typical 2-year-old become the nonstop, complex outpourings of a talkative 6-year-old.

How does such rapid cognitive development happen? How much comes from maturation and how much from education? Many young children are now taught, not merely babysat (as if adults ever merely sat) or simply cared for (as in day care or home care). This chapter describes thinking and learning from ages 2 to 6, including advances in thought, language, and education, and explores how all this develops.

>> Piaget and Vygotsky

Jean Piaget and Lev Vygotsky are justly famous for their descriptions of cognition. Their theories are "intertwined" (Fox & Riconscente, 2008, p. 373), especially when they describe young children. As you read, look for the commonalities.

Piaget: Preoperational Thought

Early childhood is the second of Piaget's four stages of cognition. He called cognitive development between about 2 and 6 years **preoperational intelligence,** a time for symbolic thought, especially language and imagination. He called this period of intelligence *pre*operational in that children do not yet use logical operations

preoperational intelligence Piaget's term for cognitive development between the ages of about 2 and 6; it includes language and imagination (which involve symbolic thought), but logical, operational thinking is not yet possible at this stage.

(reasoning processes), but they are no longer limited to senses and motor skills (sensorimotor) (Inhelder & Piaget, 1964).

symbolic thought A major accomplishment of preoperational intelligence that allows a child to think symbolically, including understanding that words can refer to things not seen and that an item, such as a flag, can symbolize something else (in this case, for instance, a country).

Piaget lauded the development of **symbolic thought,** a major accomplishment of preoperational intelligence. When a child can think symbolically, he or she becomes much more adept at pretending, and words can refer to things not seen. "Dog" can be a dog once seen, or a dog that might be seen, or an imagined dog never seen—all examples that the word *dog* has become a symbol, not simply the name of a creature within sight. Symbolic thought allows the language explosion, detailed later in this chapter, as children can talk about what they think, imagine, and remember.

Research on U.S. children of several cultural backgrounds (European, Japanese, South American) found that all infants tend to spontaneously explore objects and, as they grow older, to engage in symbolic play, as Piaget described (Cote & Bornstein, 2009). This study did not trace developmental paths from ages 2 to 6, but other scientists suggest that all children switch from sensorimotor to symbolic thinking as the result of brain maturation (experience-expectant) and social interactions (experience-dependent) (Mundy & Jarrold, 2010).

Obstacles to Logical Operations

Although symbolic thought and language are typical advances for young children everywhere, Piaget described four limitations of preoperational thought that make logic difficult until about age 6: centration, focus on appearance, static reasoning, and irreversibility.

centration A characteristic of preoperational thought in which a young child focuses (centers) on one idea, excluding all others.

Centration is the tendency to focus on one aspect of a situation to the exclusion of all others. Young children may, for example, insist that lions and tigers seen at the zoo or in picture books cannot be cats, because the children "center" on the house-pet aspect of the cats they know. Or they may insist that Daddy is a father, not a brother, because they center on the role that each family member fills for them.

egocentrism Piaget's term for children's tendency to think about the world entirely from their own personal perspective.

The daddy example illustrates a particular type of centration that Piaget called **egocentrism**—literally, "self-centeredness." Egocentric children contemplate the world exclusively from their personal perspective, as the little girl on the subway did. Egocentrism is not selfishness. Consider, for example, a 3-year-old who chose to buy a model car as a birthday present for his mother: His "behavior was not selfish or greedy; he carefully wrapped the present and gave it to his mother with an expression that clearly showed that he expected her to love it" (Crain, 2005, p. 108).

focus on appearance A characteristic of preoperational thought in which a young child ignores all attributes that are not apparent.

A second characteristic of preoperational thought is a **focus on appearance** to the exclusion of other attributes. A girl given a short haircut might worry that she has turned into a boy; a tall child is thought to be older. In preoperational thought, a thing is whatever it appears to be—evident in the joy young children have in wearing the hats or shoes of someone else.

static reasoning A characteristic of preoperational thought in which a young child thinks that nothing changes. Whatever is now has always been and always will be.

Third, preoperational children use **static reasoning,** believing that the world is unchanging, always in the state in which they currently encounter it. A young boy might want a live television show turned off while he goes to the bathroom and be furious and unbelieving when his parents tell him a particular program cannot be paused. Similarly, many children cannot imagine that their own parents were once children. Once they grasp that, they still do not understand developmental change. One preschooler told his grandmother to tell his mother to stop spanking him, because "she has to do what her mother says."

irreversibility A characteristic of preoperational thought in which a young child thinks that nothing can be undone. A thing cannot be restored to the way it was before a change occurred.

The fourth characteristic of preoperational thought is **irreversibility.** Preoperational thinkers fail to recognize that reversing a process sometimes restores whatever existed before. A young child might cry because her mother put lettuce on her sandwich. Overwhelmed by her desire to have things "just right" (explained in Chapter 8), she might reject the food even after the lettuce is removed because she believes that what is done cannot be undone.

Especially for Nutritionists How can Piaget's theory help you encourage children to eat healthy foods? (see response, page 261)

Conservation and Logic

Piaget highlighted the many ways in which preoperational intelligence overlooks logic. A famous set of experiments involved **conservation,** the notion that the amount of something remains the same (is conserved) despite changes in its appearance.

conservation The principle that the amount of a substance remains the same (i.e., is conserved) even when its appearance changes.

Suppose two identical glasses contain the same amount of liquid, and the liquid from one of these glasses is poured into a taller, narrower glass. If young children are asked whether one glass contains more liquid or both glasses contain the same amount, they will insist that the narrower glass (in which the liquid level is higher) has more.

All four characteristics of preoperational thought are evident in this mistake. Young children fail to understand conservation of liquids because they focus (*center*) on what they see (*appearance*), noticing only the immediate (*static*) condition. It does not occur to them that they could reverse the process and re-create the liquid's level of a moment earlier (*irreversibility*). (See Figure 9.1 for other examples.)

This research has many practical implications. For example, when teachers give a snack to preschoolers, all the cups should be the same size, and children will be happier with two very small crackers than one bigger one. Similarly, in a grocery store, children may be fooled by what they see, unaware that packaging is deceptive (Gaumer & Arnone, 2010).

Animism in Preoperational Thought

A final aspect of preoperational thought is called **animism,** the belief that natural objects and phenomena are alive (Piaget, 1929). Egocentric reasoning leads many children to believe that clouds, mountains, and trees have feelings, goals, and capabilities. A child might talk to a tree and ask for its protection from the rain, for instance.

animism The belief that natural objects and phenomena are alive.

Closely related to animism is treating nonhuman animals as similar to humans. For example, a dead bird discovered by a child might bring forth tears and require a burial ceremony. A dog might be told wishes and worries by a child who believes that the pet understands and sympathizes. Many children's stories—in books, cartoons, or fairy tales—include animals or objects that talk and help people. Consider the three bears, or the Pooh stories, or Teletubbies.

COURTESY OF KATHLEEN BERGER

Demonstration of Conservation My youngest daughter, Sarah, here at age 5¾, demonstrates Piaget's conservation-of-volume experiment. First, she examines both short glasses to be sure they contain the same amount of milk. Then, after the contents of one are poured into the tall glass and she is asked which has more, she points to the tall glass, just as Piaget would have expected. Later she added, "It looks like it has more because it's taller," indicating that some direct instruction might change her mind.

Tests of Various Types of Conservation

Type of Conservation	Initial Presentation	Transformation	Question	Preoperational Child's Answer
Volume	Two equal glasses of liquid.	Pour one into a taller, narrower glass.	Which glass contains more?	The taller one.
Number	Two equal lines of checkers.	Increase spacing of checkers in one line.	Which line has more checkers?	The longer one.
Matter	Two equal balls of clay.	Squeeze one ball into a long, thin shape.	Which piece has more clay?	The long one.
Length	Two sticks of equal length.	Move one stick.	Which stick is longer?	The one that is farther to the right.

FIGURE 9.1

Conservation, Please According to Piaget, until children grasp the concept of conservation at (he believed) about age 6 or 7, they cannot understand that the transformations shown here do not change the total amount of liquid, checkers, clay, and wood.

Attempts to measure children's animism find that many children simultaneously hold rational and irrational ideas (Meshcheryakov, 2005). Magical happenings and sayings are common. Wishing on a star or an eyelash, saying "Cross my heart and hope to die," holding one's breath when passing a cemetery, and much more are frequent behaviors, even if parents belittle them.

Like Piaget, adults may underestimate children and their superstitions. Many religions and cultural myths have talking animals, and most adults encourage children's faith in Santa Claus, the Tooth Fairy, and so on (Barrett, 2008). If preschoolers are cute and foolish to believe such things, what are adults who talk to their dogs?

Limitations of Piaget's Research

Notice that Piaget's original tests of conservation require the child's words, not actions or brain scans. Later research has found that when the tests of logic are simplified, young children may succeed. In many ways, children indicate that they know something via eye movements or gestures before they can say it in words (Goldin-Meadow, 2009).

Furthermore, even when words are the measure, some young children demonstrate conservation and other logical ideas in a gamelike setting, although not in Piaget's experiments (Donaldson, 1963/2003). For example, if a "naughty bear" lengthens a row of checkers, 4-year-olds say that the new row has the same number as before. That's conservation of number, a concept Piaget did not expect children to grasp until age 6.

Researchers now believe that Piaget underestimated cognition during early childhood, just as he had during infancy (Halford & Andrews, 2006). He relied on words spoken in an experimental setting rather than on nonverbal signs in a play context.

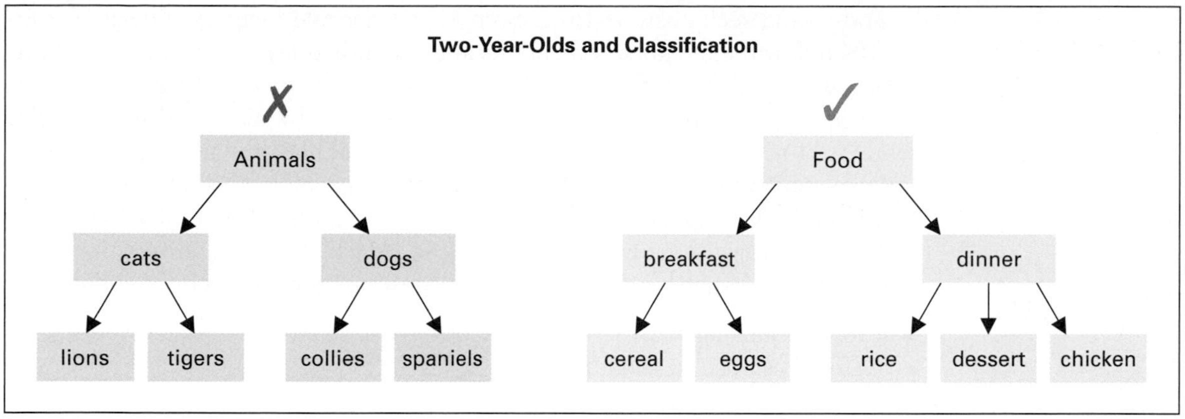

FIGURE 9.2

Everyday Categories Experience is the best teacher, especially for 2-year-olds. Many know that eating can mean a snack, or breakfast, or dinner and that particular foods belong in each of these categories. However, few know or care that tigers and lions are both cats. By the same token, humans and baboons are both primates, a subcategory of animals—something even a few adults forget.

Other experiments to distinguish preoperational thought from Piaget's next stage (concrete operational thought) show the same results. Mastery of the concept of *classification* is another example: Piaget thought that preoperational children cannot classify objects properly, that they do not firmly grasp that dogs, cats, and cows are all categories of animals. This is not necessarily accurate.

It is easy to understand why Piaget reached this conclusion. Children are confused about the relationship between superordinate categories (such as animals), subcategories (such as dogs), and further subcategories (such as collies). (Classification is discussed further in Chapter 12.) However, even 3-year-olds can classify things if the categories are ones they often use, such as that cereal and toast are part of breakfast or that ice cream and cake both belong to the dessert category (Nguyen & Murphy, 2003). (See Figure 9.2.)

Piaget was right that young children are not as logical as older children, but he did not realize how much they understand. One reason is that he did not have available the brain scans that developmentalists now use. Scans show much more early intellectual activity than was previously imagined, although they also show that Piaget was quite perceptive about early cognitive growth (Crone & Ridderinkhof, 2011).

Vygotsky: Social Learning

For decades, the magical, illogical, and self-centered aspects of early-childhood cognition dominated research; scientists were understandably awed by Piaget. His description of egocentrism was confirmed daily by anecdotes of young children's behavior. Vygotsky was the first leading developmentalist to emphasize another side of early cognition—that the thinking of young children, instead of being egocentric, is shaped by the wishes and emotions of others. He emphasized the sociocultural aspects of young children's cognition, in contrast to Piaget's emphasis on the individual.

That led Vygotsky to seek to understand cultural differences, acknowledging that "the culturally specific nature of experience is an integral part of how the person thinks and acts," as a contemporary team of developmentalists explain (Gauvain et al., 2011).

Children and Mentors

Vygotsky believed that every aspect of children's cognitive development is embedded in a social context (Vygotsky, 1934/1987). Children are curious and observant. They ask questions—about how machines work, why weather changes, where the

>> Response for Nutritionists (from page 259) Take each of the four characteristics of preoperational thought into account. Because of egocentrism, having a special place and plate might assure the child that this food is exclusively his or hers. Since appearance is important, food should look tasty. Since static thinking dominates, if something healthy is added (e.g., grate carrots into the cake, add milk to the soup), do it before the food is given to the child. In the reversibility example in the text, the lettuce should be removed out of the child's sight and the "new" hamburger presented.

sky ends—and seek answers from more knowledgeable mentors. These answers are affected by the mentors' perceptions and ethnotheories—that is, their culture.

As you remember from Chapter 2, a child is an *apprentice in thinking,* someone whose intellectual growth is stimulated and directed by older and more skilled members of society. Parents are the first mentors, although many teachers, other family members, and peers are mentors as well. For example, the verbal proficiency of children in day-care centers is affected by the language of their playmates, who teach vocabulary without consciously doing so (Mashburn et al., 2009).

According to Vygotsky, children learn because their mentors do the following:

- Present challenges
- Offer assistance (without taking over)
- Add crucial information
- Encourage motivation

guided participation The process by which people learn from others who guide their experiences and explorations.

Thinking occurs as the mentor and the child join in **guided participation,** sharing social experiences and explorations. For example, imagine a group of children learning to draw or write or dance. A teacher might perform some action first. Then the children follow the teacher but also copy one another. A child who is copied does not resent it but appreciates that someone else follows his or her lead.

Indeed, one sign of a socially attuned 3-year-old is that, when another child copies, the first child smiles and soon reciprocates, copying something the copier did. Shared joy is the result of this social interaction. Overall, the ability to learn from mentors indicates intelligence, according to Vygotsky: "What children can do with the assistance of others might be in some sense even more indicative of their mental development than what they can do alone" (1934/1987, p. 5).

CORBIS / AGE FOTOSTOCK

Words, Don't Fail Me Now Could you describe how to tie shoes? The limitations of verbal tests of cognitive understanding are apparent in many skills.

Observation Quiz What three sociocultural factors make it likely that this child will learn? (see answer, page 264)

Scaffolding

Vygotsky believed that each individual has a **zone of proximal development (ZPD).** The zone of proximal development, first described in Chapter 2, is reiterated here because ZPD is crucial for early-childhood learning. *Proximal* means "near," so the ZPD includes the ideas children are close to understanding and skills they are close to attaining but not yet able to master independently. How and when children learn depends, in part, on the wisdom and willingness of mentors to provide **scaffolding,** or temporary sensitive support, to help them within their developmental zone.

Good mentors provide plenty of scaffolding, encouraging children to look both ways before crossing the street (while holding the child's hand) or letting them stir the cake batter (perhaps the adult's hand covers the child's hand on the spoon handle, in guided participation). A preschool teacher sets up each activity in advance, with the appropriate scaffolds, and then guides each child. Scaffolding is crucial for cognitive experiences—that is, experiences that will produce better understanding of words and ideas.

zone of proximal development (ZPD) Vygotsky's term for the skills—cognitive as well as physical—that a person can exercise only with assistance, not yet independently.

scaffolding Temporary support that is tailored to a learner's needs and abilities and aimed at helping the learner master the next task in a given learning process.

The particulars of scaffolding vary by culture. Consider book-reading, for instance. In many North American families, when an adult reads to a child, the adult scaffolds—explaining, pointing, listening—within the child's zone of development. A sensitive adult reader does not tell the child to be quiet but might instead prolong the session by expanding on the child's questions and the pictures in the book.

By contrast, book-reading in middle-class Peruvian families includes teaching the child to listen when adults talk, so that a 2-year-old who interrupts is lovingly

taught to be quiet (Melzi & Caspe, 2005). Obviously, scaffolded behaviors and processes in Peru differ because the goal is a respectful child, not a talkative one. Nonetheless, everywhere adults guide children to master the ideas, skills, and behaviors of the culture.

Vygotsky Applied

Motivation is crucial in early education—one reason why sensitive social interaction is so powerful. The social learning emphasized by Vygotsky is transmitted in every culture through scaffolding (Gauvain, 2005). Toys, clothes, playground equipment, eating routines, social interactions—everything scaffolds certain skills and behaviors that children learn. Although objects help—some 2-year-olds have toy guitars, others toy brooms, others toy guns—the critical role is observation: Every child watches other people and tries to do what they do. Notice 2-year-olds who try to play the guitar: Their body movements and facial expressions copy what they have seen.

This is obvious in the research as well. For instance, a program introduced 2- and 3-year-olds to science in the sandbox: Teachers helped children experiment with sand and water. Later these children did more sandbox exploration on their own than children who did not have this apprenticeship (van Schijndel et al., 2010).

Even in conversation, scaffolding is possible and helpful. North American adults often answer young children's questions not with a simple answer but with a response that builds vocabulary and understanding (Chouinard, 2007). If a child asks, "What is that?" a teacher, instead of simply saying, "That is a truck," might say, "That is a kind of t-r-r . . ." (guiding the child to respond "truck") or "That is a garbage truck. What do you think it has inside?" Older siblings can be excellent mentors, too.

The power of scaffolding is demonstrated when 2- to 6-year-olds imitate adult actions that are irrelevant, time-consuming, and inefficient. This is called **overimitation,** evident in children from many cultures but not in other animals. Overimitation is thought to be a way that children learn from older members of their community, allowing "rapid, high-fidelity intergenerational transmission of cultural forms" (Nielsen & Tomaselli, 2010, p. 735). (See the Research Design.)

Language as a Tool

Although all the objects of a culture guide children, Vygotsky believed that words are especially pivotal. Empirical research finds this to be the case, in every culture and with children of every ability (e.g., Baker et al., 2007; Philips & Tolmie, 2007; Schick & Melzi, 2010). Just as a builder needs tools to construct a house, the mind needs language. Talking, listening, reading, and writing are tools to advance thought, and informal scaffolding leads to advances in language and cognition.

Especially for Driving Instructors
Sometimes your students cry, curse, or quit. How would Vygotsky advise you to proceed? (see response, page 265)

overimitation When a person imitates an action that is not a relevant part of the behavior to be learned. Overimitation is common among 2- to 6-year-olds when they imitate adult actions that are irrelevant and inefficient.

▶ Research Design

Scientists: Mark Nielsen and Keyan Tomaselli.

Publication: *Psychological Science* (2010).

Participants: Sixty-one 2- to 6-year-olds from Bushman communities in South Africa and Botswana; 16 young children from Brisbane, Australia; and 17 older Bushman children. The reason for these three groups of participants is that overimitation (that is, imitating unnecessary actions) has been repeatedly demonstrated among Western children, but Bushman adults rarely explicitly teach children how to use objects. Thus, if apprenticeship in learning occurs only in cultures with deliberate training, the children raised in the Bushman culture would not overimitate.

Design: Experimenters tested the children, one by one, on overimitation of irrelevant and inefficient ways to open three boxes. For example, a blue box could be easily opened by pulling a knob, but in the experimental condition, an adult (sometimes a Western scientist, sometimes a member of the local community) waved a red stick above the box three times and then used that stick to push down the knob to open the box. The children were given the stick and the box, and their actions were noted.

In the control condition, the children were simply given the stick and the box with no demonstration; again, their actions were noted. In an extension of this basic design, some of the control-group participants were shown the stick-waving demonstration after they had discovered on their own how to open the box the easy way.

Major conclusion: No matter who tested them, children of every age and culture performed the irrelevant and inefficient actions they saw, even if they had already opened the box the easy way. Apparently, children are universally predisposed to learn from mentors. If their culture does not rely on deliberate apprenticeship, then they learn via observation without adult verbal explanation. Thus, scaffolding can occur when children learn whatever routines and procedures they witness. Across cultures, "similarity of performance is profound" (p. 734). (Soon you will read applications to preschool education: Young children learn what adults encourage—imaginative play, artistic activities, social cooperation, or writing the alphabet.)

Comments: Originally, the researchers hypothesized that overimitation resulted from the practice in Western cultures whereby adults explicitly teach young children, explaining as they demonstrate. The scientists were surprised that the Bushman children imitated as often as Western children did. Such cross-cultural research discovers which aspects of cognitive development are part of Western culture and which are universal. Other developmentalists have found that a child may be selective (less likely to imitate untrustworthy adults or accidental acts). More research will "determine when children will do precisely as others have done and when they instead choose their own actions" (p. 735).

private speech The internal dialogue that occurs when people talk to themselves (either silently or out loud).

Language advances thinking in two ways, according to Vygotsky (Fernyhough, 2010). The first way is with internal dialogue, or **private speech,** in which people talk to themselves (Vygotsky, 1934/1987). Young children use private speech often, although they do not realize it (Manfra & Winsler, 2006). They talk aloud to review, decide, and explain events to themselves (and, incidentally, to anyone else within earshot).

Older preschoolers are more selective, effective, and circumspect, sometimes whispering. Audible or not, private speech aids cognition and self-reflection; adults should encourage it (Perels et al., 2009; Winsler et al., 2007). Many people of all ages talk to themselves when alone or write down ideas to help them think. That is private speech as well. Preschool curricula based on Vygotsky's ideas use games, play, social interaction, and private speech to develop executive functioning (Diamond et al., 2007).

social mediation Human interaction that expands and advances understanding, often through words that one person uses to explain something to another.

The second way in which language advances thinking, according to Vygotsky, is by mediating the social interaction that is vital to learning. This **social mediation** function of speech occurs during both formal instruction (when teachers explain things) and casual conversation. Words entice people into the zone of proximal development, as mentors guide children to learn numbers, recall memories, and follow routines.

>> Answer to Observation Quiz (from page 262) Motivation (in Spain, yellow running shoes are popular); human relationships (note the physical touching of father and son); and materials (the long laces make tying them easier).

Words, Cultures, and Math

Learning about numbers begins very early in life. Apparently, even babies have a sense of whether one, two, or three objects are in a display, although exactly what infants understand about numbers is controversial (Varga et al., 2010). However, there is no doubt that words are tools that enable many children between ages 2 and 6 to do the following:

- Count objects, with one number per item (called *one-to-one correspondence*)
- Remember times and dates (bedtime at 8 P.M., a child is 4 years old, and so on).
- Understand sequence (first child wins, last child loses)

Dozens of the cognitive accomplishments of young children—in numbers, memory, logic, and much more—have been the subject of extensive research: Mentoring and language are always found to be pivotal. What would happen if the language learned by a child had no words for numbers? Anthropologists have found a few languages in South America that lack many counting words: They use "many" for numbers higher than 2. When children and adults are tested in those languages, they have a much more difficult time with simple math examples (Gordon, 2004). By contrast, children whose parents often count out loud often become early counters and, in school, math whizzes.

Culture may affect language and therefore math knowledge, even when the language has words for trillions of numbers. English-speaking and Chinese-speaking preschoolers seem equal in their understanding of the numbers 1 to 10, but the Chinese are ahead in their understanding of 11 to 19. There are many possible explanations for this, but one is directly verbal: In Chinese, those numbers are logical and direct, the equivalent of ten-one, ten-two, ten-three, and so on. This may be easier for young children to understand than eleven, twelve, thirteen, and so on (Miller et al., 1995).

German-speaking children have an additional problem with numbers from 20 to 99, since they say the equivalent of one-and-twenty, two-and-twenty, and so on, not twenty-one, twenty-two, and so on. German 3-year-olds may become very proficient at 1 to 9, but not at 20 to 99. In these and many other ways, language and culture affect young children's understanding of math (Göbel et al., 2011).

By age 3 or 4, children's brains are mature enough to comprehend numbers, store memories, and recognize routines. Whether or not children actually demonstrate such understanding depends on what they hear and how they participate in various activities within their families, schools, and cultures. Some 2-year-olds hear sentences such as "One, two, three, takeoff," and "Here are two cookies," and "Dinner in five minutes" several times a day. Others do not—and they have a harder time with math when they reach first grade. Words are the mediator between brain potential and comprehension.

>> Response for Driving Instructors (from page 263) Use guided participation and scaffold the instruction so your students are not overwhelmed. Be sure to provide lots of praise and days of practice. If emotion erupts, do not take it as an attack on you.

A VIEW FROM SCIENCE

Witness to a Crime

One application of early cognitive competency has received attention among lawyers and judges. Some children are the only witnesses to crimes, especially of sexual abuse or domestic violence. Can a young child's words be trusted? Adults have gone to both extremes in answering this question. As one legal discussion begins:

> Perhaps as a result of the collective guilt caused by disbelieving the true victims of this abuse, in recent years the pendulum has swung in the opposite direction, to an unwavering conviction that a young child is incapable of fabricating a story of abuse, even when the tale of mistreatment is inherently incredible.
>
> *[Shanks, 2011]*

To find the right balance, the answer to the question "Is child testimony accurate?" is "sometimes." In recent years, psychologists have shown that people of all ages misremember (Frenda et al., 2011; Lyons et al., 2010) and that each age group misremembers in particular ways. Younger children, not yet imbued with stereotypes, are sometimes more accurate than older witnesses who are influenced by prejudice (Brainerd et al., 2008). However, young children want to please adults and themselves, and they may lie to do so. Even in elementary school, some children do not realize that words and memories might be false (London et al., 2011) or that enjoyable fantasies are simply imaginary and might conflict with verified facts.

Words and expressions can plant false ideas in young children, either deliberately (as an abuser might) or inadvertently (as a fearful parent might). Children's shaky grasp of reality makes them vulnerable to scaffolding memories that are imagined, not experienced (Bruck et al., 2006). This happened tragically 35 years ago in many jurisdictions, when adults suddenly realized that small children could be sexually abused and then decided that sexual abuse was rampant in preschools. For instance, 3-year-olds at Wee Care nursery school in New Jersey convinced a judge that a teacher had sexually abused them in bizarre ways (including making them lick peanut butter off her genitals) (Ceci & Bruck, 1995). In retrospect, one wonders why any adult believed what they said. Since that time, much has been learned about witnesses of all ages.

Young children are not necessarily worse than adults at recounting experiences if they are interviewed with open-ended questions by someone who does not indicate what the preferred answers are (Brainerd et al., 2008; Feltis et al., 2010). Children who have already learned to tell coherent narratives provide more accurate accounts of what happened (Kulkofsky & Klemfuss, 2008). Whether or not a child understands the difference between truth and falsehood is irrelevant to accuracy; the crucial factor is whether the interviewer is straightforward or suggestive (Lyon et al., 2008).

Guided participation can be destructive, since the guidance might lead in the wrong direction. Remember the children in the Research Design who waved the red stick before they opened the box? As Vygotsky noted, children are acutely sensitive to the culture around them, particularly to what they observe in adults. That is both a strength and a liability.

With sexual abuse in particular, a child might believe that some lewd act is OK if an adult says so. Only years later does the victim realize that it was abuse. Research on adult memory finds that sometimes adults reinterpret what happened to them, concluding only later that they were indeed abused, with genuine memories of experiences that were criminal. However, some people of all ages can be led to believe that an event, including sexual abuse, occurred when it did not (Geraerts et al., 2009).

This knowledge provides guidelines for police officers, social workers, judges, teachers, and parents. When children are witnesses, they should simply be asked to tell what happened, perhaps with eyes closed to reduce their natural attempt to please. If, instead, an adult says, "Did he touch you there?" a child might say "yes" if he thinks that is what the adult wants to hear. Preschool cognition is a mix of egocentric fantasy, social influence, and innocent honesty—care must be taken to neither automatically believe nor disbelieve what children say.

SUMMING UP

Cognition develops rapidly from ages 2 to 6. Children's active search for understanding was first recognized by Piaget, who believed that young children are generally incapable of performing logical operations (hence *pre*operational intelligence). Piaget thought that egocentrism limits understanding, as young children center on only one thing at a time, focusing on appearance. Their thinking is magical and animistic.

Vygotsky emphasized the social and cultural aspects of children's cognition. He believed that children are guided as apprentices, within their zones of proximal development. Other people are mentors, providing the scaffolding that helps children master various skills and concepts. Language is a crucial learning tool, in private speech and social mediation, a point made by Vygotsky and confirmed by recent research. ■

>> Children's Theories

Piaget and Vygotsky realized that children actively work to understand their world. No developmental scientist or teacher doubts that. The question then becomes exactly when and how does children's knowledge develop? One discovery is that children do not simply learn words and ideas—they develop theories.

Theory-Theory

theory-theory The idea that children attempt to explain everything they see and hear by constructing theories.

Humans of all ages try to explain whatever happens. The term **theory-theory** refers to the idea that children naturally construct theories to explain whatever they see and hear. In other words, the theory about how children learn is that children develop a theory:

> More than any animal, we search for causal regularities in the world around us. We are perpetually driven to look for deeper explanations of our experience, and broader and more reliable predictions about it. . . . Children seem, quite literally, to be born with . . . the desire to understand the world and the desire to discover how to behave in it.
>
> *[Gopnik, 2001, p. 66]*

According to theory-theory, the best explanation for cognition in young children is that humans always seek reasons, causes, and underlying principles to make sense of their experience. That requires displaying a lot of curiosity and thinking, which is what young children do.

Exactly how are explanations sought in early childhood? In one study, Mexican American mothers kept detailed diaries of every question their 3- to 5-year-olds asked and how they themselves responded (Kelemen et al., 2005). Most of the questions were about human behavior and characteristics (see Figure 9.3); for example, "Why do you give my mother a kiss?" "Why is my brother bad?" "Why do women have breasts?" "Why are there Black kids?" Fewer questions were about nonliving things ("Why does it rain?") or objects ("Why is my daddy's car white?").

Questions were often about the underlying purpose of whatever the child observed, although parents usually responded as if children were asking about science instead. An adult might interpret a child's one-word question "Why?" to mean "What causes X to happen?" when the child intended "Why?" to mean "I want to know more about X" (Leach, 1997). For example, if a child asks why women have breasts, the response might be about hormones and maturation, but a child-centered explanation would be that breasts are for feeding babies. From a child's egocentric perspective, any query includes "How does this relate to me?"

Percentage of Questions Asked by 3- to 5-Year-Olds, by Domain

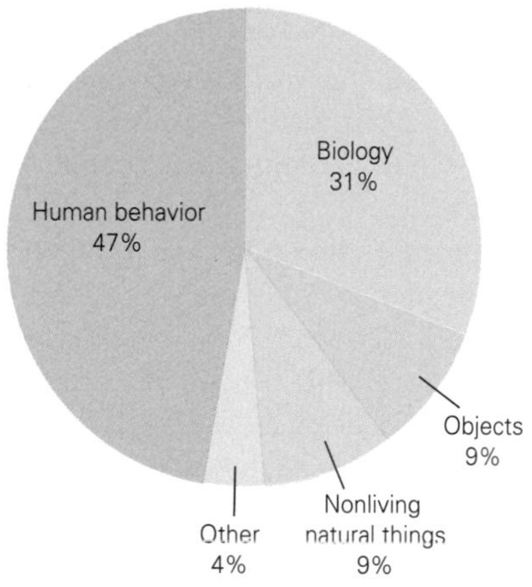

Source: Adapted from Kelemen et al., 2005.

FIGURE 9.3

Questions, Questions Parents found that most of their children's questions were about human behavior—especially the parents' behavior toward the child. Children seek to develop a theory to explain things, so the question "Why can't I have some candy?" is not satisfactorily answered by "It's almost dinnertime."

Accordingly, an adult might add that the child got his or her first nourishment from the mother's breast.

A series of experiments that explored when and how 3-year-olds imitate others provides some support for theory-theory (Williamson et al., 2008). Children seem to figure out *why* adults act as they do before deciding to copy those actions. If an adult intended to accomplish something and succeeded, a child is likely to follow the example, but if the same action and result seemed inadvertent or accidental, the child is less likely to copy it.

Indeed, even when asked to repeat something ungrammatical that an adult says, children are likely to correct the grammar based on their theory that the adult intended to speak grammatically but failed to do so (Over & Gattis, 2010). This is another example of a general principle: Children develop theories about intentions before they employ their impressive ability to imitate; they do not mindlessly copy whatever they observe. For instance, in the example in which the adult deliberately waved the stick before opening the box, the children theorized that stick-waving was somehow important.

Theory of Mind

Human mental processes—thoughts, emotions, beliefs, motives, and intentions—are among the most complicated and puzzling phenomena that we encounter every day. Adults wonder why people fall in love with the particular persons they do, or why they vote for the candidates they choose, or why they make foolish choices—from taking on a huge mortgage to buying an overripe cucumber. Children are puzzled about a playmate's unexpected anger, a sibling's generosity, or an aunt's too-wet kiss.

To know what goes on in another's mind, people develop a *folk psychology,* which includes a set of ideas about other people's thinking called **theory of mind.** Theory of mind is an emergent ability, slow to develop but typically beginning in most children at about age 4 (Sterck & Begeer, 2010).

theory of mind A person's theory of what other people might be thinking. In order to have a theory of mind, children must realize that other people are not necessarily thinking the same thoughts that they themselves are. That realization seldom occurs before age 4.

Belief and Reality: Understanding the Difference

The idea that thoughts may not reflect reality is beyond very young children, but then it occurs to each child rather suddenly sometime after age 3. This idea leads to the realization that people can be deliberately deceived or fooled—an idea that requires some theory of mind, beyond almost every 2-year-old and most 3-year-olds.

In one of several false-belief tests that researchers have developed, a child watches a doll named Max put a puppy in a red box. Then Max leaves and the child sees the puppy taken out of the red box and put in a blue box. When Max returns, the child is asked, "Where will Max look for the puppy?" Most 3-year-olds confidently say, "In the blue box"; most 6-year-olds correctly say, "In the red box," a pattern found in a dozen nations (Wellman et al., 2001).

Especially for Social Scientists Can you think of any connection between Piaget's theory of preoperational thought and 3-year-olds' errors in this theory-of-mind task? (see response, page 269)

Indeed, 3-year-olds almost always confuse what they recently learned with what they once thought and what someone else might think. Another way of describing this is to say that they are "cursed" by their own knowledge (Birch & Bloom, 2003), too egocentric to grasp others' perspectives.

Telling a Lie

The development of theory of mind can be seen in everyday life: Young children are notoriously bad at deception. They play hide-and-seek by hiding in the same place time after time, or their facial expression betrays them when they tell a fib. Parents sometimes say, "I know when you are lying," and, to the consternation of

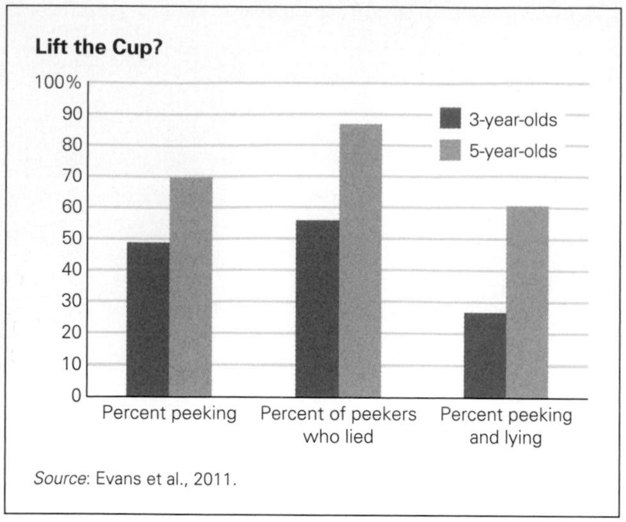

FIGURE 9.4

Better with Age? Could an obedient and honest 3-year-old become a disobedient and lying 5-year-old? Apparently, yes, as the proportion of peekers and liars in this study more than doubled over those 2 years. Does maturation make children more able to think for themselves or less trustworthy?

most 3-year-olds, parents are usually right. (This is not true at older ages because children become better at fooling their parents; knowing this, parents may be suspicious of the truth as well as of a lie.)

The development of the ability to lie was demonstrated in an experiment in which 247 children, aged 3 to 5, were left alone in a room with a cup that covered dozens of candies (Evans et al., 2011). The children were told not to peek, but 142 (75 percent) did. When they lifted the cup, the candies spilled out onto the table, and it was impossible for the children to hide the evidence before the examiner returned to ask the children how the candies got on the table. Only one-fourth of the participants (more often the younger ones) told the truth, but the lies told by the 3-year-olds were often hopeless (e.g., "The candies got out by themselves"); those told by the 4-year-olds seemed possible but unlikely (e.g., "Other children came in and knocked over the cup"). By age 5, however, most of the lies were logical and plausible (e.g. "My elbow knocked over the cup accidentally").

This particular study was done in Beijing, China, but the results seem universal: Older children are more likely to lie and they are more plausible liars. Beyond the age differences, the experimenters found that the better liars were also more advanced in theory of mind (Evans et al., 2011) (see Figure 9.4).

Closely related to young children's trouble with lying are their belief in fantasy (the magical thinking noted earlier) and their static reasoning (characteristic of preoperational thought), which make it difficult for them to change their minds. This is another example of the perseveration explained in Chapter 8.

Brain and Context

Developmentalists wonder what, precisely, strengthens theory of mind at about age 4. Is this change more nature or nurture, brain maturation or experience? There is firm evidence for nature. Age-related maturation of the prefrontal cortex seems crucial, according to brain scans of 4-, 5-, and 6-year-olds and of adults as they figured out theory-of-mind puzzles (Liu et al., 2009) (see photo). Children with autism are deficient in social understanding, particularly theory of mind: Brain imaging finds this to be neurological, not a matter of experience (Mar, 2011).

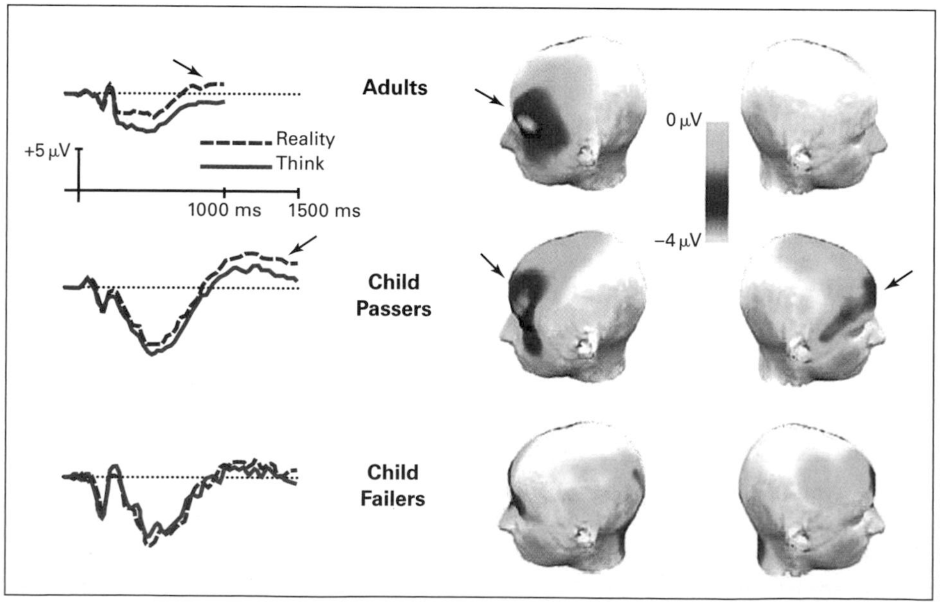

Brains at Work Neuroscience confirms the critical role of the prefrontal cortex for development of theory of mind. Adults and 4- to 6-year-olds were questioned on 40 theory-of-mind examples. The adults answered correctly, as did some 4- to 6-year-olds (passers), though not all (failers). The leftmost images are brain-wave patterns; the middle ones represent brain activity (fMRI), and the rightmost trio contrasts mental activity when distinguishing reality and belief. Adult brain waves show quick answers, and the contrast *(right)* shows that they answered quickly with little effort; but the child passers needed to think longer before they answered. The authors concluded that "social cognition and the brain develop together" (Liu et al., 2009, pp. 318, 325).

Other evidence also suggests that the prefrontal cortex is crucial. The study of lying among Chinese preschoolers also tested the children's ability to say "day" when they saw a picture of the moon and "night" when they saw a picture of the sun. This is a measure of mental flexibility, which indicates the *executive function* that occurs with maturation of the prefrontal cortex. The results confirm the importance of the brain: Children who failed the day–night tests typically told impossible lies, whereas the lies of children the same age who were high in executive function were plausible (Evans et al., 2011).

Does the crucial role of brain maturation make context irrelevant? Not at all (Sterck & Begeer, 2010). Language development is significant, especially if mother–child conversations involve thoughts and wishes (Ontai & Thompson, 2008).

Furthermore, in developing theory of mind, one expert explains, "Two older siblings are worth about a year of chronological age" (Perner, 2000, p. 383). As brothers and sisters argue, agree, compete, and cooperate, and as older siblings fool younger ones, it dawns on 3-year-olds that not everyone thinks as they do. By age 5, their theory of mind is well established: They know how to gain parental sympathy to protect themselves against their older siblings, as well as how to persuade their younger brothers and sisters to give them a toy.

Finally, culture matters. A meta-analysis of 254 studies done in China and North America found that Chinese children were about six months ahead of U.S. children (Liu et al., 2008). Another study comparing theory of mind among young children in preschools in Canada, India, Peru, Samoa, and Thailand found that the Canadian 5-year-olds were slightly more advanced and the Samoan 5-year-olds were slightly slower in passing tests of executive function (Callaghan et al., 2005). Particular aspects of culture seem relevant: In Canada, children who were often read to were more advanced than average in theory of mind compared with similar Canadian children who often watched children's television (Mar et al., 2010).

BUBBLES PHOTOLIBRARY/ALAMY

Ready to Learn When 2-year-olds quarrel, they grab toys and, if expedient, push and kick. Such fights between siblings seem to advance theory of mind: By age 4, these two may use deception to get what they want.

>> Response for Social Scientists (from page 267) According to Piaget, preschool children focus on appearance and on static conditions (so they cannot mentally reverse a process). Furthermore, they are egocentric, believing that everyone shares their point of view. No wonder they believe that they had always known the puppy was in the blue box and that Max would know that, too.

SUMMING UP

Scholars have recently noted that children develop theories to explain whatever they observe and that those theories do not necessarily spring from explanations given to them by adults. Children are interested in the underlying purpose of events; adults are more focused on scientific causes. Many researchers have explored the development of theory of mind, which is the realization at about age 4 that other people's thoughts and ideas might differ from one's own. Neurological maturation, linguistic competence, family context, and culture all affect the attainment of theory of mind. ■

>> Language Learning

Language is more than an example of symbolic thought (Piaget) and a tool for learning (Vygotsky); it is the premier cognitive accomplishment of early childhood. Two-year-olds use short, telegraphic sentences, but 6-year-olds seem able to understand and discuss almost anything (see At About This Time).

Brain maturation, myelination, scaffolding, and social interaction make early childhood the ideal time for learning language. As you remember from Chapter 1, scientists once thought that early childhood was a *critical period* for language learning—the *only* time when a first language could be mastered and the best time for learning a second or third language. It is true that the young child's brain organizes words and sounds into meaning (theory-theory), and for that reason teachers and parents should speak and listen to children many hours each day.

ALAMY

A Shared Pleasure As they read stories to young children, many adults express exaggerated surprise, excitement, worry, and relief. They realize that words are better understood and remembered when they are connected to emotions.

AT ABOUT THIS TIME
Language in Early Childhood

Approximate Age	Characteristic or Achievement in First Language
2 years	*Vocabulary:* 100–2,000 words *Sentence length:* 2–6 words *Grammar:* Plurals; pronouns; many nouns, verbs, adjectives *Questions:* Many "What's that?" questions
3 years	*Vocabulary:* 1,000–5,000 words *Sentence length:* 3–8 words *Grammar:* Conjunctions, adverbs, articles *Questions:* Many "Why?" questions
4 years	*Vocabulary:* 3,000–10,000 words *Sentence length:* 5–20 words *Grammar:* Dependent clauses, tags at sentence end (". . . didn't I?" ". . . won't you?") *Questions:* Peak of "Why?" questions; many "How?" and "When?" questions
5 years	*Vocabulary:* 5,000–20,000 words *Sentence length:* Some seem unending (". . . and . . . who . . . and . . . that . . . and . . .") *Grammar:* Complex, depending on what the child has heard. Some children correctly use the passive voice ("Man bitten by dog") and subjunctive ("If I were . . ."). *Questions:* Some about social differences (male–female, old–young, rich–poor) and many other issues

However, millions of people have learned languages after age 6; the critical-period hypothesis is false (Singleton & Munoz, 2011).

Instead, early childhood is a *sensitive period* for language learning—for rapidly and easily mastering vocabulary, grammar, and pronunciation. Young children are called "language sponges" because they soak up every drop of language they encounter. Language learning is an example of dynamic systems, in that every part of the developmental process influences every other part. To be specific, there are "multiple sensitive periods . . . auditory, phonological, semantic, syntactic, and motor systems, along with the developmental interactions among these components" (Thomas & Johnson, 2008, p. 2), all of which facilitate language learning early in life.

One of the valuable (and sometimes frustrating) traits of young children is that they talk a lot—to adults, to each other, to themselves, to their toys—unfazed by misuse, mispronunciation, stuttering, or other impediments to fluency. Language comes easily partly because young children are less self-conscious about what they say. Egocentrism has advantages; this is one of them.

The Vocabulary Explosion

Children add new words to their vocabulary rapidly. The average child knows about 500 words at age 2 and more than 10,000 at age 6 (Herschensohn, 2007). Precise estimates of vocabulary size vary because contexts are diverse; some children learn four times as many words as others. For every young child, however, vocabulary builds quickly and language potential is greater than is apparent; comprehension is more extensive than speech. Every child could become fluently bilingual given the proper circumstances.

Fast-Mapping

How does the vocabulary explosion occur? After painstakingly learning one word at a time at 12 to 18 months, children develop an interconnected set of categories for words, a kind of grid or mental map, which makes speedy vocabulary acquisition possible. The process is called **fast-mapping** (Woodward & Markman, 1998) because, rather than figuring out the exact definition after hearing a word used in several contexts, children hear a word once and quickly stick it into one of the categories in their mental language grid. That quick-sticking is fast-mapping.

fast-mapping The speedy and sometimes imprecise way in which children learn new words by tentatively placing them in mental categories according to their perceived meaning.

Like more conventional mental mapping, language mapping is not always precise. For example, if asked where Cameroon is, most adults can locate it approximately ("It's in Africa"), but few can name the six countries that border it (Nigeria, Chad, Central African Republic, Equatorial Guinea, Gabon, Congo). Similarly, children quickly map new animal names close to already-known animal names, without knowing all the precise details. Thus, *tiger* is easy to map if you know *lion*. A trip to the zoo facilitates fast-mapping of dozens of animal words, especially since zoos scaffold learning by placing similar animals near each other.

Egocentrism is an asset here—children say "tiger" for any animal that is fast-mapped in that category, from cheetah to jaguar. They do not worry that they might be wrong; they center on their own concept. Adults, however, might be silent if they cannot distinguish a lynx from an ocelot; that slows down their learning.

Fast-mapping is evident even before age 2, and it accelerates as new words are learned because each word makes it easier to map other words (Gershkoff-Stowe & Hahn, 2007). Generally, the more linguistic clues children already have, the better their fast-mapping is (Mintz, 2005). One set of experiments in vocabulary learning began in cultures whose languages had only a few counting words: the equivalents of *one, two,* and *many.* As already explained, people in such cultures were much worse at estimating quantity because they did not have the words to guide them (Gordon, 2004). Mapping and understanding a new number word, such as *nineteen,* is easier if one already knows a related word, such as *nine.*

An experiment in teaching the names of parts of objects (e.g., the spigot of a faucet) found that children learned much better if the adults named the object that had the part and then spoke of the object in the possessive (e.g., "See this butterfly? Look, this is the butterfly's thorax") (Saylor & Sabbagh, 2004). This finding shows that it is easier to map a new word when it is connected to a familiar one.

DEA / DIEGO MROSSI / PHOTOLIBRARY

Horse or Dromedary? These children might fast-map and call it a horse since it is horse-sized, horse-colored, and has a horse-like head and legs. Fast-mapping is misleading. However, if you think this is a dromedary, you made a similar mistake. All dromedaries are camels, but not all camels are dromedaries. This one is not.

Observation Quiz Is this scene set in the United States or some other country? (see answer, page 273)

Words and the Limits of Logic

Closely related to fast-mapping is a phenomenon called *logical extension:* After learning a word, children use it to describe other objects in the same category. One child told her father she had seen some "Dalmatian cows" on a school trip to a farm. He understood because he remembered that she had petted a Dalmatian dog the weekend before. Bilingual children might insert a word from another language if they don't know the word in the language they are speaking, although soon they separate one language from the other and know who speaks which—and stick to one language when speaking to a monolingual person.

Some words are particularly difficult—*who/whom, have been/had been, here/there, yesterday/tomorrow.* More than one child has awakened on Christmas morning and asked, "Is it tomorrow yet?" A child told to "stay there" or "come here" may not follow instructions because the terms are confusing. Extensive study of children's language abilities finds that fast-mapping is only one of many techniques that children use to learn language: When a word does not refer to an object on the mental map, children use other ways to master it (Carey, 2010).

Listening and Talking

Because literacy is considered crucial in the United States, a national study analyzed which activities in early childhood aided reading a few years later in elementary school. Overall, language development was found to be crucial, with both vocabulary and attention to the sounds of words (phonics) predictive of fluent reading. Based on data from about 300 published studies, five intervention efforts were discovered to be effective:

1. *Code-focused teaching.* In order for children to learn to read, they must "break the code" from the written word to the spoken word. Teaching children to recognize the letters of the alphabet and to know the sounds each makes (e.g., "A, Alligators all around" or, more conventionally, "C is for cat") is important.
2. *Book-reading.* Vocabulary as well as print familiarity build when adults read to children. It seems better when the reading includes the child asking and answering questions, not quietly listening.
3. *Parent education.* When teachers and other professionals teach parents how to stimulate cognition (as in the book-reading of #2), that predicts later literacy.

RAY AMATI / NBAE / GETTY IMAGES

Student and Teachers Children at the Lawrence, Massachusetts, YWCA show Rashon McCloud of the Boston Celtics how they use a computer to learn reading. They are participating in an NBA-sponsored program called Read to Achieve. Children are often faster than adults to catch on to technological innovations.

4. *Language enhancement.* Within each child's zone of proximal development (not too easy, not too hard) adults need to build vocabulary and grammar, expanding on what the child already knows.
5. *Preschool programs.* Children benefit from spending some time with a teacher and other children (further discussed later in this chapter).

These five measures helped children of all incomes, ages, and ethnicities. The child's age was relevant for only one item: 2- and 3-year-olds may benefit more from language-enhancement activities than 4- and 5-year-olds. Ideally, however, all young children experience all five (Shanahan & Lonigan, 2010).

Acquiring Basic Grammar

We noted in Chapter 6 that the *grammar* of language includes the structures, techniques, and rules that are used to communicate meaning. Word order and word repetition, prefixes and suffixes, intonation and emphasis—all are part of grammar.

By age 3, children understand the basics. For example, English-speaking 3-year-olds know word order (subject/verb/object), saying, "I eat the apple," not any of the 23 other sequences of those four words. They use plurals; tenses (past, present, and future); and nominative, objective, and possessive pronouns (*I/me/mine* or *my*). Some even use articles (*the, a, an*) correctly, although article use in English is bewilderingly complex (as adults learning English know all too well).

Each aspect of language (grammar, vocabulary, pronunciation, etc.) follows a particular developmental path, partly because parts of the brain myelinate at specific rates and every language has both easy and difficult constructions. In general, genes affect *expressive* (spoken or written) language more than *receptive* (heard or read) language. Thus, some children are relatively talkative or quiet because they inherit that tendency, but experience (not genes) determines which words and grammatical constructions they understand (Kovas et al., 2005). Not only do they understand most of what they hear, they believe they know more than they do (Marazita & Merriman, 2011).

overregularization The application of rules of grammar even when exceptions occur, making the language seem more "regular" than it actually is.

Sometimes children apply the rules of grammar when they should not, an error called **overregularization.** For example, English-speaking children learn to add an *s* to form the plural: Toddlers follow that rule when they ask for two *cookies* or more *blocks.* They apply this to nonsense words: If they are shown a drawing of an abstract shape, are told it is called a *wug,* and are then shown two of these shapes, they say there are two *wugs.*

However, many young children overregularize that final *s,* talking about *foots, tooths,* and *mouses.* This is evidence of increasing knowledge: Many children first say words correctly because they repeat what they have heard; later, when they grasp the grammar and try to apply it, they overregularize. Repeated exposure to exceptions is needed: At first, children assume that irregular constructions follow the regular path (Ramscar & Dye, 2011).

Learning Two Languages

Language-minority children (those who speak a language that is not the dominant language of their nation) suffer if they do not speak the majority language well. In the United States, those who are not proficient in English tend to have lower school achievement, diminished self-esteem, and inadequate employment, as well as many other problems. Fluency in English can erase these liabilities, and then fluency in another language is an asset.

In the United States in 2010, 21 percent of schoolchildren spoke a language other than English at home, with most of them (75 percent) also speaking English well. The percentage of bilingual children has been rising in the United States, but it is higher in other nations: In Canada and many African, Asian, and European nations, by sixth grade most children are at least bilingual, sometimes trilingual. When should additional languages be learned? Generally, younger is quicker.

What Is the Goal?

In thinking about learning languages, we need to clarify the goal. Is national unity crucial, and will speaking one and only one language achieve that? Is international understanding important, and will speaking several languages accomplish that? Is a nation better off with one language or with more than one official language (Switzerland has three, Canada has two)? Do individuals who speak more than one language gain in cognitive as well as linguistic development, or do they become confused?

Some say that young children need to become proficient in one, and only one, language and that children taught two languages might become semilingual, not bilingual, "at risk for delayed, incomplete, and possibly even impaired language development" (Genesee, 2008, p. 17). Others say that it is better for everyone to speak at least two languages and that "there is absolutely no evidence that children get confused if they learn two languages" (Genesee, 2008, p. 18). This second position has more research support: Soon after the vocabulary explosion, children who have heard two languages since birth usually master two distinct sets of words and grammar, along with each language's characteristic pauses, pronunciations, intonations, and even gestures (Genesee & Nicoladis, 2007).

No doubt early childhood is the best time to learn language, whether it is one, two, or three languages. Neuroscience finds that young bilingual children site both languages in the same areas of their brains yet manage to keep them separate. This separation allows them to activate one language and temporarily inhibit the other, experiencing no confusion when they speak to a monolingual person (Crinion et al., 2006). They may be a millisecond slower to respond if they must switch languages, but their brains overall function better and may even have some resistance to Alzheimer dementia in old age (Bialystok et al., 2009).

Neurological studies show that people who learn a second language in adulthood usually show different activation sites for each language and are slowed down—especially if they silently translate as they listen and speak. A few fortunate adults who learn a second language after puberty activate the same brain area for both; they tend to be unusually skilled bilingualists (Thomas & Johnson, 2008).

Pronunciation is particularly hard to master after childhood, in any language. However, do not mistake pronunciation for comprehension. From infancy on, hearing is more acute than vocalization. Almost all children have pronunciation difficulties in their first language, but they are blithely unaware of their mistakes and gradually learn to speak clearly with whatever accent they hear. Children who have spoken English all their lives, for instance, may speak with a southern accent, or a West Indian one, or a Canadian one—accents that are hard to erase when people leave their childhood home in adulthood.

In early childhood, children transpose sounds (*magazine* becomes *mazagine*), drop consonants (*truck* becomes *ruck*), and convert difficult sounds to easier ones (*father* becomes *fadder*). Mispronunciation does not impair fluency primarily because young children are more receptive than expressive—they hear better than they talk. When 4-year-old Rachel asked for a "yeyo yayipop," her father repeated, "You want a yeyo yayipop?" She replied, "Daddy, sometimes you talk funny."

To speak well, young children need to be "bathed in language," as some early-childhood educators express it. The emphasis is on hearing and speaking in every

>> Answer to Observation Quiz (from page 271) It is not in the United States. Some clues are the boys' haircuts, the girl's headscarf, and the clothes on all three—each possible in the United States, but unlikely on three U.S. children together. Another clue is that camels with two humps are rare in U.S. zoos. But one thing is definitive: the fence. By law and custom, no U.S. zoos have fences children can crawl through. Is this cultural scaffolding, leading U.S. preschoolers to fear camels more than these Italians do?

situation, just as a person taking a bath is surrounded by water. Television is a poor teacher because children need personalized, responsive instruction in the zone of proximal development. In fact, young children who watch the most television tend to be delayed in language learning (Harrison & McLeod, 2010).

Language Loss

Schools in all nations stress the dominant language, and language-minority parents fear that their children will make a *language shift,* becoming more fluent in the school language than in their home language. This is a valid fear: Language shift occurs everywhere—some language-minority children in Mexico shift to Spanish (Messing, 2007), some children from the First Nations in Canada shift to English (Allen, 2007), as do some Chinese-speaking children in the United States—but not always (Zhang, 2010). Crucial are the attitudes of the parents and the larger society about the native language.

Children may shift in talking but not in comprehending. Many 5-year-olds understand their parents' language but refuse to speak it. Nor is it unusual for immigrant adults to use a child as spokesperson and interpreter when they deal with monolingual bureaucrats. This may be a practical necessity, but the role reversal widens the generational gap between child and parent. It also reinforces the language shift, because children realize that the majority language is preferred outside the home.

Language shift and role reversal are unfortunate, not only for the cognition and mental health of the child but also for the family and society (Toppelberg et al., 2010). Having many fluently bilingual citizens is a national strength, and respect for family traditions moderates adolescent rebellion. Yet remember that young children are preoperational: They center on the immediate status of the "foreign" language, not on its global usefulness; on appearances more than history; on parental dress and customs, not on traditions and wisdom; on the present more than the past. No wonder many shift toward the dominant culture. Since language is integral to culture, if a child is to become fluently bilingual, everyone who speaks with the child should show evident appreciation of both cultures (Pearson, 2008; Snow & Kang, 2006).

Smiling Faces, Usually Everyone in this group is an immigrant, born far from his current home in Burlington, Vermont. Jean Luc Dushime escaped the 1994 genocide in Rwanda, central Africa, when he was 14. He eventually adapted to his new language, climate, surroundings, and culture. Today he helps immigrant children make the same transition.

balanced bilingual A person who is fluent in two languages, not favoring one over the other.

Especially for Immigrant Parents You want your children to be fluent in the language of your family's new country, even though you do not speak that language well. Should you speak to your children in your native tongue or in the new language? (see response, page 276)

Language Gains

Becoming a **balanced bilingual,** speaking two languages so well that no audible hint suggests the other language, is accomplished by millions of young children in many nations, to their cognitive and linguistic benefit (Bialystok & Viswanathan, 2009; Pearson, 2008). Yet millions of other children either abandon their first language or do not learn the second as well as they might. Although skills in one language can be transferred to benefit acquisition of another, "transfer is neither automatic nor inevitable" (Snow & Kang, 2006, p. 97). Scaffolding is needed.

The basics of language learning—the naming and vocabulary explosions, fast-mapping, overregularization, extensive practice—apply to every language a young child learns. Young children's vocabulary in two languages is directly connected to how much language they hear; for a child to become a balanced bilingual, adults need to expose that child to twice as much talk as usual (Hammer et al., 2011). The same practices can make a child fluently trilingual, as some 5 year-olds are. One parent might read to a child in French, for instance, and another in English, while the child attends a Spanish-speaking preschool. Thanks to theory of mind, by the time children are 5, they can understand that a particular language is understood by one person but not another, and speak accordingly.

SUMMING UP

Children aged 2 to 6 have impressive linguistic talents. They explode into speech, from about a hundred words at 24 months to thousands at 6 years, from halting baby talk to rapid, bilingual fluency. Fast-mapping and grammar are among the sophisticated devices they use, although both can backfire: Many young children misuse words or assume grammar regularities that do not exist. No other time in the entire life span is as sensitive for language learning, especially for mastering pronunciation.

Extensive exposure to two languages, with strong encouragement and repeated practice, can result in children being balanced bilinguals, which confers not only fluency but also cognitive and social benefits.

>> Early-Childhood Education

A hundred years ago, children had no formal education until first grade, which is why it was called "first" and why young children were "*pre*schoolers." Today, many 3- to 6-year-olds are in school (see Figure 9.5 for U.S. trends) not only because of changing family patterns but also because research "documents the rapid development and great learning potential of the early years" (Hyson et al., 2006, p. 6). Especially by age 3 or 4, children learn best if they have extensive practice in hearing and speaking, in fine and gross motor skills, and in literacy and numeracy, all of which most preschools provide.

Homes and Schools

A key research conclusion is that the quality of both the home and the school matter. If the home educational environment is poor, a good preschool program is especially beneficial (Hindman et al., 2010). A preschool with an inadequate curriculum is less destructive if the family provides learning opportunities and

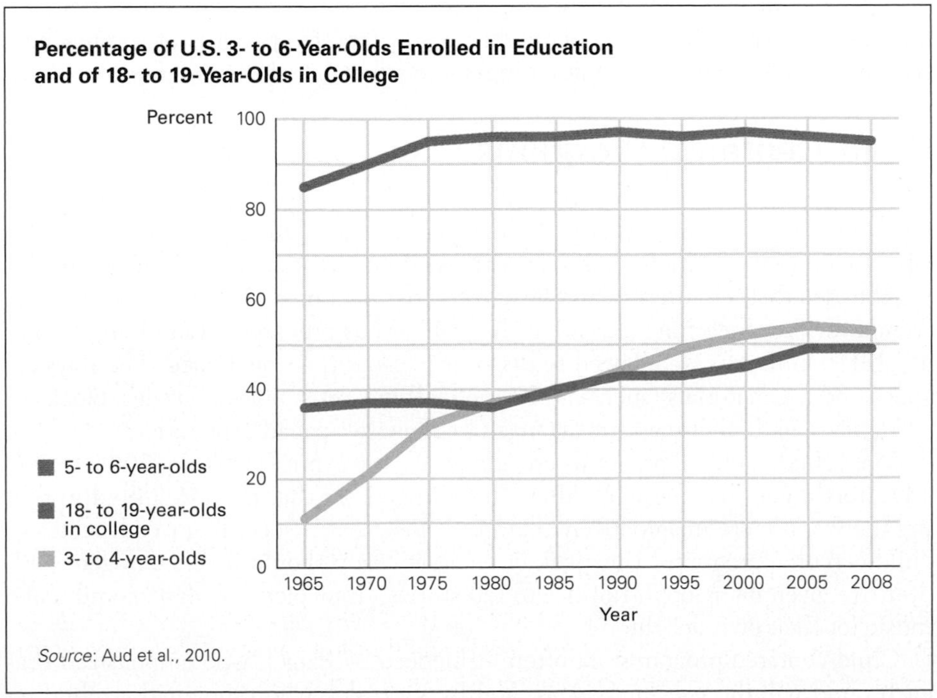

FIGURE 9.5

Changing Times As research increasingly finds that preschool education provides a foundation for later learning, most young children are enrolled in educational programs. Note the contrast with 18- to 19-year-olds in college (not shown are the 18- to 19-year-olds still in high school—about 15 percent).

Observation Quiz At what point did the percentage of 3- to 4-year-olds in school exceed that of 18- to 19-year-olds in college? (see answer, page 277)

"We teach them that the world can be an unpredictable, dangerous, and sometimes frightening place, while being careful not to spoil their lovely innocence. It's tricky."

Tricky Indeed Young children are omnivorous learners, picking up habits, curses, and attitudes that adults would rather not transmit. Deciding what to teach—by actions more than words—is essential.

encouragement every afternoon, evening, and weekend. Ideally, each child has both, partly because no home or preschool is always within the child's zone of proximal development.

It is difficult to judge both homes and schools in the United States because of the "stunning variability and fragmentation" of public and private schools (Pianta et al., 2009, p. 50). Overall, preschools foster cognition, but some programs are very weak and parents might do better in that realm. However, families do not choose home education as often as they settle for it: Access to a quality preschool is particularly difficult for middle-class families, although in some places low-income families are shut out as well.

When early-education programs are compared, the most important variables are teachers who know how to respond to the needs of young children and have time to do so. This is achieved via a combination of teacher education and experience, as well as relatively few children per teacher.

Some specific characteristics of quality day care were described in Chapter 7: safety, adequate space and equipment, a low child/adult ratio, positive social interactions among children and adults, and trained staff who stay year after year. When comparing options, one question that parents might ask is, "How long has each staff member worked here?" Even more important is to assess how effective the teachers are at implementing a curriculum that responds to the needs of each child—an assessment difficult to make even with direct observation but almost impossible for distant regulators (Pianta et al., 2009).

Educational institutions for young children are referred to by various names (preschool, nursery school, day care, pre-primary, pre-K) or structures (public, private, center, family), but these labels are not reliable indicators of the quality of an institution (Fuligni et al., 2009). Each early-childhood educational program (and sometimes each teacher) emphasizes different skills, goals, and methods (Chambers et al., 2010; Walsh & Petty, 2007). We will now consider three general categories: child-centered, teacher-directed, and intervention programs. Remember, however, that the quality of the home and the effectiveness of the teachers have more impact on young children than does the label of the program.

>> Response for Immigrant Parents (from page 274) Children learn by listening, so it is important to speak with them often. Depending on how comfortable you are with the new language, you might prefer to read to your children, sing to them, and converse with them primarily in your native language and find a good preschool where they will learn the new language. The worst thing you could do would be to restrict speech in either tongue.

Child-Centered Programs

Many programs are called *developmental,* or *child-centered,* because they stress children's development and growth. Teachers in such programs believe children need to follow their own interests rather than adult directions, for example, endorsing the idea that "children should be allowed to select many of their own activities from a variety of learning areas that the teacher has prepared" (Lara-Cinisomo et al., 2011). Children are allowed to discover ideas at their own pace. The physical space and the materials (such as dress-up clothing, art supplies, puzzles, blocks of many sizes, and other toys) are arranged to allow self-paced exploration.

Most child-centered programs encourage artistic expression (Lim, 2004). Some educators argue that young children "are all poets" in that they are gifted in seeing the world more imaginatively than older people do. According to advocates of child-centered programs, this peak of creative vision should be encouraged; children are given many opportunities to tell stories, draw pictures, dance, and make music for their own delight.

Especially for Unemployed Early-Childhood Teachers You are offered a job in a program that has 10 children for every 1 adult. You know that is too many, but you want a job. What should you do? (see response, page 279)

Child-centered programs are often influenced by Piaget, who emphasized that each child will discover new ideas, and by Vygotsky, who thought that children learn from other children, with adult guidance (Bodrova & Leong, 2005). Teachers are crucial: A child-centered program requires teachers to organize the classroom with developmentally appropriate activities for each child and then guide each child toward the activities that will advance learning (Dominguez et al., 2010).

Although children make their own choices, some aspects of the program entice children to learn words, numbers, and social skills. For example, to promote numeracy, children play games that include math (counting objects, keeping score) and follow routines that use measurements (daily calendars, schedules). Teachers also use numbers as part of managing the children (only three children in the block corner, two volunteers to get the juice).

>> Answer to Observation Quiz (from page 275) Between 1985 and 1990. The exact year (not shown) was 1988.

Montessori Schools

One type of child-centered school began a hundred years ago, when Maria Montessori opened nursery schools for poor children in Rome. She believed that children needed structured, individualized projects to give them a sense of accomplishment. They completed puzzles, used sponges and water to clean tables, traced shapes, and so on.

Like Piaget (her contemporary), Montessori (1870–1952) realized that children's thoughts and needs differ from those of adults. In her schools, children learned from activities that might seem like play. Teachers gave each child tasks that dovetailed with his or her cognitive eagerness. For example, because they have a need for order, for language learning, and for using all their senses, Montessori children are given systematic exercises that allow them to explore—such as cinnamon sticks in a paper bag, to be first smelled, then touched, then tasted. In many ways, the child's own curiosity and joy in developing and practicing various motor skills is used to aid learning.

Today's **Montessori schools** still emphasize individual pride and achievement, presenting many literacy-related tasks (such as outlining letters and looking at books) to young children (Lillard, 2005). Specific materials differ from those that Montessori developed, but the underlying philosophy is the same. Children seek out learning tasks and are not made to sit quietly while a teacher instructs them. That is what makes Montessori programs child-centered, although traditional

Montessori schools Schools that offer early-childhood education based on the philosophy of Maria Montessori, which emphasizes careful work and tasks that each young child can do.

INFOCUSPHOTOS.COM / ALAMY

Tibet, China, India, and . . . Italy? Over the past half-century, as China increased its control of Tibet, thousands of refugees fled to northern India. Tibet traditionally had no preschools, but young children adapt quickly, as here in Ladakh, India. This Tibetan boy is working a classic Montessori board.

Montessori schools exclude some activities that children enjoy (dress-up play, for example).

The goal is for all children to feel proud of themselves and engage in learning. Many aspects of Montessori's philosophy are in accord with current developmental research. That is one reason this kind of school remains popular. A study of 5-year-olds in inner-city Milwaukee who were chosen by lottery to attend Montessori programs found that the children became better at prereading and early math tasks, as well as at developing a theory of mind, than their peers in other schools (Lillard & Else-Quest, 2006). The probable explanation: Their gains in self-confidence, curiosity, and exploration transferred into more academic tasks.

Reggio Emilia

Reggio Emilia A program of early-childhood education that originated in the town of Reggio Emilia, Italy, and that encourages each child's creativity in a carefully designed setting.

Another form of early-childhood education is called **Reggio Emilia** because it began in the Italian town of that name, where virtually every young child attends preschool. In Reggio Emilia, children are encouraged to master skills that are not usually taught in North American schools until age 7 or so, such as writing and using tools. There is no large-group instruction, with formal lessons in, say, forming letters or cutting paper. Instead, "Every child is a creative child, full of potential" (Gandini et al., 2005, p. 1), with personal learning needs and artistic drive. Measurement of achievements, such as testing to see whether children have learned their letters, is not part of the core belief that each child should explore and learn in his or her own way (Lewin-Benham, 2008).

Appreciation of the arts is evident. Every Reggio Emilia school has a studio and an artist who encourages the children to be creative. The space also fosters creativity. Reggio Emilia schools have a large central room where children gather, children's art is displayed on white walls and hung from high ceilings, and floor-to-ceiling windows open to a spacious, plant-filled playground. Big mirrors are part of the school's décor—again, with the idea of fostering individuality. Reggio Emilia programs have a low child/teacher ratio, ample space, and abundant materials for creative expression.

ELIZABETH FLORES KRT / NEWSCOM

Child-Centered Pride How can Rachel Koepke, a 3-year-old from a Wisconsin town called Pleasant Prairie, seem so pleased that her hands (and cuffs) are blue? The answer arises from northern Italy—Rachel attends a Reggio Emilia preschool that encourages creative expression.

One distinctive feature of the curriculum is that a small group of children become engaged in long-term projects of their choosing. Such projects foster the children's pride in their accomplishments (which are displayed for all to admire) while teaching them to plan and work together. Children are also encouraged to investigate their physical world—plants, insects, and much more. Outdoor play space, with greenery of many kinds, is also part of the Reggio Emilio plan.

As detailed in later chapters, many nations currently emphasize children's need to learn the basics of science and math in their early years. This means a familiarity with numbers and an enthusiasm for inquiry, both of which are fostered in Reggio Emilia programs. One analysis of Reggio Emilia classrooms in the United States found "a science-rich context that triggered and supported preschoolers' inquiries, and effectively engaged preschoolers' hands, heads, and hearts with science" (Inan et al., 2010, p. 1186).

Reggio Emilia teachers are encouraged to collaborate. For six hours each week, they work without the children: planning activities, having group discussions, and talking to parents. Parents collaborate as well, teaching special subjects and learning about their child with individualized reports that include photographs, artwork, and detailed observations written by the teachers.

Teacher-Directed Programs

Unlike child-centered programs, teacher-directed preschools stress academics, usually taught by one adult to the entire group. The curriculum includes learning the names of letters, numbers, shapes, and colors according to a set timetable; every child naps, snacks, and goes to the bathroom on schedule as well. Children are taught to sit quietly and listen to the teacher. Praise and other reinforcements are given for good behavior, and time-outs (brief separation from activities) are imposed to punish misbehavior.

In teacher-directed programs, the serious work of schooling is distinguished from the unstructured play of home. Teachers endorse several ideas that indicate a teacher-directed focus, one being that children should form letters correctly before they are allowed to create a story (Lara-Cinisomo et al., 2011). Such programs occur in many nations. As one young German boy explained:

> So home is home and kindergarten is kindergarten. Here is my work and at home is off-time, understand? My mum says work is me learning something. Learning is when you drive your head, and off-time is when the head slows down.
>
> *[quoted in Griebel & Niesel, 2002, p. 67]*

The teachers' goal is to make all children "ready to learn" when they enter elementary school by teaching basic skills, including precursors to reading, writing, and arithmetic, perhaps via teachers asking questions that children answer together. Children practice forming letters, sounding out words, counting objects, and writing their names. If a 4-year-old learns to read, that is success. (In a child-centered program, early reading might arouse suspicion that the child had too little time to play or socialize.) Note that these preschools do not stress social skills, which require more informal interaction between the children. Perhaps the definition of "readiness" is too narrow (Winter, 2011).

Many teacher-directed programs were inspired by behaviorism, which emphasizes step-by-step learning and repetition. Another inspiration comes from research indicating that children who have not learned basic vocabulary and learning strategies before kindergarten often fall behind in primary school. Many state legislatures mandate that all children learn particular concepts in preschool; such specifics are best fostered by teacher-directed learning (Bracken & Crawford, 2010).

The contrast between child-centered and teacher-directed philosophies is evident not only in lessons but also in attitudes and expectations. For instance, if one child bothers another child, should the second child tell the teacher, or should the two children work it out by themselves? If one child bites another, should the biter be isolated, counseled, admonished, punished, or—as sometimes happens—should the victim be told to bite back? Preschools need rules for such situations, and rules vary because of contrasting philosophies. In a child-centered program, the offender might be asked to think of the effect of his or her actions; in a teacher-directed program, punishment might be immediate.

It may seem easier for each teacher to do whatever he or she believes is best, resulting in a happy hodgepodge of strategies, but this may confuse children and parents. According to a detailed study of early-childhood staff in the Netherlands, differences are notable among adults raised in diverse cultures. In this study, the native-born Dutch teachers emphasized individual achievement more than the adults from the Caribbean or Mediterranean, who stressed sharing and group learning (Huijbregts et al., 2009). Thus, the Dutch teachers were more child-centered, while the immigrant teachers were more teacher-directed.

>> Response for Unemployed Early-Childhood Teachers (from page 276)
It would be best for you to wait for a job in a program where children learn well, organized along the lines explained in this chapter. You would be happier, as well as learn more, in a workplace that is good for children. Realistically, though, you might feel compelled to take the 10-children-to-1-adult job. If you do, change the child/adult ratio—find a helper, perhaps a college intern or a volunteer grandmother. But choose carefully—some adults are not helpful at all. Before you take the job, remember that children need continuity: You can't leave simply because you find something better.

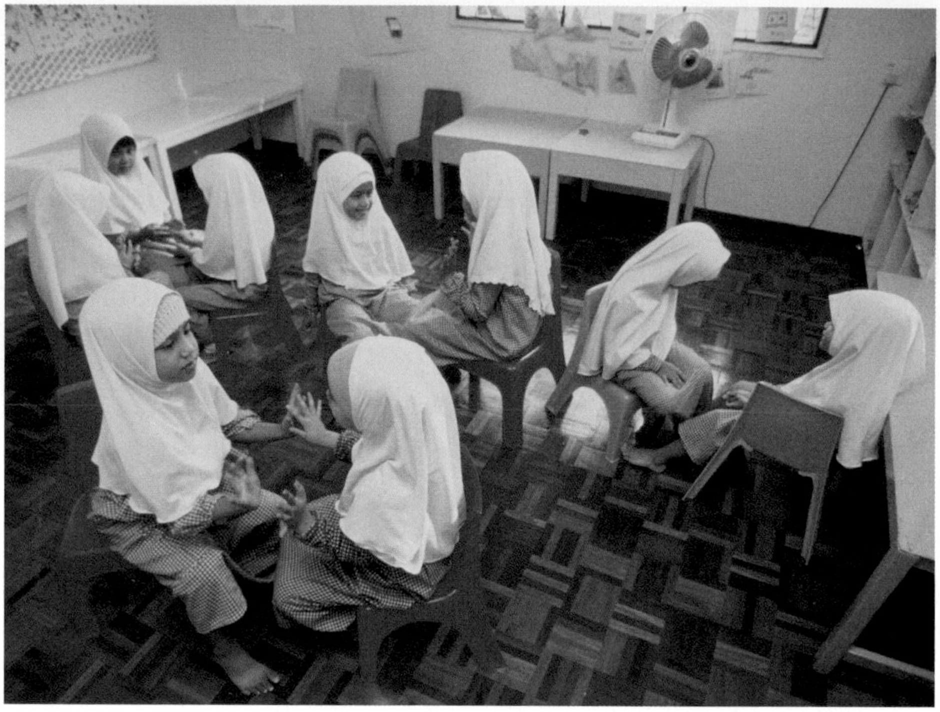
PAUL CHESLEY / STONE / GETTY IMAGES

Learning from One Another Every nation creates its own version of early education. In this scene at a nursery school in Kuala Lumpur, Malaysia, note the head coverings, uniforms, bare feet, and absence of boys. None of these elements would be found in most early-childhood-education classrooms in North America or Europe.

Observation Quiz What seemingly universal aspects of childhood are visible in this photograph? (see answer, page 282)

New teachers in those schools (and probably in all schools) were likely to believe their way was best; teachers who had worked together for years were more similar in their beliefs and practices than those who had not (Huijbregts et al., 2009). One probable reason is that they had learned from one another.

This study highlights the complexities that can result when parents, teachers, and aides are from different backgrounds, as is often the case in North American programs. As many studies have shown, children can learn whatever academic and social skills are taught to them; those who attended preschool are usually advanced in cognitive skills over those who did not (Camilli et al., 2010; Chambers et al., 2010). However, all young children need personal attention, consistency, and continuity: It does not help when each adult applies different rules and routines.

Intervention Programs

Especially for Teachers In trying to find a preschool program, what should parents look for? (see response, page 283)

Many nations try to narrow the learning gap evident between the most and least proficient kindergartner by offering early education to everyone (e.g., China, France, Italy, and Sweden). Public support for the early education of children as an intervention measure varies by cohort and culture.

First let's look at China, in some ways the opposite of the United States. When China's new regime took over in 1949, it wanted to increase national coherence and pride—not an easy task after a civil war and with a population of a billion people of many ethnicities. Accordingly, China opened thousands of preschools, emphasizing teacher-directed "collectivity and discipline," not play and individuality. Forty years later, in 1989, as educators became more influenced by Piaget and Vygotsky, the central government again imposed a curriculum, but this time it mandated a more child-centered curriculum (Xu, 2011, p. 151). The success of this curriculum is debatable, depending on what goals and standards should be measured. However, as detailed in later chapters, Chinese children have catapulted to the top in terms of scores on international achievement tests.

In Western nations, the reason for intervention has primarily been to help low-income children do better in school. By that measure, such intervention has been successful. In England, Canada, Australia, and the United States, numerous studies find that early education helps disadvantaged children (Camilli et al., 2010; Coghlan et al., 2009). Now we look at more specifics in the United States, in part to show the impact of changing policies over the decades.

Head Start

In the United States, since 1965, millions of young children were thought to need a "head start" on their formal education, to help foster better health and cognition before first grade. Consequently, the federal government funded a massive program for 4-year-olds called **Head Start.**

Head Start A federally funded early-childhood intervention program for low-income children of preschool age.

The first wave of research found dramatic improvement in children's intelligence and language; the first follow-up found that the early advances faded by second grade. Then, just as the funding was about to vanish because of diminishing returns, a third wave of research found that former Head Start students were more likely to graduate from high school and have jobs than those who had never had preschool education (Zigler & Styfco, 2004). Funding has continued: In 2009–2010, nearly a million children attended Head Start programs.

The intent of Head Start has changed over the decades, from lifting families out of poverty to promoting literacy, from providing dental care and immunizations to teaching standard English, from teaching parents better discipline methods to teaching children to solve their own conflicts. As more children speak a language other than English, literacy has become increasingly stressed; as the United States seems to fall behind other nations in science, children are encouraged to enjoy math and exploration.

Some Head Start teachers practice child-centered education while others prefer a teacher-directed approach; some consider parents to be a problem whereas others regard parents as allies (D. R. Powell, 2006). Some programs enroll only children of citizens; others allow all young children to attend.

These variations have immediate impact on children and families because young children are great learners, but what they learn depends on quite specific educational experiences. For example, many low-income 3- and 4-year-olds in the United States are not normally exposed to math. One Head Start program engaged children in a board game with numbers; their mathematical understanding advanced significantly (Siegler, 2009). Early Head Start, for children aged 3 and younger, is particularly effective for children of teenage parents of low socioeconomic status (SES). The program is thought to be effective not only because of the direct teaching in school but also because relieving some of the parents' stress allows them to provide more cognitive stimulation for their children (Ayoub et al., 2011).

ELLEN B. SENSI / IMAGE WORKS

Disaster Recovery The success of Head Start led to Early Head Start, for children such as this 2-year-old in Biloxi, Mississippi. When Hurricane Katrina destroyed most of the community, it was the first program to reemerge there. Small children recover from disasters more easily if their parents can reestablish a normal life— which is why this Head Start program is helping entire families.

Now to the present day. A recent congressional authorization of funding for Head Start included a requirement for extensive evaluation to answer two questions:

1. What difference does Head Start make to key outcomes of development and learning (in particular, school readiness) for low-income children? How does Head Start affect parental practices?
2. Under what circumstances and for whom does Head Start achieve the greatest impact?

The answers were not as dramatic as either advocates or detractors had hoped (U.S. Department of Health and Human Services, 2010). Head Start did improve children's literacy and math skills while they were in the program; their oral health

>> Answer to Observation Quiz (from page 280) Three aspects are readily apparent: These girls enjoy their friendships; they are playing a hand-clapping game, some version of which is found in every culture; and, most important, they have begun the formal education that their families want for them.

and their parents' responsiveness also improved. However, many benefits faded by first grade. One reason might be that many of the non–Head Start children in the comparison group were enrolled in other early-childhood programs—sometimes excellent ones, sometimes not.

Certain children benefited from Head Start more than others did, with benefits most apparent for children with the lowest family incomes, or those living in rural areas, or those with disabilities (U.S. Department of Health and Human Services, 2010). These were also the children least likely to find other sources of early education, which supports the notion that Head Start is better than no program at all. The strongest overall benefits were advances in language and social skills during early childhood, but those advances did not endure past kindergarten, with one exception—vocabulary. It is likely that more results will be found with long-term follow-up, a possibility shown by several small studies, reviewed now.

Four-Year-Olds in the United States, 2009

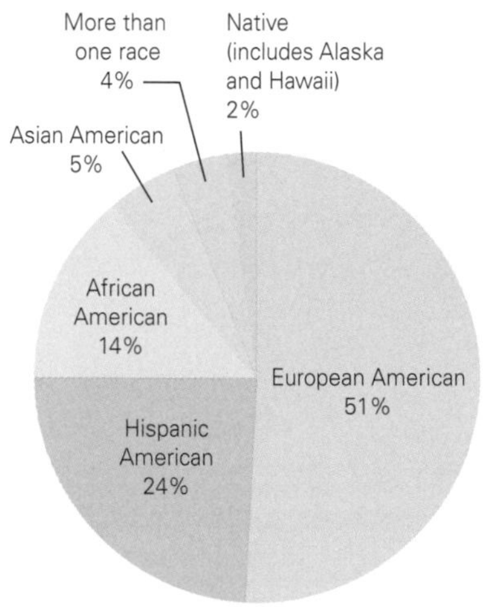

Source: U.S. Bureau of the Census, 2010.

FIGURE 9.6

Only Six Categories? Diversity in the United States is far greater than these statistics from the U.S. Census indicate. For instance, more than 50 distinct languages are spoken in U.S. homes. However, this pie chart reflects at least one cohort change: Children are more diverse than elders. Of those over age 75, 83 percent are European American.

Bilingual Education

One type of early intervention program that does seem effective is bilingual education. This is increasingly necessary worldwide, as global migration results in millions of young children speaking a language at home that is not the language of instruction in school. International research on young children who need to learn another language is limited, but results from many nations suggest that successful strategies vary depending on the child, the home background, and national values. As one review concludes, "It is highly unlikely that one approach will be equally effective for all DLLs [dual language learners]" (Hammer et al., 2011).

In the United States, the parents of about one-third of all preschoolers speak a language other than English. Most often that language is Spanish, but about 2 percent of all 4-year-olds are of Chinese background, and immigrants from other countries—especially India, Russia, the Philippines, and Korea—are also likely to speak their original language at home. Some of the parents speak English as well, and some young children are enrolled in English preschools. As a result, many 4-year-olds are fluent in more than one language.

Research has focused on the approximately 24 percent of young children of Hispanic heritage (see Figure 9.6). In general, programs that combine English

JIM WEST / ALAMY

All Together Now Socialization is part of every early-education program, in ways almost impossible for children who stay at home to benefit from. In this intervention program in Washington, D.C., children learn Spanish and English culture, with the help of a Peruvian American foster grandparent. All four are also learning computer skills—best mastered as one person shows another.

and Spanish instruction, sometimes with half a day for each, are more successful at teaching English while advancing Spanish than are programs that simply immerse the Spanish-speaking children in an English-only setting (Barnett et al., 2007). The various approaches to teaching a second language are further described in Chapter 12.

Unfortunately, for political and cultural reasons, the young children who are least likely to attend preschool in the United States are those from Spanish-speaking homes—less than half are in preschool (see Figure 9.7). These data are for 4-year-olds; the proportions of 3-year-olds from Spanish-speaking homes who are in preschools is even lower, perhaps 15 percent. Learning a second language is easiest before age 4: Most Spanish-speaking children do not have that opportunity.

As you see, the contrast between European and Hispanic Americans is most dramatic for center-based care, which includes private and state-funded preschools. The federal program, Head Start, requires that children be from low-income families, but even among such families, Hispanic children are less likely to be enrolled. One reason is fear of deportation if any member of the family is undocumented. Another reason is custom: The evidence that young children need preschool is familiar to most middle-class Americans, but not to most immigrants. An added problem is that many Head Start programs are limited to three hours a day, which limits language learning.

These data include only children who are U.S. citizens, thus excluding young children who were born in other nations and who are now living in the United States. Almost none of them are in preschool, although all of them are eligible for public education once they reach age 6. Each year, almost a million U.S. children enter first grade with poor English skills.

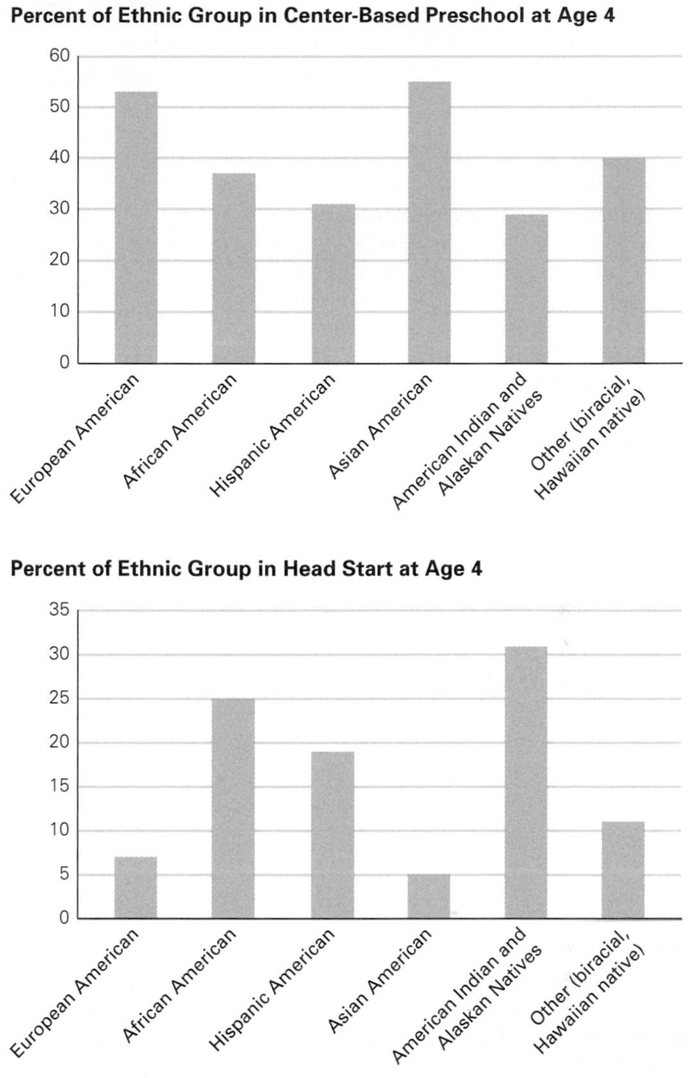

Source: Chernoff et al., 2007.

FIGURE 9.7

The Other Half Many research studies find that 4-year-olds who attend preschool are more competent in kindergarten—they have better language skills and are more likely to make friends. However, it is not known why almost half of all 4-year-olds are not in prekindergarten programs of any kind.

Long-Term Gains from Intensive Programs

Based on longitudinal evaluation, most developmentalists are convinced that early intervention can make a difference if it is sufficiently intense with effective teachers. The evidence comes from three specific programs that enrolled children full time for years, sometimes beginning with home visits in infancy, sometimes continuing in after-school programs through first grade. One program, called Perry (or High/Scope), was spearheaded in Michigan (Schweinhart & Weikart, 1997); another, called Abecedarian, got its start in North Carolina (Campbell et al., 2001); a third, called Child–Parent Centers, began in Chicago (Reynolds, 2000).

All three programs compared experimental groups of children with matched control groups, and all reached the same conclusion: Early education can have substantial long-term benefits that become most apparent when the children are in the third grade or later. Children in these three programs scored higher on math and reading achievement tests at age 10 than did other children from the same backgrounds, schools, and neighborhoods. They were less likely to be placed in special classes for slow or disruptive children or to repeat a year of school compared with other children from the same neighborhoods.

>> Response for Teachers (from page 280) Tell parents to look at the people more than the program. Parents should see the children in action and note whether the teachers show warmth and respect for each child.

FIGURE 9.8

And in Middle Age Longitudinal research found that two years in the intensive High/Scope preschool program changed the lives of dozens of children from impoverished families. The program had a positive impact on many aspects of their education, early adulthood, and middle age. (This graph does not illustrate another intriguing finding: The girls who attended High/Scope fared much better than the boys.)

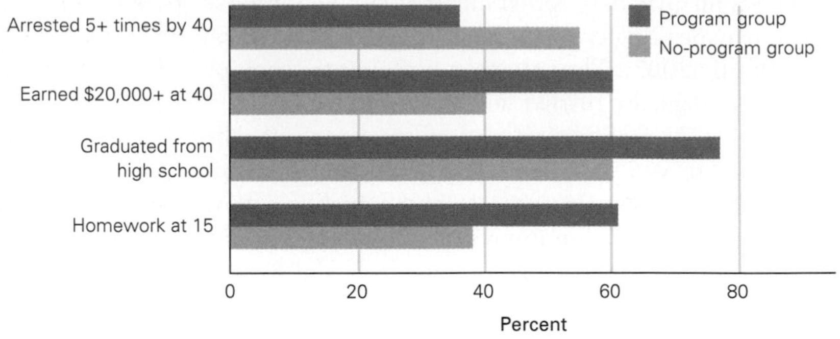

Source: Schweinhart et al., 2005, p. 196.

Benefits continued. In adolescence, the children who had undergone intensive preschool education had higher aspirations, possessed a greater sense of achievement, and were less likely to have been abused. As young adults, they were more likely to attend college and less likely to go to jail, more often paying taxes rather than being on welfare (Reynolds & Ou, 2011; Schweinhart et al., 2005). Early education affected every aspect of their adult life, as "early cognitive and scholastic advantages lead to social and motivational gains that culminate in enhanced well-being" (Reynolds & Ou, 2011, p. 578) (see Figure 9.8).

All three research projects found that providing direct cognitive training (rather than simply letting children play), with specific instruction in various school-readiness skills, was useful as long as each child's needs and talents were considered—a circumstance made possible because the child/adult ratio was low. The curricular approach was a combination of child-centered and teacher-directed. Teachers were encouraged to involve parents in their child's education, and each program included strategies to ensure this home–school connection.

These programs were expensive (ranging from $5,000 to $17,000 annually per young child in 2010 dollars). From a developmental perspective, the decreased need for special education and other social services eventually made such programs a wise investment, perhaps saving $4 for every dollar spent (Barnett, 2007). The benefits to society over the child's lifetime, including increased employment and reduced crime, are much more than that.

In fact, the greatest lifetime return came from boys from high-poverty neighborhoods in the Chicago preschool program, with a social benefit over the boys' lifetime more than 12 times the cost (Reynolds et al., 2011). The problem is that the costs are immediate and the benefits long term. Without a developmental perspective, few legislators or voters are willing to fund expensive intervention programs that do not pay off until a decade or more later. An additional problem with all successful programs is scale: Success with a small program is difficult to translate into success for a million children.

State Programs

Inspired by these intensive programs as well as by other research on young children, many U.S. developmentalists advocate early education for every child, at least by age 3. Unfortunately, in the United States overall, only about half of 3- and

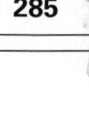

4-year-olds are enrolled in preschool, which reduces the "chance for success" in elementary school for the other half (*Education Week,* January 14, 2010).

This may be changing: 40 states sponsor public education for young children—although usually only for low-income 4-year-olds. In 2009–2010, more than a million children (1,292,310) attended state-sponsored preschools—more than double the number a decade earlier (Barnett et al., 2010). Since more than 4 million (4,268,000) children were born in 2006, that is about one-fourth of the entire cohort.

From a developmental perspective, the leading state is Oklahoma, which provides full-day kindergarten and preschool education for all children. Attendance is voluntary, but most children are enrolled. The data on the children's learning showed more gains than in Head Start or other state programs (Gormley et al., 2008). The curriculum emphasizes literacy and math; benefits are particularly strong for children whose home language is Spanish (Phillips et al., 2009).

For the 40 states that sponsor early education, the average funding is less than $5,000 per year per student. That is obviously not enough for a program with a low child/adult ratio, teachers who have college degrees, and professional mentoring in a safe, well-equipped space. The best programs include at least two adults per group, additional adults for special needs (such as an artist in Reggio Emilia or a nurse-educator in some U.S. programs), and a director who guides the program.

Only four states (Alabama, Alaska, North Carolina, and Rhode Island) have programs that developmentalists consider to be of high quality, and none of those four states have extensive programs (Barnett et al., 2010). Developmentalists agree that increasing the number of participants and improving the quality of preschool programs are prime goals; the problem is convincing legislators and the public that it must be done.

SUMMING UP

Research, particularly on preschool programs for children in low-income families, has proven that high-quality early education benefits children by improving language learning, social skills, and prospects for the future. Many different programs, including child-centered (Montessori and Reggio Emilia) and teacher-directed programs, are available—although sometimes very expensive. Massive intervention programs—such as Head Start and state-sponsored pre-kindergarten, as well as smaller ones such as High/Scope, Abecedarian, and Chicago's Child–Parent Centers—seem to improve the life course of low-income children who attend them. Nations, states, and parents differ in what they seek from early education for their children, and programs vary in teacher preparation, curriculum, physical space, and child/adult ratios. Quality matters. ■

SUMMARY

Piaget and Vygotsky

1. Piaget stressed the egocentric and illogical aspects of thought during the play years. He called this stage preoperational thought because young children often cannot yet use logical operations to think about their observations and experiences.

2. Young children, according to Piaget, sometimes focus on only one thing (centration) and see things only from their own viewpoint (egocentrism), remaining stuck on appearances and current reality. They may believe that living spirits reside in inanimate objects, a belief called animism.

3. Vygotsky stressed the social aspects of childhood cognition, noting that children learn by participating in various experiences, guided by more knowledgeable adults or peers. Such guidance assists learning within the zone of proximal development, which encompasses the knowledge and skills that the child has the potential to learn.

4. According to Vygotsky, the best teachers use various hints, guidelines, and other tools to provide the child with a scaffold for new learning. Language is a bridge that provides social mediation between the knowledge that the child already has and the learning that the society hopes to impart. For Vygotsky, words are a tool for learning.

Children's Theories

5. Children develop theories, especially to explain the purpose of life and their role in it. In fact, one theory about children's thinking is called "theory-theory"—the hypothesis that children develop theories because all humans innately seek explanations for everything they observe.

6. One example of the developmental theory is called theory of mind—an understanding of what others may be thinking. Notable advances in theory of mind occur at around age 4. Theory of mind is partly the result of brain maturation, but culture and experiences also have an impact.

Language Learning

7. Language develops rapidly during early childhood, a sensitive period but not a critical one for language learning. Vocabulary increases dramatically, with thousands of words added between ages 2 and 6. In addition, basic grammar is mastered.

8. Many children learn to speak more than one language, gaining cognitive as well as social advantages. Ideally, children become balanced bilinguals, equally proficient in two languages, by age 6.

Early-Childhood Education

9. Organized educational programs during early childhood advance cognitive and social skills, although specifics vary a great deal. Montessori and Reggio Emilia are two child-centered programs that began in Italy and are now offered in many nations. Behaviorist principles led to many specific practices of teacher-directed programs.

10. Head Start is a U.S. federal government program primarily for low-income children. Longitudinal research finds that early-childhood education reduces the risk of later problems, such as needing special education. High-quality programs increase the likelihood that a child will become a law-abiding, gainfully employed adult.

11. Many types of preschool programs are successful. It is the quality of early education that matters. Children learn best if teachers follow a defined curriculum and if the child/adult ratio is low. The training, warmth, and continuity of early-childhood teachers benefit the children in many ways.

KEY TERMS

preoperational intelligence (p. 257)
symbolic thought (p. 258)
centration (p. 258)
egocentrism (p. 258)
focus on appearance (p. 258)
static reasoning (p. 258)
irreversibility (p. 258)
conservation (p. 259)
animism (p. 259)
guided participation (p. 262)
zone of proximal development (ZPD) (p. 262)
scaffolding (p. 262)
overimitation (p. 263)
private speech (p. 263)
social mediation (p. 264)
theory-theory (p. 266)
theory of mind (p. 267)
fast-mapping (p. 270)
overregularization (p. 272)
balanced bilingual (p. 274)
Montessori schools (p. 277)
Reggio Emilia (p. 278)
Head Start (p. 281)

WHAT HAVE YOU LEARNED?

Piaget and Vygotsky

1. What are the strengths and weaknesses of preoperational thought?

2. What is the difference between egocentrism in a child and selfishness in an adult?

3. How does the animism of young children differ from the animism of adults?

4. How do the toys given to young children scaffold particular behaviors and values?

5. How does guided participation increase a child's zone of proximal development?

6. Why did Vygotsky think that talking to yourself is not a sign of illness but an aid to cognition?

Children's Theories

7. Is theory-theory as valid for adults as for children?

8. Why does a child's development of theory of mind make it more difficult to fool him or her?

9. What factors spur the development of theory of mind?

Language Learning

10. What is the evidence that early childhood is a sensitive time for learning language?

11. How does fast-mapping aid the language explosion?

12. How does overregularization signify a cognitive advance?

13. What evidence in language learning shows the limitations of logic in early childhood?

14. What are the advantages of teaching a child two languages?

15. How can language loss be avoided?

Early-Childhood Education

16. What do most preschools provide for children that most homes do not?

17. In child-centered programs, what do the teachers do?

18. What makes the Reggio Emilia program different from most other preschool programs?

19. Why are Montessori schools still functioning, 100 years after the first such schools opened?

20. What are the advantages and disadvantages of teacher-directed preschools?

21. What are the goals of Head Start?

22. Why have various evaluations of Head Start reached different conclusions?

23. What are the long-term results of intervention preschools?

APPLICATIONS

The best way to understand thinking in early childhood is to listen to a child, as applications 1 and 2 require. If some students have no access to children, they should do application 3 or 4.

1. Replicate one of Piaget's conservation experiments. The easiest one is conservation of liquids (Figure 9.1). Work with a child under age 5 who tells you that two identically shaped glasses contain the same amount of liquid. Then carefully pour one glass of liquid into a narrower, taller glass. Ask the child if one glass now contains more or if the glasses contain the same amount.

2. To demonstrate how rapidly language is learned, show a preschool child several objects and label one with a nonsense word the child has never heard. (*Toma* is often used; so is *wug*.) Or choose a word the child does not know, such as *wrench, spatula,* or the name of a coin from another nation. Test the child's fast-mapping.

3. Theory of mind emerges at about age 4, but many adults still have trouble understanding other people's thoughts and motives. Ask several people why someone in the news did whatever he or she did (e.g., a scandal, a crime, a heroic act). Then ask your informants how sure they are of their explanation. Compare and analyze the reasons as well as the degrees of certainty. (One person may be sure of an explanation that someone else thinks is impossible.)

4. Think about an experience in which you learned something that was initially difficult. To what extent do Vygotsky's concepts (guided participation, language mediation, apprenticeship, zone of proximal development) explain the experience? Write a detailed, step-by-step account of your learning process as Vygotsky would have described it.

>>ONLINE CONNECTIONS

To accompany your textbook, you have access to a number of online resources, including quizzes for every chapter of the book, flashcards (in English and Spanish), critical thinking questions, and case studies. For access to any of these links, go to www.worthpublishers.com/bergerca9e. In addition to these free resources, you'll also find links to podcasts, video clips, diagnostic quizzing with personalized study advice, and an ebook. Some of the videos and activities available online include:

- *Theory of Mind.* Watch a variety of children challenged by false-belief tasks.
- *Early-Childhood Language Development.* Six-year-olds can tell jokes and 3-year-olds engage in private speech. A variety of video clips showcase the development of children's speech through early childhood.

10

CHAPTER

Early Childhood: Psychosocial Development

WHAT WILL YOU KNOW?

1. Should children be rewarded for doing what adults want them to do?
2. What do children learn from playing with other children?
3. Should caregivers let children watch television?
4. What is the best way to teach children right from wrong?
5. Why do young children exaggerate the differences between boys and girls?

My daughter Bethany, at about age 5, challenged one of my students to a fight.

"Girls don't fight," he said, laughing.

"*Nobody* fights," I corrected him.

We were both teaching Bethany how to express emotions. She learned well; by age 6, she no longer challenged young men to fight.

I remember this incident because I am troubled by what I said. "Nobody" refers to both sexes, but would I have said the same thing if I were male? Was I teaching Bethany to be passive? Should I have asked my student to play-fight with her, as men do with young boys? Or should I have allowed him to express gender norms?

Emotional control, rough play, parenting, morality, and sex differences are all discussed in this chapter. On some aspects experts agree. For instance, no developmentalist doubts that play teaches social understanding, that parents should guide and discipline their children, that bullies should be stopped. However, other aspects are controversial. "Nobody fights" may have been wrong . . . or right.

>> Emotional Development

Children gradually learn when and how to express emotions, becoming more capable in every aspect of their lives (Buckley & Saarni, 2009; Denham et al., 2003; Morrison et al., 2010). Controlling the expression of emotions, called **emotional regulation,** is the preeminent psychosocial accomplishment between ages 2 and 6 (N. Eisenberg et al., 2004). Such regulation is virtually impossible in infancy, but when the emotional hot spots of the limbic system connect to the maturing prefrontal cortex, children become more aware of their reactions. With emotional regulation, children learn how to be angry but not explosive, frightened but not terrified, sad but not inconsolable, anxious but not withdrawn, proud but not boastful, and so on.

Initiative Versus Guilt

During Erikson's third developmental stage, **initiative versus guilt,** pride emerges from the acquisition of the skills and competencies described in the previous two chapters. "Initiative" is saying something new, extending a skill, beginning

emotional regulation The ability to control when and how emotions are expressed.

initiative versus guilt Erikson's third psychosocial crisis, in which children undertake new skills and activities and feel guilty when they do not succeed at them.

Close Connection Unfamiliar events often bring developmental tendencies to the surface, as with the curious boy and his worried brother, who are attending Colorado's Pikes Peak or Bust Rodeo breakfast. Their attentive mother keeps the livelier boy calm and reassures the shy one.

Observation Quiz Mother is obviously a secure base for both boys, who share the same family and half the same genes but are different ages: One is 2 and the other is 4. Can you tell which boy is younger? (see answer, page 292)

SEAN CAYTON / THE IMAGE WORKS

a project. Depending on the outcome (including the parents' response), children feel the emotions of pride or guilt. Usually, North American parents encourage the natural enthusiasm, effort, and pride of their 3- to 6-year-olds. If, instead, parents dismiss rather than guide a child's emotions—fear, anger, or any other feeling—that child may not learn emotional regulation (Morris et al., 2007).

self-concept A person's understanding of who he or she is, in relation to self-esteem, appearance, personality, and various traits.

Protective Optimism

Children's beliefs about their worth are connected to parental confirmation, especially when parents remind their children of their positive accomplishments (Reese et al., 2007). ("You helped Daddy sweep the sidewalk? You made it very clean.") Remember that Erikson described *autonomy* at age 2, often expressed as stubbornness, nicknamed the terrible twos. By age 3, that trait is better regulated and directed and soon becomes *initiative,* as children are eager to learn new skills (Rubin et al., 2009). In the process, a child forms a **self-concept,** an understanding of the self, which usually includes gender and size. Girls are usually happy to be girls, boys to be boys, and both are glad they aren't babies. "Crybaby" is a major insult; praise for being "a big boy" or "a big girl" is welcomed.

Erikson recognized that young children are more proud than realistic. They believe that they are strong, smart, and good-looking—and thus that any goal is achievable. Whatever they are (self-concept) is thought to be good. For instance, they believe that their nation and religion are best; they feel sorry for children who do not belong to their country or church. But don't be too critical of such narrowness: Each of Erikson's stages is appropriate for development at each age. During early childhood, a positivity bias is beneficial; it encourages children to try unfamiliar activities, make friends, begin school, and so on (Boseovski, 2010).

Research finds that many young children are confident that their good qualities will endure but that bad qualities (even biological traits such as poor eyesight) will disappear (Lockhart et al., 2002). This "protective optimism" begins at about age 3, continues through childhood, and often disappears during adolescence (Boseovski, 2010). This seems true in many nations. Modesty is valued in Asian nations, but that does not necessarily diminish children's optimism: Many Japanese children believe they could become better if they just tried hard enough (Lockhart et al., 2008).

ENIGMA / ALAMY

A Poet and We Know It She is the proud winner of a national poetry contest. Is she as surprised, humbled, and thankful as an adult winner would be?

Brain Maturation

The new initiative that Erikson describes benefits from myelination of the limbic system, growth of the prefrontal cortex, and a longer attention span, all made possible by the neurological maturation described in Chapter 8. Concentrated attention aids social competence (Murphy et al., 2007) as children practice and then master various skills. They learn to pour juice, zip pants, or climb trees, undeterred by overflowing juice, stuck zippers, or a perch too high to climb down from. Faith in themselves helps them persist.

Erikson believed that as children develop self-awareness, some begin to feel guilt if they realize their own mistakes. Many people believe that guilt is a more mature emotion than shame (as in Erikson's autonomy versus shame and doubt) because guilt is internalized (Kochanska et al., 2002; Tangney et al., 2007). Guilt comes from within the person, whereas shame comes from outside and depends on other people's opinions. Unlike guilt, shame can be based on social prejudices regarding gender, ethnicity, or background.

To counter social prejudice, many parents of minority kindergartners (Mexican American, African American, or American Indian among others) encourage ethnic pride in their children (Brown et al., 2007; Lesane-Brown et al., 2010). Although very young children raised exclusively in one ethnic group begin to prefer faces that look familiar, they do not categorize ethnicity as adults do. At about age 4, however, social awareness and self-concept become stronger, and children tend to notice categories. That is when minority families typically teach children racial pride. Meanwhile, all children begin to develop moral values via pride and guilt, not shame and doubt—discussed later in this chapter.

DANITADELONT.COM

Glad to be Navajo These sisters are about to join the procession for the annual Inter-tribal Indian Ceremonial in Gallup, New Mexico. More important, they are gaining pride in their ancestry, a key aspect of childhood emotional development.

Motivation

The idea that guilt comes from within the child highlights the distinction between *intrinsic motivation* and *extrinsic motivation*. **Intrinsic motivation** occurs when people do something for the joy of doing it: A musician might enjoy making music, even when no one else hears. **Extrinsic motivation** comes from outside, when people do something to gain praise (or some other reinforcement): A musician who plays for the reward of applause is an example. Knowing the difference is crucial in teaching young children (Cheng & Yeh, 2009).

For the most part, preschool children are intrinsically motivated. They enjoy learning, playing, and practicing whether or not someone else wants them to. Praise and prizes might be appreciated, but they are not the reason why children work at what they do. When playing a game, they might not keep score; the fun is in playing, not winning.

Intrinsic motivation is seen when children invent dialogues for their toys, concentrate on creating a work of art or architecture, and converse with **imaginary friends** who exist only in the child's imagination. The latter are rarely encouraged by adults (so the child has no extrinsic motivation to create them), but imaginary friends are nonetheless increasingly common as initiative builds from ages 3 through 7. They combat loneliness and aid emotional regulation. Children realize their imaginary friends are invisible and pretend, but conjuring them up nevertheless meets some of the child's psychosocial needs (Taylor et al., 2009).

Some imaginary friends are useful, as children need to control their tears and temper, to have a friend to provide comfort and reassurance, to learn how to share their toys, and so on (Taylor et al., 2009). Such friends have various characteristics, depending on what is needed. One girl's imaginary friend named Elephant was "7 inches tall, grey color, black eyes, wears tank top and shorts . . . sometimes

intrinsic motivation A drive, or reason to pursue a goal, that comes from inside a person, such as the need to feel smart or competent.

extrinsic motivation A drive, or reason to pursue a goal, that arises from the need to have one's achievements rewarded from outside, perhaps by receiving material possessions or another person's esteem.

imaginary friends Make-believe friends who exist only in a child's imagination; increasingly common from ages 3 through 7, they combat loneliness and aid emotional regulation.

Especially for Teachers One of your students tells you about playing, sleeping, and talking with an imaginary friend. Does this mean that that child is emotionally disturbed? (see response, page 293) is mean" (Taylor et al., 2004, p. 1178). By having an imaginary friend who is "sometimes mean," this girl was developing strategies to deal with mean people.

Especially for College Students Is extrinsic or intrinsic motivation more influential in your study efforts? (see response, page 294)

Especially for Teachers of Young Children Should you put gold stars on children's work? (see response, page 294)

An Experiment in Motivation

In a classic experiment, preschool children were given markers and paper and assigned to one of three groups who received, respectively: (1) no award, (2) an expected award (they were told *before* they had drawn anything that they would get a certificate), and (3) an unexpected award (*after* they had drawn something, they heard, "You were a big help," and got a certificate) (Lepper et al., 1973). Later, observers noted how often children in each group chose to draw on their own. Those who received the expected award were less likely to draw later than those who were unexpectedly rewarded. The interpretation was that extrinsic motivation (condition 2) undercut intrinsic motivation.

This research triggered a flood of studies seeking to understand whether, when, and how positive reinforcement should be given. The consensus is that praising or paying a person after an accomplishment sometimes encourages that behavior. However, if payment is promised in advance, that extrinsic reinforcement may backfire (Cameron & Pierce, 2002; Deci et al., 1999; Gottfried et al., 2009).

Culture and Emotional Control

Cultures differ in what emotions they expect children to regulate, and children try to follow the norms of their culture. Some research finds that specific cultures emphasize control of particular emotions and behaviors (Harkness et al., 2011; J. G. Miller, 2004; Stubben, 2001):

- Fear (United States)
- Anger (Puerto Rico)
- Pride (China)
- Selfishness (Japan)
- Impatience (many Native American communities)
- Disobedience (Mexico)
- Erratic behavior (the Netherlands)

Cultures differ in control strategies as well (Matsumoto, 2004). Shame is used when a family's reputation is a priority. Indeed, in some cultures, "pride goeth before a fall" and people who "have no shame" are considered mentally ill (Stein, 2006). Cultural differences are also apparent in emotional expression: Children may be encouraged to express their feelings, or they may be taught that emotions are best kept to oneself (Kim et al., 2008).

Of course, cultures change, parents do not always follow cultural norms, and a child's temperament may not conform to cultural expectations. Not everyone from a particular background regulates emotions in a particular way, since "cultures are inevitably more complicated than the framework that is supposed to explain them" (Harkness et al., 2011, p. 92). Sometimes Asian versus North American or other Western cultures are assumed to endorse one value over another (cooperation versus independence is often cited), but once groups within those regions are compared, many differences emerge.

There are some universals, however. In every culture, parents encourage emotional regulation, and children of depressed parents are less able to regulate their emotions (Kovacs et al., 2008). As for impulsive children, everywhere neglectful or inconsistent caregivers make their emotional problems worse, whereas nurturing caregivers guide them to be *more* competent than other children (Belsky et al., 2007; Hane & Fox, 2006).

>> Answer to Observation Quiz (from page 290) Size is not much help, since children grow slowly during these years and the heads of these two boys appear about the same size. However, emotional development is apparent. Most 2-year-olds, like the one at the right, still cling to their mothers; most 4-year-olds are sufficiently mature, secure, and curious to watch the excitement as they drink their juice.

Seeking Emotional Balance

In every culture and cohort, and at every age, developmentalists seek to prevent **psychopathology,** an illness or disorder *(-pathology)* of the mind *(psycho-)*. Although symptoms and diagnoses are influenced by culture—rebellion might be alarming in some cultures but appreciated in others—impaired emotional regulation universally signals pathology. Parents are expected to guide their young children toward cultural norms (Trommsdorff & Cole, 2011).

psychopathology An illness or disorder of the mind.

Externalizing and Internalizing Problems

Without adequate regulation, emotions are overpowering. Intense reactions occur in two seemingly opposite ways.

Some people have **externalizing problems:** Their powerful feelings burst out (exit) uncontrollably. They may externalize a feeling of rage, for example, by lashing out at other people or breaking things. Without emotional regulation, an angry child might flail at another person or lie down screaming and kicking. That externalized reaction might be accepted in a 2-year-old's temper tantrum, but 5-year-olds should have more self-control, perhaps pouting or cursing, not hitting and screaming.

externalizing problems Difficulty with emotional regulation that involves expressing powerful feelings through uncontrolled physical or verbal outbursts, as by lashing out at other people or breaking things.

Other people have **internalizing problems:** They are fearful and withdrawn, turning distress inward. Again, with maturity, the extreme fears of some 2-year-olds (e.g., terror of the bathtub drain, of an imagined tidal wave, of a stranger on crutches) diminish. They may still be afraid of the first day of kindergarten, for instance, but they bravely let go of their mother's hand. One manifestation of internalizing problems is physical illness: A child might have headaches or stomachaches. Although the cause may be psychological, the ache is real. The worst reaction would be to blame the child for the symptom: That might make internalizing worse.

internalizing problems Difficulty with emotional regulation that involves turning one's emotional distress inward, as by feeling excessively guilty, ashamed, or worthless.

Neither externalizing nor internalizing children regulate their emotions very well—or, more precisely, they do not regulate the *expression* of emotions. Either they have too little self-control or they control themselves too much (Caspi & Shiner, 2006; Hart et al., 2003). If emotional regulation is not learned in early childhood, children are likely to develop externalizing or internalizing problems in middle childhood—particularly if the emotion they never learned to regulate is anger (Morris et al., 2010). Problems get worse in adolescence, with some internalizing young children becoming externalizing teenagers.

FRANK SIMONETTI / STOCK CONNECTION / PICTUREQUEST

Who's Chicken? Genes and good parenting have made this boy neither too fearful nor too bold. Appropriate caution is probably the best approach to meeting a chicken.

Sex Differences in Emotional Regulation

Girls usually develop emotional regulation ahead of boys. This difference is especially evident with externalizing emotions; it is apparent in childhood, and then continues in adolescence, with some externalizing boys becoming violent. However, girls also increase their rate of psychopathology: As detailed in Chapter 16, teenage girls are more often depressed than teenage boys, a manifestation of internalized emotions.

One study traced internalizing and externalizing emotions from early to middle childhood. Researchers gave 5-year-olds toy figures and told them the beginning of a story (Zahn-Waxler et al., 2008). Two children (named Mark and Scott for the boys, Mary and Sarah for the girls) were said to start yelling at each other, and the 5-year-olds were asked to show what happened next.

>> Response for Teachers (from page 291) No. In fact, imaginary friends are quite common, especially among creative children. The child may be somewhat lonely, though; you could help him or her find a friend.

>> Response for College Students (from page 292) Both are important. Extrinsic motivation includes parental pressure and the need to get a good job after graduation. Intrinsic motivation includes the joy of learning. Have you ever taken a course that was not required and was said to be difficult? That was intrinsic motivation.

>> Response for Teachers of Young Children (from page 292) Perhaps, but only after the work is completed and if the child has put genuine effort into it. You do not want to undercut intrinsic motivation, as happens with older students who know a particular course will be an "easy A."

DBIMAGES / ALAMY

Learning Emotional Regulation Like this girl in Hong Kong, all 2-year-olds burst into tears when something upsets them—a toy breaks, a pet refuses to play, or it's time to go home. A mother who comforts them and helps them calm down is teaching them to regulate their emotions.

Many boys had Mark and Scott hitting and kicking each other. Boys whose behavior problems worsened between ages 5 and 9 (as rated by their teachers and parents) were the most likely to show such externalizing play-acting at age 5. By contrast, 5-year-old girls often had Mary and Sarah talk about their conflict or change the subject. Curiously, those girls whose behavior problems worsened from age 5 to 9 were more likely than the other children to engage in "reparative behavior," such as Mary hugging Sarah and saying, "I'm sorry." This response may indicate internalized guilt or shame. The authors explain:

> Gender-role stereotypes or exaggerations of masculine qualities (e.g., impulsive, aggressive, uncaring) and feminine qualities (submissive, unassertive, socially sensitive) are reflected not only in the types of problems males and females tend to develop but also in different forms of expression.
>
> *[Zahn-Waxler et al., 2008, p. 114]*

These researchers suggest that, for both sexes, extreme externalization or extreme internalization predicts future psychopathology.

The Brains of Boys and Girls

For both sexes, emotional regulation requires thinking before acting (deciding whether and how to display joy, anger, fear, or any other emotion). Such thinking occurs in the prefrontal cortex, the executive area of the brain. As you remember from Chapter 8, the prefrontal cortex regulates the limbic system (especially the amygdala), where powerful emotions form.

Normally, neurological advances in the prefrontal cortex at about age 4 or 5 make children less likely to throw a temper tantrum, provoke a physical attack, or burst into giggles during prayer (Kagan & Herschkowitz, 2005). Throughout early childhood, violent outbursts, uncontrolled crying, and terrifying phobias (irrational, crippling fears) diminish. The capacity for self-control—such as not opening a present immediately if asked to wait and not expressing disappointment at an undesirable gift—becomes more evident (Carlson, 2003; Grolnick et al., 2006).

Children of both sexes learn emotional regulation and avoid extremes of emotional imbalance, guided by their families (Grusec, 2011). However, when a family mistreats their children, emotions are dysregulated. Because of gender differences in the brain and in hormones, mistreated boys are more likely to externalize and mistreated girls to internalize. This gender difference is found in every culture and thus is probably genetic—the result of the XX or XY chromosomes—although culture and family have an impact. Neurological impairments compound the problem. For many reasons, then, by age 5, maltreated boys with immature emotional regulation are likely to throw things and vulnerable girls are likely to sob uncontrollably.

Parents are obviously crucial in helping children regulate their emotions, but preschool teachers are important as well. A program that helped Head Start teachers in 18 classrooms encourage emotional control was effective in promoting reading and math skills without changing the curriculum. The teachers learned how to set clear rules and routines and to redirect negative behavior (e.g., when one child began to hit another to get a toy, the teacher helped the first child use words to express the problem and implement turn-taking). That meant less impulsive behavior and fewer teacher–child confrontations. A control group of 17 teachers used the same curriculum, but their students did not advance as much in naming letters and understanding numbers as the students of the teachers who learned and practiced techniques to regulate emotions (Raver et al., 2011).

SUMMING UP

Erikson and many others find that pride, purpose, and initiative are integral components of the self-concept of young children, who want to try new activities. Children who have difficulty with emotional regulation may develop internalizing or externalizing problems, which may be early signs of psychopathology. Many factors—including genes, gender, brain development, culture, and hormones—influence emotional regulation. Parents and teachers can help children with emotional maturation, and this affects later school achievement. ■

>> Play

Play is timeless and universal—apparent in every part of the world for thousands of years. Many developmentalists believe that play is the most productive as well as most enjoyable activity that children undertake (Elkind, 2007; Frost, 2009), although whether play is critical or merely fun is controversial. Some educators want to reduce playtime so children will focus on reading and math skills; others predict both emotional and academic problems for children who play too rarely (Hirsh-Pasek et al., 2009; Pellegrini, 2009; Rubin et al., 2009).

Playmates

Young children play best with *peers,* that is, people of about the same age and social status. Two-year-olds are intrigued by peers but are not yet good playmates: They might throw a ball and expect another child to throw it back rather than hold it. By contrast, most 6-year-olds are quite skilled: They can gain entry to a peer group, manage conflict, take turns, find friends, and keep playmates. Over those years, peers provide practice in emotional regulation, empathy, and social understanding (Cohen, 2006).

There is an obvious task for parents: Find playmates, ideally of the same age and sex. Even the most playful parent is outmatched by another child at negotiating the rules of tag, at wrestling on the grass, at pretending to be sick, at killing a dragon. Although the specifics vary, "social play with peers is one of the most important areas in which children develop positive social skills" (Xu, 2010, p. 496).

Play Ball! In every nation, young children play with balls, but the specific games they play vary with the culture. Soccer is the favorite game in many countries, including Brazil, where these children are practicing their dribbling on Copacabana Beach in Rio de Janeiro.

REUTERS / SERGIO MORAES

Cultural Differences in Play

All young children play, whether they are on Arctic ice or desert sand. Children create dramas that reflect their culture and play games that have been passed down from older generations. Because play varies by culture, gender, and age, it teaches children values and skills required in their particular context (Sutton-Smith, 1997). Chinese children fly kites, Alaskan natives tell dreams and stories, Lapp children pretend to be reindeer, Cameroon children hunt mice, and so on. Although play is thought to be universal, not only do specifics differ but so do frequency and playmates: When adults are concerned with basic survival, they rarely play with their children. Children play with each other instead (Kalliala, 2006; Roopnarine, 2011).

As children grow older, play becomes more social, influenced not only by the availability of playmates but also by the physical setting (a small playroom, a large park, a wild hillside). One developmentalist bemoans the twenty-first century's "swift and pervasive rise of electronic media" and modern adults who lean "more toward control than freedom," while lauding children who find places to play independently and "conspire ways to elude adult management" (Chudacoff, 2007, p. 98). Many young children incorporate plots and characters that originated on television into their play, including dramas that indicate sexual awareness by age 6 (Kalliala, 2006). Not long ago, such early knowledge of sex was a sign of abuse; now it may simply mean too much television.

Before the electronic age, young children played outside with other children, often of both sexes and several ages. The youngest children learned from the older ones. The development of social play from ages 1 to 6 was described by American sociologist Mildred Parten (1932). She distinguished five kinds of play, each more interactive than the previous one:

1. *Solitary play:* A child plays alone, unaware of any other children playing nearby.
2. *Onlooker play:* A child watches other children play.
3. *Parallel play:* Children play with similar toys in similar ways, but not together.
4. *Associative play:* Children interact, observing one another and sharing material, but their play is not yet mutual and reciprocal.
5. *Cooperative play:* Children play together, creating dramas or taking turns.

As already mentioned, play is affected by culture and context, and these have changed since Parten's day. Many Asian parents teach 3-year-olds to take turns, share, and otherwise cooperate—and they do. On the other hand, many North American children, at age 6 and older, still engage in parallel play. Given all the social and economic changes over the past century, this may be developmentally appropriate (Xu, 2010).

Active Play

Children need physical activity to develop muscle strength and control. Peers provide an audience, role models, and sometimes competition. For instance, running skills develop best when children chase or race each other, not when a child runs alone. Gross motor play is favored among young children, who enjoy climbing, kicking, and tumbling (Case-Smith & Kuhaneck, 2008).

Active social play—not solitary play—correlates with peer acceptance and a healthy self-concept (Nelson et al., 2008) and may help regulate emotions (Sutton-Smith, 2011)—something adults might remember when they prefer young children to be quiet. Among nonhuman primates, deprivation of social play warps later life, rendering some monkeys unable to mate, to make friends, even to survive with other monkeys (Herman et al., 2011; Suomi, 2004).

Rough-and-Tumble Play

rough-and-tumble play Play that mimics aggression through wrestling, chasing, or hitting, but in which there is no intent to harm.

The most common form of active play is called **rough-and-tumble** because it looks quite rough and because the children seem to tumble over one another. The term was coined by British scientists who studied primates in East Africa (Blurton-Jones, 1976). They noticed that monkeys often chased, attacked, rolled over in the dirt, and wrestled quite roughly, but without hurting one another. If a young monkey wanted to play, all it had to do was come close, catch the eye of a peer, and then run a few feet, looking back. This invitation was almost always accepted, with the other monkey responding with a *play face* rather than an angry one. Puppies, kittens, and young chimpanzees similarly invite rough-and-tumble play.

When the scientists returned to their own children, they saw that human youngsters, like baby monkeys, also enjoy rough-and-tumble play (Pellegrini & Smith, 2005). They chase, wrestle, and grab each other, developing games like tag and cops-and-robbers, with play faces, lots of chasing, and various conventions, expressions, and gestures that children use to signify "just pretend."

Rough-and-tumble play appears everywhere (although cops-and-robbers can be robots-and-humans or many other iterations), particularly among young males (human and otherwise) when they are allowed to play freely with ample space and minimal supervision (Berenbaum et al., 2008; Hassett et al., 2008). Many scientists think that rough-and-tumble play helps the prefrontal cortex to develop, as children learn to regulate emotions, practice social skills, and strengthen their bodies (Pellegrini et al., 2007; Pellis & Pellis, 2011). Indeed, some believe that play in childhood, especially rough-and-tumble play between boys and their fathers, not only teaches regulation of aggression but may also prevent antisocial behavior (even murder) later on (Wenner, 2009).

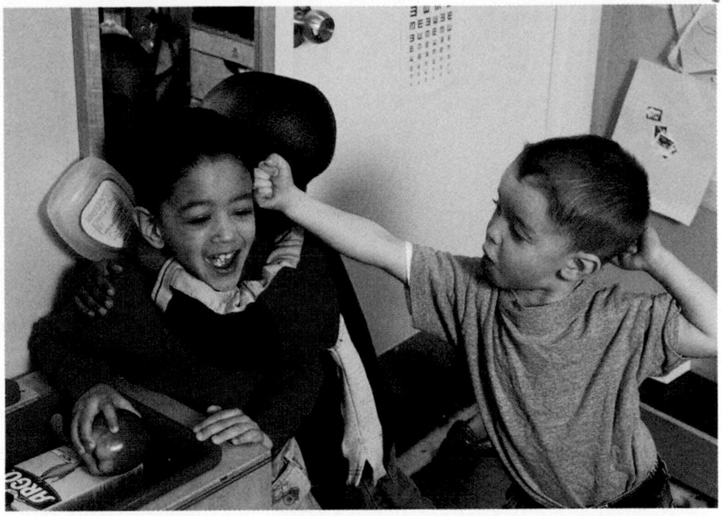

LAURA DWIGHT

Male Bonding Sometimes the only way to distinguish aggression from rough-and-tumble play is to look at the faces. The hitter is not scowling, the hittee is laughing, and the hugger is just joining in the fun. Another clue that this is rough-and-tumble play comes from gender and context. These boys are in a Head Start program, where they are learning social skills, such as how to avoid fighting.

sociodramatic play Pretend play in which children act out various roles and themes in stories that they create.

Drama and Pretending

Another major type of active play is **sociodramatic play,** in which children act out various roles and plots, taking on "any identity, role, or activity that they choose. They can be mothers, babies, Cinderella, or Captain Hook. They can make tea or fly to the moon. Or they can fight, hurt others, or kill or imprison someone" (Dunn & Hughes, 2001, p. 491).

Sociodramatic play allows children to do the following:

- Explore and rehearse social roles
- Learn how to explain their ideas and convince playmates to agree
- Practice emotional regulation by pretending to be afraid, angry, brave, and so on
- Develop self-concept in a nonthreatening context

Sociodramatic play builds on pretending and social interest, both of which emerge in toddlerhood. But preschool children do more than pretend; they combine their own imagination with that of others, advancing in theory of mind (see Chapter 9) as they do so (Kavanaugh, 2011). The beginnings of sociodramatic play are illustrated by this pair, a 3-year-old girl and a 2-year-old boy. The girl wanted to act out the role of a baby, and she persuaded the boy to play a parent.

Boy: Not good. You bad.
Girl: Why?
Boy: 'Cause you spill your milk.
Girl: No. 'Cause I bit somebody.
Boy: Yes, you did.
Girl: Say, "Go to sleep. Put your head down."
Boy: Put your head down.
Girl: No.
Boy: Yes.
Girl: No.
Boy: Yes. Okay, I will spank you. Bad boy. *[Spanks her, not hard]*
Girl: No. My head is up. *[Giggles]* I want my teddy bear.
Boy: No. Your teddy bear go away.
[At this point she asked if he was really going to take the teddy bear away.]

[from Garvey, reported in Cohen, 2006, p. 72]

Note that the girl not only directed the play but also played her part, sometimes accepting what the boy said and sometimes not. The boy took direction yet also made up his own dialogue and actions ("Bad boy").

Compare their simple plot to the play of four boys, about age 5, in a day-care center in Finland. Joni plays the role of the evil one who menaces the other boys; Tuomas directs the drama and acts in it as well.

> **Tuomas:** And now he *[Joni]* would take me and would hang me. . . . This would be the end of all of me.
> **Joni:** Hands behind.
> **Tuomas:** I can't help it. I have to. *[The two other boys follow his example.]*
> **Joni:** I would put fire all around them.
> *[All three brave boys lie on the floor with hands tied behind their backs. Joni piles mattresses on them, and pretends to light a fire, which crackles closer and closer.]*
> **Tuomas:** Everything is lost.
> *[One boy starts to laugh.]*
> **Petterl:** Better not to laugh, soon we will all be dead. . . . I am saying my last words.
> **Tuomas:** Now you can say your last wish. . . . And now I say I wish we can be terribly strong.
> *[At that point, the three boys suddenly gain extraordinary strength, pushing off the mattresses and extinguishing the fire. Good triumphs over evil, but not until the last moment, because, as one boy explains, "Otherwise this playing is not exciting at all."]*
>
> *[adapted from Kalliala, 2006, p. 83]*

Good versus evil is a favorite theme of boys' sociodramatic play. In contrast, girls often act out domestic scenes. Such gender differences are found in many cultures. In the same day-care center where Joni piles mattresses on his playmates, the girls say their play is "more beautiful and peaceful . . . [but] boys play all kinds of violent games" (Kalliala, 2006, p. 110). Although gender differences in sociodramatic play are found universally, prevalence varies. Some cultures find it frivolous and discourage it: In those places, sociodramatic play still occurs, but less often. Other cultures encourage it; parents teach toddlers to be pretend lions, or space creatures, or ladies drinking tea, and then children develop more elaborate and extensive play with each other (Kavanaugh, 2011).

MIKE GOLDWATER / ALAMY

A Toy Machine Gun These boys in Liberia are doing what young children everywhere do—following adult example. Whenever countries are at war, children play soldiers, rebels, heroes, or spies. From their perspective, there is only one problem with such play—no one wants to be the enemy.

SUMMING UP

Playing with other children is a boon for children's emotional regulation, as they learn how to get along with one another. Although play is universal, the particular form it takes varies not only by age but also by gender and culture. Many forms of play, including rough-and-tumble and sociodramatic, require social understanding and compromise. Younger children chase each other and act out simple dramas; older children have more nuanced and elaborate rules and scripts.

>> Challenges for Adults

We have seen that young children's emotions and actions are affected by many factors, including brain maturation, culture, and peers. Now we focus on another primary influence on young children: their parents and teachers.

Caregiving Styles

Although thousands of researchers have traced the effects of parenting on child development, the work of one person, 40 years ago, continues to be influential. Teachers can also be categorized in the styles identified here (Ertesvåg, 2011). In her original research, Diana Baumrind (1967, 1971) studied 100 preschool children, all from California, almost all middle-class European Americans. (The cohort and cultural limitations of this sample were not obvious at the time.)

Baumrind found that parents differed on four important dimensions:

1. *Expressions of warmth.* Some parents are warm and affectionate; others, cold and critical.
2. *Strategies for discipline.* Parents vary in whether and how they explain, criticize, persuade, ignore, and punish.
3. *Communication.* Some parents listen patiently; others demand silence.
4. *Expectations for maturity.* Parents vary in the degree of responsibility and self-control they expect from their children.

Baumrind's Three Styles of Caregiving

On the basis of the dimensions listed above, Baumrind identified three parenting styles (summarized in Table 10.1).

- **Authoritarian parenting.** The authoritarian parent's word is law, not to be questioned. Misconduct brings strict punishment, usually physical (but not so harsh as to be abusive). Authoritarian parents set down clear rules and hold high standards. They do not expect children to offer opinions; discussion about emotions is especially rare. (One adult from such a family said that "How do you feel?" had only two possible answers: "Fine" and "Tired.") Authoritarian parents love their children, but they seem cold, rarely showing affection.
- **Permissive parenting.** Permissive parents (also called *indulgent*) make few demands, hiding any impatience they feel. Discipline is lax, partly because permissive parents have low expectations for maturity. Instead, permissive parents are nurturing and accepting, listening to whatever their offspring say. They try to be helpful, but they do not feel responsible for shaping their children.
- **Authoritative parenting.** Authoritative parents set limits and enforce rules, yet they also listen to their children. They encourage maturity, but they usually forgive (not punish) if the child falls short. They consider themselves

authoritarian parenting An approach to child rearing that is characterized by high behavioral standards, strict punishment of misconduct, and little communication.

permissive parenting An approach to child rearing that is characterized by high nurturance and communication but little discipline, guidance, or control. (Also called *indulgent parenting.*)

authoritative parenting An approach to child rearing in which the parents set limits but listen to the child and are flexible.

guides, not authorities (unlike authoritarian parents) and not friends (unlike permissive parents).

neglectful/uninvolved parenting An approach to child rearing in which the parents are indifferent toward their children and unaware of what is going on in their children's lives.

A fourth style, called **neglectful/uninvolved parenting,** is sometimes mistaken for the permissive style but is actually quite different (Steinberg, 2001). The similarity is that neither permissive nor neglectful parents use physical punishment; the difference is that neglectful parents are strikingly unaware of what their children are doing—they seem not to care. By contrast, permissive parents are very involved in their children's lives: defending them from criticism, arranging play dates, and sacrificing to buy them coveted toys.

Especially for Political Scientists Many observers contend that children learn their political attitudes at home, from the way their parents treat them. Is this true? (see response, page 302)

The following long-term effects of parenting styles have been reported, not only in the United States but in many other nations as well (Baumrind, 2005, Baumrind et al., 2011; Chan & Koo, 2010; Huver et al., 2010; Rothrauff et al., 2009; Steinberg et al., 1994):

- *Authoritarian* parents raise children who are likely to become conscientious, obedient, and quiet but not especially happy. Such children tend to feel guilty or depressed, internalizing their frustrations and blaming themselves when things don't go well. As adolescents, they sometimes rebel, leaving home before age 20.
- *Permissive* parents raise unhappy children who lack self-control, especially in the give-and-take of peer relationships. Inadequate emotional regulation makes them immature and impedes friendships, which is the main reason for their unhappiness. They tend to continue to live at home, still dependent, in early adulthood. Eventually, in middle and late adulthood, they fare quite well.
- *Authoritative* parents raise children who are successful, articulate, happy with themselves, and generous with others. These children are usually liked by teachers and peers, especially in the United States and other societies in which individual initiative is valued.
- *Uninvolved* parents raise children who are immature, sad, lonely, and at risk of abuse. All children need parents who care about them because, no matter what their practices regarding punishment and expectations, "parental involvement plays an important role in the development of both social and cognitive competence" (Parke & Buriel, 2006, p. 437).

Problems with Baumrind's Styles

Baumrind's classification of caregiving styles is often criticized as too simplistic. Among the problems of her original research are the following:

- Her participants had little diversity of socioeconomic status (SES), ethnicity, or culture.
- She focused more on adult attitudes than on behavior.
- She overlooked how children affect adult behavior.
- She did not realize that some authoritarian parents are very affectionate.
- She did not realize that some permissive parents provide extensive verbal guidance (Bornstein, 2006; Lamb & Lewis, 2005; Parke & Buriel, 2006).

We now know that children's temperament and the culture's standards powerfully affect their caregivers as well as the consequences of one style or another (Cipriano & Stifter, 2010). This is as it should be. Fearful or impulsive children require particular styles (reassurance for the fearful ones and restraint for the impulsive ones). Every child needs guidance and protection, but not too much—overprotection seems to be both a cause and a consequence of childhood anxiety (McShane & Hastings, 2009).

TABLE 10.1 Characteristics of Parenting Styles Identified by Baumrind					
				Communication	
Style	Warmth	Discipline	Expectations of Maturity	Parent to Child	Child to Parent
Authoritarian	Low	Strict, often physical	High	High	Low
Permissive	High	Rare	Low	Low	High
Authoritative	High	Moderate, with much discussion	Moderate	High	High

Much depends on the particular characteristics of the child. A study of parenting at age 2 and children's competence in kindergarten (including emotional regulation and peer friendships) found "multiple developmental pathways," with the best outcomes dependent on both the child and the adult (Blandon et al., 2011). Studies such as this one suggest that advice from a textbook, or from a professional who does not know the child, may be off base: Observation of the particular interaction is needed to see how well the adult provides enough guidance without overcontrol.

Cultural Variations

The significance of the context is particularly obvious when children of various ethnic groups are compared. North American parents of Chinese, Caribbean, or African heritage are often stricter than those of European backgrounds, yet their children may develop better than if the parents were more easygoing (Chao, 2001; Parke & Buriel, 2006). Latino parents are sometimes thought to be too intrusive, other times too permissive—but their children seem to be happier than the children of North American parents who behave the same way (García & Gracia, 2009; Ispa et al., 2004). Sometimes minority and non-Western parents are categorized as authoritarian because of their punishment styles, but that label may be misapplied since many are also warm and affectionate.

In a detailed study of 1,477 instances in which Mexican American mothers of 4-year-olds tried to get their children to do something they were not doing, most of the time the mothers simply uttered a command and the children complied (Livas-Dlott et al., 2010). This simple strategy, with the mother asserting authority and the children obeying without question, might be considered authoritarian. However, almost never did the mothers use physical punishment or even harsh threats, even when the children did not immediately do as they were told—which happened 14 percent of the time. For example,

> Hailey decided to look for another doll and started digging through her toys, throwing them behind her as she dug. Maricruz [the mother]told Hailey she should not throw her toys. Hailey continued to throw toys, and Maricruz said her name to remind her to stop. Hailey continued her misbehavior, and her mother repeated "Hailey" once more. When Hailey continued, Maricruz raised her voice but calmly directed, "Hailey, look at me." Hailey continued but then looked at Maricruz as she explained, "You don't throw toys; you could hurt someone." Finally, Hailey complied and stopped.
>
> *[Livas-Dlott et al., 2010, p. 572]*

Note that the mother's first three efforts failed, and then there was a look accompanied by a calmly expressed but inaccurate explanation (in that setting, no

"He's just doing that to get attention."

one could be hurt). The researchers explain that these Mexican American families do not fit any of Baumrind's categories; respect for adult authority is rarely accompanied by a hostile mother–child relationship. Instead, the relationship shows evident *cariono* (caring) (Livas-Dlott et al., 2010).

In general, multicultural and international research has found that particular discipline methods and family rules are less important than warmth, support, and concern. Children from every ethnic group and every country benefit if they believe that they are appreciated; children everywhere suffer if they feel rejected and unwanted (Khaleque & Rohner, 2002; Maccoby, 2000).

Socioeconomic factors may be crucial. Authoritarian practices increase as income falls, perhaps because low-income families tend to be larger and thus cannot individualize their attention as authoritative families might, or perhaps because the adults want to raise obedient children who will not challenge police or employers later on. Every culture has ethnotheories about child rearing that relate to adult expectations within that society and that may differ from those of the culture of the original families Baumrind studied, as she herself acknowledges (Baumrind, 2005).

Given a multicultural perspective, developmentalists hesitate to recommend any particular parenting style (Dishion & Bullock, 2002; J. G. Miller, 2004). That does not mean that all families function equally well—far from it. Signs of trouble, including overcontrol, undercontrol, and inability to play with others, appear in children's behavior. Adults who are ineffective or uninvolved are one cause of these problems, but not the only one.

What About the Teachers?

Cohort patterns alert us to an obvious change. When Baumrind did her original research, most young children were cared for, almost exclusively, by their parents. Now most children in the United States and in many other nations have non-parental caregivers as well, who can be authoritative, authoritarian, permissive, or neglectful. Although some babysitters fall under the last two of these four styles, almost never is a preschool teacher permissive or neglectful because allowing a group of children to do whatever they want results in chaos, conflict, and perhaps even danger. Young children are not sufficiently adept at emotional regulation that they can play together, unsupervised, for long.

However, teachers can be authoritarian, setting down the law with no exceptions, or authoritative, setting guidelines that can change with discussion. Teachers with more education tend to be more authoritative, responding to each child, listening and encouraging language, and so on. This fosters more capable children, which is one reason colleges are encouraged to offer degrees for students who want to teach young children and one reason teacher education is one of the criteria used to measure program excellence (Barnett et al., 2010; Norris, 2010).

In general, young children learn more from authoritative teachers because the teachers are perceived as warmer and more loving. In fact, one study found that, compared with children who had authoritarian teachers, those children whose teachers were child-centered, noncontrolling, and very supportive scored higher on school-readiness measures (Barbarin et al., 2010). This is another example illustrating how preschool teachers who attend to the emotional climate of the classroom

>> Response for Political Scientists (from page 300) There are many parenting styles, and it is difficult to determine each one's impact on children's personalities. At this point, attempts to connect early child rearing with later political outlook are speculative.

are more successful at teaching academic skills. In this study, children learned the most if all their caregivers were authoritative, but if their parents were authoritarian and their teachers authoritative (a mismatch more likely for the African American children), that was better than having authoritarian teachers.

This result was unexpected, since usually a mismatch creates stress. Why didn't it in this case? Perhaps young children, with their preoperational focus on appearance instead of logic, feel personally rejected (recall egocentrism) if their teacher harshly punishes them—especially if the teacher is of another ethnic group. In this study, the African American children with authoritarian parents may have recognized their parents' affection within an authoritarian style, but they did not see warmth in their strict teachers.

"Why don't you get off the computer and watch some TV?"

The New Media

New challenges confront each generation. One of today's great challenges is the influence of electronic media on children. All media—television, the Internet, electronic games, and so on—can be harmful, especially when the content is violent (Anderson et al., 2007, 2008; Bailey et al., 2010; Gentile et al., 2007; Smyth, 2007).

However, most young children in the United States spend more than three hours each day using one electronic medium or another. Almost every North American family owns at least two televisions, and most preschoolers watch apart from their parents, often in their own rooms. Many children in child-care programs watch videos, play games on computers, and so on.

Electronic media are not always harmful, a topic discussed further in later chapters. During early childhood, some children may learn basic literacy from educational programs, especially if adults watch with them and reinforce the lessons. However, children rarely select educational programs over fast-paced cartoons, in which everyone hits, shoots, and kicks. Unfortunately, although many parents, teachers, and politicians are rightly concerned about children's eating and health habits, they seem oblivious to children's media diet. As a result, even health suffers: For example, in one study, one-third of the 5-year-olds were too heavy for their age and height, and hours spent watching television correlated with overweight (Kimbro et al., 2011).

Hoping Are electronic devices destructive in early childhood? Not if the girl's family are just moving into their new home, soon to turn this unfurnished room into a living or dining area and setting up the TV in the basement. And not if the boys intend to take turns playing the video game—both of which are unlikely.

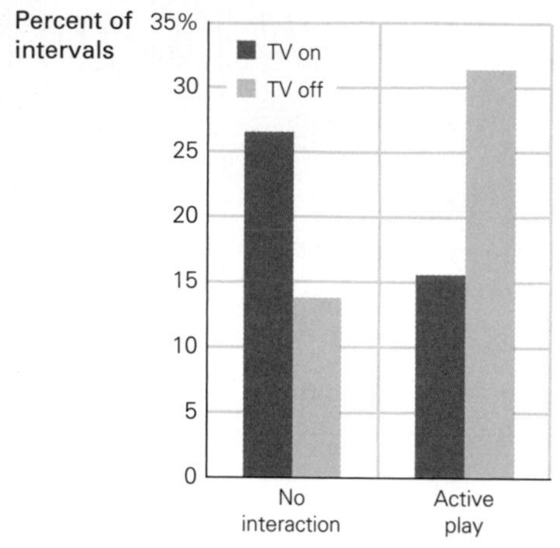

FIGURE 10.1

Don't Bother Me For dyads of 2-year-olds and their parents, having a TV on in the background reduced play by half. The effect was not as dramatic (although still evident) for 1-year-olds. Have 2-year-olds learned to be quiet when the television is on?

Research Design

Scientists: Heather L. Kirkorian, Tiffany A. Pempek, Lauren A. Murphy, Marie E. Schmidt, and Daniel R. Anderson, all at the University of Massachusetts.

Publication: *Child Development* (2009).

Participants: Fifty-one parents and their 1- to 3-year olds, mostly middle-class European Americans.

Design: Children and parents were videotaped in a well-equipped playroom for an hour, with a television in the corner showing an adult program (chosen by the parent) for half of the time. Magazines were also available for the adults to read. Parents were asked to relax, interacting with their child as they would at home. Observations of interaction were noted every 10 seconds (360 segments per parent–child dyad) and tallied for language and parental involvement by coders blind to the hypothesis of the study.

Major conclusion: Most (not all) parents interacted and spoke less when the television was on. This was true for adults of both sexes (two fathers were included), all ethnicities, and with children of all ages, especially the 2-year-olds, as shown in Figure 10.1.

Comments: This study has many strengths: detailed observation (every 10 seconds) by "blind" coders, each dyad exposed to both conditions (thus controlling for individual differences in interaction patterns), and inclusion of very young children (most earlier research assumed 1-year-olds were not affected by television). However, only 51 parent–child dyads were studied, all from one region of the United States and almost all middle class, even though background television is more prevalent in low-income families. Furthermore, the researchers were all from one university. Do any of these factors limit this study?

Good choices are particularly hard for adults to enforce because people of all ages are currently more engaged with electronic media (television, texting, e-mail, social networking) than with direct interaction. Young children learn from that example. Even when they are too young to understand television dialogue and television is merely background noise, children play less and interaction is markedly reduced when the TV is on (Kirkorian et al., 2009; Schmidt et al., 2008). Yet language development depends on conversation that is individualized to each child, and emotional regulation depends on personal guidance. (See the Research Design.)

Thus, the problem is not only that violent media teach destructive behavior but also that all media take time from constructive interactions. According to the *displacement hypothesis,* whatever time children devote to electronic media reduces time spent in social and educational activities—a hypothesis proven in school-age children and likely true in younger children as well (Weis & Cerankosky, 2010).

SUMMING UP

Over the past 40 years, Diana Baumrind and most other developmentalists have found that authoritative caregiving (warm, with guidance) is more effective than either authoritarian (very strict) or permissive (very lenient) styles. Other researchers have found that uninvolved caregivers are the least effective of all. In any culture, children thrive when their caregivers appreciate them and care about their accomplishments. The children of parents who are uninvolved, uncaring, or abusive seldom become happy, well-adjusted, and high-achieving adults.

Good caregiving is not achieved by following any one simple rule; children's temperaments vary, and so do cultural patterns. Teachers of young children are most effective when they are warm and responsive. For all adults, the media pose a particular challenge worldwide because children are attracted to colorful, fast-paced images; but violent TV programs in particular lead to more aggressive behavior. Educational television and computer games may be instructive, but all media reduce direct, one-on-one interaction, which is particularly needed when children are young. ■

>> Moral Development

Children develop increasingly complex moral values, judgments, and behaviors as they mature. The social bonds described in Chapter 7, the theory of mind described in Chapter 9, and the emotional development and social awareness described in this chapter are the foundation for morality. Piaget thought that moral development began when children learned games with rules, which he connected with concrete operational thought at about age 7 (Piaget, 1932/1997). We now know that Piaget underestimated young children: Games with rules and moral development are both evident during early childhood. Indeed, some researchers see moral judgment beginning in infancy (Narvaez & Lapsley, 2009).

Many developmentalists believe that children's attachment to their parents, and then to others, is the beginning of morality. According to evolutionary theory, humans protect, cooperate, and even sacrifice for one another precisely because social groups evolved to encourage such prosocial behavior (Krebs, 2008). With maturity and adult guidance, children develop guilt (as Erikson explained) and self-control, and that helps them behave in ethical ways (Kochanska et al., 2009; Konner, 2010).

Nature and Nurture

Debate rages over how children internalize standards, develop virtues, and avoid vices. Conflicting perspectives are taken by theories and scholars of psychology, philosophy, theology, and sociology. This conflict reflects the primal debate in developmental study—nature versus nurture:

- The "nature" perspective suggests that morality is genetic, an outgrowth of natural bonding, attachment, and cognitive maturation. That would explain why young children help and defend their parents, no matter what the parents do, and punish other children who violate moral rules.
- The "nurture" perspective contends that culture is crucial, as children learn the values of their community. Some children believe that people who eat raw fish, or hamburgers, or bacon, or crickets are immoral.

Both nature and nurture are always important, but developmentalists disagree about which is more important for morality (Killen & Smetana, 2007; Krebs, 2008; Narvaez & Lapsley, 2009; Turiel, 2006). That debate cannot be settled here, but it does seem that parents and teachers are crucial. Our discussion centers on two moral issues that arise from age 2 to age 6: First, prosocial and antisocial behavior (especially aggression), and second, the moral lessons inherent in discipline.

Empathy and Antipathy

Two moral emotions are evident as children play with one another. With increasing social experiences and decreasing egocentrism, they develop **empathy,** an understanding of other people's feelings and concerns, and **antipathy,** dislike or even hatred.

empathy The ability to understand the emotions and concerns of another person, especially when they differ from one's own.

antipathy Feelings of dislike or even hatred for another person.

Empathy is not the same as sympathy, which means feeling sorry *for* someone. Rather, empathy means feeling sorry *with* someone, experiencing the other person's pain or sadness as if it were one's own. This recalls the research with mirror neurons (see Chapter 1), which suggests that observing someone else's behavior activates the same areas in the brain of the observer as in the person performing the action. Scientists studying young humans and other primates report spontaneous efforts to help others who are hurt, crying, or in need of help: That is evidence of empathy (Warneken & Tomasello, 2009).

prosocial behavior Actions that are helpful and kind but are of no obvious benefit to oneself.

Empathy leads to **prosocial behavior,** extending helpfulness and kindness without any obvious benefit to oneself. Prosocial behavior seems to be more a result of empathy than cognition, more emotional understanding than theory of mind (Eggum et al., 2011). Expressing concern, offering to share food or a toy, and including a shy child in a game or conversation are examples of prosocial behavior among young children. Jack, age 3, showed empathy when he

> refused to bring snacks with peanuts to school because another boy had to sit alone during snack because he was allergic to nuts. Jack wanted to sit with him.
>
> *[Lovecky, 2009, p. 161]*

antisocial behavior Actions that are deliberately hurtful or destructive to another person.

Antipathy can lead to **antisocial behavior,** deliberate hurtfulness or destructiveness aimed at another person, including people who have not actually harmed the antisocial person. Antisocial actions include verbal insults, social exclusion, and physical assaults (Calkins & Keane, 2009). An antisocial 4-year-old might look another child in the eye, scowl, and then kick him hard without provocation.

Toddlers may hit, grab, pull hair, and so on, seemingly unaware that they are hurting someone. By age 4 or 5—as a result of brain maturation, theory of mind, emotional regulation, and interactions with caregivers—children can be deliberately prosocial or antisocial. When children are antisocial, adults sometimes assume that the other child's tears will make the mean child feel guilty. This is not necessarily true: Brain scans show that adults who want to punish others do so with pleasure, even if it means some loss (of money, time, or effort) to themselves (Takahashi et al., 2009). Children need to *learn* to control their aggression; most do, but this is not inevitable.

Emotional regulation, moral development, and the emergence of empathy are nowhere more apparent than in the way children learn to deal with their aggressive impulses. The gradual control of aggression is evident on close observation of rough-and-tumble play; in the fantasies of domination and submission acted out in sociodramatic play; in the increase in self-control from ages 2 to 6; and in the sharing of art supplies, construction materials, and toys (Peterson & Flanders, 2005; Utendale & Hastings, 2011).

Not surprisingly, given the moral sensibilities of young children, 5-year-olds already judge whether another child's aggression is justified or not (Etchu, 2007). As with adults, self-defense is more readily forgiven than is a deliberate, unprovoked attack. However, do not assume that bullies realize when they are wrong: At every age, aggressors feel they had a reason to do what they did.

instrumental aggression Behavior that hurts someone else because the aggressor wants to get or keep a possession or a privilege.

Researchers recognize four general types of aggression. **Instrumental aggression** is common among 2-year-olds, who often want something they do not have and who try, without thinking, to get it. The reaction of another child—crying and resisting the grab of the instrumentally aggressive child—is also more typical at age 2 than earlier or later.

reactive aggression An impulsive retaliation for another person's intentional or accidental action, verbal or physical.

Reactive aggression is common among young children as well; almost every child responds in some way when attacked by another child, with the specific response becoming better controlled as emotional regulation increases. In fact, children are less likely to react with physical aggression as they develop emotional control and theory of mind (Olson et al., 2011).

relational aggression Nonphysical acts, such as insults or social rejection, aimed at harming the social connection between the victim and other people.

Relational aggression (usually verbal) destroys another child's self-esteem and disrupts the victim's social networks, becoming more hurtful as children mature. A young child might tell another, "You can't be my friend" or "You are fat," hurting another's feelings. That is relational aggression.

The fourth and most ominous type is **bullying aggression,** done to dominate someone else. It is not rare among young children but should be stopped before school age, when it becomes particularly destructive for both victims and bullies (see Chapter 13). All forms of aggression should become less common over the years of early childhood, as the brain matures and empathy increases. Parents, peers, and preschool teachers are all pivotal mentors in this process.

bullying aggression Unprovoked, repeated physical or verbal attack, especially on victims who are unlikely to defend themselves.

Discipline

A particular issue for many developmentalists is discipline, administered when children violate a norm of their family and culture. Adult values and experiences affect when and how they discipline. Of course, values depend partly on culture. Discipline does as well.

Ideally, adults anticipate misbehavior and guide children toward patterns of behavior and internalized standards of morality, taking developmental immaturity into account, as shown in Table 10.2. However, misbehavior cannot always be prevented. In case any reader imagines that children can be cajoled to always be good, consider the results of a study of mothers and 3-year-olds during late afternoon (a stressful time). Conflicts (including verbal disagreements) arose about every two minutes (Laible et al., 2008). Here is one example:

Child: I want my other shoes.
Mother: You don't need your other shoes. You wear your Pooh sandals when we go for a walk.
Child: Noooooo.
Mother: *[Child's name]*! You don't need your other shoes.
Child: *[Cries loudly]*
Mother: No, you don't need your other shoes. You wear your Pooh sandals when we go for a walk.
Child: Ahhhh. Want pretty dress. *[Crying]*
Mother: Your pretty dress.
Child: Yeah.
Mother: You can wear them some other day.
Child: Noooooo. *[Crying]*

[quoted in Laible et al., 2008, pp. 442–443]

In this study of 64 young children and their mothers, securely attached children had as many conflicts as insecurely attached ones. However, unlike in the dialogue above, the mothers of the securely attached children were more likely to compromise and explain (Laible et al., 2008). Was that the best response? Consider the alternatives.

TABLE 10.2 Discipline and Children's Thinking

1. *Remember theory of mind.* Young children gradually come to understand things from other viewpoints. Encouraging empathy ("How would you feel if someone did that to you?") increases prosocial behavior and decreases antisocial behavior by age 5.
2. *Remember egocentrism.* Young children are developing a sense of who they are. Adults might protect that emerging self by, for example, not insisting on sharing.
3. *Remember fast-mapping.* Young children are eager to talk and think, but they say more than they understand. A child who "doesn't listen" may have not understood.
4. *Remember that young children are not logical.* Before age 5, children confuse lies and wishes, and forget why they are punished.

Many developmentalists study how children's thinking affects behavior. Here are four reminders from Chapter 9 that apply to disciplining young children. Often children believe their parents' anger, not their own misdeeds, cause punishment.

Physical Punishment

In the United States, young children are slapped, spanked, or beaten more often than are infants or older children. Many adults remember receiving such punishment and think it works. Physical punishment (called *corporal punishment* because it hurts the body) succeeds at the moment—spanking stops misbehavior—but longitudinal research finds that children who are physically punished are more likely to become bullies, delinquents, and then abusive adults, as well as slower to learn in school (Straus & Paschall, 2009).

In some nations (New Zealand is the most recent example), corporal punishment is illegal; in other nations, it is the norm. In the United States, it is illegal

URBAN ZONE / ALAMY

Smack Will the doll learn never to disobey her mother again?

(although sometimes used anyway) in most schools, especially schools for young children. Although adults might believe that physical punishment will "teach a lesson" of obedience, the lesson that children often learn is that "might makes right." When they become bigger and stronger, they'll use corporal punishment on others.

Of course, children who are spanked do not always become violent adults. Some experts believe that the correlations are merely correlations—not causes. For example, teenage mothers are more likely to spank their children, who are more likely to become delinquents who fail in school, but this does not prove that spanking is causal. Spanking may increase the risk of school failure and crime, but other factors that correlate with teen parenthood (poverty, low education, and impulsive, antisocial personality) are stronger influences.

Nonetheless, many developmentalists wonder why parents would take the chance. The only argument in favor of spanking is that alternative measures are no better, either in controlling bad behavior or increasing moral values (Larzelere et al., 2010). Before reaching that conclusion yourself, however, consider the alternatives again.

Psychological Control

psychological control A disciplinary technique that involves threatening to withdraw love and support and that relies on a child's feelings of guilt and gratitude to the parents.

Another method of discipline is called **psychological control,** in which children's shame, guilt, and gratitude are used to control their behavior (Barber, 2002). Psychological control may reduce academic achievement, just as spanking does.

Consider the results of a study of an entire cohort (the best way to obtain an unbiased sample) of children born in Finland (Aunola & Nurmi, 2004). Their parents were asked 20 questions about their approach to child rearing. The following four items, which the parents rated from 1 ("Not at all like me") to 5 ("Very much like me"), measured psychological control:

1. "My child should be aware of how much I have done for him/her."
2. "I let my child see how disappointed and shamed I am if he/she misbehaves."
3. "My child should be aware of how much I sacrifice for him/her."
4. "I expect my child to be grateful and appreciate all the advantages he/she has."

The higher the parents scored on these four measures of psychological control, the lower the children's math scores—and this connection grew stronger over time. Surprisingly, math achievement suffered most if parents were also high in affection (e.g., they frequently hugged their children), perhaps because that increased the child's guilt when the parent was disappointed (Aunola & Nurmi, 2004).

Other research finds that psychological control can depress children's achievement, creativity, and social acceptance (Soenens & Vansteenkiste, 2010). Compared to corporal punishment, children punished with psychological control seem less likely to be physical bullies but more likely to be relationally aggressive (Kuppens et al., 2009), depressed, and anxious (Gershoff et al., 2010).

Exclusion and Conversation

time-out A disciplinary technique in which a child is separated from other people for a specified time.

The disciplinary technique most often used in North America is the **time-out,** whereby an adult requires the misbehaving child to sit quietly, without toys or playmates, for a short time (Barkin et al., 2007). Time-out is favored by many experts in North American education. For example, in the large, longitudinal evaluation of Head Start highlighted in Chapter 9, an increase in use of time-out and a decrease in use of spanking were considered signs of improved parental discipline (U.S. Department of Health and Human Services, 2010).

However, research on the effectiveness of time-out is confounded by the many ways it is used. Some parents angrily put the child in a corner, yelling at him or her to stay there until the parent is no longer angry. The effect is similar to corporal punishment: The child feels rejected. To be effective, time-out must be brief; one minute for each year of the child's age is suggested.

Another alternative to physical punishment and psychological control is *induction,* in which the parents talk extensively with the offending child, getting the child to understand why his or her behavior was wrong. Conversation helps children internalize standards, but induction takes time and patience. Since 3-year-olds confuse causes with consequences, they cannot answer an angry "Why did you do that?" or appreciate a lengthy explanation. Simple induction ("You made him sad") may be more appropriate.

Induction may be best used before the child has seriously offended. In a study of parents and older siblings responding to a young child violating various norms and risking danger, the parents were more likely to talk to the child and encourage alternate behavior, while the siblings waited until the child was clearly offending and then yelled "time-out."

In general, induction is recommended if the goal is an internalized standard of right and wrong (Turiel, 2006). An interesting example comes from Japan, where physical punishment is rare and a close and protective mother–child bond is the norm: The rate of homicide is one-tenth that of the United States and one-one-hundredth that of Jamaica. Some developmentalists think inductive discipline is the reason (Guerra et al., 2011), although, again, there are dozens of explanations for this correlation.

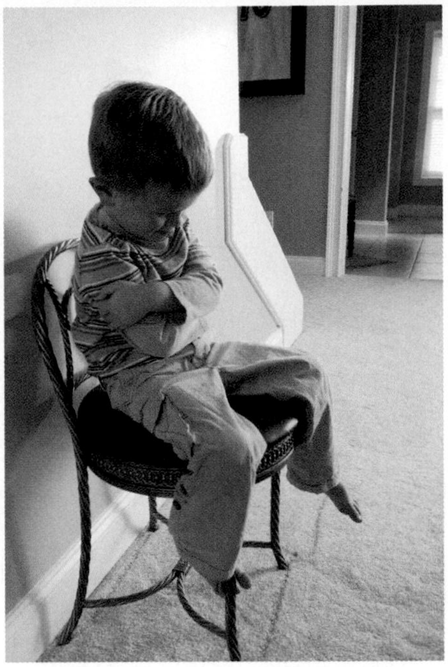

SW PRODUCTIONS / AGE FOTOSTOCK

Bad Boy or Bad Parent? For some children and cultures, sitting alone is an effective form of punishment; for others, it produces an angry child.

No Simple Answer

Methods of discipline vary in consequences and effectiveness, depending on temperament, culture, and the adult–child relationship. For example, time-out is effective *if* the child prefers to be with other people and *if* it is delivered without anger. As explained in Chapter 2, one version of time-out for older children is suspension from school. However, if a child hates school, suspension amounts to reinforcement, not punishment.

In every nation and family, adults vary in their expectations for proper behavior and in their response to transgressions. What is "rude" or "nasty" in one community is accepted, even encouraged, in another. Even family conflicts (such as between a child and an adult) are thought to require understanding and negotiation in some homes, including many in the United States, but are completely unacceptable in others.

Parents are often unaware of their ethnotheories—no wonder they do not explain them and no wonder their children disagree, disobey, and disappoint (Harkness et al., 2011). When the two parents have different childhood backgrounds or when the school culture differs from that of the home, the children are more likely to be considered disobedient and disrespectful—and indeed they are, without realizing it.

Given all this, adults might be tempted to give up and let the child alone. But remember that children need guidance in order to develop the emotional regulation and other advances

Cruel and Unusual? The PBS series *Antiques Roadshow* is popular among adults, but for a child whose sense of the finer things in life is still developing, it might be an apt punishment.

SHE USED TO HAVE 'TIME OUT' IN HER BEDROOM BUT WE FIND MAKING HER WATCH RERUNS OF THE 'ANTIQUES ROADSHOW' IS FAR MORE EFFECTIVE!
©FRAN

CARTOONSTOCK.COM

that occur during early childhood: Permissive or uninvolved caregivers have unhappy children.

All adults agree that moral development is important, and all developmentalists agree that the cognitive and emotional characteristics of young children make early childhood a critical time for teaching moral behavior. However, exactly what morals are crucial and how to achieve them is not obvious, as explained in the following. No wonder punishment is not a simple issue. One young child who was disciplined for fighting protested, "Sometimes the fight just crawls out of me." Ideally, punishment won't "just crawl out" of the adult.

A VIEW FROM SCIENCE

Culture and Punishment

Worldwide, cultural differences in child discipline are apparent. For example, only half as many Canadian parents as U.S. parents slap, pinch, or smack their children (Oldershaw, 2002). Although many U.S. school districts forbid corporal punishment in schools, the U.S. Supreme Court decided in 2004 that teachers and parents could use "reasonable force" to punish children (Bugental & Grusec, 2006). Physical punishment by anyone—parent, teacher, sibling, stranger—is illegal in many other developed nations (including Austria, Croatia, Cyprus, Denmark, Finland, Germany, Israel, Italy, Norway, New Zealand, and Sweden) because it is considered a violation of human rights (Bitensky, 2006).

Perhaps the United States has more authoritarian parents than other nations do. However, cultural differences are evident by region and income even within the United States (Giles-Sims & Lockhart, 2005). Parents in the southern states and parents in low-income families do more spanking than do parents in New England and in wealthier families.

Cultural differences may lie behind a controversy that recently arose in the United States over a recommendation by some evangelical Christians to put a drop of hot sauce (which burns) on a child's tongue as punishment for forbidden speech. This method is included in a book titled *Creative Correction* (Whelchel, 2005). Most evangelical parents as well as developmentalists consider this practice abusive. Yet opinions are strongly divided. For example, most comments (posted on Amazon.com in 2011) regarding this book were either highly favorable (90 readers rated it at 5) or highly unfavorable (66 readers rated it at 1), with only 30 in between (at 2, 3, or 4).

One woman wrote:

> Putting hot sauce on your child's tongue? I bet the author wouldn't ever dare to do that to herself & look at all the hate spewing out of her mouth. As a born-again believer & mother, I'd never follow anything in this book. It's so unchristlike that it's sickening. There's nothing "creative" about her correction ideas—it's just plain mean & a newer version of old abuse tactics that our parents used to do.

A woman who highly recommended the book wrote:

> I haven't had the need for the Tabasco trick yet, but I'm not above using it. It would make a strong impression and wouldn't require a repeat dose, I'm quite sure. Child abuse? Hardly. Giving a child free reign over the TV, internet and the house IS child abuse. Ask any elementary school teacher who her problem child is and it'll be the kid with no discipline at home. A well-behaved child grows into a well-behaved adult. This world certainly needs more of those.

Remember the study of Latino mothers and their 4-year-olds (Livas-Dlott et al., 2010)? Induction was rare and time-out was almost never used: The implicit belief was that the connection between child and mother should not be broken, even in discipline. In those Mexican American families, disobedient children needed to listen to their mothers; if they didn't comply, the child

IMAGE BAZAAR

Laughing? Pulling an ear is physical punishment—and this would be considered abuse in some cultures. Here, however, no one seems upset.

might be moved from the scene of the forbidden action or told the social reason to obey (one mother got her son to help tidy the living room by saying that she should not be the only one cleaning up). In only 3 percent of the disobedient instances did the mother lay hands on the child.

As for international comparisons, most Americans consider Japanese mothers too permissive. The Japanese almost never punish children younger than 6. Instead, they use reason, empathy, and expressions of disappointment. They might be considered permissive parents. However, although U.S. children in permissive families tend to be immature and unhappy, Japanese children raised in a permissive home usually develop well. The reason may be summed up in the word *amae,* which refers to the strong and affectionate bond that is typical of Japanese mother–child relationships (Rothbaum et al., 2000). For many Japanese children, their mother's approval is so important that no punishment is needed. Six-year-olds who, to a Western eye, might appear overly dependent on and affectionate toward their indulgent mothers seem quite normal in Japan.

The parents' underlying attitude may be crucial. One study of African American mothers found that if they disapproved of spanking but did it nonetheless, their children were likely to be depressed; however, their children were OK if spanking mothers were convinced that spanking was what they should do (McLoyd et al., 2007). Similarly, Chinese American parents who used physical punishment and shame raised children who were relatively happy and well adjusted *if* the parents used those methods because they agreed with the Chinese ideology that led to them (Fung & Lau, 2009).

Do all these observations lead to any general conclusions? Perhaps only that a multicultural understanding makes it difficult to judge which tactic is best, but that long-term as well as immediate consequences need to be considered. All children need guidance; there are many ways to provide it.

Especially for Parents Suppose you agree that spanking is destructive, but you sometimes get so angry at your child's behavior that you hit him or her. Is your reaction appropriate? (see response, page 313)

SUMMING UP

Moral development occurs throughout childhood and adolescence. During early childhood, the most powerful moral lessons—particularly the need to be appropriately prosocial, with aggression controlled—are learned. Ideally, children learn to be good friends to each other, particularly avoiding unprovoked aggression. Parents discipline their children in many ways, with each method teaching lessons about right and wrong. Induction seems most likely to lead to internalized standards of morality. ■

>> Becoming Boys and Girls

Biology determines whether a child is male or female. As you know from Chapters 3 and 4, at about 8 weeks after conception, the SRY gene on the Y chromosome directs the reproductive organs to develop externally, and then male hormones exert subtle internal control over the brain, body, and later behavior. Without that SRY gene, the fetus develops female organs, which produce other hormones, again beginning in prenatal development and affecting the brain.

However, sexual identity is more than biology, and it is during early childhood that patterns and preferences become apparent. Children become more gender conscious with every year of childhood (Ruble et al., 2006). Even 2-year-olds apply gender labels *(Mrs., Mr., lady, man)* consistently. By age 4, children are convinced that certain toys (such as dolls or trucks) are appropriate for one sex but not the other and that certain roles (not just Daddy or Mommy, but also nurse, teacher, police officer, soldier) are best for one sex or the other.

Sex and Gender

Scientists distinguish **sex differences,** which are biological differences between males and females, from **gender differences,** which are culturally prescribed roles and behaviors. In theory, this seems like a straightforward separation, but, as with every nature–nurture distinction, the interaction between sex and gender makes it hard to separate the two (Hines, 2004).

sex differences Biological differences between males and females, in organs, hormones, and body type.

gender differences Differences in the roles and behaviors of males and females that are prescribed by the culture.

PICTURE PRESS / ALAMY

DESIGN PICS / DANITADELIMONT.COM

Playing in the Sand What do you need at the beach? Depending on gender, either a man-sized shovel or a flowery raincoat. Already by age 4, girls are more likely to hold hands and boys much more likely to use construction tools.

Young children are particularly confused about gender and sex, partly because culture emphasizes gender. One little girl said she would grow a penis when she got older, and one little boy offered to buy his mother one. Ignorance about biology and sex was demonstrated by a 3-year-old who went with his father to see a neighbor's newborn kittens. Returning home, the child told his mother that there were three girl kittens and two boy kittens. "How do you know?" she asked. "Daddy picked them up and read what was written on their tummies," he replied.

In recent years, sex and gender issues have become increasingly complex as cultural acceptance of varied sexual orientations has increased—to the outrage of some and the joy of others. Adults may be lesbian, gay, bi, trans, "mostly straight," or totally heterosexual (Thompson & Morgan, 2008, p. 15). Despite the increasing acceptance of sexual diversity, at around age 5 many children become quite rigid in their ideas of sex and gender. If 5-year-old boys need new shoes, but the only ones that fit them are pink, most would rather go barefoot. In fact, by age 3 boys reject pink toys and girls prefer them (LoBue & DeLoache, 2011).

Theories of Gender-Role Development

There are many theories to explain the reasons why boys and girls, and men and women, see the sexes as they do. A dynamic-systems approach reminds us that the attitudes, the roles, and even the biology of gender differences and similarities change from one developmental period to the next; the theories about how and why this occurs change as well (Martin & Ruble, 2010).

Biologically, the differences may seem minor—a matter of only one of the 46 chromosomes. Yet that chromosome seems to affect almost everything (e.g., rough-and-tumble play, emotional regulation, parental reactions to misbehavior, to name just a few), although it determines very little, at least until puberty. For instance, the fact that boys are more likely to chase and catch each other in rough-and-tumble play does not keep millions of little girls from chasing and catching.

Nonetheless, if given many playmates to choose from, as when a child is in preschool with a dozen peers, girls usually prefer to play with the girls and boys with the boys. Despite their parents' and teachers' wishes, children of either sex might say, "No girls [or boys] allowed." Even teenagers see ethnic discrimination as more wrong than sex discrimination (Møller & Tenenbaum, 2011). How can this be explained?

Psychoanalytic Theory

Freud (1938) called the period from about ages 3 to 6 the **phallic stage** because he believed its central focus is the *phallus,* or penis. At about 3 or 4 years of age, said Freud, the process of maturation makes a boy aware of his male sexual organ. He begins to masturbate, to fear castration, and to develop sexual feelings toward his mother.

phallic stage Freud's third stage of development, when the penis becomes the focus of concern and pleasure.

These feelings make every young boy jealous of his father—so jealous, according to Freud, that every son wants to replace his dad. Freud called this the **Oedipus complex,** after Oedipus, son of a king in Greek mythology. Abandoned as an infant and raised in a distant kingdom, Oedipus later returned to his birthplace and, not realizing who they were, killed his father and married his mother. When he discovered what he had done, he blinded himself in a spasm of guilt.

Oedipus complex The unconscious desire of young boys to replace their father and win their mother's romantic love.

Freud believed that this ancient drama has been replayed in the Greek classic *Oedipus Rex* over two millennia because it dramatizes emotions that all boys feel about their parents—both love and hate. Every male feels guilty about the incestuous and murderous impulses that are buried in his unconscious. In self-defense, boys develop a powerful conscience called the **superego,** which is quick to judge and punish. That marks the beginning of morality, according to psychoanalytic theory, which contends that a young boy's fascination with superheroes, guns, kung fu, and the like arises from his unconscious impulse to kill his father. An adult man's homosexuality, homophobia, or obsession with punishment might be explained by an imperfectly resolved phallic stage. Later psychoanalytic theorists agree that morality originates from the clash between unconscious wishes and parental prohibitions in childhood (Hughes, 2007).

superego In psychoanalytic theory, the judgmental part of the personality that internalizes the moral standards of the parents.

Freud offered several descriptions of the phallic stage in girls. One centers on the **Electra complex** (also named after a figure in classical mythology). The Electra complex is similar to the Oedipus complex in that the little girl wants to eliminate the same-sex parent (her mother) and become intimate with the opposite-sex parent (her father). Girls may also develop a superego, although Freud thought it weaker than in boys.

Electra complex The unconscious desire of girls to replace their mother and win their father's romantic love.

According to psychoanalytic theory, children of both sexes cope with their guilt and fear through **identification;** that is, they try to become like the same-sex parent. Consequently, young boys copy their father's mannerisms, opinions, actions, and so on, and girls copy their mother's. Both sexes exaggerate the male or female role. Since the superego arises from the phallic stage, and since Freud believed that sexual identity and expression were crucial for mental health, his theory suggests parents should encourage boys and girls to follow appropriate sex roles, with every child accepting his or her sexual identity.

identification An attempt to defend one's self-concept by taking on the behaviors and attitudes of someone else.

Many social scientists from the mid-twentieth century onward have believed that Freud's explanation of sexual and moral development "flies in the face of sociological and historical evidence" (David et al., 2004, p. 139). In graduate school, I learned that Freud was unscientific. However, as explained in Chapter 1, developmental scientists seek to connect research, theory, and experience. My own experience has made me rethink my rejection of Freud, as the following explains.

>> Response for Parents (from page 311) No. The worst time to spank a child is when you are angry. You might seriously hurt the child, and the child will associate anger with violence. You would do better to learn to control your anger and develop other strategies for discipline and for prevention of misbehavior.

THINKING CRITICALLY

Berger and Freud

My family's first "Electra episode" occurred in a conversation with my eldest daughter, Bethany, when she was about 4 years old:

Bethany: When I grow up, I'm going to marry Daddy.
Mother: But Daddy's married to me.
Bethany: That's all right. When I grow up, you'll probably be dead.
Mother: *[Determined to stick up for myself]* Daddy's older than me, so when I'm dead, he'll probably be dead, too.
Bethany: That's OK. I'll marry him when he gets born again.

At this point, I couldn't think of a good reply. I had no idea where she had gotten the concept of reincarnation. Bethany saw my face fall, and she took pity on me:

Bethany: Don't worry, Mommy. After you get born again, you can be our baby.

The second episode was a conversation I had with Rachel when she was about 5:

Rachel: When I get married, I'm going to marry Daddy.
Mother: Daddy's already married to me.
Rachel: *[With the joy of having discovered a wonderful solution]* Then we can have a double wedding!

The third episode was considerably more graphic. It took the form of a "valentine" left on my husband's pillow by my daughter Elissa, who was about 8 years old at the time. It is reproduced here.

Finally, when my youngest daughter, Sarah, turned 5, she also expressed the desire to marry my husband. When I told her she couldn't, because he was married to me, her response revealed one more hazard of watching TV: "Oh, yes, a man can have two wives. I saw it on television."

I am not the only feminist developmentalist to be taken aback by her own children's words. Nancy Datan (1986) wrote about the Oedipal conflict: "I have a son who was once five years old. From that day to this, I have never thought Freud mistaken." As you remember from Chapter 1, however, a single example (or four daughters from another family) does not prove that Freud was correct. A behaviorist explanation would be that my daughters wanted to model themselves after me and thus naively thought that marrying my husband would do it. Cohort changes, which my two infant grandsons remind me of daily, may mean that my grandsons (no granddaughters yet) may seek someone quite unlike their mothers—or may choose to avoid marriage completely.

Or they may make me change my mind again. You have your own theories and experiences, and I still think Freud was wrong on many counts. But his description of the phallic stage seems less bizarre than I once thought.

Pillow Talk Elissa placed this artwork on my husband's pillow. My pillow, beside it, had a less colorful, less elaborate note—an afterthought. It read "Dear Mom, I love you too."

Behaviorism

In contrast to psychoanalytic theorists, behaviorists believe that virtually all roles, values, and morals are learned. To behaviorists, gender distinctions are the product of ongoing reinforcement and punishment, as well as social learning.

Some evidence supports learning theory as an explanation of gendered roles. Parents, peers, and teachers all reward behavior that is "gender appropriate" more than behavior that is "gender inappropriate" (Berenbaum et al., 2008). For example, "adults compliment a girl when she wears a dress but not when she wears pants" (Ruble et al., 2006, p. 897). According to social learning theory, children notice the ways men and women behave, and children are punished when they act inappropriately (usually not physically but with shaming words, such as "Boys don't cry" or "Be a good girl"). They internalize the standards they observe, becoming proud of themselves when they act like a "little man" or a "little lady" (Bandura & Bussey, 2004; Bussey & Bandura, 1999).

Interestingly, sex roles seem more significant for males than for females (Banerjee & Lintern, 2000; David et al., 2004). Boys are criticized for being sissies more than girls are for being tomboys. Fathers, particularly, expect their daughters to be sweet and their sons to be tough.

Behaviorists believe children learn about proper behavior not only directly (as by receiving a gender-appropriate toy or an adult's praise) but also indirectly, through *social learning.* Children model their behavior after people they perceive to be nurturing, powerful, and yet similar to themselves. For young children, those people are their parents, and men and women are usually the most sex-typed of their entire lives when they are raising young children. For instance, if ever an adult woman quits work to become a housewife, she does so when she has young children; the children do not realize that their family's arrangement, with their mother doing domestic work and their father working outside the home, is a temporary aberration.

Cognitive Theory

Cognitive theory offers an alternative explanation for the strong gender identity that becomes apparent at about age 5. Remember that cognitive theorists focus on how children understand various ideas. Children develop concepts about their experiences. In this case, a **gender schema** is the child's understanding of sex differences (Kohlberg et al., 1983; Martin et al., 2002; Renk et al., 2006).

gender schema A cognitive concept or general belief based on one's experiences—in this case, a child's understanding of sex differences.

Young children have many gender-related experiences but not much cognitive depth. They tend to see the world in simple terms. For this reason, they categorize male and female as opposites, even when evidence contradicts such a sexist view. Nuances, complexities, exceptions, and gradations about gender (as well as about everything else) are beyond the preoperational child. Furthermore, as they try to make sense of their culture, they encounter numerous customs, taboos, and terminologies that enforce the gender norms. Remember that for preoperational children, appearance is crucial and static thinking makes them believe that whatever is has always been and is irreversible.

In addition, the need to develop a self-concept leads young children to categorize themselves as male or female and then to behave in a way that fits their concept. For that reason, cognitive theorists see "Jill's claim that she is a girl because

Toy Guns for Boys, Cinderella for Girls Young boys throughout the world are the ones who aim toy guns, while young girls imagine themselves as a Disney Cinderella, waiting for her handsome prince. The question is why: Are these young monks in Laos and this girl in Mexico responding to biology or culture?

BJORN SVENSSON / ALAMY

BLICKWINKEL / ALAMY

JEFF GREENBERG / ALAMY

Imagine Halloween is a time for fantasy. Can you imagine these two boys dressed like the girl while she wore a pirate's outfit? If you can, you are not stuck in cultural norms, but you probably also realize that none of these children would be smiling if their costumes violated gender norms.

she is wearing her new frilly socks as a genuine expression of her gender identity" (David et al., 2004, p. 147). Similarly, a 3½-year-old boy whose aunt called him *cute* insisted that he should be called *handsome* instead (Powlishta, 2004). Obviously, he had developed gender-based categories, and he wanted others to see him as he conceptualized himself.

Gender and Universal Social Order

As you can see, the three grand theories differ in how they explain the young child's understanding of male and female. The newer theories have other explanations, and new research continues to find that the traditional theories themselves must change (Martin & Ruble, 2010). Evolutionary theory holds that sexual attraction is crucial for humankind's most basic urge, to reproduce; thus, males and females try to look attractive to the other sex, taking on many behaviors to do so. Sociocultural theory holds that sexual behavior depends on the culture (men holding hands with men is taboo or expected, depending on local customs) and that some of the distinctions are tied to general patterns of social organization. Therefore, evolutionary theory would encourage male–female differences and sociocultural theory would conclude that sex differences are changeable if they interfere with other values.

The theories all raise a question: What gender patterns *should* children learn? Should everyone combine the best of both sexes (called *androgyny*), and should gender stereotypes disappear with age (like Santa Claus and the Tooth Fairy)? Or should male–female distinctions be encouraged as essential for the human family? Answers vary among developmentalists as well as among mothers, fathers, and cultures. Was I right or wrong to stop my student who told Bethany, "Girls don't fight"?

SUMMING UP

Gender stereotypes are held most forcefully at about age 6. Each theory, each discipline, and probably each parent has an explanation for this phenomenon: Freud described unconscious incestuous urges; behaviorists highlight social reinforcement; cognitive theorists describe immature categorization. Moreover, people differ as to the moral response—from considering gender identification as the bedrock of morality to seeing gender stereotypes as childish and destructive. ■

SUMMARY

Emotional Development

1. Learning to regulate and control emotions is crucial during early childhood. Emotional regulation is made possible by maturation of the brain, particularly of the prefrontal cortex, as well as by experiences with parents and peers.

2. In Erikson's psychosocial theory, the crisis of initiative versus guilt occurs during early childhood. Children normally feel pride, sometimes mixed with feelings of guilt. Shame is also evident, particularly in some cultures.

3. Both externalizing and internalizing problems indicate impaired self-control. Some emotional problems that indicate psychopathology are first evident during these years.

4. Boys more often manifest externalizing behaviors and girls, internalizing behaviors. For both sexes, brain maturation and the quality of early caregiving affect emotional control.

Play

5. All young children enjoy playing—with other children of the same sex (preferably), alone, or with parents. Rough-and-tumble play teaches many social skills and occurs everywhere, especially among boys who have space to run and chase.

6. Sociodramatic play allows development of emotions and roles within a safe setting. Both sexes engage in dramatic play, with girls preferring more domestic, less violent themes.

Challenges for Adults

7. Three classic styles of parenting have been identified: authoritarian, permissive, and authoritative. Generally, children are more successful and happy when their parents express warmth and set guidelines.

8. A fourth style of parenting, uninvolved, is always harmful. The particulars of parenting reflect the culture as well as the temperament of the child.

9. Children are prime consumers of many kinds of media, usually for several hours a day and often without their parents' involvement. Content is crucial. The problems that arise from media exposure include increased aggression and less creative play.

Moral Development

10. The sense of self and the social awareness of the young child become the foundation for morality. This is evident in both prosocial and antisocial behavior.

11. There are four types of aggression: instrumental, reactive, relational, and bullying. Instrumental aggression is used by all children but becomes less common with age. Unprovoked injury (bullying) is considered wrong by children as well as by adults.

12. Parents' choice of punishment can have long-term consequences. Physical punishment may teach lessons that parents do not want their children to learn. Other forms of punishment have long-term consequences as well.

Becoming Boys and Girls

13. Even 2-year-olds correctly use sex-specific labels. Young children become aware of gender differences in clothes, toys, future careers, and playmates.

14. Freud emphasized that children are attracted to the opposite-sex parent and eventually seek to identify, or align themselves, with the same-sex parent. Behaviorists hold that gender-related behaviors are learned through reinforcement and punishment (especially for males) and social modeling.

15. Cognitive theorists note that simplistic preoperational thinking leads to gender schema and therefore stereotypes. Sociocultural theorists point to the many male–female distinctions that are apparent in every society and are taught to children.

16. Evolutionary theory contends that sex and gender differences are crucial for the survival and reproduction of the species.

KEY TERMS

emotional regulation (p. 289)
initiative versus guilt (p. 289)
self-concept (p. 290)
intrinsic motivation (p. 291)
extrinsic motivation (p. 291)
imaginary friends (p. 291)
psychopathology (p. 293)
externalizing problems (p. 293)
internalizing problems (p. 293)
rough-and-tumble play (p. 296)
sociodramatic play (p. 297)
authoritarian parenting (p. 299)
permissive parenting (p. 299)
authoritative parenting (p. 299)
neglectful/uninvolved parenting (p. 300)
empathy (p. 305)
antipathy (p. 305)
prosocial behavior (p. 306)
antisocial behavior (p. 306)
instrumental aggression (p. 306)
reactive aggression (p. 306)
relational aggression (p. 306)
bullying aggression (p. 307)
psychological control (p. 308)
time-out (p. 308)
sex differences (p. 311)
gender differences (p. 311)
phallic stage (p. 313)
Oedipus complex (p. 313)
superego (p. 313)
Electra complex (p. 313)
identification (p. 313)
gender schema (p. 315)

WHAT HAVE YOU LEARNED?

Emotional Development

1. What aspects of brain development aid emotional regulation?

2. What are the differences between shame and guilt?

3. How is initiative different from autonomy (Erikson's third and second stages, respectively)?

4. What is the connection between psychopathology and emotional regulation?

5. What emotions are hard for people to regulate and why?

6. How do children learn emotional regulation?

7. What would be an example of intrinsic versus extrinsic motivation for reading a book?

Play

8. What do children learn from rough-and-tumble play?

9. Why do children prefer to play with peers rather than adults?

10. How is the development of social play affected by culture?

11. What does sociodramatic play help children learn?

12. What are the differences in the typical play of young boys and young girls?

Challenges for Adults

13. In Baumrind's three parenting styles, how do parents differ in expectations?

14. Why are children of permissive parents often unhappy?

15. Why do many non–European American parents seem stricter than other parents?

16. What do most American child professionals advise about television and young children?

17. What is likely to be displaced when young children are using electronic media?

Moral Development

18. What did Piaget believe about the moral development of children?

19. What is the nature perspective on how people develop morals?

20. What are the differences among sympathy, empathy, and antipathy?

21. What are the advantages and disadvantages of prosocial behavior?

22. What are the similarities and differences of the four kinds of aggression?

23. Why do developmentalists hope that parents will discuss discipline with each other before their child needs it?

24. What are the advantages and disadvantages of physical punishment?

25. Why have many nations made corporal punishment illegal?

26. When is time-out an effective punishment and when is it not?

27. What are the advantages and disadvantages of using induction as punishment?

Becoming Boys and Girls

28. How and when do children learn about sex differences between males and females?

29. How and when do children learn about gender differences between boys and girls?

30. Why do many social scientists dispute Freud's theory of sex-role development?

31. What would be easy and what difficult for society if gender roles changed?

APPLICATIONS

1. Observe the interactions of two or more young children. Sort your observations into four categories: emotions, reasons, results, and emotional regulation. Note every observable emotion (expressed by laughter, tears, etc.), the reason for it, the consequences, and whether or not emotional regulation was likely. For example: "Anger: Friend grabbed toy; child suggested sharing; emotional regulation probable."

2. Ask three parents about punishment, including their preferred type, at what age, for what misdeeds, and by whom. Ask your three informants how they were punished as children and how that affected them. If your sources agree, find a parent (or a classmate) who has a different view.

3. Children's television programming has been accused of stereotyping ethnicity, gender, and morality. Watch an hour of children's TV, especially on a Saturday morning, and describe the content of both the programs and the commercials. Draw conclusions about stereotyping, citing specific evidence (rather than merely reporting your impressions).

4. Gender indicators often go unnoticed. Go to a public place (park, restaurant, busy street) and spend an hour recording and quantifying examples of gender differentiation, such as articles of clothing, mannerisms, interaction patterns, and activities.

>>ONLINE CONNECTIONS

To accompany your textbook, you have access to a number of online resources, including quizzes for every chapter of the book, flashcards (in English and Spanish), critical thinking questions, and case studies. For access to any of these links, go to www.worthpublishers.com/bergerca9e. In addition to these free resources, you'll also find links to podcasts, video clips, diagnostic quizzing with personalized study advice, and an ebook. Some of the videos and activities available online include:

- *Children at Play.* Watch video clips of children at play, identify the types of play you see, and review how each type contributes to children's development.
- *Bullying.* With video clips of bullying, this activity covers physical and relational aggression, gender differences in bullying, and the impact on victims. It presents causes and preventive measures.

PART III The Developing Person So Far:

Early Childhood

BIOSOCIAL

Body Changes Children continue to grow from ages 2 to 6, but at a slower rate. Normally, the BMI (body mass index) is lower at about ages 5 and 6 than at any other time of life. Children often eat too much unhealthy food and refuse to eat certain other foods altogether, insisting that food and other routines be "just right."

Brain Development The proliferation of neural pathways and myelination continue. Parts of the brain (e.g., the corpus callosum, prefrontal cortex, amygdala, hippocampus, and hypothalamus) connect, which allows lateralization of the brain's left and right hemispheres and better coordination of the left and right sides of the body; it also leads to a decline in impulsivity and perseveration. Gross motor skills slowly develop.

Injuries and Maltreatment Injury control is particularly necessary in these years, since far more children worldwide die of avoidable accidents than of diseases. Child abuse and neglect can occur in any family but are especially likely in homes with many children and few resources.

COGNITIVE

Piaget and Vygotsky Piaget stressed the young child's egocentric, illogical perspective, which prevents the child from grasping concepts such as conservation. Vygotsky stressed the cultural context, noting that children learn from mentors—which include parents, teachers, peers—and from the social context. Children develop their own theories, including a theory of mind, as they realize that not everyone thinks as they do.

Language Language develops rapidly. By age 6, the average child knows 10,000 words and demonstrates extensive grammatical knowledge. Young children can become balanced bilinguals during these years if their social context is encouraging.

Early-Childhood Education Young children are avid learners. Child-centered, teacher-directed, and intervention programs can all nurture learning; the outcome depends on the skill of teachers, as well as on the specifics of the curriculum.

PSYCHOSOCIAL

Emotional Development Self-esteem is usually high during early childhood. Self-concept emerges in Erikson's stage of initiative versus guilt, as does the ability to regulate emotions. Externalizing problems may be the result of too little emotional regulation; internalizing problems may result from too much control.

Parents A parenting style that is warm and encouraging, with good communication as well as high expectations (called authoritative), is most effective in promoting the child's self-esteem, autonomy, and self-control. The authoritarian and permissive styles are less beneficial. Extensive use of television and other media by children can disrupt family life.

Moral Development There is no consensus about how much of moral development is innate and how much is learned, but it is apparent that morality becomes more evident during early childhood. Empathy produces prosocial behavior; antipathy leads to antisocial actions. Aggression takes many forms; bullying aggression is ominous. Every method of parental discipline has consequences.

Becoming Boys and Girls Children develop stereotypic concepts of sex (biological) and gender (cultural). Current theories give contradictory explanations.

PART

IV

CHAPTERS 11•12•13

middle childhood

Every age has joys and sorrows, gains and losses. But if you were pushed to choose one best time, you might select ages 6 to 11, when many children experience good health and steady growth as they master new athletic skills, learn thousands of words, become less dependent on families. Usually, they appreciate their parents, make new friends, and proudly learn about their nation and religion. Life is safe and happy; the dangers of adolescence (drugs, sex, violence) are not yet on the horizon.

Yet some adults remember these years as the worst, not the best. Some children hate school; some live in destructive families; some have no permanent home; some contend with obesity, asthma, learning disabilities, or bullies. The next three chapters celebrate the joys and acknowledge the difficulties of ages 6 to 11.

11

CHAPTER

Middle Childhood: Biosocial Development

WHAT WILL YOU KNOW?

1. What would happen if more parents let their children "go out and play"?
2. Should the epidemic of childhood obesity be blamed on parents, schools, or policies?
3. Why are IQ tests not used as often as they were a few decades ago?
4. If every child is abnormal in some way, why is early diagnosis of special needs helpful?

In the middle of the second grade, my family and I moved a thousand miles. I entered a new school where my accent was odd; I was self-conscious and lonely. Cynthia had a friendly smile, freckles, and red hair. More important, she talked to me; I asked her to be my friend.

"We cannot be friends," she said, "because I am a Democrat."

"So am I," I answered. (I knew my family believed in democracy.)

"No, you're not. You are a Republican," she said.

I was stunned and sad. We never became friends.

Neither Cynthia nor I realized that all children are unusual in some way (perhaps because of appearance, culture, or family) and yet capable of friendship with children unlike themselves. Cynthia and I could have been good friends, but neither of us knew it. Her parents had told her something about my parents' politics that I did not understand. Cynthia left the school later that year, friendless; I made other friends.

This chapter describes not only the similarities among all school-age children but also differences that may become significant—in size, health, learning ability, and more. At the end of this chapter, we focus on children with special needs—who need friends but have trouble finding them.

>> A Healthy Time

Genetic and environmental factors safeguard **middle childhood** (about age 6 to 11), the period after early childhood and before adolescence. One explanation comes from the evolutionary perspective. A death during middle childhood would mean that the effort to nurture the young child was in vain (Konner, 2010). For whatever reason, few fatal diseases or accidents occur during these years. Contemporary schoolchildren have two added protections: education about risks and several doses of vaccine. All in all, middle childhood is the healthiest period of the entire life span (see Figure 11.1).

middle childhood The period between early childhood and early adolescence, approximately from ages 6 to 11.

Slower Growth, Greater Strength

Unlike infants or adolescents, school-age children's growth is slow and steady. Self-care is easy—from brushing their new adult teeth to dressing themselves, from making their own lunch to walking with friends to school. Once at school,

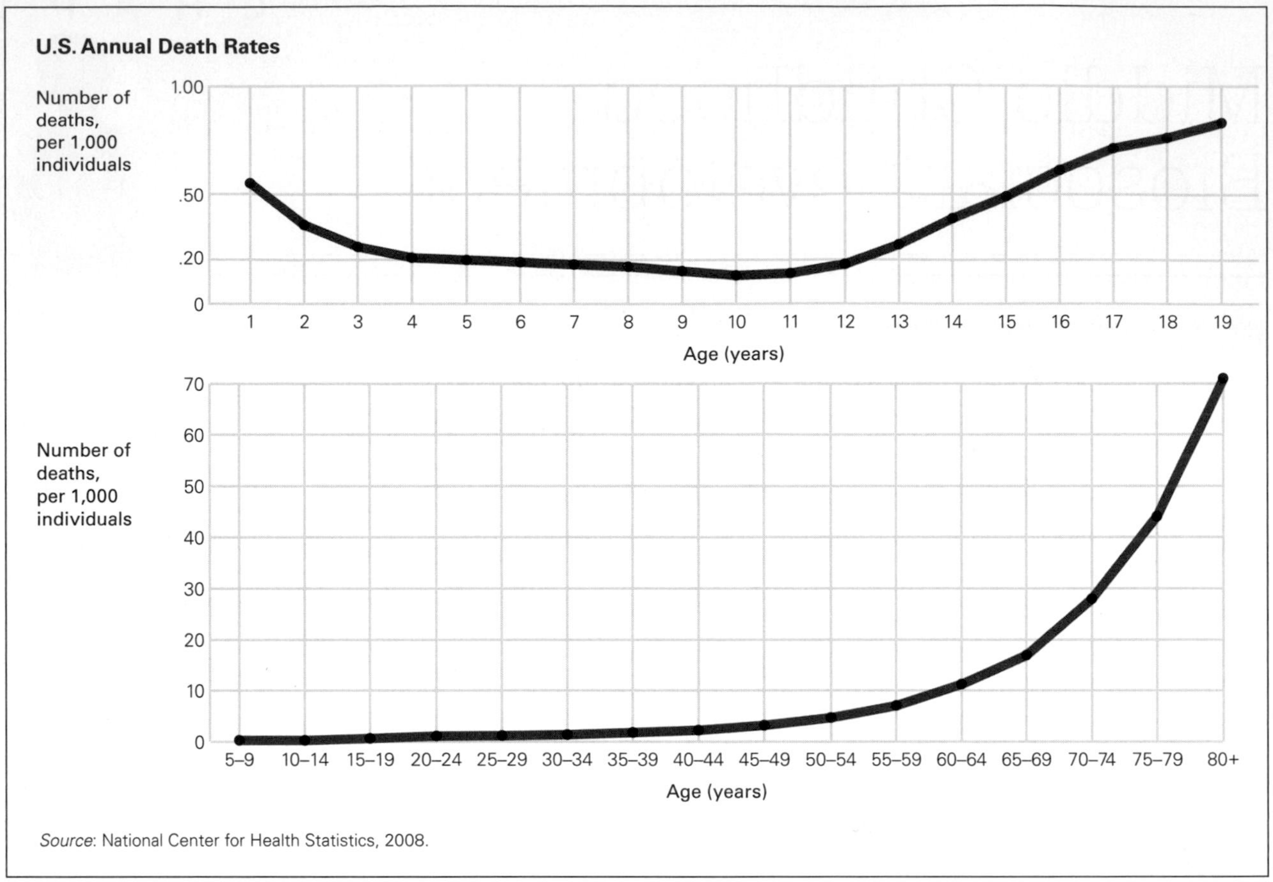

FIGURE 11.1

Death at an Early Age? Almost Never! Schoolchildren are remarkably hardy, as measured in many ways. These charts show that death rates for 6- to 11-year olds are lower than those for children under 6 or over 11 and about 100 times lower than for adults

Observation Quiz From the bottom graph, it looks as if ages 9 and 19 are equally healthy, but they are dramatically different in the top graph. What is the explanation for this? (see answer, page 326)

they can sit at their desks or tables and do their work without breaking their pencils, tearing their papers, or elbowing their classmates. In these middle years, children are quite capable and self-sufficient and are not yet buffeted by adolescent body changes and impulses.

Muscles become stronger. For example, the average 10-year-old can throw a ball twice as far as a 6-year-old can. Hearts and lungs are muscles, too, increasing in strength and capacity. Consequently, with each passing year, children run faster and exercise longer (Malina et al., 2004). Some sports valued by adults (such as basketball and football) require taller, bigger bodies than school-age children possess, but these children are far superior to their younger selves in every athletic skill.

Few are severely undernourished. As long as their entire community is not starving, school-age children feed themselves. As the "just right" obsession fades, they try new foods, especially if they are eating at a friend's house. As discussed in Chapter 8, earlier malnutrition becomes evident in height, not weight. By middle childhood, children from the poorest nations are several inches shorter than those from richer ones, with some of the short ones overweight, on the road to poor health later on (Worthman et al., 2010).

Physical Activity

Children often play joyfully, "fully and totally immersed" (Loland, 2002, p. 139). Beyond the sheer fun of playing, the benefits of physical activity—especially games with rules, which school-age children are now able to follow—can last a lifetime.

These benefits include the following:

- Better overall health
- Less obesity
- Appreciation of cooperation and fair play
- Improved problem-solving abilities
- Respect for teammates and opponents of many ethnicities and nationalities

However, there are hazards as well:

- Loss of self-esteem (teammates and coaches are sometimes cruel)
- Injuries (the infamous "Little League elbow" is one example)
- Reinforcement of prejudices (especially against the other sex)
- Increased stress (evidenced by altered hormone levels, insomnia)

Where can children reap the benefits and avoid the hazards of active play? There are three possibilities: neighborhoods, schools, and sports leagues.

DAVID MERCADO / REUTERS / CORBIS

Expert Eye–Hand Coordination The specifics of motor-skill development in middle childhood depend on the culture. These flute players are carrying on the European Baroque musical tradition that thrives among the poor, remote Guarayo people of Bolivia.

Neighborhood Games

Neighborhood play is flexible. Rules and boundaries are adapted to the context (out of bounds is "past the tree" or "behind the parked truck"). Stickball, touch football, tag, hide-and-seek, and dozens of other running and catching games go on forever—or at least until dark. The play is active, interactive, and inclusive—ideal for children. It also teaches ethics. As one scholar notes:

> Children play tag, hide and seek, or pickup basketball. They compete with one another but always according to rules, and rules that they enforce themselves without recourse to an impartial judge. The penalty for not playing by the rules is not playing, that is, social exclusion . . .
>
> *[Gillespie, 2010, p. 398]*

For school-age children, "social exclusion" is a steep price to pay for insisting on their own way. Instead, they learn to cooperate. Unfortunately, this lesson may not be learned by the current cohort of children because modern life undercuts informal neighborhood games. Vacant lots and empty fields have largely disappeared.

A century ago, 90 percent of the world's children lived in rural areas; now the majority live in cities or in shantytowns at the city's edge. The cities that have exploded most rapidly are in developing nations, where playgrounds and parks are particularly rare, but even in the slower-growing developed nations, population increases are notable. For instance, in 1990 slightly fewer than 4 million people lived in metropolitan Dallas, Texas; in 2010, nearly 7 million did.

An additional problem, especially for city children, is that their parents keep them at home because of "stranger danger"—although one expert writes that "there is a much greater chance that your child is going to be dangerously overweight from staying inside than that he is going to be abducted" (quoted in Layden, 2004, p. 86). Indoor activities like homework, television, and video games compete with outdoor play in every nation, perhaps especially in the United States. According to an Australian scholar:

> Australian children are lucky. Here the dominant view is that children's after school time is leisure time. In the United States, it seems that leisure time is available to fewer and fewer children. If a child performs poorly in school, recreation time rapidly becomes remediation time. For high achievers, after school time is often spent in academic enrichment.
>
> *[Vered, 2008, p. 170]*

IMAGE100 / ALAMY

Tree Hugging? Some adults disparage other adults who seek to preserve nature, but for children worldwide, climbing trees is a joy. Not every child has this opportunity. These fortunate boys are playing on a South African estate.

"Just remember, son, it doesn't matter whether you win or lose—unless you want Daddy's love."

Exercise in School

When opportunities for neighborhood play are scarce, physical education in school is a logical alternative. However, because schools are pressured to increase reading and math time (see Chapter 12), time for physical education and recess has declined. A study of Texas elementary schools found that 24 percent had no recess at all, and only 1 percent had recess several times a day (W. Zhu et al., 2010).

A much larger study of a U.S. cross section of more than 10,000 third-graders found that about two-thirds of all children have at least 15 minutes of recess each day. Unfortunately, those children least likely to have recess are those most likely to need it—city-dwellers who live in poor neighborhoods, where fearful parents do not let them go outside to play (Barros et al., 2009) (see the Research Design and Figure 11.2 on the next page). Many schools are required to have gym, but those classes are often too large for active play.

Not only has school time for recess and for physical education declined, but during gym class some children spend more time sitting and waiting than moving. Paradoxically, school exercise may improve academic achievement (Carlson et al., 2008). The Centers for Disease Control recommends that children be active at least half of the time in required physical education classes (Khan et al., 2009). These are minimal goals; many schools do not meet them.

>> Answer to Observation Quiz (from page 324) Look at the vertical axes. From age 1 to 20, the annual death rate is less than 1 in 1,000.

Athletic Clubs and Leagues

Private or nonprofit clubs and organizations offer additional opportunities for children to play. Culture and family affect the specifics: Some children learn golf, others tennis, others boxing. Cricket and rugby are common in England and in former British colonies such as India, Australia, and Jamaica; baseball is common in Japan, the United States, Cuba, Panama, and the Dominican Republic; soccer is central in many European, African, and Latin American nations.

The best-known organized recreation program for children is Little League. When it began in 1939, Little League had only three baseball teams of boys aged 9 to12. Now it includes girls, younger and older children, and 22,000 children with disabilities, with an annual total of 2.7 million children playing baseball or softball on more than 180,000 teams in 100 nations. Coaches are usually parent volunteers, who are not necessarily adept at encouraging every child. Nonetheless, most children enjoy it. One adult confesses:

Why Helmets? Sports organized by adults, such as this football team of 7- to 8-year-old boys sponsored by the Lyons and Police Athletic League of Detroit, may be harmful to children. The best games are those that require lots of running and teamwork—but no pushing or shoving.

> I was a lousy Little League player. Uncoordinated, small, and clueless are the accurate adjectives I'd use if someone asked politely. . . . What I did possess, though, was enthusiasm. Wearing the uniform—cheesy mesh cap, scratchy polyester shirt, old-school beltless pants, uncomfortable cleats and stirrups that never stayed up—gave me a sort of pride. It felt special and made me think that I was part of something important.
>
> *[Ryan, 2005]*

Being "part of something important" raises a problem: Many children are left out (Collins, 2003). Not all parents can pay for after-school sports or can afford the time to transport children to practices and games; many do not have the energy to cheer on the teams, much less coach them. Children from low-SES families, or those who are not well coordinated, or those who have disabilities rarely

Daily Recess in the United States for Third-Graders

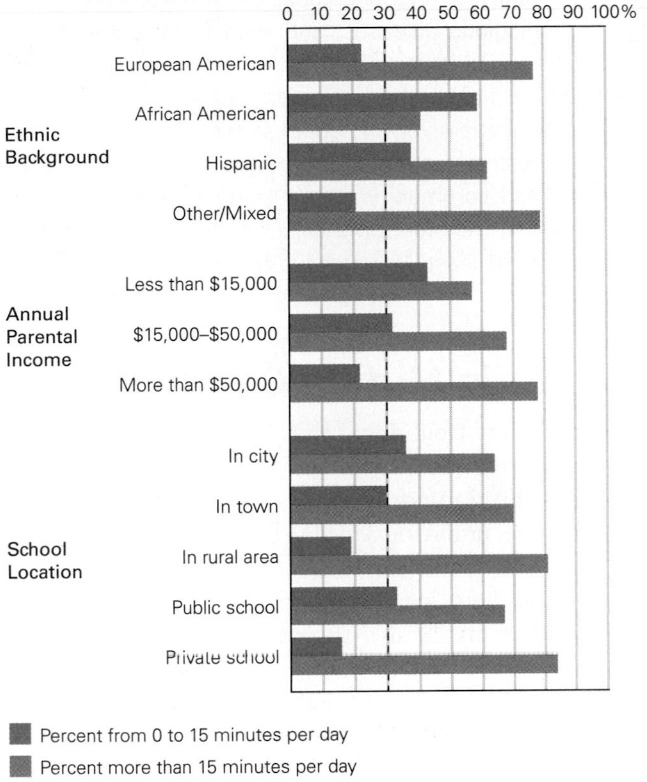

Source: Barros et al., 2009.

FIGURE 11.2

Time for Recess Although many studies find that children learn better if they have recess every day and although recess decreases obesity and increases social skills, about one-third of all children in the United States have less than 15 minutes a day of recess. This includes many schools that have no recess at all.

Observation Quiz If a child is African American, is of low SES, and attends a public school in a large city in the South, what is that child's chance of having less than 15 minutes a day of recess? (see answer, page 328)

Research Design

Scientists: Romina M. Barros, Ellen J. Silver, and Ruth E. K. Stein.

Publication: *Pediatrics* (2009).

Participants: Participants were about 11,000 8-year-olds from one part of the Early Childhood Longitudinal Study. This study began with kindergartners from many U.S. regions, of many ethnicities, and with many different levels of family income. The scientists analyzed data reported on these children in third grade. Not included were children who repeated a grade, who were immigrants, or who entered school after kindergarten. Parents and teachers were also queried.

Design: Teachers reported how much recess (unstructured play time) the children had each day. The lowest option was 0–15 minutes, chosen by 30 percent. That variable was compared to class behavior, class size, boy/girl ratio, frequency of gym class, parents' SES, and school type and location.

Results: Many significant differences were found. Less recess correlated with lower SES, classes that were "hard to manage," public schools, cities, southern states, and fewer physical education periods. Variables not associated with length of recess included class size and boy/girl ratio.

Major conclusion: Given the correlation between recess and class behavior, as well as other research on childhood learning, attention, and obesity, these researchers suggest that all children benefit from at least 20 minutes of recess each day. This is particularly important for children who have difficulty paying attention. The researchers worry that students who most need recess are least likely to have it, because "many children from disadvantaged backgrounds are not free to roam their neighborhoods or even their own yards unless they are accompanied by adults. For many of these children, recess periods may be the only opportunity for them to practice their social skills with other children" (p. 434).

These authors also note that 40 percent of U.S. schools have cut back on recess in order to spend more time on reading and math, although schools in Asia, with the highest scores on international tests of achievement, have several recess breaks totaling more than an hour each day.

Comments: Given the large, representative sample, with participants queried independently (thus avoiding the danger of researcher bias influencing results), the data reported here are probably reliable. Many adults mistakenly believe that children who misbehave and who have academic difficulties need less free play and more academic work. This study suggests the opposite—that recess not only provides exercise, it may increase academic learning.

belong to athletic clubs—yet those are the very children who could benefit most from the strength, activity, and teamwork that organized play provides.

Indeed, especially for low-income children, participation in structured sports activities correlates with academic achievement; one Canadian study found that academic performance improved for 6- and 7-year-olds who felt victimized but played sports (Perron et al., 2011). (Academic performance decreased for victimized children who did not play sports, as well as for nonvictimized sports players). Although participation in extracurricular activities, especially sports, benefits low-income children more than others, such children are less likely to join even when available after-school activities are free. The reasons are many; the consequences, sad (Dearing et al., 2009).

Especially for Physical Education Teachers A group of parents of fourth- and fifth-graders has asked for your help in persuading the school administration to sponsor a competitive sports team. How should you advise the group to proceed? (see response, page 328)

>> Answer to Observation Quiz (from page 327) The graph doesn't explicitly calculate that statistic, but since the child is in the lowest percentage of each category, any estimate between 75 and 95 percent is probably correct.

>> Response for Physical Education Teachers (from page 327) Discuss with the parents their reasons for wanting the team. Children need physical activity, but some aspects of competitive sports are better suited to adults than to children.

SUMMING UP

School-age children are usually healthy, strong, and capable. Genes as well as immunization protect them against contagious diseases, and medical care has improved over the past decades. Moreover, children's developmental advances add strength, understanding, and coordination and enable them to undertake self-care, providing a foundation that allows them to learn effectively in school as well as to have a healthy adulthood. Specific habits, and exercise overall, aid learning. Although neighborhood play, school physical education, and community sports leagues all provide needed activity, energetic play is much more likely for some children than for others; unfortunately, those who need it most are the least likely to have access to it. ■

>> Health Problems in Middle Childhood

Chronic conditions may become more troubling if they interfere with school, play, and friendship. Some worsen during the school years, including Tourette syndrome, stuttering, and allergies. Even minor problems—wearing glasses, repeatedly coughing or blowing one's nose, or having a visible birthmark—make children self-conscious.

For children with chronic conditions, learning good health habits is especially vital before adolescence: Teenagers might dye their hair green or get a tattoo, but hopefully they still take their medication and see the doctor. If adolescent rebellion includes medical noncompliance, those with serious, chronic conditions (including diabetes, phenylketonuria [PKU], epilepsy, cancer, asthma, and sickle-cell anemia) often ignore special diets, pills, and so on and get sicker (Dean et al., 2010; Suris et al., 2008). To prevent this, elementary schoolchildren need to take charge of their health, developing habits that will sustain them lifelong.

Researchers increasingly recognize that every physical and psychological problem is affected by the social context and, in turn, affects that context (Jackson & Tester, 2008). Parents and children are not merely reactive: In a dynamic-systems manner (see Chapter 1), individuals and contexts influence each other. We now focus on two examples: obesity and asthma.

Childhood Obesity

Of any age group, 5- and 6-year-olds have the least body fat and lowest **BMI (body mass index).** Yet many young children are too heavy. Childhood **overweight** is defined as having a BMI above the 85th percentile for age; childhood **obesity** is defined as having a BMI above the 95th percentile (Barlow et al., 2007). Both percentiles are measured against children's growth norms published by the U.S. Centers for Disease Control in 1980, which explains why more than 5 percent can be above the 95th percentile.

BMI (body mass index) A person's weight in kilograms divided by the square of height in meters.

overweight In a child, having a BMI above the 85th percentile, according to the U.S. Centers for Disease Control's 1980 standards for children of a given age.

obesity In a child, having a BMI above the 95th percentile, according to the U.S. Centers for Disease Control's 1980 standards for children of a given age.

Childhood obesity in all three nations of North America (Mexico, the United States, and Canada) has more than doubled since 1980. The latest U.S. data suggest the increases have stopped—but at a high level. In the United States in 2005, one-third (32 percent) of children under age 18 were overweight, half of them (16 percent) were obese and 11 percent of those obese children were extremely obese (Ogden et al., 2008). Using the same standards, 28 percent of Canadian 2- to 17-year-olds were overweight, with increases particularly in middle childhood (Shields & Tremblay, 2010).

Overweight children more often have asthma, high blood pressure, and elevated cholesterol (especially LDL, the "bad" form of cholesterol). Furthermore, on average, as excessive weight builds, school achievement decreases, self-esteem falls, and loneliness rises. This has been studied most often in the United States, where schoolchildren are more likely to reject their obese classmates, who often hate school (Zeller et al., 2008). Over time, it gets worse: If they stay heavy, obese children risk diabetes, heart disease, and strokes and are less likely to marry, to find jobs, and to live to old age. Because of obesity, today's children may be the first generation to die at younger ages than their parents did (Devi, 2008; Yajnik, 2004).

What Causes Overweight in Children?

To halt the epidemic of childhood obesity, many people search for the cause. The problem is that there is no single cause. There are "hundreds if not thousands of contributing factors" (Harrison et al., 2011, p. 51).

First, some people are genetically predisposed to high proportions of body fat. More than 200 genes affect weight by influencing activity level, food preference, body type, and metabolism (Gluckman & Hanson, 2006). Having two copies of an allele called FTO (inherited by 16 percent of all European Americans) increases the likelihood of both obesity and diabetes (Frayling et al., 2007). However, genes change little from one generation to the next and thus cannot have caused the marked increase in obesity (Harrison et al., 2011). Factors around those genes may exacerbate them—embryos that gain too little are likely to become children who weigh too much, but that seems more a matter of child rearing than of genes. One critic notes that "fat runs in families but so do frying pans" (S. Jones, 2006, p. 1879).

Especially for Teachers A child in your class is overweight, but you are hesitant to say anything to the parents, who are also overweight, because you do not want to insult them. What should you do? (see response, page 331)

Second, in many ways, parenting practices *have* changed for the worse. Obesity is more common in infants who are not breast-fed, in preschoolers who watch TV and drink soda, and in school-age children who are driven to school and rarely play outside (Institute of Medicine, 2006; Patrick et al., 2004; Rhee, 2008). Parents are crucial in all these, but during middle childhood, children themselves can change family patterns. An important factor is called "pester power"—the ability of the child to nag the parent. Usually, children pester their parents to provide calorie-dense food, but some children pester their parents in the opposite way—to play ball with them, to let them join a sports team, and so on. School health education can convince children to advocate for better diets.

A third source of childhood obesity is "embedded in social policies" (Branca et al., 2007). Communities and nations determine the quality of school lunches; the presence of snack vending machines; the prevalence of parks, bike paths, and sidewalks; and the subsidies for corn oil but not fresh vegetables. One report lists 24 specific strategies that local governments could employ to reduce overweight (Khan et al., 2009).

Particularly potent for children is food advertising. In the United States, billions of dollars are spent on ads that entice children to eat unhealthy foods. Parents rarely realize how many of those ads their children see (Linn & Novosat, 2008). Such advertising is illegal in some nations, limited in others, and unrestricted in still others—and a country's rate of childhood obesity correlates with how often children see food commercials on television (Lobstein & Dibb, 2005).

Since all three factors—genes, parents, and policies—are relevant, it is not surprising that parents blame genes or policies, while others (medical professionals, political leaders) blame parents, and the media claim that they advertise what

A Happy Meal A close look at this photograph reveals that this scene is a McDonald's in Switzerland—one of hundreds of fast-food chain branches in Europe, where many normal-weight 6-year-olds become overweight 12-year-olds.

GAETAN BALLY / KEYSTONE / COREIS

the highest bidder wants as part of freedom of speech or capitalism. Everyone may be right: It is unclear which particular measures would markedly reduce obesity.

For instance, childhood weight correlates with hours of TV watched per day (Philipsen & Brooks-Gunn, 2008)—but remember that correlation does not prove cause. If families that allow unlimited television are also likely to allow unlimited snacking, then the snacking, not the TV, might be the problem. Or maybe content is crucial: One study found that neither educational television nor commercial-free videos correlated with childhood obesity but that commercials for calorie-dense foods did (Zimmerman & Bell, 2010). As with many other aspects of child development, experimental research on children cannot *prove* that television makes children fat because we cannot compare a TV-free group with an equal group who watch several hours each day. Rather than trying to zero in on any single factor, a dynamic-systems approach is needed: Many factors, over time, make a child overweight (Harrison et al., 2011).

Especially for Parents Suppose that you always serve dinner with the television on, tuned to a news broadcast. Your hope is that your children will learn about the world as they eat. Can this practice be harmful? (see response, page 332)

Asthma

asthma A chronic disease of the respiratory system in which inflammation narrows the airways from the nose and mouth to the lungs, causing difficulty in breathing. Signs and symptoms include wheezing, shortness of breath, chest tightness, and coughing.

Asthma is a chronic inflammatory disorder of the airways that makes breathing difficult. Although asthma affects people of every age, rates are highest among school-age children, with marked increases worldwide (Cruz et al., 2010). In the United States, asthma rates among every age group of children have tripled since 1980. Parents report that 10 percent of U.S. 5- to 9-year-olds currently have asthma, with 6 percent of them having had an attack within the past year.

Ethnicity matters, either because of genes or culture (probably both). Of all U.S. children under age 18, 14 percent have been diagnosed at least once with asthma. The rate for Puerto Rican children is 26 percent; African American, 21 percent; Mexican American, 10 percent; European American, 13 percent (Bloom et al., 2009; National Center for Health Statistics, 2011).

Causes of Asthma

Many researchers seek the causes of asthma. A few alleles have been identified as potential factors, but asthma has many genetic roots, none of which act in isolation (Bossé & Hudson, 2007). Environment combined with genes is crucial (Akinbami et al., 2010). Air pollution, especially that caused by traffic congestion, increases the prevalence of asthma among vulnerable children (Gilliland, 2009).

Several aspects of modern life—carpets, pets inside the home, airtight windows, less outdoor play—also contribute to the increased rates of asthma (Tamay et al., 2007). Many allergens (pet dander, cigarette smoke, dust mites, cockroaches, and mold among them) that trigger attacks are concentrated in today's well-insulated homes.

Some experts suggest a *hygiene hypothesis,* proposing that contemporary children are kept too hygienic, overprotected from viruses and bacteria, which means they do not contract minor infections and diseases that would actually strengthen their immune systems (Busse & Lemanske, 2005; Tedeschi & Airaghi, 2006). This hypothesis is supported by data showing that (1) first-born children are more likely to develop asthma than are later-born ones and (2) farm children have much lower rates of asthma and allergies than do other children.

Pride and Prejudice In some city schools, asthma is so common that using an inhaler is a sign of prestige, as suggested by the facial expressions of these two boys. The "prejudice" is more apparent beyond the walls of this school nurse's room, in a society that allows high rates of childhood asthma to occur.

KATHY MCLAUGHLIN / THE IMAGE WORKS

However, the lower rates for farm children do not *prove* the hygiene hypothesis. Other possibilities include certain genetic factors or drinking unpasteurized milk (von Mutius & Vercelli, 2010). Surprisingly, children born by c-section have higher rates of asthma—perhaps because their birth was too sterile? One review of the hygiene hypothesis notes that "the picture can be dishearteningly complex" (Couzin-Frankel, 2010, p. 1168). The incidence of asthma seems to increase as nations get richer; at least that is dramatically true in Brazil and China. Better hygiene is one explanation, but so is increasing urbanization—which correlates with more cars, more pollution, and smaller families (Cruz et al., 2010).

>> Response for Teachers (from page 329) Speak to the parents, not accusingly (because you know that genes and culture have a major influence on body weight) but helpfully. Alert them to the potential social and health problems their child's weight poses. Most parents are very concerned about their child's well-being and will work with you to improve the child's snacks and exercise level.

Prevention of Asthma

The three levels of prevention (discussed in Chapter 8) apply to every health problem.

Primary prevention requires changes in the entire society. Better ventilation of schools and homes, less pollution, fewer cockroaches, fewer antibiotics, fewer c-sections, and more outdoor play would benefit everyone while reducing asthma.

Secondary prevention decreases asthma attacks among high-risk children. If asthma runs in the family, then prolonged breast-feeding, less dust and smoke, and no cats or cockroaches cut the onset of asthma in half (Elliott et al., 2007; Gdalevich et al., 2001).

Finally, *tertiary prevention* includes the prompt use of injections and inhalers. Using hypoallergenic materials (e.g., for mattress covers) also reduces asthma attacks—but not by much, probably because it occurs too late (MMWR, January 14, 2005). But even if tertiary prevention does not halt asthma, it can help asthmatic children, as the following illustrates.

A CASE TO STUDY

Asthma in Two Active 8-Year-Olds

A team of social scientists analyzed statistics and interviewed individuals to produce *The Measure of America,* a book comparing development in the United States and elsewhere (Burd-Sharps et al., 2008). Among their case studies were those of Sophie and Alexa, two 8-year-olds with asthma.

> Sophie is a vibrant eight-year-old who was diagnosed with severe asthma when she was two. She lives in a house in a New York City suburb with a park down the street and fresh air outside—an environment with few asthma triggers.
>
> Her family has private health insurance, a benefit of her father's job, with extensive provisions for preventative care and patient education. Her parents' jobs have personal and sick days that give them time off from work to take her to the doctor. After some early difficulty finding a suitable medication regime, she has settled into a routine of daily-inhaled medication (at a cost of $500 per month, fully covered by insurance), annual flu shots, and a special medication she takes only when she is sick with a cold. Sophie sees her pediatrician regularly and a top-flight asthma specialist yearly, to monitor her progress; has a nebulizer for quick relief in case of a serious attack; and can rely on nebulizers in her school and after-school program as well.
>
> Sophie has never had to go to the emergency room for an attack, almost always participates in gym, and misses about two or three days of school a year due to asthma-related problems.
>
> Alexa is also an active eight-year-old, first diagnosed with severe asthma at age three. She lives with her mother in a Brooklyn apartment three blocks from a waste transfer station that receives, sorts, and dispatches thirteen thousand tons of garbage each weekday. In addition to the acrid smell of garbage, the cockroaches that frequent her apartment also trigger Alexa's asthma attacks through allergens in their droppings. Her mother works at a minimum-wage job; she loses income when she takes Alexa to the doctor, fills emergency prescriptions, or stays home with Alexa when she is sick.
>
> Alexa's mother could qualify for SCHIP, which would provide health insurance for Alexa, but she has never heard of it. Instead, Alexa is officially listed as living with her grandmother, whose Medicaid coverage extends to Alexa. Alexa sees a doctor annually, though her grandmother fears Alexa is not benefitting from the latest advances in asthma care.
>
> Alexa misses twelve to fifteen days of school each year, does not participate in gym, and spends up to eight fearful nights each year in a hospital emergency room. When she misses consecutive

days of school, she struggles with schoolwork. She wishes she could run around like her classmates.

[Burd-Sharps et al., 2008, p. 67]

These cases were originally published to highlight economic disparities. Few families can afford the excellent care Sophie receives, and programs such as SCHIP do not reach every low-income child like Alexa. However, as with obesity, severe asthma in childhood can be blamed on genes, parents, schools, doctors, and neighborhoods, as well as on public policies regarding poverty and health care. Who to blame is a hotly disputed political question, but everyone agrees that Alexa should not spend "eight fearful nights" in the hospital each year. Someone, or perhaps everyone, should help her.

The increase in childhood asthma is disheartening. But improvement is possible. One hundred and thirty-three Latino (primarily Puerto Rican) adult smokers, who were caregivers for children with asthma, agreed to allow a Spanish-speaking counselor to come repeatedly to their homes (Borrelli et al., 2010). The counselor placed a smoke monitor in the child's room and a week later told the caregiver how much smoke exposure the child had experienced. Then, in three sessions, she provided specific counseling on quitting, based on the best research on addiction, with particular sensitivity to Latino values.

Three months later, one-fourth of the caregivers had quit smoking completely. Many of the rest had cut down. The average child's exposure to smoke was cut in half, and asthma problems diminished (Borrelli et al., 2010). Note that knowledge and encouragement were needed—which not all parents have. Most parents want to provide good care (many wonder how).

>> Response for Parents (from page 330) Habitual TV watching correlates with obesity, so you may be damaging your children's health rather than improving their intellect. Your children would probably profit more if you were to make dinner a time for family conversation about world events.

SUMMING UP

Some children have chronic health problems that interfere with school and friendship. Among these are obesity and asthma, both increasing in every nation and both having genetic and environmental causes. Childhood obesity may seem harmless, but it leads to social problems among classmates and severe health problems later on. Asthma's harm is more immediate: Asthmatic children often miss school and are rushed to emergency rooms, gasping for air. Family practices and lifestyle are part of the reason for increases in obesity and asthma, and many society-wide policies and cultural customs make the problems worse.

Finger Math Some teachers forbid counting with hands and fingers, yet "embodied cognition" has been part of human thought since prehistoric times. Math knowledge advanced when humans realized that counting by tens was the natural way, as this boy demonstrates.

>> Brain Development

Recall that emotional regulation, theory of mind, and left–right coordination emerge in early childhood. The maturing corpus callosum connects the hemispheres of the brain, enabling balance and two-handed coordination, while myelination speeds up thoughts and behavior. The prefrontal cortex—the executive part of the brain—begins to plan, monitor, and evaluate. All of these neurological developments continue in middle childhood and beyond. We now look at additional advances in middle childhood.

Coordinating Connections

Increasing maturation results "by 7 or 8 years of age, in a massively interconnected brain" (Kagan & Herschkowitz, 2005, p. 220). Such connections are crucial for the complex tasks that children must master (M. H. Johnson et al., 2009). One example is learning to read, perhaps the most important intellectual accomplishment of the school-age child. Reading is not instinctual: Our ancestors never did it, and until recent centuries only a few scribes and scholars were expected to make sense of those marks on paper. Consequently, the brain has no areas dedicated to reading, the way it does for talking or gesturing (Gabrieli, 2009).

How do humans read without brain-specific structures? The answer is "massive interconnections." The connections are among brain structures already described in Chapter 8, with white matter (myelination) increasing particularly in the prefrontal cortex and the corpus callosum. Those connections increase executive functioning, which in turn makes all forms of education more possible, with literacy a much-studied example.

Reading uses several parts of the brain—one for sounds, another for recognizing letters, another for sequencing, another for comprehension, and so on (Booth, 2007). Those massive interconnections are needed for many social skills as well—deciding whom to trust, figuring out what is fair, interpreting ambiguous gestures and expressions. Younger children are not proficient at interpreting social cues (that's why they are told, "Don't talk to strangers"). During middle childhood, various parts of the brain connect to allow social decision making (Crone & Westenberg, 2009). Indeed, for many activities, children use more parts of their brains than adults do, thus requiring more connections (M. H. Johnson et al., 2009).

"The path to becoming an astronaut is rougher than I thought."

CARTOONSTOCK.COM

A crucial measure of better brain coordination is the ability of the prefrontal cortex to control various impulses, as already described in the chapters on early childhood. Advances in the "mental control processes that enable self-control" (Verté et al., 2005, p. 415) allow planning for the future, which is beyond the ability of the impatient younger child. School-age children can analyze possible consequences before they lash out in anger or dissolve in tears, and they can figure out when a curse word seems advisable (on the playground to a bully, perhaps) and when it is not (in the classroom or at home). Planning for the future means they can count the days until summer vacation.

The prefrontal cortex takes decades to mature. For children who want to be rocket scientists, billionaire stock analysts, or brain surgeons, connecting those distant goals with current behavior or social reality is not yet possible. Nonetheless, connections between one part of the brain and another may be crucial because some neuroscientists believe that "social or linguistic disorders could be caused by disruptions in the pathways" of brain connections, not in the neurons themselves (Minogue, 2010, p. 747).

Think Quick; Too Slow

Advance planning and impulse control are aided by faster **reaction time,** which is how long it takes to respond to a stimulus. Thus, reaction time indicates speed of thought as an impulse travels from one neuron to another, and increasing myelination speeds reaction time every year from birth until about age 16.

reaction time The time it takes to respond to a stimulus, either physically (with a reflexive movement such as an eyeblink) or cognitively (with a thought).

A simple example is being able to kick a speeding soccer ball toward a teammate; a more complex example is being able to calculate when to utter a witty remark and when to stay quiet. Young children find both impossible; fast-thinking older children sometimes succeed; few adults can beat a teenager at a quick-paced video game.

Pay Attention

Neurological advances allow children not only to process information quickly but also to pay special heed to the most important elements of their environment. **Selective attention,** the ability to concentrate on some stimuli while ignoring

selective attention The ability to concentrate on some stimuli while ignoring others.

others, improves markedly at about age 7. School-age children not only notice various stimuli (which is one form of attention) but also select appropriate responses when several possibilities conflict (Rueda et al., 2007).

In the classroom, selective attention allows children to listen, take concise notes, and ignore distractions (all difficult at age 6, easier by age 10). In the din of the cafeteria, children can understand one another's gestures and expressions and react. On the baseball diamond, older batters ignore the other team's attempts to distract them, and older fielders start moving into position as soon as a ball is hit their way. Indeed, selective attention underlies all the abilities that gradually mature during the school years. "Networks of collaborating cortical regions" (M. H. Johnson et al., 2009, p. 151) are required because attention involves not just one brain function but three: alerting, orienting, and executive control (Posner et al., 2007).

BEN WELSH

Brains at Work Like all 10-year-olds, Luna and Carlotta love games. Playing games frequently makes some brain connections automatic, allowing players to concentrate on the most challenging aspects. Unlike the pastimes of 10-year-olds in previous generations, however, today's games usually involve small gadgets rather than big balls.

Automatic

One final advance in brain function in middle childhood is **automatization,** the process by which a sequence of thoughts and actions is repeated until it becomes automatic, or routine. At first, almost all behaviors under conscious control require careful and slow thought. After many repetitions, as neurons fire in sequence, actions become automatic and patterned. Less thinking is needed because the firing of one neuron sets off a chain reaction: That is automatization.

Consider again learning to read. At first, eyes (sometimes aided by a guiding finger) focus intensely, painstakingly making out letters and sounding out each one. This leads to the perception of syllables and then words. Eventually, the process becomes so automatic that, for instance, as you read this text, automatization allows you to concentrate on concepts without thinking about the letters. Automatization aids every skill. Learning to speak a second language, to recite the multiplication tables, and to write one's name are all slow at first but gradually become automatic.

Measuring the Mind

In ancient times, if an adult was strong and fertile, that was enough, worthy of admiration. By the twentieth century, however, cognitive abilities had become important; a stupid person, even if strong and fertile, was not admired. Because the mind became increasingly significant, many ways to measure intellect were developed.

Aptitude, Achievement, and IQ

In theory, **aptitude** is the potential to master a specific skill or to learn a certain body of knowledge. Intellectual aptitude is often measured by **IQ tests.** Originally, an IQ score was literally an intelligence quotient: Mental age (the age of a typical child who had reached a particular intellectual level) was divided by a child's chronological age, and the result of that division (the quotient) was multiplied by 100. The current method of calculating IQ is more complicated, but an IQ of 100 is still considered average (see Figure 11.3).

In theory, achievement is actual learning, not learning potential (aptitude). **Achievement tests** in school (see Chapter 12) compare scores to norms established for each grade. For example, third-grade students whose reading is typical of all third-grade students (achievement tests have national norms) would be at the third-grade level in reading achievement. Note, however, that third-graders

automatization A process in which repetition of a sequence of thoughts and actions makes the sequence routine, so that it no longer requires conscious thought.

aptitude The potential to master a specific skill or to learn a certain body of knowledge.

IQ test A test designed to measure intellectual aptitude, or ability to learn in school. Originally, intelligence was defined as mental age divided by chronological age, times 100—hence the term *intelligence quotient,* or *IQ.*

achievement test A measure of mastery or proficiency in reading, mathematics, writing, science, or some other subject.

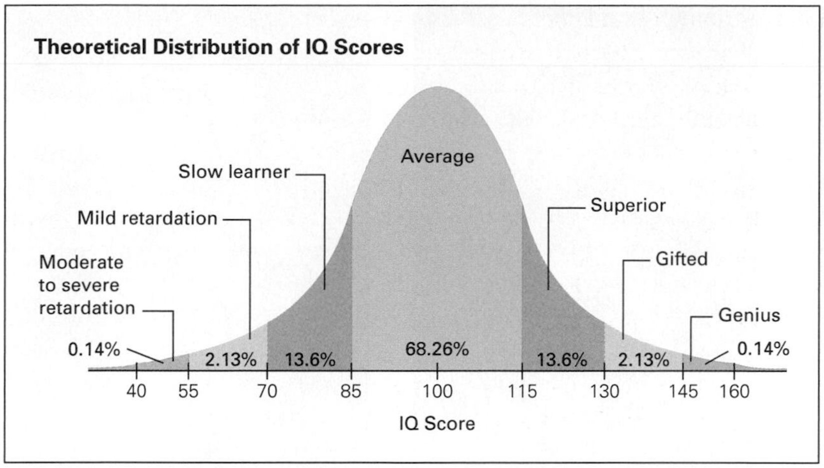

FIGURE 11.3

In Theory, Most People Are Average Almost 70 percent of IQ scores fall within the normal range. Note, however, that this is a norm-referenced test. In fact, actual IQ scores have risen in many nations; 100 is no longer exactly the midpoint. Furthermore, in practice, scores below 50 are slightly more frequent than indicated by the normal curve shown here because severe retardation is the result not of normal distribution but of genetic and prenatal factors.

Observation Quiz If a person's IQ is 110, what category is he or she in? (see answer, page 337)

who are 7, 8, or 9 years old might all be reading on grade level—achievement tests do not reflect age. The words *in theory* precede the definitions of aptitude and achievement because, although potential and accomplishment are supposed to be distinct, IQ and achievement scores are strongly correlated for individuals, for groups of children, and for nations (Lynn & Mikk, 2007).

It was once assumed that aptitude was a fixed characteristic, present at birth. Longitudinal data show that this is not the case. Children with a low IQ can become above average, or even gifted, like my nephew David (discussed in Chapter 1). Indeed, the average IQ scores of entire nations have risen substantially—a phenomenon called the **Flynn effect,** named after the researcher who first described it (Flynn, 1999, 2007).

A professor of psychology begins his attack on the hereditary view of intelligence with his personal experience:

> I began having trouble with arithmetic in the fifth grade, after I missed school for a week just when my class took up fractions. For the rest of elementary school, I never quite recovered from that setback. My parents were sympathetic, telling me that people in our family had never been very good at math. They viewed math skills as something you either had or not, for reasons having mostly to do with heredity.
>
> *[Nisbett, 2009, p. 1)*

Nisbett believes that his parents were wrong. He has gathered evidence that parents, schools, and cultures can raise a child's IQ substantially. Not every social scientist agrees with him. However, all agree that the IQ score is only a snapshot, a static view of a dynamic, developing brain.

Trial and Understanding This youngster completes one of the five performance tests of the Wechsler Intelligence Scale for Children (WISC). If her score is high, is that because of superior innate intelligence? ["Wechsler Intelligence Scale for Children" and "WISC" are trademarks, in the U.S. and/or other countries, of Pearson Education, Inc. or its affiliate(s).]

Flynn effect The rise in average IQ scores that has occurred over the decades in many nations.

Criticisms of Testing

Beyond the fact that scores change, a more fundamental question is whether any single test can measure the complexities of the human brain. This criticism has been targeted particularly at IQ tests when the underlying assumption is that there is one general thing called *intelligence* (often referred to as *g*, for general intelligence). Children may instead inherit a set of abilities, some high and some low, rather than a general intellectual ability (e.g., Q. Zhu et al., 2010). Leading developmentalists are among those who believe that humans have **multiple intelligences,** not just one.

Howard Gardner originally described seven intelligences: linguistic, logical-mathematical, musical, spatial, bodily-kinesthetic (movement), interpersonal (social

multiple intelligences The idea that human intelligence is comprised of a varied set of abilities rather than a single, all-encompassing one.

ANDREW JAMES / MIRRORPIX / NEWSCOM

CHRIS TROTMAN / GETTY IMAGES

ETHAN MILLER / GETTY IMAGES FOR ABC

High IQ? No. These three are not geniuses according to IQ tests, but they are each brilliant in their own way. *(a)* Rachel Trezise is a prize-winning Welsh novelist, *(b)* Carmelo Anthony is a star for the New York Knicks, and *(c)* Taboo is a lead singer for the Black Eyed Peas. Each excels in one of Gardner's nine multiple intelligences (respectively, linguistic, kinesthetic, and musical), but in other ways, each is simply average.

AMI VITALE / GETTY IMAGES

Genius at Work Ten-year-old Kishan Shrikanth is a Bollywood director, shown here shooting his first full-length feature film (about street children in India). He excels at some intelligences (spatial, interpersonal) but not others (kinesthetic, naturalistic). Such variations may be much more common than traditional IQ tests measure.

understanding), and intrapersonal (self-understanding), each associated with a particular brain region (Gardner, 1983). He subsequently added an eighth intelligence (naturalistic: understanding nature, as in biology, zoology, or farming) and a ninth (existential: thinking about life and death) (Gardner, 1999, 2006; Gardner & Moran, 2006). (See photos.)

Although every normal person has at least a little of all nine intelligences, Gardner believes each individual excels in some more than others. For example, someone might be gifted spatially but not linguistically (a visual artist who cannot describe her work) or might have interpersonal but not naturalistic intelligence (an astute clinical psychologist whose houseplants die).

Gardner's theory has been influential in education, especially the education of children (e.g., Armstrong, 2009; Rettig, 2005), as teachers allow children to demonstrate knowledge in their own ways—illustrating history with a drawing rather than an essay, for instance. Some children may learn by listening, others by looking, others by doing—an idea that led to research on learning styles.

Brain Scans

One way to measure the mind might be to measure the brain directly, avoiding the pitfalls of written exams or individual questions. Yet even with such measures, interpretations of brain scans, especially those of normal children, are controversial. Although it seems logical that less activation of the brain would mean less intelligence, such a conclusion would be a mistake.

In fact, many areas of a young child's brain are activated simultaneously and then, with practice, automatization reduces the need for brain activity, so the smartest children might have less active brains in some circumstances. Similarly, some research finds that a thick cortex correlates with higher ability and also that thickness develops more slowly in gifted children (Karama et al., 2009; Miller, 2006). This gifted pattern is puzzling—but so is much brain research.

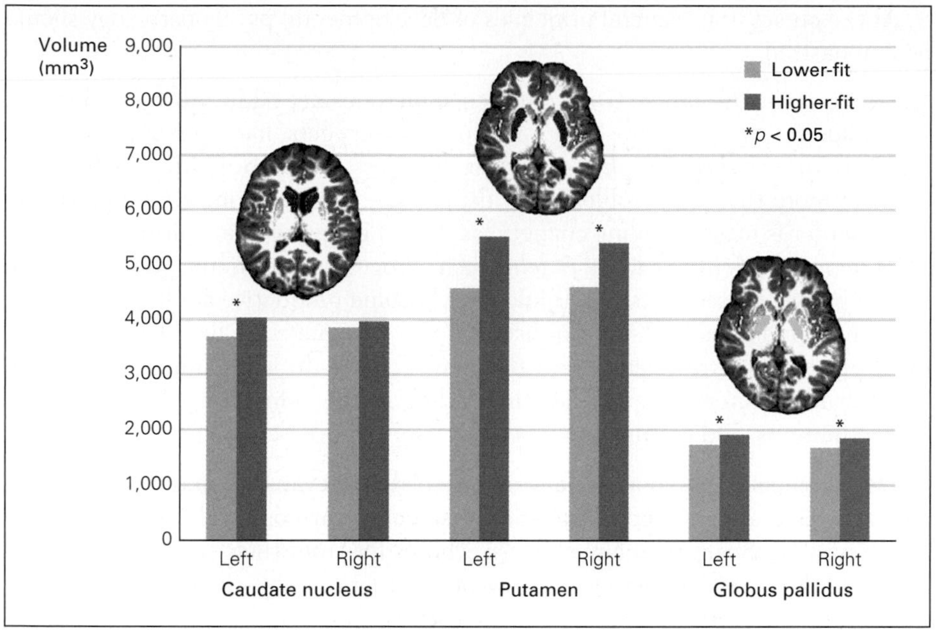

Brain Fitness Aerobic fitness was measured (by VO_2—volume of oxygen expelled after exercise) in 59 children (average age 10, none of whom had ADHD or were pubescent); then the children's brains were scanned. Overall brain size did not correlate with fitness—genes and early nutrition are more important for that. However, the volume of crucial areas for cognitive control (attention, contextualizing, planning) was significantly greater in the children who were in better shape. This is one more reason to go biking, running, or swimming with your child.

Neuroscientists agree, however, on three conclusions:

1. Brain development depends on a person's specific experiences because "brain, body, and environment are . . . dynamically coupled" (Marshall, 2009, p. 119), and thus any brain scan is accurate only for the moment it is done.
2. Brain development continues throughout life. Middle childhood is crucial, but so are developments before and after these years.
3. Children with disorders often have unusual brain patterns, and training their brains may help. However, brain complexity means that no neuroscience remediation always succeeds.

This leads to the final topic of this chapter, children with special needs.

>> **Answer to Observation Quiz** (from page 335) He or she is average. Anyone with a score between 85 and 115 is of average IQ.

SUMMING UP

During middle childhood, neurological maturation allows faster, more automatic reactions. Selective attention enables focused concentration in school and in play. Aptitude tests, including IQ tests, compare mental age to chronological age, while actual learning is measured by achievement tests. IQ scores change much more than was originally imagined, as children and cultures adapt to changing contexts. The concept that an IQ score measures one underlying aptitude is challenged by Howard Gardner and others, who believe that people have not just one type of intelligence but many. Neuroscientists see that brain activity does not reliably correlate with IQ scores. ■

Especially for Teachers What are the advantages and disadvantages of using Gardner's nine intelligences to guide your classroom curriculum? (see response, page 338)

>> Children with Special Needs

Developmental psychopathology links the study of typical development with the study of disorders (Cicchetti & Toth, 2009). Every topic already described including "genetics, neuroscience, developmental psychology . . . must be combined to understand how psychopathology develops and can be prevented" (Dodge, 2009, p. 413).

developmental psychopathology The field that uses insights into typical development to understand and remediate developmental disorders.

At the outset, four general principles of developmental psychopathology should be emphasized.

1. *Abnormality is normal.* Most children sometimes act oddly. At the same time, children with serious disorders are, in many respects, like everyone else.
2. *Disability changes year by year.* Most disorders are **comorbid,** which means that more than one problem is evident in the same person. Which particular disorder is most disabling changes, as does the degree of impairment.
3. *Life may be better or worse in adulthood.* Prognosis is difficult. Many children with severe disabilities (e.g., blindness) become productive adults. Conversely, some conditions (e.g., bipolar disorder) may become more disabling.
4. *Diagnosis and treatment reflect the social context.* In a dynamic system, each individual interacts with the surrounding setting—including family, school, community, and culture—to modify, worsen, or even create psychopathology.

comorbid Refers to the presence of two or more unrelated disease conditions at the same time in the same person.

>> Response for Teachers (from page 337) The advantages are that all the children learn more aspects of human knowledge and that many children can develop their talents. Art, music, and sports should be an integral part of education, not just a break from academics. The disadvantage is that they take time and attention away from reading and math, which might lead to less proficiency in those subjects on standard tests and thus to criticism from parents and supervisors.

Developmental psychopathology is especially relevant in middle childhood, when children are grouped by age and expected to learn on schedule. Those practices reveal problems in many children who differ from their peers. Fortunately, middle childhood is also a time when some disorders can be mitigated if treatment is early and targeted.

Therein lies a problem: Although treatment is more likely to succeed the earlier it begins, accurate diagnosis is more difficult the younger a child is, not only because many disorders are comorbid but also because symptoms differ by age. There is no simple link between cause and effect, which means that a specific behavior might be normal for children or might be an early sign of serious problems. As you remember, difference is not necessarily deficit—but this does not mean that differences are necessarily benign.

Two basic principles of developmental psychopathology are *multifinality* and *equifinality,* which lead to caution in diagnosis and treatment (Cicchetti & Toth, 2009). **Multifinality** means that one cause can have many (multiple) final manifestations (as when a child who has been flooded with stress hormones in infancy may be either hypervigilant or unusually calm, may be either easily angered or quick to cry, or may not be affected at all because of differential vulnerability). **Equifinality** (equal in final form) means that one symptom can have many causes (for instance, a 6-year-old who does not talk may be autistic, hard of hearing, mentally retarded, or electively mute).

multifinality A basic principle of developmental psychopathology that holds that one cause can have many (multiple) final manifestations.

equifinality A basic principle of developmental psychopathology that holds that one symptom can have many causes.

We focus here on only three topics (attention-deficit and bipolar disorders, learning disabilities, and autism spectrum disorder), each with many permutations. These three clusters illustrate the general principles of childhood psychopathology. (Readers interested in any specific condition are urged to read some of the extensive relevant research).

Attention-Deficit and Bipolar Disorders

These are two distinct disorders, but they are discussed together here because they are often comorbid and confused with each other (Miklowitz & Cicchetti, 2010). In childhood, equifinality is evident, in that both attention-deficit and bipolar disorders can be apparent in explosive rages and, later, deep regret.

Attention-Deficit Disorder

Perhaps 10 percent of all young children have an *attention-deficit disorder* (ADD), which means they have difficulty paying attention. Often ADD is accompanied by an uncontrollable urge to be active, in which case it is called **attention-deficit/hyperactivity disorder (ADHD).** Children with ADHD are inattentive, im-

attention-deficit/hyperactivity disorder (ADHD) A condition in which a person not only has great difficulty concentrating for more than a few moments but also is inattentive, impulsive, and overactive.

pulsive, and overactive and are thus disruptive when adults want them to be still (Barkley, 2006). About twice as many boys as girls have ADHD: Current estimates for children in middle childhood in the United States are 12 percent of boys and 6 percent of girls (National Center for Health Statistics, 2011).

A typical child with ADHD, when sitting down to do homework, might look up, ask questions, think about playing, get a drink, fidget, squirm, tap the table, jiggle his or her legs, and go to the bathroom—and then start the whole sequence again. Not surprisingly, such children tend to have academic difficulties; they are less likely to graduate from high school and college (Loe & Feldman, 2007).

SACRAMENTO BEE / LEZLIE STERLING / ZUMA PRESS

Almost Impossible The concentration needed to do homework is almost beyond Clint, age 11, who takes medication for ADHD. Note his furrowed brow, resting head, and sad face.

Observation Quiz Will he complete his homework on his own? (see answer, page 340)

The number of children diagnosed with ADHD has increased in the United States from about 5 percent in 1980 to about 10 percent currently. Rates are affected by ethnicity: More European American children than Latino ones are thought to have ADHD—at least as measured by medication use. The rate has also doubled in Europe (e.g., Hsia & Maclennan, 2009; van den Ban et al., 2010).

Bipolar Disorder

Bipolar disorder is characterized by extreme mood swings, from euphoria to deep depression. Children with bipolar disorder experience at least one episode of grandiosity. They might believe, for instance, that they are the smartest person in the school, a genius destined to save the entire world. At other times, that child might be severely depressed, unwilling or unable to read, play with friends, or go to school (Miklowitz & Cicchetti, 2010).

bipolar disorder A condition characterized by extreme mood swings, from euphoria to deep depression, not caused by outside experiences.

One U.S. study reports that medical visits for youth under age 18 with a primary diagnosis of bipolar disorder (one-third of them comorbid with attention-deficit disorder) increased 40-fold between 1995 and 2003, a period when adult diagnosis of bipolar disorder merely doubled (Moreno et al., 2007). It is virtually impossible for such a rapid increase to occur in actual psychopathology. That led critics to suggest that childhood bipolar disorder was a diagnosis in the mind of the observer, not in the moods of the child. However, careful analysis suggests that childhood bipolar disorder was often an accurate diagnosis. It is now thought that the rapid increase in diagnosis was the result of earlier misdiagnosis, not current overdiagnosis (Miklowitz & Cicchetti, 2010; Santosh & Canagaratnam, 2008).

Go Team Remember that abnormality is normal. Which of these boys has been diagnosed with a serious disability? Michael, second from the right, has bipolar disorder.

MARC ASNIN / REDUX

Distinguishing Between Disorders

Bipolar disorder "remains notoriously difficult to differentiate from other psychiatric illnesses in youth" (Phillips, 2010, p. 4). Many children diagnosed with either ADHD or bipolar disorder may be more accurately diagnosed with the other. Some symptoms are the same: Children with either disorder tend to be irritable, even rageful, when adults demand that they behave normally. Most with either condition have trouble sleeping, are sometimes notably active, and at other times are depressed.

Both disorders are more common in children whose parents have a disorder, which strongly suggests a genetic link. However, the specifics of parental disability differ.

>> Answer to Observation Quiz (from page 339) No. His mother is writing the answers for him.

Especially for Health Workers Parents ask that some medication be prescribed for their kindergarten child, who they say is much too active for them to handle. How do you respond? (see response, page 342)

Parents of children with ADHD often have learning disabilities, whereas parents of children with bipolar disorder are likely to have mood disturbances, including depression or eating disorders (also equifinal, in that not all eating disorders are related to emotional problems but many are).

Both disorders in children are also linked to unusual brain patterns, either in structures or activity, although, again, some differences may be apparent (Riccio et al., 2010; Santosh & Canagaratnam, 2008). In one study, children's brain activity was measured while they observed pictures of faces. Children with either disorder were less able to differentiate emotions than were the control-group children, but different parts of the amygdala were aroused in children with ADHD and in those with bipolar disorder (Brotman et al., 2008, 2010). There is not yet any definitive biological or neurological sign of either disorder, however.

Treatment involves (1) counseling and training for the family and the child, (2) showing teachers how to help the children learn, and (3) medication to stabilize moods for bipolar children and to quiet ADHD children. Ongoing monitoring is crucial because stimulants may help children with ADHD but harm bipolar ones. Even with accurate diagnosis, each child responds differently to each drug, and responses change with time. Psychoactive medication for children raises many issues, as the following explains.

A VIEW FROM SCIENCE

Drugs for Children

In the United States, more than 2 million children and adolescents under age 18 take prescription drugs to regulate their emotions and behavior. The rate has leveled off in recent years but remains high, with about 1 in 20 children taking psychoactive drugs in middle childhood, usually for ADHD (Scheffler et al., 2009; Vitiello et al., 2006; Zuvekas et al., 2006). In many other nations, drug use in middle childhood has recently increased (e.g., Hsia & Maclennan, 2009; van den Ban et al., 2010).

The most commonly prescribed drug is Ritalin for ADHD, but at least 20 other psychoactive drugs treat depression, anxiety, developmental delay, autism, bipolar disorder, and many other conditions in middle childhood. Younger children (ages 2 to 5) are taking these drugs at increasing rates, although their rates (about 1 child in 600) are far lower than for older children (Olfson et al., 2010). Because they have been inadequately tested for children, many drugs are prescribed "off label"—they have not been approved for patients of that age or condition. The incidence, ages, rates, and off-label uses all raise questions. Much of the American public is suspicious of any childhood psychiatric medicine (dosReis & Myers, 2008; McLeod et al., 2004; Rose, 2008).

Many child psychologists believe that drugs can be helpful, but they raise additional issues (Mayes et al., 2009). They find that some parents punish their children instead of seeking help, and developmentalists know that, for every child, finding the best drug at the right strength is difficult. Moreover, since children's weight and metabolism change, the right dose at one time is wrong at another.

Underdosing and overdosing are especially destructive when brains and habits are developing, yet only about half of all 2- to 5-year-olds who take psychoactive drugs are evaluated and monitored by a mental health professional (Olfson et al., 2010), and only half of the children diagnosed with ADHD take medication of any kind for it (National Center for Health Statistics, 2011).

Most professionals are convinced by research that finds that medication helps schoolchildren with emotional problems, particularly ADHD (Epstein et al., 2010; King et al., 2009; Scheffler et al., 2009). Some professionals also believe that contextual interventions (instructing parents and teachers on how best to manage such children) should be tried before any drug (Daley et al., 2009; Pelham & Fabiano, 2008).

By contrast, parents are less sure. One study of parents whose children were diagnosed with ADHD found that about 20 percent believed drugs should *never* be used for children, and about 29 percent believed that drugs were *necessary to* treat illnesses. The other 51 percent were in neither camp (dosReis et al., 2009). That was a small study (48 families), but a large-scale study found that only about half (56 percent) of the parents of U.S. children who are diagnosed with ADHD give them medication every day (Scheffler et al., 2009). African American children have more ADHD symptoms but are less often medicated, for reasons that include fragmented medical care and distrust of doctors (Miller et al., 2009).

The result of the discrepancy between public attitudes and research data is that some children who would benefit are never given medication, other children are given medication without the necessary monitoring, and still other children are given medication only until their symptoms subside. A group of children with ADHD from many cities in the United States and Canada were given appropriate medication, carefully calibrated. Their symptoms improved. However, eight years later, many had stopped taking their medicine. At this follow-up, both those who were still on medication and those who had stopped were likely to have learning difficulties and lower grades in school (Molina et al., 2009). Thus, the drug did not erase the problems.

What about long-term effects of taking medication? Much remains to be learned, and opinions are divided. However, two concerns—that children who take drugs in childhood will become adolescent addicts and that their growth will be stunted—seem invalid. In fact, longitudinal research comparing nonmedicated and medicated children with ADHD finds the opposite: Childhood medication reduces the risk of illegal drug use in adolescence and does not seem to adversely affect growth (Biederman et al., 2010; Faraone et al., 2003).

When appropriately used, drugs may help children make friends, learn in school, feel happier, and behave better. However, as the longitudinal study of ADHD children found, problems do not disappear: Adolescents who had childhood emotional problems were less successful academically and personally, whether or not they were medicated (Geller et al., 2008; Loe & Feldman, 2007; Molina et al., 2009). When children have special needs, parents and teachers need support and training. Drugs may help, but they are not the solution.

Learning Disabilities

Many people have some specific **learning disability** that leads to difficulty in mastering a particular skill that most other people acquire easily. Indeed, according to Gardner's view of multiple intelligences, almost everyone has a specific inadequacy or two. Perhaps one person is clumsy (low in kinesthetic intelligence), while another sings loudly but off key (low in musical intelligence).

Most such learning disabilities are not debilitating (the off-key singer learns to be quiet in chorus), but every schoolchild is expected to learn reading and math. Disabilities in either of these two subjects often undercut academic achievement and make a child feel inadequate, ashamed, and stupid. Hopefully, such children find (or are taught) ways to compensate: They learn coping strategies, and in adulthood their other abilities shine. Winston Churchill, Albert Einstein, and Hans Christian Andersen are all said to have had learning disabilities as children.

learning disability A marked delay in a particular area of learning that is not caused by an apparent physical disability, by mental retardation, or by an unusually stressful home environment.

dyslexia Unusual difficulty with reading; thought to be the result of some neurological underdevelopment.

Dyslexia

The most commonly diagnosed learning disability is **dyslexia,** unusual difficulty with reading. No single test accurately diagnoses dyslexia (or any learning disability) because every academic achievement involves many specifics (Riccio & Rodriguez, 2007). One child with a reading disability might have trouble sounding out words but might excel in comprehension and memory of printed text; another child might have the opposite problem. Dozens of types and causes of dyslexia have been identified.

Early theories hypothesized that visual difficulties—for example, reversals of letters (reading *was* instead of *saw*) and mirror writing (*b* instead of *d*)—were the cause of dyslexia, but we now know that dyslexia often originates with speech and hearing difficulties (Gabrieli, 2009). An early warning occurs if a 3-year-old does not talk clearly or has not exhibited a naming explosion (see Chapter 6). Early speech therapy might reduce or prevent later dyslexia.

© LAURENT / GLUCK

Say Ooo Most children teach themselves to talk clearly, but some need special help—as this 5-year-old does. Mirrors, mentoring, and manipulation may all be part of speech therapy.

>> Response for Health Workers (from page 340) Medication helps some hyperactive children, but not all. It might be useful for this child, but other forms of intervention should be tried first. Compliment the parents on their concern about their child, but refer them to an expert in early childhood for an evaluation and recommendations. Behavior-management techniques geared to the particular situation, not medication, will be the first strategy.

Dyscalculia

Similar suggestions apply to learning disabilities in math, called *dyscalculia.* Early help with numbers and concepts (long before first grade) can help prevent the emotional anxiety that occurs if a child is made to feel stupid (Butterworth et al., 2011). Remember that in early childhood, maybe even in infancy, most children can look at a series of dots and estimate how many there are. This basic number sense is deficient in children with dyscalculia, which provides a clue for early remediation (Piazza et al., 2010).

When a young child has trouble performing tasks that other children can do easily, such problems can be spotted in brain scans. For example, a second-grader, when asked to estimate the height of a normal room, might answer "200 feet" or, when asked whether the 5 or the 8 of hearts is higher, correctly answer 8—but only after counting the number of hearts on each card (Butterworth et al., 2011). Some success has occurred using computers to train children with dyscalculia to improve in number understanding, but—remember equifinality—this does not help every child.

Autism Spectrum Disorders

Of all the special-needs children, those with autism are probably the most troubling, not only because their problems are severe but also because the causes of and treatments for autism are hotly disputed. Most children with autism can be spotted in the first year of life, but some seem quite normal at first and then deteriorate later on.

Parents' responses vary, from irrational hope to deep despair, from blaming doctors and public policy to feeling guilty. Developmentalists generally believe that genes are one factor in autism but that parents are not to blame. Parents and teachers can be very helpful, however, if they cooperate while the child is young.

Symptoms

autism A developmental disorder marked by an inability to relate to other people normally, extreme self-absorption, and an inability to acquire normal speech.

autism spectrum disorder Any of several disorders characterized by inadequate social skills, impaired communication, and unusual play.

Autism is characterized by woefully inadequate social skills. Half a century ago, it was considered a single, rare disorder affecting fewer than 1 in 1,000 children with "an extreme aloneness that, whenever possible, disregards, ignores, shuts out anything . . . from the outside" (Kanner, 1943). Children who developed slowly but were not so withdrawn were diagnosed as being mentally retarded or as having a "pervasive developmental disorder."

Much has changed in the past decades. Now many children who would have been considered retarded are said to have an **autism spectrum disorder,** which characterizes about 1 in every 110 children (three times as many boys as girls and more European Americans than Latino, Asian, or African Americans) (Lord & Bishop, 2010). Some of these children do not seem mentally retarded at all.

There are three signs of an autism spectrum disorder: (1) delayed language; (2) impaired social responses; and (3) unusual, repetitive play. Underlying all three is a kind of emotional blindness (Scambler et al., 2007). Children with any form of autism find it difficult to understand the emotions of others, which makes them feel alien, like "an anthropologist on Mars," as Temple Grandin, an educator and writer with autism, expressed it (quoted in Sacks, 1995). Consequently, they do not want to talk, play, or otherwise interact with anyone, and they are especially delayed in developing a theory of mind (Senju et al., 2010).

Autism spectrum disorders include many symptoms of varied severity. Some children never speak, rarely smile, and often play for hours with one object (such as a spinning top or a toy train). Others are called "high-functioning" (or are said to have *Asperger syndrome*)—they are extremely talented in some specialized area, such as drawing or geometry, and their speech is close to normal. Many are brilliant in unusual ways (Dawson et al., 2007), including Grandin, a well-respected expert on animal care (Grandin & Johnson, 2009). However, social interaction is always impaired. Grandin was bewildered by romantic love.

Far more children have autism spectrum disorders now than in 1990, either because the incidence of this disorder has increased or because more children receive that diagnosis. You read earlier that currently about 1 child in 110 is autistic. This figure is based on careful assessment, but other research puts the number even higher—perhaps 1 child in 40. Underlying that estimate is the reality that no definitive measure diagnoses autism: Many people are socially inept and poor at communication—are they all somewhat autistic?

The hypothesis that the diagnosis, not the disorder, is more common is supported by a detailed study in Texas showing that in the wealthiest school districts, the number of children diagnosed with autism tripled over six years, but the number did not change in the poorest districts (Palmer et al., 2005; see the Research Design).

Research Design

Scientists: Raymond Palmer, Stephen Blanchard, and David Mandall designed the study, and C. R. Jean provided critical interpretation.

Publication: *American Journal of Public Health (2005).*

Participants: All 1,040 school districts in Texas over six school years, 1994 to 2001.

Design: The school districts were sorted into tenths according to wealth—a composite of average income, salaries, proportion of disadvantaged students, and so on. Within each tenth, the number of students designated as autistic was tallied each year.

Major conclusion: Increases in diagnosis of students with autism spectrum disorders correlated with wealth, from an increase of 300 percent in districts in the top two-tenths to no change in the bottom tenth. For every 10,000 children, 21 in the top districts and 3 in the bottom districts were designated as having autism.

Comments: These findings, covering an entire state, suggest that increases in the incidence of autism are caused by better diagnosis, more available physicians, advanced special education, and perhaps parental insistence on diagnosis and treatment.

Treatment

Equifinality certainly applies to autism: A child can have autistic symptoms for many reasons, which makes treatment difficult. An intervention that seems to help one child proves worthless for another. Biology is crucial (genes, birth complications, prenatal injury, or perhaps chemicals) and brain patterns are unusual; autism is not caused by family nurture (G. Dawson, 2010). One family factor may be influential, however: having one baby soon after another. Children born less than a year after a previous birth are more than twice as often diagnosed as autistic compared with children born 3 or more years apart (Cheslack-Postava et al., 2011).

A vast number of treatments have been used for children with autism spectrum disorders, none of them completely successful. Some parents are convinced that a particular treatment helped their child, whereas other parents say that same treatment failed. Scientists disagree as well. For instance, one popular treatment is putting the child in a hyperbaric chamber to breathe more concentrated oxygen than is found in everyday air. Two studies of hyperbaric treatments—both randomized in participant selection and both with control groups—reported contradictory results, either benefits (Rossignol et al., 2009) or no effect (Granpeesheh et al., 2010). Part of the problem may be multifinality and equifinality: Children with autism spectrum disorders have core symptoms in common, but they also differ in the cause and consequence of those symptoms.

An added problem is the gap between parents and professionals. One example concerns thimerosal, an antiseptic containing mercury that was once used in childhood immunizations. Many parents first noticed their infants' impairments after their vaccinations and believe thimerosal was the cause. No scientist who examines the evidence agrees: Extensive research has disproven the immunization hypothesis many times (Offit, 2008). Thimerosal was removed from vaccines a decade ago, but the rates of autism are still rising. Many doctors fear that parents who cling to this hypothesis are harming millions of children who suffer needless illnesses because some parents fear immunization.

Some children with autism are on special diets, take vitamin supplements, or are on medication. One drug in particular, rispridone, relieves some symptoms (although research finds side effects, including weight gain), but no treatment has

Precious Gifts Many children with autism are gifted artists. This boy attends a school in Montmoreau, France, that features workshops in which children with autism develop social, play, and learning skills.

AP PHOTO / THE TUSCALOOSA NEWS, DUSTY COMPTON

All Together Now Kiemel Lamb (top center) leads autistic children in song, a major accomplishment. For many of them, music is soothing, words are difficult, and hand-holding in a group is almost impossible.

proven successful at relieving the basic condition. As you already know, all medication use is controversial: Whether or not a child takes rispridone depends on many factors other than symptoms (Arnold et al., 2010; Rosenberg et al., 2010).

Many behavioral methods to improve talking and socialization have also been tried, again with mixed results (Granpeesheh et al., 2009; Hayward et al., 2009; Howlin et al., 2009). Early and individualized education of both the child and the parents has had some success, although the connection between disorder and special education is an uncertain one, as you will now see.

Special Education

The overlap of the biosocial, cognitive, and psychosocial domains is evident to developmentalists, who see each child's growth in every area affected by every other area. However, whether or not a child is designated as needing special education is not straightforward, nor is it closely related to specific special needs. Here, we discuss education as it pertains to developmental psychopathology, but the link between disorder and education is problematic. (Education is also discussed in every chapter on cognitive development, including the next one.)

Changing Laws and Practices

In the United States, recognition that the distinction between normal and abnormal is not clear-cut (the first principle of developmental psychopathology) led to a series of reforms in the treatment and education of children with special needs. According to the 1975 Education of All Handicapped Children Act, children with special needs must be educated in the **least restrictive environment (LRE).**

least restrictive environment (LRE) A legal requirement that children with special needs be assigned to the most general educational context in which they can be expected to learn.

Most of the time, LRE has meant educating children with special needs with other children in a regular class, sometimes called *mainstreaming,* rather than in a special classroom or school. Sometimes a child is sent to a *resource room,* with a teacher who provides targeted tutoring. Sometimes a class is an *inclusion class,* which means that children with special needs are "included" in the general classroom, with "appropriate aids and services" (usually from a trained teacher who works with the regular teacher) (Kalambouka et al., 2007).

The latest educational strategy in the United States is called **response to intervention (RTI)** (Fletcher & Vaughn, 2009; Shapiro et al., 2011). All children in the early grades who are below average in achievement (which may be half the class) are given some special intervention. Most of them respond by improving their achievement, but for those who do not, more intervention occurs. If there is no response to repeated intervention, the child is referred for testing and observation to diagnose the problem.

response to intervention (RTI) An educational strategy intended to help children in early grades who demonstrate below-average achievement by means of special intervention.

Professionals use a battery of tests (not just IQ or achievement tests) to reach their diagnosis and develop recommendations. If they find that a child has special needs, they discuss an **individual education plan (IEP)** with the parents, to specify educational goals for the child.

individual education plan (IEP) A document that specifies educational goals and plans for a child with special needs.

Cohort and Culture

Looking at Table 11.1, you can see cohort effects. More than one in four of the children with special needs in 1977 were called "mentally retarded," a category now called "intellectually disabled"; currently, of those needing special education, only about one child in 14 is designated as intellectually disabled. However, in 2010, of the special needs children, about 5 percent were designated as autistic and almost 6 percent were designated developmentally delayed (Snyder & Dillow, 2011). Neither of those two categories existed in 1977. Apparently, some children who were considered mentally retarded in the 1970s would have been called autistic or developmentally delayed if they had been diagnosed today. Labels change more quickly with the times than symptoms do.

TABLE 11.1 **Proportion of Children with Special Education Needs by Specific Designation* (percent of children)**

	1977		1997		2007	
Learning disabilities	21.5	(1.8**)	46	(5.9)	39	(5.2)
Speech impairment	35.2	(2.9)	17	(2.3)	22	(3.0)
Mentally retarded	28	(2.2)	10.0	(1.3)	7.6	(1.0)
Emotionally disturbed	7.7	(0.6)	7.7	(1.0)	6.7	(0.9)
Deafness and hearing loss	2.4	(0.2)	1.2	(0.2)	1.2	(0.2)
Blindness and low vision	1	(0.1)	0.4	(0.1)	0.4	(0.1)
Developmental delay	—	—			5.4	(0.7)
Autism spectrum	—		0.7	(0.1)	4.5	(0.6)
Orthopedic handicap	2.4	(0.2)	1.2	(0.1)	1.0	(0.1)
Other health problems***	2.8	(0.3)	3.2	(0.5)	9.7	(1.3)

*Based on evaluation by U.S. public school professionals.

**Numbers in parentheses are percentages of all public school children.

***Limited strength, vitality, or alertness due to chronic health problems, such as asthma, sickle-cell anemia, and diabetes.

Source: Snyder & Dillow (2010).

Looking internationally, the connection between special needs and education varies for cultural reasons, not child-related ones. In many African and Latin American nations, no children are designated as having special needs; in many Asian nations, the diagnosis of special needs refers primarily to the physically disabled. As a result, in Taiwan, for example, less than 1 percent of the students receive special education of any kind (Tzeng, 2007).

Gifted and Talented

Children who are unusually gifted are often thought to have special needs as well, yet they are not covered by the federal laws for the disabled. Each state of the United States selects and educates gifted and talented children, but the specifics not only vary—they are also hotly debated. A scholar writes: "The term gifted . . . has never been more problematic than it is today" (Dai, 2011, p. 8). Educators, political leaders, scientists, and everyone else argue about who is gifted and what should be done about them. Are gifted children unusually intelligent, or talented, or creative? Should they be skipped, segregated, enriched, included, or left alone?

A hundred years ago, the definition of gifted was simple: high IQ. A famous longitudinal study followed a thousand "genius" children, all of whom scored about 140 on the Stanford-Binet IQ test (Terman, 1925). Even today, some school systems define gifted as having an IQ of 130 or above (attained by 1 child in 50), or sometimes as 145 and above (1 child in 1,000).

acceleration Educating gifted children alongside other children of the same mental, not chronological, age.

A hundred years ago, the educational solution was simple, too: Educate them with children who were their mental age, not their chronological age, a practice called **acceleration.** Today this is rarely done because many of those accelerated children were bullied, unhappy, and never learned proper social skills. As one woman remembers:

> Nine-year-old little girls are so cruel to younger girls. I was much smaller than them, of course, and would have done anything to have a friend. Although I could cope with the academic work very easily, emotionally I wasn't up to it. Maybe it was my fault and I was asking to be picked on. I was a weed at the edge of the playground.
>
> *[Rachel, quoted in Freeman, 2010, p. 27]*

Weeds grow no matter where they are planted, and research on thousands of children has found that while the gifted learn differently from other children, they are neither more nor less likely to need emotional and social education. Educating the whole child, not just the mind, is required (Winner, 1996).

There is a related type of special child, often called talented instead of gifted, who is precocious in one of Gardner's nine intelligences. Mozart was such a child, composing music at age 3; so was Pablo Picasso, creating works of art at age 4. Historically, many famous musicians, artists, and scientists were child prodigies whose fathers recognized their talent (often because the father himself was in the same field) and provided special education. Mozart's father transcribed his son's earliest creations and toured Europe with his gifted son. Picasso's father removed him from school in second grade so he could create all day (Pablo said he never learned to read or write).

Although such intense early education nourished talent, neither Mozart nor Picasso had happy adult lives. Similar patterns are still apparent, as exemplified by gifted athletes (e.g., Tiger Woods and Steffi Graf) as well as those in more erudite specialties. One recent example:

> Sufiah Yusof started her maths degree at Oxford [the leading University in England] in 2000, at the age of 13. She too had been dominated and taught by her father. But she ran away the day after her final exam. She was found by police but refused to go home, demanding of her father in an email: "Has it ever crossed your mind that the reason I left home was because I've finally had enough of 15 years of physical and emotional abuse?" Her father claimed she'd been abducted and brainwashed. She refuses to communicate with him. She is now a very happy, high-class, high-earning prostitute.
>
> *[Freeman, 2010, p. 286]*

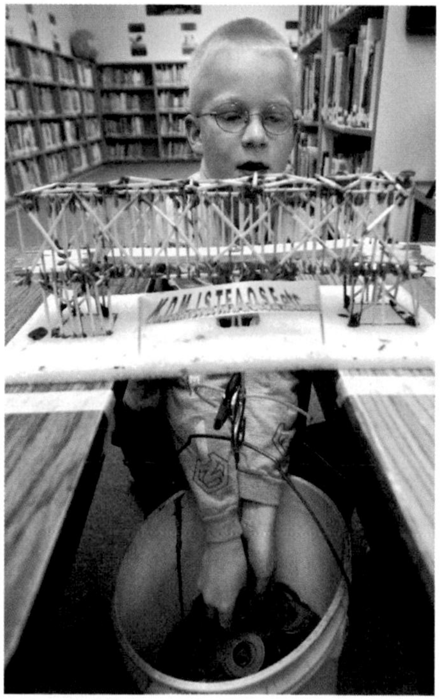

AP PHOTO / MOSCOW-PULLMAN DAILY NEWS, GEOFF CRIMMINS

Fourth Grade Challenge How much weight can a bridge hold? Thirty-three students in gifted classes at an Idaho elementary school designed and built toothpick bridges and then tested them. David Stubbens (shown here) added 61 pounds to the bucket before his bridge collapsed.

A third kind of child who might need special education is the unusually creative one (Sternberg et al., 2011). They are *divergent thinkers,* finding many solutions and even more questions for every problem. Such students joke in class, dodge drudgery, resist repetition, and bedevil their teachers. They may become innovators, inventors, and creative forces of the future.

Creative children do not conform to social standards. They are not *convergent thinkers,* who choose the correct answer on school exams. One such person was Charles Darwin, whose "school reports complained unendingly that he wasn't interested in studying, only shooting, riding, and beetle-collecting" (Freeman, 2010, p. 283). Other creative geniuses who were poor students were Einstein, Freud, Newton, and almost every contemporary innovator.

Since both acceleration and intense parental tutoring have led to later problems, a third method of educating the gifted has become popular, at least in the United States. A group of children who are bright, talented, and/or creative—all the same age but each with special abilities—are taught as a group. Ideally, such children are neither bored nor lonely; each is challenged and appreciated.

Neuroscience has recently discovered another advantage: brain development. Many studies have found that children who are allowed to practice their musical talents develop brain structures that enhance their talent. Specialized brain growth is also likely for child athletes and mathematicians, suggesting that neurological specialization in childhood may occur for every form of giftedness. As you know, a child's brain is quite plastic, and all children learn whatever their context teaches. Thus, talents may be developed, not wasted, with special education.

THINKING CRITICALLY

Fair and Reasonable Grounds?

How can a school system know which children will be geniuses? Is the class clown a creative soul who needs to be cherished or a disruptive child who needs to be disciplined? Tests of creativity have been developed, but such tests are imperfect at distinguishing the "schoolhouse gifted" from the "creative-productive gifted"; both kinds of giftedness may need specialized education, but the specifics would differ (Renzulli, 2009). Indeed, identification and then education is imperfect for all gifted children (Dai, 2010). If a child is above average (say, an IQ of 120), eventual success may depend more on motivation, personality, and good fortune than on teaching and test scores.

Furthermore, how can we be sure that the designation is valid and fair? Gifted children of lower-SES families, or those from less privileged ethnic groups, may be unfairly excluded. Bias against girls, or boys, may be problematic as well.

This concern is not abstract. Consider data from the United States in 2006 (Snyder & Dillow, 2011). Of every 150 schoolchildren, 23 in Kentucky are designated gifted and talented; only 1 in Massachusetts is designated as such. Obviously, something in the culture or politics of those states, not in the nature of the children, influences this determination.

Most states have 10 percent more girls than boys in gifted classes (sexist or biological?), yet three states (Kansas, New Mexico, and South Dakota) have about 10 percent more boys than girls in such classes (fair?). In most states, the percent of White children in gifted-and-talented classes is twice as high as the number of children from minority groups (politics or biology?), but rates are almost equal in Utah (fair?). In most states, higher proportions of African Americans than Hispanics are designated as gifted, but the opposite is true in Texas (politics or biology?).

A leading U.S. educator suggests that we scrap all designations of gifted or talented children and

> give up the notions of the "the normal," "the disabled," and "the gifted" as they are typically applied in schools, especially for the purposes of classification and grouping, and simply accept difference as the rule.
>
> *[Borland, 2003, p. 121]*

All developmentalists now see that there are many valid ways to designate and educate gifted and talented children and that the best solution reflects the cultural context. But the specifics of that best solution are far from obvious.

SUMMING UP

Many children have special learning needs that originate with problems in the development of their brains. Developmental psychopathologists emphasize that no one is typical in every way; the passage of time sometimes brings improvement to children with special needs and sometimes not. Children with attention-deficit disorders, learning disabilities, and autism spectrum disorders may function adequately or may have lifelong problems, depending on many variables such as the severity of the problem; family, school, and cultural environments; and the presence of comorbid conditions. Specifics of diagnosis, prognosis, medication, and education are debatable; no child learns or behaves exactly like another, and no educational strategy is entirely successful with every child. ■

SUMMARY

A Healthy Time

1. Middle childhood is a time of steady growth and few serious illnesses. Increasing independence and self-care allow most school-age children to be relatively happy and competent.

2. Advances in medical care have reduced childhood sickness and death. Immunization is effective, fewer children are exposed to toxins, and early diagnosis and treatment have mitigated many conditions.

3. Physical activity aids health and joy in many ways. However, current social and environmental conditions make informal neighborhood play scarce, school physical education less prevalent, and sports leagues less welcoming for some school-age children.

Health Problems in Middle Childhood

4. Childhood obesity is a worldwide epidemic. Although genes are part of the problem, less exercise and the greater availability of unhealthy foods are the main reasons today's youth are heavier than their counterparts 50 years ago. Parents and policies share the blame.

5. The incidence of asthma is increasing overall, with notable ethnic differences. The origins of asthma are genetic; the triggers are specific environmental allergens. Preventive measures include longer breast-feeding, increased outdoor play, and less air pollution, particularly from cars.

Brain Development

6. Brain development continues during middle childhood, enhancing every aspect of development. Notable are advances in reaction time and automatization, allowing faster and better coordination of many parts of the brain.

7. IQ tests quantify intellectual aptitude. Most such tests emphasize language and logical ability and predict school achievement. IQ scores sometimes change over time, partly because of maturation but primarily because of experience.

8. Achievement tests measure accomplishment, often in specific academic areas. Aptitude and achievement are correlated, both for individuals and for nations.

9. Critics contend that intelligence is manifested in multiple ways that conventional IQ tests are too limited to measure. Multiple intelligences include creative and practical abilities as well as many skills not usually valued in typical North American schools.

Children with Special Needs

10. Developmental psychopathology uses an understanding of normal development to inform the study of unusual development. Four general lessons have emerged: Abnormality is normal; disability changes over time; adolescence and adulthood may make a condition better or worse; and diagnosis depends on context.

11. Children with attention-deficit/hyperactivity disorder (ADHD) have potential problems in three areas: inattention, impulsiveness, and overactivity. Stimulant medication often helps children with ADHD to learn, but any drug use by children must be carefully monitored.

12. Children with bipolar disorder have marked mood swings, from grandiosity to depression. This disorder is often mistaken for attention-deficit/hyperactivity disorder.

13. People with learning disabilities have unusual difficulty in mastering a specific skill that other people learn easily. The most common learning disability that manifests itself during the school years is dyslexia, unusual difficulty with reading.

14. Children with autism spectrum disorders typically show odd and delayed language ability, impaired interpersonal skills, and unusual play. Many causes are hypothesized. Autism is partly genetic; no one now views autism as primarily the result of inadequate parenting. Treatments are diverse: All are controversial and none are certain to help.

15. About 13 percent of all school-age children in the United States receive special education services. These services begin with an IEP (individual education plan) and assignment to the least restrictive environment (LRE), usually the regular classroom.

KEY TERMS

middle childhood (p. 323)
BMI (body mass index) (p. 328)
overweight (p. 328)
obesity (p. 328)
asthma (p. 330)
reaction time (p. 333)
selective attention (p. 333)
automatization (p. 334)
aptitude (p. 334)
IQ test (p. 334)
achievement test (p. 334)
Flynn effect (p. 335)
multiple intelligences (p. 335)
developmental psychopathology (p. 337)
comorbid (p. 338)
multifinality (p. 338)
equifinality (p. 338)
attention-deficit/hyperactivity disorder (ADHD) (p. 338)
bipolar disorder (p. 339)
learning disability (p. 341)
dyslexia (p. 341)
autism (p. 342)
autism spectrum disorder (p. 342)
least restrictive environment (LRE) (p. 344)
response to intervention (RTI) (p. 345)
individual education plan (IEP) (p. 345)
acceleration (p. 346)

WHAT HAVE YOU LEARNED?

A Healthy Time

1. What physical abilities emerge from age 6 to age 11?

2. How do childhood health habits affect adult health?

3. What are the main advantages and disadvantages of physical play during middle childhood?

4. How do children benefit from physical education in school?

5. How do SES, gender, and culture affect after-school activities?

Health Problems in Middle Childhood

6. What are the national and cohort differences in childhood obesity?

7. Why does a thin 6-year-old not need to fatten up?

8. What roles do nature and nurture play in childhood asthma?

9. What would be primary prevention for childhood obesity?

10. Why does good tertiary prevention for childhood asthma not reach every child who needs it?

Brain Development

11. Why does quicker reaction time improve the ability to learn?

12. How do changes in brain functioning make it easier for a child to sit in a classroom?

13. When would a teacher give an aptitude test instead of an achievement test?

14. If the theory of multiple intelligences is correct, should IQ tests be discarded? Why or why not?

15. Why are some intellectual abilities valued more than others? Give examples.

16. Should brain scans replace traditional intelligence tests? Why or why not?

Children with Special Needs

17. What would be normal child behavior in one culture but not in another?

18. What examples illustrate the difference between multifinality and equifinality?

19. Why is medication recommended for children with ADHD?

20. Why might parents ask a doctor to prescribe Ritalin for their child?

21. Why is bipolar disorder hard to diagnose in children?

22. What is the difference between bipolar disorder in children and in adults?

23. What specific learning disabilities are not recognized in the United States currently?

24. How could an adult have a learning disability that has never been diagnosed?

25. If a successful adult has high-functioning autism, what kind of profession and what sort of family life would you expect him or her to have?

26. Why does the frequency of some kinds of developmental psychopathology increase while that of others decreases?

27. What are the signs of autism spectrum disorders?

APPLICATIONS

1. Compare play spaces for children in different neighborhoods—ideally, urban, suburban, and rural areas. Note size, safety, and use. How might children's weight and motor skills be affected by differences you observe?

2. Developmental psychologists believe that every teacher should be skilled at teaching children with a wide variety of needs. Does the teacher-training curriculum at your college or university reflect this goal? Should all teachers take the same courses, or should some teachers be specialized? Give reasons for your opinions.

3. Internet sources vary in quality on any topic, but this may be particularly true of Web sites designed for parents of children with special needs. Pick one childhood disability or disease and find several Web sources devoted to that condition. How might parents evaluate the information provided?

4. Special education teachers are in great demand. In your local public school, what is the ratio of regular to special education teachers? How many are in self-contained classrooms, resource rooms, and inclusion classrooms? What do your data reveal about the education of children with special needs in your community?

>>ONLINE CONNECTIONS

To accompany your textbook, you have access to a number of online resources, including quizzes for every chapter of the book, flashcards (in English and Spanish), critical thinking questions, and case studies. For access to any of these links, go to www.worthpublishers.com/bergerca9e. In addition to these free resources, you'll also find links to podcasts, video clips, diagnostic quizzing with personalized study advice, and an ebook. Some of the videos and activities available online include:

- *Autism.* This activity explores the symptoms of autism and the importance of early diagnosis. Video clips give a glimpse into the world of parents and autistic children.
- *Educating the Girls of the World.* Girls around the world talk about the challenges that hinder their enrollment in all levels of education. Highlights initiatives for change.

12

CHAPTER

Middle Childhood: Cognitive Development

WHAT WILL YOU KNOW?

1. Is it better to let children learn from experience or to teach them what they need to know?
2. Why do children change vocabulary, grammar, tone, and gestures, depending on their audience?
3. What is the best kind of school for children age 6 to 11?

At age 9, I wanted a puppy. My parents said no—we already had Dusty, our family dog. I dashed off a poem, promising "to brush his hair as smooth as silk" and "to feed him milk." (Wrong, of course: Puppies should not have cow's milk.) My father praised my poem; I got Taffy, a blonde cocker spaniel.

At age 10, my daughter Sarah wanted her ears pierced. I said no—it wouldn't be fair to her three older sisters, who had had to wait until they were teenagers before ear-piercing. Sarah wrote an affidavit and persuaded her sisters to sign it, saying that they had no objection. She got gold posts.

Sarah and I were typical, although our wishes differed by cohort and our strategies by family. Sarah knew I wouldn't budge for doggerel but that I respect signed documents. All school-age children master whatever their context presents: dividing fractions, surfing the Web, memorizing rap songs, loading rifles, or persuading parents.

This chapter describes that impressive cognitive development. We begin by examining how Piaget, Vygotsky, and information-processing theory describe cognition in middle childhood. Then we discuss applications of those theories to language, as well as the many disputes about how and what children should learn in school.

>> Building on Theory

Learning is rapid in childhood. Some children, by age 11, beat their elders at chess, play music that adults pay to hear, publish poems, win trophies. Others live on the streets or fight in civil wars, learning lessons that no child should know. How do they learn so quickly?

Piaget and School-Age Children

Piaget called the cognition of middle childhood **concrete operational thought,** characterized by concepts that enable children to use logic. *Operational* comes from the Latin word *operare,* "to work; to produce." By calling this period operational, Piaget emphasized productive thinking. The school-age child, no longer limited by egocentrism, performs logical operations. Children apply their new reasoning skills to *concrete* situations—that is, situations with visible, tangible, real

concrete operational thought Piaget's term for the ability to reason logically about direct experiences and perceptions.

AP PHOTO / THE AUGUSTA CHRONICLE CHRIS THELEN

His Science Project Concrete operational 10-year-olds like Daniel, shown here with some of his family's dairy cows, can be logical about anything they see, hear, or touch. Daniel's science experiment, on the effect of music on milk production, won first place in a Georgia regional science fair.

things (not abstractions). Children become more systematic, objective, scientific—and educable.

A Hierarchy of Categories

One logical concept is **classification,** the organization of things into groups (or *categories* or *classes*) according to some characteristic that they share. For example, *family* includes parents, siblings, and cousins. Other common classes are people, animals, toys, and food. Each class includes some elements and excludes others, and each is part of a hierarchy.

Food, for instance, is a category, with the next-lower level of that hierarchy being meat, grains, fruits, and so on. Most subclasses can be further divided: Meat includes poultry, beef, and pork, each of which can be divided again. Adults realize that items at the bottom of a classification hierarchy belong to every higher level: Bacon is always pork, meat, and food. Younger children may know that bacon is pork, but they cannot perform the mental operation of moving up and down the hierarchy.

Piaget devised many experiments to reveal children's understanding of classification. For example, an examiner shows a child a bunch of nine flowers—seven yellow daisies and two white roses (revised and published in Piaget et al., 2001). The examiner makes sure the child knows the words *flowers, daisies,* and *roses.* Then comes the pivotal question: "Are there more daisies or more flowers?" Until about age 7, most children say, "More daisies." Younger children can offer no justification for their answers, but some 6- or 7-year-olds explain that "there are more yellow ones than white ones" or that "because daisies are daisies, they aren't flowers" (Piaget et al., 2001). By age 8, most children can classify: "More flowers than daisies," they say.

classification The logical principle that things can be organized into groups (or categories or classes) according to some characteristic they have in common.

transitive inference The ability to figure out the unspoken link between one fact and another.

Other Logical Concepts

Another example of logic is the ability to grasp connections that are implied, not stated. Piaget studied **transitive inference,** the ability to figure out (infer) the unspoken link (transfer) between one fact and another. For example, "John is taller than Jim. Jim is taller than David. Who is taller, John or David?" Preoperational children are stumped. They cannot do this simple transitive inference because they know only what they have been told directly, not implications. By contrast, school-age children infer relationships.

Later research connects transitive inference to the maturation of the hippocampus, which reaches a critical point at about age 7, making inferences and other kinds of mental logic possible (DeVito et al., 2010; Zalesak & Heckers, 2009). This may seem to confirm Piaget's findings, but neurological and comparative research finds that transitive inference is both simpler and more complex than Piaget imagined (Goodwin & Johnson-Laird, 2008), with some nonhuman animals succeeding at simple versions of it.

Nonetheless, transitive inference is related to another logical concept that Piaget called *seriation,* the knowledge that things can be arranged in a logical series. Seriation is crucial for using (not merely memorizing) the alphabet or for understanding the number sequence. By age 5, most children can count up to 100, but they cannot correctly estimate where any particular two-digit number would be placed on a line that starts at 0 and ends at 100. Generally, this is possible by age 8 (Meadows, 2006).

The logical abilities of school-age children may allow them to understand arithmetic. For example, children need to understand that 12 plus 3 equals 3 plus 12 and that 15 is always 15 no matter how it was reached (conservation). Reversibility eventually allows the realization that if 5 times 7 equals 35, then 35 divided by 5 must be 7. Seriation and classification abilities correlate with math skills in primary school, although many other factors contribute to math achievement (Desoete et al., 2009).

VEER

After "Gee Whiz!" After he sees the magnified image that his classmate expects will amaze him, will he analyze his observations? Ideally, concrete operational thought enables children to use their new logic to interpret their experiences.

The Significance of Piaget's Findings

Although logic connects to math concepts, researchers have found more continuity than discontinuity in number skills. Thus, Piaget was mistaken: There is no sudden shift between preoperational and concrete operational logic. In fact, some children learn logic via math, not vice versa. As explained in Chapter 9, the ability to classify appears long before middle childhood (Halford & Andrews, 2006), and you have just read that transitive inference is not unique to humans.

Nonetheless, Piaget's experiments revealed something important. School-age children can use mental categories and subcategories more flexibly, inductively, and simultaneously than younger children can (Meadows, 2006). They are more advanced thinkers, intellectually capable in ways that younger children are not.

Vygotsky and School-Age Children

Like Piaget, Vygotsky felt that educators should consider children's thought processes, not just the outcomes. He recognized that younger children are confused by some concepts that older children understand. Children are curious, creative learners. For that reason, Vygotsky believed that an educational system based on rote memorization rendered the child "helpless in the face of any sensible attempt to apply any of this acquired knowledge" (Vygotsky, 1934/1994, pp. 356–357).

The Role of Instruction

Unlike Piaget, Vygotsky regarded instruction as crucial. He thought that peers and teachers provide the bridge between developmental potential and needed skills and knowledge, via guided participation, scaffolding, and the zone of proximal development (see Chapters 2 and 9).

Confirmation of the role of social interaction and instruction comes from children who, because of their school's entry-date cutoff, are either relatively old kindergartners or quite young first-graders. At the end of the school year, achievement scores of 6-year-old first-graders far exceed those of kindergarten 6-year-olds who are only one month younger (Lincove & Painter, 2006; NICHD, 2007). Obviously, they had learned a great deal from the first-grade teachers.

Remember that Vygotsky believed education occurs everywhere, not only in school. Children mentor one another as they play together. They learn from television, dinner with their families, people they see on the street, and every other daily experience. This education accumulates from infancy on.

For instance, a study of the reading and math achievement of more than a thousand third- and fifth-grade children from ten U.S. cities found that high-scoring primary schoolchildren were likely to have had extensive cognitive stimulation. There were three main sources of intellectual activity: their families (e.g., parents

Especially for Teachers How might Piaget's and Vygotsky's ideas help in teaching geography to a class of third-graders? (see response, page 354)

read to them daily when they were toddlers), preschool programs (e.g., a variety of learning activities), and the first grade (e.g., literacy emphasis with individual evaluation). Although children from families of low socioeconomic status (SES) were least likely to have been highly stimulated in all three contexts, achievement scores of those low-SES children who had all three influences showed even more advances than did scores of the high-SES children (Crosnoe et al., 2010).

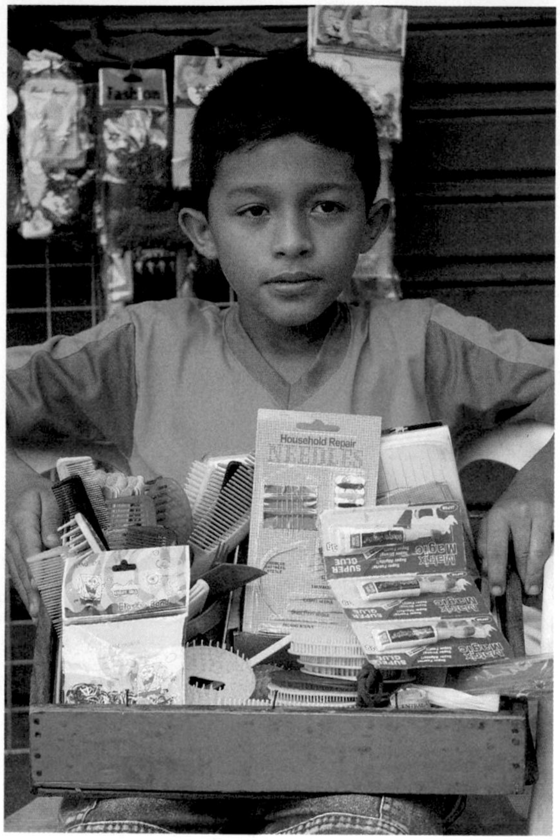

DAVID R. FRAZIER PHOTOLIBRARY, INC. / ALAMY

He Knows His Stuff Many child vendors, like this boy selling combs and other grooming aids on the streets of Manaus, Brazil, understand basic math and the give-and-take of social interaction. But, deprived of formal education, they know little or nothing about history and literature.

International Contexts

In general, Vygotsky's emphasis on sociocultural contexts contrasts with Piaget's maturational, self-discovery approach. Vygotsky believed that cultures (tools, customs, and mentors) teach. For example, a child who is surrounded by adults reading for pleasure, by full bookcases, by daily newspapers, and by street signs will read better than a child who has had little exposure to print, even if both are in the same classroom. Of course, classroom experiences matter as well, with some teachers showering children with words, spoken and written, and encouraging writing and talking from every student, whereas other teachers stress safety and silence.

The most detailed international example of the influence of context on learning comes from Brazil, where street children sell fruit, candy, and other products. Many never attend school and consequently score poorly on standard math achievement tests. This is no surprise to developmentalists, who have data from numerous nations showing that unschooled children score lower in every academic area (Rogoff et al., 2005).

However, some young Brazilian peddlers are skilled at pricing their wares and making change. Some cannot read, but they use colors and pictures to identify how many *reals* each bill is worth (Saxe, 2004). They may recalibrate selling prices daily in response to inflation, wholesale costs, and customer demand, calculating "complex markup computations . . . by using procedures that were widespread in their practice but not known to children in school" (Saxe, 1999, p. 255). Ratios and fractions, not usually taught until the end of middle childhood, are understood by young street sellers. They learn math from the following:

- The social context
- Other sellers (especially older children)
- Daily experience

None of this would surprise Vygotsky, who believed that peers are good mentors. Much other research shows that children's understanding of arithmetic depends on context: If they learn math in school, they are proficient at school math; if they learn math out of school, they are adept at problems encountered in similar situations (Abreu, 2008).

Another example of knowledge acquired from the social context comes from children in the northeast Indian district of Varanasi, many of whom have an extraordinary sense of spatial orientation—such as knowing whether they are facing north or south, even when they are inside a room with no windows. In one experiment, after children were blindfolded, spun around, and led to a second room, many of them still knew which way they were now facing (Mishra et al., 2009). This skill was learned during childhood, as adults and peers in that culture refer to the compass orientation to name the location of objects and so on. (Although the specifics differ from those of Western culture, the equivalent might be to say not that the dog is sleeping by the door but that the dog is sleeping southeast.)

This transfer of knowledge from one context to another is not automatic. The blindfolded children retained their excellent sense of direction, but a child from

>> Response for Teachers (from page 353) Here are two of the most obvious ways. (1) Use logic. Once children can grasp classification and class inclusion, they can understand cities within states, states within nations, and nations within continents. Organize your instruction to make logical categorization easier. (2) Make use of children's need for concrete and personal involvement. You might have the children learn first about their own location, then about the places where relatives and friends live, and finally about places beyond their personal experience (via books, photographs, videos, and guest speakers).

Varanasi might become disoriented in the tangle of mega-city streets—still knowing where north is, but not knowing how to get downtown.

Culture affects the methods of learning, not just the content. This was evident in a study of 80 children in California (Silva et al., 2010). All were Mexican American, similar in genetic background, but half were from families where indigenous Indian learning was the norm: Children from that culture are expected to learn by watching others and to help each other if need be. The other half were from families more acculturated to U.S. norms; the children were accustomed to direct instruction, not observational learning. They expected to work on their own, not collaboratively with their peers.

In the first session of this study, each child was shown how to make a toy while his or her sibling sat nearby. First, the younger sibling waited while the older sibling made a toy mouse and then the older sibling waited while the younger sibling made a toy frog. Each child's behavior while awaiting his or her turn was videotaped and coded every five seconds as *sustained attention* (alert and focused on the sibling's activity), as *glancing (sporadic interest, but primary focus on something else),* or as *not attending* (looking elsewhere). (See Figure 12.1 and the Research Design.)

Unexpectedly, a week later, each child was individually given the materials to make the toy his or her sibling had made but was not told how to do so (as the sibling had been told a week earlier) unless the child needed help. Children from indigenous backgrounds were more attentive in the first session and needed less help a week later (Silva et al., 2010).

Sustained Attention: Percent of 5-Second Segments

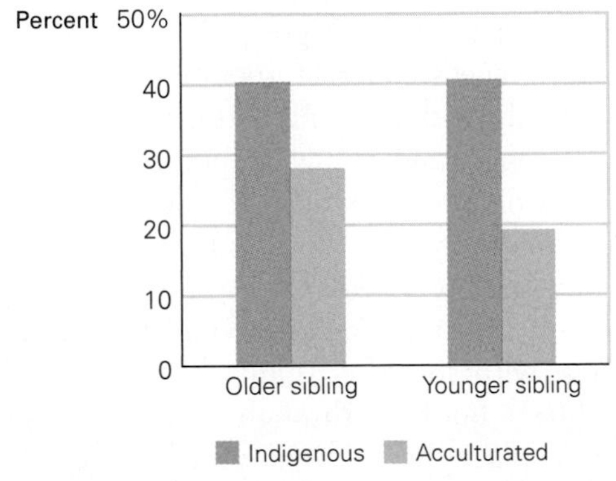

Source: Silva et al., 2010.

FIGURE 12.1

Watch Your Brother! When a brother (or sister) is learning how to make a toy, do you focus your attention on that, or do you look elsewhere? Apparently, it depends partly on what your mother has taught you, not directly but in the way she expects you to learn.

Observation Quiz Among those children accustomed to U.S. styles of learning, were older or younger siblings more likely to pay attention to their siblings? Why? (see answer, page 356)

Research Design

Scientists: Katie G. Silva, Maricela Correa-Chávez, and Barbara Rogoff.

Publication: *Child Development* (2010).

Participants: Forty 5- to 11-year-old pairs of siblings, living in southern California and attending public school. All were Mexican American, most born in the United States to families originally from rural areas in the state of Michoacán. They were divided into two groups, one closer to native Indian culture and the other more urban. For instance, the groups differed in maternal education: Some mothers were high school graduates, an accomplishment that signified more acculturation to U.S. ways of learning, while other mothers averaged six years of schooling (range 0–9) and were more indigenous (Indian) in their ways. Other indicators also showed that the two groups were different: family size (2.4 versus 3.3 children) and fathers' birthplace (half in the United States in one group versus almost all in Mexico in the other).

Design: A Spanish-speaking "toy lady" showed each child how to make a toy, with the younger sibling waiting while the older child made a mouse, and then the older child waiting while the younger child made a frog. The children were allowed to keep their toys. A week later, each child individually was given the materials to make the toy that his or her sibling had made. The toy lady ostensibly was involved in paperwork, giving hints about toy construction only when needed. Coders noted the waiting children's attention during the first session and the number of hints needed during the second. The coders and the toy ladies did not know the hypothesis, nor did they know the background of the children, who had been rated as more or less acculturated before the first session with the toy lady.

Results: Virtually none of the children were disruptive; most simply waited their turn. As they waited, the children from the indigenous backgrounds were more likely to pay close attention to the instructions and actions of their siblings; they did so in 40.4 percent of the five-second segments versus 23.6 percent for the acculturated group. Some of the indigenous siblings tried to help their brother or sister, but virtually none of the acculturated children did so. Moreover, the indigenous children remembered what they saw: A week later, they needed an average of 37 percent of the possible hints versus 47 percent for the other pairs.

Major conclusion: Even when children currently live in the same settings and attend the same schools, they follow family cultural traditions in how they learn. This is reflected in their achievement, in this case remembering how to make a toy.

Comments: This was a well-designed study. Several aspects helped all the children feel comfortable (sibling nearby, Spanish-speaking toy lady), and several measures made the data detailed and objective (videotapes, "blind" coders, five-second segments). These features suggest that the conclusion—that children from rural, lower-SES backgrounds learn better under some conditions than similar children who ordinarily are better students—is probably valid. This is useful information for all teachers and parents: Children reflect cultural ways of gathering information, and thus to teach children it is useful to know the specific ways in which they learn best.

>> Answer to Observation Quiz (from page 355) Older siblings were more attentive. The reasons are speculative—whatever reason you thought of, does it reflect your own sibling experience or your cultural values?

Information Processing

Today's educators and psychologists regard both Piaget and Vygotsky as insightful; international research confirms the merits of their theories. Piaget described universal changes; Vygotsky noted cultural impact.

A third, and more recent, approach to understanding cognition adds crucial insight. As you learned in Chapter 2, the *information-processing perspective* benefits from technology that allows much more detailed data and analysis than was possible 50 years ago. Thousands of researchers who study cognition can be said to use the information-processing approach. Not all of them would identify themselves that way, however, because "information processing is not a single theory but, rather, a framework characterizing a large number of research programs" (Miller, 2011, p. 266).

Like computers, people sense and perceive large amounts of information. They then: (1) seek specific units of information (as a search engine does), (2) analyze (as software programs do), and (3) express their conclusions so another person can understand (as a networked computer or a printout might do). By tracing the paths and links of each of these functions, scientists better understand the process of learning. This approach has become particularly useful in educating children with learning disabilities, whose processing of information is often impaired. Dyslexia or dyscalculia may be symptoms, not causes, of a learning disability (Waber, 2010), the result of some neurological roadblock in the path between input and output.

The brain's gradual growth confirms the information-processing perspective. So do data on children's school achievement: Absences, vacations, new schools, and even new teachers sometimes hinder a child's achievement because each day's learning builds on that of the previous day. Ongoing brain connections and pathways are forged from repeated experiences, allowing advances in processing. For many schoolchildren, teachers are the best facilitators, encouraging practice of exactly the next skill to be mastered. Without that, fragile connections between neurons break.

One of the leaders of the information-processing perspective is Robert Siegler (Siegler & Chen, 2008), who has studied the day-by-day details of children's cognition in math. Apparently, children do not suddenly grasp the number system, as might be expected when they reach Piaget's concrete operational stage. Instead, number understanding accrues gradually, with new and better strategies for calculation tried, ignored, half-used, abandoned, and finally adopted. Siegler compared the acquisition of knowledge to waves on a beach when the tide is rising. There is substantial ebb and flow, although eventually a new level is reached.

One specific example is children's ability to estimate where a number might fall on a number line, such as where 53 would be placed on a line from 0 to 100. U.S. kindergartners are usually lost with this task (Chinese kindergartners are somewhat better [Siegler & Mu, 2008]), but first- through third-graders gradually become more proficient. They tend to place the 53 decidedly off-center at first but then put it just above the middle on an imagined linear scale. This ability improves gradually over middle childhood and correlates with memory for numbers (such as a phone number). This has led many information-processing experts to advocate giving children practice with number lines in order to help them with other math concepts.

sensory memory The component of the information-processing system in which incoming stimulus information is stored for a split second to allow it to be processed. (Also called the *sensory register*.)

working memory The component of the information-processing system in which current conscious mental activity occurs. (Formerly called *short-term memory*.)

Memory

Many scientists who study memory take an information-processing approach. They have learned that various methods of input, storage, and retrieval affect the increasing cognitive ability of the schoolchild. Each of the three major steps in the memory process—sensory memory, working memory, and long-term memory—is affected by maturation and experience.

Sensory memory (also called the *sensory register*) is the first component of the human information-processing system. It stores incoming stimuli for a split second after they are received, with sounds retained slightly longer than sights. To use terms explained in Chapter 5, *sensations* are retained for a moment, and then some become *perceptions.* This first step of sensory awareness is already quite good in early childhood, improves slightly until about age 10, and remains adequate until late adulthood.

Once some sensations become perceptions, the brain selects those perceptions that are meaningful and transfers them to working memory for further analysis. It is in **working memory** (formerly called *short-term memory*) that current, conscious mental activity occurs. Working memory improves steadily and significantly every year from about age 4 to age 15 (Gathercole et al., 2004) as the brain matures and experiences accumulate (Baddeley, 2007). Especially significant is increased myelination and dendrite formation in the prefrontal cortex, allowing the "massive interconnections" described in Chapter 11.

AP PHOTO / THE HERALD, DAVID E. DALE

Verbs and Adverbs Erin, Ally, Paige, and Sabrina perform rap lyrics they wrote to review key concepts for an upcoming assessment test. Such mnemonic devices are beyond younger children but may be very helpful in middle childhood.

Processing, not mere exposure, is essential to getting information into working memory, which is why working memory improves markedly in middle childhood (Cowan & Alloway, 2009). Improvement in working memory during the school years includes advances in two crucial areas—one called the *phonological loop,* which stores sounds, and one called the *visual–spatial sketchpad,* which stores sights (Meadows, 2006). As the brain matures, schoolchildren use memory strategies that are not accessible to younger children (see Table 12.1).

As Siegler's metaphor of waves of cognition suggests, these strategies do not appear suddenly. Gradual improvement occurs from toddlerhood through adolescence (Schneider & Lockl, 2008), with school-age children finally knowing how to increase their working memory (Camos & Barrouillet, 2011).

TABLE 12.1 Advances in Memory from Infancy to Age 11

Child's Age	Memory Capabilities
Under 2 years	Infants remember actions and routines that involve them. Memory is implicit, triggered by sights and sounds (an interactive toy, a caregiver's voice).
2–5 years	Words are now used to encode and retrieve memories. Explicit memory begins, although children do not yet use memory strategies. Children remember things by rote (their phone number, nursery rhymes) without truly understanding them.
5–7 years	Children realize that some things should be remembered, and they begin to use simple strategies, primarily rehearsal (repeating an item again and again). This is not a very efficient strategy, but with enough repetition, automatization occurs.
7–9 years	Children use new strategies if they are taught them. Children use visual clues (remembering how a particular spelling word looks) and auditory hints (rhymes, letters), evidence of the visual–spatial sketchpad and phonological loop. Children now benefit from the organization of things to be remembered.
9–11 years	Memory becomes more adaptive and strategic as children become able to learn various memory techniques from teachers and other children. They can organize material themselves, developing their own memory aids.

Source: Based on Meadows, 2006.

The relationship among strategy, classification, and working memory was demonstrated by an experiment in which 7- and 9-year-olds memorized two lists of 10 items each (M. L. Howe, 2004). Some children had one list of toys and another of vehicles; others had the same 20 items in two mixed lists, with toys and vehicles in both. A day later, each child was asked to remember one of the two lists. Having had separate lists of toys and vehicles helped the 7-year-olds somewhat but benefited the 9-year-olds more. Those older children used the topical lists well: Not only did they surpass all the 7-year-olds, they also remembered much more than the other 9-year-olds who had mixed lists.

Older children's ability to use memory strategies is evident in other research, too. For instance, another experiment, also involving memory of lists, found that 10-year-olds did much better than 8-year-olds because fewer of them relied on rote item-by-item memory; more of them used active memory, repeating a string of items as they memorized them (Lehmann & Hasselhorn, 2010). (Stringing is similar to another way of grouping items, called *chunking,* except that in stringing, a group of items are learned in sequence). School-age children who realize this have better memories than those who do not (Cowan, 2010).

long-term memory The component of the information-processing system in which virtually limitless amounts of information can be stored indefinitely.

Finally, information from working memory may be transferred to **long-term memory,** to store it for minutes, hours, days, months, or years. The capacity of long-term memory—how much can be crammed into one brain—is very large by the end of middle childhood. Together with sensory memory and working memory, long-term memory organizes ideas and reactions. Crucial to long-term memory is not merely *storage* (how much material has been deposited) but also *retrieval* (how readily past learning can be brought into working memory). For everyone, at every age, retrieval is easier for some memories (especially memories of vivid, highly emotional experiences) than for others. And for everyone, long-term memory is imperfect: We all forget and distort memories.

Especially for Teachers How might your understanding of memory help you teach a 2,000-word vocabulary list to a class of fourth-graders? (see response, page 360)

Knowledge

knowledge base A body of knowledge in a particular area that makes it easier to master new information in that area.

According to information-processing research, the more people know, the more they learn. Having an extensive **knowledge base,** or a broad body of knowledge in a particular subject, makes it easier to master related new information.

Three factors facilitate increases in the knowledge base: past experience, current opportunity, and personal motivation. Children's knowledge base, however, is not always what their parents or teachers would like it to be. Some schoolchildren memorize words and rhythms of hit songs, know plots and characters of television programs, and can recite the names and histories of football players—yet they may not know whether World War I occurred in the nineteenth or twentieth century, or whether Afghanistan is in Asia or Africa. Motivation provides a clue for teachers: New concepts are learned best if they are connected to personal and emotional experiences (Schneider & Lockl, 2008; Wittrock, 1974/2010).

Control Processes

control processes Mechanisms (including selective attention, metacognition, and emotional regulation) that combine memory, processing speed, and knowledge to regulate the analysis and flow of information within the information-processing system. (Also called *executive processes.*)

metacognition "Thinking about thinking," or the ability to evaluate a cognitive task in order to determine how best to accomplish it, and then to monitor and adjust one's performance on that task.

The mechanisms that pull memory, processing speed, and the knowledge base together are **control processes;** they regulate the analysis and flow of information within the system. Control processes include *emotional regulation* and *selective attention,* explained in Chapters 10 and 11. Equally important is **metacognition,** sometimes defined as "thinking about thinking." Metacognition is the ultimate control process because it allows a person to evaluate a cognitive task, determine how to accomplish it, monitor performance, and then make adjustments.

Control processes require the brain to organize, prioritize, and direct mental operations, as the CEO (chief executive officer) of a business does. For that reason, control processes are also called *executive processes,* evident whenever people concentrate on only the relevant parts of a task, using their knowledge base to connect new information or apply memory strategies. Such control is more evident among 10-year-olds than among 4- or 6-year-olds (Bjorklund et al., 2009). Fourth-grade students can listen to the teacher talk about the river Nile, ignoring classmates who are chewing gum or passing notes. That's control.

Both metacognition and control processes improve with age and experience. For instance, in one study, children took a fill-in-the-blanks test and indicated how confident they were of each answer. Then they were allowed to delete some questions, thus making the remaining ones count more. Already by age 9, the children were able to estimate correctness; by age 11, they were skilled at knowing what to delete (Roebers et al., 2009). Sometimes experience is not directly related but nonetheless has an impact. This seems to be true for fluently bilingual children, who must learn to inhibit one language while using another. They are advanced in control processes, obviously in language but also in more abstract measures of control (Bialystok, 2010).

THINKING CRITICALLY

Balls Rolling Down

Should metacognition be taught, or should children develop it spontaneously when they are old enough? This question has been the focus of decades of research (Orlich et al., 2009; Pressley & Hilden, 2006), much of which has looked at both "discovery" learning (inspired by Piaget) and explicit teaching (from an information-processing perspective), always with awareness of cultural differences (as Vygotsky stressed).

The answer depends partly on the goals and methods of the culture. Some cultures value single-minded concentration, others multitasking; some stress explicit instruction, others implicit learning from observation. The latter is not necessarily inefficient, for as one commentator explained, "Simultaneous attention may be important when learning relies on observation of ongoing events" (Correa-Chavez et al., 2005, p. 665), a point made by the research cited earlier on toy-making (Silva et al., 2010).

To illustrate the impact of instruction, one study wanted children to learn that a valid scientific experiment controls all the relevant variables and measures one at a time (Klahr & Nigam, 2004). The researchers showed 112 third- and fourth-graders two balls that could roll down several ramps (see Figure 12.2). There were four variables: golf or rubber ball, steep or shallow slope, smooth or rough ramp, long or short downhill run.

First, the children were asked to design four experiments on their own: two to determine the effect of distance and two to determine the effect of steepness. Only 8 of the 112 children

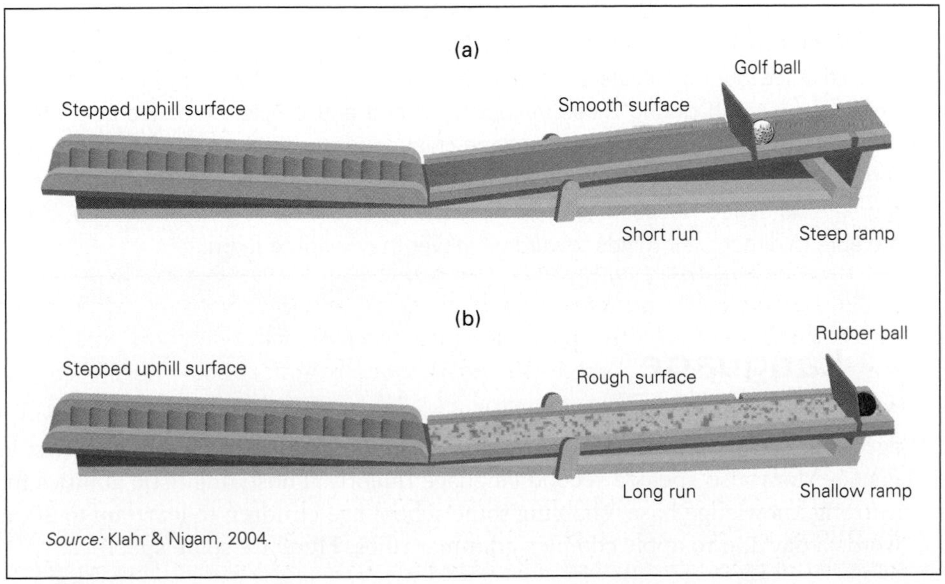

FIGURE 12.2

Design for a Confounded Experiment On each of these two ramps, children could vary the steepness, surface, and length of the ramp as well as the type of ball. The confounded experiment depicted here contrasts *(a)* a golf ball on a steep, smooth, short ramp with *(b)* a rubber ball on a shallow, rough, long ramp.

designed experiments that controlled the variables. Unless the variables were controlled, the results would be confounded (inappropriately combined). Thus, for example, a child might confound the conclusions by comparing one trial with the golf ball on a shallow ramp to a second trial with the rubber ball on a steep ramp.

The 104 children who did not spontaneously control the variables were then divided into two groups. Half were told to create their own experiments; the other half received explicit instruction by watching an experimenter create pairs of demonstrations. For that half, the experimenter asked the children whether a demonstrated pair allowed them to "tell for sure" how a particular variable affected the distance traveled by the ball. After each response, the experimenter explained the correct answer and emphasized the importance of testing a single variable at a time.

Then all 104 children were asked to design four experiments, as before. Far more children who received direct instruction (40 of 52) correctly isolated the variables than did children who explored on their own (12 of 52). A week later, to assess whether the children had really learned the importance of controlling variables, those children who seemed to understand (the 40 and the 12) were asked to examine two science posters ostensibly created by 11-year-olds. The researcher requested suggestions to make the posters "good enough to enter in a state science fair." The 40 children who had been instructed were virtually as perceptive in their critiques of the posters as the 12 who had learned through discovery. This study suggests that strategy can be taught—if the teacher actively engages the students. That is exactly what information-processing theory would predict.

Of course, scientific understanding is about more than understanding variables: It is about questioning conclusions and realizing that answers can and do change. How children develop this ability—whether by discovery and experience, as Piaget might expect, or whether by explicit instruction, as information-processing theory suggests—is a matter of intense concern to educators. Furthermore, a logical and skeptical approach to life is pivotal for scientists, but that itself may be culturally determined: Questions, critiques, and doubts may be handicapping in some communities. An understanding of human development can be helpful here. As one expert explains:

> The developmentalist can contribute knowledge of what needs to develop, sketch its course, and hopefully even gain insight into the mechanisms involved. Developmentalists and educators in collaboration can seek to identify the kinds of experiences that make it more likely to happen.
>
> *[Kuhn, 2009, p. 115]*

What experiences help children learn? Answers vary. Whatever you think about teaching metacognitive skills, Vygotsky would ask, "How does your personal experience and cultural heritage affect your answer?"

>> Response for Teachers (from page 358) Children this age can be taught strategies for remembering by forming links between working memory and long-term memory. You might break down the vocabulary list into word clusters, grouped according to root words, connections to the children's existing knowledge, applications, or (as a last resort) first letters or rhymes. Active, social learning is useful; perhaps in groups the students could write a story each day that incorporates 15 new words. Each group could read its story aloud to the class.

SUMMING UP

Every theory of cognitive development recognizes that school-age children are avid learners who actively build on the knowledge they already have. Piaget emphasized children's own logical thinking, as they come to understand classification and develop transitive inference during concrete operational thought. Research inspired by Vygotsky and the sociocultural perspective reveals that cultural differences can be powerful and that specific instruction and practical experience vary from one context to another. Therefore, each child learns different skills, guided by local culture.

An information-processing analysis highlights the many components of thinking that advance during middle childhood. Although sensory and long-term memory do not change much during these years, the speed and efficiency of working memory improve dramatically, making school-age children better thinkers as well as more strategic learners as they mature. Another advantage for older children is that they develop a greater knowledge base. As control processes and metacognition advance, children are able to direct their minds toward whatever they want to learn. ■

>> Language

As you remember, many aspects of language advance during early childhood. By age 6, children have mastered the basic vocabulary and grammar of their first language. Many also speak a second language fluently. Those linguistic abilities form a strong knowledge base, enabling some school-age children to learn up to 20 new words a day and to apply complex grammar rules. Here are some specifics.

Vocabulary

By age 6, children know the names of thousands of objects, and they use many parts of speech—adjectives and adverbs as well as nouns and verbs. As Piaget stressed, they soon become more flexible and logical; they can understand prefixes, suffixes, compound words, phrases, and figures of speech. For example, 2-year-olds know *egg,* but 10-year-olds also know *egg salad, egg-drop soup, last one in is a rotten egg.* They know that each of these expressions is connected to *egg* but is distinct from the eggs in the refrigerator.

Understanding Metaphors

Metaphors, jokes, and puns are finally comprehended. Some jokes ("What is black and white and red all over?" "Why did the chicken cross the road?") are funny only during middle childhood. Younger children don't understand why they provoke laughter, and teenagers find them lame and stale, but 6- to 11-year-olds enjoy puns, unexpected answers to normal questions, and metaphors because their new cognitive flexibility and social awareness make them funny. Indeed, a lack of metaphorical understanding, even if a child has a large vocabulary, signifies cognitive problems (Thomas et al., 2010). Humor can be a diagnostic tool.

Many adults do not realize how difficult it is for young children or adults who are learning a new language to grasp figures of speech. The humorist James Thurber remembered:

> the enchanted private world of my early boyhood. . . . In this world, businessmen who phoned their wives to say they were tied up at the office sat roped to their swivel chairs, and probably gagged, unable to move or speak except somehow, miraculously, to telephone. . . . Then there was the man who left town under a cloud. Sometimes I saw him all wrapped up in the cloud and invisible. . . . At other times it floated, about the size of a sofa, above him wherever he went. . . . [I remember]the old lady who was always up in the air, the husband who did not seem able to put his foot down, the man who lost his head during a fire but was still able to run out of the house yelling.
>
> *[Thurber, 1999, p. 40]*

Part of the problem is that metaphors are context-specific. A book written by an American who has lived in China for decades discusses dozens of cultural differences, including basic phrases having to do with baseball that U.S. children learn but that children from other cultures do not—"dropped the ball," "on the ball," "to play ball," "to throw a curve," "to strike out" (Davis, 1999). If a teacher wants a class to pay attention and says, "Keep your eye on the ball," some immigrant children might be lost.

RADIUS IMAGES / P-HOTOLIBRARY

Homework Despite first appearances, this is not teacher and student but father and daughter, as Dad becomes excited about his 7-year-old's science project. Actually, if she is as intrigued as she appears to be, he is teacher as well as father. Children learn most of their vocabulary with friends and family, not in class.

Adjusting Vocabulary to the Context

One aspect of language that advances markedly in middle childhood is **pragmatics,** the practical use of language, which includes the ability to adjust expressions to communicate with varied audiences in different contexts. This ability is obvious to linguists when they compare how children talk informally with friends (the last to arrive can be a *rotten* egg or worse) to how they talk formally with teachers (never calling them a *rotten egg*). As children master pragmatics, they become more adept. Shy 6-year-olds cope far better with the social pressures of school if they use pragmatics well (Coplan & Weeks, 2009).

Mastery of pragmatics allows children to change styles of speech, or "codes," depending on their audience. Each code includes many aspects of language—tone, pronunciation, gestures, sentence length, idioms, vocabulary, and grammar.

pragmatics The practical use of language that includes the ability to adjust language communication according to audience and context.

Especially for Parents You've had an exhausting day but are setting out to buy groceries. Your 7-year-old son wants to go with you. Should you explain that you are so tired that you want to make a quick solo trip to the supermarket this time? (see response, page 362)

CAREY KIRKELLA / GETTY IMAGES

A Good Message If he is skilled at text messaging, he understands the basics of written language. That makes learning the formal code easier, if he has a teacher who appreciates his ability.

Sometimes the switch is between *formal code* (used in academic contexts) and *informal code* (used with friends); sometimes it is between standard (or proper) speech and dialect or vernacular (used on the street). Many children use code in text messaging, with numbers (411), abbreviations (LOL), and emoticons (:-D).

Code changes are obvious when children speak one language at home and another at school. Every nation includes many such children; most of the world's 6,000 languages are not school languages. For instance, English is the language of instruction in Australia, but 17 percent of the children speak one of 246 other languages at home (Centre for Community Child Health, 2009). In the United States, an estimated one school-age child in five speaks a language other than English at home; half of them also speak English well (Passel, 2011). In addition, some children speak a dialect of English at home that is quite different from the pronunciation and grammar taught at school. All these alternate codes have distinct patterns of timing and emphasis as well as vocabulary.

Some children of every ethnicity are called **ELLs,** or **English Language Learners,** based on their proficiency in English. Among U.S. children of Hispanic heritage, those who speak English well are much better at reading than those who do not, but even they are less adept at reading than the average European American child (Garcia & Miller, 2008). Culture may be the reason, as their learning style may not be the same as their teachers', even though they are proficient in English.

ELLs (English Language Learners) Children in the United States whose proficiency in English is low—usually below a cutoff score on an oral or written test. This term replaces *ESL* (English as a Second Language) because many children who primarily speak a non-English language at home are also capable in English; they are *not* ELLs.

Differences in Language Learning

Learning to speak, read, and write the school language is pivotal for academic achievement, the foundation of all primary school education. Children differ widely in how well they use the school language. Some differences may be innate: A child with a language disability has trouble with both the school and the home language. However, most of the language gap between one child and another is the result of the social context, specifically of two factors: family income and adult expectations.

Family Poverty

Decades of research throughout the world have found a strong correlation between academic achievement and socioeconomic status. Language is a major reason. Not only do children from low-SES families usually have smaller vocabularies, but their grammar is simpler (fewer compound sentences, dependent clauses, and conditional verbs) and their sentences are shorter (Hart & Risley, 1995; E. Hoff, 2006). They fall behind their peers in talking, in reading, and then in other subjects, and even their brains signal linguistic weaknesses (Hackman & Farah, 2009).

The information-processing perspective focuses on specifics that might affect the brain and thus the ability to learn. Possibilities abound—inadequate prenatal care, exposure to lead, no breakfast, overcrowded households, few books at home, teenage parents, authoritarian child rearing, inexperienced teachers . . . The list could go on and on. All of these correlate with low SES and less learning, but none have been proven to be a major cause (not merely a correlate) of low achievement during primary school.

Three factors, however, *do* appear causal. One is limited early exposure to words. Unlike parents who attended college, many less educated parents do not provide varied and extensive language to their infants and young children. Daily

>> Response for Parents (from page 361) Your son would understand your explanation, but you should take him along if you can do so without losing patience. You wouldn't ignore his need for food or medicine; don't ignore his need for learning. While shopping, you can teach vocabulary (does he know *pimientos, pepperoni, polenta*?), categories ("root vegetables," "freshwater fish"), and math (which size box of cereal is cheaper?). Explain in advance that you need him to help you find items and carry them and that he can choose only one item that you wouldn't normally buy. Seven-year-olds can understand rules, and they enjoy being helpful.

book-reading to 2-year-olds, for instance, occurs for 24 percent of the children of mothers with less than a high school education as opposed to 70 percent of the children of mothers with at least a BA (National Center for Education Statistics, 2009) (see Figure 12.3).

As you remember from Chapter 1, book-reading is not the only way to increase language exposure in children (some families never read books to their children but may engage them in conversation about the interesting sights around them), but in the United States it often indicates how much verbal input a child is given. Another way to increase language exposure is to sing to a child, not only simple songs, but dozens of songs. Ideally, parents read and sing to each child every day, as well as provide extensive vocabulary about various activities (e.g., for a young child, "Here we are on the bumpy cobblestones. See the wilted rose, is it red or magenta or maroon? Look at the truck with six huge tires—why does it have so many tires?").

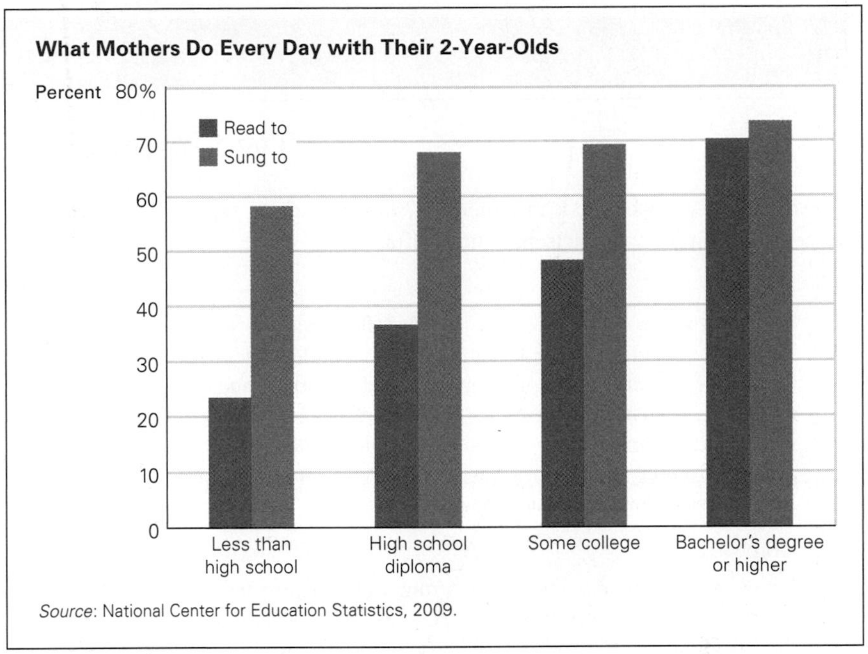

FIGURE 12.3

Red Fish, Blue Fish As you can see, most mothers sing to their little children, but the college-educated mothers are much more likely to know that book-reading is important. Simply knowing how to turn a page or hearing new word combinations (fish with a little car?) correlates with reading ability later on.

Expectations

A second cause of low achievement in middle childhood is teachers' and parents' expectations, as found in many nations (Melhuish et al., 2008; Phillipson & Phillipson, 2007; Rosenthal, 1991; Rubie-Davies, 2007). Expectations are related to another factor: whether or not a child is taught advanced words and concepts, especially the vocabulary words that are the foundation for later learning, such as *negotiate, evolve, respire, allegation, deficit* (Snow et al., 2007).

International achievement test scores (soon to be discussed) indicate that the income gap, and consequent variation in school resources and student achievement, is much greater in some nations than in others. One of the largest spreads is in the United States, where the fourth-grade reading scores among the schools with the most low-income children are 35 points below the national average. That is more than the average of 23 points in the 40 nations studied and much more than in most European nations (e.g., 11 points in France). The reason is thought to be that school systems expect too little of children from some communities, so they emphasize discipline, not academic challenge.

One of the exceptions to the SES trends is E. P. Jones, who grew up in a poor family, headed by an illiterate single mother who had high expectations for her son. Jones writes:

> For as many Sundays as I can remember, perhaps even Sundays when I was in the womb, my mother has pointed across "I" street to Seaton [school] as we come and go to Mt. Carmel [church].
>
> "You gonna go there and learn about the whole world."
>
> [*E. P. Jones, 1992/2003, p. 29*]

He did "learn about the whole world" (although he did not attend that particular school because his mother did not understand the school zones), and he won the 2004 Pulitzer Prize for his novel *The Known World* (2003).

The process works in reverse as well. Low expectations lead to low achievement, as demonstrated by Yolanda and Paul in the following.

ALASKA STOCK IMAGES

The Best of Both Worlds An Inupiat boy works at a computer keyboard in his classroom. His teachers want him and his classmates to benefit from both cultures—traditional and modern.

A CASE TO STUDY

Two Immigrants

Two children, both Mexican American, describe their experiences in their local public school in California.

Yolanda:

When I got here [from Mexico at age 7], I didn't want to stay here, 'cause I didn't like the school. And after a little while, in third grade, I started getting the hint of it and everything and I tried real hard in it. I really got along with the teachers. . . . They would start talking to me, or they kinda like pulled me up some grades, or moved me to other classes, or took me somewhere. And they were always congratulating me.

Paul:

I grew up . . . ditching school, just getting in trouble, trying to make a dollar, that's it, you know? Just go to school, steal from the store, and go sell candies at school. And that's what I was doing in the third or fourth grade. . . . I was always getting in the principal's office, suspended, kicked out, everything, starting from the third grade.

My fifth grade teacher, Ms. Nelson . . . she put me in a play and that like tripped me out. Like, why do you want me in a play? Me, I'm just a mess-up. Still, you know, she put me in a play. And in the fifth grade, I think that was the best year out of the whole six years. I learned a lot about the Revolutionary War. . . . Had good friends. . . . We had a project we were involved in. Ms. Nelson . . . just involved everyone. We made books, this and that. And I used to write, and wrote two, three books. Was in a book fair. . . . She got real deep into you. Just, you know, "Come on now, you can do it." That was a good year for me, fifth grade.

[quoted in Nieto, 2000, pp. 220, 249]

Note that initially Yolanda didn't like the United States because of school, but her teachers "kinda like pulled me up." By third grade, she was beginning to get "the hint of it." For Paul, school was where he sold stolen candy and where his third-grade teacher sent him to the principal, who suspended him. Ms. Nelson's fifth grade was "a good year," but it was too late—he had already learned he was "just a mess-up." Paul was later sent to a special school, and the text implies (but does not verify) that he was arrested and jailed by age 18. Yolanda became a successful young woman, fluently bilingual.

It would be easy to conclude that the difference was gender, since girls generally do better in school than boys. But that is too simple: Some Mexican-born boys do well in California schools—which raises the question of how teachers impact children: What could the third-grade teacher have done for Paul?

SUMMING UP

Children continue to learn language rapidly during the school years. They become more flexible, logical, and knowledgeable, figuring out the meanings of new words and grasping metaphors, jokes, and compound words. Many converse with friends using informal speech and master a more formal code to use in school. They learn whatever grammar and vocabulary they are taught, and they succeed at pragmatics, the practical task of adjusting their language to friends, teachers, or family. Millions become proficient in a second language, a process facilitated by teachers and peers. For academic achievement during middle childhood, both past exposure to language and adult expectations are influential. ▪

>> Teaching and Learning

As we have just described, school-age children are great learners, developing strategies, accumulating knowledge, expanding language, and using logic. Throughout history and worldwide, children are given new responsibility and instruction in middle childhood because that is when the human body and brain are ready. Traditionally, this occurred at home, but now more than 95 percent of the world's 7-year-olds are in school; that is where their parents and political leaders want them to be (Cohen & Malin, 2010). In 2010, for instance, India passed a law providing free education (no more school fees) to all 6- to 14-year olds, regardless of caste or income. India now has over 100 million children in primary school.

Parents rate their own children's schools more favorably than do nonparents in the same community. In one example, a U.S. survey found that nationwide people grade schools overall lower (C–) than their local schools (C+), while parents of public school children rate their local schools higher still (B–) (Snyder & Dillow, 2011). No matter what schooling children are given, parents are usually satisfied with their choice. However, educators and developmentalists are not as satisfied, as you will now see.

International Schooling

Everywhere in the world, children are taught to read, write, and do arithmetic. There are some age-based goals: Because of brain maturation and the necessity of learning in sequence, no nation teaches 6-year-olds to multiply three-digit numbers or read paragraphs fluently out loud, but every nation expects 10-year-olds to do so. Some of the sequences for reading and math that are recognized universally are listed in the accompanying At About This Time tables. Nations also want their children to be good citizens, although there is no consensus as to what that means or what developmental paths (a specific curriculum? at what age?) should be followed (Cohen & Malin, 2010).

Differences by Nation

Although literacy and numeracy (reading and math) are valued everywhere, many specifics of curriculum vary by nation, by community, and by school subject. These variations

AT ABOUT THIS TIME
Math

Age	Norms and Expectations
4–5 years	▪ Count to 20. ▪ Understand one-to-one correspondence of objects and numbers. ▪ Understand *more* and *less*. ▪ Recognize and name shapes.
6 years	▪ Count to 100. ▪ Understand *bigger* and *smaller*. ▪ Add and subtract one-digit numbers.
8 years	▪ Add and subtract two-digit numbers. ▪ Understand simple multiplication and division. ▪ Understand word problems with two variables.
10 years	▪ Add, subtract, multiply, and divide multidigit numbers. ▪ Understand simple fractions, percents, area, and perimeter of shapes. ▪ Understand word problems with three variables.
12 years	▪ Begin to use abstract concepts, such as formulas, algebra.

Math learning depends heavily on direct instruction and repeated practice, which means that some children advance more quickly than others. This list is only a rough guide, to illustrate the importance of sequence.

AT ABOUT THIS TIME
Reading

Age	Norms and Expectations
4–5 years	▪ Understand basic book concepts. For instance, children learning English and many other languages understand that books are written from front to back, with print from left to right, and that letters make words that describe pictures. ▪ Recognize letters—name the letters on sight. ▪ Recognize and spell own name.
6–7 years	▪ Know the sounds of the consonants and vowels, including those that have two sounds (e.g., *c, g, o*). ▪ Use sounds to figure out words. ▪ Read simple words, such as *cat, sit, ball, jump*.
8 years	▪ Read simple sentences out loud, 50 words per minute, including words of two syllables. ▪ Understand basic punctuation, consonant–vowel blends. ▪ Comprehend what is read.
9–10 years	▪ Read and understand paragraphs and chapters, including those with advanced punctuation (e.g., the colon). ▪ Answer comprehension questions about concepts as well as facts. ▪ Read polysyllabic words (e.g., *vegetarian, population, multiplication*).
11–12 years	▪ Demonstrate rapid and fluent oral reading (more than 100 words per minute). ▪ Vocabulary includes words that have specialized meaning in various fields. For example, in civics, *liberties, federal, parliament,* and *environment* all have special meanings. ▪ Comprehend paragraphs about unfamiliar topics. ▪ Sound out new words, figuring out meaning using cognates and context. ▪ Read for pleasure.
13+ years	▪ Continue to build vocabulary, with emphasis more on comprehension than on speech. Understand textbooks.

Reading is a complex mix of skills, dependent on brain maturation, education, and culture. The sequence given here is approximate; it should not be taken as a standard to measure any particular child.

are evident in the results of international tests; in the mix of school subjects; and in the relative power of parents, educators, and political leaders.

For example, as alluded to in Chapter 11, daily physical activity is mandated in some schools, absent in others. Many schools in Japan have swimming pools; virtually no schools in Africa or Latin America do. Geography, music, and art are essential in some places, not in others.

hidden curriculum The unofficial, unstated, or implicit rules and priorities that influence the academic curriculum and every other aspect of learning in a school.

Variation from nation to nation is even greater in aspects of the **hidden curriculum,** which refers to implicit values and assumptions evident in course selection, schedules, tracking, teacher characteristics, discipline, teaching methods, sports competition, student government, extracurricular activities, and so on. For example, if teachers differ from their students in gender, ethnicity, or economic background, the hidden message may be that education is irrelevant for these children's daily lives. If some students are in gifted classes, the message is that they are more capable of learning and that less is expected of the other students (see Chapter 11). A message regarding social values is expressed in the school's physical setting, which might include spacious classrooms, wide hallways, and large, grassy playgrounds—or cramped, poorly equipped rooms and cement play yards or play streets. In some nations, school is outdoors, with no chairs, desks, or books; school is cancelled in severe rain.

AP PHOTO / DANIEL SHANKEN

All the Same These five children all speak a language other than English at home and are now learning English as a new language at school. Although such classes should ideally be taught to true ELLs, children who already speak English are sometimes mistakenly included in such classes (like 8-year-old Elana, from Mexico).

Learning a Second Language

The questions of when, how, to whom, and whether schools should provide second-language instruction are answered in different ways from nation to nation. Some nations teach two or more languages throughout elementary school, while others punish children who utter any word in any language except the majority one.

Almost every European child speaks two languages by age 10, as does almost every Canadian child. Those African children who are talented and fortunate enough to reach high school often speak three languages. In the United States, less than 5 percent of children under age 11 study a language other than English in school (Robelen, 2011). (In secondary school, almost every U. S. student takes a year or two of a language other than English, but cognitive theory suggests that is too late for efficient learning).

immersion A strategy in which instruction in all school subjects occurs in the second (usually the majority) language that a child is learning.

bilingual schooling A strategy in which school subjects are taught in both the learner's original language and the second (majority) language.

Teaching approaches range from **immersion,** in which instruction occurs entirely in the new language (the traditional approach in the United States for children who do not already speak English), to the opposite, in which children are taught in their first language until the second language can be taught as a "foreign" tongue (a strategy rare in the United States, but common in many other nations). Between these extremes lie **bilingual schooling,** with instruction in two languages, and, in North America, ELL (formerly known as ESL, English as a Second Language) in which all non-English speakers are grouped together to be taught intensively and exclusively in English to prepare them for regular classes.

Methods for teaching a second language sometimes succeed and sometimes fail, with the research not yet clear as to which approach is best (Gandara & Rumberger, 2009). The success of any method seems to depend on the literacy of the home environment (frequent reading, writing, and listening in any language helps); the national culture; and the warmth, training, and skill of the teacher. In some schools, every teacher is bilingual; in other schools, none are—and children quickly understand the hidden curriculum. Some react to the school culture by underachieving or dropping out.

Although cognitive research leaves no doubt that school-age children *can* learn a second language if taught logically, step by step, and that they *can* maintain their original language, whether they do so is affected by factors beyond cognitive research: SES, family ethnotheories, expectations, and national policies.

International Testing

Over the past two decades, more than 50 nations have participated in at least one massive international test of educational achievement. Longitudinal data find that, if achievement rises, the national economy advances—a sequence that seems causal, not merely correlational (Hanushek & Woessmann, 2009). The probable reason is that better-educated adults become more productive workers. We focus here on results for fourth-graders, usually the youngest children tested.

Science and math achievement are tested in the **Trends in Math and Science Study (TIMSS).** East Asian nations are always at the top. Indeed, among 10-year-olds, the *average* Singapore student scores higher than the top 5 percent of U.S. students (Mullis et al., 2008).

The primary test of reading is the **Progress in International Reading Literacy Study (PIRLS).** In the most recent published study (Mullis et al., 2007), Canadian children from the western provinces were close to the top, and the United States ranked 15th out of 45 groups (most groups are nations, but some, as with the provinces of Canada, are not). Russia scored first in the PIRLS, up from 16th only five years earlier, probably because of extensive changes in education in the early grades. Only two East Asian groups took the PIRLS, Hong Kong and Singapore, where instruction is in English; they scored second and fourth among the groups. Africa and Middle Eastern groups scored low; their reading skills are, overall, no match for those of the Asians.

Trends in Math and Science Study (TIMSS) An international assessment of the math and science skills of fourth- and eighth-graders. Although the TIMSS is very useful, different countries' scores are not always comparable because sample selection, test administration, and content validity are hard to keep uniform.

Progress in International Reading Literacy Study (PIRLS) Inaugurated in 2001, a planned five-year cycle of international trend studies in the reading ability of fourth-graders.

Problems with International Benchmarks

Elaborate and extensive measures are in place to make the PIRLS and the TIMSS valid. Test items are carefully designed to be fair and culture-free; participant children are of both sexes, many incomes, many regions, and so on, to represent the entire child population of the nation. Children are compared with other schoolchildren of the same age. Consequently, these results are respected by most social scientists worldwide. However, researchers also realize that absolute equivalency is impossible, given cultural and historical differences.

Designing test items is difficult. For example, should fourth-graders be expected to understand fractions, graphs, and simple geometry, or should the test focus only on basic operations with whole numbers? Once those general questions are decided, specific items may inadvertently be culturally biased. One item testing fourth-grade math was the following:

> Al wanted to find out how much his cat weighed. He weighed himself and noted that the scale read 57 kg. He then stepped on the scale holding his cat and found that it read 62 kg. What was the weight of the cat in kilograms?
> Answer: ________ kilograms

This item requires simple subtraction. However, 40 percent of U.S. fourth-graders got it wrong. Were they unable to subtract 57 from 62, or did they not understand the example, or did the abbreviation for kilograms confuse them because—unlike children in most nations—they are more familiar with pounds? On this item, children from Yemen were at the bottom, with

"Big deal, an A in math. That would be a D in any other country."

SHEHZAD NOORANI / PETER ARNOLD, INC.

Catching Up with the West These Iranian girls are acting out a poem they have memorized from their third-grade textbook. They attend school in a UNICEF-supported Global Education pilot project. Their child-centered classes encourage maximum participation.

95 percent of them failing. Is that because few of them have cats for pets or weigh themselves on a scale?

Gender Differences in School Performance

In addition to marked national, ethnic, and economic differences, gender differences in achievement scores are reported. The PIRLS finds girls ahead of boys in verbal skills in every nation. Traditionally, boys are ahead of girls in math and science.

The most recent TIMSS finds that gender differences in math have narrowed or disappeared. Boys were slightly (10 points) higher than girls overall, but the differences were even smaller (6 points) in the United States, and girls scored higher than boys in four nations (Russia, Singapore, Algeria, and Iran) (Gonzales et al., 2009). Such results lead to a *gender-similarities hypothesis* that males and females are similar on most test measures, with "trivial" exceptions (Hyde et al., 2008, p. 494).

Classroom performance also shows gender differences in almost every nation. Girls have higher grades overall, including in math and science. Then, at puberty, girls' grades dip, especially in science. Many reasons for this drop have been suggested. One is that, since girls are ahead in physiological maturation, it is easier for young girls to sit at their desks and concentrate. Then, when they reach puberty earlier than boys, they may underachieve because they think boys will like them better if they are not too smart.

No Child Left Behind Act A U.S. law enacted in 2001 that was intended to increase accountability in education by requiring states to qualify for federal educational funding by administering standardized tests to measure school achievement.

An alternate explanation is that social prejudice favors young girls but not young women. Since most elementary school teachers are women, girls in the early grades may feel (or be) more encouraged. Then, when girls begin to prepare for adult roles, they seek the skills and jobs that characterize people of their sex, perhaps office assistants instead of engineers or physicists (Weisgram et al., 2010). For that reason, their motivation may falter in science classes.

In the United States

Although some national tests find improvements in achievement for U.S. children, when compared with other nations they have not improved much in reading or math from 1990 to 2010. Furthermore, among fourth-graders, the ethnic gap between European Americans and their Latino and African American peers is as wide as it was years ago (see Table 12.2), to the consternation of many political and educational leaders.

How Many Fingers? It looks as if teacher Alvin Yardley and fourth-grader Matthew are fully engaged in figuring out a math problem. However, U.S. fourth-graders score far below those in East Asia. Some critics blame the teachers, some the students, others the schools, and still others the culture.

AP PHOTO / JAE C. HONG

National Standards

International comparisons and disparities within the nation led to the **No Child Left Behind Act** of 2001 (NCLB), a federal law promoting high national standards for public schools. One controversial aspect of the law is the requirement for frequent testing to measure whether standards are being met. Low-scoring schools lose funding and may close. An unfortunate result is that children of middling achievement are pushed to make sure they meet the benchmark, but children far above it are ignored because they will do well enough without help. Children far below may be ignored as well because they will never attain the benchmark.

Most parents and teachers agree with the goals of NCLB (accountability and higher achievement) but not with the strategies. Strong opinions on opposite sides are common—such as those expressed in the very same issue of *Science* (Hanushek, 2009; Koretz, 2009). NCLB troubles those who value the arts, social studies, or physical education because those subjects are often squeezed out when reading and math achievement is the priority. The tests, and testing, are controversial.

Many states have created achievement tests that allow most of their schools to progress (and thus get federal funds). Federally sponsored tests called the **National Assessment of Educational Progress (NAEP)** measure achievement in reading, mathematics, and other subjects. Many critics believe that the NAEP is better than state tests (Applegate et al., 2009), a conclusion reached because fewer children are labeled proficient on the NAEP (see Figure 12.4).

Disagreement about state tests and standards led the governors of all 50 states to designate a group of experts to develop a Common Core of standards, finalized in 2010, for use nationwide. The standards, higher than most state standards, are quite explicit, with half a dozen or more specific expectations for achievement in each subject for each grade (Table 12.3 provides a sample of the specific standards). As of 2011, 45 states have adopted this Common Core.

Reading Wars, Math Wars, and Cognitive Theory

To help you understand why educators seek a common standard, consider the recent disputes about teaching reading and math. It could be that educators now have battle fatigue; they no longer want to fight over specifics of curriculum.

Clashes over teaching reading led to "serious, sometimes acrimonious debate, fueling the well-named 'reading wars'" (Keogh, 2004, p. 93). The dispute pitted advocates of the **phonics approach** (teaching letter–sound correspondence) versus advocates of the **whole-language approach** (which encourages all language—talking, listening, reading, and writing).

TABLE 12.2 TIMSS Ranking and Average Scores of Math Achievement for Fourth-Graders, 2007

Rank*	Country	Score
1.	Hong Kong	667
2.	Singapore	599
3.	China/Taipei	576
4.	Japan	568
5.	Kazakhstan	549
6.	Russian Federation	544
7.	England	541
8.	Latvia	537
9.	Netherlands	535
10.	United States	531
11.	Lithuania	530
12.	Germany	525
	Denmark	523
	Canada/Quebec	519
	Australia	516
	Hungary	516
	Canada/Ontario	512
	Italy	507
	New Zealand	492
	Iran	402
	Colombia	355
	Yemen	224

*The top 12 groups are listed in order, but after that not all the jurisdictions that took the test are listed. Some nations have improved over the past 15 years (notably, Hong Kong, England) and some have declined (Austria, Netherlands), but most continue about where they have always been.

Source: TIMSS 2007 International Mathematics Report (Mullis et al., 2008).

Rating Fourth-Graders' Reading Proficiency: The Gap Between NAEP and the States

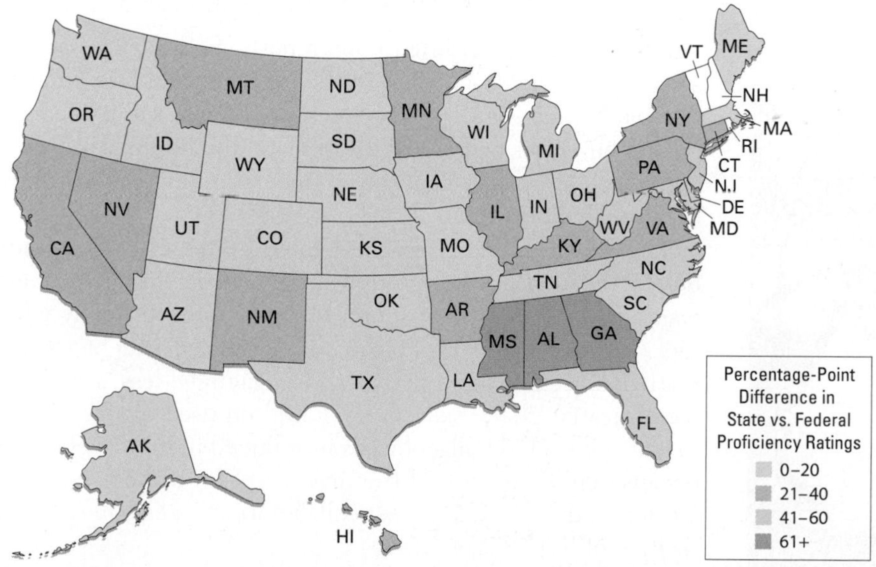

Source: EPE Research Center, in D. J. Hoff, 2007, p. 23.

National Assessment of Educational Progress (NAEP) An ongoing and nationally representative measure of U.S. children's achievement in reading, mathematics, and other subjects over time; nicknamed "the Nation's Report Card."

phonics approach Teaching reading by first teaching the sounds of each letter and of various letter combinations.

whole-language approach Teaching reading by encouraging early use of all language skills—talking and listening, reading and writing.

FIGURE 12.4

Local Standards Each state sets its own level of proficiency, which helps states in which children score low on the NAEP to obtain more federal money for education. That practice may undercut high standards for student learning in all the green and especially the purple states.

TABLE 12.3 The Common Core: Sample Items for Each Grade

Grade	Reading and Writing	Math
Kindergarten	Pronounce the primary sound for each consonant	Know number names and the count sequence
First	Decode regularly spelled one-syllable words	Relate counting to addition and subtraction (e.g., by counting 2 more to add 2)
Second	Decode words with common prefixes and suffixes	Measure the length of an object twice, using different units of length for the two measurements; describe how the two measurements relate to the size of the unit chosen
Third	Decode multisyllabic words	Understand division as an unknown-factor problem; for example, find 32×8 by finding the number that makes 32 when multiplied by 8
Fourth	Use combined knowledge of all letter–sound correspondences, syllable patterns, and morphology (e.g., roots and affixes) to read accurately unfamiliar multisyllabic words in context and out of context	Apply and extend previous understandings of multiplication to multiply a fraction by a whole number
Fifth	With guidance and support from peers and adults, develop and strengthen writing as needed by planning, revising, editing, rewriting, or trying a new approach	Graph points on the coordinate plane to solve real-world and mathematical problems

Source: National Governor's Association, 2010.

All This and More This is a small sample of the elements in the Common Core, but it is enough for you to see that the grade-by-grade standards are explicit and not easy. Teachers are encouraged to make sure all the children in each grade achieve the skills and knowledge listed for that grade.

Phonics proponents believe that decoding letters and sounds is essential to reading and that, without it, children will flounder, become frustrated, and fail. This is particularly likely if families have not prepared their children for reading. One critic said a "child-centered anti-academic" approach did not teach the basics of reading, rendering children helpless without explicit standards and foundations (Hirsch, 2008, p. 9). Basics include phonics, some educators contend.

The whole-language proponents are proud to be "child-centered." They counter that drilling children with phonics destroys motivation, reduces comprehension, and leads to the "fourth-grade slump," when 10-year-olds no longer want to learn. Whole-language educators offer children a choice of books and topics, encourage children to read their own stories to each other, and guide learners within their zone of proximal development.

Collaborative Learning Japanese children learn mathematics in a more structured and socially interactive way than are their North American counterparts.

RUSSELL D. CURTIS / PHOTO RESEARCHERS, INC.

Another battle involves math. According to one report, "U.S. mathematics instruction has been scorched in the pedagogical blaze known as the 'math wars'—a divide between those who see a need for a greater emphasis on basic skills in math and others who say students lack a broader, conceptual understanding of the subject" (Cavanagh, 2005, p. 1).

Historically, children in the United States memorized number facts, such as the multiplication tables, filling page after page of workbooks. In reaction to this approach, many educators, inspired again by Piaget and Vygotsky, sought to make math instruction more active and engaging—less a matter of memorization than of discovery. Children used blocks or marks to add and subtract; algebra was introduced in middle childhood because children enjoyed the mystery of an unknown *x* and *y*. Curiosity, discovery, and peer collaboration replace most memorization of formulas or facts.

As you read in the first half of this chapter, a newer cognitive approach is information processing, which stresses a step-

NAM Y. HUH / AP PHOTO

TED S. WARREN / AP PHOTO

Reading with Comprehension *(left)* Reading and math scores in third-grader Monica's Illinois elementary school showed improvement under the standards set by the No Child Left Behind Act. However, the principal noted a cost for this success in less time spent on social studies and other subjects. *(right)* Some experts believe that children should have their own books and be able to read them wherever and however they want. This strategy seems to be working with Josue and Cristo, two 8-year-olds who were given books through their after-school program in Rochester, Washington.

by-step sequence in learning. That might seem to support explicit, sequenced standards such as phonics and number facts. The emphasis on national and international tests and on Common Core standards can also be seen as an outcome of the information-processing approach. However, before deciding that current cognitive theory supports one side or the other of these wars, you need to remember that all children are great learners, each with particular learning needs.

Who Determines Educational Practice?

An underlying issue for both wars, for the hidden curriculum, and for international variations is the role of parental choice. In most nations, matters regarding public education—including curriculum, funding, teacher training, and so on—are set by the central government. In the United States, by contrast, local jurisdictions provide most of the funds and guidelines. Parents affect education by communicating with their child's teacher, by becoming active in parent–teacher associations (PTAs), by moving to a particular school zone. Moreover, while most U.S. parents send their children to the local zoned public school, almost one-third do not. An increasing number choose a public charter school, a private school, or home schooling (see Figure 12.5).

Especially for School Administrators Children who wear uniforms in school tend to score higher on reading tests. Why? (see response, page 373)

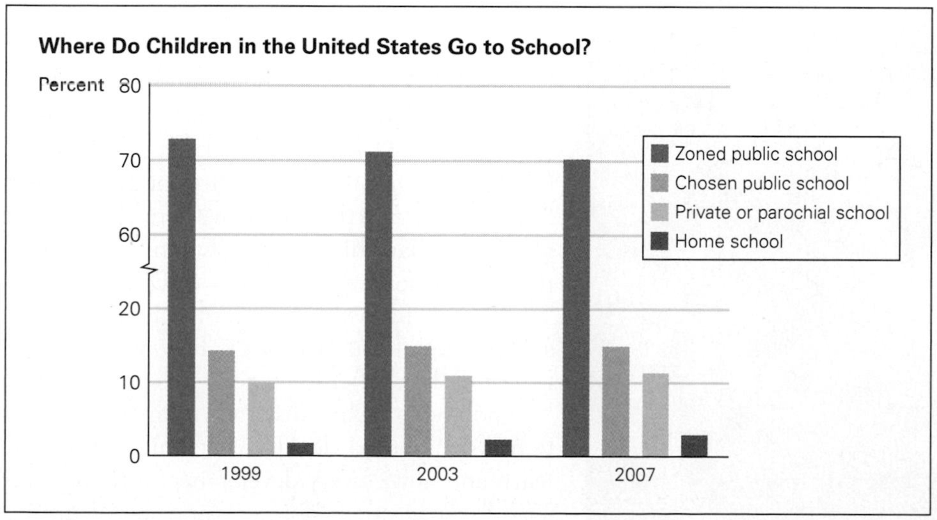

FIGURE 12.5

Where'd You Go to School? Note that although home schooling is still the least-chosen option, the number of home-schooled children is increasing, while the number of children attending zoned public schools is slightly decreasing. More detailed data indicate that, while any child might be home-schooled, the typical home-schooled child is a 7-year-old European American girl living in a rural area of the South with two parents (only one of whom is employed).

charter school A public school with its own set of standards that is funded and licensed by the state or local district in which it is located.

Charter schools are public schools, free to students and funded and licensed by states or local districts. Typically, they also have private money and sponsors. They are exempt from some regulations, especially those stipulated in contracts negotiated by unions, and they have some control over admissions and expulsions. For that reason, they often are more racially segregated and have fewer children with special needs. Typically, teachers are younger and work longer hours, and school size is smaller than that of traditional public schools.

Some charter schools are remarkably successful; others are not. A major criticism is that not every child who enters a charter school stays to graduate—one scholar says "the dropout rate for African-American males is shocking" (Miron, quoted in Zehr, 2011, p. 24). Overall, children and teachers leave charter schools more often than they leave zoned public schools, but since teachers and parents have chosen charter schools, they may be more likely to choose again, leaving if their expectations are not met.

private school A school funded by tuition charges, endowments, and often religious or other non-profit sponsors. .

Private schools are funded by tuition charges, endowments, and church sponsors. Traditionally in the United States, most private schools were organized by the Catholic Church, to educate students in religion. Tuition was relatively low since many teachers were nuns who earned little pay. In the past decades, many Catholic schools have closed, but the number of independent schools has increased.

voucher Public subsidy for tuition payment at a non-public school. Vouchers vary a great deal from place to place, not only in amount and availability, but in restrictions as to who gets them and what schools accept them.

home schooling Education in which children are taught at home, usually by their parents.

Some U.S. jurisdictions issue pay **vouchers,** with which parents may pay some or all of the tuition at a private school. This practice is controversial, not only because it decreases public school funding and enrollment but also because some families choose church-sponsored schools, which may violate separation of church and state. Proponents say that vouchers increase competition and may improve all schools, public and private.

Home schooling occurs when parents decide to avoid both public and private schools and instead educate their children at home. As Figure 12.5 shows, this solution is becoming more common, but still only a tiny minority of children are home-schooled, about 1 child in 35. Home schooling is illegal in some nations but not in the United States, where authorities set standards for what a child must learn but allow families to decide curriculum, schedules, and discipline. The major problem with home schooling is not academic (some children score high on achievement tests) but social, since children miss out on the social interactions of the classroom. To compensate, many home-schooling parents plan social activities with other home-schooling families.

Chance or Design? These third-graders are using dice to play a game that may teach them multiplication.

Observation Quiz This is a charter school in New Jersey. What three signs are visible here that few typical public schools share? (see answer, page 373)

AP PHOTO / MIKE DERER

On some issues, research clashes with parental emotions. For example, small class sizes and nightly homework can be more attractive to parents than beneficial to children. Nations whose children score high on international tests sometimes have large student/teacher ratios (Korea's average is 28 to 1) and sometimes small (Finland's is 14 to 1, as is that of the United States); and fourth-graders with no homework sometimes have higher achievement scores than those with homework (Snyder & Dillow, 2010). These data suggest that class size and homework are not the crucial variables in how much a child learns; rather, other interpretations are possible.

Underlying many disputes is another question: Who should decide what children should learn and how? Every developmental theory can lead to suggestions for teaching and learning

MICHAEL NEWMAN / PHOTOEDIT

© ANDREA RUGG / BEATEWORKS / CORBIS

Coming and Going Two U.S. elementary schools—one in Los Angeles, California *(left)*, the other in Wayzata, Minnesota *(right)*—illustrate differences in hidden curriculum. Political leaders and taxpayers often disagree with parents and teachers as to whether this affects classroom learning.

(Farrar & Al-Qatawneh, 2010), but none endorse one curriculum or method to the exclusion of all others. Parents, politicians, and developmental experts all agree that some children learn much more than others and that some teachers are more skilled than others, but adults vehemently disagree on curriculum—hidden or overt.

More quantitative and qualitative research is needed. A 19-member panel of experts seeking the best math curricula for the United States examined 16,000 studies but "found a serious lack of studies with adequate scale and design for us to reach conclusions" (Faulkner, quoted in Mervis, 2008, p. 1605). Similarly, a review of home schooling, charter schools, and vouchers complains of "the difficulty of interpreting the research literature on this topic, most of which is biased and far from approaching balanced social science" (Boyd, 2007, p. 7). The same complaint could apply to research on the reading and math wars, controversies about testing and standards, and mixed results on class size and homework: All would benefit from large-scale, controlled studies.

Fortunately, some such research is under way, and compared to even a decade ago, much more national and international interest and data are evident. School-age children are great learners: Once the strengths and weaknesses of scientific study are understood, parents and everyone else may know how best to teach them.

>> Response for School Administrators (from page 371) The relationship reflects correlation, not causation. Wearing uniforms is more common when the culture of the school emphasizes achievement and study, with strict discipline in class and a policy of expelling disruptive students.

SUMMING UP

Societies throughout the world recognize that school-age children are avid learners and that educated citizens are essential to economic development, which has led to increased enrollment: More than 95 percent of the world's children are in school of some sort, at least for a few years. Schools differ in what and how children are taught, and international tests find some nations are far more successful than others in educating their young. Test scores, as well as the nature and content of education, raise ideological and political passions: Examples are found in the reading wars, the math wars, and many other aspects of the overt and the hidden curricula. Research finds that direct instruction (in phonics; in mathematical symbols and procedures; in the vocabulary, grammar, and syntax of second languages) is useful. Also crucial are motivation, pride, and social interaction. School-age children are great learners, but they cannot learn everything. Adults must decide the specifics.

>> Answer to Observation Quiz (from page 372) Carpets and rugs, students lying down to do schoolwork, clipboards and dice—all are highly unusual for traditional schools.

SUMMARY

Building on Theory

1. According to Piaget, middle childhood is the time of concrete operational thought, when egocentrism diminishes and logical thinking begins. School-age children can understand classification and conservation, and they develop transitive inference.

2. Vygotsky stressed the social context of learning, including the specific lessons of school and learning from peers and adults. Culture affects not only what children learn but also how they learn.

3. An information-processing approach examines each step of the thinking process, from input to output, using the computer as a model. This approach is useful for understanding memory, perception, and expression.

4. Memory begins with information that reaches the brain from the sense organs. Then selection processes, benefiting from past experience, allow some information to reach working memory. Finally, long-term memory stores images and ideas indefinitely, retrieving parts when needed.

5. A broader knowledge base, logical strategies for retrieval, and faster processing advance every aspect of memory and cognition. Control processes are crucial. Children become better at controlling and directing their thinking as the prefrontal cortex matures. Metacognition improves over the years of middle childhood and beyond.

Language

6. Language learning advances in many practical ways, including expanded vocabulary as words are logically linked together and as an understanding of metaphors begins.

7. Children excel at pragmatics during middle childhood, often using one code with their friends and another in school. Many children become fluent in the school language while speaking their first language at home.

8. Children of low SES are usually lower in linguistic skills, primarily because they hear less language and because adult expectations for their learning are low. This is not inevitable for low-SES families, however.

Teaching and Learning

9. Nations and experts agree that education is critical during middle childhood. Almost all the world's children now attend primary school. Schools differ in what and how they teach, especially with regard to religion, languages, and the arts.

10. International assessments are useful as comparisons, partly because few objective measures of learning are available. Reading is assessed with the PIRLS, math and science with the TIMSS. On both measures, children in East Asia excel and children in the United States are middling.

11. In the United States, the No Child Left Behind Act and the National Assessment of Educational Progress (NAEP) attempt to raise the standard of education, with mixed success. The Common Core, developed with the sponsorship of the governors of the 50 states, is an effort to raise national standards and improve accountability.

12. The reading wars pitted advocates of phonics against advocates of the whole-language approach. A truce has been reached, however. Research finds that both methods may be needed, as children require both basic skills and more advanced thinking.

13. Disagreements about education are frequent; some parents choose charter schools, others prefer private schools, and still others opt for home schooling. However, parents value some aspects (class size, homework) more than do educators, and nations differ in how much national control they seek for public education. More research is needed to discover the best way for children to learn.

KEY TERMS

concrete operational thought (p. 351)
classification (p. 352)
transitive inference (p. 352)
sensory memory (p. 357)
working memory (p. 357)
long-term memory (p. 358)
knowledge base (p. 358)
control processes (p. 358)
metacognition (p. 358)
pragmatics (p. 361)
ELLs (English Language Learners) (p. 362)
hidden curriculum (p. 366)
immersion (p. 366)
bilingual schooling (p. 366)
Trends in Math and Science Study (TIMSS) (p. 367)
Progress in International Reading Literacy Study (PIRLS) (p. 367)
No Child Left Behind Act (p. 368)
National Assessment of Educational Progress (NAEP) (p. 369)
phonics approach (p. 369)
whole-language approach (p. 369)
charter school (p. 372)
private school (p. 372)
voucher (p. 372)
home schooling (p. 372)

WHAT HAVE YOU LEARNED?

Building on Theory

1. Why did Piaget call cognition in middle childhood *concrete operational* thought?

2. How would you express classification in categories of transportation or plants?

3. How is transitive inference the result of logic, not experience?

4. How do Vygotsky and Piaget differ in their explanation of cognitive advances in middle childhood?

5. According to Vygotsky, where and how does cognitive development occur?

6. What have developmentalists learned from child vendors in Brazil?

7. How does information processing differ from traditional theories of cognitive development?

8. According to information processing, how do children learn math concepts?

9. What aspects of memory improve markedly during middle childhood?

10. How might metacognitive skills help a student?

Language

11. How does the process of learning language differ between age 3 and age 10?

12. How is the understanding of metaphors and jokes affected by a child's age?

13. Why are prefixes and suffixes useful in expanding vocabulary?

14. Why would a child's linguistic code be criticized by teachers but admired by friends?

15. Which factors affect a child's ability to learn grammar and advanced vocabulary?

16. How and why does SES affect language learning?

Teaching and Learning

17. What do all nations have in common regarding education in middle childhood?

18. What is the difference between the overt curriculum and the hidden curriculum?

19. What are the differences in the ways that nations teach the language of the school?

20. What are the similarities and differences between the two most common international tests of achievement?

21. What are the main goals and criticisms of No Child Left Behind?

22. What gender differences are found in educational tests and school grades?

23. What problems does the Common Core attempt to solve?

24. Why are some disagreements about education called "wars," not merely differences?

25. What are the differences among charter schools, private schools, and home schooling?

26. What are the advantages and disadvantages of parental choice in how children are educated?

APPLICATIONS

1. Visit a local elementary school and look for the hidden curriculum. For example, do the children line up? Why or why not, when and how? Does gender, age, ability, or talent affect the grouping of children or the selection of staff? What is on the walls? Are parents involved? If so, how? For everything you observe, speculate about the underlying assumptions.

2. Interview a 7- to 11-year-old child to find out what he or she knows *and understands* about mathematics. Relate both correct and incorrect responses to the logic of concrete operational thought.

3. What do you remember about how you learned to read? Compare your memories with those of two other people, one at least 10 years older and the other at least 5 years younger than you are. Can you draw any conclusions about effective reading instruction? If so, what are they? If not, why not?

4. Talk to two parents of primary school children. What do they think are the best and worst parts of their children's education? Ask specific questions and analyze the results.

>>ONLINE CONNECTIONS

To accompany your textbook, you have access to a number of online resources, including quizzes for every chapter of the book, flashcards (in English and Spanish), critical thinking questions, and case studies. For access to any of these links, go to www.worthpublishers.com/bergerca9e. In addition to these free resources, you'll also find links to podcasts, video clips, diagnostic quizzing with personalized study advice, and an ebook. Some of the videos and activities available online include:

- *Conservation.* Half empty or half full? Watch as children of different ages perform the Piagetian conservation-of-liquid task and note the differences as they explain their reasoning.
- *Motivation and Learning.* Are children really "little scientists," as Piaget believed? Explores intrinsic motivation and classroom strategies that inspire it.

13

CHAPTER

Middle Childhood: Psychosocial Development

WHAT WILL YOU KNOW?

1. What helps some children thrive in difficult family or neighborhood conditions?
2. Is it better for parents to marry, risking divorce, or to avoid marriage and thus avoid divorce?
3. What can be done to stop a bully?
4. When would children lie to adults to protect a friend?

A student of mine drove to a gas station to get a flat tire fixed. She wrote:

> As I pulled up, I saw a very short boy sitting at the garage door. I imagined him to be about 8 or 9 years old and wondered why he was sitting there by himself. He directed me to park, and summoned a man who looked at my tire and spoke to the boy in a language I did not understand. This little boy then lifted my car with a jack, removed all the bolts, and fixed the flat. I was in shock. When I paid the man (who was his father), I asked how long his son had been doing this. He said about three years.
>
> *[adapted from Tiffany, personal communication, March 15, 2008]*

Adults like Tiffany are shocked to learn that many of the world's children are forced to work, in defiance of the United Nations' declaration that children have the right

> to be protected from economic exploitation and from performing any work that is likely to be hazardous or to interfere with the child's education, or to be harmful to the child's health or physical, mental, spiritual, moral, or social development.
>
> *[Convention on the Rights of the Child]*

REUTERS / ANDREW BIRAJ

"To Be Protected" Shaheen, age 10, is one of two dozen children, most of whom work 12 hours a day, employed in this aluminum factory in Dhaka, Bangladesh. Who is to blame for this "economic exploitation"—family, factory, nation, or all of us? None of them is protecting Shaheen at this moment.

The International Labour Organization (ILO) of the United Nations (Diallo et al., 2010) estimated that this right was violated for 153 million 5- to 14-year-olds worldwide, with 115 million of them (4.3 percent of all children) engaged in hazardous work.

Changing tires is not defined as hazardous, but did the work "interfere with the child's education" or was the boy harmed in any way? The answer is not obvious. With almost every aspect of middle childhood, specific details are crucial.

All children need friends, families, and skills, but some peers are destructive, some families are dysfunctional, and some skills should not be learned. This chapter describes some of the many circumstances that affect a child's "physical, mental, spiritual, moral, or social development." You will learn when child labor, peer culture, bullying, single-parent families, poverty, divorce, and so on are harmful. We begin with the children themselves and then discuss families, peers, and morality.

>> The Nature of the Child

As explained in the previous two chapters, steady growth, brain maturation, and intellectual advances make middle childhood a time when children gain independence and autonomy (see At About This Time). They acquire an "increasing ability to regulate themselves, to take responsibility, and to exercise self-control"—all strengths that make this a period of positive growth (Huston & Ripke, 2006, p. 9).

One result is that school-age children can finally care for themselves. They not only feed themselves but also make their own dinner, not only dress themselves but also pack their own suitcases, not only walk to school but also organize games with friends on the playground. They venture outdoors alone. Boys are especially likely to put some distance between themselves and their home, engaging in activities without their parents' awareness or approval (Munroe & Romney, 2006). This budding independence fosters growth.

AT ABOUT THIS TIME

Signs of Psychosocial Maturation over the Years of Middle Childhood
Children have specific chores to perform.
Children make decisions about a weekly allowance.
Children can tell time, and they have set times for various activities.
Children have homework, including some assignments over several days.
Children are less often punished physically than in early childhood.
Children try to conform to peers in clothes, language, and so on.
Children voice preferences about their after-school care, lessons, and activities.
Children use media (TV, computers, video games) without adult supervision.
Children are responsible for younger children, pets, and, in some places, work.
Children strive for independence from parents.

Industry and Inferiority

One particular characteristic of school-age children, throughout the centuries and in every culture, is that they are industrious. They busily and actively master whatever skills their culture values. Their mind and body maturation, described in the previous two chapters, makes such activity possible.

Erikson's Insights

The tension between productivity and incompetence is the fourth psychosocial crisis, **industry versus inferiority,** as described by Erik Erikson. He noted that during these years the child "must forget past hopes and wishes, while his exuberant imagination is tamed and harnessed to the laws of impersonal things," becoming "ready to apply himself to given skills and tasks" (Erikson, 1963, pp. 258, 259).

industry versus inferiority The fourth of Erikson's eight psychosocial crises, during which children attempt to master many skills, developing a sense of themselves as either industrious or inferior, competent or incompetent.

Think of learning to read and add—painstaking and boring tasks. For instance, slowly sounding out "Jane has a dog" or writing "3 + 4 = 7" for the hundredth time are not very exciting. Yet school-age children busily practice reading and math: They are intrinsically motivated to read a page, finish a worksheet, memorize a spelling word, color a map, and so on. Similarly, they enjoy collecting, categorizing, and counting whatever they accumulate—perhaps stamps, stickers, stones, or seashells. That is industry.

Overall, children judge themselves as either *industrious* or *inferior*—deciding whether they are competent or incompetent, productive or useless, winners or losers. Being productive is intrinsically joyous, and it fosters the self-control that is a crucial defense against emotional problems (Bradley & Corwyn, 2005).

A sense of industry may be a defense against early substance use as well. In a study of 509 third- and fourth-graders in Arizona over a five-month period, an increasing number said that they had tried, or were expecting to try, alcohol (from 58 percent at the start of the study to 72 percent at the end) and cigarettes (from 18 to 23 percent). Those most likely to show such upturns were the children who increasingly felt inferior, not industrious (Jones, 2011). For example, they did not agree that they "stick with things until they are finished" and they were not proud of what they did.

LINDSEY HEBBARD / WOODFIN CAMP & ASSOCIATES

Celebrating Spring No matter where they live, 7- to 11-year-olds seek to understand and develop whatever skills are valued by their culture. They do so in active, industrious ways, as described in every theory. This is illustrated here, as four friends in Assam, northeastern India, usher in spring with a Bihu celebration. Soon they will be given sweets and tea, which is the sociocultural validation of their energy, independence, and skill.

Freud on Latency

Sigmund Freud described this period as **latency,** a time when emotional drives are quiet and unconscious sexual conflicts are submerged. Some experts complain that "middle childhood has been neglected at least since Freud relegated these years to the status of an uninteresting 'latency period'" (Huston & Ripke, 2006, p. 7).

latency Freud's term for middle childhood, during which children's emotional drives and psychosexual needs are quiet (latent). Freud thought that sexual conflicts from earlier stages are only temporarily submerged, bursting forth again at puberty.

But in one sense, at least, Freud was correct: Sexual impulses are quiet. Even when children were betrothed before age 12 (rare today, but not uncommon in earlier centuries), the young husband and wife had little interaction. Everywhere, boys and girls typically choose to be with others of their own sex. Indeed, boys who write "Girls stay out!" and girls who complain that "boys stink" are quite typical. Parents sometimes worry about sexual predators. However, school-age children are not very sexual; strangers rarely attempt to seduce children who have yet to reach puberty (Wolak et al., 2008).

Self-Concept

As children mature, they develop their *self-concept*, which is their idea about themselves, including their intelligence, personality, abilities, gender, and ethnic background. As you remember, the very notion that they are individuals is a discovery in toddlerhood, and a positive, global self-concept is typical in early childhood. Not so in middle childhood. The self-concept gradually becomes more specific and logical, as one might expect, given increases in cognitive development and social awareness. As one group explains, "The cognitive ability to combine specific behavioral features of the self (I can run fast and throw far) into higher order generalizations . . . (I am athletic) appears in middle childhood . . ." (Pfeifer et al., 2010, p. 144).

As the self-concept becomes more specific and logical, it also becomes less optimistic, incorporating influences from peers and the overall society. For example, some 6-year-olds from minority ethnic groups are refreshingly unaware of prejudice against their group; by age 11, they are aware, usually taking pride in their self-concept as Latino, or whatever, in defense (García Coll & Marks, 2009).

Ideally, "children develop feelings of self-esteem, competence, and individuality during middle childhood as they begin comparing themselves with peers" (Ripke et al., 2006, p. 261). Research in many nations has found that teaching anxious children to confide in friends as well as to understand their own emotions helps them develop a better self-concept (Siu, 2007). After-school activities, particularly sports, can provide a foundation for friendship and realistic self-esteem.

effortful control The ability to regulate one's emotions and actions through effort, not simply through natural inclination.

Academic and social competence are aided by realistic self-perception. Unrealistically high self-esteem reduces **effortful control** (deliberately modifying one's impulses and emotions). A reduction of effortful control leads to lower achievement and increased aggression. The same consequences occur if self-esteem is unrealistically low, so obviously the goal is to find a middle ground—not easy, since children may be too self-critical or not self-critical enough and since cultures differ on what that middle ground is.

Not Easy Newspapers aren't the only thing being recycled here. Family values are transmitted from one generation to the next. It is easier for adults to take out the trash themselves, but having a 7-year-old do it, as shown here, develops social commitment, responsibility, and pride.

High self-esteem is not universally valued or universally criticized (Yamaguchi et al., 2007). Many cultures expect children to be modest, not prideful. For example, Australians say that "tall poppies" are cut down, and the Japanese discourage social comparison aimed at making oneself feel superior.

Although Japanese children often excel at mathematics on international tests, only 17 percent have a high opinion of their math ability. In the United States, 53 percent of the students taking the TIMSS (Trends in Math and Science Study) are very confident of their math ability, yet they score significantly lower than the Japanese do (Snyder & Dillow, 2010). In Estonia, low self-esteem correlates with high academic achievement (Pullmann & Allik, 2008).

Often in the United States, children's successes are praised and teachers are wary of being too critical, especially in middle childhood. For example, some schools issue report cards with grades ranging from "Excellent" to "Needs improvement" instead of from A to F. An opposite trend is found in the national reforms of education explained in Chapter 12, which rate some schools as failing. Obviously culture, cohort, and age all influence self-concept, with the long-term effects debatable (Heine, 2007).

Resilience and Stress

In infancy and early childhood, children depend on their immediate families for food, learning, and life itself. Then "experiences in middle childhood can sustain, magnify, or reverse the advantages or disadvantages that children acquire in the preschool years" (Huston & Ripke, 2006, p. 2). Supportive families continue to be protective, but children may escape destructive family influences by finding their own niche in the larger world.

Surprisingly, some children seem unscathed by early experiences. They have been called "resilient" or even "invincible." Current thinking about resilience (see Table 13.1), with insights from dynamic-systems theory, makes it clear that, although some children cope better than others, none are impervious to their past history or current context (Jenson & Fraser, 2006; Luthar et al., 2003). Differential sensitivity is apparent, not only for genetic reasons but also because early child rearing, preschool education, and sociocultural values may strengthen children. Some children are hardy, more like dandelions than orchids, but all are influenced by their situation (Ellis & Boyce, 2008).

resilience The capacity to adapt well to significant adversity and to overcome serious stress.

Resilience has been defined as "a dynamic process encompassing positive adaptation within the context of significant adversity" (Luthar et al., 2000, p. 543). Note the three parts of this definition:

- Resilience is *dynamic,* not a stable trait. That means a given person may be resilient at some periods but not others.
- Resilience is a *positive adaptation* to stress. For example, if parental rejection leads a child to a closer relationship with another adult, that is positive adaptation, not mere passive endurance. That child is resilient.
- Adversity must be *significant.* Some adversities are comparatively minor (large class size, poor vision), and some are major (victimization, neglect). Children need to cope with all kinds of adversities, but not all coping qualifies them as resilient.

Cumulative Stress

One important discovery is that accumulated stresses over time, including minor ones (called "daily hassles"), are more devastating than an isolated major stress. Almost every child can withstand one stressful event, but repeated stresses make resilience difficult (Jaffee et al., 2007). One example comes from research on children in New Orleans who survived Hurricane Katrina. Years after the hurricane, about half were resilient but the other half (especially those in middle childhood) were still traumatized. Their risk of developing serious psychological problems was affected not so much by the hurricane itself as by ongoing problems—frequent moves, changes in caregivers, disruption of schooling, and so on (Kronenberg et al., 2010; Viadero, 2007).

TABLE 13.1 Dominant Ideas about Challenges and Coping in Children, 1965–Present

1965	All children have the same needs for healthy development.
1970	Some conditions or circumstances—such as "absent father," "teenage mother," "working mom," and "day care"—are harmful for every child.
1975	All children are *not* the same. Some children are resilient, coping easily with stressors that cause harm in other children.
1980	Nothing inevitably causes harm. Indeed, both maternal employment and preschool education, once thought to be risk factors, usually benefit children.
1985	Factors beyond the family, both in the child (low birthweight, prenatal alcohol exposure, aggressive temperament) and in the community (poverty, violence), can be very risky for children.
1990	Risk–benefit analysis finds that some children seem to be "invulnerable" to, or even to benefit from, circumstances that destroy others. (Some do well in school despite extreme poverty, for example.)
1995	No child is invincibly resilient. Risks are always harmful—if not in educational achievement, then in emotions.
2000	Risk–benefit analysis involves the interplay among all three domains (biosocial, cognitive, and psychosocial), including factors within the child (genes, intelligence, temperament), the family (function as well as structure), and the community (including neighborhood, school, church, and culture).
2008	The focus is on strengths, not risks. Assets in the child (intelligence, personality), the family (secure attachment, warmth), the community (good schools, after-school programs), and the nation (income support, health care) must be nurtured.
2010	Strengths vary by culture and national values. Both universal ideals and local variations must be recognized and respected.
2011	Genes as well as cultural practices can be either strengths or weaknesses, with the same stress being beneficial to one child and harmful to another.

Similarly, it is a major stress for children to see their father beating their mother, but the damage to the children occurs when that stress is repeated. One study of children witnessing such abuse found that 20 percent of them were resilient, especially if their mother left the abuser, found a better life, and was not herself depressed (Graham-Bermann et al., 2009).

An international example comes from Sri Lanka, where many children were exposed to war, the 2004 tsunami, poverty, deaths of relatives, and relocation. The accumulated stresses, more than any single problem, increased pathology and decreased achievement. The authors point to "the importance of multiple contextual, past, and current factors in influencing children's adaptation" (Catani et al., 2010, p. 1188).

Coping measures reduce the impact of repeated stress. One factor is the child's own interpretation. Cortisol (the stress hormone) increased in low-income children *if* they interpreted events connected to their family's poverty as a personal threat and *if* the family lacked order and routines (thus increasing daily hassles) (E. Chen et al., 2010). When low-income children did not take things personally and their family was not chaotic, they were more resilient. Many adults who, by income standards, were poor in childhood did not consider themselves poor; thus, they were less affected by it.

In general, a child's interpretation of a family situation (poverty, divorce, and so on) determines how that situation affects him or her (Olson & Dweck, 2008). Some children consider the family they were born into a temporary hardship; they look forward to the day when they can leave childhood behind. Other children experience *parentification*: They act as parents, trying to take care of everyone, including their actual parents (Byng-Hall, 2008). Children who endured Katrina were affected by their thoughts, both positive and negative, even more than by factors one might expect, such as the distress of their caregivers (Kilmer & Gil-Rivas, 2010).

Some children develop their own friends, activities, and skills, blossoming once they are old enough, becoming "increasingly autonomous and industrious" (Pagani et al., 2006, p. 132). Many activities, from 4-H to midnight basketball, from choir to Little League, help children develop a view of themselves as industrious, not

TIM MUELLER / THE NEW YORK TIMES / REDUX

Healing Time Children who survived Hurricane Katrina participate in a fire drill at their new charter school, Lafayette Academy in New Orleans. The resumption of school routines helps them overcome the stress they experienced in the chaos of the deadly storm.

inferior. Teachers and other adult leaders can help children develop those positive self-concepts.

A 40-year study in Hawaii began with children born into poverty, often to parents who were alcoholic or mentally ill. Not surprisingly, many of these children showed signs of deprivation when they were infants (low weight, medical problems, and so on). Experts at the time predicted a troubled future for them. But that did not necessarily happen.

One such infant was Michael, born preterm, weighing less than 5 pounds. His parents were low-income teenagers; his father was absent for the first two years of his life, returning later only to impregnate Michael's mother again and again and again. When Michael was 8, both parents left him and three younger siblings with his grandparents. Yet Michael ultimately became a successful, happy, loving adult (E. Werner, 1979).

B CHILD / AP PHOTO

Grandmother Knows Best About 20,000 grandmothers in Connecticut are caregivers for their grandchildren. This 15-year-old boy and his 17-year-old sister came to live with their grandmother in New Haven after their mother died several years ago. This type of family can help children cope with stress, especially when the grandmother is relatively young and has her own house, as is the case here.

Michael was not the only resilient one. Amazingly, about one-third of the high-risk Hawaiian babies coped well. By middle childhood, they had discovered ways to avoid family stresses, to achieve in school, to make good friends, and to find adult mentors. As adults, they left family problems behind (many moved far away) and established their own healthy relationships (E. Werner & Smith, 1992, 2001).

As was true for many of these children, school and then college can be an escape. An easygoing temperament and a high IQ help (Curtis & Cicchetti, 2003), but they are not essential. In the Hawaiian study, "a realistic goal orientation, persistence, and 'learned creativity' enabled . . . a remarkable degree of personal, social, and occupational success," even for children with evident learning disabilities (E. Werner & Smith, 2001, p. 140).

Social Support and Religious Faith

Social support is a major factor that strengthens the ability to deal with stress. Compared with the homebound lives of younger children, the expanding social world of school-age children allows new possibilities (Morris & Kalil, 2006). Relatives, teachers, peers, pets, community programs (even free libraries and concerts) all help children cope with stress (Bryant & Donnellan, 2007). One study concludes:

> When children attempt to seek out experiences that will help them overcome adversity, it is critical that resources, in the form of supportive adults or learning opportunities, be made available to them so that their own self-righting potential can be fulfilled.
>
> [*Kim-Cohen et al., 2004, p. 664*]

A specific example is children's use of religion, which often provides support via adults from the same faith group (P. E. King & Furrow, 2004, p. 709). Church involvement particularly helps African American children in communities rife with social stress and racial prejudice (Akiba & García Coll, 2004). Faith is psychologically protective when it helps children reinterpret their experiences (Crawford et al., 2006).

Prayer may also foster resilience. In one study, adults were required to pray for a specific person for several weeks. Their attitude about that person changed (Lambert et al., 2010). Ethics precludes such an experiment with children, but it is known that children often pray, expecting that prayer will make them feel better, especially when they are sad or angry (Bamford & Lagattuta, 2010). As already explained, expectations and interpretations can be powerful.

BILL ARON / PHOTOEDIT, INC.

Become Like a Child Although the particulars vary a great deal, school-age children's impulses toward industriousness, stability, and dedication place them among the most devout members of every religious faith.

SUMMING UP

Children gain in maturity and responsibility during the school years. According to Erikson, the crisis of industry versus inferiority generates feelings of confidence or self-doubt. Freud thought latency enables children to master new skills. Often children develop more realistic self-concepts, with the help of their families. Resilience to major adversity is apparent in some children in middle childhood, especially if the stress is temporary and coping measures are available. Children cope with stresses not only through their own interpretations but also by becoming more independent. They use school achievement, after-school activities, supportive adults, and religious beliefs to help them overcome whatever problems they face. ■

>> Families and Children

No one doubts that genes affect personality as well as ability, that peers are vital, and that schools and cultures influence what, and how much, children learn. It has been suggested that genes, peers, and communities have so much influence that parenting has little impact—unless it is grossly abusive (Harris, 1998, 2002; McLeod et al., 2007). This suggestion arose from studies about the impact of the environment on child development.

Family Unity Thinking about any family—even a happy, wealthy family like this one—makes it apparent that each child's family experiences differ. For instance, would you expect the 5-year-old boy to be treated the same way as his two older sisters? And how about each child's feelings toward the parents? Even though the 12-year-olds are twins, one may favor her mother while the other favors her father.

MASTERFILE / RADIUS IMAGES

Shared and Nonshared Environments

Many studies have found that children are much less affected by *shared environment* (influences that arise from being in the same environment, such as for two siblings living in one home, raised by their parents) than by *nonshared environment* (e.g., the different experiences of two siblings). Careful research finds that most personality traits and intellectual characteristics can be traced to genes and nonshared environments, with little left over for the shared influence of being raised by the same parents.

Even psychopathology (Burt, 2009) and sexual orientation (Långström et al., 2010) arise primarily from genes and nonshared environment. Might parents be merely caretakers, providing basic care (food, shelter) but inconsequential no matter what rules, routines, or responses they provide?

More recent findings, however, reassert parent power. The analysis of shared and nonshared influences was correct, but the conclusion was based on a false assumption. Siblings raised together do *not* share the same environment. For example, if relocation, divorce, unemployment, or a new job occurs in a family, the impact on each child depends on each child's age, genes, resilience, and gender. Moving to another town might disturb a school-age child more than an infant, divorce harms boys more than girls, poverty may hurt the preschoolers the most, and so on.

The age and gender variations above do not apply for all siblings: Differential sensitivity means that one child is more affected, for better or worse, than another (Pluess & Belsky, 2010). Even if siblings are raised together, the mix of parental personality, genes, and gender may lead one child to become antisocial, another to have a personality disorder, and a third to be resilient, capable, and strong (Beauchaine et al., 2009).

In addition, some nonshared influences, such as school, neighborhood, after-school activity, and peers, are affected by the parents (Simpkins et al., 2006). For example, a nonshared difference would be the oldest child having attended the zoned public school and the youngest having attended a private school 10 miles away—the result of parental decisions and family income. Even identical twins, who share genes, age, sex, and home, may not share environment, as the following illustrates.

Especially for Scientists How would you determine whether or not parents treat all their children the same? (see response, page 386)

A VIEW FROM SCIENCE

"I Always Dressed One in Blue Stuff . . ."

An expert team of scientists compared 1,000 sets of monozygotic twins reared by their biological parents (Caspi et al., 2004). Obviously, the pairs were identical in genes, sex, and age. The researchers assessed each child's temperament by asking the mothers and teachers to fill out a detailed, standardized checklist. They also asked every mother to describe each twin. Maternal attitudes ranged from very positive ("my ray of sunshine") to very negative ("I wish I never had her. . . . She's a cow, I hate her") (quoted in Caspi et al., 2004, p. 153). Many mothers described personality differences between their twins. For example, one mother spoke of her identical-twin daughters:

> Susan can be very sweet. She loves babies . . . she can be insecure . . . she flutters and dances around. . . . There's not much between her ears. . . . She's exceptionally vain, more so than Ann. Ann loves any game involving a ball, very sporty, climbs trees, very much a tomboy. One is a serious tomboy and one's a serious girlie girl. Even when they were babies I always dressed one in blue stuff and one in pink stuff.
>
> *[quoted in Caspi et al., 2004, p. 156]*

Some mothers were much more cold and rejecting toward one twin than toward the other:

> He was in the hospital and everyone was all "poor Jeff, poor Jeff" and I started thinking, "Well, what about me? I'm the one's just had twins. I'm the one's going through this, he's a seven-week-old baby and doesn't know a thing about it" . . . I sort of detached and plowed my emotions into Mike.
>
> *[quoted in Caspi et al., 2004, p. 156]*

This mother blamed Jeff for favoring his father: "Jeff would do anything for Don but he wouldn't for me, and no matter what I did for either of them [Don or Jeff]it wouldn't be right" (p. 157). She said Mike was much more lovable.

In this longitudinal study, the researchers measured personality at age 5 (assessing, among other things, antisocial behavior as reported by kindergarten teachers) and then measured each twin's personality two years later. They found that if the mothers were more negative toward one of their twins, that twin *became* more antisocial than the co-twin. The rejected twins were more likely to fight, steal, and hurt others at age 7 than at age 5, after all background factors were taken into account.

These researchers acknowledge that many other nonshared factors—peers, teachers, and so on—are significant. But this difference in monozygotic twins confirms that parents matter. As every sibling knows, each child's family experiences are unique.

Family Function and Family Structure

The data reaffirm that parents are crucial, which raises the next question: What family structures make it likely (or unlikely) that families will function well? **Family structure** refers to the legal and genetic connections among related people living in the same household. **Family function** refers to how a family cares for its members.

Function is more important than structure in every developmental period. No matter what the structure, people need family love and encouragement. The ideal manifestations of that love vary by age. Infants need responsive caregiving and social interaction; teenagers need freedom and guidance; young adults need peace and privacy; the aged need respect and appreciation. But everyone needs affection in some form.

family structure The legal and genetic relationships among relatives living in the same home; includes nuclear family, extended family, stepfamily, and so on.

family function The way a family works to meet the needs of its members. Children need families to provide basic material necessities, to encourage learning, to help them develop self-respect, to nurture friendships, and to foster harmony and stability.

AMIT SHABI / LAIF / REDUX

What Must She Leave Behind? In every nation, children are uprooted from familiar places as a result of adult struggles and/or aspirations for a better life. This girl is leaving a settlement in the Gaza Strip, due to the Israeli–Palestinian conflict that has disrupted millions of lives. Worldwide, it's the children who suffer most from relocation.

Family Function in Middle Childhood

What specific forms of love and encouragement do school-age children need?

1. *Physical necessities.* Although children in middle childhood eat, dress, and go to sleep without help, families furnish food, clothing, and shelter.
2. *Learning.* These are prime learning years: Families can support, encourage, and guide education.
3. *Self-respect.* Because children at about age 6 become much more self-critical and socially aware, families can praise accomplishments and provide opportunities for success (in sports, the arts, or specific skills if academic success is difficult).
4. *Peer relationships.* Families can foster friendships, via play dates, group activities, and so on.
5. *Harmony and stability.* Families can provide protective, predictable routines with a home that is a safe haven for everyone.

No family always functions perfectly, but children worldwide fare better in families than they do in other structures (such as group residences). The final item on the list above is especially crucial in middle childhood, when children like continuity, not change.

Ironically, many parents move from one neighborhood or school to another during these years, thinking they are securing a better life for their children. To be specific, in one year (2008), 17 percent of U.S. 5- to 9-year-olds moved from one home to another, a rate four times that of adults over age 50 (U.S. Bureau of the Census, 2010). Since those data come from just one year, they suggest that over the six years from ages 5 to 11, the average child moved at least once. As with all quantitative data, some individual variations are lost. If one child moved every year (not uncommon for homeless children), the average must be balanced by five other children who stayed put. However, the basic point holds for all school-age children—change is difficult.

Lack of stability also seems to harm U.S. children in military families. Such children have several advantages: Enlisted parents tend to have higher incomes, better health care, and more education than do civilians from the same backgrounds. However, military parents repeatedly depart and return, and families typically relocate every few years (Titus, 2007). Military children (dubbed "military brats") have more emotional problems and lower school achievement than do other children of the same age and background. As one author explains:

> Military parents are continually leaving, returning, leaving again. School work suffers, more for boys than for girls, and . . . reports of depression and behavioral problems go up when a parent is deployed.
>
> *[Hall, 2008, p. 52]*

For exactly that reason, the U.S. military has instituted a special program to help children whose parents are deployed. Caregivers of such children are encouraged to avoid changes in the child's life: no new homes, new rules, or new schools (Lester et al., 2011).

Diversity of Structures

One of the many differences from one nation to another as well as one generation to another is the pattern of family structures. Worldwide, two factors—more single-parent households and fewer children per family—have changed childhood from what it was a few decades ago. The specifics vary from nation to nation (see Figure 13.1 on page 388). Most of our discussion here focuses on the United States in about 2010, partly because most of the research has been published in

>> Response for Scientists (from page 385) Proof is very difficult when human interaction is the subject of investigation, since random assignment is impossible. Ideally, researchers would find identical twins being raised together and would then observe the parents' behavior over the years.

AP PHOTO / CHARLES REX ARBOGAST

GREG ELMS / LONELY PLANET IMAGES

The Same Situation, Many Miles Apart: Happy Families The boys in both photos are about 4 years old. Roberto *(left)* lives with his single mother in Chicago. She pays $360 a month for her two children to attend a day-care center. The youngest child in the Balmedina family *(right)* lives with his nuclear family—no day care needed—in the Philippines. Which boy has the better life? The answer is not known; family function is more crucial than family structure.

that nation. Nevertheless, although the proportions differ across countries, the problems with each family structure are similar worldwide.

About two-thirds of all U.S. school-age children live in two-parent homes (see Table 13.2), most often with their biological parents—an arrangement called a **nuclear family.** In U.S. nuclear families, the parents are usually married, although in many other nations, nuclear families are headed by couples who are not legally wed. Other two-parent structures include adoptive parents, foster parents, grandparents but no parents, a biological parent with a stepparent, and same-sex couples.

In the United States, about 31 percent of all school-age children live in a **single-parent family.** Some observers may think that the single-parent percentage is actually higher than 31 percent because 40 percent of new births in the United States are to unmarried women. More than half of all contemporary U.S. children will live in a single-parent family before they reach age 18 for one of three reasons: (1) Their mother was neither married nor cohabiting when they were born, (2) their parents later separated or divorced, or (3) one parent died. However, at any given moment, less than one-third of 6-to 11-year-olds live with only one parent.

Two-parent and single-parent structures are often contrasted with the **extended family,** a three-generation family that usually includes grandparents and often aunts, uncles, and cousins. In 2010, about one in six U.S. families was an extended family—an increase from 1980 (one in eight) and a decrease from 1940 (one in five) (Pew Social Trends Staff, 2010). Such families are particularly common when children are small: By the time children reach puberty, most parents have separate households from their own parents.

Extended families are less costly and thus are more common among low-income households (the current economic picture has more poor families, which is one reason the rate of extended families is increasing). Other reasons are culture and convenience: Extended families share child care and are the norm in some other nations.

The distinction between one-parent, two-parent, and extended families is not as simple in practice as on paper. Many young parents live near relatives who provide meals, emotional support, money, and child care, functioning as an extended family. The opposite is true as well, especially in developing nations: Some families are considered extended because they share a household, but they create separate living quarters for each set of parents and children, making these units somewhat like nuclear families (Georgas et al., 2006).

In many nations, the **polygamous family** (one husband with two or more wives) is an acceptable family structure. Generally in polygamous families, income

nuclear family A family that consists of a father, a mother, and their biological children under age 18.

single-parent family A family that consists of only one parent and his or her biological children under age 18.

extended family A family of three or more generations living in one household.

polygamous family A family consisting of one man, several wives, and their children.

per child is reduced and education, especially for the girls, is limited (Omariba & Boyle, 2007). Polygamy is rare and illegal in the United States. Even in nations where it is allowed, polygamy is less common than it was 30 years ago. In Ghana, for example, men with several wives and a dozen children are now a rarity (Heaton & Darkwah, 2011).

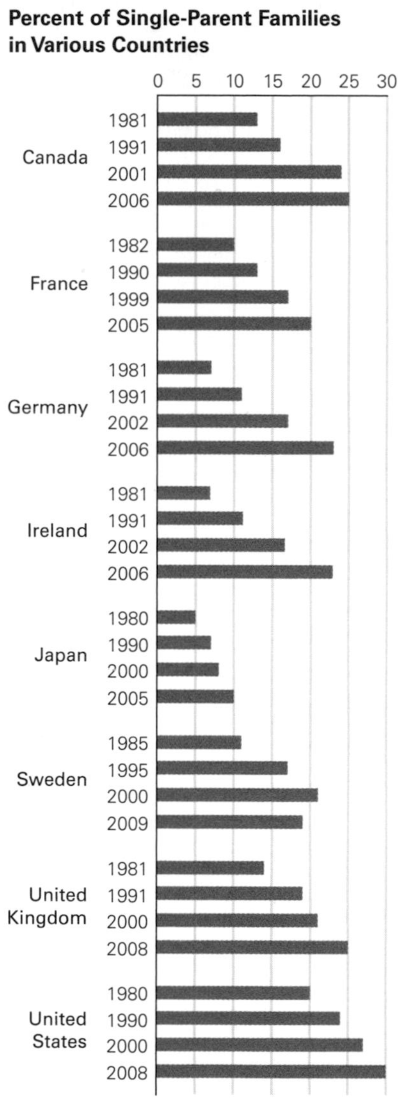

Source: U.S. Bureau of the Census, 2010.

FIGURE 13.1

Single Parents Of all the households with children, a rising percent of them are headed by a single parent. In some countries, many households are headed by two unmarried parents, which is not shown here.

TABLE 13.2 Family Structures (with percent of U.S. 6- to 11-year-olds in each type)*

Two-Parent Families (69%)

1. **Nuclear family** (55%). Named after the nucleus (the tightly connected core particles of an atom), the nuclear family consists of a man and a woman and their biological offspring under 18 years of age. About half of all school-age children live in nuclear families. Although traditionally in nuclear families, no other adults are present, about 10 percent of families headed by two biological parents include a grandparent, and often an aunt or uncle, and hence are extended families.
2. **Stepparent family** (9%). Divorced fathers usually remarry; divorced mothers remarry about half the time. When children from a former relationship live with the new couple in their home, that makes a stepparent family. If the stepparent family includes children born to two or more couples (such as children from the spouses' previous marriages and/or children of the new couple), that is called a *blended family.*
3. **Adoptive family** (2%). Although as many as one-third of infertile married couples adopt children, few adoptable children are available and so most adoptive couples have only one or two children. Thus, the number of school-age children who are adopted is only 2 percent, although the overall percentage of adoptive families is higher than that.
4. **Grandparents alone** (2%). Grandparents take on parenting for some school-age children because the children's biological parents are absent (dead, imprisoned, sick, addicted, and so on). This is increasing, especially in communities where many parents have died of AIDS.
5. **Two same-sex parents** (1%). Some two-parent families are headed by a same-sex couple, whose legal status (married, step-, adoptive) varies.

Single-Parent Families (31%)

One-parent families are increasing, but they average fewer children than two-parent families, so the number of school-age children in such families is only 31%.

1. **Single mother, never married** (12%). Almost 40 percent of all U.S. births are to unmarried mothers, but some such mothers marry by the time the child is in school. Almost half of the single-mother families also include a grandparent, and hence are extended families.
2. **Single mother—divorced, separated, or widowed** (13%). Although many marriages end in divorce (almost half in the United States, fewer in other nations), many divorcing couples have no children. Others remarry. Thus, only 13 percent of school-age children currently live with single, formerly married mothers.
3. **Single father** (5%). About 1 in 20 fathers has physical custody of his children and raises them without their mother or a new wife. This category is increasing, especially for children in middle childhood, but it is still much less common than single mother.
4. **Grandparent alone** (1%). Sometimes a single grandparent (usually the grandmother) becomes the sole caregiving adult for a child.

More Than Two Adults (15%) [Also listed as two-parent or one-parent family]

1. **Extended family** (15%). Some school-age children live with a grandparent or other relatives, as well as with one (5%) or both of their parents (10%). This pattern is most common with infants (20%) but occurs in middle childhood as well.
2. **Polygamous family** (0%). In some nations (not the United States), men can legally have several wives. This family structure is more favored by adults than children. Everywhere, polyandry (one woman, several husbands) is rare.

* Less than 1 percent of school-age children in the United States live without any adults in a parental role; they are not included here.

Source: The percentages on this table are estimates, based on data in U.S. Bureau of the Census, 2010, *Statistical Abstract* and Current Population Reports, *America's Families and Living Arrangements,* 2011; and Pew Social Trends Staff, 2010. The category "extended family" is an estimate higher than the official statistics, since some families do not tell official authorities about relatives living with them.

Connecting Family Structure and Function

More important for the children is not the structure of their family, but how that family functions. The two are related; structure influences (but does not determine) function. The crucial question for schoolchildren is whether the structure makes it more or less likely that the five family functions mentioned earlier (necessities, learning, self-respect, friendship, harmony/stability) will be fulfilled.

Benefits of Nuclear Families

In general, nuclear families function best; children in the nuclear structure tend to achieve better in school with fewer psychological problems. A scholar who summarized dozens of studies concludes: "Children living with two biological married parents experience better educational, social, cognitive, and behavioral outcomes than do other children" (Brown, 2010, p. 1062). Why? Does this mean that parents should all marry and stay married? Not exactly: Some of the benefits are correlates, not causes.

Many advantages of nuclear families begin before the wedding because education, earning potential, and emotional maturity all make it more likely that people will marry, have children, and stay married. Thus, brides and grooms bring personal assets to their new family. In other words, there is a correlation between child success and married parents partly because of the people who marry, not the fact of marriage itself.

After the marriage, ideally, mutual affection encourages both partners to become wealthier and healthier than either would be alone. Research finds that this is often true—the selection effects noted in the previous paragraph are not the entire story (Amato, 2005; Brown, 2010). For children, the *parental alliance,* when mother and father support each other in their mutual commitment to the child (as first described in Chapter 4), is crucial. Shared parenting decreases the risk of maltreatment and makes it more likely that children have someone to read to them, check their homework, invite their friends over, buy them new clothes, and save for their education.

In fact, a broad survey of parental contributions to college tuition found that the highest contributions came from nuclear families. These results might be expected when two-parent families are compared with single and divorced parents because one-parent families average less income; but remarried parents, whose family income is comparable to that of nuclear parents, nonetheless contribute less, on average, to college tuition (Turley & Desmond, 2011). This and other research find that the benefits of nuclear families continue for decades, even after children are grown.

Surprising? It should be no surprise that happy two-parent families can be of any ethnicity. Some people, however, may be surprised that a married same-sex couple can provide a well-functioning home, as this family seems to enjoy.

Other Two-Parent Families

The advantages of two-parent families are not limited to biological parents, whose genetic connections to their children might explain their commitment. Adoptive and same-sex parents typically function well for children, and single parents who then marry and thus create two-parent families often seek a new mate who will be a good stepfather or stepmother. Especially if the child is under age 2 and the stepparent forms a happy relationship with the biological parent, the children adapt to their family (Ganong et al., 2011). Of course, none of these two-parent families always function well, but the circumstances (genetic or chosen) provide a nudge in the right direction.

Considerable controversy has focused on how same-sex couples function for children. Only recently have male–male couples been

BILL ARON / PHOTOEDIT, INC.

A Comfortable Combination The blended family—husband, wife, and children from both spouses' previous marriages—often breeds resentment, depression, and rebellion in the children. That is apparently not the case for the family shown here, which provides cheerful evidence that any family structure is capable of functioning well.

able to marry and raise children; thus, longitudinal research on a large sample, with valid comparisons to male–female families of the same age and education, has not yet been published. However, research on female–female couples finds that their children develop well, emotionally and intellectually (Biblarz & Stacey, 2010). Same-sex relationships have problems similar to those of other-sex relationships, unless social prejudice disrupts family life.

The stepparent structure also has advantages and disadvantages. The primary advantage is financial, especially when compared with most single-parent families. The primary disadvantage is in meeting the fifth family function listed earlier—providing harmony and stability. Compared with other two-parent families, older stepchildren leave sooner than older biological children, new babies arrive, and marriages are more likely to dissolve (Teachman, 2008a). Harmony may also be absent, especially if the child's loyalty to both biological parents is attacked by ongoing disputes between them. A solid parental alliance is more difficult to form when it includes three adults—two of whom disliked each other enough to divorce, and a third who is a newcomer to the child's life.

Finally, when grandparents are the caretakers for children without parents present (called a *skipped-generation family*, the most common form of foster care), the hope is that grandparents provide excellent care since they are experienced, mature, and devoted to their grandchildren. Those characteristics may be present, but grandparent families average lower incomes, more health problems, and less stability than other two-parent families. They have particular difficulty obtaining adequate health care for the children, who often have special needs (such as attention-deficit or learning disabilities) because of the very circumstances that led them to live with the grandparents in the first place. Thus, skipped-generation families need special help, but they are less likely to receive it (Baker & Mutchler, 2010).

Single-Parent Families

Especially for Single Parents You have heard that children raised in one-parent families will have difficulty in establishing intimate relationships as adolescents and adults. What can you do about this possibility? (see response, page 392)

Overall, the single-parent structure functions less well for children because income and stability tend to be reduced. Most single parents fill many roles—including wage earner, daughter or son (single parents often depend on their own parents), and lover (many seek a new partner)—which makes it harder for them to provide steady emotional and academic support for their schoolchildren. If they are depressed (and many are), they are less available to meet their children's needs. Neesha is an example.

A CASE TO STUDY

How Hard Is It to Be a Kid?

Neesha's fourth-grade teacher referred her to the school guidance team because she often fell asleep in class, was late 51 days, and was absent for 15. The counselor did not have time to see Neesha at the end of the fourth grade, so she was held back and seen in the fall. Testing found Neesha at the seventh-grade level in reading and writing and at the fifth-grade level in math. Since learning was not the problem, something psychosocial might be amiss.

The counselor spoke to Tanya, Neesha's mother. Tanya was a single parent, depressed and worried about paying the rent on a tiny apartment where she had moved when Neesha's father left three years earlier to live with his girlfriend, now with a baby. Tanya said she had no problems with Neesha, who was "more like a little mother than a kid," unlike her 15-year-old son, Tyrone, who suffered from fetal alcohol effects and whose behavior worsened when his father left.

Tyrone was recently beaten up badly as part of a gang initiation, a group he considered "like a family." He was currently in juvenile detention, after being arrested for stealing bicycle parts. Note the nonshared environment here: Although the siblings grew up together and their father left them both, 12-year-old Tyrone became rebellious whereas 7-year-old Neesha became "a little mother."

Tanya said that she:

> often gets depressed, and when she isn't working evenings either she goes to bed early or cries herself to sleep. On these occasions, Neesha is very quiet and tries to comfort her mother. Tanya said that when she woke up the other morning, Neesha had placed a handmade card on her pillow. The card was decorated with hearts and bows and huge letters: "I love you, Mom. Neesha"
>
> *[Wilmhurst, 2011, pp. 150–151]*

The school counselor also spoke with Neesha.

> Neesha volunteered that she worried a lot about things and that sometimes when she worries she has a hard time falling asleep. . . . Last year she got in trouble for being late so many times, but it was hard to wake up. Her mom was sleeping late because she was working more nights cleaning the offices. Neesha said it was a very hard year. She was tired and cranky and just couldn't seem to concentrate on her work. She said she would read a page and then not remember what she had read. Neesha said she got so far behind that she just gave up. She was also having problems with the other girls in the class, who were starting to tease her about sleeping in class and not doing her work. She said they called her names like "Sleepy" and "Dummy." She said that at first it made her very sad, and then it made her very mad. That's when she started to hit them to make them stop.
>
> *[Wilmhurst, 2011, pp. 152–153]*

Neesha at age 10 is coping with poverty, a depressed mother, an absent father, a delinquent brother, and classmate bullying. The stress makes concentration difficult. Her response is parentification, hitting, and sleeping. She also shows signs of resilience—her academic achievement is impressive. Shortly after Neesha was interviewed,

> The school principal received a call from Neesha's mother, who asked that her daughter not be sent home from school because she was going to kill herself. She was holding a loaded gun in her hand and she had to do it, because she was not going to make this month's rent. She could not take it any longer, but she did not want Neesha to come home and find her dead. . . . While the guidance counselor continued to keep the mother talking, the school contacted the police, who apprehended mom while she was talking on her cell phone. . . . The loaded gun was on her lap. . . . The mother was taken to the local psychiatric facility.
>
> *[Wilmhurst, 2011, p. 154–155]*

Like many single mothers, Tanya is overwhelmed. If Neesha's father were involved, perhaps Tyrone would not need a gang family and perhaps Neesha would get to school on time. Whether Neesha's resilience will continue depends on her ability to find support beyond her mother. Social support might come from the school, but Neesha's fourth-grade teacher did not stop the bullying and failed Neesha. However, there is reason to hope:

> When asked if she would like to meet with the school psychologist once in a while, just to talk about her worries, Neesha said she would like that very much. After she left the office, she turned and thanked the psychologist for working with her, and added "You know, sometimes it's hard being a kid."
>
> *[Wilmhurst, 2011, p. 154]*

Community support for single parents makes a difference. For example, many French parents are unmarried and might be categorized as single parents in U.S. surveys, but they generally live together and share child rearing. French cohabiting parents separate less often than do married couples in the United States. Since separation and divorce are disruptive for children, this suggests that the cohabiting structure functions better in France than does the married structure in the

>> Response for Single Parents (from page 390) Do not get married mainly to provide a second parent for your child. If you were to do so, things would probably get worse rather than better. Do make an effort to have friends of both sexes with whom your child can interact.

United States. However, for U.S. children, the cohabiting structure is worse than marriage because cohabiting parents separate more often. This is one example of a general truth: Function within single-parent structures is affected by national mores (S. L. Brown, 2004).

Ethnic culture matters as well. Single parenthood is more accepted among African Americans (60 percent of African American 6- to 11-year-olds live with only one parent). In that culture, relatives and friends routinely help single parents, who might be more isolated and dysfunctional if they were of another ethnicity (Cain & Combs-Orme, 2005; Taylor et al., 2008). By contrast, only 14 percent of Asian American families are headed by single parents (U.S. Bureau of the Census, 2010). Consequently, most Asian American children have two parents to provide daily care, but those who do not may be more isolated.

All these are generalities: Contrary to the averages, thousands of nuclear families are destructive, thousands of stepparents provide excellent care, and thousands of single-parent families are wonderful. Structure and culture tend to protect or undercut healthy function, but many parents overcome structural problems to support their children.

A VIEW FROM SCIENCE

Divorce

Scientists try to provide analysis and insight, based on empirical data (of course), but the task goes far beyond reporting facts. Regarding divorce, thousands of studies and several opposing opinions need to be considered, analyzed, and combined—no easy challenge. One scholar who has done this is Andrew Cherlin. He has studied the family for over 35 years, publishing 13 books and over 200 articles since 1988.

Among the facts that need analysis are these three (Amato, 2005; Brown, 2010; Potter, 2010):

1. The United States leads the world in the rates of divorce, marriage, and remarriage. The ratio of marriage to divorce is slightly lower than it was 30 years ago, but still almost half of all marriages end in divorce. Why?
2. Single parents, cohabiting parents, and stepparent families sometimes provide the love and support children need, but, on average, children fare better in nuclear families with married parents. Why?
3. Virtually every study shows that, on average, divorce impairs children's academic achievement and psychosocial development for years, even decades. Why?

Cherlin (2009) has analyzed these facts. The problem, he contends, is that U.S. culture is conflicted: Marriage is idolized, but so is personal freedom. As a result, many people assert their independence by marrying without considering anyone else, such as their parents or community. Then, when they are overwhelmed by child care (freedom of the individual means the United States does not provide paid parental leave or extensive child care), the marriage becomes strained, so they separate. Because marriage remains the ideal, they blame their former mate or their own poor decision, not the institution, and they are eager to remarry.

Consequently, they seek another partner and, if possible, another marriage—which may lead to another divorce. (Divorced people are more likely to remarry than are other single people their age, and second marriages fail more often than first marriages.) All this is in keeping with the culture's emphasis on individual freedom, but none of it benefits the children who suffer from repeated transitions.

From this perspective, the effort to persuade unmarried parents to wed is well intentioned but shortsighted because such marriages are at high risk of divorce (Brown, 2010). Indeed, at least one longitudinal study of unwed mothers found that those who married were eventually worse off than those who did not (Lichter et al., 2006). Research on unwed parents finds that many consider marriage a much riskier commitment than childbearing (Gibson-Davis, 2009).

This leads to a related insight. Cherlin suggests that the main reason children are harmed by divorce—as well as by cohabitation, single parenthood, and stepparenthood—is not the legal status of their parents but the lack of stability.

Scholars now describe divorce as a process, with transitions and conflicts before and after the formal event (Magnuson & Berger, 2009; Potter, 2010). As you remember, resilience is difficult when the child must contend with repeated changes and ongoing hassles—yet this is what divorce brings. Coping is particularly hard when children are at a developmental transition, such as entering first grade or beginning puberty.

Given all this, despite the U. S. effort to encourage marriage, many young adults are making the opposite choice, avoiding marriage in order to avoid divorce. This strategy is working—the age at first marriage is increasing, which is one reason the divorce rate is falling even faster than the marriage rate (Amato, 2010).

Beyond analysis and insight, the other task of developmental science is to provide practical suggestions. Most scholars would agree with the following four points:

1. Marriage commitments need to be made carefully, to minimize the risk of divorce.
2. Once married, couples need to work to keep the relationship strong. Often happiness dips after the birth of the first child, then again at adolescence. Knowing that, especially during these years, couples can plan to spend time together doing what they love—dancing, traveling, praying, clubbing, and so on.
3. If divorce occurs, adults need to minimize transitions and maintain a child's relationships with both parents.
4. In middle childhood, schools can provide vital support for children who are experiencing family change. Teachers can ensure that school is a haven of stability when the home is not.

This may sound idealistic. However, another scientist, who has spent her lifetime following the patterns of divorced families, writes:

> Although divorce leads to an increase in stressful life events, such as poverty, psychological and health problems in parents, and inept parenting, it also may be associated with escape from conflict, the building of new more harmonious fulfilling relationships, and the opportunity for personal growth and individuation.
>
> [*Hetherington, 2006, p. 204*]

Not every parent should marry, not every marriage should continue, and not every child is devastated by divorce. However, every child benefits from all five family functions, including a stable and harmonious home. Adults can provide that. Scientists hope they do.

Family Trouble

Two factors interfere with family function in every structure, ethnic group, and nation: low income and high conflict. Many families experience both, because financial stress increases conflict and vice versa (McLanahan, 2009).

Poverty

Suppose a 6-year-old boy spills his milk, as every 6-year-old sometimes does. In a well-functioning, financially stable family, one parent then guides him to mop up the spill while the other parent pours more milk, perhaps encouraging family harmony by saying, "Everyone has an accident sometimes."

What if the 6-year-old lives with a single parent struggling with overdue rent, unemployment, and an older child who wants money for a school trip? What if the last of the food stamps bought that milk? Shouting, crying, and accusations are almost inevitable (perhaps the sibling claims, "He did it on purpose," to which the 6-year-old responds, "You pushed me," and a visitor adds, "You should teach him to be careful"). As in this example, poverty makes anger spill over when the milk does.

Family income correlates with both function and structure. The effects of poverty are cumulative; low socioeconomic status (SES) may be especially damaging during middle childhood if it has continued from early childhood (Duncan et al., 2010).

Many researchers want to know exactly why income affects development. Several have developed the *family-stress model,* which holds that the crucial question about any risk factor (such as low income, divorce, single parenthood, unemployment) is whether it increases stress. Poverty is less stressful *if* low income is temporary and the family's net worth (home ownership, investments, and so on) buffers the strain (Yeung & Conley, 2008). However, if economic hardship is ongoing and parents have little education, that increases stress, making adults tense and hostile toward their partners and children (Conger et al., 2002; Parke et al., 2004). Thus, the *reaction* to poverty is crucial.

Reaction to wealth may cause problems, too. Children in high-income families develop more than their share of developmental problems. One reason may

Research Design

Scientists: Greg J. Duncan, Kathleen M. Ziol-Guest, and Ariel Kalil.

Publication: *Child Development* (2010).

Participants: Individuals born between 1968 and 1975 to parents who were part of the Panel Study of Income Dynamics, a longitudinal study in the United States that traces the effect of income on families. Only people with repeated measures throughout childhood and adulthood (1,589 of them) were included. The goal of this study was to seek developmental outcomes, not merely correlates, of income.

Design: Data were collected at many stages of each person's life, incorporating detailed and repeated family economic indicators, including adult body mass index (BMI), health, education, arrests, income, employment, and psychological distress.

Major conclusion: Childhood poverty had a decided effect on adult functioning 20 and even 30 years later, particularly on work hours and earnings. This study controlled for many factors that vary with income, such as parents' education and family structure. Childhood poverty itself, especially during middle childhood, impaired well-being in adulthood.

Comments: Since low income correlates with large family size, single parenthood, low education, and so on, studies that simply link poverty to outcomes may reflect third variables. Because this study has longitudinal data on many individuals and variables, the conclusion—that childhood poverty itself impairs development—is probably valid.

be parental pressure on the children to excel, causing stress in middle childhood and creating externalizing and internalizing problems that lead to drug use, delinquency, and poor academic performance in high school (Ansary & Luthar, 2009).

Some intervention programs aim to teach parents to be more encouraging and patient (McLoyd et al., 2006). In low-income families, however, this focus may be misplaced. Poverty itself—with attendant problems such as inadequate schools, poor health, and the threat of homelessness—causes stress (see the Research Design).

Remember the dynamic-systems perspective described in Chapter 1? That perspective applies to poverty: Multigenerational research finds that poverty is both a cause and a symptom—parents with less education and immature emotional control are more likely to have difficulty finding employment and raising their children, and then low income adds to those difficulties (Schofield et al., 2011).

If that is so, more income means better family functioning. Some support for that possibility is that children in single-mother households do much better if their father pays child support, even if he is not actively involved in the child's daily life (Huang, 2009). Nations that subsidize single parents (e.g., Austria and Iceland) also have smaller achievement gaps between low- and middle-SES children on the TIMSS. This is suggestive, but controversial and value-laden. Some developmentalists report that raising income does *not,* by itself, improve parenting (L. M. Berger et al., 2009).

Conflict

There is no controversy about conflict. Every researcher agrees that family conflict harms children, particularly when adults fight about child rearing. Such fights are more common in stepfamilies, divorced families, and extended families. Of course, nuclear families are not immune: Children suffer especially if their parents abuse each other or if one parent walks out, leaving the other distraught.

Researchers are now trying to understand exactly which aspects of family conflict are harmful, as well as whether genetics has an impact. For example, according to Big Five personality research, genes make some people less agreeable and more neurotic than others. Their children may inherit those genes. Thus, if a child in a conflict-filled family has problems, the root cause could be vulnerability because of genes for neuroticism, not just the conflict.

The impact of genes on children's reaction to conflict was explored in a longitudinal study of 867 twin pairs in Sweden, all married with an adolescent child. Genetics as well as conflict could be studied, since 388 of the pairs were monozygotic and 479 were dizygotic. Each adolescent was compared to his or her cousin, the child of one parent's twin (Schermerhorn et al., 2011). The study had data from 5,202 individuals, one-third of them adult twins, one-third of them spouses of twins, and one-third of them adolescents. Conflict was assessed with a well-known questionnaire completed by all participants that included items such as, "We fight a lot in our family." The researchers found that although genes had some effect, conflict itself was the main influence on the child's well-being.

SUMMING UP

Parents influence child development. For school-age children, families serve five crucial functions: to supply basic necessities, to encourage learning, to develop self-respect, to nurture friendships, and to provide harmony and stability. Low income and family conflict interfere with these functions, no matter what the family structure.

The nuclear, two-parent family is the most common, but many families are headed by a single parent (including more than one-fourth of all families of school-age children in the United States). Families headed by two biological parents tend to provide more income, stability, and adult attention, all of which benefit children. Families that are extended, grandparent, one-parent, stepparent, same-sex parents, or adoptive sometimes raise successful children, although each type has vulnerabilities. No structure inevitably harms children, and none (even headed by married biological parents) guarantee optimal function. ■

>> The Peer Group

Peers become increasingly important in middle childhood. Younger children learn from their friends, but egocentrism buffers them from rejection. School-age children, in contrast, are painfully aware of their classmates' opinions, judgments, and accomplishments. Social comparison is one consequence of concrete operational thought.

KYUYA KAMAZAWA / HAGA / THE IMAGE WORKS

The Rules of the Game These young monks in Myanmar (formerly Burma) are playing a board game that adults also play, but the children have some of their own refinements of the general rules. Children's peer groups often modify the norms of the dominant culture, as is evident in everything from superstitions to stickball.

The Culture of Children

Peer relationships, unlike adult–child relationships, involve partners who negotiate, compromise, share, and defend themselves as equals. Consequently, children learn social lessons from one another that grown-ups cannot teach them. Adults sometimes command obedience, sometimes are subservient, but they are always much older and bigger, with the values and experiences of their own cohort, not the child's.

Child culture includes the particular rules and behaviors that are passed down to younger children from slightly older ones; it includes not only fashions and gestures but also values and rituals. Jump-rope rhymes, insults, and superstitions are often part of the peer culture. Even nursery games echo child culture. For instance, "Ring around the rosy/Pocketful of posy/Ashes, ashes/We all fall down," originated with children coping with death (Kastenbaum, 2006). (*Rosy* is short for *rosary*.)

child culture The particular habits, styles, and values that reflect the set of rules and rituals that characterize children as distinct from adult society.

Throughout the world, the child culture encourages independence from adults. Classmates pity those (especially boys) whose parents kiss them ("mama's boy"), tease children who please the teachers ("teacher's pet," "suckup"), and despise those who betray children to adults ("tattletale," "grasser," "snitch," "rat"). Keeping secrets is part of the culture of children, even as parents want to know the details of their children's lives (Gillis, 2008). A clash may develop. For instance, many children reject clothes that parents buy as too loose, too tight, too long, too short, or wrong in color, style, brand, or some other aspect that adults do not notice.

How to Play Boys teach each other the rituals and rules of engagement. The bigger boy shown here could hurt the smaller one, but he won't; their culture forbids it in such situations.

BOB DAEMMRICH / THE IMAGE WORKS

The culture of children is not always benign. For example, because children seek to communicate with their peers, parents proudly note how quickly their children come to speak a second language, but, for the same reason, parents are distressed when their children spout their peers' curses, accents, and slang. Seeking independence from parents, children find friends who defy authority (J. Snyder et al., 2005), sometimes harmlessly (passing a note during class), sometimes not (shoplifting, cigarette smoking).

Attitudes are affected by friends. Remember Yolanda and Paul (Chapter 12)? Their friends guided their lives.

> *Yolanda:*
> There's one friend . . . she's always been with me, in bad or good things. . . . She's always telling me, "Keep on going and your dreams are gonna come true."
>
> *Paul:*
> I think right now about going Christian, right? Just going Christian, trying to do good, you know? Stay away from drugs, everything. And every time it seems like I think about that, I think about the homeboys. And it's a trip because a lot of the homeboys are my family, too, you know?
>
> *[quoted in Nieto, 2000, pp. 220, 149]*

Yolanda went to college; Paul went to jail.

Friendship and Social Acceptance

Children want to be liked; they learn faster as well as feel happier when they have friends. Indeed, if they had to choose between being friendless but popular (looked up to by many peers) or having close friends but being unpopular (ignored by peers), most would choose to have friends. This is particularly true in the first years of primary school, whereas in early adolescence popularity is sometimes the priority (LaFontana & Cillessen, 2010).

Friendships become more intense and intimate as social cognition and effortful control advance. Six-year-olds are usually friends with anyone of the same sex and age who is willing to play with them cooperatively. Comparatively, 10-year-olds demand more of their friends, change friends less often, become more upset when a friendship breaks up, and find it harder to make new friends. Gender differences persist in activities (girls converse more, whereas boys play more active games), but both boys and girls want best friends. Having no close friend at age 11 predicts depression at age 13 (Brendgen et al., 2010).

Most children learn during middle childhood how to be a good friend. For example, when fifth-graders were asked how they would react if other children teased their friend, almost all said they would ask their friend to do something fun with them and would reassure the friend that "things like that happen to everyone" (Rose & Asher, 2004).

CAROL BECKWITH & ANGELA FISHER / HAGA / THE IMAGE WORKS

Friends and Culture Like children everywhere, these children—two 7-year-olds and one 10-year-old, of the Surma people in southern Ethiopia—model their appearance after that of slightly older children, in this case adolescents who apply elaborate body paint for courtship and stick-fighting rituals.

Observation Quiz Are they boys or girls? (see answer, page 398)

Popular and Unpopular Children

It seems universally true that children seek close friends, yet it also is true that culture and cohort affect what makes a child well liked or not. In North American culture, shy children are not popular, but in 1990 in Shanghai, shy children were respected and often popular (X. Chen et al., 1992).

That is a cultural difference, but a cohort difference occurred over 12 years in Shanghai. As assertiveness became more valued in Chinese culture, a survey from the same schools found that shy children were less popular than their shy predecessors had been (X. Chen et al., 2005). A third study found that, in rural China, shyness was still valued and predicted adult adjustment (X. Chen et al., 2009). Obviously, cohort and context matter.

At least in the United States, over the years of middle childhood, two types of popular children and three types of unpopular children become apparent. Throughout childhood, children who are "kind, trustworthy, cooperative" are well liked. The second type of popular children appear around fifth grade, when children who are "athletic, cool, dominant, arrogant, and . . . aggressive" are sometimes popular (Cillessen & Mayeux, 2004a, p. 147; Rodkin & Roisman, 2010).

As for the three types of unpopular children, some are *neglected,* not rejected; ignored, but not shunned. The neglected child does not enjoy school but is psychologically unharmed, especially if the child has a supportive family and outstanding talent (in music or the arts, say) (Sandstrom & Zakriski, 2004).

The other two types of unpopular children are at increased risk of depression and uncontrolled anger over the years of middle childhood. One type is **aggressive-rejected,** disliked because they are antagonistic and confrontational; the other type is **withdrawn-rejected,** disliked because they are timid and anxious. Children of these two types have much in common, often misinterpreting social situations, lacking emotional regulation, and experiencing mistreatment at home. They may become bullies and victims, a topic now discussed.

Pity the Teacher The culture of children encourages pranks, jokes, and the defiance of authorities at school. At the same time, as social cognition develops, many children secretly feel empathy for their teachers.

Bullies and Victims

From a developmental perspective, childhood bullying is connected to many other aspects of aggression, including maltreatment and delinquency (discussed in Chapters 8, 11, and 16, respectively). Here we focus on bullies and victims in school.

Bullying is defined as repeated, systematic attacks intended to harm those who are unable or unlikely to defend themselves. It occurs in every nation, in every community, and in every kind of school (religious or secular, public or private, progressive or traditional, large or small). Although adults are often unaware of it, children recognize it as common. As one girl said, "There's a little bit of bully in everyone" (Guerra et al., 2011, p. 303).

Bullying may be of four types:

- *Physical* (hitting, pinching, or kicking)
- *Verbal* (teasing, taunting, or name-calling)
- *Relational* (destroying peer acceptance)
- *Cyberbullying* (using electronic means to harm another)

The first three are common in primary school and begin even earlier, in preschool. Cyberbullying is a particularly devastating form of relational bullying, more common in secondary school and college than in primary school, and thus it is discussed in Chapter 15.

A key word in the definition of bullying is *repeated.* Almost everyone experiences an isolated attack or is called a derogatory name at some point in middle childhood. Victims of bullying, however, endure shameful experiences again and again—being forced to hand over lunch money, laugh at insults, drink milk mixed with detergent, and so on—with no one defending them. Victims tend to be "cautious, sensitive, quiet . . . lonely and abandoned at school. As a rule, they do not have a single good friend in their class" (Olweus et al., 1999, p. 15). Although it is often thought that victims are particularly ugly or odd, this is not usually the case. Victims are chosen because of their emotional vulnerability and social isolation, not their appearance, although sometimes a distinctive feature becomes the focus of teasing.

As one boy said,

> You can get bullied because you are weak or annoying or because you are different. Kids with big ears get bullied. Dorks get bullied. You can also get bullied because you think too much of yourself and try to show off. Teacher's pet gets bullied. If you say the right answer too many times in class you can get bullied. There are lots of popular groups who bully each other and other groups, but you can get bullied within your group too. If you do not want to get bullied, you have to stay under the radar, but then you might feel sad because no one pays attention to you.
>
> *[quoted in Guerra et al., 2011, p. 306]*

aggressive-rejected Rejected by peers because of antagonistic, confrontational behavior.

withdrawn-rejected Rejected by peers because of timid, withdrawn, and anxious behavior.

bullying Repeated, systematic efforts to inflict harm through physical, verbal, or social attack on a weaker person.

PETER TITMUSS / ALAMY

HENRY KING / GETTY IMAGES

Who Suffers More? The 12-year-old girl and the 10-year-old boy are both bullying younger children, but their attacks differ. Some developmentalists think a verbal assault is more painful than a physical one because it lingers for years.

bully-victim Someone who attacks others and who is attacked as well. (Also called *provocative victims* because they do things that elicit bullying.)

>> Answer to Observation Quiz (from page 396) They are all girls. Boys would not be likely to stand so close together. Also, the two 7-year-olds have decorated their soon-to-be budding breasts.

Remember the three types of unpopular children? Neglected children are not victimized, they are ignored, "under the radar." If their family relationships are good, they suffer less from bullying—true for all children who are teased, but particularly true for neglected children (Bowes et al., 2010).

Rejected victims, however, often have trouble at home as well. Most of them are withdrawn-rejected, but some are aggressive-rejected. The latter are **bully-victims** (or *provocative victims*) (Unnever, 2005), "the most strongly disliked members of the peer group," with neither friends nor sympathizers (Sandstrom & Zakriski, 2004, p. 110). One study found that teachers tend to mistreat bully-victims, making their problems worse (Khoury-Kassabri, 2009). Bully-victims suffer the most, no matter what form the bullying takes (Dukes et al., 2009).

Unlike bully-victims, most bullies are *not* rejected. Although some have low self-esteem, others are proud; they bully because they are pleased with themselves and they find bullying cool (Guerra et al., 2011). Often, bullies have a few admiring friends. They may be socially perceptive, in that they pick their victims carefully, seeking out those who are already rejected by most classmates (Veenstra et al., 2010). Over the years of middle childhood, they become skilled at avoiding adult awareness, attacking victims who will not resist effectively. This seems to be as true for relational bullying as for physical and verbal bullying.

Boys bully more than girls, and during childhood most bullies pick on their own sex. Boy bullies are often big; they target smaller, weaker boys. Girl bullies are often sharp-tongued; they harass shyer, more soft-spoken girls. Boys tend to use force (physical aggression), while girls tend to mock, ridicule, or spread rumors (verbal aggression). Both sexes may also use relational aggression, especially cyberbullying, which becomes more common with age. Interestingly, in middle childhood, the gender divide extends to bullying: Girls who bully boys are rejected whereas younger boys can sometimes be accepted by other boys if they bully girls, but this does not hold as puberty begins (about age 11), when boys who bully girls are no longer admired (Veenstra et al., 2010).

Causes and Consequences of Bullying

Bullying may originate with a genetic predisposition or a brain abnormality, but when a toddler is aggressive, parents, teachers, and peers usually teach that child to rein in those impulses and develop emotional regulation and effortful control. However, the opposite may occur (Granic & Patterson, 2006). Young children become more aggressive if their families create insecure attachment, provide a stressful home life, are ineffective at discipline, or include hostile siblings.

Peers are influential as well. Some peer groups approve of relational bullying, and children in those groups entertain their classmates as they mock and insult each other (N. E. Werner & Hill, 2010). On the other hand, when students themselves disapprove of bullying, its incidence is reduced (Guerra & Williams, 2010).

The consequences of bullying can echo for years. Many victims become depressed; many bullies become increasingly cruel. However, this is not inevitable. Both bullies and victims can be identified in first grade and "need active guidance and remediation" before their behavior patterns become truly destructive (Leadbeater & Hoglund, 2009, p. 857). Unless bullies are deterred, they and their victims risk impaired social understanding, lower school achievement, and relationship difficulties (Ma et al., 2009; Pepler et al., 2004). Bystanders suffer, too, as do adults when bullies grow up (Monks & Coyne, 2011; Nishina & Juvonen, 2005; Rivers et al., 2009).

Only an Act? Fifth-grade boys play passengers on a bus as they act out a scene in which three of them reject a fourth (at right). They are participating in a curriculum designed to increase empathy and reduce bullying.

Can Bullying Be Stopped?

Most victimized children find ways to halt ongoing bullying—by ignoring, retaliating, defusing, or avoiding. A study of older children who were bullied in one year but not in the next indicated that finding new friends was crucial (P. K. Smith et al., 2004). Friendships help individual victims, but what can be done to halt bullying altogether?

We know what does *not* work: increasing students' awareness, instituting zero tolerance for fighting, or putting troubled students together in a therapy group or a classroom (Baldry & Farrington, 2007; Monks, & Coyne, 2011). This last measure tends to make daily life easier for some teachers, but it increases aggression.

The school community itself needs to change as a whole—teachers and bystanders, parents and aides, bullies and victims. In fact, the entire school can either increase the rate of bullying or decrease it. For example, a Colorado study of children with high self-esteem found that, when the overall school climate encouraged learning and cooperation, children with high self-esteem were unlikely to be bullies; yet when the school climate was hostile, those with high self-esteem were often bullies (Gendron et al., 2011).

Peers are crucial: If they simply notice bullying, becoming aware without doing anything, that is no help. However, if they empathize with victims and refuse to admire bullies, that reduces classroom aggression (Salmivalli, 2010). Dan Olweus, a pioneer in antibullying efforts, advocates involving everyone—teachers, parents, and peers—to reduce bullying (Olweus, 1993). Efforts to change the entire school are credited with recent successful efforts to decrease bullying in 29 schools in England (e.g., Cross et al., 2011), throughout Norway, in Finland (Kärnä et al., 2011), and often in the United States (Allen, 2010; Limber, 2011). A review of all research on successful ways to halt bullying (Berger, 2007) finds the following:

- Everyone in the school must change, not just the identified bullies.
- Intervention is more effective in the earlier grades.
- Evaluation is critical: Programs that appear to be good might actually be harmful.

Especially for Parents of an Accused Bully Another parent has told you that your child is a bully. Your child denies it and explains that the other child doesn't mind being teased. (see response, page 402)

This final point merits special emphasis. Longitudinal research on whole-school efforts finds that some programs make a difference and some do not, with variations depending on the age of the children and the indicators (peer report of bullying or victimization, teacher report of incidents reported, and so on). Objective follow-up efforts suggest that bullying can be reduced but not eliminated.

SUMMING UP

School-age children develop their own culture, with customs that encourage them to be loyal to one another. All 6- to 11-year-olds want and need social acceptance and close, mutual friendships to protect against loneliness and depression. Friendship is more valued than popularity; being rejected is painful.

Most children experience occasional peer rejection. However, some children are victims, repeatedly rejected and friendless, experiencing physical, verbal, or relational bullying. Bullies are sometimes admired in middle childhood and early adolescence, but they and their victims may suffer in adulthood because of behavior patterns established in childhood. Some efforts to reduce bullying succeed and some do not; a whole-school approach seems best, with the bystanders crucial to establishing an anti-bullying culture. ■

>> Children's Moral Values

Although the origins of morality are debatable (see Chapter 10), there is no doubt that middle childhood is prime time for moral development. Ages 7 to 11 are:

> years of eager, lively searching on the part of children . . . as they try to understand things, to figure them out, but also to weigh the rights and wrongs. . . This is the time for growth of the moral imagination, fueled constantly by the willingness, the eagerness of children to put themselves in the shoes of others.
>
> *[Coles, 1997, p. 99]*

JOHN ANTHONY RIZZO / UPPERCUT IMAGES / PHOTOLIBRARY

Empathy Building Look at their facial expressions, not just their matching hats and gloves. For this 9-year-old sister and 7-year-old brother, moral development is apparent. This is not necessarily the case for all siblings, however; imagine the same behavior but with angry expressions.

That optimistic assessment seems validated by detailed research. In middle childhood, children are quite capable of making moral judgments, differentiating universal principles from mere conventional norms (Turiel, 2008). Empirical studies show that throughout middle childhood, children readily suggest moral arguments to distinguish right from wrong (Killen, 2007).

Many forces drive children's growing interest in moral issues. Three of them are (1) peer culture, (2) personal experience, and (3) empathy. As already explained, part of the culture of children involves moral values, such as being loyal to friends and protecting children from adults. A child's personal experiences also matter. For example, children in multiethnic schools are better able to argue against prejudice using moral values than are children who attend racially and ethnically homogeneous schools (Killen et al., 2006). Finally, empathy becomes stronger in middle childhood because children are more aware of one another.

This increasing perception can backfire, however. One example was just described: Bullies become adept at picking victims who are rejected by people the bullies admire (Veenstra et al., 2010). However, the increase in empathy during middle childhood at least allows the possibility of moral judgment that notices, and defends, children who are unfairly rejected.

Obviously, moral advances are not automatic. Children who are slow to develop theory of mind—which, as you remember from Chapter 9, is affected by family and culture—are also slow to develop empathy (Caravita et al., 2010). The authors of a study of 7-year-olds "conclude that moral *competence* may be a universal human characteristic, but that it takes a situation with specific demand characteristics to translate this competence into actual prosocial performance" (van IJzendoorn et al., 2010, p. 1). In other words, school-age children can think and act morally, but they do not always do so.

Moral Reasoning

Much of the developmental research on children's moral thinking began with Piaget's descriptions of the rules used by children as they play (Piaget, 1932/1997). This led to Lawrence Kohlberg's description of cognitive stages of morality (Kohlberg, 1963).

Kohlberg's Levels of Moral Thought

Kohlberg described three levels of moral reasoning and two stages at each level (see Table 13.3), with parallels to Piaget's stages of cognition.

- **Preconventional moral reasoning** is similar to preoperational thought in that it is egocentric, with children seeking their personal pleasure or avoiding pain more than focusing on social concerns.
- **Conventional moral reasoning** parallels concrete operational thought in that it relates to current, observable practices: Children watch what their parents, teachers, and friends do, and try to follow suit.
- **Postconventional moral reasoning** is similar to formal operational thought because it uses logic and abstractions, going beyond what is concretely observed in a particular society, willing to question "what is" in order to decide "what should be."

preconventional moral reasoning Kohlberg's first level of moral reasoning, emphasizing rewards and punishments.

conventional moral reasoning Kohlberg's second level of moral reasoning, emphasizing social rules.

postconventional moral reasoning Kohlberg's third level of moral reasoning, emphasizing moral principles.

According to Kohlberg, intellectual maturation advances moral thinking. During middle childhood, children's answers shift from being primarily preconventional to being more conventional: Concrete thought and peer experiences help children move past the first two stages (level I) to the next two (level II). Postconventional reasoning is not usually present until adolescence or adulthood.

Kohlberg posed moral dilemmas to school-age boys (and eventually girls, teenagers, and adults). The story of a poor man named Heinz, whose wife was dying, serves as an example. A local druggist had the only cure for the wife's illness, a drug that Heinz could not pay for and that sold for 10 times what it cost to make.

> Heinz went to everyone he knew to borrow the money, but he could only get together about half of what it cost. He told the druggist that his wife was dying and asked him to sell it cheaper or let him pay later. But the druggist said "no." The husband got desperate and broke into the man's store to steal the drug for his wife. Should the husband have done that? Why?
>
> *[Kohlberg, 1963, p. 19]*

The crucial element in Kohlberg's scheme is not the answer given but the *reasons* for it. For instance, someone might say that the husband should steal the drug because he needs his wife to care for him (preconventional), or because people will blame him if he lets his wife die (conventional), or because trying to save her life is more important than obeying the law (postconventional).

Criticisms of Kohlberg

Kohlberg has been criticized for not appreciating cultural or gender differences. His original participants were all boys, which may have led him to discount female values of nurturance and relationships (Gilligan, 1982). Kohlberg seemed to value

TABLE 13.3 Kohlberg's Three Levels and Six Stages of Moral Reasoning

Level I: Preconventional Moral Reasoning

The goal is to get rewards and avoid punishments; this is a self-centered level.

- *Stage one: Might makes right* (a punishment and obedience orientation). The most important value is to maintain the appearance of obedience to authority, avoiding punishment while still advancing self-interest. Don't get caught!
- *Stage two: Look out for number one* (an instrumental and relativist orientation). Each person tries to take care of his or her own needs. The reason to be nice to other people is so that they will be nice to you.

Level II: Conventional Moral Reasoning

Emphasis is placed on social rules; this is a community-centered level.

- *Stage three: "Good girl" and "nice boy."* Proper behavior is behavior that pleases other people. Social approval is more important than any specific reward.
- *Stage four: "Law and order."* Proper behavior means being a dutiful citizen and obeying the laws set down by society, even when no police are nearby.

Level III: Postconventional Moral Reasoning

Emphasis is placed on moral principles; this level is centered on ideals.

- *Stage five: Social contract.* Obey social rules because they benefit everyone and are established by mutual agreement. If the rules become destructive or if one party doesn't live up to the agreement, the contract is no longer binding. Under some circumstances, disobeying the law is moral.
- *Stage six: Universal ethical principles.* General, universally valid principles, not individual situations (level I) or community practices (level II), determine right and wrong. Ethical values (such as "life is sacred") are established by individual reflection and may contradict egocentric (level I) or social and community (level II) values.

abstract principles more than individual needs, but caring for people may be no less moral than impartial justice (Sherblom, 2008).

In one respect, however, Kohlberg was undeniably correct. Children use their intellectual abilities to justify their moral actions. This was shown in an experiment in which trios of children aged 8 to 18 had to decide how to divide a sum of money with another trio of children. Some groups chose to share equally; other groups were more selfish. There were no age differences in the actual decisions, but there were age differences in the arguments voiced. Older children suggested more complex rationalizations for their choices, both selfish and altruistic (Gummerum et al., 2008).

What Children Value

Many lines of research have shown that children develop their own morality, guided by peers, parents, and culture (Turiel, 2006). Some prosocial values are evident in early childhood. Among these are caring for close family members, cooperating with other children, and not hurting anyone intentionally (Eisenberg et al., 2006). Even very young children think stealing is wrong.

As children become more aware of themselves and others in middle childhood, they realize that one person's values may conflict with another's. Concrete operational cognition, which gives children the ability to observe and to use logic, propels them to think about morality and to try to behave ethically (Turiel, 2006). As part of growing up, children become conscious of immorality in their peers (Abrams et al., 2008) and, later, in their parents, themselves, and their culture.

Adults Versus Peers

When child culture conflicts with adult morality, children often align themselves with peers. A child might lie to protect a friend, for instance. On a broader level, one study found that 98 percent of a group of children believed that no child should be excluded from a sports team because of gender or race, even when adult society was less tolerant. Some of the same children, however, justified excluding another child from a friendship circle (Killen et al., 2002).

The conflict between the morality of children and that of adults is evident in the value that children place on education. Adults usually prize school, but children may encourage one another to play hooky, cheat on tests, or drop out. Peer morals sometimes outweigh adult values. Consider another comment from Paul:

> I try not to get influenced too much, pulled into what I don't want to be into. But mostly, it's hard. You don't want people to be saying you're stupid. "Why do you want to go to school and get a job? . . . Drop out."
>
> *[quoted in Nieto, 2000, p. 252]*

Not surprisingly, Paul later left school.

It is apparent that three common values among 6- to 11-year-olds are the following:

>> Response for Parents of an Accused Bully (from page 400) The future is ominous if the charges are true. Your child's denial is a sign that there is a problem. (An innocent child would be worried about the misperception instead of categorically denying that any problem exists.) You might ask the teacher what the school is doing about bullying. Family counseling might help. Because bullies often have friends who egg them on, you may need to monitor your child's friendships and perhaps befriend the victim. Talk matters over with your child. Ignoring the situation might lead to heartache later on.

- Protect your friends.
- Don't tell adults what is happening.
- Don't be too different from your peers.

These three values can explain both apparent boredom and overt defiance, as well as standards of dress that mystify adults (such as jeans so loose that they fall off or so tight that they impede digestion—both styles worn by my children, who grew up in different cohorts). Given what is known about middle childhood, it is no surprise that children do not echo adult morality.

Developing Moral Values

A detailed examination of the effect of peers on morality began with an update on one of Piaget's moral issues: whether punishment should seek *retribution* (hurting the transgressor) or *restitution* (restoring what was lost). Piaget believed the latter to be more advanced; he also found that between ages 8 and 10, children progress from retribution to restitution (Piaget, 1932/1997).

To learn how this occurs, researchers arranged for 133 9-year-olds to ponder the following:

> Late one afternoon there was a boy who was playing with a ball on his own in the garden. His dad saw him playing with it and asked him not to play with it so near the house because it might break a window. The boy didn't really listen to his dad, and carried on playing near the house. Then suddenly, the ball bounced up high and broke the window in the boy's room. His dad heard the noise and came to see what had happened. The father wonders what would be the fairest way to punish the boy. He thinks of two punishments. The first is to say: "Now, you didn't do as I asked. You will have to pay for the window to be mended, and I am going to take the money from your pocket money." The second is to say: "Now, you didn't do as I asked. As a punishment you have to go to your room and stay there for the rest of the evening." Which of these punishments do you think is the fairest?
>
> *[Leman & Björnberg, 2010, p. 962]*

The children were split equally in their answers. Then 48 of them were paired with a child who answered the other way, and each pair was asked to discuss the broken window event and try to reach agreement on the fairest punishment. As a control, the rest of the children were not paired and did not discuss the dilemma. Six pairs were boy–boy, six were boy–girl with the boy favoring restitution, six were boy–girl with the girl favoring restitution, and six were girl–girl. The conversations typically took only five minutes, and the retribution side was more often chosen—which Piaget would consider a moral backslide. However, all the children were queried again, two weeks and eight weeks later, and their responses changed toward the more advanced, restitution thinking (see Figure 13.2). This was particularly true for the children who engaged in conversation.

The main conclusion from this study was that children's "conversation on a topic may stimulate a process of individual reflection that triggers developmental advances" (Leman & Björnberg, 2010, p. 969). Parents and teachers take note: Raising moral issues, and letting children talk about them, may advance morality—not immediately, but soon.

The Morality of Child Labor

Now we are ready to reexamine the tire-changing boy from the opening vignette of this chapter. Child labor is deemed immoral by the United Nations, but that international body has had difficulty educating children about their rights and convincing nations to enforce child labor standards (Print et al., 2008). Some child labor

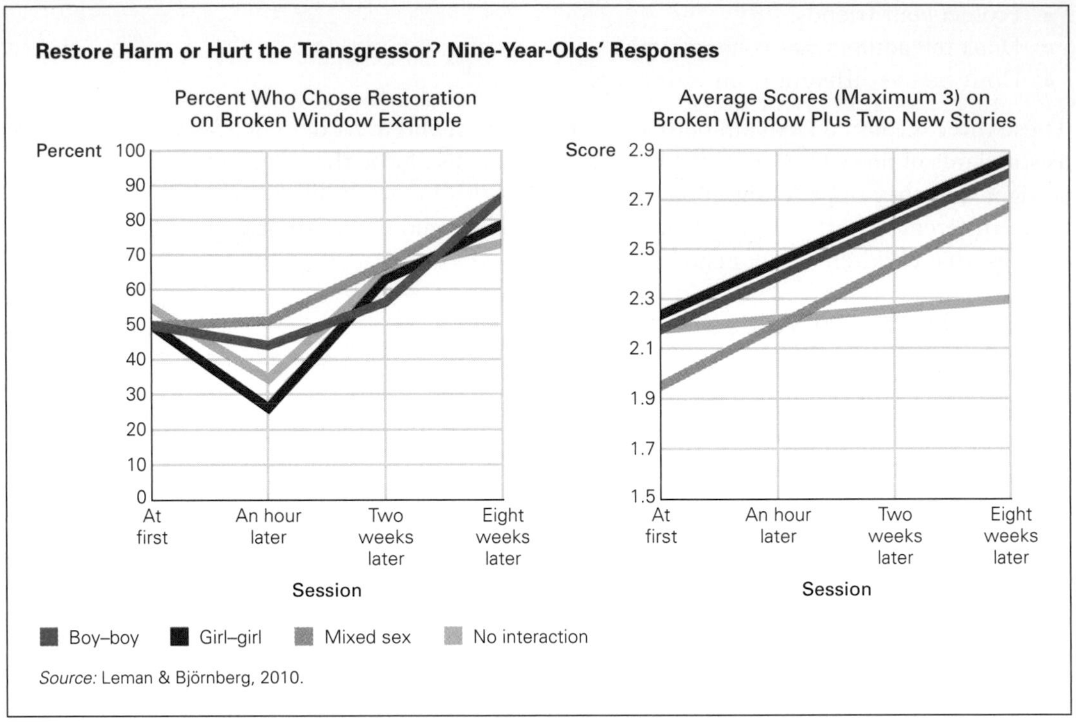

FIGURE 13.2

Benefits of Time and Talking The graph on the left shows that most children, immediately after their initial punitive response, became even more likely to seek punishment rather than to repair damage. However, after some time and reflection, they affirmed the response Piaget would consider more mature. The graph on the right indicates that children who had talked about the broken window example moved toward restorative justice even in examples they had not heard before, which was not true for those who had not talked about the first story.

is clearly hazardous, such as working in mines with cancer-causing pollutants or becoming sex workers with no opportunity for escape. Even for these examples, nations do not always protect children as they should (Diallo et al., 2010).

However, some work done by children is harder to judge. Morality is quite variable, not only among children but also among cultures. Thus, to decide whether that young boy should be helping his father would require finding out whether his life situation satisfies the five needs that are thought to be universal during middle childhood. Are his material needs met, is he learning in school, does he have friends, is he proud of himself, is his work keeping his family harmonious and stable? If the answer to all these questions is yes, then Tiffany's understandable shock, or the father's acceptance of child labor, may be more reflective of their respective cultures than of the boy's condition.

The moral lesson of this chapter, then, is that the psychosocial development of children needs to be carefully assessed, child by child. For example, married-couple families are usually good for children but not always; friends are helpful in protecting victims, but they may also encourage bullies; self-esteem is a positive attribute, but it may become too high. As with all of development, individual children, families, and cultures vary, and that must be taken into account before conclusions are drawn.

SUMMING UP

Moral issues are of great interest to school-age children, who are affected by their cultures, by their parents, and particularly by their peers. Kohlberg's stages of moral thought parallel Piaget's stages of development, suggesting that the highest level of morality goes beyond the norms of any particular nation. Children develop moral standards that they try to follow, although these may differ from adult morals. Maturation, reflection, and discussion all foster moral development.

SUMMARY

The Nature of the Child

1. All theories of development acknowledge that school-age children become more independent and capable in many ways. Erikson emphasized industry, when children busily strive to master various tasks. If they are unable to do so, they feel inferior. Freud described latency, when psychosexual needs are quiet.

2. Children develop their self-concept during these years, basing it on a more realistic assessment of their competence than they had in earlier years. High self-esteem may reduce effort and is not valued in every culture; low self-esteem is also harmful.

3. Both daily hassles and major stresses take a toll on children, with accumulated stresses more likely to impair development than any single event on its own. The child's interpretation of the situation and the availability of supportive adults and peers aid resilience.

Families and Children

4. Families influence children in many ways, as do genes and peers. Although most siblings share a childhood home and parents, each sibling experiences different (nonshared) circumstances within that family.

5. The five functions of a supportive family are to satisfy children's physical needs; to encourage learning; to support friendships; to protect self-respect; and to provide a safe, stable, and harmonious home.

6. The most common family structure worldwide is the nuclear family, usually with other relatives nearby and supportive. Other two-parent families include adoptive, same-sex, grandparent, and stepfamilies, each of which sometimes functions well for children. However, each also has vulnerabilities.

7. Generally, it seems better for children to live with two parents rather than one because a parental alliance can support their development. Single-parent families have higher rates of changes—for example, in where they live and who belongs to the family—and children are stressed by new circumstances and conditions, especially in middle childhood.

8. Income affects family function. Poor children are at greater risk for emotional and behavioral problems because the stresses that often accompany poverty hinder effective parenting. Instability and conflict are harmful.

The Peer Group

9. Peers are crucial for social development during middle childhood. Each cohort of children has a culture, passed down from slightly older children. Close friends are particularly helpful during these years.

10. Popular children may be cooperative and easy to get along with or may be competitive and aggressive. Much depends on the age and culture of the children.

11. Rejected children may be neglected, aggressive, or withdrawn. Aggressive and withdrawn children have difficulty with social cognition; their interpretation of the normal give-and-take of childhood is impaired.

12. Bullying is common among school-age children and has long-term consequences for both bullies and victims. Bullies themselves may be admired, which makes their behavior more difficult to stop. Overall, a multifaceted, long-term, whole-school approach, with parents, teachers, and bystanders working together, seems the best way to halt bullying.

Children's Moral Values

13. School-age children are very interested in differentiating right from wrong. Kohlberg described three levels of moral reasoning, each related to cognitive maturity. Although he has been criticized for focusing too much on abstractions and for ignoring cultural and gender differences in morality, it does seem that children advance in moral thinking as they mature.

14. When values conflict, children often choose loyalty to peers over adult standards of behavior. When children discuss moral issues with other children, they develop more thoughtful answers to moral questions.

KEY TERMS

industry versus inferiority (p. 378)
latency (p. 379)
effortful control (p. 380)
resilience (p. 380)
family structure (p. 385)
family function (p. 385)
nuclear family (p. 387)
single-parent family (p. 387)
extended family (p. 387)
polygamous family (p. 387)
child culture (p. 395)
aggressive-rejected (p. 397)
withdrawn-rejected (p. 397)
bullying (p. 397)
bully-victim (p. 398)
preconventional moral reasoning (p. 401)
conventional moral reasoning (p. 401)
postconventional moral reasoning (p. 401)

WHAT HAVE YOU LEARNED?

The Nature of the Child

1. How do Erikson's stages for school-age children and for preschool children differ?

2. Why is social comparison particularly powerful during middle childhood?

3. Why do cultures differ in how they value pride or modesty?

4. Why and when might minor stresses be more harmful than major stresses?

5. What factors help a child become resilient?

Families and Children

6. Why does research on nonshared environments *not* prove that parents are irrelevant?

7. Which of the five family functions is most difficult for divorcing parents to fulfill?

8. What is the difference between family function and family structure?

9. What are the advantages for children of the nuclear family structure?

10. What are the advantages and disadvantages of a stepparent family?

11. Why is a safe, harmonious home particularly important during middle childhood?

12. How can single parents fulfill the five desirable family functions for children?

13. What is the evidence that school-age children benefit from continuity?

14. What are the advantages and disadvantages for children in an extended family?

The Peer Group

15. How does the disapproval of tattletales affect bullies and victims?

16. How does what children wear reflect the culture of children?

17. How is a child's popularity affected by culture and the child's age?

18. What is the difference between being a bully and being a bully-victim?

19. Who is best able to stop a bully and why—victim, teacher, another child?

Children's Moral Values

20. What is the highest stage of morality, according to Kohlberg?

21. What are the main criticisms of Kohlberg's theory of moral development?

22. How does children's conversation impact their moral reasoning?

23. Why don't children always accept the moral standards of their parents?

APPLICATIONS

1. Go someplace where school-age children congregate (such as a schoolyard, a park, or a community center) and use naturalistic observation for at least half an hour. Describe what popular, average, withdrawn, and rejected children do. Note at least one potential conflict (bullying, rough-and-tumble play, etc.). Describe the sequence and the outcome.

2. Focusing on verbal bullying, describe at least two times when someone said something hurtful to you and two times when you said something that might have been hurtful to someone else. What are the differences between the two types of situations?

3. How would your childhood have been different if your family structure had been different, such as if you had (or had not) lived with your grandparents, if your parents had (or had not) gotten divorced, if you had (or had not) been adopted?

>>ONLINE CONNECTIONS

To accompany your textbook, you have access to a number of online resources, including quizzes for every chapter of the book, flashcards (in English and Spanish), critical thinking questions, and case studies. For access to any of these links, go to www.worthpublishers.com/bergerca9e. In addition to these free resources, you'll also find links to podcasts, video clips, diagnostic quizzing with personalized study advice, and an ebook. Some of the videos and activities available online include:

- *Moral Reasoning.* This activity reviews Kohlberg's theory of age-related changes in moral reasoning. Was he right? You can decide as you watch footage of people solving the famous Heinz dilemma.
- *Effects of Divorce and Remarriage on Children.* Learn three factors that affect a child's adjustment and what parents can do to avoid potential problems.

PART IV The Developing Person So Far:

Middle Childhood

BIOSOCIAL

A Healthy Time During middle childhood, children grow more slowly than they did earlier or than they will during adolescence. Physical play is crucial for health and happiness. Prevalent physical problems, including obesity and asthma, have genetic roots and psychosocial consequences.

Brain Development Brain maturation continues, leading to faster reactions and better self-control. Which specific skills are mastered depends largely on culture, gender, and inherited ability, all of which are reflected in intelligence tests. Children have multiple intellectual abilities, most of which are not reflected in standard IQ tests.

Special Needs Many children have special learning needs. Early recognition, targeted education, and psychological support can help them, including those with bipolar and attention-deficit disorders, specific learning disabilities, and the many disorders of the autism spectrum. Whether or not children with special needs should be educated with other children, a strategy called inclusion, is especially controversial for gifted children.

COGNITIVE

Building on Theory Piaget noted that, beginning at about age 7, children attain concrete operational thought, including the ability to understand the logical principles of classification and transitive inference. Vygotsky emphasized that children become more open to learning from mentors, both adults and peers. Information-processing abilities increase, including greater memory, knowledge, control, and metacognition.

Language Children's increasing ability to understand the structures and possibilities of language enable them to extend the range of their cognitive powers and to increase vocabulary. Children master various language codes, both formal and informal, and many become fluent in more than one language..

Education International comparisons reveal marked variations in the overt and hidden curricula, as well as in learning, between one nation and another. The emphasis in the United States on higher standards increases the importance of testing, a controversial practice. The reading and math wars pit traditional education against a more holistic approach to learning. Alternate school structures, including home schooling and charter schools, are an attempt to increase learning among U.S. schoolchildren.

PSYCHOSOCIAL

The Nature of the Child Theorists agree that many school-age children develop competencies, emotional control, and attitudes to defend against stress. Some children are resilient, coping well with problems and finding support in friends, family, school, religion, and community.

Families Parents continue to influence children, especially as they exacerbate or buffer problems in school and the community. During these years, families need to meet basic needs, encourage learning, foster self-respect, nurture friendship, and—most important—provide harmony and stability. Nuclear families often provide this, but one-parent, stepparent, same-sex, or grandparent families can also function well for children. No family structure guarantees optimal functioning. Adequate income, low conflict, and family stability benefit children of all ages, particularly in middle childhood.

Peers and Morals The peer group becomes increasingly important as children become less dependent on their parents and more dependent on friends for help, loyalty, and sharing of mutual interests. Peer rejection and bullying become serious problems. Moral development, influenced by peers, advances during these years.

P A R T

V

CHAPTERS 14•15•16

Adolescence

One observer said adolescence is like "starting turbo-charged engines with an unskilled driver" (Dahl, 2004, p. 17). Would you ride with an unskilled driver? I did. When my daughter Bethany had her learner's permit, I sought to convey confidence. Not until a terrified "Mom! Help!" did I grab the wheel to avoid hitting a subway kiosk. I should have intervened sooner, but it is hard to know at what age, and in what situations, grown daughters need their mothers. Bethany was an adolescent, neither child nor adult, sometimes wanting independence, sometimes not.

A century ago, puberty began at age 15 or so. Soon after that, most girls married and most boys found work. It is said that *adolescence begins with biology and ends with culture.* If so, then a hundred years ago adolescence lasted a few months; now it lasts a decade or more. Currently, puberty starts earlier and adulthood later, with adult responsibilities often postponed until after the next stage of development, emerging adulthood.

In the next three chapters (covering ages 11 to 18), we begin with biology (this chapter) and move toward culture (in chapter 16). Understanding adolescence is more than an abstract challenge: Those turbo-charged engines need skilled guidance. Get ready to grab the wheel.

14

CHAPTER

Adolescence: Biosocial Development

WHAT WILL YOU KNOW?

1. Since puberty normally begins anytime from age 8 to 14, is there any way to predict the onset for a particular child?
2. Why do some teenagers starve themselves and others overeat?
3. Since adolescent sexual impulses are powerful and inevitable, why is there so much variation in rates of teen pregnancy, child sexual abuse, and STIs?

I overheard a conversation among three teenagers, including my daughter Rachel, all past their awkward years, now becoming beautiful. They were discussing the imperfections of their bodies. One spoke of her fat stomach (what stomach? I could not see it), another of her long neck (hidden by her silky, shoulder-length hair). Rachel complained not only about her bent finger but also about her feet!

The reality that children grow into men and women is no shock to any adult. But for teenagers, heightened self-awareness often triggers surprise or even horror, joy or despair. Like these three, adolescents pay attention to details of their growth. This chapter describes some of those biosocial details of growing bodies and emerging sexuality. It all begins with hormones, but other invisible changes may be even more potent—such as the timing of neurological maturation that does not yet allow adolescents to realize that their minor imperfections are insignificant.

>> Puberty Begins

Puberty refers to the years of rapid physical growth and sexual maturation that end childhood, producing a person of adult size, shape, and sexuality. The forces of puberty are unleashed by a cascade of hormones that produce external growth and internal changes, including heightened emotions and sexual desires. This process normally starts between ages 8 and 14 and follows the sequence outlined in At About This Time. Most physical growth and maturation ends about four years after the first signs appear, although some individuals add height, weight, and muscle until age 20 or so.

For girls, the observable changes of puberty usually begin with nipple growth. Soon a few pubic hairs are visible, then peak growth spurt, widening of the hips, the first menstrual period (**menarche**), full pubic-hair pattern, and breast maturation (Susman et al., 2010). The average age of menarche among normal-weight girls is about 12 years, 8 months (Rosenfield et al., 2009), although variation in timing is quite normal.

For boys, the usual sequence is growth of the testes, initial pubic-hair growth, growth of the penis, first ejaculation of seminal fluid (**spermarche**), appearance of facial hair, peak growth spurt, deepening of the voice, and final pubic-hair growth (Biro et al., 2001; Herman-Giddens et al., 2001; Susman et al., 2010). The typical age of spermarche is just under 13 years, close to the age for menarche.

puberty The time between the first onrush of hormones and full adult physical development. Puberty usually lasts three to five years. Many more years are required to achieve psychosocial maturity.

menarche A girl's first menstrual period, signaling that she has begun ovulation. Pregnancy is biologically possible, but ovulation and menstruation are often irregular for years after menarche.

spermarche A boy's first ejaculation of sperm. Erections can occur as early as infancy, but ejaculation signals sperm production. Spermarche may occur during sleep (in a "wet dream") or via direct stimulation.

AT ABOUT THIS TIME

The Sequence of Puberty

Girls	Approximate Average Age*	Boys
Ovaries increase production of estrogen and progesterone**	9	
Uterus and vagina begin to grow larger	9½	Testes increase production of testosterone**
Breast "bud" stage	10	Testes and scrotum grow larger
Pubic hair begins to appear; weight spurt begins	11	
Peak height spurt	11½	Pubic hair begins to appear
Peak muscle and organ growth (also, hips become noticeably wider)	12	Penis growth begins
Menarche (first menstrual period)	12½	Spermarche (first ejaculation); weight spurt begins
First ovulation	13	Peak height spurt
Voice lowers	14	Peak muscle and organ growth (also, shoulders become noticeably broader)
Final pubic-hair pattern	15	Voice lowers; visible facial hair
Full breast growth	16	
	18	Final pubic-hair pattern

*Average ages are rough approximations, with many perfectly normal, healthy adolescents as much as three years ahead of or behind these ages.

**Estrogens and testosterone influence sexual characteristics, including reproduction. Charted here are the increases produced by the gonads (sex glands). The ovaries produce estrogens and the testes produce androgens, especially testosterone. Adrenal glands produce some of both kinds of hormones (not shown).

Unseen Beginnings

Just described are the visible changes of puberty, but the entire process begins with an invisible event, a marked hormonal increase. **Hormones** are body chemicals that regulate hunger, sleep, moods, stress, sexual desire, immunity, reproduction, and many other bodily reactions, including puberty. Hormones start the process: Menarche or spermarche is "a very late event," long after hormonal beginnings (J. L. Cameron, 2004, p. 116). Throughout adolescence, hormone levels correlate with physiological changes and self-reported developments (Shirtcliff et al., 2009).

You learned in Chapter 8 that the production of many hormones is regulated deep within the brain, where biochemical signals from the hypothalamus signal another brain structure, the **pituitary,** to go into action. The pituitary produces hormones that stimulate the **adrenal glands,** located above the kidneys at either side of the lower back. The adrenal glands produce more hormones.

Many hormones that regulate puberty follow this route, known as the **HPA (hypothalamus–pituitary–adrenal) axis** (see Figure 14.1). Abnormalities of the HPA axis in adolescence are associated with eating disorders, anxiety, and

hormone An organic chemical substance that is produced by one body tissue and conveyed via the bloodstream to another to affect some physiological function.

pituitary A gland in the brain that responds to a signal from the hypothalamus by producing many hormones, including those that regulate growth and that control other glands, among them the adrenal and sex glands.

adrenal glands Two glands, located above the kidneys, that produce hormones (including the "stress hormones" epinephrine [adrenaline] and norepinephrine).

HPA (hypothalamus–pituitary–adrenal) axis A sequence of hormone production originating in the hypothalamus and moving to the pituitary and then to the adrenal glands.

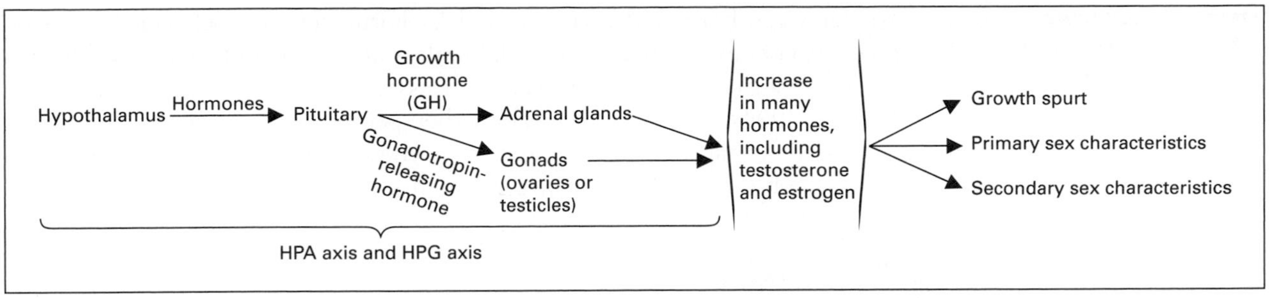

FIGURE 14.1

Biological Sequence of Puberty Puberty begins with a hormonal signal from the hypothalamus to the pituitary gland. The pituitary, in turn, signals the adrenal glands and the ovaries or testes to produce more of their hormones.

depression. These conditions and many other types of psychopathology, appearing for the first time or worsening at puberty, are connected to hormones (Dahl & Gunnar, 2009). Indeed, abnormalities of the HPA axis probably cause the sudden increases in clinical depression in early adolescence (Guerry & Hastings, 2011), and HPA disruptions are one harmful result of childhood sexual abuse (discussed later in this chapter) (Trickett et al., 2011b).

gonads The paired sex glands (ovaries in females, testicles in males). The gonads produce hormones and gametes.

HPG (hypothalamus–pituitary–gonad) axis A sequence of hormone production originating in the hypothalamus and moving to the pituitary and then to the gonads.

estradiol A sex hormone, considered the chief estrogen. Females produce much more estradiol than males do.

testosterone A sex hormone, the best known of the androgens (male hormones); secreted in far greater amounts by males than by females.

Sex Hormones

At adolescence, the pituitary activates not only the adrenal glands but also the **gonads,** or sex glands (ovaries in females; testes, or testicles, in males), following another sequence called the **HPG (hypothalamus–pituitary–gonad) axis.** One hormone in particular, GnRH (gonadotropin-releasing hormone), causes the gonads to enlarge and dramatically increase their production of sex hormones, chiefly **estradiol** in girls and **testosterone** in boys. These hormones affect the body's entire shape and functioning, including production of additional hormones that regulate stress and immunity (E. A. Young et al., 2008).

Estrogens (including estradiol) are female hormones and *androgens* (including testosterone) are male hormones, although the adrenal glands produce estrogens and androgens in everyone. The gonads, however, produce sex-specific hormones: The ovaries produce much more of the estrogens than of the androgens; the reverse is true of the testes. Testosterone skyrockets in boys—up to 20 times the prepubescent level (Roche & Sun, 2003). Estradiol increases to about 8 times a girl's childhood level (Malina et al., 2004).

The activated gonads eventually produce mature sperm or ova, released in spermarche or menarche. That signifies the potential for parenthood, although peak fertility occurs four to six years later. Hormonal increases and differences may underlie sex differences in psychopathology (Naninck et al., 2011; Steiner & Young, 2008); compared with their peers of the other sex, males are twice as likely to become schizophrenic and females are twice as likely to become depressed. For both sexes, hormones awaken and then increase interest in sex. The first sexual objects are usually unattainable—a film star, a teacher, someone's older sibling—but by mid-adolescence, fantasies may settle on another teen.

PHOTOALTO / ALAMY

Primping, Bonding, or Both? Lip gloss and eyelash-curling have the full concentration of these three, as the two "older" girls (the one on the left is 13) work on the youngest one. Critics lament society's focus on superficial appearance, but this scene may be more biological than cultural, since similar moments have occurred throughout history and in every nation.

Observation Quiz This moment was captured fairly recently, in 2007. Are these girls North American? For a clue, look at their hair. (see answer, page 415)

Especially for Parents of Teenagers
Why would parents blame adolescent moods on hormones? (see response, page 417)

Not only are brain and body affected by hormones, but behavior is as well. Surges of emotions and sudden lustful impulses are partly hormonal, but thoughts *cause* physiological and neurological processes as well as result from them (Damasio, 2003). For example, when other people react to emerging breasts, beards, or body shapes, these reactions evoke thoughts and frustrations in the adolescent, which then raise hormone levels and produce emotional outbursts, each increasing the other.

Body Rhythms

The brain of every living creature responds to the environment with natural rhythms that rise and fall by the hours, days, and seasons. For example, body weight and height are affected by time of year (children grower taller in summer and heavier in winter—by a small amount that is apparent only when thousands of children are measured very precisely). Some *biorhythms* are on a day–night cycle of biological activity that occurs approximately every 24 hours, called the **circadian rhythm.** (*Circadian* means "about a day.") Puberty affects biorhythms.

circadian rhythm A day–night cycle of biological activity that occurs approximately every 24 hours (*circadian* means "about a day").

The hypothalamus and the pituitary regulate the hormones that affect patterns of stress, appetite, sleep, and so on. These hormones cause a *phase delay* in sleep–wake cycles, making many teens wide awake and hungry at midnight but half asleep, with little appetite or energy, all morning. By contrast, many older adults are naturally alert in the morning and sleepy at night because of their circadian rhythms.

DAVID LASSMAN / SYRACUSE NEWSPAPERS / THE IMAGE WORKS

Too Early It is 8:00 A.M. on their first day of high school, and these freshmen are having trouble staying awake for orientation in their homeroom.

Added to the adolescent day–night pattern, some individuals (especially males) are naturally more alert in the evening than in the morning, a genetic trait called *eveningness.* Exacerbated by the pubescent phase delay, eveningness puts adolescents at high risk for antisocial activities (Susman et al., 2007) because they are awake when adults are sound asleep. Another result is that "teenagers are notoriously sleep deprived" (Ruder, 2008, p. 10). Uneven sleep schedules (more sleep on weekends, erratic bedtimes) decrease well-being, as does sleep deprivation (Fuligni & Hardway, 2006; Holm et al., 2009).

Sleep deprivation and irregular sleep schedules lead to several specific dangers, including insomnia, nightmares, mood disorders (depression, conduct disorder, anxiety), and falling asleep while driving. Individuals who are sleep deprived do not think or learn as well as they might when rested. The implications of that fact may be ignored by adults, as the following explains.

A VIEW FROM SCIENCE

Get Real

Some parents fight biology. They command their wide-awake teen to "go to sleep," they hang up on their child's classmates who phone after 10:00 P.M., they set curfews and stay awake until their teenagers come home, and they drag their offspring out of bed for school. (An opposite developmental clash occurs when parents tell their toddlers to stay in their cribs after dawn.) This parent–adolescent fight goes against the circadian rhythm, so sleep-deprived teenagers are likely to fall asleep in school (see Figure 14.2), have poor relationships with their parents, and abuse substances (partly to wake up or go to sleep) (Mueller et al., 2011; Patrick & Schulenberg, 2011).

Data on the adolescent phase delay convinced social scientists at the University of Minnesota to ask 17 school districts to start high school at 8:30 A.M. or later. Few parents agreed. Many (42 percent) thought high school should begin before 8:00 A.M. Some (20 percent) wanted their teenagers out of the house by

7:15 A.M., as did only 1 percent of parents with younger children (Wahlstrom, 2002).

Workers in many occupations had their own reasons for believing school should begin early. Teachers generally thought that learning was more efficient early in the morning; bus drivers hated rush hour; cafeteria workers wanted to leave by mid-afternoon; police said teenagers should be home by 4:00 P.M.; coaches needed after-school sports events to end before dark; business owners wanted teens to staff the afternoon shift; community program directors liked to use school gyms for nonschool events in the late afternoon.

Only one school district experimented. In Edina, Minnesota, high school schedules changed to 8:30 A.M. to 3:10 P.M. instead of 7:25 A.M. to 2:05 P.M. After a trial year, most parents (93 percent) and virtually all students liked the new schedule. One student said, "I have only fallen asleep in school once this whole year, and last year I fell asleep about three times a week" (quoted in Wahlstrom, 2002, p. 190). The data showed fewer absent, late, disruptive, or sick students (the school nurse became an advocate) and higher grades.

Other school districts reconsidered. Minneapolis, which had started high school at 7:15 A.M., changed the starting time to 8:40 A.M. Again, attendance improved, as did the graduation rate. School boards in South Burlington (Vermont), West Des Moines (Iowa), Tulsa (Oklahoma), Arlington (Virginia), and Milwaukee (Wisconsin) voted in favor of later starting times, switching on average from 7:45 A.M. to 8:30 A.M. (Tonn, 2006), as did one private school in Rhode Island (Owens et al., 2010). Unexpected advantages appeared: financial savings (more efficient energy use), less adolescent depression, and, at least in Tulsa, unprecedented athletic championships.

But change is hard. Many school districts stick to their old schedules. From 2006 to 2009, the community of Fairfax (Virginia) argued, forming two opposing groups: SLEEP (Start Later for Excellence in Education Proposal) versus WAKE (Worried About Keeping Extra-Curriculars). One high school sports reporter argued:

> The later start would hinder teams without lighted practice fields. Hinder kids who work after-school jobs to save for college or to help support their families. Hinder teachers who work second jobs or take late-afternoon college classes. Hinder commuters who would get stopped behind more buses during peak traffic times. Hinder kids who might otherwise seek after-school academic help, or club or team affiliation. Hinder families that depend on high school children to watch younger siblings after school. Hinder community groups that use school and park facilities in the late afternoons and evenings.
>
> *[Williams, 2009]*

This writer wrote that science was on the side of change but reality was not. To developmentalists, of course, science *is* reality. However, the school board focused on the cost of school buses in rush hour. It voted to keep high school starting time at 7:20 A.M.

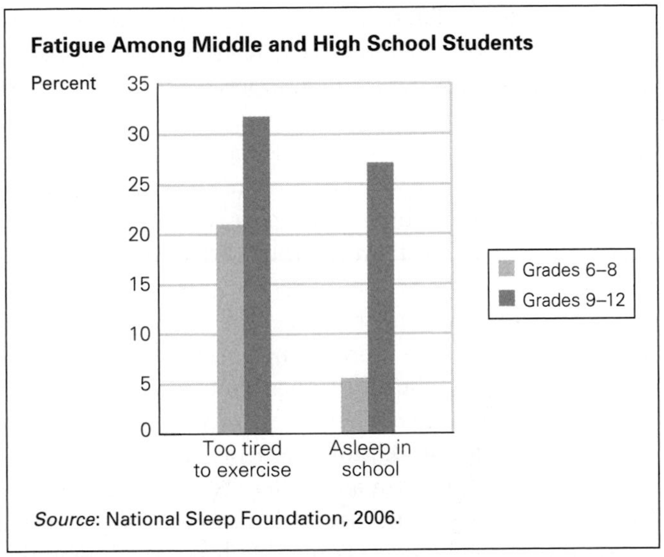

FIGURE 14.2

Dreaming and Learning? This graph shows the percentage of U.S. students who, once a week or more, fall asleep in class or are too tired to exercise. Not shown are those who are too tired overall (59 percent for high school students) or who doze in class "almost every day" (8 percent).

Age and Puberty

A practical question is: "When will adolescence begin?" Some fear *precocious puberty* (sexual development before age 8) or very late puberty (after age 16), but both are rare (Cesario & Hughes, 2007). Quite normal is hormonal activity beginning any time from age 8 to age 14, with visible signs appearing a year later. Many parents, teachers, and children want to know more precisely when puberty will occur: They want to be prepared, but not years before the events. Fortunately, genes, gender, body fat, and stress all aid in prediction.

Genes and Gender

About two-thirds of the variation in age of puberty is genetic, evident not only in families but also in ethnic groups (Ge et al., 2007; Susman et al., 2010; van den Berg

>> Answer to Observation Quiz (from page 413) This girlish behavior is universal, but the hairstyles are not. All three have braids; these girls are Argentinean.

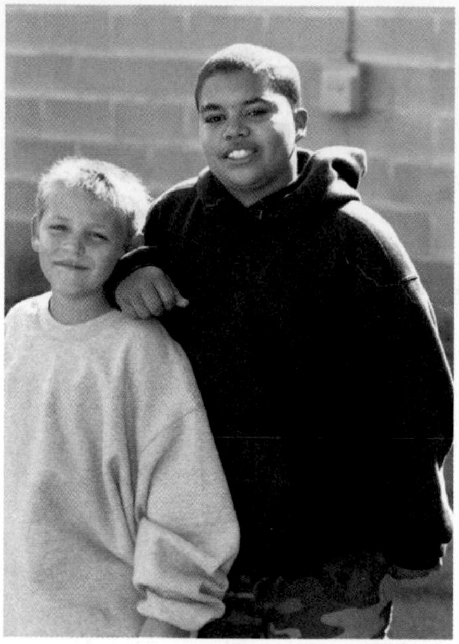

SKJOLD PHOTOGRAPHS / THE IMAGE WORKS

Both 12 The ancestors of these two Minnesota 12-year-olds came from northern Europe and West Africa, respectively. Their genes have dictated some differences between them, including the timing of puberty, but these differences are irrelevant to their friendship.

& Boomsma, 2007). African Americans reach puberty about seven months earlier than European or Hispanic Americans, while Chinese Americans average several months later. Ethnic differences are apparent on other continents as well. For instance, northern European girls reach menarche at 13 years, 4 months, on average; southern European girls do so at 12 years, 5 months (Alsaker & Flammer, 2006).

Genes on the sex chromosomes have a marked effect. In height, the average girl is about two years ahead of the average boy. However, the female height spurt occurs before menarche, whereas for boys, the increase in height is relatively late, occurring after spermarche. Thus, when it comes to hormonal and sexual changes, girls are only a few months ahead of boys (Hughes & Gore, 2007). Therefore, the sixth-grade boy with sexual fantasies about the taller girls in his class is neither perverted nor precocious; his hormones are simply ahead of his visible growth.

Body Fat

Another major influence on the onset of puberty is body fat, at least in girls. Heavy girls reach menarche years earlier than malnourished ones do. Most girls must weigh at least 100 pounds (45 kilograms) before they experience their first period (Berkey et al., 2000).

Worldwide, urban children are more often overfed and underexercised compared with rural children. That is probably why puberty starts earlier in the cities of India and China than it does in more remote villages, a year earlier in Warsaw than in rural Poland, and earlier in Athens than in other parts of Greece (Malina et al., 2004).

secular trend The long-term upward or downward direction of a certain set of statistical measurements, as opposed to a smaller, shorter cyclical variation. As an example, over the last two centuries, because of improved nutrition and medical care, children have tended to reach their adult height earlier and their adult height has increased.

Body fat also explains why youth reach puberty at age 15 or later in some parts of Africa, although their genetic relatives in North America mature much earlier. Similarly, malnutrition may explain why puberty began at about age 17 in sixteenth-century Europe. Puberty has occurred at younger ages every century since then (an example of what is called the **secular trend**): nutrition and medicine have improved, allowing not only earlier puberty but also taller average height.

One curious bit of evidence of the secular trend is that U.S. presidents are taller in recent decades than they were earlier (James Madison, the fourth president, was shortest at 5 feet, 4 inches; Barack Obama is 6 feet, 1 inch tall). Over most of the twentieth century, each generation experienced puberty a few weeks earlier and grew a centimeter or so taller than did the preceding one (Floud et al., 2011). The secular trend has stopped in developed nations, perhaps because nutrition is now sufficient for everyone to attain their genetic potential. That means that, unlike their grandparents, young men are unlikely to look down at their short fathers, or girls at their little mothers, unless they are born in Asia or Africa, where the secular trend continues.

Hormones

Of course, hormones affect sex differences, height, and weight, but there may be additional effects directly on the age of puberty. Many scientists suspect that hormones in the food supply speed the onset of puberty. As evidence, they point to the steroids fed to cattle to increase bulk and milk supply, as well as to many other substances in meat and other foods consumed by children. Steriods affect appetite, body fat, and sex hormones (Wang et al., 2005).

leptin A hormone that affects appetite and is believed to affect the onset of puberty. Leptin levels increase during childhood and peak at around age 12.

One hormone in particular has been implicated in the onset of puberty: **leptin,** which stimulates the appetite. Leptin levels in the blood show a natural increase over childhood, peaking at puberty (Rutters et al., 2008). Curiously, leptin affects appetite in females more than it does in males (Geary & Lovejoy, 2008), and body fat is more closely connected to the onset of puberty in girls than in boys. In fact,

the well-established finding that body fat precipitates puberty may not be true for boys in nations where malnutrition is rare: One study found that U.S. boys who are heavy in childhood reach puberty later, not earlier, than others (J. M. Lee et al., 2010).

It is not yet known for certain exactly what the effects of leptin are or what factors increase or decrease leptin in the bloodstream, although it is known that leptin, body fat, and puberty are connected somehow. Most of the research has been with lower animals, including mice, goats, and rabbits. Children with abnormally low levels of leptin are sometimes too thin, sometimes overweight, but often experience delayed puberty. For some, injections of leptin start puberty (Friedman, 2011), but far more research needs to occur before the effects are understood.

It also is not yet known precisely how the many chemicals in the air, water, or diet affect the human sexual-reproductive system. In general, more is known about female than male puberty, partly because menarche is easier to date than spermarche. Among adults, some toxins affect women more than men (Tomicic et al., 2011), and this may be true for adolescents as well. One conclusion is certain: For both sexes, childhood malnutrition slows growth, puberty, and reproduction. As for the specific impact and mechanisms of hormones and chemicals, many questions need answers.

>> Response for Parents of Teenagers (from page 414) If something causes adolescents to shout "I hate you," to slam doors, or to cry inconsolably, parents may decide that hormones are the problem. This makes it easy to disclaim personal responsibility for the teenager's anger. However, research on stress and hormones suggests that this comforting attribution is too simplistic.

Especially for Parents Worried About Early Puberty Suppose your cousin's 9-year-old daughter has just had her first period, and your cousin blames hormones in the food supply for this "precocious" puberty. Should you change your young daughter's diet? (see response, page 419)

Stress

There is uncertainty regarding the role of stress as well. Stress affects the sexual-reproductive system by making reproduction more difficult in adulthood and by *hastening* (not delaying) the hormonal onset of puberty. Thus, puberty arrives earlier if a child's parents are sick, addicted, or divorced or if the neighborhood is violent and impoverished.

A study of sexually abused girls found that they began puberty seven months earlier, on average, than did a matched comparison group (Trickett et al., 2011b). Puberty in some children seems unaffected by family stress, yet in children who are genetically sensitive to context, puberty comes early if their family context is stressful but late if their family is supportive (Ellis et al., 2011). Thus, specifics are influenced by the genes of the child as well as by the family situation, as differential sensitivity (explained in Chapter 1) would predict.

Corroboration comes from studies with other animals. Opossums experience earlier puberty if their environment is stressful (Warshofsky, 1999). Mice experience later puberty if their mother is highly nurturant, indicated by frequent licking and grooming during infancy, thus protecting mice against stress later on (N. M. Cameron et al., 2008).

Several longitudinal studies suggest that stress hormones directly cause early puberty. For example, one study followed 756 children from infancy to adolescence. For them, earlier puberty correlated with harsh parenting in childhood. Their parents were likely to demand quiet and respect, to spank often, and to rarely hug their children. Generally, parents punish sons more than daughters, but this study found that harsh parenting correlated with earlier puberty for daughters, not sons—especially if those daughters cried a lot as infants, which suggests that they were sensitive to stress (Belsky et al., 2007).

A further study of the same girls at age 15, controlled for genetic differences, found that harsh treatment in childhood increased sexual risk taking (e.g., more sex partners, pregnancies, diseases) but not other risks (e.g., drugs, crime) (Belsky et al., 2010). This suggests that stress targets sexual hormones more than factors that lead to overall rebellion.

Why would stress trigger puberty? Given what is known about optimal development, it makes more sense for stress to *delay* puberty. If puberty were delayed, then stressed young teens would still look and act childlike, and that might evoke adult protection, not lust or anger. Delayed puberty would be especially beneficial in conflicted or single-parent homes. But the opposite occurs. One explanation comes from evolutionary theory:

> Maturing quickly and breeding promiscuously would enhance reproductive fitness more than would delaying development, mating cautiously, and investing heavily in parenting. The latter strategy, in contrast, would make biological sense, for virtually the same reproductive-fitness-enhancing reasons, under conditions of contextual support and nurturance.
>
> *[Belsky et al., 2010, p. 121]*

In other words, in past stressful times, for species survival, stressed adolescents needed to replace themselves before they died. Of course, natural selection would postpone puberty during extreme famine (so that pregnant girls or their newborns would not die of malnutrition). But natural selection would also favor genes that hastened puberty when girls were well-fed but their families and tribes were in conflict, threatening the survival of the adolescents and adults. In that case, a new generation needed to be born before too many of the older generations went to war. By contrast, in more peaceful times and families, puberty could occur later, allowing children to benefit from years of nurturance from their parents and grandparents before having children of their own. Genes could evolve to respond differentially to war and peace.

Of course, this evolutionary rationale no longer applies. Today, early sexuality and reproduction are more likely to destroy societies than protect them. However, the genome has been shaped over millennia; timing takes centuries to change.

PHOTOLIBRARY.COM

Not Yet a Woman She may look like an attractive woman, but she is really an early-maturing girl. Notice her long and sandy feet, her relatively short torso, her thin upper arms. Her body is changing—in a photo taken two years earlier or two years later, her shape would be different.

Too Early, Too Late

For most adolescents, this speculation about hormones and evolution is irrelevant. Only one aspect of pubertal timing is important: their friends' schedules. Puberty can enhance or diminish a person's status with peers. No one wants to be too early or too late.

Girls

Think about the early-maturing girl. If she has visible breasts at age 10, the boys her age tease her; they are distressed by the sexual creature in their midst. She must fit her developing body into a school chair designed for smaller children; she might hide her breasts in large T-shirts and bulky sweaters; she might refuse to undress for gym. Early-maturing girls tend to have lower self-esteem, more depression, and poorer body image than do other girls (Compian et al., 2009). They also exercise less than their classmates, which contributes to their difficulties with self-image (Davison et al., 2007).

Sometimes early-maturing girls have older boyfriends, who are attracted to their womanly shape and girlish innocence. Having an older boyfriend gains them status—but also increases their risk of drug and alcohol use (Weichold et al., 2003), relational bullying, and victimization of physical violence (from that same boyfriend) (Schreck et al., 2007). Early-maturing girls enter abusive relationships more often than other girls do, perhaps because they are lonely and their social judgment is immature. Depression and suicide are also risks for early-maturing girls, especially if they are genetically predisposed to eveningness and are sleep deprived (Negriff et al., 2011).

Boys

Early maturation in girls has always seemed more harmful than helpful, but cohort seems crucial for boys. Early-maturing boys who were born around 1930 often became leaders in high school and more successful as adults (M. C. Jones, 1965; Taga et al., 2006). Since about 1960, however, the risks associated with early male maturation have outweighed the benefits. In the twenty-first century, early-maturing boys are more aggressive, law-breaking, and alcohol-abusing than are later-maturing boys (Biehl et al., 2007; Lynne et al., 2007) and thus are more likely to have trouble with parents, schools, and the police. For boys as well as girls, early puberty correlates with sexual activity and teenage parenthood, which in turn correlate with depression and other psychosocial problems (B. Brown, 2004; Siebenbruner et al., 2007). Not only is early puberty stressful, but speed of change is difficult as well: The boys most likely to become depressed are those for whom puberty was both early and quick (Mendle et al., 2010).

Late puberty may also be difficult, especially for boys. Slow-developing boys tend to be more anxious, depressed, and afraid of sex, at least according to research in Finland (Lindfors et al., 2007). In fact, every adolescent wants to hit puberty "on time." They are likely to overestimate or underestimate their maturation, or become depressed, if they are not average (Conley & Rudolph, 2009; Shirtcliff et al., 2009).

>> Response for Parents Worried About Early Puberty (from page 417) Probably not. If she is overweight, her diet should change, but the hormone hypothesis is speculative. Genes are the main factor; she shares only one-eighth of her genes with her cousin.

Ethnic Differences

Puberty that is late by world norms (age 14 or so) is not troubling if one's friends are late as well. Well-nourished Africans tend to experience puberty a few months earlier and Asians a few months later than Europeans, but they all develop well if their classmates are on the same schedule. However, variable timing may add to intergroup tensions in multiethnic schools. Peer approval is more important in adolescence than is approval from adults (Green et al., 2006).

For instance, in one New England high school, the shorter and thinner "quiet Asian boys" were teased, much to their dismay. When one larger Asian American fought back at an ethnic insult, he was a hero to his Asian peers, even though school authorities punished him (Lei, 2003). In a California high school, Samoan students were a small minority of the school population but advanced in puberty, which earned them respect from classmates of all backgrounds. They were accepted as peacemakers between the two more numerous groups, African and Mexican Americans (Staiger, 2006).

Size and maturation are important for many adolescents in every nation. For example, a study of more than 3,000 Australian students, primarily of English heritage, found that late developers had four times the rate of self-harm (cutting or poisoning themselves) as did other students. This is a marked indication of serious depression (Patton et al., 2007).

SUMMING UP

Puberty usually begins between ages 8 and 14 (typically around age 11) in response to a chain reaction of hormone production from the hypothalamus to the pituitary to the adrenal and sex glands. Hormones affect emotions as well as the body: Adolescent outbursts of sudden anger, sadness, and lust are caused by hormones combined with reactions from other people to the young person's changing body. Many factors, including genes, body fat, and stress, affect the onset of puberty, especially among girls. Early or late puberty is less desirable than puberty at the same age as one's peers; off-time maturation may lead to depression, drug abuse, and other problems. ■

>> Nutrition

All the changes of puberty depend on adequate nourishment, yet many adolescents do not consume enough vitamins or minerals. Teenagers often skip breakfast, eat at midnight, guzzle down soda, and munch on salty, processed snacks. One reason is that their hormones affect their diurnal rhythms, including their appetites. Another reason is that they seek independence, which may mean refusing to sit down to a family dinner.

Cohort and age are crucial. In the United States, each new generation eats less well than the previous one, and each 18-year-old tends to eat a less balanced diet than he or she did at age 10 (N. I. Larson et al., 2007). Most adolescents consume enough calories, but in 2009 only 14 percent of high school seniors ate the recommended three or more servings of vegetables a day (MMWR, June 4, 2010).

LEE SNIDER / THE IMAGE WORKS

Come Here Often? Teenagers worldwide (like this group in Yangshuo, China) are attracted by fast-food restaurants because the cheap food and public setting of such places make them ideal for snacking and socializing. However, the food—usually high in fat and low in nutrition—contributes to overweight and undernourishment in many young customers.

Diet Deficiencies

Deficiencies of iron, calcium, zinc, and other minerals are especially common during adolescence. Because menstruation depletes iron, anemia is more likely among adolescent girls than among any other age group. This is true everywhere, especially in South Asia and sub-Saharan Africa, where teenage girls rarely eat iron-rich meat and green vegetables and most are thought to be anemic. Specific data on that population are unavailable because large-scale studies that include laboratory analysis of blood iron are rare in developing nations. However, research in Saudi Arabia of 18- to 23-year-old college women (usually in good health, never pregnant, and from wealthy families) found that, despite these advantages, 26 percent had insufficient iron and another 24 percent were clinically anemic (Al-Sayes et al., 2011).

Boys may also be iron-deficient if they push their bodies in physical labor or sports: Muscles need iron for growth and strength. The cutoff for anemia is lower for boys than for girls because boys naturally require more iron to be healthy (Morón & Viteri, 2009). Many adolescents of both sexes in every nation spurn iron-rich foods (green vegetables, eggs, and meat) in favor of iron-poor chips, sweets, and fries.

Similarly, although the daily recommended intake of calcium for teenagers is 1,300 milligrams, the average U. S. teen consumes less than 500 milligrams a day. About half of adult bone mass is acquired from ages 10 to 20, which means many contemporary teenagers will develop osteoporosis (fragile bones), a major cause of disability, injury, and death in late adulthood among people of European descent.

One reason for calcium deficiency is that milk drinking has declined. In 1959, most North American children drank at least three glasses (about ¾ liter) of milk each day, providing most (about 900 milligrams) of their daily calcium requirement; by 1999, only 18 percent of U.S. children drank three glasses of milk a day. A decade after that (2009), rates for twelfth-graders were only 8 percent for girls and 20 percent for boys (MMWR, June 4, 2010). In the twenty-first century, the beverage most often consumed by 2- to 18-year-olds is soda (U.S. Department of Agriculture and U.S. Department of Health and Human Services, 2011.)

Choices Made

Many economists advocate a "nudge" to encourage people to make better choices, not only in nutrition but in all aspects of their lives (Thaler & Sunstein,

2008). Teenagers are nudged in the wrong direction. Their nutritional deficiencies result from the food choices that young adolescents are allowed, even enticed, to make.

Fast-food establishments cluster around high schools, often with extra seating that encourages teenagers to eat and socialize. This is especially true for high schools with large Hispanic populations, the teens most at risk for obesity (Taber et al., 2011). Price influences food choices, especially for adolescents (Epstein et al., 2006), and healthy foods are more expensive than unhealthy ones. To cite one specific example: In New York City in 2010, a McDonald's salad cost five times more than a hamburger ($5.59 versus $1.09).

Furthermore, nutritional deficiencies increase when schools have vending machines that offer soda and snacks, especially for middle school students (Rovner et al., 2011). A constructive nudge of higher prices, less attractive placement, and healthier selections for in-school vending machines would improve adolescent nutrition.

A more drastic strategy would be to ban the purchase of unhealthy foods in schools altogether—a strategy used by 29 percent of U.S. high schools in 2002 and 69 percent in 2008. During the same years, obesity leveled off in the United States, although school policies are only a small part of the necessary changes. Experts call for "increased efforts" at schools, in communities, and among adolescents (MMWR, October 9, 2009).

MICHAEL NEWMAN / PHOTO EDIT

Sexy? Teens of both sexes are intensely concerned with how peers view their appearance. Notice this boy's long and thin sideburns, calling attention to the earring in his right ear—a sign that he seeks a female partner.

Body Image

Another reason for poor nutrition among teenagers is anxiety about **body image**—that is, a person's idea of how his or her body looks. Few teenagers welcome every change in their bodies. Instead, they tend to focus on and exaggerate imperfections (as did the three girls in the anecdote that opens this chapter).

body image A person's idea of how his or her body looks.

Girls diet because they want to be thinner, partly because boys tend to prefer dating thin girls (Halpern et al., 2005). Boys want to look taller and stronger, a concern that increases from ages 12 to 17, partly because girls value well-developed muscles in males (D. Jones & Crawford, 2005). Thus, as the hormones of puberty awaken sexual interest, both sexes become less happy with their own bodies and more superficial in their evaluation of the other sex. This is true worldwide. A longitudinal study in Korea found that, as in the West, body image dissatisfaction began in early adolescence and increased until age 15 or so. For 10-year-old girls and 15-year-old boys, body dissatisfaction increased depression and thoughts of suicide (Kim & Kim, 2009).

In many nations, the ideal body type and facial appearance is tall, thin, and Anglo-Saxon. This is striking in places far from England, where Anglo-Saxons originated. Now teenagers in every nation are bombarded by media images that differ markedly from those their mirrors reflect (see photo at right).

Of course, few Anglo-Saxon youth achieve the media ideal, either, but the discrepancy is particularly cruel far from England. A longitudinal study in China found that adolescents in that country had anxieties about weight gain similar to those of U.S. teenagers (Chen & Jackson, 2009). Everywhere, young adolescents wish their bodies looked different, and teenagers tend to lie about their bodies—adding 3 inches and subtracting 4 pounds on average, with the boys doing more adding and the girls more subtracting (Brener et al., 2003).

African Fashion She is Anglo Saxon in almost every detail—nose, hair, eyebrows, facial shape, and body type—much like her tight-fitting strapless gown. However, she is modeling a designer dress during Africa Fashion Week in Johannesburg, South Africa, in 2010.

GABRIEL BOUYS / AFP / GETTY IMAGES

CHRISTOPHER LAMARCA / REDUX

Girl or Woman? Hannah Hartney, here age 16, has been suffering from anorexia since she was 9. Some clinicians suggest that starving oneself is a way to avoid the womanly body that develops at puberty.

anorexia nervosa An eating disorder characterized by self-starvation. Affected individuals voluntarily undereat and often overexercise, depriving their vital organs of nutrition. Anorexia can be fatal.

bulimia nervosa An eating disorder characterized by binge eating and subsequent purging, usually by induced vomiting and/or use of laxatives.

Eating Disorders

One result of dissatisfaction with body image is that many teenagers, mostly girls, eat erratically or ingest drugs (especially diet pills) to lose weight; others, mostly boys, take steroids to increase muscle mass. Eating disorders are rare in childhood but increase dramatically at puberty, accompanied by distorted body image, food obsession, and depression (Bulik et al., 2008; Hrabosky & Thomas, 2008).

Individual adolescents sometimes switch from obsessive dieting to overeating to overexercising and back again. Obesity is a problem at every age, discussed in Chapters 8 and 11. Here we describe two other eating disorders that are common in adolescence.

Anorexia Nervosa

Some individuals suffer from **anorexia nervosa,** a disorder characterized by voluntary starvation that leads to death by organ failure or suicide for between 5 and 20 percent of sufferers. If someone's body mass index (BMI) is 18 or lower, or if she (or, less often, he) loses more than 10 percent of body weight within a month or two, anorexia is suspected. According to DSM-IV, anorexia is officially diagnosed when four symptoms are evident:

1. Refusal to maintain a weight that is at least 85 percent of normal BMI
2. Intense fear of weight gain
3. Disturbed body perception and denial of the problem
4. Absence of menstruation (in adolescent and adult females)

Although anorexia existed in earlier centuries (think of the saints who refused all food), the disease was undiagnosed until about 1950, when some high-achieving, upper-class young women became so emaciated that they died. Soon anorexia became evident among younger women (the rate spikes at puberty and again in emerging adulthood), among men, and in every nation and ethnic group (Chao et al., 2008). Certain alleles increase the risk of anorexia (J. K. Young, 2010), as is evident from the higher rates among people who have a close relative, especially a monozygotic twin, with anorexia or severe depression. Probably many genes make a person more vulnerable to eating disorders, and certainly many people at genetic risk never develop anorexia: Context is pivotal.

Bulimia Nervosa

About three times as common as anorexia is **bulimia nervosa,** a disorder clinically present in 1 to 3 percent of female teenagers and young adults in the United States. The person with bulimia overeats compulsively, wolfing down thousands of calories within an hour or two, and then purges via vomiting or laxatives. Most are close to normal in weight and therefore unlikely to starve. However, they risk serious health problems, including damage to their gastrointestinal systems and cardiac arrest from electrolyte imbalance (Shannon, 2007).

Three things combine to warrant a clinical diagnosis of bulimia:

1. Bingeing and purging at least once a week for three months
2. Uncontrollable urges to overeat
3. A distorted perception of body size

These symptoms and those for anorexia are from DSM-IV, the fourth edition of the *Diagnostic and Statistical Manual of Mental Disorders,* published by the American Psychiatric Association. Many experts think that eating disorders are much more widespread among adolescents than these official statistics and listed symptoms portray. For instance, 6 percent of U.S. eleventh-grade girls and 3 percent of the boys vomited or took laxatives to lose weight in the month before a 2009 survey (MMWR, June 4, 2010). For all eating problems, treatment that begins in early adolescence has a better chance of halting the problem than treatment begun later on (Keel & Brown, 2010).

Origins of Disordered Eating

Many adolescents have unhealthy eating habits: They try new diets, go without food for 24 hours (as did 15 percent of U.S. high school girls and 7 percent of the boys in 2009), or take diet drugs (6 percent) (MMWR, June 4, 2010). Some become so hungry that they binge; some become anorexic; many eat oddly (e.g., only rice or only carrots) for awhile.

Each episode of bingeing, purging, or fasting makes the next one easier. A combination of causes leads to obesity, anorexia, or bulimia, with at least five general elements—cultural images, stress, puberty, hormones, and childhood patterns—all making disordered eating more likely (Shannon, 2007).

One family practice reduces the risk of adolescent eating disorders: eating together during childhood (Franko et al., 2008). It is not known whether family cohesion and routine are the protective factors or whether family meals directly encourage nutrition. Nonetheless, developmentalists agree that healthy eating begins with childhood habits and family routines. Some overweight or underweight infants never develop nutritional problems, but the older an overweight or underweight child is, the more likely an eating disorder will occur in adolescence.

SUMMING UP

All adolescents are vulnerable to poor nutrition; few are well nourished. Insufficient consumption of iron and calcium is particularly common, as fast food and nutrient-poor snacks often replace family meals. Both boys and girls often choose junk food instead of a balanced diet, in part because they are concerned about peer opinions regarding their appearance. The combination of nutritional deficiencies, peer culture, and anxiety about body image sometimes causes obesity, anorexia, or bulimia, influenced by heredity and childhood patterns. All adolescent nutrition problems have lifelong, potentially life-threatening, consequences. ■

>> The Transformations of Puberty

Every body part changes during puberty. For simplicity, the study of this transformation from child to adult is traditionally divided into two parts: growth and sexuality. We will use that division here. We will also describe a third transformation—changes in the adolescent brain. All three relate to adolescent cognitive and psychosocial development, described in Chapters 15 and 16, making this chapter division somewhat artificial. However, it is useful to consider each major transformation separately.

Growing Bigger and Stronger

The first set of changes is called the **growth spurt**—a sudden, uneven jump in the size of almost every body part, turning children into adults. Growth proceeds from the extremities to the core (the opposite of the earlier proximodistal growth). Thus, fingers and toes lengthen before hands and feet, hands and feet before arms and legs, arms and legs before the torso. This growth is not always symmetrical: One foot, one breast, or even one ear may grow later than the other.

growth spurt The relatively sudden and rapid physical growth that occurs during puberty. Each body part increases in size on a schedule: Weight usually precedes height, and growth of the limbs precedes growth of the torso.

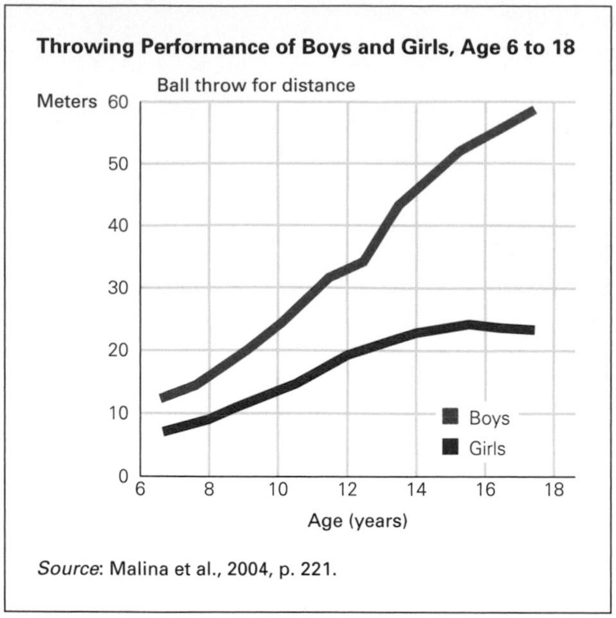

FIGURE 14.3

Big Difference All children experience an increase in muscles during puberty, but gender differences are much more apparent in some gross motor skills than in others. For instance, upper-arm strength increases dramatically only in boys.

Observation Quiz At what age does the rate of increase in the average boy's muscle strength accelerate? (see answer, page 427)

Because the torso is the last body part to grow, many pubescent children are temporarily big-footed, long-legged, and short-waisted. If young teenagers complain that their jeans don't fit, they are probably correct, even if those same jeans fit when their parents bought them a month earlier. (At least the parents had advance warning when they had to buy their children's shoes in the adult section.)

Sequence: Weight, Height, Muscles

As the bones lengthen and harden (visible on X-rays) and the growth spurt begins, children eat more and gain weight. Exactly when, where, and how much weight they gain depends on heredity, hormones, diet, exercise, and gender. For instance, at age 17, the average girl has twice the percentage of body fat as her male classmate, whose increased weight is mostly muscle (Roche & Sun, 2003).

A height spurt follows the weight spurt, then a year or two later a muscle spurt occurs. Thus, the pudginess and clumsiness of early puberty are usually gone by late adolescence. (The young teenager who took nutritional supplements or lifted weights could have simply waited a year or two.)

Arm muscles develop more in boys. On average, a boy's arm muscles are twice as strong at age 18 as at age 8, enabling him to throw a ball four times as far (Malina et al., 2004) (see Figure 14.3). Other muscles are gender-neutral. For instance, both sexes run faster with each year of adolescence, with boys not much faster than girls (unless the girls choose to slow down) (see Figure 14.4).

Organ Growth

In both sexes, organs mature. Lungs triple in weight; consequently, adolescents breathe more deeply and slowly. The heart doubles in size as the heartbeat slows, decreasing the pulse rate while increasing blood pressure (Malina et al., 2004). Consequently, endurance improves: Some teenagers can run for miles or dance for hours. Red blood cells increase in both sexes, but dramatically more in boys, which aids oxygen transport during intense exercise. By age 18, the normal boy is less likely to become winded during a long race (Malina et al., 2004).

Both weight and height increase *before* muscles and internal organs: Athletic training and weight lifting should be tailored to an adolescent's size the previous year, to protect immature muscles and organs. Sports injuries are the most common school accidents, and they increase at puberty, partly because the height spurt precedes increases in bone mass, making young adolescents particularly vulnerable to fractures (Mathison & Agrawal, 2011).

Only one organ system, the lymphoid system (which includes the tonsils and adenoids), *decreases* in size, so teenagers are less susceptible to respiratory ailments. Mild asthma, for example, often switches off at puberty (Busse & Lemanske, 2005), and teenagers have fewer colds than younger children do. This is aided by growth of the larynx, which gives deeper voices to both sexes, dramatically noticeable in boys.

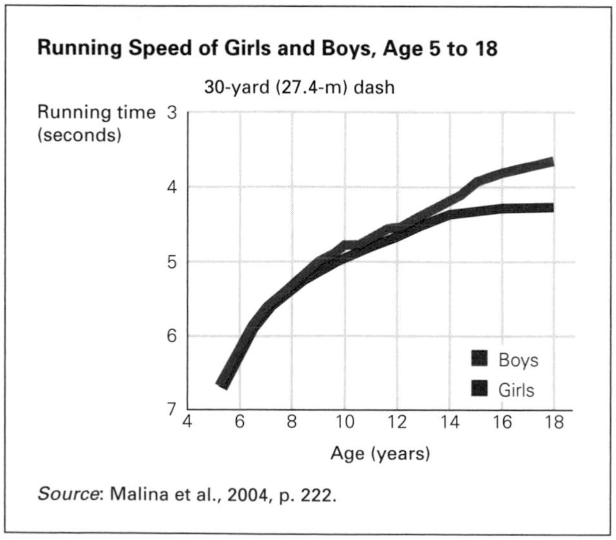

FIGURE 14.4

Little Difference Both sexes develop longer and stronger legs duing puberty.

Another organ system, the skin, becomes oilier, sweatier, and more prone to acne. Hair also changes. During puberty, hair on the head and limbs becomes coarser and darker. New hair grows under arms, on faces, and over sex organs (pubic hair, from the same Latin root as *puberty*). Visible facial and chest hair is sometimes considered a sign of manliness, although hairiness in either sex depends on genes as well as on hormones. Girls pluck or dye any facial hair they see; boys proudly shave or grow sideburns, soul patches, chinstraps, moustaches, and so on—with specifics dependent on culture and cohort. Girls shave their legs and sometimes their pubic hair before wearing a bikini.

Although everyone's hair changes texture at puberty, many teenagers use their head hair to indicate gender and autonomy. Often teenagers cut, style, or grow their hair in ways their parents do not like, as a sign of independence. To become more attractive, many adolescents spend considerable time, money, and thought on their visible hair—growing, gelling, shaving, curling, straightening, highlighting, brushing, combing, styling, dyeing, wetting, drying . . . In many ways, hair is more than a growth characteristic; it becomes a display of sexuality.

Sexual Maturation

Now we turn to the physical changes that are universal, not cultural, transforming boys into men and girls into women.

Sexual Characteristics

The body characteristics that are directly involved in conception and pregnancy are called **primary sex characteristics.** During puberty, every primary sex organ (the ovaries, the uterus, the penis, and the testes) increases dramatically in size and matures in function. By the end of the process, reproduction is possible.

primary sex characteristics The parts of the body that are directly involved in reproduction, including the vagina, uterus, ovaries, testicles, and penis.

secondary sex characteristics Physical traits that are not directly involved in reproduction but that indicate sexual maturity, such as a man's beard and a woman's breasts.

At the same time as maturation of the primary sex characteristics, secondary sex characteristics develop. **Secondary sex characteristics** are bodily features that do not directly affect fertility (hence they are secondary) but that signify masculinity or femininity. One such characteristic is shape. Young boys and girls have similar shapes, but at puberty, males widen at the shoulders and grow about 5 inches taller than females, while girls develop breasts and a wider pelvis. Breasts and broad hips are often considered signs of womanhood, but neither is required for conception; thus, they are secondary, not primary, sex characteristics.

The pattern of hair growth at the scalp line (widow's peak), the prominence of the larynx (Adam's apple), and several other anatomical features tend to differ for men and women—all secondary sex characteristics that few people notice. As just explained, facial hair increases in both sexes, but it is affected by sex hormones as well as genes and is a secondary sex characteristic.

Secondary sex characteristics are important psychologically, if not biologically. Consider breasts. Many adolescent girls buy "minimizer," "maximizer," "training," or "shaping" bras in the hope that they can conform their breasts to an idealized body image. During the same years, many boys are horrified to notice a swelling around their nipples—a normal and temporary result of the erratic hormones of early puberty. If a boy's breast growth is very disturbing, drugs can reduce the swelling, although many doctors prefer to let time, rather than tamoxifen, deal with the problem (Derman et al., 2003).

© HENRYK T. KAISER / AGE FOTOSTOCK

Competition Adolescent boys not only get arm muscles, they also have hormones that encourage them to compete—in sports, in body function, and in "scoring with girls."

Sexual Activity

The primary and secondary sex characteristics just described are not the only manifestations of the sex hormones. Fantasizing, flirting, hand-holding, staring, standing, sitting, walking, displaying, and touching are all done in particular ways to reflect gender, availability, and culture. As already explained, hormones trigger thoughts and emotions, but the social context shapes thoughts into enjoyable fantasies, shameful preoccupations, frightening impulses, or actual contact (see Figure 14.5).

FIGURE 14.5

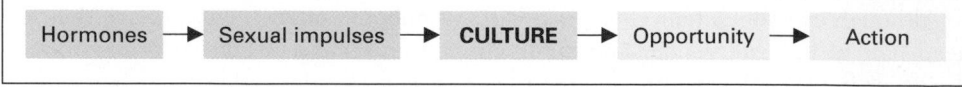

Hormones → Sexual impulses → **CULTURE** → Opportunity → Action

A recent study on sexual behaviors such as hand-holding and cuddling among young adolescents found that biological maturation was only one factor in whether or not such activities occurred: Especially among young European Americans, those girls with lower self-esteem were more likely to engage in sexual intimacy (Hipwell et al., 2010).

Regarding sex-related impulses, some experts believe that boys are more influenced by hormones and girls by culture (Baumeister & Blackhart, 2007). Perhaps. If a relationship includes sexual intimacy, girls seem more concerned than boys are about the depth of the romance (Zani & Cicognani, 2006). Girls hope their partners say, "I'll love you forever"; boys like to hear, "I want you now."

However, everyone is influenced by both hormones and society, biology and culture. All adolescents have sexual interests they did not previously have (biology), which produce behaviors that teenagers in other nations would not do (culture) (Moore & Rosenthal, 2006). Since only girls can become pregnant, their wish for long-term commitment may be a consequence of biology, not culture. If this is so, the gender difference (girls' wanting love versus boys' seeking sex) may disappear as contraception makes unwanted pregnancy rare.

The gender gap in experience is narrowing. It has already reversed in some European nations, including Norway. In 1987, Norwegian boys averaged their first coitus almost a year younger than girls did; in 2002, girls were half a year younger than boys were at the time of first intercourse (Stigum et al., 2009).

It may seem that choosing sexual partners is a private and personal matter. Yet culture rules. For example, most North American find partners who are about the same age as they are (Zani & Cicognani, 2006), but in some nations girls' first partners are significantly older, and in other nations boys' first partners are older.

KEVIN MOLONEY / THE NEW YORK TIMES / REDUX

A Daughter's Promise At a "purity ball" in Colorado, a father reads the pledge signed by his 14-year-old daughter, in which she promises that she will abstain from sex until she marries. Young adolescents who take a virginity pledge are more likely than their peers to be celibate in high school. However, they are also more likely to become parents before they graduate from college.

SPENCER GRANT / PHOTO EDIT

Nature and Nurture These twin girls pray while holding hands with their godparents as part of their quinceañera, a coming-of-age celebration for 15-year-old Latinas. However, they share chronological age and Hispanic culture—but only half of their genes. Their biological, temperamental differences may explain why they wear their nearly identical dresses in quite different ways.

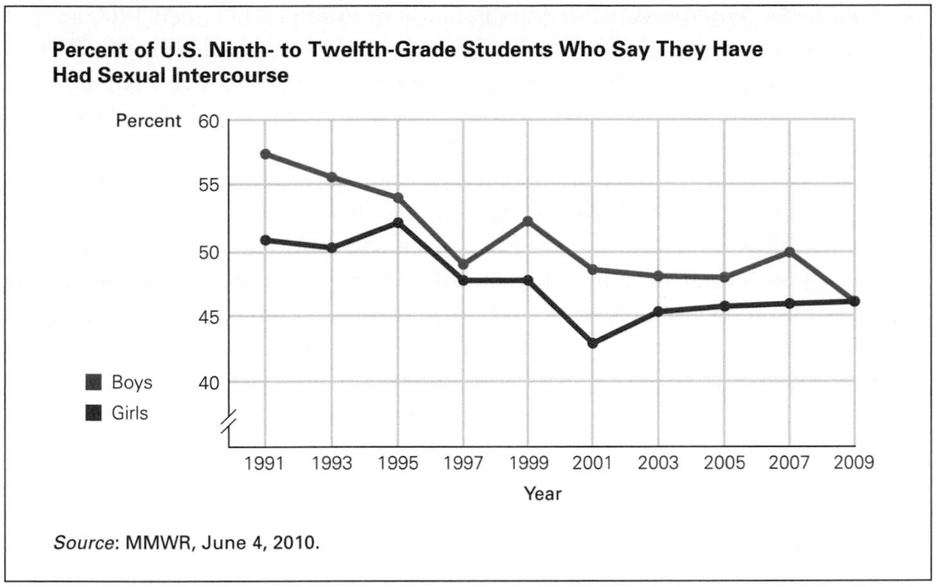

FIGURE 14.6

Boys and Girls Together Boys tend to be somewhat more sexually experienced than girls during the high school years, but since the Youth Risk Behavior Survey began in 1991, the overall trend has been toward equality in rates of sexual activity.

Cohort and culture affect sexual activity. For most of the twentieth century, surveys in North America reported sexual activity among adolescents at younger and younger ages. This trend reversed in the 1990s. In 1991, 62 percent of U.S. eleventh-graders said they had had intercourse, but in 2009 only 53 percent said so. Rates vary by state as well, from a low of 39 percent of Idaho high school students (ninth to twelfth grade) to a high of 61 percent in Mississippi (MMWR, June 4, 2010).

>> Answer to Observation Quiz (from page 424) About age 13. This is most obvious in ball throwing (Figure 14.3), but it is also apparent in the 30-yard dash (Figure 14.4).

During the same time period, the double standard (with boys expected to be more sexually active than girls) decreased, and today boys and girls are quite similar in reported sexual activity (see Figure 14.6). These gender trends are apparent within every ethnic group, but the rates of both activity and change differ. For high school students between 1991 and 2009, rates of sexual experience among African Americans decreased 16 percentage points (from 81 to 65 percent); among European Americans, they were down 8 percentage points (from 50 to 42 percent); among Latinos, down 4 percentage points (from 53 to 49 percent) (MMWR, June 4, 2010).

All these examples demonstrate that a universal experience (rising hormones) that produces another universal experience (growth of primary and secondary sex characteristics) is powerfully influenced by cohort, gender, and culture. Other research finds that for any particular adolescent of any group, the sexual activity of his or her close friends is the most powerful influence.

JIM WEST

Pin It on Him Boutonniere, corsage, formal shirt with matching tie, bare arms—all are common at U.S. high school proms, including here, at Notre Dame in Harper Woods, Michigan. Yet these sights are unknown to most 17-year-olds in other nations. Despite such cultural oddities and this once-in-a-lifetime moment, Mariel West and John Felczak are evidence of a worldwide phenomenon: sexual attraction in late adolescence.

Problems with Adolescent Sex

One of the changes in research on sexual activity is appreciation that adolescents are sexual beings. Sexual interest and interaction are normal, and researchers have found that healthy adult relationships are more likely when shame and fear do not haunt adolescent impulses (Tolman & McClelland, 2011). Teenage sexual impulses need to be channeled and guided, and reproduction controlled, but it is a mistake to make teenagers feel depraved or evil if they experience sexual urges. Before focusing specifically on hazards, we should note that several "problems" are less problematic now than in earlier decades. Here are three specifics:

- *Teen births have decreased in every nation.* For example, between 1960 and 2010, the adolescent birth rate in China was cut in half (reducing the United Nations' projections of the world's population in 2050 by about 1 billion). In the United States, in 1991, the birth rate per 1,000 girls aged 15 to 17 was 39; in 2009, it was 20.
- *The use of "protection" has risen.* Contraception, particularly condom use among adolescent boys, has increased markedly in most nations since 1990 (Santelli & Melnikas, 2010). The U.S. Youth Risk Behavior Survey found that 70 percent of sexually active ninth-grade boys had used a condom during their most recent intercourse (MMWR, June 4, 2010).
- *The teen abortion rate is down.* In the United States, the teen abortion rate is about half the rate 20 years earlier (for all girls aged 15 to 19, the rate was 15 per 1,000 in 2007) (MMWR, February 25, 2011).

Now we focus on biological problems that result from adolescent sexual activity—pregnancy and infections—and on sexual abuse.

Sex Too Soon

Sex can, of course, be thrilling and affirming, a bonding experience. However, compared to a century ago, adolescent sexual activity—especially if it results in birth—is more hazardous because four circumstances have changed:

1. Earlier puberty and weaker social taboos mean teens have sexual impulses and experiences at younger ages. Early sex correlates with depression and drug abuse.
2. Most teenage mothers have no husbands to help them. A century ago, teenage mothers were married; now, in the United States, 85 percent are unwed.
3. Raising a child has become more complex and expensive, and fewer mothers of teenagers are available to help (many are employed).
4. Sexually transmitted infections are more common and dangerous.

Rosie Will Be Fine Monica, here with her dog Rosie, is a mom-to-be—as are 13 percent of her female classmates at Timkin High School in Canton, Ohio. She is one of the fortunate ones; already a senior, she will probably earn her diploma. Plus, she is six months past conception, so the fetus is likely to be healthy. Teenagers typically welcome their unplanned babies but tend to have trouble raising them. This child will reach puberty before Monica is 30; their mutual immaturity will increase the child's risk of depression, delinquency, and another teen pregnancy.

AP TONY DEJAK

As you just read, teen births are declining, as are teen abortions. However, the U.S. rate of adolescent pregnancy is the highest of any developed nation (true among every ethnic group). If a pregnant girl is under 16 (most are not), she is more likely to experience complications—including spontaneous or induced abortion, high blood pressure, stillbirth, preterm birth, and a low-birthweight newborn—than are teenagers who are age 16 or older. The risks are reduced with age, but they do not disappear: Babies born to young parents (even as "old" as 17 or 18) have higher rates of medical, educational, and social problems lifelong.

There are many reasons in addition to maternal age for these hazards. Poverty and lack of education correlate with teenage pregnancy and with every problem just listed (Santelli & Melnikas, 2010). Beyond that, younger pregnant teenagers are often malnourished and postpone prenatal care (Borkowski et al., 2007). After birth, adolescents are less likely to be the responsive mothers that newborns need, so insecure attachment (see Chapter 7) is more common. These problems are not inevitable, but some are a direct consequence of chronological age: Immature bodies are less ready for pregnancy and birth, and it is harder to meet the nutritional needs for two growing people than for one.

Early intercourse also risks psychosocial problems later on. A study of 3,923 adult women in the United States found that those

who voluntarily had sex before age 16 were more likely to divorce later on, whether or not that early sex resulted in pregnancy and whether or not they later married that man. The same study found that adolescents of any age whose first sexual experience was unwanted (either "really didn't want" or "had mixed feelings about") were also more likely to later experience divorce (Paik, 2011). Forced sex is much worse, of course, as now explained.

Sexual Abuse

Teenage births are risky, but sexual abuse is devastating: It harms development lifelong. **Child sexual abuse** is defined as any sexual activity (including fondling) between a juvenile and an adult, with age 18 the usual demarcation (although legal age varies by state). The most common time for sexual abuse is when the first stirrings of puberty occur, with girls particularly vulnerable—although boys are also at risk. Puberty not only increases the odds for sexual abuse, it also makes the emotional consequences worse because young adolescents are typically confused about their own sexual urges and identity (Graber et al., 2010). Virtually every adolescent problem, including early pregnancy, drug abuse, eating disorders, and suicide, is more frequent in adolescents who have been sexually abused.

child sexual abuse Any erotic activity that arouses an adult and excites, shames, or confuses a child, whether or not the victim protests and whether or not genital contact is involved.

This is true worldwide. The United Nations reports that millions of girls in their early teens are forced into marriage, genital surgery, or prostitution (often across national borders) each year (Pinheiro, 2006). Exact numbers are elusive. Almost every nation has laws against child sexual abuse, but these laws are rarely enforced, and sensationalism about a single horrific case often crowds out systemic efforts to prevent, monitor, and eliminate the problem (Davidson, 2005).

In the United States, rates of sex abuse are declining (see Table 14.1), perhaps because adolescents are becoming wiser about sexual activity (Finkelhor & Jones, 2004). Evidence of their wisdom is condom use (a sign that at least one member of the couple is sexually informed and acting responsibly). Teenagers and young adults are more likely to use condoms correctly than older adults are (see Figure 14.7). (Specifics of sex education are discussed in Chapter 16.)

TABLE 14.1 Age and Sex Abuse: United States, 2007

Age	Number of Sex-Abuse Victims	Percent of Malreatment That Is Sex Abuse
Less than 1 year	315	0.3%
1–3	3,249	2.2
4–7	13,137	7.4
8–11	13,459	9.5
12–15	19,848	14.5
16–17	6,084	13.5

Source: U.S. Department of Health and Human Services, 2010.

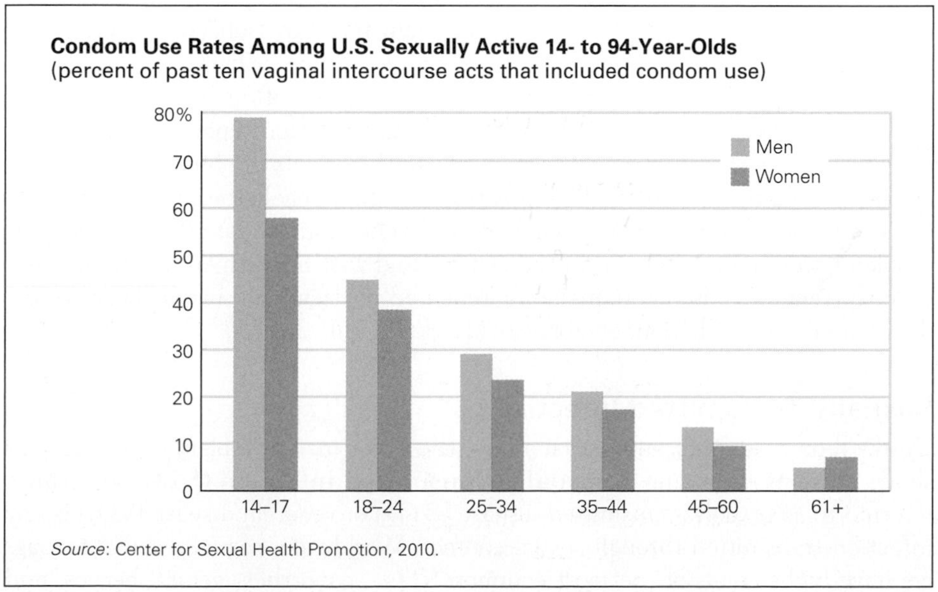

FIGURE 14.7

Pleasure and Protection Teenagers are much more likely to use condoms than are older adults, who probably never used them when they were young. This study found that sexual pleasure did not correlate with condom use. However, a negative correlation was found between condom use and having a steady partner—another reason for the age differences.

Research Design

Scientists: Penelope K. Trickett, Jennie G. Noll, and Frank W. Putnam.

Publication: *Development and Psychopathology* (2011).

Participants: The Child Protection Service in Washington, D.C., referred 84 girls, ages 6 to 16, who had recently been sexually abused. Most (70 percent) had been vaginally or anally penetrated; the abuser was usually (60 percent of the time) their father or stepfather. The scientists found a comparison group from the same neighborhoods who had not been sexually abused (16 percent of the original comparison group were excluded after the first in-depth interview because they had been sexually abused but had not reported it). They also interviewed the caretakers of the girls. In later interviews, almost half of the original sample had had children, who became participants as well.

Design: Participants were interviewed six times over 23 years, with 96 percent of the sample interviewed at least once after age 18. (This retention rate is much higher than for most longitudinal samples; the scientists used many ways to find their participants, including searching MySpace and Facebook.) Interviews lasted three to four hours, were confidential, and assessed dozens of traits and characteristics. Caregivers and offspring were also interviewed, confidentially.

Results: Every trait examined showed a far higher incidence of problems in the victims than in their nonvictimized peers. That included attitudes directly related to sex abuse (e.g., most of those abused by their biological fathers thought of sex as dirty, shameful, dangerous) and behaviors seemingly unconnected (e.g., although their body weight was in the normal range in childhood, 42 percent were obese in their 20s). Cognitive development—school achievement as well as language use—was also impaired. Among the most troubling results were much higher rates of self-harm, aggression, and repeated victimization—both sexual and physical abuse.

The children of those who had been abused often experienced problems. In fact, 3 of their 78 children died in infancy, a much higher rate than usual, and 9 were permanently removed from their mothers.

Early in this chapter, we noted that the HPA system regulates puberty and many other physiological responses. Many of the victims had signs of a breakdown in the HPA regulatory system, altering their cortisol responses. That produced heightened stress reactions in early adolescence but then abnormally low stress responses in adulthood.

Major conclusion: Severe sexual abuse damages every aspect of development, affecting victims not only in childhood and adolescence but also in adulthood. Many become victims again as well as inadequate parents. None of this is inevitable, however; a few participants escaped these problems, especially if their own caretakers were wonderful (few were).

Comments: These scientists have made major contributions to our understanding of sexual abuse, which was once ignored or considered less harmful than physical abuse. This longitudinal research on a volatile group who move frequently, are isolated, and disappear for follow-up is commendable. Part of the researchers' success is attributable to their dedication, which included sending birthday and holiday cards to their participants even when funding temporarily disappeared. These results should lead to better long-term treatment of sex-abuse victims (hopefully better than the treatment these participants received—they averaged only four visits to a therapist). The researchers believe that effective treatment would markedly reduce the rate of rape, domestic violence, and child neglect.

However, many of the youngest adolescents remain ignorant, and almost all depend on adults to protect them. Few schools teach anything about sex until high school, and even then, the curriculum may be only about the biology of sex and disease. Meanwhile, peers brag and lie about their sexual exploits, and the teen media virtually never discuss healthy sexuality (Hust et al., 2008). That leaves youth to depend on their families—the worst possible source of information and protection for sexually abused adolescents, since the abusers are almost always family members. Relatives (including the abuser) sometimes blame the child. Many children trust their family members, which makes them doubly distressed later on, when they realize what happened (Clancy, 2010).

Abusers often isolate adolescents from their peers, depriving them of the friendships and romances that aid in developing a healthy and satisfying life. As with other types of maltreatment, the consequences extend far beyond the event. Young people who are sexually exploited tend to fear sexual relationships and to devalue themselves lifelong.

A longitudinal study of reported victims (all girls) of child sex abuse traced their development for 23 years (see the Research Design). The abuse of these girls began at age 7½, on average, and continued for two years, although some of them had experienced a briefer, usually violent, rape. (Slightly older girls and boys are more often abused, but their abuse is less often reported.) In order to isolate the effects of abuse, the researchers also traced the development of girls from the same backgrounds (SES, ethnicity, and so on) who were not sexually abused. They found that all the adolescent problems were more common in the victims and that impairment continued and even worsened in adulthood, including repeated physical and sexual abuse, severe depression, drug addiction, and obesity (Trickett et al., 2011a).

Sexually Transmitted Infections

sexually transmitted infection (STI) A disease spread by sexual contact, including syphilis, gonorrhea, genital herpes, chlamydia, and HIV.

Unlike teen pregnancy and sexual abuse, the other major problem of teenage sex shows no signs of abating. A **sexually transmitted infection (STI)** (sometimes referred to as sexually transmitted disease [STD] or venereal disease [VD]) is any infection transmitted through sexual contact. Worldwide, sexually active teenagers have higher rates of the most common STIs—gonorrhea, genital herpes, and chlamydia—than do sexually active people of any other age group (World Health Organization, 2005). In the United States, 15- to 24-year-olds constitute only one-fourth of the sexually active population but account for half of all sexually transmitted infections. On average for urban U.S. teenagers, an STI is diagnosed only two years after intercourse begins (Tu et al., 2009).

Especially for Health Practitioners How might you encourage adolescents to seek treatment for STIs? (see response, page 432)

Those who have sexual intercourse before age 16 are twice as likely to catch an infection as are those who begin sexual activity at age 20 (Ryan et al., 2008). One reason is biological. Fully developed women have some natural biological defenses against STIs; this is less true for pubescent girls, who are more likely to develop any STI they are exposed to, including HIV/AIDS (World Health Organization, 2005). In addition, if symptoms appear, sexually active teens hesitate to seek diagnosis or alert their partners. In cultures or families where teenage sex is forbidden, adolescents avoid treatment for STIs until pain requires it. Adolescents with same-sex partners are especially reluctant to find treatment if their community considers homosexuality shameful.

There are hundreds of STIs (James, 2007). *Chlamydia* is the most frequently reported one; it often begins without symptoms, yet it can cause permanent infertility. A laboratory test can detect chlamydia, and it can be treated and cured, but many young people avoid doctors. Worse is *human papillomavirus (HPV)*, which has no immediate consequences but, later in life, increases a female's risk of cervical cancer and death. Immunization before the first intercourse makes contracting HPV much less likely, but many parents hesitate to immunize their virginal 11- and 12-year-olds. The interested reader is encouraged to consult Appendix A, p. A-17, as well as other sources.

play it
safe
LSC
ABCD
protect
yourself
Abstain
say no to sex
Be faithful
or true to one partner
Condom
always use one
Delay
it's worth the wait
take control!
SEAN SPRAGUE / THE IMAGE WORKS

No Safer? Educational posters and even intense educational programs have little proven effect on the incidence of AIDS among adolescents. This poster was displayed outside an HIV testing center in Windhoek, Namibia, a country that has one of the highest HIV infection rates in the world.

National variations in laws and rates of STIs are large, with rates among U.S. teenagers higher than in any other medically advanced nation. Internationally, a comparison of 30 nations found that French teenagers were among the most likely to use condoms, while those in the United States were least likely to do so (MMWR, June 4, 2010; Nic Gabhainn et al., 2009) (see Table 14.2). One reason may be that, by law, every French high school (including Catholic ones) is required to provide students with free, confidential medical care as well as condoms; by contrast, providing either medical care or condoms is illegal at many U.S. schools.

TABLE 14.2 Condom Use Among 15-Year-Olds (Tenth Grade)

Country	Sexually Active (% of total)	Used Condom at Last Intercourse (% of those sexually active)
France	20	84
Israel	14	72
Canada	23	78
United States	41	68
England	29	83
Russia	33	75

Sources: MMWR, June 4, 2010; Nic Gabhainn et al., 2009.

Neurological Development

Like the other parts of the body, different parts of the brain grow at different rates (Blakemore, 2008). The limbic system, including the amygdala, where intense fear and excitement originate, matures before the prefrontal cortex, where planning, emotional regulation, and impulse control occur. Myelination and maturation continue in the entire brain but in sequence, proceeding from the inner brain to the cortex and from back to front (Sowell et al., 2007). The result is that

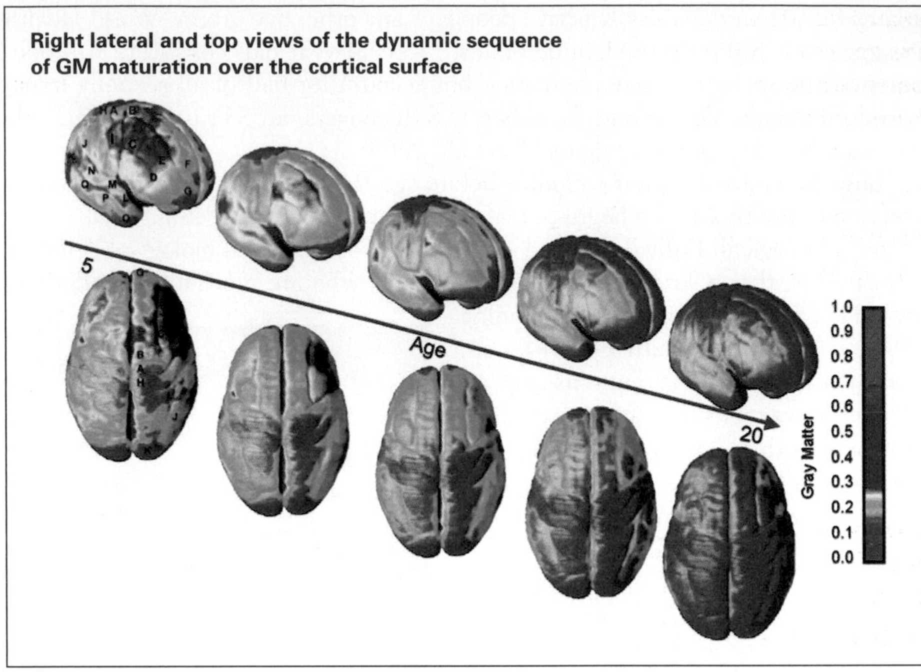

NITIN GOGTAY ET AL. / NATIONAL ACADEMY OF SCIENCES, USA

Same People, But Not the Same Brain These brain scans are part of a longitudinal study that repeatedly compares the proportion of gray matter from childhood through adolescence. Gray matter is reduced as white matter increases, in part because pruning during the teen years (the last two pairs of images here) allows intellectual connections to build. As the authors of one study that included this chart explain, teenagers may "look like an adult, but cognitively they are not there yet" (K. Powell, 2006, p. 865).

the instinctual and emotional areas of the adolescent brain develop ahead of the reflective, analytic areas. Furthermore, pubertal hormones target the amygdala directly, whereas the cortex responds more to age and experience than to hormones. As a consequence, early puberty means emotional rushes, unchecked by caution.

This is evident via brain scans. Emotional control, revealed by fMRI studies, is not fully developed until adulthood (Luna et al., 2010). When compared with 18- to 23-year-olds, 14- to 15-year-olds show heightened arousal in the brain's reward centers, making them seek excitement and pleasure (Van Leijenhorst et al., 2010).

Many types of psychopathology that originate in the brain increase at puberty. Most vulnerable are those who experience early puberty, because they must cope with the stresses of adolescence long before their prefrontal cortexes mature. As two experts explain, "The higher rates of psychopathology among early maturers are expected because their slow developing neurocognitive systems are mismatched with the fast-approaching social and affective challenges at the onset of puberty" (Ge & Natsuaki, 2009, p. 329).

Caution Needed

Adolescents are not the only ones who sometimes forget caution when excitement rises: Developmentalists, journalists, and the general public are vulnerable to the same problem. Scientists try to be careful: The same pair of researchers just quoted regarding prefrontal immaturity suggest other explanations as well (Ge & Natsuaki, 2009), although the uneven neurological maturity seems most plausible.

However, as noted in Chapter 6, the fMRI, the PET scan, and other measures of neurological activity are expensive and complex. Furthermore, "the images generated by such methods may have a power to captivate that reaches beyond their power to explain" (Miller, 2008, p. 1413). Reliable, longitudinal, multidisciplinary, replicated research on the brains of typical 10- to 17-year-olds is scarce. Probably the adolescent problem is an imbalance in the rate of growth in the various parts of the brain, not in immaturity of any one part (Casey et al., 2011).

Although caution is warranted, recent discoveries about the adolescent brain are exciting. The fact that the frontal lobes (prefrontal cortex) are the last to ma-

>> Response for Health Practitioners (from page 431): Many adolescents are intensely concerned about privacy and fearful of adult interference. This means your first task is to convince the teenagers that you are nonjudgmental and that everything is confidential.

ture may explain something that has long bewildered adults: Many adolescents are driven by the excitement of new experiences, sensations, and peers—forgetting the caution that their parents have tried to instill (Steinberg, 2008). The following is one example.

A CASE TO STUDY

"What Were You Thinking?"

Laurence Steinberg is a noted expert on adolescent thinking. He is also a father.

> When my son, Benjamin, was 14, he and three of his friends decided to sneak out of the house where they were spending the night and visit one of their girlfriends at around two in the morning. When they arrived at the girl's house, they positioned themselves under her bedroom window, threw pebbles against her windowpanes, and tried to scale the side of the house. Modern technology, unfortunately, has made it harder to play Romeo these days. The boys set off the house's burglar alarm, which activated a siren and simultaneously sent a direct notification to the local police station, which dispatched a patrol car. When the siren went off, the boys ran down the street and right smack into the police car, which was heading to the girl's home. Instead of stopping and explaining their activity, Ben and his friends scattered and ran off in different directions through the neighborhood. One of the boys was caught by the police and taken back to his home, where his parents were awakened and the boy questioned.
>
> I found out about this affair the following morning, when the girl's mother called our home to tell us what Ben had done. . . . After his near brush with the local police, Ben had returned to the house out of which he had snuck, where he slept soundly until I awakened him with an angry telephone call, telling him to gather his clothes and wait for me in front of his friend's house. On our drive home, after delivering a long lecture about what he had done and about the dangers of running from armed police in the dark when they believe they may have interrupted a burglary, I paused.
>
> "What were you thinking?" I asked.
>
> "That's the problem, Dad," Ben replied, "I wasn't."
>
> *[Steinberg, 2004, pp. 51, 52]*

Steinberg agrees with his son. As he expresses it, "The problem is not that Ben's decision-making was deficient. The problem is that it was nonexistent" (Steinberg, 2004, p. 52). In his analysis, Steinberg points out a characteristic of adolescent thought: When emotions are intense, especially when friends are nearby, the logical part of the brain shuts down. This shutdown is not reflected in questionnaires that require teenagers to respond to paper-and-pencil questions regarding hypothetical dilemmas. On those tests, most teenagers think carefully and answer correctly. They have been taught the risks of sex and drugs in biology or health classes in school. However,

> the prospect of visiting a hypothetical girl from class cannot possibly carry the excitement about the possibility of surprising someone you have a crush on with a visit in the middle of the night. It is easier to put on a hypothetical condom during an act of hypothetical sex than it is to put on a real one when one is in the throes of passion. It is easier to just say no to a hypothetical beer than it is to a cold frosty one on a summer night.
>
> *[Steinberg, 2004, p. 53]*

Ben reached adulthood safely. Some other teenagers, with less cautious police or less diligent parents, do not. Ideally, research on adolescent brains will help protect teens from their dangerous impulses (Monastersky, 2007). Brain immaturity is not the origin of every "troublesome adolescent behavior," but it is true that teenage brains have underdeveloped "response inhibition, emotional regulation, and organization" (Sowell et al., 2007, p. 59) because their prefrontal cortexes are immature.

The normal sequence of brain maturation (limbic system at puberty, then prefrontal cortex by the early 20s) combined with the early onset of puberty means that, for contemporary teenagers, emotions rule behavior for years (Blakemore, 2008; Compas, 2004). The limbic system, unchecked by the slower-maturing prefrontal cortex, makes powerful sensations—loud music, speeding cars, strong drugs—compelling.

It is not that the prefrontal cortex shuts down. In fact, it continues to mature throughout childhood and adolescence, and, when they think about it, adolescents are able to assess risks better than children are (Pfeifer et al., 2011). However, the thoughtful parts of the adolescent brain are less synchronized with the limbic system than they were earlier, and thus emotions from the amygdala are less

NORBERT SCHWERIN / THE IMAGE WORKS

Not Me! A young woman jumps into the Pacific Ocean near Santa Cruz, California, while at a friend's birthday party. The jump is illegal, yet since 1975, 52 people have died taking that leap off these cliffs. Hundreds of young people each year decide that the thrill is worth the risk, aided by what they think are sensible precautions. (Note that she is wearing shoes. Also note that the dog has apparently decided against risking a jump.) As Chapter 17 explains, slightly older adolescents now jump into the Pacific off the California coast using parachutes—even riskier since sharks also live there.

modulated than they were (Pfeifer et al., 2011). It is the balance and coordination between the various parts of the brain that is off-kilter, not the brain itself (Casey et al., 2011).

When stress, arousal, passion, sensory bombardment, drug intoxication, or deprivation is extreme, the adolescent brain is flooded with impulses that might shame adults. As further explained regarding drug abuse in Chapter 16, teenagers brag about being so drunk they were "wasted," "bombed," "smashed"—a state most adults try to avoid and would be ashamed to admit. Also, unlike adults, some teenagers choose to spend a night without sleep, go through a day without eating, exercise in pain, play football after a mild concussion. The parts of the brain dedicated to analysis may be immature until years after the first hormonal rushes and sexual urges, while teenagers have access to fast cars, lethal weapons, and dangerous drugs. As one friend said to a next-door neighbor who had given his son a red convertible for high school graduation, "Why didn't you just give him a loaded gun?"

One example of the cautious part of the brain being overwhelmed by the emotions of the moment comes from teens sending text messages while they are driving. In a survey, 64 percent of U.S. 16- to 17-year-olds say they have been in a car when the driver was texting—a practice that occurs in every state and nation even though it is illegal in many of them (Madden & Lenhart, 2009). More generally, despite quick reflexes and better vision than at later ages, by far the most common cause of teenage death is motor-vehicle accidents. Thoughtless impulses and poor decisions are almost always to blame.

Every decision, from whether to eat a peach to when and where to enroll in college, requires balancing risk and reward, caution and attraction. For everyone, experiences, memories, emotions, and the prefrontal cortex help in choosing to avoid some actions and perform others. Neurological research finds that the reward parts of adolescents' brains (the parts that respond to excitement and pleasure) are far stronger than the inhibition parts (the parts that urge caution) (Van Leijenhorst et al., 2010). That may explain many adolescent actions that seem foolhardy to adults.

Benefits of Adolescent Brain Development

It is easy to be critical of adolescent behavior and then to blame it on hormones, or brains, or the media. Yet remember from Chapter 1 that difference is not always deficit and that gains as well as losses are part of every life development. Thus, the fact that the limbic system develops faster than the prefrontal cortex has benefits as well as hazards.

With increased myelination and slower inhibition, reactions become lightning fast; such speed is valuable in many aspects of life. For instance, adolescent athletes are potential superstars, not only quick but fearless as they steal a base, tackle a fullback, or race when their lungs feel about to burst. Ideally, coaches have the wisdom to channel such bravery. Furthermore, as the reward areas of the brain activate and the production of positive neurotransmitters increases, teenagers become happier. Reaction to a new love, or a first job, or even an A on a term paper can be ecstasy, a joy to be cherished in memory lifelong.

Adolescence is a good time to question tradition and learn new things. Before the brain becomes fully mature (at about age 25) and before another wave of pruning (at about age 18), "young brains have both fast-growing synapses and sections that remain unconnected" (Ruder, 2008, p. 8). This allows new connections to facilitate acquisition of new ideas, words, memories, personality patterns, and dance steps (Keating, 2004).

Synaptic growth enhances moral development as well. Adolescents question their elders and seek to forge their own standards. Values embraced during adolescence are more likely to endure than those acquired later, after brain connections are firmly established. This is an asset if values developed during adolescence are less self-centered than those of children or are more culturally attuned than those of older generations.

In short, several aspects of adolescent brain development can be positive. The fact that the prefrontal cortex is still developing "confers benefits as well as risks. It helps explain the creativity of adolescence and early adulthood, before the brain becomes set in its ways" (Monastersky, 2007, p. A17). The emotional intensity of adolescents "intertwines with the highest levels of human endeavor: passion for ideas and ideals, passion for beauty, passion to create music and art" (Dahl, 2004, p. 21). As a practical application, those who care about the next generation must attend to the life lessons that adolescents are learning. Adults should provide "scaffolding and monitoring" until adolescents' brains can function well on their own (Dahl, quoted in Monastersky, 2007, p. A18).

EPA / CORBIS

Sacred Thread Every religion has some ritual in which young people make a public commitment to their faith. These Hindu boys are receiving the jenoi, a sacred thread that they will wear all their lives. In this initiation ceremony, they shave their heads, wear new robes, and vow to pray three times a day and to study the Vedas, which are the scriptures of Hinduism.

By age 18, not only brains but also bodies can be strong and healthy, as described in this chapter. Most 18-year-olds are capable of hard physical work, problem-free reproduction, and peak athletic performance. Growth and sexual awakening, strength and speed, emotional intensity and hormonal rushes—all of these can be wonderful. Of course, adolescent minds and contexts are not always benign, as the following chapters describe. But before learning about alienation from school, or addiction to drugs, or juvenile delinquency, pause to appreciate the transformations just described.

SUMMING UP

Three transformations of puberty—the growth spurt, sexual differentiation, and brain maturation—are dramatic. Children become men or women, first in physical and sexual growth and then in brain maturation. Growth proceeds from the extremities to the center, so the limbs grow before the internal organs. Increase in weight precedes that in height, which precedes growth of the muscles and of the internal organs. Primary sex characteristics, which are connected to reproduction, and secondary sex characteristics, which signify masculinity or femininity, develop. Both boys and girls experience an increase in sexual interest as their bodies mature and their hormone levels rise. Adolescents' sexual behavior and thoughts are powerfully affected by culture.

The brain develops unevenly, with the limbic system ahead of the prefrontal cortex and the reward centers more active than the cautionary areas. As a result, adolescents are fast and fearless, qualities that may cause trouble or may benefit society. ■

SUMMARY

Puberty Begins

1. Puberty refers to the various changes that transform a child's body into an adult one. Even before the teenage years, biochemical signals from the hypothalamus to the pituitary gland to the adrenal glands (the HPA axis) increase production of testosterone, estrogen, and various other hormones, which causes the body to develop.

2. Some emotional reactions, such as quick mood shifts and thoughts about sex, are directly caused by hormones. Others are caused by reactions (of others and then of the young person) to the physical changes of adolescence.

3. The body rhythms of life, both by the day and by the season, are regulated by hormones. In adolescence, these changes often result in sleep deprivation, partly because the natural circadian rhythm makes teenagers wide awake at night.

4. Puberty normally begins anytime from about age 8 to about age 14, most often between ages 10 and 13. The young person's sex, genetic background, body fat, and level of family stress all contribute to this variation in timing.

5. Girls generally begin and end the process of puberty before boys do, although the time gap in sexual maturity is much shorter than the two-year gender gap in reaching peak height.

6. Adolescents who reach puberty earlier or later than their friends experience additional stresses. Generally (depending on culture, community, and cohort), early-maturing girls and late-maturing boys have a particularly difficult time.

Nutrition

7. To sustain body growth, many adolescents consume large quantities of food, although they do not always make healthy choices. One reason for poor nutrition is the desire to lose (or, less often, gain) weight because of anxiety about body image.

8. Although eating disorders—overeating, anorexia, and bulimia—are not usually diagnosed until early adulthood, their precursors are evident during puberty. Many adolescents eat too much of the wrong foods or too little food overall.

The Transformations of Puberty

9. The growth spurt is an acceleration of growth in every part of the body. Peak weight usually precedes peak height, which is then followed by peak muscle growth. The lungs and the heart also increase in size and capacity.

10. Male–female differences become apparent at puberty. The maturation of primary sex characteristics means that by age 13 or so, after experiencing menarche or spermarche, teenagers are capable of reproducing.

11. Secondary sex characteristics are not directly involved in reproduction but signify that the child is becoming a man or a woman. Body shape, breasts, voice, body hair, and numerous other features differentiate males from females. Sexual activity is influenced more by culture than by physiology.

12. Among the problems that adolescents face is the tendency to become sexually active before their bodies and minds are truly ready. Pregnancy before age 16 takes a physical toll on a growing girl, and STIs at any age can lead to infertility and even death.

13. Sexual abuse, which includes any sexually provocative activity that involves a juvenile and an adult, is more likely to occur in early adolescence than at other ages. Girls are most often victims; the perpetrators are most often family members.

14. Various parts of the brain mature during puberty and the following decade. The regions dedicated to emotional arousal (including the amygdala) mature before those that regulate and rationalize emotional expression (the prefrontal cortex).

15. Because of the sequence of brain development, many adolescents seek intense emotional experiences, untempered by rational thought. For the same reasons, adolescents are quick to react, explore, and learn. As a result, adolescents take risks, bravely or foolishly, with potential for harm as well as for good.

KEY TERMS

puberty (p. 411)
menarche (p. 411)
spermarche (p. 411)
hormone (p. 412)
pituitary (p. 412)
adrenal glands (p. 412)
HPA (hypothalamus–pituitary–adrenal) axis (p. 412)
gonads (p. 413)
HPG (hypothalamus–pituitary–gonad) axis (p. 413)
estradiol (p. 413)
testosterone (p. 413)
circadian rhythm (p. 414)
secular trend (p. 416)
leptin (p. 416)
body image (p. 421)
anorexia nervosa (p. 422)
bulimia nervosa (p. 422)
growth spurt (p. 423)
primary sex characteristics (p. 425)
secondary sex characteristics (p. 425)
child sexual abuse (p. 429)
sexually transmitted infection (STI) (p. 430)

WHAT HAVE YOU LEARNED?

Puberty Begins

1. What are the first visible signs of puberty?

2. What body parts of a teenage boy or girl are the last to reach full growth?

3. How do hormones affect the physical and psychological aspects of puberty?

4. Why do adolescents have sudden, intense emotions, such as anger, ecstasy, or despair?

5. Why is the genetic trait of eveningness a particular problem during adolescence?

6. Why do parents and adolescents fight about bedtime?

7. What are the gender differences in the growth spurt?

8. What are the ethnic and cultural differences in the changes of puberty?

9. How would society be affected if puberty occurred for everyone a few years later?

10. Why is early puberty more difficult for girls than for boys?

11. Why is late puberty more difficult for boys than for girls?

Nutrition

12. Why would anyone voluntarily starve herself or himself to death?

13. Why would anyone make herself or himself throw up?

14. What problems might occur if adolescents do not get enough iron or calcium?

The Transformations of Puberty

15. Why are most adolescents unhappy with their appearance?

16. Why is body image often distorted in adolescence?

17. What are examples of the uneven growth patterns in adolescent bodies?

18. What problems result from the growth spurt sequence (weight/height/muscles)?

19. How do religion and culture affect adolescent sexual activity?

20. Among sexually active people, why do adolescents have more STIs than adults?

21. What are positive changes in adolescent sexuality over the past five decades?

22. Why is adolescent sexuality more hazardous now than it was five decades ago?

23. Why is it harmful for a young adolescent and an adult to have sex?

24. How might the timing of brain maturation during adolescence create problems?

25. In what ways is adolescent brain functioning better than adult brain functioning?

APPLICATIONS

1. Visit a fifth-, sixth-, or seventh-grade class. Note variations in the size and maturity of the students. Do you see any patterns related to gender, ethnicity, body fat, or self-confidence?

2. Interview two to four of your friends who are in their late teens or early 20s about their memories of menarche or spermarche, including their memories of others' reactions. Do their comments indicate that these events are, or are not, emotionally troubling for young people?

3. Talk with someone who became a parent before the age of 20. Were there any problems with the pregnancy, the birth, or the first years of parenthood? Would the person recommend teen parenthood? What would have been different had the baby been born three years earlier or three years later?

4. Find two or three adults who, as adolescents, acted impulsively and did something that could have potentially caused great harm to themselves and/or other people. What do they recall about their thinking at the time of the incident? How would their actions differ now? What do their answers reveal about the adolescent mind?

>>ONLINE CONNECTIONS

To accompany your textbook, you have access to a number of online resources, including quizzes for every chapter of the book, flashcards (in English and Spanish), critical thinking questions, and case studies. For access to any of these links, go to www.worthpublishers.com/bergerca9e. In addition to these free resources, you'll also find links to podcasts, video clips, diagnostic quizzing with personalized study advice, and an ebook. Some of the videos and activities available online include:

- *Brain Development: Adolescence.* There's a lot going on in a teenager's brain! Animations and illustrations highlight that development and its effect on behavior.
- *The Timing of Puberty.* Too early? Too late? Teens tell their own stories about the impact of pubertal timing. The video also reviews physical changes and gender differences in maturation.

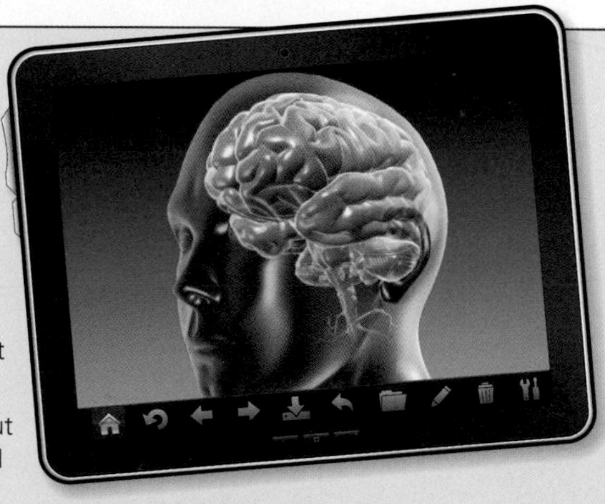

15

CHAPTER

Adolescence: Cognitive Development

WHAT WILL YOU KNOW?

1. Why do some young adolescents think everyone else is focused on them?
2. Why don't adolescents use their new cognitive ability to think logically?
3. How do computers and cell phones affect adolescent learning?
4. Which adolescents (age and background) in which schools (size and type) are likely to feel lost and ignored?

I have taught child development to thousands of college students, at four universities. Most of the content is standard, and I know it well. That allows me to update, to add examples from current events, to figure out the best strategy for each session: lecture, discussion, show of hands, group work, demonstration, video clip, pair/share, written responses, quizzes, and so on. I adjust to each class; no group is exactly like the others. Each student is unique as well: Some need encouragement to express their ideas, others need to think before they speak, some laugh easily, some are impassive. Knowing who should learn what, when, and how is the challenge—and joy—of teaching.

A few years ago, I agreed to teach a college course to advanced high school students. I was pleased: They grasped concepts quickly, they studied for tests, they completed written assignments on time. But one day I was explaining Freud's stages.

Student: I don't agree with that.
Me: You don't have to agree, you just need to learn the terms and ideas.
Student: Why should I do that?
Me: You need to understand Freud, so you can then disagree.
Student: But that's just Freud. I have my own ideas, and I like them better.

I was stunned. My college students were never so egocentric as to claim that their own ideas were so much better than Freud's that they didn't need to bother with him. Then I remembered; bright as they were, these students were adolescents.

This chapter describes adolescent cognition, sometimes impressively brilliant, sometimes surprisingly abstract, and sometimes amazingly egocentric. Taking into account the way adolescents think, we then describe how they are taught—in middle school, in high school, and around the world.

>> Logic and Self

Brain maturation, intense conversations, additional years of schooling, moral challenges, and increased independence all occur between ages 11 and 18. The combination propels impressive cognitive growth, from egocentrism to abstract logic.

Egocentrism

During puberty, young people center many of their thoughts on themselves, in part because maturation of the brain heightens self-consciousness (Sebastian et al., 2008). It is typical for young adolescents to try to understand their conflicting feelings about their parents, school, and classmates and to think deeply (but not always realistically) about their future. One reason adolescents spend so much time talking on the phone, e-mailing, and texting is that they like to ruminate about each nuance of everything they have done, are doing, and might do.

Thus, young adolescents think intensely about themselves and about what others think of them. Together these two aspects of thought are called **adolescent egocentrism,** first described by David Elkind (1967). Egocentrism is common in early adolescence among youth of both sexes and every ethnic group (Beaudoin & Schonert-Reichl, 2006). It continues throughout adolescence, especially in teenagers who have problems such as delinquency, aggression, and eating disorders, and it may increase again at the start of college (Schwartz et al., 2008).

adolescent egocentrism A characteristic of adolescent thinking that leads young people (ages 10 to 13) to focus on themselves to the exclusion of others.

In egocentrism, adolescents regard themselves as unique, special, and much more socially significant (that is, noticed by everyone) than they actually are. Accurately imagining someone else's perspective is difficult when egocentrism rules (Lapsley, 1993). For example, it seems unlikely that adolescent girls are especially attracted to boys with pimples and braces, but Edgar did not realize this, according to his older sister:

> Now in the 8th grade, Edgar has this idea that all the girls are looking at him in school. He got his first pimple about three months ago. I told him to wash it with my face soap but he refused, saying, "Not until I go to school to show it off." He called the dentist, begging him to approve his braces now instead of waiting for a year. The perfect gifts for him have changed from action figures to a bottle of cologne, a chain, and a fitted baseball hat like the rappers wear.
>
> *[adapted from Eva, personal communication, 2007]*

PICTURE PARTNERS / ALAMY

Every Detail Appearance has always been significant to young adolescents, but each cohort is distinct. Thin, waxed eyebrows, blue hair and nails, and a checkered shirt over stripes would all have been anathema to this girl's grandmother at age 15, who might have examined her rosy cheeks in a large, living room mirror.

Egocentrism leads adolescents to interpret everyone else's behavior as if it were a judgment on them. A stranger's frown or a teacher's critique could make a teenager conclude that "No one likes me" and then deduce that "I am unlovable" or even claim that "I can't leave the house." More positive casual reactions—a smile from a sales clerk or an extra-big hug from a younger brother—could lead to "I am great" or "Everyone loves me," with similarly distorted self-perception. Given the rapid mood changes described in the previous chapter, such conclusions are usually short-lived, susceptible to reversal with another offhand remark.

As an aspect of egocentrism, acute self-consciousness about one's physical appearance is probably more prevalent between ages 10 and 14 than earlier or later (Rankin et al., 2004). Young adolescents would rather not stand out from their peers, hoping instead to blend in. They also believe that everyone is as egocentric as they are. As one girl said:

> I am a real worrier when it comes to other people's opinions. I care deeply about what they say, think and do. If people are very complimentary, it can give you a big confidence boost, but if people are always putting you down you feel less confident and people can tell. A lot of advice that is given is "Do what you want and don't listen to anyone else," but I don't know one person who can do that.
>
> *[quoted in J. H. Bell & Bromnick, 2003, p. 213]*

Fables

personal fable An aspect of adolescent egocentrism characterized by an adolescent's belief that his or her thoughts, feelings, and experiences are unique, more wonderful or awful than anyone else's.

invincibility fable An adolescent's egocentric conviction that he or she cannot be overcome or even harmed by anything that might defeat a normal mortal, such as unprotected sex, drug abuse, or high-speed driving.

Elkind named several aspects of adolescent egocentrism, among them the **personal fable** and the **invincibility fable,** which often appear together. The *personal fable* is the belief that one is unique, destined to have a heroic, fabled, even legendary life. Some 12-year-olds plan to star in the NBA, or become billionaires, or cure cancer. Another example is the belief that one is destined to die a young and tragic death; thus, habits that could lead to midlife lung cancer or heart disease are no problem. In some adolescent minds, there is no contradiction between the personal fable and *invincibility,* the idea that, unless fate wills it, they will not be hurt by fast driving, unprotected sex, or addictive drugs. If they take risks and survive without harm, they feel invincible, not grateful.

In every nation, those who volunteer for military service—knowing or even hoping that they will be sent into combat—are more likely to be under age 20 than over it. Young recruits take risks more often than older, more experienced soldiers (Killgore et al., 2006). Another example comes from online chat rooms. Young teenagers reveal personal information to electronic "friends," oblivious to the dangers that adults see in such revelations (McCarty et al., 2011).

AP PHOTO

Ready for Battle? As uniformed Russian draftees, Yevgeny and Alexei might imagine that an audience sees them as tough men, but they would be mortified to know how boyishly naive they appear.

Sometimes a jolting life experience punctures the illusion of invincibility, as happened to one Pennsylvania college student when his parents ended their 19-year marriage.

> I had read a lot of things about divorce affecting children at a young age, but I was a freshman in college and did not think there would be . . . downs and corkscrews that just sent my thoughts spiraling out of control. I, the invincible wrestler, the invincible college student, had finally found that kryptonite that would weaken me. . . . I did something that was not at all a sign of invincibility: I got help.
>
> *[Pikounis, 2010, p. 14]*

The Imaginary Audience

Egocentrism creates an **imaginary audience** in the minds of many adolescents. They believe they are at center stage, with all eyes on them, and they imagine how others might react to their appearance and behavior.

imaginary audience The other people who, in an adolescent's egocentric belief, are watching and taking note of his or her appearance, ideas, and behavior. This belief makes many teenagers very self-conscious.

I witnessed this with my daughter Bethany at age 16. She was already a gifted artist. Perhaps that is why I agreed to go with her to the Metropolitan Museum of Art on a humid midsummer afternoon. When we emerged from the subway, we encountered a sudden downpour. Bethany stopped and became angry—at me!

> **She:** You didn't bring an umbrella? You should have known.
> **Me:** It's OK—we'll walk quickly. It's a warm rain.
> **She:** But we'll get all wet.
> **Me:** No problem. We'll dry.
> **She:** But people will see us with our hair all wet.
> **Me:** Honey, no one cares how we look. And we won't see anyone we know.
> **She:** That's OK for you to say. You're already married.
> **Me:** *[incredulous]* Do you think you'll meet your future husband here?
> **She:** *[exasperated]* No, of course not. But people will look at me and think, "She'll never find a husband looking like that!"

The imaginary audience can cause teenagers to enter a crowded room as if they are the most attractive human beings alive. They might put studs in their lips or blast music for all to hear, calling attention to themselves. The reverse is also possible: Unlike Edgar, they might avoid scrutiny lest someone notice a blemish on their chin or make fun of their braces. Many a 12-year-old balks at going to school with a bad haircut or the wrong shoes.

Egocentrism Reassessed

After Elkind first described adolescent egocentrism, some psychologists blamed it for every teenage problem, from drug use to pregnancy (Eckstein et al., 1999). It is still a common explanation for the risk taking evident in adolescence (Leather, 2009). However, other research has found that some adolescents do not feel invincible; in fact, some have exaggerated perceptions of risks (Mills et al., 2008).

Some developmentalists now believe that egocentrism "may signal growth toward cognitive maturity" (Vartanian, 2001, p. 378), that egocentrism may be protective "each time an individual enters into a new environmental context or dramatically new life situation" (Schwartz et al., 2008, p. 447) as the adolescent responds to culture and cohort. For example, a 13-year-old who moved to Los Angeles from a small town recalled:

> When I got to school the first day, everyone looked at me like I was from outer space or something. It was like, "Who's that? Look at her hair. Look at what she's wearing." That's all anybody cares about around here; what you look like and what you wear. I felt like a total outcast. As soon as I got home, I locked myself in my room and cried for about an hour. I was so lonely.
>
> *[Tina, quoted in R. Bell, 1998, p. 78]*

The phrase "all anybody cares about around here" applies not only to Los Angeles. The same words could have been written by a young adolescent who moved from Los Angeles to a small town or by almost any adolescent new to a school. This girl's reaction was egocentric if she imagined more scrutiny than actually occurred, but young adolescents do sometimes reject peers who dress or act in unusual ways. Self-awareness and cultural sensitivity may be helpful.

Every year, thousands of new students in middle and high schools are harassed, especially if they differ from the norm in sexual behavior, accent, or clothing. In 2010, 15-year-old Phoebe Prince killed herself three months after she moved from a small town in Ireland to Massachusetts. At first, she thought she was a star—a senior boy was romantically involved with her. Then other students called her an Irish slut and taunted her—culminating in her suicide and the indictment of nine of them. The bullies were wrong, of course. But this tragedy could have been anticipated and halted by adults if they had understood adolescent egocentrism.

Lest you conclude that young adolescents are foolhardy to think they are invincible and the subject of others' attention, we should point out that there is a positive aspect to egocentrism. Young adolescents who feel psychologically invincible (not harmed by others' judgments) tend to be resilient, less likely to be depressed (Hill et al., 2011). Without that, tragedy might occur.

Formal Operational Thought

Adolescents move past concrete operational thinking and consider abstractions. Jean Piaget described a shift to what he called **formal operational thought,** including "assumptions that have no necessary relation to reality" (Piaget, 1972, p. 148).

formal operational thought In Piaget's theory, the fourth and final stage of cognitive development, characterized by more systematic logical thinking and by the ability to understand and systematically manipulate abstract concepts.

One way to distinguish formal from concrete thinking is to compare curricula in primary school and high school. Here are three examples:

1. *Math.* Younger children multiply real numbers, such as $4 \times 3 \times 8$; adolescents can multiply unreal numbers, such as $(2x)(3y)$ or even $(25xy^2)(3zy^3)$.
2. *Social studies.* Younger children study other cultures by considering daily life—drinking goat's milk or building an igloo, for instance. Adolescents can consider "gross national product" and "fertility rate" and how these affect global politics.
3. *Science.* Younger students water plants; adolescents test H_2O in the lab.

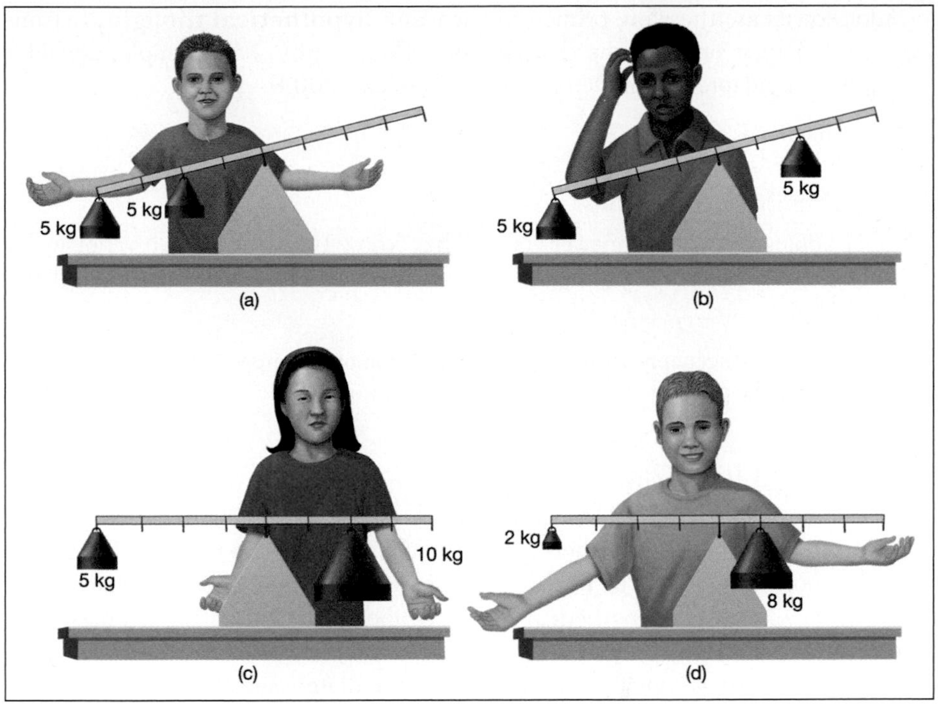

FIGURE 15.1

How to Balance a Scale Piaget's balance-scale test of formal reasoning, as it is attempted by *(a)* a 4-year-old, *(b)* a 7-year-old, *(c)* a 10-year-old, and *(d)* a 14-year-old. The key to balancing the scale is to make weight times distance from the center equal on both sides of the center; the realization of that principle requires formal operational thought.

Piaget's Experiments

Piaget and his colleagues devised a number of tasks to assess formal operational thought (Inhelder & Piaget, 1958); "in contrast to concrete operational children, formal operational adolescents imagine all possible determinants . . . [and] systematically vary the factors one by one, observe the results correctly, keep track of the results, and draw the appropriate conclusions" (P. H. Miller, 2011, p. 57).

In one experiment (diagrammed in Figure 15.1), children of many ages balance a scale by hooking weights onto the scale's arms. To master this task, they must realize that the weights' heaviness and distance from the center interact reciprocally to affect balance. Therefore, a heavier weight close to the center can be counterbalanced with a lighter weight far from the center. For example, a 12-gram weight placed 2 centimeters to the left of the center might balance a 6-gram weight placed 4 centimeters to the right.

This balancing concept was completely beyond the 3- to 5-year-olds. By age 7, children could balance the scale by putting the same amount of weight on each arm, but they didn't realize that the distance from the center mattered. By age 10, children thought about location but used trial and error, not logic. Finally, by about age 13 or 14, some children hypothesized and tested the reciprocal relationship between weight and distance and developed the correct formula (Piaget & Inhelder, 1969).

Hypothetical-Deductive Reasoning

One hallmark of formal operational thought is the capacity to think of possibility, not just reality. "Here and now" is only one of many alternatives, including "there and then," "long, long ago," "nowhere," "not yet," and "never." As Piaget said:

> The adolescent . . . thinks beyond the present and forms theories about everything, delighting especially in considerations of that which is not . . .
>
> *[Piaget, 1972, p. 148]*

hypothetical thought Reasoning that includes propositions and possibilities that may not reflect reality.

Adolescents are therefore primed to engage in **hypothetical thought,** reasoning about *if–then* propositions that do not reflect reality. For example, consider this question (adapted from De Neys & Van Gelder, 2009):

> If all mammals can walk,
> And whales are mammals,
> Can whales walk?

Younger adolescents often answer "No!" They know that whales swim, not walk, so the logic escapes them. Some adolescents answer "Yes." They understand the concept of *if.*

> *Possibility* no longer appears merely as an extension of an empirical situation or of action actually performed. Instead, it is *reality* that is now secondary to *possibility.*
>
> *[Inhelder & Piaget, 1958, p. 251; emphasis in original]*

AP PHOTO / LAS CRUCES SUN-NEWS, VLADIMIR CHALOUPKA

A Proud Teacher "Is it possible to train a cockroach?" This hypothetical question, an example of formal operational thought, was posed by 15-year-old Tristan Williams of New Mexico. In his award-winning science project, he succeeded in conditioning Madagascar cockroaches to hiss at the sight of a permanent marker. (His parents' logical reasoning about having 600 cockroaches living in their home is not known.)

Hypothetical thought transforms perceptions, not necessarily for the better. Adults sometimes become exasperated at the adolescent penchant for criticizing everything from the way their mother cooks spaghetti to why the Gregorian calendar, not the Chinese or Jewish one, is standard. They criticize what *is* precisely because of their hypothetical thinking about what might be. Adolescents' reflection about serious issues becomes complicated because they consider many possibilities, avoiding conclusions about the immediate issues (Moshman, 2005). They "naively underestimate the practical problems involved in achieving an ideal future for themselves or for society" (Miller, 2011, p. 59).

For example, a survey of U.S. teenagers' religious ideas found that most 13- to 17-year-olds considered themselves religious and thought that practicing their particular faith would help them avoid hell. However, they did not take the next logical step by trying to convince their friends to believe as they did and avoid hellfire. As one explained, "I can't speak for everybody, it's up to them. I know what's best for me, and I can't, I don't, preach" (quoted in C. Smith, 2005, p. 147).

Another said:

> I think every religion is important in its own respect. You know, if you're Muslim, then Islam is the way for you. If you are Jewish, well, that's great too. If you're Christian, well, good for you. It's just whatever makes you feel good about you.
>
> *[quoted in C. Smith, 2005, p. 163]*

deductive reasoning Reasoning from a general statement, premise, or principle, through logical steps, to figure out (deduce) specifics. (Also called *top-down reasoning.*)

inductive reasoning Reasoning from one or more specific experiences or facts to reach (induce) a general conclusion. (Also called *bottom-up reasoning.*)

In developing the capacity to think hypothetically, by age 14 or so adolescents become capable of **deductive reasoning,** or *top-down reasoning,* which begins with an abstract idea or premise and then uses logic to draw specific conclusions (Galotti, 2002; Keating, 2004). By contrast, **inductive reasoning,** or *bottom-up reasoning,* predominates during the school years, as children accumulate facts and personal experiences (the knowledge base) to aid their thought.

In essence, a child's reasoning goes like this: "This creature waddles and quacks. Ducks waddle and quack. Therefore, this must be a duck." This reasoning is inductive: It progresses from particulars ("waddles" and "quacks") to a general conclusion ("a duck"). By contrast, deduction progresses from the general to the specific: "If it's a duck, it will waddle and quack" (see Figure 15.2).

Especially for Natural Scientists Some ideas that were once universally accepted, such as the belief that the sun moved around the Earth, have been disproved. Is it a failure of inductive or deductive reasoning that leads to false conclusions? (see response, page 446)

An example of the increase in deductive reasoning comes from the ways children, adolescents, and adults change in their support of anti-racist policies in the United States. By adolescence, almost everyone in the United States is aware that racism exists—and opposes it. As one might imagine, people who are directly harmed are more aware of racism than those who merely learn about it in history books. However, children tend to think the core problem is the prejudice of individuals. Using inductive reasoning, they think that the remedy is to reduce

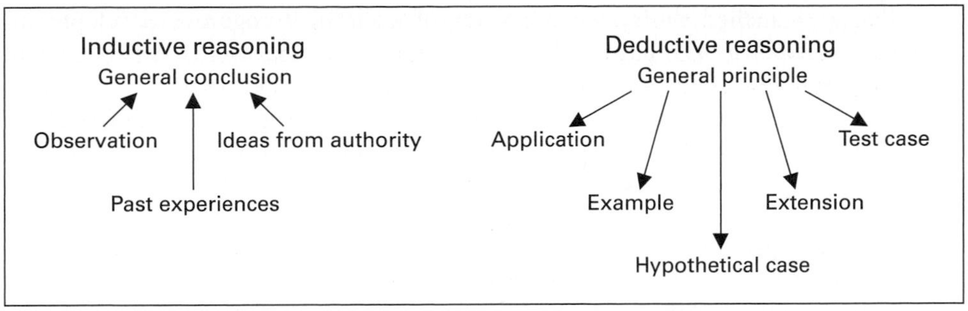

FIGURE 15.2

Bottom Up or Top Down? Children, as concrete operational thinkers, are likely to draw conclusions on the basis of their own experiences and what they have been told. This is called inductive, or bottom-up, reasoning. Adolescents can think deductively, from the top down.

racism among those people who express it, believing there will be less prejudice as individuals become more accepting of everyone. By contrast, older adolescents think, deductively, that racism is a society-wide problem that requires policy solutions.

This interpretation arises from a study of adolescent agreement or disagreement with policies to remedy racial discrimination (Hughes & Bigler, 2011). Not surprisingly, most (not all) students in an interracial U.S. high school recognized disparities between African and European Americans and believed that racism was a major cause. What was surprising to the researchers is that age made a difference. Among those who believed there were marked inequalities, older adolescents (age 16 to 17) were more likely to support systemic solutions (e.g., affirmative action and desegregation) than were younger adolescents (age 14 to 15). The authors suggest that "during adolescence, cognitive development facilitates the understanding that discrimination exists at the social-systemic level . . . racial awareness begins to inform views of race-conscious policies during middle adolescence" (Hughes & Bigler, 2011, p. 489).

Impressive Thinking "Correlating Genetic Signature with Surface Sugar Expression in Vibrio Vulnificus" is the title of Shilpa Argade's winning science project about a sometimes deadly bacteria. Like many of her peers in southern California, she is capable of deductive reasoning, but she does not always think that way.

Logical Fallacies

Many cognitive scientists study how people think, especially when logic fails. Failures are often apparent during adolescence (Albert & Steinberg, 2011).

One example is the **sunk cost fallacy.** In this fallacy, people who have spent money, time, or effort that cannot be recovered (a cost already "sunk") continue to try to achieve their desired goal because otherwise that previous effort is wasted. Sunk costs include not only monetary costs, but time and energy as well (Cunha & Caldieraro, 2009). People of all ages invest in repairing a "lemon" of a car, remaining in a class they are failing, continuing a destructive marriage, and so on.

Another common fallacy is **base rate neglect** (Barbey & Sloman, 2007). People ignore information about the frequency of a phenomenon and, influenced perhaps by a vivid experience, ignore the data. Egocentrism makes base rate neglect more likely. For instance, a teen might not wear a bicycle helmet, feeling invincible despite statistics, until a friend is brain-damaged in a biking accident. "When adolescents take unjustified risks, it is often because of the weakness of their analytic systems, which provide an inadequate check on impulsive or ill-considered decisions" (Sunstein, 2008, p. 145).

The prevalence of logical fallacies makes it apparent that formal operational thinking does not come to everyone at a certain developmental stage. On the contrary, research since Piaget has found marked variability: Some adolescents and adults still reason like concrete operational children. "No contemporary scholarly reviewer of research evidence endorses the emergence of a discrete new cognitive structure at adolescence that closely resembles . . . formal operations" (Kuhn & Franklin, 2006, p. 954).

sunk cost fallacy The mistaken belief that if money, time, or effort that cannot be recovered (a "sunk cost," in economic terms) has already been invested in some endeavor, then more should be invested in an effort to reach the goal. Because of this fallacy, people spend money trying to fix a "lemon" of a car or send more troops to fight a losing battle.

base rate neglect A common fallacy in which a person ignores the overall frequency of some behavior or characteristic (called the *base rate*) in making a decision. For example, a person might bet on a "lucky" lottery number without considering the odds that that number will be selected.

>> Response for Natural Scientists (from page 444) Probably both. Our false assumptions are not logically tested because we do not realize that they might need testing.

Piaget "launched the systematic study of adolescent cognitive development" (Keating, 2004, p. 45), but his description is not the final word. This is evident in the study just cited: Certainly adults disagree about the merits of affirmative action, for reasons that may be unrelated to whether they think inductively or deductively. Nonetheless, something shifts in cognition after puberty: Piaget was right that most older adolescents think differently than most children do.

SUMMING UP

Thinking reaches heightened self-consciousness at puberty, when adolescent egocentrism may be apparent. Some young adolescents have unrealistic notions about their place in the social world, as evidenced by the personal fable and the imaginary audience. They often imagine themselves as invincible, unique, and the center of attention. Adults often criticize this self-awareness, but it shows a cognitive advance and may be shaped by the social context.

Piaget thought the fourth and final stage of intelligence, called *formal operational thought,* begins in adolescence. He found that adolescents improve in deductive logic and hypothetical reasoning. Other scholars note logical lapses at every age and much more variability in adolescent thought than Piaget's description implies. ■

>> Two Modes of Thinking

The fact that adolescents *can* use hypothetical-deductive reasoning does not necessarily mean that they *do* use it (Kuhn & Franklin, 2006). Adolescents find it much easier and quicker to forget about logic and instead to follow their impulses. Advanced logic in adolescence is counterbalanced by the increasing power of intuitive thinking. A **dual-process model** of adolescent cognition has been formulated (Albert & Steinberg, 2011).

dual-process model The notion that two networks exist within the human brain, one for emotional and one for analytical processing of stimuli.

Intuition Versus Analysis

For adults as well as adolescents, at least two modes characterize thought. Various scholars choose different terms and sometimes distinct definitions. These two modes of thought have been called: intuitive/analytic, implicit/explicit, creative/factual, contextualized/decontextualized, unconscious/conscious, gist/quantitative, hot/cold, emotional/intellectual, experiential/rational.

The thinking described by the first half of each pair is preferred in everyday life. Sometimes, however, circumstances compel the second mode, when deeper thought is demanded. The discussion in Chapter 14 about the discrepancy between the maturation of the limbic system and the prefrontal cortex reflects this duality. Research on adolescent cognition focuses on this intuitive/analytic pair (Gerrard et al., 2008).

- **Intuitive thought** begins with a belief, assumption, or general rule (called a *heuristic*) rather than logic. Intuition is quick and powerful; it feels "right."
- **Analytic thought** is the formal, logical, hypothetical-deductive thinking described by Piaget. It involves rational analysis of many factors whose interactions must be calculated, as in the scale-balancing problem.

intuitive thought Thought that arises from an emotion or a hunch, beyond rational explanation, and is influenced by past experiences and cultural assumptions.

analytic thought Thought that results from analysis, such as a systematic ranking of pros and cons, risks and consequences, possibilities and facts. Analytic thought depends on logic and rationality.

When the two modes of thinking conflict, people sometimes use one mode and sometimes the other. Experiences and role models influence the choice. For example, one study found that when adolescents enter a multicultural high school, some rely on old stereotypes and others consider new perspectives, depending on their specific experiences and on adult attitudes (Crisp & Turner, 2011). By adulthood, people try to coordinate intuitive and analytic thought, making sure that whatever feels right is also a wise move. As one scholar expresses it, there are "two systems but one reasoner" (De Neys, 2006, p. 428).

BOB DAEMMRICH / THE IMAGE WORKS

Dual Processing Signs of both analysis and emotion are evident in these two girls at a school in south Texas. They are using wireless computers to study, perhaps analyzing information, formatting questions, and drawing logical conclusions. At the same time, intuitive thinking is also on display: The girls are sitting side by side for companionship and are dressed similarly, wearing shoes designed more for fashion than for walking.

Comparing Intuition and Analysis

Paul Klaczynski has conducted dozens of studies comparing the thinking of children, young adolescents, and older adolescents (usually 9-, 12-, and 15-year-olds) (Holland & Klaczynski, 2009; Klaczynski, 2001, 2011; Klaczynski et al., 2009). In one, he presented 19 logical problems to children and adolescents. For example:

> Timothy is very good-looking, strong, and does not smoke. He likes hanging around with his male friends, watching sports on TV, and driving his Ford Mustang convertible. He's very concerned with how he looks and with being in good shape. He is a high school senior now and is trying to get a college scholarship.
>
> *Based on this [description], rank each statement in terms of how likely it is to be true. . . . The most likely statement should get a 1. The least likely statement should get a 6.*
>
> _____ Timothy has a girlfriend.
> _____ Timothy is an athlete.
> _____ Timothy is popular and an athlete.
> _____ Timothy is a teacher's pet and has a girlfriend.
> _____ Timothy is a teacher's pet.
> _____ Timothy is popular.

In ranking these statements, most adolescents (73 percent) made at least one analytic error, ranking a double statement (e.g., popular *and* an athlete) as more likely than a single statement included in it (popular *or* an athlete). They intuitively jumped to the more inclusive statement, rather than sticking to logic. Klaczynski found that almost all adolescents were analytical and logical on some of the 19 problems but not on others. Logical thinking improved with age and education, although not with IQ.

In other words, being smarter as measured by an intelligence test did not advance logic as much as did having more experience, in school and in life. Klaczynski (2001) concluded that, even though teenagers *can* use logic, "most adolescents do not demonstrate a level of performance commensurate with their abilities" (p. 854).

AP PHOTO / GREGORY SMITH

Impressive Connections This robot is about to compete in the Robotics Competition in Atlanta, Georgia, but much more impressive are the brains of the Oregon high school team (including Melissa, shown here) who designed the robot.

Preferring Emotions

What would motivate adolescents to use—or fail to use—their formal operational thinking? Klaczynski's participants had all learned the scientific method in school, and they knew that scientists use empirical evidence and deductive reasoning. But they did not always think like scientists. Why not?

Dozens of experiments and extensive theorizing have found some answers (Albert & Steinberg, 2011). Essentially, logic is more difficult than intuition, and it requires examination of comforting, familiar prejudices. Once people of any age reach an emotional conclusion (sometimes called a "gut feeling"), they resist changing their minds. As people gain experience in making decisions and thinking things through, they become better at knowing when analysis is needed (Milkman et al., 2009). For example, in contrast to younger students, when judging the legitimacy of a rule, older adolescents are more suspicious of authority and more likely to consider mitigating circumstances (Klaczynski, 2011). Both suspicion of authority and awareness of context signify advances in reasoning, but both also complicate simple issues.

Rational judgment is difficult when egocentric emotions dominate. One psychologist discovered this firsthand when her teenage son phoned to be picked up from a party that had "gotten out of hand." The boy heard

> his frustrated father lament "drinking and trouble—haven't you figured out the connection?" Despite the late hour and his shaky state, the teenager advanced a lengthy argument to the effect that his father had the causality all wrong and the trouble should be attributed to other covariates, among them bad luck.
>
> *[Kuhn & Franklin, 2006, p. 966]*

Better Thinking

Sometimes adults conclude that more mature thought processes are wiser, since they lead to a more cautious approach (as in the father's connection between "trouble" and alcohol in the excerpt above). Adults are particularly critical when egocentrism leads an impulsive teenager to risk future addiction by experimenting with drugs or to risk pregnancy and AIDS by avoiding the awkwardness of using a condom.

But adults may themselves be egocentric in making such judgments because they assume that adolescents share their values. Parents want healthy, long-living children, and they conclude that adolescents use faulty reasoning when they risk their lives. Adolescents, however, value social warmth and friendship. A 15-year-old who is offered a cigarette might rationally choose social acceptance over the distant risk of cancer (Engels et al., 2006).

Research on how adults make complex decisions, such as whom to marry or which investment to make, finds that sometimes intuitive decisions are best and sometimes not (Dijksterhuis & Aarts, 2010). At every age, the best thinking may be "fast and frugal" (Gigerenzer, 2008). Weighing alternatives, and thinking of possibilities, could be paralyzing. The systematic, analytic thought that Piaget described is slow and costly, not fast and frugal, wasting precious time when a young person wants to act.

As the knowledge base increases and the brain matures, both modes of thought become more forceful. With maturity, adolescents avoid both extremes: They are neither paralyzed by too much analysis nor plummeted into danger via intuition. Logic increases from adolescence to adulthood (and then decreases somewhat in old age) (De Neys & Van Gelder, 2009).

Ideally, people use whatever combination of dual processing leads to good decisions (Gigerenzer, 2008). Adolescents may use formal, analytic thinking in science class and emotional, experiential thinking (which is quicker and more satisfying) for personal issues (Kuhn & Franklin, 2006).

Thinking About Religion

As you remember from Chapter 1, scientists build on previous research or theories, replicating, extending, or refuting the work of others. Scientists question assumptions, seeking empirical evidence to verify or criticize both new theories and old cultural myths. This is a formal operational approach.

Some impressionistic descriptions of teenagers and religion (e.g., Flory & Miller, 2000) emphasize cults and sects. As one observation reports, young congregants gather, "dressed as they are, piercings and all, and express their commitment by means of hip-hop and rap music, multimedia presentations, body modification, and anything else that can be infused with religious meaning" (Ream & Savin-Williams, 2003, p. 51).

This description evokes emotions—the quick, intuitive responses that judge piercings and rap to be the antithesis of religion. When another team of researchers began by "reading many published overview reports on adolescence . . . [they got] the distinct impression that American youth simply do not have religious or spiritual lives" (C. Smith, 2005, p. 4). Seeking evidence, not impressions, they surveyed 3,360 13- to 17-year-olds and their parents, tallied the quantitative results, and then added qualitative depth by interviewing 287 teenagers privately, in long, structured, conversations.

The researchers found that most adolescents (71 percent) felt close to God; believed in heaven, hell, and angels; and affirmed the same religion as their parents (78 percent Christian, 3 percent Jewish or Muslim, almost none Buddhist or Hindu). Some were agnostic (2 percent), and 16 percent said they were not religious—although many of those attended church and prayed. Less than 1 percent were "unconventional" (e.g., Wiccan). This was quite contrary to the impressionistic accounts the researchers had read.

JIM WEST

Living Their Faith? Theologians may separate faith from personal or political concerns, but few adolescents do. In a protest aimed at keeping their Catholic school open, one student leader carries a white cross with a quote from Thomas Jefferson (a deist who opposed clergy and religious doctrine); her classmate carries a bullhorn and a Bible. Secular concerns also affect adult religious thought: Despite community and student protests such as this one, the Detroit Archdiocese closed Holy Redeemer for financial reasons.

They also found that adolescents' religious beliefs were often egocentric: Faith was a personal tool to be used in times of difficulty (e.g., while taking an exam). Many (82 percent) claimed their beliefs were important in daily life. One boy explained that religion kept him from doing "bad things, like murder or something," and one girl said:

> [Religion] influences me a lot with the people I choose not to be around. I would not hang with people that are, you know, devil worshipers because that's just not my thing. I could not deal with that negativity.
>
> *[quoted in C. Smith, 2005, p. 139]*

The researchers doubt that "socializing with Satanists is a real issue in this girl's life" or that this boy "struggles with murderous tendencies" (C. Smith, 2005, p. 139). They also noted that few adolescents (less than 1 percent) used theology to guide them in the actual issues of daily life, such as seeking justice or loving one's neighbor. For most, religious beliefs were intuitive, not analytic.

What does this imply for adults who hope to instill values in the next generation? In many ways, these data are encouraging: Most children and adolescents adhere to the faith and values of their parents. However, the authors wish that adults would encourage teenagers to discuss complex spiritual issues (e.g., stewardship of the environment, economic disparity, the implications of scriptures). This would require parents and church leaders to engage in the more difficult processes of cognition.

As good scientists, the researchers surveyed the same individuals three years later. They found a "shifting away from conventional religious beliefs" (Denton et al., 2008, p. 3). But, despite less certainty about God, angels, or an afterlife, these older adolescents tended to feel they had become more, not less, religious over the three-year period. One possible reason is that "as adolescents develop and mature, they take more ownership over their own beliefs and practices so that their religiosity feels stronger and more authentic" (Denton et al., 2008, p. 32). In other words, maturation, independence, and years of questioning thought may advance cognition.

Dual Processing and the Brain

The brain maturation described in Chapter 14 seems directly related to the dual processes just explained (Steinberg, 2010). Because the limbic system is activated by puberty whereas the prefrontal cortex matures more gradually over time, it is easy to understand why adolescents are swayed by their intuition instead of logic.

New evidence for the power of impulses comes from more than 7,000 adolescents surveyed longitudinally five times between ages 12 and 24. The results were "consistent with neurobiological research indicating that cortical regions involved in impulse control and planning continue to mature through early adulthood [and that] subcortical regions that respond to emotional novelty and reward are more responsive in middle adolescence than in either children or adults" (Harden & Tucker-Drob, 2011, p. 743).

Trends in Impulsivity and Sensation Seeking

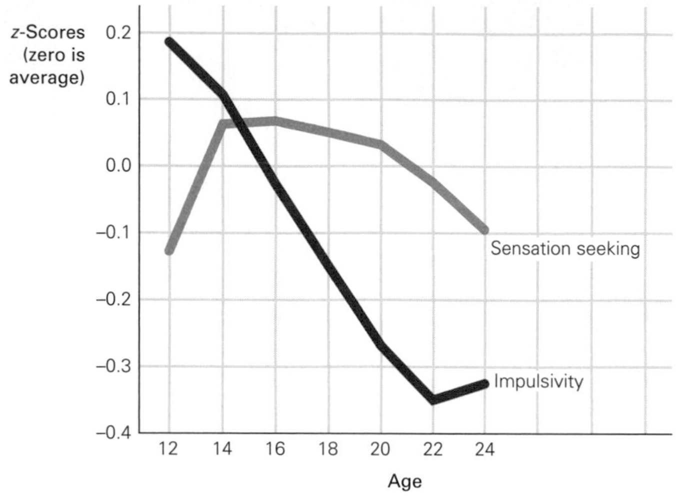

Source: Harden & Tucker-Drob, 2011.

FIGURE 15.3

Look Before You Leap As you can see, as they mature, adolescents become less impulsive, but they still enjoy the thrill of a new sensation.

To be specific, this study traced the development of sensation seeking (e.g., "I enjoy new and exciting experiences"), which seems connected to the limbic system, maturing rapidly soon after puberty. Increases in sensation seeking were notable from ages 12 to 14 (see Figure 15.3). Sensation seeking can be seen as intuitive—direct from the gut to the brain. The researchers also studied impulsivity, as indicated by agreement with statements such as "I often get in a jam because I do things without thinking." A decline in impulsive actions can be considered an increase in analytic thinking—not the fast responses of intuitive thought (Harden & Tucker-Drob, 2011).

Impulsivity declined (and therefore analytic thinking increased) as adolescents matured over the twelve years of the study. The burst of sensation seeking at puberty and the decline of impulsivity over the years of adolescence were general trends. This could be interpreted as confirming the dual-process view because each of the two modes of thought followed a distinct trajectory. In other words, there was no significant correlation between changes in sensation seeking and changes in impulsivity within individuals—a person could have a faster decline in one than in the other, or vice versa.

Indicative of this lack of correlation is that there were marked individual differences in the patterns, as found in the many personal variations in biological changes during adolescence. However, over the years of adolescence, age trends were apparent: Both sensation seeking and impulsivity eventually declined.

Those age trends could be interpreted as another example of the overall pattern of maturation of the limbic system occurring ahead of advances in the prefrontal cortex. This led one neurologist to conclude:

> The teenage brain is not just an adult brain with fewer miles on it. It's a paradoxical time of development. These are people with very sharp brains, but they're not quite sure what to do with them.
>
> *[Jensen, quoted in Ruder, 2008, p. 8]*

SUMMING UP

Current research recognizes that there are at least two modes of cognition: People sometimes use analytical thinking and other times prefer intuitive reasoning. This second kind of thinking is experiential, quicker, and more intense than formal operational thought. Both forms develop during adolescence, although sometimes intuitive processes crowd out logical ones. The logic necessary for impulse control may not increase rapidly enough when sensation seeking is strong, as the prefrontal cortex develops slowly. Each form of thinking is appropriate in some contexts. With neurological maturation, logical, reflective thinking becomes more possible, as is evident in thoughts about religion and about racism. Adolescents' impulsive and quick responses need to be guided until their logical processes can analyze and anticipate the impact of their actions. ■

>> Technology and Cognition

Is technology beneficial or harmful for adolescent cognition? Both opinions are strongly expressed, and both have research to support them (Gentile, 2011b). Adults over age 40 grew up without the World Wide Web, instant messaging, Twitter, blogs, cell phones, iPods, iPads, BlackBerries, or digital cameras. Until 2006, only students at elite colleges could join Facebook. Yet today's teenagers are "digital natives." Since childhood they have been networking, texting, and clicking for definitions, directions, and data without realizing how alien that might be for their elders. Most adolescents have cell phones, iPods, and other mobile devices within reach, day and night.

The gap between those who did and did not have computers was bemoaned a decade ago; it divided boys from girls and rich from poor (Dijk, 2005; Norris, 2001). However, in many nations, that *digital divide* has virtually disappeared. Low-income children are somewhat less likely to have high-speed Internet at home, and Hispanic households lag behind others in technology, but those divides are rapidly narrowing. Virtually every secondary school and library in every developed nation is connected to the Internet, as are many in developing nations.

Thus, today's students take technology for granted. Many own computers; some get them free from their schools (Ash, 2009). The only significant digital divide is now age: Of those over age 65, less than half (42 percent) are online (see Figure 15.4). No wonder most critics of technology are older adults.

Learning via Electronic Technology

In many schools, teachers use computers and cell phones as tools for learning. In some states (e.g., Idaho) and some school districts, students must take at least one class completely online. Internet use and video games improve visual-spatial skills and vocabulary (Greenfield, 2009). Recall that research conducted before the technology explosion found that, with education, conversation, and experience, adolescents move past egocentric thought. Social networking may speed up this process, as teens communicate daily with dozens—perhaps even hundreds or thousands—of friends via e-mail, texting, and cell phones.

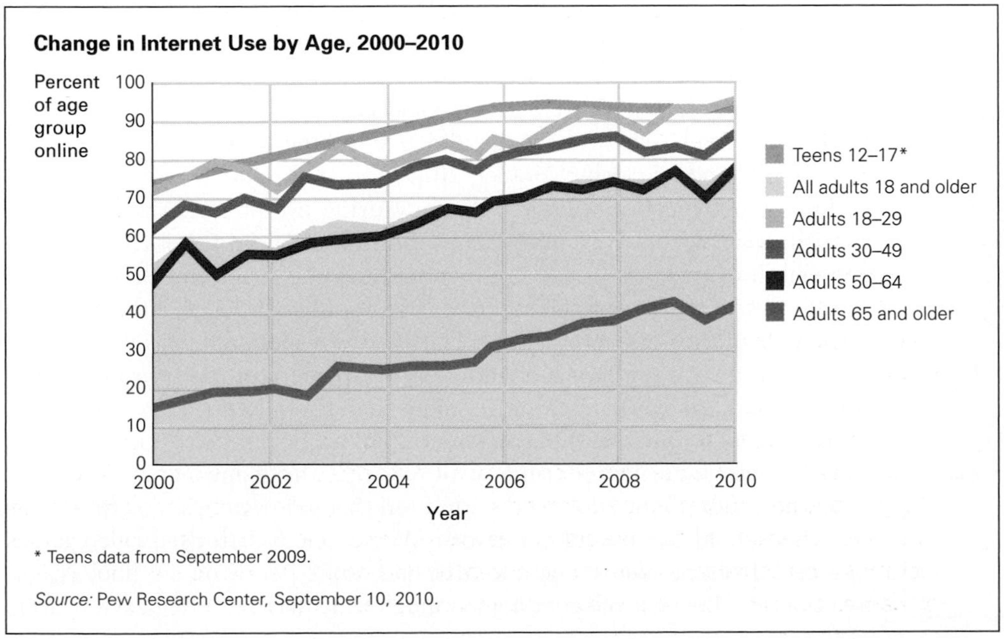

FIGURE 15.4

Almost Every Teenager Most teenagers go online every day, more often for social reasons than academic ones. The challenge for American educators is no longer access (virtually every school has Internet capability) but guidance: Adolescents need to learn appropriate Web use, including how to identify and evaluate propaganda and how to avoid plagiarism.

HERB SWANSON / THE NEW YORK TIMES

AP PHOTO / MARCELO HERNANDEZ

The Same Situation, Many Miles Apart: Where Is the Teacher? Free laptops are provided for every middle school student in Maine *(left)* and at some public schools in Uruguay *(right)*. Benefits include more active learning, collaboration, and independence—or are these liabilities instead?

Online connections bring friends closer together and reduce social isolation (Valkenburg & Peter, 2009). Although most social networking is between friends who know each other well, the Internet may be a lifeline for teenagers who are isolated because of their sexual orientation, culture, religion, or native language. For everyone, the Internet allows contact with like-minded people thousands of miles away and enables individuals to expand their knowledge on virtually any subject. Most secondary students check facts, read explanations, view videos, and thus grasp concepts they would not have known if they had grown up a few years earlier.

FIGURE 15.5

More Than Eating The average adolescent boy spends more time playing video games than reading, eating, doing homework, talking with friends, playing sports, or almost anything else except sleeping or sitting in class. Indeed, some skip school or postpone sleep to finish a game.

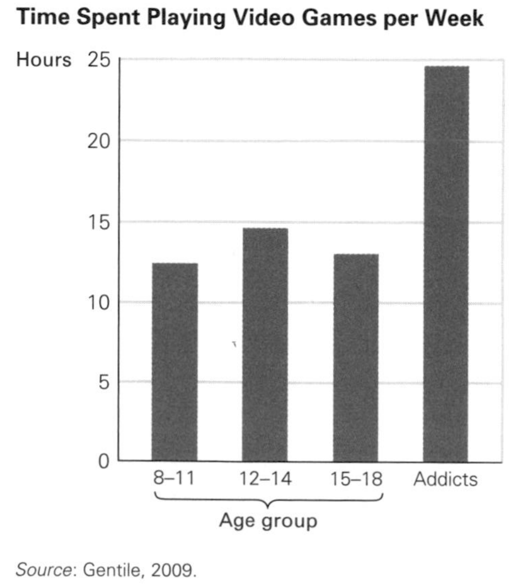

Addiction and Technology

Adults worry about sexual abuse via the Internet. There is comforting research here: Although sexual predators lurk online, most teens avoid them, just as most adults avoid distasteful ads and pornography. Sexual abuse is a serious problem, but social networking does not increase the risk (Wolak et al., 2008).

There are some dangers, however. Technology encourages rapid shifts of attention, multitasking without reflection, visual learning instead of invisible analysis (Greenfield, 2009). Video games with violent content promote aggression (Gentile, 2011b). For some adolescents, chat rooms, video games, or Internet gambling can become addictive, taking time from needed play, schoolwork, and friendship (Shuler, 2009; Yen et al., 2008).

This is not mere speculation. A study using a representative sample of 8- to 18-year-olds in the United States found that one-third of the boys and one-eighth of the girls played video games every day (see the Research Design). Most of the rest played almost as often; only 3 percent of the boys and 21 percent of the girls never played. The *average* respondent played two hours a day. Those with symptoms of addiction (12 percent of the boys and 3 percent of the girls) played, on average, more than three hours a day, with some of them (about 10 percent) playing more than six hours a day (Gentile et al., 2011a). (See Figure 15.5 for time spent playing video games, by age group.)

In this study, many adolescents admitted that video games took time away from household chores and homework. Worse, one-fourth used video games to escape from problems, and one-fifth had "done poorly on a school assignment or test" because of spending too much time playing. The heaviest users

got lower school grades and had more physical fights than did the average users. Sadly, the data from this study may underestimate the problem, since adolescents reported on themselves.

Addiction of any kind limits life experience, with the harm especially severe when the brain is still growing. Thus, adolescent video game addiction is a serious problem. This survey found that most game playing occurred at home, often in the child's own bedroom, and that only half of the parents had rules about their adolescents' play (Gentile, 2009). One conclusion is that if parents allow such games, then rule setting and monitoring are needed. As the next chapter explains, parents need to be careful: Especially with adolescents, overly restrictive parenting can backfire.

A simple solution is to ban technology from schools and bedrooms, but, as one critic writes, "Cell phones have the potential to be negative in schools. But we don't ban pencils and paper because students pass notes" (Shuler, 2009, p. 35). Some teachers confiscate computers and cell phones used in class; others include them in the curriculum.

Research Design

Scientist: Douglas Gentile.

Publication: *Psychological Science* (2009).

Participants: All were part of a Harris interactive sample, selected to be representative of youth aged 8 to 18 in the United States. The 1,178 participants (about 100 at each age) were equally divided by gender and ethnically diverse (about half non-Hispanic White; about one-sixth each African American and Latino; and the remaining mixed, Asian or Native American, or declining to specify).

Design: The participants were asked questions, via computer, about their video game use, including frequency, parental policies, and signs of possible addiction.

Results: Almost all played video games many hours a week, with boys spending about twice the time on it as girls did. For both sexes, video game frequency peaked between ages 12 and 14. Younger students played slightly less often, and older students played for a longer time at a stretch. More than half of the boys had M-rated games (rated mature, with explicit violence or sex), almost always with their parents' permission. Video game playing correlated with lower achievement and more behavior problems, especially attention-deficit disorder.

Major conclusion: Many parents, teachers, and psychologists have worried that some teenagers are addicted to video games, curtailing important aspects of their lives and using games to avoid problems. Using criteria for addiction developed by psychiatrists for other addictions (gambling, drugs, and so on), this study found an answer: 12 percent of the boys and 3 percent of girls were addicted to playing video games. Their addiction decreased their family and school involvement.

Comments: These numbers are chillingly high. One hopes those in the sample are more likely than the average teenager to be game-addicted (they were all contacted via computer) or, since this study is correlational, that low school achievement leads to video game playing, rather than vice versa. However, a later controlled study began with children whose parents intended to buy them a video game system. Half of them were given the system, and the other half had to wait. Those 6- to 9-year-old boys who received the video game system had lower reading and writing achievement than did other boys from the same population with the same characteristics who had to wait four months (Weis & Cerankosky, 2010). (A similar study with adolescents would be enlightening, but most teenage boys whose parents allow video game systems already have them.)

Cyberdanger

When a person is bullied via electronic devices, usually via e-mail, text messages, or cell phone videos, that is **cyberbullying** (Tokunaga, 2010). The adolescents most involved are usually already bullies or victims or both, with bully-victims the most likely to engage in, and suffer from, cyberbullying. Technology does not create bullies per se, but it gives them another means and wider access. It enables relational bullying, not physical bullying, and thus girls seem to engage in cyberbullying as often as boys do.

A scholar who has studied bullying in all its forms finds that cyberbullying is similar to other forms of harassment (P. K. Smith et al., 2008), a conclusion reached by numerous other social scientists. For example, a study of 1,169 15-year-olds in New Zealand found that cyberbullying correlated with physical and relational bullying (Marsh et al., 2010).

This does not mean that cyberbullying is just like other forms. Relational bullying can be more harmful when done over the Internet, since rumors can "go viral" and insults can be transmitted day and night. The imaginary audience magnifies the shame (Englander et al., 2009). An added dimension of cyberbullying comes from cell phone photos: Some adolescents photograph another in a compromising position (such as drunk, naked, or crying) and then send it to a wide audience. While the causes of all forms of bullying seem similar, each form has its own sting, and the sting of cyberbullying is worse when the self-image is forming and impulsive thoughts precede analytic ones.

All forms of bullying are affected by the school climate. When students consider their school a good place to be—with supportive teachers, friendly students, opportunities for growth (clubs, sports, theater, music) and so on—those with high self-esteem are not only less likely to engage in cyberbullying, but they also disapprove of it. That reduces the incidence overall. However, when the school climate is negative, those with high self-esteem are often bullies themselves

cyberbullying Bullying that occurs when one person spreads insults or rumors about another by means of e-mails, text messages, or cell phone videos.

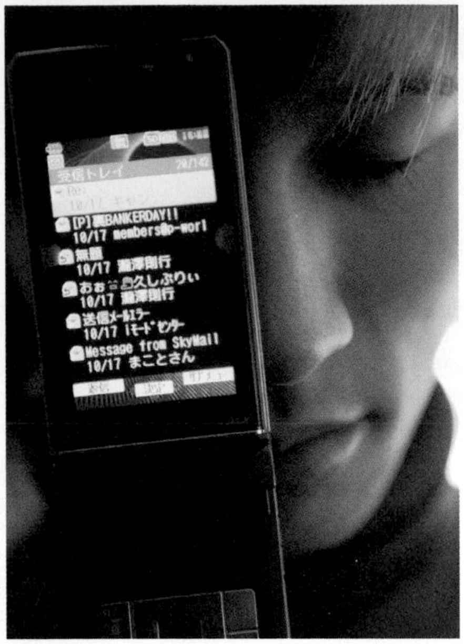

REUTERS / YURIKO NAKAO

Suicide Device High schooler Yuriko's cell phone capabilities drove him to thoughts of suicide. Fortunately, he got help to stop the mental torture he suffered from cyberbullying—a problem that may be worse in Japan because social reputation is crucial. For the same reason, young adolescents are particularly vulnerable.

cutting An addictive form of self-mutilation that is most prevalent among adolescent girls and that correlates with depression and drug abuse.

(Gendron et al., 2011). Some students believe that cyberbullying is unstoppable; however, not only schools but also some teens themselves use successful strategies, including deleting messages unread (Parris et al., 2011).

A complication is that the technology is trusted by most adolescents but misunderstood by many adults. As a result, parents and teachers are often unaware of cyberbullying, and few laws and policies are in place to prevent it. Adolescents are far more vulnerable than adults realize. This was tragically evident in the suicide of a Missouri 13-year old, Megan Meier, who believed a boy she never met named Josh Evans was her MySpace friend. When Josh turned on her, finally e-mailing that "the world would be a better place without you," she hung herself.

"Josh" was actually the mother of another girl who had been hurt by Megan. The mother was convicted of "computer fraud and abuse" in California (MySpace headquarters) but acquitted on appeal. This case is a dramatic example of a widespread problem: Electronic communication allows a dangerous mix of adult ignorance and adolescent egocentrism.

Another problem with electronic technology is less common but equally dangerous. Some teenagers use online connections to pursue a destructive action, such as extreme dieting, abusive prejudice, or self-harm. A European study of 700 adolescents in several nations found that those who were addicted to Internet use were also likely to be severely depressed (Durkee et al., 2011).

Let us look at one example in detail: self-mutilation, known as **cutting.** Over 400 Web sites are dedicated to cutting, an addictive activity (particularly among adolescent girls) that correlates with depression, drug abuse, and Internet misuse.

Analysis of a representative sample of 3,219 posts on cutting sites found that most were positive and helpful, allowing self-injuring adolescents to "establish interpersonal intimacy . . . [which is] especially difficult for young people struggling with intense shame, isolation, and distress" (Whitlock et al., 2006, p. 415). The most common theme of the messages was informal support (28 percent). Other posts described treatment (7 percent, usually positively) and emotional triggers (20 percent). Some posts, however, told how to conceal marks (9 percent) or described techniques of cutting (6 percent). Here is one exchange:

> **Poster 1:** Does anyone know how to cut deep without having it sting and bleed too much?
>
> **Poster 2:** I use box cutter blades. You have to pull the skin really tight and press the blade down really hard. You can also use a tourniquet to make it bleed more.
>
> **Poster 3:** I've found that if you press your blade against the skin at the depth you want the cut to be and draw the blade really fast it doesn't hurt and there is blood galore. Be careful, though, 'cause you can go very deep without meaning to.
>
> *[quoted in Whitlock et al., 2006, p. 413]*

Note that with both cyberbullying and cutting, the danger lies not in the computer but in the cognition of the person at the keyboard. Technology must be used with care. As with many aspects of adolescence (puberty, brain development, egocentric thought, and so on), context, adults, peers, and the adolescent's own personality and temperament "shape, mediate, and/or modify effects" of technology (Oakes, 2009, p. 1142). If a teen is intuitive, impulsive, and egocentric, he or she has difficulty analyzing the impact of whatever harmful remark is sent or limiting the emotional response to whatever destructive comment is read. Adults should know better, but all of us are sometimes illogical and emotional: It takes time and experience to use technology wisely.

SUMMING UP

In fostering adolescent cognition, technology seems to have many positive aspects: Computers are used as a tool for learning in many classrooms, and online connections can promote social cohesion and reduce isolation, especially for those who feel marginalized. Friends often connect via texting and e-mail, and social-networking sites expand the social circle. However, technology also has a dark side, evident in the frequency of cyberbullying and addiction to video games, which can interfere with education and friendship, rather than enhance them. ■

>> Teaching and Learning

What does our knowledge of adolescent thought imply about school? Educators, developmentalists, political leaders, and parents wonder exactly which curricula and school structures are best for 11- to 18-year-olds. There are dozens of options: academic knowledge or practical skills, single sex or co-ed, competitive or cooperative, large or small, public or private—and more. To further complicate matters, adolescents differ from one another in many ways. As a result, "some students thrive at school, enjoying and benefiting from most of their experiences there; others muddle along and cope as best they can with the stress and demands of the moment; and still others find school an alienating and unpleasant place to be . . ." (Eccles & Roeser, 2011, p. 225).

Given all these variations, no one school structure or style of pedagogy seems best for everyone. Various scientists, nations, schools, and teachers try many strategies, some based on opposite, but logical, hypotheses. To analyze these, we present some definitions, facts, issues, and possibilities.

Definitions and Facts

Each year of schooling advances human potential, as recognized by leaders and scholars in every nation and discipline. Adolescents are capable of deep and wide-ranging thought, no longer limited by personal experience. Yet they are often egocentric, impulsive, and intuitive. The quality of education matters: A year can propel thinking forward or can have little impact (Hanushek & Woessmann, 2010).

Secondary education—traditionally grades 7 through 12—denotes the school years after elementary or grade school (known as *primary education*) and before college or university (known as *tertiary education*). Adults are healthier and wealthier if they complete primary education, learning to read and write, and then continue on through secondary and tertiary education.

secondary education Literally, the period after primary education (elementary or grade school) and before tertiary education (college). It usually occurs from about age 12 to 18, although there is some variation by school and by nation.

Even such a seemingly unrelated condition as serious hearing loss in late adulthood is 40 percent more common among those who never graduated from high school as it is among high school graduates (National Center for Health Statistics, 2011). This statistic comes from the United States, but data on almost every ailment, from every nation and every ethnic group, confirm that high school graduation correlates with better health. Some of the reasons are only indirectly related to education (e.g., income and place of residence), but even when inadequate resources and toxic neighborhoods are taken into account, health improves with education.

Partly because political leaders recognize that educated adults advance national wealth and health, every nation is increasing the number of students in secondary schools. Education is compulsory until at least age 12 almost everywhere (UNESCO, 2010). Often, two levels of secondary education are provided.

Traditionally, secondary education was divided into junior high (usually grades 7 and 8) and senior high (usually grades 9 through 12). As the average age of puberty declined over the past century (see Chapter 14) and younger adolescents became ready for more intellectual challenge, **middle schools** were created to educate 10- to 13-year-olds (grades 6, 7, and 8). In addition, some nations have added a precollege year after grade 12.

middle school A school for children in the grades between elementary and high school. Middle school usually begins with grade 6 and ends with grade 8.

Middle School

Many developmentalists find middle schools to be "developmentally regressive" (Eccles & Roeser, 2010, p. 13)—they force children to step backward. Does this matter for later achievement? One team believes so: "Long-term academic trajectories—the choice to stay in school or to drop out and the selection in high school of academic college-prep courses versus basic-level courses—are strongly influenced by experience in grades 6–8" (Snow et al., 2007, p. 72).

For many reasons, compared to primary schools, high schools, or colleges, middle schools are the weakest link in the educational sequence, with many students feeling stressed, parents feeling worried, and teachers feeling ineffective (Meece & Eccles, 2010). The data validate such feelings. For example, a longitudinal study of 900 U.S. children, followed from birth through ninth grade, found that between grades 5 and 9 the rate of reading and math achievement was only half as rapid as between grades 3 and 5. This was true for all ethnic groups. Many explanations are possible, but less learning in middle school is one of the most likely (Hooper et al., 2010).

For many middle school students, as academic achievement slows down, behavioral problems rise. Puberty itself is part of the problem. At least for other animals, especially when under stress, learning slows down at puberty (McCormick et al., 2010).

Especially for Teachers You are stumped by a question your student asks. What do you do? (see response, page 458)

However, many experts think that the biological or psychological stresses of puberty are *not* the main reasons learning suffers in early adolescence. Instead, the organizational structure of many middle schools may undermine adolescent thought (Meece & Eccles, 2010). However, the idea that young adolescents can be taught, not merely warehoused in middle school, is supported by the experience of China. At least one team of scholars connects the Chinese economic expansion in recent years to the massive expansion of middle school education two decades ago, when millions of students learned skills that now serve their nation well (Lamb et al., 2011).

Especially for Middle School Teachers You think your lectures are interesting and you know you care about your students, yet many of them cut class, come late, or seem to sleep through it. What do you do? (see response, page 459)

What is amiss in the structure of middle schools in the West? One hypothesis is that middle schools reduce achievement because they undercut student–teacher relationships. Unlike the situation in primary school, where each teacher is responsible for one classroom of children, middle school teachers are not connected to any small group. Instead, they specialize in an academic subject, taught to hundreds of students each year. This makes them impersonal and distant: Their students learn less and risk more (Crosnoe et al., 2004).

Adolescents' relationships with their parents may change as well. Some parents feel unable to help their adult-size children. By contrast, high-achieving middle school children tend to have parents who encourage them (but do not directly help with homework) (Hill & Tyson, 2009). The particulars vary by nation. In Korea, for instance, many parents of middle school children hire tutors and keep a close watch on the tutoring process, which improves the children's school performance (Park et al., 2011). In other nations, parents are more likely to engage their children in nonacademic activities after school. If parents think that teenagers no longer need parental support and encouragement, that's a mistake. Consider James.

A CASE TO STUDY

James, the High-Achieving Dropout

A longitudinal study in Massachusetts followed children from preschool through high school. James was one of the most promising. In his early school years, he was an excellent reader whose mother took great pride in him, her only child. Once James entered middle school, however, something changed:

> Although still performing well academically, James began acting out. At first his actions could be described as merely mischievous, but later he engaged in much more serious acts, such as drinking and fighting, which resulted in his being suspended from school.
>
> *[Snow et al., 2007, p. 59]*

Family problems increased at puberty. James and his father blamed each other for their poor relationship, and his mother was uninvolved in his schooling. She bragged "about how independent James was for being able to be left alone to fend for himself," while James "described himself as isolated and closed off" (Snow et al., 2007, p. 59).

James said, "The kids were definitely afraid of me but that didn't stop them" from associating with him (Snow et al., 2007, p. 59). James's experiences with other classmates are not unusual. Generally, aggressive and drug-using students are admired in middle school more than those who are conscientious and studious—a marked difference from elementary school (Allen et al., 2005; Mayeux & Cillessen, 2007). Students dislike those who are unlike them, which may mean general antipathy toward those who excel (Laursen et al., 2010). As a consequence, some of the brightest adolescents sacrifice academics rather than risk social exclusion.

This was verified in three nations (Germany, Canada, and Israel); mathematically gifted girls were particularly likely to underachieve (Boehnke, 2008). In general, many studies find that girls are more likely to attend class and become involved in various activities but are less competitive on achievement tests. Boys are more likely to disengage from school. Data on U.S. education for the past 150 years show that more boys than girls leave school before high school graduation (Snyder & Dillow, 2011).

Puberty awakens sexual concerns, with each sex wanting to appear masculine or feminine, as the case may be. Boys particularly fear becoming a "nerd" or teacher's pet. Perhaps that is why most (60 percent) of U.S. 18- to 19-year-olds who have not completed high school are male (Snyder & Dillow, 2011). James may have been one of many "boys who choose to emphasize their masculine identities [and] may thus actively avoid literacy activities and academic success" (Snow et al., 2007, p. 64). At the end of primary school, James planned to go to college; in middle school, he said he had "a complete lack of motivation"; in tenth grade, he left school.

As with James, the early signs of a future high school dropout are found in middle school. Those students who will leave without graduating tend to be boys from minority ethnic groups and of low income, yet almost no middle school has guidance counselors or teachers who are men from those groups. Given the egocentric and intuitive way that young adolescents think, it is not surprising that many stop trying to achieve in middle school. Young adolescents are not the only ones who think egocentrically: Many school systems count as dropouts only those who begin twelfth grade but never earn diplomas—a method that puts the dropout rate at about 10 percent, much lower than the actual rate. (See Table 15.1 on ways to calculate dropouts.)

Finding Acclaim

To pinpoint the developmental mismatch between students' needs and the middle school context, note that just when egocentrism leads young people to feelings of shame or fantasies of stardom (the imaginary audience), schools typically require them to change rooms, teachers, and classmates every 40 minutes or so. That makes public acclaim and personal recognition difficult.

Personal satisfaction via academic excellence is difficult as well, because middle school teachers mark more harshly and the effort that was earlier called "outstanding" is now "average." Acclaim may also be elusive after school, since few activities

TABLE 15.1 Measuring Dropout Rates

There are three commonly used ways to measure high school dropout rates.

1. Compare the number of students in the ninth grade with the number who graduate four years later. Students who transfer out, stop out and then return, or take more than four years to graduate are counted as dropouts. This is the most rigorous method, and it is used here.
2. Determine the percentage of 16- to 24-year-olds who are not in school and have no high school diploma. (These are called *status dropouts.*) One problem with this mode is that newly arrived young-adult immigrants who have not completed high school are considered dropouts. Another problem is that General Education Diplomas are counted, although students with a GED may not have gone to high school.
3. Count only those students who formally register as school leavers, not those who simply stop coming to school. This method finds the lowest rates of dropouts but may be the least realistic.

>> Response for Teachers (from page 456) Praise a student by saying, "What a great question!" Egos are fragile, so it's best to always validate the question. Seek student engagement, perhaps asking whether any classmates know the answer or telling the student to discover the answer online. Whatever you do, don't fake it—if students lose faith in your credibility, you may lose them completely.

treat 11- to 13-year-olds appropriately, neither like children nor like adults. Finally, athletic teams become competitive, so fragile egos avoid them.

Since public acclaim is elusive, many middle school students seek acceptance from their peers. Bullying increases, appearance becomes important, status symbols are displayed (from gang colors to expensive shoes), and sexual conquests are flaunted. Of course, much depends on the cultural context, but almost every middle school student seeks peer approval in ways that adults disapprove (Véronneau & Dishion, 2010).

Coping with Middle School

One way to cope with stress is directly cognitive, that is, thinking that other people—classmates, teachers, parents, governments—are to blame. This may explain the surprising results of a Los Angeles study: Students in schools that were *more* ethnically mixed felt safer and *less* lonely. They did not necessarily have friends from other groups, but students who felt rejected could "attribute their plight to the prejudice of other people" rather than blame themselves (Juvonen et al., 2006, p. 398). Furthermore, since each group was a minority, they accepted rather than attacked one another.

Some students prevent feelings of failure by simply avoiding effort—that way, they can blame a low grade on a lack of trying ("I didn't study") rather than on stupidity. Pivotal in this is students' understanding of their own potential and how to achieve what they wish. If they believe in the **entity approach to intelligence** (i.e., that ability is innate, a fixed quantity present at birth), then they do not believe that they can improve their own intellectual ability. All they can do is accept their deficiencies, such as low math, or writing, or memory ability. They are convinced that they are innately stupid in some ways and always will be. The entity belief reduces stress but also reduces achievement: It is hopeless to try very hard.

entity approach to intelligence An approach to understanding intelligence that sees ability as innate, a fixed quantity present at birth; those who hold this view do not believe that effort enhances achievement.

By contrast, if adolescents believe in the **incremental approach to intelligence** (i.e., that intelligence can increase if they try to master whatever they seek to learn), then they will pay attention, participate in class, study, complete their homework, and so on. That is called *mastery motivation,* an example of the intrinsic motivation explained in Chapter 10.

incremental approach to intelligence An approach to understanding intelligence that holds that intelligence can be directly increased by effort; those who subscribe to this view believe they can master whatever they seek to learn if they pay attention, participate in class, study, complete their homework, and so on.

This is not just a hypothesis. In the first year of middle school, students with entity beliefs do not achieve much, whereas the achievement of those with mastery motivation improves (Blackwell et al., 2007). After one study confirmed this finding, some students in their first year of middle school were taught eight lessons designed to convey the idea that being smart was incremental; these lessons included ways to "grow your intelligence." Especially if they had formerly held the entity theory of intelligence, those students gained while students in other classes had lower grades (Blackwell et al., 2007).

Teachers themselves were surprised at the effect. Among the "typical comments" was a teacher explaining that a boy

> who never puts in any extra effort and doesn't turn in homework on time, actually stayed up late working for hours to finish an assignment early so I could review it and give him a chance to revise it. He earned a B+ . . . he had been getting C's and lower.
>
> *[quoted in Blackwell et al., 2007, p. 256]*

>> Response for Middle School Teachers (from page 456) Students need both challenge and involvement; avoid lessons that are too easy or too passive. Create small groups; assign oral reports, debates, and role-plays; and so on. Remember that adolescents like to hear one another's thoughts and their own voices.

The concept that skills and intelligence can be mastered motivates the learning of social skills as well as academic subjects (Olson & Dweck, 2008). This makes it particularly important in adolescence, when peers are so important.

The contrast between entity and incremental approaches is apparent not only for individual adolescents but also for teachers, parents, schools, and cultures. If a school is structured so that children individually compete with one another rather than being placed in cooperative groups, with each group striving for mastery, then individuals who score low are likely to cope by endorsing the entity theory (Eccles & Roeser, 2011).

According to international comparisons, educational systems that track students into higher or lower classes, expel students who are not learning, and allow competition between schools for the brightest students (all reflecting entity, not incremental, theory) also show lower average achievement and a larger gap between the scores of students at the highest and lowest score quartiles (OECD, 2010b).

The Transition to a New School

Changing schools during the growth spurt or the onset of sexual characteristics is stressful. Remember from Chapter 13 that ongoing minor stresses can become overwhelming, causing pathology if they are repeated day after day. One expert notes:

> A number of disorders and symptoms of psychopathology, including depression, self-injury behavior, substance abuse, eating disorders, bipolar disorder, and schizophrenia have striking developmental patterns corresponding to transitions in early and late adolescence.
>
> *[Masten, 2004, p. 310]*

International Communication The Russian girl on the left was one of 300 middle schoolers who crossed the border to visit a school in China, where students learn Russian and English as well as Chinese. Adolescents learn from one another, either constructively when adults structure and plan the interaction (as shown here) or destructively when adults do not engage with them.

REN YONG / XINHUA / PHOTOSHOT / NEWSCOM

Of course, transitions are not the only cause of adolescent pathology; hormones, body changes, sexual experiences, family conflict, and cultural expectations also contribute. In addition, puberty may activate genes that predispose a person to mental disorders (Erath et al., 2009), and the sequence of brain development may cause emotional difficulties. Nonetheless, many schools try to make transitions easier, with special groupings or programs for entering classes.

Some transitions are particularly difficult. When students enter a new school with classmates and customs unlike those in their old school, minority students may feel alienated, fearing failure (Benner & Graham, 2007). It is not diversity per se that is difficult; it is suddenly finding oneself in the minority, in unfamiliar circumstances. That may cause *stereotype threat,* the anxiety-producing idea that other people are judging you in stereotyped ways. Students already at risk of emotional problems may be pushed over the edge by the transition; special nurturance can help them cope (Farmer et al., 2010).

Signs of stress—absenteeism, externalizing behavior, dropping out—are not inevitable, of course. For example, a program that helped parents and other students provide support to entering Mexican American middle schoolers (a vulnerable minority, since few teachers were from Mexico or spoke Spanish) had a significant impact: Fewer of them quit school than their peers without support (Gonzales et al., 2004).

Every transition is stressful. The most difficult times are the first year of middle school, the first year of high school, and the first year of college. The larger and less personal the new institution is and the more egocentric the student is, the more difficult the change. A study of the transition from middle to high school confirmed that personal relationships are crucial: Students are less likely to drop out if they have friends in the new school as well as teachers there who encourage learning. School policies (e.g., placement in classes) can facilitate such relationships (Langenkamp, 2010).

High School

As we have seen, adolescents can think abstractly, analytically, hypothetically, and logically—as well as personally, emotionally, intuitively, and experientially. The curriculum and teaching style in high school often require the former mode. Students who need more individualized, personal attention may be left out.

The College-Bound

From a developmental perspective, the fact that high schools emphasize formal thinking makes sense, since many older high schoolers are capable of abstract logic. High school teachers typically assume that their pupils have mastered formal thinking instead of teaching them how to do it (Kuhn & Franklin, 2006).

The United States is trying to raise standards so that all high school graduates will be ready for college. One way to accomplish this has been to increase the number of students who take classes that are assessed by externally scored exams, either the IB (International Baccalaureate) or the AP (Advanced Placement). Such classes have high standards and satisfy some college requirements.

Unfortunately, merely taking the class does not necessarily lead to college readiness (Sadler et al., 2010). Some students do not sign up for the external exams, and, although 17 percent of U.S. students took AP exams in 2010, about one-third

AP PHOTO / BEBETO MATTHEWS

IMAGES OF AFRICA PHOTOBANK / ALAMY

The Same Situation, Many Miles Apart: Top Students The New York girls just won a classroom history contest, and the Kenyan boys are studying physics, a subject available only to the brightest African students.

Observation Quiz Although the two groups of winners are thousands of miles apart, there are three evident similarities between them. What are they? (see answer, page 462)

of them failed. Far fewer take the IB exams, but, again, few receive the highest scores. In 2010, only one graduate in nine earned college credit based on an AP or IB exam—and that was an improvement over prior years (Gewertz, 2011a).

Of course, college credit is not the only measure of high school rigor. Another indicator is an increase in the requirements to receive an academic diploma. (In many U.S. schools, no one is allowed to earn a vocational or general diploma unless parents request it.) Graduation requirements usually include two years of math beyond algebra, two years of laboratory science, three years of history, and four years of English. Study of a language other than English is often required as well.

In 2011, in addition to these courses, 24 U.S. states required students to pass a **high-stakes test** in order to graduate. (Any exam for which the consequences of failing are severe is called a high-stakes test.) No state had such tests a decade ago; several additional states have scheduled them to begin soon. Because the more populous states are particularly likely to have high-stakes tests, 74 percent of U.S. high school students must take exit exams before graduation.

From 2000 to 2008, the percentage of students who pass high-stakes tests increased in some states and decreased in others (Zhang, 2009). The effect of such tests on education is in dispute. High school graduation rates in the United States are inching upward, with 72 percent of ninth-grade students staying in school to graduate four years later (see Figure 15.6) (Swanson, 2011).

The concern is that those who do not graduate are discouraged about education. According to the Center on Education Policy, high-stakes tests have "a negative impact on . . . low-performing students, students of color, or students from low-income families" (2010, p. 1). Even those who pass may be less excited about education. Overall, a panel of experts in education found that too much testing reduces learning rather than advancing it (Hout & Elliot, 2011).

As reviewed in Chapter 12, two international tests, the TIMSS and the PIRLS, show many nations ahead of the United States in achievement, with no dramatic change in the U.S. since the advent of high-stakes tests. Results at grade 4 were

Especially for High School Teachers You are much more interested in the nuances and controversies than in the basic facts of your subject, but you know that your students will take high-stakes tests on the basics and that their scores will have a major impact on their futures. What should you do? (see answer, page 462)

high-stakes test An evaluation that is critical in determining success or failure. If a single test determines whether a student will graduate or be promoted, it is a high-stakes test.

FIGURE 15.6

Graduation Rates on the Rebound The U.S. graduation rate has reached its highest point thus far. Every racial and ethnic group posted solid gains for the class of 2008, marking the second straight year of across-the-board improvements. These data are based on the most conservative and probably the most accurate estimate of graduation, that is, the percentage of new ninth-grade students who earn a diploma four years later. The gap between Asian/White and the three other groups is almost always the result of differences in socioeconomic status—that is, poor families live in communities with poor schools.

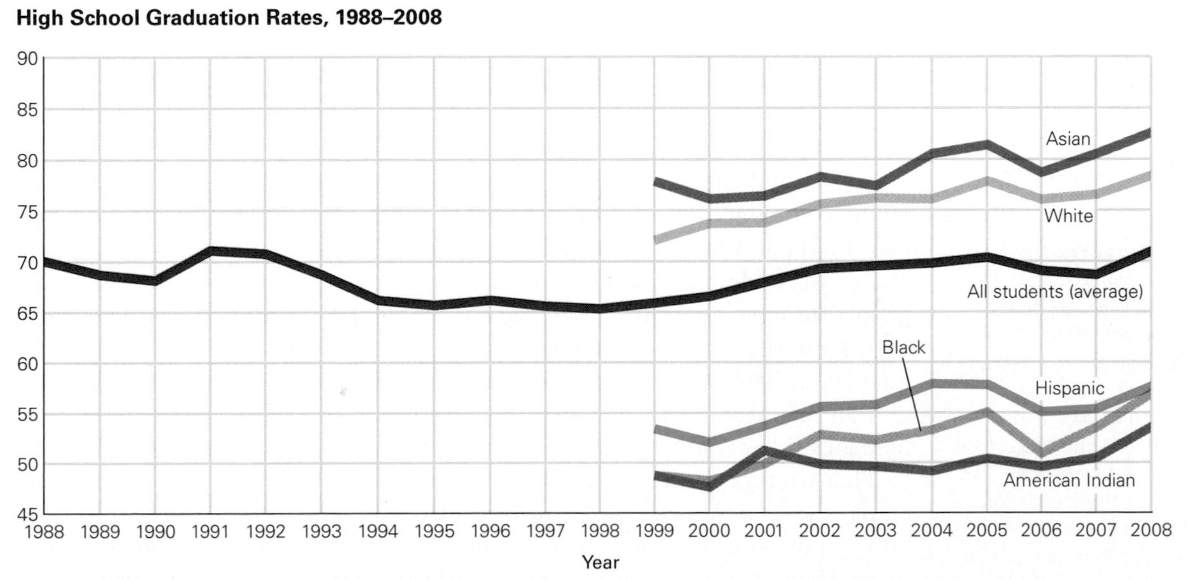

Source: Editorial Projects in Education, *Education Week*, June 9, 2011.

>> Answer to Observation Quiz (from page 460) The similarities have to do with gender, uniforms, and cooperation. Sex segregation and similar garb are evident in both photographs, although they are voluntary in U.S. public schools and compulsory in many African secondary schools. Adolescents everywhere enjoy working collaboratively.

detailed in Chapter 12; the results at grade 8 are similar. Ironically, just when more U.S. schools are raising standards, tests, and requirements, many East Asian nations, including Korea, China, and Japan, are moving in the opposite direction.

Compared to a decade ago, Japan has fewer academic requirements, Japanese schools are open five days a week instead of six, and Japanese students have less "examination hell," as their high-stakes tests had been called. The science adviser to the prime minister of Japan recommends more flexibility in education in order to promote innovation. He wants students to "study whatever they are interested in" rather than to narrow their learning so as to score high on one final test (Normile, 2007).

Those Who Do Not Go to College

In the United States, one result of pushing an academic curriculum is that most students hope to attend college, most enroll, and . . . most leave without the bachelor's degree they sought. Many high school graduates (70 percent) enter college. However, only 22 percent of those entering public community colleges complete their program within three years (Adams, 2011), and almost half of those entering public or private four-year schools do not earn degrees. Even 10 years after the usual age for high school graduation, only 32 percent of U.S. young adults have earned a bachelor's degree (Snyder & Dillow, 2011).

These sobering statistics underlie a debate among educators. Should students be encouraged to "dream big" early in high school, aspiring for tertiary learning? This suggestion originates from studies finding a correlation between dreaming big in early adolescence and going to college years later (Domina et al., 2011a, 2011b). Others suggest that college is a "fairy tale dream" that may lead to low self-esteem (Rosenbaum, 2011). If adolescents fail academic classes, will they feel bored, stupid, and disengaged? Some school systems have noncollege options for such students in high school; others do not.

In the United States, some 2,500 *career academies* (small institutions of about 300 students each) prepare students for specific jobs. Seven years after graduation, students who were in career academies earn about $100 more a month than do other students who applied but could not enroll because there was no room (Kemple, 2008). They are also more likely to be married (38 percent versus 34 percent) and living with their children (51 percent versus 44 percent). In another example, in Italy, vocational education succeeded when the learning included hands-on practical education (rare in academic courses that prepare students for college) and a personal commitment of the teachers to their students (relationships again) (Bonica & Sappa, 2010).

These programs are available to relatively few high school students. More generally, completion of secondary school is increasing worldwide, but how that is measured and what success means vary dramatically from nation to nation (Lamb et al., 2011). Meeting the needs of all secondary students is the universal goal, but people disagree about the particulars as the world economy shifts. One solution is to arrange job-training apprenticeships, whereby students earn credits toward graduation while working in local businesses. Germany placed tens of thousands of high school students in apprenticeships during the 1980s, and all were guaranteed jobs if they did well. Japan had similar success in previous decades.

That strategy succeeded when businesses needed workers. However, when unemployment increased, most employers left the program (Grollmann & Rauner, 2007). Furthermore, contrary to the intentions of the creators, students were enrolled in apprenticeship programs because their parents were of lower socioeconomic status (SES), not because they themselves were less capable of rigorous

>> Response for High School Teachers (from page 461) It would be nice to follow your instincts, but the appropriate response depends partly on pressures within the school and on the expectations of the parents and administration. A comforting fact is that adolescents can think about and learn almost anything if they feel a personal connection to it. Look for ways to teach the facts your students need for the tests as the foundation for the exciting and innovative topics you want to teach. Everyone will learn more, and the tests will be less intimidating to your students.

academic work (Lehmann, 2004). In Japan, high school graduates are no longer coveted as new employees, in part because the economy is changing (Brinton & Tang, 2010).

Choosing Vocations

A crucial question for every adolescent is what job they hope to have in adulthood. Younger children tend to want work that fewer than one in a million of them will obtain—rock star, sports hero, U.S. president—and adults often encourage such fantasies. By the teen years, however, more practical concerns arise, specifically what employment is actually available and how enjoyable, remunerative, and demanding it is. For those concerns, adults are of little help. Parents usually know only their particular work, not what labor-market projections in the next decade will be. High school guidance counselors in the United States have an *average* caseload of 270 students a year, which includes many who want to apply to a dozen colleges as well as some who need time-consuming emotional support to prevent violence, suicide, or drug addiction. Often, counselors have neither the time nor the expertise for vocational guidance (Zehr, 2011).

Some ambitious adolescents begin to think about future careers on their own. One classic tool for doing so is developmentalist John Holland's 1997 description of six possible interests (see Figure 15.7). If students develop a vision of their future and realize how high school might advance their career, then they are likely to be motivated to study and learn. Given what we know about adolescent cognition, it is no surprise that few understand the eventual importance of critical analysis, articulate speech, fluent written expression, and interpersonal understanding. Furthermore, high-stakes tests rarely measure such skills.

Students are often told that they must graduate from high school and obtain a college degree if they hope to have a good job. Given the immediate, emotional response of many adolescents, that may seem abstract and irrelevant, especially if they know someone with a degree who cannot find work or someone without a degree who earns a good living.

In that case, the base rate fallacy described on page 445 needs to be countered with facts. The data in every nation show that adults with only a high school degree are likely to be unemployed or earn low wages, that most adults with some post–high school education do better in the job market, and that people with more advanced degrees have more income and responsibility (see Figure 15.8). They need to understand that a BA is not essential: In many occupations, most workers

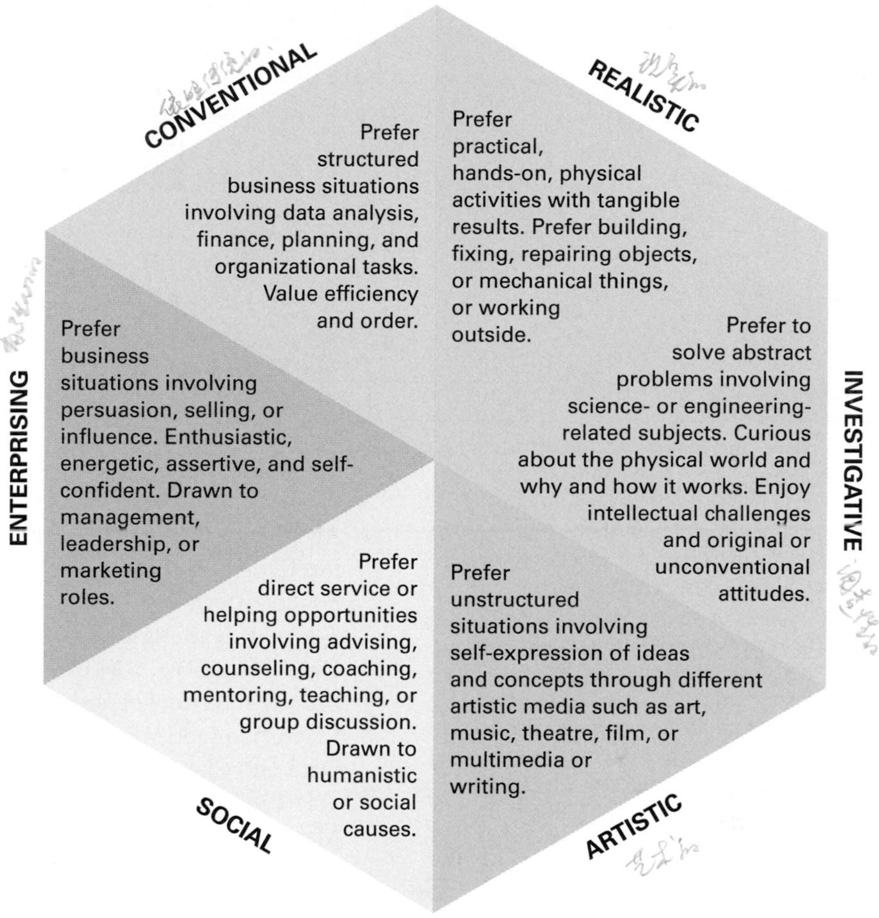

Source: http://career.sa.ucsb.edu/careerlibrary/Images/holland_codes.gif; UCSB Career Services Web Site

FIGURE 15.7

Happy at Work John Holland's six-part diagram is used to help adolescents realize that income and benefits are not the only goals of employment. Workers have healthier hearts and minds if their job fits their personal preferences.

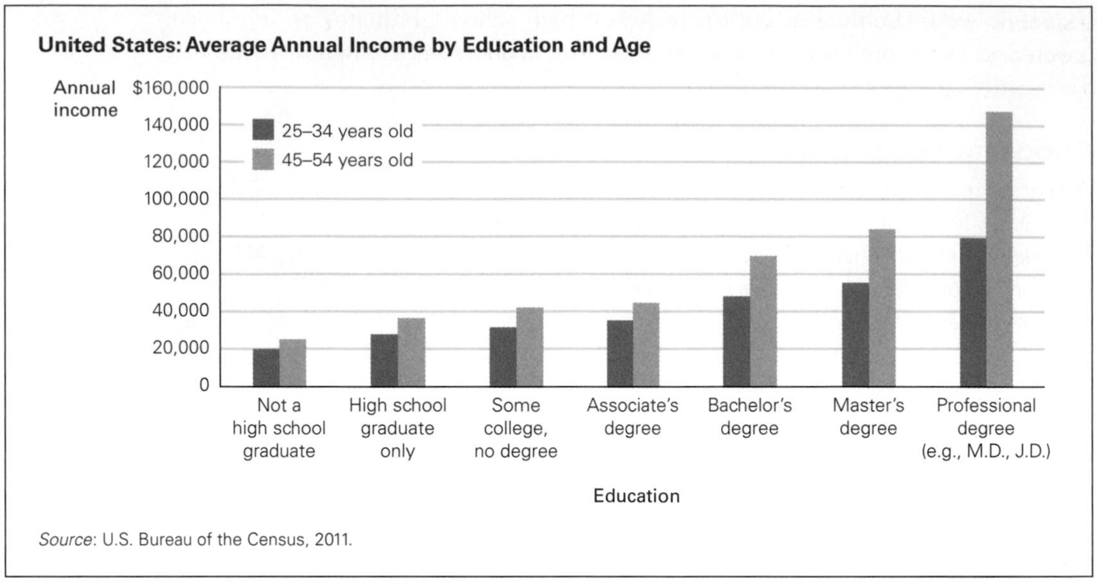

FIGURE 15.8

Older, Wiser, and Richer Adolescents find it easier to think about their immediate experiences (a boring math class) rather than their middle-age income, so some drop out of high school to take a job that will someday pay $500 a week. But over an average of 40 years of employment, someone who completes a master's degree earns half a million dollars more than someone who leaves school in eleventh grade. That translates into about $90,000 for each year of education from twelfth grade to a master's. The earnings gap is even wider than those numbers indicate because this chart compares adults who have jobs, yet finding work is more difficult for those with less education.

do not have advanced degrees (Swanson, 2011). Here are 10 such occupations, with average annual earnings:

Air traffic controller, $70,000
Firefighter, $60,000
Police officer, $58,000
Respiratory therapist, $49,000
Dental hygienist, $44,000
Payroll and timekeeping clerk, $33,000
Licensed practical nurse, $33,000
Data entry keyer, $25,000
Telephone operator, $24,000
Massage therapist, $18,000

These numbers are from 2009 in the United States as a whole: Variation is apparent not only in other nations but also in various regions of the United States. Although high school students need to know that college is not the only option, they also need to know that each of these occupations requires additional training that builds on skills mastered in high school. Understanding this may increase motivation.

Measuring Practical Cognition

Currently, employers in every nation provide on-the-job training (usually much more specific and current than high schools provide) and want their newly trained employees to know how to think, explain, write, concentrate, and get along with other people. Similar skills are necessary for the college-bound, especially if they hope to stay long enough to obtain a degree. Those skills are hard to measure on a high-stakes test or on the international tests explained in Chapter 12, the PIRLS and the TIMSS.

PISA (Programme for International Student Assessment) An international test taken by 15-year-olds in 50 nations that is designed to measure problem solving and cognition in daily life.

Another international test, the **PISA (Programme for International Student Assessment),** is designed to measure the kind of cognition needed in adult life. The PISA is taken by 15-year-olds in 50 nations, with that age picked deliberately because many students are close to the end of their formal school career. On this test, the questions are written to be practical, measuring knowledge that might apply at home or on the job. As a PISA report described it:

> The tests are designed to generate measures of the extent to which students can make effective use of what they have learned in school to deal with various problems and challenges they are likely to experience in everyday life.
>
> *[PISA, 2009, p. 12]*

For example, among the math questions is this one:

> Robert's mother lets him pick one candy from a bag. He can't see the candies. The number of candies of each color in the bag is shown in the following graph.

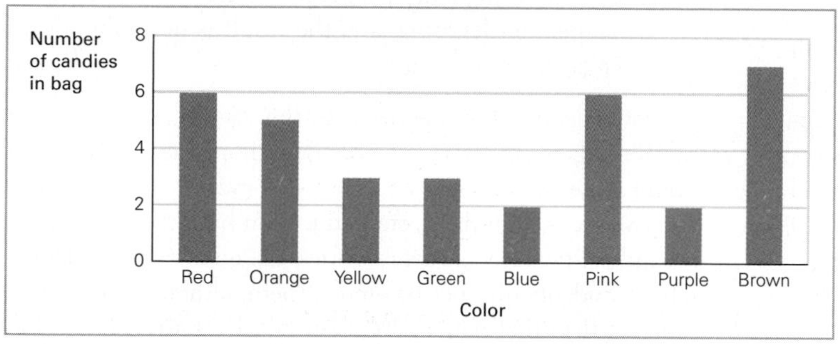

> What is the probability that Robert will pick a red candy?
>
> A. 10% B. 20% C. 25% D. 50%

For that and the other questions on the PISA, the calculations are quite simple—most 10-year-olds can do them; no calculus or complex formulas are needed. However, the mathematical reasoning may be challenging, in part because of the *base rate neglect* fallacy described in the beginning of the chapter. On this question, only one-half of the students worldwide got it right (answer B), as did fewer than one-half of the students from the United States.

Overall, the U.S. students did worse on the PISA than on the PIRLS or TIMSS. On the PISA overall (reading, science, and math), China, Finland, and Korea were at the top, Canada close to the top, and the United States average in reading and science and below average in math (see Table 15.2). Analysis of nations and scores on the PISA finds four factors that correlate with high achievement (OECD, 2010b, p. 6):

- Leaders, parents, and citizens overall value education, with individualized approaches to learning so that all students learn what they need.
- Standards are high and clear, so every student knows what he or she must do, with a "focus on the acquisition of complex, higher order thinking skills."
- Teachers and administrators are valued, given "considerable discretion . . . in determining content" and sufficient salary as well as time for collaboration.
- Learning is prioritized "across the entire system," with high-quality teachers working in the most challenging environments.

Indications from the PISA and from international comparisons of high school dropout rates suggest that secondary education can be improved for those who do not go to college. The first step seems to be to keep students engaged in school, so they do not quit. How to do that requires critical thinking, as the following explains.

Not Geography The PISA is taken by 15-year-olds in many nations. Questions are designed to measure practical applications of school knowledge in science, reading, and math. National variations are more closely tied to educational practices and values at school and home, not to geography, genes, or immigration. For instance, Finland and Norway are close on the map but not in math achievement, and although most Asian nations do very well, note that Thailand scores low. Also note that nations with a higher proportion of immigrants than the United States (e.g., Canada) or very few immigrants (e.g., Japan) seem to do equally well.

TABLE 15.2 Math Scores on the PISA, 2006/2009

Nation	Score	Nation	Score
Shanghai, China	—/600	Poland	495/495
Singapore	—/562	Hungary	491/490
Chinese Taipei	549/543	Norway	490/498
Finland	548/541	Spain	480/483
Hong Kong	547/555	Russia	476/468
South Korea	547/546	United States	474/487
Netherlands	531/526	Portugal	466/487
Switzerland	530/534	Italy	462/483
Canada	527/527	Greece	459/466
Japan	523/529	Israel	442/447
New Zealand	522/519	Uruguay	427/427
Belgium	520/515	Turkey	424/445
Australia	520/514	Thailand	417/419
Denmark	513/503	Romania	415/427
Czech Republic	510/493	Chile	411/421
Iceland	506/507	Mexico	406/419
Austria	505/496	Indonesia	391/371
Germany	504/513	Jordan	384/387
Sweden	502/494	Argentina	381/388
Ireland	501/487	Colombia	370/381
France	496/497	Brazil	370/386
United Kingdom	495/492	Tunisia	365/371

Source: PISA, 2009.

THINKING CRITICALLY

Increasing Adolescent Engagement in School

What can be done to encourage adolescents to be engaged with school? There is no single, definitive answer. However, developmental research provides three suggestions:

- *Keep high schools small.* Schools educate best if 200 to 400 students are enrolled because many teachers and staff will know every student and almost every student will be involved in some sort of team or club. That fosters a sense of belonging to the school, more personal relationships, and more engagement with education. Unfortunately, in 2010 the *average* secondary school in eight U.S. states (Florida, California, Georgia, Hawaii, Maryland, Nevada, New Jersey, and Virginia) enrolled over a thousand students.
- *Encourage extracurricular activities.* There are "developmental benefits of participation in extracurricular activities for many high school adolescents" (Fredricks & Eccles, 2006, p. 712). Athletic teams elicit positive emotions and school bonding, for the athletes and everyone else. Even activities sponsored by nonschool groups help (Glanville et al., 2008). A North Carolina study found that high schools with more varied activities, and more students in them, had fewer dropouts and higher achievement. One reason for the correlation was SES: Students from wealthier families were more likely to go to schools with many activities. But the correlation held even when student and school SES were taken into account (Stearns & Glennie, 2010). Another study of students in extracurricular activities (sponsored by school, church, or community groups) found that engagement increased when students felt competent (e.g., in drama, dance) and had positive relationships with adults or peers (Dawes & Larson, 2011).
- *Reduce harassment.* School violence is decreasing in the United States, but fear of violence is increasing. Clear rules for student behavior, rewards for attendance, and more sporting events within (not just between) schools all reduce in-school crime, according to a survey of Texas middle and high schools (Cheurprakobkit & Bartsch, 2005). Cyberbullying is particularly difficult for school policy to forbid, but it is affected by school climate. Schools can foster adult cooperation, student friendships, and respect for learning, and the result is not only safety but engagement (Stewart, 2008).

Not everyone would agree with this list, which is why critical thinking is necessary. Furthermore, implementing each item would increase school costs. Ironically, every high school dropout saves money in the overall education budget. When taxpayers and political leaders set priorities, the education of secondary school students may not be among them, although the PISA results confirm that nations in which teachers are respected and well paid are also nations in which students achieve. A positive school climate "requires explicit, targeted, and aligned change efforts at the leverage points" (McGuigan, 2008, p. 112). To agree on those levers, and pull them, requires effort.

LAURA DWIGHT

Bored or Attentive? This girl explains an aspect of history to her classmates at the small Manhattan International School. This public school's size (300 students) might increase student engagement, but the four-year graduation rate is only 60 percent, suggesting that factors beyond class size are important.

Surprisingly, students who are capable of passing their classes drop out as often as those who are less capable. Persistence, engagement, and motivation seem more crucial than intellectual ability (Archambault et al., 2009). One study that measured engagement and motivation reported that students were most motivated and engaged in primary school, somewhat engaged in college, but least engaged in secondary school (Martin, 2009).

Remember, however, that adolescents vary in every aspect and that the seriously troubled ones are a minority. A study of student emotional and academic engagement from the fifth to the eighth grade found that, as expected, the overall

direction was less engagement; but a distinctive group (about 18 percent) were highly engaged throughout, and another distinctive group (about 5 percent) experienced precipitous disengagement year by year. The 5 percent who were most turned off were typically boys from low-income families (Li & Lerner, 2011). That is tragic, for society as well as for those boys.

Secondary school teachers are hired for their academic expertise, not for their ability to engage adolescents. They model formal operational thinking—answering questions about the intricacies of theoretical physics, advanced calculus, and iambic pentameter—but they may not connect with students or understand practical vocational requirements. Furthermore, the most qualified teachers tend to gravitate to schools with more able students (where salaries are higher and class sizes smaller); even within schools, the best teachers are often assigned classes of the elite college-bound. All students learn best when a master teacher guides active discussion, debate, and exposition, but those who most need such teaching are least likely to have it (Slavin et al., 2009).

Some nations provide equally qualified teachers for every school. The disparity in teacher quality between wealthy and impoverished schools is much greater in the United States than in nations that score high on the PISA (e.g., Finland and Canada) (Cavanagh, 2007).

A final question arises for all three of the groups discussed here: the college-bound, the students who quit after they earn their diploma, and those who drop out as soon as they can (legally age 16 in most U.S. states). That question is: Does learning during adolescence matter when considering the entire life span? For individuals, the answer is a resounding yes. Not only health but also almost every other indicator of a good life—high income, stable marriage, successful children, satisfying work—correlates with education.

Beyond the benefits to the individual, entire nations gain from the quality of secondary education. A detailed calculation found that if the U.S. average PISA score increased by a mere 25 points (up to the scores for France, Ireland, or Sweden; still far below those of Finland or South Korea), that would result in an increase of $40 *trillion* in the nation's GDP (gross domestic product, a number used by economists to measure national economic production) between 2010 and 2090 (Hanushek & Woessmann, 2010). How could this be?

The cognitive skills that boost economic development are creativity, flexibility, and analytic ability; they allow innovation and mastery of new technology. When nations raise their human capital by boasting more adults who possess those skills, their economies prosper (Cohen & Soto, 2007). Scores on the PISA and other tests predict later economic development (Hanushek & Woessmann, 2010).

The cognitive abilities that nations need in the twenty-first century are exactly what adolescents can develop—with proper education and guidance. As you have read, every scientist who studies adolescent cognition notes that the logical and creative potential of the adolescent mind is not always realized, but it can be. Does this chapter end on a hopeful note?

SUMMING UP

Middle schools tend to be less personal, less flexible, and more tightly regulated than elementary schools, which may contribute to a general finding: declining student achievement. School transitions are difficult but can be made less stressful. Ideally, secondary education advances thinking, although some measures that help students connect with their schools (such as sports) are too often undervalued. High school students who do not expect to attend college may be particularly unprepared for adult life. Guidance for careers is needed, but scarce. ■

SUMMARY

Logic and Self

1. Cognition in early adolescence may be egocentric, a kind of self-centered thinking. Adolescent egocentrism gives rise to the personal fable, the invincibility fable, and the imaginary audience.

2. *Formal operational thought* is Piaget's term for the last of his four periods of cognitive development. He tested and demonstrated formal operational thought with various problems that students in a high school science or math class might encounter.

3. Piaget realized that adolescents are no longer earthbound and concrete in their thinking; they imagine the possible, the probable, and even the impossible, instead of focusing on what is real. They develop hypotheses and explore, using deductive reasoning. However, few developmentalists find that adolescents move suddenly from concrete to formal thinking.

Two Modes of Thinking

4. Intuitive thinking becomes more forceful during adolescence. Few teenagers always use logic, although they are capable of doing so. Emotional, intuitive thinking is quicker and more satisfying, and sometimes better, than analytic thought.

5. Contrary to popular belief, research has found that a large majority of adolescents consider themselves to be religious, with most following the faith of their parents. With time, they move away from traditional practices, but they believe their deeper cognition results in stronger rather than weaker faith.

6. Neurological as well as survey research finds that adolescent thinking is characterized by more rapid development of the limbic system and slower development of the prefrontal cortex. This explains the imbalance evident in dual processing.

Technology and Cognition

7. Adolescents use technology, particularly the Internet, more than people of any other age group. They reap many educational benefits, but some technology is destructive, in video game addiction, cyberbullying, and support for pathology.

Teaching and Learning

8. Secondary education—after primary education (grade school) and before tertiary education (college)—correlates with the health and wealth of individuals and nations.

9. In middle school, many students tend to be bored, difficult to teach, and hurtful to one another. One reason may be that middle schools are not structured to accommodate egocentrism or intuitive thinking.

10. Many forms of psychopathology increase during the transitions to middle school, to high school, and to college. School changes may be particularly difficult in adolescence, when young people must also adjust to biological and family changes.

11. Education in high school emphasizes formal operational thinking. In the United States, the demand for more accountability has led to increased requirements for graduation as well as more Advanced Placement (AP) classes and high-stakes testing. The concern is that this may undermine creativity and innovation.

12. A sizable number of high school students do not graduate or go on to college, and many more leave college without a degree. Current high school education does not seem to meet their needs.

13. The PISA test taken by many 15-year-olds in 50 nations measures how well they can apply the knowledge they have been taught. Students in the United States seem to have particular difficulty with such tests.

KEY TERMS

adolescent egocentrism (p. 440)
personal fable (p. 440)
invincibility fable (p. 440)
imaginary audience (p. 441)
formal operational thought (p. 442)
hypothetical thought (p. 444)
deductive reasoning (p. 444)
inductive reasoning (p. 444)
sunk cost fallacy (p. 445)
base rate neglect (p. 445)
dual-process model (p. 446)
intuitive thought (p. 446)
analytic thought (p. 446)
cyberbullying (p. 453)
cutting (p. 454)
secondary education (p. 455)
middle school (p. 456)
entity approach to intelligence (p. 458)
incremental approach to intelligence (p. 459)
high-stakes test (p. 461)
PISA (Programme for International Student Assessment) (p. 464)

WHAT HAVE YOU LEARNED?

Logic and Self

1. How does adolescent egocentrism differ from early childhood egocentrism?

2. What are the two extreme perceptions that arise from the imaginary audience?

3. Why are the personal fable and the invincibility fable called "fables"?

4. How does formal operational thinking differ from concrete operational thinking?

5. What are the advantages and disadvantages of using induction rather than deduction?

6. How certain are contemporary developmentalists that Piaget accurately described adolescent cognition?

Two Modes of Thinking

7. When might intuition and analysis lead to contrasting conclusions?

8. What mode of thinking—intuitive or analytic—do most people prefer, and why?

9. How does personal experience increase the probability of base rate neglect?

10. How does egocentrism account for the clashing priorities of parents and adolescents?

11. When is intuitive thinking better than analytic thinking?

Technology and Cognition

12. What benefits come from adolescents' use of technology?

13. How do video games affect student learning?

14. Who is most and least likely to be involved in cyberbullying?

15. If an adolescent consults the Internet regarding cutting and/ or other dangerous sites, what should adults do?

Teaching and Learning

16. Why have most junior high schools disappeared?

17. What characteristics of middle schools make them more difficult for students than elementary schools?

18. How does being a young adolescent affect a person's ability to learn?

19. Why are transitions a particular concern for educators?

20. Why is the first year of attending a new school more stressful than the second year?

21. How are educational standards changing in the United States?

22. What are the advantages and disadvantages of high-stakes testing?

23. Why is Germany's apprentice/vocational education system no longer prevalent?

24. How does the PISA differ from other international tests?

25. Why is high school achievement likely to advance the national economy?

APPLICATIONS

1. Describe a time when you overestimated how much other people were thinking about you. How was your mistake similar to and different from adolescent egocentrism?

2. Talk to a teenager about politics, families, school, religion, or any other topic that might reveal the way he or she thinks. Do you hear any adolescent egocentrism? Intuitive thinking? Systematic thought? Flexibility? Cite examples.

3. Think of a life-changing decision you have made. How did logic and emotion interact? What would have changed if you had given the matter more thought—or less?

4. Describe what happened and what you thought in the first year you attended a middle school or high school. What made it better or worse than later years in that school?

>>ONLINE CONNECTIONS

To accompany your textbook, you have access to a number of online resources, including quizzes for every chapter of the book, flashcards (in English and Spanish), critical thinking questions, and case studies. For access to any of these links, go to www.worthpublishers.com/bergerca9e. In addition to these free resources, you'll also find links to podcasts, video clips, diagnostic quizzing with personalized study advice, and an ebook. Some of the videos and activities available online include:

- *Child Soldiers and Child Peacemakers.* More than 150 wars since World War II! See the effects of armed conflict on children's development and hear how some young people take a stand for peace.
- *HIV/AIDS.* A brief history of the global spread of HIV and successful promotion of educational intervention in Sri Lanka. Videos let affected people tell their stories.

16

CHAPTER

Adolescence: Psychosocial Development

WHAT WILL YOU KNOW?

1. Why do some teenagers seem to change their appearance, their behavior, and their goals markedly from one year to the next?
2. When teenagers disagree with their parents on every issue, is it time for the parents to give up, become stricter, or something else?
3. Does knowing about sex make it more likely a teenager will be sexually active?
4. Is delinquency a sign of serious crime in adulthood or a temporary phase?
5. Since most adolescents try alcohol, why do laws forbid it?

"What does your mother do?" Emil, the head of Town Security, asked Bethany, whose summer job was as a security deputy.

"She writes books."

"How does she do that?"

"She spends a lot of time in the library, reading and writing."

"Oh, your poor mother!"

No need for pity. I enjoy my work. Each of us has our own preferences, habits, and interests, explored when we began to find our identity. Emil liked riding around town, responding to emergencies, searching for "perps." I would hate that. Even as a teenager, I enjoyed reading and writing, explaining ideas. I resented interruptions, such as those crackling on Emil's radio. I chose classes that let me figure things out with paper and pencil. Advanced math was a favorite, even though I was the only girl in the class.

In some ways, I was a rebel: I told my friends that I would never be a teacher (too conventional), and I refused the colleges my parents suggested (more of that in the epilogue). But in many ways, I was typical. For example, I was thrilled when Bill invited me to a college weekend. When his roommate said, "That's not the kind of girl you date, that's the kind of girl you marry," I was pleased. That was my plan for myself.

This chapter describes the search for identity, often a mixture of personal preferences, parental pressure, and teenage rebellion. Adults and peers influence each young person, and adolescents resist parts of their familial and cultural heritage while accepting other parts. One important topic is romance; many adolescents try to discern and express their gender identity via partners, aspirations, and sexuality. That college weekend was approved by my culture and cohort but would be less admired now. We also consider other forms of identity in this chapter, as well as dangers that threaten healthy growth.

A few adolescents plunge into despair and attempt suicide; most experiment with alcohol and minor lawbreaking—perhaps to be stopped by someone like Emil, who likes his job and would hate mine. All this is covered here, describing how 11- to 18-year-olds move through the psychosocial maze from childhood to adulthood.

>> Identity

Psychosocial development during adolescence is often understood as a search for a consistent understanding of oneself. Self-expression and self-concept become increasingly important at puberty, as the egocentrism described in Chapter 15 illustrates. Each young person wants to know, "Who am I?"

identity versus role confusion Erikson's term for the fifth stage of development, in which the person tries to figure out "Who am I?" but is confused as to which of many possible roles to adopt.

identity achievement Erikson's term for the attainment of identity, or the point at which a person understands who he or she is as a unique individual, in accord with past experiences and future plans.

According to Erik Erikson, life's fifth psychosocial crisis is **identity versus role confusion:** The complexities of finding one's own identity are the primary task of adolescence (Erikson, 1968). He said this crisis is resolved with **identity achievement,** when adolescents have reconsidered the goals and values of their parents and culture, accepting some and discarding others, discerning their own identity.

The result is neither wholesale rejection nor unquestioning acceptance of social norms (Côté, 2009). With their new autonomy, teenagers maintain continuity with the past so they can move to the future. Each person must achieve his or her own identity; the social context of each generation differs, and everyone must discover and adjust to a unique combination of genes and alleles.

Not Yet Achieved

Erikson's insights have inspired thousands of researchers. Notable among them was James Marcia, who described and measured four specific ways young people cope with this stage of life: (1) role confusion, (2) foreclosure, (3) moratorium, and finally (4) identity achievement (Marcia, 1966). Over the past half-century, major psychosocial shifts have lengthened the duration of adolescence and made identity achievement more complex (Côté, 2006; Kroger et al., 2010; Meeus, 2011). However, the three way stations on the road to identity achievement still seem evident.

role confusion A situation in which an adolescent does not seem to know or care what his or her identity is. (Sometimes called *identity* or *role diffusion.*)

Role confusion is the opposite of identity achievement. It is characterized by lack of commitment to any goals or values. Identity confusion is sometimes called *identity diffusion* instead of *role confusion,* to emphasize that some adolescents seem diffuse, unfocused, unconcerned about their future (Phillips & Pittman, 2007). Even the usual social demands—such as putting away clothes, making friends, completing school assignments, and thinking about college or career—are beyond role-confused adolescents. Instead, they might sleep too much, immerse themselves in video games or mind-numbing television, and turn from one flirtation to another. Their thinking is disorganized, they procrastinate, they avoid issues and actions (Côté, 2009).

foreclosure Erikson's term for premature identity formation, which occurs when an adolescent adopts parents' or society's roles and values wholesale, without questioning or analysis.

Identity **foreclosure** occurs when, in order to halt role confusion, young people accept traditional values (Marcia, 1966; Marcia et al., 1993). They might follow roles and customs transmitted from their parents or culture, never exploring alternatives. Or they might foreclose on an oppositional, negative identity—the direct opposite of whatever their parents want—again without thoughtful questioning. Foreclosure is comfortable. For many, it is a temporary shelter, a time for commitment to a particular identity, which will be followed by more exploration (Meeus, 2011).

moratorium An adolescent's choice of a socially acceptable way to postpone making identity-achievement decisions. Going to college is a common example.

A more mature shelter is **moratorium,** a time-out that includes some exploration, either in breadth (trying many things) or in depth (examining one path after making a tentative commitment) (Meeus, 2011). Societies provide many opportunities for moratoria, such as college or military service, that allow adolescents to postpone identity achievement. This identity status is most common at age 19, although it can occur earlier or later (Kroger et al., 2010). Many emerging adults are still in moratorium.

Several aspects of the search for identity, especially sexual and vocational identity, have become more arduous than they were when Erikson described them, and forging any personal identity is more difficult. Fifty years ago, the drive to become independent and autonomous was thought to be the "key normative psychosocial task of adolescence" (Zimmer-Gembeck & Collins, 2003, p. 177). Adolescents still struggle with identity, but now developmentalists believe that it is unusual for teenagers to resolve this crisis and reach identity achievement. Adolescents begin the search, but a review of longitudinal "studies among adults revealed that identity is a life-long process" (Meeus, 2011, p. 88).

MITCH WOJNAROWICZ / THE IMAGE WORKS

Not Just a Uniform Adolescents in moratorium adopt temporary roles to postpone achieving their final identity. High school students like these may sign up for an ROTC (Reserve Officers Training Corps) class, but few of them go on to enlist in the U.S. Marine Corps.

Four Arenas of Identity Formation

Erikson (1968) highlighted four aspects of identity: religious, political, vocational, and sexual. Terminology and emphasis have changed for all four, as has timing. In fact, if an 18-year-old is no longer open to new possibilities in any of these four areas, that may indicate foreclosure, not achievement—and identity might shift again. (My own identity is one example: I did not marry Bill, or anyone, until my mid-20s, relatively late for my cohort. At age 23, I chose teaching as my vocation.)

None of these four identity statuses occurs in social isolation: Parents and peers are influential, as detailed later in this chapter, and the ever-changing chronosystem (historical context) makes identity dynamic. Nonetheless, each of these four arenas remains integral to adolescent development.

Religious Identity

For most adolescents, their *religious identity* is similar to that of their parents and community, as noted in Chapter 15. Few adolescents totally reject religion if they've grown up following a particular faith, partly because religion provides meaning as well as coping skills that are particularly useful during stressful times (King & Roeser, 2009).

Past parental practices influence adolescent religious identity, although some adolescents express that identity in ways that their parents did not anticipate: A Muslim girl might start to wear a headscarf, or a Catholic boy might study for the priesthood, or a Baptist teenager might join a Pentecostal youth group. Such new practices are relatively minor: Almost no young Muslim converts to Judaism, and almost no teenage Baptist becomes Hindu. Most adolescents accept the broad outlines of the religious identity of their parents and culture, questioning specific beliefs as their cognitive processes allow more reflective, less concrete assumptions, but without a crisis of faith unless unusual circumstances propel it (King & Roeser, 2009).

A Religious Life These young adolescents in Ethiopia are studying to be monks. Their monastery is a haven in the midst of civil strife. Will the rituals and beliefs also provide them with a way to achieve identity?

ROB HOWARD / CORBIS

Political Identity

Parents are also influential for *political identity* in that most adolescents follow the political traditions of their parents. In the twenty-first century in the United States, party identification is weakening among adults, with more of them saying they are independent rather than Republican, Democratic, or of some other party (Pew Research Center, 2009). Their teenage children reflect this; some proudly say they do not care about politics, in which case their apolitical identity is likely to continue in adulthood (Côté, 2009).

A word here about political terrorism and religious extremism. People who are relatively young (under age 30) are often on the front lines of terrorism or are converts to groups that their elders consider cults. Fanatical political and religious movements have much in common—age of new adherents is one of them (L. L. Dawson, 2010). However, adolescents are rarely drawn to these groups unless personal loneliness or family background (such as a parent's death caused by an opposing group) compels them. It is an adult myth that every teenager is potentially a suicide bomber or willing martyr.

This does not mean that adolescents ignore their ethnicity. Especially in a multicultural society such as the United States, most adolescents identify proudly with their ethnicity—or, often, ethnicities, claiming that several labels describe them (such as African, Black, and American). One study found that the typical adolescent endorsed three such labels, with bicultural adolescents considering ethnic identities more central to themselves than monocultural adolescents did (Marks et al., 2011).

Vocational Identity

Vocational identity originally meant envisioning oneself as a worker in a particular occupation. This made sense a century ago, when most girls became wives and mothers, not employees, and most men became farmers, small businessmen, or factory workers. Those few in professions were generalists (doctors were general practitioners, lawyers handled all kinds of cases, teachers were usually unmarried women who taught all subjects). Decades ago, adolescents sought a vocational identity so they could decide whether or not to stay in high school and aim for college.

Obviously, early vocational identity is no longer relevant. Secondary education is necessary for almost everyone; no one is ready for a particular lifetime job at age 16. Nor is any teenager prepared to choose among the tens of thousands of careers; most adults change vocations (not just employers) several times. One popular reference detailing possible careers is 4,128 pages long (Ferguson Publishing, 2010). As explained in Chapter 15, adolescents are more likely to be engaged in high school if they realize that the skills they are learning will be relevant for every job, even as they realize that a college degree is not the only post–high school training they need. However, almost no one finds work during adolescence that becomes a lifelong career. Vocational identity takes years to establish.

The Same Situation, Many Miles Apart: Learning in School For these two groups of Muslim girls, the distance between their schools in Dearborn, Michigan *(left),* and Jammu, Kashmir *(right),* is more than geographical. The schools' hidden curricula teach different lessons about the roles of women.

Observation Quiz What three differences are evident? (see answer, page 476)

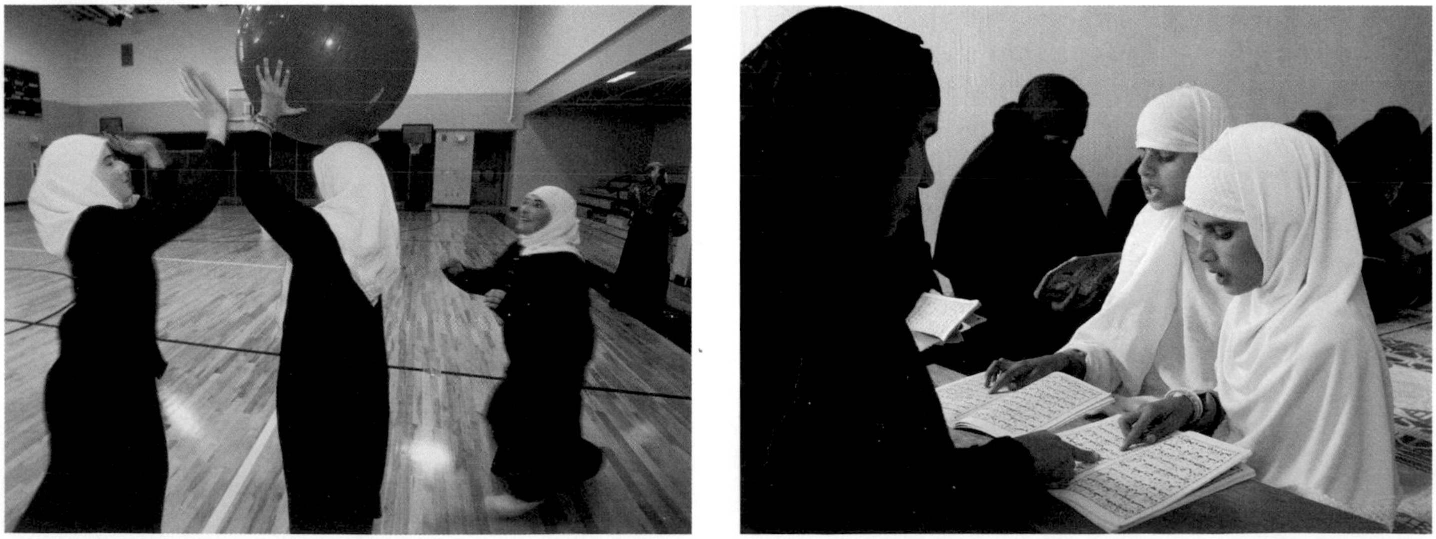

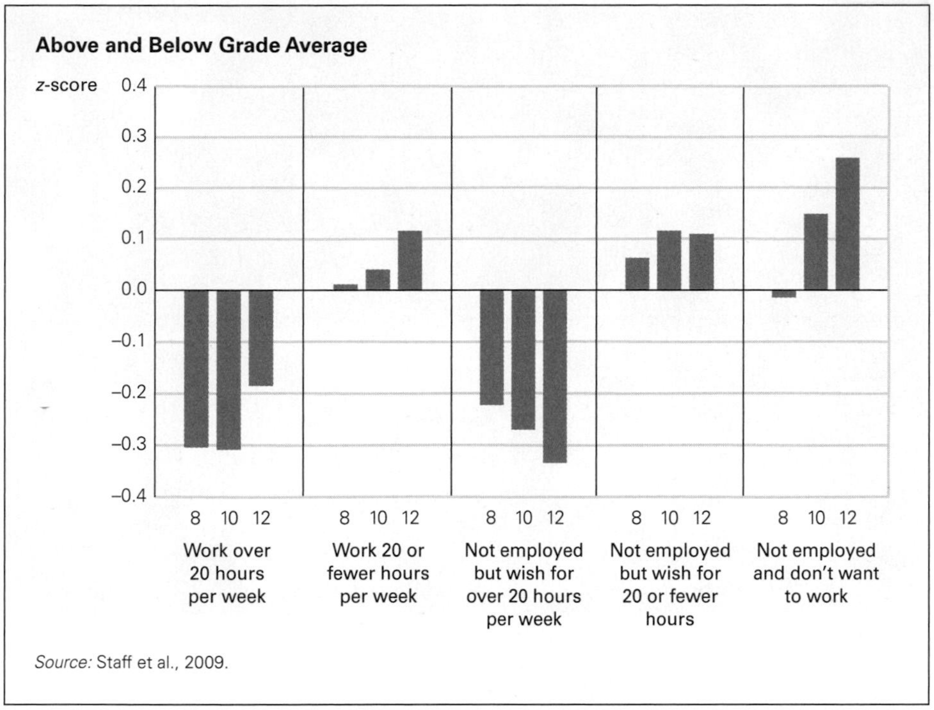

FIGURE 16.1

Don't Think About It! There was a time when high school employment correlated with saving for college and lifetime success. No longer. The surprise is that even wanting a full-time job (and the extra income that would bring) reduces achievement—or is it the other way around?

Although some adults hope that part-time employment during high school will keep teenagers out of trouble, the opposite is more likely as adolescents develop their vocational identity (Staff & Schulenberg, 2010). Working over vacations or a few hours during the school week is harmless, but adolescents who work more than 20 hours a week during the school year tend to quit school, fight with parents, smoke cigarettes, and hate their jobs—both when they are teenagers and when they become adults. Typically, they spend their wages on clothes, cars, drugs, and concerts, not family support or college savings. Grades fall: Work hours interfere with homework, extra help, and school attendance (see Figure 16.1). Only a tiny and shrinking minority—alienated from school but appreciated, mentored, and promoted at work—benefit from intense teenage employment.

Sexual Identity

Achieving *sexual identity* is also a lifelong task, in part because norms and attitudes keep changing (see Figure 16.2). Increasing numbers of young adults are single, gay, or cohabiting, providing teenagers with new role models and choices and thus making sexual identity more confusing. A half-century ago, Erikson and other theorists thought of the two sexes as opposites (P. Y. Miller & Simon, 1980). They assumed that adolescents who were confused about sexual identity would soon adopt "proper" male or female roles (Erikson, 1968; A. Freud, 1958/2000). Adolescence was once a time for "gender intensification," when people increasingly identified as male or female. No longer (Priess et al., 2009).

As you remember from Chapter 10, for social scientists *sex* and *sexual* refer to biological characteristics,

FIGURE 16.2

Young and Old Everyone knows that attitudes about same-sex relationships are changing. Less well known is that cohort differences are greater than the shift over the first decade of the twenty-first century.

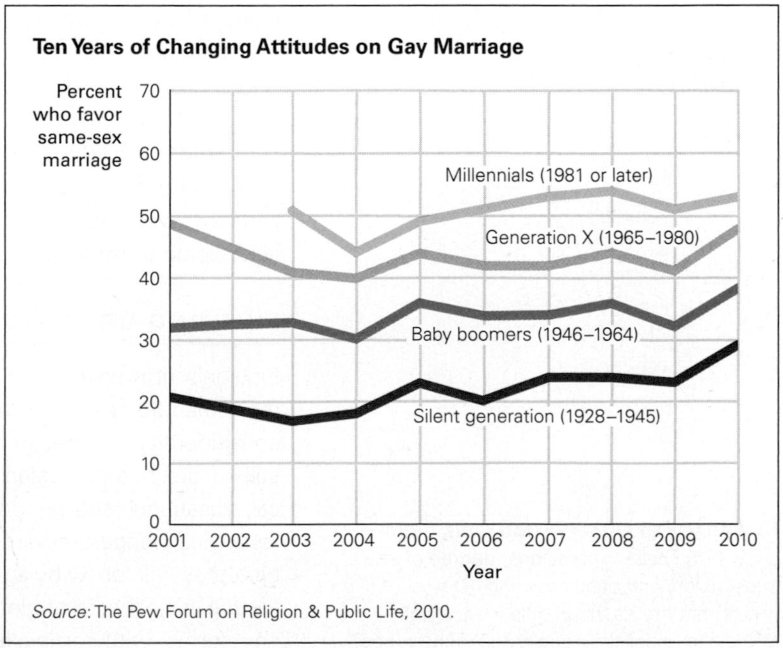

ZUMA PRESS / NEWSCOM

Who and Where? As Erikson explained in 1968, the pride of self-discovery is universal for adolescents: These could be teenagers anywhere. But a closer look reveals gay teenagers in Atlanta, Georgia, where this march could not have occurred 50 years ago.

whereas *gender* refers to cultural and social attributes that differentiate males and females. The distinction between biology and culture is not always clear-cut, since the body is affected by behavior and vice versa. Nonetheless, Erikson's term *sexual identity* has been replaced by **gender identity** (Denny & Pittman, 2007), which refers primarily to a person's self-definition as male or female. Gender identity often (not always) begins with the person's biological sex and leads to a gender role, which is a role that society considers appropriate for that gender.

gender identity A person's acceptance of the roles and behaviors that society associates with the biological categories of male and female.

Gender roles once meant that only men had jobs; they were *breadwinners* (good providers) and women were *housewives* (married to their houses). As women entered the labor market, gender roles expanded but were still apparent (nurse/doctor, secretary/businessman, pink collar/blue collar). All that continues to change today—with the degree, rate, and direction of change varying dramatically from culture to culture.

What has not changed is that adolescents experience strong sexual drives as hormones increase. As Erikson recognized, many are confused regarding when, how, and with whom to express those drives. That complicates achievement of gender identity (Baumeister & Blackhart, 2007; Gilchrist & Sullivan, 2006). Some adolescents foreclose by exaggerating male or female roles; others seek a moratorium by avoiding all sexual contact. Some of the complexities of gender-identity achievement are discussed later in this chapter, when we focus on romance.

SUMMING UP

Erikson's fifth psychosocial crisis, identity versus role confusion, was first described more than 50 years ago. Adolescence was characterized as a time to search for a personal identity in order to reach identity achievement by adulthood. The identity crisis still occurs; role confusion, foreclosure, and moratorium are apparent in religious, political, vocational, and gender identity. However, timing has changed. The identity crisis lasts much longer; fewer young people develop a firm sense of who they are and what path they will follow by age 18.

Specific aspects of identity—religious, political, vocational, and gender—have taken new forms, with complexities that Erikson did not anticipate. Settling early on an iden-

>> Answer to Observation Quiz (from page 474) Facial expressions, degree of adult supervision, and head covering. (Did you notice that the Kashmiri girls wear a tight-fitting cap under their one-piece white robes?)

tity may be a sign of foreclosure, not achievement. This is especially true for vocational identity: The vast array of possible jobs, and the training required for each one, means that adolescents need years of exploration and education. Likewise, adolescents are aware of many more possible religious, political, and gender identities than adults once recognized.

>> Relationships with Adults

Adolescence is often characterized as a period of waning adult influence, when children distance themselves from their elders. There is validity in this view, but it is not always accurate. In fact, some young people feel appreciated by their communities, trusted by teachers, and connected to parents or other adults; when they do, they usually avoid drugs, stay in school, and take good care of themselves.

Parents

The fact that parent–adolescent relationships are pivotal does not mean that they are peaceful (Eisenberg et al., 2008; Laursen & Collins, 2009). Disputes are common because the adolescent's drive for independence, arising from biological as well as psychological impulses, clashes with the parents' desire to maintain control.

Normally, parent–adolescent conflict peaks in early adolescence, especially between mothers and daughters. It usually manifests as **bickering**—repeated, petty arguments (more nagging than fighting) about routine, day-to-day concerns such as cleanliness, clothes, chores, and schedules (Eisenberg et al., 2008). One of the problems is that both generations misjudge the other: Parents think their offspring have more negative thoughts than the children have, and adolescents imagine much more intrusive control than the parents intend (Sillars et al., 2010).

bickering Petty, peevish arguing, usually repeated and ongoing.

Some bickering may indicate a healthy family, since close relationships almost always include conflict (Smetana et al., 2004). Both generations need to be more explicit—if the argument is only about the dirty socks on the floor, the teenager can put them in the laundry, but if it's about dictating personal habits, of course the child resists. With time, parents gradually grant more autonomy, and "friendship and positive affect [emotional state] typically rebound to preadolescent levels" (Collins & Laursen, 2004, p. 337). By age 18, many teenagers have reduced their impulsivity and egocentrism and can appreciate their parents, who have learned to accept less disclosure but improved communication as the young person matures (Masche, 2010).

In Chapter 10, you learned that authoritative parenting is usually best for children and that uninvolved parenting is worst. The same holds true for adolescents. Although teenagers may say they no longer need their parents, neglect is always destructive—as you saw with James in Chapter 15. Another example is Joy. When she was 16, her stepfather said: "Teens all around here [are] doing booze and doing drugs. . . . But my Joy here ain't into that stuff" (quoted in C. Smith, 2005, p. 10). In fact, however, Joy was smoking pot, drinking alcohol, and having sex with her boyfriend. She

> overdosed on a bunch of stuff once, pills or some prescription of my mom's—I took the whole bottle. It didn't work. I just went to sleep for a long time. . . . They never found out . . . pretty pitiful.
>
> *[quoted in C. Smith, 2005, p. 12]*

That suicide attempt was a clear indication that she was in far worse trouble than most "teens all around here."

ACE STOCK LIMITED / ALAMY

What Next? Crying, cursing, quitting? Hopefully not. Every close relationship has moments of conflict, which ideally lead to mutual understanding, forgiveness, and even a new way of behaving.

"So I blame you for everything—whose fault is that?"

Cultural Differences

Regarding parent–adolescent relationships, some cultures value harmony above all else, and in those places adolescents virtually never contradict their parents. Given that, some scholars wonder whether the adolescent rebellion they had taken for granted is actually a social construction (defined in Chapter 1) (Russell et al., 2010). Perhaps it is a middle-class Western assumption that adolescent rebellion is a psychosocial necessity. Or perhaps rebellion is a consequence of a competitive global economy, not a developmental universal (Larson & Wilson, 2004). This idea that rebellion is a cultural or cohort phenomenon is contrary to another idea, that bickering and the drive for autonomy are universal steps toward healthy adulthood.

More longitudinal research is needed before we can judge whether one side of this debate is more accurate than the other. But there is no doubt that culture affects the topics and methods of conflict. Because of globalization, adolescents who have never traveled far from home are aware of other ways of life, and they question why their parents do not act the same as others they have known or heard about.

Expectations vary by culture, as do justifications (Brown & Bakken, 2011). For example, Japanese youth expect autonomy in their musical choices but want parents to help them with romance (Hasebe et al., 2004), whereas U.S. teenagers resent parental interference in romance or friendship (Kakihara & Tilton-Weaver, 2009). In Chile, adolescents usually obey their parents even when they disagree, but if they do something their parents might not like, they keep it secret (Darling et al., 2008)—unlike many U.S. adolescents, who might provoke an argument by boldly announcing what they think (Cumsille et al., 2010). Filipino adolescents expect autonomy in daily choices but not in life goals: Parental advice is sought in the four aspects of identity explained earlier (Russell et al., 2010a).

Filial devotion (a child's feeling of obligation to his or her parents) is particularly strong in Asian cultures. That curbs adolescent rebellion. As a result, the independence and individuality expected for Western adolescents is not as apparent there (Russell et al., 2010b). The influence of culture was evident in a study that used language to discover prime cultural values: Hong Kong adolescents expressed more self-assertion when they spoke English than when they spoke Chinese (Wang et al., 2010). (See Figure 16.3 and the Research Design.) It was not the words themselves that mattered, of course, but rather the context evoked when a researcher spoke English or Chinese (e.g., Hong Kong's British heritage or the millennia of mainland Chinese culture).

Closeness Within the Family

More important than family conflict or independence may be family closeness, which has four aspects:

1. Communication (Do family members talk openly with one another?)
2. Support (Do they rely on one another?)
3. Connectedness (How emotionally close are they?)
4. Control (Do parents encourage or limit adolescent autonomy?)

No developmentalist doubts that the first two, communication and support, are helpful, perhaps essential. Patterns set in place during childhood continue, ideally buffering some of the turbulence of adolescence (Cleveland et al., 2005;

Research Design

Scientists: Qi Wang, Yi Shao, and Yexin Jessica Li.

Publication: *Child Development* (2010).

Participants: A total of 125 children (aged 8, 10, 12, and 14) in Hong Kong, proficient in both Chinese and English (they spoke Chinese with their parents, but their education was in English). All the children were exposed to both cultures because, in the words of these researchers, "Hong Kong is a culturally dynamic place where Western and Chinese values intertwine and where modernity and tradition coexist" (p. 557).

Design: Trained bilingual researchers asked the children to speak about memories, themselves, and their values. Children were randomly assigned to be interviewed in Chinese or English. Among the data were statements in which the adolescents said something about themselves; their statements were judged by coders (who did not know the hypothesis) as being either about the individual alone (such as "I enjoy books," "My eyes are dark") or about the individual as one of a group or as a person connected to others (such as "I am a student," "My family loves me"). The ratio of individual to social descriptions was calculated.

Results: The descriptions of those interviewed in Chinese became more social at adolescence, while those interviewed in English were more likely to refer to themselves alone. This distinction was especially apparent at age 10, which is an age characterized by accelerating hormones and increasing egocentrism.

Major conclusion: The researchers interpreted these results to mean that, at adolescence, autonomy becomes less prominent in Chinese culture but not in English culture, presumably because of the divergent cultural emphases of China and Britain. The adolescents' self-concepts seemed influenced by the context—evoked by language.

Comments: Thousands of social scientists study culture, but it is difficult to determine whether their results are objective, unaffected by translation or by the perceptions and interpretations of the scientists. These researchers randomly assigned bilingual participants to be interviewed in one language or another, a clever way to evoke cultural context. However, this study was small (about 30 adolescents at each age, 125 in total, and only two cultures); replication is needed.

Effect of Age and Language on Autonomy

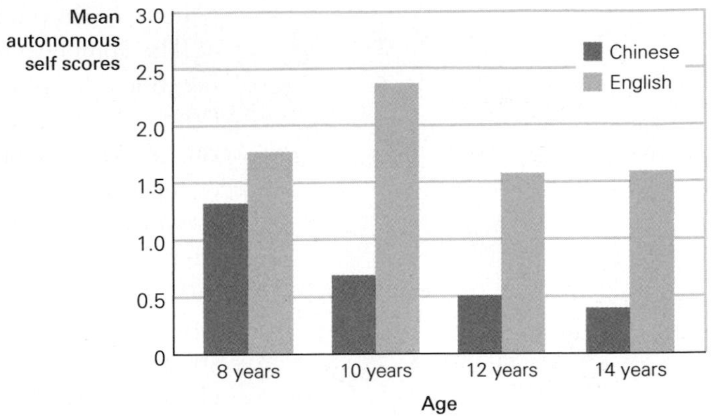

Source: Wang et al., 2010.

FIGURE 16.3

Words and Perceptions As they grew older, fluently bilingual students in Hong Kong who were interviewed in Chinese became less likely to refer to themselves as individuals distinct from their family and friends. By contrast, their classmates, who, by chance, were interviewed in English, were more self-focused—especially at age 10. Is that a shame? It depends on the culture (and maybe the language) of the observer.

Laursen & Collins, 2009). Regarding the next two, connectedness and control, consequences vary and observers differ in what they see. How do you react to this example, written by one of my students?

> I got pregnant when I was sixteen years old, and if it weren't for the support of my parents, I would probably not have my son. And if they hadn't taken care of him, I wouldn't have been able to finish high school or attend college. My parents also helped me overcome the shame that I felt when . . . my aunts, uncles, and especially my grandparents found out that I was pregnant.
>
> *[I., personal communication]*

My student is grateful to her parents, but others might wonder whether her early motherhood allowed her parents too much control and required her to remain dependent when she should have been seeking her own identity. Indeed, had they somehow allowed her to become pregnant? An added complexity is that my student's parents had emigrated from South America: Cultural expectations affected everyone's responses. A longitudinal study of nonimmigrant pregnant adolescents found that most (not all) young mothers and their children fared best if the teen's parents were supportive but did not take over child care (Borkowski et al., 2007). This may, or may not, be true for my student.

parental monitoring Parents' ongoing awareness of what their children are doing, where, and with whom.

A related issue is **parental monitoring**—that is, parental knowledge about each child's whereabouts, activities, and companions. When parental knowledge is the result of a warm, supportive relationship, children are likely to become confident, well-educated adults, avoiding drugs and risky sex (G. M. Barnes et al., 2006; Fletcher et al., 2004). That much is true, but the question broadcast to parents—"Do you know where your teenager is?"—is oversimplified.

The complication is that adolescents play an active role in their own monitoring: Some happily tell parents about their activities, whereas others are secretive (Vieno et al., 2009). Most disclose only part of the truth, selectively omitting things their parents would not approve of (Brown & Bakken, 2011). Thus, monitoring is a good sign if it indicates mutual, close interaction (Kerr et al., 2010). However, monitoring may be harmful when it derives from suspicion instead of from a warm connection.

Control is another aspect of parenting that can backfire. Adolescents expect parents to exert some control, especially over moral issues. However, overly restrictive and controlling parenting correlates with many adolescent problems, including depression (Brown & Bakken, 2011). Decreasing control over the years of adolescence is best, according to a longitudinal study of 12- to 14-year-olds in the suburbs of Chicago and Hong Kong. In both cultures, adolescents were given more autonomy over personal choices as they grew older, and in both cultures increased autonomy correlated with better emotional functioning (Qin et al., 2009).

Overall, parental reactions are crucial: Too much criticism and control might stop dialogue, not improve communication and behavior (Tilton-Weaver et al., 2010). An added complication is the personality of the adolescent and the context of the neighborhood. As one scholar who reviewed parental monitoring noted: "Some deft parental steering" is needed, but if "an adolescent is engaged in more than minor delinquent behavior, a much more structured and rule-based approach may be needed" (Capaldi, 2003, pp. 175–176).

A VIEW FROM SCIENCE

Parents, Genes, and Risks

Research on human development has practical applications. This was evident in a longitudinal study (first mentioned in Chapter 1) of African American families in rural Georgia that involved 611 parents and their 11-year-olds (Brody et al., 2009). Half of them were assigned to the control group, and the other half were invited to seven two-hour training sessions. Groups were small, and leaders were well prepared. Parents and their 11-year-olds were taught separately for an hour and then brought together.

The parents learned the following:

- The importance of being nurturing and involved
- The importance of conveying pride in being African American (called *racial socialization*)
- How monitoring and control benefit adolescents
- Why clear norms and expectations reduce substance use
- Strategies for communication about sex

The 11-year-olds learned the following:

- The importance of having household rules
- Adaptive behaviors when encountering racism
- The need for making plans for the future
- The differences between them and peers who use alcohol

After the hour during which parents and children were taught separately, the pairs were led in games, structured interactions, and modeling designed to improve family communication and cohesion. Three years later, both the experimental and control groups were reassessed regarding sex and alcohol/drug activity. The intervention helped, but the results were not dramatic.

Then, four years after the study began, the researchers read the new genetic research regarding the heightened risks for people with the short allele of the 5-HTTLPR gene. To see whether this applied to their African American teenagers, they collected and analyzed the DNA of 16-year-olds who had been, at age 11, in either the control or experimental groups. As Figure 16.4 shows, the training had no decided impact on those with the long allele, but it did have a major impact on those with the short one.

That only 14 hours or fewer of training (some families skipped sessions) had an impact is amazing, given all the other influences on these teenagers. However, since the parent–child relationship is crucial throughout adolescence, those seven sessions could have provided insights and connections that affected each vulnerable dyad from then on. Extensive research has found that postponing these three behaviors is beneficial to adolescent development in many ways, which makes these results particularly noteworthy.

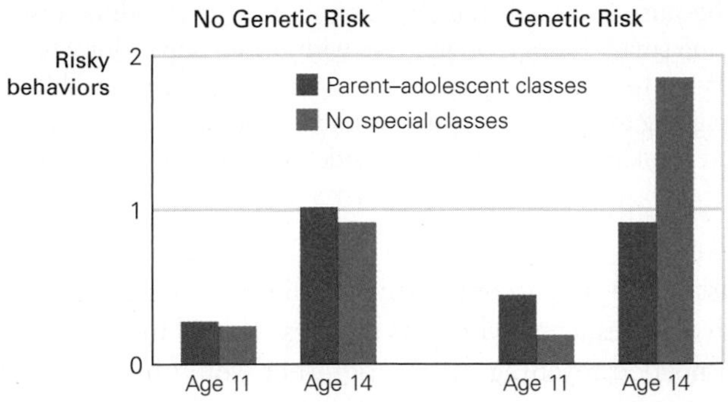

Source: Brody et al., 2009.

FIGURE 16.4

Not Yet The risk score was a simple 0 to 3, with one point for each of the following: had drunk alcohol, had smoked marijuana, had had sex. As shown, most of the 11-year-olds had done none of these. By age 14, most had done one (usually had drunk beer or wine)—except for those at genetic risk who did not have the seven-session training. Some of them had done all three, and many had done at least two. As you see, for those youth without genetic risk, the usual parental advice was no better or worse than that of the special classes; the average 14-year-old had tried only one risky behavior. But for those at genetic risk, the special program made a decided difference.

Other Adults

Parents are important to adolescents, but so are many other adults—even those with no biological relationship to the young person (Chang et al., 2010; Scales et al., 2006). For instance, consider each of the four arenas of identity development (religion, politics, vocation, gender). A church or temple youth minister can affect a young person's faith and morality; a charismatic political leader can attract devotion (especially if the adolescent's own father is absent); a school counselor or adult friend can influence vocational direction; knowing an adult with a happy and satisfying opposite- or same-sex relationship allows appreciation of sexuality (Lerner & Steinberg, 2009).

These are all examples of nonrelatives affecting adolescents. For many youth, family members—older siblings, cousins, aunts and uncles, grandparents—are even more important. Sometimes parents delegate a sibling (the adolescent's aunt or uncle) to discuss taboo topics, such as sex or delinquency (Milardo, 2009). Links between the teenager and relatives are especially common in developing nations for two reasons: (1) Relatives often live together and (2) ethnotheories make family central.

For example, a Peruvian adolescent begins a narrative of his daily life with, "It was a very beautiful day, here in my house, with my friends, my family, my cousins, my aunts and uncles, my dad, my mom . . ." In that study, and many others, family members were sometimes harmful but more often helpful (Bayer et al., 2010). Especially when adolescents are impoverished, refugee, orphaned, mistreated, and so on, nonparent relatives aid resilience. Adolescents seek out relationships—and many of them seek family members.

Grandparents can be particularly crucial, whether the parents are single, married, or remarried (Attar-Schwartz et al., 2009). Although only about 10 percent of all U.S. children currently live with their grandparents (American Community

Survey, 2009), many more are affected by them. When Jim, age 21, was asked if he had any mentors, he replied:

> My mom's father—my grandfather. A very independent guy, but a very caring guy. They [grandparents] go down to Florida every winter. And our family often goes down to spend some time with them. My grandpa really loves swimming in the ocean. So he would go out floating on his back for hours at a time. . . . When I was younger, I used to stand on the shore and watch him float out. He would disappear and come back and ask me if I wanted to go out. I did once and people were worried because I was only ten. My parents and my grandma were concerned, "Oh, he's too small," even though I was with my grandpa. But what he said to me stuck. What he said was I need to know my own limits, my abilities. Other people are going to have their opinions and worries and concerns, but being independent is taking that stuff into consideration, but then also doing what you can.
>
> *[cited in Pratt et al., 2010, p. 93]*

As with many adults whom adolescents admire, this grandfather helped his grandson affirm his own abilities, even when his parents wanted to hold him back. Of course, if young Jim needed rescuing, his grandfather would have done it, but that is not what "stuck." For many teenagers struggling to know "my own limits, my abilities," adult mentors can be crucial.

SUMMING UP

Relationships with adults are essential during adolescence. Parents and adolescents often bicker over small things, especially in early adolescence, but parental guidance and ongoing communication promote adolescents' psychosocial health. Among the signs of a healthy parent–adolescent relationship are that parents know what their child is doing (parental monitoring) and that adolescents talk with their parents about their concerns; both these factors are affected by culture, by past relationships, and by the adolescent's maturity. Parental neglect or excessive parental control can foster adolescent rebellion; authoritative parenting continues to be effective. Other relatives and even strangers have an impact in guiding adolescents, especially when parental advice is limited. ■

>> Peer Power

Adolescents rely on peers to help them navigate the physical changes of puberty, the intellectual challenges of high school, and the social changes of leaving childhood. Friendships are important at every stage, but during early adolescence popularity is most coveted (LaFontana & Cillessen, 2010). Adults are sometimes unaware of adolescents' desire for respect from their contemporaries. I did not recognize this at the time with my own children:

- Our oldest daughter wore the same pair of jeans to tenth grade, day after day. She washed them each night by hand and asked me to put them in the dryer early each morning. My husband was bewildered. "Is this some weird female ritual?" he asked. Years later, she explained that she was afraid that if she wore different pants each day, her classmates would think she cared about her clothes and then criticize her choices.
- Our second daughter, at 16, pierced her ears for the third time. When I asked if this meant she would do drugs, she laughed at my ignorance. I later noticed that many of her friends had multiple holes in their ear lobes.

- At age 15, our third daughter was diagnosed with cancer. My husband and I weighed opinions from four physicians, each explaining how to minimize the risk of death. She had her own priorities: "I don't care what you choose, as long as I keep my hair." (Her hair fell out, but now her health is good—and her hair has grown back.)
- Our youngest, in sixth grade, refused to wear her jacket (it was new; she had chosen it) even in midwinter. Not until high school did she tell me she did it so that her middle school classmates would think she was tough.

In retrospect, I am amazed that I was unaware of the power of peers.

Sometimes adults conceptualize adolescence as a time when peers and parents are at odds, or worse, that peer influence overtakes parental influence. This is not true. Relationships with parents are the prototype for peer relationships: Healthy communication and support from parents make constructive peer relationships more likely. Parents and peers are often mutually reinforcing, although many adolescents downplay the influence of their parents and many parents are unaware of the influence of peers. Only when parents are harsh or neglectful does peer influence reign alone (Bakken & Brown, 2010).

Peer Pressure

For every adolescent, the judgment of peers is important, and having friends is vital. Friends are often a positive force in a young person's life. One high school boy said:

> A lot of times I wake up in the morning and I don't want to go to school, and then I'm like, you know, I have got this class and these friends are in it, and I am going to have fun. That is a big part of my day—my friends.
>
> *[quoted in Hamm & Faircloth, 2005, p. 72]*

Adults sometimes fear **peer pressure,** that is, that peers will push an adolescent to try drugs, break the law, or other things the child would never do alone. This fear ignores the fact that "friends generally encourage socially desirable behaviors" (Berndt & Murphy, 2002, p. 281), such as playing sports, studying, quitting cigarettes, applying to college. Peers are more helpful than harmful (Audrey et al., 2006; Nelson & DeBacker, 2008), especially in early adolescence, when biological and social stresses can be overwhelming. In later adolescence, teenagers are less susceptible to peer pressure, either positive or negative (Monahan et al., 2009).

peer pressure Encouragement to conform to one's friends or contemporaries in behavior, dress, and attitude; usually considered a negative force, as when adolescent peers encourage one another to defy adult authority.

Selecting Friends

The fact that peers are often beneficial does not mean that they always encourage the behaviors that adults value. Young people *can* lead one another into trouble. Collectively, peers sometimes provide **deviancy training,** whereby one person shows another how to rebel against social norms (Dishion et al., 2001). Especially if adolescents believe that the most popular, most admired peers are having sex, doing drugs, or ignoring homework, they become more likely to take up the destructive behavior themselves (Rodgers, 2003).

deviancy training Destructive peer support in which one person shows another how to rebel against authority or social norms.

However, it is a myth that upstanding, innocent teens are routinely corrupted by deviant friends. Adolescents choose their friends and models—not always wisely, but never randomly. There is a developmental progression here: The combination of "problem behavior, school marginalization, and low academic performance" at age 11 leads to gang involvement two years later, deviancy training two years after that, and violent behavior at age 18 or 19 (Dishion et al., 2010, p. 603).

Especially for Parents of a Teenager
Your 13-year-old comes home after a sleepover at a friend's house with a new, weird hairstyle—perhaps cut or colored in a bizarre manner. What do you say and do? (see response, page 487)

SERGE J. MICHAUT / VIEWFINDER EXIS, LLC

Beach Party These laughing barefoot girls, with the boys in the background displaying manly indifference, could be partying alongside any ocean and sandy shoreline—in California, Florida, New Jersey, or several other states and nations.

Observation Quiz This photo was taken in 2007. Is it set in the United States? (see answer, page 487)

This cascade is not inevitable; adults can help disengaged 11-year-olds instead of blaming their friends years later.

To further understand the impact of peers, two concepts are helpful: *selection* and *facilitation*. Teenagers *select* a clique whose values and interests they share, abandoning former friends who follow other paths. Peers then *facilitate* destructive or constructive behaviors. It is easier to do the wrong thing ("Let's all skip school on Friday") or the right thing ("Let's study together for the chem exam") if close friends are doing it, too. Peer facilitation helps adolescents act in ways they are unlikely to act on their own.

Both selection and facilitation can work in any direction. One teenager joins a clique whose members smoke cigarettes and drink beer, and together they take the next step, perhaps sharing a joint at a party. Another teenager might choose friends who enjoy math puzzles, and, as demonstrated in this quote from Lindsay, they might all enroll in AP calculus together:

> [Companionship] makes me excited about calculus. That is a hard class, but when you need help with calculus, you go to your friends. You may think no one could be excited about calculus, but I am. Having friends in class with you definitely makes school more enjoyable.
>
> *[quoted in Hamm & Faircloth, 2005, p. 72]*

Instant Connections Ignoring the rides at Coney Island, these two girls lean on each other; both have blue bracelets, tight jeans, sleeveless shirts, and, most important, texts to read and send. As with their use of the automobile and the telephone, teens have taken an adult invention (the Internet was originally developed for military use) and turned it into a tool for increasing peer support.

FRANCES ROBERTS / ALAMY

Thus, adolescents select and facilitate, choose and are chosen. Happy, energetic, and successful teens have close friends who themselves are high achievers, with no major emotional problems. The opposite also holds: Those who are drug users, sexually active, and alienated from school choose compatible friends and support one another in continuing on that path (Crosnoe & Needham, 2004).

A study of identical twins from ages 14 to 17 found that selection typically preceded facilitation, rather than the other way around. Young teenagers who were likely to rebel chose more lawbreaking friends than did their less externalizing twin (Burt et al., 2009). A study of teenage use of cigarettes and alcohol found that, contrary to the fear of peer pressure, selection was probably more important than facilitation, especially for smoking (Kiuru et al., 2010). Peers provide opportunity and encouragement for what the adolescent already wants to do.

Approval for Risk Taking

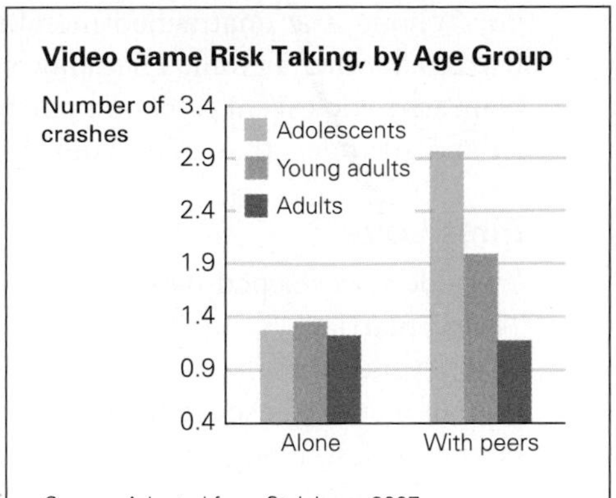

Source: Adapted from Steinberg, 2007.

FIGURE 16.5

Admire Me Everyone wants to accumulate points in a game, earn high grades, and save money—unless one is a teenager and other teens are watching. Then a desire to obtain peer admiration by taking risks may overtake caution. In this game, teenage participants chose to lose points and increase crashes when other teens were present.

Remember that adolescents must grow up, finding their own identity within a context unlike the one their parents experienced. They cannot depend exclusively on their parents; peers must be influential as well.

An experiment in peer facilitation involved adolescents (ages 13 to 16), emerging adults (ages 18 to 22), and adults (over age 24) in a video driving game (Gardner & Steinberg, 2005). As each player drove, every so often the screen would flash a yellow light, indicating that soon (within one to several seconds) a wall would appear. The goal was to drive as long as possible but brake before crashing into the wall. Points were gained for travel time; a crash erased the points from that round.

The participants were randomly assigned to one of two conditions: playing alone or with two strangers of the same sex and age as themselves. When they played alone, adolescents, emerging adults, and adults all averaged one crash per 15-round session. That single crash was enough to make them wary.

Adults were equally cautious when playing with other adults. But when the adolescents were with peers, they became bolder, crashing three times on average (see Figure 16.5) (Gardner & Steinberg, 2005; Steinberg, 2007). They chose to lose points rather than to appear cautious. Foolish? Perhaps. But although crashes lost points, they also provided an emotional connection to a peer.

The same phenomenon is evident in daily life, with teenagers driving too fast, swimming too far, or challenging authority to gain approval from others. This is especially apparent when boys want girls to admire them (see photos).

Watch Me Fall Adolescent boys in a skate park were videotaped in two circumstances: with an attractive female stranger sitting on a bench nearby and with no one watching. (The camera was hidden.) The boys took more risks, and fell more often, with the female observer present.

COURTESY RICHARD RODNAY

Romance

Contemporary adolescents often have friends of the other sex who are not their lovers. Adults sometimes worry about that, assuming that teenagers will have intercourse if unchaperoned. However, many teenagers have close, even passionate, friendships with peers of both sexes, without romantic undertones. Disruptions of friendships (either same-sex or other-sex) can cause jealousy (e.g., if the friend befriends another person) or depression (e.g., if the friend moves away). Friendship precedes romance and may be pivotal in adolescence.

Nonetheless, romance often begins in the teen years. Decades ago, Dexter Dunphy (1963) described the sequence of male–female relationships during childhood and adolescence:

1. Groups of friends, exclusively one sex or the other
2. A loose association of girls and boys, with public interactions within a crowd
3. Small mixed-sex groups of the advanced members of the crowd
4. Formation of couples, with private intimacies

Culture affects the timing and manifestation, but subsequent research in many nations validates this sequence. Youth worldwide (and even the young of other primates) avoid the other sex in childhood and are attracted to them by adulthood. This universal pattern suggests that biology underlies this sequence.

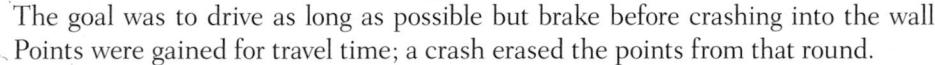

The peer group is very much involved as well. Romantic partners, especially in early adolescence, are selected not primarily for their individual traits but for the traits that are accepted by peers. If leaders of a girls' clique pair with leaders of a

© DONNA RANIERI / BLINKSTOCK

© RICHARD LORD / THE IMAGE WORKS

The Same Situation, Many Miles Apart: Teenagers in Love No matter where in the world they are, teenage couples broadcast their love in universally recognized facial expressions and body positions. Samantha and Ryan *(top)*, visiting New York City from suburban Philadelphia, are similar in many ways to the teen couple *(bottom)* in Chicute, Mozambique, even though their social contexts are dramatically different.

sexual orientation A term that refers to whether a person is sexually and romantically attracted to others of the same sex, the opposite sex, or both sexes.

boys' clique, the unattached members of the two cliques are encouraged to pair with each other as well. That allows easy double or triple dating but also helps explain why adolescent romantic partners tend to have less in common, in personality and attitudes, than adult couples do (Zimmer-Gembeck & Ducat, 2010).

First Love

In modern developed nations, where puberty begins with hormones at about age 10 and marriage occurs much later if at all, each of Dunphy's four stages typically lasts several years. Early, exclusive romances are more often a sign of social trouble than of maturity, especially for girls (Eklund et al., 2010). Unlike the norm in earlier centuries, a long-lasting commitment to a life partner does not usually occur until adulthood.

The first romances appear in high school, rarely lasting more than a year, with girls having a steady partner more often than boys do. Exclusive commitment is desired, but "cheating," flirting, and disloyalty are rife. Breakups are common; so are unreciprocated crushes. All this can be devastating to the adolescent, in part because entire high school crowds are often witnesses (Schwartz, 2006). Adolescents may despair at rejection, contemplating revenge or suicide (Fisher, 2006). In such cases, peer support can be a lifesaver. Indeed, adolescents as well as adults rely on friends, who help them cope with romantic ups and downs (Mehta & Strough, 2009).

Contrary to adult fears, many teenage romances do not include sexual intercourse. In the United States in 2009, even though one-third of all high school students were sexually experienced by the tenth grade, another one-third were virgins at high school graduation (see Figure 16.6). Every survey finds that norms vary markedly from crowd to crowd, school to school, city to city, and nation to nation. For instance, twice as many high school students in Milwaukee as in Seattle say they have had intercourse (63 percent versus 29 percent) (MMWR, June 4, 2010).

Same-Sex Romances

Some adolescents are attracted to peers of the same sex. **Sexual orientation** refers to the direction of a person's erotic desires. One meaning of *orient* is to "turn toward"; thus, sexual orientation refers to whether a person is romantically attracted to (turned on by) people of the other sex, the same sex, or both sexes. It is not known how many adolescents are romantically oriented toward people of the same sex because sexual orientation can be strong, weak, acted upon, secretive, or unconscious. Thus, asking teenagers to indicate their sexual orientation is bound to underestimate prevalence.

Currently in North America and western Europe, not just two (homosexual and heterosexual) but many gender roles and sexual orientations are evident (Denny & Pittman, 2007). Gender identity itself has become controversial; an increasing number of early adolescents do not identify with their biological sex and may be diagnosed with what the DSM-IV calls *gender-identity disorder,* the focus of an international conference in London (Asscheman, 2009). Some psychologists and psychiatrists argue that gender-identity disorder should be omitted from the DSM-5 (to be published in 2013) because they believe that gender-identity problems originate in society, not in individuals (Ross, 2009). On the other hand, nonheterosexual orientation is considered criminal as well as pathological in most nations of Africa and the Middle East.

Obviously, culture and cohort are powerful, not only in social acceptance but also in self-acceptance. Many gay youth date members of the other sex to hide their orientation, and binge drinking and suicidal thoughts remain a danger. This

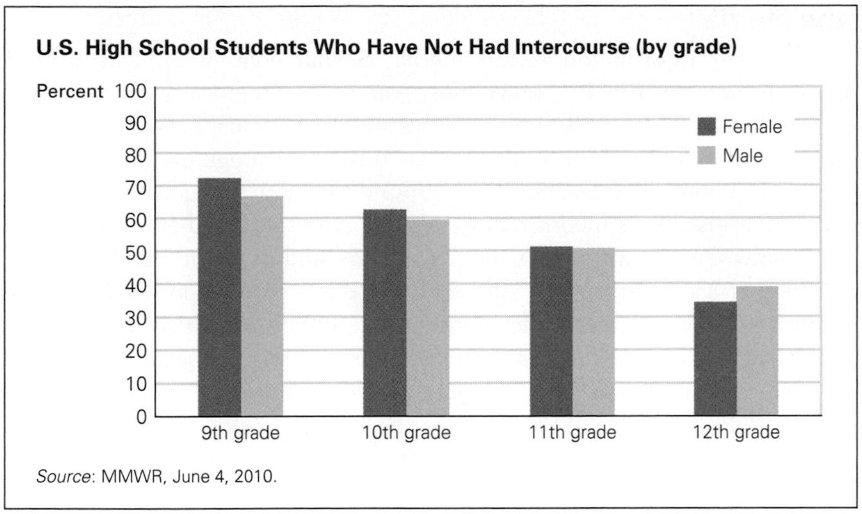

FIGURE 16.6

Many Virgins For 30 years, the Youth Risk Behavior Survey has asked high school students from all over the United States dozens of confidential questions about their behavior. As you can see, about one-third of all students have already had sex by the ninth grade, and about one-third have not yet had sex by their senior year, a group whose ranks have been increasing in recent years. Other research finds that sexual behaviors are influenced by peers, with some groups all sexually experienced by age 14 and others not until age 18 or later.

may be less common among current cohorts in nations where same-sex partnerships are accepted: Recent research finds that gay and straight adolescents have many similar problems and similar strengths (Saewyc, 2011).

Another reason it is not known how many adolescents are gay, lesbian, bisexual, or asexual is that gender identity is fluid. Girls are particularly likely to wait until they have sexual experiences to decide their identity, and many lesbian women had other-sex relationships in adolescence (Saewyc, 2011). In the mid-1990s, one large study of high school students in Massachusetts found that 1 in 200 identified as gay or lesbian (Garofalo et al., 1999). More recently, a large Dutch study of high school students found that 1 in 12 were attracted to people of their own sex (Bos et al., 2008).

Even more recently, among sexually active teenagers in New York City, 10 percent had had same-sex partners—but many of those individuals (38 percent) identified as straight (Pathela & Schillinger, 2010). In that study, those most at risk of sexual violence and sexually transmitted infections (STIs) were not those whose sexual experiences were exclusively same-sex or exclusively other-sex, but those who had partners of both sexes.

These variations reflect culture, cohort, and the words used in the surveys. Adults who care about adolescent health are advised to ask about behavior—which may differ from sexual identity or orientation (Pathela & Schillinger, 2010). When and with whom a person becomes sexually active depends on a cascade of factors, including age at puberty, parenting practices, peer pressure, and dating relationships (Longmore et al., 2009).

>> Response for Parents of a Teenager (from page 483) Remember: Communicate, do not control. Let your child talk about the meaning of the hairstyle. Remind yourself that a hairstyle in itself is harmless. Don't say "What will people think?" or "Are you on drugs?" or anything that might give your child reason to stop communicating.

Sex Education

Adults and peers both provide sex education, either explicit or implicit (through examples, expressions, silences). Many adolescents have strong sexual urges but minimal logic about pregnancy and disease, as might be expected with the differential maturation of the limbic system and prefrontal cortex or with the attraction of intuitive thought. One result is that millions of teenagers worry that they are oversexed, undersexed, or deviant, unaware that thousands, maybe millions, of people are just like them. As a result, "students seem to waffle their way through sexually relevant encounters driven both by the allure of reward and the fear of negative consequences" (Wagner, 2011, p. 193). Obviously, they have much to learn. Where do they learn it?

>> Answer to Observation Quiz (from page 484) No. They are in Halong Bay, Vietnam. Beachgoing U.S. girls would be dressed differently.

From the Media

One source of sex information is the media. Sexual content appears almost seven times per hour on the TV shows most watched by teenagers (Steinberg & Monahan, 2011). That content is almost always alluring: Almost never does a television character develop an STI, deal with an unwanted pregnancy, or mention (much less use) a condom. At least one study found that men's magazines convince teenage boys that manliness means many sexual conquests (Ward et al., 2011).

There is controversy regarding sex on TV, in film, and in music (Collins et al., 2011; Steinberg & Monahan, 2011). Although there is a correlation between adolescent exposure to media sex and adolescent sexual initiation, that correlation may reflect selection, not cause. Perhaps teenagers watch sexy TV because they are sexually active, not vice versa. One analysis concludes that "the most important influences on adolescents' sexual behavior may be closer to home than Hollywood" (Steinberg & Monahan, 2011, p. 575).

From Parents and Peers

Home is where sex education begins. Every study finds that explicit parental communication is influential (Longmore et al., 2009). However, many parents wait too long to discuss sex, utter generalities, and know little about their adolescents' romances. Three studies of quite different groups illustrate the problem.

1. Mexican American mothers told their teenagers *cuidate*, "take care of yourself," which their teenagers interpreted as advice about health, not condoms. The teens became pregnant, and the mothers wondered why (Moncloa et al., 2010).
2. Parents of 12-year-old girls were asked whether their daughters had hugged or kissed a boy "for a long time" or hung out with older boys (signs that sex information is urgently needed). Only 5 percent of the parents said yes, as did 38 percent of the girls (O'Donnell et al., 2008).
3. African and Hmong American 14- to 19-year-olds rarely tell their parents about their romantic encounters. For example, one girl said she and her girlfriend were going to the movies (true) but omitted that their boyfriends were coming, too (Brown & Bakken, 2011).

What exactly should parents say? That is the wrong question, according to a longitudinal study of thousands of adolescents. Those teens who became sexually active and who were most likely to develop an STI had parents who had talked to them about sex, warning them to stay away from it. In contrast, adolescents were more likely to remain virgins if they had a warm relationship with their parents—specific information was less important, but open communication was necessary (Deptula et al., 2010).

Especially when parents are silent, forbidding, or vague, adolescent sexual behavior is strongly influenced by peers. Many younger adolescents discuss details of romance and sex with other members of their clique, seeking advice and approval (Laursen & Mooney, 2007). Often the boys brag and the girls worry. Specifics depend on the group: All members of a clique may be virgins or all may be sexually active. Once they acquire boyfriends or girlfriends, partners teach each other. However, their lessons are more about pleasure than consequences: Only about half of U.S. adolescent couples discuss pregnancy and disease before they have sex (Ryan et al., 2007).

Especially for Sex Educators Suppose adults in your community never talk to their children about sex or puberty. Is that a mistake? (see response, page 490)

From Teachers in School

Almost all U.S. parents want their adolescents to have up-to-date sex education, including details of safe sex and contraception. Developmentalists agree that sex education belongs in the schools as well as in parent–child conversations, since adolescents need to learn from trusted and informed adults rather than misinforming each other.

Sex education varies dramatically by nation. Most northern European schools begin sex education in elementary school, and by middle school students learn about sexual responsibility, masturbation, same-sex romance, oral and anal sex—subjects rarely covered in U.S. classes. Rates of teenage pregnancy in most European nations are less than half those in the United States; perhaps curriculum is the reason. On the other hand, in Russia, although most experts believe that sex education belongs in school, few schools include it—and yet the official rate of HIV and pregnancy is lower than in the United States (Gevorgyan et al., 2011). Obviously, school sex education does not act apart from the social context.

"Smirking or Non-Smirking?"

CARTOONSTOCK.COM

Within the United States, the timing and content of sex education vary by state and community. Some high schools provide comprehensive programs, free condoms, and medical treatment; others provide nothing. Some schools begin sex education in middle school; others wait until the end of high school. This makes a difference: Many sex-education programs delay the age at which adolescents become sexually active and increase their use of condoms. However, specific information and attitudes influence the success of the curriculum—some programs have no impact (Kirby & Laris, 2009).

One controversy is whether abstinence should be taught as the only sexual strategy for adolescents, as was U.S. federal policy until 2009. It is true, of course, that abstaining from sex (including oral sex) prevents sexually transmitted infections and pregnancy, but longitudinal data four to six years after adolescents had participated in abstinence-only programs revealed that the programs did not succeed. About half of students in both experimental (abstinence-only) and control groups had had sex by age 16. The number of partners and use of contraceptives were the same with and without the special curriculum (Trenholm et al., 2007). Students in the control groups knew slightly more about preventing disease and pregnancy, but that knowledge neither slowed nor hastened their sexual initiation.

SUMMING UP

Crowds, cliques, and friends are all part of adolescence. Contrary to what some adults may think, peer pressure can be positive. Many adolescents rely on friends of both sexes to help them with the concerns and troubles of the teen years. Romances are typical in high school, but early, exclusive, long-lasting romances are more often a sign of emotional trouble than of maturity. Some adolescents are romantically attracted to others of their own sex; it is not known how often this occurs.

Given the earlier onset of puberty and the later marriages today, adolescents spend a decade or more with intense sexual drives but no enduring partner. They need accurate information about all aspects of sexuality before they become sexually active themselves. Parents are influential role models, but few provide detailed and current information before adolescents begin experimenting with sex. Most adolescents learn from personal experience with peers. School instruction may increase condom use, but not every curriculum is equally effective, and schools vary dramatically in what they teach at what age. ■

>> Response for Sex Educators (from page 488) Yes, but forgive them. Ideally, parents should talk to their children about sex, presenting honest information and listening to the child's concerns. However, many parents find it very difficult to do this because they feel embarrassed and ignorant. You might schedule separate sessions for adults over 30, for emerging adults, and for adolescents.

>> Sadness and Anger

Adolescence is usually a wonderful time, perhaps better for current generations than for any generation before. Nonetheless, troubles plague about 20 percent of youth. Most of them are *comorbid*, with several problems occurring at once. Distinguishing between normal moodiness and pathology, between behavior that is merely unsettling to adults and behavior that is seriously troubled, is complex. Many adolescents are less happy and more angry than they were as children, at least at moments—many change emotions day to day (Neumann et al., 2011). For a few, negative emotions become intense, even deadly.

Depression

The general emotional trend from late childhood through adolescence is toward less confidence. A dip in self-esteem at puberty is found for children of every ethnicity and gender (Fredricks & Eccles, 2002; Greene & Way, 2005; Kutob et al., 2009). Some studies report rising self-esteem thereafter (especially for African American girls and European American boys), but variations are many, as are individual differences.

Self-esteem is, on average, lower in girls and higher in boys, lower in Asian Americans and higher in African Americans, lower in younger adolescents and higher in older adolescents (Bachman et al., 2011). Many studies report a gradual rise in self-esteem from early adolescence through at least age 30, but all find notable variability from one person to another. Seriously depressed adolescents cannot be promised "you'll feel better soon"—severe depression may lighten, but it rarely disappears (Huang, 2010).

All studies find that parents and peers affect self-esteem (Hall-Lande et al., 2007) and that some communities have lower rates of depression because they promote strong and supportive relationships between teenagers and adults. For some adolescents, family circumstances are crucial. One factor in an individual's level of self-esteem may be the adolescents' own neurological propensity, as one might expect from differential vulnerability, explained in Chapter 1. Some adolescent girls are likely to be depressed because their mothers are belligerent, disapproving, and contemptuous; other adolescents seem protected by their brains from such parenting (Whittle et al., 2011).

Specific cultural contexts are influential as well. For Latino American youth, self-esteem and ethnic pride rise after puberty, especially if familism is strong, because their new maturity enables them to contribute in meaningful ways to their families. However, if a Latino's family is characterized by fighting and fragmentation, that reduces self-esteem even more than do similar circumstances for non-Latino adolescents (Smokowski et al., 2010). For gay adolescents, family rejection increases the rate of suicide (Saewyc, 2011). Adolescents of any background with low self-esteem turn to drugs, sex, and dieting—all of which often make depression worse (Biro et al., 2006; Trzesniewski et al., 2006).

Clinical Depression

clinical depression Feelings of hopelessness, lethargy, and worthlessness that last two weeks or more.

Some adolescents sink into **clinical depression,** a deep sadness and hopelessness that disrupts all normal, regular activities. The causes, including genes and early care, predate adolescence. Then the onset of puberty—with its myriad physical and emotional ups and downs—pushes some vulnerable children, especially girls, into despair. The rate of clinical depression more than doubles during this time, to an estimated 15 percent, affecting about 1 in 5 girls and 1 in 10 boys.

It is not known whether the reasons for these gender differences are primarily biological, psychological, or social (Alloy & Abramson, 2007). Obviously, sex hormones differ, but girls also experience social pressures from their families, peers, and cultures that boys do not. Perhaps the combination of biological and psychosocial stress causes some to slide into depression. Genes are involved as well.

One study found that the short allele of the serotonin transporter promoter gene (5-HTTLPR) increased the rate of depression among girls everywhere but increased the rate of depression among boys only if they lived in low-SES communities (Uddin et al., 2010). It is not surprising that certain genes make depression more likely, but the gender-specific neighborhood correlation is puzzling. Maybe boys are particularly likely to be depressed if they see no job prospects, and that is more likely in poor neighborhoods.

Recently, a cognitive explanation has been offered for gender differences in depression. **Rumination**—talking about, remembering, and mentally replaying past experiences—is more common among girls than boys. If unpleasant incidents are replayed, rumination often leads to depression (Ayduk & Kross, 2008).

rumination Repeatedly thinking and talking about past experiences; can contribute to depression.

Suicide

Stress can lead to depression and thoughts of suicide. Serious, distressing thoughts about killing oneself (called **suicidal ideation**) are most common at about age 15. The 2009 Youth Risk Behavior Survey revealed that one-third (33.9 percent) of U.S. high school girls felt so hopeless that they stopped doing some usual activities for two weeks or more, and one-sixth (17.4 percent) seriously thought about suicide. The corresponding rates for boys were 19.1 percent and 10.5 percent (MMWR, June 4, 2010).

suicidal ideation Thinking about suicide, usually with some serious emotional and intellectual or cognitive overtones.

Suicidal ideation can lead to **parasuicide,** also called *attempted suicide* or *failed suicide.* Parasuicide includes any deliberate self-harm that could have been lethal. *Parasuicide* is the best word to use because "failed" implies that to die is to succeed (!); "attempt" is likewise misleading because, especially in adolescence, the difference between attempt and actual suicide is difficult to discern.

parasuicide Any potentially lethal action against the self that does not result in death. (Also called *attempted suicide* or *failed suicide.*)

As you see in Table 16.1, parasuicide can be divided according to those who require medical attention (surgery, pumped stomachs, etc.) and those who do not, but any parasuicide needs to be taken seriously. Parasuicide is a flashing neon warning sign that, if there is a next time, the person may end up dead.

Internationally, rates of teenage parasuicide range between 6 and 20 percent. Among U.S. high school students in 2009, 7.9 percent of the girls and 4.6 percent of the boys said they had tried to kill themselves in the past year (MMWR, June 4, 2010; see Table 16.1).

While suicidal ideation during adolescence is common, completed suicides are not. The U.S. annual rate of completed suicide for people aged 15 to 19 (in school or not) is about 8 per 100,000, or 0.008 percent. Adolescents are *less* likely to kill

TABLE 16.1 **Suicidal Ideation and Parasuicide Among U.S. High School Students, 2009**

		Seriously Considered Suicide	Parasuicide (attempted suicide)	Parasuicide (w/medical attention)	Actual Suicide (ages 15–19)*
Overall		**13.8%**	**6.3%**	**1.9%**	Less than 0.01% (about 7.5 per 100,000)
Girls:	9th grade	20.3	10.3	2.8	
	10th grade	17.2	8.8	2.3	Girls: about 3.5 per 100,000
	11th grade	17.8	7.8	2.6	
	12th grade	13.6	4.6	1.0	
Boys:	9th grade	10.0	4.5	1.4	
	10th grade	10.0	5.2	2.0	Boys: about 11.5 per 100,000
	11th grade	11.4	4.7	1.7	
	12th grade	10.5	3.8	1.4	

*Actual suicide numbers are based on data for 2007.

Sources: MMWR, June 4, 2010; National Center for Health Statistics, 2010.

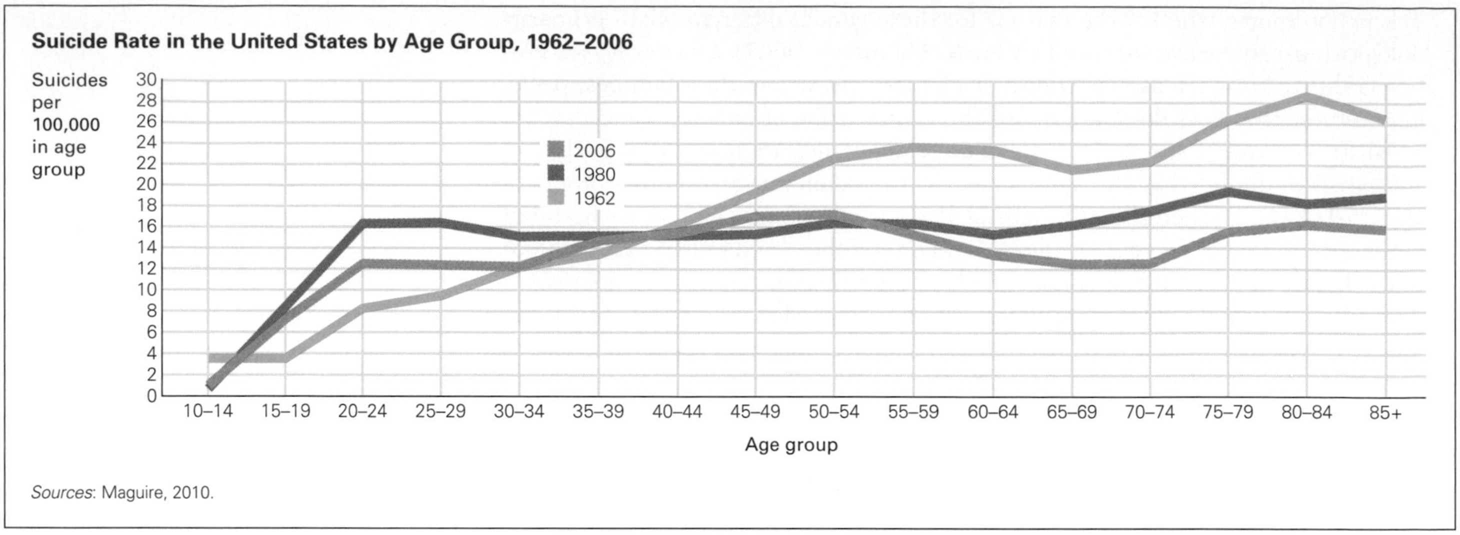

Sources: Maguire, 2010.

FIGURE 16.7

Much Depends on Age A historical look at U.S. suicide statistics reveals two trends, both of which were still apparent in 2009. First, older teenagers today are twice as likely to take their own lives as in 1960 but less likely to do so than in 1980. Second, suicide rates overall are down, but they continue to be high among elderly people.

themselves than adults are. Many people mistakenly think suicide is more frequent in adolescence for four reasons:

1. The rate, low as it is, is much higher than it appeared to be 50 years ago (see Figure 16.7).
2. Statistics on "youth" often include emerging adults aged 18 to 25, whose suicide rates are higher than those of adolescents.
3. Adolescent suicides capture media attention, and people of all ages make the logical error called base rate neglect (see Chapter 15).
4. Parasuicides may be more common in adolescence than later.

Gender differences in suicide are dramatic (see Table 16.1). Depression and parasuicide are more common among females, but completed suicide is higher for males (except in China). For instance, in the United States among 15- to 19-year-olds, boys kill themselves three times more often than girls (National Center for

KEVIN MOLONEY / THE NEW YORK TIMES / REDUX

Nothing to Do Compared with most other Americans, these three adolescents are at higher risk of diabetes, alcoholism, unemployment, and suicide. They live on the Rosebud Sioux Reservation in South Dakota. The suicide rate among Native American teenagers is more than three times as high as the rate for U.S. adolescents overall.

Health Statistics, 2010). A major reason is method: Males typically jump from high places or shoot themselves (immediately lethal), whereas females often swallow pills or cut their wrists (allowing intervention or second thoughts—common when the suicidal teen has a few minutes to reflect).

Another hypothesis is that girls talk about their emotions, allowing friends and families to get help for them. Rumination may increase depression but decrease suicide. Boys more often silently withdraw; their warning signs are less obvious. Furthermore, young men somehow think parasuicide is unmanly, so they choose deadly methods (Aseltine & DeMartino, 2004). Consider Bill.

A CASE TO STUDY

He Kept His Worries to Himself

A psychologist described an adolescent boy in these words:

> Bill is 17, a senior in high school. A good student, hard-working, some would say "driven," Bill has achieved well and is hoping to go to either Harvard or Stanford next year. He is also hopeful that his college career will lead him to medical school and a career as a surgeon like his father. Bill is a tall, handsome boy, attractive to girls but surprisingly shy among them. When he socializes, he prefers to hang out in groups rather than date; in these groups, he is likely to be seen deep in introspective discussion with one girl or another. Introspection has no place on the school football team, where this past season Bill led all receivers in pass catches. Nor does he appear at all the quiet type in his new sports car, a gift from his parents on his 17th birthday. The elder of two sons, Bill has always been close to his parents, and a "good son." Perhaps for these reasons, he has been increasingly preoccupied as verbalized threats of separation and divorce become common in his parents' increasingly frequent conflicts. These worries he has kept largely to himself.
>
> *[Berman et al., 2006, pp. 43–44]*

If you were Bill's friend, would you realize he needed professional help and make sure he got it? Unfortunately, Bill had no friends who heeded his warning signs. Even his parents did not realize he was troubled until

> Bill's body was brought to the local medical examiner's office; he put his father's .22-caliber handgun to his head and ended his life in an instant.
>
> *[Berman et al., 2006, p. 44]*

The report does not mention whether Bill's body was tested for drugs. About one-third of all U.S. suicides occur when a person has been drinking or drugging, behaviors that most high school seniors such as Bill do.

In retrospect, Bill had several risk factors and had shown danger signs—no close friends, male or female; his parents' conflicts; his foreclosure on his father's profession; his drive for perfection (Harvard or Stanford, football star); no older siblings to advise and comfort him. Did the gift of a sports car signify a problem—perhaps that Bill's parents provided material possessions instead of emotional closeness? Did his shyness around girls suggest worries about his sexuality? Had he been rejected from one of his college choices? Why did his father have a handgun, loaded and accessible?

Because they are not logical and analytical, adolescents are particularly affected when they hear about a suicide, either via media reports or from peers (Insel & Gould, 2008). That makes them susceptible to **cluster suicides,** a term for the occurrence of several suicides within a group over a brief span of time—a few weeks or months. If a high school student's "tragic end" is sentimentalized, that elicits suicidal ideation among his or her peers. Media attention increases the risk.

cluster suicides Several suicides committed by members of a group within a brief period of time.

Wealth and education decrease the incidence of many disorders, but *not* of suicide—quite the opposite. The reason may be news reports that typically highlight the lost potential of a suicidal adolescent (e.g., "Honor Student Kills Self"). This may encourage cluster suicides among, say, other honor students. Or adolescents from high-SES families may not know how to cope with a failing grade or a broken relationship.

Especially for Journalists You just heard that a teenage cheerleader jumped off a tall building and died. How should you report the story? (see response, page 494)

Since 1990, rates of adolescent suicide have fallen, especially among high-SES teenagers. One reason may be that parents spot problems and find psychotherapy,

>> Response for Journalists (from page 493) Since teenagers seek admiration from their peers, be careful not to glorify the victim's life or death. Facts are needed, as is, perhaps, inclusion of warning signs that were missed or cautions about alcohol abuse. Avoid prominent headlines or anything that might encourage another teenager to do the same thing.

which often includes antidepressants—which evidently relieve the desperate sadness that some adolescents feel (Gentile, 2010). A British study suggested that antidepressants might *increase* suicidal ideation (not suicide). However, an analysis of 27 controlled clinical trials (similar to experiments, except participants have a particular illness or disorder) found that antidepressants, especially combined with cognitive-behavioral therapy, were far more likely to relieve depression than to increase suicide (Bridge et al., 2007).

Delinquency and Disobedience

Like low self-esteem and suicidal ideation, bouts of anger are common in adolescence. In fact, the moody adolescent could be both depressed and delinquent because externalizing and internalizing behavior are more closely connected in adolescence than at any other age (Loeber & Burke, 2011). That is why teenagers jailed for assault (externalizing) are suicide risks (internalizing).

Externalizing actions are obvious. Many adolescents slam doors, defy parents, and tell friends exactly how badly other teenagers (or siblings or teachers) have behaved. Some teenagers—particularly boys—"act out" by breaking laws. They steal, damage property, or injure others.

Is such behavior normal? Some developmentalists answer yes. One was Anna Freud (Sigmund's daughter, herself a prominent psychoanalyst), who wrote that adolescent resistance to parental authority was "welcome . . . beneficial . . . inevitable." She explained:

> We all know individual children who, as late as the ages of fourteen, fifteen or sixteen, show no such outer evidence of inner unrest. They remain, as they have been during the latency period, "good" children, wrapped up in their family relationships, considerate sons of their mothers, submissive to their fathers, in accord with the atmosphere, idea and ideal of their childhood background. Convenient as this may be, it signifies a delay of their normal development and is, as such, a sign to be taken seriously.
>
> *[A. Freud, 1958/2000, p. 263]*

Contrary to Freud, many psychologists, most teachers, and almost all parents are quite happy with well-behaved, considerate teenagers. Which view is valid? Both. Adolescents vary; understanding the implications helps all of them.

Hope and Anger Adolescents and young adults everywhere demonstrate against adult authority, with varied strategies and results. In Cairo's Tahrir Square *(left)*, this young man flashes the peace sign hours before President Mubarak's resignation, but the 2011 "Arab Spring" in other nations was not as successful. French students *(right)* protested cuts in high school staff, but their demands were resisted by the government. Worldwide, social change is fueled by youthful aspirations—sometimes leading to victory, sometimes to despair.

ALAMY

PHILIPPE WOJAZER / REUTERS

Most teenagers usually obey the law, and their lawfulness does not predict a later explosion or breakdown. In fact, according to the 30-year New Zealand study first mentioned in Chapter 1, by age 26 men who had never been arrested usually earned degrees, "held high-status jobs, and expressed optimism about their own futures" (Moffitt, 2003, p. 61). Dozens of other longitudinal studies confirm that increased anger during puberty is normal but that most adolescents express their anger in acceptable ways. They yell at their parents, curse at their peers, complain about school. For a minority, anger explodes, and they break something or hurt someone. And a minority of that minority have been aggressive throughout childhood. They are the ones to be worried about.

AP PHOTO / PATRICK C. LEONARD

Some Want Her Dead But Florida law did not allow 15-year-old Morgan Leppert to be executed for murdering a 63-year-old man when she and her 22-year-old boyfriend, Toby, stole the man's car. Instead, she was sentenced to life in prison without parole. Developmentalists agree that teenage criminals are not like adult ones, but they also wonder why Morgan's mother let Toby sleep in Morgan's bedroom when she was just 14.

Breaking the Law

Both the prevalence (how widespread) and the incidence (how frequent) of criminal actions are more common during adolescence. Arrest statistics in every nation reflect this, and confidential self-reports reveal that virtually every adolescent breaks the law at least once before age 20. Only about one-fourth of young lawbreakers are caught, and most of those are warned and released (Dodge et al., 2006).

In one study of 1,559 urban seventh-graders (both sexes, all races, from parochial as well as public schools), more than three-fourths had committed at least one offense (stolen something, damaged property, or hurt someone physically). Usually, however, adolescents are not chronic offenders: In the same study, less than one-third had committed five or more such acts (Nichols et al., 2006).

Causes of Delinquency

Two clusters of factors, one from childhood (primarily brain-based) and one from adolescence (primarily contextual), predict delinquency. The first of these clusters includes a short attention span, hyperactivity, inadequate emotional regulation, slow language development, low intelligence, early and severe malnutrition, autistic tendencies, maternal cigarette smoking, and being the victim of severe child abuse. Most of these factors are more common among boys than girls, which may be one reason for the gender difference in delinquency. Neurological impairment (either inborn or caused by early experiences) increases the risk that a child will become a **life-course-persistent offender** (Moffitt et al., 2001), someone who breaks the law before and after adolescence as well as during it.

life-course-persistent offender A person whose criminal activity typically begins in early adolescence and continues throughout life; a career criminal.

The second cluster of factors that predict delinquency encompasses risk factors that are primarily psychosocial. They include having deviant friends; having few connections to school; living in a crowded, violent, unstable neighborhood; not having a job; using drugs and alcohol; and having close relatives (especially older siblings) in jail. These factors are more prevalent among low-income, urban adolescents, but adolescents at all income levels who experience them risk becoming an **adolescence-limited offender,** someone whose criminal activity stops by age 21 (Moffitt, 2003). They break the law with their friends, facilitated by their chosen antisocial clique. More boys than girls are in this group, but some lawbreaking cliques include both sexes (the gender gap in lawbreaking is narrower in late adolescence than earlier) (Moffitt et al., 2001).

adolescence-limited offender A person whose criminal activity stops by age 21.

Especially for Police Officers You see some 15-year-olds drinking beer in a local park when they belong in school. What do you do? (see response, page 498)

The criminal records of both types of teenagers may be similar. However, if adolescence-limited delinquents can be protected from various snares (such as quitting school, entering prison, drug addiction, early parenthood), they may outgrow their criminal behavior. This is confirmed by other research: Few delinquent youth who are not imprisoned continue lawbreaking in early adulthood (Monahan et al., 2009).

Of course, adolescence-limited lawbreaking is neither inevitable nor insignificant. Antisocial behavior is always dangerous, especially to other adolescents, who are victimized three times as often as adults (Baum, 2005). But maturation puts an end to adolescence-limited lawbreaking. By contrast, life-course-persistent offending begins in childhood and correlates in adulthood with more crime, less education, lower income, unhappy marriages, disobedient children, and continued violence (Huesmann et al., 2009).

Another way to analyze adolescent crime is to consider earlier patterns and stop delinquency before it reaches the point at which the police become involved. Three pathways to dire consequences can be seen:

1. Stubbornness can lead to defiance, which can lead to running away—runaways are often victims as well as criminals (e.g., prostitutes, petty thieves).
2. Shoplifting can lead to arson and burglary.
3. Bullying can lead to assault, rape, and murder.

Each of these pathways demands a different response. The rebelliousness of the first can be channeled or limited until more maturation and less impulsive anger prevail. Those on the second pathway require stronger human relationships and moral education. Those on the third present the most serious problem, with the danger of becoming more like a life-course offender than someone whose crime is adolescence-limited. For the adolescent bullies, intense treatment may deflect the pattern; if it does not, then serious penalties may be needed, with jail eventually. In all cases, early warning signs are present, and intervention is more effective earlier than later (Loeber & Burke, 2011).

Only half as many juveniles under age 18 are currently arrested for murder than was true in 1990. Although the data are solid, the explanations are not. Many possibilities have been suggested: fewer high school dropouts (more education means less crime); wiser judges (who now have community service as an option); better policing (arrests for misdemeanors are up, which may warn parents); smaller families (parents are more attentive to each of two children than each of twelve); better contraception and legal abortion (wanted children are less likely to become criminals); stricter drug laws (binge drinking and crack use increase crime); more immigrants (who are more law abiding); and more.

SUMMING UP

Compared with people of other ages, many adolescents experience sudden and extreme emotions that lead to powerful sadness and explosive anger. Supportive families, friendships, neighborhoods, and cultures usually contain and channel such feelings. For some teenagers, however, emotions are unchecked or intensified by their social contexts. This situation can lead to parasuicide (especially for girls), to minor lawbreaking (for both sexes), and, less often, to completed suicide and arrests (especially for boys). Delinquents can be adolescence-limited or life-course-persistent, a distinction that may help the justice system target the best response. Pathways to crime can be seen in childhood and early adolescence: intervention is most effective then as well. ■

>> Drug Use and Abuse

Adolescents enjoy doing something forbidden, and their hormonal surges and cognitive immaturity may cause them to be attracted to the sensations produced by drugs. But their immature bodies and brains make drug use particularly hazardous, with lifelong damage.

Variations in Drug Use

Most teenagers try *psychoactive drugs.* To a developmentalist (but not to a police officer), cigarettes, alcohol, and many prescription medicines are as addictive and damaging as illegal drugs like marijuana, cocaine, and heroin. Both prevalence and incidence of drug use increase from about ages 10 to 25 and then decrease, with use before age 18 being the best predictor of later abuse.

The one exception to this developmental increase is inhalants (fumes from aerosol containers, cleaning fluid, etc.), which are used more by younger adolescents, partly because they can be easily purchased. Sadly, the youngest adolescents are least able, cognitively, to analyze risks, and parents rarely suspect a drug problem until their child dies from breathing toxic vapors.

Variations by Place

Nations vary markedly in drug use. Consider the most common drugs: alcohol and tobacco. In most European nations, alcohol is widely used, even by children. In much of the Middle East, alcohol use is illegal, and teenagers almost never drink. In many Asian nations, anyone may smoke anywhere; in the United States, smoking is often forbidden; in Canada, cigarette advertising is outlawed. (Not surprisingly, fewer teens in Canada smoke.)

Variations within nations are marked as well. In the United States, most high school students have tried alcohol, and almost half have smoked cigarettes and marijuana—but a significant minority (about 20 percent) never use any drugs. Regional differences are apparent. For instance, 26.1 percent of high school students in Kentucky have smoked at least one cigarette in the past month, but only 14.8 New York students have (MMWR, June 4, 2010).

Variations by Generation and Gender

Cohorts vary, sometimes dramatically, as shown by a longitudinal study called Monitoring the Future that has asked thousands of young people, diverse in every way, about their recent and lifetime drug use. Use of most drugs has decreased in the United States since 1976 (as Figure 16.8 shows), but adolescent abuse of synthetic narcotics and prescription drugs has increased. During 2009, 10 percent of U.S. high school seniors used Vicodin and 6 percent used OxyContin (Johnston et al., 2010), both highly addictive and neither known to teenagers two decades ago.

With some exceptions, adolescent boys use more drugs, and use them more often, than girls do, especially outside the United States. An international survey of 13- to 15-year-olds in 131 nations found that more boys are smokers (except in a few European nations), including three times as many boys as girls in Southeast Asia (Warren et al., 2006). According to another international survey of 31 nations, almost twice as many boys as girls have tried marijuana (26 versus 15 percent) (ter Bogt et al., 2006).

These gender differences are reinforced by social constructions about proper male and female behavior. In Indonesia, for instance, 38 percent of the boys smoke

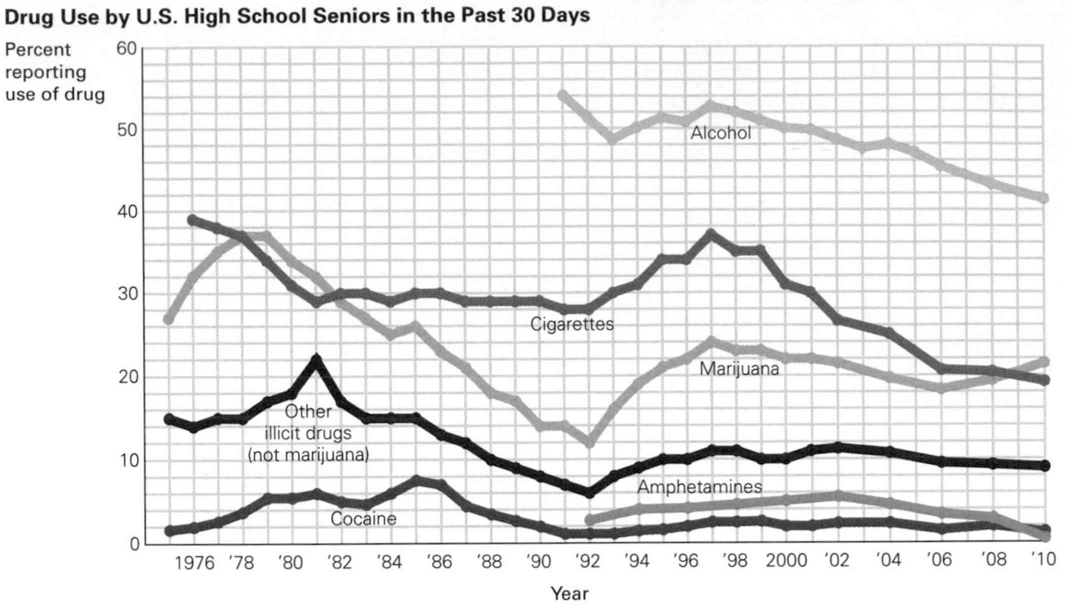

FIGURE 16.8

Rise and Fall By asking the same questions year after year, the Monitoring the Future study shows notable historical effects. It is encouraging that something in society, not in the adolescent, makes drug use increase and decrease and that the most recent data show a decline. However, as Chapter 1 emphasized, survey research cannot prove what causes change.

>> Response for Police Officers (from page 496) Avoid both extremes: Don't let them think this situation is either harmless or serious. You might take them to the police station and call their parents. These adolescents are probably not life-course-persistent offenders; jailing them or grouping them with other lawbreakers might encourage more crime.

Especially for Parents Who Drink Socially You have heard that parents should allow their children to drink at home, to teach them to drink responsibly and not get drunk elsewhere. Is that wise? (see response, page 500)

cigarettes, but only 5 percent of the girls do. One Indonesian boy explained, "If I don't smoke, I'm not a real man" (quoted in Ng et al., 2007). These worldwide gender differences are not evident in the United States, where more girls than boys smoked in the 1990s. Recent statistics show that girls smoke less than boys but are younger when they start drinking alcohol, with eighth-grade girls having notably higher rates than boys (Johnston et al., 2010). The most notable gender difference in the United States is that steroids are used by more boys and diet drugs by more girls—both a reflection of gender roles.

Harm from Drugs

Many teenagers believe that adults exaggerate the evils of drug use. That may be, but developmentalists see both immediate and long-term harm. Addiction and brain damage are among "the deleterious consequences of drug use [that] appear to be more pronounced in adolescents than in adults, a difference that has been linked to brain maturation" (Moffitt et al., 2006, p. 12). Few adolescents notice when they move past *use* (experimenting) to *abuse* (experiencing harm) and then to *addiction* (needing the drug to avoid feeling nervous, anxious, or in pain).

An obvious negative effect of *tobacco* is that it impairs digestion and nutrition, slowing down growth. This is true for bidis, cigars, pipes, and chewing tobacco as well as for cigarettes. In India, widespread tobacco use is one reason for chronic undernutrition (Warren et al., 2006). Since internal organs continue to mature after the height spurt, drug-using teenagers who appear full-grown may damage their developing hearts, lungs, brains, and reproductive systems.

Alcohol is the most frequently abused drug in North America. Heavy drinking impairs memory and self-control by damaging the hippocampus and the prefrontal cortex, perhaps distorting the reward circuits of the brain lifelong (Guerri & Pascual, 2010). Although some specifics of the impact of alcohol on the adolescent brain are still to be discovered, there is no doubt that alcohol affects adolescents more than adults because of their brain immaturity (Chin et al., 2009).

Like many other drugs, alcohol allows momentary denial of problems; worries seem to disappear when a person is under the influence. When problems get worse because they have been ignored, more alcohol is needed—a vicious cycle that often leads to addiction. Denial is a problem for all alcoholics, but particularly for teenagers who have not yet learned that they cannot drive, write, or even think after several drinks.

Marijuana affects memory, language proficiency, and motivation (Lane et al., 2005)—all of which are especially crucial during adolescence. An Australian study found that even occasional marijuana use (once a week) before age 20 affected development up to 10 years later (Degenhardt et al., 2010).

Those are correlations, which, as you know, do not reveal causation. Is it possible that adolescents who are not particularly clever or ambitious choose to smoke marijuana, rather than vice versa? Is some third variable (such as hostile parents) the cause of both the academic problems and the drug use, rendering the correlation deceptive? This seemed plausible because drug-using adolescents often distrust their parents, injure themselves, hate their schools, and break many laws.

These questions led to the hypothesis that the psychic strains of adolescence lead to drug use. In fact, however, longitudinal research suggests that drug use *causes* more problems than it solves, often *preceding* anxiety disorders, depression, and rebellion (Chassin et al., 2009; Meririnne et al., 2010). Marijuana use is particularly common among wealthier adolescents, who then become less motivated to achieve in school and more likely to develop other problems (Ansary & Luthar, 2009). Rather than lack of ambition leading to marijuana use, marijuana itself destroys ambition.

Preventing Drug Abuse: What Works?

Drug use is a progression, beginning with a social occasion and ending alone. The first use usually occurs with friends, which leads adolescents to believe that occasional use is an expression of friendship or generational solidarity. Few adolescent drug users are addicts, and, for those who are, usually they and their friends are unaware of it.

However, the Monitoring the Future study found the following: 25 percent of high school seniors report having had five drinks in a row in the past two weeks, 11 percent are daily cigarette smokers, and 5 percent are daily marijuana users (Johnston et al., 2010). These figures are ominous, suggesting that addiction is the next step. The younger a person is when beginning drug use, the more likely addiction will occur.

That may not persuade adolescents, who, as you remember, think they are exceptions to any rule. However, every psychoactive drug excites the limbic system and interferes with the prefrontal cortex. Drug users are thus more emotional (specifics vary, from ecstasy to terror, paranoia to rage) than they otherwise would be, as well as less reflective. Every hazard of adolescence—including car crashes, unsafe sex, and suicide—is more common among teens who have taken a psychoactive drug.

With harmful drugs, as with many other aspects of life, each generation prefers to learn things for themselves. A common phenomenon is **generational forgetting,** the idea that each new generation forgets what the previous generation learned (Chassin et al., 2009; Johnston et al., 2010). Mistrust of the older generation, added to loyalty to one's peers, leads not only to generational forgetting but also to a backlash. If adults say something is forbidden, that may be an incentive to try it!

generational forgetting The idea that each new generation forgets what the previous generation learned. As used here, the term refers to knowledge about the harm drugs can do.

A Man Now This boy in Tibet is proud to be a smoker—in many Asian nations, smoking is considered manly.

Some antidrug curricula and advertisements using scare tactics (such as the one that showed eggs being broken into a hot frying pan while an announcer intoned, "This is your brain on drugs") have the opposite effect from that intended, increasing rather than decreasing drug use. One reason may be that such advertisements make drugs seem exciting; another may be that adolescents recognize the exaggeration. Antismoking announcements produced by cigarette companies (such as one that showed a clean-cut young person advising viewers to think before they started smoking) actually increase use (Strasburger et al., 2008).

An added problem is that many parents do not know about their children's drug use, so their educational efforts may be too late, too general, or too ignorant. For instance, in one U.S. study, less than 1 percent of parents of sixth-graders thought their children had ever had alcohol, but 22 percent of the children said they had (O'Donnell et al., 2008). In general, adolescents follow their parents' example more than their advice.

This does not mean that trying to halt early drug use is hopeless. Massive ad campaigns in Florida and California cut adolescent smoking almost in half, in part because the publicity appealed to the young (Wakefield et al., 2003). A particularly effective ad depicted young people dumping 1,200 body bags in front of the corporate headquarters of a tobacco company to highlight the number of smoking-related deaths that occur in the United States each day (Farrelly et al., 2005). The anti-corporation message, with dramatic black-and-white footage (as if a teen had shot it a decade ago), had an impact.

Changing the social context is also helpful. Throughout the United States, higher prices, targeted warnings, and better law enforcement have led to a marked decline in cigarette smoking among younger adolescents. In 2009, only 6.5 percent of eighth-graders had smoked cigarettes in the past month, compared with 21 percent 10 years earlier (Johnston et al., 2010).

All the research confirms that parents continue to be influential on adolescent drug use. When parents forbid smoking in their homes, fewer adolescents smoke (Messer et al., 2008); when parents are careful with their own drinking, fewer teenagers abuse alcohol (Van Zundert et al., 2006). When parents provide guidance about drinking, teenagers not only drink less but use fewer other substances (Miller & Plant, 2010). Growing up with two married parents reduces cigarette and alcohol use, even when other influences (such as parental smoking and family income) are taken into account (Brown & Rinelli, 2010).

Looking broadly at the past three chapters and past 40 years in the United States, it is apparent that the universal biological processes do not lead to universal psychosocial problems. Sharply declining rates of teenage births and abortions (Chapter 14), increasing numbers graduating from high school (Chapter 15), and less use of legal and illegal drugs (Chapter 16) are apparent in many nations. Human growth starts with biology, that single sperm penetrating that single ovum, but the outcome depends on many social forces.

>> Response for Parents Who Drink Socially (from page 498) No. Alcohol is particularly harmful for young brains. It is best to drink only when your children are not around. Children who are encouraged to drink with their parents are more likely to drink when no adults are present. It is true that adolescents are rebellious, and they may drink even if you forbid it. But if you allow alcohol, they might rebel with other drugs.

SUMMING UP

Most adolescents worldwide experiment with drugs, usually cigarettes and alcohol. Variations in adolescent drug use and abuse related to age, culture, cohort, and gender are evident. Drug use in adolescence is especially risky, since many drugs reduce learning and growth as well as smooth the path to addiction and abuse. Generational forgetting is one reason each cohort has distinctive drug-use patterns, and many efforts to stop drug use have failed, but the overall trend is positive: Drug use is lower in the United States and in many other places than it was a few decades ago. ■

SUMMARY

Identity

1. Adolescence is a time for self-discovery. According to Erikson, adolescents seek their own identity, sorting through the traditions of their families and cultures.

2. Many young adolescents foreclose on their options without exploring possibilities, experience role confusion, or reach moratorium. Identity achievement takes longer for contemporary adolescents than it did half a century ago, when Erikson first described it.

3. Identity achievement occurs in many domains, including religion, politics, vocation, and sex. Each of these remains important over the life span, but timing, contexts, and often terminology have changed since Erikson and Marcia first described them.

Relationships with Adults

4. Parents continue to influence their growing children, despite bickering over minor issues. Ideally, communication and warmth remain high within the family, while parental control decreases and adolescents develop autonomy.

5. There are cultural differences in the timing of conflicts and particulars of parental monitoring. Too much parental control, with psychological intrusiveness, is harmful, as is neglect. Parents need to find a balance between granting freedom and providing guidance.

6. Adults who are not parents sometimes provide important mentoring and modeling for adolescents. Grandparents can be particularly influential.

Peer Power

7. Peers and peer pressure can be beneficial or harmful, depending on particular friends, cliques, and crowds. Adolescents select their friends, including friends of the other sex, who then facilitate constructive and/or destructive behavior.

8. Adolescents seek the approval of their peers, sometimes engaging in risky behavior for that reason.

9. Like adults, adolescents experience diverse sexual needs and may be involved in short-term or long-term romances, depending in part on their peer culture. This is a long process; early, exclusive sexual relationships are a sign of emotional immaturity.

10. The sexual orientation of some youth is toward same-sex romances. Depending on the culture and cohort, they may have a more difficult adolescence than others.

11. Most parents want schools to teach adolescents about sex, although such education often comes later than the personal experiences of the teen. No curriculum (including abstinence-only programs) markedly changes the age at which adolescents become sexually active, although some reduce pregnancy and STIs.

Sadness and Anger

12. Almost all adolescents become self-conscious and self-critical. A few become chronically sad and depressed. Many adolescents (especially girls) think about suicide, and some attempt it. Few adolescents actually kill themselves; most who do so are boys.

13. At least in Western societies, almost all adolescents become more independent and angry as part of growing up, although most still respect their parents. Lawbreaking as well as momentary rage are common; boys are more likely to be arrested for violent offenses than are girls.

14. Adolescence-limited delinquents should be prevented from hurting themselves or others; their criminal behavior will disappear with maturation. Life-course-persistent offenders are aggressive in childhood and may continue to be so in adulthood.

Drug Use and Abuse

15. Most adolescents experiment with drugs, especially alcohol and tobacco, although such substances impair growth of the body and the brain. National culture has a powerful influence on which specific drugs are used as well as on frequency of use. Age, gender, community, and parental factors are also influential.

16. Prevention and moderation of adolescent drug use and abuse are possible. Antidrug programs and messages need to be carefully designed to avoid a backlash or generational forgetting.

KEY TERMS

identity versus role confusion (p. 472)
identity achievement (p. 472)
role confusion (p. 472)
foreclosure (p. 472)
moratorium (p. 472)
gender identity (p. 476)
bickering (p. 477)
parental monitoring (p. 480)
peer pressure (p. 483)
deviancy training (p. 483)
sexual orientation (p. 486)
clinical depression (p. 490)
rumination (p. 491)
suicidal ideation (p. 491)
parasuicide (p. 491)
cluster suicides (p. 493)
life-course-persistent offender (p. 495)
adolescence-limited offender (p. 495)
generational forgetting (p. 499)

WHAT HAVE YOU LEARNED?

Identity

1. What is the relationship between the identity crisis and the past and future?

2. How does identity confusion differ from identity moratorium?

3. Why is foreclosure considered less mature than identity achievement?

4. Why is it premature for adolescents today to achieve their vocational identity?

5. What role do parents play in religious and political identity?

6. What assumptions did most adults hold 50 years ago about sexual identity?

Relationships with Adults

7. Why do parents and adolescents often bicker?

8. When is parental monitoring a sign of a healthy parent–adolescent relationship and when is it not?

9. What are the differences between the influence of parents and that of nonparent adults on adolescents?

Peer Power

10. What are the differences between the influence of peers and the influence of parents?

11. Why do many adults misunderstand the role of peer pressure?

12. What are the similarities and differences in crowds and cliques?

13. What is the role of parents, peers, and society in helping an adolescent develop an ethnic identity?

14. What are the differences in friendship during adolescence and in adulthood?

15. When is an adolescent romance healthy and when is it not?

16. How does culture affect the development of sexual orientation?

17. Where and from whom do adolescents usually learn about sex?

18. What are the variations in sex education in schools, and how does this affect adolescent sexual behavior?

Sadness and Anger

19. What is the difference between adolescent sadness and clinical depression?

20. Why do many adults think adolescent suicide is more common than it is?

21. How can rumination contribute to gender differences in depression and suicide?

22. Why are cluster suicides more common in adolescence than later?

23. What are the similarities between life-course-persistent and adolescence-limited delinquents?

24. What are the differences between life-course-persistent and adolescence-limited delinquents?

Drug Use and Abuse

25. Why are psychoactive drugs particularly attractive in adolescence?

26. Why are psychoactive drugs particularly destructive in adolescence?

27. What are the implications of national differences in drug use during adolescence?

28. What works and doesn't work in reducing adolescent drug use?

APPLICATIONS

1. Teenage cliques and crowds may be more important in large U.S. high schools than elsewhere. Interview people who spent their teenage years in U.S. schools of various sizes, or in another nation, about the peer relationships in their high schools. Describe and discuss any differences you find.

2. Locate a news article about a teenager who committed suicide. Can you find evidence in the article that there were warning signs that were ignored? Does the report inadvertently encourage cluster suicides?

3. Research suggests that most adolescents have broken the law but that few have been arrested or incarcerated. Ask 10 of your fellow students whether they broke the law when they were under 18 and, if so, how often, in what ways, and with what consequences. (Assure them of confidentiality.) What hypothesis arises about lawbreaking in your cohort?

4. Cultures have different standards for drug use among children, adolescents, and adults. Interview three people from different cultures (not necessarily from different nations; each occupation, generation, or religion can be said to have a culture) about their culture's drug-use standards. Ask your respondents to explain the reasons for any differences.

>>ONLINE CONNECTIONS

To accompany your textbook, you have access to a number of online resources, including quizzes for every chapter of the book, flashcards (in English and Spanish), critical thinking questions, and case studies. For access to any of these links, go to www.worthpublishers.com/bergerca9e. In addition to these free resources, you'll also find links to podcasts, video clips, diagnostic quizzing with personalized study advice, and an ebook. Some of the videos and activities available online include:

- *Who Am I?* The video reviews pathways to identity achievement and Marcia's dimensions of exploration and commitment. Teens talk about identity. The embedded questionnaire lets you gauge your progress in identity formation.
- *Interview with Anne Petersen.* This expert talks about the role of parents in adolescence and the need for solid community services.

PART V The Developing Person So Far: Adolescence

BIOSOCIAL

Puberty Puberty begins adolescence, as the child's body becomes much bigger (the growth spurt) and more sexual. Both sexes experience increased hormones, reproductive potential, and primary as well as secondary sexual characteristics. Brain growth, hormones, and social contexts combine to make every adolescent more interested in sexual activities, with possible hazards of early pregnancy and sexual abuse.

Nutrition The growth spurt requires adequate nutrition. Many teens do not get enough iron or calcium, since they often consume fast food and soda instead of family meals and milk. Some suffer from serious eating disorders like anorexia and bulimia.

Brain Neurological growth continues through adolescence; the limbic system typically matures faster than the prefrontal cortex. As a result, adolescents act impulsively.

COGNITIVE

Adolescent Thinking Adolescents think differently than younger children do. Piaget stressed the new ability to use abstract logic (part of formal operational thought). Adolescents think hypothetically and deductively, as they are taught to do in school. Elkind recognized adolescent egocentrism; younger teens think they are invincible or that everyone notices what they do. Intuitive thought also increases during adolescence, with emotional and experiential thinking overcoming logic at times.

Teaching and Learning Secondary education promotes individual and national success. Nations vary in how many adolescents graduate from high school. Particularly in the United States, middle schools have been considered the "low ebb" of education: Grades and achievement fall, bullying increases, and teachers and students become disenchanted with learning. International tests find marked differences in achievement. In the United States, high-stakes tests and more rigorous course requirements before high school graduation are intended to improve standards of learning.

PSYCHOSOCIAL

Identity Adolescent development includes a search for identity, as Erikson described. Adolescents combine childhood experiences, cultural values, and their unique aspirations. The contexts of identity are religion, politics/ethnicity, vocation, and sex/gender. Few adolescents achieve identity; role confusion and foreclosure are more likely.

Relationships Families continue to be influential, despite rebellion and bickering. Adolescents seek autonomy but also rely on parental support. Friends and peers of both sexes are increasingly important. Romances often begin in adolescence. About half of all U.S. teens become sexually active. Among developed nations, the United States has higher rates of teen pregnancy and less comprehensive sex education.

Sadness and Anger Depression and rebellion become serious problems for a minority of adolescents. This troubled group is at some risk of suicide (rates are lower than for adults) and violent criminality (rates are higher than for adults). Many adolescents break the law, but their delinquency is adolescence-limited; they eventually become law-abiding adults. Some, however, are life-course-persistent delinquents.

Drugs Adolescents are attracted to psychoactive drugs. Specifics of use and legality vary by nation and culture. In North America, drug use is illegal for teenagers, but most adolescents drink alcohol, and many try cigarettes and marijuana.

EPILOGUE

Emerging Adulthood

WHAT WILL YOU KNOW?

1. How can the sex drive in emerging adulthood be both a joy and a disaster?
2. Does college teach older adolescents to think like adults?
3. How do personality traits and emotional needs change between childhood and adulthood?

Consider this a review and a preview. Throughout the entire life span, genetic, prenatal, and early experiences have an impact. In this Epilogue, you will see many familiar themes—echoes of early relationships, differences among cultures, contextual and cohort effects. **Emerging adulthood** is a time of life when 18- to 25-year-olds continue their education and exploration, postponing marriage, parenthood, and career (see At About This Time).

It is not surprising that I experienced this path myself. Between ages 18 and 25, I attended four colleges or universities, changed majors five times, rejected marriage offers from four young men, lived in ten different places, and started several jobs—none lasting more than 18 months. Following that period of rapid change, I stayed put—one husband, one neighborhood, one job. What is surprising may be that similar patterns have become apparent everywhere: Young people in every nation are gaining more education and marrying later than their parents did (not always as late as I did). Emerging adulthood is a stage, or a process, worldwide (Arnett et al., 2011).

emerging adulthood The period of life between the ages of 18 and 25. Emerging adulthood is now widely thought of as a separate developmental stage.

AT ABOUT THIS TIME

Following Certain Patterns, by Average Age (U.S., 2010)
Age 17–18—Graduate from high school (about 25 percent do not do so)
Age 18–19—Enroll in college (about 30 percent of high school graduates do not)
Age 22—Earn college degree (about half of those who enter college)
Age 25—Steady employment in chosen field (rate fluctuates, depends on economy)
Age 25—Women's first birth* (for those who will have children; about 20 percent will not)
Age 26—Women's first marriage (about 18 percent never marry)
Age 28—Men's first marriage (about 25 percent never marry)

*By ethnicity: Age 23—African American or Hispanic; age 26—European American; age 29—Asian American
Source: U.S. Bureau of the Census, 2011 and previous years.

These are norms, which convey the median age for these events, each traditionally considered signs of adulthood. Note that most people do *not* achieve college graduation and that the median age for family commitment is at the end of emerging adulthood. Furthermore, many people do not follow this normative path.

>> Biosocial Development

Biologically, the years from ages 18 to 25 are prime time for hard physical work and safe reproduction. However, the fact that young adults can carry rocks, plow fields, or haul water better than older adults is no longer admired, nor is their fertility. If a contemporary young couple had a baby every year, their neighbors would be more appalled than approving. Now, during emerging adulthood, societies, families, and young adults themselves expect more education, later marriage, and fewer children than was the norm as recently as 50 years ago.

Strong and Active Bodies

Health has not changed, except maybe to improve. As always, every body system—including the digestive, respiratory, circulatory, and sexual-reproductive systems—functions optimally at the beginning of adulthood (Aspinall, 2003). Serious diseases are not yet apparent, and some childhood ailments are outgrown. For example, childhood asthma disappears as often as it continues. In a mammoth survey, 95.8 percent of young adults (aged 18 to 29) in the United States rated their health as good, very good, or excellent (National Center for Health Statistics, 2010).

However, health problems from childhood may continue. In the same survey in which only 4 percent of young adults rated their health as less than good, 15 percent said they had been told they had a chronic disease—often asthma, arthritis, or high blood pressure (National Center for Health Statistics, 2010). A comprehensive review of many studies finds that low birthweight, undernutrition in infancy, and rapid weight gain in early childhood tend to result in shorter height, reduced body functioning, and higher risk of disease (Victora et al., 2008).

Fortunately, these health problems are usually kept in check during these years. The immune system is strong, fighting off everything from the sniffles to cancer and responding well to vaccines (Grubeck-Loebenstein, 2010). Usually, teeth have no new cavities, heart rate is steady, the brain functions well, and lung capacity is sufficient. Many diagnostic tests, such as PSA (for prostate cancer), mammograms (for breast cancer), and colonoscopies (for colon cancer), are not usually recommended until age 40 or later. Death from disease is unusual (see Table EP.1).

TABLE EP.1 U.S. Deaths from the Top Three Causes (Heart Disease, Stroke, Cancer)

Age Group	Annual Rate per 100,000
15–24	7
25–34	18
35–44	65
45–54	219
55–64	561
65–74	1,313
75–84	2,971
85+	7,126

Source: National Center for Health Statistics, 2010.

Young and Healthy Young adults rarely die of diseases, including the top four: heart disease, cancer, stroke, and obstructive pulmonary disease. These are annual rates, which means that for each person, the chance of death in that decade is 10 times the yearly rate. Thus, a 15-year-old has less than 1 chance in 1,000 of dying of disease before age 25; a 75-year-old has more than 1 chance in 3 of dying of disease before age 85. (As reported later in this chapter, nondisease deaths show a different pattern.)

Observation Quiz How likely is a 90-year-old person to die in the next year? What about a 19-year-old? (see answer, page 508)

Fertility, Then and Now

As already mentioned, the sexual-reproductive system is at its strongest during emerging adulthood. Thanks to nature's wonderful mechanism for preserving the human species, young adults experience great joy from sexual interactions. During these years, orgasms are frequent; the sex drive is powerful; fertility is optimal; miscarriage is less common; serious birth complications are relatively rare. Historically, most couples had their first child when they were under age 25, and often a second and third as well.

Premarital Sex

These physiological strengths may have become liabilities. The bodies of emerging adults want sex but their minds know they are not ready for parenthood (Lefkowitz & Gillen, 2006). For many, the solution to this dilemma is sex without pregnancy, made possible by modern contraception.

According to a poll at the beginning of the twenty-first century, most U.S. 18- to 24-year-olds say premarital sex is "not wrong at all"; only 18 percent of those over age 65 agree (T. W. Smith, 2005). Those sentiments may be even stronger among the current cohort of emerging adults: Few young adults (27 percent) think living together before marriage is bad for society, although most older adults (64 percent) think it is (Pew Research Center, 2010). Even compared with young adults in 1997, fewer young adults in 2010 are married but more hope to become good parents (Wang & Taylor, 2011). (See Figure EP.1.)

Although they accept *pre*marital sex, many emerging adults (80 percent) believe that *extra*marital sex is "always wrong" (T. W. Smith, 2005). For child development, this is good news: Children fare better if they are wanted, if their parents are emotionally ready for child rearing, and if their parents are committed to each other.

The Bad News

The sexual freedom of emerging adults has a serious downside, however. Globalization accelerates every contagious disease, including sexually transmitted infections (STIs) (Herring & Swedlund, 2010). In earlier times, prostitution was local, which kept STIs local as well. Now, with international travel, an STI caught from an infected sex worker in one place quickly spreads.

This proliferation is particularly tragic with HIV/AIDS, first reported among gay men in two or three U.S. cities and then among injection drug users who shared needles. Within 30 years, primarily because of the sexual activities of young adults, HIV has become a worldwide epidemic, with more female than male victims (Davis & Squire, 2010). In nations where HIV is not yet prevalent, such as Croatia, the sexual risk taking of 18- to 25-year-olds means that many may soon become infected (Štulhofer et al., 2009). Worldwide, young adults remain the prime STI vectors (those who spread disease) as well as the new victims.

© ULANA SWITUCHA / AGE FOTOSTOCK

Anywhere In some ways, life in China is radically different from life elsewhere, but universals are also apparent. This emerging-adult couple pose in front of the Beijing stadium.

Observation Quiz One detail in the young man's hands suggests that the setting is Asia, not North America. What is it? (see answer, page 509)

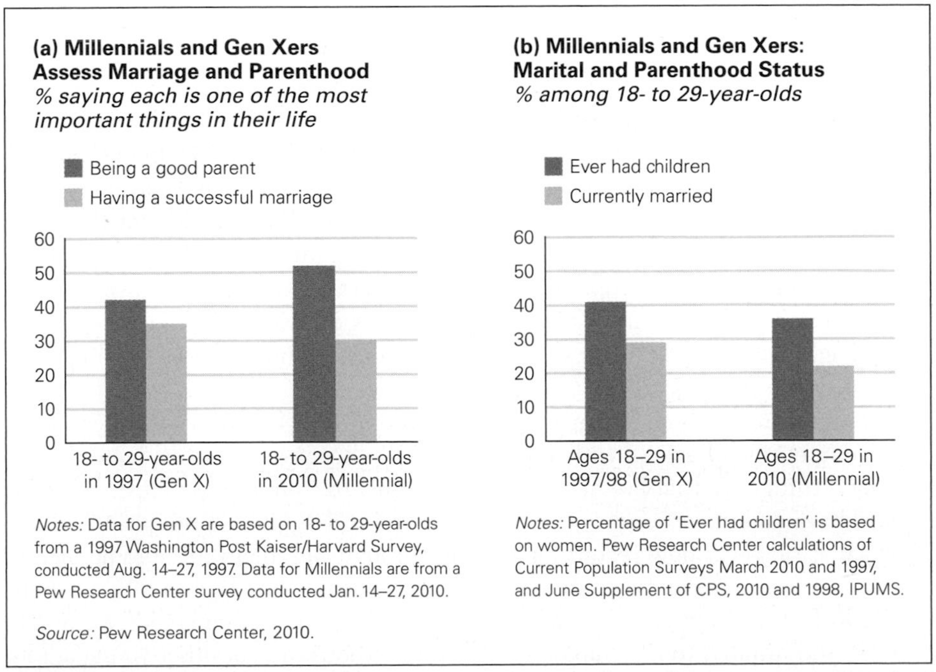

FIGURE EP.1

Children before Partners Many young adults consider parenthood more important than partnerhood. At least for previous cohorts, however, children were more likely to thrive if their parents were happily married.

ELLEN SINSI / THE IMAGE WORKS

Do They Talk? This couple in Schenectady, New York, are in a "long-term relationship," probably years from marriage. We hope they agree about what they would do if she got pregnant, or if he found someone else, or if either was offered a great job or university scholarship in another state. Few emerging adults discuss such matters until they actually happen.

Taking Risks

Remember that each age group has its own gains and losses, characteristics that can be a blessing or a burden. This is apparent with risk taking. Some emerging adults bravely, or foolishly, take risks—a behavior that is gender- and age-related, as well as genetic and hormonal. Those who are genetically impulsive *and* male *and* emerging adults are most likely to be brave and foolish.

Societies as well as individuals benefit because emerging adults take chances. Enrolling in college, moving to a new state or nation, getting married, having a baby—all these endeavors are risky. So is starting a business, filming a documentary, entering an athletic contest, enlisting in the military, and joining the Peace Corps.

Yet risk taking is often destructive. Although their bodies are strong and their reactions quick, emerging adults nonetheless have more accidents that land them in emergency rooms than do people of any other age. The low rate of serious disease between ages 18 and 25 is counterbalanced by a high rate of serious injuries (see Figure EP.2, leftmost data) and violent deaths.

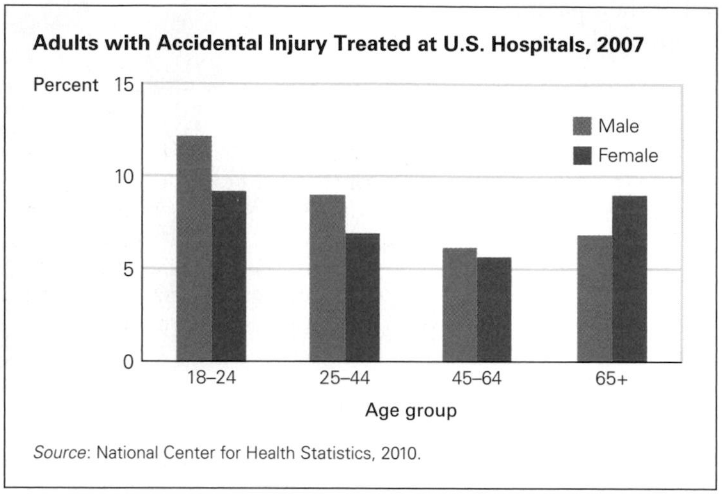

FIGURE EP.2

Send Them Home Accidents, homicides, and suicides occur more frequently during emerging adulthood than later. Note that the age range of more patients falls within the six years of emerging adulthood than within the 20 years of adulthood. Fewer young adults *stay* in the hospital, however. They are usually stitched, bandaged, injected, and sent home.

Destructive risks that are more common in emerging adulthood include unprotected sex with a new partner, driving fast without a seat belt, carrying a loaded gun, abusing drugs, and problem gambling—all done partly for an addictive rush of adrenaline (Cosgrave, 2010). Accidents, homicides, and suicides are leading causes of death among young adults—killing more young adults than all diseases combined, even where infectious diseases and malnutrition are rampant. The only exception is South Africa, where AIDS kills more young adults than suicide (but AIDS results from risk taking).

Risky Sports

Many young adults seek the rush of risk in recreation, as they climb mountains, swim in oceans, run in pain, play past exhaustion, and so on. Skydiving, bungee jumping, pond swooping, parkour, potholing (in caves), waterfall kayaking, and many more activities have been invented to satisfy the joy of risk—not that serious injury is the goal, but that high risk adds to the challenge, making preparation crucial (Brymer, 2010). Competitive **extreme sports** (such as *motocross*—motorcycle jumping off a ramp into "big air," doing tricks during the fall, and hoping to land upright) are new thrills for some emerging adults, who find golf, bowling, and so on too tame (Breivik, 2010).

extreme sports Forms of recreation that include apparent risk of injury or death and that are attractive and thrilling as a result.

This is clearer with an example. Travis Pastrana won the 2006 X Games motocross competition at age 22 with a double backflip because, as he explained, "The two main things are that I've been healthy and able to train at my fullest, and a lot of guys have had major crashes this year" (quoted in Higgins, 2006, p. D-7). Four years later, he set a new record for leaping through big air in an automobile, as he drove over the ocean from a ramp on the California shoreline to a barge more than 250 feet out. He crashed into a barrier on the boat but emerged, seemingly ecstatic and unhurt, to the thunderous cheers of thousands of other young adults on the shore (Roberts, 2010).

>> Answer to Observation Quiz (from page 506) Note that the rates are per 100,000 for the three leading diseases. This means that 1 out of every 14 90-year-olds and 1 out of every 14,000 19-year-olds will die of these diseases each year. However, people die from other causes as well. At age 90 in the United States, the rate of death doubles, meaning that a 90-year-old has about 1 chance in 7 of dying within a year. For emerging adults, the overall death rates are about 10 times higher, primarily because of violent deaths; 19-year-olds thus have an annual death rate of 1 per 1,400.

Drug Abuse

The same impulse that is admired in extreme sports can also lead to behaviors that are clearly destructive, not only for individuals but for the community. The

DAVID-YOUNG WOLFF / PHOTOEDIT INC.

>> Answer to Observation Quiz (from page 507) The cigarette, not the camera. Most young men in Canada and the United States do not smoke, especially publicly and casually, as this man does.

Higher Education College provides many benefits, but it also seems to encourage drug use. Everyone at this fraternity party appears to be using alcohol, and one young woman is drinking from a beer bong. Seeking admiration for drinking a lot in a short time is a sign that a person is at risk for alcoholism.

most studied of these is drug abuse (Reith, 2005), which can involve dozens of substances—from the perfectly legal to the extremely illegal.

By definition, **drug abuse** occurs whenever drug use harms physical, cognitive, or psychosocial well-being. Even occasional smoking or illegal drug use can be abuse, as can bingeing on alcohol (four or five drinks on one occasion). From an emerging-adult perspective, the potential for abuse is part of the attraction of drugs, especially if some authority figure disapproves: There is a special thrill in buying, carrying, and using an illegal drug, knowing that arrest is possible. Illegal drug use peaks at about age 20 and declines sharply with age (see Figure EP.3). The thrill is gone.

Surprisingly, drug abuse is more common among college students than among their peers who are not in college. For instance, college students are most likely to engage in extreme drinking, with 25 percent of young men and 5 percent of young women reporting that they consumed 10 or more drinks in a row at least once in the previous two weeks (Johnston et al., 2009). Such extremes arise from the same drive as extreme sports or other risks—with the same possible consequence: death.

drug abuse The ingestion of a drug to the extent that it impairs the user's biological or psychological well-being.

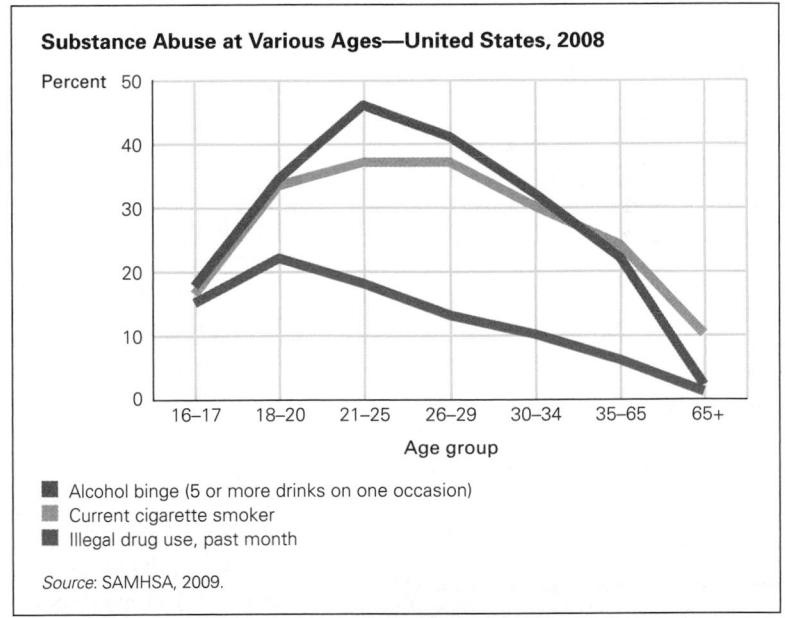

Substance Abuse at Various Ages—United States, 2008

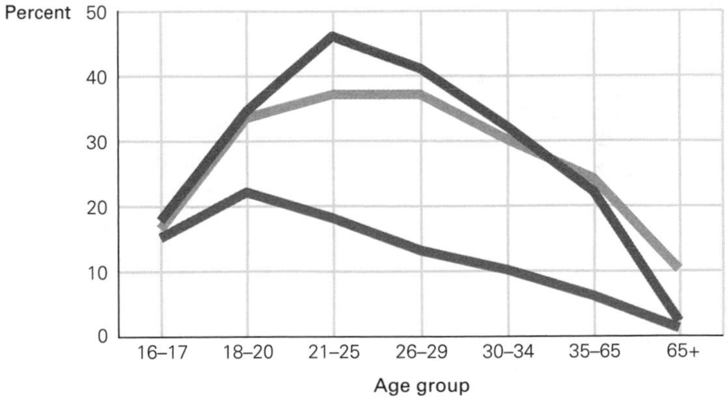

- Alcohol binge (5 or more drinks on one occasion)
- Current cigarette smoker
- Illegal drug use, past month

Source: SAMHSA, 2009.

FIGURE EP.3

Too Old for That As you can see, emerging adults are the biggest substance abusers, but illegal drug use drops much faster than do cigarette use or binge drinking.

SUMMING UP

Emerging adults are physiologically at their prime, with strong and healthy bodies. One strength is the sexual-reproductive system, which pushes many contemporary young adults to engage in premarital sex. The thrill of risk taking can become a problem, since it leads emerging adults to extreme sports, unprotected sex, drug abuse, and serious injuries. Accidents, homicide, and suicide are leading causes of death among young adults worldwide.

Especially for Substance Abuse Counselors Can you think of three possible explanations for the more precipitous drop in the use of illegal drug compared to legal ones? (see response, page 510)

>> Response for Substance Abuse Counselors (from page 509) Legal drugs could be more addictive, or the thrill of illegality may diminish with age, or the fear of arrest may increase. In any case, treatment for young-adult substance abusers may need to differ from that for older ones.

>> Cognitive Development

You remember that each of the four periods of child and adolescent development is characterized by major advances in cognition, with each advance representing a new stage, according to Piaget. Adult thinking also differs from earlier thinking: It is more practical, more flexible, and better able to coordinate objective and subjective perspectives. This may constitute a major advance, combining a new "ordering of formal operations" with a "necessary subjectivity" (Sinnott, 1998, p. 24).

Postformal Thought and Brain Development

postformal thought A proposed adult stage of cognitive development, following Piaget's four stages. Postformal thought goes beyond adolescent thinking by being more practical, more flexible, and more dialectical (i.e., more capable of combining contradictory elements into a comprehensive whole).

Many developmentalists believe that Piaget's fourth stage, formal operational thought, is inadequate to describe adult thinking. Some proposed a fifth stage, called **postformal thought,** characterized by "problem finding" not just "problem solving," wherein a person is more open to ideas and less concerned with absolute right and wrong (Yan & Arlin, 1995). As one group of scholars explained, in postformal thought, "one can conceive of multiple logics, choices, or perceptions . . . in order to better understand the complexities and inherent biases in 'truth'" (Griffin et al., 2009, p. 173).

As you remember from Chapter 15, adolescents use two modes of thought (dual processing), but they have difficulty combining them. They use formal analysis to learn science, distill principles, develop arguments, and resolve the world's problems; or, alternatively, they think spontaneously and emotionally. Rarely, however, do they coordinate both modes. They prefer quick reactions, only later realizing the consequences.

Postformal thinkers are less impulsive. They do not wait for someone else to present a problem to solve. They take a more flexible and comprehensive approach, with forethought, noting difficulties and anticipating problems, not denying, avoiding, or procrastinating. As a result, postformal thinking is more practical as well as more creative and imaginative than was thinking in previous cognitive stages (Wu & Chiou, 2008).

Many scientists doubt Piaget's stage theory of child cognition. Many more question this fifth stage. Certainly, if *stage* is taken to mean attaining a new set of intellectual abilities (such as the language explosion that distinguishes sensorimotor from preoperational thought), then adulthood has no stages. However, the prefrontal cortex is not fully mature until one's early 20s, and new dendrites grow throughout adulthood. Apparently adults tend to think in ways that adolescents do not.

Especially for Someone Who Has to Make an Important Decision Which is better: to go with your gut feelings or to consider pros and cons as objectively as you can? (see response, page 512)

For instance, one study of people aged 13 to 45 found that logical skills improved from adolescence to emerging adulthood and then stayed steady, as might be expected as analytic thought becomes established. However, social understanding continued to advance beyond early adulthood (Demetriou & Bakracevic, 2009). (Social understanding includes knowing how best to interact with other people—making and keeping good friends, responding to social slights, helping others effectively, and so on.) As another lead researcher concluded, adult thinking "can be ordered in terms of increasing levels of complexity and integration" (Labouvie-Vief et al., 2009, p. 182).

This cognitive maturation is now thought to depend partly on the brain development that continues throughout adolescence and emerging adulthood. As you remember, the limbic system matures faster than the prefrontal cortex, and not until the early 20s is the brain typically ready to analyze, plan, and coordinate impulses with the maturity expected of adults. The brain is still quite plastic in adolescence—able to learn new ideas and embark on new adventures. In emerg-

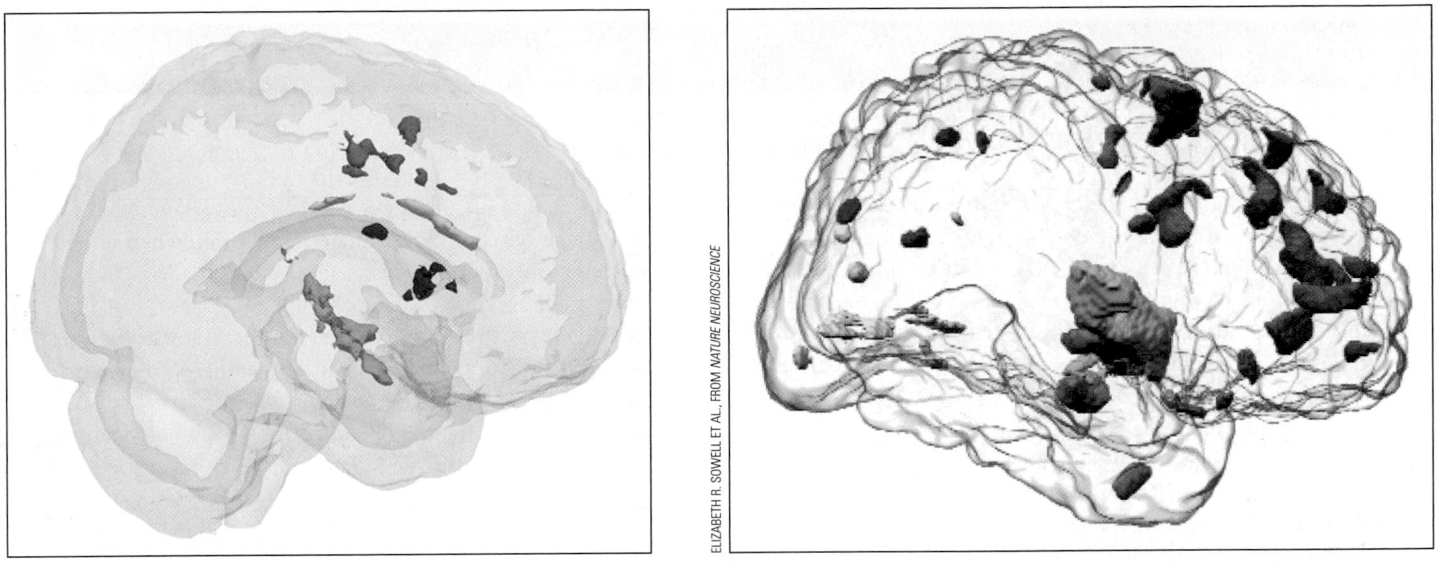

COURTESY CRAIG BENNETT & ABIGAIL BAIRD FROM *ANATOMICAL CHANGES IN THE EMERGING ADULT BRAIN*

(a)

ELIZABETH R. SOWELL ET AL., FROM *NATURE NEUROSCIENCE*

(b)

Thinking Away from Home *(a)* Entering a residential college means experiencing new foods, new friends, and new neurons. A longitudinal study of 18-year-old students at the beginning and end of their first year in college (Dartmouth) found increases in the brain areas that integrate emotion and cognition—namely, the cingulate (blue and yellow), caudate (red), and insula (orange). Researchers also studied one-year changes in the brains of students over age 25 at the same college and found no dramatic growth. *(b)* Shown here are the areas of one person's brain changes from age 14 to 25. The frontal cortex (purple) demonstrated many changes in particular parts, as did the areas for processing speech (green and blue)—a crucial aspect of young adult learning. Areas for visual processing (yellow) showed less change.

Researchers now know that brains mature in many ways between adolescence and adulthood; scientists are not yet sure of the cognitive implications.

ing adulthood, the final consolidation of various brain regions occurs (Tanner & Arnett, 2011).

Overall, many scholars find that thinking changes both qualitatively and quantitatively during adulthood (Bosworth & Hertzog, 2009). The term *fifth stage* may be a misnomer, but emerging adults can and often do reach a new cognitive level when their brains and life circumstances allow it.

Countering Stereotypes

Cognitive flexibility, particularly the ability to change one's childhood assumptions, is needed to counter stereotypes. Young adults show many signs of such flexibility in daily life. The very fact that emerging adults marry and become parents later than previous generations did suggests that, couple by couple, their thinking processes are not determined by their own childhood experiences or by traditional norms. Of course, early experiences are influential, but for postformal thinkers they are not determinative.

Research on racial prejudice is one example. Many U.S. children and adults of every ethnic group harbor implicit bias against African Americans, detectable in slower reaction times when mentally processing photos of African Americans than when processing photos of European Americans (Baron & Banaji, 2006). However, most people believe that they are not racially prejudiced, and their behavior reveals no bias (at least in explicit tests in a research laboratory). Thus, many adults have both unconscious prejudice and rational nonprejudice—a combination that illustrates dual processing. Cognitive flexibility allows people to recognize their emotional biases and to change their behaviors—both difficult without openness and flexibility.

However, people are often unaware of their own stereotypes, even when their false beliefs harm them. One of the most pernicious of these beliefs is **stereotype threat,** the worry that other people assume that you yourself are stupid, lazy, oversexed, or worse because of your ethnicity, sex, age, or appearance. Even the *possibility* of being stereotyped arouses emotions and hijacks memory, disrupting cognition (Schmader, 2010), as illustrated in the following.

stereotype threat The possibility that one's appearance or behavior will be misread to confirm another person's oversimplified, prejudiced attitudes.

A VIEW FROM SCIENCE

Stereotype Threat

One statistic has troubled social scientists for decades: African American men have lower grades in high school and earn only half as many college degrees as their genetic peers, African American women, who themselves do less well than women of other ethnic groups. This disparity has many possible causes, with most scientists blaming the context and historical discrimination (Arnett & Brody, 2008).

One African American scholar thought of another possibility, which he labeled *stereotype threat,* a "threat in the air" if not in reality (Steele, 1997). When African American males are made aware of the stereotype that they are poor scholars, they might become anxious. That anxiety would reduce their ability to focus on academics. Then, if they underachieve, they might dismiss academics in order to protect their pride. That would lead to disengagement from studying and even lower achievement (Ogbu, 2008).

Two decades of research have demonstrated that downward trajectory, but African American men are not the only ones to experience it. Hundreds of studies show that almost all humans can be harmed by stereotype threat: Women underperform in math, older people are more forgetful, bilingual students stumble with English, and every member of a stigmatized minority in every nation performs less well. Even those sometimes thought to be on top—White men—do less well in math if they think they will be negatively compared with men of Asian descent, and they do less well in some sports if they think they will be compared with men of African descent (Schmader et al., 2008). When athletes unexpectedly underperform because of stress (called choking), stereotype threat may be the cause (Hill et al., 2010).

Can stereotype threat be eliminated, or at least reduced? One group of researchers developed a hypothesis: that stereotype threat will decrease and achievement increase if African American college students *internalize* (believe wholeheartedly, not just intellectually) the idea that intelligence is plastic rather than the inalterable product of genes and gender. Using a clever combination of written material, mentoring, and video performing, these scientists convinced African Americans that their ability and hence their achievement depended on their personal efforts. That reduced stereotype threat and led to higher grades (Aronson et al., 2002).

This experiment intrigued thousands of researchers. They realized that this study required replication, since the participants were only 79 students at a highly selective university. Might other stereotyped groups respond differently? Soon thousands of other scientists replicated this study with many other groups, often targeting young adults since they may be most open to new ideas. The results confirmed, again and again, that stereotype threat is pervasive and debilitating but that it can be alleviated (Alter et al., 2010; Miyake et al., 2010; Rydell & Boucher, 2010).

>> Response for Someone Who Has to Make an Important Decision (from page 510) Both are necessary. Mature thinking requires a combination of emotions and logic. To make sure you use both, take your time (don't just act on your first impulse) and talk with people you trust. Ultimately, you will have to live with your decision, so do not ignore either intuitive or logical thought.

The Effects of College

A major reason why emerging adulthood has become a new period of development, when people postpone the usual markers of adult life (marriage, a steady job), is that many older adolescents seek further education rather than taking on adult responsibilities. However, some aspects of the impact of that education are controversial.

Massification

There is no dispute about some consequences of tertiary education: It improves health and wealth. For those reasons, every nation has recently increased the number of students in college—a phenomenon called *massification,* the idea that college could benefit everyone (the masses) (Altbach et al., 2010). The United States was the first major nation to endorse massification, but it no longer leads in this regard.

More than half of all 25- to 34-year-olds in Canada, Korea, Russia, and Japan are college graduates; the United States ranks twelfth among major nations, with about 41 percent of people in this age group having college degrees (Montgomery & Williams, 2010; UNESCO, 2009). Although not every young adult enrolls in

Especially for Those Considering Studying Abroad Given the effects of college, would it be better for a student to study abroad in the first year or last year of a college education? (see response, page 514)

college, and even fewer graduate, U.S. census data and surveys of individuals still find that college education adds about $20,000 per year to a worker's salary (see Figure 15.9).

Massification has stalled in the United States, but not elsewhere (Altbach et al., 2010). In Asia and Africa, college enrollment has more than tripled (see Figure EP.4), and the wealthiest and most capable students from those nations continue to earn degrees in North America or Europe, often returning to developing nations to work as professors. A global shift is evident: Hundreds of new universities have opened in Asia, Africa, and the Middle East. As of 2010, more college students were enrolled in China than in the United States.

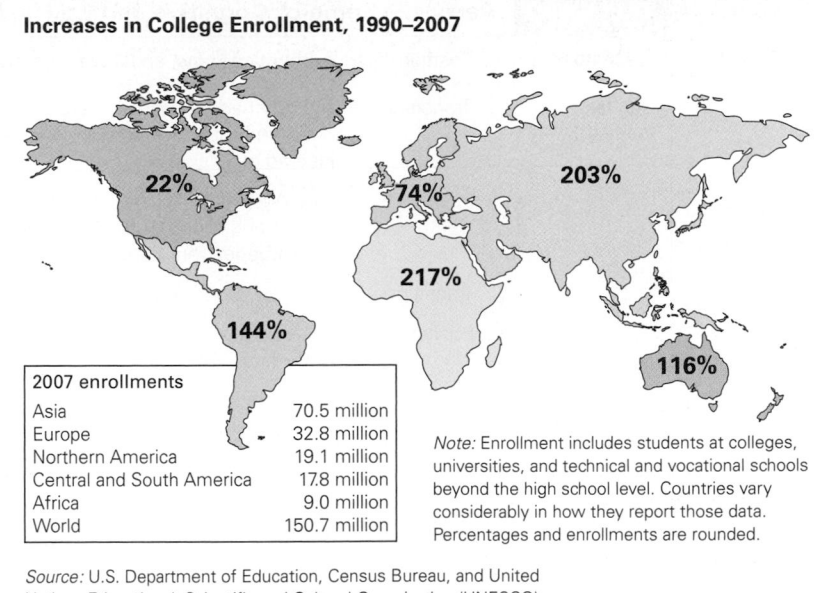

Increases in College Enrollment, 1990–2007

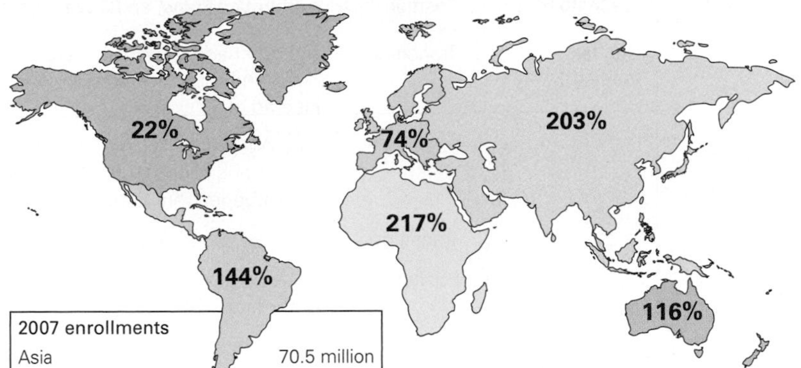

2007 enrollments	
Asia	70.5 million
Europe	32.8 million
Northern America	19.1 million
Central and South America	17.8 million
Africa	9.0 million
World	150.7 million

Note: Enrollment includes students at colleges, universities, and technical and vocational schools beyond the high school level. Countries vary considerably in how they report those data. Percentages and enrollments are rounded.

Source: U.S. Department of Education, Census Bureau, and United Nations Educational, Scientific and Cultural Organization (UNESCO).

FIGURE EP.4

Interpreting Data College-educated young adults know that maps combine facts with opinions. This map emphasizes that North America is lagging behind in college enrollment and that Africa is surging ahead, but the numbers suggest a more complex picture. Also note that eastern Europe and the Middle East are considered part of Asia and that Mexico is not included in North America. Nonetheless, one fact is obvious: Millions of students in developing nations are now attending college.

College and Cognition

For developmentalists interested in cognition, the crucial question is not about wealth, health, or numbers; it is about whether college education advances critical thinking and postformal thought. Past research has concluded that the answer is yes.

According to one classic study (Perry, 1981, 1999), thinking progresses through nine levels of complexity over the four years that lead to a bachelor's degree, moving from a simplistic dualism (right or wrong, yes or no, success or failure) to a relativism that recognizes a multiplicity of perspectives (see Table EP.2). Perry found that the college experience itself causes this progression: Peers, professors, books, and class discussion all

JEREMY WOODHOUSE / AGE FOTOSTOCK

AP PHOTO / STEPHAN SAVOIA

Education in Process These students, checking the Internet on the steps of San Miguel de Allende in Mexico *(left)* and discussing Pakistan on the quad at Brown University in the United States *(right)*, illustrate why some scholars claim that college students learn more from each other than from their professors.

TABLE EP.2 Perry's Scheme of Cognitive and Ethical Development During College

Freshmen	Position 1	Authorities know, and if we work hard, read every word, and learn Right Answers, all will be well.
Dualism modified	Transition	But what about those Others I hear about? And different opinions? And Uncertainties? Some of our own Authorities disagree with each other or don't seem to know, and some give us problems instead of Answers
	Position 2	True Authorities must be Right; the others are frauds. We remain Right. Others must be different and Wrong. Good Authorities give us problems so we can learn to find the Right Answer by our own independent thought
	Transition	But even Good Authorities admit they don't know all the answers yet!
	Position 3	Then some uncertainties and different opinions are real and legitimate temporarily, even for Authorities. They're working on them to get to the Truth.
	Transition	But there are so many things they don't know the Answers to! And they won't for a long time
Relativism discovered	Position 4a	Where Authorities don't know the Right Answers, everyone has a right to his own opinion; no one is wrong!
	Transition	Then what right have They to grade us? About what?
	Position 4b	In certain courses, Authorities are not asking for the Right Answer. They want us to think about things in a certain way, supporting opinion with data. That's what they grade us on.
	Position 5	Then all thinking must be like this, even for Them. Everything is relative but not equally valid. You have to understand how each context works. Theories are not Truth but metaphors to interpret data with. You have to think about your thinking.
	Transition	But if everything is relative, am I relative, too? How can I know I'm making the Right Choice?
	Position 6	I see I'm going to have to make my own decisions in an uncertain world with no one to tell me I'm Right.
	Transition	I'm lost if I don't. When I decide on my career (or marriage or values), everything will straighten out.
Commitments in relativism developed	Position 7	Well, I've made my first Commitment!
	Transition	Why didn't that settle everything?
	Position 8	I've made several commitments. I've got to balance them—how many, how deep? How certain, how tentative?
	Transition	Things are getting contradictory. I can't make logical sense out of life's dilemmas.
Seniors	Position 9	This is how life will be. I must be wholehearted while tentative, fight for my values yet respect others, believe my deepest values are right yet be ready to learn. I see that I shall be retracing this whole journey over and over—but, I hope, more wisely.

Source: Perry, 1981, 1999.

>> Response for Those Considering Studying Abroad (from page 512) Since one result of college is that students become more open to other perspectives while developing their commitment to their own values, foreign study might be most beneficial after several years of college. If they study abroad too early, some students might be either too narrowly patriotic (they are not yet open) or too quick to reject everything about their national heritage (they have not yet developed their own commitments).

stimulate new questions and thoughts. Other research confirmed Perry's conclusions. In general, the more years of higher education a person has, the deeper and more postformal that person's reasoning becomes (Pascarella & Terenzini, 1991).

Which aspect of college is the primary catalyst for such growth? Is it the challenging academic work, professors' lectures, peer discussions, the new setting, living away from home? All are possible. Every scientist finds that social interaction and intellectual challenge advance thinking. College students expect classes and conversations to further their thinking—which is exactly what occurs (Kuh et al., 2005). This is not surprising, since colleges were designed to foster intellectual growth. Professors themselves can advance in their thinking, passing those advances on to their students, as is evident in the following.

A CASE TO STUDY

The Academic and the Personal

One of the leading thinkers in postformal thought is Jan Sinnott, a professor and now editor of the *Journal of Adult Development.* She describes the first course she taught:

> I did not think in a postformal way. . . . Teaching was good for passing information from the informed to the uninformed. . . . I decided to create a course in the psychology of aging . . . with a fellow graduate student. Being compulsive graduate students had paid off in our careers so far, so my colleague and I continued on that path. Articles and books and photocopies began to take over my house. And having found all this information, we seem to have unconsciously sworn to use all of it. . . .
>
> Each class day, my colleague and I would arrive with reams of notes and articles and lecture, lecture, lecture. Rapidly! . . . The discussion of death and dying came close to the end of the term (naturally). As I gave my usual jam-packed lecture, the sound of note taking was intense. But toward the end of the class . . . an extremely capable student burst into tears and said she had to drop the class. . . . Unknown to me, she had been the caretaker of an older relative who had just died in the past few days. She had not said anything about this significant experience when we lectured on caretaking. . . . How could she? . . . We never stopped talking. "I wish I could tell people what it's really like," she said.
>
> [*Sinnott, 2008, pp. 54–55*]

Sinnott changed her lesson plan. In the next class, the student told her story.

> In the end, the students agreed that this was a class when they . . . synthesized material and analyzed research and theory critically.
>
> [*Sinnott, 2008, p. 56*]

Sinnott still lectures and gives multiple-choice exams, but she also includes personal stories. She combines analysis and emotion; she includes the experiences of her students. Her teaching became postformal, flexible, and responsive.

Current Contexts

But wait. You probably noticed that Perry's study was first published in 1981. Hundreds of other studies also found that college education deepens cognition, but most of that research occurred in the twentieth century. Since you know that cohort and culture are crucial influences on development, you may wonder whether those conclusions still hold.

Many recent books criticize college education on exactly those grounds. Notably, an impressive twenty-first-century longitudinal study of a cross section of U.S. college students found that students' growth in critical thinking, analysis, and communication over the four years of college was only half as much as among college students two decades ago (Arum et al., 2011). The same researchers published a detailed analysis of the first two years of college and reported that 45 percent of the students made no significant advances at all (Arum & Roksa, 2011).

Especially for High School Teachers
One of your brightest students doesn't want to go to college. She would rather keep waitressing in a restaurant, where she makes good money in tips. What do you say? (see response, page 517)

The reasons were many: Students study less, professors expect less, and students avoid classes in which they must read at least 40 pages a week or write 20 pages a semester. Administrators and faculty still hope for intellectual growth, but rigorous classes are canceled or not required.

Motivation to Attend College

An underlying problem may be that people disagree about the purpose of a college education. Developmentalists, most professors, and many college graduates believe that the main purpose is "personal and intellectual growth." However, adults who have never attended college believe that "acquiring specific skills and knowledge" is more important (see Figure EP.5). In the Arum and Roksa report (2011), students majoring in business and other career fields were less likely to gain in critical thinking compared to those in the liberal arts (courses that demand more reading and writing).

The Main Purpose of College

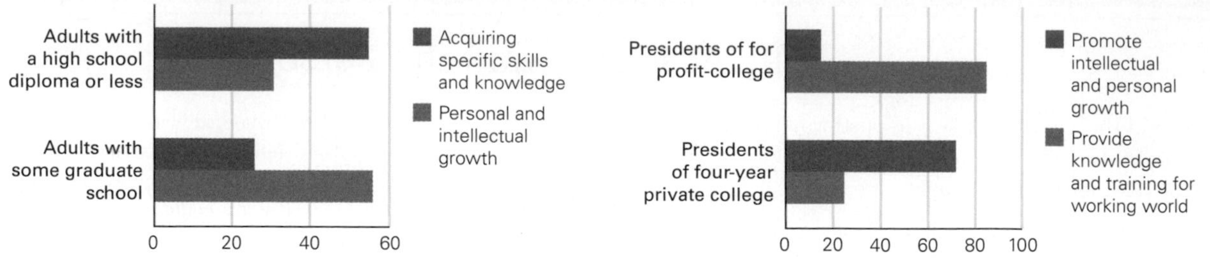

Source: Pew Social Trends Staff, 2011.

FIGURE EP.5

Intellectual or Practical Skills? As you see, people disagree as to whether a college education should foster intellectual growth or provide useful knowledge and skills. Presented here are the extremes—those with some college, and those who are leaders of community colleges, are in between these extremes.

Looking more closely at the U.S. college scene, it seems that students now attend college primarily for career reasons (see Figure EP.6). Furthermore, many select institutions for their job preparation, not their emphasis on reading and writing. Since tuition and government grants are major sources of income for colleges, institutions tend to meet the students' needs.

In 1955, most U.S. colleges were four-year institutions and most students majored in liberal arts. There were only 275 junior colleges. In 2010, there were almost 1,500 such colleges, now called community colleges, with some of them (19 in Florida) offering bachelor's degrees in careers in which jobs are available. Similarly, for-profit colleges were scarce until about 1980; now the United States has more than 1,300 of them (Chronicle of Higher Education, 2010). This is more than an increase in the number of various institutions; it signifies a shift in what people believe is the reason for college.

Students, parents, professors, and legislators disagree as to whether college should prepare people for jobs, expand their cultural understanding, or provide time and space for the development of advanced critical cognition. Depending on the goal, measurement of achievement and motivation to study will vary. No nation has reached consensus on the purpose of college.

Even in China, where the central government has fostered thousands of new institutions of higher learning, disagreement about the goals of college is evident. For instance, a new Chinese university (called South University of Science and Technology of China, SUSTC) is designed to encourage analysis and critical thinking, in deliberate contrast to the emphasis on knowledge and skills in other Chinese institutions. SUSTC does not require prospective students to take the national exam (*Gao Kao*); instead, "creativity and a passion for learning" are the admission criteria (Stone, 2011, p. 161). Faculty are supposed to nurture curiosity, not lecture. However, the Chinese government is not convinced about this educational approach: SUSTC is not yet officially accredited.

FIGURE EP.6

Cohort Shift Students in 1980 thought new ideas and a philosophy of life were prime reasons to go to college—they were less interested in jobs, careers, and money than are students in 2010. If this thinking causes a conflict between student motivation and professor's goals, who should adjust?

Reasons, listed as very important, for attending college

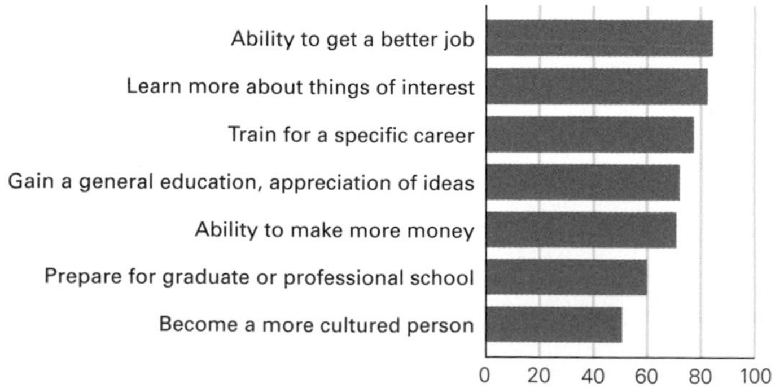

Source: Pryor et al., 2010.

The Effects of Diversity

At least one characteristic of the twenty-first-century college scene in every nation bodes well for intellectual challenges—the diversity of the student body. The most obvious change is gender: In 1970, at least two-thirds of college students were male; now in every developed nation (except Germany), most are female; and most single-sex colleges have become co-ed, even in the sex-segregated societies of the Middle East. In addition, student ethnic, economic, religious, and cultural backgrounds are more varied. Compared to 1970, more students are parents, are older than age 24, are of non-European heritage, attend part time, and live and work off-campus—all true worldwide, although the modal student is still 18 to 22 years old and attends school full time.

Discussion among people of different backgrounds and varied perspectives leads to intellectual challenge and deeper thought. Thus, the increased diversity of the student body may enhance learning. Colleges that make use of their diversity—via curriculum, class assignments, discussions, cooperative education, learning communities, and so on—help students stretch their understanding, not only of differences and similarities among people but also of themselves (Nagda et al., 2005).

Skeptical readers might question the data that link college education to a wealthier, wiser, and happier adulthood. Such skepticism is warranted, since correlation does not equal causation: Student characteristics before college may be a third variable that explains these links. However, when selection is taken into account, college still seems to aid cognitive development (Pascarella, 2005). Even the critics agree that some students at every institution advance markedly in critical thinking and analysis because of their college experience (Arum & Roksa, 2011). Now each reader of this text can try to combine objective and subjective thought—does college advance your own postformal cognition?

>> Response for High School Teachers (from page 515) Even more than ability, motivation is crucial for college success, so don't insist that she attend college. Since your student has money and a steady job (prime goals for today's college-bound youth), she may not realize what she would be missing. Ask her what she hopes for herself, in work and lifestyle, over the many decades ahead.

SUMMING UP

Emerging adults often become more flexible, creative, and coordinated thinkers than they were as adolescents, an advancement sometimes described as postformal thought. College education brings health and wealth to graduates, and nations worldwide have increased the number of students in college. Research in earlier decades in the United States finds that college also advances cognition, helping students become more critical thinkers as well as more flexible. However, some find that those cognitive effects are less evident than they were previously, especially since many current students seek skills and knowledge, not intellectual challenge. Nonetheless, for many students college broadens their perspective, as the diversity of students and the opportunity to understand and debate new ideas lead to deeper, more flexible, postformal thought. ■

>> Psychosocial Development

A theme of human development is that continuity and change are evident throughout life. In emerging adulthood, the legacy of early development is apparent amidst new achievement. Erikson recognized this ongoing process in his description of the fifth of his eight stages, identity versus role confusion. As you remember, the crisis of identity begins in adolescence, but it is not usually resolved then.

Identity Achieved

As already mentioned, Erikson believed that the outcome of earlier crises provides the foundation for each new stage of development. The identity crisis is an example (see Table EP.3). Worldwide, adults ponder all four arenas of identity—religious commitments, sex/gender roles, political/ethnic loyalties, and career options—trying to reconcile plans for the future with beliefs acquired in the past.

TABLE EP.3 Erikson's Eight Stages of Development

Stage	Virtue/Pathology	Possible in Emerging Adulthood if Not Successfully Resolved
Trust vs. mistrust	Hope/withdrawal	Suspicious of others, making close relationships difficult
Autonomy vs. shame and doubt	Will/compulsion	Obsessively driven, single-minded, not socially responsive
Initiative vs. guilt	Purpose/inhibition	Fearful, regretful (e.g., very homesick in college)
Industry vs. inferiority	Competence/inertia	Self-critical of any endeavor, procrastinating, perfectionistic
Identity vs. role diffusion	Fidelity/repudiation	Uncertain and negative about values, lifestyle, friendships
Intimacy vs. isolation	Love/exclusivity	Anxious about close relationships, jealous, lonely
Generativity vs. stagnation	Care/rejection	[In the future] Fear of failure
Integrity vs. despair	Wisdom/disdain	[In the future] No "mindfulness," no life plan

Source: Erikson, 1982.

Past as Prologue In elaborating his eight stages of development, Erikson associated each stage with a particular virtue and a type of psychopathology, as shown here. He also thought that earlier crises could reemerge, taking a specific form at each stage. Listed are some possible problems (not directly from Erikson) that could occur in emerging adulthood if earlier crises were not resolved.

Now we will focus on the two identity areas that currently seem most fluid in emerging adulthood, ethnicity and vocation.

Ethnic Identity

High school senior Natasha Scott "just realized that my race is something I have to think about." Her mother is Asian and her father is African American, which had not been an issue as she was growing up. However, college applications (and the 2010 Census) required choices regarding ethnic identity (Saulny & Steinberg, 2011).

Natasha is not the only one. In the United States and Canada, almost half of 18- to 25-year-olds are of African, Asian, Latino, or Native American heritage, and many of them have ancestors of more than one ethnic group. Usually those ancestors are long dead, but an increasing number have living parents from two groups. In 2008, 15 percent of all U.S. marriages were interethnic, a statistic from the American Community Survey, which combined many groups into a single ethnicity (e.g., no matter where they were born, Black people who were from Africa, the Caribbean, and anywhere in the United States were considered one ethnicity; Asians from Pakistan and China were similarly considered one ethnic group. Obviously, if each bride and groom were asked whether they differed in ethnicity, far more than 15 percent would say yes).

Whether one's heritage is mixed or not, ethnicity is a significant aspect of American identity (Phinney, 2006). During late adolescence and early adulthood, people are more likely to be proud, or at least accepting, of their ethnic background than younger adolescents are (Worrell, 2008). There is no doubt that "identity development . . . from the teenage years to the early 20s, if not through adulthood, . . . has been extended to explain the development of ethnic and racial identity" (Whitbourne et al., 2009, p. 1328).

As they leave their childhood homes to enroll in colleges or to find work, emerging adults, more than any other age group, find friends and acquaintances of many backgrounds. Typically, they have "both positive and negative experiences" related to their ethnic background, developing "a strong sense of ethnic identity"—true for college students of every group (Syed & Azmitia, 2010, p. 218). It may be a mistake if they either assimilate (blend in) or become alienated (isolated and antagonistic), at least according to a study of Hispanic college students. Those who resisted both assimilation and alienation fared best: They were most likely to maintain their ethnic identity, deflect stereotype threat, and become good students (Rivas-Drake & Mooney, 2009).

College classes (especially in history, ethnic studies, and sociology) attract many emerging adults who want to learn more about their culture. In addition, extracurricular groups help solidify identity because students encounter others of similar backgrounds who confront the same issues.

When it comes to sexual intimacy, although most young adults are happy to know people of other groups and most approve of interethnic romance, a study in a large multiethnic university found that students tend to choose sexual partners (from hookups to marriage) within their own group (McClintock, 2010). The reason was not prejudice against others as much as bonding with co-ethnics. Thus, ethnic identity is an example of the emerging adult's ability to combine the personal and the political, the intuitive and the analytic. Young adults accept and appreciate interracial couples, even as they usually prefer mates like themselves.

ISSEI KATO / REUTERS

Just Like Me Emerging adults of every ethnicity take pride in their culture. In Japan, adulthood begins with a celebration at age 20, to the evident joy of these young women on Coming of Age Day, a national holiday.

Vocational Identity

Developmental psychologists influenced by Erikson and emerging adults themselves consider establishing a vocational identity to be part of growing up (Arnett, 2004). Many young adults go to college not only as a moratorium but also to prepare for work. Emerging adulthood is a "critical stage for the acquisition of resources"—including the education, skills, and experience needed for family and career success lifelong (Tanner et al., 2009, p. 34).

Part of the preparation for lifetime work often includes taking temporary jobs. Between ages 18 and 27, the average U.S. worker holds eight jobs, with the college-educated changing jobs more than those who are less educated (U.S. Bureau of the Census, 2009). This illustrates the exploration that is part of the identity search, and it is also a sign that achievement has not yet occurred: The young worker is not yet climbing a particular vocational ladder, rung by rung. For most emerging adults, "the process of identifying with society's work ethic, the core of this issue [identity achievement] in Erikson's scheme, continues to evolve throughout early adulthood" (Whitbourne et al., 2009, p. 1329).

Many developmentalists wonder whether achieving a single vocational identity is still a worthy goal. Especially for young people, commitment to a particular career may limit rather than increase vocational success. Contemporary research finds that an economic recession (as apparent worldwide beginning roughly in 2008) makes vocational identity more difficult for adolescents and young adults to achieve. Research on older adults who came of age during past economic crises suggests that vocational problems may continue, affecting the current cohort when the financial picture improves (Johnson et al., 2011).

Personality in Emerging Adulthood

Continuity and change are evident in personality as well (McAdams & Olson, 2010). Of course, temperament and personality endure lifelong: The self-doubt, anxiety, depression, and so on that are present in childhood and adolescence are often still evident years later. Traits present at age 5 or 15 do not disappear by age 25.

Yet personality is not static. After adolescence, new characteristics may appear and negative traits may diminish. Emerging adults make choices that break with

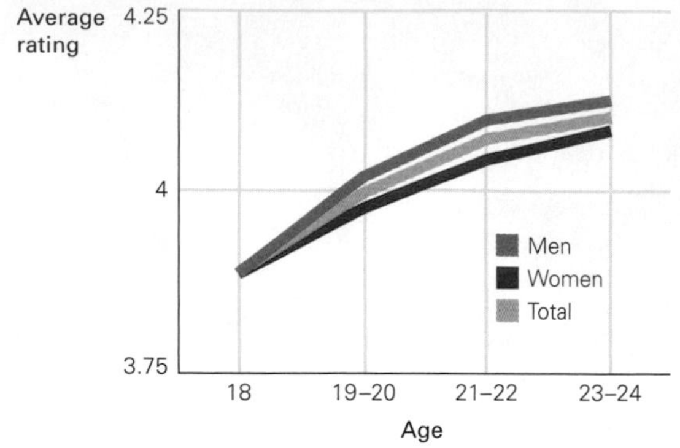

Source: Schulenberg et al., 2005, p. 424.

FIGURE EP.7

Worthy People This graph shows a steady increase in young adults' sense of well-being from age 18 to age 24, as measured by respondents' ratings of statements such as "I feel I am a person of worth." The ratings ranged from 1 (complete disagreement) to 5 (complete agreement). The average rating was already quite high at age 18, and it increased steadily over the years of emerging adulthood.

the past. This age period is now characterized by years of freedom from a settled lifestyle, which allows shifts in attitude and personality.

Rising Self-Esteem

Psychological research finds both continuity and improvement in attitudes. For example, one longitudinal study found that 17-year-olds who saw life in positive terms maintained their outlook as time went on, while those who were negative often changed for the better (Blonigen et al., 2008).

Another team of researchers traced 3,912 U.S. high school seniors until age 23 or 24. Those in college who lived away from home showed the largest gains in well-being, and those who had become single parents or who still lived with their own parents showed the least. Even the latter, however, tended to be happier than they had been in high school (see Figure EP.7; Schulenberg et al., 2005). Similarly, 404 young adults in western Canada, who were repeatedly questioned from ages 18 to 25, reported increasing self-esteem (Galambos et al., 2006).

This positive trend of increasing happiness has become more evident over recent decades, perhaps because young adults are more likely than adolescents to make their own life decisions (Twenge et al., 2008). Logically, the many stresses and transitions of emerging adulthood might reduce self-esteem, but that is not what the research finds. Psychopathology may increase and some emerging adults do develop serious disorders (Twenge et al., 2010), but most do not.

Worrisome Children Grow Up

The research just cited was conducted among North American youth, but similar conclusions come from a European longitudinal study that began with 4-year-olds who were at the extremes of either of two traits known to have strong genetic roots: extreme shyness and marked aggression. These children still tended to be shy or aggressive later in childhood (as one might expect, since genetic, familial, and cultural influences tend to be similar throughout childhood). However, by emerging adulthood most had changed for the better (Asendorpf et al., 2008).

Early traits were still evident. At age 25, those who had been aggressive 4-year-olds had more conflicts with their parents and friends and were more likely to have quit school and left jobs. (Two-thirds had dropped out of high school, as had only one-third of their nonaggressive peers.) By age 23, half had been arrested at least once, another sign of their aggressive personalities.

Yet, unexpectedly, these aggressive young adults had as many friends as their average peers did. They wanted more education, and they rated themselves as quite conscientious. They tended to be adolescence-limited offenders, and their crimes were usually minor: Only one had been sent to prison, and only one other had been arrested several times.

A closer examination of their school records found that their behavior, not their lack of ability, had caused their childhood teachers to fail them; as a result, many had repeated grades while their peers moved on. Since they were older than their classmates in high school, they quit because of the school restrictions and other peoples' assumptions, not because they hated learning. As emerging adults, most seemed to be developing well, putting their childhood problems behind them; some were employed and others had enrolled in college.

As for the emerging adults who had been inhibited as 4-year-olds, they were "cautious, reserved adults" but "with few signs of internalizing problems" (Asendorpf et al., 2008, p. 1007). They were slower than average to secure a job, choose a career, or find a romance (at age 23, two-thirds had no current partner). However, they were no more anxious or depressed than their peers, and their self-esteem was equally good. They had many friends and saw them often. Their delayed employment and later marriage were not unlike the patterns of the most successful of the emerging adults. Thus, the shyness that was considered to be a handicap in their childhood may have become an asset.

Plasticity

In the research just discussed and in other research as well, plasticity is evident. Personality is not fixed by age 5, or 15, or 20, as it was once thought to be. Emerging adults are open to new experiences (a reflection of their adventuresome spirit), and this allows personality shifts as well as eagerness for more education (McAdams & Olson, 2010; Tanner et al., 2009). The trend is toward less depression and more joy, along with more insight into the self (Galambos et al., 2006; McAdams et al., 2006).

Going to college, leaving home, paying one's way, stopping drug abuse, moving to a new city, finding satisfying work and performing it well, making new friends, committing to a partner—each of these might alter a person's life course. The feeling of self-efficacy builds with each successful accomplishment, giving people the confidence and courage to modify whatever destructive traits they may have.

Total transformation does not occur since genes, childhood experiences, and family circumstances affect people lifelong. Nor do new experiences always result in desirable changes. Indeed, it is possible that the rising self-esteem found in longitudinal research reflected historical improvements at the end of the twentieth century and that current conditions (health, the job market, the economy) may soon cause self-esteem to fall. But there is no doubt that personality *can* shift after adolescence.

Increased well-being and maturation may be the reasons for another shift: Emerging adults seem to become less self-centered and more caring of others (Eisenberg et al., 2005; Padilla-Walker et al., 2008). This can be seen as the foundation of the next psychosocial stage of development.

Intimacy

In Erikson's theory, after achieving identity, people experience the sixth crisis of development, **intimacy versus isolation.** This crisis arises from the powerful desire to share one's personal life with someone else. Without intimacy, adults suffer from loneliness and isolation. Erikson (1963) explains:

> The young adult, emerging from the search for and the insistence on identity, is eager and willing to fuse his identity with others. He is ready for intimacy, that is, the capacity to commit himself to concrete affiliations and partnerships and to develop the ethical strength to abide by such commitments, even though they call for significant sacrifices and compromises.
>
> *[p. 263]*

intimacy versus isolation The sixth of Erikson's eight stages of development. Adults seek someone with whom to share their lives in an enduring and self-sacrificing commitment. Without such commitment they risk profound loneliness and isolation.

The urge for social connection is a powerful human impulse, one reason our species has thrived. Other theorists use different words (*affiliation, affection, interdependence, communion, belonging, love*) for the same human need. Attachment experienced in infancy may well be a precursor to adult intimacy (Simpson et al., 2007). There is no doubt that all adults seek to become friends, lovers, companions, and partners.

All intimate relationships (friendship, family ties, and romance) have much in common—in both the psychic needs they satisfy and in the behaviors they require

(Reis & Collins, 2004). Intimacy progresses from attraction to close connection to ongoing commitment. Each relationship demands some personal sacrifice, including vulnerability that brings deeper self-understanding and shatters the isolation caused by too much self-protection. As Erikson (1963) explains, to establish intimacy, the emerging adult must

> face the fear of ego loss in situations which call for self-abandon: in the solidarity of close affiliations [and] sexual unions, in close friendship and in physical combat, in experiences of inspiration by teachers and of intuition from the recesses of the self. The avoidance of such experiences . . . may lead to a deep sense of isolation and consequent self-absorption.
>
> *[pp. 163–164]*

According to a more recent theory, an important aspect of close human connections is "self-expansion," the idea that each of us enlarges our understanding, our experiences, and our resources through our intimate friends and lovers (Aron et al., 2005).

Romantic Partners

Love, romance, and commitment are all of primary importance for emerging adults, although many specifics have changed. Most emerging adults are thought to be postponing, not abandoning, marriage. As one U.S. sociologist explains, "despite the culture of divorce, Americans remain optimistic about, and even eager to enter, marriages" (Hill, 2007, p. 295). One of the hottest political issues in 2011 was whether gay and lesbian couples should be allowed to marry. The very fact that gay couples want to marry, and that some other people are vehemently opposed and argue that marriage needs to be "defended," makes it clear that marriage is considered desirable.

The relationship between love and marriage depends on era and culture, with three distinct patterns evident (Georgas et al., 2006). In about one-third of the world's families, love does not lead to marriage because parents arrange marriages that will join two families together.

In another one-third of families, adolescents meet only a select group (single-sex schools keep them from meeting unsuitable mates). Parents supervise all male–female interactions. When young people decide to marry someone of that preselected group, then the young man asks the young woman's father for "her hand in marriage." Historically, if parental approval was not forthcoming, the teens parted sorrowfully or eloped—neither of which occurs as often today.

Suggesting "one-third" for each of these is a rough approximation. In former times, most marriages were of the first type; young people almost never met and married people unknown to their parents (Apostolou, 2007). Currently, in developing nations, practice often blends these two types. For example, in modern India most brides believe they have a choice, but many meet their future husbands shortly before the wedding via parental arrangement. The young man or woman can then veto the match, but usually they do not (Desai & Andrist, 2010).

The third pattern is relatively new, although familiar to most readers of this book. Young people socialize with hundreds of others and pair off but do not marry until they are able, financially and emotionally, to be independent. Their choices tilt toward personal qualities observable at the moment (physical appearance, personal hygiene, personality, sexuality, a sense of humor), not to qualities more important to parents, such as religion, ethnicity, or long-term stability—a person who has been married and divorced is seen much more negatively by parents than by unpartnered adults (Buunk et al., 2008).

For Western emerging adults, love is considered a prerequisite for marriage and then sexual exclusiveness is expected, as found in a survey of 14,121 people of many ethnic groups and orientations (Meier et al., 2009). They were asked to rate from 1 to 10 the importance of money, same racial background, long-term commitment, love, and faithfulness for a successful marriage or a serious, committed relationship. Faithfulness was the most important of all (rated 10 by 89 percent) and love was almost as high (rated 10 by 86 percent). Virtually all the rest thought faithfulness and love were very important (rated 9). By contrast, most thought being of the same race did not matter much (57 percent rated it 1, 2, or 3). Money, while important to many, was not nearly as crucial as love and fidelity.

This survey was conducted in North America, but emerging adults worldwide share many of the same values. Six thousand miles away, emerging adults in Kenya also reported that love was the primary reason for couples to connect and stay together; money was less important (Clark et al., 2010).

Finding Each Other

One major innovation of the current cohort of emerging adults is the use of social networks. Web sites such as Facebook allow individuals to post their photos and personal information on the Internet, sharing the details of their daily lives with thousands of others. Three-fourths of all 18- to 29-year-olds in the United States use social networking (Pew Research Center, 2010). Such sites often indicate whether an individual is or is not in a committed relationship. Many also use Internet matching sites to find potential partners.

One problem is that social networking may produce dozens of potential partners, increasing *choice overload* when too many options are available. Choice overload increases second thoughts after a choice is made (people wonder whether they would have been happier with another choice). Some people, overloaded with possibilities, refuse to make any selection (Iyengar & Lepper, 2000; Reutskaja & Hogarth, 2009).

EVERYSTOCKPHOTO.COM

Matched Online Karen and James met on the Internet and now enjoy their face-to-face connection—as do thousands of other social networking couples.

Choice overload has been demonstrated with consumer goods—jams, chocolates, pens, restaurants—but it has not been proven for choosing a mate. Having many complex options that require weighing both present and future advantages and disadvantages (such trade-offs are inevitable in selecting a partner) makes choice overload likely, but more research is needed (Scheibehenne et al., 2010).

Living Together

A second major innovation among emerging adults is **cohabitation,** the term for living together in a romantic partnership without being married. Cohabitation was relatively unusual 40 years ago: In the United States, less than 1 percent of all households were comprised of a cohabiting man and woman; more recently, 5 percent are (see Figure EP.8). Many couples now married were earlier in that 5 percent.

cohabitation An arrangement in which a couple live together in a committed romantic relationship but are not formally married.

Indeed, most 25-year-olds in the United States, Canada, northern Europe, England, and Australia have lived unmarried with a partner for at least a few months. Most adults in Sweden, France, Jamaica, and Puerto Rico live together and plan to stay together, never marrying. In most of the United States, committed same-sex couples are forced into this category, but not in Canada. In other nations—including Japan, Ireland, and Italy—fewer people cohabit, although the rate is rising everywhere.

FIGURE EP.8

More Together, Fewer Married As you see, the number of cohabiting male–female households in the United States has increased dramatically over the past decades. These numbers are an underestimate: Couples who do not tell the U.S. census takers that they are living together, or who cohabit within their parents' households, or who are same-sex couples (not tallied until 2000) are not included here. In addition, most emerging adults who are not now cohabiting may well be doing so within a few years.

Observation Quiz Did the rate of cohabitation increase faster before or after the year 2000? (see answer, page 526)

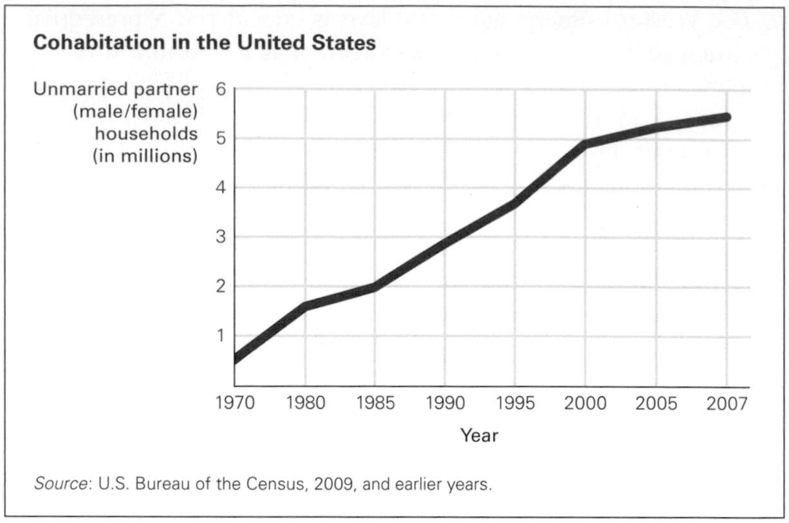

Research from 30 nations finds that acceptance of cohabitation within the nation affects the happiness of those who cohabit. Demographic differences within those 30 nations (such as education, income, age, and religion among the married and cohabitants) affect happiness as well (Soons & Kalmijn, 2009).

Research in the United States finds that people who cohabit and have children, or who cohabit and later marry (their cohabiting partner or someone else), have higher rates of separation and divorce. Furthermore, children born to cohabiting couples are more likely to have academic, health, or emotional difficulties (Schmeer, 2011; Stanley et al., 2006). Some factors—such as whether the couple is already engaged to marry before moving in together or having little or no financial stress (rare for most cohabiting couples)—mitigate such problems. However, although there are practical reasons for cohabitation—it saves money and postpones commitment—no longitudinal research has found that it improves psychosocial development. Thus, neither the popularity of cohabitation nor the immediate happiness of the participants prove that cohabitation is beneficial over the long term.

Love, Not Marriage Andrew and Jessica decided to raise their daughter together but not to marry. They live in White Bear, Minnesota, a relatively conservative area, but cohabiting couples are increasingly common everywhere.

RICHARD TSONG-TAATARII / MCT / NEWSCOM

Family Forces

It is hard to overestimate the importance of the family at any time of the life span. Although made up of individuals, a family is much more than the persons who belong to it: In dynamic synergy, children grow, adults find support, and everyone is part of an ethos that gives meaning to, and provides models for, personal aspirations and decisions.

Linked Lives

Emerging adults are said to set out independently, leaving their childhood home and parents behind. They strive for independence and avoid establishing their own families (Arnett, 2004). Thus, it might seem as if they no longer need family support and guidance. The data, however, show that parents continue to be crucial—perhaps even more so than for previous generations because many young people today rely on their parents: Compared with earlier cohorts, fewer contemporary young adults have finished their education or have started their own families and found high-paying jobs.

Especially for Family Therapists More emerging-adult children today live with their parents than ever before, yet you have learned that families often function better when young adults live on their own. What would you advise? (see response, page 527)

All members of each family have **linked lives,** meaning that the experiences and needs of family members at one stage of life are affected by those at other stages (Macmillan & Copher, 2005). We have seen this in earlier chapters: Children are affected by their parents' relationship, even if the children are not directly involved in domestic disputes, financial stresses, parental alliances, and so on. Likewise, each newborn affects every family member of every age.

linked lives Lives in which the success, health, and well-being of each family member are connected to those of other members, including members of another generation, as in the relationship between parents and children.

The same historical conditions that gave rise to this stage called emerging adulthood may have an unanticipated benefit: stronger links between parents and their adult children. Because of demographic changes over the past few decades, most parents have small families, which allows them to attend to the financial and emotional needs of their emerging-adult children since they have no younger offspring. Parental concern is intensified by several factors: Young-adult children are usually not married, not parents, and almost never vocationally secure (long gone are the days when the young took over the family business).

Strong links between emerging adults and their parents may seem counterintuitive, as emerging adults are independent and cohort changes have occurred. Nonetheless, many studies have found congruence in attitudes between parents and their young-adult children. Political and religious loyalties often link the generations.

LINDA DAVIDSON / THE WASHINGTON POST / GETTY IMAGES

Brilliant, Unemployed, and Laughing This is not an unusual combination for contemporary college graduates. Melissa, in Missoula, Montana, graduated summa cum laude from George Washington University and is now one of the many college graduates who live with their parents. The arrangement provides many financial and family benefits, but it is not known who cooked dinner and who will wash the dishes.

For instance, a detailed Dutch study found substantial agreement between parents and their adult children on issues that might, in theory, be contentious—such as cohabitation, same-sex partnerships, and divorce. Some generational differences appeared, but when parents were compared with their own children (not young adults in general), similar attitudes were apparent (Bucx et al., 2010). Adult children who still lived with their parents (about one-fourth of the sample) were more likely to agree with their parents than were adults who lived apart from them, but all groups showed "intergenerational convergence" (Bucx et al., 2010, p. 131).

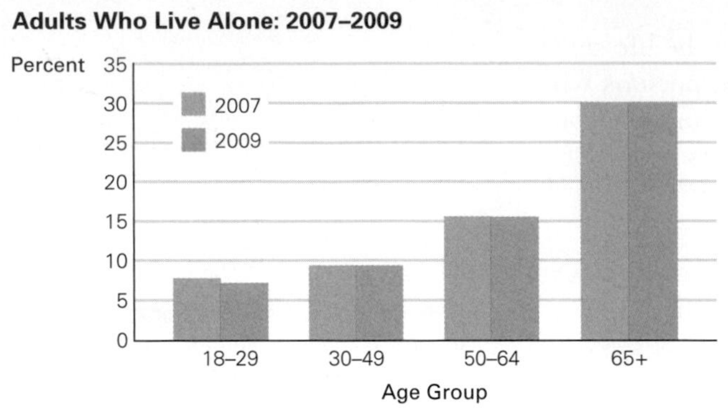

Source: Pew Research Center tabulations of Annual Social and Economic Supplement to the Current Population Survey, 2007 and 2009, U.S. Census Bureau

FIGURE EP.9

Not Lonely The assumption used to be that family affection led to multigenerational households, but that is not accurate. Financial struggle, not love, is what forces single adults to live with relatives. Young adults prefer to live with romantic partners or roommates, whereas widows and widowers favor independent households—if they can afford them.

Worldwide, many emerging adults still live with their parents, though this varies from nation to nation. Almost all unmarried young adults in Italy and Japan stay in their childhood home, as do half of those in England (Manzi et al., 2006). Fewer do so in the United States if their parents can underwrite their young-adult children's independent living (Furstenberg, 2010), but the current economic downturn has increased the number of adult children living with their parents (see Figure EP. 9).

In many nations, researchers find a connection among early attachment, adult perceptions of their current relationships with their parents, as well as adult relationships with friends, lovers, and children (Grossmann et al., 2005; Mikulincer & Goodman, 2006; Sroufe et al., 2005). Securely attached infants are more likely to become happily married adults; avoidant infants may hesitate to marry. Young adults with good family relationships are more likely to establish supportive families of their own, although they are in no hurry to do so.

A Global Perspective

Looking at many cultures, it is apparent that families can be destructive as well as helpful to emerging adults. For example, a study of enmeshment (e.g., parents insisting on knowing what their emerging-adult children are doing and thinking) found that British emerging adults were less happy or successful if their parents were too intrusive. However, emerging adults in Italy seem able to remain closely connected with their parents without hindering their own development (Manzi et al., 2006). Enmeshment can be destructive, but not always.

Some Westerners believe that family dependence is more evident in developing nations. There is some truth in this. As explained earlier, familism is a strong value in many Latino cultures. In another example, many African young adults marry someone approved by their parents and work to support their many relatives—siblings, parents, cousins, uncles, and so on. Individuals sacrifice personal goals for family concerns, and "collectivism often takes precedence and overrides individual needs and interests," which makes "the family a source of both collective identity and tension" in Africa (Wilson & Ngige, 2006, p. 248).

In cultures with arranged marriages, parents not only provide practical support (such as child care) and emotional encouragement, they may also protect their child. If the relationship is a disaster (for instance, the husband severely beats the wife, the wife refuses sex, the husband never works, or the wife never cooks), then the parents intervene. Again, each family member within each culture judges such intervention differently: What is expected in, say, Cambodia, would be unacceptable in, say, Colombia. Chinese young adults expect their parents and friends to comment on their romantic partners and, compared with U.S. young adults, they are about twice as likely to say they might stop dating someone if their parents disapproved (Zhang & Kline, 2009).

There are developmental advantages to this family involvement. Each new baby is cared for by many people, so young adults are less burdened by child care. This may be one reason why parenthood begins much earlier in African nations. By contrast, parenthood in the United States is an impediment to education and career success (Osgood et al., 2005), and thus many emerging adults postpone it (Furstenberg, 2010).

Cultural differences aside, in every nation young adults are encouraged to do well in school and to get good jobs, partly to make their families proud, partly so

>> Answer to Observation Quiz (from page 524) Before! The rate of increase from 2000 to 2005 was about 4/49, or 8 percent, whereas the rate from 1985 to 1990 was about 9/20, a 45 percent increase.

they will be able to care for their relatives when necessary, and partly for their own future. Immigrant young adults tend to be highly motivated to learn and work, and they reciprocate their parents' support. These values help them to become more successful than many native-born young adults (Mollenkopf et al., 2005).

All Together Now

When we look at actual lives, not the cultural ideal of independence or interdependence, emerging adults worldwide have much in common, including close family connections and a new freedom from parental limits (Georgas et al., 2006). It is a mistake to assume that emerging adults in Western nations abandon their parents. Just the opposite: Some studies find that family relationships *improve* when young adults leave home (Graber & Brooks-Gunn, 1996; Smetana et al., 2004). Family members continue to feel obligated to one another no matter where they live. In fact, far from ignoring the needs of their elders, parents and adult children tend to expect their own generation to be more responsive to family needs than the other generation (Bucx et al., 2010).

As we think about the experiences of emerging adults overall, it is apparent that this stage of life has many pitfalls. These years may be crucial, as "decisions made during the transition to adulthood have a particularly long-lasting influence on the remainder of the life course because they set individuals on paths that are sometimes difficult to change" (Thornton et al., 2007, p. 13).

Fortunately, most emerging adults, like humans of all ages, have strengths as well as liabilities. Many survive risks, overcome substance abuse, combat loneliness, and deal with other problems through further education, friends, family, and maturation. If they postpone marriage, prevent parenthood, and avoid a set career (all characteristics of 18- to 25-year-olds) until their identity is firmly established and their education complete, they may be preparing for adult commitments and responsibilities.

As you read on the first page of Chapter 1, the science of human development is about how people change over time. As you learned from every chapter, development occurs as individuals are influenced, supported, and guided by other people. That is exactly what occurs as emerging adults continue to be influenced by their parents and their peers while they prepare for another cycle of growth. Erikson's seventh crisis is *generativity versus stagnation,* when adults care for the new generation. Back to babies: The cycle of human development is ongoing.

THE FRESNO BEE / ZUMAPRESS.COM

PETE OXFORD / DANITADELMONT.COM

The Same Situation, Many Miles Apart: Dedication Is Universal It may seem as if the activities and clothing of the Fresno college student in the bookstore *(top)* could not differ more from those of the young mother in the doorway of her Rajastan, India, home *(bottom)*. However, both are typical emerging adults: active, healthy, and working for their futures.

SUMMING UP

Patterns of psychosocial development in emerging adulthood evidence continuity and change. Personality traits endure, but improvement is often apparent as young adults experience rising self-esteem and self-efficacy. The need for social support is lifelong, but among young adults marriage is often postponed and, at least in contemporary North America, is more often a personal choice, not a family arrangement. Parental support is ongoing, with different particulars in various nations and cultures. ■

>> Response for Family Therapists (from page 525) Remember that family function is more important than family structure. Sharing a home can work out well if contentious issues—like sexual privacy, money, and household chores—are clarified before resentments arise. You might offer a three-session preparation package, to explore assumptions and guidelines.

SUMMARY

Biosocial Development

1. Emerging adults usually have strong and healthy bodies. Death from disease is rare.

2. The sexual-reproductive system reaches a peak during these years. The sex drive is strong and orgasms frequent. Problem-free conception, pregnancy, and birth are more likely between ages 18 and 25 than earlier or later, although most current emerging adults postpone childbearing until age 25 or later.

3. Willingness to take risks is characteristic of emerging adults. This allows positive behaviors, such as entering college, meeting new people, volunteering for difficult tasks, finding new jobs. It also leads to destructive actions, such as unprotected sex and drug use.

4. Extreme sports are attractive to some emerging adults. Attempting to understand this, developmentalists posit that the risk of injury and even of death can be thrilling at this age and that boredom is to be avoided.

Cognitive Development

5. Adult thinking is more advanced than adolescent thought in that it is more flexible, better able to coordinate the objective and the subjective. Some scholars consider adult thinking a fifth stage of cognition called postformal thought.

6. The flexibility of young-adult thought allows people to reexamine stereotypes from their childhood. This is particularly important in decreasing stereotype threat, which may impair adult cognition if left unchecked.

7. Worldwide there are far more college students, especially in Asia and Africa, than there were a few decades ago. Everywhere the students' backgrounds and current situations are more diverse than formerly.

8. Although a college education has been shown to have health and income benefits, observers disagree as to how, or even whether, college improves cognition. Evidence suggests that it does, but perhaps not as much as in earlier generations.

Psychosocial Development

9. Identity continues to be worked out in emerging adulthood. Ethnic identity is particularly important in multiethnic cultures, not only for people of mixed and minority backgrounds, but also for those in the majority.

10. The current economic situation makes vocational identity even more problematic than it was a decade ago. The average emerging adult changes jobs several times.

11. Personality traits from childhood do not disappear in emerging adulthood, but many people learn to modify or compensate for whatever negative traits they have. New experiences—such as moving away from home and going to college—allow some plasticity in personality.

12. The need for social connections and relationships is lifelong. In earlier times, and in some cultures currently, emerging adults followed their parents' wishes in seeking marriage partners. Today's youth are more likely to choose their own partners and postpone marriage.

13. Cohabitation is the current norm for emerging adults in many nations. Some research finds that this increases marital and child-rearing problems later on.

14. Family members continue to be important to emerging adults. Parental support—financial as well as emotional—may be more crucial than in earlier times.

KEY TERMS

emerging adulthood (p. 505)
extreme sports (p. 508)
drug abuse (p. 509)
postformal thought (p. 510)
stereotype threat (p. 511)
intimacy versus isolation (p. 521)
cohabitation (p. 523)
linked lives (p. 525)

WHAT HAVE YOU LEARNED?

Biosocial Development

1. Why is maximum physical strength usually attained in emerging adulthood?

2. What has changed, and what has not changed, in the past decades regarding sexual and reproductive development?

3. Why are STIs more common currently than 50 years ago?

4. What are the social benefits of risk taking?

5. Why are some sports more attractive at some ages than others?

6. Why are serious accidents more common in emerging adulthood than later?

7. Why are college students more likely to abuse drugs than those not in college?

Cognitive Development

8. Why did scholars choose the term *postformal* to describe the fifth stage of cognition?

9. How does postformal thinking differ from typical adolescent thought?

10. How could the threat of a stereotype affect cognition?

11. Which groups of people are vulnerable to stereotype threat and why?

12. How do current college enrollment patterns differ from those 50 years ago?

13. Why do people disagree about the goals of a college education?

Psychosocial Development

14. How does ethnic pride change from early adolescence to adulthood?

15. Why might vocational identity be an "outdated social construction"?

16. What do emerging adults seek in a romantic partner?

17. How has the process of mate selection changed over the past decades?

18. Why do many emerging adults cohabit instead of marrying?

19. Why do people assume that emerging adults are not influenced by their parents?

20. What kinds of support do parents provide their young-adult children?

APPLICATIONS

1. Describe an incident during your emerging adulthood when taking a risk could have led to disaster. What were your feelings at the time? What would you do if you knew that a child of yours was about to do the same thing?

2. Read a biography or autobiography that includes information about the person's thinking from adolescence through adulthood. How did personal experiences, education, and maturation affect the person's thinking?

3. Statistics on cohort and culture in students and in colleges are fascinating, but only a few are reported here. Compare your nation, state, or province with another. Analyze the data and discuss causes and implications of differences.

4. Talk to three people you would expect to have contrasting views on love and marriage (differences in age, gender, upbringing, experience, and religion might affect attitudes). Ask each the same questions and then compare their answers.

>>ONLINE CONNECTIONS

To accompany your textbook, you have access to a number of online resources, including quizzes for every chapter of the book, flashcards (in English and Spanish), critical thinking questions, and case studies. For access to any of these links, go to www.worthpublishers.com/bergerca9e. In addition to these free resources, you'll also find links to podcasts, video clips, diagnostic quizzing with personalized study advice, and an ebook. Some of the videos and activities available online include:

- *Interview with Kurt Fischer.* This noted developmentalist discusses the influence of experience on brain development.
- *Transition to Parenthood.* Videos of couples in various stages of parenthood highlight the physical, emotional, social, household, and vocational changes that accompany this new responsibility.
- *Homosexuality: Genes Versus Environment.* What makes someone gay? This video shows how the nature–nurture debate plays out when applied to this question.

Appendix A

>> Supplemental Charts, Graphs, and Tables

Often, examining specific data is useful, even fascinating, to developmental researchers. The particular numbers reveal trends and nuances not apparent from a more general view. Each chart, graph, or table in this appendix contains information not generally known.

Children as a Proportion of a Nation's Population

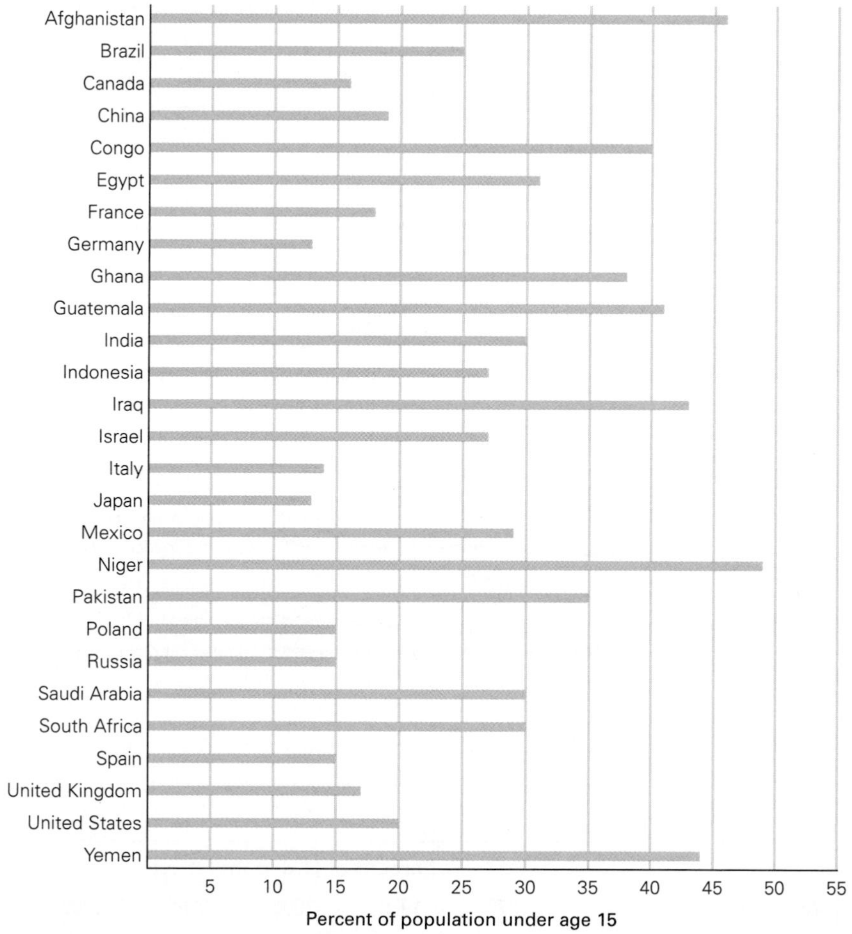

Source: United Nations Statistics Division, unstats.un.org, 2011.

More Children, Worse Schools? (Chapter 1)

Nations that have high birth rates also have high death rates, short life spans, and more illiteracy. A systems approach suggests that these variables are connected: For example, the Montessori and Reggio Emilia early-childhood education programs, said to be the best in the world, originated in Italy, and Italy has one of the lowest proportions of children under 15.

Ethnic Composition of the U.S. Population (Chapter 2)

Thinking about the ethnic makeup of the U.S. population helps explain the rising importance of sociocultural theory. If you look only at the table, you will not see dramatic differences over the past 40 years: Whites are still the majority, Native Americans (Indians) are still a tiny minority, and African Americans are still about 12 percent of the population. However, if you look at the graph, you can see why every group feels that much has changed. Because the proportions of Hispanic Americans and Asian Americans have increased dramatically, European Americans see the current non-White population at almost one-third of the total, and African Americans see that Hispanics now outnumber them.

There are also interesting regional differences within the United States; for example, the Los Angeles metropolitan area has the largest number of Native Americans (125,000) and the largest number of Asians (1.8 million). Remember that racial categories (e.g., White, Black) are often rejected by social scientists but are used in the U.S. Census and other data sources. Also note that the terms for each group vary; some people prefer one term, some another.

Observation Quiz Which ethnic group is growing most rapidly since 1980 in rate of increase (not in numbers added)? (see answer, page A-4)

Population, by Ethnic Group, 1970–2009

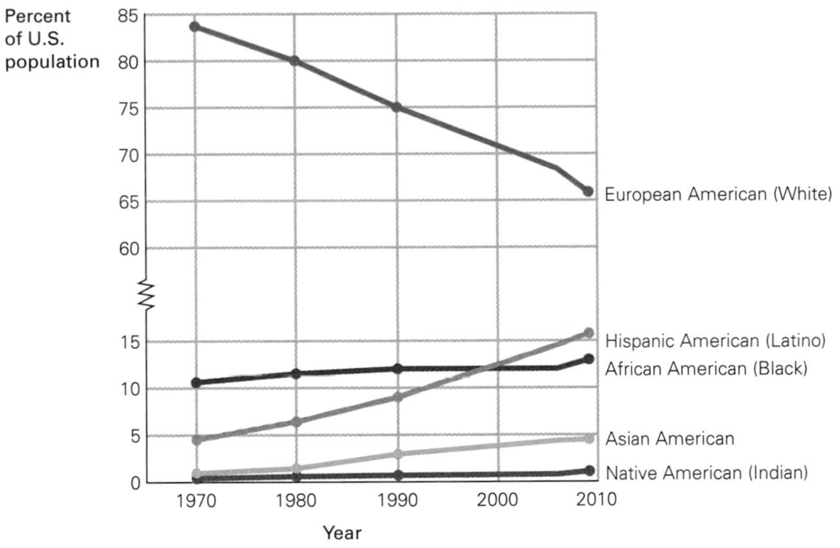

Source: U.S. Census Bureau, *State and County Quick Facts*, 2011.

	Percent of U.S. population				
Ancestry	**1970**	**1980**	**1990**	**2006**	**2009**
European (White)	83.7	80	75	68.4	65.1
African (Black)	10.6	11.5	12	12	12.9
Hispanic (Latino)	4.5	6.4	9	14.5	15.8
Asian	1.0	1.5	3	4.3	4.6
Native American (Indian)	0.4	0.6	0.7	0.82	1.0

The Genetics of Blood Types (Chapter 3)

Blood types A and B are dominant traits, and type O is recessive. The percentages given in the first column of this chart represent the odds that a child born to the parents with the various combinations of genotypes will have the genotype given in the second column.

Genotypes of Parents*	Genotype of Offspring	Phenotype	Can Donate Blood to (Phenotype)	Can Receive Blood from (Phenotype)
AA + AA (100%) AA + AB (50%) AA + AO (50%) AB + AB (25%) AB + AO (25%) AO + AO (25%)	AA (inherits one A from each parent)	A	A or AB	A or O
AA + OO (100%) AB + OO (50%) AO + AO (50%) AO + OO (50%) AB + AO (25%) AB + BO (25%)	AO	A	A or AB	A or O
BB + BB (100%) AB + BB (50%) BB + BO (50%) AB + AB (25%) AB + BO (25%) BO + BO (25%)	BB	B	B or AB	B or O
BB + OO (100%) AB + OO (50%) BO + BO (50%) BO + OO (50%) AB + AO (25%) AB + BO (25%)	BO	B	B or AB	B or O
AA + BB (100%) AA + AB (50%) AA + BO (50%) AB + AB (50%) AB + BB (50%) AO + BB (50%) AB + BO (25%) AO + BO (25%)	AB	AB	AB only	A, B, AB, O ("universal recipient")
OO + OO (100%) AO + OO (50%) BO + OO (50%) AO + AO (25%) AO + BO (25%) BO + BO (25%)	OO	O	A, B, AB, O ("universal donor")	O only

*Blood type is not sex-linked because blood type comes equally from each parent.
Source: Adapted from Hartl & Jones, 1999.

Saving Young Lives: Childhood and Adolescent Immunizations (Chapter 5)

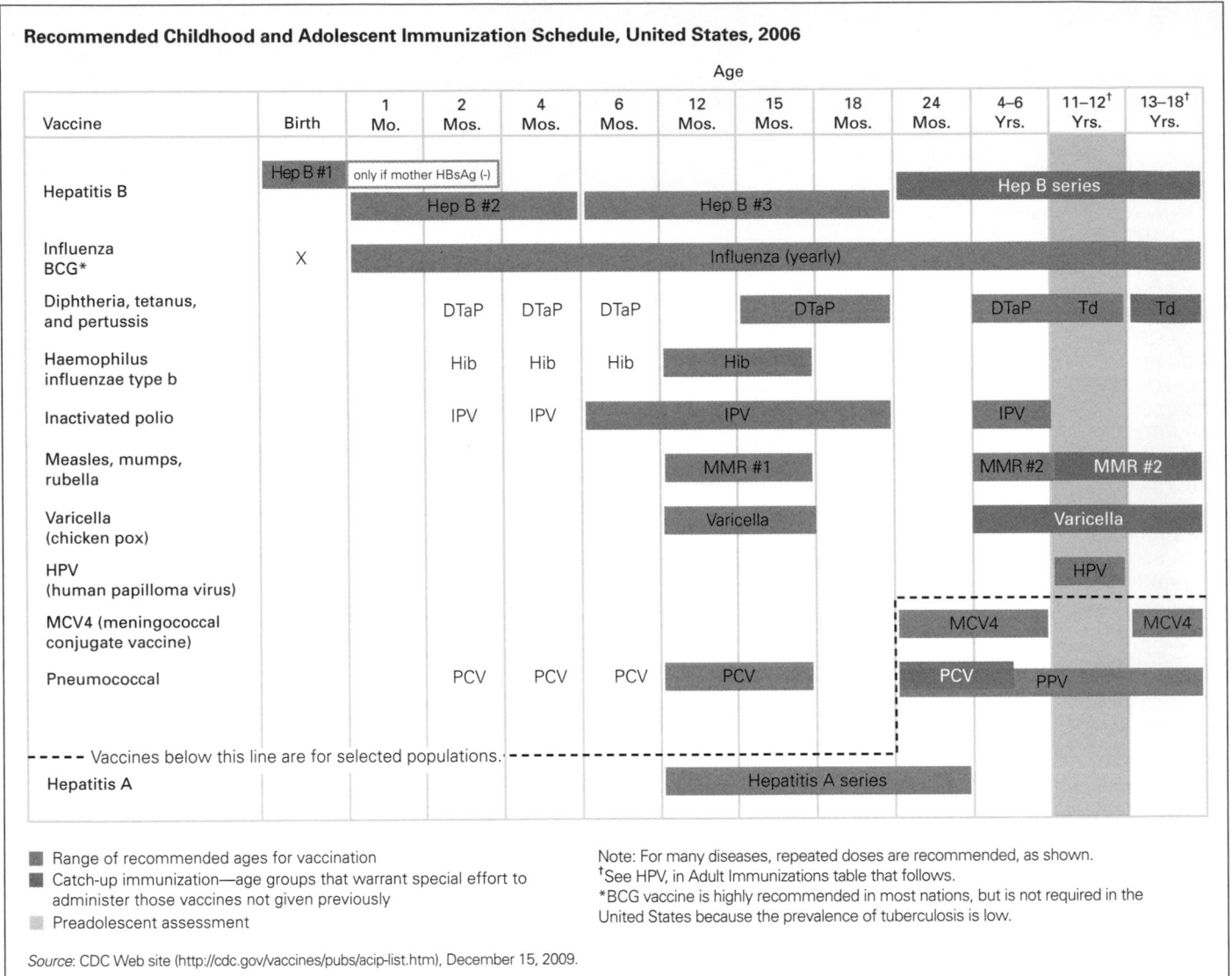

Recommended Childhood and Adolescent Immunization Schedule, United States, 2006

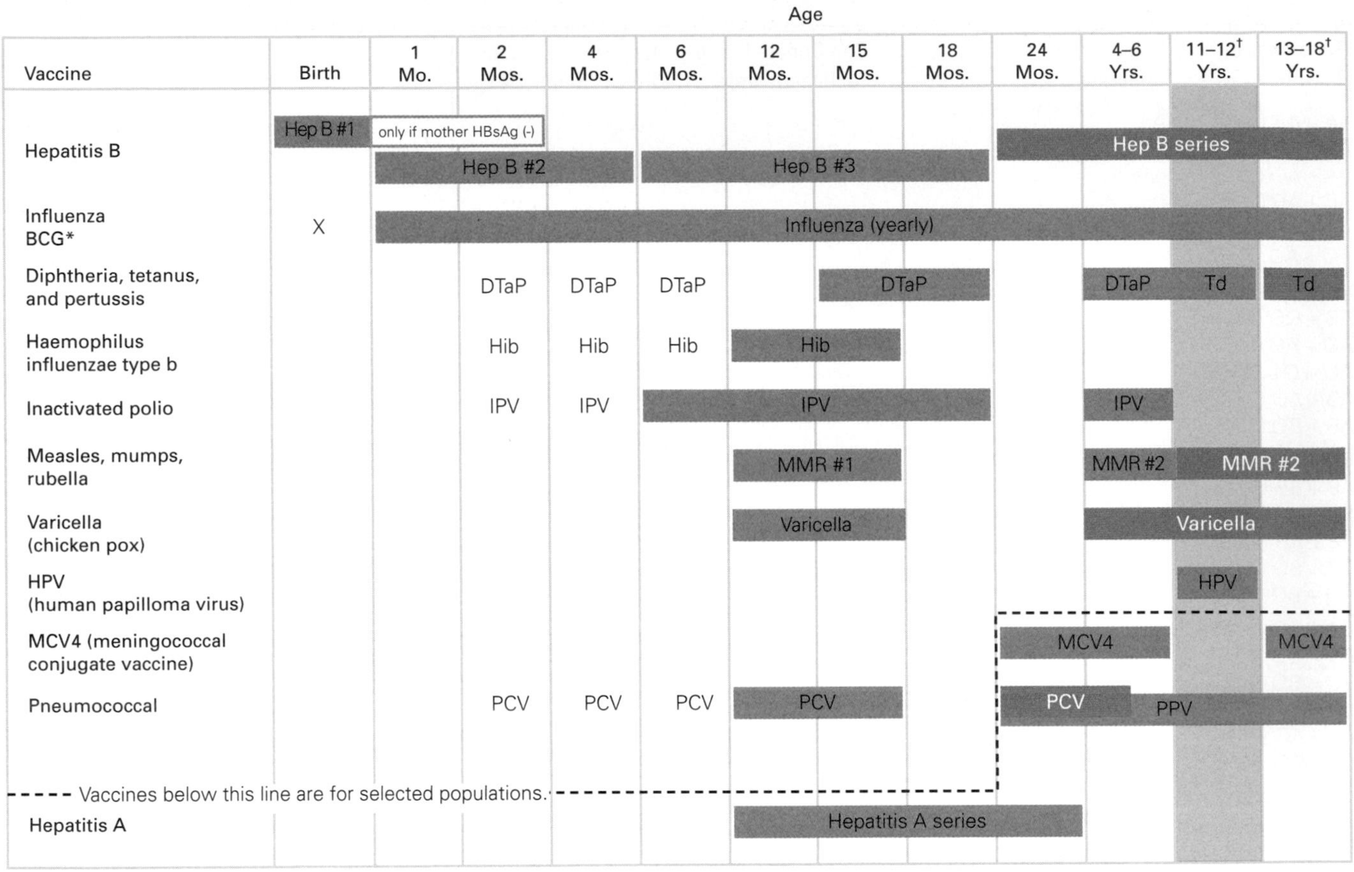
Age
Vaccine
Birth
1 Mo.
2 Mos.
4 Mos.
6 Mos.
12 Mos.
15 Mos.
18 Mos.
24 Mos.
4–6 Yrs.
11–12† Yrs.
13–18† Yrs.
Hepatitis B
Hep B #1
only if mother HBsAg (-)
Hep B #2
Hep B #3
Hep B series
Influenza
BCG*
X
Influenza (yearly)
Diphtheria, tetanus, and pertussis
DTaP
DTaP
DTaP
DTaP
DTaP
Td
Td
Haemophilus influenzae type b
Hib
Hib
Hib
Hib
Inactivated polio
IPV
IPV
IPV
IPV
Measles, mumps, rubella
MMR #1
MMR #2
MMR #2
Varicella (chicken pox)
Varicella
Varicella
HPV (human papilloma virus)
HPV
MCV4 (meningococcal conjugate vaccine)
MCV4
MCV4
Pneumococcal
PCV
PCV
PCV
PCV
PCV
PPV
Vaccines below this line are for selected populations.
Hepatitis A
Hepatitis A series

- Range of recommended ages for vaccination
- Catch-up immunization—age groups that warrant special effort to administer those vaccines not given previously
- Preadolescent assessment

Note: For many diseases, repeated doses are recommended, as shown.
†See HPV, in Adult Immunizations table that follows.
*BCG vaccine is highly recommended in most nations, but is not required in the United States because the prevalence of tuberculosis is low.

Source: CDC Web site (http://cdc.gov/vaccines/pubs/acip-list.htm), December 15, 2009.

First Sounds and First Words: Similarities Among Many Languages (Chapter 6)

	Baby's word for:	
Language	Mother	Father
English	mama, mommy	dada, daddy
Spanish	mama	papa
French	maman, mama	papa
Italian	mamma	babbo, papa
Latvian	mama	te-te
Syrian Arabic	mama	baba
Bantu	ba-mama	taata
Swahili	mama	baba
Sanskrit	nana	tata
Hebrew	ema	abba
Korean	oma	apa

>> Answer to Observation Quiz (from page A-2) Asian Americans, whose share of the U.S. population has quadrupled in the past 30 years. Latinos are increasing most rapidly in numbers, but not in proportion.

Breast-feeding in the United States (Chapter 7)

Differentiating excellent from destructive mothering is not easy, once the child's basic needs for food and protection are met. However, psychosocial development depends on responsive parent–infant relationships. Breast-feeding is one sign of intimacy between mother and infant.

Regions of the world differ dramatically in rates of breast-feeding. The highest rate is in Southeast Asia, where half of all 2-year-olds are still breast-fed. In the United States, factors that affect the likelihood of breast-feeding are ethnicity, maternal age, and education.

Breast-feeding in the United States

Sociodemographic factors	Ever breast-feeding	Breast-feeding at 6 months	Breast-feeding at 12 months	Exclusive breast-feeding* at 3 months	Exclusive breast-feeding* at 6 months
U.S. National	74.6%	44.3%	23.8%	35.0%	14.8%
Sex of baby					
Male	75.4	42.6	22.0	33.1	12.9
Female	74.6	43.5	22.8	32.9	13.7
Birth order					
First born	74.5	44.1	23.7	33.4	13.8
Not first born	75.6	41.8	20.8	32.6	12.6
Ethnicity					
Native American (Indian)	73.8	42.4	20.7	27.6	13.2
Asian or Pacific Islander	83.0	56.4	32.8	34.1	14.5
Hispanic or Latino	80.6	46.0	24.7	32.4	13.2
African American (non-Hispanic)	59.7	27.9	12.9	22.7	8.2
European (non-Hispanic)	77.7	45.1	23.6	35.3	14.4
Mother's age					
Less than 20	59.7	22.2	10.7	18.1	7.9
20–29	69.7	33.4	16.1	28.8	10.2
More than 30	79.3	50.5	27.1	36.6	15.5
Mother's education					
Less than high school	67.0	37.0	21.9	33.7	9.2
High school	66.1	31.4	15.1	25.8	8.9
Some college	76.5	41.0	20.5	34.1	14.4
College graduate	88.3	59.9	31.1	45.9	19.6
Mother's marital status					
Married	81.7	51.6	27.5	39.0	16.7
Unmarried†	61.3	25.5	11.9	20.9	6.4
Residence					
Central city	75.5	43.9	24.4	32.8	13.3
Urban	77.9	45.3	22.3	34.9	13.9
Suburban and rural	66.4	35.0	17.4	28.8	11.8

*Exclusive breast-feeding is defined as only breast milk—no solids, no water, and no other liquids.
†Unmarried includes never married, widowed, separated, and divorced.
Source: National Immunization Survey, Centers for Disease Control and Prevention, Department of Health and Human Services, 2011.

Height Gains from Birth to Age 18 (Chapters 5, 8, 11)

The range of height (on this page) and weight (see page A-7) of children in the United States. The columns labeled "50th" (the fiftieth percentile) show the average; the columns labeled "90th" (the ninetieth percentile) show the size of children taller and heavier than 90 percent of their contemporaries; and the columns labeled "10th" (the tenth percentile) show the size of children who are taller than only 10 percent of their peers. Note that girls are slightly shorter, on average, than boys.

Height by Age Percentiles: 2 to 6 Years

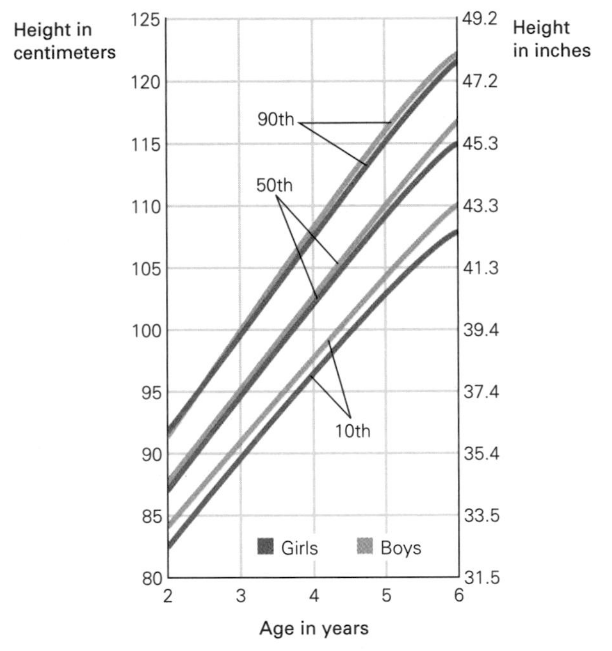

Same Data, Different Form

The columns of numbers in the table at right provide detailed and precise information about height ranges for every year of childhood. The illustration above shows the same information in graphic form for ages 2–6. The same is done for weight ranges on page A-7. Ages 2–6 are singled out because that is the period during which a child's eating habits are set. Which form of data presentation do you think is easier to understand?

Length in Centimeters (and Inches)

	Boys: percentiles			Girls: percentiles		
AGE	10th	50th	90th	10th	50th	90th
Birth	47.5 (18¾)	50.5 (20)	53.5 (21)	46.5 (18¼)	49.9 (19¾)	52.0 (20½)
1 month	51.3 (20¼)	54.6 (21½)	57.7 (22¾)	50.2 (19¾)	53.5 (21)	56.1 (22)
3 months	57.7 (22¾)	61.1 (24)	64.5 (25½)	56.2 (22¼)	59.5 (23½)	62.7 (24¾)
6 months	64.4 (25¼)	67.8 (26¾)	71.3 (28)	62.6 (24¾)	65.9 (26)	69.4 (27¼)
9 months	69.1 (27¼)	72.3 (28½)	75.9 (30)	67.0 (26½)	70.4 (27¾)	74.0 (29¼)
12 months	72.8 (28¾)	76.1 (30)	79.8 (31½)	70.8 (27¾)	74.3 (29¼)	78.0 (30¾)
18 months	78.7 (31)	82.4 (32½)	86.6 (34)	77.2 (30½)	80.9 (31¾)	85.0 (33½)
24 months	83.5 (32¾)	87.6 (34½)	92.2 (36¼)	82.5 (32½)	86.5 (34)	90.8 (35¾)
3 years	90.3 (35½)	94.9 (37¼)	100.1 (39½)	89.3 (35¼)	94.1 (37)	99.0 (39)
4 years	97.3 (38¼)	102.9 (40½)	108.2 (42½)	96.4 (38)	101.6 (40)	106.6 (42)
5 years	103.7 (40¾)	109.9 (43¼)	115.4 (45½)	102.7 (40½)	108.4 (42¾)	113.8 (44¾)
6 years	109.6 (43¼)	116.1 (45¾)	121.9 (48)	108.4 (42¾)	114.6 (45)	120.8 (47½)
7 years	115.0 (45¼)	121.7 (48)	127.9 (50¼)	113.6 (44¾)	120.6 (47½)	127.6 (50¼)
8 years	120.2 (47¼)	127.0 (50)	133.6 (52½)	118.7 (46¾)	126.4 (49¾)	134.2 (52¾)
9 years	125.2 (49¼)	132.2 (52)	139.4 (55)	123.9 (48¾)	132.2 (52)	140.7 (55½)
10 years	130.1 (51¼)	137.5 (54¼)	145.5 (57¼)	129.5 (51)	138.3 (54½)	147.2 (58)
11 years	135.1 (53¼)	143.33 (56½)	152.1 (60)	135.6 (53½)	144.8 (57)	153.7 (60½)
12 years	140.3 (55¼)	149.7 (59)	159.4 (62¾)	142.3 (56)	151.5 (59¾)	160.0 (63)
13 years	145.8 (57½)	156.5 (61½)	167.0 (65¾)	148.0 (58¼)	157.1 (61¾)	165.3 (65)
14 years	151.8 (59¾)	63.1 (64¼)	173.8 (68½)	151.5 (59¾)	160.4 (63¼)	168.7 (66½)
15 years	158.2 (62¼)	169.0 (66½)	178.9 (70½)	153.2 (60¼)	161.8 (63¾)	170.5 (67¼)
16 years	163.9 (64½)	173.5 (68¼)	182.4 (71¾)	154.1 (60¾)	162.4 (64)	171.1 (67¼)
17 years	167.7 (66)	176.2 (69¼)	184.4 (72½)	155.1 (61)	163.1 (64¼)	171.2 (67½)
18 years	168.7 (66½)	176.8 (69½)	185.3 (73)	156.0 (61½)	163.7 (64½)	171.0 (67¼)

Source: These data are those of the National Center for Health Statistics (NCHS), Health Resources Administration, DHHS. They were based on studies of The Fels Research Institute, Yellow Springs, Ohio. These data were first made available with the help of William M. Moore, M.D., of Ross Laboratories, who supplied the conversion from metric measurements to approximate inches and pounds. This help is gratefully acknowledged.

Weight Gains from Birth to Age 18 (Chapters 5, 8, 11)

These height and weight charts present rough guidelines; a child might differ from these norms and be quite healthy and normal. However, if a particular child shows a discrepancy between height and weight (for instance, at the 90th percentile in height but only the 20th percentile in weight) or is much larger or smaller than most children the same age, a pediatrician should see whether disease, malnutrition, or genetic abnormality could be part of the reason.

Weight by Age Percentiles: 2 to 6 Years

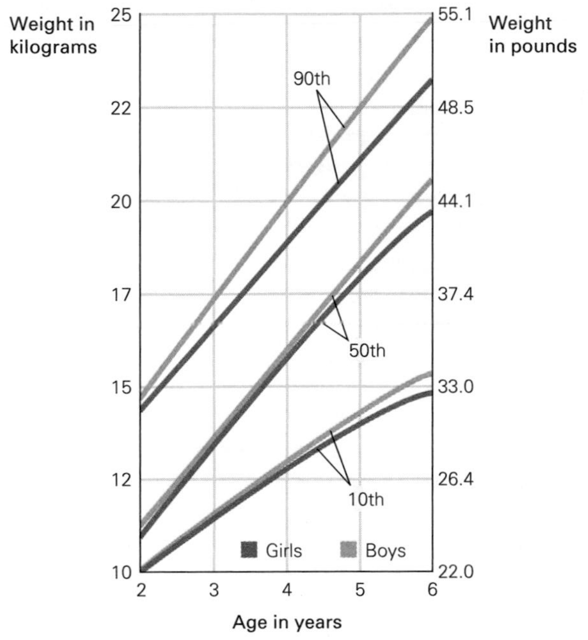

Comparisons

Notice that the height trajectories for boys and girls on page A-6 are much closer together than the weight trajectories shown above. By age 18, the height range amounts to only about 6 inches, but there is a difference of about 65 pounds between the 10th and the 90th percentiles.

Critical Thinking Question How can this discrepancy between height and weight ranges be explained? (see answer, page A-8)

Weight in Kilograms (and Pounds)

	Boys: percentiles			Girls: percentiles		
AGE	10th	50th	90th	10th	50th	90th
Birth	2.78 (6¼)	3.27 (7¼)	3.82 (8½)	2.58 (5¾)	3.23 (7)	3.64 (8)
1 month	3.43 (7½)	4.29 (9½)	5.14 (11¼)	3.22 (7)	3.98 (8¾)	4.65 (10¼)
3 months	4.78 (10½)	5.98 (13¼)	7.14 (15¾)	4.47 (9¾)	5.40 (12)	6.39 (14)
6 months	6.61 (14½)	7.85 (17¼)	9.10 (20)	6.12 (13½)	7.21 (16)	8.38 (18½)
9 months	7.95 (17½)	9.18 (20¼)	10.49 (23¼)	7.34 (16¼)	8.56 (18¾)	9.83 (21¾)
12 months	8.84 (19½)	10.15 (22½)	11.54 (25½)	8.19 (18)	9.53 (21)	10.87 (24)
18 months	9.92 (21¾)	11.47 (25¼)	13.05 (28¾)	9.30 (20½)	10.82 (23¾)	12.30 (27)
24 months	10.85 (24)	12.59 (27¾)	14.29 (31½)	10.26 (22½)	11.90 (26¼)	13.57 (30)
3 years	12.58 (27¾)	14.62 (32¼)	16.95 (37¼)	12.26 (27)	14.10 (31)	16.54 (36½)
4 years	14.24 (31½)	16.69 (36¾)	19.32 (42½)	13.84 (30½)	15.96 (35¼)	18.93 (41¾)
5 years	15.96 (35¼)	18.67 (41¼)	21.70 (47¾)	15.26 (33¾)	17.66 (39)	21.23 (46¾)
6 years	17.72 (39)	20.69 (45½)	24.31 (53½)	16.72 (36¾)	19.52 (43)	23.89 (52¾)
7 years	19.53 (43)	22.85 (50¼)	27.36 (60¼)	18.39 (40½)	21.84 (48¼)	27.39 (60½)
8 years	21.39 (47¼)	25.30 (55¾)	31.06 (68½)	20.45 (45)	24.84 (54¾)	32.04 (70¾)
9 years	23.33 (51½)	28.13 (62)	35.57 (78½)	22.92 (50½)	28.46 (62¾)	37.60 (83)
10 years	25.52 (56¼)	31.44 (69¼)	40.80 (90)	25.76 (56¾)	32.55 (71¾)	43.70 (96¼)
11 years	28.17 (62)	35.30 (77¾)	46.57 (102¾)	28.97 (63¾)	36.95 (81½)	49.96 (110¼)
12 years	31.46 (69¼)	39.78 (87¾)	52.73 (116¼)	32.53 (71¼)	41.53 (91½)	55.99 (123½)
13 years	35.60 (78½)	44.95 (99)	59.12 (130¼)	36.35 (80¼)	46.10 (101¾)	61.45 (135½)
14 years	40.64 (89½)	50.77 (112)	65.57 (144½)	40.11 (88½)	50.28 (110¾)	66.04 (145½)
15 years	46.06 (101½)	56.71 (125)	71.91 (158½)	43.38 (95¾)	53.68 (118¼)	69.64 (153¼)
16 years	51.16 (112¾)	62.10 (137)	77.97 (172)	45.78 (101)	55.89 (123¼)	71.68 (158)
17 years	55.28 (121¾)	66.31 (146¼)	83.58 (184¼)	47.04 (103¾)	56.69 (125)	72.38 (159½)
18 years	57.89 (127½)	68.88 (151¾)	88.41 (195)	47.47 (104¾)	56.62 (124¾)	72.25 (159¼)

Source: Data are those of the National Center for Health Statistics, Health Resources Administration, DHHS, collected in its Health Examination Surveys.

Children Are the Poorest Americans (Chapters 10, 11)

It probably comes as no surprise that the rate of poverty is twice as high in some states as in others. What is surprising is how much the rates vary between age groups within the same state.

Observation Quiz In which 13 states is the proportion of poor children more than twice as high as the proportion of poor people over age 65? (see answer page A-9)

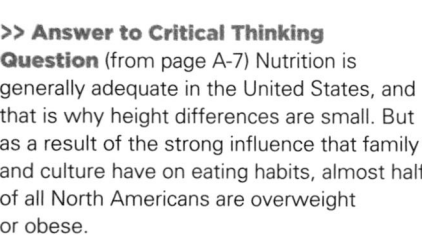

Rates of Poverty, by State and by Age Group

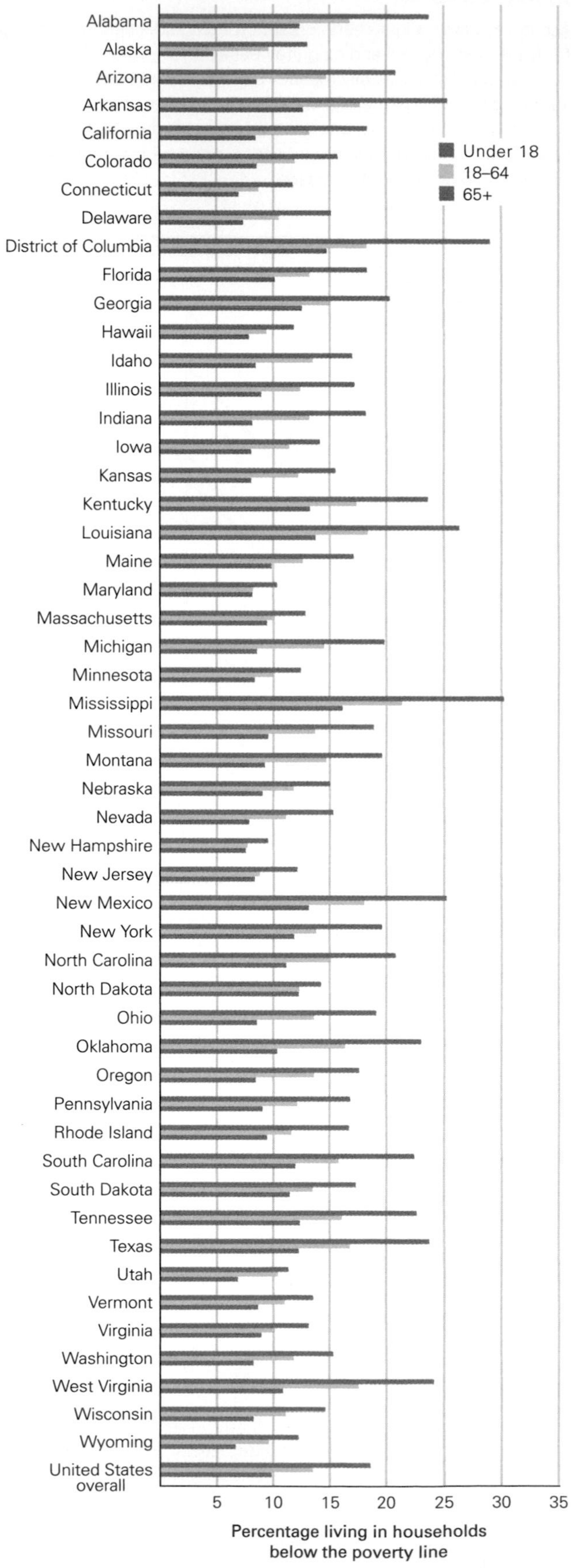

Source: 2009 American Community Survey (http://factfinder.census.gov).

>> Answer to Critical Thinking Question (from page A-7) Nutrition is generally adequate in the United States, and that is why height differences are small. But as a result of the strong influence that family and culture have on eating habits, almost half of all North Americans are overweight or obese.

DSM-IV-TR Criteria for Attention-Deficit/Hyperactivity Disorder (ADHD), Autistic Disorder, Asperger Disorder, Rett Syndrome, Reading Disability, and Math Disability (Chapter 11)

The specific symptoms for these various disorders overlap. Many other childhood disorders also have some of the same symptoms. Differentiating one problem from another is the main purpose of DSM-IV-TR. That is no easy task, which is one reason the book is now in its fourth major revision and is more than 900 pages long. Those pages include not only the type of diagnostic criteria shown here but also discussions of prevalence, age and gender statistics, cultural aspects, and prognosis for about 400 disorders or subtypes, 40 of which appear primarily in childhood. Thus, the diagnostic criteria reprinted here for five disorders represent less than 1 percent of the contents of DSM-IV-TR. Note that publication of the DSM-5 is expected in 2013, and some criteria will change.

>> **Answer to Observation Quiz** (from page A-8) Alaska, Arizona, Arkansas, California, Delaware, Idaho, Indiana, Michigan, Montana, Ohio, Oklahoma, Oregon, and West Virginia.

>> Diagnostic Criteria for Attention-Deficit/Hyperactivity Disorder

A. Either (1) or (2):

(1) Six (or more) of the following symptoms of **inattention** have persisted for at least 6 months to a degree that is maladaptive and inconsistent with developmental level:

INATTENTION

(a) often fails to give close attention to details or makes careless mistakes in schoolwork, work, or other activities
(b) often has difficulty sustaining attention in tasks or play activities
(c) often does not seem to listen when spoken to directly
(d) often does not follow through on instructions and fails to finish schoolwork, chores, or duties in the workplace (not due to oppositional behavior or failure to understand instructions)
(e) often has difficulty organizing tasks and activities
(f) often avoids, dislikes, or is reluctant to engage in tasks that require sustained mental effort (such as schoolwork or homework)
(g) often loses things necessary for tasks or activities (e.g., toys, school assignments, pencils, books, or tools)
(h) is often easily distracted by extraneous stimuli
(i) is often forgetful in daily activities

(2) Six (or more) of the following symptoms of **hyperactivity-impulsivity** have persisted for at least 6 months to a degree that is maladaptive and inconsistent with developmental level:

HYPERACTIVITY

(a) often fidgets with hands or feet or squirms in seat
(b) often leaves seat in classroom or in other situations in which remaining seated is expected
(c) often runs about or climbs excessively in situations in which it is inappropriate (in adolescents or adults, may be limited to subjective feelings of restlessness)
(d) often has difficulty playing or engaging in leisure activities quietly
(e) is often "on the go" or often acts as if "driven by a motor"
(f) often talks excessively

IMPULSIVITY

(g) often blurts out answers before questions have been completed
(h) often has difficulty awaiting turn
(i) often interrupts or intrudes on others (e.g., butts into conversations or games)

B. Some hyperactive-impulsive or inattentive symptoms that caused impairment were present before age 7 years.

C. Some impairment from the symptoms is present in two or more settings (e.g., at school [or work] and at home).

D. There must be clear evidence of clinically significant impairment in social, academic, or occupational functioning.

>> Diagnostic Criteria for Autistic Disorder

A. A total of six (or more) items from (1), (2), and (3), with at least two from (1) and one each from (2) and (3):

(1) qualitative impairment in social interaction, as manifested by at least two of the following:

(a) marked impairment in the use of multiple nonverbal behaviors such as eye-to-eye gaze, facial expression, body postures, and gestures to regulate social interaction
(b) failure to develop peer relationships appropriate to developmental level
(c) a lack of spontaneous seeking to share enjoyment, interests, or achievements with other people (e.g., by a lack of showing, bringing, or pointing out objects of interest)
(d) lack of social or emotional reciprocity

(2) qualitative impairments in communication as manifested by at least one of the following:

(a) delay in, or total lack of, the development of spoken language (not accompanied by an attempt to compensate through alternative modes of communication such as gesture or mime)
(b) in individuals with adequate speech, marked impairment in the ability to initiate or sustain a conversation with others
(c) stereotyped and repetitive use of language or idiosyncratic language
(d) lack of varied, spontaneous make-believe play or social imitative play appropriate to developmental level

(3) restricted repetitive and stereotyped patterns of behavior, interests, and activities, as manifested by at least one of the following:

(a) encompassing preoccupation with one or more stereotyped and restricted patterns of interest that is abnormal either in intensity or focus
(b) apparently inflexible adherence to specific, nonfunctional routines or rituals
(c) stereotyped and repetitive motor mannerisms (e.g., hand or finger flapping or twisting, or complex whole-body movements)
(d) persistent preoccupation with parts of objects

B. Delays or abnormal functioning in at least one of the following areas, with onset prior to age 3 years:

(1) social interaction

(2) language as used in social communication
(3) symbolic or imaginative play

C. The disturbance is not better accounted for by Rett's Disorder or Childhood Disintegrative Disorder.

>> Diagnostic Criteria for Asperger Disorder

A. Qualitative impairment in social interaction, as manifested by at least two of the following:

(1) marked impairment in the use of multiple nonverbal behaviors such as eye-to-eye gaze, facial expression, body postures, and gestures to regulate social interaction

(2) failure to develop peer relationships appropriate to developmental level

(3) a lack of spontaneous seeking to share enjoyment, interests, or achievements with other people (e.g., by a lack of showing, bringing, or pointing out objects of interest to other people)

(4) lack of social or emotional reciprocity

B. Restricted repetitive and stereotyped patterns of behavior, interests, and activities, as manifested by at least one of the following:

(1) encompassing preoccupation with one or more stereotyped and restricted patterns of interest that is abnormal either in intensity or focus

(2) apparently inflexible adherence to specific, nonfunctional routines or rituals

(3) stereotyped and repetitive motor mannerisms (e.g., hand or finger flapping or twisting, or complex whole-body movements)

(4) persistent preoccupation with parts of objects

C. The disturbance causes clinically significant impairment in social, occupational, or other important areas of functioning.

D. There is no clinically significant general delay in language (e.g., single words used by age 2 years, communicative phrases used by age 3 years).

E. There is no clinically significant delay in cognitive development or in the development of age-appropriate self-help skills, adaptive behavior (other than in social interaction), and curiosity about the environment in childhood.

F. Criteria are not met for another specific Pervasive Developmental Disorder or Schizophrenia.

>> Diagnostic Features of Learning Disorders

Learning Disorders are diagnosed when the individual's achievement on individually administered standardized tests in reading, mathematics, or written expression is substantially below that expected for age, schooling, and level of intelligence. The learning problems significantly interfere with academic achievement or activities of daily living that require reading, mathematical, or writing skills. A variety of statistical approaches can be used to establish that a discrepancy is significant.

Substantially below is usually defined as a discrepancy of more than 2 standard deviations between achievement and IQ. A smaller discrepancy between achievement and IQ (i.e., between 1 and 2 standard deviations) is sometimes used, especially in cases where an individual's performance on an IQ test may have been compromised by an associated disorder in cognitive processing, a comorbid mental disorder or general medical condition, or the individual's ethnic or cultural background. If a sensory deficit is present, the learning difficulties must be in excess of those usually associated with the deficit. Disorders may persist into adulthood.

Associated Features and Disorders

Demoralization, low self-esteem, and deficits in social skills may be associated with Learning Disorders. The school drop-out rate for children or adolescents with Learning Disorders is reported at nearly 40% (or approximately 1.5 times the average). Adults with Learning Disorders may have significant difficulties in employment or social adjustment. Many individuals (10%–25%) with Conduct Disorder, Oppositional Defiant Disorder, Attention-Deficit/Hyperactivity Disorder, Major Depressive Disorder, or Dysthymic Disorder also have Learning Disorders. There is evidence that developmental delays in language may occur in association with Learning Disorders (particularly Reading Disorder), although these delays may not be sufficiently severe to warrant the separate diagnosis of a Communication Disorder. Learning Disorders may also be associated with a higher rate of Developmental Coordination Disorder.

There may be underlying abnormalities in cognitive processing (e.g., deficits in visual perception, linguistic processes, attention, or memory, or a combination of these) that often precede or are associated with Learning Disorders. Standardized tests to measure these processes are generally less reliable and valid than other psychoeducational tests. Although genetic predisposition, perinatal injury, and various neurological or other general medical conditions may be associated with the development of Learning Disorders, the presence of such conditions does not invariably predict an eventual Learning Disorder, and there are many individuals with Learning Disorders who have no such history. Learning Disorders are, however, frequently found in association with a variety of general medical conditions (e.g., lead poisoning, fetal alcohol syndrome, or fragile X syndrome).

Specific Culture Features

Care should be taken to ensure that intelligence testing procedures reflect adequate attention to the individual's ethnic or cultural background. This is usually accomplished by using tests in which the individual's relevant characteristics are represented in the standardization sample of the test or by employing an examiner who is familiar with aspects of the individual's ethnic or cultural background. Individualized testing is always required to make the diagnosis of a Learning Disorder.

Prevalence

Estimates of the prevalence of Learning Disorders range from 2% to 10% depending on the nature of ascertainment and the definitions applied. Approximately 5% of students in public schools in the United States are identified as having a Learning Disorder.

>> Diagnostic Criteria for 315.00 Reading Disorder

A. Reading achievement, as measured by individually administered standardized tests of reading accuracy or comprehension, is substantially below that expected given the person's chronological age, measured intelligence, and age-appropriate education.

B. The disturbance in Criterion A significantly interferes with academic achievement or activities of daily living that require reading skills.

C. If a sensory deficit is present, the reading difficulties are in excess of those usually associated with it.

>> Diagnostic Criteria for 315.1 Mathematics Disorder

A. Mathematical ability, as measured by individually administered standardized tests, is substantially below that expected given the person's chronological age, measured intelligence, and age-appropriate education.

B. The disturbance in Criterion A significantly interferes with academic achievement or activities of daily living that require mathematical ability.

C. If a sensory deficit is present, the difficulties in mathematical ability are in excess of those usually associated with it.

>> Diagnostic Criteria for 299.80 Rett's Disorder

A. All of the following:
   (1) Apparently normal prenatal or perinatal development
   (2) Apparently normal psychomotor development through the first 5 months after birth
   (3) Normal head circumference at birth

B. Onset of all of the following after the period of normal development:
   (1) Deceleration of head growth between age 5 and 48 months
   (2) Loss of previously acquired purposeful hand skills between age 5 and 30 months with the subsequent development of stereotyped (e.g., hand-wringing or hand washing)
   (3) Loss of social engagement early in the course (although often social interaction develops later)
   (4) Appearance of poorly coordinated gait or trunk movements
   (5) Severely impaired expressive and receptive language development with severe psychomotor retardation

Motivation or Achievement? (Chapters 12, 15)

The PISA (Programme for International Student Assessment) is an international test of students' abilities to apply their knowledge. One explanation for the high scores of China and low scores of the United States is motivation of the students: Chinese young people are said to want to show national pride. Most experts believe that students in the United States are not as strongly motivated to learn in school—so they don't.

Science		Reading		Math	
Region	PISA Score	Region	PISA Score	Region	PISA Score
Shanghai	575	Shanghai	556	Shanghai	600
Finland	554	Korea	539	Singapore	562
Hong Kong	549	Finland	536	Hong Kong	555
Singapore	542	Hong Kong	533	Korea	546
Japan	539	Singapore	526	Taiwan	543
Korea	538	Canada	524	Finland	541
New Zealand	532	New Zealand	521	Liechtenstein	536
Canada	529	Japan	520	Switzerland	534
Estonia	528	Australia	515	Japan	529
Australia	527	Netherlands	508	Canada	527
Netherlands	522	Belgium	506	Netherlands	526
Taiwan	520	Norway	503	New Zealand	519
Germany	520	Estonia	501	Belgium	515
Liechtenstein	520	Switzerland	501	Australia	514
Switzerland	517	Poland	500	Germany	513
Britain	514	Iceland	500	Estonia	512
Slovenia	512	**United States**	**500**	Iceland	507
Poland	508	Liechtenstein	499	Denmark	503
Ireland	508	Sweden	497	Slovenia	501
Belgium	507	Germany	497	Norway	498
Hungary	503	Ireland	496	France	497
United States	**502**	France	496	Slovakia	497
AVERAGE SCORE	501	Taiwan	495	AVERAGE SCORE	497
Czech Republic	500	Denmark	495	Austria	496
Norway	500	Britain	494	Poland	495
Denmark	499	Hungary	494	Sweden	494
France	498	AVERAGE SCORE	494	Czech Republic	493
Iceland	496	Portugal	489	Britain	492
Sweden	495	Italy	486	Hungary	490
Austria	494	Latvia	484	Luxembourg	489
Latvia	494	Slovenia	483	**United States**	**487**
Portugal	493	Greece	483	Ireland	487

Changes in the Average Weekly Amount of Time Spent by 6- to 11-Year-Olds in Various Activities (Chapter 12)

Facts are the bedrock of science, but facts can be presented in many ways, with many interpretations. Your opinions about these facts reflect your values, which may be quite different from those of the parents and teachers of these children.

Total Media Use

Among all 8- to 18-year-olds, average amount of time spent with each medium in a typical day:

	2009
TV content	4:29
Music/audio	2:31
Computer	1:29
Video games	1:13
Print	:38
Movies	:25
Total Media Exposure	10:45
Multitasking proportion	29%
Total Media Use	7:38

Source: Generation M2: Media in the Lives of 8- to 18-Year-Olds, A Kaiser Family Foundation Study, January 2010.

Time Spent with Each Medium by Age

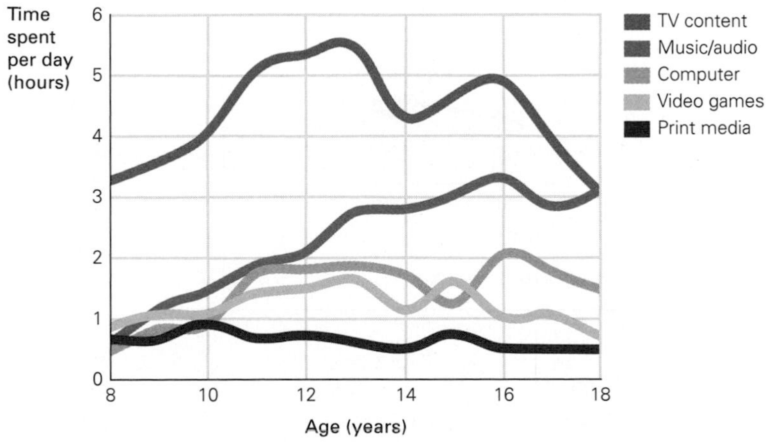

Who Is Raising the Children? (Chapter 13)

Most children still live in households with a male/female couple, who may be the children's married or unmarried biological parents, grandparents, stepparents, foster parents, or adoptive parents. However, the proportion of households headed by single parents has risen—by 350 percent for single fathers and by almost 200 percent for single mothers. (In 2008, 66 percent of U.S. households had *no* children under age 18.)

Households with Children, by Marital Status of Head, 1970–2009

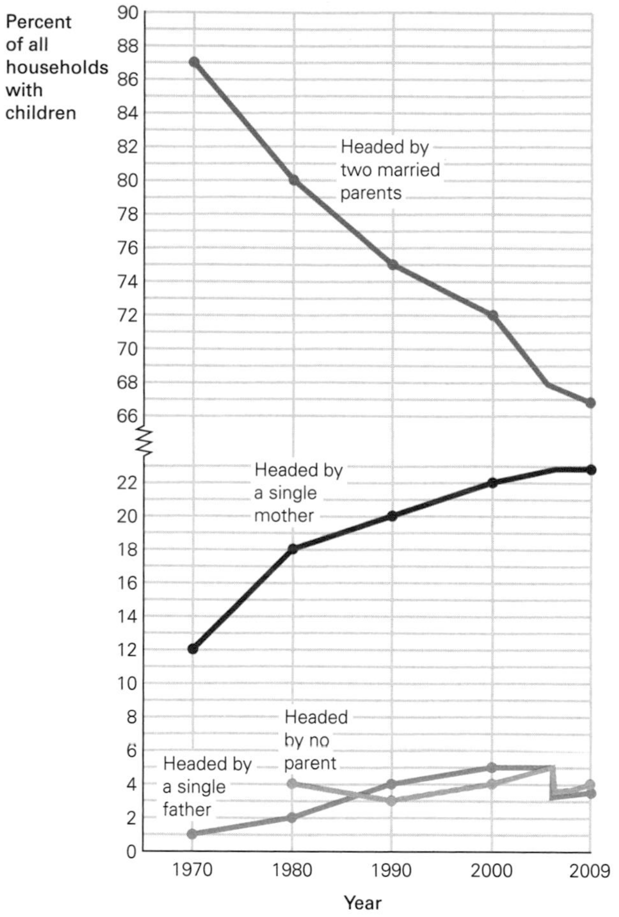

Source: U.S. Census Bureau, Current Population Survey, 2010.

Major Sexually Transmitted Infections: Some Basics (Chapter 14)

These and other STIs, if left untreated, may lead to serious reproductive and other health problems or even, as with HIV/AIDS and syphilis, to death. STIs can be avoided by consistently using condoms, having sex only in a relationship with an uninfected partner, or abstaining from sex.

Sexually Transmitted Infection (and Cause)	Symptoms	Treatment
Chlamydia (bacterium)	The most frequently reported bacterial STI in the United States. In women, abnormal vaginal discharge or burning sensation when urinating; may be followed by pain in low abdomen or low back, nausea, fever, pain during intercourse, or bleeding between menstrual periods. In men, discharge from penis or burning sensation when urinating.	Antibiotics
Genital HPV infection (virus)	One of the most common STIs in the world. Causes no symptoms or health problems in most people, but certain types may cause genital warts and others can cause cervical cancer in women and other cancers of the genitals in both sexes.	A vaccine is now available and is recommended for 11- and 12-year-old girls who are not yet sexually active.
Genital herpes (virus)	Blisters on or around the genitals or rectum that break and leave sores, which may take 2 to 4 weeks to heal; some people may experience fever, swollen glands, and other flu-like symptoms. Later outbreaks are usually less severe and shorter. Many people never have sores and may take years to realize they are infected. May lead to potentially fatal infections in babies and makes infected person more susceptible to HIV infection.	There is no vaccine or cure, but antiviral medications can shorten and prevent outbreaks.
Gonorrhea (bacterium)	Some men and most women have no symptoms. In men, a burning sensation when urinating; a white, yellow, or green discharge from the penis; painful or swollen testicles. In women, symptoms—pain or burning during urination, increased vaginal discharge, vaginal bleeding between periods—may be so mild or nonspecific that they are mistaken for a bladder or vaginal infection. May cause pelvic inflammatory disease (PID) in women and infertility in both sexes. Infected person can more easily contract HIV.	Antibiotics
Pelvic inflammatory disease (PID) (various bacteria)	A common and serious complication in women who have certain other STIs, especially chlamydia and gonorrhea. Pain in lower abdomen, fever, unusual vaginal discharge that may have a foul odor, painful intercourse, painful urination, irregular menstrual bleeding, and (rarely) pain in the right upper abdomen. May lead to blocked fallopian tubes, causing infertility.	Administration of at least two antibiotics that are effective against a wide range of infectious agents. In severe cases, surgery.
HIV/AIDS (virus)	Infection with the human immunodeficiency virus (HIV) eventually leads to acquired immune deficiency syndrome (AIDS). Infection with other STIs increases a person's likelihood of both acquiring and transmitting HIV. Soon after exposure, some people have flu-like symptoms: fever, headache, tiredness, swollen lymph glands. Months or years later, when the virus has weakened the immune system, the person may experience lack of energy, weight loss, frequent fevers and sweats, yeast infections, skin rashes, short-term memory loss. Symptoms of full-blown AIDS include certain cancers (Kaposi's sarcoma and lymphomas), seizures, vision loss, and coma. A leading cause of death among young adults in many nations.	There is no vaccine or cure, but antiretroviral drugs can slow the growth of the virus; antibiotics can cure some secondary infections, and various treatments are available to relieve painful or unpleasant symptoms.
Syphilis (bacterium)	Symptoms may not appear for years. Primary stage: One or more sores (chancres) a few days or weeks after exposure. Secondary stage: Skin rash, lesions of mucous membranes, fever, swollen lymph glands, sore throat, patchy hair loss, headaches, weight loss, muscle aches, fatigue. Latent stage: Primary and secondary symptoms disappear, but infection remains in the body. Late stage (10 to 20 years after first infection): Damage to brain, nerves, eyes, heart, blood vessels, liver, bones, and joints, progressing to difficulty coordinating muscle movements, paralysis, numbness, blindness, dementia.	Penicillin injections will kill the syphilis bacterium and prevent further damage but cannot repair damage already done.
Trichomoniasis (Trichomonas *vaginalis, a single-celled* protozoan parasite)	Most men have no symptoms, but some may temporarily have an irritation inside the penis, mild discharge, or slight burning after urination or ejaculation. Women may have a frothy, yellow-green, strong-smelling vaginal discharge and may experience discomfort during intercourse and urination; irritation and itching of the genital area; and, rarely, lower abdominal pain.	A single oral dose of metronidazole or tinidazole

Source: Centers for Disease Control and Prevention, 2009, July 14.

Sexual Behaviors of U.S. High School Students, 2009 (Chapters 14)

These percentages, as high as they may seem, are actually lower than they were in the early 1990s. (States not listed did not participate fully in the survey.) The data in this table reflect responses from students in the 9th to 12th grades. When only high school seniors are surveyed, the percentages are higher: Nationwide, 62 percent of seniors have had sexual intercourse, and 21 percent have had four or more partners.

	Ever had sexual intercourse (%)			Had first sexual intercourse before age 13 (%)			Has had four or more sex partners during lifetime (%)			Is currently sexually active (%)		
State	Female	Male	Total	Female	Male	Total	Female	Male	Total	Female	Male	Total
Alabama	51.4	61.8	**56.6**	4.1	16.2	**10.1**	14.4	25.7	**19.9**	42.0	40.9	**41.5**
Alaska	42.9	44.0	**43.5**	2.6	7.1	**5.1**	10.7	12.1	**11.4**	31.1	29.6	**30.4**
Arizona	44.8	52.1	**48.6**	2.9	7.8	**5.5**	10.4	17.4	**14.1**	34.4	34.2	**34.5**
Arkansas	51.4	55.9	**53.6**	6.7	14.3	**10.3**	15.5	20.8	**18.0**	39.9	37.6	**38.9**
Colorado	36.2	43.7	**40.0**	2.7	6.4	**4.6**	11.0	16.5	**13.8**	25.6	29.1	**27.4**
Connecticut	38.0	42.9	**40.5**	2.8	6.1	**4.6**	8.4	12.5	**10.5**	30.3	28.9	**29.6**
Delaware	57.1	57.9	**57.5**	5.8	13.4	**9.7**	18.0	23.9	**21.1**	44.2	41.5	**42.9**
Florida	47.7	53.4	**50.6**	4.3	12.0	**8.3**	11.4	21.4	**16.6**	37.0	36.8	**37.0**
Hawaii	45.8	42.7	**44.3**	4.1	7.8	**6.0**	11.3	10.9	**11.1**	33.9	27.2	**30.5**
Idaho	39.2	38.8	**39.0**	3.4	4.9	**4.2**	—	—	—	—	—	—
Illinois	43.8	52.3	**48.1**	3.6	8.9	**6.3**	10.8	18.3	**14.5**	35.4	36.9	**36.2**
Indiana	52.8	45.5	**49.2**	2.8	6.3	**4.5**	13.7	13.5	**13.7**	41.3	31.9	**36.7**
Kansas	46.2	47.0	**46.6**	1.7	7.2	**4.5**	11.8	16.4	**14.2**	35.2	33.3	**34.2**
Kentucky	47.8	49.0	**48.3**	4.0	9.3	**6.7**	10.7	14.7	**12.7**	36.1	31.2	**33.6**
Maine	45.9	45.9	**46.0**	2.8	7.3	**5.0**	10.7	13.1	**11.9**	37.1	33.3	**35.3**
Massachusetts	44.6	48.0	**46.4**	3.0	8.0	**5.4**	10.6	15.2	**12.9**	36.0	33.1	**34.6**
Michigan	44.3	46.9	**45.6**	3.0	7.2	**5.1**	11.5	15.7	**13.6**	35.6	32.6	**34.1**
Mississippi	58.2	63.9	**61.0**	8.1	18.7	**13.4**	17.6	30.1	**23.7**	44.0	45.9	**44.9**
Missouri	47.3	50.2	**48.7**	3.4	7.9	**5.7**	13.6	18.3	**16.0**	36.3	34.9	**35.5**
Montana	47.0	48.1	**47.6**	3.7	7.7	**5.7**	14.7	17.3	**16.0**	33.6	30.8	**32.2**
Nevada	45.3	52.6	**49.0**	3.4	10.0	**6.7**	10.9	20.3	**15.7**	32.8	32.5	**32.7**
New Hampshire	46.2	46.1	**46.3**	1.9	6.4	**4.3**	10.9	11.6	**11.4**	39.5	32.3	**36.3**
New Jersey	43.6	49.0	**46.3**	1.5	6.7	**4.1**	8.8	16.3	**12.5**	33.7	33.5	**33.6**
New Mexico	—	—	—	4.7	10.1	**7.4**	12.4	17.8	**15.1**	33.5	31.8	**32.6**
New York	38.4	45.6	**42.0**	3.3	8.8	**6.1**	8.4	18.4	**13.4**	29.7	33.2	**31.5**
North Carolina	48.2	54.2	**51.1**	5.1	10.1	**7.5**	12.2	19.2	**15.7**	35.7	37.5	**36.6**
North Dakota	46.7	42.3	**44.6**	2.1	4.8	**3.5**	11.6	11.7	**11.7**	37.2	29.3	**33.3**
Oklahoma	50.7	51.2	**44.6**	3.4	6.0	**4.7**	15.2	20.1	**17.6**	40.3	39.5	**39.8**
Pennsylvania	51.0	45.8	**48.3**	3.6	7.9	**5.8**	13.2	17.7	**15.4**	39.6	34.3	**36.9**
Rhode Island	42.8	45.6	**44.2**	2.4	8.0	**5.2**	8.6	13.7	**11.2**	32.6	32.0	**32.3**
South Carolina	50.7	56.3	**53.4**	6.3	12.2	**9.2**	14.8	24.9	**19.7**	37.0	40.4	**38.6**
South Dakota	46.9	47.1	**47.0**	3.7	7.6	**5.7**	14.4	16.0	**15.2**	38.9	33.7	**36.3**
Tennessee	51.2	55.6	**53.4**	3.3	11.5	**7.5**	13.3	19.8	**16.6**	38.4	39.1	**38.8**
Texas	49.3	53.9	**51.6**	3.1	9.1	**6.1**	12.7	20.3	**16.5**	38.5	36.9	**37.7**
West Virginia	54.7	53.6	**54.1**	4.6	7.5	**6.0**	14.6	16.4	**15.5**	42.4	38.2	**40.3**
Wisconsin	41.1	40.7	**40.9**	2.5	4.4	**3.4**	8.7	11.0	**9.9**	31.7	26.9	**29.3**
Wyoming	51.6	49.6	**50.6**	3.0	8.8	**5.0**	16.8	19.0	**17.9**	40.4	35.0	**37.8**
U.S. median	**46.8**	**48.5**	**48.2**	**3.3**	**7.8**	**5.7**	**11.6**	**17.3**	**14.5**	**36.2**	**33.4**	**35.4**

Source: National Center for Chronic Disease Prevention and Health Promotion, Youth Risk Behavior Surveillance System, *MMWR*, June 6, 2011.

Demographic Changes (Chapter 14)

These numbers show dramatic shifts in family planning, with teenage births continuing to fall and births after age 30 rising again. These data come from the United States, but the same trends are apparent in almost every nation. Can you tell when contraception became widely available?

Fertility by Age Cohort, 1960–2009

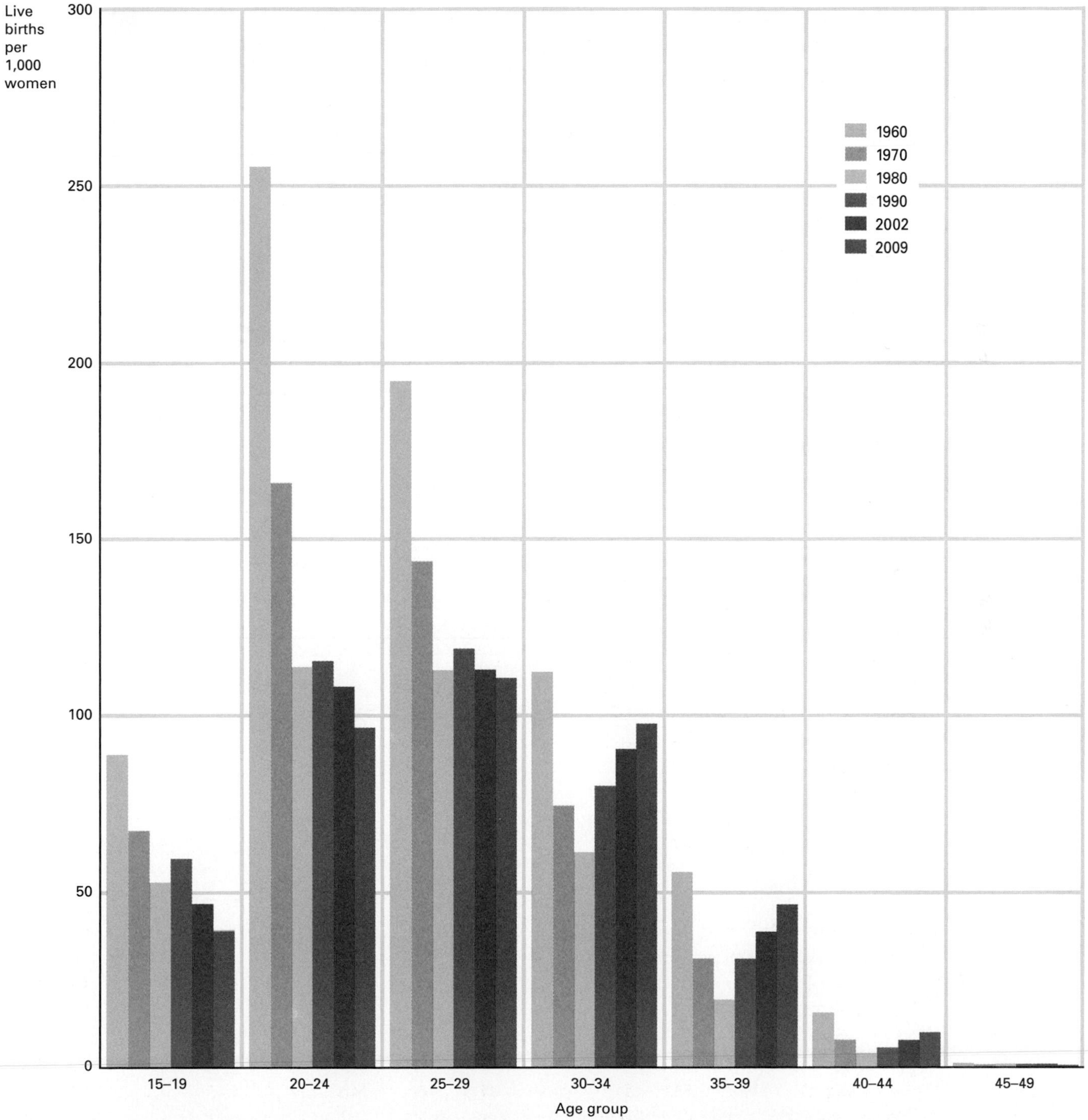

Source: CDC National Center for Health Statistics, *Vital Statistics of the United States, Preliminary Data for Dec. 21, 2010.*

Education Affects Income (Chapter 15)

Although there is some debate about the cognitive benefits of college education, there is no doubt about the financial benefits. No matter what a person's ethnicity or gender is, an associate's degree more than doubles his or her income compared to that of someone who has not completed high school. These data are for the United States; similar trends, often with steeper increases, are found in other nations.

Median Annual Income, by Educational Attainment

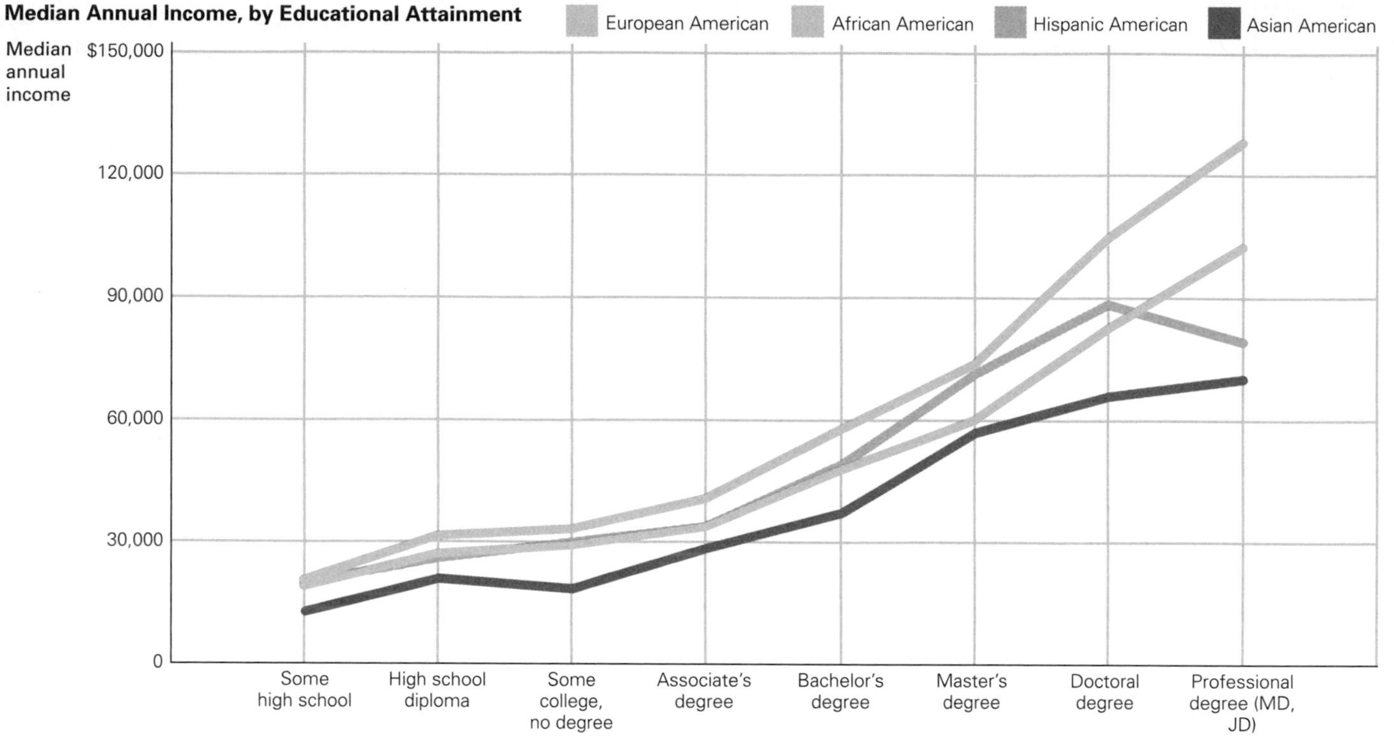

Source: U.S. Bureau of the Census, 2009.

U.S. Homicide Victim and Offender Rates, by Race and Gender, Ages 13–16 (Chapter 16)

Teenage boys are more often violent offenders than victims. The ratio of victimization to offense has varied for teenage girls over the years. The good news is that rates have decreased dramatically over the past 10 years for every category of adolescents—male and female, Black and White. (Similar declines are apparent for Asian and Hispanic Americans.) The bad news is that rates are far higher in the United States than in any other developed nation.

Number of Homicide Victims, Ages 13–16

Year	Total	Male	Female	White	Black
2001	390	291	99	190	182
2004	411	325	86	177	218
2005	467	426	41	176	272
2006	485	395	90	217	259
2007	487	380	107	206	265
2008	496	447	48	197	272
2009	400	319	81	190	199
2010	363	288	75	140	212

Source: U.S. Department of Justice—Federal Bureau of Investigation, 2011.

Number of Homicide Offenders, Ages 13–16

Year	Total	Male	Female	White	Black
2001	454	388	63	196	234
2004	480	440	39	210	256
2005	467	426	41	176	272
2006	610	560	47	213	377
2007	542	493	47	187	344
2008	496	447	48	197	272
2009	465	422	43	186	264
2010	437	395	42	153	265

Source: U.S. Department of Justice—Federal Bureau of Investigation, 2011.

The charts, graphs, and tables in this Appendix offer readers the opportunity to analyze raw data and draw their own conclusions. The same information may be presented in a variety of ways. On this page, you can create your own bar graph or line graph, depicting some noteworthy aspect of the data presented in the three tables. First, consider all the possibilities the tables offer by answering these five questions:

1. Are male or female teenagers more likely to be victims of homicide?
2. These are annual rates. How many African Americans in 1,000 were likely to commit homicide in 2010?
3. Which age group is *most* likely to commit homicide?
4. Which age group is *least* likely to be victims of homicide?
5. Of the four groups of adolescents, which has shown the greatest decline in rates of both victimization and perpetration of homicide over the past decade? Which has shown the least decline?

Answers: 1. Boys—at least 4 times as often. 2. Less than one. 3. 17–24. 4. 0–12. 5. Black males had the greatest decline, and White females had the least (but these two groups have always been highest and lowest, respectively, in every year).
Now—use the grid provided at right to make your own graph.

Overall Number of Homicides by Age, 2010, United States (Chapter 16)

Late adolescence and early adulthood are the peak times for murders—both for victims and offenders. The question for developmentalists is whether something changes before age 18 to decrease the rates in young adulthood.

Age group	Victims	Killers
0–12	627	11
13–16	363	437
17–24	3,487	4,121
25–34	3,505	2,753
35–49	2,792	1,384
50–64	1,666	651
Over 64	585	204

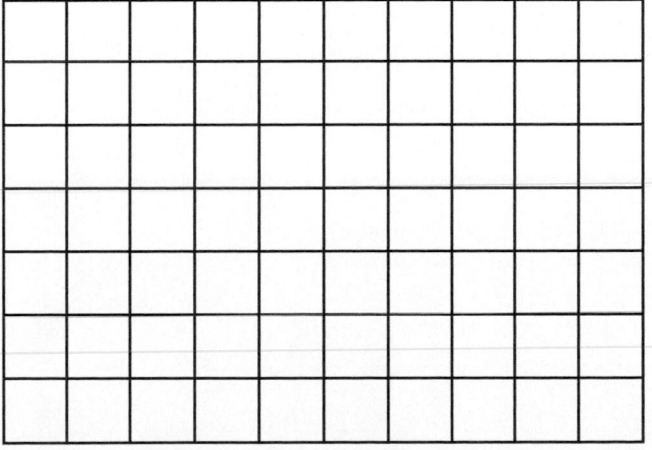

Smoking Behavior Among U.S. High School Students, 1991–2009 (Chapter 16)

The data in these two tables reveal many trends. For example, do you see that African American adolescents are much less likely to smoke than Hispanics or European Americans, but that this racial advantage is decreasing? Are you surprised to see that White females smoke more than White males?

Percentage of High School Students Who Reported Smoking Cigarettes

Smoking Behavior	1991	1995	1999	2003	2005	2007	2009
Lifetime (ever smoked)	70.1	71.3	70.4	58.4	54.3	50.3	46.3
Current (smoked at least once in past 30 days)	27.5	34.8	34.8	21.9	23.0	20.0	19.5
Current frequent (smoked 20 or more times in past 30 days)	12.7	16.1	16.8	9.7	9.4	8.1	7.3

Percentage of High School Students Who Reported Current Smoking, by Sex, Ethnicity, and Grade

Characteristic	1991	1995	1999	2003	2005	2007	2009
Sex							
Female	27.3	34.3	34.9	21.9	23.0	18.7	19.1
Male	27.6	35.4	34.7	21.8	22.9	21.3	19.8
Ethnicity							
White, non-Hispanic	30.9	38.3	38.6	24.9	25.9	23.2	22.5
Female	*31.7*	*39.8*	*39.1*	*26.6*	*27.0*	*22.5*	*22.8*
Male	*30.2*	*37.0*	*38.2*	*23.3*	*24.9*	*23.8*	*22.3*
Black, non-Hispanic	12.6	19.2	19.7	15.1	12.9	11.6	9.5
Female	*11.3*	*12.2*	*17.7*	*10.8*	*11.9*	*8.4*	*8.4*
Male	*14.1*	*27.8*	*21.8*	*19.3*	*14.0*	*14.9*	*10.7*
Hispanic	25.3	34.0	32.7	18.4	22.0	16.7	18.0
Female	*22.9*	*32.9*	*31.5*	*17.7*	*19.2*	*14.6*	*16.7*
Male	*27.9*	*34.9*	*34.0*	*19.1*	*24.8*	*18.7*	*19.4*
Grade							
9th	23.2	31.2	27.6	17.4	19.7	14.3	13.5
10th	25.2	33.1	34.7	21.8	21.4	19.6	18.3
11th	31.6	35.9	36.0	23.6	24.3	21.6	22.3
12th	30.1	38.2	42.8	26.2	27.6	26.5	25.2

Source: MMWR (2010, July 9).

Appendix B

>> Correlation of *The Developing Person Through Childhood and Adolescence, 9e* with NAEYC Standards

The following table provides an at-a-glance correlation between this text and the 2010 NAEYC Standards for Initial and Advanced Early Childhood Professional Preparation Programs. Key Elements of the Initial Standards are preceded by "(I)" and Key Elements of Advanced Standards are preceded by "(A)"; in cases in which a standard is the same for both Initial and Advanced programs, the standard is preceded by "(I and A)."

As might be expected for a textbook on child development, the strongest correlations are with Standard 1 (Promoting Child Development and Learning) and Standard 2 (Building Family and Community Relationships), which relate primarily to knowledge that an early-childhood-education candidate is required to master. There are also appropriate correlations between pertinent sections of the text and Key Elements 3a and 3b of Standard 3 (Observing, Documenting, and Assessing to Support Young Children and Families) and Key Elements 4a and 4b of Standard 4 (Using Developmentally Effective Approaches), although these standards relate more directly to the practical application of knowledge than to its acquisition.

Standard 3 (Key Elements 3c and 3d), Standard 4 (Key Elements 4c and 4d), Standard 5 (Using Content Knowledge to Build Meaningful Curriculum), Standard 6 (Becoming a Professional), and Standard 7 (Early Childhood Filed Experiences) relate to the early-childhood-education candidate's proficiency in applying knowledge and strategies and are therefore beyond the scope of a textbook to fulfill.

The NAEYC Standards were developed for educators of children up to 8 years of age. The correlations noted below apply to this age group although middle childhood is defined in the text as ages 6 to 11.

Standard 1 – Promoting Child Development and Learning **Key Elements of Standard 1** **(I and A) 1:** Knowing and understanding young children's characteristics and needs, from birth through age 8 **(I and A) 1b:** Knowing and understanding the multiple influences on early development and learning **(I and A) 1c:** Using developmental knowledge to create healthy, respectful, supportive, and challenging learning environments for young children	BIRTH TO AGE 2 Chapter 2 ▪ Presents the "grand" theories of development: psychoanalytic, behaviorism/social learning, and cognitive/information processing. Includes a Thinking Critically feature on potential impact of toilet training methods. ▪ Presents newer theories: Sociocultural (Vygotsky and beyond), humanism, and evolutionary theory. Chapter 3 ▪ Presents information about chromosomal and genetic variations that result in recognizable syndromes that effect children's biosocial, cognitive, and/or psychosocial development, including Down syndrome, hemophilia, fragile-X syndrome, sickle-cell anemia, cystic fibrosis, thalassemia. ▪ Includes a table of 20 common genetic diseases with a brief description of symptoms of each. Chapter 5 ▪ Describes physical changes from birth to age 2. ▪ Discusses normal sleep patterns as well as sleep problems and their potential effects.

- Describes normal brain development over the first two years, including basic brain structures, formation of neuronal networks, and the impact of experience on brain development.
- Discusses the effect on brain development of lack of stimulation, stress, social deprivation, and shaken baby syndrome, as well as interventions for at-risk families.
- Discusses the development and role of the five senses; the difference between sensation and perception; maturation of the language areas of the cortex and its impact on language development; adaptation of the senses to the social world; the controversy over infants' perception of pain.
- Discusses development of gross and fine motor skills, including variations in the motor skills that are encouraged in different cultures.
- Discusses infants' nutritional needs, the benefits of breast-feeding, and the physical and cognitive effects of malnutrition.

Chapter 6

- Describes cognitive development in the first two years.
- Discusses Piaget's stages of sensorimotor intelligence.
- Discusses information-processing theory and aspects of infant memory.
- Describes language development in the first two years: the universal sequence of language acquisition, the naming explosion, and major theories of language learning.

Chapter 7

- Describes emotional development in infants and toddlers in the first two years.
- Discusses infants' emotions, including smiling and laughing, anger and sadness, fear (stranger wariness and separation anxiety). Discusses toddlers' emotions, including pride, shame, guilt, embarrassment, and the development of self-awareness.
- Discusses the role of brain maturation in supporting social impulses; abnormal brain development due to stress and the consequent negative impact on emotional development.
- Discusses the four types of temperament identified by the NYLS, the continuity and discontinuity of temperament, and the impact of temperament on caregiver–child relationships (including goodness of fit).
- Discusses theories of infant psychosocial development: psychoanalytic, behaviorism/social learning, cognitive (development of working models), sociocultural (ethnotheories and the impact of proximal and distal parenting).
- Discusses the development of social bonds, including synchrony, stages of attachment, types of attachment, and social referencing.
- Discusses types of nonmaternal day care, including characteristics of high-quality day care (adequate attention to each infant, encouragement of language and sensorimotor development, attention to health and safety, and warm and responsive professional caregivers; see also Table 7.3) and the effects of day care on infants and toddlers.

AGES 2 to 6

Chapter 8

- Describes typical growth patterns in early childhood, nutritional needs, the potential effects of nutritional problems (undernutrition, overweight, and obesity) on physical growth and cognitive functioning, and the importance of oral health.
- Discusses brain development, including a detailed diagram of the major brain structures (Figure 8.2).
- Discusses myelination, which speeds thought processes and reaction time.
- Discusses lateralization and the development of the corpus callosum; covers the difference-equals-deficit error in regard to left-handedness.
- Discusses ongoing maturation of the prefrontal cortex and resultant advances in neurological control; looks at cultural differences in impulsivity and perseveration.
- Discusses the maturing limbic system, with a detailed diagram of the HPA axis (Figure 8.5), practical advice for teachers regarding children's emotional reactions, and the effect of stress on the limbic system (excessive cortisol production and permanent deficits in learning and memory).

- Discusses improvement in motor skills in early childhood, with a table listing various skills or achievements and the approximate ages at which they normally develop; reflexes and activities that aid motor development; gender differences in timing of development of motor skills.
- Discusses environmental hazards that harm growing bodies and brains (pollution, lead, pesticides, BPA, cigarette smoke, and many others), impeding balance, finger dexterity, and motivation; discusses environmental risks in different cultural settings and notes the ties between risks and SES.
- Discusses three levels of prevention of avoidable injury, including provision of safe environments.
- Discusses the short- and long-term biosocial, cognitive, and psychosocial effects of child maltreatment, including sex abuse and neglect; notes warning signs of maltreatment.

Chapter 9

- Describes cognitive development from ages 2 to 6.
- Discusses characteristics of Piaget's preoperational thought (egocentrism, centration, focus on appearance, static reasoning, irreversibility, conservation, animism).
- Discusses elements of Vygotsky's theory of cognition (guided participation, zone of proximal development, scaffolding, private speech).
- Discusses pivotal importance of mentoring and language in a child's cognitive achievements, including accomplishments in understanding of numbers, logic, memory; influence of culture on proficiency with numbers.
- Discusses cognitive advances in early childhood, including theory-theory and theory of mind; the effects of brain maturation and culture on cognitive development.
- Describes language development from ages 2 to 6 (and the influences of brain maturation, myelination, scaffolding, and social interaction); vocabulary explosion, fast-mapping, acquisition of grammar, and learning two languages.
- Discusses the influence of culture and SES on language development.
- Early Childhood Education:
  - Discusses the influence on development of home and school environments; importance of the quality of home life and effectiveness of individual teachers.
  - Discusses characteristics of child-centered and teacher-directed programs, including the educational theories that underlie each approach and practical differences in children's daily experience in each type of environment.
  - Discusses the various intervention programs (Head Start and state-sponsored programs); cultural considerations in bilingual programs; and long-term gains from intensive programs.

Chapter 10

- Discusses children's achievement of emotional regulation.
- Discusses Erikson's stage of initiative versus guilt; protective optimism; aspects of the developing self-concept.
- Ties the emergence of initiative to brain maturation (specifically to myelination of the limbic system, growth of the prefrontal cortex, and longer attention span).
- Discusses intrinsic and extrinsic motivation and ways to encourage intrinsic motivation.
- Discusses cultural differences in which emotions children are expected to regulate as well as cultural differences in control strategies.
- A section on psychopathology discusses:
  - Internalizing and externalizing problems
  - Sex differences in emotional regulation
  - The impact of maltreatment on a child's ability to regulate emotions (and differences in the way boys and girls respond—boys by externalizing and girls by internalizing).
- A section on play discusses:
  - The importance of peer relationships in development of emotional regulation, empathy, and social understanding

  - Cultural differences in play
  - Parten's five types of play
  - How active play advances planning and self-control; the theory that rough-and-tumble play advances development of the prefrontal cortex as children learn to practice social skills, regulate emotions, and strengthen their bodies.
  - The benefits of sociodramatic play (children explore and rehearse social roles; learn how to explain their ideas and convince playmates to agree; practice emotional regulation by pretending to be afraid, angry brave, etc.; and develop self-concept in a non-threatening way.)
- Discusses Baumrind's caregiving styles and their characteristics as well as the impact of each style on the child; discusses cultural variations in caregiving styles and teachers' styles of interaction.
- Discusses pros and cons young children's exposure to electronic media.
- A section on moral development discusses:
  - Factors that result in development of empathy and antipathy, prosocial and antisocial behavior
  - The four major types of aggression
  - Disciplinary measures and their effects (physical punishment, psychological control, exclusion and conversation); cultural variations in discipline
- Discusses the distinction between sex differences and gender differences.
- Discusses major theories of gender-role development (psychoanalytic, behavioral, cognitive).

AGES 6 to 11

Chapter 11

- Describes normal growth pattern (slowdown in growth and increase in strength).
- Discusses improvements in medical care and the influence of children's health habits on development.
- Discusses benefits (and potential disadvantages) of physical activity; discusses physical, cognitive, and social impact of participation in neighborhood games, school exercise, and athletic clubs and leagues.
- A section on health problems discusses:
  - The increasing prevalence, causes, and consequences of childhood obesity (includes international and SES considerations)
  - Potential causes of asthmas; treatment and prevention
- A section on brain development discusses:
  - The "massively interconnected brain" that has developed by age 7 or 8
  - The results of this brain maturation, including increased speed of thought, faster reaction time (both mental and physical), longer attention span, and automatization of thoughts and actions
- A section on measurement of cognitive potential/abilities discusses:
  - The difference between aptitude and achievement
  - Assessment of aptitude and achievement through IQ and achievement tests, criticisms of testing (including cultural bias)
  - Gardner's nine types of intelligence
  - Brain scans and what they teach us about children's brain functioning
- A section on children with special needs discusses:
  - Four general principles of developmental psychopathology: (1) abnormality is normal, (2) disability changes year by year, (3) life may be better or worse in adulthood, and (4) diagnosis and treatment reflect the social context
  - Symptoms of ADHD and bipolar disorder; potential causes; treatments (including the controversy over drug therapy)
  - Diagnosis and treatment of learning disabilities (dyslexia, dyscalculia)
  - Symptoms, treatments, and impact of autism spectrum disorder

- Changing laws and practices with regard to special education
- Educating gifted and talented children

Chapter 12

- Discusses Piaget's concrete operational thought and the child's increasing ability to use logic in thinking; classification, transitive inference, and seriation.
- Discusses Vygotsky; the roles that social interaction and instruction play in children's cognitive development.
- Discusses the influence of culture and context on what, how, and when children learn.
- Discusses information-processing theory: sensory memory, working memory, and long-term memory (see Table 12.1 for advances in memory at different ages); the influence of children's knowledge base on their learning; development of control processes and metacognition.
- A section on language discusses:
  - Advances in vocabulary and grammatical constructions (use of prefixes, suffixes, compound words, phrases, figures of speech)
  - Understanding and use of metaphors
  - Pragmatics (the child's ability to adjust speech to the social context)
  - The effect of SES on a child's exposure to and acquisition of language
  - The impact of parents' and teachers' expectations on the child's acquisition of and proficiency with language
- A section on teaching and learning discusses:
  - Differences in curriculum by nation, by community, and by school subject (evident in the results of international tests; the mix of school subjects; and the relative power of parents, educators, and political leaders)
  - Benchmarks for achievement in math and reading at different ages (see At About This Time tables on p. 365)
  - The hidden curriculum (the implicit values and assumptions evident in course selection, schedules, tracking, teacher characteristics, discipline, teaching methods, sports competition, student government, extracurricular activities, etc.)
  - Learning a second language (immersion, bilingual education, ELL)
  - Gender differences in school performance
  - The phonics approach and the whole-language approach to reading
  - Determinants of educational practice (state governments, local jurisdictions, teachers, parents)
  - Types of schools in the U.S. (public, private, charter, home schooling) and characteristics of each

Chapter 13

- Discusses Erikson's fourth psychosocial crisis (industry versus inferiority) and the child's self-assessment as industrious or inferior; the relationship between productivity and self-control.
- Discusses Freud's latency period.
- Discusses ongoing development of self-concept (which includes children's ideas about their intelligence, personality, abilities, gender, and ethnic background) as self-concept becomes more specific and logical due to advances in cognitive development and social awareness.
- Discusses resilience and stress, and the effects of cumulative stress on all aspects of development (includes section on the importance of social support and the efficacy of religious faith).
- A section on moral reasoning discusses:
  - Kohlberg's levels of moral thought and criticisms of his research
  - The influence of peers, parents, and culture on children's development of moral values
  - Alignment with peers when peer values conflict with adult values
  - The morality of child labor

Standard 2. Building Family and Community Relationships **Key Elements of Standard 2** **(I and A) 2a:** Knowing about and understanding diverse family and community characteristics **(I and A) 2b:** Supporting and engaging families and communities through respectful, reciprocal relationships **(I) 2c:** Involving families and communities in young children's development and learning	▪ The importance of establishing and nurturing ties between the family and the community is evident throughout the text. Specific examples include the following. **Chapter 1** ▪ Discusses Bronfenbrenner's ecological-systems approach and his insights about how elements of the overlapping systems affect development, and especially how elements of the microsystem—family, peer groups, classrooms, neighborhoods, houses of worship, etc.—interact to influence an individual's development. **Chapter 7** ▪ Discusses the way in which early relationships help infants develop a working model, a set of assumptions about the world and how it works, that become a frame of reference for later life. **Chapter 8** ▪ Discussion of prevention of avoidable injury includes measures that communities may take to ensure child safety. **Chapter 9** ▪ Discusses the importance of good communication between school and home. **Chapter 10** ▪ Discusses the role of communities in ensuring safe and adequate play spaces. **Chapter 11** ▪ Discusses physical, cognitive, and social impact of participation in neighborhood games, school exercise, and athletic clubs and leagues. ▪ Discusses the connections between the state governments, local jurisdictions, teachers, and parents in determining what will be taught in schools and how it will be taught. Includes discussion of the variations by school district in identifying children with special needs (those who have difficulty learning as well as those who are gifted and talented) and providing appropriate educational environments for them. **Chapter 12** ▪ Discusses Vygotsky; the roles of social interaction and instruction in children's cognitive development; the influence of culture and context on what, how, and when children learn; and the relative power of parents, educators, and political leaders in determining school curriculum. ▪ Discusses family and community influences on second-language learning and the effect that children's learning of a second language has on immigrant families. **Chapter 13** ▪ Defines family structure and family function. ▪ Discusses the five major functions that families serve for children: (1) provide physical necessities, (2) support, encourage, and guide education, (3) provide opportunities for success that encourage children's self-respect, (4) foster friendships, and (5) provide harmony and stability in the home. ▪ Discusses the diversity of family structures (Table 13.2 describes family structures—Two-parent families: nuclear, extended, polygamous, step-parent, adoptive, grandparents alone, families of same-sex couples. Single-parent families: single mother, never married; single mother, divorced, separated, or widowed; single father; one grandparent alone). ▪ Discusses the ability/challenge of different structures in meeting the five family functions. ▪ Includes A View from Science feature on aspects of divorce and its potential effects on children. ▪ Discusses the effects of poverty on the family; explains the family stress model, including stresses experienced by children in low- and high-SES families. ▪ Discusses the effects of family conflict; includes a section on the importance of networks of social support and the efficacy of affiliation with religious institutions.

<table>
<tr>
<td>Standard 3. Observing, Documenting, and Assessing to Support Young Children and Families
Key Elements of Standard 3
(I and A) 3a: Understanding the goals, benefits, and uses of assessment—including its use in development of appropriate goals, curriculum, and teaching strategies for young children
(I) 3b: Knowing about assessment partnerships with families and with professional colleagues to build effective learning environments</td>
<td>▪ The importance of careful attention to a child's development in all three domains is evident throughout the text. The At About This Time tables, which appear in many chapters, highlight the ages at which children normally achieve certain physical, cognitive, and psychosocial benchmarks, providing a framework for assessment of individual children's progress in these areas.
Chapter 12 (Academic performance)
▪ This chapter discusses the following factors that affect assessment of individual students:
▪ Differences in curriculum by nation, by community, and by school subject (evident in the results of international tests; the mix of school subjects; and the relative power of parents, educators, and political leaders)
▪ Benchmarks for achievement in math and reading at different ages (see At About This Time tables on p. 365)
▪ The hidden curriculum (the implicit values and assumptions evident in course selection, schedules, tracking, teacher characteristics, discipline, teaching methods, sports competition, student government, extracurricular activities, etc.)
▪ Learning a second language (immersion, bilingual education, ESL)
▪ Gender differences in school performance
▪ The phonics approach and the whole-language approach to reading
▪ Determinants of educational practice (state governments, local jurisdictions, teachers, parents)
▪ Types of schools in the U.S. (public, private, charter, home schooling) and characteristics of each
▪ Discusses international standardized benchmarks of achievement in reading and mathematics for fourth-grade students (PIRLS and TIMMS, respectively).
▪ Discusses goals and consequences of assessment under the No Child Left Behind Act of 2001.
▪ Discusses the federally sponsored National Assessment of Educational Progress (NAEP) achievement tests in reading, mathematics, and other subjects.</td>
</tr>
<tr>
<td>Standard 4. Using Developmentally Effective Approaches
Key Elements of Standard 3
(I and A) 4a: Understanding positive relationships and supportive interactions as the foundation of their work with young children
(I and A) 4b: Knowing and understanding effective strategies and tools for early education, including appropriate uses of technology</td>
<td>▪ The positive influence of warm, nurturing relationships and the negative influence of stressful relationships on every aspect of children's development are discussed throughout the text.
Chapter 7
▪ Discusses sociocultural theory and the importance of culture and context on children's cognitive development.
Chapter 9
▪ Discusses Vygotsky's theory of cognition, including the zone of proximal development and the efficacy of guided participation and scaffolding in supporting and encouraging children's learning.
▪ Discusses pivotal importance of mentoring and language in a child's cognitive achievements, including accomplishments in understanding of numbers, logic, memory; influence of culture on proficiency with numbers.</td>
</tr>
</table>

Glossary

23rd pair The chromosome pair that, in humans, determines sex. The other 22 pairs are autosomes; inherited equally by males and females.

A

acceleration Educating gifted children alongside other children of the same mental, not chronological, age.

accommodation The restructuring of old ideas to include new experiences.

achievement test A measure of mastery or proficiency in reading, mathematics, writing, science, or some other subject.

adolescence-limited offender A person whose criminal activity stops by age 21.

adolescent egocentrism A characteristic of adolescent thinking that leads young people (ages 10 to 13) to focus on themselves to the exclusion of others.

adoption A legal proceeding in which an adult or couple unrelated to a child is granted the joys and obligations of being that child's parent(s).

adrenal glands Two glands, located above the kidneys, that produce hormones (including the "stress hormones" epinephrine [adrenaline] and norepinephrine).

affordance An opportunity for perception and interaction that is offered by a person, place, or object in the environment.

age of viability The age (about 22 weeks after conception) at which a fetus may survive outside the mother's uterus if specialized medical care is available.

aggressive-rejected Rejected by peers because of antagonistic, confrontational behavior.

allele A variation that makes a gene different in some way from other genes for the same characteristics. Many genes never vary; others have several possible alleles.

amygdala A tiny brain structure that registers emotions, particularly fear and anxiety.

analytic thought Thought that results from analysis, such as a systematic ranking of pros and cons, risks and consequences, possibilities and facts. Analytic thought depends on logic and rationality.

animism The belief that natural objects and phenomena are alive.

anorexia nervosa An eating disorder characterized by self-starvation. Affected individuals voluntarily undereat and often overexercise, depriving their vital organs of nutrition. Anorexia can be fatal.

anoxia A lack of oxygen that, if prolonged, can cause brain damage or death.

antipathy Feelings of dislike or even hatred for another person.

antisocial behavior Actions that are deliberately hurtful or destructive to another person.

Apgar scale A quick assessment of a newborn's health. The baby's color, heart rate, reflexes, muscle tone, and respiratory effort are given a score of 0, 1, or 2 twice—at one minute and five minutes after birth—and each time the total of all five scores is compared with the maximum score of 10 (rarely attained).

apprenticeship in thinking Vygotsky's term for how cognition is stimulated and developed in people by more skilled members of society.

aptitude The potential to master a specific skill or to learn a certain body of knowledge.

assimilation The reinterpretation of new experiences to fit into old ideas.

assisted reproductive technology (ART) A general term for the techniques designed to help infertile couples conceive and then sustain a pregnancy.

asthma A chronic disease of the respiratory system in which inflammation narrows the airways from the nose and mouth to the lungs, causing difficulty in breathing. Signs and symptoms include wheezing, shortness of breath, chest tightness, and coughing.

attachment According to Ainsworth, an affectional tie that an infant forms with a caregiver—a tie that binds them together in space and endures over time.

attention-deficit/hyperactivity disorder (ADHD) A condition in which a person not only has great difficulty concentrating for more than a few moments but also is inattentive, impulsive, and overactive.

authoritarian parenting An approach to child rearing that is characterized by high behavioral standards, strict punishment of misconduct, and little communication.

authoritative parenting An approach to child rearing in which the parents set limits but listen to the child and are flexible.

autism A developmental disorder marked by an inability to relate to other people normally, extreme self-absorption, and an inability to acquire normal speech.

autism spectrum disorder Any of several disorders characterized by inadequate social skills, impaired communication, and unusual play.

automatization A process in which repetition of a sequence of thoughts and actions makes the sequence routine, so that it no longer requires conscious thought.

autonomy versus shame and doubt Erikson's second crisis of psychosocial development. Toddlers either succeed or fail in gaining a sense of self-rule over their own actions and bodies.

axon A fiber that extends from a neuron and transmits electrochemical impulses from that neuron to the dendrites of other neurons.

B

babbling An infant's repetition of certain syllables, such as *ba-ba-ba,* that begins when babies are between 6 and 9 months old.

balanced bilingual A person who is fluent in two languages, not favoring one over the other.

base rate neglect A common fallacy in which a person ignores the overall frequency of some behavior or characteristic (called the *base rate*) in making a decision. For example, a person might bet on a "lucky" lottery number without considering the odds that that number will be selected.

behavioral teratogens Agents and conditions that can harm the prenatal brain, impairing the future child's intellectual and emotional functioning.

behaviorism A grand theory of human development that studies observable behavior. Behaviorism is also called *learning theory* because it describes the laws and processes by which behavior is learned.

bickering Petty, peevish arguing, usually repeated and ongoing.

Big Five The five basic clusters of personality traits that remain quite stable throughout life: openness, conscientiousness, extroversion, agreeableness, and neuroticism.

bilingual schooling A strategy in which school subjects are taught in both the learner's original language and the second (majority) language.

binocular vision The ability to focus the two eyes in a coordinated manner in order to see one image. This ability is absent at birth.

biopsychosocial A term emphasizing the interaction of the three developmental domains (biosocial, cognitive, and psychosocial). All development is biopsychosocial, although the domains are studied separately.

bipolar disorder A condition characterized by extreme mood swings, from euphoria to deep depression, not caused by outside experiences.

BMI (body mass index) A person's weight in kilograms divided by the square of height in meters.

body image A person's idea of how his or her body looks.

Brazelton Neonatal Behavioral Assessment Scale (NBAS) A test often administered to newborns that measures responsiveness and records 46 behaviors, including 20 reflexes.

bulimia nervosa An eating disorder characterized by binge eating and subsequent purging, usually by induced vomiting and/or use of laxatives.

bullying aggression Unprovoked, repeated physical or verbal attack, especially on victims who are unlikely to defend themselves.

bullying Repeated, systematic efforts to inflict harm through physical, verbal, or social attack on a weaker person.

bully-victim Someone who attacks others and who is attacked as well. (Also called *provocative victims* because they do things that elicit bullying.)

C

carrier A person whose genotype includes a gene that is not expressed in the phenotype. The carried gene occurs in half of the carrier's gametes and thus is passed on to half of the carrier's children. If such a gene is inherited from both parents, the characteristic appears in the phenotype.

center day care Child care that occurs in a place especially designed for the purpose, where several paid adults care for many children. Usually the children are grouped by age, the day-care center is licensed, and providers are trained and certified in child development.

centration A characteristic of preoperational thought in which a young child focuses (centers) on one idea, excluding all others.

cerebral palsy A disorder that results from damage to the brain's motor centers. People with cerebral palsy have difficulty with muscle control, so their speech and/or body movements are impaired.

cesarean section (c-section) A surgical birth, in which incisions through the mother's abdomen and uterus allow the fetus to be removed quickly, instead of being delivered through the vagina. (Also called simply *section.*)

charter school A public school with its own set of standards that is funded and licensed by the state or local district in which it is located.

child abuse Deliberate action that is harmful to a child's physical, emotional, or sexual well-being.

child culture The particular habits, styles, and values that reflect the set of rules and rituals that characterize children as distinct from adult society.

child maltreatment Intentional harm to or avoidable endangerment of anyone under 18 years of age.

child neglect Failure to meet a child's basic physical, educational, or emotional needs.

child sexual abuse Any erotic activity that arouses an adult and excites, shames, or confuses a child, whether or not the victim protests and whether or not genital contact is involved.

child-directed speech The high-pitched, simplified, and repetitive way adults speak to infants and children. (Also called *baby talk* or *motherese.*)

chromosome One of the 46 molecules of DNA (in 23 pairs) that virtually each cell of the human body contains and that, together, contain all the genes. Other species have more or fewer chromosomes.

circadian rhythm A day–night cycle of biological activity that occurs approximately every 24 hours (*circadian* means "about a day").

classical conditioning The learning process in which a meaningful stimulus (such as the smell of food to a hungry animal) is connected with a neutral stimulus (such as the sound of a tone) that had no special meaning before conditioning. (Also called *respondent conditioning.*)

classification The logical principle that things can be organized into groups (or categories or classes) according to some characteristic they have in common.

clinical depression Feelings of hopelessness, lethargy, and worthlessness that last two weeks or more.

cluster suicides Several suicides committed by members of a group within a brief period of time.

code of ethics A set of moral principles or guidelines that members of a profession or group are expected to follow.

cognitive equilibrium In cognitive theory, a state of mental balance in which people are not confused because they can use their existing thought processes to understand current experiences and ideas.

cognitive theory A grand theory of human development that focuses on changes in how people think over time. According to this theory, our thoughts shape our attitudes, beliefs, and behaviors.

cohabitation An arrangement in which a couple live together in a committed romantic relationship but are not formally married.

cohort People born within the same historical period who therefore move through life together, experiencing the same events, new technologies, and cultural shifts at the same ages. For example, the effect of the Internet varies depending on what cohort a person belongs to.

cohort-sequential research A research design in which researchers first study several groups of people of different ages (a cross-sectional approach) and then follow those groups over the years (a longitudinal approach). (Also called *cross-sequential research* or *time-sequential research.*)

comorbid Refers to the presence of two or more unrelated disease conditions at the same time in the same person.

concrete operational thought Piaget's term for the ability to reason logically about direct experiences and perceptions.

conditioning According to behaviorism, the processes by which responses become linked to particular stimuli and learning takes place. The word *conditioning* is used to emphasize the importance of repeated practice, as when an athlete conditions his or her body to perform well by training for a long time.

conservation The principle that the amount of a substance remains the same (i.e., is conserved) even when its appearance changes.

control processes Mechanisms (including selective attention, metacognition, and emotional regulation) that combine memory, processing speed, and knowledge to regulate the analysis and flow of information within the information-processing system. (Also called *executive processes.*)

conventional moral reasoning Kohlberg's second level of moral reasoning, emphasizing social rules.

copy number variations Genes with various repeats or deletions of base pairs.

corpus callosum A long, thick band of nerve fibers that connects the left and right hemispheres of the brain and allows communication between them.

correlation A number between +1.0 and −1.0 that indicates the degree of relationship between two variables, expressed in terms of the likelihood that one variable will (or will not) occur when the other variable does (or does not). A correlation indicates only that two variables are somehow related, not that one variable causes the other to occur.

cortex The outer layers of the brain in humans and other mammals. Most thinking, feeling, and sensing involve the cortex. (Sometimes called the *neocortex.*)

co-sleeping A custom in which parents and their children (usually infants) sleep together in the same room.

couvade Symptoms of pregnancy and birth experienced by fathers.

critical period A time when a particular type of developmental growth (in body or behavior) must happen for normal development to occur.

cross-sectional research A research design that compares groups of people who differ in age but are similar in other important characteristics.

culture A system of shared beliefs, norms, behaviors, and expectations that persist over time and prescribe social behavior and assumptions.

cutting An addictive form of self-mutilation that is most prevalent among adolescent girls and that correlates with depression and drug abuse.

cyberbullying Bullying that occurs when one person spreads insults or rumors about another by means of e-mails, text messages, or cell phone videos.

D

deductive reasoning Reasoning from a general statement, premise, or principle, through logical steps, to figure out (deduce) specifics. (Also called *top-down reasoning.*)

deferred imitation A sequence in which an infant first perceives something done by someone else and then performs the same action hours or even days later.

dendrite A fiber that extends from a neuron and receives electrochemical impulses transmitted from other neurons via their axons.

deoxyribonucleic acid (DNA) The chemical composition of the molecules that contain the genes, which are the chemical instructions for cells to manufacture various proteins.

dependent variable In an experiment, the variable that may change as a result of whatever new condition or situation the experimenter adds. In other words, the dependent variable *depends* on the independent variable.

developmental psychopathology The field that uses insights into typical development to understand and remediate developmental disorders.

developmental theory A group of ideas, assumptions, and generalizations that interpret and illuminate the thousands of observations that have been made about human growth. A developmental theory provides a framework for explaining the patterns and problems of development.

deviancy training Destructive peer support in which one person shows another how to rebel against authority or social norms.

difference-equals-deficit error The mistaken belief that a deviation from some norm is necessarily inferior to behavior or characteristics that meet the standard.

disorganized attachment A type of attachment (type D) that is marked by an infant's inconsistent reactions to the caregiver's departure and return.

distal parenting Caregiving practices that involve remaining distant from a baby, providing toys, food, and face-to-face communication with minimal holding and touching.

dizygotic (DZ) twins Twins who are formed when two separate ova are fertilized by two separate sperm at roughly the same time. (Also called *fraternal twins.*)

dominant–recessive pattern The interaction of a heterozygous pair of alleles in such a way that the phenotype reflects one allele (the dominant gene) more than the other (the recessive gene).

doula A woman who helps with the birth process. Traditionally in Latin America, a doula was the only professional who attended childbirth. Now doulas are likely to arrive at the woman's home during early labor and later work alongside a hospital's staff.

Down syndrome A condition in which a person has 47 chromosomes instead of the usual 46, with 3 rather than 2 chromosomes at the 21st site. People with Down syndrome typically have distinctive characteristics, including unusual facial features, heart abnormalities, and language difficulties. (Also called *trisomy-21.*)

drug abuse The ingestion of a drug to the extent that it impairs the user's biological or psychological well-being.

dual-process model The notion that two networks exist within the human brain, one for emotional and one for analytical processing of stimuli.

dynamic perception Perception that is primed to focus on movement and change.

dynamic systems A view of human development as an ongoing, ever-changing interaction between the physical, cognitive, and psychosocial influences. The crucial understanding is that development is never static but is always affected by, and affects, many systems of development.

dyslexia Unusual difficulty with reading; thought to be the result of some neurological underdevelopment.

E

eclectic perspective The approach taken by most developmentalists, in which they apply aspects of each of the various theories of development rather than adhering exclusively to one theory.

ecological-systems approach A perspective on human development that considers all the influences from the various contexts of development. (Later renamed *bioecological theory.*)

effortful control The ability to regulate one's emotions and actions through effort, not simply through natural inclination.

egocentrism Piaget's term for children's tendency to think about the world entirely from their own personal perspective.

Electra complex The unconscious desire of girls to replace their mother and win their father's romantic love.

ELLs (English Language Learners) Children in the United States whose proficiency in English is low—usually below a cutoff score on an oral or written test. This term replaces *ESL* (English as a Second Language) because many children who primarily speak a non-English language at home are also capable in English; they are *not* ELLs.

embryo The name for a developing human organism from about the third through the eighth week after conception.

embryonic period The stage of prenatal development from approximately the third through the eighth week after conception, during which the basic forms of all body structures, including internal organs, develop.

emerging adulthood The period of life between the ages of 18 and 25. Emerging adulthood is now widely thought of as a separate developmental stage.

emotional regulation The ability to control when and how emotions are expressed.

empathy The ability to understand the emotions and concerns of another person, especially when they differ from one's own.

empirical Based on observation, experience, or experiment; not theoretical.

entity approach to intelligence An approach to understanding intelligence that sees ability as innate, a fixed quantity present at birth; those who hold this view do not believe that effort enhances achievement.

epigenetic Referring to environmental factors that affect genes and genetic expression—enhancing, halting, shaping, or altering the expression of genes and resulting in a phenotype that may differ markedly from the genotype.

equifinality A basic principle of developmental psychopathology that holds that one symptom can have many causes.

estradiol A sex hormone, considered the chief estrogen. Females produce much more estradiol than males do.

ethnic group People whose ancestors were born in the same region and who often share a language, culture, and religion.

ethnotheory A theory that underlies the values and practices of a culture but is not usually apparent to the people within the culture.

experience-dependent brain functions Brain functions that depend on particular, variable experiences and that therefore may or may not develop in a particular infant.

experience-expectant brain functions Brain functions that require certain basic common experiences (which an infant can be expected to have) in order to develop normally.

explicit memory Memory that is easy to retrieve on demand (as in a specific test). Most explicit memory involves consciously learned words, data, and concepts.

extended family A family of three or more generations living in one household.

externalizing problems Difficulty with emotional regulation that involves expressing powerful feelings through uncontrolled physical or verbal outbursts, as by lashing out at other people or breaking things.

extreme sports Forms of recreation that include apparent risk of injury or death and that are attractive and thrilling as a result.

extremely low birthweight (ELBW) A body weight at birth of less than 2 pounds, 3 ounces (1,000 grams).

extrinsic motivation A drive, or reason to pursue a goal, that arises from the need to have one's achievements rewarded from outside, perhaps by receiving material possessions or another person's esteem.

F

false positive The result of a laboratory test that reports something as true when in fact it is not true. This can occur for pregnancy tests, when a woman might not be pregnant even though the test says she is, or during pregnancy when a problem is reported that actually does not exist.

family day care Child care that occurs in the home of someone to whom the child is not related and who usually cares for several children of various ages.

family function The way a family works to meet the needs of its members. Children need families to provide basic material necessities, to encourage learning, to help them develop self-respect, to nurture friendships, and to foster harmony and stability.

family structure The legal and genetic relationships among relatives living in the same home; includes nuclear family, extended family, stepfamily, and so on.

fast-mapping The speedy and sometimes imprecise way in which children learn new words by tentatively placing them in mental categories according to their perceived meaning.

fetal alcohol syndrome (FAS) A cluster of birth defects, including abnormal facial characteristics, slow physical growth, and retarded mental development, that may occur in the fetus of a woman who drinks alcohol while pregnant.

fetal period The stage of prenatal development from the ninth week after conception until birth, during which the fetus gains about 7 pounds (more than 3,000 grams) and organs become more mature, gradually able to function on their own.

fetus The name for a developing human organism from the start of the ninth week after conception until birth.

fine motor skills Physical abilities involving small body movements, especially of the hands and fingers, such as drawing and picking up a coin. (The word *fine* here means "small.")

Flynn effect The rise in average IQ scores that has occurred over the decades in many nations.

fMRI Functional magnetic resonance imaging, a measuring technique in which the brain's electrical excitement indicates activation anywhere in the brain; fMRI helps researchers locate neurological responses to stimuli.

focus on appearance A characteristic of preoperational thought in which a young child ignores all attributes that are not apparent.

foreclosure Erikson's term for premature identity formation, which occurs when an adolescent adopts parents' or society's roles and values wholesale, without questioning or analysis.

formal operational thought In Piaget's theory, the fourth and final stage of cognitive development, characterized by more systematic logical thinking and by the ability to understand and systematically manipulate abstract concepts.

foster care A legal, publicly supported system in which a maltreated child is removed from the parents' custody and entrusted to another adult or family, which is reimbursed for expenses incurred in meeting the child's needs.

fragile X syndrome A genetic disorder in which part of the X chromosome seems to be attached to the rest of it by a very thin string of molecules. The cause is a single gene that has more than 200 repetitions of one triplet.

G

gamete A reproductive cell; that is, a sperm or ovum that can produce a new individual if it combines with a gamete from the other sex to make a zygote.

gender differences Differences in the roles and behaviors of males and females that are prescribed by the culture.

gender identity A person's acceptance of the roles and behaviors that society associates with the biological categories of male and female.

gender schema A cognitive concept or general belief based on one's experiences—in this case, a child's understanding of sex differences.

gene A small section of a chromosome; the basic unit for the transmission of heredity. A gene consists of a string of chemicals that provide instructions for the cell to manufacture certain proteins.

generational forgetting The idea that each new generation forgets what the previous generation learned. As used here, the term refers to knowledge about the harm drugs can do.

genetic counseling Consultation and testing by trained experts that enable individuals to learn about their genetic heritage, including harmful conditions that they might pass along to any children they may conceive.

genome The full set of genes that are the instructions to make an individual member of a certain species.

genotype An organism's entire genetic inheritance, or genetic potential.

germinal period The first two weeks of prenatal development after conception, characterized by rapid cell division and the beginning of cell differentiation.

gonads The paired sex glands (ovaries in females, testicles in males). The gonads produce hormones and gametes.

goodness of fit A similarity of temperament and values that produces a smooth interaction between an individual and his or her social context, including family, school, and community.

grammar All the methods—word order, verb forms, and so on—that languages use to communicate meaning, apart from the words themselves.

gross motor skills Physical abilities involving large body movements, such as walking and jumping. (The word *gross* here means "big.")

growth spurt The relatively sudden and rapid physical growth that occurs during puberty. Each body part increases in size on a schedule: Weight usually precedes height, and growth of the limbs precedes growth of the torso.

guided participation The process by which people learn from others who guide their experiences and explorations.

H

habituation The process of becoming accustomed to an object or event through repeated exposure to it, and thus becoming less interested in it.

Head Start A federally funded early-childhood intervention program for low-income children of preschool age.

head-sparing A biological mechanism that protects the brain when malnutrition affects body growth. The brain is the last part of the body to be damaged by malnutrition.

heritability A statistic that indicates what percentage of the variation in a particular trait within a particular population, in a particular context and era, can be traced to genes.

heterozygous Referring to two genes of one pair that differ in some way. Typically one allele has only a few base pairs that differ from the other member of the pair.

hidden curriculum The unofficial, unstated, or implicit rules and priorities that influence the academic curriculum and every other aspect of learning in a school.

high-stakes test An evaluation that is critical in determining success or failure. If a single test determines whether a student will graduate or be promoted, it is a high-stakes test.

hippocampus A brain structure that is a central processor of memory, especially memory for locations.

holophrase A single word that is used to express a complete, meaningful thought.

home schooling Education in which children are taught at home, usually by their parents.

homozygous Referring to two genes of one pair that are exactly the same in every letter of their code. Most gene pairs are homozygous.

hormone An organic chemical substance that is produced by one body tissue and conveyed via the bloodstream to another to affect some physiological function.

HPA (hypothalamus–pituitary–adrenal) axis A sequence of hormone production originating in the hypothalamus and moving to the pituitary and then to the adrenal glands.

HPG (hypothalamus–pituitary–gonad) axis A sequence of hormone production originating in the hypothalamus and moving to the pituitary and then to the gonads.

Human Genome Project An international effort to map the complete human genetic code. This effort was essentially completed in 2001, though analysis is ongoing.

humanism A theory that stresses the potential of all humans for good and the belief that all people have the same basic needs, regardless of culture, gender, or background.

hypothalamus A brain area that responds to the amygdala and the hippocampus to produce hormones that activate other parts of the brain and body.

hypothesis A specific prediction that can be tested.

hypothetical thought Reasoning that includes propositions and possibilities that may not reflect reality.

I

identification An attempt to defend one's self-concept by taking on the behaviors and attitudes of someone else.

identity achievement Erikson's term for the attainment of identity, or the point at which a person understands who he or she is as a unique individual, in accord with past experiences and future plans.

identity versus role confusion Erikson's term for the fifth stage of development, in which the person tries to figure out "Who am I?" but is confused as to which of many possible roles to adopt.

imaginary audience The other people who, in an adolescent's egocentric belief, are watching and taking note of his or her appearance, ideas, and behavior. This belief makes many teenagers very self-conscious.

imaginary friends Make-believe friends who exist only in a child's imagination; increasingly common from ages 3 through 7, they combat loneliness and aid emotional regulation.

immersion A strategy in which instruction in all school subjects occurs in the second (usually the majority) language that a child is learning.

immunization The process of protecting a person against a disease, via antibodies. Immunization can happen naturally, when someone survives a disease, or medically, usually via a small dose of the virus that stimulates the production of antibodies and thus renders a person immune. (Also called *vaccination*.)

implantation The process, beginning about 10 days after conception, in which the developing organism burrows into the placenta that lines the uterus, where it can be nourished and protected as it continues to develop.

implicit memory Unconscious or automatic memory that is usually stored via habits, emotional responses, routine procedures, and various sensations.

in vitro fertilization (IVF) Fertilization that takes place outside a woman's body (as in a glass laboratory dish). The procedure involves mixing sperm with ova that have been surgically removed from the woman's ovary. If a zygote is produced, it is inserted into a woman's uterus, where it may implant and develop into a baby.

incremental approach to intelligence An approach to understanding intelligence that holds that intelligence can be directly increased by effort; those who subscribe to this view believe they can master whatever they seek to learn if they pay attention, participate in class, study, complete their homework, and so on.

independent variable In an experiment, the variable that is introduced to see what effect it has on the dependent variable. (Also called *experimental variable*.)

individual education plan (IEP) A document that specifies educational goals and plans for a child with special needs.

inductive reasoning Reasoning from one or more specific experiences or facts to reach (induce) a general conclusion. (Also called *bottom-up reasoning*.)

industry versus inferiority The fourth of Erikson's eight psychosocial crises, during which children attempt to master many skills, developing a sense of themselves as either industrious or inferior, competent or incompetent.

information-processing theory A perspective that compares human thinking processes, by analogy, to computer analysis of data, including sensory input, connections, stored memories, and output.

initiative versus guilt Erikson's third psychosocial crisis, in which children undertake new skills and activities and feel guilty when they do not succeed at them.

injury control/harm reduction Practices that are aimed at anticipating, controlling, and preventing dangerous activities; these practices reflect the beliefs that accidents are not random and that injuries can be made less harmful if proper controls are in place.

insecure-avoidant attachment A pattern of attachment (type A) in which an infant avoids connection with the caregiver, as when the infant seems not to care about the caregiver's presence, departure, or return.

insecure-resistant/ambivalent attachment A pattern of attachment (type C) in which anxiety and uncertainty are evident, as when an infant becomes very upset at separation from the caregiver and both resists and seeks contact on reunion.

Institutional Review Board (IRB) A group within most educational and medical institutions who ensure that research follows established ethical guidelines. Unlike in prior decades, most research in human development cannot begin without IRB approval.

instrumental aggression Behavior that hurts someone else because the aggressor wants to get or keep a possession or a privilege.

internalizing problems Difficulty with emotional regulation that involves turning one's emotional distress inward, as by feeling excessively guilty, ashamed, or worthless.

intimacy versus isolation The sixth of Erikson's eight stages of development. Adults seek someone with whom to share their lives in an enduring and self-sacrificing commitment. Without such commitment they risk profound loneliness and isolation.

intrinsic motivation A drive, or reason to pursue a goal, that comes from inside a person, such as the need to feel smart or competent.

intuitive thought Thought that arises from an emotion or a hunch, beyond rational explanation, and is influenced by past experiences and cultural assumptions.

invincibility fable An adolescent's egocentric conviction that he or she cannot be overcome or even harmed by anything that might defeat a normal mortal, such as unprotected sex, drug abuse, or high-speed driving.

IQ test A test designed to measure intellectual aptitude, or ability to learn in school. Originally, intelligence was defined as mental age divided by chronological age, times 100—hence the term *intelligence quotient*, or *IQ*.

irreversibility A characteristic of preoperational thought in which a young child thinks that nothing can be undone. A thing cannot be restored to the way it was before a change occurred.

K

kangaroo care A form of newborn care in which mothers (and sometimes fathers) rest their babies on their naked chests, like kangaroo mothers that carry their immature newborns in a pouch on their abdomen.

kinship care A form of foster care in which a relative of a maltreated child, usually a grandparent, becomes the approved caregiver.

knowledge base A body of knowledge in a particular area that makes it easier to master new information in that area.

kwashiorkor A disease of chronic malnutrition during childhood, in which a protein deficiency makes the child more vulnerable to other diseases, such as measles, diarrhea, and influenza.

L

language acquisition device (LAD) Chomsky's term for a hypothesized mental structure that enables humans to learn language, including the basic aspects of grammar, vocabulary, and intonation.

latency Freud's term for middle childhood, during which children's emotional drives and psychosexual needs are quiet (latent). Freud thought that sexual conflicts from earlier stages are only temporarily submerged, bursting forth again at puberty.

lateralization Literally, sidedness, referring to the specialization in certain functions by each side of the brain, with one side dominant for each activity. The left side of the brain controls the right side of the body, and vice versa.

learning disability A marked delay in a particular area of learning that is not caused by an apparent physical disability, by mental retardation, or by an unusually stressful home environment.

least restrictive environment (LRE) A legal requirement that children with special needs be assigned to the most general educational context in which they can be expected to learn.

leptin A hormone that affects appetite and is believed to affect the onset of puberty. Leptin levels increase during childhood and peak at around age 12.

life-course-persistent offender A person whose criminal activity typically begins in early adolescence and continues throughout life; a career criminal.

linked lives Lives in which the success, health, and well-being of each family member are connected to those of other members, including members of another generation, as in the relationship between parents and children.

"little scientist" The stage-five toddler (age 12 to 18 months) who experiments without anticipating the results, using trial and error in active and creative exploration.

longitudinal research A research design in which the same individuals are followed over time, as their development is repeatedly assessed.

long-term memory The component of the information-processing system in which virtually limitless amounts of information can be stored indefinitely.

low birthweight (LBW) A body weight at birth of less than 5½ pounds (2,500 grams).

M

marasmus A disease of severe protein-calorie malnutrition during early infancy, in which growth stops, body tissues waste away, and the infant eventually dies.

menarche A girl's first menstrual period, signaling that she has begun ovulation. Pregnancy is biologically possible, but ovulation and menstruation are often irregular for years after menarche.

metacognition "Thinking about thinking," or the ability to evaluate a cognitive task in order to determine how best to accomplish it, and then to monitor and adjust one's performance on that task.

middle childhood The period between early childhood and early adolescence, approximately from ages 6 to 11.

middle school A school for children in the grades between elementary and high school. Middle school usually begins with grade 6 and ends with grade 8.

mirror neurons Cells in an observer's brain that are activated by watching an action performed by someone else as they would be if the observer had personally performed that action.

modeling The central process of social learning, by which a person observes the actions of others and then copies them.

monozygotic (MZ) twins Twins who originate from one zygote that splits apart very early in development. (Also called *identical twins.*) Other monozygotic multiple births (such as triplets and quadruplets) can occur as well.

Montessori schools Schools that offer early-childhood education based on the philosophy of Maria Montessori, which emphasizes careful work and tasks that each young child can do.

moratorium An adolescent's choice of a socially acceptable way to postpone making identity-achievement decisions. Going to college is a common example.

motor skills The learned abilities to move some part of the body, in actions ranging from a large leap to a flicker of the eyelid. (The word *motor* here refers to movement of muscles.)

multifactorial Referring to a trait that is affected by many factors, both genetic and environmental, that enhance, halt, shape, or alter the expression of genes, resulting in a phenotype that may differ markedly from the genotype.

multifinality A basic principle of developmental psychopathology that holds that one cause can have many (multiple) final manifestations.

multiple intelligences The idea that human intelligence is comprised of a varied set of abilities rather than a single, all-encompassing one.

myelination The process by which axons become coated with myelin, a fatty substance that speeds the transmission of nerve impulses from neuron to neuron.

N

naming explosion A sudden increase in an infant's vocabulary, especially in the number of nouns, that begins at about 18 months of age.

National Assessment of Educational Progress (NAEP) An ongoing and nationally representative measure of U.S. children's achievement in reading, mathematics, and other subjects over time; nicknamed "the Nation's Report Card."

nature In development, nature refers to the traits, capacities, and limitations that each individual inherits genetically from his or her parents at the moment of conception.

neglectful/uninvolved parenting An approach to child rearing in which the parents are indifferent toward their children and unaware of what is going on in their children's lives.

neurons The billions of nerve cells in the central nervous system, especially the brain.

No Child Left Behind Act A U.S. law enacted in 2001 that was intended to increase accountability in education by requiring states to qualify for federal educational funding by administering standardized tests to measure school achievement.

norm An average, or typical, standard of behavior or accomplishment, such as the norm for age of walking or the norm for greeting a stranger.

nuclear family A family that consists of a father, a mother, and their biological children under age 18.

nurture In development, nurture includes all the environmental influences that affect the individual after conception. This includes everything from the mother's nutrition while pregnant to the cultural influences in the nation.

O

obesity In a child, having a BMI above the 95th percentile, according to the U.S. Centers for Disease Control's 1980 standards for children of a given age.

object permanence The realization that objects (including people) still exist when they can no longer be seen, touched, or heard.

Oedipus complex The unconscious desire of young boys to replace their father and win their mother's romantic love.

operant conditioning The learning process by which a particular action is followed by something desired (which makes the person or animal more likely to repeat the action) or by something unwanted (which makes the action less likely to be repeated). (Also called *instrumental conditioning.*)

overimitation When a person imitates an action that is not a relevant part of the behavior to be learned. Overimitation is common among 2- to 6-year-olds when they imitate adult actions that are irrelevant and inefficient.

overregularization The application of rules of grammar even when exceptions occur, making the language seem more "regular" than it actually is.

overweight In a child, having a BMI above the 85th percentile, according to the U.S. Centers for Disease Control's 1980 standards for children of a given age.

P

parasuicide Any potentially lethal action against the self that does not result in death. (Also called *attempted suicide* or *failed suicide.*)

parental alliance Cooperation between a mother and a father based on their mutual commitment to their children. In a parental alliance, the parents support each other in their shared parental roles.

parental monitoring Parents' ongoing awareness of what their children are doing, where, and with whom.

parent–infant bond The strong, loving connection that forms as parents hold, examine, and feed their newborn.

peer pressure Encouragement to conform to one's friends or contemporaries in behavior, dress, and attitude; usually considered a negative force, as when adolescent peers encourage one another to defy adult authority.

people preference A universal principle of infant perception, specifically an innate attraction to other humans, evident in visual, auditory, and other preferences.

percentile A point on a ranking scale of 0 to 100. The 50th percentile is the midpoint; half the people in the population being studied rank higher and half rank lower.

perception The mental processing of sensory information when the brain interprets a sensation. Perception occurs in the cortex.

permanency planning An effort by child-welfare authorities to find a long-term living situation that will provide stability and support for a maltreated child. A goal is to avoid repeated changes of caregiver or school, which can be particularly harmful to the child.

permissive parenting An approach to child rearing that is characterized by high nurturance and communication but little discipline, guidance, or control. (Also called *indulgent parenting*.)

perseveration The tendency to persevere in, or stick to, one thought or action for a long time.

personal fable An aspect of adolescent egocentrism characterized by an adolescent's belief that his or her thoughts, feelings, and experiences are unique, more wonderful or awful than anyone else's.

phallic stage Freud's third stage of development, when the penis becomes the focus of concern and pleasure.

phenotype The observable characteristics of a person, including appearance, personality, intelligence, and all other traits.

phenylketonuria (PKU) A genetic disorder in which a child's body is unable to metabolize an amino acid called phenylalanine. Unless the infant immediately begins a special diet, the resulting buildup of phenylalanine in body fluids causes brain damage, progressive mental retardation, and other symptoms.

phonics approach Teaching reading by first teaching the sounds of each letter and of various letter combinations.

PISA (Programme for International Student Assessment) An international test taken by 15-year-olds in 50 nations that is designed to measure problem solving and cognition in daily life.

pituitary A gland in the brain that responds to a signal from the hypothalamus by producing many hormones, including those that regulate growth and that control other glands, among them the adrenal and sex glands.

plasticity The idea that abilities, personality, and other human characteristics can change over time. Plasticity is particularly evident during childhood, but even older adults are not always "set in their ways."

polygamous family A family consisting of one man, several wives, and their children.

polygenic Referring to a trait that is influenced by many genes.

postconventional moral reasoning Kohlberg's third level of moral reasoning, emphasizing moral principles.

postformal thought A proposed adult stage of cognitive development, following Piaget's four stages. Postformal thought goes beyond adolescent thinking by being more practical, more flexible, and more dialectical (i.e., more capable of combining contradictory elements into a comprehensive whole).

postpartum depression A new mother's feelings of inadequacy and sadness in the days and weeks after giving birth.

post-traumatic stress disorder (PTSD) An anxiety disorder that develops as a delayed reaction to having experienced or witnessed a profoundly shocking or frightening event, such as rape, severe beating, war, or natural disaster. Its symptoms may include flashbacks to the event, hyperactivity and hypervigilance, displaced anger, sleeplessness, nightmares, sudden terror or anxiety, and confusion between fantasy and reality.

pragmatics The practical use of language that includes the ability to adjust language communication according to audience and context.

preconventional moral reasoning Kohlberg's first level of moral reasoning, emphasizing rewards and punishments.

prefrontal cortex The area of cortex at the front of the brain that specializes in anticipation, planning, and impulse control.

preoperational intelligence Piaget's term for cognitive development between the ages of about 2 and 6; it includes language and imagination (which involve symbolic thought), but logical, operational thinking is not yet possible at this stage.

preterm A birth that occurs 3 or more weeks before the full 38 weeks of the typical pregnancy—that is, at 35 or fewer weeks after conception.

primary circular reactions The first of three types of feedback loops in sensorimotor intelligence, this one involving the infant's own body. The infant senses motion, sucking, noise, and other stimuli and tries to understand them.

primary prevention Actions that change overall background conditions to prevent some unwanted event or circumstance, such as injury, disease, or abuse.

primary sex characteristics The parts of the body that are directly involved in reproduction, including the vagina, uterus, ovaries, testicles, and penis.

private school A school funded by tuition charges, endowments, and often religious or other non-profit sponsors.

private speech The internal dialogue that occurs when people talk to themselves (either silently or out loud).

Progress in International Reading Literacy Study (PIRLS) Inaugurated in 2001, a planned five-year cycle of international trend studies in the reading ability of fourth-graders.

prosocial behavior Actions that are helpful and kind but are of no obvious benefit to oneself.

protein-calorie malnutrition A condition in which a person does not consume sufficient food of any kind. This deprivation can result in several illnesses, severe weight loss, and even death.

proximal parenting Caregiving practices that involve being physically close to a baby, with frequent holding and touching.

pruning When applied to brain development, the process by which unused connections in the brain atrophy and die.

psychoanalytic theory A grand theory of human development that holds that irrational, unconscious drives and motives, often originating in childhood, underlie human behavior.

psychological control A disciplinary technique that involves threatening to withdraw love and support and that relies on a child's feelings of guilt and gratitude to the parents.

psychopathology An illness or disorder of the mind.

puberty The time between the first onrush of hormones and full adult physical development. Puberty usually lasts three to five years. Many more years are required to achieve psychosocial maturity.

Q

qualitative research Research that considers qualities, not quantities. Narrative accounts and individual variations are often stressed in qualitative research.

quantitative research Research that provides data that can be expressed with numbers, such as ranks or scales.

R

race A group of people who are regarded by themselves or by others as distinct from other groups on the basis of physical appearance, typically skin color. Social scientists think race is a misleading concept, as biological differences are not signified by outward appearance.

reaction time The time it takes to respond to a stimulus, either physically (with a reflexive movement such as an eyeblink) or cognitively (with a thought).

reactive aggression An impulsive retaliation for another person's intentional or accidental action, verbal or physical.

reflex An unlearned, involuntary action or movement in response to a stimulus. A reflex occurs without conscious thought.

Reggio Emilia A program of early-childhood education that originated in the town of Reggio Emilia, Italy, and that encourages each child's creativity in a carefully designed setting.

reinforcement When a behavior is followed by something desired, such as food for a hungry animal or a welcoming smile for a lonely person.

relational aggression Nonphysical acts, such as insults or social rejection, aimed at harming the social connection between the victim and other people.

REM sleep Rapid eye movement sleep, a stage of sleep characterized by flickering eyes behind closed lids, dreaming, and rapid brain waves.

reminder session A perceptual experience that helps a person recollect an idea, a thing, or an experience.

replication Repeating a study, usually using different participants, perhaps of another age, SES, or culture.

reported maltreatment Harm or endangerment about which someone has notified the authorities.

resilience The capacity to adapt well to significant adversity and to overcome serious stress.

response to intervention (RTI) An educational strategy intended to help children in early grades who demonstrate below-average achievement by means of special intervention.

role confusion A situation in which an adolescent does not seem to know or care what his or her identity is. (Sometimes called *identity* or *role diffusion.*)

rough-and-tumble play Play that mimics aggression through wrestling, chasing, or hitting, but in which there is no intent to harm.

rumination Repeatedly thinking and talking about past experiences; can contribute to depression.

S

scaffolding Temporary support that is tailored to a learner's needs and abilities and aimed at helping the learner master the next task in a given learning process.

science of human development The science that seeks to understand how and why people of all ages and circumstances change or remain the same over time.

scientific method A way to answer questions using empirical research and data-based conclusions.

scientific observation A method of testing a hypothesis by unobtrusively watching and recording participants' behavior in a systematic and objective manner—in a natural setting, in a laboratory, or in searches of archival data.

secondary circular reactions The second of three types of feedback loops in sensorimotor intelligence, this one involving people and objects. Infants respond to other people, to toys, and to any other object they can touch or move.

secondary education Literally, the period after primary education (elementary or grade school) and before tertiary education (college). It usually occurs from about age 12 to 18, although there is some variation by school and by nation.

secondary prevention Actions that avert harm in a high-risk situation, such as stopping a car before it hits a pedestrian.

secondary sex characteristics Physical traits that are not directly involved in reproduction but that indicate sexual maturity, such as a man's beard and a woman's breasts.

secular trend The long-term upward or downward direction of a certain set of statistical measurements, as opposed to a smaller, shorter cyclical variation. As an example, over the last two centuries, because of improved nutrition and medical care, children have tended to reach their adult height earlier and their adult height has increased.

secure attachment A relationship (type B) in which an infant obtains both comfort and confidence from the presence of his or her caregiver.

selective adaptation The process by which living creatures (including people) adjust to their environment. Genes that enhance survival and reproductive ability are selected, over the generations, to become more prevalent.

selective attention The ability to concentrate on some stimuli while ignoring others.

self-awareness A person's realization that he or she is a distinct individual, whose body, mind, and actions are separate from those of other people.

self-concept A person's understanding of who he or she is, in relation to self-esteem, appearance, personality, and various traits.

self-efficacy In social learning theory, the belief of some people that they are able to change themselves and effectively alter the social context.

self-righting The inborn drive to remedy a developmental deficit; literally, to return to sitting or standing upright, after being tipped over. People of all ages have self-righting impulses, for emotional as well as physical imbalance.

sensation The response of a sensory system (eyes, ears, skin, tongue, nose) when it detects a stimulus.

sensitive period A time when a certain type of development is most likely, although it may still happen later with more difficulty. For example, early childhood is considered a sensitive period for language learning.

sensorimotor intelligence Piaget's term for the way infants think—by using their senses and motor skills—during the first period of cognitive development.

sensory memory The component of the information-processing system in which incoming stimulus information is stored for a split second to allow it to be processed. (Also called the *sensory register.*)

separation anxiety An infant's distress when a familiar caregiver leaves, most obvious between 9 and 14 months.

sex differences Biological differences between males and females, in organs, hormones, and body type.

sexual orientation A term that refers to whether a person is sexually and romantically attracted to others of the same sex, the opposite sex, or both sexes.

sexually transmitted infection (STI) A disease spread by sexual contact, including syphilis, gonorrhea, genital herpes, chlamydia, and HIV.

shaken baby syndrome A life-threatening injury that occurs when an infant is forcefully shaken back and forth, a motion that ruptures blood vessels in the brain and breaks neural connections.

single-parent family A family that consists of only one parent and his or her biological children under age 18.

small for gestational age (SGA) A term for a baby whose birthweight is significantly lower than expected, given the time since conception. For example, a 5-pound (2,265-gram) newborn is considered SGA if born on time but not SGA if born two months early. (Also called *small-for-dates.*)

social construction An idea that is built on shared perceptions, not on objective reality. Many age-related terms (such as *childhood, adolescence, yuppie,* and *senior citizen*) are social constructions, connected to biological traits but strongly influenced by social assumptions.

social learning Learning that is accomplished by observing others.

social learning theory An extension of behaviorism that emphasizes the influence that other people have over a person's behavior. Even without specific reinforcement, every individual learns many things through observation and imitation of other people. (Also called *observational learning.*)

social mediation Human interaction that expands and advances understanding, often through words that one person uses to explain something to another.

social referencing Seeking information about how to react to an unfamiliar or ambiguous object or event by observing someone else's expressions and reactions. That other person becomes a social reference.

social smile A smile evoked by a human face, normally evident in infants about six weeks after birth.

sociocultural theory A newer theory that holds that development results from the dynamic interaction of each person with the surrounding social and cultural forces.

sociodramatic play Pretend play in which children act out various roles and themes in stories that they create.

socioeconomic status (SES) A person's position in society as determined by income, occupation, education, and place of residence. (Sometimes called *social class.*)

spermarche A boy's first ejaculation of sperm. Erections can occur as early as infancy, but ejaculation signals sperm production. Spermarche may occur during sleep (in a "wet dream") or via direct stimulation.

static reasoning A characteristic of preoperational thought in which a young child thinks that nothing changes. Whatever is now has always been and always will be.

stem cells Cells from which any other specialized type of cell can form.

stereotype threat The possibility that one's appearance or behavior will be misread to confirm another person's oversimplified, prejudiced attitudes.

still-face technique An experimental practice in which an adult keeps his or her face unmoving and expressionless in face-to-face interaction with an infant.

Strange Situation A laboratory procedure for measuring attachment by evoking infants' reactions to stress in eight episodes of three minutes each.

stranger wariness An infant's expression of concern—a quiet stare, clinging to a familiar person, or sadness—when a stranger appears.

stunting The failure of children to grow to a normal height for their age due to severe and chronic malnutrition.

substantiated maltreatment Harm or endangerment that has been reported, investigated, and verified.

sudden infant death syndrome (SIDS) A situation in which a seemingly healthy infant, usually between 2 and 6 months old, suddenly stops breathing and dies unexpectedly while asleep.

suicidal ideation Thinking about suicide, usually with some serious emotional and intellectual or cognitive overtones.

sunk cost fallacy The mistaken belief that if money, time, or effort that cannot be recovered (a "sunk cost," in economic terms) has already been invested in some endeavor, then more should be invested in an effort to reach the goal. Because of this fallacy, people spend money trying to fix a "lemon" of a car or send more troops to fight a losing battle.

superego In psychoanalytic theory, the judgmental part of the personality that internalizes the moral standards of the parents.

survey A research method in which information is collected from a large number of people by interviews, written questionnaires, or some other means.

symbolic thought A major accomplishment of preoperational intelligence that allows a child to think symbolically, including understanding that words can refer to things not seen and that an item, such as a flag, can symbolize something else (in this case, for instance, a country).

synapse The intersection between the axon of one neuron and the dendrites of other neurons.

synchrony A coordinated, rapid, and smooth exchange of responses between a caregiver and an infant.

T

temperament Inborn differences between one person and another in emotions, activity, and self-regulation. Temperament is epigenetic, originating in genes but affected by child-rearing practices.

teratogens Agents and conditions, including viruses, drugs, and chemicals, that can impair prenatal development and result in birth defects or even death.

tertiary circular reactions The third of three types of feedback loops in sensorimotor intelligence, this one involving active exploration and experimentation. Infants explore a range of new activities, varying their responses as a way of learning about the world.

tertiary prevention Actions, such as immediate and effective medical treatment, that are taken after an adverse event (such as illness or injury) occurs and that are aimed at reducing the harm or preventing disability.

testosterone A sex hormone, the best known of the androgens (male hormones); secreted in far greater amounts by males than by females.

theory A comprehensive set of ideas.

theory of mind A person's theory of what other people might be thinking. In order to have a theory of mind, children must realize that other people are not necessarily thinking the same thoughts that they themselves are. That realization seldom occurs before age 4.

theory-theory The idea that children attempt to explain everything they see and hear by constructing theories.

threshold effect In prenatal development, when a teratogen is relatively harmless in small doses but becomes harmful once exposure reaches a certain level (the threshold).

time-out A disciplinary technique in which a child is separated from other people for a specified time.

transient exuberance The great but temporary increase in the number of dendrites that develop in an infant's brain during the first two years of life.

transitive inference The ability to figure out the unspoken link between one fact and another.

Trends in Math and Science Study (TIMSS) An international assessment of the math and science skills of fourth- and eighth-graders. Although the TIMSS is very useful, different countries' scores are not always comparable because sample selection, test administration, and content validity are hard to keep uniform.

trust versus mistrust Erikson's first psychosocial crisis. Infants learn basic trust if their basic needs (for food, comfort, attention, and so on) are met.

U

ultrasound An image of a fetus (or an internal organ) produced by using high-frequency sound waves. (Also called *sonogram.*)

V

very low birthweight (VLBW) A body weight at birth of less than 3 pounds, 5 ounces (1,500 grams).

visual cliff An experimental apparatus that gives the illusion of a sudden drop-off between one horizontal surface and another.

voucher Public subsidy for tuition payment at a non-public school. Vouchers vary a great deal from place to place, not only in amount and availability, but in restrictions as to who gets them and what schools accept them.

W

wasting The tendency for children to be severely underweight for their age as a result of malnutrition.

whole-language approach Teaching reading by encouraging early use of all language skills—talking and listening, reading and writing.

withdrawn-rejected Rejected by peers because of timid, withdrawn, and anxious behavior.

working memory The component of the information-processing system in which current conscious mental activity occurs. (Formerly called *short-term memory.*)

working model In cognitive theory, a set of assumptions that the individual uses to organize perceptions and experiences. For example, a person might assume that other people are always trustworthy and be surprised when this working model of human behavior is proven inadequate.

X

X-linked A gene carried on the X chromosome. If a male inherits an X-linked recessive trait from his mother, he expresses that trait because the Y from his father has no counteracting gene. Females are more likely to be carriers of X-linked traits but are less likely to express them.

XX A 23rd chromosome pair that consists of two X-shaped chromosomes, one each from the mother and the father. XX zygotes become females.

XY A 23rd chromosome pair that consists of an X-shaped chromosome from the mother and a Y-shaped chromosome from the father. XY zygotes become males.

Z

zone of proximal development In sociocultural theory, a metaphorical area, or "zone," surrounding a learner that includes all the skills, knowledge, and concepts that the person is close ("proximal") to acquiring but cannot yet master without help.

zygote The single cell formed from the union of two gametes, a sperm and an ovum.

References

Aarnoudse-Moens, Cornelieke S. H., Smidts, Diana P., Oosterlaan, Jaap, Duivenvoorden, Hugo J., & Weisglas-Kuperus, Nynke. (2009). Executive function in very preterm children at early school age. *Journal of Abnormal Child Psychology, 37,* 981–993.

Abrams, Dominic, Rutland, Adam, Ferrell, Jennifer M., & Pelletier, Joseph. (2008). Children's judgments of disloyal and immoral peer behavior: Subjective group dynamics in minimal intergroup contexts. *Child Development, 79,* 444–461.

Abreu, Guida de. (2008). From mathematics learning out-of-school to multicultural classrooms: A cultural psychology perspective. In Lyn D. English, Maria Bartolini Bussi, Graham A. Jones, Richard A. Lesh, & Bharath Sriraman (Eds.), *Handbook of international research in mathematics education* (2nd ed., pp. 323–353). New York, NY: Routledge.

Abrevaya, Jason. (2009). Are there missing girls in the United States? Evidence from birth data. *American Economic Journal: Applied Economics, 1,* 1–34.

Accardo, Pasquale. (2006). Who's training whom? *The Journal of Pediatrics, 149,* 151–152.

Ackerman, Joshua M., & Kenrick, Douglas T. (2009). Cooperative courtship: Helping friends raise and raze relationship barriers. *Personality and Social Psychology Bulletin, 35,* 1285–1300.

Adam, Emma K., Klimes-Dougan, Bonnie, & Gunnar, Megan R. (2007). Social regulation of the adrenocortical response to stress in infants, children, and adolescents: Implications for psychopathology and education. In Donna Coch, Geraldine Dawson, & Kurt W. Fischer (Eds.), *Human behavior, learning, and the developing brain: Atypical development* (pp. 264–304). New York, NY: Guilford Press.

Adams, Caralee J. (2011, June 9). Popularity offers challenges for community colleges. *Education Week,* pp. 14–17.

Adamson, Lauren B., & Bakeman, Roger. (2006). Development of displaced speech in early mother-child conversations. *Child Development, 77,* 186–200.

Adolph, Karen E., & Berger, Sarah E. (2005). Physical and motor development. In Marc H. Bornstein & Michael E. Lamb (Eds.), *Developmental science: An advanced textbook* (5th ed., pp. 223–281). Mahwah, NJ: Erlbaum.

Adolph, Karen E., Vereijken, Beatrix, & Shrout, Patrick E. (2003). What changes in infant walking and why. *Child Development, 74,* 475–497.

Afifi, Tracie O., Enns, Murray W., Cox, Brian J., Asmundson, Gordon J. G., Stein, Murray B., & Sareen, Jitender. (2008). Population attributable fractions of psychiatric disorders and suicide ideation and attempts associated with adverse childhood experiences. *American Journal of Public Health, 98,* 946–952.

Ahmed, Parvez, & Jaakkola, Jouni J. K. (2007). Maternal occupation and adverse pregnancy outcomes: A Finnish population-based study. *Occupational Medicine, 57,* 417–423.

Ainsworth, Mary D. Salter. (1973). The development of infant-mother attachment. In Bettye M. Caldwell & Henry N. Ricciuti (Eds.), *Review of child development research* (Vol. 3, pp. 1–94). Chicago, IL: University of Chicago Press.

Akiba, Daisuke, & García Coll, Cynthia. (2004). Effective interventions with children of color and their families: A contextual developmental approach. In Timothy B. Smith (Ed.), *Practicing multiculturalism: Affirming diversity in counseling and psychology* (pp. 123–144). Boston, MA: Pearson/Allyn and Bacon.

Akinbami, Lara J., Lynch, Courtney D., Parker, Jennifer D., & Woodruff, Tracey J. (2010). The association between childhood asthma prevalence and monitored air pollutants in metropolitan areas, United States, 2001–2004. *Environmental Research, 110,* 294–301.

Al-Sayes, Fatin, Gari, Mamdooh, Qusti, Safaa, Bagatian, Nadiah, & Abuzenadah, Adel. (2011). Prevalence of iron deficiency and iron deficiency anemia among females at university stage. *Journal of Medical Laboratory and Diagnosis, 2,* 5–11.

Albert, Dustin, & Steinberg, Laurence. (2011). Judgment and decision making in adolescence. *Journal of Research on Adolescence, 21,* 211–224.

Alexander, Robin. (2000). *Culture and pedagogy: International comparisons in primary education.* Malden, MA: Blackwell.

Allen, Elizabeth, Bonell, Chris, Strange, Vicki, Copas, Andrew, Stephenson, Judith, Johnson, Anne, et al. (2007). Does the UK government's teenage pregnancy strategy deal with the correct risk factors? Findings from a secondary analysis of data from a randomised trial of sex education and their implications for policy. *Journal of Epidemiology & Community Health, 61,* 20–27.

Allen, Joseph P., Porter, Maryfrances R., McFarland, F. Christy, Marsh, Penny, & McElhaney, Kathleen Boykin. (2005). The two faces of adolescents' success with peers: Adolescent popularity, social adaptation, and deviant behavior. *Child Development, 76,* 747–760.

Allen, Kathleen P. (2010). A bullying intervention system in high school: A two-year school-wide follow-up. *Studies In Educational Evaluation, 36,* 83–92.

Allen, Nicholas J. (2008). *Early human kinship: From sex to social reproduction.* Malden, MA: Blackwell.

Allen, Shanley. (2007). The future of Inuktitut in the face of majority languages: Bilingualism or language shift? *Applied Psycholinguistics, 28,* 515–536.

Alloy, Lauren B., & Abramson, Lyn Y. (2007). The adolescent surge in depression and emergence of gender differences: A biocognitive vulnerability-stress model in developmental context. In Daniel Romer & Elaine F. Walker (Eds.), *Adolescent psychopathology and the developing brain: Integrating brain and prevention science* (pp. 284–312). New York, NY: Oxford University Press.

Alm, Bernt. (2007). To co-sleep or not to sleep. *Acta Pædiatrica, 96,* 1385–1386.

Almond, Douglas. (2006). Is the 1918 influenza pandemic over? Long-term effects of in utero influenza exposure in the post-1940 U.S. population. *Journal of Political Economy, 114,* 672–712.

Alsaker, Françoise D., & Flammer, August (2006). Pubertal development. In Sandy Jackson & Luc Goossens (Eds.), *Handbook of adolescent development* (pp. 30–50). Hove, East Sussex, UK: Psychology Press.

Altbach, Philip G., Reisberg, Liz, & Rumbley, Laura E. (2010, March/April). Tracking a global academic revolution. *Change: The Magazine of Higher Learning, 42,* 30–39.

Alter, Adam L., Aronson, Joshua, Darley, John M., Rodriguez, Cordaro, & Ruble, Diane N. (2010). Rising to the threat: Reducing stereotype threat by reframing the threat as a challenge. *Journal of Experimental Social Psychology, 46,* 166–171.

Amato, Paul R. (2005). The impact of family formation change on the cognitive, social, and emotional well-being of the next generation. *Future of Children, 15*(2), 75–96.

Amato, Paul R. (2010). Research on divorce: Continuing trends and new developments. *Journal of Marriage and Family, 72,* 650–666.

Ambady, Nalini, & Bharucha, Jamshed. (2009). Culture and the brain. *Current Directions in Psychological Science, 18,* 342–345.

American Community Survey. (2009). *2005–2009 American Community Survey 5-year estimates: S1002. Grandparents.* Retrieved from http://www.factfinder.census.gov/servlet/STTable?_bm=y&-geo_id=01000US&-qr_name=ACS_2009_5YR_G00_S1002&-ds_name=ACS_2009_5YR_G00_&-_lang=en&-_caller=geoselect&-state=st&-format=

American Psychological Association. (2010). *Ethical principles of psychologists and code of conduct 2002: 2010 amendments.* Retrieved from http://www.apa.org/ethics/code/index.aspx

Anderson, Craig A., Gentile, Douglas A., & Buckley, Katherine E. (2007). *Violent video game effects on children and adolescents: Theory, research, and public policy.* New York, NY: Oxford University Press.

Anderson, Craig A., Sakamoto, Akira, Gentile, Douglas A., Ihori, Nobuko, Shibuya, Akiko, Yukawa, Shintaro, et al. (2008). Longitudinal effects of violent video games on aggression in Japan and the United States. *Pediatrics, 122,* e1067–1072. doi:10.1542/peds.2008–1425

Andrade, Susan E., Gurwitz, Jerry H., Davis, Robert L., Chan, K. Arnold, Finkelstein, Jonathan A., Fortman, Kris, et al. (2004). Prescription drug use in pregnancy. *American Journal of Obstetrics and Gynecology, 191,* 398–407.

Andreassen, Carol, & West, Jerry. (2007). Measuring socioemotional functioning in a national birth cohort study. *Infant Mental Health Journal, 28,* 627–646.

Ansary, Nadia S., & Luthar, Suniya S. (2009). Distress and academic achievement among adolescents of affluence: A study of externalizing and internalizing problem behaviors and school performance. *Development and Psychopathology, 21,* 319–341.

Apgar, Virginia. (1953). A proposal for a new method of evaluation of the newborn infant. *Current Researches in Anesthesia and Analgesia, 32,* 260–267.

Apostolou, Menelaos. (2007). Sexual selection under parental choice: The role of parents in the evolution of human mating. *Evolution and Human Behavior, 28,* 403–409.

Applegate, Anthony J., Applegate, Mary DeKonty, McGeehan, Catherine M., Pinto, Catherine M., & Kong, Ailing. (2009). The assessment of thoughtful literacy in NAEP: Why the states aren't measuring up. *Reading Teacher, 62,* 372–381.

Appoh, Lily Yaa. (2004). Consequences of early malnutrition for subsequent social and emotional behaviour of children in Ghana. *Journal of Psychology in Africa, 14,* 87–94.

Appoh, Lily Yaa, & Krekling, Sturla. (2004). Effects of early childhood malnutrition on cognitive performance of Ghanaian children. *Journal of Psychology in Africa: South of the Sahara, the Caribbean, and Afro-Latin America, 14,* 1–7.

Archambault, Isabelle, Janosz, Michel, Fallu, Jean-Sebastien, & Pagani, Linda S. (2009). Student engagement and its relationship with early high school dropout. *Journal of Adolescence, 32,* 651–670.

Armstrong, Thomas. (2009). *Multiple intelligences in the classroom* (3rd ed.). Alexandria, VA: Association of Supervision and Curriculum Development.

Arnett, Jeffrey Jensen. (2004). *Emerging adulthood: The winding road from the late teens through the twenties.* New York, NY: Oxford University Press.

Arnett, Jeffrey Jensen, & Brody, Gene H. (2008). A fraught passage: The identity challenges of African American emerging adults. *Human Development, 51,* 291–293.

Arnett, Jeffrey Jensen, Kloep, Marion, Hendry, Leo B., & Tanner, Jennifer L. (2011). *Debating emerging adulthood: Stage or process?* New York, NY: Oxford University Press.

Arnold, L. Eugene, Farmer, Cristan, Kraemer, Helena Chmura, Davies, Mark, Witwer, Andrea, Chuang, Shirley, et al. (2010). Moderators, mediators, and other predictors of risperidone response in children with autistic disorder and irritability. *Journal of Child and Adolescent Psychopharmacology, 20,* 83–93.

Aron, Arthur. (2010). Behavior, the brain, and the social psychology of close relationships. In Christopher R. Agnew, Donald E. Carlston, William G. Graziano, & Janice R. Kelly (Eds.), *Then a miracle occurs: Focusing on behavior in social psychological theory and research* (pp. 283–298). New York, NY: Oxford University Press.

Aronson, Joshua, Fried, Carrie B., & Good, Catherine. (2002). Reducing the effects of stereotype threat on African American college students by shaping theories of intelligence. *Journal of Experimental Social Psychology, 38,* 113–125.

Arum, Richard, & Roksa, Josipa. (2011). *Academically adrift: Limited learning on college campuses.* Chicago, IL: University of Chicago Press.

Arum, Richard, Roksa, Josipa, & Cho, Esther. (2011). *Improving undergraduate learning: Findings and policy recommendations from the SSRC-CLA Longitudinal Project.* New York, NY: Social Science Research Council.

Aseltine, Robert H., Jr., & DeMartino, Robert. (2004). An outcome evaluation of the SOS suicide prevention program. *American Journal of Public Health, 94,* 446–451.

Asendorpf, Jens B., Denissen, Jaap J. A., & van Aken, Marcel A. G. (2008). Inhibited and aggressive preschool children at 23 years of age: Personality and social transitions into adulthood. *Developmental Psychology, 44,* 997–1011.

Ash, Caroline, Jasny, Barbara R., Roberts, Leslie, Stone, Richard, & Sugden, Andrew M. (2008, February 8). Reimagining cities. *Science, 319,* 739.

Ash, Katie. (2009, October 21). Maine 1-to-1 effort moves forward: Student laptop program expands into high schools *Education Week's Digital Directions, 3,* 14–15.

Aspinall, Richard J. (2003). *Aging of organs and systems.* Boston, MA: Kluwer Academic.

Asscheman, Henk. (2009). Gender identity disorder in adolescents. *Sexologies, 18,* 105–108.

Atkinson, Janette, & Braddick, Oliver. (2003). Neurobiological models of normal and abnormal visual development. In Michelle De Haan & Mark H. Johnson (Eds.), *The cognitive neuroscience of development* (pp. 43–71). New York, NY: Psychology Press.

Attar-Schwartz, Shalhevet, Tan, Jo-Pei, Buchanan, Ann, Flouri, Eirini, & Griggs, Julia. (2009). Grandparenting and adolescent adjustment in two-parent biological, lone-parent, and step-families. *Journal of Family Psychology, 23,* 67–75.

Aud, Susan, Hussar, William, Planty, Michael, Snyder, Thomas, Bianco, Kevin, Fox, Mary Ann, et al. (2010). *The condition of education 2010.* Washington, DC: National Center for Education Statistics, Institute of Education Sciences, U.S. Department of Education.

Audrey, Suzanne, Holliday, Jo, & Campbell, Rona. (2006). It's good to talk: Adolescent perspectives of an informal, peer-led intervention to reduce smoking. *Social Science & Medicine, 63,* 320–334.

Aunola, Kaisa, & Nurmi, Jari-Erik. (2004). Maternal affection moderates the impact of psychological control on a child's mathematical performance. *Developmental Psychology, 40,* 965–978.

Austad, Steven N. (2010). Methusaleh's zoo: How nature provides us with clues for extending human health span. *Journal of Comparative Pathology, 142*(Suppl. 1), S10–21.

Ayduk, Özlem, & Kross, Ethan. (2008). Enhancing the pace of recovery. *Psychological Science, 19,* 229–231.

Ayoub, Catherine, Vallotton, Claire D., & Mastergeorge, Ann M. (2011). Developmental pathways to integrated social skills: The roles of parenting and early intervention. *Child Development, 82,* 583–600.

Azrin, Nathan H., & Foxx, Richard M. (1974). *Toilet training in less than a day.* New York, NY: Simon and Schuster.

Bachman, Jerald G., O'Malley, Patrick M., Freedman-Doan, Peter, Trzesniewski, Kali H., & Donnellan, M. Brent. (2010). Adolescent self-esteem: Differences by race/ethnicity, gender, and age. *Self and Identity.* Advance online publication. doi:10.1080/15298861003794538

Badaloo, Asha V., Forrester, Terrence, Reid, Marvin, & Jahoor, Farook. (2006). Lipid kinetic differences between children with kwashiorkor and those with marasmus. *American Journal of Clinical Nutrition, 83,* 1283–1288.

Baddeley, Alan D. (2007). *Working memory, thought, and action.* New York, NY: Oxford University Press.

Bagner, Daniel M., Pettit, Jeremy W., Lewinsohn, Peter M., & Seeley, John R. (2010). Effect of maternal depression on child behavior: A sensitive period? *Journal of the American Academy of Child and Adolescent Psychiatry, 49,* 699–707.

Bailey, Kira, West, Robert, & Anderson, Craig A. (2010). A negative association between video game experience and proactive cognitive control. *Psychophysiology, 47,* 34–42.

Baillargeon, Renée. (2000). How do infants learn about the physical world? In Darwin Muir & Alan Slater (Eds.), *Infant development: The essential readings* (pp. 195–212). Malden, MA: Blackwell.

Baillargeon, Renée, & DeVos, Julie. (1991). Object permanence in young infants: Further evidence. *Child Development, 62,* 1227–1246.

Baker, Jason K., Fenning, Rachel M., Crnic, Keith A., Baker, Bruce L., & Blacher, Jan. (2007). Prediction of social skills in 6-year-old children with and without developmental delays: Contributions of early regulation and maternal scaffolding. *American Journal on Mental Retardation, 112,* 375–391.

Baker, Jeffrey P. (2000). Immunization and the American way: 4 childhood vaccines. *American Journal of Public Health, 90,* 199–207.

Baker, Lindsey A., & Mutchler, Jan E. (2010). Poverty and material hardship in grandparent-headed households. *Journal of Marriage and Family, 72,* 947–962.

Baker, Susan P. (2000). Where have we been and where are we going with injury control? In Dinesh Mohan & Geetam Tiwari (Eds.), *Injury prevention and control* (pp. 19–26). London, England: Taylor & Francis.

Bakken, Jeremy P., & Brown, B. Bradford. (2010). Adolescent secretive behavior: African American and Hmong adolescents' strategies and justifications for managing parents' knowledge about peers. *Journal of Research on Adolescence, 20,* 359–388.

Baldry, Anna C., & Farrington, David P. (2007). Effectiveness of programs to prevent school bullying. *Victims & Offenders, 2,* 183–204.

Baldwin, Dare A. (1993). Infants' ability to consult the speaker for clues to word reference. *Journal of Child Language, 20,* 395–418.

Bamford, Christi, & Lagattuta, Kristin Hansen. (2010). A new look at children's understanding of mind and emotion: The case of prayer. *Developmental Psychology, 46,* 78–92.

Bandura, Albert. (1977). *Social-learning theory.* Englewood Cliffs, NJ: Prentice-Hall.

Bandura, Albert. (1986). *Social foundations of thought and action: A social cognitive theory.* Englewood Cliffs, NJ: Prentice-Hall.

Bandura, Albert. (1997). The anatomy of stages of change. *American Journal of Health Promotion, 12,* 8–10.

Bandura, Albert. (2006). Toward a psychology of human agency. *Perspectives on Psychological Science, 1,* 164–180.

Bandura, Albert, Barbaranelli, Claudio, Caprara, Gian Vittorio, & Pastorelli, Concetta. (2001). Self-efficacy beliefs as shapers of children's aspirations and career trajectories. *Child Development, 72,* 187–206.

Bandura, Albert, & Bussey, Kay. (2004). On broadening the cognitive, motivational, and sociostructural scope of theorizing about gender development and functioning: Comment on Martin, Ruble, and Szkrybalo (2002). *Psychological Bulletin, 130,* 691–701.

Banerjee, Robin, & Lintern, Vicki. (2000). Boys will be boys: The effect of social evaluation concerns on gender-typing. *Social Development, 9,* 397–408.

Bansal, Vishal, Fortlage, Dale, Lee, Jeanne, Costantini, Todd, Potenza, Bruce, & Coimbra, Raul. (2009). Hemorrhage is more prevalent than brain injury in early trauma deaths: The golden six hours. *European Journal of Trauma and Emergency Surgery, 35,* 26–30.

Barbarin, Oscar, Downer, Jason T., Head, Darlene, & Odom, Erica. (2010). Home-school differences in beliefs, support, and control during public pre-kindergarten and their link to children's kindergarten readiness. *Early Childhood Research Quarterly, 25,* 358–372.

Barber, Brian K. (Ed.). (2002). *Intrusive parenting: How psychological control affects children and adolescents.* Washington, DC: American Psychological Association.

Barbey, Aron K., & Sloman, Steven A. (2007). Base-rate respect: From ecological rationality to dual processes. *Behavioral and Brain Sciences, 30,* 241–254.

Barinaga, Marcia. (2003, January 3). Newborn neurons search for meaning. *Science, 299,* 32–34.

Barkin, Shari, Scheindlin, Benjamin, Ip, Edward H., Richardson, Irma, & Finch, Stacia. (2007). Determinants of parental discipline practices: A national sample from primary care practices. *Clinical Pediatrics, 46,* 64–69.

Barkley, Russell A. (2006). *Attention-deficit hyperactivity disorder: A handbook for diagnosis and treatment* (3rd ed.). New York, NY: Guilford Press.

Barlow, Sarah E., & the Expert Committee. (2007). Expert Committee recommendations regarding the prevention, assessment, and treatment of child and adolescent overweight and obesity: Summary report. *Pediatrics, 120*(Suppl. 4), S164–S192.

Barnes, Grace M., Hoffman, Joseph H., Welte, John W., Farrell, Michael P., & Dintcheff, Barbara A. (2006). Effects of parental monitoring and peer deviance on substance use and delinquency. *Journal of Marriage and Family, 68,* 1084–1104.

Barnett, Kylie J., Finucane, Ciara, Asher, Julian E., Bargary, Gary, Corvin, Aiden P., Newell, Fiona N., et al. (2008). Familial patterns and the origins of individual differences in synaesthesia. *Cognition, 106,* 871–893.

Barnett, Mark, Watson, Ruth, & Kind, Peter. (2006). Pathways to barrel development. In Reha Erzurumlu, William Guido, & Zoltán Molnár (Eds.), *Development and plasticity in sensory thalamus and cortex* (pp. 138–157). New York, NY: Springer.

Barnett, W. Steven. (2007). The importance of demographic, social, and political context for estimating policy impacts: Comment on "Implementing New York's universal prekindergarten program." *Early Education and Development, 18,* 609–616.

Barnett, W. Steven, Epstein, Dale J., Carolan, Megan E., Fitzgerald, Jen, Ackerman, Debra J., & Friedman, Allison H. (2010). *The state of preschool 2010.* New Brunswick, NJ: National Institute for Early Education Research.

Barnett, W. Steven, Yarosz, Donald J., Thomas, Jessica, Jung, Kwanghee, & Blanco, Dulce. (2007). Two-way and monolingual English immersion in preschool education: An experimental comparison. *Early Childhood Research Quarterly, 22,* 277–293.

Baron, Andrew Scott, & Banaji, Mahzarin R. (2006). The development of implicit attitudes: Evidence of race evaluations from ages 6 and 10 and adulthood. *Psychological Science, 17,* 53–58.

Barrett, Justin L. (2008). Why Santa Claus is not a god. *Journal of Cognition and Culture, 8,* 149–161.

Barrett, Karen Caplovitz. (2005). The origins of social emotions and self-regulation in toddlerhood: New evidence. *Cognition & Emotion, 19,* 953–979.

Barry, Patrick. (2007, September 8). Genome 2.0: Mountains of new data are challenging old views. *Science News, 172,* 154.

Bates, Gillian, Harper, Peter S., & Jones, Lesley (Eds.). (2002). *Huntington's disease* (3rd ed.). Oxford, UK: Oxford University Press.

Bates, Lisa M., Acevedo-Garcia, Dolores, Alegria, Margarita, & Krieger, Nancy. (2008). Immigration and generational trends in body mass index and obesity in the United States: Results of the National Latino and Asian American Survey, 2002–2003. *American Journal of Public Health, 98,* 70–77.

Bateson, Patrick. (2005, February 4). Desirable scientific conduct. *Science, 307,* 645.

Bauer, Patricia J. (2006). Event memory. In William Damon & Richard M. Lerner (Series Eds.) & Deanna Kuhn & Robert S. Siegler (Vol. Eds.), *Handbook of child psychology: Vol. 2. Cognition, perception, and language* (6th ed., pp. 373–425). Hoboken, NJ: Wiley.

Bauer, Patricia J., San Souci, Priscilla, & Pathman, Thanujeni. (2010). Infant memory. *Wiley Interdisciplinary Reviews: Cognitive Science, 1,* 267–277.

Baum, Katrina. (2005). *Juvenile victimization and offending, 1993–2003* (NCJ 209468). Washington, DC: U.S. Department of Justice, Office of Justice Programs.

Baumeister, Roy F., & Blackhart, Ginnette C. (2007). Three perspectives on gender differences in adolescent sexual development. In Rutger C. M. E. Engels, Margaret Kerr, & Håkan Stattin (Eds.), *Friends, lovers, and groups: Key relationships in adolescence* (pp. 93–104). Hoboken, NJ: Wiley.

Baumrind, Diana. (1967). Child care practices anteceding three patterns of preschool behavior. *Genetic Psychology Monographs, 75,* 43–88.

Baumrind, Diana. (1971). Current patterns of parental authority. *Developmental Psychology, 4*(1, Pt. 2), 1–103.

Baumrind, Diana. (2005). Patterns of parental authority and adolescent autonomy. *New Directions for Child and Adolescent Development, 2005,* 61–69.

Baumrind, Diana, Larzelere, Robert E., & Owens, Elizabeth B. (2010). Effects of preschool parents' power assertive patterns and practices on adolescent development. *Parenting, 10,* 157–201.

Bayer, Angela M., Gilman, Robert H., Tsui, Amy O., & Hindin, Michelle J. (2010). What is adolescence?: Adolescents narrate their lives in Lima, Peru. *Journal of Adolescence, 33,* 509–520.

Bayer, Jordana K., Hiscock, Harriet, Hampton, Anne, & Wake, Melissa. (2007). Sleep problems in young infants and maternal mental and physical health. *Journal of Paediatrics and Child Health, 43,* 66–73.

Beal, Susan. (1988). Sleeping position and sudden infant death syndrome. *Medical Journal of Australia, 149,* 562.

Beauchaine, Theodore P., Klein, Daniel N., Crowell, Sheila E., Derbidge, Christina, & Gatzke-Kopp, Lisa. (2009). Multifinality in the development of personality disorders: A Biology × Sex × Environment interaction model of antisocial and borderline traits. *Development and Psychopathology, 21,* 735–770.

Beaudoin, Kathleen M., & Schonert-Reichl, Kimberly A. (2006). Epistemic reasoning and adolescent egocentrism: Relations to internalizing and externalizing symptoms in problem youth. *Journal of Youth and Adolescence, 35,* 999–1014.

Beck, Melinda. (2009, May 26). How's your baby? Recalling the Apgar score's namesake. Wall Street Journal, pp. D-1.

Beck, Martha Nibley. (1999). *Expecting Adam: A true story of birth, rebirth, and everyday magic.* New York, NY: Times Books.

Begos, Kevin. (2010, Winter). A wounded hero. *CR, 5,* 30–35, 62–63.

Behne, Tanya, Carpenter, Malinda, Call, Josep, & Tomasello, Michael. (2005). Unwilling versus unable: Infants' understanding of intentional action. *Developmental Psychology, 41,* 328–337.

Beilin, Lawrence, & Huang, Rae-Chi. (2008). Childhood obesity, hypertension, the metabolic syndrome and adult cardiovascular disease. *Clinical and Experimental Pharmacology and Physiology, 35,* 409–411.

Belfield, Clive R., Nores, Milagros, Barnett, Steve, & Schweinhart, Lawrence. (2006). The High/Scope Perry Preschool Program: Cost benefit analysis using data from the age-40 followup. *Journal of Human Resources, 41,* 162–190.

Bell, Aleeca F., White-Traut, Rosemary, & Medoff-Cooper, Barbara. (2010). Neonatal neurobehavioral organization after exposure to maternal epidural analgesia in labor. *Journal of Obstetric, Gynecologic, & Neonatal Nursing, 39,* 178–190.

Bell, Joanna H., & Bromnick, Rachel D. (2003). The social reality of the imaginary audience: A ground theory approach. *Adolescence, 38,* 205–219.

Bell, Ruth. (1998). *Changing bodies, changing lives: A book for teens on sex and relationships* (Expanded 3rd ed.). New York, NY: Times Books.

Belsky, Jay. (2011). The determinants of parenting in GxE perspective: A case of differential susceptibility? In Alan Booth, Susan M. McHale, & Nancy S. Landale (Eds.), *Biosocial foundations of family processes* (pp. 61–68). New York, NY: Springer Science + Business Media.

Belsky, Jay, Bakermans-Kranenburg, Marian J., & Van IJzendoorn, Marinus H. (2007). For better and for worse: Differential susceptibility to environmental influences. *Current Directions in Psychological Science, 16,* 300–304.

Belsky, Jay, & Pluess, Michael. (2009). The nature (and nurture?) of plasticity in early human development. *Perspectives on Psychological Science, 4,* 345–351.

Belsky, Jay, Steinberg, Laurence, Houts, Renate M., Halpern-Felsher, Bonnie L., & The NICHD Early Child Care Research Network. (2010). The development of reproductive strategy in females: Early maternal harshness → earlier menarche → increased sexual risk taking. *Developmental Psychology, 46,* 120–128.

Benacerraf, Beryl R. (2007). *Ultrasound of fetal syndromes* (2nd ed.). Philadelphia, PA: Churchill Livingstone/Elsevier.

Benjamin, Georges C. (2004). The solution is injury prevention. *American Journal of Public Health, 94,* 521.

Benner, Aprile D., & Graham, Sandra. (2007). Navigating the transition to multi-ethnic urban high schools: Changing ethnic congruence and adolescents' school-related affect. *Journal of Research on Adolescence, 17,* 207–220.

Bentley, Gillian R., & Mascie-Taylor, C. G. Nicholas. (2000). Introduction. In Gillian R. Bentley & C. G. Nicholas Mascie-Taylor (Eds.), *Infertility in the modern world: Present and future prospects* (pp. 1–13). Cambridge, England: Cambridge University Press.

Berenbaum, Sheri A., Martin, Carol Lynn, Hanish, Laura D., Briggs, Phillip T., & Fabes, Richard A. (2008). Sex differences in children's play. In Jill B. Becker, Karen J. Berkley, Nori Geary, Elizabeth Hampson, James P. Herman, & Elizabeth Young (Eds.), *Sex differences in the brain: From genes to behavior* (pp. 275–290). New York, NY: Oxford University Press.

Berg, Sandra J., & Wynne-Edwards, Katherine E. (2002). Salivary hormone concentrations in mothers and fathers becoming parents are not correlated. *Hormones & Behavior, 42,* 424–436.

Berger, Kathleen Stassen. (2007). Update on bullying at school: Science forgotten? *Developmental Review, 27,* 90–126.

Berger, Lawrence M., Paxson, Christina, & Waldfogel, Jane. (2009). Income and child development. *Children and Youth Services Review, 31,* 978–989.

Berkey, Catherine S., Gardner, Jane D., Frazier, A. Lindsay, & Colditz, Graham A. (2000). Relation of childhood diet and body size to menarche and adolescent growth in girls. *American Journal of Epidemiology, 152,* 446–452.

Berlin, Lisa J., Appleyard, Karen, & Dodge, Kenneth A. (2011). Intergenerational continuity in child maltreatment: Mediating mechanisms and implications for prevention. *Child Development, 82,* 162–176.

Berman, Alan L., Jobes, David A., & Silverman, Morton M. (2006). *Adolescent suicide: Assessment and intervention* (2nd ed.). Washington, DC: American Psychological Association.

Bernard, Kristin, & Dozier, Mary. (2010). Examining infants' cortisol responses to laboratory tasks among children varying in attachment disorganization: Stress reactivity or return to baseline? *Developmental Psychology, 46,* 1771–1778.

Berndt, Thomas J., & Murphy, Lonna M. (2002). Influences of friends and friendships: Myths, truths, and research recommendations. In Robert V. Kail (Ed.), *Advances in child development and behavior* (Vol. 30, pp. 275–310). San Diego, CA: Academic Press.

Bernstein, Mary. (2005). Identity politics. *Annual Review of Sociology, 31,* 47–74.

Bhattacharjee, Yudhijit. (2008, February 8). Choking on fumes, Kolkata faces a noxious future. *Science, 319,* 749.

Bhutta, Zulfiqar A., Ali, Samana, Cousens, Simon, Ali, Talaha M., Haider, Batool Azra, Rizvi, Arjumand, et al. (2008). Interventions to address maternal, newborn, and child survival: What difference can integrated primary health care strategies make? *Lancet, 372,* 972–989.

Bialystok, Ellen. (2010). Global-local and trail-making tasks by monolingual and bilingual children: Beyond inhibition. *Developmental Psychology, 46,* 93–105.

Bialystok, Ellen, & Viswanathan, Mythili. (2009). Components of executive control with advantages for bilingual children in two cultures. *Cognition, 112,* 494–500.

Biblarz, Timothy J., & Stacey, Judith. (2010). How does the gender of parents matter? *Journal of Marriage and Family, 72,* 3–22.

Biederman, Joseph, Spencer, Thomas J., Monuteaux, Michael C., & Faraone, Stephen V. (2010). A naturalistic 10-year prospective study of height and weight in children with attention-deficit hyperactivity disorder grown up: Sex and treatment effects. *The Journal of Pediatrics, 157,* 635–640.e1.

Biehl, Michael C., Natsuaki, Misaki N., & Ge, Xiaojia. (2007). The influence of pubertal timing on alcohol use and heavy drinking trajectories. *Journal of Youth and Adolescence, 36,* 153–167.

Bienvenu, Thierry. (2005). Rett syndrome. In Merlin Gene Butler & F. John Meaney (Eds.), *Genetics of developmental disabilities* (pp. 477–519). Boca Raton, FL: Taylor & Francis.

Bijou, Sidney W., & Baer, Donald M. (1978). *Behavior analysis of child development.* Englewood Cliffs, NJ: Prentice-Hall.

Birch, Susan A. J., & Bloom, Paul. (2003). Children are cursed: An asymmetric bias in mental-state attribution. *Psychological Science, 14,* 283–286.

Birdsong, David. (2006). Age and second language acquisition and processing: A selective overview. *Language Learning, 56*(Suppl. 1), 9–49.

Birney, Damian P., Citron-Pousty, Jill H., Lutz, Donna J., & Sternberg, Robert J. (2005). The development of cognitive and intellectual abilities. In Marc H. Bornstein & Michael E. Lamb (Eds.), *Developmental science: An advanced textbook* (5th ed., pp. 327–358). Mahwah, NJ: Erlbaum.

Biro, Frank M., McMahon, Robert P., Striegel-Moore, Ruth, Crawford, Patricia B., Obarzanek, Eva, Morrison, John A., et al. (2001). Impact of timing of pubertal maturation on growth in black and white female adolescents: The National Heart, Lung, and Blood Institute Growth and Health Study. *Journal of Pediatrics, 138,* 636–643.

Biro, Frank M., Striegel-Moore, Ruth H., Franko, Debra L., Padgett, Justina, & Bean, Judy A. (2006). Self-esteem in adolescent females. *Journal of Adolescent Health, 39,* 501–507.

Bisiacchi, Patrizia Silvia, Mento, Giovanni, & Suppiej, Agnese. (2009). Cortical auditory processing in preterm newborns: An ERP study. *Biological Psychology, 82,* 176–185.

Bitensky, Susan H. (2006). *Corporal punishment of children: A human rights violation.* Boston, MA: Brill.

Bjorklund, David F., Dukes, Charles, & Brown, Rhonda Douglas. (2009). The development of memory strategies. In Mary L. Courage & Nelson Cowan (Eds.), *The development of memory in infancy and childhood* (2nd ed., pp. 145–175). New York, NY: Psychology Press.

Blackwell, Lisa S., Trzesniewski, Kali H., & Dweck, Carol Sorich. (2007). Implicit theories of intelligence predict achievement across an adolescent transition: A longitudinal study and an intervention. *Child Development, 78,* 246–263.

Blair, Peter S., & Ball, Helen L. (2004). The prevalence and characteristics associated with parent-infant bed-sharing in England. *Archives of Disease in Childhood, 89,* 1106–1110.

Blakemore, Sarah-Jayne. (2008). Development of the social brain during adolescence. *The Quarterly Journal of Experimental Psychology, 61,* 40–49.

Blandon, Alysia Y., Calkins, Susan D., & Keane, Susan P. (2010). Predicting emotional and social competence during early childhood from toddler risk and maternal behavior. *Development and Psychopathology, 22,* 119–132.

Blonigen, Daniel M., Carlson, Marie D., Hicks, Brian M., Krueger, Robert F., & Iacono, William G. (2008). Stability and change in personality traits from late adolescence to early adulthood: A longitudinal twin study. *Journal of Personality, 76,* 229–266.

Bloom, Barbara, Cohen, Robin A., & Freeman, Gulnur. (2009). Summary health statistics for U.S. children: National Health Interview Survey, 2008. *Vital and Health Statistics, 10*(244).

Bloom, Lois. (1993). *The transition from infancy to language: Acquiring the power of expression.* New York, NY: Cambridge University Press.

Bloom, Lois. (1998). Language acquisition in its developmental context. In William Damon (Series Ed.) & Deanna Kuhn & Robert S. Siegler (Vol. Eds.), *Handbook of child psychology: Vol. 2. Cognition, perception, and language* (5th ed., pp. 309–370). New York, NY: Wiley.

Blum, Deborah. (2002). *Love at Goon Park: Harry Harlow and the science of affection.* Cambridge, MA: Perseus.

Blum, Nathan J., Taubman, Bruce, & Nemeth, Nicole. (2003). Relationship between age at initiation of toilet training and duration of training: A prospective study. *Pediatrics, 111*(4, Pt. 1), 810–814.

Blurton-Jones, Nicholas G. (1976). Rough-and-tumble play among nursery school children. In Jerome S. Bruner, Alison Jolly, & Kathy Sylva (Eds.), *Play: Its role in development and evolution* (pp. 352–363). New York, NY: Basic Books.

Bodrova, Elena, & Leong, Deborah J. (2005). High quality preschool programs: What would Vygotsky say? *Early Education and Development, 16,* 435–444.

Boehnke, Klaus. (2008). Peer pressure: A cause of scholastic underachievement? A cross-cultural study of mathematical achievement among German, Canadian, and Israeli middle school students. *Social Psychology of Education, 11,* 149–160.

Boles, David B., Barth, Joan M., & Merrill, Edward C. (2008). Asymmetry and performance: Toward a neurodevelopmental theory. *Brain and Cognition, 66,* 124–139.

Bonica, Laura, & Sappa, Viviana. (2010). Early school-leavers' microtransitions: Towards a competent self. *Education + Training, 52,* 368–380.

Booth, James R. (2007). Brain bases of learning and development of language and reading. In Donna Coch, Kurt W. Fischer, & Geraldine Dawson (Eds.), *Human behavior, learning, and the developing brain: Typical development* (pp. 279–300). New York, NY: Guilford.

Borke, Jörn, Lamm, Bettina, Eickhorst, Andreas, & Keller, Heidi. (2007). Father-infant interaction, paternal ideas about early child care, and their consequences for the development of children's self-recognition. *Journal of Genetic Psychology, 168,* 365–379.

Borkowski, John G., Farris, Jaelyn Renee, Whitman, Thomas L., Carothers, Shannon S., Weed, Keri, & Keogh, Deborah A. (2007). *Risk and resilience: Adolescent mothers and their children grow up.* Mahwah, NJ: Erlbaum.

Bornstein, Marc H. (2002). Parenting infants. In Marc H. Bornstein (Ed.), *Handbook of parenting: Vol. 1. Children and parenting* (2nd ed., pp. 3–43). Mahwah, NJ: Erlbaum.

Bornstein, Marc H. (2006). Parenting science and practice. In William Damon & Richard M. Lerner (Series Eds.) & K. Ann Renninger & Irving E. Sigel (Vol. Eds.), *Handbook of child psychology: Vol. 4. Child psychology in practice* (6th ed., pp. 893–949). Hoboken, NJ: Wiley.

Bornstein, Marc H., Arterberry, Martha E., & Mash, Clay. (2005). Perceptual development. In Marc H. Bornstein & Michael E. Lamb (Eds.), *Developmental science: An advanced textbook* (5th ed., pp. 283–325). Mahwah, NJ: Erlbaum.

Bornstein, Marc H., Mortimer, Jeylan T., Lutfey, Karen, & Bradley, Robert. (2011). Theories and processes in life-span socialization. In Karen Fingerman, Cynthia Berg, Jacqui Smith, & Toni Antonucci (Eds.), *Handbook of life-span development* (pp. 27–56). New York, NY: Springer.

Bornstein, Marc H., Putnick, Diane L., Suwalsky, Joan T. D., Venuti, Paola, de Falco, Simona, Galperín, Celia Zingman de, et al. (2010). Emotional relationships in mothers and infants: Culture-common and community-specific characteristics of dyads from rural and metropolitan settings in Argentina, Italy, and the United States. *Journal of Cross-Cultural Psychology.* Advance online publication. doi:10.1177/0022022110388563

Borrelli, Belinda, McQuaid, Elizabeth L., Novak, Scott P., Hammond, S. Katharine, & Becker, Bruce. (2010). Motivating Latino caregivers of children with asthma to quit smoking: A randomized trial. *Journal of Consulting and Clinical Psychology, 78,* 34–43.

Bortz, Walter M. (2005). Biological basis of determinants of health. *American Journal of Public Health, 95,* 389–392.

Bos, Henny M. W., Sandfort, Theo G. M., de Bruyn, Eddy H., & Hakvoort, Esther M. (2008). Same-sex attraction, social relationships, psychosocial functioning, and school performance in early adolescence. *Developmental Psychology, 44,* 59–68.

Boseovski, Janet J. (2010). Evidence for "rose-colored glasses": An examination of the positivity bias in young children's personality judgments. *Child Development Perspectives, 4,* 212–218.

Bossé, Yohan, & Hudson, Thomas J. (2007). Toward a comprehensive set of asthma susceptibility genes. *Annual Review of Medicine, 58,* 171–184.

Bosworth, Hayden B., & Hertzog, Christopher. (2009). *Aging and cognition: Research methodologies and empirical advances.* Washington, DC: American Psychological Association.

Bower, Bruce. (2007, February 17). Net heads. *Science News, 171,* 104–106.

Bowers, Jeffrey S., Mattys, Sven L., & Gage, Suzanne H. (2009). Preserved implicit knowledge of a forgotten childhood language. *Psychological Science, 20,* 1064–1069.

Bowes, Lucy, Maughan, Barbara, Caspi, Avshalom, Moffitt, Terrie E., & Arseneault, Louise. (2010). Families promote emotional and behavioural resilience to bullying: Evidence of an environmental effect. *Journal of Child Psychology and Psychiatry, 51,* 809–817.

Bowlby, John. (1969). *Attachment and loss: Vol. 1. Attachment.* New York, NY: Basic Books.

Bowlby, John. (1973). *Attachment and loss: Vol. 2. Separation: Anxiety and anger.* New York, NY: Basic Books.

Bowlby, John. (1988). *A secure base: Clinical applications of attachment theory.* London, England: Routledge.

Boyce, W. Thomas, Essex, Marilyn J., Alkon, Abbey, Goldsmith, H. Hill, Kraemer, Helena C., & Kupfer, David J. (2006). Early father involvement moderates biobehavioral susceptibility to mental health problems in middle childhood. *Journal of the American Academy of Child and Adolescent Psychiatry, 45,* 1510–1520.

Boyd, William L. (2007). The politics of privatization in American education. *Educational Policy, 21,* 7–14.

Bracken, Bruce A., & Crawford, Elizabeth. (2010). Basic concepts in early childhood educational standards: A 50–state review. *Early Childhood Education Journal, 37,* 421–430.

Bradley, Robert H., & Corwyn, Robert F. (2005). Productive activity and the prevention of behavior problems. *Developmental Psychology, 41,* 89–98.

Brainerd, Charles J., Reyna, Valerie F., & Ceci, Stephen J. (2008). Developmental reversals in false memory: A review of data and theory. *Psychological Bulletin, 134,* 343–382.

Branca, Francesco, Nikogosian, Haik, & Lobstein, Tim (Eds.). (2007). *The challenge of obesity in the WHO European Region and the strategies for response.* Copenhagen, Denmark: WHO Regional Office for Europe.

Brandone, Amanda C., & Wellman, Henry M. (2009). You can't always get what you want. *Psychological Science, 20,* 85–91.

Braun, Joe M, & Hauser, Russ. (2011). Bisphenol A and children's health. *Current Opinion in Pediatrics, 23,* 233–239.

Brazelton, T. Berry, & Sparrow, Joshua D. (2006). *Touchpoints: Birth to 3: Your child's emotional and behavioral development* (2nd ed.). Cambridge, MA: Da Capo Press.

Breivik, Gunnar. (2010). Trends in adventure sports in a post-modern society. *Sport in Society: Cultures, Commerce, Media, Politics, 13,* 260–273.

Brendgen, Mara, Lamarche, Véronique, Wanner, Brigitte, & Vitaro, Frank. (2010). Links between friendship relations and early adolescents' trajectories of depressed mood. *Developmental Psychology, 46,* 491–501.

Brener, Nancy D., McManus, Tim, Galuska, Deborah A., Lowry, Richard, & Wechsler, Howell. (2003). Reliability and validity of self-reported height and weight among high school students. *The Journal of Adolescent Health : Official Publication of the Society for Adolescent Medicine, 32,* 281–287.

Brennan, Arthur, Ayers, Susan, Ahmed, Hafez, & Marshall-Lucette, Sylvie. (2007). A critical review of the Couvade syndrome: The pregnant male. *Journal of Reproductive and Infant Psychology, 25,* 173–189.

Bretherton, Inge. (2010). Fathers in attachment theory and research: A review. *Early Child Development and Care, 180,* 9–23.

Brickhouse, Tegwyn H., Rozier, R. Gary, & Slade, Gary D. (2008). Effects of enrollment in Medicaid versus the State Children's Health Insurance Program on kindergarten children's untreated dental caries. *American Journal of Public Health, 98,* 876–881.

Bridge, Jeffrey A., Iyengar, Satish, Salary, Cheryl B., Barbe, Remy P., Birmaher, Boris, Pincus, Harold Alan, et al. (2007). Clinical response and risk for reported suicidal ideation and suicide attempts in pediatric antidepressant treatment: A meta-analysis of randomized controlled trials. *Journal of the American Medical Association, 297,* 1683–1696.

Briggs, Gerald G., Freeman, Roger K., & Yaffe, Sumner J. (2008). *Drugs in pregnancy and lactation: A reference guide to fetal and neonatal risk* (8th ed.). Philadelphia, PA: Lippincott Williams & Wilkins.

Brinton, Mary C., & Tang, Zun. (2010). School–work systems in postindustrial societies: Evidence from Japan. *Research in Social Stratification and Mobility, 28,* 215–232.

Brody, Gene H., Beach, Steven R. H., Philibert, Robert A., Chen, Yi-fu, & Murry, Velma McBride. (2009). Prevention effects moderate the association of 5–HTTLPR and youth risk behavior initiation: Gene × environment hypotheses tested via a randomized prevention design. *Child Development, 80,* 645–661.

Bronfenbrenner, Urie. (1977). Toward an experimental ecology of human development. *American Psychologist, 32,* 513–531.

Bronfenbrenner, Urie, & Morris, Pamela A. (2006). The bioecological model of human development. In William Damon & Richard M. Lerner (Series Eds.) & Richard M. Lerner (Vol. Ed.), *Handbook of child psychology: Vol. 1. Theoretical models of human development* (6th ed., pp. 793–828). Hoboken, NJ: Wiley.

Bronte-Tinkew, Jacinta, Moore, Kristin A., Matthews, Gregory, & Carrano, Jennifer. (2007). Symptoms of major depression in a sample of fathers of infants: Sociodemographic correlates and links to father involvement. *Journal of Family Issues, 28,* 61–99.

Brooker, Robert J. (2009). *Genetics: Analysis & principles* (3rd ed.). New York, NY: McGraw-Hill.

Brotman, Melissa A., Guyer, Amanda E., Lawson, Evin S., Horsey, Sarah E., Rich, Brendan A., Dickstein, Daniel P., et al. (2008). Facial emotion labeling deficits in children and adolescents at risk for bipolar disorder. *American Journal of Psychiatry, 165,* 385–389.

Brotman, Melissa A., Rich, Brendan A., Guyer, Amanda E., Lunsford, Jessica R., Horsey, Sarah E., Reising, Michelle M., et al. (2010). Amygdala activation during emotion processing of neutral faces in children with severe mood dysregulation versus ADHD or bipolar disorder. *American Journal of Psychiatry, 167,* 61–69.

Brown, B. Bradford. (2004). Adolescents' relationships with peers. In Richard M. Lerner & Laurence D. Steinberg (Eds.), *Handbook of adolescent psychology* (2nd ed., pp. 363–394). Hoboken, NJ: Wiley.

Brown, B. Bradford, & Bakken, Jeremy P. (2011). Parenting and peer relationships: Reinvigorating research on family–peer linkages in adolescence. *Journal of Research on Adolescence, 21,* 153–165.

Brown, B. Bradford, & Larson, James. (2009). Peer relationships in adolescence, *Handbook of adolescent psychology: Vol. 2. Contextual influences on adolescent development* (3rd ed., pp. 74–103). Hoboken, NJ: Wiley.

Brown, Christia Spears, Alabi, Basirat O., Huynh, Virginia W., & Masten, Carrie L. (2011). Ethnicity and gender in late childhood and early adolescence: Group identity and awareness of bias. *Developmental Psychology, 47,* 463–471.

Brown, Christia Spears, & Bigler, Rebecca S. (2005). Children's perceptions of discrimination: A developmental model. *Child Development, 76,* 533–553.

Brown, Susan L. (2004). Family structure and child well-being: The significance of parental cohabitation. *Journal of Marriage and Family, 66,* 351–367.

Brown, Susan L. (2010). Marriage and child well-being: Research and policy perspectives. *Journal of Marriage and Family, 72,* 1059–1077.

Brown, Susan L., & Rinelli, Lauren N. (2010). Family structure, family processes, and adolescent smoking and drinking. *Journal of Research on Adolescence, 20,* 259–273.

Brown, Tony N., Tanner-Smith, Emily E., Lesane-Brown, Chase L., & Ezell, Michael E. (2007). Child, parent, and situational correlates of familial ethnic/race socialization. *Journal of Marriage and Family, 69,* 14–25.

Bruce, Susan, & Muhammad, Zayyad. (2009). The development of object permanence in children with intellectual disability, physical disability, autism, and blindness. *International Journal of Disability, Development and Education, 56,* 229–246.

Bruck, Maggie, Ceci, Stephen J., & Principe, Gabrielle F. (2006). The child and the law. In William Damon & Richard M. Lerner (Series Eds.) & K. Ann Renninger & Irving E. Sigel (Vol. Eds.), *Handbook of child psychology: Vol. 4. Child psychology in practice* (6th ed., pp. 776–816). Hoboken, NJ: Wiley.

Bruschweiler-Stern, Nadia. (2009). Moments of meeting: Pivotal moments in mother, infant, father bonding: Switzerland. In Kevin J. Nugent, Bonnie J. Petrauskas, & T. Berry Brazelton (Eds.), *The newborn as a person: Enabling healthy infant development worldwide* (pp. 70–84). Hoboken, NJ: Wiley.

Bryant, Brenda K., & Donnellan, M. Brent. (2007). The relation between socio-economic status concerns and angry peer conflict resolution is moderated by pet provisions of support. *Anthrozoös, 20,* 213–223.

Bryant, Gregory A., & Barrett, H. Clark. (2007). Recognizing intentions in infant-directed speech: Evidence for universals. *Psychological Science, 18,* 746–751.

Brymer, Eric. (2010). Risk and extreme sports: A phenomenological perspective. *Annals of Leisure Research, 13,* 218–239.

Buccino, Giovanni, & Amore, Mario. (2008). Mirror neurons and the understanding of behavioural symptoms in psychiatric disorders. *Current Opinion in Psychiatry, 21,* 281–285.

Buckhalt, Joseph A., El-Sheikh, Mona, & Keller, Peggy. (2007). Children's sleep and cognitive functioning: Race and socioeconomic status as moderators of effects. *Child Development, 78,* 213–231.

Buckley, Kristi A., & Tobey, Emily A. (2011). Cross-modal plasticity and speech perception in pre- and postlingually deaf cochlear implant users. *Ear and Hearing, 32,* 2–15.

Buckley, Maureen, & Saarni, Carolyn. (2009). Emotion regulation: Implications for positive youth development. In Rich Gilman, E. Scott Huebner, & Michael J. Furlong (Eds.), *Handbook of positive psychology in schools* (pp. 107–118). New York, NY: Routledge/Taylor & Francis.

Bucx, Freek, Raaijmakers, Quinten, & van Wel, Frits. (2010). Life course stage in young adulthood and intergenerational congruence in family attitudes. *Journal of Marriage and Family, 72,* 117–134.

Bugental, Daphne Blunt, & Grusec, Joan E. (2006). Socialization theory. In William Damon & Richard M. Lerner (Series Eds.) & Nancy Eisenberg (Vol. Ed.), *Handbook of child psychology: Vol. 3. Social, emotional, and personality development* (6th ed., pp. 366–428). Hoboken, NJ: Wiley.

Bugental, Daphne Blunt, & Happaney, Keith. (2004). Predicting infant maltreatment in low-income families: The interactive effects of maternal attributions and child status at birth. *Developmental Psychology, 40,* 234–243.

Bugental, Daphne Blunt, & Schwartz, Alex. (2009). A cognitive approach to child mistreatment prevention among medically at-risk infants. *Developmental Psychology, 45,* 284–288.

Bulbulia, Joseph A. (2007). Evolution of religion. In R. I. M. Dunbar & Louise Barrett (Eds.), *Oxford handbook of evolutionary psychology* (pp. 621–636). New York, NY: Oxford University Press.

Bulik, Cynthia M., Thornton, Laura, Pinheiro, Andréa Poyastro, Plotnicov, Katherine, Klump, Kelly L., Brandt, Harry, et al. (2008). Suicide attempts in anorexia nervosa. *Psychosomatic Medicine, 70,* 378–383.

Burd-Sharps, Sarah, Lewis, Kristen, & Martins, Eduardo Borges. (2008). *The measure of America: American human development report, 2008–2009.* New York, NY: Columbia University Press.

Burkitt, Esther. (2004). Drawing conclusions from children's art. *The Psychologist, 17,* 566–568.

Burt, S. Alexandra. (2009). Rethinking environmental contributions to child and adolescent psychopathology: A meta-analysis of shared environmental influences. *Psychological Bulletin, 135,* 608–637.

Burt, S. Alexandra, McGue, Matt, & Iacono, William G. (2009). Nonshared environmental mediation of the association between deviant peer affiliation and adolescent externalizing behaviors over time: Results from a cross-lagged monozygotic twin differences design. *Developmental Psychology, 45,* 1752–1760.

Buss, David M. (2003). *The evolution of desire: Strategies of human mating* (Revised ed.). New York, NY: Basic Books.

Buss, David M., Haselton, Martie G., Shackelford, Todd K., Bleske, April L., & Wakefield, Jerome C. (1998). Adaptations, exaptations, and spandrels. *American Psychologist, 53,* 533–548.

Busse, William W., & Lemanske, Robert F. (Eds.). (2005). *Lung biology in health and disease: Vol. 195. Asthma prevention.* Boca Raton, FL: Taylor & Francis.

Bussey, Kay, & Bandura, Albert. (1999). Social cognitive theory of gender development and differentiation. *Psychological Review, 106,* 676–713.

Butler, Merlin Gene, & Meaney, F. John. (2005). *Genetics of developmental disabilities.* Boca Raton, FL: Taylor & Francis.

Butterworth, Brian, Reeve, R., & Reynolds, F. (2011). Using mental representations of space when words are unavailable: Studies of enumeration and arithmetic in indigenous Australia. *Journal of Cross-Cultural Psychology, 42*(4), 630–638.

Buunk, Abraham P., Park, Justin H., & Dubbs, Shelli L. (2008). Parent-offspring conflict in mate preferences. *Review of General Psychology, 12,* 47–62.

Byers-Heinlein, Krista, Burns, Tracey C., & Werker, Janet F. (2010). The roots of bilingualism in newborns. *Psychological Science, 21,* 343–348.

Byng-Hall, John. (2008). The significance of children fulfilling parental roles: Implications for family therapy. *Journal of Family Therapy, 30,* 147–162.

Cabrera, Natasha J., Shannon, Jacqueline D., West, Jerry, & Brooks-Gunn, Jeanne. (2006). Parental interactions with Latino infants: Variation by country of origin and English proficiency. *Child Development, 77,* 1190–1207.

Cain, Daphne S., & Combs-Orme, Terri. (2005). Family structure effects on parenting stress and practices in the African American family. *Journal of Sociology & Social Welfare, 32,* 19–40.

Calkins, Susan D., & Keane, Susan P. (2009). Developmental origins of early antisocial behavior. *Development and Psychopathology, 21,* 1095–1109.

Callaghan, Tara, Rochat, Philippe, Lillard, Angeline, Claux, Mary Louise, Odden, Hal, Itakura, Shoji, et al. (2005). Synchrony in the onset of mental-state reasoning: Evidence from five cultures. *Psychological Science, 16,* 378–384.

Calvert, Karin. (2003). Patterns of childrearing in America. In Willem Koops & Michael Zuckerman (Eds.), *Beyond the century of the child: Cultural history and developmental psychology* (pp. 62–81). Baltimore, MD: University of Pennsylvania Press.

Cameron, Judy, & Pierce, W. David. (2002). *Rewards and intrinsic motivation: Resolving the controversy.* Westport, CT: Bergin & Garvey.

Cameron, Judy L. (2004). Interrelationships between hormones, behavior, and affect during adolescence: Understanding hormonal, physical, and brain changes occurring in association with pubertal activation of the reproductive axis. Introduction to Part III. In Ronald E. Dahl & Linda Patia Spear (Eds.), *Adolescent brain development: Vulnerabilities and opportunities* (Vol. 1021, pp. 110–123). New York, NY: New York Academy of Sciences.

Cameron, Nicole M., Fish, Eric W., & Meaney, Michael J. (2008). Maternal influences on the sexual behavior and reproductive success of the female rat. *Hormones and Behavior, 54,* 178–184.

Camilli, Gregory, Vargas, Sadako, Ryan, Sharon, & Barnett, W. Steven. (2010). Meta-analysis of the effects of early education interventions on cognitive and social development. *Teachers College Record, 112,* 579–620.

Camos, Valérie, & Barrouillet, Pierre. (2011). Developmental change in working memory strategies: From passive maintenance to active refreshing. *Developmental Psychology, 47,* 898–904.

Campbell, Frances A., Pungello, Elizabeth P., Miller-Johnson, Shari, Burchinal, Margaret, & Ramey, Craig T. (2001). The development of cognitive and academic abilities: Growth curves from an early childhood educational experiment. *Developmental Psychology, 37,* 231–242.

Camras, Linda A., & Shutter, Jennifer M. (2010). Emotional facial expressions in infancy. *Emotion Review, 2,* 120–129.

Capaldi, Deborah M. (2003). Parental monitoring: A person-environment interaction perspective on this key parenting skill. In Ann C. Crouter & Alan Booth (Eds.), *Children's influence on family dynamics: The neglected side of family relationships* (pp. 171–179). Mahwah, NJ: Lawrence Erlbaum.

Caravita, Simona C. S., Di Blasio, Paola, & Salmivalli, Christina. (2010). Early adolescents' participation in bullying: Is ToM involved? *The Journal of Early Adolescence, 30,* 138–170.

Carey, Susan. (2010). Beyond fast mapping. *Language Learning and Development, 6,* 184–205.

Carlson, Susan A., Fulton, Janet E., Lee, Sarah M., Maynard, L. Michele, Brown, David R., Kohl, Harold W., III, et al. (2008). Physical education and academic achievement in elementary school: Data from the early childhood longitudinal study. *American Journal of Public Health, 98,* 721–727.

Carlson, Stephanie M. (2003). Executive function in context: Development, measurement, theory and experience. *Monographs of the Society for Research in Child Development, 68*(3, Serial No. 274), 138–151.

Carpendale, Jeremy I. M., & Lewis, Charlie. (2004). Constructing an understanding of mind: The development of children's social understanding within social interaction. *Behavioral and Brain Sciences, 27,* 79–96.

Case-Smith, Jane, & Kuhaneck, Heather Miller. (2008). Play preferences of typically developing children and children with developmental delays between ages 3 and 7 years. *OTJR: Occupation, Participation and Health, 28,* 19–29.

Casey, B. J., Jones, Rebecca M., & Somerville, Leah H. (2011). Braking and accelerating of the adolescent brain. *Journal of Research on Adolescence, 21,* 21–33.

Caspi, Avshalom, McClay, Joseph, Moffitt, Terrie, Mill, Jonathan, Martin, Judy, Craig, Ian W., et al. (2002, August 2). Role of genotype in the cycle of violence in maltreated children. *Science, 297,* 851–854.

Caspi, Avshalom, Moffitt, Terrie E., Morgan, Julia, Rutter, Michael, Taylor, Alan, Arseneault, Louise, et al. (2004). Maternal expressed emotion predicts children's antisocial behavior problems: Using monozygotic-twin differences to identify environmental effects on behavioral development. *Developmental Psychology, 40,* 149–161.

Caspi, Avshalom, & Shiner, Rebecca L. (2006). Personality development. In William Damon & Richard M. Lerner (Series Eds.) & Nancy Eisenberg (Vol. Ed.), *Handbook of child psychology: Vol. 3. Social, emotional, and personality development* (6th ed., pp. 300–365). Hoboken, NJ: Wiley.

Cassia, Viola Macchi, Kuefner, Dana, Picozzi, Marta, & Vescovo, Elena. (2009). Early experience predicts later plasticity for face processing: Evidence for the reactivation of dormant effects. *Psychological Science, 20,* 853–859.

Castle, David J., & Morgan, Vera. (2008). Epidemiology. In Kim T. Mueser & Dilip V. Jeste (Eds.), *Clinical handbook of schizophrenia* (pp. 14–24). New York, NY: Guilford Press.

Catani, Claudia, Gewirtz, Abigail H., Wieling, Elizabeth, Schauer, Elizabeth, Elbert, Thomas, & Neuner, Frank. (2010). Tsunami, war, and cumulative risk in the lives of Sri Lankan schoolchildren. *Child Development, 81,* 1176–1191.

Cavanagh, Sean. (2005, January 5). Poor math scores on world stage trouble U.S. *Education Week,* pp. 1, 18.

Cavanagh, Sean. (2007, December 13). Poverty's effect on U.S. scores greater than for other nations. *Education Week, 27,* 1, 13.

CBS News. (2005, Feb 8). *World's smallest baby goes home: Cellphone-sized baby is discharged from hospital.* Retrieved from http://www.cbsnews.com/stories/2005/02/08/health/main672488.shtml

CDC (Centers for Disease Control and Prevention) (Ed.). (2007). *Epidemiology and prevention of vaccine-preventable diseases* (10th ed.). Washington, DC: Public Health Foundation.

Ceci, Stephen J., & Bruck, Maggie. (1995). *Jeopardy in the courtroom: A scientific analysis of children's testimony.* Washington, DC: American Psychological Association.

Center for Sexual Health Promotion. (2010). *National Survey of Sexual Health and Behavior (NSSHB).* Retrieved from http://nationalsexstudy.indiana.edu/

Center on Education Policy. (2010). *State high school tests: Exit exams and other assessments.* Washington, DC: Author.

Centre for Community Child Health and Telethon Institute for Child Health Research. (2009). *A snapshot of early childhood development in Australia: Australian Early Development Index (AEDI) national report 2009.* Retrieved from Australian Government Department of Education website: http://www.rch.org.au/aedi/media/Snapshot_of_Early_Childhood_DevelopmentinAustralia_AEDI_National_Report.pdf

Cesario, Sandra K., & Hughes, Lisa A. (2007). Precocious puberty: A comprehensive review of literature. *Journal of Obstetric, Gynecologic, & Neonatal Nursing, 36,* 263–274.

Chaddock, Laura, Erickson, Kirk I., Prakash, Ruchika Shaurya, VanPatter, Matt, Voss, Michelle W., Pontifex, Matthew B., et al. (2010). Basal ganglia volume is associated with aerobic fitness in preadolescent children. *Developmental Neuroscience, 32,* 249–256.

Chafen, Jennifer J. Schneider, Newberry, Sydne J., Riedl, Marc A., Bravata, Dena M., Maglione, Margaret, Suttorp, Marika J., et al. (2010). Diagnosing and managing common food allergies. *Journal of the American Medical Association, 303,* 1848–1856.

Chaignat, Evelyne, Yahya-Graison, Emilie Aït, Henrichsen, Charlotte N., Chrast, Jacqueline, Schütz, Frédéric, Pradervand, Sylvain, et al. (2011). Copy number variation modifies expression time courses. *Genome Research, 21,* 106–113.

Chambers, Bette, Cheung, Alan C., Slavin, Robert E., Smith, Dewi, & Laurenzano, Mary. (2010). *Effective early childhood education programs: A systematic review.* Baltimore, MD: Johns Hopkins University, Center for Research and Reform in Education.

Champagne, Frances A., & Curley, James P. (2010). Maternal care as a modulating influence on infant development. In Mark S. Blumberg, John H. Freeman, & Scott R. Robinson (Eds.), *Oxford handbook of developmental behavioral neuroscience* (pp. 323–341). New York, NY: Oxford University Press.

Chan, Cheri C. Y., Brandone, Amanda C., & Tardif, Twila. (2009). Culture, context, or behavioral control? English- and Mandarin-speaking mothers' use of nouns and verbs in joint book reading. *Journal of Cross-Cultural Psychology, 40,* 584–602.

Chan, David W., & Zhao, Yongjun. (2010). The relationship between drawing skill and artistic creativity: Do age and artistic involvement make a difference? *Creativity Research Journal, 22,* 27–36.

Chan, Siu Mui, Bowes, Jennifer, & Wyver, Shirley. (2009). Parenting style as a context for emotion socialization. *Early Education & Development, 20,* 631–656.

Chan, Tak Wing, & Koo, Anita. (2010). Parenting style and youth outcomes in the UK. *European Sociological Review.* Advance online publication. doi:10.1093/esr/jcq013

Chang, Esther S., Greenberger, Ellen, Chen, Chuansheng, Heckhausen, Jutta, & Farruggia, Susan P. (2010). Nonparental adults as social resources in the transition to adulthood. *Journal of Research on Adolescence, 20,* 1065–1082.

Chao, Ruth K. (2001). Extending research on the consequences of parenting style for Chinese Americans and European Americans. *Child Development, 72,* 1832–1843.

Chao, Y. May, Pisetsky, Emily M., Dierker, Lisa C., Dohm, Faith-Anne, Rosselli, Francine, May, Alexis M., et al. (2008). Ethnic differences in weight control practices among U.S. adolescents from 1995 to 2005. *International Journal of Eating Disorders, 41,* 124–133.

Chaplin, Lan Nguyen, & John, Deborah Roedder. (2007). Growing up in a material world: Age differences in materialism in children and adolescents. *Journal of Consumer Research, 34,* 480–493.

Chassin, Laurie, Hussong, Andrea, Barrera, Manuel, Jr., Molina, Brooke S. G., Trim, Ryan, & Ritter, Jennifer. (2004). Adolescent substance use. In Richard M. Lerner & Laurence D. Steinberg (Eds.), *Handbook of adolescent psychology* (2nd ed., pp. 665–696). Hoboken, NJ: Wiley.

Chassin, Laurie, Hussong, Andrea, & Beltran, Iris. (2009). Adolescent substance use. In Richard M. Lerner & Laurence Steinberg (Eds.), *Handbook of adolescent psychology: Individual bases of adolescent development* (3rd ed., pp. 723–763). Hoboken, NJ: Wiley.

Chattopadhyay, Amit. (2008). Oral health disparities in the United States. *Dental Clinics of North America, 52,* 297–318.

Chein, Isidor. (2008). *The science of behavior and the image of man.* New Brunswick, NJ: Transaction.

Chen, Edith, Cohen, Sheldon, & Miller, Gregory E. (2010). How low socioeconomic status affects 2-year hormonal trajectories in children. *Psychological Science, 21,* 31–37.

Chen, Hong, & Jackson, Todd. (2009). Predictors of changes in weight esteem among mainland Chinese adolescents: A longitudinal analysis. *Developmental Psychology, 45,* 1618–1629.

Chen, Xinyin, Cen, Guozhen, Li, Dan, & He, Yunfeng. (2005). Social functioning and adjustment in Chinese children: The imprint of historical time. *Child Development, 76,* 182–195.

Chen, Xinyin, Wang, Li, & Wang, Zhengyan. (2009). Shyness-sensitivity and social, school, and psychological adjustment in rural migrant and urban children in China. *Child Development, 80,* 1499–1513.

Cheng, Diana, Kettinger, Laurie, Uduhiri, Kelechi, & Hurt, Lee. (2011). Alcohol consumption during pregnancy: Prevalence and provider assessment. *Obstetrics & Gynecology, 117,* 212–217.

Cheng, Yi-Chia, & Yeh, Hsin-Te. (2009). From concepts of motivation to its application in instructional design: Reconsidering motivation from an instructional design perspective. *British Journal of Educational Technology, 40,* 597–605.

Cherlin, Andrew J. (2009). *The marriage-go-round: The state of marriage and the family in America today.* New York, NY: Knopf.

Chernoff, Jodi Jacobson, Flanagan, Kristin Denton, McPhee, Cameron, & Park, Jennifer. (2007). *Preschool: First findings from the preschool*

follow-up of the Early Childhood Longitudinal Study, Birth Cohort (ECLS-B) (NCES 2008–025). Washington, DC: National Center for Education Statistics.

Cheslack-Postava, Keely, Liu, Kayuet, & Bearman, Peter S. (2011). Closely spaced pregnancies are associated with increased odds of autism in California sibling births. *Pediatrics, 127,* 246–253.

Cheung, Benjamin Y., Chudek, Maciej, & Heine, Steven J. (2011). Evidence for a sensitive period for acculturation. *Psychological Science, 22,* 147–152.

Cheurprakobkit, Sutham, & Bartsch, Robert A. (2005). Security measures on school crime in Texas middle and high schools. *Educational Research, 47,* 235–250.

Chiao, Joan Y., & Blizinsky, Katherine D. (2010). Culture-gene coevolution of individualism-collectivism and the serotonin transporter gene. *Proceedings of the Royal Society B: Biological Sciences, 277,* 529–537.

Children's Bureau. (2010). *Child maltreatment 2008*. Washington, DC: U.S. Department of Health and Human Services, Administration for Children and Families, Administration on Children, Youth and Families.

Chin, Vivien S., Skike, Candice E. Van, & Matthews, Douglas B. (2010). Effects of ethanol on hippocampal function during adolescence: A look at the past and thoughts on the future. *Alcohol, 44,* 3–14.

Chomsky, Noam. (1968). *Language and mind*. New York, NY: Harcourt Brace & World.

Chomsky, Noam. (1980). *Rules and representations*. New York, NY: Columbia University Press.

Chouinard, Michelle M. (2007). Children's questions: A mechanism for cognitive development. *Monographs of the Society for Research in Child Development, 72*(1, Serial No. 286), vii–112.

Christian, Cindy W., Block, Robert, & and the Committee on Child Abuse and Neglect. (2009). Abusive head trauma in infants and children. *Pediatrics, 123,* 1409–1411.

Chronicle of Higher Education. (2010). *Almanac of higher education 2010–2011*. Washington, DC: Author.

Chua, Amy. (2011). *Battle hymn of the tiger mother*. New York, NY: Penguin.

Chudacoff, Howard P. (2007). *Children at play: An American history*. New York: New York University Press.

Cicchetti, Dante, Rogosch, Fred A., & Sturge-Apple, Melissa L. (2007). Interactions of child maltreatment and serotonin transporter and monoamine oxidase A polymorphisms: Depressive symptomatology among adolescents from low socioeconomic status backgrounds. *Development and Psychopathology, 19,* 1161–1180.

Cicchetti, Dante, & Toth, Sheree L. (2009). The past achievements and future promises of developmental psychopathology: The coming of age of a discipline. *Journal of Child Psychology and Psychiatry, 50,* 16–25.

Cillessen, Antonius H. N., & Mayeux, Lara. (2004). From censure to reinforcement: Developmental changes in the association between aggression and social status. *Child Development, 75,* 147–163.

Cipriano, Elizabeth A., & Stifter, Cynthia A. (2010). Predicting preschool effortful control from toddler temperament and parenting behavior. *Journal of Applied Developmental Psychology, 31,* 221–230.

Claas, Marieke J., de Vries, Linda S., Bruinse, Hein W., van Haastert, Ingrid C., Uniken Venema, Monica M. A., Peelen, Linda M., et al. (2011). Neurodevelopmental outcome over time of preterm born children ≤750g at birth. *Early Human Development, 87,* 183–191.

Clancy, Susan A. (2010). *The trauma myth: The truth about the sexual abuse of children—and its aftermath*. New York, NY: Basic Books.

Clark, Nina Annika, Demers, Paul A., Karr, Catherine J., Koehoorn, Mieke, Lencar, Cornel, Tamburic, Lillian, et al. (2009). Effect of early life exposure to air pollution on development of childhood asthma. *Environmental Health Perspectives, 118,* 284–290.

Clark, Shelley, Kabiru, Caroline, & Mathur, Rohini. (2010). Relationship transitions among youth in urban Kenya. *Journal of Marriage and Family, 72,* 73–88.

Cleland, Verity, Timperio, Anna, Salmon, Jo, Hume, Clare, Telford, Amanda, & Crawford, David. (2011). A longitudinal study of the family physical activity environment and physical activity among youth. *American Journal of Health Promotion, 25,* 159–167.

Cleveland, Michael J., Gibbons, Frederick X., Gerrard, Meg, Pomery, Elizabeth A., & Brody, Gene H. (2005). The impact of parenting on risk cognitions and risk behavior: A study of mediation and moderation in a panel of African American adolescents. *Child Development, 76,* 900–916.

Coghlan, Misia, Bergeron, Caroline, White, Karen, Sharp, Caroline, Morris, Marian, & Rutt, Simon. (2009). *Narrowing the gap in outcomes for young children through effective practices in the early years*. London, England: Centre for Excellence and Outcomes in Children and Young People's Services.

Cohen, David. (2006). *The development of play* (3rd ed.). New York, NY: Routledge.

Cohen, David. (2010). Probabilistic epigenesis: An alternative causal model for conduct disorders in children and adolescents. *Neuroscience & Biobehavioral Reviews, 34,* 119–129.

Cohen, Daniel, & Soto, Marcelo. (2007). Growth and human capital: Good data, good results. *Journal of Economic Growth, 12,* 51–76.

Cohen, Jon. (2007, September 7). DNA duplications and deletions help determine health. *Science, 317,* 1315–1317.

Cohen, Jon. (2007, March 9). Hope on new AIDS drugs, but breast-feeding strategy backfires. *Science, 315,* 1357.

Cohen, Joel E., & Malin, Martin B. (Eds.). (2010). *International perspectives on the goals of universal basic and secondary education*. New York, NY: Routledge.

Cohen, Larry, Chávez, Vivian, & Chehimi, Sana. (2007). *Prevention is primary: Strategies for community well-being*. San Francisco, CA: Jossey-Bass.

Cohen, Leslie B., & Cashon, Cara H. (2006). Infant cognition. In William Damon & Richard M. Lerner (Series Eds.) & Deanna Kuhn & Robert S. Siegler (Vol. Eds.), *Handbook of child psychology: Vol. 2. Cognition, perception, and language* (6th ed., pp. 214–251). Hoboken, NJ: Wiley.

Cole, Claire, & Winsler, Adam. (2010). Protecting children from exposure to lead: Old problem, new data, and new policy needs. *Social Policy Report, 24,* 3–29.

Coles, Robert. (1997). *The moral intelligence of children: How to raise a moral child*. New York, NY: Random House.

Collins, Juliet, Johnson, Susan L., & Krebs, Nancy F. (2004). Screen for and treat overweight in 2- to 5-year-olds? Yes! *Contemporary Pediatrics, 21,* 60–74.

Collins, Michael F. (with Kay, Tess). (2003). *Sport and social exclusion*. London, England: Routledge.

Collins, W. Andrew, & Laursen, Brett. (2004). Parent-adolescent relationships and influences. In Richard M. Lerner & Laurence D. Steinberg (Eds.), *Handbook of adolescent psychology* (2nd ed., pp. 331–361). Hoboken, NJ: Wiley.

Compas, Bruce E. (2004). Processes of risk and resilience during adolescence: Linking contexts and individuals. In Richard M. Lerner & Laurence D. Steinberg (Eds.), *Handbook of adolescent psychology* (2nd ed., pp. 263–296). Hoboken, NJ: Wiley.

Compian, Laura J., Gowen, L. Kris, & Hayward, Chris. (2009). The interactive effects of puberty and peer victimization on weight concerns and depression symptoms among early adolescent girls. *The Journal of Early Adolescence, 29,* 357–375.

Conboy, Barbara T., & Thal, Donna J. (2006). Ties between the lexicon and grammar: Cross-sectional and longitudinal studies of bilingual toddlers. *Child Development, 77,* 712–735.

Conger, John J. (1975). Proceedings of the American Psychological Association, Incorporated, for the year 1974: Minutes of the annual meeting of the Council of Representatives. *American Psychologist, 30,* 620–651.

Conger, Rand D., Wallace, Lora Ebert, Sun, Yumei, Simons, Ronald L., McLoyd, Vonnie C., & Brody, Gene H. (2002). Economic pressure in African American families: A replication and extension of the family stress model. *Developmental Psychology, 38,* 179–193.

Conley, Colleen S., & Rudolph, Karen D. (2009). The emerging sex difference in adolescent depression: Interacting contributions of puberty and peer stress. *Development and Psychopathology, 21,* 593–620.

Conley, Dalton, & Glauber, Rebecca. (2008). All in the family? Family composition, resources, and sibling similarity in socioeconomic status.

Research in Social Stratification and Mobility, 26, 297–306.

Cooper, Carey E., McLanahan, Sara S., Meadows, Sarah O., & Brooks-Gunn, Jeanne. (2009). Family structure transitions and maternal parenting stress. *Journal of Marriage and Family, 71,* 558–574.

Coovadia, Hoosen M., & Wittenberg, Dankwart F. (Eds.). (2004). *Paediatrics and child health: A manual for health professionals in developing countries* (5th ed.). New York, NY: Oxford University Press.

Coplan, Robert J., & Weeks, Murray. (2009). Shy and soft-spoken: Shyness, pragmatic language, and socio-emotional adjustment in early childhood. *Infant and Child Development, 18,* 238–254.

Corballis, Michael C. (2010). Mirror neurons and the evolution of language. *Brain and Language, 112,* 25–35.

Corballis, Michael C. (2011). *The recursive mind: The origins of human language, thought, and civilization.* Princeton, NJ: Princeton University Press.

Correa-Chavez, Maricela, Rogoff, Barbara, & Arauz, Rebeca Mejia. (2005). Cultural patterns in attending to two events at once. *Child Development, 76,* 664–678.

Cosgrave, James F. (2010). Embedded addiction: The social production of gambling knowledge and the development of gambling markets. *Canadian Journal of Sociology, 35,* 113–134.

Côté, James E. (2006). Emerging adulthood as an institutionalized moratorium: Risks and benefits to identity formation. In Jeffrey Jensen Arnett & Jennifer Lynn Tanner (Eds.), *Emerging adults in America: Coming of age in the 21st century* (pp. 85–116). Washington, DC: American Psychological Association.

Côté, James E. (2009). Identity formation and self-development in adolescence. In Richard M. Lerner & Laurence Steinberg (Eds.), *Handbook of adolescent psychology: Vol. 1. Individual bases of adolescent development* (3rd ed., pp. 266–304). Hoboken, NJ: Wiley.

Cote, Linda R., & Bornstein, Marc H. (2009). Child and mother play in three U.S. cultural groups: Comparisons and associations. *Journal of Family Psychology, 23,* 355–363.

Côté, Sylvana M., Borge, Anne I., Geoffroy, Marie-Claude, Rutter, Michael, & Tremblay, Richard E. (2008). Nonmaternal care in infancy and emotional/behavioral difficulties at 4 years old: Moderation by family risk characteristics. *Developmental Psychology, 44,* 155–168.

Courage, Mary L., & Setliff, Alissa E. (2010). When babies watch television: Attention-getting, attention-holding, and the implications for learning from video material. *Developmental Review, 30,* 220–238.

Couzin-Frankel, Jennifer. (2011, February 11). What would you do? *Science, 331,* 662–665.

Cowan, Nelson (Ed.). (1997). *The development of memory in childhood.* Hove, East Sussex, UK: Psychology Press.

Cowan, Nelson. (2010). The magical mystery four. *Current Directions in Psychological Science, 19,* 51–57.

Cowan, Nelson, & Alloway, Tracy. (2009). Development of working memory in childhood. In Mary L. Courage & Nelson Cowan (Eds.), *The development of memory in infancy and childhood* (2nd ed., pp. 303–342). New York, NY: Psychology Press.

Coward, Fiona. (2008, March 14). Standing on the shoulders of giants. *Science, 319,* 1493–1495.

Cramer, Robert, Lipinski, Ryan, Bowman, Ashley, & Carollo, Tanner. (2009). Subjective distress to violations of trust in Mexican American close relationships conforms to evolutionary principles. *Current Psychology, 28,* 1–11.

Crawford, Emily, Wright, Margaret O'Dougherty, & Masten, Ann S. (2006). Resilience and spirituality in youth. In Eugene C. Roehlkepartain, Pamela Ebstyne King, Linda Wagener, & Peter L. Benson (Eds.), *The handbook of spiritual development in childhood and adolescence* (pp. 355–370). Thousand Oaks, CA: Sage Publications.

Crinion, Jenny, Turner, R., Grogan, Alice, Hanakawa, Takashi, Noppeney, Uta, Devlin, Joseph T., et al. (2006, June 9). Language control in the bilingual brain. *Science, 312,* 1537–1540.

Crisp, Richard J., & Turner, Rhiannon N. (2011). Cognitive adaptation to the experience of social and cultural diversity. *Psychological Bulletin, 137,* 242–266.

Crone, Eveline A., & Ridderinkhof, K. Richard. (2011). The developing brain: From theory to neuroimaging and back. *Developmental Cognitive Neuroscience, 1,* 101–109.

Crone, Eveline A., & Westenberg, P. Michiel. (2009). A brain-based account of developmental changes in social decision making. In Michelle de Haan & Megan R. Gunnar (Eds.), *Handbook of developmental social neuroscience* (pp. 378–396). New York, NY: Guilford.

Crosnoe, Robert, Johnson, Monica Kirkpatrick, & Elder, Glen H., Jr. (2004). Intergenerational bonding in school: The behavioral and contextual correlates of student-teacher relationships. *Sociology of Education, 77,* 60–81.

Crosnoe, Robert, Leventhal, Tama, Wirth, Robert John, Pierce, Kim M., Pianta, Robert C., & NICHD Early Child Care Research Network. (2010). Family socioeconomic status and consistent environmental stimulation in early childhood. *Child Development, 81,* 972–987.

Crosnoe, Robert, & Needham, Belinda. (2004). Holism, contextual variability, and the study of friendships in adolescent development. *Child Development, 75,* 264–279.

Cross, Donna, Monks, Helen, Hall, Marg, Shaw, Thérèse, Pintabona, Yolanda, Erceg, Erin, et al. (2010). Three-year results of the Friendly Schools whole-of-school intervention on children's bullying behaviour. *British Educational Research Journal, 37,* 105–129.

Cruz, Alvaro A., Bateman, Eric D., & Bousquet, Jean. (2010). The social determinants of asthma. *European Respiratory Journal, 35,* 239–242.

Cruz-Inigo, Andres E., Ladizinski, Barry, & Sethi, Aisha. (2011). Albinism in Africa: Stigma, slaughter and awareness campaigns. *Dermatologic Clinics, 29,* 79–87.

Cuijpers, Pim, Brännmark, Jessica G., & van Straten, Annemieke. (2008). Psychological treatment of postpartum depression: A meta-analysis. *Journal of Clinical Psychology, 64,* 103–118.

Cumsille, Patricio, Darling, Nancy, & Martínez, M. Loreto. (2010). Shading the truth: The patterning of adolescents' decisions to avoid issues, disclose, or lie to parents. *Journal of Adolescence, 33,* 285–296.

Cunha, Marcus, Jr., & Caldieraro, Fabio. (2009). Sunk-cost effects on purely behavioral investments. *Cognitive Science, 33,* 105–113.

Currie, Janet, & Widom, Cathy Spatz. (2010). Long-term consequences of child abuse and neglect on adult economic well-being. *Child Maltreatment, 15,* 111–120.

Curtis, W. John, & Cicchetti, Dante. (2003). Moving research on resilience into the 21st century: Theoretical and methodological considerations in examining the biological contributors to resilience. *Development & Psychopathology, 15,* 773–810.

D'Angelo, Denise, Williams, Letitia, Morrow, Brian, Cox, Shanna, Harris, Norma, Harrison, Leslie, et al. (2007). Preconception and interconception health status of women who recently gave birth to a live-born infant—Pregnancy Risk Assessment Monitoring System (PRAMS), United States, 26 reporting areas, 2004. *MMWR Surveillance Summaries, 56*(SS10), 1–35.

Daddis, Christopher. (2010). Adolescent peer crowds and patterns of belief in the boundaries of personal authority. *Journal of Adolescence, 33,* 699–708.

Dahl, Ronald E. (2004). Adolescent brain development: A period of vulnerabilities and opportunities. Keynote address. In Ronald E. Dahl & Linda Patia Spear (Eds.), *Adolescent brain development: Vulnerabilities and opportunities* (Vol. 1021, pp. 1–22). New York, NY: New York Academy of Sciences.

Dahl, Ronald E., & Gunnar, Megan R. (2009). Heightened stress responsiveness and emotional reactivity during pubertal maturation: Implications for psychopathology. *Development and Psychopathology, 21,* 1–6.

Dai, David Yun. (2010). *The nature and nurture of giftedness: A new framework for understanding gifted education.* New York, NY: Teachers College Press.

Daley, Dave, Jones, Karen, Hutchings, Judy, & Thompson, Margaret. (2009). Attention deficit hyperactivity disorder in pre-school children: Current findings, recommended interventions and future directions. *Child: Care, Health and Development, 35,* 754–766.

Dalman, Christina, Allebeck, Peter, Gunnell, David, Harrison, Glyn, Kristensson, Krister, Lewis, Glyn, et al. (2008). Infections in the

CNS during childhood and the risk of subsequent psychotic illness: A cohort study of more than one million Swedish subjects. *American Journal of Psychiatry, 165,* 59–65.

Damasio, Antonio R. (2003). *Looking for Spinoza: Joy, sorrow, and the feeling brain*. Orlando, FL: Harcourt.

Damasio, Antonio R. (2010). *Self comes to mind: Constructing the conscious brain*. New York, NY: Pantheon Books.

Danel, Isabella, Berg, Cynthia, Johnson, Christopher H., & Atrash, Hani. (2003). Magnitude of maternal morbidity during labor and delivery: United States, 1993–1997. *American Journal of Public Health, 93,* 631–634.

Darling, Nancy, Cumsille, Patricio, & Martinez, M. Loreto. (2008). Individual differences in adolescents' beliefs about the legitimacy of parental authority and their own obligation to obey: A longitudinal investigation. *Child Development, 79,* 1103–1118.

Daro, Deborah. (2002). Public perception of child sexual abuse: Who is to blame? *Child Abuse & Neglect, 26,* 1131–1133.

Darwin, Charles. (1859). *On the origin of species by means of natural selection*. London, England: J. Murray.

Dasen, Pierre R. (2003). Theoretical frameworks in cross-cultural developmental psychology: An attempt at integration. In T. S. Saraswati (Ed.), *Cross-cultural perspectives in human development: Theory, research, and applications* (pp. 128–165). New Delhi, India: Sage.

Datan, Nancy. (1986). Oedipal conflict, platonic love: Centrifugal forces in intergenerational relations. In Nancy Datan, Anita L. Greene, & Hayne W. Reese (Eds.), *Life-span developmental psychology: Intergenerational relations* (pp. 29–50). Hillsdale, NJ: Erlbaum.

David, Barbara, Grace, Diane, & Ryan, Michelle K. (2004). The gender wars: A self-categorization perspective on the development of gender identity. In Mark Bennett & Fabio Sani (Eds.), *The development of the social self* (pp. 135–157). Hove, East Sussex, England: Psychology Press.

Davidson, Julia O'Connell. (2005). *Children in the global sex trade*. Malden, MA: Polity.

Davis, Elysia Poggi, Parker, Susan Whitmore, Tottenham, Nim, & Gunnar, Megan R. (2003). Emotion, cognition, and the hypothalamic-pituitary-adrenocortical axis: A developmental perspective. In Michelle de Haan & Mark H. Johnson (Eds.), *The cognitive neuroscience of development* (pp. 181–206). New York, NY: Psychology Press.

Davis, Linell (1999). *Doing culture: Cross-cultural communication in action*. Beijing, China: Foreign Language Teaching & Research Press.

Davis, Mark, & Squire, Corinne (Eds.). (2010). *HIV treatment and prevention technologies in international perspective*. New York, NY: Palgrave Macmillan.

Davis-Kean, Pamela E., Jager, Justin, & Collins, W. Andrew (2009). The self in action: An emerging link between self-beliefs and behaviors in middle childhood. *Child Development Perspectives, 3,* 184–188.

Davison, Kirsten Krahnstoever, Werder, Jessica L., Trost, Stewart G., Baker, Birgitta L., & Birch, Leann L. (2007). Why are early maturing girls less active? Links between pubertal development, psychological well-being, and physical activity among girls at ages 11 and 13. *Social Science & Medicine, 64,* 2391–2404.

Dawes, Nickki Pearce, & Larson, Reed. (2011). How youth get engaged: Grounded-theory research on motivational development in organized youth programs. *Developmental Psychology, 47,* 259–269.

Dawson, Geraldine. (2010). Recent advances in research on early detection, causes, biology, and treatment of autism spectrum disorders. *Current Opinion in Neurology, 23,* 95–96.

Dawson, Lorne L. (2010). The study of new religious movements and the radicalization of home-grown terrorists: Opening a dialogue. *Terrorism and Political Violence, 22,* 1–21.

Dawson, Michelle, Soulières, Isabelle, Gernsbacher, Morton Ann, & Mottron, Laurent. (2007). The level and nature of autistic intelligence. *Psychological Science, 18,* 657–662.

De Dreu, Carsten K. W., Nijstad, Bernard A., & van Knippenberg, Daan. (2008). Motivated information processing in group judgment and decision making. *Personality and Social Psychology Review,* 22–49.

de Haan, Amaranta D., Prinzie, Peter, & Dekovic, Maja. (2009). Mothers' and fathers' personality and parenting: The mediating role of sense of competence. *Developmental Psychology, 45,* 1695–1707.

de Heering, Adelaide, de Liedekerke, Claire, Deboni, Malorie, & Rossion, Bruno. (2010). The role of experience during childhood in shaping the other-race effect. *Developmental Science, 13,* 181–187.

de Jonge, Ank, van der Goes, Birgit Y., Ravelli, Anita C. J., Amelink-Verburg, Marianne P., Mol, Ben Willem, Nijhuis, Jan G., et al. (2009). Perinatal mortality and morbidity in a nationwide cohort of 529,688 low-risk planned home and hospital births. *BJOG: An International Journal of Obstetrics & Gynaecology, 116,* 1177–1184.

De Lee, Joseph Bolivar. (1938). *The principles and practice of obstetrics* (7th ed.). Philadelphia, PA: Saunders.

De Neys, Wim. (2006). Dual processing in reasoning: Two systems but one reasoner. *Psychological Science, 17,* 428–433.

De Neys, Wim, & Van Gelder, Elke. (2009). Logic and belief across the lifespan: The rise and fall of belief inhibition during syllogistic reasoning. *Developmental Science, 12,* 123–130.

de Schipper, Elles J., Riksen-Walraven, J. Marianne, & Geurts, Sabine A. E. (2006). Effects of child-caregiver ratio on the interactions between caregivers and children in child-care centers: An experimental study. *Child Development, 77,* 861–874.

Dean, Angela J, Walters, Julie, & Hall, Anthony. (2010). A systematic review of interventions to enhance medication adherence in children and adolescents with chronic illness. *Archives of Disease in Childhood, 95,* 717–723.

Dearing, Eric, Wimer, Christopher, Simpkins, Sandra D., Lund, Terese, Bouffard, Suzanne M., Caronongan, Pia, et al. (2009). Do neighborhood and home contexts help explain why low-income children miss opportunities to participate in activities outside of school? *Developmental Psychology, 45,* 1545–1562.

Decety, Jean. (2011). Dissecting the neural mechanisms mediating empathy. *Emotion Review, 3,* 92–108.

Deci, Edward L., Koestner, Richard, & Ryan, Richard M. (1999). A meta-analytic review of experiments examining the effects of extrinsic rewards on intrinsic motivation. *Psychological Bulletin, 125,* 627–668.

Degenhardt, Louisa, Coffey, Carolyn, Carlin, John B., Swift, Wendy, Moore, Elya, & Patton, George C. (2010). Outcomes of occasional cannabis use in adolescence: 10-year follow-up study in Victoria, Australia. *The British Journal of Psychiatry, 196,* 290–295.

DeLoache, Judy S., Chiong, Cynthia, Sherman, Kathleen, Islam, Nadia, Vanderborght, Mieke, Troseth, Georgene L., et al. (2010). Do babies learn from baby media? *Psychological Science, 21,* 1570–1574.

Demetriou, Andreas, & Bakracevic, Karin. (2009). Reasoning and self-awareness from adolescence to middle age: Organization and development as a function of education. *Learning and Individual Differences, 19,* 181–194.

Denham, Susanne A., Blair, Kimberly A., DeMulder, Elizabeth, Levitas, Jennifer, Sawyer, Katherine, Auerbach-Major, Sharon, et al. (2003). Preschool emotional competence: Pathway to social competence. *Child Development, 74,* 238–256.

Denny, Dallas, & Pittman, Cathy. (2007). Gender identity: From dualism to diversity. In Mitchell S. Tepper & Annette Fuglsang Owens (Eds.), *Sexual health: Vol. 1. Psychological foundations* (pp. 205–229). Westport, CT: Praeger/Greenwood.

Denton, Melinda Lundquist, Pearce, Lisa D., & Smith, Christian. (2008). *Religion and spirituality on the path through adolescence* (Research Report Number 8). Chapel Hill, NC: National Study of Youth and Religion, University of North Carolina at Chapel Hill.

Deptula, Daneen P., Henry, David B., & Schoeny, Michael E. (2010). How can parents make a difference? Longitudinal associations with adolescent sexual behavior. *Journal of Family Psychology, 24,* 731–739.

Desai, Sonalde, & Andrist, Lester. (2010). Gender scripts and age at marriage in India. *Demography, 47,* 667–687.

DesJardin, Jean L., Ambrose, Sophie E., & Eisenberg, Laurie S. (2009). Literacy skills in children with cochlear implants: The importance of early oral language and joint storybook reading. *Journal of Deaf Studies and Deaf Education, 14,* 22–43.

Desoete, Annemie, Stock, Pieter, Schepens, Annemie, Baeyens, Dieter, & Roeyers, Herbert. (2009). Classification, seriation, and counting in grades 1, 2, and 3 as two-year longitudinal predictors for low achieving in numerical facility and arithmetical achievement? *Journal of Psychoeducational Assessment, 27,* 252–264.

Devi, Sharmila. (2008). Progress on childhood obesity patchy in the USA. *Lancet, 371,* 105–106.

DeVito, Loren M., Kanter, Benjamin R., & Eichenbaum, Howard. (2010). The hippocampus contributes to memory expression during transitive inference in mice. *Hippocampus, 20,* 208–217.

Diallo, Yacouba, Hagemann, Frank, Etienne, Alex, Gurbuzer, Yonca, & Mehran, Farhad (2010). *Global child labour developments: Measuring trends from 2004 to 2008.* Geneva, Switzerland: International Labour Office, International Programme on the Elimination of Child Labour.

Diamanti-Kandarakis, Evanthia, Bourguignon, Jean-Pierre, Giudice, Linda C., Hauser, Russ, Prins, Gail S., Soto, Ana M., et al. (2009). Endocrine-disrupting chemicals: An endocrine society scientific statement. *Endocrine Society, 30,* 293–342.

Diamond, Adele, & Amso, Dima. (2008). Contributions of neuroscience to our understanding of cognitive development. *Current Directions in Psychological Science, 17,* 136–141.

Diamond, Adele, Barnett, W. Steven, Thomas, Jessica, & Munro, Sarah. (2007, November 30). Preschool program improves cognitive control. *Science, 318,* 1387–1388.

Diamond, David M., Dunwiddie, Thomas V., & Rose, Gregory M. (1988). Characteristics of hippocampal primed burst potentiation in vitro and in the awake rat. *Journal of Neuroscience, 8,* 4079–4088.

Diamond, Lisa M., & Fagundes, Christopher P. (2010). Psychobiological research on attachment. *Journal of Social and Personal Relationships, 27,* 218–225.

Diamond, Mathew E. (2007). Neuronal basis of perceptual intelligence. In Flavia Santoianni & Claudia Sabatano (Eds.), *Brain development in learning environments: Embodied and perceptual advancements* (pp. 98–108). Newcastle, UK: Cambridge Scholars.

Diener, Marissa. (2000). Gift from the gods: A Balinese guide to early child rearing. In Judy S. DeLoache & Alma Gottlieb (Eds.), *A world of babies: Imagined childcare guides for seven societies* (pp. 96–116). New York, NY: Cambridge University Press.

Dietrich, Anne. (2008). *When the hurting continues: Revictimization and perpetration in the lives of childhood maltreatment survivors.* Saarbrücken, Germany: VDM Verlag.

DiGirolamo, Ann, Thompson, Nancy, Martorell, Reynaldo, Fein, Sara, & Grummer-Strawn, Laurence. (2005). Intention or experience? Predictors of continued breastfeeding. *Health Education & Behavior, 32,* 208–226.

Dijk, Jan A. G. M. van. (2005). *The deepening divide: Inequality in the information society.* Thousand Oaks, CA: Sage.

Dijksterhuis, Ap, & Aarts, Henk. (2010). Goals, attention, and (un)consciousness. *Annual Review of Psychology, 61,* 467–490.

Dilworth-Bart, Janean E., & Moore, Colleen F. (2006). Mercy mercy me: Social injustice and the prevention of environmental pollutant exposures among ethnic minority and poor children. *Child Development, 77,* 247–265.

DiPietro, Janet A., Hilton, Sterling C., Hawkins, Melissa, Costigan, Kathleen A., & Pressman, Eva K. (2002). Maternal stress and affect influence fetal neurobehavioral development. *Developmental Psychology, 38,* 659–668.

Dirix, Chantal E. H., Nijhuis, Jan G., Jongsma, Henk W., & Hornstra, Gerard. (2009). Aspects of fetal learning and memory. *Child Development, 80,* 1251–1258.

Dishion, Thomas J., & Bullock, Bernadette Marie. (2002). Parenting and adolescent problem behavior: An ecological analysis of the nurturance hypothesis. In John G. Borkowski, Sharon Landesman Ramey, & Marie Bristol-Power (Eds.), *Parenting and the child's world: Influences on academic, intellectual, and social-emotional development* (pp. 231–249). Mahwah, NJ: Erlbaum.

Dishion, Thomas J., Poulin, François, & Burraston, Bert. (2001). Peer group dynamics associated with iatrogenic effects in group interventions with high-risk young adolescents. In William Damon (Series Ed.) & Douglas W. Nangle & Cynthia A. Erdley (Vol. Eds.), *New Directions for Child and Adolescent Development: No. 91. The role of friendship in psychological adjustment* (pp. 79–92). San Francisco, CA: Jossey-Bass.

Dishion, Thomas J., Véronneau, Marie-Hélène, & Myers, Michael W. (2010). Cascading peer dynamics underlying the progression from problem behavior to violence in early to late adolescence. *Development and Psychopathology, 22,* 603–619.

Dobson, Velma, Candy, T. Rowan, Hartmann, E. Eugenie, Mayer, D. Luisa, Miller, Joseph M., & Quinn, Graham E. (2009). Infant and child vision research: Present status and future directions. *Optometry & Vision Science, 86,* 559–560.

Dodge, Kenneth A. (2009). Mechanisms of gene–environment interaction effects in the development of conduct disorder. *Perspectives on Psychological Science, 4,* 408–414.

Dodge, Kenneth A., Coie, John D., & Lynam, Donald R. (2006). Aggression and antisocial behavior in youth. In William Damon & Richard M. Lerner (Series Eds.) & Nancy Eisenberg (Vol. Ed.), *Handbook of child psychology: Vol. 3. Social, emotional, and personality development* (6th ed., pp. 719–788). New York, NY: Wiley.

Domina, Thurston, Conley, AnneMarie, & Farkas, George. (2011a). The case for dreaming big. *Sociology of Education, 84,* 118–121.

Domina, Thurston, Conley, AnneMarie, & Farkas, George. (2011b). The link between educational expectations and effort in the college-for-all era. *Sociology of Education, 84,* 93–112.

Dominguez, Ximena, Vitiello, Virginia E., Maier, Michelle F., & Greenfield, Daryl B. (2010). A longitudinal examination of young children's learning behavior: Child-level and classroom-level predictors of change throughout the preschool year. *School Psychology Review, 39,* 29–47.

Donaldson, Margaret C. (2003). *A study of children's thinking.* New York, NY: Routledge. (Original work published 1963)

dosReis, Susan, Mychailyszyn, Matthew P., Evans-Lacko, Sara E., Beltran, Alicia, Riley, Anne W., & Myers, Mary Anne. (2009). The meaning of attention-deficit/hyperactivity disorder medication and parents' initiation and continuity of treatment for their child. *Journal of Child and Adolescent Psychopharmacology, 19,* 377–383.

dosReis, Susan, & Myers, Mary Anne. (2008). Parental attitudes and involvement in psychopharmacological treatment for ADHD: A conceptual model. *International Review of Psychiatry, 20,* 135–141.

Dowling, John E. (2004). *The great brain debate: Nature or nurture?* Washington, DC: Joseph Henry Press.

Drover, James, Hoffman, Dennis R., Castañeda, Yolanda S., Morale, Sarah E., & Birch, Eileen E. (2009). Three randomized controlled trials of early long-chain polyunsaturated fatty acid supplementation on means-end problem solving in 9-month-olds. *Child Development, 80,* 1376–1384.

Dukes, Richard L., Stein, Judith A., & Zane, Jazmin I. (2009). Effect of relational bullying on attitudes, behavior and injury among adolescent bullies, victims and bully-victims. *The Social Science Journal, 46,* 671–688.

Duncan, Greg J., Ziol-Guest, Kathleen M., & Kalil, Ariel. (2010). Early-childhood poverty and adult attainment, behavior, and health. *Child Development, 81,* 306–325.

Duncan, Jhodie R., Paterson, David S., Hoffman, Jill M., Mokler, David J., Borenstein, Natalia S., Belliveau, Richard A., et al. (2010). Brainstem serotonergic deficiency in sudden infant death syndrome. *Journal of the American Medical Association, 303,* 430–437.

Dunn, Judy, & Hughes, Claire. (2001). "I got some swords and you're dead!": Violent fantasy, antisocial behavior, friendship, and moral sensibility in young children. *Child Development, 72,* 491–505.

Dunphy, Dexter C. (1963). The social structure of urban adolescent peer groups. *Sociometry, 26,* 230–246.

Durkee, Tony, Kaess, Michael, Floderus, Birgitta, Carli, Vladimir, & Wasserman, Danuta. (2011). Adolescent internet behavior and its correlation to depression, self-harm and suicidal behavior in European pupils. *European Psychiatry, 26*(Suppl. 1), 1863.

Dweck, Carol S. (2007). Is math a gift? Beliefs that put females at risk. In Stephen J. Ceci & Wendy M. Williams (Eds.), *Why aren't* *more women in science: Top researchers debate the evidence* (pp. 47–55). Washington, DC: American Psychological Association.

Eccles, Jacquelynne. (2011). Gendered educational and occupational choices: Applying the Eccles et al. model of achievement-related choices. *International Journal of Behavioral Development, 35,* 195–201.

Eccles, Jacquelynne C., & Roeser, Robert W. (2010). An ecological view of schools and development. In Judith L. Meece & Jacquelynne S. Eccles (Eds.), *Handbook of research on schools, schooling, and human development* (pp. 6–22). New York, NY: Routledge.

Eccles, Jacquelynne S., & Roeser, Robert W. (2011). Schools as developmental contexts during adolescence. *Journal of Research on Adolescence, 21,* 225–241.

Eckstein, Daniel G., Rasmussen, Paul R., & Wittschen, Lori. (1999). Understanding and dealing with adolescents. *Journal of Individual Psychology, 55,* 31–50.

Education Week. (2010, January 14). *Chance for success* [Table]. Retrieved from http://www.edweek.org/media/ew/qc/2010/17sos.h29.chance.pdf

Edwards, Judge Leonard. (2010). Relative placement in child protection cases: A judicial perspective. *Juvenile and Family Court Journal, 61,* 1–44.

Eggum, Natalie D., Eisenberg, Nancy, Kao, Karen, Spinrad, Tracy L., Bolnick, Rebecca, Hofer, Claire, et al. (2011). Emotion understanding, theory of mind, and prosocial orientation: Relations over time in early childhood. *The Journal of Positive Psychology, 6,* 4–16.

Eisenberg, Nancy, Cumberland, Amanda, Guthrie, Ivanna K., Murphy, Bridget C., & Shepard, Stephanie A. (2005). Age changes in prosocial responding and moral reasoning in adolescence and early adulthood. *Journal of Research on Adolescence, 15,* 235–260.

Eisenberg, Nancy, Fabes, Richard A., & Spinrad, Tracy L. (2006). Prosocial development. In William Damon & Richard M. Lerner (Series Eds.) & Nancy Eisenberg (Vol. Ed.), *Handbook of child psychology: Vol. 3. Social, emotional, and personality development* (6th ed., pp. 646–718). Hoboken, NJ: Wiley.

Eisenberg, Nancy, Hofer, Claire, Spinrad, Tracy L., Gershoff, Elizabeth T., Valiente, Carlos, Losoya, Sandra, et al. (2008). Understanding mother-adolescent conflict discussions: Concurrent and across-time prediction from youths' dispositions and parenting. *Monographs of the Society for Research in Child Development,* 73(2, Serial No. 290), vii–viii, 1–160.

Eisenberg, Nancy, Spinrad, Tracy L., Fabes, Richard A., Reiser, Mark, Cumberland, Amanda, Shepard, Stephanie A., et al. (2004). The relations of effortful control and impulsivity to children's resiliency and adjustment. *Child Development, 75,* 25–46.

Eklund, Jenny M., Kerr, Margaret, & Stattin, Håkan. (2010). Romantic relationships and delinquent behaviour in adolescence: The moderating role of delinquency propensity. *Journal of Adolescence, 33,* 377–386.

Elder, Glen H., Jr,, & Shanahan, Michael J. (2006). The life course and human development. In William Damon & Richard M. Lerner (Series Eds.) & Richard M. Lerner (Vol. Ed.), *Handbook of child psychology: Vol. 1. Theoretical models of human development* (6th ed., pp. 665–715). Hoboken, NJ: Wiley.

Elia, Josephine, & Vetter, Victoria L. (2010). Cardiovascular effects of medications for the treatment of attention-deficit hyperactivity disorder: What is known and how should it influence prescribing in children? *Pediatric Drugs, 12,* 165–175.

Elkind, David. (1967). Egocentrism in adolescence. *Child Development, 38,* 1025–1034.

Elkind, David. (2007). *The power of play: How spontaneous, imaginative activities lead to happier, healthier children.* Cambridge, MA: Da Capo Press.

Elliott, Leslie, Arbes, Samuel J., Jr., Harvey, Eric S., Lee, Robert C., Salo, Päivi M., Cohn, Richard D., et al. (2007). Dust weight and asthma prevalence in the National Survey of Lead and Allergens in Housing (NSLAH). *Environmental Health Perspectives, 115,* 215–220.

Ellis, Bruce J., & Boyce, W. Thomas. (2008). Biological sensitivity to context. *Current Directions in Psychological Science, 17,* 183–187.

Ellis, Bruce J., Shirtcliff, Elizabeth A., Boyce, W. Thomas, Deardorff, Julianna, & Essex, Marilyn J. (2011). Quality of early family relationships and the timing and tempo of puberty: Effects depend on biological sensitivity to context. *Development and Psychopathology, 23,* 85–99.

Else-Quest, Nicole M., Hyde, Janet Shibley, Goldsmith, H. Hill, & Van Hulle, Carol A. (2006). Gender differences in temperament: A meta-analysis. *Psychological Bulletin, 132,* 33–72.

Engelberts, Adèle C., & de Jonge, Guus A. (1990). Choice of sleeping position for infants: Possible association with cot death. *Archives of Disease in Childhood, 65,* 462–467.

Engels, Rutger C. M. E., Scholte, Ron H. J., van Lieshout, Cornelis F. M., de Kemp, Raymond, & Overbeek, Geertjan. (2006). Peer group reputation and smoking and alcohol consumption in early adolescence. *Addictive Behaviors, 31,* 440–449.

Englander, Elizabeth, Mills, Elizabeth, & McCoy, Meghan. (2009). Cyberbullying and information exposure: User-generated content in post-secondary education. *International Journal of Contemporary Sociology, 46,* 213–230.

Enserink, Martin. (2011, February 18). Can this DNA sleuth help catch criminals? *Science, 331,* 838–840.

Epps, Chad, & Holt, Lynn. (2011). The genetic basis of addiction and relevant cellular mechanisms. *International Anesthesiology Clinics, 49,* 3–14.

Epstein, Jeffery N., Langberg, Joshua M., Lichtenstein, Philip K., Altaye, Mekibib, Brinkman, William B., House, Katherine, et al. (2010). Attention-deficit/hyperactivity disorder outcomes for children treated in community-based pediatric settings. *Archives of Pediatrics & Adolescent Medicine, 164,* 160–165.

Epstein, Leonard H., Handley, Elizabeth A., Dearing, Kelly K., Cho, David D., Roemmich, James N., Paluch, Rocco A., et al. (2006). Purchases of food in youth: Influence of price and income. *Psychological Science, 17,* 82–89.

Erath, Stephen A., Keiley, Margaret K., Pettit, Gregory S., Lansford, Jennifer E., Dodge, Kenneth A., & Bates, John E. (2009). Behavioral predictors of mental health service utilization in childhood through adolescence. *Journal of Developmental & Behavioral Pediatrics, 30,* 481–488.

Erikson, Erik H. (1963). *Childhood and society* (2nd ed.). New York, NY: Norton.

Erikson, Erik H. (1968). *Identity: Youth and crisis.* New York, NY: Norton.

Erikson, Erik H. (1969). *Gandhi's truth: On the origins of militant nonviolence.* New York, NY: Norton.

Erikson, Erik H. (1982). *The life cycle completed: A review.* New York, NY: Norton.

Ertesvåg, Sigrun K. (2011). Measuring authoritative teaching. *Teaching and Teacher Education, 27,* 51–61.

Ertmer, David J., Young, Nancy M., & Nathani, Suneeti. (2007). Profiles of vocal development in young cochlear implant recipients. *Journal of Speech, Language, and Hearing Research, 50,* 393–407.

Etchu, Koji. (2007). Social context and preschoolers' judgments about aggressive behavior: Social domain theory. *Japanese Journal of Educational Psychology, 55,* 219–230.

Evans, Angela D., Xu, Fen, & Lee, Kang. (2011). When all signs point to you: Lies told in the face of evidence. *Developmental Psychology, 47,* 39–49.

Evans, David W., & Leckman, James F. (2006). Origins of obsessive-compulsive disorder: Developmental and evolutionary perspectives. In Dante Cicchetti & Donald J. Cohen (Eds.), *Developmental psychopathology: Vol. 3. Risk, disorder, and adaptation* (2nd ed., pp. 404–435). Hoboken, NJ: Wiley.

Evans, David W., Leckman, James F., Carter, Alice, Reznick, J. Steven, Henshaw, Desiree, King, Robert A., et al. (1997). Ritual, habit, and perfectionism: The prevalence and development of compulsive-like behavior in normal young children. *Child Development, 68,* 58–68.

Eyer, Diane E. (1992). *Mother-infant bonding: A scientific fiction.* New Haven, CT: Yale University Press.

Fagard, Jacqueline, & Lockman, Jeffrey J. (2010). Change in imitation for object manipulation between 10 and 12 months of age. *Developmental Psychobiology, 52,* 90–99.

Falbo, Toni, Kim, Sunghun, & Chen, Kuan-yi. (2009). Alternate models of sibling status effects on health in later life. *Developmental Psychology, 45,* 677–687.

Falk, Dean. (2004). Prelinguistic evolution in early hominins: Whence motherese? *Behavioral and Brain Sciences, 27,* 491–503.

Farahani, Mansour, Subramanian, S. V., & Canning, David. (2009). The effect of changes in health sector resources on infant mortality in the short-run and the long-run: A longitudinal econometric analysis. *Social Science & Medicine, 68,* 1918–1925.

Faraone, Stephen V., Sergeant, Joseph, Gillberg, Christopher, & Biederman, Joseph. (2003). The worldwide prevalence of ADHD: Is it an American condition? *World Psychiatry, 2,* 104–113.

Farmer, Thomas W., Hamm, Jill V., Petrin, Robert A., Robertson, Dylan, Murray, Robert A., Meece, Judith L., et al. (2010). Supporting early adolescent learning and social strengths: Promoting productive contexts for students at-risk for EBD during the transition to middle school. *Exceptionality, 18,* 94–106.

Farrar, Ruth D., & Al-Qatawneh, Khalil S. (2010). Interdisciplinary theoretical foundations for literacy teaching and learning. *European Journal of Social Sciences, 13,* 56–66.

Farrelly, Matthew C., Davis, Kevin C., Haviland, M. Lyndon, Messeri, Peter, & Healton, Cheryl G. (2005). Evidence of a dose-response relationship between "truth" antismoking ads and youth smoking prevalence. *American Journal of Public Health, 95,* 425–431.

Fazzi, Elisa, Signorini, Sabrina Giovanna, Bomba, Monica, Luparia, Antonella, Lanners, Josée, & Balottin, Umberto. (2011). Reach on sound: A key to object permanence in visually impaired children. *Early Human Development, 87,* 289–296.

Fechter-Leggett, Molly O., & O'Brien, Kirk. (2010). The effects of kinship care on adult mental health outcomes of alumni of foster care. *Children and Youth Services Review, 32,* 206–213.

Feldman, Ruth. (2007). Parent-infant synchrony and the construction of shared timing; Physiological precursors, developmental outcomes, and risk conditions. *Journal of Child Psychology and Psychiatry, 48,* 329–354.

Feldman, Ruth, & Eidelman, Arthur I. (2004). Parent-infant synchrony and the social-emotional development of triplets. *Developmental Psychology, 40,* 1133–1147.

Feldman, Ruth, Weller, Aron, Sirota, Lea, & Eidelman, Arthur I. (2002). Skin-to-skin contact (kangaroo care) promotes self-regulation in premature infants: Sleep-wake cyclicity, arousal modulation, and sustained exploration. *Developmental Psychology, 38,* 194–207.

Feltis, Brooke B., Powell, Martine B., Snow, Pamela C., & Hughes-Scholes, Carolyn H. (2010). An examination of the association between interviewer question type and story-grammar detail in child witness interviews about abuse. *Child Abuse & Neglect: The International Journal, 34,* 407–413.

Fenson, Larry, Bates, Elizabeth, Dale, Philip, Goodman, Judith, Reznick, J. Steven, & Thal, Donna. (2000). Measuring variability in early child language: Don't shoot the messenger. *Child Development, 71,* 323–328.

Fentiman, Linda C. (2009). Pursuing the perfect mother: Why America's criminalization of maternal substance abuse is not the answer—A comparative legal analysis. *Michigan Journal of Gender & Law, 15.*

Ferber, Sari Goldstein, & Makhoul, Imad R. (2004). The effect of skin-to-skin contact (kangaroo care) shortly after birth on the neurobehavioral responses of the term newborn: A randomized, controlled trial. *Pediatrics, 113,* 858–865.

Ferguson Publishing. (2007). *Encyclopedia of careers and vocational guidance* (14th ed.). New York, NY: Author.

Fernyhough, Charles. (2010). Vygotsky, Luria, and the social brain. In Bryan W. Sokol, Ulrich Müller, Jeremy I. M. Carpendale, Arlene R. Young, & Grace Iarocci (Eds.), *Self and social regulation: Social interaction and the development of social understanding and executive functions* (pp. 56–79). New York, NY: Oxford University Press.

Fewtrell, Mary, Wilson, David C., Booth, Ian, & Lucas, Alan. (2011). Six months of exclusive breast feeding: How good is the evidence? *British Medical Journal, 342,* c5955. doi:10.1136/bmj.c5955

Finkelhor, David, & Jones, Lisa M. (2004). *Explanations for the decline in child sexual abuse cases.* Retrieved from Office of Juvenile Justice and Delinquency Prevention website: http://www.ncjrs.gov/html/ojjdp/199298/contents.html

Fisher, Helen E. (2006). Broken hearts: The nature and risks of romantic rejection. In Ann C. Crouter & Alan Booth (Eds.), *Romance and sex in adolescence and emerging adulthood: Risks and opportunities* (pp. 3–28). Mahwah, NJ: Erlbaum.

Fletcher, Anne C., Steinberg, Laurence, & Williams-Wheeler, Meeshay. (2004). Parental influences on adolescent problem behavior: Revisiting Stattin and Kerr. *Child Development, 75,* 781–796.

Fletcher, Jack M., & Vaughn, Sharon. (2009). Response to intervention: Preventing and remediating academic difficulties. *Child Development Perspectives, 3,* 30–37.

Flory, Richard W., & Miller, Donald E. (2000). *GenX religion.* New York, NY: Routledge.

Floud, Roderick, Fogel, Robert W., Harris, Bernard, & Hong, Sok Chul. (2011). *An overview of the changing body: Health, nutrition, and human development in the Western world since 1700.* Cambridge, MA: Cambridge University Press.

Floud, Roderick, Fogel, Robert W., Harris, Bernard, & Hong, Sok Chul. (2011). *The changing body: Health, nutrition, and human development in the western world since 1700.* Cambridge, UK: Cambridge University Press.

Flynn, James R. (1999). Searching for justice: The discovery of IQ gains over time. *American Psychologist, 54,* 5–20.

Flynn, James R. (2007). *What is intelligence? Beyond the Flynn effect.* New York, NY: Cambridge University Press.

Forget-Dubois, Nadine, Dionne, Ginette, Lemelin, Jean-Pascal, Pérusse, Daniel, Tremblay, Richard E., & Boivin, Michel. (2009). Early child language mediates the relation between home environment and school readiness. *Child Development, 80,* 736–749.

Fortuna, Keren, & Roisman, Glenn I. (2008). Insecurity, stress, and symptoms of psychopathology: Contrasting results from self-reports versus interviews of adult attachment. *Attachment & Human Development, 10,* 11–28.

Foster, Eugene A., Jobling, M. A., Taylor, P. G., Donnelly, P., de Knijff, P., Mieremet, Rene, et al. (1998, November 5). Jefferson fathered slave's last child. *Nature, 396,* 27–28.

Fox, Emily, & Riconscente, Michelle. (2008). Metacognition and self-regulation in James, Piaget, and Vygotsky. *Educational Psychology Review, 20,* 373–389.

Fox, Nathan A., Henderson, Heather A., Rubin, Kenneth H., Calkins, Susan D., & Schmidt, Louis A. (2001). Continuity and discontinuity of behavioral inhibition and exuberance: Psychophysiological and behavioral influences across the first four years of life. *Child Development, 72,* 1–21.

Fox, Sharon E., Levitt, Pat, & Nelson, Charles A., III. (2010). How the timing and quality of early experiences influence the development of brain architecture. *Child Development, 81,* 28–40.

Fragouli, Elpida, & Wells, Dagan. (2011). Aneuploidy in the human blastocyst. *Cytogenetic and Genome Research, 133,* 149–159.

Frankenburg, William K., Dodds, Josiah, Archer, Philip, Shapiro, Howard, & Bresnick, Beverly. (1992). The Denver II: A major revision and restandardization of the Denver Developmental Screening Test. *Pediatrics, 89,* 91–97.

Franko, Debra L., Thompson, Douglas, Affenito, Sandra G., Barton, Bruce A., & Striegel-Moore, Ruth H. (2008). What mediates the relationship between family meals and adolescent health issues. *Health Psychology, 27*(Suppl. 2), S109–S117.

Franks, Paul W., Hanson, Robert L., Knowler, William C., Sievers, Maurice L., Bennett, Peter H., & Looker, Helen C. (2010). Childhood obesity, other cardiovascular risk factors, and premature death. *New England Journal of Medicine, 362,* 485–493.

Frayling, Timothy M., Timpson, Nicholas J., Weedon, Michael N., Zeggini, Eleftheria, Freathy, Rachel M., Lindgren, Cecilia M., et al. (2007, May 11). A common variant in the FTO gene is associated with body mass index and predisposes to childhood and adult obesity. *Science, 316,* 889–894.

Frazier, Thomas W., & Hardan, Antonio Y. (2009). A meta-analysis of the corpus callosum in autism. *Biological psychiatry, 66,* 935–941.

Fredricks, Jennifer A., & Eccles, Jacquelynne S. (2002). Children's competence and value beliefs from childhood through adolescence: Growth trajectories in two male-sex-typed domains. *Developmental Psychology, 38,* 519–533.

Fredricks, Jennifer A., & Eccles, Jacquelynne S. (2006). Is extracurricular participation associated with beneficial outcomes? Concurrent and longitudinal relations. *Developmental Psychology, 42,* 698–713.

Freeman, Elisabeth. (2010). *Run for your life* (Book Three). Time to Heal Ministries Publishing.

Frenda, Steven J., Nichols, Rebecca M., & Loftus, Elizabeth F. (2011). Current issues and advances in misinformation research. *Current Directions in Psychological Science, 20,* 20–23.

Freud, Anna. (2000). Adolescence. In James B. McCarthy (Ed.), *Adolescent development and psychopathology* (Vol. 13, pp. 29–52). Lanham, MD: University Press of America. (Reprinted from *Psychoanalytic Study of the Child,* pp. 255–278, 1958, New Haven, CT: Yale University Press)

Freud, Sigmund. (1935). *A general introduction to psychoanalysis* (Joan Riviere, Trans.). New York, NY: Liveright.

Freud, Sigmund. (1938). *The basic writings of Sigmund Freud* (A. A. Brill, Ed. and Trans.). New York, NY: Modern Library.

Freud, Sigmund. (1949). *An outline of psychoanalysis* (James Strachey, Trans.). New York, NY: W. W. Norton. (Original work published 1940)

Freud, Sigmund. (1964). An outline of psychoanalysis. In James Strachey (Ed. and Trans.), *The standard edition of the complete psychological works of Sigmund Freud* (Vol. 23, pp. 144–207). London, England: Hogarth Press. (Original work published 1940)

Friedman, Jeffrey M. (2011). Leptin and the regulation of body weight. *Keio Journal of Medicine, 60,* 1–9.

Fries, Alison B. Wismer, & Pollak, Seth D. (2007). Emotion processing and the developing brain. In Donna Coch, Kurt W. Fischer, & Geraldine Dawson (Eds.), *Human behavior, learning, and the developing brain. Typical development* (pp. 329–361). New York, NY: Guilford Press.

Frost, Joe L. (2009). *A history of children's play and play environments: Toward a contemporary child-saving movement.* New York, NY: Routledge.

Fuligni, Andrew J., & Hardway, Christina. (2006). Daily variation in adolescents' sleep, activities, and psychological well-being. *Journal of Research on Adolescence, 16,* 353–378.

Fuligni, Andrew J., Hughes, Diane L., & Way, Niobe. (2009). Ethnicity and immigration. In Richard M. Lerner & Laurence Steinberg (Eds.), *Handbook of adolescent psychology: Vol. 2. Contextual influences on adolescent development* (3rd ed., pp. 527–569). Hoboken, NJ: Wiley.

Fuligni, Allison Sidle, Howes, Carollee, Lara-Cinisomo, Sandraluz, & Karoly, Lynn A. (2009). Diverse pathways in early childhood professional development: An exploration of early educators in public preschools, private preschools, and family child care homes. *Early Education and Development, 20,* 507–526.

Fung, Joey J., & Lau, Anna S. (2009). Punitive discipline and child behavior problems in Chinese-American immigrant families: The moderating effects of indigenous child-rearing ideologies. *International Journal of Behavioral Development, 33,* 520–530.

Furstenberg, Frank F., Jr. (2010). On a new schedule: Transitions to adulthood and family change. *Future of Children, 20,* 67–87.

Gabrieli, John D. E. (2009, July 17). Dyslexia: A new synergy between education and cognitive neuroscience. *Science, 325,* 280–283.

Gaertner, Bridget M., Spinrad, Tracy L., Eisenberg, Nancy, & Greving, Karissa A. (2007). Parental childrearing attitudes as correlates of father involvement during infancy. *Journal of Marriage and Family, 69,* 962–976.

Galambos, Nancy L., Barker, Erin T., & Krahn, Harvey J. (2006). Depression, self-esteem, and anger in emerging adulthood: Seven-year trajectories. *Developmental Psychology, 42,* 350–365.

Gallese, Vittorio, Fadiga, Luciano, Fogassi, Leonardo, & Rizzolatti, Giacomo. (1996). Action recognition in the premotor cortex. *Brain, 119,* 593–609.

Galotti, Kathleen M. (2002). *Making decisions that matter: How people face important life choices.* Mahwah, NJ: Erlbaum.

Gandara, Patricia, & Rumberger, Russell W. (2009). Immigration, language, and education: How does language policy structure opportunity? *Teachers College Record, 111,* 750–782.

Gandini, Leila, Hill, Lynn, Cadwell, Louise, & Schwall, Charles (Eds.). (2005). *In the spirit of the studio: Learning from the atelier of Reggio Emilia.* New York, NY: Teachers College Press.

Gangestad, Steven W., & Simpson, Jeffry A. (2007). *The evolution of mind: Fundamental questions and controversies.* New York, NY: Guilford Press.

Ganong, Lawrence H., Coleman, Marilyn, & Jamison, Tyler. (2011). Patterns of stepchild–stepparent relationship development. *Journal of Marriage and Family, 73,* 396–413.

García Coll, Cynthia T., & Marks, Amy Kerivan. (2009). *Immigrant stories: Ethnicity and academics in middle childhood.* New York, NY: Oxford University Press.

Garcia, Eugene E., & Miller, L. Scott. (2008). Findings and recommendations of the National Task Force on Early Childhood Education for Hispanics. *Child Development Perspectives, 2,* 53–58.

García, Fernando, & Gracia, Enrique. (2009). Is always authoritative the optimum parenting style? Evidence from Spanish families. *Adolescence, 44,* 101–131.

Garcia-Segura, Luis Miguel. (2009). *Hormones and brain plasticity.* New York, NY: Oxford University Press.

Gardner, Howard. (1983). *Frames of mind: The theory of multiple intelligences.* New York, NY: Basic Books.

Gardner, Howard. (1999). Are there additional intelligences? The case for naturalist, spiritual, and existential intelligences. In Jeffrey Kane (Ed.), *Education, information, and transformation: Essays on learning and thinking* (pp. 111–131). Upper Saddle River, NJ: Merrill.

Gardner, Howard. (2006). *Multiple intelligences: New horizons in theory and practice* (Completely rev. and updated ed.). New York, NY: Basic Books.

Gardner, Howard, & Moran, Seana. (2006). The science of multiple intelligences theory: A response to Lynn Waterhouse. *Educational Psychologist, 41,* 227–232.

Gardner, Margo, & Steinberg, Laurence. (2005). Peer influence on risk taking, risk preference, and risky decision making in adolescence and adulthood: An experimental study. *Developmental Psychology, 41,* 625–635.

Garofalo, Robert, Wolf, R. Cameron, Wissow, Lawrence S., Woods, Elizabeth R., & Goodman, Elizabeth. (1999). Sexual orientation and risk of suicide attempts among a representative sample of youth. *Archives of Pediatrics & Adolescent Medicine, 153,* 487–493.

Gaskins, Suzanne. (1999). Children's daily lives in a Mayan village: A case study of culturally constructed roles and activities. In Artin Goncu (Ed.), *Children's engagement in the world: Sociocultural perspectives* (pp. 25–60). New York, NY: Cambridge University Press.

Gathercole, Susan E., Pickering, Susan J., Ambridge, Benjamin, & Wearing, Hannah. (2004). The structure of working memory from 4 to 15 years of age. *Developmental Psychology, 40,* 177–190.

Gathwala, Geeta, Singh, Bir, & Balhara, Bharti. (2008). KMC facilitates mother baby attachment in low birth weight infants. *The Indian Journal of Pediatrics, 75,* 43–47.

Gaumer, Carol J., & Arnone, Carol. (2009). Grocery store observation: Parent-child interaction in family purchases. *Journal of Food Products Marketing, 16,* 1–18.

Gauvain, Mary. (2005). Scaffolding in socialization. *New Ideas in Psychology, 23,* 129–139.

Gauvain, Mary, Beebe, Heidi, & Zhao, Shuheng. (2011). Applying the cultural approach to cognitive development. *Journal of Cognition and Development, 12,* 121–133.

Gdalevich, Michael, Mimouni, Daniel, & Mimouni, Marc. (2001). Breast-feeding and the risk of bronchial asthma in childhood: A systematic review with meta-analysis of prospective studies. *Journal of Pediatrics, 139,* 261–266.

Ge, Xiaojia, & Natsuaki, Misaki N. (2009). In search of explanations for early pubertal timing effects on developmental psychopathology. *Current Directions in Psychological Science, 18,* 327–331.

Ge, Xiaojia, Natsuaki, Misaki N., Neiderhiser, Jenae M., & Reiss, David. (2007). Genetic and environmental influences on pubertal timing: Results from two national sibling studies. *Journal of Research on Adolescence, 17,* 767–788.

Geary, Nori, & Lovejoy, Jennifer. (2008). Sex differences in energy metabolism, obesity, and eating behavior. In Jill B. Becker, Karen J. Berkley, Nori Geary, Elizabeth Hampson, James P. Herman, & Elizabeth Young (Eds.), *Sex differences in the brain: From genes to behavior* (pp. 253–274). New York, NY: Oxford University Press.

Geller, Barbara, Tillman, Rebecca, Bolhofner, Kristine, & Zimerman, Betsy. (2008). Child bipolar I disorder: Prospective continuity with adult bipolar I disorder; characteristics of second and third episodes; predictors of 8-year outcome. *Archives of General Psychiatry, 65,* 1125–1133.

Gendron, Brian P., Williams, Kirk R., & Guerra, Nancy G. (2011). An analysis of bullying among students within schools: Estimating the effects of individual normative beliefs, self-esteem, and school climate. *Journal of School Violence, 10,* 150–164.

Genesee, Fred. (2008). Early dual language learning. *Zero to Three, 29,* 17–23.

Genesee, Fred, & Nicoladis, Elena. (2007). Bilingual first language acquisition. In Erika Hoff & Marilyn Shatz (Eds.), *Blackwell handbook of language development* (pp. 324–342). Malden, MA: Blackwell.

Gentile, Douglas. (2009). Pathological video-game use among youth ages 8 to 18. *Psychological Science, 20,* 594–602.

Gentile, Douglas A. (2011b). The multiple dimensions of video game effects. *Child Development Perspectives, 5,* 75–81.

Gentile, Douglas A., Choo, Hyekyung, Liau, Albert, Sim, Timothy, Li, Dongdong, Fung, Daniel, et al. (2011a). Pathological video game use among youths: A two-year longitudinal study. *Pediatrics.* Advance online publication. doi:10.1542/peds.2010–1353

Gentile, Douglas A., Saleem, Muniba, & Anderson, Craig A. (2007). Public policy and the effects of media violence on children. *Social Issues and Policy Review, 1,* 15–61.

Gentile, Salvatore. (2010). Antidepressant use in children and adolescents diagnosed with major depressive disorder: What can we learn from published data? *Reviews on Recent Clinical Trials 5,* 63–75.

Georgas, James, Berry, John W., van de Vijver, Fons J. R., Kagitçibasi, Çigdem, & Poortinga, Ype H. (2006). *Families across cultures: A 30–nation psychological study.* Cambridge, UK: Cambridge University Press.

Geraerts, Elke, Lindsay, D. Stephen, Merckelbach, Harald, Jelicic, Marko, Raymaekers, Linsey, Arnold, Michelle M., et al. (2009). Cognitive mechanisms underlying recovered-memory experiences of childhood sexual abuse. *Psychological Science, 20,* 92–98.

Gernsbacher, Morton Ann. (2010). Stigma from psychological science: Group differences, not deficits—Introduction to stigma special section. *Perspectives on Psychological Science, 5,* 687.

Gerrard, Meg, Gibbons, Frederick X., Houlihan, Amy E., Stock, Michelle L., & Pomery, Elizabeth A. (2008). A dual-process approach to health risk decision making: The prototype willingness model. *Developmental Review, 28,* 29–61.

Gershkoff-Stowe, Lisa, & Hahn, Erin R. (2007). Fast mapping skills in the developing lexicon. *Journal of Speech, Language, and Hearing Research, 50,* 682–696.

Gershoff, Elizabeth T., Grogan-Kaylor, Andrew, Lansford, Jennifer E., Chang, Lei, Zelli, Arnaldo, Deater-Deckard, Kirby, et al. (2010). Parent discipline practices in an international sample: Associations with child behaviors and moderation by perceived normativeness. *Child Development, 81,* 487–502.

Gettler, Lee T., & McKenna, James J. (2010). Never sleep with baby? Or keep me close but keep me safe: Eliminating inappropriate safe infant sleep rhetoric in the United States. *Current Pediatric Reviews, 6,* 71–77.

Gevorgyan, Ruzanna, Schmidt, Elena, Wall, Martin, Garnett, Geoffrey, Atun, Rifat, Maksimova, Svetlana, et al. (2011). Does Russia need sex education? The views of stakeholders in three Russian regions. *Sex Education, 11,* 213–226.

Gewertz, Catherine. (2011a, February 22). AP passing rates rose for last year's seniors. *Education Week,* p. 5.

Gewertz, Catherine. (2011b, June 9). 'College for all' reconsidered: Are four-year degrees for all? *Education Week,* pp. 6–8.

Giardino, Angelo P., & Alexander, Randell. (2011). *Child maltreatment* (4th ed.). St. Louis, MO: G. W. Medical.

Gibson, Eleanor J. (1969). *Principles of perceptual learning and development.* New York, NY: Appleton-Century-Crofts.

Gibson, Eleanor J. (1988). Exploratory behavior in the development of perceiving, acting, and the acquiring of knowledge. *Annual Review of Psychology, 39,* 1–42.

Gibson, Eleanor J. (1997). An ecological psychologist's prolegomena for perceptual development: A functional approach. In Cathy Dent-Read & Patricia Zukow-Goldring (Eds.), *Evolving explanations of development: Ecological approaches to organism-environment systems* (pp. 23–54). Washington, DC: American Psychological Association.

Gibson, Eleanor J., & Walk, Richard D. (1960). The "visual cliff." *Scientific American, 202,* 64–71.

Gibson, James Jerome. (1979). *The ecological approach to visual perception.* Boston, MA: Houghton Mifflin.

Gibson-Davis, Christina M. (2009). Money, marriage, and children: Testing the financial expectations and family formation theory. *Journal of Marriage and Family, 71,* 146–160.

Gibson-Davis, Christina M., & Brooks-Gunn, Jeanne. (2006). Couples' immigration status and ethnicity as determinants of breastfeeding. *American Journal of Public Health, 96,* 641–646.

Gigerenzer, Gerd. (2008). Why heuristics work. *Perspectives on Psychological Science, 3,* 20–29.

Gilchrist, Heidi, & Sullivan, Gerard. (2006). The role of gender and sexual relations for young people in identity construction and youth suicide. *Culture, Health & Sexuality, 8,* 195–209.

Giles, Amy, & Rovee-Collier, Carolyn. (2011). Infant long-term memory for associations formed during mere exposure. *Infant Behavior and Development, 34,* 327–338.

Giles-Sims, Jean, & Lockhart, Charles. (2005). Culturally shaped patterns of disciplining children. *Journal of Family Issues, 26,* 196–218.

Gillespie, Michael Allen. (2010). Players and spectators: Sports and ethical training in the American university. In Elizabeth Kiss & J. Peter Euben (Eds.), *Debating moral education: Rethinking the role of the modern university* (pp. 293–316). Durham, NC: Duke University Press.

Gilliam, Mary, Stockman, Michael, Malek, Meaghan, Sharp, Wendy, Greenstein, Deanna, Lalonde, Francois, et al. (2011). Developmental trajectories of the corpus callosum in attention-deficit/hyperactivity disorder. *Biological Psychiatry, 69,* 839–846.

Gilligan, Carol. (1982). *In a different voice: Psychological theory and women's development.* Cambridge, MA: Harvard University Press.

Gilliland, Frank D. (2009). Outdoor air pollution, genetic susceptibility, and asthma management: Opportunities for intervention to reduce the burden of asthma. *Pediatrics, 123*(Suppl. 3), S168–173.

Gillis, John R. (2008). The islanding of children: Reshaping the mythical landscapes of childhood. In Marta Gutman & Ning De Coninck-Smith (Eds.), *Designing modern childhoods: History, space, and the material culture of children* (pp. 316–329). New Brunswick, NJ: Rutgers University Press.

Gintis, Herb, Bowles, Samuel, Boyd, Robert, & Fehr, Ernst. (2007). Explaining altruistic behaviour in humans. In R. I. M. Dunbar & Louise Barrett (Eds.), *Oxford handbook of evolutionary psychology* (pp. 605–620). New York, NY: Oxford University Press.

Glanville, Jennifer L., Sikkink, David, & Hernández, Edwin I. (2008). Religious involvement and educational outcomes: The role of social capital and extracurricular participation. *Sociological Quarterly, 49,* 105–137.

Gluckman, Peter D., & Hanson, Mark A. (2006). *Developmental origins of health and disease.* Cambridge, England: Cambridge University Press.

Göbel, Silke M., Shaki, Samuel, & Fischer, Martin H. (2011). The cultural number line: A review of cultural and linguistic influences on the development of number processing. *Journal of Cross-Cultural Psychology, 42,* 543–565.

Goldberg, Wendy A., Prause, JoAnn, Lucas-Thompson, Rachel, & Himsel, Amy. (2008). Maternal employment and children's achievement in context: A meta-analysis of four decades of research. *Psychological Bulletin, 134,* 77–108.

Goldin-Meadow, Susan. (2006). Nonverbal communication: The hand's role in talking and thinking. In William Damon & Richard M. Lerner (Series Eds.) & Deanna Kuhn & Robert S. Siegler (Vol. Eds.), *Handbook of child psychology: Vol.*

2. *Cognition, perception, and language* (6th ed., pp. 336–369). Hoboken, NJ: Wiley.

Goldin-Meadow, Susan. (2009). How gesture promotes learning throughout childhood. *Child Development Perspectives, 3,* 106–111.

Goldstein, Michael H., Schwade, Jennifer A., & Bornstein, Marc H. (2009). The value of vocalizing: Five-month-old infants associate their own noncry vocalizations with responses from caregivers. *Child Development, 80,* 636–644.

Goldston, David B., Molock, Sherry Davis, Whitbeck, Leslie B., Murakami, Jessica L., Zayas, Luis H., & Hall, Gordon C. Nagayama. (2008). Cultural considerations in adolescent suicide prevention and psychosocial treatment. *American Psychologist, 63,* 14–31.

Golinkoff, Roberta Michnick, & Hirsh-Pasek, Kathy. (2008). How toddlers begin to learn verbs. *Trends in Cognitive Sciences, 12,* 397–403.

Gonzales, Nancy A., Dumka, Larry E., Deardorff, Julianna, Carter, Sara Jacobs, & McCray, Adam. (2004). Preventing poor mental health and school dropout of Mexican American adolescents following the transition to junior high school. *Journal of Adolescent Research, 19,* 113–131.

Gonzales, Patrick, Williams, Trevor, Jocelyn, Leslie, Roey, Stephen, Kastberg, David, & Brenwald, Summer. (2009). *Highlights from TIMSS 2007: Mathematics and science achievement of U.S. fourth- and eighth-grade students in an international context.* Washington, DC: National Center for Education Statistics, U.S. Department of Education.

Goodman, Judith C., Dale, Philip S., & Li, Ping. (2008). Does frequency count? Parental input and the acquisition of vocabulary. *Journal of Child Language, 35,* 515–531.

Goodman, Sherryl H., & Gotlib, Ian H. (2002). *Children of depressed parents: Mechanisms of risk and implications for treatment.* Washington, DC: American Psychological Association.

Goodwin, Geoffrey P., & Johnson-Laird, Philip. N. (2008). Transitive and pseudo-transitive inferences. *Cognition, 108,* 320–352.

Gopnik, Alison. (2001). Theories, language, and culture: Whorf without wincing. In Melissa Bowerman & Stephen C. Levinson (Eds.), *Language acquisition and conceptual development* (pp. 45–69). Cambridge, UK: Cambridge University Press.

Gopnik, Alison, & Schulz, Laura. (2007). *Causal learning: Psychology, philosophy, and computation.* New York, NY: Oxford University Press.

Gordis, Elana B., Granger, Douglas A., Susman, Elizabeth J., & Trickett, Penelope K. (2008). Salivary alpha amylase-cortisol asymmetry in maltreated youth. *Hormones and Behavior, 53,* 96–103.

Gordon, Peter. (2004, August 19). Numerical cognition without words: Evidence from Amazonia. *Science, 306,* 496–499.

Gormley, William T., Jr., Phillips, Deborah, & Gayer, Ted. (2008, June 27). Preschool programs can boost school readiness. *Science, 320,* 1723–1724.

Gottesman, Irving I., Laursen, Thomas Munk, Bertelsen, Aksel, & Mortensen, Preben Bo. (2010). Severe mental disorders in offspring with 2 psychiatrically ill parents. *Archives of General Psychiatry, 67,* 252–257.

Gottfried, Adele Eskeles, Marcoulides, George A., Gottfried, Allen W., & Oliver, Pamella H. (2009). A latent curve model of parental motivational practices and developmental decline in math and science academic intrinsic motivation. *Journal of Educational Psychology, 101,* 729–739.

Gottlieb, Alma. (2000). Luring your child into this life: A Beng path for infant care. In Judy S. DeLoache & Alma Gottlieb (Eds.), *A world of babies: Imagined childcare guides for seven societies* (pp. 55–90). New York, NY: Cambridge University Press.

Gottlieb, Gilbert. (2002). *Individual development and evolution: The genesis of novel behavior.* Mahwah, NJ: Erlbaum. (Original work published 1992)

Gottlieb, Gilbert. (2007). Probabilistic epigenesis. *Developmental Science, 10,* 1–11.

Gottlieb, Gilbert. (2010). Normally occurring environmental and behavioral influences on gene activity. In Kathryn E. Hood, Carolyn Tucker Halpern, Gary Greenberg, & Richard M. Lerner (Eds.), *Handbook of developmental science, behavior, and genetics* (pp. 13–37). Malden, MA: Wiley-Blackwell.

Goymer, Patrick. (2007). Genes know their left from their right. *Nature Reviews Genetics, 8,* 652.

Graber, Julia A., & Brooks-Gunn, Jeanne. (1996). Expectations for and precursors to leaving home in young women. In Julia A. Graber & Judith Semon Dubas (Eds.), *Leaving home: Understanding the transition to adulthood* (pp. 21–38). San Francisco, CA: Jossey-Bass.

Graber, Julia A., Nichols, Tracy R., & Brooks-Gunn, Jeanne. (2010). Putting pubertal timing in developmental context: implications for prevention. *Developmental psychobiology, 52,* 254–262.

Graham-Bermann, Sandra A., Gruber, Gabrielle, Howell, Kathryn H., & Girz, Laura. (2009). Factors discriminating among profiles of resilience and psychopathology in children exposed to intimate partner violence (IPV). *Child Abuse & Neglect: The International Journal, 33,* 648–660.

Grandin, Temple, & Johnson, Catherine. (2009). *Animals make us human: Creating the best life for animals.* Boston, MA: Houghton Mifflin Harcourt.

Granic, Isabela, & Patterson, Gerald R. (2006). Toward a comprehensive model of antisocial development: A dynamic systems approach. *Psychological Review, 113,* 101–131.

Granpeesheh, Doreen, Tarbox, Jonathan, & Dixon, Dennis R. (2009). Applied behavior analytic interventions for children with autism: A description and review of treatment research. *Annals of Clinical Psychiatry, 21,* 162–173.

Granpeesheh, Doreen, Tarbox, Jonathan, Dixon, Dennis R., Wilke, Arthur E., Allen, Michael S., & Bradstreet, James Jeffrey. (2010). Randomized trial of hyperbaric oxygen therapy for children with autism. *Research in Autism Spectrum Disorders, 4,* 268–275.

Gray, John. (2004). *Men are from Mars, women are from Venus: A practical guide for improving communication and getting what you want in your relationships* (Paperback ed.). New York, NY: HarperCollins. (Original work published 1992)

Gray, John. (2010). *Venus on fire, Mars on ice: Hormonal balance—The key to life, love and energy.* Coquitlam, British Columbia, Canada: Mind.

Greely, Henry T. (2011, January 20). Get ready for the flood of fetal gene screening. *Nature, 469,* 289–291.

Green, Melinda A., Scott, Norman A., DeVilder, Elizabeth L., Zeiger, Amanda, & Darr, Stacy. (2006). Relational-interdependent self-construal as a function of bulimic symptomatology. *Journal of Clinical Psychology, 62,* 943–951.

Greene, Melissa L., & Way, Niobe. (2005). Self-esteem trajectories among ethnic minority adolescents: A growth curve analysis of the patterns and predictors of change. *Journal of Research on Adolescence, 15,* 151–178.

Greenfield, Patricia M. (2009, January 2). Technology and informal education: What is taught, what is learned. *Science, 323,* 69–71.

Greenhalgh, Susan. (2008). *Just one child: Science and policy in Deng's China.* Berkeley, CA: University of California Press.

Greenough, William T., & Volkmar, Fred R. (1973). Pattern of dendritic branching in occipital cortex of rats reared in complex environments. *Experimental Neurology, 40,* 491–504.

Greenwood, Charles R., Thiemann-Bourque, Kathy, Walker, Dale, Buzhardt, Jay, & Gilkerson, Jill. (2010). Assessing children's home language environments using automatic speech recognition technology. *Communication Disorders Quarterly.*

Gregg, Christopher. (2010, November 5). Parental control over the brain. *Science, 330,* 770–771.

Griebel, Wilfried, & Niesel, Renate. (2002). Co-constructing transition into kindergarten and school by children, parents, and teachers. In Hilary Fabian & Aline-Wendy Dunlop (Eds.), *Transitions in the early years: Debating continuity and progression for young children in early education* (pp. 64–75). New York, NY: RoutledgeFalmer.

Griffin, James, Gooding, Sarah, Semesky, Michael, Farmer, Brittany, Mannchen, Garrett, & Sinnott, Jan. (2009). Four brief studies of relations between postformal thought and non-cognitive factors: Personality, concepts of God, political opinions, and social attitudes. *Journal of Adult Development, 16,* 173–182.

Grobman, Kevin H. (2008). *Learning & teaching developmental psychology: Attachment theory, infancy, & infant memory development.* Retrieved from DevPsy.Org website: http://www.devpsy.org/questions/attachment_theory_memory.html

Grollmann, Philipp, & Rauner, Felix. (2007). Exploring innovative apprenticeship: Quality and costs. *Education + Training, 49,* 431–446.

Grolnick, Wendy S., McMenamy, Jannette M., & Kurowski, Carolyn O. (2006). Emotional self-regulation in infancy and toddlerhood. In Lawrence Balter & Catherine S. Tamis-LeMonda (Eds.), *Child psychology: A handbook of contemporary issues* (2nd ed., pp. 3–25). New York, NY: Psychology Press.

Grossmann, Klaus E., Grossmann, Karin, & Waters, Everett (Eds.). (2005). *Attachment from infancy to adulthood: The major longitudinal studies.* New York, NY: Guilford Press.

Grosvenor, Theodore. (2003). Why is there an epidemic of myopia? *Clinical and Experimental Optometry, 86,* 273–275.

Grubeck-Loebenstein, Beatrix. (2010). Fading immune protection in old age: Vaccination in the elderly. *Journal of Comparative Pathology, 142*(Suppl. 1), S116–S119.

Grusec, Joan E. (2011). Socialization processes in the family: Social and emotional development. *Annual Review of Psychology, 62,* 243–269.

Guerra, Nancy G., Graham, Sandra, & Tolan, Patrick H. (2011). Raising healthy children: Translating child development research into practice. *Child Development, 82,* 7–16.

Guerra, Nancy G., & Williams, Kirk R. (2010). Implementing bullying prevention in diverse settings: Geographic, economic, and cultural influences. In Eric M. Vernberg & Bridget K. Biggs (Eds.), *Preventing and treating bullying and victimization* (pp. 319–336). New York, NY: Oxford University Press.

Guerra, Nancy G., Williams, Kirk R., & Sadek, Shelly. (2011). Understanding bullying and victimization during childhood and adolescence: A mixed methods study. *Child Development, 82,* 295–310.

Guerri, Consuelo, & Pascual, María. (2010). Mechanisms involved in the neurotoxic, cognitive, and neurobehavioral effects of alcohol consumption during adolescence. *Alcohol, 44,* 15–26.

Guerry, John, & Hastings, Paul. (2011). In search of HPA axis dysregulation in child and adolescent depression. *Clinical Child and Family Psychology Review, 14,* 135–160.

Gummerum, Michaela, Keller, Monika, Takezawa, Masanori, & Mata, Jutta. (2008). To give or not to give: Children's and adolescents' sharing and moral negotiations in economic decision situations. *Child Development, 79,* 562–576.

Guo, Sufang, Padmadas, Sabu S., Zhao, Fengmin, Brown, James J., & Stones, R. William. (2007). Delivery settings and caesarean section rates in China. *Bulletin of the World Health Organization, 85,* 755–762.

Haas, David M., Gallauresi, Beverly, Shields, Kristine, Zeitlin, Deborah, Clark, Shannon M., Hebert, Mary F., et al. (2011). Pharmacotherapy and pregnancy: Highlights from the Third International Conference for Individualized Pharmacotherapy in Pregnancy. *Clinical and Translational Science, 4,* 204–209.

Hackman, Daniel A., & Farah, Martha J. (2009). Socioeconomic status and the developing brain. *Trends in Cognitive Sciences, 13,* 65–73.

Haden, Catherine A. (2010). Talking about science in museums. *Child Development Perspectives, 4,* 62–67.

Halford, Graeme S., & Andrews, Glenda. (2006). Reasoning and problem solving. In William Damon & Richard M. Lerner (Series Eds.) & Deanna Kuhn & Robert S. Siegler (Vol. Eds.), *Handbook of child psychology: Vol. 2. Cognition, perception, and language* (6th ed., pp. 557–608). Hoboken, NJ: Wiley.

Hall, Lynn K. (2008). *Counseling military families: What mental health professionals need to know.* New York, NY: Taylor and Francis.

Hall-Lande, Jennifer A., Eisenberg, Marla E., Christenson, Sandra L., & Neumark-Sztainer, Dianne. (2007). Social isolation, psychological health, and protective factors in adolescence. *Adolescence, 42,* 265–286.

Halpern, Carolyn Tucker, King, Rosalind Berkowitz, Oslak, Selene G., & Udry, J. Richard. (2005). Body mass index, dieting, romance, and sexual activity in adolescent girls: Relationships over time. *Journal of Research on Adolescence, 15,* 535–559.

Hamerton, John L., & Evans, Jane A. (2005). Sex chromosome anomalies. In Merlin Gene Butler & F. John Meaney (Eds.), *Genetics of developmental disabilities* (pp. 585–650). Boca Raton, FL: Taylor & Francis.

Hamm, Jill V., & Faircloth, Beverly S. (2005). The role of friendship in adolescents' sense of school belonging. *New Directions for Child and Adolescent Development, 107,* 61–78.

Hammer, Carol Scheffner, Jia, Gisela, & Uchikoshi, Yuuko. (2011). Language and literacy development of dual language learners growing up in the United States: A call for research. *Child Development Perspectives, 5,* 4–9.

Hammond, Christopher J., Andrew, Toby, Mak, Ying Tat, & Spector, Tim D. (2004). A susceptibility locus for myopia in the normal population is linked to the PAX6 gene region on chromosome 11: A genomewide scan of dizygotic twins. *American Journal of Human Genetics, 75,* 294–304.

Hanania, Rima. (2010). Two types of perseveration in the dimension change card sort task. *Journal of Experimental Child Psychology, 107,* 325–336.

Hane, Amie Ashley, & Fox, Nathan A. (2006). Ordinary variations in maternal caregiving influence human infants' stress reactivity. *Psychological Science, 17,* 550–556.

Hannan, Claire, Buchanan, Anna DeBlois, & Monroe, Judy. (2009). Maintaining the vaccine safety net. *Pediatrics, 124*(Suppl. 5), S571–572.

Hanoch, Yaniv, Miron-Shatz, Talya, & Himmelstein, Mary. (2010). Genetic testing and risk interpretation: How do women understand lifetime risk results? *Judgment and Decision Making, 5,* 116–123.

Hanushek, Eric A. (2009, November 6). Building on No Child Left Behind. *Science, 326,* 802–803.

Hanushek, Eric A., & Woessmann, Ludger. (2009). *Do better schools lead to more growth? Cognitive skills, economic outcomes, and causation* (IZA Discussion Paper 4575). Bonn, Germany: Institute for the Study of Labor.

Hanushek, Eric A., & Woessmann, Ludger. (2010). *The high cost of low educational performance: The long-run economic impact of improving PISA outcomes.* Paris, France: Organisation for Economic Co-operation and Development.

Harden, K. Paige, & Tucker-Drob, Elliot M. (2011). Individual differences in the development of sensation seeking and impulsivity during adolescence: Further evidence for a dual systems model. *Developmental Psychology, 47,* 739–746.

Harden, K. Paige, Turkheimer, Eric, & Loehlin, John. (2007). Genotype by environment interaction in adolescents' cognitive aptitude. *Behavior Genetics, 37,* 273–283.

Hare, Kelly M., & Cree, Alison. (2010). Incidence, causes and consequences of pregnancy failure in viviparous lizards: Implications for research and conservation settings. *Reproduction, Fertility and Development, 22,* 761.

Harjes, Carlos E., Rocheford, Torbert R., Bai, Ling, Brutnell, Thomas P., Kandianis, Catherine Bermudez, Sowinski, Stephen G., et al. (2008, January 18). Natural genetic variation in Lycopene Epsilon Cyclase tapped for maize biofortification. *Science, 319,* 330–333.

Harkness, Sara, Super, Charles M., & Mavridis, Caroline Johnston. (2011). Parental ethnotheories about children's socioemotional development, *Socioemotional development in cultural context* (pp. 73–98). New York, NY: Guilford Press.

Harlor, Allen D. Buz, Jr., & Bower, Charles. (2009). Hearing assessment in infants and children: Recommendations beyond neonatal screening. *Pediatrics, 124,* 1252–1263.

Harris, Judith Rich. (1998). *The nurture assumption: Why children turn out the way they do.* New York, NY: Free Press.

Harris, Judith Rich. (2002). Beyond the nurture assumption: Testing hypotheses about the child's environment. In John G. Borkowski, Sharon Landesman Ramey, & Marie Bristol-Power (Eds.), *Parenting and the child's world: Influences on academic, intellectual, and social-emotional development* (pp. 3–20). Mahwah, NJ: Erlbaum.

Harrison, Denise, Bueno, Mariana, Yamada, Janet, Adams-Webber, Thomasin, & Stevens, Bonnie. (2010). Analgesic effects of sweet-tasting solutions for infants: Current state of equipoise. *Pediatrics, 126,* 894–902.

Harrison, Kristen, Bost, Kelly K., McBride, Brent A., Donovan, Sharon M., Grigsby-Toussaint, Diana S., Kim, Juhee, et al. (2011). Toward a developmental conceptualization of contributors to overweight and obesity in childhood: The Six-Cs model. *Child Development Perspectives, 5,* 50–58.

Harrison, Linda J., & McLeod, Sharynne. (2010). Risk and protective factors associated with speech and language impairment in a nationally representative sample of 4- to 5-year-old children. *Journal of Speech, Language, and Hearing Research, 53,* 508–529.

Hart, Betty, & Risley, Todd R. (1995). *Meaningful differences in the everyday experience of young American children.* Baltimore, MD: Brookes.

Hart, Daniel, Atkins, Robert, & Fegley, Suzanne. (2003). Personality and development in childhood: A person-centered approach. *Monographs of the Society for Research in Child Development, 68*(Serial No. 272), vii–109.

Harter, Susan. (2006). The self. In William Damon & Richard M. Lerner (Series Eds.) & Nancy Eisenberg (Vol. Ed.), *Handbook of child psychology: Vol. 3. Social, emotional, and personality development* (6th ed., pp. 505–570). Hoboken, NJ: Wiley.

Hartmann, Donald P., & Pelzel, Kelly E. (2005). Design, measurement, and analysis in developmental research. In Marc H. Bornstein & Michael E. Lamb (Eds.), *Developmental science: An advanced textbook* (5th ed., pp. 103–184). Mahwah, NJ: Erlbaum.

Hasebe, Yuki, Nucci, Larry, & Nucci, Maria S. (2004). Parental control of the personal domain and adolescent symptoms of psychopathology: A cross-national study in the United States and Japan. *Child Development, 75,* 815–828.

Hassett, Janice M., Siebert, Erin R., & Wallen, Kim. (2008). Sex differences in rhesus monkey toy preferences parallel those of children. *Hormones and Behavior, 54,* 359–364.

Hastie, Peter A. (2004). Problem-solving in teaching sports. In Jan Wright, Lisette Burrows, & Doune MacDonald (Eds.), *Critical inquiry and problem-solving in physical education* (pp. 62–73). London, UK: Routledge.

Hawthorne, Joanna. (2009). Promoting development of the early parent-infant relationship using the Neonatal Behavioural Assessment Scale. In Jane Barlow & P. O. Svanberg (Eds.), *Keeping the baby in mind: Infant mental health in practice* (pp. 39–51). New York, NY: Routledge/Taylor & Francis Group.

Haydon, Jo. (2007). *Genetics in practice: A clinical approach for healthcare practitioners.* Hoboken, NJ: Wiley.

Hayes, Rachel A., & Slater, Alan. (2008). Three-month-olds' detection of alliteration in syllables. *Infant Behavior & Development 31,* 153–156.

Hayne, Harlene, & Simcock, Gabrielle. (2009). Memory development in toddlers. In Mary L. Courage & Nelson Cowan (Eds.), *The development of memory in infancy and childhood* (2nd ed., pp. 43–68). New York, NY: Psychology Press.

Hayward, Diane W., Gale, Catherine M., & Eikeseth, Svein. (2009). Intensive behavioural intervention for young children with autism: A research-based service model. *Research in Autism Spectrum Disorders, 3,* 571–580.

Heaton, Tim B., & Darkwah, Akosua. (2011). Religious differences in modernization of the family: Family demographics trends in Ghana. *Journal of Family Issues.* Advance online publication. doi:10.1177/0192513x11398951

Heine, Steven J. (2007). Culture and motivation: What motivates people to act in the ways that they do? In Shinobu Kitayama & Dov Cohen (Eds.), *Handbook of cultural psychology* (pp. 714–733). New York, NY: Guilford Press.

Hemminki, Kari, Sundquist, Jan, & Lorenzo Bermejo, Justo. (2008). Familial risks for cancer as the basis for evidence-based clinical referral and counseling. *The Oncologist, 13,* 239–247.

Henning, Anne, & Striano, Tricia. (2011). Infant and maternal sensitivity to interpersonal timing. *Child Development, 82,* 916–931.

Herek, Gregory M. (2010). Sexual orientation differences as deficits: Science and stigma in the history of American psychology. *Perspectives on Psychological Science, 5,* 693–699.

Herman, Khalisa N., Paukner, Annika, & Suomi, Stephen J. (2011). Gene × environment interactions and social play: Contributions from rhesus macaques. In Anthony D. Pellegrini (Ed.), *The Oxford handbook of the development of play* (pp. 58–69). New York, NY: Oxford University Press.

Herman-Giddens, Marcia E., Wang, Lily, & Koch, Gary. (2001). Secondary sexual characteristics in boys: Estimates from the National Health and Nutrition Examination Survey III, 1988–1994. *Archives of Pediatrics & Adolescent Medicine, 155,* 1022–1028.

Herring, Ann, & Swedlund, Alan C. (Eds.). (2010). *Plagues and epidemics: Infected spaces past and present.* New York, NY: Berg.

Herrmann, Esther, Call, Josep, Hernàndez-Lloreda, María Victoria, Hare, Brian, & Tomasello, Michael. (2007, September 7). Humans have evolved specialized skills of social cognition: The cultural intelligence hypothesis. *Science, 317,* 1360–1366.

Herschensohn, Julia Rogers. (2007). *Language development and age.* New York, NY: Cambridge University Press.

Hetherington, E. Mavis. (2006). The influence of conflict, marital problem solving and parenting on children's adjustment in nondivorced, divorced and remarried families In Alison Clarke-Stewart & Judy Dunn (Eds.), *Families count: Effects on child and adolescent development* (pp. 203–237). New York, NY: Cambridge University Press.

Higgins, Matt. (2006, August 7). A series of flips creates some serious buzz. *New York Times,* p. D7.

Higuchi, Susumu, Matsushita, Sachio, Muramatsu, Taro, Murayama, Masanobu, & Hayashida, Motoi. (1996). Alcohol and aldehyde dehydrogenase genotypes and drinking behavior in Japanese. *Alcoholism: Clinical and Experimental Research, 20,* 493–497.

Hill, Denise M., Hanton, Sheldon, Matthews, Nic, & Fleming, Scott. (2010). Choking in sport: A review. *International Review of Sport and Exercise Psychology, 3,* 24–39.

Hill, Nancy E., Bush, Kevin R., & Roosa, Mark W. (2003). Parenting and family socialization strategies and children's mental health: Low-income, Mexican-American and Euro-American mothers and children. *Child Development, 74,* 189–204.

Hill, Nancy E., & Tyson, Diana F. (2009). Parental involvement in middle school: A meta-analytic assessment of the strategies that promote achievement. *Developmental Psychology, 45,* 740–763.

Hill, Patrick L., Duggan, Peter M., & Lapsley, Daniel K. (2011). Subjective invulnerability, risk behavior, and adjustment in early adolescence. *The Journal of Early Adolescence.* Advance online publication. doi:10.1177/0272431611400304

Hill, Shirley A. (2007). Transformative processes: Some sociological questions. *Journal of Marriage and Family, 69,* 293–298.

Hillier, Dawn. (2003). *Childbirth in the global village: Implications for midwifery education and practice.* New York, NY: Routledge.

Hillman, Richard. (2005). Expanded newborn screening and phenylketonuria (PKU). In Merlin Gene Butler & F. John Meaney (Eds.), *Genetics of developmental disabilities* (pp. 651–664). Boca Raton, FL: Taylor & Francis.

Hilton, Irene V., Stephen, Samantha, Barker, Judith C., & Weintraub, Jane A. (2007). Cultural factors and children's oral health care: A qualitative study of carers of young children. *Community Dentistry and Oral Epidemiology, 35,* 429–438.

Hindman, Annemarie H., Skibbe, Lori E., Miller, Alison, & Zimmerman, Marc. (2010). Ecological contexts and early learning: Contributions of child, family, and classroom factors during Head Start, to literacy and mathematics growth through first grade. *Early Childhood Research Quarterly, 25,* 235–250.

Hines, Melissa. (2004). *Brain gender.* Oxford, UK: Oxford University Press.

Hipwell, Alison E., Keenan, Kate, Loeber, Rolf, & Battista, Deena. (2010). Early predictors of sexually intimate behaviors in an urban sample of young girls. *Developmental Psychology, 46,* 366–378.

Hirsch, Eric Donald, Jr. (2008). Plugging the hole in state standards. *American Educator, 32,* 8–12.

Hirsh-Pasek, Kathy, Golinkoff, Roberta Michnick, Berk, Laura E., & Singer, Dorothy G. (2009). *A mandate for playful learning in preschool: Presenting the evidence.* New York, NY: Oxford University Press.

Ho, Caroline, Bluestein, Deborah N., & Jenkins, Jennifer M. (2008). Cultural differences in the relationship between parenting and children's behavior. *Developmental Psychology, 44,* 507–522.

Ho, Emily S. (2010). Measuring hand function in the young child. *Journal of Hand Therapy, 23,* 323–328.

Hofer, Scott M., & Piccinin, Andrea M. (2010). Toward an integrative science of life-span development and aging. *The Journals of Gerontology: Series B: Psychological Sciences and Social Sciences, 65B,* 269–278.

Hoff, David J. (2007, April 18). Not all agree on meaning of NCLB proficiency. *Education Week,* pp. 1, 23.

Holden, Constance. (2009, October 16). Fetal cells again? *Science, 326,* 358–359.

Holland, James D., & Klaczynski, Paul A. (2009). Intuitive risk taking during adolescence. *Prevention Researcher, 16,* 8–11.

Holland, John L. (1997). *Making vocational choices: A theory of vocational personalities and work environments* (3rd ed.). Odessa, FL: Psychological Assessment Resources.

Hollich, George. (2010). Early language. In J. Gavin Bremner & Theodore D. Wachs (Eds.), *The Wiley-Blackwell Handbook of Infant Development* (pp. 426–449). Oxford, UK: Wiley-Blackwell.

Hollich, George J., Hirsh-Pasek, Kathy, Golinkoff, Roberta Michnick, Brand, Rebecca J., Brown, Ellie, Chung, He Len, et al. (2000). Breaking the language barrier: An emergentist coalition model for the origins of word learning. *Monographs of the Society for Research in Child Development, 65*(3, Serial No. 262), v–123.

Holm, Stephanie M., Forbes, Erika E., Ryan, Neal D., Phillips, Mary L., Tarr, Jill A., & Dahl, Ronald E. (2009). Reward-related brain function and sleep in pre/early pubertal and mid/late pubertal adolescents. *The Journal of Adolescent Health, 45,* 326–334.

Holodynski, Manfred, & Friedlmeier, Wolfgang. (2006). *Development of emotions and emotion regulation.* New York, NY: Springer.

Holsti, Liisa, Grunau, Ruth E., & Shany, Eilon. (2011). Assessing pain in preterm infants in the neonatal intensive care unit: Moving to a brain-oriented approach. *Pain Management, 1,* 171–179.

Holtzman, Jennifer. (2009). Simple, effective—and inexpensive—strategies to reduce tooth decay in children. *ICAN: Infant, Child, & Adolescent Nutrition, 1,* 225–231.

Hooper, Stephen R., Roberts, Joanne, Sideris, John, Burchinal, Margaret, & Zeisel, Susan. (2010). Longitudinal predictors of reading and math trajectories through middle school for African American versus Caucasian students across two samples. *Developmental Psychology, 46,* 1018–1029.

Hormann, Elizabeth. (2007). Sleeping with your baby: A parent's guide to co-sleeping. *Birth, 34,* 355–356.

Horowitz, Frances Degen, Subotnik, Rena F., & Matthews, Dona J. (Eds.). (2009). *The development of giftedness and talent across the life span.* Washington, DC: American Psychological Association.

Hougaard, Karin S., & Hansen, Åse M. (2007). Enhancement of developmental toxicity effects of chemicals by gestational stress. A review. *Neurotoxicology and Teratology, 29,* 425–445.

Hout, Michael, & Elliott, Stuart W. (Eds.). (2011). *Incentives and test-based accountability in education.* Washington, DC: National Academies Press.

Howe, Mark L. (2004). The role of conceptual recoding in reducing children's retroactive interference. *Developmental Psychology, 40,* 131–139.

Howell, Diane M., Wysocki, Karen, & Steiner, Michael J. (2010). Toilet training. *Pediatrics in Review, 31,* 262–263.

Howlin, Patricia, Magiati, Iliana, Charman, Tony, & MacLean, William E., Jr. (2009). Systematic review of early intensive behavioral interventions for children with autism. *American Journal on Intellectual and Developmental Disabilities, 114,* 23–41.

Hrabosky, Joshua I., & Thomas, Jennifer J. (2008). Elucidating the relationship between obesity and depression: Recommendations for future research. *Clinical Psychology: Science and Practice, 15,* 28–34.

Hrdy, Sarah B. (2009). *Mothers and others: The evolutionary origins of mutual understanding.* Cambridge: Harvard University Press.

Hsia, Yingfen, & Maclennan, Karyn. (2009). Rise in psychotropic drug prescribing in children and adolescents during 1992–2001: A population-based study in the UK. *European Journal of Epidemiology, 24,* 211–216.

Huang, Chiungjung. (2010). Mean-level change in self-esteem from childhood through adulthood: Meta-analysis of longitudinal studies. *Review of General Psychology, 14,* 251–260.

Huang, Chien-Chung. (2009). Mothers' reports of nonresident fathers' involvement with their children: Revisiting the relationship between child support payment and visitation. *Family Relations, 58,* 54–64.

Huesmann, L. Rowell, Dubow, Eric F., & Boxer, Paul. (2009). Continuity of aggression from childhood to early adulthood as a predictor of life outcomes: Implications for the adolescent-limited and life-course-persistent models. *Aggressive Behavior, 35,* 136–149.

Hugdahl, Kenneth, & Westerhausen, René. (2010). *The two halves of the brain: Information processing in the cerebral hemispheres.* Cambridge, MA: MIT Press.

Hughes, Julie Milligan, & Bigler, Rebecca S. (2011). Predictors of African American and European American adolescents' endorsement of race-conscious social policies. *Developmental Psychology, 47,* 479–492.

Hughes, Sonya M., & Gore, Andrea C. (2007). How the brain controls puberty, and implications for sex and ethnic differences. *Family & Community Health, 30*(Suppl. 1), S112–S114.

Huijbregts, Sanne K., Tavecchio, Louis, Leseman, Paul, & Hoffenaar, Peter. (2009). Child rearing in a group setting: Beliefs of Dutch, Caribbean Dutch, and Mediterranean Dutch caregivers in center-based child care. *Journal of Cross-Cultural Psychology, 40,* 797–815.

Huntsinger, Carol S., Jose, Paul E., Krieg, Dana Balsink, & Luo, Zupei. (2011). Cultural differences in Chinese American and European American children's drawing skills over time. *Early Childhood Research Quarterly, 26,* 134–145.

Hussey, Jon M., Chang, Jen Jen, & Kotch, Jonathan B. (2006). Child maltreatment in the United States: Prevalence, risk factors, and adolescent health consequences. *Pediatrics, 118,* 933–942.

Hust, Stacey J. T., Brown, Jane D., & L'Engle, Kelly Ladin. (2008). Boys will be boys and girls better be prepared: An analysis of the rare sexual health messages in young adolescents' media. *Mass Communication and Society, 11,* 3–23.

Huston, Aletha C., & Aronson, Stacey Rosenkrantz. (2005). Mothers' time with infant and time in employment as predictors of mother-child relationships and children's early development. *Child Development, 76,* 467–482.

Huston, Aletha C., & Ripke, Marika N. (2006). Middle childhood: Contexts of development. In Aletha C. Huston & Marika N. Ripke (Eds.), *Developmental contexts in middle childhood: Bridges to adolescence and adulthood* (pp. 1–22). New York, NY: Cambridge University Press.

Huver, Rose M. E., Otten, Roy, de Vries, Hein, & Engels, Rutger C. M. E. (2010). Personality and parenting style in parents of adolescents. *Journal of Adolescence, 33,* 395–402.

Hyde, Janet Shibley. (2007). New directions in the study of gender similarities and differences. *Current Directions in Psychological Science, 16,* 259–263.

Hyde, Janet S., Lindberg, Sara M., Linn, Marcia C., Ellis, Amy B., & Williams, Caroline C. (2008, July 25). Gender similarities characterize math performance. *Science, 321,* 494–495.

Hyson, Marilou, Copple, Carol, & Jones, Jacqueline. (2006). Early childhood development and education. In William Damon & Richard M. Lerner (Series Eds.) & K. Ann Renninger & Irving E. Sigel (Vol. Eds.), *Handbook of child psychology: Vol. 4. Child psychology in practice* (6th ed., pp. 3–47). Hoboken, NJ: Wiley.

Iacoboni, Marco. (2009). Imitation, empathy, and mirror neurons. *Annual Review of Psychology, 60,* 653–670.

Iacovidou, Nicoletta, Varsami, Marianna, & Syggellou, Angeliki. (2010). Neonatal outcome of preterm delivery. In George Creatsas & George Mastorakos (Eds.), *Annals of the New York Academy of Sciences: Vol. 1205. Women's health and disease* (pp. 130–134). Malden, MA: Blackwell.

Imai, Mutsumi, Kita, Sotaro, Nagumo, Miho, & Okada, Hiroyuki. (2008). Sound symbolism facilitates early verb learning. *Cognition, 109,* 54–65.

Inan, Hatice Zeynep, Trundle, Kathy Cabe, & Kantor, Rebecca. (2010). Understanding natural sciences education in a Reggio Emilia-inspired preschool. *Journal of Research in Science Teaching, 47,* 1186–1208.

Inhelder, Bärbel, & Piaget, Jean. (1958). *The growth of logical thinking from childhood to adolescence: An essay on the construction of formal operational structures.* New York, NY: Basic Books.

Inhelder, Bärbel, & Piaget, Jean. (1964). *The early growth of logic in the child.* New York, NY: Harper & Row.

Insel, Beverly J., & Gould, Madelyn S. (2008). Impact of modeling on adolescent suicidal behavior. *Psychiatric Clinics of North America, 31,* 293–316.

Institute of Medicine, Committee on Food Marketing and the Diets of Children and Youth. (2006). *Food marketing to children and youth: Threat or opportunity?* Washington, DC: National Academies Press.

Irwin, Scott, Galvez, Roberto, Weiler, Ivan Jeanne, Beckel-Mitchener, Andrea, & Greenough, William. (2002). Brain structure and the functions of FMR1 protein. In Randi Jenssen Hagerman & Paul J. Hagerman (Eds.), *Fragile X syndrome: Diagnosis, treatment, and research* (3rd ed., pp. 191–205). Baltimore, MD: Johns Hopkins University Press.

Ispa, Jean M., Fine, Mark A., Halgunseth, Linda C., Harper, Scott, Robinson, JoAnn, Boyce, Lisa, et al. (2004). Maternal intrusiveness, maternal warmth, and mother-toddler relationship outcomes: Variations across low-income ethnic and acculturation groups. *Child Development, 75,* 1613–1631.

Iverson, Jana M., & Fagan, Mary K. (2004). Infant vocal-motor coordination: Precursor to the gesture-speech system? *Child Development, 75,* 1053–1066.

Iyengar, Sheena S., & Lepper, Mark R. (2000). When choice is demotivating: Can one desire too much of a good thing? *Journal of personality and social psychology, 79,* 995–1006.

Izard, Carroll E. (2009). Emotion theory and research: Highlights, unanswered questions, and emerging issues. *Annual Review of Psychology, 60,* 1–25.

Izard, Carroll E., Fine, Sarah, Mostow, Allison, Trentacosta, Christopher, & Campbell, Jan. (2002). Emotion processes in normal and abnormal development and preventive intervention. *Development & Psychopathology, 14,* 761–787.

Jackson, Richard J. J., & Tester, June. (2008). Environment shapes health, including children's mental health. *Journal of the American Academy of Child & Adolescent Psychiatry, 47,* 129–131.

Jacob, Jenet I. (2009). The socio-emotional effects of non-maternal childcare on children in the USA: A critical review of recent studies. *Early Child Development and Care, 179,* 559–570.

Jacobson, Matthew Frye. (1998). *Whiteness of a different color: European immigrants and the alchemy of race.* Cambridge, MA: Harvard University Press.

Jaffe, Eric. (2004). Mickey Mantle's greatest error: Yankee star's false belief may have cost him years. *Observer, 17*(9), 37.

Jaffee, Sara R., Caspi, Avshalom, Moffitt, Terrie E., Polo-Tomás, Monica, & Taylor, Alan. (2007). Individual, family, and neighborhood factors distinguish resilient from non-resilient maltreated children: A cumulative stressors model. *Child Abuse & Neglect, 31,* 231–253.

James, Raven. (2007). Sexually transmitted infections. In Annette Fuglsang Owens & Mitchell S. Tepper (Eds.), *Sexual health: Vol. 4. State-of-the-art treatments and research* (pp. 235–267). Westport, CT: Praeger/Greenwood.

Jansen, Jarno, Beijers, Roseriet, Riksen-Walraven, Marianne, & de Weerth, Carolina. (2010). Cortisol reactivity in young infants. *Psychoneuroendocrinology, 35,* 329–338.

Jenson, Jeffrey M., & Fraser, Mark W. (2006). *Social policy for children & families: A risk and resilience perspective.* Thousand Oaks, CA: Sage.

Johnson, Elizabeth K., & Tyler, Michael D. (2010). Testing the limits of statistical learning for word segmentation. *Developmental Science, 13,* 339–345.

Johnson, Mark H. (2005). Developmental neuroscience, psychophysiology and genetics. In Marc H. Bornstein & Michael E. Lamb (Eds.), *Developmental science: An advanced textbook* (5th ed., pp. 187–222). Mahwah, NJ: Erlbaum.

Johnson, Mark H., Grossmann, Tobias, & Kadosh, Kathrin Cohen. (2009). Mapping functional brain development: Building a social brain through interactive specialization. *Developmental Psychology, 45,* 151–159.

Johnson, Mark H. with Michelle de Haan. (2011). *Developmental cognitive neuroscience: An introduction* (3rd ed.). Malden, MA: Wiley-Blackwell.

Johnson, Monica Kirkpatrick, Crosnoe, Robert, & Elder, Glen H. (2011). Insights on adolescence from a life course perspective. *Journal of Research on Adolescence, 21,* 273–280.

Johnson, Susan C., Dweck, Carol S., Chen, Frances S., Stern, Hilarie L., Ok, Su-Jeong, & Barth, Maria. (2010). At the intersection of social and cognitive development: Internal working models of attachment in infancy. *Cognitive Science, 34,* 807–825.

Johnson, Scott P., & Shuwairi, Sarah M. (2009). Learning and memory facilitate predictive tracking in 4-month-olds. *Journal of Experimental Child Psychology, 102,* 122–130.

Johnson, Teddi Dineley. (2011). Report calls for examination of chemical safety: National coalition notes difficulty determining exposures. *The Nation's Health, 41,* 9.

Johnson, Wendy. (2010). Understanding the genetics of intelligence: Can height help? Can corn oil? *Current Directions in Psychological Science, 19,* 177–182.

Johnston, Lloyd D., O'Malley, Patrick M., Bachman, Jerald G., & Schulenberg, John E. (2008). *Monitoring the Future national results on adolescent drug use: Overview of key findings, 2007* (NIH Publication No. 08–6418). Bethesda, MD: National Institute on Drug Abuse.

Johnston, Lloyd D., O'Malley, Patrick M., Bachman, Jerald G., & John E. Schulenberg. (2010). *Monitoring the Future national results on adolescent drug use: Overview of key findings, 2009* (NIH Publication No. 10–7583). Bethesda, MD: National Institute on Drug Abuse.

Johnston, Lloyd D., O'Malley, Patrick M., Bachman, Jerald G., & Schulenberg, John E. (2009). *Monitoring the Future national survey results on drug use, 1975–2008: Vol. II. College students and adults ages 19–50* (NIH Publication No. 09–7403). Bethesda, MD: National Institute on Drug Abuse.

Jones, Diane, & Crawford, Joy. (2005). Adolescent boys and body image: Weight and muscularity concerns as dual pathways to body dissatisfaction. *Journal of Youth and Adolescence, 34,* 629–636.

Jones, Edward P. (2003). *The known world.* New York, NY: Amistad.

Jones, Edward P. (2003). *Lost in the city: Stories.* New York, NY: Amistad. (Original work published 1992)

Jones, Mary Cover. (1965). Psychological correlates of somatic development. *Child Development, 36,* 899–911.

Jones, Randall M. (2011). Psychosocial development and first substance use in third and fourth grade students: A short-term longitudinal study. *Child Development Research, 2011.* doi:10.1155/2011/916020

Jones, Steve. (2006, December 22). Prosperous people, penurious genes. *Science, 314,* 1879.

Jong, Jyh-Tsorng, Kao, Tsair, Lee, Liang-Yi, Huang, Hung-Hsuan, Lo, Po-Tsung, & Wang, Hui-Chung. (2010). Can temperament be understood at birth? The relationship between neonatal pain cry and their temperament: A preliminary study. *Infant Behavior and Development, 33,* 266–272.

Juan, Shan. (2010, January 14). *C-section epidemic hits China.* Retrieved from http://www.chinadaily.com.cn/index.html

Juvonen, Jaana, Nishina, Adrienne, & Graham, Sandra. (2006). Ethnic diversity and perceptions of safety in urban middle schools. *Psychological Science, 17,* 393–400.

Kagan, Jerome. (2008). In defense of qualitative changes in development. *Child Development, 79,* 1606–1624.

Kagan, Jerome. (2011). Three lessons learned. *Perspectives on Psychological Science, 6,* 107–113.

Kagan, Jerome, & Herschkowitz, Elinore Chapman. (2005). *Young mind in a growing brain.* Mahwah, NJ: Erlbaum.

Kagan, Jerome, & Norbert Herschkowitz (with Herschkowitz, Elinore Chapman). (2005). *A young mind in a growing brain.* Mahwah, NJ: Erlbaum.

Kagan, Jerome, Snidman, Nancy, Kahn, Vali, & Towsley, Sara. (2007). The preservation of two infant temperaments into adolescence. *Monographs of the Society for Research in Child Development, 72*(Serial No. 287), 1–95.

Kagitcibasi, Cigdem. (2003). Human development across cultures: A contextual-functional analysis and implications for interventions. In T. S. Saraswati (Ed.), *Cross-cultural perspectives in human development: Theory, research, and applications* (pp. 166–191). New Delhi, India: Sage.

Kahana-Kalman, Ronit, & Walker-Andrews, Arlene S. (2001). The role of person familiarity in young infants' perception of emotional expressions. *Child Development, 72,* 352–369.

Kakihara, Fumiko, & Tilton-Weaver, Lauree. (2009). Adolescents' interpretations of parental control: Differentiated by domain and types of control. *Child Development, 80,* 1722–1738.

Kalambouka, Afroditi, Farrell, Peter, Dyson, Alan, & Kaplan, Ian. (2007). The impact of placing pupils with special educational needs in mainstream schools on the achievement of their peers. *Educational Research, 49,* 365–382.

Kalliala, Marjatta. (2006). *Play culture in a changing world*. Maidenhead, England: Open University Press.

Kalra, Suleena Kansal, & Barnhart, Kurt T. (2011). In vitro fertilization and adverse childhood outcomes: What we know, where we are going, and how we will get there. A glimpse into what lies behind and beckons ahead. *Fertility and Sterility, 95,* 1887–1889.

Kanner, Leo. (1943). Autistic disturbances of affective contact. *Nervous Child, 2,* 217–250.

Karabinus, David S. (2009). Flow cytometric sorting of human sperm: MicroSort® clinical trial update. *Theriogenology, 71,* 74–79.

Karama, Sherif, Ad-Dab'bagh, Yasser, Haier, Richard J., Deary, Ian J., Lyttelton, Oliver C., Lepage, Claude, et al. (2009). Positive association between cognitive ability and cortical thickness in a representative US sample of healthy 6 to 18–year-olds. *Intelligence, 37,* 145–155.

Kärnä, Antti, Voeten, Marinus, Little, Todd D., Poskiparta, Elisa, Kaljonen, Anne, & Salmivalli, Christina. (2011). A large-scale evaluation of the KiVa antibullying program: Grades 4–6. *Child Development, 82,* 311–330.

Kärtner, Joscha, Keller, Heidi, & Yovsi, Relindis D. (2010). Mother infant interaction during the first 3 months: The emergence of culture-specific contingency patterns. *Child Development, 81,* 540–554.

Kärtner, Joscha, Keller, Heidi, & Yovsi, Relindis D. (2010). Mother–infant interaction during the first 3 months: The emergence of culture-specific contingency patterns. *Child Development, 81,* 540–554.

Kastenbaum, Robert. (2006). *Death, society, and human experience* (9th ed.). Boston, MA: Allyn and Bacon.

Kavanaugh, Robert D. (2011). Origins and consequences of social pretend play. In Anthony D. Pellegrini (Ed.), *The Oxford handbook of the development of play* (pp. 296–307). New York, NY: Oxford University Press.

Keating, Daniel P. (2004). Cognitive and brain development. In Richard M. Lerner & Laurence D. Steinberg (Eds.), *Handbook of adolescent psychology* (2nd ed., pp. 45–84). Hoboken, NJ: Wiley.

Keating, Daniel P. (Ed.). (2011). *Nature and nurture in early child development*. New York, NY: Cambridge University Press.

Kedar, Yarden, Casasola, Marianella, & Lust, Barbara. (2006). Getting there faster: 18- and 24-month-old infants' use of function words to determine reference. *Child Development, 77,* 325–338.

Keel, Pamela K., & Brown, Tiffany A. (2010). Update on course and outcome in eating disorders. *International Journal of Eating Disorders, 43,* 195–204.

Keil, Frank C. (2011, February 25). Science starts early. *Science, 331,* 1022–1023.

Kelemen, Deborah, Callanan, Maureen A., Casler, Krista, & Perez-Granados, Deanne R. (2005). Why things happen: Teleological explanation in parent-child conversation. *Developmental Psychology, 41,* 251–264.

Keller, Heidi, Borke, Jörn, Chaudhary, Nandita, Lamm, Bettina, & Kleis, Astrid. (2010). Continuity in parenting strategies: A cross-cultural comparison. *Journal of Cross-Cultural Psychology, 41,* 391–409.

Keller, Heidi, Lamm, Bettina, Abels, Monika, Yovsi, Relindis, Borke, Jörn, Jensen, Henning, et al. (2006). Cultural models, socialization goals, and parenting ethnotheories: A multicultural analysis. *Journal of Cross-Cultural Psychology, 37,* 155–172.

Keller, Heidi, Yovsi, Relindis, Borke, Joern, Kärtner, Joscha, Jensen, Henning, & Papaligoura, Zaira. (2004). Developmental consequences of early parenting experiences: Self-recognition and self-regulation in three cultural communities. *Child Development, 75,* 1745–1760.

Kellman, Philip J., & Arterberry, Martha E. (2006). Infant visual perception. In William Damon & Richard M. Lerner (Series Eds.) & Deanna Kuhn & Robert S. Siegler (Vol. Eds.), *Handbook of child psychology: Vol. 2. Cognition, perception, and language* (6th ed., pp. 109–160). Hoboken, NJ: Wiley.

Kempe, Ruth S., & Kempe, C. Henry. (1978). *Child abuse*. Cambridge, MA: Harvard University Press.

Kemple, James J. (with Cynthia J. Willner). (2008). *Career academies: Long-term impacts on labor market outcomes, educational attainment, and transitions to adulthood.* Retrieved from MDRC website: http://www.mdrc.org/publications/482/full.pdf

Kempner, Joanna, Perlis, Clifford S., & Merz, Jon F. (2005, February 11). Forbidden knowledge. *Science, 307,* 854.

Kennedy, Colin R., McCann, Donna C., Campbell, Michael J., Law, Catherine M., Mullee, Mark, Petrou, Stavros, et al. (2006). Language ability after early detection of permanent childhood hearing impairment. *New England Journal of Medicine, 354,* 2131–2141.

Keogh, Barbara K. (2004). The importance of longitudinal research for early intervention practices. In Peggy D. McCardle & Vinita Chhabra (Eds.), *The voice of evidence in reading research* (pp. 81–102). Baltimore, MD: Brookes.

Kéri, Szabolcs. (2009). Genes for psychosis and creativity: A promoter polymorphism of the neuregulin 1 gene is related to creativity in people with high intellectual achievement. *Psychological Science, 20,* 1070–1073.

Kerns, Kathryn A., Brumariu, Laura E., & Seibert, Ashley. (2011). Multi-method assessment of mother-child attachment: Links to parenting and child depressive symptoms in middle childhood. *Attachment & Human Development, 13,* 315–333.

Kerr, Margaret, Stattin, Håkan, & Burk, William J. (2010). A reinterpretation of parental monitoring in longitudinal perspective. *Journal of Research on Adolescence, 20,* 39–64.

Keysers, Christian, & Gazzola, Valeria. (2010). Social neuroscience: Mirror neurons recorded in humans. *Current Biology, 20,* R353–R354.

Khaleque, Abdul, & Rohner, Ronald P. (2002). Perceived parental acceptance-rejection and psychological adjustment: A meta-analysis of cross-cultural and intracultural studies. *Journal of Marriage & the Family, 64,* 54–64.

Khan, Laura Kettel, Sobush, Kathleen, Keener, Dana, Goodman, Kenneth, Lowry, Amy, Kakietek, Jakub, et al. (2009, July 24). Recommended community strategies and measurements to prevent obesity in the United States. *Morbidity and Mortality Weekly Report Recommendations and Reports,* 58(RR07), 1–26.

Khanna, Sunil K. (2010). *Fetal/fatal knowledge: New reproductive technologies and family-building strategies in India*. Belmont, CA: Wadsworth/Cengage Learning.

Khoury-Kassabri, Mona. (2009). The relationship between staff maltreatment of students and bully-victim group membership. *Child Abuse & Neglect: The International Journal, 33,* 914–923.

Kiang, Lisa, & Harter, Susan. (2008). Do pieces of the self-puzzle fit? Integrated/fragmented selves in biculturally-identified Chinese Americans. *Journal of Research in Personality, 42,* 1657–1662.

Kiang, Lisa, Witkow, Melissa, Baldelomar, Oscar, & Fuligni, Andrew. (2010). Change in ethnic identity across the high school years among adolescents with Latin American, Asian, and European backgrounds. *Journal of Youth and Adolescence, 39,* 683–693.

Killen, Melanie. (2007). Children's social and moral reasoning about exclusion. *Current Directions in Psychological Science, 16,* 32–36.

Killen, Melanie, Kelly, M., Richardson, C., Crystal, D., & Ruck, M. (2010). European-American children's and adolescents' evaluations of interracial exclusion. *Group Processes and Intergroup Relations, 13,* 283–300.

Killen, Melanie, Lee-Kim, Jennie, McGlothlin, Heidi, & Stangor, Charles. (2002). How children and adolescents evaluate gender and racial exclusion. *Monographs of the Society for Research in Child Development,* 67(4, Serial No. 271).

Killen, Melanie, Margie, Nancy Geyelin, & Sinno, Stefanie. (2006). Morality in the context of intergroup relationships. In Melanie Killen & Judith G. Smetana (Eds.), *Handbook of moral development* (pp. 155–183). Mahwah, NJ: Erlbaum.

Killen, Melanie, & Smetana, Judith. (2007). The biology of morality: Human development and moral neuroscience. *Human Development, 50,* 241–243.

Killgore, William D. S., Vo, Alexander H., Castro, Carl A., & Hoge, Charles W. (2006). Assessing risk propensity in American soldiers: Preliminary reliability and validity of the Evaluation of Risks (EVAR) scale-English version. *Military Medicine, 171,* 233–239.

Kilmer, Ryan P., & Gil-Rivas, Virginia. (2010). Exploring posttraumatic growth in children impacted by Hurricane Katrina: Correlates of the phenomenon and developmental considerations. *Child Development, 81,* 1211–1227.

Kim, Dong-Sik, & Kim, Hyun-Sun. (2009). Body-image dissatisfaction as a predictor of suicidal ideation among Korean boys and girls in different stages of adolescence: A two-year longitudinal study. *The Journal of Adolescent Health, 45,* 47–54.

Kim, Geunyoung, Walden, Tedra A., & Knieps, Linda J. (2010). Impact and characteristics of positive and fearful emotional messages during infant social referencing. *Infant Behavior and Development, 33,* 189–195.

Kim, Heejung S., Sherman, David K., & Taylor, Shelley E. (2008). Culture and social support. *American Psychologist, 63,* 518–526.

Kim-Cohen, Julia, Moffitt, Terrie E., Caspi, Avshalom, & Taylor, Alan. (2004). Genetic and environmental processes in young children's resilience and vulnerability to socioeconomic deprivation. *Child Development, 75,* 651–668.

Kimbro, Rachel Tolbert, Brooks-Gunn, Jeanne, & McLanahan, Sara. (2011). Young children in urban areas: Links among neighborhood characteristics, weight status, outdoor play, and television watching. *Social Science & Medicine, 72,* 668–676.

King, Pamela Ebstyne, & Furrow, James L. (2004). Religion as a resource for positive youth development: Religion, social capital, and moral outcomes. *Developmental Psychology, 40,* 703–713.

King, Pamela Ebstyne, & Roeser, Robert W. (2009). Religion and spirituality in adolescent development. In Richard M. Lerner & Laurence Steinberg (Eds.), *Handbook of adolescent psychology: Vol. 1. Individual bases of adolescent development* (3rd ed., pp. 435–478). Hoboken, NJ: Wiley.

King, Sara, Waschbusch, Daniel A., Pelham, William E., Frankland, Bradley W., Corkum, Penny V., & Jacques, Sophie. (2009). Subtypes of aggression in children with attention deficit hyperactivity disorder: Medication effects and comparison with typical children. *Journal of Clinical Child and Adolescent Psychology, 38,* 619–629.

Kinney, Hannah C., & Thach, Bradley T. (2009). The sudden infant death syndrome. *New England Journal of Medicine, 361,* 795–805.

Kirby, Douglas, & Laris, B. A. (2009). Effective curriculum-based sex and STD/HIV education programs for adolescents. *Child Development Perspectives, 3,* 21–29.

Kirkorian, Heather L., Pempek, Tiffany A., Murphy, Lauren A., Schmidt, Marie E., & Anderson, Daniel R. (2009). The impact of background television on parent-child interaction. *Child Development, 80,* 1350–1359.

Kiuru, Noona, Burk, William J., Laursen, Brett, Salmela-Aro, Katariina, & Nurmi, Jari-Erik. (2010). Pressure to drink but not to smoke: Disentangling selection and socialization in adolescent peer networks and peer groups. *Journal of Adolescence, 33,* 801–812.

Klaczynski, Paul, Daniel, David B., & Keller, Peggy S. (2009). Appearance idealization, body esteem, causal attributions, and ethnic variations in the development of obesity stereotypes. *Journal of Applied Developmental Psychology, 30,* 537–551.

Klaczynski, Paul A. (2001). Analytic and heuristic processing influences on adolescent reasoning and decision-making. *Child Development, 72,* 844–861.

Klaczynski, Paul A. (2011). Age differences in understanding precedent-setting decisions and authorities' responses to violations of deontic rules. *Journal of Experimental Child Psychology, 109,* 1–24.

Klahr, David, & Nigam, Milena. (2004). The equivalence of learning paths in early science instruction: Effects of direct instruction and discovery learning. *Psychological Science, 15,* 661–667.

Klassen, Terry P., Kiddoo, Darcie, Lang, Mia E., Friesen., Carol, Russell, Kelly, Spooner, Carol, et al. (2006). *The effectiveness of different methods of toilet training for bowel and bladder control* (AHRQ Publication No. 07–E003). Rockville, MD: Agency for Healthcare Research and Quality.

Klaus, Marshall H., & Kennell, John H. (1976). *Maternal-infant bonding: The impact of early separation or loss on family development.* St. Louis, MO: Mosby.

Kleinspehn-Ammerlahn, Anna, Riediger, Michaela, Schmiedek, Florian, von Oertzen, Timo, Li, Shu-Chen, & Lindenberger, Ulman. (2011). Dyadic drumming across the lifespan reveals a zone of proximal development in children. *Developmental Psychology, 47,* 632–644.

Kline, Kathleen Kovner. (2008). *Authoritative communities: The scientific case for nurturing the whole child.* New York, NY: Springer.

Klöppel, Stefan, Vongerichten, Anna, Eimeren, Thilo van, Frackowiak, Richard S. J., & Siebner, Hartwig R. (2007). Can left-handedness be switched? Insights from an early switch of handwriting. *Journal of Neuroscience, 27,* 7847–7853.

Klug, William, Cummings, Michael, Spencer, Charlotte, & Palladino, Michael. (2008). *Concepts of genetics* (9th ed.). San Francisco, CA: Pearson/Benjamin Cummings.

Kochanska, Grazyna, Aksan, Nazan, Prisco, Theresa R., & Adams, Erin E. (2008). Mother-child and father-child mutually responsive orientation in the first 2 years and children's outcomes at preschool age: Mechanisms of influence. *Child Development, 79,* 30–44.

Kochanska, Grazyna, Barry, Robin A., Jimenez, Natasha B., Hollatz, Amanda L., & Woodard, Jarilyn. (2009). Guilt and effortful control: Two mechanisms that prevent disruptive developmental trajectories. *Journal of Personality and Social Psychology, 97,* 322–333.

Kochanska, Grazyna, Gross, Jami N., Lin, Mei-Hua, & Nichols, Kate E. (2002). Guilt in young children: Development, determinants, and relations with a broader system of standards. *Child Development, 73,* 461–482.

Kogan, Michael D., Blumberg, Stephen J., Schieve, Laura A., Boyle, Coleen A., Perrin, James M., Ghandour, Reem M., et al. (2009). Prevalence of parent-reported diagnosis of autism spectrum disorder among children in the US, 2007. *Pediatrics, 124,* 1395–1403.

Kohl, Patricia L., Jonson-Reid, Melissa, & Drake, Brett. (2009). Time to leave substantiation behind. *Child Maltreatment, 14,* 17–26.

Kohlberg, Lawrence. (1963). The development of children's orientations toward a moral order: I. Sequence in the development of moral thought. *Vita Humana, 6,* 11–33.

Kohlberg, Lawrence, Levine, Charles, & Hewer, Alexandra. (1983). *Moral stages: A current formulation and a response to critics.* New York, NY: Karger.

Kolb, Bryan, & Whishaw, Ian Q. (2008). *Fundamentals of human neuropsychology* (6th ed.). New York, NY: Worth.

Kolling, Thorsten, Goertz, Claudia, Frahsek, Stefanie, & Knopf, Monika. (2009). Stability of deferred imitation in 12- to 18-month-old infants: A closer look into developmental dynamics. *European Journal of Developmental Psychology, 6,* 615–640.

Konner, Melvin. (2007). Evolutionary foundations of cultural psychology. In Shinobu Kitayama & Dov Cohen (Eds.), *Handbook of cultural psychology* (pp. 77–105). New York, NY: Guilford Press.

Konner, Melvin. (2010). *The evolution of childhood: Relationships, emotion, mind.* Cambridge, MA: Harvard University Press.

Kopp, Claire B. (2011). Development in the early years: Socialization, motor development, and consciousness. *Annual Review of Psychology, 62,* 165–187.

Koretz, Daniel. (2009, November 6). Moving past No Child Left Behind. *Science, 326,* 803–804.

Kovacs, Maria, Joormann, Jutta, & Gotlib, Ian H. (2008). Emotion (dys)regulation and links to depressive disorders. *Child Development Perspectives, 2,* 149–155.

Kovas, Yulia, Hayiou-Thomas, Marianna E., Oliver, Bonamy, Dale, Philip S., Bishop, Dorothy V. M., & Plomin, Robert. (2005). Genetic influences in different aspects of language development: The etiology of language skills in 4.5-year-old twins. *Child Development, 76,* 632–651.

Krebs, Dennis L. (2008). Morality: An evolutionary account. *Perspectives on Psychological Science, 3,* 149–172.

Krebs, John R. (2009). The gourmet ape: Evolution and human food preferences. *American Journal of Clinical Nutrition, 90,* 707S-711S.

Krentz, Ursula C., & Corina, David P. (2008). Preference for language in early infancy: The human language bias is not speech specific. *Developmental Science, 11,* 1–9.

Kroger, Jane, Martinussen, Monica, & Marcia, James E. (2010). Identity status change during adolescence and young adulthood: A meta-analysis. *Journal of Adolescence, 33,* 683–698.

Kronenberg, Mindy E., Hansell, Tonya Cross, Brennan, Adrianne M., Osofsky, Howard J., Osofsky, Joy D., & Lawrason, Beverly. (2010). Children of Katrina: Lessons learned about postdisaster symptoms and recovery patterns. *Child Development, 81,* 1241–1259.

Kruger, Daniel J., & Polanski, Stephen P. (2011). Sex differences in mortality rates have increased in China following the single-child law. *Letters on Evolutionary Behavioral Science, 2,* 1–4.

Kruk, Margaret E., Prescott, Marta R., & Galea, Sandro. (2008). Equity of skilled birth attendant utilization in developing countries: Financing and policy determinants. *American Journal of Public Health, 98,* 142–147.

Kryzer, Erin M., Kovan, Nikki, Phillips, Deborah A., Domagall, Lindsey A., & Gunnar, Megan R. (2007). Toddlers' and preschoolers' experience in family day care: Age differences and behavioral correlates. *Early Childhood Research Quarterly, 22,* 451–466.

Kuehn, Bridget M. (2011). Scientists find promising therapies for fragile X and Down syndromes. *The Journal of the American Medical Association, 305,* 344–346.

Kuh, George D., Gonyea, Robert M., & Williams, Julie M. (2005). What students expect from college and what they get. In Thomas E. Miller, Barbara E. Bender, John H. Schuh, & Associates (Eds.), *Promoting reasonable expectations: Aligning student and institutional views of the college experience* (pp. 34–64). San Francisco, CA: Jossey-Bass.

Kuhn, Deanna. (2009). The importance of learning about knowing: Creating a foundation for development of intellectual values. *Child Development Perspectives, 3,* 112–117.

Kuhn, Deanna, & Franklin, Sam. (2006). The second decade: What develops (and how). In William Damon & Richard M. Lerner (Series Eds.) & Deanna Kuhn & Robert Siegler (Vol. Eds.), *Handbook of child psychology: Vol. 2. Cognition, perception, and language* (6th ed., pp. 953–993). Hoboken, NJ: Wiley.

Kuhn, Louise, Sinkala, Moses, Thea, Don, Kankasa, Chipepo, & Aldrovandi, Grace. (2009). HIV prevention is not enough: Child survival in the context of prevention of mother to child HIV transmission. *Journal of the International AIDS Society, 12,* 36.

Kulkofsky, Sarah, & Klemfuss, J. Zoe. (2008). What the stories children tell can tell about their memory: Narrative skill and young children's suggestibility. *Developmental Psychology, 44,* 1442–1456.

Kun, Jürgen F. J., May, Jürgen, & Noedl, Harald. (2010). Surveillance of malaria drug resistance: Improvement needed? *Future Medicine, 7,* 3–6.

Kuppens, Sofie, Grietens, Hans, Onghena, Patrick, & Michiels, Daisy. (2009). Associations between parental control and children's overt and relational aggression. *British Journal of Developmental Psychology, 27,* 607–623.

Kutob, Randa M., Senf, Janet H., Crago, Marjorie, & Shisslak, Catherine M. (2010). Concurrent and longitudinal predictors of self-esteem in elementary and middle school girls. *Journal of School Health, 80,* 240–248.

Kwok, Sylvia Y. C. Lai, & Shek, Daniel T. L. (2010). Hopelessness, parent-adolescent communication, and suicidal ideation among Chinese adolescents in Hong Kong. *Suicide and Life-Threatening Behavior, 40,* 224–233.

LaBar, Kevin S. (2007). Beyond fear: Emotional memory mechanisms in the human brain. *Current Directions in Psychological Science, 16,* 173–177.

Labouvie-Vief, Gisela, Grühn, Daniel, & Mouras, Harold. (2009). Dynamic emotion-cognition interactions in adult development: Arousal, stress, and the processing of affect. In Hayden B. Bosworth & Christopher Hertzog (Eds.), *Aging and cognition: Research methodologies and empirical advances* (pp. 181–196). Washington, DC: American Psychological Association.

LaFontana, Kathryn M., & Cillessen, Antonius H. N. (2010). Developmental changes in the priority of perceived status in childhood and adolescence. *Social Development, 19,* 130–147.

Laible, Deborah, Panfile, Tia, & Makariev, Drika. (2008). The quality and frequency of mother-toddler conflict: Links with attachment and temperament. *Child Development, 79,* 426–443.

Lamb, Michael E. (1982). Maternal employment and child development: A review. In Michael E. Lamb (Ed.), *Nontraditional families: Parenting and child development* (pp. 45–69). Hillsdale, NJ: Erlbaum.

Lamb, Michael E. (Ed.). (2010). *The role of the father in child development* (5th ed.). Hoboken, NJ: Wiley.

Lamb, Michael E., & Lewis, Charlie (2005). The role of parent-child relationships in child development. In Marc H. Bornstein & Michael E. Lamb (Eds.), *Developmental science: An advanced textbook* (5th ed., pp. 429–468). Mahwah, NJ: Erlbaum.

Lamb, Stephen, Markussen, Eifred, Teese, Richard, Sandberg, Nina, & Polesel, John (Eds.). (2011). *School dropout and completion: International comparative studies in theory and policy.* New York, NY: Springer.

Lambert, Nathaniel M., Fincham, Frank D., Stillman, Tyler F., Graham, Steven M., & Beach, Steven R. H. (2010). Motivating change in relationships. *Psychological Science, 21,* 126–132.

Lamm, Bettina, Keller, Heidi, Yovsi, Relindis D., & Chaudhary, Nandita. (2008). Grandmaternal and maternal ethnotheories about early child care. *Journal of Family Psychology, 22,* 80–88.

Lane, Scott D., Cherek, Don R., Pietras, Cynthia J., & Steinberg, Joel L. (2005). Performance of heavy marijuana-smoking adolescents on a laboratory measure of motivation. *Addictive Behaviors, 30,* 815–828.

Langenkamp, Amy G. (2010). Academic vulnerability and resilience during the transition to high school. *Sociology of Education, 83,* 1–19.

Långström, Niklas, Rahman, Qazi, Carlström, Eva, & Lichtenstein, Paul. (2010). Genetic and environmental effects on same-sex sexual behavior: A population study of twins in Sweden. *Archives of Sexual Behavior, 39,* 75–80.

Lapsley, Daniel K. (1993). Toward an integrated theory of adolescent ego development: The "new look" at adolescent egocentrism. *American Journal of Orthopsychiatry, 63,* 562–571.

Lara, Marielena, Akinbami, Lara, Flores, Glenn, & Morgenstern, Hal. (2006). Heterogeneity of childhood asthma among Hispanic children: Puerto Rican children bear a disproportionate burden. *Pediatrics, 117,* 43–53.

Lara-Cinisomo, Sandraluz, Fuligni, Allison Sidle, & Karoly, Lynn A. (2011). Preparing preschoolers for kindergarten. In DeAnna M. Laverick & Mary Renck Jalongo (Eds.), *Transitions to early care and education* (Vol. 4, pp. 93–105). New York, NY: Springer.

Laraway, Kelly A., Birch, Leann L., Shaffer, Michele L., & Paul, Ian M. (2010). Parent perception of healthy infant and toddler growth. *Clinical Pediatrics, 49,* 343–349.

Larson, Nicole I., Neumark-Sztainer, Dianne, Hannan, Peter J., & Story, Mary. (2007). Trends in adolescent fruit and vegetable consumption, 1999–2004: Project EAT. *American Journal of Preventive Medicine, 32,* 147–150.

Larson, Reed, & Wilson, Suzanne. (2004). Adolescence across place and time: Globalization and the changing pathways to adulthood. In Richard M. Lerner & Laurence D. Steinberg (Eds.), *Handbook of adolescent psychology* (2nd ed., pp. 299–330). Hoboken, NJ: Wiley.

Larzelere, Robert, Cox, Ronald, & Smith, Gail. (2010). Do nonphysical punishments reduce antisocial behavior more than spanking? A comparison using the strongest previous causal evidence against spanking. *BMC Pediatrics, 10,* 10.

Lassiter, G. Daniel, & Meissner, Christian A. (Eds.). (2010). *Police interrogations and false confessions: Current research, practice, and policy recommendations.* Washington, DC: American Psychological Association.

Laursen, Brett, Bukowski, William M., Nurmi, Jari-Eri, Marion, Donna, Salmela-Aro, Katariina, & Kiuru, Noona. (2010). Opposites detract: Middle school peer group antipathies. *Journal of Experimental Child Psychology, 106,* 240–256.

Laursen, Brett, & Collins, W. Andrew. (2009). Parent-child relationships during adolescence. In Richard M. Lerner & Laurence Steinberg (Eds.), *Handbook of adolescent psychology: Vol. 2. Contextual influences on adolescent development* (3rd ed., pp. 3–42). Hoboken, NJ: Wiley.

Laursen, Brett, & Mooney, Karen S. (2007). Individual differences in adolescent dating and adjustment. In Rutger C. M. E. Engels, Margaret Kerr, & Håkan Stattin (Eds.), *Friends, lovers, and* *groups: Key relationships in adolescence* (pp. 81–92). Hoboken, NJ: Wiley.

Lavelli, Manuela, & Fogel, Alan. (2005). Developmental changes in the relationship between the infant's attention and emotion during early face-to-face communication: The 2-month transition. *Developmental Psychology, 41,* 265–280.

Layden, Tim. (2004, November 15). Get out and play! *Sports Illustrated, 101,* 80–93.

Leach, Penelope. (1997). *Your baby & child: From birth to age five* (3rd ed.). New York, NY: Knopf.

Leach, Penelope. (2009). *Child care today: Getting it right for everyone*. New York, NY: Knopf.

Leadbeater, Bonnie J., & Hoglund, Wendy L. G. (2009). The effects of peer victimization and physical aggression on changes in internalizing from first to third grade. *Child Development, 80,* 843–859.

Leather, Nicola C. (2009). Risk-taking behaviour in adolescence: A literature review. *Journal of Child Health Care, 13,* 295–304.

Lee, Joyce M., Kaciroti, Niko, Appugliese, Danielle, Corwyn, Robert F., Bradley, Robert H., & Lumeng, Julie C. (2010). Body mass index and timing of pubertal initiation in boys. *Archives of Pediatric and Adolescent Medicine, 164,* 139–144.

Leerkes, Esther M., Blankson, A. Nayena, & O'Brien, Marion. (2009). Differential effects of maternal sensitivity to infant distress and non-distress on social-emotional functioning. *Child Development, 80,* 762–775.

Lefkowitz, Eva S., & Gillen, Meghan M. (2006). "Sex is just a normal part of life": Sexuality in emerging adulthood. In Jeffrey Jensen Arnett & Jennifer Lynn Tanner (Eds.), *Emerging adults in America: Coming of age in the 21st century* (pp. 235–255). Washington, DC: American Psychological Association.

Lehmann, Martin, & Hasselhorn, Marcus. (2010). The dynamics of free recall and their relation to rehearsal between 8 and 10 years of age. *Child Development, 81,* 1006–1020.

Lehmann, Wolfgang. (2004). "For some reason, I get a little scared": Structure, agency, and risk in school-work transitions. *Journal of Youth Studies, 7,* 379–396.

Lei, Joy L. (2003). (Un)necessary toughness?: Those "loud black girls" and those "quiet Asian boys". *Anthropology & Education Quarterly, 34,* 158–181.

Leman, Patrick J., & Björnberg, Marina. (2010). Conversation, development, and gender. A study of changes in children's concepts of punishment. *Child Development, 81,* 958–971.

Lengner, Christopher J. (2010). iPS cell technology in regenerative medicine. In Mone Zaidi (Ed.), *Annals of the New York Academy of Sciences: Vol. 1192. Skeletal biology and medicine* (pp. 38–44). Boston, MA: Blackwell.

Lenneberg, Eric H. (1967). *Biological foundations of language*. New York, NY: Wiley.

Lenroot, Rhoshel K., & Giedd, Jay N. (2008). The changing impact of genes and environment on brain development during childhood and adolescence: Initial findings from a neuroimaging study of pediatric twins. *Development and Psychopathology, 20,* 1161–1175.

Lepper, Mark R., Greene, David, & Nisbett, Richard E. (1973). Undermining children's intrinsic interest with extrinsic reward: A test of the "overjustification" hypothesis. *Journal of Personality & Social Psychology, 28,* 129–137.

Lerner, Claire, & Dombro, Amy Laura. (2004). Finding your fit: Some temperament tips for parents. *Zero to Three, 24,* 42–45.

Lerner, Richard M., & Steinberg, Laurence D. (2009). *Handbook of adolescent psychology* (3rd ed.). Hoboken, NJ: Wiley.

Lesane-Brown, Chase L., Brown, Tony N., Tanner-Smith, Emily E., & Bruce, Marino A. (2010). Negotiating boundaries and bonds: Frequency of young children's socialization to their ethnic/racial heritage. *Journal of Cross-Cultural Psychology, 41,* 457–464.

Lester, Patricia, Leskin, Gregory, Woodward, Kirsten, Saltzman, William, Nash, William, Mogil, Catherine, et al. (2011). Wartime deployment and military children: Applying prevention science to enhance family resilience. In Shelley MacDermid & David S. Riggs (Eds.), *Risk and resilience in U.S. military families* (pp. 149–174). New York, NY: Springer.

Leung, Angel Nga-Man, Wong, Stephanie Siu-fong, Wong, Iris Wai-yin, & McBride-Chang, Catherine. (2010). Filial piety and psychosocial adjustment in Hong Kong Chinese early adolescents. *The Journal of Early Adolescence, 30,* 651–667.

Levi Setti, Paolo E., Albani, Elena, Cesana, Amalia, Novara, Paola Vittoria, Zannoni, Elena, Baggiani, Annamaria M., et al. (2011). Italian Constitutional Court modifications of a restrictive assisted reproduction technology law significantly improve pregnancy rate. *Human Reproduction, 26,* 376–381.

Lewallen, Lynne Porter. (2011). The importance of culture in childbearing. *Journal of Obstetric, Gynecologic, & Neonatal Nursing, 40,* 4–8.

Lewin, Kurt. (1943). Psychology and the process of group living. *Journal of Social Psychology, 17,* 113–131.

Lewin, Tamar (2009, October 23). No Einstein in your crib? Get a refund. *New York Times,* p. A1.

Lewin-Benham, Ann. (2008). *Powerful children: Understanding how to teach and learn using the Reggio approach*. New York, NY: Teachers College Press.

Lewis, Charlotte W., Linsenmayer, Kristi A., & Williams, Alexis. (2010). Wanting better: A qualitative study of low-income parents about their children's oral health. *Pediatric Dentistry, 32,* 518–524.

Lewis, Lawrence B., Antone, Carol, & Johnson, Jacqueline S. (1999). Effects of prosodic stress and serial position on syllable omission in first words. *Developmental Psychology, 35,* 45–59.

Lewis, Michael. (2008). The emergence of human emotions. In Michael Lewis, Jeannette M. Haviland-Jones, & Lisa Feldman Barrett (Eds.), *Handbook of emotions* (3rd ed., pp. 304–319). New York, NY: Guilford Press.

Lewis, Michael, & Brooks, Jeanne. (1978). Self-knowledge and emotional development. In Michael Lewis & L. A. Rosenblum (Eds.), *Genesis of behavior: Vol. 1. The development of affect* (pp. 205–226). New York, NY: Plenum Press.

Lewis, Michael, & Ramsay, Douglas. (2005). Infant emotional and cortisol responses to goal blockage. *Child Development, 76,* 518–530.

Lewkowicz, David J. (2010). Infant perception of audio-visual speech synchrony. *Developmental Psychology, 46,* 66–77.

Li, Yibing, & Lerner, Richard M. (2011). Trajectories of school engagement during adolescence: Implications for grades, depression, delinquency, and substance use. *Developmental Psychology, 47,* 233–247.

Libertus, Melissa E., & Brannon, Elizabeth M. (2009). Behavioral and neural basis of number sense in infancy. *Current Directions in Psychological Science, 18,* 346–351.

Lichter, Daniel T., Qian, Zhenchao, & Mellott, Leanna M. (2006). Marriage or dissolution? Union transitions among poor cohabiting women. *Demography, 43,* 223–240.

Lillard, Angeline, & Else-Quest, Nicole. (2006, September 29). Evaluating Montessori education. *Science, 313,* 1893–1894.

Lillard, Angeline Stoll. (2005). *Montessori: The science behind the genius*. New York, NY: Oxford University Press.

Lim, Boo Yeun. (2004). The magic of the brush and the power of color: Integrating theory into practice of painting in early childhood settings. *Early Childhood Education Journal, 32,* 113–119.

Limber, Susan P. (2011). Development, evaluation, and future directions of the Olweus Bullying Prevention Program. *Journal of School Violence, 10,* 71–87.

Lincove, Jane A., & Painter, Gary (2006). Does the age that children start kindergarten matter? Evidence of long-term educational and social outcomes. *Educational Evaluation and Policy Analysis, 28,* 153–179

Lindfors, Kaj, Elovainio, Marko, Wickman, Sanna, Vuorinen, Risto, Sinkkonen, Jari, Dunkel, Leo, et al. (2007). Brief report: The role of ego development in psychosocial adjustment among boys with delayed puberty. *Journal of Research on Adolescence, 17,* 601–612.

Linn, Susan, & Novosat, Courtney L. (2008). Calories for sale: Food marketing to children in the twenty-first century. In Amy B. Jordan (Ed.), *Annals of the American Academy of Political and Social Science: Vol. 615. Overweight and obesity in America's children: Causes, consequences, solutions* (pp. 133–155). Thousand Oaks, CA: Sage.

Lipton, Jennifer S., & Spelke, Elizabeth S. (2003). Origins of number sense: Large-number discrimination in human infants. *Psychological Science, 14,* 396–401.

Liszkowski, Ulf, Schäfer, Marie, Carpenter, Malinda, & Tomasello, Michael. (2009). Prelinguistic infants, but not chimpanzees, communicate about absent entities. *Psychological Science, 20,* 654–660.

Liszkowski, Ulf, & Tomasello, Michael. (2011). Individual differences in social, cognitive, and morphological aspects of infant pointing. *Cognitive Development, 26,* 16–29.

Liu, David, Sabbagh, Mark A., Gehring, William J., & Wellman, Henry M. (2009). Neural correlates of childrens theory of mind development. *Child Development, 80,* 318–326.

Liu, David, Wellman, Henry M., Tardif, Twila, & Sabbagh, Mark A. (2008). Theory of mind development in Chinese children: A meta-analysis of false-belief understanding across cultures and languages. *Developmental Psychology, 44,* 523–531.

Livas-Dlott, Alejandra, Fuller, Bruce, Stein, Gabriela L., Bridges, Margaret, Mangual Figueroa, Ariana, & Mireles, Laurie. (2010). Commands, competence, and *cariño*: Maternal socialization practices in Mexican American families. *Developmental Psychology, 46,* 566–578.

Lloyd-Fox, Sarah, Blasi, Anna, Volein, Agnes, Everdell, Nick, Elwell, Claire E., & Johnson, Mark H. (2009). Social perception in infancy: A near infrared spectroscopy study. *Child Development, 80,* 986–999.

Lobstein, T., & Dibb, S. (2005). Evidence of a possible link between obesogenic food advertising and child overweight. *Obesity Reviews, 6,* 203–208.

LoBue, Vanessa, & DeLoache, Judy S. (2011). Pretty in pink: The early development of gender-stereotyped colour preferences. *British Journal of Developmental Psychology, 29,* 656–667.

Lockhart, Kristi L., Chang, Bernard, & Story, Tyler. (2002). Young children's beliefs about the stability of traits: Protective optimism? *Child Development, 73,* 1408–1430.

Lockhart, Kristi L., Nakashima, Nobuko, Inagaki, Kayoko, & Keil, Frank C. (2008). From ugly duckling to swan? Japanese and American beliefs about the stability and origins of traits. *Cognitive Development, 23,* 155–179.

Loe, Irene M., & Feldman, Heidi M. (2007). Academic and educational outcomes of children with ADHD. *Journal of Pediatric Psychology, 32,* 643–654.

Loeb, Susanna, Bridges, Margaret, Bassok, Daphna, Fuller, Bruce, & Rumberger, Russell. (2005). *How much is too much? The influence of preschool centers on children's social and cognitive development.* Retrieved from National Bureau of Economic Research website: http://www.nber.org/papers/w11812

Loeber, Rolf, & Burke, Jeffrey D. (2011). Developmental pathways in juvenile externalizing and internalizing problems. *Journal of Research on Adolescence, 21,* 34–46.

Loland, Sigmund. (2002). *Fair play in sport: A moral norm system.* London, England: Routledge.

Loman, Michelle M., & Gunnar, Megan R. (2010). Early experience and the development of stress reactivity and regulation in children. *Neuroscience & Biobehavioral Reviews, 34,* 867–876.

London, Kamala, Bruck, Maggie, Poole, Debra Ann, & Melnyk, Laura. (2011). The development of metasuggestibility in children. *Applied Cognitive Psychology, 25,* 146–155.

Longmore, Monica, Eng, Abbey, Giordano, Peggy, & Manning, Wendy. (2009). Parenting and adolescents' sexual initiation. *Journal of Marriage and Family, 71,* 969–982.

Lord, Catherine, & Bishop, Somer L. (2010). Autism spectrum disorders: Diagnosis, prevalence, and services for children and families. *Social Policy Report, 24*(2), 1–26.

Losin, Elizabeth A. Reynolds, Dapretto, Mirella, & Iacoboni, Marco. (2009). Culture in the mind's mirror: How anthropology and neuroscience can inform a model of the neural substrate for cultural imitative learning. *Progress in Brain Research, 178,* 175–190.

Lovecky, Deirdre V. (2009). Moral sensitivity in young gifted children. In Tracy Cross & Don Ambrose (Eds.), *Morality, ethics, and gifted minds* (pp. 161–176). New York, NY: Springer.

Lowell, Darcy I., Carter, Alice S., Godoy, Leandra, Paulicin, Belinda, & Briggs-Gowan, Margaret J. (2011). A randomized controlled trial of Child FIRST: A comprehensive home-based intervention translating research into early childhood practice. *Child Development, 82,* 193–208.

Lucast, Erica K. (2007). Informed consent and the misattributed paternity problem in genetic counseling. *Bioethics, 21,* 41–50.

Luna, Beatriz, Padmanabhan, Aarthi, & O'Hearn, Kirsten. (2010). What has fMRI told us about the development of cognitive control through adolescence? *Brain and Cognition, 72,* 101–113.

Luthar, Suniya S., Cicchetti, Dante, & Becker, Bronwyn. (2000). The construct of resilience: A critical evaluation and guidelines for future work. *Child Development, 71,* 543–562.

Luthar, Suniya S., D'Avanzo, Karen, & Hites, Sarah. (2003). Maternal drug abuse versus other psychological disturbances: Risks and resilience among children. In Suniya S. Luthar (Ed.), *Resilience and vulnerability: Adaptation in the context of childhood adversities* (pp. 104–129). New York, NY: Cambridge University Press.

Lynn, Richard, & Mikk, Jaan. (2007). National differences in intelligence and educational attainment. *Intelligence, 35,* 115–121.

Lynne, Sarah D., Graber, Julia A., Nichols, Tracy R., Brooks-Gunn, Jeanne, & Botvin, Gilbert J. (2007). Links between pubertal timing, peer influences, and externalizing behaviors among urban students followed through middle school. *Journal of Adolescent Health, 40,* 181.e187–181.e113.

Lyon, Thomas D., Malloy, Lindsay C., Quas, Jodi A., & Talwar, Victoria A. (2008). Coaching, truth induction, and young maltreated children's false allegations and false denials. *Child Development, 79,* 914–929.

Lyons, Kristen E., Ghetti, Simona, & Cornoldi, Cesare. (2010). Age differences in the contribution of recollection and familiarity to false-memory formation: A new paradigm to examine developmental reversals. *Developmental Science, 13,* 355–362.

Lyons-Ruth, Karlen, Bronfman, Elisa, & Parsons, Elizabeth. (1999). IV. Maternal frightened, frightening, or atypical behavior and disorganized infant attachment patterns. *Monographs of the Society for Research in Child Development, 64*(3, Serial No. 258), 67–96.

Ma, Lang, Phelps, Erin, Lerner, Jacqueline V., & Lerner, Richard M. (2009). Academic competence for adolescents who bully and who are bullied: Findings from the 4-H Study of Positive Youth Development. *The Journal of Early Adolescence, 29,* 862–897.

Maas, Carl, Herrenkohl, Todd I., & Sousa, Cynthia. (2008). Review of research on child maltreatment and violence in youth. *Trauma, Violence & Abuse, 9,* 56–67.

Maccoby, Eleanor E. (2000). Parenting and its effects on children: On reading and misreading behavior genetics. *Annual Review of Psychology, 51,* 1–27.

Macgregor, Stuart, Lind, Penelope A., Bucholz, Kathleen K., Hansell, Narelle K., Madden, Pamela A. F., Richter, Melinda M., et al. (2009). Associations of ADH and ALDH2 gene variation with self report alcohol reactions, consumption and dependence: An integrated analysis. *Human Molecular Genetics, 18,* 580–593.

MacMillan, Harriet L., Wathen, C. Nadine, Barlow, Jane, Fergusson, David M., Leventhal, John M., & Taussig, Heather N. (2009). Interventions to prevent child maltreatment and associated impairment. *Lancet, 373,* 250–266.

Macmillan, Ross, & Copher, Ronda. (2005). Families in the life course: Interdependency of roles, role configurations, and pathways. *Journal of Marriage and Family, 67,* 858–879.

Madden, Mary, & Lenhart, Amanda. (2009). *Teens and distracted driving: Texting, talking and other uses of the cell phone behind the wheel.* Washington, DC: Pew Internet & American Life Project.

Magnuson, Katherine, & Berger, Lawrence M. (2009). Family structure states and transitions: Associations with children's well-being during middle childhood. *Journal of Marriage and Family, 71,* 575–591.

Maguire, Kathleen. (2010). *Sourcebook of criminal justice statistics.* Washington, DC: U.S. Department of Justice.

Mahler, Margaret S., Pine, Fred, & Bergman, Anni. (1975). *The psychological birth of the human infant: Symbiosis and individuation.* New York, NY: Basic Books.

Mahmoud, Adel. (2004, July 9). The global vaccination gap. *Science, 305,* 147.

Majercsik, Eszter. (2005). Hierachy of needs of geriatric patients. *Gerontology, 51,* 170–173.

Makimoto, Kiyoko. (1998). Drinking patterns and drinking problems among Asian-Americans and Pacific Islanders. *Alcohol Health and Research World, 22,* 270–275.

Malina, Robert M., Bouchard, Claude, & Bar-Or, Oded. (2004). *Growth, maturation, and*